EDITED BY LAWRENCE BOOTH

WISDEN

CRICKETERS' ALMANACK

2021

158th EDITION

John Wisden & Co

An imprint of Bloomsbury Publishing Plc

WISDEN
Bloomsbury Publishing Plc
50 Bedford Square, London, WC1B 3DP, UK
29 Earlsfort Terrace, Dublin 2, Ireland

BLOOMSBURY, WISDEN and the wood-engraving device are trademarks of Bloomsbury Publishing Plc

First published in Great Britain 2021

WISDEN CRICKETERS' ALMANACK

Editor **Lawrence Booth**
Co-editor **Hugh Chevallier**
International editor **Steven Lynch**
Statistical editor **Harriet Monkhouse**
Digital editor **Richard Whitehead**
Production co-ordinator **Matt Boulton**
Statisticians **Philip Bailey** and **Andrew Samson**
Proofreader **Charles Barr**
Database and typesetting **James Parsisson**
Publisher **Katy McAdam**
Consultant publisher **Christopher Lane**

Reader feedback: almanack@wisdenalmanack.com
www.wisdenalmanack.com
www.wisdenrecords.com
Follow Wisden on Twitter @WisdenAlmanack
and on Facebook at Wisden Sports

A catalogue record for this book is available from the British Library

Library of Congress Cataloguing-in-Publication data has been applied for

Hardback 978-1-4729-7547-8 £55
Soft cover 978-1-4729-7548-5 £55
Large format 978-1-4729-7549-2 £75
Leatherbound 978-1-4729-9085-3 £295
The Shorter Wisden (eBook) 978-1-4729-8815-7 £15

2 4 6 8 10 9 7 5 3 1

Every reasonable effort has been made to trace copyright holders of material reproduced in this book, but if any have been inadvertently overlooked the publishers would be glad to hear from them.

Typeset in Times New Roman and Univers by DLxml, a division of RefineCatch Ltd, Bungay, Suffolk
Printed and bound in Italy by L.E.G.O. S.p.A.

Bloomsbury Publishing Plc makes every effort to ensure that the papers used in the manufacture of our books are natural, recyclable products made from wood grown in well-managed forests. Our manufacturing processes conform to the environmental regulations of the country of origin.

To find out more about our authors and books visit www.wisdenalmanack.com and sign up for our newsletters.

A Taste of Wisden 2021

Wisden pointed out that, for Middlesex, unbeaten until nearly a month after the assassination of Archduke Franz Ferdinand in Sarajevo on June 28, "the declaration of War quite upset the county's plans".

When the cricket stops, page 43

* * *

He was holding the ball aloft, not to acknowledge the crowd, since there was none, but in dedication to his father, Bob, who had recently died at a Leicester care home from Covid-related illnesses.

Five Cricketers of the Year, page 73

* * *

More than 80 years on, sheltering from the 2020 pandemic in Jersey, he pronounces himself "delighted" to have his glory days remembered.

Wisden Schools Cricketers of the Year, page 129

* * *

His batting, like a racehorse being turned into a steeplechaser, was designed for the turf not the air.

Retirements, page 193

* * *

By 1968 he was chairman of selectors, and controversially chose himself for a (later cancelled) tour of England.

Obituaries, page 298

* * *

But this was West Indies' moment: players and backroom staff, on one knee, right fists sporting black gloves raised to the sky.

England v West Indies in 2020, page 333

* * *

There were no snakes of plastic beer cups, no fancy-dress nuns, no Barmy Army chants, no Pakistan flags, no raucous cheers from home supporters when another drive from Buttler or Woakes crossed the rope.

England v Pakistan in 2020, page 363

* * *

At the Bay Oval he entered during the first over, and made the greentop seem a red herring.

New Zealand v Pakistan in 2020-21, page 715

LIST OF CONTRIBUTORS

Timothy Abraham
Ujjwal Acharya
Andrew Alderson
Tanya Aldred
James Anderson
Chris Aspin
Scott Bailey
Vaneisa Baksh
Marcus Berkmann
Benedict Bermange
Scyld Berry
Edward Bevan
Paul Bird
Paul Bolton
Daniel Brettig
Liam Brickhill
Colin Bryden
Ian Callender
Brian Carpenter
Daniel Cherny
James Coyne
Liam Cromar
Jon Culley
John Curtis
Debasish Datta
Geoffrey Dean
Tim de Lisle
Peter Della Penna
William Dick
George Dobell
Rory Dollard
Patrick Eagar
Paul Edwards
Syd Egan
Mark Eklid
Matthew Engel
Peter English
John Etheridge
Melinda Farrell
Warwick Franks
Nick Friend
Daniel Gallan
Alan Gardner
Mark Geenty
Pat Gibson
Richard Gibson
Haydn Gill
James Gingell
Julian Guyer
Gideon Haigh
Duncan Hamilton
Kevin Hand
Graham Hardcastle
Philip Hardman
David Hardy
Shahid Hashmi
Douglas Henderson
Andrew Hignell
Paul Hiscock
Richard Hobson
Michael Holding
Tom Holland
Jon Hotten
Nick Hoult
Steve James
Emma John
Quentin Jones
Abid Ali Kazi
Patrick Kidd
Richard Latham
Jack Leach
Geoff Lemon
Jonathan Liew
Richard Logan
Will Macpherson
Neil Manthorp
Vic Marks
Ali Martin
Mazher Arshad
Kalika Mehta
Peter Miller
Mohammad Isam
R. Mohan
Benj Moorehead
Chetan Narula
Paul Newman
Raf Nicholson
Andrew Nixon
Harry Pearson
Mark Pennell
Derek Pringle
Paul Radley
Richard Rae
Ebony Rainford-Brent
Matt Roller
Osman Samiuddin
Helge Schutz
Neville Scott
Shadi Khan Saif
Sreshth Shah
Jack Shantry
Utpal Shuvro
Simon Sinclair
Brendan Smith
Rob Smyth
Garfield Sobers
Richard Spiller
Clive Stafford Smith
Fraser Stewart
Andy Stockhausen
Chris Stocks
Pat Symes
Bruce Talbot
Sa'adi Thawfeeq
Dave Tickner
Sharda Ugra
Phil Walker
John Ward
Tim Wigmore
Freddie Wilde
Simon Wilde
Marcus Williams
Dean Wilson
Robert Winder
Alex Winter
Dominic Wood
Andrew Wu
Andy Zaltzman
Lungani Zama

Cartoons by Nick Newman. Contributors to the **Round the World** section are listed after their articles.

The editor also acknowledges with gratitude assistance from the following: Robin Abrahams, Clare Adams, Emily Banting, Peter Bather, Mike Bechley, Jack Birkenshaw, Mike Brearley, Derek Carlaw, Stephen Chalke, Barry Chambers, Simon Charles, Xeena Cooper, Matt Cornford, Mike Coward, Stephen Cubitt, Prakash Dahatonde, Nigel Davies, Gulu Ezekiel, M. L. Fernando, Ric Finlay, Alan Fordham, David Frith, Evan Gray, Nigel Hancock, Clive Hitchcock, Anthony Hyde, Christopher Jarrey, David Kendix, Nigel King, Barry Knight, Sam Knowles, Rajesh Kumar, John Leather, Edward Liddle, Daniel Lightman, Richard Logan, Malcolm Lorimer, Ernie McDade, Brian McKenzie, Mahendra Mapagunaratne, Barry Mason, Kate Matheve, Jeff Medlock, Garry Morgan, Dan Nice, Caroline Nyamande, Michael Owen-Smith, Rachel Pagan, Francis Payne, Toby Pettman, Maggie Phillips, Ken Piesse, Peter Pollock, Qamar Ahmed, Danny Reuben, David Rimmer, Janet Rouse, Andy Rushton, Steven Stern, Jeremy Tagg, Bob Thomas, Mike Vockins, Chris Walmsley, Keith Walmsley.

The production of *Wisden* would not be possible without the support and co-operation of many other cricket officials, county scorers, writers and lovers of the game. To them all, many thanks.

PREFACE

For some of last year, it looked as if "Cricket match takes place" might become a candidate for our index of unusual occurrences. In the event, plenty of matches did happen, though – inevitably – fewer than usual. This year's Almanack is about 20% slimmer than its recent predecessors, but longer than any edition before 1980. The coronavirus *Wisden* should be easy to spot on the shelves. We hope there will not be a companion volume, though at the time of writing it was hard to be sure.

The only annual award scuppered by the pandemic was the Schools Cricketer of the Year. It has been running since 2007, when Jonny Bairstow (who averaged 218 for St Peter's, York) got the nod. Instead, we have named a schools winner for every year before that, back to 1900. The process gave rise to one piece of especially heart-warming news: George Knight, in the year he turned 100, could take delight in being rewarded for his stellar performance for Victoria College, Jersey, in 1939. Good things come to those who wait.

We have also embarked on a project which will carry us through towards the end of the decade. Patrick Eagar, helped by Bob Thomas and Nigel Davies, has chosen three cricket images from the 1950s. Next year, attention will turn to the 1960s, and so on. The choices are a reminder of how much the game has changed – and, in the spectators' enthusiasm, stayed the same.

Special thanks go to the editorial team, who took the year's strangeness in their stride. Hugh Chevallier, our co-editor, pulled the strings with customary deftness; without him, this Almanack wouldn't be what it is. International editor Steven Lynch ticked off 35 years as a Wisden employee in one guise or another; statistical editor Harriet Monkhouse completed 30 with the Almanack alone. Both are indispensable. We look forward to Richard Whitehead's continued contributions to the obituaries, while Matt Boulton did another sterling job as production co-ordinator.

Christopher Lane, our consultant publisher, was his usual fount of good sense; Charles Barr remained a keen-eyed proofreader, and Philip Bailey and Andrew Samson the sharpest of statisticians. James Parsisson at DLxml typeset the book with skill and patience. Thanks, too, to Katy McAdam, Lizzy Ewer and Katherine Macpherson at Bloomsbury, and to my colleagues at the *Daily Mail* and *The Mail on Sunday*, Marc Padgett, Paul Newman, Richard Gibson and Mike Richards. Danny Reuben, the ECB's genial head of team communications, took the cover shot of a masked Stuart Broad, for which we are most grateful. Clare Adams presided diligently over our photograph competition, which has an interesting winner.

My wife, Anjali, had to deal with more than usual during the days of lockdown, and no words can convey my love or thanks. Our second daughter, Anoushka, arrived in May, and it shouldn't be more than a few years before she is playing with her sister Aleya's new bat and ball.

LAWRENCE BOOTH
Barnes, February 2021.

CONTENTS

Part One – Comment

Part Two – The Wisden Review

Part Three – English International Cricket

Part Four – English Domestic Cricket

Statistics

Bob Willis Trophy

Vitality T20 Blast

Other English Cricket

Part Five – Overseas Cricket

CRICKET IN ZIMBABWE

OTHER OVERSEAS INTERNATIONAL CRICKET

Part Six – Overseas Twenty20 Franchise Cricket

Part Seven – Women's Cricket

WORLD TABLES, RANKINGS AND AVERAGES

TWENTY20 WORLD CUP

INTERNATIONAL SERIES

DOMESTIC CRICKET

Part Eight – Records and Registers

Part Nine – The Almanack

SYMBOLS AND ABBREVIATIONS

*	In full scorecards and lists of tour parties signifies the captain. In short scorecards, averages and records signifies not out.
†	In full scorecards signifies the designated wicketkeeper. In averages signifies a left-handed batsman.
‡	In short scorecards signifies the team who won the toss.
DLS	Signifies where the result of a curtailed match has been determined under the Duckworth/Lewis/Stern method.

Other uses of symbols are explained in notes where they appear.

First-class matches Men's matches of three or more days are first-class unless otherwise stated. All other matches are not first-class, including one-day and T20 internationals.

Scorecards Where full scorecards are not provided in this book, they can be found at Cricket Archive (www.cricketarchive.co.uk) or ESPNcricinfo (www.cricinfo.com). Full scorecards from matches played overseas can also be found in the relevant *ACS Overseas First-Class Annuals*. In Twenty20 scorecards, the first figure in a bowling analysis refers to balls bowled, not overs, and the second to dot balls, not maidens (as in first-class or List A games).

Records The Records section (pages 926–1076) is online at www.wisdenrecords.com. The database is regularly updated and, in many instances, more detailed than in *Wisden 2021*.

PART ONE

Comment

Wisden Honours

THE LEADING CRICKETERS IN THE WORLD

Ben Stokes (page 97)
Beth Mooney (page 96)

The Leading Cricketers in the World are chosen by the editor of *Wisden* in consultation with some of the world's most experienced writers and commentators. Selection is based on a player's class and form shown in all cricket during the calendar year, and is merely guided by statistics rather than governed by them. There is no limit to how many times a player may be chosen. A list of past winners can be found on page 98. A list of notional past winners, backdated to 1900, appeared on page 35 of *Wisden 2007*.

THE LEADING TWENTY20 CRICKETER IN THE WORLD

Kieron Pollard (page 824)

This award exactly mirrors those above, but is based solely on performances in Twenty20 cricket, both international and domestic – and may be won by a male or female player.

FIVE CRICKETERS OF THE YEAR

Zak Crawley (page 65)
Jason Holder (page 67)
Mohammad Rizwan (page 69)
Dominic Sibley (page 71)
Darren Stevens (page 73)

The Five Cricketers of the Year are chosen by the editor of *Wisden*, and represent a tradition that dates back to 1889, making this the oldest individual award in cricket. Excellence in and/or influence on the previous English summer are the major criteria for inclusion. No one can be chosen more than once. A list of past winners can be found on page 1178.

WISDEN SCHOOLS CRICKETER OF THE YEAR

There is no Schools Cricketer of the Year for 2020, but a list of notional past winners, backdated to 1900, appears on page 127.

WISDEN BOOK OF THE YEAR

This is Cricket by Daniel Melamud (page 173)

The Book of the Year is selected by *Wisden's* guest reviewer; all cricket books published in the previous calendar year and submitted to *Wisden* for possible review are eligible. A list of past winners can be found on page 174.

WISDEN CRICKET PHOTOGRAPH OF THE YEAR

was won by Steve Waugh (whose entry appears opposite page 64)

The Cricket Photograph of the Year is chosen by a panel of independent experts; all images on a cricket theme photographed in the previous calendar year are eligible.

WISDEN'S WRITING COMPETITION

was won by Philip Hardman (page 93)

Wisden's Writing Competition is open to anyone (other than previous winners) who has not been commissioned to write for, or has a working relationship with, the Almanack. Full details appear on page 94.

Full details of past winners of all these honours can be found at www.wisdenalmanack.com

NOTES BY THE EDITOR

Cricket has never been less important than in 2020 – and never more. As coronavirus spread, it seemed frivolous to wonder when the season might start, or whether anyone would be there to watch; months later, with the UK's death toll into six figures, even writing about runs and wickets felt wrong.

But this is a sports book, so let us start with what we know best. Cricket, like everything else, had its heart ripped out, and its soul very nearly crushed (for once, soul struck the right note). It lost family and friends. It made compromises in order to survive, and may take years to recover. The story is far from over.

The pace of events was dizzying, shocking. David Hodgkiss was the Lancashire chairman when *Wisden 2020* was printing; by publication, he had died. And the obituaries this year include at least 15 others linked to Covid-19.

They were all ages, and from every corner of the game. Lee Nurse was just 43, and had played for Berkshire. Riaz Sheikh, a former leg-spinner who was 51, once dismissed Inzamam-ul-Haq. Phil Wright, aged 60, was Leicestershire's popular dressing-room attendant. The 73-year-old Chetan Chauhan will always be four decades younger, dragged by Sunil Gavaskar towards the pavilion after an lbw decision in a Test at Melbourne. Ken Merchant, a member of The Cricket Society, died at the age of 81, on the same day as his wife, in the same Southend hospital ward. Peter Edrich, cousin of Bill and John, was 93.

How did cricket go on? The trite answer is it had to; those above would have had it no other way. And in the game's continuance came a kind of salvation.

From the abyss

In early 2019, the ECB's annual report identified two threats to cricket beyond their control: terrorism, and national mourning. A year later, shortly after the World Health Organisation declared a "public health emergency of international concern", the ECB added a third: communicable disease. This coincided with the first confirmed cases of Covid-19 in the UK, though it was still regarded, more or less, as a problem for China. Within days, cricket was facing its greatest disruption since the Second World War.

The ECB rose to the challenge. Swift measures taken by chief executive Tom Harrison spared the English game the worst of the financial damage. The biosecure bubble organised by director of events Steve Elworthy proved unburstable, allowing England's men to fulfil all 18 home internationals in the space of ten strange weeks. With the domestic fixture list looking like a ghost town, the counties squeezed in two competitions. It was faintly miraculous.

The board might have done one thing differently. They had allowed their reserves to dwindle from £73m in 2015-16 to £17m four years later, which suggested they had been paying lip service to the possibility of bombs disrupting a money-spinning visit by India, or the death of the monarch. It's also true that their obsession with The Hundred – delayed by 12 months because of the pandemic, and missed by few – had cost them more than planned. But, as Boris Johnson bragged about shaking hands in hospitals, then dithered over a start date for cricket while snooker fans were allowed inside the Crucible, there was more decisive governance coming from Lord's than the Commons.

The price was still huge. The women's game, it was made clear, was expendable, and spared a wipeout only by the decision of West Indies to visit Derby in September. Funding was cut further down the ladder, and may not return. The ECB slashed 20% of their workforce. After initial fears cricket might lose £380m, a shortfall of around £110m was almost a triumph. But it was sobering, even so.

That, though, was only one way of looking at it – the modern way, with its gaze never far from the bottom line. There was another, too. Cricket's absence in April, May and June had left everyone bereft, for reasons that took a while to sink in. We could all agree we missed the matches, the drama, the ebb and flow. But there was a more profound silence: gone was the reassuring buzz of an English summer, a sense that, somewhere, there was a game going on, a tale in the making, honey still for tea. For cricket lovers, checking the score is a comforting ritual; its loss was impossible to measure.

The pandemic had more serious repercussions than the cancellation of sport. Yet it doesn't diminish personal tragedy to point out the cruelty of the timing. The previous summer had left optimism in the air: England were world champions, Ben Stokes the Colossus of Leeds. There was hope cricket might overcome the disadvantage of the TV paywall. In early 2020, Stokes was at it again, inspiring a series victory in South Africa. England headed for Sri Lanka in March, and the new season could not start quickly enough.

Instead, cricket again shrank in the national mind. Until now, the lack of a satellite dish hadn't necessarily left the game out of reach: fans could always buy a ticket, assuming they could afford one. But playing behind closed doors removed that option, and so – initially – cricket's relationship with its TV paymasters became more pliant than ever. The game was happening for one reason alone: broadcasting contracts. Sky's coverage remained peerless, but when pundits were analysing Rory Burns's front-foot technique in an empty stadium, sport's eternal balance between importance and irrelevance was too fine for comfort.

And yet cricket has always adapted: not for the first time, it came back from the brink. With precious little else going on, even empty grounds began to resemble hives of activity. Fans found ways of staying in touch. During the 2019 World Cup, *Test Match Special* received 11.3m "online listening requests"; last summer, it was 14.5m, despite the Test opponents being neither Australia nor India. The increasingly slick live-streaming offered by the counties was lapped up by millions and, when Sky Sports broadcast the final of the Bob Willis Trophy on their YouTube channel, 967,000 logged on. There has always been an audience. Obliged to find different ways of reaching it, cricket actually looked ahead of the game.

There was also a glimpse of humanity. Players raised money for various charities and the NHS. Some used lockdown to study for online degrees, connecting with a world beyond county contracts. Others spent time with their young families. Everyone took pay cuts, many willingly.

Administrators, too, could take stock. There were still fixtures to fulfil, and TV deals to honour, but the new ICC chairman, New Zealand's Greg Barclay, reached a conclusion that had proved beyond his predecessors: the schedule was "unsustainable". The ECB evidently agreed, reacting to the prospect of 17 England Tests in 2021, plus a T20 World Cup, by getting serious about rest and rotation. That meant fans could not watch the best players all the time, but most understood that Covid was changing expectations.

The ECB's policy was also a humane response to the nightmare of life in a bubble. West Indies took 54 hours to fly to New Zealand, spent a fortnight in quarantine (and were told off for socialising in hotel corridors), then lost almost every game. Towards the end of the IPL, Jofra Archer said he was "counting down the days". South Africa's Kagiso Rabada spoke of a "luxury prison". Australia's Steve Smith said he hadn't slept in his own bed for five months. Worryingly, the Professional Cricketers' Association reported a big increase in the number of players seeking help for mental health issues – and a lack of funds to provide it. After the pandemic subsides, this cannot go on.

Naturally, there were other problems. When Archer popped home to Hove in between bubbles, he was told he had only gone and jeopardised the entire financial wellbeing of English cricket. Counties who had heeded the advice to spruce up their grounds, and host concerts and conferences, were harder hit than those who relied on their ECB handout, which seemed no sort of reward. But the return of crowds in Australia and New Zealand, where the virus had been kept in check, acted as world cricket's vaccine jab. And an all-time classic between Australia and India was pure adrenalin.

By the time England had won 2–0 on their return to Sri Lanka in January, we had another reminder – of the capacity of Test cricket to carry us along, to enthral and absorb us and, perhaps most importantly, to distract us. Boris Johnson had described the cricket ball as a "natural vector of disease". He was missing the point: last year, it carried more hope than threat. There was sadness in 2020, but that was only part of the story.

Inequality street

Jason Holder's West Indians were among the summer's heroes, swapping the calm of the Caribbean for the claustrophobia of UK hotel life, with its cordoned-off dining areas and endless bottles of hand sanitiser. Had it not been for their courage, Ireland, Pakistan and Australia, as well as the West Indian women, might have stayed away, and the ECB's finances would have been in tatters, not merely frayed.

Yet Holder and Co offered more than philanthropy (more, in a bit, of his contribution to Black Lives Matter). At the tour's end, he spoke passionately about inequality in the game, and demolished one of the early platitudes about the virus's spread – that it was indiscriminate, affecting pauper and prince alike. The figures proved this was not the case, and so did cricket.

A predictable theme emerged. England had been grateful for the visits of others, then left South Africa in a hurry, even after two positive Covid-19 tests in their own camp proved false. Australia snubbed Bangladesh, Zimbabwe, West Indies and Afghanistan – but travelled to England, and moved heaven and earth to accommodate India (who had already cancelled series against Zimbabwe and Sri Lanka). At the last minute, the Australians then called off a Test tour of South Africa, who had bowed to numerous demands. The Sri Lankans – who *did* visit South Africa – insisted on strict quarantine rules for Bangladesh, who stayed at home, but relaxed them for England. Ireland were left with almost nothing, and hoped to play their next Test in December, two and a half years after their last. (Crazily, this is saving them money.) Zimbabwe had three Tests in 2020, Bangladesh two, Afghanistan none. New Zealand went top of the rankings, despite only eight overseas Tests since October 2016. As for the West Indians who helped prop up England, they took a 50% pay cut.

Behind the widespread relief that the sport stayed on the tracks, dangers lurk. The IPL now openly dictates the calendar, with inevitable consequences for international cricket: excluding the two eras worst affected by world wars, the 2010s were the first decade to contain fewer Tests than the previous one (despite the existence of more teams than ever). The BCCI, after a period of enforced introspection, were throwing their weight around again, and cosying up to India's politicians. Money, more than ever, is the name of the game. Had England not rearranged their tour of Sri Lanka, or shoehorned in another two-Test series at home to New Zealand, all their Tests in 2021 would have been against India or Australia.

We always knew the playing field wasn't level, but cricket seems happy to ram home the point.

Enough of the excuses

On July 8, at a near-deserted Rose Bowl, the West Indian and England teams took a knee. They were paying tribute to George Floyd, who had died at the hands of Minneapolis police a few weeks earlier, and to the Black Lives Matter message. The West Indians also wore a black glove on a raised fist, just as the American sprinters Tommie Smith and John Carlos had at the 1968 Mexico Olympics. It was quiet, dignified and powerful – and one of the images of the year.

Also that morning, Michael Holding and Ebony Rainford-Brent gave moving accounts on Sky Sports of their own experiences of racism. It was a moment to pause, and reflect. Players past and present had already begun telling stories of prejudice; the trickle became a torrent. The rule of thumb was simple, and brutal: if you weren't white, you had suffered.

For a while, cricket said and did the right things. The ECB admitted they had let things slip, and promised action. And when Ireland visited for three one-day internationals, players on both sides took a knee once more. The idea

The new masters?

On dark mornings in the bleak midwinter came sunshine from a distant land: Australia v India, now reliably the most gripping Test series of the lot. Australia had once avoided the fixture: not until more than 15 years after India's maiden Test, at Lord's in 1932, did Don Bradman's side deign to play them. But recent clashes have been a battle of empires: the game's historical superpower against a team with the potential to oust them. In the other-worldly light of a southern summer, anything seemed possible.

India's 2–1 victory rubbed shoulders with other epic Test series: Australia v West Indies in 1960-61, India v Australia in 2000-01, the Ashes in 2005. Those, though, were all won by the hosts. This was won by a team battling on many fronts: quarantine, Virat Kohli's paternity leave, an injury list that required a second side of A4, crass sledging, and racial abuse from the crowd. Any of these alone might derail a touring side; that India overcame all five made it the most astonishing fightback in Test history.

The transformation was a thing of wonder. At Adelaide, they had been bowled out for 36, and immediately condemned by pundits to a whitewash. By the Fourth Test at Brisbane, where Australia hadn't lost since Bob Hawke was prime minister, India were missing so many bowlers that their attack had over 1,000 Test wickets fewer than their opponents'. To cap it all, they chased down 328.

It shouldn't have been a contest, yet India's strength in depth became the story of the tour, quite possibly of the sport. It was as if they had achieved the ultimate piece of cricketing alchemy, turning the base metals of a huge population and an unrivalled love of the game into gold. In 1992, Francis Fukuyama argued that Western liberal democracy had finally won politics. At the Gabba, it was tempting to imagine India had finally won cricket.

Play the man, not the bauble

Since its creation for the 1963 England–West Indies series, the Wisden Trophy has never been namechecked by the players as often as last summer. The lure of retaining it with a drawn series might even have encouraged Jason Holder to protect his lead: twice bowling first at Old Trafford looked defensive. And then, just like that, one of international cricket's oldest bilateral baubles was gone. In its place would be the Richards–Botham Trophy, after Mike Atherton argued cricket could "do better".

Richards and Botham are names to conjure with. But one was already attached to a Test series: South Africa and West Indies have contested the Sir Vivian Richards Trophy for 20 years. And the other is now attached to one of the few series he never bent to his will: in 20 Tests against West Indies, Ian Botham averaged 21 with the bat and 35 with the ball. In the era of the *Windrush* scandal and the toppling of statues connected to the slave trade, the explanation that their friendship symbolised the link between the Caribbean and Britain was simplistic.

If change really was necessary, there was a more elegant solution. The two men behind the Wisden Trophy were Ken Medlock (whose obituary appears in these pages) and Learie Constantine, the trailblazing Trinidadian all-rounder who rose above racial hostility to settle in Lancashire, and became the UK's first black peer. He was a giant who straddled both cultures, and instinctively grasped the complexity of Anglo-Caribbean relations. The Learie Constantine Trophy would have been perfect.

Parent power

The headline from the women's T20 World Cup final at Melbourne in March was an attendance of 86,174 – the perfect answer to those who say no one watches women's sport. Almost as refreshing was the identity of one of the spectators: fast bowler Mitchell Starc had been given permission to leave Australia's one-day series in South Africa to watch his wife, Alyssa Healy, open the batting. Good decision: she scored a match-winning 75 from 39 balls.

Not long ago, Starc would have been mocked. But cricket is waking up to domestic responsibility. Last summer, Joe Root missed the First Test against West Indies to attend the birth of his second child. Over the winter, Kane Williamson followed suit, skipping New Zealand's Second Test against West Indies for the birth of his daughter. India captain Virat Kohli went even further, flying home to prepare for fatherhood after the first of the four Tests in Australia. As recently as 2003, this Almanack published a piece entitled "Don't marry a cricketer". These days, we might not be so proscriptive.

Hello, old friend

And then there was none. When Ian Bell signed off from first-class cricket with 50 and 90 for Warwickshire at Cardiff in September, it meant every player from the 2005 Ashes had retired. This went beyond nostalgia: among current England cricketers, only James Anderson – who has been an international cricketer since 2002-03, but missed that series – had played a Test on free-to-air television.

The gods of TV scheduling woke up: in February 2021, Channel 4 – for ever linked with the summer of '05 – acquired the rights to England's Test series in India. Providing punditry from a hurriedly assembled studio in London was Alastair Cook, whose entire Test career – 161 games and 12,472 runs – had taken place behind the paywall. Over in Chennai, his successor as England captain, Joe Root, lived up to the occasion, uniquely marking his 100th Test with a double-century, and a memorable win. Channel 4 were spoiling their viewers all over again.

The station's last-minute re-entry into the big time was low on frills, but high on significance. Despite little time to plan their broadcast or spread the word to fans who had almost forgotten watching an England Test on free-to-air telly, they secured a peak first-day audience of 1.1m – more than twice what Sky managed during England's tour of Sri Lanka. By day three, the figure had risen to 1.7m. In all, nearly 6m tuned in. Meanwhile, 44% of viewers were said to come from homes without a Sky subscription. However you spun the numbers – and there were one or two hoping Channel 4 would fall flat on their face – live Test cricket was now more accessible. And with the rights fee going to the BCCI, no one could say the move had cost English cricket anything.

There was concern that the viewership was skewed towards the over-35s, (as if teenagers were going to crawl out of bed at four in the morning). But the understandable clamour for youth has obscured a wider point: cricket is our national summer sport, and over-35s should be able to watch it too. For an older audience, sheltering at home, and less likely than other generations to watch subscription channels, the coverage must have been especially welcome.

Defenders of the paywall regularly employ a straw man argument: English cricket would be nowhere without Sky's money. Yet few argue for a wholesale return to the old times – just a bit more balance. In Channel 4's heyday, Sky would exclusively broadcast one of the home Tests. Why not return the favour?

Anyone up there?

If an England prospect scores a century in front of an empty press box at Grace Road or Riverside, was it ever really scored at all? Journalists are not known for understating their influence, but a decision by the ECB to cut their County Reporters' Network from 18 to six threatened to have more serious consequences for the domestic game than they appeared to realise.

The network itself was an imperfect solution to an intractable problem: with newspapers losing interest in county cricket, the board stepped in to finance the reporting. That fostered a perception that journalists were no longer fully independent, but it was probably a price worth paying. Now, the cost-cutting triggered by Covid-19 has led to an inexorable conclusion – and the possibility that some Championship games in 2021 will not be covered in person at all.

At the time of writing, some counties were planning to fill the holes by paying reporters themselves, which raises more questions about independence. If the people who run the game are less accountable, and the reporting less vivid, the readers will soon lose interest. As for the players, who among them with international ambitions will want to play for a county that lacks media attention? There is already a gap between the haves and the have-nots of the domestic game. It must not become a chasm.

Say Grace

The bronze statue of W. G. Grace at Lord's is not to be sniffed at, but cricket might have missed a trick last summer after a statue of a slave trader, Edward Colston, was torn down by protestors and tossed into Bristol Harbour. As the former *Times* cricket writer Richard Hobson tweeted, the plinth might easily have been filled instead by one of the city's most famous residents. Not Banksy or Cary Grant, but WG, one of Victorian England's biggest celebrities, yet still a peripheral figure in the place he called home.

Better late than never

A year ago, we urged the ICC to reconsider the status of England's five games in 1970 against the Rest of the World, and treat them like Tests – just as those who played in them did. The ICC's position is that the matches were not sanctioned as Tests – only marketed as such by the English authorities, in the hope they would pass muster. But sentimentality, it turns out, is not dead. Fifty years to the day after he made what he thought was his Test debut, Glamorgan's Alan Jones – who didn't play for England again – was surprised on Zoom by a phalanx of ECB officials and old team-mates, and presented with a navy blue cap. He was now, officially, England's 696th Test cricketer. His speechlessness spoke volumes.

It went that way...

An unexpected side-effect of the pandemic was to remind the world's best players how it all began. Was any sight more democratic than Joe Root or Ben Stokes ferreting around in the stands to look for the ball, just as countless village players do every weekend in the shrubbery? As for playing in front of no one, join the club. Our star cricketers can seem remote, but there were moments last year when they were as reassuringly unglamorous as the rest of us.

CRICKET AND CORONAVIRUS

Scraps of comfort

DUNCAN HAMILTON

At various stages during spring and summer, particularly before the season's first ball was bowled, I found myself fretting about the welfare of a stranger. I had come across him the previous September. He was sitting beside the sightscreen at Grace Road. Leicestershire against Northamptonshire was no one's idea of a marquee occasion. It was such a murky, dank morning that the floodlights were soon ablaze. And there were so few people that I could have shaken hands with all of them in less than 15 minutes. This man, however, was conspicuous, to say the least.

Having checked my notes, I have to confess my inadequacies as a news reporter. I'm afraid I can't tell you his name or age (older than me, for certain), or give much of a physical description ("greyish hair" and "thick sweater" is all I scribbled down). I offer a feeble excuse: I was taken aback by what I saw. He was punctiliously recording every ball. And he was relying on old technology: pens, pencils, pencil sharpener, rubber, scorebook pages clipped to a pale brown board. It was like being whisked back into that bygone era, quaintly antiquarian now, when you rubbed linseed oil on your bat, and Blanco on your pads, and F. S. Trueman was a summariser on *Test Match Special*.

I admired his discipline and commitment, both of which demonstrated the seminal role cricket surely plays in his life. I may be hopelessly wide of the stumps here – projecting my own addict's devotion on to someone else – but I am guessing he possesses no ordinary love for it. I am guessing the fixtures, published each winter, are the route map through all his summers. I am also guessing that, as one season ends, he is already hankering after the next.

Snap.

When lockdown was announced, the first round of the County Championship was three weeks away. At this juncture, I have to stop, and then stress that every lovely violin lament for the matches we lost demands perspective. Next to the suffering elsewhere, the local difficulties cricket experienced shrink into insignificance. At the beginning of the pandemic, when it was difficult to absorb the shock of everything, I didn't care whether Essex would retain their title, and I didn't dwell on who might triumph in the War of the Roses at Scarborough. I turned back to cricket only when I couldn't take any more of the present, which made the past the safest place to be. By then, we had become accustomed to that austerely Orwellian term "the new normal". Along with "self-isolation" and "furlough", it had slipped so easily into usage that we seemed to have been saying it for years, and enduring it almost for ever. I longed for the old normal, which is why I took refuge in old books and old matches, scavenged from YouTube.

Duncan Hamilton

Cut, paste... and carry on: Duncan Hamilton's desk, and the tools of his trade.

You'll remember that Mother Nature was absolutely no help. She mocked us from early April until late May, providing unbroken weeks of immaculate sunshine that would have guaranteed hard pitches, big scores, and blisters for any bowler. Like Browning, I've never wanted to be anywhere other than in England during those months, but the fabulous skies and the white blossom only reminded me of what I was missing, and where I ought to have been: Trent Bridge, the sun on my face. I knew others would be feeling what I felt: an ache that was not unlike homesickness. It made me think of the man at Grace Road. How was he bearing up? How had he filled in the blank weeks so far?

Several scenarios crossed my mind. When it seemed distinctly possible that no matches would be played at all, some found unlikely solace in Subbuteo Table Cricket. You would hardly credit the three-figure sums paid on eBay for a game which, devised back in the 1950s, has no graphics or sound effects, and in which nothing gets blown up or shot down. Perhaps he'd been one of the bidders who had beaten me in the auction. One thing common among cricket obsessives is that we covet ephemera. Perhaps he was sorting out his own collection, box by buff-coloured box, as I was mine. Or perhaps he was reliving games through his meticulous scorecards? Hopefully, one day, I'll find out.

I flung myself into full nerd mode: I put together a scrapbook – partly for something to do, partly to preserve the swirl of events, and partly, given the bleak circumstances, as a sort of therapy. The friends I confided in were impeccably polite, but I read their minds: I had gone benignly doolally. I like to think the man at Grace Road, bless him, would have understood my motivation immediately. The scrapbook was the best work I did during the

VILLAGE CRICKET LEAVES LOCKDOWN

Dodging the Sandwich of Doom

MARCUS BERKMANN

My team of crocks and incompetents, the Rain Men, would normally expect to play around 20 games a year, winning at least one. But in 2020, Covid-19 struck. We were all kept indoors for months, watching our DVDs of the 2005 Ashes over and over again. Games were cancelled, and every email referred to "these strange times". I quite enjoyed not having to get 11 players out every Sunday, and had several more hours in the day to do some real work.

But then lockdown was eased, cricket became feasible, and I had to rearrange the fixture list in a rush. We are a travelling team, utterly reliant on the hospitality and good cheer of opponents who will beat us, usually by eight wickets. But with a little nifty footwork, I was able to put together a revised list of 14 games, of which we eventually played all but one.

There were severe limitations on behaviour, many of which seemed faintly ridiculous as time wore on. Because so much hand sanitising had to be done, games started half an hour earlier than usual, and sometimes earlier than that. Pavilions were closed, except for access to the loos, because viruses, while rife in dressing-rooms, prefer to give the lavatorial facilities a miss. Teas could not be provided, in case someone inadvertently ingested the Sandwich of Doom. We tended to follow the lead of our hosts, some of whom used hand sanitiser in industrial quantities, some of whom did not. But everyone was more relaxed by the end of the season than at the start, as it became clear cricket was a sport for which the term social distancing could have been invented. I have been social distancing down at third man for the best part of 40 years.

Our squad, if you can call them that, comprise around 25 to 30 men (and one woman), of whom very few are still as young and vibrant as Wilfred Rhodes the last time he played Test cricket. Last season, maybe a third of our squad turned out very rarely or not at all, while other, more occasional, cricketers started to play more often. So the team altered, or mutated, in the course of the shortened summer, and became more tight-knit than before – and, actually, friendlier as well.

Like most cricket teams (because it's the sort of game that attracts them), we have had a few troublemakers over the years, and one or two out-and-out lunatics who have done well to escape the clutches of the funny farm. But none of these people appeared last year. As well as being more amiable, the team became better at playing the game. We won two matches, and might have won more.

I myself have given up playing because I have developed a tremor in both hands (not Parkinson's, I'm happy to report), which made me drop catches and get out for nought even more than before. But I often go along because I love cricket, and the team are my friends, and I tend to take a long walk in the surrounding countryside while they are fielding. What keeps them all going, I realise, is the knowledge that time is short, that they may injure themselves tomorrow beyond repair, and that every game could be their last. We are all driven by the dying of the light, and in our case we are now 15-watt bulbs. And it's better than playing golf. Anything's better than playing golf.

chaos. Ludicrous as it may sound, the simple task of cutting out newsprint and pasting it into an A3 hardback made me feel closer to cricket – especially when the season was stuck in limbo, and I feared it might not escape.

For one reason or another, every summer is crucial for our game, which is always on a tightrope between relative prosperity and relative penury. Last season would have been no different, except in one vital regard: it was full of possibility. We were travelling optimistically, certain 2020 was about to make the most of the inheritance 2019 had bequeathed. We had won the World Cup, the high drama of the final so defying rational belief that it seems hallucinatory even now. We had relished the Ashes, which rose to sublimity at Headingley, and was so watchable throughout that our gallant failure to snatch the urn didn't take the shine off the series.

We had poster boys – Stokes and Archer – and we would have paid a premium rate just to see them in the nets. Of course, The Hundred was also floating towards us on a cloud of hype. For the sake of purists like me, who can't say its name without choking, I won't linger on the matter. Instead, I'll plagiarise Donald Bradman who, during the Centenary Test at Melbourne, used curt diplomacy to avoid confronting the ghosts of Bodyline: "I will pass over [it]."

You can extrapolate to your heart's content about what might have happened to cricket if Covid-19 hadn't sent the world askew. What *did* happen was this: affection for the game grew abundantly, surprising us all. This isn't a romantic view. The evidence is among the headlines in my scrapbook. Here's what I learned.

Clichés survive as a convenient, brisk shorthand. The headline writers reached for the hoariest of them: the "scent of cut grass"; the "sound of leather on willow"; the cry of "Howzat!", trailing its fat exclamation mark behind it. The clichés evoked what a much plainer headline more memorably described as "Our Beautiful Game". The appreciation of just how beautiful it is, and where it sits in our summer, spread steadily, until few disputed the claim.

The absence of cricket made us more aware of the part it plays culturally and socially, and (though more modestly) in shaping our heritage, our character, our national identity. The return of cricket was so welcome and so consoling that even many of those with a scant or tangential interest in the game forged a connection to it.

Neville Cardus was instrumental in that, almost half a century after his death. He considered himself a slacker, which is hard to comprehend when you tot up the copy he shifted. His work counts as a bespoke product churned out on an industrial scale. I calculate that every season during his Golden Age, which spanned the interwar years, he wrote around 12,000 words a week for *The Manchester Guardian* and a battalion of magazines, illustrious and obscure. In 2020, his entire oeuvre, comprising several million words, was reduced to ten. Would the old boy have minded? I don't think so. Like Oscar Wilde, he regarded not being talked about as purgatory.

You'll know what's coming next. If it hasn't been done already, I suspect we're about to find this sentence emblazoned on T-shirts, tea-towels, coffee mugs and assorted kitsch. *There can be no summer in this land without cricket.*

Stu Forster, Getty Images

Gloveman: Jack Leach carries out twelfth-man duties, wearing PPE – and a smile.

knocked me back – and almost made me feel more ill than I was. But I was confident my fitness levels reduced those risks too. Once I'd got my head round that, I found it easier to deal with. The closest I came to breaching protocols was when I was on twelfth man duty – which I was a lot – and forgot to wear gloves as I ran out with the drinks. I'll never make it as a waiter…

I was also determined to make the most of the situation, and worked hard on my game. I've always used setbacks as motivation, and I wanted to make sure I emerged a better bowler, with a stronger action. As a cricketer, you often feel as if you're on a conveyor belt, with little free time to improve your skills. I think I did that, so my time in lockdown didn't feel like a waste, and I really enjoyed bowling for Somerset in the final of the Bob Willis Trophy. I can't say I missed the bubble.

Jack Leach was talking to Lawrence Booth.

Even the sceptical, who assumed Cardus had been exaggerating, cottoned on. Cricket is not some great triviality, but integral to the fabric of the country: a summer without it is only half-dressed.

Cardus can't take all the credit. Cricket and cricketers seldom made a song and dance out of the crisis. The posture adopted by those governing the game and those playing it was near perfect. In the initial weeks after Covid-19 struck, when everything seemed suspended in unreality, Premier League football found cover in the biosecure bubble of its colossal ego. It indulged in wishy-washy prevarication, and appeared intransigent, self-serving and rapacious, hoarding money the way the rest of us were hoarding loo roll. Cricket was different, but then you could argue it has an unfair advantage: unlike football, it still lives on the same planet as those who pay to watch it. This helped cricket understand from the off what the situation demanded: everyone had to muck in, and compromise. Even the England players took pay cuts.

MCC annually invite some luminary to Lord's to give a lecture on The Spirit of Cricket. That spirit means different things to different people; it is too nebulous to pin down. But how cricket reacted last summer expressed what we've been trying, but failing, to articulate through language alone.

“The least I can do now is support Stanmore, give something back,” says Fraser

If you or I had won a World Cup, we'd have hired bodyguards to protect the shirt we wore. Jos Buttler auctioned his, raising more than £65,000 to treat patients with the virus. Graham Gooch ferried food to hospitals in Essex. Heather Knight signed up for the NHS's volunteer scheme. Sam Billings, also on behalf of the NHS, shaved his head to inspire donations; he was dashing around supermarket aisles too, shopping for anyone in Canterbury unable to leave the house. I could go on listing charitable deeds, each motivated by a willingness to put someone else first, but even *Wisden* can't accommodate the number of pages required to do them all justice.

The story I liked best dug into the grassroots. Angus Fraser picked up a brush and went off to paint the pavilion at Stanmore, the 167-year-old club where he auditioned for his professional career. In the photograph, Fraser seemed to have as much paint on himself as on the walls. He said of Stanmore: “The least I can do now is support it, give something back.” The decency you routinely find in cricket shone through the simplicity of the sentiment. In moments like that, the game stacked up a lot of credit – perhaps more than it realises – just by being itself.

In recent seasons, I have punched away at the ECB, who behave as though the County Championship is one of those products they bought expensively on a whim, and would now like to return to the shop, and swap for something else. But you'd have to be pernickety to find fault in how resourcefully they got the show back on the road, then crammed so much into so few weeks. The ECB were even nobly stoic after Boris Johnson claimed the ball was “a natural vector of disease”. Aware as he spoke, apparently off the cuff, that his claim might not be entirely accurate, our prime minister hastily added "potentially", an inadequate get-out clause. The damage was already done. He'd made a £30 Dukes Select sound as dangerous as an M67 grenade. No wonder we were so gloomy. No wonder our relief was so blissful when England and West Indies came on to the field at the Rose Bowl. The sight was solemn, but uplifting and magnificent enough to melt your eyes. You shut out, if only fleetingly, the Lowry-grey sky and the banks of empty seating.

Vector protector? Nick Newman's cartoon from *The Cricketer.*

The first day of that First Test was too brief a treat: less than an hour and a half's play before the rain squalls turned nasty. We were glad of anything, grateful for the glimpse. We gave the Test due deference because its symbolic nature was obvious. A cricket match – something so reassuringly ordinary – was exactly what we needed. It brought a semblance of order and stability to the summer.

Cricket has always had more support than can be adequately measured. There are fans in absentia, scarcely perceptible, who follow what's going on but seldom declare their interest publicly by walking through the gate. This is only a hunch, which I'd be prepared nonetheless to back with a minor wager: the game accumulated a lot more of them after the attitude it adopted, the sacrifices it made, and the publicity it got.

Helpfully, cricket stepped out from the semi-darkness of the paywall. A Twenty20 international against Pakistan, shown live on BBC, hit a satisfying peak of 2.8m viewers. Who could possibly have forecast that allowing licence-fee payers to sample cricket again would increase awareness of the game? Even if we had to mute the sound to save our ears from the monotonous, bee-like hum of the artificial crowd noise, we couldn't resist the nostalgia of the opening titles. The marimba solo of "Soul Limbo" was suddenly the sweetest music imaginable.

For me, the season's supreme irony was that the truncated Championship, rebranded the Bob Willis Trophy, commanded more media coverage than I can remember since the late 1980s. Perish the thought, but some counties have often given the impression that the rank-and-file stalwart membership, who generally prefer the red ball to the white, are a nagging pain to be tolerated, like mild myalgia. Many members were still unswervingly loyal, donating their subscriptions rather than asking for them back.

While newspapers cranked out endless colour pieces about the novelty of playing matches without them, the members (and, later, all of us) were sitting at home enjoying the brilliant online streaming that brought the action directly to laptop or phone. Again, it broadened cricket's audience, recruiting the

Mike Hewitt, AFP/Getty Images

Official coverage: umpires Richard Kettleborough, Richard Illingworth and a masked Alex Wharf survey a wet Rose Bowl as the season endures – in one respect – a traditional start.

previously unconverted. Some of those who logged on had never been to a four-day game. In fact, if everyone watching had actually been inside the ground at the same time, rather than parked on their sofa, attendances would have been high enough by Championship standards to count as startling. I was even among the 1,500 who caught the climax of the village final at Lord's.

Amid all that good news, and despite all the goodwill cricket generated, I can't pretend the game is about to sweep into a period of renaissance. Far from it. A real struggle lies ahead to repair the rip in its finances, which runs from the top tier to the foundations. I've never noticed a magic money tree in the Harris Garden.

Eventually, history's long gaze will settle on last summer, and reach conclusions we are unable to comprehend now, because it is still too close. The picture we have is in bits, so jumbled it resembles an abstract portrait by Picasso in which the nose is where the mouth ought to be.

But there's one thing we don't have to wait for historians to tell us. What 2020 proved was how much cricket matters, how much we need it, and how dearly we have to protect it. If you still don't believe me, there's a spot you should visit beside the sightscreen at Grace Road. Ask the man you'll find there what he thinks. You'll pick him out quite easily. He'll have a pencil in his hand, and a scoresheet across his lap.

Duncan Hamilton has won the Wisden Book of the Year award three times.

TIMELINE OF A PANDEMIC

Positives and negatives

Mar 3 England say fist-bumps will replace handshakes during the tour of Sri Lanka.

Mar 11 Two World XI v Asia XI matches in Bangladesh on March 21 and 22 are postponed.

England will refuse selfies and autographs in Sri Lanka.

Mar 12 MCC announce formation of Coronavirus Risk Management Group.

Mar 13 ECB postpone Test series in Sri Lanka. "You could see looking at the players that their minds were elsewhere," says England captain Joe Root.

MCC scrap Champion County match, due to start at Galle on March 24.

After one of the crowd tests positive the previous day, Cricket Australia chief executive Kevin Roberts denies it was irresponsible for the women's T20 World Cup final (March 8) to have 86,000 at the MCG.

Australia women's tour of South Africa is called off.

Two remaining India–South Africa ODIs are postponed.

IPL is postponed, at least until April 15.

West Indies suspend their domestic season.

Mar 14 The day after a behind-closed-doors one-day international at Sydney, the Australia–New Zealand ODI series is cancelled; a return T20 series in New Zealand is postponed.

Mar 15 Last round of Sheffield Shield matches is scrapped.

Mar 16 One ODI and one Test in Karachi between Pakistan and Bangladesh are called off.

So are last two rounds of New Zealand's Plunket Shield; Wellington named champions.

All sporting activity is suspended in South Africa.

Mar 17 Sheffield Shield final is cancelled; New South Wales named champions.

Pakistan Super League is suspended after Alex Hales (Karachi Kings) has symptoms.

Mar 18 ECB suspend all recreational cricket indefinitely.

Mar 19 A gin distillery owned by Shane Warne turns production to hand sanitiser.

Mar 20 County season delayed until at least May 28, say ECB.

Former Scotland off-spinner Majid Haq tests positive.

Mar 21 All domestic cricket postponed in Sri Lanka after fears that a match between St Thomas's College and Royal College, attended by thousands, helped spread the virus.

Mar 22 Eight arrested in Kalyan, near Mumbai, for playing cricket during a curfew.

Mar 24 Cricket West Indies call off rest of domestic season; Barbados named champions.

Mar 25 ECB offer home training packages – including ropes, resistance bands and medicine balls – to England men and women players.

Jed Leicester, Getty Images

The time is out of joint: captains at Lynton & Lynmouth CC heed the Covid-19 advice to touch elbows rather than shake hands.

Mar 26 Travel restrictions strand England internationals Lauren Winfield and Amy Jones in Australia – Winfield on honeymoon on Great Barrier Reef, Jones in Perth. They agree not to leave each other behind when flights resume.

Yorkshire furlough a "large proportion" of their staff.

Mar 30 Lancashire chairman David Hodgkiss dies aged 71 after contracting Covid-19; he had attended the Cheltenham racing festival (March 10–13).

Mar 31 ECB announce £61m aid package: counties, county boards and MCC share £40m, with £21m in interest-free loans for grassroots clubs. "The biggest challenge the ECB have faced," says chief executive Tom Harrison.

Apr 3 England's men will make an "initial donation" of £500,000 to ECB and selected good causes. The women take a voluntary salary reduction for April, May and June.

Edgbaston will become Covid-19 testing centre.

Apr 7 Between 20 and 30 men are seen playing cricket at the Chandos recreation ground in Edgware, north London, but run off when police approach.

Apr 13 Zafar Sarfraz, a first-class cricketer for Peshawar, dies from Covid-19, aged 50.

Three jailed in Mumbai (and three on the run), after they are seen playing cricket.

Apr 24 The English season is delayed until at least July 1.

Apr 26 Foreign secretary Dominic Raab, standing in for prime minister Boris Johnson (in hospital with Covid-19), says it is "very difficult" to see outdoor amateur sport before the end of summer, raising the possibility of no recreational cricket in 2020.

Apr 29 Launch of The Hundred is postponed until 2021.

May 5 Harrison says ECB losses could reach £380m. To the parliamentary Digital, Culture, Media and Sport committee, he denies he has "bet the house" on The Hundred.

MCC will not refund 2020 subscriptions.

May 7 ECB announce League Emergency Loan Scheme to provide open-age and junior leagues with loans of up to £50,000, to fund the cost of balls and unrecoverable expenses, such as ground hire, printing of handbooks, and equipment.

May 21 England bowlers train at Chester-le-Street, Edgbaston, Hove, Old Trafford, Taunton, The Oval and Trent Bridge, with strict social distancing and hygiene measures; players have to bring their own balls. "It will be safer than going to the supermarket," says director of cricket Ashley Giles.

May 28 ECB announce there will be no domestic cricket before August 1.

May 29 England name a squad of 55 players for the international programme. Substitutes may be allowed for players suffering symptoms.

May 30 Guernsey stages the summer's first match in the British Isles: a T20 game to raise money for the Covid-19 appeal. A live stream attracts over 84,000 views.

Oliver Dowden, secretary of state at DCMS, says professional sport can return behind closed doors.

Jun 3 The day after West Indies confirm their trip to England, Darren Bravo, Shimron Hetmyer and Keemo Paul elect not to tour, because of concerns over Covid-19.

Jun 9 West Indies land in Manchester, and head to biosecure hotel at Old Trafford for two weeks' isolation.

ICC confirm saliva must not be used to shine the ball.

Jun 12 India call off tour of Zimbabwe the day after cancelling the tour of Sri Lanka.

Jun 13 Former Pakistan all-rounder Shahid Afridi reveals he has contracted Covid-19.

Jun 16 Roberts resigns as chief executive amid dissatisfaction at CA's handling of the crisis.

Jun 17 Batting coach Graeme Hick is among 40 CA redundancies, announced after arrival of Nick Hockley as interim CEO.

Jun 22 England v West Indies will be named the #raisethebat series, with England players wearing the names of key workers with cricket connections on training shirts.

Three of Pakistan squad for England – Haider Ali, Shadab Khan and Haris Rauf – test positive.

Cricket South Africa test 100 players, support staff and board workers: seven positives.

Jun 23 Seven more Pakistan players – Fakhar Zaman, Imran Khan, Kashif Bhatti, Mohammad Hafeez, Mohammad Hasnain, Mohammad Rizwan and Wahab Riaz – test positive. PCB chief executive Wasim Khan says "the tour to England is very much on track".

Prime minister Johnson eases lockdown, but recreational cricket cannot return: "The ball is a natural vector of the disease."

Jun 24 Surrey and Middlesex announce plans for a red-ball match at The Oval on July 26–27.

Jun 29 ECB confirm county cricket will return on August 1.

Jul 1 Conde Riley, president of Barbados Cricket Association, calls for the sacking of Phil Simmons as West Indies coach, after he attends the funeral of his father-in-law.

HOW CRICKET HELPED

Playing for the team

- Durham seamer Chris Rushworth launches a YouTube channel, giving demonstrations of basic cricket skills, aimed at keeping children active. He later runs a half-marathon to raise money for the Solan Connor Fawcett Family Cancer Trust.
- The Tooting branch of Sam's Chicken, owned by Sussex all-rounder Ravi Bopara, offers free food to NHS staff.
- Brothers Irfan and Yusuf Pathan offer free surgical masks to help India's effort. Their father runs a charity that has helped flood victims in Kerala and Gujarat.
- Surrey spinner Amar Virdi joins volunteers from Khalsa Aid, a humanitarian relief organisation, to deliver Punjabi food to staff in the A&E department of Watford General Hospital.
- Umpire Aleem Dar offers free food to the unemployed at his Dar's Delighto restaurant in Lahore.
- Sachin Tendulkar donates 50 lakh rupees (about £50,000) to the Prime Minister's Relief Fund and the Chief Minister of Maharashtra's Relief Fund, set up by the Indian government.
- England captain Heather Knight signs up for the NHS volunteer scheme: "My brother and his partner are doctors, and I have a few friends in the NHS, so I know how hard they are working and how difficult it is for everyone."
- Kent captain Sam Billings says he will shave his head to raise money for the NHS.
- Surrey all-rounder Rikki Clarke becomes an NHS volunteer, delivering shopping and medicine to the vulnerable.
- Jos Buttler puts his World Cup final shirt on eBay to raise funds for the Royal Brompton & Harefield Hospitals Charity. It attracts 82 bids, and sells for £65,100.
- Brisbane Heat's Laura Harris volunteers as an emergency nurse at a hospital in Queensland.
- Afghanistan all-rounder Mohammad Nabi delivers food and basic commodities to the destitute, while leg-spinner Rashid Khan provides food. "We don't need to have deep pockets or be rich to help the needy and poor people," he says. "We just need a heart."
- Commentator Isa Guha says she will stream a weekly Bengali cook-along, using recipes from her late mother's book, *Roma's Recipes*. Proceeds go to Rennie Grove Hospice, the NHS and The British Asian Trust.
- Former England captain Graham Gooch delivers food to NHS workers in 13 hospitals in Essex. "It's been very humbling," he says. "Some of these nurses have been working all hours of the day, so they're the heroes." Essex players help with preparation and delivery of the meals.
- Ben Stokes says he will run his first half-marathon to raise funds for the NHS and Chance to Shine. He was inspired by three trainee army officers – Rob Cross, Rob Treasure and Charlie Newman – who completed half-marathons in their gardens by running up and down the length of a cricket pitch 2,387 times, wearing full kit and carrying a bat.
- A T-shirt designed by then coach Jim Troughton featuring the county's bear-and-ragged-staff badge is marketed by Warwickshire. Proceeds go to Birmingham's Queen Elizabeth Hospital and the NSPCC's Childline service.
- Former South Africa captain Faf du Plessis and his wife, Imari, are involved in a scheme to buy food for 35,000 children affected by the pandemic.
- A bracelet worn during his career by former Bangladesh captain Mashrafe bin Mortaza, now an MP, fetches $50,000 at auction. The money will help build a hospital in Narail, his constituency. The highest bidder immediately returns the bracelet to Mortaza.

Alex Davidson, Getty Images

Safe hands: a player from Indian Gymkhana is thrown the team bottle of sanitiser.

Jul 3 Johnson shifts position on recreational cricket during a phone-in on LBC. "The risk is not so much the ball, though that may be a factor – it's the teas, it's the changing-rooms." He later allows recreational cricket to resume on July 11: "The third umpire has been invoked. Having been stumped on the radio this morning... I sought scientific advice."

Jul 5 *Test Match Special* producer Adam Mountford tweets that his commentary team will not be able to receive cakes from listeners during the biosecure Tests.

Jul 8 International cricket returns after four months: England v West Indies at Southampton.

Jul 16 Jofra Archer is dropped for the Second Test after breaching England's biosecurity bubble by going to his home in Hove. "The ripple effect from this small act could have cost us tens of millions of pounds," says Giles.

Jul 19 During the Second Test, at Old Trafford, the umpires disinfect the ball with wipes after England's Dom Sibley absent-mindedly uses saliva to polish it.

Jul 20 ICC postpone men's T20 World Cup, due to start in Australia in October. India's women pull out of their tour of England.

Jul 22 Surrey women win the London Cup against Middlesex, the summer's first match at The Oval, broadcast on Facebook.

Jul 26 Attendance at Oval friendly between Surrey and Middlesex men is limited to 1,000. Observers from the Sports Grounds Safety Authority, and DCMS, monitor the crowd.

Jul 27 Up to 2,500 will be allowed to watch first two days of two Bob Willis Trophy matches: Surrey v Middlesex at The Oval, and Warwickshire v Northamptonshire at Edgbaston.

Jul 31 Government announce continuation of lockdown restrictions: July 27 plans are shelved.

Aug 7 ICC postpone women's 50-over World Cup, scheduled for New Zealand in February, and move men's T20 World Cup in Australia from 2020-21 to 2022-23. (The 2021-22 tournament remains in India.)

England's white-ball tour of India (September and October) postponed.

Aug 11 Jordan Cox of Kent goes into self-isolation after posing for a photo with fans following a double-hundred against Sussex.

Aug 12 Pakistan's Mohammad Hafeez also goes into self-isolation after posing for a photo with a 90-year-old woman on the Rose Bowl golf course. He rejoins the team bubble a day later after testing negative.

Aug 14 Government lift ban on spectators, raising hopes they will be allowed at T20 Blast games.

Aug 18 South Africa's women pull out of their tour of England.

Aug 25 West Indies' women agree a five-match T20 series at Derby, starting on September 21.

Sep 3 Surrey's T20 Blast match v Hampshire at The Oval has 2,500 Surrey members – the only live audience for a competitive county fixture all year.

Sep 6 The BWT match between Gloucestershire and Northamptonshire is abandoned on the first day after Northamptonshire's Ben Curran tests positive. Though not with the squad in Bristol, he had been in contact with other players.

Sep 19 IPL starts six months late, and in the UAE.

Sep 22 Government restrictions prevent ECB from admitting fans to T20 Blast knockout games.

Sep 25 CA postpone their first Test against Afghanistan, planned for Perth in November.

Sep 28 Bangladesh's three-Test tour of Sri Lanka is off after boards disagree over quarantine.

BCCI president Sourav Ganguly says India still intend to host England in the new year, despite suggestions the tour might move to the UAE.

Cricket South Africa postpone the T20 Mzansi Super League.

Oct 1 ECB confirm Sussex seamer Mitch Claydon missed T20 quarter-final v Lancashire as part of a nine-match ban for applying hand sanitiser to the ball during a BWT match v Middlesex in August. On October 14, Sussex are retrospectively docked 24 points.

Oct 13 Aspiring young cricketers in Bangladesh must send in videos after the board rule face-to-face trials too risky.

Oct 14 England leg-spinner Sarah Glenn reveals she had the virus in April, possibly after a man bumped into her while shopping. "I came home so angry," she says. "I said to my parents: 'If I get ill next week, I'm going to be fuming.' And there I was next week in bed."

Oct 20 Ben Lister, a seamer for Auckland, is cricket's first Covid substitute after replacing Mark Chapman ahead of a four-day game against Otago. Chapman reported feeling unwell, but takes his place on the second day after testing negative.

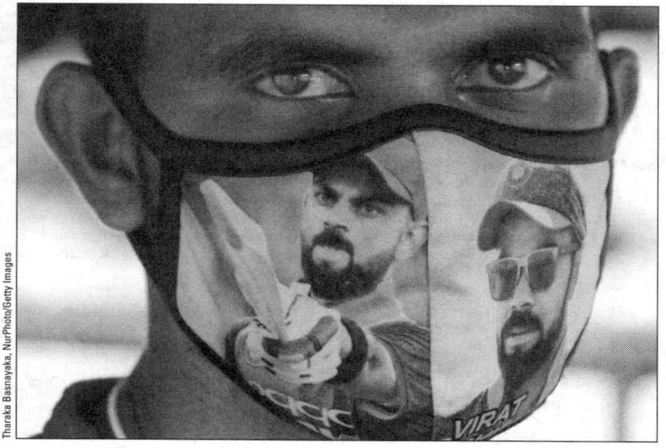

Tharaka Basnayaka, NurPhoto/Getty Images

My inspiration: a fan makes his allegiance clear.

Oct 22 Zimbabwe players Regis Chakabva and Timycen Maruma test positive after sharing a room at the Zimbabwe Cricket Academy at Harare.

India's tour of Australia is set to go ahead after the New South Wales government allow the touring team, and Australian players returning from the IPL, to quarantine in Sydney.

Oct 23 England's 19 centrally contracted men's players agree a 15% pay cut.

Oct 26 The Victoria premier, Daniel Andrews, says he is "very confident" fans will be allowed in to the MCG for the Boxing Day Test after the state lifts a four-month lockdown.

Oct 30 West Indies' tour party begin a fortnight's quarantine in Christchurch, having spent 54 hours travelling from Barbados, via London, Dubai and Auckland.

Nov 2 In South Africa, Warriors withdraw six players from their four-day fixture with Knights at Bloemfontein after two test positive and four more come into contact with them. Warriors miss their transformation targets for the match, fielding only five "players of colour" (not the stipulated six), of whom two are black Africans (not three).

Nov 9 Hampshire's James Vince becomes second Multan Sultans player ruled out of the delayed PSL play-offs because of a positive test, 24 hours after Bangladesh's Mahmudullah.

Nov 10 Bangladesh's Test captain, Mominul Haque, tests positive, showing mild symptoms.

Nov 12 West Indies coach Phil Simmons apologises to the "New Zealand public and the government" after members of the touring party shared food and socialised during a 14-day quarantine. "It's embarrassing," he says.

Nov 18 South Africa isolate Andile Phehlukwayo before their T20 series v England when he tests positive. Close contacts Temba Bavuma and Kagiso Rabada enter self-isolation.

Nov 20 Pakistan seamer Sohail Tanvir and Canadian batsman Ravinderpal Singh test positive after arriving in Sri Lanka for the T20 Lanka Premier League.

ICC change World Test Championship points system after many fixtures succumb to the pandemic. Teams will be ranked on points percentage: India drop to second, behind Australia, whom they had led on points (360 to 296) but not percentage (75 to 82).

Nov 21 A second South African player, David Miller, tests positive.

Nov 26 Six of Pakistan's touring party test positive, two days after arriving in New Zealand. The NZ health ministry say the tourists have been given a "final warning" after breaches of protocol – including socialising in hallways, sharing food and not wearing masks – were caught on CCTV. "I don't know how many times they did that, but it only needs once for us to take a dim view," says Dr Ashley Bloomfield, director-general of health. PCB chief executive Wasim Khan warns his players: "They have told me in clear terms that if we commit one more breach, they'll send us home."

Nov 27 Australia meet India in first ODI, watched by around 24,000, roughly half SCG capacity.

Nov 28 A seventh Pakistani tests positive in New Zealand following a second batch of testing.

Nov 30 Pakistan spinner Raza Hasan is "expelled" from the first-class Quaid-e-Azam Trophy after leaving his hotel without permission.

Dec 2 An eighth Pakistan tourist tests positive.

Dec 4 The first ODI between South Africa and England at Cape Town is called off less than an hour before the toss after a home player, Heinrich Klaasen, tests positive.

Dec 6 The rescheduled first ODI, now in Paarl, is cancelled after two of the England squad receive unconfirmed positive results.

Dec 7 England call off their tour.

Dec 8 England are cleared to fly home after the two unconfirmed positives turn out negative.

Dec 14 A four-day match in South Africa between Titans and Dolphins at Centurion is called off before the start of the second day after a Dolphins player tests positive.

Dec 15 Chris Lynn and Essex batsman Dan Lawrence are fined $A10,000 each, and their Big Bash team Brisbane Heat $50,000, for breaching Covid protocols on an evening out in Canberra. They sat inside without masks, agreed to a selfie with a fan, and took a taxi.

Dec 17 South Africa halt first-class season with two rounds to go, after a string of positive cases.

Dec 18 Two South Africans removed from Test squad to face Sri Lanka after testing positive.

Dec 22 Former India batsman Suresh Raina is arrested in Mumbai after police claim he and 33 others violated a Covid-related curfew. He is taken into custody, then released on bail.

WHEN THE CRICKET STOPS

Hitler, Hedley and Hove

PATRICK KIDD

Had Benjamin Franklin been born 150 years later, and spent more time on his off-cutter than taunting lightning with a kite, he would surely have written of life's three certainties: death, taxes and *Wisden* every spring. But what to do when there is little cricket to fill the pages? No matter how grim the Covid-hit summer of 2020, at least there *was* a season, even if it began in July and ended in October; English professional cricket had not been played so late since 1864 (the year of the first Almanack). Half a century on, though, after war had stopped the game almost everywhere except at school, it was tradition alone that forced the proprietors' hand. "The question of coming out at all was seriously considered," wrote the editor, Sydney Pardon, in the preface to *Wisden 1916*.

Filling it was a challenge, even when reduced from 791 pages to 299. The first *Wisden* had included the rules of quoits, dates from the Wars of the Roses, and a list of canals in Britain and Ireland more than 30 miles long. Between 1916 and 1919, the book was full of death, showing "how great is the number of famous cricketers and of those of great promise who have given their lives for the Empire," as E. B. Noel wrote in his chapter on schools cricket in the 1916 edition. More than 80 pages were devoted to obituaries of the war dead, including Capt. Fergus Bowes-Lyon, the brother of the future Queen Mother, and Sub-Lt Rupert C. Brooke, who headed the bowling averages at Rugby in 1906, and had "gained considerable reputation as a poet".

There were a poignant six lines for Ernest Allen, a staff member of the Cricket Reporting Agency, which put *Wisden* together. He had joined the Scots Guards in the first week of war, and was killed on January 1, 1915. It is possible his death was known when Pardon wrote that year's preface, which mentioned Allen signing up. Either way, the Almanack's convention of recording deaths only from the previous calendar year meant Allen's was not formally noted until 1916. Longer obituaries appeared for A. E. Stoddart, the former England captain who had killed himself, and the Australian hero Victor Trumper, dead from Bright's disease at 37. Meanwhile, 45 pages were spent on the feats of W. G. Grace, who had died at home in south-east London. Legend has it he had been shaking his fists at the Zeppelins, cursing that they were the first opponents he couldn't see.

It was on Dr Grace's urging that cricket had ceased in 1914. On August 3, the day before Britain declared war, Jack Hobbs made 226 in four hours 20 minutes against Nottinghamshire at The Oval. The title was given to Surrey with two of their fixtures unplayed. *Wisden* pointed out that, for Middlesex, unbeaten until nearly a month after the assassination of Archduke Franz Ferdinand in Sarajevo on June 28, "the declaration of War quite upset the county's plans".

The plans of many young men were upset too. The obituaries in 1915 include Lt A. E. J. Collins, killed at Ypres; as a 13-year-old in 1899 he had made 628 not out in a house match at Clifton. Not every detail was accurate. *Wisden* reported that the Rev. A. H. C. Fargus, a navy chaplain and former Gloucestershire fast bowler, had died in the sinking of HMS *Monmouth*. In fact, he had not been on board, having missed a train. Fargus, who took 12 for 87 against Middlesex in 1900, then a record for a Championship debutant, did not die until 1963, but *Wisden* failed to note it until 1994.

For some, war was apparently the least of their worries. The 1915 edition had an advert for Dr J. Collis Browne's Chlorodyne, a remedy for coughs, colds, asthma, bronchitis, spasms, palpitation, hysteria, neuralgia, toothache, rheumatism, gout, fever, croup and ague. It was said to act "like a charm in diarrhoea, colic and other bowel complaints". Whether it was effective against trench foot was unclear.

A sign of the growing gloom can be seen in *Wisden's* reporting on the international game. In 1915, it said Australia were due to tour England in 1916, followed by the visit of South Africa a year later. "This scheme has been upset by the War," it reported. The same information appeared the next year, with one addition: "This scheme has been completely upset by the War." A brutal adverb.

The 1915 Notes by the Editor were pessimistic. "Never before has the game been in such a plight," wrote Pardon. The Notes vanished in 1916 and 1917 (their only absence in the Almanack's history since Pardon introduced them in 1901), so he transferred the gloom to the preface. In 1916, he wrote: "As regards the future the outlook is dark enough." And in 1917, "the outlook for the game" was "as dark as possible". That year's edition was "of necessity a rather mournful volume". Among the obituaries in 1918 was Kent's slow left-armer Colin Blythe, the leading wicket-taker in the season before war.

Still, the old saw prevailed that *dulce et decorum est pro patria mori* (it is sweet and fitting to die for one's country). Lord Hawke, president of MCC, was reported as saying: "When we are once more at peace and able to enjoy our games, the crowd will not discuss what such and such a sportsman did on the playing fields before the War, but what he did for his country during the War." In too many cases, they simply died.

Yet cricket survived, of course. "The long nightmare of the War has come to an end," Pardon wrote in his 1919 Notes, but in its place was something purists also found horrific: reform. As today, ideas for "brightening" cricket buzzed around, such as penalising the batting side for every maiden, ruling a batsman out unless he scored at a set rate, or moving the boundaries in. "Many people seem to regard cricket purely as a spectacle," Pardon complained. And he meant it to sting.

Twenty years later, war again stopped play. On the day Hitler invaded Poland, Hedley Verity, the Yorkshire left-arm spinner, took seven for nine at Hove. "I wonder if I'll ever bowl here again," he said to a team-mate. Verity died of wounds received in action in Italy. Editor Hubert Preston set aside 13 pages for him in 1944.

Long appreciations of the "doings" of the greats – Sutcliffe, Leyland, Hammond and Verity, two years before his death – were one way *Wisden* padded out these war years. And an analysis of all Hobbs's centuries, first-class and otherwise, revealed he first got to three figures in 1901, for Ainsworth against Cambridge Liberals, and was still raising his bat 40 years later, for the Fathers' XI against Kimbolton School.

Pagination again suffered, falling from 875 in 1940 to 343 by 1944. A paper shortage, as well as the publishers' premises being bombed, made this a testing time. Yet the Second World War editions feel different from the First. There is less of the Hawkeian spirit, and not such an overpowering sense of death, in space or tone. Perhaps this reflects a new type of soldier at the front: fewer public schoolboys volunteering to be mown down *pro patria*.

Humour played a greater part, too. A sign was pinned to the gate of "a certain South Coast ground" after a bombing: "Each peardrop which fell on this ground saved lives and property. We shall carry on. Nothing which falls from the skies will deter us except RAIN." *Wisden* readers might also have enjoyed learning of some rare failures in the 1940-41 Australian season for Don Bradman, which moved the Almanack to employ an uncharacteristic exclamation mark: "Twice he was out first ball!"

One reason for the change in tone between the wars was the amount of cricket for the star players. There may have been no Tests or County Championship, but the best cricketers regularly turned out for clubs, services teams and representative sides such as London Counties or the British Empire XI. Ernest Bevin, the labour minister, requested MCC to send a team to the North, saying it would be good for morale.

The 1942 Notes lamented that "cricket without competition [is] a snack, not a meal", but there were thrilling matches. Eton beat Harrow by one wicket in 1940: with the scores tied, three maidens were bowled, two balls seemed to pass through the stumps, and a catch was dropped. In 1942, Cambridge

CONTENTS.

Book of record: deaths, including a tribute to WG, took up almost half *Wisden 1916*.

beat Oxford from the penultimate delivery. A year later, the British Empire XI beat the RAF by one run off the last.

As before, *Wisden* rebuked those who sought to use the war to reform the game. Lancashire proposed a regional championship, and others a Lord's final, a scheme that took eight decades to come to fruition. A one-day competition was also mooted, an idea the Almanack compared to "the new clockwork monkey in the nursery". While some might delight in seeing the ball hit "far, high and often", the Notes grumbled, "such spectators are, frankly, not wanted at county cricket". R. C. Robertson-Glasgow, an eloquent harrumpher, returned to this theme in 1945, writing that, for his money, seeing 20 for no wicket was a finer way to spend an hour than 60 for five. "The three-day match is a thing of hope," he pleaded.

And here is the biggest difference between *Wisden's* two wartime periods. In the 1940s, there is a much greater optimism. With reduced expenses, and many members still paying their subscriptions, nearly all the counties ended the war in a healthier financial position, whereas the first conflict had almost seen the end of some, notably Gloucestershire and Worcestershire. This message shines out in an essay by H. S. Altham, the cricket historian, in 1940. He ends by describing a visit to Lord's, sandbags everywhere, the Long Room stripped bare. And yet: "The turf was a wondrous green, old Time on the Grand Stand was gazing serenely at the nearest balloon, and one felt that somehow it would take more than totalitarian war to put an end to cricket."

Since all *Wisden* readers obviously enjoyed a classical education, he concluded with a line – in Latin only – from Horace, the poet who had also written the *dulce et decorum est* mantra that inspired the Great War generals. Altham's choice was more positive: *Merses profundo, pulchrior evenit* (You may drown it in the depths, but it rises the more glorious). So it was for cricket in 1940, so it will be 80 years later.

Patrick Kidd is editor of the Times's *Diary column, and author of* The Weak are a Long Time in Politics.

THE 1918–20 SPANISH FLU PANDEMIC

The silent killer

STEVEN LYNCH

Long before lockdowns, masks and R-numbers ruled our lives, there was Spanish flu, a pandemic that took hold from 1918 to 1920 in three distinct waves. Despite its name, it originated in America: the Spanish king, Alfonso, was an early high-profile sufferer, while the press in neutral Spain, unfettered by wartime restrictions, gave it greater coverage, creating the impression that it was the epicentre of the disease. Around a third of the world's population was infected, and estimates of deaths range from 17 to 100 million. One casualty was the infant twin brother of a New Yorker who died 100 years later of Covid-19.

Some sports were badly hit: in the United States, the Major League Baseball programme was cut short in 1918, and ice hockey's Stanley Cup abandoned mid-finals the following year. But British sport, particularly cricket, seems to have carried on. One reason was that, after four grim years of conflict, sport's resumption conveyed a return to something like normality. Indeed, the flu may have hastened the end of the Great War, since its effects were more keenly felt on the European mainland. Even so, an estimated 228,000 Britons succumbed to the virus.

You might expect contemporary *Wisdens* to have given the Spanish flu some space – but it is hardly mentioned. Sydney Pardon, in his Notes in 1919, is too exercised by the "sad blunder" of restricting the first post-war Championship to two days, with longer playing hours. The pandemic also goes unremarked in the county section, but the schools reviewer did thank the masters who had helped him, "some of them with influenza in their houses".

Around 20 obituaries in the 1919 and 1920 Almanacks cite "influenza" as the cause of death; since other illnesses are rarely mentioned, it seems safe to assume most of these were Spanish flu victims. Much the most famous was Reggie Schwarz, one of a phalanx of South African googly bowlers who had overwhelmed Plum Warner's England 4–1 in 1905-06. Schwarz, who was born in Kent and played rugby for England, died in France just seven days after the Armistice in November 1918, aged 43. Two other first-class players look likely casualties: Arthur Houssemayne du Boulay, who played nine games for Kent, Gloucestershire and MCC, and once scored 402 not out for the School of Military Engineering; and Hugh Jones, who never got the chance to add to his solitary appearance for Gloucestershire in 1914.

It might now seem odd that *Wisden* underplayed the pandemic a century ago. But it no doubt reflected the national mood: amid the euphoria surrounding the end of the war, an outbreak of illness – however widespread – was not going to get in the way.

STUART BROAD TAKES 500 TEST WICKETS

Almost like telepathy

JAMES ANDERSON

It seemed written in the stars. Over the past decade and more, our careers have become so intertwined that Stuart's 500th Test victim just had to be Kraigg Brathwaite, the man I dismissed to reach the same milestone in 2017.

After the first innings of the final Test against West Indies in Manchester last summer, there was chat in our dressing-room about whether it really would be Brathwaite. Stuart was on 497, so a lot had to fall into place, but we all had a feeling it was going to happen, and that grew when he claimed the first two wickets on the third evening – with Brathwaite still there. When Stuart trapped him leg-before on the final morning, after rain washed out the fourth day, it was amazing to be out in the middle, so much so that the Covid-19 protocols went out of the window: I had to give him a hug. We have shared many experiences, but none more special than that.

It's true, I believe, that you don't really think about your own numbers: they are simply part of maintaining focus on what you are trying to achieve. But when it's your mate, you feel proud. It probably provided me with an insight into how he was feeling when I got my 500th, or when Azhar Ali edged to slip

THE DOUBLE ACT

	T	*Balls*	*Wkts*	*Avge*
Broad (with Anderson)	120	24,719	435	28.02
Broad (without Anderson)	24	4,441	82	25.13
Anderson (with Broad)	120	26,457	484	25.01
Anderson (without Broad)	37	7,474	122	32.92

Their combined total of 919 wickets in Tests played together is exceeded only by Shane Warne and Glenn McGrath (1,001). The next-best by a pair of fast bowlers is 762, by Curtly Ambrose and Courtney Walsh.

for my 600th at the end of the Third Test against Pakistan. What matters more than statistics is being in the dressing-room with the guys after amazing wins like the one over the Pakistanis in Manchester. That's why we play the game: to create memories, and cherish them. One day, we will look back on everything over a glass or two of red wine.

People will have their own thoughts on Stuart's best spells, and the eight for 15 in the 2015 Ashes win at Trent Bridge was outstanding. For me, though, that was a scenario loaded in his favour: the first morning of a Test, at his home ground, in bowler-friendly conditions. Don't get me wrong: it was an amazing performance. But, in my view, the spells that really stand out have occurred when England have needed someone to change the course of the match. That's when he has risen to the occasion.

Gareth Copley, Getty Images

Select band: Stuart Broad takes the wicket of Kraigg Brathwaite, his 500th in Tests.

The Oval in 2009 springs to mind. The game felt as if it was drifting away; then Stuart came on. He trapped Shane Watson, bowled Ricky Ponting, and had Mike Hussey lbw, one of those streaks for which he has become renowned: five for 37 in all, and suddenly we had control of the match – and the series. Then there was Durham 2013, another Ashes match. Again, the game was not going for us, but he blew Australia's batting away in the fourth innings. I took the final catch at mid-off to dismiss Peter Siddle, and Stuart finished with a six-for. It says something about a player's ability and character when the performances team-mates can recall most readily took place with the game in the balance, or the opposition on top.

Another example came earlier in 2013, when we were bowling together against New Zealand at Lord's. They were chasing 239, but Stuart got seven for 44, and we dismissed them for 68. It was one of those days when I knew he was on a roll. He went at four an over, but looked a threat every ball, and it was my job to dry up the runs at the other end to allow him to keep attacking. That was a good example of how our partnership works at its best.

A lot of people talk about leading an attack, the implication being that it is one bowler who does the job. But I believe we have done it together, trying to get the team into a good position early in every innings. The first time it struck me how we could complement each other was at the start of the 2010-11 Ashes, when we combined really well at Brisbane. We didn't take a wicket in that spell, but Hussey said afterwards it was one of the toughest he had faced in Test cricket. That gave us a huge amount of confidence. Stuart got injured as we went 1–0 up at Adelaide, and missed the rest of the series, but it felt like the start of something: we were working out what we wanted to achieve as a pair.

BROAD IN NUMBERS

The seizer and shaper

ANDY ZALTZMAN

Stuart Broad's dismissal of West Indies' Kemar Roach on the third evening of the Third Test at Old Trafford was not the wicket that attracted most attention last summer. It was understandable: a nightwatchman, an empty stadium, Broad still one short of 500. Statisticians, though, banged their abacuses in appreciation: it took his average below 28 for the first time, in his 140th Test. For much of his career, he has in fact been a mid-20s bowler: from 2011 until the end of last summer, he took 415 wickets at 25. But his career average hovered above 30 for more than 70 Tests, then pottered around in the high 20s. All the while, Broad evolved into one of cricket's greatest game-changers, a seizer and shaper of pivotal moments. Beneath the cloak of that career average (27.56 after the Sri Lankan tour in early 2021) lurk some extraordinary figures.

His numerical narrative can be split into four phases – two moderate, two exceptional. They tell a story of improvement and persistence similar to James Anderson, his partner in the exclusive Half-a-Thousand-Wickets club. The Broad of Phase 1, from his debut at 21 in 2007-08 until an injury-ruined 2010-11 Ashes, was unremarkable, despite some sumptuous lower-order runs. His bowling average (35), not helped by learning his craft in an era of batting dominance, was the 19th-best of the 25 Test seamers who took most wickets in that period. Seldom a major influence, he claimed less than three per Test,

THE STUART BROAD PHASEBOOK

		T	*O*	*R*	*W*	*BB*	*5I*	*10M*	*Avge*
1	Dec 2007 to Dec 2010	34	1,115.3	3,489	99	6-91	3	0	35.24
2	May 2011 to Feb 2016	57	2,032	6,056	234	8-15	12	2	25.88
3	May 2016 to Jan 2018	23	774.4	2,161	66	4-21	0	0	32.74
4	Mar 2018 to Jan 2021	30	937.5	2,544	118	6-31	3	1	21.55
		144	**4,860**	**14,250**	**517**	**8-15**	**18**	**3**	**27.56**

and averaged almost the same in victory (27 in 16 matches) as defeat (28 in five). Yet within his prolonged apprenticeship came the first of the golden-armed eruptions that define his career – an Ashes-winning rout, in his 22nd Test, of Australia's top order at The Oval in 2009.

The improved, Phase 2 Broad – finally able to ditch his unhelpful "enforcer" tag, and bowl a fuller length – emerged in 2011: a haul of 25 wickets at 13 against India, followed by 13 at 20 against Pakistan in the UAE, the first overseas series in which he averaged below 30. In Phase 2, which lasted until 2015-16, his average of 25 was the fifth-best of the 25 leading seamers. He averaged over four wickets per Test, dominated at home (152 wickets at 24 in five summers), and did pretty well on tour (82 at 28).

His performances had become central to England's fortunes. In victory, Broad took 5.3 wickets per match, and averaged 17 (Anderson's figures were 4.5 and 22); in defeat, he averaged 34. (Curiously, his one-day career slid in the opposite direction: Phase 1 Broad took 111 ODI wickets at 23; Phase 2 Broad 48 at 42. That was the end of his white-ball international career.) But the influence and regularity of his eruptions set him apart. He took four or more wickets in a spell on nine occasions, including another two Ashes-winning masterpieces: Chester-le-Street in 2013, Trent Bridge in 2015. England's other seamers managed five such spells between them: Steven Finn twice; Anderson, Tim Bresnan and Chris Jordan once each. Broad's hot streaks have scorched as toastily as any bowler. Fifty men have taken four wickets in a Test innings 25 times or more. Broad's average of ten in his 41 four-wicket innings is the best of the lot, pipping Curtly Ambrose and S. F. Barnes. When he takes six or more, he averages seven – the best of the 26 bowlers with at least eight six-fors. He has been exceptional among the exceptional.

Phase 3 Broad, from the 2016 summer to an ineffective 2017-18 Ashes, was significantly diminished. Anderson was at his peak and, while there was a shift in the Test game towards bowlers, Broad's figures drifted towards Phase 1 levels. He had the 17th-best average (32) of the 25 leading seamers, and was again taking less than three wickets per Test. He had no five-wicket haul in two years. A spate of dropped catches hardly helped; nor did a tendency to bowl back of a length with the new ball. The magic, it seemed, had gone.

Once more, he rewarded the selectors' patience. The launch of Phase 4 Broad, from the tour of New Zealand early in 2018, was gradual at first. But after shortening his run-up in search of more rhythm, and making his action more side-on in search of extra swing, he picked up 30 wickets in the summer of 2019, including Australian opener David Warner seven times – a surgical, round-the-wicket demolition. A good winter followed: 18 at 24, his second-best average for a Test winter, behind 2015-16. Despite his frugality, however, bowling averages around the world were tumbling too. And, in the continuing absence of those Broadian eruptions, his omission from the First Test against West Indies in Southampton was not the most unreasonable selectorial axe his family had ever suffered (see father Chris's dropping in 1988).

His response was sensational: 29 wickets at 13, the best home-summer average by an England bowler (with at least 25) since Derek Underwood's 30 at ten in 1969. In seven consecutive innings, Broad picked up three or more, one short of the England record, held by Barnes and Maurice Tate.

Time will tell whether the last five Tests of the 2020 summer marked the high point of Phase 4 Broad, or the beginning of Phase 5, in which he combines those incandescent spells with the relentless pressure of a technical and tactical master. Either way, he has been an outstanding Test bowler, one half of an extraordinary partnership. Peak Stuart Broad has been one of the best of his generation. Peak-peak Stuart Broad has been one of the most destructive, highest-impact bowlers in Test history.

Andy Zaltzman is a comedian, podcaster and Test Match Special *scorer and statistician.*

BROAD'S LANDMARK WICKETS

				Test No.	Career average	Avge for last 100
1	W. P. U. J. C. Vaas	v Sri Lanka at Colombo (SSC)	2007-08	1	73.00	–
100	N. L. T. C. Perera	v Sri Lanka at Cardiff	2011	35	35.94	35.94
200	M. J. Clarke	v Australia at Manchester	2013	60	31.54	27.14
300	C. J. L. Rogers	v Australia at Nottingham	2015	83	29.57	25.65
400	T. W. M. Latham	v New Zealand at Auckland	2017-18	115	29.30	28.50
500	K. C. Brathwaite	v West Indies at Manchester	2020	140	27.98	22.70

And it really has been as a pair, because I don't think I would have got anywhere near 600 without him. Our relationship has been that important. We work out opposition batsmen and conditions together; sometimes it's almost like telepathy. It might sound like a small thing, but having him at mid-off when I'm bowling, and vice versa, makes a huge difference. When I first played Test cricket in 2003, bowlers would drift down to fine leg between overs, and leave the guy at the other end to get on with it. Nasser Hussain, the captain, was at mid-off, and he was the one you would take instructions from. But I feel it makes more sense to have the other bowler there, to make sure you are both doing the right thing. The constant input – throwing ideas around, sharing information – is invaluable. Is the ball swinging? Is it moving off the seam? When should I use the bouncer?

Stuart also senses the slightest doubt in a batsman's eyes, and can pounce. David Warner was struggling against him during the 2019 Ashes, and Stuart played it perfectly. Even before play, Warner would ask him: "Mate, are you trying to swing the ball, nip it back, or what?" Stuart just replied: "Dunno, mate." He relished Warner's uncertainty – and got him seven times at a cost of 35 runs. When a batsman comes up to you and starts talking like that, you know you have a grip on him.

I've referred to Stuart as a streak bowler, and that's partly to do with his belief that he can get anyone out at any time. But he is a lot more consistent than that: you don't get 500 Test wickets by going on the odd streak. Yes, the

ENGLAND'S 200-WICKET SEAMERS, HOME AND AWAY

		Home			Away			
W		*T*	*W*	*Avge*	*T*	*W*	*Avge*	*Diff*
606	**J. M. Anderson**	**89**	**384**	**23.83**	**68**	**222**	**31.39**	**7.55**
517	**S. C. J. Broad**	**82**	**334**	**25.54**	**62**	**183**	**31.24**	**5.70**
383	I. T. Botham	59	226	27.54	43	157	29.63	2.09
325	R. G. D. Willis	41	176	23.50	49	149	27.20	3.70
307	F. S. Trueman	47	229	20.04	20	78	26.08	6.04
252	J. B. Statham	37	148	22.77	33	104	27.79	5.02
248	M. J. Hoggard	33	122	30.73	34	126	30.26	–0.47
236	A. V. Bedser	32	167	21.55	19	69	32.98	11.43
234	A. R. Caddick	33	128	30.07	29	106	29.70	–0.37
229	D. Gough	32	124	29.66	26	105	26.90	–2.76
222	S. J. Harmison	32	133	28.47	30	89	37.12	8.65
219	A. Flintoff	40	109	36.11	38	110	30.60	–5.51
202	J. A. Snow	37	140	29.21	12	62	20.91	–8.30

Only two England spinners have taken 200 wickets: D. L. Underwood (297) and G. P. Swann (255).

Patrick Eagar, Popperfoto/Getty Images

Hot streak: Ricky Ponting, bowled for eight at The Oval in 2009, was wicket No. 60.

that's part of what makes him so dangerous: I don't know if he always feels it, or if it is simply instinctive, but he clearly loves the big occasion. Yet his all-round ability as a bowler should not be undersold.

In his early days, there was talk of him being England's enforcer. But whether it has been roughing batsmen up, as he did back then, or outwitting them with the skills he can call on now – an ability to swing the ball, and nip it off the seam – he is able to adapt to any surface or situation. In Test cricket, you cannot sit still. For example, he's used wobble seam for a while, but there are different types of wobble. Some bowlers use scrambled seams, where the ball might land either on the seam or on the leather, and the bounce becomes unpredictable. Then there is a variation in which the ball goes a fraction off straight. He's worked hard on both.

In the last couple of years, he's also put in a lot of work on his action and run-up, to get the ball to swing away from the right-hander; it was something he spent hours on in the nets with Peter Moores during lockdown. As a consequence of challenging the outside edge, he has tended to bowl fuller, and we saw that pay dividends against West Indies and Pakistan.

He has kept developing, and I would argue that only now is he approaching his peak. He's 34, so people may think he's on the other side of the hill, but that need not be the case. I got better after I turned 34: there's no reason he can't go on to greater things. And, like me, he is fortunate in the way he is built: bowling doesn't seem to take a huge amount out of him. He doesn't wake up stiff and sore after long spells in the field.

He also has an ability to channel emotions, and use them positively. Being left out of the First Test against West Indies last summer hit him hard. He was upset and angry. Had I been in his position, I think I would have felt the same. To be left out after a brilliant couple of years – a successful Ashes, and an amazing tour of South Africa, where he led the attack superbly – meant he felt let down.

But, characteristically, he was determined to show the selectors that they had made the wrong decision: the next five Tests brought 29 wickets at 13. If I had to name the quality I admire most, it would be resilience. His bloody-mindedness is extraordinary. Whenever there has been a question mark placed next to him over the past 15 years, he has answered it.

That's the Stuart Broad I know and love: never better than when he's proving the world wrong.

By January 2021, James Anderson had played 120 of his 157 Tests with Stuart Broad. He was talking to Richard Gibson.

250 YEARS OF CRICKET BATS

Where there's a willow...

JON HOTTEN

In late September 1771 at Laleham Burway, Thomas "Daddy" White of Chertsey walked out to face the bowlers of Hambledon lugging an unusual bat. It was half as wide as it was long – broad enough, once he took guard, to obscure the entire wicket. Perhaps he was being serious, maybe mischievous, even satirical; 250 years on, his precise intent remains misty.

What we do know is that Hambledon and Chertsey met seven days later on Broadhalfpenny Down, and the bat did not appear again – then or ever. That afternoon at Laleham Burway had shown the game a path it should not – *could not* – contemplate. The match had been a good old dust-up: two days long, with each team putting £50 into a winner-takes-all kitty, and far heavier gambling among the crowd; Hambledon triumphed by "a single notch".

Next day, blood was still high, mostly over Daddy and his bat. The counter-attack was led, naturally, by a bowler, Thomas Brett, "beyond all comparison, the fastest as well as straitest ever known", as John Nyren would describe him half a century later. Brett's letter of protest was endorsed by the signatures of "The General" Richard Nyren – father of John, proprietor of the Bat & Ball Inn and captain of Hambledon – and of John Small, star batsman of the day.

Patrick Eagar, Popperfoto/Getty Images

Not tempted? At Old Trafford in 1976, John Edrich passes an outsize bat to West Indies' Deryck Murray after a member of the crowd had given it to him; umpire Lloyd Budd seems perplexed.

(Four years later, Small was rushing Hambledon to victory at the Artillery Ground, this time alongside Daddy White, in a five-a-side game against Kent, when "Lumpy" Stevens got one past his bat, and neatly through the gap between the two stumps. It happened twice more. Lumpy cursed his luck; another new regulation was needed.)

Brett's letter consisted of a single, deadly sentence: "In view of the performance of one White of Ryegate on September 23rd that ffour and a quarter inches shall be the breadth forthwith." The word "performance" works as sharply as a stiletto; indignation remains in that misspelled "ffour". The bat slipped into history, only to reappear as a practical joke. In the heat and fury of the Old Trafford Test against West Indies in 1976, a member of the crowd handed John Edrich a bat as wide as the stumps, while Brian Close looked on. Then, before the 1997 Ashes, the *Daily Mirror* manufactured a gotcha photograph of the out-of-form Australian captain Mark Taylor next to a metre-wide bat; in the First Test, after 21 innings without a half-century, he made 129.

Man and willow go back perhaps 10,000 years

Meanwhile, The General ordered construction of "an iron frame, of the statute width… kept by the Hambledon club". It was the game's first bat gauge. Four and a quarter inches was written into the 1774 edition of the Laws, and has held fast ever since.

The bat had not long been straight, its form responding to the urges of a game in which underarm bowlers skimmed a "three-quarter length", a new strategy where the ball bounced rather than rolled, and one that demanded to be met. Small had led the way, compiling scores that, by the rickety standards of the 18th century, set him apart. And he was not simply a batsman but a batmaker, literally shaping the future of the game. The weight of the cudgels that came from his workshop in Petersfield, Hampshire, was a daunting 5lb. But Small was, according to John Nyren, "as active as a hare", and noted for wristy strokeplay. Batsman and bat had begun their symbiotic journey.

England offers the damp soil and moderate climate in which *salix alba*, the white willow, can flourish. Man and willow go back perhaps 10,000 years, when basic tools were fashioned from its tough but pliable wood. Among its cultivars is *salix alba caerulea*, a supreme piece of natural engineering, its trunk a network of tubes that draw sustenance from root to leaf as efficiently as possible. It grows quickly, over a metre a year, and the fabled grains that run the length of the bat are the growth circles of the tree, each representing a year of life: the closer they are, the slower the growth. Veteran batmakers can pick the hotter summers by the depth of colour in the grain. Other types of willow, and wood with similar density, such as poplar, have been tried. But *salix alba* is uniquely suited to cricket. That said, *caerulea* cuttings sent to Australia grew too quickly in the drier climate, producing a brittle wood. In New Zealand, stronger winds fatally weakened the trees as they matured. From *salix alba caerulea* grown in England comes every high-grade cricket bat in the world.

Small used white willow for his bats but, as batmakers would for the next century or so, he took the dark heartwood from the centre of the cleft – the dead, heavy part of the tree that gave early bats their weight and colour.

Topical Press Agency/Getty Images

Logging an interest: Jack Hobbs selects the raw material for a new bat, 1922.

A sporting goods firm belonging to Victorian industrialist George Gibson Bussey began using the sapwood from the outer part of the trunk, much lighter in colour and density. It was a leap forward. A slender blade, easier to manipulate, coincided with the revolution in technique brought about by W. G. Grace and the Golden Age. "There was a prevailing idea at the time that, as long as a bowler was straight, a batsman could do nothing against him," said Grace. "That idea I determined to test."

Grace sensed the personality of a good bat. When a favourite broke, he wrote to its maker, L. J. Nicolls of Robertsbridge, plaintive over its loss. Bussey called one model the "Demon Driver". Jack Hobbs sold bats from his shop in Fleet Street embossed with his name. Bill Ponsford christened his beefy blade "Big Bertha". Here were the first hints of a deepening connection between batsman and bat, of an idea that it was not merely a physical tool but a psychological one, too.

That notion would take perhaps a century to coalesce, as the bat entered an evolutionary hibernation, a simple form that a good pod-shaver could produce in a couple of hours. Decades passed: the war-ruined 1940s, the monochrome 1950s, the stolid 1960s. And then it came, the bat's cultural revolution, a decade or so after everyone else.

The atom-splitting moment emerged from golf, where new hollow-backed irons were found to be more forgiving to the amateur player than the small clubfaces used by the pros. Arthur Garner, a South African golf club engineer, and his business partner Barrie Wheeler, went to Gray-Nicolls with the idea that a hollow back might also create a larger sweet spot on a cricket bat. John Newbery, a young batmaker, shaped a prototype, while Robert "Swan" Richards expanded the brand in Australia, talking Ian Chappell into using a Scoop during the 1974-75 Ashes. An era began.

The GN100, as the Scoop was officially named, remade the emotional connection between batsman and bat. Its sleek, futuristic design, capped by the idea of painting the hollowed-out part of the spine red, made it an object of desire. Like cars and guitars, the Scoop started to tap its market. New and daring experiments followed. Stuart Surridge came up with the Jumbo, a great shark's fin of extra willow left on its back. Duncan Fearnley made the Magnum, a railway sleeper created to bludgeon bowling into oblivion. Slazenger enhanced the spine to create the V12, which sounded like a missile. The bright flare of Australia's St Peter, with its bold SP logo on a bat whose back was flattened down, burned briefly, and was paired with its trademark mitten gloves; the marketing campaign was led by an almost naked Tony Greig.

This carnival of innovation reached a mad high point at Perth

These bats fell into the hands of newer, cooler cricketers, who grew their hair, wore sweatbands and gold chains and open shirts, joined Kerry Packer, and played under floodlights in coloured clothes and space-age helmets. A once sepulchral, black-and-white world was alive again. The imperious Vivian Richards spun the Jumbo in his hands as he walked out to bat. Ian Botham swung Fearnley's Magnum, and Viv later joined him. Graham Gooch used both. The Scoop had generations of swashbuckling acolytes, from the immortal Hampshire opening combo of Barry Richards and Gordon Greenidge, to Brian Lara, who used it for his 375 and 501 epics.

Gray-Nicolls carved a bat with four scoops instead of one; with it, David Gower hit his first ball in Test cricket to the boundary. Newbery, now with his own eponymous marque, invented the Excalibur, with its shoulders shaved away, brandished by the mighty Lance Cairns. Bob Willis adopted Fearnley's offbeat Run Reaper, a bat with tiny holes drilled through, on an aerodynamic whim. This carnival of innovation reached a mad high point at Perth in 1979-80, when Dennis Lillee hurled his aluminium ComBat across the field after the umpires upheld a complaint from Mike Brearley that it was damaging the ball. More than 200 years after Daddy, Lillee led to another rewriting of the Laws: the bat's blade must be made of wood.

We are now living through a third, perhaps final, revolution. It began in India a few years into the new millennium, when bats began to put on muscle, a reaction to a muscular new game. Batting's greatest technical advance since Grace was urged by short-form cricket, specifically T20's mantra that every ball is an event. Innings such as Chris Gayle's 57-ball 117 at the 2007 World T20, Yuvraj Singh's six sixes off Stuart Broad a week later, and Brendon McCullum's 158 on the first night of the IPL in 2008, opened eyes. This revolution occurred first in the minds of players who believed new things were possible, even in an ancient game. Once again, the bat responded.

Patrick Eagar, Popperfoto/Getty Images

Armed to the teeth: Ian Chappell and his Scoop, 1974.

Prime willow was pressed more lightly, durability sacrificed for thick, sweeping edges that curved like ellipses, taking weight from the shoulders to pack girth behind the sweet spot. (In 2017, MCC responded to complaints that miscues were flying for six by limiting the edge to 4cm.) Faces were flattened, even concave, to make them appear broader (Daddy White would have smiled). As players glanced down at their bat, they saw something that *looked* as if it was going to hit the ball a long way. The batmaker Chris King once said, "fast cars look fast", which summed up the new confluence of psychological and physical aggression. Spectators and commentators were flummoxed at first. "These big, heavy bats" became a way of explaining how hard and far the ball was being hit. Except the bats weren't heavier. If anything, they were lighter: the wood that makes them is less compacted, drier and more voluminous, sprung with the trampolining force that powers the ball from the blade. A good one may last a pro anywhere between 200 and 1,000 runs. A top batsman may once have taken two on a winter tour; now, it may be a dozen.

As a physical object, the bat might have been pushed as far as it can go. It works at the maximum efficiency that can be had from a natural substance; unlike golf clubs or tennis racquets, it is constrained by the materials that can be used. Its future lies in the psychological, in how its look and language make its users feel.

Its look may change a little with novel interpretations of old themes. Its language is nothing short of a fecund lingua franca, the bat's size and shape fetishised as deep, sleek, massive. The names of bats are like the names of cars, strange and suggestive: the Recurve, the Uzi, the Finback, the Gladiator, the Colossus, the Mjolnir, the Oblivion Slayer, the Rogue, the Rumpus, the Ghost… They imply not just what the bat is and what it does, but chime with the self-image of its purchaser. The bat in your hand says something about how you play – and possibly even who you are.

Jon Hotten is the author of several books, including Bat, Ball and Field, *forthcoming from HarperCollins.*

THE END OF KOLPAKS – THE ENGLISH VIEW

Closing the loophole

ALAN GARDNER

Heard the one about the Slovak handball player who overturned two complex cricketing ecosystems half a world apart? If you're a follower of the game in England or South Africa, you might have thought you would never hear the end of it. But two decades on, the UK's departure from the European Union has drawn a line under the legacy left to cricket by Maroš Kolpak's decision to pursue his employment rights, via his country's associate agreement with the EU.

Brexit succeeded where numerous attempts by the ECB had failed: it closed the loophole that allowed players from a collection of nations – chiefly South Africa, Zimbabwe and many Caribbean islands – to appear in county cricket while effectively considered locals. Not a slogan worth putting on the side of a bus, perhaps. But with Kolpak registrations now impossible, it allowed English cricket to take back control over what constitutes a domestic player.

Both bane and cure could be filed under the law of unintended consequences. When Kolpak, a goalkeeper plying his trade in Germany with Östringen, won his case at the European Court in 2003, he had no thought for the impact on other sports. He laughed when told by *Wisden* a year later that cricketers who took advantage of the ruling were known as Kolpaks (they could just as easily have been Cotonous, after the treaty in question). Presumably, he would find the idea of a retrospective piece on the era equally baffling.

The path first trodden by Claude Henderson, the South African left-arm spinner, on his way to Leicestershire for the 2004 season became well worn, as did arguments about the merits or otherwise of Kolpak signings. Many were viewed as mercenaries, obstacles to young British talent. In fact, the term became a de facto insult, briefly imbued with other connotations after Yorkshire captain Andrew Gale referred to Lancashire's Ashwell Prince as a "Kolpak fucker" during an on-field contretemps in 2014. The ECB subsequently dropped a charge of racist abuse, though Gale was barred from lifting the Championship trophy, handed a four-match ban and required to undergo anger-management training.

Tempers on the subject ran high. Fears about Afrikaans becoming the lingua franca in certain dressing-rooms peaked in 2008, following a fixture at Grace Road between Leicestershire and Northamptonshire that became symbolic of the "Kolpakshire" malaise. Thirteen of the 22 players were born outside the UK, with five South Africans on either side; only one official overseas cricketer was involved. For a while, Northamptonshire's T20 nickname came with a twist: the Steelbacks were the Steelboks.

"Both we and Northants were guilty of over-egging the pudding," says Paul Nixon, the former England wicketkeeper who captained Leicestershire in that

Ross Kinnaird, Getty Images

More or Leics: in 2008, of Leicestershire's nine senior players (seated) four were Kolpaks – Garnett Kruger (second left), Claude Henderson (fourth left), Hylton Ackerman (third right) and Jermaine Lawson (far right). Two more were born overseas – James Allenby (fourth right) and Jacques du Toit (second right). In the middle is Paul Nixon.

game. But Nixon, now their head coach, does not believe the period threatened the foundations of English cricket. Far from it: he describes Kolpak signings as a "brilliant option", while emphasising the importance of bringing in players who would contribute to the club, rather than simply collect their pay cheque. "The right Kolpak players strengthened our game, and gave to our system."

But plenty were concerned about counties exploiting the ruling for short-term gain. David Ripley, who in 2008 was involved with Northamptonshire's youth set-up, and later oversaw Kolpak signings as head coach, viewed the Grace Road encounter as proof the balance had tipped too far. "There was a time when it became a bit too easy to sign a Kolpak," he says. "They weren't the kind of bums-on-seats players who would vastly improve your squad – but they were better than an 18- or 19-year-old lad in the Academy."

If those two counties were seen as leading the initial South African market sweep, the rest were not far behind – despite one or two conscientious objectors. Surrey and Glamorgan initially refused to countenance Kolpak signings (both changed their minds), while Worcestershire prioritised homegrown players during Steve Rhodes's decade in charge. "It had to be a moral decision not to play Kolpaks," says Rhodes. By and large, he argues, "they were no better than good county players who were missing out".

A tightening of the regulations meant only those with a valid work permit or recent international experience remained eligible, while the ECB introduced payments to encourage the use of young, England-qualified players. But the trickle threatened to become a flood once again after the 2016 referendum set the clock ticking on Britain's EU membership.

Yet what of the charge that relying on imports to pad out the domestic game would hurt the national team? By a crude measurement, during the 16-year period in question, England won five Ashes series out of nine, rose to the ICC's No. 1 ranking in all three formats, and lifted both the 20- and 50-over

World Cups. Leicestershire could point to the emergence of Stuart Broad, James Taylor and Harry Gurney, and Northamptonshire to Monty Panesar, Ben Duckett and David Willey, as evidence that those who were good enough would still make it. They could also claim that the poaching of those players by wealthier counties was partly why they had turned to Kolpaks in the first place. And few would deny that the presence of players such as Simon Harmer – instrumental in helping Essex to three first-class titles in four seasons – and Kyle Abbott at Hampshire raised domestic standards.

Many made a lasting impression at their counties, and are fondly remembered. Henderson played in each of Leicestershire's three T20 triumphs, and mentored Jigar Naik; Prince spent six prolific seasons at Lancashire, three as a Kolpak; Martin van Jaarsveld managed more than 13,000 runs for Kent, Alfonso Thomas more than 500 wickets for Somerset (his 33 T20 Cup wickets in 2010 remains a record).

Some might say those players could have made similar contributions in an overseas slot – and that is probably what will happen now, with the allowance going back up to two. After the hue and cry, there is every chance the English system, which has always found room for itinerant talent, won't look so different. Things change, things stay the same, though at least Maroš Kolpak won't have to answer any more questions about county cricket.

Alan Gardner is a deputy editor at ESPNcricinfo.

THE END OF KOLPAKS – THE SOUTH AFRICAN VIEW

Branded with a K

DANIEL GALLAN

Not many will shed a tear: Kolpak cricketers had long been seen as keener to inflate their bank accounts than serve their country. An over-simplification, of course, but sporting nationalism leaves little room for shades of grey. And no cricketing country was affected by the Kolpak ruling quite as much as South Africa.

When Claude Henderson moved to Leicestershire, he was barely known to most South African fans. But, as the years progressed, higher-profile names went north. Some, such as Shaun Pollock and Lance Klusener, did so once their international careers had petered out. Others, such as Faf du Plessis and Jacques Rudolph, treated cricket in England as a finishing school: when the national selectors came calling, they obediently returned home, equipped with new skills.

Matters took a turn for the frantic when the United Kingdom voted to leave the European Union in June 2016. That November, Hardus Viljoen, Simon Harmer and Stiaan van Zyl all signed Kolpak deals before their 30th birthdays. A year later, Kyle Abbott, Rilee Rossouw and Marchant de Lange joined them.

Cameron Spencer, Getty Images

Fight or flight? Of the three seamers who steered South Africa to victory over Australia in 2016-17, Kyle Abbott (centre) and Vernon Philander (right) chose the Kolpak path; not so Kagiso Rabada.

Several factors rankled with both Cricket South Africa and the average fan. There was the impression that players were using their status as international cricketers as a stepping stone for personal gain. The vast investment in their development was not being repaid with runs and wickets for the Proteas, but for counties with pounds to spare. Fast bowler Duanne Olivier reportedly earned not far off £150,000 a season with Yorkshire, three times the value of his central contract with CSA. The exodus not only weakened the national team, but deprived emerging talent in the domestic set-up of the chance to rub shoulders with more experienced professionals. And no matter how many opportunities these vacancies provided, the perception was that South African cricket was diminished.

"A lot has been lost," says Ashwell Prince, who extended his stay at Lancashire by becoming a Kolpak in 2013, after his Test career ended. "A lot of players took the easier option of leaving, rather than fight for their place in the national team. Maybe they didn't believe they had the quality."

On a deeper level, too, the Kolpak conundrum was a painful reminder that all was not well in South Africa, a generation after its first democratic vote. The promises made by Nelson Mandela's African National Congress party in 1994 had not been kept. State corruption and poor governance have entrenched divisions already cut along racial lines: according to the World Bank, South Africa is now the world's most unequal country. Desperately poor people have few options. Gender-based violence is a scourge, violent crime a familiar reality. The evils of apartheid linger.

Of the 40-odd South African Kolpaks to have played in England (Vernon Philander and Farhaan Berhardien had their plans scuppered by Covid), 36 were white. Most were products of elite all-boy schools that remain oases of privilege amid the struggle and squalor. For many critics, they embodied a wide migration of disgruntled and disaffected whites who turned their back on their homeland. Following Rossouw's departure for Hampshire, former national coach Russell Domingo spoke for many: "We backed him when he made five noughts. If that had been a player of colour, everyone would have said 'transformation'." As it turned out, Rossouw's last five innings for South Africa – all during a home one-day series against Australia late in 2016 – produced 311 runs at 77.

Rossouw might have added middle-order experience following the retirement of A. B. de Villiers after the home Test win over Australia early in 2018 – just as Abbott, another Hampshire recruit, could have stepped in for Morne Morkel, who quit international cricket at the age of 33 to join Surrey. Harmer's off-spin, meanwhile, would have been useful during South Africa's drubbings in India in 2019-20. Instead, he was winning trophies with Essex, and briefly wondering whether he might qualify for England.

Yet in the vacuums they left behind, others have flourished. In the 2019 Boxing Day Test against England at Centurion, Rassie van der Dussen made his debut at 30; now he looks secure in the top order. When Dale Steyn struggled with fitness, Kagiso Rabada assumed the role of spearhead, bringing Lungi Ngidi and Anrich Nortje along in his wake, part of the seemingly ceaseless production line of talent in South African sport. Some were still green when thrown into the maw of Test cricket, but most have survived.

The tumbling repercussions of Maroš Kolpak's legal dispute may soon be remembered as a quirk. But if there are any winners from Brexit, CSA may be among them. No coach or captain wants to look longingly at cards he cannot use. With a major barrier removed, an organisation desperate to put a difficult period in the past can finally play something resembling their strongest hand.

The Kolpak players must now navigate new waters. Some will return to South Africa. Others will do what they can to play in the UK in an overseas slot. Whatever their decision, they will for ever be branded with a scarlet K. "I believe that the people who know cricket understood why we did it," says Abbott, who early in 2021 signed a contract with the Titans in South Africa's one-day competition, and will represent Hampshire as an overseas player. "I've been called a coward and a traitor. I knew I was going to upset people. Ultimately, I did what was best for me."

Daniel Gallan is a freelance journalist from Johannesburg, based in London.

THE WISDEN CRICKET PHOTOGRAPH OF 2020 Steve Waugh wins the award for his picture of an early-morning game in the Thar Desert, near Osian in Rajasthan, September 30.

Steve Waugh

The 11th Wisden Cricket Photograph of the Year competition attracted over 300 entries. First prize was £1,000, and the two runners-up received £400. Any image with a cricket theme taken during 2020 was eligible. The independent judging panel, chaired by former *Sunday Times* chief photographer Chris Smith, comprised award-winning photographer Patrick Eagar, former art director of *The Cricketer*, Nigel Davies, and Clare Adams, MCC's filming and photography manager. For more details, go to wisden.com/photographoftheyear

THE WISDEN CRICKET PHOTOGRAPH OF 2020 Jed Leicester is one of two runners-up, for his shot of a socially distanced spectator at Lynton & Lynmouth CC in north Devon, August 9.

Jed Leicester

THE WISDEN CRICKET PHOTOGRAPH OF 2020 The other runner-up is Darrian Traynor, who captured Jordan Silk of Sydney Sixers making a valiant attempt at a catch, Hobart, December 10. He had to settle for saving a six.

Darrian Traynor

Adrian Dennis, AFP/Getty Images

FIVE CRICKETERS OF THE YEAR Jason Holder

Stu Forster, Getty Images

FIVE CRICKETERS OF THE YEAR Mohammad Rizwan

Visionhaus, Getty Images

FIVE CRICKETERS OF THE YEAR Dominic Sibley

James Chance, Getty Images

FIVE CRICKETERS OF THE YEAR Darren Stevens

Stu Forster, Getty Images

FIVE CRICKETERS OF THE YEAR Zak Crawley

FIVE CRICKETERS OF THE YEAR

The Five Cricketers of the Year represent a tradition that dates back in Wisden *to 1889, making this the oldest individual award in cricket. The Five are picked by the editor, and the selection is based, primarily but not exclusively, on the players' influence on the previous English season. No one can be chosen more than once. A list of past Cricketers of the Year appears on page 1178.*

Zak Crawley

TIM DE LISLE

On August 21, as England warmed up for the Third Test against Pakistan at Southampton, several things were not happening to Zak Crawley. He was not about to be voted Young Cricketer of the Year by the Cricket Writers' Club, or Young Player of the Year by the PCA. He was not a shoo-in for *Wisden's* Five, or the cover of *Playfair*. By 4.30 on August 22, all these honours were in the bag. It's amazing what you can achieve just by scoring 267.

This was Crawley's eighth Test, and his seventh as a stand-in. He had shown promise, but his height (6ft 5in) was more striking than his average (28). Now, at 22, he was the understudy who stole the show. It's the storyline of *All About Eve*, the classic film revived as a stage hit. In the 2020 remake, *All About Zak*, the plot came with a twist: the novice was not a nasty piece of work.

He agreed to meet at his home ground, Canterbury, on a November Thursday, which turned out to be day one of England's second lockdown. Kent's office was closed ("Please deliver all parcels and letters to Sainsbury's"). But here was Crawley, unruffled, loping across the car park with a smile. He apologised for being late; it had been a full five minutes. In two circuits of the St Lawrence ground, he retraced his whole career.

For the first lockdown, he had moved back to his parents', near Sevenoaks, and spent the long blank days running and reading. This time, he was staying put at the flat he shares with a team-mate, Grant Stewart. "Up there," Crawley said. He really does live above the shop. He moved in after reading that the great footballer Johan Cruyff had lived at Ajax's stadium in Amsterdam. While some players struggled with the biosecure bubble, gazing out at their workplace every night, Crawley was very much at home.

ZAK CRAWLEY was born in Bromley on February 3, 1998. His background looks stereotypical – commuter belt, comfortable home, private school – but again there's a twist. His father, Terry, was a carpet fitter who became a futures trader, earned millions and had his day in *The Sun*, under the headline "Rugs to riches". He was a scratch golfer, while Zak's mother, Lisa, and sister, India, played netball and lacrosse. But he inherited more than an eye for a ball. "My dad always said I wasn't working hard enough at my sport," he told *The Times*. "Without realising it, I was soon working harder than other people my age."

At seven, Zak played for Sevenoaks District Under-10s as a seamer; at ten, for Kent Under-11s when someone dropped out (the story of his life). By 11, he was a batsman, and had been to the final day of the 2009 Ashes at The Oval – "Flintoff's run-out and Swann taking the last wicket". But he wanted to be Kevin Pietersen. "I can relate to his height, not his playing style." By 15, he was in the Tonbridge XI and the Kent Academy. "I'd go to the indoor school" – he points across the outfield – "three times a week for five years." It made him a back-foot player. "It's really quick in there, so I felt decent against pace."

He missed out on England's teenage teams, but landed a county contract at 17. "I was better at 17 than 18." Why? "This horrendous trigger movement – going across, getting lbw. A bit of natural talent meant I could get away with it." At 19, statuesque again, he made his first-class debut against the West Indians at Canterbury. "Got 60-odd, batted nicely." Watching Tests on Sky, he reached two conclusions: the best players shone against pace and spin; and, of England's teams, the Test side were "probably the easiest" to break into. He went to Perth to be coached by Neil "Noddy" Holder, and spent a week facing spinners in Mumbai, observed by his mentor, Rob Key. "Found a way of using my feet and my wrists a bit more. Being wooden and English doesn't work."

In 2019, he made 111 against Nottinghamshire at Tunbridge Wells – "probably the best innings I've played". He also hit 69 at The Oval, against Morne Morkel and Sam Curran. The national selector, Ed Smith, who was there, felt Crawley improved as the standard rose. Playing for the Lions against the Australians – at Canterbury – he scored 43. When Smith rang to say he was going on tour, Crawley assumed he meant the Lions. "Then he mentioned Chris Silverwood." He called his father, and walked round to tell his mother, who had come to watch him. Those were the days.

On tour in New Zealand, Jos Buttler hurt his back in the gym, handing Crawley a Test debut, at No. 6. He made only one, but landed another chance in South Africa, when Rory Burns was injured playing football. Opening with his friend Dom Sibley, Crawley began with four, 25, 44 and 66 – going up and up, if not away. After lockdown, deputising for Joe Root, he stroked a classy 76 against West Indies, only to collect a golden duck when he finally made the first-choice XI. Squeezed out for two Tests because Ben Stokes couldn't bowl, he studied the Pakistan attack on video. When Stokes flew to New Zealand for family reasons, Crawley made 53. Then, suddenly, the strands of his life came together – Tonbridge and Canterbury, Perth and Mumbai, Key's guidance and Smith's belief, his own talent and drive. He mastered pace and spin, reaching 67 as England wobbled, and making 200 more after being joined by Buttler. When nerves struck in the nineties, and again on 197, he kept Crawley calm. He hit 34 fours and a single six, a sublime chip over mid-off. As he passed 221, Key's Test best, "Mark Wood shouted from the boundary." In a full ground, the shout would have gone unheard.

When Crawley was stumped, it was the first time he'd not minded being out. He had the biggest score by an England No. 3 since Wally Hammond in 1932-33, but the highlight had been simply reaching three figures. "All the nets I'd done, all the times I'd gone on my own to hit some balls – it all seemed worth it." Back at Kent, he rattled up big Twenty20 runs at high speed, including another century at Southampton. Crawley was living the dream, but when had the dreaming begun? As a boy, after a game, Zak had a ritual: lobbing his socks at the laundry basket in his bedroom. If they went in, he told himself, he'd play for England. Did they go in? "It was quite a big basket."

Jason Holder

GEORGE DOBELL

In a year partially defined by racial divide, a group of West Indian cricketers came to England's rescue. When they arrived on June 9, there was barely any team sport going on in the world. And while the Caribbean had been largely untouched by Covid-19, in the UK concert halls and conference centres became emergency hospitals and morgues. Faced with weeks in lockdown, the West Indies players would receive only 50% of their normal tour fees because their board were grappling with the implications of the virus. Who could have blamed them had they stayed at home?

But they came. And, after they proved the viability of sport in a bio-bubble, Ireland, Pakistan and Australia followed. For English cricket, contemplating financial disaster, it should not be forgotten that West Indies came first. Leading from the front was their captain, Jason Holder. With his soft voice, old-world manners and a physique that wouldn't shame a superhero, he had something of the Golden Age Hollywood star. Now, he graduated into a statesman.

For the tour had another context: the recent murder of George Floyd in Minneapolis. American police had killed black people before, but Floyd's death sparked global outrage. Former England opener Michael Carberry was the first to make the Black Lives Matter movement relevant to cricket. His testimony of a sport "rife with racism" won support from black players past and present. Within weeks, it became apparent cricket had a significant issue. Holder and his squad were determined to show solidarity. After discussions with the England management, both teams wore a BLM logo on their shirts, while the squads, plus backroom staff and officials, would take a knee before the first ball in each game. It was a rare example of cricket uniting in a humanitarian gesture – and a defining image of the summer.

"It was about educating," says Holder. "The world needed to understand what was going on. A lot of people might not have experienced racism, but there are many from the Caribbean who have. We've guys in our team who have been racially abused. We needed to stand behind those people, and show we supported the movement. We knew it would have a massive impact."

West Indies' players also raised a gloved fist – a nod towards the civil-rights-inspired protest at the Mexico Olympics of 1968, though Holder had also raised a clenched fist on reaching his maiden Test century, in April 2015, as a mark of respect to Nelson Mandela. But West Indies weren't in town just for the gestures: they had a series to win.

"We felt our message was enforced by playing solid cricket," says Holder. "In the past, we haven't started series well, but we drew on it for motivation.

It sparked something within the group. We've always had that 'flamboyant' tag. We've always been seen as saga boys. But I want people to know we're more than that. Living in the bubble, and standing up for injustice, brought us closer. We were proud to be standing shoulder to shoulder with our brother."

JASON OMAR HOLDER was born in Bridgetown, Barbados, on November 5, 1991. Although his parents divorced before he went to primary school, they remained on good terms, and played a full role in his upbringing. "Manners come first," was the mantra of his mother, Denise. School reports tell of "a dignified bearing and spirit… stirred by intellectual curiosity" at an age when other boys were still running around with untied shoelaces. Physically and metaphorically, he was head and shoulders above the rest.

The Holders were not a cricket family. With his height (6ft 7in) and ability, Jason could have chosen a different sport: his elder brother, Andre, a couple of inches taller, won a basketball scholarship to the US. But his father, Ronald, enrolled him on a summer programme at the Empire Club aged eight, before his mother took him to the prestigious Wanderers Club. Between there and The St Michael School, where West Indies seamer Ezra Moseley was coach, his gifts were nurtured. At nine, he made the Barbados Under-13 side; even then, he was the tallest. By 17, he was playing first-class cricket.

When Holder was offered the West Indies one-day captaincy, at 23, Denise urged him not to accept. But Clive Lloyd, who made the offer, reasoned that West Indies had a man who could lead them for a decade. Within a year, and without any first-class captaincy experience, he had the Test job, too. He dismisses the idea this may have compromised his development, but there have been moments when a willingness to take responsibility has hurt him. During the 2015 World Cup, he assumed the role of death bowler, and against South Africa leaked 64 in his last two overs after his first five had cost nine. An analysis of one for 104 remains the most expensive in West Indies history.

It was a wiser, better, cricketer who flew to England in 2020 – the No. 1 all-rounder in the Test rankings and, after one match, No. 2 in the bowling. His career-best six for 42 in Southampton helped inflict on England their only Test defeat of the year. Moving the ball both ways, from a nagging line and length, it was a masterful demonstration. England hit back. No side had won a Test at Old Trafford after inserting the opposition; Holder attempted it, in vain, twice. But he insists it was the *execution* that went awry. And it is true that, late on the fourth day of the Second Test, West Indies were 242 for four, perhaps an hour or two from securing a draw and, with it, the Wisden Trophy.

Asked if he could move into politics like Sir Frank Worrell, he says, with feeling: "No chance." But as the conversation moves on, the potential politician, the embryonic statesman, the natural leader with a sense of justice, returns to the surface. "More has to be done so world cricket doesn't die," he says. "Smaller territories are going to feel the financial brunt of Covid-19 most. The ICC have to step in. And if they're not prepared to distribute revenues from global events more evenly, then the touring team should be entitled to a portion of revenue from bilateral series."

One way or another, you suspect Holder will still be a giant, still striving to make a difference, still leading from the front, well beyond the boundary.

Mohammad Rizwan

OSMAN SAMIUDDIN

A little like goalkeepers and the Ballon d'Or, it isn't often wicketkeepers are Wisden Cricketers of the Year. Since the first players were chosen in 1889, they have accounted for only one in 15. And many of those were chosen for their batting as much as their glovework.

There is a paradox here. Like goalkeepers, the less attention wicketkeepers attract, the better we imagine they have performed. And there is a theme among some of the Almanack's recent wicketkeeping winners: Mark Boucher's "unpretentious" style, Matt Prior going "unnoticed", and the same adjective for Jack Russell, "until the rare fumble". Even a purist such as Chris Read might have missed out had he not led Nottinghamshire to the Championship.

It says something about the modern accent on a keeper's batting that Mohammad Rizwan's work behind the stumps last summer *was* noticed, precisely for its expertise. Few wicketkeepers emerge well from an England tour, because of the late wobble, the often low bounce, the murky light. And Rizwan's five catches and a stumping in three Tests does not sound like a rich haul; his England counterpart, Jos Buttler, caught nine. Yet there was an adroitness to Rizwan's work. Those numbers hide more than they tell.

His grab to dismiss Ben Stokes on the final day at Old Trafford was spectacular: Yasir Shah's googly, from round the wicket, pitched in the rough, spat at the batsman, brushed his glove and climbed further, so that Rizwan parried it from around his left shoulder, before recovering to complete the catch. Then there was his balance while pulling off a diving take in front of first slip to dismiss Joe Root at Southampton, possible even after a step to leg because the ball was so straight. And the anticlimactic end to the monumental 267 from Zak Crawley, who fell to Asad Shafiq's part-time off-spin, dimmed a sparkling leg-side stumping.

There were runs, too, harking back in manner and tone to a pre-Gilchristian age. Scored in a crisis, of course, but nuggety; malleable enough to accommodate the strengths or limitations of the partner; sensitive to the need of the hour. Wicketkeeping, though, was Rizwan's superpower, all the more remarkable given he had done the job only once before in England – the most difficult country, he says, for keepers. But he was well prepared, thanks to years of practising when he had least motivation.

"I believe I have a few things in my control, one of which is how hard I can work," he says. "Work that, deep inside, I don't want to do. I would wake up very early, right after *Fajr* [dawn] prayers, when you really don't want to wake up, and then do two hours of keeping. In Ramadan, I would practise at noon for a couple of hours before a game."

Beyond that, beyond tips from mentors such as Rashid Latif and Steve Rixon, and beyond the conditioning work of Grant Bradburn, there was an unshakable resolve. "My attitude was, I don't care where the ball hits me: it can't go past me. The pain from being hit will go away. But the pain of letting through four byes will never go. Those runs will never come back. You can break fingers or your mouth, so my aim was: 'OK, break them, but just don't let it get through you.'"

MOHAMMAD RIZWAN was born in Peshawar on June 1, 1992, the middle of three brothers among six siblings. His father, Akhter Parvez, didn't approve of his cricket as a child, though his grandfather was greatly encouraging. In early tape-ball games, Rizwan – honing his reflexes and wit – became known as "Jonty" because of his willingness to dive on any surface. He had no wicketkeeping hero, but he does remember wanting gloves when others wanted bats and pads. He became so renowned that teams would call him up to keep in one-off tape-ball finals. But it was when he joined the esteemed Islamia College, and Shama Club, one of the region's best, that his rise acquired a sharper gradient. By 2007, he was playing for Peshawar Under-19.

Thereafter, Rizwan's progress slowed a touch, partly because Pakistan's cricket gaze was only just starting to spread beyond Karachi and Punjab. His first-class debut took another 18 months, but the grounding was useful: in 2008-09, he hit five fifties (four unbeaten) in his first seven innings. Yet had it not been for a finger injury to Riaz Afridi – elder brother of current Test seamer Shaheen Shah Afridi – Peshawar might have remained Rizwan's ceiling.

Against Sui Northern Gas Pipelines Limited, the scene's dominant side, in 2011-12, Rizwan came on as substitute, and took a spectacular catch at third slip, attracting the attention of Sui Northern coach Basit Ali. When, a few weeks later – against Sui Northern once more – Rizwan held eight catches and scored a vital 46, Basit had seen enough. A formal offer followed. Worried about breaking into such a strong XI, Rizwan prevaricated; but once he understood how much he could learn from being around Test cricketers, he made the move. In his first first-class game for his new side, he made 68.

If it took him a while to break into the Pakistan team, it was because of the omnipresence, until 2019, of Sarfraz Ahmed. A few white-ball internationals here, a lone Test in New Zealand there (playing as a batsman at Hamilton, he was bounced out first ball by Neil Wagner). But Sarfraz's demise changed Rizwan's fortunes so much that, when Azhar Ali was removed as Test captain late last year, Rizwan was one of two candidates to replace him. Ultimately, the job went to Babar Azam, but the selectors had been taken with Rizwan's pristine 37 and 95 at the Gabba in 2019-20, his second Test, three years after his first. Two fifties in difficult conditions in England sealed his standing. And when Babar was injured in New Zealand at the end of 2020, Rizwan took charge, scoring 71, 60 and 61 in a 2–0 defeat.

In an era of terrible, underprepared pitches in Pakistan, he had a first-class average of 43, displaying cussedness all the way. "This England attack, they have swing *and* pace, and I got hit by Jofra Archer. I was nervous until then, but once I got hit, I thought: 'I'm set now.' Nothing worse can happen."

In fact, only good things did.

Dominic Sibley

ROB SMYTH

Dom Sibley knew he wouldn't get much sleep. Two or three hours probably, four if he was lucky. It had always been this way. Adrenalin and anticipation mean that, if he is unbeaten overnight, he is likely to be not out in more ways than one. "When I bat, I can't switch off," he says. "I'm excited, especially if I'm near a hundred."

On the night of July 16, Sibley was 86 not out against West Indies at Old Trafford, tantalisingly close to satisfying his new craving: Test hundreds. Six months earlier, in Cape Town, he had been on 85 overnight, before reaching his maiden century. Never mind the nervous nineties: in 2020, Sibley had to deal with the eternal eighties.

His natural tempo can make the journey to a century a long one – he doesn't use the motorway – but he keeps getting there. A breakthrough innings at Grace Road in September 2018 was the first of 12 first-class hundreds in under two years, more than anyone else in the world over the same period. For a man with Sibley's substance-to-style ratio, that's an important badge of honour. The sequence includes those two Test centuries, in his first year as an England opener. "I know what it takes to score a Test hundred now," he said. "It's draining and it's tough work, but it's the best feeling in the world."

Sibley got the 14 runs he needed against West Indies, and went on to bat over nine hours for 120. A mighty partnership of 260 with Ben Stokes was the foundation of victory in the match and the series, and the highlight of a summer in which Sibley was England's chief bricklayer.

DOMINIC PETER SIBLEY, born on September 5, 1995, in Epsom, has been scoring runs for as long as anyone can remember. Cricket was part of his family life, and his father, Mark, was briefly the ECB's commercial director. Dom joined Surrey at the age of nine, and his potential was soon being spoken of in hushed tones. He was first mentioned in *Wisden* for hitting six sixes in an over for Whitgift School Under-13s, but it was not until 2011 that he started to think a career in cricket might be possible. He won five awards at the Bunbury Festival and, two days later, smashed a double-hundred in the Surrey Championship for Ashtead against a Weybridge attack including former England seamer Jimmy Ormond. Sibley was 15.

He enjoyed other sports, especially rugby, but the case for focusing on cricket was irresistible. In 2013, he became the youngest (18 years 21 days) since W. G. Grace in 1866 to score a first-class double-century in England – 242 for Surrey against Yorkshire. But the fairytale turned into a cautionary tale. "I thought I'd cracked it, and my career would be a smooth ride. That's why cricket is such a great game, because there are so many ups and downs. Mother Cricket keeps you on your toes."

A lack of confidence, new signings at Surrey, and the weight of expectation made the next few years a struggle. A fresh start at Warwickshire in 2017 didn't help. Then, the following year, before that trip to Leicester, Jonathan

Trott suggested he open his stance. Sibley tried it in the nets, and felt more balanced. It was his Eureka moment. On the day Alastair Cook scored a century in his final Test, Sibley made 106 against Leicestershire – the first of six hundreds in consecutive first-class matches across two summers. In between, he resisted the lure of club cricket in Perth, and spent the winter in England, grooving his new technique. "I wanted to film myself, and understand what had made me score those hundreds. It was a case of homing in on that, and doing the dark, dingy hours."

A Test call-up became inevitable. Sibley was picked on sheer weight of runs, not to mention balls faced: 3,024 in the 2019 Championship, more than 1,000 clear of any Division One rival. With Chris Silverwood replacing Trevor Bayliss as England coach, Sibley was a symbolic departure from the limited-overs Test cricket they had been playing. Last summer, he was at it again, facing 941 balls in Tests, over 100 more than anybody else. England's average score when he was dismissed was 92; the figure for Cook, Andrew Strauss and Geoffrey Boycott over their careers was in the eighties. By seeing the shine off the new ball, and taking the spring out of the bowlers' step, Sibley made life easier for an explosive middle order. He was frustrated by unconverted starts – "I should have scored another century in South Africa, and maybe another in the summer" – but they were valuable innings, the batting equivalent of bowling a long spell into the wind.

While he is reluctant to accept praise for thirties and forties, he was surprised by the criticism of his scoring-rate after his Old Trafford century, especially as it took place in favourable bowling conditions: "Getting negative comments after a Test hundred was a bit of an eye-opener." Oddly, life in the bubble made it even harder to escape the outside world, because he had no access to his inner circle. "Usually I like to go out for food, or see friends and get away from the game. We couldn't do that, so I ended up reading on my phone more than I normally would."

The critics of Sibley's tempo – and bottom-handed technique – were guilty of looking a gift plodder in the mouth. His approach was just what England needed, and his team-mates told him as much in the dressing-room during a rainy third day. Further validation came when England squared the series, just as they had at Cape Town. In their six Test victories of 2020, only Stokes scored more runs. Sibley is desperate for more – not just centuries, but centuries in wins. After his false dawn in 2013, he will never take good form for granted again. He nets compulsively, and his self-improvement regime extended to losing almost two stone during the spring lockdown, a response to watching team-mates train in the humidity of Sri Lanka.

While his physical fitness needed work, his mental strength is God-given. Yet Sibley is as intrigued as anyone by his old-fashioned ability to bat for hours. "Honestly, I don't know where it comes from. At school I couldn't concentrate at all! When I was younger, I got some big scores, and people said I could bat for long periods of time, so I just kept trying to do that."

Doesn't he ever get bored? "Ah mate, you don't get tired of batting. If I'm still out there at 6pm, I'm where I want to be." If it means a few more sleepless nights, he can live with that.

Darren Stevens

MARK PENNELL

The dismissal itself was typical enough, yet for Darren Stevens it was unforgettable. In early August, against Sussex at Canterbury, he skidded one down the Nackington Road slope to the left-handed George Garton; it pitched on middle, hit the seam, and clattered off stump. Stevens wheeled away to celebrate his 27th first-class five-for. Business as usual? Not quite. He was holding the ball aloft, not to acknowledge the crowd, since there was none, but in dedication to his father, Bob, who had recently died at a Leicester care home from Covid-related illnesses.

"My dad loved cricket, loved watching me play, loved walking round at Canterbury," he says. "I knew he'd be up there, watching me bowl, with a pint at his right hand. When dad died, there was some talk about a few county games being played, but I wasn't bothered about cricket going ahead or not. My priority was the family, my mum especially: she was self-isolating for a fortnight after dad passed.

"I spent that time living in a tiny caravan on my cousin's driveway in Leicester to try and be near her. That way, I could visit mum, speak to her through the window and show her she wasn't alone. I so wanted to give her a hug, but we couldn't – it was horrible. Then we had the funeral, which was dreadful too, because we had to restrict the numbers.

"So when the cricket did finally come, it was a welcome distraction. I considered not playing, but then I thought again of my dad, who'd have been telling me to get on with it. If ever I'd had an injury niggle, he used to say: 'Your grandad would play with a broken leg.' Dad would have wanted me to play on. So I did."

The Sussex game provided the first of Stevens's three five-wicket returns as Kent came second in the South Group of the Bob Willis Trophy. He finished the competition with 29 wickets at 15; only Essex off-spinner Simon Harmer and Somerset's Craig Overton took more. For the second year running, Stevens convinced the club to extend his contract, and was set to play into his 46th year – his 17th with Kent, and 25th in all. There were no plans to call time on a career that, across three formats, has reaped 27,323 runs and 820 wickets.

Wisden hasn't chosen an older Cricketer of the Year since Leicestershire's Ewart Astill in 1933. Among players in their forties, only W. G. Grace had previously taken ten wickets in a match and scored a double-hundred in the same English season, as Stevens did in 2019. He is now the oldest bowler to regularly open Kent's attack since Edgar Willsher in the 1870s. And he is the county's first non-international to be recognised by the Almanack since Jack Bryan in 1922. Not bad for a colour-blind cricketer who struggles to differentiate between browns, reds and greens.

DARREN IAN STEVENS was born in Leicester on April 30, 1976. Both his father, who ran a cleaning company, and his grandfather Reg played club cricket, while his mother, Maddy, worked as a seamstress for hosiery firms, and helped make the teas. At school, Stevens loved football and even dabbled with baseball but, thanks to his father's persistence, he went for cricket.

He joined Leicestershire in 1997, scoring the first of his four Championship centuries for them against Sussex at Arundel, as an opener; to mark the occasion, Colin Cowdrey presented him with an oil painting of the ground. But after eight seasons he was struggling to keep his place, having gained a reputation for "pretty thirties". He hit 105 and 70 in his penultimate home game, in 2004, against a Hampshire attack including Chris Tremlett and Shane Warne, but was released a fortnight later. He joined Kent, where he became an instant favourite for his aggressive but stylish batting, and sharp slip catching.

Yet not until surgery for a chronic ankle issue did he become a relentlessly accurate seamer. Stevens credits Rob Key, his former county captain, for his epiphany. During an early-season draw with Lancashire on a sluggish Old Trafford pitch in 2010, Key – keen to manage the workload of his frontline seamers – threw the second new ball to Stevens, who finished with four for 44. A year later came six for 60 (the first of 29 hauls of five or more) as Essex were beaten at Chelmsford. His best return is eight for 75, against his former county, at Canterbury in 2017 – a summer that produced a career-best first-class tally of 63.

His longevity as a seamer may owe something to the fact that he rarely bowled for Leicestershire: 105.3 overs produced six first-class wickets at 67, with a best of two for 50, in his final game. Though occasionally derided as a Division Two trundler, Stevens has two match hauls of ten or more: 11 for 70 as Kent drubbed Surrey at Canterbury in 2011, then ten for 92 at Trent Bridge in 2019. A week later, he took five for 20 against Yorkshire, having hit 237. That was one of 34 first-class hundreds – he has also made seven in one-day matches – that mark him out as a rare breed: a genuine all-rounder, good enough to hold his place as batsman or bowler. His ability to destroy an attack also made him a central figure in Kent's white-ball teams until early 2019. The high point came in 2007, when he clattered the winning boundary against Gloucestershire in a tight Twenty20 Cup final at Edgbaston – Kent's first trophy in six years.

During the close season, Stevens has played club cricket in South Africa, New Zealand and Australia, and starred for T20 franchises in Zimbabwe, New Zealand and Bangladesh, where his team, Dhaka Gladiators, won back-to-back titles. After the second of those triumphs, in 2012-13, he became embroiled in match-fixing allegations; charged with failing to report a corrupt approach, he was later exonerated. The next two Bangladesh Premier Leagues were cancelled, but he returned in 2015-16 to play for Comilla Victorians: three tidy overs in the final helped clinch his third BPL title out of three.

But Kent is where the heart is, and his enthusiastic description of the wicket that had him acknowledging his dad that afternoon at Canterbury tells of a passion that hasn't waned. "It was a good ball. We spoke about trying to hit Garton on the pads, because he gets across with his front foot. I swung everything into him and, once he started staying leg side, I ran one down the slope. The plan worked." It often has.

CRICKET AND RACISM

Yes, we can

EBONY RAINFORD-BRENT

There wasn't much good news around in 2020, but out of the darkness came a ray of hope: cricket finally faced up to its lack of diversity. It's true that this took a freakish, tragic sequence of events: if the coronavirus had not already begun its spread, and if George Floyd had not died at the hands of Minnesota police in May, the issue would almost certainly have remained under the carpet. But the pandemic put the world on hold, and allowed time for reflection. When Floyd was murdered, the reflection turned to anger.

I felt honoured to be part of Sky Sports' broadcast on the first morning of the Test series between England and West Indies in July, when Mikey Holding and I spoke from the heart about our experiences. I know what we said stopped a lot of viewers in their tracks. Its power was incredible, and it stirred people up, in good ways and bad. Michael Carberry had already spoken passionately about racism in cricket, and the Sky broadcast created more space for people like Azeem Rafiq, the former England Under-19 captain, to open up about racist abuse he said he had suffered at Yorkshire.

As black and Asian players revealed the prejudice they had faced, one thing became clear: there could be no going back. The conversation has begun, administrators have acknowledged the problem, and cricket is pulling together. The written media played their part in creating pressure to ensure the stories were told: there was no hiding. I'm more hopeful now than I have ever been that the English game understands the importance of fully representing every member of its community – black, Asian, the white working-class and, yes, the public-school system.

When we first started talking about an African-Caribbean Engagement programme in 2019, the aim was not to sideline areas of the game that have done so much for cricket in England down the years. After all, public schools have supplied so many talented players. Our aim was simple: to persuade people that cricket was a sport for everyone. And to do that, we had to break down some damaging preconceptions.

One of the most common was that black people in this country don't like cricket. At least that was one of the reasons we kept being given for the lack of African-Caribbean players in the county game. Sure, the older generation of West Indian immigrants in Britain *loved* cricket. But the youngsters? Too busy playing football…

This had always struck me as suspect, and I'm not just talking as a black woman who fell in love with the game the moment I first hit a ball aged ten as part of a state-school scheme run by the London Community Cricket Association. I played with up to 50 kids every Saturday from the community at Stockwell Park School; many remain close friends, and still love the game.

Tom Jenkins, Getty Images

House of Stewart: Ebony Rainford-Brent, Surrey's director of women's cricket, in the Oval Long Room.

Ever since, I have known that black people do care about cricket. It's just that cricket hasn't cared about them. That knowledge – based on countless conversations down the years – became even more tangible when we launched ACE last year. The response was overwhelming.

In Lambeth, south London – my neck of the woods – 42% of ten-to-19-year-olds are black. That's 33,000 kids or young adults walking past the gates of The Oval every day. At ACE, it was no surprise the phone rang off the hook. The vibe was clear: "We've been in love with this game for so long, but we've not felt welcomed." Some older members of the community felt especially pushed out during the 1990s, when musical instruments were banned from grounds, depriving places like The Oval of the atmosphere that had made West Indies Tests so joyous. Tickets grew more expensive, pricing many black fans out of the market.

Chris Grant, a board member of Sport England, summed it up recently when he described that period as a divorce between an entire community and the sport they loved. And yet, here we were, taking calls from youngsters who – in spite of everything – just wanted to play cricket. So, please: don't tell me they're not interested.

Surrey accepted action was needed, and I'm grateful to my club, in particular to chief executive Richard Gould, who is just as impatient to see change. What we've heard hasn't been easy, but then systemic change rarely is. During my chats with players on the ACE scheme, a pattern emerged: when it came to selection crunch points, especially for age-group teams, black youngsters were being pushed aside. I'd ask them how they felt they had performed, and they'd often say they were doing as well as the other kids, if not better. So what's been going on? Research shows unconscious bias is heavily present in our game, and we are a long way from a meritocracy.

The message this sends to cricket-loving black youngsters is that, to be chosen, you have to be exceptional. You can't simply be performing at the same level as others: you have to be a Jofra Archer or a Chris Jordan. It's heart-breaking to sit down with a 16- or 17-year-old who says they hate the game, and gave it up because of how they were treated.

But there are uplifting stories, too. Idris Otto-Mian had already been playing club cricket for Shepherds Bush, but he got involved with ACE, and last summer represented the Surrey Elite Player Pathway against Kent Under-17s. He was off to university after that, but we hope we can support him through the next phase of his development. A few years ago, he might have slipped through the net.

It's great that diversity is now on the ECB's agenda, but I would like to see change happen more quickly and more visibly, with more black faces in positions of power. The danger, as we've seen, is that cricket's authorities make a strong statement, and launch an initiative. For a while, the heat disappears. But it's not long before old behaviour returns.

The debate around taking a knee was an example. I was happy that cricket adopted the gesture before the England–West Indies series. But I was disappointed it stopped when Pakistan arrived. Cricket has to be more conscious of its historical role, and its use as a colonising tool: probably more than any sport, it has to examine its racial politics closely. If ever there was a chance to make a statement, this was it. Had I been in the ECB boardroom discussing whether to carry on taking a knee, I'd have said: "Look, guys, precisely *because* we're cricket, we have to go the extra mile – not jump off the train as soon as possible." I appreciate we can't take a knee for ever, but to stop halfway through the summer, at a time when we're trying to shift public consciousness? That didn't sit comfortably with me.

Eoin Morgan and Aaron Finch explained they weren't going to take a knee before the England–Australia white-ball matches because they wanted to focus on education, not protest. I could accept that. But what education has there been since then? It made me think it had all been a token gesture. Not everyone will feel the same way, but the time to tiptoe round the subject has gone.

The events of last year have also brought to the fore how the language we use really does matter. Take the BAME acronym: Black, Asian and Minority Ethnic. I understand why it was important to use the term when few were thinking about diversity. However, in that category are countless different groups, each with unique needs. Instead, they're getting lumped together. In my view, BAME has served its purpose as a piece of terminology. It has to go.

Cricket, perhaps without even realising it, has been dealing with something similar. The South Asian Action Plan, launched by the ECB in 2018, is an excellent initiative: it targets an audience who love the sport, and previously felt unwelcomed by the English game. But I do feel it allowed administrators and coaches to say: "Look, we've got more BAME players now." What they meant was: "Look we've got more British-Asian players." Different communities need treating differently. We are not boxes to be ticked.

I include in that white working-class kids, who have been neglected by the system too. It is important we become, like football, an all-access game. I want

THE PREJUDICE LAID BARE

What's the difference between me and him?

"I've almost come close to making a coach spit 32 [teeth] out on the ground for stuff that he said to me. 'I couldn't see you in the dark', and 'What are the brothers having tonight? Bit of fried chicken, and rice and peas?' I had to drag him out on the balcony, and say: 'Listen, let me ask you something, mate. How much time have you spent in black company?' And he literally wet his pants. He literally hung his head like a little child." *Former England batsman Michael Carberry on the Cricket Badger podcast.*

"Growing up, I knew I had to be a lot better than the rest. My father knew that as well. He would push me in that sense: 'You've got to train harder than everybody. You've got to make sure you're better than everybody.'" *England leg-spinner Adil Rashid on the ECB's* No Boundaries *documentary series.*

"Look at the facts and figures. Look at a squad photograph. Look at the coaches. How many non-white faces do you see? Despite the ethnic diversity of the cities in Yorkshire, despite the love for the game from Asian communities, how many people from those backgrounds are making it into the first team? It's obvious there's a problem." *Former Yorkshire all-rounder Azeem Rafiq on ESPNcricinfo.* *See also page 542.*

"Some of the abuse I have taken over the past few days on Instagram has been racist, and I have decided that enough is enough." *England fast bowler Jofra Archer in the* Daily Mail *after he broke coronavirus protocols by visiting his home in Hove. He forwarded the abuse to the ECB.*

"Is every cricketer, regardless of race or colour, being given an equal opportunity of playing for their country? If the people making those decisions give an honest answer to that question, then fair enough, but they are the only ones who can answer it." *Hampshire all-rounder Keith Barker in* The Daily Telegraph.

"There are a lot of Asian kids who play a lot of cricket in London. And I find it amazing that a London club doesn't have many people coming through the ranks and representing Middlesex." *Former Middlesex and England batsman Owais Shah in* The Daily Telegraph.

"You look at some of the players who did get signed, you see their record, and you think: 'What's the difference between me and him? I've got a better record, so why did he get more opportunities than me?' And then it comes back to this: is there another reason? It would be easy to draw the conclusion that it was race. It could have been. I don't know, I don't know. But it's one of those things that, to my last day, I'll think: 'Well, why not?'" *Former Northamptonshire all-rounder Mark Nelson in* The Guardian.

"At Trent Bridge in 2006, I hit three boundaries in a row. I went for a fourth, missed it, and the bowler said to me: 'All you lot play the same.'" *Nelson again.*

"In 2002, I was playing a charity game at the Bunbury Festival. This guy drops a catch, and everyone starts laughing, and he turns to me and says: 'You look like you've just come from robbing a car, I better mind my stereo.'" *Surrey all-rounder Chris Thompson in* The Guardian.

"A man from the ECB spoke about what the board could do to get more black players in the game. He explained: 'I've checked out your stats, I've spoken to your coaches, and players you played with. I can tell you the reason you weren't signed wasn't that you weren't good enough, but because of the colour of your skin.'" *Thompson again.*

"I'm someone who is quite sociable, quite talkative, quite jovial, and I find that for me, personally, in cricket that comes across as: 'He doesn't take the game seriously, he's a joker.' But if there are white players who are like that, who are maybe not performing, it's more a case of: 'Oh yeah, he's good for the team, he has great banter, and it's great for the culture.'" *Former Gloucestershire batsman James Pearson in* The Guardian.

"You have that old saying that politics and sport don't mix, which I've never quite understood because there's politics in sport. I've always been against that saying." *Moeen Ali in* Wisden Cricket Monthly.

"Every time I went for any major roles, it was: 'Sorry – you lack experience.' My answer was always: 'Well, how are you going to get experience if you don't get the opportunity?'" *Former England all-rounder Phil DeFreitas, in* The Daily Telegraph, *on the lack of black coaches in county cricket.*

"The numbers are disgusting. A lot of black guys get a lot of kudos for the physical attributes, but not a lot for their strategic and mental attributes. That thinking needs to change." *Former Gloucestershire captain and coach Mark Alleyne in* The Daily Telegraph *on the same subject.*

"Racist notes were slipped under my hotel door. My coffin was filled with orange juice and milk. Years later, former players hugged me, and said that they wished they had done something to help." *Former England and Surrey batsman Monte Lynch in* The Cricketer.

"Black kids don't expect to participate in certain sports, like cricket or golf or horse racing – they're perceived as very white, very hard-to-access sports. Do you want cricket to be known as a sport like golf, that is sort of members-only exclusive, and black people don't feel part of?" *Abi Sakande, former Sussex fast bowler, in* The Cricketer.

"My son, Jaden, is 14 now, and I have taken him around the country since he was nine, right through the age groups. He's been on tours, played at festivals, all around, and the most baffling thing is that, in travelling all these years, I can't recall one black boy other than him." *Former England fast bowler Devon Malcolm in the* Daily Mail.

"It is now 11 years since my retirement and ten for Vanburn [Holder], and no other non-white umpires have been added to the panel, yet many have graced the game. My suspicion is that there has been a definite policy of only employing whites for this position. There needs to be a transparent policy related to selecting, training and mentoring umpires, which presently does not exist." *Former Test umpire John Holder in a statement via Stump Out Racism. Holder and fellow umpire Ismail Dawood sued the ECB for alleged racial discrimination.*

"Having worked in different progressive sectors to cricket, I feel the ECB is the last colonial outpost; it is archaic, and any change is mere marketing rhetoric." *Dawood.*

"It's personally very hurtful to go through this process and hear these stories, from the very people we're trying to make this game better for." *ECB chief executive Tom Harrison in the* Daily Mail.

ACE/Surrey CCC

At home again: Surrey welcome young black Londoners back to The Oval.

cricketers to be scouted from the inner cities as well as from the public-school circuit, and from leagues that use non-turf pitches. If we look more widely for talent, the whole game benefits.

We had about 100 kids attending our first ACE trials last year, and initially we were going to offer only 16 scholarships. But the interest and the standard were so high we upped it to 25. The big breakthrough came in October, when ACE received £540,000 over three years from Sport England – enough to employ four full-time staff. Crucially, that allows us to build a talent pathway. In theory, if we do it right, there'll be nothing to stop a young black cricketer with no prior interest in the game from getting discovered and, if they have the talent, progressing through the system. Sport England have also encouraged us to spread beyond London – and the ECB have given us funds to set up in Birmingham.

I do believe people are finally ready to listen, in a way that hasn't happened before. That alone is a major milestone; until now, the game hasn't been ready to properly explore the issue of race. To see the shift within counties, to hear the conversations taking place, to realise there is a willingness to change – that's all great. The speed is not quick enough for me, but then I'm impatient. Things are moving.

Looking at my own career, I was one of the lucky ones. The London Community Cricket Association were brilliant, and I remember being backed by a woman called Jenny Wostrack. At the time, I had no idea about her heritage, partly because she looked more white than anything. But it turned out she was a niece of Frank Worrell, the first black man to captain West Indies. And that, I guess, is why she took an interest in me. Without Jenny, who died in 2013, I probably wouldn't have made it in cricket. She drove me everywhere, helped me get scholarships, fought the battles that needed fighting on my behalf. Like I say, I was lucky, and I'll always be grateful.

But young black cricketers should not have to be lucky to forge a career in the sport they love. Talent should be enough. And they should be able to trust that the system will then embrace them and nurture them and make them feel wanted. Yes, the ultimate winner will be English cricket. But it's about far more than that. Only when all members of our community are operating on a level playing field will we be able to say cricket is truly inclusive. I'm optimistic that 2020 will be regarded as the year things changed for the better.

Ebony Rainford-Brent is the director of women's cricket at Surrey, and the chair of the African-Caribbean Engagement programme. She played 29 limited-overs internationals between 2001 and 2010. She was talking to Lawrence Booth.

BLACK LIVES MATTER

"No one is born a racist"

MICHAEL HOLDING

The following is an edited extract from comments made by Michael Holding on Sky Sports on July 8 – first during a pre-recorded interview, then live on air, in conversation with Ian Ward and Nasser Hussain.

I know of a story about a gentleman on a road where I grew up in Jamaica. His name was Evon Blake. He went to a hotel in downtown Kingston that only ex-pats and white Jamaicans went to. And he decided he was going to break the law, as far as they were concerned. He went to the swimming pool and jumped in – and of course everyone jumped out. The hotel called the police, who escorted him out of the property. And they drained the pool before a white person went back in.

I went to Australia on my first tour, 1975-76, and I never experienced any racism on the field. But I heard comments when I was fielding down on the boundary. You just think: "These people are sick." Then I came to England in 1976, and it started again. But, again, I told myself: "Mikey, you are here for the summer. You are going back home in September." And that was my attitude. Once no one touched me physically, I said to myself: "That's their problem, not my problem."

That tour was when Tony Greig made the comment on the BBC about making West Indies grovel. I saw it live. It was the word "grovel" that caused the problems. Tony Greig, with his South African background, in the middle of the apartheid era, using that word against a team that was mainly black – it made everyone stand up and think: "Is this man trying to be racist, is he saying that we black boys… is he going to be putting his foot on us, and we're going to be grovelling?" Obviously, as time went on, I discovered that Tony Greig was not racist. But it was the connotations around the word "grovel" that made us get fired up whenever he came to the crease. Us fast bowlers in particular, we were ready. A lot of the English batsmen didn't like batting with Tony Greig.

The blackwash series was 1984 – my third tour to England. I can understand totally why the West Indians called it "blackwash". I got to meet the West Indians who lived here, and to understand exactly what they went through in this country, what it meant to them to win. And I can understand them saying: "What is this whitewash thing? Why does everything good have to be white? We're going to call this 'blackwash'." I was happy they could identify with something, and call it whatever they wanted.

As for the rebel tours [to South Africa], obviously I didn't go on any. I was never, ever going to support the apartheid regime. I fell out with a lot of the guys who did go. I made some very caustic remarks at the time. Looking back now, perhaps I could have been a little bit more diplomatic. But that's not me.

Patrick Eagar, Popperfoto/Getty Images

Ashley Vlotman, Gallo Images/Getty Images

Fast and forthright: Michael Holding in 1976, and in 2020.

I tell you exactly how I think and feel. And there's absolutely no way I would have gone to South Africa under the apartheid regime. People may say they tried to go down there and make changes. I don't see it that way at all. Whether you are black, white, pink, green – if you went to South Africa during the apartheid regime, you were supporting it.

People could see life slowly ebbing out of the man [George Floyd]. People could see the look on the police officer's face, and the look on the faces of the other police officers, as if they did not care if this man dies – it's just another black man. Technology has caught up with the racists in America. This thing has been going on for decades – for a very, very long time. But people were getting away with it, because they were not being filmed.

Racism is taught. No one is born a racist. But the environment in which you grow, the society in which you live, encourages and teaches racism. Everybody has heard about the American lady in the park, who was asked by a black man to put her dog on a leash, which is the law. She threatened this black man with her whiteness, saying she was going to call the police and say there's a black man threatening her. If the society in which she was living did not empower her to think that she had that power of being white, and could call the police on a black man, she would not have done it. It's an automatic reaction because of the society in which she lives. If you don't educate people, you'll not get meaningful change.

I hope people recognise that this Black Lives movement is not trying to get black people above white people. It's all about equality. And when you say to somebody "black lives matter", and they tell you "all lives matter" or "white lives matter" – please, we black people know white lives matter. I don't think you know that black lives matter. So don't shout back at us about "all lives matter". It is obvious: the evidence is clearly there that white lives matter. We want black lives to matter now. Simple as that.

We have been brainwashed – not just black people, but white people. Look at Jesus Christ. The image they give you of him is pale skin, blond hair, blue eyes. Where Jesus came from, who in that part of the world looks that way? But that's brainwashing, to show you this is what the image of perfection is. If you look at the plays of those days, Judas is black – brainwashing people into thinking he's the bad man.

Go back in history. Thomas Edison invented a light bulb with a paper filament. It burned out in no time at all. Can you tell me who invented the filament that makes these lights continue to shine? Nobody knows, because it was a black man, Lewis Howard Latimer, and it was not taught in schools.

I was never taught anything good about black people. You cannot have a society that only teaches what's convenient to the teacher. History is written by the conqueror, not by those who are conquered, by those who do the harm, not by those who get harmed. We need to go back and teach both sides of history. Until we do that, and educate the entire human race, this thing will not stop.

They keep telling me there is no such thing as white privilege. Give me a break. I don't see white people going into a store in Oxford Street, and be followed. A black man walks in, and is followed everywhere he goes. That is basic white privilege.

Michael Holding played 60 Tests for West Indies between November 1975 and February 1987, taking 249 wickets at 23. Of his 16 Test series, West Indies won 12, including the two "blackwashes" of England, in 1984 and 1985-86.

CRICKET AND SLAVERY

Artefact – or fiction?

TOM HOLLAND

In June 1988, a series of stamps was issued to celebrate the 60th anniversary of the first Test match played by West Indies. The postmasters general of Barbados, Jamaica and Trinidad & Tobago had teamed up to make it possible. Each of the 15 stamps featured the same design – a bat, a ball, three stumps – and boasted the image of a celebrated cricketer. The players were carefully selected, and constituted a gallery of famous faces spanning the sweep of West Indies Test history. They ranged from George Challenor, who at Lord's in 1928 had faced the first ball bowled to a West Indian in a Test match, to Michael Holding, who had retired from international cricket only the previous year. Issued during the heyday of Viv Richards's captaincy, the stamps told a triumphant story: an ascent from scratchy, provincial beginnings to peerless, all-conquering pomp.

Cricket in the West Indies, however, reached back much further than 1928. Each of the stamps acknowledged this, featuring something more unexpected: the image of a batsman on an antique belt buckle. The shot he was playing – perhaps a leg glance – was very much not in the tradition of Worrell, or Sobers, or Richards. The ball, far from skimming across the outfield, was hitting middle stump. Beyond the boundary stood a hut and a windmill, and beyond the buildings what appeared to be tropical vegetation. Admittedly, the image was worn. But the scene, even so, seemed appropriate to a celebration of West Indies cricket. Flying stumps and palm trees: what could be more Caribbean?

The buckle, however, had not been found in the West Indies. Instead, it had been unearthed nine years previously in chillier climes – beside the River Tweed on the Scottish border. Clive Williams, a lawyer who had made the discovery while metal-detecting on holiday, had not initially appreciated just what an intriguing artefact he had found. Returning home, he consigned it to his sock drawer. Four years later, while cleaning his wife's jewellery, he gave the delicate piece of metal – "like the lid of a sardine tin" – a second polish. Now Williams could make out more precise detail. A confirmed cricket lover, he was sufficiently intrigued to take the buckle to various specialists.

A botanist at Kew Gardens informed him that a leaf on the rim was most likely from a cabbage palm indigenous to Barbados. Analysis of the metal at Oxford University suggested the buckle might be pre-Victorian. An expert at the National Portrait Gallery floated the possibility that the image of the batsman was "a specific example of portraiture". But, if a portrait, then of whom? *The Times* repeated an astounding possibility, already mooted by specialist magazines: "According to Arnon Adams, a West Indian historian consulted by Mr Williams, the batsman looks like a well-fed, well-muscled mulatto, probably the offspring of a white overseer and a black slave mother."

Stamp of approval? Barbados placed the belt buckle beside figures from its cricketing past: Manny Martindale, George Challenor, Harold Austin and Frank Worrell.

If so, the implications of the scene on the buckle were becoming clear. The buildings shown on the boundary could only be a wattle-and-daub hut and a windmill used to crush sugar cane. The faded detail around the batsman's neck could only be a slave collar. The batsman himself could only be a slave. If indeed, as the growing consensus suggested, the buckle dated from some time between 1780 and 1810, then it was the oldest known cricket artefact to have originated outside Britain. By 2012, when Bonhams said they would put it up for auction with a guide price of £100,000–150,000, the possibility that the first portrayal of a non-indigenous person playing sport in the Americas had been a black slave was hardening into an established fact. Caribbean cricket had a new icon. It was as though, redeemed from the silt of the River Tweed, a mirror had been found in which we could glimpse a scene at once familiar and repellently, terrifyingly strange: the very beginnings of cricket in the West Indies.

These – much like the beginnings of cricket itself – have long been obscure. The brilliance with which cricket has blazed in the Caribbean over the past century renders the murk of its beginnings only the more frustrating and tantalising. The research of Sir Hilary Beckles has established that the earliest known mention of a match in a West Indian newspaper appeared as late as 1809. It was to be played, so the *Barbados Mercury and Bridgetown Gazette* announced, "between the Officers of the Royal West Indies Rangers and Officers of the Third West Indian Regiment for 55 guineas a side on the Grand Parade on Tuesday, September 19". That it was a military fixture comes as little surprise. Garrisons and cricket pitches were widely viewed as a natural fit; the Duke of Wellington was not alone in his conviction that battles were won on playing fields. An Englishman was likelier to take an interest in war, so the joke went, if it could be compared to a game. Cricket – "the truly British, and manly sport", according to the newspaper's editor in 1838 – enjoyed pride of place: an officer who ranked as a decent cricketer could be trusted to stand steady when faced by the French.

And not only the French. There were other potential adversaries in the Caribbean. Between the British colonies of Barbados and Jamaica lay the island of Hispaniola. Here, in 1804, a 13-year rebellion by slaves in the colony of Saint-Domingue had culminated in the overthrow of French rule, and the establishment of an independent black empire. The existence of Haiti, as its first emperor had renamed the colony, stirred contradictory emotions among the British. The Royal Navy had played a key role in the success of the Haitian Revolution, and the destruction of the French empire in the Caribbean had been a signal triumph for British policy. Even so, the existence across the waters from Jamaica of a state founded by former slaves gave pause to plantation owners everywhere in the West Indies. It demonstrated just how far a rebellion might go, given half a chance – and how fundamental naval power was to the maintenance of slavery. Unlike the French officers in Saint-Domingue, the British officers playing cricket in Barbados could be confident of receiving reinforcements in the event of an insurrection. Cricket in the Caribbean served as a marker of military virility. It flourished, in the final reckoning, for the same reason that slavery in Barbados and Jamaica flourished: because Britannia ruled the waves.

Perhaps it is telling, then, that the enthusiastically received attempt to explain how the Barbados Cricket Buckle ended up beside the River Tweed should come with a naval tang. "Lo and behold," *The Times* proclaimed, "from research at the British Museum and the National Maritime Museum at Greenwich there emerged on the Tweed, upstream from where the buckle was found, a branch of the Hothams ("o" pronounced as in mother), a noted naval family with records of service in the Caribbean in the 18th and 19th centuries…"

The report did not exaggerate the prowess of the Hothams. They did indeed seem figures conjured from the pages of a Patrick O'Brian novel. A pair of cousins, Henry and William, had both played cricket to a high level as schoolboys, served during the Napoleonic Wars in the Caribbean, and were elevated to the Admiralty. They in turn had been following a trail blazed by their uncle, the 1st Baron Hotham, whose peerage had been reward for an impressive record of service: one that, like his nephews, had seen him excel at cricket, repeatedly fight the French, and patrol the waters off Barbados. Any of these three Hothams might have organised a cricket match in the Caribbean; any might have commissioned a decorated buckle to mark the occasion.

Admittedly, as *The Times* acknowledged, the theory "must remain speculative"; and yet even without substantive proof it has served a valuable purpose. The focus which interest in the Barbados Cricket Buckle has placed on the Hothams has drawn attention to the high profile cricket enjoyed among naval officers. That cricket served the British in the Caribbean as a marker of their identity has long been appreciated; much clearer now is the degree to which it served them too as a marker of their power.

This was something to which their colonial rivals were alert. In 1778, an official in Demerara, a Dutch colony on the South American mainland (now part of Guyana), wrote to his superior in Amsterdam that English planters were settling there "who play a game with a small ball and sticks". When, 18 years later, Britain annexed Demerara, the agents of the British state were following

Clasping at straws? The origin and subject of the belt buckle found in the River Tweed are debated.

where the cricket-playing slave owners had led. Power in the West Indies was not vested solely in redcoats or commodores. Plantation owners, too, depended for their status on the construction of rigid hierarchies. An Englishman who transplanted the appurtenances of the motherland to the different climes of the Caribbean was not merely flaunting his wealth and privilege, but firming up the foundations on which they depended. It was no simple matter to maintain a cricket ground where sugar cane had once grown, to have a decent wicket rolled, to fashion out of some foreign field a corner that had the look of England. It required wealth; and it required labour. Lots of labour. Playing cricket in the West Indies, like taking a carriage, or hosting a ball, or attending a playhouse, was a pastime that did not come cheap.

The truest mark of status, of course, was to leave the Caribbean altogether, and play cricket back in England. Philip Dehany, vice-chair of the London Society of West India Planters and Merchants, an organisation founded in 1780 to defend the interests of British slaveholders, was an active member of the Hampshire County Cricket Club. Other members of the Society were even more passionate cricketers. The full name of a second Dehany, George, appears only once in the minutes of the Society's meetings – perhaps because he seems to have spent his summers turning out for pretty much any exclusive cricket club that would have him. In 1793 alone, he played for Surrey and Sussex, the Earl of Winchilsea's XI and England; such were the opportunities open to a planter with deep pockets. In Britain, George Dehany could feel himself not a grubby purveyor of sugar, but a sportsman, a gentleman. There were no slave huts ringing the boundary, no windmills full of crushing machines. No need to part the veil drawn by the Society of West India Planters and Merchants across what it actually meant to have made a fortune out of sugar cane.

In the Caribbean itself, of course, this was not an option. When, on June 11, 1778, Thomas Thistlewood – the owner of a 160-acre plantation in Jamaica – recorded in his diary that "Mr Beckford and Mr John Lewis, etc, played at cricket", there would have been no hiding the cost in human suffering that made such an evening possible. Thistlewood, the son of a Lincolnshire farmer, was many rungs down the social ladder from the Dehanys. He had no prospect of playing for the Earl of Winchilsea. He could not even afford a sugar plantation. Instead, he grew crops which he sold to the owners of sugar estates, and hired out the slaves he had purchased during his career as an overseer. Thistlewood, far from closing his eyes to the systematic brutalisation on which his income and status were built, revelled in it. Even by the standards of a society founded on dehumanisation, his talent for cruelty was exceptional.

Male slaves who offended him might be flayed with a whip, then have "salt pickle, lime juice & bird pepper" rubbed into their wounds; be smeared with molasses, locked in irons and exposed to mosquitoes; have other slaves shit in their mouth before being gagged. Female slaves were systematically tortured and raped. Some were murdered. All this happened without a peep of complaint or interference from the colonial authorities. The rudimentary codes which made the killing of a slave a criminal offence were simply ignored. It made the carefully tended field on which, with his fellow plantation owners, Thistlewood "played at cricket" in the cool of the Jamaican evening a perfect metaphor for the society which the British had come to preside over in the West Indies.

Inside a ground cleared of sugar cane and weeds, only whites were permitted, there to enjoy their leisure time by playing a team game redolent of England, and governed by scrupulously detailed laws. Beyond the ground, in the sugar cane fields, no laws applied, save that which allowed whites to do as they pleased to the human chattels in their possession – the "negroes", as Thistlewood termed his slaves. Legal it may have been to starve rebellious Africans to death in cages, to break their limbs on wheels, to mutilate their corpses and leave them to rot in public. But it most certainly wasn't cricket.

All of which explains why the Barbados Cricket Buckle, when it came to the attention of historians of cricket and slavery, should have attracted such excitement. If indeed it portrays a black slave, then it is a good deal more subversive than it might at first appear. "Negroes" were not allowed on cricket pitches, except to weed the outfield or to roll the wicket. During matches, their task was to stand beyond the boundary, and chase any ball hit into the sugar cane field. And when a slave found a ball, and held it in his hand? Clem Seecharan, in his aptly named study of cricket and education in the West

Indies, *Muscular Learning*, has vividly imagined what happened next. “Many of the slaves,” he writes, “were robust men with splendid physique, long-limbed, with the ability to throw the ball astounding distances. The simple motion of demonstrating this gift contained a more deep-seated, if submerged, aspiration – releasing the body, symbolically, from the thraldom of bondage and dispossession of self.” In time, during those fleeting moments when slaves were exempted from the supervision that otherwise marked their entire lives, there were some who would copy what they had seen their masters doing, and play at cricket. Reactions to this among plantation owners varied. Many – the majority, no doubt – were appalled. But some saw opportunity.

It was tiring to bowl in the Caribbean heat. In the West Indies as in England, batsmanship was viewed as the lordly art, and net bowlers as cannon fodder. Why not, then, put slaves to giving their masters some batting practice? Their whole existence was toil and sweat and exhaustion, after all. And so, for the first time, black men were given cricket balls, and encouraged to bowl them as fast as they could at white men; perhaps, if they were not sending stumps flying, they might have their masters duck, and weave, and flinch. To make a master hop was not, of course, to make him grovel – but it did hint at what a world might look like in which the traditional hierarchies of race and class had been suspended. And maybe, on rare occasions, this sense of disorientation was pushed to further extremes. Such, at any rate, is what some wanted the Barbados Cricket Buckle to suggest. Yes, the slave is losing his middle stump. The significance of the scene, however, lies not in the batsman’s performance, but in his presence at the wicket. It is not done well; but you are surprised to find it done at all.

James saw an image capable of “enriching the whole world”

“On the cricket field,” wrote C. L. R. James in *Beyond a Boundary*, “all men, whatever their colour or status, were theoretically equal.” No one better understood the ambivalences and ambiguities of the sport that slave-owning white men had introduced to the West Indies. He had fathomed the monstrousness of slavery so unflinchingly that even today, more than 80 years after he wrote it, *The Black Jacobins* remains the classic account of the Haitian Revolution. He had exposed, with the scalpel of a pathologist, the role played by cricket in upholding values to which he was opposed with every fibre of his being: racism, capitalism, empire. Yet James knew as well – as only a man in love with both cricket and the culture that had given it birth truly could – that this was not the whole story.

In a slave holding a bat on an antique belt buckle he saw an image capable of “enriching the whole world”. A sport introduced to the West Indies by slave owners, and played by officers who served as sentinels of empire, seemed to have provided a black slave with the chance, however fleeting, to compete with his masters as an equal. Over the course of the two centuries that followed, centuries that witnessed the abolition of slavery, the emergence of cricket as the Caribbean’s first expression of popular mass culture, and the ascent of West Indies to a pinnacle unsurpassed in Test history, the wicket provided the supreme stage on which the descendants of slaves were able to demonstrate

Roy Milligan, *Daily Express*/Getty Images

Expression of freedom: C. L. R. James at Speakers' Corner, August 1967.

their liberation, and to assert their humanity. Cricket, to adapt a phrase, was not just a matter of life and death. It was more important than that.

This, no doubt, is why so many should have such emotional investment in the Barbados Cricket Buckle. Too much investment, perhaps. Celebrated though Williams's discovery has become, the engraving on it is not unique. A buckle found as far as can be imagined from the River Tweed, in New South Wales, bears an identical design. The notion that the buckle is a distinctive artefact, designed originally to commemorate a distinctive occasion, and portraying a distinctive person, seems hard to sustain – and the identification of the batsman with "a well-fed, well-muscled mulatto" equally implausible. How are such conclusions to be derived from such a faded die impression? Might the detail around the batsman's neck not be a gentleman's collar and tie? Might the hut and windmill not be bucolic details appropriate to an English scene? Might the leaf not after all be just a leaf? Were these the kind of questions, back in 2012, that prompted the withdrawal of the buckle from the Bonhams sale?

It is the measure of a tradition precious to people that those who love it will yearn to know more about its beginnings than the sources afford. "Things not known to exist should not be postulated as existing." So John Major, with the ruthlessness of the accountant he once was, dealt with the supposed evidence for the playing of cricket in the Middle Ages. Even so, the desire to believe that the beginnings of cricket can indeed be traced back to eighth-century monks, or to the reign of Edward I, is in itself suggestive. It bears witness, not to the origins of the sport, but to the hold that it has on those who love it, and to the peculiar potency of its history.

What is true of cricket in England is true as well of cricket in the West Indies. Even more so, perhaps – for in the Caribbean the origins of the sport are bound up indissolubly with urgent and sensitive issues. People have been ready to believe that the buckle found beside the River Tweed portrays a slave at the wicket because they want to believe it. Far from diminishing the significance of the artefact, it serves – if anything – to enhance it. While it may tell us nothing about the beginnings of cricket in the West Indies, it tells us a great deal about what cricket has become. Indeed, as an emblem of the ambivalences and complexities of that story, and of the anxieties and the fantasies that have shadowed it, there may be little to rival it.

In *Beyond a Boundary*, James describes how he "worshipped at the shrine" of two batsmen. The first, W. G. Grace, remains the archetype of the great cricketer: the man who, more than any other, transformed cricket from an elite pastime to a sport with mass appeal. The second, Matthew Bondman, would be forgotten today had James not written about him: "He was generally dirty. He would not work. His eyes were fierce, his language was violent and his voice loud." Walking the roads, he did so barefoot. To James, he embodied poverty and marginalisation. "But that is not why I remember Matthew. For ne'er-do-well, in fact vicious character, as he was, Matthew had one saving grace – Matthew could bat."

At the wicket, Bondman cast off his bonds. No longer was he shackled to the legacy of slavery. He was transformed into an example of "that *genus Britannicus*, a fine batsman". James's formulation was striking – and intended to be. It was a tribute paid to the origins of cricket in England, and to the status of Grace, the model of "a fine batsman", as the man who had transfigured it radically, and for good. By coupling the most famous sportsman in Victorian England with a Trinidadian bum, James was dignifying the latter, to be sure. But he was also suggesting that Bondman, like Grace, represented cricket's capacity to transform itself, to undermine hierarchies as well as to uphold them, to subvert the *status quo* as well as to maintain it.

James, like those who enshrined the Barbados Cricket Buckle as an emblem of the sport's beginnings in the Caribbean, was joining dots that some may dispute existed. But he was at the same time articulating a perspective profound and true. A perspective without which, he might well have suggested, cricket would barely rank as cricket at all.

Tom Holland is a historian and broadcaster. His most recent book is Dominion: The Making of the Western Mind. *He was once described by* The Times *as "a leading English cricketer".*

WISDEN WRITING COMPETITION IN 2020

Every picture tells a story

PHILIP HARDMAN

Just weeks before the release of Rod Stewart's acclaimed third album, I bought my first cricket book: *Playfair Cricket Annual 1971*. While its back cover advertises the maiden post-decimalisation *Wisden* (£2.15 including postage), the front features an uncredited photograph of John Snow. Over the years, it has thrilled me as much as Beldam's Trumper or Fishwick's Hammond have many others.

Shot roughly from midwicket, Snow is captured at the apogee of his follow-through: left arm broom-handle straight addressing the heavens; right whipped tight across an oblique torso; feet off the ground; gaze still mercilessly fixed on a winning length, off stump and the outside edge; energy catapulting from potential to kinetic. The frozen image radiates a cocktail of propulsion, supreme control, icy calculation and speed. An eye-blink later, and this taut ferocity collapses into those haphazard movements typical of fierce deceleration and regaining the perpendicular. An eye-blink earlier, the threat is present, the venom not – witness Jofra Archer on the 2020 cover.

Behind Snow, the stumps. An executive might today brand them "vanilla" – unencumbered by logos, cameras or Zing bails. But, to me, they are simply the father of the stumps I used to whack into the ground with the full face of my Size 5 Woolies bat at the washing-line end of the garden every May, and uproot the day after the Gillette Cup final. Last, and barely in frame, is an unmistakable figure. Sleeveless sweater, cuffs tightly buttoned, a lounging coiled spring, the oxymoron more apt here than for any other: Sobers, batting for the Rest of the World.

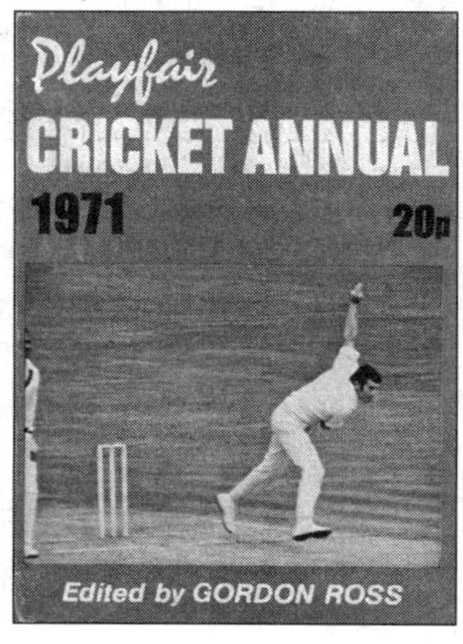

Childhood aside, the photo evokes much: the tours from which Snow was harshly omitted; the run-up laden with the insatiable purpose of a tidal bore; his collision with Gavaskar; the 50-odd (yes, 50) eight-ball overs he sent down at Brisbane; the brooding introspection of the return to his mark; and, on my Test debut as a spectator, at Old Trafford in 1972, waiting for him to bowl. The photo evokes some of his peers: the rapid, enigmatic and sadly brittle Alan Ward; Peter Lever's voracious, bounding stride; the nobility of J. S. E. Price's curved approach to the bowling crease, an odyssey which could as readily have been the prelude to the state opening of parliament as the delivery of a cricket ball.

Finally, the picture has me ponder John Snow's place in the pace-bowling firmament. *Playfair* captions him "the finest fast bowler in the world", and yet nowadays I detect he is often casually neglected. For me, his Test endeavours, hostility and aura transcended his figures – very good though they are – not least during his tours de force in the Caribbean in 1967-68, and Australia three winters later. Though he may not shine as the brightest star of the modern (loosely, colour-television) era, as do Lillee, Hadlee, Marshall, Wasim, McGrath and Steyn, assuredly Snow belongs in their immediate shadow, alongside Procter, Imran, Holding, Ambrose, Waqar and Anderson.

Philip Hardman is retired and lives in Salford. He has his dad, "Owzthat" and Jack Bond's Lancashire to thank for his love of the game.

THE COMPETITION

In a year of fewer distractions, Wisden received 193 entries for its ninth writing competition. The geographical range of the entrants was impressive – they came, as one might expect, from Australia, Bangladesh, India, Pakistan and New Zealand, and also from Belgium, Canada and the Virgin Islands. They came from all corners of the UK, with particular knots around Bristol and Kettering. The standard was exceptionally high, and special mention should be made of 13-year-old Jordi Blake's account of listening to an Ashes Test from Phoenix Park. Wisden much appreciates the imagination and hard work of all entrants. The first submission arrived in April, while others came closer to the deadline at the end of November – **a deadline which this year comes a month earlier, at the end of October**. Every entry was read by the editorial team, and judging gets harder each year. The first prize is publication, adulation, and invitation to the launch dinner, held at Lord's in April. The winner, as well as a small number of runners-up, receives a year's subscription to *The Nightwatchman* (which will also publish the shortlisted entries). Circumstances beyond Wisden's control may force cancellation of the dinner, as happened in 2020.

The rules are largely unchanged. Anyone who has never been commissioned by Wisden can take part. Entries, which should not have been submitted before (and are restricted to a maximum of two per person), must be:

1. the entrant's own work
2. unpublished in any medium
3. received by the end of **October 2021**
4. between 480 and 500 words (excluding the title)
5. neither libellous nor offensive
6. related to cricket, but not a match report

Articles should be sent to competitions@wisdenalmanack.com, with "Writing Competition 2021" as the subject line. (Those without access to email may post their entry to Writing Competition 2021, John Wisden & Co, 13 Old Aylesfield, Golden Pot, Alton, Hampshire GU34 4BY, *though email is much preferred.*) Please provide your name, address and telephone number. All entrants will be contacted by the end of November 2021, and the winner informed by the end of January 2022. (Please contact Wisden if your entry has not been acknowledged by the start of December.) Past winners of this competition, Bloomsbury staff and those who in the editor's opinion have a working relationship with Wisden are ineligible. The editor's decision is final.

THE 2020 ENTRANTS

Abdullah Haider, Arjunan Ahilan, Auni Akhter, Philip Albery, Oliver Alcock, Adam Allies, Mike Almond, Martin Austin, Steve Baker, Peter Bales, Jim Barclay, Thomas Barclay, Andrew Barker, David Baxter, Matt Becker, David Beere, Lisa Best, Sean Beynon, Sam Blackledge, Jordi Blake, Adrian Booth, Daniel Booth, David Bown, Andrew Broomfield, Brenda Brown, Michael Brown, Peter Brown, Sam Bruning, Lee Burman, Michael Burton, Megan Cantle, Andrew Carr, Paul Caswell, Mark Catley, Sarthak Chugh, Tom Churton, Michael Claughton, Paul Clifford, Quentin Colborn, Hamish Colley, Richard Conway, Isaac Cooper, Xeena Cooper, Peter Coulson, Orla Dalby, Peter Danks, Elwyn Davies, Richard Davies, Pranav Dayanand, Paul Dennett, Andrew Farthing, Ben Fawkes, Roseline Fernandes, William Flight, Daniel Forman, David Fraser, Mark Gannaway, Sushain Ghosh, Ed Gibb, Steve Green, David Gwynne, Hugo Gye, Steven Haigh, Jonathan Hall, Roger Hall, Matthew Hard, Philip Hardman, Paul Harrison, Stephen Hart, Jack Harwood, Max Hill, Anthony Hodges, Thomas Hooker, Paul Hopper, Richard Hunter, Francesca Jackson, Joel Jackson, Marco Jackson, Kenneth Jarvis, Ramakanth Josyula, Peter Joyce, Junaed Kabir, Colin Keal, John Kirby, John Kirkaldy, John Lewis, John Locke, Christopher Lowe, Anthony McKenna, Duncan McLeish, Steve McVeagh, David Markey, Dan Marsik, Mark Meyrick, Tim Mickleburgh, David Miles, Keith Miller, David Milne, Jack Mitchell, Stephen Moore, Rhodri Morgan, Anthony Morrissey, K. O. Nair, Brian Northfield, Simon Parham, Stephen Pickles, Richard Pierce, David Potter, D. P. Prashant, Gordon Price, Simon Pringle, Tawhid Qureshi, Rajiv Radhakrishnan, Niharika Raina, Raisan Kabir Raahim, Martin Randall, Richard Reardon, Shubhankar Reddy, Edward Reece, Jon Reynolds, Paul Reynolds, Timothy Reynolds, Abbie Rhodes, John Rigg, Kenneth Rignall, John Riley, Tim Robertson, Darryl Robinson, Chris Roche, Andy Ryan, Mark Sanderson, Simon Sargent, Abhijato Sensarma, Neil Shah, Christopher Sharp, Andrew Shenton, David Sim, Christy Simson, Abi Slade, John Sleigh, Joe Smith, Peter Smith, Srikrishnan Srinivasan, Andy Stevens, Andrew Stone, Peter Stone, Suman DC, Andrew Thomas, Joshua Thomas, Seth Thomas, Patrick Thompson, Luke Thorne, Dave Thornton, Bill Udy, Bob Usherwood, Nauman Vania, George Varley, Dilan Vithlani, Matt Waghorn, David Walsh, Edmund Waterhouse, Rod Wickens, Andy Willis, Anthony Wilson, David Windram, Leo Winkley, Jo Wright, Tim Wye, Zahoor Reza.

WINNERS

2012	Brian Carpenter	2017	Robert Stanier
2013	Liam Cromar	2018	Nick Campion
2014	Peter Casterton	2019	Jonathan Foulkes
2015	Will Beaudouin	**2020**	**Philip Hardman**
2016	John Pitt		

LEADING WOMAN CRICKETER IN THE WORLD IN 2020

Beth Mooney

RAF NICHOLSON

Beth Mooney hates blowing her own trumpet. Her aim, she says, is to play her best cricket, but remain out of the spotlight – which is easier said than done. When she found out she had won this award, her initial reaction was discomfort: "I don't want that tag. I just want to be me, and fly under the radar." She had felt the same way in March, when she was Player of the Tournament at the T20 World Cup, after scores of 81 not out, 60, 28 and a calm but combative 54-ball 78 not out against India in the final. "I wondered if they'd made a mistake." They hadn't. A day later, the ICC rankings proved it: Mooney was now officially the No. 1 T20 batter in the world.

Mooney, who grew up in Shepparton, Victoria, and moved to Queensland aged ten, made her state debut four days after turning 16. She had to bide her time to rise to the top. In 2014, months after quitting a teaching degree to focus on cricket, she was called up to the national side – though as reserve keeper for a World T20 warm-up. Eventually, aged 22, she made her debut, against India in a T20 at Adelaide in January 2016. But trying to bag a place as a specialist batter in the most successful women's side of all time was a struggle.

A T20 century in 2017-18 Ashes was the turning point. Between then and the end of last year, she scored more runs in 20-over internationals – 1,350 – than anyone in the world, of either sex. Given that her batting relies on timing and placement rather than biffing sixes, that points to a phenomenal consistency. Asked what has changed, she mentions a renewed focus on fitness, and "staying neutral and balanced, managing my emotions".

One innings typified Mooney's new resilience. It came in the final of the Women's Big Bash League in January 2019. Suffering from flu and heat exhaustion, she scored 65 from 46 balls – pausing between overs to dry-retch – and won the game for Brisbane Heat. In December that year, as the Heat defended their title, she was Player of the Match in the final once more. A move to Perth Scorchers for 2020-21 meant only more of the same: Mooney topped the charts with 551, and overtook Ellyse Perry as the leading run-scorer in WBBL history, with 3,127 at 46, including 30 scores of 50-plus in 89 innings. The tournament, she says, "showed me and everyone else that I am good enough to make it on the big stage".

That, combined with top-scoring in a World Cup final in front of 86,000 at the MCG, means "flying under the radar" proved tricky. But then it was only a matter of time before everyone sat up and took notice.

WISDEN'S LEADING WOMAN CRICKETER IN THE WORLD

2014 Meg Lanning (Aus)
2015 Suzie Bates (NZ)
2016 Ellyse Perry (Aus)
2017 Mithali Raj (India)
2018 Smriti Mandhana (Ind)
2019 Ellyse Perry (Aus)
2020 Beth Mooney (Australia)

Pankaj Nangia, Sportzpics for BCCI

BUT CLASS IS PERMANENT After a lean 2020, Joe Root enjoyed a phenomenal start to 2021, making 228 and 186 in Galle, and 218 in Chennai.

Matt King, Getty Images

THE SKIES HAVE IT   Cricket in a time of pandemic may have lost spectators, but the drama of the setting remains: the Sydney Cricket Ground in March, and the Rose Bowl in August.

Gareth Copley, Getty Images

Ryan Redman

SOMETHING'S MISSING Hampshire played their first-class matches at Arundel, where the lack of a crowd adds to the rural feel; at Edgbaston, the lack of a crowd sets a fielder a puzzle.

Mike Egerton, PA Images/Alamy

Asanka Brendon Ratnayake

HEAD DOWN Marnus Labuschagne makes a meal of things in the Melbourne Test against India, while a club umpire finds a moment for yoga during a hand-sanitising break.

Dave Vokes

Michael Steele, Getty Images

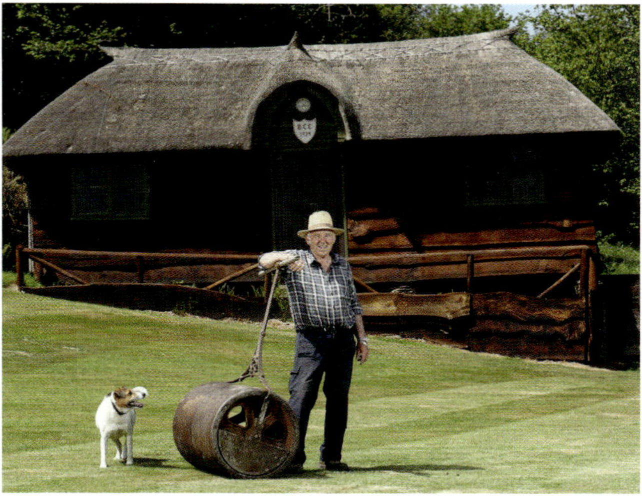

ONE MAN AND HIS DOG – AND HIS CAP Doug Sherring and his companion Jack keep the ground at Bridgetown Cricket Club (Somerset) in trim during lockdown. Elsewhere, Alan Jones earns recognition 50 years after representing England against the Rest of the World.

Chris Fairweather/Huw Evans Agency

Atul Kamble

THE DREAMING Children play on a Mumbai beach at sunset, while at Canberra in December, the Australia Twenty20 team wear shirts inspired by indigenous art.

Cameron Spencer, Getty Images

Jed Leicester

IN THE DEEP   A stag in the long grass at cow corner, Bushy Park, south-west London.

Lee Smith, Getty Images

THE LEADING CRICKETERS IN THE WORLD   Ben Stokes and Beth Mooney

Cameron Spencer, Getty Images

THE LEADING CRICKETER IN THE WORLD IN 2020

Ben Stokes

DEAN WILSON

Sportsmen are often painted as modern-day gladiators, the cut and thrust of their deeds entertaining the masses. For those at the centre of it all, it can be life-affirming stuff. But sometimes it means more. When Ben Stokes took the final three wickets in the rousing finale of the Second Test in Cape Town in January 2020, gladiator and crowd – at least those cheering for England – were as one. Social media was awash with videos of celebration as Ollie Pope took the winning catch. Yet the day's arresting image was of Stokes.

Game won and memories secured, he turned to the camera, raised his left hand and bent his middle finger – a gesture to his father, who had come on tour to watch him, but now lay in a Johannesburg hospital, having suffered a stroke shortly before Christmas. Gerard Stokes – "Ged" to most – a former rugby league player and coach who had once chosen to lose most of his finger rather than undergo an operation that would have delayed his return to action, had recovered enough to follow the game on TV. And he was beaming just as brightly when his son hit 120 to help win the next Test, at Port Elizabeth.

"Ben knows how much joy Gerard got from watching him play," said his mum, Deborah. "At Cape Town, I thought that every run, every wicket, every catch was for his dad." The series finished in Johannesburg, where Stokes was again able to visit him, as well as contribute to a third and final victory. Far from failing to live up to his performances in 2019, he was sustaining them – despite issues beyond his control.

For now, though, the good news was that his dad was well enough to travel back home to New Zealand, where he could convalesce among friends and family. Stokes could look ahead to an English summer, a T20 World Cup at the end of the year, and regular updates that dad was making good progress.

Coronavirus turned the world upside down and, when England resumed, behind closed doors in July, Stokes faced extra responsibility: with Joe Root on paternity leave, he was captain for the First Test against West Indies. England lost by four wickets but, back in the ranks, Stokes made a patient 176 in the first innings of the Second Test in Manchester, then a quickfire unbeaten 78 in the second, when he opened the batting, proving there was little he couldn't do on the cricket field. Tireless spells of bouncers from round the wicket helped square the series, then claim the Wisden Trophy. By now, he had overtaken West Indies captain Jason Holder as the ICC's top-ranked Test all-rounder.

Off the field, things were less rosy. Ged had been diagnosed with brain cancer; by the middle of the summer, he knew it was terminal. The last thing Ben wanted was to leave his team-mates after only one Test against Pakistan. But family came first: after helping set up victory with two important wickets again in Manchester, he flew to New Zealand.

"I knew he would come without any prompting," said Deborah. "It was the best thing for him, because it allowed him to spend real quality time with his dad. They had a ball. I told him this would be the most important time he would ever have with his dad, and that proved the case."

In seven Tests in 2020, Stokes averaged 58 with the bat, having scored more runs (641) than anyone in the world, and 18 with the ball. He had already become only the second England player to win this award, after Andrew Flintoff; now, he is the third of any nationality, after Virender Sehwag and Virat Kohli, to win it in successive years. All the while, his mind could justifiably have been elsewhere.

"Once you get out on the field and into the competition, that is where all your focus is at, and that is where I enjoy my work most," he said. "Every now and again, you will have thoughts about other things, but being on a cricket field, in whites or colours, is one of the happy places I have."

It was a wrench for Stokes to leave New Zealand and return to action at a rescheduled Indian Premier League in October, but a 59-ball century for Rajasthan Royals against Mumbai Indians showed his skills remained sharp. And his appearance in a 3–0 T20 victory in South Africa meant that, across two international formats in 2020, he had won five series out of five.

On December 8, with the England squad preparing to fly home early from South Africa because of another Covid scare, news arrived that his father had passed away. Ben had spent the previous two years winning more than anyone could have imagined. In the end, he lost the greatest supporter he ever had.

THE LEADING CRICKETER IN THE WORLD

2003	Ricky Ponting (Australia)	2012	Michael Clarke (Australia)
2004	Shane Warne (Australia)	2013	Dale Steyn (South Africa)
2005	Andrew Flintoff (England)	2014	Kumar Sangakkara (Sri Lanka)
2006	Muttiah Muralitharan (Sri Lanka)	2015	Kane Williamson (New Zealand)
2007	Jacques Kallis (South Africa)	2016	Virat Kohli (India)
2008	Virender Sehwag (India)	2017	Virat Kohli (India)
2009	Virender Sehwag (India)	2018	Virat Kohli (India)
2010	Sachin Tendulkar (India)	2019	Ben Stokes (England)
2011	Kumar Sangakkara (Sri Lanka)	**2020**	**Ben Stokes (England)**

A list of notional past winners from 1900 appeared in Wisden 2007, *page 32.*

THREE PHOTOGRAPHS OF THE 1950s

"Is it the Ashes? Yes..."

HUGH CHEVALLIER

Wisden has a long history of celebrating excellence. In 1889, Charles Pardon selected Six Great Bowlers of the Year, an honour that ultimately settled into the now-familiar Five Cricketers. More recently, awards have been added for writers of books and essays, as well as new accolades for players. And in 2011, the Almanack introduced a competition that recognised the best cricket photography of the previous year, publishing the winning entry and two runners-up. Images from the annual award now comprise the beginnings of a library of the game's greatest photographs. The winners from the 11th contest form the opening of the colour section found between pages 64 and 65.

Other than in *Wisden 2000*, though, where Patrick Eagar chose an image from each decade of the 20th century, there has been no broad retrospective of photographs taken before 2011. In a modest way, that now changes. During the quiet, cricketless days of last spring, the idea was hatched that Eagar might revisit the decades from the 1950s onwards, and select three images from each: essentially, a scaled-down recreation of the photography competition, organised in ten-year chunks. So this edition of *Wisden* reproduces three pictures from the 1950s; the next from the 1960s, and so on. As with the annual award, Eagar has enjoyed the help of knowledgable and experienced figures from the world of photography – in this instance Bob Thomas, who runs Popperfoto, and Nigel Davies, the former art director of *The Cricketer*.

WINNERS OF THE WISDEN PHOTOGRAPH OF THE YEAR

2010	Scott Barbour	2016	Saqib Majeed
2011	S. L. Shanth Kumar	2017	Stu Forster
2012	Anthony Au-Yeung	2018	Phil Hillyard
2013	Atul Kamble	2019	Gareth Copley
2014	Matthew Lewis	**2020**	**Steve Waugh**
2015	Robert Cianflone		

Inevitably, some of the images Eagar chose at the start of the millennium reappear, but quality bears repetition every 20 or so years. And while readers may recognise the moment Denis Compton and Bill Edrich sprint from the Oval square in August 1953, the Ashes in their metaphorical pockets, they may not know the other images selected by the panel. By coincidence, one – of young lads risking injury to catch a glimpse of the action – comes from the same day and the same venue, even if the perspective is different. And the third, from 1950, is of cricket's greatest triumvirate: the Three Ws.

THE PHOTOGRAPHS

PATRICK EAGAR

Central Press, Getty Images

This is Denis Compton and Bill Edrich at The Oval in 1953 – coronation year. They've just beaten the Aussies, and everything's right about the picture: the moment of victory; the most glamorous batsmen in English cricket. We're not sure who took it, but Central Press, who had the exclusive right to photography at The Oval, probably had three men at the ground. It looks as though this is from the first floor of the pavilion, so he's spotted the huge crowd pouring on to the pitch and automatically picked up the camera with a shorter lens so the photo can convey the numbers.

It's unthinkable now – and not just because of Covid – to have so many people swarming round the players. There are a couple of dozen police in uniform rather than stewards in high-vis jackets, and so much of life is laid out before us: the lad in school cap in the lower left balancing on the barrier; the bowler hat in the centre near the bottom; people at the cricket in collar and tie; the all-pervading sense of jubilation.

Timing is so important. Whoever took it would have been using 5×4 sheet film, and there'd have been only one opportunity to press the button. Getting another plate ready would have taken at least 15 seconds – and the batsmen would have gone. So he's waited, and chosen his moment to perfection.

Daily Mirror, Mirrorpix/Getty Images

Meanwhile, outside the ground, the rest of Fleet Street have sent photographers to glean what they can of the pervading atmosphere. Again, we don't know who pressed the shutter release on August 19, 1953, though we do know he is working for the *Daily Mirror*. This picture is almost dead square, and I doubt it's been cropped, so it's been taken on a 2¼-inch Rolleiflex TLR (or twin-lens reflex) – the sort of box camera where you look down at the viewfinder. There were 12 pictures in a roll of film, and the temptation was to compose the shot for the square, which didn't always work.

Here we have the lad in the left bottom corner, though the interest lies elsewhere. The photographer's keen to get the top of the lamp-post in, so we're looking up and – once again – the timing is crucial, because the boy who has somehow shinned up the lamp-post is caught mid-leap, his hand on the point of letting go of the curving steel, his foot about to land on the wall. He's oblivious to the camera, yet the photographer is a presence in the picture because the fellow in the white shirt, as well as the one with the stout plank, have spotted the camera. If photography is all about capturing the moment, here is a great example.

Roger Wood, ArenaPAL

And then there are the Three Ws: Frank Worrell, Clyde Walcott, Everton Weekes – the cream of Caribbean batting. The photo is unlike the other two, as it's posed, but it's remarkable in having the trio together in a cricket context. Finding two is easy enough, but not a complete set. This time, we can give credit where it's due: Roger Wood, primarily a photographer of ballet and theatre, had an interest in cricket. We think this was taken at the end of the busy 1950 tour of England, which was a triumph for West Indies in general – they won the Test series 3–1 – and the Ws in particular. Between them, they hit 5,759 first-class runs at 67, with 20 hundreds; in the Tests, they totted up 1,106 at 65. It's an ordinary portrait in a way, yet it has tremendous appeal: they're sitting informally on the grass, as if entirely at ease with Wood; we can see the tools of their trade, and they're smiling just the right amount. They're looking great – it's a photograph I'd love to have taken. Wood probably had 12 shots with his Rolleiflex, and this was the best. And it's not bad.

Patrick Eagar took his first photograph of international cricket – of Weekes and Bruce Pairaudeau – in July 1957, aged 13. He was talking to Hugh Chevallier.

M. S. DHONI RETIRES FROM INTERNATIONAL CRICKET

The pan-Indian hero

SHARDA UGRA

Pick an all-format, all-time Indian XI, and – for many – Mahendra Singh Dhoni would be first in. Recency bias means Virat Kohli next, then Sachin Tendulkar and Kapil Dev. Foremost, though, it's Dhoni – as captain, too.

Through the course of a 15-year international career, formally brought to a close last August, M. S. Dhoni maximised his all-round abilities. In Tests, that meant high-quality keeping, and middle-order attack or defence. In limited-overs cricket, he had – in his prime – an innate sense of how to manoeuvre a chase, or cut off his opponent's path to a target; he remained in calm control of the high-speed decision-making needed in T20. At his best, he stayed ahead of a game's tempo.

India will continue to churn out eye-catching batsmen and a kaleidoscope of bowlers, fast and slow. But will we ever see Dhoni's like again? In the national pantheon, he occupies a unique space, ahead even of Kapil, in many ways his 20th-century precursor. Kapil, from humble Haryana, was the first Indian cricket superstar to emerge from outside the traditional urban power centres.

DHONI IN FIGURES

	M	*R*	*HS*	*100*	*Avge*	*SR*	*Ct*	*St*
Tests	90	4,876	224	6	38.09	59.11	256	38
ODIs	350	10,773	183*	10	50.57	87.56	321	123
T20Is	98	1,617	56	0	37.60	126.13	57	34
As captain								
Tests	60	3,454	224	5	40.63	57.82	187	24
ODIs	200	6,641	139*	6	53.55	86.21	185	73
T20Is	72	1,112	48*	0	37.06	122.60	40	22

Dhoni took one wicket for 31 in ODIs, and none for 67 in Tests.

As his country's first fast-bowling all-rounder, he also tore up stereotypes; he also captained them to World Cup victory. But, in an India very different from the one Kapil dominated, Dhoni's is the overpowering story.

His impact on Indian life, cricketing and cultural, is full of layers. He began as an unorthodox, genre-busting product of the grassroots, a torchbearer for small-town energy and ambition, and became a pan-Indian hero, straddling worlds. As Jharkhand's most famous citizen, he brought attention to a neglected state, where tribal identity tussles with a powerful mining industry. And he is a son of the hardy Kumaoni hill people, his family originally from Lawali, in the Himalayan state of Uttarakhand. Today, Dhoni is an unexpected Tamil pop

Captain Cool: M. S. Dhoni wins the 2011 World Cup with a six; Yuvraj Singh is quick to celebrate.

icon, affectionately referred to as *Thala* ("the leader" in Tamil) because of his association with Chennai Super Kings. Then there is the name that arose from the 2007 World T20, which India won: Captain Cool.

Dhoni as gun-wielding combat man makes sporadic appearances too, a product of his boyhood dream of joining the Indian army. A dagger insignia on his wicketkeeping gloves at the 2019 World Cup, with the word *balidaan* (sacrifice), belongs to the Indian army's special forces, and was banned by the ICC because of its political edge. Dhoni was given the rank of honorary lieutenant colonel in India's Territorial Army in November 2011 – a perfect fit for a hypernationalistic country forever on the lookout for old heroes and new enemies. In 2018, he completed a five-jump certification with the TA paratroop regiment and, dressed in his uniform and beret, received a civilian honour from Ram Nath Kovind, the president of India. He is a life member of the National Rifle Association of India and, after the 2019 World Cup, pulled out of a tour of the West Indies to spend two months with his TA regiment. He loves machinery, and motorbikes. Combat man is hardly a smaller part of his identity than Captain Cool.

Dhoni's announcement on August 16 belonged to Cool School, and came on Instagram: "Thanks a lot for ur love and support throughout. From 1929 hrs consider me as Retired." It featured an evocative slideshow of career snapshots to a soulful Hindi song about fleeting fame and public recall, written by Sahir Ludhianvi, one of Indian poetry's modern greats. And it hit social media just as Dhoni headed out for a training session with CSK.

This was the third time a major piece of personal news had felt like a throwaway remark, as if he didn't care about trappings or formalities – ironic, perhaps, given how often he was protected in the game's corridors of power. In December 2014, captain Dhoni had used a BCCI media release to retire from Test cricket in the middle of a series in Australia, citing the "strain of playing all formats". In January 2017, around ten days before an ODI series against England, he stepped down from the captaincy of the limited-overs teams, again via press release. (The first we heard of his reasoning was September 2018: during a motivational speech to the Central Industrial Security Force, he said he had wanted to give Kohli time to prepare a team for the 2019 World Cup.) Now came the Instagram announcement. Each decision has reinforced his brand as a strong-and-silent man's man.

Early on, his detached demeanour was welcomed as a departure from Indian cricket's overheated environment; historian and commentator Mukul Kesavan called him "India's first adult captain since Pataudi". As the years passed, Dhoni's healthy distance from the media only added to the mystique, and became his shield from answering questions, cricketing or otherwise. Potential subjects included heavy defeats in away Test series, and on-field decisions such as the batting order, or how he had chosen to finish a game. But there were also issues that struck deep, such as the 2013 IPL corruption scandal in which a CSK team official, Gurunath Meiyappan – son-in-law of the BCCI president, N. Srinivasan – was accused of having links to the (illegal) betting industry. CSK were banned for two years, yet when Dhoni was asked about it by journalists, he smiled beatifically, and allowed the media minder to step in. His most public comment on the matter was enigmatic: "The biggest crime I can commit is not a murder, it is match-fixing." For some, his stance was unsettling, and remained so.

With India, he was as detached as he chose to be. It was only in CSK yellow that he acted out of character: distraught after losing an IPL final to Mumbai Indians, hollering at a bowler for overstepping, storming on to the field to argue with the umpires for overturning a no-ball in a last-over finish. In the tournament's 2020 edition, he was at it again, apparently persuading an umpire to change his mind about a wide.

Yet even in the ranks, Dhoni remained an enormous presence in the Indian team, with his glovework and spatial instincts behind the wicket, his canny nuggets – audible over the stump mike – to bowlers, and as counsel, guru and field-setter for Kohli. Not being captain was perfect: no press conferences, no carrying the load as representative sage of his country's cricket ecosystem.

In his toughest days, he was protected by the board and, above all, by Srinivasan, CSK's uber-owner. In January 2012, after 4–0 wipeouts in England and Australia, the selectors wanted Dhoni sacked as skipper, but Srinivasan used his veto as BCCI president to nix the decision. That September, Mohinder Amarnath, chief of selectors, was removed from the panel.

Nothing dimmed Dhoni's lustre in the eyes of his fans. Haters will hate, they scoffed. A from-the-jaws-of-defeat 2013 Champions Trophy victory was his last major title as captain. But it reminded India why Dhoni, from the moment he made his debut in December 2004, had been so loved. Not just for his carefree, unschooled strokeplay – epitomised by the wristy helicopter shot that sent full-length balls on off stump whistling over long-on – but for an

Manan Vatsyayana, AFP/Getty Images

Top gear: Dhoni gives Player of the Match Harbhajan Singh a ride on his prize, after beating England in a one-day international at Delhi, 2005-06.

indefatigable appetite for the impossible: as batsman, to chase what looked too large; as captain, to defend what appeared too small. He had rewritten the script of chasing targets by going deep into a game, turning cricket into a mano-a-mano contest. The pitch became boxing ring. It was heady stuff.

In the second half of his career, even as his impact as a finisher diminished, his cult grew. Two World Cups (the World T20 in 2007 and the 50-over edition in 2011, sealed with a Dhoni six), plus that Champions Trophy, had earned him an everlasting layer of Teflon. It was just as well. Between late 2015 and his international retirement, Dhoni's hand in chases, win or lose, went from clear-eyed to befuddled. Two of his last three innings for India were at the 2019 World Cup: 42 not out from 54 balls as India, five wickets in hand, lost by 31 runs to England; then a painful 72-ball 50 during the semi-final defeat by New Zealand. Both lacked a carefully calibrated counter-attack, as if he had lost his hold on the game's tempo, and kept missing the beat.

Regardless, any talk about him quitting was considered blasphemy. Last year, Dhoni joked in a TV advert: "Everyone's really worried about my retirement." As much as the R word, his jagged performances in white-ball death overs acquired holy-cow status among the commentariat. Few called it what it was: the fading of both his enormous hitting power, and his control over acceleration. Instead, his most repetitive tactical oversight – a refusal to bat higher up the order – was hastily retrofitted to suit the Dhoni brand.

The latest stumbles, in last year's IPL, were interpreted as part of Dhoni's far-seeing plan to give the team's young players a chance to fit into CSK's

MOST TEST WINS AS INDIAN CAPTAIN

Wins	*T*		
33	56	V. Kohli	2014-15 to 2020-21
27	**60**	**M. S. Dhoni**	**2007-08 to 2014-15**
21	49	S. C. Ganguly	2000-01 to 2005-06
14	47	M. Azharuddin	1989-90 to 1998-99
9	40	Nawab of Pataudi jnr	1961-62 to 1974-75
9	47	S. M. Gavaskar	1975-76 to 1984-85
8	25	R. Dravid	2003-04 to 2007
6	22	B. S. Bedi	1975-76 to 1978-79
4	5	A. M. Rahane	2016-17 to 2020-21
4	16	A. L. Wadekar	1970-71 to 1974
4	25	S. R. Tendulkar	1996-97 to 1999-2000
4	34	Kapil Dev	1982-83 to 1986-87

As at January 19, 2021.

superhero uniforms of the future. He himself said the team had not seen "the kind of spark" in the youngsters that could have prompted change. An old fable about an emperor's clothes came to mind. There were more shabby chases, with Dhoni – who totalled a modest 200 runs in the competition at 25, with a strike-rate of just 116 – often giving up the ghost too early, and CSK missing out on the play-offs for the first time. Not that he showed any sign of stepping down as captain.

And so he has morphed from a long-haired, devil-may-care, six-hitting, small-town hero into a percentage-playing man of the Establishment. A Dhoni admirer, far removed from the cricket world, pithily described the distance covered by this most original of Indian cricketers: Dhoni the batsman, she observed, had gone "from dreamer to realist to cynic".

The best of his cricket belonged to the wide, open spaces of possibility and imagination. Final over, batsman versus bowler, you versus me, let everyone see what we're made of. It is probably where M. S. Dhoni should be left. Shoulders rolling, all muscle and intent, eyes narrowed to the sun as the bowler runs in, breeze blowing. The match is on the line, the series is in the balance, India need 16, and Dhoni is on strike.

Sharda Ugra spent three decades reporting sport as required by tabloids, broadsheets, news magazines and websites. Now she lives in Bangalore, and writes to suit herself.

FIFTY YEARS OF ONE-DAY INTERNATIONAL CRICKET

Natural selection

LAWRENCE BOOTH

On January 5, 1971, Australia and England played a one-day game at Melbourne of such apparent meaninglessness that *Wisden* declined to provide a match report or full scorecard – an oversight now remedied. The sniffiness came as no surprise: the match was hurriedly arranged to ease the financial burden after the Third Test had been abandoned, and players on both sides struggled to take it seriously. Watched by a curious crowd of 46,000, more than twice the expected number (a hint, there, for the future), the cricket proved low-key: Geoff Boycott made eight in 37 balls, England managed seven boundaries in 40 eight-ball overs, and Australia ambled home with five to spare. And when Ray Illingworth's side regained the Ashes six weeks later, the MCG experiment seemed forgotten.

History has been kinder: that game was quickly anointed as the first one-day international, and its 50-year anniversary passed in January, by which time a further 4,266 had come and gone. To mark the occasion, *Wisden* has named Five Cricketers with a difference: one for each decade of the format's existence. The quintet comprises three batsmen, a seam-bowling all-rounder and a spinner; three Indians, a West Indian and a Sri Lankan. They are five giants of the limited-overs game – and of Test cricket, as it happens, confirming the suspicion that the best players thrive wherever they lay their bat.

Condensing so huge a cast into a handful will provoke debate. Australia have won five of the 12 men's one-day World Cups, yet go unrepresented. There is no room for Kumar Sangakkara, whose haul of 14,234 ODI runs is second only to Sachin Tendulkar; nor for Wasim Akram, the only bowler other than Muttiah Muralitharan to pass 500 wickets; nor Joel Garner, who was among the first to nail the one-day yorker, and who conceded barely three an over. There is no Ricky Ponting, no Waqar Younis, no Chaminda Vaas.

Others, too, would have been in contention if we were choosing an all-time XI. Dean Jones was an early master of the chase, paving the way for Michael Bevan and Virat Kohli, our ODI cricketer of the 2010s. Adam Gilchrist was both a pinch-hitter – after Kris Srikkanth, Mark Greatbatch and Sanath Jayasuriya had smoothed the path – and a proper batsman, as well as a wicketkeeper. In the field, M. S. Dhoni was a master puppeteer, whose last-over sixes underlined his sense of drama. And any one-day podium that has no room for A. B. de Villiers must be pretty strong.

Two unexpected England players might have stood a chance in the 1970s but for Viv Richards. No one scored as many ODI hundreds that decade as Dennis Amiss (four), and no bowler came within nine wickets of Chris Old (41). Old, by the way, went for 3.41 an over in his 32 ODIs. As Harold Pinter wrote of Len Hutton: another time, another time.

Patrick Eagar, Popperfoto/Getty Images

Patrick Eagar, Popperfoto/Getty Images

Off their own bat: Viv Richards bestrides the 1979 World Cup final at Lord's, while Kapil Dev entertains Tunbridge Wells in 1983.

The 1970s: Viv Richards

There were two showcase one-day internationals in the 1970s, and Viv Richards lit up both. In 1975, in the first World Cup final, he helped West Indies beat Australia by pulling off three run-outs – Alan Turner, Greg Chappell and Ian Chappell, the first two with direct hits, the second from point, aiming at a single stump. Four years later, West Indies returned to Lord's and defended their title, after Richards smashed an unbeaten 138 against a helpless England. There have been few more dismissive strokes on the biggest stage than his last-ball six that afternoon, a flick over square leg off Mike Hendrick. These days, such strokes are two a penny; back then, they were pure gold.

By the end of the decade, Richards was outscoring almost everyone, more quickly, more violently, more memorably. Of those who topped 500 ODI runs, only his captain Clive Lloyd had a higher strike-rate than his 87, but at an average barely half Richards's 73; and only Greg Chappell totalled more than his 883, but at a lower average (54) and strike-rate (74). Even without a helmet, Richards intimidated bowlers, his gum-chewing swagger to the wicket somewhere between an act of theatre and a declaration of war. The IPL marketeers would have had a field day, just as their World Series Cricket predecessors did in the late 1970s: in limited-overs internationals played under Kerry Packer's banner, Richards scored 1,063 runs, more than any of his West Indian colleagues. If nothing else, it was a useful net.

AUSTRALIA v ENGLAND

The first one-day international

At Melbourne, January 5, 1971. Australia won by five wickets. Toss: Australia. One-day international debuts: all.

The match subsequently recognised as the first one-day international was hastily added to the 1970-71 Ashes tour after the Third Test was washed out. The England players were upset they had not been consulted: "The manager just had a chat with Don Bradman, and all they were interested in was making some brass for Australian cricket," said Ray Illingworth, the captain. "There was nearly a riot in the dressing-room." According to Illingworth, England "didn't take the game particularly seriously. We were there to win the Ashes, and I didn't want anyone to get injured." Greg Chappell, who had just started his international career, was less damning: "It didn't have the same feel as a Test match, but I think it was still seen as a contest between England and Australia, so it was still important." After winning the toss in a game of 40 eight-ball overs, Bill Lawry had a hand in the first wicket, taking a smart catch at square leg off Geoff Boycott, whose innings of eight used up 37 balls. The bowler, Alan "Froggy" Thomson, had a peculiar wrong-footed action, and delivered around 25 bouncers in his eight-over spell. The spinners applied the brakes, and removed six batsmen: Keith Stackpole's rusty leg-breaks never claimed another ODI wicket. Thanks almost entirely to John Edrich, whose 82 included four of the innings' seven fours, England reached 190. "A score of 220 would have been a challenge, so the general feeling was that England had underperformed," said Chappell. "The pitch was slowish, so getting the spinners away wasn't easy. Had Derek Underwood played, it might have been a different story." Australia cruised home with five overs to spare, after Ian Chappell and Doug Walters countered Illingworth, England's sole spinner. Charlie Elliott, the visiting English umpire, gave the $A200 individual award to Edrich, reasoning that without him "there'd have been no match". Despite the late notice and its being on a Tuesday, 46,006 spectators turned up, clogging the roads around the MCG. "There is clearly a great future for this sort of thing," said E. W. Swanton. The next Ashes, in England in 1972, included three one-day internationals, and more than 4,200 have now been played. STEVEN LYNCH

Player of the Match: J. H. Edrich.

England

G. Boycott c Lawry b Thomson	8
J. H. Edrich c Walters b Mallett	82
K. W. R. Fletcher c G. S. Chappell b Mallett	24
B. L. D'Oliveira run out (I. M. Chappell/Marsh)	17
J. H. Hampshire c McKenzie b Mallett	10
M. C. Cowdrey c Marsh b Stackpole	1
*R. Illingworth b Stackpole	1
†A. P. E. Knott b McKenzie	24
J. A. Snow b Stackpole	2
K. Shuttleworth c Redpath b McKenzie	7
P. Lever not out	4
B 1, lb 9	10
1/21 (1) 2/87 (3) 3/124 (4) 4/144 (5) 5/148 (6) 6/152 (7) 7/156 (2) 8/171 (9) 9/183 (10) 10/190 (8) (39.4 overs)	190

McKenzie 7.4–0–22–2; Thomson 8–2–22–1; Connolly 8–0–62–0; Mallett 8–1–34–3; Stackpole 8–0–40–3.

Australia

*W. M. Lawry c Knott b Illingworth	27
K. R. Stackpole c and b Shuttleworth	13
I. M. Chappell st Knott b Illingworth	60
K. D. Walters c Knott b D'Oliveira	41
I. R. Redpath b Illingworth	12
G. S. Chappell not out	22
†R. W. Marsh not out	10
Lb 4, w 1, nb 1	6
1/19 (2) 2/51 (1) 3/117 (4) 4/158 (5) 5/165 (3) (5 wkts, 34.6 overs)	191

A. A. Mallett, G. D. McKenzie, A. N. Connolly and A. L. Thomson did not bat.

Snow 8–0–38–0; Shuttleworth 7–0–29–1; Lever 5.6–0–30–0; Illingworth 8–1–50–3; D'Oliveira 6–1–38–1.

Umpires: T. F. Brooks and L. P. Rowan.

The match was scheduled as 40 eight-ball overs per side.

His maiden ODI hundred had come in 1976, in one of only two men's internationals played at Scarborough; the third century, 153 not out, was at the MCG, six months after the 1979 final. But Richards, like all greats, transcended his sport – in his own mind, and others'. He later described his innings in that final as "the turning point in West Indian cricket history", since it meant the 1975 win could not be disregarded as a one-off. The team, he felt, now had "no reason at all to feel inferior".

He was ahead of his times, too, seeing in those triumphs over the old guard of Australia and England a point made not just by a cricket team but by an entire culture. "I may be wrong," he wrote in his aptly entitled 1991 autobiography, *Hitting Across the Line*, "but I sense that winning an ultimate contest like that is more important for a black person than anyone else." Nearly three decades before most of the world woke up, Richards knew black lives mattered.

His one-day aura shone deep into the next decade, never more brightly than when he made 189 not out at Old Trafford in 1984, in a total of 272 for nine (next-best was 26, by Eldine Baptiste). But by then, the West Indian story had shifted to Test cricket – a narrative foretold, as Richards suggested, by their one-day dominance. And no one embodied that more than he did.

The 1980s: Kapil Dev

Like Richards, Kapil Dev had the ability and the charisma to shift cricket's tectonic plates. And while it's true that India's seismic victory in the 1983 World Cup was not solely his work, they might never have got close without him. An old-school Test nation, India might not have embraced the joys of limited-overs cricket, and the global game might have taken much longer to realise its economic potential.

Kapil's running catch over his shoulder to send back Richards on a magical day at Lord's, where India defended 183 to prevent a West Indian World Cup hat-trick, was *the* symbolic moment of 1980s one-day cricket, a wresting of the baton by one champion from another. But his most crucial intervention had come a week earlier at Tunbridge Wells. At 17 for five against Zimbabwe, India were in danger of going out. Kapil responded with what *Wisden* called "one of the most spectacular innings played in this form of cricket": an unbeaten 175 from 138 balls, with 16 fours and six sixes. India made 266 for eight, and won. The absence of TV cameras has burnished the mythology: only those who were really there can say how often he disturbed the rhododendrons. Seven days later at Lord's, India came up roses.

Events that summer led John Woodcock to describe Kapil as "the Severiano Ballesteros of the game, a man capable of heroics". *India Today* had a grander scope in mind. Surveying the "personal rivalries, inner tensions, regional loyalties" that had besmirched the Indian game, the newspaper declared: "One man, in the short space of time as captain, counsellor and friend, has altered all that – mainly by personal example."

Kapil was no one-trick pony. Across the 1980s, he took 168 wickets in one-day internationals, 24 clear of his nearest rival, Imran Khan. And he scored 2,869 runs at a strike-rate of nearly 102, practically unheard of back then.

Andrew Biraj, Reuters

Eras overlap: Virat Kohli and Sachin Tendulkar, Mirpur, 2012.

Among regulars, only New Zealand's Lance Cairns bettered that, though his tally was just 792. Richards, meanwhile, had a strike-rate of 91.

If Kapil wasn't always at the crease for a long time (he averaged 26, and suffered 11 ducks, more than anyone during the decade), he was undoubtedly there for a good time. And it was infectious: when Australia hosted the World Championship of Cricket early in 1985 to celebrate the 150th anniversary of the founding of the state of Victoria, India saw off the other six Test-playing nations to lift the trophy. Kapil's new-ball incisions in the final against Pakistan at the MCG were crucial.

Twenty-four years after India fell for one-day cricket, the nation's heads were turned by victory at the inaugural World T20, in South Africa. Soon after came the IPL. Kapil's place in that lineage is as proud as anyone's.

The 1990s: Sachin Tendulkar

Selecting a purple patch from Tendulkar's one-day career is as fraught as picking a favourite child. To plump for the 1990s ignores more than half his 18,426 ODI runs. Yet his pre-eminence in that period – especially in its second half – is startling. He made 24 hundreds, 20 from the start of 1996, and nine in 1998 alone. What for most batsmen would have been the work of a lifetime was for Tendulkar the spoils of 12 months. Even now, no one has scored as many ODI hundreds in a calendar year.

Only a World Cup eluded him (and would until 2011), yet Tendulkar's personal triumphs became a storyline in themselves, so distracting that India's lack of silverware scarcely mattered. Take the 1999 tournament in England, where they finished bottom of the Super Six table, below Zimbabwe. Instead, his fans recall how he returned from a trip home for his father's funeral to score an unbeaten 140 against Kenya at Bristol.

It's also true he wasn't averse to cashing in: four of his hundreds in the 1990s were scored off Zimbabwe, three off Kenya (against whom he averaged 385). But there were five against Australia and five against Sri Lanka, two of the decade's world champions. Tough runs, easier runs: for Tendulkar, they were much the same.

Long before Covid-19, his great gift was being able to succeed in a bubble. Despite the hullabaloo that accompanied his every gesture, despite the demands of a fast-growing country itching for global clout, despite propping up a shaky Test team, he took a deep breath and got on with it – always armed with a bat that seemed too big, and usually from the top of the order. A strike-rate of 86 lost out to few in comparison.

His decade had started slowly. By September 8, 1994, after 77 one-day appearances in the 1990s, he had scored 2,126 runs at 33, with 17 fifties and no century. Next day, against Australia in Colombo, he made 110. And while that innings was followed by three ducks, it was also the start of a broader trend: from September 9 until the decade's end, Tendulkar scored an ODI hundred roughly every six innings – as close to inevitability as anyone since Bradman.

The high point came in Sharjah in April 1998, during the Coca-Cola Cup, a tournament that might otherwise have passed into obscurity. In three days, he hit two hundreds against Australia. The first – 143, then a career-best – occurred after a sandstorm had wiped four overs off India's allocation. (In a typical twist, India lost, but qualified for the final on net run-rate, so the innings was deified anyway.) The second, 134, helped win the trophy. It was his 25th birthday, and this was his 15th ODI hundred; *Wisden* hailed his "genius", no doubt wondering what feats lay ahead.

The 2000s: Muttiah Muralitharan

These days, it's taken as read that slow bowlers win white-ball matches. In Muttiah Muralitharan's era, not so much. He did, though, possess the ingredient widely regarded as the one-day spinner's *sine qua non*: he had mystery, thanks to an unusually pliable wrist, which gave his off-breaks added value. When he retired from international cricket after Sri Lanka's defeat by India in the 2011 World Cup final, Murali had hoovered up 534 ODI wickets – a haul that, a decade later, is still 32 clear of the competition.

The first ten years of the new millennium were an extended heyday. Already a World Cup winner, and with the no-ball controversies at the hands of Australian umpires behind him, he was into his impish stride. He formed chalk-and-cheese partnerships, first with the left-arm swing and seam of Chaminda Vaas, then with the slingy thunderbolts of Lasith Malinga. Swift enough through the air to discourage batsmen from taking liberties with their footwork, but devilish off the pitch if they weren't reading him from the hand, Murali claimed 335 ODI wickets – the most in any decade by any bowler (next, with 324, also in the 2000s, is Brett Lee).

The previous decade, when he had considered quitting the game because of the furore over his action, had not exactly been unprofitable: 177 wickets at 27. In October 2000, he laid down a marker for the new millennium: a then world

Patrick Eagar, Popperfoto/Getty Images

Gripping stuff: Muttiah Muralitharan gives it everything in the 2003 World Cup.

record seven for 30 against India in the Coca-Cola Champions Trophy at Sharjah, followed two days later by three for six in the final (India 54 all out).

On an average day, Murali might take two for 35. The problem for batsmen was that he was a lot better than average, and the next couple of years brought one example after another: five for 30 in Napier, a combined seven for 40 in successive matches against England, five for nine out of a New Zealand total of 218 for eight at Sharjah. *Wisden*, briefly sounding like Geoffrey Boycott, said the batsmen "might as well have been playing with sticks of rhubarb". All the mastery made his figures of none for 99 at Sydney in 2005-06, then the most runs conceded from ten overs in ODI history, one of cricket's most incongruous analyses.

Mainly, though, he was relentless, conceding an average of 3.74 from the 1,836.1 overs he bowled that decade; only South Africa's metronome Shaun Pollock (3.62) was harder to hit. As for Murali's haul of wickets, one measure of its magnitude was that the next spinner, New Zealand's Daniel Vettori, had 112 fewer.

Some still grumbled about his elbow, whose natural kink was made to look worse by the whirling wrist. But the ICC had long since cleared his action, leaving Muralitharan – who was meanwhile racking up 800 Test wickets – to enjoy the bouquets of all but a few.

The 2010s: Virat Kohli

In 2011, Virat Kohli hoisted Sachin Tendulkar on to his shoulders as India's cricketers celebrated their World Cup triumph on the outfield of Mumbai's Wankhede Stadium. Kohli explained that Tendulkar had "carried the burden of the nation for 21 years". He finished with the kind of flourish that was beginning to characterise his batting: "It was time we carried him."

By the end of the decade, it was as if Kohli had decided to carry the burden himself. India might not have won another World Cup, but his performances in 50-over cricket were among the greatest by any player in any format. (And all the while, he was excelling in Tests and Twenty20.)

Kohli's one-day tally in the 2010s was 11,125. Daylight, as they say, was second, and Rohit Sharma third, with 8,249. Even accounting for Kohli's tirelessness – he alone appeared in over 200 ODIs – his numbers took white-ball batting into unexplored territory. He made 42 centuries (Sharma came next, with 28), at an average over 60 (second only among regulars to A. B. de Villiers's 64), and a strike-rate of 94.

He redefined what was possible in run-chases. There had been great finishers before: Australians Dean Jones and Michael Bevan, then Kohli's own World Cup-winning captain, M. S. Dhoni. But Kohli was something else. He batted in 82 of India's 94 victorious chases, scoring 5,076 runs at an average of 95, with 21 hundreds and 20 fifties. His competitiveness meant it was not enough simply to lead his team towards the finishing line: he had to breast the tape himself; there were 29 not-outs. While Kohli was at the crease, India were in the game. And he made his runs with a lightness of touch that was supposed to be going out of fashion. He could clear the ropes when he had to, but he also picked gaps and turned ones into twos.

Unlike Jones and Bevan, Kohli performed under the gaze of the world's most demanding fans. Unlike Dhoni, he batted up the order, and often needed to see off the new ball before he could contemplate the conclusion. And he was ruthless, making the most of good form: four hundreds in five innings in 2012 against Sri Lanka and Pakistan; five in nine in 2017-18 against New Zealand and South Africa; three in a row against West Indies in seven days in October 2018. Like all the greats, his hot streaks were hotter and longer than his rivals'.

No team kept him quiet. He made nine centuries against West Indies, eight against Australia, seven against Sri Lanka, five against New Zealand. Only England took his wicket at an average below 50. For opposition bowlers, that was as good as it got.

THE END OF FIRST-CLASS UNIVERSITY CRICKET

All academic now

DEREK PRINGLE

Amid the turmoil of Covid-19 came the demise of first-class status for university cricket. Almost unnoticed, Cambridge beat Oxford by 249 runs at Fenner's in early September. And that was it. Few mourned the declassification, though its passing was brutal. O my Cowdrey and my Dexter long ago…

Oxford and Cambridge had been playing matches now described as first-class since the early 19th century, predating most of the county clubs. But the ECB's decision was no surprise; most wondered why it had taken so long. The answer probably lay in the stranglehold over public life enjoyed by their alumni. When you have dominated every corridor of the Establishment for centuries, it is easy to keep old and ailing friends at the feast.

Wisden had been among the first to question the true merit of university cricket, removing its traditional list of Oxbridge Blues in 1993. Matthew Engel, the editor, was widely condemned; one critic tartly observed he was a "political scientist from Manchester University". But Engel, with some justification, felt the roll call had become the "biggest anachronism in the book". He added: "Even the *Oxford Mail* and *Cambridge Evening News* stopped sending reporters."

A Blue had once denoted more than a first-class career: it opened doors. A job at the Sudan Civil Service, for instance, required either a first-class degree, or a Blue plus a second – which is how Guy Pawson, Oxford's captain in 1910, got in. Nor had the cachet shown any signs of abating after the Second World War. Years later, *The Guardian* recalled: "In 1948 the Varsity Match was in its high summer. It was a social occasion to match Henley, Wimbledon and Royal Ascot. From early on Saturday, the toppers and morning coats paraded through the Grace Gates, and all day Lord's overflowed."

Even if the pandemic had not kept spectators away in 2020, there is little chance Fenner's would have overflowed (the match had not been at Lord's since 2000). Reasons for the decline are several, starting in the 1960s, with the gradual disregard for sporting excellence from admissions tutors more concerned with league tables of an academic kind. The number of universities was now expanding, spreading the cricket talent more thinly. Then, when most colleges became mixed in the 1970s and 1980s, came a reduction in male students. And with no empire to administer, perhaps the focus shifted to winning Nobel prizes. Certainly, Oxford captains were no longer considered quite the catch they once were. As John Claughton, captain in 1978, prepared for life on the outside, *The Guardian* noted: "The one firm offer he has received is a job with IBM." He later taught at Eton.

You could almost understand the prejudice against sporting types if it were true that playing games depresses grades. But a recent study by the University of Cambridge Sports Service showed that students who play sport generally

Popperfoto/Getty Images

First-class honours: the Cambridge team of 1921 were particularly strong, though they lost by an innings to Warwick Armstrong's Australians. The two students standing are Charles "Father" Marriott and Percy Chapman. The large figure in the middle is Armstrong, and to his left is Gilbert Ashton, his opposite number. In front of them is Tom Lowry, New Zealand's first Test captain.

gain better degrees than those who do not, and most enjoy better mental health. As if to prove the point, six of the 2019 Oxford team took firsts. Despite that, a good university cricket team went from being a priority to an ambivalence, and finally an encumbrance.

This seemed more the case at Oxford and Cambridge than elsewhere, as Steve James, also of Glamorgan and England, discovered in 1989, when a Combined Universities side including him, Michael Atherton and Nasser Hussain reached the quarter-finals of the Benson and Hedges Cup. But whereas Durham University allowed Hussain – and wicketkeeper Martin Speight – to sit a finals exam a day early in order to play Somerset, Cambridge did not afford the same courtesy to James, who missed the game. Atherton took four wickets with his leg-breaks, and Hussain scored a century, but the students lost three wickets in the final over, bowled by Peter Roebuck, and the game by three runs. It is easy to forget that Oxford had their own team in the 1973 B&H (beating Northamptonshire), and Cambridge in both 1972 and 1974.

One former headmaster, an Oxford Blue, told me that sporty Oxbridge candidates from his school were advised "not to mention the cricket". Rowing is still indulged, because of the global publicity brought by the Boat Race. But other sports are woefully under-resourced, with recent Oxford XIs having to raise funds to pay groundstaff their overtime. In my time at Cambridge (1979–82), players had to buy their own lunch at Fenner's. The bill – and bar tab – had to be settled at the end of term.

And yet it would not have taken much to improve the cricket of recent university sides. For the past two years, I have coached the pace bowlers at Cambridge, and been impressed by their quality and commitment; perhaps half would have won Blues in other eras too. What the team have lacked are two or three cricketers of county standard. But even if admissions tutors suddenly became sympathetic, talented schoolboy players might still be lured by a county. Alastair Cook was offered a place by Cambridge and Durham, but preferred Essex CCC.

Academic work was more or less voluntary for the university sportsman of yesteryear, but today's students are expected to clock up 45 hours a week. Imagine Ted Dexter worrying about that as he teed off at the Gog Magog golf club near Cambridge. Dexter had joined Jesus College in 1955, supposedly to read French and Italian, but later changed to English, which he felt offered a better chance of "scraping through". He admitted: "I was to distinguish myself by failing to attend one lecture all the time I was there." He left without a degree (but with a foot in the door at Sussex).

Meanwhile, the Fenner's pitches have grown faster and bouncier, which is a double whammy for students: county batsmen *and* bowlers prefer such conditions to the old featherbeds. Without the protection of what one county bowler used to call "Cyril Coote's slow nothings" (Coote was the legendary groundsman at Fenner's from 1936 until 1980), the gap grew.

It was not always thus. One hundred years ago, Cambridge – captained by Gilbert Ashton, the eldest of three brothers in the team – had one of the strongest sides in England. That season, they won nine of their 12 first-class matches; one of their two defeats was by Warwick Armstrong's Australians, who claimed that summer's Ashes 3–0. Pitches were uncovered, so the students might have caught opponents on a wet or drying surface. But you don't beat Lancashire, Yorkshire or Warwickshire (twice) by fluke, or count two players – Hubert Ashton and John Bryan – among *Wisden's* Five. Of that team, Percy Chapman and Charles "Father" Marriott both played Test cricket for England; a third, Tom Lowry, for New Zealand. Chapman captained in 17 Tests, and oversaw a 4–1 triumph in Australia in 1928-29; Marriott won a single cap, taking 11 for 96 with his leg-breaks against West Indies at The Oval in 1933. Eight of the other nine regulars enjoyed distinguished first-class careers.

There have been two other heydays at Cambridge: 1878–82 and 1949–52. The first could even claim to be a golden age, since they twice beat the Australians. Oxford did so in 1884, but lost to them in 1886: needing 64 to win at the Christ Church Ground, they managed 38, with Frederick Spofforth taking 15 for 36.

Back then, Cambridge fielded Edward and Alfred Lyttelton, Ivo Bligh (recipient of the original Ashes urn), Allan Steel, and the Studd brothers, Charles and George, who became missionaries. Five of the six had gone to Eton (Steel attended Marlborough), and only Edward Lyttelton did not play Test cricket. If the 1882 team were predominantly public school, so was Cambridge's intake. This had not changed by the early 1950s, when the university could last claim some of the best cricketers in the land. David Sheppard, Peter May, Hubert Doggart and John Dewes, all privately educated,

Patrick Eagar, Popperfoto/Getty Images

Press pass: Derek Pringle (26 not out and two for 82) of Cambridge University, and Jonathan Agnew (two runs and none for 45) of Leicestershire, in 1980.

played for England while undergraduates. (So did team-mate J. J. Warr, a grammar-school boy – and a bowler.) Today's Oxbridge teams are mainly drawn from public schools too, despite the universities' drive to become more egalitarian. Cricket in state schools, however, has all but vanished.

It has not been the only imbalance. While batsmen have racked up over 1,000 Test caps, bowlers are in the low hundreds. *Oxford and Cambridge Cricket*, by Doggart and George Chesterton, contains a statistical section on great Oxbridge batsmen, but nothing on great bowlers, despite the likes of Imran Khan (who attended Oxford after Cambridge turned him down), Trevor Bailey and Phil Edmonds. Yet bowlers win matches, especially in three-day cricket. In 1950, with Warr their only bowler of consistent quality, Cambridge won just once against county opposition. But they lost only once, too, because their batting kept them out of trouble: in five seasons, Sheppard, May, Doggart and Dewes scored 37 hundreds between them.

Those post-war sides, at least until 1960, possessed another advantage: players who had already completed National Service, and were older, stronger and mostly wiser than the undergrads who followed. Men versus men gradually became men versus boys – the more so once gap years fell out of fashion. And, after amateur status ended in 1963, younger students also had to face all-professional county sides, who could no longer afford to cruise: come the season's end, with contracts at stake, a hundred or a five-wicket haul at Fenner's or the Parks might just stay the axe. (Not that Mike Procter, Gloucestershire's South African captain, was fooled: on studying the averages, he discounted anything against the students.)

Wins over counties became scarce. After 1960, when each won three games, Cambridge have recorded just 12, and Oxford 17. Captained by Alan Smith, who also led Warwickshire and played six Tests, Oxford were bolstered that year by the Nawab of Pataudi and Abbas Ali Baig from India, and Pakistan's Javed Burki. Through Rhodes scholarships, a legacy that no longer dares speak its name, talented cricketers from former colonies, such as South Africa's Murray Hofmeyr (captain in 1951) and Australia's Alan Dowding (captain in 1953), strengthened many an Oxford side.

Were university cricket a business, accountants would have closed it down long ago. But matches against the counties served a purpose. Cambridge's 1977 side, for instance, included eight who had played, or would play, at first-class domestic level, and two who would represent England. Mike Howat, who opened the bowling that year, reckons the addition of three overseas players, as some counties had that season, would have made them competitive in the Championship (and, he happily admits, squeezed him out of the team).

Back then, if you switched subject – as I did, from geography to land economy – you could wangle a fourth year. Although contracted to Essex in my gap year, and for the second half of each university summer, I was in no rush to join the club full-time. They were a settled side, difficult to break into. Rather than languish in the Seconds, I extended my time at Cambridge, where my cricketing education, against county and Test players, advanced far more quickly. Had I been at Essex, I could have hidden behind the likes of John Lever, Keith Fletcher, Graham Gooch and Ken McEwan. At Cambridge, I had to take responsibility, and stood out to the extent that I was picked for England in 1982 – the first undergraduate to be selected since Peter May, against South Africa in 1951. It was a bold gambit by the chairman of selectors – May.

In my first year at university alone, I played against nine county sides, encountering David Gower, Clive Rice, Kepler Wessels and Geoff Lawson. In my second, I faced the great West Indians, batting against Andy Roberts, Malcolm Marshall and Colin Croft, and bowling to Desmond Haynes, Gordon Greenidge and Lawrence Rowe. These days, "privilege" has become a dirty word, but as expert tutorials go it was unbeatable, especially as some opponents dispensed their knowledge afterwards in the bar.

Yet with no points – or prize money – at stake, most pros saw the matches as glorified nets. Certainly, the question of why they needed to play the universities arose every year at the county captains' meeting. But timing was everything. As Lever, Essex's premier bowler of the era, put it: "Spending five to six hours a day in the field early season was ideal to get match-hardened. It was better than nets. But going to the Parks in June, say – that was a waste of time."

During my time at Cambridge, we beat Lancashire in 1982, and might well have added Glamorgan had I not miscalculated the run-rate at a crucial juncture in the chase (maths was not a strong point). The victory over Lancashire, by seven wickets, was seen by a large crowd, as word got round town that something was afoot. The night before, as we met our opponents for a drink, Lancashire's Frank Hayes had me in a headlock, and instructed me not to blow our advantage. Not everyone saw the funny side. David Lloyd, deputising for Clive Lloyd as captain, was hauled before the club committee. His response:

Hugh Chevallier

Spring fever: Oxford University at home in the Parks in 2015.

they hadn't lost any Championship points, and nobody had died. He didn't lead Lancashire very often after that. In my final year, I was offered the captaincy of both Glamorgan and Worcestershire, which I felt sure wouldn't have happened without the Cambridge connection.

England players continued to emerge from university cricket after the early 1980s. Atherton, James, Tim Curtis, John Crawley, Ed Smith and Zafar Ansari all played Tests between 1988 and 2016 after attending Cambridge; Oxford's sole internationals in that time were Jason Gallian and Jamie Dalrymple. Atherton captained England in 54 Tests, a record until Cook overtook him. Of England's 81 Test captains, 34 have been to Oxford or Cambridge – among them Douglas Jardine, May and Mike Brearley. While no Oxbridge cricketer has held the office since Atherton, Durham University has filled the breach, thanks to Hussain and Andrew Strauss. They could be the last graduates to do so.

With standards continuing to slide, attempts were made at the start of the century to justify first-class status. Oxford and Cambridge merged with the former polytechnics in their cities, and the hybrid sides played as University Centres of Cricketing Excellence. Others formed at Durham, Loughborough, Leeds/Bradford and Cardiff – a safety-in-numbers approach to camouflage the fact that Oxford and Cambridge had retained their rank. The move, essentially an Elastoplast before an amputation, was not welcomed by all. Graeme Fowler, the former England opener who coached the Durham students, felt first-class status would be "a stick for critics to beat university cricket with". He fears for its future under the auspices of the ECB. The emphasis, he believes, "seems to have shifted from excellence to participation".

In 2004, MCC took over sponsorship of the UCCEs, later rebranding them MCC University teams. The prestige of first-class status, though not a stipulation, did persuade MCC to fund the enterprise, to the tune of £7.5–8m over 15 years.

OXBRIDGE CAPTAINS OF ENGLAND

Thirteen England Test captains have attended **Oxford University**:

	Appointed		*Appointed*
Lord Harris (4 Tests as captain) . .	1878-79	R. T. Stanyforth (4).	1927-28
T. C. O'Brien (1).	1895-96	G. T. S. Stevens (1).	1927-28
P. F. Warner (10).	1903-04	D. R. Jardine (15)	1931
R. E. Foster (3)	1907	D. B. Carr (1).	1951-52
F. L. Fane (5).	1907-08	M. C. Cowdrey (27)	1959
H. D. G. Leveson Gower (3).	1909-10	M. J. K. Smith (25)	1963-64
C. B. Fry (6)	1912		

Eight other Oxford students have become Test captains: H. M. Taberer (SA, 1, 1902-03); A. Melville (SA, 10, 1938-39); Nawab of Pataudi snr (I, 3, 1946); A. H. Kardar (P, 23, 1952-53); C. B. van Ryneveld (SA, 8, 1956-57); Nawab of Pataudi jnr (I, 40, 1961-62); Javed Burki (P, 5, 1962); Imran Khan (P, 48, 1982).

Twenty-one have attended **Cambridge University**:

	Appointed		*Appointed*
Hon. I. F. W. Bligh (4)	1882-83	R. W. V. Robins (3).	1937
A. G. Steel (4)	1886	N. W. D. Yardley (14).	1946-47
C. A. Smith (1)	1888-89	F. G. Mann (7).	1948-49
Lord Hawke (4).	1895-96	F. R. Brown (15)	1949
Hon. F. S. Jackson (5).	1905	D. S. Sheppard (2).	1954
A. O. Jones (2).	1907-08	P. B. H. May (41)	1955
F. T. Mann (5)	1922-23	E. R. Dexter (30).	1961-62
A. E. R. Gilligan (9)	1924	A. R. Lewis (8)	1972-73
A. P. F. Chapman (17).	1926	J. M. Brearley (31)	1977
Hon. F. S. G. Calthorpe (4).	1929-30	M. A. Atherton (54).	1993
G. O. B. Allen (11)	1936		

Seven other Cambridge students have become Test captains: F. Mitchell (SA, 3, 1912); T. C. Lowry (NZ, 7, 1929-30); G. C. Grant (WI, 12, 1930-31); R. S. Grant (WI, 3, 1939); F. C. M. Alexander (WI, 18, 1957-58); Majid Khan (P, 3, 1972-73); D. L. Murray (WI, 1, 1979-80).

Oxford alumni have captained England in 105 Tests; Cambridge alumni in 271. In all Tests, the figures are 243 and 318.

Two England Test captains attended Durham: N. Hussain (45, 1999) and A. J. Strauss (50, 2006).

Around 150 UCCE and MCCU players went on to county cricket, with a dozen appearing for England – most recently Rory Burns and Jack Leach (both Cardiff) and Sam Billings (Loughborough). By that measure, the enterprise was fairly successful. But MCC felt there were better uses for their money.

The ECB have now agreed to fund each of the six university centres £50,000 a year, though the sums are not guaranteed, given the enormous cost of the Covid-19 pandemic – which also robbed the MCCUs of their final first-class matches – is yet to wash through budgets. With the original sum insufficient to sustain even a full-time coach, you have to worry whether every student team will be able to operate a fixture list, let alone return to the glory days when the Varsity Match packed out Lord's.

In 33 first-class games for Cambridge University, Derek Pringle scored 1,929 runs at 50, and took 79 wickets at 25. When he led them to victory over Lancashire, he had match figures of 45.1–20–87–9, and hit 24 and 61 not out. He still lives a quick stroll from Fenner's.

THE THREE Ws

The Knights of St Michael

GARFIELD SOBERS

The year was 1950, and West Indies were in England on one of the most celebrated tours in cricket history. I was 13 when it started, and would leave home at seven in the morning to try to catch snatches of commentary on my way to Bay Street Boys' School in Bridgetown. My father had died at sea during the war when I was five – he was a merchant seaman, and his ship was torpedoed – and my mother did not have a radio, so I used to stop outside people's houses and press my ear to their doors or windows to listen in until they shooed me away.

I remember that famous victory at Lord's – West Indies' first in England – when Sonny Ramadhin and Alf Valentine were immortalised in calypso. And I can still hear the voice of the English commentator describing the batting of my boyhood heroes, Frank Worrell, Clyde Walcott and Everton Weekes, as we went on to win the series.

Worrell, said the voice, batted so delicately that when he stroked the ball to the boundary, it got there just before the fielder, who tired himself out chasing it. Walcott was the Bully Beef of the West Indies batting, because he hit the ball with such power that the fielder took his hands out of the way.

Bob Thomas, Popperfoto/Getty Images

Two Ws and a Garry… The West Indians take on T. N. Pearce's XI at Scarborough, September 1957: Andy Ganteaume, Everton Weekes, Rohan Kanhai, Alf Valentine, Garry Sobers, Clyde Walcott, Gerry Alexander, Nyron Asgarali, Collie Smith, Tom Dewdney and Roy Gilchrist.

And Weekes was so quick-footed and graceful, so neat and tidy, that the fielders could only stand and admire his strokeplay. That voice, I later discovered, belonged to John Arlott, and his words made a lasting impression. It was not long before I had the opportunity to tell him so.

The Three Ws were all born in the parish of St Michael in the south-west of Barbados. So was I, but I did not really get to know them until I was selected to play for West Indies less than four years later. As a boy, I used to put the numbers up on the scoreboard at Bay Pasture, the Wanderers ground, so I had the perfect vantage point to watch and study them when they were playing for their clubs. I did not get the chance to play against them, though, because by the time Denis Atkinson, later to become one of my Test captains, got me into the Police team, they were spending most of their time off the island, touring with West Indies or playing in the Lancashire Leagues.

THE WWW FACTOR

Sir Clyde Leopold Walcott (January 17, 1926–August 26, 2006) 44 Tests

Runs 3,798 at 56.68 *Hundreds* 15 *Ct/St* 53/11 *Wickets* 11 at 37.09

His five centuries in the 1954-55 home series against Australia remain a Test record. First black chairman of the ICC, 1993–1997.

Sir Everton de Courcy Weekes (February 26, 1925–July 1, 2020) 48 Tests

Runs 4,455 at 58.61 *Hundreds* 15 *Ct* 49 *Wickets* 1 at 77.00

His five successive hundreds (against England in 1947-48 and India in 1948-49) remain a Test record. The sequence ended when he was controversially given run out for 90 at Madras.

Sir Frank Mortimer Maglinne Worrell (August 1, 1924–March 13, 1967) 51 Tests

Runs 3,860 at 49.48 *Hundreds* 9 *Ct* 43 *Wickets* 69 at 38.72

Became West Indies' first regular black captain when appointed for the 1960-61 tour of Australia, an exhilarating series that started with the first tied Test.

I had made a bit of a name for myself when I was 13 or 14 playing against much older fellows, and I first appeared for Barbados against the Indian touring team at 16. But, little over a year later, I was still playing cricket in the street with my friends, as I did most evenings, when a message came to my home summoning me to Jamaica for the Fifth Test against England. I was amazed. Two or three days later, I got to Sabina Park, where the players were practising, and saw Worrell, Walcott and Weekes in the dressing-room, as well as the great George Headley. I said to myself: "Oh boy, you have really arrived."

Because Valentine was sick, I had been selected as a left-arm spinner batting at No. 9, and I picked up four wickets in England's first innings. Len Hutton got a double-hundred, and they won easily. But everybody was kind and complimentary, although I don't think they realised I had some ability as a batsman until I was asked to open in the Third Test against Australia the following year. Jeff Stollmeyer, the captain, had apparently trodden on a ball and twisted his ankle, though I was led to believe he had other reasons for not facing Ray Lindwall and Keith Miller.

Three Ws: Frank Worrell, Everton Weekes and Clyde Walcott, with Sonny Ramadhin beyond, 1957.

I went in thinking I wasn't really an opening batsman, so I wasn't going to try and play like one. I took guard and looked around the field: no one in front of me except Miller, the bowler. I said to myself: "Don't look behind and, if you see red, just throw the bat." I hit him for four fours in his first over. Then Ian Johnson came on to bowl his off-breaks: I had a sweep, and was caught at backward square leg for 43.

I never batted at No. 9 again, but I knew I still had a lot to learn. I will always say that it was Atkinson who did most to set me on my path, because he spotted me as a little boy, and would send the groundsman to take me on his bicycle and bowl to him at the Wanderers. But Frank, Clyde and Everton helped me in so many ways.

There are some places where the senior players don't want to see the youngsters – they want them out of the room – but those fellows were nothing like that. Forget about their standing as three of the greatest players the game had seen: they always had time for you.

I used to see a lot of Frank when I went to England to play for Radcliffe in the Central Lancashire League. He lived near me, and I used to go to his house and ask for information and advice about the pitches I would play on, and the players I would face. One of them was Cec Pepper, the great Australian all-rounder, and the only player around who bowled a flipper. The first time I faced him, I was batting reasonably well, but got a bit carried away when he sent down a short one. I was halfway through my pull shot when I suddenly remembered what Frank had said about his flipper, and dropped the bat quickly. The ball hit it, and fell safely to the ground. Cec, who was renowned for his salty language, came marching down the pitch: "You've been talking to that so-and-so Worrell, haven't you!" Or words to that effect.

Frank also taught me how to supplement my income. I got £500 for the entire league season, and out of that I had to pay for my digs and keep myself tidy. The professional could make extra cash by scoring 50, at which point a collection box would go round the ground. The pennies, shillings and sometimes pounds would stop going in if you were out, and Frank drummed it into me: "Don't get out until the last penny drops." He had a lasting influence on West Indies cricket when he became captain, and I was honoured to succeed him.

I was lucky to have Clyde at the other end when I was scoring the world record 365 not out against Pakistan at Sabina Park in 1958. He came down the wicket, and said just what I wanted to hear: "You get the runs, and I'll keep you going." He was as good as his word, finishing unbeaten on 88.

Everton became a lifelong friend. We had played a bit of dominoes and bridge together before we started travelling the world, and we did so regularly when we were back in Barbados. I enjoyed sitting on top of the pavilion at Kensington watching cricket with him. He was always such a cheerful person, and a very nice man.

They have all gone now: Frank from leukaemia at the age of 42 in 1967, Clyde aged 80 in 2006, and Everton last year at 95. Yet they will never be forgotten, not just in the Caribbean, but all round the world. They were great players and great ambassadors for West Indies cricket. They were also great people.

Sir Garfield Sobers was talking to Pat Gibson.

WISDEN SCHOOLS CRICKETERS OF THE YEAR

Always sunny when you're young

ROBERT WINDER

In 2007, *Wisden* introduced a new award: the Schools Cricketer of the Year. The selectors had clear eyes: the first winner was **Jonny Bairstow**, the second **James Taylor**, the third **Jos Buttler**. It had long been known that serious cricket talent tended to reveal itself at a young age. Here was proof.

In the Covid-hit season of 2020, the Almanack decided to delve into its archive and compile a list of those who might have been earlier winners, from 1900 on. There followed much sifting, weighing, debating and selecting. Clearly, future glories were irrelevant. But how to cope with so many variables – the weather, the strength of a fixture list, the quality of the square, changes in format, the shifting nature of the game itself? What was the balance between runs and wickets? A century ago, 80 wickets might equate to 1,000 runs; today, with bowling restrictions, especially for seamers, a 50-wicket season is a rare beast. And what should be made of eye-witness testimony?

In the end, the judges relied chiefly on numbers, given the impracticality of juggling those considerations. Of course, a match-winning 40 in harsh conditions might be a greater achievement than a patient century on a tame surface; a series of maidens against a fierce attack greater than a blizzard of sixes against declaration lobs. And how should wicketkeeping be quantified? But the figures could not be ignored: they spoke for themselves.

The list reminds us that schooldays play a part in any sporting biography, and that cricket has survived many storms. In marking the game's return after the war, *Wisden 1919* barely mentioned the raging flu pandemic that would kill 228,000 Britons. Instead the editor noted a silver lining for schoolboys looking to graduate to the first-class game: "The demand for fresh talent is almost certain to exceed the supply."

At the going down of the sun, *Wisden* kept its eye firmly on the ball.

On August 12, 1939, as shadows lengthened over the two-day Young Amateurs v Young Professionals fixture at Lord's, the game stood on a knife-edge. With three minutes remaining, the Professionals needed three runs, the Amateurs one wicket. The bowler was **George Knight**, and the match had started on his 19th birthday. That season, he had hit 1,250 runs at 59 and taken 89 wickets at nine for Victoria College, Jersey. His coach, the Surrey professional Bert Geary, thought him exceptional.

Knight later called it the highlight of his life: "To play at Lord's – it doesn't come much better than that." But it did. With war casting a dark cloud over the summer, Knight claimed the final scalp: Young Amateurs won by two runs.

It is impossible to judge the value of runs scored so long ago. The pitch at Victoria College is not the biggest: for a strong batsman, it is a friendly venue.

WISDEN SCHOOLS CRICKETERS OF THE YEAR

1900 E. W. Dillon Rugby School 620 runs at 56.36; 33 wkts at 17.90
Capped by Kent in 1901, and led them in 1909–13; won four caps at rugby union for England.

1901 J. E. Raphael Merchant Taylors', Northwood 1,397 at 69.85; 76 at 14.09
Cricket for Oxford University and Surrey, and rugby for England; killed in the First World War.

1902 S. A. Trick Merchant Taylors', Northwood 759 at 58.38; 55 at 17.09
Hit 157 against Epsom College; later played for Essex. His nephew appeared for Glamorgan.

1903 G. T. Branston Charterhouse 708 at 78.66; 30 at 22.20
Played for Oxford U and Notts; 194 v Cambridge U in 1908. Toured NZ with MCC in 1906-07.*

1904 H. C. Tebbutt The Leys School 1,443 at 60.12; 72 at 16.97
A stellar season included eight centuries; no first-class cricket, but a regular for Cambridgeshire.

1905 J. N. Crawford Repton School 766 at 85.11; 51 at 12.96
England's first teenage Test cricketer, at Johannesburg in January 1906.

1906 C. Gimson Oundle School 349 at 38.77; 50 at 9.54
Tall all-rounder. Eight matches in 1921 for Leicestershire; long-serving committee-man there.

1907 G. H. Francis Chatham House School 662 at 28.78; 123 at 7.23
Only Farrelly (1913) has taken more wickets in a school season, according to Wisden's *records.*

1908 H. M. Bannister Tonbridge School 649 at 59.00; 47 at 12.38
The school's "crack" player, said Wisden*; played occasionally for Leicestershire, wearing glasses.*

1909 P. G. H. Fender St Paul's School 734 at 48.93; 34 at 15.97
Innovative Surrey captain 1921–31, and scorer of fastest authentic first-class century, in 35 minutes.

1910 F. H. Knott Tonbridge School 1,126 at 80.43; 18 at 25.22
Capped by Kent later in 1910, having scored 114 against Worcestershire in his third match.

1911 F. C. W. Newman Bedford Modern School 898 at 89.80; 15 at 20.82
Organised Sir Julien Cahn's XI (a first-class team 1929–39) and hit a century for them.

1912 F. W. H. Nicholas Forest School 875 runs at 97.22
Essex 1912–29, scoring 140 v Surrey in 1926; football for GB at 1920 Olympics; grandfather of Mark.

1913 F. J. Farrelly Stonyhurst College 134 wkts at 5.39
Highest number of wickets recorded in Wisden *for a school season. First-class cricket in South Africa.*

1914 A. E. R. Gilligan Dulwich College 508 at 36.28; 78 at 8.80
Captained Sussex from 1922 to 1929, and England in the 1924-25 Ashes; later president of MCC.

1915 A. D. Denton Wellingborough School 894 at 68.76; 21 at 15.95
Four matches for Northants before Great War – and three after, despite losing a leg on Western Front.

1916 J. D. Wyatt-Smith Sherborne School 575 at 57.50; 19 at 7.15
Killed in a plane crash serving with the Royal Flying Corps in Italy in 1918.

1917 G. T. S. Stevens University College School 640 at 58.27; 66 at 8.65
A leg-spinning all-rounder, chosen for the Gentlemen while at school; won ten Test caps.

But Knight, as we have seen, had another string to his bow: his "medium-pace off-spinners". He claimed a pair of hat-tricks, and against an All-Island XI pulled off one of cricket's golden feats (achieved by John Wisden himself) by bagging all ten wickets – in ten overs, for 24 runs.

Who can say what sort of career he might have enjoyed had war not broken out? Hampshire were interested, but Knight was stranded in the German-occupied Channel Islands, before becoming – according to the *Jersey Evening Post* in a 100th-birthday tribute last August – "the most outstanding all-round cricketer this island has produced". More than 80 years on, sheltering from the 2020 pandemic in a Jersey care home, he pronounces himself "delighted" to have his glory days remembered.

Courtesy of *Jersey Evening Post*

Jersey royal: George Knight, star of Channel Islands cricket before and after the war.

In 1953, a schoolboy named **Robert Barber** went one better. In a record-breaking season for Ruthin School, in Denbighshire, Barber achieved the grand double of 1,000 runs and 100 wickets. As the only person on the list opposite to accomplish this, he could claim to be the leading schools cricketer of the 20th century.

He could, but he doesn't. From his home in Switzerland, Bob Barber – who in January 1966 would score a masterly 185 for England against Australia in Sydney – is quick to point out that this exclusive club has two other members. One, Mike Taylor, was an older boy at Ruthin when Barber arrived: "My inspiration, actually." The other, back in 1929, was John Rogers of Birkenhead School. Neither Ruthin nor Birkenhead submitted records to *Wisden* for the relevant years, but – proof it could scent eminence in the mist – the summary in the 1930 Almanack did record that Rogers "took 100 wickets and scored 1,000 runs the second season in succession". While noting that "he played in many matches and the opposition was not always strong", *Wisden* believed this was a record "likely to last for many years". (There is a fourth known to have done the double: in 1895, Gilbert Jessop combined 1,058 runs at 132 with 100 wickets at 2.44 for Beccles College. He was, however, aged 21, and a teacher.)

Barber recalls his schooldays with palpable affection. "Cricket mattered more back then. It really was the national game. In the evenings, the fields were full of us all just playing cricket until it got dark." The fixture list was the usual blend of rival schools and wandering men's sides. "It wasn't an unbeaten season: we lost to Ruthin Cricket Club. I don't think the headmaster was too pleased."

Thanks to Taylor, Barber knew of the precious double, though it didn't cross his mind until "right at the end" – those last few wickets were hard-

1918	**N. E. Partridge**	Malvern College	514 at 102.80; 32 at 11.56

Against Repton, he scored 229 and took 11 wickets; later played 100 matches for Warwickshire.*

1919	**A. T. Lay**	Fettes College	1,259 at 57.22; 49 at 11.37

Retains Fettes run record. All-round sportsman and pianist, interned in China during the war.

1920	**G. J. Bryan**	Wellington College	699 at 116.50; 10 at 4.70

Youngest of three brothers who played for Kent; debut in 1920, aged 17, and scored 124 v Notts.

1921	**L. S. H. Summers**	Emanuel School	624 at 34.67; 101 at 7.77

A leg-spinner. "I can scarcely think of a better cricketer not seen in county cricket" – E. W. Swanton.

1922	**R. E. H. Hudson**	Haileybury College	956 runs at 68.28

Career army officer who hit 217 for them v RAF in 1932, and 181 v West Indian tourists in 1933.

1923	**K. S. Duleepsinhji**	Cheltenham College	576 at 52.36; 35 at 18.40

Nephew of Ranji – and, like him, scored a century in his first Ashes Test, in 1930.

1924	**R. W. V. Robins**	Highgate School	791 at 49.44; 54 at 10.29

Leg-spinning all-rounder who captained Middlesex, and England in three of his 19 Tests.

1925	**M. J. L. Turnbull**	Downside School	1,323 runs at 94.50

Glamorgan's captain throughout 1930s, when he also won nine Test caps; killed in France in 1944.

1926	**S. A. Block**	Marlborough College	698 at 53.69; 15 at 24.73

Scored first-class centuries for Cambridge University and Surrey. Represented England at hockey.

1927	**L. R. W. Salmon**	Allhallows School	427 at 19.40; 100 at 12.23

One of the few bowlers recorded in Wisden *as having taken 100 wickets in a school season.*

1928	**E. Ingram**	Belvedere College, Dublin	1,011 at 59.47; 52 at 4.59

Nineteen first-class games for Ireland, 12 for Middlesex; 1,008 runs and 85 wickets for school in 1929.

1929	**J. H. Cameron**	Taunton School	108 wkts at 8.06

Prolific school leg-spinner, born in Jamaica, and vice-captain of the 1939 West Indian tourists.

1930	**D. F. Surfleet**	University College School	767 at 40.36; 83 at 8.86

Broke Greville Stevens's school batting records; ten matches for Middlesex.

1931	**C. R. N. Maxwell**	Brighton College	1,037 at 69.13; 35 dismissals

"Above the average as a school wicketkeeper". Played for Notts, Middlesex and Worcs.

1932	**N. S. Mitchell-Innes**	Sedbergh School	689 at 62.63; 33 at 9.96

Long association with Somerset – and one Test for England, against South Africa in 1935.

1933	**N. W. D. Yardley**	St Peter's School, York	973 at 88.45; 40 at 11.90
1934	**N. W. D. Yardley**	St Peter's School, York	584 at 48.66; 31 at 12.29

Captained Yorkshire from 1948 to 1955; led England in 14 of his 20 Tests, including the 1948 Ashes.

1935	**G. E. Hewan**	Marlborough College	914 at 60.93; 30 at 21.66

Hit 205 v Free Foresters, and 176 and 98 v Rugby at Lord's; played for Cambridge U and Berkshire.

1936	**P. J. Dickinson**	KCS, Wimbledon	948 at 118.50; 22 at 14.86
1937	**P. J. Dickinson**	KCS, Wimbledon	1,061 at 81.61; 47 at 14.76

Century in 1939 Varsity Match for Camb U, and another for Bombay in 1947. Played for Surrey.

earned. The highlight? In another year it might have been taking all ten for 27 against Llandovery. But in 1953 it was trumped by the day he scored 136 not out against Rydal (a tense local derby), then picked up nine for 40. A busy afternoon.

Yet it isn't these spectacular figures – "irrelevant numerals", says Barber – that make him smile. Nor is it the fact that this was his penultimate year; the following season he broke his foot, leaving him free to focus on the A-Levels (chemistry, physics and biology) that took him to Cambridge, where he studied natural sciences. "It was happy cricket, that was the thing. I strongly believe that if you want people to play well they've got to be happy, and we were. I don't remember any stress. That big green field at Ruthin – it's always sunny when you're young, isn't it?"

The schools section of the Almanack strikes some as an anachronism. In the meritocratic and professional-minded modern world, it seems odd there should be any call to record the performances of schoolboys – especially since, in practice, this usually means *public* schoolboys. Yet stories such as Knight and Barber confirm that, far from being a nostalgic indulgence, the schools section is rich in cricket history. The roll call of famous names whose youthful exploits it has preserved reminds us that this is not a matter of opinion, preference, or even tradition. The schools have long been a substantial component of England's cricket heritage.

Nor does it follow (to gloss the most common argument) that the public schools are exercising an unjust grip on English cricket. Many recent international regulars – such as Bairstow, Buttler, Rory Burns, Tom and Sam Curran, Chris Jordan, Joe Root and Dom Sibley – attended public school on sports scholarships. It could be claimed that the schools they went to were not embedding privilege so much as operating a de facto national cricket academy.The opacity of post-war education policy makes it hard to be sure, but it is telling that of the schools listed opposite, all bar two or three are privately funded. It is also striking that of the England XI who faced Pakistan in the Second Test in 2020, all but James Anderson and Chris Woakes went to

---

AN ALL-ROUND EDUCATION

1,000 runs and 50 wickets in a school season in the British Isles (as recorded in *Wisden*):

	Runs	*Wickets*	
J. E. Raphael (*Merchant Taylors', Northwood*)	1,397	76	1901
H. C. Tebbutt (*The Leys School*)	1,443	72	1904
E. Ingram (*Belvedere College, Dublin*)	1,011	52	1928
E. Ingram (*Belvedere College, Dublin*)	1,008	85	1929
G. W. Knight (*Victoria College, Jersey*)	1,250	89	1939
R. W. Barber (*Ruthin School*)	1,012	108	1953
P. D. Johnson (*Nottingham HS*)	1,038	91	1969
I. R. Payne (*Emanuel School*)	1,144	79	1976
M. A. Atherton (*Manchester GS*)	1,013	61	1984
N. J. Lenham (*Brighton College*)	1,534	50	1984
Bazid Khan (*Brighton College*)	1,481	50	1999

All tables refer to 1900 onwards.

1938 J. M. Leiper Chigwell School 911 at 65.07; 77 at 7.96
Opening bowler who played two first-class matches for Essex in 1950. Father of the 1979 winner.

1939 G. W. Knight Victoria College, Jersey 1,250 at 59.52; 89 at 9.46
A regular in Jersey's annual match against Guernsey; celebrated his 100th birthday in August 2020.

1940 H. E. Watts Downside School 938 at 104.22; 36 at 12.81
Played for Somerset in 1939, aged 17, and received his county cap in 1946. Cambridge Blue 1947.

1941 T. E. Bailey Dulwich College 851 at 121.57; 41 at 12.65
1942 T. E. Bailey Dulwich College 635 at 52.91; 66 at 6.16
A great England all-rounder; more than 28,000 first-class runs and 2,000 wickets, plus 61 Test caps.

1943 J. G. Dewes Aldenham School 418 at 69.66; 20 at 9.10
1944 J. G. Dewes Aldenham School 518 at 74.00; 20 at 7.70
Chosen for an England XI in the Victory Tests of 1945, aged 18; later played five official Tests.

1945 P. D. S. Blake Eton College 778 runs at 86.44
Five centuries, and "eclipsed the record of any previous Etonian"; played for Sussex, before ordination.

1946 I. P. Campbell Canford School 1,277 runs at 116.09
Hit 222 v Marlborough, and 237 in 106 minutes v Old Canfordians; played for Kent and Oxford U.*

1947 P. B. H. May Charterhouse 651 runs at 81.37
Captained in 41 of his 66 Test matches, and led Surrey to two Championships.

1948 M. J. D. Bower Radley College 788 at 71.63; 40 at 12.82
Hit a school-record 207 v St Edward's, and captained Public Schools at Lord's.*

1949 M. C. Cowdrey Tonbridge School 893 at 55.81; 49 at 13.77
1950 M. C. Cowdrey Tonbridge School 1,033 at 79.46; 47 at 14.72
Played for Tonbridge at Lord's in 1946, aged 13, and scored 75; first to appear in 100 Tests.

1951 R. G. Woodcock RGS, Worcester 600 at 30.00; 93 at 6.81
Left-arm spinner; he took 53 first-class wickets for Oxford U and hit 57 v New Zealanders in 1958.

1952 R. A. Gale Bedford Modern School 725 at 90.26; 36 at 10.36
"A tall, elegant left-handed opening batsman," Gale scored more than 11,000 runs for Middlesex.

1953 R. W. Barber Ruthin School 1,012 at 67.46; 108 at 4.30
Recorded the rare schoolboy double; played 28 Tests for England.

1954 G. W. Cook Dulwich College 810 runs at 81.00
Struck two centuries for Cambridge Univ in 1957, including one v Oxford; also played for Kent.

1955 P. J. Sharpe Worksop College 1,251 at 113.72; 23 at 17.39
Five centuries and two doubles; long Yorkshire career as batsman (and superb slip); 12 Test caps.

1956 R. A. G. Luckin Felsted School 872 at 72.66; 10 at 20.60
Hit 235 v Old Felstedians; shared Essex-record sixth-wicket stand of 206 with Barry Knight in 1962.

1957 C. D. Drybrough Highgate School 706 at 78.44; 32 at 13.06
Australian-born all-rounder; captain of Oxford in the 1961 and 1962 Varsity Matches, also Middlesex.

1958 Nawab of Pataudi Winchester College 683 at 62.09; 14 at 22.21
Led India in 40 Tests, despite losing an eye in an accident in 1961. Also 88 matches for Sussex.

Courtesy of Ruthin School

Annus mirabilis: Bob Barber leads the 1953 Ruthin team; seated, second left, is wicketkeeper, future neurosurgeon and lifelong friend Glenn Neil-Dwyer; he helped Barber's leg-spin accrue 108 wickets.

independent schools. This cannot be put down to a blinkered selection policy: the national sorting hat had already done its work.

If there is scandal here, it lies in the paucity of facilities – and the culture that goes with them – available to state pupils. This is a political policy matter, not an editorial oversight. *Wisden* issues frequent appeals for state and girls' schools to submit averages, but few can maintain the infrastructure or fixture list required. When Liam Plunkett helped launch an ECB cricket-in-schools initiative in 2019, he revealed that in his own school career he "probably only ever played two games".

It is common knowledge that public schools possess enviable cricket grounds. Yet the real problem lies where they are absent. London's East End, home to hundreds of thousands of fervent cricket lovers of Asian descent, does not boast a single high-quality pitch. We can be dismayed, or angered; but it is hardly a false picture of English cricket's class-conscious heritage.

In some ways the list hides as much as it reveals. The following names, for instance, shone within *Wisden's* pages – Percy Chapman, Douglas Jardine, Gubby Allen, Freddie Brown, David Sheppard, Ted Dexter, M. J. K. Smith, Tom Graveney, Mike Brearley, David Gower, Alec Stewart, Nasser Hussain, Andrew Strauss and Joe Root – yet none did well enough to win a retrospective award. And this is to name only future England captains. Many modern stars also missed out. In 2016, Ollie Pope scored 904 runs for Cranleigh, and Zak Crawley 897 for Tonbridge; both were pipped by **A. J. Woodland**, who amassed 1,026 for St Edward's, Oxford.

1959 D. I. Yeabsley Exeter School 476 at 47.60; 86 at 4.15
Helped his school win 14 of their 17 matches; a prolific Minor Counties wicket-taker for Devon.

1960 E. J. Craig Charterhouse 1,106 runs at 92.16
In four years, he made 2,803 runs at 62 for the school, then scored seven centuries for Cambridge U.

1961 M. G. Griffith Marlborough College 1,070 runs at 97.27
Batsman and wicketkeeper who captained Sussex, and followed his father as MCC president.

1962 M. D. Mence Bradfield College 846 at 70.50; 84 at 10.61
"An all-rounder quite out of the ordinary". Played for Warwicks, Glos and frequently MCC.

1963 R. K. Paull Millfield School 1,009 at 100.90; 19 at 13.57
Leg-spinning all-rounder who played six matches for Somerset; Cambridge Blue in 1967.

1964 R. W. Elviss Leeds Grammar School 420 at 26.25; 64 at 8.68
Off-spinner who took 65 first-class wickets for Oxford U, including four five-fors against counties.

1965 D. R. Aers Tonbridge School 914 at 70.30; 41 at 15.78
Slow left-armer who played for Cambridge U; professor of English at Duke University, North Carolina.

1966 C. Johnson Pocklington School 668 at 111.33; 31 at 12.00
Made 88 for The Rest v Southern Schools at Lord's; 100 matches for Yorkshire in a decade from 1969.*

1967 D. R. Owen-Thomas KCS, Wimbledon 815 at 58.21; 48 at 12.91
Stylish batsman for Cambridge U and Surrey. Cricket writers' Young Cricketer of the Year 1972.

1968 P. D. Johnson Nottingham High School 1,061 at 70.73; 75 at 8.90
1969 P. D. Johnson Nottingham High School 1,038 at 54.63; 91 at 11.19
Took 473 wickets at 12 in eight seasons in the first team. Also played for Cambridge U and Notts.

1970 B. R. Weedon King's School, Canterbury 1,084 at 98.54; 48 at 12.70
South African-born; he made 203 against the Buccaneers, but never played first-class cricket.*

1971 W. Snowden Merchant Taylors', Crosby 1,018 runs at 127.25
Won four Blues at Cambridge, but never played county cricket; later taught geography at Harrow.

1972 C. J. Tavaré Sevenoaks School 794 at 113.42; 18 at 12.00
1973 C. J. Tavaré Sevenoaks School 1,036 at 94.18; 23 at 15.17
Also tough to dislodge for Kent, Somerset and England; Sevenoaks were unbeaten in both seasons.

1974 P. G. Ingham Ashville College, Harrogate 645 at 129.00; 33 at 10.06
Played eight first-class matches for Yorkshire, often as an opener when Geoff Boycott was on Test duty.

1975 C. S. Cowdrey Tonbridge School 966 at 80.50; 30 at 13.86
Son of the 1949–50 winner; captained Kent and (briefly) England.

1976 I. R. Payne Emanuel School 1,144 at 52.00; 79 at 8.68
Played for Surrey and Gloucestershire. Two one-day caps for England Young Cricketers in 1977.

1977 D. R. Pringle Felsted School 830 at 92.22; 53 at 11.94
Won 11 trophies in 16 seasons with Essex. Played the first of his 30 Tests while at Cambridge.

1978 J. W. Slingsby Abingdon School 1,003 runs at 91.18
Went into teaching after a prolific school career, and organised the sport at Ampleforth College.

Many have been good enough to play county cricket while still in school uniform: Barber, for example, pulled on a Lancashire sweater. But only one represented his country. In 1971, the 18-year-old Imran Khan made his Test debut for Pakistan at Edgbaston before spending winter in the nets at Worcester Royal Grammar, developing the scorching action that brought so much glory. *Wisden* described him as an "unusual schoolboy" who "understandably monopolised the batting and the bowling". Yet this was not enough to make him 1972's leading player. Instead, **Chris Tavaré** won the first of his two awards for hitting 794 runs for Sevenoaks.

The fact that a further 11 England captains (Gilligan, Stevens, Robins, Yardley, May, Cowdrey, Cowdrey, Atherton, Cook, plus Buttler and Taylor in ODIs), as well as 28 Test and 79 county players *do* appear opposite underlines the value of schools cricket in the national game (not just the English game, since the **Nawab of Pataudi jnr** is a notable presence).

There is equal pleasure to be had foraging in the small print. In 1984, we find a remarkable bowling effort by a young Nasser Hussain (Forest School), who took six for five against Westminster in a season that yielded 48 wickets and 1,070 runs. But that was arguably bettered by **Michael Atherton** of Manchester Grammar School, who collected 61 wickets (with what *Wisden* called his "all-conquering" leg-spin) and 1,013 runs. The pair met in the Southern Schools v The Rest match too: Atherton was snared twice by Hussain, while Hussain was caught behind off what may have been Atherton's mystery ball.

Yet here is the thing. *Both* these outstanding schoolboys were outshone by **Neil Lenham** of Brighton College, whose 50 wickets and 1,534 runs (then an all-time English schools record) made him that year's top performer.

There are even smaller nuggets. At Wrekin College, in 2000, a "South African exchange student" named Jean-Paul Duminy "made an immediate impact when he dropped a skyer off the first ball of the season"; he made a

---

HEAVY BATS

1,350 runs in a school season in the British Isles (as recorded in *Wisden*):

	I	*NO*	*Runs*	*HS*	*Avge*	
I. J. Sutcliffe (*Leeds GS*)	24	8	1,623	161	101.43	1993
G. R. Treagus (*King Edward VI, Southampton*)	25	6	1,613	134*	84.89	1993
C. G. Taylor (*Colston's School*)	18	3	1,597	278*	106.46	1995
N. J. Lenham (*Brighton College*)	21	2	1,534	207	80.73	1984
R. W. Nowell (*Trinity School, Croydon*)	25	6	1,505	170	79.21	1992
Bazid Khan (*Brighton College*)	23	7	1,481	169	92.56	1999
H. C. Tebbutt (*The Leys School*)	24	0	1,443	154	60.12	1904
S. E. P. Davies (*Bradford GS*)	26	3	1,424	143*	61.91	1995
E. T. D. Casterton (*RGS High Wycombe*)	21	5	1,423	267*	88.93	2017
D. Grundy (*Merchant Taylors', Northwood*)	26	9	1,419	158*	83.47	1995
T. Köhler-Cadmore (*Malvern College*)	15	1	1,409	186	100.64	2013
J. E. Raphael (*Merchant Taylors', Northwood*)	26	6	1,397	175*	69.85	1901
J. A. Haynes (*Malvern College*)	25	4	1,393	177*	66.33	2018
C. N. Gates (*Brighton College*)	22	3	1,378	178*	72.52	1990
C. M. Jaggard (*Merchant Taylors', Northwood*)	25	3	1,364	145	62.00	1990
M. J. Chilton (*Manchester GS*)	16	3	1,361	143	104.69	1995
M. A. Thornely (*Brighton College*)	21	6	1,360	182*	90.66	2005
C. J. Warde (*Dauntsey's School*)	21	3	1,352	103	75.11	2000

1979	**R. J. Leiper**	Chigwell School	1,031 at 85.91; 11 at 9.09

Son of 1938 winner. Two first-class games for Essex; three caps for England Young Cricketers, 1980.

1980	**A. Seymour**	Plymouth College	342 at 28.50; 70 at 8.44

Left-arm spinner who took two hat-tricks. Gave up cricket soon after school to become a GP.

1981	**H. Morris**	Blundell's School	923 runs at 184.60
1982	**H. Morris**	Blundell's School	1,032 at 129.00; 25 at 17.56

Reached 50 in 23 of 28 school innings 1981–82; long career for Glamorgan; three Tests for England.

1983	**M. A. Roseberry**	Durham School	826 at 75.09; 48 at 8.45

Opening batsman for Middlesex and Durham in 17-year career. Toured Australia with England A.

1984	**N. J. Lenham**	Brighton College	1,534 at 80.73; 50 at 11.20

Played 14 seasons for Sussex, finishing with more than 10,000 first-class runs, and 20 centuries.

1985	**M. A. Atherton**	Manchester Grammar School	748 at 187.00; 21 at 15.76

Collected 1,013 runs and 61 wickets in 1984. Led in 54 of 115 Tests, before moving into the media.

1986	**M. A. Crawley**	Manchester Grammar School	1,123 at 112.30; 31 at 19.51

Played for Oxford U, Lancs and Notts, with less impact than his brother, the 1989 winner.

1987	**H. A. M. Marcelline**	Bishop's Stortford College	1,166 at 145.75; 32 at 15.34

A Sri Lankan-born opener, Hareen Marcelline scored five centuries in the school season.

1988	**N. Shahid**	Ipswich School	937 at 85.18; 67 at 10.49

Six years with Essex, then ten at The Oval; nine first-class centuries and two in one-day games.

1989	**J. P. Crawley**	Manchester Grammar School	940 runs at 156.66

Long career with Lancs and Hants produced nearly 25,000 runs; 54 centuries – and 37 Test caps.

1990	**C. J. Eyers**	RGS, Worcester	932 at 49.05; 51 at 15.15

Five seasons with Worcestershire, but never played first-class cricket.

1991	**M. G. N. Windows**	Clifton College	615 runs at 123.00

Injured for half the season. Followed his father into the Glos side, and scored over 9,000 runs.

1992	**R. W. Nowell**	Trinity School, Croydon	1,505 at 79.21; 64 at 14.92

Only 16, he hit seven centuries; played 12 first-class games for Surrey; worked in cricket sponsorship.

1993	**I. J. Sutcliffe**	Leeds Grammar School	1,623 runs at 101.43

Highest seasonal aggregate recorded in Wisden*; later played for Oxford U and three counties.*

1994	**L. J. Botham**	Rossall School	774 at 70.36; 54 at 10.00

Ian Botham's son, 16, led the school; later played cricket for Hants, and professional rugby.

1995	**C. G. Taylor**	Colston's School	1,597 at 106.46; 31 at 18.87

Hit 278 against Hutton GS. A long career with Gloucestershire; later England's fielding coach.*

1996	**R. Wilkinson**	Worksop College	1,161 at 82.92; 33 at 14.33

Played one first-class match for Yorkshire in 1998; captained the Academy side.

1997	**R. S. Clinton**	Colfe's School	963 runs at 107.00

Outstanding opening batsman, aged 15. Played for Essex and Surrey – a first-class century for each.

Courtesy of Stonyhurst College

Strength in numbers: the Stonyhurst first team of 1913 boasted two 100-wicket bowlers. Roderick Riley (seated, second left) claimed 103, and Francis Farrelly (seated, far right) 134.

more lasting impact with a batting average of 150. At Bedford School, **Alastair Cook** "hinted at impressive powers of concentration" in 2002, while two years later a not-so-young touring New Zealander in search of match practice turned out for King's, Macclesfield. Daniel Vettori, aged 25, bowled a tidy if unpenetrating ten overs, and impressed spectators by helping shove the sightscreens to and fro.

Peter Johnson of Nottingham High, winner in 1968 and 1969, has the astonishing distinction of appearing in the *Wisden* schools section for eight editions. Johnson – who reportedly never missed a match – left with a jaw-dropping haul of 473 wickets, seeing off **John Cameron's** 425 (for Taunton School in seven seasons between 1927 and 1933). There are other astonishing tales: "Fowler's match" of 1910, when Eton captain Robert Fowler scored 64 in the follow-on to set Harrow 55 to win, then took eight for 23 to seize victory by nine runs; or the Tonbridge v Clifton clash of 1946, when the 13-year-old Colin Cowdrey – "reputed to be the youngest player to appear in a match at Lord's", said *Wisden* (who also called him "Michael") – steered Tonbridge to a two-run win with match tallies of 119 runs and eight wickets.

Overseas tours feature, too – as in 1987, when the English schoolboys competing in the Sir Garfield Sobers International Schools Tournament came up against a diminutive but promising batsman from Trinidad's Fatima College: Brian Lara.

The list trembles with more solemn echoes. The 1901 winner, **John Raphael**, scored five first-class centuries, stood as a Liberal candidate in 1909

1998 P. J. S. Spencer Brighton College 602 at 37.62; 77 at 8.92
Leg-spinner helped by the presence of future England keeper Matt Prior behind the stumps.

1999 Bazid Khan Brighton College 1,481 at 92.56; 50 at 19.52
Eventually followed his father (Majid Khan) and grandfather (Jahangir Khan) as a Test player.

2000 G. J. Muchall Durham School 1,003 at 167.16; 15 at 29.73
Hit 254 for England Under-19 in 2002; nearly 8,000 first-class runs for Durham, with 14 hundreds.

2001 T. B. Huggins Kimbolton School 1,069 at 106.90; 36 at 15.30
His runs included 700 in a week, for once out; later played for Northamptonshire and Suffolk.

2002 A. N. Cook Bedford School 1,126 at 93.83; 22 at 16.27
2003 A. N. Cook Bedford School 1,287 runs at 160.87
Went on to score 12,472 runs, with 33 centuries, in 161 Tests – all England records.

2004 J. Cole Merchant Taylors', Crosby 959 at 119.87; 10 at 18.70
His runs included five centuries; he played for Lancashire's Second XI, and Cumberland.

2005 D. B. Pheloung Felsted School 61 wkts at 12.22
A 16-year-old leg-spinner, who broke Derek Pringle's school wickets record.

2006 P. L. Mommsen Gordonstoun School 1,062 at 151.71; 15 at 13.06
South African-born, but went on to play for Scotland, and captained them at the 2015 World Cup.

Formal award inaugurated

2007	**J. M. Bairstow**	St Peter's School, York	654 at 218.00; 16 at 23.62
2008	**J. W. A. Taylor**	Shrewsbury School	898 runs at 179.60
2009	**J. C. Buttler**	King's College, Taunton	554 runs at 61.55
2010	**W. G. R. Vanderspar**	Eton College	1,286 runs at 80.37
2011	**D. J. Bell-Drummond**	Millfield School	801 runs at 133.50
2012	**T. B. Abell**	Taunton School	1,156 at 192.66; 19 at 15.68
2013	**T. Köhler-Cadmore**	Malvern College	1,409 at 100.64; 10 at 33.10
2014	**D. E. Budge**	Woodhouse Grove School	731 runs at 121.83
2015	**B. A. Waring**	Felsted School	68 wkts at 9.23
2016	**A. J. Woodland**	St Edward's, Oxford	1,026 at 85.50; 12 at 19.08
2017	**E. T. D. Casterton**	RGS, High Wycombe	1,423 at 88.93; 14 at 27.64
2018	**N. J. Tilley**	Reed's School	1,256 runs at 139.55
2019	**T. S. Muyeye**	Eastbourne College	1,112 at 69.50; 23 at 16.73
2020	**No award**		

The winners of the awards were decided by Douglas Henderson, the Almanack's schools correspondent since 2005, in conjunction with Wisden staff.

Schools reports and averages from every edition of Wisden *can be found at schoolscricketonline.co.uk/ wisden-archive* and, a year later, led a British representative rugby team to Argentina, before falling, like hundreds of others in *Wisden's* pre-war schools' pages, on the Western Front. He is buried in a military cemetery in Belgium, the country of his birth. And the Lancelot Hingley who scored 741 runs for Rugby in 1940 cropped up again in 1941, when he played for MCC against his old school. *Wisden* ran a photograph of the teams, explaining Hingley's absence by saying he "arrived late after bombing German factories up to 5am". He made a final entry, in *Wisden 1944*, in the obituaries – aged 21.

Of all the near misses, two stand out. The unluckiest bowler was Roderick Riley, who in 1913 took an extraordinary 103 wickets for Stonyhurst (where Arthur Conan Doyle had learned the game). But he was outdone by a team-mate, **Francis Farrelly**, who took 134 – an amazing figure, even if Stonyhurst cricket was sometimes 13-a-side. The most unfortunate batsman, meanwhile, must be Glyn Treagus, who in 1993 totted up 1,613 runs for King Edward VI, Southampton, only to find that **Iain Sutcliffe** had scored ten more for Leeds Grammar. These are the only two to have topped 1,600 – and both did it in the same school season. Cricket, eh?

But no one ever said luck wasn't part of the game. John Barclay, who enjoyed a long career with Sussex, had cause to groan after taking nine for 57 for Public Schools at Lord's in 1970, only for the English Schools Cricket Association to ruin what *Wisden* called a "once-in-a-lifetime chance" by a "somewhat unchivalrous" declaration.

There are plenty of signs that cricket runs in families. David Gower's father, Richard (King's, Canterbury), was a strong contender in 1935, while **Frederick Nicholas** (grandfather of Mark, and "an exceptionally good bat") *did* stand out in 1912. **Liam Botham** scored 774 runs and took 54 wickets for Rossall in 1994, before deciding to shun his father's footsteps and play rugby. **Mark Crawley** (1986) and brother **John** (1989) followed Mike Atherton's (1985) example at Manchester GS. And **Bazid Khan**, the 1999 winner for a superlative season comprising 1,481 runs and 50 wickets for Brighton College, had more than just a famous father (Majid Khan) as inspiration: uncle Imran may also have been a useful role model.

UNPLAYABLE

90 wickets in a school season in the British Isles (as recorded in *Wisden*):

	O	*M*	*R*	*W*	*Avge*	
F. J. Farrelly (*Stonyhurst College*)	350	76	723	134	5.39	1913
G. H. Francis (*Chatham House, Ramsgate*)	298	70	890	123	7.23	1907
R. W. Barber (*Ruthin School*)	210.2	62	465	108	4.30	1953
J. H. Cameron (*Taunton School*)	310.3	51	871	108	8.06	1929
R. R. Riley (*Stonyhurst College*)	284	60	502	103	4.87	1913
L. S. H. Summers (*Emanuel School*)	328.4	76	785	101	7.77	1921
L. R. W. Salmon (*Allhallows School*)	393.1	72	1,223	100	12.23	1927
R. G. Woodcock (*RGS, Worcester*)	334.5	97	634	93	6.81	1951
J. A. I. Watts (*Newton College*)	231	14	918	93	9.87	1912
W. P. Lipscomb (*KCS, Wimbledon*)	–	–	754	92	8.19	1905
J. H. Cameron (*Taunton School*)	208	29	636	91	6.98	1930
P. D. Johnson (*Nottingham HS*)	435.3	138	1,019	91	11.19	1969
F. W. M. Draper (*Merchant Taylors', Northwood*)	342.5	63	1,175	91	12.91	1901

Trinity Mirror/Mirrorpix/Alamy

Nature *and* nurture: Chris and Colin Cowdrey, winners for 1975, 1949 and 1950.

The list throws up two father-and-son pairings (the **Cowdreys** of Tonbridge and the **Leipers** of Chigwell), and nearly a third. In 1970, the "schoolboy cricketer of the year," in the words of E. M. Wellings, *Wisden's* hard-to-impress reviewer, "was undoubtedly Bairstow". This was David Bairstow, father of Jonny and a brilliant wicketkeeper for Hanson Grammar in Bradford. He caught the eye playing at Lord's for England Young Cricketers against their West Indian counterparts, though by then he had already made a splash. Having been given dispensation to take his English literature A-level at 7am, he made his debut for Yorkshire against Gloucestershire that morning, and took five catches in the game. But Hanson did not appear in *Wisden's* list of schools, so he registered only a distant blip on the schoolboy-of-the-year radar.

Fittingly, *Wisden* often adopted a schoolmasterly tone with its annual crop of youngsters, chiding them for "bad eating and sleeping habits", or for having the "wrong attitude" in "this lazy modern age". Bairstow had not been the only young player to catch the Wellings eye at Lord's. Of Richard Brown, son of England captain Freddie, he wrote: "Brown's approach to the job of batting was splendidly uncomplicated. But why must he handicap himself by sporting his hair so long? A hairnet might have been more useful to him than his cap, which perched on top of the shrub without any permanence… Such luxuriant growth of hair is as much a handicap to a cricketer as long fingernails." *Wisden* – and from 1945 until 1972 that meant Wellings – also handed out tips: "He

Patrick Eagar, Popperfoto/Getty Images

Stacks of laughs: Micky Stewart and Christopher Martin-Jenkins in the Great Portland Street office.

But, by the 1960s, with Warner and Langford soldiering on, *The Cricketer* was often tawdry in content and appearance, every cover a garish lime green and red, evoking two of the game's colours. It was deemed not sufficiently profitable, and would have been wound up were it not for an alert cricket devotee on the board. Ben Brocklehurst had overcome steeper obstacles: mauled by a bear in Kashmir, put in command of 2,000 Japanese POWs, and in 1953 saddled with the captaincy of Somerset. In 1972, he bought the magazine, and resolved to run it with his wife, Belinda, from their home near Tunbridge Wells.

By now, E. W. Swanton wore the crown, though he would always be editorial director, not editor. In 1967, the Cambridge graduate Christopher Martin-Jenkins had been hired for £700 a year – "slave labour it was to be too" – and within a month he found himself promoted to assistant editor after Irving Rosenwater flounced out of the Great Portland Street offices on a point of statistical principle. Many a journalist or historian was admonished during Rosenwater's lifelong pursuit of accuracy, and it seems even relations with the lordly Swanton were a price worth paying.

The Cricketer's freelance rate was one guinea per 100 words "for all our contributors, great and small". At least they saved on budget when Richie Benaud's Australia tour preview failed to arrive in spring 1968; CMJ ended up writing it under Benaud's byline, "affecting a certain racy Aussie style".

Swanton's many years of service to "the paper" for a few hundred quid a year – as with Anthony Howard and the *New Statesman*, it was always "the paper" – no doubt fostered a sense of entitlement. But it is unfair to write him off as a fusty reactionary. His columns had injected *The Cricketer* with a forceful tone, complemented by superb action shots from the twentysomething photographer Patrick Eagar, whom he had accidentally discovered in 1965. Swanton had been visiting Mike Griffith, son of Billy (both would become president of MCC), at Magdalene College, Cambridge, where his room shared a landing with Eagar's. Swanton knew the name – Desmond Eagar had captained Hampshire – and knocked on his door to confirm he was "Desmond's son". They got talking, and Swanton suggested Eagar take some photos for his magazine. He started with a feature on Fenner's, and followed it up with one on Canterbury. So began the most famous career in cricket photography.

In 1972, two years after the magazine had gone monthly, John Arlott suggested David Frith to Swanton as his next day-to-day man. "Swanton called me up to the gantry underneath the Oval press box in between commentary stints during the last Test of the summer," says Frith. "It was supposed to be an informal chat, but we both knew it was an interview. He asked who Jimmy Cannon was. 'Oh, he was Tityrus, who wrote *Wickets and Goals*,' I said confidently. 'No, no, no,' he roared. 'That was Jimmy Catton. Cannon was the chief clerk at Lord's.' He was chuckling away, and I knew I had the job. He could be a disgraceful bully: I saw him once harangue a young Australian journalist in the press box. But you had to respect his knowledge and his war experience. He had a set of rules to protect the game at all costs, and you can't help but line up with that."

Frith acquired the Wisden name for a royalty of 2p per copy

One of Swanton's rules was that under no circumstances would the sweep shot be illustrated – even though Denis Compton had spread such joy with the stroke years earlier, and the Mohammad brothers had started *reverse*-sweeping. Frith broke the dictum almost immediately with a Tony Lewis cover image in February 1973.

It was discord with Brocklehurst and his advertising man Christopher Bazalgette that led to Frith's sacking in 1978. "I'm still waiting for an explanation," he growls. His response? To start his own magazine. It would be unthinkable now. *The Cricketer* had the market to itself after swallowing the snazzier *Playfair Cricket Monthly* in 1973, aping their better ideas and pocketing their subscribers. Brocklehurst and Bazalgette had embarked on several ventures to keep the business viable. At one point, five recreational competitions were run in-house, plus celebrity-branded tours to Corfu, where The Cricketer taverna still stands. By 1984, around 30,000 people across Britain had played in one of the magazine's competitions; circulation climbed to 45,000.

The debut issue of Frith's *Wisden Cricket Monthly*, in June 1979, sold more than 58,000, and was reprinted. "It took me a year to pull it together, but I bloody showed them how to do it," he says. He feels his timing was fortunate: the Packer rebels had rejoined the mainstream, and English cricket was on the cusp of the Botham boom.

Frith's masterstroke was to acquire the Wisden name for a royalty of 2p per copy sold. And although sales plateaued into a monthly slugfest against *The Cricketer*, the new magazine, glory be, made money – if not as much as its rival, after Brocklehurst's careful budgeting. Frith targeted big-name

Bob Thomas Sports Photography/Getty Images

Talking shop: E. W. Swanton signs a copy of *Follow On* for David Frith, November 1977.

columnists: Bob Willis ("willing, but lacking in ideas"), David Gower ("disappointingly indolent, but I knew he sold magazines"), Ted Dexter and Arlott ("no one could have replaced the void left by his son, Jim, but I'd like to think I went as far as anyone"). Eagar was signed up on an exclusive deal. It was reflective of some kind of philosophical split that Arlott and Swanton were going up against each other every month – *WCM* coming out on the fourth Wednesday, two days ahead of *The Cricketer*.

They were subtly different. Frith concluded there was little hope of doing justice to all the cricket played in Britain: it was easier to direct focus (and funds) towards the pointy end of the game, where the glamour lay. Steven Lynch, Frith's deputy from 1985 to 1996 (and now the *Almanack's* international editor), recalls: "I seem to remember it being said, 'Why would we cover the Surrey Championship when only people from Surrey will be interested in reading about it?'" *WCM* developed in Frith's image: concerned primarily with England and Australia, then the game's powers, and his two homes; without censor in its Editorial and Letters; crotchety on international issues and administration (both he and the trenchant E. M. Wellings opposed South Africa's isolation); adoring towards history and the game's great figures, many of whom Frith knew personally; and reflecting his own obsession with memorabilia.

With photos gradually supplanting adverts on the front of *The Cricketer* from 1952, the cover became a balance between catching eyes on the news-stand and not alienating loyal subscribers. When Basil D'Oliveira struck his century at The Oval in 1968, only to be initially left out of England's tour party

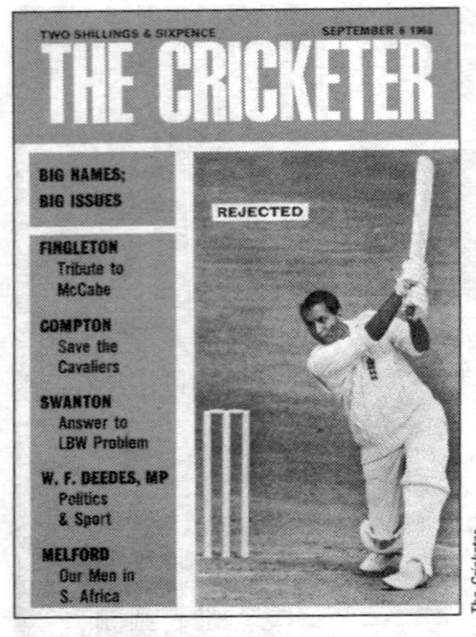

Cover drive: CMJ's one-word comment on Basil D'Oliveira's exclusion.

for South Africa, Martin-Jenkins stuck "Rejected" on the cover over Dolly's square-drive. Swanton disapproved, but wasn't there on deadline to make his feelings known. He did so in the following winter annual, mixing his sorrow at the suspension of a sporting rivalry with his "reavowed detestation" for apartheid.

The Cricketer was cerebral enough in the 1970s to produce covers exhibiting Jacques Sablet's painting of Thomas Hope, bat in hand, on the Grand Tour and, to herald the Centenary Test, a fetching orange collage of James Lillywhite's inaugural Test side. No other high-street cricket magazine would have made a cover star of Fiji's Ilikena Vuli, as *The Cricketer* did in July 1979 ahead of the ICC Trophy. But sales dipped for the *WCM* issue led by George Beldam's great picture of Victor Trumper winding up for a drive, and containing an imaginary interview between Frith and Trumper (dead since 1915).

Instead, in the monthly landgrab, a well-known international player was plonked on the front, no matter how tenuous his mention inside (it was almost always a he). Though *The Cricketer* had Jan Brittin square-cutting in culottes in November 1984, and *WCM* – now edited by Tim de Lisle – dressed Isabelle Duncan in an MCC sweater for October 1998 to signal their stance on the membership debate, putting a woman on the front has generally been avoided on commercial grounds. (Only with *All Out Cricket*, initially published by the Professional Cricketers' Association, and rebranded as *Wisden Cricket Monthly* in 2017, did a magazine make women's cricket a badge of honour.) Frith, meanwhile, was told by someone in the industry that "black faces don't sell"; even though he never liked West Indies' bouncer-heavy approach, he ignored the advice several times over.

One of Frith's regrets is that a trunkload of suggested articles, which he deemed worthy of publication but couldn't fit into 60 pages, went unused. These days, they might go online. Yet an unsolicited submission that *was* used cost him his job. In 1995, he ran an article by Robert Henderson headlined "Is it in the Blood?", which claimed foreign-born players were incapable of committing wholeheartedly to the England team. *WCM* ended up paying substantial damages to Phil DeFreitas, Devon Malcolm and Chris Lewis.

Perhaps only so much checking was possible by a skeleton staff on their hands and knees in a room in Guildford, piecing together pages with scissors, spatulas and Cow Gum. "I don't know what was in the gum," says Lynch, "but after one of my first deadlines I spent a day in a darkened room shaking off a thumping headache." Incorporating overseas tour photos from Eagar or David Munden relied on begging a returning newspaperman to pack umpteen rolls of film in his luggage. Finally, in 1997, under the lateral-thinking editorship of de Lisle, *WCM* fell into the orbit of a major publisher (John Brown, in west London), and was put together on computer; *The Lady* was thought to be the last major British magazine still battling with pots of glue.

The digital revolution has changed magazine production beyond recognition. It is one of the reasons why *The Wisden Cricketer*, edited for its eight years by John Stern, was so superb. About the only clumsy thing about it was the name, an amalgam of *WCM* and *The Cricketer*, after both proprietors decided in 2003 it was futile to keep fighting each other. (How many club subscribers were lost when only one of Brocklehurst's competitions, the National Village Cup, retained the magazine's backing?) Ownership by Paul Getty, and later Rupert Murdoch, did no harm to the editorial budget. This was clear from the glittering array of freelance contributors to *TWC* – with perhaps just two-thirds of a page set aside for columns by such eminences as Frith, Scyld Berry or Matthew Engel – and the seemingly unlimited use of Eagar's picture archive.

EDITORS OF THE CRICKETER

Sir Pelham Warner	1921–61
Peter Morris	1962–64
A. W. T. Langford	1964–66
E. W. Swanton (*editorial director*)	1966–83
David Frith	1973–78
Reg Hayter	1978–81
Christopher Martin-Jenkins (*editorial director* 1988–1991)	1981–88
Peter Perchard	1988–2003
Richard Hutton (*editorial director*)	1991–98
The Wisden Cricketer	
John Stern	2003–11
The Cricketer	
John Stern	2011
Andrew Miller	2012–14
Alec Swann	2014–16
Simon Hughes	2016–

The internet is both saviour and threat. It provides all the tools to make a compelling magazine, though the ten-day lag between deadline and publication still exists. Back in the 1980s, the earnest cricket watcher might carry *The Cricketer* or *WCM* in their satchel alongside *The Times*, *Telegraph* or *Guardian*; now, they can get their fix on ESPNcricinfo or Twitter, or consume the action live via BBC Sport or Sky Go. In the last few years, thecricketer.com and wisden.com have become impressive presences, and helped spread the gospel about their heritage title to a younger audience. But the lucrative adverts seen in older magazines, perhaps for cigarettes or E-Type Jags, are long gone.

Patrick Eagar, Popperfoto/Getty Images

Required reading: John Edrich, David Steele, John Snow and Tony Greig, Lord's, 1975.

News-stand sales were on the wane before Covid-19 – how often do you see someone thumbing a paid-for magazine on a train? – but there are still around 30,000 who pay less than £45 a year to subscribe to either *The Cricketer* or *WCM*. Would it be easier to put it all online? Perhaps, yet it is more complex than that. Ask fans to pay for web journalism and – unless it's Mike Atherton or Gideon Haigh – they often recoil. There is a feeling that what you read on one website is already on another, or rushed, or confected in the pursuit of clicks.

The task of Warner or Swanton was to draw together the cricketing world in an authoritative way. Now magazines have to listen to their readers – and rightly so – the Letters pages of *The Cricketer* are rich with varied and thoughtful feedback, even if the hearts of many remain firmly with the traditional red-ball county game. *The Cricketer* – and in summer, the weekly *Cricket Paper* – seem to have taken on the job of regular county news which newspapers abandoned after the last recession.

So a delicate balance persists: give loyal readers enough of what they like, but cast a discerning eye on changes in the game they might not. The only sensible solution, as Frith says, is to "do what isn't done elsewhere, or do it better". And even when sales are healthy, there's always the fear of what lies round the corner – until you open an email from a reader telling you the magazine has never been better. You *could* put it all online, but that just wouldn't be the same…

James Coyne is assistant editor of The Cricketer.

WISDEN – THE PREQUEL?

Turning over an old leaf

JON HOTTEN

There is something very 2020 about three men standing around outside a bank wearing masks. It's a wet day in October in Hemel Hempstead, the mizzle heavy enough to drench us all. One of the men is Nigel King, a dealer in rare books; the second is Robert Winder, author of *The Little Wonder* (a history of this Almanack); the third is me.

We're not about to rob the place, but we are here to enrich ourselves in other ways. From the vault where it lives, stuffed inside a couple of supermarket carrier bags, appears something that King bought at an auction in Amersham in March 2016, and that has come to dominate his life. He pulls it from the bags, and lays it on the table in the bank. It is an old book, bound in red leather, and its 250 or so pages – gilt-edged and luminously beautiful – are not printed, but handwritten. Seemingly unconcerned by its fragile loveliness or the yellowing sticky tape around its spine, King flips it open, riffles through the pages, and begins.

"See here," he says, jabbing a finger under a line of tiny cursive script. "Wisden… first mention."

Nigel King is a maverick figure, used to living on his wits. At auction, he buys on a mix of knowledge and intuition. Viewing opportunities for the diary were limited but, in the minutes available, he noticed in the neat handwriting John Wisden's name as one of those present at a shoot. King is not a follower of cricket, but Wisden, and the appearance of scorecards and match reports, persuaded him to bid. He won't say what he paid – "hundreds rather than thousands" – though he knew he had done well when Rupert Powell, a rare-books expert for *Antiques Roadshow*, approached him as he left, dismayed he had arrived too late to view it himself.

In the weeks that followed, King examined the diary more closely. It appeared to be "three or four manuscripts in one". There were day-to-day entries running from January to September 1863; a record of the Victorian sporting season that began with shooting, and included rowing, horse racing and lots of cricket; a series of other reports and records; and several missing pages, largely at the back, that seemed to have been cut with scissors or a scalpel. The first half of the diary contained a series of miniature, sometimes exquisite, pen and wash illustrations reminiscent of William Blake. As well as plenty of time, the author had talent. But who was he?

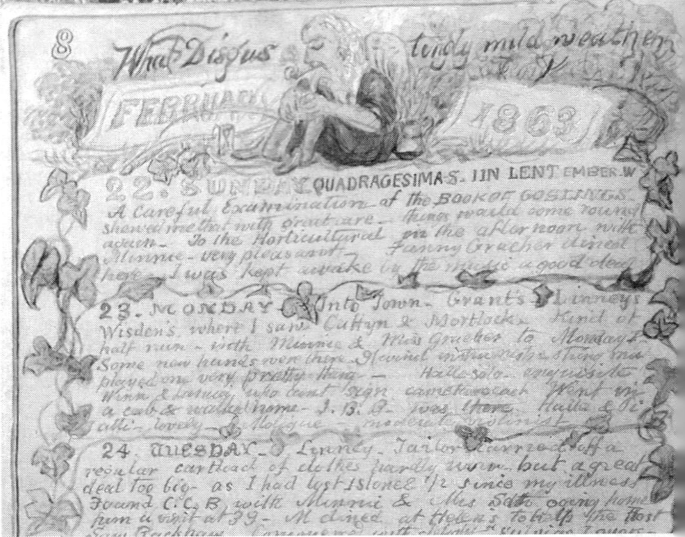

8 What Disgus tingly mild weather

FEBRUARY 1863

22. SUNDAY QUADRAGESIMA S. 1 IN LENT EMBER W

A Careful Examination of the BOOK OF GOSLINGS showed me that with great care – things would come round again. To the Horticultural in the afternoon with Minnie – very pleasant – Fanny Gracher dined here – I was kept awake by the music a good deal

23. MONDAY Into Town – Grant's Linney's Wisden's where I saw Caffyn & Mortlock

24. TUESDAY – Linney – Tailor carried off a regular cartload of clothes hardly worn but a great deal too big – as I had lost 1 stone 1/2 since my illness

Francis Emilius Carey Elwes was not, as his initials might suggest, a future England captain, even if he was born, in August 1828, into circumstances that ensured good prospects. The Elweses, one of England's oldest families, were a grand collection of landowners, soldiers and politicians (and later actors, artists and musicians). His father, Robert, cut a dashing figure in the best social circles, and bred two Derby winners, Mameluke in 1827 and Cossack in 1847. Francis's own talents do not appear to have found expression beyond his diary, which is a window into a vanished life: moneyed and time-rich, with long days filled by pleasure. "Walked around a bit," reads one entry, "then went to Lord's."

Were the diary no more than a sharply observed amble through the mid-19th century, it would still be a valuable document. But when King read more closely, another story emerged. John Wisden appeared in the diary not just once, but frequently – sometimes several times on a page. Wasn't it curious that the lofty, aristocratic Elwes was friendly with a man like Wisden, the son of a builder? How might their paths have crossed, and why would Elwes invite him shooting at Egton, the vast estate near Whitby owned by his half-brother, or go to dinner with him in London?

King had never seen the first Almanack, so he went to the library at Lord's. He was surprised to find that the book John Wisden billed as *The Cricketer's Almanack for the Year 1864* contained no match reports, just a range of scorecards and ephemera such as the phases of the moon, a list of canals, the

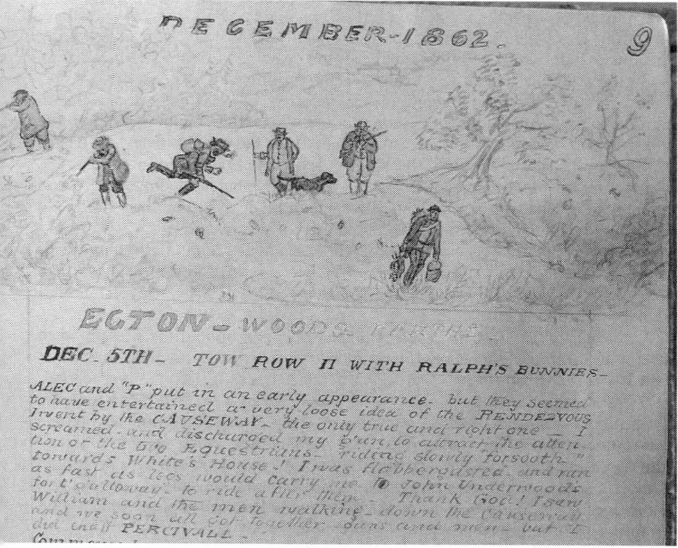
DECEMBER - 1862. 9

EGTON - WOODS [illegible]

DEC. 5TH - TOW ROW II WITH RALPH'S BUNNIES -

ALEC and "P" put in an early appearance. but they seemed
to have entertained a very loose idea of the RENDEZVOUS
I went by the CAUSEWAY - the only true and right one - I
screamed - and discharged my gun, to attract the attention of the two Equestrians - riding slowly "forsooth"
towards White's House -! I was flabbergasted - and ran
as fast as legs would carry me to John Underwoods
for t'galloway - to ride after them - Thank God! I saw
William and the men walking - down the Causeway
and we soon all got together - guns and men - but I
did [illegible] PERCIVALL -

rules of quoits and the dates of the Crusades. The emphasis was as much on almanack as cricket. It was a flimsier and less detailed production than the diary Elwes had created in 1863, which contained lengthy match reports, as well as more informative scorecards.

Then, on page 108 of the Almanack, King noticed a section headed "University Rowing Matches". It was almost identical to a list that appeared in the diary. Elwes, who had rowed for Magdalene College, Cambridge, seems to have based his information on the *Rowing Almanack and Oarsman's Companion*, founded in 1861. The matter is not entirely straightforward, but in recording the times for the races of 1861, 1862 and 1863, Elwes has departed from the *Rowing Almanack*. What makes this intriguing is that the times given in the first *Wisden* match Elwes verbatim. For King, this is a smoking gun: Wisden had sight of Elwes's diary.

King combed it for connections, spending almost 18 months transcribing every page. He found more threads to pull on, such as Elwes's deep love of horse racing – and the first Almanack's list of Classic winners.

The diary offers plenty on the relationship between Elwes and Wisden, which might have stretched back to Wisden's time coaching at Harrow, where generations of Elweses were educated. There can be no doubt cricket meant a great deal to Francis, a member at Lord's and The Oval, and the connection came with benefit to both parties. When Wisden enjoyed his ten days' shooting at Egton, he brought his friend and fellow star George Parr. Elwes writes later of "going to Wisden's", of the "grog and sandwiches" they consumed. King speculates that one of Elwes's engaging line drawings might even be Wisden – a figure at dinner who wears a familiar hat, puffing on a pipe.

Did their relationship extend to the creation of the first Almanack, an entrepreneurial endeavour that exploited new printing technology and the emergence of professional cricket? Wisden had both the reputation and the means to sell and distribute the book through his sporting goods shop in Haymarket. His former business partner Fred Lillywhite had been producing guides and annuals for a decade or so. Perhaps Elwes, with his love of the diary form, and an eye on the main chance, nudged the old cricketer into action?

"It's possible," says Robert Winder, who had not encountered Francis Elwes in his research for *The Little Wonder*. "There's no doubt that there is a connection between them, and that Wisden saw the diary. Beyond that, I suspect we'll never know, but I don't think it matters."

A note at the front of the 1864 Almanack reads: "Should the present work meet with but moderate success, it is intended next year to present our readers with a variety of other matches…" Moderate success has certainly been his. Elwes and his diary had a more melancholy fate. As 1863 wears on, the illustrations disappear, the writing loses its snap, and completion becomes a chore, then a trial. The handwriting deteriorates, and crossings-out – almost entirely absent early on – grow frequent. Elwes, who may have been a syphilitic, is never in good health in the diary, and his downward slide ends four years later, at the age of 39. He dies in Sussex, at Ticehurst House Hospital, a sprawling Victorian asylum for wealthy patients (and now part of The Priory chain).

Nigel King's dogged pursuit of Elwes and Wisden probably ends here, too. For a while he was obsessed, sitting in the road outside Lord's during the 2019 World Cup with home-made placards about "Wisden's Secret", and creating a website that seemed to be searching for conclusive proof of a crime – plagiarism, presumably – that quite possibly never existed. But he has given Francis Elwes and his diary a place in Wisden history, a despatch from the past that refracts new light on old, beautiful, pages.

Jon Hotten is the author of several books, including Bat, Ball and Field, *forthcoming from HarperCollins.*

After dinner ALL England sent in Willsher and Caesar to the bowling of Griffith and Atkinson as before. Griffith in his 3d over floor-
ed Caesar and the 4th sent Willsher back. 2 wkts - 9 runs. and
then Stephenson and Hayward and ran up the score to 52 when
Stephenson gave a chance to long leg which was well taken
by Newman - Hayward's stumps were lowered next over.
Stephenson's bold innings composed a 4 four 3's, two 2s. Hay
played well for his 14. Daft came in to hit but skyed one
to short leg. but put on 11. not bad a maimed man. Parr
was caught by the long stop after getting 9 - in which was one
good cut for 4. Hodgson and Caffyn were now exchanged for
Atkinson and Griffith - somewhat tired - Tom shewed great skill
in his management. Hodgson and Caffyn bowled extremely
well and destroyed the remaining wickets - a great victory ensu-
ing for the UNITED. The law 10 was fairly carried out and
the only man that seemed inclined to raise his hand was Woot-
ton. May they have a better wicket next year. I believe that every
man nearly received some little punishment

First-hand knowledge: Francis Elwes was at Lord's on May 26 to watch the United England XI defeat the All-England XI by 70 runs.

LEARIE CONSTANTINE AND THE WISDEN TROPHY

Peer pressure

HARRY PEARSON

When the ECB announced that the Wisden Trophy was to be replaced, a number of wise commentators suggested this might be the ideal opportunity to honour Learie Constantine, the great West Indies all-rounder. Without his intervention it's doubtful the trophy would have come into existence.

When the Almanack reached its 100th edition in 1963, John Wisden & Co chairman Ken Medlock was keen to commemorate the milestone, and it was Constantine, a long-time family friend, who suggested a trophy for the winner of England–West Indies Test series. Constantine knew from experience how the game had the power to forge bonds and dismantle prejudice. The Wisden Trophy would be a celebration of the sporting and cultural ties between Britain and the Caribbean, of commonality rather than difference. But Medlock's approach to MCC was politely rebuffed, and Constantine, a man whose influence stretched far beyond cricket – by then he was Trinidad & Tobago's high commissioner in London, and had recently been knighted – petitioned the West Indies Cricket Board of Control. MCC swiftly reconsidered.

There was more to it than that, though. The trophy was inaugurated in the summer of Martin Luther King's March on Washington. In 2020, when the

Trinity Mirror/Mirrorpix, Alamy

Source of wonder: Learie Constantine and young admirers.

Black Lives Matter movement was given fresh worldwide impetus by the brutal death of George Floyd, Constantine's achievements in battling racial injustice would have merited lasting recognition from those who run the game he loved and adorned.

Born on a cocoa plantation in rural Trinidad, and the grandson of a slave, Constantine was the first true star of Caribbean cricket. He bowled with electric pace and hostility, clobbered the ball with exuberance, and fielded with such acrobatic panache that reports from West Indies' first tour of Australia in 1930-31 suggested he had taken a catch in the covers while turning a cartwheel. Constantine's dash and charisma encouraged the apocryphal, and few who saw him in action ever forgot. In 1928, playing for the West Indians on their first tour as a Test team, he created a sensation against Middlesex at Lord's, taking a seven-for with his ferocious bowling, and smashing a century in an hour – including one blow that ricocheted off Father Time. Shortly after, Constantine signed to play as the professional for Nelson in the Lancashire League, becoming one of the highest-paid sportsmen in Britain. Soon, he would be one of the nation's first black celebrities, too.

On the field, he was a first-class cricketer; off it, a third-class citizen

Constantine came to play in Lancashire not only for financial betterment, but to escape the deeply rooted racial discrimination of the colonial Caribbean. In Trinidad, the darker a person's skin, the narrower the field of opportunities. Constantine was, in the jargon of the time and place, a "black man", and at the bottom of a hierarchy topped by whites. On the field, he was a first-class cricketer; off it, a third-class citizen.

His arrival in Nelson caused a stir: he and his family were the first black people most Lancashire folk had seen. Children queued to peep through the Constantines' kitchen window and watch them eating. Initially, Learie found the curiosity unbearable, but his wife, Norma – always a calming influence – counselled forbearance: "They will get used to us."

"Nearly all the prejudice I have ever encountered," Constantine would later write, "was based on ignorance." It was a situation he worked hard to rectify. When not playing cricket or studying for a law degree, he toured the North – often accompanied by his friend C. L. R. James. They gave lectures about the West Indies, and made the case for home rule at a time when the prevailing opinion was, at best, that West Indians were cheerful but unruly children who needed a firm – white – hand to guide them.

Though Norma was right, in the main, prejudice did not evaporate, even in the part of Lancashire where people came to embrace Constantine as one of their own. There was a rancorous encounter with East Lancashire's South African pro, Jim Blanckenberg, an unapologetic racist who refused to shake his hand. Meanwhile, the former Derbyshire player Archie Slater, the pro at Colne, tried to unsettle Constantine with racially charged sledging. In both cases the response was a furious barrage of bouncers that left Blanckenberg covered in bruises, and Colne seeking peace talks.

If the actions of Slater and Blanckenberg seem unconscionable today, they reflected the attitude of certain first-class professionals of the era. When

Keystone Press/Alamy

Lords debut, 1969: Lord Constantine is welcomed to Westminster by Lord Cholmondeley, Lord Brockway (sponsor), the Duke of Norfolk and Lord Beswick (sponsor).

Australian fast bowler Ted McDonald left Lancashire in 1931, Constantine appeared an obvious replacement. However, after an initial approach, the club committee dropped the idea when their pros let it be known they would oppose his appointment. "It would have seemed wrong seeing a black man sitting where an Englishman should have been," one later commented.

His rip-roaring success at Nelson – who won the Lancashire League seven times while he was there – paved the way for scores of top-class West Indians to make a living playing in northern England at a time when there was no professional cricket in the Caribbean. Among those who benefited was West Indies' first regular black captain, Frank Worrell, who led his side to victory in the inaugural Wisden Trophy.

Constantine's career as an international cricketer – he played in 18 Tests, helping West Indies to their first victories over England and Australia – ended at The Oval in August 1939. When war broke out, he might have returned to the safety of Trinidad; instead, with typical integrity, he remained in England. Working for the ministry of labour as a welfare officer, he helped the great influx of Caribbean workers who had come to aid the war effort settle in an alien – and sometimes hostile – land.

He was awarded an MBE for his work, but not everybody in England was appreciative. In 1943, the Constantines tried to check into the Imperial Hotel in London, having booked a room and paid a deposit. When they arrived, however, the manager refused – describing them, within earshot, in the most offensive terms. Incensed, Constantine resolved to act. Since there were no laws against racial discrimination in Britain at the time, he sued for breach of contract. His victory in *Constantine v Imperial Hotels* was a landmark in the politics of the UK. He would go on to help dozens of other black and Asian immigrants bring similar cases, giving a redress against bigotry to those who had previously been powerless.

In the 1950s, Constantine returned to Trinidad and, as a key figure in the People's National Movement, helped lead his nation to the self-rule he had so often championed to audiences in northern England. He came back to the UK as his country's first high commissioner. In 1963, the year of the first Wisden

TEST CRICKETERS TO SIT IN THE HOUSE OF LORDS

George Robert Canning Harris (4th Baron Harris)	1872
Martin Bladen Hawke (7th Baron Hawke)	1887
Ivo Francis Walter Bligh (8th Earl of Darnley)	1900
Lionel Hallam Tennyson (3rd Baron Tennyson)	1928
Learie Nicholas Constantine (Baron Constantine of Maraval and Nelson)	1969
David Stuart Sheppard (Baron Sheppard of Liverpool)	1980
Michael Colin Cowdrey (Baron Cowdrey of Tonbridge)	1997
Rachael Heyhoe Flint (Baroness Heyhoe Flint of Wolverhampton)	2011
Ian Terence Botham (Baron Botham of Ravensworth)	2020

The first four were hereditary peers, and the date is of their succession to the title. The other five were life peers, and the date is of their appointment.

Trophy, he involved himself publicly – and at the cost of his diplomatic position – in the acrimonious Bristol Bus Company dispute, which had begun when the firm banned the hiring of black or Asian crews. His tactful negotiations helped end the ban, and his consultations with Harold Wilson's Labour government during the affair led to the passing of the 1965 Race Relations Act.

In 1969, he was elevated to the House of Lords, the upper chamber's first black member. Fittingly for a man who was a hero in both the West Indies and England, he included in his title Maraval, the village in which he had grown up, and Nelson, the cotton town he had come to think of as home.

Constantine was a sparkling cricketer, yet it was his achievements off the field as an amiable, good-humoured but forceful campaigner for equality that remain his true legacy. Like Jackie Robinson, Muhammad Ali and Colin Kaepernick, Learie Constantine is an athlete whose refusal to be cowed by bigotry changed the way we look at the world. Perhaps his name deserves to be attached to something more important than a cricket trophy.

Harry Pearson is the author of Connie: The Marvellous Life of Learie Constantine *(Little, Brown). He lives in Hexham, the birthplace of Kent seamer Norman Graham, and is almost as tall.*

PART TWO

The Wisden Review

CRICKET BOOKS IN 2020

A green and pleasant land?

EMMA JOHN

Nostalgia, eh? They say it ain't what it used to be, yet sports fans continually prove them wrong. During long days of lockdown, broadcasters who had run out of fresh produce were forced to spoon-feed us long-life staples from the larder, fare with no best-before date: Borg v McEnroe at Wimbledon, the 2005 Ashes, a variety pack of medal highlights from the London Olympics. We devoured them all, and went back for seconds.

It was an ever-tempting prospect, during 2020, to retreat into rose-tinted history rather than face present woes. Happily for cricket lovers, the bookshelves were already stocked with remembrance of things past. We had been primed for a different existential threat – the invasion of The Hundred, due to land on the English season "like a grand piano falling from space", as Duncan Hamilton puts it in **One Long and Beautiful Summer**. "Everything has a last time," he writes, "and I knew those of us devoted to the Championship must wring out, drop by drop, what is left." It was to be ripped along its centre-seam, and restuffed with a toxic mix of city franchises and five-ball overs. Spooked by this Frankenstein's teddy of a future, Hamilton travelled the counties in 2019, composing an elegy to a game, and a way of life, he feared doomed.

Michael Henderson also set out to capture what remained of the English game's soul "before cricket shatters into a thousand fragments". In **That Will Be England Gone**, he too constructs a personal fixture list that thoughtfully blends county matches with other traditions – village games, league games. **Cricket on the Edge**, a by-the-numbers diary of the English season, spends less time at the grounds than in front of the screen. But its author, Tim Cawkwell, was similarly inspired to bear some kind of final witness.

Hamilton and Henderson are both masters of prose, and of the past; they have written books that weave a cashmere-cosy blanket of memory and anecdote. Henderson meanders between history, literature, art and music, waxing erudite about everything from Azharuddin's six sixes over the sightscreen at Chesterfield, to Chaucer, Anouilh, and Powell and Pressburger at Canterbury Week. Hamilton encounters the ghosts of Hobbs and Larwood at Welbeck CC, where Nottinghamshire are taking on Hampshire at the smallest ground ever to host a Championship match, "camouflaged by the shallow rise of lush fields, tall plump trees and high hedges".

The fact that the World Cup exiled many counties to historic outgrounds was a blessing to both men's adventures (they overlap at Scarborough). It is not so much the game they are lamenting, but an ideal of it – a vision of Englishness that the sport has always enabled and encouraged. Henderson kicks off with a description of the Malvern Hills so vivid you can practically hear the strings in the background, pouring out an Elgar serenade.

It is tempting to believe, when wallowing in their descriptions, that everything – cricket, beer, education – was better in the old days. That we who live now are in the death grip of greying modernity, just as Philip Larkin described it in the poem that inspires Henderson's title: "...all that remains/ For us will be concrete and tyres". Cricket has fertilised its mythology in this way for generations. Henderson mentions Cardus's part in the charade; Hamilton hat-tips Edmund Blunden, whose *Cricket Country* paid much the same melancholy tribute in 1944 as Hamilton does now. And as Hamilton did ten years ago, when he wrote *A Last English Summer*.

While he and Henderson were getting their gloom on at a Championship circuit that has been sparsely attended for decades, a thrilling World Cup was being played to ecstatic, multicultural crowds. An Ashes series was turning Ben Stokes into the sporting personality of the year. Hamilton has the awareness to admit he sounds like "a croaky and whiskery veteran". Henderson doubles down on the grumpy old man schtick, whinging about "diversity", "accessibility" and players wearing their caps the wrong way round.

What I take issue with is not the dislike of The Hundred's superficial silliness (agree), the appreciation of the county game's subtle beauty (strongly agree), or even the notion that some of cricket's charms are slipping into quiet oblivion (as they have ever since the moment someone added a third stump). It's the despairing tone, and the faint noxious whiff that England is losing her identity. Real ale good, craft beer bad.

Our tendency as cricket lovers to romanticise the past and to decry the future isn't just habit, it's a full-blown pathology. We should, when necessary, call it out. Does county cricket really reflect a national "patience, forbearance and tolerance", as Hamilton suggests? The claim rings a little false in a year when black and Asian cricketers have spoken out about decades of prejudice.

Polarisation is the poison of our times, and there's no need for us to up the ante. If Henderson wants to mount an argument of how public-school privilege benefits us all, that's his hill to die on. If he thinks culture is in a race to the bottom, it won't touch those of us who feel blessed to live in the age of Michaela Coel or Steve McQueen or Phoebe Waller-Bridge. Nor will his out-of-touch suggestion that today's young cricket writers lack the wit of their predecessors find much sympathy here – but hey, if he doesn't get their jokes, I'm happy to explain them.

These books are the outpouring of a common human feeling, the one we all share as we witness the world change in ways we do not control, never wanted, and cannot prevent. In 2020, Hamilton and Henderson were far from the only men in their sixties grieving a "loss of identity".

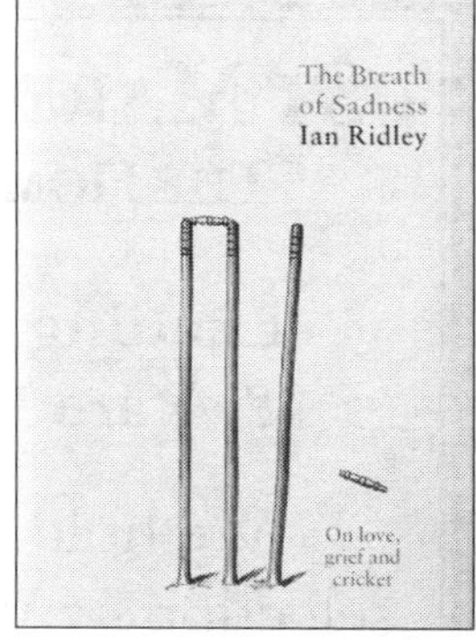

Two more titles, following the domestic season in similar style, continue the note of elegy. In Richard Clarke's **Last-Wicket Stand** and Ian Ridley's **The Breath of Sadness**, the county game's old-fashioned rhythms and quiet spaces became a place of balm – for a mid-life depression in Clarke's case and, in Ridley's, for the devastation of losing his wife.

Vikki Orvice was a pioneering sportswriter of sparkling charisma and generosity; her loss from cancer at the age of 56 was felt by all who knew her. When she died, at the start of 2019, Ridley became enveloped in a mania of grief. Living alone, and seeking a way to bear his perpetual heartache, he looked to cricket for a reason to leave the house, visiting grounds and towns that had held meaning for him and Orvice. It was no miracle cure. Often the sorrow was so intense he couldn't abide as much as a day away from home, "the familiarity of Vikki. Her clothes. The growing collection of photographs of her, and us, that I'd framed. Her very presence." The book is a moving and bleakly honest account of the mind-rending effect of losing a beloved.

The cricket (deckchair days at Hove, the inevitable trip to Scarborough) tends to be the least compelling narrative element. Sometimes the game serves as a metaphor for Ridley's feelings, with its "moods, its ebbing and flowing, its lassitude and inactivity before huge waves, of emotion as well as action". Later, as he looks back on his turbulent summer, he decides that grief, like the game he loved, "rewarded sticking with it"; that "gradually understanding its intricacies induced a comfort".

The poignancy lies in the rendering of county cricket as a refuge for a single, lonely, older man. "The thing about going to cricket on your own is that it doesn't matter if you are among fellow loners and losers," writes Ridley, and it's a sentiment shared in both *Last-Wicket Stand* and *One Long and Beautiful Summer*. The background mumbles create a soothing space for both Clarke and Hamilton, when accompanied by the black dog of depression, to find some peace.

While we're in sombre mood, **A Cricketer and a Gentleman** pays touching tribute to Bob Willis, who died at the end of 2019. Through its anthology of interviews and anecdotes, along with unpublished essays by Willis himself, a lovely portrait emerges, quite different from the grumbly figure he presented on commentary stints, or the desk-thumping fulminator of Sky Sports' *Cricket Debate*.

No wonder the book became a bestseller. Willis's career – England's then-highest wicket-taker, and sometime captain, not to mention the under-sung

architect of Headingley '81 – is worth sashaying through in its own right. But it's the personal moments that make this a special pleasure: from his brother David's explaining the origin of his idiosyncratic run-up, to a 21-year-old Ian Botham's first meeting with him on Test debut, or John Major's endearing observation that "I sometimes wish that Bob had been less laconic, and more proud of his achievements." It's like being at the wake with his closest friends.

It is hard for biography to shed light on the best-known players. And when it does, it feels worthy of celebration. How many of us knew, for instance, that Brian Close was a maths whizz, or a prolific letter-writer? A large cache of his correspondence has been uncovered and collected by veteran Yorkshire cricket reporter David Warner in a volume named after Close's usual opening gambit, **Just A Few Lines…**

The contents cover the early part of his career, from schoolboy prodigy to 1955-56 MCC tour of Pakistan; it's a nice opportunity to hear his unfiltered voice recount the daily incidents that make up his life. He chases girls in London during the 1948 Olympics, goes to a lot of films, and shares racy magazines with Fred Trueman that "don't half set your blood tickling". At one stage, he plays such a good game of football that he feels as though he's just had sex with Lana Turner.

He's not a bad match reporter, either. His descriptions of the 1950-51 Ashes tour, on which he was frequently sidelined, are entertainment in their own right, especially the low-scoring First Test at Brisbane ("Alec, who had been sent in as nightwatchman, took a swing at one and was caught… the b—— fool"). Even more intriguing is his relationship with the chief recipient of these letters, John Anderson, a best friend since boyhood who was afflicted with polio. Although we don't see the other side of the correspondence, John's jealous need for Close's attention is a constant theme ("For God's sake," Close writes, "stop being so damned moody"). Even Anderson's sister Margery admits John was "quite upset" when Brian met Vivien, his wife-to-be. John died a few weeks after Close; he arranged himself a funeral that matched his friend's to the last detail.

Close lived to 84 years and 202 days. Last year, his sometime England team-mate Ted Dexter celebrated *his* life to date in **85 Not Out**, which looks back not just on a storied career for Sussex and England, but on a beleaguered time as chairman of selectors. It also includes a number of chapters on his financial ventures, PR business, golf-playing and retirement to France. Not to mention the activities of his various family members, which are bafflingly included.

Still, the first half of the book can be captivating. Some of the stuff charting a post-war boyhood spent between the Home Counties and northern Italy, where his father worked, is almost magical. For a while, it suggests a counter to the "lordly" label that's always stuck to him, revealing a personality that found it hard to settle to anything, even cricket. And yet he can be careless in the way he speaks about people – including old friends such as Reg Hayter, or Clifford Makins, the former sports editor of *The Observer* who helped him write his previous autobiography, *Ted Dexter Declares*, back in 1966.

The Archie Jackson Story: Cricket's Tragic Genius was first written by David Frith in 1974. His revised edition updates this biography of the Keats of Australian cricket with new material, gleaned across the past half-century, without changing it in any significant regard. It requires little comment other than this: Frith's beautifully wistful memorial to the Bradman-that-never-was remains an essential read for anyone who likes cricket, or words.

And so, seamlessly, we come to **Oi, Key**, the autobiography of a Kent captain turned chatty TV pundit. I'd make a joke about moving from the sublime to the ridiculous, but I can't, because Rob Key's book is actually one of the biographies I've enjoyed most all year. Lord knows, I am not a fan of #bantz, and once made a dig at the feller in print, comparing his unrelenting style of commentary with the more debonair David Gower. But the longer Key has sat behind the mike, the more he has become a rare observer of the game – and an excellent communicator of its intricacies.

What can I say: the man's grown on me. His take on the life of a minor England/senior county figure is unsurprisingly honest, not least in discussions of fitness, fatness and professional cricket's drinking culture. But his insights into strategy and team dynamics – "give me a coach who has no influence" – stand out. Key cuts through bullshit buzzwords and training techniques to the things that actually matter, like recognising your best players. He lays bare a fundamental problem of youth cricket: if you're not good, it's usually no fun. "You stand in a field, you don't bowl, and you don't bat," he says, pointing out that in most set-ups the majority of kids are "simply there to facilitate the game". And yeah, if you want LOL late-night drinking tales of rooming with Freddie and Swanny and Owaisy, you can get them here too.

You may have noticed by now that 2020 lacked books by or about current England players: a consequence, no doubt, of the rush to market at the end of a World Cup winning year. The exception comes from Nick Hoult and Steve James, who have composed a long-lens view of the one-day team's achievements, with a title that sums up their effort far better than I can – **Morgan's Men: The Inside Story of England's Rise from Cricket World Cup Humiliation to Glory**.

Back in 2014, Graeme Swann prophesied, with deadly accuracy, that England would crash and burn in the 2015 tournament. It was from these metaphorical cinders that Eoin Morgan and his men began their rebuilding. This book revisits that period alongside a match-by-match retelling of the 2019 tournament itself. Thanks to the familiarity of Hoult and James with the team and their processes, it becomes more than the sum of its occasionally well-known quotes. New angles emerge on pivotal moments – such as the late-night Bristol incident that landed Ben Stokes and Alex Hales in trouble – and insights from England's support staff give a broader sense of how today's elite teams achieve success. The development of tactics from Nathan Leamon's data analysis – including the decision to "take down" the new ball – helps explain an England one-day team that were, for the first time, ahead of the curve.

Mike Brearley's latest book, **Spirit of Cricket**, begins with a confession. "When I first heard the phrase the 'spirit of cricket', I was suspicious of it." This review also starts with a confession: I did not quite get this book. Brearley's brilliance has been established beyond doubt, in multiple fields, so it is certain the problem is mine rather than his. I tried my best to keep up amid the scholarly grappling with the titular concept – for example, the abstruse line between "demoralising" opponents with sledging, and "disintegrating" them, or whether there's something Freudian about ball-tampering. But I got to the end unsure what conclusions I was supposed to reach, or whether not reaching conclusions was the point.

I feel terrible about this and, if philosophy is your thing, you will engage with it more fruitfully. Brearley's direction of travel is very much towards forgiveness and mercy – a message that cannot be heard enough right now. And while we're on the subject, forgiveness and mercy are what you'll feel for Mohammad Amir by the end of **The Thin White Line**, Nick Greenslade's fine account of the spot-fixing crimes of 2010. The headlines may have been unforgettable, but the book shows how little detail of the seismic scandal is commonly known. His is a true behind-the-scenes narrative, told from the vantage point of the Fleet Street reporters and operators who ran the sting that exposed Amir, Salman Butt and Mohammad Asif. It not only documents the

meticulous work that goes into such an investigation – culminating in the drama of a secretly filmed cash exchange – but builds a sense of the painfully mundane details and decisions that can lead to an 18-year-old prodigy being sentenced to six months in a young offenders institution. There runs through the book an admiration for the dark arts of tabloid journalism which not every reader will share. But it is an original and well-told piece of reportage, approached with the kind of legwork of which any newspaper editor would approve.

The hiatus that the pandemic brought upon us – in cricket, in sport, in everything – meant reflection was less a lifestyle choice (if you reached mid-April without downloading a mindfulness app, all power to you) than a global mandate. There was plenty to reflect on. As the Black Lives Matter movement gathered pace, it issued a call – and offered an opportunity – for us all to consider whose voices we listen to, and whose stories we tell.

Those of us who love cricket's history and literature are well aware of the dominant narrative of colonialism: for more than a century it has shaped both the game and the way we think about it. Surely this is why C. L. R. James's *Beyond a Boundary* is regarded as one of the greatest cricket books. Beautifully written and powerfully argued, it was among the first works to cast a perspective on the game that didn't belong to the Europeans who ran it.

Ramachandra Guha – whose **The Commonwealth of Cricket** is a delightfully whimsical memoir of his cricket life and loves – has authored works that are vital to broadening the understanding of the game in the subcontinent, as have Mihir Bose, Osman Samiuddin and Prashant Kidambi. They have overlaid the traditionally Eurocentric standpoint, of a British officer class that gifted the game to the colonies, with that of Indians, Pakistanis and Sri Lankans who fought to make it their own. But the long-standing imbalance in the way we tell cricket's story still requires much redress.

Beyond the Pale, by Andy Carter, sets out "to look at cricket, race and identity through the experiences of non-white cricketers in England between 1868 and 1939", and the result isn't half as heavy as it sounds. The book was conceived as a podcast series, and Carter uses his admirable research to turn each chapter into a readable story – be it the Aboriginal team who were the first Australians to tour England, or Alfred Holsinger, a Ceylonese club pro who plied his trade on the Isle of Wight at the turn of the 20th century. The tone is even-handed, pointing out injustices and inconsistencies with acerbity rather than emotion: the British Gymkhana in Bombay, for instance, "saw no irony" when they considered themselves the "home team" against the city's Parsees. It also acts as a check on more wishful thinking about the past. Michael Henderson says in *That Will Be England Gone* that Learie Constantine "encountered occasional puzzlement" in Lancashire, "but no hostility". Carter says Constantine received letters telling him to go home, was racially abused by a team-mate, and considered breaking his contract after his first season, wondering "whether he would ever be fully accepted in an English town".

Racism is one of the most painful and difficult topics that cricket – like wider society – has faced. We know it is wrong, and yet we know it happens. If we have not experienced it, fellow cricket lovers and players have. One of the reasons it continues is that those unaffected by prejudice have often failed to recognise it, and ignored its less obvious forms. Sometimes we even outsource that responsibility – to institutions we are not part of, to countries other than our own, or to generations before us.

Last year marked the 50th anniversary of the furore surrounding South Africa's planned tour of England, and of the Rest of the World series that replaced it. At so great a distance, it is easy to shake our heads at the obvious wrongs committed under apartheid, safe in the knowledge we are on the right side of history. A raft of books tied to the 1970 controversies may encourage us to better understand not only what took place, but how the oppressive power structures shaped by a 500-year tale of Western conquest still inform society and sport.

Chief among them is **Pitch Battles** by Peter Hain and André Odendaal, which documents "the making of the most racist sports system in the world", and the "six-decade-long struggle to overthrow… its effects". It is the ultimate insiders' guide to the fight for a sporting boycott of South Africa, jointly written by the man who founded the Stop the Seventy Tour protest movement, and a first-class cricketer and anti-apartheid activist who has become one of South Africa's pre-eminent historians.

They start by reclaiming some of the stories of the non-white cricketers who were, quite literally, written out of the past. Men like Krom Hendricks, the "Spofforth of South Africa" and the first player banned from playing for the country because of his skin colour. If you want to know more about Hendricks, **Too Black to Wear Whites** by Jonty Winch and Richard Parry provides a sobering side read. It tells how he was hounded out by the prime minister of the Cape Colony, Cecil Rhodes – just one way in which the ugly pursuit of white supremacy under apartheid can be traced back to European colonisation.

The D'Oliveira affair, the pitch invasions that plagued the Springboks' rugby tour of the British Isles, the vandalism of county grounds, the political brinkmanship between MCC and home secretary James Callaghan – *Pitch Battles* takes a well-known narrative and combines it with chilling detail from life in an apartheid police state. It is a heavy but rewarding read, a deep dive into the workings of the various groups lobbying for and against South Africa's place on the world's sporting stage, as well as Hain's prosecution for conspiracy after the tour was called off.

Arunabha Sengupta's **Apartheid: A Point to Cover** follows a similar path, although its inclusion of Hain's origin story – fuelled by the extraordinary activism of his parents, and the execution of a family friend – is moving. **Tour de Farce**, by Mark Rowe, focuses on the police and media attitudes that prevailed towards the turbulent 1960s landscape of protest.

The English cricket establishment's reluctance to take a moral stand looks shabby in every version of this tale (and *Wisden* doesn't look so innocent, either). Glamorgan's Wilf Wooller receives notably more ire in Rowe's book than the MCC pair of Billy Griffith and Gubby Allen, the traditional villains. More instructive are the huge numbers of ordinary people who would rather have seen the South African team play than listen to the ethical debate against it, the county members who put their names to petitions, and collected for a "Support the Tour" fund, on the principle that sport and politics shouldn't mix. Poor judgment abounded, thanks to the self-interested response of cricket's leadership, a heightened atmosphere of social division, and a general ignorance of the facts. The idea that sport and politics shouldn't mix has been proven inadequate many times over.

"The story of the cancellation is not really a cricket story," writes Colin Shindler in **Barbed Wire and Cucumber Sandwiches**. "If anything it is the story of generations in conflict." His book places the narrative in the context of the 1960s struggles for civil rights, and senses similarities with the societal fault line exposed by Brexit. Little did Shindler know his book would be published two weeks before George Floyd's death unleashed passionate protests across the United States. Nor that a tidal wave of global solidarity would prompt a backlash from those who would rather not believe structural racism exists.

As a white man who grew up in an apartheid-supporting family, yet became a trusted ally of Nelson Mandela, Odendaal seems pertinent here. The decision to join his black countrymen's fight for freedom was not born of a bravery beyond the rest of us, but of a willingness to allow his own sense of self to be challenged by empathy for others; to move "from a life and ideas informed by a white colonial… paradigm to a framework which… identified with the oppressed, and demanded a certain humility".

It's that humility we all need now, the preparedness to listen to voices other than those which continually echo and reinforce our own limited view of the world. Perhaps this is one of the motivations behind **The Unforgiven: Mercenaries or Missionaries?**, in which Ashley Gray tracks down and interviews the players who went on the West Indian rebel tours of South Africa in the 1980s. This is not the first journalistic effort about the men who broke their countries' ban, but it is the most complete and best researched. Gray builds up a sense both of characters and tour action, devoting a chapter to each squad member. Many were vilified for their involvement, and several shunned by friends, family and employers on their return home. Everton Mattis, David Murray and Richard Austin all fell into drug addiction; Herbert Chang had a breakdown.

The majority, happy to say, have found a second act to their lives – several in the US – and it is notable how many stand by their decision. For most, it was a payday they couldn't turn down, at a time when fighting your way into the West Indies side was a difficult process. "It was hard enough being born with the wrong skin colour into second-world poverty," Gray notes, "let alone being forced to wear criticism for trying to escape it."

Three more books deserve a mention for fresh perspectives. **Englistan**, by Kamran Abbasi, explores the cricketing obsession of a British Asian; his

exasperated devotion to the Pakistan team will resonate with many. Raf Nicholson's **Ladies and Lords** is the most far-reaching and academically rigorous history of women's cricket yet published, revealing the sport as a cradle of feminism against all the odds. Meanwhile, **A New Innings**, written by Simon Hughes and Manoj Badale, co-owner of Rajasthan Royals, gleans the important lessons from the commercial and popular success of the IPL. Arguably, it is the one cricket book published in 2020 whose contents were made *more* relevant by the pandemic, offering a timely outlook on where cricket can go from here.

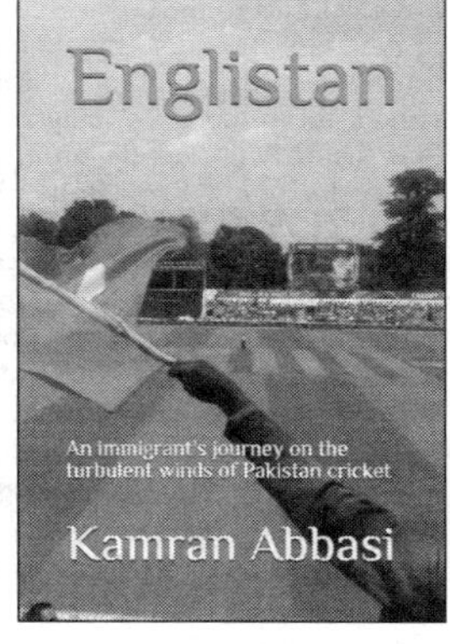

It is a tough break for authors when their carefully crafted creations are born into surroundings so different from those in which they were written. England win the World Cup, and publishers can turn out Ben Stokes stocking fillers by Christmas. But a pandemic – or Floyd's killing in Minneapolis – makes the presses seem to grind exceeding slow. There was nothing published in 2020 that feels like *the* cricket book we need right now.

But there is one that presents a great deal of something we could all do with: joy. This was not, I'll admit, a publication I gave much thought to when I first heard about it. Then it arrived on my doorstep with a self-satisfied thump, and I needed both hands to pick it up. The title sounded a little off, but it was a cricket art-book published in New York, so what did I expect? I opened it. And from that point, I couldn't tear myself away.

I have seen plenty of collections of cricket photography before. **This is Cricket: In the Spirit of the Game** was the first that pricked my eyes with tears. To someone starved, all year, of the real-life sights and sounds and smells of the game, this glorious 368-page compendium, its spreads the size of a modest paving slab, was almost too rich, a feast of images that threatened to overwhelm the senses.

To list what I saw does not do the experience any justice: Clive Lloyd in the nets in his salmon-pink World Series gear; Kapil Dev and Mohinder Amarnath laughing on the Lord's balcony; Jan Brittin smashing a square cut to the boundary. Some are famous pictures you've ached to have a copy of – Botham with his cigar, Buttler running out Guptill. Many capture moments you'll recognise, in ways you don't; and plenty more are simply photographs from the cricketing landscape that you've never seen. All come screaming off the page.

After months of isolation, they transported me to unfamiliar times and places, made me weep with pleasure over games played before I was born. The book is irresistible – a tactile treat I keep coming back to, carefully turning its luxuriant pages for a glimpse of whites, a whiff of grass.

I notice, with delight, how magnificent the book's many women look; how, under the lens, their power and art achieve parity with their male peers. I find myself drawn to the crowd scenes, appreciating, for the first time, the marvel of the mass spectator experience, from Antigua to Pune to the MCG. Several times I gasped – at a broken-armed Paul Terry trying to dig out a Joel Garner yorker, for instance – or laughed out loud. And dammit, it felt good.

In *One Long and Beautiful Summer*, Hamilton talks of a photograph of Worcester's New Road from 1972 that he looks at every day. Here, Test and county grounds, village greens, the Oval Maidan, and more, bleed their green and pleasant land to the very edges of the page. And as I gaze at them, I am awash with gratitude. Not just to the photographers who took these pictures, or author Daniel Melamud for curating them in a way that can give me so many feels. But to the sport I love, simply for existing. The Wisden Book of the Year is *This is Cricket*. And nostalgics are going to love it.

Emma John is the author of Following On, *which was the Wisden Book of the Year in 2017. She has since written two more books,* Wayfaring Stranger: A Musical Journey in the American South, *and* Self-Contained: Scenes from a Single Life.

WISDEN BOOK OF THE YEAR

Since 2003, *Wisden's* reviewer has selected a Book of the Year. The winners have been:

2003 *Bodyline Autopsy* by David Frith
2004 *No Coward Soul* by Stephen Chalke and Derek Hodgson
2005 *On and Off the Field* by Ed Smith
2006 *Ashes 2005* by Gideon Haigh
2007 *Brim Full of Passion* by Wasim Khan
2008 *Tom Cartwright: The Flame Still Burns* by Stephen Chalke
2009 *Sweet Summers: The Classic Cricket Writing of J. M. Kilburn* edited by Duncan Hamilton
2010 *Harold Larwood: The Authorised Biography of the World's Fastest Bowler* by Duncan Hamilton
2011 *The Cricketer's Progress: Meadowland to Mumbai* by Eric Midwinter
2012 *Fred Trueman: The Authorised Biography* by Chris Waters
2013 *Bookie Gambler Fixer Spy: A Journey to the Heart of Cricket's Underworld* by Ed Hawkins
2014 *Driving Ambition* by Andrew Strauss
2015 *Wounded Tiger: A History of Cricket in Pakistan* by Peter Oborne
2016 *The Test: My Life, and the Inside Story of the Greatest Ashes Series* by Simon Jones and Jon Hotten
2017 *Following On: A Memoir of Teenage Obsession and Terrible Cricket* by Emma John
2018 *A Clear Blue Sky* by Jonny Bairstow and Duncan Hamilton
2019 *Steve Smith's Men* by Geoff Lemon
2020 *Cricket 2.0: Inside the T20 Revolution* by Tim Wigmore and Freddie Wilde
2021 ***This is Cricket: In the Spirit of the Game*** **by Daniel Melamud**

OTHER AWARDS

The Cricket Society and MCC Book of the Year Award has been presented since 1970 to the author of the cricket book judged best of the year. The 2020 award was shared by Christopher Sandford for **The Final Innings: The Cricketers of Summer 1939** (The History Press) and Duncan Hamilton for **The Great Romantic: Cricket and the Golden Age of Neville Cardus** (Hodder & Stoughton). Hamilton's book also won the Cricket Writers' Club award.

In July, Tim Wigmore and Freddie Wilde won the cricket category at the British Sports Book Awards for **Cricket 2.0: Inside the T20 Revolution** (Polaris).

BOOKS RECEIVED IN 2020

GENERAL

Abbasi, Kamran **Englistan** An immigrant's journey on the turbulent winds of Pakistan cricket (Jadoo Books, paperback, £12.99, details from kamabbasi@gmail.com)

Badale, Manoj and Hughes, Simon **A New Innings** How the IPL's reinvention of cricket provides lessons for the business of sport (Clink Street, £19.99)

Battersby, David **"A Nail-Biter in Lydney"** Gloucestershire versus Glamorgan, John Player League, July 13th 1975 (limited-edition paperback; details from dave@talbot.force9.co.uk)

Battersby, David **Glamorgan CCC's First Ever Game** Glamorgan v Warwickshire at Cardiff Arms Park June 21st and 22nd 1889 (limited-edition paperback)

Battersby, David **New Zealand – The 1927 Tour of the United Kingdom** (limited-edition paperback)

Blow, Thomas **The Honorary Tyke** Inside Sachin Tendulkar's Summer at Yorkshire CCC (Vertical Editions, paperback, £11.99)

Brearley, Mike **Spirit of Cricket** Reflections on Play and Life (Constable, £20)

Brenkley, Stephen **Small Town, Big Dreams** The Life and Times of Barnard Castle Cricket Club (Baliol Books, £25) *Off-beat and affectionate history of Barnard Castle CC ("Barney"), founded in 1832; written by former* Independent *cricket correspondent.*

Brooks, Tim **A Corner of Every Foreign Field** Cricket's Journey from English Game to Global Sport (Pitch, paperback, £12.99)

Carter, Andy **Beyond the Pale** Early Black and Asian Cricketers in Britain 1868–1945 (Troubador, paperback, £15)

Cawkwell, Tim **Cricket on the edge** (Sforzinda Books, paperback, £9.90; details from www.timcawkwell.co.uk/my-books)

Clarke, Richard **Last-Wicket Stand** Searching for redemption, revival and a reason to persevere in English county cricket (Pitch, paperback, £12.99)

Clement, Kevin **Flashes of brilliance** A History of Bedfordshire County Cricket Club (details from kpaclement@yahoo.co.uk, £10 + p&p)

Gray, Ashley **The Unforgiven** Mercenaries or Missionaries? The untold stories of the rebel West Indian cricketers who toured apartheid South Africa (Pitch, £19.99)

Greenslade, Nick **The Thin White Line** The Inside Story of Cricket's Greatest Scandal (Pitch, £19.99)

Guha, Ramachandra **The Commonwealth of Cricket** A Lifelong Love Affair with the Most Subtle and Sophisticated Game Known to Humankind (William Collins, £20)

Hain, Peter and Odendaal, André **Pitch Battles** Sport, Racism and Resistance (Rowman & Littlefield, £25)

Hamilton, Duncan **One Long and Beautiful Summer** A short elegy for red-ball cricket (Riverrun, £16.99)

Henderson, Michael **That Will Be England Gone** The Last Summer of Cricket (Constable, £20)

Hignell, Andrew **Cricketscapes** (ACS, shop.acscricket.com, paperback, £15)

Hoult, Nick and James, Steve **Morgan's Men** The Inside Story of England's Rise from Cricket World Cup Humiliation to Glory (Allen & Unwin, £18.99)

Lonsdale, Jeremy **A Game Divided** Triumphs and troubles in Yorkshire cricket in the 1920s (ACS, paperback, £15) *The third volume of Lonsdale's Yorkshire history focuses on a falling-out with Middlesex which symbolised the divisions between north and south, professional and amateur.*

Moulton, Roger **A Tale of Three Managers** The Old Hurst Johnian Cricket Week 1920 to 2020 (ACS, paperback, £18)

Nicholson, Rafaelle **Ladies and Lords** A History of Women's Cricket in Britain (Peter Lang, paperback, £46)

Peel, Mark **The Hollow Crown** England Captains from 1945 to the present (Pitch, £19.99)

Rice, Jonathan **Notes by the Editors** 120 Years of Wisden Opinion (John Wisden, £12.99)

Rowe, Mark **Tour de Farce** Anti-apartheid protest and South Africa's cancelled 1970 cricket tour of England (ACS, paperback, £18)

Sengupta, Arunabha **Apartheid: A Point to Cover** South African cricket 1948–1970 and the Stop the Seventy Tour campaign Foreword by Peter Hain (CricketMASH, paperback, £10.99)

Shindler, Colin **Barbed Wire and Cucumber Sandwiches** The Controversial South Africa Cricket Tour of 1970 Foreword by Sir Michael Parkinson (Pitch, £19.99)

Warner, David and Deaton, Ron (ed.) **Just A Few Lines…** The unseen letters and memorabilia of Brian Close (Great Northern, £20)

Waters, Chris **The Men Who Raised the Bar** The evolution of the highest individual score in Test cricket (John Wisden, £12.99)

Watson, Malcolm **Much More Wit and Wisdom of an Ordinary Subject** (privately published, paperback, £8.99)

Williams, Mark and Wigmore, Tim **The Best** How Elite Athletes Are Made Foreword by Matthew Syed (Nicholas Brealey Publishing, £20)

BIOGRAPHY

Bindman, Steve **Schooled in Cricket** The Johnny Lawrence Story (ACS, paperback, £16)

Francis, Bill **Second Only to Bradman** The Life of Stewie Dempster Foreword by Bruce Edgar (The Cricket Publishing Company, paperback, $A50.00) *Elegant paperback about New Zealand's first century-maker, who averaged 65 in Tests and later did well for Leicestershire. Of those who played more than four Tests, only the Don had a higher average.*

Frith, David **Archie Jackson** Cricket's Tragic Genius (Slattery Media Group, £15)

Heavens, Roger **A Cuckfield Life** Ernest Attwater 1888–1918 Soldier, Sportsman, Gentleman (Roger Heavens, paperback, £5; details from shop.acscricket.com)

Hignell, Andrew **A Tall Story** The life of Nigel Plews (ACS, paperback, £15)

Murtagh, Andrew **If Not Me, Who?** The Story of Tony Greig, the Reluctant Rebel (Pitch, £19.99)

Ogden, Geoff **Born in Bolton** The First-Class Cricketers born in Bolton (Max Books, paperback, £9.95)

Peel, Mark **Cricketing Caesar** A Biography of Mike Brearley (Pitch, £19.99) *A diligent attempt to examine one of England's greatest captains. Strong on his leadership and batting struggles, but ultimately fails to get close to the man.*

Rigby, Vic **A Voice from the Golden Age** The Remarkable R. P. Keigwin (J. W. McKenzie, paperback, £15)

Shenton, Kenneth **O My Hornby and My Barlow Long Ago** The Life of the Poet Francis Thompson 1859–1907 (Max Books, paperback, £9.95)

Willis, David, ed. **Bob Willis** A Cricketer and a Gentleman Foreword by Sir Ian Botham (Hodder & Stoughton, £20)

Winch, Jonty and Parry, Richard **Too Black to Wear Whites** The Remarkable Story of Krom Hendricks, a Cricket Hero who was Rejected by Cecil John Rhodes's Empire (Pitch, £19.99)

AUTOBIOGRAPHY

Dexter, Ted **85 Not Out** (Quiller, £20)

Fletcher, Luke **Tales from the Front Line** (Pitch, £16.99) *Tries hard to provide chucklesome dressing-room insight, but much of it is banal. Fletcher's encounter with Ricky Ponting hits the spot, though.*

Gould, Ian **Gunner** My Life in Cricket (Pitch, £19.99) *Lively account of the life of wicketkeeper-turned-international umpire. Unafraid to criticise – on match referees: "Basically, if you knew where your bread was buttered, you had to suck up to them… Once I got good feedback for my performance on the field, but was marked down because the referee felt I smoked too much!"*

Harrison, Richard **Stumped** One Cricket Umpire, Two Countries (privately published, paperback, £12.99, details from contact@richardharrison.com.au)

Key, Rob **"Oi, Key"** Tales of a Journeyman Cricketer (White Owl, £20)

Radhakrishnan, Rajiv **A Life in Cricket 1986–2019** (privately published, paperback, details from rajivradhakrishnan@hotmail.co.uk)

Ridley, Ian **The Breath of Sadness** On love, grief and cricket (Floodlit Dreams, £13.99)

ILLUSTRATED

Melamud, Daniel **This is Cricket** In the Spirit of the Game (Rizzoli, £50)

Milton, Howard, with Francis, Peter **Kent County Cricket Grounds** 150 Years of Cricket across the Garden of England (Pitch, for Kent CCC, £25)

ANTHOLOGY

Walker, Phil, Harman, Jo and Thacker, Matt, ed. **Golden Summers** Personal reflections from cricket's glorious past (Fairfield, £21)

STATISTICAL

Lawton Smith, Julian, ed. **The Minor Counties Championship 1914** (ACS, paperback, £17)
Lynch, Steven, ed. **The Wisden Book of Test Cricket 2014–2019** (John Wisden, £40)
Walmsley, Keith, ed. **First-Class Matches: West Indies 1989/90 to 1998/99** (ACS, paperback, £27)

HANDBOOKS AND ANNUALS

Bailey, Philip, ed. **ACS International Cricket Year Book 2020** (ACS, paperback, £37)
Bryant, John, ed. **ACS Overseas First-Class Annual 2020** (ACS, paperback, £60) *Full scorecards for first-class matches outside England in 2019-20.*
Bryden, Colin, ed. **South African Cricket Annual 2020** (Blue Weaver, R270, info@blueweaver.co.za)
Colliver, Lawrie, ed. **Australian Cricket Digest 2020-21** (paperback, \$A35; details from lawrie.colliver@gmail.com)
Marshall, Ian, ed. **Playfair Cricket Annual 2020** (Headline, paperback, £9.99)
Moorehead, Benj, ed. **The Cricketers' Who's Who 2020** Foreword by Katherine Brunt (Jellyfish, £19.99)
Parkinson, Paul, Clayton, Howard, and Gerrish, Keith ed. **First-Class Counties Second Eleven Annual 2020** (ACS, paperback, £13)
Payne, Francis and Smith, Ian, ed. **2020 New Zealand Cricket Almanack** (Upstart Press, \$NZ55)
Piesse, Ken, ed. **Pavilion 2021** (Australian Cricket Society, paperback, \$A10, www.cricketbooks.com.au)

REPRINTS AND UPDATES

John Wisden's Cricketers' Almanack for 1864 to **1878** and **1916** to **1919** (John Wisden, facsimile editions, hardbacks from £33 to £48 each, paperbacks from £12 to £26)
O'Brien, Christopher **Cardus Uncovered** Neville Cardus: The Truth, the Untruth and the Higher Truth (Second edition, revised with a new chapter. Whitethorn Range Publishing, paperback, £10 + £2.50 p&p; details from chris.obrien.uk@gmail.com)

PERIODICALS

The Cricketer (monthly) ed. Simon Hughes (The Cricketer Publishing, £5.50; £44.99 for 12 print issues, £44.99 digital, £49.99 print & digital. Subscriptions: www.thecricketer.com)
The Cricket Paper (weekly) ed. Jon Couch (Greenways Publishing, £1.80; £20 for ten issues inc p&p, £49.99 for one year digital, www.thecricketpaper.com)
The Cricket Statistician (quarterly) ed. Simon Sweetman (ACS, £3.50 to non-members)
The Journal of the Cricket Society ed. Nigel Hancock (twice yearly) (from D. Seymour, 13 Ewhurst Road, Crofton Park, London SE4 1AG, £5 to non-members, www.cricketsociety.com, details from nigelhancock@cricketsociety.com)
The Nightwatchman The Wisden Cricket Quarterly ed. Tanya Aldred, Jon Hotten and Benj Moorehead (TriNorth, £10 print, £5 digital; from £29.95 for four print issues exc p&p, from £15 digital, www.thenightwatchman.net)
Wisden Cricket Monthly ed. Phil Walker (TriNorth, £4.95; £39.99 for 12 print issues, £17.99 digital. Subscriptions: www.wisdensubs.com)

CRICKET AND THE MEDIA IN 2020

Light-bulb moment

RICHARD HOBSON

Seldom can the cricket media have been so moulded by events more suited to the front pages. The season was putty in the hands of a virus that determined what could be played, where, when and by whom. Then, as the more traditional enemies of rain and bad light delayed the international restart on its first morning, the year's second big theme made itself felt.

Stories stemming from the Black Lives Matter movement had preceded the opening Test in July. Michael Carberry's claims of racism gained traction at ESPNcricinfo. Barney Ronay, in *The Observer*, heard the one-time Surrey wicketkeeper Lonsdale Skinner reveal discrimination in the 1970s. In *The Daily Telegraph*, Nick Hoult reported that MCC had removed portraits of their first secretary, the slave-owning Benjamin Aislabie.

But none of this prepared us for a short documentary on Sky Sports in which Michael Holding and a tearful Ebony Rainford-Brent outlined their shocking experiences. Nor for what followed. Because of the rain, the subject could now be discussed properly; fair weather might not have allowed the luxury. Holding was at the top of his mark. He spoke of the "dehumanisation of the black race", of history being written by the harmers not the harmed, and of forgotten achievements of black men and women, such as Lewis Howard Latimer, inventor of the carbon-filament light bulb. Ian Ward's question had long been forgotten as Holding crescendoed. "When you see somebody react to Black Lives Matter with 'all lives matter', please, we black people know that white lives matter. I don't think you know that black lives matter."

Often, arguments are lost in anger. Speakers become tongue-tied; their point degenerates into a rant. What was striking was Holding's reason, calm, detail, dignity, knowledge, authority; the wisdom of age and experience. It felt a seminal moment, like Princess Diana's ITV interview 25 years earlier, which gripped the nation with its searing honesty. At just under five minutes, Holding's speech was shorter than "Bohemian Rhapsody" but longer than the Gettysburg Address. By the end, you wanted to leap from the settee, and clap.

Holding and Rainford-Brent continued to speak out, with Rainford-Brent generating more publicity through the African-Caribbean Engagement programme in south London. "The game's been shaken up," she told Andy Bull in *The Guardian*. "The spotlight's been shone, and the stories have been heard. What's clear is that there's no going back." The scale of the challenge was highlighted by Richard Gibson and Matt Hughes in the *Daily Mail*. Their research found only 33 BAME (Black, Asian and Minority Ethnic) players across the 18 counties, and six coaches in a total of 93.

Perhaps the climate emboldened Azeem Rafiq to make public alleged discrimination at Yorkshire. He spoke first to Wisden.com, claiming he had

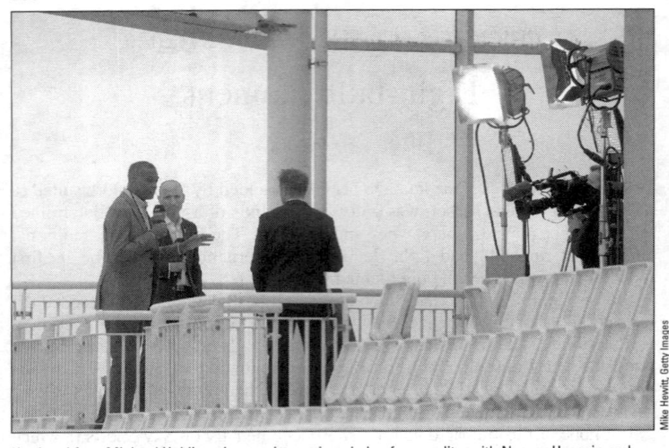

Mike Hewitt, Getty Images

Hard and fast: Michael Holding gives an impassioned plea for equality, with Nasser Hussain and Ian Ward at the Rose Bowl, before the start of the First Test.

played under an "openly racist" captain. The club refused to comment. A week later, Rafiq had another go, in an interview on the Cricket Badger podcast with James Buttler, a former Yorkshire media officer. Again, nothing from the club. Only after a piece with George Dobell on ESPNcricinfo did Yorkshire respond, and launch an inquiry. Here was an insight into the modern media, a story that gained legs via a website rather than a paper, and confirmed Dobell's heft.

The international matches felt low-key without spectators. There were only 12 spaces in socially distanced press boxes at Old Trafford and the Rose Bowl, but in *Dawn*, the Pakistan daily, the veteran writer Qamar Ahmed bemoaned the absence of overseas journalists. Later, Daniel Brettig on ESPNcricinfo rued the lack of Australian media covering their white-ball matches in England: news that Steve Smith had been hit on the head at nets did not emerge until the toss the following day.

A couple of landmarks enjoyed good space as Stuart Broad reached 500 Test wickets, and James Anderson 600. "Yet again," wrote John Etheridge in *The Sun*, he "showed why he is the greatest England bowler of his generation." There was even a leader column in *The Times*, which spoke of "incontrovertible proof that Anderson has matured into England's greatest bowler". Mike Atherton, their cricket correspondent, named Anderson as the best English seamer in his memory, followed by Ian Botham and Darren Gough.

But had England missed an opportunity to promote younger talent with the 2021-22 Ashes in mind? "Management retreated into the safe and familiar embrace of their 85mph seamers," wrote the ever-provocative Jonathan Liew in *The Guardian*. Scyld Berry also criticised England's selection, refusing to rest easy on his laptop, despite stepping down as *Telegraph* correspondent; the paper had appointed Hoult, after a decade of ferreting as Berry's No. 2. It was the first time they had filled the august post with a writer from a news background since Peter Deeley, over 30 years earlier. Not that Hoult's pounding the mean streets of Northampton as a cub reporter quite matched Deeley's experience of the Troubles in Northern Ireland or the Afghan war. At the end of the year, a second correspondent left his job, when Vic Marks retired from *The Guardian* as the paper identified sport as an area for cuts.

Given an enviably broad canvas, Berry – now chief cricket writer – wandered the counties, and wrote with his characteristic mix of off-beat and erudite. At his favourite Taunton for an early Bob Willis Trophy match, he revealed that Somerset's live stream had attracted 126,000 views on the third day against Glamorgan. As well as using two cameras installed for analysis, Somerset employed a further three (plus one for slow motion), grasping the potential to reach their membership, and well beyond. *The Times* reported some 1.5m views for the first round of fixtures. India, Pakistan and Bangladesh provided plenty of them; Adele Madsen watched from Durban as her son, Wayne, helped Derbyshire beat Nottinghamshire at Trent Bridge. Ivo Tennant, in *The Times*, discovered that John Cleese had rung the switchboard at Worcester to find out why he could not follow play when they entertained Somerset. The headline blamed a "Fawlty" feed.

"I'm almost embarrassed to be watching this," Atherton said, hiding his eyes

What a relief after lockdown to have something to write about. The preceding months had proved that cricket does its history better – or at least more thoroughly – than any other sport. Not an all-time XI went unpicked, or a great game undissected. Sky Sports needed particular enterprise to fill their cricket channel, showing not just highlights but complete Test matches. They also pulled protagonists together to reflect on real-time reruns in that "Celebrity Squares" layout now familiar from Zoom calls. Best of all was the discussion between Atherton and Allan Donald of the 1998 Trent Bridge Test. "I'm almost embarrassed to be watching this," Atherton said, hiding his eyes as umpire Steve Dunne missed his gloved catch behind. "I'm running out of words," added Donald, with that familiar girder-melting glare.

The success of these programmes owed much to the interplay of Atherton and his old sparring partner Nasser Hussain, which stopped just the right side of chumminess. "A few empty seats in the background there," Atherton noted. "That's probably because Nasser was batting." In the event, the most memorable joke was on Atherton. To mark the return of club cricket, Sky asked viewers to tweet their performances in the recreational game. "Hugh Jardon, six for nine at Cockermouth," Atherton read out. "That's Ben Stokes's old club, isn't it?" Fellow commentators Rob Key and Ian Ward were unable to respond, since they were too busy corpsing. Atherton laughed sheepishly, perhaps taking solace from giving cricket an overdue smile.

The BBC were anything but tentative in dipping a toe into the water for their first live action since the 1999 World Cup. "Clear your diary and sit down for three hours of thrill-a-minute cricket," ran the PR guff. "And, just like in 1999,

CRICKET PODCASTS IN 2020

Hobby horses and hang-ups

JAMES GINGELL

In early spring, Covid-19 seemed to have inverted economic doctrine, with US oil prices going negative, and a Conservative chancellor paying people not to work. Podcasters seemed gripped by market madness, too: while listeners dropped by as much as a fifth – probably caused by a drastic reduction in commuting – the number of new podcasts shot up.

It made for much surplus. Mark Nicholas named his show **Rain Delay**, presumably to steel his audience for the hours of aimlessness and frustration. It doesn't take long to forget that Nicholas is an excellent sports broadcaster, or to recall that Alan Partridge began life in a similar vocation. "Great Wall of China or Great Barrier Reef?" he asks one guest, apparently not joking. "Churchill or Thatcher?" "Oranges or apples?" "Boxers or briefs?" Only terror alleviates the tedium. At one stage, he invites Piers Morgan to role-play a prime minister tackling Covid; he made even the incumbent look good. Still, Geoffrey Boycott's **Corridor of Certainty**, three and a half hours of the same old hobby horses and hang-ups, was somehow worse.

Others were welcome. Peter Oborne and Richard Heller's **On Cricket** evokes the plum and dust of parliamentary tearooms – never more than when Lord Jeffrey Archer of Weston-super-Mare claims Ian Botham was Victoria Cross material – only with far more open-minded hosts. Tim Wigmore persuades them Twenty20 does have nuance, Mihir Bose that cricket is the only world sport run by non-white people. It's outwardly fusty, inwardly modern, social and political as much as sporting; in some ways it was the Almanack to the **Wisden Cricket Podcast's** monthly magazine. There was further heft in the **Caribbean Cricket** podcast, hosted by Machel St Patrick Hewitt and Santokie Nagulendran, particularly their fascinating discussion of Indo-Caribbean culture; and in James Buttler's **Cricket Badger**, Michael Carberry's stories of structural racism deserved even more headlines than they received.

Some true documentaries popped up, too, including Jarrod Kimber's excellent **Double Century**, a chronicle of ramp shots, googlies and more. **Calling The Shots**, by Adam Collins and Dan Norcross, was better still, a slick history of cricket broadcasting that revealed, with Reithian ideals, everything from Brian Johnston's conflict with Andy Pandy to Cricinfo's battles with bankruptcy, and Big Brother. It cemented Collins's standing as the doyen: his other shows, **The Final Word** (with Geoff Lemon) and **The Greatest Season That Was** (with Dan Brettig and Shannon Gill) maintained exceptional standards.

In dark times, the joy was often the sense of eavesdropping on friends. The selling point of **No Balls** was intimacy more than information: hosts Kate Cross and Alex Hartley, both England cricketers, speak candidly about their friendship, mental health, families and failures – and occasionally their careers. Elsewhere there was **Two Hacks, One Pro** (Vithushan Ehantharajah, Will Macpherson and Sam Northeast) for those wanting gossip and tales from the counties, the **Cricviz Podcast** (Ben Jones and Freddie Wilde) for deep technical analysis, **The 80s and 90s Cricket Show** (Gary Naylor) for syrupy nostalgia. Cricket journalists, long comfortable with business illogic, saw the unwelcoming market conditions, and dived in. Of course, most of these enterprises had little to do with economics; these were simply mates who wanted to talk about their lives, their loves, and something other than the great pall.

James Gingell is a civil servant whose only partiality is to Somerset CCC.

Console-ation prize: *The Cricketer* managed to air some action, even if it wasn't quite the real thing.

the BBC is the place to watch it." If they thought so much of cricket, why had they not tried harder to win the broadcast rights? Anyway, come the big day, a T20 against Pakistan, the BBC team were soon forgetting the first rule of television commentary – add to the picture, don't repeat it – and never spoke when they could shout. Benaud and West it was not. But the insight of Anderson augured well for his post-playing career, while Phil Tufnell's comic timing transferred easily from radio. The Beeb also screened the third match of the women's T20 series between England and West Indies; with Sky, they helped attract around 2m viewers across the five games.

The Quarantine Cup had been a cheerful initiative devised by Sam Morshead at *The Cricketer*: a five-over, virtual tournament, with counties represented by one of their players on a games console. Glamorgan (Roman Walker) beat Hampshire (Mason Crane) in the final, and Adam Collins provided good value on commentary. "My oh my! Has Nathan Lyon dropped the Quarantine Cup?" he screamed, as the hapless fielder (or his avatar) missed a dolly from Marnus Labuschagne – confirmation after Headingley 2019 that Lyon just couldn't cope with pressure. Dan Douthwaite hit the winning single. "For the first time since 2004, Glamorgan will hold a trophy high," Collins said. Thanks to lockdown, the scenes at Cardiff had to be imagined.

Walker's heroics were not rewarded with a first-class debut. Collins, though, went from strength to strength as a smart addition to *Test Match Special,* imposing his own style and passion, while respecting the brand's tradition. As usual, the programme had its critics. Simon Heffer, who is not one of the game's modernisers, referred in the *Telegraph* to "painful stretches of commentary consisting of little beyond banalities of a sort an Arlott or a Mosey would never have dreamt of inflicting". Meanwhile, in a letter to *The Cricketer* from Mr Stuart Manger, statistician Andy Zaltzman was accused of helping *TMS* "descend into a 'show' – nay a music hall stand-up stage for rampant egos". Presumably in his day job as a comedian, Zaltzman is criticised for using

too many stats. *TMS* has always enjoyed a sense of fun, no one more so than Brian Johnston, among Heffer's favourites. It is all about balance. With Isa Guha, Alison Mitchell and Rainford-Brent, *TMS* is more balanced than ever.

One famous figure was missing. After 14 years, it was decided Geoffrey Boycott, at 79, was too old to summarise from grounds during a pandemic. In reality, we all knew this was more *adieu* than *à bientôt* – not that Boycott has a love of the French. Naturally, he had his say on developments. The BBC was now "all about political correctness, gender and race". Or, as he put it later in the *Telegraph*: "Nothing has changed except the political climate and my age." Ah, that's the trouble with the political climate: it changes. Marie Antoinette must have lamented the same thing as her head was dropping into the basket.

The key is to move with the times. Take Andrew Flintoff, who has adjusted from cricket to television and showbiz. *Freddie Flintoff: Living with Bulimia* (BBC1) was his finest hour since 2005, when it turned out he was plotting the quietest times and routes from the England dressing-room to the toilet so he could throw up unnoticed. He has suffered from bulimia since 2000, when *The Sun* said he was heavier than boxer Lennox Lewis. "I played all right for a fat lad," Flintoff said after winning a match award, apparently deflecting criticism with self-deprecation. The documentary was stark stuff. Confused and concerned, he struggled to articulate his thoughts as he listened to the experiences of others, including a mother whose son had died of the illness. By the end, he agreed to seek therapy.

It is easy to think Flintoff and Holding were putting the game in perspective. So they were, but let's not forget cricket has a significant role in itself. There must have been psychological benefits to clubbies nationwide when the recreational game was allowed to resume. Despite what the *Telegraph* said, this was no thanks to their campaign urging the prime minister to rethink his unexpected decision to block a July return. All the time, Tom Harrison and ECB colleagues had been working hard behind the scenes; cue much scepticism when the paper claimed credit for the inevitable volte-face. At least they produced one gem when Tim Wigmore revealed that, while Britain was at a standstill, in Germany they were already back playing the game. Bloody Germans! Now they were even doing cricket better than we were.

Amid this, one gesture transcended all cynicism. Employees at TriNorth Communications, whose publications include *Wisden Cricket Monthly* and *The Nightwatchman*, donated 20% of their wages to fund a digital magazine, *The Pinch Hitter*, written by struggling freelancers. But the problems for cricket writers didn't end after lockdown. When the ECB revealed that their reporter network would shrink from 18 to six, it meant some games in 2021 might be played without a single member of the written media present. Those live streams have come just in time.

Richard Hobson is a freelance cricket writer. He covered the game for more than 20 years at The Times, *and now gives guided tours of Oxford.*

CRICKET AND SOCIAL MEDIA IN 2020

Eight hours later…

DAVE TICKNER

For a large chunk of the summer, cricket on social media faced the same problem as cricket everywhere else: there wasn't any. With other sports, that led to a reduction in content; with cricket, not so much.

Leading the way was Surrey commentator Mark Church, who began producing new descriptions of classic moments. These were a big hit and – long story short – he also ended up playing an entire season of international cricket (Tests, ODIs, T20s) in his garden against assorted items of furniture. As well as the matches themselves, we had press conferences before and after play. Twitter being Twitter, cricket being cricket, and #CricketTwitter being #CricketTwitter, we also saw people compiling scorecards and statistics to record the games for posterity. For a while, it looked as if these might be the summer's only stats. A shame, really, to get all that actual cricket to fill *Wisden*: the thought of readers, years from now, taking this book from the shelf to check how Little Garden Bench or Petrol Mower went in the summer of 2020 was appealing.

While the absence of cricket sent some in wildly unpredictable directions, others simply did more of the same, but with greater meaning. Top of the list was Rob Moody and his incomprehensibly vast, self-curated library of footage. He was already a hero for his robelinda2 Twitter account and YouTube channels – a rich source of cricketing gems, and as good a reason as any to pop online for a few minutes, only to spend eight hours watching videos of right-handers batting left-handed. I almost wrote "wasted eight hours", but that time is not wasted. Left-handed Ian Bell cover-driving right-arm Mitchell Johnson is why the internet was invented.

Novelties such as those, or painstaking highlights packages where Rob has – ridiculously, magnificently – matched up "12th Man" skits to the closest available real-life action, are wonderful. You're going to look them up now rather than finish this piece, and rightly so. Yet the deepest joy comes from the sheer scale of his back catalogue, and his ability to locate the most obscure events – things you've never heard of, things you'd assume were lost. Some come from a collection of almost every cricket video ever released, but there are uncountable hours of footage he has recorded himself during the last 30 years. His system is simple: tape it all – full live coverage, not just highlights. If you remember anything from a televised game, no matter how trivial, chances are Rob can find it. We're used to seeing the same old highlights during rain delays. If lockdown was one long break in play, Rob filled it with novelty. Chris Adams blasting the 1997 Australians around Derby in a tour match? Naturally. Jason Gillespie and Glenn McGrath putting on 43 against West Indies at Sydney in 1996-97? But of course.

CRICKET AND BLOGS IN 2020

Saluting Chris Tavaré

BRIAN CARPENTER

In the sun-drenched spring and early summer, it often felt as though the most memorable aspect of the English cricket season might be that it contained no cricket at all. The game's late rebirth did produce moments of magnificence: Stuart Broad's bowling, Zak Crawley's batting, Maxwell and Carey at Old Trafford. But the impression left by the game's bloggers was of a sport that had come to an unexpected and painful halt.

In April, as the peak of the pandemic's first wave coincided with what would have been the early rounds of the County Championship, Sean Buckley, at *Being Outside Cricket* (**beingoutsidecricket.com**), wrote movingly of the role of cricket in his life, and the effect of its absence – a feeling to which any other follower of the game could relate: "The thing about sport is it can act as a comfort blanket when things are a bit rubbish, it can make you turn from a normal human being into a quivering wreck… it can take you to a place that is out of your reality. Sport is in our psyche, it's a chance to catch up with old friends and make new ones, it's a chance to immerse yourself in the action… it's a chance to live unfulfilled dreams invested in others, and of course it's the perfect opportunity to debate, dissect or argue about the outcome."

Gary Naylor, at *99.94* (**nestaquin.wordpress.com**), shared those feelings, but saw his lifelong love of cricket as good preparation for the longueurs of lockdown: "These are strange days indeed as we sit, confined to barracks, while a virus flits its fatal paths in the outside world. We may never have had more ways to distract ourselves, to hold back the boredom, to ease the passage of long days that we can't quite fill. But it's still tough, as March dragged into April, and April slides on towards May. But for some of us, it's not so bad. And for that, Chris Tavaré, I salute you."

There was some fine writing about elements of the game which were lent greater significance as they faded from the realm of direct experience into memory. *CricketMASH* (**cricmash.com**) and *81 All Out* (**81allout.com**) gave an Asian perspective on cricket's past, present and future, while the voice of the sport in South Africa, Neil Manthorp, charted the waning fortunes of his nation, on field and off, at *Manners on Cricket* (**manners-on-cricket.com**).

Cameron Ponsonby's debut article at *The Full Toss* (**thefulltoss.com**) drew on personal experience and interviews with professional batsmen to dissect the business of facing fast bowling. It was ambitious, enlightening and evocative. To read Michael Carberry relive the act of taking on Mitchell Johnson at Adelaide in 2013-14 was a reminder of what cricket had been, and would be again.

From America's Midwest, Matt Becker observes the game through the prism of genuine love, and his writing at his personal blog, *Limited Overs* (**limitedovers.com**), is distinctively personal, elegiac and often beautiful: "This is the power of sport. To pick us up and place us down somewhere else. There are days when I think of it as a gift. And there are days when I do not. But it brings memories like cannon fire, because those losses are always in the fall, when all we know is loss and decay, when we cannot see the green that will come, cannot even imagine it. We grieve collectively, always, all the time. And then we move on. We look out the window, and wait for spring."

Last year, more than ever before, cricket waited for spring.

In 2013, Brian Carpenter was the inaugural winner of Wisden's writing competition.

It's worth taking a moment (or eight hours) to scroll through Rob's Twitter mentions and see how many niche requests he receives, and how many he meets. It's all tremendous fun, except when cricket reverts to stereotype. Our sport is lucky to have Rob. It should be showering him with gratitude. The ICC should give him a job. But instead of slapping him on the back, cricket punches him in the face. His YouTube channel is frequently threatened with closure, as takedown notices roll in from rights holders. It's not as simple as giving Rob, or anyone else, a free pass with what is mostly copyrighted footage. But for cricket to treat one of its most enthusiastic promoters this way is a spectacular own goal.

Talking of goals, the biggest cricket phenomenon of the year on social media was provided by Dele Alli, Harry Kane, Joe Hart and especially Eric Dier, but *especially* Sergio Reguilon, as Tottenham's footballers developed a sudden yet deep obsession with the game. It started during what looked like an impromptu hit in the gym – although Dier's use of proper wicketkeeping gloves pointed to something more serious. Alli took a nonchalant catch after flicking the ball up with his foot and, knowing exactly where the CCTV cameras were, he channelled his inner Rob Moody to compile a video, with half-decent production values. His tweet of the catch means nobody can ever again respond to cricketers warming up playing football by claiming you wouldn't see footballers warming up playing cricket.

There was much more. By the end of the week, Spurs had put a two-minute video on Twitter, and a nine-minute one on YouTube. New signing Hart, a gifted youth cricketer who – 4,875 tweeters were keen to tell anyone who would listen – had been at the Worcestershire Academy, was widely seen as the ringleader. He bowled eye-catching left-arm pace, while it was clear other members of the squad (Ben Davies and, inevitably, Yorkshireman Jack Clarke) had played a bit; some (Dier, Kane) were just alphas who could turn their hand to any sport.

But the star was Spain international Reguilon. His tweets feigned indifference to cricket, claiming not to get it, but the footage told another story. A cheerleader in the field, where he used random gym equipment as rudimentary bongos, he would greet the fall of a wicket with an enthusiastic knee slide that will probably earn him a demerit point from the ICC once Football Gym Cricket becomes established.

To any cricket tragic, the signs were clear. We've seen it all before, and we've been there ourselves: that moment this sport grabs you. It has Reguilon now, and will never let go. In five years, he'll be batting against furniture in the back garden. Ten years, and he'll be uploading videos of a left-handed Kane facing a right-arm Hart. Welcome to the gang, Sergio.

Dave Tickner is editor of Cricket365.com, and can generally be found posting the same three or four tired jokes on Twitter as @tickerscricket.

RETIREMENTS IN 2020

Tastes of the big time

JACK SHANTRY

Graham Onions played nine Tests, marking his debut with a five-wicket haul against West Indies at Lord's in 2009, and would almost certainly have played more if not for a serious back injury. A fast-medium seamer with the ability to move the ball both ways, he appeared destined to become a fixture in the England line-up – not least after removing Shane Watson and Mike Hussey with the first two balls of the second day of the 2009 Edgbaston Ashes Test; a few overs later, he bounced out Ricky Ponting. But after the injury in early 2010, Onions was selected for only one more Test, leaving him with an average of 29 – lower than Stuart Broad (43) or James Anderson (34) after nine matches. More improbably, he helped secure a 1–1 draw in South Africa in 2009-10 by twice batting out time from No. 11, at Centurion and Cape Town.

Stu Forster, Getty Images

Golden Graham: Onions at Edgbaston in 2012.

There was a period after his last Test, in 2012, when he could be unplayable. That summer, he finished with 72 first-class wickets at 14, then 73 at 18 in 2013: c Mustard b Onions became one of county cricket's most familiar dismissals. In all, he took at least 50 wickets in a first-class season eight times during a career spanning 17 years, including all three of Durham's title-winning summers. If county colleagues such as Steve Harmison, Mark Wood and Ben Stokes all spent longer in an England shirt, there was scarcely a tougher test for an opening batsman than facing Onions and Chris Rushworth on an overcast morning at Chester-le-Street. Onions was a nice guy off the field, but his game face was a different matter.

He was known predominantly for his skills with a red Dukes, though his record in the shorter format was better than most. While he was often rested from limited-overs matches –

Durham wanted to preserve him for the Championship – he had a miserly T20 economy-rate of 6.86. It looked as if he would see out his career at Riverside, a one-county man, but Durham's reluctance to offer a multi-year deal meant Onions moved to Old Trafford in 2018. He enjoyed an Indian summer, forming a formidable partnership with Tom Bailey. But he injured his spine bending down to pick up a ball shortly before Lancashire's opening Bob Willis Trophy match last season, and was warned by specialists that more cricket could lead to permanent damage. He chose to become Lancashire's bowling coach.

Another who enjoyed his best days after being discarded by England was **Tim Ambrose**. A natural gloveman, he faced a battle with Matt Prior during the first part of his career, both for Sussex and England. Ambrose had won the match award for scoring a hundred, full of fierce square cuts, at Wellington's Basin Reserve in his second Test, in March 2008. A year later, at the age of 26, he had played his final international. He battled with depression, and briefly considered retirement after losing the England gloves to Prior. But Warwickshire showed faith, and their patience was rewarded as Ambrose became a mainstay of the Championship-winning team of 2012, and the victorious T20 side in 2014.

Also leaving Edgbaston was **Jeetan Patel**, for many years rated the best spinner in the county game. Patel started his career with his native Wellington, and began playing for Warwickshire in 2009. His sharp turn and combative nature made him a star performer in all formats, and he finished with 473 first-class wickets for the club at just 26, as well as 269 in white-ball games; there were also 24 Tests, 43 ODIs and 11 T20s for New Zealand. After captaining Warwickshire towards the end of his career, he became involved as a spin coach with England.

Ollie Rayner, a 6ft 5in off-spinner, was much loved on the county circuit for his gregarious nature, and fans of both Sussex and Middlesex held him in great esteem. A victim of the paucity of first-class matches in high summer, and of the preponderance of seamer-friendly pitches, he was often reduced to holding down an end. There were Lions tours, but no England call-up, despite several eye-catching performances. They included 15 for 118 against Surrey at The Oval in 2013, and 51 wickets at 23 to help Middlesex secure the Championship three years later. A more than useful batsman, with two first-class centuries, he also had spells with Kent and Hampshire.

A prodigious swinger of the ball, **Tony Palladino** was the go-to bowler of the Derbyshire attack for the better part of a decade. His "Never say die" tattoo reflected his attitude on the pitch over 17 years in the professional game, which started at Chelmsford and also saw him represent Cambridge UCCE and British Universities. During his eight seasons at Essex, he provided evidence that led to the conviction of team-mate Mervyn Westfield for match-fixing, the first such prosecution in county cricket.

Back trouble forced **Stuart Whittingham** to retire at 26. A Scotland international, he joined Gloucestershire from Sussex in 2018, but injury meant he never played first-team cricket for his new county. A product of the Sussex Academy, he had burst on to the scene by dismissing Derbyshire's New Zealand Test batsman Hamish Rutherford twice on Championship debut.

IAN BELL RETIRES

Not merely a matter of how many

SCYLD BERRY

It is often said "we shall not see his like again". If said about Ian Bell, it may well prove true. He was the embodiment of orthodoxy, the coaching book incarnate. Of England Test batsmen since the Second World War, Bell, Geoffrey Boycott and Len Hutton can be ranked as the supreme technicians; and to finish among England's ten highest Test run-scorers rounded off an outstanding career.

Every young batsman now wants to hit 360 degrees, and as high and far as he or she can. But only towards the end of his career, as T20 proliferated, did Bell overcome his conditioned instincts to hit along the ground. His batting, like a racehorse being turned into a steeplechaser, was designed for the turf not the air. In this new pursuit of maximum effectiveness, elegance such as Bell's is lost. It is when the batsman has his head over the ball, for instance to cover-drive, that he assumes the power position, the most aesthetic male posture. Leaning back, to get under the ball, may thrill but does not please.

Bell's Test debut, at The Oval in 2004 against West Indies, told us he had the temperament, too. He was pummelled by Fidel Edwards, but emerged, baptised, with 70. For any England cricketer to be called great, he must dominate an Ashes series, and Bell did so in 2013. Having weighed in only after someone else had made a century, he became the prime mover in the Test line-up. He had also been a slow starter in series – and dropped because of it in the West Indies in 2008-09 – but in 2013 he scored a hundred in the First Test (when England won by 14 runs), the Second and the Fourth. His feat should be remembered; it tended to be forgotten, as greedy administrators arranged another Ashes three months later, and England were Mitchell Johnsoned 5–0.

Cameron Spencer, Getty Images

For the purists: another Ian Bell cover-drive.

Could he have scored more than 7,727 Test runs? Yes, had he been more driven by ego, the desire to be the centre of attention, like Kevin Pietersen. But the technique would have been less pure. On that dire day at Adelaide in 2006-07, when England, having hit 551 in their first innings, collapsed and lost, Bell edged a ball to third man. He promptly rehearsed the stroke, to diagnose what had gone wrong in his pursuit of perfection. The non-striker was yelling at him to run, until Bell looked up from his analysis. We are all wired differently. For Bell, the means to scoring was as important as the end. It was never merely a matter of how many.

Seldom is it feasible to make such a close comparison between two top cricketers as it is between Bell and Jonathan Trott, contemporaries for much of their Warwickshire and England careers. Trott averaged 44 in Tests, batting mainly at No. 3; Bell averaged 42, and was his most prolific at five or six. Trott will be remembered for his obduracy, obsessiveness and shovelling through midwicket; Bell for the orthodoxy and elegance of his strokeplay, especially the cover-drive. No one innings of Bell's stands out, because every one – so far as it went – was a model of red-ball batsmanship.

Mark Nolan, Getty Images

Final answer? Laura Marsh pleads for lbw at the climax of the 2009 World Cup.

Another Sussex seamer, left-armer **Chris Liddle** was a canny limited-overs specialist, who also had stints with Leicestershire and Gloucestershire. He retired to become bowling coach at Northamptonshire.

Laura Marsh retired with three World Cup winners' medals, and 193 international white-ball wickets, more than any other England spinner. Her off-breaks were hard to hit (she went for 3.89 in ODIs and 5.29 in T20s), and she was the leading wicket-taker at the 2008-09 World Cup in Australia, which England won. Incredibly, that came not long after she had switched from seam to spin because of an injury.

Paul Horton was a combative top-order batsman for Lancashire and Leicestershire. Born in Sydney, but with a UK passport, he was a vital part of Lancashire's 2011 Championship-winning team, adept at batting time, and finishing with 1,040 runs, more than any of his team-mates. An excellent slip fielder, he captained Leicestershire in 2018 and 2019.

Kent's Zimbabwe-born keeper **Adam Rouse** has the curious honour of playing one first-class match for three counties. He started with a game for Hampshire, in 2013, and finished with one-off appearances for Surrey and Sussex against touring A-Teams. In between, he played briefly for Gloucestershire, before finding a more permanent home at Canterbury – though he could never quite displace Sam Billings behind the stumps.

Craig Meschede retired at the age of 28 because of a biceps injury. A powerful all-rounder with Somerset and Glamorgan, he also represented Germany, qualifying through his father. **Calum Haggett** overcame open-heart surgery to represent Kent more than 100 times. A right-arm seamer and left-handed batsman, he played age-group cricket for Somerset; his condition was discovered during routine screening with England Under-19.

Daryn Smit joined Derbyshire in 2017, having made his name with KwaZulu-Natal and Dolphins. He was used predominantly as a wicketkeeper-batsman, though his leg-spin claimed over 100 first-class wickets in his native South Africa. **Craig Cachopa** was also born there, but grew up in New Zealand and used his Portuguese passport to move to Hove, after Luke Wright talent-spotted his batting during their time together at Auckland. He last played for Sussex in 2016, after which he captained Auckland's one-day team.

Jack Shantry made 255 appearances in a ten-year career for Worcestershire. He retired in 2018, aged 30, and has taken up umpiring.

CAREER FIGURES

Players not expected to appear in county cricket in 2021

(minimum 25 first-class appearances)

BATTING

	M	*I*	*NO*	*R*	*HS*	*100*	*Avge*	*1,000r/ season*
T. R. Ambrose	251	383	34	11,349	251*	18	32.51	–
I. R. Bell	312	524	55	20,440	262*	57	43.58	5
M. J. Cosgrove	221	393	22	14,976	233	36	40.36	4
H. Z. Finch	53	89	6	2,166	135*	3	26.09	–
C. J. Haggett	41	54	13	926	80	–	22.58	–
G. J. Harte	25	46	4	1,201	114	3	28.59	–
P. J. Horton	218	373	26	12,308	209	24	35.46	3
C. A. J. Meschede	70	101	13	2,250	107	2	25.56	0
M. Morkel	153	192	35	2,062	82*	–	13.13	–
C. D. Nash	208	359	20	12,552	184	24	37.02	4
R. I. Newton	98	172	13	5,675	202*	15	35.69	1
G. Onions	193	248	86	2,100	65	–	12.96	–
A. P. Palladino	166	239	50	2,915	106	1	15.42	–
S. D. Parry	28	34	2	456	44	–	14.25	–
J. S. Patel	293	391	78	6,695	120*	3	21.38	–
O. P. Rayner	151	201	32	3,432	143	2	20.30	–
N. J. Rimmington	53	76	16	1,221	102*	1	20.35	–
A. P. Rouse	36	51	4	1,103	95*	–	23.46	–
D. Smit	137	208	37	6,077	156*	9	35.53	0+1
I. A. A. Thomas	35	46	23	117	13	–	5.08	–
G. G. Wagg	164	246	26	5,904	200	5	26.83	–

0+1 indicates one season in South Africa; other instances of 1,000 in a season are in England.

BOWLING AND FIELDING

	R	*W*	*BB*	*Avge*	*5I*	*10M*	*Ct/St*
T. R. Ambrose	1	1	1-0	1.00	–	–	678/43
I. R. Bell	1,615	47	4-4	34.36	–	–	238
M. J. Cosgrove	2,393	52	3-3	46.01	–	–	132
H. Z. Finch	118	2	1-9	59.00	–	–	68
C. J. Haggett	3,008	89	4-15	33.79	–	–	10
G. J. Harte	635	15	4-15	42.33	–	–	6
P. J. Horton	80	2	2-6	40.00	–	–	201/1
C. A. J. Meschede	5,310	142	5-84	37.39	1	–	23
M. Morkel	14,416	567	6-23	25.42	20	2	51
C. D. Nash	3,309	81	4-12	40.85	–	–	123
R. I. Newton	107	1	1-82	107.00	–	–	28
G. Onions	18,583	723	9-67	25.70	31	3	35
A. P. Palladino	13,255	464	7-53	28.56	17	1	40
S. D. Parry	1,926	58	5-23	33.22	2	–	7
J. S. Patel	29,239	892	8-36	32.77	38	7	155
O. P. Rayner	10,411	313	8-46	33.26	10	1	196
N. J. Rimmington	4,235	134	5-27	31.60	3	–	15
A. P. Rouse	–	–	–	–	–	–	112/4
D. Smit	3,501	106	7-27	33.02	3	–	362/22
I. A. A. Thomas	2,260	74	5-91	30.54	1	–	9
G. G. Wagg	16,034	465	6-29	34.48	12	1	54

CRICKETANA IN 2020

To cap it all

MARCUS WILLIAMS

While much of the world adjusted during the pandemic to the novelty of remote communication, auctioneers had long been trading this way. Postal and telephone bids were commonplace well before the internet took over as the dominant source of customers. Inevitably, Covid produced challenges, but the answer usually lay in small tweaks. Every lot now had to be photographed and described in more detail, with particular emphasis on its condition; a venue might need to be changed, perhaps making it impossible to view an item, or attend a sale, in person. But there was no shortage of material, and much sourced from renowned names.

In Australia, the year began with a different challenge. For months, bushfires had devastated swathes of the country, at great cost to life, wildlife and livelihood. To raise funds for the affected communities – human and animal – Shane Warne joined a number of sports stars keen to do their bit when he put his cherished Baggy Green, celebratory beer splashes and all, up for auction in January. "It means the world to me," he said. "To give it up wasn't easy, but I wanted to help out as much as possible."

Boosted by being part of the Australian Red Cross Disaster Relief and Recovery Fund, Warne's cap fetched $A1,007,500 (around £530,000); the winning bid came from the Commonwealth Bank of Australia. It went on a national tour of schools, cricket clubs and community centres to raise more money, before the scheme was cut short by Covid; the cap now has a permanent home at the Bradman Museum in Bowral as part of a collection of 30 Baggy Greens that extend back to the 19th century.

The previous record for a Baggy Green was the $425,000 paid in 2003 for the 1948 "Invincibles" tour cap worn by Don Bradman. That sum was bettered in December 2020, when the Don's first Baggy Green, dating from 1928, was bought by a Sydney businessman for $450,000, after failing to make its reserve at auction. It had been put up for sale after the owner, Peter Dunham, a 76-year-old accountant, was jailed for eight years and two months for swindling investors out of $1.3m. The cap, which Dunham had been given by Bradman as a boy, and cannot be removed from Australia, was sold at the behest of a trustee, Oracle Insolvency Services, after his estate was declared bankrupt. (Baggy Greens, limited since 1993 to one a career, were once given out more frequently.)

Covid, or the combating of it, was also the spur for a charitable gesture by Jos Buttler. In late March, at the height of the first wave, he put on eBay the long-sleeved shirt he had worn when keeping wicket in the 2019 World Cup final at Lord's – and thus as he completed the run-out of Martin Guptill in the super over. Like Warne's cap, Buttler's shirt bore testimony to alcoholic

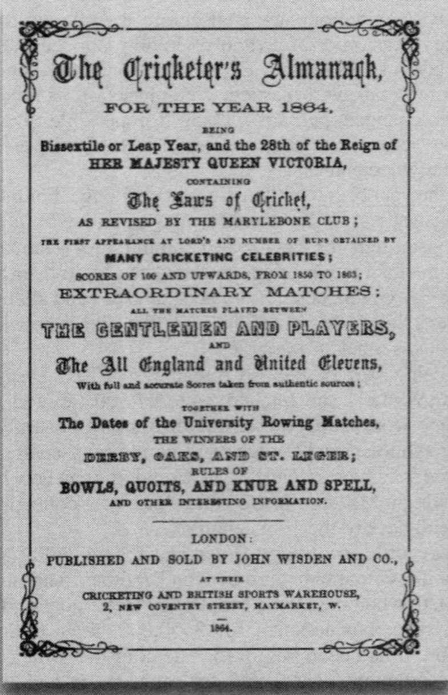

The Cricketer's Almanack,
FOR THE YEAR 1864,
BEING
Bissextile or Leap Year, and the 28th of the Reign of
HER MAJESTY QUEEN VICTORIA,
CONTAINING
The Laws of Cricket,
AS REVISED BY THE MARYLEBONE CLUB;
THE FIRST APPEARANCE AT LORD'S AND NUMBER OF RUNS OBTAINED BY
MANY CRICKETING CELEBRITIES;
SCORES OF 100 AND UPWARDS, FROM 1850 TO 1863;
EXTRAORDINARY MATCHES;
ALL THE MATCHES PLAYED BETWEEN
THE GENTLEMEN AND PLAYERS,
AND
The All England and United Elevens,
With full and accurate Scores taken from authentic sources;
TOGETHER WITH
The Dates of the University Rowing Matches,
THE WINNERS OF THE
DERBY, OAKS, AND ST. LEGER;
RULES OF
BOWLS, QUOITS, AND KNUR AND SPELL,
AND OTHER INTERESTING INFORMATION.

LONDON:
PUBLISHED AND SOLD BY JOHN WISDEN AND CO.,
AT THEIR
CRICKETING AND BRITISH SPORTS WAREHOUSE,
2, NEW COVENTRY STREET, HAYMARKET, W.
1864.

celebration, especially since he kept it on until almost 12 hours after the match had ended. Signed by the England team, it made £65,100, which Buttler donated to the Royal Brompton and Harefield Hospitals emergency appeal.

While these selfless one-offs grabbed media attention, the headline sale of the year came near its end when 130 lots of Geoffrey Boycott's memorabilia were offered in a three-week online auction held by Christie's. Total realisation was £207,625 (inclusive of buyer's premium).

Christie's

Online on-drive: Patrick Eagar's photo of a moment of Boycott glory eclipsed its estimate.

The prime item was Lot 100, the Hunts County bat with which Boycott scored 191 against Australia at Headingley in 1977 – his 100th first-class hundred. It raised £43,750. On the back was a signed inscription stating it had also been used for his 99th (104 for Yorkshire against Warwickshire). Other items associated with the occasion attracted much interest: one of the stumps made £5,625, while a Patrick Eagar photograph of the on-drive with which Boycott reached his landmark, signed by the batsman and framed, soared from its estimate of £100–200 to £3,000. Two more stumps, this time from the 1981 Ashes series, also attracted keen bidding: one, from the miracle at Headingley, fetched £8,125, and another, from the thriller at Edgbaston, £4,375.

Boycott explained to *The Cricketer* his reasons for selling the collection: "The bat's been with Yorkshire in their museum, but… the museum is only open on match days, so very few people see it. For many years, [my mementos and memorabilia] have been in boxes and suitcases not seen by anyone. Better cricket lovers, admirers and collectors have the opportunity to enjoy them."

Other bats featured prominently in the sale, which included the one he used in his final innings for Yorkshire, against Northamptonshire at Scarborough in 1986 (run out for 61), and another with which he scored 105 against India at Delhi, an innings that made him the leading Test run-scorer. The bats made £4,750 each.

A pair of Boycott's caps attracted keen competition, selling well ahead of estimate at £11,250. One, a ceremonial black version with white piping and tassel, was embroidered with his name and the numbers 422/1, representing his positions in England's Test and one-day international rolls (Boycott faced the first ball in the first one-day game). The other was a familiar blue Test cap.

The collection also included Viv Richards's 1980 maroon West Indies cap, which was bid up to £10,625, as well as Greg Chappell's Baggy Green, which fetched £7,500. It was Chappell who bowled the ball in the Eagar photograph.

Caught for posterity: the timing of Herbert Fishwick's photograph of Frank Woolley clinging on at slip to remove Tommy Andrews is perfection.

At the same time as the Boycott sale, Knights' autumn auction included several superb lots. Of great historical value was an archive of 71 photographs taken at all five Tests of the 1924-25 Ashes series by Herbert Henry Fishwick, widely regarded as the father of modern sports photography. Each photo bears Fishwick's handwritten captions on the rear. An Englishman who emigrated to Australia, he revolutionised the way cricket was photographed by introducing a telescopic lens, which enabled clear, close-up action shots taken from the boundary, rather than distant panoramas. This unique collection, featuring the likes of Hobbs, Sutcliffe, Tate, Ponsford, Gregory and Mailey, fetched £13,020.

Fred Spofforth, the Australian fast bowler of the 1870s and 1880s nicknamed "the Demon", was also a pioneer: the first to 50 Test wickets, and to claim a Test hat-trick. His early prowess ensured his autograph commanded a premium of £1,017 in the same Knights sale, far ahead of Larwood (£31), Tate (£37) and even Jessop (£93).

Top price in the Knights auction was the £14,880 paid for a scarce first hardback *Wisden* of 1896; it was in exceptional condition, but for a minor tear to one of its 524 pages. In terms of pounds per word, it was outshone by the £1,798 paid for a single sheet of paper that contained 46 lines of printed verse, called "A Cricketer's Prologue". Its subheading was "Spoken in the Kentish Dialect, before the Play of *The Poor Gentlemen*, at the Theatre, Canterbury, during the Great Cricket Match, August 1st, 1842." The game gave birth to the hardiest perennial of the county calendar: Canterbury Week.

CRICKET AND THE WEATHER IN 2020

The unhappy trio of Ellen, Francis and Alex

ANDREW HIGNELL

In the sunniest spring on record, there were no weather interruptions to county games in April, May, June or July. Trouble was, thanks to Covid-19, there were no county games to interrupt then either. The azure skies had come courtesy of a high-pressure cell that lasted for much of April and May, and the first spell of significant rain did not arrive until June 3.

After the wettest ever February, the three spring months saw 626 hours of sunshine, far above the average of 436. April temperatures were also the highest since records began, in 1659, and the country experienced only around 15% of average rainfall: the jet stream in the upper atmosphere swept the moisture-bearing fronts north of the UK.

The summer weather was not so well behaved. On July 8, it delayed the start of the international season by a session, and was particularly irksome during the Second Test against Pakistan – also at Southampton – when just 134.3 overs were possible, the fewest in a home Test since 1987. The disruption, mainly for light, prompted officials to adopt a more flexible attitude to start and finish times for the last match.

The first two rounds of the inaugural Bob Willis Trophy, held in early August, benefited from more high pressure, and for six days temperatures reached 34°C, the longest stretch since 1961. However, the next two rounds were afflicted by storms Ellen and Francis – a named weather system is a rarity in August – causing loss of play. Another Atlantic depression hampered the T20 Blast when it began late in the month: five of the opening nine games were abandoned; just one reached a result. Conditions improved for the rest of the group matches – September was globally the warmest ever – but finals day, shunted into October, was marred by storm Alex. The Saturday was the wettest day the country has ever endured, with the equivalent of Loch Ness falling on the UK. Alex relented enough to squeeze in three curtailed games next day.

The lack of early-season cricket gave time for the analysis of some county meteorological data. The county least affected by the weather this millennium has been Sussex, followed by Essex, winners of the 2019 Championship and the BWT. Lancashire, to no great surprise, fare worst, though Hampshire's poor show is less expected.

AVERAGE HOURS LOST IN CHAMPIONSHIP SEASON, 2000–2019

County	Hours	County	Hours	County	Hours
Derbyshire	62.25	Kent	57.50	Somerset	60.75
Durham	58.65	Lancashire	65.00	Surrey	58.50
Essex	55.75	Leicestershire	63.00	Sussex	48.00
Glamorgan	61.00	Middlesex	56.00	Warwickshire	56.00
Gloucestershire	63.00	Northamptonshire	57.50	Worcestershire	61.00
Hampshire	63.75	Nottinghamshire	60.75	Yorkshire	61.50

The Shorter Wisden

The Shorter Wisden eBook is a compelling distillation of the most enticing features of its bigger (printed) brother.

It includes the Notes by the Editor, the obituaries, every front-of-book article and review, plus reports of all England's Test matches in the previous year.

To order, visit wisdenalmanack.com

Tour to Oz 2021

The Cricket Society

You love cricket so why not join the Cricket Society

Do you want to:

- Hear from great speakers including current and former cricketers at regular events both in person and online
- Celebrate cricket at our Annual Awards Lunch at The Oval and our Book of the Year event at Lord's
- Receive exclusive and informative publications about cricket
- Watch cricket at home, and follow England on affordable tours abroad
- Play cricket to a good standard with the wandering Cricket Society XI

Then join the Society today! Visit our website to find out how: www.cricketsociety.com

CRICKET PEOPLE

Tales from lockdown

RICHARD WHITEHEAD

In a year of extraordinary challenges, cricket provided a source of comfort and inspiration for **Dr Samara Afzal**. In February, her husband, Nasir Jamshed – a former Pakistan opener – was sentenced to 17 months in prison for his role in a plot to fix matches in the Pakistan Super League. Soon after, as a GP in the West Midlands, she faced the daunting impact of the Covid-19 pandemic.

"Cricket was the best thing in the summer," said Afzal. "It came back at just at the right time to stop everything getting too depressing." There was another piece of cheering news with the announcement that, as part of the #raisethebat initiative, the England players would have the names of NHS key workers on their training shirts during the summer Tests. Afzal was put forward by the National Asian Cricket Council, and Chris Woakes wore her name on his kit.

"I have met Chris, so it was really nice that he was the one to wear my name," she said. "It was picked up by the Pakistan media, and it was good to have some positive coverage there." Afzal, who bowls seam for Walmley CC (also Woakes's club) and represented Warwickshire over a decade ago, managed a few games herself, but thought it wise not to play every week. "I couldn't always be sure who I had come into contact with, and I didn't want to pass anything on." She described the early weeks of the pandemic as "quite stressful", and added: "You never knew what would be coming through the door. I was in contact with a couple of patients who tested positive for Covid, but I was fortunate not to catch it." She has been active in using social media to alert the public to the dangers of the disease.

Her first exposure to cricket was during the 1992 World Cup, when the family home would host boisterous parties during Pakistan matches. "I used to go along when my dad and cousins were playing in the park on Saturday afternoons. At first they only let me fetch the ball and throw it back – but eventually I was allowed to bowl and bat." Older family members disapproved: "They didn't think it was appropriate for a girl to be playing cricket." Reassured by her father's determination, she ignored them.

It was not just lockdown that made May in Manchester feel oddly different – the fact that there was barely any rain that month added to the discombobulation. For Old Trafford groundsman **Matt Merchant**, however, it proved a godsend.

With pitches subject to the sort of scrutiny given to a newly discovered medieval manuscript or an arms-reduction treaty, the life of a Test groundsman is fraught at the best of times. England's redrafted behind-closed-doors schedule upped the ante. "We were told we were having the Second and Third Tests against West Indies," Merchant said. "Preparing one Test pitch is stressful enough, but preparing two – oh my god."

Then life got even more demanding. "When we were preparing those strips, the confirmation came through that Pakistan were coming over as well." Two became three. "We have a small square compared with other counties, and only five TV pitches, so we knew we were going to be using pitches that had never been used for a Test before." Every groundsman at a major venue knows the stomach-churning tension of watching the first over of a Test match. "Going through that three times was pretty stressful. Fortunately, you tend to relax a bit once the first over has been bowled."

There were also white-ball matches against Pakistan and Australia: in all, Merchant prepared pitches for nine internationals. "It was not just physically tiring, but mentally as well," he said. "You had to fill in a questionnaire on an app about how you were feeling. Then, at the ground, you had to go through a temperature tent. This was all before you even got in to do any work – and this was every day from June until the end of September."

Merchant has been at Old Trafford since 1990, the last 12 seasons as head groundsman, after succeeding Peter Marron. "Peter told me it would get easier after the first couple of years – after turning the square around in 2010-11, hosting the World Cup in 2019, and now this, I'm still waiting for it to happen."

The honours and accolades came thick and fast for **Captain Sir Tom Moore** in 2020 – a knighthood, a No. 1 record, the freedom of the City of London, and the publication of his autobiography, to mention just a few. Moore, a Second World War veteran and retired businessman, became a focus of national attention in the spring lockdown when he set out to complete 100 sponsored laps of his garden before his 100th birthday at the end of April. When the last of the donations came in, he had raised around £33m for NHS charities.

His birthday celebrations included being installed as an official member of the England cricket team. In bestowing the award, former captain Michael Vaughan called him "the nation's heartbeat". He also had two Zoom calls with fellow Yorkshireman Joe Root, where the mutual appreciation was obvious. "I feel extremely privileged to get the chance to speak to you," said Root. "You're a huge inspiration to the nation." Moore said: "I was in awe, because I've watched Joe play such magnificent cricket in the past few years."

There were other invitations. Root wanted Moore to deliver a pre-Test team talk to his players, and he had also been asked to ring the five-minute bell at Lord's after becoming an honorary member of MCC. "That must be the greatest honour you can have in the cricket world."

Sadly, the honour was never his. In early February 2021 came news that Moore had died, shortly after contracting Covid-19. In a statement, his daughters, Hannah Ingram-Moore and Lucy Teixeira, said: "The last year of our father's life was nothing short of remarkable. He was rejuvenated, and experienced things he'd only ever dreamed of."

CRICKET AND THE LAW OF THE LAND IN 2020

Beware sixes: court rules against walker

A woman awarded £17,000 damages after being struck in the eye by a cricket ball hit for six in a London park had the verdict in her favour reversed on appeal. Phoebe Lewis, a cricket fan and MCC member, had argued the authorities at Battersea Park should have erected warning signs. She also said that, although she was aware of the game, she assumed the ball would be soft.

This argument, accepted by the Recorder in the County Court, was rejected by Mr Justice Stewart on November 26: "What I frankly fail to understand is how the Recorder could envisage that a cricket match played by adult men could be assumed by any reasonable passer-by to be using a soft ball... This would have been particularly so if they were wearing whites and therefore playing what would appear to be a serious match."

Ms Lewis had sued Wandsworth Council after the incident, which occurred in 2014. "I was not focused on the cricket at all as I was chatting to my friend," she said. "But I can't deny I might have seen the players." The appeal judge cited the case of *Bolton* v *Stone* (1951), which concerned a woman injured outside the ground used by Cheetham CC in Manchester. The House of Lords then unanimously ruled that the injury was not the result of negligence.

Stewart added: "In the circumstances which obtained, allowing pedestrians to walk along the path when a cricket match was taking place was reasonably safe, the prospects of an accident (albeit nasty if it occurred) being remote."

HEAVY FINE FOR FAKING MCC MEMBERSHIP

A Bournemouth businessman was fined £10,000 after he admitted faking an MCC membership card and securing access to the Lord's Pavilion. James Lattimer, 51, bought a card on eBay that belonged to a dead member, glued on his picture and hid the date. Lattimer's trick was discovered at the 2019 Ashes Test at Lord's after a woman – who accused him of sexual assault at an earlier match – pointed him out to police. Judge Michael Grieve QC said at Southwark Crown Court on March 11 that forging the ticket was "despicable", adding: "You acquired the privilege people wait half a lifetime to acquire." Lattimer had earlier pleaded not guilty to the assault charge, and was acquitted because the identification could not be proven. For the fraud, he was given a suspended ten-month prison sentence, and ordered to do 150 hours' unpaid work.

DOG STEALS BALL... NINE MEN GET LIFE SENTENCE

Nine men were jailed for life in Mumbai for their part in the death of Anil Pandey, 30, an alleged gangster. A dispute erupted in 2015 when Pandey was walking his pet Dobermann past an informal cricket match; the dog took the ball, refused to drop it, then bit 18-year-old Saurabh Khopade, the youngest of the nine. At 2am, the men broke into Pandey's house and attacked him with knives and swords. He died in hospital. (See also *Wisden 2016*, page 1541)

TEST PLAYER'S BROTHER JAILED

Arsalan Khawaja, 40-year-old brother of Australian batsman Usman, was jailed for a minimum of two and half years by the New South Wales District Court on November 5, after attempting to frame two perceived love rivals by linking them with terrorism. Khawaja filled a notebook belonging to a colleague with suspicious threats, one of them to the Boxing Day Test in Melbourne, and handed it to a manager. The colleague was arrested and held in a maximum security jail. Khawaja, who in 2017 made anonymous calls to a police hotline implicating another man in terrorist activity, had been in custody for almost two years. He will be eligible for parole in June 2021.

EX-COUNTY PLAYER ADMITS STALKING

Former Gloucestershire batsman Grant Hodnett, 38, narrowly escaped jail after he admitted sending derogatory messages about his ex-girlfriend to her friends, family and business contacts. This followed his discovery that she worked in adult modelling. The victim said his actions had started to increase, and was scared what might happen next. Hodnett's solicitor, Mark Haslam, said: "The defendant accepts that his conduct was not just inappropriate, but totally unacceptable. It was not for him to go on a moral crusade." South African-born Hodnett was told by Warrington magistrates on September 23 that only his previous good character spared him from prison. He was given a suspended sentence for "stalking involving serious alarm or distress", and a two-year community order, involving unpaid work and rehabilitation. He now plays for Grappenhall CC, Cheshire, and works as a personal trainer.

COUNTY BATSMAN BANNED AFTER FOUR-CAR PILE-UP

Gloucestershire batsman George Hankins was banned from driving for 22 months after a bizarre accident during lockdown in April. He went out for hay-fever tablets while his alcohol level was more than double the legal limit. On his return, he crashed into two cars in one drive, which were shunted into two cars next door, which were pushed into a house, causing £15,000 damage. Hankins, 23, who was staying in Surrey at the time, pleaded guilty to drink-driving at Staines Magistrates' Court. He was also fined £600. Mark Haslam, defending, said: "We have here a thoroughly decent, capable and well-regarded young man who made a quite ridiculous decision to drive."

ENGLAND PLAYER RECORDS HUNDRED

Nottinghamshire batsman Ben Duckett was banned from driving after doing 106mph on the A43 in Northamptonshire. But his punishment was reduced because Covid restrictions – forcing players to travel separately – would have stopped him from getting to away matches if still in force in 2021. Northampton magistrates reduced the normal six-month ban to three, and fined him £817. Duckett was disqualified in 2015 for drink-driving.

THE LAWS OF THE GAME

I do declare – again

FRASER STEWART

Even in a quiet year, there were plenty of Laws-related conundrums to prompt people to contact MCC. In Port Elizabeth in January, Joe Root declared England's first innings at 467 for nine when Mark Wood was caught off Kagiso Rabada. But once replays showed a no-ball, Root was allowed to withdraw the declaration, which came soon after, at 499 for nine.

Law 15.3 states that a declaration cannot be changed once the opposing captain and umpires have been notified; strictly, Root's retraction should not have stood. However, since ICC playing regulations allow no-ball decisions to be overturned, the umpires looked favourably on his position, presumably concluding that, had they called the no-ball in the first place, he would not have declared. The right decision was probably reached, even if the letter of the Law was not followed. It is, in fact, rare for a captain to "notify" his opposite number and the umpires: in practice, declarations are usually signalled from the pavilion.

Following two incidents in Australia's Big Bash League, MCC examined whether a Law change, or at least clarification, was needed regarding fielders moving backwards before the ball has reached the striker. Playing for Sydney Thunder against Hobart Hurricanes, Alex Hales was on the edge of the 30-yard ring at mid-off when he started walking backwards as soon as the bowler released the ball. Next day, Melbourne Stars' Adam Zampa took a catch just outside the ring at short fine leg, having moved back on seeing Sydney Sixers' Moises Henriques shape to ramp the ball over him.

Hales, who was criticised on air by former Australian captain Ricky Ponting, argued his action was similar to a slip fielder moving to the leg side because the batsman is about to sweep – and such anticipatory movement was permitted in a Law change in 2015. Law 28.6 allows "movement *towards* the striker that does not significantly alter the position of the fielder" (in other words, walking in), or "movement by any fielder in response to the stroke that the striker is playing, or that his/her actions suggest he/she intends to play". Hales thought Hobart's Simon Milenko would try to hit the ball over his head, though his movement was potentially at odds with the intention of the BBL playing condition about the number of fielders in the ring.

MCC decided no change was required, but felt Law 28.6 was being used to circumvent the playing condition limiting where fielders can stand. They thought this could be looked at by the governing bodies who write the playing conditions, and who should decide whether the requirement of having a fielder within the ring takes priority over the fielder's ability to react to the striker's movement. A tweak to such conditions could, for example, insist that the fielder remains within the ring until the ball reaches the striker.

During the Third Test between England and Pakistan at Southampton in August, Azhar Ali batted throughout the third day, and was unbeaten on 141 when his team's last wicket fell, with only a few overs remaining. England enforced the follow-on, and Azhar – normally a No. 3 – decided he would open in the second innings, since his eye was in. He walked out with Shan Masood but, before play had been called by the umpire, the light was deemed too bad, and the game ended for the day.

Did Azhar still have to open next morning, as he had already walked out on to the field? Law 25.2 states: "The innings of the first two batsmen, and that of any new batsman on the resumption of play after a call of Time, shall commence at the call of Play. At any other time, a batsman's innings shall be considered to have commenced when that batsman first steps on to the field of play." So when Azhar and Masood walked out to bat, play was not in progress, and the match effectively at a standstill. This is different from the fall of a wicket, when play is in progress. Since neither of their innings had started, Pakistan were free to choose their openers next morning, and Azhar batted at No. 3, as usual.

At the IPL in October, Sunrisers Hyderabad's Rashid Khan seemed to be out both hit wicket and caught off the same delivery, against Chennai Super Kings: his back foot dislodged the bails moments before he was held at long-on. Law 33.5 states that caught takes precedence over all other forms of dismissal, except bowled. However, Law 20.1.1.3 states that the ball becomes dead once a batsman is dismissed, and Law 31.2 clarifies that a batsman is dismissed once he has been given out by an umpire following an appeal. In Rashid's case, the square-leg umpire upheld CSK's appeal for hit wicket before the catch was taken, so the ball was dead before it reached the fielder. The dismissal was correctly recorded as hit wicket. Had the umpire waited until the catch was held, Rashid would have been out caught, potentially affecting who would face the next delivery if the batsmen had crossed with the ball in the air.

In the Bob Willis Trophy game between Leicestershire and Lancashire, following a straight-drive from Lancashire batsman Danny Lamb, the bowler Dieter Klein fielded the ball and threw it back at him. Lamb had not left his ground, and had shown no intention of running. The ball struck him hard on the leg; he was fortunate to escape serious injury. The umpires rightly invoked Law 42.3, which forbids "throwing the ball at a player, umpire or another person in an inappropriate and dangerous manner", and awarded five penalty runs to Lancashire. It is important that bowlers are aware of this Law and its implications, as well as the fact that the ball does not have to make contact with the other person for it to be breached. If the striker has left his ground, and a run-out is possible, the bowler is entitled to throw the ball at the stumps. However, it is sometimes thrown – often in a fit of pique – when the striker is within his ground, and such petulance should not go unpunished.

Fraser Stewart is Laws manager at MCC.

CRICKET AND TECHNOLOGY IN 2020

Come on, feel the noise

LIAM CROMAR

Anyone familiar with cricket will know its soundtrack extends far beyond the cliché of leather on willow. So a behind-closed-doors broadcast presented a problem: without crowds, it would – in the words of Bryan Henderson, Sky's director of cricket – be "eerily quiet and cold". For fans who have grown used to audio-free online streams of county games – or even for those who, before the coronavirus, attended those games – such silence might not have been unusual. But it risked alienating the more casual viewer.

Sky's innovations mitigated the impact on the visual spectacle: the use of a remote-controlled camera buggy (nicknamed "Little Wardy", after roving reporter Ian Ward) for player interviews; drones shooting from areas that would have been off-limits with crowds; high-wire cameras that would normally have blocked spectators' views; shots chosen to avoid empty stands. Yet without background noise, the aural canvas would have been blank. Sound supervisor Jason Watts described the lack of a crowd as "an immense technical challenge. Our whole coverage strategy is based on getting a huge, lively, atmospheric crowd sound."

The solution: pipe in the noise from a past game. And even though Lord's had no Tests in 2020, all six Tests had Lord's, since the audio was drawn from the Ashes match there a year earlier, with the ground chosen because of its unique hum. For the white-ball games, recordings from an England–India one-day international, also at Lord's, were added to the mix. A different clip was used on a loop for the three sessions – each lasting 80 seconds, and taken from a Test-match day's three drinks breaks, to avoid PA announcements and match sounds. Volume was slowly increased during the day, and commentators instructed to boost their intensity at dramatic moments. The in-ground PA man was asked to up the level of his announcements, and any music. All this served to take the edge off the unreality of proceedings – though some suspension of disbelief was required on the listener's part.

Naturally, there were challenges. As Watts observed, turning stump microphones up increased the trickiness of "keeping the wicketkeeper under control", with regard to both volume and content – traditionally a concern for the captain rather than the sound crew. Thanks to their efforts, broadcast incidents of industrial language were rare.

With background audio successfully produced, Sky were left considering how far to go. In the end, with the focus on the Tests, event-specific cheering was left largely unexplored, though the ECB added it to their online streaming of the T20 Blast knockout stages. This was a whisper of what was to come.

IPL broadcasters Star, who had much longer to prepare than Sky, took the idea to a new level, having tested their system on knockout matches at the

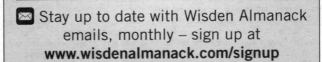

Caribbean Premier League. Since specific fixtures and individual players generate their own crowd sounds, a bank of over 400 elements was compiled. These were not merely extracted from previous games: fans were recruited to record themselves remotely and, in partnership with audio specialists Dolby, fresh chants were processed to give the impression of a cast of thousands.

The IPL was able to feature not only cheers on-tap – singles, boundaries, wickets and near-misses all had their own tracks – but specific mixes for teams, players and match situations. Cheers for Virat Kohli hitting a six for Royal Challengers Bangalore at the death would, for example, be different from David Warner doing so for Sunrisers Hyderabad in the powerplay. This was developed during the competition: a new chant was recorded for Rajasthan Royals' Rahul Tewatia, after his unanticipated heroics during a win over Kings XI Punjab.

The sound was also played inside the grounds, with Chennai Super Kings' Australian batsman Shane Watson claiming the "white noise of the crowd" had a "huge impact". Yet it was not about the whims of the producer: chants were triggered by fans using the Cheer@home facility on Disney+ Hotstar, a subscription streaming service owned by Star India. Viewers sent live emoji reactions, such as the one for M. S. Dhoni; the audio producer monitored trends, and fired up chants in response.

Another feature, Virtual Match Ticket, allowed a limited number of fans to attend games via webcam, their reactions visible to the players on in-ground LED screens. At a time of widespread isolation, extra engagement was a positive step. But subtle ethical issues arise. How much should a broadcaster be allowed to influence a player's performance? And if augmented audio is used in internationals, should the host broadcaster weight cheering to provide home advantage?

Then there's the audience: at what point does a broadcast cease to represent what is taking place at the ground? Sanjog Gupta, head of sports at Star, was clear there was no intention to "mislead viewers at home. We at no point suggested there are fans inside the stadium." Furthermore, enhanced crowd noise is not new: football broadcasting has for some years fed it in to cover offensive chanting. But to what extent are the audience entitled to see and hear what is actually going on?

As the lines blur between remote and in-person viewing, and with innovations developed for the year of Covid-19 available in future, broadcasters – and viewers – will have to decide an appropriate level of integration. Perhaps the main issue is disclosure: if the audience are informed of enhancements, a happy fiction can be maintained. A sound idea?

Liam Cromar freelances in cricket at @LiamCromar, and in code at @SpinnerWebs.

CRICKET AND THE ENVIRONMENT IN 2020

Think twice before setting off

TANYA ALDRED

In the sudden surprise of long-unheard birdsong, the emergence of the Himalayan peaks to those in northern Punjab for the first time in over 30 years or the 7% fall in fossil-fuel burning, there were flickers of hope amid the global lockdown.

And yet the level of CO_2 in the earth's atmosphere reached record levels in 2020. It was the joint-hottest year recorded – matched only by 2016, when temperatures were boosted by El Niño. The wildfires that burned uncontrolled through the 2019-20 Australian cricketing summer were mirrored in California and even Siberia, and there were a record 29 tropical storms in the Atlantic.

Cricket, like everything else, had to bed down in the Covid-19 pandemic. Around the world, airports lay empty as borders closed. Emissions from aviation were an estimated 40% down on 2019, though expected to bounce back. A November report concluded that 1% of the world's population emitted 50% of commercial aviation's CO_2, and that only 2–4% had flown internationally in 2018. Flying is an elite pursuit; flying a lot is niche-elite, and sports stars slot right in. Cricketers fly to series, and (except in England and Sri Lanka) within series; so do umpires, backroom staff, media and the rest. A small number of players, who ride the T20 tournament merry-go-round, fly even more. But international cricket relies on aeroplanes for its very existence. So, what to do?

Ritesh Uttamchandani, *Hindustan Times*/Getty Images

Done by the flight: kids at Dharavi, beside Mumbai airport; the slum is home to around a million.

It is a sensitive subject. The first UK Climate Assembly called, among other things, for a tax on frequent flyers. Aviation makes up only 2.5% of global CO_2 emissions – similar to the amount given off to power the internet, but less than, say, cement (3%) or livestock (14.5%). But since 1960, emissions from aircraft have gone up by a factor of 6.8 – and pre-pandemic predictions envisaged a further tripling by 2050, flying in the face of attempts to reach net zero.

Carbon offsetting is one solution, but problematic. Many see it as a licence to pollute, and it is no substitute for trying to reduce emissions: a tree takes years to absorb the amount of carbon promised by schemes. As Greenpeace point out, there is always the risk that even this offsetting will be wiped out by drought, wildfire, tree disease or deforestation. There are also issues in separating UN-certified offsetters from what even EasyJet have called "snake-oil salesmen".

Gold-standard offsetting would seem a useful tool to reduce the damage caused by flights that absolutely must be taken, though this is not something the ICC or member states currently do. But who decides what is necessary? In international sport, greed is king. Games equal broadcasting rights equal money. Rare is the administrator who says enough is enough.

Change may come from cricketers themselves, not with an environmental hat on (climate chaos is yet to become a common topic in dressing-rooms), but for reasons of burnout. The pressures of living in a bubble in 2020 brought to the surface issues that have been simmering – players play too much, with boards trying to squeeze every last buck from every last bang. West Indies captain Jason Holder spoke for many: "It's been really tough being sat in the room seeing the same walls. Every time you leave and come back, the room feels a bit smaller." There is, though, a sniff of change in the air: Greg Barclay, the new ICC chairman, declared the cricket calendar "unsustainable".

So the onus is on the ICC and individual boards to keep the number of games in check to protect player health – but also to keep emissions to a minimum. Covid has provided breathing space, an opportunity to reset, to think smarter. Does cricket really need so many tournaments, so many series? The ICC say they are "conscious of the environmental impact of our sport more broadly, and in recent years have made a number of changes to the way ICC events operate to ensure we are taking a more sustainable approach". Sustainability will be part of the bidding criteria for the 28 tournaments planned between 2023 and 2031. But, tellingly perhaps, concrete details or pledges are not forthcoming.

As a matter of urgency, bilateral tours – the domain of national boards, not the ICC – should be planned in a responsible manner, to avoid constant zig-zagging. Flying direct from Heathrow to Perth at the start of an Ashes tour, for example, would reduce the fuel burned in take-off and landing.

Covid has proved that, in an emergency, cricket can transform how it operates. Yet nothing is more important than the climate crisis, as the protesters who invaded the pitch during the first ODI between Australia and India at Sydney in November understood. They were railing against the proposed Adani coalmine in Queensland, dubbed by *Rolling Stone* "the most insane

THE EXTINCTION REBELLION CRICKET CLUB

The Westminster Test

HUGH CHEVALLIER

It seems an unlikely marriage: cricket and Extinction Rebellion (XR), the non-violent, direct-action protest group founded to draw attention to the climate crisis. But as these pages have shown in recent years, the game is especially vulnerable to global heating, and a growing number are discovering they share a love of cricket and a desire to mitigate damage to the planet.

In Bristol, a group of 30 or more such activists have coalesced to form XRCC. Two of the driving forces are Xeena Cooper and Steve Dunk. Xeena attended the London rebellion of spring 2018, where she saw theatre, music, art – but no cricket. She and Steve resolved to change that. By the time they went to London for another XR event in October 2019, the club were starting to take shape. They brought along basic kit and, on the trafficless tarmac of Parliament Square, XRCC found a pitch that guaranteed publicity for what they call their "First Test". Pictures appeared in several papers – and in the colour section of *Wisden 2020*.

Fergus MacGregor

Xeena, as keen about the history of cricket as for playing it, is adamant it was no short-form game. "Our goals in XR are long-term, so we play Tests – we're in for the long haul. I could see some of the police were itching to join in with us, but I realise that's difficult."

As it turned out, the club needed patience, since the next cricket was delayed by Covid-19 until September 2020, when they took on the splendidly named Easton Cuttlefish, also from Bristol. This looked more like the conventional game than the Westminster Test and, though they lost, XRCC did not embarrass themselves. The pandemic also scuppered closer links with Gloucestershire CCC. A talk at the County Ground explaining the nature of the environmental threat – and its effect on Bristol communities – had to be shelved, as were plans for XRCC to have net sessions at Nevil Road.

Though enthusiastic at the growth of the club, and how they have been a force for good, Xeena also strikes a sombre note, at the core of XR concerns: "It's a love of the game that's brought us all together – and it's a deep sorrow that a world so full of beauty is threatened. We must act for change now."

energy project on the planet". Amid the imminent threat, especially to the global south, with disrupted monsoons, extreme weather and killer air pollution, cricket cannot sit idly by.

The pandemic also introduced the concept of online meetings to cricket administrators. The ECB offices at Lord's were shut in March, and communication done remotely; the ICC also shut their offices in Dubai, though they stress the importance of occasional face-to-face meetings. MCC have embraced the world of Zoom, while their AGM took place on YouTube, and over 2,000 members logged in. Even cricket societies have joined the digital revolution, with winter speakers beamed into members' homes from beside their own Christmas trees.

Mark Kolbe, Getty Images

Coal board: an SCG protestor makes his point.

The fast-approaching COP26 – the UN Climate Summit, due to be held in Glasgow in November 2021 – has heightened awareness throughout governments and businesses. At the ECB, attitudes seem to be changing, too. The pandemic forced them to cut 20% of their workforce and freeze recruitment, but they made an exception for the post of sustainability manager, which they were close to filling in 2020 before lockdown intervened. Controversial in some quarters, the sustainability budget has also been protected from the cuts that have scythed through other departments.

All 18 first-class counties have undergone a carbon audit, while the ECB were being audited by Enworks, experts in environmental business issues. They scrutinised everything from flights and train journeys, to the board's offices at Lord's, Loughborough, Edgbaston and Old Trafford. The aim was to form the basis of a sustainability policy for the whole game.

There have already been efforts to lessen cricket's carbon footprint further down the food chain. Over the last six years, the ECB have encouraged leagues to localise, and reduce the average travel time from 90 minutes to half an hour. The regional structure of the Bob Willis Trophy in 2020 minimised travel for county cricketers as well. And Gloucestershire became the first UK club to join the UN Sports for Climate Action Framework.

There is a balance to be struck, between the social benefits of playing and watching sport, and the carbon it emits. With nearly 39m flights taken worldwide in 2019 (the figure dropped dramatically during the pandemic), cricket's contribution, even with associated tourism, is a fraction of a percent. But everyone carries the responsibility to reduce their footprint. Covid has presented a chance to build back better.

Tanya Aldred is a freelance writer and editor, and founder of @TheNextTest.

CRICKET AND TELEVISION IN 2020

Prime cuts

GIDEON HAIGH

The Test is an ambitious documentary series tracing the highs and lows of the Australian team from the middle of 2018 to the end of the 2019 Ashes. For sale on Amazon Prime, it is also a piece of official Cricket Australia merchandise, whose scarcely obscure aim is to help rebuild public faith in, and affinity with, CA's premier sporting product.

The two concerns are in tension through *The Test's* eight episodes, but ultimately rub along together pretty well. As a wardrobe account of the Australians' fight to reconstruct their shattered XI under the coaching of Justin Langer and the captaincy of Tim Paine, it would be hard to improve this polished, well-paced, sharply edited series, boiled down from 2,300 hours of footage. And *The Test* rebuilds a brand tarnished by the shame of Sandpapergate. When seduction is inevitable, well, why not lie back and enjoy it?

The dressing-room, of course, is usually a cricket team's *sanctum sanctorum*, shrouded in mystery and prestige. It was no small matter for the Australian team to condone cameraman Andre Mauger in their midst so long, or trust director Adrian Brown to craft the final result. Who knew how the team would fare, and which members would last the distance, as Australia defended both the World Cup and the Ashes?

There are hints of a rift in the lute, as the players try to cope with Langer's intensity

The only comparable series, Netflix's *Cricket Fever* (2019), which followed Mumbai Indians as they sought to defend their IPL title, blanched when the team hit trouble, and the producers had to recalibrate for failure. There must have been times in the making of *The Test* when the temptation, on both sides, was to look away.

The first half of the series is Australia being flogged, in ODIs in England, in Tests in the Gulf, and at home in the Border–Gavaskar Trophy. Langer is for much of it an ersatz narrator, because he spans the three formats. But there are hints of a genuine rift in the lute, as the players try to cope with Langer's intensity. In episode four, after Australia's heavy defeat by India in the Boxing Day Test, Usman Khawaja says the coach is causing him to think negatively, fearful of error, rather than freely, according to his nature. Shot in indifferent light with quiet audio, it makes you feel like you're listening at a keyhole.

The coach struggles with his own team-baking, bin-kicking candour. His expressions as he watches Virat Kohli are exquisite: exasperation, torment, awe. His wisdom is pungent: "None of you are good enough to have theories yet"; "You can't sugarcoat shit." What Langer says out of the camera's range is an interesting speculation. He relates that, before the third morning of the Sydney Test, when Australia were at their nadir, his wife burst into tears over breakfast. "It was a wake-up call," he says. "It was really tough. It really got to me." He looks chastened, temporarily at least.

Not quite the yin to Langer's yang, although sometimes close, is Paine. We encounter, perhaps, the contrast between the former player who can see the totality of the action but not influence it in real time, and the current player caught up in the run of events but with a sense of the fickleness of fortune and the fog of war. Langer, for example, seethes at the hostility of the crowd at Edgbaston. Paine is more sanguine: "You don't play against the ground."

The dynamic is similar in the wake of the Headingley Test. Paine tries to soothe his colleagues' disappointment at being single-handedly bested by Ben Stokes: "We didn't panic. We didn't shit ourselves. We tried our best. We had a crack. A bloke had a day out." Langer, meanwhile, wishes them, including Paine, to stare their failures in the face. Watching the team watch themselves on a screen, reliving the match's final hour, is uncomfortable viewing, as though one is intruding on a private grief.

It's not actually clear whose view prevails – to know that, we would need to climb into each player's head. But Australia regrouped proudly to win in Manchester and retain the Ashes. And it's Paine's prediction, just minutes after the loss at Leeds, that stands out in hindsight for its quiet authority: "The process we've got in place is going to win it."

Also vividly conveyed are cricket's occasional random cruelties. Sequences showing injuries to Khawaja and Shaun Marsh during the World Cup feel almost voyeuristic. We see Khawaja's tears – the only ones, he says, he has ever shed over cricket. We see Marsh's blank acknowledgment that his arm is broken, the distress of colleagues. "I just wanted to cry for him," admits Nathan Coulter-Nile.

The alarm in the dressing-room when Steve Smith is felled by Jofra Archer in the Test at Lord's is admirably captured, as is the solicitous way team-mates keep their distance when he is out. Smith, whose post-Sandpapergate return to the colours with David Warner and Cameron Bancroft is seen as disarmingly low-key and practical, remains rather hard to know – a kind of batting savant, blurred by his tics and tricks. Or maybe he just spent so long in the middle, or taking throwdowns, that the documentary makers could not quite pin him down.

"We're a newish side trying to find our identity," Pat Cummins remarks during a pre-World Cup bonding trip to Gallipoli. It is a comment on the strangeness of the lives that modern athletes lead that both a pilgrimage to the site of a First World War battle, and a full-dress documentary series under the auspices of a global retailing giant, are experienced as natural ways to explore it.

Gideon Haigh's latest book is Shelf Life: Journalism 2000–2020.

OBITUARIES

AHMED, RAZIA FARID, died when a landslide triggered by heavy rain engulfed her home in the village of Mawnei in north-eastern India on September 25. She was 25, and played several matches for Meghalaya in the national state competition, often opening the batting. Another keen female club player, Ferozia Khan, died during the deluge.

ANDERSON, ROBERT GEOFFREY, died on May 3, aged 81. A seamer from Dunedin who usually took the new ball, Geoff Anderson played 16 matches for Otago in the early 1960s, claiming 43 wickets, though never more than three in an innings. His last game for Otago, in 1964-65, was the first for two distinguished cricketers: Glenn Turner (whose catch provided Anderson with his final first-class wicket) and Billy Ibadulla.

ANDERTON, REV. FREDERIC MICHAEL, died on April 28, aged 88. Born in Agra, within sight of the Taj Mahal, Michael Anderton led a remarkably varied life: after initially studying medicine, he graduated in history and economics, joined the clergy – one of his first churches was in St John's Wood, next to Lord's – and eventually became a psychoanalyst, before retiring to Winchester. He had been a fine all-round sportsman (and head boy) at Sherborne, before national service, which the *Church Times* suggested he enjoyed: "He filled the next two years with cricket – his first love – eating and drinking in the officers' mess, going to the opera, and writing cars off." While up at Cambridge he played rugby and cricket. He made three first-class appearances for the university in 1953, scoring 38 in the first, against Middlesex at Fenner's.

ANGULUGAHA, KODITUWAKKU ARACHCHIGE PRASAD SENAKA, died of blood poisoning on February 2, aged 60. A medium-pacer from Colombo, Senaka Angulugaha played 13 first-class matches for the Sri Lanka Air Force, taking four for 42 against Burgher Sports Club in January 1990, three coming as he and Rohan Weerakkody reduced them to 18 for five. He later did development work for the Sri Lankan board.

ASLAM QURESHI, who died of Covid-19 on June 6, aged 66, was a seamer who claimed 120 wickets for Habib Bank and various Karachi teams. His best return was eight for 75, to spirit Karachi Greens to a narrow victory over Sargodha at Lyallpur (now Faisalabad) in 1971-72. He also took seven for 36 – and 11 for 69 in the match, his victims including five Test players – as Habib Bank beat United Bank at Karachi in 1979-80. Qureshi played league cricket in Lancashire and Birmingham, and later became a groundsman, employed by the Pakistan board to oversee pitches in Karachi.

ATKINS, NORMAN, MBE, who died on March 16, aged 81, was a lifelong cricket enthusiast who became a Minor Counties umpire. He was associated with the St Margaret's club in Ipswich for nearly 60 years, and was Suffolk's chairman from 1994 to 2009, before a term as president.

AUTY, GILES AINSWORTH, who died on September 24, aged 85, was an art critic for the *New Statesman* and *The Spectator*, and an artist himself, exhibiting in London – and Newlyn, in Cornwall, near where he was brought up. He eventually moved to Australia, where he lived in the Blue Mountains outside Sydney and wrote on various subjects. In the 1970s, he had opened the bowling for Dorset and Cornwall in the Minor Counties Championship.

BAKER-WHITE, ROBIN JOHN, who died on December 28, aged 88, was Kent's president in 1996, and also president of Street End CC, who play on land owned by his family. He was descended from William de Chair Baker, one of the founders of Canterbury Week.

BARKER, ANTONY ROYSTON PAUL, died on April 20, aged 72. Roy Barker played 27 matches for Worcestershire between 1967 and 1969, usually filling in when Tom Graveney and Basil D'Oliveira were on England duty. He did not have much success with

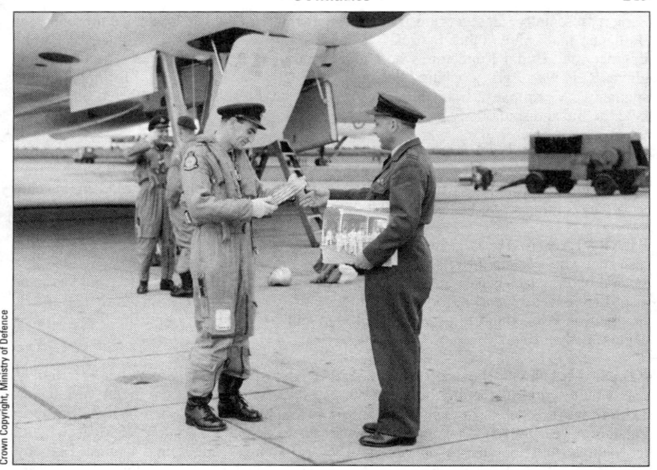

Crown Copyright, Ministry of Defence

Hold the back page: Mike Beavis inspects his cricket cargo, 1961.

the bat, although he fought well for 67 at Southport in 1969, defying Lancashire's new-ball pair of Peter Lever and Ken Higgs. After his first-class career, Barker played for Staffordshire, and made 117 against a Lincolnshire side including Sonny Ramadhin in 1970; he remained a force in club cricket, captaining Kidderminster to the Birmingham League title in 1975. "Roy was a smashing bloke who maintained a keen and enthusiastic interest in how Worcestershire were doing," said former county seamer Paul Pridgeon.

BASHIR SHANA, who died on May 20, aged 78, scored more than 2,000 runs in 40 first-class matches in Pakistan. His 208 against Public Works Department in 1973-74 remains Hyderabad's highest first-class score; he made three other centuries.

BEAVIS, Air Chief Marshal Sir MICHAEL GORDON, KCB, CBE, AFC, who died on June 7, aged 90, joined the RAF in 1949 and rose to become commander-in-chief of Support Command in 1981. Mike Beavis captained the first plane to fly non-stop from England to Australia, in June 1961: his Vulcan bomber completed the trip to Sydney in just over 20 hours, thanks to four tricky mid-air refuellings over Cyprus (where he would live in retirement), Karachi, and north and south Malaysia. Beavis had a lifelong interest in sport – his last job before joining up was with *Boxing News* – so was happy that the cargo for his historic flight included photographs and film from the touring Australians' match at Canterbury, which had ended in a close draw the day they took off.

BECK, NEIL, who died on January 1, aged 72, was a familiar sight at Sussex matches, where he ran a well-stocked bookstall, which eventually acquired semi-permanent premises at Hove. He started at Eastbourne in 1985, and went full-time – as Castle Cricket Books – after retiring as a librarian in 1998. Beck, who sold memorabilia as well as books, said: "*Wisdens* are the bread and butter of this business."

BELLIAPPA, PATAMADA KARAMBIAH, who died on February 19, aged 79, was a long-serving wicketkeeper for Madras (later Tamil Nadu), captaining them in the 1967-68 Ranji Trophy final, won by serial champions Bombay. He was also a regular in the South

Zone representative side, scoring 104 as an opener against the 1963-64 MCC touring team. Belliappa made three other first-class centuries, but was never able to displace Farokh Engineer and Budhi Kunderan, who had a decade-long battle for India's wicketkeeping gloves. "He was a gritty opening batsman and very good keeper," said former Test leg-spinner V. V. Kumar, a frequent team-mate. "He was a self-made cricketer, and off the field the life and soul of any party."

BEZUIDENHOUT, DENZIL HILARY, who died on June 20, aged 86, was an umpire from Natal who oversaw 53 first-class and 43 one-day games from 1973-74. South Africa were excluded from international cricket during his career, but he stood in matches involving touring sides; his last, in 1986-87, involved Kim Hughes's rebel Australians.

BHARATAN, RAJU, who died on February 7, aged 86, was a cricket writer and film historian who worked for *The Illustrated Weekly of India* for over 40 years. He produced several books, starting as a teenager with an account of India's 1952 tour of England, and also directed *The Victory Story*, about India's first series win in England, in 1971. "He reported on cricket and films with equal elan and commitment," said the former Indian captain Bishan Bedi.

BHASKARAN, DR CHANDROTH KALYADAN, who died on November 21, aged 79, was a hard-working opening bowler from Kerala who played an unofficial Test against Ceylon at Ahmedabad in January 1965, in an Indian side captained by the Nawab of Pataudi. A year later, he took a career-best seven for 86 against Andhra. He then switched to Madras, and hit 76 not out in the 1967-68 Ranji Trophy final against Bombay. Bhaskaran, who became a dermatologist in the United States, was an ardent Olympics fan, and attended every Games from Munich in 1972 to Rio de Janeiro in 2016.

BHIMANI, KISHORE, who died of Covid-19 on October 15, aged 80, was a respected Indian journalist from Calcutta, and also a radio commentator, whose assignments included the tie between India and Australia at Madras in 1986-87. He had written an account of India's eventful tour of the West Indies early in 1976. His son, Gautam, followed in his footsteps: a colleague pointed out after India won the 2014 Lord's Test that their first victory there – in 1986 – had also featured a Binny on the field and a Bhimani in the press box.

George Lipman, Fairfax Media/Getty Images

Away from the limelight: Wendy Blunsden.

BLUNSDEN, WENDY ANN, who died on August 1, aged 77, played seven Tests for Australia in the 1970s, and also appeared in the first World Cup in 1973. An accurate off-spinner from Adelaide who went for less than 1.5 an over in Tests, Blunsden took eight for 16 in 19 overs against Western Australia in 1973-74. Two seasons earlier, she had played her first Test, against New Zealand in Melbourne; Blunsden said receiving the letter advising of her selection was "the best day of my life, but no one was home, so I celebrated with the dog". She captained in her next Test, in 1974-75, but did not enjoy the politics that accompanied the job, and found life back in the ranks – for tours of England and the West Indies in 1976 – more congenial. She became a teacher.

BOLUS, JOHN BRIAN, died on May 6, aged 86. Brian Bolus might have hit the first ball he faced in both first-class and Test cricket for four, but he was no cavalier. Instead, he was a grafting opener, and only occasionally revealed a sense of adventure. The statistics of a 20-year career were impressive, though: 25,598 runs, with 39 hundreds. And a Test average of 41 suggests he was unlucky to play only seven.

Bolus forced his way into the England team in 1963, having batted like a man on a mission at Nottinghamshire after being released by Yorkshire. Playing a more expansive game, he was the leading run-scorer in the country by the time of the Fourth Test against West Indies, and made a hometown debut at Headingley. He on-drove his first ball, from Wes Hall, for a boundary; in the same over, he late-cut another. Ian Wooldridge observed: "The crowd was up near 30,000 again and, from the noise they made as Bolus cracked his first ball in Test cricket away for four between midwicket and long-on, most of them seemed to be his cousins or uncles."

Bolus made just 14 before Hall had his revenge, but hit 43 in the second innings, then 33 and 15 at The Oval. He earned selection for the trip to India, where he was England's leading scorer both in the Tests (391 at 48) and overall (752 at 50). "Bolus scored with splendid consistency," wrote E. M. Wellings in *Wisden*. "He fully proved his temperament and fighting spirit, a good ally in times of adversity."

After that, he might have expected a crack at Australia in 1964. For MCC against the tourists at Lord's in May, he opened with Geoffrey Boycott, whose emergence at Yorkshire had been one of the reasons behind his release. Bolus outscored him in the match (by one run), but when the Ashes began Boycott was opening. Bolus did not play Test cricket again, though he departed with a statistic yet to be eclipsed: in 12 innings, he never made a single-figure score.

Bolus was born in Whitkirk, Leeds, and attended nets at Headingley, where he became "consumed with theory". As he put it: "I was concentrating so hard on whether my hands and feet were doing the right thing that I hardly saw the ball coming back down the wicket." Two years of national service cleared his mind, and he made his first-class debut against MCC at Lord's in April 1956. But he made little impact until 1959, when he hit 91 in a low-scoring match at Bristol.

The breakthrough came the next year, when he totalled 1,245 runs in a second successive Championship-winning season. Against Hampshire at Portsmouth, he made his first century, an unbeaten 146. And in 1961, now capped, Bolus scored 1,970 at 35, with four hundreds. He recalled a conversation with Essex opener Gordon Barker. "You've got too many runs this year, Bolly." Bolus was taken aback. "How can anyone score too many runs?" Barker replied: "They'll expect that every year now – when I get to 1,500, I call it off."

It proved prescient. Yorkshire's autocratic cricket chairman Brian Sellers warned that two capped players would be culled before the end of the 1962 season. Under pressure, Bolus struggled. "You had six batsmen fighting for four places, and that made people cautious," said Ray Illingworth. "Before that, Brian had been quite an attacking player." He was opening with

PA Images/Alamy

Nottinghamshire exile: Brian Bolus in 1969.

Boycott for the Second XI when news of the axe came through. Illingworth believes Bolus was not too despondent: "Brian was married with children by then, and wanted to be paid the salary of a senior capped player. In those days, that made a massive difference to what you earned." He turned down Essex and Kent ("Don't sign for anyone south of the Trent," Sellers had told him), and joined Nottinghamshire.

Armed with the security of a three-year contract, he flourished. With 2,190, he was the country's leading run-scorer of 1963. His five hundreds included a career-best 202 against Glamorgan. "I was determined to do well," he said. "But I never had animosity towards Yorkshire." Returning for the first time, he carried his bat for 100 out of 159 during the first round of the new Gillette Cup, at Middlesbrough. Later that summer, he hit 114 at Bradford. "The Yorkshire spectators cheered him all the way to the pavilion," said *The Times*.

His England call-up brought a tart response from Sellers: "He might be good enough for England, but he wasn't good enough for Yorkshire." But in the First Test at Madras, he batted five minutes short of seven hours for 88, and came back to Trent Bridge a different player. "Gone was the carefree strokeplay of 1963, to be replaced by batting much more in the Boycott mould," wrote the Nottinghamshire historian Peter Wynne-Thomas. Bolus had his own explanation. "The theory started to kick in again. Instead of playing my natural game, I became bogged down with technical issues." Mike Smedley, another Yorkshire exile at Trent Bridge, said: "Brian was a good cover-driver, and he used to hook, but mainly he was an accumulator who spent a lot of time at the crease."

His cautious approach did not impress the Nottinghamshire hierarchy, but in 1964 he made 1,961 runs, and in all passed 1,000 in 11 successive seasons. He was known for wearing large, bright-white pads – and for using them. "He would give a bat–pad catch to cover," said Illingworth. Smedley recalled: "He used to get the dressing-room attendant to whiten his pads as close to the start of play as possible. Then he would go out to bat with them still damp, and bits of whitener would appear on the ball. That used to really annoy bowlers."

He captained Nottinghamshire in 1972, when Garry Sobers returned exhausted from the Caribbean, but "failed to gain much response from the men under him, and one depressing result followed another", said *Wisden*. Nottinghamshire announced his release before the season's end, although within five days he had been appointed captain of Derbyshire, becoming the first to lead two counties in consecutive summers.

Derbyshire had just finished bottom, but Bolus raised morale. "He liked to do things properly," said the journalist Neil Hallam. "He didn't like anyone who wasn't a proper pro." Against Yorkshire at Chesterfield in June 1973, he was at the centre of a front-page story when seamer Alan Ward, beset by poor form and no-ball worries, refused to bowl. Bolus ordered him off the field, but didn't relish it: "He always said it was the worst thing that happened to him in a game of cricket," said Hallam.

He resigned as captain early in the summer of 1975, and retired at its conclusion, though he continued in the leagues beyond his 50th birthday. Bolus became recreation officer for a local authority but, with the endorsement of Illingworth, now chairman of selectors, joined the selection committee in 1994. He was quickly at loggerheads with Mike Atherton, who described him in his autobiography as "a man to whom I took a fairly immediate and visceral dislike. I got the immediate impression that he didn't think I ought to be England captain."

Bolus was chairman of the England management advisory committee from 1998 until 2002, and continued to irk captains. "Bolus was an extraordinary character," wrote Nasser Hussain. "I think he's got a screw loose." A regular complaint was that he regularly leaked the contents of meetings to journalists. England coach David Lloyd revealed that he referred to ECB chairman Lord MacLaurin, former chief executive of Tesco, as "the grocer". After leaving the selection panel, Bolus continued as a scout for Illingworth. "He was a very good judge of a player – but he probably spoke to the press a bit too much."

He served on the Nottinghamshire committee, and as president in 2004 and 2005. For many years, he was a regular on the after-dinner circuit, always starting with the same line: "For those of you who saw me bat, let me apologise."

PA Images/Alamy

Cutter's arc: Brian Booth clips another behind the wicket. John Murray is the keeper.

BOOTH, BRIAN JOSEPH, who died on December 14, aged 85, was a consistent performer for Lancashire and Leicestershire who collected his 1,000 runs almost every season between 1961 and 1969 (he made 936 in 1963). He signed at Old Trafford as a 15-year-old leg-spinner after some promising displays for Darwen CC, but Lancashire already had future Test players Tommy Greenhough and Bob Barber to bowl leg-breaks, so Booth concentrated more on his batting. "He was a gutsy sort of opener, not flamboyant – he nudged it around a bit," said team-mate Jack Birkenshaw. "He was a good cutter, got a lot of runs through third man – he knew his scoring areas. Brian was a quiet bloke, very calm in the dressing-room."

After serving his apprenticeship – he scored seven hundreds for the Second XI – Booth broke through in 1961, when a career-best haul of 1,752 runs included an undefeated 183 against Oxford University, the highest of his 18 first-class centuries. Another good season followed, but it was a time of upheaval at Lancashire. In 1964, Booth moved to Leicestershire, and immediately chalked up another 1,000-run summer.

At Lord's in 1965, he hit twin hundreds against Middlesex, though another century – at The Oval in 1966 – had a painful ending. "As he was raising his bat to celebrate, Stewart Storey threw the ball in from third man," remembered Birkenshaw. "Arnold Long, Surrey's keeper, shouted: 'Look out, Brian!' But it hit him full in the face. His nose was in a terrible state, and he had to retire hurt."

Booth rarely bowled for Leicestershire, but did make an early mark when given the last over against Gloucestershire, with two wickets needed: he struck with the third and fifth deliveries to clinch victory. Five years earlier, in 1959, he had taken seven for 143 (and nine in the match) for Lancashire against Worcestershire at Southport. "He was a very decent leg-spinner, with a good googly," said Birkenshaw.

Team-mates and opponents remembered a whimsical character. "He used to whistle all the time when he was batting," said Somerset's Peter Robinson. Booth owned greyhounds for a while. His Leicestershire captain Maurice Hallam recalled: "Brian would go to the dogs on a Saturday night. Then he'd go to church on Sunday to get back in His good books." Booth's good humour even survived a horror start to the 1970 season: four runs in six innings, beginning with four ducks, three against Lancashire. Fleet Street was beset by industrial action, so he asked: "Are the newspapers still on strike? In that case I'll ring home and tell them I scored 50."

BOOTH, JENNIFER EVELYN, who died on November 12, aged 78, was one half of a partnership – with husband Keith – who frequently undertook the scoring at The Oval, although she was more often in charge of the Surrey Second XI book. They scored 15 Tests in tandem, and several white-ball internationals. "She would wrestle with recalcitrant computers and dodgy wifi connections, which rarely if ever got the better of her," recalled Richard Spiller, *Wisden's* Surrey correspondent. The Booths also co-authored books about the Surrey players Jack Crawford and Tom Hayward, and were presented with honorary county caps after retiring in 2017.

BORTHWICK, MARGARET, died on February 8, aged 77. Known in Durham for her peerless pies, which she would also present to the press, "Nana" Borthwick fed generations of cricketers, including her grandson, Scott, an all-rounder for Durham, Surrey and England. "For me and my sister growing up, it was a case of, if you want a good feed, you go there," he told David Hopps in 2016. "She does everything – good old-fashioned northern grub."

BOUGH, FRANCIS JOSEPH, died on October 21, aged 87. Frank Bough was a reassuring presence for a generation as the anchorman of BBC TV's Saturday-afternoon sports programme *Grandstand*, which often featured Test cricket, between 1968 and 1983. He was also a familiar face in the early days of the BBC's coverage of Sunday cricket, and was among the first to undertake pitchside interviews with players. "If my life depended on the smooth handling of a TV show," said Michael Parkinson in 1988, "Frank Bough would be my first choice to be in charge." When breakfast television started, Bough was chosen as one of the hosts, known for his patterned pullovers. Twice tabloids revealed other penchants; the first forced a move from the BBC, the second ended his television career. He had won a football Blue at Oxford, but his heart lay elsewhere: "He was a mad cricketer – loved his cricket," said Stephen, one of his sons. A regular club player in his youth, Bough later turned out for the Lord's Taverners.

BRACHE, NOEL, died on March 24, aged 65. Born on Christmas Day in 1954, he was a member of a well-known Cape Town sporting family, particularly associated with the Avendale club, where he enjoyed success, and later coached. A left-hander, Brache played three matches now considered first-class for Western Province's non-white side in 1974-75.

BREAM, JULIAN ALEXANDER, CBE, who died on August 14, aged 87, was one of the most celebrated classical guitarists of the 20th century, and also helped revive interest in the lute. Over a long and varied career, he won four Grammy awards from the US Recording Academy, and received a lifetime achievement award from *Gramophone* magazine. Bream was also passionate about cricket, and staged matches at his home in Wiltshire, wearing batting gloves in the field to protect his fingers. A 1976 BBC documentary included scenes of him "stringing up cricket nets so his team of arty friends could prepare to be thrashed by the local village", according to *The Guardian*. In 1995, he performed the first classical guitar recital in the Long Room at Lord's.

BROMFIELD, HARRY DUDLEY, who died on December 27, aged 88, was an economical off-spinner from Western Province who played nine Tests in the 1960s as South Africa were searching for a replacement for Hugh Tayfield. "He didn't spin the ball much, but he was deadly accurate, and bowled little drifters that snared many a wicket," wrote occasional clubmate Robin Jackman, who also died in December.

Tall, with glasses and a pencil moustache which gave him a schoolmasterly air, Bromfield made his first-class debut in 1956-57 against the England tourists, dismissing Peter May in both innings. But he had to wait five seasons for his international debut, against New Zealand, after Tayfield finally retired. He kept the runs down, but took only eight wickets in five Tests. Fast bowler Peter Pollock made his debut alongside Bromfield at Durban: "He was one of those flat, accurate off-spinners, and an exceptionally good gully fieldsman – great pair of hands. He was a quiet, likeable character with quite a sharp, dry sense of humour."

Recalled for the Third Test against England in 1964-65 after taking five wickets against them for Western Province, Bromfield wheeled down 57.2 overs in the first innings on his home Cape Town pitch, his five for 88 including Geoff Boycott, Ted Dexter and skipper Mike Smith (for 121); the first 28 overs cost just 28. He struck only once in each of the last two Tests but, allied to smart catching, it was enough to secure a place for the return tour of England. However, he had a quiet time, before rounding off the trip with five for 42 against Lancashire. He did play at Lord's – his only overseas Test – and nabbed Bob Barber and Fred Titmus after they had reached half-centuries. He had one more season for WP at home, and made a surprise return for one match in January 1969, again keeping it tight, with 25–13–44–1 against Transvaal. It meant Bromfield had an economy-rate of just 2.1 in his 62-match career, with a best of seven for 60 against Transvaal at Newlands in 1960-61.

BROOKE-TAYLOR, TIMOTHY JULIAN, OBE, died of complications from Covid-19 on April 12, aged 79. Tim Brooke-Taylor was one of several bright young comedians who emerged from Oxbridge – in his case, Pembroke College, Cambridge – in the 1960s. He was probably best known for being one of the comedy trio *The Goodies*, which ran to nine television series between 1970 and 1982, a marginally less anarchic rival of *Monty Python's Flying Circus*. The Tim character usually wore a Union Jack waistcoat, revered Margaret Thatcher, and espoused British traditions. One episode, set in the future, found the Goodies' descendants trying to resurrect the ancient sport of cricket, helped by a rallying poem which began: "There's a deathly hush at Lord's tonight. | The pitch lies covered in weeds, | Willow and leather crack no more together, | But that's what the country needs." Competing against the violent rival sport of roller-egg, some ageing MCC members manage to "inherit the Earth and retain the Ashes". Brooke-Taylor, whose cousin and uncle both played for Derbyshire, was a panellist on the radio comedy *I'm Sorry I*

Daily Express/Hulton Archive/Getty Images

Serious business: students (and at least one don) at Cambridge stage a re-enactment of a game of cricket from 1774. Tim Brooke-Taylor lies on the left; Kingsley Amis stands in the middle (white shirt).

Haven't A Clue for nearly 50 years. A long-time member of the Lord's Taverners, in 1986 he produced *Tim Brooke-Taylor's Cricket Box*, a suitably zany manual which promised to take cricket out of the Long Room and into the lunatic asylum.

BROWN, ANTHONY STEPHEN, died on May 27, aged 83. The roll call of Gloucestershire all-rounders includes some of cricket's greatest names – W. G. Grace, Gilbert Jessop, Wally Hammond, Mike Procter. Tony Brown might easily slip under the radar, but his figures are compelling: only he, WG and John Mortimore have 12,000 runs and 1,200 wickets for the county.

Born in Bristol, Brown made his Gloucestershire debut aged 17 in 1953, and retired to become secretary in 1976. A tall, athletic swing bowler, he had a limitless capacity for hard work, but could produce explosive spells: at Bristol in 1959, he routed Yorkshire with seven for 11. He could be equally destructive as a middle-order batsman. And he was a magnificent catcher, at slip or close in on the leg side. Against Nottinghamshire at Trent Bridge in 1966, he held seven in an innings, a record for a non-wicketkeeper he shares with Micky Stewart and Rikki Clarke.

From 1969, Brown excelled in eight seasons as captain. In the Championship, Gloucestershire finished second once, and third twice, and they lifted the Gillette Cup in 1973 – the club's first honour since an unofficial Championship in 1877. "He could lead by example and inspiration, and also by logic and persuasion," wrote team-mate David Green. Another, David Graveney, added: "He gave me my debut, and took me under his wing. But if you did something wrong, he would fix you with those steely blue eyes."

Brown was given three games in 1953, a tough baptism, since two were against Yorkshire. He did not bowl, and had a top score of six, but returned from national service to make 20 appearances in 1957; he soon became a regular. He was, though, still a dressing-room junior, often touring the Bristol shops to collect purchases made by Tom Graveney's wife – then returning them next day after she changed her mind. In 1959, he took 110 wickets at 23, hit 799 runs, and held 40 catches. In a tied match against Essex at Leyton, he had match figures of seven for 126, then smashed 91 in a tense chase, with four sixes and ten fours. His innings was "superbly steeled in technique, temper and judgment," wrote Denys Rowbotham in *The Guardian*.

He performed consistently during the 1960s, and passed 1,000 runs in 1964. "He was the mainstay of a team that was often up against it," said the former Gloucestershire chairman John Light. Arthur Milton told the writer Stephen Chalke: "He was a good driver, but he never scored as many runs as he should have done." His bowling workload was finally eased by the arrival of Procter in 1968.

Brown was a stickler for standards, and his first initiative after succeeding Milton as captain was to improve fitness levels. David Allen recalled: "He decided to run us around Failand, near Redwood Lodge. We'd never been out of the County Ground before! It was quite hilly, and Browny was about a hundred yards in front, leading the way, the rest of us struggling along." The backmarker was David Shepherd, who hitched a lift on a milk float and overtook his captain, waving regally. "Browny was furious, but he did see the funny side of it," said Allen. On the field, there was a dramatic improvement: Gloucestershire rose from 16th to second in the Championship, and were sixth in the Sunday League.

10,000 RUNS AND 500 WICKETS FOR GLOUCESTERSHIRE

	M	*Runs*	*Avge*	*Wkts*	*Avge*	*Ct*	*Career*
A. S. Brown	**489**	**12,684**	**18.14**	**1,223**	**25.47**	**489**	**1953–1976**
W. G. Grace	360	22,808	40.51	1,339	18.48	377	1870–1899
W. R. Hammond	405	33,664	57.05	504	29.36	552	1920–1951
G. L. Jessop	345	18,936	32.53	620	22.34	357	1894–1914
J. B. Mortimore	594	14,918	18.32	1,696	22.69	320	1950–1975
M. J. Procter	259	14,441	36.19	833	19.56	209	1965–1981
R. A. Sinfield	423	15,562	25.89	1,165	24.37	174	1924–1939

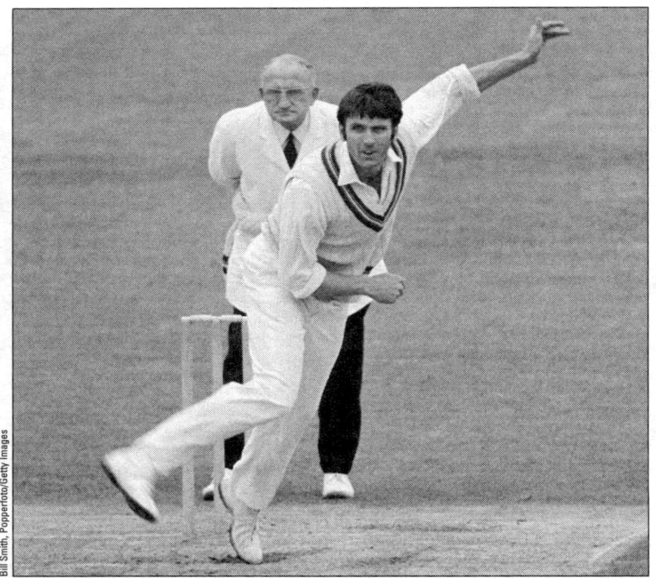
Bill Smith, Popperfoto/Getty Images

Bristol fashion: Tony Brown in 1971. Tom Spencer is the umpire.

While most captains approached the new 40-over competition defensively, Brown's instinct was to attack; he always posted at least two close catchers.

His approach was rewarded in 1973, when Gloucestershire beat Sussex in the Gillette Cup in their first one-day final. "We had a team meeting beforehand, which was very unusual in those days, and decided to target Mike Buss's left-arm seam," said David Graveney. They were soon 27 for three, with Buss removing Sadiq Mohammad and Zaheer Abbas. Procter and Brown rebuilt with 74 for the sixth wicket, then Brown hit 46 out of 68 in the last eight overs, twice pulling Tony Greig for six, to finish unbeaten on 77. "He has always been a fine striker of the ball, but never finer than this," wrote John Woodcock. Gloucestershire won by 40 runs, and Brown edged out Procter for the match award.

After six years as club secretary, he joined Somerset in a similar capacity. In August 1986, he was embroiled in a huge row after the committee decided not to offer new contracts to Viv Richards and Joel Garner; Ian Botham left in high dudgeon. "Tony ran the club efficiently," said former Somerset captain Brian Rose. "But in terms of his relationships with the players, especially the more experienced ones, he either could not handle them, or did not want to handle them."

Even so, Brown had been asked to manage England's tour of India in 1984-85. Within hours of their arrival, prime minister Indira Gandhi was assassinated. He led the negotiations with the British High Commission, the government and the Indian cricket authorities, which led to the team seeking temporary sanctuary in Sri Lanka. On their return to Bombay just before the First Test, the British deputy high commissioner Percy

Norris was murdered, the morning after he had hosted a party for the squad. At a tense team meeting, Allan Lamb voiced concerns about security. Brown waved his passport in the air: "Here it is if you want it." Brown told the press: "We have two choices. We play the game, or we go home. Some of the players are apprehensive but, with all the security, being out in the middle might be the safest place." In *Wisden's* tour review, he was praised for keeping "his sense of perspective".

After leaving Somerset in 1988, he joined the TCCB as assistant secretary. "He used to joke that he had the job of telling Ian Botham he was no longer captain of Somerset, and Dickie Bird he was off the Test umpires list," said Light. He left in 1997, immediately after he had publicly criticised Lord MacLaurin's proposed reforms of the domestic game. Back at Bristol, he became chairman of the cricket committee from 1999 to 2007, and relished the club's run of one-day trophies at the turn of the century. But politics intervened again when he was caught in the middle of a power struggle between coach John Bracewell and a group of players led by Kim Barnett. Brown also served as president from 2008 to 2011.

His name will be installed on the Legends Walkway at the County Ground. Andy Brassington, a former team-mate, said: "In my last conversation with him, when it became clear that this was the last time I would talk to him, I simply thanked him, on behalf of all players, past and present, for his enormous contribution to Gloucestershire cricket. He will be remembered very fondly by so many people."

BRUCE, JOHN, died on December 13, aged 56. Johnny Bruce played 999 matches for the north London side Hornsey over 34 years, finishing with 19,419 runs and 886 wickets. The figures are exact because, as the club historian, he produced a 1,574-page *Hornsey Almanack* in 2015. He was also an authority on, among other things, the London Underground, the assassination of President Kennedy, the history of *Wisden*, and Woolacombe tide tables.

BUSHBY, MICHAEL HOWARD, died on February 8, aged 88. On a sunlit evening at Fenner's in 1953, Cambridge University opener Mike Bushby took on Australia's Ray Lindwall, then the best fast bowler in the world, and produced a minor gem of an innings. "Some of his strokes off his legs to the pace attack were beautifully timed," wrote Geoffrey Green, cricket correspondent of *The Times*. In his tour book, *The Ashes Crown the Year*, Jack Fingleton went further: "I am enthralled by the batting of Bushby. I have never seen Lindwall played better. Erect, Bushby stands with his bat well into his legs, and picks and forces the ball to the on side in a fascinating manner." It was a cameo: he made 34, before Lindwall had him lbw in the last over of the day. But it supported the view that he could have made a career in county cricket. Instead, he spent his working life at Tonbridge School, where he became an institution.

The son of an insurance salesman – his father had made one Minor Counties appearance for Cheshire – and a schoolteacher, Bushby won a scholarship to Dulwich College, where he excelled at cricket and rugby. After national service, he read history at Queens' College. He made his first-class debut against Leicestershire in 1952, and stayed in the team for the rest of the season. In the Varsity Match, he opened with David Sheppard, making 19 in his only innings. He began the following summer with a maiden century, against Sussex, but against Oxford – now opening with his great friend Dennis Silk – he contributed just ten and 21 to Cambridge's two-wicket victory.

Bushby captained the university in his final year, hitting 57 against the touring Pakistanis, and a dogged career-best 113 against Lancashire. In the 1954 Varsity Match, he struck a deal with his opposite number, Colin Cowdrey, to rid the fixture of its habitual caution: they agreed to forgo the tea interval on the final day in an effort to force a result, but the game was drawn after M. J. K. Smith's unbeaten double-century for Oxford. Bushby again failed to make an impact with the bat. After that, he played in just three first-class matches, all for MCC in Ireland in the 1960s.

At Tonbridge, he taught history and ran the school's cricket from 1956 to 1972, usually wearing white-coated Hush Puppies while coaching rather than cricket boots. Roger

Tonbridge School

Tonbridge past and future: Colin Cowdrey and Mike Bushby at the toss of the 1954 Varsity Match.

Prideaux captained one of his early teams, and Chris Cowdrey played in Bushby's final year. "He was an incredible enthusiast – he loved cricket and was obsessed with it," said Cowdrey. Having been outstanding in the covers himself, Bushby placed a high premium on fielding. "The way he communicated was so infectious: he wanted us to be the best fielding school in the country." He retired in 1991, and moved to a house 200 yards from the school, where he remained a familiar figure on the boundary. Cowdrey summed up: "He was one of the most influential people in my life."

CAMPBELL, BLAIR MAESMORE, who died on November 3, aged 74, was a left-arm wrist-spinner from Melbourne's Prahran club. He played eight matches for Victoria in 1969-70 and, around a decade later, 11 for Tasmania. Campbell never improved on the five for 53 he took on debut, against Queensland at the MCG in December 1969, although he did take four for 59 against them ten years later, at Hobart. He also played Australian Rules football for Richmond and Melbourne, where he was remembered as an early exponent of the swinging banana (or boomerang) kick.

CAPEL, DAVID JOHN, died on September 2, aged 57, two years after first undergoing surgery for a brain tumour. David Capel belonged to a line of players – including George Thompson, Percy Davis and Brian Reynolds – who embodied Northamptonshire cricket. Raised in the village of Roade, half a dozen miles south of the County Ground, he even worked as a cobbler, the town's traditional trade, and produced bowling boots for Mike Hendrick and Graham Dilley, before joining the club in 1980 aged 17. It was the start of a mutual love affair lasting 32 years, first as yeoman all-rounder, then as coach. Along the way, he earned 15 Test caps at a time when England were obsessively casting around for "the next Ian Botham".

The comparisons were not always helpful. A Championship match against Worcestershire in 1989 was billed as Capel v Botham; even the tabloids sent reporters. There was only one winner: Botham took 11 wickets, including his supposed heir (twice), and

Northamptonshire lost by an innings. Capel was far better off focusing on being himself, a wholehearted amalgam of punchy but correct middle-order batting and brisk awayswing that brought him over 12,000 first-class runs and nearly 550 wickets.

On Test debut against Pakistan at Headingley in 1987 – the first Northamptonshire-born England cricketer since Thompson, 77 years earlier – he walked out at 31 for five, with Imran Khan and Wasim Akram wreaking havoc. His first partner was Botham: they added 54, and Capel top-scored with 53. (They never again appeared in the same Test.) In Pakistan that winter, after scores of nought, nought, one and two, he fought his way to 98 at Karachi, despite having little idea how to read Abdul Qadir. Jack Russell pulled out his camera in anticipation but, before Capel could add another run, he fell to Qadir's googly.

That would remain his highest Test score, though perhaps not his fondest memory. In the spring of 1990, Capel was part of Graham Gooch's England side that stunned West Indies at Sabina Park, where they had not lost for 35 years. His contribution to a nine-wicket win – his only victory as a Test cricketer – was to remove Richie Richardson and Carlisle Best cheaply in the first innings. Then, in Trinidad, he made an important 40 – "an innings of considerable courage at a vulnerable time", said *Wisden* – and was batting again on the last afternoon with Russell when, after blatant West Indian time-wasting, the game was called off in near-lethal light. England, five down, were 31 short of going 2–0 up with two to play. The sight of Capel gesturing frantically to the dressing-room for guidance in the gloom summed up the chaos. England lost the series, though not before he had dismissed Viv Richards twice in Barbados (Richards would finish as his official Test bunny, providing three of his 21 wickets). To Capel's pride, he was warned in Antigua, in what proved his final Test, for intimidatory bowling to Curtly Ambrose, despite being the least terrifying seamer on either side.

At international level, that was part of the problem. Yet in the domestic game – his first Championship victim, in 1982, was Geoff Boycott – Capel could be potent. He never quite struck a balance between his own desire to be a batsman who bowled, and the ambitions of coaches and team-mates keen on the reverse, though there were days when they had a point: seven for 62 against Lancashire at Lytham in 1985 was followed by seven for 86 at Derby in 1986, then seven for 46 against Yorkshire at Wantage Road in 1987. Eight years later, with Northamptonshire pushing for a first Championship, he collected a career-best seven for 44 in the first innings against title rivals Warwickshire at Edgbaston, then sealed a pulsating seven-run win by trapping Tim Munton. But it made no odds: Warwickshire finished top, and Middlesex pushed Northamptonshire into third.

It was a familiar near miss. Between 1976 and 1996, they appeared in ten Lord's finals, but won only three; Capel's personal ratio was one out of six, no disappointment greater than the double blow of 1987. In the B&H final in July, he made 97, then leaked 66 in 11 overs; the scores were tied, but Yorkshire had lost one wicket fewer. Less than two months later, Northamptonshire were on top in the NatWest Trophy final against Nottinghamshire, only for the game to go into a second day, when Richard Hadlee hit a match-winning unbeaten 70, including a last-over six off Capel.

Yet his game was flourishing. In 1989, his best all-round season, he scored 1,311 first-class runs, twin centuries at Hove among them, and took 57 wickets. In 1990, he averaged 47 with bat and 28 with ball. In 1992, he produced three maidens in a tight spell to help win the NatWest final against Leicestershire. But his career was interrupted when Malcolm Marshall broke his left arm the following summer; injury and illness turned 1994 into a write-off.

Next year, raring to go once more, Capel was at the forefront of Northamptonshire's raucous assault on that elusive Championship, finishing with 885 runs at 38, and 47 wickets at 24, as they won 12 out of 17. There was even talk of an England recall, but it was hard to look beyond what had gone before: Test averages of 15 and 50, plus 23 largely forgettable one-day internationals. Those who knew him felt the numbers remained a source of regret.

His county captain Allan Lamb, who was better at bravado, thought he should have fretted less: "If he could relax and just play instead of worrying about it, he would have

Bob Thomas Sports Photography/Getty Images

Utter enthusiast: David Capel in Rawalpindi, at the start of England's 1987-88 tour of Pakistan.

played more Test cricket." Another former Northamptonshire team-mate, ECB chief executive Tom Harrison, remembered a "complex and private man on the surface, a kind and gentle one to those who knew him well". And almost everyone described him, fondly, as "intense", though Mal Loye – another colleague – said: "It was more that he had an incredible love for the game. I enjoyed his passion and openness." Alan Fordham, who opened the batting with Capel during the club's run to the 1996 B&H final, said: "His intensity about cricket was matched by his gentleness away from the game. He was just the kindest person." But he hated not being taken seriously at the top of the order, once telling the dressing-room: "They don't call Mark Waugh a pinch-hitter!"

Above all, Capel cared. After retiring from the first-class game in 1998, he was soon running the club's Academy, taking under his wing a new generation of Northamptonshire cricketers, treating them like extended family. As late as 2006, aged 43, he turned out for the Second XI at Bristol as a non-bowling No. 11. That July, after a player revolt brought to an end Kepler Wessels's stormy reign as coach, Capel stepped in, and set about restoring harmony, as perhaps only a local could. He just wasn't very good at the awkward stuff. Having tempted Loye back for a second stint at Wantage Road, he soon found himself having to sack him. "He started welling up," remembered Loye. "I said: 'At least give me the chance to cry first.' That was the sort of guy he was – very caring."

Midway through a difficult 2012 season, Capel himself was sacked – "like Lear banishing Cordelia", wrote Matthew Engel in *The Guardian* – but went on to enjoy spells in the women's game: assistant coach with England, head coach with Bangladesh. He never could quite shake the home ties: four years later, he was charging in for Northamptonshire's Over-50s. In 2018, he had a brain tumour removed, but remained full of beans. "He thought it would be decades, not years," said David Ripley, Capel's successor as Northamptonshire coach. "When he had a second operation in 2019, he didn't really talk about it, but he was a glass-half-full kind of guy. As a player, he had this habit of thinking he could do anything."

Capel would have enjoyed that tribute, just as he would a tweet following his death that called his enthusiasm for the game "second to none". It was from Ian Botham.

CAPLE, ROBERT GRAHAM, died in December 2019, aged 80. Bob Caple started with Middlesex, playing against both universities in 1959 while still a teenager, before moving to Hampshire. In his first Championship match, in August 1963, he hit 31 during a stand of 117 with the rampaging Roy Marshall, and the following year made an unbeaten 64, also against Surrey; that remained his highest score. It was a similarly low-key story with the ball: he took five for 54 with his off-breaks against Oxford University in 1966 but, in a side well stocked with spinners, claimed only 13 wickets in 57 Championship matches. He became a successful coach in England (working for some time at Bedford School) and South Africa.

CATLEY, RUSSELL JAMES, died on December 1, aged 47, having been diagnosed with a brain tumour in 2004. A batsman and useful leg-spinner, Catley scored three centuries for Suffolk in the Minor Counties Championship, the highest an unbeaten 130 against Buckinghamshire in 1998. His brothers Matt and Tim also represented Suffolk: the three played together several times.

CHAMANLAL, MALHOTRA, who died on February 14, aged 84, had a long first-class career in India, scoring four centuries, the highest an unbeaten 141 while captaining Northern Punjab against Railways in Ludhiana in 1964-65. He took a career-best four for 46 in the same match. Chamanlal had made a splash at university in 1956, slamming 502 not out for Mohindra College, in Patiala, against Rupar's Government College. He had an "insatiable appetite for runs on matting wickets", according to Bishan Bedi, an early team-mate. "The cut and the pull were his favourite scoring shots. He would terrorise the bowlers all over Punjab."

CHAUHAN, CHETANDRA PRATAP SINGH, died of complications from Covid-19 on August 16, aged 73. An adhesive opening batsman, Chetan Chauhan was in danger of missing out on a long international career after his first five Tests produced a highest score of 34. Then, eight years after his debut, he was recalled in 1977-78, and settled into a productive opening partnership with Sunil Gavaskar that yielded ten century stands, plus another down the order after Chauhan picked up an injury. Their 3,010 runs together in 59 innings as openers stood as an Indian record until Virender Sehwag and Gautam Gambhir passed it in November 2010.

Gavaskar was ideally placed to dissect his technique. "His top hand was around the handle, the back of his palm would face him, and the top hand would get locked up as a result," he wrote. "It meant his leg-side game was a touch restricted, and he would score a lot more on the off side, with that rasping back-and-across square cut his attacking shot."

Chauhan won his first cap in 1969-70 against New Zealand, and took 25 minutes to get off the mark, before smacking seamer Bruce Taylor for four and six (his only one in 40 Tests). He had made his first two centuries the previous season, the second an eye-catching knock for West Zone against an array of international bowlers. In 1972-73, Chauhan hit 203 for Maharashtra against Gujarat – having won a brief Test recall against England after three years out – and 207 against Vidarbha, when he shared an opening stand of 405 with Madhukar Gupte.

Patrick Eagar, Popperfoto/Getty Images

In the lions' den: Chetan Chauhan, en route to 93 at Lahore in October 1978, is watched by Wasim Bari.

He seemed reinvigorated when his work with a bank took him to Delhi in 1975. His first two seasons for his new team produced nearly 1,000 runs apiece, including an undefeated 158, despite a broken jaw, against a Haryana attack led by the young Kapil Dev; in his next two games, he made 150 and 200. Haryana off-spinner Sarkar Talwar said: "He took Ranji Trophy matches as seriously as Tests."

This run of form earned Chauhan a second recall, for India's 1977-78 tour of Australia, who were weakened by defections to Kerry Packer's World Series Cricket; it led to a seesaw encounter, which Australia – led by the returning veteran Bob Simpson – shaded 3–2. After an eight-and-a-half-hour 157 against Victoria at the MCG, Chauhan was picked for the Second Test at Perth. He made a gritty 88 – and stayed at the top of the order almost unchallenged, until the emergence of Kris Srikkanth in 1981-82. At The Oval in 1979, he put on 213 with Gavaskar as India made a heroic attempt to chase down 438 – they finished nine short with two wickets left. Gavaskar, however, felt their stand of 192 against Pakistan in Lahore the previous October was better, coming in front of a hostile crowd of 40,000. Both fell in the nineties – a rarity for Gavaskar, who would finish with 34 hundreds, but more familiar for his partner, who got to 70 ten times in Tests, but never three figures. Chauhan observed: "You are the century-maker, not me."

The pair's adventures included a near walk-off, at Melbourne in 1980-81, after Gavaskar was incensed at being given lbw to a ball from Dennis Lillee he thought he had edged. He beckoned his partner to leave the field with him, but they were met near the boundary by India's manager, who told Chauhan to go back.

He retired after the 1984-85 Ranji Trophy final, which Delhi lost to Bombay. Characteristically, he just missed a century, dismissed by Ravi Shastri for 98. He did make 21 first-class hundreds, though, and averaged 40. He also occasionally bowled off-breaks, and surprised Gujarat with six for 26 for Maharashtra in December 1971.

A member of the BJP, Chauhan had two spells as an MP, and latterly had a seat in the Uttar Pradesh legislative assembly. He had perhaps been given a taste for politics by an early encounter with India's finance minister, when he and Gavaskar successfully petitioned for tax reductions for match fees. Chauhan was also heavily involved in cricket administration, and had spells as a selector and as India's team manager, where his diplomatic approach helped defuse a racism row during the 2007-08 tour of Australia:

MOST TEST RUNS WITHOUT A CENTURY

		T	*I*	*NO*	*HS*	*50*	*Avge*
3,154	S. K. Warne (A)	145	199	17	99	12	17.32
2,163	D. P. D. N. Dickwella (SL)	41	74	4	92	16	30.90
2,084	**C. P. S. Chauhan (I)**	**40**	**68**	**2**	**97**	**16**	**31.57**
1,993	D. L. Murray (WI)	62	96	9	91	11	22.90
1,810	M. D. Marshall (WI)	81	107	11	92	10	18.85
1,779	V. D. Philander (SA)	64	94	20	74	8	24.04
1,713	J. E. Emburey (E)	64	96	20	75	10	22.53
1,699	H. M. R. K. B. Herath (SL)	93	144	28	80*	3	14.64
1,690	T. G. Southee (NZ)	77	109	11	77*	5	17.24
1,596	M. A. Starc (A)	61	91	19	99	10	22.16
1,534	T. D. Paine (A)	35	57	10	92	9	32.63
1,507	K. D. Mackay (A)	37	52	7	89	13	33.48

As at January 25, 2021.

Andrew Symonds claimed the Indian off-spinner Harbhajan Singh had called him a monkey. Sourav Ganguly paid tribute to "a tough opening batsman, and a person with a tremendous sense of humour and tremendous attachment to Indian cricket".

CHOPRA, ASHWINI KUMAR, who died on January 18, aged 63, was an Indian journalist, notably for the Hindi newspaper *Punjab Kesari*, which was founded by his grandfather; his editorials usually appeared in bold on the front page. In 2014, he became an MP, entering the Lok Sabha as the ruling BJP's member for Karnal in Haryana, winning the seat by a majority of over 360,000. Suffering from cancer, he did not contest the 2019 election. He had played first-class cricket, as Ashwini Minna, making his debut for the Rest of India against Ranji Trophy champions Bombay in 1975-76; his first wicket was Sunil Gavaskar. After taking nine for 70 in the match with his leg-spin for Punjab against Services in December 1976, he was touted as a Test possible, but managed only two wickets in two tour games against Tony Greig's England side. Two seasons later, he took six for 15 and six for 35 against Jammu & Kashmir at Srinagar.

CLARKE, JONATHAN KIRKWOOD, died on June 2, aged 76. The bespectacled Jono Clarke made a superb start to his first-class career, becoming the first to make a century on debut for Rhodesia (now Zimbabwe). After a first-innings duck, he made a fighting unbeaten 112 against Western Province at Cape Town in December 1967. Strong off the back foot, he added 130 against Orange Free State in his third game, sharing an opening stand of 268 with Ray Gripper, still a record for the national team. But Clarke could not sustain this form: a dozen further matches produced a best of 56. He emigrated to Australia.

COCHRANE, JOHN LOWRY, who died on March 11, aged 91, was a considerable figure in cricket in Ireland's north-west, playing for Donemana and Coleraine for over 30 years: he hit seven centuries, the last when he was 45, and twice took eight wickets in an innings with his left-arm seamers. Indifferent performances in trial games meant he was passed over for Ireland selection – until 1969, when he was 41 and already a grandfather. After dismissing Hanif Mohammad when a touring Pakistan International Airways side met North-West Ireland at Strabane, Cochrane was chosen for the trip to England that followed, and played in a two-day game against MCC at Lord's.

COCKETT, JOHN ASHLEY, who died on February 16, aged 92, was an excellent all-round sportsman who won a Blue at Cambridge in 1951, alongside future England batsmen Peter May, David Sheppard and Raman Subba Row. Cockett secured his place for Lord's with a boundary-studded 121 against Sussex at Worthing, but bagged a pair in the Varsity Match. Two years later, now with Buckinghamshire, he had a final first-class game, for Minor Counties against the touring Australians – but collected another pair, bowled by Ray Lindwall (on his way to seven for 20) and Ron Archer. Cockett taught maths at

Felsted School, and ran the cricket there for almost 30 years. He was a member of the Great Britain hockey teams that won the bronze medal at the 1952 Olympics in Helsinki, and narrowly missed another, at Melbourne in 1956.

COLEMAN, RICHARD, died on June 21, aged 77. After retiring from teaching in 1999, Rick Coleman became a hugely popular tour guide at Edgbaston, and at Birmingham City's ground, St Andrews. He was Warwickshire's welfare officer for a while, and provided temporary shelter for several new signings. "Everyone who came into contact with Rick will remember his beaming smile, his enthusiasm for his work and his passion for the Bears," said Warwickshire's media spokesman Tom Rawlings.

COOPER, TERRY WILLIAM, who died on January 31, aged 79, was the last remaining journalist to have worked for the Cricket Reporting Agency, which was responsible for compiling *Wisden* from 1887 to 1965. The operation was taken over by the Press Association, and Cooper went on to become one of PA's top cricket and rugby correspondents. PA sell news to other media outlets, and the main requirements are speed and accuracy. Cooper was a master of both, able to phone through a coherent instant account of play without note or stumble. In 1980, with the two sports' seasons starting to overlap, he was forced to choose: his heart said cricket, his conscience as a family man said rugby. But he remained a presence at home Tests until 1990, and continued as *Wisden's* Middlesex correspondent almost every summer between 1968 and 1993. Agency work offers little public profile, but he was not a reticent man, and took no nonsense from officials. "Why did your team play so badly?" he once asked Saracens' Australian head coach Rod Kafer after a rugby defeat. "I only answer specific questions," replied Kafer. "*Specifically*," said Cooper, "why did your team play so badly?" He was prone to theatrical press-box rages, to which the pressure of his job entitled him. However, these usually produced gales of laughter from his colleagues – and, eventually, from Terry.

COPPS, DENNIS EDWARD ARTHUR, who died on April 22, aged 91, umpired 36 first-class matches, 13 of them Tests, and stood in New Zealand's first official List A game, in 1970-71. He was born in Tooting, south London, and worked for the Admiralty before emigrating in 1956, and settling in Wellington.

CORNELL, PATRICK CLIVE, who died on February 24, aged 87, was an all-rounder who played 20 first-class matches in South Africa. His highest score was 80, for Border against Griqualand West in 1954-55, and six seasons later – now playing for Eastern Province, for whom 16-year-old Graeme Pollock stroked 54 on debut – he hit 61 not out against a Border side containing his brother. Pat Cornell's enthusiastic seamers accounted for 17 batsmen in first-class cricket, including New Zealand's John Reid in a tour game in 1953-54 – although he was reportedly more proud of a return catch that sent back the future Test player Tiger Lance in 1960. He later became mayor of Pietermaritzburg.

COWDREY, THE HON. GRAHAM ROBERT, died of sepsis on November 10, aged 56. For Graham Cowdrey, there was little point trying to emulate his father's flowing cover-drives or coaching-manual defence. Instead, he hit the ball hard, and often. In full cry, he could leave an attack in ruins. "Graham realised his destiny in life was not to try and play classically and with finesse, but simply to belt the daylights out of every loose ball that came his way," said his friend and Kent team-mate Aravinda de Silva.

Cowdrey acknowledged his name could be a burden. "I might have played for England if I'd been Graham Smith and not Graham son-of-Colin Cowdrey," he said. But he also recognised his limitations: "I had the talent, I think, to be a top player, a really top player, but mentally I wasn't quite there." Nevertheless, for a decade from the mid-1980s, he was one of the mainstays of an enterprising Kent side. He passed 1,000 runs for three successive seasons from 1990, averaging over 50 in 1992.

In a different era, his explosive one-day batting might have earned international recognition. His brother Chris recalled a 76-ball Sunday League century against Leicestershire on a stodgy pitch at Folkestone in 1989, and an unbroken ten-over partnership of 115 in another Sunday game at Northampton the following year. "I thought I was playing quite well, but at the other end the ball kept disappearing. I remember one shot that went high up into the old football floodlights – the Northamptonshire players had never seen the ball hit that far." Chris felt he would have been an outstanding T20 batsman. "He was the most devastating striker of the ball, who could turn a game in three overs."

But it was not just his batting, or superb fielding in the covers, that earned his team-mates' affection. Although private and not a big drinker, he was often the hub of dressing-room humour. "He could take over a day or an evening in the life of a team, and make it entirely his own," wrote Ed Smith, now the national selector. "Impressions of team-mates, re-enactments of funny moments from the field, uncanny mimicry – when the force was with him he was irresistibly funny." Another master of the art, the comedian Rory Bremner, made Cowdrey his best man: "He made me laugh more than anybody I have ever met."

He was also known for his love of the arts and devotion to the singer/songwriter Van Morrison: he saw him live more than 250 times. Sometimes Morrison would peer into the audience between songs, and ask: "Is Graham here?" They became friends, and Cowdrey acted as his driver on one tour. "I was in groupie heaven," he said. On his death, Morrison sent a letter of condolence.

The youngest of Colin's four children, Graham played for Young England against Australia in 1983, along with Neil Fairbrother, Hugh Morris, Steve Rhodes and Peter Such. "He's only here because he's a bloody Cowdrey," he heard a spectator say after a second cheap dismissal. Next season came his debut for Kent, and he had a short run in the first team in 1985, hitting a maiden fifty against the Australians at Canterbury. Another followed swiftly against Worcestershire, but his first hundred did not arrive until 1988, when Kent finished second in the Championship. They were runners-up again in 1992, but their main strength lay in the one-day competitions.

Cowdrey had made an early impact in the Benson and Hedges Cup in 1986, scoring an unbeaten 60 at Southampton to earn the match award. "He looks to have a lot of talent and his father's temperament," said adjudicator Len Hutton. In the final against Middlesex, he top-scored with 58, but narrowly failed to steer Kent to victory. They also lost B&H finals to Hampshire in 1992, Lancashire in 1995 and Surrey in 1997, and were Sunday League runners-up in 1993 and 1997. They shed the bridesmaid's tag to win the title on run-rate in 1995, Cowdrey leading their batting with 593 runs at 53, but the lack of reward for the team's potential was a lasting regret. "For a long time, we were the favourites for the one-day tournaments every year," he said. "We could have won four or five trophies."

He was introduced to cricket in a net at the family home in Limpsfield, Surrey, and attended Wellesley House prep school before moving on to Tonbridge, where his father and brothers had been educated. He felt under pressure to follow the family tradition, and join Kent. "A schedule was laid out for me, and I had arguments with masters at Tonbridge," he recalled in Ivo Tennant's book *The Cowdreys*. He went to Durham University to read general arts, but left after a year when he failed an anthropology exam. He opted for cricket, though not without equivocation: "I was questioning myself as to whether it was my decision, or made by other people."

In 1987, he missed most of the season after Michael Holding broke his jaw at Derby. "I was never quite the same," he said. "I never really pulled or hooked after that." Yet his most prolific seasons lay ahead, and he relished batting with de Silva in 1995. Against Derbyshire at Maidstone, they put on 368, then a Kent record for any wicket, and still their highest for the fourth.

As early as 1986, he had been grumbling about the county treadmill, and did not enjoy aspects of the team environment. Nor did he welcome the increased emphasis on fitness in the 1990s. Passing Smith on the dressing-room stairs during one pre-season, he asked: "Could you just pop over to the outfield and check the fitness trainers have left? If they're still here, I'll be in the loos." He retired in 1998, soon after a depressing Second XI match at Taunton. "I played and missed a dozen times when this young pup in the slips says: 'Jeez, I think we'd better tie a bell on it for the old codger.' I should have been annoyed, but he was right."

Bob Thomas Sports Photography/Getty Images

"A lot of talent": Graham Cowdrey hits 60 for Kent at Northlands Road, Southampton, May 1986.

Cowdrey married the amateur jockey Maxine Juster, who became assistant to his stepmother, the trainer Lady Herries. After cricket, he worked in corporate hospitality for spread-betting companies, and set up a fundraising silent-auction business. But when that – and his marriage – failed, he lived a hand-to-mouth existence, sofa-surfing and sometimes sleeping in his car.

He was welcomed back into cricket in 2015, when he became an ECB liaison officer, a role he enjoyed, and continued to fulfil during the shortened 2020 season. During the spring lockdown, he had worked as an Amazon delivery driver. On his death, Matthew Fleming, one of his former Kent team-mates, wrote: "I am numb with shock and sadness that the brilliant, generous, funny and complex friend who lit up so many cricket grounds, on and off the pitch, has slipped away."

COWLES, SHIRLEY DAWN (*née* McCaw), who died on March 5, aged 80, played the first of her seven Tests for New Zealand against England at Hagley Oval in March 1969; her second-innings 46 remained her highest in Tests, although she equalled it against Young England during the inaugural World Cup in 1973. She was one of seven children in an unusual family: all four girls, but none of the three boys, liked cricket. Team-mates remembered a good fielder, who was speedy between the wickets.

COZIER, JILLIAN GORDON, who died on May 10, aged 76, was the widow of Tony Cozier, the Caribbean's foremost cricket journalist; they had been married for more than 50 years at the time of his death in 2016. An accomplished sportswoman, she kept the home fires burning while Cozier was on the road with the West Indian team, and helped him entertain visitors back in Barbados, where their parties for the press in a small wooden beach house at Conset Bay, on the island's east coast, acquired legendary status: the place was difficult to find, then many could not remember how they got back home. "A very generous host, as was Tony," said the former *Wisden* editor Scyld Berry. Their son Craig is a cricket statistician and TV producer who has also contributed to *Wisden*.

CRIMP, GRAHAM CHARLES, MBE, who died on April 14, aged 91, was a tireless worker for cricket in Wales. He was secretary and later president of Penarth CC, and long-serving treasurer of the Welsh Cricket Association, then of the Welsh Cricket Board when it was set up in 1996.

CRONJE, NICOLAAS EVERHARDUS, died on May 11, aged 80. Raised on a farm not far from Bloemfontein, and a product of Grey College, where he later taught and coached, Ewie Cronje was a God-fearing man, like most of his peers. His faith was sorely tested in 2000, when his son Hansie – South Africa's Test captain – staggered the cricket world by admitting fixing matches for money, and was banned for life. Two years later, Hansie was killed in a plane crash; Ewie was a pall-bearer at the funeral. He had been a combative all-rounder for Orange Free State throughout the 1960s, often as captain, and made 112 – his only century – against Griqualand West at Kimberley in 1966-67. A few weeks later, he hung around for four and a half hours, scoring 70 not out and sharing a last-wicket stand of 91, to stave off the follow-on against the Australian tourists (it was the state's highest score against them until Hansie hammered 251 against Mark Taylor's team in 1993-94). Another son, Frans, also played for Free State, while daughter Hester married Gordon Parsons, a team-mate of Hansie during a spell at Leicestershire. Cronje senior was heavily involved with cricket administration: president of the Free State Cricket Union between 1983 and 1990, he received a lifetime award from the South African board in 2012.

CROOK, FRANK, who died on May 8, aged 81, was a journalist and radio host who specialised in cricket for a time: he covered Ashes tours for the Sydney *Sun*, and in 1981 broke the story of Dennis Lillee and Rod Marsh betting against Australia at odds of 500-1 at Headingley, which made him unpopular with the players. Although he described himself as "technologically dyslexic", at the 1984 Los Angeles Olympics he used a revolutionary new device called an acoustic coupler, which sent his words in the form of sound tones – essentially an early modem. According to the *Sydney Morning Herald*, Crook "spent much of his time in the Olympics press room explaining how it worked to awed American reporters".

CROUCH, MAURICE WILLIAM, who died in June, aged 89, was a wicketkeeper from Letchworth CC who played 47 Minor Counties Championship matches for Bedfordshire over a decade from 1955.

DASTANE, UMESH MANOHAR, who died from Covid-19 on August 2, aged 63, was a batsman who played one Ranji Trophy match for Maharashtra, before moving to Railways, for whom he made his solitary century, against Rajasthan at Gorakhpur in 1983-84.

DAVIES, HAYDN, who died on March 10, aged 84, was a tireless worker for schools cricket in Essex, where he taught maths. In 2014, he received an award at Lord's to mark 50 years of involvement with junior cricket, presented by Nasser Hussain, one of several prominent players who first made a mark for Davies's Essex Schools teams. "For every cricketer there is a story of someone behind the scenes who helped them along the way," said Hussain. In his youth, Davies played for Glamorgan's Second XI as a batsman and off-spinner.

DEWAR, ARTHUR, who died in January 2020, aged 85, was a seamer from the strong Perthshire CC. He took seven for 71 for Scotland against Warwickshire – including Billy Ibadulla and Tom Cartwright – at Edgbaston in May 1961. Dewar's other four first-class games for Scotland were less memorable, bringing him just four more wickets.

DHARSI, SHIRAZ KASSAM, who died on July 23, aged 78, had an unusual cricket career. A batsman who could also keep wicket, he made 104 for Railways against Delhi in 1968-69, the season after being a standby player for India's tour of Australasia. "He was my captain in the Bombay University team," remembered Sunil Gavaskar. "He opened with Sudhir Naik, and I batted at No. 3." Dharsi's work took him to Pakistan, where he played for various teams and scored three centuries in three matches for the Public Works Department in 1972-73, including a career-best 149 against Karachi Blues. Later still, he went to teach in Britain, first living near Lord's, then moving to Scotland, where he represented Dunfermline and played a few games for the national team, before taking up coaching. Against the 1980 West Indians in Dundee, he saw off the new-ball attack of Colin Croft and Malcolm Marshall, only to fall to the lesser pace of Collis King.

DIBB, PETER, who was found dead in woods at Farnley Tyas, Yorkshire, on May 10, aged 86, was a club cricketer who collected more than 12,000 runs and 2,000 wickets in the Huddersfield League, for nine clubs over 62 seasons from 1948. He won the league's batting prize in 1953, and the bowling equivalent 30 years later.

DLADLA, BEN, who died of cancer on December 27, aged 57, was a recent candidate for the presidency of the troubled South African board. He had been president of the KwaZulu-Natal Cricket Union since 2018.

DOBAL, SANJAY, who died of Covid-19 on June 29, aged 53, was a familiar figure in club and coaching circles in Delhi. His older son, Siddhant, plays for Rajasthan, while Dobal had overseen his younger son Ekansh's progress with Delhi Under-23s.

D'SOUZA, WALTER A., who died on April 9, aged 93, scored 50 and 77 for Gujarat in their first Ranji Trophy final, in 1950-51, but could not prevent defeat by Holkar. Shortly before, he made his highest score of 91 against Bombay. Gujarat did not win the Ranji until 2016-17, when D'Souza – thought to be the first Goan to play in the tournament – was an honoured guest at the celebrations.

DUCKWORTH, CECIL, CBE, who died on November 15, aged 83, had been Worcestershire's president since March 2019. A prominent local businessman whose engineering company helped invent the combiboiler, he formerly owned the Worcester Warriors top-flight rugby club. On T20 finals day in 2019, he went to watch the Warriors' rugby match in between Worcestershire's semi and final at Edgbaston.

DUNKLEY, FREDERICK DAVID, died on May 20, aged 79. David Dunkley was a long-time Lancashire committee member, serving as treasurer for ten years from 2003, and latterly a vice-president. He was closely involved with the Liverpool Competition – for over 30 years as a player with Liverpool CC (and briefly Cheshire), then as an administrator known to many as "The Cricket Ball Man", as he organised the balls used in the league. His grandfather, Jack Sharp, played for Lancashire and England.

DU PREEZ, JOHN HARCOURT, died on April 8, aged 77. Jackie du Preez was a whippy leg-spinner from Salisbury (now Harare), who had a successful career for Rhodesia when they took part in the Currie Cup. At a time when South Africa were looking for good slow bowlers, he played two Tests against Australia in 1966-67. His first wicket, as the home side pressed in vain for victory in the rain-affected Fourth Test at Johannesburg, was a good one, as former national captain Jackie McGlew described: "In his second over, du Preez tossed one well up, drew [Bob] Cowper forward on the drive and bowled him with the fourth ball." His three cheap scalps also included Keith Stackpole, but South Africa had no more Tests for three years, and du Preez missed out when they played again.

He was also a useful batsman, who scored 112 and 70 against Eastern Province at Port Elizabeth in December 1966, putting on 210 with Rhodesia's captain Tony Pithey. That helped him into the South African side, though both his Test innings ended in ducks. He remained a force for Rhodesia, claiming eight for 92 and six for 74 in successive innings in 1967-68. And although his bowling lost a little sting, as late as 1974-75 he took six for 102 to bowl Rhodesia to victory over a strong Western Province side captained by Eddie Barlow. In all, du Preez played 112 first-class matches for Rhodesia, taking 277 wickets and scoring almost 4,000 runs. Former team-mate Stuart Robertson said: "In all the time he played – 18 years – I never heard anyone say a bad word about him, team-mates or opposition." A tobacco farmer, he later became a national selector, and had a spell as the Zimbabwe team manager.

DURY, PETER, MBE, who died on January 18, aged 84, never progressed beyond Nottinghamshire's Second XI – but carved out a name for himself as a groundsman, and later an expert in the construction of synthetic pitches. He started with Southport & Birkdale CC in 1961, and eventually became a director of Notts Sport, who were leading providers of artificial strips, which required less maintenance for cash-strapped schools and clubs. Dury was also a consultant to the ECB. In 2018, he became the first person to receive a second lifetime award from the Institute of Groundsmanship.

DYKES, ROSS ALEXANDER, who died on November 30, aged 75, was a notable figure in cricket in New Zealand, first as a polished wicketkeeper who could bat a bit – for Auckland, he made 82 against Wellington at Eden Park in 1981-82 – and then as an administrator. He was a national selector from 1990 to 2005, later as chairman, before taking charge of Otago's cricket board. "He was across everything in New Zealand cricket," said former Test captain Brendon McCullum. "He always made you feel as if the game was meant to be enjoyed for what it was." The national team wore black armbands in Dykes's memory in a T20 match against West Indies at Mount Maunganui.

DYSON, EDWARD MARTIN, died on December 22, 2019, aged 84. A polished batsman from Wakefield, Martin Dyson was given several opportunities at Oxford University, but managed only three half-centuries, all in 1960. His Blue had come two years previously, when he plugged a troublesome opening spot and sealed a place with a first-wicket stand of 104 against Middlesex; in the 1958 Varsity Match, he opened with Alan Smith and made 34. He also played a few games for Yorkshire's Second XI. Dyson, who had one final first-class match for MCC in 1968, became a teacher at St Paul's, Eton and Ludgrove preparatory school. After the death of his wife, he lived in the Grade I listed almshouses at St Cross, near Winchester.

EBRAHIM, ISMAIL, died on July 18, aged 73. A classy slow left-armer from Durban, "Baboo" Ebrahim would surely have played Test cricket had he not been confined to South Africa's non-white leagues until well past 30; by readmission, he was in his mid-forties. He was quicker than some, but still found spin: Mike Procter remembered a bowler "who turned the ball, and never gave anything away". In April 1976, he had showed what might have been when he bowled a South African Invitation XI to victory over the touring International Wanderers at Kingsmead; his six for 66 was composed entirely of Test players, including Greg Chappell and Mike Denness. "Just think what we've been missing," said Test all-rounder Eddie Barlow, while Barry Richards thought it a significant moment: "The day he won the game for 'South Africa' was another step towards the end of our exile." One of the first non-white cricketers to play in the Currie Cup, Ebrahim took seven for 50 (and 11 in the match) in Natal B's innings victory over Griqualand West in 1979-80. He also had a season for Radcliffe in the Central Lancashire League, taking 62 wickets at 14.

EDRICH, JOHN HUGH, MBE, who died on December 23, aged 83, was impassive and unflinching in the face of the world's most hostile bowlers. In his first full season for Surrey, he had fingers broken by Fred Trueman and Frank Tyson; on his Test debut, he took on Wes Hall and Charlie Griffith; later, he was hit on the head by Peter Pollock, and batted with broken ribs against Dennis Lillee and Jeff Thomson. His Test career ended in

1976 when, aged 39, he was caught in West Indies' crosshairs at Old Trafford. Fearless, tough and brave – three words that cropped up frequently.

But Edrich collected more than bruises. In over 20 summers with Surrey, and on six England tours, he emerged with a magnificent record – 39,790 first-class runs at 45, and 103 hundreds, 12 for England, seven in the Ashes. His unbeaten 310 against New Zealand in 1965 is England's fifth-highest score. "He was one of the greatest run-scorers of my lifetime," said his former county and Test opening partner Micky Stewart. "He scored runs when they were needed." Edrich was no crowd pleaser and, unlike many left-handers, earned few marks for artistic merit. Early on, he worked out which shots carried little risk, and did not expand his repertoire. When he reached 30,000 first-class runs, Surrey team-mate Robin Jackman – who died two days after Edrich – joked that 28,000 had come through third man.

"He had the ideal temperament," said his former England captain Ray Illingworth. "If he played and missed a few times, it did not bother him. He could miss three in a row, then hit the next three for four. He always played the next ball." Edrich was 5ft 8in, but physically strong, having worked on the family sugar-beet farm in Norfolk. His beefy forearms helped him drive powerfully through the off side, and loft straight sixes; he used the pace of the ball to score behind square. "He had a method," said Keith Fletcher. "Being left-handed helped, but it was a successful method." Fred Titmus rated him the best punisher of the slightly bad ball: "I got fed up conceding eight runs an over after beating him four times in it." Edrich's maxim was simple: "You can do absolutely nothing about what has gone before – either the previous day, or the ball you have just missed."

He came from blue-blooded cricket stock. Cousins Bill, Brian, Eric and Geoff were all first-class players, with Bill a superstar for Middlesex and England. Yet John was determined to go his own way. He knew the family name would be a burden at Middlesex, turning down Bill's offer of an introduction. When he arrived at The Oval in April 1955, he had never seen a first-class game. At Second XI nets, his method was the subject of derision. "Come and look at this bloke," said one first-teamer. "I can't decide whether he's supposed to be a bowler or a wicketkeeper. He's certainly not a batsman." They spent 15 minutes sniggering, until batsman Bernie Constable cut in. "I don't know what you're laughing at: he hasn't missed a ball yet."

Les Lee, *Daily Express*/Hulton Archive/Getty Images

In demand: John Edrich and young admirers, 1964.

Surrey coach Andrew Sandham saw the same qualities. They worked together for hours, disagreeing only when Edrich refused to try a higher backlift. In general, though, the approach was uncomplicated: "Andrew told me it didn't matter how I got my runs, just to get them." And Sandham rammed home one crucial message: "Once I got to 40, I had to go on to get a hundred." After a summer in the Second XI, he began his national service, and made his first-class debut for Combined Services in 1956. His Championship debut came against Worcestershire in September 1958, when he made an unbeaten 24 in a second-innings total of just 57. Over eight months later, in his second Championship match, Edrich was promoted to open at Trent Bridge: he hit 112 and 124.

He soon made it four hundreds in seven innings, and by early July had added three more, before Trueman hit him on the hand with successive deliveries at Bradford, breaking a knuckle. He returned three weeks later, only for Tyson to inflict a similar injury when Northamptonshire visited The Oval in September. Despite the setbacks, an aggregate of 1,799 first-class runs at 52 marked a first full season *Wisden* described as "astonishing". He spent part of the winter in plaster, after having a small piece of leg bone grafted on to his knuckle.

Yet the selectors proved hard to impress. In 1962, he was the leading run-scorer in the country with 2,482 at 51, but still didn't make the Ashes touring party. Eventually, he got the call for the First Test of the 1963 series against West Indies, opening with Stewart. On the first morning, they had a visit from selector Walter Robins: "I couldn't sleep for thinking about you poor buggers facing that pace attack." Edrich made just 66 in four innings and was dropped, faring little better when he was recalled for the Fifth Test. After a tour of India on which he struggled with illness, he achieved his ambition of playing against Australia, in the Second Test at Lord's in 1964. The match was ruined by rain, but Edrich hit 120 in England's only innings. He relished a partnership of 41 with former Norfolk Colts team-mate Peter Parfitt, but didn't excite all the critics. In *The Guardian*, Denys Rowbotham described his innings as "an assertion of stern character rather than an exercise of effortless resource".

Edrich missed out in the run-gluts of the next two Tests, and was dropped again; nor was he chosen for the tour of South Africa. But he began the 1965 season with a remarkable burst of scoring and, with Geoffrey Boycott and Ted Dexter injured, was recalled for the Third Test against New Zealand at Headingley. Edrich regarded it as his last chance, and was contemplating retirement. "I knew that to secure a decent standard of living I had to be playing Test cricket and going on tours," he said. He took 25 minutes to get off the mark, but by the close was unbeaten on 194, with Ken Barrington on 152. "Never in my life had I been timing the ball so well," said Edrich. "I never thought I'd get out." Next day, he had moved to 310 off 450 balls with 52 fours and five sixes – "a ruthlessly methodical piece of batting," wrote John Woodcock – when England declared. It was his ninth consecutive 50-plus score, an aggregate of 1,311 at 218. Many thought captain Mike Smith should have allowed him to break Garry Sobers's Test-record 365: "Edrich was robbed", screamed the *Daily Mirror*.

He was hit on the head by Pollock in the First Test against South Africa at Lord's, but he finished the summer with 2,319 at 62 (including 49 sixes), and was named a Wisden Cricketer of the Year. Edrich also secured a place in the 1965-66 Ashes squad. He batted at No. 3 to avoid disturbing Boycott's opening partnership with Bob Barber, and enjoyed the bounce of Australian wickets, scoring centuries in the Second and Third Tests, though *Wisden* was grudging: "Seldom can a batsman have played and missed so often, have so often threatened to get out and yet scored so well in Australia." The selectors seemed to agree. He made just three Test appearances in the next two summers, before being chosen for the 1967-68 tour of the Caribbean, where he scored a century off 340 balls at Bridgetown. Back in England, against Australia, he enjoyed his best Test summer yet: 554 runs in nine innings, including 164 in the Fifth Test victory at The Oval. He was named Man of the Series.

It turned out to be a good tune-up for the 1970-71 series in Australia. Again, he dropped to No. 3, this time to allow Brian Luckhurst to open with Boycott, before scoring centuries

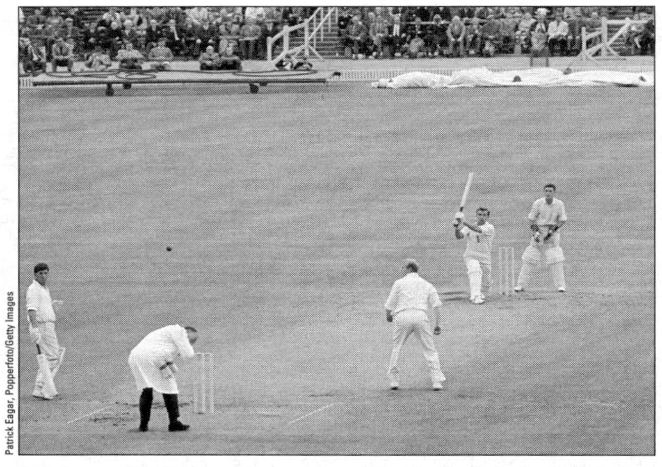

Patrick Eagar, Popperfoto/Getty Images

Beefy forearms: John Edrich en route to an unbeaten 310, against New Zealand at Headingley in 1965. Ken Barrington, who made 163, looks on. Umpire Charles Elliott ducks for cover.

at Perth and Adelaide en route to 648 runs at 72. Only Walter Hammond, Alastair Cook, Herbert Sutcliffe, Jack Hobbs and Boycott (on the same tour) have scored more for England in an away Ashes series. It was a peak he could not scale again. He was 34 that June and, while still prolific at county level, the Test returns dwindled. He took on the Surrey captaincy in 1973, and wrestled with the demands of one-day cricket – though he had been Man of the Match in the historic first ODI at Melbourne in January 1971, after becoming the first to hit a half-century in the format.

But he was appointed Mike Denness's vice-captain for the Ashes defence in 1974-75. Lillee broke his hand in the First Test and, by the Fourth, at Sydney, England were in full retreat. Denness stood down, handing the reins to Edrich, who responded with a typically defiant 50 off 177 balls in the first innings. With the urn slipping away, he had to retire in the second after being hit in the ribs by Lillee; despite breathing difficulties, he returned to defy Australia, making 33 not out, and taking England to within 43 balls of a heroic draw. "My ribs hurt when I talk. They hurt when I laugh, and they hurt when I move," he said. "But what really hurts is that we've lost."

Back in England the following summer, he had a measure of revenge with 175 at Lord's. "It was great to see Lillee on his knees after the hammering we'd taken from him a few months earlier," he told the writer Pat Murphy. In his final Test, in 1976, he opened with the 45-year-old Brian Close at Old Trafford, and the pair were subjected to a withering 80-minute assault by Andy Roberts, Michael Holding and Wayne Daniel on the Saturday evening. Somehow, they reached stumps at 21 without loss – Edrich even managed two fours while ducking and diving. "Courageous beyond the call of duty," wrote Robin Marlar in *The Sunday Times*. "Some like steak tartare, but this cricket was too raw for my stomach." Edrich was disillusioned: "I couldn't see the point in standing out there for hours, waiting to get my head knocked off, and wondering if I'd get a chance to score."

In his first season as Surrey captain, he had guided them to second in the Championship. The Benson and Hedges Cup was won in 1974 – with Edrich taking the match award –

MOST RUNS FROM BOUNDARIES IN A TEST INNINGS

	4	*6*			
238	**52**	**5**	**J. H. Edrich (310*)**	**England v New Zealand at Leeds**	**1965**
218	38	11	M. L. Hayden (380)	Australia v Zimbabwe at Perth	2003-04
206	38	9	Inzamam-ul-Haq (329)	Pakistan v New Zealand at Lahore	2002
202	40	7	V. Sehwag (293)	India v Sri Lanka at Mumbai (Brabourne)	2009-10
198	42	5	V. Sehwag (319)	India v South Africa at Chennai	2007-08
196	34	10	W. R. Hammond (336*)	England v New Zealand at Auckland	1932-33
196	43	4	B. C. Lara (400*)	West Indies v England at St John's	2003-04
194	47	1	V. Sehwag (254)	India v Pakistan at Lahore	2005-06
192	39	6	V. Sehwag (309)	India v Pakistan at Multan	2003-04
190	43	3	G. A. Gooch (333)	England v India at Lord's	1990
190	34	9	C. H. Gayle (333)	West Indies v Sri Lanka at Galle	2010-11
186	30	11	B. A. Stokes (258)	England v South Africa at Cape Town	2015-16
184	46	0	D. G. Bradman (334)	Australia v England at Leeds	1930
184	43	2	D. G. Bradman (304)	Australia v England at Leeds	1934
180	45	0	B. C. Lara (375)	West Indies v England at St John's	1993-94

but the team gradually slipped down the table. "He rarely showed any empathy, and we became accustomed to the sight of him, hands on hips, kicking the turf in disgust when a youngster bowled a half-volley," recalled Alan Butcher. "Playing cricket became a joyless exercise, to the point where the team looked forward to John joining England." There was a rebellion, but Edrich gatecrashed the conspirators' meeting. Jackman stood his ground, and demanded he resign. Roger Knight returned to take over the captaincy in 1978.

The rancorous atmosphere overshadowed the milestone of his 100th century, in July 1977. In sharp contrast to the ballyhoo when Boycott reached the landmark a month later in an Ashes Test at Headingley, Edrich got there at the fag-end of a draw with Derbyshire at The Oval, becoming the 17th batsman – and the third left-hander, after Philip Mead and Frank Woolley – to achieve the feat. He had been stuck on 99 since September 1976, and only made it because the visiting captain, Eddie Barlow, agreed to an extra half-hour. "Eddie said he liked a glass of champers now and again, and he didn't mind staying on the field," Edrich said. His response to the low-key moment was typical. "It's not the 100th hundred that counts, it's the previous 99."

He retired in 1978 with a formidable record; only Hobbs, Tom Hayward and Sandham scored more than his 29,305 runs for Surrey. He became the marketing manager for a bank in Jersey, and later lived in Cape Town. After the death of his son in a car crash, he moved to Aberdeenshire. In 1999, he was diagnosed with a supposedly incurable form of leukaemia, but recovered, he believed, thanks to injections of mistletoe extract. Edrich's involvement in cricket became sporadic. He played a second season of Minor Counties cricket for Norfolk in 1979, 25 years after his first; he had one summer as a Test selector in 1981, and was briefly England batting coach in the mid-1990s. He was Surrey president in 2006-07, and opened the Edrich Gates at The Oval in 2015. In a poll to mark the club's 175th anniversary in 2020, he was chosen to open the batting in an all-time XI with Hobbs. As Illingworth put it: "I wished I'd had 11 like him in the team."

EDRICH, PETER GEORGE, who died of Covid-19 on April 22, aged 93, was a member of the famous Norfolk family, which produced two Test cricketers (his cousins Bill and John) and three other first-class players (Brian, Eric and Geoff). A fast bowler and handy lower-order batsman, Peter made two Minor Counties Championship appearances for Norfolk in 1951. He was also a stalwart of the South Walsham club, where he opened the bowling with George C. Edrich, his brother. Their father – George H. – would bowl spin. An annual highlight was the Edrich family XI matches against Lord's Taverners teams, which were held for a number of years at Ingham CC in Norfolk. "There would be big crowds, parking their cars and setting up their picnics around the boundary," recalled

Steven Edrich

Keeping it in the family: a team made up entirely of Edriches at Ingham, Norfolk, 1964.
Standing: Barry, Brian, Fred, Alan S., Peter, George C., Arthur, Geoff, Alan.
Seated: Eric, George H., Bill, William, Edith, John, Millie, Edwin, Midge.

Peter's son, Steven. "It's a tree-lined ground with short boundaries, and I remember cars being peppered with sixes. We seemed to spend a lot of the time looking for lost balls in the woods." Peter worked for the family livestock auction business for more than 50 years, and was instrumental in setting up the Norfolk Wildlife Trust. In his nineties, he moved into a care home in Blofield, in what had been his grandfather's house.

EDWARDS, GRAHAM NEIL, died on April 6, aged 64. Local legend has it that the chunky New Zealander Jock Edwards once hit a ball about 40 miles – he sent it soaring out of Nelson's Trafalgar Park, into the back of a passing lorry bound for Blenheim. On another occasion, he slapped Test seamer Ewen Chatfield out of the picturesque Pukekura Park ground in New Plymouth and into a nearby lake.

Big hitting came naturally to Edwards, who vaulted to national attention in February 1977 with innings of 49 and 99 – despite a nasty blow on the elbow from Dennis Lillee – for Central Districts against the Australians; he made his Test debut a week later. Early in his onslaught, Edwards missed a hook. "Where did you learn to hook, your back yard?" snarled Lillee. Shortly afterwards, Edwards smashed him for six. "Must've been a bloody big back yard," murmured Rod Marsh behind the stumps.

Edwards made 51 in his second Test, but was hamstrung later on in international cricket by being saddled with the wicketkeeping gloves. Recalled for the Third Test against England at Auckland in March 1978, he made 55 and 54 – and was the only keeper for the tour of England that followed. He had a torrid time, and played little representative cricket afterwards. Trevor Bailey was typically acerbic on *Test Match Special*: "He's committed errors you'd have the school Third XI keeper running round the field for." Others felt Edwards had been sold a hospital pass: "It was a poor selection to take him as sole keeper, as that was not his forte," said the Test slow left-armer Evan Gray. "Jock should have been there on merit as a batsman. He'd have made a killing in T20."

Edwards remained a favourite with Central Districts, for whom he made all his five first-class centuries, the highest an undefeated 177 against Wellington early in 1981. That won him a final international recall, by which time Ian Smith – who also hailed from Nelson – had secured the gloves. "Jock was the wicketkeeper when I first joined Central

Districts," wrote Smith. "I would stand in the slips and be amazed how this short, rotund man could be so quick on his feet. He was one of the most natural cricketers I've ever met – he had such a great eye, and loved to hit the ball hard and often."

These sentiments were echoed by the Test opener John Wright. "Jock would be the most talented New Zealander I've seen when it comes to striking a cricket ball," he said. "He was such a natural it was a shame he never really fulfilled his potential – he got caught halfway between batting and wicketkeeping. Unfortunately he never played in an era which emphasised fitness, and was always carrying a little bit of excess… in England he once let four byes through at five minutes to one, and a spectator told him to stop thinking about lunch."

ELLMAN-BROWN, DAVID ALAN, who died on December 31, aged 82, was a long-serving administrator, who started as treasurer of the Mashonaland Cricket Association in the 1960s, and later filled most of Zimbabwean cricket's senior posts. He was the board's treasurer, chief executive, vice-president and president, and as late as June 2019 was put in charge of the interim committee that ran Zimbabwe Cricket after the original board were suspended by the government. Ellman-Brown was also the manager of the Zimbabwe team that took part in the World Cup for the first time, in England in 1983, defeating Australia in their first match and reducing eventual champions India to 17 for five at Tunbridge Wells before a stunning innings from Kapil Dev turned the tables. For the next few years he worked tirelessly to transform Zimbabwe into a Test-playing nation, a dream that came true in 1992. "I don't believe we would ever have got Test status without him," said *Wisden's* local correspondent John Ward.

FAY, STEPHEN FRANCIS JOHN, who died on May 12, aged 81, had an unusual career as a cricket writer. He was already in his fifties when he stepped into a press box, after a successful and varied career as a reporter, editor and author – including many years as a star writer at *The Sunday Times* in its heyday. After he had two stints as deputy editor of *The Independent on Sunday*, an imaginative sports editor, Neil Morton, asked Fay if he might like to indulge his enthusiasm for cricket, and sent him to the Tests to work alongside the paper's correspondent, Stephen Brenkley – a partnership that would last 15 years. "We argued a lot, but we never fell out," says Brenkley. "I did my job better for having him alongside me." Fay was new to the inner workings of the game, and brought a fresh eye, while already a journalistic master craftsman. He was both erudite and constantly curious: as John Woodcock put it, "he elevated the press box". And he was always a congenial companion for après-cricket. Fay edited *Wisden Cricket Monthly* from 2000 to 2003 with his customary professionalism, good ideas and editorial rigour. In 2005, he wrote *Tom Graveney at Lord's*, an account of a once-rebellious figure's year as MCC president, and in 2018 collaborated with the historian David Kynaston on *Arlott, Swanton and The Soul of English Cricket*, a triumphant merger of talents to dissect two of the most significant figures in 20th-century cricket.

FERROW, DESMOND JOSEPH, died on December 5, aged 87. Des Ferrow arrived in Auckland from his native Australia in January 1954, and went "looking for a hit-up" the same day. His off-breaks proved fruitful for the Bay of Plenty team and, after taking 20 wickets in four innings, he was selected for Northern Districts' first match in the Plunket Shield, which started on Christmas Day 1956. Ferrow took four for 50 in a rain-affected draw with Auckland, and added three for 77 in 40 overs a few days later against Central Districts. He played only two more first-class games, although he remained a wicket-taker for Bay of Plenty for another decade. In November 1960, he took seven for 35 and six for 16 in a two-day game against King County. He became a prominent businessman in Tauranga.

FLINTOFT, THOMAS, died on June 30, aged 86. One of the most astute signings Durham made in their ascent to first-class status in 1992 was not a player but a groundsman: Tom Flintoft, who was enticed away from Southampton to create a new pitch out of scrubland in the shadow of Lumley Castle at Chester-le-Street. He found the type of soil he wanted at nearby Wynyard Hall, the home of Newcastle United owner Sir John Hall, and transported 1,000 tons of clay-based loam to what became an international stadium. "I sowed the first seeds on the Riverside outfield at what was then just a green oasis," said Flintoft. Ten years on, in 2000, the ground staged its first Test. Flintoft had retired two years earlier, unusually being granted a benefit season by a grateful county. "He threw himself into an incredible job," said Geoff Cook, Durham's first director of cricket, "and undoubtedly made a brilliant contribution to some memorable early years." While still at Hampshire, he had won the Groundsman of the Year award in 1990, and remained in demand as a pitch consultant for the ECB and several league clubs in Durham.

FOLEY, JACK CLIFFORD, who died on November 23, aged 89, was Kent's official scorer from 1987 to 2011, only their eighth since the club were founded in the 1870s. After 40 years working in insurance, Foley soon became a cheery presence in the Canterbury press box, where the scorers occupied the front row; he was occasionally joined by his wife, Eunice, known to Kent's players as "Waqar". According to Frank Keating, "roly-poly jolly Jack Foley is any casting director's perfect double for Mr

KENT'S OFFICIAL SCORERS

1874–1896	J. Crow	1956–1958	W. Handsford
1897–1924	W. Hearne	1959–1988	C. Lewis
1925–1939	A. Hearne	**1987–2011**	**J. C. Foley**
1946	G. D. Fenner	2012–	L. A. R. Hart
1947–1955	E. R. S. Hoskin		

Pickwick watching All-Muggleton take on Dingley Dell from the boundary edge". And former captain Rob Key recalled: "Such a nice man. He used to sit at the front of the bus telling John Wright [Kent's coach] what shares he should buy. I can't remember a time I didn't see him laughing." Foley's only regret was that Kent never won the Championship during his time. "I experienced many changes of competitions, rules, Duckworth/Lewis and computer scoring," he said on retirement. "But I loved every minute."

FREEMAN, ERIC WALTER, OAM, who died on December 14, aged 76, was a true all-rounder – an explosive batsman who hit his second ball in Tests for six, a lively seamer, and an Australian Rules footballer so valuable that he was met off the plane after the 1968 Ashes tour by his Port Adelaide coach, and told to get ready for the play-offs.

Freeman broke into the Australian side as a fast-medium bowler with a late outswinger, plus a cutter he often deployed into the wind at Adelaide Oval; his methods were similar to his state and Test team-mate Neil Hawke, a notable Aussie Rules footballer himself. "He had a really strong shoulder action, which took advantage of his build," said Ian Chappell. Freeman had first played for South Australia in 1964-65, but did not make much impression until two seasons later, when he took seven for 52 against Queensland. He finished the 1966-67 season with 35 wickets, which won him a trip to New Zealand with what would now be called Australia A.

The New Zealanders made a return trip later in 1967, and needed only 188 to beat South Australia at Adelaide – but Freeman ripped them apart, finishing with a career-best eight for 47, which followed a maiden fifty. With Australia looking for a reliable partner for Graham McKenzie, Freeman was picked for the Third Test against India at Brisbane. He removed Abid Ali with his third ball, and Farokh Engineer with his tenth. Four more wickets in the next Test secured a spot in Bill Lawry's 1968 Ashes team in England, where Freeman took five wickets at Edgbaston, including John Edrich twice and – after a century in his 100th Test – Colin Cowdrey. "Freeman may not be the most skilful bowler in the world, but no one puts more heart and soul into their efforts," wrote Bob

PA Images/Alamy

Heart and soul: Eric Freeman, 1968.

Simpson, Lawry's predecessor as captain. Freeman also smashed 116 in 90 minutes against Northamptonshire, after taking five for 78.

He continued to chip in against West Indies in 1968-69, clouting a Test-best 76 at Sydney – "he plonked one into the second level of the members' stand," remembered Chappell – and collecting 13 wickets in four games. There were also runs and wickets in the deciding match as South Australia won the Sheffield Shield for the first time in 16 years. But his only notable contribution in India soon after was four for 54 to set up victory at Calcutta. Then, like many others, he ran out of puff in the South African tour that followed.

Freeman was still expected to feature in the 1970-71 Ashes, but injury kept him out. His Test career was over, though there was time for another crucial Shield show-stopper: after five wickets in the first innings of the last match, against New South Wales, he had painkilling injections in a hamstring, then went out and ensured another title with eight for 64.

Freeman had three more seasons at State level, without threatening an international return. He worked in banking for more than 30 years, before becoming executive director of the South Australian Lacrosse Federation, and was also a regular on TV and radio for the ABC in Adelaide, covering cricket and Aussie Rules. He was awarded the Medal of the Order of Australia in 2002 for services to sport as a player, administrator and commentator. His private life was touched by tragedy: his son, David, took his own life in 1999; three years later, his 19-year-old grandson died of sepsis.

GAWLI, SHEKHAR MADHUKAR, died on September 2, aged 45, after falling into a deep gorge while trekking in India's Western Ghats mountains, near his birthplace of Nashik. A leg-spinner, Gawli played twice for Maharashtra in the Ranji Trophy, collecting three wickets; he had been the fitness trainer of the state team in 2018-19, before taking charge of the Under-23s.

GAYLE, JOHN RICHARD, died on September 14, aged 96. Johnny Gayle was a Jamaican umpire who stood in 34 first-class matches, three of them Tests. He also featured in a strange incident in 1977-78, when the final Test of Australia's tour was interrupted by a disorderly crowd, with West Indies in trouble late on the final day. With 6.2 overs of the last hour still to bowl, and one wicket to take, the Australians argued the match should be concluded next morning – but one of the umpires, Ralph Gosein, disagreed. Gayle was asked to stand by as a replacement, but after further discussions no play took place, and the match was left drawn. Gayle spent his working life in Jamaica's ministry of agriculture, and was an expert on pimentos, an important local crop.

GEAREY, KEVIN, who died on December 23, aged 66, worked for the BBC for 32 years, mostly as a sports reporter widely admired for his ability to convey the news with a light touch. Gearey's role meant he covered several England cricket tours. "Old school in many ways, and a brilliant writer of short, sharp, frequently witty TV reports," said *The Sun's* John Etheridge.

GILLETT, PHILIP JOHN SAFFORD, collapsed during an Over-60s county final in Cambridge on September 23, and died in hospital. He had turned 60 two months earlier. An enthusiastic medium-pacer, Phil Gillett played for his local club, Waresley, in Huntingdonshire, for 47 years, and many others besides. He had one outing for Northamptonshire's Second XI, at Chelmsford in May 1978, but his three overs disappeared for 38; Gillett consoled himself with the thought that his bowling had helped Graham Gooch – who biffed 87 – regain some form. Three weeks later, Gooch returned to the Test side after three years, and made 54 against Pakistan.

GOEL, RAJINDER, who died on June 21, aged 77, was among the finest bowlers never to play Test cricket: his 637 wickets in India's Ranji Trophy makes him easily the most prolific, over 100 clear of Srinivas Venkataraghavan. Yet slow left-armer Goel could not force his way past Bishan Bedi into the Test side: the nearest he came was against West Indies at Bangalore in 1974-75, after Bedi was dropped for disciplinary reasons. Even then, Goel was left out at the last minute: he did briefly make it on to the field, to tell the players who should take over as captain when Mansur Ali Khan Pataudi was injured, since the selectors had not appointed an official deputy. "I think I was born at the wrong time," said Goel. "Bedi was a great bowler, so I have no regrets about it. It was not written in my fate to play Test cricket."

Goel went back to the domestic circuit, and continued to churn out the wickets: his best season – 54 victims – was in 1979-80, when he was 37. That included eight for 87 for Haryana against his former team Delhi, where he had jostled for a place alongside Bedi for a decade. Finally unchallenged as his side's No. 1 spinner, Goel took 391 wickets at 15 for Haryana, including a career-best eight for 55 against Railways in 1973-74, and helped them to three Ranji semi-finals, although the last step proved beyond them until after his retirement in 1984-85. Haryana were not Goel-less for long: two years later his son, Nitin – another left-hander, but a batsman – made his debut, and played for more than a decade.

Bedi himself knew there was not much to choose between them. "I think it was a matter of getting a break, and I was fortunate to get one," he said. "Goel was almost robotic in his bowling pattern, and a captain's delight. He would go about his job with mechanical precision. The only people who had to be on their toes were the batsmen."

GOMES, SHELDON ANTHONY, who died on September 15, aged 69, was close to emulating Larry, one of his nine siblings, in playing for West Indies – but was restricted to several stints as a substitute, taking three catches in the 1970-71 home series against India. (The only other uncapped player to take three Test catches is Iqbal Sikander, though he did appear in one-day internationals for Pakistan.) Test wicketkeeper Deryck Murray recalled: "He would volunteer to go to bat–pad or silly point in the days when protection wasn't around, so it was just sheer bravery." Gomes was also a skilful batsman, whose five centuries for Trinidad included 213 against Jamaica at Montego Bay in 1976-77, when he and Murray put on 140. The following season he defied the fearsome pace of Sylvester Clarke and Colin Croft during centuries against Barbados and Guyana. He later lived in the United States, and died in Las Vegas.

GOSWAMI, SUBIMAL, died on April 30, aged 82. Chuni Goswami was perhaps the closest thing India have ever had to a double international at cricket and football, in which he led the national side that won the gold medal at the 1962 Asian Games. A striker who scored nine goals in 30 appearances for India, he also played first-class cricket for Bengal for ten years, latterly as captain, making 103 against Bihar in 1971-72 before losing in the Ranji Trophy final. Three seasons earlier, also in the final, Goswami scored 96 and 84, although Bombay prolonged their long winning streak thanks to a first-innings lead. Bengal's future Indian slow left-armer Dilip Doshi, then in his first season, recalled: "His will to fight was infectious, and as youngsters we learned about fitness and attitude." Goswami was also a handy medium-pacer, and took five for 47 as Central & East Zones beat the 1966-67 West Indian tourists at Indore, including Rohan Kanhai, his "most-prized scalp".

GREEN, DAVID JOHN, who died on May 12, aged 84, was an accomplished batsman, who often opened, and made his first-class debut at 17 in 1953, while still at Burton Grammar School. He was one of several amateurs Derbyshire shuffled in and out of their side, although there was rarely the irritation among the pros that this engendered at other counties. "We had some very good amateur cricketers in the 1950s," remembered off-spinner Edwin Smith. "It was a good mix, and I can honestly say I cannot remember any trouble in those years." Green struggled at first – there was only one double-figure score in his first eight innings – though he later made 59 against the 1956 Australian tourists. The following year he went up to Cambridge, and played under fellow golf enthusiast Ted Dexter in the Varsity Match. He captained Cambridge himself in 1959, losing at Lord's to Oxford (who had their own David Green, the future Lancashire and Gloucestershire batsman), before a final season playing for Derbyshire in the school holidays. Green often looked good, but his returns remained modest: he averaged just 15 for Derbyshire, and his only first-class century came in one of his last matches, for the Free Foresters against Cambridge at Fenner's in 1960. Derbyshire had facilitated a teaching post at Denstone College, to allow him to continue playing for them, but in 1962 he moved to Marlborough, and stayed 33 years, running the cricket for most of the time, as well as teaching history. The switch ended his first-class career, but he did turn out for Wiltshire in the Minor Counties Championship.

GROWDEN, GREGORY PAUL, who died of cancer on November 14, aged 60, was the chief rugby correspondent of the *Sydney Morning Herald* from 1987 to 2012, and then worked for ESPN; he was one of only two writers to attend the first eight Rugby World Cups. Growden also made two important contributions to cricket literature. In 1991 he produced *A Wayward Genius*, after becoming fascinated with the rise and fall of the 1930s Australian spinner "Chuck" Fleetwood-Smith, whose struggles with alcoholism meant he spent a time sleeping under the bridges of Melbourne. Sixteen years later, Growden wrote a biography of Jack Fingleton – Test opener turned cricket writer and political journalist – which examined his often turbulent relationship with Don Bradman.

HADDRICK, RONALD NORMAN, AM, MBE, died on February 11, aged 90. Ron Haddrick, from Adelaide, was probably the only man to give up first-class cricket to accept an invitation to perform with what became the Royal Shakespeare Company. He stayed in Stratford-upon-Avon for five years before returning home in 1959 to become one of Australia's best-known stage actors, with frequent forays into television. As a cricketer, he had opened for Glenelg with the future Test batsman Gavin Stevens, and played three first-class matches for South Australia in 1952. Another Glenelg player, Australian captain Ian Chappell, spoke at Haddrick's memorial service.

HAMILTON, BRUCE GLANVILLE, who died on May 8, aged 87, played just one first-class match – but it was important, since a five-wicket victory over Canterbury at Palmerston North in 1953-54 confirmed Central Districts' first Plunket Shield title. Hamilton made only five, and returned to club cricket, where he made a dozen appearances for Wanganui in the challenge match for the Hawke Cup, for New Zealand's minor associations. In those, he hit 110 against Wairarapa in February 1954, and 93 against Southland the following January as Wanganui retained the trophy. He became a respected teacher.

HARTRIDGE, JOHN FORTESCUE, who died on November 12, aged 89, was Sussex's scorer from 2002 until 2006, after several years with the Second XI. He was in charge of the book for Sussex's first County Championship title, in 2003.

HAZARIKA, ANWAR HUSSAIN, who died on July 6, aged 75, scored 120 on his first-class debut, for Assam against Orissa at Cuttack in December 1965. He added 58 in the second innings, but managed only one more half-century in 15 matches.

HENDRICKS, EMRAAN, died on March 21, aged 87. "Rani" Hendricks was a leading all-rounder in South Africa's non-white competitions in the 1970s and '80s. He scored 668 runs and took 63 wickets for Eastern Province, often playing alongside future national

Visionhaus, Corbis/Getty Images

Shake on it: David Hodgkiss congratulates Jos Buttler, Old Trafford, 2018.

administrators Khaya Majola and Haroon Lorgat. Hendricks, who was a useful football and squash player, took five for 14 against Transvaal in February 1979, and two years later hit 71, also against them.

HEWITSON, DONALD, died on March 10, aged 74. New Zealander Don Hewitson was credited with transforming British attitudes to wine-drinking, starting with his ownership of the Cork & Bottle wine bar in London's Leicester Square. "I'd heard that the situation in Britain was bad, but I was shocked," he said. "I chucked all the wines out and only purchased genuine stuff." He was an avid cricket fan, and when in London rarely missed a day's play at Lord's – where, *The Times* reported, "The first bottle of champagne would be opened along with the batting at 11am."

HODGKISS, DAVID MICHAEL WILLIAM, OBE, who died of complications from Covid-19 on March 29, aged 71, had been on Lancashire's board for 22 years, as chairman since April 2017, after an earlier spell as treasurer. He was the chief executive of the Hare Group, a leading independent steel-fabricating company. One of his earliest connections with Lancashire was as chairman of Mike Watkinson's benefit committee, and he recalled taking the collection box round to a group of Yorkshire supporters during a one-day semi-final at Old Trafford: "I think I collected 5p, and was lucky to get out alive. It didn't help that during the collection Mike took two wickets! But I enjoyed the banter."

HOWARD, BARRY JOHN, who died on April 27, 2019, aged 92, was a member of a prominent Lancashire cricket family: his father, Rupert, was the county's secretary from 1932 to 1948, while his older brother, Nigel, captained them from 1949 to 1953, and England in four Tests in India in 1951-52. A stylish batsman, Barry won his county cap after making two centuries in 1947, but struggled to hold down a regular place, although he remained a heavy scorer in the Second XI, who won the Minor Counties title in 1948. Howard made a final first-class century for MCC against Essex at Lord's in 1949. He was Lancashire's president in 1987–88.

HUGHES, RICHARD CLIVE, who died on March 5, aged 93, was a left-arm seamer who played ten matches for Worcestershire in 1951, after one the previous season. He was the last survivor of a famous win at Scarborough, which harmed Yorkshire's Championship chances (they eventually finished behind Warwickshire). Worcestershire won by eight runs, despite being bowled out for 92 in their second innings. Hughes's single wicket was his last in county cricket; he asked to be released from his contract after the season to concentrate on his insurance business. He played for Hertfordshire in the Minor Counties Championship, taking six for 46 against Buckinghamshire in 1955. "Although my time at Worcester was very short," said Hughes, "I found the whole experience wonderful, meeting and playing with famous cricketers, something I never, ever contemplated."

HUMPHRIES, DAVID JOHN, died on July 14, aged 66. For much of the 1970s, Worcestershire's wicketkeeping gloves were swapped between Rodney Cass and Gordon Wilcock, but the arrival of David Humphries from Leicestershire in 1977 changed that: for eight seasons, he was the undoubted first choice. His less-than-svelte figure inspired the nickname "Humpty", but did not seem to affect his glovework. "In today's era of shuttle runs and bleep tests he might have struggled, but fitness to play cricket was never an issue," remembered Worcestershire's then-secretary Mike Vockins. "He was a good all-round keeper, as adept standing up to the stumps when the wily Norman Gifford was bowling as taking acrobatic catches off the quicks."

Humphries had started with Shropshire, helping them to their only Minor Counties title in 1973. Apart from his wicketkeeping, he was also a useful left-hand batsman, whose four first-class centuries included an undefeated 133 against Derbyshire at New Road in 1984. Two years before, he made 852 runs, his best in a season. "He was an extremely hard hitter," said former team-mate Paul Pridgeon. "Opponents would put fielders all round the boundary. He was a gentle, affable soul, one of the good guys, and never happier than with a cigarette and a pint – an old-fashioned cricketer and a very good one."

The signing of Steve Rhodes from Yorkshire in 1985 put a sudden end to his first-team career. Humphries captained Worcestershire's Second XI that summer, but left at the end of the season. He went to work for the Severn Trent Water Authority.

HUNTER, WILLIAM RAYMOND, died on December 9, aged 82. Ray Hunter from Belfast played 11 first-class matches for Ireland as a seam-bowling all-rounder between 1958 and 1965, taking five for 22 against MCC in Dublin in 1961; two years earlier, in a two-day game at Lord's, he scored 43 and 68, both not out, against an MCC attack including the Australians Keith Miller and George Tribe. In 1963, he took advantage of a sporting pitch at Dublin's Trinity College to take five for 36 against the West Indian tourists. Hunter was better known as a rugby player: a winger, he won ten caps for Ireland, and toured South Africa with the British Lions in 1962.

IMTIAZ AHMED, SYED, who died on February 14, aged 65, was a batsman who played 12 Ranji Trophy matches for Karnataka, but never improved on the 72 he made on debut, against Tamil Nadu at Bangalore in January 1976. He started a cricket academy in Bangalore with the former Test batsman Brijesh Patel, and later ran it on his own after they fell out. Players who trained there included Rahul Dravid and Venkatesh Prasad.

IRRFAN KHAN (Sahabzade Irfan Ali Khan), who died of cancer on April 29, aged 53, was one of India's leading actors, best known to a wider public from the successful 2008 film *Slumdog Millionaire*, in which he played a police inspector, and from the Oscar-winning *Life of Pi*. But it might have been very different. "I wanted to become a cricketer," he told India's *Telegraph*. "I was an all-rounder, and the youngest one in my team in Jaipur. I was selected for the C. K. Nayudu tournament [India's Under-22 championship], but I needed 600 rupees and didn't know who to ask. That day I decided I cannot pursue it." It was a good move: "There are only 11 players… But there is no age limit in acting."

ISMAIL IBRAHIM, who died on June 15, aged 87, was an all-rounder who played eight first-class matches in Pakistan in the 1950s. His highest score (66) and best figures (five for 54) came in the same game, for Karachi C v Karachi A in 1957-58. Two seasons earlier, he had been part of an unusual hat-trick for MCC's Tony Lock while playing for the Amir of Bahawalpur's XI: Ibrahim was the last man out in the first innings after top-scoring with 45, then Lock dismissed Test players Wallis Mathias and Khan Mohammad with his first two deliveries in the second.

JACKMAN, ROBIN DAVID, died on December 25, aged 75. For a man whose first ambition was to be an actor, it was a sad irony that the pinnacle of Robin Jackman's fame came in a non-speaking role. He was the centrepiece of a drama that convulsed world cricket and made ripples beyond: the Jackman affair.

In February 1981, Jackman was flown out to join England's tour of the West Indies to replace the injured Bob Willis. Unfortunately, the team were then in politically volatile Guyana. He was far from the only player in the party who had links with South Africa, still under white minority rule, and an international pariah. But the arrival of Jackman – who wintered there regularly – galvanised Guyanese militants. Three days after he arrived, the government ordered his deportation. The whole England party left with him, and it required frantic diplomacy to ensure the tour continued. It worked out well enough for Jackman. He was already 35 and, after 15 years of outstanding bowling for Surrey, he finally made his Test debut a fortnight later in Barbados, played again in Jamaica, and twice more against Pakistan in 1982. He performed respectably, as he always did, without commanding the attention achieved on his brief visit to Guyana.

On the circuit, he was a personality. Alan Gibson, whose much-loved county reports in *The Times* mixed wisdom, whimsy and a little cricket, called him The Shoreditch Sparrow, placing him in the pantheon of The Oval's lively Londoners. In fact, Jackman was not a Londoner at all. He was born in India, where his father was an officer in the Gurkhas until he lost a leg in an accident. Invalided out, Colonel Jackman brought the family home to a 16-acre spread in Surrey, and bowled to his younger son tirelessly on his prosthetic limb in a net in the garden. Aged 11, he was advised against the stage by his actor-uncle Patrick Cargill; he took the hint.

At St Edmund's School, Canterbury, he topped the batting and bowling averages, but saw himself mainly as a batsman. He appeared for Surrey's Second XI aged 18, and the bowling started to take precedence. His first-team debut came in 1966, and he began to turn in some eye-catching performances, but with too many bad balls. Keen to improve, he arranged a close season in Cape Town where he fell in love for ever with the place, the life, and a trainee nurse, Yvonne, who became his wife. He also learned to bowl and bowl – in one club match he had a 57-over spell, interrupted only by lunch and tea. In 1970s England he was among the leading wicket-takers year after year, an occasional pick for the small number of one-day internationals then played, and the regular subject of Test speculation.

THE OLDEST SWINGERS IN TOWN

The oldest specialist seamers to make a Test debut for England since 1930:

Yrs	*Days*			
36	145	G. H. Pope	v South Africa at Lord's	1947
36	87	T. F. Smailes	v India at Lord's	1946
35	316	N. I. Thomson	v South Africa at Durban	1964-65
35	**212**	**R. D. Jackman**	**v West Indies at Bridgetown**	**1980-81**
35	107	A. W. Wellard	v New Zealand at Manchester	1937
34	136	H. J. Butler	v South Africa at Leeds	1947
34	131	R. Pollard	v India at Manchester	1946
33	197	J. E. Benjamin	v South Africa at The Oval	1994
33	103	A. D. G. Matthews	v New Zealand at The Oval	1937

Bob Thomas Sports Photography/Getty Images

"In your face the whole time": Robin Jackman makes his Test debut at Bridgetown, March 1981.

"He was unbelievably competitive," recalled Mike Selvey, the Middlesex seamer who became cricket correspondent of *The Guardian*. "In your face the whole time. He sledged mercilessly. And he was always at you with the ball. Very tight to the stumps, skiddy, moving it away. He was certainly quick enough, whatever anyone says about his pace." And he was still an actor-manqué. As Gibson put it: "He dashes about, waves his arms furiously, appeals loudly, scratches himself, and bends himself into knots to examine the soles of his boots."

In 1976, Jackman was convinced he was about to be called to Old Trafford as cover for John Snow, but was hurt in a car crash; Selvey got the call instead. In 1980, he had his year of years: 121 wickets at 15, including a county-best eight for 58 against Lancashire – helped, as he readily acknowledged, by the presence of the ferocious Sylvester Clarke at the other end – and a place in the England squad for the Centenary Test against Australia at Lord's. He got the bad news unofficially from the hotel receptionist when he checked in: "Ah, yes, sir. Just the three nights, I believe." Nothing else was said until next day, when the captain, Ian Botham, returned from the toss. "Oh, sorry, Jackers, I forgot to tell you. You're carrying the drinks I'm afraid, mate."

But his day did come – his first three Test wickets in Barbados were Gordon Greenidge, Desmond Haynes and Clive Lloyd – and in 1982 he bowled well in a tense win over Pakistan at Headingley, which ensured his place on the Ashes tour. This made him relieved about a snub several months earlier: even though he was already in South Africa, and the enterprise was run by a pal of his, he was ignored for the rebel tour led by Graham Gooch. But for that, he would have been ineligible for Australia. There was a lot of drinks-carrying there too, which was hard on a 37-year-old, and the prospect of a new job in the Cape led to a retirement announcement before the tour was over. He finished with 1,402 first-class wickets, 1,206 of them for Surrey, putting him 11th on their all-time list.

The job itself did not go to plan, but he had a successful stint coaching Western Province (he had played several seasons for Rhodesia), and later found a new niche. He had done a few BBC stints on radio and television, and eventually emerged as a star of TV commentary in South Africa. When he died, the *Cape Times* praised his out-of-fashion Benaudesque ability to let the pictures speak for themselves. His playing contemporaries liked him a lot (except as an opponent), but never saw silence as his main attribute.

A heavy smoker in his playing days, Jackman was diagnosed with throat cancer in 2012, and suffered further health problems before testing positive for Covid-19 as Christmas

2020 approached. He died two days after John Edrich, his long-time Surrey team-mate (and captain); they were both in the side that won the Championship in 1971, Surrey's first since the glory days of the 1950s. Jackman was a Wisden Cricketer of the Year in 1981.

JAHANZEB KHAN, who died on December 5, aged 68, was a seamer who played 60 first-class matches in Pakistan, mainly for National Bank: his 92 wickets for them included five for 41 (and nine for 80 in the match) as Habib Bank were skittled for 78 and 85 in the Quaid-e-Azam Trophy final in January 1979. In his next match, against Hyderabad, Jahanzeb improved his career-best to five for 24.

JARMAN, BARRINGTON NOEL, OAM, died on July 17, aged 84. Barry Jarman might easily have enjoyed a decade as Australia's Test wicketkeeper, after he and Wally Grout, both uncapped, toured South Africa in 1957-58 following the retirement of Gil Langley. Jarman, from South Australia, was nine years younger, a better batsman, and good with the gloves – but Grout, from Queensland, was an even better keeper, equalled the Test record at the time with six catches in an innings in the first match, and guarded his spot jealously until he retired after the 1965-66 Ashes. He often played with injuries, reasoning he might not get his place back. "Never give a sucker an even break," he would say. "And Barry Jarman is no sucker."

Instead, Jarman had to be content with crumbs: even Grout could not ignore a broken jaw, courtesy of an awkwardly bouncing rocket from Queensland's overseas fast bowler Wes Hall, and missed the first three Tests of the 1962-63 Ashes. Jarman performed well, especially when he latched on to Geoff Pullar's leg-side nudge at Melbourne ("Catch in a Million", ran one headline). But when Grout was fit, back he came. "How I blessed the seeming inconsistencies of selectors everywhere," he wrote. "I tried to feel sorry for Barry Jarman, but couldn't." By the time Grout retired, Jarman had only four other caps to show from several tours, including two to England. He was then forced to sit out the 1966-67 South African trip as his wife was ill, which gave an even break to another non-sucker, Brian Taber of New South Wales. Jarman was finally installed as Australia's No. 1 for India's visit in 1967-68 – and the carping started that, always a big man, he had slowed down a little and was past his prime.

But he performed efficiently enough against India, scoring important runs early in the series, and made his third Ashes tour in 1968 as Bill Lawry's deputy. He broke a finger in Australia's collapse to 78 all out at Lord's – Taber deputised in the next Test – but was back for the Fourth at Headingley, as one of two stand-in captains: Lawry had also broken a finger, while Colin Cowdrey had injured his leg, so Tom Graveney took charge for England. A draw ensured Australia kept the urn, and Jarman brushed off criticism of negative tactics: "My job was to make sure we didn't lose the Ashes, and we didn't."

Back in Australia, he played in the first four Tests of a high-scoring series against West Indies. He shelled three chances in the third match, and was retained, despite a "Jarman Must Go" campaign by a Sydney newspaper. But he was dropped for the last, hearing of his axing on the radio. Only 32, he retired at the end of the season, ending up with 560 dismissals: among Australians, only Grout (587) and Bert Oldfield (662) had more at the time. Jarman's last match, against NSW at Sydney, sealed another Sheffield Shield

Bill Smith, Popperfoto/Getty Images

No sucker: Barry Jarman, Arundel, 1964.

TWO AND ONLY

Tests featuring two one-time captains:

South Africa (O. R. Dunell) v England (C. A. Smith) at Port Elizabeth	1888-89
West Indies (G. A. Headley) v England (K. Cranston) at Bridgetown.........	1947-48
England (T. W. Graveney) v Australia (B. N. Jarman) at Leeds	**1968**

title for South Australia, his second (after 1963-64). Eric Freeman, a state and Test team-mate, said: "Barry played a major role in South Australia winning the Shield in 1968-69. We had some younger players coming through, and BJ and the captain Les Favell were the elder statesmen of the team."

Over the years, Jarman's batting improved, and he made five first-class centuries, the highest at Adelaide in December 1965. "He seemed to get over-anxious in Test cricket, but I remember his top first-class score well," said Ian Chappell, often alongside him at first slip. "He got 196 against a strong NSW team, and I've never again seen a bloke cramp up in every muscle in his body."

Jarman ran a sports shop in Adelaide, and was one of the early ICC referees, overseeing 28 one-day internationals and 25 Tests, including England's at Centurion early in 2000, which gained notoriety when it emerged that the South African captain, Hansie Cronje, had accepted gifts (including a leather jacket) for ensuring against a draw. "We were all saying what a great match, and cricket was the winner," remembered Jarman. "Little did I know the bookmakers might have wanted a result." He was more disposed than some to query controversial bowling actions, and reported Muttiah Muralitharan and Shahid Afridi.

In retirement, Jarman was not bitter about his treatment by the selectors. "Don't forget, I did have the chance to captain Australia."

JAYAMOHAN THAMPI, KRISHNANKUTTY, died on June 8, aged 64, after an argument over money with his son, who was later charged with murder. A bank official, he played six Ranji Trophy matches for Kerala, with a highest score of 32 against Tamil Nadu in 1980-81.

JENKINS, GORDON GRAHAM, who died on May 4, aged 90, was the manager of the MCC indoor school from 1984 to 1995, after two years running its equipment shop. He moved from Wales to London in 1951, and worked for over 30 years as an engineer before going full-time at Lord's. He had already coached Brondesbury CC and Middlesex Young Cricketers, among others. A twinkling eye hid a regard for correct behaviour, but for the MCC cricket staff – which for some years included Gary, one of his four children – Jenkins remained a trusted adviser, ready with a word of encouragement in what could be an unforgiving, competitive environment.

JOHNSON, HUBERT LAURENCE, died on February 4, aged 92. Laurie Johnson came to England soon after the war from his native Barbados, and worked in a Derby factory that made sugar-processing machinery. He had arrived with his friend Michael Frederick, another white Bajan who had attended The Lodge, one of Bridgetown's leading schools. They did well for the Swarkestone club, and played a few matches for Derbyshire before returning to the Caribbean. Frederick won a Test against England in 1953-54, but Johnson came back in 1955, after playing just one game in three years while working in British Guiana, and rejoined Derbyshire as a professional. He gave sterling service as an attacking batsman and fine fielder, and even deputised occasionally as wicketkeeper. For around a decade, Derbyshire regularly included both H. L. Johnson and H. L. Jackson (the feared seamer, Les).

Johnson had trouble adapting his front-foot game, developed on sun-drenched Bajan pitches, to seaming tracks in England. It meant he was a late bloomer in county cricket: in four seasons from 1955, he averaged around 20, and failed to make a century. But he hit 1,480 runs in 1959 and, already 32, finally reached three figures, against Essex at Derby in

June 1960. He finished that summer with four centuries, and 1,870 runs, his best return. "Once he got the measure of the English wickets, his cover-driving was typically Caribbean and very powerful, while his fielding at point was world-class," remembered Derbyshire off-spinner Edwin Smith. "He had a bullet-like throw, which I suppose you would expect from someone who once held the junior world record for throwing a cricket ball!"

For one match the team stayed in a Bristol hotel right next to the railway, and some of the players were woken around four in the morning when shunting began. One leaned out of the window and asked the passing crew for a light. "The fireman got a small ember from the firebox in his tongs and held it up to the window," recalled Johnson.

Always a good driver and cutter, he cracked 154 at Leicester in 1962, dominating a stand of 181 with Billy Oates, and added five centuries two years later, including Derbyshire's first against an Australian touring team. Johnson had a benefit in 1965 (it raised £2,383, not a bad sum for the day), and passed 1,000 runs again, but left the staff following a low-key summer in 1966. After retirement he lived quietly in Birmingham, and was Derbyshire's oldest cricketer when he died.

JONES, DEAN MERVYN, AM, died of a heart attack on September 24, aged 59; he was in Mumbai, where he was part of the official IPL commentary team. Whether dancing down the pitch to smite the ball over the infield, dashing to turn an easy single into two, or needling the opposition (and sometimes his team-mates), Dean Jones was rarely out of the action. He was remarkably popular around Australia, especially in his home state, where a "Bring back Deano" campaign raged for years after he was jettisoned by the selectors. "He was an entertainer," said former Test captain Bill Lawry, "and Victorians are very, very loyal."

Jones was born in the Melbourne suburb of Coburg – although his mother, Gaynor, used to tease him that the reason he had so much to say was that he was conceived in Canberra, the political capital. An uncompromising attitude was instilled by his father, Barney, who played for Carlton, one of Melbourne's leading clubs; like his son, he died of heart trouble, aged 65. Dean was also schooled there by the Test opener Keith Stackpole. "He was what I would term my 'mental mentor'," said Jones. "He was the toughest bloke I ever came across in training and in technical aspects of the game."

An aggressive batsman, strong off the front foot, who might have been designed with limited-overs cricket in mind, Jones was instantly recognisable from a jaunty walk and an almost permanent smudge of zinc cream across his lips. He hit 11 centuries in Tests, and seven in one-day internationals, but was finally dropped from the Test team in 1992, amid suggestions that most of his runs came when the pressure was off. He did average 50 in drawn Tests – but also 53 in matches Australia won. It is probably nearer the mark to say that, as an unabashed Victorian, he was an outsider in a team usually captained by New South Welshmen.

There was certainly no shortage of pressure during Jones's first Test century, in boiling heat at Madras in 1986-87. It was just his third Test, more than two years after his second, and started with a long partnership with David Boon. By the second afternoon, Jones was approaching 170, in severe distress, dehydrated and occasionally vomiting near the pitch. He told Allan Border, his captain and batting partner, that he would have to retire: in an attempt to make him carry on, Border said he'd have to get someone tough out there, like a Queenslander. Jones took the hint: "Stick it up your bum, AB, I'm staying here!" He eventually fell for 210, in 502 enervating minutes – but could not remember the last part of his innings, and had to spend the night on a hospital drip. He returned to the ground to resume his place in what became the second tied Test. The experience may have permanently affected his health: in later life, he often struggled in hot conditions.

After being a productive member of the team which pulled off a surprise victory in the 1987 World Cup – he scored 33 in the final, as Australia beat England by seven runs – Jones made 566 runs in the 1989 Ashes, with 157 spread over four days at a soggy Edgbaston. "His driving was again of the highest class," said team-mate Geoff Lawson,

Patrick Eagar, Popperfoto/Getty Images

The entertainer: Dean Jones swashbuckles against England at the MCG, Boxing Day, 1986.

"using the slow pace of the wicket to hit balls on off stump through midwicket with complete safety." Jones added 122 in the final Test at The Oval. A few months earlier, he had reeled off a Test-best 216 against West Indies at Adelaide. He was named a Wisden Cricketer of the Year, and seemed a fixture – but just three years later was dropped, from the five-day team at least. Form was not the problem: his previous Test innings in Australia was an unbeaten 150, against India at Perth in February 1992, and in his last series, in Sri Lanka a few months later, he had successive scores of 57, 77 and 100 not out.

Jones remained a one-day favourite, and famously riled Curtly Ambrose in a one-day final at Sydney in January 1993, asking him to take off his white wristbands when he bowled, claiming they made it hard to see the white ball. Jones was suffering from a broken thumb, and had hoped to put Ambrose off, but succeeded only in making him steam in more ferociously. After copping a couple of bruises – and watching Mark Taylor parry a snorter to gully – he said: "You can put them back on now."

After the South African tour of 1993-94, he was dropped for good. Border might have goaded him in Madras, but remained an admirer: "He was unbelievable at Test level, but his one-day aggression will be remembered for ever." Jones finished with 6,068 runs at 44 in ODIs; at the time, only Viv Richards had made more at a higher average.

Jones concentrated instead on domestic cricket, making a career-best 324 not out – the score matched his Australian shirt number – for Victoria against South Australia in one of the earliest first-class floodlit games, at the MCG in February 1995, and resuming the county career he had started in 1992. He had been an inspired choice for Durham's maiden first-class season, but did not return as it was wrongly assumed he would be in the following year's Ashes squad. "He made an instant impression," remembered fellow Durham newbie Simon Hughes. "In our first match, a Sunday League game against Lancashire, he strode out at No. 3, took guard outside his crease and slapped the bowlers – including Paul Allott, Phillip DeFreitas and Danny Morrison – all around the place for a brilliant hundred. After that, he reeled off six successive Sunday League fifties."

In 1996, Jones reappeared as captain of Derbyshire and, to start with, energised the squad again: they mountaineered 12 places in the Championship and finished second behind Leicestershire, their best since their only title, in 1936. He ended up with 1,502 runs at 51, including a ninth and last double-century, at Sheffield. But trouble was brewing. Some senior players were unhappy at being marginalised by Jones and the Australian coach Les Stillman, and the fallout led him to quit at the end of June 1997, with a parting shot at others' lack of commitment. "Dean cocked up a declaration, and we lost to Hampshire at Chesterfield," remembered Chris Adams, a Jones supporter who also left Derbyshire after that seismic season. "But the incident that made his mind up took place not on a cricket field but the golf course." Jones had asked if anyone fancied 18 holes, and Adams was the only taker. On the first green they heard some familiar voices, and spotted four other players on the course. "Dean didn't say anything, but his expression told me he was absolutely devastated… He probably started packing his bags that night."

Jones bowed out at home after making an undefeated 100 – and a duck – in his final game for Victoria, against Tasmania at Melbourne in March 1998. It was his 55th first-class century, and left him with an average nudging 52. Two years earlier, in a match to mark the centenary of the Victorian Cricket Association at the MCG, Jones faced his former Australian team-mates for an unofficial World XI, and purred to a vintage 103. It helped them to a competitive total after being 114 for six, and allowed the local *Herald Sun* to run the headline "Deano saves the World".

After retiring from playing, Jones combined coaching with commentary. In 2006, thinking he was off air, he referred to Hashim Amla, the bearded South African Muslim, as a "terrorist" during a Test in Colombo. He was immediately sacked by the network, and work dried up for a while – but Jones re-established himself, inventing the character of "Professor Deano", who explained tactics, complete with mortar-board, ring-binder and cane. He kept up the coaching, too, and rebuilt his reputation and popularity on the subcontinent: he inspired Islamabad United to the first Pakistan Super League title in 2016, and again in 2018. Players and officials from Karachi Kings and Multan Sultans formed a giant "D" on the outfield before the start of their PSL play-off in November. Karachi, whom he had coached at the start of 2020, went on to lift the trophy.

Jones had dropped occasional hints about helping the Australian white-ball teams – and Justin Langer, the current coach, admitted he was in the mix. "He eagerly sought information, and used it to enhance other cricketers' performances," said Ian Chappell.

A restless mind meant that, even in retirement, Jones was always thinking about cricket, and how to improve it. He was among the first to suggest the third umpire should call front-foot no-balls, and felt that, where technology was available, hits over 85 metres should be worth eight rather than six. Unlike some broadcasters, he mixed eagerly with the written press when off duty. "He respected and made an effort with everyone, whether ex-cricketer or no-name journo at your first game," recalled Brydon Coverdale, the Australian TV personality who formerly wrote for ESPNcricinfo.

Jones was under no illusions. "I've been a lucky boy," he told *Wisden Cricket Monthly* not long before his death. "If you'd said to me after my first Test series in the West Indies – where I got absolutely ripped apart mentally, physically and technically – that I would play 52 Test matches and 164 ODIs, and that I would play in Ashes series, win a World Cup, and stuff like that, I'd have thought you were on drugs." Not everyone was a fan: a long-time feud with former team-mate Merv Hughes, which started when Jones thought Hughes was being too careful after an injury, was never resolved.

After calling an IPL match – taking place in the UAE – on September 23, Jones was in a Mumbai hotel when he suffered a cardiac arrest. Brett Lee, his fellow Test-player-turned-commentator, tried in vain to revive him. News of his death stunned Australia. "When you first get a message like that, you don't quite believe it," said Mark Taylor. "You think somehow the lines of communication have been blurred." A fortnight later, Jones's hearse made a final lap around the MCG, the scene of many of his more raucous triumphs – but now, because of Covid-19, hauntingly empty.

There was one last farewell. On the first day of the Boxing Day Test against India, Jones's widow, Jane, and daughters, Augusta and Phoebe, as well as Allan Border, placed his Baggy Green and bat by the stumps, while the Australian players wore zinc on their lower lip in his honour. Cricket Victoria reinstated Jones's life membership, which he had handed back after criticising their administration, and renamed the state's annual one-day award after him. "Dean was one of Victoria's greatest players, and we want his cricket legacy to live on," said chairman David Maddocks.

JONES, JOHN GARETH, died on November 9, aged 69. Rhodesia-born "Robin" Jones had a sobering introduction to big cricket: picked at 17 for South African Schools against Natal in Pietermaritzburg in January 1969, he was one of five victims for the menacing Vintcent van der Bijl, who finished with 10–8–4–5. Jones later played three first-class matches for Rhodesia in 1975-76 – twice coming off second-best against van der Bijl again – which were sandwiched by two seasons in the Lancashire League as the professional for Bacup, for whom he scored 117 against Todmorden.

KASPER, RONALD JOHN, died on January 20, aged 73. The versatile John Kasper forced his way into a strong Auckland side as a batsman in 1966-67, before trying his luck in grade cricket in Australia, then moving to South Africa. In his first match for Natal B he made an unbeaten 122, which remained his highest first-class score, and soon graduated to the A-Team. He also switched from occasional off-breaks to seamers, and took six for 110 against Transvaal B in Ladysmith in December 1971. "He was a hard-working all-rounder," recalled the South African fast bowler Vintcent van der Bijl. "It was difficult to get the ball out of his hand after a few wickets!" Finally, back in New Zealand, Kasper hit two more centuries for Auckland, the last in his penultimate match, in 1978-79, against a Canterbury attack led by Richard Hadlee. He remained involved in cricket, playing and coaching at Cornwall CC in Auckland.

KASTURIRANGAN, GOPALASWAMY IYENGER, who died on August 19, aged 89, was an industrious seamer with a wrong-footed action, who came tantalisingly close to Test selection in 1952-53. He was chosen for India's first tour of the West Indies, but withdrew, reportedly with a groin injury – although it seems more likely he dropped out as a friend he considered more deserving of a place was not picked. Kasturirangan continued at domestic level for Mysore (now Karnataka) for another ten years, recording his best figures of six for 42 as Hyderabad were dismantled for 85 in August 1961. Later that season, captaining a South Zone side containing five Test players, he dismissed MCC's Eric Russell and Ken Barrington cheaply; in the Calcutta Test which preceded that game, he caught Peter Parfitt while on as a substitute. He became involved with administration, and had a spell in charge of pitch preparation at Bangalore's Chinnaswamy Stadium.

KENNEDY, DR JAMES HENRY, died on October 26, aged 71. A left-arm seamer from the Clydesdale club, the bespectacled Jim Kennedy played four matches for Scotland, two first-class, against Ireland in 1970 and Pakistan in 1971. He also took three for 51 in a three-day game against Warwickshire in 1970, when his victims included the former England captain Mike Smith. He became a consultant gynaecologist.

KHALID WAZIR, SYED, who died on June 27, aged 84, was a surprise selection for Pakistan's first tour of England, in 1954: he had played only two first-class matches at home, although his seamers had accounted for Imtiaz Ahmed and the Mohammad brothers, Hanif and Wazir. Tall and slim, with a rakish moustache, he had a quiet time in England, playing in two of the Tests but not bowling a ball; he took only nine wickets on the tour, to go with 253 runs, which included a half-century against Derbyshire. He decided to stay on in England and, with that, his first-class career was over before he turned 19 – unique for a Test player. He lived in Chester, where he worked in insurance and played for various clubs, including Lowerhouse in the Lancashire League. According to some accounts, he came close to a surprise international comeback when, in 1962, the Pakistan tourists ran into injury problems – but did not actually take the field after meeting up with the team. His father, Wazir Ali, and uncle, Nazir Ali, played Tests for India in the 1930s.

KING, IAN METCALFE, who died on March 31, aged 88, was a slow left-armer who spent the first half of the 1950s on the staff at Edgbaston, then had a season with Essex. "I didn't play for Warwickshire for that long," he said, "because back then cricketers were so poorly paid it was hard to make a living, so I went and did other things. I was paid £6 a week, but got another £2 if we won and another £1 if we got a first-innings lead. It wasn't lucrative, but it was a great way to spend the summer."

King had to take his chances alongside Eric Hollies, the veteran leg-spinner who collected a record 2,201 wickets for Warwickshire. "Eric was a brilliant bowler," he said. "He didn't spin the ball miles, but could put it on a sixpence for hours on end. His figures say it all. Mind you, I remember one game at Trent Bridge when it was a great batting wicket – Tom Dollery threw the ball to him, and Eric said: 'Not today, Tom, give the young lad a go instead.' He didn't want to get smashed around!"

His best figures, five for 59, came against Essex in 1954, the victims including Trevor Bailey and Doug Insole; possibly they remembered this when signing King for the 1957 season. He played 28 matches for Essex that year, but his gentle spin claimed only 34 victims, and he finally went off and did those other things. "But I wouldn't have missed it for the world."

KNOTT, SIDNEY, died on December 8, aged 87. Sid Knott was a brisk seamer and handy batsman who appeared regularly for the South African province of Border for a dozen seasons from 1951-52, latterly as captain. He took seven for 34 against North Eastern Transvaal at Benoni in December 1952, and a few weeks later ten in the match against Griqualand West. On New Year's Day 1954, he hit his highest score of 79 against Orange Free State. Knott took five for 40 as Natal were bowled out for 90 at East London in December 1959; among his scalps were the Test openers Jackie McGlew and Trevor Goddard, and Roy McLean. But that was the end of the good news: Border were skittled for 16 and 18, the lowest two-innings aggregate in a first-class match. Knott's son, David, later played for Border as well.

LACY SCOTT, DAVID GEFFREY, who died on February 2, aged 99, might – but for the Second World War – have become a notable all-rounder for Kent. His school career at Marlborough College certainly promised much: he scored over 500 runs in his first two seasons, and was captain in his last, in 1939, when *Wisden* singled him out as one of the leading public-school all-rounders. By then, he had already appeared for Kent's Second XI, opening with the future county batsman and *Observer* journalist Tony Pawson. In 1939, less than a month before war was declared, he scored 93 for Public Schools against the Army at Lord's. Born in India, he returned there in 1940 to join the Central India Horse, and was invalided out with the rank of captain five years later. Lacy Scott finally made his first-class debut for Cambridge University in 1946. He had a top score of 36, against Middlesex, and took five for 35 against Free Foresters, enough to earn a Blue. His solitary first-class appearance for Kent came against Sussex at Hastings that summer. A chartered accountant, he worked in London as well as in India, Rhodesia and Spain.

LARTER, LORNA (later Mrs Beal), who died on August 10, aged 96, began playing cricket on the streets of Depression-era Melbourne in the 1930s, and joined Hawthorn Ladies at the age of 15 in 1938. She went on to keep wicket in Australia's first seven Tests after the war, being "full of agile anticipation to the spinners", according to team-mate Norma Whiteman. She did little with the bat, but did make a century in England in 1951, against East Women at St Albans. Larter met Roy Beal on the voyage to England, and retired from cricket when they married soon after returning home.

LAWRENCE, BERNARD, died on August 13, aged 81. A Goan Christian whose day job was at a Karachi advertising agency, Ben Lawrence was also a keen cricket statistician, and the scorer for Pakistan radio and television for more than 20 years from the 1970s. He contributed to several books, and compiled *Pakistan Test Cricket 1952-53 to 1988-89*.

LEE, GRAHAM DAVID, died of cancer on June 11, aged 52. Left-arm spinner "Chubby" Lee was an inveterate club cricketer, mainly for Torrisholme and nearby Morecambe. His array of cricketing friends included South African Test batsman Ashwell Prince, who lodged with Lee during a two-year stint with Morecambe. "He had an incredible bowling style," said Radio Lancashire's Mike Latham. "You might say he was deceptively slow, but he used to get overseas professionals out who had never seen anything like it. He dismissed a lot of top batsmen – you could probably pick a Test team out of them."

LEGARD, EDWIN, died on January 29, aged 84. Wicketkeeper Eddie Legard surfaced at the wrong time to play for his native Yorkshire: Jimmy Binks had not long established himself behind the stumps, and stayed there for all 412 County Championship matches between his debut in 1955 and retirement in 1969. Legard played well over 100 games for the Second XI, but eventually moved to Warwickshire. He was second-choice there too, this time to A. C. Smith, but at least got the chance to play 20 first-class matches, although only four in the Championship. Legard's batting proved fragile, bringing a highest score of 21 – but he had his moments at lower levels. He had started at Barnsley, alongside Dickie Bird, who told the tale of a game against Hull where they went in first, after Geoff Boycott said: "Let someone else go in and knock the shine off the ball, then I'll go in and finish it off." The makeshift openers cruised past a target of 187.

LEWIS, ANTHONY JOHN, MBE, died on March 15, aged 78. Tony Lewis was a mathematician whose name entered cricket's vocabulary after he joined forces with statistician Frank Duckworth to devise a fairer formula for deciding the results of rain-shortened limited-overs matches.

In 1992, a colleague showed Lewis a paper Duckworth had given to the Royal Statistical Society: "A fair result in foul weather". He immediately appreciated the theory – that revisions to the target should take account of wickets lost, as well as overs, and reflect how many runs a team could be expected to score from their position when the game was interrupted. His particular interest was in mathematics' practical applications, so he set a student to analyse several hundred *Wisden* scorecards to see how it might work, and continued to experiment with the data himself. Lewis and Duckworth approached Tim Lamb, then cricket secretary at the TCCB, and were invited to Lord's to show him and ICC chief executive David Richards what they were calling the "Lancastrian method", as both hailed from Lancashire. By the time they presented it to the ICC Board, they had settled on "Duckworth/Lewis method".

The system was first used on New Year's Day 1997, when England fell short of a D/L target in Harare, and was adopted for the following English domestic season. It swiftly spread, and by 1999 was incorporated into ICC playing conditions. Despite complaints

Dave Rogers, Getty Images

Method actors: Tony Lewis (right) and Frank Duckworth, 2003.

from the press that they could not follow the maths – the professional version relies on a computer, rather than the original lengthy tables – the underlying principle is generally accepted as much fairer than previous alternatives.

The pair continued to refine their method to take account of rising scoring-rates and the Twenty20 revolution, but in 2014 handed over custody to Australian statistician Steven Stern. The fame remained theirs, even if Lewis – in his youth "a fairly dour opening batsman" for Grimsargh, near Preston – was sometimes confused with his namesake, the former Glamorgan and England captain. One unexpected tribute was a pop duo from Ireland who called themselves The Duckworth Lewis Method.

LUDVIKSSON, LUDVIK, who died from heart disease on May 22, aged 48, was one of 22 native Icelanders who took part in the country's first modern-day cricket match, in July 2000. A slow bowler, he played for Kylfan CC (now Reykjavík) in the Icelandic Cricket Cup, and made one appearance for the national team, in 2003.

LŪSIS, JĀNIS, who died on April 29, aged 80, was a Latvian athlete who, competing for the Soviet Union, achieved a rare full set of medals in one Olympic event, taking gold in the javelin in 1968, silver in 1972, and bronze in 1964. Lūsis has long featured in *Wisden's* Miscellaneous Records section, as he is rumoured to have thrown a cricket ball 150 yards while in England during the 1960s – a world record if true. Asked about it for *Wisden 2020* (see page 1119), he said: "It's possible – I've thrown stones further than that."

McNAMEE, BASIL THOMSON, who died on April 17, aged 81, was the president of Cricket Ireland in 2010-11, his tenure including a World Twenty20 and a 50-over World Cup. A distinguished cardiologist, he had a long career as a player, mainly for the Dungannon club in Tyrone, for whom he took 399 wickets. In 1989, when he was 50, he played alongside his three sons as Victoria were bowled out for 26.

MACKERETH, ERIC GEORGE, who died on June 21, aged 81, was the first chairman of the Shropshire Cricket League, after one appearance in the Minor Counties Championship in 1964. He played for Shrewsbury and Wroxeter, among others, and organised a tour to

Devon for around 30 years. He was also a good rugby player, golfer and skier – and a guitarist confident enough to try his luck on *Opportunity Knocks* in the 1950s. After a period as a journalist, including with the *Daily Mail*, he ran several successful business ventures.

MADAN MOHAN, Dr KOYIPPILLIL, who died on January 8, aged 74, was a batsman from Trivandrum who had modest success in a long career with Kerala, latterly as captain. In 32 matches, Madan Mohan made only four half-centuries – all against Hyderabad, the highest 72 in January 1965. Two seasons later, his 71 not out coaxed Kerala to their first victory over Hyderabad, by one wicket. He became a noted paediatric surgeon.

MALLOCH, TREVOR STUART, who died on November 2, aged 91, was a seamer who had two matches for Wellington in 1953-54, starting against Central Districts on Christmas Day. Although that was the extent of his first-class career, he remained active in club cricket, and opened the bowling against the 1960-61 MCC tourists at Palmerston North. He was Wellington's oldest player when he died.

MANNERS, Lieutenant Commander JOHN ERROL, dsc, who died on March 7, aged 105, was the longest-lived first-class cricketer and the last survivor of the pre-war county game. Some thought he had the technique for Test cricket. "Not only was he potentially prolific, but his strokeplay was brilliant," wrote John Arlott. But he had long been destined for a career in the Royal Navy: his father, an admiral, was Commodore of Convoys during the Second World War.

Manners himself had an eventful war. After various scrapes and escapes – and his wedding to an actress in a church near Lord's – by April 1945 he was commanding HMS *Viceroy*, which was leading a convoy off the coast near Newcastle when it was attacked by a German U-boat. Manners dropped depth charges, which found their target, although the explosions also caused a few problems above water: "The *Viceroy* did a big shudder, leapt a foot or two in the sea and blacked out, as all the electric switches were thrown off, leaving everything in darkness… Shortly, the switches were refixed, and we were back in

PA Images/Alamy

Calm under fire: John Manners on his way to an unbeaten 107 for the Navy at Lord's, 1951; the Army wicketkeeper is Keith Andrew.

action." Among the debris was a large grey cylinder, which Manners hoisted aboard, in case of survivors. It contained 72 bottles of brandy, "fortunately none of which were damaged". One was sent to the prime minister's office: the ship soon received the thanks of Winston Churchill, who said he intended to keep the "interesting souvenir".

As a 15-year-old cadet at Dartmouth, Manners had taken three wickets in a schools match at Lord's in 1930. Six years later – by now in the Navy – he had a taste of county cricket. He was serving on the Royal Yacht but, "since the King [Edward VIII] didn't want to go to Cowes that year, we had nothing to do". So he was allowed to play for Hampshire against Gloucestershire at the United Services ground in Portsmouth – and scored 81, becoming one of seven victims for off-spinner Reg Sinfield after being asked to push the score along on the second day. "I cracked a ball hard into my foot, and it trickled slowly back on to the stumps," he recalled. He had a few more matches that season – against Surrey, Yorkshire and the Indian tourists – but naval commitments intervened, and he did not appear again for more than ten years. "I was saving up lots of leave to have a summer of cricket in 1940, but then war was declared."

In his second match back, in 1947, Manners hit 121 against Kent, showing off what *Wisden* called "perfect strokeplay, drives, cuts and hooks". But, as a serving officer, his availability was limited. That innings at Canterbury remained his only county century, though he did make three more in first-class cricket for the Combined Services, including 123 against the New Zealand tourists in 1949.

After retiring from the Navy in 1958, Manners became bursar at Dauntsey's School in Wiltshire, where he was fondly remembered. His advice, though, might have landed him in trouble when the odd-job man, complaining about interference in his domain by a member of staff, was told: "Next time she does it, give her a working-over with your blowlamp." There was a rather more serious incident in 1964, when Manners was briefly suspended after pupils organised a strike in protest at the food. "They left their meat pie and rice pudding lunch uneaten," gasped the *Daily Express*. He was reinstated after a week, helped by a letter of support signed by all but one of the teaching staff.

Manners became a dedicated amateur photographer, contributed to *Country Life*, produced four books on country crafts, and visited his daughter in Australia every year until he was past his century. *Wisden 2016* tracked down the last two men who had appeared in pre-war county cricket in England (the other was Leo Harrison, another Hampshire player, who died later in 2016, aged 94). The story related how Manners would march "up the High Street for a pint of milk or something from the butcher". He was 100 at the time.

MARSLAND, GEOFFREY PETER, who died on August 25, 2016, aged 84, played 17 matches for Oxford University, clinching his Blue in 1954 by scoring 74 against Middlesex, in an opening stand of 138 with Mike Smith. It was a strong side, captained by Colin Cowdrey, although they could not quite force a win in the Varsity Match, despite Smith's unbeaten 201. Marsland later taught at Eton, briefly alongside David Cornwell, who found fame as the novelist John le Carré.

MEDLOCK, GEORGE KENNETH, OBE, JP, DL, died on May 1, aged 105. Ken Medlock was a businessman who rescued John Wisden & Co from the brink of extinction. His love of cricket began early: he was taken to the 1921 Headingley Test as a six-year-old, and went on to captain Birch Vale CC in Derbyshire. In 1960, he had just been promoted to the main board of the Co-operative Wholesale Society, without knowing that, during the war, it had acquired Wisden. Then, at his first meeting, he saw an agenda item about liquidating this loss-making subsidiary. Medlock successfully argued against destroying such a famous name. He revived Wisden's declining sports-goods business (although that was ultimately doomed), staved off any threat to the Almanack, and became a much-liked and effective chairman of John Wisden for the next eight years, until the Co-op sold the company on. With Learie Constantine, he was the driving force behind instituting the now-abandoned Wisden Trophy for England–West Indies Tests. After leaving the Co-op, Medlock was the first chairman of Liverpool-based Radio City (one of Britain's most

Jeff Medlock

To the victor... Ken Medlock hands a miniature Wisden Trophy to Derek Underwood after England defeated West Indies in the 1969 Test series. In the background are Ray Illingworth and Alan Knott.

successful commercial stations) from 1973 to 1985, was involved with numerous charities, and remained indefatigable even in alleged old age. He wrote his autobiography, *A Good Innings*, aged 97, and travelled down from the Wirral for the Wisden dinner aged 98. His marriage to Edna lasted 78 years until she died, aged 102, in 2018. "He had my absolute trust," said the writer Gillian Reynolds, who worked with him at Radio City. "And when there was good news, his twinkle would rival Blackpool Illuminations."

MENON, GOPAL KRISHNA, who died on August 11, aged 93, was a well-respected Bombay journalist, primarily for *The Times of India* and *The Indian Express*. He covered a lot of cricket, including the Test against Australia at the Brabourne Stadium early in 1970 which was interrupted when spectators lit fires in one of the stands in protest against an umpiring decision; Menon went on to the field to tell the umpires that the smoke was preventing the official scorers from seeing their signals, earning a rebuke from the visiting captain, Bill Lawry. He was also involved in coaching, and had a part in the development of the Indian opening bowler Ramakant "Tiny" Desai.

MERCHANT, KENNETH FRANCIS CHARLES, died of Covid-19 on April 2, aged 81; his wife, Joan, died of the virus the same day, in the adjacent bed at Southend Hospital. A keen cricket watcher and collector, Ken Merchant was a long-time member of The Cricket Society, and a trustee of their charitable trust from 1992 to 2019.

MILLER, STANLEY, who died on July 20, aged 81, was a Manchester journalistic legend who reported Lancashire cricket from the 1950s to the 1990s. Most of the legend was forged at his other workplace, the city magistrates' court, where he hoovered up news stories and kept tabs on everyone and everything. "Stan will know," was the mantra from the bench downwards. An essential trick was working out how long cases might last, so that – in summer, with Lancashire at home – he could rush over to cover the day's play on behalf of the reporting agency he co-owned, Stewart & Hartley. A big, humorous man with a curly mop, Stan made the grubby shack that housed the old press box very welcoming. He rarely reported from the other Old Trafford: he preferred to spend his Saturdays playing high-standard football himself – at one stage for New Mills in Derbyshire.

MOHAMMAD BASHIR, who died on November 18, aged 79, was a groundsman at the Gaddafi Stadium in Lahore for over 50 years. As a junior, he was there for the ground's first Test, against Australia in 1959-60, and watched it develop into a modern stadium that can hold 60,000: "It has been like seeing your own child grow up in front of you." Haji Bashir also helped out with pitch preparation at other Pakistan grounds and in the UAE, and a luxuriant beard meant he was a familiar sight on television. "All Pakistan pitches have his sweat and blood," said journalist Shahid Hashmi.

MOHAMMAD MUNAF, who died on January 28, aged 84, was a stocky seamer who worked up good pace from a low-slung action for various sides in Pakistan. His total of four Test caps would have been more but for Fazal Mahmood, an automatic new-ball choice throughout the 1950s, and a leg injury which kept him out of the 1962 tour of England. When Ted Dexter's side visited Pakistan the previous winter, he had taken four for 42 in the first innings of the First Test at Lahore, and dismissed Geoff Pullar for a pair. He showed what might have been in England during a Pakistan Eaglets tour in 1963, with a career-best eight for 84 against Kent. Along with his schoolmate Hanif Mohammad and other promising youngsters, Munaf was supported early on by the Pir of Pagaro, a cricket-loving spiritual leader. He had a narrow escape one day after felling his patron in the nets with a ball to the groin, at which point several of the Pir's followers rushed towards the bowler brandishing sticks. Fortunately, the Pir staggered to his feet just in time to call them off.

MOHAMMAD SOZIB HOSEN, who hanged himself at home in Rajshahi on November 15, aged 21, was a batsman who represented Bangladesh's Under-19 side in 2016 and 2017, and played a few List A matches for Shinepukur. Friends suspected depression after he had been left out of a local T20 tournament.

MORDAUNT, DAVID JOHN, who died on November 28, aged 83, was a tall, attacking batsman and seam bowler who had an eventful first-class debut for Sussex against Oxford University in 1958: a duck followed by 96 when he holed out aiming for a fourth six. That remained his highest score in a total of 19 county appearances, before he devoted himself to teaching, first at Stowe, then at Wellington College, his old school, where he had once broken an umpire's nose with a straight-drive. "He was a lovable fellow – good eye, ball sense, a lot of natural talent, but it didn't quite work out for him at County Championship level," remembered Sussex batsman Les Lenham. "He used to drive into the ground in a 1920s Morris Oxford saloon which was so large it took up a couple of spaces in the car park."

Mordaunt played Minor Counties cricket for Berkshire and, in their first Gillette Cup match, against Somerset at Reading in 1965, his rapid 60 included four sixes off Bill Alley, whose reaction was probably audible back in Taunton. He went on several MCC tours to far-flung places, scoring 134 against Philadephia in September 1959, and 109 against Argentina in January 1965. "He thumped the ball out of sight, and pocketed close catches with the same ease and safety as he holed the golf ball on countless greens throughout Canada," said *The Cricketer* of the first trip. These visits may have sharpened his appetite for travel: Mordaunt organised three expeditions to the Arctic, and in 1983 led a Royal Geographical Society trip through Nepal to the base of Annapurna.

MORGAN, DOUGLAS WAUGH, died on April 4, aged 73. Scrum-half Dougie Morgan won 21 rugby caps for Scotland, captaining them in the 1978 Five Nations; the previous year he played for the British Lions in South Africa. He later coached Scotland. Morgan was also a useful cricketer, who appeared in junior representative matches and later for Melville College Former Pupils; his unbeaten 154 against Brunswick in 1972 was an East of Scotland League record. Although he never played for the national side, he did take a catch for them at Lord's, as twelfth man against MCC in 1968.

MOUNTFORD, STUART GEORGE ELLIOTT, who died on February 22, aged 96, was connected with Bovey Tracey CC in Devon for more than 80 years, starting as a teenager in 1938 and playing until 1973, then helping around the ground into old age. He represented Devon for ten years from 1947, scoring 79 against Gloucestershire Second XI at Plymouth in the Minor Counties Championship in 1950. Four years later, he was part of the side which contested the Challenge Match after finishing second in the Minor Counties table: Devon took a first-innings lead at The Oval – Mountford, who sometimes kept wicket, stumped his opposite number, the future England keeper Roy Swetman – but couldn't force the win they needed to deny Surrey Second XI the title. Mountford's Devon cap (he was the first Bovey Tracey player to receive one) was placed on his coffin.

MURCH, STEWART NIGEL CLIFFORD, died on July 15, aged 76. Nine matches for Victoria over four seasons in the 1960s, and a bowling average above 50, suggest a player on the margins. Yet Nigel Murch was a dynamic presence for St Kilda in Melbourne grade cricket for 15 years, taking 376 wickets with his aggressive fast bowling, and adding nearly 3,000 pugnacious runs. He spent the northern summer of 1968 at Northampton, and played against Cambridge University. As a captain, Murch courted controversy, once given out for blocking an opposition wicketkeeper trying to take a skyer; he was also no-balled for throwing. "He was great on the talking side of it – he would intimidate a lot of batsmen," recalled Tony Beer, from the rival Malvern club. Murch's son, James, married Cathy Freeman, Australia's iconic 400m gold medallist at the 2000 Sydney Olympics, who hailed her father-in-law as "a man in a billion".

MURPHY, DR EDWARD GORDON, who died in May, aged 98, was the son of a prominent communist and trade union leader, Jack Murphy, who in 1926 moved his family to Minsk, in what is now Belarus. Even so, he sent his son to Bedales, a public school in Hampshire, after which he qualified as a doctor. While doing national service in the RAF, Murphy opened the batting in two first-class matches for Combined Services in 1948; in between, he scored 101 not out against the Minor Counties in a non-first-class game at Jesmond. Two years later, Murphy emigrated to Canada, where he had a long career in paediatric medicine. He was married, to Nadia, for 73 years.

MURRAY, KINGSTON ANTHONY, who died of Covid-19 on April 4, aged 69, was a fast bowler from Grenada who made a splash in London club cricket, helping Mitcham to their most recent Surrey Championship title, in 1978. Before moving to England in search of better job prospects, Murray often took the new ball for the Grenadian national team, and shook up a touring Glamorgan side early in 1970 with three quick wickets.

MUSTAFI, ASHOKE, who died on July 30, aged 86, played two Ranji Trophy matches for Bengal in 1958-59, then coached for many years in Kolkata. His charges included the young Sourav Ganguly, who arranged some of Mustafi's medical care during his final illness.

NADKARNI, RAMESHCHANDRA GANGARAM, died on January 17, aged 86. "Bapu" Nadkarni was a mesmerisingly accurate left-arm spinner, best remembered for an astonishing performance in the First Test of India's 1963-64 home series against England at Madras. He wheeled down 21 successive maidens – a world record – and finished with figures of 32–27–5–0. England did have an excuse for their go-slow on the third day: several players had food poisoning. As Nadkarni recalled: "They had absolutely bad tummies – four or five or six people were down." *The Times* delicately described the problem as "internal misfortunes". With a rest day coming up, Brian Bolus and Ken Barrington – two of the most obdurate batsmen England have ever produced – dug in, to give their team-mates a chance to recover. There were only 27 runs between lunch and tea, and a further 59 in the final session, most while Nadkarni was having a rest. "Much as I hate such things on the cricket field," wrote John Woodcock, "there is no denying that England had some justification for their tactics."

On a pitch taking slow turn, ball after ball was patted back to the bowler or the close fielders: one 19-over spell from Nadkarni produced just a single, from his final delivery. His usual style was to fire the ball in at the right-hander's pads, as Barry Knight – one of the recovering invalids – confirmed: "He was a flat left-arm spinner, like Derek Underwood. He didn't exactly loop it up." Nadkarni said: "The basic principle was to be accurate to the point of perfection."

Central Press, Getty Images

Giving nothing away: "Bapu" Nadkarni, 1967.

His feat at Madras was not a one-off: against Pakistan at Delhi in 1960-61 – another series in which all five Tests were drawn – he had followed 34–24–24–1 in the first innings with 52.4–38–43–4. In total, he had an economy-rate of 1.67 in Tests, the second-lowest by anyone bowling more than 500 overs (0.03 of a run behind the South African left-arm medium-pacer Trevor Goddard), and was even more miserly in first-class cricket (1.64). Of Nadkarni's 1,527 overs in Tests, 665 were maidens.

He had made his Test debut in 1955-56, failing to take a wicket against New Zealand, and was part of India's dispiriting tour of England in 1959, when they lost 5–0. Nadkarni, though, finished the trip with 55 wickets and 945 runs. Back at Madras in 1964-65, he took 11 against Australia, but was on the losing side again. By then, India were ushering in a new generation of spinners, with Bishan Bedi the left-armer of choice, and Nadkarni missed out on another England tour in 1967. But, at the urging of the Nawab of Pataudi, he returned for a final hurrah in Australasia in 1967-68. He retired at the end, signing off in a 272-run victory at Auckland with trademark figures of 14–6–16–1 and 2–1–1–1. He finished with 88 wickets in his 41 Tests, and exactly 500 in first-class cricket.

Nadkarni was also a very useful left-hand batsman, with 14 first-class centuries and an average of 40. That included an unbeaten seven-hour 122 as India followed on in the Fifth Test of that 1963-64 series, to ensure the fifth draw. In the 1960-61 Ranji Trophy semi-final, in his first season after joining Bombay from Maharashtra, he made 283 not out against Delhi, then 96 against Rajasthan in the final, to help seal the first of his six Ranji titles.

After four productive seasons for Ramsbottom in the Lancashire League, Nadkarni filled various administrative roles at home, including a stint as a Test selector, and accompanied several tours as assistant manager. He became a sounding board for a

MOST SUCCESSIVE MAIDENS IN FIRST-CLASS CRICKET

21	**R. G. Nadkarni**	**India v England at Madras**	**1963-64**
20	M. B. Majithia	Madhya Pradesh v Railways at Indore	1999-2000
17	H. L. Hazell	Somerset v Gloucestershire at Taunton	1949
17	G. A. R. Lock	MCC v Governor-General's XI at Karachi	1955-56
17	R. A. Jadeja	India v South Africa at Delhi	2015-16
16	J. M. Cole	Natal v Eastern Province at Port Elizabeth	1963-64
15	W. S. Haig	Otago v Wellington at Dunedin	1956-57
15	M. C. Carew	West Indies v England at Port-of-Spain	1967-68
15	D. Wilson	Yorkshire v Lancashire at Sheffield	1969

Six-ball overs. For South Africa v England at Durban in 1956-57, H. J. Tayfield bowled 14 successive maiden eight-ball overs. He delivered 137 successive dot balls, Nadkarni 131.

generation of players, as Sunil Gavaskar recalled: "He was very encouraging. His favourite term was *chhoddo matt* [hang in there]. And he was very helpful in terms of strategy – he would say bring this bowler on, or ask that one to bowl round the wicket. Indian cricket has lost a real champion."

NAIK, RAJIV MANUBHAI, died of a heart attack while undergoing cancer treatment on February 20, aged 52. An aggressive batsman, Raju Naik scored two one-day hundreds for his native Baroda. He followed the second, in January 1995, with 70 from 78 balls in a Ranji Trophy match against Bombay, for whom Sachin Tendulkar replied with 175. Naik played only six first-class games, reining himself in to make 87 in 269 minutes against Saurashtra in 1992-93.

NAJEEB TARAKAI, who died on October 6, aged 29, after a road accident in Jalalabad, was an attacking opener who played 13 white-ball internationals for Afghanistan, hitting 90 in a T20 match against Ireland early in 2017. He also made six first-class centuries, four in successive games in April 2019, including 200 for Speen Ghar against Mis Ainak in Asadabad, studded with 19 sixes (only two first-class innings have contained more). Fellow players paid warm tributes – Mohammad Nabi said Najeeb's death left them "stunned and speechless" – and national captain Asghar Afghan was a pall-bearer.

NEWDICK, GRAHAM ANTHONY, who died on August 25, aged 71, was a determined opening batsman who came close to New Zealand selection during a ten-year career for Wellington. "Nudes" came to prominence with 143 – his highest score – in his fifth match, against Auckland in January 1971, and played for New Zealand Under-23 a few weeks later. He made three further centuries, and forged a solid partnership with Bruce Edgar, who remembered "not a self-centred batsman by any means – he and I shared some great opening partnerships. Overall, he was a top bloke." Newdick, who worked as a carpenter, spent his final years in England, after moving to be closer to his two sons, who had both played in Wellington age-group teams.

NURSE, LEE HARVEY, who died of Covid-19 on April 9, aged 43, was a hard-hitting batsman for Finchampstead and for the Basingstoke & North Hants club, which he captained for a time. Nurse, whose great-uncle Seymour played for West Indies, also represented Berkshire, winning the match award for his 81 in a NatWest Trophy victory over the Sussex Cricket Board in May 2000. "He was small in stature, but huge in character," remembered clubmate Julian Wood, who played for Hampshire.

OPATHA, ANTONY RALPH MARINON, died on September 11, aged 72. A tall seamer who swung the ball both ways, Tony Opatha was a pillar of Sri Lanka's national team in the 1970s. Early in 1975, he shot out Roy Fredericks, Alvin Kallicharran, Viv Richards and Clive Lloyd as the West Indians crashed to 32 for four in a tour game in Colombo. Later that year, Opatha appeared in the first World Cup, and returned for the second in 1979, but had announced his retirement by the time Sri Lanka earned Test status. Even so, he was included in a trial game before the inaugural Test, against England in February 1982, took five wickets – and was then excluded from the squad for the big match. "It hurt me," he said. "I had never been dropped in my whole life." Soon after, Opatha was involved in organising a rebel Sri Lankan tour of South Africa, ending up as player/manager of a modest side seduced by the cash. All earned 25-year bans; Opatha spent more than two decades playing and coaching in the Netherlands. Earlier, he had taken six for 91 in an unofficial Test against Pakistan at Lahore in March 1974. He accounted for Zaheer Abbas and Imran Khan in a World Cup game in 1975, and four years later took three for 31 in a historic victory against India.

OWEN, PAUL ANDREW, died of a haemorrhage on June 10, the day after his 51st birthday. Born in Canada, slow left-armer Owen was plucked from Minor Counties cricket with Bedfordshire to play for Gloucestershire in 1990, while David Graveney was recovering from a hand injury. His first-class career lasted 11 days, but included three matches, all at Cheltenham College; his four victims were all top-seven batsmen, and included Rob Bailey and Ian Greig. Owen returned to Bedfordshire, for whom he took 64 wickets; he then moved to Cheshire, where he claimed over 450 for Woodford CC.

Dan Callister Online USA Inc/Getty Images

Just a minute... Nicholas Parsons prepares to bat for the Lord's Taverners, 1999.

PARSONS, CHRISTOPHER NICHOLAS, CBE, died on January 28, aged 96. As the suave host of BBC Radio's comedy game show *Just a Minute* for more than 50 years, Nicholas Parsons became one of the most recognisable voices on the airwaves. He was also a regular on screen: straight man to comedian Arthur Haynes, part of Benny Hill's supporting cast, and host of ITV quiz *Sale of the Century*, which once attracted an audience of 21m. The son of a Clapham doctor, he often visited The Oval as a schoolboy (he could recite the pre-war Surrey team), and was there in 1948 for Don Bradman's duck in his final Test innings. Parsons turned out frequently for the Lord's Taverners; he was president in 1998 and 1999. At Lord's, he once went on the offensive against Lancashire's Jack Simmons, who eventually bowled him with an "unplayable" ball. "I thought you'd had your fun," said Simmons as Parsons walked off. And, though an occasional bowler, he dismissed Dennis Lillee at Stocketts Manor in Surrey. In 1978, he took a Taverners team to Corfu. Ken Barrington, Jack Robertson and John Price were the professionals, while celebrities included John Cleese, Brian Rix and Willie Rushton. *Mad Dogs and Cricketers*, the documentary Parsons made about the trip, is on YouTube.

PATIL, SADASHIV RAOJI, who died on September 15, aged 86, was a seamer from Maharashtra who played one Test for India, against New Zealand in 1955-56, after taking seven wickets against them for West Zone in a tour match. Patil picked up two wickets – John Reid twice – but was never called on again, although his first-class career extended to December 1963. He had made a splash on debut, against Ranji Trophy champions Bombay in 1952-53, taking five for 65, and improved on that ten years later with five for 38 against Gujarat. He also had two productive seasons in the Lancashire League.

PERERA, AJITH CHRYSANTHA STEPHEN, who died on October 29, aged 64, was on the verge of becoming an international umpire at the age of 35 when a tree fell on his car during a storm in Colombo in November 1992, and left him a paraplegic. He had been due to stand in a Test between Sri Lanka and New Zealand a few days later. Perera rebuilt his life, working to improve facilities for the disabled, writing a book about Sri Lanka's 1996 World Cup triumph, and qualifying as a scorer and an umpiring instructor. He was featured in "Cricket People" in *Wisden 2000*.

PHILLIPS, EDMUND FREDERICK, who died on February 18, aged 88, played 32 matches for Leicestershire towards the end of the 1950s, but managed only one half-century, 55 against Essex at Grace Road in July 1959. In all, he spent nine years on the Leicestershire staff, signing off with 100 not out and 92 for the Second XI in 1963.

PICKLES, DAVID, who died on June 22, aged 84, made his debut for Yorkshire at 21, and was briefly spoken of as the quickest bowler in the country. "He was so terrifyingly fast, opposing batsmen used to want to face Fred Trueman from the other end," said TV sports commentator John Helm, president of Pickles's old club Baildon. In August 1957,

THE WOMEN WISDEN MISSED

No nonsense

POLLARD, MARJORIE ANNE, JP, OBE, died on March 21, 1982, aged 82. In the 1939 edition of *Girl's Own Annual*, Marjorie Pollard laid down her philosophy: "Do girls play cricket? Can they play cricket? Should they play cricket? The answer is, without any hesitation, Yes! Yes!! Yes!!!" The exclamation marks summed up her approach: vigour, enthusiasm, unswerving commitment.

Pollard was one of the key figures in establishing women's cricket in England in the late 1920s, and ensured it prospered. She was also a talented player: for Midlands Women against the touring Australians at Edgbaston in 1937, she hit a fifty in both innings. The following summer, for the Home Counties against The Rest at Northampton, she made 75.

In the late summer of 1926, she had been among a group of women who took part in a "cricket holiday" to play matches at Malvern College. "After play was over, we sat in the Park Hotel at Colwall and discussed how cricket could become real for us – no longer to be an illusive thing that one played half afraid of ridicule. We pondered, mused, talked." That led, in October, to the formation of the Women's Cricket Association. Pollard was one of 19 present at the inaugural meeting.

She had been introduced to the game in backyard matches at home in Rugby with her father, a train driver. He delivered a message that remained ingrained, whether she was playing cricket, hockey or golf. "He always said as the ball pitched: 'Smell it, girl, smell it.' He was wiser than he knew." She attended teacher-training college, and became headmistress of the village infants' school in Boughton, Northamptonshire. On June 17, 1929, she played in the first public women's match – London & District v The Rest at Beckenham. She was out for nought, but took two wickets.

Bampton Community Archive

Marjorie's menagerie: with Jessica the donkey and a Jacob sheep.

Netta Rheinberg, who covered women's cricket for *Wisden*, described her vividly: "When bowling, she ran towards the wicket in leisurely fashion, slightly pigeon-toed, but batsmen soon found out that this was deceptive, her head and her capacious hand working intelligently in unison. As a player she was a mighty hitter, fine fielder and a resourceful captain." Pollard described her own strengths: "I am 5ft 7in in height. I am strong, and I try to get most of my runs in front of the wicket."

It was in her work as a journalist and broadcaster that she made perhaps her greatest contribution. She launched *Women's Cricket* magazine in 1929, and was editor until 1950. Its mission was to counter ignorance and patronising coverage in the mainstream media. In 1934, she wrote and published *Cricket for Women and Girls*, an introductory guide to the game. Pollard was also the first female BBC sports commentator and reporter, making her first appearance behind the microphone at a men's match in 1935. Two years later, she covered the first women's

Best of The Rest: Marjorie Pollard (front row, second left) scored an unbeaten 53 for The Rest against England Women at The Oval in June 1935. Her team-mates were, back row: Betty Belton, Megan Lowe, Joyce Haddelsey, Joan Davis, Lorna Green, Margaret Tetley. Front row: Con Holden, Pollard, Amy Bull, Violet Straker, Olive Andrews.

Tests in England, against Australia, for BBC radio. In 1951, she commentated on the first televised women's match: England v Australia at The Oval. And in 2020, a blue plaque was unveiled on the site of her former school, Peterborough County Grammar, marking her pioneering role in sports broadcasting. She also covered women's sport for *The Times*, *The Guardian*, *The Observer* and London's *Evening News*.

While international recognition eluded her at cricket, in hockey she was a star. Between 1921 and 1937, she played for England 41 times, and was a prodigious goalscorer. In 1926, she scored 13 against Wales, five against Scotland, eight against Germany and seven against Ireland. She ran *Hockey Field* magazine for 34 years, and was instrumental in bringing international matches to Wembley Stadium in the 1950s. She made a series of coaching films, which were donated to the Hockey Museum at Woking in 2017.

Pollard had clearly defined views on the development of women's cricket: no matches involving men, nor on Sundays; no league competitions nor county championships. And definitely no trousers. "I have never seen, or wish to see, a women's cricket team so garbed," she said. Her opinions did not make her universally popular. She recalled overhearing a player say: "Come on, we'd better be quick over tea, Pollard's here."

In later years, she lived in Oxfordshire, becoming the first woman to chair Witney Rural District Council. She was also a JP, and kept a herd of Jacob sheep. But in 1982, depressed by ill health, the death of her companion and the possibility of losing her house, she shot herself. She was the only female player in David Frith's 2001 study of cricket suicides, *Silence of the Heart*. Despite her impact and influence, her original *Wisden* obituary ran to just seven lines.

For too long, these obituaries largely ignored women's cricket. In the coming years, Wisden *will publish details of significant figures whose death was overlooked.*

he destroyed Somerset at Taunton with seven for 61 and five for 72. "Pickles does not move like a cricketer," wrote John Woodcock in *The Times*, "but he bowled with plenty of life." He rounded off the summer with six wickets against MCC at Scarborough, including Doug Insole and Ted Dexter for ducks. After 37 wickets at 15, he added 42 at 20 the following season – but the comet was showing signs of burning out. Pickles had apparently never been coached before arriving at Headingley and, as various people tinkered with his action, he lost rhythm and confidence. "He got some bad advice one winter about crossing his legs at delivery, and was never the same again," remembered team-mate Don Wilson. "But for a while he was a real threat to Trueman's eminence – and Fred knew it." Pickles made only eight appearances in 1959 and one in 1960 – Yorkshire won the Championship both years – and eventually left the staff.

POORE, MATT BERESFORD, who died on June 11, aged 90, was an off-spinning all-rounder who played 14 Tests for New Zealand without finishing on the winning side. In his first, against South Africa at Auckland in March 1953, he scored 45 and took two wickets in each innings – but never improved on these performances, despite touring South Africa and the subcontinent. Poore had better luck at home with Canterbury, making 142 against Central Districts at Lancaster Park on New Year's Eve 1954, and 103 against Auckland two seasons later. Poore had an eventful time in India in 1955-56. In one game, he seemed to fall asleep in the field, a reaction to medication, and later had to undergo regular rabies shots after being bitten by a dog during a game in Bangalore. "Matt had a stomach injection every day for 14 days, during which he was playing a Test – not the most comfortable preparation," wrote New Zealand's captain, John Reid. "All and sundry had a jab at his stomach at some stage, and it got to be quite a little game – except, of course, for Matt." There seemed to be no lasting effects: Poore ended the tour with a career-best five for 27, against Indian Universities, though never appeared for New Zealand again.

POWELL, PETER WILLIAM GEORGE, who died on April 19, aged 94, was an architect and town planner who oversaw large-scale projects in Baghdad and Dacca, before becoming a planning and housing advisor for the whole of Pakistan. While in Lahore he met his future wife, and converted to Islam before they returned to England in 1966. A lifelong cricket enthusiast whose cousin was Tom Graveney, Powell co-wrote the *Wisden Guide to Cricket Grounds* with his son, William, and the journalist Alex Bannister.

PRASADIKA LIYANAGE, GUSTHINGHA LIYANAGE POOJANI, died in a road accident in Kurunegala on June 15, aged 33. Leg-spinner Poojani Prasadika Liyanage played for Sri Lanka A in a tri-series against Australia A and the England Academy in 2015-16, and not long after took six for 19 for Colts CC against the Army. She had also played for Colombo CC, and took up scoring after helping Galle win the Women's Super Provincial Tournament in December 2018.

PRESTON, Dr DAVID GEORGE, who died on June 22, aged 80, was the son and grandson of *Wisden* editors, Norman and Hubert, who between them were in charge of the Almanack from 1944 to 1980. David did not continue the dynasty, but remained a huge enthusiast for both the book and the game, while teaching languages, mainly in Reading. Perhaps his life's most significant work was closer to the real Bible: a devout Nonconformist, he reworked all 150 psalms, many of them published in *The Book of Praises* and *Praise!* The Christian writer Christopher Idle called them "meticulously crafted… accurate and truly poetic".

PRITCHARD, GRAHAM CHARLES, who died on October 26, 2019, aged 77, was a seamer who played several matches for Cambridge University, winning a Blue under the captaincy of Mike Brearley in 1964. At Lord's, opening the bowling with Richard Hutton, he took three wickets as Oxford were dismissed for 142. The previous year, Pritchard's three wickets and a run-out reduced Surrey to five for four at Guildford; he finished with a career-best six for 51. "He was a strong young man, with a big stride when he bowled – he put a lot of effort into it," said Brearley, who also recalled a notable victim when the

Australians visited Fenner's in 1964. "He bowled Bill Lawry for seven, behind his legs, I think. The ball ran down to fine leg, and Lawry ran two, but the bail was on the ground. He looked a bit flummoxed, but left the field without a protest. No one seemed quite sure what had happened. Afterwards he admitted that when he 'looked back and saw the bail lying on the ground, the outlook wasn't too rosy'." Pritchard later played occasionally for Essex. A genuine No. 11, he averaged four in first-class cricket, his last six innings being scoreless.

PROCTER, ANTHONY WILFRED, died on March 21, aged 76. A medium-paced all-rounder who batted left-handed, Anton Procter played four first-class matches in South Africa in 1966-67, three alongside his more famous younger brother, Mike; their father, Woodrow, also played first-class cricket. "We grew up holding the feistiest of battles in our yard," wrote Mike. Anton was long involved in horse racing, as an owner, trainer and breeder – plus a hectic period as a bookmaker.

PROVERBS, NIGEL GORDON, died while watching the World Cup on television on July 12, 2019, aged 95. A member of a famous Bajan sporting family, Gordon Proverbs played six first-class matches at a time of spasmodic inter-island competition. His highest score of 84 came in Barbados's record total, 753 against Jamaica at Bridgetown in January 1952. He later lived in New Zealand, and played club cricket in Nelson.

RAFI NASIM, COLONEL, who died on December 7, aged 90, was a colourful figure in Pakistan cricket. A request to help produce a souvenir for MCC's visit in 1951-52 was the first assignment of a career in cricket journalism that lasted more than 50 years, and survived a stint in the army. After two spells as the Pakistan board's secretary, he was also an approachable media manager. He was popular with the players – at least until a spat with Imran Khan during a one-day international against West Indies at Peshawar in 1985-86. It concerned the quality of the umpiring, prompting Rafi to ask which officials the captain would prefer – and Imran, a long-time advocate of neutral umpires, ordered him out of the dressing-room. Rafi demanded an apology, but never received one. His second spell as board secretary ended not long afterwards.

RAIJI, VASANT NAISADRAI, who died on June 20, aged 100, was steeped in every aspect of cricket. His fascination dated from December 1933, when as a teenager he watched Lala Amarnath score India's maiden century in their first home Test, against England at the Bombay Gymkhana. Raiji was a good enough batsman to play for the powerful Bombay side in the Ranji Trophy, and later represented Baroda, making 68 and 53 against Maharashtra at Poona in 1944-45. A chartered accountant, he also wrote several books – prized by collectors – on famous players, including Ranjitsinhji, Duleepsinhji, C. K. Nayudu and Victor Trumper, as well as general cricket history. Sachin Tendulkar and Steve Waugh paid a visit to mark Raiji's 100th birthday early in 2020, and helped him cut a large cake. "Steve and I had a wonderful time listening to some amazing cricket stories about the past," said Tendulkar.

RAJASINGHAM, MURUGIAH, who died on September 8, in his late eighties, was the assistant secretary of the Sri Lankan board from 1973 to 1978. He was the liaison officer during Sri Lanka's inaugural Test, against England early in 1982, and assistant manager on their first Test tour of England in 1984. Born in Kandy, he represented Colts CC and the Sinhalese Sports Club, and was also a good hockey player.

RAJESH, MADRAS PRASANTH, died of a heart attack on October 5, aged 35. Prasanth Rajesh was a leg-spinner and excellent fielder who played for Tamil Nadu's age-group teams and in its leagues, alongside Ravichandran Ashwin. His three first-class appearances all came in domestic cricket in Sri Lanka, for Badureliya in January 2018; he took five for 41 against the Army in the second, and finished with eight in the match.

RAJPUT, SUSHANT SINGH, was found hanged at his Mumbai home on June 14. He was 34. Rajput was an Indian actor best known for his portrayal of the title character in the 2016 biopic *M. S. Dhoni: The Untold Story*, which earned him a nomination for Bollywood's

Filmfare awards. Not a natural cricketer, he practised for ten months with the former Test wicketkeeper Kiran More, once straining his back attempting to replicate Dhoni's signature helicopter shot. Rajput was often seen at IPL matches, and became friendly with several of the players; reports suggested he had been suffering from depression.

RAKA, TUKU, died on March 29, aged 56. Energetic fast-bowling all-rounder "Thunder" Raka followed his father into the Papua New Guinea side, and played for them at five ICC Trophy tournaments, the first in England in 1986. In the 1990 edition, he slapped 59 not out from No. 9 against Argentina, then took three for 28. Seven years later, in Malaysia, he claimed four early wickets as Bermuda dipped to 42 for five. "Tuku was regarded as the country's No. 1 bowler from 1986 to 2001," said the local board. Raka also helped his Port Moresby club, Hoods, win several titles.

RAMCHAND GOALA, who died on June 19, aged 79, was a coach in Mymensingh, in Bangladesh, and an early mentor of Test all-rounder Mahmudullah. A slow left-armer, Goala had a few matches for the national team in the 1980s, when already past 40 – he dismissed Arjuna Ranatunga when Sri Lanka toured in 1984-85 – and played high-standard club cricket into his fifties.

RANAWEERA, TANAWEERA ACHCHIGE VAJIRA HEMANTHA KUMARA, died of a heart attack on April 28, aged 51. An enthusiastic fast bowler, Vajira Ranaweera played 96 first-class matches for Colombo's Police Sports Club over a dozen seasons from 1995-96. His best performance came in January 1998, when eight for 95 against Bloomfield included a number of future Sri Lankan internationals. He also once took seven for six in a club game against Bloomfield. He claimed more first-class wickets (255) than he scored runs (234). Ranaweera qualified as an umpire, but had little time for it as his police duties increased; he rose to the rank of chief inspector.

RANDALL, CHARLES ALFRED, died on January 31, aged 71. Charlie Randall was on the sports staff of *The Daily Telegraph* from 1979 to 2006, latterly spending his summers on the cricket circuit. In the rumbustious press boxes of the era, he was self-contained, and perceived as rather earnest. One day, when he was covering a Hampshire match at Bournemouth and mooching with colleagues near the boundary, the ball raced towards him. Still carrying on the conversation, he nonchalantly picked it up and sent it fizzing into the keeper's gloves. From that moment he won respect. In fact, he was a very fine batsman in Hertfordshire club cricket and scored heavily for Radlett over many years, making his final century while captaining the Fifth XI aged 64. He began in journalism as sports editor of *The Herts Advertiser*; his innate modesty, it was said, obliged him to censor his own high scores from the match reports. After leaving the *Telegraph* he maintained his love of club cricket, acting as "writer-in-residence" for the Club Cricket Conference and running his own lively blog, concentrating on the recreational game.

RAYMENT, ALAN WILLIAM HARRINGTON, who died on October 27, aged 92, carved out an unusual career: county cricketer and dance instructor. It gave him an original take on his fellow professionals: "Derek Shackleton, when he ran up and bowled, was wonderfully upright and elegant, like Fred Astaire, whereas Fred Trueman was down and muscular, like Gene Kelly." Rayment spent ten summers with Hampshire, where his run-scoring rarely did justice to his talent. But, whether batting, or prowling the covers, his footwork always drew admiration.

Born in Finchley, he was on the staff at Middlesex when he caught Hampshire's eye in a Second XI match at Bournemouth in June 1948. He resisted the wiles of slow left-armer Reg Dare to hit 40, and ran out county coach Arthur Holt with a direct hit. It led to a two-year, £5-a-week contract the following summer, although he had an early reprimand from captain and coach Desmond Eagar for smiling, regardless of how he had fared: "That sort of thing doesn't go down well in Hampshire, you know."

Admirable footwork: Alan Rayment, county cricketer and dance instructor, 1954.

Back at Bournemouth in September 1950, he made 58 and 94, as Gloucestershire's Tom Goddard and Sam Cook spun Hampshire to defeat. John Arlott thought them the two best innings by a young player he had seen that season: "He never played a reckless stroke at a good ball [and] never failed to punish a bad ball." But his first hundred did not come until 1952, when he passed 1,000 runs for the first time.

Rayment, always known as "Punchy", and his wife, Betty, were both qualified dance teachers, and set up a school in a hotel near Northlands Road. He often went straight there to take a class after close of play. Team-mates would sometimes turn up; only Peter Sainsbury persevered, though he drew the line at the tango. "He thought it was a bit too sexy," said Rayment. Later, Alan and Betty branched out into rock and roll, and opened a ballroom in the city centre.

Perhaps his best innings came at Weston-super-Mare in August 1955, when he hit 104 against Somerset, who were bowled out for 37 (Shackleton eight for four) and 98 (Shackleton six for 25). "I danced up and down the wicket a bit," he said. He made exactly 1,000 runs in 1956, but retired two years later, having never averaged more than 23 in a season. He spent the next summer on the coaching staff at Lord's, turning down the post of head coach. After divorce from Betty, and the end of the dance business, he embarked on a remarkably diverse career: prep-school teacher, estate agent, social worker, psychotherapist, bereavement counsellor. In 2013, he published *Punchy Through the Covers*, a 384-page autobiography that took his story as far as 1949. Friends are planning to publish volume two. "I have always had a curiosity about life and people," he told the writer Stephen Chalke. "And curiosity is the key to learning."

RAZICK, GNANI SHEIKHABDULCADER MOHAMED SHENI ABDUL, died on October 26, 2019, aged 76. All-rounder Ghulam Razick, from the Moors club, played five first-class matches for Ceylon teams in the 1960s, including against the 1968-69 MCC tourists. He took the first three wickets – John Edrich, Roger Prideaux and Keith Fletcher – in a 60-over game in Colombo.

REID, JOHN FULTON, who died on December 28, aged 64, was a left-hander from Auckland, attractive and adhesive, who had a short but successful Test career for New Zealand. It started during his breakthrough season of 1978-79, which included a maiden century against Northern Districts. Propelled into the Test side after scoring 85 and 40 for a Young New Zealand XI against the Pakistan tourists, he began with a duck against Imran Khan. Recalled two years later, he soon collected 123 not out in more than seven hours against India at Christchurch.

Reid could be difficult to shift: he converted six of his eight Test fifties into hundreds (there was also a 97). His 180 in scorching conditions in Colombo in March 1984 occupied 685 minutes, New Zealand's fourth-longest innings. "I loved his poise, calmness and lateness of stroke," wrote Martin Crowe. "He was as fine a player of spin as you could ever bat with."

Early in 1985, Reid reached 1,000 Test runs in his 20th innings – a New Zealand record later equalled by Mark Richardson – during an eight-hour undefeated 158 to set up an innings victory over Pakistan at Auckland. Shortly afterwards, he missed a tour of the Caribbean to concentrate on his job as a geography teacher, which some put down to a reluctance to face

HIGHEST TEST AVERAGES FOR NEW ZEALAND

		T	*I*	*NO*	*Runs*	*HS*	*100*	*50*	*Debut*
65.72	C. S. Dempster	10	15	4	723	136	2	5	1929-30
54.31	K. S. Williamson	83	144	13	7,115	251	24	32	2010-11
52.90	M. P. Donnelly	7	12	1	582	206	1	4	1937
46.28	**J. F. Reid**	**19**	**31**	**3**	**1,296**	**180**	**6**	**2**	**1978-79**
45.83	L. R. P. L. Taylor	105	183	22	7,379	290	19	34	2007-08
45.36	M. D. Crowe	77	131	11	5,444	299	17	18	1981-82
44.77	M. H. Richardson	38	65	3	2,776	145	4	19	2000-01
44.64	G. M. Turner	41	73	6	2,991	259	7	14	1968-69
44.27	A. H. Jones	39	74	8	2,922	186	7	11	1986-87
43.91	H. M. Nicholls	37	55	6	2,152	174	7	10	2015-16

As at January 25, 2021. Qualification: 10 innings.

West Indies. But Martin Snedden, an Auckland and New Zealand team-mate, disagreed: "You always heard sceptical backroom chat about John's ability to play fast bowling at that level, but look at his Test record – it's unbelievable against good pace and spin attacks."

Reid returned later that year for a memorable jaunt across the Tasman Sea, when one of New Zealand's greatest teams won a series in Australia for the first (and still only) time. They were spearheaded by Richard Hadlee, but Reid's 108 – in a partnership of 224 with Crowe – helped establish an impregnable position in the First Test at Brisbane, where Hadlee took 15 wickets. "It wasn't an easy, flat pitch, and I proved I could score a hundred outside subcontinent or spin-dominated attacks," Reid told *The New Zealand Herald*.

He played in the return series at home but then, barely 30, returned to teaching. His retirement meant he missed the 1986 tour of England, opponents he never faced in a Test match. He was tempted out of the schoolroom a few years later, becoming the first chief executive of Auckland Cricket, before running New Zealand's high-performance scheme, and a brief spell as the national team's caretaker coach. "He was the most lovely, engaging man, who inspired all those around him, including generations of young men and women cricketers," said NZC's chief executive, David White.

He was not related to New Zealand's other John Reid (below), but was a cousin of Australia's left-arm seamer Bruce Reid, who dismissed him in a Test at Wellington in 1985-86.

REID, JOHN RICHARD, CNZM, OBE, died on October 14, aged 92. If John Reid had been born in Australia, he might have been a superstar; instead, he settled for becoming the cornerstone of a New Zealand team which, in his time, often lacked depth. From his debut in 1949, he played in 58 successive Tests until he retired after the 1965 tour of England. For the previous ten years he had been captain, and led his country to their first Test victory – over West Indies at Auckland in 1955-56 – after 26 years of trying. New Zealand journalist John Mehaffey wrote: "Through his unflagging enthusiasm and drive, Reid helped keep the faltering flame of New Zealand cricket alight in the dark days of the 1950s, when the nation's Test status was questioned after they were dismissed for 26 by England."

Richard Hadlee, one of the few rivals to Reid's status as his country's greatest player, said: "If he was playing today, he certainly would have made a wonderful one-day international cricketer and would have done pretty well in the Twenty20 format. The impact he had on the game during his time was extraordinary."

Like many of his compatriots, Reid was drawn to rugby – but two bouts of rheumatic fever meant he eventually concentrated on cricket. He started as a fast bowler, before a knee injury caused him to throttle back, and he was always an agile fielder. But it was his batting that took the eye, initially as the 20-year-old baby of the strong New Zealand side that toured England in 1949. Accorded only three-day Tests, they drew all four; from then until 2019, Tests in England were scheduled for at least five days. Reid had played only seven previous first-class matches, scoring a maiden century in the last trial game before selection, but added four more on the way to nearly 1,500 runs in England, including 188 not out against Cambridge University, when he shared a stand of 324 with Merv Wallace. He made 50 on debut in the Third Test, and top-scored with 93 in the Fourth at The Oval, where he showed his versatility by keeping wicket. "Reid grew noticeably in stature as the tour progressed," wrote John Arlott, adding presciently: "He should be a considerable pillar of New Zealand batting for 20 years to come."

Chances to improve, at international level at least, were few: New Zealand's home Tests were usually afterthoughts once a tired touring team had taken on Australia. Overseas trips were also rare, although Reid did manage a maiden Test century at Cape Town in 1953-54. The following season, he was part of the side that collapsed to that Test-low of 26 at Auckland, after starting their second innings only 46 behind England. "It was a freak occasion," he recalled. "We thought we had a sniff of a victory, and ended up being beaten by an innings. Frank Tyson just steamed in and let it go at you at frightening pace – we'd never been subjected to that sort of pace. But let's not forget, he had destroyed the Australian batting too that summer."

Around this time, Reid was spending the northern summers with Heywood in the Central Lancashire League, but he knocked back several approaches to qualify for English counties, which would probably have ended his Test career. "During my time in the leagues, I received five offers (from Leicester, Northants, Worcester, Gloucester, Warwick) but preferred to play my cricket in New Zealand during those league off-seasons."

After an enervating tour of India in 1955-56 – he made centuries at Delhi and Calcutta – Reid took over as captain during the home series against West Indies which produced the long-awaited win. His 84 set up a crucial lead of 110 at Auckland, before West Indies were skittled for 77. "For once, it wasn't us that bowled the one loose ball each over, or dropped the vital catch," said a relieved Reid. One sadness was that Bert Sutcliffe, New Zealand's

---

TOP OF THE CLASS

New Zealand's Test records when John Reid retired in 1965:

Most caps		**Most wickets**	
J. R. Reid	58	**J. R. Reid**	85
B. Sutcliffe	42	A. R. MacGibbon	70
A. R. MacGibbon	26	F. J. Cameron	62
Most runs		**Most catches in the field**	
J. R. Reid	3,428	**J. R. Reid**	39
B. Sutcliffe	2,727	B. Sutcliffe	20
G. T. Dowling	995	A. R. MacGibbon	13

PA Images/Alamy

Warm reception: John Reid, captain of the touring New Zealanders, meets Learie Constantine, 1965.

only other Test-class batsman during Reid's time, missed the match through illness; he never finished on the winning side in his 42 Tests. "If Sutcliffe wasn't playing, I was the only player in the team who could score a Test century," said Reid. "In the 1980s, they had six or seven. You do feel it's all on you, and that can weigh you down."

New Zealand's next overseas venture, to England in 1958, was a disaster: only rain at The Oval prevented a 5–0 defeat, as callow batting failed to cope with the left-arm spin of Tony Lock, who took 34 wickets at seven apiece on helpful pitches. Reid, at least, had a satisfactory trip, scoring more than 1,400 runs, and was one of Wisden's Five Cricketers of the Year.

It was more than three years before they toured again, to South Africa. Now aged 33, and at his peak, Reid hammered 1,915 runs at 68 in all matches on the trip, setting an aggregate record for a South African season that still stands. Of those, 546 came in an absorbing Test series in which his side twice came from behind to draw 2–2. A measured 142 at Johannesburg – after both openers fell for ducks – was the highest of his six Test centuries. "I wrote that Reid was 'another Stan McCabe'," said R. S. Whitington, the Australian journalist. "Indeed, I now seriously doubt whether that was a fitting description of the Reid of 1961-62. Perhaps 'a Compton–McCabe combined' would have approached nearer to adequacy." John Waite, South Africa's long-serving wicketkeeper, was similarly impressed: "John is one of the strongest, if not *the* strongest batsman I have seen." Reid himself admitted he was "a bit of a thumper".

He took his form home: the following season, he blitzed 296 in 220 minutes for Wellington against Northern Districts. His 15 sixes were a world record until 1995, when Andrew Symonds hit 16 in a county game at Abergavenny. Among the opposition bowlers that day at the Basin Reserve was a frustrated Don Clarke, better known as a granite-hard full-back for the All Blacks. He unleashed a head-high beamer at Reid, who coolly hooked it out of the ground: onlookers remember it pinging off a nearby floodlight pylon with the sound of a tuning fork.

The final chapter of Reid's career was an ambitious ten-Test tour of India, Pakistan and England that occupied the first seven months of 1965: not for nothing did he call his 1966 autobiography *A Million Miles of Cricket*. At Calcutta, the Indian seamer Ramakant "Tiny" Desai started with a bouncer barrage. "Desai tried to knock my head off," said Reid. "He was a medium-pacer, a little wee fellow. Wrong guy. Four sixes in ten balls before lunch."

Even so, New Zealand lost both series in Asia, and it was a familiar story on juicy tracks in England: all three Tests were lost. Reid nursed a dodgy knee through the trip, and retired at the end, aged 37. "I had devoted my time and energy to cricket almost from the day I left school," he said, "and in recent years such application had been increasingly difficult." He was a popular visitor, and was touched when BBC viewers voted for him to captain a World XI for an end-of-season festival match.

In retirement, Reid set up a sports complex at home in Wellington which helped popularise squash in New Zealand, and was a national selector. He then lived in South Africa for a while, and was later one of the first ICC referees; he oversaw 50 Tests, reporting Shoaib Akhtar's bowling action, and 98 ODIs, enraging Pakistan by banning Waqar Younis for ball-tampering. Reid had been the oldest surviving New Zealand Test player, a mantle that passed to Trevor McMahon. His son, Richard, played nine one-day internationals.

One of Reid's stranger claims to fame was his participation in the first organised cricket at the South Pole, in 1969; the wicket was the barber-shop-style post that marked the Pole itself. The game ended when a big Reid hit was lost in a snowdrift; it was noted that wherever he hit the ball, it travelled north.

REZA-E-KARIM, who died on March 22, aged 82, was the first secretary of the Bangladesh Cricket Board, in 1976-77, having helped restart cricket in the country after Independence in 1971. He was buried in the Martyred Intellectuals Graveyard in Mirpur, near the national stadium.

RIAZ SHEIKH, who died of Covid-19 on June 2, aged 51, was a leg-spinning all-rounder who played 43 first-class matches in Pakistan. He took seven for 71 in his second, in 1986-87, and a career-best eight for 60 for Karachi Whites against Multan in the third, his haul including the young Inzamam-ul-Haq. Riaz also hit three centuries, the highest 132 against Islamabad in 1998-99. He had captained the future Test wicketkeeper Moin Khan in age-group cricket, and became head coach at Moin's academy in Karachi.

RICHARDSON, BERTRAM HAROLD, died on September 24, aged 88. Slow left-armer Bert Richardson was given a chance by Derbyshire in 1950, when only 18, after taking ten wickets in a Second XI match against Warwickshire. He claimed eight Hampshire wickets at Derby that July, including a career-best four for 39, but generally proved unpenetrative. Not helped by a slipped disc in 1951, he left the staff two years later, with 33 wickets from 27 matches.

RICHARDSON, BRIAN DOUGLAS, who died on April 28, aged 87, was a member of a prominent Hobart sporting family: his father, uncle and four brothers also played interstate cricket. Tasmania had few first-class opportunities before joining the Sheffield Shield in 1977-78, but Richardson grabbed one of his: 112 against Mike Smith's 1965-66 England touring team at Launceston. "One look at him as he came in, embedded in a long-sleeve sweater when everyone else was too hot in shirtsleeves, revealed a stubborn streak," wrote John Woodcock in *The Times*. "He was an irritating little man to bowl at, yet before long a good eye was enabling him to go along at quite a lively rate." A horticulturist, Richardson worked for the Department of Agriculture for 40 years, ten in Kashmir as director of a World Bank aid project.

RIKA, JOSEFA FALANI, died on February 3 of complications after an asthma attack, aged 32. A left-hander who also bowled serviceable off-spin, Joe Rika first played for Fiji in 2006, and the following year, while captaining their Under-19s, hammered 257 off 145 balls against Japan. He led Fiji until 2015, and had been working as their high performance manager. "He was one of the best cricketers to come out of the Pacific islands," said the Fijian board's chief executive, Alex Konrote. "The face of Cricket Fiji for more than a decade."

ROBSON, BRIAN, who died on May 1, aged 84, was Nottinghamshire's secretary from 1982 to 2000, after three years as the club's accountant. They had been in a poor financial state, but under his stewardship turnover rose from around £250,000 a year to £4m, and the Radcliffe and Hound Road stands at Trent Bridge were redeveloped. When Robson retired, Nottinghamshire's president Albert Bocking observed: "His ability to remain diplomatic, courteous and retain a dry sense of humour in endless committee meetings was a rare talent."

ROSEBERRY, MATTHEW, died on February 6, aged 75. A successful local businessman, Matty Roseberry was one of the guiding hands behind Durham's rise to first-class status in 1992. One of his early cricket ventures was an indoor school in Houghton-le-Spring, near Sunderland, which he set up with the former England rugby international Mike Weston; both had two sons who went on to play first-class cricket. Mike Roseberry, who scored 2,044 runs for Middlesex in 1992, moved to Durham three years later as captain, despite being advised against it by his father. It ended in tears when Mike was relieved of the job late in 1996 (he eventually returned to Lord's), and Matty left the county's board. His other son, Andrew, played a few matches for Leicestershire and Glamorgan.

RUSSELL, ROBERT PAUL, died on January 20, 2018, aged 69. In 2006, after securing funding from the local city council, Glamorgan's chairman Paul Russell announced: "We're bringing the Ashes to Cardiff!" Three years later, the 2009 series started at the remodelled Sophia Gardens; England secured a draw, thanks to heroic resistance from James Anderson and Monty Panesar. Russell stepped down in 2011, after eight years in the Glamorgan hot seat. He was also an influential president of Ebbw Vale rugby club, guiding them through the seismic changes that accompanied rugby union's move to professionalism. Russell's brother, Marcus, was the manager of rock group Oasis.

SCOTT, MALCOLM ERNEST, who died on September 11, aged 84, was a gifted all-round sportsman who played football and county cricket. A centre-half, he made his debut for Newcastle United against Manchester United at Old Trafford in January 1957 and, though never a regular, stayed at St James' Park until 1961, later playing for Darlington and York City. His cricket career started with Durham when he was 17. Three years later, in 1956, he flourished for the Minor Counties XI against the touring Australians at Jesmond: 53 and 59, with four sixes off fellow slow left-armer Jack Wilson, and the wickets of Richie Benaud and Ron Archer.

National service intervened, but Northamptonshire showed an interest, and Scott made his Championship debut in 1960, not long after taking ten wickets against Cambridge University at Wantage Road. He was still playing football, but gradually cricket took over, and he was capped by Northamptonshire in 1964, his best season. His 113 wickets that year included seven for 32 (and 13 for 94 in the match, both career-bests) against Sussex at Hastings, with Ted Dexter dismissed twice. Keith Andrew, his captain and wicketkeeper, remembered: "Malcolm was extremely accurate, and he had a lovely loop to his flight. His trouble was that he didn't have a positive enough attitude. He wasn't aggressive. I never appealed unless I thought the batsman was out – but Malcolm never appealed at all."

Injuries restricted him over the next couple of summers, before a bombshell in 1967. Scott recalled: "My left shoulder was giving me problems, and a lot of pain even after receiving treatment. At the same time, one or two of my colleagues alerted me that my quicker-ball delivery was getting very jerky at the elbow." It wasn't just his colleagues: umpires reported Scott to Lord's and, at a time when suspect actions were seen as a worldwide problem, he was suspended late in the season. Several others had their actions reported, but Scott was the only one singled out for a ban: "It seemed Lord's wanted a scapegoat." He returned in 1968, but collected only 46 wickets in 23 matches, and left the county after playing a few games in 1969. He coached sport in schools for many years.

SEDGLEY, JOHN BRIAN, died on November 29, aged 81. Jack Sedgley never quite made the step up from Worcestershire's Second XI, for whom he hit three centuries. He did score 95 against Derbyshire in June 1960, but there was just one other half-century, and he played only twice in 1961 before returning to the Birmingham League, where he remained a heavy scorer for West Bromwich Dartmouth and Old Hill, among others. Sedgley finished at Dudley, where he had a lucky escape at their old Tipton Road ground in 1985: while he was manning the heavy roller before a match, an 80-foot hole opened up over some former mine workings. One of the players recalled: "We arrived, and there was Jack staring into a huge abyss that was meant to be the outfield." Dudley had to pull out of the league, and never played at the ground again.

SEMMENCE, DEREK JOHN, who died on March 29, aged 81, made just 35 appearances for Sussex, but claimed a record that remains intact. At Trent Bridge in July 1956, aged 18 years 85 days, he became the county's youngest first-class centurion. But the potential displayed in his elegant strokeplay that damp Saturday was never fulfilled. "He was an attractive player, a very good striker of the ball," said team-mate Jim Parks, the previous holder of the record. "But we had a pretty good side, and it was hard work getting into the team. In another era, he would have played more."

It did not stop Semmence becoming an instantly recognisable figure in Sussex cricket. He was coach at Hurstpierpoint College for 29 years – his pupils included the county's future wicketkeeper-batsman Martin Speight – captain of the Over-50s, 60s and 70s teams, and a familiar face at Hove and Arundel. "He was a wonderful man, a fine cricketer, superb coach and always so generous, modest and understated," said the former Sussex captain John Barclay.

Semmence made 18 appearances in 1956. Without passing 50, he had made some promising scores (and collected a pair against Brian Statham) before his century at Nottingham. "He sorted out the one to hit, and drove with a fluent swing, and his cutting was firm and clean," wrote H. L. V. Day in *The Sunday Times*.

But his progress was disrupted by national service, and he played only a handful of games, with modest results, on his full-time return to Sussex in 1959. He did not get on with the coach George Cox, and his contract was cancelled after Cox wrote to the cricket committee saying he would not listen to advice. Semmence always regretted that this fractious relationship had cost him his first-class career.

He made one appearance for Essex in 1962, before returning to Sussex to play six games in 1967 and 1968. He also played in the Minor Counties Championship for Devon, Northumberland and Cambridgeshire.

In 1959, Prince Y. S. Shatrusalyasinhji, a descendant of Ranjit and Duleep, had a brief trial at Sussex; he and Semmence quickly formed a friendship. Shatrusalyasinhji became the last Jam Saheb of Nawanagar, and Semmence made more than 30 trips to India, where he lived in royal palaces, and played and coached as the maharajah's guest. Teams from Hurstpierpoint contested two-day matches against Rajkumar College. "Over Christmas in 1985-86, we beat them for the first time," said Speight. "We won a big silver trophy, but then struggled to get it out past Indian customs because it was a valuable heirloom."

Semmence coached Bangladesh in the 1990s, before Test status, and in 2007 was

Sussex Cricket Museum

Youthful potential: Derek Semmence, May 1956.

asked by IPL founder Lalit Modi to coach junior squads in Rajasthan. "He taught the basics without stifling natural ability," said Speight. "He became a mentor to me, always the first on the phone if I was having a bad patch. I would not have become a first-class cricketer if I had not been coached by Derek."

SEWARD, DAVID GEORGE, who died on October 12, aged 76, was a popular secretary of Somerset and Surrey, who oversaw the construction of the vast Bedser Stand at The Oval's pavilion end. After leaving Surrey in 1992, he worked at Woking FC, before going to live in Australia. Seward was an accomplished musician, and played the organ at the memorial service for Geoffrey Howard, another Surrey secretary, at St Mark's Church near The Oval in 2003.

SHAHID MAHMOOD, who died on December 13, aged 81, was a left-handed all-rounder from Karachi who was one of only seven men whose CV boasted a first-class double-century and a ten-for. A good off-side player, he hit 220 for Karachi University against Peshawar University; more than a decade later, he took ten for 58 for Karachi Whites against Khairpur at the National Stadium in September 1969, mixing his usual left-arm medium-pacers with

A MAGNIFICENT SEVEN

Players to score a double-century and take ten wickets in an innings in first-class cricket:

	First 200	*First 10-for*
T. E. Bailey	205 (1947)	10-90 (1949)
G. Giffen	203 (1887-88)	10-66 (1883-84)
W. G. Grace	224* (1866)	10-92 (1873)
V. W. C. Jupp	217* (1914)	10-127 (1932)
F. A. Tarrant	206 (1907-08)	10-90 (1918-19)
Shahid Mahmood	**220 (1958-59)**	**10-58 (1969-70)**
S. M. J. Woods	215 (1895)	10-69 (1890)

Grace scored 13 double-centuries in all, and took ten wickets in an innings twice. Giffen and Tarrant scored four doubles.

the occasional spinner. He was the first Pakistani to take all ten in a first-class game, although he had done it before in a lesser match – in England in 1958, for the touring Pakistan Eaglets against the Isle of Wight (where he also scored a hundred).

Shahid won one Test cap, at Trent Bridge in 1962: he opened in the first innings with Hanif Mohammad, making 16, and adding nine down the order in the second. He had started the tour with a century in a one-day game at Eastbourne, but had a quiet time after that, although he did make an unbeaten 77 against Lancashire. He eventually settled in the United States, where he ran a successful advertising business, and advised presidents Reagan and Bush senior on issues concerning the Islamic community in America.

SINCLAIR, IAN McKAY, who died on August 25, 2019, aged 86, was an off-spinner from Canterbury who played two Tests for New Zealand in 1955-56. He took only one wicket, but it was distinguished: Everton Weekes, after he made 103 at Christchurch. Both matches were lost, and Sinclair was left out for the final Test, at Auckland, so missed New Zealand's first victory, although he was on hand as twelfth man. He had clinched a place with four wickets in the tourists' match against Canterbury, including Garry Sobers, which followed a good Plunket Shield season – 22 wickets at 18, with a career-best five for 65 against Central Districts. Sinclair played only three more first-class games after that summer, though in club cricket he captained Riccarton to the local title in 1962-63. He was married, to Azalea, for 63 years.

SINGH, DR HARJIT, who died on October 19, aged 70, was a tireless worker for cricket in Malaysia. After graduating from university in India, he returned home and captained the national team in 1980. He played for many years for Johor province, and as the association's president from 1986 oversaw the construction of a new ground, which hosted several matches in the Under-19 World Cup in 2007-08, and of its indoor school, the first in south-east Asia. According to *Free Malaysia Today*, "he honed, toned and burnished cricket to an A-list shine".

SMITH, CLEON, who died of a heart condition on May 28, aged 60, had been the head coach of the Jamaican women's team – several times regional champions – for ten years, bringing on the likes of Stafanie Taylor and Shanel Daley. "He dedicated his life to coaching the game at community, school and regional levels," said Jimmy Adams, the former Test captain who is now West Indies' director of cricket.

SMITH, COLIN MILNER, died on July 10, aged 83. A wicketkeeper, he had the misfortune to be at Oxford at the same time as the future Test keeper A. C. Smith, and played just one first-class game, against Sussex in 1958. An old boy of Tonbridge School, he was on the winning side in the Cricketer Cup finals of 1976 (when he put on 80 with Colin Cowdrey) and 1979 (alongside Chris Cowdrey). His brother, Martin, captained in those finals, and also played one first-class match, for Cambridge University in 1961. Colin's distinguished career culminated in 1991 in his appointment as a circuit judge.

SMITH, JACK, who died on May 7, aged 84, captained Bedfordshire between 1962 and 1973, a spell that included their only two outright Minor Counties Championship titles. Smith's accurate off-breaks, allied to the leg-spin of Graham Jarrett, played a big part in those successes: they shared 97 wickets in 1970, and 74 in 1972. Overall, Smith took 463 wickets at 17 for Bedfordshire, while for the Minor Counties XI against the Australians in 1964, he had figures of 21.1–11–22–3, his first victim being Bill Lawry. The following year, he played his only first-class match, against the South Africans – and took four wickets, including Denis Lindsay (twice) and Colin Bland. Smith was also a rugby regular for Bedford at full-back, and represented the Barbarians. A car dealer, he was jailed for four years in 1981 for insurance fraud.

SMITH, ROY, who died on September 22, aged 90, was snapped up by Somerset after taking 117 wickets at eight with his slow left-armers for the Devon club Instow while still in his teens. At Taunton, Smith became more of a batsman, and after national service he was briefly a regular. His best season was 1953, when he made 100 against Worcestershire at Frome – earning his county cap – and an unbeaten 77 against the Australian tourists to help Somerset recover from 19 for four. He finished with 1,176 runs. But his form fell away, and he left the staff after no first-team appearances in 1956. He became a maths teacher, ran the cricket and football at his old school, Huish's GS, and played for Devon, hitting 150 against Cornwall in 1959.

SOOD, MAN MOHAN, who died on January 19, aged 80, was a batsman from Delhi who was a surprise inclusion in India's side for the Fourth Test against Australia in 1959-60. He was 20, and had played only seven first-class matches – but he had just made an attractive 73, his maiden half-century, for the Board President's XI against the tourists. At Madras he batted at No. 9 and did not bowl. In the first innings he was stumped for a duck, Alan Davidson's only such victim in Tests. "Wally Grout had noticed Sood's tendency to overbalance slightly after attempting a drive," recalled Davidson. "Wally gave me the nod and moved up behind the stumps. I really began to wonder if I'd slowed down… but Sood lifted his back foot next ball, and Wally flicked off the bails. It was a superb piece of wicketkeeping." He made three in the second innings, becoming Davidson's 100th Test wicket (bowled this time). Sood never got another cap, although he did extend his only century, against Southern Punjab the following season, to 170. He later served on the Delhi association's board, and was a national selector in the 1980s.

SPEED, STEWART RAYMOND, who died on June 22, aged 77, came close to Test selection in the 1960s after polished performances behind the stumps for Auckland. He was an attacking batsman, who scored 88 against a strong Canterbury side at Eden Park in February 1965. Speed was part of the Auckland team which romped to the Plunket

Shield title in 1968-69, but also excelled at other sports. "It mattered not the size of the ball – as long as it was round, he pretty much mastered each art," said the former Test captain Mark Burgess, who also remembered Speed's sense of style: "Stew brought a special level of elegance and fashion that most of us didn't dare try to emulate. It was very brave in the early '60s turning up to an Eden football dressing-room smelling of Old Spice."

SPENCER, CHARLES TERENCE, died on February 1, aged 88. England's first innings in the Test trial against the Rest at Edgbaston in May 1953 had thrown up contrasting fortunes for two national servicemen hoping to play against Australia. Fred Trueman, the leading contender, had none for 58 from 22 uninspiring overs. But his new-ball partner, Leicestershire's Terry Spencer, had three for 51 from 23. "The youthful Spencer, of medium-fast pace and upright action, was altogether the more impressive," wrote Geoffrey Green in *The Times*. "He was always forcing the batsman into the more hurried strokes, while he twice brought the ball back very sharply to hit the middle stumps of May and Compton." In the second innings, he dismissed Reg Simpson; Trueman went wicketless again.

Although Len Hutton regarded Spencer as "one of the best young prospects", that was the closest he came to Test cricket. "The wickets I took were all coming in to the bat," he said. "They seemed to think the ball coming in wouldn't be such a good ploy against the Australians." But he had no regrets. At Leicestershire, he was part of the furniture: in more than two decades, Spencer took 1,320 first-class wickets (third on the county's all-time list) in 496 appearances (fourth). "This is more than a job," he said. "I'd play cricket if I had to pay to do so, and there's not many people could say that about their work."

Tall and strongly built, he loved to charge down the hill at Grace Road. "He was a hit-the-deck bowler," said team-mate Jack Birkenshaw. "His action suggested he would move the ball away, but he usually nipped it back off the pitch." Competitive and often grumpy – he chuntered about the number of Yorkshire imports at Leicestershire – Spencer expected high standards from himself and his colleagues. "When Willie Watson was captain, he'd take 'Spenner' off if he bowled poorly in his first couple of overs," said Birkenshaw. "He'd get angry with himself, so Willie would send him down to third man or fine leg to seethe for a bit. Then, after half an hour, he'd bring him back on."

Bill Smith, Popperfoto/Getty Images

More than a job: Terry Spencer, 1972.

Spencer took centre stage in an extraordinary match at Huddersfield in June 1954. Yorkshire gained a first-innings lead of 23 but, before the second-day close, Spencer bowled Frank Lowson and had Hutton caught behind. Next morning, he was irresistible: 23 overs unchanged in all, and nine for 63, seven bowled. According to J. M. Kilburn in *The Yorkshire Post*, he found enough swing to leave "experienced batsmen strokeless". Needing 137, Leicestershire were soon 29 for five, with four for Trueman. They recovered but, by the time Johnny Wardle began the final over, Spencer and limping last man Brian Boshier were nine short. Despite Boshier's sciatica, they ran two singles, then Spencer lofted the fourth ball into a nearby cemetery to bring the scores level. Wardle fired the next one in, and Spencer could not find a gap. Before the last ball, he told Boshier: "Whatever you do, get out of your trap quickly." Boshier obliged, but Spencer's

MOST FIRST-CLASS WICKETS FOR LEICESTERSHIRE

		M	*R*	*BB*	*5I*	*10W*	*Avge*	*Career*
2,131	W. E. Astill	628	49,399	9-41	127	21	23.18	1906–39
1,759	G. Geary	454	34,705	10-18	110	27	19.72	1912–38
1,320	**C. T. Spencer**	**496**	**35,508**	**9-63**	**45**	**5**	**26.90**	**1952–74**
1,127	J. E. Walsh	279	27,335	8-40	96	25	24.25	1937–56
1,100	J. H. King	502	27,780	8-17	64	10	25.25	1895–1925
1,076	H. A. Smith	341	27,968	8-40	66	11	25.99	1925–39
930	V. E. Jackson	322	22,462	8-43	43	7	24.15	1938–56
908	J. Birkenshaw	420	24,058	8-94	37	3	26.49	1961–80
816	J. S. Savage	281	19,969	8-50	42	7	24.47	1953–56
650	W. W. Odell	172	15,219	8-20	39	4	23.41	1901–14
632	J. P. Agnew	205	18,144	9-70	36	6	28.70	1978–90

off-drive was not wide enough of Wardle, who ran him out with a direct hit. It remains Leicestershire's only Championship tie.

Spencer was born in Braunstone, near Aylestone Road, the club's HQ before Grace Road. He did not have to look far for a role model: his uncle Haydon Smith was a seamer for the county and took over 1,000 wickets between 1925 and 1939. But Spencer was no prodigy. He played at school without great success, then gave the game up for a year. Another uncle persuaded him to turn out for the wandering Leicester Veronique club, however, and he soon progressed to the Leicestershire nets.

He made his debut against Cambridge University at Fenner's in April 1952 – David Sheppard was his first victim, lbw for 148 – and in his second appearance, against the touring Indians, he dismissed Polly Umrigar, Pankaj Roy and Dattu Phadkar. "I was playing local cricket one year, and for the county the next, bowling against all the great batsmen," he told the writer Stephen Chalke. Barely 21, he finished the season with almost 850 overs under his belt, taking 80 wickets at 30. A template had been set. "He was a workhorse," said team-mate Maurice Hallam. "He never shirked anything."

Two years of national service were spent as an equipment repairer, but Spencer was not short of cricket. "One year, I went four months before I got back to draw my army pay," he recalled. After the success of Frank Tyson and Brian Statham in Australia in 1954-55, he made the mistake of straining for extra speed: "You try to bowl quicker, and your action tends to go a bit." Once back on track, he took over 80 wickets in six consecutive seasons; his best summer was 1961, when he claimed 123 at 19. MCC asked about his availability for the tour of India and Pakistan, but he was not selected. He often made useful contributions down the order, with a top score of 90 against Essex at Leicester in 1964, and was a brilliant close fielder. His 377 catches for the county place him fourth on their list.

He retired from first-class cricket at the end of 1969, but in 1970 played a handful of one-day games, then returned in both formats until 1974, helping Leicestershire to their first trophy, the Benson and Hedges Cup in 1972. He captained the Second XI in the mid-1970s. After leaving Grace Road, he was on the first-class umpires' list from 1979 until 1983. Later, he ran his own window-fitting business. "He was a Leicester man through and through, and took a great interest in the county and the city's sports teams," said Birkenshaw. "At old players' reunions, he could get quite emotional."

SPRINGALL, JOHN DENIS, died on June 26, aged 87. A Londoner who arrived at Trent Bridge from the Lord's groundstaff, Springall enjoyed two good seasons for Nottinghamshire. He did not have a good start. "Who signed this bloke?" asked Reg Simpson on spotting him in the nets. "He can't play." But four years later, in 1959, he collected 1,488 runs, with his only two centuries, both unbeaten – 107 against Leicestershire and 100 at Northamptonshire's expense, during a hundred partnership with the mollified Simpson. He added 1,413 in 1960, when he was capped. A useful change seamer, Springall claimed 74 of his 80 first-class wickets in those two summers: he took six for 43 against Surrey at

The Oval in 1959, and eight wickets in a victory over Somerset at Bath in 1960. After that, the returns fell off, perhaps sparked by a change of captain, from Simpson to John Clay. His last first-class match was in 1963, but he made a surprise return four years later for a Gillette Cup game, by which time he was on the Nottinghamshire committee and playing for Walkden in the Central Lancashire League. He was a cousin of the comedian Charlie Drake, whose real surname was Springall.

STAMP, ROBERT, died on March 23, aged 97. Bob Stamp was involved in youth cricket for more than 40 years, serving as chairman of the Lancashire Schools Cricket Association from 1993 to 2002 after an initial spell in 1989, and also acting as a selector.

STEWART, TREVOR GEORGE, died on May 20, aged 80. Born in the isolated inland mining town of Mount Isa, Stewart was a seamer who played six matches for Queensland in the early 1960s, collecting 13 wickets. Against Victoria at the MCG in 1963-64, he dismissed three future Test batsmen in Ian Redpath, Bob Cowper and Keith Stackpole.

STILES, NORBERT PETER PATRICK PAUL, MBE, died on October 30, aged 78. Balding, short-sighted and dentally challenged, Nobby Stiles did not look like a sporting hero – but he was a key member of the England side that won the football World Cup for the only time, in 1966: photographs of him skipping deliriously around Wembley with the Cup are still instantly recognisable. An uncompromising enforcer in midfield, he performed a similar role in over 300 matches for Manchester United, helping them win the European Cup in 1968, before winding down at Middlesbrough and Preston North End. Stiles was also a keen cricket fan, and spent a lot of time as a youth at the other Old Trafford. "My heroes were Brian Statham and Roy Tattersall," he told *Test Match Special* in 1997. "A few years later I had lunch with them, and I must have driven 'em daft, talking about the Roses match I'd seen them play in 1950. Much later I'd come one stop on the Metro and just sit there and watch on my own." He had trials with Manchester Boys, but wasn't helped by poor eyesight: contact lenses, a relatively new innovation, made soccer possible. Stiles's later years were clouded by dementia – brought on, his family believed, by years of heading heavy leather footballs.

Trinity Mirror/Mirrorpix/Alamy

A bigger stage awaits: Nobby Stiles (with bat) and England team-mates Alan Ball, Peter Bonetti, Jimmy Greaves and Bobby Charlton relax before a looming game against West Germany, July 1966.

STRACHAN, GEORGE ROBSON, who died on March 8, aged 87, was a seamer from West Lothian who played two first-class matches for Scotland in 1965. In the second, in Dublin, a lead of 47 proved sufficient for an innings victory when Ireland were skittled for 25, though Strachan did not bowl. It was the lowest total against Scotland until February 2019, when Oman made 24. In his other match, against MCC in Glasgow, he had dismissed the England all-rounder Barry Knight. In club cricket, Strachan – a chartered surveyor – scored over 6,000 runs and took nearly 1,000 wickets, including four in four balls against Ayr in 1957.

SUMMERFIELD, DAVID, who died on August 16, aged 81, was a familiar sight at the St Lawrence ground in Canterbury, where he and his son Keith ran a bookstall for more than 30 years, dispensing secondhand cricket titles, cheery badinage and chummy gossip. They also operated at Kent's outgrounds, and made guest appearances around Essex and as far afield as Scarborough.

SURESH KUMAR, MANI, who was found hanged at home in India on October 9, aged 47, was a slow left-armer who had a long career with Kerala, and four seasons with Railways. His 196 wickets included 12 in Kerala's first victory over Tamil Nadu, at Palakkad in 1994-95, and a hat-trick against Rajasthan at Delhi in January 1996. A useful batsman, he also made a century against Andhra in 2000-01. Suresh Kumar had played for India Under-19s alongside Rahul Dravid, who mentioned him in his Bradman Oration speech in Canberra in 2011: "We had two bowlers, one from the north Indian state of Uttar Pradesh who spoke Hindi, and Suresh Kumar from Kerala in the deep south, who spoke only the state's regional language, Malayalam. In one game, they came together at the crease – and in the dressing-room we were in stitches, wondering how they were going to manage the business of calling for runs or sharing the strike. Neither man could understand a word the other was saying. This could only happen in Indian cricket. And these guys came up with a 100-run partnership."

TAUFIQ TIRMIZI, SYED, who died of a heart attack on April 9, aged 59, was a leg-spinner from Karachi who played 12 first-class matches, with a best of five for 63 for the House Building Finance Corporation in 1980-81. He continued to play cricket on the seniors circuit, and appeared occasionally on television.

TAYLOR, REGINALD GEORGE, died on May 26, aged 86. Reg Taylor followed 34 years as a civil engineer for Rolls-Royce with a stint as Derbyshire's chief executive from 1993 to 1996, and then joined their committee. He captained Aston-on-Trent CC.

THORNTON, JULIAN, who died on March 24, aged 84, was a seasoned administrator from Durban, who performed many roles for Natal, from team manager to president of the provincial association. When the United Cricket Board of South Africa were set up in 1991, Thornton was treasurer. Ali Bacher, the managing director, remembered: "He was an accountant by profession, and a very able treasurer, but it was his love of the game that was key. He was also a wonderful man, without a mean bone in his body."

TILLARD, JOHN ROBERT, died on December 16, 2019, aged 95. Rob Tillard was a good all-round sportsman who played football for the Oxbridge side Pegasus and cricket for Sussex. His solitary first-class match, in 1949, was not a success: he made three and nought as Oxford University overwhelmed them by an innings. He did manage half-centuries for the Second XI against Essex and Surrey, and later played for the Army, in which he remained until 1958. Late in life, Tillard became embroiled in an argument with his local church, in Chailey, East Sussex, after challenging their decision to replace 150-year-old oak pews with chairs. He had worshipped there for over 80 years, and his family had contributed to the costs of extensions. Early in 2019, Tillard lost the protracted case, incurring costs of around £3,000, but said he was "too old and too tired" to appeal; he died later in the year.

TIWARI, KARAN, hanged himself at his home in Mumbai on August 10. He was 27, and apparently depressed at his failure to secure a professional contract. A seamer who had modelled his delivery on Dale Steyn – his friends called him "Junior Steyn" – Tiwari bowled tirelessly in the nets, often at the Mumbai Indians IPL team. But after an unsuccessful trial for Delhi Capitals "the spark had gone out of his life", according to his brother Avinash. "He would shut himself in his room and barely speak."

TRAFFORD, STANLEY JOHN, died on November 19, aged 74. Stan Trafford, who was associated with Leek CC in Staffordshire for around 60 years, appeared in four Minor Counties Championship matches, and scored 68 against Cheshire in 1976. He also played football for Port Vale, and remembered an early match in the FA Youth Cup against Aston Villa: "There were five youth internationals in their team, and all us lot were local lads from the Vale. We scored first – and ended up losing 12–1."

TYNAN, JOHN CHRISTOPHER, died on August 23, aged 94. New Zealand's hockey captain at the 1956 Olympics, Jack Tynan had previously played four first-class cricket matches for Wellington as a batsman who bowled occasional off-breaks. He had been Wellington's oldest surviving player, a distinction that briefly passed to John Reid.

VENKATARAMAN, R., who died on August 6, aged 86, was a batsman who played five Ranji Trophy matches – three for Madhya Pradesh and two for Vidarbha – alongside his brother, R. "Challah" Narasimhan. Venkat made an unbeaten 52 in his first match, against Uttar Pradesh in December 1954, but never again passed 11.

WALKER, PETER MICHAEL, MBE, who died on April 4, aged 84, was so brilliant a close fielder that it often overshadowed all else. An aggressive middle-order batsman, and a hard-working left-armer who switched between seam and spin, Peter Walker was one of the leading all-rounders in county cricket. Yet any discussion about him always came back to fielding. "He was the greatest catcher of a cricket ball I ever saw," said former Glamorgan captain Tony Lewis.

At 16, Walker ran away from home in South Africa, and spent a wild year as a merchant seaman, escaping a knife-wielding assailant in the Suez Canal, and living on his wits in a tough New York neighbourhood. After retiring as a player, he fronted the BBC's coverage of the Sunday League, and co-founded a TV production company. He played the clarinet, hunted crocodiles, fished for sharks and filmed a gunpoint interview with South African white supremacists. He also found time to write an erotic novel. His statistics underscore his place in Glamorgan history: fourth on their list of first-class appearances, ninth among run-scorers, 12th among wicket-takers. He passed 1,000 runs in a season 11 times, and took over 50 wickets seven times, completing the double in 1961. But his 656 outfield catches for the county were unrivalled, and his 697 overall placed him 11th in all first-class cricket.

ALL AT ONCE

Most matches by those achieving their highest score and best bowling in the same first-class game:

651	J. W. H. T. Douglas (210* and 9-47)	Essex v Derbyshire at Leyton	1921
469	**P. M. Walker (152* and 7-58)**	**Glamorgan v Middlesex at Lord's**	**1962**
422	B. Hedges (182 and 1-16)	Glamorgan v Oxford University at Oxford	1967
363	T. F. Shepherd (277* and 6-78)	Surrey v Gloucestershire at The Oval	1927
314	E. M. Grace (192* and 10-69)	Gents of MCC v Gents of Kent at Canterbury	1862
277	P. A. Cottey (203 and 4-49)	Glamorgan v Leicestershire at Swansea	1996
258	K. D. Walters (253 and 7-63)	New South Wales v S. Australia at Adelaide	1964-65
256	A. P. Lucas (145 and 6-10)	England XI v Cambridge U. at Cambridge	1882
201	A. N. Connolly (40 and 9-67)	Victoria v Queensland at Brisbane	1964-65
193	M. H. Yardy (257 and 5-83)	Sussex v Bangladeshis at Hove	2005
193	R. N. ten Doeschate (259* and 6-20)	Netherlands v Canada at Pretoria	2006-07

Walker was born in Bristol, of Welsh stock, and his family moved to South Africa when he was two. As music and literary editor of *The Star* in Johannesburg, his father was involved in liberal politics; Nelson Mandela was smuggled home for clandestine meetings. In his teens, Walker was coached by the Glamorgan trio of Allan Watkins and the two Davieses, Emrys and Dai. Watkins, a superb close catcher, imparted a love of fielding. One of Walker's proudest possessions was the sunhat Watkins wore when he caught Dudley Nourse at Durban in 1948-49.

After telling his parents he was going camping, Walker joined the crew of a Swedish oil tanker bound for the Persian Gulf. During a short break from the seas, he spent a freezing winter with his grandparents in Cardiff, but was soon off again – this time on a Finnish tanker, sailing from Rotterdam to Los Angeles via the Middle East. He struck up a friendship with a Dutch crew member, Benny Laros, and every day they would raid the ship's potato stores, hurling them at each other across deck. "Potatoes come in all shapes and sizes, demanding flexibility and sure hands," said Walker. "Catching a potato became the single most important preoccupation in our lives. Irrespective of its size, weight or shape, if one had to take a tumble to reach a low catch, in the process taking a heavy fall on the metal deck, so be it." So many went overboard that the supply ran out.

His itinerant lifestyle ended after he contracted jaundice, and wound up in a New York seaman's hospital. But in August 1953, now back in the UK, he knocked on the door of the Glamorgan club offices, and asked for a trial. Watkins remembered him, and he was given a £4-a-week contract for two summers, though he did not make his debut until June 1956, against Leicestershire at Llanelli. He caught Maurice Hallam off Don Shepherd – the beginning of a formidable alliance. By 1958, he was a regular, passing 1,000 runs and taking 36 wickets. The press noted his "flypaper fingers", and he received some key advice from wicketkeeper Haydn Davies. "What do you catch with, Peter?" he asked. "Obvious isn't it, my hands," Walker replied. "No, you pillock, it's your eyes. They tell you where your hands should go. That's why I keep after you to stand still, to give your eyes a chance." His skills were also enhanced by rigorous training. "When we went back to nets in April, everybody would bat and bowl, and then start to head home at about 4.30," said opener Alan Jones. "But Peter always wanted me to stay on to hit catches at him."

Walker was proficient in the deep, but it was close in that he made his reputation, despite ending up there almost by accident. Against Warwickshire at Cardiff Arms Park in 1957, he asked a grumpy Wilf Wooller where he should field. "Spit in the air and see where it lands," came the response. Walker did as he was told, and stationed himself at short square leg. Two balls later, he took a low, sprawling catch. "I spent the majority of the next 16 years in that position."

Though 6ft 3in, Walker was able to crouch low for hours; only Brian Close among his contemporaries stood as near to the batsman. "He wore no protection, but never moved or

---

IT'S CATCHING

Most catches by an outfielder off the same bowler in first-class cricket:

Ct	*M*	*Fielder*	*Bowler*
237	285	W. R. Hammond	C. W. L. Parker
222	499	F. E. Woolley	A. P. Freeman
199	300	J. Tunnicliffe	W. Rhodes
175	**420**	**P. M. Walker**	**D. J. Shepherd**
171	265	A. Mitchell	H. Verity
164	326	J. Seymour	C. Blythe
155	599	D. Denton	W. Rhodes
147	615	G. H. Hirst	W. Rhodes
145	482	C. P. Mead	J. A. Newman
141	431	W. H. Ashdown	A. P. Freeman

On form: Peter Walker hits out against Surrey, 1964. Stewart Storey is slip, Arnold Long the keeper.

flinched," said Jones. Shepherd's accuracy increased his sense of security. With Roger Davis and Euros Lewis, Glamorgan boasted an outstanding close-catching unit. "I always let Peter organise the catchers," said Tony Lewis. At Chesterfield in 1961, Walker noticed Derbyshire's Bill Oates leaving his crease. In the second innings, he began to move with him, crouching all the while. Oates was soon out, caught bat and pad. "It was one of the catches that gave me the most pleasure," said Walker.

In 1960, he was selected for the First Test against South Africa at Edgbaston. He top-scored in England's second innings with 37, and held two catches. "Walker has all the gifts to make a Test all-rounder," wrote John Arlott in *The Guardian*. At Lord's, he made a fifty, hitting Trevor Goddard for successive sixes. But he did not bowl and, after hitting 30 in his only innings at Trent Bridge and bowling just three overs, he was dropped.

His Test appearances came amid a poor run of form. He slid into depression, and was accused in the dressing-room of not applying himself. After another loose shot led to a cheap dismissal at Bath, he spent a night on a pew in the abbey. Next day, he told Wooller he was resigning, but he was persuaded to stay. Fully recovered in 1961, he enjoyed his best season – 1,347 runs and 101 wickets, both at 24, and 73 catches. He remained a key figure when Glamorgan were champions in 1969. "Every day he contributed something with one of his skills," said Lewis.

Walker had first tried his hand at journalism in the 1960s, and was on duty with BBC Wales in October 1966 when news came through that a coal tip had slipped down a hillside in Aberfan. He joined a team of reporters at the scene but, overwhelmed by the scale of the disaster, put down his tape recorder and helped with the rescue efforts. He covered rugby for national newspapers, and contributed to *The Cricketer*; a profile of Garry Sobers earned compliments from Neville Cardus. After his last season with Glamorgan, in 1972, he replaced Frank Bough as presenter of Sunday-afternoon cricket on BBC Two, fronting the coverage for 18 years. He was later Glamorgan president, but resigned in November 2010 after the sacking of captain Jamie Dalrymple and the departure of coach Matthew Maynard.

In 1985, he helped establish Merlin Television in Cardiff. They tackled assignments all over the world, including a fraught operation to provide coverage of West Indies v India for Indian TV. He later became director of development for the Cricket Board of Wales, spending three years reorganising the grassroots game. "Whatever he did, he wanted to be the best," said Jones. Walker's autobiography, *It's not just Cricket*, was published in 2006. Another literary outing was *Breakaway: A Female Fantasy Week*, written under the pseudonym Ceri Megane. "It was a remarkable life," said Lewis. "And he was always looking for a remarkable life."

WAQAR HASAN MIR, who died on February 10, aged 87, was the last survivor of Pakistan's inaugural Test, at Delhi in October 1952. Waqar, 20 at the time, made little impact in that match, or in Pakistan's stunning innings victory in the Second Test, to square the rubber at Lucknow – but he scored 81 and 65 (in five and a half hours) in the Third in Bombay, and added 97 in another vigil to help save the Fifth at Calcutta, top-scoring with 357 runs in the series. "The childlike enthusiasm of being a part of the first-ever team to tour as a Test-playing nation was glaringly visible on everyone's faces," he wrote.

In England in 1954 – "the stylist of the side", according to *Wisden* – he had little success in the Tests, but collected 1,263 runs overall, including 123 against county champions Surrey. And he was part of the joyous band that won the final Test at The Oval. He later added wins over Australia and New Zealand at home. At Lahore in 1955-56, Waqar made 189 – his only Test century – and put on 308 (still a record partnership for Pakistan's seventh wicket) with Imtiaz Ahmed, which rescued them from 111 for six against New Zealand. "Neat on his feet, Waqar is essentially a back-foot player, and also revels in executing pulsating drives through the covers," enthused the Pakistan writer Qamaruddin Butt. "He sends the ball away with a parting flick of pliant wristwork."

Dennis Oulds, Central Press/Getty Images

Stylist: Waqar Hasan, May 1954.

In 1953-54, Waqar had scored the first double-century in first-class cricket in Pakistan; three seasons earlier, while at Lahore's Government College, he hammered

337 in 250 minutes in a university game. Although his last Test was in 1959-60, he played on for Karachi until 1965-66. He set up a food and spice business, which became the multimillion-dollar conglomerate National Foods. He married Jamila Razzaq, a film star, and published an autobiography, *For Cricket and Country*, in 2002. One of his brothers, slow left-armer Pervez Sajjad, later played 19 Tests.

WATSON, GRAEME DONALD, who died on April 24, aged 75, was a combative all-rounder who played five Tests for Australia, and the first to appear for three different states in the Sheffield Shield. Watson, whose fashionable mop of hair earned him the nickname "Beatle", recovered from a horrific injury early in 1972 to open the batting in the Ashes in England six months later, though he did not feature again after some hesitant performances.

The injury occurred during the unofficial Test between Australia and a World XI at Melbourne in January 1972. Not long after Garry Sobers had completed a stupendous 254, Watson was batting. Tony Greig sent down an unintentional beamer – his hand hit the stumps as he delivered the ball – and Watson top-edged it into his face, breaking his nose. He spent three weeks in hospital. An artery had been damaged, and he needed around 40 pints of blood. "He was very unfortunate, as the ball would have hit him in the chest if his attempted pull shot had missed," said Ian Chappell, the non-striker. "It was only when I met one of his nurses at a social function that I found out Beatle had actually stopped breathing for a while when he was in hospital. It was typical of him to say very little about the incident – he made light of any injury, and at times was too brave for his own good."

An attacking batsman and enthusiastic seamer, Watson had played first-grade cricket for Melbourne when he was 16, and in 1965-66 scored a maiden century in his first full season as Victoria successfully chased 387 to beat Queensland at the MCG. Soon after, he followed 80 against South Australia with six for 61 and, when Doug Walters had to withdraw from the following season's tour of South Africa to do national service, Watson was called up. Still only 21, he played in three of the five Tests, but faded after a bright 50 on debut at Cape Town, where he shared a seventh-wicket stand of 128 with Keith Stackpole that helped Australia win their only match of a series lost 3–1.

Bill Smith, Popperfoto/Getty Images

Beatle: Graeme Watson in 1972.

With Walters reclaiming his place, Watson faded from the selectors' thoughts, until he was revived by a move to Western Australia in 1971 (he had gone to Perth to manage a nightclub). He started for his new state with 145 against Queensland, which ended when he walked off, convinced he had been caught at point; the umpire thought it was not out, and instructed the scorers to record it as "retired out".

Watson added 89 for WA against the World XI, before 122 in Queensland clinched the return to the Australian team which ended in the intensive-care unit. He worked hard to regain fitness in time for the tour of England, and started with a career-best 176 in a rollicking opening stand of 301 against Hampshire, outscoring the usually aggressive Stackpole. But in the First Test at Old Trafford, down at No. 5, Watson spooned a John Snow bouncer back to the bowler, and departed for a duck. "He shaped to hook it and then, in a reaction to his injury, stopped his bat halfway through the swing," said Stackpole. "He hit the ball slowly back to Snow, as if to say 'Catch me.' I felt sorry for him, since it was clear from that moment he could never be the same batsman again."

His international career was effectively over, though he hit 13 and six at The Oval. But Watson helped Western Australia win three Sheffield Shield titles in four seasons, before moving to New South Wales, the third team he represented in the Shield. It might have been four: he had a season of grade cricket in Queensland before joining World Series Cricket, in which his bowling fared better than his batting.

Watson eventually returned to his career as an architect, and worked on some of the infrastructure for the Sydney Olympics in 2000. He went to live in Don Bradman's home town of Bowral with his fourth wife, Jan. When she needed a kidney transplant, he offered to donate one – but the preparations revealed the cancer which eventually claimed his life.

WATSON, ROY CLARENCE WILLIAM, who died on April 10, aged 86, was a wicketkeeper from Fremantle who played seven first-class matches for Western Australia, including two against the 1958-59 MCC tourists. The previous season, he scored 28 and 21 – both not out – and took seven catches in a victory over South Australia at Perth. He also represented his state at baseball.

WEEKES, SIR EVERTON DE COURCY, GCM, OBE, died on July 1, aged 95. No West Indies cricket lover could have easily chosen between the Three Ws. But despite the elegance of Frank Worrell and the power of Clyde Walcott, plenty believed the ruthless run-gathering of Everton Weekes gave him a hair's-breadth advantage. In the early 1950s, he and Neil Harvey were the most exciting batsmen in the world, but Weekes's pursuit of big scores meant comparisons were more often made with Don Bradman. "He attacked the bowlers from the start," said Sonny Ramadhin. "He never gave them a chance."

Richie Benaud and Keith Miller reckoned Weekes had the edge over his compatriots, and statistics support them: he scored more Test runs (4,455), at a higher average (58), than Worrell or Walcott, and tied with Walcott on 15 centuries, to Worrell's nine. Small in stature, Weekes was predominantly a back-foot player. "He was a fierce hooker, puller and square-cutter, but at the same time a terrific driver," said Benaud. He also had nimble footwork. "He was down the pitch in a trice once the spinners came on, sometimes even before they did," wrote John Woodcock. C. L. R. James thought Weekes played a defensive shot only when he had exhausted his attacking options. And he was an outstanding fielder: safe close to the wicket, electrifying in the deep. "He had a fantastic arm from the boundary," said Ramadhin.

Weekes's figures retain their lustre. Among batsmen whose Test careers are complete (and comprised at least 20 innings), he has the eighth-highest average, and the second-highest for West Indies, behind George Headley. He reached 1,000 Test runs in 12 innings, a record shared with Herbert Sutcliffe. But his significance went deeper than sport. From a childhood of poverty, he fought his way through the strict racial divisions in West Indies cricket, breaking down decades of prejudice and exclusion for the black population of Barbados. In March 2020, he overtook Andy Ganteaume as West Indies' longest-lived Test cricketer.

The Three Ws were born within a mile of each other in the parish of St Michael, Weekes arriving six months after Worrell and 11 before Walcott; it was said the same midwife delivered them all. He was named after his father's favourite English football team – "It's a good job he didn't support West Bromwich Albion," quipped Jim Laker – but was brought up by his mother and elder sister while his father was working in Trinidad. The house was 300 yards from Kensington Oval, home of the whites-only Pickwick club; access was possible only if he turned up early to help the groundstaff. In January 1935, aged nine, Weekes lingered after completing his duties, and saw both Headley and Wally Hammond bat on the opening day of the First Test against England.

William Vanderson, Getty Images

Masters of the art: Frank Worrell and Everton Weekes at Fenner's, Cambridge, June 1950. Worrell made 160, and Weekes 304 not out; they put on 350.

Football was Everton's first sporting love, and he represented Barbados. Racism, though, was ingrained in the island's sporting institutions. Weekes said: "I could not think of anyone of colour apart from George Headley who played cricket professionally. It was said that a line was drawn, and you were not supposed to be in parts of your own country at certain times of the day." Leaving school at 14 with no qualifications, he took a less trodden route to first-class cricket, via the Barbados Cricket League. (Worrell and Walcott had things easier, attending secondary schools with links to the established Spartan and Empire clubs.)

Weekes prospered after joining the Barbados Regiment during the Second World War: no active service, but plenty of cricket. "The first time I got on to a properly prepared pitch, I wondered just how do you get out." In February 1945, two days before his 20th birthday, he made his first-class debut for Barbados against Trinidad, and was stumped for a duck. His first hundred came against British Guiana at Georgetown in September 1946, and the following season he was called up for a Test debut against Gubby Allen's understrength England.

He made a steady but unspectacular start, scoring between 20 and 36 in each of his first five innings. Initially dropped for the Fourth Test at Kingston, he was reprieved by an injury to Headley. But an unscheduled stop in Puerto Rico delayed his arrival. Flying into Jamaica, he could see the game going on below and, when he got to Sabina Park, he found local favourite John Holt fielding in his place; after Weekes came on instead, the crowd booed every time he touched the ball. When West Indies batted, he was dropped on nought by Godfrey Evans, and needed to be coaxed by Worrell through a spell of left-arm spin from Dick Howorth. Weekes hit 141, and was carried off in triumph.

That innings was the start of an extraordinary run. Later that year in India, he made 128 at Delhi, 194 at Bombay, then 162 and 101 at Calcutta: five successive Test centuries remains a record. He rated the 162 his best: "Everywhere I tried to hit the ball, I hit it." In the Fourth Test at Madras, Weekes had 90 when Gerry Gomez called him through for a single. "I got into the crease – I watched the whole thing happen. The umpire's hand went up. We didn't have all this technology, we didn't have replays. It was rather doubtful." He finished the series with 779 runs at 111.

In 1950, Weekes embarked on a triumphal procession around England, although only after Headley had agreed to take over his Lancashire League contract with Bacup. It was a seminal trip for West Indies, who won their first series there. Ramadhin and Alf Valentine cast a spell on the English batsmen, and the Three Ws hammered 20 first-class centuries, with Weekes contributing seven in his 2,310 tour runs at 79.

At The Oval, he made 232 against Surrey, demonstrating a new-found ability to hook and sweep. A few days later, in reply to Cambridge University's 594 for four on a Fenner's featherbed, he made a career-best unbeaten 304 in under five and a half hours, as the West Indians ran up 730 for three. As he approached the triple-century, his concentration lapsed, and he was overheard chastising himself: "Play carefully in the nineties, Weekes man." Against Nottinghamshire he hit 279 in 235 minutes; against Hampshire 246 not out in 245. At Leicester in mid-July, Weekes reached three figures in 65 minutes – the fastest hundred of the season – on his way to an undefeated 200.

His only Test century of the tour came in the third match, at Trent Bridge. His fourth-wicket partnership of 283 with Worrell was then the highest for any West Indian wicket. "It is many a long day since I saw an English Test attack thrashed so unmercifully," wrote Charles Bray in the *Daily Herald*. Along with Ramadhin, Valentine and Worrell, Weekes was named a Wisden Cricketer of the Year.

There were memorable innings to come, though he was never again so consistent. In the First Test against Australia at Brisbane in 1951-52, he injured his thigh, and was troubled for the rest of his career; even so, at home against India he was soon back to his punishing best. The visit of Len Hutton's Ashes winners in 1953-54 was hyped as a battle to decide the best team in the world. A sulphurous series produced some compelling cricket, with England recovering from 2–0 down to draw. Weekes averaged nearly 70, and hit 206 at Port-of-Spain, but his 94 in the Third Test at Georgetown was his most memorable contribution. "Brian Statham was bowling brilliantly," said Ramadhin. "He was bowling off-cutters and the like, but Everton made it look so easy. In the end, Brian just had to smile."

Following a trail blazed by Learie Constantine and Headley, the Three Ws all spent English summers in the Lancashire leagues. They would meet for a drink in Manchester on Friday evenings, but not much more: "There were no nightclubs," said Weekes. He played for Bacup for seven seasons between 1949 and 1958, and was worth every penny of the club's annual £500 investment, passing 1,000 runs each time. His average – 91 from 150 innings – is the highest in league history. In 1951, he totalled 1,518 runs, surpassing his own record of two years earlier; it has been bettered only three times since. When Bacup suspended him for playing for a Commonwealth XI without permission, supporters daubed slogans on the pavilion roof calling for his reinstatement. "He was a great cricketer, a great man and a great ambassador for race relations in the town," said Peter Steen of Rossendale Borough Council. The local authority plan to name a new market square after him.

West Indies lost 3–0 at home to Australia in 1954-55, but Weekes scored 469 runs at 58, and at Port-of-Spain managed the only two sixes of his Test career. His reluctance to hit in the air dated back to boyhood games in confined spaces: a shot into neighbouring gardens could mean a broken window and a confiscated ball. He carried his form to New Zealand in 1955-56, making a hundred in each of his first five first-class innings, but West Indies' return to England in 1957 proved a letdown. They were beaten by an innings three times, and Weekes scored just one century, against T. N. Pearce's XI at Scarborough, in his last match of the tour. Laid low by sinus trouble, he had to settle for an aggregate of 1,096, but he batted through the pain of a broken finger to hit a brilliant 90 in the Lord's Test; MCC secretary Ronny Aird wrote him a note of appreciation on behalf of the members.

Eyes on the ball: Everton Weekes during his century against England at Trent Bridge in 1950. Godfrey Evans is behind the stumps, Gilbert Parkhouse at slip.

There was one more series, against Pakistan in 1957-58. In the opening match, he scored 197 at Bridgetown, his only Test score above 50 at his home ground. He celebrated his 33rd birthday during the Third Test, and retired at the end of the series: "I wasn't enjoying the cricket and I wasn't enjoying the administration." Weekes became the first regular black captain of Barbados in 1959-60, leading them until his retirement from the international game in 1964. The following year, aged 40, he hit 105 for a Barbados Colts XI against the touring Australians.

He remained involved in cricket, as coach, selector and West Indies team manager in home series. He was briefly an ICC match referee in 1994, but perhaps the role that suited him best was as a TV summariser alongside Tony Cozier. He also represented Barbados at bridge – "It's like golf: once you get into it, you get addicted" – and took up poker. One of his four children is David Murray, who played 19 Tests as wicketkeeper for West Indies before being banned for touring South Africa. Murray's son, Ricky Hoyte, also kept wicket for Barbados.

Weekes's funeral took place at Kensington Oval; he was buried alongside Worrell and Walcott on the Cave Hill campus at the University of the West Indies in Barbados, where the ground is the Three Ws Oval. In Manchester and Southampton, West Indies and England players held a minute's silence during their intra-squad warm-up matches. Perhaps the greatest tribute had come 70 years earlier, from Nottinghamshire's George Gunn, after Weekes's 279 at Trent Bridge. "I have seen them all since Victor Trumper, including Bradman, but I have never seen a more brilliant array of strokes, nor heard the ball so sweetly struck."

WEERASINGHE, DHANASIRI H. A., who died on July 7, aged 84, was a batsman from Ananda College who played 12 first-class matches for Ceylon. By 1968 he was chairman of selectors, and controversially chose himself for a (later cancelled) tour of England. He showed it was a reasonable selection in the annual Gopalan Trophy match against Madras in March 1969, with a career-best 92 as captain. He went to live in Australia in 1974.

WEIR, WENDY MARGARET, AM, who died on November 28, aged 72, was a left-arm spinner who played two Tests for Australia, going wicketless in the first but taking four in Sydney in January 1979, including New Zealand's captain Trish McKelvey in both innings. She was also part of Australia's squad for the inaugural women's World Cup, in 1973, although her only match – against an International XI at Swansea – was rained off after 22 minutes. Weir later had a spell as a national selector, and was president of Women's Cricket New South Wales, where she helped transform the sport from a genteel pastime. "She was one of those pioneers who set up what we're seeing now," said the former Australian captain Lisa Sthalekar. Weir was made a Member of the Order of Australia in 2002 for services to cricket.

Lee, Fairfax Media/Getty Images

Force for change: Wendy Weir, 1974.

WELD, ANTHONY EDWARD JOSEPH, died on May 19, aged 95. Hampshire's scorer from 2005 to 2014 – he took on the job in his eighties – the popular Tony Weld also accompanied touring teams from Australia, New Zealand, Pakistan, South Africa and West Indies around England, and did the scoring in several Test series and other internationals. He had been a keen club player, and then an umpire who stood in the first Hampshire League match, in 1973. Fellow scorers remembered Weld's cribbage board, which he would produce during rain breaks.

WILKINSON, ROBERT WILLIAM, who died on March 19, aged 80, was prevented by serious illness from fulfilling the promise he had shown in the late 1950s. A great-nephew of the Surrey and England batsman Bobby Abel (and, like him, born in Rotherhithe in south-east London), Wilkinson was an aggressive batsman and useful swing bowler. After excelling in schools cricket, he was given a Second XI debut by Kent in 1956, aged 16, and identified – with Brian Luckhurst – as the club's most promising youngster. He was given his chance in the first team in 1959, and often contributed quick runs down the order. But poor form and a broken hand got in the way; then, in the winter of 1960-61 he contracted tuberculosis. By 1962 he was playing again, and rejoined Kent the following summer; impressive figures for the Seconds led to a final first-class appearance. Acting on medical advice, he gave up trying to forge a professional career, though subsequent performances in club cricket suggested the prognosis had been hasty.

WOOLER, CHARLES ROBERT DUDLEY, who died on April 26, 2017, aged 86, was a Bulawayo-born medium-pacer who spent three seasons with Leicestershire after being spotted by their Australian spinner Vic Jackson while coaching in Rhodesia. Wooler took 50 wickets in both 1950 and 1951, but then returned home and played a few games for Rhodesia. His best figures – five for 47, and eight in the match – came in his penultimate game for Leicestershire, against Kent at Grace Road in August 1951. He rounded off his first-class career by dismissing Denis Compton during England's visit in 1956-57.

WRIGHT, PHILLIP, died of complications from Covid-19 on November 12, aged 60. "Big Phil" was a popular dressing-room attendant at Grace Road for 35 years. "He was loved by everyone," said Leicestershire coach Paul Nixon. "When we won a game, he would be the happiest man on the ground; if we lost, he would have some words of comfort."

WUITE, PIM, was one of five swimmers drowned in freak conditions off Scheveningen, the Netherlands, on May 11. He was 24, and an experienced surfer and coach. Wuite was also a keen cricketer for the HBS club in The Hague.

YOUNUS ATA, who died of Covid-19 on May 5, aged 60, made an unbeaten 70 on first-class debut, for Baluchistan against Sind in January 1979, then 90 and 70 in his next match – almost five years later – for Quetta against Sukkur. He played only three more games. His older brother, Tariq Ata, was an umpire who stood in Pakistan's Test against Australia at Faisalabad in September 1988, before dying of cancer the following year.

ZAFAR SARFRAZ, who died of Covid-19 on April 13, aged 50, was a left-hander who played 15 matches for Peshawar, with a best of 69 against Faisalabad in 1994-95. His brother, Akhtar Sarfraz, who died of cancer in 2019, played four one-day internationals for Pakistan.

ZAIDI, AHMAD RAZA, who died of a heart attack on April 24, aged 63, combined his job as a civil servant with a sideline as an English-language commentator on Pakistan TV and radio for nearly 30 years, including many overseas tours.

ZAVERI, PANKAJ NAVINCHANDRA, who died on May 1, aged 75, picked up 140 wickets for Gujarat in a long career that began in 1965-66; latterly he captained them. He usually took the new ball with his mixture of brisk off-cutters and off-breaks, and made a splash in only his second match, with five for 86 against Maharashtra, including Test batsman Chandu Borde. Many years later, against Saurashtra in 1974-75, he improved his career-best to seven for 51.

The obituaries include those who died, or whose deaths were notified, in 2020. Wisden *always welcomes information about those who might be included: please send details to almanack@wisdenalmanack.com, or to John Wisden & Co, 13 Old Aylesfield, Golden Pot, Alton, Hampshire GU34 4BY.*

BRIEFLY NOTED

The following, whose deaths were noted during 2020, played or umpired in a small number of first-class (fc) matches.

	Died	*Age*	*Main team(s)*
ABELL, Roy Beverley	30.6.2020	89	Warwickshire
Moseley CC leg-spinner: one fc match in 1967, taking four wickets against Cambridge University.			
BRADBURY, Leslie	5.2020	82	Derbyshire
Seamer: one fc match, aged 33, in 1971. Once took all ten in an innings for Matlock CC.			
BROWN, Andrew John Trevor	16.6.2020	84	Combined Services
Left-hand batsman: two fc matches in 1960, 40 v Cambridge Univ. Also played for Devon.*			
BRYANT, Christopher	11.11.2020	75	Umpire
Magistrate, and chairman of Stone CC; stood in 2019 Village final at Lord's.			
DUNNING, Michael Lindsay	13.8.2020	79	Combined Services
Windsor-born Old Etonian: two fc matches, 42 and 85 on debut v Cambridge University in 1962.			
DWYER, Kevin Francis	12.7.2020	91	Auckland
Batsman who played seven fc matches: 56 and 49 against Otago at Eden Park in 1952-53.			
GRAHAM, Colin Gordon	26.3.2020	90	Otago
Batsman from Dunedin: five fc matches, 46 v Auckland in 1955-56.			
HENDERSON, Dr Andrew William	18.8.2020	98	Scotland
Seamer from Selkirk whose one fc match, against Ireland in 1953, was affected by rain.			
LEWIS, Kevin John	27.9.2020	72	South Australia
West Torrens leg-spinner who played three fc matches in 1981-82.			
McCULLOUGH, Robert Bruce	22.3.2020	76	Wellington
Left-arm seamer from Hawkes Bay who played one fc match in 1971-72.			

McTAVISH, Christopher Russell 22.2.2020 76 Rhodesia
Opened the batting in his only fc match, against Worcestershire at Bulawayo in 1964-65.

MARSH, Alan Geoffrey 8.7.2020 86 Umpire
Played (wicketkeeper) and later umpired at Devon's Sidmouth CC for around 70 years.

MARTIN, Geoffrey Bernard ("Paddy") 12.6.2020 92 Tasmania
One fc match in 1950-51; notable local Aussie Rules footballer. His father also played for Tasmania.

MURRAY, William Walter Bruce 16.4.2020 90 Victoria
Left-arm seamer from Prahran CC: four fc matches in 1957-58, took 3-72 against South Australia.

NICHOLSON, Colin Ross 4.2.2020 80 Canterbury/Otago
Left-arm seamer from Ashburton in Canterbury: two fc matches, no wickets.

PEOPLES, Joseph 15.6.2020 76 Umpire
Undertaker, later a publican; well-known official in Ireland's North West Cricket Union.

REBBECK, Phillip Douglas 29.9.2020 72 South Australia
Batsman from Adelaide: five fc matches, 55 on debut, against Victoria at Adelaide in 1971-72.

ROLFE, Douglas John 1.6.2020 67 Victoria/S. Australia
Batsman from Melbourne who made 83 on debut for South Australia v Tasmania in 1979-80.

SARMA, Dr Ananda Chandra 19.5.2020 90 Assam
Opener who played one Ranji Trophy match in 1955-56; doctor and medical administrator.

SILVA, Sripal 27.2.2020 59 Moratuwa
Opened the bowling in one fc match, in January 1996, and took 1-26.

SMITH, John Phillips 10.2.2020 83 Victoria
Opening bowler for Hawthorn–East Melbourne: 4-76 in only fc match, v 1963-64 South Africans.

STEVENS, Lyndon James 1.9.2020 79 Umpire
First Tasmanian to umpire a full international – Australia v England ODI at the SCG in 1979-80.

STUBBS, John Robert Marshall 14.8.2020 88 Western Australia
Leg-spinner: three fc matches between 1956-57 and 1961-62.

TARR, Graeme Maxwell 8.12.2020 84 Northern Districts
Batsman from Hamilton who played eight fc matches: 38 against Canterbury in 1957-58.

TATTERSALL, Roger Hartley 24.4.2020 68 Lancashire
Left-arm seamer from Nelson: two fc matches in 1971.

WILLIAMS, Neville Rhodri 4.5.2020 81 Rhodesia
Seamer who played seven fc matches: 3-38 on debut v Griqualand West in 1963-64.

A LIFE IN NUMBERS

	Runs	*Avge*	*Wkts*	*Avge*
Anderson, R. G.	307	13.34	43	26.58
Angulugaha, K. A. P. S.	217	12.76	30	23.63
Aslam Qureshi	800	16.00	120	24.56
Barker, A. R. P.	544	31.60	–	–
Bashir Shana	2,412	34.95	3	63.00
Belliappa, P. K.	4,060	29.42	2	50.00
Bhaskaran, C. K.	580	11.60	106	29.05
Bolus, J. B.	**25,598**	**34.03**	**24**	**36.91**
Booth, B. J.	15,298	27.91	146	32.03
Brache, N.	9	2.25	–	–
Bromfield, H. D.	**374**	**6.33**	**205**	**25.63**
Brown, A. S.	12,851	18.12	1,230	25.64
Bushby, M. H.	1,919	24.92	1	11.00
Campbell, B. M.	312	13.56	32	36.56
Capel, D. J.	**12,202**	**29.68**	**546**	**32.18**
Caple, R. G.	1,581	18.38	34	36.32
Chamanlal, M.	2,418	37.78	42	38.30
Chauhan, C. P. S.	**11,143**	**40.22**	**51**	**34.13**
Chopra, A. K.	155	8.61	73	23.04
Clarke, J. K.	719	26.62	–	–
Cockett, J. A.	311	23.92	–	–
Cornell, P. C.	626	20.19	17	21.64
Cowdrey, G. R.	8,858	34.73	12	72.66
Cronje, N. E.	1,164	29.10	38	34.36
Dastane, U. M.	747	32.47	13	48.15
Dewar, A.	15	5.00	11	33.27
Dharsi, S. K.	2,288	32.22	1	18.00
D'Souza, W. A.	821	35.69	7	44.57
du Preez, J. H.	**4,063**	**23.76**	**296**	**31.13**
Dykes, R. A.	723	20.08	–	–
Dyson, E. M.	819	18.20	0	–
Ebrahim, I.	520	10.19	179	21.33
Edrich, J. H.	**39,790**	**45.47**	**0**	**–**
Edwards, G N.	**4,589**	**29.41**	**0**	**–**
Ferrow, D. J.	16	3.20	9	24.44
Freeman, E. W.	**2,244**	**19.17**	**241**	**27.75**
Gawli, S. M.	2	1.00	3	52.66
Goel, R.	1,037	9.34	750	18.58
Gomes, S. A.	2,645	32.65	0	–
Goswami, S.	1,592	28.42	47	24.08
Green, D. J.	2,929	20.20	1	99.00
Haddrick, R. N.	69	13.80	–	
Hamilton, B. G.	5	5.00	–	–
Hazarika, A. H.	567	18.29	–	–
Hendricks, E.	668	16.70	63	17.07
Hughes, R. C.	47	5.87	15	46.26
Humphries, D. J.	5,116	24.83	–	–
Hunter, W. R.	202	11.22	19	23.42

	Runs	Avge	Wkts	Avge
Imtiaz Ahmed, S.	348	24.85	3	22.33
Ismail Ibrahim	296	29.60	15	16.73
Jackman, R. D.	**5,685**	**17.71**	**1,402**	**22.80**
Jahanzeb Khan	312	5.67	120	29.63
Jarman, B. N.	**5,615**	**22.73**	**3**	**32.66**
Jayamohan Thampi, K.	114	11.40	–	–
Johnson, H. L.	14,286	26.40	21	39.14
Jones, D. M.	**19,188**	**51.85**	**27**	**57.22**
Jones, J. G.	33	6.60	0	–
Kasper, R. J.	1,742	29.52	23	37.78
Kasturirangan, G. I.	421	15.03	94	22.02
Kennedy, J. H.	7	7.00	1	99.00
Khalid Wazir	**271**	**15.05**	**14**	**53.28**
King, I. M.	476	8.35	129	28.72
Knott, S.	1,222	14.37	194	21.59
Lacy Scott, D. G.	294	14.00	9	29.77
Legard, E.	144	11.07	–	–
Madan Mohan, K.	828	14.78	5	59.60
Malloch, T. S.	19	9.50	6	30.33
Manners, J. E.	1,162	31.40	0	–
Marsland, G. P.	448	16.00	2	69.00
Mohammad Munaf	**1,356**	**17.61**	**180**	**24.22**
Mordaunt, D. J.	599	23.03	24	25.04
Murch, S. N. C.	215	17.91	17	51.05
Murphy, E. G.	24	6.00	–	–
Mustafi, A.	61	30.50	–	–
Nadkarni, R. G.	**8,880**	**40.36**	**500**	**21.37**
Naik, R. M.	265	24.09	1	15.00
Najeeb Tarakai	2,030	47.20	21	38.47
Newdick, G. A.	3,292	30.48	5	26.80
Opatha, A. R. M.	790	17.17	111	30.74
Owen, P. A.	2	1.00	4	59.75
Patil, S. R.	**848**	**26.50**	**83**	**30.60**
Phillips, E. F.	629	13.38	–	–
Pickles, D.	74	3.70	96	21.47
Poore, M. B.	**2,336**	**23.12**	**68**	**26.66**
Pritchard, G. C.	111	4.11	56	36.75
Procter, A. W.	67	11.16	5	25.20
Proverbs, N. G.	268	26.80	–	–
Raiji, V. N.	277	23.08	0	–
Rajesh, M. P.	64	16.00	19	16.80
Ranaweera, T. H. V. H. K.	234	3.25	255	26.25
Rayment, A. W. H.	6,338	20.31	19	40.63
Razick, G. S. M. S. A.	80	10.00	2	102.50
Reid, J. F.	**5,650**	**38.17**	**6**	**36.83**
Reid, J. R.	**16,128**	**41.35**	**466**	**22.60**
Riaz Sheikh	1,803	30.05	116	31.12
Richardson, B. D.	142	17.75	0	–
Richardson, B. H.	279	11.16	33	30.39
Scott, M. E.	2,445	12.86	461	24.72
Sedgley, J. B.	389	15.56	–	–
Semmence, D. J.	890	14.59	1	123.00
Shahid Mahmood	**3,117**	**31.80**	**89**	**21.64**
Sinclair, I. M.	**264**	**14.66**	**41**	**27.34**
Smith, C. M.	16	8.00	–	–
Smith, J.	17	8.50	4	24.75
Smith, R.	2,600	17.10	19	57.00
Sood, M. M.	**1,214**	**28.23**	**2**	**77.50**
Speed, S. R.	904	25.11	–	–
Spencer, C. T.	5,871	10.77	1,367	26.68
Springall, J. D.	5,176	25.88	80	41.40
Stewart, T. G.	120	20.00	13	44.92
Strachan, G. R.	17	–	2	17.00
Suresh Kumar, M.	1,657	19.49	196	27.77
Taufiq Tirmizi	245	15.31	16	39.75
Tillard, J. R.	3	1.50	–	–
Tynan, J. C.	80	11.42	2	24.00
Venkataraman, R.	84	10.50	0	–
Walker, P. M.	**17,650**	**26.03**	**834**	**28.63**
Waqar Hasan	**4,741**	**35.64**	**2**	**86.00**
Watson, G. D.	**4,674**	**32.68**	**186**	**25.31**
Watson, R. C. W.	115	19.16	–	–
Weekes, E. D.	**12,010**	**55.34**	**17**	**43.00**
Weerasinghe, D. H. A.	446	23.47	0	–
Wilkinson, R. W.	635	19.84	10	62.60
Wooler, C. R. D.	832	10.80	130	31.00
Younus Ata	326	36.22	0	–
Zafar Sarfraz	616	28.00	0	–
Zaveri, P. N.	972	14.72	140	25.45

*Test players are in **bold**; their career figures can be found on page 1077.*

Belliappa made 93 catches and 46 stumpings; Dharsi 67 and 26; Dykes 57 and 24; Edwards 126 and 16; Humphries 294 and 60; Jarman 431 and 129; Johnson 217 and two; Legard 33 and nine; J. F. Reid 116 and nine; J. R. Reid 239 and seven; C. M. Smith one and one; Speed 61 and 12; R. C. W. Watson 23 and none.

PART THREE

English International Cricket

THE ENGLAND TEAM IN 2020

Bubbling up

STEVE JAMES

On March 13, it became clear this was to be a year like no other for England's cricketers. After tea on the second day of a warm-up match in Sri Lanka, they were fielding at the P. Sara Oval when Joe Root walked off to speak on the phone to Ashley Giles, England's director of cricket. The match and the tour were abandoned – and the consequences of the Covid-19 pandemic were starting to unfold. The United Kingdom went into lockdown ten days later, and international cricket felt a distant dream.

That a revised, and delayed, home schedule of six Tests, six one-day internationals and six T20s became possible – behind closed doors at Southampton and Manchester – was little short of miraculous, and testimony to some determined work by the ECB, led by Steve Elworthy. When the year ended with the postponement of a three-match ODI series in South Africa because of Covid-19 concerns, it merely emphasised the meticulousness of the ECB's work.

ENGLAND IN 2020

	Played	*Won*	*Lost*	*Drawn/No result*
Tests	9	6	1	2
One-day internationals	9	4	4	1
Twenty20 internationals	12	8	3	1

Month	Fixtures	Reference
DECEMBER / JANUARY / FEBRUARY	4 Tests, 3 ODIs and 3 T20Is (a) v South Africa	(see *Wisden 2020*, page 440)
MARCH		
APRIL		
MAY		
JUNE		
JULY / AUGUST / SEPTEMBER	3 Tests (h) v West Indies	(page 327)
	3 ODIs (h) v Ireland	(page 349)
	3 Tests and 3 T20Is (h) v Pakistan	(page 355)
	3 ODIs and 3 T20Is (h) v Australia	(page 378)
OCTOBER		
NOVEMBER	3 T20Is (a) v South Africa	(page 387)
DECEMBER		

Stu Forster, Getty Images

After the Tests, before the testing: England celebrate a 3–1 victory in South Africa in January 2020.

There had not been one positive test in the three summer months of international cricket, and only one blemish, when Jofra Archer (whose 85 days in the bubble was the longest of all England's players) breached protocols by returning home between the first two Tests against West Indies. His error, which forced him into self-isolation and briefly cost him his place, underlined the fragility of the operation; Giles said it could have been a "disaster" for the finances of English cricket. ECB chief executive Tom Harrison had already spelled out the maths: a £380m loss for the game if no cricket took place, and over £100m out of pocket even if all England's fixtures were fulfilled.

Despite that, they could finish the year reasonably satisfied with their work, losing only one series in ten across the formats – a first ODI defeat since January 2017, thanks to a record-breaking partnership between Australia's Glenn Maxwell and Alex Carey at Old Trafford. Eyes, though, were already turning towards the next T20 World Cup, even if the tournament scheduled for Australia in autumn 2020 was postponed a year, and moved to India. England beat South Africa twice (both away), and Australia, and drew with Pakistan, as white-ball selection became T20-focused – most obviously when Archer, Ben Stokes and Sam Curran, who had all appeared between September and November at the rescheduled IPL, were rested from the one-day squad for South Africa. Amid the chaos inflicted on the fixture list by the pandemic, England ended the year top of the rankings in both 50- and 20-over cricket.

They also consolidated the forward strides made in South Africa earlier in the year by winning home Test series against West Indies and Pakistan – though they finished 2020 fourth in the World Test Championship behind Australia, India and New Zealand, and in danger of missing out on the Lord's final in 2021. But they had continued to espouse the mantra of new head coach Chris Silverwood in batting for longer periods, and had not won three consecutive Test series since Andrew Strauss's team went No. 1 in the world in 2011. There were special moments for Stuart Broad, who claimed his 500th Test wicket, for James Anderson, who became the first fast bowler to 600, and for 22-year-old Zak Crawley, whose maiden Test century, against Pakistan at Southampton, blossomed into an astonishing 267.

That Stokes played a leading role was little surprise. He was England's highest Test run-scorer in 2020, despite missing the last two games – as well as nine white-ball matches against Pakistan and Australia – to be with his father, Ged, who had been diagnosed with brain cancer in New Zealand. He died in early December.

With Root attending the birth of his second child, Stokes had captained England for the first time, in the First Test against West Indies – a game preceded by a memorable tribute from both sides to the Black Lives Matter movement. England lost by four wickets after making just 204 in their first innings, but Stokes produced an all-round masterclass in the Second Test, ushering them to a thrilling 113-run victory with two very different innings: 176 from 356 balls, having needed 255 for his slowest first-class century, and 78 not out from 57 when promoted up the order, having needed 36 for England's fastest Test fifty by an opener. Those innings showed his adaptability, and his class. Just for good measure, he took three key wickets. It all prompted Root – no doubt grateful in part because he was struggling for runs himself – to suggest his team were "in the presence of greatness". Stokes, he said, was England's "Mr Incredible".

Dan Mullan, Getty Images

Job done: Jos Buttler cracks Adam Zampa for six to clinch the T20 series against Australia.

Just as incredible was the sixth-wicket partnership of 139 between Jos Buttler and Chris Woakes that pinched the First Test at Old Trafford from Pakistan's grasp. Chasing 277 on a wearing pitch suited to the wrist-spin and reverse-swing strengths of their opponents' attack, England had slumped to 117 for five. Buttler, who had missed three chances behind the stumps, later admitted he was playing for his place, and had the added burden of learning the night before that his father was ill. Woakes's ten most recent Test scores, meanwhile, had been 5, 1, 2, 6, 0, 32, 0, 0, 1 and 19. Yet together they fashioned a famous win, with Woakes remaining unbeaten on 84, after Buttler had fallen for 75. The partnership set the pair up for fantastic summers, with both having a credible claim to being England's outstanding player.

Buttler's keeping will always have its critics, and Surrey's Ben Foakes was always there in England's bubble as a reminder of the romantics' wishes. But he is a hugely respected figure in the dressing-room, and his 152 – and partnership of 359 with Crawley – in the final Test of the summer against Pakistan, was confirmation he was adjusting to the demands of the red ball. Buttler also opened the batting in the first two T20 internationals against Australia, both won, smashing 44 in the first, then a magisterial 77 not out from 54 balls in the second, closing the match with a straight six off leg-spinner Adam Zampa. That ended the debate about whether he was an opener or a finisher: he could be both. Opening once more, he made 67 not out in the final game of the year, in South Africa.

The ever cheerful and underrated Woakes took 20 wickets in six Tests at 21, and in ODIs was England's most economical bowler, going at 4.51 an over (he also averaged 43 with the bat). His most telling one-day intervention was in the second match against Australia at Old Trafford, where he and Archer dragged England back from the brink of defeat: with the tourists 144 for two, and cantering towards a modest target of 232, they took four for three in 21 balls. As captain Eoin Morgan put it: "Jofra is an ace, and so is Woakesy. You bowl them in the most important parts of the game."

Archer is indeed an ace, highlighted by his selection as the IPL's Most Valuable Player, but this was not an auspicious year for him in Test cricket. He was still learning his trade, and was clearly more effective – and faster, because of the lesser requirements – in the shorter formats. With the Ashes on the horizon, Root and the management were eager to wring more from his talent.

It was perhaps with that trip in mind that Archer was selected alongside Mark Wood in the First Test against West Indies – one of England's fastest pairings of all time. The ploy did not work, though, and it proved Wood's only Test of the summer. It irked Broad no end, too. Left out of a home Test for the first time in eight years, he expressed his dissatisfaction in a mid-match interview on Sky Sports. "It is quite a hard decision to understand," he said. "I have probably bowled the best I have ever bowled in the last couple of years. I felt like it was my shirt."

England did not repeat the mistake. Broad played the remaining five Tests, reaching the 500 milestone when he dismissed West Indies' Kraigg Brathwaite to join Anderson, Glenn McGrath and Courtney Walsh as the only fast bowlers in an elite club. He was comfortably England's leading Test wicket-taker, with 38 at just 14, a staggeringly good return. His had been a point well made, as undue fascination surrounded the Ashes, and whether Broad (aged 34) and Anderson (38) could both make the trip. Anderson was second to Broad, with

Stu Forster, Getty Images

Indefatigable: Phil Neale (right), who stepped down as operations manager after more than two decades, and coach Chris Silverwood.

23 at 20, reaching 600 when he induced an edge from Pakistan captain Azhar Ali on the final afternoon of the summer's final, rain-ravaged Test.

Dominic Sibley bowled some filthy leg-spin that day, but had a year to remember. His 615 Test runs were second only to Stokes, and his second century, 120 off 372 balls against West Indies, was another example of his resilience. He, Rory Burns and Crawley looked a traditional Test-match top order in their approach, though the quirky techniques of the openers were another matter. Crawley has a wonderfully simple way of batting, with a small forward press by way of a trigger movement, and a free flow of the bat. His game, with a strong back-foot element, is ideally set up for Test cricket, which might explain his modest county record: the domestic game is more distanced from the top level than ever. Sibley showed off an unusual method, mainly eschewing the off side, and a chink down the leg side that might be exposed by quicker bowlers on bouncier pitches. But he was now a proven run-scorer at every level.

If only the same could be said of off-spinner Dom Bess as a wicket-taker. He played all six summer Tests, and had improved since his initial forays in 2018, but claimed just eight victims. It was no surprise he was offered only an incremental contract. With Moeen Ali's decline in all formats – he did at least captain England for the first time, in the third T20 against Australia – the search for a Test-class slow bowler went on. Leg-spinner Adil Rashid remained England's best white-ball bowler, while dampening speculation, because of a rickety shoulder, about a Test return.

It was inevitably an odd year for the one-day world champions, with a bubble of players separate from the Test squad necessary for the first home

ODIs – three against Ireland – since their 2019 triumph. At least there was always something to play for, since those matches signalled the start of the ICC World Cup Super League to determine qualification for the 2023 tournament. There were opportunities for the likes of Sam Billings (who made a maiden ODI century, against Australia) and Tom Banton, as well as a brief shot at redemption for David Willey after his World Cup omission.

In T20 cricket, Dawid Malan continued an astounding run of form, taking his tally of scores of 50-plus to ten from 19 innings, at a strike-rate of almost 150. That lifted him to the top of the world rankings, and the highest points score ever (915). Yet before the three-match series in South Africa in November, he was still no certain pick. There remained concerns about his slow starts – and maybe even his selfishness, given that Morgan had publicly berated him after he had not run a bye off the final ball of a T20 in New Zealand in 2019-20. But in the last match of the series in Cape Town, he went off like a train, and finished 99 not out to cement his place, and buttress England's aspirations of T20 World Cup glory. With Stokes back, and Jonny Bairstow in a new role at No. 4, they won 3–0.

The effects of so much time in bubbles took its toll, though, with Banton and Tom Curran pulling out of Big Bash contracts. Earlier, Archer had also opted out, saying: "I'm not sure how many more bubbles I've got left in me." And though two England positive Covid-19 tests were revealed as false, the South Africa ODI series was postponed essentially because of player anxiety.

It promised to be another challenging year in 2021, when England's backroom team will be without the indefatigable Phil Neale, the former Worcestershire captain who had been their operations manager for 21 years. He had worked on a remarkable 257 Tests, 422 ODIs and 110 T20Is, before retiring in October.

ENGLAND PLAYERS IN 2020

LAWRENCE BOOTH

The following 31 players (there were 38 in 2019, and 35 in 2018) appeared in 2020, when England played nine Tests, nine one-day internationals and 12 Twenty20 internationals. Statistics refer to the full year, not the 2020 season.

MOEEN ALI — Worcestershire

Alarmed by Ali's admission that he had been "coasting", Morgan did everything possible to reignite his spark, handing him the vice-captaincy for the Ireland ODIs, then the captaincy itself for the final T20 against Australia. But, with the exception of a blast-from-the-past 61 off 33 deliveries in a losing T20 cause against Pakistan, Ali just couldn't find his bearings, with bat or ball. At 33, he was running out of time to relocate them. Reselected for the Test tour of Sri Lanka in early 2021, he promptly caught Covid-19.

5 ODIs: 24 runs @ 8.00, SR 64.86; 1 wicket @ 216.00, ER 4.80.
9 T20Is: 157 runs @ 22.42, SR 168.81; 2 wickets @ 55.50, ER 8.53.

JAMES ANDERSON — Lancashire

There were moments when it was easy to forget that Anderson was nearing an unprecedented milestone: 600 Test wickets for a seamer. And after match figures of one for 97 against Pakistan in Manchester – his worst at home for five years – he felt obliged to scotch rumours of retirement. At that point, with critics agonising over what role he might play in Australia in 2021-22, he still needed ten wickets from two games. Despite a flurry of drops, he got there on the last afternoon of a Test summer in which one narrative (international seamers can't be as old as 38) yielded to another (in English conditions, Anderson still had it). The decision about the Ashes could wait.

6 Tests: 36 runs @ 9.00; 23 wickets @ 20.47.

JOFRA ARCHER — Sussex

After starring in his first year with England in 2019, Archer had his best moments at the IPL, where his new-ball incisions and six-hitting for Rajasthan Royals made him the tournament's MVP. For his country, he was more rank and file, partly because – with Anderson fit again – he had the new ball in Tests only once, almost undermining West Indies' run-chase at the Rose Bowl. Root and Silverwood insisted he rattle the speedgun; Archer insisted it wasn't so simple. He seemed more at home (and faster) spearheading the white-ball attacks under Morgan, and was all over Australia's David Warner – a dynamic that continued at the IPL. But, in a summer when travel was taboo, it was Archer's detour from Southampton to his home at Hove, a breach of coronavirus protocol, that attracted the loudest headlines, and cost him a Test cap.

4 Tests: 42 runs @ 10.50; 8 wickets @ 45.00.
3 ODIs: 14 runs without dismissal, SR 116.66; 7 wickets at 21.57, ER 5.20.
6 T20Is: 5 wickets @ 37.40, ER 8.13.

JONNY BAIRSTOW **Yorkshire**

For the first time since his Test debut in 2012, Bairstow went a calendar year without red-ball cricket for England – the consequence of averaging just 27 across the previous three. Instead, he settled down to burnishing his white-ball reputation: more 50-over runs than any team-mate (plus the best strike-rate of the specialist batsmen), and more 20-over runs than any bar Malan. As ever, no Bairstow story was complete without the suggestion that he was at his best with a point to prove: in this case, an unbeaten 86 from 48 balls to win a T20 at Cape Town in November after being lowered to No. 4. Soon after, he was in the Test squad for Sri Lanka – the latest twist in a career full of them.

9 ODIs: 346 runs @ 43.25, SR 100.87.
12 T20Is: 329 runs @ 32.90, SR 150.91.

TOM BANTON **Somerset**

These were early days, but there was enough to set the pulse racing: 137 in three T20 innings against Pakistan off just 89 balls, plus a maiden ODI half-century against Ireland, batting out of position in the middle order. Reality couldn't always match expectation: 12 runs in three T20 innings against Australia, and five lbws among his 11 dismissals of the summer. Taken later to South Africa as a batting spare, he then pulled out of the Big Bash League, citing bubble fatigue – in more ways than one, a very modern cricketer.

6 ODIs: 134 runs @ 26.80, SR 92.41.
6 T20Is: 149 runs @ 24.83, SR 136.69.

DOMINIC BESS **Somerset/Yorkshire**

Success in South Africa, plus Leach's health problems and Ali's Test exile, thrust Bess into the lone spinner's role for the summer – with modest results. He wasn't helped by a dearth of left-handers in the West Indian and Pakistani line-ups, nor by Buttler's fragile keeping. But neither did he nail his length. The odd highlight – a dipping, turning off-break to bowl West Indies captain Jason Holder as England squared the series in Manchester – couldn't mask a sense of futility: in two of the home Tests, he didn't bowl at all. Success in Galle in early 2021 lifted his spirits.

8 Tests: 112 runs @ 22.40; 16 wickets @ 40.62.

SAM BILLINGS **Kent**

Billings began to look the business again. After stylishly making 132 runs off 133 balls for once out in the one-dayers against Ireland, he almost turned a lost cause into victory against Australia with a sparkling maiden international century, followed two games later by 57. He had his eye on the finisher's role at No. 6; for the first time in years, the ambition felt realistic.

6 ODIs: 315 runs @ 78.75, SR 95.74.
4 T20Is: 43 runs @ 14.33, SR 113.15.

STUART BROAD **Nottinghamshire**

Dropped for the First Test against West Indies, Broad let off steam during an interview with Sky, then took it out on the opposition. The summer's remaining five Tests produced 29 wickets at 13, including ten for 67 as England won the decider against West Indies, and his 500th in all. A fuller length, for so long regarded with suspicion, now seemed ingrained; the lbws flowed. His batting, too, had a new lease of life. After working in the nets with Peter Moores, the Nottinghamshire coach, he was giving himself room to free his arms, and hitting good-length balls over extra cover. Cameos became the norm: 43 off 28 in Johannesburg in January, then 62 off 45 against the West Indians, and an unbeaten 29 against Pakistan. Only Stokes hit more than his eight Test sixes, and he even earned a promotion to No. 8. Irked to be placed in the same age bracket as Anderson, the 34-year-old Broad was learning new tricks.

8 Tests: 177 runs @ 35.40; 38 wickets @ 14.76.

RORY BURNS — Surrey

A mixed summer threw up renewed questions about his quirky technique. Against West Indies, Burns averaged 46, and in four innings out of five batted over two hours. But his failure to convert any of his starts into hundreds felt costly when Shaheen Shah Afridi exposed a tendency to play around his front pad: against Pakistan, he averaged five, prompting the kind of commentary-box dissection players dread.

6 Tests: 254 runs @ 28.22.

JOS BUTTLER — Lancashire

By his own admission, Buttler walked out to bat on the fourth afternoon of the First Test against Pakistan with his career in the balance. By the evening, he and Woakes had secured an improbable win, and Buttler's flakiness with the gloves – and lone half-century in 16 innings – had been forgotten. Two games later, he batted for 311 balls (having never faced more than 200 in a Test) for a career-best 152, and looked as close as ever to being England's long-term Test keeper. In T20s, he was typically unfettered, securing series against Australia and South Africa.

9 Tests: 497 runs @ 38.23; 30 catches as wicketkeeper.
3 ODIs: 12 runs @ 4.00, SR 38.70; 6 catches and 1 stumping as wicketkeeper.
8 T20Is: 291 runs @ 48.50, SR 150.77; 8 catches and 1 stumping as wicketkeeper.

ZAK CRAWLEY — Kent

A year of four quarters peaked in a sublime 267 against Pakistan at the Rose Bowl, as Crawley nudged his way, almost from nowhere, into a variety of tables and records. Not many had seen it coming while he operated as a stand-in opener in South Africa (Burns was injured), then as a stand-in No. 4 for the First Test against West Indies (Root was on paternity leave). Crawley was dropped again for the Third (Stokes couldn't bowl, so England needed an extra seamer). When Stokes joined his family in New Zealand, Crawley got another chance at No. 3, against Pakistan, making 53 in the rain-ruined Second Test – a useful recce. After he batted for nine hours in the summer's final Test, all the upheaval seemed worth it, only for a struggle against Sri Lanka spinner Lasith Embuldeniya in the New Year.

7 Tests: 580 runs @ 52.72.

SAM CURRAN **Surrey**

Curran spent a year in which his IPL captain M. S. Dhoni described him as a "complete cricketer" serving up bits and pieces for England. He kept playing in victorious Test teams, and had won 13 of his 19 by the summer's end; his canny left-armers brought a balance England craved. But individual moments were thin on the ground: a couple of batting cameos, the crucial wicket of Shamarh Brooks in the final session of the Second Test against West Indies, then three for 28 opening in the first T20 at Cape Town. Still, at 22 it was all good experience.

5 Tests: 118 runs @ 19.66; 9 wickets @ 40.11.
3 ODIs: 8 runs @ 4.00, SR 34.78; 3 wickets @ 26.33, ER 4.93.
3 T20Is: 8 runs @ 8.00, SR 100.00; 3 wickets @ 29.00, ER 9.66.

TOM CURRAN **Surrey**

A chastening T20 series in South Africa late in the year summed up Curran's struggles: 10–0–116–2, and the suspicion that batsmen were wising up to his variations. With 20-over World Cups scheduled this year and next, the timing felt ominous. A lone 50-over wicket at exorbitant cost did little to lift the gloom, though a tight performance helped square the series with Australia in Manchester. Like Banton, he withdrew from the BBL because of the demands of life in the bubble.

7 ODIs: 114 runs @ 38.00, SR 82.01; 1 wicket @ 261.00; ER 5.11.
12 T20Is: 18 runs @ 9.00, SR 90.00; 10 wickets @ 39.40, ER 9.85.

JOE DENLY **Kent**

Denly's curio of an England career hit the buffers. He reached double figures in six of his seven Test innings, but couldn't breach 38, and was dropped after the first Test of the summer, almost certainly for good. He later admitted he had got "bogged down" in his role at No. 3. In white-ball cricket, he was a habit the selectors seemed unsure whether to kick: after helping square the 50-over series in South Africa in February, he was ignored in England, only to be recalled for a dead T20 against Australia.

4 Tests: 176 runs @ 25.14; 2 wickets @ 35.50.
3 ODIs: 153 runs @ 76.50, SR 84.06; no wicket for 41 runs, ER 6.83.
3 T20Is: 33 runs @ 16.50, SR 132.00; no wicket for 8 runs, ER 8.00.

CHRIS JORDAN **Sussex**

Now 32, Jordan had settled on his England role: senior statesman of the 20-over attack. (A trio of ODIs in South Africa in February 2020, his first for three and a half years, had confirmed he was better suited to the shortest format.) No team-mate claimed more than his dozen T20 wickets, though a few were less expensive. But Morgan still trusted him at both ends of the innings, and his yorker – when he landed it properly – remained potent. And in December, he passed Broad's national record of 65 T20I wickets – the first non-white cricketer to top one of England's runs or wickets charts in any format.

3 ODIs: 1 run without dismissal, SR 20.00; 2 wickets @ 45.00, ER 6.27.
12 T20Is: 31 runs @ 10.33, SR 124.00; 12 wickets @ 30.91, ER 9.16.

DAWID MALAN **Yorkshire**

By the time he was smashing an unbeaten 99 from 47 balls at Cape Town in December, to take England to a 3–0 T20 drubbing of South Africa and back to the top of the rankings, it seemed absurd there had ever been a debate over Malan's worth. Some fretted over his steady starts, but his eventual numbers brooked little argument, and left him with a record ICC T20 rating. Perhaps being on the periphery had kept him sharp – just like his strokeplay, which was precise but punishing, ferocious without being frantic.

10 T20Is: 397 runs @ 49.62, SR 142.29.

EOIN MORGAN **Middlesex**

If his stats tailed off a little after the *annus mirabilis* of 2019, they spoke of a player who, even at 34, was keeping the youngsters honest. A one-day century against his native Ireland came in defeat, and his cleanest hitting was reserved for T20: a strike-rate bettered among team-mates only by Ali, and an unmatched 17 sixes. His 33-ball 66 to marshal an imposing chase against Pakistan was vintage Morgan, who later in the year was happy to slip down the order from No. 4. All the while, he exuded an authority born of lifting a World Cup: if the Test team felt like a joint production between Root and coach Chris Silverwood, the white-ball stage was all Morgan's.

9 ODIs: 250 runs @ 35.71, SR 97.65.
11 T20Is: 276 runs @ 34.50, SR 168.29.

OLLIE POPE **Surrey**

A stunning tour of South Africa gave way to a modest summer, concerns about the claustrophobia of life in the bubble, and a second dislocation of his left shoulder, ruling him out of the 2020-21 tour of Sri Lanka. Pope's sparkling performances in wins at Cape Town, Port Elizabeth and Johannesburg had felt like his breakthrough. But while he shone with successive half-centuries in Manchester – against West Indies and Pakistan – he didn't pass 12 in seven home innings either side. He did receive a jaffa or two, but was made to look mortal by Yasir Shah.

9 Tests: 481 runs @ 43.72.

ADIL RASHID **Yorkshire**

To watch Rashid take control of the middle overs of white-ball matches was now an established treat – and his googly to bowl Australia's Aaron Finch in the third T20 in Southampton arguably the ball of the summer. His 24 limited-overs wickets were ten clear of the English pack; if another Australian, Glenn Maxwell, took advantage of a short boundary in Manchester to collar him in the deciding ODI, Rashid alone among England bowlers conceded less than eight an over in T20 matches. Mainly, he was so masterful that excited talk of resurrecting his Test career had to be quietened by reminders of a frail shoulder.

7 ODIs: 56 runs @ 18.66, SR 105.66; 12 wickets @ 30.16, ER 5.37.
12 T20Is: 5 runs @ 5.00, SR 62.50; 12 wickets @ 26.33, ER 7.52.

JOE ROOT **Yorkshire**

By one measure, Root was doing better than fine: wins of South Africa, West Indies and Pakistan meant that, among those to have captained England at least 20 times, only Mike Brearley had a higher win percentage than his 52. (He even missed England's only defeat of the year, because of paternity leave.) But his batting remained a source of frustration. It wasn't that he kept failing: not once in Tests was he dismissed in single figures. But by reaching 20 in ten of his 13 innings without passing 68, he was unable to silence those who feared big runs were incompatible with leadership. Too often, he played a rash stroke where Kohli, Smith or Williamson would not; uncharacteristically, he appeared frantic. An average of 42 was hardly a disaster – but, like his quiet time in one-day cricket, he could do so much more. And in early 2021, he did, spectacularly – scoring 228 and 186 in wins at Galle, then 218 in the victory at Chennai.

8 Tests: 464 runs @ 42.18; 5 wickets @ 41.20.
6 ODIs: 106 runs @ 21.20, SR 67.08; 4 wickets @ 31.75, ER 5.52.

JASON ROY **Surrey**

Few England players were more badly thrown by lockdown than Roy, who never rediscovered the rhythm established during a strong T20 series in South Africa in February. Six home ODIs against Ireland and Australia, interrupted by a side injury, yielded 49 runs. Then another three T20s in South Africa produced 30. The harder he searched for fluency, the scratchier he grew. For the first time since he was dropped during the 2017 Champions Trophy, Roy – so central to England's World Cup success – was glancing over his shoulder.

9 ODIs: 102 runs @ 12.75, SR 87.17.
6 T20Is: 147 runs @ 24.50, SR 138.67.

DOMINIC SIBLEY **Warwickshire**

Even while averaging 47, Sibley felt there was more to come: six of his 14 innings ended between 32 and 44, amid talk of a curious weakness down the leg side. And yet the overall impression was of a stability so lacking in recent England openers: more often than not, Sibley – who shed two stone during lockdown after observing team-mates' fitness in Sri Lanka – took the shine off the new ball. Against West Indies in Manchester, with England 1–0 down, he did far more than that, adding 120 to the unbeaten 133 he had made at Cape Town six months earlier, and putting on 260 with Stokes. If his technique remained a riddle wrapped in an enigma, then the stats were clear enough.

9 Tests: 615 runs @ 47.30; no wicket for seven runs.

BEN STOKES **Durham**

Despite personal anguish, Stokes ensured 2020 would not be the calm after the storm of 2019. Runs and wickets to seal a Test series in South Africa were followed by a monumental 176 and (as opener) 78 not out, plus tireless spells of round-the-wicket bouncers, to help square one with West Indies. No longer simply England's best all-rounder, he was their best batsman too. For a while, his body rebelled, but he returned from the canvas to take two cheap wickets as Pakistan collapsed in Manchester. By now, though, his mind was elsewhere:

his father, Ged, was gravely ill in Christchurch. Stokes flew to the city of his birth to join him, delaying his entrance at the IPL. He was in South Africa when Ged died in early December, his son at the peak of his powers.

7 Tests: 641 runs @ 58.27; 19 wickets @ 18.73.
6 T20Is: 126 runs @ 31.50, SR 141.57; 6 wickets @ 19.16, ER 8.21.

CHRIS WOAKES — Warwickshire

Once again, there were few team men quite like Woakes. After helping win a series with the ball, taking a five-for in the decisive Test against West Indies, he effectively won another with the bat, scoring an unbeaten 84 to rescue England's run-chase with Buttler in the only game against Pakistan not to finish drawn. His figures were impeccable, even though he was usually armed with the old ball; and in his lone Test with the new one, against West Indies at Manchester, he had a match analysis of 37–13–76–5. To underline the point, his one-day economy-rate was the team's meanest.

6 Tests: 176 runs @ 29.33; 20 wickets @ 21.65.
5 ODIs: 129 runs @ 43.00, SR 98.47; 7 wickets @ 27.71, ER 4.51.

MARK WOOD — Durham

When he did get a chance, he was rapid. But nine wickets at the Wanderers in January faded as he played only one summer Test – the one England lost, against West Indies at Southampton. Partly, the selectors were reluctant to pair him up with Archer, reasoning that two bowlers of extreme pace were unnecessary once Broad started going on the rampage. But Wood – story of his life – was never quite as fit as he hoped, and he was limited to some fiery but unproductive white-ball spells in late season. He was, it seemed, being saved for Australian pitches in 2021-22.

3 Tests: 102 runs @ 25.50; 14 wickets @ 19.50.
2 ODIs: did not bat; 3 wickets @ 31.33, ER 4.94.
6 T20Is: did not bat; 7 wickets @ 30.28, ER 9.63.

AND THE REST...

Given the new ball in two of the three Ireland ODIs and both the Pakistan T20s, **Saqib Mahmood** (Lancashire; 4 ODIs, 3 T20Is) never quite stated his case, and was left out of the end-of-year trip to South Africa. England desperately wanted **James Vince** (Hampshire; 3 ODIs) to succeed but, against Ireland, innings of 25, 16 and 16 – full of elegance and fragility – were all too familiar. **David Willey** (Yorkshire; 3 ODIs) was delighted to be recalled for that series more than a year after his World Cup omission, and responded with a first international five-for and crucial runs – only to be dropped again when the Australians arrived. **Matt Parkinson** (Lancashire; 2 ODIs) played just twice, in South Africa in February and did not take a wicket. The injury-plagued **Reece Topley** (Surrey; 1 ODI) bowled well against Ireland in his first England game since March 2016, and earned selection for the white-ball tour of South Africa. The highlight of the T20 series against Pakistan for **Lewis Gregory** (Somerset; 3 T20Is) was being the most economical bowler on either side in the high-scoring second match; but, overall, he went wicketless, and never went past 12.

ENGLAND TEST AVERAGES IN CALENDAR YEAR 2020

BATTING AND FIELDING

		T	*I*	*NO*	*R*	*HS*	*100*	*50*	*Avge*	*SR*	*Ct*
1	†B. A. Stokes	7	12	1	641	176	2	2	58.27	62.17	14
2	Z. Crawley	7	11	0	580	267	1	3	52.72	56.86	4
3	D. P. Sibley	9	14	1	615	133*	2	2	47.30	37.89	4
4	O. J. D. Pope	9	14	3	481	135*	1	4	43.72	57.05	9
5	J. E. Root	8	13	2	464	68*	0	4	42.18	56.44	14
6	J. C. Buttler	9	14	1	497	152	1	2	38.23	53.44	30
7	†S. C. J. Broad	8	9	4	177	62	0	1	35.40	112.02	4
8	C. R. Woakes	6	7	1	176	84*	0	1	29.33	63.08	4
9	†R. J. Burns	6	9	0	254	90	0	2	28.22	43.56	4
10	M. A. Wood	3	5	1	102	42	0	0	25.50	103.03	2
11	J. L. Denly	4	7	0	176	38	0	0	25.14	33.91	2
12	D. M. Bess	8	10	5	112	31*	0	0	22.40	52.33	2
13	†S. M. Curran	5	6	0	118	44	0	0	19.66	80.27	1
14	J. C. Archer	4	4	0	42	23	0	0	10.50	52.50	1
15	†J. M. Anderson	6	5	1	36	11	0	0	9.00	50.00	4

BOWLING

		Style	*O*	*M*	*R*	*W*	*BB*	*5I*	*Avge*	*SR*
1	S. C. J. Broad	RFM	242.5	77	561	38	6-31	1	14.76	38.34
2	B. A. Stokes	RFM	125.4	30	356	19	4-49	0	18.73	39.68
3	M. A. Wood	RF	92.3	17	273	14	5-46	1	19.50	39.64
4	J. M. Anderson	RFM	198	57	471	23	5-40	2	20.47	51.65
5	C. R. Woakes	RFM	164	39	433	20	5-50	1	21.65	49.20
6	S. M. Curran	LFM	115	25	361	9	2-39	0	40.11	76.66
7	D. M. Bess	OB	249.1	65	650	16	5-51	1	40.62	93.43
8	J. E. Root	OB/LB	70.2	21	206	5	4-87	0	41.20	84.40
9	J. C. Archer	RF	125.4	23	360	8	3-45	0	45.00	94.25

Also bowled: J. L. Denly (LB) 25–5–71–2; D. P. Sibley (LB) 1–0–7–0.

> "Buttler's shirt bore testimony to alcoholic celebration, especially since he kept it on until almost 12 hours after the match had ended. Signed by the England team, it made £65,100, which he donated to the Royal Brompton and Harefield Hospitals emergency appeal."
>
> Cricketana, page 197

ENGLAND ONE-DAY INTERNATIONAL AVERAGES IN CALENDAR YEAR 2020

BATTING AND FIELDING

		M	*I*	*NO*	*R*	*HS*	*100*	*50*	*Avge*	*SR*	*Ct/St*
1	S. W. Billings	6	6	2	315	118	1	2	78.75	95.74	3
2	J. M. Bairstow	9	8	0	346	112	1	2	43.25	100.87	5
3	C. R. Woakes	5	4	1	129	53*	0	1	43.00	98.47	1
4	T. K. Curran	7	5	2	114	38*	0	0	38.00	82.01	1
5	†E. J. G. Morgan	9	8	1	250	106	1	0	35.71	97.65	3
6	T. Banton	6	5	0	134	58	0	1	26.80	92.41	2
7	J. E. Root	6	5	0	106	49	0	0	21.20	67.08	0
8	J. M. Vince	3	3	0	57	25	0	0	19.00	87.69	1
9	A. U. Rashid	7	5	2	56	35*	0	0	18.66	105.66	1
10	J. J. Roy	9	8	0	102	32	0	0	12.75	87.17	1
11	†M. M. Ali	5	4	1	24	17*	0	0	8.00	64.86	0
12	J. C. Buttler	3	3	0	12	8	0	0	4.00	38.70	6/1

Played in four matches: S. Mahmood 12 (1ct). Played in three matches: J. C. Archer 8*, 6* (1ct); †S. M. Curran 7, 1; J. L. Denly 87, 66; C. J. Jordan 1*, 0*; †D. J. Willey 47*, 51 (1ct). Played in two matches: M. W. Parkinson did not bat, M. A. Wood did not bat (1ct). Played in one match: R. J. W. Topley did not bat (1ct).

BOWLING

		Style	*O*	*M*	*R*	*W*	*BB*	*4I*	*Avge*	*SR*	*ER*
1	D. J. Willey	LFM	28.4	4	148	8	5-30	1	18.50	21.50	5.16
2	J. C. Archer	RF	29	2	151	7	3-34	0	21.57	24.85	5.20
3	S. M. Curran	LFM	16	0	79	3	3-35	0	26.33	32.00	4.93
4	C. R. Woakes	RFM	43	1	194	7	3-32	0	27.71	36.85	4.51
5	A. U. Rashid	LB	67.2	4	362	12	3-34	0	30.16	33.66	5.37
6	S. Mahmood	RFM	32.5	2	156	5	2-36	0	31.20	39.40	4.75
7	M. A. Wood	RF	19	1	94	3	3-54	0	31.33	38.00	4.94
8	J. E. Root	OB	23	0	127	4	2-46	0	31.75	34.50	5.52

Also bowled: M. M. Ali (OB) 45–0–216–1; T. K. Curran (RFM) 51–4–261–1; J. L. Denly (LB) 6–0–41–0; C. J. Jordan (RFM) 14.2–0–90–2; M. W. Parkinson (LB) 10.4–0–63–0; R. J. W. Topley (LFM) 9–1–31–1; J. M. Vince (RM) 7–0–38–1.

"In March 1996, he faced his former Australian team-mates for a World XI, and purred to a vintage 103. It helped them to a competitive total after being 114 for six, and allowed the local *Herald Sun* to run the headline 'Deano saves the World'."

Obituaries, page 259

ENGLAND TWENTY20 INTERNATIONAL AVERAGES IN CALENDAR YEAR 2020

BATTING AND FIELDING

		M	*I*	*NO*	*R*	*HS*	*50*	*Avge*	*SR*	*4*	*6*	*Ct/St*
1	†M. M. Ali	9	9	2	157	61	1	22.42	**168.81**	12	10	1
2	†E. J. G. Morgan	11	10	2	276	66	3	34.50	**168.29**	21	17	4
3	J. M. Bairstow	12	11	1	329	86*	3	32.90	**150.91**	31	15	3
4	J. C. Buttler	8	8	2	291	77*	3	48.50	**150.77**	33	11	8/1
5	†D. J. Malan	10	10	2	397	99*	4	49.62	**142.29**	46	10	2
6	†B. A. Stokes	6	5	1	126	47*	0	31.50	**141.57**	7	8	5
7	J. J. Roy	6	6	0	147	70	1	24.50	**138.67**	13	7	0
8	T. Banton	6	6	0	149	71	1	24.83	**136.69**	13	6	2
9	J. L. Denly	3	3	1	33	29*	0	16.50	**132.00**	4	0	1
10	L. Gregory	3	3	1	14	12	0	7.00	**127.27**	2	0	0
11	C. J. Jordan	12	7	4	31	14*	0	10.33	**124.00**	1	1	6
12	S. W. Billings	4	4	1	43	26	0	14.33	**113.15**	4	1	1
13	T. K. Curran	12	5	3	18	8*	0	9.00	**90.00**	0	1	5
14	A. U. Rashid	12	3	2	5	3*	0	5.00	**62.50**	0	0	2

Played in six matches: J. C. Archer did not bat; M. A. Wood did not bat. Played in three matches: †S. M. Curran 7*, 1; S. Mahmood did not bat.

BOWLING

		Style	*Balls*	*Dots*	*R*	*W*	*BB*	*4I*	*Avge*	*SR*	*ER*
1	A. U. Rashid	LB	252	86	316	12	3-21	0	26.33	21.00	**7.52**
2	J. C. Archer	RF	138	53	187	5	2-33	0	37.40	27.60	**8.13**
3	B. A. Stokes	RFM	84	23	115	6	2-26	0	19.16	14.00	**8.21**
4	C. J. Jordan	RFM	243	68	371	12	2-28	0	30.91	20.25	**9.16**
5	M. A. Wood	RF	132	51	212	7	2-39	0	30.28	18.85	**9.63**
6	S. M. Curran	LFM	54	14	87	3	3-28	0	29.00	18.00	**9.66**
7	T. K. Curran	RFM	240	68	394	10	2-33	0	39.40	24.00	**9.85**

Also bowled: M. M. Ali (OB) 78–20–111–2; J. L. Denly (LB) 6–1–8–0; L. Gregory (RFM) 42–11–63–0; S. Mahmood (RFM) 48–11–75–0.

> “Sibley is as intrigued as anyone by his old-fashioned ability to bat for hours. ‘Honestly, I don’t know where it comes from. At school I couldn’t concentrate at all! When I was younger, I got some big scores, and people said I could bat for long periods of time, so I just kept trying to do that.’”
>
> Five Cricketers of the Year, page 72

SRI LANKA v ENGLAND IN 2019-20

RORY DOLLARD

On departure for Sri Lanka, Joe Root described the unfolding outbreak of coronavirus as "an evolving situation", which would be dealt with – initially, at least – by banning handshakes. Yet it soon became clear that circumstances were not so much evolving as spiralling out of control, and would require considerably more than the introduction of fist-bumps. Little more than a week later, the World Health Organisation decreed a pandemic; within 72 hours, England were flying home.

The tour lasted 12 days, five taken up by cricket, and ended abruptly when Root shuttled a message from player to player at drinks on the second afternoon of the four-day game with a Board President's XI at the P. Sara Oval in Colombo. Having just concluded a phone call on the boundary with ECB managing director of cricket Ashley Giles and chief executive Tom Harrison, who had been leading intensive discussions back at Lord's, Root was passing on the news that the match was being abandoned, and the tour postponed. The decision had been announced a couple of minutes earlier, leaving leg-spinner Matt Parkinson to send down the final over, unaware the tour had already been scrubbed from the calendar. Little did he, or anyone, know quite how long it would be before the next delivery was sent down by an England bowler.

Turn and flight: Matt Parkinson bowls in Colombo; within hours, England were on a plane to London.

The travelling party had arrived in Sri Lanka fully briefed by their doctor, Gurjit Bhogal, who issued immunity packs containing hand sanitiser, disinfectant wipes and throat spray. Meanwhile, the presence of thermal-imaging scanners at the airport, malls and hotels was an early sign this was not business as usual. Yet, at that stage, Sri Lanka remained virtually untouched by Covid-19, and the players were bothered more by the closure of the Table One restaurant at the Shangri-La hotel on Colombo's Galle Face: it had been a firm favourite during England's previous tour, in late 2018, but was now under reconstruction after being targeted by suicide bombers during the attacks of Easter 2019.

Briefly, the most pressing issues were professional matters. Offering 60 points apiece, the scheduled Tests in Galle and Colombo represented glittering prizes in the World Test Championship. Much, though, had changed since England's 3–0 triumph here 16 months earlier.

> With worldwide coronavirus infections growing exponentially, a heavy shadow was falling

Both sides had new coaches: Chris Silverwood and Mickey Arthur. Meanwhile, spinners Moeen Ali and Adil Rashid, who between them had accounted for half the 60 wickets England took in the whitewash, were watching from afar. Ali was continuing a curious hiatus from Test cricket, while Rashid's ongoing shoulder problem had nudged him further towards limited-overs specialism.

Jack Leach was primed to take the lead, a precarious plan given he had been fighting off a calf problem. He also had better reason than most to fear infection, because of a recent brush with sepsis and a compromised immune system brought about by treatment for Crohn's disease. He was backed by his puckish Somerset team-mate, Dom Bess, and Lancashire's uncapped Parkinson. It was a greener unit than the one Leach had joined two years earlier.

England's first warm-up, in Katunayake, was both useful workout and red herring. They managed four half-centuries, and acclimatised in the heat, but the pitch was suspiciously grassy, and there was a prevalence of seam in the opposition ranks. Despite that, Parkinson and Bess shared figures of seven for 122. It was around this time that England became early adopters of social distancing, media interactions taking place with a strict two-metre buffer zone. For at least two days, that was enforced by a chunky blue table, sourced at short notice from the pavilion. Fans due to join the tour in Galle were informed that no selfies or autographs would be possible, which played firmly against type for a friendly team, though the warning was soon rendered irrelevant.

On day one of the final warm-up, the increasingly impressive Zak Crawley made an assured hundred, before Root and Ollie Pope cashed in. But, behind the scenes, things had escalated. With worldwide infections growing exponentially, and high-profile sporting events being cancelled on an hourly basis, a heavy shadow was falling. England lost their last seven wickets in a rush on the second day, with Root later explaining that concerns over the

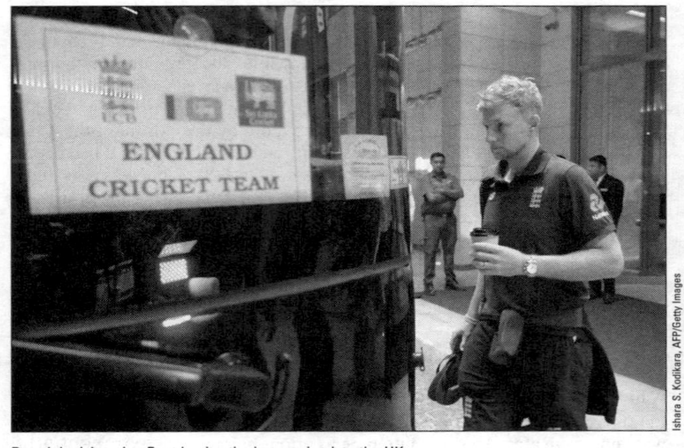

Ishara S. Kodikara, AFP/Getty Images

Board decision: Joe Root begins the journey back to the UK.

welfare of the players' families back home, and a desire to be reunited with them, had become an overwhelming distraction. An advance look at what to expect from Sri Lanka's quarantine arrangements also had an unsettling effect.

By the time Arthur abandoned a scouting mission to attend emergency talks with the Sri Lankan board, it was only a matter of time. Soon, the teams were shaking hands – or bumping fists – and heading towards an uncertain future.

ENGLAND TOURING PARTY

*J. E. Root (Yorkshire), D. M. Bess (Somerset), S. C. J. Broad (Nottinghamshire), J. C. Buttler (Lancashire), Z. Crawley (Kent), S. M. Curran (Surrey), J. L. Denly (Kent), B. T. Foakes (Surrey), K. K. Jennings (Lancashire), M. J. Leach (Somerset), S. Mahmood (Lancashire), M. W. Parkinson (Lancashire), O. J. D. Pope (Surrey), D. P. Sibley (Warwickshire), B. A. Stokes (Durham), C. R. Woakes (Warwickshire).

M. A. Wood (Durham) was originally selected, but withdrew with a side strain and was replaced by Mahmood.

Head coach: C. E. W. Silverwood. *Assistant coaches:* P. D. Collingwood, G. P. Thorpe. *Spin consultant:* J. S. Patel. *Fielding coach:* C. D. Hopkinson. *Team manager:* P. A. Neale. *Analyst:* R. Lewis. *Doctor:* G. Bhogal. *Physiotherapist:* C. A. de Weymarn. *Masseur:* M. Saxby. *Strength and conditioning:* R. Ahmun. *Security manager:* S. Dickason. *Head of team communications:* D. M. Reuben. *Digital editor:* G. R. Stobart.

At Katunayake, March 7–9, 2020 (not first-class). **Drawn.** **‡England XI 316** (85.3 overs) (J. E. Root 78, J. C. Buttler 79; S. M. L. D. Samarakoon 3-63) **and 320-7** (79.1 overs) (Z. Crawley 91, O. J. D. Pope 77); **Sri Lanka Cricket XI 245** (80 overs) (S. M. A. Priyanjan 77; D. M. Bess 3-54, M. W. Parkinson 4-68). *The tourists, who rotated their whole squad (apart from Jack Leach), had the better of a draw against a Sri Lanka Cricket XI, who picked from 15. First-day seventies from a fluent Joe Root and a more careful Jos Buttler helped England recover from 142-5 on a green pitch to 316, before spinners Dom Bess and Matt Parkinson earned them a lead of 71. Zak Crawley extended their advantage with 91 off 99 balls, while Ollie Pope continued his exciting winter with 77.*

At Colombo (PSO), March 12–15, 2020 (not first-class). **Drawn.** ‡**England XI 463** (117.4 overs) (Z. Crawley 105, J. E. Root 102, O. J. D. Pope 95; N. G. R. P. Jayasuriya 6-164); **Sri Lanka Board President's XI 150-3** (40 overs) (H. D. R. L. Thirimanne 88*). *The game – and the tour – was abandoned 11 overs after tea on the second day of the scheduled four. Though instances of Covid-19 in Sri Lanka remained scarce, Root's team were concerned about the possibility of being quarantined thousands of miles from their families; the ECB agreed there could be only one course of action. In the cricket that was possible, there were hundreds for Crawley and for Root, who then put on 190 for the fourth wicket in just 43 overs with Pope. Slow left-armer Prabath Jayasuriya finished with six for 164. But English thoughts were drifting homeward: on the second morning, they lost seven for 94. Woakes removed Pathum Nissanka Silva with the first ball of the President's XI reply, and quickly added Sadeera Samarawickrama. It was all immaterial. The match had originally been first-class, only for Parkinson to replace Stokes, who had an abdominal strain, on the second day. After much debate, it was decided to remove the game's first-class status, because the substitution was not caused by concussion.*

First Test At Galle, March 19–23, 2020. Cancelled.

Second Test At Colombo (RPS), March 26–30, 2020. Cancelled.

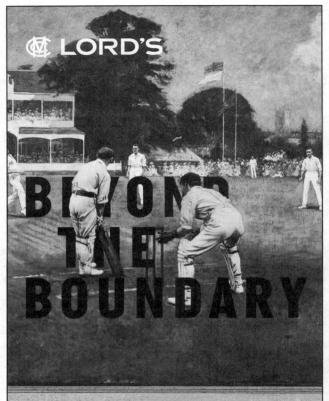

ENGLAND v WEST INDIES IN 2020

REVIEW BY SIMON WILDE

Test matches (3): England 2 (80pts), West Indies 1 (40pts)

West Indies failed in their attempt to win a first Test series in England since 1988, but they gave it a decent shot. And, by agreeing to be the first touring side to put themselves through the ordeal of biosecure cricket, they earned the lasting gratitude of the global game. After four months in the desert, here was the first oasis.

Jason Holder and his team were thankful for the opportunity to play for the first time since early March in Sri Lanka, though seven weeks inside Old Trafford and the Rose Bowl, both equipped with hotels, was not easy. Yet they endured their trial with good grace. All but ten days were spent in Manchester, where a 25-man squad began with two weeks in quarantine, before playing a pair of internal warm-up matches. Then, after a brief sojourn south for the First Test, they returned north for the Second and Third.

"It has been challenging," Holder said at the end. "Mentally, some of the guys are worn out. We had a change of environment at Southampton, which we really enjoyed, but then we had to come back here to see the same people, the same place, the same rooms." It hardly helped that Manchester's weather was at its most fickle, wiping three full days from the schedule: the first day of their second warm-up match, and one in each of the Tests. That took to 31 the days of Test cricket washed out at Old Trafford, cementing its huge lead at the top of the global rain-chart.

Stuart Broad, England's Player of the Series, saluted the West Indians: "They've been the heroes of this summer." When Holder suggested England repay the favour with a tour of the Caribbean before the end of the year, he was being optimistic, but the sentiment was understandable. Without West Indies' willingness to fly to a country beset by the coronavirus, the ECB's losses – already huge – would have spiralled out of control.

They had been due to arrive in mid-May, take on England Lions and Worcestershire, then play a three-Test series, starting on June 4, at The Oval, Edgbaston and Lord's. But their arrival was put back to June 9, by which time some professional sport was allowed behind closed doors, and the Tests to July 8. In the absence of a sponsor, the series was branded #raisethebat in recognition of key workers during the pandemic; on the first morning, England's players trained in shirts bearing some of the workers' names.

WINNING A THREE-TEST SERIES AFTER LOSING THE FIRST

England beat Australia in England . . .	1888
South Africa beat New Zealand in SA	1994-95
Pakistan beat Zimbabwe in Zimbabwe	1994-95
Sri Lanka beat Pakistan in Pakistan . . .	1995-96
Sri Lanka beat New Zealand in SL . . .	1997-98
England beat Sri Lanka in Sri Lanka . .	2000-01
India beat Australia in India	2000-01
South Africa beat India in SA	2006-07
South Africa beat West Indies in SA . .	2007-08
England beat New Zealand in NZ	2007-08
India beat Sri Lanka in Sri Lanka.	2015-16
England beat West Indies in England	**2020**

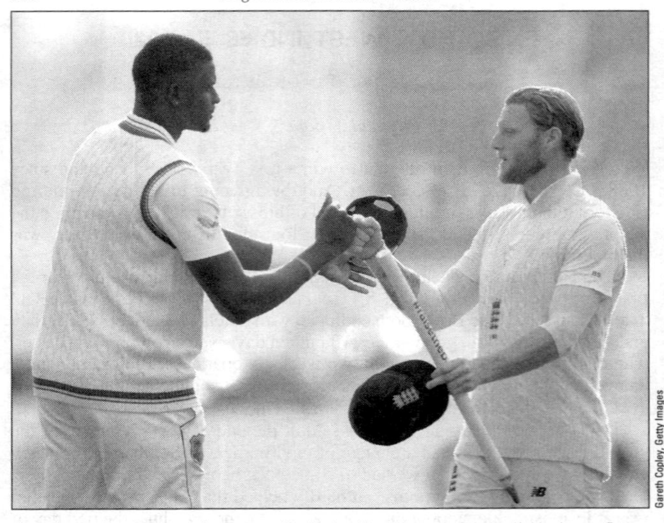
Gareth Copley, Getty Images

All to play for: Ben Stokes grabs a stump after England level the series; Jason Holder bumps fists.

Cricket West Indies were kept closely informed about the plans drawn up by the ECB in consultation with the government, and expressed few reservations. A key moment was a virtual presentation on May 1 to the managements of both teams, as well as Holder and Joe Root, about how the matches would operate. The ECB did all they could to sugar the pill, paying for chartered flights that brought the West Indies players together in Antigua, then on to Manchester; laying on well-equipped games rooms at the two venues; and even providing a short-term loan of £2.4m after CWI were hit by a delay in emergency funding from the ICC.

Players on both sides were given the choice to opt out if they had concerns; a week before departure, batsmen Darren Bravo and Shimron Hetmyer, and fast bowler Keemo Paul, did just that. All three had faced England in the Caribbean in early 2019, and the absence of Bravo and Hetmyer significantly reduced the strength of the batting. Meanwhile, head coach Phil Simmons left the bubble during the warm-up phase to attend a funeral, then isolated for five days before rejoining his players.

No England player withdrew, but Root's wife, Carrie, gave birth to their second child shortly before the First Test; having left the bubble in Southampton to be with her, he had insufficient time to self-isolate, and missed the match, allowing Ben Stokes to become England's 81st Test captain.

More sensationally, the day after doing more than anyone with the ball to try (unsuccessfully) to prevent England from losing the opening Test for the

THE BIOSECURE BUBBLE

"Like an open prison"

ALI MARTIN

After a home World Cup and Ashes in 2019, Steve Elworthy – the ECB's director of special projects – might have expected a quieter 12 months, give or take the scheduled launch of The Hundred. Instead, after England's tour of Sri Lanka was abandoned in March, he and medical director Dr Nick Peirce were plunged into the complex world of biosecurity in a bid to save the summer.

Tom Harrison, the ECB chief executive, had warned of a £380m hit – the bulk of it broadcast revenue – in the event of no cricket at all. The original June start for the three-Test series against West Indies had been rendered impossible, as had the notion of crowds. But this gave Elworthy and Peirce more time to evaluate every element of hosting major matches through what Elworthy called "the prism of Covid-19".

A plan came together to pare cricket back to a made-for-TV product. The Rose Bowl and Old Trafford, which both have hotels, would be turned into "bubbles", and host the entire men's international schedule. (Later, Derby stepped in to host West Indies women, after both India and South Africa had opted out of touring.) Players, support staff and match officials would be forced to live on site for weeks on end, while subject to a rigorous testing regime, daily temperature checks and a Bluetooth tracking system to retrace interactions in the event of an outbreak.

Perimeter controls were drawn up, and venues divided into zones and one-way systems in order to reduce contact with workers at the grounds. A typical headcount of 1,500 match-day personnel, including the broadcasters and written media, was slashed below 300; each group had their own zone. Personal protective equipment was procured privately, so as not to deprive the NHS. Hand-sanitiser stations were everywhere, including on the boundary, and touch points – such as light switches and door handles – marked with red stickers to direct regular cleaning.

It still required willing teams and serious logistics. In May, a group of 55 England players for all formats returned to individual training at 11 county grounds, and had their first taste of the stringent protocols. Each was allocated his own box of balls, which only he could touch, and had to arrive and leave in his kit. On a charter flight paid for by the ECB, a 25-strong West Indies party landed on June 9 to begin a fortnight's quarantine at Old Trafford; Pakistan arrived three weeks later and headed for Worcester, though with ten of their intended 29 initially missing after testing positive for the virus.

An England squad trimmed down to 30 entered the Rose Bowl on June 23, ahead of an intra-squad warm-up game. After testing, and a 24-hour spell in their rooms awaiting results (all negative), they began a lifestyle of eating at separate tables, facing away from each other in lifts, training in shifts, and observing a two-metre distance where possible. West Indies, already au fait with the new regime at their Manchester base, then joined them in Southampton before the First Test.

"It's like an open prison," said one of the inmates, although stepping out – the so-called "bridge to the outside" – was possible under the detailed protocols. But while West Indies coach Phil Simmons and England captain Joe Root had permission to attend, respectively, a family funeral and the birth of a daughter, Jofra Archer, who took a detour to his flat in Hove between the first two Tests, did not. He was confined to his room during the Second; some felt it all a bit extreme. Ultimately, though, Test cricket was back – and the television money could flow.

MOST SUCCESSIVE HOME TESTS FOR ENGLAND

89†	A. N. Cook	2006–2018	**48**	**J. E. Root**	**2013–2019**
61†	A. J. Strauss	2004–2012	44	I. T. Botham	1978–1985
51	**S. C. J. Broad**	**2012–2019**	38	M. A. Atherton	1992–1998
50	A. P. E. Knott	1967–1977	37	M. J. Prior	2009–2014
49	A. J. Stewart	1996–2003	34	I. R. Bell	2011–2015

† *Complete home Test career.*

fifth series in a row, Jofra Archer took a detour – en route from Southampton to Manchester – to his home in Hove, breaking protocols. He came into contact with only one person, who subsequently tested negative for Covid-19. But Ashley Giles, managing director of England cricket, was unequivocal: "This could have been a disaster. The ripple effect… through the whole summer could have cost us tens of millions of pounds."

Archer spent almost all the Second Test in his hotel room; he was fined the equivalent of a match fee, and handed a written warning. He then let off steam about unfair treatment from mainstream and social media in his *Daily Mail* column two days before the Third. "Some of the abuse I have taken over the past few days on Instagram has been racist, and I have decided that enough is enough… I will not allow anything to pass, so I have forwarded on my complaints to the ECB." In an early version of the column which appeared in the paper's Irish edition, Archer even said he was considering taking a break from cricket, but he played in the final Test. Giles confirmed that details of the abuse had been passed to the police – for the second time in Archer's short international career, following an incident in New Zealand in November 2019.

Gareth Copley, Getty Images

Precautionary tale: Jofra Archer, in mask and gloves, heads for the nets during the Second Test, at Old Trafford.

The cricket itself was more exciting and memorable than anyone could have dared hope, given the eerie silence in which it was played. The fate of the Wisden Trophy – in its final outing before being replaced by the Richards–Botham Trophy – hung in the balance until the end. For the best part of nine days, West Indian prospects of retaining it had been strong; then came a turnaround on the penultimate evening of the Second Test, when they had been only four down in their first innings, seemingly assured of safety. Broad picked up three wickets in 14 deliveries with the second new ball, and England were unstoppable. No one could say the players were trying any less for the absence of spectators.

When the series had begun, the focus was on Holder and Stokes as rival all-rounders – and, in the first match, as captains. Simmons suggested it held the key to the outcome, and for two Tests it appeared he would be right. In the First, a career-best six for 42 from Holder meant Stokes's bold decision to bat in bowler-friendly conditions backfired, as England were dismissed for 204; despite his own runs and wickets, it was a position from which they never quite recovered. But he responded with an astonishing performance in Manchester, batting painstakingly for eight hours for 176 to help post a match-shaping 469 for nine, then smashing 78 not out off 57 balls to buy time to dismiss West Indies in their second innings. These efforts might have drained lesser men, but he also bowled two aggressive 11-over spells with the old ball to suck the life out of his opponents.

Neither man had much to give by the decider, which Stokes played purely as a batsman after his efforts in the previous game left him carrying a thigh strain (he still finished the series averaging 90 with the bat, and 16 with the

MOST TEST WICKETS FOR ENGLAND AGAINST WEST INDIES

		T	*Runs*	*BB*	*5I*	*10M*	*Avge*
87	**J. M. Anderson**	**22**	**1,967**	**7-42**	**5**	**0**	**22.60**
86	F. S. Trueman	18	2,018	7-44	6	2	23.46
73	**S. C. J. Broad**	**19**	**1,818**	**7-72**	**3**	**2**	**24.90**
72	J. A. Snow	14	1,917	7-49	4	1	26.62
70	A. R. C. Fraser	17	1,659	8-53	5	1	23.70
61	I. T. Botham	20	2,146	8-103	3	0	35.18
60	S. J. Harmison	14	1,539	7-12	3	0	25.65
53	A. R. Caddick	14	1,355	6-65	5	0	25.56
51	J. C. Laker	13	1,551	7-103	1	0	30.41

For West Indies, C. E. L. Ambrose took 164 wickets against England, C. A. Walsh 145, M. D. Marshall 127, G. S. Sobers 102 and L. R. Gibbs 100.

ball, to Holder's 22 and 30). Holder again chose to bowl, and England again began with what proved the biggest total of the match.

The show was stolen by Broad, a man on a mission ever since his axing from the First Test. On the third morning of that game, he had voiced his fury during an interview in Sky's new player zone. "I felt like it was my shirt," he said. "When I get that opportunity again, you can bet I'll be on the money." Sure enough, he took six wickets at crucial moments during the Second Test, and in the decider struck 62 off 45 balls, before claiming match figures of ten for 67, benefiting from the repeated refusal of the West Indian batsmen to get on to the front foot. His ninth wicket was also his 500th in Tests. His father, Chris, witnessed the milestone: he was the match referee because Covid-19 restrictions had ruled out overseas officials, and he was the sole Englishman on the ICC's elite panel.

It was a series of slow and low scoring, with only two centuries, by Stokes and Dom Sibley, both in the Second Test. Stokes's hundred was the slowest of

Dan Mullan, Getty Images

#raisetheball: Kemar Roach celebrates his 200th Test wicket.

his ten in Tests, and Sibley's the longest recorded by minutes (465) in England. This suited the patient, platform-laying approach Root wanted to cultivate. The dropping of Joe Denly after one game, following a lengthy but unsatisfactory run at the top of the order, aided the process: in the Third Test, England managed century stands for the first two wickets in the same innings for the first time since Abu Dhabi in 2015-16.

Meanwhile, no West Indian scored a century during a series in England for the first time since their inaugural Test tour, in 1928. Kraigg Brathwaite, Jermaine Blackwood and Shamarh Brooks all played notably for half-centuries, but Shai Hope was a grave disappointment after his Headingley heroics of 2017 and, like opener John Campbell, averaged under 20. Blackwood played courageously for 95 on the final day at Southampton to give West Indies their first lead in England for 20 years, but he was granted several let-offs – most critically on 20, when Jos Buttler spilled a leg-side chance. Buttler's struggles as batsman-keeper generated debate, though he struck 67 in the first innings of the final match.

It was also a series dominated by fast bowlers. England found themselves in the unusual position of having six specialists to choose from, and started – mistakenly, in hindsight – by teaming up Archer and Mark Wood for the first time in Tests, possibly the fastest pairing in their history. Archer topped 90mph, and bowled an incisive opening spell on the last day, and Wood hit 94.5, but they were generally underwhelming. Wood did not play another Test all summer.

The West Indies pacemen began the better, and the persevering Shannon Gabriel won the match award in the First, with nine wickets. Despite the

FIVE STATS YOU MAY HAVE MISSED

BENEDICT BERMANGE

- When he dismissed Ben Stokes in the First Test, Jason Holder equalled Imran Khan's record of removing nine captains during his Test career. Imran accounted for Viv Richards, Gordon Greenidge and Desmond Haynes (West Indies), Mike Gatting and David Gower (England), Sunil Gavaskar and Kris Srikkanth (India), John Wright (New Zealand) and Duleep Mendis (Sri Lanka); Holder had dismissed Stokes and Joe Root (England), Angelo Mathews and Suranga Lakmal (Sri Lanka), Graeme Cremer (Zimbabwe), Virat Kohli (India), Misbah-ul-Haq (Pakistan), Rashid Khan (Afghanistan) and Shakib Al Hasan (Bangladesh).

- In the Second Test, Dominic Sibley's 120 included only five fours, one-sixth of his score. Only two England batsmen have made as many with a lower boundary percentage:

%	*4*			
6.66	2	P. A. Gibb (120)	v South Africa at Durban	1938-39
16.39	5	L. Hutton (122*)	v Australia at Sydney	1946-47
16.66	**5**	**D. P. Sibley (120)**	**v West Indies at Manchester**	**2020**

- In the same game, Roston Chase became only the third West Indian spinner to complete five-wicket hauls against England home and away, after Sonny Ramadhin in the 1950s and Lance Gibbs in the 1960s. Chase took eight for 60 at Bridgetown in 2018-19.

- England used four different openers in the Second Test, for the first time since 1953-54, against West Indies at Kingston (L. Hutton, T. E. Bailey, T. W. Graveney, W. Watson), and the first time at home since the 1921 Ashes Test at Manchester (A. C. Russell, G. Brown, C. Hallows, C. H. Parkin).

- Also in the Second Test, Ben Stokes became the fifth to score 250 runs and take three wickets in the same Test:

F. M. M. Worrell (261; 3-40, 0-30)	West Indies v England at Nottingham	1950
M. H. Mankad (72, 184; 5-196, 0-35)	India v England at Lord's	1952
S. T. Jayasuriya (340; 3-45)	Sri Lanka v India at Colombo (RPS)	1997-98
T. M. Dilshan (162, 143; 4-10)	Sri Lanka v Bangladesh at Chittagong	2008-09
B. A. Stokes (176, 78*; 1-29, 2-30)	**England v West Indies at Manchester**	**2020**

Benedict Bermange is the statistician for Sky Sports.

staying power of Kemar Roach, who passed 200 Test wickets in the Third, they lacked England's depth, and stuck with the same line-up for the next game. By the Third, Gabriel was struggling to stay on the field. In contrast, Broad and Chris Woakes, who also sat out the opener, grew stronger, taking 27 of the last 36 West Indies wickets, and keeping them below 200 in their final three innings.

On this most extraordinary of assignments, Holder and his players deserved special praise for their response to the Black Lives Matter movement, which was at its height when they arrived. Both sides agreed to have a BLM logo on their shirt collars, and it also became clear England would join West Indies in taking a knee at the start of the series. There were some powerful and moving words from Michael Holding and Ebony Rainford-Brent on Sky. But this was West Indies' moment: players and backroom staff, down on one knee, right fists sporting black gloves raised to the sky.

WEST INDIAN TOURING PARTY

*J. O. Holder, J. Blackwood, N. E. Bonner, K. C. Brathwaite, S. S. J. Brooks, J. D. Campbell, R. L. Chase, R. R. S. Cornwall, S. O. Dowrich, S. T. Gabriel, C. K. Holder, S. D. Hope, A. S. Joseph, R. A. Reifer, K. A. J. Roach.

D. M. Bravo, S. O. Hetmyer and K. M. A. Paul declined invitations to join the tour. S. W. Ambris, J. Da Silva, K. J. Harding, P. A. S. McSween, K. R. Mayers, M. J. Mindley, S. A. R. Moseley, A. Phillip, O. R. Thomas and J. A. Warrican accompanied the team as standby players. Gabriel was initially part of this back-up squad, but was added to the main party after proving his fitness.

Coach: P. V. Simmons. *Manager:* R. N. Lewis. *Assistant coaches:* R. O. Estwick and R. Griffith. *Batting coach:* F. L. Reifer. *Team doctor:* Praimanand Singh. *Strength and conditioning:* R. Rogers. *Physiotherapists:* N. Barry and D. Byam. *Massage therapists:* N. Meade and Z. Nicholas. *Team psychologist:* D. LaGuerre. *Analyst:* A. R. Srikkanth. *Media and content:* D. Barthley.

TEST MATCH AVERAGES

ENGLAND – BATTING AND FIELDING

	T	*I*	*NO*	*R*	*HS*	*100*	*50*	*Avge*	*Ct*
†B. A. Stokes	3	5	1	363	176	1	1	90.75	2
D. M. Bess	3	4	3	83	31*	0	0	83.00	1
†R. J. Burns	3	5	0	234	90	0	2	46.80	1
D. P. Sibley	3	5	0	226	120	1	2	45.20	0
J. E. Root	2	4	1	130	68*	0	1	43.33	4
O. J. D. Pope	3	5	1	134	91	0	1	33.50	2
J. C. Buttler	3	5	0	151	67	0	1	30.20	12
Z. Crawley	2	4	0	97	76	0	1	24.25	0
†J. M. Anderson	2	3	1	25	11	0	0	12.50	2
J. C. Archer	2	3	0	26	23	0	0	8.66	1

Played in two Tests: †S. C. J. Broad 11*, 62 (1 ct); C. R. Woakes 0, 1 (1 ct). Played in one Test: †S. M. Curran 17; J. L. Denly 18, 29; M. A. Wood 5, 2.

BOWLING

	Style	*O*	*M*	*R*	*W*	*BB*	*5I*	*Avge*
S. C. J. Broad	RFM	60.1	17	175	16	6-31	1	10.93
B. A. Stokes	RFM	52	13	147	9	4-49	0	16.33
C. R. Woakes	RFM	66	15	183	11	5-50	1	16.63
J. M. Anderson	RFM	64	23	150	5	3-62	0	30.00
S. M. Curran	LFM	28	7	100	3	2-70	0	33.33
D. M. Bess	OB	65.1	13	208	5	2-51	0	41.60
J. C. Archer	RF	66	8	202	4	3-45	0	50.50

Also bowled: J. E. Root (OB) 2.2–2–0–0; M. A. Wood (RF) 34–2–110–2.

WEST INDIES – BATTING AND FIELDING

	T	*I*	*NO*	*R*	*HS*	*100*	*50*	*Avge*	*Ct*
J. Blackwood	3	6	0	211	95	0	2	35.16	1
S. S. J. Brooks	3	6	0	195	68	0	2	32.50	0
K. C. Brathwaite	3	6	0	176	75	0	2	29.33	1
R. L. Chase	3	6	0	157	51	0	1	26.16	0
J. O. Holder	3	6	1	114	46	0	0	22.80	5
S. O. Dowrich	3	6	0	126	61	0	1	21.00	7
A. S. Joseph	2	3	0	59	32	0	0	19.66	2
S. D. Hope	3	6	0	105	31	0	0	17.50	3
†J. D. Campbell	3	6	1	84	32	0	0	16.80	1
K. A. J. Roach	3	5	2	15	5*	0	0	5.00	1
S. T. Gabriel	3	5	3	4	4	0	0	2.00	0

Played in one Test: R. R. S. Cornwall 10, 2 (2 ct).

BOWLING

	Style	*O*	*M*	*R*	*W*	*BB*	*5I*	*Avge*
J. O. Holder	RFM	111.5	31	301	10	6-42	1	30.10
S. T. Gabriel.	RF	98.1	14	355	11	5-75	1	32.27
R. L. Chase.	OB	94	14	340	10	5-172	1	34.00
K. A. J. Roach	RFM	116.4	31	292	8	4-72	0	36.50
A. S. Joseph	RFM	56.1	11	182	3	2-45	0	60.66

Also bowled: K. C. Brathwaite (OB) 6.5–0–18–0; R. R. S. Cornwall (OB) 46–7–164–0.

At Manchester, June 23–25 (not first-class). **Drawn. K. C. Brathwaite's XI 275** (79 overs) (K. C. Brathwaite 84, S. D. Hope 83; S. T. Gabriel 3-32, A. S. Joseph 4-60) **and 231-4 dec** (51 overs) (S. S. J. Brooks 66*, S. O. Dowrich 56*); **‡J. O. Holder's XI 193** (51.1 overs) (S. W. Ambris 52; M. J. Mindley 3-27, R. A. Reifer 5-60) **and 149-3** (44 overs) (S. A. R. Moseley 83*). *All 25 members of the extended touring squad took part in the first behind-closed-doors warm-up of the trip (Jomel Warrican played for both sides). Kraigg Brathwaite's team owed much to his own partnership of 103 for the third wicket with Shai Hope, although from 273-5 they lost five for two. Jason Holder's side also stuttered, from 90-1 to 111-7, with left-arm seamer Raymon Reifer collecting five in 11 balls. John Campbell, who had made a 26-minute duck in the first innings, found some form with 49 in an opening stand of 88 with Brathwaite, after which four wickets tumbled for 12; Shamarh Brooks and Shane Dowrich rebuilt with a stand of 131*. Holder's team needed a fanciful 314, but Bajan left-hander Sheyne Moseley prevented any embarrassment with 83*.*

At Manchester, June 29–July 2 (not first-class). **Drawn. ‡J. O. Holder's XI 272** (76.5 overs) (J. Da Silva 133*; P. A. S. McSween 3-28) **and 171-4** (51 overs) (J. Da Silva 56*); **K. C. Brathwaite's XI 178** (34 overs) (K. R. Mayers 74*; S. T. Gabriel 4-42). *The weather washed out the first day and allowed only 34 overs on the second. After Moseley fell to the match's first ball, from Oshane Thomas, Trinidadian wicketkeeper Joshua Da Silva carried his bat for just over six hours; from 108-5, he put on 71 with Reifer (22 from 107 balls) and 77 with Alzarri Joseph (38 from 36). Preston McSween, a left-arm seamer from Barbados, rounded off the innings with three in seven balls, all bowled. Brathwaite's XI slumped to 49-5 before an aggressive 74* from Kyle Mayers, another left-handed Bajan, who thumped nine fours and three sixes from 56 balls. With Da Silva adding an unbeaten half-century in the second innings, after useful knocks from Jermaine Blackwood (43) and Nkrumah Bonner (47), it meant the bulk of the runs had come from the standbys rather than the official touring party, although Shannon Gabriel took four wickets to prove his fitness for the Tests.*

At Southampton, July 1–3 (not first-class). **Drawn. J. C. Buttler's XI 287-5 dec** (90 overs) (J. R. Bracey 85, D. W. Lawrence 58) **and 200-6 dec** (41.4 overs) (O. J. D. Pope 55*; M. J. Leach 3-82); **‡B. A. Stokes's XI 233** (87.5 overs) **and 157-4** (30.2 overs). *Down on the South Coast, England played an intra-squad match of their own, using 28 players, but not Joe Root, who had left the bubble for the birth of his second child, or Olly Stone, who had tweaked a hamstring. James Bracey compiled 85 in 267 minutes for Jos Buttler's team on the first day, adding 98 with Joe Denly (48) and 53 with Dan Lawrence, who made a half-century. Ben Stokes's side found runs harder to come by. Zak Crawley top-scored with 43, but Mark Wood had figures of 11–4–14–1, and Ollie Robinson extracted Moeen Ali and Lewis Gregory in a double-wicket-maiden. Buttler's XI went for quick runs on the third day, with Ollie Pope's 55* helping swell the target to 255. Jonny Bairstow (39) and Dom Sibley (38) put on 70 in 16 overs, then Crawley (34) and Stokes (33* from 17, with three sixes and a reverse-swept four in one Matt Parkinson over) enjoyed themselves. Sam Curran was placed in self-isolation after a stomach upset on the first day; a Covid-19 test proved negative.*

ENGLAND v WEST INDIES

First #raisethebat Test

WILL MACPHERSON

At Southampton, July 8–12. West Indies won by four wickets. West Indies 40pts. Toss: England.

By the time Roach ran in to Burns on July 8, Test cricket had been away for 127 days, and first-class cricket for 113, its longest absence since 1944. No formal matches had been played in England since September 26. Summer was late on parade by three months.

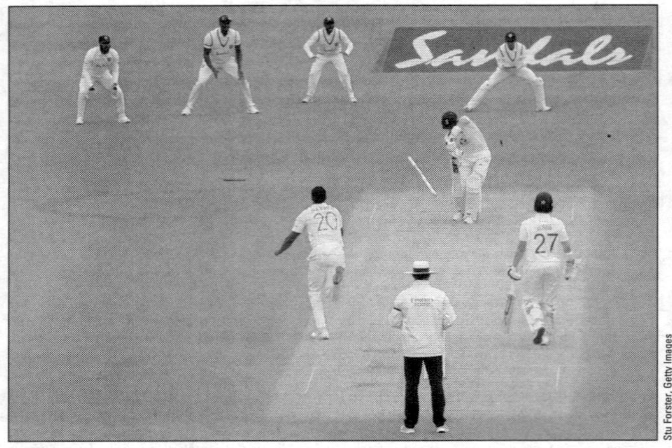

Stu Forster, Getty Images

You gotta go, Joe: Shannon Gabriel proves too good for Joe Denly.

With just a couple of hundred essential staff and media allowed in because of the biosecure protocols, the cricket sounded and looked different; and, with the use of saliva on the ball outlawed for health reasons, it probably tasted different too. But Test cricket did not return quietly: the game brought a strong stand for racial equality, selection issues, explosive interviews, fiery fast bowling, and drama until the final evening. Above all, a win for West Indies set the series up perfectly.

This being England, dank and dreary weather delayed the start. But after so long away, what were three more hours? It proved among the most significant rain breaks in memory, as Sky broadcast powerful testimony on racism from commentators Michael Holding, from Jamaica, and Ebony Rainford-Brent, from south London. Holding cast a broader eye over society, while Rainford-Brent relayed her experiences in the English game, and a "constant drip, drip" that had eroded her spirit. The killing of George Floyd by Minnesota police had forced the world – cricket included – to face up to some uncomfortable questions. But, on a morning when so many fans had tuned in for sport, they got so much more, as two popular and ebullient characters rawly revealed their emotion and anger. Even in a thrilling series, no moment was shared more widely on social media.

Both sets of players had already agreed to do their bit and, after two minute's silences for victims of the pandemic and for Everton Weekes, who had died a few days earlier, they took a knee – a gesture that began when Colin Kaepernick, the San Francisco 49ers quarterback, knelt during the US national anthem before a game in 2016 in protest at police brutality and racism. West Indies players also wore black gloves on their raised right fists. No one referred to it as a Black Power gesture, but the echo of the 1968 Olympics in Mexico City, when American sprinters Tommie Smith and John Carlos had performed a similar salute on the podium, was unmistakable.

The toss had been limited to the captains – with Joe Root on paternity leave, ending a sequence of 77 Tests, Stokes was leading England for the first time – plus match referee Chris Broad (the only family member, it turned out, who made it on the field). After Holder called incorrectly, he instinctively stuck out a hand: Stokes responded with a

FALSE STARTS

Summers when the English Test season began with a wicket rather than a run:

Year	*Batsman*	*Bowler*	
1888	A. C. Bannerman . . .	G. A. Lohmann . . .	Australia v England at Lord's
1999	R. G. Twose	A. D. Mullally	New Zealand v England at Birmingham
2020	**D. P. Sibley**	**S. T. Gabriel**.	**England v West Indies at Southampton**

Bannerman and Sibley fell to the tenth ball of the summer, Twose to the third.

smile and a fist-bump. His decision to bat was brave: the skies were leaden, the West Indian strength lay in their four-pronged pace attack, and England had their least experienced top four since the Trent Bridge Ashes Test of 1989, when Tim Curtis, Martyn Moxon, Mike Atherton and Robin Smith boasted 19 caps between them. The pitch, though, seemed unlikely to hold demons until late on, when Stokes hoped Bess's off-breaks might have a say.

He had presided over a brave selection call, too, when Stuart Broad was left out of a home Test for the first time in eight years. England wanted to pair the pace of Archer and Wood, and manage the transition away from Broad and Anderson. It was a decision that had at least one eye on Brisbane 2021-22, though England were adamant the focus was on Southampton 2020. Broad did not slink off quietly. On the second day, he tweeted analysis – "tremendous English bowling conditions" – from his hotel room, which had a view of the ground. Next morning, he let rip in Sky Sports' "Zone", a new facility for chatting to players at a social distance which resembled *Big Brother's* diary room. "To say I'm disappointed would be an understatement," he said. "I've been frustrated, angry, gutted, because it's quite a hard decision to understand." It was great television, and showed Broad's passion remained undimmed. But not everyone in the camp was delighted.

Meanwhile, England were falling behind. The opening two days had been bitty, with only 17.4 overs possible on the first, when Sibley shouldered arms to Gabriel's fourth ball. Burns and Denly muddled through to stumps, but a superb performance from the West Indies attack next morning left England reeling at 87 for five. Gabriel dismissed the two overnight batsmen, though not before Burns became the first England opener to pass 1,000 Test runs since Alastair Cook in 2006-07. Holder then did for Crawley and Pope. Umpires Kettleborough and Illingworth – because of Covid travel restrictions, the first pair of Englishmen to stand in an England Test since Merv Kitchen and Barrie Meyer at The Oval in 1993 – were having a tough time. Burns, Crawley and, later, Archer all fell lbw only after West Indies had asked for reviews.

Stokes and Buttler steadied England with a stand of 67, which ended when Stokes – dropped on 14 and 32 – advanced at Holder, and was caught behind by Dowrich as he tried to work to leg. Buttler fell to the same combination soon after, and it needed a perky

BEST TEST FIGURES BY A CAPTAIN AGAINST ENGLAND

7-40	Imran Khan.	for Pakistan at Leeds.	1987
7-52	Imran Khan.	for Pakistan at Birmingham	1982
7-100	M. A. Noble	for Australia at Sydney.	1903-04
6-42	**J. O. Holder**.	**for West Indies at Southampton**	**2020**
6-70	R. Benaud.	for Australia at Manchester	1961
6-71	B. S. Bedi	for India at Bangalore.	1976-77
6-87	E. P. Nupen.	for South Africa at Johannesburg	1930-31
6-115	R. Benaud.	for Australia at Brisbane.	1962-63
6-129	Imran Khan.	for Pakistan at Birmingham	1987
6-155	G. Giffen.	for Australia at Melbourne	1894-95

Stu Forster, Getty Images

Best foot forward: Jermaine Blackwood pulls West Indies towards victory.

innings from Bess to drag the total beyond 200. Holder's relentless lines typified his team's approach: three batsmen were bowled, three lbw, three caught at the wicket. He finished with a career-best six for 42, surpassing Chris Tremlett's six for 48 against Sri Lanka in 2011 as the best Test figures at the Rose Bowl. For a man who had bowled only five overs during the warm-up matches because of an ankle injury, it was some feat.

The West Indies reply showed the benefits of their preparation. Brathwaite, Chase and Dowrich played late and delicately, chiselling out partnerships and ensuring wickets did not fall in clusters. Dowrich, from No. 7, scored more than twice as many as he had in the entire series in England three years earlier. And, for all the talk about Archer, Wood and a new generation of English pace, it was the wiles of Anderson and the variety of Stokes that proved most effective. With little movement on offer (sweat was evidently less helpful than saliva), Anderson relied on accuracy, while Stokes removed Brathwaite for 65 – his first Test half-century in 22 innings – and Dowrich for 61. His eventual four for 49 were the best figures by an England captain since Bob Willis picked up five for 35 against New Zealand at Headingley in 1983, and took Stokes past 150 Test wickets. Bess kept things tight, and benefited from wild drives by Hope and Blackwood, whose dismissal, caught at mid-off, Bess described as "rogue". When Wood, who had been fast but occasionally wayward, bowled Gabriel, West Indies' lead was 114.

Conditions seemed kinder for batting now, and Burns and Sibley – having survived ten overs on the third evening – put on a stately 72 at two an over. But with lunch approaching on the fourth day, Burns cut Chase to point, his first wicket against England in 58 overs since he managed eight for 60 at Bridgetown in 2018-19. Sibley ground out a half-century from 161 balls, and took England to within two runs of parity when he was bowled by Gabriel – only for replays to show a marginal no-ball. No matter: two deliveries later, Gabriel strangled Sibley down the leg side. When Denly fell softly for 29 – a career characterised – Stokes joined Crawley, and the pair put on a sunny 98, the highest stand of the match.

At 249 for three, England led by 135, but couldn't make it count. Stokes fell to Holder for the second time, shuffling across his stumps and poking to one of two gullies; once more, his departure triggered a collapse. Crawley went tamely in the next over for a Test-best 76, prodding a return catch to Joseph, who then bowled Buttler. When Gabriel, who could barely move in the field, somehow charged in with venom to bowl Bess and Pope, England had lost five for 30, and entered the final day with a lead of 170. Gabriel removed Wood and Archer to finish with five for 75, and nine in the match, and leave West Indies needing a neat 200.

If England seemed slight favourites, that took no account of West Indies' fourth-innings record: set 200 or fewer on 60 previous occasions, they had won 54 and lost none. But now England's pace came to the fore. Archer crunched Campbell's toe, forcing him to retire hurt, then bowled Brathwaite off the edge, and pinned Brooks in front. When Wood bowled Hope, the top four had been removed – one way or another – for 27.

West Indies would not lie down. Chase got stuck in, and Blackwood gave it some welly, as well as some chances, the simplest a drop down the leg side by Buttler off Stokes when he had 20. A stand of 73 came to an end when Chase was bounced out during a brilliantly hostile spell from Archer, but Blackwood was unperturbed by the short stuff (and Stokes's sledging), and built another vital partnership, this time 68 with Dowrich.

Stokes suggested one last twist by dismissing both but, by the time Blackwood, on 95, was caught at mid-off once more, just 11 were required. Campbell hobbled back out to finish the job. After so long, perhaps any old Test match would have done. It was much better than that.

Player of the Match: S. T. Gabriel.

Close of play: first day, England 35-1 (Burns 20, Denly 14); second day, West Indies 57-1 (Brathwaite 20, Hope 3); third day, England 15-0 (Burns 10, Sibley 5); fourth day, England 284-8 (Archer 5, Wood 1).

England

R. J. Burns lbw b Gabriel	30	– c Campbell b Chase	42
D. P. Sibley b Gabriel	0	– c Dowrich b Gabriel	50
J. L. Denly b Gabriel	18	– c Holder b Chase	29
Z. Crawley lbw b Holder	10	– c and b Joseph	76
*B. A. Stokes c Dowrich b Holder	43	– c Hope b Holder	46
O. J. D. Pope c Dowrich b Holder	12	– b Gabriel	12
†J. C. Buttler c Dowrich b Holder	35	– b Joseph	9
D. M. Bess not out	31	– b Gabriel	3
J. C. Archer lbw b Holder	0	– c Dowrich b Gabriel	23
M. A. Wood c Hope b Holder	5	– c Dowrich b Gabriel	2
J. M. Anderson b Gabriel	10	– not out	4
Lb 6, w 2, nb 2	10	B 4, lb 10, nb 3	17
1/0 (2) 2/48 (3) 3/51 (1) (67.3 overs)	204	1/72 (1) 2/113 (2) (111.2 overs)	313
4/71 (4) 5/87 (6) 6/154 (5)		3/151 (3) 4/249 (5)	
7/157 (7) 8/157 (9) 9/174 (10) 10/204 (11)		5/253 (4) 6/265 (7) 7/278 (8)	
		8/279 (6) 9/303 (10) 10/313 (9)	

Roach 19–6–41–0; Gabriel 15.3–3–62–4; Joseph 13–4–53–0; Holder 20–6–42–6. *Second innings*—Roach 22–8–50–0; Gabriel 21.2–4–75–5; Holder 22–8–49–1; Chase 25–6–71–2; Joseph 18–2–45–2; Brathwaite 3–0–9–0.

West Indies

K. C. Brathwaite lbw b Stokes	65	– b Archer	4
J. D. Campbell lbw b Anderson	28	– not out	8
S. D. Hope c Stokes b Bess	16	– b Wood	9
S. S. J. Brooks c Buttler b Anderson	39	– lbw b Archer	0
R. L. Chase lbw b Anderson	47	– c Buttler b Archer	37
J. Blackwood c Anderson b Bess	12	– c Anderson b Stokes	95
†S. O. Dowrich c Buttler b Stokes	61	– c Buttler b Stokes	20
*J. O. Holder c Archer b Stokes	5	– not out	14
A. S. Joseph b Stokes	18		
K. A. J. Roach not out	1		
S. T. Gabriel b Wood	4		
Lb 21, nb 1	22	Lb 7, w 5, nb 1	13
1/43 (2) 2/102 (3) 3/140 (1) (102 overs)	318	1/7 (1) (6 wkts, 64.2 overs)	200
4/173 (4) 5/186 (6) 6/267 (5)		2/7 (4) 3/27 (3)	
7/281 (8) 8/306 (9) 9/313 (7) 10/318 (11)		4/100 (5) 5/168 (7) 6/189 (6)	

In the second innings J. D. Campbell, when 1, retired hurt at 6-0 and resumed at 189-6.

Anderson 25–11–62–3; Archer 22–3–61–0; Wood 22–2–74–1; Stokes 14–5–49–4; Bess 19–5–51–2. *Second innings*—Anderson 15–3–42–0; Archer 17–3–45–3; Wood 12–0–36–1; Bess 10–2–31–0; Stokes 10.2–1–39–2.

Umpires: R. K. Illingworth and R. A. Kettleborough. Third umpire: M. A. Gough. Referee: B. C. Broad.

ENGLAND v WEST INDIES

Second #raisethebat Test

LAWRENCE BOOTH

At Manchester, July 16–20. England won by 113 runs. England 40pts. Toss: West Indies.

Three days after the teams headed north, the focus switched to the one player who had headed east. Instead of following instructions and driving straight from Southampton to Manchester, Jofra Archer popped along the coast to his home in Hove to visit his girlfriend. It was a thoughtless act, with potentially disastrous consequences for the series and the summer, had he brought the coronavirus into the team bubble. When he let news of the detour slip to the team psychologist on the eve of this Test, England had no option but to enact the protocol: bar a quick net session in mask and gloves on the fourth day of the game, Archer would spend the match quarantined in his room at Old Trafford's in-house Hilton. It felt unavoidably cruel – especially since, when he dared open his curtains, he could see at close quarters what he was missing. Quite a lot, as it happened.

The game belonged – as many do – to Stokes, back in the ranks after standing in for Root at the Rose Bowl. Then, he had twice fallen impetuously in the forties. Now, he adapted assiduously to demand, first Boycottian, then Bothamesque: 176 in over eight hours as England made Holder regret inviting them to bat; and 78 not out in 57 balls as they brushed aside a third-day washout. He took three crucial wickets, too, and on the last afternoon could be seen haring to long-off to field off his own bowling; the batsmen ran four, but that was hardly the point. Root later said his team-mates were "in the presence of greatness". When the ICC readjusted their rankings, Stokes had ousted Holder as the No. 1 all-rounder, and risen to joint-third in the batting, behind only Steve Smith and Virat Kohli.

Root had been in less generous mood five days earlier when he was told about Archer, forcing England to make four changes, one more than planned: Joe Denly had already been dropped from the squad, freeing up No. 3 for his Kent colleague Crawley; James Anderson and Mark Wood were rested. As well as their captain, England welcomed back

Jon Super, AFP/Getty Images

Turning their way: Dom Sibley and Ben Stokes revive England from an uncertain 81 for three.

Sam Curran, Woakes and Broad, still smouldering after his omission at Southampton. West Indies, needing only a draw to retain the Wisden Trophy, were unchanged.

When play began, 90 minutes late because of overnight rain, the West Indian seamers looked creaky after Holder had become the first captain to choose to field at Old Trafford since Graham Gooch against Australia in 1993. Even under grey Mancunian skies – the edge of the Peak District dimly visible in the distance – it was a spinner who broke through. In the last over before lunch, Chase had Burns lbw, playing for non-existent turn; first ball after, Crawley tickled to leg slip, as if unaware of the lurking Holder. Root averted a hat-trick, but appeared fidgety, while Sibley left alone whenever possible; his first four, an upper-cut off Gabriel, took 91 balls. But moments after mid-afternoon drinks, Joseph offered width to Root, who offered a catch to Holder at second slip: 81 for three.

Stung by a pair of collapses in the First Test, England carefully set about preventing another, which suited Sibley: his half-century came from 164 deliveries, and only when he was badly dropped by Holder off Gabriel on 68 did he venture from his shell. For Stokes, so much self-denial was less natural, though West Indies' plan was clear: dangle it wide of off stump, and wait for him to take the bait. He refused. At stumps, England were a sackcloth-and-ashes 207 for three.

The second day was to have marked the start of The Hundred, a competition not created with Sibley in mind. A straight-drive for three off Joseph to bring up his first Test century at home was from his 312th ball (and lured Archer on to his balcony). His 465 minutes beat Keith Fletcher's 458 against Pakistan at The Oval in 1974 as the slowest Test hundred recorded on English soil. The morning session, which ended with Stokes on 99, had brought Sibley 15 runs. Immediately after lunch, Stokes moved to the slowest of his ten Test hundreds (255 deliveries), then launched Joseph over midwicket for six with barely a checked drive. Runs began to flow, before Sibley lofted Chase to deep midwicket on 120, made in nine hours 16 minutes, with five fours. That ended a stand of 260, the second-highest for any wicket in a Manchester Test, behind 267 by Michael Vaughan and Graham Thorpe against Pakistan in 2001.

Pope came and went, before Stokes – eyeing a second Test double – tried to reverse-swat Roach, and edged behind for 176. At 356 balls, this was his longest Test innings by a distance, beating 235 against India at Rajkot in 2016-17. It was also Roach's first Test wicket in 87 overs since removing India's K. L. Rahul and Kohli in successive deliveries in Jamaica the previous September. Now he celebrated with another two-in-two, Woakes poking low to gully for a golden duck. Buttler hit an inventive 40, before Bess and Broad extended matters by an irksome 42. England's 469 for nine was their highest first-innings total after being put in since 575 for nine against Sri Lanka at Lord's six years earlier. And in 14 overs before stumps, Curran overturned umpire Illingworth's not-out verdict to have Campbell leg-before. Had he reviewed another lbw shout, against nightwatchman Joseph from the evening's penultimate ball, West Indies would have been two down.

A rain-ruined third day was dominated by the news that Archer had been fined the equivalent of his match fee (a little under £15,000); since he also missed out on his fee for this game, he was nearly £30,000 out of pocket. He apologised in a statement, though later in a newspaper column he questioned his treatment; he also revealed he had suffered racial abuse on social media.

For much of the fourth day, his absence also looked costly for his team-mates. Pundits muttered that, without Archer, the only variety in the attack came from Curran's left-armers. And England kept fluffing their lines: Stokes dropped Joseph in the slips off Woakes, while Sibley spurned a chance to run him out. Sibley then confessed to the

HIGHEST PARTNERSHIPS FOR ENGLAND v WEST INDIES

411	for 4th	P. B. H. May (285*)/M. C. Cowdrey (154) at Birmingham	1957
303	for 3rd	M. A. Atherton (135)/R. A. Smith (175) at St John's	1993-94
291	for 2nd	A. J. Strauss (137)/R. W. T. Key (221) at Lord's	2004
266	for 2nd	P. E. Richardson (126)/T. W. Graveney (258) at Nottingham	1957
264	for 3rd	L. Hutton (165*)/W. R. Hammond (138) at The Oval	1939
260	**for** 4th	**D. P. Sibley (120)/B. A. Stokes (176) at Manchester**	**2020**
249	for 4th	A. Sandham (325)/L. E. G. Ames (149) at Kingston	1929-30
248	for 4th	L. Hutton (196)/D. C. S. Compton (120) at Lord's	1939
248	for 3rd	A. N. Cook (243)/J. E. Root (136) at Birmingham	2017
237	for 4th	E. H. Hendren (205*)/L. E. G. Ames (105) at Port-of-Spain	1929-30

umpires shortly before lunch that he had absent-mindedly applied saliva to the ball. The new Covid-19 regulations did give officials – and players – some leeway: two warnings, then a five-run penalty. In this instance, Illingworth and Gough settled for a gentle rebuke, and a disinfectant wipe.

Curran soon out-thought Hope with an off-cutter, while Stokes thundered in for an 11-over spell of short stuff, mainly from round the wicket. The tactic finally paid off when the adhesive Brathwaite, on 75, provided a return catch off the leading edge. Still, at 242 for four, with less than four sessions to go, and Brooks in fluent touch, West Indies seemed an hour from safety.

Enter Broad. In 14 deliveries with the second new ball, he trapped Brooks and Dowrich, either side of bowling Blackwood with one that kept low – each wicket evidence of his new preference for a fuller length, which was well suited to a grudging pitch. When Woakes got Holder, playing away from his body, West Indies were eight down and still ten short of avoiding the follow-on. Chase took care of that, but Woakes removed him and Gabriel in one over: six had fallen for 45, and England – armed with an unexpected lead of 182 – had eight overs and a day to force a result. There was nothing for it but to go for broke: out walked Stokes and Buttler, as if for a World Cup final super over. Roach quickly cleaned up Buttler and Crawley, but Stokes was in the mood. The last day was set up beautifully.

Next morning, reprieved by Campbell at deep cover on 29, Stokes proved unstoppable, walloping the quickest half-century by an England opener, from 36 balls. In all, the total advanced by 92 in 11 overs for the loss of Root, a sacrificial run-out. By the time West

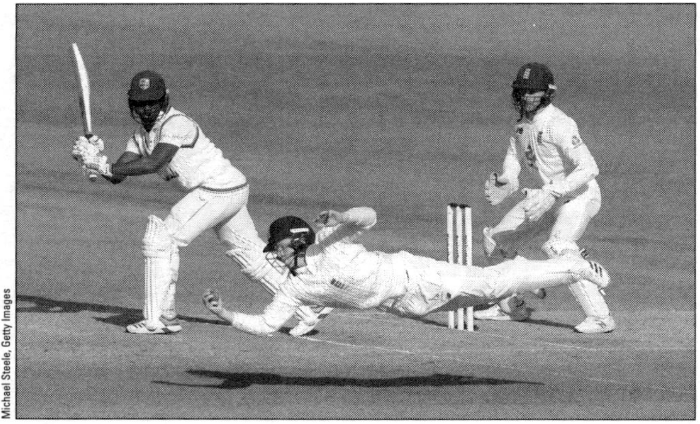
Michael Steele, Getty Images

Flat out: Ollie Pope holds on, and England draw level.

Indies had been set 312 in 85, Stokes had made 254 across two innings out of 443 while at the crease. His batting had moved to another level, if that were possible after 2019.

Broad helped reduce West Indies to 37 for four soon after lunch, but batting had been tricky throughout the game against the new ball, less so against the old. Brooks and Blackwood settled in, Brooks surviving England's failure to review a catch behind – ball brushed glove – off Woakes on 17. With Bess struggling for rhythm, West Indies were once more inching towards safety; once more, they couldn't quite get there. The tireless Stokes was goading Blackwood with words and bouncers. Three balls before tea, the stand worth 100, he induced the indiscretion he was after – a leg-side flap at a rib-tickler, and a running, tumbling catch by Buttler. England poured through the breach.

Woakes inflicted a pair on Dowrich, his 100th Test wicket, before Curran angled one in to the pads of Brooks, out in the sixties for the second time in 24 hours. Bess at last got it right, producing a gorgeous off-break to bowl Holder, and Joseph slashed Stokes to point. The scene was set for a Stokes *coup de grace* but, after four balls at No. 11 Gabriel, he walked off clutching his side. Indigestion, it transpired: the man was mortal after all.

Instead, victory came from the first ball of the final 15 overs: Roach turned Bess to leg, and Pope – fielding under the helmet – launched himself to his left, holding a stunning catch at the second attempt. Hardly anyone was there to witness it, but that didn't bother England. In four days' time, at the same venue, the teams would do it all over again – and this time they would both have a chance to win the Wisden Trophy.

Player of the Match: B. A. Stokes.

Close of play: first day, England 207-3 (Sibley 86, Stokes 59); second day, West Indies 32-1 (Brathwaite 6, Joseph 14); third day, no play; fourth day, England 37-2 (Stokes 16, Root 8).

> "For one reason or another, every summer is crucial for our game, which is always on a tightrope between relative prosperity and relative penury."
>
> Cricket and Coronavirus, page 28

England

First innings		Second innings	
R. J. Burns lbw b Chase	15		
D. P. Sibley c Roach b Chase	120		
Z. Crawley c Holder b Chase	0	– b Roach	11
*J. E. Root c Holder b Joseph	23	– run out (Dowrich/Joseph/Holder)	22
B. A. Stokes c Dowrich b Roach	176	– (1) not out	78
O. J. D. Pope lbw b Chase	7	– (5) not out	12
†J. C. Buttler c Joseph b Holder	40	– (2) b Roach	0
C. R. Woakes c Hope b Roach	0		
S. M. Curran c Brathwaite b Chase	17		
D. M. Bess not out	31		
S. C. J. Broad not out	11		
B 4, lb 7, w 10, nb 8	29	B 1, lb 1, w 3, nb 1	6
1/29 (1) 2/29 (3) 3/81 (4) 4/341 (2) 5/352 (6) 6/395 (5) 7/395 (8) 8/426 (7) 9/427 (9) (9 wkts dec, 162 overs)	469	1/1 (2) 2/17 (3) 3/90 (4) (3 wkts dec, 19 overs)	129

Roach 33–9–58–2; Gabriel 26–2–79–0; Joseph 23.1–5–70–1; Holder 32–10–70–1; Chase 44–3–172–5; Brathwaite 3.5–0–9–0. *Second innings*—Roach 6–0–37–2; Gabriel 7–0–43–0; Holder 4–0–33–0; Joseph 2–0–14–0.

West Indies

First innings		Second innings	
K. C. Brathwaite c and b Stokes	75	– lbw b Woakes	12
J. D. Campbell lbw b Curran	12	– c Buttler b Broad	4
A. S. Joseph c Pope b Bess	32	– (10) c Bess b Stokes	9
S. D. Hope c Buttler b Curran	25	– (3) b Broad	7
S. S. J. Brooks lbw b Broad	68	– (4) lbw b Curran	62
R. L. Chase lbw b Woakes	51	– (5) lbw b Broad	6
J. Blackwood b Broad	0	– (6) c Buttler b Stokes	55
†S. O. Dowrich lbw b Broad	0	– (7) lbw b Woakes	0
*J. O. Holder c Root b Woakes	2	– (8) b Bess	35
K. A. J. Roach not out	5	– (9) c Pope b Bess	5
S. T. Gabriel b Woakes	0	– not out	0
B 1, lb 12, w 2, nb 2	17	Lb 3	3
1/16 (2) 2/70 (3) 3/123 (4) 4/199 (1) 5/242 (5) 6/248 (7) 7/252 (8) 8/260 (9) 9/287 (6) 10/287 (11) (99 overs)	287	1/7 (2) 2/19 (1) 3/23 (3) 4/37 (5) 5/137 (6) 6/138 (7) 7/161 (4) 8/183 (8) 9/192 (10) 10/198 (9) (70.1 overs)	198

Broad 23–7–66–3; Woakes 21–10–42–3; Curran 20–4–70–2; Bess 21–3–67–1; Root 1–1–0–0; Stokes 13–3–29–1. *Second innings*—Broad 15–5–42–3; Woakes 16–3–34–2; Curran 8–3–30–1; Bess 15.1–3–59–2; Stokes 14.4–4–30–2; Root 1.2–1–0–0.

Umpires: M. A. Gough and R. K. Illingworth. Third umpire: R. A. Kettleborough.
Referee: B. C. Broad.

ENGLAND v WEST INDIES

Third #raisethebat Test

GEORGE DOBELL

At Manchester, July 24–28. England won by 269 runs. England 40pts. Toss: West Indies.

It was fitting that Stuart Broad should have the final word. Even when he wasn't playing, he had dominated the series, which had started with his omission, and now ended with his claiming the wicket that sealed an England victory. From the moment he had taken the second new ball on the fourth afternoon of the Second Test, he had controlled the destiny of the Wisden Trophy.

Broad's performance here completed a remarkable turnaround, both for him and the team: as in South Africa at the start of the year, England had won after going 1–0 down. He produced his best innings figures since 2015-16, and his best match figures and highest score since the 2013 Ashes. In the process, he became only the seventh player to reach 500 Test wickets, and won his first Player of the Series award since India toured in 2011.

If the wicket that clinched the win was unbeautiful – Blackwood caught down the leg side off a stiff loosener – his bowling in the rest of the match was almost faultless. Gone was the Broad whose default response to any challenge was the short ball. In its place was a 34-year-old who had lost a little pace, but learned new skills, pitching the ball fuller to demand a stroke and threaten both edges. He had now finished three of the last four series as England's leading wicket-taker. His former captain, Andrew Strauss, was among those to wonder if he had ever bowled better.

Broad's heroics in the Second Test meant there was no doubt about his inclusion here, though England were forced to make changes. The exertions of that game had taken their toll on Stokes, who had sore quad muscles and played as a specialist batsman. As a result, Zak Crawley was omitted to make space for four frontline seamers and the spin of Bess, who never bowled. Anderson and Archer returned, with Sam Curran also missing out.

WE'LL HAVE A BOWL... AGAIN

Most successive decisions to field first after winning the toss in Tests:

8	G. P. Howarth (New Zealand)	1979-80 to 1983
8	**J. O. Holder (West Indies)**	**2018-19 to 2020-21**
7	A. Ranatunga (Sri Lanka)	1989-90 to 1992-93
7	K. S. Williamson (New Zealand)	2016 to 2017-18
6	J. V. Coney (New Zealand)	1985-86 to 1986-87
5	C. L. Hooper (West Indies	2001-02 to 2002
5	S. T. Jayasuriya (Sri Lanka)	1999-2000

Howarth chose to bowl first the first eight times he won the toss in Tests, Ranatunga the first seven.

There was a change for West Indies, too, as the mountainous off-spinning all-rounder Rahkeem Cornwall came in for the injured seamer Alzarri Joseph. But while no member of England's attack bowled in more than two of the three Tests, West Indies kept faith with their main trio – Roach, Gabriel and Holder. There were moments when it showed: as early as his fourth over, Gabriel left the field for treatment.

Holder also kept faith with his tactic at the toss: no team had ever won a Test in Manchester after choosing to bowl, but he attempted it for the second time in nine days. Sibley fell in the first over, and Root was superbly run out by Chase's direct hit from short third man. Stokes, forced by Roach into his crease by a pair of bouncers – one struck his helmet – was then bowled by a beauty that seamed between bat and pad. And when Burns was instinctively caught at slip by Cornwall after edging a cut off Chase, England were 122 for four. Holder could feel quietly satisfied.

If Chase had hit the stumps again, when Pope had 21, or if Pope's edge had carried to slip when he had 24, West Indies might have taken control. Instead, Pope went on to produce the most fluent batting of the series. With Buttler, who contributed his first half-century in 15 Test innings, he added 136 by stumps, moving to 91. As the stand grew, so did West Indian tiredness. Pope unfurled a series of elegant drives and deft cuts that drew comparison with Ian Bell. That evening, he spoke of his relief at scoring runs, after 43 in

Quite a pair: Stuart Broad joins his new-ball partner Jimmy Anderson in reaching 500 Test wickets.

four innings; the claustrophobia of the biosecure environment, he said, had been hard to deal with.

The value of that partnership was put in relief by events on the second morning. England quickly lost four for 18, with Pope unable to add to his overnight score, and Roach – when he dismissed Woakes – becoming the ninth West Indian to claim 200 Test wickets, and the first since Curtly Ambrose in 1993-94. But, from 280 for eight, West Indies were thwarted by Broad. Giving himself room – a tactic he had been honing with Nottinghamshire coach Peter Moores – and throwing everything at it, he middled some, edged a few, and ended up with England's joint-third-quickest half-century, from 33 balls. Since the tourists had passed 318 only once in their previous 12 Tests, England's eventual 369 looked daunting.

So it proved. As the four-pronged seam attack exploited a dry, crusty surface offering movement and variable bounce, West Indies subsided to 110 for six. Again, it was Broad who inflicted the early damage, taking the vital wicket of Brathwaite in his first over with a ball that bounced, and left him. Campbell spliced a brute from Archer to gully, before Anderson produced two terrific deliveries: Hope edged one that moved away, Brooks one that nipped back. Broad then trapped Chase with an inducker, and Woakes unlocked Blackwood's gate. West Indies' batting had looked fragile all series but, in these conditions, against this attack, more celebrated line-ups would have struggled.

It seemed, for a while, as if the follow-on might feature. And while enforcing it has gone out of fashion, regular showers and a grim forecast suggested it could offer England's best hope. But Holder and Dowrich added 68 to avert that possibility, before Broad, still gaining lateral movement in both directions, claimed the final four wickets in 22 deliveries on the third morning.

Comforted by a lead of 172, Sibley and Burns compiled England's first century opening stand in a home Test since Alastair Cook and Alex Hales in 2016. And if one or two grumbled about the pace of scoring – their partnership of 114 ended in the 41st over – England still had the luxury of declaring their second innings with eight wickets in hand before the close. Sibley contributed his third score of 50 or more in the series, while Burns

MOST TEST SIX-FORS FOR ENGLAND

	T			*T*	
12	27	S. F. Barnes	5	14	T. Richardson
12	**144**	**S. C. J. Broad**	5	19	C. Blythe
10	86	D. L. Underwood	5	33	J. Briggs
10	102	I. T. Botham	5	46	J. C. Laker
7	18	G. A. Lohmann	5	49	G. A. R. Lock
7	51	A. V. Bedser	5	60	G. P. Swann
6	50	M. S. Panesar	5	62	A. R. Caddick
6	67	F. S. Trueman	**5**	**157**	**J. M. Anderson**

accelerated selflessly, eventually top-edging a slog-sweep off Chase on 90. He was caught by the uncapped Joshua Da Silva, a Trinidadian of Portuguese descent who was operating as a substitute wicketkeeper because Dowrich, after a torrid time behind the stumps, had been hit in the face by a delivery from Gabriel. In the company of the industrious Root, and against weary seamers and ineffective spinners (Cornwall finished with match figures of none for 164), Burns had recorded England's third hundred partnership of the Test.

By stumps, West Indies were reeling at ten for two, and Broad was within a wicket of his landmark, after Campbell and nightwatchman Roach were both caught in the cordon. He was made to wait for the 500th. Rain wiped out the fourth day, offering West Indies an escape route. But England were not to be denied. In the eighth over of the final morning, he got there with the wicket of Brathwaite (as Anderson had at Lord's three years earlier), struck on the back pad. Briefly forgetting about social distancing, Broad held the match ball aloft to a deserted ground, then hugged Anderson.

With rain still threatening – there were three interruptions on the final day – West Indian ambitions of achieving the draw they needed to retain the Wisden Trophy remained intact. But Hope's grim series ended with a bizarrely aggressive pull to mid-on, Chase was run out by a direct hit from Bess, and Woakes's seam movement accounted in quick succession for Holder, Dowrich and Cornwall, all lbw.

Spare a thought for Woakes. If Broad has spent much of his life in the shadow of Anderson, Woakes has been George Harrison to their Lennon and McCartney. He had rarely been an automatic pick, but his five-wicket haul (his fourth in Tests, and first away from Lord's) sustained his record of having a lower average than both men in home Tests. In another era, he might have taken the new ball for England for the best part of a decade.

Broad wrapped up the innings for 129. Moments later, rain returned, prompting the thought that, had West Indies been able to hold out for another hour, it might have been enough. You sense, though, that whatever the elements had thrown at Manchester, Broad would have found an answer.

Player of the Match: S. C. J. Broad.

Players of the Series: England – S. C. J. Broad; West Indies – R. L. Chase.

Close of play: first day, England 258-4 (Pope 91, Buttler 56); second day, West Indies 137-6 (Holder 24, Dowrich 10); third day, West Indies 10-2 (Brathwaite 2, Hope 4); fourth day, no play.

Dan Mullan, Getty Images

Mission accomplished: Joe Root, the last captain to receive the Wisden Trophy.

England

First innings		Second innings	
R. J. Burns c Cornwall b Chase	57	– c sub (†J. Da Silva) b Chase	90
D. P. Sibley lbw b Roach	0	– lbw b Holder	56
*J. E. Root run out (Chase)	17	– not out	68
B. A. Stokes b Roach	20		
O. J. D. Pope b Gabriel	91		
†J. C. Buttler c Holder b Gabriel	67		
C. R. Woakes b Roach	1		
D. M. Bess not out	18		
J. C. Archer c Holder b Roach	3		
S. C. J. Broad c Blackwood b Chase	62		
J. M. Anderson c Cornwall b Holder	11		
B 12, lb 4, nb 6	22	B 6, lb 3, nb 3	12
1/1 (2) 2/47 (3) 3/92 (4) 4/122 (1) 5/262 (5) 6/267 (7) 7/272 (6) 8/280 (9) 9/356 (10) 10/369 (11) (111.5 overs)	369	1/114 (2) 2/226 (1) (2 wkts dec, 58 overs)	226

Roach 25.4–4–72–4; Gabriel 23.2–5–77–2; Holder 24.5–5–83–1; Cornwall 27–5–85–0; Chase 11–3–36–2. *Second innings*—Roach 11–4–34–0; Gabriel 5–0–19–0; Holder 9–2–24–1; Chase 14–2–61–1; Cornwall 19–2–79–0.

West Indies

First innings		Second innings	
K. C. Brathwaite c Root b Broad	1	– lbw b Broad	19
J. D. Campbell c Burns b Archer	32	– c Root b Broad	0
S. D. Hope c Buttler b Anderson	17	– (4) c Broad b Woakes	31
S. S. J. Brooks c Buttler b Anderson	4	– (5) c Buttler b Woakes	22
R. L. Chase lbw b Broad	9	– (6) run out (Bess)	7
J. Blackwood b Woakes	26	– (7) c Buttler b Broad	23
*J. O. Holder lbw b Broad	46	– (8) lbw b Woakes	12
†S. O. Dowrich c Woakes b Broad	37	– (9) lbw b Woakes	8
R. R. S. Cornwall lbw b Broad	10	– (10) lbw b Woakes	2
K. A. J. Roach c Root b Broad	0	– (3) c Buttler b Broad	4
S. T. Gabriel not out	0	– not out	0
B 4, lb 5, w 5, nb 1	15	Lb 1	1
1/1 (1) 2/44 (2) 3/58 (3) 4/59 (4) 5/73 (5) 6/110 (6) 7/178 (7) 8/188 (9) 9/188 (10) 10/197 (8) (65 overs)	197	1/0 (2) 2/6 (3) 3/45 (1) 4/71 (4) 5/79 (5) 6/87 (6) 7/99 (8) 8/117 (9) 9/119 (10) 10/129 (7) (37.1 overs)	129

Anderson 16–5–28–2; Broad 14–4–31–6; Archer 17–1–72–1; Woakes 18–2–57–1. *Second innings*—Anderson 8–4–18–0; Broad 8.1–1–36–4; Woakes 11–0–50–5; Archer 10–1–24–0.

Umpires: M. A. Gough and R. A. Kettleborough. Third umpire: R. K. Illingworth.
Referee: B. C. Broad.

ENGLAND v IRELAND IN 2020

LAWRENCE BOOTH

One-day internationals (3): England 2 (20pts), Ireland 1 (10pts)

Ireland's first full series of any kind in England was rescued from anonymity by one of the great run-chases. At 2–0 down against the world champions, who were playing at home for the first time since lifting the trophy a year earlier, the Irish risked going unnoticed in the small window between England's Test series against West Indies and Pakistan. But not even the absence of spectators – or seven of the 11 England players from the World Cup final – could detract from centuries by opener Paul Stirling and captain Andrew Balbirnie as Ireland knocked off 329, emphatically opening their account in the first matches to count towards the ICC's new Super League. The ultimate prize, for the league's top eight, was direct qualification for the 2023 World Cup in India. No matter that the series was already lost: the euphoria echoing around an empty Rose Bowl confirmed that victory over England – nine years on from Ireland's only other win against them, in India – mattered as much as ever.

The three matches had been scheduled for mid-September, at Trent Bridge, Edgbaston and The Oval. But with the ECB trying to juggle fixtures amid the pandemic, and a planned visit by the Australians in July pushed back by two months, Ireland were offered a one-stop trip to Southampton. They gladly accepted, bringing a squad of 22, with 14 named for each game. England's biosecure one-day bubble included 24, though leg-spinner Matt Parkinson pulled out with an ankle injury; Joe Denly was a late addition, having been released from the Test party, only to suffer a back spasm that ruled him out of the series. He was the lone transfer between the Test and one-day groups. To keep them otherwise separate, Paul Collingwood assumed the head coach's role, with Chris Silverwood in charge of the Test squad in Manchester.

England won the first game with 22 overs to spare, and the second with 17. But complacent strokeplay meant they twice needed the steadying influence of Sam Billings, playing because of Denly's injury. James Vince was especially culpable (though always elegant), squandering his latest crack at international

HIGHEST SUCCESSFUL ODI CHASES AGAINST ENGLAND

356-7 (48.1 overs)	India (*chasing 351*) at Pune	2016-17
339-5 (49.3)	New Zealand (*336*) at Dunedin	2017-18
334-8 (49.2)	Australia (*334*) at Sydney	2010-11
329-3 (49.5)	**Ireland (*329*) at Southampton**	**2020**
329-7 (49.1)	Ireland (*328*) at Bangalore	2010-11
326-8 (49.3)	India (*326*) at Lord's	2002
324-2 (37.3)	Sri Lanka (*322*) at Leeds	2006
319-3 (46.2)	South Africa (*319*) at Centurion	2015-16
317-8 (49.4)	India (*317*) at The Oval	2007
312-1 (47.2)	Sri Lanka (*310*) at Wellington	2014-15

New Zealand made 340-7 to tie with England at Napier in 2007-08.

Philip Brown, Popperfoto/Getty Images

Effort ball: David Willey's left-arm pace claimed eight wickets in the series.

cricket by making 25, 16 and 16. In the second game, Jonny Bairstow – still smarting from his omission from the Test squad – belted 82 off 41. But the series award went to another aggrieved Yorkshire cricketer, David Willey, who had been replaced in the World Cup squad at the last minute by Jofra Archer. In his first appearance since then, he helped reduce Ireland to 28 for five; in his second, he took two more early wickets, and hit an unbeaten 47; in his third, he made 51 from 42. Now aged 30, he said he was determined to enjoy his new lease of life – and it showed.

When Eoin Morgan scored a 78-ball hundred in the third game to rescue England from 44 for three, a whitewash looked inevitable. But Stirling and Balbirnie put on a blistering 214, the seventh-highest stand against England in ODIs, before Kevin O'Brien – who had starred in Ireland's previous win against them – supplied the finishing touches with 20-year-old Harry Tector. Another newcomer, 21-year-old Curtis Campher – a South African-born all-rounder who owed his Irish passport to a grandmother from Londonderry – made a half-century in each of the first two matches, and claimed five wickets with his bustling seamers. Both players summed up Ireland's desire to give a new generation a chance as they built towards 2023. Their 35-year-old former captain, William Porterfield, didn't get a game, while 36-year-old seamer Boyd Rankin missed out after suffering a recurrence of a back injury.

England also had an eye on the future. Tom Banton, aged 21, played all three games, registering a maiden international fifty, and there was a recall in the second match for left-arm seamer Reece Topley, after an injury-hit gap of more than four years; he was promptly ruled out of the third with a groin strain. Moeen Ali was handed the vice-captaincy, and took charge in the field after Morgan tweaked his groin while making his hundred. But he could do nothing to halt Stirling or Balbirnie, completing a quiet few days in which he notched more runs (one) than wickets.

IRELAND TOURING PARTY

*A. Balbirnie, M. R. Adair, C. Campher, P. K. D. Chase, G. J. Delany, G. H. Dockrell, J. J. Garth, T. E. Kane, J. B. Little, A. R. McBrine, B. J. McCarthy, J. A. McCollum, K. J. O'Brien, W. T. S. Porterfield, W. B. Rankin, S. Singh, P. R. Stirling, H. T. Tector, S. R. Thompson, L. J. Tucker, G. C. Wilson, C. A. Young. *Coach:* G. X. Ford.

At Southampton, July 21. **M. M. Ali's XI won by 100 runs. M. M. Ali's XI 325-9** (40 overs) (J. M. Bairstow 127, M. M. Ali 85; A. U. Rashid 4-65); **E. J. G. Morgan's XI 225** (32.3 overs) (B. M. Duckett 68; M. M. Ali 3-40). *Blistering innings from Jonny Bairstow (127 off 88 balls, with 16 fours and seven sixes) and Moeen Ali (85 off 45, with seven and six) took Ali's own team out of reach in a game reduced to 40 overs a side. All the bowlers suffered, none more than Saqib Mahmood, whose eight overs cost 76; Adil Rashid picked up four wickets, but went for 65 off seven. In reply, only Ben Duckett passed 33 for Eoin Morgan's XI. Tom Banton played for both sides, while Sam Hain and Liam Livingstone batted twice for Ali's team, which in effect had only nine players.*

At Southampton, July 22. **Ireland A won by three wickets. ‡Ireland 307-6** (50 overs) (W. T. S. Porterfield 57, H. T. Tector 54, A. R. McBrine 51*); **Ireland A 310-7** (48.2 overs) (K. J. O'Brien 126*, S. Singh 71; C. A. Young 3-69). *A chaotic intra-squad warm-up was decided by 126* off 128 balls from Kevin O'Brien, who put on 127 for the fifth wicket with Simi Singh to break the back of the Ireland A chase. In the Ireland innings, six of the seven players used had scored at least 30 (Gary Wilson batted twice); for Ireland A, Lorcan Tucker made up for a second-ball duck at No. 4 by hitting 18* after returning at the fall of the seventh wicket. To further confuse matters, James McCollum opened for both teams, scoring nine for Ireland, and none for Ireland A.*

At Southampton, July 24. **J. M. Vince's XI won by six wickets. M. M. Ali's XI 108** (28.4 overs) (L. Gregory 3-29, L. A. Dawson 4-21); **J. M. Vince's XI 109-4** (17.4 overs) (T. Banton 57*). *Only 46.2 overs of a possible 100 were bowled as Ali's XI – for whom Phil Salt batted twice to make up the numbers – were skittled by the seam of Lewis Gregory and the spin of Liam Dawson. David Willey removed Duckett and Sam Billings with the first two balls of the chase and, when Tom Curran trapped James Vince for another duck, Vince's side were 4-3. Banton steadied the ship, first with Laurie Evans (24), then with Dawson (21*).*

At Southampton, July 26 (day/night). **England Lions won by seven wickets. ‡Ireland 296** (49.4 overs) (P. R. Stirling 53, A. Balbirnie 60, H. T. Tector 55; T. G. Helm 3-49, H. J. H. Brookes 3-52); **England Lions 297-3** (34.4 overs) (P. D. Salt 100, J. M. Vince 66, S. W. Billings 54*). *Phil Salt battered a century from 58 balls before retiring in a 12-a-side game, helping England Lions make mincemeat of a respectable target. James Vince also retired, after hitting 66 from 43, while Sam Billings (54* off 36) rounded off a chase that had begun with the first-ball dismissal of Jason Roy. Josh Little bowled 6.4 overs for 71. Ireland had reached 210-3 in the 39th, thanks to half-centuries from Paul Stirling and Andy Balbirnie. Harry Tector added another, but Tom Helm and Henry Brookes chipped away to keep the target below 300.*

ENGLAND v IRELAND

First Royal London One-Day International

At Southampton, July 30 (day/night). England won by six wickets. England 10pts. Toss: England. One-day international debuts: C. Campher, H. T. Tector.

Two players who enjoyed 2019 rather less than their compatriots settled the game decisively in England's favour. Willey, belatedly squeezed out of the World Cup squad, collected his first international five-for, while Billings, whose hopes of playing in that tournament had been ended by a dislocated shoulder, hit a career-best unbeaten 67. In the first match of the ICC World Cup Super

League, it looked as if Ireland would be blown away completely: invited to bat, they staggered to 28 for five, with Willey picking up four wickets in his first 21 balls. But debutant Curtis Campher, a South African armed with an Irish passport, put on 51 with O'Brien, then – from 79 for seven – a further 66 with McBrine. His 59 was the second-highest score on ODI debut for Ireland, behind 99 (run out) by Eoin Morgan against Scotland at Ayr in 2006. Willey removed Young to finish with five for 30 and, though Ireland's last five wickets had added 144, England needed just 173 to win their first home ODI as world champions. They briefly made a meal of it, even after McCarthy had limped off in his opening over: when Banton top-edged a pull off Campher's medium-pace, it was 78 for four. But Billings was in glittering touch on a tacky pitch, twice in an over reverse-sweeping Singh to the boundary, and taking four fours in seven balls off Campher as he went on to his first ODI half-century since March 2017. Morgan played second fiddle, until he hastened victory with two late sixes.

Player of the Match: D. J. Willey.

Ireland

P. R. Stirling c Morgan b Willey	2	B. J. McCarthy c Vince b Mahmood	3
G. J. Delany c Banton b Willey	22	C. A. Young c Roy b Willey	11
*A. Balbirnie c Bairstow b Willey	3		
H. T. Tector b Mahmood	0	B 4, lb 2, w 4	10
K. J. O'Brien c Willey b Rashid	22		—
†L. J. Tucker lbw b Willey	0	1/2 (1) 2/7 (3) 3/28 (4) (44.4 overs)	172
C. Campher not out	59	4/28 (2) 5/28 (6) 6/79 (5)	
S. Singh run out (Banton/Bairstow)	0	7/79 (8) 8/145 (9) 9/156 (10)	
A. R. McBrine c Billings b Curran	40	10/172 (11)	10 overs: 37-5

Willey 8.4–2–30–5; Mahmood 9–1–36–2; Rashid 10–3–26–1; Curran 7–0–37–1; Ali 10–0–37–0.

England

J. J. Roy lbw b Young	24	*E. J. G. Morgan not out	36
†J. M. Bairstow lbw b McBrine	2	Lb 6, w 2, nb 1	9
J. M. Vince c Tucker b Young	25		—
T. Banton c Tucker b Campher	11	1/12 (2) 2/34 (1) (4 wkts, 27.5 overs)	174
S. W. Billings not out	67	3/59 (3) 4/78 (4)	10 overs: 59-3

M. M. Ali, D. J. Willey, T. K. Curran, A. U. Rashid and S. Mahmood did not bat.

McCarthy 0.5–0–3–0; Stirling 0.1–0–1–0; Young 8–0–56–2; McBrine 8–0–47–1; Campher 5–0–26–1; Singh 3.5–0–23–0; Delany 2–0–12–0.

Umpires: M. Burns and A. G. Wharf. Third umpire: M. J. Saggers.
Referee: P. Whitticase.

ENGLAND v IRELAND

Second Royal London One-Day International

At Southampton, August 1 (day/night). England won by four wickets. England 10pts. Toss: Ireland.

A belligerent 82 from 41 balls by Bairstow almost went to waste as the second game developed along similar lines to the first. Ireland were again in an early pickle, before Campher rescued them; England again stumbled in their chase, before Billings eased them home. Set 213, they had lost Roy in the first over, only for Bairstow to bludgeon a 21-ball half-century, equalling Morgan's England record (against Australia at Trent Bridge in 2018 during their world-record 481 for six). He soon lost Vince and Banton, both to Campher. But at 131 for three in the 16th, with Bairstow equalling another England record (72 innings for 3,000 ODI runs, level with Joe Root), a mauling was on the cards. Instead, left-arm quick Josh Little responded with three wickets in six balls, sending off Bairstow with language that breached the ICC's code of conduct, then removing Morgan and Ali, captain and vice-captain, for ducks. Still 76 short, England were thankful for the class of Billings and the brawn of Willey, who deposited two sixes over fine leg in a run-a-ball unbeaten 47. Earlier, he had made quick incisions once more, while Vince picked up his first international wicket when Balbirnie edged a wide long hop. The match also saw the return of left-arm seamer Reece Topley, who had last played for England at the World T20 in India in

March 2016; he was unfortunate to collect only one wicket, from the final ball of the innings. Rashid bowled intelligently to take three, but Ireland were revived by an inventive 68 from Campher, who became their first player to record a half-century in each of his first two ODIs.

Player of the Match: J. M. Bairstow.

Ireland

P. R. Stirling c Banton b Willey	12
G. J. Delany lbw b Willey	0
*A. Balbirnie c Bairstow b Vince	15
H. T. Tector c Mahmood b Rashid	28
K. J. O'Brien b Rashid	3
†L. J. Tucker c Topley b Rashid	21
C. Campher c Rashid b Mahmood	68
S. Singh c Bairstow b Mahmood	25
A. R. McBrine c Bairstow b Topley	24
C. A. Young not out	2
B 4, lb 5, w 4, nb 1	14
1/12 (2) 2/15 (1) 3/39 (3) 4/44 (5) 5/78 (4) 6/91 (6) 7/151 (8) 8/207 (7) 9/212 (9) — (9 wkts, 50 overs)	212
10 overs: 20-2	

J. B. Little did not bat.

Willey 10–1–48–2; Topley 9–1–31–1; Ali 8–0–27–0; Vince 4–0–18–1; Rashid 10–0–34–3; Mahmood 9–0–45–2.

England

J. J. Roy c Delany b Young	0
†J. M. Bairstow c Tucker b Little	82
J. M. Vince b Campher	16
T. Banton lbw b Campher	15
S. W. Billings not out	46
*E. J. G. Morgan c Campher b Little	0
M. M. Ali c Tucker b Little	0
D. J. Willey not out	47
B 2, w 6, nb 2	10
1/0 (1) 2/71 (3) 3/98 (4) 4/131 (2) 5/137 (6) 6/137 (7) — (6 wkts, 32.3 overs)	216
10 overs: 77-2	

A. U. Rashid, R. J. W. Topley and S. Mahmood did not bat.

Young 9–0–68–1; Little 10–3–60–3; McBrine 5–0–33–0; Campher 6.3–1–50–2; Singh 2–0–3–0.

Umpires: D. J. Millns and A. G. Wharf. Third umpire: M. Burns.
Referee: P. Whitticase.

ENGLAND v IRELAND

Third Royal London One-Day International

At Southampton, August 4 (day/night). Ireland won by seven wickets. Ireland 10pts. Toss: Ireland.

Nine years after Ireland's only previous victory over England, at Bangalore in the World Cup, they did it again, with Kevin O'Brien – their hero that night – scoring the winning run in the last over. But the plaudits belonged to Stirling and Balbirnie: each hit a century during a second-wicket stand of 214, Ireland's second-highest for any ODI wicket (behind 227 for the fourth between O'Brien and William Porterfield against Kenya in Nairobi in 2006-07), and each played out of his skin. In 2011, Ireland had needed 328; now it was 329, more than any team had successfully chased to beat England on their own turf. Willey bowled Delany behind his legs for 12, but by then Ireland had 50, and Stirling had hit successive sixes off Mahmood; he would add three off Rashid, and an outrageous mow on one knee off Willey, all over the shorter leg-side boundary. Balbirnie was relatively measured, yet his well-crafted hundred still came at a run a ball. Stirling, who had never reached 50 in 13 innings against England in all formats, was dropped twice by Vince, on 95 and 139, and eventually run out for 142 off 128; soon, Balbirnie lifted Rashid to long-off. Bravely, Ireland had sent in Tector at No. 4 and, after an initial struggle, he and O'Brien added the decisive 50 off 5.2 overs – helped by above-waist-height no-balls from Willey and Mahmood. On a true surface (not the one used for the first two games), England's total had been less imposing than it seemed. At 44 for three, after Roy had fallen for the 15th time in the first over, nine more than anyone else since his debut, they were in trouble. But Morgan counter-attacked thrillingly, and put on 146 with Banton, who scored his first international half-century. Morgan reached his 14th ODI hundred – and third at the Rose Bowl – from just 78 balls, but his demise started a collapse of four for 26, and it needed the

Adrian Dennis, Pool/AFP/Getty Images

Legging it: Paul Stirling pulls en route to a match-winning 142.

nous of Willey and Curran to cajole 112 from the last three wickets. That, though, showed the true nature of the pitch – and Stirling was in the mood.

Player of the Match: P. R. Stirling. *Player of the Series:* D. J. Willey.

England

J. J. Roy c Balbirnie b Young	1
†J. M. Bairstow b Adair	4
J. M. Vince c Tucker b Young	16
*E. J. G. Morgan c Tector b Little	106
T. Banton lbw b Delany	58
S. W. Billings c Adair b Young	19
M. M. Ali c Stirling b Campher	1
D. J. Willey c Balbirnie b Campher	51
T. K. Curran not out	38
A. U. Rashid run out (Tucker)	3
S. Mahmood c Balbirnie b Little	12
Lb 10, w 7, nb 2	19
1/2 (1) 2/14 (2) 3/44 (3) 4/190 (4) 5/202 (5) 6/203 (7) 7/216 (6) 8/289 (8) 9/298 (10) 10/328 (11) (49.5 overs)	328
10 overs: 59-3	

Young 10–1–53–3; Adair 7–0–45–1; Little 8.5–0–62–2; Campher 10–1–68–2; McBrine 8–0–61–0; Delany 6–0–29–1.

Ireland

P. R. Stirling run out (Roy/Curran)	142
G. J. Delany b Willey	12
*A. Balbirnie c Billings b Rashid	113
H. T. Tector not out	29
K. J. O'Brien not out	21
Lb 2, w 7, nb 3	12
1/50 (2) 2/264 (1) 3/279 (3) (3 wkts, 49.5 overs)	329
10 overs: 55-1	

†L. J. Tucker, C. Campher, M. R. Adair, A. R. McBrine, C. A. Young and J. B. Little did not bat.

Willey 10–1–70–1; Mahmood 9.5–0–58–0; Curran 10–0–67–0; Ali 7–0–51–0; Rashid 10–1–61–1; Vince 3–0–20–0.

Umpires: D. J. Millns and M. J. Saggers. Third umpire: A. G. Wharf.
Referee: P. Whitticase.

ENGLAND v PAKISTAN IN 2020

REVIEW BY NICK HOULT

Test matches (3): England 1 (66pts), Pakistan 0 (26pts)
Twenty20 internationals (3): England 1, Pakistan 1

After English cricket had gone to the expense of creating a biosecure bubble, conducting thousands of Covid-19 tests, laying on charter flights, and locking players away for several weeks, this three-Test series hinged on a couple of hours at Old Trafford.

Pakistan had dominated the first seven sessions of the First Test, but on the fourth afternoon they let slip their advantage, and allowed Jos Buttler and Chris Woakes, both with points to prove, to master a run-chase that sealed a memorable victory for England. Their sixth-wicket partnership, eventually worth 139, might have lacked the edge-of-your-seat drama of Ben Stokes at Headingley 12 months earlier, but it was still gripping to watch the pressure shift from batsmen to bowlers – and painful to see Azhar Ali, the fielding captain, lose control so badly.

Thanks to the Southampton weather, the rest of the series did not catch fire. The Second Test was reduced to discussions over bad light, while rain meant the Third became about the statistical feats of Zak Crawley and James Anderson, at opposite ends of their careers. It was the first time England had drawn successive home Tests in the same series since hosting Sri Lanka in 2011, but a 1–0 win was their first victory over Pakistan in a decade. Crawley's breathtaking 267 in the final Test – the highest maiden century by

Philip Brown, Popperfoto/Getty Images

Down, but not out: Stuart Broad tries to remove Azhar Ali; he survives, and his unbeaten century helps Pakistan save the Third Test – though not the series.

FIVE STATS YOU MAY HAVE MISSED

BENEDICT BERMANGE

- When England held the First Test at Manchester, they became the first side to play three successive Tests at the same venue since Zimbabwe played five at the Harare Sports Club between April 2013 and August 2014. Only Lord's had previously held three in an English summer: in the Triangular Tournament of 1912, and again in 2010, when Pakistan, unable to play at home, used the ground for a Test against Australia. In 2020, Old Trafford and the Rose Bowl staged three each. The last time England played three in a row at one venue was at the Old Wanderers in Johannesburg in 1905-06.

- In the First Test, Naseem Shah became, at 17 years 174 days, the third-youngest to take a Test wicket in England, behind two other Pakistanis: Khalid Hassan was 16 years 353 days at Nottingham in 1954, and Ata-ur-Rehman 17 years 72 days at Birmingham in 1992.

- Zak Crawley's 267 was the highest Test innings to end in a stumping; the record had been Seymour Nurse's 258 (in his final innings) for West Indies v New Zealand at Christchurch in 1968-69. The highest scores for each dismissal are:

Caught	380	M. L. Hayden	Australia v Zimbabwe at Perth	2003-04
Bowled	374	D. P. M. D. Jayawardene	Sri Lanka v South Africa at Colombo (SSC)	2006
Run out	277	B. C. Lara	West Indies v Australia at Sydney	1992-93
Stumped	**267**	**Z. Crawley**	**England v Pakistan at Southampton**	**2020**
Hit wicket	266	W. H. Ponsford	Australia v England at The Oval	1934
Lbw	266	D. L. Houghton	Zimbabwe v Sri Lanka at Bulawayo	1994-95
Handled ball	133	G. A. Gooch	England v Australia at Manchester	1993
Obstructing field	27	L. Hutton	England v South Africa at The Oval	1951

The highest score by a batsman retiring out is 201 by M. S. Atapattu for Sri Lanka v Bangladesh at Colombo (SSC) in 2001-02. No one has been timed out in a Test.

- Only two batsmen have scored more Test runs in a day for England against Pakistan than Crawley's 171 on the first day of the Third Test. Denis Compton hit 273 on the second at Nottingham in 1954, and Colin Cowdrey 182 on the first at The Oval in 1962.

- James Anderson reached 600 wickets in the Third Test with his 33,717th ball in Test cricket: only Muttiah Muralitharan was quicker, by six (33,711). Shane Warne needed 34,919, and Anil Kumble 38,494. It was Anderson's 156th Test match; Murali reached the landmark in 101, Kumble 124 and Warne 126.

an England batsman for 116 years – was a huge moment for the development of Joe Root's team, though some argued it was offset by the continued reliance on Anderson and Stuart Broad, who took a combined 24 at 19 at a combined age of 72; their team-mates took 17 at 39.

The Covid-19 pandemic had cast its shadow over the tour before it started, when ten of Pakistan's squad of 29 tested positive. Each had to return two negative tests before travelling to England, where they would spend four weeks acclimatising in Worcester and Derby, staying at the hotels attached to the grounds, and playing intra-squad games. "Cricket and Covid-19 will have to co-exist," said Wasim Khan, CEO of the Pakistan Cricket Board. "We went ahead with the tour to play our important part in the restoration of world cricket." Khan and Ehsan Mani, the PCB chairman, insisted the trip was not part of a quid pro quo, but later in the year England accepted an invitation to play two Twenty20 matches in Karachi in October 2021; they also said the

Alastair Grant, AFP/Getty Images

On the up: Zak Crawley scores freely during his Southampton double-hundred.

next Test series against England (in 2022-23) should be in Pakistan. "I don't think there will be any reason for England not to come," said Mani. "I'm very clear: we play in Pakistan, or we won't play."

At the end of the series, Root made the right noises: "I'd love to go and visit Pakistan. The wickets look nice and flat, which will be a nice change to what we have just played on." His tongue was in his cheek after another disappointing series in which he averaged 31, with a best of 42 – his second successive home summer without a Test hundred. For the last two games, he also had to cope without his deputy, Ben Stokes, who flew to New Zealand to be with his sick father, Ged. Stokes admitted his focus was missing in Manchester, where he took two crucial wickets late on the third day, but failed twice with the bat and dropped an easy slip catch off Anderson.

Had it been anyone else, Anderson would have boiled over; instead, he simmered. For much of a First Test in which he took one for 97 – his worst home figures for five years – he was fuming with the world, and himself. Perhaps he was hampered by a ban on putting saliva on the ball. Whatever the reason, he struggled to find his usual swing and seam. The day after the game, he was working on his follow-through; and, angered by rumours he was over the hill and about to retire, he called a press conference. "I want to keep playing for as long as I possibly can," he said. "I think the frustration is that after one bad game, whispers go around, and I don't think that is really fair."

England felt obliged to give him a chance to prove his performance had been a one-off; so when weather ruined the Second Test, he kept his place for the Third, despite suggestions he would play only four of the summer's six matches as the fast bowlers were rested and rotated. Typically, Anderson responded with five wickets in Pakistan's first innings. But Mark Wood never played, while Jofra Archer remained first or second change, and was less potent without the new ball. And so another summer ticked by with England dependent on Anderson and Broad, and little progress was made towards building an attack for the 2021-22 Ashes. In fact, it was only the third English summer in which Test cricket had been played without an England debut, after 1953 and 2011 – and the first without a Test debut for any side.

Anderson, now 38, was frustrated that his age had been thrown at him, yet his summer's haul of 16 wickets was among his lowest. His 600th in Tests did not arrive until the final day of the series – and only after team-mates had dropped three catches the evening before. Heavy overnight rain delayed the restart until 4.15, and it all felt for one purpose. Anderson took only 14 balls to turn the millstone into a milestone, removing Azhar to become the first seamer, and the fourth in all – after Shane Warne, Muttiah Muralitharan and Anil Kumble – to reach the landmark.

There was less pressure on Broad, who had cemented his place against West Indies, and carried on where he left off, taking 13 wickets at 16. Woakes was England's most threatening swing bowler until he faded in the final Test, but spin was again a problem. Dom Bess was sparky and combative, but his lack

HIGHEST MAIDEN TEST CENTURIES

365*	G. S. Sobers	West Indies v Pakistan at Kingston	1957-58
311	R. B. Simpson	Australia v England at Manchester	1964
303*	K. K. Nair	India v England at Chennai	2016-17
287	R. E. Foster†	England v Australia at Sydney	1903-04
277	B. C. Lara	West Indies v Australia at Sydney	1992-93
274	Zaheer Abbas	Pakistan v England at Birmingham	1971
267	**Z. Crawley**	**England v Pakistan at Southampton**	**2020**
256	R. B. Kanhai	West Indies v India at Calcutta	1958-59
255*	D. J. McGlew	South Africa v New Zealand at Wellington	1952-53
251	W. R. Hammond	England v Australia at Sydney	1928-29
250	S. F. A. F. Bacchus	West Indies v India at Kanpur	1978-79

† *On debut.*

of experience was exposed; not helped by the shortage of left-handers in Pakistan's gifted top seven, he never proved a threat, even if he was let down by his fielders. Strangely, Jack Leach, his Somerset team-mate, played no part.

Buttler came of age as a Test batsman, but his keeping was shaky, especially off Bess. On the first evening of the series, as he walked across the Old Trafford outfield toward the team hotel after missing two opportunities to dismiss Shan Masood on 45, he was consoled by Bruce French, England's wicketkeeping coach. Masood went on to make a big hundred and, when England conceded a 107-run lead on first innings, Pakistan were in control. Set 277 on a worn pitch, England looked beaten at 117 for five, but this was a situation tailored to Buttler's one-day strengths: he had a target in a set amount of time, and expectations were low. He went after Yasir Shah, the fifty stand with Woakes took 49 balls, and Azhar quickly became defensive. After that, England were able to coast.

Lee Smith, AFP/Getty Images

Power play: Mohammad Rizwan hits out during the First Test; Ollie Pope cowers at short leg.

Woakes had not passed 37 in Tests in the two years since a century against India at Lord's, suffering as teams targeted him with the short ball. Yet, despite the pace of Naseem Shah and Shaheen Shah Afridi, Pakistan bowled him only one bouncer, allowing Woakes to play off the front foot and grow in confidence; his timing matched Buttler's. Twelve months on from the Heist at Headingley, England had pulled off the Miracle at Manchester. "After last summer, it is very hard to stop believing," said Root. "We know anything is possible. We never give up." The result also ended England's run of five defeats in the opening Test of a series. For once, they were not playing catch-up.

Buttler did not look back, and credited a small technical change – pointing his front foot straighter down the wicket – for his improved balance, which culminated in a brilliantly crafted career-best 152 in the last match. Above all, it proved he could pace a Test innings, and start under pressure: coming in at 127 for four, he added 359 with Crawley, sweeping past an England fifth-wicket record that had stood for nearly five decades.

Crawley had been left out for two Tests – the Third against West Indies and the First here – on tactical grounds, with Stokes playing purely as a batsman. But an opening emerged when Stokes departed. A strong back-foot player, and increasingly adept against spin, Crawley appeared to have all the attributes of a successful Test batsman. He showed mental toughness after being dropped, and provided the attacking instinct at No. 3 that Trevor Bayliss had craved during his four years as head coach. In making the tenth-highest Test score by an Englishman, he showed immense powers of concentration.

Others had more concerns over their future, especially knowing Stokes would return. Rory Burns fell three times to Afridi, and averaged five, his technique out of sync. During a similar rut in 2019, he had turned to his schoolboy coach,

Neil Stewart, but circumstances prevented outside help, and he looked lost by the end of the series. His opening partner, Dom Sibley, had a quiet time too, but was able to stick around: for England, only Buttler and Crawley faced more balls than his 264, and he made progress against spin. Ollie Pope played just one innings of significance and, worryingly, required a second operation on a dislocated left shoulder after diving in the field in the Third Test.

Pakistan relied too heavily on the runs of Mohammad Rizwan, whose glovework was irresistible, and never found the right balance. They had started with an extra bowler – the leg-spinning all-rounder Shadab Khan – but quickly abandoned that plan, and picked the extra batting of Fawad Alam, plucked from obscurity for his first Test cap in 11 years. Neither tactic worked. Masood's 156 was remarkable, given he went into the series averaging 16 against England, and had been dismissed six times by Anderson. He somehow survived a new-ball examination at Old Trafford, but reverted to type against the moving Dukes, and made just 23 runs in the next four innings. By the end, his overall record against Anderson was eight dismissals and 40 runs. Babar Azam began with a sparkling 69 to encourage talk that he had joined the upper echelon of Test batsmen, but passed 50 once thereafter.

Azhar faced huge criticism in Pakistan for his tactics in the First Test. He placed much hope in his two young fast bowlers, but they faded as the series wore on. The 17-year-old Naseem arrived with a burgeoning reputation, and produced stunning deliveries to dismiss Pope and Root, but totalled three wickets at 69. Yasir Shah, their frontline leg-spinner, took eight at Old Trafford, but England played him better at the Rose Bowl, and he took only three more at 67 apiece. Azhar salvaged his reputation a little in the final Test with an unbeaten hundred, and headed home ruing one bad passage of play: "Unfortunately, the session that mattered the most, we lost."

The T20 series in Manchester was hit by the weather too, though Pakistan restored some pride by winning the final game to draw 1–1. The second had been shown on the BBC, the first match they had broadcast live since 1999. An audience of 2.7m showed the pulling power of free-to-air television.

In the end, though, the greatest result for English cricket was that the tour went ahead at all. "You boys owe Pakistan cricket, and the country, a lot," said their former fast-bowling great Wasim Akram. Few could argue.

PAKISTAN TOURING PARTY

*Azhar Ali (T), Abid Ali (T), Asad Shafiq (T), Babar Azam (T/20), Fahim Ashraf (T), Fakhar Zaman (20), Fawad Alam (T), Haider Ali (20), Haris Rauf (20), Iftikhar Ahmed (20), Imad Wasim (20), Imam-ul-Haq (T), Imran Khan (T), Kashif Bhatti (T), Khushdil Shah (20), Mohammad Abbas (T), Mohammad Amir (20), Mohammad Hafeez (20), Mohammad Hasnain (20), Mohammad Rizwan (T/20), Naseem Shah (T/20), Sarfraz Ahmed (T/20), Shadab Khan (T/20), Shaheen Shah Afridi (T/20), Shan Masood (T), Shoaib Malik (20), Sohail Khan (T), Usman Shinwari (T), Wahab Riaz (T/20), Yasir Shah (T).

Pakistan named a 29-man touring party on June 12, but ten tested positive for Covid-19 and could not travel until returning negative results; Musa Khan and Rohail Nazir were added to the squad. Haris Rauf failed further tests and was replaced for the T20 leg by Mohammad Amir. Rauf was eventually cleared to join the tour. Kashif Bhatti tested positive in England, rejoining the squad after a period of isolation. Mohammad Hafeez briefly had to self-isolate after breaching biosecure protocols: he was photographed with a fan on the Rose Bowl golf course. The official Test squad was trimmed to 20 (though the other players remained), and a T20 squad of 17, with Babar Azam as captain, was announced on August 21.

Coach: Misbah-ul-Haq. *Manager:* Mansoor Rana. *Assistant coach:* Shahid Aslam. *Batting coach:* Younis Khan. *Bowling coach:* Waqar Younis. *Spin-bowling coach:* Mushtaq Ahmed. *Fielding coach:* Abdul Majeed. *Team doctor:* Sohail Saleem. *Trainer:* Mohammad Yasir Malik. *Physiotherapist:* W. A. Deacon. *Masseur:* Malang Ali. *Analyst:* Mohammad Ejaz. *Security manager:* Usman Rifat Anwari. *Media manager:* Raza Rashid Kitchlew.

TEST MATCH AVERAGES

ENGLAND – BATTING AND FIELDING

	T	*I*	*NO*	*R*	*HS*	*100*	*50*	*Avge*	*Ct*
J. C. Buttler	3	4	1	265	152	1	1	88.33	9
C. R. Woakes	3	3	1	143	84*	0	1	71.50	1
J. E. Root	3	4	1	94	42	0	0	31.33	6
D. M. Bess	3	3	2	28	27*	0	0	28.00	0
†S. C. J. Broad	3	3	1	51	29*	0	0	25.50	0
D. P. Sibley	3	4	0	98	36	0	0	24.50	3
O. J. D. Pope	3	4	0	81	62	0	1	20.25	0
†R. J. Burns	3	4	0	20	10	0	0	5.00	3

Played in three Tests: †J. M. Anderson 7. Played in two Tests: J. C. Archer 16; Z. Crawley 53, 267 (1 ct). Played in one Test: †S. M. Curran did not bat; †B. A. Stokes 0, 9 (2 ct).

BOWLING

	Style	*O*	*M*	*R*	*W*	*BB*	*5I*	*Avge*
S. C. J. Broad	RFM	94	31	214	13	4-56	0	16.46
J. M. Anderson	RFM	97	19	258	11	5-56	1	23.45
C. R. Woakes	RFM	67	14	165	6	2-11	0	27.50
J. C. Archer	RF	59.4	15	158	4	3-59	0	39.50
D. M. Bess	OB	71	12	236	3	1-40	0	78.66

Also bowled: S. M. Curran (LFM) 18–3–44–1; J. E. Root (OB) 12–0–42–1; D. P. Sibley (LB) 1–0–7–0; B. A. Stokes (RFM) 4–1–11–2.

PAKISTAN – BATTING AND FIELDING

	T	*I*	*NO*	*R*	*HS*	*100*	*50*	*Avge*	*Ct/St*
Azhar Ali	3	5	1	210	141*	1	0	52.50	0
Babar Azam	3	5	1	195	69	0	2	48.75	1
Mohammad Rizwan	3	4	0	161	72	0	2	40.25	5/1
†Shan Masood	3	5	0	179	156	1	0	35.80	1
Abid Ali	3	5	0	139	60	0	1	27.80	0
Yasir Shah	3	4	0	63	33	0	0	15.75	1
Asad Shafiq	3	5	0	67	29	0	0	13.40	3
†Fawad Alam	2	3	1	21	21	0	0	10.50	1
†Shaheen Shah Afridi	3	4	1	14	9*	0	0	4.66	0
Mohammad Abbas	3	4	1	6	3*	0	0	2.00	0
Naseem Shah	3	4	1	5	4	0	0	1.66	0

Played in one Test: Shadab Khan 45, 15 (2 ct).

BOWLING

	Style	O	M	R	W	BB	5I	Avge
Yasir Shah	LB	98	9	368	11	4-66	0	33.45
Mohammad Abbas	RFM	78	23	179	5	2-28	0	35.80
Shaheen Shah Afridi	LFM	76.5	13	258	5	2-121	0	51.60
Naseem Shah	RF	61	14	208	3	1-44	0	69.33

Also bowled: Asad Shafiq (OB) 7–0–24–1; Azhar Ali (RM) 0.1–0–0–0; Fawad Alam (SLA) 12–0–46–2; Shadab Khan (LB) 11.3–0–47–2; Shan Masood (RM) 6–1–25–0.

At Derby, July 17–20 (not first-class). **Pakistan Greens won by six wickets. ‡Pakistan Whites 249** (93.5 overs) (Mohammad Rizwan 54*; Mohammad Abbas 3-42, Naseem Shah 5-55) **and 284-5 dec** (83.4 overs) (Haider Ali 51, Babar Azam 58, Mohammad Rizwan 100*); **Pakistan Greens 181** (65.1 overs) (Asad Shafiq 51; Shaheen Shah Afridi 3-33, Sohail Khan 5-50) **and 354-4** (88.1 overs) (Fakhar Zaman 99, Azhar Ali 120, Asad Shafiq 67). *Mohammad Rizwan made the most of this intra-squad game, batting more than six hours in all, and making sure he retained his Test place behind the stumps ahead of former captain Sarfraz Ahmed, one of five to fall cheaply to Sohail Khan in the Greens' first innings. Before that, Naseem Shah had collected 5-55. Azhar Ali made a satisfying century as the Greens, chasing 353, won with five balls remaining; Fakhar Zaman fell just short after smiting six sixes. Abid Ali was taken off the field in an ambulance and tested for concussion after being hit on the head at short leg by a shot from Haider Ali on the third day. Pakistan Greens chose from 14 players, the Whites from 12.*

PAKISTAN GREENS v PAKISTAN WHITES

At Derby, July 24–27. Drawn. Toss: Pakistan Whites.

Adherence to 11-a-side meant this match was given first-class status, but bad weather hampered Pakistan's practice. Only seven overs were possible on the second day, and none on the fourth. On the first, 36-year-old seamer Sohail Khan had reprised his five-for in the previous warm-up – but still could not force his way into the side for the Tests. Pakistan Greens scraped to 113, and the Whites struggled in turn, before Fawad Alam fought 205 minutes for 43. Imam-ul-Haq, who retired hurt after being struck on the left hand by Naseem Shah late on the first day, resumed on the third and made an unbeaten 41 – he batted for three and a half hours, as his side filched a lead of 85. The Greens lost two wickets clearing the deficit, but rain prevented what might have been an interesting conclusion.

Close of play: first day, Pakistan Whites 88-3 (Fawad Alam 18, Sarfraz Ahmed 6); second day, Pakistan Whites 108-3 (Fawad Alam 21, Sarfraz Ahmed 13); third day, Pakistan Greens 133-3 (Babar Azam 25, Asad Shafiq 0).

Pakistan Greens

First innings		Second innings	
Shan Masood lbw b Sohail Khan	9	– b Imran Khan	49
Abid Ali c Sarfraz Ahmed b Sohail Khan	1	– lbw b Fahim Ashraf	16
*Azhar Ali lbw b Sohail Khan	6	– lbw b Sohail Khan	28
Babar Azam c Sarfraz Ahmed b Imran Khan	32	– not out	25
Asad Shafiq c Iftikhar Ahmed b Fahim Ashraf	9	– not out	0
†Mohammad Rizwan b Fahim Ashraf	18		
Shadab Khan b Sohail Khan	11		
Yasir Shah not out	8		
Shaheen Shah Afridi lbw b Sohail Khan	3		
Mohammad Abbas run out (Fawad Alam)	4		
Naseem Shah c and b Kashif Bhatti	2		
B 8, nb 2	10	B 5, lb 1, w 5, nb 4	15
1/3 (2) 2/10 (1) 3/23 (3) 4/45 (5) 5/64 (4) 6/86 (7) 7/92 (6) 8/97 (9) 9/111 (10) 10/113 (11) (47.1 overs)	113	1/47 (2) 2/78 (1) 3/133 (3) (3 wkts, 48 overs)	133

Sohail Khan 16–4–37–5; Imran Khan 10–0–35–1; Usman Shinwari 5–1–14–0; Fahim Ashraf 12–5–16–2; Iftikhar Ahmed 1–1–0–0; Kashif Bhatti 3.1–1–3–1. *Second innings*—Sohail Khan 12–4–29–1; Imran Khan 9–1–28–1; Usman Shinwari 8–2–34–0; Fahim Ashraf 9–1–17–1; Iftikhar Ahmed 6–2–9–0; Kashif Bhatti 4–0–10–0.

Pakistan Whites

Imam-ul-Haq not out	41
Fakhar Zaman lbw b Naseem Shah	22
Haider Ali c Shadab Khan b Shan Masood	7
Iftikhar Ahmed st Mohammad Rizwan b Yasir Shah	7
Fawad Alam b Mohammad Abbas	43
*†Sarfraz Ahmed lbw b Shaheen Shah Afridi	26
Fahim Ashraf c Asad Shafiq b Shaheen Shah Afridi	0
Kashif Bhatti b Naseem Shah	11
Sohail Khan c Mohammad Rizwan b Naseem Shah	2
Usman Shinwari b Naseem Shah	0
Imran Khan c Mohammad Abbas b Shaheen Shah Afridi	2
B 5, lb 22, w 5, nb 5	37
1/41 (2) 2/50 (3) 3/77 (4) (78.3 overs)	198
4/138 (6) 5/160 (5) 6/161 (7)	
7/183 (8) 8/195 (9) 9/195 (10) 10/198 (11)	

Imam-ul-Haq, when 19, retired hurt at 50-2 and resumed at 138-4.

Shaheen Shah Afridi 19.3–3–47–3; Mohammad Abbas 30–11–53–1; Naseem Shah 21–5–52–4; Shan Masood 3–0–12–1; Yasir Shah 5–0–7–1.

Umpires: S. J. O'Shaughnessy and A. G. Wharf.

ENGLAND v PAKISTAN

First #raisethebat Test

VIC MARKS

At Manchester, August 5–8. England won by three wickets. England 40pts. Toss: Pakistan.

This was a thrilling Test match that was surely beyond the expectations of all who had spent so long plotting a summer of behind-closed-doors cricket. Pakistan were in charge for most of it, but England won on the fourth afternoon, thanks to a bold, sparkling partnership of 139 between Buttler and Woakes on a dry, deteriorating surface. It would prove the critical passage of play in the series.

More significant than the result, however, was a potent demonstration that Test cricket can captivate onlookers like few other sporting activities. There was, of course, no one in the stands as the drama unfolded, except for a few stray stewards and photographers. There were no snakes of plastic beer cups, no fancy-dress nuns, no Barmy Army chants, no Pakistan flags, no raucous cheers from home supporters when another drive from Buttler

Buttler fingers: Shan Masood survives after Jos Buttler fluffs a stumping.

HIGHEST FOURTH-INNINGS STANDS IN AN ENGLAND VICTORY

210	for 3rd	A. Ward/J. T. Brown	v Australia at Melbourne	1894-95
181	for 3rd	M. A. Butcher/N. Hussain	v Australia at Leeds	2001
167*	for 2nd	A. N. Cook/K. P. Pietersen	v Bangladesh at Mirpur	2009-10
154	for 1st	J. M. Brearley/G. Boycott	v Australia at Nottingham	1977
152	for 2nd	M. A. Atherton/N. Hussain	v South Africa at Nottingham	1998
142*	for 2nd	A. N. Cook/G. S. Ballance	v West Indies at St George's	2014-15
139*	for 4th	N. Hussain/G. P. Thorpe	v New Zealand at Lord's	2004
139	**for 6th**	**J. C. Buttler/C. R. Woakes**	**v Pakistan at Manchester**	**2020**
132	for 5th	A. N. Cook/I. R. Bell	v West Indies at Lord's	2012
129	for 1st	M. A. Atherton/A. J. Stewart	v West Indies at Port-of-Spain	1997-98

or Woakes crossed the rope. Yet viewers and listeners were mesmerised as the game reached its climax. It seemed the pandemic had helped us appreciate the virtues of a tight Test match, which offered a timely reminder that it is the game, not the gimmicks, that has an audience entranced.

When Woakes joined Buttler eight overs before tea on the fourth day, England had slumped to 117 for five in pursuit of 277; they had never successfully chased more than 219, at Headingley in 1982, to win a Test against Pakistan. Stokes and Pope had just been undone by deliveries that leapt devilishly. If Buttler and Woakes, an undemonstrative, softly spoken pair, needed any encouragement to play their shots, those two dismissals had provided it: they were both minded to attack from the start. Once they had middled a few, the surface mysteriously seemed more trustworthy.

Buttler drove and swept in a variety of ways with superb judgment and timing. He had done this on a regular basis in limited-overs cricket, and after the game acknowledged that he might have been helped by having a target, preferably before the advent of the second new ball. So, at last, he was able to transfer his one-day skills to the final scenes of a Test match. It was an opportune intervention, not just in terms of the result, because he had endured a torrid time behind the stumps, and the hue and cry for him to be replaced was growing louder and more widespread. This innings of 75, and this victory, offered his critics significant pause for thought. Even so, Buttler was realistic enough to admit that his place had been in jeopardy.

The innings from Woakes was more startling still. Logic hardly suggested he would be one of the batsmen to rescue England. His ability had long been recognised, but in his last nine Test innings he had passed six only once. Yet here he timed the ball exquisitely from the off, with a stream of glorious cover-drives against every type of bowler. His unbeaten 84 was surely his best knock for England – though it helped that Pakistan failed to test out an old nervousness against the short ball. Back home, the captaincy of Azhar Ali came under renewed scrutiny.

Woakes had been retained at No. 7 as England opted to play an extra bowler for the second match in succession, since Stokes was reckoned fit enough only to bat. Pakistan also took a bold course, picking a second leg-spinner, Shadab Khan, rather than a sixth specialist batsman. The first day, interrupted by rain, belonged to Pakistan. There may have been moisture in the air at the toss, but the pitch was surprisingly dry, and Azhar opted to bat. They were soon 43 for two, before Babar Azam demonstrated his class. His footwork was sharp and precise, his strokeplay crisp and sure. Opener Shan Masood was not so convincing, though he was resolute, except when facing the off-spin of Bess: on 45, he offered two chances, but Buttler dropped an edge, then missed a stumping.

On the second morning, Babar fell in Anderson's first over, but Masood gradually prospered, with some impish support from Shadab. They sprinted between the wickets, and Shadab in particular welcomed Root's decision to use himself alongside Bess immediately after lunch, with the new ball imminent. The pair put on 105 for the sixth wicket, before Shadab slogged Bess to mid-on. Masood was ninth out for 156, becoming the second, after

India's Vinod Kambli, to score three Test hundreds in successive innings against different opponents (following centuries against Sri Lanka at Karachi, and Bangladesh at Rawalpindi). It was a formidable innings in the conditions, and one that seemed likely to decide the match, especially when England slumped to 12 for three against the contrasting challenges posed by Shaheen Shah Afridi and Mohammad Abbas. The delivery from Abbas to Stokes, standing out of his crease to counter any swing, was a pearler, beating the outside edge and hitting the top of off stump; Stokes departed open-mouthed. Before the end of the second day, Root had gone too, edging an injudicious cut off Yasir Shah.

From 62 for four, England did relatively well to reach 219 against a beguiling attack: after the opening bowlers came the prodigy Naseem Shah, and Yasir's ebullient wrist-spin. Pope made a sparky 62, Buttler's 38 was increasingly notable for its self-denial, while Broad suggested it was not just his bowling that was undergoing a renaissance, biffing an unbeaten 29.

Pakistan had a lead of 107, substantial but not decisive as wickets tumbled on a frenetic third afternoon. Broad removed Masood immediately, caught down the leg side, then Abid Ali was dropped by Stokes off Anderson, who kicked the turf angrily in the manner of Angus Fraser in his pomp. Anderson was frustrated by the blemish, and by his own

HIGHEST SCORE FROM No. 7 IN A SUCCESSFUL TEST CHASE

149*	A. C. Gilchrist	Australia v Pakistan at Hobart	1999-2000
104	G. L. Jessop	England v Australia at The Oval	1902
87*	A. Ranatunga	Sri Lanka v Zimbabwe at Colombo (SSC)	1997-98
84*	**C. R. Woakes**	**England v Pakistan at Manchester**	**2020**
80*	D. A. S. Gunaratne	Sri Lanka v Zimbabwe at Colombo (RPS)	2017
73*	V. V. S. Laxman	India v Australia at Mohali	2010-11
65	D. Williams	West Indies v England at Port-of-Spain	1997-98
60*	S. O. Dowrich	West Indies v Pakistan at Sharjah	2016-17
57*	Kamran Akmal	Pakistan v South Africa at Port Elizabeth	2006-07
55	B. J. Haddin	Australia v South Africa at Johannesburg	2011-12
53	Nawab of Pataudi jnr	India v Australia at Bombay (Brabourne)	1964-65

bowling, which he later acknowledged did not reach its usual standards. He had also become the first to be no-balled under new regulations, whereby the TV umpire (Michael Gough) monitored the front line from his screen.

Next, Woakes delivered a potent five-over spell in which he removed the most likely Pakistan run-scorers, Babar and Azhar. It was curious that Root did not call on him again. Sibley's direct hit from cover accounted for Asad Shafiq, before Stokes did his Lazarus act by indicating he was now fit to bowl, and snatched two wickets at the end of an action-packed Friday. Pakistan closed on 137 for eight, a lead of 244 on a surface that seemed on the verge of disintegration.

On Saturday morning, it took England just 16 deliveries to bowl them out, but only after conceding 32 as Yasir swung with abandon. Broad sent him on his way with an expletive, earning a fine from the match referee – his dad, Chris. England's pursuit started sedately. They lost Burns, lbw to the relentless Abbas, but Sibley and Root took the score to 86 for one, after which all serenity vanished. Sibley was caught at slip off Yasir, and the ball began to misbehave. Root received a beauty from Naseem, but the deliveries that accounted for Stokes and Pope were unplayable: Yasir got a googly to rear at Stokes, superbly caught off the glove by Rizwan at the second attempt, before a brute of a ball from Afridi took the shoulder of Pope's bat and looped to gully.

Unless Buttler could produce something magical, the game was up. He opened with two fluent cover-drives against Yasir, and Azhar was quick to spread the field; it seemed he was as interested in keeping Buttler quiet as in dismissing him, which was probably a mistake. Woakes warmed to the task, having decided that there was only one way to play.

Dan Mullan, Getty Images

In control: Chris Woakes glides England towards victory.

Azhar switched his bowlers anxiously. England were scoring so freely that the second new ball was unlikely to be relevant. In the 78th over, with 21 required, Buttler was lbw, reverse-sweeping at Yasir, ending England's highest sixth-wicket stand in the fourth innings of a Test (their 139 beat the 131 between Mike Gatting and Jack Richards at Sydney in 1986-87). England promoted Broad, not a ploy they had been minded to adopt in recent years, and he swatted a boundary, before also falling lbw to a sweep. But Woakes was still there, and two fours off Afridi – an exquisite straight-drive followed by an edge to third man – sealed a stunning victory, which prompted much elbow-pumping.

Player of the Match: C. R. Woakes.

Close of play: first day, Pakistan 139-2 (Shan Masood 46, Babar Azam 69); second day, England 92-4 (Pope 46, Buttler 15); third day, Pakistan 137-8 (Yasir Shah 12, Mohammad Abbas 0).

Pakistan

First innings		Second innings	
Shan Masood lbw b Broad	156	– c Buttler b Broad	0
Abid Ali b Archer	16	– c Woakes b Bess	20
*Azhar Ali lbw b Woakes	0	– lbw b Woakes	18
Babar Azam c Root b Anderson	69	– c Stokes b Woakes	5
Asad Shafiq c Stokes b Broad	7	– run out (Sibley)	29
†Mohammad Rizwan c Buttler b Woakes	9	– lbw b Stokes	27
Shadab Khan c Root b Bess	45	– lbw b Broad	15
Yasir Shah lbw b Archer	5	– c Buttler b Broad	33
Mohammad Abbas c Root b Archer	0	– (10) not out	3
Shaheen Shah Afridi not out	9	– (9) c Burns b Stokes	2
Naseem Shah c Buttler b Broad	0	– b Archer	4
B 1, lb 7, nb 2	10	B 4, lb 5, nb 4	13
1/36 (2) 2/43 (3) 3/139 (4) 4/150 (5) 5/176 (6) 6/281 (7) 7/291 (8) 8/291 (9) 9/317 (1) 10/326 (11) (109.3 overs)	326	1/6 (1) 2/33 (2) 3/48 (4) 4/63 (3) 5/101 (5) 6/120 (6) 7/122 (7) 8/137 (9) 9/158 (8) 10/169 (11) (46.4 overs)	169

Anderson 19–6–63–1; Broad 22.3–9–54–3; Woakes 20–6–43–2; Archer 22–4–59–3; Bess 20–4–74–1; Root 6–0–25–0. *Second innings*—Anderson 9–2–34–0; Broad 10–3–37–3; Archer 6.4–0–27–1; Bess 12–2–40–1; Woakes 5–1–11–2; Stokes 4–1–11–2.

England

R. J. Burns lbw b Shaheen Shah Afridi	4	– lbw b Mohammad Abbas	10
D. P. Sibley lbw b Mohammad Abbas	8	– c Asad Shafiq b Yasir Shah	36
*J. E. Root c Mohammad Rizwan b Yasir Shah	14	– c Babar Azam b Naseem Shah	42
B. A. Stokes b Mohammad Abbas	0	– c Mohammad Rizwan b Yasir Shah	9
O. J. D. Pope c Shadab Khan b Naseem Shah	62	– c Shadab Khan b Shaheen Shah Afridi	7
†J. C. Buttler b Yasir Shah	38	– lbw b Yasir Shah	75
C. R. Woakes b Yasir Shah	19	– not out	84
D. M. Bess c Asad Shafiq b Yasir Shah	1	– (9) not out	0
J. C. Archer c Mohammad Rizwan b Shadab Khan	16		
S. C. J. Broad not out	29	– (8) lbw b Yasir Shah	7
J. M. Anderson lbw b Shadab Khan	7		
B 8, lb 4, w 1, nb 8	21	Lb 2, nb 5	7
1/4 (1) 2/12 (2) 3/12 (4) (70.3 overs)	219	1/22 (1) (7 wkts, 82.1 overs)	277
4/62 (3) 5/127 (5) 6/159 (6)		2/86 (2) 3/96 (3)	
7/161 (8) 8/170 (7) 9/197 (9) 10/219 (11)		4/106 (4) 5/117 (5) 6/256 (6) 7/273 (8)	

Shaheen Shah Afridi 18–4–51–1; Mohammad Abbas 15–6–33–2; Naseem Shah 16–4–44–1; Yasir Shah 18–2–66–4; Shadab Khan 3.3–0–13–2. *Second innings*—Shaheen Shah Afridi 15.1–1–61–1; Mohammad Abbas 16–4–36–1; Naseem Shah 13–4–45–1; Yasir Shah 30–2–99–4; Shadab Khan 8–0–34–0.

Umpires: R. K. Illingworth and R. A. Kettleborough. Third umpire: M. A. Gough.
Referee: B. C. Broad.

ENGLAND v PAKISTAN

Second #raisethebat Test

JOHN ETHERIDGE

At Southampton, August 13–17. Drawn. England 13pts, Pakistan 13pts. Toss: Pakistan.

A total of just 134.3 overs were bowled – the fewest in a Test in England since 1987 – but it should have been more. Bad light and rain, and the apparent inertia shown by the umpires, as well as by the groundstaff, became the main discussion point of a match that ended Root's sequence of six victories as Test captain.

Such was the criticism from broadcast and written media – not to mention fans on Twitter – that an immediate response followed. Both boards and teams, the ICC, the match officials and broadcasters all agreed to a more flexible approach in the Third Test beginning four days later. Essentially, that meant starting half an hour earlier, at 10.30, if time had to be made up, as long as the morning forecast was good. The umpires were also told that light should be "monitored to maximise playing time while it is still safe to do so".

SHORTEST TEST MATCHES IN ENGLAND

Balls	*Opposition*			*Balls*	*Opposition*		
104	Australia	Nottingham	1926	792‡	Australia	Lord's	1888
228	Australia	Lord's	1902	**807**	**Pakistan**	**Southampton**	**2020**
401	South Africa	Manchester	1924	815†	South Africa	The Oval	1912
426	New Zealand	Manchester	1931	941†	West Indies	Leeds	2000
635	Australia	Manchester	1912	958	Pakistan	Leeds	1978
677	Pakistan	Lord's	1987	976†	South Africa	Leeds	1907
788†	Australia	Manchester	1888	976†	Sri Lanka	Leeds	2016

† *Won by England.* ‡ *Won by Australia.*
Excludes Manchester Ashes Tests of 1890 and 1938, which were abandoned without a ball bowled.

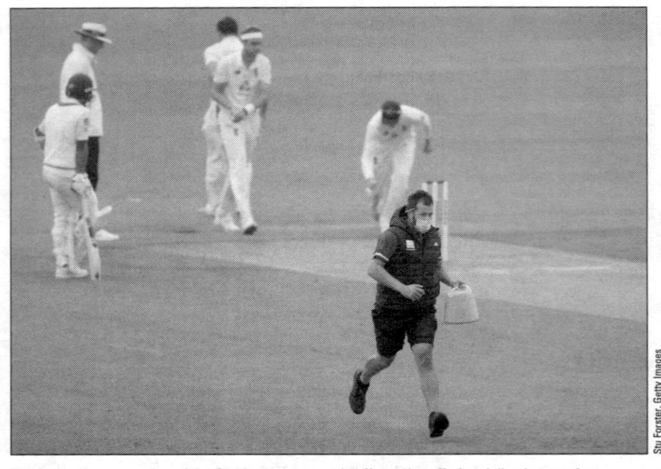

Stu Forster, Getty Images

Delayed action: a member of the Southampton groundstaff scurries off after delivering sawdust.

After three blocks of heavy rain restricted play to 45.4 overs on the first day, the real problems began on the second. The start was delayed by an hour and a half, yet lunch was taken only an hour later, wasting 40 minutes' potential playing time. Bad light then intervened shortly before tea and, after it, only nine balls were deemed possible, even though the floodlights were on. In all, just 40.2 overs were bowled on day two. Meanwhile, the Pakistan Twenty20 squad were playing on the adjoining nursery ground without the aid of floodlights, and with Wahab Riaz steaming in.

Former players, television pundits – Nasser Hussain and Mike Atherton were particularly vocal – radio analysts and cricket writers were virtually unanimous in their belief that Michael Gough and Richard Kettleborough were being unduly cautious, and adhering too closely to ICC guidelines regarding light. (Kettleborough had been less assiduous on the first morning, when he wore a smartwatch, in contravention of anti-corruption rules; he alerted the ACU himself, and no action was taken.) The work involved in creating a biosecure bubble had been immense, and players had been in lockdown for weeks. And yet, in this summer of all summers, the cricket was halted because it was a tad gloomy.

In fact, the playing regulations for the ICC World Test Championship state that conditions should "not be regarded as either dangerous or unreasonable merely because they are not ideal". If anything, they were not following the rubric closely enough. The seed of negativity had been planted, and perhaps observers began looking for reasons to criticise the umpires. They did not have far to look.

The third day was washed out, despite little rain. For several hours, it was spitting at most, the sort of weather in which play does not often start, but usually continues. Yet the lack of activity in the middle was startling. Neither Super Soppers nor a rope were used to dry the covers or the outfield; for hours, nothing happened. Pre-emptive action would surely have hastened a start time if the drizzle had ceased.

Then came day four. The first ball was delayed by a minute or two as a member of the groundstaff trotted to the middle with a bucket of sawdust. Nobody had thought to take it out before play. It was a small but symbolic vignette: were people actually thinking about how to maximise the cricket? Just 10.2 overs, either side of a change of innings (Pakistan's first had stretched into the fourth morning), were possible before bad light and rain struck again. The players did not return. The rain stopped around 3.10, but not until 3.45 did three of the four umpires speak to the groundsman. Oddly, each had his umbrella up – a negative look seen more than once in recent summers. Play was called off, even though no one had been to the middle to check conditions. Soon after, clouds gave way to bright sunshine. The consensus was that play could have started by six o'clock at the latest, perhaps earlier.

A ferocious overnight storm and morning rain allowed just 38.1 overs on the last day. But the difference in approach was striking: the groundstaff's lethargy had become urgency. Somebody had had a word. Play eventually began, and the match petered out to its inevitable draw. It should be noted that the ECB made it clear, privately at least, that they placed no blame on head groundsman Simon Lee and his team. Throughout, the ECB insisted, the groundstaff had followed instructions from the match officials; there were said to be no issues, either, with the drainage or the number of helpers. Perhaps there would have been more play had the ground been full of jeering spectators.

Suggestions for maximising cricket ranged from pink (or lighter-red) balls, better floodlights, light-enhancing glasses and illuminated sightscreens. Surely, however, the answer was simply a willingness to play more in adverse conditions, with less paranoia over legal action in case of injury.

In the cricket that was possible, Anderson bowled better after being "frustrated and emotional" with his performance in Manchester, and raised his career aggregate to 593 wickets. Broad took three or more for the seventh consecutive Test innings – the first England bowler to do so since Graeme Swann in 2009, and only their seventh in all.

Stance and deliver? Fawad Alam's idiosyncratic technique does not bring instant rewards.

Fawad Alam, playing his first Test for 11 years, attracted plenty of comment for his eccentric, Chanderpaul-like open stance, and was dismissed for a fourth-ball duck by Woakes. Mohammad Rizwan batted skilfully and friskily, and helped Pakistan's last two wickets put on 60; England, not for the first time, found themselves in a tangle over whether to get a lesser batsman on strike, or to try to dismiss the senior partner. Sibley (straightforward) and Burns (a dolly) dropped chances in the slips, while wicketkeeper Buttler (not difficult) also failed to cling on. Pakistan's 236 was not such a bad effort.

England had entered the match without their two fastest bowlers, Jofra Archer and Mark Wood – or their three fastest, if you counted Ben Stokes, who was preparing to fly to New Zealand to visit his unwell father. His absence meant a recall for Crawley, who made 53 on the final day. By then, Burns had been caught at second slip for nought. It was the fourth duck by an England opener in 2020 – the joint-most in a home summer alongside 1989. Sibley was once more caught down the leg side, while Yasir Shah outfoxed Pope. Statisticians noted that no captain had declared a Test innings in England for fewer than 110 for four. After five futile days, it felt aptly academic.

Player of the Match: Mohammad Rizwan.

Close of play: first day, Pakistan 126-5 (Babar Azam 25, Mohammad Rizwan 4); second day, Pakistan 223-9 (Mohammad Rizwan 60, Naseem Shah 1); third day, no play; fourth day, England 7-1 (Sibley 2, Crawley 5).

Pakistan

Shan Masood lbw b Anderson	1
Abid Ali c Burns b Curran	60
*Azhar Ali c Burns b Anderson	20
Babar Azam c Buttler b Broad	47
Asad Shafiq c Sibley b Broad	5
Fawad Alam lbw b Woakes	0
†Mohammad Rizwan c Crawley b Broad	72
Yasir Shah c Buttler b Anderson	5
Shaheen Shah Afridi run out (Sibley)	0
Mohammad Abbas lbw b Broad	2
Naseem Shah not out	1
B 9, lb 12, w 1, nb 1	23
1/6 (1) 2/78 (3) 3/102 (2) (91.2 overs)	236
4/117 (5) 5/120 (6) 6/158 (4)	
7/171 (8) 8/176 (9) 9/215 (10) 10/236 (7)	

Anderson 27–5–60–3; Broad 27.2–9–56–4; Curran 18–3–44–1; Woakes 19–3–55–1.

England

R. J. Burns c Asad Shafiq b Shaheen Shah Afridi	0
D. P. Sibley c Mohammad Rizwan b Mohammad Abbas	32
Z. Crawley lbw b Mohammad Abbas	53
*J. E. Root not out	9
O. J. D. Pope lbw b Yasir Shah	9
†J. C. Buttler not out	0
Lb 3, w 1, nb 3	7
1/0 (1) 2/91 (3) (4 wkts dec, 43.1 overs)	110
3/92 (2) 4/105 (5)	

C. R. Woakes, S. M. Curran, D. M. Bess, S. C. J. Broad and J. M. Anderson did not bat.

Shaheen Shah Afridi 10–3–25–1; Mohammad Abbas 14–5–28–2; Naseem Shah 5–0–10–0; Yasir Shah 11–2–30–1; Shan Masood 3–0–14–0; Azhar Ali 0.1–0–0–0.

Umpires: M. A. Gough and R. A. Kettleborough. Third umpire: R. K. Illingworth.
Referee: B. C. Broad.

ENGLAND v PAKISTAN

Third #raisethebat Test

JONATHAN LIEW

At Southampton, August 21–25. Drawn. England 13pts, Pakistan 13pts. Toss: England.

A giddy levity overcomes the English cricketing public whenever a batsman makes a very large score. The blood flows a little more quickly, and so does the ink. Commentators adopt a tone of hushed excitement. Lists are hastily compiled, cropped, screen-grabbed; Almanacks lustily thumbed. Cricket Twitter drowns in arcane trivia: the seventh-highest this, a record (in home Tests) that, the first something or other against Pakistan on a Saturday since 1992. These days, the great innings don't merely generate runs. They generate content.

This is doubly true when we are confronted with a feat so surprising that it makes little sense. Such was the case with Zak Crawley's epic here: a glorious anomaly, scarcely portended by a modest first-class average of 30. His career may yet reverse-engineer some semblance of logic to his innings, in the way Brian Lara's 277 at Sydney in 1992-93 would become the prologue to a much richer tale. But whatever Crawley goes on to achieve, we should not forget the shocking freshness of this initial statement: how a tall 22-year-old with seven Tests to his name dismantled one of the world's best attacks, as if it was what he had been doing all his life.

And so this would be a match defined by big numbers. Broad's 500th Test wicket earlier in the summer had been commemorated with a presentation on the outfield; now, as the weather drew the sting from this game, attention turned to Anderson's quest for 600. After a maddening wait, he got there on the final day: a monumental and warmly received achievement that no fast bowler may ever match.

In between came Crawley's magnum opus. Perhaps the curious part of his knock was that he batted not like a player averaging 28 in Tests and fighting for his place, but one with 5,000 runs in the bank, an MBE and his own winter coaching academy. It was an innings that created its own rationale as it went along: inconceivable at its outset, inevitable at its conclusion. Such was his assurance from the moment he clipped his first ball for four. Such was the range and audacity of his strokeplay, from the disdainful drives at the start, to the flips and sweeps that took him through the 100s and 200s. Such was the blithe conviction that led him to declare afterwards, without a scintilla of arrogance, that by the time he had reached 25, he already sensed it was going to be his day.

Crawley's 267 was the second-highest score by an England No. 3, after Wally Hammond's 336 not out at Auckland in 1932-33, and the biggest maiden century for England since "Tip" Foster hit 287 at Sydney in 1903-04. He became the fifth-youngest

Alastair Grant, AFP/Getty Images

Six hundred and out: Joe Root holds the catch that gives Jimmy Anderson another Test landmark; Azhar Ali is the victim.

to score a Test 250, after Sobers, Bradman, Hutton and Graeme Smith. His partnership of 359 with Buttler, whose best Test innings passed almost unnoticed, was England's highest for the fifth wicket, surpassing the 254 of Keith Fletcher and Tony Greig at Bombay in 1972-73. Yet for all the historical footnotes, Crawley's innings had a vibrant immediacy, marking not just his coming of age, but the instant at which England's intractable No. 3 problem apparently evaporated. It also sweetened the pill of failing to secure victory, as a combination of bad weather, tame bowling and mature batting helped Pakistan to safety.

The match had begun in windy conditions under cloudy skies. Root had no hesitation in choosing to bat on a tacky, underprepared pitch. And though England lost Burns in the fifth over, Crawley wasted no time in building a platform, quickly overtaking Sibley, and bringing up his fifty with a confident straight-drive from the last ball before lunch. As he progressed to only his fourth first-class century, it was his adaptability and problem-solving that caught the eye: advancing down the pitch to smother the lateral movement of

HIGHEST PARTNERSHIPS FOR ENGLAND IN TESTS

411	for 4th	P. B. H. May/M. C. Cowdrey	v West Indies at Birmingham	1957
399	for 6th	B. A. Stokes/J. M. Bairstow	v South Africa at Cape Town	2015-16
382	for 2nd	L. Hutton/M. Leyland	v Australia at The Oval	1938
370	for 3rd	W. J. Edrich/D. C. S. Compton	v South Africa at Lord's	1947
369	for 2nd	J. H. Edrich/K. F. Barrington	v New Zealand at Leeds	1965
359	for 1st	L. Hutton/C. Washbrook	v South Africa at Johannesburg	1948-49
359	**for 5th**	**Z. Crawley/J. C. Buttler**	**v Pakistan at Southampton**	**2020**
351	for 2nd	G. A. Gooch/D. I. Gower	v Australia at The Oval	1985
350	for 3rd	I. R. Bell/K. P. Pietersen	v India at The Oval	2011
332	for 8th	I. J. L. Trott/S. C. J. Broad	v Pakistan at Lord's	2010

Mohammad Abbas, messing with Yasir Shah's length by cutting and sweeping him to distraction, using his height to ride the pace and bounce of Naseem Shah, counter-attacking against the left-arm swing of Shaheen Shah Afridi. He raised and lowered the tempo as required. On a rain-interrupted second morning, he was made to wait almost two hours to add to his overnight 171. Later, as Pakistan began to fray, he tucked into a tiring attack with greed and relish.

Buttler, meanwhile, was already making his own surprising statement: a century of attrition rather than aggression, patience rather than violence, a support act rather than a star turn. He had arrived at 127 for four, with England again responding to the absence of Ben Stokes by playing an extra bowler, Archer replacing Sam Curran. The situation demanded discretion. After judiciously milking the old ball on day one, slotting into Crawley's slipstream, Buttler applied the brakes on day two: his three fifties came off 85, 104 and 118 balls. In a game full of weird and wonderful statistics, perhaps the most outlandish was that, on the second afternoon, one of the world's most fearless batsmen went more than two and a half hours without a boundary. This was just his second Test hundred.

His stoicism put Crawley's breezy enterprise into perspective. This was not quite the batsman's paradise a cursory glance at the scorecard might suggest, the surface more conducive to survival than to self-expression. Plenty managed to score; only Crawley did so with any freedom. He eventually perished just before tea on the second day, stumped down the leg side to provide Asad Shafiq's very occasional off-breaks with a third Test wicket, and left to warm congratulations from the Pakistan fielders. He had batted a minute over nine hours, and hit 34 fours and a six. Buttler, having played his longest first-class innings – nearly seven and a half hours – offered a tired return catch soon after reaching 150. Woakes, Bess and Broad thrashed England towards the declaration and, when Anderson prised out three wickets with the new ball, taking his haul to 596, Pakistan's resolve seemed broken.

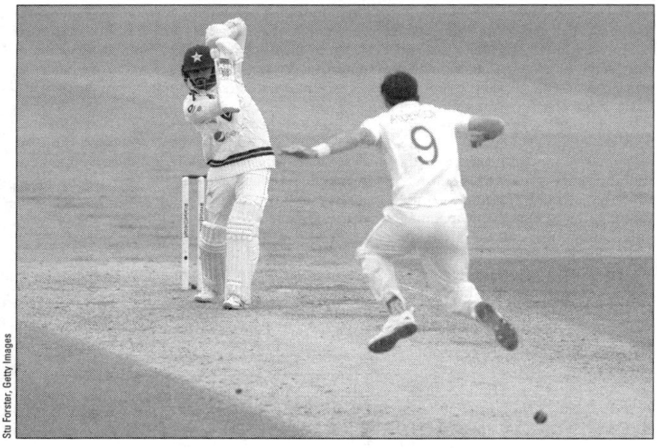

Stu Forster, Getty Images

Jumping to his tune: Jimmy Anderson leaps clear of a straight-drive from Azhar Ali.

That they anaesthetised the game said a lot about their attitude, and a little about England's. Azhar Ali's gritty century, his first in an away Test for more than three years, not only eased the pressure on his captaincy (and lifted him past 6,000 Test runs), but held together Pakistan's fragile resistance. He defended beautifully, cut and pulled delightfully and picked his moments to attack Bess. Mohammad Rizwan supported him well before tickling Woakes down the leg side, the first of two superb tumbling catches by Buttler.

It was around this point that England began to take their eye off the ball, figuratively and literally. To Anderson's chagrin, three routine catches went down off the second new ball: one to Burns at second slip, one to Crawley at fourth, and a sitter to mid-on, where Broad dropped the chance, but recovered in time to run out Abbas. By the time Anderson dismissed Naseem to end the Pakistan innings, move to 598 and complete his 29th five-wicket haul (level with Glenn McGrath), he was still too disgruntled to do more than grimace. And in retrospect this was where the game began to slip away from England, distracted from their processes by the spectre of Anderson's milestone, and the frequent delays for the weather.

Despite being made to follow on, Pakistan saved the game at a relative canter. Much of the fourth afternoon was lost to rain, and an overnight downpour prevented any play until 4.15 on the fifth. Yet in the interim England looked bereft of ideas against a team content to plug away at less than two an over. Broad tried leg theory from round the wicket. Archer bowled short spells of telegraphed bouncers, in keeping with the brief Root and Chris Silverwood had assigned him. Bess was flat and innocuous. But at least there was time for Anderson to claim his 600th wicket, surprising Azhar with extra bounce, and raising the ball to empty stands after Root had pouched the catch at slip.

But England decided life was draining from the game, even after Shafiq turned Root to short leg. At that point, more than 18 overs remained – a potential 15 with a new ball – to claim six more wickets, and precious Test Championship points. But, one ball into the final hour, elbows were bumped, and stumps drawn. For Pakistan, another tentative sign of progress: evidence of a robust mentality and robust techniques, even if their attack had again let them down at key moments. For all the smiles in the England camp – Anderson's landmark, Crawley's breakthrough, the satisfaction of a first series win over Pakistan since 2010 – legitimate questions remained. A haul of 14 wickets in 176 overs was hardly a ringing endorsement of their potency on flat surfaces. The continuing reliance on Anderson and Broad was a mixed blessing – a nod to the past and a doubling-down on the present, but without clarity on how this might all play out in the future.

Maybe these were not the questions concerning Root or England for now. A remarkable Test summer had ended without a series defeat for the sixth consecutive season. And for all the weirdness of the setting – the absence of crowds, the masks and the gloves and the Covid protocols, the vague sense of dystopian disorientation – this also felt like a time to revel in the banal. A brittle top order. Anderson and Broad scampering in from either end. Long, listless hours spent moaning about the weather. If you weren't watching closely, you could almost pretend things were normal.

Player of the Match: Z. Crawley.

Players of the Series: England – J. C. Buttler; Pakistan – Mohammad Rizwan.

Close of play: first day, England 332-4 (Crawley 171, Buttler 87); second day, Pakistan 24-3 (Azhar Ali 4); third day, Pakistan 273; fourth day, Pakistan 100-2 (Azhar Ali 29, Babar Azam 4).

England

R. J. Burns c Shan Masood b Shaheen Shah Afridi	6
D. P. Sibley lbw b Yasir Shah	22
Z. Crawley st Mohammad Rizwan b Asad Shafiq	267
*J. E. Root c Mohammad Rizwan b Naseem Shah	29
O. J. D. Pope b Yasir Shah	3
†J. C. Buttler c and b Fawad Alam	152
C. R. Woakes c Yasir Shah b Fawad Alam	40
D. M. Bess not out	27
S. C. J. Broad b Shaheen Shah Afridi	15
B 4, lb 13, w 1, nb 4	22
1/12 (1) 2/73 (2) 3/114 (4) 4/127 (5) 5/486 (3) 6/530 (6) 7/547 (7) 8/583 (9) — (8 wkts dec, 154.4 overs)	583

J. C. Archer and J. M. Anderson did not bat.

Shaheen Shah Afridi 33.4–5–121–2; Mohammad Abbas 33–8–82–0; Yasir Shah 39–3–173–2; Naseem Shah 27–6–109–1; Fawad Alam 12–0–46–2; Shan Masood 3–1–11–0; Asad Shafiq 7–0–24–1.

Pakistan

First innings	Runs	Second innings	Runs
Shan Masood lbw b Anderson	4	lbw b Broad	18
Abid Ali c Sibley b Anderson	1	lbw b Anderson	42
*Azhar Ali not out	141	c Root b Anderson	31
Babar Azam lbw b Anderson	11	not out	63
Asad Shafiq c Root b Anderson	5	c sub (J. R. Bracey) b Root	21
Fawad Alam c Buttler b Bess	21	not out	0
†Mohammad Rizwan c Buttler b Woakes	53		
Yasir Shah c Root b Broad	20		
Shaheen Shah Afridi c Buttler b Broad	3		
Mohammad Abbas run out (Broad)	1		
Naseem Shah c Sibley b Anderson	0		
B 2, lb 7, w 2, nb 2	13	Lb 9, nb 3	12
1/6 (1) 2/11 (2) 3/24 (4) 4/30 (5) 5/75 (6) 6/213 (7) 7/241 (8) 8/247 (9) 9/261 (10) 10/273 (11) — (93 overs)	273	1/49 (1) 2/88 (2) 3/109 (3) 4/172 (5) — (4 wkts, 83.1 overs)	187

Anderson 23–3–56–5; Broad 20–5–40–2; Archer 17–3–58–0; Woakes 15–2–42–1; Bess 18–2–68–1. *Second innings*—Anderson 19–3–45–2; Broad 14.1–5–27–1; Woakes 8–2–14–0; Archer 14–8–14–0; Bess 21–4–54–0; Root 6–0–17–1; Sibley 1–0–7–0.

Umpires: M. A. Gough and R. K. Illingworth. Third umpire: R. A. Kettleborough.
Referee: B. C. Broad.

TWENTY20 INTERNATIONAL REPORTS BY JULIAN GUYER

ENGLAND v PAKISTAN

First Vitality Twenty20 International

At Manchester, August 28 (floodlit). No result. Toss: Pakistan.

After ruining the Tests in Southampton, rain spoiled the first of the three T20s in Manchester, though not before Banton had scored his maiden fifty at this level. In his preferred opening position following a side injury to Jason Roy, and with Jos Buttler unavailable after England chose not to select their Test players, Banton overcame a relatively slow start to produce a sparkling array of shots. Reprieved on five when Iftikhar Ahmed dropped the textbook definition of a regulation slip catch off Shaheen Shah Afridi, Banton added 71 for the second wicket with Malan. He soon slog-swept consecutive sixes off leg-spinner Shadab Khan, and completed a 33-ball fifty, before scooping fast bowler Haris Rauf for an audacious six over fine leg. But his dismissal for 71, slicing Shadab to extra cover, sparked a collapse of four for 14 in 19 balls, all to spin. With England's innings in the balance at 131 for six off 16.1 overs, rain intervened. The umpires, whose Test colleagues had been much criticised for not taking all possible steps to resume play, held a lengthy inspection, before concluding shortly after nine o'clock that the outfield was too wet.

England

		B	*4/6*
1 T. Banton *c 8 b 6*	71	42	4/5
2 †J. M. Bairstow *c and b 8*	2	4	0
3 D. J. Malan *run out (3/6)*	23	23	2
4 *E. J. G. Morgan *lbw b 5*	14	10	1/1
5 M. M. Ali *c 7 b 6*	8	7	1
6 S. W. Billings *not out*	3	5	0
7 L. Gregory *st 7 b 8*	2	3	0
8 C. J. Jordan *not out*	2	3	0
Lb 4, w 2	6		
6 overs: 34-1 (16.1 overs)	131-6		

1/3 2/74 3/109 4/118 5/120 6/123

9 T. K. Curran, 10 A. U. Rashid and 11 S. Mahmood did not bat.

Imad Wasim 24–7–31–2; Shaheen Shah Afridi 12–8–10–0; Mohammad Amir 13–5–14–0; Haris Rauf 18–3–32–0; Shadab Khan 24–9–33–2; Iftikhar Ahmed 6–2–7–1.

Pakistan

1 *Babar Azam, 2 Fakhar Zaman, 3 Mohammad Hafeez, 4 Shoaib Malik, 5 Iftikhar Ahmed, 6 Shadab Khan, 7 †Mohammad Rizwan, 8 Imad Wasim, 9 Mohammad Amir, 10 Shaheen Shah Afridi and 11 Haris Rauf did not bat.

Umpires: M. Burns and A. G. Wharf. Third umpire: M. J. Saggers.
Referee: W. M. Noon.

ENGLAND v PAKISTAN

Second Vitality Twenty20 International

At Manchester, August 30. England won by five wickets. Toss: England.

It was hard to disagree with Morgan when he said he was batting better than ever following a blistering 66 off 33 balls as England made light work of a target of 196. It was the highest successful T20 chase against Pakistan, surpassing the 192 Australia knocked off in the 2010 World Twenty20 semi-final in St Lucia. Coming in on a hat-trick against Shadab Khan, Morgan put on a decisive 112 with Malan – equalling England's highest stand for any wicket against Pakistan (Morgan also put on an unbroken 112 with Kevin Pietersen at Dubai in 2009-10). He might have been lbw second ball to Shadab, but Martin Saggers said not out, and Pakistan's review revealed umpire's call on impact. Morgan was quickly into his stride against an attack weakened when Mohammad Amir went off with a hamstring injury after his second over, and dominated a 55-ball century stand, of which

Malan's share was 34. By the time he picked out deep backward square, England needed only 18 from 19 balls. Ali went tamely, and Billings with the scores level, before Malan finished things off with five deliveries to spare, having completed his seventh fifty in 12 T20 internationals. Earlier, Babar Azam and Mohammad Hafeez punished an attack that again failed to take a powerplay wicket and, Rashid apart, lacked penetration. Pakistan's 195 for four was their highest T20 score against England, surpassing 173 for six at Cardiff the previous summer. There was no denying the entertainment in the first England fixture broadcast live on BBC television since 1999 – several years before the birth of professional T20 cricket, and at a time when the idea of an Irish white-ball specialist leading the side would have seemed equally outlandish.

Player of the Match: E. J. G. Morgan.

Pakistan

		B	*4/6*
1 *Babar Azam *c 6 b 10*	56	44	7
2 Fakhar Zaman *c 1 b 10*	36	22	5/1
3 Mohammad Hafeez *c 4 b 9*	69	36	5/4
4 Shoaib Malik *c 4 b 8*	14	11	1
5 Iftikhar Ahmed *not out*	8	9	0
6 Shadab Khan *not out*	0	0	0
Lb 6, w 4, nb 2	12		
6 overs: 51-0 (20 overs)	195-4		

1/72 2/112 3/162 4/194

7 †Mohammad Rizwan, 8 Imad Wasim, 9 Mohammad Amir, 10 Shaheen Shah Afridi and 11 Haris Rauf did not bat.

12th man: Khushdil Shah.

Mahmood 24–7–38–0; Ali 6–0–10–0; Jordan 24–4–41–1; Curran 24–5–46–1; Rashid 24–6–32–2; Gregory 18–5–22–0.

England

		B	*4/6*
1 T. Banton *lbw b 6*	20	16	0/1
2 †J. M. Bairstow *c 8 b 6*	44	24	4/2
3 D. J. Malan *not out*	54	36	6/1
4 *E. J. G. Morgan *c 12 b 11*	66	33	6/4
5 M. M. Ali *c 1 b 6*	1	2	0
6 S. W. Billings *c 2 b 11*	10	5	2
7 L. Gregory *not out*	0	0	0
Lb 1, w 2, nb 1	4		
6 overs: 65-0 (19.1 overs)	199-5		

1/66 2/66 3/178 4/182 5/195

8 C. J. Jordan, 9 T. K. Curran, 10 A. U. Rashid and 11 S. Mahmood did not bat.

Imad Wasim 18–4–30–0; Shaheen Shah Afridi 19–3–44–0; Mohammad Amir 12–2–25–0; Shadab Khan 24–6–34–3; Iftikhar Ahmed 18–3–31–0; Haris Rauf 24–7–34–2.

Umpires: D. J. Millns and M. J. Saggers. Third umpire: M. Burns.
Referee: W. M. Noon.

ENGLAND v PAKISTAN

Third Vitality Twenty20 International

At Manchester, September 1 (floodlit). Pakistan won by five runs. Toss: England. Twenty20 international debut: Haider Ali.

Pakistan's 66th day in the bubble saw them win at the last, and square the series. Victory was built on a partnership of 100 between 19-year-old debutant Haider Ali and 39-year-old Hafeez, though it was hard to tell who was the veteran. In at two for one, Haider slog-swept his second ball, from Ali, for six, and sent Gregory's opening delivery over the longest boundary, at midwicket. His fifty, from 28 deliveries, was the first on T20 international debut by a Pakistani. Haider was eventually bowled by Jordan, but Hafeez carried on, having launched two of his six sixes in consecutive deliveries off the unusually expensive Rashid. Needing five runs fewer than two days earlier, England were soon 69 for four, with Malan brilliantly caught by a leaping Fakhar Zaman at deep midwicket, and Morgan run out following confusion with Banton, whose enterprising 46 ended five balls later. Ali, until this innings hopelessly out of touch, led a rally, adding 57 with Billings, but Wahab Riaz produced a superb 19th over, with England needing 20. He ran out Jordan, cramped Ali with a short ball, and conceded just a wide and two singles. The equation was down to 12 off two deliveries when Curran smashed a slower ball from Haris Rauf over extra cover for six, but he could do nothing about the next, a 90mph yorker. A campaign notably free of rancour, with both sides conscious of the wider issues at stake amid the pandemic, ended with Rauf rowing with his team-mates about allowing Curran his late chance at glory.

Player of the Match: Mohammad Hafeez. *Player of the Series:* Mohammad Hafeez.

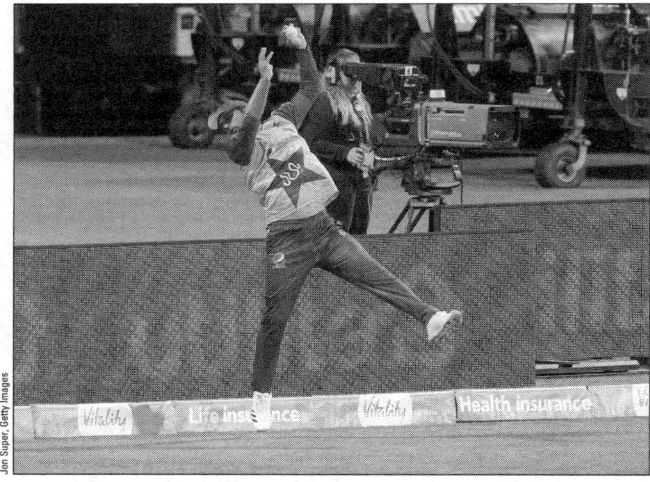

Jon Super, Getty Images

Life on the edge Fakhar Zaman catches Dawid Malan.

Pakistan

		B	*4/6*
1 *Babar Azam *b 9*	21	18	3
2 Fakhar Zaman *b 5*	1	3	0
3 Haider Ali *b 8*	54	33	5/2
4 Mohammad Hafeez *not out*	86	52	4/6
5 Shadab Khan *c 9 b 8*	15	11	2
6 Imad Wasim *not out*	6	4	0
Lb 1, w 5, nb 1	7		
6 overs: 47-2 (20 overs)	190-4		

1/2 2/32 3/132 4/177

7 Shoaib Malik, 8 †Sarfraz Ahmed, 9 Wahab Riaz, 10 Shaheen Shah Afridi and 11 Haris Rauf did not bat.

Mahmood 24–4–37–0; Ali 6–1–10–1; Jordan 24–9–29–2; Curran 24–8–32–1; Gregory 24–6–41–0; Rashid 18–5–40–0.

England

		B	*4/6*
1 T. Banton *lbw b 11*	46	31	8
2 †J. M. Bairstow *b 10*	0	3	0
3 D. J. Malan *c 2 b 6*	7	8	1
4 *E. J. G. Morgan *run out (11/8)*	10	5	0/1
5 M. M. Ali *c and b 9*	61	33	4/4
6 S. W. Billings *c 6 b 9*	26	24	2/1
7 L. Gregory *b 10*	12	8	2
8 C. J. Jordan *run out (9)*	1	2	0
9 T. K. Curran *not out*	8	5	0/1
10 A. U. Rashid *not out*	3	3	0
B 5, lb 2, w 2, nb 2	11		
6 overs: 54-2 (20 overs)	185-8		

1/1 2/26 3/65 4/69 5/126 6/170 7/172 8/174

11 S. Mahmood did not bat.

Shaheen Shah Afridi 24–12–28–2; Imad Wasim 24–11–35–1; Haris Rauf 24–7–41–1; Wahab Riaz 24–9–26–2; Shadab Khan 24–6–48–0.

Umpires: M. Burns and D. J. Millns. Third umpire: A. G. Wharf.
Referee: W. M. Noon.

ENGLAND v AUSTRALIA IN 2020

CHRIS STOCKS

Twenty20 internationals (3): England 2, Australia 1
One-day internationals (3): England 1 (10pts), Australia 2 (20pts)

A tour that meant all 18 men's international fixtures were fulfilled during the summer produced a gripping conclusion, with Australia becoming the first visiting team to win a one-day series in England since they had done so five years earlier. The tourists, who had collapsed chasing moderate targets in two of the first five games across the limited-overs formats, were indebted to a partnership for the ages between Alex Carey and Glenn Maxwell, as they came back from 73 for five to knock off a target of 303 in the 50-over decider at Old Trafford. Before the trip, Maxwell had not played for his country for ten months, yet his 108 during a stand of 212 with Carey, who also scored a century, made him the Player of the Series in the ODIs.

England's powerful batting was largely negated by tricky, made-to-order pitches – Eoin Morgan wanted his side to learn how to "win ugly" in preparation for the T20 World Cup in India in 2021-22 – but there was consolation in having already claimed the 20-over series. Australia had begun as the format's No. 1 team, before England ousted them with victory in the first two matches; a win for the Australians in the third returned them to the top of the rankings. Yet with the postponement of the T20 World Cup in Australia – originally scheduled to start the following month – those games lacked a wider context.

Playing behind closed doors at least spared the Australians their usual interactions with English crowds. "It was the first time I've been here and not got abuse," said David Warner after the first of the three T20s at the Rose Bowl. "It was quite nice." Instead, he had to contend with Jofra Archer, who removed him four times in five games, three times for single figures.

That opening T20 match had witnessed the first of the Australian implosions, as they lost five for 24 chasing 163, and the game by two runs. England would also steal the second of the three one-day internationals in Manchester after the tourists lost seven for 32. It left Australia's coach, Justin Langer, fielding questions about his players' mental fragility, though Maxwell and Carey provided the perfect riposte.

There was no argument from Langer, though, when Michael Holding criticised both sides for not taking a knee in support of the Black Lives Matter movement – as England had done during their series with West Indies and Ireland, though not Pakistan. "To be completely honest, we could've talked more about it perhaps, leading up to that first game," said Langer. That followed pre-series comments from Australian captain Aaron Finch, who argued that "the education around it is more important than the protest". Later, Archer insisted England had not forgotten about BLM, and were working with the ECB on projects to promote equality and diversity.

With the Test summer over, England had the majority of their all-format players back. Yet they were still without Ben Stokes, whose father, Ged – based

Stu Forster, Getty Images

From the unlikeliest of positions: Glenn Maxwell masterminds a recovery from 73 for five in the decisive one-day game – and Australia steal the series.

in New Zealand – had been diagnosed with brain cancer. Australia also had a significant absentee from the ODIs, after Steve Smith suffered a blow to the head from an errant throwdown in the nets on the eve of the first game. Unlike the previous summer's Ashes, when he had been felled by Archer at Lord's, there were few witnesses, since reporters were barred from practice sessions because of coronavirus protocols. Smith's absence from the first match was announced only at the toss. With Archer and Mark Wood bowling consistently above 90mph, it was perhaps no surprise he ended up missing the entire series.

Despite the heroics of Maxwell and Carey, Australia's victory in the one-dayers owed much to the excellence of their bowlers – none more so than Josh Hazlewood, who in 2019 had been rested for the World Cup in preparation for the Ashes. His haul of four wickets at 30 looked unspectacular, but an economy-rate of four – as well as five maidens in his 30 overs – told a tale. Leg-spinner Adam Zampa recovered from a mauling in the T20s, when he was the most expensive bowler on either side, to collect ten ODI wickets at 14 apiece while conceding just 4.73 an over.

For England, Chris Woakes excelled in the 50-over matches, averaging 44 with the bat and 22 with the ball. Had the pendulum swung the other way at the last, he – not Maxwell – might have been the Player of the Series. Sam Billings made a breakthrough century in the first ODI, while Jonny Bairstow followed 84 in that game with 112 in the third. But England regularly struggled against Australia's Test-hardened new-ball attack: Jason Roy, who missed the T20s because of a side injury, completed a quiet international summer with 24 runs in three innings, while Joe Root totalled 40. In the third ODI, Mitchell Starc removed both with the first two balls of the game. Earlier, Dawid Malan had replaced Pakistan's Babar Azam at the top of the T20 rankings after scores of 66, 42 and 21.

That the tour had gone ahead at all was a triumph of perseverance and planning. Australia's home one-day series against New Zealand in March, abandoned after one match, had been the last international cricket played before the pandemic was declared. Events in the interim, particularly the closure of some state borders in Australia, meant the challenge of getting a party to the UK was significant. Originally scheduled for July, the trip was signed off by the Australian government only ten days before the team's departure on August 23, with Cricket Australia receiving clearance for a final squad of 21 to assemble in Perth for a charter flight.

Different restrictions across the states meant different levels of preparation. Western Australians such as Mitchell Marsh and Marcus Stoinis were able to go about their daily lives largely unrestricted; Finch and Maxwell, whose state, Victoria, had been in a strict lockdown for months, could leave their homes

HIGHEST ODI PARTNERSHIPS CONCEDED BY ENGLAND AT HOME

286	for 1st	W. U. Tharanga/S. T. Jayasuriya	for Sri Lanka at Leeds	2006
214	**for 2nd**	**P. R. Stirling/A. Balbirnie**	**for Ireland at Southampton**	**2020**
212	**for 6th**	**A. T. Carey/G. J. Maxwell**	**for Australia at Manchester**	**2020**
206	for 3rd	K. S. Williamson/L. R. P. L. Taylor	for New Zealand at Southampton	2015
187	for 2nd	C. H. Gayle/R. R. Sarwan	for West Indies at Lord's	2004
183	for 1st	A. M. Rahane/S. Dhawan	for India at Birmingham	2014
175	for 3rd	S. Chanderpaul/M. N. Samuels	for West Indies at Birmingham	2007
172*	for 4th	H. M. Amla/A. B. de Villiers	for South Africa at Nottingham	2012
172	for 2nd	T. M. Dilshan/K. C. Sangakkara	for Sri Lanka at Lord's	2014
170	for 3rd	†R. Dravid/V. Kohli	for India at Cardiff	2011

† *Dravid and Kohli were the only pair who went on to lose.*

only to train with each other. Even then, getting out of Australia proved tricky, since Qantas's entire international fleet was grounded. In the end, CA sourced a jet from Paris through a boutique French airline, La Compagnie. Because of a small fuel load, it had to stop in Colombo and Dubai during the 19-hour journey to East Midlands Airport.

Unlike West Indies and Pakistan, Australia did not have to quarantine on arrival in the UK, thanks to the travel corridor agreed between the countries. But, with England's final Test against Pakistan at the Rose Bowl in progress when they landed, they did have to spend three nights in a Travelodge next to Derbyshire's County Ground before they were free to head to Southampton. Given the efforts made to get them into the country, and the cricket that followed, it was a small price to pay.

AUSTRALIAN TOURING PARTY

*A. J. Finch, S. A. Abbott, A. C. Agar, A. T. Carey, P. J. Cummins, J. R. Hazlewood, M. Labuschagne, N. M. Lyon, M. R. Marsh, G. J. Maxwell, R. P. Meredith, J. R. Philippe, K. W. Richardson, D. R. Sams, S. P. D. Smith, M. A. Starc, M. P. Stoinis, A. J. Tye, M. S. Wade, D. A. Warner, A. Zampa.

Gareth Copley, Getty Images

Pace, precision and purpose: Jofra Archer tears past David Warner, his serial victim.

England

J. J. Roy run out (Stoinis)	21
J. M. Bairstow c Carey b Starc	0
J. E. Root c Finch b Zampa	39
*E. J. G. Morgan lbw b Zampa	42
†J. C. Buttler lbw b Cummins	3
S. W. Billings b Zampa	8
C. R. Woakes c Carey b Hazlewood	26
S. M. Curran c Carey b Starc	1
T. K. Curran b Marsh	37
A. U. Rashid not out	35
J. C. Archer not out	6
Lb 5, w 8	13
1/20 (2) 2/29 (1) 3/90 (3) 4/107 (5) 5/117 (4) 6/140 (6) 7/143 (8) 8/149 (7) 9/225 (9) — (9 wkts, 50 overs)	231
10 overs: 32-2	

Starc 10–1–38–2; Hazlewood 10–2–27–1; Cummins 10–3–56–1; Marsh 8–1–49–1; Stoinis 2–0–20–0; Zampa 10–0–36–3.

Australia

D. A. Warner c Buttler b Archer	6
*A. J. Finch b Woakes	73
M. P. Stoinis c Buttler b Archer	9
M. Labuschagne lbw b Woakes	48
M. R. Marsh b Archer	1
†A. T. Carey st Buttler b Rashid	36
G. J. Maxwell b Woakes	1
P. J. Cummins b S. M. Curran	11
M. A. Starc c Buttler b S. M. Curran	0
A. Zampa c Archer b S. M. Curran	2
J. R. Hazlewood not out	7
Lb 11, w 1, nb 1	13
1/9 (1) 2/37 (3) 3/144 (4) 4/145 (5) 5/145 (2) 6/147 (7) 7/166 (8) 8/166 (9) 9/176 (10) 10/207 (6) — (48.4 overs)	207
10 overs: 44-2	

Woakes 10–1–32–3; Archer 10–2–34–3; T. K. Curran 10–2–28–0; Rashid 9.4–0–67–1; S. M. Curran 9–0–35–3.

Umpires: M. A. Gough and M. J. Saggers. Third umpire: R. K. Illingworth.
Referee: B. C. Broad.

ENGLAND v AUSTRALIA

Third Royal London One-Day International

At Manchester, September 16 (day/night). Australia won by three wickets. Australia 10pts. Toss: England.

At 73 for five, chasing 303, Australia required something remarkable to win the series. Carey and Maxwell provided it, putting on 212, the third-highest sixth-wicket stand in one-day internationals, to

WICKETS WITH THE FIRST TWO BALLS OF AN ODI INNINGS

Bowler	*Batsmen out*		
T. M. Alderman...	Ramiz Raja/Aamer Malik.........	A v P at Brisbane	1988-89
W. P. U. J. C. Vaas	Hannan Sarkar/Mohammad Ashraful	SL v B at Pietermaritzburg	2002-03
Mohammad Irfan..	H. M. Amla/C. A. Ingram	P v S Africa at Durban	2012-13
M. A. Starc......	**J. J. Roy/J. E. Root.............**	**A v E at Manchester ....**	**2020**

Vaas completed a hat-trick by dismissing Ehsanul Haque and, after a four and a wide, removed Sanwar Hossain with the fifth legal delivery of the match.

---

leave England ruing two missed chances. Carey had only nine when he upper-cut Archer to third man, momentarily leaving Australia 87 for six. But Archer had overstepped, his first no-ball in ODIs. Then Maxwell was dropped by Buttler off Rashid on 44, with the total 164. Carey went on to make his first ODI hundred, and Maxwell his second. Maxwell in particular exploited the short leg-side boundary towards the giant red Point building, hitting seven sixes in all, three off Rashid. Only once before had Nos 6 and 7 each made a hundred in the same ODI innings: Mahela Jayawardene and M. S. Dhoni for the Asia XI against Africa at Chennai in 2007. By the time Maxwell top-edged Rashid, Australia needed 18 from 15 balls, which became ten from six when Archer dismissed Carey with the final delivery of the penultimate over. Morgan handed the last to Rashid – rather than Wood or Curran – but Starc hit the first ball straight for six, then heaved the fourth for four. Earlier, he had taken wickets with the first two balls of the match. Bairstow's first ODI hundred since the World Cup helped England recover, and half-centuries from Billings and Woakes, who made an unbeaten 53 from 39 balls, lifted them to a good total on a fresh pitch. Yet this match was all about one of the great one-day partnerships, inspiring Australia to the highest successful ODI chase at Old Trafford, and condemning England to their first bilateral series defeat since touring India in January 2017.

Player of the Match: G. J. Maxwell. *Player of the Series:* G. J. Maxwell.

England

J. J. Roy c Maxwell b Starc	0
J. M. Bairstow b Cummins	112
J. E. Root lbw b Starc	0
*E. J. G. Morgan c Starc b Zampa	23
†J. C. Buttler c Finch b Zampa	8
S. W. Billings c Marsh b Zampa	57
C. R. Woakes not out	53
T. K. Curran b Starc	19
A. U. Rashid not out	11
Lb 8, w 10, nb 1	19
1/0 (1) 2/0 (3) 3/67 (4) 4/96 (5) 5/210 (6) 6/220 (2) 7/266 (8) (7 wkts, 50 overs)	302
10 overs: 67-2	

J. C. Archer and M. A. Wood did not bat.

Starc 10–0–74–3; Hazlewood 10–0–68–0; Cummins 10–0–53–1; Zampa 10–0–51–3; Marsh 6–0–25–0; Maxwell 4–0–23–0.

Australia

D. A. Warner b Root	24
*A. J. Finch lbw b Woakes	12
M. P. Stoinis c Morgan b Woakes	4
M. Labuschagne run out (Billings/Buttler)	20
M. R. Marsh c Buttler b Root	2
†A. T. Carey c Wood b Archer	106
G. J. Maxwell c Curran b Rashid	108
P. J. Cummins not out	4
M. A. Starc not out	11
Lb 5, w 8, nb 1	14
1/21 (2) 2/31 (3) 3/51 (1) 4/55 (5) 5/73 (4) 6/285 (7) 7/293 (6) (7 wkts, 49.4 overs)	305
10 overs: 47-2	

A. Zampa and J. R. Hazlewood did not bat.

Woakes 10–0–46–2; Archer 9–0–60–1; Wood 9–1–40–0; Root 8–0–46–2; Curran 6–1–40–0; Rashid 7.4–0–68–1.

Umpires: R. K. Illingworth and A. G. Wharf. Third umpire: R. A. Kettleborough.
Referee: B. C. Broad.

SOUTH AFRICA v ENGLAND IN 2020-21

NEIL MANTHORP

Twenty20 internationals (3): South Africa 0, England 3

Positive Covid-19 tests on players and hotel staff led to the last-minute postponement of the first one-day international, then its cancellation, and finally England's return home halfway through their six-match tour. After enormous effort by Cricket South Africa to create a biosecure environment – including exclusive use for both teams of the four-star Vineyard Hotel in Cape Town, and strict security at Newlands and Paarl's Boland Park – local disappointment was immense.

The trip, originally scheduled for the northern spring of 2021, had already been brought forward at the ECB's request, because of concerns about fixture overload. For a while, tension between South Africa's government and cricket board threatened to scupper the tour, with sports minister Nathi Mthethwa urging the board to step down amid accusations of mismanagement. But it was clear that cancellation suited no one – and might even have bankrupted CSA, who hoped to net £3.5m in TV revenue from England's visit.

While South Africa's internal squabble inevitably resolved itself, with the entire board standing down on October 26, and replaced by an interim committee, the ECB dealt behind the scenes with Graeme Smith, CSA's director of cricket. The ECB had paid for the charter flights that brought West Indies and Pakistan to the UK during the summer but, conscious of the hosts' precarious finances, now funded their own travel. And so, on November 16, a squad of 23, and almost as many management and coaching staff, flew to Cape Town for ten days of semi-quarantine, during which they played two intra-squad matches, and plenty of golf – a condition of touring, not simply a request.

For the two teams, those ten days could not have been more contrasting. Before they entered the mini-lockdown, South Africa were already isolating three players – Andile Phehlukwayo, who had contracted the virus outside the bubble and, as a precaution, "close contacts" Temba Bavuma and Kagiso Rabada. None of the trio was originally named. Next day, the South Africans called off a practice match after David Miller – again unnamed – tested positive too. They also ceded all common areas of the hotel to the England players, including the gym and swimming pool, and for six days made use of goods entrances and fire exits, until the entire squad had tested negative three times.

England's warm-ups, between Team Morgan and Team Buttler, were intense and entertaining, with Buttler's XI comfortably winning both, across 40 overs at Newlands, and 20 at Paarl. South Africa did not even have a middle practice, with their non-IPL contingent – which was most of them – having played no white-ball cricket for almost nine months. The fact that they were competitive in the first two T20 internationals was surprising, though they lost the series 3–0.

Then, the day before the first ODI, another South African player, Heinrich Klaasen, tested positive; two days later, so did two of the hotel staff, including

Shaun Botterill, Getty Images

Coach party: the South African bus waits outside the Vineyard Hotel, Cape Town.

one who had been working in England's section of the accommodation. The tourists were en route to Newlands when the game was postponed. Meanwhile, when news emerged that England had apparently broken their own strict protocols by using the nets behind the stands at Newlands, rather than those set up for them on the square, there was danger of a tit-for-tat row. England insisted they had been granted permission to use the nets, but the SA Police Service brigadier in charge of biosecurity was so incensed he threatened to press charges, until pacified by CSA. The South African team had been denied permission to use the nets.

The original schedule of three ODIs in six days was always tight but, displaying an admirable willingness to continue, England agreed to three in four days – then, after the first was cancelled, two in two. But when two of their own party had returned unconfirmed positive tests, the tourists were spooked. And even though the two positive tests proved negative 12 hours later, they had had enough. Next day, the tour was called off.

CSA's chief medical officer, Dr Shuaib Manjra, was "devastated" by the decision, and said expectations had been "unrealistic" – probably because the ECB had managed to get through a condensed home summer involving five touring teams without a single positive case. "In some ways, they were a victim of their own success, and set the bar unrealistically high," he said. "They spent millions, and created more of a vacuum than a biosecure environment. It was obvious they were experiencing some bubble fatigue, so we tried to incorporate some leeway, without compromising their health and safety."

Manjra cited England's request to play golf – the players were driven straight to the first tee at prearranged courses, bypassing the clubhouses – as evidence of their desire to be a bit more relaxed. "None of the smaller nations outside the Big Three can afford to spend the money the ECB did, and nobody can guarantee there will be no infections, in any environment," he said. "What matters is how you manage the infections."

He believed it was safe and reasonable for England to have played at least the second and third ODIs. Just days after the tour was abandoned, the ECB's own medical team joined a conference call between CSA and Sri Lanka Cricket to assure the Sri Lankans that everything had been done to keep the players safe, and that they should have no doubts about visiting South Africa for two Tests shortly after England's departure. After initial concerns, SLC played ball.

Graeme Smith and ECB chief executive Tom Harrison agreed the one-day series would be rescheduled "within the current cycle" of World Cup Super League matches building up to the 2023 World Cup, and the tourists would pick up the £400,000 hotel bill. The fact that they stayed on for the full scheduled duration of the tour was seen by locals as indicative of the danger they really believed they were in.

As for the cricket that *was* played, England captain Eoin Morgan gave his team "seven out of ten, maybe eight for the last game". Nonetheless, the series win moved them to the top of the T20 rankings, while more clinical batting from Dawid Malan, twice named Player of the Match, confirmed they also had the format's top-ranked batsman.

ENGLAND TOURING PARTY

*E. J. G. Morgan (Middlesex; 50/20), M. M. Ali (Worcestershire; 50/20), J. C. Archer (Sussex; 20), J. M. Bairstow (Yorkshire; 50/20), S. W. Billings (Kent; 50/20), J. C. Buttler (Lancashire; 50/20), S. M. Curran (Surrey; 20), T. K. Curran (Surrey; 50/20), L. Gregory (Somerset; 50), C. J. Jordan (Sussex; 20), L. S. Livingstone (Lancashire; 50), D. J. Malan (Yorkshire; 20), A. U. Rashid (Yorkshire; 50/20), J. E. Root (Yorkshire; 50), J. J. Roy (Surrey; 50/20), B. A. Stokes (Durham; 20), O. P. Stone (Warwickshire; 50), R. J. W. Topley (Surrey; 50/20), C. R. Woakes (Warwickshire; 50), M. A. Wood (Durham; 50/20).

J. T. Ball (Nottinghamshire), T. Banton (Somerset) and T. G. Helm (Middlesex) travelled with the squad as reserve players.

Head coach: C. E. W. Silverwood. *Assistant coaches:* G. P. Thorpe, P. D. Collingwood. *Bowling coach:* J. Lewis. *Batting consultant:* M. E. Trescothick. *Spin consultant:* J. S. Patel. *Wicketkeeping consultant:* J. S. Foster. *Team manager:* A. W. Bentley. *Analyst:* N. A. Leamon. *Doctor:* Moiz Moghal. *Physiotherapists:* S. Griffin, B. Langley. *Masseur:* M. Saxby. *Strength and conditioning:* R. Ahmun. *Security manager:* W. Carr. *Head of team communications:* D. M. Reuben. *Digital editor:* W. Turner.

At Cape Town, November 21, 2020. **J. C. Buttler's XI won by 50 runs.** ‡**J. C. Buttler's XI 255** (39.1 overs) (J. E. Root 77, S. W. Billings 52; M. A. Wood 3-48, T. K. Curran 4-25); **E. J. G. Morgan's XI 205** (35.5 overs) (C. R. Woakes 55; L. Gregory 3-18). *Jos Buttler's side easily won this 40-over intra-squad warm-up, with Joe Root's run-a-ball 77 – and stand of 103 with Sam Billings – setting up an imposing total on a sluggish pitch. Eoin Morgan's team never got close: even though the top nine all reached double figures, they had to be rescued by Chris Woakes (55 off 41) and Tom Curran, who put on 79 for the seventh wicket. Buttler's side chose from 12 players.*

At Paarl, November 23, 2020 (floodlit). **J. C. Buttler's XI won by six wickets. E. J. G. Morgan's XI 139-9** (20 overs) (M. M. Ali 41; O. P Stone 3-12); **J. C. Buttler's XI 141-4** (12.4 overs) (J. E. Root 45*, S. M. Curran 45*). *Morgan's side failed again, despite Ben Stokes (three and 10*) and Jonny Bairstow (11 and 10*) both having two innings, after being dismissed early on by Olly Stone, who took three wickets in eight balls. The first over of the chase, from Reece Topley, went for 17 – but Buttler's team were 50-4, before Root and Sam Curran clonked 91* in seven overs.*

SOUTH AFRICA v ENGLAND

First Twenty20 International

At Cape Town, November 27, 2020 (floodlit). England won by five wickets. Toss: England. Twenty20 international debut: G. F. Linde.

South Africa's total was 20 above par for Newlands, and England's chase appeared to be going to the wire: 51 required from four overs, with six wickets in hand. But left-arm seamer Hendricks buckled against the aggression of Bairstow and Morgan, and delivered a nine-ball 17th over: it cost 28 and, effectively, the game. Bairstow, at No. 4 for the first time in more than five years after England chose to open with Roy and Buttler, was bullish from the moment he arrived at 27 for two in the fifth – soon 34 for three when Malan fell to left-arm spinner George Linde, who had already removed Roy with his second ball in T20 internationals. Bairstow's counter-attack was matched by Stokes during a fourth-wicket stand of 85, and his improvisation – particularly slicing wide yorkers to the boundary – unnerved the South Africans; he finished with a career-best unbeaten 86 from 48 balls. Earlier, du Plessis had steered the South African innings after a cautious start, and van der Dussen hit three sixes, but neither was able to dominate the bowlers – except when du Plessis took 24 off the fifth over, from Tom Curran, who finished with his most expensive analysis in T20 internationals. By contrast, his brother Sam claimed a career-best three for 28, while Rashid conceded only one boundary. The teams declined to take a knee before the game, but wore black armbands in this match and the next, in recognition of gender-based violence and Covid-19.

Player of the Match: J. M. Bairstow.

South Africa

		B	*4/6*
1 T. Bavuma *c 2 b 7*	5	5	1
2 *†Q. de Kock *c 6 b 8*	30	23	2/1
3 F. du Plessis *c 8 b 7*	58	40	4/2
4 H. E. van der Dussen *c 3 b 11*	37	28	0/3
5 H. Klaasen *c 2 b 7*	20	12	2
6 P. J. van Biljon *not out*	7	6	0
7 G. F. Linde *b 9*	12	6	1/1
Lb 1, w 9	10		
6 overs: 57-1 (20 overs)	179-6		

1/6 2/83 3/110 4/147 5/161 6/179

8 K. Rabada, 9 B. E. Hendricks, 10 L. T. Ngidi and 11 T. Shamsi did not bat.

S. M. Curran 24–9–28–3; Archer 24–8–28–1; T. K. Curran 24–6–55–1; Rashid 24–6–27–0; Jordan 24–5–40–1.

England

		B	*4/6*
1 J. J. Roy *c 2 b 7*	0	2	0
2 †J. C. Buttler *c 5 b 10*	7	6	1
3 D. J. Malan *c 8 b 7*	19	20	3
4 J. M. Bairstow *not out*	86	48	9/4
5 B. A. Stokes *c 7 b 11*	37	27	1/3
6 *E. J. G. Morgan *c 1 b 10*	12	10	0/1
7 S. M. Curran *not out*	7	3	0/1
Lb 3, w 12	15		
6 overs: 34-3 (19.2 overs)	183-5		

1/0 2/27 3/34 4/119 5/159

8 C. J. Jordan, 9 T. K. Curran, 10 A. U. Rashid and 11 J. C. Archer did not bat.

Linde 24–13–20–2; Rabada 24–10–32–0; Hendricks 24–6–56–0; Ngidi 20–6–31–2; Shamsi 18–5–27–1; Klaasen 6–2–14–0.

Umpires: A. T. Holdstock and A. Paleker. Third umpire: B. P. Jele.
Referee: A. J. Pycroft.

SOUTH AFRICA v ENGLAND

Second Twenty20 International

At Paarl, November 29, 2020. England won by four wickets. Toss: England.

Malan later wondered whether he had "mistimed the run-chase a little bit", after reaching 25 off 30 balls, with England requiring more than ten an over on a slow, low pitch. But he slapped Ngidi to the point boundary, and took successive fours off Nortje in the 16th over. With 29 needed off three, Malan – at the ground where he had made his first-class debut, for Boland, nearly 15 years earlier – then showed he had acquired a taste for Ngidi's pace, hitting him for 14 in three deliveries, before falling on the boundary for 55 from 40. With Morgan also in the groove, the back of the chase had been broken – though a scratchy innings from Sam Curran meant England contrived to win with only a ball to spare. Earlier, de Kock had given South Africa a quick start with 30 from 18, but van der Dussen was befuddled by the conditions and the bowling, particularly Archer and Rashid, and finished with a boundaryless 25 not out from 29. Linde produced a late cameo, but a target of 147 was unlikely to prevent England from clinching the series – though left-arm wrist-spinner Shamsi made life hard for them with a career-best three for 19.

Player of the Match: D. J. Malan.

South Africa

		B	4/6
1 T. Bavuma *b 11*	13	10	2
2 *†Q. de Kock *c 9 b 8*	30	18	3/1
3 R. R. Hendricks *b 10*	16	18	2
4 F. du Plessis *st 2 b 10*	11	11	1
5 H. E. van der Dussen *not out*	25	29	0
6 H. Klaasen *c 5 b 9*	7	10	0
7 G. F. Linde *run out (5/8)*	29	20	2/1
8 K. Rabada *not out*	5	4	1
B 1, w 9	10		
6 overs: 50-2 (20 overs)	146-6		

1/33 2/48 3/65 4/75 5/95 6/139

9 A. A. Nortje, 10 L. T. Ngidi and 11 T. Shamsi did not bat.

S. M. Curran 12–2–24–0; Archer 24–12–18–1; T. K. Curran 24–6–37–1; Jordan 24–7–29–1; Rashid 24–10–23–2; Stokes 12–4–14–0.

England

		B	4/6
1 J. J. Roy *c 6 b 10*	14	19	2
2 †J. C. Buttler *b 11*	22	15	4
3 D. J. Malan *c 3 b 10*	55	40	7/1
4 J. M. Bairstow *c 3 b 11*	3	7	0
5 B. A. Stokes *c 2 b 11*	16	13	1/1
6 *E. J. G. Morgan *not out*	26	17	3/1
7 S. M. Curran *b 8*	1	5	0
8 C. J. Jordan *not out*	3	3	0
Lb 4, w 3	7		
6 overs: 41-1 (19.5 overs)	147-6		

1/25 2/51 3/55 4/83 5/134 6/144

9 T. K. Curran, 10 A. U. Rashid and 11 J. C. Archer did not bat.

Linde 24–10–27–0; Rabada 23–9–25–1; Nortje 24–12–21–0; Ngidi 24–8–51–2; Shamsi 24–10–19–3.

Umpires: S. George and A. T. Holdstock. Third umpire: A. Paleker.
Referee: A. J. Pycroft.

SOUTH AFRICA v ENGLAND

Third Twenty20 International

At Cape Town, December 1, 2020 (floodlit). England won by nine wickets. Toss: South Africa.

England bared their teeth after two close games, pulling off a record chase at Newlands – and a 3–0 whitewash – with 14 balls in hand. The only anticlimactic moment in Malan's clinical exhibition came with the scores level, when he called for a quick single on 98; few would have begrudged him the use of an extra delivery or two to hit a boundary. Nortje had trapped Roy in the fourth over, but such was Malan's fluency that Buttler was initially happy to play a supporting role, before finishing with an unbeaten 67 from 46 balls in a stand of 167 in 14 overs. Malan managed 99 off 47; each hit five sixes, though Malan scored 11 fours to Buttler's three. Only once before had an England pair shared a higher partnership, when Malan and Morgan put on 182 for the third wicket against New Zealand at Napier in November 2019. Asked whether he had confirmed his status as the world's No. 1 T20 batsman, and finally established himself in England's best XI, Malan replied: "I'm still coming to terms with that – I'd like to think I'll be on the next tour." England's bowlers had suffered too, shipping 84 from the last five overs of South Africa's innings, exceeding the 80 they conceded to India at the 2007 World T20, when Yuvraj Singh hit Stuart Broad for six sixes. Archer and Jordan each went for at least 20 in their final over, and Sam Curran 17, as van der Dussen and du Plessis feasted on a rash of missed lengths. Their stand of 127 in 10.3 overs was the second-highest for the

---

ONE SHORT: 99 NOT OUT IN A T20 INTERNATIONAL

L. J. Wright	England v Afghanistan at Colombo (RPS)	2012-13
D. J. Malan	**England v South Africa at Cape Town**	**2020-21**
Mohammad Hafeez	**Pakistan v New Zealand at Hamilton**	**2020-21**

A. D. Hales is the only man to be dismissed for 99 (England v West Indies at Nottingham in 2012).

Rodger Bosch, AFP/Getty Images

Booking a place: Dawid Malan proves himself invaluable to the England batting machine.

fourth wicket in T20 internationals. Morgan later defended the use of coded messages placed by team analyst Nathan Leamon on the dressing-room balcony to help with decision-making. The messages, comprising a number and a letter, each on a clipboard, had been cleared in advance with match referee Andy Pycroft, and Morgan insisted they were "100% within the spirit of the game".

Player of the Match: D. J. Malan. *Player of the Series:* D. J. Malan.

South Africa

		B	*4/6*
1 *†Q. de Kock *c 9 b 8*	17	12	1/1
2 T. Bavuma *c 8 b 5*	32	26	1/2
3 R. R. Hendricks *c 2 b 5*	13	14	2
4 F. du Plessis *not out*	52	37	5/3
5 H. E. van der Dussen *not out*	74	32	5/5
W 2, nb 1	3		
6 overs: 44-1 (20 overs)	191-3		

1/34 2/61 3/64

6 P. J. van Biljon, 7 G. F. Linde, 8 A. A. Nortje, 9 L. L. Sipamla, 10 L. T. Ngidi and 11 T. Shamsi did not bat.

S. M. Curran 18–3–35–0; Archer 24–8–44–0; Jordan 24–6–42–1; T. K. Curran 12–3–24–0; Rashid 24–12–20–0; Stokes 18–6–26–2.

England

		B	*4/6*
1 J. J. Roy *lbw b 8*	16	14	1/1
2 †J. C. Buttler *not out*	67	46	3/5
3 D. J. Malan *not out*	99	47	11/5
B 4, w 5, nb 1	10		
6 overs: 56-1 (17.4 overs)	192-1		

1/25

4 J. M. Bairstow, 5 B. A. Stokes, 6 *E. J. G. Morgan, 7 S. M. Curran, 8 C. J. Jordan, 9 T. K. Curran, 10 A. U. Rashid and 11 J. C. Archer did not bat.

Linde 24–11–26–0; Nortje 24–8–37–1; Sipamla 16–2–45–0; Ngidi 18–7–23–0; Shamsi 24–3–57–0.

Umpires: B. P. Jele and A. Paleker. Third umpire: A. T. Holdstock. Referee: A. J. Pycroft.

First one-day international At Paarl, December 6, 2020. **Cancelled.**

Second one-day international At Cape Town, December 7, 2020. **Cancelled.**

Third one-day international At Cape Town, December 9, 2020. **Cancelled.**

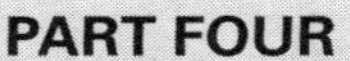

PART FOUR

English Domestic Cricket

FIRST-CLASS AVERAGES IN 2020

BATTING AND FIELDING

(Qualification: 5 innings)

		M	I	NO	R	HS	100	50	Avge	Ct/St
1	†D. J. Malan (*Yorks*)	3	5	0	332	219	1	1	66.40	2
2	S. J. Croft (*Lancs*)	4	5	2	199	63	0	3	66.33	6
3	Z. Crawley (*Kent & England*)	5	8	0	522	267	2	2	65.25	2
4	J. M. Cox (*Kent*)	4	6	1	324	238*	1	0	64.80	6
5	†B. A. Stokes (*England*)	4	7	1	372	176	1	1	62.00	4
6	†B. T. Slater (*Leics & Notts*)	5	7	0	425	172	2	1	60.71	2
7	A. J. A. Wheater (*Essex*)	6	9	4	291	83*	0	2	58.20	17/3
8	†A. N. Cook (*Essex*)	6	11	1	563	172	2	1	56.30	10
9	†B. M. Duckett (*Notts*)	5	8	1	394	150	2	0	56.28	3
10	D. M. Bess (*England*)	6	7	5	111	31*	0	0	55.50	1
11	J. D. Libby (*Worcs*)	5	9	0	498	184	1	3	55.33	2
12	C. N. Ackermann (*Leics*)	5	9	2	379	94	0	4	54.14	6
13	T. T. Bresnan (*Warwicks*)	4	6	2	214	105	1	0	53.50	5
14	†W. M. H. Rhodes (*Warwicks*)	5	9	1	423	207	1	0	52.87	2
15	B. L. D'Oliveira (*Worcs*)	5	8	1	367	174	1	1	52.42	2
16	J. C. Buttler (*England*)	6	9	1	416	152	1	2	52.00	21
17	†T. A. Lammonby (*Somerset*)	6	11	2	459	116	3	0	51.00	4
18	Babar Azam (*Pakistan Greens & Pakistan*)	4	7	2	252	69	0	2	50.40	1
19	†L. A. Procter (*Northants*)	4	6	2	200	112*	1	0	50.00	1
20	F. J. Hudson-Prentice (*Derbys*)	3	5	2	145	91*	0	1	48.33	1
21	†A. Z. Lees (*Durham*)	5	8	0	386	106	1	3	48.25	4
22	A. L. Davies (*Lancs*)	5	8	1	337	86	0	4	48.14	7
23	T. C. Fell (*Worcs*)	5	9	2	336	110*	1	1	48.00	3
24	†J. A. Thompson (*Yorks*)	5	6	1	234	98	0	2	46.80	2
25	†L. M. Reece (*Derbys*)	4	7	1	277	122	1	2	46.16	4
26	O. B. Cox (*Worcs*)	5	8	3	225	45*	0	0	45.00	25
27	C. O. Thurston (*Northants*)	5	8	0	357	115	1	2	44.62	2
28	J. A. Tattersall (*Yorks*)	5	7	1	265	71	0	3	44.16	9
29	J. J. Weatherley (*Hants*)	5	7	1	263	98	0	2	43.83	2
30	†N. R. T. Gubbins (*Middx*)	4	8	0	350	192	1	1	43.75	1
31	M. K. O'Riordan (*Kent*)	5	8	3	216	52*	0	1	43.20	1
32	H. C. Brook (*Yorks*)	5	7	1	258	66*	0	3	43.00	4
33	D. K. H. Mitchell (*Worcs*)	5	9	0	384	110	1	2	42.66	7
34	†J. L. du Plooy (*Derbys*)	5	7	0	296	130	1	1	42.28	5
35	G. J. Harte (*Durham*)	5	8	2	250	72	0	1	41.66	0
36	†S. C. J. Broad (*England*)	5	5	2	124	62	0	1	41.33	1
	B. A. Raine (*Durham*)	4	7	4	124	31	0	0	41.33	0
38	J. A. Haynes (*Worcs*)	5	9	2	285	51	0	2	40.71	1
39	Azhar Ali (*Pakistan Greens & Pakistan*)	4	7	1	244	141*	1	0	40.66	0
40	†S. M. Davies (*Somerset*)	6	10	2	320	123*	1	1	40.00	19
41	J. A. Leaning (*Kent*)	5	8	1	279	220*	1	0	39.85	9
42	A. M. Rossington (*Northants*)	3	6	1	196	135*	1	0	39.20	8
43	M. J. J. Critchley (*Derbys*)	5	7	1	234	63	0	1	39.00	4
44	H. Hameed (*Notts*)	5	7	0	272	87	0	3	38.85	8
45	T. B. Abell (*Somerset*)	6	11	1	386	119	2	1	38.60	5
46	†P. I. Walter (*Essex*)	5	9	2	266	46	0	0	38.00	2
47	H. J. Swindells (*Leics*)	5	7	2	188	52*	0	1	37.60	11
48	J. M. Clarke (*Notts*)	5	8	1	263	133	1	1	37.57	0
49	J. E. Root (*England*)	5	8	2	224	68*	0	1	37.33	10
50	J. Overton (*Somerset & Surrey*)	5	7	0	261	120	1	2	37.28	9
51	†R. J. Burns (*Surrey & England*)	7	11	0	409	103	1	3	37.18	6

		M	*I*	*NO*	*R*	*HS*	*100*	*50*	*Avge*	*Ct/St*
52	J. J. Bohannon (*Lancs*)	5	7	0	257	94	0	2	36.71	4
53	P. D. Salt (*Sussex*)	4	8	0	290	80	0	3	36.25	6
54	D. P. Sibley (*England*)	6	9	0	324	120	1	2	36.00	3
	C. R. Woakes (*England*)	5	5	1	144	84*	0	1	36.00	2
56	Mohammad Rizwan (*Pak Greens & Pakistan*)	4	5	0	179	72	0	2	35.80	6/2
57	†J. A. Simpson (*Middx*)	5	9	2	250	53	0	1	35.71	19/1
58	D. J. Vilas (*Lancs*)	5	7	0	247	90	0	1	35.28	5
59	R. G. White (*Middx*)	3	5	0	176	99	0	1	35.20	1
60	J. Blackwood (*West Indies*)	3	6	0	211	95	0	2	35.16	1
61	†Shan Masood (*Pakistan Greens & Pakistan*)	4	7	0	237	156	1	0	33.85	1
62	S. J. Mullaney (*Notts*)	5	7	0	235	67	0	2	33.57	10
63	H. R. Hosein (*Derbys*)	4	6	1	167	84	0	2	33.40	13/1
64	M. de Lange (*Glam*)	3	5	1	131	113	1	0	32.75	2
65	C. B. Cooke (*Glam*)	5	10	1	294	82	0	3	32.66	16/2
66	S. S. J. Brooks (*West Indies*)	3	6	0	195	68	0	2	32.50	0
67	G. A. Bartlett (*Somerset*)	4	6	1	160	100*	1	0	32.00	2
68	†W. T. Root (*Glam*)	5	10	1	286	118	1	1	31.77	1
69	†R. S. Vasconcelos (*Northants*)	5	8	1	222	58	0	2	31.71	13/1
70	D. G. Bedingham (*Durham*)	5	8	0	253	96	0	2	31.62	3
71	†A. Lyth (*Yorks*)	5	8	1	220	103	1	1	31.42	5
72	†G. P. Balderson (*Lancs*)	5	7	2	156	61*	0	1	31.20	0
73	R. N. ten Doeschate (*Essex*)	5	7	0	218	78	0	1	31.14	0
74	W. G. Jacks (*Surrey*)	5	10	2	248	84*	0	2	31.00	6
	C. Overton (*Somerset*)	6	10	2	248	66	0	2	31.00	7
76	G. L. van Buuren (*Glos*)	5	8	0	244	72	0	2	30.50	3
77	J. L. Smith (*Surrey*)	5	10	1	274	80	0	1	30.44	8
78	W. L. Madsen (*Derbys*)	5	8	1	213	103	1	1	30.42	10
79	S. R. Patel (*Notts*)	5	7	0	210	80	0	2	30.00	2
80	†M. D. E. Holden (*Middx*)	5	10	0	299	72	0	1	29.90	4
81	†B. J. Curran (*Northants*)	4	8	0	238	82	0	2	29.75	5
82	S. T. Evans (*Leics*)	3	5	0	148	85	0	1	29.60	3
83	†T. J. Moores (*Notts*)	5	7	0	207	106	1	0	29.57	15/1
84	K. C. Brathwaite (*West Indies*)	3	6	0	176	75	0	2	29.33	1
85	D. W. Lawrence (*Essex*)	4	6	1	144	60	0	1	28.80	0
86	L. J. Evans (*Surrey*)	3	6	0	172	65	0	1	28.66	1
87	M. K. Andersson (*Middx*)	5	9	1	227	92	0	2	28.37	3
88	†B. A. Godleman (*Derbys*)	5	8	0	226	86	0	3	28.25	2
89	J. A. Brooks (*Somerset*)	5	7	2	139	72	0	1	27.80	1
90	†T. J. Haines (*Sussex*)	5	10	1	249	117	1	0	27.66	1
91	B. C. Brown (*Sussex*)	5	10	0	270	98	0	2	27.00	10/1
92	O. J. D. Pope (*England*)	6	9	1	215	91	0	2	26.87	2
93	R. L. Chase (*West Indies*)	3	6	0	157	51	0	1	26.16	0
94	†H. E. Dearden (*Leics*)	5	9	0	234	70	0	1	26.00	1
	†K. K. Jennings (*Lancs*)	5	8	1	182	81	0	1	26.00	8
	M. G. Hogan (*Glam*)	4	7	4	78	33*	0	0	26.00	1
97	H. Z. Finch (*Sussex*)	5	10	0	259	69	0	2	25.90	6
98	S. A. Northeast (*Hants*)	5	7	0	181	81	0	2	25.85	0
99	J. A. R. Harris (*Middx*)	4	7	2	128	41	0	0	25.60	0
100	B. G. F. Green (*Somerset*)	3	5	0	127	54	0	1	25.40	0
101	E. J. H. Eckersley (*Durham*)	5	8	2	152	78*	0	1	25.33	3
102	†D. M. W. Rawlins (*Sussex*)	5	10	0	252	65	0	1	25.20	0
103	F. I. N. Khushi (*Essex*)	4	5	0	125	66	0	1	25.00	5
104	R. F. Higgins (*Glos*)	5	8	1	173	51	0	1	24.71	2
105	†E. J. Byrom (*Somerset*)	6	11	0	271	117	1	0	24.63	3
106	T. van der Gugten (*Glam*)	4	7	3	98	30*	0	0	24.50	3
107	†C. D. J. Dent (*Glos*)	4	7	0	170	92	0	2	24.28	4
108	†E. N. Gay (*Northants*)	4	6	1	121	77*	0	1	24.20	4
109	S. D. Robson (*Middx*)	5	10	1	215	82*	0	1	23.88	8
110	†T. P. Alsop (*Hants*)	5	7	0	164	87	0	1	23.42	5
111	D. J. Bell-Drummond (*Kent*)	5	9	1	185	45	0	0	23.12	3

		M	*I*	*NO*	*R*	*HS*	*100*	*50*	*Avge*	*Ct/St*
112	I. R. Bell (*Warwicks*)	5	8	0	184	90	0	2	23.00	5
	O. G. Robinson (*Kent*)	5	6	0	138	78	0	1	23.00	22
114	J. O. Holder (*West Indies*)	3	6	1	114	46	0	0	22.80	5
115	Abid Ali (*Pakistan Greens & Pakistan*)	4	7	0	156	60	0	1	22.28	0
116	G. F. B. Scott (*Glos*)	4	6	2	87	44*	0	0	21.75	0
117	N. J. Selman (*Glam*)	5	10	0	215	73	0	2	21.50	10
	G. Stewart (*Kent*)	4	6	0	129	58	0	1	21.50	0
119	S. C. Meaker (*Sussex*)	3	6	1	106	42	0	0	21.20	0
120	S. O. Dowrich (*West Indies*)	3	6	0	126	61	0	1	21.00	7
	E. G. Barnard (*Worcs*)	5	6	2	84	48*	0	0	21.00	5
122	J. C. Hildreth (*Somerset*)	4	6	0	124	45	0	0	20.66	10
123	L. D. McManus (*Hants*)	5	7	0	142	50	0	1	20.28	11/2
124	B. A. Carse (*Durham*)	3	5	0	100	41	0	0	20.00	0
	G. G. Wagg (*Glam*)	3	6	1	100	54	0	1	20.00	3
126	B. W. M. Mike (*Leics*)	4	6	1	99	51*	0	1	19.80	2
127	M. H. Wessels (*Worcs*)	5	8	0	157	88	0	1	19.62	4
128	†S. G. Borthwick (*Surrey*)	5	10	0	192	92	0	2	19.20	5
129	P. Coughlin (*Durham*)	4	6	0	114	90	0	1	19.00	2
130	J. H. Davey (*Somerset*)	6	9	3	113	28	0	0	18.83	1
131	A. D. Thomason (*Sussex*)	3	6	0	111	49	0	0	18.50	1
132	S. R. Hain (*Warwicks*)	5	8	0	146	65	0	2	18.25	5
	A. T. Thomson (*Warwicks*)	5	8	0	146	46	0	0	18.25	1
134	T. Köhler-Cadmore (*Yorks*)	5	8	1	127	41	0	0	18.14	2
135	†M. H. Azad (*Leics*)	5	8	0	144	58	0	1	18.00	3
136	D. A. Douthwaite (*Glam*)	5	10	1	160	86	0	1	17.77	3
137	†N. L. J. Browne (*Essex*)	4	8	0	142	61	0	1	17.75	4
	Yasir Shah (*Pakistan Greens & Pakistan*)	4	5	1	71	33	0	0	17.75	1
139	S. D. Hope (*West Indies*)	3	6	0	105	31	0	0	17.50	3
140	T. Westley (*Essex*)	6	11	1	172	51	0	1	17.20	3
141	†R. M. Yates (*Warwicks*)	5	9	1	137	88	0	1	17.12	2
142	M. G. K. Burgess (*Warwicks*)	5	8	0	135	39	0	0	16.87	15/1
143	G. H. Roderick (*Glos*)	4	7	1	101	39	0	0	16.83	12
144	†J. D. Campbell (*West Indies*)	3	6	1	84	32	0	0	16.80	1
145	S. S. Eskinazi (*Middx*)	5	10	1	151	29	0	0	16.77	7
146	G. H. Rhodes (*Leics*)	4	7	2	83	22*	0	0	16.60	4
147	I. G. Holland (*Hants*)	5	7	0	115	42	0	0	16.42	4
148	G. T. Hankins (*Glos*)	5	8	0	130	69	0	1	16.25	7
149	M. E. Milnes (*Kent*)	4	6	0	96	43	0	0	16.00	1
150	L. Gregory (*Somerset*)	3	5	0	78	37	0	0	15.60	1
151	†G. H. S. Garton (*Sussex*)	4	8	1	109	54*	0	1	15.57	4
152	R. P. Jones (*Lancs*)	3	5	0	77	23	0	0	15.40	3
	†M. E. Claydon (*Sussex*)	4	8	3	77	24	0	0	15.40	0
154	J. K. Fuller (*Hants*)	4	5	1	61	30	0	0	15.25	2
155	R. Clarke (*Surrey*)	3	6	0	91	30	0	0	15.16	4
156	P. D. Trego (*Notts*)	5	8	0	116	39	0	0	14.50	1
157	J. T. A. Burnham (*Durham*)	3	5	0	72	31	0	0	14.40	1
158	J. T. Ball (*Notts*)	3	5	1	56	34	0	0	14.00	3
159	S. R. Harmer (*Essex*)	6	9	1	111	32	0	0	13.87	10
160	†T. G. R. Clark (*Sussex*)	4	8	0	110	65	0	1	13.75	2
161	K. S. Carlson (*Glam*)	4	8	0	109	79	0	1	13.62	2
162	R. I. Keogh (*Northants*)	4	6	0	80	31	0	0	13.33	1
	T. N. Cullen (*Glam*)	3	6	0	80	26	0	0	13.33	6
164	†M. D. Stoneman (*Surrey*)	4	8	0	106	45	0	0	13.25	1
	D. Klein (*Leics*)	4	5	1	53	27	0	0	13.25	0
166	†B. G. Charlesworth (*Glos*)	4	6	0	78	51	0	1	13.00	0
	†R. S. Patel (*Surrey*)	3	6	0	78	44	0	0	13.00	5
168	D. I. Stevens (*Kent*)	5	6	0	77	36	0	0	12.83	3
169	Asad Shafiq (*Pakistan Greens & Pakistan*)	4	7	1	76	29	0	0	12.66	4
170	S. R. Dickson (*Durham*)	5	8	0	97	56	0	1	12.12	4
171	R. E. van der Merwe (*Somerset*)	4	6	1	57	30	0	0	11.40	4

		M	I	NO	R	HS	100	50	Avge	Ct/St
172	H. T. Crocombe (*Sussex*)	4	8	4	45	15	0	0	11.25	1
173	C. Rushworth (*Durham*)	4	7	2	54	25	0	0	10.80	0
174	†A. P. Beard (*Essex*)	5	6	2	43	17	0	0	10.75	1
	†O. J. Hannon-Dalby (*Warwicks*)	5	7	3	43	19	0	0	10.75	1
176	C. R. Hemphrey (*Glam*)	3	6	0	62	20	0	0	10.33	3
177	H. R. C. Came (*Hants*)	4	5	0	49	25	0	0	9.80	1
178	J. Leach (*Worcs*)	5	6	1	47	17	0	0	9.40	1
179	B. Muzarabani (*Northants*)	4	5	2	27	15	0	0	9.00	1
	C. N. Miles (*Warwicks*)	3	5	2	27	13*	0	0	9.00	0
181	†T. J. Murtagh (*Middx*)	4	5	2	26	11*	0	0	8.66	1
182	M. D. Taylor (*Glos*)	5	7	2	43	19*	0	0	8.60	0
183	F. S. Organ (*Hants*)	5	7	0	60	16	0	0	8.57	1
184	J. P. A. Taylor (*Surrey*)	3	5	1	34	22	0	0	8.50	1
185	M. S. Crane (*Hants*)	4	5	1	33	25*	0	0	8.25	0
186	J. A. Porter (*Essex*)	6	8	4	30	13	0	0	7.50	3
187	A. W. Finch (*Surrey*)	3	5	1	29	10	0	0	7.25	1
188	†S. A. Zaib (*Northants*)	4	5	0	36	23	0	0	7.20	2
189	J. Shaw (*Glos*)	5	7	0	50	21	0	0	7.14	0
	K. A. Bull (*Glam*)	4	8	1	50	23	0	0	7.14	1
191	J. J. Carson (*Sussex*)	4	8	0	57	21	0	0	7.12	1
192	S. J. Cook (*Essex*)	5	5	1	26	15*	0	0	6.50	0
193	D. A. Payne (*Glos*)	4	5	1	24	14	0	0	6.00	0
194	†M. P. Dunn (*Surrey*)	3	6	1	28	12	0	0	5.60	2
195	†T. N. Walallawita (*Middx*)	5	6	2	22	11	0	0	5.50	0
196	G. S. Virdi (*Surrey*)	5	9	4	26	12	0	0	5.20	1
197	K. A. J. Roach (*West Indies*)	3	5	2	15	5*	0	0	5.00	1
198	C. T. Steel (*Durham*)	3	5	0	22	11	0	0	4.40	0
199	†Shaheen Shah Afridi (*Pak Greens & Pakistan*)	4	5	1	17	9*	0	0	4.25	0
200	Hamidullah Qadri (*Kent*)	4	5	2	11	5	0	0	3.66	0
201	Mohammad Abbas (*Pak Greens & Pakistan*)	4	5	1	10	4	0	0	2.50	1
202	S. T. Gabriel (*West Indies*)	3	5	3	4	4	0	0	2.00	0
203	Naseem Shah (*Pakistan Greens & Pakistan*)	4	5	1	7	4	0	0	1.75	0

BOWLING

(Qualification: 5 wickets)

		Style	O	M	R	W	BB	5I	Avge
1	B. O. Coad (*Yorks*)	RFM	69	28	87	12	5-18	1	7.25
2	J. C. Vitali (*Cambridge Univ*)	RM	32.5	7	92	10	6-34	1	9.20
3	Sohail Khan (*Pakistan Whites*)	RFM	28	8	66	6	5-37	1	11.00
4	O. E. Robinson (*Sussex*)	RFM/OB	73.1	22	175	14	5-29	1	12.50
5	T. J. Murtagh (*Middx*)	RFM	145.5	48	318	25	5-34	2	12.72
6	F. S. Organ (*Hants*)	OB	27	3	90	7	4-42	0	12.85
7	S. C. J. Broad (*England*)	RFM	154.1	48	389	29	6-31	1	13.41
8	C. Overton (*Somerset*)	RFM	196.2	66	403	30	5-26	2	13.43
9	M. S. Crane (*Hants*)	LB	60.4	8	190	14	3-19	0	13.57
10	J. H. Davey (*Somerset*)	RFM	150.2	55	331	24	4-25	0	13.79
11	J. P. Morley (*Lancs*)	SLA	40	15	71	5	4-62	0	14.20
12	D. A. Payne (*Glos*)	LFM	95	29	199	14	5-31	1	14.21
13	B. A. Stokes (*England*)	RFM	56	14	158	11	4-49	0	14.36
14	R. Clarke (*Surrey*)	RFM	88	23	190	13	5-20	1	14.61
15	B. W. Sanderson (*Northants*)	RFM	55.1	14	166	11	5-28	1	15.09
16	D. I. Stevens (*Kent*)	RM	209	64	452	29	5-37	3	15.58
17	B. A. J. Fisher (*Oxford Univ*)	RFM	21.2	1	79	5	3-37	0	15.80
18	S. R. Harmer (*Essex*)	OB	257.1	81	603	38	8-64	3	15.86
19	H. W. Podmore (*Kent*)	RFM	117.3	30	307	19	5-43	1	16.15
20	J. A. Thompson (*Yorks*)	RFM	104	25	246	15	5-31	1	16.40
21	P. J. Flanagan (*Cambridge Univ*)	RFM	31.1	11	83	5	3-30	0	16.60

		Style	*O*	*M*	*R*	*W*	*BB*	*5I*	*Avge*
22	D. J. Lamb (*Lancs*)	RFM	68.1	13	203	12	4-55	0	16.91
23	J. Overton (*Somerset & Surrey*)	RFM	89.1	27	256	15	5-48	1	17.06
24	N. Botha (*Cambridge Univ*)	OB	44	19	87	5	4-43	0	17.40
25	I. G. Holland (*Hants*)	RFM	129	41	297	17	6-60	1	17.47
26	L. Gregory (*Somerset*)	RFM	102.3	22	318	18	6-72	1	17.66
27	M. K. Andersson (*Middx*)	RFM	75.5	15	250	14	4-38	0	17.85
28	S. A. Patterson (*Yorks*)	RFM	106.3	37	197	11	3-27	0	17.90
29	M. D. Fisher (*Yorks*)	RFM	67	22	180	10	4-54	0	18.00
30	L. S. Livingstone (*Lancs*)	LB	21.3	2	92	5	3-79	0	18.40
31	S. J. Cook (*Essex*)	RFM	140	39	318	17	5-76	1	18.70
32	N. L. Buck (*Northants*)	RFM	64	21	173	9	3-42	0	19.22
33	J. A. Brooks (*Somerset*)	RFM	89.5	23	254	13	4-40	0	19.53
34	C. White (*Northants*)	RFM	88	20	260	13	4-35	0	20.00
35	D. T. Moriarty (*Surrey*)	SLA	98.2	15	342	17	6-70	3	20.11
36	T. H. S. Pettman (*Oxford Univ*)	RFM	43	9	121	6	4-53	0	20.16
37	C. R. Woakes (*England*)	RFM	133	29	348	17	5-50	1	20.47
38	J. A. Porter (*Essex*)	RFM	185.5	48	553	27	5-60	1	20.48
39	R. A. Stevenson (*Hants*)	RFM	32	8	103	5	4-70	0	20.60
40	M. L. Cummins (*Middx*)	RF	92.1	28	269	13	5-62	1	20.69
41	O. J. Hannon-Dalby (*Warwicks*)	RFM	196.3	53	523	25	6-33	2	20.92
42	E. G. Barnard (*Worcs*)	RFM	148.5	40	390	18	4-25	0	21.66
43	T. E. Bailey (*Lancs*)	RFM	111.4	44	282	13	3-11	0	21.69
44	C. Rushworth (*Durham*)	RFM	104	14	358	16	7-108	1	22.37
45	C. A. J. Morris (*Worcs*)	RFM	99.3	21	315	14	5-80	1	22.50
46	D. Y. Pennington (*Worcs*)	RFM	90.1	22	248	11	3-30	0	22.54
47	J. J. Carson (*Sussex*)	OB	108.1	17	340	15	5-93	1	22.66
	B. A. Hutton (*Northants*)	RFM	39	8	136	6	4-77	0	22.66
49	R. F. Higgins (*Glos*)	RFM	148.4	41	391	17	7-42	1	23.00
50	G. H. S. Garton (*Sussex*)	LFM	70.3	13	282	12	5-26	1	23.50
51	M. E. Milnes (*Kent*)	RFM	119.3	29	355	15	4-46	0	23.66
52	M. Carter (*Notts*)	OB	149.2	54	263	11	4-76	0	23.90
53	C. F. Parkinson (*Leics*)	SLA	79.3	22	192	8	3-30	0	24.00
54	A. P. Beard (*Essex*)	RFM	78.1	17	265	11	4-21	0	24.09
55	M. de Lange (*Glam*)	RF	81.2	17	218	9	4-84	0	24.22
56	S. M. Curran (*Surrey & England*)	LFM	85.5	17	268	11	4-39	0	24.36
57	W. M. H. Rhodes (*Warwicks*)	RFM	79.4	16	245	10	4-46	0	24.50
58	G. G. Wagg (*Glam*)	SLA/LM	73	14	272	11	3-38	0	24.72
59	B. Muzarabani (*Northants*)	RFM	70.5	17	278	11	4-29	0	25.27
60	J. M. Anderson (*England*)	RFM	161	42	408	16	5-56	1	25.50
61	J. Leach (*Worcs*)	RFM	169.3	44	490	19	4-67	0	25.78
62	G. S. Virdi (*Surrey*)	OB	179	26	570	22	6-101	1	25.90
63	J. C. Tongue (*Worcs*)	RFM	117.1	26	363	14	3-38	0	25.92
64	L. J. Hurt (*Lancs*)	RFM	48	6	182	7	4-27	0	26.00
65	L. M. Reece (*Derbys*)	LM	132.3	40	340	13	3-51	0	26.15
66	M. E. Claydon (*Sussex*)	RFM	102	25	294	11	3-23	0	26.72
67	A. W. Finch (*Surrey*)	RM	74.1	9	215	8	4-38	0	26.87
68	M. J. J. Critchley (*Derbys*)	LB	128.4	14	457	17	6-73	1	26.88
69	M. A. R. Cohen (*Derbys*)	LFM	44.2	7	191	7	3-47	0	27.28
70	T. T. Bresnan (*Warwicks*)	RFM	116	36	275	10	4-99	0	27.50
71	C. J. C. Wright (*Leics*)	RFM	57	21	141	5	2-39	0	28.20
72	P. D. Trego (*Notts*)	RM	134.3	44	342	12	3-33	0	28.50
73	K. H. D. Barker (*Hants*)	LFM	66	13	201	7	2-44	0	28.71
74	Z. J. Chappell (*Notts*)	RFM	131.2	30	431	15	4-59	0	28.73
75	D. R. Melton (*Derbys*)	RFM	70	13	233	8	4-22	0	29.12
76	M. E. T. Salisbury (*Durham*)	RFM	53.1	14	148	5	4-57	0	29.60
77	S. R. Patel (*Notts*)	SLA	156.2	36	388	13	4-80	0	29.84
78	M. D. Taylor (*Glos*)	LM	115	22	330	11	3-43	0	30.00
79	J. O. Holder (*West Indies*)	RFM	111.5	31	301	10	6-42	1	30.10
80	T. van der Gugten (*Glam*)	RFM	119	31	362	12	3-45	0	30.16
81	B. W. M. Mike (*Leics*)	RFM	88.1	13	279	9	4-39	0	31.00

		Style	O	M	R	W	BB	5I	Avge
82	Yasir Shah (*Pakistan Greens & Pakistan*)	LB	103	9	375	12	4-66	0	31.25
83	J. A. R. Harris (*Middx*)	RFM	89	19	284	9	2-46	0	31.55
84	M. K. O'Riordan (*Kent*)	OB	62.1	5	255	8	3-50	0	31.87
85	S. T. Gabriel (*West Indies*)	RF	98.1	14	355	11	5-75	1	32.27
86	J. K. Fuller (*Hants*)	RFM	70	12	293	9	4-17	0	32.55
87	G. P. Balderson (*Lancs*)	RFM	104	23	296	9	3-63	0	32.88
88	J. T. Ball (*Notts*)	RFM	112.5	30	336	10	3-71	0	33.60
89	D. A. Douthwaite (*Glam*)	RFM	121.1	16	473	14	3-42	0	33.78
90	G. K. Berg (*Northants*)	RFM	47	9	203	6	4-64	0	33.83
91	R. L. Chase (*West Indies*)	OB	94	14	340	10	5-172	1	34.00
92	B. A. Raine (*Durham*)	RFM	105.1	25	308	9	3-53	0	34.22
93	B. W. Aitchison (*Derbys*)	RFM	78	20	211	6	3-55	0	35.16
94	G. T. Griffiths (*Leics*)	RFM	61.5	13	181	5	3-52	0	36.20
95	D. Olivier (*Yorks*)	RFM	91	18	364	10	3-29	0	36.40
96	S. Conners (*Derbys*)	RFM	94.2	23	328	9	3-63	0	36.44
97	K. A. J. Roach (*West Indies*)	RFM	116.4	31	292	8	4-72	0	36.50
98	D. Klein (*Leics*)	LFM	95	10	332	9	3-44	0	36.88
99	Naseem Shah (*Pakistan Greens & Pakistan*)	RF	82	19	260	7	4-52	0	37.14
100	Shaheen Shah Afridi (*Pak Grns & Pakistan*)	LFM	96.2	16	305	8	3-47	0	38.12
101	Mohammad Abbas (*Pak Greens & Pakistan*)	RFM	108	34	232	6	2-28	0	38.66
102	B. T. J. Wheal (*Hants*)	RFM	61	21	203	5	2-11	0	40.60
103	T. N. Walallawita (*Middx*)	SLA	88.2	28	245	6	3-28	0	40.83
104	J. Shaw (*Glos*)	RFM	99.5	17	328	8	3-13	0	41.00
105	T. A. I. Taylor (*Leics*)	RFM	93	25	247	6	2-49	0	41.16
106	T. E. Barber (*Notts*)	LFM	79	9	289	7	3-42	0	41.28
107	R. N. Sidebottom (*Warwicks*)	RFM	88	12	331	8	3-37	0	41.37
108	J. C. Archer (*England*)	RF	125.4	23	360	8	3-45	0	45.00
109	M. P. Dunn (*Surrey*)	RFM	70.4	16	239	5	3-53	0	47.80
110	M. G. Hogan (*Glam*)	RFM	139	32	397	8	3-59	0	49.62
111	K. A. Bull (*Glam*)	OB	102.3	4	462	9	3-112	0	51.33
112	B. L. D'Oliveira (*Worcs*)	LB	95	13	312	6	2-31	0	52.00
113	T. W. Hartley (*Lancs*)	SLA	111	28	324	6	3-79	0	54.00
114	D. M. Bess (*England*)	OB	136.1	25	444	8	2-51	0	55.50
115	G. Stewart (*Kent*)	RFM	95.5	19	299	5	3-48	0	59.80

BOWLING STYLES

LB	Leg-breaks (5)	**RF**	Right-arm fast (5)
LFM	Left-arm fast medium (8)	**RFM**	Right-arm fast medium (74)
LM	Left-arm medium (3)	**RM**	Right-arm medium (4)
OB	Off-breaks (11)	**SLA**	Slow left-arm (7)

Note: The total comes to 117 because O. E. Robinson and G. G. Wagg have two styles of bowling.

INDIVIDUAL SCORES OF 100 AND OVER

There were **50** three-figure innings in 54 first-class matches in 2020, which was 155 fewer than in 2019, when 149 matches were played. Of these, five were double-hundreds, compared with 11 in 2019. The list includes 43 in the Bob Willis Trophy.

T. A. Lammonby (3)
101* Somerset v Glos, Taunton
107* Somerset v Worcs, Worcester
116 Somerset v Essex, Lord's

T. B. Abell (2)
119 Somerset v Glam, Taunton
101* Somerset v Glos, Taunton

A. N. Cook (2)
129* Essex v Hants, Arundel
172 Essex v Somerset, Lord's

Z. Crawley (2)
267 England v Pakistan, Southampton
105 Kent v Hants, Canterbury

B. M. Duckett (2)
116 Notts v Lancs, Nottingham
150 Notts v Durham, Nottingham

B. T. Slater (2)
172 Leics v Lancs, Worcester
142 Notts v Lancs, Nottingham

The following each played one three-figure innings:

Azhar Ali, 141*, Pakistan v England, Southampton.

G. A. Bartlett, 100*, Somerset v Glos, Taunton; T. T. Bresnan, 105, Warwicks v Northants, Birmingham; R. J. Burns, 103, Surrey v Sussex, The Oval; J. C. Buttler, 152, England v Pakistan, Southampton; E. J. Byrom, 117, Somerset v Essex, Lord's.

J. M. Clarke, 133, Notts v Durham, Nottingham; J. M. Cox, 238*, Kent v Sussex, Canterbury.

P. D. Daneel, 125, Cambridge Univ v Oxford Univ, Cambridge; S. M. Davies, 123*, Somerset v Warwicks, Birmingham; M. de Lange, 113, Glam v Northants, Northampton; B. L. D'Oliveira, 174, Worcs v Glam, Worcester; J. L. du Plooy, 130, Derbys v Notts, Nottingham.

T. C. Fell, 110*, Worcs v Northants, Northampton; B. T. Foakes, 118, Surrey v Kent, The Oval.

N. R. T. Gubbins, 192, Middx v Surrey, The Oval.

T. J. Haines, 117, Sussex v Surrey, The Oval.

H. G. Kuhn, 140, Kent v Essex, Chelmsford.

J. A. Leaning, 220*, Kent v Sussex, Canterbury; A. Z. Lees, 106, Durham v Yorks, Chester-le-Street; J. D. Libby, 184, Worcs v Glam, Worcester; A. Lyth, 103, Yorks v Lancs, Leeds.

W. L. Madsen, 103, Derbys v Leics, Leicester; D. J. Malan, 219, Yorks v Derbys, Leeds; D. K. H. Mitchell, 110, Worcs v Warwicks, Worcester; T. J. Moores, 106, Notts v Yorks, Nottingham.

J. Overton, 120, Somerset v Warwicks, Birmingham.

L. A. Procter, 112*, Northants v Warwicks, Birmingham.

L. M. Reece, 122, Derbys v Durham, Chester-le-Street; W. M. H. Rhodes, 207, Warwicks v Worcs, Worcester; W. T. Root, 118, Glam v Worcs, Worcester; A. M. Rossington, 135*, Northants v Warwicks, Birmingham.

Shan Masood, 156, Pakistan v England, Manchester; D. P. Sibley, 120, England v West Indies, Manchester; B. A. Stokes, 176, England v West Indies, Manchester.

C. Z. Taylor, 106, Glam v Northants, Northampton; C. O. Thurston, 115, Northants v Glam, Northampton.

FASTEST HUNDREDS BY BALLS...

Balls		
62	M. de Lange	Glamorgan v Northamptonshire, Northampton.
84	J. Overton	Somerset v Warwickshire, Birmingham.
88	C. Z. Taylor	Glamorgan v Northamptonshire, Northampton.
94	Z. Crawley	Kent v Hampshire, Canterbury.
112	R. J. Burns	Surrey v Sussex, The Oval.

...AND THE SLOWEST

Balls		
312	D. P. Sibley	England v West Indies, Manchester.
258	W. T. Root	Glamorgan v Worcestershire, Worcester.
255	B. A. Stokes	England v West Indies, Manchester.
253	A. Z. Lees	Durham v Yorkshire, Chester-le-Street.
251	Shan Masood	Pakistan v England, Manchester.

TEN WICKETS IN A MATCH

There were **six** instances of bowlers taking ten or more wickets in a first-class match in 2020, which was 17 fewer than in 2019. Four were in the Bob Willis Trophy.

The following each took ten wickets in a match on one occasion:

S. C. J. Broad, 10-67, England v West Indies, Manchester.
O. J. Hannon-Dalby, 12-110, Warwicks v Glos, Bristol; S. R. Harmer, 14-131, Essex v Surrey, Chelmsford; R. F. Higgins, 11-96, Glos v Warwicks, Bristol.
D. T. Moriarty, 11-224, Surrey v Sussex, The Oval.
J. C. Vitali, 10-92, Cambridge Univ v Oxford Univ, Cambridge.

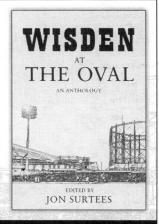

BOB WILLIS TROPHY IN 2020

NEVILLE SCOTT

1 Essex 2 Somerset

Mocked by the sunniest April since records began, the County Championship failed to start as scheduled on the 12th – a day when Covid-19 deaths in British hospitals passed 10,000, and the prime minister, who could have been one of them, was discharged from St Thomas's, barely a mile from The Oval. The Championship was later abandoned, and a short replacement, the Bob Willis Trophy, cleared to open on August 1. The new competition, named after the former Test bowler and commentator who had died in December 2019, split the counties into three regional groups of six, playing five matches each, with a final for the two group winners with most points.

Reporting on matches, you recalled the first line of Orwell's celebrated wartime essay: "As I write, highly civilised human beings are flying overhead, trying to kill me." If it was pathogens not bombs this time, cricket, in unguarded moments, could still seem irrelevant – almost impertinent.

BOB WILLIS TROPHY TABLES

Central Group

						Bonus pts			
		M	*W*	*L*	*D*	*Bat*	*Bowl*	*Pen*	*Pts*
1	SOMERSET	5	4	0	1	10	15	0	97
2	Worcestershire	5	2	1	2	14	12	0	74
3	Warwickshire	5	0	1	4	7	14	0	53
4	Northamptonshire	5	1	2	2	4	13	0	49
5	Gloucestershire	5	1	2	2	3	10	0	45
6	Glamorgan	5	0	2	3	6	13	0	43

North Group

						Bonus pts			
		M	*W*	*L*	*D*	*Bat*	*Bowl*	*Pen*	*Pts*
1	Yorkshire	5	3	0	2	11	12	0	87
2	Derbyshire	5	2	1	2	13	13	0	74
3	Lancashire	5	2	1	2	7	11	0	66
4	Nottinghamshire	5	0	2	3	20	15	0	59
5	Leicestershire	5	1	2	2	4	13	0	49
6	Durham	5	0	2	3	7	10	0	41

South Group

						Bonus pts			
		M	*W*	*L*	*D*	*Bat*	*Bowl*	*Pen*	*Pts*
1	ESSEX	5	4	0	1	6	12	0	90
2	Kent	5	3	1	1	12	15	1	82
3	Middlesex	5	2	2	1	8	14	0	62
4	Hampshire	5	2	2	1	4	13	0	57
5	Surrey	5	1	4	0	8	12	0	36
6	Sussex	5	1	4	0	9	11	24	12

Win = 16pts; draw = 8pts.

Kent had 1pt deducted for a slow over-rate against Surrey. Sussex had 24pts deducted after Mitchell Claydon applied hand sanitiser to the ball in their match with Middlesex.

Somerset and Essex advanced to the final as the two group leaders with most points.

And yet, and yet. It soon became clear that lovers of the county game, while excluded from grounds for safety reasons, drew a rare solace from play. Via the media, through online live streaming or county websites, hundreds of thousands found honest release in some semblance of history resumed. The county clubs had voted only 11–7 in favour of the tournament, understandably perhaps, for most faced deep financial difficulty. But the players, often uncertain of their futures, committed fully.

Their efforts were selfless, yet claims that the format showed how lowly clubs could hold their own were needlessly romantic. That we had any domestic cricket at all was the relief. No fewer than 55 players had been summoned into biosecure bubbles by England, overseas imports were widely absent, and there was a reluctance to risk injury to key bowlers lacking pre-season preparation. Though counties played only five games, Lancashire granted as many red-ball debuts to bowlers alone; six of Sussex's 16 men had made just four Championship appearances between them; Northamptonshire fielded 19 in all, Surrey required 21 (their six England players totalled five matches). Settled squads sought a place in the final; others, while respecting the competition, used it more as a testing ground, making the T20 Blast their priority. Of the six teams to claim top-two places in the three BWT groups, only Kent reached the T20 quarter-finals, where they were hammered by Surrey, whose stars were finally available.

Essex and **Somerset**, the 2019 county champions and runners-up, won the South and Central Groups respectively, and contested the final. **Yorkshire**, claiming wickets more cheaply than all save this pair, took the North Group; but, with one fewer win, they finished four points shy of qualification.

Ironically, Somerset benefited from having three seamers (Lewis Gregory and the Overton twins) in England camps. When released, they proved the fittest of trios: just one of Somerset's group-stage scalps fell to spin, and slow left-armer Jack Leach's three wickets on September 27, the last day of the final, were his first in competitive cricket since November 2019.

Somerset trounced Glamorgan, Northamptonshire and Gloucestershire; thanks to the regional groups, it was the first time since 2007 they had played Glamorgan and Gloucestershire. (They are scheduled to meet Leicestershire this year, closing a gap of one season more, the longest between established first-class counties since Derbyshire, admitted to the Championship in 1895, were granted a match against Middlesex 34 years later.) They would have routed **Warwickshire**, too, but for rain in Birmingham – where Somerset's Jamie Overton made a rampant 120, a score bettered only once by an English No. 10, after being goaded by Oliver Hannon-Dalby's parody of his aggressive bowling demeanour. Even in a vast, damp and empty Edgbaston, his batting delighted sear hacks, watching from afar with "admit to Outer Zone" passes round their necks.

In a season of loans and deals, Overton joined Surrey two rounds later, but Somerset's attack remained penetrative. There were only three half-centuries in 109 individual innings against them in the group phase, the highest Chris Cooke's 82 for Glamorgan. That came in a total of 166, which was the most they conceded until the last round, when their closest rivals, **Worcestershire**,

Bitter taste: Will Buttleman douses Feroze Khushi (far left) in beer, bringing unwelcome attention to Essex celebrations.

mustered 200 and 184, but lost by 60 runs. Worcestershire were an admirably cohesive, home-nurtured unit of just a dozen players, fighting to the end.

The other key game had come in the opening round, when Essex beat **Kent**, fourth in 2019 and once again playing above their apparent ability. Essex forced their way home by two wickets, despite an 89-run first-innings deficit, with Alastair Cook hitting 66 on the final day. Had Kent prevailed, they would almost certainly have reached the final.

Darren Stevens, at 44, took almost a third of their wickets, a proportion matched by 39-year-old Tim Murtagh for **Middlesex**, who ended third ahead of a depleted **Hampshire** (their home games played at Arundel), Surrey and Sussex. Although August hosted 36 of the 45 matches, seam-friendly, low-scoring pitches remained the norm. Indeed, average runs per wicket across the South and Central Groups, at 25.84, were lower than in any of the 28 seasons of purely four-day play; only the more run-heavy North Group, where six of the 15 games significantly lost direction through rain, carried the overall average above 27, marginally beating 2018's 26.69, the weakest to date.

With Somerset bowling only six overs of spin at Taunton, there was one exception to the seamers' pitches: Chelmsford. When Essex concluded their group matches, overwhelming Middlesex on September 8, they had won all 11 of their home games since losing to Surrey two years and two days earlier. In that sequence, South African off-spinner Simon Harmer boasted 87 wickets at 13. There waited at Lord's, however, a grudging pitch, offering lavish aid to none. It inspired instead a masterly vigil from Cook, whose 172 in a rain-hit final, scheduled for five days but effectively reduced to four, secured a first-innings lead of 36, enough to decide the trophy in the event of a draw. Cook was in his 18th season, Tom Lammonby in his first. A 20-year old Devonian of Australian parentage, Lammonby proved the batting find of the year; his third hundred in five innings moved Somerset towards a last-morning declaration that set 237 in 81 overs. Essex, holding their nerve, reached 179 for six, and their third red-ball prize in four summers.

In 2021, they will be defending two titles: this one, and the Championship they won in 2019. Anticipating that Covid could still be an issue, the ECB devised a modified form of the Championship, with counties playing ten rounds in three seeded conference groups, before being sorted into three divisions on the basis of those results. The winners of Division One would be County Champions, but the Bob Willis Trophy was retained as a one-off fixture for the champions and runners-up.

Derbyshire proved surprise performers: their hopes of unexpected glory lingered until they lost their final game, to **Lancashire**. For the first time since 1976, when a tenancy dispute with the council kept them out, they did not play at the County Ground, as it became a biosecure base for touring squads and England's women. Permanently nomadic, Derbyshire pulled off the season's biggest shock, at Trent Bridge, by making 365 in the fourth innings to win.

COUNTY CHAMPIONSHIP 2021

Group 1	Group 2	Group 3
Derbyshire	Gloucestershire	Glamorgan
Durham	Hampshire	Kent
Essex	Leicestershire	Lancashire
Nottinghamshire	Middlesex	Northamptonshire
Warwickshire	Somerset	Sussex
Worcestershire	Surrey	Yorkshire

Each county will play ten matches, home and away, within their group. The top two in each group will advance to Division One, the middle two to Division Two, and the bottom two to Division Three. Each will carry forward half the points earned in their two games against the fellow qualifier from their group, and play a further four matches against the other qualifiers. The winners of Division One will be county champions, and also play the runners-up for the Bob Willis Trophy.

Ben Slater, on loan to Leicestershire in that round, returned to **Nottinghamshire** to complete his second century against Lancashire in 14 days for two different teams, totalling 425 in seven innings, despite three ducks. Nottinghamshire continued a run now comprising 27 first-class games without victory, but still finished ten points ahead of **Leicestershire**, who had beaten Lancashire on the back of Slater's century, and **Durham**, also winless.

So were **Glamorgan**, at the bottom of the Central Group. Like Durham, they relied heavily on non-English (and non-Welsh) players; Marchant de Lange (from Transvaal) completed a century in 62 balls, Glamorgan's fastest, against **Northamptonshire**. Earlier in the game, Callum Taylor (from Newport) had scored a debut hundred, but they still lost.

At the bottom of the South Group, **Surrey** and **Sussex** managed only 36 points, fewer than Durham or Glamorgan, and Sussex had 24 of those deducted by a disciplinary panel. The ruling was announced in mid-October, more than seven weeks after seamer Mitch Claydon used hand sanitiser to doctor the ball. A further 12 points were to be deducted from Sussex's total in the 2021 Championship but, citing possible conflicts of interest for one member of the panel, Sussex successfully challenged the additional penalty. It is hard to see how the amended punishment was a deterrent.

They had earlier gone down by an innings in a remarkable game in which Kent lost only one wicket. (Admittedly, their innings closed after 120 overs, under competition rules. But, discounting forfeitures in rain-hit games, it was only the ninth instance of victory in county cricket with one or no wicket lost). In his seventh first-class innings, 19-year-old Jordan Cox reached 238, sharing an unbroken 423-run partnership with Jack Leaning; it was an all-wicket record for Kent, and the second-highest for the second wicket in county cricket, after an unbroken 465 by John Jameson and Rohan Kanhai for Warwickshire against Gloucestershire in 1974.

That tale was not done. After play, Cox innocently agreed to pose with young fans for a photo, breaching virus protocols. He spent the next game in quarantine confinement. Against the odds, however, only one actual fixture fell foul of the rules, in the final round. In a poignant last act, after 41 years as player and umpire, Jerry Lloyds pulled stumps at lunch on the first day of **Gloucestershire's** match with Northamptonshire in Bristol; the visiting players had been in contact the day before with a colleague now found to be infected.

Would that this game had been the summer's sole loss.

FINAL

ESSEX v SOMERSET

PAUL NEWMAN

At Lord's, September 23–27. Drawn. Essex won the Bob Willis Trophy by virtue of their first-innings lead. Toss: Essex.

Nothing summed up the success of five absorbing days better than centuries of the highest class from two left-handers at opposite ends of their careers. Two years after his Test retirement, Alastair Cook demonstrated that his quality, commitment and desire to score runs and win trophies remained undimmed, making a momentous hundred that was to prove decisive in the outcome of cricket's newest prize. Not far behind was a century of such promise from 20-year-old Tom Lammonby that Somerset could take some consolation from another near miss.

In that respect, the climax to a competition that had salvaged the red-ball season provided familiar stories: as well as Somerset frustration, there was Essex silverware – a fourth honour in four years, although they benefited from the unsatisfactory tie-breaker of first-innings lead. (In the group stage, Somerset collected 97 points to Essex's 90.)

Cook's innings was full of sublime strokeplay and uncharacteristic fluency, with many of the 26 fours in his 67th first-class hundred coming from sumptuous drives. When Craig Overton, employing a refined run-up and action, was bowling at him with the new ball, the quality and hostility of the battle between the country's two most consistently successful teams resembled a Test. And the old master was on top. Cook needed to be at his best, too, after Somerset – inserted in autumnal conditions, with bitter cold and a biting wind persisting for a lot of the first five-day county game in England since 1834 – had made an above-par 301. It owed much to Zimbabwe-born Eddie Byrom, who drove almost as well as Cook while making his third first-class century (but first against county opposition), and added 127 for the sixth wicket with Overton. Sam Cook overshadowed the bigger names of Harmer and Porter by taking five wickets with his lively seamers.

Rain and bad light meant Essex did not start their reply until the third morning, and such was their reliance on Alastair Cook that he had made 172 out of 266 when he was sixth out. It needed Wheater's experience to settle their nerves, and ensure the crucial lead before tournament regulations ended the innings after 120 overs. While Gregory took six for 72, six team-mates managed two for 249.

Somerset knew only victory would now suffice, and they had to make all the running. Following a third-ball duck in the first innings, Lammonby hit his third century in successive matches. But, after setting Essex 237 in what became 81 overs, they were denied by a combination of a flat Lord's pitch and stubborn batting. Only when Cook was contentiously given out caught behind off Gregory by umpire Warren to make it 68 for three in the 24th did Somerset hopes rise. Leach toiled away for his first first-class wickets since England's Test series in New Zealand in November 2019, but Essex had no need to chase the target, and ten Doeschate – their 40-year-old former captain – calmly ate up 164 minutes for his 46, adding 48 in 27 overs with Wheater.

Essex received a trophy designed and presented by Bob Willis's widow, Lauren Clark, though the celebrations brought the game's only sour note, when young reserve Will Buttleman emptied a bottle of beer over team-mate Feroze Khushi, a Muslim, on the dressing-room balcony. Essex pledged to "work harder" on their players' cultural education, while captain Tom Westley apologised on social media. Those close to both players blamed Buttleman's actions on over-exuberance; Khushi, who had given his blessing to alcohol being sprayed during the celebrations, was said not to be offended, though he was concerned about how his family and friends would react. It was unfortunate that a county who do more than most to engage with their South Asian communities had some of the gloss taken off their triumph. But the overwhelming message after the first Bob Willis Trophy final was a positive one for county cricket.

Close of play: first day, Somerset 119-4 (Byrom 51, Davies 13); second day, Somerset 301; third day, Essex 271-6 (Porter 5, Wheater 0); fourth day, Somerset 227-7 (Overton 17, Davey 2).

Alex Davidson, Getty Images

Masters of the draw: Essex captain Tom Westley holds the Bob Willis Trophy after a first-innings lead – thanks to Alastair Cook – secures the title. In the middle is Lauren Clark, Willis's widow.

Somerset

B. G. F. Green b S. J. Cook	24	– c A. N. Cook b Beard	41
T. A. Lammonby lbw b S. J. Cook	0	– lbw b Harmer	116
*T. B. Abell c Wheater b Beard	19	– c Browne b Porter	15
E. J. Byrom lbw b S. J. Cook	117	– b Porter	1
G. A. Bartlett c A. N. Cook b Porter	12	– c Westley b Porter	5
†S. M. Davies c Wheater b S. J. Cook	27	– c A. N. Cook b Harmer	19
C. Overton lbw b Porter	66	– (8) not out	45
L. Gregory lbw b S. J. Cook	9	– (7) c A. N. Cook b Porter	1
J. H. Davey not out	17	– not out	16
M. J. Leach lbw b Harmer	3		
J. A. Brooks b Harmer	0		
B 1, lb 4, nb 2	7	Lb 11, nb 2	13
1/0 (2) 2/34 (3) 3/52 (1) (102 overs)	301	1/105 (1) (7 wkts dec, 76 overs)	272
4/94 (5) 5/139 (6) 6/266 (7)		2/155 (3) 3/167 (4)	
7/270 (4) 8/279 (8) 9/301 (10) 10/301 (11)		4/187 (5) 5/187 (2) 6/188 (7) 7/224 (6)	

Porter 29–9–85–2; S. J. Cook 32–10–76–5; Beard 11–1–68–1; Harmer 20–6–36–2; Lawrence 1–0–2–0; Walter 9–1–29–0. *Second innings*—Porter 23–4–73–4; S. J. Cook 16–2–56–0; Harmer 32–9–101–2; Walter 1–0–3–0; Beard 4–0–28–1.

Essex

N. L. J. Browne c Overton b Gregory	8	– c Abell b Gregory	13
A. N. Cook c Overton b Gregory	172	– c Davies b Gregory	31
*T. Westley c Abell b Lammonby	51	– lbw b Overton	0
D. W. Lawrence c Lammonby b Gregory	6	– lbw b Leach	35
P. I. Walter lbw b Gregory	0	– lbw b Leach	21
R. N. ten Doeschate lbw b Overton	21	– c Bartlett b Leach	46
J. A. Porter b Gregory	13		
†A. J. A. Wheater not out	26	– (7) not out	14
S. R. Harmer c Overton b Gregory	0	– (8) not out	0
A. P. Beard not out	14		
B 4, lb 12, nb 10	26	B 1, lb 10, nb 8	19
1/27 (1) 2/197 (3) (8 wkts, 120 overs)	337	1/25 (1) (6 wkts, 80.3 overs)	179
3/208 (4) 4/208 (5) 5/264 (6)		2/26 (3) 3/68 (2)	
6/266 (2) 7/303 (7) 8/303 (9)		4/98 (4) 5/131 (5) 6/179 (6)	

S. J. Cook did not bat.

Overton 29–6–66–1; Davey 23–3–70–0; Gregory 27–5–72–6; Brooks 9–3–25–0; Abell 2–0–10–0; Leach 22–4–52–0; Lammonby 8–2–26–1. *Second innings*—Overton 17–7–37–1; Davey 9–3–18–0; Gregory 21.3–5–52–2; Brooks 8–3–11–0; Leach 22–10–38–3; Byrom 1–0–4–0; Lammonby 2–1–8–0.

Umpires: R. J. Bailey and R. J. Warren. Referee: D. A. Cosker.

Pre-season betting (Ladbrokes): 9-2 Somerset; 5-1 ESSEX; 7-1 Yorkshire; 8-1 Lancashire; 10-1 Warwickshire; 12-1 Hampshire and Surrey; 14-1 Nottinghamshire; 20-1 Kent; 25-1 Middlesex, Northamptonshire, Sussex and Worcestershire; 28-1 Gloucestershire; 33-1 Durham; 50-1 Derbyshire, Glamorgan and Leicestershire.

Prize money

£35,000 for winners: ESSEX.
£10,000 for other group winners: SOMERSET and YORKSHIRE.

£2,500 for Most Valuable Player of Bob Willis Trophy: C. Overton (Somerset).
£5,000 for Most Valuable Player in overall county cricket (BWT and Blast): S. R. Harmer (Essex).

Leaders: *Central Group* – from August 4 Worcestershire; August 9 Somerset; August 18 Worcestershire; August 25 Somerset.
North Group – from August 4 Leicestershire; August 10 Derbyshire; September 9 Yorkshire.
South Group – from August 4 Middlesex; August 11 Essex.

Bottom place: *Central Group* – from August 4 Glamorgan and Gloucestershire; August 11 Northamptonshire; August 25 Glamorgan.
North Group – from August 4 Durham.
South Group – from August 4 Hampshire and Surrey; August 11 Surrey; September 9 Sussex.

Scoring of Points in Bob Willis Trophy Group Games

(*a*) For a win, 16 points plus any points scored in the first innings.
(*b*) In a tie, each side score eight points, plus any points scored in the first innings.
(*c*) In a drawn match, each side score eight points, plus any points scored in the first innings.
(*d*) If the scores are equal in a drawn match, the side batting in the fourth innings score eight points, plus any points scored in the first innings, and the opposing side score five points, plus any points scored in the first innings.
(*e*) First-innings points (awarded only for performances in the first 110 overs of each first innings and retained whatever the result of the match):

(i) A maximum of five batting points to be available: 200 to 249 runs – 1 point; 250 to 299 runs – 2 points; 300 to 349 runs – 3 points; 350 to 399 runs – 4 points; 400 runs or over – 5 points. Penalty runs awarded within the first 110 overs of each first innings count towards the award of bonus points.

(ii) A maximum of three bowling points to be available: 3 to 5 wickets taken – 1 point; 6 to 8 wickets taken – 2 points; 9 to 10 wickets taken – 3 points.

(*f*) If a match is abandoned without a ball being bowled, each side score eight points.
(*g*) The side who have the highest aggregate of points at the end of the group stage shall be the group winner. Should any sides in a group be equal on points, the following tie-breakers will be applied in the order stated: most wins, fewest losses, team achieving most points in head-to-head contests, most wickets taken, most runs scored.
(*h*) The two best-placed group winners shall compete in a five-day final. The tie-breakers above shall apply across groups to split teams finishing on the same number of points. If the final is drawn, and both first innings are completed, the winner shall be the team that scored most runs in the first innings. Should the scores in completed first innings be equal or if both first innings are not completed, the trophy shall be shared. If the final is tied, the trophy shall be shared.
(*i*) The minimum over-rate to be achieved by counties will be 15 overs per hour. Overs will be calculated at the end of the match, and penalties applied on a match-by-match basis. For each over (ignoring fractions) that a side have bowled short of the target number, one point will be deducted from their group total.
(*j*) Penalties for poor and unfit pitches are at the discretion of the Cricket Discipline Commission.

Under ECB playing conditions, two extras were awarded for every no-ball bowled, whether scored off or not, and one for every wide. With no-balls, any runs off the bat were credited to the batsman, and leg-byes and byes were counted as such, in addition to the initial two extras; runs scored off wides, including byes, were counted as wides, in addition to the initial one-run extra. Any penalties off no-balls or wides were counted as penalty runs, in addition to the initial extras.

CONSTITUTION OF COUNTY CHAMPIONSHIP

At least four possible dates have been given for the start of county cricket in England. The first, patchy, references began in 1825. The earliest mention in any cricket publication is in 1864, and eight counties have come to be regarded as first-class from that date, including Cambridgeshire, who dropped out after 1871. For many years, the County Championship was considered to have started in 1873, when regulations governing qualification first applied; indeed, a special commemorative stamp was issued by the Post Office in 1973. However, the Championship was not formally organised until 1890, and before then champions were proclaimed by the press; sometimes publications differed in their views, and no definitive list of champions can start before that date. Eight teams contested the 1890 competition – Gloucestershire, Kent, Lancashire, Middlesex, Nottinghamshire, Surrey,

Sussex and Yorkshire. Somerset joined the following year, and in 1895 the Championship began to acquire something of its modern shape, when Derbyshire, Essex, Hampshire, Leicestershire and Warwickshire were added. At that point, MCC officially recognised the competition's existence. Worcestershire, Northamptonshire and Glamorgan were admitted in 1899, 1905 and 1921 respectively, and are regarded as first-class from these dates. An invitation in 1921 to Buckinghamshire to enter the Championship was declined, owing to the lack of necessary playing facilities, and an application by Devon in 1948 was unsuccessful. Durham were admitted in 1992, and granted first-class status prior to their pre-season tour of Zimbabwe.

In 2000, the Championship was split for the first time into two divisions, on the basis of counties' standings in the 1999 competition. From 2000 onwards, the bottom three teams in Division One were relegated at the end of the season, and the top three teams in Division Two promoted. From 2006, this was changed to two teams relegated and two promoted. In 2016, two were relegated and one promoted, to create divisions of eight and ten teams. In 2019, one was relegated and three promoted, to change the balance to ten teams in Division One and eight in Division Two.

There was no County Championship in 2020, however, because of the Covid-19 pandemic; it was replaced by an alternative competition, the Bob Willis Trophy. In 2021, the Championship was to be played in two phases: three conference groups, followed by three divisions based on the group results. The winners of Division One would be champions, but would also play the runners-up for the Bob Willis Trophy.

COUNTY CHAMPIONS

The title of champion county is unreliable before 1890. In 1963, *Wisden* formally accepted the list of champions "most generally selected" by contemporaries, as researched by Rowland Bowen (see *Wisden 1959*, page 91). This appears to be the most accurate available list but has no official status. The county champions from 1864 to 1889 were, according to Bowen: 1864 Surrey; 1865 Nottinghamshire; 1866 Middlesex; 1867 Yorkshire; 1868 Nottinghamshire; 1869 Nottinghamshire and Yorkshire; 1870 Yorkshire; 1871 Nottinghamshire; 1872 Nottinghamshire; 1873 Gloucestershire and Nottinghamshire; 1874 Gloucestershire; 1875 Nottinghamshire; 1876 Gloucestershire; 1877 Gloucestershire; 1878 undecided; 1879 Lancashire and Nottinghamshire; 1880 Nottinghamshire; 1881 Lancashire; 1882 Lancashire and Nottinghamshire; 1883 Nottinghamshire; 1884 Nottinghamshire; 1885 Nottinghamshire; 1886 Nottinghamshire; 1887 Surrey; 1888 Surrey; 1889 Lancashire, Nottinghamshire and Surrey.

1890 Surrey
1891 Surrey
1892 Surrey
1893 Yorkshire
1894 Surrey
1895 Surrey
1896 Yorkshire
1897 Lancashire
1898 Yorkshire
1899 Surrey
1900 Yorkshire
1901 Yorkshire
1902 Yorkshire
1903 Middlesex
1904 Lancashire
1905 Yorkshire
1906 Kent
1907 Nottinghamshire
1908 Yorkshire
1909 Kent
1910 Kent
1911 Warwickshire
1912 Yorkshire
1913 Kent
1914 Surrey
1919 Yorkshire
1920 Middlesex
1921 Middlesex
1922 Yorkshire
1923 Yorkshire
1924 Yorkshire
1925 Yorkshire
1926 Lancashire
1927 Lancashire
1928 Lancashire
1929 Nottinghamshire
1930 Lancashire
1931 Yorkshire
1932 Yorkshire
1933 Yorkshire
1934 Lancashire
1935 Yorkshire
1936 Derbyshire
1937 Yorkshire
1938 Yorkshire
1939 Yorkshire
1946 Yorkshire
1947 Middlesex
1948 Glamorgan
1949 Middlesex / Yorkshire
1950 Lancashire / Surrey
1951 Warwickshire
1952 Surrey
1953 Surrey
1954 Surrey
1955 Surrey
1956 Surrey
1957 Surrey
1958 Surrey
1959 Yorkshire
1960 Yorkshire
1961 Hampshire
1962 Yorkshire
1963 Yorkshire
1964 Worcestershire
1965 Worcestershire
1966 Yorkshire
1967 Yorkshire
1968 Yorkshire
1969 Glamorgan
1970 Kent
1971 Surrey
1972 Warwickshire
1973 Hampshire
1974 Worcestershire
1975 Leicestershire
1976 Middlesex
1977 Middlesex / Kent
1978 Kent
1979 Essex
1980 Middlesex

1981	Nottinghamshire	1994	Warwickshire	2007	Sussex
1982	Middlesex	1995	Warwickshire	2008	Durham
1983	Essex	1996	Leicestershire	2009	Durham
1984	Essex	1997	Glamorgan	2010	Nottinghamshire
1985	Middlesex	1998	Leicestershire	2011	Lancashire
1986	Essex	1999	Surrey	2012	Warwickshire
1987	Nottinghamshire	2000	Surrey	2013	Durham
1988	Worcestershire	2001	Yorkshire	2014	Yorkshire
1989	Worcestershire	2002	Surrey	2015	Yorkshire
1990	Middlesex	2003	Sussex	2016	Middlesex
1991	Essex	2004	Warwickshire	2017	Essex
1992	Essex	2005	Nottinghamshire	2018	Surrey
1993	Middlesex	2006	Sussex	2019	Essex

Notes: Since the Championship was constituted in 1890, it has been won outright as follows: Yorkshire 32 times, Surrey 19, Middlesex 11, Essex and Lancashire 8, Warwickshire 7, Kent and Nottinghamshire 6, Worcestershire 5, Durham, Glamorgan, Leicestershire and Sussex 3, Hampshire 2, Derbyshire 1. Gloucestershire, Northamptonshire and Somerset have never won.

The title has been shared three times since 1890, involving Middlesex twice, Kent, Lancashire, Surrey and Yorkshire.

There was no County Championship in 2020 because of the Covid-19 pandemic. An alternative competition, the Bob Willis Trophy, was won by Essex.

Wooden spoons: Since the major expansion of the Championship from nine teams to 14 in 1895, the counties have finished outright bottom as follows: Derbyshire 16, Leicestershire 14, Somerset 12, Glamorgan and Northamptonshire 11, Gloucestershire 9, Nottinghamshire and Sussex 8, Worcestershire 6, Durham and Hampshire 5, Warwickshire 3, Essex and Kent 2, Yorkshire 1. Lancashire, Middlesex and Surrey have never finished bottom. Leicestershire have also shared bottom place twice, once with Hampshire and once with Somerset.

From 1977 to 1983 the Championship was sponsored by Schweppes, from 1984 to 1998 by Britannic Assurance, from 1999 to 2000 by PPP healthcare, in 2001 by Cricinfo, from 2002 to 2005 by Frizzell, from 2006 to 2015 by Liverpool Victoria (LV), and from 2016 to 2019 by Specsavers. LV were to return in 2021.

COUNTY CHAMPIONSHIP – FINAL POSITIONS, 1890–2019

	Derbyshire	Durham	Essex	Glamorgan	Gloucestershire	Hampshire	Kent	Lancashire	Leicestershire	Middlesex	Northamptonshire	Nottinghamshire	Somerset	Surrey	Sussex	Warwickshire	Worcestershire	Yorkshire
1890	–	–	–	–	6	–	3	2	–	7	–	5	–	1	8	–	–	3
1891	–	–	–	–	9	–	5	2	–	3	–	4	5	1	7	–	–	8
1892	–	–	–	–	7	–	7	4	–	5	–	2	3	1	9	–	–	6
1893	–	–	–	–	9	–	4	2	–	3	–	6	8	5	7	–	–	1
1894	–	–	–	–	9	–	4	4	–	3	–	7	6	1	8	–	–	2
1895	5	–	9	–	4	10	14	2	12	6	–	12	8	1	11	6	–	3
1896	7	–	5	–	10	8	9	2	13	3	–	6	11	4	14	12	–	1
1897	14	–	3	–	5	9	12	1	13	8	–	10	11	2	6	7	–	4
1898	9	–	5	–	3	12	7	6	13	2	–	8	13	4	9	9	–	1
1899	15	–	6	–	9	10	8	4	13	2	–	10	13	1	5	7	12	3
1900	13	–	10	–	7	15	3	2	14	7	–	5	11	7	3	6	12	1
1901	15	–	10	–	14	7	7	3	12	2	–	9	12	6	4	5	11	1
1902	10	–	13	–	14	15	7	5	11	12	–	3	7	4	2	6	9	1
1903	12	–	8	–	13	14	8	4	14	1	–	5	10	11	2	7	6	3
1904	10	–	14	–	9	15	3	1	7	4	–	5	12	11	6	7	13	2
1905	14	–	12	–	8	16	6	2	5	11	13	10	15	4	3	7	8	1
1906	16	–	7	–	9	8	1	4	15	11	11	5	11	3	10	6	14	2

	Derbyshire	Durham	Essex	Glamorgan	Gloucestershire	Hampshire	Kent	Lancashire	Leicestershire	Middlesex	Northamptonshire	Nottinghamshire	Somerset	Surrey	Sussex	Warwickshire	Worcestershire	Yorkshire
1907	16	–	7	–	10	12	8	6	11	5	15	1	14	4	13	9	2	2
1908	14	–	11	–	10	9	2	7	13	4	15	8	16	3	5	12	6	1
1909	15	–	14	–	16	8	1	2	13	6	7	10	11	5	4	12	8	3
1910	15	–	11	–	12	6	1	4	10	3	9	5	16	2	7	14	13	8
1911	14	–	6	–	12	11	2	4	15	3	10	8	16	5	13	1	9	7
1912	12	–	15	–	11	6	3	4	13	5	2	8	14	7	10	9	16	1
1913	13	–	15	–	9	10	1	8	14	6	4	5	16	3	7	11	12	2
1914	12	–	8	–	16	5	3	11	13	2	9	10	15	1	6	7	14	4
1919	9	–	14	–	8	7	2	5	9	13	12	3	5	4	11	15	–	1
1920	16	–	9	–	8	11	5	2	13	1	14	7	10	3	6	12	15	4
1921	12	–	15	17	7	6	4	5	11	1	13	8	10	2	9	16	14	3
1922	11	–	8	16	13	6	4	5	14	7	15	2	10	3	9	12	17	1
1923	10	–	13	16	11	7	5	3	14	8	17	2	9	4	6	12	15	1
1924	17	–	15	13	6	12	5	4	11	2	16	6	8	3	10	9	14	1
1925	14	–	7	17	10	9	5	3	12	6	11	4	15	2	13	8	16	1
1926	11	–	9	8	15	7	3	1	13	6	16	4	14	5	10	12	17	2
1927	5	–	8	15	12	13	4	1	7	9	16	2	14	6	10	11	17	3
1928	10	–	16	15	5	12	2	1	9	8	13	3	14	6	7	11	17	4
1929	7	–	12	17	4	11	8	2	9	6	13	1	15	10	4	14	16	2
1930	9	–	6	11	2	13	5	1	12	16	17	4	13	8	7	15	10	3
1931	7	–	10	15	2	12	3	6	16	11	17	5	13	8	4	9	14	1
1932	10	–	14	15	13	8	3	6	12	10	16	4	7	5	2	9	17	1
1933	6	–	4	16	10	14	3	5	17	12	13	8	11	9	2	7	15	1
1934	3	–	8	13	7	14	5	1	12	10	17	9	15	11	2	4	16	5
1935	2	–	9	13	15	16	10	4	6	3	17	5	14	11	7	8	12	1
1936	1	–	9	16	4	10	8	11	15	2	17	5	7	6	14	13	12	3
1937	3	–	6	7	4	14	12	9	16	2	17	10	13	8	5	11	15	1
1938	5	–	6	16	10	14	9	4	15	2	17	12	7	3	8	13	11	1
1939	9	–	4	13	3	15	5	6	17	2	16	12	14	8	10	11	7	1
1946	15	–	8	6	5	10	6	3	11	2	16	13	4	11	17	14	8	1
1947	5	–	11	9	2	16	4	3	14	1	17	11	11	6	9	15	7	7
1948	6	–	13	1	8	9	15	5	11	3	17	14	12	2	16	7	10	4
1949	15	–	9	8	7	16	13	11	17	1	6	11	9	5	13	4	3	1
1950	5	–	17	11	7	12	9	1	16	14	10	15	7	1	13	4	6	3
1951	11	–	8	5	12	9	16	3	15	7	13	17	14	6	10	1	4	2
1952	4	–	10	7	9	12	15	3	6	5	8	16	17	1	13	10	14	2
1953	6	–	12	10	6	14	16	3	3	5	11	8	17	1	2	9	15	12
1954	3	–	15	4	13	14	11	10	16	7	7	5	17	1	9	6	11	2
1955	8	–	14	16	12	3	13	9	6	5	7	11	17	1	4	9	15	2
1956	12	–	11	13	3	6	16	2	17	5	4	8	15	1	9	14	9	7
1957	4	–	5	9	12	13	14	6	17	7	2	15	8	1	9	11	16	3
1958	5	–	6	15	14	2	8	7	12	10	4	17	3	1	13	16	9	11
1959	7	–	9	6	2	8	13	5	16	10	11	17	12	3	15	4	14	1
1960	5	–	6	11	8	12	10	2	17	3	9	16	14	7	4	15	13	1
1961	7	–	6	14	5	1	11	13	9	3	16	17	10	15	8	12	4	2
1962	7	–	9	14	4	10	11	16	17	13	8	15	6	5	12	3	2	1
1963	17	–	12	2	8	10	13	15	16	6	7	9	3	11	4	4	14	1
1964	12	–	10	11	17	12	7	14	16	6	3	15	8	4	9	2	1	5
1965	9	–	15	3	10	12	5	13	14	6	2	17	7	8	16	11	1	4
1966	9	–	16	14	15	11	4	12	8	12	5	17	3	7	10	6	2	1
1967	6	–	15	14	17	12	2	11	2	7	9	15	8	4	13	10	5	1
1968	8	–	14	3	16	5	2	6	9	10	13	4	12	15	17	11	7	1
1969	16	–	6	1	2	5	10	15	14	11	9	8	17	3	7	4	12	13

	Derbyshire	Durham	Essex	Glamorgan	Gloucestershire	Hampshire	Kent	Lancashire	Leicestershire	Middlesex	Northamptonshire	Nottinghamshire	Somerset	Surrey	Sussex	Warwickshire	Worcestershire	Yorkshire
1970	7	–	12	2	17	10	1	3	15	16	14	11	13	5	9	7	6	4
1971	17	–	10	16	8	9	4	3	5	6	14	12	7	1	11	2	15	13
1972	17	–	5	13	3	9	2	15	6	8	4	14	11	12	16	1	7	10
1973	16	–	8	11	5	1	4	12	9	13	3	17	10	2	15	7	6	14
1974	17	–	12	16	14	2	10	8	4	6	3	15	5	7	13	9	1	11
1975	15	–	7	9	16	3	5	4	1	11	8	13	12	6	17	14	10	2
1976	15	–	6	17	3	12	14	16	4	1	2	13	7	9	10	5	11	8
1977	7	–	6	14	3	11	1	16	5	1	9	17	4	14	8	10	13	12
1978	14	–	2	13	10	8	1	12	6	3	17	7	5	16	9	11	15	4
1979	16	–	1	17	10	12	5	13	6	14	11	9	8	3	4	15	2	7
1980	9	–	8	13	7	17	16	15	10	1	12	3	5	2	4	14	11	6
1981	12	–	5	14	13	7	9	16	8	4	15	1	3	6	2	17	11	10
1982	11	–	7	16	15	3	13	12	2	1	9	4	6	5	8	17	14	10
1983	9	–	1	15	12	3	7	12	4	2	6	14	10	8	11	5	16	17
1984	12	–	1	13	17	15	5	16	4	3	11	2	7	8	6	9	10	14
1985	13	–	4	12	3	2	9	14	16	1	10	8	17	6	7	15	5	11
1986	11	–	1	17	2	6	8	15	7	12	9	4	16	3	14	12	5	10
1987	6	–	12	13	10	5	14	2	3	16	7	1	11	4	17	15	9	8
1988	14	–	3	17	10	15	2	9	8	7	12	5	11	4	16	6	1	13
1989	6	–	2	17	9	6	15	4	13	3	5	11	14	12	10	8	1	16
1990	12	–	2	8	13	3	16	6	7	1	11	13	15	9	17	5	4	10
1991	3	–	1	12	13	9	6	8	16	15	10	4	17	5	11	2	6	14
1992	5	18	1	14	10	15	2	12	8	11	3	4	9	13	7	6	17	16
1993	15	18	11	3	17	13	8	13	9	1	4	7	5	6	10	16	2	12
1994	17	16	6	18	12	13	9	10	2	4	5	3	11	7	8	1	15	13
1995	14	17	5	16	6	13	18	4	7	2	3	11	9	12	15	1	10	8
1996	2	18	5	10	13	14	4	15	1	9	16	17	11	3	12	8	7	6
1997	16	17	8	1	7	14	2	11	10	4	15	13	12	8	18	4	3	6
1998	10	14	18	12	4	6	11	2	1	17	15	16	9	5	7	8	13	3
1999	9	8	12	14	18	7	5	2	3	16	13	17	4	1	11	10	15	6
2000	**9**	**8**	*2*	*3*	*4*	**7**	**6**	**2**	**4**	*8*	*1*	*7*	**5**	**1**	*9*	*6*	*5*	**3**
2001	*9*	*8*	**9**	**8**	*4*	*2*	**3**	**6**	**5**	*5*	**7**	*7*	**2**	**4**	*1*	*3*	*6*	**1**
2002	*6*	*9*	*1*	*5*	*8*	**7**	**3**	**4**	**5**	*2*	*7*	*3*	**8**	**1**	**6**	**2**	*4*	**9**
2003	*9*	*6*	**7**	*5*	*3*	*8*	**4**	**2**	**9**	**6**	*2*	**8**	*7*	**3**	**1**	**5**	*1*	*4*
2004	*8*	*9*	*5*	*3*	**6**	*2*	**2**	**8**	*6*	**4**	**9**	*1*	*4*	**3**	**5**	**1**	**7**	*7*
2005	*9*	*2*	*5*	**9**	**8**	**2**	**5**	*1*	*7*	**6**	*4*	**1**	*8*	**7**	**3**	**4**	*6*	*3*
2006	*5*	**7**	*3*	*8*	*7*	**3**	**5**	**2**	*4*	**9**	*6*	**8**	*9*	*1*	**1**	**4**	*2*	**6**
2007	*6*	**2**	*4*	*9*	*7*	**5**	**7**	**3**	*8*	*3*	*5*	*2*	*1*	**4**	**1**	**8**	**9**	**6**
2008	*6*	**1**	*5*	*8*	*9*	**3**	**8**	**5**	*7*	*3*	*4*	**2**	**4**	**9**	**6**	*1*	*2*	**7**
2009	*6*	**1**	*2*	*5*	*4*	**6**	*1*	**4**	*9*	*8*	*3*	**2**	**3**	*7*	**8**	**5**	**9**	**7**
2010	*9*	**5**	**9**	*3*	*5*	**7**	**8**	**4**	*4*	*8*	*6*	**1**	**2**	*7*	*1*	**6**	*2*	**3**
2011	*5*	**3**	*7*	*6*	*4*	**9**	*8*	**1**	*9*	*1*	*3*	**6**	**4**	*2*	**5**	**2**	**7**	**8**
2012	*1*	**6**	*5*	*6*	*9*	*4*	*3*	**8**	*7*	**3**	*8*	**5**	**2**	**7**	**4**	**1**	**9**	*2*
2013	**8**	**1**	*3*	*8*	*6*	*4*	*7*	*1*	*9*	**5**	*2*	**7**	**6**	**9**	**3**	**4**	*5*	**2**
2014	*4*	**5**	*3*	*8*	*7*	*1*	*6*	**8**	*9*	**7**	**9**	**4**	**6**	*5*	**3**	**2**	*2*	**1**
2015	*8*	**4**	*3*	*4*	*6*	**7**	*7*	*2*	*9*	**2**	*5*	**3**	**6**	*1*	**8**	**5**	**9**	**1**
2016	*9*	**4**	*1*	*8*	*6*	**8**	*2*	**7**	*7*	**1**	*5*	**9**	**2**	**5**	*4*	**6**	*3*	**3**
2017	*8*	*9*	**1**	*7*	*6*	**5**	*5*	**2**	*10*	**7**	*3*	*2*	**6**	**3**	*4*	**8**	*1*	**4**
2018	*7*	*8*	**3**	*10*	*5*	**5**	*2*	**7**	*6*	*4*	*9*	**6**	**2**	**1**	*3*	*1*	**8**	**4**
2019	*7*	*5*	**1**	*4*	*3*	**3**	**4**	*1*	*10*	*8*	*2*	**8**	**2**	**6**	*6*	**7**	*9*	**5**

2020 *The County Championship was replaced by the Bob Willis Trophy, and won by Essex.*

For the 2000–2019 Championships, Division One placings are in bold, Division Two in italic.

MATCH RESULTS, 1864–2020

County	*Years of Play*	*Played*	*Won*	*Lost*	*Drawn*	*Tied*	*% Won*
Derbyshire	1871–87; 1895–2020	2,592	635	958	998	1	24.49
Durham	1992–2020	456	124	189	143	0	27.19
Essex	1895–2020	2,557	761	732	1,058	6	29.76
Glamorgan	1921–2020	2,082	456	723	903	0	21.90
Gloucestershire	1870–2020	2,835	830	1,037	966	2	29.27
Hampshire	1864–85; 1895–2020	2,665	703	891	1,067	4	26.37
Kent	1864–2020	2,950	1,056	880	1,009	5	35.79
Lancashire	1865–2020	3,027	1,116	629	1,278	4	36.86
Leicestershire	1895–2020	2,522	560	925	1,036	1	22.20
Middlesex	1864–2020	2,732	992	697	1,038	5	36.31
Northamptonshire	1905–2020	2,289	577	780	929	3	25.20
Nottinghamshire	1864–2020	2,862	862	790	1,209	1	30.11
Somerset	1882–85; 1891–2020	2,565	632	980	949	4	24.63
Surrey	1864–2020	3,107	1,208	696	1,199	4	38.87
Sussex	1864–2020	3,001	859	1,019	1,117	6	28.62
Warwickshire	1895–2020	2,537	709	723	1,103	2	27.94
Worcestershire	1899–2020	2,474	640	866	966	2	25.86
Yorkshire	1864–2020	3,130	1,352	557	1,219	2	43.19
Cambridgeshire	1864–69; 1871	19	8	8	3	0	42.10
		23,201	14,080	14,080	9,095	26	

Matches abandoned without a ball bowled are excluded. Figures include the Bob Willis Trophy.

Counties participated in the years shown, except that there were no matches in 1915–1918 and 1940–1945; Hampshire did not play inter-county matches in 1868–1869, 1871–1874 and 1879; Worcestershire did not take part in the Championship in 1919.

BOB WILLIS TROPHY STATISTICS FOR 2020

	For			Runs scored	Against		
County	*Runs*	*Wickets*	*Avge*	*per 100 balls*	*Runs*	*Wickets*	*Avge*
Derbyshire (*2*)	2,076	59	35.18	50.01	2,334	71	32.87
Durham (*6*)	1,910	77	24.80	43.32	1,746	42	41.57
Essex (W)	2,416	83	29.10	49.34	2,049	97	21.12
Glamorgan (**6**)	2,113	94	22.47	49.41	2,555	73	35.00
Gloucestershire (**5**)	1,415	76	18.61	42.08	1,721	56	30.73
Hampshire (4)	1,408	66	21.33	47.13	1,700	76	22.36
Kent (2)	2,114	64	33.03	58.26	2,245	89	25.22
Lancashire (*3*)	1,929	61	31.62	48.02	1,978	71	27.85
Leicestershire (*5*)	1,930	68	28.38	52.57	1,901	57	33.35
Middlesex (3)	2,170	78	27.82	51.51	1,807	77	23.46
Northamptonshire (**4**)	1,790	70	25.57	53.89	1,817	70	25.95
Nottinghamshire (*4*)	2,374	69	34.40	64.31	2,521	81	31.12
Somerset (**R**)	2,864	95	30.14	59.30	1,825	112	16.29
Surrey (5)	2,002	94	21.29	48.03	2,428	82	29.60
Sussex (6)	2,175	100	21.75	52.74	2,113	67	31.53
Warwickshire (**3**)	1,993	72	27.68	49.61	2,425	71	34.15
Worcestershire (**2**)	2,540	64	39.68	57.13	2,315	86	26.91
Yorkshire (*1*)	1,862	60	31.03	54.78	1,601	72	22.23
	37,081	1,350	27.46	51.78	37,081	1,350	27.46

2020 Bob Willis Trophy positions are shown in brackets; Central Group in bold, North Group in italic, South Group in roman. W = winners; R = runners-up.

COUNTY CAPS AWARDED IN 2020

Durham*	D. G. Bedingham, S. R. Dickson.
Essex	S. J. Cook, A. J. A. Wheater.
Gloucestershire*.	T. C. Lace, T. J. Price, G. F. B. Scott.
Northamptonshire. . . .	L. A. Procter.
Nottinghamshire.	H. Hameed.
Warwickshire	W. M. H. Rhodes, O. P. Stone.
Worcestershire*	J. D. Libby.

* *Durham and Gloucestershire now award caps to all first-class players; Worcestershire have replaced caps with colours awarded to all Championship players (or, in 2020, the Bob Willis Trophy).*

No caps were awarded by the other 11 counties.

COUNTY TESTIMONIALS AWARDED FOR 2021

Glamorgan	*M. G. Hogan.
Hampshire	F. H. Edwards.
Lancashire	*S. D. Parry.
Middlesex.	*E. J. G. Morgan.
Northamptonshire .	*A. G. Wakely.
Surrey.	R. Clarke.
Yorkshire	*A. Lyth.

* *Testimonial originally awarded for 2020, but extended because of the Covid-19 crisis.*

None of the other 11 counties awarded a testimonial for 2021.

DERBYSHIRE

Celebrations on ice

MARK EKLID

The 150th anniversary of the meeting at the Derby Guildhall that led to the formation of Derbyshire County Cricket Club was to have been marked by a year of celebration. Instead, the club did not play a single match within the county borders.

That is not to say they hosted no cricket. As sport emerged from lockdown in July, it turned into a busy summer for club staff. Derby was selected by the ECB to become a biosecure bubble: a training base for the men's squads from Pakistan and Australia, and later for the women of England and West Indies, who contested five Twenty20 internationals there in September.

Investment in facilities in recent years, and a hotel close enough to minimise the risk of infection from outside the bubble, meant Derbyshire played a key role in salvaging the international season. That brought some monetary compensation, but the real reward, according to chief executive Ryan Duckett, was the bigger picture.

"It was important to give the club a bit of financial upside, but the big thing for us was to do what we could to safeguard the whole game," he said. "Because we played our part in making sure the Pakistan and Australia series went ahead, the ECB could fulfil their broadcasting commitments, and ensure the appropriate funding filtered down, not only through the professional game but the recreational game as well."

A further consequence was to condemn Derbyshire's first-team players and coaches to a nomadic existence for two months. Though they made a temporary base at Repton School, about ten miles south-west of Derby, for training and practice, there was no alternative but to hit the road for their five Bob Willis Trophy matches, plus all ten in the Vitality Blast. It was the first time in 80 years they had not played any home games; even during the Second World War (except for 1940), some representative cricket had been staged in the county.

Despite the disruption, Derbyshire did surprisingly well: heading into their last first-class fixture, against Lancashire at Liverpool, they had a chance of qualifying for the Lord's final. The tone had been set in their first match when, led by an undefeated 91 from Fynn Hudson-Prentice, they scored 365 against Nottinghamshire – Derbyshire's largest fourth-innings total to beat another county. They also won their second, against Leicestershire, to move top of the North Group. Draws in the next two meant they were still the leaders as they took the field at Aigburth. Though defeat allowed Yorkshire to overtake them, it had been an encouraging few weeks, especially as the Derbyshire attack was without its two most experienced members. Tony Palladino was unavailable because of mental health issues, and left at the end of the summer after nine outstanding years with the club, while Ravi Rampaul stayed at home in the West Indies.

Jan Kruger, Getty Images

Luis Reece

Academy graduate Sam Conners, Zimbabwe-born Dustin Melton (a Kolpak, though he re-signed as an overseas player for 2021), new recruits Michael Cohen and Ben Aitchison, plus Ed Barnes, on loan from Yorkshire, had played only six first-class matches in England between them (though Cohen had played 15 in his native South Africa). But all provided valuable seam support for the durable Luis Reece. The pick of the attack, however, was leg-spinner Matt Critchley, whose 17 wickets earned the club's Player of the Year award. Long regarded as a good prospect, he enjoyed his most mature summer yet. Reece's all-round value was demonstrated by 13 wickets, second only to Critchley, and 277 runs, behind only Leus du Plooy – and Reece played four games to their five.

The Vitality Blast proved more sobering. Derbyshire had prepared to follow up the heady achievement of 2019, when they made their first appearance at finals day, by recruiting two Australians, fast bowler Sean Abbott and wicketkeeper-batsman Ben McDermott. But in April the decision was made to defer both players' contracts until 2021. Rampaul, the competition's top wicket-taker in 2019, was also badly missed, and the batting line-up's top four – Reece, Billy Godleman, Wayne Madsen and du Plooy – were far less effective than the previous year. Derbyshire won only one of their ten games, and finished bottom of the group.

With much of the compensation for turning Derby into a biosecure bubble spent on the increased cost of playing all matches away, the club could not escape the realities facing county cricket. The cushion of a record £402,000 surplus in 2019 undoubtedly helped, but as the year ended it was unclear whether the financial limitations of the post-Covid world – or Australia's international plans – would allow Abbott to join them, though McDermott's white-ball contract was confirmed in November.

All may not be lost, however, and hopes remain that Derbyshire's 150th anniversary may yet be suitably commemorated. It had been decided to mark 2020, because the meeting that led to the club's formation was in November 1870. The revised plan is to celebrate 2021, and the sesquicentenary of the maiden first-class match, in May 1871: a thumping victory over Lancashire by an innings and 11 runs.

"That voice, I later discovered, belonged to John Arlott, and his words made a lasting impression. It was not long before I had the opportunity to tell him so."
The Three Ws, page 124

DERBYSHIRE RESULTS

Bob Willis Trophy matches – Played 5: Won 2, Lost 1, Drawn 2.
Vitality Blast matches – Played 8: Won 1, Lost 7. Abandoned 2.

Bob Willis Trophy, 2nd in North Group;
Vitality Blast, 6th in North Group.

BOB WILLIS TROPHY AVERAGES

BATTING AND FIELDING

Cap		*Birthplace*	*M*	*I*	*NO*	*R*	*HS*	*100*	*Avge*	*Ct/St*
	F. J. Hudson-Prentice	*Haywards Heath*	3	5	2	145	91*	0	48.33	1
2019	†L. M. Reece	*Taunton*	4	7	1	277	122	1	46.16	4
	†M. A. R. Cohen††	*Cape Town, SA*	2	3	2	43	30*	0	43.00	0
	†J. L. du Plooy††	*Pretoria, SA*	5	7	0	296	130	1	42.28	5
2019	M. J. J. Critchley	*Preston*	5	7	1	234	63	0	39.00	4
	A. K. Dal	*Newcastle-u-Tyne*	4	4	1	108	78*	0	36.00	2
	H. R. Hosein	*Chesterfield‡*	4	6	1	167	84	0	33.40	13/1
2011	W. L. Madsen	*Durban, SA*	5	8	1	213	103	1	30.42	10
2015	†B. A. Godleman	*Islington*	5	8	0	226	86	0	28.25	2
	M. H. McKiernan	*Billinge*	2	4	0	103	52	0	25.75	3
	S. Conners	*Nottingham*	4	4	2	45	21	0	22.50	0
	D. R. Melton††	*Harare, Zimbabwe*	3	3	1	11	11	0	5.50	0

Also batted: B. W. Aitchison (*Southport*) (3 matches) 8 (2 ct); E. Barnes (*York*) (2 matches) 4; B. D. Guest (*Manchester*) (1 match) did not bat; A. L. Hughes (*Wordsley*) (cap 2017) (2 matches) 27, 13; T. A. Wood (*Derby‡*) (1 match) 26.

‡ *Born in Derbyshire.* †† *Other non-England-qualified.*

BOWLING

	Style	*O*	*M*	*R*	*W*	*BB*	*5I*	*Avge*
L. M. Reece	LFM	132.3	40	340	13	3-51	0	26.15
M. J. J. Critchley	LB	128.4	14	457	17	6-73	1	26.88
M. A. R. Cohen	LFM	44.2	7	191	7	3-47	0	27.28
D. R. Melton	RFM	70	13	233	8	4-22	0	29.12
B. W. Aitchison	RFM	78	20	211	6	3-55	0	35.16
E. Barnes	RFM	32	6	107	3	2-24	0	35.66
S. Conners	RFM	94.2	23	328	9	3-63	0	36.44

Also bowled: A. K. Dal (RFM) 43–10–95–2; J. L. du Plooy (SLA) 9–1–41–2; F. J. Hudson-Prentice (RFM) 34–8–105–1; A. L. Hughes (RM) 21–2–79–1; M. H. McKiernan (LB) 10.2–2–48–2; W. L. Madsen (OB) 1–0–4–0.

LEADING VITALITY BLAST AVERAGES (70 runs/10 overs)

Batting	*Runs*	*HS*	*Avge*	*SR*	*Ct*
J. L. du Plooy	138	53*	19.71	**139.39**	4
W. L. Madsen	192	68	24.00	**138.12**	0
A. L. Hughes	116	36*	19.33	**130.33**	1
M. H. McKiernan	71	25	11.83	**126.78**	2
M. J. J. Critchley	154	44	19.25	**111.59**	1
L. M. Reece	110	42	15.71	**103.77**	2
B. A. Godleman	166	49	20.75	**101.21**	2

Bowling	*W*	*BB*	*Avge*	*ER*
M. H. McKiernan	2	2-22	65.50	**7.27**
W. L. Madsen	2	1-25	56.50	**7.53**
M. J. J. Critchley	4	1-21	58.75	**7.79**
A. L. Hughes	4	2-34	41.00	**7.80**
D. R. Melton	4	2-37	31.00	**9.53**
S. Conners	3	2-38	40.00	**10.00**
L. M. Reece	3	2-31	50.33	**10.06**
M. A. R. Cohen	3	2-23	45.33	**10.46**

FIRST-CLASS COUNTY RECORDS

Highest score for	274	G. A. Davidson v Lancashire at Manchester	1896
Highest score against	343*	P. A. Perrin (Essex) at Chesterfield	1904
Leading run-scorer	23,854	K. J. Barnett (avge 41.12)	1979–98
Best bowling for	10-40	W. Bestwick v Glamorgan at Cardiff	1921
Best bowling against	10-45	R. L. Johnson (Middlesex) at Derby	1994
Leading wicket-taker	1,670	H. L. Jackson (avge 17.11)	1947–63
Highest total for	801-8 dec	v Somerset at Taunton	2007
Highest total against	677-7 dec	by Yorkshire at Leeds	2013
Lowest total for	16	v Nottinghamshire at Nottingham	1879
Lowest total against	23	by Hampshire at Burton-upon-Trent	1958

LIST A COUNTY RECORDS

Highest score for	173*	M. J. Di Venuto v Derbys County Board at Derby	2000
Highest score against	158	R. K. Rao (Sussex) at Derby	1997
Leading run-scorer	12,358	K. J. Barnett (avge 36.67)	1979–98
Best bowling for	8-21	M. A. Holding v Sussex at Hove	1988
Best bowling against	8-66	S. R. G. Francis (Somerset) at Derby	2004
Leading wicket-taker	246	A. E. Warner (avge 27.13)	1985–95
Highest total for	366-4	v Combined Universities at Oxford	1991
Highest total against	369-6	by New Zealanders at Derby	1999
Lowest total for	60	v Kent at Canterbury	2008
Lowest total against	42	by Glamorgan at Swansea	1979

TWENTY20 COUNTY RECORDS

Highest score for	111	W. J. Durston v Nottinghamshire at Nottingham	2010
Highest score against	158*	B. B. McCullum (Warwickshire) at Birmingham	2015
Leading run-scorer	**2,998**	**W. L. Madsen (avge 30.59, SR 134.31)**	**2010–20**
Best bowling for	5-27	T. Lungley v Leicestershire at Leicester	2009
Best bowling against	5-14	P. D. Collingwood (Durham) at Chester-le-Street	2008
Leading wicket-taker	**53**	**A. L. Hughes (avge 34.58, ER 8.01)**	**2011–20**
Highest total for	222-5	v Yorkshire at Leeds	2010
	222-5	v Nottinghamshire at Nottingham	2017
Highest total against	249-8	by Hampshire at Derby	2017
Lowest total for	72	v Leicestershire at Derby	2013
Lowest total against	84	by West Indians at Derby	2007

ADDRESS

The Incora County Ground, Nottingham Road, Derby DE21 6DA; 01332 388 101; info@derbyshireccc.com; www.derbyshireccc.com. Twitter: @DerbyshireCCC.

OFFICIALS

Captain B. A. Godleman
Head of cricket D. L. Houghton
Head of talent pathway D. Smit
Assistant coach (batting) M. B. Loye
2020 (bowling) S. P. Kirby
Twenty20 coach D. G. Cork

President J. G. Wright
Chairman R. I. Morgan
Chief executive R. Duckett
Head groundsman N. Godrich
Scorer J. M. Brown

DERBYSHIRE v NOTTINGHAMSHIRE

At Nottingham, August 1–4. Derbyshire won by three wickets. Derbyshire 20pts, Nottinghamshire 6pts. Toss: Derbyshire. First-class debut: B. W. Aitchison. County debuts: M. A. R. Cohen; T. E. Barber, H. Hameed, P. D. Trego.

Derbyshire completed victory with a ball to spare after making 365 for seven, their highest winning fourth-innings total against another county. Hudson-Prentice, unable to field the day before because of a thigh injury, led them home with an unbeaten 91; he shared half-century stands with McKiernan and Michael Cohen, a South African left-arm seamer who marked his county debut – and 22nd birthday – by striking the winning runs. They had trailed by 85 on first innings, but it would have

DERBYSHIRE'S HIGHEST FOURTH-INNINGS TOTALS

396	v Leicestershire (*set 425*) at Leicester	2007
371-9	v Australians (*371*) at Derby	1997
365-7	**v Nottinghamshire (*365*) at Nottingham**	**2020**
365	v Surrey (*408*) at Chesterfield	2010
350-3	v Northamptonshire (*347*) at Derby	1982
344	v Hampshire (*364*) at Southampton	1911
336-7	v Worcestershire (*335*) at Worcester	1985
336	v Australians (*344*) at Chesterfield	1968
331-8	v Leicestershire (*341*) at Derby	2015
328-7	v Nottinghamshire (*331*) at Ilkeston	1974
328	v Northamptonshire (*494*) at Chesterfield	2011

been far more without 130 from du Plooy, who scored more than half his runs in a stand of 80 with Conners, a Derbyshire tenth-wicket record in this fixture. For Nottinghamshire, Hameed made two half-centuries, in his first match since leaving Old Trafford; so did No. 8 Patel, whose second-innings 80 was his highest first-class score for three years. Though staged at Trent Bridge, this was classified as a home game for Derbyshire, who had handed over their ground to the ECB as a biosecure base for touring teams.

Close of play: first day, Derbyshire 9-0 (Reece 0, Godleman 9); second day, Nottinghamshire 84-3 (Hameed 30, Mullaney 27); third day, Derbyshire 129-1 (Godleman 69, Madsen 27).

Nottinghamshire

C. D. Nash lbw b Conners	59	– b Conners	0
H. Hameed lbw b Reece	68	– c McKiernan b Aitchison	52
B. M. Duckett c du Plooy b Aitchison	9	– c Hosein b Conners	23
J. M. Clarke c Hosein b Cohen	8	– lbw b Conners	2
*S. J. Mullaney c McKiernan b Reece	6	– c McKiernan b Reece	48
P. D. Trego c Hosein b Cohen	1	– c Critchley b Aitchison	8
†T. J. Moores c Hosein b Hudson-Prentice	15	– c Reece b Cohen	7
S. R. Patel c Madsen b Cohen	63	– lbw b Critchley	80
J. D. M. Evison c Godleman b McKiernan	38	– c Critchley b Aitchison	31
J. T. Ball b McKiernan	34	– c Hosein b Cohen	22
T. E. Barber not out	0	– not out	0
B 10, lb 3, w 2, nb 8	23	B 1, lb 4, w 1	6
1/111 (1) 2/124 (3) 3/147 (4) 4/159 (2) 5/160 (5) 6/160 (6) 7/192 (7) 8/253 (8) 9/321 (9) 10/324 (10) (77.2 overs)	324	1/0 (1) 2/39 (3) 3/41 (4) 4/116 (5) 5/127 (6) 6/140 (7) 7/150 (2) 8/224 (9) 9/279 (8) 10/279 (10) (83.2 overs)	279

Conners 15–3–69–1; Aitchison 18–3–57–1; Reece 15–3–45–2; Hudson-Prentice 11–2–44–1; Cohen 9–1–47–3; Critchley 8–0–46–0; McKiernan 1.2–0–3–2. *Second innings*—Conners 15–3–63–3; Aitchison 23–4–55–3; Reece 23–6–61–1; Cohen 13.2–2–51–2; Critchley 7–1–31–1; McKiernan 2–0–13–0.

Derbyshire

First innings		Second innings	
L. M. Reece c Moores b Ball	0	– c Ball b Trego	24
*B. A. Godleman c Moores b Ball	18	– lbw b Evison	86
W. L. Madsen c Nash b Ball	0	– lbw b Ball	43
J. L. du Plooy c Evison b Patel	130	– lbw b Mullaney	7
M. J. J. Critchley run out (Mullaney)	45	– st Moores b Patel	35
†H. R. Hosein lbw b Evison	1	– b Ball	3
F. J. Hudson-Prentice lbw b Evison	8	– not out	91
M. H. McKiernan c Hameed b Evison	0	– b Ball	20
M. A. R. Cohen b Barber	7	– not out	30
B. W. Aitchison c Mullaney b Barber	8		
S. Conners not out	5		
Lb 7, w 6, nb 4	17	B 6, lb 12, w 6, nb 2	26
1/14 (1) 2/19 (2) 3/26 (3) 4/119 (5) 5/120 (6) 6/132 (7) 7/134 (8) 8/149 (9) 9/159 (10) 10/239 (4) (71 overs)	239	1/33 (1) 2/146 (2) 3/165 (4) 4/180 (3) 5/192 (6) 6/234 (5) 7/299 (8) (7 wkts, 120.5 overs)	365

Ball 20–3–71–3; Trego 13–3–36–0; Evison 11–3–38–3; Mullaney 8–2–12–0; Barber 15–1–71–2; Patel 4–1–4–1. *Second innings*—Ball 33.5–9–98–3; Trego 19–7–52–1; Evison 11.5–1–36–1; Barber 13–0–53–0; Patel 23.1–2–74–1; Mullaney 20–8–34–1.

Umpires: N. A. Mallender and P. R. Pollard. Referee: S. Cummings.

At Leicester, August 8–10. DERBYSHIRE beat LEICESTERSHIRE by nine wickets. *Derbyshire replace Leicestershire at the head of the North Group.*

At Leeds, August 15–18. DERBYSHIRE drew with YORKSHIRE.

DERBYSHIRE v DURHAM

At Chester-le-Street, August 22–25. Drawn. Derbyshire 14pts, Durham 12pts. Toss: Derbyshire. County debut: B. D. Guest.

Storm Francis wiped out the final day, but the bowlers had little reason to feel they could force a result on an increasingly placid pitch. In another supposed home fixture, Derbyshire had enjoyed some early success, but Durham fought back from 32 for three through century stands between Lees and Harte, then Eckersley and Coughlin. Their 157 was a seventh-wicket record for Durham against Derbyshire; Coughlin, who hit a career-best 90, had also featured in the previous record, 130 with Paul Collingwood here in 2017. Eckersley declared after rain ended play three overs into the second afternoon; on the third, Derbyshire took the lead – plus four batting points, which kept them top of the North Group – for the loss of only four wickets, following Reece's seventh first-class century. Even Poynter bowled, his first overs in any senior cricket, as Durham's hopes dwindled. Ben Aitchison injured his ankle ligaments while practising during lunch on day three; he was out for the rest of Derbyshire's season.

Close of play: first day, Durham 219-6 (Eckersley 22, Coughlin 42); second day, Durham 337-9 (Eckersley 78, Rushworth 2); third day, Derbyshire 355-4 (Critchley 46, Hudson-Prentice 26).

Durham

A. Z. Lees b Reece	84	M. E. T. Salisbury c Madsen b Barnes	4
S. R. Dickson lbw b Conners	0	C. Rushworth not out	2
M. A. Jones lbw b Reece	2		
D. G. Bedingham c and b Aitchison	9	B 2, lb 13, nb 2	17
G. J. Harte c Reece b Critchley	44		—
S. W. Poynter lbw b Critchley	7	1/7 (2) 2/14 (3) (9 wkts dec, 114 overs)	337
*†E. J. H. Eckersley not out	78	3/32 (4) 4/143 (5)	
P. Coughlin b Critchley	90	5/155 (6) 6/155 (1) 7/312 (8)	
M. J. Potts b Critchley	0	8/312 (9) 9/323 (10) 110 overs: 313-8	

Conners 15–3–44–1; Reece 26–9–60–2; Aitchison 20–6–56–1; Hudson-Prentice 15–4–39–0; Barnes 11–2–43–1; Dal 9–1–27–0; Critchley 18–0–53–4.

Derbyshire

L. M. Reece c Potts b Rushworth	122	F. J. Hudson-Prentice not out	26
*B. A. Godleman c Jones b Potts	51	B 3, lb 5, nb 10	18
W. L. Madsen b Salisbury	52		—
J. L. du Plooy b Harte	40	1/98 (2) 2/222 (3) (4 wkts, 98 overs)	355
M. J. J. Critchley not out	46	3/244 (1) 4/313 (4)	

†B. D. Guest, A. K. Dal, B. W. Aitchison, E. Barnes and S. Conners did not bat.

Rushworth 18–2–53–1; Potts 21–4–50–1; Salisbury 18–7–42–1; Harte 16–0–80–1; Coughlin 20–2–94–0; Lees 1–0–7–0; Poynter 4–0–21–0.

Umpires: S. J. O'Shaughnessy and N. Pratt. Referee: W. R. Smith.

At Liverpool, September 6–9. DERBYSHIRE lost to LANCASHIRE by 178 runs. *Derbyshire's hopes of a Lord's final disappear.*

DURHAM

Disenchanted April

SIMON SINCLAIR

April at Riverside is a time when Chris Rushworth should be bounding in off 20 paces. But in 2020 he was training for a half-marathon in his garden for the Solan Connor Fawcett Family Cancer Trust. Wicketkeeper Ned Eckersley should have been behind the stumps, bellowing orders; instead, he was volunteering at London's Royal Free Hospital, bagging groceries for NHS staff.

As Covid-19 spread throughout the UK, everyone was forced to adjust. The South African-born Brydon Carse had enjoyed a breakthrough in 2019 – the year he qualified for England – and earned selection for the Lions on their unbeaten tour of Australia. But his hopes of another strong season, and perhaps of pushing his way into the senior England squad, were frustrated. Instead, he joined Eckersley and the million volunteers who pledged to help the NHS.

David Bedingham – also from South Africa, but allowed to play on a UK visa – had signed a one-year deal with Durham, after three seasons in the Nottinghamshire leagues; he hoped to secure his spot in the middle order of a team under reconstruction. But he had to cope with three months' solitude in the North-East, while his partner and family stayed in South Africa.

By June, Carse had resumed individual training, along with Ben Stokes and Mark Wood as they prepared for the visits of West Indies and Pakistan; Carse eventually joined the one-day squad at the Rose Bowl ahead of a series with Ireland, though there was no England debut. Three Bob Willis Trophy wickets at 81 apiece did not help.

Meanwhile, the rest of the Durham squad returned for practice, in a new world of temperature checks and Covid-19 tests, as a truncated domestic season was arranged to begin in August. With the County Championship's two divisions replaced by the Bob Willis Trophy's three regional groups, Durham found themselves one of six teams in the North Group, facing Yorkshire and Lancashire, who would have been in Division One. The previous season's captain, Cameron Bancroft, was unable to travel from Australia, so Eckersley, who had stood in for him at the end of 2019, was appointed to lead the first-class side.

Showers and sunshine greeted cricket's return to Riverside in August, though there was little atmosphere as Durham and Yorkshire took the field in front of empty stands. Durham began with two familiar collapses – bowled out for 103 on the first day, then folding against Matthew Fisher, after Alex Lees had fought back with a second-innings century. They struggled even more in their next game – an innings defeat by Lancashire – drew the remaining three, and finished bottom of the North Group.

Rushworth, at least, secured his place among the great seamers of the county circuit by passing 500 first-class wickets. He claimed 16 in four matches, to

Ian Horrocks, Getty Images

Chris Rushworth

end the season with 505 for Durham at an average of just 22, in striking distance of Graham Onions's club record 527. Lees was the other success story, scoring 386 runs at 48; against his old team, Yorkshire, he made Durham's only century.

There were sporadic highlights from Bedingham and Gareth Harte, who both reached 250; Ben Raine bowled well, without enjoying the success he deserved (though only Rushworth surpassed his nine wickets), and averaged 41 with the bat. Sean Dickson arrived from Kent, initially on loan, but managed only one fifty.

It was evident that coach James Franklin and director of cricket Marcus North were still some way from fashioning a team capable of competing for first-class honours again. The departure of seamer James Weighell and leg-spinner Richard Whitehead was announced in July; they were followed by Twenty20 captain Nathan Rimmington, Sol Bell and Josh Coughlin, while Scott Steel moved to Leicestershire.

Initially, Durham's Blast campaign followed a similar pattern to the Bob Willis Trophy. They lost four of their first five matches (the other was abandoned), conceding hundreds to Keaton Jennings and Joe Clarke, and an unbeaten 85 to Tom Köhler-Cadmore. But the tide turned in mid-September. Raine struck eight sixes to help Durham reach 223, their second-highest Twenty20 total, and beat Derbyshire. Matty Potts then took centre-stage to lead a charge towards the quarter-finals, improving his career-best in three successive victories. As in 2019, Durham fell short when it mattered, losing their final fixture to Nottinghamshire, the eventual winners. Farhaan Behardien, a South African Kolpak, achieved little.

Still, in a year where the cricket was put into perspective, underwhelming returns in a short and extraordinary season were no great blemish on a team in transition. The shoots of recovery were boosted by the return of Scott Borthwick after four years with Surrey. Lees's form provided solid foundations that Durham have sorely missed. If Bancroft returns in 2021, the batting will boast a top three with tremendous potential, paired with an impressive stock of seamers. The building blocks were in place; they needed to be backed up with performances on the field.

Off it, a profitable year in 2019, when the club hosted three World Cup matches, helped mitigate the inevitable losses in 2020 – and left Durham well placed for whatever lay in store in 2021.

"By 1968 he was chairman of selectors, and controversially chose himself for a (later cancelled) tour of England."
Obituaries, page 298

DURHAM RESULTS

Bob Willis Trophy matches – Played 5: Lost 2, Drawn 3.
Vitality Blast matches – Played 9: Won 4, Lost 5. Abandoned 1.

Bob Willis Trophy, 6th in North Group;
Vitality Blast, 4th in North Group.

BOB WILLIS TROPHY AVERAGES

BATTING AND FIELDING

Cap		*Birthplace*	*M*	*I*	*NO*	*R*	*HS*	*100*	*Avge*	*Ct*
2018	†A. Z. Lees	*Halifax*	5	8	0	386	106	1	48.25	4
2018	G. J. Harte	*Johannesburg, SA*	5	8	2	250	72	0	41.66	0
2011	†B. A. Raine	*Sunderland‡*	4	7	4	124	31	0	41.33	0
2020	D. G. Bedingham††	*George, SA*	5	8	0	253	96	0	31.62	3
2018	M. A. Jones	*Ormskirk*	2	3	0	84	82	0	28.00	2
2019	E. J. H. Eckersley	*Oxford*	5	8	2	152	78*	0	25.33	3
2016	B. A. Carse	*Port Elizabeth, SA*	3	5	0	100	41	0	20.00	0
2016	S. W. Poynter††	*Hammersmith*	2	3	0	58	50	0	19.33	0
2012	P. Coughlin	*Sunderland‡*	4	6	0	114	90	0	19.00	2
2015	J. T. A. Burnham	*Durham‡*	3	5	0	72	31	0	14.40	1
2020	S. R. Dickson	*Johannesburg, SA*	5	8	0	97	56	0	12.12	4
2010	C. Rushworth	*Sunderland‡*	4	7	2	54	25	0	10.80	0
2017	C. T. Steel	*Greenbrae, USA*	3	5	0	22	11	0	4.40	0
2017	M. J. Potts	*Sunderland‡*	2	3	0	10	10	0	3.33	1
2018	M. E. T. Salisbury	*Chelmsford*	3	3	0	5	4	0	1.66	0

‡ *Born in Durham.* †† *Other non-England-qualified.*

Durham now award caps on first-class debut for the county.

BOWLING

	Style	*O*	*M*	*R*	*W*	*BB*	*5I*	*Avge*
C. Rushworth	RFM	104	14	358	16	7-108	1	22.37
M. E. T. Salisbury	RFM	53.1	14	148	5	4-57	0	29.60
B. A. Raine	RFM	105.1	25	308	9	3-53	0	34.22
B. A. Carse	RF	49	4	245	3	2-110	0	81.66
P. Coughlin	RFM	78.4	9	304	3	3-46	0	101.33

Also bowled: G. J. Harte (RM) 50.4–5–206–2; A. Z. Lees (LB) 2–0–19–1; M. J. Potts (RFM) 36–9–94–2; S. W. Poynter (OB) 4–0–21–0; C. T. Steel (LB) 2–0–8–1.

LEADING VITALITY BLAST AVERAGES (70 runs/10 overs)

Batting	*Runs*	*HS*	*Avge*	*SR*	*Ct/St*
G. Clark	261	68	29.00	**171.71**	5
B. A. Carse	172	35	28.66	**154.95**	2
B. A. Raine	167	71	33.40	**146.49**	1
P. Coughlin	78	22*	15.60	**132.20**	2
A. Z. Lees	365	77*	52.14	**125.86**	4
D. G. Bedingham	97	33	13.85	**108.98**	7/1
F. Behardien	71	26	14.20	**87.65**	1

Bowling	*W*	*BB*	*Avge*	*ER*
S. Steel	6	3-20	29.16	**7.29**
M. J. Potts	13	3-8	18.07	**7.34**
L. Trevaskis	10	2-17	25.40	**7.69**
B. A. Carse	3	1-18	66.33	**7.96**
N. J. Rimmington	9	2-31	29.22	**8.76**
P. Coughlin	13	3-22	16.23	**10.55**

FIRST-CLASS COUNTY RECORDS

Highest score for	273	M. L. Love v Hampshire at Chester-le-Street	2003
Highest score against	501*	B. C. Lara (Warwickshire) at Birmingham	1994
Leading run-scorer	12,030	P. D. Collingwood (avge 33.98)	1996–2018
Best bowling for	10-47	O. D. Gibson v Hampshire at Chester-le-Street	2007
Best bowling against	9-34	J. A. R. Harris (Middlesex) at Lord's	2015
Leading wicket-taker	527	G. Onions (avge 25.58)	2004–17
Highest total for	648-5 dec	v Nottinghamshire at Chester-le-Street	2009
Highest total against	810-4 dec	by Warwickshire at Birmingham	1994
Lowest total for	61	v Leicestershire at Leicester	2018
Lowest total against	18	by Durham MCCU at Chester-le-Street	2012

LIST A COUNTY RECORDS

Highest score for	164	B. A. Stokes v Nottinghamshire at Chester-le-St	2014
Highest score against	174	J. M. Bairstow (Yorkshire) at Leeds	2017
Leading run-scorer	6,007	P. D. Collingwood (avge 33.00)	1995–2018
Best bowling for	7-32	S. P. Davis v Lancashire at Chester-le-Street	1983
Best bowling against	6-22	A. Dale (Glamorgan) at Colwyn Bay	1993
Leading wicket-taker	298	N. Killeen (avge 23.96)	1995–2010
Highest total for	353-8	v Nottinghamshire at Chester-le-Street	2014
Highest total against	361-7	by Essex at Chelmsford	1996
Lowest total for	72	v Warwickshire at Birmingham	2002
Lowest total against	63	by Hertfordshire at Darlington	1964

TWENTY20 COUNTY RECORDS

Highest score for	108*	P. D. Collingwood v Worcestershire at Worcester	2017
Highest score against	127	T. Köhler-Cadmore (Worcs) at Worcester	2016
Leading run-scorer	3,206	P. Mustard (avge 25.04, SR 121.99)	2003–16
Best bowling for	5-6	P. D. Collingwood v Northants at Chester-le-St	2011
Best bowling against	5-11	J. W. Shutt (Yorkshire) at Chester-le-Street	2019
Leading wicket-taker	93	G. R. Breese (avge 21.56, ER 6.76)	2004–14
Highest total for	225-2	v Leicestershire at Chester-le-Street	2010
Highest total against	225-6	by Worcestershire at Worcester	2016
Lowest total for	78	v Lancashire at Chester-le-Street	2018
Lowest total against	47	by Northamptonshire at Chester-le-Street	2011

ADDRESS

Emirates Riverside, Chester-le-Street, County Durham DH3 3QR; 0191 387 1717; reception@durhamcricket.co.uk; www.durhamcricket.co.uk. Twitter: @DurhamCricket.

OFFICIALS

Captain E. J. H. Eckersley
(Twenty20) N. J. Rimmington
Director of cricket M. J. North
High performance coach J. E. C. Franklin
Academy director J. B. Windows

Chairman Lord Botham
Chief operating officer R. Dowson
Chief executive T. J. Bostock
Head groundsman V. Demain
Scorer W. R. Dobson

DURHAM v YORKSHIRE

At Chester-le-Street, August 1–4. Yorkshire won by six wickets. Yorkshire 19pts, Durham 3pts. Toss: Durham. First-class debut: J. W. Shutt. County debuts: D. G. Bedingham, S. R. Dickson; D. J. Malan.

A brilliant burst from Fisher set up Yorkshire's victory. When he came on, Durham were 215 for three in their second innings, leading by 119, and Lees had just reached a century against his old team. But Fisher, armed with the second new ball, bowled him and Burnham, then trapped Eckersley and Coughlin, in a devastating spell of 6–3–9–4. In all, the final seven fell for 45, and Yorkshire required only 171. Rushworth gave Durham hope, extracting the three men he needed for 500 first-class wickets (495 for the county, five for MCC). But Malan and Brook took control; after a last-morning washout, they raced to the target, which Brook brought up with a four and two sixes. Yorkshire had taken the early advantage, bowling out Durham for 103 on the opening day. The home attack fought back, depriving them of a batting point and keeping the deficit to 96, which looked less daunting when Lees and David Bedingham – one of two South Africans on county debut, along with Sean Dickson – guided them past 200 in a stand worth 136. But once Patterson parted them, the stage was set for Fisher.

Close of play: first day, Yorkshire 84-4 (Malan 14, Brook 2); second day, Durham 106-2 (Lees 58, Bedingham 18); third day, Yorkshire 103-3 (Malan 50, Brook 23).

Durham

First innings		Second innings	
A. Z. Lees lbw b Fisher	8	– b Fisher	106
S. R. Dickson c Tattersall b Coad	11	– c Tattersall b Patterson	14
C. T. Steel c Tattersall b Thompson	9	– run out (Coad/Tattersall)	11
D. G. Bedingham c Fisher b Thompson	8	– lbw b Patterson	77
G. J. Harte not out	33	– not out	29
J. T. A. Burnham b Coad	7	– b Fisher	2
*†E. J. H. Eckersley lbw b Patterson	6	– lbw b Fisher	0
P. Coughlin lbw b Thompson	3	– lbw b Fisher	0
B. A. Raine lbw b Fisher	7	– b Thompson	0
M. J. Potts c Fisher b Coad	10	– c Köhler-Cadmore b Thompson	0
C. Rushworth c and b Coad	0	– lbw b Patterson	14
Lb 1	1	B 4, lb 9	13
1/13 (1) 2/25 (2) 3/34 (3) (58.4 overs)	103	1/47 (2) 2/71 (3) (109.2 overs)	266
4/41 (4) 5/61 (6) 6/68 (7)		3/207 (4) 4/221 (1)	
7/77 (8) 8/86 (9) 9/103 (10) 10/103 (11)		5/225 (6) 6/225 (7) 7/229 (8)	
		8/231 (9) 9/239 (10) 10/266 (11)	

Coad 16.4–6–23–4; Fisher 16–5–43–2; Patterson 13–3–20–1; Thompson 13–6–16–3. *Second innings*—Coad 25–12–23–0; Fisher 26–9–54–4; Patterson 24.2–5–62–3; Thompson 19–2–53–2; Shutt 8–0–41–0; Brook 6–1–17–0; Lyth 1–0–3–0.

Yorkshire

First innings		Second innings	
A. Lyth c Dickson b Rushworth	10	– lbw b Rushworth	4
T. Köhler-Cadmore b Raine	41	– lbw b Rushworth	24
W. A. R. Fraine lbw b Coughlin	14	– lbw b Rushworth	0
D. J. Malan c Eckersley b Rushworth	30	– c Dickson b Lees	73
*S. A. Patterson lbw b Coughlin	0		
H. C. Brook c Burnham b Potts	41	– (5) not out	66
†J. A. Tattersall b Raine	17	– (6) not out	2
J. A. Thompson lbw b Raine	1		
M. D. Fisher c Lees b Rushworth	1		
B. O. Coad c Eckersley b Coughlin	28		
J. W. Shutt not out	7		
B 4, lb 5	9	Lb 3	3
1/32 (1) 2/66 (2) 3/68 (3) (62.4 overs)	199	1/4 (1) (4 wkts, 44.4 overs)	172
4/68 (5) 5/120 (4) 6/154 (6)		2/4 (3) 3/56 (2)	
7/157 (8) 8/164 (7) 9/164 (9) 10/199 (10)		4/154 (4)	

Rushworth 17–1–69–3; Potts 9–3–19–1; Raine 20–8–53–3; Harte 2–1–3–0; Coughlin 14.4–3–46–3. *Second innings*—Rushworth 15–3–52–3; Potts 6–2–25–0; Raine 14–3–32–0; Coughlin 8–2–31–0; Lees 1–0–12–1; Harte 0.4–0–17–0.

Umpires: G. D. Lloyd and N. Pratt. Referee: J. J. Whitaker.

DURHAM v LANCASHIRE

At Chester-le-Street, August 8–10. Lancashire won by an innings and 18 runs. Lancashire 22pts, Durham 3pts. Toss: Durham. County debut: L. Wood.

Lancashire secured an emphatic win in eight sessions. The in-form Lees batted nearly four and a half hours for 66, but the next-best score in Durham's first innings was 37 from Extras. Gleeson, who had been part of England's white-ball squad in Southampton, collected three for 32 on his return to county cricket. In Lancashire's reply, Bohannon provided a platform for aggressive lower-order contributions from Luke Wood, making his debut for his fourth county, and Bailey. A total of 308 gave them three batting points and a lead of 128, and they smelled blood. Now sharing the new ball, Bailey and Wood reduced Durham to 21 for four by lunch – this time, Lees was bowled for a duck. When Hurt hurtled in from the Finchale End to dismiss Eckersley and Carse with consecutive deliveries on his way to a career-best four for 27, it was 49 for seven.

Close of play: first day, Lancashire 33-0 (Jennings 14, Davies 8); second day, Lancashire 284-9 (Bailey 18, Gleeson 2).

Durham

A. Z. Lees run out (Vilas/Tattersall)	66	– b Bailey	0
S. R. Dickson c Davies b Bailey	2	– c Davies b Bailey	3
C. T. Steel lbw b Wood	1	– lbw b Wood	0
D. G. Bedingham c Davies b Gleeson	5	– lbw b Bailey	25
G. J. Harte run out (Balderson)	18	– c Croft b Wood	3
J. T. A. Burnham lbw b Gleeson	5	– b Hurt	27
*†E. J. H. Eckersley c Jennings b Balderson	8	– c Croft b Hurt	5
B. A. Carse c Vilas b Hurt	11	– c Croft b Hurt	0
B. A. Raine not out	24	– not out	25
M. E. T. Salisbury lbw b Gleeson	1	– c Livingstone b Hurt	0
C. Rushworth c Davies b Livingstone	2	– c Davies b Livingstone	11
B 10, lb 5, nb 22	37	B 4, lb 3, nb 4	11
1/3 (2) 2/14 (3) 3/42 (4) 4/94 (5) 5/111 (6) 6/132 (1) 7/141 (7) 8/165 (8) 9/177 (10) 10/180 (11) (78.3 overs)	180	1/0 (1) 2/3 (2) 3/5 (3) 4/21 (5) 5/35 (4) 6/49 (7) 7/49 (8) 8/78 (6) 9/86 (10) 10/110 (11) (42.1 overs)	110

Bailey 15–8–14–1; Wood 16–4–40–1; Hurt 16–1–44–1; Gleeson 14–4–32–3; Balderson 13–4–26–1; Livingstone 4.3–0–9–1. *Second innings*—Bailey 9–4–11–3; Wood 12–2–31–2; Hurt 10–3–27–4; Gleeson 4–0–20–0; Balderson 5–2–10–0; Livingstone 2.1–0–4–1.

Lancashire

K. K. Jennings c Lees b Rushworth	18
†A. L. Davies c Bedingham b Raine	8
J. J. Bohannon b Salisbury	75
*D. J. Vilas c Dickson b Harte	32
L. S. Livingstone c Bedingham b Raine	23
S. J. Croft lbw b Salisbury	16
G. P. Balderson c Bedingham b Rushworth	11
L. Wood b Salisbury	46
L. J. Hurt c Eckersley b Raine	2
T. E. Bailey not out	38
R. J. Gleeson lbw b Salisbury	6
B 3, lb 5, w 5, nb 20	33
1/33 (2) 2/43 (1) 3/99 (4) 4/136 (5) 5/184 (6) 6/200 (7) 7/241 (3) 8/250 (9) 9/276 (8) 10/308 (11) (105.1 overs)	308

Rushworth 25–6–47–2; Carse 17–1–93–0; Raine 25–7–62–3; Salisbury 23.1–5–57–4; Harte 15–2–41–1.

Umpires: N. A. Mallender and N. Pratt. Referee: S. Cummings.

At Leicester, August 15–18. DURHAM drew with LEICESTERSHIRE.

At Chester-le-Street, August 22–25. DURHAM drew with DERBYSHIRE. *This was officially a home match for Derbyshire.*

At Nottingham, September 6–9. DURHAM drew with NOTTINGHAMSHIRE. *Chris Rushworth becomes the third bowler to take 500 first-class wickets for Durham.*

ESSEX

Harmering it home

PAUL HISCOCK

Essex reinforced their position as county cricket's premier first-class side by winning the inaugural Bob Willis Trophy, to follow the County Championship titles of 2017 and 2019. They had now lost only one of their last 23 four-day games, and took their winning streak at Chelmsford to 11.

Victory by virtue of a first-innings lead over Somerset in the five-day Lord's final meant that Tom Westley – who had taken over as captain from Ryan ten Doeschate – lifted the new trophy. "Given the format, we knew we needed three or four wins to get to the final," said head coach Anthony McGrath. "To win four out of five, with the other rained off – you can't ask for much more." Essex qualified with 90 points, narrowly pipping Yorkshire (87), and behind only Somerset (97), the two other group winners.

Simon Harmer was once again the country's leading wicket-taker, with 38 at 15 apiece in the six BWT matches, eight more than anyone else. With Kolpak contracts ended by Brexit, he simply switched to being an overseas player. It is possible that Harmer – who had contemplated qualifying for England – will return to international cricket with South Africa, since he is eligible again to add to the five Test caps he won in 2015. Still only 32, he is undoubtedly a better bowler now.

He was helped by the club's new-ball pair. Jamie Porter steamed past 350 first-class wickets in only his seventh season, while Sam Cook picked up five for 76 in the first innings of the final. With the Australian Peter Siddle unable to take his place in the seam attack because of the pandemic, Aaron Beard claimed some important wickets.

Alastair Cook continued to flourish, a superb 172 at Lord's – his 67th first-class century – ensuring that vital lead over Somerset. He finished with 563 runs in the BWT, which meant Essex had the competition's top run-scorer too, and looked set to continue for years. Despite the knighthood and 161 England caps, he was still only 35 when the season ended.

Cook was pipped in the averages by wicketkeeper Adam Wheater, who had an excellent all-round season: his determined rearguard on the last day of the final ensured Essex won the trophy. Paul Walter proved a reliable middle-order contributor, although his bowling fell away, while ten Doeschate was as consistent as ever. Dan Lawrence came close to an international call-up, then left the England bubble to bolster the batting in four matches, before eventually making a promising Test debut in Sri Lanka in January 2021. But Nick Browne made little impression, and Westley's only half-century came during a stand of 170 with Cook at Lord's.

It was a less cheerful story in the T20 Blast. Essex never threatened to repeat their 2019 triumph, and were all but eliminated after six matches brought only two points, from a no-result and a tie. In contrast to their red-ball dominance at Chelmsford, they lost all their completed home games. They did manage a couple of late victories, to avoid bottom place in their group, by which time they were trying out youngsters from the Academy, including seamers Ben Allison and Jack Plom, and batsmen Feroze Khushi and Robin Das. Khushi, a Muslim, found himself the unwitting centre of controversy when, during the BWT celebrations on the Lord's balcony, fellow reserve Will Buttleman tipped a bottle of beer over him. Essex swiftly apologised, and introduced a new cultural awareness programme for their players.

Nick Wood, Getty Images

Adam Wheater

Most of the squad will come back in 2021, including ten Doeschate, who agreed a new one-year deal, and turns 41 in June. It is hoped Siddle can take up his spot as a second permitted overseas player, while the South African Cameron Delport's ancestry visa continues to allow him to play as English-qualified; he hoped to return for a third season as a T20 specialist. Batsman Rishi Patel, meanwhile, moved to Leicestershire in search of first-team opportunities.

Off the field, Essex tried several initiatives to help locked-down locals. Former captain Graham Gooch, now an ambassador for the club, joined Harmer and Westley at the Supporting Humanity charity, providing hot meals for vulnerable people and key workers in 13 nearby hospitals. Ronnie Irani, the cricket committee chairman, delivered fruit and vegetables, and other players and coaches made contact with over 1,000 elderly or vulnerable Essex members to check their wellbeing. The young were not forgotten either: junior members received personalised birthday greetings. Essex also launched the "Alternative Cricket Tea Campaign", in support of Chelmsford's food bank, to provide for locals in need.

The pandemic had a huge effect on finances. Players and staff were initially furloughed and, though the players came out of the scheme in July, some staff missed the whole season. "We have to be looking at wage cuts across the board, including players, but hopefully that will be a temporary measure," said Derek Bowden, who stepped down as chief executive in October, after eight seasons in the post. "We have had to dip into our reserves, and will continue to do so in 2021. We're fortunate that we have such reserves – many counties do not."

> "His batting, like a racehorse being turned into a steeplechaser, was designed for the turf not the air."
> Retirements, page 193

ESSEX RESULTS

Bob Willis Trophy matches – Played 6: Won 4, Drawn 2.
Vitality Blast matches – Played 10: Won 2, Lost 6, Tied 1, No result 1.

Bob Willis Trophy, winners;
Vitality Blast, 5th in South Group.

BOB WILLIS TROPHY AVERAGES

BATTING AND FIELDING

Cap		*Birthplace*	*M*	*I*	*NO*	*R*	*HS*	*100*	*Avge*	*Ct/St*
2020	A. J. A. Wheater	*Leytonstone‡*	6	9	4	291	83*	0	58.20	17/3
2005	†A. N. Cook	*Gloucester*	6	11	1	563	172	2	56.30	10
	†P. I. Walter	*Basildon‡*	5	9	2	266	46	0	38.00	2
2006	R. N. ten Doeschate	*Port Elizabeth, SA*	5	7	0	218	78	0	31.14	0
2017	D. W. Lawrence	*Leytonstone‡*	4	6	1	144	60	0	28.80	0
	F. I. N. Khushi	*Leytonstone‡*	4	5	0	125	66	0	25.00	5
2018	V. Chopra	*Barking‡*	2	4	0	89	41	0	22.25	4
2015	†N. L. J. Browne	*Leytonstone‡*	4	8	0	142	61	0	17.75	4
2013	T. Westley	*Cambridge*	6	11	1	172	51	0	17.20	3
2018	S. R. Harmer††	*Pretoria, SA*	6	9	1	111	32	0	13.87	10
	†A. P. Beard	*Chelmsford‡*	5	6	2	43	17	0	10.75	1
2015	J. A. Porter	*Leytonstone‡*	6	8	4	30	13	0	7.50	3
2020	S. J. Cook	*Chelmsford‡*	5	5	1	26	15*	0	6.50	0

Also batted: M. R. Quinn†† (*Auckland, NZ*) (2 matches) 0, 13.

‡ *Born in Essex.* †† *Other non-England-qualified.*

BOWLING

	Style	*O*	*M*	*R*	*W*	*BB*	*5I*	*Avge*
S. R. Harmer	OB	257.1	81	603	38	8-64	3	15.86
S. J. Cook	RFM	140	39	318	17	5-76	1	18.70
J. A. Porter	RFM	185.5	48	553	27	5-60	1	20.48
A. P. Beard	RFM	78.1	17	265	11	4-21	0	24.09
M. R. Quinn	RFM	55.3	10	156	3	1-19	0	52.00

Also bowled: D. W. Lawrence (OB) 2–1–2–0; R. N. ten Doeschate (RM) 6–0–14–1; P. I. Walter (LM) 15–1–53–0.

LEADING VITALITY BLAST AVERAGES (70 runs/14 overs)

Batting	*Runs*	*HS*	*Avge*	*SR*	*Ct*
P. I. Walter	147	76	21.00	**144.11**	7
T. Westley	191	51	27.28	**137.41**	4
R. N. ten Doeschate	255	52	51.00	**137.09**	3
D. W. Lawrence	190	81	27.14	**136.69**	3
C. S. Delport	222	64	24.66	**133.73**	2
S. R. Harmer	73	23	14.60	**121.66**	9
A. J. A. Wheater	135	63	33.75	**118.42**	0
V. Chopra	84	41	16.80	**107.69**	2

Bowling	*W*	*BB*	*Avge*	*ER*
P. I. Walter	7	2-13	16.14	**6.64**
S. R. Harmer	10	2-21	28.10	**7.20**
J. H. Plom	7	3-32	18.42	**7.74**
A. S. S. Nijjar	8	3-22	31.37	**7.84**
M. R. Quinn	10	2-24	21.30	**7.93**
D. W. Lawrence	4	2-3	28.00	**8.00**
C. S. Delport	4	2-22	29.25	**8.16**
S. Snater	4	2-22	32.00	**8.53**

FIRST-CLASS COUNTY RECORDS

Highest score for	343*	P. A. Perrin v Derbyshire at Chesterfield	1904
Highest score against	332	W. H. Ashdown (Kent) at Brentwood	1934
Leading run-scorer	30,701	G. A. Gooch (avge 51.77)	1973–97
Best bowling for	10-32	H. Pickett v Leicestershire at Leyton	1895
Best bowling against	10-40	E. G. Dennett (Gloucestershire) at Bristol	1906
Leading wicket-taker	1,610	T. P. B. Smith (avge 26.68)	1929–51
Highest total for	761-6 dec	v Leicestershire at Chelmsford	1990
Highest total against	803-4 dec	by Kent at Brentwood	1934
Lowest total for	20	v Lancashire at Chelmsford	2013
Lowest total against	14	by Surrey at Chelmsford	1983

LIST A COUNTY RECORDS

Highest score for	201*	R. S. Bopara v Leicestershire at Leicester	2008
Highest score against	158*	M. W. Goodwin (Sussex) at Chelmsford	2006
Leading run-scorer	16,536	G. A. Gooch (avge 40.93)	1973–97
Best bowling for	8-26	K. D. Boyce v Lancashire at Manchester	1971
Best bowling against	7-29	D. A. Payne (Gloucestershire) at Chelmsford	2010
Leading wicket-taker	616	J. K. Lever (avge 19.04)	1968–89
Highest total for	391-5	v Surrey at The Oval	2008
Highest total against	373-5	by Nottinghamshire at Chelmsford	2017
Lowest total for	57	v Lancashire at Lord's	1996
Lowest total against	41	by Middlesex at Westcliff-on-Sea	1972
	41	by Shropshire at Wellington	1974

TWENTY20 COUNTY RECORDS

Highest score for	152*	G. R. Napier v Sussex at Chelmsford	2008
Highest score against	153*	L. J. Wright (Sussex) at Chelmsford	2014
Leading run-scorer	3,405	R. S. Bopara (avge 28.85, SR 129.36)	2003–19
Best bowling for	6-16	T. G. Southee v Glamorgan at Chelmsford	2011
Best bowling against	5-11	Mushtaq Ahmed (Sussex) at Hove	2005
	5-11	T. G. Helm (Middlesex) at Lord's	2017
Leading wicket-taker	126	R. S. Bopara (avge 25.66, ER 7.57)	2003–19
Highest total for	242-3	v Sussex at Chelmsford	2008
Highest total against	226-3	by Sussex at Chelmsford	2014
Lowest total for	74	v Middlesex at Chelmsford	2013
Lowest total against	82	by Gloucestershire at Chelmsford	2011

ADDRESS

The Cloudfm County Ground, New Writtle Street, Chelmsford CM2 0PG; 01245 252420; administration@essexcricket.co.uk; www.essexcricket.org.uk. Twitter: @EssexCricket.

OFFICIALS

Captain T. Westley
(Twenty20) S. R. Harmer
Head coach A. McGrath
President D. L. Acfield
Chairman 2020 J. L. Faragher

Chief executive 2020 D. W. Bowden
Executive chairman 2021 J. L. Faragher
Chairman, cricket advisory group R. C. Irani
Head groundsman S. G. Kerrison
Scorer A. E. Choat

ESSEX v KENT

At Chelmsford, August 1–4. Essex won by two wickets. Essex 21pts, Kent 7pts. Toss: Kent. First-class debut: F. I. N. Khushi. County debuts: Hamidullah Qadri, J. A. Leaning.

Kent were in charge for the first half of an exciting match, before the pendulum swung dramatically in the second innings. A superb 140 from Kuhn, his maiden first-class century for Kent, and his partnerships of 150 with Robinson and 80 with Stevens had ensured an imposing first-day total. Although Kuhn went without adding to his overnight score, Kent's bowlers secured a lead of 89, which would have been more but for tenacious efforts from Browne and ten Doeschate. The game changed on the third afternoon, as Kent's last six wickets tumbled for 26, Harmer filleting the middle order. Chasing 202, Essex were on course while Alastair Cook and the 21-year-old debutant Feroze Khushi were adding 86. But Thomas – who missed the entire 2019 season after knee surgery – set nerves jangling with four wickets in 17 balls. An hour of application, however, from Wheater and Sam Cook, on his 23rd birthday, carried Essex to victory. Before the match, the players observed a minute's silence for Covid-19 victims, and then applauded key workers; after the umpires called play, both squads took a knee in solidarity with the Black Lives Matter movement.

Close of play: first day, Kent 344-6 (Kuhn 140, O'Riordan 20); second day, Essex 179-5 (ten Doeschate 22, Wheater 24); third day, Essex 0-0 (Porter 0, Browne 0).

Kent

*D. J. Bell-Drummond lbw b S. J. Cook	6	– c Wheater b Porter	5
J. M. Cox c Wheater b Porter	15	– b S. J. Cook	29
J. A. Leaning c Khushi b S. J. Cook	0	– lbw b S. J. Cook	6
†O. G. Robinson c Wheater b Porter	78	– c Harmer b Quinn	14
H. G. Kuhn lbw b Porter	140	– c Browne b Harmer	17
D. I. Stevens c Browne b Porter	36	– c Westley b Harmer	13
G. Stewart lbw b ten Doeschate	37	– c Wheater b Porter	7
M. K. O'Riordan not out	42	– lbw b Harmer	1
M. E. Milnes c Porter b Harmer	19	– c Khushi b Harmer	5
Hamidullah Qadri c Chopra b Harmer	0	– c Wheater b S. J. Cook	0
I. A. A. Thomas c Harmer b Quinn	0	– not out	3
Lb 10, nb 4	14	B 8, nb 4	12
1/15 (1) 2/23 (2) 3/23 (3) 4/173 (4) 5/253 (6) 6/306 (7) 7/344 (5) 8/381 (9) 9/386 (10) 10/387 (11) (104.3 overs)	387	1/6 (1) 2/13 (3) 3/36 (4) 4/65 (5) 5/86 (6) 6/95 (7) 7/100 (8) 8/100 (2) 9/100 (10) 10/112 (9) (49.1 overs)	112

Porter 26–4–107–4; S. J. Cook 21–3–70–2; Quinn 23.3–1–76–1; Harmer 28–1–110–2; ten Doeschate 6–0–14–1. *Second innings*—Porter 12–5–31–2; S. J. Cook 10–2–19–3; Quinn 9–5–19–1; Harmer 18.1–5–35–4.

Essex

N. L. J. Browne b Stevens	61	– (2) c Stevens b Hamidullah Qadri	25
A. N. Cook lbw b Milnes	8	– (3) lbw b Thomas	66
*T. Westley c Kuhn b Stevens	13	– (4) c Robinson b Stewart	0
V. Chopra b O'Riordan	41	– (5) c Robinson b Stewart	9
F. I. N. Khushi c Cox b O'Riordan	2	– (6) c Robinson b Thomas	45
R. N. ten Doeschate c Leaning b Milnes	78	– (7) lbw b Thomas	5
†A. J. A. Wheater run out (Kuhn)	37	– (8) not out	26
S. R. Harmer lbw b O'Riordan	29	– (9) c Robinson b Thomas	0
S. J. Cook c O'Riordan b Milnes	8	– (10) not out	15
J. A. Porter not out	2	– (1) c Bell-Drummond b Stewart	3
M. R. Quinn c Kuhn b Milnes	0		
B 4, lb 3, nb 12	19	Nb 8	8
1/19 (2) 2/41 (3) 3/120 (4) 4/124 (5) 5/144 (1) 6/213 (7) 7/281 (8) 8/289 (6) 9/298 (9) 10/298 (11) (108.2 overs)	298	1/11 (1) 2/48 (2) 3/49 (4) 4/61 (5) 5/147 (3) 6/152 (6) 7/171 (7) 8/171 (9) (8 wkts, 69.4 overs)	202

Milnes 20.2–8–46–4; Stevens 27–9–57–2; Stewart 15–4–39–0; Hamidullah Qadri 14–3–34–0; Thomas 7–1–42–0; O'Riordan 23–3–71–3; Leaning 2–1–2–0. *Second innings*—Milnes 15–4–32–0; Stevens 15–1–27–0; Stewart 13–2–48–3; O'Riordan 8–0–39–0; Hamidullah Qadri 10.4–2–24–1; Thomas 8–1–32–4.

Umpires: N. L. Bainton and B. J. Debenham. Referee: S. J. Davis.

ESSEX v SURREY

At Chelmsford, August 8–11. Essex won by 169 runs. Essex 21pts, Surrey 3pts. Toss: Essex. First-class debut: A. A. P. Atkinson. County debut: A. W. Finch.

A towering performance from Harmer, who became the first bowler to take a third career-haul of 14 wickets or more since Derek Underwood in 1970, spun Essex to an emphatic victory. Only Jamie Smith, who top-scored in Surrey's second innings, was not dismissed by him. Essex had begun uncertainly, losing Browne in the debutant seamer Gus Atkinson's fifth over, and slipping to 98 for four before a mature maiden half-century from Khushi and 52 from Wheater helped them pass 250. Clarke, who took three late wickets, conceded just one boundary in 21 overs. Surrey were severely understrength: with 14 players absent through injury, international calls or travel restrictions, they included loanees Laurie Evans (Sussex), playing his first match for them since 2010 and Adam Finch (from Worcestershire). Patel fell in the first over and Borthwick in the third, both to Porter, before Harmer took control. Jacks was dropped three times in a spirited 70, but there were six single-figure dismissals in a disappointing total. The sun was blazing – the temperature hit 33°C – but Essex made heavy weather of building on a lead of 75: five players reached 33, but none 50. Still, Surrey needed an unlikely 337, and Harmer proved irresistible again. He took the first six wickets, including Evans, stumped for a second-ball duck, before catching the seventh (Smith) with a stunning low dive at second slip. Harmer finished with eight for 64, bowling 30 overs unchanged on the final day, despite a muscle strain. "I'll take that catch and an eight-for any day," he said. "When the wicket is turning, I'm going to cash in as much as I can."

Close of play: first day, Essex 253-7 (Harmer 16, Beard 1); second day, Essex 13-0 (Browne 4, A. N. Cook 8); third day, Surrey 27-1 (Patel 10).

Essex

N. L. J. Browne c Stoneman b Atkinson	8	– c Smith b Finch	4
A. N. Cook c Clarke b Virdi	42	– lbw b Atkinson	42
*T. Westley c Smith b Taylor	10	– c Borthwick b Virdi	34
V. Chopra c Borthwick b Taylor	0	– c Patel b Finch	39
F. I. N. Khushi c Patel b Virdi	66	– c Patel b Clarke	11
P. I. Walter b Borthwick	33	– b Virdi	46
†A. J. A. Wheater c Evans b Clarke	52	– c Borthwick b Finch	33
S. R. Harmer c Patel b Atkinson	19	– lbw b Virdi	14
A. P. Beard c Smith b Clarke	1	– c Smith b Virdi	17
S. J. Cook lbw b Clarke	3	– lbw b Finch	0
J. A. Porter not out	0	– not out	0
Lb 6, nb 22	28	B 2, lb 3, nb 16	21
1/21 (1) 2/49 (3) 3/49 (4) 4/98 (2) 5/165 (5) 6/222 (6) 7/248 (7) 8/256 (9) 9/262 (10) 10/262 (8) (95.4 overs)	262	1/22 (1) 2/69 (2) 3/105 (3) 4/122 (5) 5/167 (4) 6/209 (6) 7/237 (8) 8/255 (7) 9/255 (10) 10/261 (9) (75.4 overs)	261

Finch 17–3–44–0; Atkinson 14.4–2–57–2; Clarke 21–6–26–3; Taylor 8–2–31–2; Patel 6–0–17–0; Virdi 24–5–65–2; Borthwick 5–1–16–1. *Second innings*—Clarke 7–1–17–1; Virdi 27.4–2–85–4; Finch 12–1–38–4; Atkinson 11–0–45–1; Taylor 10–0–42–0; Borthwick 2–0–12–0; Jacks 6–0–17–0.

Surrey

*M. D. Stoneman c A. N. Cook b Harmer	5	– lbw b Harmer	16
R. S. Patel c Harmer b Porter	0	– c Porter b Harmer	19
S. G. Borthwick c Khushi b Porter	0	– c Wheater b Harmer	5
W. G. Jacks c Beard b Harmer	70	– lbw b Harmer	21
†J. L. Smith b Porter	8	– c Harmer b Beard	45
L. J. Evans b Porter	41	– st Wheater b Harmer	0
R. Clarke c Chopra b Harmer	15	– c Chopra b Harmer	14
A. A. P. Atkinson c Chopra b Harmer	1	– b Harmer	15
A. W. Finch c Westley b Harmer	6	– not out	7
J. P. A. Taylor c Browne b Harmer	22	– c Khushi b Beard	0
G. S. Virdi not out	6	– c Porter b Harmer	12
B 4, lb 6, w 1, nb 2	13	B 5, lb 4, nb 4	13
1/1 (2) 2/1 (3) 3/35 (1) 4/54 (5) 5/134 (4) 6/136 (6) 7/137 (8) 8/154 (7) 9/169 (9) 10/187 (10) (75.3 overs)	187	1/27 (1) 2/35 (3) 3/48 (2) 4/99 (4) 5/99 (6) 6/117 (7) 7/141 (5) 8/145 (8) 9/150 (10) 10/167 (11) (75.1 overs)	167

Porter 16–3–53–4; S. J. Cook 13–5–21–0; Harmer 31.3–11–67–6; Beard 12–3–26–0; Walter 3–0–10–0. *Second innings*—Porter 16–5–29–0; S. J. Cook 13–4–21–0; Harmer 34.1–15–64–8; Beard 10–3–33–2; Walter 2–0–11–0.

Umpires: B. J. Debenham and C. M. Watts. Referee: P. M. Such.

At Hove, August 15–18. ESSEX beat SUSSEX by three wickets.

At Arundel, August 22–25. ESSEX drew with HAMPSHIRE. *Only 78 overs are possible.*

ESSEX v MIDDLESEX

At Chelmsford, September 6–8. Essex won by nine wickets. Essex 20pts, Middlesex 3pts. Toss: Middlesex.

Middlesex were rarely in the hunt on a pitch that helped the bowlers, and the match was over inside seven sessions, as Essex ensured their place in the inaugural Bob Willis Trophy final. Fifteen wickets had gone down on the first day – 12 to the seamers, and three to the inevitable Harmer, who extracted turn straight away. Middlesex, with five players whose T20 Blast match at The Oval the previous evening had finished at 9.20, scraped into three figures thanks to 34 from Harris at No. 8; Essex were then rescued from 87 for five by Wheater. He had earlier taken five catches, and now put on 72 with Harmer, after ten Doeschate retired hurt with back trouble (he later resumed with a runner). Wheater's 83, his highest first-class score against county opposition for three years, stretched the lead to 98, and Middlesex lost five wickets clearing the deficit, with Beard taking three for four on the way to career-best figures. Although Simpson hung around for more than two hours, the eventual target was a modest 53; Robson and Gubbins bowled in their caps.

Close of play: first day, Essex 108-5 (ten Doeschate 28, Wheater 18); second day, Middlesex 123-6 (Simpson 16, Harris 3).

Middlesex

	First innings		Second innings	
S. D. Robson b Porter	15	–	(2) c Harmer b S. J. Cook	6
M. D. E. Holden c Wheater b S. J. Cook	0	–	(1) b Beard	37
N. R. T. Gubbins lbw b Porter	2	–	lbw b Harmer	16
*S. S. Eskinazi c Wheater b S. J. Cook	15	–	b Beard	5
R. G. White c A. N. Cook b Porter	12	–	lbw b Harmer	23
M. K. Andersson c Khushi b Harmer	5	–	c Harmer b Beard	3
†J. A. Simpson c Wheater b Harmer	12	–	not out	26
J. A. R. Harris lbw b S. J. Cook	34	–	b S. J. Cook	3
B. C. Cullen c Wheater b Harmer	11	–	c Wheater b S. J. Cook	4
T. N. Walallawita c Wheater b S. J. Cook	4	–	b Beard	7
T. J. Murtagh not out	11	–	st Wheater b Harmer	5
Lb 13, nb 4	17		Lb 15	15
1/2 (2) 2/5 (3) 3/18 (1) 4/38 (4) 5/50 (6) 6/56 (5) 7/76 (7) 8/110 (8) 9/120 (10) 10/138 (9) (53.3 overs)	138		1/29 (2) 2/58 (3) 3/63 (4) 4/70 (1) 5/84 (6) 6/120 (5) 7/123 (8) 8/133 (9) 9/143 (10) 10/150 (11) (69.5 overs)	150

Porter 15–3–55–3; S. J. Cook 15–5–27–4; Beard 5–2–9–0; Harmer 18.3–5–34–3. *Second innings*—Porter 10–2–32–0; S. J. Cook 20–8–28–3; Harmer 28.5–12–54–3; Beard 10–3–21–4; Lawrence 1–1–0–0.

Essex

	First innings		Second innings	
P. I. Walter b Harris	43	–	not out	20
A. N. Cook c Eskinazi b Cullen	6	–	b Murtagh	21
*T. Westley b Murtagh	8	–	not out	10
D. W. Lawrence c Simpson b Murtagh	0			
F. I. N. Khushi lbw b Harris	1			
R. N. ten Doeschate c Simpson b Andersson	43			
†A. J. A. Wheater not out	83			
S. R. Harmer lbw b Andersson	32			
A. P. Beard c Eskinazi b Andersson	1			
S. J. Cook c Robson b Andersson	0			
J. A. Porter c Simpson b Murtagh	3			
B 6, lb 5, w 1, nb 4	16		B 1, lb 1	2
1/18 (2) 2/35 (3) 3/43 (4) 4/44 (5) 5/87 (1) 6/194 (8) 7/203 (9) 8/203 (10) 9/227 (6) 10/236 (11) (73 overs)	236		1/41 (2) (1 wkt, 13.5 overs)	53

In the first innings ten Doeschate, when 31, retired hurt at 122-5 and resumed at 203-8.

Murtagh 19–4–50–3; Cullen 13–2–46–1; Walallawita 18–7–30–0; Harris 12–1–61–2; Andersson 11–0–38–4. *Second innings*—Murtagh 6–1–17–1; Andersson 3–0–14–0; Cullen 3–1–13–0; Robson 1–0–6–0; Gubbins 0.5–0–1–0.

Umpires: P. R. Pollard and R. J. Warren. Referee: P. M. Such.

At Lord's, September 23–27. ESSEX drew with SOMERSET. *Essex win the trophy by virtue of a first-innings lead, set up by 172 from Alastair Cook* *(**report on page 406**).*

GLAMORGAN

Not enough Cookes

EDWARD BEVAN

There was little to savour from Glamorgan's performances after the season finally got under way in August. They finished bottom of their Bob Willis Trophy group, losing two matches, and might have lost the other three but for the weather and an over-cautious declaration. They were similarly lacklustre in the Vitality Blast, before three late victories brightened the mood.

The main problem lay in the batting. Glamorgan had relied heavily on the Australian Marnus Labuschagne in 2019, and in his absence there was rarely anyone to back up the captain, Chris Cooke, although Billy Root did manage a century against Worcestershire. It meant Glamorgan were seldom in a position to dictate terms. Only in the final match, against Warwickshire, did they take a first-innings lead – yet still ended up hanging on for a draw, nine down. They were thrashed by Somerset in the first game, and would surely have lost the second had Worcestershire not batted on after lunch on the final day to set an improbable 358 in 51 overs. Glamorgan were soon five for three, but were saved by Cooke's three-hour 74.

They were fortunate to survive against Gloucestershire after the first day was washed out; then came further defeat, at Northampton, though not before two rousing rearguards. In the first innings, Callum Taylor, a 22-year-old all-rounder from Newport making his first-class debut, was joined by No. 11 Michael Hogan at 135 for nine. They added 124, with Taylor making 106 from 94 balls, including six sixes. In the second, Marchant de Lange – entering at a calamitous 60 for eight – went even quicker, reaching his maiden hundred from just 62 balls, the fastest in Glamorgan's history, beating Gary Butcher (64 balls) against Oxford University in 1997. De Lange and Dan Douthwaite put on 168 in 19.3 overs. Despite these stunning efforts, Glamorgan lost again. It was reassuring that Labuschagne was scheduled to return in 2021.

The bowling attack were no more than adequate. Timm van der Gugten was leading wicket-taker across the formats, with 26, though Hogan, whose testimonial was ruined by Covid-19 (and deferred by a year, even though he will be 40 in May 2021), claimed his 600th first-class wicket.

Colin Ingram, stuck in South Africa, was a notable absentee in the Blast (though he hoped to be available in 2021), while all-rounder David Lloyd broke his foot in a pre-season game; he did return for the last five T20 matches, after which Glamorgan's fortunes improved. Lloyd and fellow opener Nick Selman both hit a half-century, while Andrew Balbirnie, the Ireland captain, proved a shrewd signing: he was the leading run-scorer with 255, and just missed a century against Gloucestershire. He had 98 when the last over started, but Douthwaite was on strike until the last ball, when Balbirnie could manage only a single.

Head coach Matthew Maynard was often critical of the fielding, and made a plea for a specialist coach after Somerset's Babar Azam was dropped twice during a T20 century for Somerset. In the present financial climate, however, he is unlikely to get his wish. The squad were trimmed in the autumn: youngsters Connor Brown, Kieran Bull and Owen Morgan were released, while 37-year-old all-rounder Graham Wagg reluctantly departed after ten years in Wales. Another all-rounder, Craig Meschede, was forced to retire by a shoulder injury. Then came news that de Lange, who had been playing courtesy of his wife's British passport, had joined Somerset as an overseas player. In October, the county signed seam-bowling all-rounder Michael Neser. The future of Doncaster-born batsman Charlie Hemphrey, though, was in doubt after the ECB ruled he was not qualified to represent England because he had gained Australian residency a few years earlier.

Harry Trump, Getty Images

Chris Cooke

Hugh Morris, Glamorgan's chief executive, was not alone in calling the 2020 season "extraordinary". He thanked members who waived subscription refunds, saving the club £120,000. Much of that was invested in the live-streaming service, which drew 587,000 viewers and peaked at 21,000 for the T20 Blast game against Somerset at Sophia Gardens. More gloomily, Morris reported that conference sales and bookings for Christmas 2020 were zero. But somehow he kept the bank happy, and was investigating the possibility of further grants from Sport Wales.

Not long after the season ended, he had to contend with a newspaper story about Mohsin Arif, who played two Second XI games for Glamorgan in 2005, and Imran Hassan, who last appeared for the Seconds in 2016. They accused the club of racism, with Arif claiming coaches had lost interest in him and other non-white cricketers. Glamorgan have two British Asian members on their board, and quickly issued a statement saying they were "obviously saddened by Mohsin's and Imran's experiences, and are actively taking steps… to make cricket more accessible, inclusive and diverse for all". The club set up a working group, which included Hassan.

On April 5, Glamorgan lost one of their greatest all-rounders, when Peter Walker died at the age of 84. He played over 500 matches for them, and three Tests for England in 1960. There was no public funeral, but the club said there would be a memorial service when restrictions were lifted.

There was one morsel of good news. In June, Alan Jones, a long-time team-mate of Walker, was finally awarded his England cap, 50 years after his only appearance, against the Rest of the World team which stepped in after the proposed South African tour was cancelled. The 1970 matches were marketed as Tests at the time, but subsequently deemed unofficial, leaving Jones out in the cold. His cap was presented by England captain Joe Root during a conference call on Zoom with ECB officials and former Glamorgan players.

GLAMORGAN RESULTS

Bob Willis Trophy matches – Played 5: Lost 2, Drawn 3.
Vitality Blast matches – Played 9: Won 4, Lost 5. Abandoned 1.

Bob Willis Trophy, 6th in Central Group;
Vitality Blast, 5th in Central Group.

BOB WILLIS TROPHY AVERAGES

BATTING AND FIELDING

Cap		*Birthplace*	*M*	*I*	*NO*	*R*	*HS*	*100*	*Avge*	*Ct/St*
	C. Z. Taylor	*Newport‡*	2	4	0	153	106	1	38.25	0
2019	M. de Lange††	*Tzaneen, SA*	3	5	1	131	113	1	32.75	2
2016	C. B. Cooke	*Johannesburg, SA*	5	10	1	294	82	0	32.66	16/2
	†W. T. Root	*Sheffield*	5	10	1	286	118	1	31.77	1
2013	M. G. Hogan††	*Newcastle, Aus*	4	7	4	78	33*	0	26.00	1
2018	T. van der Gugten††	*Sydney, Australia*	4	7	3	98	30*	0	24.50	3
	N. J. Selman	*Brisbane, Australia*	5	10	0	215	73	0	21.50	10
2013	G. G. Wagg	*Rugby*	3	6	1	100	54	0	20.00	3
	D. A. Douthwaite	*Kingston-u-Thames*	5	10	1	160	86	0	17.77	3
	K. S. Carlson	*Cardiff‡*	4	8	0	109	79	0	13.62	2
	T. N. Cullen	*Perth, Australia*	3	6	0	80	26	0	13.33	6
	†J. M. Cooke	*Hemel Hempstead*	2	4	0	48	23	0	12.00	1
	C. R. Hemphrey††	*Doncaster*	3	6	0	62	20	0	10.33	3
	K. A. Bull	*Haverfordwest‡*	4	8	1	50	23	0	7.14	1

Also batted: L. J. Carey (*Carmarthen‡*) (1 match) 23, 11 (1 ct); A. O. Morgan (*Swansea‡*) (1 match) 28, 0; R. A. J. Smith (*Glasgow*) (1 match) 23, 3.

‡ *Born in Wales.* †† *Other non-England-qualified.*

BOWLING

	Style	*O*	*M*	*R*	*W*	*BB*	*5I*	*Avge*
R. A. J. Smith	RM	14	4	41	3	3-41	0	13.66
M. de Lange	RF	81.2	17	218	9	4-84	0	24.22
G. G. Wagg	SLA/LM	73	14	272	11	3-38	0	24.72
L. J. Carey	RFM	24.5	4	82	3	3-54	0	27.33
T. van der Gugten	RFM	119	31	362	12	3-45	0	30.16
D. A. Douthwaite	RFM	121.1	16	473	14	3-42	0	33.78
M. G. Hogan	RFM	139	32	397	8	3-59	0	49.62
K. A. Bull	OB	102.3	4	462	9	3-112	0	51.33

Also bowled: K. S. Carlson (OB) 1–0–2–0; C. R. Hemphrey (OB) 9–0–37–0; A. O. Morgan (SLA) 11.5–0–43–1; C. Z. Taylor (OB) 26–2–81–2.

LEADING VITALITY BLAST AVERAGES (60 runs/10 overs)

Batting	*Runs*	*HS*	*Avge*	*SR*	*Ct/St*
D. A. Douthwaite	75	23*	18.75	**178.57**	2
A. Balbirnie	255	99*	36.42	**144.88**	3
D. L. Lloyd	160	56	32.00	**139.13**	1
M. de Lange	68	28*	17.00	**128.30**	2
N. J. Selman	176	78	29.33	**123.94**	0
C. B. Cooke	221	72	31.57	**123.46**	6/3
C. Z. Taylor	76	23	12.66	**84.44**	4

Bowling	*W*	*BB*	*Avge*	*ER*
P. Sisodiya	10	3-26	23.20	**6.44**
T. van der Gugten	14	3-17	14.92	**7.46**
M. de Lange	5	2-23	33.60	**7.75**
R. A. J. Smith	5	2-13	35.60	**8.09**
A. G. Salter	10	4-20	29.30	**8.13**
G. G. Wagg	3	3-34	47.66	**8.93**

FIRST-CLASS COUNTY RECORDS

Highest score for	309*	S. P. James v Sussex at Colwyn Bay	2000
Highest score against	322*	M. B. Loye (Northamptonshire) at Northampton	1998
Leading run-scorer	34,056	A. Jones (avge 33.03)	1957–83
Best bowling for	10-51	J. Mercer v Worcestershire at Worcester	1936
Best bowling against	10-18	G. Geary (Leicestershire) at Pontypridd	1929
Leading wicket-taker	2,174	D. J. Shepherd (avge 20.95)	1950–72
Highest total for	718-3 dec	v Sussex at Colwyn Bay	2000
Highest total against	750	by Northamptonshire at Cardiff	2019
Lowest total for	22	v Lancashire at Liverpool	1924
Lowest total against	33	by Leicestershire at Ebbw Vale	1965

LIST A COUNTY RECORDS

Highest score for	169*	J. A. Rudolph v Sussex at Hove	2014
Highest score against	268	A. D. Brown (Surrey) at The Oval	2002
Leading run-scorer	12,278	M. P. Maynard (avge 37.66)	1985–2005
Best bowling for	7-16	S. D. Thomas v Surrey at Swansea	1998
Best bowling against	7-30	M. P. Bicknell (Surrey) at The Oval	1999
Leading wicket-taker	356	R. D. B. Croft (avge 31.96)	1989–2012
Highest total for	429	v Surrey at The Oval	2002
Highest total against	438-5	by Surrey at The Oval	2002
Lowest total for	42	v Derbyshire at Swansea	1979
Lowest total against	59	by Combined Universities at Cambridge	1983
	59	by Sussex at Hove	1996

TWENTY20 COUNTY RECORDS

Highest score for	116*	I. J. Thomas v Somerset at Taunton	2004
Highest score against	117	M. J. Prior (Sussex) at Hove	2010
Leading run-scorer	2,031	C. A. Ingram (avge 38.32, SR 159.29)	2015–19
Best bowling for	5-14	G. G. Wagg v Worcestershire at Worcester	2013
Best bowling against	6-5	A. V. Suppiah (Somerset) at Cardiff	2011
Leading wicket-taker	100	D. A. Cosker (avge 30.32, ER 7.79)	2003–16
Highest total for	240-3	v Surrey at The Oval	2015
Highest total against	239-5	by Sussex at Hove	2010
Lowest total for	44	v Surrey at The Oval	2019
Lowest total against	81	by Gloucestershire at Bristol	2011

ADDRESS

Sophia Gardens, Cardiff CF11 9XR; 029 2040 9380; info@glamorgancricket. co.uk; www.glamorgancricket.com. Twitter: @GlamCricket.

OFFICIALS

Captain C. B. Cooke
2020 (50-over) D. L. Lloyd
Head coach M. P. Maynard
Director of cricket M. A. Wallace
Head of talent development R. V. Almond

President G. Elias
Chairman G. Williams
Chief executive H. Morris
Head groundsman R. Saxton
Scorer/archivist A. K. Hignell

At Taunton, August 1–4. GLAMORGAN lost to SOMERSET by 289 runs.

At Worcester, August 8–11. GLAMORGAN drew with WORCESTERSHIRE.

GLAMORGAN v GLOUCESTERSHIRE

At Cardiff, August 15–18. Drawn. Glamorgan 11pts, Gloucestershire 11pts. Toss: Gloucestershire. County debut: T. C. Lace.

After a long rearguard to save the game at New Road, Cooke did it again, defying the Gloucestershire attack for four and a half hours, latterly in the company of van der Gugten, described by Cooke as "probably the best No. 10 in the tournament". He had arrived at 138 for eight, with Glamorgan 73 ahead, and 37 overs remaining – but survived for 103 minutes and 86 balls, before Cooke and Gloucestershire captain Dent shook hands with 13 overs left. It was a lucky escape for Glamorgan, who had been polished off for 116 in their first innings after the first day was washed out, and the second cut in half. Seamers Payne, Taylor – both left-armers – and Shaw relished the spicy conditions, combining for nine for 57 from 36.3 overs; on the second day, Glamorgan managed only two boundaries in front of the wicket. In reply, Lace, who had just joined from Middlesex, and Higgins both battled into the forties, but the last five wickets fell for 44, restricting Gloucestershire's advantage to 65. Selman's studious half-century took Glamorgan to 92 for three, but five tumbled for 46, before Cooke and van der Gugten stopped the rot.

Close of play: first day, no play; second day, Glamorgan 80-5 (Root 18, Douthwaite 6); third day, Glamorgan 23-0 (Selman 17, Hemphrey 6).

Glamorgan

N. J. Selman c Hankins b Shaw	11	– lbw b Higgins	55
C. R. Hemphrey b Shaw	12	– lbw b Taylor	6
K. S. Carlson c Roderick b Taylor	8	– b Taylor	0
W. T. Root c Hankins b Payne	19	– c Hankins b Payne	13
*†C. B. Cooke lbw b Payne	4	– not out	59
T. N. Cullen c Roderick b Scott	16	– b Taylor	10
D. A. Douthwaite not out	30	– c Hankins b Payne	1
G. G. Wagg c Higgins b Payne	8	– c Roderick b Payne	0
K. A. Bull c Roderick b Payne	0	– b van Buuren	7
T. van der Gugten lbw b Payne	1	– not out	30
M. de Lange c Roderick b Shaw	2		
Lb 5	5	B 8, lb 2, nb 6	16
1/27 (1) 2/30 (2) 3/42 (3) (59.3 overs)	116	1/23 (2) (8 wkts, 91 overs)	197
4/50 (5) 5/71 (6) 6/81 (4)		2/23 (3) 3/49 (4)	
7/91 (8) 8/91 (9) 9/113 (10) 10/116 (11)		4/92 (1) 5/109 (6)	
		6/117 (7) 7/121 (8) 8/138 (9)	

Payne 17–7–31–5; Higgins 17–5–41–0; Taylor 10–4–13–1; Shaw 9.3–1–13–3; Scott 6–3–13–1. *Second innings*—Payne 20–6–30–3; Higgins 25–11–32–1; Shaw 13–3–49–0; Taylor 19–5–43–3; Charlesworth 3–1–19–0; Scott 5–1–7–0; van Buuren 6–4–7–1.

Gloucestershire

B. G. Charlesworth lbw b Wagg	8	D. A. Payne c and b Bull	8
*C. D. J. Dent c Cooke b van der Gugten	0	J. Shaw c Selman b de Lange	2
G. L. van Buuren b van der Gugten	32	M. D. Taylor not out	0
T. C. Lace c Cooke b Wagg	42	B 6, lb 3, nb 10	19
G. T. Hankins c Selman b Wagg	3		——
R. F. Higgins c de Lange b Bull	48	1/0 (2) 2/31 (1) 3/74 (3) (64.2 overs)	181
†G. H. Roderick c Cooke b Douthwaite	9	4/89 (5) 5/116 (4) 6/137 (7)	
G. F. B. Scott c Cooke b de Lange	10	7/155 (8) 8/173 (6) 9/181 (10) 10/181 (9)	

De Lange 17–4–31–2; van der Gugten 11–4–24–2; Douthwaite 13–2–31–1; Wagg 13–4–38–3; Bull 10.2–0–48–2.

Umpires: I. D. Blackwell and J. H. Evans. Referee: R. M. Ellison.

At Northampton, August 22–25. GLAMORGAN lost to NORTHAMPTONSHIRE by six wickets. *Marchant de Lange enters at 60-8, and hits a 62-ball century, Glamorgan's fastest.*

GLAMORGAN v WARWICKSHIRE

At Cardiff, September 6–9. Drawn. Glamorgan 12pts, Warwickshire 11pts. Toss: Glamorgan.

As neither team were in contention for the final, the interest centred on the last appearance of Warwickshire's Ian Bell, who had announced his retirement the day before the start. "Physically, where I am now, I just don't think I would have got through the whole of next season," he explained. After only 44 runs in his previous six first-class innings, he finished on a high, with an elegant 50 in the first innings, and a silky 90 in the second. There was general disappointment from the 80 or so present – team squads, stewards and media – when he chopped an inducker from van der Gugten into his stumps, ten short of a 58th first-class century. He narrowly missed a win, too: after Mousley's maiden fifty helped set a lofty target of 331 on a pitch that had flattened out, Glamorgan looked safe as Selman settled in for five and a half hours, but a clatter of wickets meant the last pair had to see out the final 17 balls to force another draw. There was another farewell: Welsh umpire Jeff Evans retired after 20 seasons on the first-class list.

Close of play: first day, Glamorgan 4-1 (J. M. Cooke 2, van der Gugten 0); second day, Glamorgan 203; third day, Glamorgan 9-0 (Selman 7, J. M. Cooke 2).

Warwickshire

R. M. Yates c Cullen b Carey	11	– c Selman b van der Gugten	9
*W. M. H. Rhodes b van der Gugten	2	– c Selman b Hogan	30
S. R. Hain lbw b van der Gugten	4	– c Cullen b Douthwaite	65
I. R. Bell c Cullen b Douthwaite	50	– b van der Gugten	90
D. R. Mousley lbw b Carey	31	– c J. M. Cooke b Douthwaite	71
†M. G. K. Burgess c Selman b Carey	13	– c Cullen b Morgan	11
A. T. Thomson c Cullen b van der Gugten	6	– c van der Gugten b Taylor	36
E. A. Brookes c Selman b Douthwaite	6	– not out	15
L. C. Norwell c Carey b Douthwaite	12	– not out	7
O. J. Hannon-Dalby c Cullen b Hogan	19		
R. N. Sidebottom not out	13		
B 5, lb 12, nb 2	19	B 8, lb 2, w 1, nb 2	13
	——		——
1/3 (2) 2/17 (3) 3/23 (1) (66.3 overs)	186	1/20 (1) (7 wkts dec, 88.5 overs)	347
4/93 (5) 5/117 (6) 6/132 (4)		2/53 (2) 3/196 (3)	
7/138 (8) 8/138 (7) 9/154 (9) 10/186 (10)		4/217 (4) 5/234 (6) 6/314 (7) 7/335 (5)	

Van der Gugten 19–8–45–3; Carey 19–4–54–3; Hogan 14.3–7–27–1; Douthwaite 13–1–42–3; Taylor 1–0–1–0. *Second innings*—van der Gugten 21–4–70–2; Carey 5.5–0–28–0; Hogan 21–1–75–1; Douthwaite 13.1–0–61–2; Taylor 16–0–60–1; Morgan 11.5–0–43–1.

Glamorgan

N. J. Selman c Bell b Norwell	2 – lbw b Hannon-Dalby	73
J. M. Cooke c Burgess b Norwell	4 – c Burgess b Sidebottom	23
T. van der Gugten c Burgess b Norwell	17 – (9) not out	19
A. O. Morgan b Rhodes	28 – (3) b Sidebottom	0
*C. B. Cooke c Burgess b Rhodes	27 – (4) c Burgess b Hannon-Dalby	32
W. T. Root not out	51 – (5) c Hain b Hannon-Dalby	5
C. Z. Taylor c Bell b Norwell	16 – (6) c Mousley b Rhodes	31
D. A. Douthwaite b Sidebottom	11 – (7) c Burgess b Sidebottom	13
†T. N. Cullen b Sidebottom	10 – (8) lbw b Thomson	26
L. J. Carey b Rhodes	23 – c Hain b Hannon-Dalby	11
M. G. Hogan c Hannon-Dalby b Rhodes	0 – not out	5
B 4, lb 6, nb 4	14 B 6, lb 14, w 1, nb 6	27

1/3 (1) 2/12 (2) 3/29 (3) (68.4 overs) 203
4/82 (5) 5/83 (4) 6/116 (7)
7/138 (8) 8/162 (9) 9/193 (10) 10/203 (11)

1/35 (2) (9 wkts, 95 overs) 265
2/35 (3) 3/96 (4)
4/112 (5) 5/179 (6) 6/187 (1)
7/220 (8) 8/220 (7) 9/256 (10)

Hannon-Dalby 22–4–56–0; Norwell 20–5–43–4; Rhodes 12.4–3–46–4; Sidebottom 14–2–48–2. *Second innings*—Norwell 24–5–52–0; Hannon-Dalby 25–6–59–4; Sidebottom 19–4–37–3; Rhodes 13–2–52–1; Brookes 3–1–13–0; Thomson 11–0–32–1.

Umpires: J. H. Evans and R. A. White. Referee: D. A. Cosker.

GLOUCESTERSHIRE

Cancel culture

ANDY STOCKHAUSEN

To suggest Gloucestershire's anniversary celebrations, 150 years after their first first-class match, did not go according to plan would be a gross understatement. An early sign that this might be a season like no other came in March, when – with the coronavirus pandemic taking hold in parts of mainland Europe – the club cancelled a training camp at the Spanish resort of La Manga. With the advent of the national lockdown, the pace of change quickened. Gloucestershire's annual meeting was postponed, junior and Academy cricket put on ice, the County Ground at Bristol shut down, and the majority of employees placed on furlough. Only a skeleton office staff remained, and they were encouraged to work remotely.

Grim announcements came thick and fast, including the cancellation of a money-spinning one-day international against Australia in July, the annual Cheltenham Festival and, with it, numerous fundraising events earmarked for midsummer. Although income fell by about £1.5m, Gloucestershire came out of lockdown in better financial shape than others, since 2019 had been a bumper year, leaving a significant surplus. Even anticipating a worst-case scenario of no cricket at all, chief executive Will Brown had been bullish about the prospect of at least breaking even, at a time when many counties were suffering horribly. It helped that more than 500 members donated the cost of their 2020 season ticket to the club coffers, an act of generosity which aided cashflow during the challenging months of May and June.

In preparation for their first season in Division One of the Championship since 2005 – a longer absence than any county bar Glamorgan and Leicestershire – Gloucestershire had picked up all-rounder George Scott from Middlesex, and fast-tracked the promising seamer Tom Price, following a successful season in the Second XI. They had also signed three high-profile overseas players. Yet once it became apparent that experienced Indian batsman Cheteshwar Pujara, West Indies fast bowler Jerome Taylor and Afghanistan leg-spinner Qais Ahmad would not be available, the bubble of excitement burst. Of the three, Taylor – who had signed a three-year contract before the pandemic spread, and turns 37 in June – was set to be at Bristol in 2021 as an overseas player.

Hampered by modest numbers, which makes player rotation tricky, the county also sought strength in depth closer to home, enticing batsman Tom Lace from Middlesex in August, then former England Under-19 seamer Jared Warner from Yorkshire on a three-year deal in September. Meanwhile, Gloucestershire secured their base, with influential red-ball captain Chris Dent, long-serving left-arm seamer David Payne, experienced slow left-armer Tom Smith and top-order batsman Miles Hammond all signing new contracts.

GLOUCESTERSHIRE AT 150

Gloucestershire played their inaugural first-class match, against Surrey on Durdham Down in Bristol, in 1870, having been founded by Dr Henry Mills Grace, WG's father. But it wasn't until 1871, when the earlier Cheltenham & County of Gloucester club were wound up, and their leading officials absorbed by Gloucestershire, that the club truly represented the whole county.

1874 Having been joint champion county with Nottinghamshire the previous year, Gloucestershire claimed the title to themselves, although the Championship did not become official until 1890. Their unofficial success was repeated in 1876 and 1877, but never since.

1876 In three consecutive innings, W. G. Grace totalled 839 runs. He hit a career-best 344 for MCC against Kent at Canterbury, 177 for Gloucestershire against Nottinghamshire at Clifton College, and 318 not out (the county record for 128 years) against Yorkshire at Cheltenham College.

1878 First Cheltenham cricket week was held at the college ground.

1880 Three of the Grace brothers, Edward, WG and Fred, played against Australia in the first Test on English soil, at The Oval. Edward and WG hit an opening stand of 91, WG went on to make 152, and England won by five wickets after enforcing the follow-on.

1889 Bristol County Ground at Ashley Down, still Gloucestershire's home today, hosted its first first-class match in July, against Lancashire, who won by an innings; in Gloucestershire's second, WG carried his bat for 37 in a total of 87.

1906 Left-arm spinner George Dennett recorded Gloucestershire's best first-class figures, bowling unchanged through Essex's first innings at Bristol to take ten for 40; in the second, uninterrupted again, he took five for 48. Gloucestershire won by nine wickets.

1907 Gloucestershire bowled out Northamptonshire for 12, the joint-lowest score in first-class cricket, at the Spa Ground, Gloucester. Dennett took eight for nine, and match figures of 15 for 21 – all on the second day. With the third washed out, the game was drawn.

1927 Wally Hammond made his England debut at Johannesburg in December, having hit 1,042 runs before the end of May. The next summer he held 63 catches, a club record for a fielder.

1935 Slow left-armer Charlie Parker retired after 602 Gloucestershire appearances and 3,170 wickets – both club records.

1937 Off-spinner Tom Goddard finished the season with 222 wickets, the most by a Gloucestershire bowler. He equalled his record in 1947. Goddard, Parker and WG are all among first-class cricket's top six wicket-takers.

1951 Hammond retired from first-class cricket, having scored 113 centuries and 33,664 runs for Gloucestershire, both club records.

1958 Arthur Milton became the first Gloucestershire player since WG to score a century on Test debut, making 104 against New Zealand at Headingley. Milton had represented England at football in 1951.

1973 Gloucestershire won their first trophy: Tony Brown led them to a 40-run victory over Sussex in the Gillette Cup final at Lord's. The club would win the same competition, under its various guises, in 1999, 2000, 2003 and 2004.

1977 The Benson and Hedges Cup was won for the first time, Mike Procter lifting the trophy after a 64-run win over Kent. The success was repeated in 1999 and 2000.

1983 Bristol hosted its first one-day international: New Zealand v Sri Lanka in the World Cup.

1988 Team-mates Jack Russell and David Lawrence made their England debuts against Sri Lanka at Lord's.

2000 Gloucestershire completed the one-day treble – Benson and Hedges Cup, NatWest Trophy and Norwich Union Sunday League – under coach John Bracewell and captain Mark Alleyne.

2004 New Zealander Craig Spearman beat WG's record, scoring 341 against Middlesex at Archdeacon Meadow, Gloucester. "You are talking about the father of cricket, as he is known the world over," said Spearman, "so it is quite something."
The County Ground was bought back from Royal and Sun Alliance, having been sold to Phoenix Assurance in 1976.

2015 Gloucestershire won the Royal London Cup in Richard Dawson's first season as coach, beating Surrey in the final.

2019 Promotion was secured to the first division of the County Championship after 14 seasons in the second. But then came the pandemic.

RICHARD LATHAM

Australian seamer Dan Worrall was due to return in 2021 as an overseas player.

But wicketkeeper-batsman Gareth Roderick ended his eight-year stay, after opting to join former team-mate Alex Gidman, now head coach at neighbouring Worcestershire. Academy product George Drissell, a 21-year-old off-spinner, was released after just seven first-class appearances over four summers, while Scottish international seamer Stuart Whittingham was forced into early retirement at the age of 26 because of back trouble.

Ian Cockbain

After thriving in 2019, wicketkeeper-batsman James Bracey, all-rounder Ben Charlesworth and head coach Richard Dawson were all singled out for recognition. Chosen by the England selectors to be part of the 30-man behind-closed-doors training group at the Rose Bowl, Bracey distinguished himself with 85 in a three-day warm-up match, and was a reserve during the Test series against West Indies. Before that, Charlesworth, another graduate of the Academy, represented England at the Under-19 World Cup in South Africa, while Dawson oversaw a successful England Lions tour of Australia.

Even following the resumption of county cricket in August, Covid-19 continued to cast its shadow, as Gloucestershire's home Bob Willis Trophy fixture against Northamptonshire became the only game of the delayed season to be abandoned because of the pandemic. Stumps were pulled shortly after lunch on the first day after Ben Curran, a member of the visiting squad – not playing at Bristol, but self-isolating at home after feeling unwell – received a positive test. Because he had been in contact with two members of the team who had travelled to Nevil Road, officials from both clubs contacted the ECB, who called the match off. Of the four games that were completed, Gloucestershire won only one, at home to Warwickshire, with Ryan Higgins returning a career-best 11 for 96. Failure to pass 300 even once did not help.

In the Vitality Blast, Gloucestershire reached finals day for the first time since 2007. Their batting was powered by Ian Cockbain (399 runs at 44) and Dent (371 at 33). Models of consistency with the white ball, Higgins and Payne took 16 wickets apiece, while spinners Smith and Graeme van Buuren claimed 26 between them to underpin a six-match winning streak and first place in the Central Group. Northamptonshire were thrashed in a one-sided quarter-final at Bristol, but Surrey proved too strong in a rain-affected semi at Edgbaston, a six-wicket defeat ending Gloucestershire's latest quest for a first Blast title.

> "The night before, as we met our opponents for a drink, Lancashire's Frank Hayes had me in a headlock, and instructed me not to blow our advantage."
>
> The End of First-Class University Cricket, page 120

GLOUCESTERSHIRE RESULTS

Bob Willis Trophy matches – Played 5: Won 1, Lost 2, Drawn 2.
Vitality Blast matches – Played 11: Won 8, Lost 3. Abandoned 1.

Bob Willis Trophy, 5th in Central Group;
Vitality Blast, semi-finalists.

BOB WILLIS TROPHY AVERAGES

BATTING AND FIELDING

Cap		Birthplace	M	I	NO	R	HS	100	Avge	Ct
2016	G. L. van Buuren††	Pretoria, SA	5	8	0	244	72	0	30.50	3
2018	R. F. Higgins	Harare, Zimbabwe	5	8	1	173	51	0	24.71	2
2010	†C. D. J. Dent	Bristol	4	7	0	170	92	0	24.28	4
2020	G. F. B. Scott	Hemel Hempstead	4	6	2	87	44*	0	21.75	0
2020	T. C. Lace	Hammersmith	3	4	0	73	42	0	18.25	1
2010	J. M. R. Taylor	Banbury	2	4	0	71	34	0	17.75	1
2013	G. H. Roderick††	Durban, SA	4	7	1	101	39	0	16.83	12
2016	G. T. Hankins	Bath	5	8	0	130	69	0	16.25	7
2018	†B. G. Charlesworth	Oxford	4	6	0	78	51	0	13.00	0
2013	M. D. Taylor	Banbury	5	7	2	43	19*	0	8.60	0
2016	J. Shaw	Wakefield	5	7	0	50	21	0	7.14	0
2011	D. A. Payne	Poole	4	5	1	24	14	0	6.00	0

Also batted: †J. R. Bracey (*Bristol*) (cap 2016) (1 match) 4; †M. A. H. Hammond (*Cheltenham‡*) (cap 2013) (1 match) 14, 9 (1 ct); T. J. Price (*Oxford*) (cap 2020) (1 match) 0, 0; T. M. J. Smith (*Eastbourne*) (cap 2013) (2 matches) 24*, 6.

‡ *Born in Gloucestershire.* †† *Other non-England-qualified.*

Gloucestershire award caps on first-class debut.

BOWLING

	Style	O	M	R	W	BB	5I	Avge
D. A. Payne	LFM	95	29	199	14	5-31	1	14.21
R. F. Higgins	RFM	148.4	41	391	17	7-42	1	23.00
M. D. Taylor	LM	115	22	330	11	3-43	0	30.00
J. Shaw	RFM	99.5	17	328	8	3-13	0	41.00
G. F. B. Scott	RM	44	9	129	3	2-34	0	43.00

Also bowled: B. G. Charlesworth (RM) 27–6–103–1; T. J. Price (RM) 18–1–80–1; T. M. J. Smith (SLA) 5–0–10–0; J. M. R. Taylor (OB) 0.1–0–4–0; G. L. van Buuren (SLA) 21–5–60–1.

LEADING VITALITY BLAST AVERAGES (70 runs/10 overs)

Batting	Runs	HS	Avge	SR	Ct/St
B. A. C. Howell	96	49*	48.00	**213.33**	5
I. A. Cockbain	399	89	44.33	**169.78**	6
G. L. van Buuren	79	53	26.33	**161.22**	1
C. D. J. Dent	371	87	33.72	**153.30**	5
J. R. Bracey	125	39*	17.85	**134.40**	1/5
R. F. Higgins	200	30*	28.57	**130.71**	3
J. M. R. Taylor	133	31*	22.16	**117.69**	5
M. A. H. Hammond	210	49	21.00	**116.66**	3

Bowling	W	BB	Avge	ER
T. M. J. Smith	14	5-16	17.35	**5.92**
G. L. van Buuren	12	3-15	18.66	**6.78**
D. A. Payne	16	3-18	18.68	**7.90**
B. A. C. Howell	7	3-16	20.85	**8.11**
R. F. Higgins	16	4-34	20.56	**9.49**
M. D. Taylor	8	3-29	29.62	**9.80**

FIRST-CLASS COUNTY RECORDS

Highest score for	341	C. M. Spearman v Middlesex at Gloucester	2004
Highest score against	319	C. J. L. Rogers (Northants) at Northampton	2006
Leading run-scorer	33,664	W. R. Hammond (avge 57.05)	1920–51
Best bowling for	10-40	E. G. Dennett v Essex at Bristol	1906
Best bowling against	10-66	A. A. Mailey (Australians) at Cheltenham	1921
	10-66	K. Smales (Nottinghamshire) at Stroud	1956
Leading wicket-taker	3,170	C. W. L. Parker (avge 19.43)	1903–35
Highest total for	695-9 dec	v Middlesex at Gloucester	2004
Highest total against	774-7 dec	by Australians at Bristol	1948
Lowest total for	17	v Australians at Cheltenham	1896
Lowest total against	12	by Northamptonshire at Gloucester	1907

LIST A COUNTY RECORDS

Highest score for	177	A. J. Wright v Scotland at Bristol	1997
Highest score against	190	J. M. Vince (Hampshire) at Southampton	2019
Leading run-scorer	7,825	M. W. Alleyne (avge 26.89)	1986–2005
Best bowling for	7-29	D. A. Payne v Essex at Chelmsford	2010
Best bowling against	6-16	Shoaib Akhtar (Worcestershire) at Worcester	2005
Leading wicket-taker	393	M. W. Alleyne (avge 29.88)	1986–2005
Highest total for	401-7	v Buckinghamshire at Wing	2003
Highest total against	496-4	by Surrey at The Oval	2007
Lowest total for	49	v Middlesex at Bristol	1978
Lowest total against	48	by Middlesex at Lydney	1973

TWENTY20 COUNTY RECORDS

Highest score for	126*	M. Klinger v Essex at Bristol	2015
Highest score against	116*	C. L. White (Somerset) at Taunton	2006
Leading run-scorer	**3,064**	**I. A. Cockbain (avge 32.94, SR 131.16)**	**2011–20**
Best bowling for	**5-16**	**T. M. J. Smith v Warwickshire at Birmingham**	**2020**
Best bowling against	5-16	R. E. Watkins (Glamorgan) at Cardiff	2009
Leading wicket-taker	**116**	**B. A. C. Howell (avge 18.93, ER 7.08)**	**2012–20**
Highest total for	254-3	v Middlesex at Uxbridge	2011
Highest total against	250-3	by Somerset at Taunton	2006
Lowest total for	68	v Hampshire at Bristol	2010
Lowest total against	97	by Surrey at The Oval	2010

ADDRESS

County Ground, Nevil Road, Bristol BS7 9EJ; 0117 910 8000; reception@glosccc.co.uk; www.gloscricket.co.uk. Twitter: @Gloscricket.

OFFICIALS

Captain (first-class) C. D. J. Dent
(Twenty20) J. M. R. Taylor
Head coach R. K. J. Dawson
Assistant head coach I. J. Harvey
Head of talent pathway T. H. C. Hancock

President R. A. Gibbons
Chairman J. A. Hollingdale
Chief executive W. G. Brown
Head groundsman S. P. Williams
Scorer A. J. Bull

GLOUCESTERSHIRE v WORCESTERSHIRE

At Bristol, August 1–4. Worcestershire won by eight wickets. Worcestershire 22pts, Gloucestershire 3pts. Toss: Gloucestershire. First-class debut: T. J. Price. County debut: J. D. Libby.

Worcestershire's discipline paid dividends on a surface conducive to attritional cricket. Seamers Morris and Tongue claimed six wickets each, while Leach made the second new ball sing on the fourth day, taking four for 12 in 30 balls to set up a comfortable chase. Gloucestershire had squandered the position built up on the first by Dent and van Buuren, who added 127 for the second wicket. D'Oliveira broke the partnership and, from a powerful 205 for two, the last eight tumbled for 62. Mitchell and Libby began Worcestershire's reply with a stand of 152, before Mitchell provided a maiden first-class wicket for debutant seamer Tom Price. But all the top five ended up facing over 100 balls; 19-year-old Jack Haynes scored his first first-class fifty, while D'Oliveira and Cox eventually thrashed 124 in 13.4 overs to earn a lead of 161. Dent managed another authoritative half-century, and Hankins resisted for over four and a half hours; those who followed were less resolute.

Close of play: first day, Gloucestershire 246-8 (Roderick 7, Shaw 3); second day, Worcestershire 223-2 (Fell 32, Haynes 20); third day, Gloucestershire 135-3 (Hankins 38, Shaw 0).

Gloucestershire

M. A. H. Hammond c Cox b Tongue	14	– (2) c Mitchell b Morris	9
*C. D. J. Dent b D'Oliveira	92	– (1) c Cox b Morris	67
G. L. van Buuren b D'Oliveira	60	– lbw b Tongue	9
G. T. Hankins b Morris	30	– lbw b Tongue	69
R. F. Higgins lbw b Morris	18	– (6) lbw b Mitchell	6
J. M. R. Taylor c Wessels b Tongue	0	– (7) c Mitchell b Leach	23
†G. H. Roderick not out	25	– (8) lbw b Leach	9
T. J. Price b Morris	0	– (9) lbw b Leach	0
D. A. Payne c Cox b Leach	1	– (10) b Leach	14
J. Shaw c Cox b Tongue	3	– (5) lbw b Tongue	21
M. D. Taylor c Cox b Morris	1	– not out	19
Lb 3, w 10, nb 10	23	B 13, lb 2, w 3, nb 6	24
1/23 (1) 2/150 (3) 3/205 (2) 4/228 (4) 5/233 (6) 6/239 (5) 7/239 (8) 8/243 (9) 9/246 (10) 10/267 (11) (96.3 overs)	267	1/26 (2) 2/46 (3) 3/134 (1) 4/163 (5) 5/183 (6) 6/214 (4) 7/234 (8) 8/236 (9) 9/239 (7) 10/270 (10) (104.3 overs)	270

Leach 19–4–48–1; Morris 22.3–6–52–4; Tongue 21–3–75–3; Barnard 17–6–32–0; D'Oliveira 17–1–57–2. *Second innings*—Leach 26.3–4–72–4; Morris 22–8–52–2; Tongue 20–5–65–3; Barnard 16–6–36–0; D'Oliveira 11–2–23–0; Mitchell 9–4–7–1.

Worcestershire

D. K. H. Mitchell b Price	80	– b Shaw	20
J. D. Libby c Dent b Payne	77	– c Hammond b Shaw	25
T. C. Fell lbw b Shaw	39	– not out	32
J. A. Haynes lbw b Higgins	51	– not out	28
B. L. D'Oliveira not out	91		
M. H. Wessels c van Buuren b M. D. Taylor	19		
†O. B. Cox not out	45		
B 4, lb 12, w 2, nb 8	26	B 1, lb 1, nb 6	8
1/152 (1) 2/180 (2) 3/233 (3) 4/281 (4) 5/304 (6) (5 wkts, 120 overs)	428	1/41 (1) 2/60 (2) (2 wkts, 26.1 overs)	113
110 overs: 332-5			

E. G. Barnard, *J. Leach, J. C. Tongue and C. A. J. Morris did not bat.

Payne 22–6–54–1; Higgins 25–6–72–1; M. D. Taylor 20.4–2–83–1; Price 17–1–69–1; Shaw 23.2–3–94–1; van Buuren 12–1–40–0. *Second innings*—Payne 6–1–9–0; Higgins 7–1–24–0; Shaw 5–0–26–2; M. D. Taylor 4–1–24–0; Price 1–0–11–0; van Buuren 3–0–13–0; J. M. R. Taylor 0.1–0–4–0.

Umpires: J. W. Lloyds and M. Newell. Referee: D. A. Cosker.

GLOUCESTERSHIRE v WARWICKSHIRE

At Bristol, August 8–11. Gloucestershire won by 78 runs. Gloucestershire 20pts, Warwickshire 4pts. Toss: Warwickshire. County debut: G. F. B. Scott.

Higgins produced figures of seven for 42 in Warwickshire's second innings, and 11 for 96 in the match – both career-bests – as Gloucestershire staged a superb last-day fightback. They had begun it with a lead of 160 and only four wickets intact, but were indebted to George Scott, one of four brothers who have played for Hertfordshire. His unbeaten 44 on county debut helped set a target of 239 in a minimum of 65 overs. Higgins took centre stage, producing a triple-wicket maiden in his second over; from four for three, Warwickshire never got back on an even keel. Defeat was tough on Hannon-Dalby, who returned match figures of 12 for 110 in sweltering heat, including a career-best six for 33 in the first innings. Lamb top-scored with 65 as Warwickshire forged a lead of 37, which looked even more useful when Gloucestershire slipped to 30 for three second time round. But van Buuren and the ubiquitous Higgins added 110 as the balance of power shifted once more. Then Higgins made sure with the ball.

Close of play: first day, Gloucestershire 191-8 (Smith 15, Shaw 3); second day, Warwickshire 230-8 (Bresnan 34, Miles 5); third day, Gloucestershire 197-6 (J. M. R. Taylor 23, Scott 2).

Gloucestershire

B. G. Charlesworth c Hain b Rhodes	51	– lbw b Hannon-Dalby	14
*C. D. J. Dent c Burgess b Hannon-Dalby	2	– b Bresnan	0
G. L. van Buuren c Bell b Miles	33	– c Hain b Brookes	72
G. T. Hankins lbw b Hannon-Dalby	11	– c Bresnan b Hannon-Dalby	0
R. F. Higgins lbw b Hannon-Dalby	1	– c Burgess b Brookes	51
J. M. R. Taylor lbw b Rhodes	14	– lbw b Hannon-Dalby	34
†G. H. Roderick st Burgess b Rhodes	39	– c Lamb b Miles	13
G. F. B. Scott lbw b Hannon-Dalby	17	– not out	44
T. M. J. Smith not out	24	– lbw b Hannon-Dalby	6
J. Shaw c sub (D. R. Mousley) b Hannon-Dalby	13	– b Hannon-Dalby	11
M. D. Taylor b Hannon-Dalby	0	– c Bresnan b Hannon-Dalby	8
Lb 2, w 1, nb 2	5	B 8, lb 4, nb 10	22
1/9 (2) 2/76 (3) 3/102 (1) 4/102 (4) 5/103 (5) 6/155 (6) 7/160 (7) 8/178 (8) 9/210 (10) 10/210 (11) (96.3 overs)	210	1/2 (2) 2/22 (1) 3/30 (4) 4/140 (3) 5/155 (5) 6/190 (7) 7/213 (6) 8/249 (9) 9/267 (10) 10/275 (11) (95 overs)	275

Hannon-Dalby 23.3–11–33–6; Bresnan 15–1–39–0; Brookes 17–5–52–0; Miles 22–7–51–1; Thomson 6–0–15–0; Rhodes 13–4–18–3. *Second innings*—Hannon-Dalby 23–5–77–6; Bresnan 23–12–38–1; Miles 21–7–51–1; Brookes 18–1–66–2; Rhodes 6–1–21–0; Thomson 4–0–10–0.

Warwickshire

R. M. Yates lbw b Higgins	0	– c van Buuren b Higgins	2
*W. M. H. Rhodes b Charlesworth	41	– c Roderick b Higgins	48
S. R. Hain lbw b M. D. Taylor	8	– lbw b Higgins	0
I. R. Bell c Hankins b Scott	13	– c Roderick b Higgins	0
M. J. Lamb c Dent b Higgins	65	– b Shaw	14
†M. G. K. Burgess b Scott	28	– lbw b Higgins	15
T. T. Bresnan c Roderick b Higgins	38	– not out	22
A. T. Thomson b M. D. Taylor	15	– c J. M. R. Taylor b M. D. Taylor	3
H. J. H. Brookes b M. D. Taylor	0	– lbw b M. D. Taylor	0
C. N. Miles not out	13	– c Dent b Higgins	12
O. J. Hannon-Dalby c Hankins b Higgins	0	– c Roderick b Higgins	18
B 8, lb 12, nb 6	26	B 10, lb 10, nb 6	26
1/4 (1) 2/15 (3) 3/55 (4) 4/93 (2) 5/162 (6) 6/190 (5) 7/223 (8) 8/223 (9) 9/241 (7) 10/247 (11) (90.3 overs)	247	1/4 (1) 2/4 (3) 3/4 (4) 4/50 (5) 5/80 (2) 6/101 (6) 7/109 (8) 8/109 (9) 9/130 (10) 10/160 (11) (60.1 overs)	160

Higgins 24.3–6–54–4; M. D. Taylor 22–4–53–3; Shaw 18–5–44–0; Scott 13–3–34–2; Charlesworth 12–3–40–1; Smith 1–0–2–0. *Second innings*—Higgins 19.1–7–42–7; M. D. Taylor 15–6–27–2; Scott 8–1–26–0; Shaw 7–1–22–1; Smith 4–0–8–0; Charlesworth 7–2–15–0.

Umpires: I. D. Blackwell and R. J. Warren. Referee: R. M. Ellison.

At Cardiff, August 15–18. GLOUCESTERSHIRE drew with GLAMORGAN.

At Taunton, August 22–25. GLOUCESTERSHIRE lost to SOMERSET by 314 runs. *Gloucestershire are dismissed for 76 and 70.*

GLOUCESTERSHIRE v NORTHAMPTONSHIRE

At Bristol, September 6. Drawn. Gloucestershire 8pts, Northamptonshire 10pts. Toss: Northamptonshire. First-class debut: H. O. M. Gouldstone.

The game was abandoned on the first day after it emerged that Northamptonshire's Ben Curran had tested positive for Covid-19. Curran had not travelled to Bristol, but had been in close contact with several team-mates in the previous 48 hours. At first, no explanation was provided for the players' failure to reappear after lunch. But, after a delay of an hour, during which both counties consulted the ECB, umpires Ian Blackwell and Jeremy Lloyds emerged from the pavilion with the two captains and the ground manager; Lloyds removed a stump to signal the end of the match. No interviews were given, and Curran's identity was not officially revealed. Neither side were in contention for a place in the final, but the abandonment helped Gloucestershire out of a tricky position, after their batting had imploded on a green-tinged pitch, under cloudy skies.

Gloucestershire

†J. R. Bracey c Gouldstone b Muzarabani	4
B. G. Charlesworth c Vasconcelos b Hutton	1
G. L. van Buuren c Gay b White	22
T. C. Lace c Gay b Procter	2
G. T. Hankins b White	6
R. F. Higgins not out	13
G. F. B. Scott c Vasconcelos b Kerrigan	11
B 1, lb 4, nb 2	7
1/7 (2) 2/17 (1) 3/34 (3) 4/34 (4) 5/46 (5) 6/66 (7) (6 wkts, 29.4 overs)	66

T. M. J. Smith, *D. A. Payne, M. D. Taylor and J. Shaw did not bat.

Hutton 9–2–22–1; Muzarabani 5–3–5–1; White 8–3–18–2; Procter 6–1–15–1; Kerrigan 1.4–0–1–1.

Northamptonshire

E. N. Gay, *R. S. Vasconcelos, C. O. Thurston, L. A. Procter, R. I. Keogh, S. A. Zaib, †H. O. M. Gouldstone, B. A. Hutton, S. C. Kerrigan, B. Muzarabani, C. J. White.

Umpires: I. D. Blackwell and J. W. Lloyds. Referee: R. M. Ellison.

HAMPSHIRE

Passing the Test

PAT SYMES

Hampshire were among the few beneficiaries of the Covid-19 pandemic. All England's home matches were held at either Southampton or Manchester, where on-site hotels enabled the creation of biosecure bubbles. It meant the Rose Bowl hosted nine internationals – three Tests (one against West Indies, two against Pakistan), three one-dayers (Ireland) and three Twenty20s (Australia).

The matches came pell-mell – a daunting task for new groundsman Simon Lee and his staff. Recruited from Taunton in 2019, Lee became the focus of international attention, but produced a succession of quality pitches. Only in the drawn Second Test against Pakistan, when long delays for rain or bad light – both beyond his control – held up play, were there rumblings of discontent.

Overall, the Hampshire management came through the extraordinary situation with credit, answering the call from a nation desperate for cricket. In so doing, they proved conclusively that the Rose Bowl – which had previously hosted three Tests in nine seasons – is an international venue of genuine quality. It could only help long-held aspirations of hosting an Ashes Test.

The other side of the coin was that Lee had yet to produce a Championship wicket. With the ground given over to internationals, Hampshire decamped across the border to Sussex, swapping their up-to-the-minute facilities for the rural charms of Arundel. There they played two home fixtures in the Bob Willis Trophy, before returning to headquarters for the Vitality Blast. Not that it did them much good: once the powerhouse of domestic T20 cricket, Hampshire won two and lost seven, and finished last in their group.

Before the virus rendered all pre-season planning futile, Hampshire believed they had assembled a team capable of winning the Championship for the first time since 1973. The big announcement was the signing of Australia's Nathan Lyon, arguably the best spinner in the world. Meanwhile, Kyle Abbott and Fidel Edwards, who between them claimed 119 wickets in 2019, had committed to return. Fellow seamer Keith Barker, who took 37, was also available. With James Vince, Sam Northeast and Liam Dawson forming the heart of the batting, there was reason to believe the optimism was not misplaced.

But hope quickly evaporated. Lyon, Abbott, Edwards and white-ball specialist Rilee Rossouw were marooned abroad, Dawson managed only one BWT match before rupturing an Achilles tendon, and Vince's contribution was reduced – by England commitments and the birth of his second child – to six largely unproductive T20 games.

So the youthful squad led by Northeast in Vince's absence was cobbled together from the previous year's Second XI, or players such as Felix Organ, Tom Alsop and Joe Weatherley, who had points to prove. The new-look

Alex Davidson, Getty Images

Simon Lee

Hampshire won twice in the BWT: two mature half-centuries from Weatherley inspired a three-wicket win over Middlesex at Radlett; and a James Fuller hat-trick was the highlight of an innings victory over Surrey at Arundel. But insipid performances against Sussex and Kent brought defeat and, come the end of the first-class season, little had been learned about the inexperienced newcomers.

There were debuts for Scott Currie, Tom Scriven and Ajeet Dale, while Harry Came – a great-grandson of Walter Robins, and a concussion substitute in 2019 – started for the first time. In October, however, both he and batsman Oli Soames were released. Hampshire were also hindered by a season-ending foot injury to Barker, as well as Aneurin Donald's long-term lay-off after knee surgery. Weatherley's 98 at Radlett was the club's top score in either format, while only Ian Holland managed five wickets in a first-class innings: his six for 60 was as important in beating Surrey as Fuller's hat-trick. But leg-spinner Mason Crane returned from a lengthy rehabilitation from a severe back injury to take 14 cheap first-class wickets, plus nine in the Blast. In January, he was one of seven stand-by players in England's Test squad in Sri Lanka.

Not much had gone right for Hampshire's T20 side before the final match, at home against Middlesex, but Pakistan left-armer Shaheen Shah Afridi ensured the season ended in a blaze of glory when he grabbed the last four wickets in four balls, the seventh such instance in T20 cricket. That gave him a Hampshire-record six for 19, all bowled; in six previous games, he had taken one for 191. The only other win had come against a powerful Essex at Chelmsford, when Holland hit the winning run off the penultimate ball. But the T20 weaknesses were obvious. Before Afridi's six-for, Hampshire had taken 28 wickets in nine matches; across the season, there were just five half-centuries, including two from Fuller – more bowler than all-rounder, but the leading scorer in 2020. In December, left-arm seamer Chris Wood, who had played throughout the Blast, was given a two-month suspended ban by the ECB after placing nine bets on matches in 2011 and 2016. Earlier in the year, he had spoken openly about a gambling addiction.

Hampshire have produced only a handful of international-class players through their youth schemes, but in Vince, the club captain, supporters believed they had a true champion. To their exasperation, his latest failures against Ireland may mean the world will never see the outstanding talent Hampshire know him to be. Vince said they had been overtaken in the limited-overs game, and there had to be a big improvement in 2021. Few disagreed.

The club donated over £50,000 to Southampton Hospitals Charity from fund-raising during the pandemic. The money was to go towards the construction of a rehabilitation area for the ICU department of the city's University Hospital.

HAMPSHIRE RESULTS

Bob Willis Trophy matches – Played 5: Won 2, Lost 2, Drawn 1.
Vitality Blast matches – Played 10: Won 2, Lost 7, No result 1.

Bob Willis Trophy, 4th in South Group;
Vitality Blast, 6h in South Group.

BOB WILLIS TROPHY AVERAGES

BATTING AND FIELDING

Cap		*Birthplace*	*M*	*I*	*NO*	*R*	*HS*	*100*	*Avge*	*Ct/St*
	J. J. Weatherley	*Winchester‡*	5	7	1	263	98	0	43.83	2
	†K. H. D. Barker	*Manchester*	2	4	2	63	28*	0	31.50	1
	T. A. R. Scriven	*Oxford*	2	3	0	84	68	0	28.00	1
2019	S. A. Northeast	*Ashford, Kent*	5	7	0	181	81	0	25.85	0
	B. T. J. Wheal††	*Durban, SA*	3	3	2	24	14*	0	24.00	0
	†T. P. Alsop	*High Wycombe*	5	7	0	164	87	0	23.42	5
	L. D. McManus	*Poole*	5	7	0	142	50	0	20.28	11/2
	I. G. Holland	*Stevens Point, USA*	5	7	0	115	42	0	16.42	4
	J. K. Fuller	*Cape Town, SA*	4	5	1	61	30	0	15.25	2
	H. R. C. Came	*Basingstoke‡*	4	5	0	49	25	0	9.80	1
	F. S. Organ	*Sydney, Australia*	5	7	0	60	16	0	8.57	1
	M. S. Crane	*Shoreham-by-Sea*	4	5	1	33	25*	0	8.25	0
	A. S. Dale	*Slough*	2	4	1	7	6	0	2.33	0

Also batted: S. W. Currie (*Poole*) (1 match) 38, 0 (2 ct); L. A. Dawson (*Swindon*) (cap 2013) (1 match) 43* (3 ct); R. A. Stevenson (*Torquay*) (2 matches) 0.

‡ *Born in Hampshire.* †† *Other non-England-qualified.*

BOWLING

	Style	*O*	*M*	*R*	*W*	*BB*	*5I*	*Avge*
F. S. Organ	OB	27	3	90	7	4-42	0	12.85
M. S. Crane	LB	60.4	8	190	14	3-19	0	13.57
I. G. Holland	RFM	129	41	297	17	6-60	1	17.47
A. S. Dale	RFM	21	4	73	4	3-20	0	18.25
S. W. Currie	RFM	17	4	58	3	3-42	0	19.33
R. A. Stevenson	RFM	32	8	103	5	4-70	0	20.60
T. A. R. Scriven	RFM	21	3	79	3	2-24	0	26.33
K. H. D. Barker	LFM	66	13	201	7	2-44	0	28.71
J. K. Fuller	RFM	70	12	293	9	4-17	0	32.55
B. T. J. Wheal	RFM	61	21	203	5	2-11	0	40.60

Also bowled: L. A. Dawson (SLA) 16.5–5–39–2.

LEADING VITALITY BLAST AVERAGES (70 runs/10 overs)

Batting	*Runs*	*HS*	*Avge*	*SR*	*Ct/St*
J. K. Fuller	205	53*	34.16	**131.41**	2
I. G. Holland	161	65	32.20	**130.89**	0
J. J. Weatherley	185	68	20.55	**121.71**	2
T. P. Alsop	197	51	24.62	**110.05**	2/1
J. M. Vince	93	48	15.50	**98.93**	2
S. A. Northeast	149	37	16.55	**98.67**	2
L. D. McManus	79	26	9.87	**95.18**	2/1

Bowling	*W*	*BB*	*Avge*	*ER*
M. S. Crane	9	3-18	22.00	**6.60**
I. G. Holland	3	1-25	54.00	**7.30**
Shaheen Shah Afridi	7	6-19	30.00	**8.07**
C. P. Wood	6	2-29	44.66	**8.12**
R. A. Stevenson	3	1-25	77.33	**9.40**

FIRST-CLASS COUNTY RECORDS

Highest score for	316	R. H. Moore v Warwickshire at Bournemouth	1937
Highest score against	303*	G. A. Hick (Worcestershire) at Southampton	1997
Leading run-scorer	48,892	C. P. Mead (avge 48.84)	1905–36
Best bowling for	9-25	R. M. H. Cottam v Lancashire at Manchester	1965
Best bowling against	10-46	W. Hickton (Lancashire) at Manchester	1870
Leading wicket-taker	2,669	D. Shackleton (avge 18.23)	1948–69
Highest total for	714-5 dec	v Nottinghamshire at Southampton	2005
Highest total against	742	by Surrey at The Oval	1909
Lowest total for	15	v Warwickshire at Birmingham	1922
Lowest total against	23	by Yorkshire at Middlesbrough	1965

LIST A COUNTY RECORDS

Highest score for	190	J. M. Vince v Gloucestershire at Southampton	2019
Highest score against	203	A. D. Brown (Surrey) at Guildford	1997
Leading run-scorer	12,034	R. A. Smith (avge 42.97)	1983–2003
Best bowling for	7-30	P. J. Sainsbury v Norfolk at Southampton	1965
Best bowling against	7-22	J. R. Thomson (Middlesex) at Lord's	1981
Leading wicket-taker	411	C. A. Connor (avge 25.07)	1984–98
Highest total for	371-4	v Glamorgan at Southampton	1975
Highest total against	360-7	by Somerset at Southampton	2018
Lowest total for	43	v Essex at Basingstoke	1972
Lowest total against	61	by Somerset at Bath	1973
	61	by Derbyshire at Portsmouth	1990

TWENTY20 COUNTY RECORDS

Highest score for	124*	M. J. Lumb v Essex v Southampton	2009
Highest score against	116*	L. J. Wright (Sussex) at Southampton	2014
Leading run-scorer	**3,930**	**J. M. Vince (avge 31.95, SR 134.58)**	**2010–20**
Best bowling for	**6-19**	**Shaheen Shah Afridi v Middlesex at Southampton**	**2020**
Best bowling against	6-28	J. K. Fuller (Middlesex) at Southampton	2018
Leading wicket-taker	**137**	**C. P. Wood (avge 26.79, ER 8.28)**	**2010–20**
Highest total for	249-8	v Derbyshire at Derby	2017
Highest total against	220-4	by Somerset at Taunton	2010
Lowest total for	85	v Sussex at Southampton	2008
Lowest total against	67	by Sussex at Hove	2004

ADDRESS

The Ageas Bowl, Botley Road, West End, Southampton SO30 3XH; 023 8047 2002; enquiries@ageasbowl.com; www.ageasbowl.com. Twitter: @hantscricket.

OFFICIALS

Captain J. M. Vince
Cricket operations manager T. M. Tremlett
Director of cricket G. W. White
First-team manager A. V. Birrell
Head of player development C. R. M. Freeston

President N. E. J. Pocock
Chairman R. G. Bransgrove
Chief executive D. Mann
Head groundsman S. Lee
Scorer K. R. Baker

At Hove, August 1–3. HAMPSHIRE lost to SUSSEX by 94 runs.

At Radlett, August 8–11. HAMPSHIRE beat MIDDLESEX by three wickets.

HAMPSHIRE v SURREY

At Arundel, August 15–18. Hampshire won by innings and 52 runs. Hampshire 21pts, Surrey 3pts. Toss: Surrey. First-class debut: T. A. R. Scriven.

Hampshire achieved a crushing victory after dismissing Surrey for 74 on a hectic last day. Only 40 overs had been bowled over the first two – rain interrupted all four – and despite a tricky pitch, a result looked improbable when Surrey began their second innings, 126 adrift, on the final afternoon. The turning point was a dynamic spell of medium-pace from Fuller, whose hat-trick reduced Surrey to 51 for eight; it was the first in the Bob Willis Trophy, and Fuller's second, after one for Gloucestershire in 2013. Two others to have taken a hat-trick for Hampshire were present: Billy Taylor was umpiring, Kevan James commentating. The damage done, leg-spinner Crane wrapped up the tail. Thanks to the weather and the defiance of Evans, the Surrey first innings had stretched into the third day; Holland's career-best six for 60 kept Hampshire on top. Virdi's off-spin troubled their reply, but tenacious eighties from Alsop and Northeast set up a lead – and the unexpected finale. Arundel, around 16 miles into West Sussex, became Hampshire's 15th home ground in first-class cricket because the Rose Bowl was being used for the England–Pakistan Test series.

Close of play: first day, Surrey 79-5 (Smith 3, Evans 39); second day, Surrey 130-8 (Morkel 0, Dunn 0); third day, Hampshire 198-3 (Alsop 52, Came 0).

FIRST-CLASS HAT-TRICKS FOR HAMPSHIRE

A. W. Ridley	v Sussex at Hove	1875
J. A. Newman	v Australians at Soton	1909
A. S. Kennedy	v Glos at Soton	1920
A. S. Kennedy	v Somerset at Bournemouth	1920
A. S. Kennedy	v Glos at Soton	1924
G. S. Boyes	v Surrey at Portsmouth	1925
G. S. Boyes	v Warwicks at Birmingham	1926
O. W. Herman	v Glam at Portsmouth	1938
T. A. Dean	v Worcs at Bournemouth	1939
D. W. White	v Sussex at Portsmouth	1961
D. W. White	v Sussex at Hove	1962
J. W. Holder	v Kent at Soton	1972
M. D. Marshall	v Somerset at Taunton	1983
K. J. Shine	v Lancs at Manchester	1992
K. D. James	v Indians at Soton	1996
C. T. Tremlett	v Notts at Nottingham	2005
B. V. Taylor	v Middx at Soton	2006
K. J. Abbott	v Worcs at Worcester	2018
J. K. Fuller	**v Surrey at Arundel**	**2020**

Of the hat-tricks at Southampton, all were taken at Northlands Road except Taylor's (Rose Bowl).

Surrey

*M. D. Stoneman lbw b Holland	21	– c Alsop b Wheal	3
R. S. Patel b Holland	6	– c McManus b Wheal	5
S. G. Borthwick c McManus b Holland	0	– lbw b Crane	5
W. G. Jacks lbw b Wheal	4	– lbw b Holland	0
J. J. Roy lbw b Holland	4	– lbw b Fuller	14
†J. L. Smith c McManus b Scriven	18	– not out	22
L. J. Evans lbw b Holland	65	– c Alsop b Fuller	6
A. A. P. Atkinson lbw b Holland	5	– lbw b Fuller	0
M. Morkel lbw b Crane	33	– b Fuller	0
M. P. Dunn not out	2	– lbw b Crane	5
G. S. Virdi st McManus b Crane	5	– lbw b Crane	0
B 7, nb 2	9	B 4, lb 6, nb 4	14
1/18 (2) 2/18 (3) 3/31 (4) 4/31 (1) 5/36 (5) 6/120 (7) 7/130 (6) 8/130 (8) 9/166 (9) 10/172 (11) (49 overs)	172	1/5 (2) 2/10 (1) 3/15 (4) 4/27 (3) 5/39 (5) 6/51 (7) 7/51 (8) 8/51 (9) 9/64 (10) 10/74 (11) (32.4 overs)	74

Wheal 15–5–60–1; Holland 20–7–60–6; Fuller 2–1–17–0; Scriven 8–1–20–1; Crane 4–1–8–2. *Second innings*—Wheal 8–5–11–2; Holland 9–1–17–1; Crane 8.4–2–19–3; Fuller 7–4–17–4.

Hampshire

F. S. Organ b Atkinson	16
J. J. Weatherley lbw b Virdi	36
T. P. Alsop c Borthwick b Virdi	87
*S. A. Northeast lbw b Virdi	81
H. R. C. Came lbw b Virdi	12
J. K. Fuller lbw b Dunn	1
†L. D. McManus c Roy b Virdi	8
I. G. Holland b Dunn	6
T. A. R. Scriven b Virdi	8
M. S. Crane not out	25
B. T. J. Wheal b Dunn	1
B 1, lb 12, nb 4	17
1/18 (1) 2/68 (2) 3/189 (4) (80.4 overs)	298
4/249 (3) 5/250 (5) 6/250 (6)	
7/258 (8) 8/268 (7) 9/273 (9) 10/298 (11)	

Morkel 14–7–28–0; Dunn 16.4–4–53–3; Atkinson 10–3–26–1; Patel 4–0–37–0; Virdi 26–1–101–6; Borthwick 10–1–40–0.

Umpires: B. J. Debenham and B. V. Taylor. Referee: P. M. Such.

HAMPSHIRE v ESSEX

At Arundel, August 22–25. Drawn. Hampshire 9pts, Essex 9pts. Toss: Hampshire.

Few had cause to look back on this soggy match with much satisfaction other than Alastair Cook. Rain, often heavy, permitted 78 overs, Hampshire's shortest home game since they hosted Yorkshire at Basingstoke in 1987, which comprised 45. There was no play on either the first or last day, ending Essex's perfect start to the season. Asked to bat, they were just short of a second batting point when the weather intervened for the final time. Conditions were never easy, but the watchful Cook was immovable; his 66th first-class century was the 50th at Arundel. In a risk-free innings, he reached 24,000 runs as Hampshire failed to make the most of winning the toss.

Close of play: first day, no play; second day, Essex 146-2 (A. N. Cook 75, Porter 0); third day, Essex 249-3 (A. N. Cook 129, Lawrence 37).

Essex

P. I. Walter c Alsop b Holland	43
A. N. Cook not out	129
*T. Westley c McManus b Crane	18
J. A. Porter lbw b Stevenson	8
D. W. Lawrence not out	37
B 2, lb 10, nb 2	14
1/83 (1) 2/144 (3) (3 wkts, 78 overs)	249
3/171 (4)	

F. I. N. Khushi, R. N. ten Doeschate, †A. J. A. Wheater, S. R. Harmer, A. P. Beard and S. J. Cook did not bat.

Wheal 14–2–62–0; Holland 17–6–25–1; Stevenson 13–2–33–1; Fuller 13–1–65–0; Crane 19–2–47–1; Organ 2–0–5–0.

Hampshire

F. S. Organ, J. J. Weatherley, T. P. Alsop, *S. A. Northeast, H. R. C. Came, I. G. Holland, †L. D. McManus, J. K. Fuller, R. A. Stevenson, M. S. Crane, B. T. J. Wheal.

Umpires: I. J. Gould and B. V. Taylor. Referee: S. J. Davis.

At Canterbury, September 6–8. HAMPSHIRE lost to KENT by seven wickets.

KENT

Method in his madness

MARK PENNELL

It was meant to be a season of celebration, to mark the 150th anniversary of Kent's formation. If Covid-19 put paid to that, there was still cause for cheer in the blossoming of Zak Crawley. Barely three years after making a half-century on first-class debut – against the West Indians during Canterbury Week – he hit a sublime, nine-hour double-hundred in the last Test of the summer, against Pakistan at Southampton.

Uplifted by his flawless 267, Crawley returned to Kent a fortnight later and stroked a 94-ball century that sped them to a three-day victory over Hampshire. A week later, Hampshire suffered again when he went back to Southampton and hammered an unbeaten 108 from 54 balls, his maiden T20 century. Once more, Kent romped home.

So it was no surprise when Crawley, still just 22, was named the Professional Cricketers' Association Player of the Month for September; nor when he picked up the PCA Young Player of the Year award. Rob Key, the former Kent and England batsman turned commentator, described him as the best to progress from Canterbury to the Test team since Colin Cowdrey. Like Cowdrey and Ed Smith – the national selector – Crawley honed his elegant cover-drives on the shirtfronts of The Head, the Tonbridge School ground.

Polite and softly spoken, Crawley is quick to blush at his own jokes, or flash a boyish smile – but that hides a fierce determination. After a busy winter with England and the Lions, he went straight into lockdown at his parents' west Kent home, where he tried to fill his days usefully: "I found myself measuring out a pitch on the lawn, picking up my bat and gloves and practising running between the wickets. Anyone watching might have thought I was crazy, but I thought I should work on my turns and changing the bat between hands as you swivel round. It doesn't get much madder than that, does it?"

Lockdown proved a demanding time for many. Kent's executive directors took a 20% pay cut, and renegotiated a loan with Canterbury City Council. Hanging on to membership fees sparked some whinging, though other members clubbed together to donate £31,000, as Kent froze all capital spending.

The majority of players, coaches and administrators joined the government's job retention scheme, leaving Sam Billings and Joe Denly – who was contracted to England – to carry out community liaison duties with youth groups and cricket clubs. Staff from Kent supported The Rainbow Run, and raised £15,000 for health charities, while the club made conference rooms at Canterbury and Beckenham available for blood donor sessions and NHS meetings. Later, the St Lawrence Ground became a vaccination centre.

Eventually, cricket resumed on August 1 and, though it was behind closed doors, a total of 604,000 watched home games on the internet via the club's

Alex Davidson, Getty Images

Jordan Cox

excellent live feed. The figure for the Vitality Blast derby with Essex alone was 145,191. Playing regulations for the Bob Willis Trophy, meanwhile, meant teams used facilities on opposite sides of the ground. Kent shared the home and away dressing-rooms next to the pavilion; opponents changed in the two-tier Leslie Ames Stand at the Nackington Road End.

With overseas and Kolpak players largely unavailable, a new-look Kent side finished second in their group, with three wins and a draw. Their only defeat, by two wickets at Chelmsford to eventual champions Essex, came in their first match. As it turned out, victory would have been enough to send them to the final.

Jordan Cox, a 19-year-old wicketkeeper-batsman, and one of several young players to make a mark, hit 238 not out against Sussex – the highest maiden century for Kent – but posed for a photo with a fan, and spent the next game in self-isolation. He was the leading scorer with 324 runs at 64 and, in the absence of Billings, ousted the highly regarded Ollie Robinson to keep wicket in six T20 games. Marcus O'Riordan, a 22-year-old Tonbridge School team-mate of Crawley, showed potential as an off-spinner, and mettle as a batsman. Thrust occasionally into the role of emergency opener, he was one of four to pass 200 runs. Winter recruit Jack Leaning did so in a single innings, when he shared a Kent-record unbroken stand of 423 with Cox in a total of 530 for one during the demolition of Sussex.

All the while, the 44-year-old Darren Stevens was snatching 29 wickets at 15, to earn another year's contract extension. Stevens – who had to cope with the Covid-related death of his father during the summer – and Crawley were both among Wisden's Five Cricketers of the Year. Harry Podmore, another to sign a new deal, finished with 19 at 16, while Matt Milnes took 15 at 23, despite injury niggles.

As in 2019, Kent's Twenty20 challenge faded badly. They clung on to finish third in the group, but were heavily defeated by Surrey in the quarter-finals. Fred Klaassen (13) and Imran Qayyum (11) were the only bowlers to take more than seven wickets; Crawley and Daniel Bell-Drummond, making up for a disappointing red-ball season, led the batting.

Kent signed Zimbabwe-born seamer Nathan Gilchrist from Somerset, but lost Sean Dickson to Durham; keeper-batsman Adam Rouse retired, aged 28. In October, seamers Ivan Thomas and Calum Haggett were released. Head coach Matt Walker was given a two-year deal, but difficult times lie ahead. The club confirmed in September that a fifth of administrative and management roles were under threat; negotiations over further salary cuts continued.

In December, Kent retrospectively awarded 51 caps to women players, dating back to their first match in 1935, from Carol Valentine to Fran Wilson.

KENT RESULTS

Bob Willis Trophy matches – Played 5: Won 3, Lost 1, Drawn 1.
Vitality Blast matches – Played 11: Won 5, Lost 4, Tied 1, No result 1.

Bob Willis Trophy, 2nd in South Group;
Vitality Blast, quarter-finalists.

BOB WILLIS TROPHY AVERAGES

BATTING AND FIELDING

Cap		*Birthplace*	*M*	*I*	*NO*	*R*	*HS*	*100*	*Avge*	*Ct*
2018	H. G. Kuhn††	*Piet Retief, SA*	2	4	1	202	140	1	67.33	5
	J. M. Cox	*Margate‡*	4	6	1	324	238*	1	64.80	6
	M. K. O'Riordan	*Pembury‡*	5	8	3	216	52*	0	43.20	1
	J. A. Leaning	*Bristol*	5	8	1	279	220*	1	39.85	9
2019	H. W. Podmore	*Hammersmith*	3	3	1	79	47	0	39.50	2
2015	D. J. Bell-Drummond	*Lewisham‡*	5	9	1	185	45	0	23.12	3
	O. G. Robinson	*Sidcup‡*	5	6	0	138	78	0	23.00	22
	G. Stewart††	*Kalgoorlie, Australia*	4	6	0	129	58	0	21.50	0
	M. E. Milnes	*Nottingham*	4	6	0	96	43	0	16.00	1
2005	D. I. Stevens	*Leicester*	5	6	0	77	36	0	12.83	3
	Hamidullah Qadri	*Kandahar, Afghanistan*	4	5	2	11	5	0	3.66	0

Also batted: S. W. Billings (*Pembury‡*) (cap 2015) (2 matches) 20 (2 ct); Z. Crawley (*Bromley‡*) (cap 2019) (1 match) 0, 105 (1 ct); J. L. Denly§ (*Canterbury‡*) (cap 2008) (1 match) 89 (1 ct); N. N. Gilchrist (*Harare, Zimbabwe*) (1 match) 25, 13; T. D. Groenewald (*Pietermaritzburg, SA*) (1 match) did not bat; F. J. Klaassen (*Haywards Heath*) (1 match) 0* (1 ct); I. A. A. Thomas (*Greenwich‡*) (2 matches) 0, 3*.

‡ *Born in Kent.* § *ECB contract.* †† *Other non-England-qualified.*

BOWLING

	Style	*O*	*M*	*R*	*W*	*BB*	*5I*	*Avge*
D. I. Stevens	RM	209	64	452	29	5-37	3	15.58
H. W. Podmore	RFM	117.3	30	307	19	5-43	1	16.15
F. J. Klaassen	LFM	27	6	80	4	4-44	0	20.00
M. E. Milnes	RFM	119.3	29	355	15	4-46	0	23.66
M. K. O'Riordan	OB	62.1	5	255	8	3-50	0	31.87
I. A. A. Thomas	RFM	30	3	136	4	4-32	0	34.00
G. Stewart	RFM	95.5	19	299	5	3-48	0	59.80

Also bowled: D. J. Bell-Drummond (RM) 5–0–22–0; J. L. Denly (LB) 2–0–12–0; N. N. Gilchrist (RFM) 9–1–52–0; T. D. Groenewald (RFM) 28–5–119–2; Hamidullah Qadri (OB) 38.4–7–104–1; J. A. Leaning (OB) 2–1–2–0.

LEADING VITALITY BLAST AVERAGES (70 runs/9 overs)

Batting	*Runs*	*HS*	*Avge*	*SR*	*Ct/St*
Z. Crawley	342	108*	38.00	**156.88**	3
D. J. Bell-Drummond	423	89	42.30	**154.94**	5
J. L. Denly	152	38	25.33	**142.05**	1
J. A. Leaning	201	55*	33.50	**138.62**	2
A. J. Blake	171	52*	21.37	**134.64**	7
S. W. Billings	86	50	28.66	**132.30**	3
J. M. Cox	75	39*	18.75	**122.95**	5/2
H. G. Kuhn	104	42*	17.33	**118.18**	2
G. Stewart	79	21*	13.16	**98.75**	1

Bowling	*W*	*BB*	*Avge*	*ER*
J. L. Denly	3	1-19	55.33	**7.90**
T. D. Groenewald	4	2-31	29.75	**7.93**
I. Qayyum	11	3-25	29.90	**8.02**
G. Stewart	6	2-28	54.83	**8.73**
M. E. Milnes	7	3-19	48.28	**9.13**
F. J. Klaassen	13	3-36	28.76	**9.19**
C. J. Haggett	2	1-28	46.50	**10.33**

FIRST-CLASS COUNTY RECORDS

Highest score for	332	W. H. Ashdown v Essex at Brentwood	1934
Highest score against	344	W. G. Grace (MCC) at Canterbury	1876
Leading run-scorer	47,868	F. E. Woolley (avge 41.77)	1906–38
Best bowling for	10-30	C. Blythe v Northamptonshire at Northampton	1907
Best bowling against	10-48	C. H. G. Bland (Sussex) at Tonbridge	1899
Leading wicket-taker	3,340	A. P. Freeman (avge 17.64)	1914–36
Highest total for	803-4 dec	v Essex at Brentwood	1934
Highest total against	676	by Australians at Canterbury	1921
Lowest total for	18	v Sussex at Gravesend	1867
Lowest total against	16	by Warwickshire at Tonbridge	1913

LIST A COUNTY RECORDS

Highest score for	150*	J. L. Denly v Glamorgan at Canterbury	2018
Highest score against	167*	P. Johnson (Nottinghamshire) at Nottingham	1993
Leading run-scorer	7,814	M. R. Benson (avge 31.89)	1980–95
Best bowling for	8-31	D. L. Underwood v Scotland at Edinburgh	1987
Best bowling against	6-5	A. G. Wharf (Glamorgan) at Cardiff	2004
Leading wicket-taker	530	D. L. Underwood (avge 18.93)	1963–87
Highest total for	384-6	v Berkshire at Finchampstead	1994
	384-8	v Surrey at Beckenham	2018
Highest total against	380-5	by Middlesex at Canterbury	2019
Lowest total for	60	v Somerset at Taunton	1979
Lowest total against	60	by Derbyshire at Canterbury	2008

TWENTY20 COUNTY RECORDS

Highest score for	127	J. L. Denly v Essex at Chelmsford	2017
Highest score against	151*	C. H. Gayle (Somerset) at Taunton	2015
Leading run-scorer	**3,510**	**J. L. Denly (avge 30.00, SR 127.40)**	**2004–20**
Best bowling for	5-11	A. F. Milne v Somerset at Taunton	2017
Best bowling against	5-17	G. M. Smith (Essex) at Chelmsford	2012
Leading wicket-taker	119	J. C. Tredwell (avge 28.46, ER 7.32)	2003–17
Highest total for	231-7	v Surrey at The Oval	2015
	231-5	v Somerset at Canterbury	2018
Highest total against	250-6	by Surrey at Canterbury	2018
Lowest total for	72	v Hampshire at Southampton	2011
Lowest total against	82	by Somerset at Taunton	2010

ADDRESS

The Spitfire Ground, St Lawrence, Old Dover Road, Canterbury CT1 3NZ; 01227 456886; feedback@kentcricket.co.uk; www.kentcricket.co.uk. Twitter: @KentCricket.

OFFICIALS

Captain S. W. Billings
Director of cricket P. R. Downton
Head coach M. J. Walker
Head of talent pathway M. M. Patel
President Sir Timothy Laurence

Chairman S. R. C. Philip
Chief executive S. Storey
Head groundsman A. Llong
Scorer L. A. R. Hart

At Chelmsford, August 1–4. KENT lost to ESSEX by two wickets.

KENT v SUSSEX

At Canterbury, August 8–10. Kent won by an innings and 25 runs. Kent 24pts, Sussex 3pts. Toss: Sussex. County debuts: T. D. Groenewald; S. C. Meaker.

It was hard to overstate Kent's dominance – despite Sussex appearing content with a total of 332 early on day two. The visitors had depended on a dogged 98 from Brown and a stylish 65 from the teenage Tom Clark; the seam of Podmore and off-spin of O'Riordan kept the score within bounds. From then on, it was all Kent. Claydon, back in the county he had served for seven seasons, did remove Bell-Drummond, but that simply brought together Cox and Leaning. On a belting pitch, Cox – who had played beside Clark for England Under-19 – betrayed no nerves as he approached landmark after landmark; he moved to his maiden hundred with a six, and converted it into a chanceless double. In all, he faced 345 balls, batted almost eight hours, and hit 27 fours and three sixes. The only teenager to have made a higher score in English first-class cricket was Dom Sibley,

HIGHEST FIRST-CLASS TOTALS LOSING ONE WICKET OR FEWER

561-1	Karachi Whites v Quetta at Karachi	1976-77
555-1	Yorkshire v Essex at Leyton	1932
549-1	Rhodesia v Orange Free State at Bloemfontein	1967-68
530-1	**Kent v Sussex at Canterbury**	**2020**
517-1	England v Australia at Brisbane	2010-11
503-1	Cricket Australia XI v New Zealanders at Sydney (Blacktown)	2015-16
501-1	Worcestershire v Warwickshire at Worcester	1982
493-1	Yorkshire v Hampshire at Sheffield	1939
485-1	Habib Bank v WAPDA at Karachi	2016-17
481-1	Delhi v Himachal Pradesh at Delhi	1987-88

All innings were declared, apart from the game at Canterbury.

HIGHEST FIRST-CLASS PARTNERSHIPS FOR KENT

423* for 2nd	**J. M. Cox/J. A. Leaning**	**v Sussex at Canterbury**	**2020**
382 for 2nd	S. R. Dickson/J. L. Denly	v Northamptonshire at Beckenham	2017
368 for 4th	P. A. de Silva/G. R. Cowdrey	v Derbyshire at Maidstone	1995
366 for 2nd	S. G. Hinks/N. R. Taylor	v Middlesex at Canterbury	1990
352 for 2nd	W. H. Ashdown/F. E. Woolley	v Essex at Brentwood	1934
346 for 6th	S. W. Billings/D. I. Stevens	v Yorkshire at Leeds	2019
323 for 3rd	R. W. T. Key/M. van Jaarsveld	v Surrey at Tunbridge Wells	2005
321* for 3rd	A. Hearne/J. R. Mason	v Nottinghamshire at Nottingham	1899
315 for 6th	P. A. de Silva/M. A. Ealham	v Nottinghamshire at Nottingham	1995
309 for 3rd	G. O. Jones/M. van Jaarsveld	v Glamorgan at Canterbury	2009

who hit 242 for Surrey against Yorkshire in 2013. Nimble on his feet, Cox committed one error, on 134, when he took a painful blow on the chest after ducking into a Meaker bouncer. Leaning, dropped at long leg on 19, reached his own maiden double with a five – thanks to overthrows – from his 289th delivery, and Kent had twin scores of 200-plus for only the second time: in 1934, Bill Ashdown (332) and Les Ames (202 not out) had steered them to 803 for four against Essex at Brentwood. The stand of 423 was the highest by any team at Canterbury. Under tournament regulations, Kent's innings ended after 120 overs, so there were almost five sessions left; Sussex lasted less than two. Only Finch offered any fight as Stevens – with a five-for – and Podmore hastened victory. Kent had never before won a full match for the loss of one wicket.

Close of play: first day, Sussex 320-9 (Brown 90, Claydon 10); second day, Kent 338-1 (Cox 167, Leaning 110).

Sussex

P. D. Salt c Robinson b Stevens	19 – c Leaning b Podmore	0
T. J. Haines c Cox b Groenewald	21 – lbw b Stevens	17
H. Z. Finch c Stevens b O'Riordan	37 – c Billings b Podmore	66
T. G. R. Clark c Podmore b O'Riordan	65 – c Robinson b Stevens	0
*†B. C. Brown b Podmore	98 – lbw b Stevens	2
D. M. W. Rawlins c Robinson b Podmore	20 – b Stevens	19
G. H. S. Garton c Robinson b Podmore	4 – b Stevens	6
J. J. Carson c Leaning b Podmore	16 – c Billings b Podmore	0
H. T. Crocombe lbw b O'Riordan	15 – c Robinson b Groenewald	2
S. C. Meaker run out (Hamidullah Qadri/Stevens)	5 – not out	31
M. E. Claydon not out	14 – c Robinson b O'Riordan	24
B 4, lb 5, w 1, nb 8	18 B 4, lb 2	6
1/27 (1) 2/77 (2) 3/90 (3) (94.3 overs)	332 1/0 (1) 2/35 (2) (46.1 overs)	173
4/173 (4) 5/215 (6) 6/221 (7)	3/43 (4) 4/59 (5)	
7/253 (8) 8/284 (9) 9/293 (10) 10/332 (5)	5/89 (6) 6/99 (7) 7/102 (8)	
	8/113 (3) 9/113 (9) 10/173 (11)	

Podmore 23.3–3–85–4; Stevens 23–8–56–1; Groenewald 19–5–66–1; Thomas 11–0–48–0; O'Riordan 13–0–50–3; Hamidullah Qadri 5–1–18–0. *Second innings*—Podmore 14–5–28–3; Stevens 15–3–50–5; Groenewald 9–0–53–1; O'Riordan 4.1–1–22–1; Thomas 4–1–14–0.

Kent

D. J. Bell-Drummond c Finch b Claydon	43
J. M. Cox not out	238
J. A. Leaning not out	220
B 6, lb 5, w 2, nb 16	29
1/107 (1) (1 wkt, 120 overs)	530
110 overs: 455-1	

*S. W. Billings, †O. G. Robinson, D. I. Stevens, M. K. O'Riordan, T. D. Groenewald, H. W. Podmore, Hamidullah Qadri and I. A. A. Thomas did not bat.

Claydon 24–4–86–1; Crocombe 16–0–89–0; Garton 20–4–79–0; Haines 5–0–19–0; Meaker 21–1–114–0; Carson 16–1–59–0; Rawlins 18–0–73–0.

Umpires: N. J. Llong and M. Newell. Referee: S. J. Davis.

KENT v MIDDLESEX

At Canterbury, August 15–18. Drawn. Kent 11pts, Middlesex 13pts. Toss: Kent. First-class debut: J. L. B. Davies.

A game that lost 118 overs of its first two days to rain and – despite floodlights – murk, sparked briefly into flame. But caution, and a lifeless pitch, prevented a result. Middlesex, an uncertain 123 for six at the start of the third day, were steered to a useful 269 thanks mainly to Robbie White. He fell one short of a maiden hundred when Leaning clung on to a slip catch at the third attempt. Klaassen found more bounce than most to claim a career-best four wickets, while Stevens grabbed his 28th five-for. The pace of Cummins soon caused problems. Without the confident Denly, just released by England, Kent – who lost their last five for 23 on the final morning – would have been much more than 78 adrift. Middlesex needed quick runs but, while Holden cracked 72 off 81 balls, Robson dawdled to an unbeaten 82 off 143. Eskinazi's eventual declaration set Kent a notional 248 in a session. Bell-Drummond and makeshift opener O'Riordan – Jordan Cox was self-isolating because he had posed for a photograph with fans after his heroics against Sussex – saw off Cummins's new-ball burst. Middlesex were also missing a top-order regular for similar reasons: Nick Gubbins had possibly come into contact with someone who tested positive for Covid-19.

Close of play: first day, Middlesex 22-1 (Robson 17, Eskinazi 2); second day, Middlesex 123-6 (White 36); third day, Kent 146-5 (Denly 70, Milnes 4).

Middlesex

S. D. Robson c Bell-Drummond b Klaassen	36	– (2) not out	82
M. D. E. Holden c and b Milnes	2	– (1) c Denly b O'Riordan	72
*S. S. Eskinazi c Robinson b Stevens	9	– not out	10
R. G. White c Leaning b Stevens	99		
M. K. Andersson c and b Klaassen	2		
J. L. B. Davies lbw b Stevens	13		
†J. A. Simpson c Robinson b Klaassen	10		
J. A. R. Harris b Stevens	41		
E. R. Bamber not out	24		
M. L. Cummins b Klaassen	1		
T. N. Walallawita lbw b Stevens	11		
B 1, lb 12, nb 8	21	B 1, lb 2, w 2	5
1/11 (2) 2/32 (3) 3/54 (1) 4/68 (5) 5/108 (6) 6/123 (7) 7/216 (4) 8/249 (8) 9/250 (10) 10/269 (11) (108 overs)	269	1/143 (1) (1 wkt dec, 40 overs)	169

Milnes 28–8–61–1; Stevens 31–9–79–5; Stewart 17–4–26–0; Klaassen 20–6–44–4; Hamidullah Qadri 7–1–20–0; Denly 2–0–12–0; O'Riordan 3–1–14–0. *Second innings*—Milnes 5–0–24–0; Stevens 11–1–25–0; Klaassen 7–0–36–0; Stewart 5–0–21–0; O'Riordan 8–0–42–1; Bell-Drummond 4–0–18–0.

Kent

D. J. Bell-Drummond c Simpson b Cummins	14	– not out	31
M. K. O'Riordan c Andersson b Cummins	11	– not out	34
J. L. Denly b Harris	89		
J. A. Leaning c Holden b Bamber	4		
*S. W. Billings c Simpson b Cummins	20		
†O. G. Robinson c Eskinazi b Andersson	17		
M. E. Milnes b Cummins	16		
D. I. Stevens c Robson b Andersson	4		
G. Stewart c Holden b Harris	1		
F. J. Klaassen not out	0		
Hamidullah Qadri c Andersson b Cummins	5		
Lb 1, w 1, nb 8	10	B 5	5
1/18 (1) 2/37 (2) 3/57 (4) 4/96 (5) 5/132 (6) 6/168 (7) 7/182 (3) 8/186 (8) 9/186 (9) 10/191 (11) (64.1 overs)	191	(no wkt, 14 overs)	70

Cummins 19.1–5–62–5; Bamber 17–5–56–1; Andersson 12–4–23–2; Harris 14–4–46–2; Walallawita 2–0–3–0. *Second innings*—Cummins 4–1–12–0; Bamber 4–1–23–0; Andersson 3–0–22–0; Harris 2–0–8–0; Walallawita 1–1–0–0.

Umpires: N. L. Bainton and N. J. Llong. Referee: G. R. Cowdrey.

At The Oval, August 22–25. KENT beat SURREY by 17 runs.

KENT v HAMPSHIRE

At Canterbury, September 6–8. Kent won by seven wickets. Kent 19pts, Hampshire 3pts. Toss: Kent. First-class debut: S. W. Currie.

Crawley atoned for an eight-ball duck in the first innings with a graceful 94-ball century as Kent completed an ultimately comfortable three-day win. The first two days, though, had been hard-fought. Weatherley and Holland put on 69 for Hampshire's first wicket but, once a breach was made, Stevens was quick to capitalise under heavy cloud. His five-for was his eighth in 11 matches (and his four wickets in the second innings would take his record at Canterbury in 2020 to 20 wickets at 14). Robinson held six catches behind the stumps. Kent found batting no easier, bundled out inside 61 overs to trail by 21: only Kuhn, O'Riordan and No. 11 Podmore made it to the thirties, though not beyond. Hampshire's 19-year-old debutant, Scott Currie, who had earlier hit a diligent 38, took three of the first four wickets. But then Kent exerted control. Between them, Podmore and Stevens claimed nine cheap wickets, and without Tom Scriven – who arrived at 23 for five – and McManus, Kent might have been chasing fewer than 100. A target of 181 was trickier, though O'Riordan, reprising his role as stand-in opener after Cox fell ill, and his former Tonbridge School team-mate Crawley settled the issue in a second-wicket partnership of 157.

Close of play: first day, Kent 21-2 (Milnes 1, Crawley 0); second day, Hampshire 108-5 (McManus 50, Scriven 42).

Hampshire

First innings		Second innings	
J. J. Weatherley lbw b Podmore	37	– (2) c Crawley b Podmore	7
I. G. Holland c Kuhn b Milnes	42	– (1) lbw b Podmore	2
T. P. Alsop c Kuhn b Stevens	8	– c Leaning b Podmore	4
*S. A. Northeast c Robinson b Stevens	16	– lbw b Stevens	2
F. S. Organ lbw b Stevens	0	– b Stevens	0
†L. D. McManus c Robinson b Stevens	17	– c Leaning b Podmore	50
T. A. R. Scriven c Robinson b Milnes	8	– c Podmore b Stevens	68
S. W. Currie c Robinson b Podmore	38	– c Kuhn b Podmore	0
M. S. Crane c Robinson b Milnes	0	– c Cox b Stevens	8
B. T. J. Wheal not out	14	– not out	9
A. S. Dale c Robinson b Stevens	0	– c Robinson b Stewart	6
Lb 7, nb 4	11	Lb 1, nb 2	3
1/69 (2) 2/85 (1) 3/99 (3) 4/99 (5) 5/126 (4) 6/127 (6) 7/144 (7) 8/144 (9) 9/190 (8) 10/191 (11) (75 overs)	191	1/6 (1) 2/10 (3) 3/13 (4) 4/13 (5) 5/23 (2) 6/110 (6) 7/120 (8) 8/139 (9) 9/146 (7) 10/159 (11) (64.1 overs)	159

Podmore 21–6–49–2; Stevens 27–15–37–5; Milnes 15–5–54–3; Stewart 12–2–44–0. *Second innings*—Podmore 23–8–43–5; Stevens 22–8–35–4; Stewart 13.1–2–50–1; Milnes 5–0–26–0; Bell-Drummond 1–0–4–0.

Kent

First innings		Second innings	
*D. J. Bell-Drummond b Holland	16	– b Holland	7
J. M. Cox c Alsop b Currie	2		
M. E. Milnes c and b Currie	6		
Z. Crawley lbw b Currie	0	– (3) lbw b Crane	105
J. A. Leaning c McManus b Scriven	14	– (4) b Dale	0
H. G. Kuhn c Holland b Wheal	34	– (5) not out	11
†O. G. Robinson c Weatherley b Scriven	12		
M. K. O'Riordan lbw b Crane	37	– (2) not out	52
D. I. Stevens c Currie b Holland	0		
G. Stewart c Scriven b Wheal	4		
H. W. Podmore not out	30		
Lb 11, nb 4	15	Lb 6, nb 4	10
1/20 (2) 2/20 (1) 3/21 (4) 4/30 (3) 5/64 (5) 6/76 (7) 7/107 (6) 8/114 (9) 9/123 (10) 10/170 (8) (61 overs)	170	1/8 (1) 2/165 (3) 3/170 (4) (3 wkts, 41.5 overs)	185

Wheal 15–6–34–2; Holland 20–12–26–2; Currie 13–3–42–3; Dale 2–0–16–0; Scriven 8–2–24–2; Crane 3–0–17–1. *Second innings*—Holland 9–2–38–1; Wheal 9–3–36–0; Scriven 5–0–35–0; Currie 4–1–16–0; Crane 8.5–1–30–1; Organ 1–0–2–0; Dale 5–0–22–1.

Umpires: N. J. Llong and B. V. Taylor. Referee: G. R. Cowdrey.

LANCASHIRE

An exit and six entrances

PAUL EDWARDS

Lancashire's first match at Old Trafford in 2020 took place on September 17, when they defeated Yorkshire by seven runs in a T20 game on a perfect late-summer evening. But neither the weather nor the cricket lingered in the mind. Rather it was the memory of the club's staff lining the boundary to pay their respects to David Hodgkiss, Lancashire's chairman, who had died in March after contracting Covid-19. Chief executive stood next to cook, steward next to media officer. High in the pavilion the journalists stood too, as did the players of both sides on the outfield. Applause rang out in the warm air; a few folk were not ready for the rawness of the moment, or the indomitability of it all. No one at Lancashire needed telling that the virus would cost more than money, more than sport.

There was sport, though. And even if five Bob Willis Trophy matches and 12 Vitality Blast games were rather hard commons beside the banquet of a normal summer, they were more than had seemed possible in the wretched spring. The revised schedule necessitated changes. Contracts with overseas players were cordially cancelled, though Lancashire were one of only two counties (along with Surrey) who did not furlough their cricketers, and Old Trafford's transformation into a biosecure international venue meant they played just three late T20 matches there. They opened their programme with a (home) first-class fixture at Worcester, in August. Injuries to Graham Onions and Richard Gleeson, and England call-ups for Saqib Mahmood and Liam Livingstone, further reduced the pool of professionals available, especially for four-day games. Yet out of this ticklish predicament emerged the distinguishing feature of the season: fresh talent.

Six Lancashire players made their first-class debuts in the Bob Willis Trophy, the most for any team in competitive county cricket since Essex in the 1962 Championship. In that opening game at Worcester, George Balderson, Tom Hartley and Ed Moulton appeared against Leicestershire. Three weeks later, George Burrows arrived, in the Roses match at Headingley; Jack Morley and George Lavelle joined the ranks at Aigburth, where Lancashire ended their red-ball programme with victory over Derbyshire.

Watching these debutants in 2020 was almost like studying the 18th-century British monarchy: three very different Georges (though none went barmy). Balderson, a seam-bowling all-rounder, took to four-day cricket with unnerving self-possession, and Lavelle's wicketkeeping at Liverpool – only four byes in 184.1 overs – was assured. The best of the six newcomers was probably slow left-armer Hartley, who was selected for all but one of Lancashire's 16 matches. In the Blast semi-final, the climax of the county's season, he dismissed Nottinghamshire's Tom Moores and Joe Clarke within four balls.

Mark Fletcher, MI News/NurPhoto/Getty Images
Alex Davies

Lancashire were not the only team to bring on apprentices, and would not have relied on them so much but for the circumstances. Yet no county's selectors grabbed the chance more enthusiastically, or saw more clearly that the long-term benefits would outweigh the immediate gains of importing players on short-term contracts. And it would be unfair to blame the freshmen for a relatively modest showing in the Bob Willis Trophy. Although Onions or Gleeson would have strengthened the attack against Leicestershire – the only defeat – the failure of Dane Vilas's side to reach the final owed as much to a poor performance at Trent Bridge and bad weather at Leeds. The best batsmen in both formats were Alex Davies and Steven Croft. Davies scored seven fifties in 18 innings, and was voted the members' Player of the Year; Croft yet again married hard-won experience with the enthusiasm of a colt. But no Lancashire batsman made a first-class century and, though Keaton Jennings reached a 60-ball hundred on the Blast's opening day, the failure of the middle order was a regular feature in four T20 defeats.

The bowling was more consistent. Tom Bailey took 13 wickets in four first-class appearances; Danny Lamb, who had previously struggled to get a game, a dozen. But Onions, who had collected 102 in two Championship seasons with Lancashire, injured his back, never played, and announced his retirement in September; in January, he was appointed bowling coach. The spinners had few first-class opportunities until the Derbyshire match, but were integral to the team's progress to finals day in the Blast. Parkinson took 15 wickets; Hartley curbed batsmen's attempts to attack.

The pandemic was never far away, its melancholy impact manifest in the deserted grounds. But there were still chances to smile. During lockdown, many club staff telephoned members who were isolating, to reassure them they were not forgotten. Former captain Warren Hegg found one in fine fettle. "I spoke to a gentleman and asked him about the best spinner he had seen at Old Trafford," Hegg recalled. "He mentioned Jim Laker and Shane Warne, and I came back with Muttiah Muralitharan. 'Oh yes, I remember sitting behind you when you were keeping to him,' he replied. 'Don't worry, I couldn't pick him either.'" David Hodgkiss would have enjoyed that one.

Treasurer Les Platts acted as chairman during the summer, but in November Lancashire appointed Andy Anson, the chief executive of the British Olympic Association, to succeed Hodgkiss; he warned that "we can't plan for anything but uncertainty". Opener Luke Wells was signed from Sussex, and seamer Jack Blatherwick from Nottinghamshire. There were departures too, with Brooke Guest moving to Derbyshire, Toby Lester released, and Stephen Parry leaving after 16 years with Lancashire – though the club announced that his testimonial, scheduled for 2020, would be carried over.

LANCASHIRE RESULTS

Bob Willis Trophy – Played 5: Won 2, Lost 1, Drawn 2.
Vitality Blast matches – Played 11: Won 6, Lost 4, No result 1. Abandoned 1.

Bob Willis Trophy, 3rd in North Group;
Vitality Blast, semi-finalists.

BOB WILLIS TROPHY AVERAGES

BATTING AND FIELDING

Cap		*Birthplace*	*M*	*I*	*NO*	*R*	*HS*	*100*	*Avge*	*Ct*
2010	S. J. Croft	*Blackpool‡*	4	5	2	199	63	0	66.33	6
2017	A. L. Davies	*Darwen‡*	5	8	1	337	86	0	48.14	7
	J. J. Bohannon	*Bolton‡*	5	7	0	257	94	0	36.71	4
2018	D. J. Vilas††	*Johannesburg, SA*	5	7	0	247	90	0	35.28	5
	†T. W. Hartley	*Ormskirk‡*	4	4	3	35	13*	0	35.00	2
	D. J. Lamb	*Preston‡*	3	4	1	104	50*	0	34.66	1
	†G. P. Balderson	*Manchester‡*	5	7	2	156	61*	0	31.20	0
2018	†K. K. Jennings	*Johannesburg, SA*	5	8	1	182	81	0	26.00	8
2018	T. E. Bailey	*Preston‡*	4	4	1	47	38*	0	15.66	0
	R. P. Jones	*Warrington*	3	5	0	77	23	0	15.40	3

Also batted: G. D. Burrows (*Wigan‡*) (2 matches) 1; R. J. Gleeson (*Blackpool‡*) (1 match) 6; L. J. Hurt (*Preston‡*) (2 matches) 2, 1; G. I. D. Lavelle (*Ormskirk‡*) (1 match) 13, 7 (2 ct); L. S. Livingstone (cap 2017) (*Barrow-in-Furness*) (2 matches) 23, 14 (1 ct); †J. P. Morley (*Rochdale‡*) (1 match) 3; E. H. T. Moulton (*Preston‡*) (1 match) 0, 0; †L. Wood (*Sheffield*) (2 matches) 46, 6.

‡ *Born in Lancashire.* †† *Other non-England-qualified.*

BOWLING

	Style	*O*	*M*	*R*	*W*	*BB*	*5I*	*Avge*
J. P. Morley	SLA	40	15	71	5	4-62	0	14.20
D. J. Lamb	RFM	68.1	13	203	12	4-55	0	16.91
R. J. Gleeson	RFM	18	4	52	3	3-32	0	17.33
L. S. Livingstone	LB	21.3	2	92	5	3-79	0	18.40
T. E. Bailey	RFM	111.4	44	282	13	3-11	0	21.69
L. J. Hurt	RFM	48	6	182	7	4-27	0	26.00
G. D. Burrows	RFM	40	8	127	4	2-20	0	31.75
G. P. Balderson	RFM	104	23	296	9	3-63	0	32.88
L. Wood	LFM	44	8	118	3	2-31	0	39.33
T. W. Hartley	SLA	111	28	324	6	3-79	0	54.00

Also bowled: S. J. Croft (RFM/OB) 1–0–6–0; K. K. Jennings (RM) 15–3–28–1; R. P. Jones (LB) 3–2–4–0; E. H. T. Moulton (RFM) 27–4–110–0.

LEADING VITALITY BLAST AVERAGES (60 runs/10 overs)

Batting	*Runs*	*HS*	*Avge*	*SR*	*Ct/St*
L. S. Livingstone	192	69	27.42	**156.09**	2
K. K. Jennings	233	108	58.25	**134.68**	0
S. J. Croft	272	58	30.22	**125.92**	3
D. J. Vilas	144	44*	20.57	**122.03**	9
A. L. Davies	299	82	29.90	**121.54**	6/6
R. P. Jones	77	38*	25.66	**105.47**	7
D. J. Lamb	69	29*	69.00	**104.54**	0

Bowling	*W*	*BB*	*Avge*	*ER*
T. E. Bailey	10	5-17	11.10	**6.93**
S. J. Croft	4	2-29	19.25	**7.00**
T. W. Hartley	6	2-21	42.66	**7.11**
L. Wood	7	3-21	20.42	**7.52**
L. S. Livingstone	9	4-23	21.22	**7.53**
M. W. Parkinson	15	3-9	20.66	**7.68**
S. Mahmood	4	1-14	29.00	**7.73**
D. J. Lamb	7	1-14	32.28	**8.07**

FIRST-CLASS COUNTY RECORDS

Highest score for	424	A. C. MacLaren v Somerset at Taunton	1895
Highest score against	315*	T. W. Hayward (Surrey) at The Oval	1898
Leading run-scorer	34,222	E. Tyldesley (avge 45.20)	1909–36
Best bowling for	10-46	W. Hickton v Hampshire at Manchester	1870
Best bowling against	10-40	G. O. B. Allen (Middlesex) at Lord's	1929
Leading wicket-taker	1,816	J. B. Statham (avge 15.12)	1950–68
Highest total for	863	v Surrey at The Oval	1990
Highest total against	707-9 dec	by Surrey at The Oval	1990
Lowest total for	25	v Derbyshire at Manchester	1871
Lowest total against	20	by Essex at Chelmsford	2013

LIST A COUNTY RECORDS

Highest score for	166	D. J. Vilas v Nottinghamshire at Nottingham	2019
Highest score against	186*	C. G. Greenidge (West Indians) at Liverpool	1984
Leading run-scorer	11,969	N. H. Fairbrother (avge 41.84)	1982–2002
Best bowling for	6-10	C. E. H. Croft v Scotland at Manchester	1982
Best bowling against	8-26	K. D. Boyce (Essex) at Manchester	1971
Leading wicket-taker	480	J. Simmons (avge 25.75)	1969–89
Highest total for	406-9	v Nottinghamshire at Nottingham	2019
Highest total against	417-7	by Nottinghamshire at Nottingham	2019
Lowest total for	59	v Worcestershire at Worcester	1963
Lowest total against	52	by Minor Counties at Lakenham	1998

TWENTY20 COUNTY RECORDS

Highest score for	**108**	**K. K. Jennings v Durham at Chester-le-Street**	**2020**
Highest score against	108*	I. J. Harvey (Yorkshire) at Leeds	2004
Leading run-scorer	**3,680**	**S. J. Croft (avge 29.20, SR 123.61)**	**2006–20**
Best bowling for	5-13	S. D. Parry v Worcestershire at Manchester	2016
Best bowling against	6-19	T. T. Bresnan (Yorkshire) at Leeds	2017
Leading wicket-taker	**118**	**S. D. Parry (avge 24.88, ER 7.14)**	**2009–20**
Highest total for	231-4	v Yorkshire at Manchester	2015
Highest total against	211-5	by Derbyshire at Derby	2017
Lowest total for	**83**	**v Durham at Manchester**	**2020**
Lowest total against	53	by Worcestershire at Manchester	2016

ADDRESS

Emirates Old Trafford, Talbot Road, Manchester M16 0PX; 0161 282 4000; enquiries@lancashirecricket.co.uk; www.lancashirecricket.co.uk. Twitter: @lancscricket.

OFFICIALS

Captain D. J. Vilas
Director of cricket P. J. W. Allott
Head coach G. Chapple
Performance director/asst coach M. J. Chilton
Head of talent pathway C. T. Benbow
President Sir Howard Bernstein

Acting chairman 2020 L. M. Platts
Chairman 2021 A. E. Anson
Chief executive D. Gidney
Head groundsman M. Merchant
Scorers C. Rimmer and G. L. Morgan

LANCASHIRE v LEICESTERSHIRE

At Worcester, August 1–4. Leicestershire won by seven wickets. Leicestershire 22pts, Lancashire 4pts. Toss: Lancashire. First-class debuts: G. P. Balderson, T. W. Hartley, E. H. T. Moulton. County debut: B. T. Slater.

Ackermann inspired Leicestershire's first first-class win over Lancashire since 2005. With Old Trafford a biosecure international venue, and Lancashire uneasy about Leicester – then a Covid-19 hotspot – the match moved to Worcester, where a slow pitch appeared likely to frustrate attempts to force victory. But Ackermann scored 167 in all, and managed his bowlers skilfully; he was at the crease when Taylor hit Bailey for four to reach a target of 150 in 17 overs with eight balls to spare. On the first day, Vilas and Croft had put on 130 for Lancashire's fifth wicket, and their total was later boosted by a five-run penalty after Klein threw the ball at Lamb "in an inappropriate and dangerous manner". But Slater began his fortnight on loan from Nottinghamshire with a career-best 172, putting on 153 with Azad and 165 with Ackermann, a third-wicket record for Leicestershire in this fixture. Their lead of 87 proved vital as the bowlers patiently worked through Lancashire's second innings. Requiring nearly nine an over, they triumphed through Ackermann's enterprising 73 in 41 balls, and Dearden's three sixes. Lancashire fielded three first-class debutants for the first time since 2005, when Croft, Gareth Cross and Tom Smith appeared against Oxford UCCE – and the first time against another county since Charles de Trafford, John Heap and Hugh McIntyre at Derby in 1884.

Close of play: first day, Lancashire 265-6 (Balderson 13, Lamb 2); second day, Leicestershire 183-2 (Slater 104, Ackermann 15); third day, Lancashire 96-3 (Jones 13, Vilas 7).

HOME – AND AWAY

BWT matches officially declared home fixtures for a county playing at an away or neutral ground:

At Nottingham, August 1–4	Derbyshire beat Nottinghamshire by three wickets
At Worcester, August 1–4	Lancashire lost to Leicestershire by seven wickets
At Arundel, August 15–18	Hampshire beat Surrey by an innings and 52 runs
At Nottingham, August 15–18	Lancashire drew with Nottinghamshire
At Chester-le-Street, August 22–25	Derbyshire drew with Durham
At Arundel, August 22–25	Hampshire drew with Essex

Middlesex played their home games at Radlett in Hertfordshire, a regular venue since 2013.

Lancashire

K. K. Jennings lbw b Taylor	5	– c Rhodes b Wright	8
†A. L. Davies c Rhodes b Klein	21	– lbw b Parkinson	54
J. J. Bohannon c Swindells b Klein	44	– lbw b Mike	3
R. P. Jones b Klein	12	– c Rhodes b Wright	16
*D. J. Vilas c Azad b Taylor	90	– b Parkinson	43
S. J. Croft lbw b Ackermann	63	– not out	52
G. P. Balderson c Ackermann b Wright	29	– lbw b Parkinson	4
D. J. Lamb b Parkinson	27	– lbw b Mike	19
T. E. Bailey c Taylor b Wright	5	– c Swindells b Mike	0
T. W. Hartley not out	5	– lbw b Ackermann	5
E. H. T. Moulton lbw b Parkinson	0	– lbw b Mike	0
B 10, lb 2, nb 4, p 5	21	B 5, lb 23, nb 4	32
1/5 (1) 2/44 (2) 3/82 (4) 4/97 (3) 5/227 (5) 6/258 (6) 7/283 (7) 8/289 (9) 9/322 (8) 10/322 (11) (107.5 overs)	322	1/35 (1) 2/59 (3) 3/83 (2) 4/101 (4) 5/155 (5) 6/163 (7) 7/206 (8) 8/206 (9) 9/230 (10) 10/236 (11) (109.1 overs)	236

Wright 24–9–52–2; Taylor 23–4–64–2; Klein 20–0–81–3; Mike 17–0–55–0; Parkinson 18.5–4–32–2; Ackermann 5–2–21–1. *Second innings*—Taylor 20–9–40–0; Wright 21–11–39–2; Parkinson 25–14–30–3; Mike 17.1–3–39–4; Klein 19–3–54–0; Ackermann 7–5–6–1.

Leicestershire

M. H. Azad c Jones b Hartley	58		
B. T. Slater c Bohannon b Bailey	172	– c Vilas b Bailey	25
H. E. Dearden c Vilas b Balderson	0	– (4) c and b Lamb	33
*C. N. Ackermann run out (Jennings)	94	– (3) not out	73
G. H. Rhodes c Vilas b Bailey	11	– (1) c Jones b Bailey	8
T. A. I. Taylor lbw b Balderson	15	– (5) not out	6
†H. J. Swindells b Hartley	5		
B. W. M. Mike c Bohannon b Hartley	16		
D. Klein not out	21		
C. F. Parkinson not out	8		
Lb 1, nb 8	9	B 1, lb 4	5
1/153 (1) 2/156 (3) (8 wkts dec, 119 overs)	409	1/16 (1) (3 wkts, 15.4 overs)	150
3/321 (2) 4/333 (5) 5/359 (4)		2/62 (2) 3/133 (4)	
6/360 (6) 7/364 (7) 8/399 (8) 110 overs: 335-4			

C. J. C. Wright did not bat.

Bailey 25–9–63–2; Moulton 25–4–94–0; Hartley 33–5–117–3; Lamb 15–1–53–0; Balderson 20–1–75–2; Croft 1–0–6–0. *Second innings*—Bailey 6.4–0–63–2; Moulton 2–0–16–0; Hartley 5–0–43–0; Lamb 2–0–23–1.

Umpires: N. G. B. Cook and R. White. Referee: A. J. Swann.

At Chester-le-Street, August 8–10. LANCASHIRE beat DURHAM by an innings and 18 runs.

LANCASHIRE v NOTTINGHAMSHIRE

At Nottingham, August 15–18. Drawn. Lancashire 9pts, Nottinghamshire 16pts. Toss: Lancashire.

Lancashire opted to bowl, then served up some rare tripe that set the tone for a game they were lucky not to lose: Nottinghamshire, playing an away fixture at their own ground, took eight bonus points to Lancashire's one. Neither Slater nor Duckett objected to the bowlers' generosity on the opening day. Slater reached his second century against Lancashire in a fortnight, following his 172 in 401 minutes while on loan to Leicestershire with 142 in 408. His classical technique complemented Duckett's improvisations as they added 178 for the second wicket. After the next day was washed out, Lancashire's bowlers performed more capably on the third morning, with Bailey the pick. But they could not prevent Nottinghamshire collecting five batting points, and lost six wickets during a 44-over evening session, three to Chappell's well-directed aggression. On the last morning, Croft finally fell for an obdurate fifty, and the tail did not hang around; Mullaney immediately enforced the follow-on. But he was thwarted by bad light, and by Jennings and Davies, who displayed the competence lacking in the first innings.

Close of play: first day, Nottinghamshire 268-2 (Slater 111, Clarke 4); second day, no play; third day, Lancashire 129-6 (Croft 37, Hartley 6).

HUNDREDS FOR TWO COUNTIES IN ONE SEASON

A. J. Strauss	3 for Middlesex and 1 for Somerset	2011
J. W. A. Taylor	2 for Nottinghamshire and 1 for Sussex	2013
J. D. Libby	1 for Northamptonshire and 1 for Nottinghamshire	2016
B. T. Slater	**1 for Leicestershire and 1 for Nottinghamshire**	**2020**

Strauss appeared as a guest for Somerset v Indians and Taylor for Sussex v Australians. Nottinghamshire loaned Libby to Northamptonshire and Slater to Leicestershire. Only Slater scored centuries against the same team.

Nottinghamshire

B. T. Slater c Croft b Bailey	142
H. Hameed lbw b Balderson	22
B. M. Duckett lbw b Bailey	116
J. M. Clarke b Balderson	57
*S. J. Mullaney c sub (R. P. Jones) b Livingstone	67
P. D. Trego c Davies b Bailey	1
†T. J. Moores c Vilas b Hurt	18
S. R. Patel c Croft b Livingstone	0
M. Carter c Hartley b Hurt	22
Z. J. Chappell c Bohannon b Livingstone	0
T. E. Barber not out	2
B 2, lb 8, w 1, nb 14	25
(119.5 overs)	472

1/78 (2) 2/256 (3) 3/343 (1) 4/373 (4) 5/378 (6) 6/425 (7) 7/425 (8) 8/453 (9) 9/455 (10) 10/472 (5) 110 overs: 405-5

Bailey 30–10–91–3; Wood 16–2–47–0; Hurt 22–2–111–2; Balderson 19–1–73–2; Livingstone 14.5–2–79–3; Hartley 11–0–47–0; Jennings 7–1–14–0.

Lancashire

K. K. Jennings c Hameed b Chappell	10	– not out 37
†A. L. Davies c Moores b Trego	26	– not out 69
J. J. Bohannon c and b Chappell	1	
L. S. Livingstone b Mullaney	14	
*D. J. Vilas c Moores b Chappell	26	
S. J. Croft c sub (L. A. Patterson-White) b Barber	59	
G. P. Balderson c Chappell b Trego	8	
T. W. Hartley not out	13	
L. Wood c Slater b Barber	6	
T. E. Bailey c Duckett b Barber	4	
L. J. Hurt c Moores b Trego	1	
B 5	5	B 4, lb 8, nb 2 14
(64.3 overs)	173	(no wkt, 40 overs) 120

1/23 (1) 2/37 (2) 3/37 (3) 4/59 (4) 5/109 (5) 6/121 (7) 7/158 (6) 8/168 (9) 9/172 (10) 10/173 (11)

Trego 14.3–2–33–3; Chappell 17–5–48–3; Mullaney 7–1–23–1; Barber 10–2–42–3; Carter 16–7–22–0. *Second innings*—Trego 9–3–15–0; Chappell 4–1–15–0; Barber 9–0–32–0; Mullaney 4–1–12–0; Patel 6–2–17–0; Carter 7–2–15–0; Duckett 1–0–2–0.

Umpires: P. K. Baldwin and R. T. Robinson. Referee: J. J. Whitaker.

At Leeds, August 22–25. LANCASHIRE drew with YORKSHIRE.

LANCASHIRE v DERBYSHIRE

At Liverpool, September 6–9. Lancashire won by 178 runs. Lancashire 20pts, Derbyshire 3pts. Toss: Lancashire. First-class debuts: G. I. D. Lavelle, J. P. Morley.

Derbyshire arrived as North Group leaders, but their hopes of a Lord's final all but disappeared when they failed to gain a batting point. Still, their resilience was typical of their tournament: they came within half an hour of their first unbeaten first-class season since 1874. Finally playing a home match on home soil, Lancashire lost both openers leg-before without scoring. Then Bohannon batted five hours for 94 – following an unbeaten 98 on his previous first-class visit to Aigburth – and Balderson helped him repair the innings, though Reece restricted the total to 219. Derbyshire also started shakily: Lamb and Balderson reduced them to 17 for four, which became 61 for seven, before Hosein and McKiernan shared a century stand. But two debutants, slow left-armer Jack Morley and keeper George Lavelle, combined to remove Hosein, and Derbyshire just missed that batting point. Second time round, they bowled poorly: Jennings and Davies put on 138, while Balderson and Lamb completed maiden fifties. Needing 381, Derbyshire collapsed to the spin of Morley and Hartley, losing six for 17, before McKiernan and Conners held firm for 36 overs. With Lancastrian nerves beginning to fray, Morley trapped Conners; McKiernan was last out for his own first half-century, giving Lamb career-best match figures of seven for 72.

Close of play: first day, Lancashire 206-8 (Hartley 5, Morley 0); second day, Derbyshire 120-7 (Hosein 44, McKiernan 19); third day, Lancashire 312-6 (Balderson 56, Lamb 16).

Lancashire

Batsman	First innings		Second innings	
K. K. Jennings lbw b Conners	0	–	c Godleman b Critchley	81
A. L. Davies lbw b Reece	0	–	c Dal b Critchley	86
J. J. Bohannon c Hudson-Prentice b Melton	94	–	c Madsen b Reece	35
R. P. Jones c du Plooy b Melton	23	–	c Madsen b Critchley	5
*D. J. Vilas c Hosein b Reece	5	–	c Reece b Critchley	10
†G. I. D. Lavelle lbw b Melton	13	–	lbw b Reece	7
G. P. Balderson c Madsen b Conners	36	–	not out	61
D. J. Lamb c du Plooy b Critchley	8	–	not out	50
T. W. Hartley not out	12			
J. P. Morley c Hosein b Dal	3			
G. D. Burrows c Madsen b Reece	1			
B 8, lb 10, nb 6	24		B 4, lb 7, w 2, nb 8	21
1/0 (1) 2/2 (2) 3/58 (4) 4/72 (5) 5/108 (6) 6/169 (3) 7/197 (7) 8/197 (8) 9/214 (10) 10/219 (11) (101.3 overs)	219		1/138 (2) 2/201 (1) 3/214 (4) 4/230 (3) 5/230 (5) 6/246 (6) (6 wkts dec, 72.2 overs)	356

Conners 16–6–32–2; Reece 29.3–12–54–3; Melton 17–4–46–3; Hudson-Prentice 8–2–22–0; Critchley 22–8–39–1; Dal 9–5–8–1. *Second innings*—Conners 9.2–0–56–0; Reece 13–2–49–2; Dal 10–2–22–0; Critchley 26–0–126–4; Melton 7–0–60–0; McKiernan 7–2–32–0.

Derbyshire

Batsman	First innings		Second innings	
L. M. Reece c Lavelle b Lamb	2	–	c Jennings b Morley	69
*B. A. Godleman c Jennings b Lamb	6	–	c Jones b Lamb	4
W. L. Madsen lbw b Balderson	4	–	lbw b Lamb	9
J. L. du Plooy lbw b Lamb	0	–	lbw b Hartley	34
M. J. J. Critchley lbw b Burrows	14	–	b Morley	7
F. J. Hudson-Prentice c Hartley b Balderson	19	–	c Jennings b Hartley	1
†H. R. Hosein c Lavelle b Morley	84	–	lbw b Morley	6
A. K. Dal c Jennings b Balderson	2	–	lbw b Hartley	3
M. H. McKiernan lbw b Burrows	31	–	lbw b Lamb	52
S. Conners not out	10	–	lbw b Morley	9
D. R. Melton b Lamb	11	–	not out	0
B 2, lb 3, w 1, nb 6	12		B 2, lb 6	8
1/5 (1) 2/15 (2) 3/15 (4) 4/17 (3) 5/44 (5) 6/59 (6) 7/61 (8) 8/163 (9) 9/178 (7) 10/195 (11) (93.3 overs)	195		1/4 (2) 2/20 (3) 3/118 (1) 4/118 (4) 5/122 (6) 6/126 (5) 7/131 (8) 8/135 (7) 9/195 (10) 10/202 (9) (90.4 overs)	202

Balderson 25–6–63–3; Lamb 22.3–3–60–4; Burrows 11–3–20–2; Hartley 25–8–38–0; Morley 10–5–9–1. *Second innings*—Balderson 7–2–19–0; Lamb 5.4–3–12–3; Hartley 37–15–79–3; Burrows 8–2–18–0; Morley 30–10–62–4; Jones 3–2–4–0.

Umpires: G. D. Lloyd and S. J. O'Shaughnessy. Referee: A. J. Swann.

LEICESTERSHIRE

Misfield of nightmares

RICHARD RAE

The domestic playing field was levelled in 2020, in a way that no one could have foreseen. But Leicestershire, accustomed to financial restrictions, did their best to make the most of it – and, to some extent, succeeded.

Head coach Paul Nixon found himself with the county's least experienced squad for years: Paul Horton and Mark Cosgrove, who was marooned in Australia and later released after five seasons, did not play. Captain in 2019, Horton was expected to retire at the end of 2020 but, after the first-class season was reduced to five games, he accepted the club's decision to concentrate on younger players. When Leicestershire drew with Nottinghamshire in the Bob Willis Trophy in August, the new captain, 29-year-old Colin Ackermann, was the oldest member of the XI – a novel experience for him – though a couple of over-30s (Dieter Klein and Chris Wright) appeared in other matches.

But with most counties deprived of their overseas signings, Leicestershire – who put South African batsman Janneman Malan on hold – had a better chance of competing against richer clubs.

They briefly led the Bob Willis Trophy's North Group after beating Lancashire in the opening round, thanks to 172 from Ben Slater, on a short-term loan from Nottinghamshire, plus two half-centuries from Ackermann. A fortnight later, Ackermann was on 61, and seemed to be steering his side towards victory over Durham, when the weather intervened. In the following game, his second-innings 65 was vital in extending Nottinghamshire's long wait for a first-class win. When he failed to reach 50 – against Derbyshire and Yorkshire – Leicestershire lost.

They did miss the runs and nous that Cosgrove and Horton might have contributed. Harry Dearden and the previous year's leading scorer, Hassan Azad, started well, but fell away. Dearden scored half his 234 runs against Derbyshire, while Azad attracted some debatable decisions – though his determination to play positively rendered him more vulnerable. He needs to find the right balance between quick scoring and the obduracy that brought him success in 2019.

Slater's return to Trent Bridge after two games meant Sam Evans was brought in to open. Scores of 85 against Durham and 48 against Nottinghamshire should earn further opportunities, though the signing of more young batsmen, Zimbabwean Nick Welch (who appeared in the Blast), Rishi Patel from Essex (initially on loan) and Scott Steel from Durham, adds welcome competition. Seamer Ed Barnes arrived from Yorkshire after a loan spell with Derbyshire. There was also encouragement from the growing confidence of 21-year-old wicketkeeper-batsman Harry Swindells, and the potential of all-rounder Ben

Alex Pantling, Getty Images

Colin Ackermann

Mike, who turned 22 in August. Swindells scored a maiden first-class fifty, while Mike continued to have an impact with the ball.

That said, the loss of Wright to a knee injury after two games severely reduced Leicestershire's seam options. For the most part, duties were shared by Mike, Klein, Gavin Griffiths and Tom Taylor (who later moved to Northamptonshire); Alex Evans – still a teenager when the season started – came in for the last two games. None made an immediate impression, or took more than nine first-class wickets, though no frontline bowler played all five matches.

They peaked early in the Bob Willis Trophy, but Leicestershire left their best until last in the Vitality Blast, where they came heartbreakingly close to reaching finals day for the first time since winning the Twenty20 trophy in 2011. To scrape into the quarter-finals, they had needed to beat North Group leaders Nottinghamshire at home, and second-placed Lancashire at Old Trafford, in their last two qualifying games. They did just that, earning a rematch with Nottinghamshire at Trent Bridge, where the scores were tied and the hosts went through on a better total in the powerplay. But for late misfields by Arron Lilley and Klein, Leicestershire would have been in the last four.

Making the knockouts was an admirable effort by this young team. Left-arm spinner Callum Parkinson, with ten wickets and an economy-rate of 6.56, proved every bit as talented as his leg-spinning twin, Matt, at Lancashire. Ackermann and Lilley scored heavily, while Ireland all-rounder Gareth Delany was a useful signing. In January, the club picked up South Africa all-rounder Wiaan Mulder as an overseas player for 2021.

The leanest of the first-class counties before the Covid-19 pandemic, Leicestershire furloughed 33 of their 44 full-time staff, including all 17 members of the first-team squad – for three months from the start of April. New chief executive Sean Jarvis said that no club sponsors requested refunds, and only 13% of members asked for subscriptions to be returned.

The fact that 92% of the club's income derives from the ECB, sponsors and members meant their revenue stream was less affected than some other counties; even so, around £1m was lost. By the end of Leicestershire's financial year in September 2020, a projected £300,000 profit had turned into a loss of £50,000.

But fund-raising by Friends of Grace Road covered one substantial expense: the complete renovation of the fine old manual scoreboard. One of only two remaining on county grounds, it outshines Canterbury through its splendid Cupola Clock.

LEICESTERSHIRE RESULTS

Bob Willis Trophy matches – Played 5: Won 1, Lost 2, Drawn 2.
Vitality Blast matches – Played 9: Won 4, Lost 4, No result 1. Abandoned 2.

Bob Willis Trophy, 5th in North Group;
Vitality Blast, quarter-finalists.

BOB WILLIS TROPHY AVERAGES

BATTING AND FIELDING

Cap		*Birthplace*	*M*	*I*	*NO*	*R*	*HS*	*100*	*Avge*	*Ct*
2019	C. N. Ackermann††	*George, SA*	5	9	2	379	94	0	54.14	6
	†B. T. Slater	*Chesterfield*	2	4	0	197	172	1	49.25	0
	T. A. I. Taylor	*Stoke-on-Trent*	3	3	1	78	57	0	39.00	1
	H. J. Swindells	*Leicester‡*	5	7	2	188	52*	0	37.60	11
	S. T. Evans	*Leicester‡*	3	5	0	148	85	0	29.60	3
	†H. E. Dearden	*Bury*	5	9	0	234	70	0	26.00	1
	G. T. Griffiths	*Ormskirk*	3	3	2	23	11*	0	23.00	1
	C. F. Parkinson	*Bolton*	3	3	1	42	21	0	21.00	0
	B. W. M. Mike	*Nottingham*	4	6	1	99	51*	0	19.80	2
	†M. H. Azad	*Quetta, Pakistan*	5	8	0	144	58	0	18.00	3
	G. H. Rhodes	*Birmingham*	4	7	2	83	22*	0	16.60	4
	D. Klein††	*Lichtenburg, SA*	4	5	1	53	27	0	13.25	0
	†H. A. Evans	*Bedford*	2	3	0	16	15	0	5.33	1

Also batted: W. S. Davis (*Stafford*) (2 matches) 20, 8; A. M. Lilley (*Tameside*) (1 match) 5, 13 (1 ct); R. K. Patel (*Chigwell*) (1 match) 19, 5; †W. J. Weighell (*Middlesbrough*) (1 match) 23; C. J. C. Wright (*Chipping Norton*) (2 matches) 10*, 23.

‡ *Born in Leicestershire.* †† *Other non-England-qualified.*

BOWLING

	Style	*O*	*M*	*R*	*W*	*BB*	*5I*	*Avge*
A. M. Lilley	OB	6	1	21	3	3-21	0	7.00
C. N. Ackermann	OB	35	12	92	4	2-24	0	23.00
C. F. Parkinson	SLA	79.3	22	192	8	3-30	0	24.00
C. J. C. Wright	RFM	57	21	141	5	2-39	0	28.20
B. W. M. Mike	RFM	88.1	13	279	9	4-39	0	31.00
W. S. Davis	RFM	30	6	106	3	2-75	0	35.33
G. T. Griffiths	RFM	61.5	13	181	5	3-52	0	36.20
D. Klein	LFM	95	10	332	9	3-44	0	36.88
T. A. I. Taylor	RFM	93	25	247	6	2-49	0	41.16
H. A. Evans	RFM	35.2	7	140	3	2-59	0	46.66

Also bowled: M. H. Azad (OB/LB) 2.1–0–15–1; S. T. Evans (OB) 3–0–22–0; W. J. Weighell (RM) 6–0–29–0.

LEADING VITALITY BLAST AVERAGES (70 runs/10 overs)

Batting	*Runs*	*HS*	*Avge*	*SR*	*Ct/St*
B. W. M. Mike	70	22*	17.50	**179.48**	3
G. J. Delany	193	68	21.44	**139.84**	1
A. M. Lilley	278	69	30.88	**139.00**	3
C. N. Ackermann	246	67*	30.75	**122.38**	5
N. R. Welch	101	43	20.20	**103.06**	1
L. J. Hill	83	22	11.85	**102.46**	2/2
H. E. Dearden	120	36*	17.14	**88.88**	1

Bowling	*W*	*BB*	*Avge*	*ER*
C. F. Parkinson	10	3-21	21.00	**6.56**
D. Klein	2	1-22	33.00	**6.60**
C. N. Ackermann	8	3-18	18.75	**7.14**
T. A. I. Taylor	2	1-7	43.00	**7.81**
G. T. Griffiths	10	4-35	18.00	**7.82**
G. J. Delany	6	2-26	24.66	**8.70**
W. S. Davis	7	3-38	26.57	**8.71**

FIRST-CLASS COUNTY RECORDS

Highest score for	309*	H. D. Ackerman v Glamorgan at Cardiff	2006
Highest score against	355*	K. P. Pietersen (Surrey) at The Oval	2015
Leading run-scorer	30,143	L. G. Berry (avge 30.32)	1924–51
Best bowling for	10-18	G. Geary v Glamorgan at Pontypridd	1929
Best bowling against	10-32	H. Pickett (Essex) at Leyton	1895
Leading wicket-taker	2,131	W. E. Astill (avge 23.18)	1906–39
Highest total for	701-4 dec	v Worcestershire at Worcester	1906
Highest total against	761-6 dec	by Essex at Chelmsford	1990
Lowest total for	25	v Kent at Leicester	1912
Lowest total against	24	by Glamorgan at Leicester	1971
	24	by Oxford University at Oxford	1985

LIST A COUNTY RECORDS

Highest score for	201	V. J. Wells v Berkshire at Leicester	1996
Highest score against	201*	R. S. Bopara (Essex) at Leicester	2008
Leading run-scorer	8,216	N. E. Briers (avge 27.66)	1975–95
Best bowling for	6-16	C. M. Willoughby v Somerset at Leicester	2005
Best bowling against	6-21	S. M. Pollock (Warwickshire) at Birmingham	1996
Leading wicket-taker	308	K. Higgs (avge 18.80)	1972–82
Highest total for	406-5	v Berkshire at Leicester	1996
Highest total against	458-4	by India A at Leicester	2018
Lowest total for	36	v Sussex at Leicester	1973
Lowest total against	62	by Northamptonshire at Leicester	1974
	62	by Middlesex at Leicester	1998

TWENTY20 COUNTY RECORDS

Highest score for	113	B. A. Raine v Warwickshire at Birmingham	2018
Highest score against	103*	A. N. Petersen (Lancashire) at Leicester	2016
Leading run-scorer	1,579	M. J. Cosgrove (avge 27.22, SR 132.24)	2005–19
Best bowling for	7-18	C. N. Ackermann v Warwickshire at Leicester	2019
Best bowling against	**5-17**	**T. E. Bailey (Lancashire) at Leicester**	**2020**
Leading wicket-taker	69	C. W. Henderson (avge 26.95, ER 6.92)	2004–12
Highest total for	229-5	v Warwickshire at Birmingham	2018
Highest total against	255-2	by Yorkshire at Leicester	2019
Lowest total for	90	v Nottinghamshire at Nottingham	2014
Lowest total against	72	by Derbyshire at Derby	2013

ADDRESS

Fischer County Ground, Grace Road, Leicester LE2 8EB; 0116 283 2128; enquiries@leicestershireccc.co.uk; www.leicestershireccc.co.uk. Twitter: @leicsccc.

OFFICIALS

Captain C. N. Ackermann
Head coach P. A. Nixon
Head of talent pathway A. J. Maiden
President J. Birkenshaw

Chairman M. Duke
Chief executive S. M. Jarvis
Head groundsman A. B. Ward
Scorer P. J. Rogers

At Worcester, August 1–4. LEICESTERSHIRE beat LANCASHIRE by seven wickets. *Leicestershire's first first-class victory over Lancashire for 15 years.*

LEICESTERSHIRE v DERBYSHIRE

At Leicester, August 8–10. Derbyshire won by nine wickets. Derbyshire 24pts, Leicestershire 3pts. Toss: Leicestershire. First-class debut: E. Barnes.

A fine pitch and cloudless skies prompted Ackermann to bat, but his team failed to take advantage. They were undone by accurate bowling from Derbyshire's attack (which had three changes from the previous week), scrambled thinking – Azad, batting outside his crease, was stumped by Hosein lobbing the ball into the stumps from 15 yards back – and poor shot selection. It did not help when Dearden, who had played beautifully for 70, was given lbw to a delivery pitching some way outside leg. Madsen's 30th hundred for Derbyshire (only Kim Barnett and John Morris had more) and half-centuries from Reece, du Plooy and Hosein gave them a lead of 209, and earned them full bonus points. Then Critchley demonstrated how his leg-spin had developed: he picked up a career-best six for 73, including three in five balls, as Leicestershire crumbled from 104 for two to 140 for eight. Derbyshire's second straight win meant they replaced their opponents at the top of the North Group.

Close of play: first day, Derbyshire 101-1 (Reece 50, Madsen 37); second day, Leicestershire 2-0 (Parkinson 0, Azad 0).

Leicestershire

M. H. Azad st Hosein b Reece	6	– (2) lbw b du Plooy	40
B. T. Slater c Critchley b Conners	0	– (3) c Madsen b Barnes	0
H. E. Dearden lbw b Conners	70	– (4) c Reece b Critchley	47
*C. N. Ackermann c du Plooy b Melton	12	– (5) c Madsen b Critchley	22
G. H. Rhodes c Hosein b Hughes	5	– (6) lbw b Melton	8
†H. J. Swindells b Melton	21	– (7) not out	41
B. W. M. Mike b Melton	14	– (8) c du Plooy b Critchley	0
C. F. Parkinson c Hosein b Reece	21	– (1) b Barnes	13
D. Klein b Melton	0	– c Hosein b Critchley	0
W. S. Davis c Hosein b Reece	20	– c Madsen b Critchley	8
C. J. C. Wright not out	10	– b Critchley	23
B 4, lb 8, nb 8	20	B 5, lb 1, nb 12	18
1/9 (2) 2/15 (1) 3/38 (4) (68 overs)	199	1/34 (1) 2/34 (3) (80.3 overs)	220
4/84 (5) 5/115 (3) 6/138 (7)		3/104 (4) 4/112 (2)	
7/154 (6) 8/154 (9) 9/180 (8) 10/199 (10)		5/138 (6) 6/140 (5) 7/140 (8)	
		8/140 (9) 9/168 (10) 10/220 (11)	

Conners 16–5–43–2; Reece 17–6–51–3; Melton 13–5–22–4; Barnes 10–0–40–0; Hughes 5–1–16–1; Critchley 7–1–15–0. *Second innings*—Reece 9–2–20–0; Conners 8–3–21–0; Barnes 11–4–24–2; Melton 14–2–25–1; Hughes 6–0–35–0; Critchley 25.3–3–73–6; du Plooy 7–1–16–1.

Derbyshire

L. M. Reece run out (Klein)	56	– not out	4
*B. A. Godleman c Azad b Wright	3	– c Swindells b Parkinson	4
W. L. Madsen b Davis	103	– not out	2
J. L. du Plooy c Swindells b Klein	55		
M. J. J. Critchley c Swindells b Ackermann	24		
A. L. Hughes c Rhodes b Ackermann	27		
†H. R. Hosein not out	66		
A. K. Dal lbw b Klein	25		
E. Barnes c Swindells b Davis	4		
S. Conners c Mike b Parkinson	21		
D. R. Melton lbw b Parkinson	0		
B 1, lb 3, w 2, nb 18	24	Lb 2	2
1/9 (2) 2/116 (1) 3/211 (4) (106.4 overs)	408	1/9 (2) (1 wkt, 4 overs)	12
4/253 (3) 5/270 (5) 6/311 (6)			
7/350 (8) 8/371 (9) 9/408 (10) 10/408 (11)			

Wright 12–1–50–1; Klein 23–3–79–2; Mike 19–2–82–0; Davis 20–4–75–2; Parkinson 23.4–2–94–2; Ackermann 9–3–24–2. *Second innings*—Parkinson 2–0–5–1; Ackermann 2–0–5–0.

Umpires: T. Lungley and P. R. Pollard. Referee: J. J. Whitaker.

LEICESTERSHIRE v DURHAM

At Leicester, August 15–18. Drawn. Leicestershire 10pts, Durham 10pts. Toss: Leicestershire.

After 186 overs were lost to rain across the first three days, Leicestershire were set 292 off 82 after a declaration – Durham were gifted runs by opening batsmen Evans and Azad (who accidentally bowled Carse) – and two forfeits. Back in his usual job, Evans reached 85, his highest county score, passing a concussion test after being struck on the helmet on 70. A shower trimmed two overs, but the target was down to a gettable 84 from 16, with seven wickets in hand and the classy Ackermann 61 not out on a benign pitch, when the rain returned. By the time the covers had been cleared with the help of the coaching staff, there was little point in a resumption. On the opening day, Lees and Bedingham had put on 159 for Durham's third wicket, with Bedingham dismissed just short of a maiden hundred in England (he had seven in South Africa).

Close of play: first day, Durham 176-3 (Lees 62, Harte 0); second day, Durham 227-6 (Eckersley 0, Coughlin 0); third day, Durham 250-7 (Eckersley 7, Carse 14).

Durham

A. Z. Lees c Swindells b Taylor	64
S. R. Dickson c Swindells b Klein	4
C. T. Steel c Azad b Griffiths	1
D. G. Bedingham c Ackermann b Taylor	96
G. J. Harte c Swindells b Griffiths	17
J. T. A. Burnham c Ackermann b Davis	31
*†E. J. H. Eckersley not out	22
P. Coughlin c Evans b Griffiths	0
B. A. Carse b Azad	17
B. A. Raine not out	18
B 6, lb 11, w 2, nb 2	21
1/14 (2) (8 wkts dec, 89.1 overs)	291

2/17 (3) 3/176 (4) 4/181 (1) 5/227 (6) 6/227 (5) 7/227 (8) 8/258 (9)

M. E. T. Salisbury did not bat.

Taylor 21–7–49–2; Klein 15–0–57–1; Griffiths 23–6–52–3; Davis 10–2–31–1; Parkinson 10–2–31–0; Ackermann 5–1–17–0; Evans 3–0–22–0; Azad 2.1–0–15–1.

Durham forfeited their second innings.

Leicestershire

Leicestershire forfeited their first innings.

M. H. Azad b Carse	19
S. T. Evans c Lees b Steel	85
H. E. Dearden lbw b Raine	23
*C. N. Ackermann not out	61
G. H. Rhodes not out	10
Lb 4, nb 6	10
1/34 (1) 2/69 (3) (3 wkts, 63.5 overs)	208

3/196 (2)

T. A. I. Taylor, †H. J. Swindells, C. F. Parkinson, D. Klein, G. T. Griffiths and W. S. Davis did not bat.

Raine 16.5–3–46–1; Salisbury 12–2–49–0; Coughlin 15–0–52–0; Carse 12–2–34–1; Harte 6–1–15–0; Steel 2–0–8–1.

Umpires: N. G. B. Cook and N. A. Mallender. Referee: T. J. Boon.

LEICESTERSHIRE v NOTTINGHAMSHIRE

At Leicester, August 22–25. Drawn. Leicestershire 11pts, Nottinghamshire 14pts. Toss: Nottinghamshire. County debut: W. J. Weighell.

Twice Nottinghamshire seemed on their way to ending a run of 25 first-class matches without victory. On the first morning, they reduced Leicestershire to 54 for five, the evergreen Trego bowling a 16-over spell into a strong wind either side of lunch. But all-rounders Taylor and Mike hit back with attacking half-centuries, and dragged their team to 222, which just about kept them in the game; it helped that Nottinghamshire dropped five catches. Then, on the second evening, Slater and Hameed touched gloves after raising 200 – a county first-wicket record against Leicestershire, and the biggest partnership for any opening pair in the 2020 season. Next morning, however, pressing for quick runs in an attempt to dodge a dire final-day forecast and force a three-day win, Nottinghamshire lost six wickets, and Mullaney declared at lunch with a lead of just 121. Their hopes rose with two early strikes, but Evans and Ackermann wiped off the deficit in a stand of 93. Storm Francis allowed only 22 overs on the fourth day, enough for Swindells to score a lively maiden fifty.

Close of play: first day, Nottinghamshire 48-0 (Slater 12, Hameed 34); second day, Nottinghamshire 221-2 (Duckett 17, Clarke 2); third day, Leicestershire 143-3 (Ackermann 58, Rhodes 4).

Leicestershire

First innings		Second innings	
M. H. Azad c Slater b James	4	– c Moores b Trego	6
S. T. Evans c James b Trego	4	– c Hameed b Patel	48
H. E. Dearden c Patel b Trego	7	– lbw b Mullaney	16
*C. N. Ackermann c Mullaney b Trego	4	– lbw b Trego	65
G. H. Rhodes c Moores b Chappell	19	– not out	22
†H. J. Swindells lbw b Patel	33	– not out	52
T. A. I. Taylor c Chappell b Barber	57		
B. W. M. Mike not out	51		
W. J. Weighell b Chappell	23		
G. T. Griffiths c Moores b Barber	8		
H. A. Evans b Patel	1		
B 1, lb 5, w 5	11	B 20, lb 3, w 5	28
1/7 (2) 2/15 (3) 3/21 (4) 4/25 (1) 5/54 (5) 6/135 (6) 7/137 (7) 8/181 (9) 9/215 (10) 10/222 (11) (74.1 overs)	222	1/14 (1) 2/36 (3) 3/129 (2) 4/150 (4) (4 wkts, 91.2 overs)	237

Trego 22–9–46–3; Chappell 20–5–54–2; James 9–0–43–1; Barber 12–1–48–2; Patel 11.1–3–25–2. *Second innings*—Trego 17–4–63–2; Chappell 18.2–8–34–0; James 7–2–12–0; Mullaney 12–6–37–1; Barber 20–5–43–0; Patel 17–8–25–1.

Nottinghamshire

B. T. Slater c Ackermann b Taylor	86
H. Hameed lbw b H. A. Evans	87
B. M. Duckett c Dearden b Mike	37
J. M. Clarke c Griffiths b Mike	2
*S. J. Mullaney b Mike	18
S. R. Patel b Taylor	13
P. D. Trego c H. A. Evans b Griffiths	22
†T. J. Moores b Griffiths	5
L. W. James not out	36
B 9, lb 7, w 7, nb 14	37
1/200 (2) 2/210 (1) 3/221 (4) 4/258 (3) 5/260 (5) 6/282 (6) 7/293 (8) 8/343 (7) (8 wkts dec, 99.5 overs)	343

Z. J. Chappell and T. E. Barber did not bat.

Taylor 29–5–94–2; H. A. Evans 17–2–73–1; Griffiths 20.5–4–64–2; Mike 20–6–48–3; Weighell 6–0–29–0; Ackermann 7–1–19–0.

Umpires: N. G. B. Cook and Hassan Adnan. Referee: J. J. Whitaker.

At Leeds, September 6–9. LEICESTERSHIRE lost to YORKSHIRE by ten wickets.

MIDDLESEX

The stand is full of shades

KEVIN HAND

For a while it seemed Middlesex might not play a single match at Lord's, for the first time (excluding the war years) since 1876. MCC, the ground owners, had put most of their staff on furlough, meaning it was unavailable. In the end, arrangements were made for all five home T20 Blast games to be played there, though they were conducted in front of ghostly spectator-free stands, and an empty Pavilion.

Middlesex also furloughed most of their staff, including the players, until the announcement of the shortened season. The ramifications of the loss of gate and commercial revenue will be felt for years, even though they are one of the better-off clubs. The uncertainty meant that ambitious plans for Middlesex to build their own stadium, on a site at Barnet Copthall on the northern outskirts of London, were unlikely to progress.

Various activities helped the players fill their time before the restart. Some helped out with food deliveries, others with different outreach programmes. The online team churned out extensive interviews with ex-players (current ones were not allowed to contribute while on furlough), in an attempt to provide something for the members and fans. Director of cricket Angus Fraser, along with his family, repainted the pavilion at his old club, Stanmore.

With Middlesex's indoor school in Finchley also closed, a biosecure environment was set up at Radlett, where they have played the odd game since 2013. Both home Bob Willis Trophy matches were staged there, and were seesaw affairs on a pitch that played tricks later on. Hampshire won the first by three wickets, while Middlesex shaded the second, against Sussex, by five wickets after an uncertain start. In the T20 Blast, they recorded only three victories, and were well adrift in their group, finishing fourth of six.

The club had lost Dawid Malan, the 2019 captain, to Yorkshire, and also had to do without his successor, the Australian Peter Handscomb, who was stuck at home; his two-year stint was now scheduled to start in 2021. Stevie Eskinazi stepped in for the four-day games, and did a capable job; he also batted fluently in the T20s, top-scoring in all five home matches.

In what looked a strong South Group in the BWT, Middlesex did well to make it to the final game with an outside chance of finishing top, but a feeble performance against eventual champions Essex scotched that. Stuart Law, Middlesex's coach, warned that changes might be needed if they were to compete for the title in 2021. So members were irked that the promising young batsman Tom Lace was released from his contract to join Gloucestershire in August, though it emerged that Middlesex had been unable to guarantee him regular first-team action. Another batsman, Dan Lincoln, who played in six of the Blast matches, was also released.

One of the batting successes was Martin Andersson, who also bowled well, taking 14 BWT wickets with his medium-pace. Law saw hints of Jacques Kallis and Mark Waugh in his game, and he made a career-best 92 against Hampshire at Radlett. Nick Gubbins, out of sorts for three years, made a welcome return to form, hitting 192 in the first match, against Surrey at The Oval. He finished as the leading run-scorer with 350, despite missing the game with Kent because of concerns he had come into contact with someone who had tested positive for Covid-19. No one else managed a century, though at Canterbury Robbie White fell one short of a maiden first-class hundred.

James Chance, Getty Images

Martin Andersson

Along with several other counties, Middlesex handed opportunities to promising youngsters who might not have played if the squad had been at full strength. One was the 22-year-old slow left-armer Thilan Walallawita, who was born in Sri Lanka but came to England when he was 12, having narrowly survived the 2004 tsunami. He had been connected with Middlesex for eight years and, finally given a chance, showed impressive control in the Bob Willis Trophy. Another bonus was the white-ball form of Luke Hollman, an aggressive batsman and promising leg-break bowler, who might have missed out if the Afghan spinner Mujeeb Zadran – one of Middlesex's overseas T20 specialists – had been able to take up his place.

The leading wicket-taker, though, was a familiar name: Tim Murtagh, aged 39, and with his Ireland days reluctantly behind him, took 25 wickets in four red-ball matches at just 12 apiece. Fourteen came in the two games Middlesex won, against Surrey and Sussex. Steven Finn sat out the four-day competition, but did well as captain in the T20s, and was the county's leading wicket-taker with 14, to Tom Helm's 12. But Finn's absence from the longer format gave an opportunity to the lanky teenager Blake Cullen, a fluent and seemingly effortless quick bowler.

It remains to be seen whether Miguel Cummins, the West Indian who joined Middlesex as a Kolpak signing for 2020, is retained as a fully fledged overseas player alongside Handscomb for 2021. He did his cause no harm with five for 62 against Kent at Canterbury. In all, Middlesex lost over £1.6m because of shortfalls in membership, sponsorship and gate receipts.

> "At just under five minutes, Holding's speech was shorter than 'Bohemian Rhapsody' but longer than the Gettysburg Address. By the end, you wanted to leap from the settee, and clap."
>
> Cricket and the Media in 2020, page 179

MIDDLESEX RESULTS

Bob Willis Trophy matches – Played 5: Won 2, Lost 2, Drawn 1.
Vitality Blast matches – Played 10: Won 3, Lost 5, Tied 1, No result 1.

Bob Willis Trophy, 3rd in South Group;
Vitality Blast, 4th in South Group.

BOB WILLIS TROPHY AVERAGES

BATTING AND FIELDING

Cap		*Birthplace*	*M*	*I*	*NO*	*R*	*HS*	*100*	*Avge*	*Ct/St*
2016	†N. R. T. Gubbins	*Richmond*	4	8	0	350	192	1	43.75	1
2011	†J. A. Simpson	*Bury*	5	9	2	250	53	0	35.71	19/1
	R. G. White	*Ealing‡*	3	5	0	176	99	0	35.20	1
	†M. D. E. Holden	*Cambridge*	5	10	0	299	72	0	29.90	4
	M. K. Andersson	*Reading*	5	9	1	227	92	0	28.37	3
2015	J. A. R. Harris	*Morriston*	4	7	2	128	41	0	25.60	0
2013	S. D. Robson	*Paddington, Aus*	5	10	1	215	82*	0	23.88	8
2018	S. S. Eskinazi	*Johannesburg, SA*	5	10	1	151	29	0	16.77	7
	B. C. Cullen	*Hounslow‡*	2	3	0	49	34	0	16.33	1
	N. A. Sowter††	*Penrith, Australia*	2	4	2	25	20	0	12.50	5
2008	†T. J. Murtagh††	*Lambeth*	4	5	2	26	11*	0	8.66	1
	†T. N. Walallawita	*Colombo, SL*	5	6	2	22	11	0	5.50	0

Also batted: E. R. Bamber (*Westminster‡*) (1 match) 24*; †M. L. Cummins†† (*St Michael, Barbados*) (3 matches) 1, 25; †J. L. B. Davies (*Reading*) (1 match) 13; T. G. Helm (*Stoke Mandeville*) (cap 2019) (1 match) 28, 1.

‡ *Born in Middlesex.* †† *Other non-England-qualified.*

BOWLING

	Style	*O*	*M*	*R*	*W*	*BB*	*5I*	*Avge*
T. J. Murtagh	RFM	145.5	48	318	25	5-34	2	12.72
M. K. Andersson	RFM	75.5	15	250	14	4-38	0	17.85
M. L. Cummins	RF	92.1	28	269	13	5-62	1	20.69
J. A. R. Harris	RFM	89	19	284	9	2-46	0	31.55
B. C. Cullen	RFM	30	5	110	3	2-51	0	36.66
N. A. Sowter	LB	52.5	16	120	3	1-4	0	40.00
T. N. Walallawita	SLA	88.2	28	245	6	3-28	0	40.83

Also bowled: E. R. Bamber (RFM) 21–6–79–1; N. R. T. Gubbins (LB) 1.3–0–2–0; T. G. Helm (RFM) 24.3–7–66–1; S. D. Robson (LB/RM) 4–3–6–2.

LEADING VITALITY BLAST AVERAGES (70 runs/10 overs)

Batting	*Runs*	*HS*	*Avge*	*SR*	*Ct/St*
J. B. Cracknell	123	50	30.75	**148.19**	0
S. S. Eskinazi	413	84	41.30	**148.02**	6
L. B. K. Hollman	139	46	34.75	**139.00**	2
M. D. E. Holden	220	102*	27.50	**134.96**	3
J. A. Simpson	288	48	36.00	**132.71**	5/1
N. R. T. Gubbins	87	53	21.75	**117.56**	1
M. K. Andersson	94	24	10.44	**103.29**	7

Bowling	*W*	*BB*	*Avge*	*ER*
T. J. Murtagh	7	2-20	17.00	**6.61**
L. B. K. Hollman	9	3-18	18.11	**6.79**
N. A. Sowter	10	3-30	26.20	**7.27**
S. T. Finn	14	3-18	19.00	**8.06**
T. G. Helm	12	2-12	22.75	**8.44**
M. L. Cummins	3	1-26	51.00	**9.66**
J. A. R. Harris	1	1-46	131.00	**13.10**

FIRST-CLASS COUNTY RECORDS

Highest score for	331*	J. D. B. Robertson v Worcestershire at Worcester	1949
Highest score against	341	C. M. Spearman (Gloucestershire) at Gloucester	2004
Leading run-scorer	40,302	E. H. Hendren (avge 48.81)	1907–37
Best bowling for	10-40	G. O. B. Allen v Lancashire at Lord's	1929
Best bowling against	9-38	R. C. Robertson-Glasgow (Somerset) at Lord's	1924
Leading wicket-taker	2,361	F. J. Titmus (avge 21.27)	1949–82
Highest total for	642-3 dec	v Hampshire at Southampton	1923
Highest total against	850-7 dec	by Somerset at Taunton	2007
Lowest total for	20	v MCC at Lord's	1864
Lowest total against	31	by Gloucestershire at Bristol	1924
	31	by Glamorgan at Cardiff	1997

LIST A COUNTY RECORDS

Highest score for	166	M. D. E. Holden v Kent at Canterbury	2019
Highest score against	166	L. J. Wright (Sussex) at Lord's	2019
Leading run-scorer	12,029	M. W. Gatting (avge 34.96)	1975–98
Best bowling for	7-12	W. W. Daniel v Minor Counties East at Ipswich	1978
Best bowling against	6-27	J. C. Tredwell (Kent) at Southgate	2009
Leading wicket-taker	491	J. E. Emburey (avge 24.68)	1975–95
Highest total for	380-5	v Kent at Canterbury	2019
Highest total against	368-2	by Nottinghamshire at Lord's	2014
Lowest total for	23	v Yorkshire at Leeds	1974
Lowest total against	41	by Northamptonshire at Northampton	1972

TWENTY20 COUNTY RECORDS

Highest score for	129	D. T. Christian v Kent at Canterbury	2014
Highest score against	123	I. A. Cockbain (Gloucestershire) at Bristol	2018
Leading run-scorer	3,318	D. J. Malan (avge 32.85, SR 128.00)	2006–19
Best bowling for	6-28	J. K. Fuller v Hampshire at Southampton	2018
Best bowling against	**6-19**	**Shaheen Shah Afridi (Hampshire) at Southampton**	**2020**
Leading wicket-taker	**97**	**S. T. Finn (avge 22.34, ER 8.13)**	**2008–20**
Highest total for	227-4	v Somerset at Taunton	2019
Highest total against	254-3	by Gloucestershire at Uxbridge	2011
Lowest total for	92	v Surrey at Lord's	2013
Lowest total against	74	by Essex at Chelmsford	2013

ADDRESS

Lord's Cricket Ground, London NW8 8QN; 020 7289 1300; enquiries@middlesexccc.com; www.middlesexccc.com. Twitter: @Middlesex_CCC.

OFFICIALS

Captain S. S. Eskinazi
(Twenty20) S. T. Finn
Managing director of cricket A. R. C. Fraser
Head coach S. G. Law
Head of youth cricket R. I. Coutts

President M. W. W. Selvey
Chairman M. I. O'Farrell
Secretary/chief executive R. J. Goatley
Head groundsman K. McDermott
Scorer D. K. Shelley

At The Oval, August 1–4. MIDDLESEX beat SURREY by 190 runs.

MIDDLESEX v HAMPSHIRE

At Radlett, August 8–11. Hampshire won by three wickets. Hampshire 21pts, Middlesex 4pts. Toss: Hampshire.

Middlesex looked likelier winners when Hampshire, chasing 158, slipped to 108 for seven on the final morning, on a pitch showing signs of wear. Murtagh and the young slow left-armer Thilan Walallawitta, in his second first-class match, had taken three wickets apiece. But opener Weatherley held firm with a hobbling Barker, putting on 53 in 12 overs to seal a hard-earned victory. It was Weatherley's second important contribution: in the first innings, he lasted more than five hours for 98, and his 162 runs in the match included 25 fours. Middlesex had made a poor start, and were indebted to Andersson, who made a workmanlike career-best 92 after being dropped by Dawson at slip when 23. Northeast and Dawson helped Weatherley establish a lead of 44, before Hampshire's depleted attack restricted Middlesex to 201, even though the top seven all reached double figures. They were without Dawson, who ruptured his Achilles tendon while batting, and was stretchered off. So too was Stevenson, following career-best figures in the first innings, when he gashed his leg on the edge of the wooden floor of the players' dining marquee after a sliding stop on the boundary. Northeast tried Organ's off-breaks instead, and was rewarded with four wickets, while Sowter was superbly snaffled at cover, one of three catches for substitute Brad Wheal.

Close of play: first day, Hampshire 27-2 (Weatherley 6, Alsop 4); second day, Hampshire 279-7 (McManus 14, Fuller 1); third day, Hampshire 60-2 (Weatherley 23, Northeast 8).

Middlesex

S. D. Robson b Barker	0	– (2) c Weatherley b Holland	21
M. D. E. Holden c Holland b Barker	36	– (1) c McManus b Barker	26
N. R. T. Gubbins c Organ b Fuller	8	– lbw b Fuller	46
*S. S. Eskinazi lbw b Stevenson	18	– c sub (B. T. J. Wheal) b Organ	29
M. K. Andersson lbw b Fuller	92	– b Fuller	12
†J. A. Simpson c Dawson b Stevenson	28	– lbw b Organ	23
J. A. R. Harris c Holland b Dawson	8	– c sub (B. T. J. Wheal) b Organ	23
N. A. Sowter c Dawson b Stevenson	20	– c sub (B. T. J. Wheal) b Holland	3
T. G. Helm c and b Dawson	28	– b Organ	1
T. N. Walallawita c McManus b Stevenson	0	– not out	0
T. J. Murtagh not out	2	– c Alsop b Barker	8
Lb 7, w 1, nb 4	12	B 1, lb 8	9
1/6 (1) 2/15 (3) 3/41 (4) 4/85 (2) 5/178 (6) 6/191 (7) 7/201 (5) 8/244 (8) 9/244 (10) 10/252 (9) (73.5 overs)	252	1/34 (1) 2/70 (2) 3/124 (3) 4/128 (4) 5/142 (5) 6/172 (6) 7/181 (8) 8/186 (9) 9/193 (7) 10/201 (11) (53 overs)	201

Barker 14–3–44–2; Fuller 14–3–54–2; Stevenson 19–6–70–4; Holland 10–1–38–0; Dawson 16.5–5–39–2. *Second innings*—Barker 14–1–53–2; Fuller 11–0–58–2; Holland 15–3–39–2; Organ 13–1–42–4.

Hampshire

F. S. Organ c Sowter b Harris	11	– c Simpson b Harris	10
J. J. Weatherley lbw b Murtagh	98	– not out	64
K. H. D. Barker b Harris	6	– (9) not out	28
T. P. Alsop c Simpson b Helm	4	– (3) c Eskinazi b Walallawita	13
*S. A. Northeast c Sowter b Walallawita	51	– (4) c Holden b Murtagh	8
L. A. Dawson retired hurt	43		
I. G. Holland c Robson b Murtagh	22	– (5) c Sowter b Murtagh	17
H. R. C. Came lbw b Sowter	5	– (6) c Robson b Murtagh	1
†L. D. McManus c Robson b Murtagh	16	– (7) b Walallawita	13
J. K. Fuller not out	16	– (8) c Simpson b Walallawita	0
R. A. Stevenson c Simpson b Murtagh	0		
B 4, lb 8, w 8, nb 4	24	B 5, lb 1, w 1	7
1/17 (1) 2/23 (3) 3/28 (4) (111 overs)	296	1/29 (1) (7 wkts, 61.3 overs)	161
4/167 (5) 5/204 (2) 6/255 (7)		2/48 (3) 3/61 (4)	
7/277 (8) 8/292 (9) 9/296 (11) 110 overs: 295-8		4/85 (5) 5/87 (6) 6/104 (7) 7/108 (8)	

In the first innings Dawson retired hurt at 261-6.

Murtagh 30–13–61–4; Helm 18–6–41–1; Harris 25–5–66–2; Andersson 13–0–41–0; Sowter 17–2–52–1; Walallawita 8–3–23–1. *Second innings*—Murtagh 18–3–41–3; Helm 6.3–1–25–0; Sowter 11–4–34–0; Harris 10–2–27–1; Walallawita 16–6–28–3.

Umpires: N. L. Bainton and R. A. White. Referee: A. J. Swann.

At Canterbury, August 15–18. MIDDLESEX drew with KENT.

MIDDLESEX v SUSSEX

At Radlett, August 22–24. Middlesex won by five wickets. Middlesex 20pts, Sussex –19pts (after 24pt penalty). Toss: Sussex. First-class debuts: B. C. Cullen; W. A. Sheffield.

Neither team could reach the final, but this match gained significance a fortnight later, when it emerged that the Sussex opening bowler Mitchell Claydon had applied hand sanitiser to the ball. Sussex imposed a six-match ban, later extended by the ECB to nine. Claydon was found guilty of "unfair and improper conduct… prejudicial to the interests of cricket and likely to bring the game into disrepute". Sussex were subsequently penalised 24 points. The match itself was not dissimilar to the previous one at Radlett: this time it was Middlesex's turn to win from an unpromising position, overcoming a sizeable first-innings deficit to triumph late on the third evening. After a battling 69 from Finch and a run-a-ball 46 from Rawlins pushed Sussex towards 293, Middlesex plummeted to 80 for six. But Simpson put on 70 with debutant Blake Cullen, who resisted for two and a half hours against Claydon and the promising teenage off-spinner Carson. Sussex were soon in disarray at four for four, with Murtagh taking three in eight balls; Brown and Rawlins put on 55, but the seamers mopped up. Requiring 193, Middlesex lost Holden and Gubbins to successive balls from Robinson, who then removed Robson in his next over. Eskinazi and White steadied the ship, before falling at the same score, and both Andersson and Simpson were dropped in the slips: they made Sussex pay, completing victory with an unbroken stand of 63.

Close of play: first day, Sussex 293; second day, Sussex 33-4 (Brown 9, Rawlins 19).

Sussex

First innings		Second innings	
P. D. Salt c Cullen b Andersson	42	– b Murtagh	1
T. J. Haines not out	31	– (7) c Simpson b Murtagh	1
H. Z. Finch c Simpson b Cullen	69	– lbw b Murtagh	2
T. G. R. Clark c Robson b Cullen	8	– c Eskinazi b Murtagh	0
*†B. C. Brown c White b Murtagh	26	– c Simpson b Andersson	45
A. D. Thomason lbw b Andersson	10	– (2) lbw b Cummins	0
D. M. W. Rawlins c Gubbins b Andersson	46	– (6) c and b Murtagh	33
O. E. Robinson lbw b Cummins	19	– c Simpson b Andersson	3
J. J. Carson lbw b Cummins	0	– c Simpson b Cummins	9
M. E. Claydon c Eskinazi b Andersson	14	– not out	3
W. A. Sheffield b Murtagh	6	– c Eskinazi b Andersson	1
B 5, lb 4, w 1, nb 12	22	Lb 2, nb 2	4
1/56 (1) 2/108 (4) 3/171 (5) 4/201 (3) 5/211 (6) 6/246 (8) 7/246 (9) 8/284 (7) 9/286 (10) 10/293 (11) (87.5 overs)	293	1/2 (1) 2/4 (3) 3/4 (4) 4/4 (2) 5/59 (6) 6/71 (7) 7/74 (8) 8/97 (5) 9/99 (9) 10/102 (11) (35.5 overs)	102

In the first innings Haines, when 29, retired hurt at 84-1 and resumed at 284-8.

Murtagh 21.5–7–41–2; Cummins 19–7–62–2; Cullen 14–2–51–2; Walallawita 14.2–3–52–0; Andersson 18–5–77–4; Gubbins 0.4–0–1–0. *Second innings*—Murtagh 13–3–34–5; Cummins 15–4–45–2; Andersson 7.5–2–21–3.

Middlesex

First innings		Second innings	
S. D. Robson lbw b Robinson	2	– (2) c Clark b Robinson	15
M. D. E. Holden c Salt b Sheffield	7	– (1) c Brown b Robinson	28
N. R. T. Gubbins lbw b Carson	26	– c Brown b Robinson	0
*S. S. Eskinazi lbw b Robinson	3	– lbw b Robinson	26
R. G. White lbw b Claydon	7	– lbw b Haines	35
M. K. Andersson lbw b Carson	17	– not out	27
†J. A. Simpson b Claydon	48	– not out	32
B. C. Cullen lbw b Claydon	34		
M. L. Cummins b Carson	25		
T. N. Walallawita not out	0		
T. J. Murtagh lbw b Carson	0		
B 10, lb 8, nb 16	34	B 9, lb 5, nb 16	30
1/2 (1) 2/33 (2) 3/36 (4) 4/55 (5) 5/63 (3) 6/80 (6) 7/150 (7) 8/201 (8) 9/203 (9) 10/203 (11) (68 overs)	203	1/48 (1) 2/48 (3) 3/57 (2) 4/130 (5) 5/130 (4) (5 wkts, 54 overs)	193

Robinson 21–4–56–2; Claydon 14–6–23–3; Sheffield 13–0–45–1; Carson 15–2–46–4; Rawlins 5–2–15–0. *Second innings*—Robinson 18–6–54–4; Carson 12–0–44–0; Claydon 13–3–41–0; Sheffield 2–0–9–0; Haines 8–1–24–1; Rawlins 1–0–7–0.

Umpires: B. J. Debenham and R. T. Robinson. Referee: P. M. Such.

At Chelmsford, September 6–8. MIDDLESEX lost to ESSEX by nine wickets.

NORTHAMPTONSHIRE

Singapore, and sadness

ALEX WINTER

It might have been a year of progress. Northamptonshire were back in Division One of the Championship after five seasons, had their largest playing staff since 2014, were set to pay off the last of their loan from the local council, and had taken the first step of their ambitious Global Partnership Strategy with a pre-season tour to Singapore. But that trip, part of a new link with the Singapore Cricket Association as chief executive Ray Payne looked to turn Northamptonshire into a "globally recognised brand", was curtailed as Covid-19 took its grip, and the squad returned home early to a world of uncertainty. Payne admitted that, five years previously, the club would not have survived a summer without crowds or events at Wantage Road; now, their finances transformed, they could absorb the hit of around £1m.

Nothing, though, could soften the blow that arrived on September 2, when David Capel died following a brain tumour, at the age of 57. He was one of the county's own – born in Northampton, and involved with the club from his Second XI debut in 1979 until his tenure as head coach ended in 2012. Less than four months before his death, he had been inducted into Northamptonshire's Hall of Fame. He also played 38 times for England. With numbers limited at the funeral in his home village of Bugbrooke, over 100 people lined the procession route, and raised bats to an all-rounder admired as much for his loyalty to his roots as his determination on the field.

Northamptonshire attempted to honour him with another Twenty20 title as they prioritised the Vitality Blast in a rejigged summer. Pakistan's Fahim Ashraf and West Indian Kieron Pollard were unable to fulfil their contracts but, in Ireland batsman Paul Stirling, they did secure one of the few overseas players in the competition. All-rounder Tom Taylor then joined on a three-year deal from Leicestershire in September – a coup, given that bigger counties were also interested.

The minimum target was to reach a first quarter-final since 2016, which they did. But, after four consecutive victories, they were almost derailed when Ben Curran tested positive for Covid-19 midway through the group stage. It caused the abandonment, on the first day, of the final Bob Willis Trophy match, against Gloucestershire, and disrupted selection and training schedules for the second half of the Blast. Northamptonshire lost their next four T20 games, and it took a combination of a miraculous run-chase in the final match, at Edgbaston – where Taylor smashed a 27-ball fifty on debut – and Gloucestershire's last-ball win over Somerset moments later, to secure a place in the last eight. But, 11 days later, they were hopeless in the quarter-final at Bristol.

Familiar batting failures had resurfaced when conditions were not to their liking. The order was front-loaded with power, but none of Stirling, Richard

David Rogers, Getty Images

Charlie Thurston

Levi, Josh Cobb or Adam Rossington rose to the occasion, totalling 740 between them, with only three half-centuries from 37 innings. Perhaps the tactic was too one-dimensional, and a lack of craft or guile was often exposed – glaringly so at Cardiff, where Northamptonshire surrendered for 98. Then, in that quarter-final, they were rolled for 113. What really rankled was an absence of fight with the ball: in their most important limited-overs match for four years, they allowed Gloucestershire to romp home with more than eight overs unused.

It left a feeling of dissatisfaction after their red-ball ambitions had been sacrificed on the altar of T20. Northamptonshire were among a number of counties with reservations about bringing players off furlough for four-day cricket, and used the competition to develop their squad, in particular the batting. But the policy did not sit well with many members, whose correspondence caused sleepless nights for head coach David Ripley.

With Somerset in the same group, reaching the final always looked difficult. But, given the other opponents, three home fixtures and Northamptonshire's 2019 form, a first-choice XI might have stood a chance. It was never selected, and only one game, against Glamorgan, was won. They had their moments against Somerset and Worcestershire, but batting collapses and, crucially, a failure to polish off the lower order, proved costly. It was also folly that both matches were played on wickets that heavily assisted seam bowling, hindering one of the goals of the summer – for inexperienced batsmen to learn to build an innings.

The four-day side lacked a frontline spinner, so left-armer Simon Kerrigan was brought in from the wilderness, on a two-year deal; against Glamorgan, he played his first professional match since appearing on loan for the club in 2017. In that game, Charlie Thurston scored his maiden county hundred. He had also made 96 at Edgbaston, helping save the opening BWT fixture after Northamptonshire had trailed by 227 on first innings, and secured a two-year contract. Curran was offered the same terms, as was seamer Jack White. The club's latest signing from the National Counties – he had been playing for Cheshire – White made his debut at Edgbaston aged 28, and took 13 wickets at 20, suggesting he could follow Ben Sanderson and Richard Gleeson as late developers at Wantage Road.

In October, the bowling group lost Brett Hutton, who returned to Nottinghamshire, and Zimbabwean Blessing Muzarabani, who left with a year remaining on his contract because Kolpak registrations had ended. Rob Newton, who scored over 7,000 runs for the club, and Scotland international all-rounder Tom Sole, were also released. But a late boost came in December, when Afghanistan's Mohammad Nabi, No. 1 in the ICC's T20 all-rounder rankings, was signed for the 2021 Blast.

NORTHAMPTONSHIRE RESULTS

Bob Willis Trophy matches – Played 5: Won 1, Lost 2, Drawn 2.
Vitality Blast matches – Played 10: Won 5, Lost 5. Abandoned 1.

Bob Willis Trophy, 4th in Central Group;
Vitality Blast, quarter-finalists.

BOB WILLIS TROPHY AVERAGES

BATTING AND FIELDING

Cap		*Birthplace*	*M*	*I*	*NO*	*R*	*HS*	*100*	*Avge*	*Ct/St*
2020	†L. A. Procter	*Oldham*	4	6	2	200	112*	1	50.00	1
	C. O. Thurston	*Cambridge*	5	8	0	357	115	1	44.62	2
2019	A. M. Rossington	*Edgware*	3	6	1	196	135*	1	39.20	8
	†R. S. Vasconcelos††	*Johannesburg, SA*	5	8	1	222	58	0	31.71	13/1
	N. L. Buck	*Leicester*	2	3	1	61	32	0	30.50	0
	†B. J. Curran	*Northampton‡*	4	8	0	238	82	0	29.75	5
	†E. N. Gay	*Bedford*	4	6	1	121	77*	0	24.20	4
	G. K. Berg	*Cape Town, SA*	2	4	0	63	45	0	15.75	3
2019	R. I. Keogh	*Dunstable*	4	6	0	80	31	0	13.33	1
	B. Muzarabani††	*Harare, Zimbabwe*	4	5	2	27	15	0	9.00	1
2018	B. W. Sanderson	*Sheffield*	2	3	0	23	23	0	7.66	0
	†S. A. Zaib	*High Wycombe*	4	5	0	36	23	0	7.20	2
	†C. J. White	*Kendal*	4	4	2	9	7*	0	4.50	0

Also batted: B. D. Glover†† (*Johannesburg, SA*) (1 match) 0, 0; H. O. M. Gouldstone (*Kettering‡*) (1 match) did not bat (1 ct); B. A. Hutton (*Doncaster*) (2 matches) 9 (1 ct); S. C. Kerrigan (*Preston*) (2 matches) 1 (1 ct); R. E. Levi†† (*Johannesburg, SA*) (cap 2017) (1 match) 11, 8 (1 ct); A. G. Wakely (*Hammersmith*) (cap 2012) (1 match) 9, 2 (1 ct).

‡ *Born in Northamptonshire.* †† *Other non-England-qualified.*

BOWLING

	Style	*O*	*M*	*R*	*W*	*BB*	*5I*	*Avge*
B. W. Sanderson	RFM	55.1	14	166	11	5-28	1	15.09
N. L. Buck	RFM	64	21	173	9	3-42	0	19.22
C. J. White	RFM	88	20	260	13	4-35	0	20.00
S. A. Zaib	SLA	28	5	84	4	2-11	0	21.00
B. A. Hutton	RFM	39	8	136	6	4-77	0	22.66
B. D. Glover	RFM	24	5	94	4	2-45	0	23.50
B. Muzarabani	RFM	70.5	17	278	11	4-29	0	25.27
S. C. Kerrigan	SLA	23.3	4	89	3	2-54	0	29.66
G. K. Berg	RFM	47	9	203	6	4-64	0	33.83

Also bowled: R. I. Keogh (OB) 38–10–112–1; L. A. Procter (RM) 30–5–130–2.

LEADING VITALITY BLAST AVERAGES (70 runs/10 overs)

Batting	*Runs*	*HS*	*Avge*	*SR*	*Ct/St*
T. A. I. Taylor	77	50*	77.00	**183.33**	0
G. G. White	96	37*	32.00	**171.42**	2
P. R. Stirling	232	80*	25.77	**152.63**	4
S. A. Zaib	116	30	19.33	**131.81**	6
R. E. Levi	196	50	19.60	**130.66**	5
A. M. Rossington	156	51	22.28	**118.18**	1/1
J. J. Cobb	156	49	17.33	**94.54**	3
A. G. Wakely	91	36*	15.16	**84.25**	1

Bowling	*W*	*BB*	*Avge*	*ER*
J. J. Cobb	3	1-17	53.00	**6.11**
L. A. Procter	2	1-11	32.00	**6.40**
G. G. White	12	3-28	24.91	**7.50**
G. K. Berg	4	2-31	24.00	**8.00**
B. W. Sanderson	12	3-11	22.25	**8.38**
N. L. Buck	10	4-29	25.00	**8.92**
B. D. Glover	7	2-32	22.14	**9.11**

FIRST-CLASS COUNTY RECORDS

Highest score for	331*	M. E. K. Hussey v Somerset at Taunton	2003
Highest score against	333	K. S. Duleepsinhji (Sussex) at Hove	1930
Leading run-scorer	28,980	D. Brookes (avge 36.13)	1934–59
Best bowling for	10-127	V. W. C. Jupp v Kent at Tunbridge Wells	1932
Best bowling against	10-30	C. Blythe (Kent) at Northampton	1907
Leading wicket-taker	1,102	E. W. Clark (avge 21.26)	1922–47
Highest total for	781-7 dec	v Nottinghamshire at Northampton	1995
Highest total against	701-7 dec	by Kent at Beckenham	2017
Lowest total for	12	v Gloucestershire at Gloucester	1907
Lowest total against	33	by Lancashire at Northampton	1977

LIST A COUNTY RECORDS

Highest score for	172*	W. Larkins v Warwickshire at Luton	1983
Highest score against	184	M. J. Lumb (Nottinghamshire) at Nottingham	2016
Leading run-scorer	11,010	R. J. Bailey (avge 39.46)	1983–99
Best bowling for	7-10	C. Pietersen v Denmark at Brøndby	2005
Best bowling against	7-35	D. E. Malcolm (Derbyshire) at Derby	1997
Leading wicket-taker	251	A. L. Penberthy (avge 30.45)	1989–2003
Highest total for	425	v Nottinghamshire at Nottingham	2016
Highest total against	445-8	by Nottinghamshire at Nottingham	2016
Lowest total for	41	v Middlesex at Northampton	1972
Lowest total against	56	by Leicestershire at Leicester	1964
	56	by Denmark at Brøndby	2005

TWENTY20 COUNTY RECORDS

Highest score for	111*	L. Klusener v Worcestershire at Kidderminster	2007
Highest score against	161	A. Lyth (Yorkshire) at Leeds	2017
Leading run-scorer	**2,597**	**A. G. Wakely (avge 26.23, SR 117.67)**	**2009–20**
Best bowling for	6-21	A. J. Hall v Worcestershire at Northampton	2008
Best bowling against	5-6	P. D. Collingwood (Durham) at Chester-le-Street	2011
Leading wicket-taker	73	D. J. Willey (avge 19.45, ER 7.42)	2009–15
Highest total for	231-5	v Warwickshire at Birmingham	2018
Highest total against	260-4	by Yorkshire at Leeds	2017
Lowest total for	47	v Durham at Chester-le-Street	2011
Lowest total against	86	by Worcestershire at Worcester	2006

ADDRESS

County Ground, Abington Avenue, Northampton NN1 4PR; 01604 514455; reception@nccc.co.uk; www.northantscricket.com. Twitter: @NorthantsCCC.

OFFICIALS

Captain A. M. Rossington
(ltd-overs) J. J. Cobb
Head coach D. Ripley
Academy director K. J. Innes
President Lord Naseby

Chairman G. G. Warren
Chief executive R. Payne
Head groundsman C. Harvey
Scorer A. C. Kingston

At Birmingham, August 1–4. NORTHAMPTONSHIRE drew with WARWICKSHIRE.

NORTHAMPTONSHIRE v SOMERSET

At Northampton, August 8–9. Somerset won by 167 runs. Somerset 19pts, Northamptonshire 3pts. Toss: Somerset. County debut: B. D. Glover.

On a pitch offering seam movement and bounce, both batting line-ups struggled, and an unsatisfactory game was over on the second evening. The difference between the sides was the lower order: while Somerset's last four wickets added 258 across both innings, Northamptonshire's managed just eight. From 114 for nine after Sanderson's 13th five-for, Somerset still made enough to fashion a first-innings lead of 99, with No. 11 Brooks chancing his arm to top-score with 36 from 23 balls. He then ran out Vasconcelos, prompting a ridiculous collapse of nine for 21 as Northamptonshire slumped to their lowest total in any format against Somerset, below 95 at Bath in 1913; only Curran reached double figures. The visitors' top order failed again and, when their sixth wicket fell, they led by 152. But Craig Overton and van der Merwe added a raucous 67, before Jamie Overton hoisted four sixes in a 43-ball 68 – a career-best (for a week). Northamptonshire needed an implausible 322 and, though Vasconcelos at one stage struck six fours in ten balls, Jamie Overton and Brooks brought about a second outrageous collapse: six for six in 24 deliveries.

Close of play: first day, Somerset 15-1 (Byrom 2, Abell 12).

Somerset

First innings		Second innings	
E. J. Byrom c Rossington b Glover	6	– c Vasconcelos b Sanderson	20
T. A. Lammonby b Sanderson	1	– lbw b Glover	0
*T. B. Abell c Rossington b Glover	0	– c Rossington b Sanderson	12
J. C. Hildreth c Rossington b Sanderson	32	– lbw b Berg	17
T. Banton b Berg	18	– c Rossington b Berg	2
†S. M. Davies b Sanderson	13	– b Berg	0
C. Overton c Berg b Sanderson	16	– c Curran b Berg	53
R. E. van der Merwe not out	20	– c Vasconcelos b Glover	30
J. Overton c Procter b Sanderson	11	– c Rossington b Sanderson	68
J. H. Davey c Berg b Procter	1	– c Muzarabani b Sanderson	5
J. A. Brooks c Rossington b Muzarabani	36	– not out	2
B 1, lb 6, w 1, nb 4	12	B 1, lb 12	13
1/7 (1) 2/7 (2) 3/7 (3) 4/36 (5) 5/74 (6) 6/77 (4) 7/96 (7) 8/110 (9) 9/114 (10) 10/166 (11) (47.2 overs)	166	1/0 (2) 2/15 (3) 3/50 (4) 4/50 (1) 5/52 (5) 6/53 (6) 7/120 (8) 8/151 (7) 9/187 (10) 10/222 (9) (39.1 overs)	222

Sanderson 15–7–28–5; Glover 15–3–49–2; Muzarabani 7.2–1–37–1; Berg 7–0–36–1; Procter 3–0–9–1. *Second innings*—Sanderson 13.1–3–61–4; Glover 9–2–45–2; Berg 10–0–64–4; Muzarabani 5–0–26–0; Procter 2–1–13–0.

Northamptonshire

First innings		Second innings	
B. J. Curran c C. Overton b Davey	35	– c J. Overton b Davey	10
E. N. Gay c Davies b C. Overton	0	– c Hildreth b J. Overton	16
R. S. Vasconcelos run out (Brooks)	7	– c J. Overton b Davey	52
R. I. Keogh lbw b Davey	2	– c and b Brooks	1
C. O. Thurston lbw b Brooks	1	– c Davies b J. Overton	34
L. A. Procter lbw b Davey	5	– c C. Overton b J. Overton	26
*†A. M. Rossington c Davies b C. Overton	9	– lbw b J. Overton	0
G. K. Berg c Hildreth b J. Overton	0	– c Hildreth b Brooks	0
B. W. Sanderson c and b C. Overton	0	– lbw b Brooks	0
B. Muzarabani not out	0	– not out	1
B. D. Glover b C. Overton	0	– c van der Merwe b Brooks	0
Lb 2, w 6	8	B 3, lb 5, nb 6	14
1/9 (2) 2/46 (3) 3/50 (1) 4/53 (4) 5/53 (5) 6/65 (6) 7/67 (7) 8/67 (8) 9/67 (9) 10/67 (11) (32 overs)	67	1/21 (1) 2/46 (2) 3/51 (4) 4/104 (3) 5/148 (5) 6/148 (7) 7/153 (8) 8/153 (9) 9/153 (6) 10/154 (11) (43 overs)	154

C. Overton 11–6–12–4; Davey 10–4–23–3; J. Overton 5–2–14–1; Brooks 6–1–16–1. *Second innings*—C. Overton 12–3–40–0; Davey 10–4–23–2; J. Overton 8–3–26–4; Brooks 11–2–40–4; Abell 2–0–17–0.

Umpires: R. J. Bailey and N. G. B. Cook. Referee: T. J. Boon.

NORTHAMPTONSHIRE v WORCESTERSHIRE

At Northampton, August 15–18. Worcestershire won by 78 runs. Worcestershire 20pts, Northamptonshire 4pts. Toss: Northamptonshire.

Tom Fell made his first first-class century since having surgery for testicular cancer in 2015. Until his decisive and disciplined 110 not out in Worcestershire's second innings, batsmen on both sides had apparently determined that aggression was the only way to score runs at a venue where 66 wickets had fallen in the equivalent of four days. But Fell reaped the rewards of a sound technique, and helped Worcestershire build on a slender lead to set Northamptonshire 263 in 68 overs. It proved more than enough, as the hosts' top order failed yet again. Wessels's hitting had rescued Worcestershire from 84 for five in the first innings; in reply, it took Berg's county-best 45, and a chancy knock from Buck, to prevent a large deficit. Buck then took three wickets and, when Cox was sixth out, Worcestershire led by 179. But Fell and Barnard survived the first hour of the final day, then slammed 29 in two overs to set up the declaration.

Close of play: first day, Worcestershire 93-5 (Wessels 5, Cox 4); second day, Northamptonshire 90-4 (Thurston 20, Zaib 19); third day, Worcestershire 177-6 (Fell 81, Barnard 3).

Worcestershire

D. K. H. Mitchell c Berg b Buck	7	– lbw b White	39
J. D. Libby c Wakely b Buck	0	– c Vasconcelos b Buck	3
T. C. Fell c Curran b Muzarabani	10	– not out	110
J. A. Haynes b Buck	38	– c Vasconcelos b Zaib	32
B. L. D'Oliveira c Curran b Berg	24	– c Rossington b Buck	5
M. H. Wessels b Zaib	88	– b Buck	5
†O. B. Cox b Muzarabani	39	– c Levi b Zaib	2
E. G. Barnard c Curran b Zaib	0	– not out	48
*J. Leach lbw b Muzarabani	5		
J. C. Tongue not out	1		
D. Y. Pennington c Vasconcelos b Muzarabani	0		
B 2, lb 5	7	B 4, lb 2, w 3, nb 2	11
1/5 (2) 2/8 (1) 3/43 (3) 4/84 (4) 5/84 (5) 6/212 (6) 7/212 (7) 8/218 (8) 9/219 (9) 10/219 (11) (64.3 overs)	219	1/11 (2) 2/78 (1) 3/137 (4) 4/142 (5) 5/148 (6) 6/172 (7) (6 wkts dec, 86 overs)	255

Buck 19–6–67–3; White 14–5–47–0; Muzarabani 12.3–4–29–4; Berg 14–2–58–1; Zaib 5–1–11–2. *Second innings*—Buck 19–7–42–3; White 16–1–54–1; Berg 16–7–45–0; Muzarabani 15–1–51–0; Zaib 20–4–57–2.

Northamptonshire

B. J. Curran c Haynes b Tongue	14	– lbw b Leach	17
R. S. Vasconcelos c Fell b Leach	4	– lbw b Tongue	31
A. G. Wakely c Wessels b Barnard	9	– c Leach b Tongue	2
C. O. Thurston c Cox b Tongue	21	– c Cox b Barnard	11
R. E. Levi c Mitchell b Barnard	11	– c Barnard b Pennington	8
S. A. Zaib c Wessels b Leach	23	– c Cox b Pennington	5
*†A. M. Rossington c Fell b Tongue	4	– c Cox b Leach	44
G. K. Berg c Cox b Leach	45	– b Tongue	18
N. L. Buck c Mitchell b Barnard	32	– not out	24
B. Muzarabani c Fell b Barnard	15	– c Cox b Pennington	11
C. J. White not out	7	– b Barnard	0
B 8, lb 10, w 1, nb 8	27	B 1, lb 8, nb 4	13
1/6 (2) 2/28 (1) 3/44 (3) 4/60 (5) 5/92 (4) 6/100 (6) 7/100 (7) 8/159 (9) 9/193 (10) 10/212 (8) (61 overs)	212	1/48 (1) 2/52 (2) 3/55 (3) 4/71 (4) 5/77 (5) 6/94 (6) 7/130 (8) 8/150 (7) 9/177 (10) 10/184 (11) (40.4 overs)	184

Leach 14–2–54–3; Pennington 12–4–33–0; Tongue 15–3–42–3; Barnard 17–4–46–4; D'Oliveira 3–0–19–0. *Second innings*—Leach 12–2–62–2; Pennington 9–1–30–3; D'Oliveira 1–0–7–0; Tongue 10–1–38–3; Barnard 8.4–1–38–2.

Umpires: R. J. Bailey and R. A. White. Referee: A. J. Swann.

NORTHAMPTONSHIRE v GLAMORGAN

At Northampton, August 22–25. Northamptonshire won by six wickets. Northamptonshire 22pts, Glamorgan 5pts. Toss: Northamptonshire. First-class debut: C. Z. Taylor. County debut: J. M. Cooke.

Northamptonshire's first victory in the Bob Willis Trophy was delivered by four inexperienced players, quietening the voices who had questioned their development policy for the competition. Thurston scored his maiden hundred for the club, Curran fell one short of equalling his career-best, White claimed eight wickets, and Gay ticked off his first half-century. Northamptonshire should have won by a greater margin, but again failed to deal with a gung-ho lower order – twice. On the first day, Glamorgan had slumped to 135 for nine, before Callum Taylor made a whirlwind 88-ball century, and put on 124 in 11.2 overs with Michael Hogan, the county's tenth-wicket record against Northamptonshire. Taylor was only the fourth Glamorgan player to score a hundred on first-class debut. Then, after Curran and Thurston helped the hosts secure a lead of 73, Glamorgan broke the ninth-wicket record for the fixture, thanks to some remarkable hitting from de Lange. Coming in at 60 for eight, he thrashed a 62-ball maiden hundred, and put on 168 in less than 20 overs with Douthwaite. In all, de Lange hit nine sixes and six fours in 78 deliveries in the highest score by a Glamorgan No. 10, beating Johnnie Clay's 101 not out against Worcestershire at Swansea in 1929. That left Northamptonshire, who suddenly needed 189, to wonder if Storm Francis would clear on the final day. It did, and the matter was settled by a stand of 106 between Gay and Thurston, though Hogan did pick up his 600th first-class wicket.

Close of play: first day, Northamptonshire 82-1 (Curran 31, Thurston 30); second day, Northamptonshire 288-5 (Vasconcelos 31, Zaib 6); third day, Northamptonshire 62-1 (Gay 23, Thurston 25).

FASTEST FIRST-CLASS HUNDREDS FOR GLAMORGAN

Balls			
62	**M. de Lange (113)**	**v Northamptonshire at Northampton**	**2020**
64	G. P. Butcher (101*)	v Oxford University at Oxford	1997
79	W. G. A. Parkhouse (105)	v Northamptonshire at Northampton	1961
80	Majid Khan (113)	v Warwickshire at Birmingham	1972

Parkhouse and Majid both reached their centuries in 70 minutes, Glamorgan's joint-fastest by time. Butcher's century was his only one in first-class cricket. Ball-by-ball information is not known for many early matches.

Research by Andrew Hignell

Glamorgan

N. J. Selman c Vasconcelos b White	42	– c Vasconcelos b Muzarabani	1
J. M. Cooke lbw b White	18	– lbw b White	3
K. S. Carlson c Kerrigan b Muzarabani	8	– lbw b Hutton	1
W. T. Root c Zaib b Hutton	16	– c Vasconcelos b Muzarabani	3
*†C. B. Cooke b Hutton	2	– c Hutton b White	14
C. Z. Taylor c Thurston b White	106	– c Curran b Muzarabani	0
D. A. Douthwaite c Vasconcelos b White	11	– st Vasconcelos b Kerrigan	86
T. van der Gugten c Vasconcelos b Muzarabani	4	– c Thurston b White	4
K. A. Bull c Vasconcelos b Hutton	0	– b White	4
M. de Lange c Zaib b Hutton	0	– c Keogh b Kerrigan	113
M. G. Hogan not out	33	– not out	21
B 16, lb 1, nb 2	19	B 4, lb 3, nb 4	11
1/31 (2) 2/68 (3) 3/86 (1) 4/90 (4) 5/93 (5) 6/106 (7) 7/113 (8) 8/123 (9) 9/135 (10) 10/259 (6) (67 overs)	259	1/1 (1) 2/2 (3) 3/7 (4) 4/15 (2) 5/16 (6) 6/28 (5) 7/42 (8) 8/60 (9) 9/228 (7) 10/261 (10) (53.5 overs)	261

Hutton 17–2–77–4; Muzarabani 14–5–63–2; White 18–4–48–4; Procter 5–1–20–0; Kerrigan 13–3–34–0. *Second innings*—Hutton 13–4–37–1; Muzarabani 12–3–67–3; White 12–4–35–4; Procter 4–0–45–0; Kerrigan 8.5–1–54–2; Keogh 4–1–16–0.

Northamptonshire

B. J. Curran c Selman b van der Gugten	82	– c and b van der Gugten	12
E. N. Gay c and b de Lange	15	– not out	77
C. O. Thurston b Taylor	115	– lbw b Douthwaite	64
L. A. Procter c Douthwaite b van der Gugten	3	– c C. B. Cooke b Hogan	25
R. I. Keogh b Douthwaite	20	– run out (Carlson)	0
*†R. S. Vasconcelos c van der Gugten b de Lange	58	– not out	4
S. A. Zaib c Selman b van der Gugten	8		
B. A. Hutton c Selman b de Lange	9		
S. C. Kerrigan c C. B. Cooke b Douthwaite	1		
B. Muzarabani b de Lange	0		
C. J. White not out	0		
B 8, lb 6, w 1, nb 6	21	B 2, lb 3, w 1, nb 4	10
1/26 (2) 2/202 (1) 3/210 (4) (108.2 overs)	332	1/27 (1) (4 wkts, 42.3 overs)	192
4/234 (3) 5/273 (5) 6/291 (7)		2/133 (3) 3/176 (4)	
7/320 (8) 8/321 (9) 9/328 (6) 10/332 (10)		4/187 (5)	

Van der Gugten 22–4–64–3; Hogan 25–2–78–0; de Lange 23.2–6–84–4; Douthwaite 22–4–47–2; Bull 6–1–23–0; Carlson 1–0–2–0; Taylor 9–2–20–1. *Second innings*—Hogan 11.3–1–48–1; van der Gugten 11–3–53–1; de Lange 10–2–31–0; Bull 3–0–22–0; Douthwaite 7–1–33–1.

Umpires: R. J. Warren and C. M. Watts. Referee: S. Cummings.

At Bristol, September 6. NORTHAMPTONSHIRE drew with GLOUCESTERSHIRE. *The game is abandoned after one session because Ben Curran – who did not travel to Bristol – tested positive for Covid-19.*

NOTTINGHAMSHIRE

The wait goes on, but what a Blast!

JON CULLEY

Compared with 2019, when the ignominy of relegation in the Championship was amplified by an extraordinary one-run defeat in the semi-final of the Vitality Blast, this truncated season was one of joy and optimism for Nottinghamshire. It's true that their five matches in the Bob Willis Trophy did not yield a win – the county have now played 27 consecutive first-class fixtures without one – but they did show signs of a recovery in the red-ball game. And they returned to Edgbaston on the last day of the season to exorcise memories of the previous summer's dashed hopes: for the second time in four years, they were crowned Twenty20 champions.

After Nottinghamshire finished 2019 without a first-class victory, for the first time since 1967, another zero in the wins column might suggest more of the same. But other statistics reflected progress. They collected 20 batting points, six more than any other county, and 15 for bowling, equalled only by Kent and finalists Somerset. And they took the lead in all five games: their average first-innings total was 383, their opponents' 238.

Failing to turn any of those leads into a win was down to a number of factors. Against Derbyshire, who successfully chased 365 in the fourth innings, and Yorkshire, who routed Nottinghamshire for 97 when they needed a modest 188, the mental burden of two years without a victory almost certainly came into play. Yet there was no evidence of negativity in the remaining three matches. In rain-affected draws, they forced Lancashire to follow on, and had the upper hand against Leicestershire; they also dominated Durham, until thwarted by late resistance from the tail.

The recruits who had been so disappointing a year earlier were much more productive. Ben Duckett began to look like the batsman whose phenomenal 2016 season with Northamptonshire and England Lions made him a Wisden Cricketer of the Year. He rediscovered his panache to score 394 runs at 56, with hundreds against Lancashire and Durham, played a vital role in the Blast, where his four half-centuries included a match-winning unbeaten 53 in the final, and was named the club's Player of the Season. There were also two centuries for Ben Slater, though one was for Leicestershire: after a career-best 172 against Lancashire while on loan, he returned to Trent Bridge reinvigorated, replaced Chris Nash as opener, and punished Lancashire's bowlers again, with 142. Joe Clarke, who was troubled during his first season with Nottinghamshire by the conviction of a former Worcestershire team-mate for rape, made two hundreds against Durham – from 44 balls in the Blast, and in the Bob Willis Trophy ten days later.

A double-century opening stand against Leicestershire showed the potential of Slater and Haseeb Hameed, who was seeking a fresh beginning after his rise

Stu Forster, Getty Images

Ben Duckett

at Lancashire mystifyingly stalled; he passed 50 three times in seven innings. Wicketkeeper Tom Moores improved his glovework, and turned a cautious start into an exuberant century against Yorkshire. He needed more consistency in both disciplines but, at 24, had time on his side.

Zak Chappell, who had not been able to find a wicket in any format in his injury-troubled first season at Trent Bridge, had undergone minor ankle surgery, and tweaked his run-up with no loss of pace: he collected 15 in the Bob Willis Trophy. After a long run of injuries, Jake Ball was the Blast's leading wicket-taker with 19, supplemented by ten in three first-class games. Samit Patel's left-arm spin was also effective, and the decision to snap up Peter Trego after his release by Somerset was rewarded when he claimed 12 wickets in his 40th year. Tall off-spinner Matt Carter continued to improve, and 18-year-old all-rounder Joey Evison showed promise in the opening match, before a foot injury curtailed his season. Luke Fletcher, their most successful bowler in 2019, missed the first-class tournament with abdominal trouble.

The enduring image of the club's previous Blast campaign had been of a distraught Duckett, after he failed to connect for a last-ball single that would have put his side in the final. So it was fitting that he struck the winning four when Nottinghamshire defeated Surrey by a comfortable six wickets on a damp Sunday evening in October. This time, Duckett was lifted off his feet in a bear hug from his captain and batting partner, the Australian Dan Christian.

In a deep batting line-up, Duckett and Clarke scored 711 T20 runs between them. Along with Ball – who made up for Harry Gurney's absence with a shoulder problem – they helped Nottinghamshire achieve the best qualifying record. After stumbling through their quarter-final with Leicestershire, they swept aside Lancashire and Surrey on finals day.

If the future on the field was looking brighter, it was more difficult to plan ahead in a broader sense. As the Covid-19 crisis struck, many employees, including players, were placed on furlough, and all staff agreed pay cuts. The club asked members to consider donating their 2020 subscriptions, and a majority agreed.

In September, it was announced that the 37-year-old Nash and 22-year-old seamer Jack Blatherwick would not be offered new contracts; Blatherwick found a home at Old Trafford. Brett Hutton returned after three seasons with Northamptonshire, and the club also signed Oxford University captain Toby Pettman, a seamer, and Zimbabwe Under-19 wicketkeeper Dane Schadendorf, who has a British passport.

NOTTINGHAMSHIRE RESULTS

Bob Willis Trophy matches – Played 5: Lost 2, Drawn 3.
Vitality Blast matches – Played 11: Won 10, Lost 1. Abandoned 2.

Bob Willis Trophy, 4th in North Group;
Vitality Blast, winners.

BOB WILLIS TROPHY AVERAGES

BATTING AND FIELDING

Cap		*Birthplace*	*M*	*I*	*NO*	*R*	*HS*	*100*	*Avge*	*Ct/St*
	†B. T. Slater	*Chesterfield*	3	3	0	228	142	1	76.00	2
2019	†B. M. Duckett	*Farnborough, Kent*	5	8	1	394	150	2	56.28	3
2020	H. Hameed	*Bolton*	5	7	0	272	87	0	38.85	8
	J. M. Clarke	*Shrewsbury*	5	8	1	263	133	1	37.57	0
2013	S. J. Mullaney	*Warrington*	5	7	0	235	67	0	33.57	10
2008	S. R. Patel	*Leicester*	5	7	0	210	80	0	30.00	2
	†T. J. Moores	*Brighton*	5	7	0	207	106	1	29.57	15/1
	C. D. Nash	*Cuckfield*	2	4	0	78	59	0	19.50	1
	M. Carter	*Lincoln*	3	4	1	50	22	0	16.66	3
	P. D. Trego	*Weston-super-Mare*	5	8	0	116	39	0	14.50	1
2016	J. T. Ball	*Mansfield‡*	3	5	1	56	34	0	14.00	3
	Z. J. Chappell	*Grantham*	4	4	1	1	1	0	0.33	3
	T. E. Barber	*Poole*	3	3	3	2	2*	0	–	0

Also batted: J. D. M. Evison (*Peterborough*) (1 match) 38, 31 (1 ct); L. W. James (*Worksop‡*) (1 match) 36* (1 ct).

‡ *Born in Nottinghamshire.* †† *Other non-England-qualified.*

BOWLING

	Style	*O*	*M*	*R*	*W*	*BB*	*5I*	*Avge*
C. D. Nash	OB	11.2	1	38	3	3-20	0	12.66
J. D. M. Evison	RM	22.5	4	74	4	3-38	0	18.50
M. Carter	OB	149.2	54	263	11	4-76	0	23.90
P. D. Trego	RFM	134.3	44	342	12	3-33	0	28.50
Z. J. Chappell	RFM	131.2	30	431	15	4-59	0	28.73
S. R. Patel	SLA	156.2	36	388	13	4-80	0	29.84
J. T. Ball	RFM	112.5	30	336	10	3-71	0	33.60
T. E. Barber	LFM	79	9	289	7	3-42	0	41.28
S. J. Mullaney	RM	80	22	183	4	1-23	0	45.75

Also bowled: B. M. Duckett (OB) 1–0–2–0; L. W. James (RFM) 16–2–55–1.

LEADING VITALITY BLAST AVERAGES (70 runs/10 overs)

Batting	*Runs*	*HS*	*Avge*	*SR*	*Ct/St*
J. M. Clarke	371	100*	37.10	**175.00**	2
A. D. Hales	202	49	18.36	**164.22**	11
D. T. Christian	173	33*	28.83	**144.16**	3
B. M. Duckett	340	86*	42.50	**137.65**	6
T. J. Moores	188	51	26.85	**135.25**	4/2
C. D. Nash	185	55	23.12	**122.51**	4

Bowling	*W*	*BB*	*Avge*	*ER*
S. J. Mullaney	9	2-17	21.44	**7.14**
Imad Wasim	8	2-24	28.87	**7.21**
S. R. Patel	11	2-19	26.00	**7.52**
J. T. Ball	19	3-28	13.63	**7.58**
D. T. Christian	9	4-23	30.88	**7.94**
M. Carter	7	2-16	27.28	**8.68**
L. J. Fletcher	8	5-43	18.50	**9.86**

FIRST-CLASS COUNTY RECORDS

Highest score for	312*	W. W. Keeton v Middlesex at The Oval	1939
Highest score against	345	C. G. Macartney (Australians) at Nottingham	1921
Leading run-scorer	31,592	G. Gunn (avge 35.69)	1902–32
Best bowling for	10-66	K. Smales v Gloucestershire at Stroud	1956
Best bowling against	10-10	H. Verity (Yorkshire) at Leeds	1932
Leading wicket-taker	1,653	T. G. Wass (avge 20.34)	1896–1920
Highest total for	791	v Essex at Chelmsford	2007
Highest total against	781-7 dec	by Northamptonshire at Northampton	1995
Lowest total for	13	v Yorkshire at Nottingham	1901
Lowest total against	16	by Derbyshire at Nottingham	1879
	16	by Surrey at The Oval	1880

LIST A COUNTY RECORDS

Highest score for	187*	A. D. Hales v Surrey at Lord's	2017
Highest score against	191	D. S. Lehmann (Yorkshire) at Scarborough	2001
Leading run-scorer	11,237	R. T. Robinson (avge 35.33)	1978–99
Best bowling for	6-10	K. P. Evans v Northumberland at Jesmond	1994
Best bowling against	7-41	A. N. Jones (Sussex) at Nottingham	1986
Leading wicket-taker	291	C. E. B. Rice (avge 22.60)	1975–87
Highest total for	445-8	v Northamptonshire at Nottingham	2016
Highest total against	425	by Northamptonshire at Nottingham	2016
Lowest total for	57	v Gloucestershire at Nottingham	2009
Lowest total against	43	by Northamptonshire at Northampton	1977

TWENTY20 COUNTY RECORDS

Highest score for	113*	D. T. Christian v Northants at Northampton	2018
Highest score against	111	W. J. Durston (Derbyshire) at Nottingham	2010
Leading run-scorer	**3,602**	**S. R. Patel (avge 27.28, SR 127.36)**	**2003–20**
Best bowling for	5-22	G. G. White v Lancashire at Nottingham	2013
Best bowling against	5-13	A. B. McDonald (Leicestershire) at Nottingham	2010
Leading wicket-taker	**165**	**S. R. Patel (avge 26.76, ER 7.33)**	**2003–20**
Highest total for	227-3	by Derbyshire at Nottingham	2017
Highest total against	227-5	by Yorkshire at Leeds	2017
Lowest total for	91	v Lancashire at Manchester	2006
Lowest total against	90	by Leicestershire at Nottingham	2014

ADDRESS

County Cricket Ground, Trent Bridge, Nottingham NG2 6AG; 0115 982 3000; questions@nottsccc.co.uk; www.trentbridge.co.uk. Twitter: @TrentBridge.

OFFICIALS

Captain (Ch'ship/one-day) S. J. Mullaney
(Twenty20) D. T. Christian
Director of cricket M. Newell
Head coach P. Moores
President S. B. Hassan

Chairman R. W. Tennant
Chief executive L. J. Pursehouse
Chairman, cricket committee D. J. Bicknell
Head groundsman S. Birks
Scorers R. Marshall and A. Cusworth

At Nottingham, August 1–4. NOTTINGHAMSHIRE lost to DERBYSHIRE by three wickets. *Classified as a home game for Derbyshire, since the ECB were using their ground as a biosecure bubble.*

NOTTINGHAMSHIRE v YORKSHIRE

At Nottingham, August 8–11. Yorkshire won by 90 runs. Yorkshire 21pts, Nottinghamshire 7pts. Toss: Yorkshire. First-class debut: D. J. Leech.

Seemingly in sight of their first first-class victory for more than two years, Nottinghamshire slid to a ninth defeat in ten matches. A career-best 106 from Moores had put them 91 ahead, before Chappell and Carter claimed four wickets apiece to engineer a last-day chase of 188. They managed barely half that. An eight-day-old pitch offered no appreciable advantage to the Yorkshire bowlers, who simply capitalised on batting fragility. On the first day, Thompson had scored a mature 98 for them, when Nash bowled Brook with his first delivery in first-class cricket since 2018 – and soon had another two. Moores built steadily, then accelerated boldly, reverse-sweeping Lyth and Malan for six, and completing his second fifty in 38 balls. When Yorkshire batted again, Bairstow reached 75 before being undone by Hameed's brilliant one-handed catch at short leg, off Carter's off-spin. Chappell, who had taken no wickets in any format in his first, injury-ravaged, season at Trent Bridge, finished with six in the match; Mullaney caught seven, equalling the county record for a fielder, held by Arthur Jones (1908) and Bill Voce (1929). Yet it all came to nothing: Nottinghamshire folded inside 30 overs, as Thompson followed his highest score with a career-best three for six.

Close of play: first day, Nottinghamshire 13-1 (Hameed 4); second day, Nottinghamshire 355; third day, Yorkshire 259-7 (Tattersall 41, Olivier 8).

Yorkshire

A. Lyth lbw b Ball	4	– c Mullaney b Patel	50
T. Köhler-Cadmore c Mullaney b Carter	21	– c Carter b Chappell	0
†J. M. Bairstow c Patel b Chappell	5	– c Hameed b Carter	75
D. J. Malan c Moores b Chappell	9	– c Hameed b Carter	1
H. C. Brook b Nash	62	– c Mullaney b Patel	30
J. A. Tattersall lbw b Patel	31	– c Mullaney b Carter	53
J. A. Thompson c Mullaney b Nash	98	– c Carter b Chappell	33
*S. A. Patterson c Mullaney b Nash	11	– c Moores b Chappell	4
D. Olivier lbw b Patel	5	– c Moores b Chappell	8
J. W. Shutt lbw b Carter	0	– (11) not out	0
D. J. Leech not out	0	– (10) c Mullaney b Carter	1
B 12, lb 2, nb 4	18	B 13, lb 8, nb 2	23
1/6 (1) 2/23 (3) 3/33 (4) 4/44 (2) 5/136 (6) 6/176 (5) 7/218 (8) 8/231 (9) 9/232 (10) 10/264 (7) (81.2 overs)	264	1/4 (2) 2/135 (1) 3/135 (3) 4/136 (4) 5/186 (5) 6/240 (7) 7/246 (8) 8/262 (9) 9/267 (10) 10/278 (6) (108.2 overs)	278

Ball 14–5–41–1; Chappell 13–3–64–2; Mullaney 4–0–9–0; Carter 27–8–44–2; Patel 17–3–72–2; Nash 6.2–0–20–3. *Second innings*—Ball 3–1–5–0; Chappell 17–3–59–4; Trego 10–3–26–0; Carter 40.2–14–76–4; Mullaney 7–1–16–0; Patel 26–5–57–2; Nash 5–1–18–0.

Nottinghamshire

C. D. Nash b Patterson	8	– lbw b Olivier	11
H. Hameed c Lyth b Leech	21	– c Bairstow b Leech	1
B. M. Duckett c Lyth b Olivier	4	– c Malan b Olivier	19
J. M. Clarke run out (Thompson)	35	– c and b Olivier	18
*S. J. Mullaney lbw b Lyth	50	– c Bairstow b Patterson	5
P. D. Trego c Brook b Olivier	39	– lbw b Shutt	7
†T. J. Moores b Patterson	106	– b Thompson	8
S. R. Patel c Brook b Malan	38	– c Malan b Shutt	14
Z. J. Chappell c Bairstow b Thompson	1	– c Shutt b Thompson	0
J. T. Ball c Lyth b Malan	0	– (11) not out	0
M. Carter not out	15	– (10) lbw b Thompson	7
B 11, lb 9, w 6, nb 12	38	Lb 1, nb 6	7
1/13 (1) 2/30 (3) 3/55 (2) 4/115 (4) 5/163 (5) 6/187 (6) 7/286 (8) 8/293 (9) 9/294 (10) 10/355 (7) (95.1 overs)	355	1/16 (1) 2/16 (2) 3/46 (3) 4/61 (4) 5/61 (5) 6/74 (7) 7/82 (6) 8/89 (9) 9/97 (10) 10/97 (8) (29.2 overs)	97

Olivier 19–4–88–2; Patterson 21.1–10–38–2; Leech 10–2–42–1; Thompson 16–5–37–1; Brook 2–0–5–0; Shutt 8–0–49–0; Lyth 13–1–52–1; Malan 6–1–24–2. *Second innings*—Olivier 10–4–29–3; Leech 4–1–20–1; Patterson 7–1–27–1; Thompson 5–1–6–3; Shutt 3.2–0–14–2.

Umpires: J. D. Middlebrook and R. T. Robinson. Referee: W. R. Smith.

At Nottingham, August 15–18. NOTTINGHAMSHIRE drew with LANCASHIRE. *Another away game on home soil.*

At Leicester, August 22–25. NOTTINGHAMSHIRE drew with LEICESTERSHIRE. *Slater and Hameed share a double-century opening stand.*

NOTTINGHAMSHIRE v DURHAM

At Nottingham, September 6–9. Drawn. Nottinghamshire 16pts, Durham 13pts. Toss: Durham.

Both sides ended the first-class season without a victory; for Nottinghamshire, it was their 27th winless match since June 2018. Yet they had the better of it until a stubborn rearguard denied them. Durham had recovered from Chappell's early strikes on the first day, but centuries for Duckett and Clarke established a home ascendancy. Duckett, whose second hundred of the competition took him past 6,000 runs, was sure-footed almost throughout; Clarke rode his luck, surviving chances on 16 and 23, before growing in flair. Their stand of 195, a third-wicket record between these sides, set up a lead of 128 that might have been bigger but for Rushworth. His seven for 108 made him the third bowler to take 500 for Durham, and Nottinghamshire's last five fell for 15. Then, as nightwatchman, he batted over an hour on the final morning, helping Scotland's Michael Jones to a maiden first-class fifty, after 24 runs in his seven other first-class innings. But it was a last-wicket stand of 45 between Carse and Raine that ensured the draw. When they came together, Durham were only 156 ahead, with more than 30 overs to go. They raised the target to 202 from 17: too tall an order, despite Trego's lusty hitting.

Close of play: first day, Durham 275-8 (Carse 35, Raine 23); second day, Nottinghamshire 251-2 (Duckett 146, Clarke 74); third day, Durham 131-2 (Jones 39, Rushworth 0).

Durham

First innings		Second innings	
A. Z. Lees c Moores b Ball	31	– lbw b Trego	27
S. R. Dickson lbw b Chappell	7	– b Patel	56
M. A. Jones c Carter b Chappell	0	– c Moores b Ball	82
D. G. Bedingham c Duckett b Chappell	4	– (5) lbw b Trego	29
G. J. Harte b Mullaney	72	– (6) c Hameed b Carter	34
S. W. Poynter c Moores b Carter	50	– (7) b Trego	1
*†E. J. H. Eckersley c Ball b Carter	25	– (8) c Mullaney b Patel	8
P. Coughlin c Hameed b Carter	21	– (9) c Moores b Patel	0
B. A. Carse c Duckett b Chappell	41	– (10) c Ball b Patel	31
B. A. Raine c Trego b Ball	31	– (11) not out	19
C. Rushworth not out	0	– (4) c Hameed b Carter	25
B 1, lb 2, w 5, nb 4	12	B 5, lb 6, nb 6	17
1/16 (2) 2/29 (3) 3/33 (4) 4/66 (1) 5/167 (5) 6/180 (6) 7/204 (8) 8/227 (7) 9/294 (9) 10/294 (10) (103 overs)	294	1/67 (1) 2/128 (2) 3/183 (4) 4/226 (3) 5/240 (5) 6/254 (7) 7/278 (6) 8/279 (9) 9/284 (8) 10/329 (10) (140 overs)	329

Ball 20–6–58–2; Chappell 23–3–92–4; Trego 11–4–37–0; Carter 26–10–43–3; Patel 14–2–34–0; Mullaney 9–1–27–1. *Second innings*—Ball 22–6–63–1; Chappell 19–2–65–0; Trego 19–9–34–3; Patel 38–10–80–4; Carter 33–13–63–2; Mullaney 9–2–13–0.

Nottinghamshire

First innings		Second innings	
B. T. Slater lbw b Rushworth	0		
H. Hameed c Coughlin b Rushworth	21		
B. M. Duckett c Jones b Carse	150	– (2) not out	36
J. M. Clarke c Dickson b Rushworth	133	– (3) not out	8
*S. J. Mullaney b Rushworth	41		
S. R. Patel lbw b Carse	2		
†T. J. Moores lbw b Raine	48		
P. D. Trego lbw b Rushworth	4	– (1) b Raine	34
M. Carter c Lees b Rushworth	6		
Z. J. Chappell not out	0		
J. T. Ball c Coughlin b Rushworth	0		
Lb 1, nb 16	17	Lb 2, nb 2	4
1/0 (1) 2/65 (2) 3/260 (3) 4/328 (5) 5/332 (6) 6/407 (4) 7/411 (8) 8/417 (7) 9/421 (9) 10/422 (11) (101 overs)	422	1/69 (1) (1 wkt, 9.2 overs)	82

Rushworth 26–2–108–7; Coughlin 21–2–81–0; Raine 25–4–72–1; Carse 18–1–110–2; Harte 11–1–50–0. *Second innings*—Rushworth 3–0–29–0; Raine 4.2–0–43–1; Carse 2–0–8–0.

Umpires: N. G. B. Cook and I. N. Ramage. Referee: T. J. Boon.

SOMERSET

Excuse my French

RICHARD LATHAM

Somerset followers might have ended an extraordinary season by reaching for the phrase *plus ça change, plus c'est la même chose*. For all the upheaval brought about by Covid-19, one statistic was wearingly familiar: their team finished second, for the sixth time in 11 seasons.

On this occasion, the runners-up tag came with a difference. The five-day final of the Bob Willis Trophy at Lord's had ended in a rain-affected draw, leaving Essex – who had pipped Somerset to the County Championship in 2019 – as winners because of a first-innings lead that owed almost everything to Alastair Cook's vintage 172. Somerset, who had lost an important toss, were arguably in the better position after declaring their second innings on 272 for seven on a testing pitch. But Essex knew a draw would be enough and, having been 131 for five chasing 237, batted out time.

The silver lining for Somerset, who had won four of their five games in the Central Group (and would have secured a fifth victory but for bad weather at Edgbaston), came in the shape of impressive centuries in the final from two Academy products. Eddie Byrom in the first innings, and Tom Lammonby in the second, each demonstrated the technique and the temperament for the big occasion; Lammonby finished the tournament with three hundreds, more than anyone in the country.

With the experienced James Hildreth ruled out of the final by a hamstring injury, and Tom Banton at the Indian Premier League, Ben Green – another Academician – opened with Lammonby and scored 24 and 41. Craig Overton, meanwhile, contributed 111 runs (and was dismissed only once). Earlier in the competition, George Bartlett, yet another Academy graduate, hit an unbeaten century in a thumping win over Gloucestershire, while captain Tom Abell confirmed his growing maturity with hundreds both in that game and against Glamorgan. It was all a source of encouragement for head coach Jason Kerr, after batting had been a recent Achilles heel for an otherwise powerful team.

Hopes that Somerset can mount another strong challenge for a first Championship title in 2021 are based on greater competition for batting places, and a bowling attack that will remain among the strongest in the country, despite the departures of seamer Jamie Overton to Surrey, and England off-spinner Dom Bess to Yorkshire. Overton wanted to take the new ball, and Bess to emerge from the shadow of Jack Leach (at club level, at least), though Kerr regretted losing two players the coaching staff had worked hard to develop.

But Somerset will still be able to call on a potent pace department, which in the five BWT group games never conceded more than 200; Northamptonshire were skittled for 67, and Gloucestershire for 76 and 70. Craig Overton, who added speed to his repertoire and managed 30 wickets at 13, more than any seamer in the competition, to earn the PCA's Most Valuable Player award, was well supported by the probing Josh Davey (24 at 13), a natural wicket-taker in Lewis Gregory, and the wily Jack Brooks. In October, South African quick Marchant de Lange signed a two-year deal as an overseas player, having spent much of the previous four seasons at Glamorgan. They will all work under new bowling coach Steve Kirby, who arrived from Derbyshire. If Leach can continue to put behind him a forgettable 2020 marred by illness and injury, Somerset will have all bases covered in their quest for the title long-suffering fans now refer to as the "Holy Grail", though Test selection may get in the way. The club will also have to overcome an eight-point penalty – revised from 12, and deferred a year because of the pandemic – after the Taunton pitch for the 2019 Championship decider against Essex was ruled to have shown "excessive unevenness of bounce".

Philip Brown, Popperfoto/Getty Images

Tom Lammonby

While the Bob Willis Trophy brought frustration, Somerset's performance in the Vitality Blast was nothing short of lamentable. They went into the competition confident that Pakistan's Babar Azam, then the world's top-ranked T20 batsman, would lead them to the knockout stages. Instead, his four appearances at Taunton brought a total of 20 runs, even if a brilliant century against Glamorgan at Cardiff kept Somerset in with a chance of the quarter-finals. Had they limited Gloucestershire to a single from the last ball of their last group game, they would have qualified; instead, Tom Smith hit Ollie Sale to the midwicket boundary, and Somerset were out.

Kerr admitted getting the balance of the team wrong at times, but could take heart from the emergence of talent. Eighteen-year-old Will Smeed hit 82 against Gloucestershire on only his second appearance, while Lewis Goldsworthy, a year older, marked his debut with 38 not out against Glamorgan, and claimed five wickets in three games with his left-arm spin. But 20-year-old seamer Nathan Gilchrist opted to join Kent.

The pandemic meant a challenging start for Somerset's new chief executive, Gordon Hollins, the ECB's former chief operating officer and managing director of county cricket. He started in March, and one of his first tasks was to furlough 67 of the club's 76 staff, including players. In an open letter to supporters, he pointed out that the closure of Somerset's conference and events business alone was costing around £75,000 a month, while lost revenue from match-day ticket sales amounted to £600,000. It was later estimated that the overall loss for the season was £1m: ten members of staff paid with their jobs. While the club hoped prompt action taken to reduce expenditure, and financial support from the ECB, would help ride out the storm, the future was uncertain.

On a more positive note, Somerset supported their local NHS by raising £5,000 through the production and sale of a special commemorative shirt, and allowed the County Ground to be used as a Covid-19 testing site.

SOMERSET RESULTS

Bob Willis Trophy matches – Played 6: Won 4, Drawn 2.
Vitality Blast matches – Played 9: Won 4, Lost 5. Abandoned 1.

Bob Willis Trophy, finalists;
Vitality Blast, 4th in Central Group.

BOB WILLIS TROPHY AVERAGES

BATTING AND FIELDING

Cap		*Birthplace*	*M*	*I*	*NO*	*R*	*HS*	*100*	*Avge*	*Ct*
	†T. A. Lammonby	*Exeter*	6	11	2	459	116	3	51.00	4
2017	†S. M. Davies	*Bromsgrove*	6	10	2	320	123*	1	40.00	19
2018	T. B. Abell	*Taunton‡*	6	11	1	386	119	2	38.60	5
2019	J. Overton	*Barnstaple*	4	6	0	206	120	1	34.33	7
	G. A. Bartlett	*Frimley*	4	6	1	160	100*	1	32.00	2
2016	C. Overton	*Barnstaple*	6	10	2	248	66	0	31.00	7
	J. A. Brooks	*Oxford*	5	7	2	139	72	0	27.80	1
	B. G. F. Green	*Exeter*	3	5	0	127	54	0	25.40	0
	†E. J. Byrom††	*Harare, Zimbabwe*	6	11	0	271	117	1	24.63	3
2007	J. C. Hildreth	*Milton Keynes*	4	6	0	124	45	0	20.66	10
	J. H. Davey††	*Aberdeen*	6	9	3	113	28	0	18.83	1
2015	L. Gregory	*Plymouth*	3	5	0	78	37	0	15.60	1
2018	R. E. van der Merwe††	*Johannesburg, SA*	4	6	1	57	30	0	11.40	4
	T. Banton	*Chiltern*	2	3	0	33	18	0	11.00	0
2017	†M. J. Leach§	*Taunton‡*	2	3	0	29	21	0	9.66	1

‡ *Born in Somerset.* § *ECB contract.* †† *Other non-England-qualified.*

BOWLING

	Style	*O*	*M*	*R*	*W*	*BB*	*5I*	*Avge*
J. Overton	RFM	68.1	24	186	15	5-48	1	12.40
C. Overton	RFM	196.2	66	403	30	5-26	2	13.43
J. H. Davey	RFM	150.2	55	331	24	4-25	0	13.79
T. B. Abell	RM	16.2	5	50	3	3-4	0	16.66
L. Gregory	RFM	102.3	22	318	18	6-72	1	17.66
J. A. Brooks	RFM	89.5	23	254	13	4-40	0	19.53
M. J. Leach	SLA	52	17	112	3	3-38	0	37.33

Also bowled: E. J. Byrom (OB) 1–0–4–0; T. A. Lammonby (LM) 12–3–38–2; R. E. van der Merwe (SLA) 6–2–8–1.

LEADING VITALITY BLAST AVERAGES (70 runs/10 overs)

Batting	*Runs*	*HS*	*Avge*	*SR*	*Ct*
T. A. Lammonby	121	43*	40.33	**177.94**	0
R. E. van der Merwe	127	41*	42.33	**176.38**	4
L. Gregory	118	50	23.60	**157.33**	9
J. C. Hildreth	119	34*	39.66	**141.66**	2
Babar Azam	218	114*	36.33	**137.97**	6
T. B. Abell	227	74*	32.42	**136.74**	6
S. M. Davies	182	60	20.22	**131.88**	4
W. C. F. Smeed	94	82	18.80	**117.50**	2

Bowling	*W*	*BB*	*Avge*	*ER*
M. T. C. Waller	8	3-18	26.50	**6.23**
R. E. van der Merwe	3	2-15	69.66	**7.20**
L. P. Goldsworthy	5	2-21	17.20	**7.81**
J. H. Davey	11	4-41	11.18	**8.20**
C. Overton	6	3-36	22.83	**9.23**
L. Gregory	9	2-18	19.55	**9.26**
O. R. T. Sale	13	3-32	23.15	**10.14**

FIRST-CLASS COUNTY RECORDS

Highest score for	342	J. L. Langer v Surrey at Guildford	2006
Highest score against	424	A. C. MacLaren (Lancashire) at Taunton	1895
Leading run-scorer	21,142	H. Gimblett (avge 36.96)	1935–54
Best bowling for	10-49	E. J. Tyler v Surrey at Taunton	1895
Best bowling against	10-35	A. Drake (Yorkshire) at Weston-super-Mare	1914
Leading wicket-taker	2,165	J. C. White (avge 18.03)	1909–37
Highest total for	850-7 dec	v Middlesex at Taunton	2007
Highest total against	811	by Surrey at The Oval	1899
Lowest total for	25	v Gloucestershire at Bristol	1947
Lowest total against	22	by Gloucestershire at Bristol	1920

LIST A COUNTY RECORDS

Highest score for	184	M. E. Trescothick v Gloucestershire at Taunton	2008
Highest score against	167*	A. J. Stewart (Surrey) at The Oval	1994
Leading run-scorer	7,374	M. E. Trescothick (avge 36.87)	1993–2014
Best bowling for	8-66	S. R. G. Francis v Derbyshire at Derby	2004
Best bowling against	7-39	A. Hodgson (Northamptonshire) at Northampton	1976
Leading wicket-taker	309	H. R. Moseley (avge 20.03)	1971–82
Highest total for	413-4	v Devon at Torquay	1990
Highest total against	429-9	by Nottinghamshire at Taunton	2017
Lowest total for	58	v Essex at Chelmsford	1977
	58	v Middlesex at Southgate	2000
Lowest total against	60	by Kent at Taunton	1979

TWENTY20 COUNTY RECORDS

Highest score for	151*	C. H. Gayle v Kent at Taunton	2015
Highest score against	122*	J. J. Roy (Surrey) at The Oval	2015
Leading run-scorer	**3,694**	**J. C. Hildreth (avge 24.46, SR 124.25)**	**2004–20**
Best bowling for	6-5	A. V. Suppiah v Glamorgan at Cardiff	2011
Best bowling against	5-11	A. F. Milne (Kent) at Taunton	2017
Leading wicket-taker	137	A. C. Thomas (avge 20.17, ER 7.67)	2008–15
Highest total for	250-3	v Gloucestershire at Taunton	2006
Highest total for	231-5	by Kent at Canterbury	2018
Lowest total for	82	v Kent at Taunton	2010
Lowest total against	73	by Warwickshire at Taunton	2013

ADDRESS

Cooper Associates County Ground, St James's Street, Taunton TA1 1JT; 0845 337 1875; enquiries@somersetcountycc.co.uk; www.somersetcountycc.co.uk. Twitter: @SomersetCCC.

OFFICIALS

Captain T. B. Abell
(Twenty20) L. Gregory
Director of cricket A. Hurry
Head coach J. I. D. Kerr
Academy director S. D. Snell

President B. C. Rose
Chairman G. M. Baird
Chief executive G. M. Hollins
Head groundsman S. Hawkins
Scorer P. Rhodes

SOMERSET v GLAMORGAN

At Taunton, August 1–4. Somerset won by 289 runs. Somerset 21pts, Glamorgan 3pts. Toss: Somerset. First-class debut: T. A. Lammonby.

The first pitch produced for a competitive match by Somerset's new head groundsman, Scott Hawkins, offered pace and bounce for the seamers – and Glamorgan's reduced the home side to 189 for nine. But last man Brooks contributed a belligerent 58-ball 72 to a tenth-wicket stand of 107 with Davies. Craig Overton, released by England after attending their training camp at the Rose Bowl, then responded to a challenge from the selectors to add a yard of pace without sacrificing accuracy, and claimed five for 38 from the River End as Somerset gained a lead of 165. With Glamorgan a bowler light because of a hamstring injury to Smith (who batted twice with a runner), Somerset captain Abell cemented his side's position with his sixth first-class hundred, and first at Taunton since 2015. Ben Green, a concussion replacement for Bartlett – struck on the head by de Lange on the first day – hit his maiden half-century. Set 456, Glamorgan collapsed against Jamie Overton, whose impending departure for Surrey had been announced just before the game.

Close of play: first day, Glamorgan 8-0 (Selman 4, Hemphrey 0); second day, Somerset 131-2 (Abell 44, Hildreth 45); third day, Glamorgan 126-5 (Cooke 67).

Somerset

First innings		Second innings	
E. J. Byrom b Wagg	22	– c Cooke b de Lange	27
T. A. Lammonby lbw b Hogan	41	– c Cooke b Wagg	8
*T. B. Abell b de Lange	3	– c sub (C. Z. Taylor) b Bull	119
J. C. Hildreth c Carlson b Douthwaite	16	– c Cooke b Hogan	45
G. A. Bartlett c Carlson b Smith	23		
†S. M. Davies not out	81	– b Bull	18
C. Overton lbw b Douthwaite	2	– not out	6
R. E. van der Merwe lbw b Smith	0	– (9) c Selman b Bull	2
J. Overton c Hemphrey b Smith	3	– (8) c Hemphrey b Douthwaite	0
J. H. Davey c Douthwaite b de Lange	20		
J. A. Brooks c and b Wagg	72		
B. G. F. Green (did not bat)		– (5) c Wagg b Douthwaite	54
Lb 7, nb 6	13	B 4, lb 1, nb 6	11
1/36 (1) 2/41 (3) 3/75 (4) 4/95 (2) 5/139 (5) 6/142 (7) 7/143 (8) 8/149 (9) 9/189 (10) 10/296 (11) (81 overs)	296	1/26 (2) 2/38 (1) 3/131 (4) 4/257 (3) 5/278 (6) 6/282 (5) 7/282 (8) 8/290 (9) (8 wkts dec, 80.1 overs)	290

Green replaced Bartlett, as a concussion substitute.

Hogan 17–9–37–1; Smith 14–4–41–3; de Lange 17–3–37–2; Wagg 14–2–59–2; Douthwaite 12–0–79–2; Bull 7–0–36–0. *Second innings*—Hogan 16–5–42–1; Wagg 15–4–36–1; Douthwaite 16–3–60–2; de Lange 14–2–35–1; Bull 19.1–0–112–3.

Glamorgan

First innings		Second innings	
N. J. Selman lbw b Davey	9	– lbw b C. Overton	0
C. R. Hemphrey c Lammonby b C. Overton	7	– c and b J. Overton	20
K. S. Carlson c van der Merwe b C. Overton	7	– c J. Overton b C. Overton	4
*†C. B. Cooke c J. Overton b C. Overton	0	– (5) c Hildreth b J. Overton	82
W. T. Root c J. Overton b Davey	1	– (4) b van der Merwe	26
D. A. Douthwaite c van der Merwe b C. Overton	2	– lbw b J. Overton	6
G. G. Wagg c Hildreth b C. Overton	28	– c Davies b J. Overton	1
K. A. Bull lbw b Brooks	23	– b J. Overton	9
M. de Lange c Davey b J. Overton	8	– (10) not out	8
R. A. J. Smith c Davies b J. Overton	23	– (9) c van der Merwe b Davey	3
M. G. Hogan not out	2	– c J. Overton b Brooks	0
B 12, lb 7, nb 2	21	Lb 5, nb 2	7
1/15 (2) 2/23 (1) 3/33 (3) 4/34 (4) 5/34 (5) 6/38 (6) 7/91 (7) 8/100 (9) 9/107 (8) 10/131 (10) (46.1 overs)	131	1/0 (1) 2/10 (3) 3/29 (2) 4/95 (4) 5/126 (6) 6/140 (7) 7/153 (5) 8/158 (9) 9/158 (8) 10/166 (11) (64.2 overs)	166

C. Overton 17–5–38–5; Davey 12–7–34–2; Brooks 8–1–24–1; J. Overton 9.1–2–16–2. *Second innings*—C. Overton 17–4–31–2; Davey 12–5–26–1; Brooks 10.2–3–41–1; J. Overton 17–6–48–5; van der Merwe 6–2–8–1; Abell 2–0–7–0.

Umpires: I. D. Blackwell and R. J. Warren. Referee: R. M. Ellison.

At Northampton, August 8–9. SOMERSET beat NORTHAMPTONSHIRE by 167 runs. *Somerset take 20 wickets in 75 overs.*

At Birmingham, August 15–18. SOMERSET drew with WARWICKSHIRE. *Jamie Overton hits a century from No. 10.*

SOMERSET v GLOUCESTERSHIRE

At Taunton, August 22–25. Somerset won by 314 runs. Somerset 20pts, Gloucestershire 3pts. Toss: Gloucestershire.

George Bartlett's fourth first-class century, laced with scything back-foot shots through the off side, rescued Somerset from 89 for five on the opening day of a match that raised smiles at the club's Academy. A fellow graduate of the youth set-up, Tom Lammonby, notched his maiden hundred in the second innings. With Somerset's seamers putting on another potent display, it all proved too much for Gloucestershire, who were skittled for 76 and 70 in a total of 73.5 overs. They had last been dismissed twice in double figures in a game in 1989, by Essex at Bristol (and by Somerset only once, at Bristol in 1909). The fiery Craig Overton and the persistent Davey shared 16 wickets, aided by a little seam movement and inept batting from a line-up more used to Division Two attacks. The highest score by a Gloucestershire batsman was 21 – three fewer than Somerset No. 11 Brooks managed in the first innings. And when Abell matched Lammonby's unbeaten 101 to set a target of 385 on the second evening, the only threat to his side came from the weather, which delayed an emphatic victory until the final afternoon.

Close of play: first day, Gloucestershire 13-4 (Lace 1, Taylor 3); second day, Gloucestershire 14-3 (van Buuren 1); third day, Gloucestershire 63-8 (Scott 5, Shaw 0).

Somerset

E. J. Byrom b Payne	0	– c van Buuren b Payne	6
T. A. Lammonby c Lace b Higgins	24	– not out	101
*T. B. Abell c Roderick b Shaw	10	– not out	101
J. C. Hildreth lbw b Higgins	13		
G. A. Bartlett not out	100		
†S. M. Davies c Roderick b Payne	16		
C. Overton lbw b Higgins	32		
R. E. van der Merwe c Hankins b Payne	1		
J. Overton c Roderick b Payne	4		
J. H. Davey c Dent b Higgins	0		
J. A. Brooks c Higgins b Taylor	24		
B 1, lb 8, nb 4	13	B 1, lb 4, nb 10	15
1/4 (1) 2/29 (3) 3/44 (4) (72.2 overs)	237	1/12 (1) (1 wkt dec, 54 overs)	223
4/57 (2) 5/89 (6) 6/164 (7)			
7/165 (8) 8/169 (9) 9/176 (10) 10/237 (11)			

Payne 19–6–44–4; Higgins 20–4–72–4; Shaw 13–4–41–1; Taylor 14.2–0–53–1; Scott 6–1–18–0. *Second innings*—Payne 11–3–31–1; Higgins 11–1–54–0; Shaw 11–0–39–0; Taylor 10–0–34–0; Scott 6–0–31–0; Charlesworth 5–0–29–0.

Gloucestershire

B. G. Charlesworth c Hildreth b Davey	3	– c Davies b Davey	1
*C. D. J. Dent lbw b C. Overton	5	– lbw b C. Overton	4
G. L. van Buuren c Davies b C. Overton	1	– c Davies b Davey	15
J. Shaw lbw b Davey	0	– (10) c Bartlett b C. Overton	0
T. C. Lace b Brooks	21	– (4) b Davey	8
M. D. Taylor c Lammonby b Davey	12	– (11) c Lammonby b Brooks	3
G. T. Hankins c C. Overton b J. Overton	6	– (5) b C. Overton	5
R. F. Higgins c Davies b C. Overton	15	– (6) lbw b C. Overton	21
†G. H. Roderick lbw b C. Overton	6	– (7) c Byrom b Davey	0
G. F. B. Scott c Davies b Lammonby	0	– (8) not out	5
D. A. Payne not out	0	– (9) c Hildreth b C. Overton	1
Lb 5, nb 2	7	Lb 5, nb 2	7
1/7 (2) 2/9 (1) 3/9 (3) 4/9 (4) 5/29 (6) 6/48 (7) 7/56 (5) 8/71 (9) 9/76 (10) 10/76 (8) (38.2 overs)	76	1/5 (1) 2/5 (2) 3/14 (4) 4/23 (5) 5/49 (3) 6/49 (7) 7/61 (6) 8/63 (9) 9/67 (10) 10/70 (11) (35.3 overs)	70

C. Overton 13.2–4–25–4; Davey 12–7–21–3; J. Overton 6–1–12–1; Brooks 5–2–9–1; Lammonby 2–0–4–1. *Second innings*—C. Overton 13–6–26–5; Davey 11–3–25–4; J. Overton 5–3–6–0; Brooks 6.3–2–8–1.

Umpires: P. K. Baldwin and I. D. Blackwell. Referee: R. M. Ellison.

At Worcester, September 6–9. SOMERSET beat WORCESTERSHIRE by 60 runs. *Somerset ensure top spot in the Central Group, and a place in the final.*

At Lord's, September 23–27. SOMERSET drew with ESSEX. *Essex win the Bob Willis Trophy by virtue of their first-innings lead* *(see page 406).*

SURREY

The best-laid schemes…

RICHARD SPILLER

Not for the first time, a landmark summer went awry for Surrey. In 1945, their centenary year, The Oval was turned into a prisoner of war camp. Now, the club's 175th anniversary season was ruined by the coronavirus, before Surrey narrowly missed out on the T20 Blast, losing to Nottinghamshire in the final.

The pandemic was just starting to take hold when a dinner to celebrate Surrey's birthday was staged on March 6. For many present, it was their only visit to the ground in 2020. Surrey did not furlough their players, who found new ways of filling their time. Rikki Clarke became an NHS volunteer responder, Amar Virdi delivered meals for a Sikh charity, and Sam Curran raised over £13,000 for health workers. Others rang elderly members: one said it "absolutely made my day" to receive a call from Tom Curran.

Chief executive Richard Gould was justifiably proud of a £6.3m pre-tax profit in 2019. But he spent much of his tenth year in charge staving off the inevitable consequences of a lack of crowds: for the first time since 1945 (excluding 1970 and the Rest of the World) there was no Oval Test. It led to a predicted loss approaching £4m. Despite this, members were offered a 25% subscription refund at the end of the season, though some felt it should have been more. Construction of the new One Oval Square development continued (it was due for completion early in 2021).

When the season eventually got going, Surrey hosted a pilot scheme for spectators, with more than 1,000 watching both days of the friendly against Middlesex in July, and another 2,500 at a Blast game in September – the summer's only competitive match with a crowd. In between, though, plans to do the same for the Bob Willis Trophy were scuppered by a change of heart by the government. The online team's slick coverage drew over 2m views.

On the playing side, director of cricket Alec Stewart implemented a major change before the players returned: Michael Di Venuto, their Australian head coach, was released early from the fifth and final year of his contract. Stewart praised his contribution to restoring Surrey as a power in the Championship. The contracts of overseas players Michael Neser, Shadab Khan and D'Arcy Short were also cancelled.

Vikram Solanki was a popular choice to succeed Di Venuto – and the first British-Asian to coach a county side – but he found himself up against it when injuries, international calls and the absence of South Africans Hashim Amla and Morne Morkel (both delayed abroad) led to a severe player shortage. It showed: in the Bob Willis Trophy, Surrey pushed their opening match, against Middlesex, into the final hour, but still lost by 190 runs. Another heavy loss followed to Essex, before a low point – 74 all out and an innings defeat – against Hampshire.

Will Jacks

By then Stewart had embraced the loan system, borrowing Laurie Evans from Sussex, a move which became permanent, and Worcestershire seamer Adam Finch, who collected four-wicket hauls against Essex and Kent. Surrey lost the second of those games by 17 runs – the first time they had lost four successive first-class matches since 1994. Ben Foakes's escape from inactivity in the England bubble was marked by a century against Kent, while the eventual arrival of Amla, and the return of Rory Burns after a disappointing international season, were key factors in a consolation victory over a youthful Sussex. Morkel's comeback, however, was limited to one match, before he trod on a ball and injured his ankle. Surrey initially shared bottom spot in the South Group with Sussex, who later lost points for ball-tampering.

The Vitality Blast had an equally uninspiring start – no-result, tie, defeat – before a spectacular run of seven victories powered them to the top of the group. They brushed off Kent in the quarter-final, and Gloucestershire in the semi, before coming a cropper in the final.

The T20 attack was dominated by the spinners, with 20-year-old left-armer Daniel Moriarty showing impressive control: after 17 wickets in his two BWT matches, where he formed a promising partnership with Virdi, he managed 17 more in the Blast. With the official T20 captain, Jade Dernbach, missing the whole tournament through injury, 42-year-old off-spinner Gareth Batty called the shots.

Lambeth-born Evans, who had last played for Surrey in 2010, showed the experience he had gained elsewhere with 363 rapid runs, yet was outshone by Will Jacks, whose 309 included three half-centuries. He also took 13 wickets with his off-spin, and was named the Blast's Most Valuable Player by the PCA.

Jamie Overton arrived from Somerset, also initially on loan: his bat thundered, but he struck just once (in the Blast) with the ball. Reece Topley and Liam Plunkett recovered from ailments to play major roles in the T20 run. But in the final they were without Ollie Pope, who injured his shoulder on England duty, and both Currans (international and IPL calls).

Although he had a year left on his contract, Scott Borthwick was allowed to return to Durham for 2021. His batting had been enigmatic and his leg-spin erratic, but his catching in the slips was sublime, and his sunny personality will be missed. Amla was expected to return as an overseas player, but Morkel's time in county cricket appears to be over. Now 36, he will be remembered at The Oval for his stellar contribution (59 wickets at 14) to the 2018 Championship title.

A difficult year ended on a sad note, with the deaths of two of Surrey's finest players, John Edrich and Robin Jackman, who were instrumental in winning the 1971 Championship.

SURREY RESULTS

Bob Willis Trophy matches – Played 5: Won 1, Lost 4.
Vitality Blast matches – Played 13: Won 10, Lost 1, Tied 1, No result 1.

Bob Willis Trophy, 5th in South Group;
Vitality Blast, finalists.

BOB WILLIS TROPHY AVERAGES

BATTING AND FIELDING

Cap		*Birthplace*	*M*	*I*	*NO*	*R*	*HS*	*100*	*Avge*	*Ct/St*
2016	B. T. Foakes	*Colchester*	2	4	1	227	118	1	75.66	4/1
	W. G. Jacks	*Chertsey‡*	5	10	2	248	84*	0	31.00	6
	J. L. Smith	*Epsom‡*	5	10	1	274	80	0	30.44	8
	L. J. Evans	*Lambeth‡*	3	6	0	172	65	0	28.66	1
2018	†S. G. Borthwick	*Sunderland*	5	10	0	192	92	0	19.20	5
2005	R. Clarke	*Orsett*	3	6	0	91	30	0	15.16	4
2018	†M. D. Stoneman	*Newcastle-u-Tyne*	4	8	0	106	45	0	13.25	1
	†R. S. Patel	*Sutton‡*	3	6	0	78	44	0	13.00	5
	J. P. A. Taylor	*Stoke-on-Trent*	3	5	1	34	22	0	8.50	1
	A. W. Finch	*Wordsley*	3	5	1	29	10	0	7.25	1
	†M. P. Dunn	*Egham‡*	3	6	1	28	12	0	5.60	2
	A. A. P. Atkinson	*Chelsea*	2	4	0	21	15	0	5.25	0
	G. S. Virdi	*Chiswick*	5	9	4	26	12	0	5.20	1
	†D. T. Moriarty	*Reigate‡*	2	3	0	1	1	0	0.33	0

Also batted: H. M. Amla†† (*Durban, SA*) (1 match) 26, 18 (1 ct); †R. J. Burns§ (*Epsom‡*) (cap 2014) (1 match) 103, 52 (2 ct); J. Clark (*Whitehaven*) (1 match) 1, 7; †S. M. Curran§ (*Northampton*) (cap 2018) (1 match) 21, 14; †M. Morkel†† (*Vereeniging, SA*) (cap 2018) (1 match) 33, 0; J. Overton (*Barnstaple*) (1 match) 55 (2 ct); J. J. Roy§ (*Durban*) (cap 2014) (1 match) 4, 14 (1 ct).

‡ *Born in Surrey.* § *ECB contract.* †† *Other non-England-qualified.*

BOWLING

	Style	*O*	*M*	*R*	*W*	*BB*	*5I*	*Avge*
R. Clarke	RFM	88	23	190	13	5-20	1	14.61
S. M. Curran	LFM	39.5	7	124	7	4-39	0	17.71
D. T. Moriarty	SLA	98.2	15	342	17	6-70	3	20.11
G. S. Virdi	OB	179	26	570	22	6-101	1	25.90
A. W. Finch	RFM	74.1	9	215	8	4-38	0	26.87
A. A. P. Atkinson	RFM	35.4	5	128	4	2-57	0	32.00
J. P. A. Taylor	RFM	46	6	171	4	2-31	0	42.75
M. P. Dunn	RFM	70.4	16	239	5	3-53	0	47.80

Also bowled: S. G. Borthwick (LB) 43–3–161–2; J. Clark (RM) 11–3–30–0; W. G. Jacks (OB) 6–0–17–0; M. Morkel (RF) 14–7–28–0; J. Overton (RFM) 21–3–70–0; R. S. Patel (RM) 14–1–72–0.

LEADING VITALITY BLAST AVERAGES (70 runs/10 overs)

Batting	*Runs*	*HS*	*Avge*	*SR*	*Ct/St*
J. Overton	103	40*	34.33	**194.33**	10
L. J. Evans	363	88*	45.37	**153.16**	2
W. G. Jacks	309	65	34.33	**149.27**	7
J. J. Roy	206	72	41.20	**131.21**	2
R. J. Burns	141	56*	23.50	**127.02**	8
H. M. Amla	271	75	38.71	**124.88**	1
B. T. Foakes	141	60*	23.50	**110.15**	5/4
J. L. Smith	89	38*	29.66	**97.80**	4

Bowling	*W*	*BB*	*Avge*	*ER*
G. J. Batty	10	3-18	19.60	**6.46**
W. G. Jacks	13	4-15	16.07	**6.46**
D. T. Moriarty	17	3-25	18.29	**6.91**
L. E. Plunkett	7	3-12	16.28	**7.12**
R. J. W. Topley	15	4-20	19.40	**7.27**
M. P. Dunn	4	2-24	25.00	**8.00**
A. A. P. Atkinson	7	2-18	28.57	**9.52**
J. Overton	1	1-29	173.00	**10.17**

FIRST-CLASS COUNTY RECORDS

Highest score for	357*	R. Abel v Somerset at The Oval	1899
Highest score against	366	N. H. Fairbrother (Lancashire) at The Oval	1990
Leading run-scorer	43,554	J. B. Hobbs (avge 49.72)	1905–34
Best bowling for	10-43	T. Rushby v Somerset at Taunton	1921
Best bowling against	10-28	W. P. Howell (Australians) at The Oval	1899
Leading wicket-taker	1,775	T. Richardson (avge 17.87)	1892–1904
Highest total for	811	v Somerset at The Oval	1899
Highest total against	863	by Lancashire at The Oval	1990
Lowest total for	14	v Essex at Chelmsford	1983
Lowest total against	16	by MCC at Lord's	1872

LIST A COUNTY RECORDS

Highest score for	268	A. D. Brown v Glamorgan at The Oval	2002
Highest score against	187*	A. D. Hales (Nottinghamshire) at Lord's	2017
Leading run-scorer	10,358	A. D. Brown (avge 32.16)	1990–2008
Best bowling for	7-30	M. P. Bicknell v Glamorgan at The Oval	1999
Best bowling against	7-15	A. L. Dixon (Kent) at The Oval	1967
Leading wicket-taker	409	M. P. Bicknell (avge 25.21)	1986–2005
Highest total for	496-4	v Gloucestershire at The Oval	2007
Highest total against	429	by Glamorgan at The Oval	2002
Lowest total for	64	v Worcestershire at Worcester	1978
Lowest total against	44	by Glamorgan at The Oval	1999

TWENTY20 COUNTY RECORDS

Highest score for	131*	A. J. Finch v Sussex at Hove	2018
Highest score against	129	C. S. Delport (Essex) at Chelmsford	2019
Leading run-scorer	**3,183**	**J. J. Roy (avge 30.90, SR 148.32)**	**2008–20**
Best bowling for	6-24	T. J. Murtagh v Middlesex at Lord's	2005
Best bowling against	5-16	S. T. Finn (Middlesex) at Lord's	2019
Leading wicket-taker	114	J. W. Dernbach (avge 26.76, ER 8.37)	2005–19
Highest total for	250-6	v Kent at Canterbury	2018
Highest total against	240-3	by Glamorgan at The Oval	2015
Lowest total for	88	v Kent at The Oval	2012
Lowest total against	44	by Glamorgan at The Oval	2019

ADDRESS

The Kia Oval, Kennington, London SE11 5SS; 0844 375 1845; enquiries@surreycricket.com; www.surreycricket.com. Twitter: @surreycricket.

OFFICIALS

Captain R. J. Burns
(Twenty20) J. W. Dernbach
Director of cricket A. J. Stewart
Head coach V. S. Solanki
Assistant coach R. L. Johnson
Academy director G. T. J. Townsend

President K. D. Schofield
Chairman R. W. Thompson
Chief executive R. A. Gould
Head groundsman L. E. Fortis
Scorer 2020 P. J. Makepeace

SURREY v MIDDLESEX

At The Oval, August 1–4. Middlesex won by 190 runs. Middlesex 22pts, Surrey 3pts. Toss: Middlesex. First-class debuts: D. T. Moriarty; T. N. Walallawita. County debut: J. P. A. Taylor.

Middlesex held the upper hand throughout, although it took them until the final hour to seal victory, as they took advantage of a second Surrey meltdown. Gubbins's impressive 192, after only two Championship centuries in three seasons, led the way as Middlesex made the most of a benign pitch and shoddy fielding. He shared three-figure stands with Holden and Simpson, but he missed a double-century in a vain hunt for a fourth batting point. Surrey's reply started well. Borthwick fell just short of a third successive century at The Oval, but put on 105 with the feisty Smith. From 254 for three, seven wickets tumbled for 28, with Murtagh taking four for four in six overs. Gubbins and the enterprising Andersson helped stretch the lead to 313 an hour into the final day; both were dismissed by 20-year-old slow left-armer Dan Moriarty, who displayed good control on his debut. Surrey were soon 20 for three, but Patel and Smith dug in, then Clarke and Clark held the fort for 23 overs. But Robson claimed two wickets in two balls with his occasional leg-breaks – his fifth and sixth first-class wickets, in his 158th game – and Cummins blew away the tail.

Close of play: first day, Middlesex 264-4 (Gubbins 150, Simpson 19); second day, Surrey 189-3 (Borthwick 73, Smith 15); third day, Middlesex 184-3 (Gubbins 49, Andersson 35).

Middlesex

First innings		Second innings	
S. D. Robson c Smith b Clarke	7	– (2) c Smith b Moriarty	31
M. D. E. Holden c Smith b Virdi	48	– (1) c Clarke b Moriarty	43
N. R. T. Gubbins c Jacks b Clarke	192	– b Moriarty	60
*S. S. Eskinazi c Dunn b Moriarty	18	– c Jacks b Moriarty	18
M. K. Andersson lbw b Clarke	18	– c Patel b Moriarty	51
†J. A. Simpson lbw b Borthwick	53	– c Dunn b Virdi	18
J. A. R. Harris not out	2	– not out	17
N. A. Sowter not out	0	– not out	2
B 8, lb 1	9	B 4, lb 2, nb 2	8
1/7 (1) 2/118 (2) 3/155 (4) 4/211 (5) 5/342 (3) 6/346 (6) (6 wkts dec, 111.3 overs) 110 overs: 344-5	347	1/70 (1) 2/81 (2) 3/113 (4) 4/202 (3) 5/213 (5) 6/245 (6) (6 wkts dec, 70.2 overs)	248

T. N. Walallawita, M. L. Cummins and T. J. Murtagh did not bat.

Dunn 15–3–40–0; Clarke 19–4–48–3; Clark 11–3–30–0; Taylor 14–1–49–0; Virdi 18–2–60–1; Moriarty 18.3–4–54–1; Patel 3–1–14–0; Borthwick 13–0–43–1. *Second innings*—Dunn 7–2–24–0; Clarke 9–0–24–0; Taylor 5–1–12–0; Patel 1–0–4–0; Virdi 23–2–102–1; Moriarty 23.2–3–64–5; Borthwick 2–0–12–0.

Surrey

First innings		Second innings	
M. D. Stoneman c Andersson b Walallawita	45	– lbw b Murtagh	4
R. S. Patel c Simpson b Murtagh	4	– c Sowter b Harris	44
S. G. Borthwick c Robson b Andersson	92	– c Simpson b Walallawita	1
W. G. Jacks lbw b Harris	36	– b Murtagh	0
†J. L. Smith c Sowter b Cummins	80	– c Simpson b Cummins	40
*R. Clarke c Simpson b Sowter	1	– st Simpson b Sowter	22
J. Clark c Simpson b Murtagh	1	– c and b Robson	7
D. T. Moriarty lbw b Murtagh	0	– lbw b Robson	0
J. P. A. Taylor not out	5	– (10) b Cummins	4
M. P. Dunn b Murtagh	1	– (9) c Holden b Cummins	0
G. S. Virdi lbw b Murtagh	0	– not out	0
B 6, lb 3, nb 8	17	B 1	1
1/9 (2) 2/80 (1) 3/149 (4) 4/254 (3) 5/261 (6) 6/263 (7) 7/269 (8) 8/281 (5) 9/282 (10) 10/282 (11) (101 overs)	282	1/14 (1) 2/19 (3) 3/20 (4) 4/84 (2) 5/94 (5) 6/119 (7) 7/119 (8) 8/119 (9) 9/123 (10) 10/123 (6) (62.5 overs)	123

Murtagh 25–13–47–5; Cummins 21–5–58–1; Harris 19–5–56–1; Walallawita 18–6–76–1; Sowter 15–3–30–1; Andersson 3–1–6–1. *Second innings*—Murtagh 13–4–27–2; Cummins 14–6–30–3; Walallawita 11–2–33–1; Harris 7–2–20–1; Sowter 9.5–7–4–1; Andersson 5–3–8–0; Robson 3–3–0–2.

Umpires: R. J. Bailey and N. J. Llong. Referee: P. M. Such.

At Chelmsford, August 8–11. SURREY lost to ESSEX by 169 runs.

At Arundel, August 15–18. SURREY lost to HAMPSHIRE by an innings and 52 runs.

SURREY v KENT

At The Oval, August 22–25. Kent won by 17 runs. Kent 21pts (after 1pt penalty), Surrey 5pts. Toss: Surrey. First-class debut: N. N. Gilchrist.

Kent's last-gasp victory kept alive their hopes of a place in the Lord's final. They had the better of the first two days once Stewart and Podmore counter-attacked enterprisingly for the seventh wicket, before Milnes and Nathan Gilchrist, a Zimbabwe-born debutant seamer, helped the last four double the score. Adam Finch, on loan from Worcestershire, deserved his four wickets. On a pitch that played occasional tricks, Surrey made an indifferent start, and were indebted to Foakes, who timed the ball well for a man confined to the nets for the previous couple of months in the England bubble. The match lurched Surrey's way on the third afternoon when Clarke – half-fit, and bowling within himself – swung the ball alarmingly and claimed three wickets in his first three overs. Sam Curran, another bubble escapee, offered excellent support, and Surrey needed 192 from 62 overs. They dipped to 20 for four, three to Stevens, who returned later to account for the dangerous Evans. Again it was left to Foakes to organise the tail but, when he fell to a smart leg-side catch from his opposite number Robinson, the game was up.

Close of play: first day, Kent 295-8 (Milnes 22, Gilchrist 1); second day, Surrey 239-7 (Foakes 88, Finch 9); third day, Kent 118-9 (Gilchrist 4, Hamidullah Qadri 4).

Kent

*D. J. Bell-Drummond lbw b Finch	45	– lbw b Curran	18
J. M. Cox lbw b Dunn	8	– b Clarke	32
J. A. Leaning c Virdi b Curran	21	– lbw b Clarke	14
†O. G. Robinson lbw b Curran	17	– b Clarke	0
M. K. O'Riordan c Foakes b Curran	30	– c Clarke b Curran	9
D. I. Stevens c Foakes b Clarke	24	– c Borthwick b Dunn	0
G. Stewart b Virdi	58	– lbw b Clarke	22
H. W. Podmore c Jacks b Finch	47	– c Jacks b Clarke	2
M. E. Milnes c Smith b Finch	43	– lbw b Curran	7
N. N. Gilchrist c Foakes b Finch	25	– c Clarke b Curran	13
Hamidullah Qadri not out	2	– not out	4
B 1, lb 14, w 1, nb 6	22	Lb 2, nb 4	6
1/17 (2) 2/75 (3) 3/97 (1) (103.1 overs)	342	1/18 (1) 2/63 (3) (46.5 overs)	127
4/99 (4) 5/154 (6) 6/170 (5)		3/63 (4) 4/68 (2)	
7/243 (8) 8/292 (7) 9/333 (10) 10/342 (9)		5/69 (6) 6/100 (7) 7/102 (5)	
		8/102 (8) 9/114 (9) 10/127 (10)	

Dunn 20–6–68–1; Curran 25–2–85–3; Clarke 18–5–55–1; Finch 23.1–4–69–4; Virdi 11–2–37–1; Borthwick 6–1–13–0. *Second innings*—Curran 14.5–5–39–4; Dunn 12–1–54–1; Borthwick 1–0–1–0; Virdi 1–1–0–0; Finch 4–1–11–0; Clarke 14–7–20–5.

Surrey

*M. D. Stoneman lbw b Podmore	2 – c Cox b Podmore	10
S. G. Borthwick c Cox b Stevens	26 – c Bell-Drummond b Stevens	2
J. L. Smith b Milnes	28 – c Leaning b Stevens	0
W. G. Jacks c Leaning b Stevens	5 – c Robinson b Stevens	6
†B. T. Foakes c Cox b Stewart	118 – c Robinson b Podmore	57
L. J. Evans b Milnes	18 – c and b Stevens	42
S. M. Curran c Robinson b Podmore	21 – b Milnes	14
R. Clarke c Leaning b Stevens	30 – b Milnes	9
A. W. Finch lbw b Podmore	10 – lbw b Milnes	6
M. P. Dunn lbw b Milnes	8 – b Milnes	12
G. S. Virdi not out	0 – not out	3
B 1, lb 1, nb 10	12 B 2, w 1, nb 10	13

1/2 (1) 2/58 (3) 3/64 (2) (91.4 overs) 278
4/83 (4) 5/134 (6) 6/181 (7)
7/220 (8) 8/245 (9) 9/278 (10) 10/278 (5)

1/6 (2) 2/6 (3) (48.1 overs) 174
3/20 (1) 4/20 (4)
5/77 (6) 6/94 (7) 7/116 (8)
8/136 (9) 9/164 (5) 10/174 (10)

Podmore 22–7–61–3; Stevens 25–10–45–3; Milnes 16–2–55–3; Stewart 15.4–3–51–1; Gilchrist 8–1–39–0; Hamidullah Qadri 2–0–8–0; O'Riordan 3–0–17–0. *Second innings*—Podmore 14–1–41–2; Stevens 13–0–41–4; Milnes 15.1–2–57–4; Stewart 5–2–20–0; Gilchrist 1–0–13–0.

Umpires: N. L. Bainton and N. J. Llong. Referee: G. R. Cowdrey.

SURREY v SUSSEX

At The Oval, September 6–9. Surrey won by six wickets. Surrey 22pts, Sussex 6pts. Toss: Sussex. First-class debut: J. M. Coles.

Led by Moriarty's 11 wickets, Surrey restored some honour after four defeats, admittedly against a Sussex side containing three teenagers: all-rounder Jamie Coles, Irish off-spinner Jack Carson and seamer Henry Crocombe. At 16 years 157 days, Coles was their second-youngest player after Hamilton Hoare (two days younger in 1853). Haines's patient century had dominated the first day. Virdi and Moriarty kept the brakes on, despite a short boundary on one side, before Wiese cut loose

YOUNGEST TO TAKE TEN WICKETS IN A MATCH FOR SURREY

Yrs	*Days*			
17	269	J. N. Crawford (10-78)	v Gloucestershire at Cheltenham	1904
18	236	Waqar Younis (11-128)	v Warwickshire at The Oval	1990
19	255	P. I. Pocock (10-84)	v Somerset at Bath	1966
19	345	S. M. Curran (10-101)	v Yorkshire at The Oval	2018
19	347	G. A. Lohmann (12-29)	v Hampshire at The Oval	1885
20	135	N. H. Peters (10-67)	v Warwickshire at The Oval	1988
20	197	T. K. Curran (10-176)	v Northamptonshire at The Oval	2015
20	223	Saqlain Mushtaq (10-128)	v Durham at The Oval	1997
20	271	N. A. Knox (11-147)	v Lancashire at Liverpool	1905
20	**281**	**D. T. Moriarty (11-224)**	**v Sussex at The Oval**	**2020**
20	361	G. S. Virdi (14-139)	v Nottinghamshire at Nottingham	2019

next day, striking three sixes in his 47-ball 57. Burns rediscovered his touch, mislaid in the Pakistan Tests, before becoming one of four wickets in 19 balls, but a mature innings from Jacks and an enterprising one from Overton – in his first first-class match for Surrey – closed the gap, even as Carson picked up a maiden five-for. With a reused pitch growing capricious, Moriarty gained sharp turn, and became the first English bowler to take three successive five-wicket hauls in his first two inter-county first-class matches. Virdi supported him well, taking his own match haul to seven for 120, and it was left to Meaker, on his return to The Oval, to give Sussex hope from 62 for eight; his 42 meant Surrey needed 156. Coles snaffled Smith and Burns in the same over, but Foakes and Jacks ensured there were no more alarms. Surrey had not won after conceding as many as 415 in the opening innings of a match since 1947.

Close of play: first day, Sussex 239-3 (Haines 105, Brown 9); second day, Surrey 171-4 (Amla 6, Foakes 0); third day, Sussex 109-9 (Meaker 32, Crocombe 0).

Sussex

A. D. Thomason lbw b Moriarty	49	– st Foakes b Moriarty	9
T. J. Haines lbw b Virdi	117	– c Amla b Moriarty	8
H. Z. Finch lbw b Virdi	1	– c Burns b Moriarty	13
D. M. W. Rawlins c Jacks b Virdi	65	– c Taylor b Virdi	9
*†B. C. Brown c Foakes b Taylor	51	– lbw b Virdi	7
J. M. Coles lbw b Taylor	11	– lbw b Virdi	10
D. Wiese c Finch b Moriarty	57	– c Overton b Moriarty	4
G. H. S. Garton lbw b Moriarty	12	– lbw b Moriarty	1
S. C. Meaker b Moriarty	12	– c Overton b Virdi	42
J. J. Carson c Jacks b Moriarty	21	– c Burns b Moriarty	6
H. T. Crocombe not out	5	– not out	9
Lb 5, w 1, nb 8	14	B 10	10

1/102 (1) 2/109 (3) 3/225 (4)	(118.3 overs) 415	1/9 (1) 2/30 (2)	(38.2 overs) 128
4/262 (2) 5/305 (6) 6/310 (5)		3/31 (3) 4/46 (5)	
7/333 (8) 8/357 (9) 9/410 (7)		5/47 (4) 6/58 (6) 7/59 (8)	
10/415 (10)	110 overs: 355-7	8/62 (7) 9/102 (10) 10/128 (9)	

Overton 18–2–62–0; Finch 18–0–53–0; Taylor 9–2–37–2; Virdi 32–9–80–3; Moriarty 37.3–3–154–5; Borthwick 4–0–24–0. *Second innings*—Overton 3–1–8–0; Moriarty 19–5–70–6; Virdi 16.2–2–40–4.

Surrey

*R. J. Burns lbw b Carson	103	– st Brown b Coles	52
S. G. Borthwick lbw b Carson	50	– c Garton b Carson	11
H. M. Amla lbw b Rawlins	26	– c Finch b Rawlins	18
J. L. Smith b Crocombe	0	– b Coles	33
A. W. Finch lbw b Crocombe	0		
†B. T. Foakes b Coles	39	– (5) not out	13
W. G. Jacks not out	84	– (6) not out	22
J. Overton c Haines b Wiese	55		
J. P. A. Taylor c Wiese b Carson	3		
D. T. Moriarty b Carson	1		
G. S. Virdi c Finch b Carson	0		
B 9, lb 14, w 2, nb 2	27	B 3, lb 5	8

1/164 (2) 2/169 (1) 3/170 (4)	(113.5 overs) 388	1/28 (2)	(4 wkts, 44.5 overs) 157
4/170 (5) 5/213 (3) 6/256 (6)		2/55 (3) 3/119 (4)	
7/368 (8) 8/379 (9) 9/388 (10)		4/120 (1)	
10/388 (11)	110 overs: 383-8		

Garton 12–0–68–0; Crocombe 19–7–36–2; Carson 34.5–8–93–5; Wiese 13–3–32–1; Rawlins 20–1–78–1; Meaker 13–3–55–0; Coles 2–0–3–1. *Second innings*—Crocombe 4–0–11–0; Carson 12–2–46–1; Rawlins 17.5–3–60–1; Coles 11–0–32–2.

Umpires: N. L. Bainton and B. J. Debenham. Referee: S. J. Davis.

SUSSEX

Teenage ticks

BRUCE TALBOT

Early in March 2020, as he made his way from Adelaide to Cape Town for Sussex's pre-season tour, head coach Jason Gillespie was entitled to feel bullish about the summer ahead. He had acquired the experience of Travis Head, Ravi Bopara, Stuart Meaker and Mitch Claydon and, having agreed a contract extension up to 2022, he had the time to build his legacy.

Seven bewildering months later, Gillespie was heading home for good, after accepting the opportunity to coach South Australia. Sussex delayed naming his replacement while they assessed the financial impact of Covid-19, but in November they announced that spin-bowling coach Ian Salisbury and fast-bowling coach James Kirtley, both former club favourites, would share duties – Salisbury in charge of the first-class and one-day teams, Kirtley of the T20 side.

The club were disappointed to see Gillespie go, though they understood his reasons. The verdict on his three years depended on whose view was canvassed. Some of the squad, notably Ollie Robinson and Jofra Archer, improved during his tenure, and his openness made him a popular figure with players and supporters. Sussex reached the knockouts of the Blast three times, and the final once. But, as he acknowledged, they stood still in four-day cricket, winning only a third of their 33 matches under his watch.

Unsurprisingly, given the loss of £3m in revenue because of the pandemic, his wasn't the only high-profile departure. Laurie Evans and Danny Briggs, frustrated at a lack of red-ball cricket, left for Surrey and Warwickshire, while Luke Wells joined Lancashire. Harry Finch and Will Sheffield were released. Gillespie and captain Ben Brown gave youth its head in the Bob Willis Trophy, reasoning there was little chance of winning a group containing the county champions, Essex, and three more Division One sides. It wasn't a universally popular strategy, but Gillespie happily tackled his critics on social media.

Although they finished bottom, and picked up fewer points than any county bar Surrey, Sussex were competitive in each game – except for a chastening defeat at Canterbury, where they conceded 530 for one, the fourth-highest single-wicket score in history. By their last match, a defeat by Surrey, Gillespie and Brown nevertheless felt their policy vindicated. Off-spinner Jack Carson was leading wicket-taker with 15, and seamer Henry Crocombe, who also played four games, showed potential; both signed two-year contracts. Tom Clark hit a maiden half-century, while a fourth teenager, James Coles, a batting all-rounder from Oxfordshire, became Sussex's youngest first-class cricketer for 167 years; he was aged 16 years and 157 days, and shaped up well. Another Academy product, Tom Haines, hit his second first-class hundred in the same game, the club's only century of the summer. Jamie Atkins, an 18-year-old

George Garton

fast bowler clocked at 88mph in a Young Lions game, also signed a two-year deal, while left-arm seamer Sean Hunt, 19, moved south from Surrey.

Sussex were unable to call on Archer or Rashid Khan in the Blast, yet still fielded a useful team, and finished runners-up in their group – despite winning only twice at home. They struggled again at Hove in the quarter-final, where they were flummoxed by Lancashire. Luke Wright, the white-ball captain, made 411 runs, but Sussex relied too much on him. Bopara, meanwhile, failed to match his billing as a middle-order finisher, and made 122 in 11 innings. Of the other arrivals, Meaker pulled up no trees in three BWT games, while Claydon, who chipped in with a few wickets, was lucky not to have been sacked. Against Middlesex, he was found to have brought the game into disrepute by trying to alter the condition of the ball with hand sanitiser, and was given a nine-match ban. Sussex were docked 24 points, but successfully challenged an extra 12-point penalty for 2021 after the ECB admitted a "procedural irregularity" relating to a potential conflict of interest for a member of the disciplinary panel; a suspended fine of £10,000 was also removed.

Few have eclipsed Ollie Robinson in recent years, but the Player of the Season was left-arm seamer George Garton. In 2017-18, he helped England prepare for the Ashes, but two side strains set him back. Now, by cutting his run-up and sacrificing speed for accuracy, he reaped the rewards. He was leading wicket-taker in the Blast, with 14, and balanced the red-ball team with runs in the lower middle order; against Essex, he had match figures of nine for 76. Haines and Delray Rawlins showed enough promise to be handed new contracts. Head and Stiaan van Zyl were expected to be the overseas players for 2021.

Like most counties, Sussex furloughed staff and cut costs to mitigate the financial effects of Covid-19. Members donated £140,000, while live streams of matches attracted more than 2m views. And there was much to admire in the club's response in their community. They raised 26% of the £35,217 for the nationwide Together Through This Test auction, and provided 1,200 meals to local families, working with Brighton & Hove Food Partnership. Webinars during lockdown attracted around 100 local clubs each week, and Sussex's community department helped more than 50 secure £350,000 in government funding to ensure grounds were safe when the recreational game resumed.

But perhaps the biggest symbol of Sussex's determination to look to the future came when demolition of the Sussex Cricketer pub started in the winter; it makes way for 37 flats, a bar and a restaurant, as well as office space and parking. Phase one should be complete in 2022, when the County Ground celebrates its 150th anniversary. "We have a clear plan to cope with whatever is thrown at us over the next 12 months and beyond," said chief executive Rob Andrew.

SUSSEX RESULTS

Bob Willis Trophy matches – Played 5: Won 1, Lost 4.
Vitality Blast matches – Played 11: Won 6, Lost 4, No result 1.

Bob Willis Trophy, 6th in South Group;
Vitality Blast, quarter-finalists.

BOB WILLIS TROPHY AVERAGES

BATTING AND FIELDING

Cap		*Birthplace*	*M*	*I*	*NO*	*R*	*HS*	*100*	*Avge*	*Ct/St*
	P. D. Salt	*Bodelwyddan*	4	8	0	290	80	0	36.25	6
	†T. J. Haines	*Crawley‡*	5	10	1	249	117	1	27.66	1
2014	B. C. Brown	*Crawley‡*	5	10	0	270	98	0	27.00	10/1
	H. Z. Finch	*Hastings‡*	5	10	0	259	69	0	25.90	6
	†D. M. W. Rawlins	*Bermuda*	5	10	0	252	65	0	25.20	0
	S. C. Meaker	*Pietermaritzburg, SA*	3	6	1	106	42	0	21.20	0
	A. D. Thomason	*Birmingham*	3	6	0	111	49	0	18.50	1
	†G. H. S. Garton	*Brighton‡*	4	8	1	109	54*	0	15.57	4
	†M. E. Claydon	*Fairfield, Australia*	4	8	3	77	24	0	15.40	0
2019	O. E. Robinson	*Margate*	2	4	0	56	23	0	14.00	0
	†T. G. R. Clark	*Haywards Heath‡*	4	8	0	110	65	0	13.75	2
	H. T. Crocombe	*Eastbourne‡*	4	8	4	45	15	0	11.25	1
	J. J. Carson	*Craigavon, Ireland*	4	8	0	57	21	0	7.12	1

Also batted: J. M. Coles (*Aylesbury*) (1 match) 11, 10; †W. A. Sheffield (*Haywards Heath‡*) (1 match) 6, 1; D. Wiese†† (*Roodepoort, SA*) (cap 2016) (1 match) 57, 4 (1 ct).

‡ *Born in Sussex.* †† *Other non-England-qualified.*

BOWLING

	Style	*O*	*M*	*R*	*W*	*BB*	*5I*	*Avge*
J. M. Coles	SLA	13	0	35	3	2-32	0	11.66
O. E. Robinson	RFM/OB	73.1	22	175	14	5-29	1	12.50
J. J. Carson	OB	108.1	17	340	15	5-93	1	22.66
G. H. S. Garton	LFM	70.3	13	282	12	5-26	1	23.50
M. E. Claydon	RFM	102	25	294	11	3-23	0	26.72
H. T. Crocombe	RFM	71	13	245	3	2-36	0	81.66
D. M. W. Rawlins	SLA	69.5	8	261	3	1-14	0	87.00

Also bowled: T. J. Haines (RM) 25–3–72–2; S. C. Meaker (RFM) 46.5–5–225–2; W. A. Sheffield (LFM) 15–0–54–1; D. Wiese (RFM) 13–3–32–1.

LEADING VITALITY BLAST AVERAGES (70 runs/10 overs)

Batting	*Runs*	*HS*	*Avge*	*SR*	*Ct*
P. D. Salt	211	56	26.37	**167.46**	2
D. Wiese	281	79*	40.14	**145.59**	4
L. J. Wright	411	83	37.36	**137.00**	2
D. M. W. Rawlins	208	62*	20.80	**132.48**	3
A. D. Thomason	73	47	36.50	**125.86**	0
G. H. S. Garton	101	34*	25.25	**116.09**	5
C. S. MacLeod	102	40	14.57	**95.32**	6
R. S. Bopara	122	24	12.20	**93.84**	2

Bowling	*W*	*BB*	*Avge*	*ER*
D. R. Briggs	12	3-17	20.75	**6.55**
D. M. W. Rawlins	8	3-21	13.25	**7.06**
G. H. S. Garton	14	4-21	16.50	**7.70**
T. S. Mills	11	2-23	22.54	**8.00**
R. S. Bopara	0	0-10	–	**8.36**
W. A. T. Beer	4	3-34	33.00	**8.80**
O. E. Robinson	9	2-25	33.44	**9.12**
D. Wiese	1	1-7	113.00	**10.11**

FIRST-CLASS COUNTY RECORDS

Highest score for	344*	M. W. Goodwin v Somerset at Taunton	2009
Highest score against	322	E. Paynter (Lancashire) at Hove	1937
Leading run-scorer	34,150	J. G. Langridge (avge 37.69)	1928–55
Best bowling for	10-48	C. H. G. Bland v Kent at Tonbridge	1899
Best bowling against	9-11	A. P. Freeman (Kent) at Hove	1922
Leading wicket-taker	2,211	M. W. Tate (avge 17.41)	1912–37
Highest total for	742-5 dec	v Somerset at Taunton	2009
Highest total against	726	by Nottinghamshire at Nottingham	1895
Lowest total for	19	v Surrey at Godalming	1830
	19	v Nottinghamshire at Hove	1873
Lowest total against	18	by Kent at Gravesend	1867

LIST A COUNTY RECORDS

Highest score for	171	D. Wiese v Hampshire at Southampton	2019
Highest score against	198*	G. A. Gooch (Essex) at Hove	1982
Leading run-scorer	7,969	A. P. Wells (avge 31.62)	1981–96
Best bowling for	7-41	A. N. Jones v Nottinghamshire at Nottingham	1986
Best bowling against	8-21	M. A. Holding (Derbyshire) at Hove	1988
Leading wicket-taker	370	R. J. Kirtley (avge 22.35)	1995–2010
Highest total for	399-4	v Worcestershire at Horsham	2011
Highest total against	377-9	by Somerset at Hove	2003
Lowest total for	49	v Derbyshire at Chesterfield	1969
Lowest total against	36	by Leicestershire at Leicester	1973

TWENTY20 COUNTY RECORDS

Highest score for	153*	L. J. Wright v Essex at Chelmsford	2014
Highest score against	152*	G. R. Napier (Essex) at Chelmsford	2008
Leading run-scorer	**4,517**	**L. J. Wright (avge 32.97, SR 149.02)**	**2004–20**
Best bowling for	5-11	Mushtaq Ahmed v Essex at Hove	2005
Best bowling against	5-14	A. D. Mascarenhas (Hampshire) at Hove	2004
	5-14	K. J. Abbott (Middlesex) at Hove	2015
Leading wicket-taker	**97**	**W. A. T. Beer (avge 26.67, ER 7.45)**	**2008–20**
Highest total for	242-5	v Gloucestershire at Bristol	2016
Highest total against	242-3	by Essex at Chelmsford	2008
Lowest total for	67	v Hampshire at Hove	2004
Lowest total against	85	by Hampshire at Southampton	2008

ADDRESS

The 1st Central County Ground, Eaton Road, Hove BN3 3AN; 0844 264 0202; info@sussexcricket.co.uk; www.sussexcricket.co.uk. Twitter: @SussexCCC.

OFFICIALS

Captain B. C. Brown
(Twenty20) L. J. Wright
Director of cricket K. Greenfield
Head coach 2020 J. N. Gillespie
2021 R. J. Kirtley/I. D. K. Salisbury
Academy director R. G. Halsall

President Sir Rod Aldridge
Chairman R. C. Warren
CEO/chair cricket committee C. R. Andrew
Head groundsman B. J. Gibson
Scorer G. J. Irwin

SUSSEX v HAMPSHIRE

At Hove, August 1–3. Sussex won by 94 runs. Sussex 19pts, Hampshire 3pts. Toss: Sussex. First-class debuts: J. J. Carson, H. T. Crocombe; A. S. Dale. County debut: M. E. Claydon.

On a pitch that behaved better than the scores suggest, a Sussex team containing nine Academy graduates possessed the two key players in Salt (home-grown) and Robinson (a Kent import). Salt hit twin half-centuries, demonstrating defensive discipline and – when the chance arose – customary aggression. Robinson, raring to go after a month in England's Test bubble, exposed frail technique, especially in Hampshire's second innings: he took the first four wickets, including three in 15 balls, and ended with five for 29. For Hampshire, set 245, no one made more than 30, and first-team manager Adrian Birrell seemed charitable when describing several dismissals as soft. Sussex's Jack Carson, a debutant off-spinner from Armagh, exploited the rough created by the left-armers, and in both innings took a wicket with his second ball; he also visited the hospitality box (doubling as the umpires' room) for a ticking-off after showing dissent when given out in the second innings. The other debutants were seamers: Ajeet Dale, from Slough, took three wickets; Henry Crocombe, from Eastbourne, did not break through.

Close of play: first day, Hampshire 77-4 (Northeast 14); second day, Sussex 155-6 (Rawlins 11, Garton 1).

Sussex

First innings		Second innings	
P. D. Salt c and b Fuller	68	– c Fuller b Organ	80
T. J. Haines lbw b Barker	14	– lbw b Holland	20
H. Z. Finch lbw b Holland	8	– lbw b Holland	10
T. G. R. Clark c Barker b Dale	2	– c McManus b Barker	4
*†B. C. Brown c McManus b Dale	0	– c Came b Organ	25
D. M. W. Rawlins lbw b Holland	0	– (7) c McManus b Barker	13
G. H. S. Garton not out	54	– (8) lbw b Crane	13
O. E. Robinson b Dale	11	– (9) c Holland b Organ	23
J. J. Carson lbw b Crane	5	– (6) c McManus b Crane	0
H. T. Crocombe st McManus b Crane	2	– not out	11
M. E. Claydon b Crane	3	– b Crane	16
B 2, lb 6, w 1	9	B 2, lb 2, w 2	6
1/33 (2) 2/56 (3) 3/64 (4) 4/64 (5) 5/73 (6) 6/108 (1) 7/125 (8) 8/140 (9) 9/156 (10) 10/176 (11) (61.1 overs)	176	1/60 (2) 2/90 (3) 3/99 (4) 4/142 (5) 5/143 (6) 6/143 (1) 7/157 (7) 8/186 (9) 9/199 (8) 10/221 (11) (71 overs)	221

Barker 20–5–45–1; Fuller 11–2–53–1; Holland 13–3–27–2; Dale 10–3–20–3; Crane 7.1–2–23–3. *Second innings*—Barker 18–4–59–2; Fuller 12–1–29–0; Dale 4–1–15–0; Holland 16–6–27–2; Organ 11–2–41–3; Crane 10–0–46–3.

Hampshire

First innings		Second innings	
F. S. Organ b Claydon	14	– c Garton b Robinson	9
J. J. Weatherley c Brown b Carson	19	– c Garton b Robinson	2
T. P. Alsop b Robinson	21	– b Carson	27
*S. A. Northeast c Salt b Claydon	21	– b Robinson	2
M. S. Crane c Brown b Robinson	0	– (10) c Brown b Carson	0
H. R. C. Came c Finch b Garton	25	– (5) c Salt b Robinson	6
I. G. Holland b Garton	13	– (6) b Carson	13
†L. D. McManus lbw b Robinson	10	– (7) c Carson b Garton	28
J. K. Fuller c Garton b Claydon	14	– (8) c Crocombe b Rawlins	30
K. H. D. Barker c Salt b Carson	4	– (9) not out	25
A. S. Dale not out	1	– c Brown b Robinson	0
Lb 3, nb 8	11	B 5, lb 1, nb 2	8
1/25 (1) 2/61 (2) 3/73 (3) 4/77 (5) 5/98 (4) 6/119 (6) 7/134 (8) 8/136 (7) 9/149 (9) 10/153 (10) (62.2 overs)	153	1/11 (2) 2/16 (1) 3/20 (4) 4/38 (5) 5/56 (6) 6/71 (3) 7/113 (7) 8/125 (8) 9/137 (10) 10/150 (11) (43.1 overs)	150

Robinson 21–9–36–3; Claydon 14–3–31–3; Crocombe 9–1–31–0; Garton 11–3–37–2; Carson 7.2–2–15–2. *Second innings*—Robinson 13.1–3–29–5; Claydon 8–2–31–0; Crocombe 4–1–11–0; Carson 11–2–37–3; Garton 5–0–22–1; Rawlins 2–0–14–1.

Umpires: I. J. Gould and B. V. Taylor. Referee: G. R. Cowdrey.

At Canterbury, August 8–10. SUSSEX lost to KENT by an innings and 25 runs. *Sussex take only one Kent wicket.*

SUSSEX v ESSEX

At Hove, August 15–18. Essex won by three wickets. Essex 19pts, Sussex 3pts. Toss: Essex.

A young Sussex side gave high-flying Essex a fright, before Walter calmly sealed their third successive win, with six overs of a much-interrupted match to spare. Bowlers on both teams enjoyed uneven bounce and, while it was no surprise Essex's old firm of Harmer and Porter each took eight wickets, there was encouragement for Sussex, too: left-arm seamer Garton sacrificed raw pace for swing and accuracy, and claimed career-best match figures of nine for 76, including Cook twice. Sussex, asked to bat in the best conditions of the game, should have gone well beyond 200, though Garton's maiden five-for ensured a handy lead of 54. They had stretched it to 111 before losing their second wicket to the last ball of the third day. That lifted Essex spirits, and a lack of experience soon became clear against the class of Harmer. Sussex plugged away, but Lawrence and Walter made batting look relatively straightforward.

Close of play: first day, Sussex 93-2 (Finch 20, Clark 0); second day, Sussex 155-6 (Thomason 14, Garton 8); third day, Sussex 57-2 (Salt 18).

Sussex

First innings		Second innings	
P. D. Salt c Harmer b Porter	57	– c Wheater b Porter	23
T. J. Haines c Harmer b Porter	14	– c Harmer b Porter	6
H. Z. Finch c Cook b Porter	21	– c Wheater b Beard	32
T. G. R. Clark c sub (F. I. N. Khushi) b Beard	21	– lbw b Harmer	10
*†B. C. Brown c Walter b Harmer	11	– st Wheater b Harmer	5
A. D. Thomason c Cook b Harmer	30	– c Walter b Quinn	13
D. M. W. Rawlins c Cook b Harmer	7	– lbw b Harmer	40
G. H. S. Garton c Wheater b Porter	18	– lbw b Harmer	1
S. C. Meaker c Harmer b Porter	10	– b Harmer	6
H. T. Crocombe not out	0	– b Porter	1
M. E. Claydon c Cook b Beard	1	– not out	2
B 1, lb 1, nb 2	4	Lb 2	2
1/38 (2) 2/81 (1) 3/98 (3) 4/113 (5) 5/131 (4) 6/142 (7) 7/167 (8) 8/183 (9) 9/193 (6) 10/194 (11) (77.1 overs)	194	1/7 (2) 2/57 (3) 3/62 (1) 4/72 (4) 5/79 (5) 6/119 (6) 7/120 (8) 8/128 (9) 9/137 (7) 10/141 (10) (56.5 overs)	141

Porter 24–7–60–5; Quinn 12–2–39–0; Beard 14.1–3–45–2; Harmer 27–11–48–3. *Second innings*—Porter 14.5–6–28–3; Quinn 11–2–22–1; Beard 12–2–35–1; Harmer 19–6–54–5.

Essex

N. L. J. Browne b Claydon	4	– lbw b Garton	19
A. N. Cook lbw b Garton	20	– c Salt b Garton	26
*T. Westley c Clark b Crocombe	4	– b Meaker	24
D. W. Lawrence c Brown b Garton	6	– c Brown b Garton	60
R. N. ten Doeschate c Salt b Haines	13	– c Thomason b Garton	12
P. I. Walter b Garton	33	– not out	27
†A. J. A. Wheater c Brown b Meaker	6	– c Brown b Claydon	14
S. R. Harmer lbw b Claydon	17	– c Finch b Claydon	0
A. P. Beard c Finch b Garton	0	– not out	10
J. A. Porter not out	1		
M. R. Quinn b Garton	13		
B 1, lb 9, w 5, nb 8	23	B 4, lb 1, nb 2	7
1/4 (1) 2/15 (3) 3/29 (4) (55.3 overs)	140	1/44 (2) (7 wkts, 45.5 overs)	199
4/50 (2) 5/60 (5) 6/90 (7)		2/49 (1) 3/118 (3)	
7/119 (6) 8/121 (9) 9/121 (8) 10/140 (11)		4/142 (5) 5/153 (4) 6/172 (7) 7/172 (8)	

Claydon 15–5–32–2; Crocombe 10–3–25–1; Haines 8–2–18–1; Garton 10.3–5–26–5; Meaker 7–1–17–1; Rawlins 5–2–12–0. *Second innings*—Claydon 14–2–50–2; Crocombe 9–1–42–0; Garton 12–1–50–4; Haines 4–0–11–0; Rawlins 1–0–2–0; Meaker 5.5–0–39–1.

Umpires: I. J. Gould and M. Newell. Referee: S. J. Davis.

At Radlett, August 22–24. SUSSEX lost to MIDDLESEX by five wickets. *Sussex are later docked 24pts after Mitchell Claydon is found guilty of trying to alter the condition of the ball.*

At The Oval, September 6–9. SUSSEX lost to SURREY by six wickets. *Sussex endure a fourth straight defeat, despite making 415 in the first innings.*

WARWICKSHIRE

It tolls for three

PAUL BOLTON

There was a constant reminder of the coronavirus threat throughout an abbreviated season of farewells and frustration at Edgbaston: part of the car park was transformed into one of the first NHS drive-through testing stations. It had a steady flow of visitors – but cricket watchers were excluded for all but a friendly against Worcestershire in July. All the competitive cricket took place in a deserted, eerily quiet stadium; only the chants of three diehard supporters, who used a stepladder to get a glimpse of the T20 action from a perimeter wall on the Edgbaston Road, added to the players' shouts and claps.

It meant Ian Bell, Jeetan Patel and Tim Ambrose all shuffled into retirement without the farewell they deserved. Bell's decision to end a career that had started in the last season of the one-division County Championship in 1999, came barely two months after he had signed a contract extension for 2021. Niggling injuries, which he had generally avoided down the years, took their toll. Having scraped only 85 runs from his first nine innings in all competitions, he announced the news the day before the last first-class match of the season, in Cardiff. He signed off with two half-centuries, falling ten short in his final innings of what would have been his 58th first-class hundred. Bell played 383 matches for Warwickshire, making 17,757 runs with 38 centuries, and leaves a hole that will be hard to fill.

Patel's retirement for a career in coaching was more planned. He had been due to spend the first part of the summer with England as a spin-bowling coach, but work-permit complications prevented him from travelling from his native New Zealand until mid-August. He sat out the Bob Willis Trophy, but played all the T20 Blast games, although there was no fairytale end for the man who rivalled Rohan Kanhai or Allan Donald as the county's most popular overseas player. Patel took 473 first-class wickets for Warwickshire – 140 more than for Wellington – plus 269 in white-ball cricket, and added enormous value as a role model to younger team-mates. In the 2010s, he took 701 first-class wickets, more than anyone else in the decade.

Everyone had hoped his swansong would come on T20 finals day, at Edgbaston. Warwickshire had one foot in the quarter-finals until Northamptonshire's Graeme White thumped three sixes in what became Patel's final over in senior cricket. It turned into a low-key farewell: he was applauded off by his team-mates – and the Northamptonshire players, in the visiting teams' temporary changing-rooms at the opposite end of the ground.

Nothing was seen of former Test wicketkeeper Ambrose after he announced his retirement just before the revised season began. He slipped quietly into married life, fatherhood and the golf course, while Warwickshire gave opportunities to Michael Burgess and, when he fell ill, Vikai Kelley from the

Academy. Burgess, like Ambrose, had joined Warwickshire from Sussex in pursuit of regular first-team cricket, and soon discovered he had big gloves to fill. Although Burgess kept tidily enough, his batting – supposedly his stronger suit – was disappointing: he failed to reach 40 in 16 innings in all cricket.

Philip Brown, Popperfoto/Getty Images

Will Rhodes

In October came news that head coach Jim Troughton had been sacked, ending a 30-year association with Warwickshire. Sports director Paul Farbrace felt a coaching team comprised entirely of club old boys – Troughton, Graeme Welch, Tony Frost and Ian Westwood – was too cosy. They became the first county to apply the Rooney Rule, whereby the interviewees had to include a BAME candidate – though the job eventually went to Mark Robinson, former coach of England's women.

It all left Chris Woakes as the only survivor of Warwickshire's 2012 Championship-winning side – and he played no county cricket in 2020 because of England commitments. Dom Sibley featured in three T20 matches – which produced two ducks and four runs – after he returned from international duty. Warwickshire will need more top-order runs, particularly from Sam Hain, now the senior batsman. He struggled at first when he returned from England's white-ball bubble, but found form in the Blast.

Will Rhodes followed a series of cameos with a maiden double-century, against Worcestershire, and made a favourable impression in his first season as captain, helped by the arrival of Tim Bresnan from Yorkshire. Bresnan made a century on debut, against Northamptonshire, and formed an accurate new-ball partnership with Olly Hannon-Dalby, another Yorkshire exile. But the back-up seamers were less reliable, with Henry Brookes, Craig Miles and Ryan Sidebottom expensive at times, and Liam Norwell and Olly Stone again troubled by injuries. Warwickshire won none of their five BWT matches – one of only four sides to end empty-handed – but still finished third in the Central Group. Two young left-hand batsmen, Rob Yates and Dan Mousley, made red-ball progress, at the expense of Liam Banks, who was released, and Adam Hose, who responded with a century in the T20 defeat by Northamptonshire.

Ed Pollock's 61 runs in five Blast innings – which meant just one T20 score over 40 since September 2017 – silenced the chatter about a career strike-rate of almost 170; his discomfort against slow bowling was exploited by opposition captains. Warwickshire's own problems in the spin department were also exposed in Patel's absence. Alex Thomson took only four wickets in the Bob Willis Trophy, but experienced left-armer Danny Briggs was recruited from Sussex at the end of the season.

Off the field, it was a challenging first season for Mark McCafferty, the new chairman, and Stuart Cain, who joined from Wasps rugby club as chief executive just in time for the government to pull the plug on another pilot crowd scheme planned for the first two days of the Northamptonshire match.

WARWICKSHIRE RESULTS

Bob Willis Trophy – Played 5: Lost 1, Drawn 4.
Vitality Blast matches – Played 9: Won 5, Lost 4. Abandoned 1.

Bob Willis Trophy, 3rd in Central Group;
Vitality Blast, 3rd in Central Group.

BOB WILLIS TROPHY AVERAGES

BATTING AND FIELDING

Cap		*Birthplace*	*M*	*I*	*NO*	*R*	*HS*	*100*	*Avge*	*Ct/St*
	T. T. Bresnan	*Pontefract*	4	6	2	214	105	1	53.50	5
2020	†W. M. H. Rhodes	*Nottingham*	5	9	1	423	207	1	52.87	2
	†D. R. Mousley	*Birmingham‡*	2	3	0	149	71	0	49.66	1
	M. J. Lamb	*Wolverhampton*	3	4	0	101	65	0	25.25	1
2001	I. R. Bell	*Walsgrave‡*	5	8	0	184	90	0	23.00	5
2018	S. R. Hain	*Hong Kong*	5	8	0	146	65	0	18.25	5
	A. T. Thomson	*Macclesfield*	5	8	0	146	46	0	18.25	1
	†R. M. Yates	*Solihull‡*	5	9	1	137	88	0	17.12	2
	M. G. K. Burgess	*Epsom*	5	8	0	135	39	0	16.87	15/1
2019	†O. J. Hannon-Dalby	*Halifax*	5	7	3	43	19	0	10.75	1
	C. N. Miles	*Swindon*	3	5	2	27	13*	0	9.00	0
	H. J. H. Brookes	*Solihull‡*	2	4	0	23	12	0	5.75	1

Also batted: E. A. Brookes (*Solihull‡*) (1 match) 6, 15*; L. C. Norwell (*Bournemouth*) (1 match) 12, 7*; R. N. Sidebottom†† (*Shepparton, Australia*) (3 matches) 0*, 13*; O. P. Stone (*Norwich*) (cap 2020) (1 match) 36* (1 ct).

‡ *Born in Warwickshire.* †† *Other non-England-qualified.*

BOWLING

	Style	*O*	*M*	*R*	*W*	*BB*	*5I*	*Avge*
O. P. Stone	RF	17	3	49	4	4-39	0	12.25
O. J. Hannon-Dalby	RFM	196.3	53	523	25	6-33	2	20.92
L. C. Norwell	RFM	44	10	95	4	4-43	0	23.75
W. M. H. Rhodes	RFM	79.4	16	245	10	4-46	0	24.50
T. T. Bresnan	RFM	116	36	275	10	4-99	0	27.50
R. N. Sidebottom	RFM	88	12	331	8	3-37	0	41.37
C. N. Miles	RFM	74	17	265	4	1-51	0	66.25
A. T. Thomson	OB	100	14	276	4	2-3	0	69.00

Also bowled: E. A. Brookes (RFM) 3–1–13–0; H. J. H. Brookes (RFM) 51–6–203–2; D. R. Mousley (OB) 9–1–37–0; R. M. Yates (OB) 22–9–37–0.

LEADING VITALITY BLAST AVERAGES (60 runs/9 overs)

Batting	*Runs*	*HS*	*Avge*	*SR*	*Ct*
R. M. Yates	89	37	22.25	**158.92**	1
A. J. Hose	268	119	29.77	**154.02**	4
S. R. Hain	284	73*	56.80	**139.21**	1
H. J. H. Brookes	72	31*	24.00	**130.90**	0
D. R. Mousley	101	58*	50.50	**126.25**	1
W. M. H. Rhodes	120	46	13.33	**117.64**	1
E. J. Pollock	61	21	12.20	**115.09**	0
M. G. K. Burgess	64	17*	12.80	**108.47**	5

Bowling	*W*	*BB*	*Avge*	*ER*
J. B. Lintott	10	3-11	18.90	**6.30**
J. S. Patel	6	2-27	46.83	**8.51**
O. P. Stone	14	3-45	17.50	**8.75**
W. M. H. Rhodes	0	0-12	–	**8.77**
T. T. Bresnan	12	3-25	19.33	**8.98**
H. J. H. Brookes	11	2-24	26.09	**9.25**

FIRST-CLASS COUNTY RECORDS

Highest score for	501*	B. C. Lara v Durham at Birmingham	1994
Highest score against	322	I. V. A. Richards (Somerset) at Taunton	1985
Leading run-scorer	35,146	D. L. Amiss (avge 41.64)	1960–87
Best bowling for	10-41	J. D. Bannister v Combined Services at Birmingham	1959
Best bowling against	10-36	H. Verity (Yorkshire) at Leeds	1931
Leading wicket-taker	2,201	W. E. Hollies (avge 20.45)	1932–57
Highest total for	810-4 dec	v Durham at Birmingham	1994
Highest total against	887	by Yorkshire at Birmingham	1896
Lowest total for	16	v Kent at Tonbridge	1913
Lowest total against	15	by Hampshire at Birmingham	1922

LIST A COUNTY RECORDS

Highest score for	206	A. I. Kallicharran v Oxfordshire at Birmingham	1984
Highest score against	172*	W. Larkins (Northamptonshire) at Luton	1983
Leading run-scorer	11,254	D. L. Amiss (avge 33.79)	1963–87
Best bowling for	7-32	R. G. D. Willis v Yorkshire at Birmingham	1981
Best bowling against	6-27	M. H. Yardy (Sussex) at Birmingham	2005
Leading wicket-taker	396	G. C. Small (avge 25.48)	1980–99
Highest total for	392-5	v Oxfordshire at Birmingham	1984
Highest total against	415-5	by Nottinghamshire at Nottingham	2016
Lowest total for	59	v Yorkshire at Leeds	2001
Lowest total against	56	by Yorkshire at Birmingham	1995

TWENTY20 COUNTY RECORDS

Highest score for	158*	B. B. McCullum v Derbyshire at Birmingham	2015
Highest score against	115	M. M. Ali (Worcestershire) at Birmingham	2018
Leading run-scorer	**2,152**	**I. R. Bell (avge 30.74, SR 127.63)**	**2003–20**
Best bowling for	5-19	N. M. Carter v Worcestershire at Birmingham	2005
Best bowling against	7-18	C. N. Ackermann (Leicestershire) at Leicester	2019
Leading wicket-taker	**141**	**J. S. Patel (avge 24.76, ER 6.99)**	**2009–20**
Highest total for	242-2	v Derbyshire at Birmingham	2015
Highest total against	231-5	by Northamptonshire at Birmingham	2018
Lowest total for	73	v Somerset at Taunton	2013
Lowest total against	96	by Northamptonshire at Northampton	2011
	96	by Gloucestershire at Cheltenham	2013

ADDRESS

Edgbaston Stadium, Birmingham B5 7QU; 0844 635 1902; info@edgbaston.com; www.edgbaston.com. Twitter: @WarwickshireCCC.

OFFICIALS

Captain W. M. H. Rhodes
Sport director P. Farbrace
First-team coach 2020 J. O. Troughton
2021 M. A. Robinson
Elite development manager P. Greetham
President Earl of Aylesford

Chairman M. McCafferty
Chief executive 2020 N. Snowball
2020-21 S. Cain
Head groundsman G. Barwell
Scorer M. D. Smith

WARWICKSHIRE v NORTHAMPTONSHIRE

At Birmingham, August 1–4. Drawn. Warwickshire 14pts, Northamptonshire 10pts. Toss: Warwickshire. First-class debut: C. J. White. County debut: T. T. Bresnan.

Feckless in their first innings, when Stone demolished their middle order, Northamptonshire displayed greater fortitude in the second to pass 500 for the first time against Warwickshire, and earn a deserved draw against an attack now weakened by Stone's absence, following a side strain late on the second day. A home win had looked assured after lunch on the third, when Bresnan inflicted a pair on Zaib to reduce Northamptonshire to 148 for five. But Thurston, who fell just short of a maiden county century when he was lbw in the second over with the new ball, and Rossington led the resistance. They put on 159 – a record for Northamptonshire's sixth wicket against Warwickshire – before Rossington, who curbed his attacking instincts to face 399 balls in more than eight hours, batted throughout the last day with Procter in an unbroken partnership of 200. Procter's century was his first in four years, and first for Northamptonshire, as Warwickshire were left to rue erratic bowling and catching. Earlier, they had claimed a lead of 227 thanks to composed innings from Yates and Bresnan, who marked his debut following his move from Yorkshire with a century. Plans to admit 2,500 spectators on each of the first two days were aborted on government instructions, even though Edgbaston had successfully staged a crowd pilot with 800 for the first day of a recent friendly against Worcestershire.

Close of play: first day, Warwickshire 130-4 (Yates 63, Burgess 30); second day, Northamptonshire 19-0 (Curran 10, Gay 9); third day, Northamptonshire 317-6 (Rossington 60, Procter 5).

Northamptonshire

B. J. Curran b Hannon-Dalby	10	– lbw b Rhodes	58
E. N. Gay c Rhodes b Stone	2	– c Bresnan b Hannon-Dalby	11
R. S. Vasconcelos c Burgess b Bresnan	24	– c Bell b Thomson	42
R. I. Keogh b Sidebottom	26	– c Yates b Bresnan	31
C. O. Thurston c Bell b Stone	15	– lbw b Bresnan	96
S. A. Zaib c Burgess b Stone	0	– c Burgess b Bresnan	0
*†A. M. Rossington c Burgess b Stone	4	– not out	135
L. A. Procter not out	29	– not out	112
N. L. Buck c Stone b Sidebottom	5		
B. W. Sanderson lbw b Thomson	23		
C. J. White b Thomson	2		
Lb 2	2	B 6, lb 11, w 1, nb 4	22
1/12 (1) 2/12 (2) 3/49 (4) (51 overs)	142	1/26 (2) (6 wkts dec, 175 overs)	507
4/70 (5) 5/70 (6) 6/76 (7)		2/105 (1) 3/136 (3)	
7/86 (3) 8/91 (9) 9/140 (10) 10/142 (11)		4/148 (4) 5/148 (6) 6/307 (5)	

Hannon-Dalby 12–4–30–1; Stone 14–3–39–4; Bresnan 12–4–22–1; Sidebottom 10–1–46–2; Thomson 3–1–3–2. *Second innings*—Hannon-Dalby 32–7–94–1; Stone 3–0–10–0; Thomson 44–9–116–1; Bresnan 26–11–37–3; Sidebottom 25–2–129–0; Rhodes 23–5–67–1; Yates 22–9–37–0.

Warwickshire

R. M. Yates c Gay b White	88	O. P. Stone not out	36
*W. M. H. Rhodes lbw b Sanderson	2	O. J. Hannon-Dalby not out	5
S. R. Hain lbw b White	6	Lb 30, w 3	33
I. R. Bell c sub (J. J. Cobb) b Buck	9		
M. J. Lamb c Gay b Buck	0	1/27 (2) 2/59 (3) (8 wkts, 120 overs)	369
†M. G. K. Burgess b Sanderson	39	3/77 (4) 4/85 (5)	
T. T. Bresnan b Keogh	105	5/141 (6) 6/220 (1)	
A. T. Thomson b Buck	46	7/324 (8) 8/328 (7)	110 overs: 318-6

R. N. Sidebottom did not bat.

Sanderson 27–4–77–2; Buck 26–8–64–3; White 20–3–58–2; Procter 10–2–28–0; Keogh 34–9–96–1; Zaib 3–0–16–0.

Umpires: Hassan Adnan and R. T. Robinson. Referee: T. J. Boon.

At Bristol, August 8–11. WARWICKSHIRE lost to GLOUCESTERSHIRE by 78 runs. *Olly Hannon-Dalby takes 12 wickets.*

WARWICKSHIRE v SOMERSET

At Birmingham, August 15–18. Drawn. Warwickshire 11pts, Somerset 16pts. Toss: Warwickshire.

Rain wiped out all but 94 balls of the last day, and denied Somerset a victory that appeared certain once their powerful seam attack flattened Warwickshire on the first. With Lamb unlikely to bat after breaking a toe in the first innings, Somerset probably needed only one more wicket to complete a third straight emphatic win – but heavy downpours on the final afternoon saturated the outfield. More than half the second day had also been lost. Warwickshire's bowling lacked Somerset's depth and, although the accuracy of Hannon-Dalby and Bresnan made the batsmen work hard, Miles and Brookes absorbed heavy punishment from Jamie Overton, who clobbered a maiden century from 84 balls; 96 of his eventual 120 came in boundaries. Early on, he was taunted by Hannon-Dalby, who mimicked Overton's aggressive follow-through. It may have been intended in jest, but it backfired: Overton had the last laugh as he bludgeoned the second-highest score by an English No. 10, behind Derbyshire's John Chapman, with 165 against Warwickshire at Blackwell in 1910. Davies contributed a patient but valuable century, his second in two matches at Edgbaston, and was part of a ninth-wicket stand of 180, a record in this fixture.

Close of play: first day, Somerset 80-2 (Abell 16, Hildreth 1); second day, Somerset 214-6 (Davies 56, Gregory 14); third day, Warwickshire 104-6 (Thomson 9, Brookes 0).

Warwickshire

R. M. Yates c Davies b C. Overton	3	– b Davey	1
*W. M. H. Rhodes run out (Abell)	10	– c and b Gregory	41
S. R. Hain b C. Overton	1	– c Hildreth b J. Overton	7
I. R. Bell c Davies b Gregory	15	– c Davies b Gregory	6
M. J. Lamb b C. Overton	22		
†M. G. K. Burgess b Gregory	15	– (5) c Abell b Davey	13
T. T. Bresnan not out	32	– (6) c Hildreth b Davey	0
A. T. Thomson run out (Banton)	0	– (7) c Davies b J. Overton	26
H. J. H. Brookes c Hildreth b Abell	11	– (8) b Gregory	12
C. N. Miles c Davies b Abell	0	– (9) not out	2
O. J. Hannon-Dalby c Davies b Abell	0	– (10) not out	0
B 1, lb 5, w 2, nb 4	12	B 6, lb 10, w 6, nb 10	32
1/12 (1) 2/15 (3) 3/15 (2) (45.2 overs)	121	1/3 (1) 2/24 (3) (8 wkts, 56 overs)	140
4/59 (4) 5/65 (5) 6/88 (6)		3/39 (4) 4/58 (5)	
7/88 (8) 8/113 (9) 9/113 (10) 10/121 (11)		5/58 (6) 6/104 (2) 7/138 (8) 8/138 (7)	

C. Overton 14–6–17–3; Davey 11–2–22–0; Gregory 8–1–30–2; J. Overton 9–2–42–0; Abell 3.2–2–4–3. *Second innings*—C. Overton 17–5–31–0; Davey 12–5–21–3; J. Overton 9–5–22–2; Gregory 16–5–50–3; Abell 2–2–0–0.

Somerset

E. J. Byrom c Bresnan b Hannon-Dalby	30
T. A. Lammonby c Hain b Hannon-Dalby	33
*T. B. Abell c Burgess b Miles	41
J. C. Hildreth c Thomson b Bresnan	1
T. Banton lbw b Hannon-Dalby	13
†S. M. Davies not out	123
C. Overton lbw b Bresnan	25
L. Gregory c Brookes b Bresnan	14
R. E. van der Merwe c Burgess b Hannon-Dalby	4
J. Overton c Burgess b Bresnan	120
J. H. Davey not out	5
Lb 3, w 1	4
1/56 (1) 2/67 (2) (9 wkts dec, 99 overs)	413
3/80 (4) 4/101 (5)	
5/130 (3) 6/191 (7)	
7/215 (8) 8/226 (9)	
9/406 (10)	

Hannon-Dalby 33–7–104–4; Bresnan 26–3–99–4; Brookes 16–0–85–0; Miles 13–2–82–1; Rhodes 5–1–14–0; Thomson 6–1–26–0.

Umpires: T. Lungley and R. J. Warren. Referee: D. A. Cosker.

At Worcester, August 22–25. WARWICKSHIRE drew with WORCESTERSHIRE. *Will Rhodes scores 207.*

At Cardiff, September 6–9. WARWICKSHIRE drew with GLAMORGAN. *Ian Bell makes 50 and 90 in his last match before retirement.*

WORCESTERSHIRE

Twelve good men and true

JOHN CURTIS

Worcester's winter floods, some of the worst in the club's history, left New Road under water for more than 60 days between November and February. The upshot was that the opening game was – in theory – shifted to Kidderminster. It was worryingly reminiscent of 2007, when floods in mid-June stopped cricket at HQ for the rest of the summer, with financial implications that lasted several years.

In March, though, such soggy concerns were dwarfed by another threat, less visible but more sinister. Covid-19 prevented cricket anywhere, flood or no flood. In May, in a welcome break from the lockdown regime, players – male and female – and coaches embraced the Rapids Relay, in which they covered a total of more than 1,000km in a week, via 84 one-hour solo runs; it raised £17,000 for Acorns Children's Hospice.

The squad returned from furlough on June 22, a week sooner than many counties, and the benefits of a winter programme focused on improving red-ball cricket quickly became clear. That had been identified by head coach Alex Gidman as the area most in need of change, after Worcestershire were relegated from Division One in 2018, and finished last but one in Division Two a year later. Back at their winter base in Malvern College two months earlier than usual, the players embarked on technical work – with the emphasis on batting for long periods, bowling a disciplined line and length, and avoiding costly mini-sessions that ceded control.

When competitive cricket eventually took place in August, Worcestershire fared well, despite their Bob Willis Trophy group including four Division One counties, and remained in contention for the Lord's final until the last afternoon. But, in a seesaw encounter at New Road, they were edged aside by Somerset. After the disappointment had worn off, there was much encouragement to be drawn from the five games: the hoped-for upturn in four-day cricket saw them finish second.

Unable to command a regular place in Nottinghamshire's Championship side, Jake Libby – signed on a three-year deal – quickly showed his potential. He finished the group stages as the highest run-scorer in the tournament, and his 498 (at 55) was not overtaken until Alastair Cook hit a century in the final. He brought resilience and calmness to the top of the order, which permeated the rest of the batting. The stability also helped Daryl Mitchell (384 at 42), who had put up with five different opening partners the previous year. In all, only 12 players appeared in the BWT.

In 2019, Worcestershire had broached 400 in their first game, and never again in the next 13. In 2020, they did so three times in their opening four matches – against a stronger set of opponents. Six batsmen averaged 40

Michael Steele, Getty Images

Jake Libby

or more, including Tom Fell, who hit his first first-class hundred since September 2015, just weeks before undergoing surgery for testicular cancer. Reaching the landmark (against Northamptonshire at Wantage Road) was an emotional occasion, greeted with rapturous applause from his team-mates. He had resumed that morning on 81, having barely slept. It was the prelude to a second BWT victory, after Gloucestershire were thumped in the opening round.

Jack Haynes, who played in the Under-19 World Cup earlier in the year, was consistent rather than prolific: he made between 21 and 51 in eight of his nine innings. But he did not look out of place at senior level, and must now turn starts into hundreds. The other notable run-scorers were Brett D'Oliveira and Ben Cox, whose exceptional keeping was backed up by smart slip catching from Mitchell and Riki Wessels.

Worcestershire had many seam options. The captain, Joe Leach, was the leading wicket-taker, with 19, including four-fors against Gloucestershire and Glamorgan. He enjoyed excellent support: Ed Barnard claimed 18, while Charlie Morris – who collected five for 80 against Warwickshire – and Josh Tongue both took 14. And with Dillon Pennington managing 11, it was hardly a surprise that Adam Finch was loaned to Surrey, though he did return for the Vitality Blast.

The missing cog, though, was a frontline spinner. D'Oliveira bowled his leg-spin with modest results, while Libby's occasional off-breaks gained a couple of victims. But slow left-armer Ben Twohig was released – as was batsman Olly Westbury.

After two successful years in the Blast, Worcestershire plummeted to the bottom of the Central Group. They badly missed T20 captain Moeen Ali, who was on England duty, and Wayne Parnell, stuck in South Africa; with Kolpaks a thing of the past, he will not return in 2021. Pat Brown, so influential in recent seasons, looked rusty when the tournament began in late August. The weakened attack leaked runs, and the standard of fielding was lower than usual. Too often, opponents sped past decent totals or set daunting targets. New Zealander Hamish Rutherford and Libby both scored freely, but there was only so much they could do.

Worcestershire have strengthened the batting for 2021 by recruiting Gareth Roderick, well-known to Gidman from his playing days at Gloucestershire; the hope is he can blossom like Libby. And with key contributors such as Morris and Fell committing to the club, there is genuine optimism, at least for the red-ball future.

And, as it turned out, the first game of the season *was* at New Road, though not quite as envisaged, since it was nominally a home match for Lancashire against Leicestershire – in August. It was a strange season.

WORCESTERSHIRE RESULTS

Bob Willis Trophy matches – Played 5: Won 2, Lost 1, Drawn 2.
Vitality Blast matches – Played 9: Won 2, Lost 7. Abandoned 1.

Bob Willis Trophy, 2nd in Central Group;
Vitality Blast, 6th in Central Group.

BOB WILLIS TROPHY AVERAGES

BATTING AND FIELDING

Colours		*Birthplace*	*M*	*I*	*NO*	*R*	*HS*	*100*	*Avge*	*Ct*
2020	J. D. Libby	*Plymouth*	5	9	0	498	184	1	55.33	2
2012	B. L. D'Oliveira	*Worcester*‡	5	8	1	367	174	1	52.42	2
2013	T. C. Fell	*Hillingdon*	5	9	2	336	110*	1	48.00	3
2009	O. B. Cox	*Wordsley*‡	5	8	3	225	45*	0	45.00	25
2005	D. K. H. Mitchell	*Badsey*‡	5	9	0	384	110	1	42.66	7
2019	J. A. Haynes	*Worcester*‡	5	9	2	285	51	0	40.71	1
2015	E. G. Barnard	*Shrewsbury*	5	6	2	84	48*	0	21.00	5
2019	M. H. Wessels	*Maroochydore, Aust*	5	8	0	157	88	0	19.62	4
2012	J. Leach	*Stafford*	5	6	1	47	17	0	9.40	1
2018	D. Y. Pennington	*Shrewsbury*	3	4	2	15	11*	0	7.50	1
2017	J. C. Tongue	*Redditch*‡	4	3	2	1	1*	0	1.00	0

Also batted: C. A. J. Morris (*Hereford*) (cap 2014) (3 matches) did not bat.

‡ *Born in Worcestershire.* †† *Other non-England-qualified.*

Worcestershire award colours to all Championship/Bob Willis Trophy players.

BOWLING

	Style	*O*	*M*	*R*	*W*	*BB*	*5I*	*Avge*
E. G. Barnard	RFM	148.5	40	390	18	4-25	0	21.66
C. A. J. Morris	RFM	99.3	21	315	14	5-80	1	22.50
D. Y. Pennington	RFM	90.1	22	248	11	3-30	0	22.54
J. Leach	RFM	169.3	44	490	19	4-67	0	25.78
J. C. Tongue	RFM	117.1	26	363	14	3-38	0	25.92
B. L. D'Oliveira	LB	95	13	312	6	2-31	0	52.00

Also bowled: J. D. Libby (OB) 14.4–2–46–2; D. K. H. Mitchell (RM) 31–7–63–1.

LEADING VITALITY BLAST AVERAGES (70 runs/10 overs)

Batting	*Runs*	*HS*	*Avge*	*SR*	*Ct*
H. D. Rutherford	352	100	39.11	**160.00**	1
J. A. Haynes	149	41	21.28	**137.96**	2
J. D. Libby	318	75*	39.75	**137.06**	1
R. A. Whiteley	118	25	16.85	**131.11**	6
O. B. Cox	176	56*	29.33	**129.41**	4
B. L. D'Oliveira	143	61	28.60	**128.82**	3
M. H. Wessels	79	30	13.16	**102.59**	3

Bowling	*W*	*BB*	*Avge*	*ER*
D. K. H. Mitchell	6	3-35	36.33	**7.78**
B. L. D'Oliveira	3	1-11	62.33	**8.50**
E. G. Barnard	10	3-44	26.00	**8.66**
A. W. Finch	4	1-22	36.75	**9.18**
C. A. J. Morris	6	2-44	32.16	**9.98**
D. Y. Pennington	5	2-27	42.20	**10.04**
P. R. Brown	8	3-39	41.62	**10.85**

FIRST-CLASS COUNTY RECORDS

Highest score for	405*	G. A. Hick v Somerset at Taunton	1988
Highest score against	331*	J. D. B. Robertson (Middlesex) at Worcester	1949
Leading run-scorer	34,490	D. Kenyon (avge 34.18)	1946–67
Best bowling for	9-23	C. F. Root v Lancashire at Worcester	1931
Best bowling against	10-51	J. Mercer (Glamorgan) at Worcester	1936
Leading wicket-taker	2,143	R. T. D. Perks (avge 23.73)	1930–55
Highest total for	701-6 dec	v Surrey at Worcester	2007
Highest total against	701-4 dec	by Leicestershire at Worcester	1906
Lowest total for	24	v Yorkshire at Huddersfield	1903
Lowest total against	30	by Hampshire at Worcester	1903

LIST A COUNTY RECORDS

Highest score for	192	C. J. Ferguson v Leicestershire at Worcester	2018
Highest score against	161*	S. R. Hain (Warwickshire) at Worcester	2019
Leading run-scorer	16,416	G. A. Hick (avge 44.60)	1985–2008
Best bowling for	7-19	N. V. Radford v Bedfordshire at Bedford	1991
Best bowling against	7-15	R. A. Hutton (Yorkshire) at Leeds	1969
Leading wicket-taker	370	S. R. Lampitt (avge 24.52)	1987–2002
Highest total for	404-3	v Devon at Worcester	1987
Highest total against	399-4	by Sussex at Horsham	2011
Lowest total for	58	v Ireland v Worcester	2009
Lowest total against	45	by Hampshire at Worcester	1988

TWENTY20 COUNTY RECORDS

Highest score for	127	T. Köhler-Cadmore v Durham at Worcester	2016
Highest score against	141*	C. L. White (Somerset) at Worcester	2006
Leading run-scorer	2,589	M. M. Ali (avge 29.08, SR 141.47)	2007–19
Best bowling for	5-24	A. Hepburn v Nottinghamshire at Worcester	2017
Best bowling against	6-21	A. J. Hall (Northamptonshire) at Northampton	2008
Leading wicket-taker	**98**	**D. K. H. Mitchell (avge 29.51, ER 7.66)**	**2005–20**
Highest total for	227-6	v Northamptonshire at Kidderminster	2007
Highest total against	233-6	by Yorkshire at Leeds	2017
Lowest total for	53	v Lancashire at Manchester	2016
Lowest total against	93	by Gloucestershire at Bristol	2008

ADDRESS

New Road, Worcester WR2 4QQ; 01905 748474; info@wccc.co.uk; www.wccc.co.uk. Twitter: @WorcsCCC.

OFFICIALS

Captain J. Leach
(ltd-overs) E. G. Barnard
First-team coach A. P. R. Gidman
Assistant/bowling coach A. Richardson
Head of player development K. Sharp
Academy coach E. J. Wilson

President 2020 C. Duckworth
Chairman F. Hira
Chief executive TBC
Head groundsman T. R. Packwood
Scorers S. M. Drinkwater and P. M. Mellish

At Bristol, August 1–4. WORCESTERSHIRE beat GLOUCESTERSHIRE by eight wickets.

WORCESTERSHIRE v GLAMORGAN

At Worcester, August 8–11. Drawn. Worcestershire 15pts, Glamorgan 12pts. Toss: Worcestershire.

Glamorgan captain and wicketkeeper Chris Cooke had a day to remember as Worcestershire were left to rue delaying their declaration until half an hour after lunch on the last. Having equalled the Glamorgan record for most dismissals in a match, he dug in to stave off defeat. His side were five for three, needing 358, when Cooke arrived but, on a flat pitch, he hung around for three hours; when he departed for 74, the draw was almost guaranteed. Earlier, Libby had marked his home debut with a career-best 184; his stand of 318 with D'Oliveira was an all-wicket record between Worcestershire and Glamorgan. They had come together at 70 for three, all to the excellent Hogan, though he remained on 599 first-class wickets for the rest of the match. A remarkable third-morning spell of 7–5–3–4 from Leach reduced Glamorgan from an overnight 181 for two to 203 for six, but Root batted responsibly, and found an ally in Wagg; they avoided the follow-on, before a stunning one-handed catch away to his left by keeper Cox ended Root's 284-ball innings. Mitchell fell six short of a century, before Leach declared with seven an over needed. Worcestershire head coach Alex Gidman described the timing as "spot on".

MOST DISMISSALS IN A FIRST-CLASS MATCH FOR GLAMORGAN

9 (9 ct)	C. P. Metson	v Worcestershire at Worcester	1993
9 (9 ct)	C. P. Metson	v Surrey at The Oval	1995
9 (9 ct)	M. A. Wallace	v Derbyshire at Colwyn Bay	2016
9 (9 ct)	M. A. Wallace	v Worcestershire at Worcester	2016
9 (7 ct, 2 st)	**C. B. Cooke**	**v Worcestershire at Worcester**	**2020**

There are nine instances of a Glamorgan wicketkeeper making eight dismissals in a match, including five by Wallace and one by Metson.

Close of play: first day, Worcestershire 309-3 (Libby 142, D'Oliveira 123); second day, Glamorgan 181-2 (Carlson 76, Root 53); third day, Worcestershire 98-2 (Mitchell 48).

Worcestershire

D. K. H. Mitchell c Cooke b Hogan	0	– st Cooke b Bull	94
J. D. Libby st Cooke b Bull	184	– c Cooke b Douthwaite	44
T. C. Fell c Cooke b Hogan	8	– (4) c Cooke b van der Gugten	36
J. A. Haynes c Douthwaite b Hogan	21	– (5) not out	30
B. L. D'Oliveira c Cooke b Wagg	174	– (6) c Cooke b Wagg	22
M. H. Wessels c and b Wagg	4	– (7) c Cooke b Wagg	0
†O. B. Cox not out	23	– (8) not out	33
E. G. Barnard c Hogan b Wagg	7		
*J. Leach c Root b Bull	17	– (3) c Hemphrey b Bull	0
D. Y. Pennington not out	0		
B 5, lb 2, nb 10	17	B 1, lb 10, nb 6	17
1/0 (1) 2/22 (3) 3/70 (4) (8 wkts, 120 overs)	455	1/97 (2) (6 wkts dec, 71 overs)	276
4/388 (2) 5/405 (6) 6/410 (5)		2/98 (3) 3/183 (4)	
7/424 (8) 8/453 (9) 110 overs: 404-4		4/197 (1) 5/232 (6) 6/232 (7)	

C. A. J. Morris did not bat.

Hogan 22–4–59–3; van der Gugten 21–6–55–0; Douthwaite 18–1–99–0; Wagg 19–3–66–3; Bull 31–3–132–2; Hemphrey 9–0–37–0. *Second innings*—Hogan 12–3–31–0; van der Gugten 14–2–51–1; Douthwaite 7–4–21–1; Wagg 12–1–73–2; Bull 26–0–89–2.

Glamorgan

N. J. Selman c Cox b Barnard	22	– lbw b Leach	0
C. R. Hemphrey lbw b Barnard	16	– lbw b Leach	1
K. S. Carlson c Mitchell b Leach	79	– c Cox b Pennington	2
W. T. Root c Cox b Morris	118	– c Cox b Pennington	34
*†C. B. Cooke c Barnard b Leach	0	– b Libby	74
T. N. Cullen c Mitchell b Leach	1	– lbw b Morris	17
D. A. Douthwaite c D'Oliveira b Leach	0	– lbw b Libby	0
G. G. Wagg c Cox b Barnard	54	– not out	9
K. A. Bull c Cox b Morris	7	– not out	0
T. van der Gugten not out	23		
M. G. Hogan c Barnard b Pennington	17		
B 14, lb 10, w 3, nb 10	37	B 1, lb 3	4
1/39 (1) 2/44 (2) 3/185 (3) (116.3 overs)	374	1/0 (1) (7 wkts, 50.4 overs)	141
4/189 (5) 5/203 (6) 6/203 (7)		2/5 (3) 3/5 (2)	
7/321 (4) 8/329 (9) 9/333 (8)		4/87 (4) 5/125 (6)	
10/374 (11) 110 overs: 333-8		6/126 (7) 7/141 (5)	

Leach 26–9–67–4; Morris 21–2–86–2; Pennington 24.3–5–66–1; Barnard 21–5–54–3; D'Oliveira 21–3–63–0; Mitchell 3–0–14–0. *Second innings*—Leach 7–4–12–2; Pennington 11–6–13–2; Morris 8–2–26–1; D'Oliveira 5–1–21–0; Libby 13.4–2–45–2; Barnard 4–0–16–0; Mitchell 2–0–4–0.

Umpires: G. D. Lloyd and J. W. Lloyds. Referee: D. A. Cosker.

At Northampton, August 15–18. WORCESTERSHIRE beat NORTHAMPTONSHIRE by 78 runs.

WORCESTERSHIRE v WARWICKSHIRE

At Worcester, August 22–25. Drawn. Worcestershire 13pts, Warwickshire 13pts. Toss: Worcestershire.

A flat and sluggish pitch discouraged both run-scoring and wicket-taking. Worcestershire captain Joe Leach said last-day rain had come as a relief, and that he had known within ten minutes the game would end in a draw. Only as the 120-over first-innings cut-off approached did batsmen take risks, or bowlers see much reward. Even so, Rhodes scored his first century since replacing Jeetan Patel as Warwickshire captain – and converted it into a maiden double. Adapting sensibly to the conditions, he batted more than eight hours, sharing hundred stands with Hain, who ended a run of five single-figure scores, and Mousley. In the 107th over, the total was 307 for three, but Morris, rewarded for perseverance, claimed his sixth five-for, as Warwickshire declined to 355 all out. Mitchell also dropped anchor, going on to his first century against them; only Surrey were now missing from his county set. Fifties from Libby, Fell and Haynes guided Worcestershire towards 400, for the third time in four games; in 2019, they had done so once in 14. Hannon-Dalby's patience and control brought three wickets. Warwickshire had now gone 20 years since a first-class defeat in the local derby.

Close of play: first day, Warwickshire 228-3 (Rhodes 142, Mousley 18); second day, Worcestershire 170-0 (Mitchell 85, Libby 80); third day, Warwickshire 68-0 (Yates 21, Rhodes 42).

Warwickshire

R. M. Yates c Wessels b Morris	2	– not out	21
*W. M. H. Rhodes c Cox b Morris	207	– not out	42
S. R. Hain c Cox b Barnard	55		
I. R. Bell c Barnard b Leach	1		
D. R. Mousley c Cox b Morris	47		
†M. G. K. Burgess c Cox b Barnard	1		
T. T. Bresnan c Libby b Morris	17		
A. T. Thomson c Cox b Tongue	14		
C. N. Miles c D'Oliveira b Morris	0		
O. J. Hannon-Dalby not out	1		
R. N. Sidebottom not out	0		
Lb 1, w 5, nb 4	10	B 1, nb 4	5
1/13 (1) 2/178 (3) (9 wkts dec, 119.1 overs)	355	(no wkt, 23 overs)	68

3/179 (4) 4/307 (5)
5/308 (6) 6/331 (7) 7/354 (2)
8/354 (8) 9/354 (9) 110 overs: 319-5

Leach 23–3–80–1; Morris 23–3–80–5; Barnard 28–5–84–2; Tongue 23.1–5–69–1; D'Oliveira 6–0–14–0; Mitchell 16–3–27–0. *Second innings*—Tongue 4–2–6–0; Leach 3–1–12–0; D'Oliveira 7–2–23–0; Morris 3–0–19–0; Barnard 5–1–6–0; Libby 1–0–1–0.

Worcestershire

D. K. H. Mitchell c Yates b Miles	110
J. D. Libby c Bresnan b Hannon-Dalby	84
T. C. Fell b Hannon-Dalby	55
J. A. Haynes c Rhodes b Sidebottom	51
B. L. D'Oliveira lbw b Bresnan	15
M. H. Wessels b Hannon-Dalby	0
†O. B. Cox lbw b Rhodes	43
E. G. Barnard not out	29
*J. Leach not out	2
B 8, lb 2, w 5, nb 6	21
1/177 (2) 2/214 (1) (7 wkts, 120 overs)	410

3/303 (4) 4/317 (3) 5/317 (6)
6/325 (5) 7/407 (7) 110 overs: 351-6

J. C. Tongue and C. A. J. Morris did not bat.

Hannon-Dalby 26–9–70–3; Miles 18–1–81–1; Sidebottom 20–3–71–1; Bresnan 14–5–40–1; Thomson 26–3–74–0; Mousley 9–1–37–0; Rhodes 7–0–27–1.

Umpires: R. J. Bailey and J. W. Lloyds. Referee: A. J. Swann.

WORCESTERSHIRE v SOMERSET

At Worcester, September 6–9. Somerset won by 60 runs. Somerset 21pts, Worcestershire 4pts. Toss: Somerset.

Somerset sealed their place at Lord's after winning a topsy-turvy game between the group's leaders. On the first day, they stumbled from 120 for two to 134 for six, threatening to squander a resolute fifty from Abell. But the lower order wagged vigorously on a green pitch, and a total of 251 proved much the highest of the game. No team in 2020 had made more than 166 against Somerset's formidable attack and, though Worcestershire scraped 200, that was a let-down from 123 for one. A rain break had brought a shift in momentum: the Somerset bowlers regrouped, and shared the wickets

YOUNGEST TO CARRY THEIR BAT FOR SOMERSET

Yrs	*Days*					
20	**98**	**T. A. Lammonby**	**107***	**(193)**	**v Worcestershire at Worcester**	**2020**
21	102	T. B. Abell	76*	(200)	v Nottinghamshire at Taunton	2015
22	20	A. D. E. Rippon	87*	(194)	v Kent at Taunton	1914
22	74	L. C. H. Palairet	22*	(58)	v Lancashire at Manchester	1892
23	279	P. A. Slocombe	93*	(210)	v Lancashire at Bath	1978
23	315	R. P. Northway	21*	(43)†	v Yorkshire at Bradford	1930

† *One man absent.* *First instance only.* *Figures in brackets show team total.*

around. Then Lammonby, in only his fifth first-class match, batted with tremendous composure. Content to knuckle down against the newer ball, he took 102 deliveries over his first 21 runs, before accelerating: his second hundred in successive matches came, with a six, from his 205th ball. For the second time, Somerset were indebted to runs from their bowlers, as 82 for six became 193 – and a target of 245. The loss of Mitchell and Libby before the end of the third day tipped the scales towards Somerset and, though five of the top seven made at least 20, none could emulate Lammonby. Absent Somerset supporters took a keen interest in the game, including former comedian John Cleese, who called New Road for help in viewing the live video.

Close of play: first day, Worcestershire 14-0 (Mitchell 8, Libby 2); second day, Somerset 16-1 (Lammonby 9, Abell 7); third day, Worcestershire 58-2 (Fell 18, Haynes 12).

Somerset

B. G. F. Green run out (Barnard)	8	– b Leach	0
T. A. Lammonby b Pennington	28	– not out	107
*T. B. Abell c Cox b Pennington	59	– c Cox b Leach	7
G. A. Bartlett b Tongue	18	– lbw b Barnard	2
E. J. Byrom c Barnard b Pennington	30	– lbw b Barnard	12
†S. M. Davies b D'Oliveira	9	– b D'Oliveira	14
C. Overton c Mitchell b Barnard	1	– b D'Oliveira	2
L. Gregory c Pennington b D'Oliveira	37	– c Libby b Pennington	17
J. H. Davey c sub (J. J. Dell) b Barnard	28	– c sub (J. J. Dell) b Barnard	21
M. J. Leach lbw b Barnard	21	– lbw b Barnard	5
J. A. Brooks not out	4	– c Cox b Pennington	1
B 5, lb 3	8	Lb 5	5
1/18 (1) 2/93 (2) 3/120 (4) 4/120 (3) 5/131 (6) 6/134 (7) 7/195 (8) 8/203 (5) 9/242 (9) 10/251 (10) (83.1 overs)	251	1/4 (1) 2/16 (3) 3/28 (4) 4/42 (5) 5/78 (6) 6/82 (7) 7/121 (8) 8/176 (9) 9/190 (10) 10/193 (11) (70.4 overs)	193

Leach 20–4–59–0; Tongue 12–3–40–1; Pennington 20–5–49–3; Barnard 15.1–3–53–3; D'Oliveira 15–3–31–2; Mitchell 1–0–11–0. *Second innings*—Leach 19–11–24–2; Pennington 13.4–1–57–2; Barnard 17–9–25–4; Tongue 12–4–28–0; D'Oliveira 9–1–54–2.

Worcestershire

D. K. H. Mitchell lbw b Gregory	31	– b Gregory	3
J. D. Libby c Davies b Brooks	58	– b Gregory	23
T. C. Fell b Brooks	26	– lbw b Gregory	20
J. A. Haynes b Gregory	4	– lbw b Davey	30
B. L. D'Oliveira lbw b Overton	8	– lbw b Overton	28
M. H. Wessels c Byrom b Overton	32	– c Byrom b Davey	9
†O. B. Cox c Abell b Overton	8	– c Davies b Davey	32
E. G. Barnard b Davey	0	– c Abell b Overton	0
*J. Leach c Leach b Davey	6	– lbw b Brooks	17
D. Y. Pennington not out	11	– lbw b Brooks	4
J. C. Tongue b Davey	0	– not out	0
Lb 12, nb 4	16	B 12, lb 4, nb 2	18
1/57 (1) 2/123 (3) 3/128 (4) 4/128 (2) 5/164 (5) 6/181 (6) 7/182 (8) 8/182 (7) 9/190 (9) 10/200 (11) (62 overs)	200	1/5 (1) 2/30 (2) 3/72 (3) 4/96 (4) 5/108 (6) 6/126 (5) 7/132 (8) 8/176 (9) 9/184 (10) 10/184 (7) (71.2 overs)	184

Overton 16–4–40–3; Davey 14–4–32–3; Gregory 13–1–49–2; Leach 8–3–22–0; Brooks 11–4–45–2. *Second innings*—Overton 20–10–40–2; Davey 14.2–8–16–3; Gregory 17–5–65–3; Brooks 15–2–35–2; Abell 5–1–12–0.

Umpires: R. J. Bailey and N. A. Mallender. Referee: S. Cummings.

YORKSHIRE

Knocked out by the virus

GRAHAM HARDCASTLE

Yorkshire took one step forward, two steps back. They won the North Group of the Bob Willis Trophy, only to miss out on the Lord's final, then declined from a position of relative health midway through the Vitality Blast.

Before travelling to Grace Road for their sixth Twenty20 fixture, on September 11, they sat third in the table, two points behind Nottinghamshire and Lancashire, and in the reckoning for the knockouts. But they lost to Leicestershire, failing to defend 189 when Ben Mike hit Adam Lyth for a straight six off the final ball. Then things unravelled.

Three days later – just before a Roses clash at Headingley – T20 captain David Willey, Matthew Fisher, Tom Köhler-Cadmore and Josh Poysden were all omitted, in accordance with Covid-19 guidelines, after Willey's wife reported symptoms. All four were later ruled out for the remaining three group matches; Willey had tested positive and, having been in close contact away from cricket, the other three had to self-isolate for 14 days. Starting at Leicester, Yorkshire lost four successive games, and finished next to bottom of their group. "We had the heart of our team ripped out," said coach Andrew Gale.

It added to a wretched few weeks for the club, who had been accused of "deep-rooted institutional racism" by their former spinner Azeem Rafiq – a claim later supported by Rana Naved-ul-Hasan and Tino Best, two of Yorkshire's overseas players. The county asked an independent law firm to conduct an investigation into Rafiq's allegations, but in December, with the results still awaited, he filed a legal claim against them with Leeds Employment Tribunal.

Back on the field, there were still positive moments in the Blast. Lyth was both the club's leading run-scorer and most economical bowler, while Test captain Joe Root enhanced his standing as a T20 player with four sixties and seven wickets in five appearances. He shared an unbroken stand of 91 with Harry Brook in a consolation victory over Derbyshire in the final game – though Root was overshadowed by the 21-year-old Brook's 50 off 29 balls. He was one of a number of young players who pressed their case in both formats after the departure of stalwart Tim Bresnan to Warwickshire at the end of June, a few weeks before the belated launch of the domestic season. During the two months of cricket that were possible, seven players – Ben Birkhead, George Hill, Dom Leech, Matthew Revis, Jack Shutt, James Wharton and Sam Wisniewski – made four-day or T20 debuts.

But the prime example was Jordan Thompson, a 23-year-old all-rounder who had played for the first team sporadically since 2018. He would not have started the summer had Matthew Waite not suffered a shoulder injury shortly before the opening Bob Willis Trophy fixture at Chester-le-Street. Thompson

AZEEM RAFIQ ACCUSES YORKSHIRE OF RACISM

"I lost faith in humanity"

Aug 17 Azeem Rafiq, a 29-year-old former England Under-19 captain and Yorkshire all-rounder, alleges he was the victim of racial abuse during his career at the club, which ran from 2008 to 2018. Speaking to wisden.com, he says: "There's one comment that stands out for me… It was around the time of my debut. There was me, Adil Rashid, Ajmal Shahzad and Rana Naved-ul-Hasan. We're walking on to the field, and one player said: 'There's too many of you lot. We need to have a word about that.' You can imagine the sort of thing that leaves on you, and you hear these things all day, every day." Yorkshire decline to comment.

Aug 24 In an interview with the Cricket Badger podcast, Rafiq says he spoke up about racism in the Yorkshire dressing-room, "and my life was made hell after that… Do I think there is institutional racism? It's at its peak, in my opinion."

Sep 2 Rafiq tells ESPNcricinfo that his experience left him considering suicide, and he "lost faith in humanity" following his release by the club in 2018, not long after the stillbirth of his son. "I took my son straight from the hospital to the funeral… Yorkshire told me they would look after me professionally and personally. But all I heard after that was a short email… The way it was done was horrible."

Sep 3 Yorkshire promise a full independent inquiry into Rafiq's comments and their own "policies and culture". Chairman Roger Hutton says: "Any allegation of this nature is hugely concerning to everyone, from the board to the playing staff here, and we take the reports very seriously."

The chairman of the Yorkshire South Premier League, Roger Pugh, uses a blog to describe Rafiq as "discourteous and disrespectful". He adds: "I am not a religious man, but a biblical quote seems to me apt here. It is, 'as ye sow, so shall ye reap'." Pugh later deletes the post.

Sep 5 Yorkshire appoint law firm Squire Patton Boggs to lead the inquiry.

Sep 9 The club appoint an inquiry subcommittee, chaired by Dr Samir Pathak, a trustee of the MCC Foundation. Also on it are Gulfraz Riaz, chairman of the National Asian Cricket Council, Stephen Wills, chief financial officer of Durham University, and Hanif Malik, an independent director at Yorkshire. Malik later pulls out; Rafiq claims he had previously outlined his grievances to him, but no action was taken.

In an open letter to the club on change.org, British Asians Against Racism express their concern over the handling of the case.

Sep 27 Pugh resigns "with immediate effect" as chairman of the Yorkshire South Premier League, but makes no reference to his blog.

Oct 1 Rafiq calls for witness anonymity in the inquiry, after former team-mates call him to apologise.

Oct 2 Yorkshire say there "must be no repercussions" for any witness. Two more are added to the subcommittee: Rehana Azib, a barrister, and Helen Hyde, former personnel director at Waitrose.

Oct 23 Gulfraz Riaz steps down from the subcommittee after it emerges he is due to provide a witness statement. He is replaced by NACC vice-chair Mesba Ahmed.

Nov 13 Speaking on video link to the inquiry, Rafiq says he was "bullied and targeted because of my race". He says Asian players at Yorkshire were referred to as "Pakis" and "elephant washers", and told to "go back to where you came from".

Nov 25 Yorkshire say they will appoint a head of diversity, equality and inclusion, and admit "there is much more we can do".

Dec 4 Taj Butt, a former community development officer at the Yorkshire Cricket Foundation, tells the inquiry there were "continuous references to taxi drivers and restaurant workers when referring to [the] Asian community. They called every person of colour 'Steve'. Even Cheteshwar Pujara, who joined as an overseas professional, was called Steve, because they could not pronounce his name."

Dec 15 Rafiq files a separate legal claim against Yorkshire, citing "direct discrimination and harassment on the grounds of race", and "victimisation and detriment as a result of his efforts to address racism at the club". Yorkshire decline to comment while the independent investigation is ongoing. The date for his employment tribunal hearing is later set for February 18.

grabbed his chance, scoring 234 runs at 46 in five first-class matches as a powerful lower-middle-order left-hander, while his bustling right-arm seamers made him the team's leading first-class wicket-taker, with 15; he also contributed in the field. His best performance with the bat was a first-innings 98 against Nottinghamshire, a game Yorkshire won by 90 runs defending 188; with the ball, five for 31 to wrap up Leicestershire's second innings, and ensure a third victory.

Alex Pantling, Getty Images

Jordan Thompson

A marquee signing from Middlesex, Dawid Malan headed the run-charts with 332 in three matches, including a superb 219 against Derbyshire. His performances went some way to filling the void left by the absence of the prolific Gary Ballance, who missed the entire season through illness and anxiety heightened by the Covid-19 lockdown.

Despite heading the North Group by 13 points, Yorkshire were kept out of the Bob Willis Trophy final by Somerset and Essex, who scored more points in winning their groups. The failure was largely down to losing 460 overs to weather in their three home games: they drew with Derbyshire and Lancashire, before that last-round victory over Leicestershire. But being unbeaten across the five matches gave an emerging squad confidence they could mount a strong challenge when the Championship returned in 2021. For that campaign, Yorkshire signed Test off-spinner Dom Bess from Somerset on a four-year contract. Young seamers Jared Warner and Ed Barnes departed for Gloucestershire and Leicestershire respectively, and slow left-armer James Logan was released.

Yorkshire were one of 16 counties who put their players on furlough during the first half of the summer; they also cancelled overseas contracts for Keshav Maharaj, Ravichandran Ashwin and Nicholas Pooran. The coaching staff were furloughed, too, with only director of cricket Martyn Moxon and operations manager Cecilia Allen remaining in post, along with four groundstaff and some senior officials.

Fast bowler Fisher used the time to undertake several online courses with the Open University: he studied accounting, nutrition, and athlete recovery and psychology. Moxon and chief executive Mark Arthur made phone calls to chat to elderly members isolated through lockdown. Gale signed up as a volunteer for the NHS, but his services were not required. Or, as he put it: "I didn't make the eleven."

YORKSHIRE RESULTS

Bob Willis Trophy matches – Played 5: Won 3, Drawn 2.
Vitality Blast matches – Played 8: Won 3, Lost 5. Abandoned 2.

Bob Willis Trophy, 1st in North Group;
Vitality Blast, 5th in North Group.

BOB WILLIS TROPHY AVERAGES

BATTING AND FIELDING

Cap		*Birthplace*	*M*	*I*	*NO*	*R*	*HS*	*100*	*Avge*	*Ct*
	†D. J. Malan	*Roehampton*	3	5	0	332	219	1	66.40	2
	†J. A. Thompson	*Leeds‡*	5	6	1	234	98	0	46.80	2
	J. A. Tattersall	*Harrogate‡*	5	7	1	265	71	0	44.16	9
	H. C. Brook	*Keighley‡*	5	7	1	258	66*	0	43.00	4
2011	J. M. Bairstow§	*Bradford‡*	2	3	0	102	75	0	34.00	5
2010	†A. Lyth	*Whitby‡*	5	8	1	220	103	1	31.42	5
2019	T. Köhler-Cadmore	*Chatham*	5	8	1	127	41	0	18.14	2
	D. Olivier††	*Groblersdal, SA*	4	4	1	33	20*	0	11.00	3
	W. A. R. Fraine	*Huddersfield‡*	3	4	0	32	14	0	8.00	1
	J. W. Shutt	*Barnsley‡*	3	4	3	7	7*	0	7.00	2
2012	S. A. Patterson	*Beverley‡*	4	4	0	23	11	0	5.75	0

Also batted: B. O. Coad (*Harrogate‡*) (cap 2018) (2 matches) 28, 4 (1 ct); M. D. Fisher (*York‡*) (2 matches) 1, 1 (2 ct); G. C. H. Hill (*Keighley‡*) (2 matches) 4*, 29; D. J. Leech (*Middlesbrough‡*) (2 matches) 0*, 1; T. W. Loten (*York‡*) (2 matches) 0, 11; J. D. Warner (*Wakefield‡*) (1 match) 4.

‡ *Born in Yorkshire.* § *ECB contract.* †† *Other non-England-qualified.*

BOWLING

	Style	*O*	*M*	*R*	*W*	*BB*	*5I*	*Avge*
B. O. Coad	RFM	69	28	87	12	5-18	1	7.25
J. A. Thompson	RFM	104	25	246	15	5-31	1	16.40
S. A. Patterson	RFM	106.3	37	197	11	3-27	0	17.90
M. D. Fisher	RFM	67	22	180	10	4-54	0	18.00
D. J. Leech	RFM	34	5	134	4	2-72	0	33.50
D. Olivier	RFM	91	18	364	10	3-29	0	36.40

Also bowled: H. C. Brook (RM) 14.1–1–49–0; G. C. H. Hill (RFM) 25–8–54–1; A. Lyth (OB) 23–3–75–2; D. J. Malan (LB) 6–1–24–2; J. W. Shutt (OB) 19.2–0–104–2; J. D. Warner (RFM) 9–0–23–1.

LEADING VITALITY BLAST AVERAGES (60 runs/12 overs)

Batting	*Runs*	*HS*	*Avge*	*SR*	*Ct*
W. A. R. Fraine	163	44*	27.16	**187.35**	4
A. Lyth	308	71	38.50	**157.94**	4
J. A. Thompson	89	44	14.83	**148.33**	4
H. C. Brook	189	50*	27.00	**145.38**	7
J. E. Root	278	65	69.50	**144.79**	2
T. Köhler-Cadmore	110	85*	36.66	**137.50**	3
J. A. Tattersall	63	22*	31.50	**114.54**	6

Bowling	*W*	*BB*	*Avge*	*ER*
A. Lyth	3	2-28	41.66	**6.57**
J. E. Root	7	2-7	16.00	**6.58**
M. D. Fisher	8	3-21	15.25	**8.13**
B. O. Coad	6	3-40	21.50	**8.60**
J. E. Poysden	5	3-32	22.80	**8.76**
J. W. Shutt	2	1-24	53.50	**8.91**
J. A. Thompson	8	2-25	25.50	**9.27**

FIRST-CLASS COUNTY RECORDS

Highest score for	341	G. H. Hirst v Leicestershire at Leicester	1905
Highest score against	318*	W. G. Grace (Gloucestershire) at Cheltenham	1876
Leading run-scorer	38,558	H. Sutcliffe (avge 50.20)	1919–45
Best bowling for	10-10	H. Verity v Nottinghamshire at Leeds	1932
Best bowling against	10-37	C. V. Grimmett (Australians) at Sheffield	1930
Leading wicket-taker	3,597	W. Rhodes (avge 16.02)	1898–1930
Highest total for	887	v Warwickshire at Birmingham	1896
Highest total against	681-7 dec	by Leicestershire at Bradford	1996
Lowest total for	23	v Hampshire at Middlesbrough	1965
Lowest total against	13	by Nottinghamshire at Nottingham	1901

LIST A COUNTY RECORDS

Highest score for	191	D. S. Lehmann v Nottinghamshire at Scarborough	2001
Highest score against	177	S. A. Newman (Surrey) at The Oval	2009
Leading run-scorer	8,699	G. Boycott (avge 40.08)	1963–86
Best bowling for	7-15	R. A. Hutton v Worcestershire at Leeds	1969
Best bowling against	7-32	R. G. D. Willis (Warwickshire) at Birmingham	1981
Leading wicket-taker	308	C. M. Old (avge 18.96)	1967–82
Highest total for	411-6	v Devon at Exmouth	2004
Highest total against	375-4	by Surrey at Scarborough	1994
Lowest total for	54	v Essex at Leeds	2003
Lowest total against	23	by Middlesex at Leeds	1974

TWENTY20 COUNTY RECORDS

Highest score for	161	A. Lyth v Northamptonshire at Leeds	2017
Highest score against	111	D. L. Maddy (Leicestershire) at Leeds	2004
Leading run-scorer	**2,927**	**A. Lyth (avge 27.35, SR 144.61)**	**2008–20**
Best bowling for	6-19	T. T. Bresnan v Lancashire at Leeds	2017
Best bowling against	**5-43**	**L. J. Fletcher (Nottinghamshire) at Nottingham**	**2020**
Leading wicket-taker	118	T. T. Bresnan (avge 24.72, ER 8.09)	2003–19
Highest total for	260-4	v Northamptonshire at Leeds	2017
Highest total against	231-4	by Lancashire at Manchester	2015
Lowest total for	90-9	v Durham at Chester-le-Street	2009
Lowest total against	90	by Glamorgan at Cardiff	2016

ADDRESS

Emerald Headingley, Leeds LS6 3DP; 0344 504 3099; cricket@yorkshireccc.com; www.yorkshireccc.com. Twitter: @YorkshireCCC.

OFFICIALS

Captain S. A. Patterson
(Twenty20) D. J. Willey
Director of cricket M. D. Moxon
First-team coach A. W. Gale
2nd XI coach/Academy director I. M. Dews

President G. A. Cope
Chairman C. N. R. Hutton
Chief executive M. A. Arthur
Head groundsman A. Fogarty
Scorer J. T. Potter

At Chester-le-Street, August 1–4. YORKSHIRE beat DURHAM by six wickets.

At Nottingham, August 8–11. YORKSHIRE beat NOTTINGHAMSHIRE by 90 runs.

YORKSHIRE v DERBYSHIRE

At Leeds, August 15–18. Drawn. Yorkshire 15pts, Derbyshire 13pts. Toss: Derbyshire. First-class debut: G. C. H. Hill.

Under slate-grey skies, Malan lit up his home debut for Yorkshire with a sparkling 219 in 244 balls. But rain and bad light severely restricted the match between the North Group's top two. Coming in on the first morning, Malan drove handsomely in challenging conditions; he moved from 145 to 153 during the second day's only over, and reached a maiden double-century on the third (he had scored 199, also against Derbyshire, for Middlesex in 2019). He added 200 with Tattersall, a fifth-wicket record between these counties, and was caught at long-off trying to hit du Plooy for a third successive six to bring up 400 and maximum batting points. George Hill, Yorkshire's third first-class debutant in three games, achieved the goal a few minutes later. Patterson immediately declared, and produced a miserly spell of 16–8–16–3 that evening as Derbyshire slipped to 174 for six, still 27 short of saving the follow-on. Critchley and Dal calmly averted danger, taking their stand to 104 after the final morning was lost. Derbyshire declared at 300 for seven, to deny Yorkshire a third bowling point, but their lead had narrowed to two.

Close of play: first day, Yorkshire 280-4 (Malan 145, Tattersall 64); second day, Yorkshire 288-4 (Malan 153, Tattersall 64); third day, Derbyshire 198-6 (Critchley 31, Dal 15).

Yorkshire

A. Lyth c Hosein b Cohen	31
T. Köhler-Cadmore c Critchley b Aitchison	0
†J. M. Bairstow c Hosein b Dal	22
D. J. Malan c Aitchison b du Plooy	219
H. C. Brook c Madsen b Cohen	0
J. A. Tattersall c Dal b Critchley	66
J. A. Thompson not out	36
G. C. H. Hill not out	4
B 8, lb 7, w 5, nb 2	22
1/2 (2) 2/40 (3) 3/106 (1) 4/106 (5) 5/306 (6) 6/395 (4) (6 wkts dec, 101.1 overs)	400

*S. A. Patterson, D. Olivier and D. J. Leech did not bat.

Cohen 22–4–93–2; Aitchison 17–7–43–1; Melton 19–2–80–0; Dal 15–2–38–1; Hughes 10–1–28–0; Critchley 15.1–1–74–1; du Plooy 2–0–25–1; Madsen 1–0–4–0.

Derbyshire

T. A. Wood c and b Thompson	26
*B. A. Godleman c Bairstow b Patterson	54
W. L. Madsen lbw b Patterson	0
J. L. du Plooy c Köhler-Cadmore b Patterson	30
M. J. J. Critchley b Leech	63
A. L. Hughes c Olivier b Leech	13
†H. R. Hosein c Bairstow b Olivier	7
A. K. Dal not out	78
M. A. R. Cohen not out	6
B 4, lb 7, w 6, nb 6	23
1/58 (1) 2/58 (3) 3/126 (4) 4/127 (2) 5/152 (6) 6/174 (7) 7/278 (5) (7 wkts dec, 107.1 overs)	300

B. W. Aitchison and D. R. Melton did not bat.

Olivier 25–8–83–1; Leech 20–2–72–2; Thompson 18–3–45–1; Patterson 22–9–27–3; Hill 13–4–27–0; Lyth 3–1–8–0; Brook 6.1–0–27–0.

Umpires: P. J. Hartley and J. D. Middlebrook. Referee: S. Cummings.

YORKSHIRE v LANCASHIRE

At Leeds, August 22–25. Drawn. Yorkshire 11pts, Lancashire 11pts. Toss: Yorkshire. First-class debut: G. D. Burrows.

Yorkshire opener Lyth ended a wait of nearly two years since his last hundred in any format, and Lancashire's bustling seamer Lamb claimed a career-best four for 55. But there was little else to celebrate in this rainy stalemate. Only 13 balls were bowled on the first day, much of the second afternoon was washed out, and the match was abandoned on the final morning. The third day, however, was sunny and uninterrupted, giving Lyth, who was particularly strong to leg, the chance to move from his overnight 86 to 103. Yorkshire were all out for 260 shortly before lunch, and afterwards Davies scored a fluent 73; Lancashire closed on 195 for five. The draw ended their hopes of a Lord's final, though Yorkshire's remained alive. Ten players (six for the home side, four for the visitors) were playing their first first-class Roses match – only the second time since 1867 there had been so many newcomers in this fixture.

Close of play: first day, Yorkshire 8-0 (Lyth 0, Köhler-Cadmore 4); second day, Yorkshire 178-6 (Lyth 86, Hill 9); third day, Lancashire 195-5 (Croft 9, Balderson 7).

Yorkshire

A. Lyth c Jennings b Bailey 103
T. Köhler-Cadmore c Jennings b Bailey . . . 18
W. A. R. Fraine c Davies b Lamb 5
T. W. Loten lbw b Lamb 0
H. C. Brook c Bohannon b Burrows 6
†J. A. Tattersall c Croft b Jennings 25
J. A. Thompson b Burrows 4
G. C. H. Hill b Lamb 29
*S. A. Patterson c Jennings b Lamb 8
D. Olivier not out 20
J. D. Warner lbw b Balderson 4
B 5, lb 27, w 2, nb 4 38

1/53 (2) 2/61 (3) 3/61 (4) (93 overs) 260
4/78 (5) 5/139 (6) 6/164 (7)
7/219 (1) 8/221 (8) 9/234 (9) 10/260 (11)

Bailey 26–13–40–2; Burrows 21–3–89–2; Balderson 15–7–30–1; Lamb 23–6–55–4; Jennings 8–2–14–1.

Lancashire

K. K. Jennings lbw b Lyth 23
†A. L. Davies lbw b Patterson 73
J. J. Bohannon c Tattersall b Warner 5
R. P. Jones c Tattersall b Hill 21
*D. J. Vilas lbw b Olivier 41
S. J. Croft not out 9
G. P. Balderson not out 7
Lb 7, w 1, nb 8 16

1/104 (1) 2/112 (3) (5 wkts, 69 overs) 195
3/112 (2) 4/177 (5)
5/177 (4)

D. J. Lamb, T. E. Bailey, T. W. Hartley and G. D. Burrows did not bat.

Patterson 19–9–23–1; Olivier 13–0–65–1; Warner 9–0–23–1; Thompson 10–1–38–0; Hill 12–4–27–1; Lyth 6–1–12–1.

Umpires: P. J. Hartley and J. D. Middlebrook. Referee: T. J. Boon.

YORKSHIRE v LEICESTERSHIRE

At Leeds, September 6–9. Yorkshire won by ten wickets. Yorkshire 21pts, Leicestershire 3pts. Toss: Yorkshire. County debut: R. K. Patel.

A third victory meant Yorkshire topped the North Group, but did not reach the Lord's final, since they had fewer points than the other group leaders, Essex and Somerset. The loss of 460 overs across three home games cost them dear. Their objective here was a maximum 24 points (as it turned out, that would have put them level with Essex, though they would have lost the tie-breaker, as Essex had four wins). Part one went smoothly: led by the skilful Coad, they routed Leicestershire for 124. In his first game since tearing a muscle in the opening round, he claimed five for 18, including his 150th first-class wicket in 38 matches. Despite a second-day washout, part two – full batting points – was still on at 237 for five. Then disaster struck: Mike and off-spinner Lilley extracted Yorkshire's last five in 29 balls before tea. They scraped just two batting points. Leicestershire slumped to 78 for five, still 50 behind, by the close. Ackermann's determined 47 avoided an innings defeat, though Thompson collected a maiden five-wicket haul, and Coad eight for 41 in the match. Yorkshire's openers strolled past a target of 34.

Close of play: first day, Yorkshire 36-2 (Fraine 11, Loten 7); second day, no play; third day, Leicestershire 78-5 (Ackermann 23, Lilley 10).

Leicestershire

M. H. Azad lbw b Fisher	0	– (2) c Tattersall b Thompson	11
S. T. Evans lbw b Coad	7	– (1) lbw b Coad	4
H. E. Dearden c and b Olivier	20	– c Tattersall b Thompson	18
*C. N. Ackermann lbw b Fisher	1	– b Thompson	47
R. K. Patel c Lyth b Coad	19	– c Shutt b Thompson	5
†H. J. Swindells c Tattersall b Coad	36	– c Tattersall b Fisher	0
A. M. Lilley lbw b Coad	5	– c Fraine b Coad	13
B. W. M. Mike c Brook b Fisher	17	– lbw b Coad	1
D. Klein c Brook b Olivier	5	– c Thompson b Olivier	27
G. T. Griffiths not out	4	– not out	11
H. A. Evans c Lyth b Coad	0	– b Thompson	15
B 2, lb 6, nb 2	10	B 1, lb 2, nb 6	9
1/7 (1) 2/11 (2) 3/12 (4) 4/36 (3) 5/59 (5) 6/65 (7) 7/98 (8) 8/115 (9) 9/124 (6) 10/124 (11) (48.2 overs)	124	1/4 (1) 2/34 (2) 3/35 (3) 4/47 (5) 5/53 (6) 6/84 (7) 7/92 (8) 8/135 (9) 9/139 (4) 10/161 (11) (51 overs)	161

Coad 13.2–6–18–5; Fisher 12–4–29–3; Thompson 12–5–20–0; Olivier 11–0–49–2. *Second innings*—Coad 14–4–23–3; Fisher 13–4–54–1; Thompson 11–2–31–5; Olivier 13–2–50–1.

Yorkshire

*A. Lyth c Swindells b Klein	4	– not out	14
T. Köhler-Cadmore c S. T. Evans b H. A. Evans	0	– not out	23
W. A. R. Fraine c Mike b Klein	13		
T. W. Loten c Swindells b Klein	11		
H. C. Brook c Ackermann b H. A. Evans	53		
†J. A. Tattersall b Mike	71		
J. A. Thompson lbw b Lilley	62		
M. D. Fisher c and b Lilley	1		
B. O. Coad c S. T. Evans b Mike	4		
D. Olivier c Ackermann b Lilley	0		
J. W. Shutt not out	0		
B 2, lb 18, w 9, nb 4	33		
1/4 (2) 2/4 (1) 3/38 (3) 4/46 (4) 5/121 (5) 6/237 (6) 7/239 (8) 8/250 (7) 9/250 (10) 10/252 (9) (69 overs)	252	(no wkt, 6.2 overs)	37

Klein 15–3–44–3; H. A. Evans 18–5–59–2; Griffiths 15–3–53–0; Mike 15–2–55–2; Lilley 6–1–21–3. *Second innings*—Klein 3–1–17–0; Griffiths 3–0–12–0; H. A. Evans 0.2–0–8–0.

Umpires: P. J. Hartley and J. D. Middlebrook. Referee: J. J. Whitaker.

VITALITY BLAST IN 2020

MATT ROLLER

1 Nottinghamshire 2 Surrey 3= Gloucestershire, Lancashire

The T20 Blast, which was supposed to play second fiddle in the summer of 2020, took on a crucial role – and all it needed was a pandemic. The tournament had been due to start in late May, with a Hundred-sized gap between the group stage and the knockouts. But once The Hundred was postponed for a year, the Blast simply had to be protected.

The ECB's plan was to push the dates back as far as possible, in the hope that the virus would have been contained sufficiently by autumn for supporters and members to attend. In fact, the total attendance was just 2,500, since the government hastily scrapped their pilot scheme to allow fans into grounds, following a trial at Surrey's home game against Hampshire. That meant the knockout stage – which saw county cricket in October for the first time since 1864 – remained behind closed doors.

Finals day therefore provided an odd spectacle, not least because of a 24-hour delay thanks to the wettest recorded day in the country's history. With the threat of bowl-outs looming, the four counties involved practised hitting the stumps, but were relieved when the weather relented (the ECB had hastily added a second reserve day to avoid a farcical finale).

As in the Bob Willis Trophy, the Blast's pared-down format – three groups of six for the first time since 2013 – worked well, with the best two teams, Nottinghamshire and Surrey, reaching the final. Nottinghamshire took their

Jordan Mansfield, Getty Images

Crowded out: Surrey host Hampshire in front of 2,500 socially distanced spectators, the only ones to be let in to a competitive match all summer.

second T20 crown in four years, losing only one of their 11 completed matches. Their two blips had come against unfancied Leicestershire, first in a group-stage defeat at Grace Road, then in a dramatic tied quarter-final. After convincing wins for Surrey, Gloucestershire and Lancashire earlier in the day, the game was following a similar pattern when Leicestershire limped to 22 for three. But they recovered to a competitive 139 for seven, before pegging Nottinghamshire back with regular wickets. However, a couple of misfields – not helped by a soaking-wet ball – allowed Samit Patel and Imad Wasim to level the scores. Having lost the same number of wickets, Nottinghamshire progressed by virtue of a higher powerplay total. A super over was available in the knockouts only if the match was weather-affected and DLS had been brought into play.

Dan Christian became the third player in a row – following Ben Cox and Simon Harmer – to lift the trophy after winning the match award twice on finals day. In the 11-over semi against Lancashire, Christian struck four sixes in four balls off Liam Livingstone – all into an eerily empty Eric Hollies Stand – to "knock the game on its head", as he put it. In the final, he took four for 11 in two late overs, before watching from the non-striker's end as Ben Duckett pulled the winning runs. They became the third and fourth players to win the competition three times.

Nottinghamshire were the Blast's most experienced side, and fulfilled Christian's pre-season prediction that "old blokes win stuff", thanks to a long batting line-up, which often featured Imad – sometimes No. 6 for Pakistan – at No. 9. That allowed the youth wing to attack at will, with Duckett and Joe Clarke enjoying excellent seasons in the middle order. In Jake Ball, Nottinghamshire also had the leading wicket-taker; an indication of their bench strength was that he might not have played had Harry Gurney been fit. They were the only side to employ two overseas players – there were nine across the competition in total – and their decision was vindicated by coach Peter Moores's third white-ball trophy in four summers.

Surrey enjoyed their best season since winning the inaugural competition in 2003, recording nine successive victories, before falling at the last. At first, they struggled to get 11 men on the field, because of injuries and international calls, but the arrival of Laurie Evans and Jamie Overton (both on loan ahead of permanent moves), and the return of their England players, meant they had enough depth to leave Hashim Amla out of the semi-final. In Will Jacks, Surrey had the tournament's MVP: he contributed quickfire runs and vital wickets, bowling his brisk off-breaks in the powerplay.

Gloucestershire rued a frenetic batting effort in a shortened semi-final after dominating the Central Group, with Ian Cockbain's runs complemented by David Payne's new-ball swing and the left-arm spin of Tom Smith and Graeme van Buuren. Lancashire, the other beaten semi-finalists, never quite clicked, though their spin-heavy attack blew Sussex away in the quarters.

Five of the last eight had been known before the final round of group games. Sussex – their destiny in their own hands – qualified with a win at Chelmsford, while on a remarkable afternoon Northamptonshire and Leicestershire squeezed through from the Central Group at the expense of Somerset and Warwickshire.

Alex Davidson, Getty Images

Jacks of all trades: off-spin at quite a lick – the second string to his bow – brought Will Jacks of Surrey ten wickets at less than 6.5 an over.

Northamptonshire had a bizarre season, with a no-result and four wins from their first five games, before a positive Covid-19 test for Ben Curran sent two first-choice players into self-isolation; their next four matches were lost. Much of their last group game, at Edgbaston, reflected the story of their campaign: they reduced Warwickshire to 20 for four, watched Adam Hose's maiden hundred help the hosts recover to 191 for five, then slumped to 71 for six in reply. But Tom Taylor, making his debut after a mid-season move from Leicestershire, hit an unbeaten 50 from 27 balls, and No. 9 Graeme White blasted 37 off 12 to complete a miraculous win. When, moments later, Gloucestershire beat Somerset with a last-ball four at Bristol, Northamptonshire were through. That result might have taken Warwickshire through, too, only for Leicestershire's Colin Ackermann to rescue an improbable predicament in Manchester, and earn his side qualification as one of the best third-placed teams.

Other sides also suffered a Covid crisis: Hampshire were depleted by self-isolation for a dead rubber, and Yorkshire lost Matt Fisher, Tom Köhler-Cadmore, Josh Poysden and David Willey for their last four games, after Willey and his wife tested positive. And so, at the end of a competition in which Joe Root, desperate to prove his short-form credentials, had upstaged his England rival Dawid Malan, the ICC's new No. 1-ranked T20 batsman, Yorkshire were forced to field Academy players.

Spinners were more influential than ever, accounting for more than two-fifths of the overs, and proved particularly successful in the powerplay. With no fans to entertain, counties were happy to push the boundary ropes all the way back, and prepare slower surfaces, and scoring-rates fell slightly: 8.25 per over, compared with 8.34 in 2019.

An underlying theme was the success of players who had missed out in the Hundred draft, with Ball, Cockbain, Kent's Daniel Bell-Drummond and Stevie Eskinazi of Middlesex all citing it as motivation. The Blast still looked set to retreat into the shadows in 2021 when The Hundred finally launches – but this season proved a reminder of its worth.

FINAL GROUP TABLES

	Central Group	*P*	*W*	*L*	*T*	*NR*	*Pts*	*NRR*
1	GLOUCESTERSHIRE	10	7	2	0	1	15	1.01
2	NORTHAMPTONSHIRE	10	5	4	0	1	11	0.05
3	Warwickshire	10	5	4	0	1	11	–0.63
4	Somerset	10	4	5	0	1	9	0.65
5	Glamorgan	10	4	5	0	1	9	–0.30
6	Worcestershire	10	2	7	0	1	5	–0.78

	North Group	*P*	*W*	*L*	*T*	*NR*	*Pts*	*NRR*
1	NOTTINGHAMSHIRE	10	7	1	0	2	16	1.31
2	LANCASHIRE	10	5	3	0	2	12	–0.25
3	LEICESTERSHIRE	10	4	3	0	3	11	–0.18
4	Durham	10	4	5	0	1	9	0.42
5	Yorkshire	10	3	5	0	2	8	0.29
6	Derbyshire	10	1	7	0	2	4	–1.58

	South Group	*P*	*W*	*L*	*T*	*NR*	*Pts*	*NRR*
1	SURREY	10	7	1	1	1	16	0.65
2	SUSSEX	10	6	3	0	1	13	0.37
3	KENT	10	5	3	1	1	12	0.10
4	Middlesex	10	3	5	1	1	8	–0.29
5	Essex	10	2	6	1	1	6	0.00
6	Hampshire	10	2	7	0	1	5	–0.80

Where counties finished tied on points, positions were decided by (a) most wins, (b) net run-rate.

Prize money

£250,000 for winners: NOTTINGHAMSHIRE.
£110,000 for runners-up: SURREY.
£30,000 for losing semi-finalists: GLOUCESTERSHIRE and LANCASHIRE.
£7,500 for losing quarter-finalists: KENT, LEICESTERSHIRE, NORTHAMPTONSHIRE, SUSSEX.
Match-award winners received: £2,500 in the final, £1,000 in the semi-finals, £500 in the quarters, and £225 in group games. The Most Valuable Player (Will Jacks of Surrey) received £2,500.

VITALITY BLAST AVERAGES

BATTING (220 runs)

		M	*I*	*NO*	*R*	*HS*	*100*	*50*	*Avge*	*SR*	*4*	*6*
1	J. M. Clarke (*Notts*)	11	11	1	371	100*	1	2	37.10	**175.00**	35	22
2	G. Clark (*Durham*)	10	9	0	261	68	0	2	29.00	**171.71**	29	10
3	I. A. Cockbain (*Glos*)	11	11	2	399	89	0	3	44.33	**169.78**	31	22
4	†H. D. Rutherford (*Worcs*)	9	9	0	352	100	1	1	39.11	**160.00**	33	19
5	†A. Lyth (*Yorks*)	8	8	0	308	71	0	3	38.50	**157.94**	31	12
6	Z. Crawley (*Kent*)	11	11	2	342	108*	1	1	38.00	**156.88**	43	7
7	D. J. Bell-Drummond (*Kent*)	11	11	1	423	89	0	3	42.30	**154.94**	53	12
8	A. J. Hose (*Warwicks*)	9	9	0	268	119	1	0	29.77	**154.02**	27	13
9	†C. D. J. Dent (*Glos*)	11	11	0	371	87	0	4	33.72	**153.30**	48	9

		M	I	NO	R	HS	100	50	Avge	SR	4	6
10	L. J. Evans (*Surrey*)	11	11	3	363	88*	0	3	45.37	**153.16**	28	15
11	P. R. Stirling (*Northants*) .	10	10	1	232	80*	0	1	25.77	**152.63**	26	11
12	W. G. Jacks (*Surrey*)	13	12	3	309	65	0	3	34.33	**149.27**	33	9
13	S. S. Eskinazi (*Middx*) . . .	10	10	0	413	84	0	4	41.30	**148.02**	31	17
14	D. Wiese (*Sussex*).	10	9	2	281	79*	0	1	40.14	**145.59**	20	13
15	A. Balbirnie (*Glam*)	9	9	2	255	99*	0	2	36.42	**144.88**	25	7
16	J. E. Root (*Yorks*)	5	5	1	278	65	0	4	69.50	**144.79**	32	4
17	S. R. Hain (*Warwicks*) . . .	9	9	4	284	73*	0	3	56.80	**139.21**	25	10
18	A. M. Lilley (*Leics*)	9	9	0	278	69	0	1	30.88	**139.00**	19	14
19	†B. M. Duckett (*Notts*)	11	11	3	340	86*	0	4	42.50	**137.65**	41	4
20	R. N. ten Doeschate (*Essex*)	9	8	3	255	52	0	1	51.00	**137.09**	15	9
21	J. D. Libby (*Worcs*)	9	9	1	318	75*	0	2	39.75	**137.06**	30	5
22	L. J. Wright (*Sussex*)	11	11	0	411	83	0	2	37.36	**137.00**	53	7
23	T. B. Abell (*Somerset*) . . .	9	9	2	227	74*	0	2	32.42	**136.74**	23	3
24	†M. D. E. Holden (*Middx*) .	9	9	1	220	102*	1	0	27.50	**134.96**	19	8
25	†K. K. Jennings (*Lancs*) . . .	7	6	2	233	108	1	0	58.25	**134.68**	22	3
26	†C. S. Delport (*Essex*)	10	10	1	222	64	0	1	24.66	**133.73**	28	8
27	†J. A. Simpson (*Middx*) . . .	10	10	2	288	48	0	0	36.00	**132.71**	13	14
28	S. J. Croft (*Lancs*).	10	9	0	272	58	0	1	30.22	**125.92**	12	16
29	†A. Z. Lees (*Durham*)	10	9	2	365	77*	0	4	52.14	**125.86**	32	6
30	H. M. Amla (*Surrey*)	8	8	1	271	75	0	3	38.71	**124.88**	27	5
31	C. B. Cooke (*Glam*)	9	9	2	221	72	0	2	31.57	**123.46**	12	9
32	C. N. Ackermann (*Leics*) .	9	9	1	246	67*	0	2	30.75	**122.38**	17	8
33	A. L. Davies (*Lancs*)	11	10	0	299	82	0	3	29.90	**121.54**	32	6

BOWLING (10 wickets, economy-rate 8.50)

		Style	Balls	Dots	R	W	BB	4I	Avge	SR	ER
1	T. M. J. Smith (*Glos*)	SLA	246	84	243	14	5-16	1	17.35	17.57	**5.92**
2	J. B. Lintott (*Warwicks*) . .	SLW	180	68	189	10	3-11	0	18.90	18.00	**6.30**
3	P. Sisodiya (*Glam*)	SLA	216	88	232	10	3-26	0	23.20	21.60	**6.44**
4	G. J. Batty (*Surrey*).	OB	182	61	196	10	3-18	0	19.60	18.20	**6.46**
5	W. G. Jacks (*Surrey*).	OB	194	73	209	13	4-15	1	16.07	14.92	**6.46**
6	D. R. Briggs (*Sussex*)	SLA	228	80	249	12	3-17	0	20.75	19.00	**6.55**
7	C. F. Parkinson (*Leics*) . . .	SLA	192	82	210	10	3-21	0	21.00	19.20	**6.56**
8	G. L. van Buuren (*Glos*) . .	SLA	198	63	224	12	3-15	0	18.66	16.50	**6.78**
9	D. T. Moriarty (*Surrey*). . .	SLA	270	92	311	17	3-25	0	18.29	15.88	**6.91**
10	T. E. Bailey (*Lancs*)	RFM	96	47	111	10	5-17	1	11.10	9.60	**6.93**
11	S. R. Harmer (*Essex*).	OB	234	83	281	10	2-21	0	28.10	23.40	**7.20**
12	N. A. Sowter (*Middx*)	LB	216	62	262	10	3-30	0	26.20	21.60	**7.27**
13	R. J. W. Topley (*Surrey*). .	LFM	240	109	291	15	4-20	1	19.40	16.00	**7.27**
14	M. J. Potts (*Durham*)	RFM	192	87	235	13	3-8	0	18.07	14.76	**7.34**
15	T. van der Gugten (*Glam*) . .	RFM	168	56	209	14	3-17	0	14.92	12.00	**7.46**
16	G. G. White (*Northants*) . .	SLA	239	74	299	12	3-28	0	24.91	19.91	**7.50**
17	S. R. Patel (*Notts*)	SLA	228	70	286	11	2-19	0	26.00	20.72	**7.52**
18	J. T. Ball (*Notts*)	RFM	205	70	259	19	3-28	0	13.63	10.78	**7.58**
19	M. W. Parkinson (*Lancs*) . .	LB	242	68	310	15	3-9	0	20.66	16.13	**7.68**
20	L. Trevaskis (*Durham*) . . .	SLA	198	72	254	10	2-17	0	25.40	19.80	**7.69**
21	G. H. S. Garton (*Sussex*) . .	LFM	180	69	231	14	4-21	2	16.50	12.85	**7.70**
22	G. T. Griffiths (*Leics*)	RFM	138	53	180	10	4-35	1	18.00	13.80	**7.82**
23	D. A. Payne (*Glos*)	LFM	227	88	299	16	3-18	0	18.68	14.18	**7.90**
24	M. R. Quinn (*Essex*)	RFM	161	56	213	10	2-24	0	21.30	16.10	**7.93**
25	T. S. Mills (*Sussex*).	LF	186	75	248	11	2-23	0	22.54	16.90	**8.00**
26	I. Qayyum (*Kent*)	SLA	246	63	329	11	3-25	0	29.90	22.36	**8.02**
27	S. T. Finn (*Middx*).	RFM	198	65	266	14	3-18	0	19.00	14.14	**8.06**
28	A. G. Salter (*Glam*).	OB	216	60	293	10	4-20	1	29.30	21.60	**8.13**
29	J. H. Davey (*Somerset*) . . .	RFM	90	39	123	11	4-41	1	11.18	8.18	**8.20**
30	B. W. Sanderson (*Nhants*) . .	RFM	191	65	267	12	3-11	0	22.25	15.91	**8.38**
31	T. G. Helm (*Middx*)	RFM	194	80	273	12	2-12	0	22.75	16.16	**8.44**

LEADING WICKETKEEPERS

Dismissals	*M*	
12 (6ct, 6st)	9	A. L. Davies (*Lancs*)
9 (6ct, 3st)	9	C. B. Cooke (*Glam*)
9 (5ct, 4st)	12	B. T. Foakes (*Surrey*)
8 (6ct, 2st)	7	J. A. Tattersall (*Yorks*)
6 (4ct, 2st)	6	J. M. Cox (*Kent*)
6 (5ct, 1st)	7	D. G. Bedingham (*Durham*)
6 (5ct, 1st)	10	J. A. Simpson (*Middx*)
6 (1ct, 5st)	11	J. R. Bracey (*Glos*)
6 (4ct, 2st)	11	T. J. Moores (*Notts*)

A. L. Davies played two further matches when not keeping wicket, but took no catches; D. G. Bedingham took two catches in three matches, and J. M. Cox one in two, when not keeping wicket.

LEADING FIELDERS

Ct	*M*	
11	11	A. D. Hales (*Notts*)
10	11	J. Overton (*Surrey*)
9	7	L. Gregory (*Somerset*)
9	10	S. R. Harmer (*Essex*)
9	11	D. J. Vilas (*Lancs*)
8	13	R. J. Burns (*Surrey*)

CENTRAL GROUP

GLAMORGAN

At Cardiff, August 27 (floodlit). **Glamorgan v Worcestershire. Abandoned.**

At Cardiff, August 30. **Warwickshire won by six wickets.** ‡**Glamorgan 140-9** (20 overs) (C. B. Cooke 72; T. T. Bresnan 3-33); **Warwickshire 141-4** (18.5 overs) (A. J. Hose 38, S. R. Hain 35*). *PoM:* C. B. Cooke. *County debut:* J. B. Lintott (Warwickshire). *As in the Bob Willis Trophy, Glamorgan captain Chris Cooke lacked support: his 72 from 56 balls was more than half the total, and of the others only Dan Douthwaite (15) managed double figures. Although Ed Pollock fell to the second ball, Warwickshire paced their reply well, with Ian Bell (28) enjoying his promotion to open. With two wanted, Sam Hain pulled Timm van der Gugten for six, but the delivery was a high full toss, so the runs did not count: the two-run penalty for the no-ball had already ended the game.*

At Cardiff, September 13. **Glamorgan won by seven wickets.** ‡**Northamptonshire 98** (17.2 overs) (P. Sisodiya 3-26, T. van der Gugten 3-17); **Glamorgan 99-3** (16 overs) (D. L. Lloyd 40). *PoM:* D. L. Lloyd. *Glamorgan ended a run of four defeats after Northamptonshire, never recovering from losing the openers in the first seven balls, failed to reach three figures. Tom Sole top-scored with 25; slow left-armer Prem Sisodiya took three wickets, as did van der Gugten. David Lloyd hit 40 from 29 as the chase became a formality.*

At Cardiff, September 16 (floodlit). **Somerset won by 66 runs. Somerset 183-3** (20 overs) (Babar Azam 114*, L. P. Goldsworthy 38*); ‡**Glamorgan 117** (15.5 overs) (C. Overton 3-36). *PoM:* Babar Azam. *County debut:* L. P. Goldsworthy (Somerset). *Babar Azam made the most of being dropped twice to plunder a 62-ball 114*, his fourth, and highest, T20 century. He put on 110* for the fourth wicket in 10.4 overs with the 18-year-old debutant Lewis Goldsworthy. Glamorgan then lost Lloyd and Cooke in the second over, from Roelof van der Merwe.*

At Cardiff, September 18 (floodlit). **Glamorgan won by 17 runs.** ‡**Glamorgan 188-4** (20 overs) (D. L. Lloyd 41, A. Balbirnie 99*); **Gloucestershire 171-6** (20 overs) (C. D. J. Dent 55, J. R. Bracey 37; G. G. Wagg 3-34). *PoM:* A. Balbirnie. *Ireland captain Andy Balbirnie came close to registering Glamorgan's first home T20 century, to go with six on English soil. But, after starting the final over on 98, he was denied the strike until the last ball, and managed only a single. His innings, which included stands of 61 with Lloyd and 79 in 28 balls with Cooke (24), set up a total which Gloucestershire threatened only while Chris Dent was making 55 from 36. Three wickets for the accurate Graham Wagg ensured a home win.*

HIGHEST T20 SCORES FOR GLAMORGAN

116*	I. J. Thomas	v Somerset at Taunton	2004
114	C. A. Ingram	v Essex at Chelmsford	2017
105	J. Allenby	v Middlesex at Richmond	2014
101*	J. A. Rudolph	v Gloucestershire at Bristol	2015
101	C. A. Ingram	v Essex at Chelmsford	2016
101*	C. A. Ingram	v Sussex at Arundel	2017
99*	**A. Balbirnie**	**v Gloucestershire at Cardiff**	**2020**
98	H. H. Gibbs	v Northamptonshire at Northampton	2008
97*	D. L. Lloyd	v Kent at Cardiff	2016
96*	J. Allenby	v Somerset at Taunton	2014
96	C. A. Ingram	v Somerset at Taunton	2015
91	C. A. Ingram	v Surrey at The Oval	2015

Glamorgan away matches

August 29: beat Gloucestershire by 15 runs.
September 1: lost to Somerset by eight wickets.
September 3: lost to Northamptonshire by four wickets.
September 11: lost to Warwickshire by 13 runs.
September 20: beat Worcestershire by six wickets.

GLOUCESTERSHIRE

At Bristol, August 27. **Gloucestershire v Northamptonshire. Abandoned.**

At Bristol, August 29. **Glamorgan won by 15 runs. Glamorgan 150-7** (20 overs) (C. B. Cooke 51*; R. F. Higgins 3-29); **‡Gloucestershire 135** (20 overs) (G. F. B. Scott 33, G. L. van Buuren 53; A. G. Salter 4-20). *PoM:* A. G. Salter. *County debut:* A. Balbirnie (Glamorgan). *Andrew Salter claimed 4-20 after opening the bowling with fellow spinner Prem Sisodiya (4–16–12–1). They reduced Gloucestershire to 49-5 after ten overs, rendering inconsequential Graeme van Buuren's 27-ball 53. Earlier, Chris Cooke had made an authoritative 51* off 35 on a slow pitch as Glamorgan recovered from 88-5; they were troubled only by Ryan Higgins's clever variations.*

At Bristol, September 4. **Gloucestershire won by 30 runs. Gloucestershire 181-4** (20 overs) (C. D. J. Dent 87, J. R. Bracey 39*; E. G. Barnard 3-44); **‡Worcestershire 151-9** (20 overs) (J. D. Libby 33; R. F. Higgins 4-34). *PoM:* C. D. J. Dent. *Chris Dent, a regular again after three seasons out of the T20 side, crafted a superb career-best 87 off 52 balls. James Bracey's 39* off 20 helped them to an above-par total, before Matt Taylor removed the Worcestershire openers, and Higgins dismantled the middle order. The visitors remained winless after five games.*

At Bristol, September 15. **Gloucestershire won by 50 runs. ‡Gloucestershire 173-6** (20 overs) (M. A. H. Hammond 49, C. D. J. Dent 39, I. A. Cockbain 44); **Warwickshire 123** (17.1 overs) (S. R. Hain 43*; G. L. van Buuren 3-33, M. D. Taylor 3-29). *PoM:* I. A. Cockbain. *After hitting 84* at Edgbaston a fortnight earlier, Ian Cockbain crashed 44 off 21 balls – including all four of his side's sixes – as Gloucestershire recorded a sixth straight win. Their progress to the quarter-finals was confirmed later in the day, when Northamptonshire lost to Worcestershire. Dent and Miles Hammond had laid the foundations with an opening stand of 88. Taylor and van Buuren took three wickets each as Warwickshire were shot out in 17 overs.*

At Bristol, September 20. **Gloucestershire won by two wickets. ‡Somerset 161-7** (20 overs) (S. M. Davies 31, Babar Azam 42, L. Gregory 50); **Gloucestershire 163-8** (20 overs) (I. A. Cockbain 89; O. R. T. Sale 3-32, J. H. Davey 3-24). *PoM:* I. A. Cockbain. *Gloucestershire eliminated arch-rivals Somerset in a thrilling finish, mainly thanks to Cockbain's brilliant 89 off 57 balls. When he fell to the penultimate delivery of the 19th over, his team still needed 15, which became four off the last ball after Ollie Sale removed Benny Howell. But Tom Smith, who had earlier been the pick of the Gloucestershire attack with 2-25, calmly found the midwicket boundary, to set up a home quarter-final against Northamptonshire, who qualified instead of Somerset. The visitors' 161-7 had relied on late hitting from captain Lewis Gregory (50 off 28).*

Gloucestershire away matches

August 31: beat Worcestershire by 22 runs.
September 2: beat Warwickshire by 57 runs.
September 11: beat Northamptonshire by 35 runs.
September 13: beat Somerset by 11 runs.
September 18: lost to Glamorgan by 17 runs.

NORTHAMPTONSHIRE

At Northampton, August 30. **Northamptonshire won by nine runs. Northamptonshire 171-6** (20 overs) (J. J. Cobb 42, A. M. Rossington 51); ‡**Somerset 162-8** (20 overs) (J. C. Hildreth 34, R. E. van der Merwe 41*; B. W. Sanderson 3-36). *PoM:* S. A. Zaib. *Adam Rossington's 51 from 31 and a late burst from Saif Zaib (28* from 13) proved too much for Somerset; a ninth-wicket stand of 46* between Roelof van der Merwe and Ollie Sale only limited the margin of defeat. Earlier, a delivery from Sale had struck Rossington on the hand, preventing him from taking the field for the reply, and leaving Ricardo Vasconcelos to assume the wicketkeeping duties; he caught Eddie Byrom and stumped Ben Green.*

At Northampton, September 1 (floodlit). **Northamptonshire won by 38 runs. Northamptonshire 158-7** (20 overs) (R. E. Levi 35, R. S. Vasconcelos 34, S. A. Zaib 30); ‡**Warwickshire 120** (19.5 overs) (H. J. H. Brookes 31*; B. W. Sanderson 3-11). *PoM:* N. L. Buck. *County debut:* V. V. Kelley (Warwickshire). *The spin of Jake Lintott and Jeetan Patel, and two stumpings for Vikai Kelley on his professional debut (and the eve of his 18th birthday), dragged back a bright start to Northamptonshire's innings, in which Richard Levi blazed four sixes in an 18-ball 35. But Warwickshire never recovered from a double-wicket maiden by Nathan Buck in the fourth over, and Ben Sanderson wrapped things up.*

At Birmingham, September 3 (floodlit). **Northamptonshire won by four wickets. Glamorgan 160-7** (20 overs) (N. J. Selman 35, A. Balbirnie 58; N. L. Buck 4-29); ‡**Northamptonshire 161-6** (19.2 overs) (A. G. Wakely 36*). *PoM:* N. L. Buck. *This home fixture was relocated in Birmingham to allow Sky Sports to broadcast successive matches at the same venue (Somerset had played Worcestershire earlier in the day). Ireland captain Andy Balbirnie made his first fifty for Glamorgan, but Buck picked up four wickets, and Zaib pulled off two sensational boundary catches. Northamptonshire were coasting at 113-3 from 13, but stumbled slightly, leaving Alex Wakely and Graeme White to score 20 from 14 balls; two missed chances helped them to their fourth successive win. The players wore black armbands in memory of the former Northamptonshire all-rounder David Capel, who had died the previous day; on-field umpires Rob Bailey and Nick Cook had been his team-mates.*

At Northampton, September 11. **Gloucestershire won by 35 runs. Gloucestershire 185-6** (20 overs) (C. D. J. Dent 50, I. A. Cockbain 40; G. G. White 3-28); ‡**Northamptonshire 150-6** (20 overs) (P. R. Stirling 32; G. L. van Buuren 3-15). *PoM:* G. L. van Buuren. *Chris Dent and Ian Cockbain thrashed 90 in 45 balls for Gloucestershire's second wicket to set Northamptonshire a challenging total, before Graeme van Buuren reduced them from 51-0 in 5.1 overs to 58-3 in 7.5. Fellow slow left-armer Tom Smith (1-18) also proved hard to get away, and the chase petered out. Gloucestershire's fourth straight win took them above their previously undefeated opponents.*

At Northampton, September 15 (floodlit). **Worcestershire won by eight runs.** ‡**Worcestershire 178-6** (20 overs) (H. D. Rutherford 62); **Northamptonshire 170-7** (20 overs) (R. E. Levi 50, A. M. Rossington 45). *PoM:* E. G. Barnard. *A third consecutive defeat left Northamptonshire's qualification hopes in the balance. Levi's 27-ball half-century had put them in control of the chase, before Rossington and Zaib added 57 for the sixth wicket in 5.3 overs. But miserly spells from Barnard (2-15 off four overs) and Mitchell (1-17 off three) left them with too much to do. The meat in Worcestershire's decent total of 178 came from New Zealander Hamish Rutherford (62 off 37).*

Northamptonshire away matches

August 27: no result v Gloucestershire.
August 29: beat Worcestershire by nine wickets.
September 13: lost to Glamorgan by seven wickets.
September 18: lost to Somerset by seven wickets.
September 20: beat Warwickshire by three wickets.

SOMERSET

At Taunton, September 1 (floodlit). **Somerset won by eight wickets. Glamorgan 133-8** (20 overs) (C. B. Cooke 42; B. G. F. Green 4-26); ‡**Somerset 134-2** (16.1 overs) (J. C. Hildreth 34*, T. B. Abell 74*). *PoM:* B. G. F. Green. *Somerset's sixth bowler, Ben Green, claimed four wickets, including Chris Cooke, Glamorgan's captain and top-scorer; Green had not taken more than one in an innings in his previous seven first-team games. Tom Abell's 45-ball 74*, packed with textbook strokes, and a stand of 110* with James Hildreth, ensured a comfortable win.*

At Taunton, September 4 (floodlit). **Warwickshire won by four runs** (DLS). **Warwickshire 107-4** (12 overs) (S. R. Hain 55*); ‡**Somerset 120-7** (12 overs) (T. A. Lammonby 43*). *PoM:* S. R. Hain. *Rain interrupted play with Warwickshire 85-4 off 11 overs, turning the game into a 12-over contest. On resumption, Sam Hain (55* off 31) plundered 15 from an Ollie Sale over that cost 22, leaving Somerset with a revised target of 125. They slipped to 52-6 in the seventh, before a late assault from Tom Lammonby (43* off 20) and Roelof van der Merwe (25 off 14) gave them hope. Needing 23 off the last, bowled by Henry Brookes, Lammonby managed 18.*

At Taunton, September 11 (floodlit). **Worcestershire won by three runs.** ‡**Worcestershire 168-4** (20 overs) (H. D. Rutherford 46, J. D. Libby 48, O. B. Cox 56*); **Somerset 165-8** (20 overs) (T. B. Abell 60; P. R. Brown 3-39). *PoM:* O. B. Cox. *County debut:* W. C. F. Smeed (Somerset). *Worcestershire's first group win was set up by sweet striking from Hamish Rutherford (46 off 29, with four sixes) and Ben Cox (56* off 34, with three). Charlie Morris trapped Babar Azam with the first ball of the reply, but Abell's elegant 60 off 39 kept Somerset in the hunt. When Craig Overton swung Pat Brown over deep square leg from the second ball of the last over, they needed six off four. But Brown conceded only two singles, either side of dismissing van der Merwe.*

At Taunton, September 13. **Gloucestershire won by 11 runs. Gloucestershire 203-6** (20 overs) (I. A. Cockbain 50, J. M. R. Taylor 31*, B. A. C. Howell 49*; M. T. C. Waller 3-18); ‡**Somerset 192-8** (20 overs) (W. C. F. Smeed 82, L. Gregory 38; R. F. Higgins 3-47). *PoM:* W. C. F. Smeed. *Over a year after his previous appearance, Benny Howell marked his return from injury with 49* off 18 balls from No. 8, including five sixes, to inspire Gloucestershire to their fifth win in a row. That followed 50 off 27 from Ian Cockbain, who helped take 30 off a chaotic ninth over: Abell was removed from the attack after consecutive no-balls above waist height, and was replaced by Sale, who was hit for three sixes by Cockbain. Leg-spinner Max Waller, who opened the bowling, managed 3-18. In reply, Dent ran out Abell and Bartlett, each attempting a second, but Will Smeed, an 18-year-old Academy product, biffed five sixes in a 49-ball 82. It still wasn't enough.*

At Taunton, September 18 (floodlit). **Somerset won by seven wickets.** ‡**Northamptonshire 140-9** (20 overs) (J. J. Cobb 49); **Somerset 146-3** (18 overs) (S. M. Davies 45, T. B. Abell 42*, T. A. Lammonby 43*). *PoM:* T. A. Lammonby. *Somerset inflicted a fourth successive defeat on Northamptonshire to draw level with them, and stay in the race for the quarter-finals. The visitors had been 82-2 from ten, but lost their way against Somerset's spinners, and managed only three more boundaries. A stand of 65* in seven overs between Abell and Lammonby polished off the chase.*

Somerset away matches

August 28: no result v Warwickshire.
August 30: lost to Northamptonshire by nine runs.
September 3: beat Worcestershire by 16 runs.
September 16: beat Glamorgan by 66 runs.
September 20: lost to Gloucestershire by two wickets.

WARWICKSHIRE

At Birmingham, August 28 (floodlit). **Warwickshire v Somerset. Abandoned.**

At Birmingham, September 2 (floodlit). **Gloucestershire won by 57 runs. Gloucestershire 157-3** (12 overs) (M. A. H. Hammond 41, I. A. Cockbain 84*); ‡**Warwickshire 100** (11.1 overs) (T. M. J. Smith 5-16). *PoM:* I. A. Cockbain. *Rain restricted this to a 12-over contest – enough for Gloucestershire to complete a thumping victory. Their big total was built around Ian Cockbain's explosive 35-ball 84*, which contained seven sixes and six fours. Then left-arm spinner Tom Smith took over, with county-record figures of 18–11–16–5. From 55-1 after four overs, Warwickshire lost five for seven in 15 balls – three in Smith's first over, including a run-out – as Gloucestershire's fielders backed up their bowlers.*

BEST T20 FIGURES FOR GLOUCESTERSHIRE

5-16	**T. M. J. Smith**	**v Warwickshire at Birmingham**	**2020**
5-18	B. A. C. Howell	v Glamorgan at Cheltenham	2019
5-24	D. A. Payne	v Middlesex at Richmond	2015
5-35	G. J. McCarter	v Sussex at Hove	2014
5-39	T. M. J. Smith	v Essex at Bristol	2015

At Birmingham, September 11 (floodlit). **Warwickshire won by 13 runs.** ‡**Warwickshire 142-9** (20 overs) (W. M. H. Rhodes 46; T. van der Gugten 3-27); **Glamorgan 129-8** (20 overs) (A. Balbirnie 30, T. van der Gugten 34*; T. T. Bresnan 3-26, J. B. Lintott 3-11). *PoM:* J. B. Lintott. *Glamorgan's chase was initially derailed by Tim Bresnan, who took the first three wickets, then – after Andy Balbirnie had steered them to 79-4 – by the left-arm spin of Jake Lintott, as four tumbled in ten balls. Will Rhodes's format-best 46 from 31 proved decisive, after Dom Sibley had fallen for a golden duck in his first county appearance of the season following Test duty.*

At Birmingham, September 18 (floodlit). **Warwickshire won by 16 runs.** ‡**Warwickshire 179-6** (20 overs) (R. M. Yates 37, S. R. Hain 61, D. R. Mousley 40); **Worcestershire 163-8** (20 overs) (H. D. Rutherford 45, B. L. D'Oliveira 61). *PoM:* S. R. Hain. *Sam Hain, who had hit 73* from 44 balls five days earlier, again enjoyed himself at Worcestershire's expense, this time hammering 61 from 33, and putting on 80 – a fifth-wicket record in this fixture – with Dan Mousley. Helped by scruffy fielding, Warwickshire plundered 107 from their last ten overs. Worcestershire struggled to put partnerships together, despite Brett D'Oliveira's feisty 40-ball 61.*

At Birmingham, September 20. **Northamptonshire won by three wickets.** ‡**Warwickshire 191-5** (20 overs) (A. J. Hose 119, D. R. Mousley 58*); **Northamptonshire 193-7** (18.5 overs) (P. R. Stirling 38, R. I. Keogh 37, T. A. I. Taylor 50*, G. G. White 37*; T. T. Bresnan 3-25). *PoM:* G. G. White. *County debut:* T. A. I. Taylor (Northamptonshire). *Warwickshire needed a win to qualify for the quarter-finals, with the carrot of an appearance at home on finals day – but were thwarted by Tom Taylor, making an eventful debut for Northamptonshire after a move from Leicestershire. He had managed only 43 runs in five previous innings in the competition, all this season, but now flayed 50* from 27 balls to ensure Northamptonshire finished ahead of Warwickshire on net run-rate. When news came through that Gloucestershire had beaten Somerset, Northamptonshire were into the last eight, too. From 71-6, Taylor put on 69 with Rob Keogh – a county seventh-wicket record – then 53* in 19 balls with Graeme White, who thumped three sixes in what turned out to be Jeetan Patel's final over in professional cricket. Earlier, Taylor had taken two wickets in his first over, after Rob Yates pulled his first delivery for six. From 20-4, Adam Hose, who hit nine fours and seven sixes from 64 balls, became only Warwickshire's third T20 centurion (after Brendon McCullum and Ian Bell), and put on 171 with Mousley, who weighed in with a maiden fifty.*

Warwickshire away matches

August 30: beat Glamorgan by six wickets.
September 1: lost to Northamptonshire by 38 runs.
September 4: beat Somerset by four runs (DLS).
September 13: beat Worcestershire by six wickets.
September 15: lost to Gloucestershire by 50 runs.

WORCESTERSHIRE

At Worcester, August 29. **Northamptonshire won by nine wickets. Worcestershire 124-7** (20 overs) (J. A. Haynes 41); ‡**Northamptonshire 128-1** (15.1 overs) (R. E. Levi 33, P. R. Stirling 80*). *PoM:* P. R. Stirling. *County debut:* P. R. Stirling (Northamptonshire). *On his Northamptonshire debut, Paul Stirling hit 80* off 48 balls to reproduce the form which brought him 142 in Ireland's one-day win at the Rose Bowl earlier in the month. He then took two cheap wickets with his off-breaks as the visitors sent down 15 overs of spin on a slow pitch that proved taxing for Worcestershire, led for the first time by Ed Barnard. The exception was 19-year-old Jack Haynes, who made 41 from 27 on T20 debut, and managed six of his side's nine boundaries. Stirling and Richard Levi began the chase with 107 inside 13 overs, and Northamptonshire romped home.*

At Worcester, August 31. **Gloucestershire won by 22 runs.** ‡**Gloucestershire 197-3** (20 overs) (M. A. H. Hammond 48, C. D. J. Dent 60, R. F. Higgins 30*); **Worcestershire 175-8** (20 overs) (H. D. Rutherford 30, M. H. Wessels 30; D. A. Payne 3-32). *PoM:* T. M. J. Smith. *After a first-ball duck against Glamorgan two days earlier in his first T20 game for four years, Chris Dent cracked a 33-ball 60 to set up a Gloucestershire win. He and Miles Hammond (48 off 38) started with 82 in 8.3 overs, and the momentum was maintained as Pat Brown – released from England's white-ball bubble – conceded 57. Needing 198, Worcestershire reached 89-1 in the eighth, but spinners Tom Smith and Graeme van Buuren combined for 48–11–43–3 to strangle the middle order.*

At Birmingham, September 3. **Somerset won by 16 runs. Somerset 229-8** (20 overs) (Babar Azam 42, S. M. Davies 60; D. K. H. Mitchell 3-35); ‡**Worcestershire 213-7** (20 overs) (J. D. Libby 75*, D. K. H. Mitchell 45; J. H. Davey 4-41). *PoM:* S. M. Davies. *Somerset achieved their highest T20 score away from Taunton, after former Worcestershire player Steve Davies (60 off 35) and Pakistan's Babar Azam (42 off 35) began with 90 inside ten overs. They were aided by wayward bowling, which culminated in Barnard (18–3–55–0) being banned from the attack after successive head-high full tosses were hit for four and six by Roelof van der Merwe at the start of the 19th; completed by Adam Finch, it cost 29. Jake Libby hit a career-best 75* off 46, and Daryl Mitchell a late 22-ball 45, but Worcestershire never threatened victory; Josh Davey finished with four wickets. Earlier, Mitchell had become his side's leading T20 wicket-taker, passing Jack Shantry's tally of 92. The game was played at Edgbaston as part of a TV double-header also involving Northamptonshire v Glamorgan.*

SOMERSET'S HIGHEST T20 TOTALS

250-3	v Glos at Taunton	2006	226-5	v Middx at Taunton	2019
235-5	v Middx at Taunton	2011	225-2	v Essex at Chelmsford	2011
229-6	v Middx at Taunton	2018	225-6	v Essex at Chelmsford	2019
229-8	**v Worcs at Birmingham**	**2020**	224-7	v Kent at Taunton	2015
228-5	v Glos at Taunton	2005	220-4	v Hants at Taunton	2010
226-5	v Kent at Canterbury	2018	219-5	v Glam at Taunton	2006

All totals from 20 overs except for 220-4 v Hampshire (18 overs).

At Worcester, September 13. **Warwickshire won by six wickets.** ‡**Worcestershire 178-4** (20 overs) (H. D. Rutherford 41, J. D. Libby 63, O. B. Cox 46*; O. P. Stone 3-45); **Warwickshire 181-4** (19.1 overs) (A. J. Hose 43, S. R. Hain 73*). *PoM:* S. R. Hain. *Warwickshire won the West Midlands derby for the first time since 2017, thanks to a punishing 73* off 44 balls from Sam Hain. Charlie Morris had struck with his first ball for the second time in three days, adding the scalp of Dom Sibley to Somerset's Babar Azam – but Brett D'Oliveira conceded 22 in his first over, and Hain kept Warwickshire ahead of the rate. Worcestershire had lost momentum in their innings, after Henry Brookes began the 19th over by removing Libby (63 off 40), then completed a wicket-maiden with five dots to Ross Whiteley. Ben Cox (46* off 28) was starved of the strike. A fifth defeat in six all but put paid to the hosts' quarter-final ambitions.*

At Worcester, September 20. **Glamorgan won by six wickets.** ‡**Worcestershire 190-3** (20 overs) (H. D. Rutherford 100, J. D. Libby 47; T. van der Gugten 3-28); **Glamorgan 196-4** (19.4 overs) (D. L. Lloyd 56, N. J. Selman 78). *PoM:* H. D. Rutherford. *Winners in 2018 and runners-up in 2019, Worcestershire picked up the Central Group's wooden spoon, despite a raucous 62-ball 100 from Hamish Rutherford. But with Glamorgan chasing 191, Brown – so central to Worcestershire's previous successes – went for 63, the club's most expensive performance (beating 2-58 by John Hastings at Headingley in 2017). Amid the carnage, though, he found himself on a hat-trick as Glamorgan – who had started with 120 inside 13 overs from David Lloyd (56 off 38) and Nick Selman (78 from 53) – lost three for five in seven balls. But, with 13 needed off the last over, Dan Douthwaite hit Brown for three sixes in four deliveries. It left Worcestershire without a win at New Road in any cricket in 2020.*

Worcestershire away matches

August 27: no result v Glamorgan.
September 4: lost to Gloucestershire by 30 runs.
September 11: beat Somerset by three runs.
September 15: beat Northamptonshire by eight runs.
September 18: lost to Warwickshire by 16 runs.

NORTH GROUP

DERBYSHIRE

At Leicester, August 27 (floodlit). **Derbyshire v Leicestershire. Abandoned.**

At Leeds, August 31 (floodlit). **Lancashire won by four runs.** ‡**Lancashire 178-5** (20 overs) (A. L. Davies 82, S. J. Croft 38); **Derbyshire 174-7** (20 overs) (L. M. Reece 39, W. L. Madsen 44, M. J. J. Critchley 32). *PoM:* A. L. Davies. *Alex Davies's powerful 82 off 56 was the defining innings, though Matt Critchley nearly upstaged him. Needing 19 off the final over, he struck 12 off the first three balls, but was run out off the fifth; with six required off the last, Derbyshire managed a single. Earlier, their seamer Ed Barnes took two wickets on T20 debut, after Davies had put on 63 with Keaton Jennings and 74 with Steven Croft. This was the second half of a televised double-header at Headingley, following Leicestershire v Durham.*

At Chester-le-Street, September 2 (floodlit). ‡**Derbyshire v Durham. Abandoned.** *County debut:* F. Behardien (Durham). *Rain relented to allow the toss, but soon returned.*

At Nottingham, September 13. **Nottinghamshire won by 13 runs.** ‡**Nottinghamshire 198-6** (20 overs) (A. D. Hales 49, J. M. Clarke 57, T. J. Moores 31); **Derbyshire 185-6** (20 overs) (W. L. Madsen 68, M. J. J. Critchley 44, A. L. Hughes 36*). *PoM:* J. M. Clarke. *Joe Clarke passed 50 for the third time in the tournament, and a late flurry took Nottinghamshire to 198. Derbyshire openers Luis Reece and Billy Godleman suffered first-ball ducks, though Wayne Madsen and Critchley kept them in contention. Alex Hughes pulled level with Tim Groenewald as Derbyshire's leading T20 wicket-taker when Clarke became his 51st victim.*

At Leeds, September 20. **Yorkshire won by six wickets.** ‡**Derbyshire 167-6** (20 overs) (T. A. Wood 67, B. A. Godleman 49; B. O. Coad 3-40); **Yorkshire 171-4** (20 overs) (J. E. Root 60*, H. C. Brook 50*). *PoM:* J. E. Root. *Harry Brook hit the final ball for four to seal victory, and reach his first T20 fifty; he and Joe Root had revived Yorkshire from 80-4, with 91* in 8.2 overs. Earlier, Tom Wood brought up his own maiden half-century with a six during an opening stand of 109 with Godleman, which had promised a stronger Derbyshire total; they lost five for 32 in the last four overs. The teams who led the North Group in the Bob Willis Trophy filled the bottom places in the Blast.*

Derbyshire away matches

August 30: lost to Yorkshire by 99 runs.
September 4: lost to Lancashire by eight wickets.
September 11: lost to Durham by 55 runs.
September 15: beat Leicestershire by four runs.
September 17: lost to Nottinghamshire by eight wickets.

DURHAM

At Chester-le-Street, August 27 (floodlit). **Lancashire won by 27 runs.** ‡**Lancashire 190-3** (20 overs) (A. L. Davies 65, K. K. Jennings 108); **Durham 163-7** (20 overs) (A. Z. Lees 51, D. G. Bedingham 33, B. A. Carse 35). *PoM:* K. K. Jennings. *Keaton Jennings returned to haunt his old club, scoring a maiden T20 century from 60 balls. His 108, and an opening stand of 170 with Alex Davies, were both county records, propelling Lancashire to a big total. Alex Lees hit a fifty in response, but Durham were well beaten.*

At Chester-le-Street, August 29. **Nottinghamshire won by six wickets.** ‡**Durham 181-3** (20 overs) (A. Z. Lees 53, G. Clark 60, B. A. Carse 32*); **Nottinghamshire 185-4** (16.2 overs) (C. D. Nash 55, J. M. Clarke 100*). *PoM:* J. M. Clarke. *Joe Clarke powered Nottinghamshire to their first win of the summer. He scored his second T20 century – both against Durham – from only 44 balls; his eighth six, down the ground, clinched victory (and later the Walter Lawrence Trophy for the season's fastest hundred). Durham slumped to another defeat, despite half-centuries from Lees and Graham Clark.*

At Chester-le-Street, September 4 (floodlit). **Yorkshire won by 29 runs. Yorkshire 198-3** (20 overs) (T. Köhler-Cadmore 85*, W. A. R. Fraine 36*); ‡**Durham 169** (19.1 overs) (G. Clark 68; D. J. Willey 3-26, J. E. Poysden 3-32). *PoM:* T. Köhler-Cadmore. *Tom Köhler-Cadmore scored a match-winning 85*, then claimed he was not at his best. Though playing the anchor role, he cleared the rope five times, including a straight six into the car park. Late fireworks from Harry Brook and Will Fraine propelled Yorkshire to 198. Clark hit back with 68 in 39, but the spin of Josh Poysden and Joe Root (who dismissed both openers) slowed Durham down, before David Willey sank them.*

At Chester-le-Street, September 11 (floodlit). **Durham won by 55 runs.** ‡**Durham 223-2** (20 overs) (A. Z. Lees 77*, G. Clark 45, B. A. Raine 71); **Derbyshire 168-5** (20 overs) (L. M. Reece 42, J. L. du Plooy 53*). *PoM:* B. A. Raine. *Durham finally chalked up their first win of 2020, thanks to their second-highest T20 total. Ben Raine struck eight sixes in his 39-ball 71, despatching an inexperienced attack around the ground in a second-wicket stand of 123 with Lees. Earlier, Clark scored a devastating 45 in 20, and Brydon Carse's late cameo (17* off six) put the game out of Derbyshire's reach; they were always off the pace, despite Leus du Plooy's 53* in 32.*

At Chester-le-Street, September 13. **Durham won by six wickets.** ‡**Leicestershire 130-9** (20 overs) (A. M. Lilley 45, H. E. Dearden 30; M. J. Potts 3-19); **Durham 132-4** (15.2 overs) (G. Clark 35, B. A. Raine 50*). *PoM:* M. J. Potts. *County debut:* N. R. Welch (Leicestershire). *Outstanding bowling from Matty Potts and Liam Trevaskis (2-17) paved the way for a comfortable victory. Trevaskis set the tone, removing Gareth Delany for a duck, and Potts claimed his then-best T20 return to restrict Leicestershire to 130-9. Clark scored 21 runs in the first over, and his 35 from 14 got Durham ahead of the rate; Raine finished things off with a six.*

Durham away matches

August 31: lost to Leicestershire by 30 runs.
September 2: no result v Derbyshire.
September 16: beat Yorkshire by 43 runs.
September 18: beat Lancashire by 74 runs.
September 20: lost to Nottinghamshire by 18 runs.

LANCASHIRE

At Liverpool, September 2. **Lancashire v Nottinghamshire. Abandoned.**

At Liverpool, September 4. **Lancashire won by eight wickets. Derbyshire 98-7** (20 overs) (A. L. Hughes 32); ‡**Lancashire 102-2** (17.2 overs) (A. L. Davies 36, K. K. Jennings 49*). *PoM:* K. K. Jennings. *After losing an important toss, Derbyshire slumped to 18-4 in the sixth over, though Alex Hughes steered them to 98 on a turning pitch. An opening stand of 61 between Alex Davies and Keaton Jennings – their third in succession over 60 – confirmed Lancashire's dominance. Dane Vilas completed victory with a six, only the second of the match.*

At Manchester, September 17 (floodlit). **Lancashire won by seven runs.** ‡**Lancashire 167-6** (20 overs) (L. S. Livingstone 69, S. J. Croft 58); **Yorkshire 160-6** (20 overs) (A. Lyth 45, J. E. Root 64). *PoM:* L. S. Livingstone. *County debut:* S. A. Wisniewski (Yorkshire). *With barely a fortnight of the season left, Lancashire played their first fixture at Old Trafford, the night after England completed their international season. They celebrated with their fifth successive T20 Roses victory, clinching a quarter-final place – and eliminating Yorkshire, despite Joe Root's contributions. Liam Livingstone and Steven Croft added 130, an all-wicket T20 Roses record. But Root (one of five Yorkshire spinners) helped engineer the loss of five for 16. The pursuit reached 115-1 before Adam Lyth and Root were run out; Lyth accused his team of "schoolboy cricket" after they failed to score 53 off seven overs with eight wickets in hand.*

At Manchester, September 18 (floodlit). **Durham won by 74 runs.** ‡**Durham 157-5** (20 overs) (A. Z. Lees 67*); **Lancashire 83** (15 overs) (M. J. Potts 3-8, S. Steel 3-20). *PoM:* A. Z. Lees. *Two days after destroying Yorkshire's top order at Headingley, Matty Potts did it again: in five balls, he dismissed Croft, Vilas and Rob Jones for ducks, leaving Lancashire 9-4. A total of 83 was their lowest in T20 cricket, and Potts improved his career-best for the third game running. A fourth successive win kept Durham's knockout ambitions alive, and justified Alex Lees's patience: he batted through the innings, with only three fours. They were later boosted by a five-run penalty for Livingstone's abusive language on dismissal.*

At Manchester, September 20. **Leicestershire won by 22 runs.** ‡**Leicestershire 154-5** (20 overs) (N. R. Welch 43, A. M. Lilley 49); **Lancashire 132-5** (20 overs) (A. L. Davies 52, S. J. Croft 36; C. N. Ackermann 3-18). *PoM:* C. N. Ackermann. *Leicestershire joined Lancashire in the last eight, and dashed their chances of a home quarter-final. Nick Welch's hitting enlivened the powerplay, before Arron Lilley's steadier 49 – and the donation of 30 off the last two overs – gave them a defendable total. Although Davies and Croft put on 74, Lancashire needed 43 off 27 once they fell to successive deliveries from Colin Ackermann; Josh Bohannon and Vilas promptly went without scoring.*

Lancashire away matches

August 27: beat Durham by 27 runs.
August 29: no result v Leicestershire.
August 31: beat Derbyshire by four runs.
September 11: lost to Nottinghamshire by six wickets.
September 14: beat Yorkshire by six wickets.

LEICESTERSHIRE

At Leicester, August 29. **No result. Leicestershire 150-9** (20 overs) (H. E. Dearden 31; T. E. Bailey 5-17) **v ‡Lancashire.** *County debut:* G. J. Delany (Leicestershire). *Tom Bailey's best T20 figures, supported by outstanding catching and fielding – Dane Vilas held three – helped Lancashire restrict Leicestershire on a good pitch. Rain prevented any reply.*

At Leeds, August 31. **Leicestershire won by 30 runs. ‡Leicestershire 177-6** (20 overs) (G. J. Delany 68, A. M. Lilley 69); **Durham 147-8** (20 overs) (A. Z. Lees 36; C. F. Parkinson 3-21). *PoM:* A. M. Lilley. *Leicestershire claimed their first victory after two no-results, in a home game switched to Headingley as the first half of a televised double-header with Derbyshire v Lancashire. A second-wicket partnership of 88 between Arron Lilley and Ireland's Gareth Delany set up a total which they defended with ease; slow left-armer Callum Parkinson picked up three wickets.*

At Leicester, September 11 (floodlit). **Leicestershire won by three wickets. Yorkshire 188-6** (20 overs) (A. Lyth 71, J. A. Thompson 44); **‡Leicestershire 192-7** (20 overs) (G. J. Delany 64, A. M. Lilley 30, C. N. Ackermann 58; M. D. Fisher 3-35). *PoM:* G. J. Delany. *Adam Lyth's 46-ball 71 laid the platform for a challenging 188, but Leicestershire seemed to have a straightforward victory in sight after half-centuries from Delany and Colin Ackermann. Then they lost five in five overs, and found themselves needing nine off the last. David Willey called up Lyth, who had not yet bowled; he conceded only six from his first five deliveries, before Ben Mike hit him back over his head for six.*

At Leicester, September 15 (floodlit). **Derbyshire won by four runs. ‡Derbyshire 147-8** (20 overs) (B. A. Godleman 34, W. L. Madsen 33; G. T. Griffiths 4-35); **Leicestershire 143-4** (20 overs) (N. R. Welch 32, G. H. Rhodes 30*, H. E. Dearden 36*). *PoM:* A. L. Hughes. *Gavin Griffiths picked up three wickets in Derbyshire's final over to earn his best figures, and restrict them to an apparently beatable 147. But, after Nick Welch made a promising home debut, George Rhodes and Harry Dearden found boundaries hard to come by. None at all was scored in the final three overs, as Michael Cohen and Dustin Melton turned the screw to steal Derbyshire's only win of the tournament. Alex Hughes followed 25 in 14 by dismissing Ackermann – his 52nd T20 victim, a Derbyshire record.*

At Leicester, September 18 (floodlit). **Leicestershire won by four wickets. ‡Nottinghamshire 162-7** (20 overs) (B. M. Duckett 53, T. J. Moores 51; W. S. Davis 3-38); **Leicestershire 163-6** (19.5 overs) (A. M. Lilley 34, C. N. Ackermann 67*). *PoM:* C. N. Ackermann. *Nottinghamshire were 42-3 when Parkinson bowled Alex Hales with superb turn, but Ben Duckett and Tom Moores added 102, before Will Davis's three late wickets thwarted any acceleration. In the first over of Leicestershire's chase, they were awarded five runs for "fake fielding", under the recent Law 41.5 on deliberately deceiving the batsman: Steven Mullaney simulated sliding and grabbing the ball. Ackermann inflicted Nottinghamshire's only defeat with one ball to spare, keeping open his own team's chance of making the quarter-finals.*

Leicestershire away matches

August 27: no result v Derbyshire.
September 2: no result v Yorkshire.
September 4: lost to Nottinghamshire by five wickets.
September 13: lost to Durham by six wickets.
September 20: beat Lancashire by 22 runs.

NOTTINGHAMSHIRE

At Nottingham, August 31. **Nottinghamshire won by six wickets. ‡Yorkshire 190** (20 overs) (A. Lyth 53, J. E. Root 65, H. C. Brook 39; J. T. Ball 3-36, L. J. Fletcher 5-43); **Nottinghamshire 194-4** (19.2 overs) (C. D. Nash 51, B. M. Duckett 86*). *PoM:* B. M. Duckett. *Adam Lyth (53 from 29) and Joe Root dominated a Yorkshire innings that ended with three eventful overs, yielding 30 runs and seven wickets. Five of the wickets came in ten balls from Luke Fletcher, the fifth Nottinghamshire bowler to claim a T20 five-for. Alex Hales equalled another county record, with four catches – before he and Joe Clarke fell in the first two overs of the reply. Chris Nash and Ben Duckett stemmed the tide, adding 85; Duckett remained unbeaten as they got home.*

BEST T20 FIGURES FOR NOTTINGHAMSHIRE

5-22	G. G. White	v Lancashire at Nottingham	2013
5-25	D. J. Pattinson	v Warwickshire at Birmingham	2011
5-26	R. J. Logan	v Lancashire at Nottingham	2003
5-30	H. F. Gurney	v Derbyshire at Derby	2019
5-43	**L. J. Fletcher**	**v Yorkshire at Nottingham**	**2020**

At Nottingham, September 4 (floodlit). **Nottinghamshire won by five wickets. ‡Leicestershire 123-8** (20 overs); **Nottinghamshire 124-5** (15 overs) (A. D. Hales 44, D. T. Christian 33*). *PoM:* D. T. Christian. *Nottinghamshire completed a straightforward win after restricting Leicestershire to 123. Jake Ball (2-17) conceded one boundary in four overs; left-arm spinner Imad Wasim (2-24) bowled 12 dots. The outcome was clear once Hales smashed 44 off 16 balls, including 16 in an over, twice – off Gavin Griffiths and Gareth Delany, who dismissed him with his next delivery.*

At Nottingham, September 11 (floodlit). **Nottinghamshire won by six wickets. Lancashire 167-5** (20 overs) (L. S. Livingstone 33, K. K. Jennings 33, S. J. Croft 37, D. J. Vilas 31); **‡Nottinghamshire 169-4** (17 overs) (J. M. Clarke 77, T. J. Moores 31*). *PoM:* J. M. Clarke. *Lancashire were 65-1 from the powerplay, but could not keep up the pace; they had no one to match Nottinghamshire's Clarke, whose 77 off 36 balls included five sixes – three in four deliveries from medium-pacer Danny Lamb in the sixth over, which cost 27. Clarke dominated a stand of 82 in seven overs with Hales (19); his hitting was emulated by Tom Moores (31* in 19).*

At Nottingham, September 17 (floodlit). **Nottinghamshire won by eight wickets. Derbyshire 142-8** (20 overs) (B. A. Godleman 47; J. T. Ball 3-28); **‡Nottinghamshire 143-2** (14.1 overs) (C. D. Nash 40*, B. M. Duckett 57*). *PoM:* B. M. Duckett. *Nottinghamshire beat Derbyshire for the second time in five days. A 98-run partnership between Duckett and Nash – playing his 500th match across three formats – carried them to their sixth straight win, with almost six overs to spare. Hales had launched the chase with 22 from seven deliveries. Earlier, Billy Godleman batted into Derbyshire's 16th over, but found limited support. Ball's fine form took him to 12 wickets from six games.*

At Nottingham, September 20. **Nottinghamshire won by 18 runs. Nottinghamshire 150-6** (20 overs); **‡Durham 132** (19.1 overs) (L. Trevaskis 31*). *PoM:* Imad Wasim. *Nottinghamshire's seventh victory confirmed them as group winners. Durham's pursuit of a modest target never recovered from a catastrophic fifth over, bowled by Imad Wasim: Ben Raine was caught at mid-off, Alex Lees sharply stumped, and David Bedingham run out. From 84-8, Liam Trevaskis supervised the addition of 48 – in vain. Earlier, Nottinghamshire had wobbled when Moores and Duckett departed to consecutive balls after putting on 49, but Imad and Steven Mullaney took 31* off the last three.*

Nottinghamshire away matches

August 27: no result v Yorkshire.
August 29: beat Durham by six wickets.
September 2: no result v Lancashire.
September 13: beat Derbyshire by 13 runs.
September 18: lost to Leicestershire by four wickets.

YORKSHIRE

At Leeds, August 27 (floodlit). **Yorkshire v Nottinghamshire. Abandoned.**

At Leeds, August 30. **Yorkshire won by 99 runs. ‡Yorkshire 220-5** (20 overs) (A. Lyth 61, J. E. Root 64, W. A. R. Fraine 44*); **Derbyshire 121-9** (20 overs) (M. D. Fisher 3-21). *PoM:* A. Lyth. *Yorkshire ended a run of six defeats by Derbyshire in style. Half-centuries for Adam Lyth and Joe Root, in his first county game of 2020 after leaving England's Test bubble, plus a 16-ball 44* from Will Fraine, pummelling wayward death bowling, helped them reach 220. Root's triumphant return also included two wickets as he and Matthew Fisher reduced Derbyshire to 20-4; Matt Critchley's 26 was their top score.*

At Leeds, September 2 (floodlit). **Yorkshire v Leicestershire. Abandoned.** *Yorkshire suffered their second no-result in four group games, and Leicestershire their third.*

At Leeds, September 14 (floodlit). **Lancashire won by six wickets.** ‡**Yorkshire 145-9** (20 overs) (A. Lyth 36; L. Wood 3-21, M. W. Parkinson 3-25); **Lancashire 148-4** (17.5 overs) (D. J. Vilas 44*, R. P. Jones 38*). *PoM:* M. W. Parkinson. *County debut:* J. H. Wharton (Yorkshire). *Four Yorkshire players – Fisher, Tom Köhler-Cadmore, Josh Poysden and captain David Willey – were omitted after Willey's wife, Carolynne, reported Covid symptoms; all four had been in contact two days earlier. They sat in separate cars outside Headingley, hoping Willey's test would prove negative and allow them to play, but the result did not arrive in time. Though Lancashire dropped three catches, Yorkshire stuttered after acting-captain Lyth's brisk 36 led them to 78-1 in eight overs. Matt Parkinson and Luke Wood took three apiece, exposing an inexperienced middle order. Lancashire looked shaky at 77-4, but Dane Vilas and Robert Jones added 71* to secure a fourth win; they were now just two points behind group leaders Nottinghamshire.*

At Leeds, September 16 (floodlit). **Durham won by 43 runs. Durham 147** (19.3 overs); ‡**Yorkshire 104** (16.4 overs) (M. J. Potts 3-14, P. Coughlin 3-22). *PoM:* M. J. Potts. *The four Yorkshire players omitted from the previous game were withdrawn for their last three fixtures; Willey and his wife had tested positive, so all had to self-isolate for 14 days. Durham's third successive victory lifted them from fifth place to third; Yorkshire's third successive defeat all but knocked them out. Durham had slipped from 46-0 in five overs to 147 all out (Duanne Olivier 2-16). But Yorkshire were rolled over inside 17, after Matty Potts ripped out their top three in seven balls – Dawid Malan chopped on for a golden duck.*

Yorkshire away matches

August 31: lost to Nottinghamshire by six wickets.
September 4: beat Durham by 29 runs.
September 11: lost to Leicestershire by three wickets.
September 17: lost to Lancashire by seven runs.
September 20: beat Derbyshire by six wickets.

SOUTH GROUP

ESSEX

At Chelmsford, August 27. **No result. Middlesex 184-5** (20 overs) (M. D. E. Holden 102*); ‡**Essex 10-0** (1.3 overs). *Missed on two and 27, Max Holden batted through the Middlesex innings for his maiden T20 century, on one of Chelmsford's hybrid pitches, with synthetic fibres implanted in the loam. A shower meant Essex's target was revised to 156 in 16 overs, but a downpour ended play after nine deliveries.*

T20 HUNDREDS FOR MIDDLESEX

129	D. T. Christian	v Kent at Canterbury	2014
117	D. J. Malan	v Surrey at The Oval	2019
115*	D. J. Malan	v Sussex at Hove	2015
109	P. R. Stirling	v Surrey at The Oval	2018
106	A. C. Gilchrist	v Kent at Canterbury	2010
103	D. J. Malan	v Lancashire at The Oval	2008
102*	**M. D. E. Holden**	**v Essex at Chelmsford**	**2020**

At Chelmsford, September 1. **Hampshire won by five wickets. Essex 139-6** (20 overs) (C. S. Delport 36, R. N. ten Doeschate 37*; M. S. Crane 3-18); ‡**Hampshire 140-5** (19.5 overs) (H. G. Munsey 32). *PoM:* M. S. Crane. *Playing again on a hybrid pitch, Essex struggled to score quickly: Ryan ten Doeschate worked the ball around, his 37* occupying 29 balls, but the target was modest. Harry Munsey and Tom Alsop started with 51 in 7.3 overs, and the chase was always in hand, although Hampshire cut it fine: Ian Holland collected the winning single from the penultimate delivery.*

At The Oval, September 5. **Kent won by 29 runs.** ‡**Kent 192-6** (20 overs) (D. J. Bell-Drummond 81, A. J. Blake 52*); **Essex 163-7** (20 overs) (V. Chopra 41, R. N. ten Doeschate 42; I. Qayyum 3-25). *PoM:* D. J. Bell-Drummond. *This match was played at The Oval as the first part of a televised double-header with Surrey v Middlesex. Kent took early control: Daniel Bell-Drummond (81 from*

45 balls) put on 83 in 6.3 overs with Zak Crawley (28), then 64 for the third wicket with Alex Blake, whose 52 came from 35 balls. Cameron Delport gave Essex a decent start with 28 from 17 but, once Varun Chopra fell, making it 94-5 in the 13th – a third wicket for slow left-armer Imran Qayyum – the game was up.*

At Chelmsford, September 11. **Surrey won by four wickets.** ‡**Essex 195-8** (20 overs) (C. S. Delport 64, A. J. A. Wheater 63; R. J. W. Topley 3-38, D. T. Moriarty 3-36); **Surrey 198-6** (20 overs) (L. J. Evans 88*, R. J. Burns 30, J. Overton 30; A. P. Beard 3-41). *PoM:* L. J. Evans. *Back on a hybrid pitch, Essex lost their way from 144-1 – Delport and Adam Wheater had kicked off with 105 inside nine overs – and at one point surrendered five for 23 in 18 balls. Slow left-armer Dan Moriarty took the first three, and former Essex left-arm seamer Reece Topley the last three, in nine balls – although arguably the best spell came from Surrey's 42-year-old captain Gareth Batty (2-23). Surrey lost Hashim Amla first ball, but Laurie Evans put them back on track with 88* from 65, adding 54 with Will Jacks, and 68 with Rory Burns. With two needed, Gus Atkinson slapped Sam Cook to the boundary.*

At Chelmsford, September 20. **Sussex won by four wickets. Essex 136-9** (20 overs) (P. I. Walter 76; G. H. S. Garton 4-21); ‡**Sussex 137-6** (18.2 overs) (P. D. Salt 42, C. S. MacLeod 40, G. H. S. Garton 34*). *PoM:* G. H. S. Garton. *County debuts:* B. M. J. Allison, R. J. Das (Essex). *Paul Walter batted sensibly for a format-best 76 from 45 balls. But his team-mates floundered, particularly against left-armer George Garton, whose lively pace was mixed with some telling slower deliveries: after four balls, Essex were 0-2, with Delport and Feroze Khushi gone for ducks. Garton then starred with the bat: Sussex had dipped to 59-5, but he and Calum MacLeod put on 71 in ten overs, and were separated only with victory in sight. This match was not played on a hybrid pitch.*

Essex away matches

August 30: tied with Surrey.
September 3: lost to Middlesex by 11 runs.
September 14: beat Sussex by 12 runs.
September 16: beat Hampshire by 54 runs.
September 18: lost to Kent by four wickets.

HAMPSHIRE

At Southampton, September 10 (floodlit). **Sussex won by 13 runs. Sussex 159-5** (20 overs) (L. J. Wright 83, D. Wiese 41); ‡**Hampshire 146-6** (20 overs) (T. P. Alsop 43). *PoM:* L. J. Wright. *County debuts:* C. G. Harrison (Hampshire); C. S. MacLeod (Sussex). *Hampshire had started with four away games, as the Rose Bowl was accommodating England, but – now at home – they slumped to a third defeat. Sussex made a circumspect start (39-2 in the powerplay), but Luke Wright batted right through before holing out to the last delivery for 83 from 59 balls. Ravi Bopara fell to the debutant South African leg-spinner Calvin Harrison, who also spilled three return catches of varying difficulty; Hampshire grassed six in all, after running out Sussex's new signing, Scotland's Calum MacLeod, in the first over. Hampshire were 59-1 in the eighth, but Danny Briggs kept his old county in check with a miserly 2-20.*

At Southampton, September 14. **Kent won by eight wickets. Hampshire 182-6** (20 overs) (J. M. Vince 48, S. A. Northeast 37, J. K. Fuller 50*); ‡**Kent 183-2** (17.1 overs) (Z. Crawley 108*, J. L. Denly 38). *PoM:* Z. Crawley. *Back on the ground where he had scored 267 for England three weeks previously, Zak Crawley made his second century against Hampshire in seven days (following 105 in the Bob Willis Trophy at Canterbury). His maiden T20 century took 54 balls, and he dominated a stand of 121 in 11 overs with Joe Denly, which made a testing target look simple. Earlier, Hampshire had scooted to their highest total of the season, thanks to aggressive contributions from James Vince and James Fuller, who carted Fred Klaassen's last ball of the innings for six to reach 50* from 23. Hampshire's fifth defeat in seven matches meant they were eliminated.*

At Southampton, September 16. **Essex won by 54 runs.** ‡**Essex 168-3** (20 overs) (C. S. Delport 31, T. Westley 51, D. W. Lawrence 49*); **Hampshire 114-9** (20 overs) (A. S. S. Nijjar 3-22). *PoM:* A. S. S. Nijjar. *After Tom Westley and Dan Lawrence took advantage of mediocre bowling, Essex slow left-armer Aron Nijjar was given the new ball, and struck with his fourth delivery, well caught by Sam Cook at third man as George Munsey attempted a third reverse sweep. Nijjar returned to dismiss Joe Weatherley and Lewis McManus in three balls to reduce Hampshire to 38-6. At the other end, seamer Jack Plom took his first wicket for Essex when Vince collected his fourth golden duck against them in T20s, and finished with 24–15–18–2.*

At Southampton, September 18. **Surrey won by nine wickets. Hampshire 138-8** (20 overs) (I. G. Holland 65; R. J. W. Topley 4-20); ‡**Surrey 143-1** (15.2 overs) (W. G. Jacks 56*, L. J. Evans 81*). *PoM:* L. J. Evans. *Surrey were on top from the first ball, when Munsey became the first of Reece Topley's four wickets on his return to the Rose Bowl. Four Hampshire players were self-isolating, while wicketkeeper McManus had undergone an appendix operation. It needed Ian Holland's 65 from 51 to avoid embarrassment. But Will Jacks and Laurie Evans put on 118* for the second wicket as Surrey eased to their sixth win – Hampshire's sixth successive defeat.*

At Southampton, September 20. **Hampshire won by 20 runs.** ‡**Hampshire 141-9** (20 overs) (S. A. Northeast 31; T. N. Walallawita 3-19, N. A. Sowter 3-30); **Middlesex 121** (18 overs) (J. A. Simpson 48; Shaheen Shah Afridi 6-19). *PoM:* Shaheen Shah Afridi. *Chasing a modest 142, Middlesex were 121-6 in the 18th over, at which point Shaheen Shah Afridi became only the second bowler to take four wickets in four balls in the English T20 competition. After only one wicket in six matches for Hampshire, he finally got his yorker going, and castled John Simpson, Steven Finn, Thilan Walallawita and Tim Murtagh to finish with 6-19, all bowled. Earlier, spinners Walallawita (in his first senior T20 match), Luke Hollman (2-25) and Nathan Sowter had restricted the Hampshire scoring with combined figures of 8-74.*

FOUR WICKETS IN FOUR BALLS IN A T20 MATCH

J. Allenby (5-21)	Leicestershire v Lancashire at Manchester	2008
A. D. Russell (4-45)	West Indies A v India A at Bangalore	2013-14
Al-Amin Hossain (5-17)	Bangladesh Cricket Board XI v Abahani at Sylhet	2013-14
Rashid Khan (5-27)	Afghanistan v Ireland at Dehradun	2018-19
S. L. Malinga (5-6)	Sri Lanka v New Zealand at Pallekele	2019
A. Mithun (5-39)	Karnataka v Haryana at Surat	2019-20
Shaheen Shah Afridi (6-19)	**Hampshire v Middlesex at Southampton**	**2020**

Hampshire away matches

August 27: no result v Kent.
August 30: lost to Sussex by six wickets.
September 1: beat Essex by five wickets.
September 3: lost to Surrey by nine wickets (DLS).
September 12: lost to Middlesex by 19 runs.

KENT

At Canterbury, August 27. **No result. Hampshire 139-6** (20 overs) (J. J. Weatherley 68; M. E. Milnes 3-19); ‡**Kent 52-0** (4.1 overs). *County debuts:* S. W. Currie, H. G. Munsey (Hampshire). *Regulations regarding what constituted a match came under scrutiny when rain ended the game 25 balls into Kent's reply. Their position could hardly have been stronger and, had they reached the same score from five balls more, they would have won. As it was, the good work of Matt Milnes (a career-best 3-19), Zak Crawley (22* from nine) and Daniel Bell-Drummond (28* from 16) counted for naught. Joe Weatherley had revived the Hampshire innings from 28-3 with 68, another career-best.*

At Canterbury, September 1. **Kent won by five wickets. Surrey 161-4** (20 overs) (H. M. Amla 75, R. J. Burns 56*); ‡**Kent 162-5** (18.3 overs) (Z. Crawley 32, H. G. Kuhn 42*; D. T. Moriarty 3-25). *PoM:* H. G. Kuhn. *County debut:* R. J. W. Topley (Surrey). *Despite the absence of England internationals Sam Billings and Joe Denly, Kent swept Surrey aside. Crawley (32 off 21) and acting-captain Bell-Drummond (25 off 18) had begun the chase with 49 inside five overs and, despite three wickets for slow left-armer Dan Moriarty, Heino Kuhn saw Kent home with a calm 42* off 31 – days after the birth of his first child, Abigail. Surrey had been 28-3 after four, before Hashim Amla (75 off 56) and Rory Burns (a career-best 56* off 49) put on 127 – too steadily, it turned out.*

At Canterbury, September 12. **Sussex won by eight wickets. Kent 141-8** (20 overs) (J. L. Denly 32; D. R. Briggs 3-27); ‡**Sussex 145-2** (15.4 overs) (L. J. Wright 45, D. M. W. Rawlins 62*). *PoM:* D. M. W. Rawlins. *Sussex replaced Kent at the top of the group, thanks to the all-round efforts of Delray Rawlins. He began with 2-25, as he and fellow slow left-armer Danny Briggs (3-27) limited the hosts to 141-8 – an anticlimax from 90-2 in the 11th. Then, after Sussex captain Luke Wright departed for a lively 27-ball 45, Rawlins clubbed 62* from 33 to complete a thumping win.*

At Canterbury, September 16. **Middlesex won by two runs. Middlesex 184-6** (20 overs) (J. B. Cracknell 50, J. A. Simpson 46, L. B. K. Hollman 46); ‡**Kent 182-7** (20 overs) (D. J. Bell-Drummond 89, J. M. Cox 39*). *PoM:* L. B. K. Hollman. *Tom Helm held his nerve in the final over: Kent required nine, but Bell-Drummond picked out deep cover with the first ball, to depart for a powerful 89 off 54, and Grant Stewart was run out from the fifth. Needing four, Milnes could only edge a single. Earlier, Joe Cracknell – a 20-year-old from Enfield on his third first-team appearance – slammed a 22-ball 50 (with 42 in boundaries); John Simpson (from 34 balls) and Luke Hollman (from 26) each hit 46. Kent had looked out of it at 94-5 in the 13th, before Jordan Cox (39* off 21) put on 82 with Bell-Drummond.*

At Canterbury, September 18. **Kent won by four wickets.** ‡**Essex 167-9** (20 overs) (T. Westley 39, R. N. ten Doeschate 52; F. J. Klaassen 3-36); **Kent 171-6** (19.4 overs) (J. A. Leaning 55*; J. H. Plom 3-32). *PoM:* J. A. Leaning. *A 32-ball 55* from Jack Leaning – his first T20 half-century in seven innings since moving from Yorkshire – secured Kent's place in the knockouts. At 80-5, with Billings a third victim for Essex's former England Under-19 seamer Jack Plom, the hosts had needed 88 from 55 balls. But Leaning added 67 with Alex Blake (29 off 19), then 24* in nine balls with Stewart, who won the game with a mighty six off Plom over midwicket. Essex had managed 167, built around opener Tom Westley's 39 off 19, and Ryan ten Doeschate's 52 off 33.*

Kent away matches

August 29: tied with Middlesex.
September 3: beat Sussex by one run.
September 5: beat Essex by 29 runs.
September 14: beat Hampshire by eight wickets.
September 20: lost to Surrey by six wickets.

MIDDLESEX

At Lord's, August 29. **Tied. Middlesex 209-4** (20 overs) (S. S. Eskinazi 84, N. R. T. Gubbins 53); ‡**Kent 209-5** (20 overs) (Z. Crawley 31, D. J. Bell-Drummond 72). *PoM:* D. J. Bell-Drummond. *Cricket returned to Lord's after 11 months, although the stands were empty for a classic. Tom Helm ran in with Sussex needing five off the last; not for the first time, he kept a cool head. After a bye and a wide, Grant Stewart was bowled, and Ollie Robinson could not score from the next two balls, before squeezing a single. That left Jack Leaning needing two – but he could only scamper a bye to force a tie. It was tough on Kent captain Daniel Bell-Drummond, who had ransacked 72 from 32 balls, after a rapid opening stand of 89 with Zak Crawley. Earlier, Middlesex owed much to Stevie Eskinazi (84 from 52) and Nick Gubbins (53 from 33), who put on 111 for the third wicket.*

At Lord's, September 1 (floodlit). **Sussex won by three wickets. Middlesex 165-5** (20 overs) (S. S. Eskinazi 79, J. A. Simpson 46); ‡**Sussex 168-7** (19.2 overs) (D. Wiese 79*). *PoM:* D. Wiese. *County debut:* L. B. K. Hollman (Middlesex). *Eskinazi gave Middlesex another brisk start with 79 from 48, but canny T20 specialists Tymal Mills (2-33) and Danny Briggs (2-21) slowed the scoring. Sussex seemed out of it at 67-5 in the tenth, 19-year-old leg-spinner Luke Hollman marking an impressive debut with the wickets of Delray Rawlins and Ravi Bopara, but the big-hitting David Wiese wrenched back the initiative. Helm could not repeat his last-over heroics, with Wiese hitting the second ball for four to finish with 79* from 46, his highest T20 score in his 229th match.*

At Lord's, September 3 (floodlit). **Middlesex won by 11 runs. Middlesex 167-7** (20 overs) (S. S. Eskinazi 51, M. D. E. Holden 46); ‡**Essex 156-8** (20 overs) (R. N. ten Doeschate 32; S. T. Finn 3-18). *PoM:* S. T. Finn. *A third successive half-century from Eskinazi – a transformed white-ball batsman after being pushed up to open – underpinned a lop-sided Middlesex innings: 97-0 at halfway, they managed only 70-7 in the second ten as Simon Harmer (2-23) and Cameron Delport (2-31) applied the brakes. But with Essex, the defending champions, in shaky form, it proved enough. Steven Finn, Middlesex's T20 captain, took three wickets and, with Hollman (2-26) again catching the eye, a formidable bowling unit appeared to be taking shape.*

At Lord's, September 12. **Middlesex won by 19 runs.** ‡**Middlesex 142-6** (20 overs) (S. S. Eskinazi 33, J. A. Simpson 30*); **Hampshire 123** (18.5 overs) (T. P. Alsop 43, J. K. Fuller 34; S. T. Finn 3-27). *PoM:* T. G. Helm. *Another excellent Middlesex bowling performance made up for a middling display with the bat, in which Eskinazi top-scored again. But with the exception of Tom Alsop and James Fuller, who put on 71, Hampshire's batsmen were at sea: no one else reached double figures, as Finn, Helm (2-12) and Tim Murtagh (2-20) scuttled the visitors.*

At Lord's, September 14 (floodlit). **Surrey won by 30 runs. Surrey 218-5** (20 overs) (W. G. Jacks 55, H. M. Amla 67); ‡**Middlesex 188-5** (20 overs) (S. S. Eskinazi 77, J. A. Simpson 31). *PoM:* W. G. Jacks. *County debut:* J. B. Cracknell (Middlesex). *A savage onslaught by Surrey's batsmen ensured victory, and damaged Middlesex's run-rate. Openers Will Jacks, whose 30-ball 55 included five sixes, and Hashim Amla kicked off with 101, then Rory Burns (25 from ten) and Jamie Overton (29 from 12) kept up the barrage as Surrey equalled the highest total in any T20 match at Lord's, their own 218-7 in 2006. Eskinazi rounded off his prolific Lord's season (324 runs in five innings) with six sixes in his 44-ball 77, top-scoring for the fifth home game in five. But Middlesex still needed 61 when he was run out at the end of the 17th. Earlier, 20-year-old left-hander Jack Davies, in only his third senior T20 match, pinged Overton for a six that punched a hole in the panels just below Father Time.*

Middlesex away matches

August 27: no result (DLS) v Essex.
September 5: lost to Surrey by six wickets.
September 16: beat Kent by two runs.
September 18: lost to Sussex by three wickets.
September 20: lost to Hampshire by 20 runs.

SURREY

At The Oval, August 30. **Tied. Essex 143-6** (20 overs) (R. N. ten Doeschate 35, A. J. A. Wheater 32); ‡**Surrey 143-8** (20 overs) (J. L. Smith 30, B. T. Foakes 44). *PoM:* B. T. Foakes. *Needing one from two balls, Surrey blew it: Ben Foakes top-edged Matt Quinn to fine leg, then James Taylor missed the final delivery, lingered in his crease while partner Matt Dunn hurtled towards him, and was run out. Essex relied on Ryan ten Doeschate's 35, and a late blast from Paul Walter (23* from 13), to reach a competitive total.*

At The Oval, September 3 (floodlit). **Surrey won by nine wickets** (DLS). **Hampshire 77-5** (11 overs) (S. A. Northeast 31); ‡**Surrey 81-1** (10.4 overs) (W. G. Jacks 45*). *PoM:* W. G. Jacks. *County debuts:* J. Overton (Surrey); Shaheen Shah Afridi (Hampshire). *Slow left-armer Dan Moriarty bowled superbly in a rain-reduced match, finishing with 2-12 from three overs; his second wicket (Joe Weatherley) came courtesy of a sprawling catch in the deep by Rory Burns. The match started late, initially as 17 overs a side; further rain meant another reduction, to 11, with Surrey's target revised slightly to 80. They were always on track: openers Hashim Amla (29) and Will Jacks (45* from 31) put on 64 from 8.2 overs. Their first win for more than a year was watched by that 2020 rarity – a crowd, numbering 2,500.*

At The Oval, September 5 (floodlit). **Surrey won by six wickets.** ‡**Middlesex 113-9** (20 overs) (G. J. Batty 3-18); **Surrey 116-4** (18.1 overs) (B. T. Foakes 60*, J. L. Smith 38*). *PoM:* B. T. Foakes. *A partnership of 93* between Foakes and Jamie Smith transformed a low-scoring match, the second half of a televised double-header (earlier, Kent had beaten Essex). Middlesex had been kept to 113-9, Max Holden top-scoring with 29; Gareth Batty's figures of 24–13–18–3 included his 100th T20 wicket for Surrey, after 41 for Worcestershire. Surrey limped to 23-4 in the fifth, with Steven Finn and Nathan Sowter both striking twice, before Foakes and Smith stopped the rot.*

At The Oval, September 16 (floodlit). **Surrey won by four wickets. Sussex 165-7** (20 overs) (L. J. Wright 45, D. Wiese 33); ‡**Surrey 167-6** (19.1 overs) (W. G. Jacks 65, J. Overton 40*; W. A. T. Beer 3-34). *PoM:* W. G. Jacks. *Having taken 2-29 with his off-breaks, Jacks blitzed 65 from 39 balls, but leg-spinner Will Beer induced a few palpitations before Jamie Overton's late burst ensured Surrey's fifth win, and a place in the quarter-finals. Sussex had found scoring difficult, but David Wiese (33 from 23 balls) and Ravi Bopara (24 from nine) cracked 59 from the last five.*

At The Oval, September 20. **Surrey won by six wickets. Kent 159-8** (20 overs) (D. J. Bell-Drummond 37, S. W. Billings 50; L. E. Plunkett 3-19); ‡**Surrey 161-4** (18.4 overs) (J. J. Roy 72, L. J. Evans 73). *PoM:* L. J. Evans. *Jason Roy, whose nine innings for Surrey and England in the summer had produced 73 runs, returned to form with a boundary-studded 72, from 52 balls. He put on 135 for the second wicket with Laurie Evans, who skated along even more quickly – 73 from 45 – as Surrey, who needed to score at least 127 to top the table and guarantee a home quarter-final, romped to their seventh win of the group stage. Earlier, Sam Billings had lacked support as the England seamers Liam Plunkett and Reece Topley (1-30) took control: the last five overs yielded only 32.*

Surrey away matches

August 28: no result v Sussex.
September 1: lost to Kent by five wickets.
September 11: beat Essex by four wickets.
September 14: beat Middlesex by 30 runs.
September 18: beat Hampshire by nine wickets.

SUSSEX

At Hove, August 28. **No result. Sussex 116-5** (15.2 overs) (P. D. Salt 40, L. J. Wright 31) **v ‡Surrey.** *County debut:* R. S. Bopara (Sussex). *Surrey had fought back strongly when rain arrived: Sussex, from 83-1 in the ninth, lost four for 12 in 20 balls. The collapse included Phil Salt for a 22-ball 40, and Ravi Bopara, on his county debut, for a single. Salt had peppered the short boundary by the scoreboard, taking 28 off James Taylor's first over in T20 cricket.*

At Hove, August 30. **Sussex won by six wickets. Hampshire 176-5** (20 overs) (T. P. Alsop 51, J. K. Fuller 53*, I. G. Holland 36*; D. R. Briggs 3-17); **‡Sussex 177-4** (19.5 overs) (L. J. Wright 82, D. Wiese 43*). *PoM:* L. J. Wright. *A thunderous 82 off 55 balls by Luke Wright set up victory, although it wasn't until the penultimate ball that David Wiese (43* off 31), playing after a fortnight's quarantine, hit the winning boundary. Earlier, James Fuller smashed the window of a hospitality box (as, later, did Wright) during a 31-ball 53* that included five sixes, as he and Ian Holland (36* off 22) turned a Hampshire score of 88-5 into a challenging total; Danny Briggs managed 3-17. Fuller's first over then cost 29, as Salt and Wright put on 87 in eight for Sussex's first wicket.*

At Hove, September 3. **Kent won by one run. Kent 195-5** (20 overs) (Z. Crawley 67, A. J. Blake 41, J. A. Leaning 37*); **‡Sussex 194-7** (20 overs) (P. D. Salt 33, L. J. Wright 40, D. M. W. Rawlins 30, D. Wiese 38). *PoM:* Z. Crawley. *Needing nine off seven balls with six wickets in hand, Sussex fluffed their lines. First, Wiese fell to Adam Milnes; then, with two needed off two, Bopara was caught behind off Fred Klaassen, and Ollie Robinson run out scrambling for a bye that would have earned a tie. Bowlers on both sides had suffered on a flat pitch, not least Kent's Grant Stewart, who briefly had figures of 0.1–0–13–0: his first delivery, a no-ball, was hit for six by Salt; his second was a wide; his third (and first legitimate delivery) went for four. The Kent total was boosted by Zak Crawley's 67 off 49, while Salt and Wright got Sussex off to another flyer – 56 in four overs.*

At Hove, September 14. **Essex won by 12 runs. Essex 197-5** (20 overs) (T. Westley 39, D. W. Lawrence 81, M. S. Pepper 34*); **‡Sussex 185-8** (20 overs) (A. D. Thomason 47, D. M. W. Rawlins 37, D. Wiese 30). *PoM:* D. W. Lawrence. *After just 57 runs in five T20 innings, Dan Lawrence smashed 81 off 44 balls, with six fours and six sixes, to earn Essex their first win. On a flat pitch, the Sussex attack – already without Chris Jordan, who had flown to the UAE for the IPL – had struggled; Tymal Mills left the field with back trouble before he could complete his allocation at the death. At 119-2 after 13, they were in the hunt, only for Lawrence to take two big wickets in his only over: the dangerous Delray Rawlins (37 off 20) and opener Aaron Thomason (47 off 36).*

At Hove, September 18. **Sussex won by three wickets. Middlesex 155-8** (20 overs) (J. B. Cracknell 37, J. A. Simpson 46, L. B. K. Hollman 35; G. H. S. Garton 4-27, D. M. W. Rawlins 3-21); **‡Sussex 158-7** (19.2 overs) (P. D. Salt 56; L. B. K. Hollman 3-18). *PoM:* L. B. K. Hollman. *With his parents watching from the flat he owns overlooking the ground, George Garton had a day to remember, as Sussex stayed on track for the quarter-finals. He took a brilliant return catch from the third ball of the game to dismiss Max Holden, before picking up three more wickets, including the fluent Luke Hollman (35 off 21). Then, after Sussex had slipped from 70-0 to 121-6, with Hollman's leg-breaks collecting 3-18, Garton hit 22 off five balls from Steven Finn in the penultimate over to all but settle the game. Earlier, Rawlins managed a career-best 3-21 with his slow left-armers.*

Sussex away matches

September 1: beat Middlesex by three wickets.
September 10: beat Hampshire by 13 runs.
September 12: beat Kent by eight wickets.
September 16: lost to Surrey by four wickets.
September 20: beat Essex by four wickets.

QUARTER-FINALS

At Bristol, October 1. **Gloucestershire won by seven wickets. ‡Northamptonshire 113** (19.4 overs) (B. A. C. Howell 3-16, R. F. Higgins 3-24); **Gloucestershire 114-3** (11.5 overs) (C. D. J. Dent 40, I. A. Cockbain 30*). *PoM:* B. A. C. Howell. *Gloucestershire produced a Twenty20 masterclass to overwhelm Northamptonshire, and reach finals day for the first time since 2007. Benny Howell and Ryan Higgins took three wickets each as the visitors were shot out for 113; Tom Taylor top-scored with 27, including three of his side's feeble haul of seven boundaries. Chris Dent made an assured 40 from 25, and Ian Cockbain 30* off 20, to usher Gloucestershire to an eighth win in nine, with more than eight overs in hand.*

At The Oval, October 1. **Surrey won by 56 runs. Surrey 169-2** (20 overs) (J. J. Roy 56, H. M. Amla 73*); **‡Kent 113-7** (20 overs) (J. A. Leaning 34; W. G. Jacks 4-15). *PoM:* W. G. Jacks. *Kent paid dearly for giving Surrey first use of a tired pitch: Jason Roy and Hashim Amla piled on an opening stand of 114, and Amla stayed to the end, placing the ball beautifully in his 73* from 53 balls. Will Jacks's sparky 23* provided a late spurt to 169-2, which proved more than enough. Imran Qayyum's 2-32 had shown that spin might play a part, and Jacks struck twice with his off-breaks in the second over, removing Kent's prolific opening pair, Daniel Bell-Drummond and Zak Crawley, thanks to excellent catches by keeper Ben Foakes. Only Jack Leaning made it past 20. Jacks finished with career-best figures of 24–15–15–4.*

At Hove, October 1. **Lancashire won by 45 runs. Lancashire 140-8** (20 overs) (S. J. Croft 41, D. J. Vilas 40; G. H. S. Garton 3-28); **‡Sussex 95** (17.2 overs) (L. J. Wright 36; M. W. Parkinson 3-9, L. S. Livingstone 4-23). *PoM:* L. S. Livingstone. *Jason Gillespie's final match as Sussex coach was an anticlimax. He felt Lancashire's total was 15–20 below par, but Sussex showed little method against their three spinners on a dry, turning surface. They returned combined figures of 8-50, with Matt Parkinson taking three wickets in four balls, which ensured the pragmatic batting of Steven Croft and Dane Vilas was not wasted.*

At Nottingham, October 1 (floodlit). **Tied. Nottinghamshire won by virtue of a higher score in the powerplay. Leicestershire 139-7** (20 overs) (C. N. Ackermann 43, H. J. Swindells 58); **‡Nottinghamshire 139-7** (20 overs) (J. M. Clarke 35; C. N. Ackermann 3-27, G. T. Griffiths 3-21). *PoM:* S. R. Patel. *Nottinghamshire scraped through to finals day with a generous slice of luck, after Leicestershire had fought back in defence of an apparently inadequate total. Tied down by seam and spin, with Callum Parkinson producing a beauty to bowl Alex Hales, Nottinghamshire ended up needing 17 from seven deliveries, which would have been beyond them but for two misfields. The first was by Arron Lilley, who let Samit Patel's pull slip through his legs for four at midwicket. Then Dieter Klein should have kept Imad Wasim to a single from his mistimed pull to mid-on off the last – but he took his eye off the slippery ball, allowing a scurried second. A tie did not lead to a super over in the knockouts, as the regulations permitted one only in matches affected by DLS. The first tie-breaker was wickets lost but, as both sides had lost seven, it went down to the higher powerplay score – and Nottinghamshire had made 42-1 to Leicestershire's 22-2. It meant Joe Clarke's early 35 from 22 balls was the match-winning innings, trumping the higher scores of Leicestershire's Colin Ackermann and Harry Swindells.*

FINALS DAY REPORTS BY NICK FRIEND

SEMI-FINALS

GLOUCESTERSHIRE v SURREY

At Birmingham, October 3–4. Surrey won by six wickets. Toss: Surrey.

It was fitting that, at the end of an exceptional summer, finals day should begin even later than planned. After a nationwide deluge, a reserve day was called on for the first time in the competition's history. Even that took place only because of the heroism of Edgbaston's groundstaff. The worst-case scenario of Sunday-evening bowl-outs was alleviated by the addition of a second reserve day, for the following Wednesday, just in case. Fortunately, it was not required, with 11-over semi-finals beginning at 3.15pm – 28 hours later than scheduled. Asked to bat on their first finals-day appearance since 2007, Gloucestershire struggled for boundaries. Hammond used up a sixth of the shortened innings in making a single, missing a string of attempted reverse sweeps off Jacks, before Cockbain, who earlier in the competition had hit an unbeaten 84 off 35 balls at Edgbaston against Warwickshire, went without scoring. Dent, Higgins and Howell all attempted to provide impetus, but were fighting a losing battle, and Plunkett picked up three wickets in two overs. Surrey made light work of their task, picking up three boundaries in the first over (Gloucestershire had needed 47 balls to hit as many). Payne struck three times, but Foakes ensured Surrey remained ahead of a modest rate, and they eased to their ninth T20 win in a row, with eight balls to spare.

Player of the Match: L. E. Plunkett.

Gloucestershire

		B	4/6
1 M. A. H. Hammond *c 4 b 10*	1	11	0
2 C. D. J. Dent *c 1 b 11*	17	13	2
3 I. A. Cockbain *c 1 b 2*	0	3	0
4 R. F. Higgins *c 11 b 8*	19	14	1
5 *J. M. R. Taylor *c 2 b 8*	3	4	0
6 B. A. C. Howell *c 2 b 8*	21	12	1/2
7 †J. R. Bracey *not out*	4	5	0
8 G. L. van Buuren *c 6 b 10*	3	4	0
Lb 2, w 3	5		
3.2 overs: 12-1 (11 overs)	73-7		

1/12 2/12 3/24 4/33 5/59 6/65 7/73

9 T. M. J. Smith, 10 D. A. Payne and 11 J. Shaw did not bat.

Topley 18–10–15–2; Jacks 12–9–5–1; Moriarty 12–1–24–1; Batty 12–2–15–0; Plunkett 12–6–12–3.

Surrey

		B	4/6
1 J. J. Roy *c 6 b 10*	6	5	1
2 W. G. Jacks *b 10*	16	11	3
3 L. J. Evans *c 9 b 6*	12	12	1
4 †B. T. Foakes *c 7 b 10*	20	20	0/1
5 R. J. Burns *not out*	12	9	2
6 J. Overton *not out*	4	1	1
Lb 3, w 1	4		
3.2 overs: 28-1 (9.4 overs)	74-4		

1/15 2/28 3/41 4/70

7 J. Clark, 8 L. E. Plunkett, 9 *G. J. Batty, 10 R. J. W. Topley and 11 D. T. Moriarty did not bat.

Van Buuren 6–2–13–0; Payne 16–7–18–3; Shaw 6–3–7–0; Smith 12–4–12–0; Howell 12–5–12–1; Higgins 6–1–9–0.

Umpires: M. Burns and A. G. Wharf. Third umpire: M. J. Saggers.
Referee: S. Cummings.

LANCASHIRE v NOTTINGHAMSHIRE

At Birmingham, October 3–4. Nottinghamshire won by five wickets. Toss: Lancashire.

The two best teams in the North Group met on a pitch that had flattened out while the sun was making a belated appearance. Lancashire, as had been their tournament strategy, opted to bat, and Davies, Livingstone and Croft all made quickfire contributions. But their innings fell away: from 61 for one in the seventh, they added just 33 from the final 27 deliveries. Nottinghamshire's attack had plenty of nous: Imad Wasim, Ball, Patel and Christian had all played T20 internationals. In the previous year's semi-final, they had blown it against Worcestershire. This time, there was little such drama, even after Hales was bowled by a beauty from leg-spinner Matt Parkinson, three days after being similarly undone by his twin, Leicestershire's slow left-armer Callum. His dismissal was followed by some colourful expletives, earning a team warning for bad language from umpire Saggers, and the threat of five penalty runs. But by the end of the third over, Duckett, Hales and Clarke had all hit a six; even as Lancashire fought back through the spin of Hartley and Parkinson, runs continued to flow. Moores and Clarke followed in quick succession, to make it 61 for four after six, but Christian eased any concerns, slog-sweeping four consecutive sixes off Livingstone into the Hollies Stand.

Player of the Match: D. T. Christian.

Lancashire

		B	4/6
1 †A. L. Davies *c 9 b 6*	15	11	2
2 L. S. Livingstone *c 11 b 10*	22	15	2/1
3 S. J. Croft *c 12 b 11*	33	22	2/2
4 *D. J. Vilas *lbw b 10*	5	6	0
5 K. K. Jennings *not out*	9	7	0
6 R. P. Jones *not out*	6	5	0
Lb 1, w 3	4		
3.2 overs: 32-1 (11 overs)	94-4		

1/18 2/61 3/75 4/78

7 D. J. Lamb, 8 L. Wood, 9 T. W. Hartley, 10 S. Mahmood and 11 M. W. Parkinson did not bat.

Imad Wasim 18–3–20–0; Ball 12–2–20–1; Patel 12–4–17–1; Christian 12–2–20–0; Carter 12–6–16–2.

Nottinghamshire

		B	4/6
1 B. M. Duckett *c 3 b 10*	13	7	0/1
2 A. D. Hales *b 11*	29	17	2/2
3 J. M. Clarke *b 9*	17	8	0/2
4 †T. J. Moores *c 4 b 9*	1	3	0
5 *D. T. Christian *st 1 b 11*	30	13	0/4
6 S. R. Patel *not out*	1	1	0
7 Imad Wasim *not out*	4	1	1
3.2 overs: 41-1 (8.2 overs)	95-5		

1/30 2/50 3/59 4/61 5/91

8 C. D. Nash, 9 S. J. Mullaney, 10 M. Carter and 11 J. T. Ball did not bat.

12th man: Z. J. Chappell.

Hartley 12–3–21–2; Wood 6–1–11–0; Mahmood 6–2–14–1; Livingstone 12–3–37–0; Parkinson 14–6–12–2.

Umpires: D. J. Millns and M. J. Saggers. Third umpire: A. G. Wharf.
Referee: S. Cummings.

FINAL

NOTTINGHAMSHIRE v SURREY

At Birmingham, October 4. Nottinghamshire won by six wickets. Toss: Nottinghamshire.

It all came down to this: Surrey and Nottinghamshire, defeated once each en route to the final, in a 16-over-a-side, night-time showpiece. Three hours later, under the Edgbaston floodlights, Nottinghamshire emerged as dominant champions. For the club, it was a second title in four years. For Duckett, unbeaten in an ultimately clinical chase, it swept away the demons from the previous season's semi-final against Worcestershire, when Nottinghamshire choked. Then, he ended the match crouched on his haunches. Now, he leapt into the dark sky with a punch of the air.

Alex Davidson, Getty Images

Christian, up and smite them! Dan Christan launches another.

It is one thing to claim to have learned from a chastening experience; another to prove it on the big stage. He was now a three-time Blast winner by the age of 25, having been victorious with Northamptonshire in 2013 and 2016. For Christian, captain and overseas player, this was an eighth T20 title around the globe – evidence, as he had tweeted in August, that "old blokes win stuff".

In a chase that had begun unconvincingly, Duckett soon imposed himself. "I think I've come on a long way since then," he said, recalling the events of 2019. "I'd be lying if I said it wasn't in the back of my mind." This was reward for sheer hard work, and a fresh emphasis on fitness; it was no coincidence that his white-ball success was matched by 394 runs – more than 100 clear of his nearest team-mate – in the Bob Willis Trophy.

Set 128, Nottinghamshire had lost Hales first ball, pulling Topley to deep square leg, and it was soon 19 for three when Jacks removed Clarke and Patel. But Duckett and the 39-year-old Trego, playing his first Twenty20 game since July 2019 – and his first for Nottinghamshire, after 163 for Somerset (and four for Kent) –

added a buccaneering 63 in 5.3 overs. Still, when Trego, selected after Chris Nash was injured during the semi-final, departed with 46 needed in seven, Surrey sensed an opening. Those hopes were soon extinguished by Christian, who cracked three boundaries in another momentum-shifting cameo.

Earlier, he had elected to field, confident in his side's experience and depth: Patel, down on the card at No. 8 (though he went in at No. 4), was the sixth-highest T20 run-scorer in county history. Amla was recalled after sitting out the semi, but struggled for timing: he and Jacks – later named the Blast's MVP – fell early to Patel and Ball. A pre-tournament injury to Harry Gurney had freed up a place, and Ball ended the competition as its leading wicket-taker, with 19. He also accounted for Roy, who played imperiously during a 90-run partnership with Evans. But Evans's departure triggered a match-defining collapse: five for 13 in the final 16 balls, four to Christian, placing Nottinghamshire in command.

Once primed, Duckett asserted control, eventually hitting the winning runs and passing 50 in the process with consecutive boundaries. And just like that, this abbreviated, 65-day county season was over.

Player of the Match: D. T. Christian. *Player of the Tournament:* W. G. Jacks.

Surrey

		B	*4/6*
1 J. J. Roy *lbw b 11*	66	47	7/1
2 H. M. Amla *c 6 b 4*	3	10	0
3 W. G. Jacks *c 6 b 11*	3	4	0
4 L. J. Evans *c 2 b 6*	43	23	3/2
5 J. Overton *c 7 b 6*	0	1	0
6 R. J. Burns *not out*	5	5	0
7 †B. T. Foakes *c 2 b 6*	1	3	0
8 L. E. Plunkett *c 1 b 6*	4	3	0
Lb 2	2		
4.5 overs: 24-2 (16 overs)	127-7		

1/18 2/24 3/114 4/115 5/119 6/122 7/127

9 *G. J. Batty, 10 R. J. W. Topley and 11 D. T. Moriarty did not bat.

Patel 24–12–25–1; Ball 18–6–17–2; Imad Wasim 18–7–28–0; Carter 12–2–19–0; Mullaney 6–0–13–0; Christian 18–4–23–4.

Nottinghamshire

		B	*4/6*
1 A. D. Hales *c 4 b 10*	0	1	0
2 B. M. Duckett *not out*	53	38	8
3 J. M. Clarke *c 5 b 3*	3	6	0
4 S. R. Patel *c 6 b 3*	7	6	1
5 P. D. Trego *lbw b 11*	31	21	5/1
6 *D. T. Christian *not out*	21	11	3
Lb 2, w 6, nb 6	14		
4.5 overs: 32-3 (13.2 overs)	129-4		

1/0 2/4 3/19 4/82

7 †T. J. Moores, 8 S. J. Mullaney, 9 Imad Wasim, 10 M. Carter and 11 J. T. Ball did not bat.

Topley 18–10–25–1; Jacks 18–5–32–2; Moriarty 18–9–20–1; Plunkett 6–2–13–0; Overton 6–1–16–0; Batty 14–5–21–0.

Umpires: M. Burns and D. J. Millns. Third umpire: A. G. Wharf.
Referee: S. Cummings.

T20 BLAST FINALS

2003 SURREY beat Warwickshire by nine wickets at Nottingham.
2004 LEICESTERSHIRE beat Surrey by seven wickets at Birmingham.
2005 SOMERSET beat Lancashire by seven wickets at The Oval.
2006 LEICESTERSHIRE beat Nottinghamshire by four runs at Nottingham.
2007 KENT beat Gloucestershire by four wickets Birmingham.
2008 MIDDLESEX beat Kent by three runs at Southampton.
2009 SUSSEX beat Somerset by 63 runs at Birmingham.
2010 HAMPSHIRE beat Somerset by losing fewer wickets with the scores tied at Southampton.
2011 LEICESTERSHIRE beat Somerset by 18 runs at Birmingham.
2012 HAMPSHIRE beat Yorkshire by ten runs at Cardiff.
2013 NORTHAMPTONSHIRE beat Surrey by 102 runs (D/L) at Birmingham.
2014 WARWICKSHIRE beat Lancashire by four runs at Birmingham.
2015 LANCASHIRE beat Northamptonshire by 13 runs at Birmingham.
2016 NORTHAMPTONSHIRE beat Durham by four wickets at Birmingham.
2017 NOTTINGHAMSHIRE beat Warwickshire by 22 runs at Birmingham.
2018 WORCESTERSHIRE beat Sussex by five wickets at Birmingham.
2019 ESSEX beat Worcestershire by four wickets at Birmingham.
2020 NOTTINGHAMSHIRE beat Surrey by six wickets at Birmingham.

T20 BLAST RECORDS

Highest score	161	A. Lyth	Yorkshire v Northants at Leeds	2017
	158*	B. B. McCullum	Warwicks v Derbys at Birmingham	2015
	153*	L. J. Wright	Sussex v Essex at Chelmsford	2014
Fastest 50 – balls	13	M. E. Trescothick	Somerset v Hampshire at Taunton	2010
Fastest 100 – balls	34	A. Symonds	Kent v Middlesex at Maidstone	2004
Most sixes – innings	16	G. R. Napier	Essex v Sussex at Chelmsford	2008
Most runs – season	710	J. M. Vince (avge 59.16, SR 134.46) for Hampshire		2015
Most sixes – season	34	C. J. Anderson for Somerset		2018
Most runs – career	**4,498**	**L. J. Wright (avge 33.07, SR 148.98)**		**2004 to 2020**
	4,079	**J. L. Denly (avge 28.92, SR 125.08)**		**2004 to 2020**
	4,035	**M. H. Wessels (avge 29.45, SR 140.98)**		**2005 to 2020**
Most 100s – career	7	M. Klinger		2013 to 2019
Best SR – career*	182.97	C. H. Gayle (505 runs, avge 84.16)		2015 to 2016
Most sixes – career	**168**	**L. J. Wright**		**2004 to 2020**
Best bowling	7-18	C. N. Ackermann	Leics v Warwicks at Leicester	2019
	6-5	A. V. Suppiah	Somerset v Glamorgan at Cardiff	2011
	6-16	T. G. Southee	Essex v Glamorgan at Chelmsford	2011
Most econ four overs	2-5	A. C. Thomas	Somerset v Hants at Southampton	2010
	3-5	D. R. Briggs	Hampshire v Kent at Canterbury	2010
Most expensive analysis	0-77	B. W. Sanderson	Northants v Yorkshire at Leeds	2017
Most wickets – season	33	A. C. Thomas (avge 13.93, ER 6.31) for Somerset		2010
Most wickets – career	**172**	**D. R. Briggs (avge 21.34, ER 7.16)**		**2010 to 2020**
	165	**S. R. Patel (avge 26.76, ER 7.33)**		**2003 to 2020**
	156	Yasir Arafat (avge 21.10, ER 8.09)		2006 to 2016
Best ER – career	5.64	J. Botha (300 balls, avge 23.50)		2011
Highest total	260-4	Yorkshire v Northamptonshire at Leeds		2017
	255-2	Yorkshire v Leicestershire at Leicester		2019
	254-3	Gloucestershire v Middlesex at Uxbridge		2011
Lowest total	44	Glamorgan v Surrey at The Oval		2019
	47	Northamptonshire v Durham at Chester-le-Street		2011
	53	Worcestershire v Lancashire at Manchester		2016
Highest successful chase	227-4	Middlesex v Somerset at Taunton		2019
Highest match aggregate	462-10	Warwickshire v Northamptonshire at Birmingham		2018

* *Career strike-rate: minimum 500 runs.* † *Career economy-rate: minimum 300 balls.*

THE UNIVERSITIES IN 2020

The final season of first-class university cricket in England – a tradition dating back to 1817 – was ruined by Covid-19, which obliterated the whole of the MCC Universities programme. When the pandemic showed signs of easing, it proved possible at least to salvage the four-day Varsity Match, which was switched from the Parks in July to Fenner's in September.

"Four of our players had technically graduated, including me, but were allowed to come back and play," said Oxford's captain Toby Pettman, a tall seamer who signed for Nottinghamshire for 2021. "The most unusual aspects were playing without any crowd – we had a live stream instead on the boundary edge – and only one person allowed in the changing-room, which made it interesting when people were padding up. We were temperature-tested on arrival each day, and had all our food in pre-packaged containers. But when we were on the pitch, everything felt relatively normal. We felt very lucky to be playing."

"It was nice to go out with an emphatic victory," said the Cambridge captain, Nick Taylor, who had played alongside Pettman for Oxford in 2017. "Many protocols had to be put in place. The whole occasion was a logistical nightmare – so it was very pleasing to get such a good outcome, if it really was the last first-class game at Fenner's."

Derek Pringle's reflections on university cricket appear on page 116.

THE UNIVERSITY MATCHES IN 2020

At Oxford, September 1. **Oxford University won by 78 runs.** ‡**Oxford University 262-8** (50 overs) (G. T. Hargrave 100, T. R. W. Gnodde 72); **Cambridge University 184** (43 overs) (A. K. Agedah 35, Extras 31). *In a game switched from Lord's because of the pandemic, Oxford's batting proved too strong, and they completed their eighth successive victory in the Varsity one-day match, to stretch their overall lead to 17–9. After a cautious opening, as a lively pitch – and the 10.30 start – caused problems, George Hargrave made his way to a superb century. Tom Gnodde hammered five sixes in his 58-ball 72 to swell the total, and Cambridge had no way back after dipping to 12-3 in the sixth over. There was no Varsity 20-over match in 2020 (Cambridge lead 5–4 since the first in 2008; two were no-results, and one was abandoned).*

CAMBRIDGE UNIVERSITY v OXFORD UNIVERSITY

At Cambridge, September 3–6. Cambridge University won by 249 runs. Toss: Cambridge University. First-class debuts: A. K. Agedah, J. S. Dhariwal, P. J. Flanagan, J. E. Gillespie; D. J. de Silva, B. A. J. Fisher, T. R. W. Gnodde, J. C. A. Job, A. W. Livingstone, W. D. N. von Behr.

Cambridge rounded off the first-class history of the Varsity Match with a thumping victory – their second-highest by runs in the 175 games – thanks to a century from the South African Pieter Daneel, and ten wickets from James Vitali, a seamer from Salisbury. Their batsmen had battled through the first day. Eight reached double figures, but the top score was wicketkeeper Edward Hyde's 55; as the Oxford bowlers exhibited understandable signs of rustiness, there were also 54 extras in a total of 307. Vitali soon inflicted two ducks and, from 108 for five, Oxford lost their last five for 21; Vitali finished with six for 34. Shortly before the second-day close, Cambridge were in a spot of bother at 84 for five, but next day Daneel grafted to a maiden century, putting on 86 for the seventh wicket with Jovan Dhariwal as the lead climbed. Set 436, Oxford were soon 41 for four, after two wickets for off-spinner Neil Botha, another South African. The later batsmen pushed the match into the fourth day, with left-hander Freddie Foster biffing a lively unbeaten 50 from No. 9, but Vitali soon took the last two wickets to round off his ten-for. Padraic Flanagan and Will von Behr were the first graduates of Dublin's Trinity College to feature in the Varsity Match since Thomas Babington Jones in 1874.

Close of play: first day, Cambridge University 282-8 (Hyde 54, Vitali 5); second day, Cambridge University 95-5 (Daneel 39, Hyde 4); third day, Oxford University 165-8 (Foster 39, Fisher 0).

Cambridge University

*N. P. Taylor c Gnodde b Fisher	20	– lbw b Pettman	0
J. E. Gillespie lbw b Fisher	4	– b Pettman	16
A. K. Agedah b Pettman	14	– c Job b Searle	7
P. D. Daneel lbw b Livingstone	22	– c Job b Pettman	125
A. J. Moen c Foster b Pettman	41	– lbw b Fisher	15
N. Botha lbw b von Behr	31	– b Fisher	7
†E. R. B. Hyde c Job b Livingstone	55	– c Foster b von Behr	9
A. R. Amin c Job b von Behr	23	– (9) c Job b Pettman	0
J. S. Dhariwal c Foster b Searle	27	– (8) b Foster	34
J. C. Vitali not out	8	– not out	15
P. J. Flanagan b Fisher	8	– b Foster	2
B 9, lb 7, w 12, nb 26	54	B 9, lb 10, w 6, nb 2	27
1/29 (2) 2/40 (1) 3/55 (3) (96.2 overs)	307	1/0 (1) 2/19 (3) (77.2 overs)	257
4/96 (4) 5/128 (5) 6/167 (6)		3/33 (2) 4/70 (5)	
7/203 (8) 8/272 (9) 9/285 (7) 10/307 (11)		5/84 (6) 6/132 (7) 7/218 (8)	
		8/219 (9) 9/246 (4) 10/257 (11)	

Pettman 22–6–68–2; Searle 18–5–45–1; Fisher 10.2–0–37–3; Livingstone 13–1–60–2; Foster 12–3–43–0; von Behr 21–8–38–2. *Second innings*—Pettman 21–3–53–4; Searle 12–1–52–1; von Behr 18–6–37–1; Fisher 11–1–42–2; Livingstone 5–1–21–0; Foster 10.2–2–33–2.

Oxford University

D. J. de Silva c Hyde b Vitali	0	– lbw b Vitali	1
G. T. Hargrave c Daneel b Flanagan	25	– c Hyde b Botha	10
†J. C. A. Job lbw b Vitali	0	– c Daneel b Botha	22
M. A. Naylor c Hyde b Flanagan	14	– c Amin b Flanagan	0
W. D. N. von Behr c Daneel b Botha	14	– lbw b Botha	22
T. R. W. Gnodde lbw b Vitali	45	– b Vitali	21
C. J. Searle c Daneel b Vitali	8	– b Flanagan	26
*T. H. S. Pettman c Amin b Vitali	0	– lbw b Botha	18
F. J. H. Foster c Hyde b Vitali	1	– not out	50
B. A. J. Fisher not out	13	– c Botha b Vitali	10
A. W. Livingstone b Flanagan	3	– lbw b Vitali	0
B 3, lb 1, w 2	6	Lb 1, w 5	6
1/0 (1) 2/0 (3) 3/39 (2) (47.1 overs)	129	1/5 (1) 2/32 (2) (70.5 overs)	186
4/42 (4) 5/72 (5) 6/108 (6)		3/35 (4) 4/41 (3)	
7/108 (8) 8/111 (7) 9/114 (9) 10/129 (11)		5/79 (6) 6/84 (5) 7/116 (7)	
		8/163 (8) 9/176 (10) 10/186 (11)	

Vitali 14–3–34–6; Flanagan 13.1–4–30–3; Botha 18–6–44–1; Amin 1–0–10–0; Dhariwal 1–0–7–0. *Second innings*—Flanagan 18–7–53–2; Vitali 18.5–4–58–4; Botha 26–13–43–4; Amin 8–0–31–0.

Umpires: T. Lungley and C. M. Watts.

Cambridge University *N. P. Taylor *(The Perse School, St Catherine's College, Oxford, and Clare)*, A. K. Agedah *(Bancroft's School and Selwyn)*, A. R. Amin *(Merchant Taylors' School, Northwood, and Emmanuel)*, N. Botha *(Paul Roos Gymnasium, Stellenbosch University and St Catharine's)*, P. D. Daneel *(Paul Roos Gymnasium, Stellenbosch University and Jesus)*, J. S. Dhariwal *(King Edward VI School, Southampton, and Magdalene)*, P. J. Flanagan *(St Michael's College, Trinity College, Dublin, and St Catharine's)*, J. E. Gillespie *(Malmesbury School, Nottingham University and Wolfson)*, E. R. B. Hyde *(Tonbridge School and Jesus)*, A. J. Moen *(Tonbridge School and Magdalene)*, J. C. Vitali *(Sherborne School, University College, London, and Christ's)*.

THE SCORER'S VIEW

Fenner's, or Fort Knox?

QUENTIN JONES

It was nothing short of a miracle that the 2020 Varsity Match happened at all. Originally, it was planned for the University Parks at Oxford but, even with a rescheduled fixture list, the game was never going to take place there – it's impossible to put a biosecure bubble around a ground in a public park that attracts people in droves. The only option was to switch it to Fenner's – although that bald statement does not hint at the effort that went into hosting the last first-class edition of this historic match.

The Cambridge University administrators, working closely with the ECB, swung into action. After endless calls, by phone and on Zoom, email exchanges with officials, paramedics and other medical personnel, the game was given the all-clear. It was like a military operation. When I arrived at the main gate, to do the scoring for Oxford, I had my temperature checked and was asked several questions before my name was ticked off the approved list, and I was allowed in. Once inside, I could not leave until close of play, and the gate was electronically locked behind me. Fenner's had turned into Fort Knox.

The mammoth logistical operation paid off, and play in the 175th University Match finally got under way. Three days later, at 10.48 on September 6, James Vitali struck Angus Livingstone on the pad, and went up for lbw: umpire Chris Watts, standing at the Gresham Road End, gave it some quick thought and raised his finger. That was it. The end of 193 years of history. I felt a profound sense of loss and sadness as I entered the data on the laptop, and pencilled one final "W" on my back-up linear sheet.

I love both Fenner's and the Parks, but I will be gobsmacked if either sees another first-class match. All that history. What special places.

T. W. Balderson *(Cheadle Hulme High School and Downing)* and K. Suresh *(Cranleigh School and Wolfson)* replaced Flanagan and Gillespie in the 50-over match.

Oxford University *T. H. S. Pettman *(Tonbridge School and Jesus)*, D. J. de Silva *(Harrow School and Exeter)*, B. A. J. Fisher *(Bishop Wordsworth's School, Salisbury, and Magdalen)*, F. J. H. Foster *(Eltham College and St Cross)*, T. R. W. Gnodde *(Eton College and Pembroke)*, G. T. Hargrave *(Shrewsbury School and Hertford)*, J. C. A. Job *(Cranleigh School and St Hilda's)*, A. W. Livingstone *(Ipswich School and Worcester)*, M. A. Naylor *(Finham Park School, Coventry, and St Cross)*, C. J. Searle *(Hampton School and Worcester)*, W. D. N. von Behr *(Marlborough College, Trinity College, Dublin, and Wolfson)*.

J. A. Curtis *(St Edward's School, Oxford, and Keble)* replaced Livingstone in the 50-over match.

UNIVERSITY MATCH FIRST-CLASS RECORDS

The University Match dates back to 1827. Altogether there have been 175 official matches, Cambridge winning 61 and Oxford 58, with 56 drawn (the 1988 fixture was abandoned without a ball bowled). The match was usually staged at Lord's, though Oxford also hosted it five times (four at the Magdalen Ground and one at Bullingdon Green) between 1829 and 1850. The first-class fixture was moved from Lord's in 2001, to be staged alternately at Cambridge and Oxford, with a one-day game played at Lord's instead.

D. W. Jarrett (Oxford 1975, Cambridge 1976), S. M. Wookey (Cambridge 1975 and 1976, Oxford 1978), G. Pathmanathan (Oxford 1975 to 1978, Cambridge 1983), J. A. Lodwick (Oxford 2010, Cambridge 2012), A. D. J. Kennedy (Cambridge 2010 to 2012, Oxford 2013 and 2014) and

N. P. Taylor (Oxford 2017, Cambridge 2019 and 2020) gained Blues for both universities. R. P. Moulding (Oxford 1978 to 1983) and J. J. N. Heywood (Cambridge 2003 to 2008) both made a record six appearances.

A full list of Blues from 1837 may be found in *Wisdens* published between 1923 and 1939; the lists were thereafter curtailed, covering more recent years only, and dropped after 1992.

Highest scores

313*	S. S. Agarwal (Oxford) at Cambridge	2013
247	S. Oberoi (Oxford) at Cambridge	2005
238*	Nawab of Pataudi snr (Oxford) at Lord's	1931
236*	J. W. M. Dalrymple (Oxford) at Cambridge	2003
211	G. Goonesena (Cambridge) at Lord's	1957
202	M. A. Naylor (Oxford) at Oxford	2018
201*	M. J. K. Smith (Oxford) at Lord's	1954
201	A. Ratcliffe (Cambridge) at Lord's	1931
200	Majid Khan (Cambridge) at Lord's	1970

Ratcliffe's 201 was a record for a day, before being beaten by Pataudi's 238.*

Altogether 138 hundreds were scored, 71 by Oxford and 67 by Cambridge. Only M. J. K. Smith (Oxford) and R. J. Boyd-Moss (Cambridge) made three hundreds, and only Boyd-Moss two in a match (139 and 124 at Lord's in 1983).

Most Runs

489	R. J. Boyd-Moss (Cambridge)	1980–83
477	M. J. K. Smith (Oxford)	1954–56
469	S. S. Agarwal (Oxford)	2010–13
466	J. W. M. Dalrymple (Oxford)	2001–03
457	Nawab of Pataudi snr (Oxford)	1929–31
452	A. S. Ansari (Cambridge)	2008–13

Highest Partnerships

259	for 1st	D. A. King/S. S. Agarwal (Oxford) at Oxford	2010
226	for 2nd	W. G. Keighley/H. A. Pawson (Oxford) at Lord's	1947
408	for 3rd	S. Oberoi/D. R. Fox (Oxford) at Cambridge	2005
250	for 4th	C. M. Gupte/C. J. Hollins (Oxford) at Lord's	1994
267	for 5th	D. A. Escott/M. A. Naylor (Oxford) at Oxford	2018
216	for 6th	A. S. Ansari/N. M. H. Whittington (Cambridge) at Oxford	2008
289	for 7th	G. Goonesena/G. W. Cook (Cambridge) at Lord's	1957
112	for 8th	H. E. Webb/A. W. H. Mallett (Oxford) at Lord's	1948
97*	for 9th	J. F. Marsh/F. J. V. Hopley (Cambridge) at Lord's	1904
90	for 10th	W. J. H. Curwen/E. G. Martin (Oxford) at Lord's	1906

Most Wickets in an Innings

10-38	S. E. Butler (Oxford)	1871
9-?	G. B. Lee (Oxford)	1839
8-44	G. E. Jeffery (Cambridge)	1873
8-52	G. J. Toogood (Oxford)	1985
8-62	A. G. Steel (Cambridge)	1878
8-66	R. H. B. Bettington (Oxford)	1923
8-68	E. M. Kenney (Oxford)	1868
8-99	P. R. le Couteur (Oxford)	1911
8-161	J. C. Hartley (Oxford)	1896
8-?	G. E. Yonge (Oxford)	1845

All instances were at Lord's. Full analyses are not recorded in some 19th-century games.

Most Wickets in a Match

15-95	S. E. Butler (Oxford)	1871	13-75	W. N. Powys (Cambridge)	1872
14-119	E. M. Kenney (Oxford)	1868	13-88	E. L. Fellowes (Oxford)	1866
14-?	H. E. Moberly (Oxford)	1843	13-130	A. H. Evans (Oxford)	1881
13-73	A. G. Steel (Cambridge)	1878	13-237	I. A. R. Peebles (Oxford)	1930

All instances were at Lord's except for Moberly, who took his 14 wickets at Bullingdon Green in Oxford; his full analysis is not recorded.

Hat-Tricks

F. C. Cobden (Cambridge)	1870	J. F. Ireland (Cambridge)	1911
A. G. Steel (Cambridge)	1879	R. G. H. Lowe (Cambridge)	1926
P. H. Morton (Cambridge)	1880		

All instances were at Lord's. Cobden dismissed Oxford's last three to win the match by two runs.

Most Wickets

43	G. E. Yonge (Oxford)	1844–48	36	A. H. Evans (Oxford)	1878–81
40	C. D. B. Marsham (Oxford)	1854–58	36	S. M. J. Woods (Cambridge)	1888–91
38	A. G. Steel (Cambridge)	1878–81			

Highest Totals

611-5 dec	Oxford at Oxford	2010	533-7 dec	Oxford at Oxford	2018
610-5 dec	Oxford at Cambridge	2005	522-7 dec	Oxford at Cambridge	2003
604	Cambridge at Oxford	2002	513-6 dec	Oxford at Lord's	1996
550-7 dec	Oxford at Cambridge	2013	503	Oxford at Lord's	1900

The highest fourth-innings total was 384 by Cambridge (who lost by 45 runs) in 1939; the highest fourth-innings total to win was Oxford's 330-6 in 1896.

Lowest Totals

32	Oxford at Lord's	1878	52‡	Cambridge at Lord's	1836
39	Cambridge at Lord's	1858	55†	Cambridge at Oxford (Magdalen)	1850
42	Oxford at Lord's	1890	55	Oxford at Lord's	1883
47†	Cambridge at Lord's	1838	56	Oxford at Lord's	1847

† *One man absent.* ‡ *Two men absent.*

Largest Victories

Largest innings victories

Inns & 227 runs	Oxford (422) v Cambridge (59 & 136) at Lord's	1923
Inns & 213 runs	Oxford (610-5 dec) v Cambridge (129 & 268) at Cambridge	2005
Inns & 186 runs	Cambridge (424-7 dec) v Oxford (92 & 146) at Lord's	1957
Inns & 186 runs	Oxford (550-7 dec) v Cambridge (119 & 245) at Cambridge	2013
Inns & 166 runs	Cambridge (388) v Oxford (72 & 150) at Lord's	1872

Largest victories by runs

268 runs	Oxford (259 & 291) v Cambridge (137 & 145) at Lord's	1903
266 runs	Cambridge (182 & 254) v Oxford (106 & 64) at Lord's	1893
249 runs	**Cambridge (307 & 257) v Oxford (129 & 186) at Cambridge**	**2020**
238 runs	Cambridge (168 & 229) v Oxford (127 & 32) at Lord's	1878

Oxford won by ten wickets in 1877 and 1976, and Cambridge in 2009.

MCC IN 2020

STEVEN LYNCH

For much of the year, it seemed likely Lord's would see no cricket at all: the ground was closed down, and most of the staff furloughed in March. The first professional cricket was played on August 29, and the season rounded off by the Bob Willis Trophy final in late September – but no spectators were allowed.

While the lack of cricket caused all grounds financial problems, MCC's were particularly severe: the recent decision to fund ambitious building projects without accepting help from developers was based on Lord's staging two Test matches most years. Faced with a huge hole in the budget, the committee decided not to offer subscription rebates, which irked some members, and also cranked up an old idea – used in the 1920s and 1990s to fund building projects – by offering life membership for a lump sum, which varied according to age. The scheme proved a great success, with around 10% of the 18,000 members taking up the offer.

It was also possible for candidates to bypass the long waiting list, for around £45,000; home secretary Priti Patel was among those to jump the queue. In all, around £26m was raised – but future subscription income will be reduced, which could signal steep rises in years to come (after 2021, as the rates were frozen).

Although building continued – the new Compton and Edrich Stands at the Nursery End were almost complete by the end of the year – there were also inevitable economies. Some long-serving staff accepted redundancy or early-retirement packages; further departures were expected.

Kumar Sangakkara, the prolific Sri Lankan batsman who had become MCC's first president from overseas, captained an MCC tour of Pakistan in February, but had little opportunity after that to spread his wings during the lockdown, and was asked to carry on for another year. When he does step down, it will be to make way for another first: he will be succeeded by the former England women's captain, Clare Connor, who will become MCC's first female president. In another change at the top, Gerald Corbett was succeeded as club chairman by Bruce Carnegie-Brown, the chairman of Lloyds of London.

The usual programme of more than 400 out-matches was badly affected. The Cricket Office, which organises the games, moved from the Pavilion to the manager's spare room, and eventually MCC got back on the field on August 2, against the Kent Academy. In all, they played 107 men's matches by the start of October; 58 were won, 31 lost, and 18 drawn or abandoned. Women's teams played six matches, winning three and losing one.

THE NATIONAL COUNTIES IN 2020

HUGH CHEVALLIER AND RICHARD LOGAN

"Nearly everything will be different in Minor Counties cricket in 2020", began this review a year ago. Shame about that first word, but otherwise the forecast held true. *Wisden* imagined it was referring to a new structure: the introduction of tiers, including promotion and relegation, within the two existing geographic divisions of the Championship; a greater emphasis on 50-over cricket; and incorporation as a limited company. The loss of the familiar Minor Counties name, mourned by some, was a small part of the sweeping changes. But other forces blew the first National Counties season off course.

The bottom line was that the coronavirus pandemic prevented any competitive cricket in 2020. In July, having played a long waiting game, the National Counties Cricket Association abandoned plans for limited-overs tournaments after an 11–9 vote among the 20 clubs. Considerations included the lack of catering facilities, the availability of grounds, and the need for players and officials to travel independently, perhaps already in their kit. The Championship programme – reduced under the new arrangements to four three-day games per team – had already been called off in June. After an immense amount of hard work to ensure government biosecurity guidelines were met, some counties did manage to play friendlies against local rivals.

One of the year's keenest losses was the new "showcase" game, with all 20 counties hosting a first-class neighbour in a 50-over match. It was a welcome throwback to the first round of the NatWest Trophy, though unlike the old system there was no competitive framework. Still, the prospect of top-class players returning to some of the country's loveliest off-the-beaten-track grounds was not to be sniffed at.

It remains to be seen how the bigger counties treat these fixtures. And if they blood promising youngsters, they will be playing the National Counties at their own game. Governance introduced for the NCCA requires each side to field eight under-25s, as well as eight with strong ties to the county.

With little or no cricket, there was plenty of time for regular online meetings, which allowed clear lines of communication within and beyond the counties to be established. An interim board have been in place since the company was formed in November 2019, and an official board were due to take over after the first annual general meeting, scheduled for February 2021. Late in 2020, it was announced that full funding would be available for the year ahead.

An NCCA website (nationalcountiesca.co.uk) was launched, and looked an informative resource. Getting the new name known is, of course, a challenge: type NCCA into Google and you are transported to the home page of the National Carpet Cleaners Association.

The retiring president, John Pickup, gave sterling service, and makes way for a familiar name: Philip August was for 17 editions the Minor Counties correspondent for this Almanack.

LEAGUE CRICKET IN 2020

Vector ludorum

GEOFFREY DEAN

The government allowed some amateur sports to restart much sooner – golf resumed in mid-May – but recreational cricket lost the first three months of the season to Covid-19, with prime minister Boris Johnson suggesting the ball could be "a natural vector of disease". The first permitted day of competition in England and Wales was July 11: only the Derbyshire League, which by chance had targeted that as a possible resumption date during lockdown, were ready to start. Several other leagues cranked up the following week, and most continued deep into September.

The formats varied. Normally, around a third of the 29 premier leagues play declaration cricket for part or all of the season, but in 2020 it was all limited-overs games, as it was felt they should combine brevity with meaning. Most were 40-over contests, though a few went for the traditional premier-league length of 50, and there were also some T20 matches. The reductions proved popular, since over-rates were significantly slower than usual because of enforced hygiene breaks and the unavailability of dressing-rooms. Also, with bars generally closed and socialising reduced, players were keen to get home quickly after games finished.

There was one constant: none of the premier leagues had relegation or promotion. "It would have been nonsensical," said Paul Bedford, the ECB's national manager for leagues and competitions. "What you got was an old-fashioned way of playing whoever you were drawn against. You go and have a decent game of cricket, and play your best – and you all come back next week, rather than get too clever about what league position you are in. It could also have driven the wrong behaviour, such as people with Covid not declaring it."

The 12 clubs in the North Yorkshire & South Durham League managed to play each other, with Richmondshire retaining their title. The ten Middlesex League clubs did the same, and Teddington celebrated a notable triple – their first, second and third teams all won their respective divisions, a feat achieved previously only by Ealing in 2008. In the Surrey Championship, no winner was officially declared, although Wimbledon came out on top of an eight-strong posse of clubs, two fewer than normal. The Birmingham League, like several others, split into groups, with play-offs and a final.

Other leagues divided in two by geographical location, respecting government advice on unnecessary travel. This was particularly the case in the regional leagues spread across more than one county, such as the Home Counties and the Southern. In the West of England League, Somerset-based clubs opted to play only against sides within the county boundary. Meanwhile, in rural Surrey, a group of seven clubs situated close together – including

TALE OF AN ESSEX TEN-FOR

Shak attack

PHIL WALKER

Shaker Ullah Wasiq had only been with us a few weeks, so naturally we'd gone with "Shak", the kind of guttural monosyllable that travels well across a barren London rec on a Saturday afternoon. Shak was playing his third game for Gidea Park & Romford CC, who in normal seasons take part in the Shepherd Neame Essex League. He had debuted in the threes, bowled an over in the ones, and was now playing his second game with us, the moody blues, in a hastily arranged cup competition.

We lost the toss, in the dirt. Goresbrook batted, and Shak was thrown the new ball. He chose the right end: downhill, with a tailwind on his back. History tends to happen slowly in cricket. This took 44 deliveries. We knew he was good. I'd already heard the story: how Shak and his younger brother, Waleullah, had found the club online, and rocked up one night hoping to rent a net; how it was training night, so they'd been asked to join in, and how Shak's fifth ball cleaned up our first-team skipper. Shak was unsure how many months – eight or nine, perhaps – he and Waleullah had been in England, since the boys and their mother had made the journey from Kunar, a province north-west of Kabul, Afghanistan, to join up with their father, who had found work in east London.

The family needed to get out of Kunar. "There is no peace, no justice, just poverty," he said. "Innocent people are killed, but the important thing is justice is not there. My family… it's very hard in Afghanistan." Cricket, he said, was everything. Cricket in the streets. Tape-ball cricket. Inter-province games. Village scraps. And then this.

The first seven were all bowled. Out they strode, back they went. The pitch was lively, but it was that skidding, spitting length that took them down. Shak is not tall, but everything in his action comes through straight. The feet point down the track; the chest opens out to the target. And the arm: the arm is fast. Seven down, 18 on the board, a policeman watching from his patrol car at wide third man, and something in the air. The eighth to fall is the first catch of the day, a bouncer fended off the grille. The next is caught at mid-off: 31 for nine. By now, Shak has bowled six of his allocated eight overs. At the other end, we've installed a canny operator who knows his role: hold an end up, don't ruin it.

Shak's seventh over is a stinker: too short and wide, down on pace. At the end of it, I go up to him at long leg. No pressure, old boy, but you've got six balls to make history. From there, we stumble into one of those mid-pitch team meetings in which it's agreed that, in the event of a chance coming anyone's way next over, we are to respectfully shell it. Adam, the old stooge, bowls a serenely bland maiden.

Their last man is on strike. A fierce wind drives across the Dagenham plains. The first ball is edged wide of third slip. Crouching at second, I become aware we're all suffering our own psychodramas, caught between a desire to be part of history, and a mortal fear of being the pillock who drops it.

We needn't have worried. The second ball is fast, arcing towards the bootstraps. Everyone goes up. The finger follows. Social-distancing measures are momentarily abandoned. Shak is the calmest among us. He walks off holding the ball, looking down and smiling at it: 7.2–1–26–10. For a photo by the scoreboard, he puts on a crisp new white shirt.

Later, back at the club, he says: "I feel very happy here. The English people are very kind." Does he hope to play for a long time at Gidea Park? "I don't know. In the future, I would like to play for England cricket team."

A version of this article first appeared on wisden.com.

Guildford, Cranleigh and Normandy – played each other, despite being from three different divisions.

The ECB make an annual grant to each premier league, usually in the region of £10,000, although amounts vary. For 2020, there was general agreement that this would have to be reduced, and around 30% was dispensed. The ECB also offered interest-free loans to clubs needing money to pay for balls, equipment or umpires; the leagues decided not to charge clubs their annual affiliation fees. "I was very pleased by that," said Bedford. "All the leagues bent over backwards to help clubs as best they could."

There are no additions to the ranks of premier leagues in 2021, although a couple of aspiring candidates may be accorded that status in 2022 if they satisfy the necessary criteria. ECB grants to leagues may have to be reduced this year as a result of coronavirus cutbacks, but the recreational game deserves credit for its fortitude in the face of the pandemic.

Chris Aspin writes: The Lancashire League replaced its traditional competitions with a President's Cup, which was contested during August and early September. Four groups played 40-over games to provide the semi-finalists. Five clubs fielded contracted professionals who were living in the UK, but the rest were unable to bring players from abroad. There was the odd unusual problem: local lockdowns in Blackburn and Pendle briefly prevented East Lancashire and Nelson from playing at home, so one round of fixtures was reversed.

In the final, Ramsbottom – playing at home – needed 15 off the last over to beat Church, but managed 11. The bowler was Neil Hornbuckle, a South African who had been engaged as pro just for this match; he top-scored for Church with 43, then took two for 40. Kieren Grimshaw made an unbeaten 60 for Ramsbottom. Church last gained a major trophy in 1945, when they won the league. Clitheroe triumphed in the junior competition, beating Walsden in the final.

When Ramsbottom beat Littleborough, both sides' South African professionals – Daryn Smit and Travis Townsend – made hundreds. The season's amateur century-makers were Jimmy Whitehead (124 for Lowerhouse v Darwen, when he shared a second-wicket stand of 167 with Charlie Cottam), Josh Gale (101 for Walsden v Lowerhouse) and Connor Reed, who hit 100 as Haslingden made the highest total of the season, 264 for six against Rawtenstall. It was not the only good news for Haslingden: an anonymous donor left the club £65,000 in his will.

When Ramsbottom beat Middleton, Grimshaw top-scored with 49 and then claimed six for three, including a hat-trick. Ockert Erasmus, Burnley's professional, took six for four against Middleton, and Tom Walker of Accrington five for five against Great Harwood.

Nineteen-year-old Alice Clarke became the first woman to play for a senior Lancashire League side when she opened the batting and kept wicket for Accrington against Rishton. She faced 43 balls and scored ten; later she took a catch and did not concede a bye. At the end of the season, Liberty Heap, just 16, was chosen on merit to play for Lowerhouse in a friendly at Colne. An off-spinner, she did not take a wicket in her eight overs, but did have two catches put down – one by her father, Ben, Lowerhouse's captain.

Greenmount will join the second division next season. The former Bolton League club, a founder member of the Greater Manchester Competition, will fill the gap left by Milnrow, who resigned from the Lancashire League during 2019, and rejoined the Manchester Competition.

The death of the great West Indian batsman Everton Weekes rekindled memories of his successes for Bacup, where he became a folk hero. In seven seasons between 1949 and 1958 (he missed two as West Indies were touring England), he made 32 centuries, seven in 1951; three years later, he averaged 158. Rossendale Borough Council were considering a lasting memorial, possibly naming a new market square in Bacup after him.

ECB PREMIER LEAGUES IN 2020

No recreational cricket was allowed in England until July 11, after which it could proceed with caution. The ECB gave the 29 premier leagues free rein to organise their seasons, with no stipulations about playing conditions. Around half played a reduced version of their normal competition.

Birmingham and District League
The 12-team Premier League did not happen, but the Graham Williamson Trophy (the usual cup competition) did, with four groups of six teams contesting 40-over matches. Barnt Green beat West Bromwich Dartmouth by five wickets in the final.

Bradford Premier League
Ten of the 12 teams contested a reduced league, playing eight 40-over matches each. Townville finished with 134 points, and Hanging Heaton 126. Woodville, the 2019 champions, did not take part.

Cheshire County League Premier Division
Two groups of six played mostly T20 games. Neston won the West Group, and beat East winners Didsbury by two runs in the 20-over final. The 2019 champions, Chester Boughton Hall, finished equal on points with Nantwich in the West, despite bowling them out for 26 in one match.

Cornwall Premier League
Two groups of six played ten matches apiece, before semi-finals and a final, for the Bond Timber Trophy. Penzance, the 2019 champions, topped the West Group ahead of St Just, while Werrington led the East Group with 130. In the final, Penzance bowled out St Just for 86, and won by eight wickets.

Derbyshire Premier League
The 12 teams were split into two groups, each club playing ten matches. Denby finished top of the North Group with 207 points, while Spondon – the 2019 champions – led the South with 188. Spondon were bowled out for 100 in the 40-over play-off final, and Denby won by four wickets.

Devon Premier League
Bradninch, Heathcoat, Plymouth and Sidmouth finished top of four groups of four (including six clubs outside the scheduled Premier League). Making the most of home advantage in the final, Sidmouth beat 2019 champions Heathcoat, helped by an opening stand of 127 between the former Somerset batsman Alex Barrow and Josh Bess, one of three cousins of England off-spinner Dominic in the side.

East Anglian Premier League
Two groups of six were topped by newcomers Sawston & Babraham (who won nine of their ten matches) and Swardeston; 2019 champions Frinton-on-Sea finished bottom of the South Group. Jordan Taylor's unbeaten 97 took Swardeston home in the final, after his brother Callum's three wickets helped restrict Sawston & Babraham to 162.

Essex League Premier Division
The league was renamed the "Gooch Division" for 2020, and ten teams played each other once. Wanstead & Snaresbrook, who had finished second in 2019, pipped champions Brentwood – 152 points to 136 – after beating them by four wickets in the last round.

Hertfordshire League Premier Division
The division's ten teams played each other once. Potters Bar, who won seven and tied one, finished top with 198 points, ahead of Totteridge Milhillians (180) and 2019 champions Radlett (163).

Home Counties Premier League
The previous year's top two divisions played eight matches apiece in a combined league. Wokingham finished top with 131 points; Chesham, High Wycombe and Oxford Downs all collected 120, and progressed to the semi-finals of the John Goodman Cup, named after a local administrator and scorer who had died in 2019. High Wycombe edged Oxford Downs by one run in the final.

Kent League Premier Division
The Kent Premier Division clubs played no competitive cricket in 2020.

Leics and Rutland League Premier Division
The league's top two divisions were amalgamated and split into three groups of six, and one of five; they included three Second XIs. Each of the groups led to finals, which were won by Kegworth Town (who beat table toppers Loughborough Town), Barrow Town, Kibworth, and Loughborough Town Second XI (who beat Ashby Hastings).

Lincolnshire Cricket Board Premier League
The teams split into two groups, with some cross-pool matches to ensure everyone played seven. Grantham (26 points) topped the South Group, and Lindum (24) the North. In the final of what was named the "Covid Cup", Lindum beat Grantham by 46 runs.

Liverpool and District Competition
The competition's 26 teams were split into seven groups. Liverpool, who headed Group E, won all eight of their matches. Other group winners were Southport & Birkdale, Formby, Hightown St Mary's, Rainford, Wallasey and Leigh. After the league stage, each group contested play-offs among themselves, the finals being won by Southport Trinity (who had lost all six of their group games), Northern, Hightown St Mary's, Rainhill (who upset Rainford), Liverpool, New Brighton and Leigh.

Middlesex County League Division One
The division's ten clubs played each other once: Teddington, who won seven of their eight completed matches (plus a no-result), finished with 71 points, ahead of Richmond (63) and Shepherds Bush (53). North Middlesex, the 2019 champions, were one of three teams on 52.

Northamptonshire League Premier Division
The division's ten teams played seven league games apiece before a knockout phase. The 2019 champions, Peterborough Town, topped the table with 120 points, and went on to beat Old Northamptonians in the final.

North East Premier League
The top two divisions' 24 teams were split into three groups of eight, leading to a knockout phase. Chester-le-Street defeated 2019 champions Burnmoor in the final to win the Banks Salver, which is usually awarded for the league's cup competition.

North Staffordshire & South Cheshire League Premier Division
The league's 12 teams managed to fit in matches against all 11 opponents. Porthill Park, the champions of 2019, finished top again with 152 points, three ahead of Longton, who lost their last match heavily to third-placed J&G Meakin.

North Wales League Premier Division
The league was split into groups, playing what was described as "non-competitive matches"; not everyone met each other. The groups were topped by Menai Bridge and Gresford.

North Yorkshire & South Durham League Premier Division
The league's 12 teams managed to fit in matches against all 11 opponents. Richmondshire, the 2019 champions, just came out on top again, finishing with 201 points – one more than Middlesbrough, with Hartlepool (192) third.

Northern Premier League
The Northern Premier League clubs played no competitive cricket in 2020.

Nottinghamshire Cricket Board Premier League
The top two teams in two groups of six progressed to a knockout phase. Kimberley Institute won the North Division, and Radcliffe-on-Trent the South, but both lost in the semis. Cavaliers & Carrington beat Papplewick & Linby by 44 runs in the final.

South Wales Premier League Division One

The South Wales Premier League clubs played no competitive cricket in 2020.

Southern Premier League

Two groups of nine, including some non-Premier clubs: St Cross Symondians Seconds won the East Group, and Bournemouth the West, ahead of St Cross's first team, with 2019 champions Bashley (Rydal) fourth.

Surrey Championship Premier Division

Eight teams contested a reduced league, called the Challenge Cup: Wimbledon won all seven of their matches to finish top, with 2019 champions East Molesey second.

Sussex League Premier Division

Two groups of six played five matches apiece: Preston Nomads (sixth in 2019) and Eastbourne (seventh) won all five in their respective divisions. Eastbourne beat East Grinstead by 12 runs in the final.

West of England Premier League

A "Covid League" included five groups of eight, plus one of seven. Some Second XIs were included: in Group A, Bath's reserves topped the table ahead of their first team (the match between them was a no-result). The other group winners were Bedminster, Taunton Deane, North Perrott, Potterne (2019 champions) and Cheltenham.

Yorkshire North Premier League

Ten of the usual 12 teams contested a 40-over league. Dunnington won seven of their nine games, and finished with 28 points, ahead of Stamford Bridge (25), Clifton Alliance (24) and 2019 champions Sheriff Hutton Bridge (21).

Yorkshire South Premier League

Two groups of six played ten matches apiece: 2019 champions Doncaster Town won the Eastern Group, and Whitley Hall the Western, before going on to win the final. They overhauled Doncaster's modest 167 with four wickets and 7.3 of their 40 overs remaining.

Lancashire League (not an ECB Premier League)

The 23 clubs in the League's two divisions divided into four groups, leading to a knockout stage. Ramsbottom (who finished ahead of 2019 champions Burnley), Church, Clitheroe and Walsden topped the groups, and Church edged Ramsbottom by three runs in the final to win the President's Cup.

THE CRICKETER VILLAGE CUP IN 2020

BENJ MOOREHEAD

By the time the Village Cup finally began in late August, entrants had dwindled from 308 to 141. Matches took place weekly, not fortnightly – and a post-match pint, already under threat, became impossible.

Yet in the end, to the credit of the organisers, Covid-19 was confined to little more than a footnote. This was just another year of the Village Cup, with scenes of heroic failure and incandescent triumph, teams haring across the country to discover how the rain falls elsewhere, local greens encircled by nail-chewing spectators (socially distanced, of course). And it was crowned by a humdinger of a Lord's final. Though denied its traditional partisan crowd, it had the allure of being the only non-professional match played at Lord's in 2020, and one of just seven in all. Roll on this summer's 50th edition.

Colwall, whose lovely Herefordshire ground sits under the Malvern Hills, won the competition for the first time. Because of a lopsided draw, they had only four fixtures before the final, two of which were spoiled by the weather: the first was a washout, and settled by the toss of a coin, while their semi-final was decided on run-rate. But you couldn't begrudge Colwall their success: they have been front-runners in this competition for most of the last 50 years, coming within a boundary of a Lord's final in 1982.

Several players have ties to Malvern College, including pupil Oliver Cox and housemaster Richard Howitt, who said: "Olly has called me 'Sir' or 'Mr Howitt' for the whole summer. I did say to him, 'When we're at Lord's, you can call me Richard.'" Mr Howitt, who played six first-class games for Cambridge University in 2000, scoring an unbeaten hundred against Middlesex, made key contributions at the top of the order, but his most crucial intervention came during the semi-final in East Yorkshire, when he dismissed Carlton Towers's Tom Collins for 27. In 2018, Collins put on 340 with team-mate Mark Holmes during a Snaith Evening League T20 game, and had plundered an astonishing 497 runs off 379 balls at an average of 165 leading up to the match. Howitt's feat was squeezed between his housemaster duties: "I went to bed at 3am. Got up at 5.30. Drove to Yorkshire. Got Tom Collins out lbw. Drove home. And was on duty until 10.30pm."

Redbourn, the runners-up from Hertfordshire who celebrate their bicentenary in 2022 and still play on the local common, were making their first appearance in the Village Cup. Six of their seven matches before the final were away from home, including trips to the South Downs and the Somerset–Dorset border. "I think that's one of the best things about the competition," said Ed Hales, Redbourn's 22-year-old captain, opening batsman and wicketkeeper. "You go to different places, where you'd never normally play, and sample village cricket elsewhere." Hales scored five half-centuries in seven innings before Lord's, including a stinging 71 from 48 balls against North Perrott in the semi-final, where he and his brother, William, shared an opening stand of 120. Then, in the final, he let rip with an 83-ball 119 that began with an impudent six pulled into the Grand Stand. His was the sixth hundred in Village finals, and the only one in a losing cause.

The first national round of the competition had been beset by storms, and produced four bowl-outs which really should have been read out by James Alexander Gordon: Bearsted 2, Glynde & Beddingham 3; Easton Socon 3, Blackheath 1; Weekly & Warkton 2, Milford Hall 3; Frocester 2, Yelverton Bohemians 0. Poor Yelverton made a 300-mile round trip from Dartmoor to the Cotswolds for the sake of less than two overs' play and a sodden bowl-out, in which they failed in all ten attempts to hit the stumps.

FINAL

COLWALL v REDBOURN

At Lord's, September 19. Colwall won by six runs. Toss: Colwall.

This was a novel final: without a crowd, streamed online for the first time, played on a central wicket usually reserved for a Test and, bucking a recent trend, thrilling to the last. Redbourn seemed destined to win after a brilliant, free-flowing hundred by opener Ed Hales. He swatted his first ball for six, carved the second through gully, and never looked back. His trademark shot was a leg-side whip, but a cover-drive brought his fifty, and he eased through the nineties with a perfect reverse-sweep. By the time he was dismissed, Redbourn needed 70 from 86 balls with seven wickets in hand. But Colwall's spin–seam tandem of Ben Febery and Michael Gooch applied the squeeze, conceding just 15 in a six-over spell, and 11 off the last proved too much, as Redbourn fell six short of what would have been a record chase of 230. The Colwall innings had been a mirror image, starting slowly after two early wickets, before Richard Howitt's composed half-century set up a violent assault by Ben Wheeler, a Herefordshire Second XI wicketkeeper whose 33-ball 72 included seven sixes, three dumped into cow corner in the final over. Redbourn's four spinners bowled 32 of the 40 overs. Conor Yorath (leg-breaks) and Daniel Darvell (slow left-arm) were effective with the new ball, but no one could contain Wheeler.

Player of the Match: B. P. Wheeler.

Colwall

O. H. Cox b Darvell	4
B. M. Cooke b Yorath	11
R. W. J. Howitt b Darvell	58
F. A. D. Cameron c Craig b Arnold	23
J. J. Abel b Darvell	21
†B. P. Wheeler not out	72
B. G. Febery st E. S. Hales b Yorath	7
A. G. O. Robertson not out	8
B 4, lb 6, w 12, nb 3	25
1/9 (1) 2/24 (2) 3/93 (4) 4/130 (5) 5/152 (3) 6/195 (7) (6 wkts, 40 overs)	229

*J. K. F. Wagstaff, M. J. Gooch and L. S. Dalley did not bat.

Yorath 8–2–23–2; Darvell 8–0–31–3; Moyle 4–0–26–0; Arnold 8–0–43–1; Roe 8–0–39–0; Richards 1–0–15–0; Craig 3–0–42–0.

Redbourn

*†E. S. Hales lbw b Febery	119
W. M. Hales c Gooch b Howitt	11
C. A. Yorath c Febery b Dalley	2
D. M. Roe c Cameron b Febery	32
H. J. I. Craig not out	19
S. H. Richards c Cooke b Dalley	22
A. J. Pritchard not out	1
B 1, lb 10, w 5, nb 1	17
1/58 (2) 2/77 (3) 3/160 (1) 4/187 (4) 5/218 (6) (5 wkts, 40 overs)	223

G. L. Cutler, J. Arnold, C. A. Moyle and D. F. Darvell did not bat.

Gooch 8–1–35–0; Robertson 4–0–30–0; Dalley 8–2–33–2; Howitt 8–0–47–1; Wagstaff 4–0–27–0; Febery 8–0–40–2.

Umpires: A. J. Anthony and R. Patel.

DISABILITY CRICKET IN 2020

The next generation

HUGH CHEVALLIER

No area of the game survived the global pandemic unscathed, and an early casualty was the Blind Ashes, initially scheduled for Worcester in August. England, who won the trophy in Adelaide on Australia Day 2016, will now defend them in August 2021. Another postponement was the Deaf Cricket T20 World Cup, due to be staged in the UAE last November, and provisionally rearranged for early 2022. Domestic cricket also suffered beyond the strict lockdown period. Many players have underlying health conditions, and so – even after the recreational game was allowed to restart – it made no sense for them to travel across the country to compete in county matches.

Instead, England's Physical Disability squad focused on fundraising. Left-arm amputee Matt Askin from Staffordshire, shielding at home because of asthma, completed the ball-tap challenge in aid of the Ruth Strauss Foundation. Later in the summer, the squad – led by batsman Callum Flynn – ran a marathon between them in order to raise money for the Lord's Taverners Super 1s programme. "It's a privilege for us as England players to raise money to support a program that will hopefully provide the next generation," said Flynn. The squad raised over £4,000.

By way of a thank you, the Taverners challenged the England Physical Disability squad to a match as restrictions were eased. They may or may not have known what they were letting themselves in for: the England team enjoyed a comfortable seven-wicket victory.

With so little cricket happening, focus turned to the structure and governance of the sport. In the deepest financial crisis in their history, the ECB felt it was vital to protect their ambitious "Inspiring Generations" strategy, the five-year plan that aimed "to connect communities, and inspire current and future generations through cricket". Rigorous reviews were undertaken, and tough decisions made. The Disability Performance Programme is now under the remit of Ashley Giles, managing director of English cricket. Meanwhile, the Participation Programme now comes within the recreational game department. Greater attention to equality, diversity and inclusion should bring benefits for disability cricket, as the ECB seek to prove it is indeed a game for all.

In October, Devon's Dan Bowser was named the Lords Taverners/Cricket Writers' Club Disabled Player of the Year. He was a member of the ECB Learning Disabilities side, and had steered England to a crushing 8–0 victory over their Australian counterparts a year earlier (see *Wisden 2020*, page 812). And in the Queen's birthday honours in 2020, there was an MBE for Bill Higginson. A former chair of the British Association for Cricketers with Disabilities, he had devoted many years of his supposed retirement to helping players make the most of their talents.

SCHOOLS CRICKET IN 2020

DOUGLAS HENDERSON

The last time outdoor school sport was cancelled for an entire term was the Big Freeze of early 1963. Cricket, spared back then, was not so lucky in 2020, when coronavirus struck. As always, though, those running the game in schools rose to a challenge – in this case even more daunting than revision mania.

September, more often the last gasp of summer than the first stirring of autumn, came to the rescue. Students returned after months and, for four or five weeks, enjoyed an array of cricket practice, plus a few games. Most were internal: as well as the usual house matches, there were a few arranged by "franchise", perhaps in imitation of the IPL. Some, though, were against other schools. They tended mainly to involve boys, with hockey taking precedence for girls. The 100-ball format proved popular. MCC did their bit by arranging 56 schools fixtures. With the weather not always obliging, and several falling prey to Covid-19, not all made it to the square. One, against St Peter's, York, was cancelled on the morning of the game because of a small outbreak.

The unluckiest players were the 2020 leavers, deprived of the climax to their school cricket career. In a bid to rectify that injustice, some in charge of cricket ensured leavers played at least one match. It was a bittersweet experience for Ben Spink, Marlborough's captain: bowled for 99 in his only innings.

A few head teachers understandably chose not to risk external fixtures, leading to late cancellation. Clifton, however, had ten in September, even if they were shorter matches than usual. And while most schools organised bubbles by year group, several in the West Country opted to select a first team from a mix of years, and make them their own bubble.

Every establishment made use of technology. Some hosted Q&A sessions with alumni who had gone on to England careers. Eastbourne College, meanwhile, created their own app (Preview/Prepare/Perform) to teach skills, such as how a batsman should judge line and length.

There was a welcome rise in links with local clubs, with several providing venue and opposition. These games began late in the summer term – such as it was – and continued in the holidays. Skinners' School, in Kent, played 16, and Cheadle Hulme, in Cheshire, ten. Groundstaff also worked non-stop, maintaining a usable square for months when cricket was impossible – as well as weeks in September when winter preparation would normally begin.

The ECB have long dreamed of schools cricket in the autumn, but conflict with rugby, for example, which demands long grass, has militated against it. Yet 2020 has shown it is possible, and one school described the deep feeling of regret when cricket training yielded to rugby. Eton played cricket seven days a week, while others believe Sunday matches in September can work.

With the announcement in January that GCSE and A-level exams were cancelled in 2021, there is the prospect of a summer in which schools cricket can flourish. The longer-term future remains uncertain. But, at least in 2020, September cricket helped foster *mens sana in corpore sano*.

PART FIVE

Overseas Cricket

INTERNATIONALS CANCELLED OR POSTPONED BY THE PANDEMIC

Mar 2020	Australia v New Zealand – 2nd and 3rd ODIs
	India v South Africa – 2nd and 3rd ODIs
	Sri Lanka v England – 2 Tests (played Jan 2021)
	Asia XI v World XI in Bangladesh – 2 T20Is
	New Zealand v Australia – 3 T20Is
Mar–Apr 2020	South Africa Women v Australia Women – 3 ODIs and 3 T20Is
Apr 2020	Zimbabwe v Ireland – 3 T20Is and 3 ODIs
	Pakistan v Bangladesh – 1 ODI and 2nd Test
	Sri Lanka Women v New Zealand Women – 3 ODIs
May 2020	Ireland v Bangladesh – 3 ODIs and 4 T20Is
Jun 2020	Scotland v New Zealand – 1 T20I and 1 ODI
	Bangladesh v Australia – 2 Tests
	Netherlands v New Zealand – 1 T20I
	Scotland v Australia – 1 T20I
	Sri Lanka v South Africa – 3 ODIs and 3T20Is
	Sri Lanka v India – 3 ODIs and 3T20Is
Jun–Jul 2020	Ireland v New Zealand – 3 T20Is and 3 ODIs
	England Women v India Women – 2 T20Is and 4 ODIs
Jul 2020	Women's World Cup Qualifier in Sri Lanka (postponed to Jul 2021)
	Netherlands v Pakistan – 3 ODIs
	West Indies v New Zealand – 3 ODIs and 3 T20Is
	Ireland v Pakistan – 2 T20Is
	Netherlands v West Indies – 3 ODIs
Jul–Aug 2020	West Indies v South Africa – 2 Tests and 5 T20Is
Aug 2020	Australia v Zimbabwe – 3 ODIs
	Zimbabwe v India – 3 ODIs
Aug–Sep 2020	Bangladesh v New Zealand – 2 Tests
Sep 2020	England Women v South Africa Women – 2 T20Is and 4 ODIs
	Zimbabwe v Netherlands – 3 ODIs
Oct 2020	Australia v West Indies – 3 T20Is
	Sri Lanka v Zimbabwe – 3 ODIs and 2 T20Is
	Sri Lanka v Bangladesh – 3 Tests
Oct–Nov 2020	MEN'S T20 WORLD CUP IN AUSTRALIA (postponed to India, Oct–Nov 2021)
Nov 2020	Australia v Afghanistan – 1 Test
	Ireland Women v Scotland Women (in Spain) – 3 T20Is
Dec 2020	South Africa v England – 3 ODIs
	Bangladesh v Sri Lanka – 3 ODIs
Jan 2021	UAE v Ireland – 2nd and 3rd ODIs (of 4)
	Namibia Women v Zimbabwe Women – 4 T20Is
Jan–Feb 2021	Australia v New Zealand – 3 ODIs and 1 T20I
Feb 2021	Zimbabwe Women v Pakistan Women – 3 T20Is
	New Zealand v Sri Lanka – 3 ODIs
	Afghanistan v Zimbabwe – 2 Tests and 3 T20Is
Feb–Mar 2021	WOMEN'S WORLD CUP IN NEW ZEALAND (postponed to Mar–Apr 2021)
Mar 2021	South Africa v Australia – 3 Tests
	India v Afghanistan – 3 ODIs

Series that were postponed, but played later in the same season, are not included.

WORLD TEST CHAMPIONSHIP 2019–2021

Australia's decision at the start of February 2021 to postpone their tour of South Africa because of the Covid-19 situation meant New Zealand became the first team to qualify for the final of the World Test Championship.

The pandemic had halted the Championship in March 2020, just after New Zealand leapt into third place, collecting a maximum 120 points on defeating the then leaders India 2–0. Though it resumed in July, when England met West Indies, the ICC soon concluded it would be impossible to fit in all the postponed fixtures before the scheduled final in June 2021. Rather than extend the timetable by a year, they changed the rules mid-term: the rankings would now be determined by the percentage of possible points earned by each team in the series they managed to play.

As the Border–Gavaskar Trophy reached its climax at Brisbane in January 2021, Australia led the table. Had they won or drawn that Test, they would have stayed top, but India's triumphant run-chase meant they reclaimed pole position; Australia dropped to third, a fraction of a percentage below New Zealand, who had claimed full points at home to West Indies and Pakistan. England's 2–0 win in Sri Lanka the following week put them just behind Australia.

Only three percentage points separated the top four, with the other five also-rans. Everything hinged on the four-Test India–England series starting in February. Either could meet New Zealand in the final: India had to take the series with at least two wins, England with at least three. But if the series was drawn, or the winners failed to secure enough victories, their percentages would both fall below Australia, who would join New Zealand.

A maximum of 120 points are available for each series in the Championship, with the number for individual matches varying according to how many games are played (see table below). The tournament, running from 2019 to 2021, was designed to give context to (most) Tests, and features the nine teams who led the Test rankings in March 2018. Before Covid intervened (in the middle of the Pakistan–Bangladesh series), each side were meant to play six qualifying series of at least two Tests. Series involving Afghanistan, Ireland and Zimbabwe are not included.

CHAMPIONSHIP TABLE

		Series	*Tests*	*W*	*L*	*D*	*Pen*	*Pts*	*Potential points*	*%*
1	India	5	13	9	3	1	0	430	600	71.66
2	New Zealand	5	11	7	4	0	0	420	600	70.00
3	Australia	4	14	8	4	2	4	332	480	69.16
4	England	5	17	10	4	3	0	412	600	68.66
5	South Africa	3	9	3	6	0	6	144	360	40.00
6	Pakistan	4.5	10	2	5	3	0	166	540	30.74
7	Sri Lanka	4	8	1	6	1	0	80	480	16.66
8	West Indies	3	7	1	6	0	0	40	360	11.11
9	Bangladesh	1.5	3	0	3	0	0	0	180	0.00

Penalties are deducted for slow over-rates. If teams finish tied on percentage, they are separated by runs-per-wicket ratio (runs scored per wicket lost, divided by runs conceded per wicket taken).

To January 25, 2021.

HOW THE POINTS WORK

Up to 120 points are available for each series. How they are awarded for each match depends on the number of individual Tests played:

	Win	*Draw*	*Tie*
Five-Test series	24	8	12
Four-Test series	30	10	15
Three-Test series	40	13	20
Two-Test series	60	20	30

WORLD CUP SUPER LEAGUE 2020–2022

In 2020, the ICC introduced another league, for one-day internationals, to serve as a qualifying tournament for the men's World Cup in 2023. It features 13 teams – the 12 Full Members plus the Netherlands, who won the last World Cricket League Championship in December 2017. India, the hosts in 2023, and the other top seven will qualify automatically for the World Cup, while the bottom five will join teams from lower leagues in a further qualifier.

Each Super League team are due to play three ODIs against eight other sides – four series at home, and four away, a total of 24 ODIs worth ten points each (ten for a win, five for a no-result). As in the World Test Championship, the fixtures fit into the existing system of bilateral series; teams can arrange more than three matches, but only the designated three count in the league.

The programme was supposed to begin in May 2020, but the pandemic delayed the launch until July, when England met Ireland at Southampton – and split the points 20–10. Australia played England in Manchester and India at home, winning both series 2–1, to finish the year on top of the table with 40 points. England's next series, in South Africa, was called off at the last minute after staff at their hotel tested positive for Covid. Meanwhile, Pakistan won two games against Zimbabwe, who got off the mark thanks to a super over in the third. In January 2021, Bangladesh whitewashed West Indies, and Afghanistan did the same to Ireland in Abu Dhabi.

SUPER LEAGUE TABLE

		M	*W*	*L*	*Pts*	*NRR*
1	Australia	6	4	2	40	0.34
2	Bangladesh	3	3	0	30	1.89
3	England	6	3	3	30	0.79
4	Afghanistan	3	3	0	30	0.52
5	Pakistan	3	2	1	20	0.74
6	Zimbabwe	3	1	2	10	–0.74
7	Ireland	6	1	5	10	–1.07
8	India	3	1	2	9*	–0.69
9	West Indies	3	0	3	0	–1.89

* *1pt deducted for slow over-rate.*

To January 26, 2021. Yet to play: Netherlands, New Zealand, South Africa and Sri Lanka.

MRF TYRES ICC TEAM RANKINGS

TEST RANKINGS (As at January 25, 2021)

		Matches	*Points*	*Rating*
1	New Zealand	27	3,198	118
2	India	32	3,765	118
3	Australia	31	3,498	113
4	England	44	4,734	108
5	South Africa	26	2,499	96
6	Sri Lanka	33	2,742	83
7	Pakistan	23	1,890	82
8	West Indies	25	1,937	77
9	Bangladesh	17	939	55
10	Zimbabwe	8	144	18

Afghanistan had a rating of 57 and Ireland 0, but neither had played sufficient Tests to achieve a ranking.

ONE-DAY RANKINGS (As at December 31, 2020)

		Matches	*Points*	*Rating*
1	England	44	5,405	123
2	India	52	6,102	117
3	New Zealand	32	3,716	116
4	Australia	39	4,344	111
5	South Africa	31	3,345	108
6	Pakistan	35	3,490	100
7	Bangladesh	34	2,989	88
8	Sri Lanka	39	3,297	85
9	West Indies	43	3,285	76
10	Afghanistan	28	1,549	55
11	Ireland	24	1,256	52

Remaining rankings: 12 Netherlands (44), 13 Zimbabwe (42), 14 Oman (40), 15 Scotland (26), 16 Nepal (18), 17 United Arab Emirates (17), 18 Namibia (17), 19 USA (13), 20 Papua New Guinea (0).

TWENTY20 RANKINGS (As at December 31, 2020)

		Matches	*Points*	*Rating*
1	England	25	6,877	275
2	Australia	25	6,800	272
3	India	38	10,186	268
4	Pakistan	29	7,516	259
5	South Africa	20	5,047	252
6	New Zealand	28	6,952	248
7	Sri Lanka	23	5,293	230
8	Bangladesh	20	4,583	229
9	Afghanistan	17	3,882	228
10	West Indies	26	5,885	226
11	Ireland	29	5,513	190
12	Zimbabwe	21	3,984	190
13	United Arab Emirates	23	4,288	186
14	Scotland	17	3,096	182
15	Nepal	23	4,148	180
16	Papua New Guinea	21	3,769	179
17	Netherlands	26	4,618	178
18	Oman	18	3,169	176

Remaining rankings: 19 Namibia (157), 20 Singapore (142), 21 Canada (130), 22 Qatar (130), 23 Hong Kong (119), 24 Kenya (116), 25 Jersey (115), 26 Kuwait (110), 27 Italy (110), 28 Saudi Arabia (107), 29 Denmark (98), 30 Bermuda (92), 31 Uganda (90), 32 Malaysia (88), 33 Germany (87), 34 USA (79), 35 Ghana (77), 36 Guernsey (72), 37 Botswana (72), 38 Austria (69), 39 Nigeria (67), 40 Norway (62), 41 Romania (60), 42 Spain (59), 43 Sweden (56), 44 Tanzania (56), 45 Cayman Islands (54), 46 Argentina (51), 47 Belgium (50), 48 Philippines (48), 49 Bahrain (47), 50 Vanuatu (47), 51 Belize (42), 52 Hungary (41), 53 Malawi (40), 54 Fiji (35), 55 Peru (33), 56 Panama (32), 57= Costa Rica (32), Japan (32), 59 Samoa (31), 60 Czech Republic (30), 61 Mexico (29), 62 Luxembourg (25), 63 Portugal (25), 64 Finland (23), 65 Bulgaria (22), 66 Thailand (21), 67 Isle of Man (20), 68 South Korea (20), 69 Malta (17), 70 Mozambique (14), 71 Brazil (14), 72 Bhutan (13), 73 Sierra Leone (12), 74 Maldives (10), 75 Chile (9), 76 St Helena (9), 77 Indonesia (5), 78 Myanmar (4), 79= China (0), Gambia (0), Gibraltar (0), Lesotho (0), Rwanda (0), Swaziland (0), Turkey (0).

The ratings are based on all Test series, one-day and Twenty20 internationals completed since May 1, 2017.

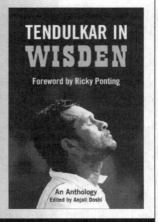

MRF TYRES ICC PLAYER RANKINGS

Introduced in 1987, the rankings have been backed by various sponsors, but were taken over by the ICC in January 2005. They rank cricketers on a scale up to 1,000 on their performances in Tests. The rankings take into account playing conditions, the quality of the opposition and the result of the matches. In August 1998, a similar set of rankings for one-day internationals was launched, and Twenty20 rankings were added in October 2011.

The leading players in the Test rankings on January 25, 2021, were:

	Batsmen	*Points*		*Bowlers*	*Points*
1	K. S. Williamson (NZ)	919	1	P. J. Cummins (A)	908
2	S. P. D. Smith (A)	891	2	S. C. J. Broad (E)	839
3	M. Labuschagne (A)	878	3	N. Wagner (NZ)	825
4	V. Kohli (I)	862	4	J. R. Hazlewood (A)	816
5	J. E. Root (E)	823	5	T. G. Southee (NZ)	811
6	Babar Azam (P)	781	6	J. M. Anderson (E)	807
7	C. A. Pujara (I)	760	7	K. Rabada (SA)	786
8	A. M. Rahane (I)	748	8	R. Ashwin (I)	760
9	H. M. Nicholls (NZ)	747	9	J. J. Bumrah (I)	757
10	B. A. Stokes (E)	744	10	J. O. Holder (WI)	753

The leading players in the one-day international rankings on December 31, 2020, were:

	Batsmen	*Points*		*Bowlers*	*Points*
1	V. Kohli (I)	870	1	T. A. Boult (NZ)	722
2	R. G. Sharma (I)	842	2	Mujeeb Zadran (Afg)	701
3	Babar Azam (P)	837	3	J. J. Bumrah (I)	700
4	L. R. P. L. Taylor (NZ)	818	4	C. R. Woakes (E)	675
5	A. J. Finch (A)	791	5	K. Rabada (SA)	665
6	F. du Plessis (SA)	790	6	J. R. Hazlewood (A)	660
7	D. A. Warner (A)	773	7	Mohammad Amir (P)	647
8	K. S. Williamson (NZ)	765	8	P. J. Cummins (A)	646
9	Q. de Kock (SA)	755	9	M. J. Henry (NZ)	641
10	J. M. Bairstow (E)	754	10	J. C. Archer (E)	637

The leading players in the Twenty20 international rankings on December 31, 2020, were:

	Batsmen	*Points*		*Bowlers*	*Points*
1	D. J. Malan (E)	915	1	Rashid Khan (Afg)	736
2	Babar Azam (P)	820	2	Mujeeb Zadran (Afg)	730
3	K. L. Rahul (I)	816	3	A. U. Rashid (E)	700
4	A. J. Finch (A)	808	4	A. Zampa (A)	685
5	H. E. van der Dussen (SA)	744	5	T. Shamsi (SA)	680
6	G. J. Maxwell (A)	701	6	A. C. Agar (A)	664
7	V. Kohli (I)	697	7	T. G. Southee (NZ)	636
8	C. Munro (NZ)	695	8	S. S. Cottrell (WI)	634
9	T. L. Seifert (NZ)	685	9	M. J. Santner (NZ)	628
10	Hazratullah Zazai (Afg)	676	10	C. J. Jordan (E)	618

INTERNATIONAL RESULTS IN 2020

TEST MATCHES

	Tests	*W*	*L*	*D*	*% won*	*% lost*	*% drawn*
New Zealand	6	5	1	0	**83.33**	16.66	0.00
England	9	6	1	2	**66.66**	11.11	22.22
Australia	3	2	1	0	**66.66**	33.33	0.00
Bangladesh	2	1	1	0	**50.00**	50.00	0.00
Sri Lanka	3	1	1	1	**33.33**	33.33	33.33
India	4	1	3	0	**25.00**	75.00	0.00
South Africa	4	1	3	0	**25.00**	75.00	0.00
Pakistan	5	1	2	2	**20.00**	40.00	40.00
West Indies	5	1	4	0	**20.00**	80.00	0.00
Zimbabwe	3	0	2	1	**0.00**	66.66	33.33
Totals	22	19	19	3	**86.36**	86.36	13.63

Afghanistan and Ireland played no Tests in 2020.

ONE-DAY INTERNATIONALS (Full Members only)

	ODIs	*W*	*L*	*NR*	*% won*	*% lost*
Bangladesh	3	3	0	0	**100.00**	0.00
Sri Lanka	3	3	0	0	**100.00**	0.00
South Africa	6	4	1	1	**80.00**	20.00
New Zealand	4	3	1	0	**75.00**	25.00
Pakistan	3	2	1	0	**66.66**	33.33
England	9	4	4	1	**50.00**	50.00
West Indies	6	3	3	0	**50.00**	50.00
Australia	13	6	7	0	**46.15**	53.84
India	9	3	6	0	**33.33**	66.66
Ireland	6	1	5	0	**16.66**	83.33
Zimbabwe	6	1	5	0	**16.66**	83.33
Totals	34	33	33	1		

Afghanistan played no ODIs in 2020. Zimbabwe's win came in a super over after they tied with Pakistan. The following also played official ODIs in 2020, none against Full Members: Oman (P6 W5 L1); United Arab Emirates (P3 W2 L1); Nepal (P4 W2 L2); Namibia (P3 W1 L2); USA (P4 L4).

TWENTY20 INTERNATIONALS (Full Members only)

	T20Is	*W*	*L*	*NR*	*% won*	*% lost*
India	11	9	1	1	**90.00**	10.00
England	12	8	3	1	**72.72**	27.27
Pakistan	11	7	3	1	**70.00**	30.00
Afghanistan	3	2	1	0	**66.66**	33.33
West Indies	8	3	3	2	**50.00**	50.00
Bangladesh	4	2	2	0	**50.00**	50.00
Australia	9	4	5	0	**44.44**	55.55
New Zealand	11	4	6	1	**40.00**	60.00
Ireland	6	2	3	1	**40.00**	60.00
South Africa	9	2	7	0	**22.22**	77.77
Sri Lanka	5	0	4	1	**0.00**	100.00
Zimbabwe	5	0	5	0	**0.00**	100.00
Totals	47	43	43	4		

All white-ball matches between Full Members only. Ties settled by a tie-breaker are counted as wins and losses; the % won/lost excludes no-results. With the extension of Twenty20 international status to all Associate Members of the ICC, a further 24 teams also played official T20Is in 2020.

TEST AVERAGES IN CALENDAR YEAR 2020

BATTING (200 runs)

		T	I	NO	R	HS	100	50	Avge	SR	Ct/St
1	A. D. Mathews (SL)	2	3	1	277	200*	1	1	138.50	39.85	2
2	K. S. Williamson (NZ)	4	6	0	498	251	2	1	83.00	54.66	1
3	†S. C. Williams (Z)	2	4	1	217	107	1	1	72.33	64.01	1
4	†Mominul Haque (B)	2	3	0	203	132	1	0	67.66	52.59	0
5	Babar Azam (P)	4	6	1	338	143	1	2	67.60	59.92	1
6	M. Labuschagne (A)	3	6	0	403	215	1	1	67.16	53.94	2
7	†B. A. Stokes (E)	7	12	1	641	176	2	2	58.27	62.17	14
8	B. K. G. Mendis (SL)	3	5	1	230	116*	1	1	57.50	46.93	2
9	Z. Crawley (E)	7	11	0	580	267	1	3	52.72	56.86	4
10	†H. M. Nicholls (NZ)	5	7	1	284	174	1	1	47.33	50.98	2
11	D. P. Sibley (E)	9	14	1	615	133*	2	2	47.30	37.89	4
12	†D. Elgar (SA)	4	7	0	317	95	0	2	45.28	51.04	6
13	†C. R. Ervine (Z)	3	6	0	267	107	1	1	44.50	50.37	1
14	O. J. D. Pope (E)	9	14	3	481	135*	1	4	43.72	57.05	9
15	Mohammad Rizwan (P)	5	7	0	302	72	0	4	43.14	43.64	12/1
16	F. du Plessis (SA)	4	7	0	301	199	1	0	43.00	50.41	4
17	J. Blackwood (WI)	5	10	0	427	104	1	3	42.70	63.07	1
18	J. E. Root (E)	8	13	2	464	68*	0	4	42.18	56.44	14
19	Azhar Ali (P)	5	8	1	287	141*	1	0	41.00	38.57	1
20	A. M. Rahane (I)	4	8	1	272	112	1	0	38.85	42.36	5
21	†Q. de Kock (SA)	4	7	0	269	76	0	3	38.42	57.60	19
22	J. C. Buttler (E)	9	14	1	497	152	1	2	38.23	53.44	30
23	†T. W. M. Latham (NZ)	6	10	1	342	86	0	4	38.00	46.84	10
24	Sikandar Raza (Z)	3	6	0	219	72	0	1	36.50	51.40	1
25	†Shan Masood (P)	5	8	0	289	156	2	0	36.12	46.53	3
26	B. R. M. Taylor (Z)	3	6	0	215	67	0	2	35.83	71.66	1
27	L. R. P. L. Taylor (NZ)	6	9	2	237	70	0	1	33.85	56.02	8
28	H. E. van der Dussen (SA)	4	7	0	232	98	0	2	33.14	39.25	9
29	†R. J. Burns (E)	6	9	0	254	90	0	2	28.22	43.56	4
30	T. A. Blundell (NZ)	6	10	1	250	64	0	2	27.77	41.05	4
31	J. O. Holder (WI)	5	10	2	217	61	0	1	27.12	51.05	9
32	S. S. J. Brooks (WI)	5	10	0	248	68	0	2	24.80	42.98	2
33	K. C. Brathwaite (WI)	5	10	0	231	75	0	2	23.10	42.00	2

Mushfiqur Rahim (Bangladesh) scored 203 (strike-rate 63.83) in his only Test innings of 2020.*

BOWLING (7 wickets)

		Style	O	M	R	W	BB	5I	Avge	SR
1	K. A. Jamieson (NZ)	RFM	159.2	56	361	25	5-34	2	14.44	38.24
2	S. C. J. Broad (E)	RFM	242.5	77	561	38	6-31	1	14.76	38.34
3	R. A. S. Lakmal (SL)	RFM	87	32	151	10	4-27	0	15.10	52.20
4	J. R. Hazlewood (A)	RFM	51	16	116	7	5-8	1	16.57	43.71
5	Nayeem Hasan (B)	OB	62	15	152	9	5-82	1	16.88	41.33
6	T. G. Southee (NZ)	RFM	187.5	52	511	30	5-32	2	17.03	37.56
7	P. J. Cummins (A)	RF	96.3	29	244	14	4-21	0	17.42	41.35
8	B. A. Stokes (E)	RFM	125.4	30	356	19	4-49	0	18.73	39.68
9	N. M. Lyon (A)	OB	98.3	20	263	14	5-50	2	18.78	42.21
10	M. A. Wood (E)	RF	92.3	17	273	14	5-46	1	19.50	39.64
11	M. A. Starc (A)	LF	87	17	240	12	4-53	0	20.00	43.50
12	J. M. Anderson (E)	RFM	198	57	471	23	5-40	2	20.47	51.65
13	R. Ashwin (I)	OB	114.1	18	276	13	4-55	0	21.23	52.69
14	C. R. Woakes (E)	RFM	164	39	433	20	5-50	1	21.65	49.20
15	Abu Jayed (B)	RFM	57	13	161	7	4-71	0	23.00	48.85
16	N. Wagner (NZ)	LFM	167.1	39	436	18	4-66	0	24.22	55.72

		Style	O	M	R	W	BB	5I	Avge	SR
17	J. J. Bumrah (I)	RFM	132.4	30	379	14	4-56	0	27.07	56.85
18	T. A. Boult (NZ)	LFM	189	43	579	20	4-28	0	28.95	56.70
19	Sikandar Raza (Z)	OB	121	20	349	12	7-113	1	29.08	60.50
20	Mohammad Abbas (P)	RFM	154.4	54	313	10	2-19	0	31.30	92.80
21	S. T. Gabriel (WI)	RF	149.1	27	537	17	5-75	1	31.58	52.64
22	A. A. Nortje (SA)	RF	128.1	14	520	16	5-110	1	32.50	48.06
23	K. Rabada (SA)	RF	67.5	12	234	7	3-68	0	33.42	58.14
24	L. Embuldeniya (SL)	SLA	130.3	28	451	13	5-114	1	34.69	60.23
25	Yasir Shah (P)	LB	180.2	18	643	18	4-58	0	35.72	60.11
26	Shaheen Shah Afridi (P)	LFM	161.4	29	506	14	4-53	0	36.14	69.28
27	K. A. J. Roach (WI)	RFM	146.4	38	406	11	4-72	0	36.90	80.00
28	Naseem Shah (P)	RF	122.5	20	446	12	4-26	0	37.16	61.41
29	Taijul Islam (B)	SLA	93	14	307	8	4-78	0	38.37	69.75
30	C. B. R. L. S. Kumara (SL)	RFM	101.1	23	315	8	3-32	0	39.37	75.87
31	S. M. Curran (E)	LFM	115	25	361	9	2-39	0	40.11	76.66
32	D. M. Bess (E)	OB	249.1	65	650	16	5-51	1	40.62	93.43
33	R. L. Chase (WI)	OB	132	15	503	12	5-172	1	41.91	66.00
34	J. O. Holder (WI)	RFM	169.5	49	446	10	6-42	1	44.60	101.90
35	J. C. Archer (E)	RF	125.4	23	360	8	3-45	0	45.00	94.25
36	A. S. Joseph (WI)	RFM	109.1	21	390	7	3-109	0	55.71	93.57
37	K. A. Maharaj (SA)	SLA	153	36	502	8	5-180	1	62.75	114.75

MOST DISMISSALS BY A WICKETKEEPER

Dis		T	
30	(30ct)	9	J. C. Buttler (E)
25	(25ct)	5	B-J. Watling (NZ)
19	(19ct)	4	Q. de Kock (SA)
14	(13 ct, 1st)	3	T. D. Paine (A)
13	(10ct, 3st)	3	D. P. D. N. Dickwella (SL)
13	(12ct, 1st)	5	Mohammad Rizwan (P)
12	(12ct)	3	R. R. Pant (I)
10	(9ct, 1st)	3	R. W. Chakabva (Z)

MOST CATCHES IN THE FIELD

Ct	T	
14	7	B. A. Stokes (E)
14	8	J. E. Root (E)
10	6	T. W. M. Latham (NZ)
9	4	H. E. van der Dussen (SA)
9	5	J. O. Holder (WI)
9	9	O. J. D. Pope (E)

"He is a life member of the National Rifle Association of India and, after the 2019 World Cup, pulled out of a tour of the West Indies to spend two months with his Territorial Army regiment. He loves machinery, and motorbikes."

M. S. Dhoni Retires From International Cricket, page 104

ONE-DAY INTERNATIONAL AVERAGES IN CALENDAR YEAR 2020

BATTING (200 runs)

		M	I	NO	R	HS	100	50	Avge	SR	4	6
1	H. Klaasen (SA)	3	3	2	242	123*	1	2	242.00	105.67	20	5
2	Liton Das (B)	3	3	1	311	176	2	0	155.50	118.70	31	10
3	†Tamim Iqbal (B)	3	3	1	310	158	2	0	155.00	107.63	29	9
4	Babar Azam (P)	3	3	1	221	125	1	1	110.50	101.84	23	3
5	H. H. Pandya (I)	3	3	1	210	92*	0	2	105.00	114.75	15	6
6	†E. Lewis (WI)	3	3	1	208	102	1	1	104.00	96.74	20	7
7	Aaqib Ilyas (Oman)	6	6	2	400	109*	2	2	100.00	82.30	40	4
8	S. W. Billings (E)	6	6	2	315	118	1	2	78.75	95.74	38	4
9	G. J. Maxwell (A)	6	6	1	353	108	1	3	70.60	145.26	20	22
10	W. I. A. Fernando (SL)	3	3	0	206	127	1	1	68.66	97.16	20	1
11	S. P. D. Smith (A)	10	9	0	568	131	3	2	63.11	106.56	55	9
12	†S. C. Williams (Z)	5	5	1	241	118*	1	1	60.25	86.37	31	2
13	†S. Dhawan (I)	6	5	0	290	96	0	3	58.00	91.48	39	2
14	A. J. Finch (A)	13	13	1	673	114	2	5	56.08	81.67	65	14
15	†R. A. Jadeja (I)	9	7	3	223	66*	0	2	55.75	98.67	12	8
16	K. L. Rahul (I)	9	9	1	443	112	1	3	55.37	106.23	29	16
17	M. J. Guptill (NZ)	4	4	0	217	79	0	2	54.25	90.79	16	8
18	†H. M. Nicholls (NZ)	4	4	0	209	80	0	2	52.25	78.57	26	0
19	V. Kohli (I)	9	9	0	431	89	0	5	47.88	92.29	35	5
20	S. D. Hope (WI)	6	6	0	282	115	1	2	47.00	75.00	24	0
21	J. M. Bairstow (E)	9	8	0	346	112	1	2	43.25	100.87	39	11
22	†Zeeshan Maqsood (Oman)	6	6	1	215	109	1	1	43.00	84.98	25	4
23	†D. A. Warner (A)	12	12	1	465	128*	1	3	42.27	95.28	51	7
24	S. S. Iyer (I)	9	9	1	331	103	1	2	41.37	95.38	41	3
25	†N. Pooran (WI)	6	6	1	204	52	0	2	40.80	95.32	20	3
26	P. R. Stirling (Ire)	6	6	0	239	142	1	1	39.83	86.90	20	7
27	B. R. M. Taylor (Z)	6	6	0	237	112	1	1	39.50	84.34	28	5
28	M. Labuschagne (A)	13	12	0	473	108	1	3	39.41	91.13	32	0
29	†Q. de Kock (SA)	6	6	0	228	107	1	1	38.00	87.69	19	5
	A. Balbirnie (Ire)	6	6	0	228	113	1	1	38.00	86.36	24	3
31	W. N. Madhevere (Z)	6	6	0	227	55	0	2	37.83	90.80	26	1
32	†E. J. G. Morgan (E)	9	8	1	250	106	1	0	35.71	97.65	32	7
33	Sikandar Raza (Z)	6	6	0	200	66	0	2	33.33	105.26	17	5
34	†A. T. Carey (A)	13	11	1	287	106	1	0	28.70	91.11	23	3

BOWLING (7 wickets)

		Style	O	M	R	W	BB	4I	Avge	SR	ER
1	Mohammad Saifuddin (B)	RM	13.3	0	63	7	4-41	1	9.00	11.57	4.66
2	S. Bhari (Nepal)	SLA	30.2	3	103	11	4-5	1	9.36	16.54	3.39
3	Aaqib Ilyas (Oman)	OB	31	2	122	10	4-36	1	12.20	18.60	3.93
4	Ahmed Raza (UAE)	SLA	27	3	88	7	5-26	1	12.57	23.14	3.25
5	J. J. Smit (Namibia)	LFM	22	1	109	8	5-44	1	13.62	16.50	4.95
6	A. S. Joseph (WI)	RFM	60	2	265	18	4-32	3	14.72	20.00	4.41
7	K. C. Karan (Nepal)	RFM	28.1	4	119	8	4-15	2	14.87	21.12	4.22
8	Zeeshan Maqsood (Oman)	SLA	52.1	7	198	13	4-15	1	15.23	24.07	3.79
9	L. T. Ngidi (SA)	RFM	34	2	193	12	6-58	1	16.08	17.00	5.67
10	Bilal Khan (Oman)	LFM	53	5	227	14	4-49	1	16.21	22.71	4.28
11	D. J. Willey (E)	LFM	28.4	4	148	8	5-30	1	18.50	21.50	5.16
12	S. Lamichhane (Nepal)	LB	36	4	153	8	6-16	1	19.12	27.00	4.25
13	B. Muzarabani (Z)	RFM	27	1	136	7	5-49	1	19.42	23.14	5.03
14	H. R. Walsh (WI)	LB	36	0	171	8	4-36	1	21.37	27.00	4.75
15	J. C. Archer (E)	RF	29	2	151	7	3-34	0	21.57	24.85	5.20

		Style	O	M	R	W	BB	4I	Avge	SR	ER
16	Mohammad Nadeem (Oman)	RFM	38	1	211	9	3-43	0	23.44	25.33	5.55
17	A. Zampa (A).	LB	128	0	641	27	4-54	2	23.74	28.44	5.00
18	C. R. Woakes (E).	RFM	43	1	194	7	3-32	0	27.71	36.85	4.51
19	T. Shamsi (SA)	SLW	40	0	195	7	3-38	0	27.85	34.28	4.87
20	S. S. Cottrell (WI)	LFM	49	2	284	10	4-67	1	28.40	29.40	5.79
21	A. U. Rashid (E)	LB	67.2	4	362	12	3-34	0	30.16	33.66	5.37
22	J. R. Hazlewood (A)	RFM	98.3	8	493	16	3-26	0	30.81	36.93	5.00
23	Mohammed Shami (I)	RFM	55.5	0	393	12	4-63	1	32.75	27.91	7.03
24	C. A. Young (Ire).	RFM	36	1	234	7	3-53	0	33.42	30.85	6.50
25	C. T. Mumba (Z)	RFM	35	0	259	7	3-69	0	37.00	30.00	7.40
26	Y. S. Chahal (I)	LB	39	1	265	7	3-47	0	37.85	33.42	6.79
27	P. J. Cummins (A)	RF	103	8	592	15	3-25	0	39.46	41.20	5.74
28	S. N. Thakur (I)	RFM	43.1	2	321	7	3-51	0	45.85	37.00	7.43
29	M. A. Starc (A)	LF	103.3	1	651	12	3-56	0	54.25	51.75	6.28
30	R. A. Jadeja (I).	SLA	88	1	472	7	2-44	0	67.42	75.42	5.36

MOST DISMISSALS BY A WICKETKEEPER

Dis		M	
15	(14ct, 1st)	6	S. D. Hope (WI)
15	(15ct)	13	A. T. Carey (A)
12	(10ct, 2st)	8	K. L. Rahul (I)
11	(11ct)	6	L. J. Tucker (Ire)
7	(6ct, 1st)	3	J. C. Buttler (E)
7	(6ct, 1st)	4	B. Bhandari (Nepal)
7	(6ct, 1st)	6	Q. de Kock (SA)

Rahul played one further one-day international when not keeping wicket, but took no catches.

MOST CATCHES IN THE FIELD

Ct	M	
10	11	M. A. Starc (A)
7	6	G. J. Maxwell (A)
6	6	Khawar Ali (Oman)
5	9	V. Kohli (I)
5	10	S. P. D. Smith (A)

TWENTY20 INTERNATIONAL AVERAGES IN CALENDAR YEAR 2020

BATTING (200 runs)

		M	I	NO	R	HS	100	50	Avge	SR	4	6
1	Shaheryar Butt (Belgium)	4	4	2	236	125*	1	1	118.00	**212.61**	18	17
2	†Q. de Kock (SA).	9	9	0	285	70	0	2	31.66	**170.65**	18	21
3	†E. J. G. Morgan (E).	11	10	2	276	66	0	3	34.50	**168.29**	21	17
4	B. R. S. de Silva (Kuwait)	5	5	1	219	84*	0	2	54.75	**165.90**	23	12
5	K. S. Williamson (NZ) . .	5	5	1	218	95	0	3	54.50	**155.71**	20	11
6	Mohammad Hafeez (P) .	10	8	3	415	99*	0	4	83.00	**152.57**	36	20
7	J. M. Bairstow (E)	12	11	1	329	86*	0	3	32.90	**150.91**	31	15
8	J. C. Buttler (E).	8	8	2	291	77*	0	3	48.50	**150.77**	33	11
9	Babar Azam (P)	8	6	1	276	82	0	4	55.20	**144.50**	34	3
10	†D. J. Malan (E)	10	10	2	397	99*	0	4	49.62	**142.29**	46	10
11	V. Kohli (I).	10	9	1	295	85	0	1	36.87	**141.82**	18	10
12	K. L. Rahul (I)	11	10	1	404	57*	0	4	44.88	**140.76**	34	13
13	H. E. van der Dussen (SA)	9	9	3	288	74*	0	1	48.00	**140.48**	17	14
14	T. L. Seifert (NZ)	11	10	3	352	84*	0	4	50.28	**140.23**	31	16
15	A. J. Finch (A)	8	8	0	271	55	0	1	33.87	**138.97**	34	7
16	S. S. Iyer (I)	10	9	3	203	58*	0	1	33.83	**135.33**	12	11
17	Kamran Khan (Qatar) . . .	7	7	0	335	88	0	3	47.85	**135.08**	24	22
18	S. P. D. Smith (A).	9	9	1	217	46	0	0	27.12	**131.51**	13	9

		M	*I*	*NO*	*R*	*HS*	*100*	*50*	*Avge*	*SR*	*4*	*6*
19	C. Suri (UAE)	5	5	1	239	75	0	3	59.75	**130.60**	24	5
20	†Syed Aziz (Malaysia)	9	8	2	222	51*	0	2	37.00	**130.58**	18	9
21	Ahmed Faiz (Malaysia)	8	7	0	234	58	0	1	33.42	**120.61**	25	5
22	†Virandeep Singh (Malaysia)	9	9	1	253	50	0	1	31.62	**119.33**	24	11

BOWLING (10 wickets)

		Style	*B*	*D*	*R*	*W*	*BB*	*4I*	*Avge*	*SR*	*ER*
1	Pavandeep Singh (Malaysia)	SLA	198	82	206	12	3-18	0	17.16	16.50	**6.24**
2	Haroon Arshad (Hong Kong)	RFM	109	54	115	11	5-16	2	10.45	9.90	**6.33**
3	M. N. M. Aslam (Kuwait)	SLA	120	36	128	12	4-5	2	10.66	10.00	**6.40**
4	Aftab Hussain (Hong Kong)	SLA	204	83	225	15	3-14	0	15.00	13.60	**6.61**
5	Iqbal Hussain (Qatar)	RM	161	23	178	12	4-16	1	14.83	13.41	**6.63**
6	A. C. Agar (A)	SLA	144	49	162	13	5-24	1	12.46	11.07	**6.75**
7	Syazrul Idrus (Malaysia)	RM	168	74	194	14	3-17	0	13.85	12.00	**6.92**
8	Awais Malik (Qatar)	RFM	144	13	167	12	3-28	0	13.91	12.00	**6.95**
9	Mohammed Nadeem (Qatar)	SLA	156	14	183	12	3-27	0	15.25	13.00	**7.03**
10	Aizaz Khan (Hong Kong)	RFM	204	87	241	12	2-15	0	20.08	17.00	**7.08**
11	Khizar Hayat (Malaysia)	OB	198	61	244	13	5-4	1	18.76	15.23	**7.39**
12	A. U. Rashid (E)	LB	252	86	316	12	3-21	0	26.33	21.00	**7.52**
13	A. Zampa (A)	LB	194	57	256	11	2-9	0	23.27	17.63	**7.91**
14	Haris Rauf (P)	RFM	258	86	372	16	3-29	0	23.25	16.12	**8.65**
15	T. G. Southee (NZ)	RFM	207	78	304	12	4-21	1	25.33	17.25	**8.81**
16	S. Muniandy (Malaysia)	RM	179	53	268	10	4-13	1	26.80	17.90	**8.98**
17	S. N. Thakur (I)	RFM	186	76	281	15	3-23	0	18.73	12.40	**9.06**
18	C. J. Jordan (E)	RFM	243	68	371	12	2-28	0	30.91	20.25	**9.16**
19	T. K. Curran (E)	RFM	240	68	394	10	2-33	0	39.40	24.00	**9.85**
20	L. T. Ngidi (SA)	RFM	200	63	349	17	3-30	0	20.52	11.76	**10.47**

Details of dot balls are incomplete for Aslam, Iqbal Hussain, Awais Malik and Mohammad Nadeem.

MOST DISMISSALS BY A WICKETKEEPER

Dis		*M*	
11	(10ct, 1st)	11	T. L. Seifert (NZ)
9	(5ct, 4st)	7	Mohammad Rizlan (Qatar)
9	(8ct, 1st)	8	J. C. Buttler (E)
9	(6ct, 3st)	10	Mohammad Rizwan (P)
8	(6ct, 2st)	5	U. Patel (Kuwait)
8	(8ct)	8	N. Pooran (WI)
8	(4ct, 4st)	9	Virandeep Singh (Malaysia)

MOST CATCHES IN THE FIELD

Ct	*M*	
12	9	Nizakat Khan (Hong Kong)
9	9	T. G. Southee (NZ)
8	9	M. J. Santner (NZ)
8	9	S. P. D. Smith (A)
7	6	D. A. Miller (SA)

ICC UNDER-19 MEN'S WORLD CUP IN 2019-20

SRESHTH SHAH

1 Bangladesh 2 India 3 Pakistan

This tournament will live long in the memory for several reasons. India's latest batting prodigy, Yashasvi Jaiswal, lit up the competition with his strokeplay, hitting five 50-plus scores in six games, and finishing with 400 runs at 133. The dominance of spin suggested the art was in safe hands: eight of the top 11 wicket-takers were slow bowlers. Nigeria and Japan both made their first appearance in a global competition, and impressed onlookers with their enthusiasm, if not their batting: between them, their highest total in the group games was Nigeria's 61 all out against Australia. And, despite ugly scenes that marred the end of an electrifying final, there were heartening examples of sportsmanship.

But two strands stood out. One was the manner in which South Africans embraced the tournament, helping make it an outstanding success. The other was the triumph of Bangladesh over holders and favourites India in the final. Their first victory in an ICC event offered genuine hope that, in the coming years, they would land punches at senior level too.

With England's Test tour taking place at the major venues, the Under-19 World Cup visited less prominent grounds. In Kimberley, schoolchildren turned out every day, whoever was playing: when Afghanistan thumped South Africa in the opener, they applauded each time Shafiqullah Ghafari took a wicket. They were delighted when West Indies' Nyeem Young smashed England to the tune of 66 from 41 balls, then picked up five wickets. And they thrilled to a last-ball finish that eliminated England at the group stage: Australia's ninth-wicket pair put on an unbroken 47.

In Bloemfontein, there was sympathy for Sri Lanka when New Zealand's Kristian Clarke knocked them out with a final-over six. When Japan played India, children ran round the ground with a Japanese flag; only ten Japan fans, all relations of the team, were present, but the locals made it feel like more. When the action moved to Potchefstroom, which staged most of the knockout games, college students replaced schoolkids, the atmosphere more beer and braai.

In the quarters, Australia were humbled by India, New Zealand inched past West Indies, South Africa were thrashed by Bangladesh, and Pakistan overcame Afghanistan. Pakistan then lost to India, causing some to rue the absence of 16-year-old Test seamer Naseem Shah: the PCB preferred to give a chance to a player yet to prove himself. But it was the second semi that caught the eye: Bangladesh thumped New Zealand to reach their first World Cup final.

Some episodes reflected well on the players. In the quarter-final, West Indies batsman Kirk McKenzie, who had earlier retired hurt with cramp, was last out for 99 and – unable to move – carried off by New Zealand captain Jesse Tashkoff and Joey Field. And when Noor Ahmad, the Afghanistan spinner, Mankaded the Pakistan batsman Mohammad Huraira in another quarter-final, Huraira admitted his error in prematurely leaving his crease.

Matthew Lewis, ICC/Getty Images

Boiling point: leg-spinner Ravi Bishnoi was one of five charged after an ill-tempered final.

All this made it more regrettable that five members of the Australian squad posted messages on team-mate Jake Fraser-McGurk's Instagram account using language described as inappropriate by Cricket Australia. The messages were written in broken English, and appeared to mock fans from South Asia; one Indian journalist accused the players of "casual racism".

The conclusion of the final, meanwhile, was marred by verbal confrontations and physical contact between jubilant Bangladesh players, who invaded the ground en masse, and their Indian opponents. Five players – three Bangladeshi, two Indian – were sanctioned by the ICC. Akbar Ali, the Bangladesh captain, said: "It shouldn't happen. We have to show respect to the opponent; we should have respect for the game."

The atmosphere was charged throughout, with several robust exchanges on the field, and tension in the stands, where Bangladesh supporters were in the majority. It had, though, been a tremendous contest. When Rakibul Hasan flicked Atharva Ankolekar to deep midwicket for the winning run, it completed a triumph for solid teamwork over individual brilliance. Bangladesh's most prolific batsman, Mahmudul Hasan (184 at 46), finished 15th in the run table, while their most successful bowler, slow left-armer Rakibul Hasan, was joint-sixth in the list of wicket-takers. But they made up for a lack of star quality in other ways, especially at the pinch points in the final, when Akbar was outstanding.

As he raised the trophy under grey skies, it seemed possible that this was the arrival of a new superpower. And, as the crowds that greeted the Bangladeshis on their return home demonstrated, the victory gave unbridled joy to a country more used to disappointment than success.

NATIONAL SQUADS

* *Captain.* † *Did not play.*

Afghanistan *Farhan Zakhil, Abdul Rahman, Abid Mohammadi, †Abidullah Taniwal, Asif Musazai, Fazal Haque, Ibrahim Zadran, Imran Mir, Jamshid Khan, Mohammad Ishaq, Noor Ahmad, Rahmanullah, Sediqullah Atal, Shafiqullah Ghafari, Zohaib Ahmadzai.

Australia *M. W. G. Harvey, C. P. L. Connolly, O. Davies, S. T. Fanning, J. Fraser-McGurk, L. D. Hearne, C. Kelly, L. F. Marshall, T. R. Murphy, P. J. Rowe, T. Sangha, L. A. H. Scott, B. Simpson, C. Sully, M. G. Willans.

Bangladesh *Akbar Ali, Avishek Das, Hasan Murad, Mahmudul Hasan, †Meharab Hasan, Mrittunjoy Chowdhury, Parvez Hossain, †Prantik Nawroz, Rakibul Hasan, Shahadat Hossain, †Shahin Alam, Shamim Hossain, Shoriful Islam, Tanzid Hasan, Tanzim Hasan Sakib, Towhid Hridoy.

Mrittunjoy Chowdhury injured his shoulder during the tournament and was replaced by Meharab Hasan.

Canada *A. Deosammy, H. S. Bedi, B. F. Calitz, †A. S. Dhaliwal, G. S. Gosal, R. R. Joshi, A. Kumar, N. A. Manohar, Muhammad Kamal, M. Patel, R. S. Sandhu, E. Sensarma, R. O. Shamsudeen, A. Verma, U. S. Walia.

England *G. P. Balderson, K. L. Aldridge, B. G. Charlesworth, T. G. R. Clark, J. M. Cox, B. C. Cullen, S. W. Currie, H. G. Duke, J. D. M. Evison, L. P. Goldsworthy, Hamidullah Qadri, J. A. Haynes, G. C. H. Hill, D. R. Mousley, S. J. Young.

India *P. K. Garg, Akash Singh, A. V. Ankolekar, R. Bishnoi, S. Hegde, Y. B. Jaiswal, D. C. Jurel, K. Kushagra, S. S. Mishra, V. Patil, S. G. Rawat, D. A. Saxena, N. T. Tilak Varma, K. Tyagi, S. A. Veer.

D. S. Joshi was originally selected but dislocated his shoulder and was replaced by Veer.

Japan *M. Thurgate, T. Chaturvedi, M. Clements, N. S. Date, K. K. O. Dobell, I. Fartyal, S. Ichiki, L. Mehlig, M. Morita, S. Noguchi, Y. J. Retharekar, D. Sahoo, R. Suto, K. Takahashi, A. Thurgate.

New Zealand *J. M. Tashkoff, A. Ashok, K. D. C. Clarke, H. B. Dickson, J. F. A. Field, D. B. Hancock, S. B. Keene, F. F. Lellman, N. J. Lidstone, R. A. Mariu, W. P. O'Rourke, B. J. Pomare, Q. L. M. Sunde, B. R. Wheeler-Greenall, O. J. White.

Nigeria *S. A. Okpe, R. Abolarin, P. Aho, M. E. Akhigbe, S. I. Audu, I. Danladi, M. K. Ikaige, A. E. Isesele, A. A. Jimoh, S. Mba, T. A. Mohammed, B. E. Oche, O. E. Olaleye, S. Runsewe, I. C. Uboh.

Pakistan *Rohail Nazir, Aamir Ali, †Aarish Ali Khan, Abbas Afridi, Abdul Bangalzai, Fahad Munir, Haider Ali, Irfan Khan, Mohammad Amir Khan, Mohammad Haris, Mohammad Huraira, Mohammad Shehzad, Mohammad Wasim, Qasim Akram, Tahir Hussain.

Naseem Shah was originally selected, but had already made his Test debut, and was eventually withdrawn to concentrate on his senior career; he was replaced by Mohammad Wasim.

Scotland *A. S. Guy, D. O. Cairns, J. S. Cairns, B. J. Davidson, J. J. Davidson, S. K. Fischer-Keogh, C. R. Grant, R. J. R. Hanley, E. P. McBeth, T. S. S. Mackintosh, L. R. Naylor, C. D. Peet, L. J. Robertson, K. A. Sajjad, S. M. U. Shah.

D. C. Mackay-Champion was originally selected but fractured a finger and was replaced by Robertson.

South Africa *B. R. Parsons, L. J. Beaufort, J. A. Bird, M. R. Brett, A. B. Cloete, G. W. Coetzee, K. Cotani, T. Karelse, M. K. Khumalo, J. P. Lees, A. W. Louw, L. M. Manje, O. Modimokoane, P. K. K. Moletsane, T. M. van Vuuren.

Sri Lanka *N. D. Perera, A. A. Daniel, D. A. O. de Silva, W. R. R. de Silva, G. S. Dinusha, T. A. Kahaduwaarachchi, L. M. D. Madushanka, R. V. P. K. Mishara, Mohamed Shamaz, K. Nadeeshan, N. D. Paranavithana, M. Pathirana, W. A. A. Sachintha, D. S. Thilakaratne, M. A. C. P. Wijesinghe.

United Arab Emirates *A. Lakra, Akasha Tahir, Ali Naseer, V. Aravind, C. D. H. G. Chethiya, J. J. Figy, K. P. Meiyappan, Muhammad Farazuddin, R. Mukherjee, Osama Hassan, A. Sharafu, S. M. Sharma, K. Smith, Syed Haider, A. Tandon.

West Indies *K. S. Melius, K. A. Anderson, D. J. Beckford, M. W. Forde, J. M. James, †M. N. A Joseph, L. J. A. Julien, K. S. A. McKenzie, †A. Mahabirsingh, A. R. D. Morris, A. R. Nedd, M. J. S Patrick, J. N. T. Seales, R. R. Simmonds, N. R. J. Young.

Zimbabwe *D. N. Myers, E. T. Bawa, P. T. Chesa, G. F. Chirawu, A. R. Ebrahim, D. J. Grant, W. N. Madhevere, T. R. Marumani, S. Ndlela, N. Nungu, T. M. Nyangani, L. D. Oldknow, D. J. Schadendorf, M. Shumba, T. T. Tugwete.

B. M. James and S. T. Ruwisi were originally selected but James injured his shoulder and Ruwisi his back; they were replaced by Ndlela and Nungu.

Group A

At Potchefstroom (University), January 18, 2020. **No result. New Zealand 195-2** (28.5 overs) (R. A. Mariu 51, O. J. White 80) **v ‡Japan.** *Japan's first appearance at any World Cup – and first full Under-19 international – was ruined by the weather. New Zealand were on course for a huge total, after openers Rhys Mariu and Ollie White put on 119 inside 16 overs.*

At Bloemfontein, January 19, 2020. **India won by 90 runs. India 297-4** (50 overs) (Y. B. Jaiswal 59, P. K. Garg 56, D. C. Jurel 52*); **‡Sri Lanka 207** (45.2 overs) (N. D. Perera 50). *PoM:* S. A. Veer. *A team effort ensured a comfortable win for the defending champions. Five of India's batsmen made between 44 and 59, while six bowlers took at least one wicket. All-rounder Siddesh Veer, a late inclusion in the squad, followed 44* from 27 balls with 2-34 for his off-breaks. Sri Lanka had been well placed at 106-1 in the 23rd over, but the rate climbed, and their last nine tumbled for 101.*

At Bloemfontein, January 21, 2020. **India won by ten wickets. Japan 41** (22.5 overs) (K. Tyagi 3-10, R. Bishnoi 4-5); **‡India 42-0** (4.5 overs). *PoM:* R. Bishnoi. *Japan's small group of supporters arrived at the ground with a banner urging their team to "Play without fear". But they hardly had time to absorb the message, bowled out for 41, with ducks for Nos 3–7, unprecedented in a men's game. Only Scotland (22 against Australia at Chittagong in 2003-04) had been dismissed for fewer at an Under-19 World Cup. Japan's batsmen found the leg-breaks and googlies of Ravi Bishnoi (8–3–5–4) unfathomable. Extras top-scored with 19; no one passed the seven made by opener Shu Noguchi and No. 8 Kento Dobell. India knocked off the runs in 29 balls.*

At Bloemfontein, January 22, 2020. **New Zealand won by three wickets. Sri Lanka 242-9** (50 overs) (W. A. A. Sachintha 64; A. Ashok 3-38); **‡New Zealand 243-7** (49.5 overs) (R. A. Mariu 86, B. R. Wheeler-Greenall 80). *PoM:* B. R. Wheeler-Greenall. *With six needed off two balls, Kristian Clarke carted left-arm seamer Dilshan Madushanka high over midwicket to take New Zealand through to the quarter-finals at Sri Lanka's expense. His team had almost botched a testing chase: from 217-3 with three overs to go, they lost four for 12, including Beckham Wheeler-Greenall, who had put on 111 for the third wicket with Mariu. The Sri Lankan batsmen had stumbled too, from 106-2 to 141-6, before Ahan Wickramasinghe Sachintha plundered 64 off 48.*

At Bloemfontein, January 24, 2020. **India won by 44 runs** (DLS). **India 115-0** (23 overs) (Y. B. Jaiswal 57*, D. A. Saxena 52*); **‡New Zealand 147** (21 overs) (R. Bishnoi 4-30, A. V. Ankolekar 3-28). *PoM:* R. Bishnoi. *India topped the group after New Zealand fell well short of a revised target of 192 in 23 overs. At 83-1 in the ninth, they had a chance, but the leg-spin of Bishnoi and Atharva Ankolekar's slow left-armers accounted for seven wickets; the last nine fell for just 64. Earlier, India's openers, Yashasvi Jaiswal and Divyaansh Saxena, made unbeaten fifties before rain ended the innings.*

At Potchefstroom (University), January 25, 2020. **Sri Lanka won by nine wickets. Japan 43** (18.3 overs); **‡Sri Lanka 47-1** (8.3 overs). *PoM:* N. D. Paranavithana. *For the second time in five days, Japan were dismissed in the forties; as against India, no one reached double figures. The Japanese did at least take a wicket this time, Dobell bowling Navod Paranavithana for nine, before Sri Lanka completed the easiest of chases in a game reduced to 22 overs a side.*

INDIA 6pts, NEW ZEALAND 3pts, Sri Lanka 2pts, Japan 1pt.

Group B

At Kimberley (Diamond Oval), January 18, 2020. **West Indies won by three wickets. Australia 179** (35.4 overs) (J. Fraser-McGurk 84; M. W. Forde 3-24, J. N. T. Seales 4-49); **‡West Indies 180-7** (46 overs) (N. R. J. Young 61; T. Sangha 4-30). *PoM:* N. R. J. Young. *Rain delayed the game by an hour, pinching an over from each innings, had push come to shove. Australia rallied after an unlucky start – twice the non-striker was run out by a deflection – and, thanks to a 91-run stand between Jake Fraser-McGurk and Patrick Rowe, were doing nicely at 158-4 in the 31st. But both departed to seamer Jayden Seales as the innings went into a tailspin: the last six wickets fell for 21.*

Australian leg-spinner Tanveer Sangha then reduced West Indies to 92-5. Once they had seen him off, though, they were heading for victory, despite the late wickets of all-rounders Matthew Forde, who had taken three in the earlier melee, and Nyeem Young.

At Kimberley (Country Club), January 20, 2020. **Australia won by ten wickets.** ‡**Nigeria 61** (30.3 overs) (B. Simpson 3-11, T. Sangha 5-14); **Australia 62-0** (7.4 overs). *PoM:* T. Sangha. *The star of this one-sided match was Sangha: two days after claiming four West Indies wickets, he snatched 5-14 against Nigeria, like Japan playing their first full Under-19 international. They struggled to lay bat on his leg-spin and, in a wicket-to-wicket spell of 5-8 in 6.5 overs, all eight came from wides. The only Nigerian to make much impression was Elijah Olaleye, who battled to 21 from 53 balls, before becoming Sangha's second victim; no one else made double figures. Australia boosted their net run-rate by zipping home at eight an over.*

At Kimberley (Diamond Oval), January 20, 2020. **West Indies won by 71 runs** (DLS). **West Indies 267-7** (50 overs) (K. A. Anderson 86*, N. R. J. Young 66); ‡**England 184-9** (43.4 overs) (N. R. J. Young 5-45). *PoM:* N. R. J. Young. *With only Nigeria still to play, West Indies effectively guaranteed top spot with another convincing win. Put in, they progressed steadily until off-spinner Hamidullah Qadri broke through in the ninth over, his first. In came Kevlon Anderson, whose calm 86* helped guide West Indies back from the brink at 138-5; he and the aggressive Young, whose 66 came from 41 balls, put on 101 in 13 overs. Slow left-armer Lewis Goldsworthy took 2-28 from his ten, but a target of 268 looked demanding. England were 120-2 at the start of the 30th, and needed to pick up speed; instead they lost wickets, including five to the seam of Young. At 151-8 in the 39th, the die was cast. When rain ended play early, England were put out of their misery.*

At Kimberley (Diamond Oval), January 23, 2020. **Australia won by two wickets. England 252-7** (50 overs) (B. G. Charlesworth 82, D. R. Mousley 51*); ‡**Australia 253-8** (50 overs) (M. W. G. Harvey 65). *PoM:* C. Sully. *Defeat in this crackerjack match – a must-win for both teams – condemned England to the Plate competition. But it was tight: Australia were 213-8, with 40 needed from 16 balls, when No. 9 Connor Sully crashed Blake Cullen for three sixes and a four. Eight came from the next over, the 49th, so the requirement was ten from the 50th, bowled by Joey Evison. Australia brought the equation down to three from two, and levelled the scores when a misfield allowed a second; Sully brought victory with a single off the last. Earlier, Ben Charlesworth at the top of the order and Dan Mousley, with a brisk 51* from No. 7, sustained England. At 153-2 after 30 overs, with Mackenzie Harvey going well on 65, Australia seemed to have done the heavy lifting, but spinners Hamidullah and Goldsworthy took four in five overs, to set up the tense conclusion.*

At Kimberley (Country Club), January 23, 2020. **West Indies won by 246 runs.** ‡**West Indies 303-8** (50 overs) (K. S. Melius 65, M. J. S. Patrick 68); **Nigeria 57** (21.4 overs) (J. N. T. Seales 4-19, A. R. Nedd 3-11). *PoM:* M. J. S. Patrick. *The match ended in crushing defeat, yet there were crumbs of comfort for Nigeria, who never let West Indies run riot on a true pitch. The most fluent scoring came from Matthew Patrick and Joshua James (43), who added 90 after coming together at 199-6. There was also 46 from Extras, including 26 in wides. A total of 303, though, was light years beyond Nigeria. The pacy Seales bowled the openers for ducks, en route to 4-19, while Patrick (off-breaks) and Ashmead Nedd (slow left-arm) had combined figures of 5-27. The two Nigerians to scrape double figures, captain Sylvester Okpe and Abdulrahman Jimoh, had earlier claimed two wickets each.*

At Kimberley (Diamond Oval), January 25, 2020. **England won by eight wickets.** ‡**Nigeria 58** (27.5 overs) (G. C. H. Hill 4-12, Hamidullah Qadri 4-24); **England 64-2** (11 overs). *PoM:* G. C. H. Hill. *Another game, another hiding for Nigeria, whose three totals were nothing if not consistent: 61, 57 and now 58. As against Australia, Okpe chose to bat, with predictable results: a steady fall of wickets, and a string of modest scores. Okpe was alone in reaching double figures. George Hill, a seamer playing his first game of the tournament, and the reliable Hamidullah took four wickets each; Goldsworthy had figures of 5–2–6–0. Sam Young, also on tournament debut, struck 39*, hitting the winning six from his 33rd delivery.*

WEST INDIES 6pts, AUSTRALIA 4pts, England 2pts, Nigeria 0pts.

Group C

At Potchefstroom (Senwes Park), January 18, 2020. **Bangladesh won by nine wickets** (DLS). **Zimbabwe 137-6** (28.1 overs); ‡**Bangladesh 132-1** (11.2 overs) (Parvez Hossain 58*). *PoM:* Parvez Hossain. *Bangladesh made a confident start, their five bowlers taking a wicket apiece as Zimbabwe were restricted to 137-6 before rain ended their innings. After a long delay, Bangladesh were set*

130 in 22 overs, and steamed home with few alarms. Tanzid Hasan fired off a ten-ball 32, then Parvez Hossain (58 from 33) and Mahmudul Hasan (38*) completed the job in a hurry.*

At Potchefstroom (University), January 19, 2020. **Pakistan won by seven wickets. ‡Scotland 75** (23.5 overs) (Tahir Hussain 3-23, Mohammad Wasim 5-12); **Pakistan 77-3** (11.4 overs). *PoM:* Mohammad Wasim. *Pakistan brushed Scotland aside in around three hours. Only Tom Mackintosh (17) and Uzzair Shah (20) reached double figures for the Scots – four made ducks, including both openers, bowled in Tahir Hussain's first over – as seamer Mohammad Wasim claimed five wickets. Pakistan also lost both openers cheaply, but were rescued from 4-2 by captain/wicketkeeper Rohail Nazir (27) and Irfan Khan (38*). This was Scotland's first official Under-19 ODI since the last-but-one World Cup in February 2016; all 11 players were making their debuts.*

At Potchefstroom (Witrand), January 21, 2020. **Bangladesh won by seven wickets. ‡Scotland 89** (30.3 overs) (Rakibul Hasan 4-20); **Bangladesh 93-3** (16.4 overs) (S. K. Fischer-Keogh 3-27). *PoM:* Rakibul Hasan. *Scotland again failed to make the match last past halfway, succumbing for 89 against a varied attack, in which slow left-armer Rakibul Hasan took a hat-trick, and left-arm seamer Mrittunjoy Chowdhury 1-8 in five overs. Tanzid fell to the first ball of the chase – one of three wickets for Sean Fischer-Keogh – but Mahmudul (35*) calmed any nerves from 35-3.*

At Potchefstroom (Witrand), January 22, 2020. **Pakistan won by 38 runs. Pakistan 294-9** (50 overs) (Fahad Munir 53, Qasim Akram 54, Mohammad Haris 81; D. J. Grant 3-46); **‡Zimbabwe 256** (46.3 overs) (W. N. Madhevere 53, M. Shumba 58; Tahir Hussain 3-42, Abbas Afridi 3-55). *PoM:* Mohammad Haris. *At 208-3 in the 39th, Zimbabwe looked well placed for an upset, but Abbas Afridi removed top-scorer Milton Shumba and the dangerous Tadiwanashe Marumani in three balls, and Tahir grabbed three late wickets. Pakistan had earlier found scoring difficult, apart from Mohammad Haris, who pounded 81 from 48, with four sixes.*

At Potchefstroom (Senwes Park), January 24, 2020. **No result. Bangladesh 106-9** (25 overs) (Mohammad Amir Khan 4-30, Abbas Afridi 3-20) **v ‡Pakistan.** *After a late start reduced this to a 37-over match, Pakistan seemed set to claim bragging rights in the group as Bangladesh slipped from 51-2 to 69-6; seamers Afridi and Mohammad Amir Khan finished with a combined 7-50. But rain swept in, leaving Bangladesh on top of the table on net run-rate (5.00 to Pakistan's 2.70).*

At Potchefstroom (Witrand), January 25, 2020. **Zimbabwe won by eight wickets. Scotland 140** (37.2 overs) (K. A. Sajjad 68; S. Ndlela 4-27); **‡Zimbabwe 146-2** (17.1 overs) (T. R. Marumani 85). *PoM:* T. R. Marumani. *Scotland made another poor start in a wooden-spoon match reduced to 42 overs. Seamer Sakhumuzi Ndlela sent them crashing to 18-4, though they did finally make it into three figures, thanks to No. 7 Kess Sajjad, who hit seven of the Scots' nine boundaries, four of them sixes. But Zimbabwe sailed home, opener Marumani belting 85 from 55 balls, and putting on 121 in 14 overs with Shumba, who made a run-a-ball 37*.*

BANGLADESH 5pts, PAKISTAN 5pts, Zimbabwe 2pts, Scotland 0pts.

Group D

At Kimberley (Diamond Oval), January 17, 2020. **Afghanistan won by seven wickets. ‡South Africa 129** (29.1 overs) (Shafiqullah Ghafari 6-15); **Afghanistan 130-3** (25 overs) (Ibrahim Zadran 52, Imran Mir 57). *PoM:* Shafiqullah Ghafari. *Afghanistan – semi-finalists two years earlier – beat the hosts in little more than half the allotted 100 overs. Bryce Parsons chose to bat, but his 42-ball 40 was the only innings of substance as South Africa lurched from 62-2 to 90-8. Leg-spinner Shafiqullah Ghafari claimed 6-15 (including four bowled), which would remain the best return of this tournament, and conceded a single boundary in 9.1 overs; only a rapid 38 from tailender Gerald Coetzee lifted South Africa to three figures. Ibrahim Zadran, who had already played two Tests, after appearing in the previous Under-19 World Cup as a 16-year-old, and Imran Mir hit fifties to ensure an Afghan victory.*

At Bloemfontein, January 18, 2020. **United Arab Emirates won by eight wickets. Canada 231-8** (50 overs) (M. Patel 90; S. M. Sharma 3-42); **‡United Arab Emirates 232-2** (38.4 overs) (A. Lakra 66, J. J. Figy 102*). *PoM:* J. J. Figy. *Mihir Patel and Randhir Sandhu (35) gave Canada a solid start of 82. Despite a middle-order wobble, when Sanchit Sharma dismissed three of his partners in seven deliveries, Patel advanced to 90 as they reached a respectable 231, boosted by a late 31 off 17 from Muhammad Kamal. But Johnny Figy, who had spent two years at Winchester College – and already made his ODI debut – put on 149 for the UAE's second wicket with captain Aryan Lakra, and completed a run-a-ball century as victory arrived with more than 11 overs to spare.*

At Potchefstroom (University), January 22, 2020. **Afghanistan won by 160 runs. ‡Afghanistan 265-6** (50 overs) (Ibrahim Zadran 87, Rahmanullah 81); **United Arab Emirates 105** (32.4 overs) (Noor Ahmad 3-30, Shafiqullah Ghafari 5-23). *PoM:* Shafiqullah Ghafari. *Afghanistan's second win, which ensured their place in the quarter-finals, contained many of the same elements as the first, though this time they won the toss and batted. There was another half-century for Ibrahim Zadran, who shared a 112-run stand with Rahmanullah for the third wicket. And Shafiqullah collected five more wickets (plus a run-out), which gave him 11-38 from 17.1 overs in two games, backed up by three from 15-year-old left-arm wrist-spinner Noor Ahmad. Figy followed his century against Canada with a three-ball duck as the UAE slipped from 61-0 to 78-6.*

At Potchefstroom (Senwes Park), January 22, 2020. **South Africa won by 150 runs. South Africa 349-8** (50 overs) (J. A. Bird 54, B. R. Parsons 121, T. Karelse 60*; A. Kumar 4-56); **‡Canada 199** (41.1 overs) (B. F. Calitz 62*). *PoM:* B. R. Parsons. *South Africa relaunched their campaign by amassing 349, thanks to 121 in 91 balls from their captain, Parsons, the highest individual score in this tournament and only eight short of their team total against Afghanistan. He was involved in three of four successive half-century partnerships. Facing an asking-rate of seven an over, Canada managed 69-2 in their first ten, but lost momentum. Only Ben Calitz passed 26, standing firm as they declined from 120-3 to 164-9.*

At Potchefstroom (Ibbies), January 24, 2020. **Afghanistan v Canada. Abandoned.** *The point Afghanistan took from a washout guaranteed they would head the group.*

At Bloemfontein, January 25, 2020. **South Africa won by 23 runs** (DLS). **‡South Africa 299-8** (50 overs) (B. R. Parsons 84, L. J. Beaufort 85; S. M. Sharma 3-57, A. Lakra 3-48); **United Arab Emirates 112-3** (23.5 overs). *PoM:* B. R. Parsons. *The group's second qualifying spot awaited the winners: South Africa made sure of it in a game halted by a dust storm and ended by rain. Parsons led the way again after Lakra had removed both openers in the 11th over. He scored 84 in 83 balls, sharing a third-wicket stand of 152 with Luke Beaufort before both fell to Sharma. The UAE made a bold start and were 65-2 in the tenth over, ahead of the rate, but another wicket slowed them down and left them behind on DLS when the weather struck.*

AFGHANISTAN 5pts, SOUTH AFRICA 4pts, United Arab Emirates 2pts, Canada 1pt.

Quarter-finals

At Potchefstroom (Senwes Park), January 28, 2020. **India won by 74 runs. India 233-9** (50 overs) (Y. B. Jaiswal 62, A. V. Ankolekar 55*); **‡Australia 159** (43.3 overs) (S. T. Fanning 75; K. Tyagi 4-24, Akash Singh 3-30). *PoM:* K. Tyagi. *When India posted a less-than-formidable 233, it was game on. Five balls into Australia's reply, it felt like game over. Fraser-McGurk was run out without facing from the first delivery, then a fired-up Kartik Tyagi struck twice to make it 4-3. When Tyagi removed Oliver Davies soon after, it was 17-4. Opener Sam Fanning and Liam Scott, batting as a concussion substitute after Corey Kelly was injured in the field, put on 81, but Fanning's dismissal was the first of three in three balls, including the run-out of Sully. Earlier, Jaiswal had continued his good form, and Ankolekar's aggressive 55* ensured India passed 200.*

At Benoni, January 29, 2020. **New Zealand won by two wickets. ‡West Indies 238** (47.5 overs) (K. S. A. McKenzie 99; K. D. C. Clarke 4-25); **New Zealand 239-8** (49.4 overs) (A. R. Nedd 3-33). *PoM:* K. D. C. Clarke. *New Zealand and West Indies reprised their Old Trafford thriller at the senior World Cup seven months earlier – and New Zealand squeaked home again. Chasing 239, they were on the ropes at 153-8, but Joey Field and Kristian Clarke added 86* to complete victory with two balls to spare. With four overs left, they had still needed 45, but cashed in on some nervy death bowling. West Indies had started poorly after opting to bat, but Kirk McKenzie supervised a recovery, sharing partnerships of 78 for the third wicket and 73 for the fourth. But 183-3 became 205-8 against the bowling of Clarke and captain Jesse Tashkoff. McKenzie returned after retiring with cramp, but could not move after he was last out for 99, a fourth wicket for Clarke; Tashkoff and Field carried him off.*

At Potchefstroom (Senwes Park), January 30, 2020. **Bangladesh won by 104 runs. Bangladesh 261-5** (50 overs) (Tanzid Hasan 80, Towhid Hridoy 51, Shahadat Hossain 74*); **‡South Africa 157** (42.3 overs) (L. J. Beaufort 60; Rakibul Hasan 5-19). *PoM:* Rakibul Hasan. *Bangladesh booked a semi-final against New Zealand with a comprehensive victory. Rakibul was the architect of*

South Africa's downfall, with a cheap five-four that included top-scorers Beaufort and opener Jono Bird (35); the last six wickets fell for just 44. After Bangladesh had been put in, Shahadat Hossain's 74 off 76 built on the foundations laid by opener Tanzid Hasan (80 off 84).*

At Benoni, January 31, 2020. **Pakistan won by six wickets.** ‡**Afghanistan 189** (49.1 overs) (Mohammad Amir Khan 3-58); **Pakistan 190-4** (41.1 overs) (Mohammad Huraira 64). *PoM:* Mohammad Huraira. *Afghanistan paid the price for an impetuous batting display, failing to make the most of a promising start. "The batsman did not take any responsibility," said their coach, Raees Ahmadzai. "Six gave their wickets freely." In all, seven reached double figures, but none surpassed the 40 made by captain and opener Farhan Zakhil. Pakistan's response relied on debutant opener Mohammad Huraira, who reached 64 before he was Mankaded by Noor Ahmad.*

Semi-finals

At Potchefstroom (Senwes Park), February 4, 2020. **India won by ten wickets.** ‡**Pakistan 172** (43.1 overs) (Haider Ali 56, Rohail Nazir 62; S. S. Mishra 3-28); **India 176-0** (35.2 overs) (Y. B. Jaiswal 105*, D. A. Saxena 59*). *PoM:* Y. B. Jaiswal. *Just as they had in the semi-final at Christchurch two years earlier, India thrashed Pakistan with lordly ease. Jaiswal underlined their superiority by completing the win – and his century – with a six, his fourth of a dominant innings. It was India's 11th successive Under-19 World Cup victory, and the first by ten wickets in the knockout stages in the competition's history. Jaiswal – whose tournament average soared to 156 – received excellent support from Saxena, who had earlier taken a magnificent catch to remove Mohammad Haris, and trigger a collapse of six for 26.*

At Potchefstroom (Senwes Park), February 6, 2020. **Bangladesh won by six wickets. New Zealand 211-8** (50 overs) (B. R. Wheeler-Greenall 75*; Shoriful Islam 3-45); ‡**Bangladesh 215-4** (44.1 overs) (Mahmudul Hasan 100). *PoM:* Mahmudul Hasan. *Mahmudul Hasan's hundred steered Bangladesh to their first global final at any level. Mahmudul, who had been in poor form, consolidated after the early departure of both openers, putting on 68 with Towhid Hridoy (40) and 101 with Shahadat Hossain (40*). By the time Mahmudul was dismissed, the ball after reaching three figures, Bangladesh were ready to start the celebrations. Their win also owed much to a cohesive effort by the bowlers, who kept New Zealand on a tight leash. It took Wheeler-Greenall's 75* off 83 to give their total respectability.*

FINAL

BANGLADESH v INDIA

At Potchefstroom (Senwes Park), February 9, 2020. Bangladesh won by three wickets (DLS). Toss: Bangladesh.

Amid high drama and mutual antagonism, Bangladesh clinched their first World Cup. After 23 overs, they were 102 for six, before opener Parvez Hossain – having retired with cramp – re-emerged, and put on 41 with his captain, Akbar Ali, who then found a solid ally in Rakibul Hasan. With rain having reduced the target to 170 in 46 overs, they added an unbroken 27, sparking a jubilant pitch invasion by the entire squad. There was pushing and shoving between the teams, scenes the ICC later described as "unedifying". Five players – Towhid Hridoy, Shamim Hossain and Rakibul for Bangladesh, and India's Ravi Bishnoi and Akash Singh – were found guilty of bringing the game into disrepute, while Bishnoi was also reprimanded for his reaction to the wicket of Avishek Das. India's captain, Priyam Garg, called the Bangladeshi reaction "dirty"; Akbar apologised on his team's behalf. India had been 156 for three before opener Yashasvi Jaiswal departed for 88 – the first of seven to tumble for 21. Bangladesh then reached 50 without loss in the ninth over, only for Bishnoi – making liberal use of his googly – to induce panic during a high-class spell of four for five in 21 balls. At 65 for four, with Parvez retired hurt, Bangladesh were in trouble; at the fall of their sixth wicket, they still needed 76. Rain trimmed eight from the target and, when play resumed, they required seven off 30. Rakibul lofted the winning single to deep midwicket, triggering joy – and more niggle.

Player of the Match: Akbar Ali. *Player of the Tournament:* Y. B. Jaiswal.

India Under-19

Y. B. Jaiswal c Tanzid Hasan b Shoriful Islam . 88
D. A. Saxena c Mahmudul Hasan b Avishek Das . 2
N. T. T. Varma c Shoriful Islam b Tanzim Hasan Sakib . 38
*P. K. Garg c Tanzid Hasan b Rakibul Hasan 7
†D. C. Jurel run out (Shamim Hossain/Akbar Ali) . 22
S. A. Veer lbw b Shoriful Islam 0
A. V. Ankolekar b Avishek Das 3
R. Bishnoi run out (Shoriful Islam) 2
S. S. Mishra c Shoriful Islam b Tanzim Hasan Sakib . 3
K. Tyagi c Akbar Ali b Avishek Das 0
Akash Singh not out 1
Lb 1, w 10 11

1/9 (2) 2/103 (3) (47.2 overs) 177
3/114 (4) 4/156 (1) 5/156 (6)
6/168 (5) 7/170 (8) 8/170 (7)
9/172 (10) 10/177 (9) 10 overs: 23-1

Shoriful Islam 10–1–31–2; Tanzim Hasan Sakib 8.2–2–28–2; Avishek Das 9–0–40–3; Shamim Hossain 6–0–36–0; Rakibul Hasan 10–1–29–1; Towhid Hridoy 4–0–12–0.

Bangladesh Under-19

Parvez Hossain c Akash Singh b Jaiswal . . 47
Tanzid Hasan c Tyagi b Bishnoi 17
Mahmudul Hasan b Bishnoi 8
Towhid Hridoy lbw b Bishnoi 0
Shahadat Hossain st Jurel b Bishnoi 1
*†Akbar Ali not out 43
Shamim Hossain c Jaiswal b Mishra 7
Avishek Das c Tyagi b Mishra 5
Rakibul Hasan not out 9
B 8, lb 4, w 19, nb 2 33

1/50 (2) 2/62 (3) (7 wkts, 42.1 overs) 170
3/62 (4) 4/65 (5)
5/85 (7) 6/102 (8) 7/143 (1) 10 overs: 55-1

Tanzim Hasan Sakib and Shoriful Islam did not bat.

Parvez Hossain, when 25, retired hurt at 62-2 and resumed at 102-6.

Tyagi 10–2–33–0; Mishra 7–0–25–2; Akash Singh 8–1–33–0; Bishnoi 10–3–30–4; Ankolekar 4.1–0–22–0; Jaiswal 3–0–15–1.

Umpires: A. T. Holdstock and S. J. Nogajski. Third umpire: R. R. Wimalasiri.
Referee: G. F. Labrooy.

UNDER-19 WORLD CUP FINALS

1987-88 AUSTRALIA beat Pakistan by five wickets at Adelaide.
1997-98 ENGLAND beat New Zealand by seven wickets at Johannesburg.
1999-2000 INDIA beat Sri Lanka by six wickets at Colombo (SSC).
2001-02 AUSTRALIA beat South Africa by seven wickets at Lincoln.
2003-04 PAKISTAN beat West Indies by 25 runs at Dhaka.
2005-06 PAKISTAN beat India by 38 runs at Colombo (RPS).
2007-08 INDIA beat South Africa by 12 runs (D/L) at Kuala Lumpur.
2009-10 AUSTRALIA beat Pakistan by 25 runs at Lincoln.
2012 INDIA beat Australia by six wickets at Townsville.
2013-14 SOUTH AFRICA beat Pakistan by six wickets at Dubai.
2015-16 WEST INDIES beat India by five wickets at Mirpur.
2017-18 INDIA beat Australia by eight wickets at Mount Maunganui.
2019-20 BANGLADESH beat India by three wickets (DLS) at Potchefstroom.

Third-place Play-off

At Benoni, February 8, 2020. **New Zealand v Pakistan. Abandoned.** *As at the previous tournament, Pakistan finished third, after a washout, because they had a better qualifying record.*

Fifth-place Play-off

Semi-final At Potchefstroom (Senwes Park), February 1, 2020. **West Indies won by four wickets.** ‡**South Africa 143** (38.2 overs); **West Indies 147-6** (41.4 overs). *PoM:* M. J. S. Patrick. *West Indies came through a drab, low-scoring encounter, after twice threatening to make a mess of a small chase. At 11-2, then 66-4, they had left the door ajar for South Africa, before Patrick – after two cheap wickets for his off-spin – slammed it shut. The South Africans had collapsed from 98-3, losing seven for 45, including two to the miserly slow left-armer Nedd, whose ten overs cost just 18.*

Semi-final At Potchefstroom (University), February 2, 2020. **Australia won by four wickets.** ‡**Afghanistan 191-7** (50 overs) (Farhan Zakhil 91*; T. Sangha 4-41); **Australia 195-6** (49.5 overs) (S. T. Fanning 62; Abdul Rahman 3-49). *PoM:* T. Sangha. *Sangha held Afghanistan at bay, taking four wickets with his leg-breaks, then hitting 46* from 40 balls after Australia had tottered to 123-6 in pursuit of 192. With his side needing three off two, he pummelled Ibrahim Zadran – bowling his first over of the innings – for six. The Afghans had looked down and out at 56-5, but Zakhil hung around for 91* to give his bowlers a chance. Australia slipped to 3-2, before Fanning and Lachlan Hearne (48) rebuilt. Four wickets for 24 changed the mood, only for Rowe (22*) and Sangha to put on 72* in 11.4 overs. Australia were without Fraser-McGurk, sent home for precautionary medical treatment after a monkey scratched him on the face during a visit to a wildlife reserve.*

Final At Benoni, February 7, 2020. **No result. Australia 319-8** (50 overs) (L. A. H. Scott 66, L. D. Hearne 58, C. P. L. Connolly 64; M. J. S. Patrick 3-43); ‡**West Indies 62-1** (12.3 overs). *Rain handed fifth place to West Indies, by virtue of their higher finish in Group B, where they had beaten Australia. The Australians might have fancied their chances of revenge, after all their top six made at least 20. West Indies opener and captain, Kimani Melius (39), fell to the last ball possible before the weather closed in.*

Seventh-place Play-off

At Benoni, February 5, 2020. **Afghanistan won by five wickets.** ‡**South Africa 154** (39.3 overs) (Fazal Haque 3-33, Shafiqullah Ghafari 4-15); **Afghanistan 158-5** (40.2 overs) (Ibrahim Zadran 73*). *PoM:* Shafiqullah Ghafari. *Just as in the opening game, leg-spinner Shafiqullah shepherded Afghanistan to victory over South Africa. This time he took four wickets, giving him ten for 30 in the two matches. The hosts were 40-3 when Bird, then on 22, retired after being hit on the elbow. And when three Shafiqullah wickets rattled the middle order, South Africa were on the ropes at 91-7. Merrick Brett and Mondli Khumalo added 51, but 154 was plainly inadequate. Ibrahim Zadran anchored the chase.*

Ninth-place Play-off (Plate)

Quarter-final At Potchefstroom (Witrand), January 27, 2020. **England won by nine wickets. Japan 93** (38.4 overs) (S. W. Currie 3-15, Hamidullah Qadri 3-17); ‡**England 94-1** (11.3 overs) (D. R. Mousley 57*). *PoM:* D. R. Mousley. *Three more wickets for Hamidullah, who now had 11 at 11 apiece, helped England to a straightforward victory – though making 93 was an achievement for Japan, dismissed for 41 and 43 in their two previous games. Indeed, at 78-2 after 29 overs, and with Debashish Sahoo on 24, they had looked set to sail past three figures, only for Evison to take two in two – and initiate a collapse of eight for 15. Mousley walloped 57* from 36 balls as England cantered home in the 12th.*

Quarter-final At Potchefstroom (Ibbies), January 27, 2020. **Sri Lanka won by 233 runs. Sri Lanka 306-7** (50 overs) (Mohamed Shamaz 56, W. R. R. de Silva 102*); ‡**Nigeria 73** (17.3 overs) (L. M. D. Madushanka 5-36, K. Nadeeshan 3-6). *PoM:* W. R. R. de Silva. *The mainstay of the Sri Lankan innings was Ravindu Rasantha de Silva, who reached his century in the 50th over, from his 109th ball. He shared three partnerships of 50 or more: a steady 89 with opener Mohamed Shamaz, a brisker 56 with Nipun Perera (37) and a swift 81 with Sonal Dinusha (43). Nigeria seamer Rasheed Abolarin took 2-50. Left-armer Madushanka immediately cut a swathe through the Nigerian batting: he finished with five wickets – four bowled and one lbw. Leg-spinner Kavindu Nadeeshan was almost as destructive. Extras top-scored, with 23.*

Quarter-final At Potchefstroom (Ibbies), January 28, 2020. **Zimbabwe won by 95 runs.** ‡**Zimbabwe 271-7** (50 overs) (T. T. Tugwete 50, E. T. Bawa 105*, G. F. Chirawu 54*; A. Kumar 3-63); **Canada 176** (47.3 overs). *PoM:* E. T. Bawa. *Zimbabwe's acting-captain Wesley Madhevere's decision to bat looked misguided at 54-5 in the 16th over. But striding to the crease was 16-year-old Emannuel Bawa, who proved their saviour. First he put on 84 with Taurayi Tugwete and then, after two quick wickets, 130* in 15 overs with Gareth Chirawu. It was, by 28 runs, the highest eighth-wicket stand in Under-19 one-day internationals. Canada's Akhil Kumar picked up three wickets. Initially, the chase followed a similar path, with Canada slipping to 69-5 – but there the parallel ended. Once again, Extras (28) top-scored. All 11 bowlers across the two innings claimed at least one wicket.*

Quarter-final At Potchefstroom (Witrand), January 28, 2020. **Scotland won by seven wickets. United Arab Emirates 249** (49 overs) (V. Aravind 61, Osama Hassan 81; D. O. Cairns 4-32); ‡**Scotland 250-3** (44.2 overs) (S. M. U. Shah 71, T. S. S. Mackintosh 57). *PoM:* S. M. U. Shah. *This game followed the pattern for the Plate quarter-finals, with one team running away with it. The surprise, given that the UAE had beaten New Zealand in a warm-up, was that the comfortable winners were Scotland. Fifties from Vriitya Aravind and Osama Hassan had steered the Emiratis towards a decent score, though they struggled against the off-spin of Daniel Cairns, and failed to bat out their overs. In response, the Scots top five were all in the runs. Shah made 71 from 77 and Mackintosh 57 from 50, allowing Jasper Davidson and Angus Guy to stroll home.*

Semi-final At Potchefstroom (University), January 30, 2020. **Sri Lanka won by 97 runs** (DLS). ‡**Sri Lanka 277-6** (50 overs) (N. D. Paranavithana 54, N. D. Perera 66, W. A. A. Sachintha 59); **Scotland 149-8** (40 overs) (M. A. C. P. Wijesinghe 3-31). *PoM:* N. D. Perera. *A shower meant Scotland's target was revised to 247 in 40 overs, but they were never in touch after a fourth-wicket stand of 103 between captain Nipun Dananjaya Perera and Wickramasinghe Sachintha had helped Sri Lanka reach 277.*

Semi-final At Kimberley (Diamond Oval), January 31, 2020. **England won by 75 runs.** ‡**England 286-9** (50 overs) (J. M. Cox 59, G. C. H. Hill 90; W. N. Madhevere 4-42); **Zimbabwe 211** (40.5 overs) (W. N. Madhevere 52, T. T. Tugwete 58; G. P. Balderson 3-29). *PoM:* G. C. H. Hill. *England made an uncertain start against the off-breaks of Madhevere, but were rescued by Jordan Cox and Hill, before skipper George Balderson hit 45* from 30 balls. Balderson then took two early wickets, including his opposite number Dion Myers first ball. Madhevere clouted 52 from 45 before he was run out, and Zimbabwe were reasonably placed at 148-4 after 30 overs, but the loss of Tugwete – to another run-out – left the tail too much to do.*

Plate Final At Benoni, February 3, 2020. **England won by 152 runs. England 279-7** (50 overs) (D. R. Mousley 111, J. A. Haynes 68, J. D. M. Evison 59); ‡**Sri Lanka 127** (31 overs) (W. R. R. de Silva 66; L. P. Goldsworthy 5-21). *PoM:* D. R. Mousley. *England salvaged some pride by winning the Plate final convincingly. His opening partner Young fell for a duck, but Mousley dug in for 111. Contrasting fifties from Jack Haynes and Evison (who slapped three sixes) swelled the total, before Sri Lanka also lost an opener in the first over. Cornish slow left-armer Goldsworthy then got among the wickets – his 5-21 was England's best at an Under-19 World Cup – and slick fielding produced three run-outs; only Rasantha de Silva made more than 15.*

Eleventh-place Play-off

At Kimberley (Diamond Oval), February 2, 2020. **Zimbabwe won by 172 runs.** ‡**Zimbabwe 354-8** (50 overs) (T. R. Marumani 90, M. Shumba 69, E. T. Bawa 56); **Scotland 182** (33.4 overs) (D. O. Cairns 58; P. T. Chesa 5-49). *PoM:* P. T. Chesa. *Zimbabwe reprised their group-stage thumping of Scotland, with Marumani's even-paced 90 setting up a huge total. Cairns followed two wickets with a defiant 58, but Priviledge Chesa – in his first match of the tournament – befuddled five Scots with his leg-breaks.*

Thirteenth-place Play-off

Semi-final At Potchefstroom (Ibbies), January 30, 2020. **Canada won by 182 runs. Canada 300-7** (50 overs) (N. A. Manohar 101); ‡**Japan 118** (29.4 overs) (N. S. Date 59; A. Kumar 6-46). *PoM:* A. Kumar. *Nicholas Manohar scored a rapid hundred in Canada's large total, but was upstaged by seamer Kumar. He took the tournament's second six-for as Japan lost nine for 45 from a promising 73-1.*

Semi-final At Potchefstroom (Witrand), January 30, 2020. **United Arab Emirates won by seven wickets. Nigeria 145** (46.4 overs) (A. Lakra 3-20, R. Mukherjee 4-35); ‡**United Arab Emirates 146-3** (29.2 overs) (A. Sharafu 59*). *PoM:* A. Sharafu. *Nigeria battled gamely to their highest total of the competition (previously 73 against Sri Lanka), but were no match for the UAE. Off-spinner Rishabh Mukherjee and slow left-armer Lakra picked up seven wickets between them, before an unbeaten half-century from Alishan Sharafu took the UAE home with more than 20 overs to spare.*

Final At Potchefstroom (Witrand), February 1, 2020. **Canada won by four wickets. United Arab Emirates 174** (44.1 overs) (A. Sharafu 65*; A. Kumar 3-37, U. S. Walia 3-16); ‡**Canada 180-6** (42.2 overs) (U. S. Walia 51*; R. Mukherjee 3-55). *PoM:* U. S. Walia. *A stand of 87* between Harmanjeet Bedi (31*) and Udaybir Walia took Canada over the line. Walia, bowling for the first time in the competition, had earlier taken three in 19 balls.*

Fifteenth-place Play-off

At Potchefstroom (Ibbies), February 1, 2020. **Nigeria won by eight wickets.** ‡**Japan 115** (42 overs) (I. C. Uboh 5-23); **Nigeria 116-2** (22.4 overs) (S. I. Runsewe 56*). *PoM:* I. C. Uboh. *The newcomers – bloodied but unbowed – ended their first global tournament in a tussle to avoid the wooden spoon. Nigeria seamer Ifeanyi Uboh made the key contribution: his five-for ensured Japan fell four short of their highest total of the tournament. Wicketkeeper Sulaimon Runsewe stroked 56* to ease Nigeria home.*

Final rankings

1 Bangladesh 2 India 3 Pakistan 4 New Zealand 5 West Indies 6 Australia 7 Afghanistan 8 South Africa 9 England 10 Sri Lanka 11 Zimbabwe 12 Scotland 13 Canada 14 United Arab Emirates 15 Nigeria 16 Japan

AFGHANISTAN CRICKET IN 2020

Imran Khan gives hope

SHAHID HASHMI

It was a quiet year on the field. The national team's only matches came early on, during a Twenty20 series in March against Ireland, which Afghanistan won 2–0. Other encounters were swept away by the pandemic: the most notable casualty was a tour of Australia, planned for November, including a Test match in Perth. The Afghanistan Cricket Board were left with ample time to reappraise their domestic structure and administration.

The lack of cricket and a shortage of sponsors forced the board to part ways with their long-time guide and motivator, the former Warwickshire batsman Andy Moles, who had played a significant role in the Afghan game's development during his six-year association. The news, in August, came four months after Moles had the lower part of his left leg amputated, after being infected with MRSA.

His replacement as director of cricket was Raees Ahmadzai, a batsman who played in some of Afghanistan's earliest official internationals in 2009-10.

AFGHANISTAN IN 2020

	Played	*Won*	*Lost*	*Drawn/No result*
Tests	–	–	–	–
One-day internationals	–	–	–	–
Twenty20 internationals	3	2	1	–

JANUARY		
FEBRUARY		
MARCH	3 T20Is (in India) v Ireland	(page 620)
APRIL		
MAY		
JUNE		
JULY		
AUGUST		
SEPTEMBER		
OCTOBER		
NOVEMBER		
DECEMBER		

For a review of Afghanistan domestic cricket from the 2019-20 season, see page 622.

Mohammad Nabi, the experienced off-spinner, joined the set-up, with a brief to help unearth new talent.

The board also halved the salaries of the coaching staff, who were led by Lance Klusener, with H. D. Ackerman, another South African, the batting coach. On the administrative front, chief executive officer Lutfullah Stanikzai was sacked, after allegations of mismanagement. A panel sifted through 45 applicants, and Rahmatullah Qureishi – with 23 years' experience at organisations such as the World Bank and the United Nations – took over in November. "Our aim will be to further serve and develop the game of cricket, as it is a source of joy for our country," he said. "We want to improve the infrastructure as more and more kids are attracted towards the game."

Around the same time, Pakistan's prime minister Imran Khan visited Kabul, on a mission to reduce tension between the countries, and invited Afghanistan to tour Pakistan in the near future. Such a trip should help rebuild relations. Pakistan helped Afghanistan immeasurably as they began their climb up the cricketing ladder, but recent meetings have been fraught – notably at the 2019 World Cup, when their match at Headingley was marred by crowd trouble.

Wasim Khan, the Pakistan board's chief executive, said: "We have played a major role in their cricket development, and are still open to extending our support whenever required. Afghanistan playing Pakistan has a big commercial potential and a big viewership."

Afghanistan also took a big step towards forming a national women's team. A camp for 40 female players was held in October and November; following practice matches, 25 were selected for central contracts. The board took cultural sensitivities and Islamic traditions into account, and hoped to set up more women-only facilities in major cities.

On the debit side, the menace of match-fixing made an unwelcome appearance in Afghanistan. Shafiqullah Shinwari, a talented wicketkeeper-batsman who played 70 white-ball internationals over a decade from 2009, was banned for six years, and junior coach Noor Mohammad for five. Shafiqullah admitted trying to influence the outcome of matches in the domestic T20 league in 2018. The board vowed to continue educating the players through lectures and monitoring.

There was even more sad news in October, when Najeeb Tarakai, 29, died after being knocked down by a car in Jalalabad. An off-spinning all-rounder with a first-class batting average of 47, Najeeb played the most recent of his 13 white-ball internationals in September 2019. "It was something very shocking to hear," said Rashid Khan, who was playing at the time in the IPL, where his Sunrisers Hyderabad team-mates wore black armbands in tribute. "He was a good friend to all of us."

AFGHANISTAN v IRELAND IN INDIA IN 2019-20

SHADI KHAN SAIF

Twenty20 internationals (3): Afghanistan 2, Ireland 1

This exciting Twenty20 series finished the day before the World Health Organisation declared a pandemic, though India – which hosted the games – would not enter lockdown for another fortnight. Afghanistan won 2–1, thanks to quality spin bowling, but continued to grapple with selection issues that had emerged before the 2019 World Cup. Even so, it was refreshing to see some young talent thrive. The 18-year-old Rahmanullah Gurbaz was the only player on either side to top 100 runs overall, while leg-spinner Qais Ahmad, a year older, picked up three wickets in his first T20 international, including the prize scalp of Kevin O'Brien. Familiar names prospered too. Rashid Khan took five wickets at 14, and conceded only a run a ball; Mujeeb Zadran also finished with five.

At times, Ireland struggled to adjust to the conditions in Greater Noida, and their opponents' high-class spin. Paul Stirling managed 60 off 41 balls in the first match – the only half-century in the series on either side – but no one totalled more than Harry Tector's 97 runs. After losing the first two games, the Irish pinched the third following a super over, settled by O'Brien's last-ball six off Rashid – their first T20 victory over Afghanistan in their last 13 attempts stretching back to November 2013. It was a thrilling game, so it was a pity the cricket took place before such thin crowds.

IRELAND TOURING PARTY

*A. Balbirnie, G. J. Delany, G. H. Dockrell, S. T. Doheny, S. C. Getkate, J. B. Little, B. J. McCarthy, K. J. O'Brien, W. B. Rankin, S. Singh, P. R. Stirling, H. T. Tector, L. J. Tucker, C. A. Young. *Coach:* G. X. Ford.

Doheny replaced G. C. Wilson, who had originally been selected but withdrew after falling ill during Ireland Wolves' tour of South Africa.

First Twenty20 international At Greater Noida, March 6, 2020. **Afghanistan won by 11 runs** (DLS). ‡**Ireland 172-6** (20 overs) (P. R. Stirling 60, K. J. O'Brien 35; Rashid Khan 3-22); **Afghanistan 133-5** (15 overs) (Najibullah Zadran 42*). *PoM:* Rashid Khan. *Afghanistan were ahead when rain came, thanks to a blistering 21-ball 42* from Najibullah Zadran, who helped his side recover from a collapse of four for 16. Not even the loss to the last ball possible of Samiullah Shenwari, who missed a slog off Boyd Rankin, could affect the outcome. Ireland had been given a flyer by Paul Stirling (60 off 41) and Kevin O'Brien (35 off 17), who helped them to 111-1 in the 13th. But Rashid Khan slowed the scoring, and it needed a 17-ball flourish from the 20-year-old Harry Tector (29*) to reinject momentum. Afghanistan also began well, and had 50 on the board after four overs, before off-spinner Simi Singh removed both openers, then ran out captain Asghar Afghan, who had not faced a ball. At 70-4, the game was in the balance, only for Najibullah to tilt it his side's way.*

Second Twenty20 international At Greater Noida, March 8, 2020. **Afghanistan won by 21 runs.** ‡**Afghanistan 184-4** (20 overs) (Rahmanullah Gurbaz 35, Asghar Afghan 49); **Ireland 163-6** (20 overs) (A. Balbirnie 46, H. T. Tector 37; Mujeeb Zadran 3-38). *PoM:* Mujeeb Zadran. *Afghanistan claimed the series with their 12th straight T20 win over Ireland (excluding an abandonment), following some ferocious late hitting. Having won the toss, they overcame a sluggish start to belt 99*

CONSECUTIVE T20 WINS AGAINST ONE OPPONENT

14	***Pakistan v Zimbabwe**	**2008-09 to 2020-21**
12	**Afghanistan v Ireland**	**2016-17 to 2019-20**
11	Kent v Somerset	2014 to 2019
10	Delhi v Jammu & Kashmir	2006-07 to 2018-19
9	Essex v Surrey	2005 to 2010
9	Auckland v Wellington	2005-06 to 2011-12
9	*Odisha v Tripura	2006-07 to 2017-18
9	*Bengal v Tripura	2006-07 to 2017-18
9	Madhya Pradesh v Railways	2009-10 to 2017-18
9	**Nottinghamshire v Derbyshire**	**2015 to 2020**

* *All matches between these teams.*

from the last seven overs: Asghar took 20 off four balls from Craig Young in the 16th, while Najibullah and Gulbadeen Naib each hit two sixes in the 20th, bowled by Josh Little. It cost 26 – precisely the number required by Ireland when they began their last over. Instead, left-arm opening bowler Shapoor Zadran conceded four singles, leaving Andy Balbirnie's 35-ball 46 in the shade.

Third Twenty20 international At Greater Noida, March 10, 2020. **Ireland won the super over, after a tie.** ‡**Ireland 142-8** (20 overs) (G. J. Delany 37, H. T. Tector 31; Naveen-ul-Haq 3-21, Qais Ahmad 3-25); **Afghanistan 142-7** (20 overs) (Rahmanullah Gurbaz 42, Asghar Afghan 32). *PoM:* K. J. O'Brien. *PoS:* Rahmanullah Gurbaz. *T20I debut:* Qais Ahmad (Afghanistan). *In a game that went to a super over, O'Brien's last-ball six off Rashid finally ended Ireland's losing sequence against the Afghans. Earlier, Rashid seemed to have dashed Irish hopes once more. With Afghanistan needing 13 off three to complete a whitewash, he launched Little for six in between a pair of wides; then, after a dot ball, he carved the last over cover for four. Young limited Afghanistan to eight in the eliminator, before Stirling hit Rashid for four from the second ball of the reply. But when Rashid trapped him lbw, then conceded only one run from the next two balls, O'Brien needed three from the last. He hit a six over long-off. At 92-2 in the 13th, Afghanistan had been on course. But Barry McCarthy bowled Karim Janat, and Singh removed Mohammad Nabi and Najibullah in successive balls. Two more wickets set up the pulsating conclusion. Ireland should have made more than 142 after reaching 74-2 from nine, but seamer Naveen-ul-Haq and leg-spinner Qais Ahmad, in his first T20I, finished with three wickets each to drag things back.*

DOMESTIC CRICKET IN AFGHANISTAN IN 2020

Like so many of their counterparts, the Afghanistan Cricket Board were forced, in March 2020, to postpone their domestic tournaments. But the government's Covid-19 emergency committee agreed in July that domestic cricket could resume. Although it was initially assumed that this would be without spectators, when the Shpageeza T20 Tournament began in September, the grounds were allowed to admit crowds of up to 30% of their capacity, with social distancing enforced, and masks handed out by the ACB.

Mis Ainak, who won two limited-overs trophies the previous year, the Shpageeza and the one-day Ghazi Amanullah Khan tournament, again reached both finals. They surrendered the Shpageeza title to **Kabul Eagles**, but remained 50-over champions when they defeated leaders Amo.

The Ahmad Shah Abdali Four-Day Tournament, which ran from April to December 2019, was covered in Wisden 2020 *(page 873).*

GHAZI AMANULLAH KHAN REGIONAL TOURNAMENT IN 2020

50-over league plus knockout

	P	*W*	*L*	*Pts*	*NRR*
AMO	4	4	0	8	1.17
MIS AINAK	4	3	1	6	–0.16
BAND-E-AMIR	4	2	2	4	0.59
Speen Ghar	4	1	3	2	–0.04
Boost	4	0	4	0	–1.43

2nd v 3rd play-off: Mis Ainak beat Band-e-Amir by seven wickets.

Final At Kandahar, October 22, 2020. **Mis Ainak won by seven wickets. Amo 260-7** (50 overs) (Abdul Malik 107); ‡**Mis Ainak 261-3** (46.1 overs) (Rahmanullah Gurbaz 128). *Mis Ainak retained their one-day title, as Amo slipped up after winning all four qualifying games. Opener Abdul Malik led Amo's recovery after Ziaur Rahman made two early strikes, adding 111 with Afsar Zazai (46) on his way a maiden one-day century. But Mis Ainak captain Rahmanullah Gurbaz hit five sixes in a 100-ball 128, leading his team to 193-1, and Shahidullah (36*) completed the job with nearly four overs to spare.*

AUSTRALIAN CRICKET IN 2020

Overturned by Covid – and India

DANIEL BRETTIG

On March 8, the MCG was host to 86,174 spectators for the glorious climax of the women's Twenty20 World Cup. Meg Lanning's Australian team won out handsomely over India, after a tense struggle to reach the final. They celebrated their achievement alongside singer Katy Perry, in joyous scenes beamed all around the world. As a moment in time for Australian cricket, it was hard to beat, underlining efforts to broaden the game from the old white male territory it has generally occupied.

It was later revealed there had been a case of Covid-19 in the members' reserve that night, around six weeks after the country's first reported instance. Over the months that followed, Australian cricket would join the rest of the

AUSTRALIA IN 2020

	Played	*Won*	*Lost*	*Drawn/No result*
Tests	3	2	1	–
One-day internationals	13	6	7	–
Twenty20 internationals	9	4	5	–

DECEMBER / JANUARY	3 Tests (h) v New Zealand	(see *Wisden 2020*, page 896)
	3 ODIs (a) v India	(page 675)
FEBRUARY / MARCH	3 ODIs and 3 T20Is (a) v South Africa	(page 743)
	1 ODI (h) v New Zealand	(page 627)
APRIL		
MAY		
JUNE		
JULY		
AUGUST		
SEPTEMBER	3 ODIs and 3 T20Is (a) v England	(page 378)
OCTOBER		
NOVEMBER / DECEMBER / JANUARY	4 Tests, 3 ODIs and 3 T20Is (h) v India	(page 630)

For a review of Australian domestic cricket from the 2019-20 season, see page 656.

Daniel Kalisz, Getty Images

Treading carefully: Justin Langer and Tim Paine, Adelaide, December 2020.

world in being overturned by the virus. And it was also left with some sobering lessons on the field once the international caravan resumed.

Within a few days of that final – and a packed celebration in Melbourne's Federation Square the following afternoon – a men's limited-overs series against New Zealand was called off after a single game at an empty SCG. Kevin Roberts, Cricket Australia's chief executive, oversaw the cancellation of the closing rounds and final of the Sheffield Shield, which was left in the hands of New South Wales, the league leaders.

Roberts said CA's concern was now: "How do we guarantee the continuity of our business?" The corporate-speak turned out to be a veiled reference to massive and clumsy cost-cutting, partly in response to threats from broadcasters about the continuation of the $A1.18bn contract that had been signed off in 2018. Seven West Media, it turned out, had been looking at ways to slash costs even before coronavirus, but it was curious to watch CA wrestle publicly with such issues when there were still so many months before another season. By contrast, Australia's winter football codes were almost immediately thrust into a fight to survive.

In April, Roberts – who had given little indication of what lay ahead during his almost daily video-conference addresses to staff – received the green light from his board to furlough the vast majority of the workforce until July, on 20% pay; to start financial renegotiations with CA's state associations and players' union partners; and to seek a multimillion-dollar loan from National Australia Bank. Meanwhile, the men's tour of Bangladesh was postponed, a brief Zimbabwe series pushed back, and the white-ball tour of England delayed.

These moves unleashed a slew of unresolved tensions with Roberts from all sides – players who distrusted him after his role in a 2017 pay dispute, states wary of accepting any reductions in their lucrative annual grants, and staff unhappy about being stood down on vastly reduced salaries, while CA's well-paid executives were not. The scar tissue was so widespread it was soon obvious Roberts's position was untenable. His predecessor, James Sutherland,held the job for 18 years; in June, Roberts resigned after little more than 18 months. Even so, the cuts had to go on, causing enormous damage to community cricket in some states.

The interim chief executive, Nick Hockley, formerly head of the T20 World Cup local organising committee, was left to work with CA chairman Earl Eddings on rebuilding these bridges. He was also left to manage issues such as the postponement of the men's T20 World Cup (scheduled for Australia in October and November), biosecurity plans for the tour of England, and the shift of the IPL – with its many Australian participants – into October.

Financial reporting season in August brought to the fore Channel Seven's campaign for a rights-fee reduction. The dispute escalated: requests for arbitration, the network's temporary refusal to pay a full instalment of their fees, and the threat of court proceedings. All this, capped by the publication of an affidavit in which private exchanges between Seven and CA executives were daubed across back pages, made cricket's return something of a relief. For all their table-thumping, there was never any question of Seven not broadcasting the matches they had paid for.

Australia's white-ball players got back on the field in September, after a charter flight to England and a stretch in quarantine were followed by the new phenomenon of the biosecure bubble. They did reasonably well, considering England had the advantage of being in season. A narrow loss in the T20 series was followed by a dramatic and topsy-turvy 50-over bout. A collapse in sight of victory in the second ODI provoked some of Justin Langer's harshest words since he became coach, but then a sublime chase from a position of weakness by Alex Carey and Glenn Maxwell meant the tourists won 2–1 in a series of fine margins – 19 runs, 24 runs, three wickets.

Back home, at the end of September, the women played the first international matches of any kind in Australia since the start of Covid-19, comfortably defeating New Zealand in one-day and T20 series in front of managed crowds at Brisbane's Allan Border Field. Star all-rounder Ellyse Perry missed out: she had pulled a hamstring during the World Cup, then tweaked it again before New Zealand arrived.

Sydney Thunder, well marshalled by Rachael Haynes, won the women's Big Bash League, defeating the vastly improved Melbourne Stars in the final. The entire competition was held in Sydney, as much thanks to draconian state border restrictions as Covid case numbers. Langer, for example, was forced to serve consecutive 14-day spells of quarantine in Adelaide and Perth after his return from the UK.

India's arrival had been shrouded in doubt until a few days before they finally touched down in Sydney, after negotiations fell through with the state governments of South Australia and Queensland. This meant the white-ball matches were played at the SCG and Canberra's Manuka Oval. The early exchanges were occasionally misleading – Steve Smith's pair of 62-ball centuries in consecutive ODIs suggested a domination he would not repeat in the Tests – but also showed up the resilience and depth of India, who claimed the T20s 2–1.

Then, under lights in Adelaide, the opening Test seesawed until Pat Cummins and Josh Hazlewood made a fearful mess of India's batting on the third afternoon, razing them for 36, and turning a possible defeat into a remarkably swift victory. This match was the end of Virat Kohli's contribution, as he flew home to attend the birth of his first child, leaving the captaincy in the hands of Ajinkya Rahane. He executed plans hatched by coach Ravi Shastri and his assistant Bharat Arun, then drilled into all members of the touring squad.

What followed, complicated by a Covid-19 outbreak on Sydney's northern beaches that left arrangements for the Tests at Melbourne, Sydney and Brisbane in doubt, was a gradual and dramatic dismantling of any semblance of comfort that Langer, captain Tim Paine and his team had in their methods on home soil. Paradoxically, the injuries that forced India into repeated changes meant they looked a more mentally refreshed and tactically vital unit as the tour progressed, after Rahane's century underpinned a series-equalling win at the MCG.

In Sydney, they fought their way to a draw, despite needing to survive four sessions in the fourth innings. Paine's frustrations were clear when he was overheard on the stump mike calling Ravichandran Ashwin a dickhead. Next over, he dropped his third catch of the day, which might even then have allowed the Australians to scramble home. Paine felt compelled to make a public apology after the Test, and was unable to rouse his troops to better efforts at the Gabba, where an unbeaten streak that had lasted since 1988-89 was brought to a shuddering stop by India's audacious chase. Conversations soon turned to leadership, and the balance of power between Paine and Langer, who found his coaching methods under media scrutiny.

As in life, 2020 was a year in which Australian cricket tackled the loss of certainty on just about every front imaginable. Even Lanning's team could not build on their T20 World Cup win as envisaged: the Rose Bowl internationals against New Zealand were the only ones the women managed after that magical night at the MCG.

AUSTRALIA v NEW ZEALAND IN 2019-20

ANDREW WU

One-day internationals (3): Australia 1, New Zealand 0

The Chappell–Hadlee series had originally been scheduled for January, at the end of Australia's 3–0 Test whitewash of New Zealand, but India's insistence on hosting the Australians around that time pushed this trip back two months. The build-up to the one-day series had been underwhelming, as international cricket in Australia in March often is, with many fans turning their focus towards the football codes. But the sight of an empty SCG for the first game had nothing to do with a lack of interest. A force had intervened that was even greater than the BCCI: Covid-19.

Hours before the start of the scheduled three-match series, Cricket Australia took the drastic measure of banning crowds, part of a strategy to minimise the public's exposure to the virus. (That morning, Melbourne's Grand Prix was called off.) Seamer Kane Richardson missed the game after reporting a mild sore throat, but tested negative, while interviews at the toss and after the match were conducted via Spidercam. Out of habit, Aaron Finch tried to shake his opposite number's hand at the toss, before realising his mistake: Kane Williamson smiled, and proffered an elbow, which Finch punched playfully. By the end of the game – won, almost incidentally, by Australia – the New Zealand fast bowler Lockie Ferguson also reported a sore throat; he, too, tested negative.

Matt King, Getty Images

Stand clear: a statue of Yabba, the SCG's legendary barracker, sits alone during the only game of the series to survive the pandemic.

But the crisis was developing fast. The following day, the New Zealand government imposed stricter border controls, saying they would subject those entering the country from Australia to a mandatory 14-day self-isolation period. With the controls coming into force at midnight, the New Zealanders had to head home immediately to avoid quarantine. The final two matches of the series could not be played, leaving the trophy – and cricket – in limbo. This was the last senior international match played anywhere until July 8, when the England v West Indies Test series began at Southampton.

NEW ZEALAND TOURING PARTY

*K. S. Williamson, T. A. Blundell, T. A. Boult, C. de Grandhomme, L. H. Ferguson, M. J. Guptill, M. J. Henry, K. A. Jamieson, T. W. M. Latham, J. D. S. Neesham, H. M. Nicholls, M. J. Santner, I. S. Sodhi, T. G. Southee, L. R. P. L. Taylor. *Coach:* G. R. Stead.

AUSTRALIA v NEW ZEALAND

First One-Day International

At Sydney, March 13, 2020 (day/night). Australia won by 71 runs. Toss: Australia.

Crushed by Australia in the Tests two months earlier, New Zealand had taken a turn for the better, defeating India at home in both the one-day and Test series. Australia, meanwhile, were showing signs of fatigue after a hectic 12 months, and had just lost three ODIs in South Africa. But, in a stadium empty because of coronavirus – the World Health Organisation had declared a pandemic two days earlier – the New Zealanders came up well short. They were chasing the game almost from the start, as Warner and Finch put on 124. Santner led a fightback, removing Finch and Smith in successive overs, and finishing with a frugal two for 34, while fellow spinner Sodhi kept the middle order quiet. But Labuschagne's 52-ball 56 gave his team something to work with, and New Zealand's batting line-up was no match for Australia's seamers. Cummins and Marsh each picked up three cheap wickets, though not before Zampa had breached Williamson's defences with a beautiful googly. The experience of playing behind closed doors produced differing reactions. "It was unique playing cricket in front of half a dozen people and the journos," said Finch. "But, all in all, I think it was a pretty good result, compared with what is happening around the world, with sporting events being cancelled." Sodhi sounded less enthusiastic: "Every time you tried to speak it echoed around the ground. It was a little bit bizarre." And things were about to get odder still.

Player of the Match: M. R. Marsh.

Australia

D. A. Warner c Sodhi b Ferguson	67	P. J. Cummins not out	14
*A. J. Finch c Latham b Santner	60	M. A. Starc not out	9
S. P. D. Smith b Santner	14	Lb 3, nb 2	5
D. J. M. Short c Nicholls b Sodhi	5		
M. Labuschagne c Taylor b Ferguson	56	1/124 (1) 2/145 (2) (7 wkts, 50 overs)	258
M. R. Marsh c Guptill b Sodhi	27	3/146 (3) 4/165 (4)	
†A. T. Carey c Boult b Sodhi	1	5/224 (6) 6/226 (7) 7/248 (5) 10 overs: 51-0	

A. Zampa and J. R. Hazlewood did not bat.

Boult 10–0–37–0; Ferguson 9–0–60–2; Neesham 7–0–44–0; Santner 10–0–34–2; de Grandhomme 6–0–29–0; Sodhi 8–0–51–3.

New Zealand

M. J. Guptill c Smith b Cummins	40	L. H. Ferguson b Marsh	1
H. M. Nicholls c Carey b Hazlewood	10	T. A. Boult c and b Cummins	5
*K. S. Williamson b Zampa	19		
L. R. P. L. Taylor c Starc b Marsh	4	Lb 5, w 4	9
†T. W. M. Latham c Short b Hazlewood	38		
J. D. S. Neesham c Carey b Cummins	8	1/28 (2) 2/64 (3) 3/69 (4) (41 overs)	187
C. de Grandhomme c Starc b Zampa	25	4/82 (1) 5/96 (6) 6/147 (5)	
M. J. Santner c Cummins b Marsh	14	7/160 (7) 8/170 (8) 9/180 (10)	
I. S. Sodhi not out	14	10/187 (11)	10 overs: 28-1

Starc 7–0–33–0; Hazlewood 10–0–37–2; Cummins 8–2–25–3; Marsh 7–0–29–3; Zampa 8–0–50–2; Smith 1–0–8–0.

Umpires: M. Erasmus and P. Wilson. Third umpire: R. K. Illingworth.
Referee: R. S. Madugalle.

Second one-day international At Sydney, March 15, 2020. **Australia v New Zealand.** Cancelled.

Third one-day international At Hobart, March 20, 2020. **Australia v New Zealand.** Cancelled.

A return series of three Twenty20 internationals in New Zealand the following week was also cancelled.

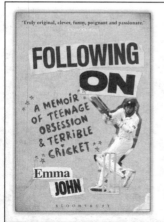

AUSTRALIA v INDIA IN 2020-21

GEOFF LEMON

One-day internationals (3): Australia 2 (20pts), India 1 (9pts)
Twenty20 internationals (3): Australia 1, India 2
Test matches (4): Australia 1 (36pts), India 2 (70pts)

To decide if something qualifies as great, we hold it up to other examples and seek commonality. Yet India's Test series win in Australia was an anomaly: patently great in its drama and skill, but in a manner unlike almost any other. A revered series usually has consistency at its centre, an ongoing struggle between a few titans. This was the opposite, as match after match saw India lose players to injury, departure, or poor form. Instead, a succession of new names and lesser lights each made a contribution to one of the most stirring comebacks the game has known.

Two years earlier, India had won in Australia for the first time in 12 attempts across 71 years, as an immaculately drilled outfit hit almost every mark. Never before had India enjoyed a fast-bowling cartel: then, Ishant Sharma, Mohammed Shami and Jasprit Bumrah had Umesh Yadav and Bhuvneshwar Kumar in support. Captaining with ferocity was Virat Kohli. The Australians were led by an emergency appointee in wicketkeeper Tim Paine, after suspending their two best batsmen, Steven Smith and David Warner. Their ball-tampering snafu

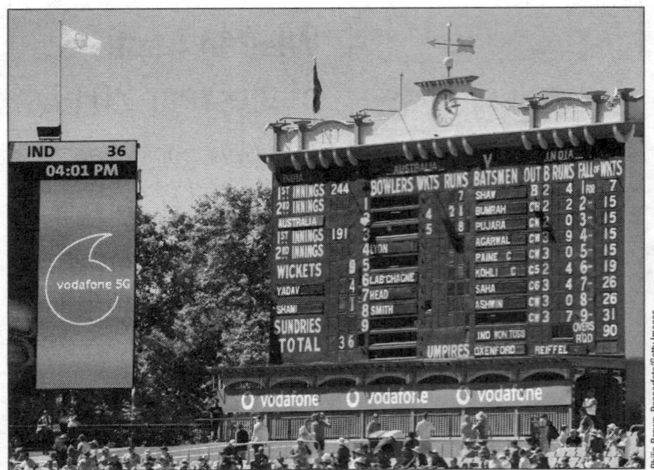

Philip Brown, Popperfoto/Getty Images

Nadir: India crash to 36 all out at Adelaide – and the only way is up.

earlier in 2018 had brought condemnation at home and abroad, leaving the team and Australian cricket badly shaken.

The 2020-21 series was supposed to be a return to normal. Smith and Warner were back, Paine had become a credible leader, the callow batting had mature graduates in Marnus Labuschagne and Travis Head, all-rounder Cameron Green was the talk of the town, and Australia had a point to prove. India had become the side short-staffed: injury ruled Ishant and Bhuvneshwar out of the tour, batsman Rohit Sharma from the first two Tests, and all-rounder Hardik Pandya after the short-form matches, unable to bowl because of a back injury. Kohli, meanwhile, would leave after one Test for the birth of his daughter.

The other major player was the Covid-19 pandemic. Entering Australia required a fortnight's quarantine, eliminating India's chance of summoning mid-tour reinforcements. An extended Test squad using white-ball players as net bowlers had to suffice. There was constant doubt about venues, because of shifting state-border protocol: the ODIs and T20s were slated for Brisbane before moving to Sydney and Canberra; the Boxing Day Test was confirmed for Melbourne only once a viral wave had been suppressed; the First and Third Tests were imperilled after outbreaks in Adelaide and Sydney; so was the Fourth, because of restrictions travelling from Sydney to Brisbane.

Spending months in hotels was nothing new for either squad, but the constraints were more onerous. Players were supposed to mix only with their own group – stepping out of the rain or taking a photo with a fan could constitute a biosecurity breach, with major financial consequences. Justin Langer and Ravi Shastri, the head coaches, had to keep their squads mentally steady from mid-November to mid-January. When a video of five members of the touring party dining together at a Melbourne restaurant was posted on Twitter, the BCCI launched an investigation; all five tested negative.

The portents were grim for India when Smith started the tour with his two fastest centuries in one-day cricket – both from 62 balls – to win the opening two matches at a canter, though Warner injured his groin, ruling him out until the New Year. But India won the third, and the first two T20s.

Then came the day/night Adelaide Test. Batting wasn't easy against the pink ball, but India couldn't blame the twilight when they collapsed under sunny skies to 36 all out. The match went from contested to decided within an hour, as Patrick Cummins and Josh Hazlewood bowled them out for their lowest ever score. Kohli went home, as did Shami, whose arm had been broken at the end of the rout. Umesh was injured in the Second Test, then Bumrah, Ravichandran Ashwin, Ravindra Jadeja and Hanuma Vihari in the Third. Opening bats Prithvi Shaw and Mayank Agarwal, plus wicketkeeper Wriddhiman Saha, were dropped. By the Fourth, India had called on 20 players, the most by any side away from home. Only Cheteshwar Pujara and Ajinkya Rahane appeared in all four matches.

And yet. At Melbourne, a week after the embarrassment at Adelaide, Rahane – captain in Kohli's absence – set aggressive fields, marshalled his bowlers with skill, then made a century. India levelled the series inside four days. At Sydney, a team halved by injury held on for a draw in the shadows.

Daniel Pockett, Cricket Australia/Getty Images

Captain hook: Ajinkya Rahane provides the runs and the nous to bring about India's resurrection.

At Brisbane, one of the least experienced sides to represent India chased down 328, to win both match and series, and retain the Border–Gavaskar Trophy.

It was an unthinkable achievement. Missing were their five best fast bowlers, two best spinners, two first-choice batsmen (including first-choice captain), and best all-rounder – ten certain picks. A result those players might never have achieved was driven by the audacity of youth: Shubman Gill, Rishabh Pant, Mohammed Siraj, Washington Sundar, Shardul Thakur, Navdeep Saini, Thangarasu Natarajan. Their senior help came from Rahane, a leader so different from Kohli in style, and Pujara, who soaked up every blow the fast bowlers could deliver, and faced 928 balls in the series, 366 more than any of his team-mates.

For Australia, it was just as unthinkable: a Test defeat in Brisbane for the first time since 1988-89, a second series loss in a row at home to India, and with no allowance this time for missing personnel. They had the two top run-scorers and the top two wicket-takers. After Adelaide, they won all three tosses. They set two daunting targets, and closed out neither. Perhaps a lack of enforced change became a hindrance: the adaptability Langer had used so well in England in 2019 was abandoned, and the same four bowlers contested all four matches. Cummins and Hazlewood were rarely less than outstanding, but Starc's 11 wickets cost 40, and Lyon's nine an unflattering 55, leaving him on 399.

Australia's administrators and public had accepted the loss in 2018-19, perhaps as a form of post-sandpaper penance. But 2020-21 brought heat on Paine, captain on both occasions. He had lowered his colours late in the Sydney Test, losing his temper as he sledged a stonewalling Ashwin. It raised doubts about Paine's three-year mission to change Australia's historical causticity, but his outburst was notable in its isolation, and the directness of his apology next day was unlike anything his predecessors would have offered. In any case, his punishment was karmic: "I can't wait to get you to the Gabba, Ash," will go down as a famous story of comeuppance.

Words fully deserving of condemnation came from spectators, after a Cricket Australia investigation found several Indian players were racially abused on the third day at Sydney. Other spectators were ejected on the fourth, for taunts later cleared of racism. It was this fraught environment that made Paine's outburst on the fifth so clanging in tone.

SUCCESSIVE TEST SERIES WINS BY TEAMS TOURING AUSTRALIA

3	England	1884-85 to 1887-88
3	West Indies	1984-85 to 1992-93
3†	South Africa	2008-09 to 2016-17
2	England	1928-29 and 1932-33
2†	**India**	**2018-19 and 2020-21**

† *Run ongoing.*

The emblem of the tour was Siraj, the bearded pace bowler, his long hair swept up in a topknot. When his father died in late November, quarantine issues meant he chose to stay on and pursue his dream of playing Test cricket, rather than attend the funeral. Despite no guarantee of being anything more than a net bowler, he won his debut in Melbourne, and wept during the anthem. In Sydney, he had the courage to halt a Test match to report crowd behaviour. By Brisbane, he was the attack leader, and took a five-for. He sent down nearly 135 overs, and was one run from equalling the best figures at the Gabba by an Indian seamer.

Yet, for India, everyone contributed, in a tight series in which neither team passed 369. Nobody needed to be dominant, because each new inclusion had an influence. For all the talk of cricket as a team sport, results usually rely on an exceptional few; in celebrity culture, attention stays on them, even when their performances don't warrant it. But this was team sport in its truest incarnation, a team shorn of superstars, and somehow harder to tackle because of it. This is what will be celebrated, as its own special strand of greatness.

INDIAN TOURING PARTY

*V. Kohli (T/50/20), M. A. Agarwal (T/50/20), R. Ashwin (T), J. J. Bumrah (T/50/20), Y. S. Chahal (50/20), D. L. Chahar (20), S. Dhawan (50/20), S. Gill (T/50), S. S. Iyer (50/20), R. A. Jadeja (T/50/20), Mohammed Shami (T/50/20), T. Natarajan (T/50/20), M. K. Pandey (50/20), H. H. Pandya (50/20), R. R. Pant (T), C. A. Pujara (T), A. M. Rahane (T). K. L. Rahul (T/50/20), W. P. Saha (T), N. Saini (T/50/20), S. V. Samson (50/20), R. G. Sharma (T), P. P. Shaw (T), M. Siraj (T), S. N. Thakur (T/50/20), G. H. Vihari (T), M. S. Washington Sundar (T/20), K. Yadav (T/50), U. T. Yadav (T). *Coach:* R. J. Shastri.

Kohli returned home after the First Test for the birth of his first child; Rahane took over as captain. V. V. Chakravarthy was originally selected for the T20 squad, but failed to recover from a shoulder injury and was replaced by Natarajan. Pant and R. G. Sharma sat out the white-ball matches as they were recovering from injuries suffered during the IPL. Jadeja was concussed during the first T20, and later fractured his thumb in the Third Test. Mohammed Shami broke his arm in the First Test, and returned home; Natarajan and Thakur were added to the Test squad. U. T. Yadav injured his calf during the Second Test, while Rahul sprained his wrist before the Third. Both missed the rest of the series, and Saini and Washington Sundar were added to the Test squad. Bowlers K. L. Nagarkoti, I. C. Porel and K. Tyagi also accompanied the tour to assist at practice; Natarajan started as part of this group, but ended up playing in all three formats.

TEST MATCH AVERAGES

AUSTRALIA – BATTING AND FIELDING

	T	*I*	*NO*	*R*	*HS*	*100*	*50*	*Avge*	*Ct*
M. Labuschagne	4	8	0	426	108	1	2	53.25	2
S. P. D. Smith	4	8	1	313	131	1	2	44.71	6
T. D. Paine	4	7	2	204	73*	0	2	40.80	17
C. D. Green	4	7	0	236	84	0	1	33.71	5
†M. S. Wade	4	8	0	173	45	0	0	21.62	5
J. A. Burns	2	4	1	63	51*	0	1	21.00	0
†T. M. Head	2	3	0	62	38	0	0	20.66	2
†M. A. Starc	4	6	2	81	24	0	0	20.25	2
†D. A. Warner	2	4	0	67	48	0	0	16.75	1
P. J. Cummins	4	6	1	61	28*	0	0	12.20	3
N. M. Lyon	4	6	0	70	24	0	0	11.66	2
†J. R. Hazlewood	4	6	2	43	11	0	0	10.75	1

Played in one Test: †M. S. Harris 5, 38; W. J. Pucovski 62, 10.

BOWLING

	Style	*O*	*M*	*R*	*W*	*BB*	*5I*	*Avge*
J. R. Hazlewood	RFM	144.4	49	329	17	5-8	2	19.35
P. J. Cummins	RF	162.1	51	421	21	4-21	0	20.04
M. A. Starc	LF	137	29	448	11	4-53	0	40.72
N. M. Lyon	OB	187	47	496	9	3-72	0	55.11

Also bowled: C. D. Green (RFM) 44–7–118–0; M. Labuschagne (LB) 11–3–36–0.

INDIA – BATTING AND FIELDING

	T	*I*	*NO*	*R*	*HS*	*100*	*50*	*Avge*	*Ct*
†R. R. Pant	3	5	1	274	97	0	2	68.50	8
S. Gill	3	6	1	259	91	0	2	51.80	2
A. M. Rahane	4	8	1	268	112	1	0	38.28	6
C. A. Pujara	4	8	0	271	77	0	3	33.87	3
R. G. Sharma	2	4	0	129	52	0	1	32.25	5
R. Ashwin	3	5	1	78	39*	0	0	19.50	1
G. H. Vihari	3	5	1	72	23*	0	0	18.00	1
M. A. Agarwal	3	6	0	78	38	0	0	13.00	4
M. Siraj	3	3	1	19	13	0	0	9.50	2
U. T. Yadav	2	3	1	19	9	0	0	9.50	0
N. Saini	2	3	1	8	5	0	0	4.00	1
J. J. Bumrah	3	4	1	6	4*	0	0	2.00	1

Played in two Tests: †R. A. Jadeja 57, 28* (2 ct). Played in one Test: V. Kohli 74, 4 (2 ct); Mohammed Shami 0, 1*; †T. Natarajan 1*; W. P. Saha 9, 4; P. P. Shaw 0, 4; S. N. Thakur 67, 2 (2 ct); †M. S. Washington Sundar 62, 22 (1 ct).

BOWLING

	Style	O	M	R	W	BB	5I	Avge
R. A. Jadeja	SLA	37.3	9	105	7	4-62	0	15.00
S. N. Thakur	RFM	43	8	155	7	4-61	0	22.14
R. Ashwin	OB	134.1	19	346	12	4-55	0	28.83
J. J. Bumrah	RFM	117.4	29	323	11	4-56	0	29.36
M. Siraj	RFM	134.2	32	384	13	5-73	1	29.53
U. T. Yadav	RF	39.4	8	133	4	3-40	0	33.25
T. Natarajan	LFM	38.2	7	119	3	3-78	0	39.66
M. S. Washington Sundar	OB	49	7	169	4	3-89	0	42.25
N. Saini	RFM	41.5	5	172	4	2-54	0	43.00

Also bowled: Mohammed Shami (RFM) 17–4–41–0; R. G. Sharma (OB) 0.1–0–1–0.

AUSTRALIA v INDIA

First One-Day International

At Sydney, November 27, 2020 (day/night). Australia won by 66 runs. Australia 10pts, India –1pt (after 1pt penalty). Toss: Australia.

As the tour approached, a casual observer might have thought the contest was Australia v Kohli. His abbreviated stay made local media desperate to siphon his star power while they could, and shortened the head-to-head between him and Smith, rival claimants to being the best Test batsman in the world. In ODIs there was no competition: Kohli had 43 hundreds and an average of 59, to Smith's nine hundreds and average of 42. And while Kohli had IPL gears, Smith was generally a run-a-ball accumulator. Now, in front of a crowd of 17,821 – the first at a men's international since March 11, at Mirpur – the hometown boy cut loose. After Finch and Warner gave him a base of 156 in 28 overs, Smith repeatedly used a snap of his wrists to clatter the pickets at midwicket and cover. His charge to a 62-ball century – the quickest of his ten in ODIs – was accompanied first by Finch's 17th hundred, then by Maxwell's carnivalesque 45 from 19 balls: reverse-sweeping for six, helicoptering yorkers, square-driving on one knee at the edge of the cut strip, and playing reverse laps through fine third man. Australia's 374 for six was (for two days) their highest total against India, beating 359 (which they had made four times, including at the 2003 World Cup final in Johannesburg). Hazlewood soon reduced the tourists to 80 for three and, while Dhawan and Pandya kept the chase alive with a fifth-wicket stand of 128, Zampa smothered any hope. The game did not finish until 11.10, more than an hour after the scheduled close, and beyond the supposed curfew for the SCG floodlights. India were fined 20% of their match fee.

Player of the Match: S. P. D. Smith.

Australia

D. A. Warner c Rahul b Mohammed Shami	69
*A. J. Finch c Rahul b Bumrah	114
S. P. D. Smith b Mohammed Shami	105
M. P. Stoinis c Rahul b Chahal	0
G. J. Maxwell c Jadeja b Mohammed Shami	45
M. Labuschagne c Dhawan b Saini	2
†A. T. Carey not out	17
P. J. Cummins not out	1
B 1, lb 6, w 12, nb 2	21
1/156 (1) 2/264 (2) 3/271 (4) 4/328 (5) 5/331 (6) 6/372 (3) (6 wkts, 50 overs)	374
10 overs: 51-0	

M. A. Starc, A. Zampa and J. R. Hazlewood did not bat.

Mohammed Shami 10–0–59–3; Bumrah 10–0–73–1; Saini 10–0–83–1; Chahal 10–0–89–1; Jadeja 10–0–63–0.

India

M. A. Agarwal c Maxwell b Hazlewood	22	Mohammed Shami b Starc	13
S. Dhawan c Starc b Zampa	74	J. J. Bumrah not out	0
*V. Kohli c Finch b Hazlewood	21	Lb 2, w 15, nb 3	20
S. S. Iyer c Carey b Hazlewood	2		—
†K. L. Rahul c Smith b Zampa	12	1/53 (1) 2/78 (3) (8 wkts, 50 overs)	308
H. H. Pandya c Starc b Zampa	90	3/80 (4) 4/101 (5)	
R. A. Jadeja c Starc b Zampa	25	5/229 (2) 6/247 (6)	
N. Saini not out	29	7/281 (7) 8/308 (9)	10 overs: 80-3

Y. S. Chahal did not bat.

Starc 9–0–65–1; Hazlewood 10–0–55–3; Cummins 8–0–52–0; Zampa 10–0–54–4; Stoinis 6.2–0–25–0; Maxwell 6.4–0–55–0.

Umpires: S. J. Nogajski and R. J. Tucker. Third umpire: P. R. Reiffel.
Referee: D. C. Boon.

AUSTRALIA v INDIA

Second One-Day International

At Sydney, November 29, 2020 (day/night). Australia won by 51 runs. Australia 10pts. Toss: Australia.

Another day at the SCG, another big stand between Warner and Finch, another 62-ball hundred for Smith, and another win for Australia. This was the openers' 12th century partnership – and their last for the season, as Warner suffered a groin strain in the field. Seven other ODI opening pairs had put on more than their 3,638 together, but none of them at a better average than their 52. Smith then equalled his own fastest century, unfurling an array of straight-drives, airborne and grounded. He even threw in an acrobatic scoop, diving towards point into a forward roll to get the ball over his shoulder to fine leg.

FASTEST ODI HUNDREDS FOR AUSTRALIA

Balls			
51	G. J. Maxwell (102)	v Sri Lanka at Sydney	2014-15
57	J. P. Faulkner (116)	v India at Bangalore	2013-14
62	**S. P. D. Smith (105)**	**v India at Sydney (first ODI)**	**2020-21**
62	**S. P. D. Smith (104)**	**v India at Sydney (second ODI)**	**2020-21**
66	M. L. Hayden (101)	v South Africa at Basseterre†	2006-07
67	A. C. Gilchrist (122)	v Sri Lanka at Brisbane	2005-06
69	S. R. Watson (185*)	v Bangladesh at Mirpur	2010-11
71	R. T. Ponting (164)	v South Africa at Johannesburg	2005-06
72	A. C. Gilchrist (149)	v Sri Lanka at Bridgetown†	2006-07
73	A. C. Gilchrist (103)	v World XI at Melbourne (Docklands)	2005-06

† *World Cup (Gilchrist's innings was in the final).*

Maxwell was devastating again, finishing unbeaten on 63 from 29, while Labuschagne contributed a relatively quiet 70. Once more, Australia had their highest total against India, who this time made a better fist of the chase, with Kohli threatening a century of his own. But Hazlewood picked him up on the pull shot, courtesy of a miraculous diving catch from Henriques, who on his return to the side also contributed some frugal overs and a wicket. Rahul belted five sixes in a 66-ball 76, but the quality of Cummins and Zampa told thereafter, and Australia clinched the series.

Player of the Match: S. P. D. Smith.

Australia

D. A. Warner run out (Iyer)	83	M. C. Henriques not out	2
*A. J. Finch c Kohli b Mohammed Shami	60		
S. P. D. Smith c Mohammed Shami b Pandya	104	Lb 2, w 4, nb 1	7
M. Labuschagne c Agarwal b Bumrah	70	1/142 (2) 2/156 (1) (4 wkts, 50 overs)	389
G. J. Maxwell not out	63	3/292 (3) 4/372 (4) 10 overs: 59-0	

†A. T. Carey, P. J. Cummins, M. A. Starc, A. Zampa and J. R. Hazlewood did not bat.

Mohammed Shami 9–0–73–1; Bumrah 10–1–79–1; Saini 7–0–70–0; Chahal 9–0–71–0; Jadeja 10–0–60–0; Agarwal 1–0–10–0; Pandya 4–0–24–1.

India

M. A. Agarwal c Carey b Cummins	28	J. J. Bumrah lbw b Zampa	0
S. Dhawan c Starc b Hazlewood	30	Y. S. Chahal not out	4
*V. Kohli c Henriques b Hazlewood	89		
S. S. Iyer c Smith b Henriques	38	W 8, nb 2	10
†K. L. Rahul c Hazlewood b Zampa	76		
H. H. Pandya c Smith b Cummins	28	1/58 (2) 2/60 (1) (9 wkts, 50 overs)	338
R. A. Jadeja c Maxwell b Cummins	24	3/153 (4) 4/225 (3)	
N. Saini not out	10	5/288 (5) 6/321 (7) 7/321 (6)	
Mohammed Shami c and b Maxwell	1	8/326 (9) 9/328 (10) 10 overs: 67-2	

Starc 9–0–82–0; Hazlewood 9–0–59–2; Cummins 10–0–67–3; Zampa 10–0–62–2; Henriques 7–0–34–1; Maxwell 5–0–34–1.

Umpires: G. A. Abood and P. R. Reiffel. Third umpire: B. N. J. Oxenford.
Referee: D. C. Boon.

AUSTRALIA v INDIA

Third One-Day International

At Canberra, December 2, 2020 (day/night). India won by 13 runs. India 10pts. Toss: India. One-day international debuts: C. D. Green; T. Natarajan.

Australia's first ODI at Manuka Oval in four years brought a change of personnel – and a change of fortune for India. Cummins and Starc were rested, while 21-year-old all-rounder Cameron Green made his international debut, and Sean Abbott played his second ODI, more than six years after his first. Even so, Australia's reshaped attack had India 152 for five when Kohli fell to Hazlewood for the third time in the series, after another composed half-century. But the hosts had no answers to an unbeaten partnership of 150 between Pandya and Jadeja, a record for India's sixth wicket against Australia. Pandya surged powerfully to a career-best 92 not out from 76 balls, while Jadeja added late flair: after 43 overs, he had 18 from 31, before thrashing 48 from his next 19. Abbott's last three overs cost 49. With Warner injured, Labuschagne opened, and provided a first wicket for left-arm seamer Thangarasu Natarajan, another debutant. Thakur also came in, and picked up Smith cheaply. Green made a solid 21, but no one could keep Maxwell company for long, as he took his series tally to 167 from 86 balls, with 12 fours and 11 sixes. When he was undone by Bumrah's pace, Australia needed 35 from 33, but with only three wickets in hand. It proved beyond Agar and the rest of the lower order.

Player of the Match: H. H. Pandya. *Player of the Series:* S. P. D. Smith.

India

S. Dhawan c Agar b Abbott	16	R. A. Jadeja not out	66
S. Gill lbw b Agar	33	B 1, lb 1, w 4, nb 2	8
*V. Kohli c Carey b Hazlewood	63		—
S. S. Iyer c Labuschagne b Zampa	19	1/26 (1) 2/82 (2) (5 wkts, 50 overs)	302
†K. L. Rahul lbw b Agar	5	3/114 (4) 4/123 (5)	
H. H. Pandya not out	92	5/152 (3) 10 overs: 49-1	

S. N. Thakur, K. Yadav, J. J. Bumrah and T. Natarajan did not bat.

Hazlewood 10–1–66–1; Maxwell 5–0–27–0; Abbott 10–0–84–1; Green 4–0–27–0; Agar 10–0–44–2; Zampa 10–0–45–1; Henriques 1–0–7–0.

Australia

M. Labuschagne b Natarajan	7	A. Zampa lbw b Bumrah	4
*A. J. Finch c Dhawan b Jadeja	75	J. R. Hazlewood not out	7
S. P. D. Smith c Rahul b Thakur	7		
M. C. Henriques c Dhawan b Thakur	22	Lb 6, w 9, nb 2	17
C. D. Green c Jadeja b Yadav	21		—
†A. T. Carey run out (Kohli/Rahul)	38	1/25 (1) 2/56 (3) 3/117 (4) (49.3 overs)	289
G. J. Maxwell b Bumrah	59	4/123 (2) 5/158 (5) 6/210 (6)	
A. C. Agar c Yadav b Natarajan	28	7/268 (7) 8/278 (9) 9/278 (8)	
S. A. Abbott c Rahul b Thakur	4	10/289 (10) 10 overs: 51-1	

Bumrah 9.3–0–43–2; Natarajan 10–1–70–2; Thakur 10–1–51–3; Yadav 10–0–57–1; Jadeja 10–0–62–1.

Umpires: B. N. J. Oxenford and P. Wilson. Third umpire: R. J. Tucker.
Referee: D. C. Boon.

AUSTRALIA v INDIA

First Twenty20 International

At Canberra, December 4, 2020 (floodlit). India won by 11 runs. Toss: Australia. Twenty20 international debut: T. Natarajan.

On a mild Canberra night, the Australian men's team turned out for the first time wearing the Indigenous-artwork kit designed by Courtney Hagen and Aunty Fiona Clarke – a tribute to the 1868 Aboriginal team that toured England, and included Clarke's great-great-grandfather. Starc returned to rattle Dhawan's timbers early, while leg-spinner Swepson – flown in for the injured Ashton Agar to play his second T20I, two and a half years after his first – dismissed Kohli. Henriques, the sixth bowler used, picked up a career-best three for 22, including top-scorer Rahul. But, from 92 for five, Jadeja smoked a career-best 44 not out from 23 balls. In the final over, he was hit on the back of the helmet by Starc and, though he batted out the innings, hitting Starc for successive fours, India requested a concussion substitute at the break. Match referee David Boon approved leg-spinner Yuzvendra Chahal, which an angry Justin Langer argued was not like-for-like – though Jadeja would normally bowl four overs with his slow left-armers, and was replaced by a spinner who turned the ball the same way. Australian annoyance grew when Chahal removed Finch, Smith and Wade; Natarajan, on T20 debut, also took three, as the hosts fell short. Given that Australia had hit Chahal for 160 in 19 overs in the two Sydney ODIs, perhaps their discontent should have been with their own batting. Jadeja was later ruled out of the remaining two games with concussion.

Player of the Match: Y. S. Chahal.

India

		B	4/6
1 †K. L. Rahul *c 7 b 5*	51	40	5/1
2 S. Dhawan *b 8*	1	6	0
3 *V. Kohli *c and b 9*	9	9	1
4 S. V. Samson *c 9 b 5*	23	15	1/1
5 M. K. Pandey *c 11 b 10*	2	8	0
6 H. H. Pandya *c 3 b 5*	16	15	0/1
7 R. A. Jadeja *not out*	44	23	5/1
8 M. S. Washington Sundar *c 7 b 8*	7	5	1
9 D. L. Chahar *not out*	0	0	0
Lb 2, w 5, nb 1	8		
6 overs: 42-1 (20 overs)	161-7		

1/11 2/48 3/86 4/90 5/92 6/114 7/152

10 Mohammed Shami, 11 T. Natarajan and 12 Y. S. Chahal did not bat.

Chahal replaced Jadeja, as a concussion substitute.

Starc 24–9–34–2; Hazlewood 24–8–39–0; Zampa 24–9–20–1; Abbott 12–2–23–0; Swepson 12–3–21–1; Henriques 24–11–22–3.

Australia

		B	4/6
1 D. J. M. Short *c 6 b 11*	34	38	3
2 *A. J. Finch *c 6 b 12*	35	26	5/1
3 S. P. D. Smith *c 4 b 12*	12	9	0/1
4 G. J. Maxwell *lbw b 11*	2	3	0
5 M. C. Henriques *lbw b 9*	30	20	1/1
6 †M. S. Wade *c 3 b 12*	7	9	0
7 S. A. Abbott *not out*	12	8	0/1
8 M. A. Starc *b 11*	1	2	0
9 M. J. Swepson *not out*	12	5	1/1
Lb 4, w 1	5		
6 overs: 53-0 (20 overs)	150-7		

1/56 2/72 3/75 4/113 5/122 6/126 7/127

10 A. Zampa and 11 J. R. Hazlewood did not bat.

Chahar 24–10–29–1; Washington Sundar 24–13–16–0; Mohammed Shami 24–7–46–0; Natarajan 24–7–30–3; Chahal 24–7–25–3.

Umpires: S. A. J. Craig and R. J. Tucker. Third umpire: P. Wilson.
Referee: D. C. Boon.

At Sydney (Drummoyne Oval), December 6–8, 2020. **Drawn. ‡Indians 247-9 dec** (93 overs) (C. A. Pujara 54, A. M. Rahane 117*; J. L. Pattinson 3-58) **and 189-9 dec** (61 overs) (W. P. Saha 54*; M. T. Steketee 5-37); **Australia A 306-9 dec** (95 overs) (C. D. Green 125*; U. T. Yadav 3-48, M. Siraj 3-83) **and 52-1** (15 overs). *While India's T20 side were in action at the SCG, the Test specialists were involved in a warm-up game across town. Tim Paine kept wicket for Australia A, while Travis Head captained. A century from Ajinkya Rahane rescued the Indians after openers Prithvi Shaw and Shubman Gill fell for ducks. Australia A took a lead of 59, mainly thanks to Cameron Green's fifth first-class century, which clinched his Test debut a few days later. At 129-7 on the third day, the tourists were only 70 in front and in danger of defeat – but Wriddhiman Saha prolonged the innings for another 20 overs. That ensured a draw, though there was time for opener Will Pucovski to retire hurt with mild concussion after being clanged on the helmet by Kartik Tyagi.*

AUSTRALIA v INDIA

Second Twenty20 International

At Sydney, December 6, 2020 (floodlit). India won by six wickets. Toss: India. Twenty20 international debut: D. R. Sams.

Wade had been prolific as an opener in the Big Bash League, but for Australia was nearly always asked to bat in the middle. Now, with Finch missing because of a muscle strain, Wade was handed the captaincy for the first time, and immediately promoted himself. It worked a charm, as he blasted 58 from 32, until Kohli dropped a catch in the circle but recovered in time to run him out. Smith helped carry the score to 194, before India set off in spirited pursuit, Rahul and Dhawan putting on

56 in five overs. Samson hit a six into the SCG's second tier, but was stopped by the frugal leg-spin of Swepson; Kohli was crisp, and took Tye to the cleaners, before debutant Daniel Sams had him caught behind (Starc was missing the last two T20s because of a family illness). With India needing 46 from 23, Australia were on top, but again Pandya drove them home, pillaging two sixes from Sams in the final over, to win the series with a game to spare.

Player of the Match: H. H. Pandya.

Australia

		B	4/6
1 *†M. S. Wade *run out (3/1)*	58	32	10/1
2 D. J. M. Short *c 6 b 11*	9	9	1
3 S. P. D. Smith *c 5 b 10*	46	38	3/2
4 G. J. Maxwell *c 7 b 8*	22	13	0/2
5 M. C. Henriques *c 1 b 11*	26	18	0/1
6 M. P. Stoinis *not out*	16	7	0/1
7 D. R. Sams *not out*	8	3	1
Lb 1, w 8	9		
6 overs: 59-1 (20 overs)	194-5		

1/47 2/75 3/120 4/168 5/171

8 S. A. Abbott, 9 A. J. Tye, 10 M. J. Swepson and 11 A. Zampa did not bat.

Chahar 24–6–48–0; Washington Sundar 24–7–35–0; Thakur 24–7–39–1; Natarajan 24–8–20–2; Chahal 24–5–51–1.

India

		B	4/6
1 †K. L. Rahul *c 10 b 9*	30	22	2/1
2 S. Dhawan *c 10 b 11*	52	36	4/2
3 *V. Kohli *c 1 b 7*	40	24	2/2
4 S. V. Samson *c 3 b 10*	15	10	1/1
5 H. H. Pandya *not out*	42	22	3/2
6 S. S. Iyer *not out*	12	5	1/1
Lb 1, w 2, nb 1	4		
6 overs: 60-1 (19.4 overs)	195-4		

1/56 2/95 3/120 4/149

7 M. S. Washington Sundar, 8 S. N. Thakur, 9 D. L. Chahar, 10 Y. S. Chahal and 11 T. Natarajan did not bat.

Sams 22–8–41–1; Abbott 12–3–17–0; Tye 24–10–47–1; Maxwell 6–0–19–0; Swepson 24–7–25–1; Henriques 6–1–9–0; Zampa 24–4–36–1.

Umpires: S. J. Nogajski and P. Wilson. Third umpire: R. J. Tucker.
Referee: D. C. Boon.

AUSTRALIA v INDIA

Third Twenty20 International

At Sydney, December 8, 2020 (floodlit). Australia won by 12 runs. Toss: India.

Finch returned, but was out second ball, while Wade kept his spot at the top and blasted a career-best 80 off 53. He was spared an lbw dismissal on 50, when India were too slow to review Natarajan's appeal, while Maxwell was caught on 19 off a Chahal no-ball, and survived caught-behind reviews on 35 and 37; he finished with a typically zany 54 from 36. He was then a surprise choice to bowl the first over, and had Rahul caught at deep midwicket second ball, then Kohli badly dropped by Smith on nine in the same position. Australia almost paid for the error, as Kohli assembled a masterful 85 from 61. He was stopped by a stunning catch from Sams at deep backward point, one more piece of brilliance in the field: Samson and Smith had already produced superb airborne efforts to prevent sixes. India fell short by 13, despite an attractive flurry from Thakur and Washington Sundar – a partnership that foreshadowed the Gabba Test six weeks later.

Player of the Match: M. J. Swepson. *Player of the Series:* H. H. Pandya.

Australia

		B	4/6
1 †M. S. Wade *lbw b 8*	80	53	7/2
2 *A. J. Finch *c 6 b 7*	0	2	0
3 S. P. D. Smith *b 7*	24	23	1
4 G. J. Maxwell *b 11*	54	36	3/3
5 M. C. Henriques *not out*	5	2	1
6 D. J. M. Short *run out (12/1)*	7	3	1
7 D. R. Sams *not out*	4	2	1
Lb 1, w 10, nb 1	12		
6 overs: 51-1 (20 overs)	186-5		

1/14 2/79 3/169 4/175 5/182

8 S. A. Abbott, 9 A. J. Tye, 10 M. J. Swepson and 11 A. Zampa did not bat.

Chahar 24–8–34–0; Washington Sundar 24–9–34–2; Natarajan 24–8–33–1; Chahal 24–3–41–0; Thakur 24–6–43–1.

India

		B	4/6
1 †K. L. Rahul *c 3 b 4*	0	2	0
2 S. Dhawan *c 7 b 10*	28	21	3
3 *V. Kohli *c 7 b 9*	85	61	4/3
4 S. V. Samson *c 3 b 10*	10	9	0
5 S. S. Iyer *lbw b 10*	0	1	0
6 H. H. Pandya *c 2 b 11*	20	13	1/2
7 M. S. Washington Sundar *c 9 b 8*	7	6	1
8 S. N. Thakur *not out*	17	7	0/2
9 D. L. Chahar *not out*	0	0	0
B 1, w 6	7		
6 overs: 55-1 (20 overs)	174-7		

1/0 2/74 3/97 4/100 5/144 6/151 7/164

10 Y. S. Chahal and 11 T. Natarajan did not bat.

12th man: M. K. Pandey.

Maxwell 18–3–20–1; Abbott 24–4–49–1; Sams 12–2–29–0; Tye 24–10–31–1; Swepson 24–4–23–3; Zampa 18–3–21–1.

Umpires: G. A. Abood and R. J. Tucker. Third umpire: P. Wilson.
Referee: D. C. Boon.

At Sydney, December 11–13, 2020 (day/night). **Drawn. ‡Indians 194** (48.3 overs) (J. J. Bumrah 55*; S. A. Abbott 3-46, J. D. Wildermuth 3-13) **and 386-4 dec** (90 overs) (M. A. Agarwal 61, S. Gill 65, G. H. Vihari 104*, R. R. Pant 103*); **Australia A 108** (32.2 overs) (Mohammed Shami 3-29, N. Saini 3-19) **and 307-4** (75 overs) (B. R. McDermott 107*, A. T. Carey 58, J. D. Wildermuth 111*). *First-class debut:* P. J. Rowe. *Twenty wickets tumbled on the first day, when the Indians lurched from 102-2 to 123-9, before a last-wicket stand of 71 between No. 10 Jasprit Bumrah – whose maiden fifty more than tripled his previous first-class highest of 16* – and Mohammed Siraj. Australia A then collapsed under lights against the pink ball. Cameron Green and New South Wales seamer Harry Conway were both hit on the head, and replaced by concussion substitutes Pat Rowe (the Australia Under-19 wicketkeeper, making his first-class debut) and Mark Steketee. The Indians batted much better on the second day, with Hanuma Vihari and Rishabh Pant putting on 147*. The last over of the day started with Pant on 81: after a dot he smacked Jack Wildermuth for 44644 to reach his hundred from 73 balls, with six sixes. Australia A needed 473 on the final day: Wildermuth gained some revenge with a century of his own, during a match-saving stand of 165* with Ben McDermott.*

AUSTRALIA v INDIA

First Test

At Adelaide, December 17–19, 2020 (day/night). Australia won by eight wickets. Australia 30pts. Toss: India. Test debut: C. D. Green.

Adelaide might have been a comfortable starting point for India. In 2014-15, Kohli made twin hundreds here, and set off after 364 on the fifth day like it was no big thing. India fell 49 short, but his performance seemed the start of a bolder era. In 2018-19, India began their tour in Adelaide by outbowling Australia on their way to a 31-run win. But

Philip Brown, Popperfoto/Getty Images

Break point? Mohammed Shami fails to evade a vicious ball from Pat Cummins, and India's innings is ended for 36.

this was a day/night Test, with a pink Kookaburra. India had only one experience of the format, against Bangladesh at Kolkata in November 2019, while Australia had seven – all at home, all won.

In the previous Adelaide Test, a little over a year earlier, Warner had racked up 335, before Pakistan tailender Yasir Shah clouted a century. Curator Damien Hough had not enjoyed seeing bowlers so toothless, and now left eight millimetres of grass on the pitch, two more than usual. It worked. From a distance, the track looked a batsman-friendly straw colour, but that was because the grass tips had dried out, concealing what lay beneath. In the event, moisture helped both sets of bowlers during a modest first two innings.

Starc started with swing to knock over Shaw second ball of the match, while Hazlewood and Cummins found plenty of seam movement. Pujara held Australia at bay for over three and a half hours, but the bowlers avoided anything straight, and runs came at a trickle. He didn't hit a boundary until his 148th ball, collected another from his 149th, and was out to his 160th – all off Lyon. Still, his spadework helped Kohli and Rahane, who took India to 188 for three under lights. Then things came undone, with Rahane calling "yes" for a sharp single, but bailing out with Kohli halfway down. His run-out for 74 felt like a match-changing moment. Rahane was pinned on the back pad soon after by Starc and the second new ball, and Vihari fell shortly before stumps. Next day, the last four tumbled for 11.

Australia were in trouble themselves before long. Burns had endured a wretched first-class season but, given Warner's injury, had been retained, alongside Wade as a stopgap opener. Bumrah started with a purr, and nabbed both lbw for eight. Much had been made of Ashwin's modest record in Australia, and the record of touring off-spinners in general: this time he bowled like a dream to get Smith, Head and Green on his way to four for 55, his best figures in the country. His teasing line to have Smith edge a non-turning delivery to slip was a work of art. Only a rash of dropped catches kept Australia in the game: three

INDIA'S LOWEST TEST TOTALS

36†	**v Australia at Adelaide**	**2020-21**	76	v South Africa at Ahmedabad	2007-08
42†	v England at Lord's	1974	81	v West Indies at Bridgetown	1996-97
58	v Australia at Brisbane	1947-48	81†	v New Zealand at Wellington	1975-76
58	v England at Manchester	1952	82	v England at Manchester	1952
66	v South Africa at Durban	1996-97	83	v New Zealand at Mohali	1999-2000
67	v Australia at Melbourne	1947-48	83†	v England at Madras	1976-77
75	v West Indies at Delhi	1987-88			

† *One batsman absent or retired hurt.*

off Labuschagne and one off Paine, who counterpunched with the tail through the second evening session to limit the deficit to 53. In the few overs left, Cummins removed Shaw with a beauty that seamed back through the gate.

The third day began with the match poised. India moved to 15 for one before Bumrah, the nightwatchman, popped a catch back to Cummins. But imagine suggesting he would be the first of six to face a ball before the next run came. Four wickets fell in 33 scoreless deliveries; eight wickets, and an innings-ending injury – Mohammed Shami having his arm broken by Cummins – in 13.3 overs, for the addition of 21 runs. India had been bowled out for 36, their lowest Test total. For the first time in a Test innings, all 11 batsmen and Extras failed to reach double figures (when South Africa were bowled out for 30 at Edgbaston in 1930, Extras top-scored with 11).

There was nothing outrageous in the pitch, just pace, bounce and movement. But every ball hit the spot, and every chance was held, Cummins and Hazlewood bowling a length that required shots but created catches; five went to Paine. Starc bowled three overs on the day, Lyon none in the innings. Kohli tried to counter-attack, but was held in the gully, completing his only calendar year without an international century since his debut in 2008. Hazlewood finished with five for eight, and claimed his 200th Test wicket. Cummins finished with four for 21, including his 150th.

Australia needed just 90 to win, and the opening stand brought 70, before Saha freakishly ran out Wade, backhanding the ball after a deflection from short leg. Burns brought up the win, and a half-century, by hooking a six, parried over fine leg by Bumrah. With the bowlers impossible to separate, Paine was given the match award for his batting and keeping. Kohli had not previously lost any of the 25 Tests in which he had won the toss. Now, with India's captain heading home, most pundits agreed they would lose 4–0.

Player of the Match: T. D. Paine.

Close of play: first day, India 233-6 (Saha 9, Ashwin 15); second day, India 9-1 (Agarwal 5, Bumrah 0).

CHEAPEST TEST FIVE-FORS

5-2	E. R. H. Toshack	Australia v India at Brisbane	1947-48
6-3	J. J. C. Lawson	West Indies v Bangladesh at Dhaka	2002-03
5-6	H. Ironmonger	Australia v South Africa at Melbourne	1931-32
8-7	G. A. Lohmann	England v South Africa at Port Elizabeth	1895-96
6-7	A. E. R. Gilligan	England v South Africa at Birmingham	1924
5-7	V. D. Philander	South Africa v New Zealand at Cape Town	2012-13
5-7	J. J. Bumrah	India v West Indies at North Sound	2019
6-8	D. W. Steyn	South Africa v Pakistan at Johannesburg	2012-13
5-8	K. A. J. Roach	West Indies v Bangladesh at North Sound	2018
5-8	**J. R. Hazlewood**	**Australia v India at Adelaide**	**2020-21**
6-9	M. J. Clarke	Australia v India at Mumbai	2004-05
5-9	T. B. A. May	Australia v West Indies at Adelaide	1992-93

India

P. P. Shaw b Starc	0	– b Cummins	4
M. A. Agarwal b Cummins	17	– c Paine b Hazlewood	9
C. A. Pujara c Labuschagne b Lyon	43	– (4) c Paine b Cummins	0
*V. Kohli run out (Hazlewood/Lyon)	74	– (5) c Green b Cummins	4
A. M. Rahane lbw b Starc	42	– (6) c Paine b Hazlewood	0
G. H. Vihari lbw b Hazlewood	16	– (7) c Paine b Hazlewood	8
†W. P. Saha c Paine b Starc	9	– (8) c Labuschagne b Hazlewood	4
R. Ashwin c Paine b Cummins	15	– (9) c Paine b Hazlewood	0
U. T. Yadav c Wade b Starc	6	– (10) not out	4
J. J. Bumrah not out	4	– (3) c and b Cummins	2
Mohammed Shami c Head b Cummins	0	– retired hurt	1
B 2, lb 8, w 1, nb 7	18		
1/0 (1) 2/32 (2) 3/100 (3) 4/188 (4) 5/196 (5) 6/206 (6) 7/233 (8) 8/235 (7) 9/240 (9) 10/244 (11) (93.1 overs)	244	1/7 (1) 2/15 (3) 3/15 (4) 4/15 (2) 5/15 (6) 6/19 (5) 7/26 (8) 8/26 (9) 9/31 (7) (21.2 overs)	36

In the second innings Mohammed Shami retired hurt at 36-9.

Starc 21–5–53–4; Hazlewood 20–6–47–1; Cummins 21.1–7–48–3; Green 9–2–15–0; Lyon 21–2–68–1; Labuschagne 1–0–3–0. *Second innings*—Starc 6–3–7–0; Cummins 10.2–4–21–4; Hazlewood 5–3–8–5.

Australia

M. S. Wade lbw b Bumrah	8	– run out (Saha)	33
J. A. Burns lbw b Bumrah	8	– not out	51
M. Labuschagne lbw b Yadav	47	– c Agarwal b Ashwin	6
S. P. D. Smith c Rahane b Ashwin	1	– not out	1
T. M. Head c and b Ashwin	7		
C. D. Green c Kohli b Ashwin	11		
*†T. D. Paine not out	73		
P. J. Cummins c Rahane b Yadav	0		
M. A. Starc run out (Shaw/Saha)	15		
N. M. Lyon c Kohli b Ashwin	10		
J. R. Hazlewood c Pujara b Yadav	8		
Lb 3	3	Lb 1, nb 1	2
1/16 (1) 2/29 (2) 3/45 (4) 4/65 (5) 5/79 (6) 6/111 (3) 7/111 (8) 8/139 (9) 9/167 (10) 10/191 (11) (72.1 overs)	191	1/70 (1) 2/82 (3) (2 wkts, 21 overs)	93

Yadav 16.1–5–40–3; Bumrah 21–7–52–2; Mohammed Shami 17–4–41–0; Ashwin 18–3–55–4. *Second innings*—Yadav 8–1–49–0; Bumrah 7–1–27–0; Ashwin 6–1–16–1.

Umpires: B. N. J. Oxenford and P. R. Reiffel. Third umpire: R. J. Tucker.
Referee: D. C. Boon.

AUSTRALIA v INDIA

Second Test

At Melbourne, December 26–29, 2020. India won by eight wickets. India 30pts, Australia -4pts (after 4pt penalty). Toss: Australia. Test debuts: S. Gill, M. Siraj.

You don't want to be asked to bowl on Boxing Day. For a decade, the Melbourne pitch had been a slab of rolled mud, making it hard to score runs but even harder to get out. In 2020, though, curator Matt Page had managed to Frankenstein it with life. With Kohli now on paternity leave, India – under the captaincy of Rahane – did not turn up like a humbled team hoping to make good. They brought measured aggression to their selections, fielding positions and bowling plans, and turned the series around.

Shaw was gone after one Test, bowled twice too often, and replaced by another young sensation, 21-year-old debutant Shubman Gill. Saha gave way to Pant, a lesser keeper but more aggressive batsman. Kohli's absence was covered not by a batsman, but by Jadeja, the spinning all-rounder at No. 7. Only the inclusion of Mohammed Siraj, another debutant, for the injured Shami was driven by necessity rather than boldness.

Bumrah led the line, working over Burns for nine balls of misery, and a duck. Wade smoked shots through cover, before a brain fade against Ashwin. The catch, though, was memorable, Jadeja made up 40 metres at full sprint from mid-on to deep midwicket, while Gill ran a converging line, heedless of his team-mate's calls; Jadeja held on while looking over his shoulder, and anticipating contact, which came when Gill crashed into his chest. On an Aussie Rules football ground, it was a contested mark, well held at half-forward kicking to the City End. Ashwin then had Smith caught at leg slip for only his fifth duck in 134 Test innings. Australia were 38 for three.

Labuschagne and Head put on a restorative 86, before Bumrah removed Head. Siraj had Labuschagne caught at leg gully, and set up Green – width and away movement, then an inducker. He held two good outfield catches as Australia's tail swung for the seats: 195 all out. At tea, the late local hero Dean Jones, who died in September, aged 59, was celebrated as his family brought out his bat, cap and sunglasses to the middle. Fellow Victorian James Pattinson and India's K. L. Rahul then took the items to the dugout, so Jones could be present in spirit.

HOMES FROM HOME

Most Test wins for India on overseas grounds:

W	*T*		*W*	*T*	
4	**14**	**Melbourne**	2	5	Auckland
3	9	Colombo (SSC)	2	5	Johannesburg
3	13	Port-of-Spain	2	5	Galle
3	13	Kingston	2	5	Colombo (PSO)
2	2	Bulawayo	2	6	Leeds
2	2	Mirpur	2	7	Nottingham
2	2	North Sound	2	13	Adelaide
2	3	Dhaka	2	18	Lord's

Starc got rid of Agarwal with the sixth ball of the reply, but Gill played his shots on the second morning, while Pujara batted time. Cummins dismissed them in successive overs, however, and Australia produced three hours of suffocating bowling. Averting another collapse was Rahane, with a perfectly paced century – soaking up those hours, opening up as the day wore on. From a shaky 116 for four after lunch, Pant reminded Rahane that they could score against this attack, making a brisk 29 in a partnership of 57, before becoming Starc's 250th Test wicket and Paine's 150th dismissal. By now, India trailed by just 22, and Jadeja joined Rahane to build a lead. They reversed the pressure, then accelerated against the second new ball, and pushed a stand eventually worth 121 into the third day. It ended with the run-out of Rahane, attempting to bring up Jadeja's fifty, but India finished 131 in front.

Burns looked scrambled, ended up flat on his face keeping out a yorker, then asked for a review when caught behind. The wicket was Yadav's last contribution before straining his calf. That didn't slow India: Ashwin tickled Labuschagne's edge, and Bumrah kissed leg stump as Smith stepped across the crease. Paine fumed when given caught behind, after DRS showed evidence of a noise, but not one that sounded like a nick. Australia were 99 for six, and still behind.

The job of setting a target was left to Green – standing 6ft 6in, and with breadth to match – who put on 57 in 35 overs with Cummins. Green was powerful through the off side, including a square cut on one knee which was a shot entirely his own, yet nimble on his feet to the spinners. He eventually fell to a leaping catch from Jadeja at midwicket on the fourth morning. His dismissal for 45 meant that, for the first time since losing to West Indies at Melbourne in 1988-89, no Australian would score a half-century in a home Test. To add to their disarray, they lost four points in the World Test Championship for their slow over-rate.

Now it was India's turn to chase a token target. Gill enjoyed a gallop and, if there were any tremors when a couple of wickets fell, Rahane was on hand to steer them to the 70 they needed – and 1–1.

Player of the Match: A. M. Rahane.

Close of play: first day, India 36-1 (Gill 28, Pujara 7); second day, India 277-5 (Rahane 104, Jadeja 40); third day, Australia 133-6 (Green 17, Cummins 15).

Australia

J. A. Burns c Pant b Bumrah	0	– (2) c Pant b Yadav	4
M. S. Wade c Jadeja b Ashwin	30	– (1) lbw b Jadeja	40
M. Labuschagne c Gill b Siraj	48	– c Rahane b Ashwin	28
S. P. D. Smith c Pujara b Ashwin	0	– b Bumrah	8
T. M. Head c Rahane b Bumrah	38	– c Agarwal b Siraj	17
C. D. Green lbw b Siraj	12	– c Jadeja b Siraj	45
*†T. D. Paine c Vihari b Ashwin	13	– c Pant b Jadeja	1
P. J. Cummins c Siraj b Jadeja	9	– c Agarwal b Bumrah	22
M. A. Starc c Siraj b Bumrah	7	– not out	14
N. M. Lyon lbw b Bumrah	20	– c Pant b Siraj	3
J. R. Hazlewood not out	4	– b Ashwin	10
B 10, w 1, nb 3	14	Lb 5, nb 3	8
1/10 (1) 2/35 (2) 3/38 (4) 4/124 (5) 5/134 (3) 6/155 (6) 7/155 (7) 8/164 (9) 9/191 (10) 10/195 (8) (72.3 overs)	195	1/4 (2) 2/42 (3) 3/71 (4) 4/98 (1) 5/98 (5) 6/99 (7) 7/156 (8) 8/177 (6) 9/185 (10) 10/200 (11) (103.1 overs)	200

Bumrah 16–4–56–4; Yadav 12–2–39–0; Ashwin 24–7–35–3; Jadeja 5.3–1–15–1; Siraj 15–4–40–2. *Second innings*—Bumrah 27–6–54–2; Yadav 3.3–0–5–1; Siraj 21.3–4–37–3; Ashwin 37.1–6–71–2; Jadeja 14–5–28–2.

India

M. A. Agarwal lbw b Starc	0	– c Paine b Starc	5
S. Gill c Paine b Cummins	45	– not out	35
C. A. Pujara c Paine b Cummins	17	– c Green b Cummins	3
*A. M. Rahane run out (Labuschagne/Paine)	112	– not out	27
G. H. Vihari c Smith b Lyon	21		
†R. R. Pant c Paine b Starc	29		
R. A. Jadeja c Cummins b Starc	57		
R. Ashwin c Lyon b Hazlewood	14		
U. T. Yadav c Smith b Lyon	9		
J. J. Bumrah c Head b Lyon	0		
M. Siraj not out	0		
B 12, lb 6, w 2, nb 2	22		
1/0 (1) 2/61 (2) 3/64 (3) 4/116 (5) 5/173 (6) 6/294 (4) 7/306 (7) 8/325 (9) 9/325 (8) 10/326 (10) (115.1 overs)	326	1/16 (1) 2/19 (3) (2 wkts, 15.5 overs)	70

Starc 26–5–78–3; Cummins 27–9–80–2; Hazlewood 23–6–47–1; Lyon 27.1–4–72–3; Green 12–1–31–0. *Second innings*—Starc 4–0–20–1; Cummins 5–0–22–1; Hazlewood 3–1–14–0; Lyon 2.5–0–5–0; Labuschagne 1–0–9–0.

Umpires: B. N. J. Oxenford and P. R. Reiffel. Third umpire: P. Wilson.
Referee: D. C. Boon.

AUSTRALIA v INDIA

Third Test

At Sydney, January 7–11, 2021. Drawn. Australia 10pts, India 10pts. Toss: Australia. Test debuts: W. J. Pucovski; N. Saini.

For the first Test of the New Year, it was all change. Warner and Sharma, among the highest run-scorers in IPL history, faced off in Tests again, as Sharma replaced Mayank Agarwal, and the fit-again Warner pushed out Travis Head, releasing Wade back down the order. Australia could no longer persist with Joe Burns, so Will Pucovski made his long-awaited debut, after problems with head injuries and mental health. For India, seamer Navdeep Saini debuted for the injured Umesh Yadav.

Batting first on a placid track, Australia finally clicked. Warner fell early to a wild drive, but Pucovski made 62, after being dropped twice by Pant, and spared a run-out by the dozing Bumrah. His was the only other wicket on a rainy first day of 55 overs, after he added 100 with Labuschagne, who added 100 with Smith.

Labuschagne's straight-drives were the feature of his 91, before he edged a back-foot force off Jadeja to slip on the second morning. Smith's series had brought him ten runs, his worst four-innings sequence, but he ended it with his 27th Test century, and eighth against India, his attacking shots through cover and point radiating confidence. He paced it like his Edgbaston marvel in 2019: careful early, accelerating with each wicket, last man out. Wrestling him was Jadeja, who prised out four of Smith's partners, then lopped off his final flourish, tearing in from deep backward square and nailing the stumps with a direct hit. Rahane supported Jadeja with a long spell and the right field; keeping Australia to 338 was a decent result from 206 for two. But, after a fluent stand of 70, Sharma and Gill fell before stumps.

On the third day, India's wheels fell off. Australia produced three run-outs, including Hazlewood's diving stunner from mid-off to dismiss Vihari. Pujara battled to his slowest Test fifty, 174 balls, but Cummins got him and Rahane with a relentless line. He also smashed Pant on the elbow, while Jadeja had his left thumb bent back by Starc; both were incapacitated for the next day. Out for 244, trailing by 94, and two players down, India looked in strife.

Except it wasn't just two. Ashwin's back was seizing up, and Bumrah had an abdominal strain. Even though Australia's openers fell cheaply on the third evening, they started day four 197 ahead. Second ball of the morning, Labuschagne worked Bumrah to square leg, where Vihari dropped a sitter. After that, it was all Australia. Smith missed out on twin tons, but still made plenty, and Green had licence to swing four sixes in his 84. Bumrah had another catch dropped, but kept smiling. Paine declared at tea, 406 in front. Amid this plunder, Siraj halted the match to report crowd abuse, with Rahane – who had reported racist abuse the day before – willing to leave the field. His young bowler was visibly upset, but remained upright.

As in the first innings, India's openers looked good, putting on 71, but were gone by stumps. Lyon had been dangerous throughout, drawing reams of false shots, especially from Pujara. Early on the fifth day, he looked to have made the decisive blow, Rahane caught at short leg. But that brought Pant to the middle. Wriddhiman Saha had kept wicket the previous day, and held four catches – equalling the record for a substitute, by outfield Younis Khan for Pakistan against Bangladesh in 2001-02. Now, however, Pant was promoted up the order, despite a bruised arm, to give India a left–right combination. He had a dramatic effect. Twice Lyon drew his edge, but Paine dropped both. In between, while Pujara gave support, Pant took on the spinner in buccaneering style, skipping down the pitch, bashing anything too straight over midwicket, going back to cut anything wide. In three hours he had 97 but, looking for a century, sliced Lyon to gully.

Until then, India had actually been on track to win – 250 for three, needing 157 more at three an over. Pujara took up the cause, peeling off three consecutive boundaries from Cummins, who had the second new ball. But Vihari tore a hamstring taking a run, and next over Pujara received an unplayable delivery from Hazlewood that decked away to take off stump. Ashwin came out, hobbled by his back injury, Jadeja was padded up, but with a broken thumb, and three other bowlers were rabbits. With 43 overs left, the only option was to survive.

That's what India did. Ashwin got bombed, and was hit in the ribs. Yet, with Vihari barely walking, he hoarded the strike. They began sharing a chest guard. When Lyon bowled, they settled into an arrangement: Vihari, unable to get a stride in, faced pace, and Ashwin spin. At tea, Ashwin stayed on his feet, because his back was too sore to sit. First ball after it, he was given out caught behind, but overturned the decision – not glove but arm-guard. Sean Abbott, on as substitute, dropped Ashwin at square leg. The clock ticked down.

With 11 overs to go, Paine's frustration boiled over. His jibes at Ashwin were tame by historical standards, but they were childish, and directed into the stump microphones. Ashwin repeatedly refused to face until Paine was quiet. Next over, a wayward Starc got his line right from around the wicket, and drew Vihari's edge. Paine dived, and dropped it. The 9.1 overs left could have been enough for four more wickets. Instead, the final partnership was 62 runs from 43 overs, battered but unbroken, and India had saved the match. For all the blocking, they were only 73 short of a win. Avoid defeat at Brisbane, and the Border–Gavaskar Trophy would remain theirs.

Player of the Match: S. P. D. Smith.

Close of play: first day, Australia 166-2 (Labuschagne 67, Smith 31); second day, India 96-2 (Pujara 9, Rahane 5); third day, Australia 103-2 (Labuschagne 47, Smith 29); fourth day, India 98-2 (Pujara 9, Rahane 4).

Australia

W. J. Pucovski lbw b Saini	62	– (2) c sub (†W. P. Saha) b Siraj	10
D. A. Warner c Pujara b Siraj	5	– (1) lbw b Ashwin	13
M. Labuschagne c Rahane b Jadeja	91	– c sub (†W. P. Saha) b Saini	73
S. P. D. Smith run out (Jadeja)	131	– lbw b Ashwin	81
M. S. Wade c Bumrah b Jadeja	13	– c sub (†W. P. Saha) b Saini	4
C. D. Green lbw b Bumrah	0	– c sub (†W. P. Saha) b Bumrah	84
*†T. D. Paine b Bumrah	1	– not out	39
P. J. Cummins b Jadeja	0		
M. A. Starc c Gill b Saini	24		
N. M. Lyon lbw b Jadeja	0		
J. R. Hazlewood not out	1		
B 4, w 1, nb 5	10	B 1, lb 4, nb 3	8
1/6 (2) 2/106 (1) 3/206 (3) 4/232 (5) 5/249 (6) 6/255 (7) 7/278 (8) 8/310 (9) 9/315 (10) 10/338 (4) (105.4 overs)	338	1/16 (2) 2/35 (1) 3/138 (3) 4/148 (5) 5/208 (4) 6/312 (6) (6 wkts dec, 87 overs)	312

Bumrah 25.4–7–66–2; Siraj 25–4–67–1; Ashwin 24–1–74–0; Saini 13–0–65–2; Jadeja 18–3–62–4. *Second innings*—Bumrah 21–4–68–1; Siraj 25–5–90–1; Saini 16–2–54–2; Ashwin 25–1–95–2.

India

R. G. Sharma c and b Hazlewood	26 – c Starc b Cummins	52
S. Gill c Green b Cummins	50 – c Paine b Hazlewood	31
C. A. Pujara c Paine b Cummins	50 – b Hazlewood	77
*A. M. Rahane b Cummins	22 – c Wade b Lyon	4
G. H. Vihari run out (Hazlewood)	4 – (6) not out	23
†R. R. Pant c Warner b Hazlewood	36 – (5) c Cummins b Lyon	97
R. A. Jadeja not out	28	
R. Ashwin run out (Cummins/Labuschagne)	10 – (7) not out	39
N. Saini c Wade b Starc	3	
J. J. Bumrah run out (Labuschagne)	0	
M. Siraj c Paine b Cummins	6	
Lb 2, w 5, nb 2	9	Lb 3, w 2, nb 6 11
1/70 (1) 2/85 (2) 3/117 (4) (100.4 overs)	244	1/71 (2) (5 wkts, 131 overs) 334
4/142 (5) 5/195 (6) 6/195 (3)		2/92 (1) 3/102 (4)
7/206 (8) 8/210 (9) 9/216 (10) 10/244 (11)		4/250 (5) 5/272 (3)

Starc 19–7–61–1; Hazlewood 21–10–43–2; Cummins 21.4–10–29–4; Lyon 31–8–87–0; Labuschagne 3–0–11–0; Green 5–2–11–0. *Second innings*—Starc 22–6–66–0; Hazlewood 26–12–39–2; Cummins 26–6–72–1; Lyon 46–17–114–2; Green 7–0–31–0; Labuschagne 4–2–9–0.

Umpires: P. R. Reiffel and P. Wilson. Third umpire: B. N. J. Oxenford.
Referee: D. C. Boon.

AUSTRALIA v INDIA

Fourth Test

At Brisbane, January 15–19, 2021. India won by three wickets. India 30pts. Toss: Australia. Test debuts: T. Natarajan, M. S. Washington Sundar.

In advance, Paine talked up the intimidating properties of the Gabba, which was strange, since he seemed to be buying into hype he didn't believe. In England in 2019, he had shut down any attempt to make Edgbaston a psychological hurdle. "We don't play the ground," he said, when asked about the home side's record there. Nor was the Gabba scary, not really. For decades, it had mostly been a batting track, whose concession to bowlers was

THE FORTRESSES

Longest Test unbeaten streaks on one ground:

34	Pakistan at Karachi (W17, D17)	1954-55 to 1999-2000
31	**Australia at Brisbane (W24, D7)**	**1989-90 to 2019-20**
27	West Indies at Bridgetown (W16, D11)	1947-48 to 1992-93
25	England at Manchester (W8, D17)	1905 to 1954
19	West Indies at Kingston (W11, D8)	1957-58 to 1988-89
18	England at The Oval (W10, D8)	1884 to 1929
18	Australia at Lord's (W9, D9)	1938 to 2005
18	New Zealand at Wellington (W6, D12)	1968-69 to 1992-93
17	West Indies at Port-of-Spain (W10, D7)	1977-78 to 1997-98
16	England at Birmingham (W9, D7)	1902 to 1974
15	Australia at Sydney (W7, D8)	1979-80 to 1992-93

The longest unbroken runs by the end of January 2021 were 12 Tests by England at Durban (since 1930-31), and by India at Delhi (1992-93) and Mohali (1997-98).

Patrick Hamilton, AFP/Getty Images

Fixed intent: Mohammed Siraj tears past Tim Paine.

bounce and early swing. Australia's unbeaten streak owed a lot to their strength during that period, as well as the fact that Brisbane usually hosted the first match of the summer, before visitors had acclimatised.

In any case, a win should not have been beyond them. Australia's only change was Harris for Will Pucovski, who had hurt his shoulder. India made four. Agarwal replaced Hanuma Vihari in the middle order, having been dropped one match earlier. Ashwin, Jadeja and Bumrah were all injured. Thangarasu Natarajan and Washington Sundar – playing his first first-class game for over three years – were on debut, while Shardul Thakur had played one Test, over two years earlier (when he tweaked his groin after ten balls). India's five main bowlers had 11 wickets between them. Australia's four had 1,013, with Lyon – playing his 100th – on 396.

But India's selections were positive. They could have gone with Pant at No. 7, three quicks and left-arm wrist-spinner Kuldeep Yadav. Instead, they wanted five bowlers – and a shot at victory. Sundar was known as a T20 spinner, but was picked at seven because he could bat, which allowed four seamers. Just as well: on day one, Saini suffered a groin injury of his own.

The plan worked: bowling first, Natarajan, Thakur and Sundar each collected three wickets. Australia's 369 was a good score; as at Sydney, dropped catches featured, two to reprieve Labuschagne, who made his fifth Test hundred. A storm shortened the second day, but on the third India were in trouble at 186 for six. Thakur joined Sundar, and got off the mark by hooking Cummins for six, followed up with sumptuous drives. They went shot for shot in a glorious partnership of 123, each making his first Test fifty. By the time the frustrated Australians cleaned up the tail, their lead was down to 33.

Australia, needing victory to regain the Border–Gavaskar Trophy, piled on 294 in 75 overs, with a fast start from Warner and Harris, and another Smith fifty; Siraj took his first five-wicket haul. India needed 328 from nearly four sessions. Rain wiped out 23 overs, leaving 98 on the fifth day, which they began on four without loss. No visitors had chased over 170 to win at the Gabba. But, at Sydney, India had enjoyed a dress rehearsal.

It was Gill, in his third Test, who went after it. Unbothered by the early loss of Sharma, he stood tall to hook and pull, or nonchalantly punch quality fast bowling through cover; inexplicably, he was using an unsponsored bat. His partner barely needed to score, though after lunch Gill's example coaxed Pujara into an upper-cut, the pair sacking 20 from one Starc over. When Gill edged Lyon to slip for 91, India needed another 196. Rahane took over as aggressor, then Pant. The approach was masterful: from one end, Gill and company batted to win; from the other, Pujara batted to draw. If others got out, Pujara could try to save the game. If Pujara got out, India might be close enough to the target to make Australia sweat.

Pujara set another record for his slowest fifty – 196 balls this time – and got bashed for his trouble. Not trusting the bounce from one end, he kept his gloves down, and protected his wicket at the cost of his body. Eleven times he was hit: shoulder, forearm, elbow, fingers; two blows to the head were glancing. The one on his glove was anything but, smushing his fingers against the handle like a poached egg on to toast. He was out after tea to Cummins – who else? – when DRS projected a sliver of ball meeting a sliver of stump, to uphold the umpire's decision.

By then, Pant was set, despite some streaky moments, and India needed 100 from 20 overs. Pujara had been counselling caution, encouraging his left-handed partner to leave when Lyon bowled wide of off stump. But now came the time to move. Pant hit T20 mode, slog-sweeping, falling across his stumps to scoop, playing a pull that landed him on his back. Agarwal came and went, but the energy was going one way when Sundar hooked Cummins, the world's best fast bowler, for six. Australia scrapped two more wickets, but this young Indian team were full of bravado, and not to be denied. Pant drove them home with three overs to spare, taking his team to the top of the World Test Championship.

The huge, extended squad ran on to the field. Spared the need to bat, Siraj beamed with delight. A shower so localised that it fell between the centre square and the Members Stand, but nowhere else, encouraged the feeling that this was a slightly magic day.

INDIA'S HIGHEST SUCCESSFUL TEST RUN-CHASES

406-4	v West Indies at Port-of-Spain	1975-76	256-8	v Australia at Bombay . . .	1964-65
387-4	v England at Chennai.	2008-09	233-6	v Australia at Adelaide . . .	2003-04
329-7	**v Australia at Brisbane . . . .**	**2020-21**	216-9	v Australia at Mohali	2010-11
276-5	v West Indies at Delhi	2011-12	207-3	v Australia at Bangalore . .	2010-11
264-3	v Sri Lanka at Kandy	2001	203-4	v Pakistan at Delhi	2007-08
262-5	v New Zealand at Bangalore .	2012-13	200-5	v New Zealand at Dunedin	1967-68
258-5	v Sri Lanka at Colombo (PSO)	2010			

Lyon would be remembered for creeping from 390 wickets to 399 in the series, but his many chances could have gone differently. The quicks were finished by the final session. "The ball was new, but the bowlers were worn," wrote Greg Baum in *The Age*. "They had punched themselves out on Pujara." As on his last Australian visit, he had faced the most balls in the series.

At Headingley in 2019, Ben Stokes had to belt sixes because it was England's one chance of escape. At Brisbane, India didn't have to chase the runs, but had a go anyway. The T20 generation is a misnomer, given the format has been around nearly 20 years, but a T20 mindset can make a player look at a target, and ask: "Why not?" For India, there seemed fewer mottos more fitting.

Player of the Match: R. R. Pant. *Player of the Series:* P. J. Cummins.

Close of play: first day, Australia 274-5 (Green 28, Paine 38); second day, India 62-2 (Pujara 8, Rahane 2); third day, Australia 21-0 (Harris 1, Warner 20); fourth day, India 4-0 (Sharma 4, Gill 0).

Australia

First innings		Second innings	
D. A. Warner c Sharma b Siraj	1	– (2) lbw b Washington Sundar	48
M. S. Harris c Washington Sundar b Thakur	5	– (1) c Pant b Thakur	38
M. Labuschagne c Pant b Natarajan	108	– c Sharma b Siraj	25
S. P. D. Smith c Sharma b Washington Sundar	36	– c Rahane b Siraj	55
M. S. Wade c Thakur b Natarajan	45	– c Pant b Siraj	0
C. D. Green b Washington Sundar	47	– c Sharma b Thakur	37
*†T. D. Paine c Sharma b Thakur	50	– c Pant b Thakur	27
P. J. Cummins lbw b Thakur	2	– not out	28
M. A. Starc not out	20	– c Saini b Siraj	1
N. M. Lyon b Washington Sundar	24	– c Agarwal b Thakur	13
J. R. Hazlewood b Natarajan	11	– c Thakur b Siraj	9
B 4, lb 5, w 5, nb 6	20	B 5, lb 2, w 2, nb 4	13
1/4 (1) 2/17 (2) 3/87 (4) 4/200 (5) 5/213 (3) 6/311 (7) 7/313 (6) 8/315 (8) 9/354 (10) 10/369 (11) (115.2 overs)	369	1/89 (1) 2/91 (2) 3/123 (3) 4/123 (5) 5/196 (4) 6/227 (6) 7/242 (7) 8/247 (9) 9/274 (10) 10/294 (11) (75.5 overs)	294

Siraj 28–10–77–1; Natarajan 24.2–3–78–3; Thakur 24–6–94–3; Saini 7.5–2–21–0; Washington Sundar 31–6–89–3; Sharma 0.1–0–1–0. *Second innings*—Siraj 19.5–5–73–5; Natarajan 14–4–41–0; Washington Sundar 18–1–80–1; Thakur 19–2–61–4; Saini 5–1–32–0.

India

First innings		Second innings	
R. G. Sharma c Starc b Lyon	44	– c Paine b Cummins	7
S. Gill c Smith b Cummins	7	– c Smith b Lyon	91
C. A. Pujara c Paine b Hazlewood	25	– lbw b Cummins	56
*A. M. Rahane c Wade b Starc	37	– c Paine b Cummins	24
M. A. Agarwal c Smith b Hazlewood	38	– (6) c Wade b Cummins	9
†R. R. Pant c Green b Hazlewood	23	– (5) not out	89
M. S. Washington Sundar c Green b Starc	62	– b Lyon	22
S. N. Thakur b Cummins	67	– c Lyon b Hazlewood	2
N. Saini c Smith b Hazlewood	5	– not out	0
M. Siraj b Hazlewood	13		
T. Natarajan not out	1		
B 5, lb 7, nb 2	14	B 18, lb 8, nb 3	29
1/11 (2) 2/60 (1) 3/105 (3) 4/144 (4) 5/161 (5) 6/186 (6) 7/309 (8) 8/320 (9) 9/328 (7) 10/336 (10) (111.4 overs)	336	1/18 (1) 2/132 (2) 3/167 (4) 4/228 (3) 5/265 (6) 6/318 (7) 7/325 (8) (7 wkts, 97 overs)	329

Starc 23–3–88–2; Hazlewood 24.4–6–57–5; Cummins 27–5–94–2; Green 8–1–20–0; Lyon 28–9–65–1; Labuschagne 1–1–0–0. *Second innings*—Starc 16–0–75–0; Hazlewood 22–5–74–1; Cummins 24–10–55–4; Green 3–1–10–0; Lyon 31–7–85–2; Labuschagne 1–0–4–0.

Umpires: B. N. J. Oxenford and P. Wilson. Third umpire: P. R. Reiffel.
Referee: D. C. Boon.

ENGLAND LIONS IN AUSTRALIA IN 2019-20

A-Team Test (1): Australia A 0, England Lions 1

England's second-string side enjoyed perhaps their most successful tour since Alan Wells led England A to victory in all three Tests against India in 1994-95. Never before had the Lions – or their equivalent – beaten their Australian counterparts: excluding an abandonment, six previous A-Team internationals had produced two draws and four defeats. Now, thanks to hundreds by Dominic Sibley and the prolific Dan Lawrence, and 13 wickets for the new-ball pairing of Craig Overton and Ollie Robinson, the Lions dominated the four-day floodlit match at the MCG, Australian cricket's spiritual home. When they escaped with a rainy draw against a New South Wales XI at Wollongong, the tourists completed a triumphant unbeaten trip in a country where the senior side had lost the previous two Ashes series 5–0 and 4–0.

The results reflected well on the leadership of Richard Dawson, the Gloucestershire coach who was taking charge of his first Lions tour following Andy Flower's departure from the ECB, and captain Lewis Gregory, the Somerset all-rounder; injury ruled him out at Melbourne, where Keaton Jennings led instead. Gregory was especially indebted to Lawrence, the sparkling 22-year-old Essex batsman, who racked up 493 runs at 98 across the formats – 268 ahead of the next best (Sibley). His success followed a decision towards the end of the 2019 domestic season to stand stiller at the crease. "I've cut down my trigger a lot," he said. Not content with scoring runs every time he went to the middle, including 190 against a Cricket Australia XI at Hobart and 125 against Australia A, Lawrence picked up 11 wickets with his perky off-breaks, making him the Lions' joint-leading wicket-taker, with Overton.

Others chipped in. There were hundreds for Sibley at Hobart and Melbourne, and for Jennings at Hobart; both had already been selected for the Test trip to Sri Lanka. Warwickshire's Sam Hain, meanwhile, confirmed why he had a List A average touching 60 when he stamped his mark on the tour opener, a 50-over match against a Cricket Australia XI, with a match-winning unbeaten 122. For Tom Abell, who led the side in Gregory's continued absence for the final game, runs proved harder to come by. But that was a minor detail from a happy few weeks.

ENGLAND LIONS TOURING PARTY

*L. Gregory (Somerset; FC/50), T. B. Abell (Somerset; FC), D. M. Bess (Somerset; FC/50), J. R. Bracey (Gloucestershire; FC/50), H. J. H. Brookes (Warwickshire; 50), B. A. Carse (Durham; FC/50), S. J. Cook (Essex; FC), O. B. Cox (Worcestershire; 50), M. S. Crane (Hampshire; 50), Z. Crawley (Kent; FC), L. J. Evans (Sussex; 50), R. J. Gleeson (Lancashire; FC/50), S. R. Hain (Warwickshire; FC/50), W. G. Jacks (Surrey; 50), K. K. Jennings (Lancashire; FC), T. Köhler-Cadmore (Yorkshire; FC/50), D. W. Lawrence (Essex; FC/50), M. E. Milnes (Kent; 50), T. J. Moores (Nottinghamshire; 50), S. A. Northeast (Hampshire; FC), C. Overton (Somerset; FC/50), O. E. Robinson (Sussex; FC), O. G. Robinson (Kent; FC), D. P. Sibley (Warwickshire; FC), G. S. Virdi (Surrey; FC). *Coach:* R. K. J. Dawson.

S. Mahmood (Lancashire) was originally selected for the four-day matches, but hurt his knee during England's T20 series in South Africa, and returned home. Cox joined the white-ball squad after an injury to Moores, but did not play. Cook was called up for the final two matches after Gregory suffered a calf injury, and Gleeson flew home after injuring his shoulder in the first red-ball game.

At Carrara, February 2, 2020. **England Lions won by six wickets.** **‡Cricket Australia XI 281-8** (50 overs) (M. A. Bryant 102); **England Lions 285-4** (48.2 overs) (S. R. Hain 122*, L. J. Evans 94, D. W. Lawrence 50*). *PoM:* S. R. Hain. *Sam Hain guided the Lions to an impressive win after a shaky start to their chase. From 32-3, he put on 154 with Laurie Evans, then 99* in 11 overs with Dan Lawrence. The CA XI had looked set for more than 281 when Max Bryant was thrashing 102 of their 127-1 in just 17 overs. But his dismissal, to his 60th ball, drained the life from their innings. With spinners Mason Crane (1-44) and Lawrence (1-35) imposing control, the next 33 overs yielded 154-7. The Australians' captain, Will Pucovski (23), retired with concussion after he tripped over his bat as he attempted a single. He was replaced by Xavier Crone, who neither batted nor bowled, but did catch Evans.*

At Carrara, February 4, 2020. **England Lions won by four wickets.** **‡Cricket Australia XI 179** (46.4 overs) (X. A. Crone 66; D. W. Lawrence 4-28, B. A. Carse 3-17); **England Lions 180-6** (41 overs). *PoM:* D. W. Lawrence. *The game was decided by a calamitous CA XI collapse of five for four in 22 balls, leaving them 50-6 in the 15th. Lawrence claimed the first three in four balls with his off-breaks, including Jake Lehmann – captain in place of the injured Pucovski – for a golden duck. Seamer Brydon Carse then struck twice in the same over. Crone supervised a recovery, helping squeeze 103 from the last three wickets, but 179 was barely competitive. James Bracey began the chase with a 47-ball 49, and Lawrence added 35, as the Lions eased home.*

At Carrara, February 6, 2020. **Cricket Australia XI v England Lions. Abandoned.**

At Sydney (Drummoyne Oval), February 9, 2020. **New South Wales XI v England Lions. Abandoned.**

At Sydney (Drummoyne Oval), February 11, 2020. **England Lions won by 52 runs.** **England Lions 293-9** (50 overs) (L. Gregory 55; G. A. West 3-58); **‡New South Wales XI 241** (42.1 overs) (R. J. Gibson 87; M. S. Crane 3-56). *A hard-hit 55 off 34 balls, including four sixes, by Lions captain Lewis Gregory ensured a match-winning total, after his top five had all been dismissed between 24 and 48. At 108-2 in the 17th, the New South Wales XI were in the game. But Crane removed Nicholas Bertus – the first of his three wickets against the state he briefly represented in the 2016-17 Sheffield Shield – and Lawrence trapped the captain, Ryan Gibson, for an 80-ball 87. For the hosts, it was the beginning of the end.*

At Hobart, February 15–18, 2020 (not first-class). **Drawn.** **England Lions 613-8 dec** (133.4 overs) (D. P. Sibley 103, K. K. Jennings 141, D. W. Lawrence 190, J. R. Bracey 58; B. J. Doggett 4-60) **and 116-3** (31 overs); **‡Cricket Australia XI 546** (157.2 overs) (J. J. S. Sangha 72, J. S. Lehmann 150, J. R. Edwards 192; C. Overton 3-100, D. W. Lawrence 3-94). *PoM:* D. W. Lawrence. *The first red-ball game was a 12-a-side high-scoring draw, in which Dominic Sibley and Keaton Jennings celebrated selection for England's tour of Sri Lanka with centuries. They were joined by the in-form Lawrence, whose 190 occupied only 194 balls, and set up the second-highest total by the Lions (or equivalent), behind 624-8 against South Africa A at Paarl in 2014-15. Seamer Brendan Doggett claimed 4-60; seven team-mates managed 4-542, including leg-spinner Lloyd Pope, who had figures of 33–0–190–1, two years after demolishing England Under-19 with 8-35 in a World Cup game. Injuries to Richard Gleeson and Gregory damaged the Lions' chances of forcing a result, with Lehmann and Jack Edwards, last out for 192, taking advantage as the Australians limited the deficit to 67. Dom Bess bowled 50 wicketless overs for 120.*

AUSTRALIA A v ENGLAND LIONS

At Melbourne, February 22–25, 2020 (day/night). England Lions won by nine wickets. Toss: Australia A.

England Lions pulled off their first win over Australia A in seven attempts. The platform in this pink-ball game was laid by Sibley and Lawrence, who added 219 for the fourth wicket after the Lions had been in a spot of bother at 55 for three on the first day; as at Hobart, each made a century. Bracey then contributed 65 as the bowlers tired. The Australians, whose top five all had Test experience, were bundled out for 176, and followed on, 252 behind. Patterson held firm, but Bess removed Harris and Henriques in successive overs to make it 85 for four, and Craig Overton and

Robinson chipped away, finishing with four wickets each. That left the Lions needing just 20, which they achieved for the loss of Sibley.

Close of play: first day, England Lions 274-3 (Sibley 108, Lawrence 125); second day, Australia A 103-5 (Inglis 13, Wildermuth 11); third day, Australia A 180-5 (Patterson 43, Wildermuth 16).

England Lions

Z. Crawley c Inglis b Bird	18	– not out	10
D. P. Sibley c Inglis b Steketee	116	– c Khawaja b Bird	3
*K. K. Jennings c and b Wildermuth	14	– not out	5
S. A. Northeast c and b Wildermuth	1		
D. W. Lawrence c Inglis b Steketee	125		
†J. R. Bracey c Maddinson b Swepson	65		
T. B. Abell c Wildermuth b Steketee	3		
D. M. Bess c Inglis b Steketee	29		
C. Overton lbw b Swepson	4		
B. A. Carse not out	30		
O. E. Robinson c Maddinson b Swepson	13		
Lb 6, w 2, nb 2	10	B 2	2
1/24 (1) 2/51 (3) 3/55 (4) (140.2 overs)	428	1/5 (2) (1 wkt, 7.4 overs)	20
4/274 (5) 5/295 (2) 6/305 (7)			
7/369 (8) 8/378 (9) 9/391 (6) 10/428 (11)			

Bird 31–12–81–1; Neser 27–3–108–0; Swepson 31.2–1–97–3; Steketee 32–13–75–4; Wildermuth 18–3–59–2; Maddinson 1–0–2–0. *Second innings*—Bird 4–2–4–1; Steketee 3.4–0–14–0.

Australia A

M. S. Harris c Lawrence b Robinson	6	– (2) b Bess	24
U. T. Khawaja c Bracey b Overton	30	– (1) lbw b Overton	4
N. J. Maddinson lbw b Overton	1	– c Northeast b Overton	52
K. R. Patterson c Overton b Carse	11	– not out	94
*M. C. Henriques c Bracey b Robinson	25	– c Overton b Bess	4
†J. P. Inglis b Robinson	40	– c Jennings b Robinson	35
J. D. Wildermuth not out	50	– c Abell b Overton	37
M. G. Neser c Bracey b Abell	6	– lbw b Overton	2
J. M. Bird c Bracey b Abell	0	– b Robinson	9
M. T. Steketee c Lawrence b Carse	1	– c Sibley b Robinson	0
M. J. Swepson c Abell b Carse	0	– c Jennings b Robinson	3
B 4, nb 2	6	Lb 2, w 3, nb 2	7
1/22 (1) 2/23 (3) 3/41 (4) (59.3 overs)	176	1/4 (1) 2/81 (3) (73.4 overs)	271
4/71 (2) 5/80 (5) 6/146 (6)		3/81 (2) 4/85 (5)	
7/169 (8) 8/169 (9) 9/170 (10) 10/176 (11)		5/150 (6) 6/217 (7) 7/227 (8)	
		8/254 (9) 9/254 (10) 10/271 (11)	

Overton 17–6–34–2; Robinson 22–5–66–3; Carse 12.3–3–50–3; Abell 8–1–22–2. *Second innings*—Overton 20–3–67–4; Robinson 21.4–5–81–4; Carse 12–0–57–0; Bess 18–3–57–2; Lawrence 1–0–5–0; Abell 1–0–2–0.

Umpires: G. A. Abood and S. J. Nogajski.
Referee: D. J. Harper.

At Wollongong, March 2–5, 2020 (not first-class). **Drawn.** **‡New South Wales XI 405-8 dec** (129.5 overs) (R. P. Hackney 95, J. J. S. Sangha 85, D. R. Sams 80); **England Lions 202-5** (74.2 overs) (D. W. Lawrence 52, S. A. Northeast 77*). *Rain helped the Lions end their tour unbeaten, allowing only 26.2 overs on the third day, and none on the fourth – though they were also grateful for a sixth-wicket stand of 83* in 31 overs between Sam Northeast and Carse (44*). NSW's grunt work was performed by opener Ryan Hackney, who fell in the 82nd over for 95. No. 4 Jason Sangha had already come and gone for 85, while Daniel Sams made a fluent 80 down the order. In reply, Lawrence ticked off one last half-century of a profitable tour.*

DOMESTIC CRICKET IN AUSTRALIA IN 2019-20

PETER ENGLISH

A summer shrouded in smoke and ash was killed off by the threat of disease. Poor air quality and the haze from devastating bushfires on Sydney's outskirts endangered games at the SCG in December; in March, with one qualifying round of the Sheffield Shield to go, Cricket Australia cancelled the remaining matches, including the final, because of coronavirus. It was the first time the season had been cut short since the war.

A couple of days later, **New South Wales** were declared the Shield winners. While there was no doubt they were the leading team – with six victories and an unbeatable 12-point lead – the cancellation meant their superiority could not be tested in a final; supporters of Victoria, the defending champions who finished second, were keen to remind them their success came with an asterisk. The title decision was announced by CA's chief executive (and former New South Wales batsman) Kevin Roberts. Soon after, he stood down most of CA's employees, with 80% pay cuts, citing financial worries caused by Covid-19 – despite it being the off-season, when the game generates little income anyway. But Roberts's tumultuous tenure since replacing James Sutherland in October 2018 ended when his own departure was announced in June. A day later, 40 CA staff lost their jobs.

Given the lockdown, celebrations of New South Wales's first Shield since 2013-14 were muted – doubly so for Steve O'Keefe, who was not offered a new contract, despite 16 wickets in five matches. That gave him 224 for them in a dozen seasons of mesmerising slow left-arm. Seamers Trent Copeland and Harry Conway collected 25 each; Copeland passed 300 Shield victims between shifts of international commentary. The batting was led by Daniel Hughes (665), Moises Henriques (512) and the emerging Daniel Solway, whose 498 runs at 55 included a century on debut.

The Shield's top run-scorer was **Victoria's** Nic Maddinson, catapulted by a career-high 224 to 780 runs at 86; he shared the Shield Player of the Year award with Henriques. His team-mate Peter Siddle announced his international retirement but remained a force in domestic cricket, taking 32 wickets at 19, before moving to Tasmania in hope of a swansong. The MCG pitch, often devoid of life, had too much when a match against Western Australia was called off on the opening day because the visiting batsmen kept being struck by good-length deliveries, and had to be tested for concussion.

Queensland went close in the Shield and the one-day competition. They had the Shield's leading wicket-taker in Cameron Gannon – 38 victims at 20 – plus the joint-second in Michael Neser, who took 33 in only six games. Experienced opener Joe Burns collected 515 runs when not on Test duty, while new batsman Bryce Street showed promise with two lively centuries; he was elevated to the first team after an innings of 345, a record in the Second XI competition.

In **Tasmania**, George Bailey passed 10,000 first-class runs in his 160th match, then retired after his 161st. He was bowled first ball in his final innings, and trudged off to join the national selection panel. Test captain Tim Paine scored his second first-class century, 13 years after his first; both came against Western Australia at the WACA. Jackson Bird remained the outstanding bowler in the seaming local conditions, with 28 wickets, but life was tough for batsmen.

Shaun Marsh guided **Western Australia** to victory in the final of the Marsh One-Day Cup, with an unbeaten 101. He had also made a double-century in the Shield, and scored 724 in all, despite three successive ducks in February. The 20-year-old all-rounder Cameron Green contributed three composed hundreds, amassing 699 at 63.

Last for the eighth time in 11 campaigns, **South Australia** lost their coach just before the season was called off, when former batting favourite Jamie Siddons stepped down. They did end a run of 18 matches without victory, and there were signs of brightness from Tom Cooper (765 runs), the dependable seamer Chadd Sayers, whose 31 victims helped him past 300 first-class wickets, and Wes Agar, who claimed 33 in his debut season.

FIRST-CLASS AVERAGES IN 2019-20

BATTING (400 runs)

		M	*I*	*NO*	*R*	*HS*	*100*	*Avge*	*Ct/St*
1	†D. A. Warner (*NSW/Australia*)	7	12	3	927	335*	4	103.00	7
2	M. Labuschagne (*Queensland/Aus*)	10	16	1	1,182	215	4	78.80	4
3	†N. J. Maddinson (*Victoria/Australia A*)	8	12	1	833	224	2	75.72	6
4	C. D. Green (*Western Australia*)	8	15	4	699	158*	3	63.54	4
5	D. L. Solway (*New South Wales*)	7	12	3	498	133*	1	55.33	4
6	T. L. W. Cooper (*South Australia*)	8	15	1	765	271*	1	54.64	7
7	†M. S. Wade (*Tasmania/Australia*)	9	14	3	570	89	0	51.81	3
8	†S. E. Marsh (*Western Australia*)	9	17	2	724	214	2	48.26	15
9	M. C. Henriques (*NSW/Australia A*)	8	14	2	541	124	2	45.08	1
10	†D. P. Hughes (*New South Wales*)	9	18	3	665	136	2	44.33	0
11	S. P. D. Smith (*NSW/Australia*)	8	12	0	486	106	2	40.50	14
12	†T. M. Head (*S Australia/Aus A/Aus*)	12	19	1	713	114	2	39.61	6
13	J. A. Burns (*Queensland/Aus A/Aus*)	12	21	1	782	135	1	39.10	16
14	†M. S. Harris (*Victoria/Australia A*)	9	14	1	508	116	1	39.07	3
15	†J. B. Weatherald (*South Australia*)	9	17	0	660	198	2	38.82	9
16	B. J. Webster (*Tasmania*)	7	13	1	459	187	1	38.25	8
17	†B. E. Street (*Queensland*)	8	15	2	489	115	2	37.61	12
18	P. M. Nevill (*New South Wales*)	9	13	2	411	88*	0	37.36	28/3
19	T. D. Paine (*Tasmania/Australia*)	11	15	2	479	121	1	36.84	53/4
20	A. J. Doolan (*Tasmania*)	9	17	1	575	170*	2	35.93	5
21	B. R. McDermott (*Tasmania*)	8	14	0	459	89	0	32.78	7
22	N. C. R. Larkin (*New South Wales*)	8	15	2	421	91	0	32.38	6
23	C. J. Ferguson (*South Australia*)	7	14	0	451	123	1	32.21	5
24	H. J. Hunt (*South Australia*)	9	17	0	487	132	1	28.64	7

BOWLING (15 wickets, average 35.00)

		Style	*O*	*M*	*R*	*W*	*BB*	*5I*	*Avge*
1	J. R. Hazlewood (*NSW/Australia*)	RFM	144.3	39	347	21	6-35	1	16.52
2	N. T. Ellis (*Tasmania*)	RFM	96.3	17	301	18	6-43	2	16.72
3	M. A. Starc (*NSW/Australia*)	LF	281.5	66	797	46	6-66	4	17.32
4	W. J. Sutherland (*Victoria*)	RFM	121.3	33	317	18	6-67	2	17.61
5	P. M. Siddle (*Victoria*)	RFM	278.2	77	636	32	5-49	1	19.87
6	M. G. Neser (*Queensland/Aus A*)	RFM	300.2	96	747	37	5-56	1	20.18
7	H. N. A. Conway (*NSW*)	RFM	197.5	56	518	25	5-15	3	20.72
8	C. J. Gannon (*Queensland*)	RFM	295	95	795	38	5-94	1	20.92
9	P. J. Cummins (*NSW/Australia*)	RF	204.2	51	529	24	5-28	1	22.04
10	S. N. J. O'Keefe (*New South Wales*)	SLA	145.3	21	356	16	5-80	1	22.25
11	N. Wagner (*New Zealand*)	LFM	157.3	33	387	17	4-83	0	22.76
12	J. M. Bird (*Tasmania/Australia A*)	RFM	256.5	76	711	30	5-78	1	23.70
13	M. T. Steketee (*Queensland/Aus A*)	RFM	267.1	77	754	31	5-19	1	24.32
14	W. A. Agar (*South Australia*)	RF	291.5	81	803	33	5-53	1	24.33
15	J. D. Wildermuth (*Queensld/Aus A*)	RFM	174.3	56	409	16	3-17	0	25.56
16	G. T. Bell (*Tasmania*)	RM	189.1	58	531	20	4-45	0	26.55
17	J. L. Pattinson (*Victoria/Australia*)	RFM	198	43	536	20	4-66	0	26.80
18	N. M. Lyon (*NSW/Australia*)	OB	433.2	109	1,155	42	5-50	3	27.50
19	C. J. Sayers (*South Australia*)	RFM	331.3	94	877	31	8-64	2	28.29
20	M. L. Kelly (*Western Australia*)	RFM	252.1	53	769	27	5-63	2	28.48
21	M. J. Swepson (*Queensland/Aus A*)	LB	205.3	41	538	17	4-75	0	31.64
22	T. A. Copeland (*New South Wales*)	RFM	304.4	89	797	25	5-63	1	31.88
23	R. P. Meredith (*Tasmania/Aus A*)	RFM	163.4	23	702	22	5-98	1	31.90
24	J. M. Mennie (*South Australia*)	RFM	187.4	37	645	19	6-103	1	33.94
25	C. P. Tremain (*Victoria*)	RFM	257.3	61	662	19	4-45	0	34.84

SHEFFIELD SHIELD IN 2019-20

					Bonus pts			
	P	*W*	*L*	*D*	*Bat*	*Bowl*	*Adj*	*Pts*
New South Wales	9	6	2	1	6.16	7.6	–	50.76
Victoria	9	3	3	3*	7.59	6.6	3.34	38.53
Queensland	9	4	3	2	3.31	7.6	–	36.91
Tasmania	9	3	4	2	4.79	7.5	–	32.29
Western Australia	9	2	3	4*	6.53	5.2	3.64	31.37
South Australia	9	2	5	2	8.54	6.0	–	28.54

Outright win = 6pts; draw = 1pt. Bonus points awarded for the first 100 overs of each team's first innings: 0.01 batting points for every run over the first 200; 0.1 bowling points for each wicket taken.

* *Victoria v Western Australia on December 7–10 was called off because of a substandard pitch. Both teams were awarded 4.64pts, the average earned by the other teams in that round; this included 1pt for a draw and the 0.3 bonus pts earned by Victoria in the play possible.*

Because of the Covid-19 pandemic, the last round of the Sheffield Shield and the final were cancelled; New South Wales were declared winners by virtue of heading the table.

SHEFFIELD SHIELD WINNERS

1892-93	Victoria	1929-30	Victoria	1968-69	South Australia
1893-94	South Australia	1930-31	Victoria	1969-70	Victoria
1894-95	Victoria	1931-32	New South Wales	1970-71	South Australia
1895-96	New South Wales	1932-33	New South Wales	1971-72	Western Australia
1896-97	New South Wales	1933-34	Victoria	1972-73	Western Australia
1897-98	Victoria	1934-35	Victoria	1973-74	Victoria
1898-99	Victoria	1935-36	South Australia	1974-75	Western Australia
1899-1900	New South Wales	1936-37	Victoria	1975-76	South Australia
1900-01	Victoria	1937-38	New South Wales	1976-77	Western Australia
1901-02	New South Wales	1938-39	South Australia	1977-78	Western Australia
1902-03	New South Wales	1939-40	New South Wales	1978-79	Victoria
1903-04	New South Wales	1940–46	*No competition*	1979-80	Victoria
1904-05	New South Wales	1946-47	Victoria	1980-81	Western Australia
1905-06	New South Wales	1947-48	Western Australia	1981-82	South Australia
1906-07	New South Wales	1948-49	New South Wales	1982-83	New South Wales*
1907-08	Victoria	1949-50	New South Wales	1983-84	Western Australia
1908-09	New South Wales	1950-51	Victoria	1984-85	New South Wales
1909-10	South Australia	1951-52	New South Wales	1985-86	New South Wales
1910-11	New South Wales	1952-53	South Australia	1986-87	Western Australia
1911-12	New South Wales	1953-54	New South Wales	1987-88	Western Australia
1912-13	South Australia	1954-55	New South Wales	1988-89	Western Australia
1913-14	New South Wales	1955-56	New South Wales	1989-90	New South Wales
1914-15	Victoria	1956-57	New South Wales	1990-91	Victoria
1915–19	*No competition*	1957-58	New South Wales	1991-92	Western Australia
1919-20	New South Wales	1958-59	New South Wales	1992-93	New South Wales
1920-21	New South Wales	1959-60	New South Wales	1993-94	New South Wales
1921-22	Victoria	1960-61	New South Wales	1994-95	Queensland
1922-23	New South Wales	1961-62	New South Wales	1995-96	South Australia
1923-24	Victoria	1962-63	Victoria	1996-97	Queensland*
1924-25	Victoria	1963-64	South Australia	1997-98	Western Australia
1925-26	New South Wales	1964-65	New South Wales	1998-99	Western Australia*
1926-27	South Australia	1965-66	New South Wales	1999-2000	Queensland
1927-28	Victoria	1966-67	Victoria	2000-01	Queensland
1928-29	New South Wales	1967-68	Western Australia	2001-02	Queensland

2002-03	New South Wales*	2008-09	Victoria	2014-15	Victoria
2003-04	Victoria	2009-10	Victoria	2015-16	Victoria*
2004-05	New South Wales*	2010-11	Tasmania	2016-17	Victoria
2005-06	Queensland	2011-12	Queensland	2017-18	Queensland
2006-07	Tasmania	2012-13	Tasmania	2018-19	Victoria
2007-08	New South Wales	2013-14	New South Wales	2019-20	New South Wales†

New South Wales have won the title 47 times, Victoria 32, Western Australia 15, South Australia 13, Queensland 8, Tasmania 3.

The tournament was the Pura Milk Cup in 1999-2000, and the Pura Cup from 2000-01 to 2007-08.

* *Second in table but won final. Finals were introduced in 1982-83.*

† *There was no final in 2019-20.*

MARSH ONE-DAY CUP IN 2019-20

50-over league plus final

	P	*W*	*L*	*Bonus*	*Pts*	*NRR*
QUEENSLAND	7	5	2	2	22	0.75
WESTERN AUSTRALIA	7	5	2	2	22	0.48
South Australia	7	4	3	2	18	0.07
Tasmania	7	3	4	1	12*	–0.03
Victoria	7	3	4	0	12	–0.78
New South Wales	7	1	6	1	5	–0.48

* *One point deducted for a slow over-rate.*

Win = 4pts; 1 bonus point awarded for achieving victory with a run-rate 1.25 times that of the opposition, and 2 bonus points for victory with a run-rate twice that of the opposition.

Final At Brisbane (Allan Border Field), November 26, 2019. **Western Australia won by four wickets. Queensland 205** (49.3 overs); ‡**Western Australia 210-6** (48 overs) (S. E. Marsh 101*). *Table leaders Queensland lost half their side for 56 to Jhye Richardson and Nathan Coulter-Nile, who finished with three wickets apiece, before Jimmy Peirson scored 79 off 83 balls and raised the target to 206. Though Western Australia lost three early wickets, Shaun Marsh steadied their innings in a stand of 97 with Marcus Stoinis, and his unbeaten century took them home with two overs to spare.*

The KFC T20 Big Bash League has its own section (page 826).

BANGLADESH CRICKET IN 2020

A full stop. And a farewell

UTPAL SHUVRO

When Bangladesh left the field at the Sher-e-Bangla Stadium in Mirpur on March 11, after completing an all-format clean sweep over Zimbabwe, no one could have imagined they had played their last cricket of the year.

The final leg of a tour of Pakistan was the first casualty of the pandemic. It was already a complicated trip, which went ahead only after prolonged discussions about security; former captain Mushfiqur Rahim declined to travel. Pakistan had won the two completed T20 matches, and romped home in the First Test, in Rawalpindi in February. Bangladesh were due to return in April for another Test and a one-day international, but Covid-19 put paid to that.

All the other planned matches were, eventually, postponed, although not without more long-winded negotiations. Bangladesh were supposed to play three Tests in Sri Lanka in July, later put back to October. The players were summoned to a training camp, and preparations were in full swing – but the two countries could not agree about quarantine requirements. The Sri Lankan

BANGLADESH IN 2020

	Played	*Won*	*Lost*	*Drawn/No result*
Tests	2	1	1	–
One-day internationals	3	3	–	–
Twenty20 internationals	4	2	2	–

JANUARY, FEBRUARY	1 Test and 2 T20Is (a) v Pakistan	(page 729)
FEBRUARY, MARCH	1 Test, 3 ODIs and 2 T20Is (h) v Zimbabwe	(page 663)
APRIL		
MAY		
JUNE		
JULY		
AUGUST		
SEPTEMBER		
OCTOBER		
NOVEMBER		
DECEMBER		

For a review of Bangladesh domestic cricket from the 2019-20 season, see page 667.

Leaving on a high: Mashrafe bin Mortaza is chaired off after his last game for Bangladesh.

health authorities insisted the Bangladeshis would have to be confined to their hotel rooms for 14 days, but Nazmul Hasan, the BCB president, said "what they are insisting is not quarantine, but full isolation".

It later emerged that the England touring squad were not subjected to such strict measures, but the Sri Lankan concern was understandable: their Covid-19 situation was largely under control by then, thanks to stringent border controls, whereas in Bangladesh the virus was still spreading. Several high-profile players tested positive, including Mahmudullah, Mominul Haque, Abu Jayed and Saif Hasan, as did former captains Habibul Bashar (now a selector) and Mashrafe bin Mortaza.

To ensure some international cricket for 2021, the board were forced to arrange some domestic matches to show potential touring sides that the country was safe for cricket. A one-day BCB President's Cup took place in October, with three teams chosen by the selectors, followed by a Twenty20 competition. This was dedicated to Bangladesh's first president, Sheikh Mujibur Rahman – "Bangabandhu" – whose birth centenary fell in March; the tournament, which replaced two planned matches between Asia and a World XI, was named the Bangabandhu T20 Cup. Khulna, led by Mahmudullah, beat Chittagong in the final in December. Back in January, Khulna Tigers had come up short in the final of the Bangladesh Premier League, losing to Rajshahi Royals, captained by the West Indian Andre Russell.

The measures paid off. West Indies fulfilled their tour early in 2021, though with a second-string squad. Bangladesh won the Twenty20 series easily, before losing the Tests.

There was a notable farewell in 2020, as Mortaza stepped down from the captaincy of the 50-over team after ten years in charge. He had been widely expected to retire following a miserable World Cup in England in 2019, when he took one wicket for 361; the board were even planning a special match for him. But Mortaza soldiered on, determined to go out on his own terms, and finally announced his decision before the third one-dayer against Zimbabwe in Sylhet in March. After another victory – his 50th in 88 ODIs as captain – the team all wore shirts with his name on the back, and hoisted him on their shoulders for a lap of honour.

There was one other major success story before the coronavirus changed everything. Bangladesh pulled off a stunning victory in the Under-19 World Cup – their first global trophy of any kind – in South Africa in January and February. It was the result of meticulous planning over more than two years. They were lucky that rain allowed them to escape from a dire position in their qualifier against Pakistan, but wicketkeeper-batsman Akbar Ali led them to rousing victories over South Africa in the quarter-final and New Zealand in the semi, before a highly charged victory over India. Several of the team are expected to feature in full internationals before long: the BCB awarded them all two-year contracts, and announced a new Under-21 unit to prepare them for the challenges ahead.

BANGLADESH v ZIMBABWE IN 2019-20

MOHAMMAD ISAM

Test match (1): Bangladesh 1, Zimbabwe 0
One-day internationals (3): Bangladesh 3, Zimbabwe 0
Twenty20 internationals (2): Bangladesh 2, Zimbabwe 0

Bangladesh were in desperate need of a tonic, which Zimbabwe obligingly provided. A poor year on the field in 2019 had been accompanied by conflict between the Bangladeshi players and the board, the seismic suspension on corruption charges of Shakib Al Hasan, and an ongoing debate over the future of Mashrafe bin Mortaza. However, their problems paled alongside Zimbabwe's, and the gulf between the teams was huge: Bangladesh won all six matches, five by a wide margin.

Recent games against Zimbabwe had often provided opponents with a chance to buff up their career statistics, and so it proved again. One of the chief beneficiaries was Liton Das, who across the formats hit two centuries and three fifties. The Test, meanwhile, was a personal triumph for Mushfiqur Rahim, who hit his third double-hundred, and second against Zimbabwe. It gave him four entries in Bangladesh's top ten scores. There was also a century for Mominul Haque, in his first home Test as captain, while teenage off-spinner Nayeem Hasan collected nine wickets.

Liton and a back-in-form Tamim Iqbal both passed 300 runs in the ODIs, while Liton was easily the leading scorer in the two-match Twenty20 series. With seven wickets at nine, seamer Mohammad Saifuddin returned from a back injury to finish as the most successful bowler in the 50-over games.

For Zimbabwe, there was little to lift the gloom. A shaft of light was provided by the 19-year-old all-rounder Wesley Madhevere, who made his international debut soon after appearing in his third Under-19 World Cup. He made useful middle-order runs in the one-dayers, and deployed some varied off-breaks. Craig Ervine – captain for the first time while Sean Williams stayed at home to be with his wife, who was expecting their first child – hit his third Test hundred. Sikandar Raza scored a couple of one-day fifties, and shouldered a big workload with his off-spin. But Chamu Chibhabha, the new white-ball captain, split the webbing in his hand in the first ODI, and was ruled out of the rest; Williams, who arrived in time to take part in the one-day series, deputised.

The continuing dysfunction in Bangladesh cricket was demonstrated after the Test when board president Nazmul Hassan criticised Mushfiqur's decision to opt out of the split tour of Pakistan, due to resume in April. "Players have to think about the country, and not just themselves," he said, contradicting earlier comments that players were free to make up their own minds. Mushfiqur, who was subsequently dropped for the third ODI, said his family did not think it was safe to play there.

Meanwhile, the approaching shadow of the Covid-19 pandemic prompted the BCB to put in measures to reduce attendances at the T20 matches.

ZIMBABWE TOURING PARTY

*C. R. Ervine (T/50/20), R. W. Chakabva (T/50/20), C. J. Chibhabha (50/20), T. S. Kamunhukamwe (50/20), K. T. Kasuza (T), W. N. Madhevere (50/20), T. Maruma (T/50/20), P. S. Masvaure (T), C. B. Mpofu (T/50/20), B. S. Mudzinganyama (T), C. T. Mumba (T/50/20), C. T. Mutombodzi (T/50/20), R. Mutumbami (50/20), A. Ndlovu (T/50/20), V. M. Nyauchi (T), Sikandar Raza (T/50/20), B. R. M. Taylor (T/50/20), D. T. Tiripano (T/50/20), C. K. Tshuma (T/50/20), S. C. Williams (50/20).

Chibhabha was named as the ODI and T20 captain, but was ruled out by a hand injury after the first match. Williams took over.

BANGLADESH v ZIMBABWE

Only Test

At Mirpur, February 22–25, 2020. Bangladesh won by an innings and 106 runs. Toss: Zimbabwe. Test debut: C. K. Tshuma.

After 15 months without a Test win, Bangladesh completed a comfortable victory before tea on the fourth day. Their batsmen looked in good form, and the bowlers were penetrative, but the crushing margin owed much to the opposition.

Yet the match had begun encouragingly for Zimbabwe, when Ervine's decision to bat seemed vindicated by a lunchtime score of 80 for one. Leading the team because Sean Williams was on paternity leave, he put on 111 for the second wicket with Prince Masvaure. But their alliance could not soothe Zimbabwe's nerves. The last nine fell for 147, including Ervine for 107, to a combination of the swing of Abu Jayed and the spin of Nayeem Hasan. Jayed's four for 71 were his best Test figures, reward for a bowler who had once contemplated moving to the United States after years on the domestic circuit.

Bangladesh were batting before lunch on the second day, and gradually eased themselves into an unassailable position. After Nazmul Hossain fell for 71 – a maiden Test wicket for Charlton Tshuma – Mominul Haque and Mushfiqur Rahim put on 222 for the fourth wicket, with Mominul reaching his ninth Test century (all at home), and first since becoming captain. Mushfiqur then added 111 for the sixth wicket with Liton Das. He carried remorselessly on to his third Test double-hundred, in 315 balls, with 28 fours, and was eyeing his own landmark of 219, Bangladesh's highest Test score, when Mominul declared with a lead of 295 shortly before the third-day close. The threat of rain influenced his decision, but Mushfiqur was miffed. "I wasn't aware we would be declaring today," he said. "There wasn't any discussion about a declaration during the tea interval." Even so, 560 for six was Bangladesh's third-highest total, and the biggest between these sides.

But any argument was ended when Nayeem dismissed Masvaure and nightwatchman Tiripano with the second and third balls of Zimbabwe's second innings. On the fourth morning, under grey skies and occasional drizzle, Nayeem and Taijul Islam pushed Bangladesh towards victory. There was some middle-order resistance, but in general Zimbabwe batted with little regard for the discipline needed to save the match, or for the inclement forecast. The Bangladesh spinners had men round the bat, though reckless shots

---

HIGHEST TEST SCORES FOR BANGLADESH

219*	Mushfiqur Rahim	v Zimbabwe at Mirpur	2018-19
217	Shakib Al Hasan	v New Zealand at Wellington	2016-17
206	Tamim Iqbal	v Pakistan at Khulna	2014-15
203*	**Mushfiqur Rahim**	**v Zimbabwe at Mirpur**	**2019-20**
200	Mushfiqur Rahim	v Sri Lanka at Galle	2012-13
190	Mohammad Ashraful	v Sri Lanka at Galle	2012-13
181	Mominul Haque	v New Zealand at Chittagong	2013-14
176	Mominul Haque	v Sri Lanka at Chittagong	2017-18
161	Mominul Haque	v Zimbabwe at Mirpur	2018-19
159	Mushfiqur Rahim	v New Zealand at Wellington	2016-17

meant three catches were held in the deep. Nayeem finished with match figures of nine for 152. It was Bangladesh's second innings victory, having beaten West Indies by an innings and 184 at the same venue in 2018-19.

Player of the Match: Mushfiqur Rahim.

Close of play: first day, Zimbabwe 228-6 (Chakabva 9, Tiripano 0); second day, Bangladesh 240-3 (Mominul Haque 79, Mushfiqur Rahim 32); third day, Zimbabwe 9-2 (Kasuza 8, Taylor 1).

Zimbabwe

First innings		Second innings	
P. S. Masvaure c and b Nayeem Hasan	64	– b Nayeem Hasan	0
K. T. Kasuza c Nayeem Hasan b Abu Jayed	2	– c Mithun Ali b Taijul Islam	10
*C. R. Ervine b Nayeem Hasan	107	– (5) run out (Mominul Haque)	43
B. R. M. Taylor b Nayeem Hasan	10	– c Taijul Islam b Nayeem Hasan	17
Sikandar Raza c Liton Das b Nayeem Hasan	18	– (6) c Mushfiqur Rahim b Taijul Islam	37
T. Maruma lbw b Abu Jayed	7	– (7) c Tamim Iqbal b Nayeem Hasan	41
†R. W. Chakabva c Nayeem Hasan b Taijul Islam	30	– (8) c Tamim Iqbal b Taijul Islam	18
D. T. Tiripano c Liton Das b Abu Jayed	8	– (3) c Liton Das b Nayeem Hasan	0
A. Ndlovu lbw b Abu Jayed	0	– lbw b Nayeem Hasan	4
C. K. Tshuma lbw b Taijul Islam	0	– lbw b Taijul Islam	3
V. M. Nyauchi not out	6	– not out	7
B 4, lb 4, w 5	13	B 9	9
1/7 (2) 2/118 (1) 3/134 (4) 4/174 (5) 5/199 (6) 6/226 (3) 7/240 (8) 8/244 (9) 9/245 (10) 10/265 (7) (106.3 overs)	265	1/0 (1) 2/0 (3) 3/15 (2) 4/44 (4) 5/104 (5) 6/121 (6) 7/165 (8) 8/170 (9) 9/181 (7) 10/189 (10) (57.3 overs)	189

Ebadat Hossain 17–8–26–0; Abu Jayed 24–6–71–4; Nayeem Hasan 38–9–70–4; Taijul Islam 27.3–1–90–2. *Second innings*—Nayeem Hasan 24–6–82–5; Taijul Islam 24.3–7–78–4; Abu Jayed 4–3–4–0; Ebadat Hossain 5–1–16–0.

Bangladesh

Tamim Iqbal c Chakabva b Tiripano	41
Saif Hasan c Chakabva b Nyauchi	8
Nazmul Hossain c Chakabva b Tshuma	71
*Mominul Haque c and b Ndlovu	132
Mushfiqur Rahim not out	203
Mithun Ali c Chakabva b Ndlovu	17
†Liton Das c Chakabva b Sikandar Raza	53
Taijul Islam not out	14
B 8, lb 3, w 5, nb 5	21
1/18 (2) 2/96 (1) 3/172 (3) 4/394 (4) 5/421 (6) 6/532 (7) (6 wkts dec, 154 overs)	560

Nayeem Hasan, Abu Jayed and Ebadat Hossain did not bat.

Tiripano 30–6–96–1; Nyauchi 27–3–87–1; Sikandar Raza 30–2–111–1; Tshuma 25–2–85–1; Ndlovu 42–4–170–2.

Umpires: P. R. Reiffel and J. S. Wilson. Third umpire: H. D. P. K. Dharmasena.
Referee: J. J. Crowe.

First one-day international At Sylhet, March 1, 2020 (day/night). **Bangladesh won by 169 runs.** ‡**Bangladesh 321-6** (50 overs) (Liton Das 126*, Mahmudullah 32, Mithun Ali 50); **Zimbabwe 152** (39.1 overs) (W. N. Madhevere 35; Mohammad Saifuddin 3-22). *PoM:* Liton Das. *ODI debut:* W. N. Madhevere (Zimbabwe). *Bangladesh recorded their largest victory – surpassing their 163-run defeat of Sri Lanka at Mirpur in 2017-18 – on the back of Liton Das's second ODI century. Heat and humidity troubled him more than the Zimbabwe attack, and he retired with cramp on 126* off 105 balls in the 37th over, after hitting his second six. But, powered by Mithun Ali (50 off 41) and Mohammad Saifuddin (28* off 15), Bangladesh plundered 94 from the last ten. Saifuddin then took 2-6 in his opening five-over burst. In a miserable effort from Zimbabwe, teenage debutant Wesley Madhevere top-scored with 35. Chamu Chibhabha, in his first ODI since July 2018 after being promoted to captain, suffered a hand injury that ended his series.*

Second one-day international At Sylhet, March 3, 2020 (day/night). **Bangladesh won by four runs.** ‡**Bangladesh 322-8** (50 overs) (Tamim Iqbal 158, Mushfiqur Rahim 55, Mahmudullah 41, Mithun Ali 32*); **Zimbabwe 318-8** (50 overs) (T. S. Kamunhukamwe 51, W. N. Madhevere 52,

Sikandar Raza 66, C. T. Mutombodzi 34, D. T. Tiripano 55*; Taijul Islam 3-52). *PoM:* Tamim Iqbal. *ODI debut:* C. K. Tshuma (Zimbabwe). *When Zimbabwe lost their seventh wicket in the 42nd over, they were still 98 short of victory, and apparently destined for another heavy defeat. But Tino Mutombodzi and Donald Tiripano put on 80 in 7.3 overs to induce anxiety among the Bangladeshis. Even after Mutombodzi holed out off the second ball of the final over, Tiripano slammed his fourth and fifth sixes to bring up a maiden international half-century, from just 26 deliveries, and leave Zimbabwe needing six from two. But Al-Amin Hossain held his nerve, and sealed a series-clinching win. Until then, the day had belonged to Tamim Iqbal, who helped his team to their joint-sixth-highest total, one more than they had made two days earlier. Ending a spell of 23 ODIs without a hundred, he hit 158 off 136, surpassing his own national record – 154 against the same opponents at Bulawayo in 2009. He also became the first Bangladeshi to reach 7,000 ODI runs.*

Third one-day international At Sylhet, March 6, 2020 (day/night). **Bangladesh won by 123 runs** (DLS). **Bangladesh 322-3** (43 overs) (Tamim Iqbal 128*, Liton Das 176; C. T. Mumba 3-69); ‡**Zimbabwe 218** (37.3 overs) (R. W. Chakabva 34, S. C. Williams 30, W. N. Madhevere 42, Sikandar Raza 61; Mohammad Saifuddin 4-41). *PoM:* Liton Das. *PoS:* Liton Das and Tamim Iqbal. *ODI debuts:* Afif Hossain, Mohammad Naim (Bangladesh). *In a riot of record-breaking, Bangladesh ensured Mashrafe bin Mortaza's reign as captain ended with an emphatic victory, his 50th in 88 ODIs in charge, and a 3–0 whitewash. Despite the loss of seven overs to rain, Bangladesh matched their total (off 50 overs) from the second game, with a second century in the series for both Tamim and Liton, who put on 292 inside 41 overs. Tamim finished on 128* from 109, with seven fours and six sixes, but lost the national record he had set three days earlier: Liton racked up 176 from 143, with 16 fours and eight sixes (another national record, breaking the seven hit by Tamim against Zimbabwe at Chittagong in 2010-11; the openers' combined 14 sixes was another best for a Bangladesh innings). Zimbabwe, who added to their problems with a slapdash display in the field, had their target revised to 342 in 43 overs, but they were never in the hunt. In tribute to Mortaza, who had first captained the one-day team nearly a decade earlier, the Bangladesh players wore "thank you captain" and his number (2) on their shirts at the post-match presentation.*

HIGHEST OPENING PARTNERSHIPS IN AN ODI

365	J. D. Campbell /S. D. Hope	West Indies v Ireland at Clontarf	2019
304	Imam-ul-Haq/Fakhar Zaman	Pakistan v Zimbabwe at Bulawayo	2018
292	**Tamim Iqbal/Liton Das**	**Bangladesh v Zimbabwe at Sylhet**	**2019-20**
286	W. U. Tharanga/S. T. Jayasuriya	Sri Lanka v England at Leeds	2006
284	D. A. Warner/T. M. Head	Australia v Pakistan at Adelaide	2016-17
282*	Q. de Kock/H. M. Amla	South Africa v Bangladesh at Kimberley	2017-18
282	W. U. Tharanga/T. M. Dilshan	Sri Lanka v Zimbawe at Pallekele	2010-11
274	J. A. H. Marshall/B. B. McCullum	New Zealand v Ireland at Aberdeen	2008
258*	**D. A. Warner/A. J. Finch**	**Australia v India at Mumbai**	**2019-20**
258	S. C. Ganguly/S. R. Tendulkar	India v Kenya at Paarl	2001-02

First Twenty20 international At Mirpur, March 9, 2020 (floodlit). **Bangladesh won by 48 runs. Bangladesh 200-3** (20 overs) (Tamim Iqbal 41, Liton Das 59, Soumya Sarkar 62*); ‡**Zimbabwe 152** (19 overs) (Mustafizur Rahman 3-32, Aminul Islam 3-34). *PoM:* Soumya Sarkar. *T20I debuts:* T. S. Kamunhukamwe, W. N. Madhevere, C. T. Mumba (Zimbabwe). *Amid fears over the coronavirus, attendance was kept to a fifth of capacity, but that did not affect the hosts' in-form openers, Tamim and Liton. They cracked 92 in 10.2 overs – Bangladesh's best first-wicket T20 stand – before Soumya Sarkar, back from a break to get married, hammered a career-best 62* off 32, hitting five of his team's 12 sixes, equalling the national record. In pursuit of Bangladesh's third-highest total, Zimbabwe went on the offensive: five reached 20, but no one managed more than opener Tinashe Kamunhukamwe's 28.*

Second Twenty20 international At Mirpur, March 11, 2020 (floodlit). **Bangladesh won by nine wickets. Zimbabwe 119-7** (20 overs) (B. R. M. Taylor 59*); ‡**Bangladesh 120-1** (15.5 overs) (Liton Das 60*, Mohammad Naim 33). *PoM:* Liton Das. *PoS:* Liton Das. *T20I debuts:* Hasan Mahmud (Bangladesh); C. K. Tshuma (Zimbabwe). *With attendance restrictions again in place, Zimbabwe's wretched tour came to an appropriately downbeat end. Brendan Taylor found some form at last, with 59* off 48, but Craig Ervine's 29 was the only other significant contribution. Bangladesh sailed home with 25 balls to spare, with the irrepressible Liton making 60* off 45.*

DOMESTIC CRICKET IN BANGLADESH IN 2019-20

UTPAL SHUVRO

The latest edition of the National Cricket League was billed as a battle between Khulna and Rajshahi, who had six titles apiece, but it turned out to be no contest. **Khulna** led from the start, and were crowned champions for a record seventh time; Rajshahi, who had won the previous tournament, were relegated.

Though Khulna dominated throughout, the title was not decided until the final round, when they faced their nearest challengers, Dhaka. Trailing by nearly six points, Dhaka had to win, but Nurul Hasan blasted an unbeaten 150 to give Khulna a 100-run first-innings lead. Dhaka's unconvincing second innings left a target of 117; Khulna cantered home inside 26 overs, losing only one wicket. The match witnessed a shocking incident, when Dhaka pace bowler Shahadat Hossain assaulted team-mate Arafat Sunny, who had refused to shine the ball for him; he had to be restrained by other team-mates. Shahadat, ignored by the national team since 2015 – when he was charged with the torture of an 11-year-old housemaid, briefly jailed, then acquitted – was banned for five years, with two suspended; Sunny and another colleague, Mohammad Shahid, who allegedly provoked Shahadat, were handed one-year suspended bans.

Like the title, Rajshahi's relegation was settled in the last round. They led opponents Rangpur by more than five points, and a draw would have kept them up, but – chasing 249 – they were bundled out for 93.

The Bangladesh Cricket Board ordered each team to pick at least one leg-spinner in every NCL match, in an attempt to strengthen that department of the national side. Two coaches, Jahangir Alam of Dhaka and Rangpur's Masud Pervez Razan, were sacked for failing to comply, though Dhaka escaped punishment when they did it again.

It was a memorable season for Khulna's captain, 37-year-old left-arm spinner Abdur Razzak. Despite missing their final game, he was the NCL's leading wicket-taker, with 31 – no one else managed 20 – and became the first Bangladeshi to 600 first-class wickets when he captured 12 for 140 against Rangpur in the tournament's best match. In a dramatic finish, Khulna completed only the second one-wicket victory in the NCL's history; Razzak had also played in the first, when Khulna beat Sylhet in 2002-03.

But the most remarkable bowling performance came from Sylhet's 18-year-old seamer Ruyel Miah: his eight for 26 against Chittagong was the best innings return by a Bangladeshi quick, and his match haul of 13 for 65 the third-best by any Bangladeshi. **Sylhet** crushed Chittagong in two days to clinch promotion for the first time since two tiers were introduced in 2015-16. Taibur Rahman of Dhaka and Anamul Haque of Khulna were the tournament's leading batsmen: Taibur scored 523 at 58, Anamul 506 at 72. Anamul also passed 500 runs in the franchise-based Bangladesh Cricket League, and scored twin hundreds in both competitions. Sylhet tailender Imran Ali equalled a world record with ducks in six consecutive innings going back to October 2017.

Anamul and Razzak were the vital cogs who ensured **South Zone's** third successive BCL title. Razzak topped this league's bowling list too, with 22 wickets. Due to time constraints, the BCL teams played three league matches, down from six. Players were picked by draft, though plans to make the five-day final a day/night game with a pink ball were discarded. South beat East with a day to spare.

Tamim Iqbal, Bangladesh's most successful batsman, broke a national record in his only BCL match. Playing for East against Central, he smashed the highest first-class score by a Bangladeshi, an unbeaten 334, surpassing Raqibul Hasan's 313 not out for Barisal against Sylhet in 2006-07. Raqibul, fielding for Central, was the first to congratulate him. It was also the highest score on Bangladesh soil, beating 319 by Sri Lanka's Kumar Sangakkara in the Chittagong Test of 2013-14.

In March, only two days of the Dhaka Premier League were played before the Covid-19 pandemic forced the rest to be postponed.

FIRST-CLASS AVERAGES IN 2019-20

BATTING (400 runs)

		M	*I*	*NO*	*R*	*HS*	*100*	*Avge*	*Ct/St*
1	†Tamim Iqbal (*Chittagong/EZ/Bang*)	3	4	1	451	334*	1	150.33	2
2	Anamul Haque (*Khulna/South Zone*)	9	17	4	1,007	151*	4	77.46	6
3	†Nazmul Hossain (*Rajshahi/CZ/Bang*)	6	10	1	617	253*	1	68.55	1
4	Yasir Ali (*Chittagong/East Zone*)	5	9	1	532	165	2	66.50	9
5	Nurul Hasan (*Khulna/South Zone*)	9	13	4	584	155	2	64.88	25/6
6	Mushfiqur Rahim (*Bang/Rajshahi/NZ*)	6	11	1	608	203*	2	60.80	4
7	Marshall Ayub (*Dhaka Met/C Zone*)	7	9	1	473	163	3	59.12	4
8	Shamsur Rahman (*Dhaka Met/S Zone*)	10	15	1	766	133	4	54.71	7
9	†Imrul Kayes (*Khulna/East Zone*)	6	11	2	488	202*	1	54.22	6
10	Saif Hasan (*Dhaka/C Zone/Bang*)	6	9	1	422	220*	1	52.75	1
11	†Taibur Rahman (*Dhaka/Central Zone*)	8	14	1	678	110	2	52.15	4
12	Mahmudullah (*Bang/Dhaka Met/SZ*)	5	9	1	400	111	2	50.00	6
13	Raqibul Hasan (*Dhaka/Central Zone*)	9	16	1	678	99	0	45.20	4
14	Tanveer Haider (*Rangpur/North Zone*)	8	14	2	537	177	1	44.75	8
15	Nasir Hossain (*Rangpur/East Zone*)	8	14	2	513	161*	1	42.75	8
16	Mohammad Ashraful (*Barisal/E Zone*)	8	13	2	463	150*	1	42.09	0
17	†Pinak Ghosh (*Chittagong/East Zone*)	10	18	2	671	121	2	41.93	7
18	†Fazle Mahmud (*Barisal/South Zone*)	10	14	0	587	141	2	41.92	1
19	Suhrawadi Shuvo (*Rangpur/C Zone*)	7	12	1	430	105	1	39.09	6
20	Naeem Islam (*Rangpur/North Zone*)	9	16	0	567	135	1	35.43	2
21	Ariful Haque (*Rangpur/North Zone*)	8	14	1	449	58*	0	34.53	3
22	†Shahriar Nafees (*Barisal/South Zone*)	8	14	1	418	111	1	32.15	6
23	Shuvagata Hom (*Dhaka/Central Zone*)	9	16	1	469	122	2	31.26	10
24	†Junaid Siddique (*Rajshahi/North Zone*)	9	18	0	417	61	0	23.16	21

BOWLING (15 wickets)

		Style	*O*	*M*	*R*	*W*	*BB*	*5I*	*Avge*
1	Ruyel Miah (*Sylhet/East Zone*)	LFM	71.2	13	246	18	8-26	2	13.66
2	Ifran Hossain (*Chittagong/C Zone*)	RM	92.2	16	330	21	6-57	2	15.71
3	Nayeem Hasan (*Bang/Ch'gong/EZ*)	OB	313.2	72	818	44	8-107	4	18.59
4	Taskin Ahmed (*Dhaka Met/N Zone*)	RFM	171.1	34	536	27	5-54	1	19.85
5	Shafiul Islam (*Rajshahi/South Zone*)	RFM	159.1	28	441	22	6-40	1	20.04
6	Ariful Haque (*Rangpur/North Zone*)	RFM	124.2	30	374	17	6-41	1	22.00
7	Farhad Reza (*Rajshahi/South Zone*)	RFM	145.2	32	405	18	6-48	1	22.50
8	Salauddin Sakil (*Dhaka/N Zone*)	LM	168.3	35	534	23	4-77	0	23.21
9	Abdur Razzak (*Khulna/South Zone*)	SLA	416.1	68	1,261	53	7-69	3	23.79
10	Mehedi Hasan snr (*Khulna/S Zone*)	OB	255	63	747	31	5-46	2	24.09
11	Abu Jayed (*Sylhet/East Zone/Bang*)	RFM	134.1	40	422	17	4-49	0	24.82
12	Sumon Khan (*Dhaka/North Zone*)	RM	194.5	42	557	22	5-50	1	25.31
13	Taijul Islam (*Bang/Rajshahi/EZ*)	SLA	301.4	60	856	31	5-58	2	27.61
14	Suhrawadi Shuvo (*Rangpur/CZ*)	SLA	144.4	28	460	16	6-55	1	28.75
15	Rejaur Rahman (*Sylhet/East Zone*)	RM	148.5	16	593	20	5-60	1	29.65
16	Hasan Mahmud (*Chittagong/EZ*)	RM	173.1	36	540	18	4-35	0	30.00
17	Sanjamul Islam (*Rajshahi/N Zone*)	SLA	269	47	776	23	7-115	2	33.73
18	Shuvagata Hom (*Dhaka/C Zone*)	OB	285.4	56	789	23	5-46	1	34.30
19	Arafat Sunny (*Dhaka Met/C Zone*)	SLA	229.3	46	658	19	6-87	2	34.63
20	Shahidul Islam (*Dhaka Met/C Zone*)	RM	183.2	40	601	17	4-29	0	35.35
21	Enamul Haque (*Sylhet/North Zone*)	SLA	160.2	24	576	15	3-85	0	38.40
22	Nazmul Islam (*Dhaka*)	SLA	302.3	59	763	18	5-65	1	42.38

WALTON LED TV NATIONAL CRICKET LEAGUE IN 2019-20

Tier One	*P*	*W*	*L*	*D*	*Pts*
Khulna	6	3	0	3	39.81
Dhaka	6	1	1	4	24.39
Rangpur	6	1	2	3	21.46
Rajshahi	6	1	3	2	18.65

Tier Two	*P*	*W*	*L*	*D*	*Pts*
Sylhet	6	3	2	1	36.04
Dhaka Metropolis	6	1	1	4	25.79
Barisal	6	1	1	4	21.35
Chittagong	6	1	2	3	20.92

Outright win = 8pts; draw = 2pts. Bonus points awarded for the first 100 overs of each team's first innings, when each team have had the chance to face 100 overs or been bowled out: 0.01 batting points for every run over the first 250; 0.5 bowling points for the fifth, seventh and ninth wicket taken.

Sylhet were promoted, and Rajshahi relegated.

NATIONAL CRICKET LEAGUE WINNERS

†1999-2000	Chittagong
2000-01	Biman Bangladesh Airlines
2001-02	Dhaka
2002-03	Khulna
2003-04	Dhaka
2004-05	Dhaka
2005-06	Rajshahi
2006-07	Dhaka
2007-08	Khulna
2008-09	Rajshahi
2009-10	Rajshahi
2010-11	Rajshahi
2011-12	Rajshahi
2012-13	Khulna
2013-14	Dhaka
2014-15	Rangpur
2015-16	Khulna
2016-17	Khulna
2017-18	Khulna
2018-19	Rajshahi
2019-20	Khulna

† *The National Cricket League was not first-class in 1999-2000.*

Khulna have won the title 7 times, Rajshahi 6, Dhaka 5, Biman Bangladesh Airlines, Chittagong and Rangpur 1.

BANGLADESH CRICKET LEAGUE IN 2019-20

	P	*W*	*L*	*D*	*Bonus pts Bat*	*Bonus pts Bowl*	*Pts*
East Zone	3	2*	1	0	2.47	4.0	23.47
South Zone	3	1†	0	2	2.39	4.5	19.89
Central Zone	3	1	1	1	0.00	1.5	11.50
North Zone	3	0	2	1	0.22	4.0	6.22

* *One win by an innings.* † *One win by ten wickets.*

Outright win = 8pts; draw = 2pts. Bonus points awarded for the first 100 overs of each first innings, when each team have had the chance to face 100 overs or been bowled out: 0.01 batting points for every run over the first 250; 0.5 bowling points for the fifth, seventh and ninth wicket taken. A further bonus point was awarded for winning by an innings or by ten wickets.

At Chittagong, February 22–25, 2020. **South Zone won by 105 runs. South Zone 486** (Farhad Reza 103*) **and 140; ‡East Zone 273** (Abdur Razzak 7-102) **and 248.** *South Zone retained their title with a day to spare, thanks to a big first-innings total. They faltered from 189-1 to 283-6, but that brought in Farhad Reza, who scored 103* from No. 8. Slow left-armer Abdur Razzak collected seven wickets, including his 50th of the season, to bowl out East Zone, 213 behind. Though South's second innings was disappointing – No. 8 top-scored again, though this time it was Mehedi Hasan snr, with 53 – they had enough of a cushion to defeat East comfortably on the fourth day.*

The Bangladesh Premier League has its own section (page 831).

INDIAN CRICKET IN 2020

History made – and in the making

SHARDA UGRA

At Brisbane in January 2021, the last hour of the last day of the last Test produced India's greatest result. And because the Border–Gavaskar Trophy against Australia followed months shredded by the pandemic, the game at the Gabba was extra cause for celebration. India's second successive series victory in Australia, after achieving none in 11 visits stretching back to 1947-48, meant everything – to the fans, to the history books and to what the future may hold. The series easily slotted into Test cricket's greatest hits, and became the latest, gleaming advertisement for a format threatened by the runaway popularity of franchise cricket.

Until that series, or rather until its Second Test, India had endured an underwhelming year. Before Boxing Day, they had lost all their three Tests in the calendar year (two in New Zealand, one – harrowingly – at Adelaide),

INDIA IN 2020

	Played	*Won*	*Lost*	*Drawn/No result*
Tests	4	1	3	–
One-day internationals	9	3	6	–
Twenty20 internationals	11	9	1	1

JANUARY	3 T20Is (h) v Sri Lanka 3 ODIs (h) v Australia	(page 673) (page 675)
FEBRUARY / MARCH	2 Tests, 3 ODIs and 5 T20Is (a) in New Zealand	(page 693)
APRIL		
MAY		
JUNE		
JULY		
AUGUST		
SEPTEMBER		
OCTOBER		
NOVEMBER / DECEMBER / JANUARY	4 Tests, 3 ODIs and 3 T20Is (a) v Australia	(page 630)

For a review of Indian domestic cricket from the 2019-20 season, see page 680.

David Gray, AFP/Getty Images

Lining up nicely: Ajinkya Rahane, Jasprit Bumrah, Ravichandran Ashwin, Wriddhiman Saha and Shubman Gill at Sydney, January 2021.

and six of their nine ODIs. Success in T20, with nine wins from ten completed games – two after a super over in New Zealand – was meant to serve as preparation for the T20 World Cup in Australia, only for it to be postponed because of the pandemic. It made space for the IPL, which moved to the UAE.

For more than two years, head coach Ravi Shastri had been saying he was working with the best team India had fielded – but the results had not quite caught up with the branding. At the start of 2020, New Zealand produced Test-match greentops, and presented India with a triple whammy: the head-spinning whirlabout of swing, sideways movement and short stuff. Faced with four seamers in Wellington and five in Christchurch, India didn't pass 242, averaged 180, and managed only four individual half-centuries. Virat Kohli averaged 9.50. In the ODIs, India were blanked 3–0, with New Zealand recording their highest successful chases against them – 348 at Hamilton and 300 at Mount Maunganui. Against Australia in November, India couldn't haul in two big totals at Sydney, but had a consolation win at Canberra. For a team which took pride in their bowling stock, the portents were grim. They also lacked a big hitter. Hardik Pandya was expected to fill the role, but injury problems meant he didn't come to life until some white-ball fireworks in Australia.

The team's year-end resurrection meant these sobering memories were cast aside. The opening Test in Adelaide had begun with the emptiest afternoon for Indian cricket, a full-strength batting line-up shot out for 36, undercutting their previous low of 42, at Lord's in 1974. It was brought about by an Australian bowling performance of exceptional precision and well-deserved fortune: every ball past the bat caught a nick, every nick found safe hands. The Test ended with the first of many injuries, as Pat Cummins broke No. 11 Mohammed Shami's forearm. The talismanic Kohli's pre-planned departure for paternity leave was meant to signal the onset of doom.

In an extraordinary series of events, whose story arc would be slashed off a film script as too improbable, India instead rode their perfect storm. Only two played in all four Tests: stand-in captain Ajinkya Rahane and the indestructible Cheteshwar Pujara. Nine first-team players pulled out of the series at one point or other through injury, a decimation that would have destroyed most other teams, and India used 20 in all. Thanks to the pandemic, they were ready on standby and instantly available. Before their call-ups, each had been a net bowler, an understudy, a drinks carrier, a nobody. What stunned Australia was their composure and capability in the thick of the fight.

Whenever a crisis arose, a player emerged, as if born for that very day. Mohammed Siraj's decision to carry on after hearing of the death of his father made for an emotional debut at Melbourne, where Rahane's century helped square the series. Ravichandran Ashwin and the hamstrung Hanuma Vihari then defended to the death at Sydney. At Brisbane, the second-highest partnership of the series (123) came at the hands of India's Nos 7 and 8, Washington Sundar and Shardul Thakur. There was the smooth, noiseless ascent of Shubman Gill at the top of the order, and the mocking mirth of Rishabh Pant's bat, mangling bowling, scoreboard and expectation.

The most poignant truth after the stunning finish to Brisbane was that the Indian XI who pulled off the boldest heist in modern memory may never play together again. A combination of circumstances ensured that team had between them 13 wickets (including two from opener Rohit Sharma) to Australia's 1,033. Their 329 was the highest successful chase at the ground, where the hosts had not lost since 1988-89.

The reasons behind Indian resilience and recovery were several. The IPL had thrown up cricketers who were no stranger to pressure. They play with or against the world's best for two months a year, blunting any intimidation from overseas opposition. A steady supply of A-tours has led to a familiarity with foreign conditions: other than left-arm paceman Thangarasu Natarajan, all the replacements in Australia were part of the India A set-up, and between them had travelled the world. The white-ball specialists were able to revel in the altered equation of Test cricket, where the bowler is the aggressor.

The series also served as an illustration of the power of sound cricketing fundamentals – practical selections, on-field alertness, smart tactical switches – that are often ignored amid the bluster and marketing of major contests. The lack of these had previously cost India vital victories overseas. If ever Indian cricket needed a shake-up to respect the value of cricketing intelligence, it came in the understated, underrated presence and nous of Rahane.

The victory was also an unplanned, but successful experiment of what could happen if the scale, breadth and depth of Indian cricket is put to use. The decade ahead could ensure multi-format domination by India, of the kind seen only from cricket's two most legendary teams – West Indies and Australia. Despite Shastri's declarations, an Indian side of that stature have yet to show up. But if, five years from now, they do, we will know where it all began.

INDIA v SRI LANKA IN 2019-20

CHETAN NARULA

Twenty20 internationals (3): India 2, Sri Lanka 0

India won their fourth Twenty20 series out of five, overwhelming an inexperienced Sri Lanka. The hosts looked in fine fettle for the T20 World Cup in Australia, scheduled for later in the year, though the prospects for the Sri Lankans seemed less rosy. "The coaching staff and players have got some serious work to do in terms of game plans, match awareness and playing the big moments," said coach Mickey Arthur.

Sri Lanka had stepped in, after Zimbabwe, originally expected to tour, were briefly suspended by the ICC. They had been encouraged when a callow squad won 3–0 in Pakistan in October, but that was followed by a whitewash in Australia, and this was another tough assignment they failed to negotiate. There were a few promising performances to encourage Arthur, but not much more.

With one eye on a busy programme, India rested vice-captain Rohit Sharma and fast bowler Mohammed Shami. It merely underlined the riches at their disposal. Delhi seamer Navdeep Saini was Player of the Series, and prospered thanks as much to his variations as his pace; his five wickets were matched by Shardul Thakur. Jasprit Bumrah appeared for the first time since India's tour of the Caribbean in August 2019 and, after a rusty start, finished the series close to his best. K. L. Rahul, opening in Sharma's absence, made two important contributions.

A short tour was further abbreviated when the first game in Guwahati was abandoned: water had run on to the pitch from the covers, and the groundsmen could not salvage it in the wintry evening conditions, despite deploying irons and hairdryers. Sri Lankan highlights were sparse. At Pune, left-arm wrist-spinner Lakshan Sandakan took three wickets, and Dhananjaya de Silva made their only half-century of the series. In the same match, Angelo Mathews played his first T20 international since August 2018, and reminded everyone he was far from a spent force by hitting 31 off 20 balls.

SRI LANKA TOURING PARTY

*S. L. Malinga, D. M. de Silva, P. W. H. de Silva, D. P. D. N. Dickwella, B. O. P. Fernando, W. I. A. Fernando, M. D. Gunathilleke, C. B. R. L. S. Kumara, A. D. Mathews, B. K. G. Mendis, M. D. K. J. Perera, P. B. B. Rajapaksa, C. A. K. Rajitha, P. A. D. L. R. Sandakan, M. D. Shanaka, I. Udana. *Coach:* J. M. Arthur.

First Twenty20 international At Guwahati, January 5, 2020 (floodlit). **Sri Lanka v ‡India. Abandoned.**

Second Twenty20 international At Indore, January 7, 2020 (floodlit). **India won by seven wickets. Sri Lanka 142-9** (20 overs) (M. D. K. J. Perera 34; S. N. Thakur 3-23); **‡India 144-3** (17.3 overs) (K. L. Rahul 45, S. Dhawan 32, S. S. Iyer 34, V. Kohli 30*). *PoM:* N. Saini. *Shardul Thakur and Navdeep Saini (2-18) compensated for a low-key return by Jasprit Bumrah, fit again after a stress fracture of the back. They took five cheap wickets, while spinners Washington Sundar (1-29) and Kuldeep Yadav (2-38) played their part by claiming top-order scalps. Kusal Perera briefly prospered* *for Sri Lanka, before perishing in search of a fourth six as the run-rate flagged. India's openers, K. L. Rahul and Shikhar Dhawan, then raced to 54 in the powerplay, and Sri Lanka were hampered by the absence of seamer Isuru Udana, who injured his back in the fourth over while fielding.*

Third Twenty20 international At Pune, January 10, 2020 (floodlit). **India won by 78 runs. India 201-6** (20 overs) (K. L. Rahul 54, S. Dhawan 52, M. K. Pandey 31*; P. A. D. L. R. Sandakan 3-35); ‡**Sri Lanka 123** (15.5 overs) (A. D. Mathews 31, D. M. de Silva 57; N. Saini 3-28). *PoM:* S. N. Thakur. *PoS:* N. Saini. *India tinkered with their middle order, but two familiar names swept them to a series-clinching win. Rahul and Dhawan put on 97, before four wickets fell swiftly, left-arm wrist-spinner Lakshan Sandakan taking three for 16 in seven chaotic balls. But Manish Pandey hit 31* off 18, and Virat Kohli 26 off 17 from No. 6 (only once before, against Ireland in June 2018, had he batted so low in a T20 international). Sri Lanka then stumbled to 26-4, with Bumrah moving to an Indian-record 53 T20O wickets, before Angelo Mathews and Dhananjaya de Silva (57 off 36) put on 68 in six overs. India's bowlers snuffed out hopes of a revival, however, as the last six fell for 29; Thakur and Saini again collected five between them.*

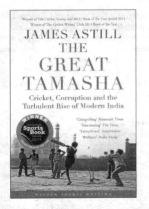

INDIA v AUSTRALIA IN 2019-20

SCOTT BAILEY

One-day internationals (3): India 2, Australia 1

Despite a roasting in the first game, India displayed a resilience that explained why no visiting team had won successive one-day series in the country in a decade. After winning 3–2 the previous March, and by ten wickets in the first game this time, at Mumbai, Australia were on course to set that record straight. But the home batsmen reasserted their authority to give India victories in Rajkot and Bangalore – and the series.

Shikhar Dhawan, Virat Kohli and Rohit Sharma – the usual suspects – all averaged more than 50, maintaining their habit of performing well against Australia. Dhawan top-scored in the first two games, before a shoulder injury sustained in the field prevented him from opening in the decider. Not that his side missed him: Sharma hit a smart century, Kohli made 89, and India won by seven wickets. K. L. Rahul proved himself Mr Fix-It, hitting 146 runs at a strike-rate of 104 from Nos 3, 5 and 2. He also took the gloves in all three games, after designated wicketkeeper Rishabh Pant suffered concussion when batting at Mumbai.

With the ball, India's success was built around Mohammed Shami. He was superb at the death in the two must-win games, and finished with seven wickets, the most on either side. His opening partner, Jasprit Bumrah, claimed only one, but an economy-rate of 4.58 – easily the best of the series – underlined his worth. Spinners Kuldeep Yadav and Ravindra Jadeja took crucial wickets in the second and third games, when they dominated the batsmen during the middle overs.

Australia rarely leave home in the southern summer, but their form batsmen had few problems in adapting to the different surroundings. David Warner continued his magnificent run with a century at Mumbai – the fifth since his disastrous Ashes series – though he contributed little in the two defeats. Meanwhile, Marnus Labuschagne successfully made the transition from red ball to white, and hit 100 busy runs in his two innings. He shared partnerships of 96 and 127 with Steve Smith, arguably Australia's best batsman on this trip. At Bangalore, he hit a magnificent 131, three years to the day since his previous ODI hundred.

If Australia's strength was their top four – captain Aaron Finch weighed in with 162 at 81, and won all three tosses – their weakness was their bottom seven. Ashton Turner hit 13 and four, and was dropped for the trip to South Africa that started in February, while the other Ashton, Agar, claimed only two expensive wickets (Rahul, twice). Leg-spinner Adam Zampa grabbed most – five at 29 – while costing less than five an over. On largely batsmen-friendly surfaces, Australia's opening pair of Mitchell Starc and Pat Cummins struggled after a superb effort in the Wankhede. Combined figures of five for 100 there preceded a collective none for 261 in the defeats.

AUSTRALIA TOURING PARTY

*A. J. Finch, A. C. Agar, A. T. Carey, P. J. Cummins, P. S. P. Handscomb, J. R. Hazlewood, M. Labuschagne, K. W. Richardson, D. J. M. Short, S. P. D. Smith, M. A. Starc, A. J. Turner, D. A. Warner, A. Zampa. *Coach:* J. L. Langer.

S. A. Abbott was named in the original party, but withdrew with a side injury, and was replaced by Short.

INDIA v AUSTRALIA

First One-Day International

At Mumbai, January 14, 2020 (day/night). Australia won by ten wickets. Toss: Australia. One-day international debut: M. Labuschagne.

Finch and Warner gave Australia the perfect start to the series by completing their first ten-wicket demolition of India. Their 258 was the highest for any wicket against India, and the second-highest opening stand for Australia – Warner had put on 284 with Travis Head against Pakistan at Adelaide in 2016-17. Finch began the quicker, though Warner, continuing the sparkling white-ball form that had begun at the World Cup, soon overtook him. Since his return to international cricket the previous June, he had now totted up 1,062 limited-overs runs for Australia at an average of 106. He reached his fifty from 40 balls, and his hundred from 88. In one of Australia's most polished limited-overs performances in years, victory came with 74 balls to spare, and even the normally parsimonious Bumrah went for more than seven an over. Cummins had earlier put Australia on top with a typically tight two for 44 from ten – hitting Pant on the helmet and preventing him from keeping wicket – while Starc finished with three as India stumbled from a healthy 134 for one in the 28th to a sickly 255 all out. Seemingly all of Finch's bowling changes brought a wicket, while categorically none of Kohli's did. The manner of the defeat piled pressure on India's batting, with many questioning the wisdom of placing Rahul higher than Kohli. Play was held up near the end of the Indian innings when a kite – part of the Hindu festival of Makar Sankranti – became tangled in Spidercam.

Player of the Match: D. A. Warner.

India

R. G. Sharma c Warner b Starc	10
S. Dhawan c Agar b Cummins	74
K. L. Rahul c Smith b Agar	47
*V. Kohli c and b Zampa	16
S. S. Iyer c Carey b Starc	4
†R. R. Pant c Turner b Cummins	28
R. A. Jadeja c Carey b Richardson	25
S. N. Thakur b Starc	13
Mohammed Shami c Carey b Richardson	10
K. Yadav run out (Smith)	17
J. J. Bumrah not out	0
Lb 3, w 8	11
1/13 (1) 2/134 (3) 3/140 (2) 4/156 (4) 5/164 (5) 6/213 (7) 7/217 (6) 8/229 (8) 9/255 (10) 10/255 (9) — (49.1 overs)	255
10 overs: 45-1	

Starc 10–0–56–3; Cummins 10–1–44–2; Richardson 9.1–0–43–2; Zampa 10–0–53–1; Agar 10–1–56–1.

Australia

D. A. Warner not out	128
*A. J. Finch not out	110
B 4, lb 7, w 9	20
(no wkt, 37.4 overs)	258
10 overs: 84-0	

S. P. D. Smith, M. Labuschagne, †A. T. Carey, A. J. Turner, A. C. Agar, P. J. Cummins, M. A. Starc, K. W. Richardson and A. Zampa did not bat.

Mohammed Shami 7.4–0–58–0; Bumrah 7–0–50–0; Thakur 5–0–43–0; Yadav 10–0–55–0; Jadeja 8–0–41–0.

Umpires: M. A. Gough and C. Shamshuddin. Third umpire: R. A. Kettleborough.
Referee: R. S. Madugalle.

INDIA v AUSTRALIA

Second One-Day International

At Rajkot, January 17, 2020 (day/night). India won by 36 runs. Toss: Australia.

The restoration of Kohli to No. 3 paid immediate dividends: his controlled 76-ball 78 helped settle the Indian batting powerhouse, and a total of 340 was enough to set up a decider. Runs came from the word go, with openers Sharma and Dhawan both flourishing, before Rahul blasted 80 from 52 at his new position of No. 5. (He also kept the gloves because Pant had not recovered.) The pitch had little in it for the bowlers, and Starc suffered his worst figures in ODIs. Only Zampa had much joy: he removed Kohli for the fifth time in international cricket in less than a year. Warner fell early when an airborne Pandey held a sensational one-handed catch at cover, but Australia stayed in the hunt with a third-wicket stand of 96. At 178 for two in the 31st, with Labuschagne taking to ODI cricket like a duck to water, and Smith apparently heading for another hundred, the game was evenly poised. But both fell to spin as landmarks beckoned, and the game turned. The lower order could not find the firepower to see Australia home.

Player of the Match: K. L. Rahul.

India

R. G. Sharma lbw b Zampa	42
S. Dhawan c Starc b Richardson	96
*V. Kohli c Starc b Zampa	78
S. S. Iyer b Zampa	7
†K. L. Rahul run out (Carey)	80
M. K. Pandey c Agar b Richardson	2
R. A. Jadeja not out	20
Mohammed Shami not out	1
B 5, lb 4, w 5	14
1/81 (1) 2/184 (2) 3/198 (4) 4/276 (3) 5/280 (6) 6/338 (5) (6 wkts, 50 overs)	340
10 overs: 55-0	

K. Yadav, N. Saini and J. J. Bumrah did not bat.

Cummins 10–1–53–0; Starc 10–0–78–0; Richardson 10–0–73–2; Zampa 10–0–50–3; Agar 8–0–63–0; Labuschagne 2–0–14–0.

Australia

D. A. Warner c Pandey b Mohammed Shami	15
*A. J. Finch st Rahul b Jadeja	33
S. P. D. Smith b Yadav	98
M. Labuschagne c Mohammed Shami b Jadeja	46
†A. T. Carey c Kohli b Yadav	18
A. J. Turner b Mohammed Shami	13
A. C. Agar lbw b Saini	25
P. J. Cummins b Mohammed Shami	0
M. A. Starc c Rahul b Saini	6
K. W. Richardson not out	24
A. Zampa c Rahul b Bumrah	6
Lb 10, w 10	20
1/20 (1) 2/82 (2) 3/178 (4) 4/220 (5) 5/221 (3) 6/259 (6) 7/259 (8) 8/274 (7) 9/275 (9) 10/304 (11) (49.1 overs)	304
10 overs: 55-1	

Bumrah 9.1–2–32–1; Mohammed Shami 10–0–77–3; Saini 10–0–62–2; Jadeja 10–0–58–2; Yadav 10–0–65–2.

Umpires: R. A. Kettleborough and V. K. Sharma. Third umpire: M. A. Gough.
Referee: R. S. Madugalle.

INDIA v AUSTRALIA

Third One-Day International

At Bangalore, January 19, 2020 (day/night). India won by seven wickets. Toss: Australia.

India clinched the series with a relatively comfortable win, thanks in the main to Sharma and Kohli. On a slow pitch, Sharma walloped 119, his eighth century against Australia, taking his average against them beyond 60. He and Kohli, who fell a couple of blows short of a ninth hundred against these opponents, added 137 in 24 overs, and broke the back of the chase. Despite Sharma hitting six sixes, there was no unseemly haste, and victory came with 15 balls to spare. Spinners Agar and Zampa imposed more control than their swifter colleagues, with Cummins conspicuously expensive.

Australia were left to rue a lack of oomph at the end of their own innings. After Smith and Labuschagne had taken them to 173 for two in the 32nd, a total north of 300 seemed likely. But the promotion of Starc did not pay off, and only four boundaries came in the last nine overs, all from Smith's bat. Not for the first time, Bumrah's accuracy bought wickets for Shami.

Player of the Match: R. G. Sharma. *Player of the Series:* V. Kohli.

Australia

D. A. Warner c Rahul b Mohammed Shami	3
*A. J. Finch run out (Jadeja/Iyer/Mohammed Shami)	19
S. P. D. Smith c Iyer b Mohammed Shami	131
M. Labuschagne c Kohli b Jadeja	54
M. A. Starc c sub (Y. S. Chahal) b Jadeja	0
†A. T. Carey c Iyer b Yadav	35
A. J. Turner c Rahul b Saini	4
A. C. Agar not out	11
P. J. Cummins b Mohammed Shami	0
A. Zampa b Mohammed Shami	1
J. R. Hazlewood not out	1
Lb 14, w 13	27
1/18 (1) 2/46 (2) 3/173 (4) 4/173 (5) 5/231 (6) 6/238 (7) 7/273 (3) 8/276 (9) 9/282 (10) — (9 wkts, 50 overs)	286
10 overs: 56-2	

Bumrah 10–0–38–0; Mohammed Shami 10–0–63–4; Saini 10–0–65–1; Yadav 10–0–62–1; Jadeja 10–1–44–2.

India

R. G. Sharma c Starc b Zampa	119
†K. L. Rahul lbw b Agar	19
*V. Kohli b Hazlewood	89
S. S. Iyer not out	44
M. K. Pandey not out	8
Lb 2, w 8	10
1/69 (2) 2/206 (1) 3/274 (3) — (3 wkts, 47.3 overs)	289
10 overs: 61-0	

S. Dhawan, R. A. Jadeja, Mohammed Shami, K. Yadav, N. Saini and J. J. Bumrah did not bat.

Cummins 7–0–64–0; Starc 9–0–66–0; Hazlewood 9.3–1–55–1; Agar 10–0–38–1; Zampa 10–0–44–1; Labuschagne 1–0–11–0; Finch 1–0–9–0.

Umpires: M. A. Gough and V. K. Sharma. Third umpire: R. A. Kettleborough.
Referee: R. S. Madugalle.

INDIA v SOUTH AFRICA IN 2019-20

DEBASISH DATTA

One-day internationals (3): India 0, South Africa 0

India were raring to go when South Africa returned five months after playing the Test and Twenty20 legs of this tour (see *Wisden 2020*, page 939). In the meantime, Virat Kohli's side had been hammered in their Tests and one-day matches in New Zealand, though they had won the T20s 5–0. They were itching to get back to winning ways, and close the gap on England at the top of the ODI rankings, ahead of the IPL which was due to start at the end of March. With Shikhar Dhawan, Hardik Pandya and Bhuvneshwar Kumar back after injury, they were set to unleash a full-strength side.

But first rain – a seemingly constant companion to cricket in Dharamsala – washed out the opening match. And then, after initial thoughts that the remaining two games could be played behind closed doors as the coronavirus spread, it was decided to call them off, with the Indian board suggesting the series could be rescheduled (the IPL was later postponed until September). It was an abrupt end to Quinton de Kock's first overseas assignment as South Africa's permanent white-ball captain.

SOUTH AFRICAN TOURING PARTY

*Q. de Kock, T. Bavuma, F. du Plessis, B. E. Hendricks, H. Klaasen, G. F. Linde, K. A. Maharaj, J. N. Malan, D. A. Miller, L. T. Ngidi, A. A. Nortje, A. L. Phehlukwayo, L. L. Sipamla, J. T. Smuts, H. E. van der Dussen, K. Verreynne. *Coach:* M. V. Boucher.

T. Shamsi was originally selected, but withdrew for the birth of his first child and was replaced by Linde. Malan was a late addition to the squad.

First one-day international At Dharamsala, March 12, 2020 (day/night). Abandoned. *Persistent rain washed out the match, echoing the fate of the Twenty20 international between these teams here the previous September.*

Second one-day international At Lucknow, March 15, 2020 (day/night). Cancelled.

Third one-day international At Kolkata, March 18, 2020 (day/night). Cancelled.

DOMESTIC CRICKET IN INDIA IN 2019-20

R. MOHAN

After losing three finals in the previous seven seasons, **Saurashtra** won their maiden Ranji Trophy, having secured a first-innings lead over Bengal on the fifth morning of a match which concluded in front of empty stands, for fear of spreading the coronavirus. Next day, as concerns about the pandemic grew, the BCCI cancelled the rest of the domestic season, including the following week's Irani Cup match, in which Saurashtra would have met the Rest of India.

Saurashtra's triumph continued a 21st-century trend in which the trophy is no longer monopolised by the traditional powerhouses of Indian cricket. They were the sixth first-time winners since 2001-02, though two of their forerunners – Nawanagar, the princedom where Ranjitsinhji himself was once maharajah, and Western India – had won the title before the formation of the state of Saurashtra in 1948.

Left-arm fast bowler Jaydev Unadkat spearheaded their campaign with 67 wickets, one short of the record for a Ranji tournament set by Ashutosh Aman the previous season. Unadkat, who in 2018 had become the most expensive bowler in an IPL auction, was also a key performer in the Duleep Trophy final, where he helped **India Red** beat India Green by an innings. The one-day Deodhar Trophy was won by **India B**, led by Parthiv Patel, who defeated Shubman Gill's India C by 51 runs in the final.

Karnataka claimed a white-ball double by winning two finals against Tamil Nadu. In the 50-over Vijay Hazare Trophy, they cantered to victory in a run-chase halted by rain, after a hat-trick by their seamer Abhimanyu Mithun. A few weeks later, they won the Twenty20 Syed Mushtaq Ali Trophy – by a single run.

Wasim Jaffer retired just short of his 42nd birthday. He finished as the Ranji Trophy's highest scorer, with 12,038 runs, the maker of most centuries (40), the fielder with most catches (200), and the most appearances (156, for Mumbai and Vidarbha).

With the Ranji Trophy now containing 38 teams – Chandigarh had joined since the expansion of the previous season – there was greater opportunity for creating records, especially in the Plate League, for the weaker sides. Rahul Dalal of Arunachal Pradesh scored 1,340 runs, a tournament aggregate second only to V. V. S. Laxman's 1,415 for Hyderabad in 1999-2000. No other player reached 1,000. Santha Moorthy was 40 when

FIVE IN AN INNINGS BY OVER-40s ON FIRST-CLASS DEBUT

Years	*Days*				
51	62	*W. Brown	7-42, 8-31	Tasmania v Victoria at Hobart	1857-58
48	321	*J. Hughes	2-48, 7-46	South v MCC at Lord's	1874
45	308	*L. N. Jones	2-14, 5-8	Minor Counties v Ireland at Rathmines	1937
44	150	A. E. Sellers	5-22, 2-53	Scotland v Ireland at Edinburgh	1920
44	102	W. A. Hay	8-70, 4-48	Otago v Southland at Dunedin	1917-18
42	332	J. A. Doig	7-46, 0-19	Southland v Otago at Invercargill	1914-15
42	141	W. Henty	4-52, 5-26	†Tasmania v Victoria at Launceston	1850-51
41	323	*R. G. Smith	5-94, 0-4	Burma v MCC at Rangoon	1926-27
40	**158**	***S. Moorthy**	**2-51, 5-79**	**Puducherry v Nagaland at Puducherry**	**2019-20**
40	49	F. Wright	5-78, 1-68	Leics v Derbys at Leicester	1895

* *His only first-class match.* † *The first first-class match played in Australia.*

All matches except Moorthy's (Ranji Trophy) and Wright's (County Championship) were friendlies.

The oldest debutant to bowl was C. J. Vels, aged 60 years 269 days, for Orange Free State v MCC at Bloemfontein in 1927-28. The oldest debutant to take a wicket was T. Morris, aged 52 years 262 days, for Players of the USA v Gentlemen of Philadelphia at Belmont in 1893, his only first-class match.

Research: Keith Walmsley

he picked up five for 79 in the second innings of his debut for Puducherry, which made him the oldest player to take five wickets on first-class debut in a major competition. Another newcomer, 28-year-old left-armer Ravi Yadav, achieved a unique feat, bagging a hat-trick in his first over on first-class debut, for Madhya Pradesh against Uttar Pradesh in Elite Group B. In the same group, Mumbai's Sarfaraz Khan hit one of the tournament's three triple-hundreds, but his side won only once.

In November 2019, the Himalayan state of Uttarakhand, one of nine teams admitted to the Ranji Trophy a year earlier, became the first state association in India to provide annual contracts for their senior cricketers, as well as providing scholarships for junior players (male and female), and pledging to open two training centres. Even so, Uttarakhand were relegated back into the Plate League from which they had just been promoted.

Non-playing curiosities of the season included a snake delaying the start of the first-round Ranji game between Andhra Pradesh and Vidarbha, when it slithered on to the pitch at Vijayawada, and the visit of US president Donald Trump to Gujarat in February for the inauguration of the world's largest cricket stadium in Motera. The Sardar Patel Stadium had been completely rebuilt, doubling its capacity, and 110,000 watched Trump join Indian prime minister Narendra Modi on stage, and make a speech mentioning Virat Kohli and "Soochin" Tendulkar.

FIRST-CLASS AVERAGES IN 2019-20

BATTING (650 runs, average 40.00)

		M	*I*	*NO*	*R*	*HS*	*100*	*Avge*	*Ct/St*
1	S. N. Khan (*Mumbai*)	6	9	3	928	301*	3	154.66	5
2	R. Dalal (*Arunachal Pradesh*)	9	17	3	1,340	267*	4	95.71	11/2
3	G. Satish (*Vidarbha*)	8	11	2	727	237	3	80.77	1
4	P. Dogra (*Puducherry*)	9	13	1	967	200	4	80.58	16
5	T. Kohli (*Mizoram*)	9	16	2	998	307*	3	71.28	4
6	†H. S. Bhatia (*India Red/Chhattisgarh*)	9	13	1	855	221	4	71.25	8
7	P. Bisht (*Meghalaya*)	9	15	1	976	250	2	69.71	27/4
8	Mandeep Singh (*Punjab*)	8	13	3	696	204*	2	69.60	4
9	M. A. Agarwal (*India/Karnataka*)	7	10	0	682	243	3	68.20	2
10	S. K. Patel (*Goa*)	10	14	2	799	236	3	66.58	20/2
11	†A. A. Verma (*Goa*)	10	14	1	848	148	4	65.23	6
12	M. D. Rahmatullah (*Bihar*)	9	15	4	695	140	4	63.18	0
13	A. R. Bawne (*Ind Bl/Ind A/Maha'tra*)	11	20	7	785	204*	2	60.38	2
14	A. P. Majumdar (*Bengal*)	8	13	1	704	157	2	58.66	5
15	C. A. Pujara (*India/Saurashtra*)	11	15	0	829	248	1	55.26	7
16	†A. L. Menaria (*Rajasthan*)	8	13	1	660	119*	2	55.00	7
17	Babul Kumar (*Bihar*)	9	15	0	822	195	2	54.80	16
18	†A. V. Vasavada (*Saurashtra*)	10	16	2	763	139	4	54.50	2
19	S. P. Jackson (*Saurashtra*)	10	18	2	809	186	3	50.56	5
20	M. K. Tiwary (*Bengal*)	11	16	2	707	303*	1	50.50	8
21	K. B. Pawan (*Mizoram*)	9	16	2	706	129*	4	50.42	12
22	S. S. Mundhe (*Nagaland*)	9	15	0	753	166	2	50.20	2
23	K. K. Nair (*Ind Red/Ind A/Karnataka*)	13	21	3	870	166*	1	48.33	11
24	†Iqbal Abdulla (*Sikkim*)	9	15	1	673	135	1	48.07	1
25	Yashpal Singh (*Sikkim*)	9	16	1	692	155	2	46.13	8
26	†M. K. Lomror (*India Red/Rajasthan*)	10	16	1	684	126	2	45.60	4

BOWLING (37 wickets)

		Style	*O*	*M*	*R*	*W*	*BB*	*5I*	*Avge*
1	R. Vinay Kumar (*Puducherry*)	RFM	180.2	46	509	45	6-32	4	11.31
2	S. P. Udeshi (*Puducherry*)	SLA	234.2	86	545	45	6-50	3	12.11
3	R. Sanjay Yadav (*Meghalaya*)	SLA	277.5	69	696	55	9-52	5	12.65
4	H. V. Patel (*Haryana*)	RFM	235.2	48	753	52	7-29	4	14.48

		Style	O	M	R	W	BB	5I	Avge
5	J. D. Unadkat (*Ind Red/Saurashtra*)	LFM	394.2	92	1,123	76	7-56	7	14.77
6	Gurender Singh (*Chandigarh*)	SLA	218.2	60	607	40	6-24	3	15.17
7	A. A. Verma (*Goa*)	LB	209.1	45	677	43	6-52	4	15.74
8	D. G. Pathania (*India Blue/Services*)	RM	352.3	78	899	56	5-36	4	16.05
9	M. B. Murasingh (*Tripura*)	RM	293.5	86	834	49	7-63	3	17.02
10	A. Aman (*Bihar*)	SLA	364.4	97	887	49	6-66	5	18.10
11	A. R. Nagwaswalla (*Gujarat*)	LM	269.2	70	753	41	5-50	3	18.36
12	R. Ashwin (*India/Tamil Nadu*)	OB	356.2	87	911	47	7-145	2	19.38
13	K. Gowtham (*India A/Karnataka*)	OB	261	65	737	38	8-60	3	19.39
14	K. V. Sasikanth (*Andhra*)	RM	300.4	76	750	38	5-38	3	19.73
15	Aavesh Khan (*Ind Red/Madhya Pr*)	RM	259.1	55	774	39	5-52	1	19.84
16	J. S. Saxena (*Ind Blue/Ind A/Kerala*)	OB	394.2	62	993	49	7-51	4	20.26
17	S. Pandey (*Services*)	RM	297.1	76	853	41	5-56	1	20.80
18	S. S. Bachhav (*Maharashtra*)	SLA	259.1	36	778	37	5-55	1	21.02
19	R. L. Mali (*Assam*)	RFM	279.3	72	832	39	6-24	3	21.33
20	Ashish Kumar (*Jharkhand*)	RM	250.2	59	806	37	6-79	3	21.78
21	I. H. Chaudhary (*Sikkim*)	RFM	284.2	49	1,093	49	6-39	6	22.30
22	I. M. Lemtur (*Nagaland*)	LM	296.5	69	922	41	7-25	4	22.48
23	Saurabh Kumar (*Ind Blue/Uttar Pr*)	SLA	409.5	86	1,075	45	6-55	5	23.88
24	S. B. Pradhan (*Odisha*)	RM	302.5	46	1,034	40	6-36	3	25.85
25	D. A. Jadeja (*Ind Green/Saurashtra*)	SLA	481.4	104	1,296	39	5-92	1	33.23

DULEEP TROPHY IN 2019-20

	P	W	L	D	1st-inns pts	Pts	Quotient
INDIA RED	2	0	0	2	4	6	1.14
INDIA GREEN	2	0	0	2	0	2	1.19
India Blue	2	0	0	2	0	2	0.63

Outright win = 6pts; draw = 1pt; first-innings lead in a draw = 2pts. India Green qualified by virtue of their superior quotient (runs scored per wicket divided by runs conceded per wicket).

Final At Bangalore, September 4–7, 2019. **India Red won by an innings and 38 runs. ‡India Green 231 and 119** (A. A. Wakhare 5-13); **India Red 388** (A. R. Easwaran 153). *Left-armer Jaydev Unadkat claimed four wickets as India Green slumped to 112-8, but Mayank Markande scored a career-best 76* as the last two wickets more than doubled the total. Opener Abhimanyu Easwaran led India Red's reply, batting seven hours; no one else reached 40, but they took a 157-run lead, before off-spinner Akshay Wakhare rolled over Green for 119 to seal a Red win with a day to spare.*

RANJI TROPHY IN 2019-20

Elite A	P	W	L	D	1st-inns pts	Bonus	Pts	Quotient
GUJARAT	8	5	0	3	2	0	35	1.23
BENGAL	8	4	1	3	4	1	32	1.47
ANDHRA	8	4	2	2	0	1	27	1.17
Punjab	8	3	3	2	2	2	24	1.27
Delhi	8	2	1	5	4	0	21	1.00
Vidarbha	8	2	2	4	4	1	21	1.15
Rajasthan	8	2	4	2	2	1	17	0.84
Kerala	8	1	5	2	2	0	10	0.77
Hyderabad	8	1	6	1	0	0	7	0.50

Elite B	*P*	*W*	*L*	*D*	*1st-inns pts*	*Bonus*	*Pts*	*Quotient*
KARNATAKA	8	4	0	4	2	1	31	1.04
SAURASHTRA	8	3	1	4	8	1	31	1.23
Tamil Nadu	8	2	2	4	2	2	20	1.14
Uttar Pradesh	8	2	1	5	2	1	20	1.09
Himachal Pradesh	8	2	1	5	2	0	19	0.98
Mumbai	8	1	2	5	6	0	17	1.19
Railways	8	1	4	3	6	1	16	0.86
Baroda	8	2	4	2	0	0	14	0.67
Madhya Pradesh	8	0	2	6	6	0	12	0.88
Elite C								
JAMMU & KASHMIR	9	6	1	2	0	1	39	1.46
ODISHA	9	5	2	2	2	4	38	1.21
Services	9	5	2	2	2	2	36	1.04
Haryana	9	5	2	2	2	2	36	1.27
Maharashtra	9	5	3	1	2	1	34	1.10
Jharkhand	9	3	3	3	2	1	24	0.91
Chhattisgarh	9	2	2	5	4	2	23	1.34
Assam	9	1	4	4	4	1	15	0.71
Tripura	9	0	6	3	6	0	9	0.82
Uttarakhand	9	0	7	2	0	0	2	0.53
Plate								
GOA	9	7	0	2	2	4	50	2.34
Puducherry	9	7	1	1	0	5	48	2.33
Chandigarh	9	4	0	5	10	4	43	3.49
Meghalaya	9	5	3	1	0	3	34	1.30
Bihar	9	3	1	5	6	1	30	1.19
Nagaland	9	2	3	4	2	1	19	0.76
Manipur	9	2	7	0	0	0	12	0.39
Mizoram	9	1	6	2	4	0	12	0.42
Sikkim	9	1	5	3	2	0	11	0.70
Arunachal Pradesh	9	0	6	3	0	0	3	0.45

Outright win = 6pts; draw = 1pt; first-innings lead in a draw = 2pts; bonus for winning by an innings or ten wickets = 1pt. Teams tied on points were ranked on most wins, then on head-to-head result, and then on quotient (runs scored per wicket divided by runs conceded per wicket).

The five teams with most points across Elite A and B, the top two from Elite C and the top Plate team advanced to the quarter-finals.

Quarter-finals Bengal drew with Odisha but qualified by virtue of their first-innings lead; Gujarat beat Goa by 464 runs; Karnataka beat Jammu & Kashmir by 167 runs; Saurashtra drew with Andhra but qualified by virtue of their first-innings lead.

Semi-finals Bengal beat Karnataka by 174 runs; Saurashtra beat Gujarat by 92 runs.

Final At Rajkot, March 9–13, 2020. **Drawn. Saurashtra won by virtue of their first-innings lead. ‡Saurashtra 425** (A. V. Vasavada 106) **and 105-4; Bengal 381**. *Saurashtra, losing finalists the previous year, claimed their first Ranji Trophy in an empty stadium: the last day was played behind closed doors because of the worsening Covid-19 pandemic. Cheteshwar Pujara, who had retired on the opening day with a fever, resumed on the second morning, and helped his childhood friend Arpit Vasavada add 142 for the sixth wicket. Saurashtra's total of 425 looked vulnerable as Bengal reached 354-6 on the fourth day, and it became clear the title would be settled on first innings. But Jaydev Unadkat made the crucial breakthroughs on the final morning, and Saurashtra led by 44. For part of the second day, umpire K. N. Ananthapadmanabhan stood at both ends, after his colleague Chettithody Shamshuddin was struck by a ball and taken to hospital. Yeshwant Barde arrived to stand from the third day onwards.*

RANJI TROPHY WINNERS

1934-35	Bombay	1963-64	Bombay	1992-93	Punjab
1935-36	Bombay	1964-65	Bombay	1993-94	Bombay
1936-37	Nawanagar	1965-66	Bombay	1994-95	Bombay
1937-38	Hyderabad	1966-67	Bombay	1995-96	Karnataka
1938-39	Bengal	1967-68	Bombay	1996-97	Mumbai
1939-40	Maharashtra	1968-69	Bombay	1997-98	Karnataka
1940-41	Maharashtra	1969-70	Bombay	1998-99	Karnataka
1941-42	Bombay	1970-71	Bombay	1999-2000	Mumbai
1942-43	Baroda	1971-72	Bombay	2000-01	Baroda
1943-44	Western India	1972-73	Bombay	2001-02	Railways
1944-45	Bombay	1973-74	Karnataka	2002-03	Mumbai
1945-46	Holkar	1974-75	Bombay	2003-04	Mumbai
1946-47	Baroda	1975-76	Bombay	2004-05	Railways
1947-48	Holkar	1976-77	Bombay	2005-06	Uttar Pradesh
1948-49	Bombay	1977-78	Karnataka	2006-07	Mumbai
1949-50	Baroda	1978-79	Delhi	2007-08	Delhi
1950-51	Holkar	1979-80	Delhi	2008-09	Mumbai
1951-52	Bombay	1980-81	Bombay	2009-10	Mumbai
1952-53	Holkar	1981-82	Delhi	2010-11	Rajasthan
1953-54	Bombay	1982-83	Karnataka	2011-12	Rajasthan
1954-55	Madras	1983-84	Bombay	2012-13	Mumbai
1955-56	Bombay	1984-85	Bombay	2013-14	Karnataka
1956-57	Bombay	1985-86	Delhi	2014-15	Karnataka
1957-58	Baroda	1986-87	Hyderabad	2015-16	Mumbai
1958-59	Bombay	1987-88	Tamil Nadu	2016-17	Gujarat
1959-60	Bombay	1988-89	Delhi	2017-18	Vidarbha
1960-61	Bombay	1989-90	Bengal	2018-19	Vidarbha
1961-62	Bombay	1990-91	Haryana	2019-20	Saurashtra
1962-63	Bombay	1991-92	Delhi		

Bombay/Mumbai have won the Ranji Trophy 41 times, Karnataka 8, Delhi 7, Baroda 5, Holkar 4, Bengal, Hyderabad, Madras/Tamil Nadu, Maharashtra, Railways, Rajasthan and Vidarbha 2, Gujarat, Haryana, Nawanagar, Punjab, Saurashtra, Uttar Pradesh and Western India 1.

IRANI CUP IN 2019-20

Ranji Trophy Champions (Saurashtra) v Rest of India

At Rajkot, March 18–22, 2020. **Cancelled.** *Called off because of the Covid-19 pandemic.*

VIJAY HAZARE TROPHY IN 2019-20

Four 50-over leagues plus knockout

Quarter-finals Gujarat beat Delhi by six wickets (VJD); Karnataka beat Puducherry by eight wickets; Chhattisgarh v Mumbai, and Punjab v Tamil Nadu, were no-results, but Chhattisgarh and Tamil Nadu went through on better qualifying record.

Semi-finals Karnataka beat Chhattisgarh by nine wickets; Tamil Nadu beat Gujarat by five wickets.

Final At Bangalore, October 25, 2019. **Karnataka won by 60 runs** (VJD). **Tamil Nadu 252** (49.5 overs) (A. Mithun 5-34); ‡**Karnataka 146-1** (23 overs). *When rain ended play, Karnataka were way ahead of a par score of 86. Abhinav Mukund (85) and Baba Apparajith (66) had steered Tamil Nadu to 148-2, before medium-pacer Abhimanyu Mithun collected career-best figures, finishing off the innings with a hat-trick. K. L. Rahul (52*) and Mayank Agarwal (69*) shared a stand of 112* before rain ended the game.*

DEODHAR TROPHY IN 2019-20

50-over league for India A, India B and India C, plus final

Final At Ranchi, November 4, 2019. **India B won by 51 runs.** ‡**India B 283-7** (50 overs) (I. C. Porel 5-43); **India C 232-9** (50 overs). *Seventeen-year-old Yashasvi Jaiswal (54) dominated the first half of India B's innings, and Kedar Jadhav, twice his age, the second, with 86 from 94 balls before becoming Ishan Porel's fifth victim. Priyam Garg, who would be Jaiswal's captain in the Under-19 World Cup a few months later, made 74 from 77 in reply, but could not find enough support to challenge B's total.*

SYED MUSHTAQ ALI TROPHY IN 2019-20

Five 20-over leagues, two super leagues, plus semis and final

Semi-finals Karnataka beat Haryana by eight wickets; Tamil Nadu beat Rajasthan by seven wickets.

Final At Surat, December 1, 2019 (floodlit). **Karnataka won by one run. Karnataka 180-5** (20 overs); ‡**Tamil Nadu 179-6** (20 overs). *First-time winners the previous season, Karnataka retained their title, despite a first-ball duck for Mayank Agarwal, their hero in the 2018-19 final. Captain Manish Pandey hit 60* in 45 balls to lift them to 180; Baba Apparajith (40) and Vijay Shankar (44) took Tamil Nadu's run-chase from 80-4 to 151, but they fell just short.*

The Dream11 Indian Premier League has its own section (page 835).

IRISH CRICKET IN 2020

Toppling the world champions – twice

IAN CALLENDER

For the second year running, a game against world champions England was the highlight for Irish cricket – and this time they had a victory to savour. A successful run-chase, in the last of three World Cup Super League matches in Southampton, was Ireland's first away win against England, and completed a satisfactory, if much curtailed, year which also included victory over West Indies, the T20 world champions, in the Caribbean, and a first T20 win over Afghanistan in more than six years.

The games against England were Ireland's last of the year, after the pandemic struck in March and wiped out their entire home fixture list. Series against Bangladesh, New Zealand and Pakistan were to be rearranged, as well as visits to Zimbabwe and Sri Lanka. Quite when Ireland would next play a Test, however, was uncertain: their last was at Lord's in July 2019, since when matches against Afghanistan, Zimbabwe and Bangladesh had been postponed even before Covid-19, because of the cost. A proposed Test away to

IRELAND IN 2020

	Played	*Won*	*Lost*	*Drawn/No result*
Tests	–	–	–	–
One-day internationals	6	1	5	–
Twenty20 internationals	6	2	3	1

JANUARY	3 ODIs and 3 T20Is (a) v West Indies	(page 777)
FEBRUARY		
MARCH	3 T20Is (in India) v Afghanistan	(page 620)
APRIL		
MAY		
JUNE		
JULY / AUGUST	3 ODIs (a) v England	(page 349)
SEPTEMBER		
OCTOBER		
NOVEMBER		
DECEMBER		

For a review of Irish domestic cricket from the 2019-20 season, see page 689.

Mike Hewitt, Getty Images

School of hard knocks: captain Andy Balbirnie and his deputy, Paul Stirling, go back a long way.

Afghanistan in January 2021 went the same way, leaving a Test in Sri Lanka in December as the only one on the slate. Yet savings made from *not* playing will stand Cricket Ireland in good stead after a year when they had to place staff on furlough, and turnover shrank by almost 40%.

Ireland started 2020 with a new captain, Andrew Balbirnie, while his great friend Paul Stirling – they had come through every age group together since the Under-13s – was appointed vice-captain. They did not have an auspicious start in the Caribbean in January. West Indies won the first and third 50-over matches with time to spare, and in between Ireland squandered a wonderful chance of victory, missing two run-out opportunities in the last over, before West Indies crossed the line with a six off the penultimate ball.

There was delight, however, in the first match of the T20 series, when the 20-year-old left-arm seamer Josh Little held his nerve. With West Indies needing five from the last three balls, Little conceded none, and dismissed Dwayne Bravo. After the second game was washed out, West Indies tied the series with a nine-wicket win in St Kitts.

In March, there was a feeling of déjà vu as Afghanistan won the first two matches of a T20 series, taking their winning run over Ireland to 12. But finally the Irish hit back, skilfully defending a modest target of 143. Little could not quite repeat his final-over heroics: ten (plus a wide) came from his last three deliveries as Afghanistan tied the scores. But Ireland triumphed in the super over, with Kevin O'Brien hitting Rashid Khan's last delivery for six. The following day, the World Health Organisation declared a pandemic.

It was more than four months before Ireland made it on to the field again, in biosecure conditions at the Rose Bowl. In the first two matches, England were untroubled by totals of 172 and 212 – and Ireland got that many only thanks to fifties from new cap Curtis Campher, a 21-year-old Irish passport-holder from South Africa who had not even played club cricket in Ireland. In the final match, Eoin Morgan thumped a century against his former countrymen as England racked up 328 – one more than they had managed during the 2011 World Cup, when they were banjaxed in Bangalore. Ireland had made 329 that day, and did so again. Stirling and Balbirnie both scored a century, sharing a second-wicket stand of 214, and Kevin O'Brien – the hero of Bangalore – hit the winning run off the penultimate ball.

Six of the winning team in Southampton were under 25, including Harry Tector, who was with O'Brien at the end. He had made his ODI debut in the first game at the expense of William Porterfield – and, when a 16-man squad was chosen for another series against Afghanistan early in 2021, the former captain was a notable absentee. However, Porterfield does have a full-time contract for 2021, with Campher, Little and 23-year-old David Delany the new names on an 18-man list. Missing were Stuart Thompson, Tyrone Kane and Boyd Rankin, after 118 internationals in two spells dating back to 2007, either side of a flirtation with England.

There was a change in the coaching staff too. Rob Cassell, who accepted a post with Rajasthan Royals in the IPL, was replaced by Stuart Barnes, who had also been head coach Graham Ford's assistant during his two-year spell with Surrey.

Balbirnie, Stirling and Gareth Delany played for English counties in the T20 Blast, all with some success. It was invaluable experience for players who will be key to Ireland's white-ball prospects in a future which – pandemic permitting – includes two T20 World Cups just 12 months apart.

Ireland's women have a 50-over World Cup qualifier to look forward to in Sri Lanka in July, but 2020 was a year to forget. They did not play a single international match.

DOMESTIC CRICKET IN IRELAND IN 2020

IAN CALLENDER

There was no first-class cricket in Ireland in 2020. Because of the Covid-19 crisis, the game was not given the go-ahead until the middle of July, when Cricket Ireland took the decision to cancel the three-day Interprovincial Championship, and restricted all matches at club level to the Twenty20 format.

The provincial teams did not take the field until August, when the T20 Interprovincial Trophy began, and the 50-over Interprovincial Cup finally started in mid-September. It had been scheduled to expand to six matches for each of the three sides, but reverted to the usual four. The first two fixtures, between **Northern Knights** and **North West Warriors**, were rained off, and **Leinster Lightning** won all four of the remaining games; they have won the competition every year, apart from the inaugural season in 2013 (and also regained the T20 trophy). Five of their batsmen passed 100 runs: the uncapped Stephen Doheny hit 79 in the first match against Northern, and was the leading run-scorer with 142 at 47. Simi Singh headed the averages with 104 at 52, helped by an unbeaten 63 in the return game with the Knights; he also led the bowlers' lists, his off-spin claiming ten wickets at 13.

The women's Super Series was cut from three teams to two, who played eight 50-over games – unscathed by the weather – though the T20 fixtures were dropped. **Typhoons** and **Scorchers** won four matches each; Typhoons, led by Ireland captain Laura Delany, clinched the title on net run-rate.

TEST TRIANGLE INTERPROVINCIAL CUP IN 2020

50-over league

	P	*W*	*L*	*NR*	*Bonus*	*Pts*	*NRR*
Leinster	4	4	0	0	2	18	1.42
Northern.	4	0	2	2	0	4	–1.33
North West.	4	0	2	2	0	4	–1.55

Winners of Irish Leagues and Cups

All-Ireland T20 Cup **YMCA**. Leinster League Cup **YMCA**. Munster T20 Blast **Cork County**. Northern League Cup **North Down**. Northern T20 Cup **CIYMS**. North West Senior Cup **Donemana**.

The Test Triangle Interprovincial Trophy appears on page 868.

NEW ZEALAND CRICKET IN 2020

Kane and able

ANDREW ALDERSON

New Zealand led the world in their response to Covid-19, and by the start of 2021 their cricketers were on top too: the Test side were ranked No. 1 for the first time in history. In short, they made the most of a crisis, thanks to a balanced pace attack, and the batting of Kane Williamson, who welded together the top order.

After an unbeaten home run was extended to a record 17 Tests, the robust strains of the team song emanating from the dressing-room at Christchurch's Hagley Oval on January 6 marked a cycle of redemption. It was a big contrast to the emergency summit eight years earlier, in former captain Brendon McCullum's Cape Town hotel room, to discuss how the side – then ranked eighth – could rekindle their soul after being routed by South Africa. Now, fans cherish a team built on inclusivity, humility and the relentless pursuit of excellence. As Williamson noted: "Under Brendon and Hess [former coach

NEW ZEALAND IN 2020

	Played	*Won*	*Lost*	*Drawn/No result*
Tests	6	5	1	–
One-day internationals	4	3	1	–
Twenty20 internationals	11	4	6	1

DECEMBER JANUARY	3 Tests (a) v Australia	(see *Wisden 2020*, page 896)
JANUARY FEBRUARY MARCH	2 Tests, 3 ODIs and 5 T20Is (h) v India	(page 693)
	1 ODI (a) v Australia	(page 627)
APRIL		
MAY		
JUNE		
JULY		
AUGUST		
SEPTEMBER		
OCTOBER		
NOVEMBER DECEMBER	2 Tests and 3 T20Is (h) v West Indies	(page 707)
DECEMBER JANUARY	2 Tests and 3 T20Is (h) v Pakistan	(page 714)

For a review of New Zealand domestic cricket from the 2019-20 season, see page 722.

Michael Bradley, AFP/Getty Images

Triple-centurion: Tim Southee ended the Pakistan series on 302 Test wickets; Trent Boult had 281.

Mike Hesson] there were drastic changes in culture, and from our perspective it's been building, growing and adjusting that."

While chaos raged overseas, in New Zealand packed embankments enjoyed the privilege of watching cricket at boutique grounds. For most of the year, isolation hotels stood between the pandemic and the community. The West Indian and Pakistan players grappled with social distancing in quarantine. When they emerged, they were just as ill-equipped to cope with a juggernaut of runs and a barrage of pace. New Zealand claimed uncharted territory with six straight Test wins, against India, West Indies and Pakistan. Only one – the first against Pakistan – went to a fifth day.

Individual highlights built team victories. Williamson's 360-degree catalogue of strokes delivered 498 Test runs at 83 for the calendar year, including a career-best 251 against West Indies at Hamilton (he started 2021 pretty well too, with 238 against Pakistan at Christchurch). His captaincy also sparkled: he marshalled his bowlers deftly, declared strategically at Mount Maunganui, and enforced the follow-on at Hamilton. However, he made his best decision ahead of the Wellington Test, which he sat out to prepare for parenthood with his wife, Sarah. Their daughter was born during the match.

Tim Southee, Williamson's chief lieutenant, became the third New Zealander to 300 Test wickets, after Richard Hadlee and Daniel Vettori, with Trent Boult (281) not far behind. In 2020, Southee took 30 at 17, generating enough nagging movement at 80mph to keep batsmen guessing. He was matched by heir apparent Kyle Jamieson, who made the most of his 6ft 8in. Steepling bounce contributed towards 25 wickets at 14; he also averaged 49 with the bat, suggesting that all-rounder status was within reach. Neil Wagner continued to steam in, and took 18 wickets at 24 in his four Tests, finishing the year with 219.

One-day internationals were less of a priority, since Twenty20s had been the focus ahead of the World Cup, which was eventually postponed. Back at the start of the year, New Zealand lost all five T20s to India, suffering yet more super-over anguish, twice. Given the later riches, it is remarkable to recall the rants when coach Gary Stead took what the board described as a "planned break" after eight straight defeats across formats. Phone-ins ran red-hot, and former captain Jeremy Coney said: "If it's too much for them... you can go and get a job in a hardware store and see your family every night." But the criticism melted away when India were despatched 3–0 in the ODIs, starting with a Ross Taylor-led record chase of 348, before both Tests were won as well. The 2019-20 summer finished prematurely, with the echoes of balls hitting hoardings at an empty Sydney Cricket Ground as lockdown loomed.

When play resumed, new talent emerged during T20 wins over West Indies and Pakistan. Tim Seifert, Glenn Phillips and Johannesburg-born Devon Conway – who became eligible on August 28 – shone with the bat, and Jacob Duffy showed promise with the ball. Injuries stymied Lockie Ferguson, although he did claim five for 21, New Zealand's second-best T20 figures, to ensure victory over West Indies at Auckland.

The women's team struggled, despite the energy of new captain Sophie Devine and the experience of new coach Bob Carter. In January, they lost a one-day series to South Africa for the first time. Form remained elusive after the enforced break, too – crushed 3–0 by Australia, including a 232-run thumping. New Zealand did win the T20 series against South Africa in February, and pinched a game off Australia in September, but sank at the World Cup, where they finished third in their group.

Lockdown did at least offer a glimpse of players operating beyond their usual trade. Williamson fed his dog backyard slip catches, all applauded on social media; Colin de Grandhomme reconnected with his electrician apprenticeship; Ferguson developed a speedball radar app. Commercial future-proofing also took place. New Zealand Cricket signed with new local broadcasters for the first time this century: telecoms giant Spark and TVNZ replaced Sky on the television front, and Mediaworks swooped on the radio rights when NZME failed to renew their contract.

Infrastructure improvements included the erection of floodlights at Hagley Oval, and the development of a training hub at Mount Maunganui's Bay Oval. That has plans for an all-weather, 24-pitch greenhouse, where bespoke conditions can be dialled up using technology adapted from the Central Otago fruit-growing industry.

NZC's budgeted \$2.4m loss somehow morphed into a \$1.5m net surplus, mainly thanks to operating savings, including a staff restructure, which were enacted mid-year. Inbound tours were largely unaffected by Covid-19, though the various bubbles required by government protocols ramped up the costs.

In the boardroom, New Zealand gained international clout. Former NZC chairman Greg Barclay took up a similar role at the ICC, while the players' association boss Heath Mills was appointed executive chairman of FICA, the international parent body.

NEW ZEALAND v INDIA IN 2019-20

ANDREW ALDERSON

Twenty20 internationals (5): New Zealand 0, India 5
One-day internationals (3): New Zealand 3, India 0
Test matches (2): New Zealand 2 (120pts), India 0 (0pts)

These teams seemed to be heading in different directions as the tour began. India had despatched allcomers since New Zealand beat them in the World Cup semi-final in July 2019: West Indies (twice), South Africa, Bangladesh, Sri Lanka and Australia were seen off in various formats. New Zealand, meanwhile, were reeling from a whitewash in Australia – who won all three Tests by more than 240 runs – dousing speculation that this was their finest team.

The Twenty20s continued the trend: India's IPL muscle memory kept them unbeaten. Their batting heroes were K. L. Rahul, who collected 224 runs despite being lumbered with the wicketkeeping gloves, and Shreyas Iyer, who made 153; they would lead the way in the 50-over matches too, with 204 and 217 respectively. However, the 5–0 scoreline disguised the level of drama in a series that featured later than usual starts after New Zealand Cricket acceded to Indian television demands: the fourth match, at Wellington, ended after midnight. New Zealand could not escape their cricketing kryptonite, the super over, which had proved a step too far in the World Cup final and November's T20 decider against England. Now, in the third and fourth matches, they endured two more.

Kane Williamson was forced to admit that super overs "certainly haven't been our friend" as his side stumbled to two more agonising defeats. As the angst grew, radio phone-ins brimmed with callers relieved that the Super Rugby competition was beginning earlier than normal. Critics had a handy target: after eight successive defeats, head coach Gary Stead then took what NZC described as a planned break, sitting out the one-day series. Conspiracy theories abounded, and the former Test captain Jeremy Coney fanned the flames: "Would you call it desertion, or would you just say it's a really bad look?"

The criticism dissolved when India's juggernaut was halted in the 50-over matches, starting with a Ross Taylor-led chase of 348. That performance turned the tables: Jasprit Bumrah failed to take a wicket in 30 overs (though he was India's most economical seamer), while Virat Kohli's footwork struggled to counter a dogged short-of-a-length line outside off stump, too full to pull and too short to drive. He made 51 in the opening ODI, but fell away alarmingly, and dragged the Indian batting down with him; he averaged less than ten in the Tests, his second-lowest in a series. Kohli also lost his cool in the Second Test: he seemingly mouthed a Hindi insult after Williamson's dismissal in the first innings, and swore at the crowd following Tom Latham's departure. He jousted with the media when asked if he should be setting a better example.

Michael Bradley, AFP/Getty Images

Taking flight: K. L. Rahul was India's leading scorer on the tour.

The yin of Kohli's batting and general attitude was balanced by the yang of Kyle Jamieson, a 25-year-old Aucklander who made his one-day and Test debuts, and earned match awards in both series. At 6ft 8in, he was the tallest man to represent New Zealand, and found awkward bounce to take nine Test wickets at 16. More surprisingly, his batting proved useful in a low-scoring series: down at No. 9, he hit 44 at Wellington and 49 at Christchurch, demoralising the Indians. Jamieson's contribution with the ball was trumped only by Tim Southee, who showed what a blunder it had been to rest him from the Third Test in Sydney at the start of the year. He took 14 wickets at 13 in the Tests, which suggested he had recovered from the strain of bowling all three dispiriting super overs during the New Zealand summer.

INDIAN TOURING PARTY

*V. Kohli (T/50/20), M. A. Agarwal (T/50), R. Ashwin (T), J. J. Bumrah (T/50/20), Y. S. Chahal (50/20), S. R. Dube (50/20), S. Gill (T), S. S. Iyer (50/20), R. A. Jadeja (T/50/20), K. M. Jadhav (50), Mohammed Shami (T/50/20), M. K. Pandey (50/20), R. R. Pant (T/50/20), C. A. Pujara (T), A. M. Rahane (T), K. L. Rahul (50/20), W. P. Saha (T), N. Saini (T/50/20), S. V. Samson (20), I. Sharma (T), R. G. Sharma (20), P. P. Shaw (T/50), S. N. Thakur (50/20), G. H. Vihari (T), M. S. Washington Sundar (20), K. Yadav (50/20), U. T. Yadav (T). *Coach:* R. J. Shastri.

S. Dhawan was originally named in both white-ball squads, but injured his shoulder shortly before departure, and was replaced by Samson for the T20s and Shaw for the ODIs. R. G. Sharma was originally selected for the 50-over series, but tore a calf muscle in the final T20 match, and was replaced by Agarwal.

NEW ZEALAND v INDIA

First Twenty20 International

At Auckland, January 24, 2020 (floodlit). India won by six wickets. Toss: India. Twenty20 international debut: H. K. Bennett.

The self-belief bred by the IPL was exemplified by Shreyas Iyer, a fringe player anxious to nail down a permanent spot in the powerful Indian line-up. Entering at halfway after Rahul's rapid 56, he also rattled along at two a ball, unperturbed by the loss of Kohli to a full-length dive by Guptill at deep midwicket – a brilliant effort which partly made up for the team's earlier comedic failure to run out Rahul, despite two attempts to throw the stumps down. India never panicked, even though New Zealand had earlier scored quickly themselves: Williamson thwacked 51 from 26, including successive sixes off Thakur, and three fours in four balls to dent the figures of leg-spinner Chahal. Both sides hit ten sixes in all.

Player of the Match: S. S. Iyer.

New Zealand

		B	*4/6*
1 M. J. Guptill *c 1 b 5*	30	19	4/1
2 C. Munro *c 9 b 8*	59	42	6/2
3 *K. S. Williamson *c 3 b 9*	51	26	4/4
4 C. de Grandhomme *c 5 b 7*	0	2	0
5 L. R. P. L. Taylor *not out*	54	27	3/3
6 †T. L. Seifert *c 4 b 11*	1	2	0
7 M. J. Santner *not out*	2	2	0
Lb 1, w 5	6		
6 overs: 68-0 (20 overs)	203-5		

1/80 2/116 3/117 4/178 5/181

8 T. G. Southee, 9 I. S. Sodhi, 10 B. M. Tickner and 11 H. K. Bennett did not bat.

Bumrah 24–8–31–1; Thakur 18–5–44–1; Mohammed Shami 24–6–53–0; Chahal 24–8–32–1; Dube 18–7–24–1; Jadeja 12–2–18–1.

India

		B	*4/6*
1 R. G. Sharma *c 5 b 7*	7	6	0/1
2 †K. L. Rahul *c 8 b 9*	56	27	4/3
3 *V. Kohli *c 1 b 10*	45	32	3/1
4 S. S. Iyer *not out*	58	29	5/3
5 S. R. Dube *c 8 b 9*	13	9	1/1
6 M. K. Pandey *not out*	14	12	0/1
W 10, nb 1	11		
6 overs: 65-1 (19 overs)	204-4		

1/16 2/115 3/121 4/142

7 R. A. Jadeja, 8 S. N. Thakur, 9 Y. S. Chahal 10 Mohammed Shami and 11 J. J. Bumrah did not bat.

Southee 24–5–48–0; Santner 24–5–50–1; Bennett 24–3–36–0; Tickner 18–4–34–1; Sodhi 24–6–36–2.

Umpires: C. M. Brown and S. B. Haig. Third umpire: A. Mehrotra.
Referee: B. C. Broad.

NEW ZEALAND v INDIA

Second Twenty20 International

At Auckland, January 26, 2020 (floodlit). India won by seven wickets. Toss: New Zealand.

India's Republic Day was celebrated in style, with victory set up by superb death bowling from Bumrah. Only 12 runs came from the 18th and 20th overs as he mixed up yorkers, good-length deliveries and slower balls. The closest New Zealand came to momentum was when Munro unintentionally bumped into Thakur while attempting a quick single in the powerplay, which rugby aficionados joked should have earned him a yellow card. The hosts did not manage a boundary between the ninth and 16th overs – Jadeja whisked through his spell without conceding one – and a total of 132 never looked enough, even when Sharma departed to the sixth delivery. The pivotal over was the 15th, bowled by Bennett: Rahul top-edged a six, a wayward bouncer shot away for five wides, then New Zealand missed a run-out. India needed a run a ball, and strolled home despite the loss of Iyer, to a diving catch from Southee, after a stand of 86.

Player of the Match: K. L. Rahul.

New Zealand

		B	4/6
1 M. J. Guptill *c 3 b 8*	33	20	4/2
2 C. Munro *c 3 b 5*	26	25	2/1
3 *K. S. Williamson *c 9 b 7*	14	20	0
4 C. de Grandhomme *c and b 7*	3	5	0
5 L. R. P. L. Taylor *c 1 b 11*	18	24	0
6 †T. L. Seifert *not out*	33	26	1/2
7 M. J. Santner *not out*	0	0	0
Lb 1, w 4	5		
6 overs: 48-1 (20 overs)	132-5		

1/48 2/68 3/74 4/81 5/125

8 T. G. Southee, 9 I. S. Sodhi, 10 B. M. Tickner and 11 H. K. Bennett did not bat.

Thakur 12–8–21–1; Mohammed Shami 24–11–22–0; Bumrah 24–9–21–1; Chahal 24–5–33–0; Dube 12–4–16–1; Jadeja 24–9–18–2.

India

		B	4/6
1 R. G. Sharma *c 5 b 8*	8	6	2
2 †K. L. Rahul *not out*	57	50	3/2
3 *V. Kohli *c 6 b 8*	11	12	1
4 S. S. Iyer *c 8 b 9*	44	33	1/3
5 S. R. Dube *not out*	8	4	0/1
W 7	7		
6 overs: 40-2 (17.3 overs)	135-3		

1/8 2/39 3/125

6 M. K. Pandey, 7 R. A. Jadeja, 8 S. N. Thakur, 9 Y. S. Chahal, 10 Mohammed Shami and 11 J. J. Bumrah did not bat.

Southee 21–12–20–2; Bennett 18–8–29–0; Tickner 18–3–34–0; Santner 24–10–19–0; Sodhi 24–5–33–1.

Umpires: C. M. Brown and S. B. Haig. Third umpire: A. Mehrotra.
Referee: B. C. Broad.

NEW ZEALAND v INDIA

Third Twenty20 International

At Hamilton, January 29, 2020 (floodlit). India won the super over, after a tie. Toss: New Zealand.

A magnificent 48-ball 95 from Williamson, who pinged eight fours and six sixes, looked to have dragged New Zealand back into the series. But with two required from four deliveries, his attempted dab off Mohammed Shami between keeper and gully was hauled in by Rahul. After a dot ball, Seifert pinched a bye, Taylor chopped the last ball into his stumps, and New Zealand faced another super over, their third in six months. Again they lost: although Williamson took his match aggregate to 106 as Bumrah's over cost 17, in reply Sharma powered the last two balls, half-volleys from Southee, over long-on and long-off for sixes. It was his second stunning burst of the day: he had lit the blue touch-paper in the sixth over of the match, smashing successive balls from Bennett for six, six, four, four and six. "I thought we were down and out," said a relieved Kohli after clinching the series.

Player of the Match: R. G. Sharma.

India

		B	4/6
1 R. G. Sharma *c 9 b 11*	65	40	6/3
2 †K. L. Rahul *c 2 b 5*	27	19	2/1
3 S. R. Dube *c 10 b 11*	3	7	0
4 *V. Kohli *c 9 b 11*	38	27	2/1
5 S. S. Iyer *st 7 b 4*	17	16	0/1
6 M. K. Pandey *not out*	14	6	1/1
7 R. A. Jadeja *not out*	10	5	0/1
B 1, lb 2, w 2	5		
6 overs: 69-0 (20 overs)	179-5		

1/89 2/94 3/96 4/142 5/160

8 S. N. Thakur, 9 Y. S. Chahal, 10 Mohammed Shami and 11 J. J. Bumrah did not bat.

12th man: S. V. Samson.

Southee 24–7–39–0; Bennett 24–4–54–3; Kuggeleijn 12–5–10–0; Santner 24–5–37–1; Sodhi 24–8–23–0; de Grandhomme 12–3–13–1.

New Zealand

		B	4/6
1 M. J. Guptill *c 12 b 8*	31	21	2/3
2 C. Munro *st 2 b 7*	14	16	2
3 *K. S. Williamson *c 2 b 10*	95	48	8/6
4 M. J. Santner *b 9*	9	11	1
5 C. de Grandhomme *c 3 b 8*	5	12	0
6 L. R. P. L. Taylor *b 10*	17	10	1/1
7 †T. L. Seifert *not out*	0	2	0
B 6, lb 2	8		
6 overs: 51-1 (20 overs)	179-6		

1/47 2/52 3/88 4/137 5/178 6/179

8 S. C. Kuggeleijn, 9 T. G. Southee, 10 I. S. Sodhi and 11 H. K. Bennett did not bat.

Thakur 18–10–21–2; Mohammed Shami 24–9–32–2; Bumrah 24–8–45–0; Chahal 24–8–36–1; Jadeja 24–11–23–1; Dube 6–0–14–0.

Super over: **New Zealand 17-0** (Williamson 11*, Guptill 5*, Extras 1; Bumrah 6–1–16–0): **India 20-0** (Sharma 15*, Rahul 5*; Southee 6–0–20–0).

Umpires: C. M. Brown and S. B. Haig. Third umpire: K. D. Cotton.
Referee: B. C. Broad.

NEW ZEALAND v INDIA

Fourth Twenty20 International

At Wellington (Westpac Stadium), January 31, 2020 (floodlit). India won the super over, after a tie. Toss: New Zealand.

Another day, another super over: in the first T20 international in New Zealand to end after midnight, the hosts' hopes went pumpkin-shaped after they lost four wickets in the final over of the match proper, from Thakur. That undid the good work of Munro and Seifert (the second of the last-over victims), who had put on 74 for the second wicket. Defending 13, and seemingly stuck in a recurring nightmare, Southee bowled the super over – and, although Rahul went six, four, out, Kohli

---

NEW ZEALAND'S NOT-SO-SUPER OVERS

Four extra-time defeats in six months:

July 14, 2019 (ODI)	Lord's	England won the World Cup on boundary count
November 10, 2019 (T20)	Auckland	England won, to take the series 3–2
January 29, 2020 (T20)	**Hamilton**	**India won, to clinch the series**
January 31, 2020 (T20)	**Wellington**	**India won, to make it 4–0**

calmly swatted the winning boundary from the fifth ball. New Zealand could have done with the cool head of Williamson, but he was absent with a shoulder niggle that would keep him on the sidelines until the third ODI. India had looked in trouble at 88 for six in the 12th over, but were rescued by a half-century from Pandey, who was making the most of a rare opportunity.

Player of the Match: S. N. Thakur.

India

		B	*4/6*
1 †K. L. Rahul *c 7 b 10*	39	26	3/2
2 S. V. Samson *c 7 b 8*	8	5	0/1
3 *V. Kohli *c 7 b 11*	11	9	2
4 S. S. Iyer *c 3 b 10*	1	7	0
5 S. R. Dube *c 4 b 10*	12	9	2
6 M. K. Pandey *not out*	50	36	3
7 M. S. Washington Sundar *b 7*	0	3	0
8 S. N. Thakur *c 9 b 11*	20	15	2
9 Y. S. Chahal *c 3 b 9*	1	2	0
10 N. Saini *not out*	11	9	2
B 2, lb 3, w 6, nb 1	12		
6 overs: 51-2 (20 overs)	165-8		

1/14 2/48 3/52 4/75 5/84 6/88 7/131 8/143

11 J. J. Bumrah did not bat.

Southee 24–7–28–1; Kuggeleijn 24–12–39–1; Santner 24–11–26–1; Bennett 24–7–41–2; Sodhi 24–8–26–3.

New Zealand

		B	*4/6*
1 M. J. Guptill *c 1 b 11*	4	8	0
2 C. Munro *run out (8/3)*	64	47	6/3
3 †T. L. Seifert *run out (1)*	57	39	4/3
4 T. C. Bruce *b 9*	0	3	0
5 L. R. P. L. Taylor *c 4 b 8*	24	18	2
6 D. J. Mitchell *c 5 b 8*	4	3	1
7 M. J. Santner *run out (2/1)*	2	2	0
8 S. C. Kuggeleijn *not out*	0	0	0
Lb 7, w 3	10		
6 overs: 39-1 (20 overs)	165-7		

1/22 2/96 3/97 4/159 5/163 6/164 7/165

9 *T. G. Southee, 10 I. S. Sodhi and 11 H. K. Bennett did not bat.

Thakur 24–9–33–2; Saini 24–12–29–0; Bumrah 24–11–20–1; Chahal 24–4–38–1; Washington Sundar 12–3–24–0; Dube 12–3–14–0.

Super over: **New Zealand 13-1** (Seifert 8, Munro 5*, Taylor 0*; Bumrah 6–1–13–1); **India 16-1** (Rahul 10, Kohli 6*, Samson 0*; Southee 5–1–16–1).

Umpires: C. M. Brown and S. B. Haig. Third umpire: A. Mehrotra.
Referee: B. C. Broad.

NEW ZEALAND v INDIA

Fifth Twenty20 International

At Mount Maunganui, February 2, 2020 (floodlit). India won by seven runs. Toss: India.

India completed an unprecedented Twenty20 5–0 sweep, with New Zealand unable to recover from slumps at the start and end of their chase. Rahul and Sharma had provided the spine of India's total, putting on 88, although Sharma – captain for the day, with Kohli resting – eventually succumbed to a calf strain during the 17th over. Chasing 164, New Zealand stumbled to 17 for three, before Seifert and Taylor, in his 100th T20 international, biffed 99 in nine overs, which included 34 from the tenth, bowled by medium-pacer Dube. But then, with Bumrah's yorkers proving almost unplayable, six wickets tumbled for 25. Sodhi hoisted Thakur for two sixes, but New Zealand fell short again.

Player of the Match: J. J. Bumrah. *Player of the Series:* K. L. Rahul.

Fiona Goodall, Getty Images

R&R: Virat Kohli (resting) and Kane Williamson (recuperating) chat at Mount Maunganui; Rishabh Pant listens in.

India

		B	*4/6*
1 †K. L. Rahul *c 7 b 11*	45	33	4/2
2 S. V. Samson *c 7 b 8*	2	5	0
3 *R. G. Sharma *retired hurt*	60	41	3/3
4 S. S. Iyer *not out*	33	31	1/2
5 S. R. Dube *c 4 b 8*	5	6	1
6 M. K. Pandey *not out*	11	4	1/1
Lb 1, w 6	7		
6 overs: 53-1 (20 overs)	163-3		

1/8 2/96 3/148

7 M. S. Washington Sundar, 8 S. N. Thakur, 9 Y. S. Chahal, 10 N. Saini and 11 J. J. Bumrah did not bat.

Sharma retired hurt at 138-2.

Southee 24–5–52–0; Kuggeleijn 24–14–25–2; Bennett 24–11–21–1; Sodhi 24–9–28–0; Santner 24–5–36–0.

New Zealand

		B	*4/6*
1 M. J. Guptill *lbw b 11*	2	6	0
2 C. Munro *b 7*	15	6	2/1
3 †T. L. Seifert *c 2 b 10*	50	30	5/3
4 T. C. Bruce *run out (2/1)*	0	3	0
5 L. R. P. L. Taylor *c 1 b 10*	53	47	5/2
6 D. J. Mitchell *b 11*	2	4	0
7 M. J. Santner *c 6 b 8*	6	7	0
8 S. C. Kuggeleijn *c 7 b 8*	0	1	0
9 *T. G. Southee *b 11*	6	5	1
10 I. S. Sodhi *not out*	16	10	0/2
11 H. K. Bennett *not out*	1	2	0
Lb 1, w 3, nb 1	5		
6 overs: 41-3 (20 overs)	156-9		

1/7 2/17 3/17 4/116 5/119 6/131 7/132 8/133 9/141

Washington Sundar 18–9–20–1; Bumrah 24–16–12–3; Saini 24–14–23–2; Thakur 24–8–38–2; Chahal 24–7–28–0; Dube 6–0–34–0.

Umpires: C. M. Brown and S. B. Haig. Third umpire: A. Mehrotra.
Referee: B. C. Broad.

NEW ZEALAND v INDIA

First One-Day International

At Hamilton, February 5, 2020 (day/night). New Zealand won by four wickets. Toss: New Zealand. One-day international debuts: T. A. Blundell; M. A. Agarwal, P. P. Shaw.

After eight straight defeats, and an India total of 347, New Zealand had every right to feel vulnerable. They had never chased so many and won, and Williamson was still nursing a shoulder injury. And yet, inspired by Taylor's 21st ODI century, and boundary-filled innings from Nicholls and Latham, they cantered home with 11 deliveries to spare. The result changed the mood of the tour. Positive footwork and crisp sweeping were the hallmarks of a fourth-wicket stand of 138 in just 79 balls between Taylor and stand-in captain Latham, which brought the target within reach. New Zealand's previous-best successful chase was also at Seddon Park, in 2006-07, when a boundary with the scores level knocked off Australia's 346. For the first half of the day, India seemed to be reprising their T20 dominance. The openers, both debutants, put on 50 inside eight overs, then Iyer – who went on to a maiden ODI century – put on 102 with Kohli (gated by Sodhi's googly) and 136 with Rahul, whose unbeaten 88 included six sixes from 64 balls. The new-ball pair of Southee and Bennett were caned for 162 between them, and only de Grandhomme exerted much control. But, on a consistent pitch, New Zealand's batsmen were undaunted. Guptill and Nicholls, strong off the hips, set the platform with a stand of 85, and Taylor's 73-ball hundred ensured their work was not wasted.

Player of the Match: L. R. P. L. Taylor.

India

P. P. Shaw c Latham b de Grandhomme	20	K. M. Jadhav not out	26
M. A. Agarwal c Blundell b Southee	32	Lb 7, w 19, nb 1	27
*V. Kohli b Sodhi	51		
S. S. Iyer c Santner b Southee	103	1/50 (1) 2/54 (2) (4 wkts, 50 overs)	347
†K. L. Rahul not out	88	3/156 (3) 4/292 (4) 10 overs: 55-2	

R. A. Jadeja, S. N. Thakur, Mohammed Shami, K. Yadav and J. J. Bumrah did not bat.

Southee 10–1–85–2; Bennett 10–0–77–0; de Grandhomme 8–0–41–1; Neesham 8–0–52–0; Santner 10–0–58–0; Sodhi 4–0–27–1.

New Zealand

M. J. Guptill c Jadhav b Thakur	32	C. de Grandhomme run out (Iyer/Kohli)	1
H. M. Nicholls run out (Kohli)	78	M. J. Santner not out	12
T. A. Blundell st Rahul b Yadav	9		
L. R. P. L. Taylor not out	109	Lb 4, w 24, nb 1	29
*†T. W. M. Latham c Mohammed Shami b Yadav	69	1/85 (1) 2/109 (3) (6 wkts, 48.1 overs)	348
J. D. S. Neesham c Jadhav b Mohammed Shami	9	3/171 (2) 4/309 (5) 5/328 (6) 6/331 (7) 10 overs: 54-0	

T. G. Southee, I. S. Sodhi and H. K. Bennett did not bat.

Bumrah 10–1–53–0; Mohammed Shami 9.1–0–63–1; Thakur 9–0–80–1; Jadeja 10–0–64–0; Yadav 10–0–84–2.

Umpires: S. B. Haig and L. Rusere. Third umpire: B. N. J. Oxenford.
Referee: B. C. Broad.

NEW ZEALAND v INDIA

Second One-Day International

At Auckland, February 8, 2020 (day/night). New Zealand won by 22 runs. Toss: India. One-day international debut: K. A. Jamieson.

Jadeja and Saini kept India in the hunt before the lofty seamer Kyle Jamieson – the tallest New Zealand international at 6ft 8in (203cm), just shading "Two-Metre Peter" Fulton – knocked back Saini's leg stump in the 45th over to end an eighth-wicket partnership of 76. Soon Jadeja holed out, and New Zealand clinched the 50-over series. They had taken the early advantage in a fluctuating encounter, with Guptill and Nicholls sharing an opening stand of 93 which mixed boundaries with drop-and-run singles on a drop-in pitch. The Indian fielders, initially at least, were on their heels as the ball held up on the lush Eden Park rugby-season turf. But from 142 for one in the 27th, New

Zealand lost seven for 55 before Taylor and Jamieson cracked 76 from the last 51 balls. India's frustration was palpable: Bumrah flicked off the bails after another wicketless spell, and Kohli remonstrated with anyone who would pay attention – including the crowd. Iyer contributed another useful knock but, when he fell, India were well behind the rate at 129 for six. Jamieson took two wickets to clinch the match award, but Southee's two for 41 despite a dodgy stomach also deserved plaudits. Illness had spread through the home dressing-room to such an extent that the injured Williamson ran the drinks, and assistant coach Luke Ronchi fielded for a while as a substitute.

Player of the Match: K. A. Jamieson.

New Zealand

M. J. Guptill run out (Thakur/Rahul)	79
H. M. Nicholls lbw b Chahal	41
T. A. Blundell c Saini b Thakur	22
L. R. P. L. Taylor not out	73
*†T. W. M. Latham lbw b Jadeja	7
J. D. S. Neesham run out (Jadeja)	3
C. de Grandhomme c Iyer b Thakur	5
M. S. Chapman c and b Chahal	1
T. G. Southee c Saini b Chahal	3
K. A. Jamieson not out	25
B 4, lb 4, w 6	14
1/93 (2) 2/142 (3) 3/157 (1) 4/171 (5) 5/175 (6) 6/185 (7) 7/187 (8) 8/197 (9) (8 wkts, 50 overs)	273
10 overs: 52-0	

H. K. Bennett did not bat.

Thakur 10–1–60–2; Bumrah 10–0–64–0; Saini 10–0–48–0; Chahal 10–0–58–3; Jadeja 10–0–35–1.

India

P. P. Shaw b Jamieson	24
M. A. Agarwal c Taylor b Bennett	3
*V. Kohli b Southee	15
S. S. Iyer c Latham b Bennett	52
†K. L. Rahul b de Grandhomme	4
K. M. Jadhav c Nicholls b Southee	9
R. A. Jadeja c de Grandhomme b Neesham	55
S. N. Thakur b de Grandhomme	18
N. Saini b Jamieson	45
Y. S. Chahal run out (Neesham/Latham)	10
J. J. Bumrah not out	0
Lb 4, w 12	16
1/21 (2) 2/34 (1) 3/57 (3) 4/71 (5) 5/96 (6) 6/129 (4) 7/153 (8) 8/229 (9) 9/251 (10) 10/251 (7) (48.3 overs)	251
10 overs: 59-3	

Bennett 9–0–58–2; Southee 10–1–41–2; Jamieson 10–1–42–2; de Grandhomme 10–1–54–2; Neesham 9.3–0–52–1.

Umpires: C. M. Brown and B. N. J. Oxenford. Third umpire: L. Rusere.
Referee: B. C. Broad.

NEW ZEALAND v INDIA

Third One-Day International

At Mount Maunganui, February 11, 2020 (day/night). New Zealand won by five wickets. Toss: New Zealand.

New Zealand's composure in chasing down 297 ensured India's first one-day series whitewash since 2006-07, when they lost 4–0 in South Africa. Rahul's 112, and his stand of 100 with the consistent Iyer, set up a reasonable total, although the bustling Bennett limited the late damage with three wickets in five balls. He had earlier peppered Kohli with short deliveries outside off, eventually persuading him to upper-cut to Jamieson, running in from third man. Guptill and Nicholls made another good start – 106 in 16 overs this time – and although the returning Williamson fell for 22, New Zealand were generally in charge. When Neesham fell in the 40th over, 77 were still required. But, with Latham looking on, de Grandhomme bludgeoned 58 from 28 balls – 33 off nine from Thakur – to complete the 3–0 sweep.

Player of the Match: H. M. Nicholls. *Player of the Series:* L. R. P. L. Taylor.

India

P. P. Shaw run out (de Grandhomme/Latham)	40	S. N. Thakur c de Grandhomme b Bennett	7
M. A. Agarwal b Jamieson	1	N. Saini not out	8
*V. Kohli c Jamieson b Bennett	9		
S. S. Iyer c de Grandhomme b Neesham	62	B 1, w 6	7
†K. L. Rahul c Jamieson b Bennett	112		
M. K. Pandey c Santner b Bennett	42	1/8 (2) 2/32 (3) 3/62 (1) 4/162 (4) 5/269 (5) 6/269 (6) 7/280 (8) — (7 wkts, 50 overs)	296
R. A. Jadeja not out	8	10 overs: 56-2	

Y. S. Chahal and J. J. Bumrah did not bat.

Southee 9–0–59–0; Jamieson 10–0–53–1; Bennett 10–1–64–4; de Grandhomme 3–0–10–0; Neesham 8–0–50–1; Santner 10–0–59–0.

New Zealand

M. J. Guptill b Chahal	66	C. de Grandhomme not out	58
H. M. Nicholls c Rahul b Thakur	80	B 1, lb 2, w 6, nb 2	11
*K. S. Williamson c Agarwal b Chahal	22		
L. R. P. L. Taylor c Kohli b Jadeja	12	1/106 (1) 2/159 (3) 3/186 (4) 4/189 (2) 5/220 (6) — (5 wkts, 47.1 overs)	300
†T. W. M. Latham not out	32		
J. D. S. Neesham c Kohli b Chahal	19	10 overs: 65-0	

M. J. Santner, T. G. Southee, K. A. Jamieson and H. K. Bennett did not bat.

Bumrah 10–0–50–0; Saini 8–0–68–0; Chahal 10–1–47–3; Thakur 9.1–0–87–1; Jadeja 10–0–45–1.

Umpires: C. M. Brown and L. Rusere. Third umpire: B. N. J. Oxenford.
Referee: B. C. Broad.

NEW ZEALAND v INDIA

First Test

At Wellington, February 21–24, 2020. New Zealand won by ten wickets. New Zealand 60pts. Toss: New Zealand. Test debut: K. A. Jamieson.

A dominant debut, a swashbuckling tail, and precision pace ensured New Zealand kept the upper hand to force their 100th Test victory. It injected hope into their Test Championship campaign, and dented India's after seven successive victories.

The issue of whether the visiting team should be allowed to choose what to do, without a toss, was raised by a juicy Basin Reserve pitch that offered the bowlers early incentives. In reality, the result hinged on New Zealand's strengths: an attack offering minimal respite, and a determined if occasionally unorthodox batting order. After India rolled over for 165, Williamson top-scored with 89 as his side amassed a first-innings lead of 183, before Southee and Boult dismantled India again. It meant New Zealand extended a decade-long sequence – 17 home matches without defeat after winning the toss, since Pakistan triumphed on this ground in December 2009.

Neil Wagner missed the match for the birth of his first child, which meant a Test debut for Kyle Jamieson. As in the one-dayers, he grabbed his opportunity with both hands, following figures of four for 39 with an attacking innings as the lead mushroomed. He bowled mainly from the Vance Stand End with a northerly breeze behind him, and forced batsmen on to the back foot by generating bounce off a good length, before paralysing them on the crease with fuller deliveries. His first victims formed a distinguished trio: Pujara, Kohli and Vihari. Rahane showed the most pluck, scrapping to 46 in 199 minutes.

Early on the third day, with the new ball looming, New Zealand were teetering at 225 for seven, before Jamieson entered to play his part with the bat. He thumped four sixes and a four on his way to 44, the highest score by a New Zealand No. 9 on debut (previously Graham Vivian's 43 against India at Calcutta in 1964-65). Jamieson used his height to pull and hook Bumrah and Mohammed Shami, and thumped Ashwin over cow corner towards the refurbished, earthquake-strengthened and well-patronised Museum Stand, which had lain derelict since 2012.

The final three wickets added 123 to swing the match in New Zealand's favour. Ishant Sharma, in his third Test on the ground, used his experience to take five for 68, although his figures were dented during a merry stand between Patel and No. 11 Boult, whose 38 was the highest Test score by a batsman making all the runs while he was at the crease. That beat Kapil Dev's 36 for India against Sri Lanka in Colombo in 1985-86, when Sunil Gavaskar was the silent partner.

India laboured to 144 for four by the end of the third day, still 39 behind. Agarwal scored a bright 58, but Boult made inroads, including Kohli – edging to a gleeful Watling – for another disappointing score. After Boult added Rahane in the third over next day, Southee took up the cudgels, removing Vihari and going on to finish with five wickets – nine in the match. India's last three crashed in 11 balls, just after the innings defeat was averted. Latham and Blundell wasted no time in finishing things off.

The victory had special significance for Taylor, who became the fourth New Zealander to appear in 100 Tests – and the first from anywhere to chalk up a century in all three formats. He had received a standing ovation when he went in to bat – he made an important 44 – after two of his three children, daughter Mackenzie and son Jonty, stood alongside him for the national anthem, while mum Ann, wife Victoria and his other daughter, Adelaide, watched from the stands.

Player of the Match: T. G. Southee.

Close of play: first day, India 122-5 (Rahane 38, Pant 10); second day, New Zealand 216-5 (Watling 14, de Grandhomme 4); third day, India 144-4 (Rahane 25, Vihari 15).

India

First innings		Second innings	
P. P. Shaw b Southee	16	– c Latham b Boult	14
M. A. Agarwal c Jamieson b Boult	34	– c Watling b Southee	58
C. A. Pujara c Watling b Jamieson	11	– b Boult	11
*V. Kohli c Taylor b Jamieson	2	– c Watling b Boult	19
A. M. Rahane c Watling b Southee	46	– c Watling b Boult	29
G. H. Vihari c Watling b Jamieson	7	– b Southee	15
†R. R. Pant run out (Patel)	19	– c Boult b Southee	25
R. Ashwin b Southee	0	– lbw b Southee	4
I. Sharma c Watling b Jamieson	5	– lbw b de Grandhomme	12
Mohammed Shami c Blundell b Southee	21	– not out	2
J. J. Bumrah not out	0	– c sub (D. J. Mitchell) b Southee	0
Lb 1, w 3	4	W 2	2
1/16 (1) 2/35 (3) 3/40 (4) 4/88 (2) 5/101 (6) 6/132 (7) 7/132 (8) 8/143 (5) 9/165 (9) 10/165 (10) (68.1 overs)	165	1/27 (1) 2/78 (3) 3/96 (2) 4/113 (4) 5/148 (5) 6/148 (6) 7/162 (8) 8/189 (9) 9/191 (7) 10/191 (11) (81 overs)	191

Southee 20.1–5–49–4; Boult 18–2–57–1; de Grandhomme 11–5–12–0; Jamieson 16–3–39–4; Patel 3–2–7–0. *Second innings*—Southee 21–6–61–5; Boult 22–8–39–4; de Grandhomme 16–5–28–1; Jamieson 19–7–45–0; Patel 3–0–18–0.

New Zealand

	First innings		Second innings
T. W. M. Latham c Pant b Sharma	11	– not out	7
T. A. Blundell b Sharma	30	– not out	2
*K. S. Williamson c sub (R. A. Jadeja) b Mohammed Shami	89		
L. R. P. L. Taylor c Pujara b Sharma	44		
H. M. Nicholls c Kohli b Ashwin	17		
†B-J. Watling c Pant b Bumrah	14		
C. de Grandhomme c Pant b Ashwin	43		
T. G. Southee c Mohammed Shami b Sharma	6		
K. A. Jamieson c Vihari b Ashwin	44		
A. Y. Patel not out	4		
T. A. Boult c Pant b Sharma	38		
B 1, lb 1, w 6	8		
1/26 (1) 2/73 (2) 3/166 (4) 4/185 (3) 5/207 (5) 6/216 (6) 7/225 (8) 8/296 (9) 9/310 (7) 10/348 (11) (100.2 overs)	348	(no wkt, 1.4 overs)	9

Bumrah 26–5–88–1; Sharma 22.2–6–68–5; Mohammed Shami 23–2–91–1; Ashwin 29–1–99–3. *Second innings*—Sharma 1–0–8–0; Bumrah 0.4–0–1–0.

Umpires: Aleem Dar and R. A. Kettleborough. Third umpire: M. A. Gough.
Referee: R. S. Madugalle.

NEW ZEALAND v INDIA

Second Test

At Christchurch, February 29–March 2, 2020. New Zealand won by seven wickets. New Zealand 60pts. Toss: New Zealand.

On a helpful Hagley Park pitch, New Zealand completed their sixth successive series win at home. An emerald carpet was unveiled before the toss, prompting the former Test opener Mark Richardson to deliver a pitch report predicting batting travails. The Indian board's official Twitter account got in on the act, captioning their photo of the surface "spot the pitch". Rupert Bool, the groundsman, defended his handiwork, saying it would play as it had before – but in the event the bowlers enjoyed a deck that probably had Sir Richard Hadlee's moustache twitching as he sat in the pavilion named after his family.

The predictions were right: only 218 overs – fewer than half the available 450 – were needed, and the umpires never had to hand over a second new ball. New Zealand recalled Wagner, meaning Jadeja was the only specialist spinner on either side, and even he might not have played had Ishant Sharma been fit (he was replaced by Umesh Yadav).

The pitch was soon pockmarked by divots. Many of the 33 wickets to fall were bowled, lbw or caught in the cordon, although some were down to hesitation, or the ball swinging in the air rather than moving off the surface. A crucial passage of play came on the third (and final) day, when New Zealand's Tom–Tom opening partnership – Latham and

Kai Schwoerer, Getty Images

Tall story: the 6ft 8in Kyle Jamieson, playing his second Test, helps deliver a New Zealand victory.

Blundell – ticked off 103 of the 132 needed to win. That was 22 more than any other pair had managed all match, and ensured local fans did not require the defibrillator.

Contrasting innings by Shaw, who needed just 61 balls to reach his fifty, and Pujara, who required 117, had given India a decent start, but both eventually fell to Jamieson, while Southee swept away Kohli and Rahane. Vihari hit ten fours in a sparkling 55, but Jamieson did for the tail after tea to finish with five for 45; Latham and Blundell reduced the deficit to 179 by stumps. Bumrah had Williamson caught behind early on the second day, and later removed Watling and Southee in a single over: New Zealand were clinging on at 153 for seven, but Jamieson played another important innings – 49 from 63 balls – and with Wagner put on 51. The stand ended with a superb one-handed catch by Jadeja on the run at deep square to see off Wagner. The crowd, thinking the ball was flying to the boundary, started to applaud, but gasped when it was plucked from the air, and redoubled their applause when Jadeja's agility was replayed on the big screen. Still, the damage was done: India's lead was a measly seven.

Boult and Southee got into the swing again, helped by the freshly mulleted de Grandhomme, who pinned Kohli for 14: he finished the Tests with just 38 runs. Wagner crashed one through Rahane's defences, and the only real resistance came from Pujara, who faced 88 balls, more than twice as many as anyone else. By the end of a second day on which 16 wickets fell for 262, India were reeling at 90 for six.

Only the jack-in-the-box Jadeja made it into double figures on the third morning, when Vihari fell to a superb catch by Watling. Boult finished with four for 28 – and also ran out last man Bumrah – while Southee was not far behind. New Zealand were left with what might have been a tricky target, but Latham and Blundell, who had put on 66 in the first innings, motored past three figures. It was New Zealand's 13th straight home Test without defeat, dating back to March 2017, when South Africa won in Wellington. The last Test anywhere before lockdown secured a 2–0 series win, and 120 precious World Championship points.

Player of the Match: K. A. Jamieson. *Player of the Series:* T. G. Southee.

Close of play: first day, New Zealand 63-0 (Latham 27, Blundell 29); second day, India 90-6 (Vihari 5, Pant 1).

India

P. P. Shaw c Latham b Jamieson	54	– c Latham b Southee	14
M. A. Agarwal lbw b Boult	7	– lbw b Boult	3
C. A. Pujara c Watling b Jamieson	54	– b Boult	24
*V. Kohli lbw b Southee	3	– lbw b de Grandhomme	14
A. M. Rahane c Taylor b Southee	7	– b Wagner	9
G. H. Vihari c Watling b Wagner	55	– (7) c Watling b Southee	9
†R. R. Pant b Jamieson	12	– (8) c Watling b Boult	4
R. A. Jadeja c Boult b Jamieson	9	– (9) not out	16
U. T. Yadav c Watling b Jamieson	0	– (6) b Boult	1
Mohammed Shami b Boult	16	– c Blundell b Southee	5
J. J. Bumrah not out	10	– run out (Boult/Williamson)	4
B 4, lb 6, w 5	15	B 9, lb 12	21
1/30 (2) 2/80 (1) 3/85 (4) (63 overs)	242	1/8 (2) 2/26 (1) (46 overs)	124
4/113 (5) 5/194 (6) 6/197 (3)		3/51 (4) 4/72 (5)	
7/207 (7) 8/207 (9) 9/216 (8) 10/242 (10)		5/84 (3) 6/89 (6) 7/97 (7)	
		8/97 (8) 9/108 (10) 10/124 (11)	

Southee 13–5–38–2; Boult 17–2–89–2; de Grandhomme 9–2–31–0; Jamieson 14–3–45–5; Wagner 10–2–29–1. *Second innings*—Southee 11–2–36–3; Boult 14–4–28–4; Jamieson 8–4–18–0; de Grandhomme 5–3–3–1; Wagner 8–1–18–1.

New Zealand

T. W. M. Latham b Mohammed Shami	52	– c Pant b Yadav	52
T. A. Blundell lbw b Yadav	30	– b Bumrah	55
*K. S. Williamson c Pant b Bumrah	3	– c Rahane b Bumrah	5
L. R. P. L. Taylor c Yadav b Jadeja	15	– not out	5
H. M. Nicholls c Kohli b Mohammed Shami	14	– not out	5
†B-J. Watling c Jadeja b Bumrah	0		
C. de Grandhomme b Jadeja	26		
T. G. Southee c Pant b Bumrah	0		
K. A. Jamieson c Pant b Mohammed Shami	49		
N. Wagner c Jadeja b Mohammed Shami	21		
T. A. Boult not out	1		
B 20, lb 4	24	B 1, lb 8, nb 1	10
1/66 (2) 2/69 (3) 3/109 (4) (73.1 overs)	235	1/103 (1) (3 wkts, 36 overs)	132
4/130 (1) 5/133 (5) 6/153 (6)		2/112 (3) 3/121 (2)	
7/153 (8) 8/177 (7) 9/228 (10) 10/235 (9)			

Bumrah 22–5–62–3; Yadav 18–2–46–1; Mohammed Shami 23.1–3–81–4; Jadeja 10–2–22–2. *Second innings*—Bumrah 13–2–39–2; Yadav 14–3–45–1; Mohammed Shami 3–1–11–0; Jadeja 5–0–24–0; Kohli 1–0–4–0.

Umpires: M. A. Gough and R. A. Kettleborough. Third umpire: Aleem Dar.
Referee: R. S. Madugalle.

NEW ZEALAND v WEST INDIES IN 2020-21

MARK GEENTY

Twenty20 internationals (3): New Zealand 2, West Indies 0
Test matches (2): New Zealand 2 (120pts), West Indies 0 (0pts)

Jason Holder, West Indies' Test captain, sat at a microphone-laden table in the indoor nets beneath the Basin Reserve's R. A. Vance Stand in Wellington, and smiled ruefully. "It has been a tough year," he said. "Not just for the team, but for me personally. I haven't seen home in six months now. I have been going non-stop. We have had pay cuts..." Asked when he would next set foot in his Barbados home, Holder said he didn't know. He took his leave, and prepared for another flight, to Australia, for a cameo in the Big Bash. A fortnight later, it was announced he would not join the tour of Bangladesh, beginning in January.

Holder and several of his players had indeed endured a sapping year: they first donned their masks back in June, to fly to England for a long incarceration in a biosecure bubble, then contested the CPL and the IPL in hotel lockdown, before the long journey to Christchurch and another bout of isolation. It was hardly a surprise that they endured a tough time in New Zealand, losing the T20 and Test series 2–0, with both Tests ending in innings defeats.

But the hosts were grateful for the sacrifices. The virus had apparently been seen off in New Zealand, thanks to a hard lockdown in March and April. It was a close-run thing, but New Zealand Cricket were able to stage their first international cricket with unrestricted crowds since the pandemic struck – and fans visited Eden Park for the T20 opener on November 27. It was barely 24 hours since West Indies' T20 captain Kieron Pollard, and a handful of returning IPL players from each side, had completed their 14 days' managed isolation at a Christchurch hotel (at a cost to the board of $NZ7,000 per person). There had been a kerfuffle when some of the earlier arrivals were spotted socialising and sharing food in the hotel corridors, which broke the strict regulations; for a while, the whole squad were stopped from practising.

Kane Williamson and Trent Boult were among those returning from the IPL, and were excused the Twenty20 series to go home briefly before the Tests. New Zealand won both completed T20s, before the third was washed out, with Lockie Ferguson producing some searing deliveries on the way to series figures of seven for 56. There was also a promising start for Devon Conway, the 29-year-old South African-born left-hander, who followed 41 from 29 balls on debut with an unbeaten 65 from 37 in his second match. But that was overshadowed by Glenn Phillips, who – despite a dodgy knee – blasted a 46-ball century, New Zealand's fastest in T20s.

Meanwhile, most of West Indies' Test squad were experiencing the delights of Queenstown for their warm-up matches, free of restrictions. When the Test team left for Hamilton, the reserves for both squads were transformed into West Indies A, and played two more first-class matches.

At home in Hamilton: Kane Williamson moves towards his fifth and highest century at Seddon Park.

David Rowland, AFP/Getty Images

There were still hardships: on the eve of the First Test, Kemar Roach was told his father had died. He played at Hamilton – both sides wore black armbands – but returned home immediately afterwards, along with the injured Shane Dowrich.

Williamson had no first-class preparation, but it hardly showed. He stroked a classy 251 at Hamilton, his highest Test score, and a perfect demonstration of his single-minded pursuit of excellence. After victory at Wellington in the Second Test, New Zealand's unbeaten run at home stretched to 15 games since South Africa upset them there in March 2017, and they edged ever closer to the top of the world rankings.

The lanky Kyle Jamieson continued his rapid ascent, and was named Player of the Series. He brought a new dimension to New Zealand's pace attack, with steep bounce and vicious swing, which compounded West Indies' batting woes in the Tests. Across four innings, their top five totalled just 267, which Williamson would probably have outdone on his own had he not missed the Second Test to be at the birth of his first child, a daughter.

There were a few umpiring decisions that raised eyebrows during both series, which led to question marks about the use of two home officials for internationals during the pandemic. Holder understood the reasons, but said: "If we can travel and do a quarantine, I don't see why an overseas umpire can't."

WEST INDIAN TOURING PARTY

*J. O. Holder (T), F. A. Allen (20), J. Blackwood (T), K. C. Brathwaite (T), D. M. Bravo (T), S. S. J. Brooks (T), J. D. Campbell (T), R. L. Chase (T), R. R. S. Cornwall (T), S. S. Cottrell (20), J. Da Silva (T), S. O. Dowrich (T), A. D. S. Fletcher (20), S. T. Gabriel (T), S. O. Hetmyer (T/20), C. K. Holder (T), A. S. Joseph (T), B. A. King (20), K. R. Mayers (20), K. M. A. Paul (T/20), K. A. Pollard (20), N. Pooran (20), R. Powell (20), K. A. J. Roach (T), R. Shepherd (20), O. R. Thomas (20), H. R. Walsh (20), K. O. K. Williams (20). *Coach:* P. V. Simmons.

Pollard captained in the T20s. D. J. Bravo was originally selected for the T20 squad, but failed to recover from a groin injury, and was replaced by Shepherd. N. E. Bonner, P. A. S. McSween, S. A. R. Moseley, R. A. Reifer and J. N. T. Seales travelled with the team as standby players; Da Silva was originally part of this group, but was added to the Test squad when Dowrich went home with a finger injury after the First Test. Roach also returned home then, following the death of his father.

At Queenstown, November 26–29, 2020. **Drawn.** ‡**West Indians 571** (162.1 overs) (K. C. Brathwaite 246, D. M. Bravo 93, J. Blackwood 53; C. E. McConchie 3-130); **New Zealand A 440-8 dec** (149 overs) (H. R. Cooper 54, R. Ravindra 52, W. A. Young 133, C. E. McConchie 124*; C. K. Holder 3-100). *West Indies' Test players warmed up in picturesque Queenstown while the T20 series got under way in Auckland. After a three-day game against New Zealand A in which the tourists rotated 16 players, the sides reconvened for a first-class match, on what turned out to be a batsman's paradise. Kraigg Brathwaite accumulated a career-best 246, in 552 minutes from 400 balls, which included stands of 111 with John Campbell, 189 with Darren Bravo and 107 with Jermaine Blackwood. Off-spinner Cole McConchie, the home captain, took some tap during his 36.1 overs, while slow left-armer Rachin Ravindra sent down 35, claiming 2-102. McConchie got some revenge as New Zealand A batted out the rest of the match, scoring a century of his own and putting on 170 for the fifth wicket with Will Young, who earned himself a Test debut with a six-hour 133.*

First Twenty20 international At Auckland, November 27, 2020 (floodlit). **New Zealand won by five wickets** (DLS). **West Indies 180-7** (16 overs) (A. D. S. Fletcher 34, K. A. Pollard 75*, F. A. Allen 30; L. H. Ferguson 5-21); ‡**New Zealand 179-5** (15.2 overs) (D. P. Conway 41, J. D. S. Neesham 48*, M. J. Santner 31*). *PoM:* L. H. Ferguson. *T20I debuts:* D. P. Conway, K. A. Jamieson (New Zealand). *Rarely, if ever, have a West Indian team in New Zealand faced such fearsome fast bowling as Lockie Ferguson produced, aided by a bouncy drop-in pitch spiced up by light rain. Consistently over 90mph, he finished with 5-21, New Zealand's second-best figures in T20s, behind Tim Southee's 5-18 against Pakistan at Auckland on Boxing Day 2010. West Indies had sprinted to 58-0 from 20 balls, but lost four wickets without addition, and another at 59. They were rescued by Kieron Pollard, their captain, who muscled eight sixes in his 37-ball 75*; Fabian Allen helped put on 84, and West Indies reached 180-7 during a rain-shortened innings. New Zealand's target was adjusted to 176 in 16, but they lost Martin Guptill in the first over, and were 63-4 in the seventh. The debutant Devon Conway put them back on track, adding 77 with Jimmy Neesham. Glenn Phillips – who, like Neesham and Mitchell Santner, hit three sixes – earlier cracked 22 from seven balls, but collapsed in agony after one big hit: he had dislocated a kneecap, which had to be eased back into place by medical staff.*

Second Twenty20 international At Mount Maunganui, November 29, 2020. **New Zealand won by 72 runs. New Zealand 238-3** (20 overs) (M. J. Guptill 34, D. P. Conway 65*, G. D. Phillips 108); ‡**West Indies 166-9** (20 overs). *PoM:* G. D. Phillips. *T20I debut:* K. R. Mayers (West Indies). *Phillips again had knee trouble, but it hardly slowed him down: he thrashed New Zealand's fastest T20 century, from 46 balls, one quicker than Colin Munro (also against West Indies at the Bay Oval, in January 2018). Phillips hit eight sixes and ten fours, and his stand of 184 in 13.3 overs with Conway raised a total the visitors never threatened. Five reached 20, but Pollard's 28 (which contained four sixes) was the highest. They were haunted again by Phillips, who ignored his problematic patella to run out Andre Fletcher with a direct hit from side on, then dived to catch the debutant Kyle Mayers on the midwicket boundary. Earlier, Keemo Paul's four overs had disappeared for 64, West Indies' most expensive T20 analysis; his seven in the series cost 103.*

Third Twenty20 international At Mount Maunganui, November 30, 2020 (floodlit). **No result. West Indies 25-1** (2.2 overs) **v** ‡**New Zealand.** *PoS:* L. H. Ferguson. *Only 14 deliveries were possible before rain set in, although there was time for Ferguson to remove Brandon King.*

NEW ZEALAND v WEST INDIES

First Test

At Hamilton, December 3–6, 2020. New Zealand won by an innings and 134 runs. New Zealand 60pts. Toss: West Indies. Test debut: W. A. Young.

When the coin landed the right way for Holder, and Gabriel bustled in to try to exploit an even more verdant Seddon Park strip than usual, things were looking up for West Indies. Gabriel soon broke through, as the debutant Will Young – thrust into the opening role when a hamstring injury to wicketkeeper B-J. Watling caused a New Zealand reshuffle – was trapped in front. But that was as good as it got.

The arrival of Williamson signalled the start of a suffocation which gradually drained the life from the attack. New Zealand's captain began watchfully, soft hands in defence taking the sting out of any threatening deliveries, while others whizzed past the edge. The pressure applied by the bowlers was not prolonged enough to bother him, and he bedded down for ten hours 24 minutes to make 251, his highest Test score. After a second-wicket partnership of 154 with Latham, Williamson virtually did it on his own: until Jamieson's late cameo, the best of the rest was Taylor's 38. Even as Gabriel and the grieving Roach, whose father had died shortly before the match, worked their way through the middle order, Williamson was immovable; then he shifted up the gears. His 22nd Test hundred was one of his best.

When Jamieson started swinging hard, Williamson joined in the fun, and they rattled up 94 for the seventh wicket. Just as the talk turned to whether he might join Brendon McCullum in the Test triple-centurions' club, Williamson holed out to deep midwicket. He waited for Jamieson to complete his maiden Test fifty, then declared at 519 for seven.

In general, the West Indians had bowled too short to make the most of the conditions: Holder, the captain, was among the culprits, with 31 economical but wicketless overs.

HIGHEST TEST SCORES AT HAMILTON

251	**K. S. Williamson**	**New Zealand v West Indies**	**2020-21**
226	J. E. Root	England v New Zealand	2019-20
200*	K. S. Williamson	New Zealand v Bangladesh	2018-19
192	S. P. Fleming	New Zealand v Pakistan	2003-04
190	R. Dravid	India v New Zealand	1998-99
189	M. J. Guptill	New Zealand v Bangladesh	2009-10
185	B. B. McCullum	New Zealand v Bangladesh	2009-10
176	K. S. Williamson	New Zealand v South Africa	2016-17
170	S. L. Campbell	West Indies v New Zealand	1999-2000
161	T. W. M. Latham	New Zealand v Bangladesh	2018-19
160	S. R. Tendulkar	India v New Zealand	2008-09

Injuries did not help. Wicketkeeper Dowrich suffered a tour-ending finger injury on the first day, while Darren Bravo was helped off with a tweaked Achilles tendon. Bravo did pad up later, and survived gamely for 50 minutes.

For the second successive Test, after a dominant win over India at Christchurch in March, New Zealand had not chosen a specialist spinner, going instead with their Fab Four pacemen: Southee, Boult, Wagner and Jamieson, with Mitchell in support, instead of the injured Colin de Grandhomme. The mix was just right: after a stubborn two-hour opening stand between Brathwaite and Campbell on the second evening, the West Indian batsmen found the cocktail too hot to handle. Next day, with the ball swinging, Southee hit an impeccable line and length, daring the batsmen to chase him. His four wickets, helped by a lack of discipline, meant West Indies were shot out for 138. They had lasted only 64 overs, so the bowlers were still fresh: with a lead of 381, Williamson enforced the follow-on. If the visitors were not on their knees already, they soon were – two wickets from Wagner helped reduce them to 27 for four, and New Zealand sensed a three-day win.

Counter-attack was the only way to limit the damage. Blackwood, with one century from his previous 31 Tests, made the home bowlers toil. From 89 for six, he put on 155 with Joseph, which stretched the match an hour into the fourth day. Blackwood lifted his side's spirits, and had the small home crowd relishing a contest at last. Joseph, whose previous-highest in Tests was 34, clattered three sixes on his way to 86, while Blackwood hit two – and 11 fours – in that elusive second ton.

For once, Williamson was searching for solutions. Jamieson finally provided one, having Joseph caught when he toe-ended a flourishing drive, and Wagner did the rest, removing Blackwood with a bouncer pulled to backward square, and shattering Gabriel's stumps in the same over. So often New Zealand's short-ball enforcer, Wagner showed he could also cause problems by pitching the ball up; he finished with six wickets in the match. West Indies' two innings lasted less than 123 overs. They had watched a Williamson masterclass for much of the first two days, yet none of the batsmen heeded the lesson.

Player of the Match: K. S. Williamson.

Close of play: first day, New Zealand 243-2 (Williamson 97, Taylor 31); second day, West Indies 49-0 (Brathwaite 20, Campbell 22); third day, West Indies 196-6 (Blackwood 80, Joseph 59).

New Zealand

T. W. M. Latham b Roach	86
W. A. Young lbw b Gabriel	5
*K. S. Williamson c Chase b Joseph	251
L. R. P. L. Taylor c †Brooks b Gabriel	38
H. M. Nicholls c Holder b Roach	7
†T. A. Blundell lbw b Gabriel	14
D. J. Mitchell c Holder b Roach	9
K. A. Jamieson not out	51
T. G. Southee not out	11
B 11, lb 23, w 1, nb 12	47
1/14 (2) (7 wkts dec, 145 overs)	519
2/168 (1) 3/251 (4)	
4/281 (5) 5/353 (6) 6/409 (7) 7/503 (3)	

N. Wagner and T. A. Boult did not bat.

Roach 30–7–114–3; Gabriel 25–6–89–3; Holder 31–12–60–0; Joseph 31–8–99–1; Chase 25–0–109–0; Brathwaite 3–0–14–0.

West Indies

K. C. Brathwaite c Blundell b Boult	21	– c Blundell b Southee	10
J. D. Campbell c Williamson b Southee	26	– c Latham b Boult	2
S. S. J. Brooks c Taylor b Southee	1	– (4) c sub (D. P. Conway) b Wagner	2
D. M. Bravo b Jamieson	9	– (3) c Southee b Wagner	12
R. L. Chase lbw b Wagner	11	– lbw b Jamieson	6
J. Blackwood c Latham b Southee	23	– c Southee b Wagner	104
*J. O. Holder not out	25	– lbw b Mitchell	8
A. S. Joseph c Mitchell b Southee	0	– c sub (M. J. Santner) b Jamieson	86
K. A. J. Roach b Jamieson	2	– not out	0
S. T. Gabriel lbw b Wagner	1	– b Wagner	0
†S. O. Dowrich absent hurt		– absent hurt	
B 8, lb 7, w 1, nb 3	19	Lb 7, w 8, nb 2	17
1/53 (2) 2/55 (3) 3/55 (1) (64 overs)	138	1/4 (2) 2/25 (3) (58.5 overs)	247
4/79 (4) 5/79 (5) 6/119 (6)		3/27 (4) 4/27 (1) 5/53 (5)	
7/119 (8) 8/135 (9) 9/138 (10)		6/89 (7) 7/244 (8) 8/247 (6) 9/247 (10)	

Southee 19–7–35–4; Boult 17–5–30–1; Jamieson 13–3–25–2; Wagner 15–3–33–2. *Second innings*—Southee 15–2–62–1; Boult 15–1–63–1; Wagner 13.5–0–66–4; Jamieson 12–2–42–2; Mitchell 3–0–7–1.

Umpires: C. B. Gaffaney and W. R. Knights. Third umpire: C. M. Brown.
Referee: J. J. Crowe.

NEW ZEALAND v WEST INDIES

Second Test

At Wellington, December 11–14, 2020. New Zealand won by an innings and 12 runs. New Zealand 60pts. Toss: West Indies. Test debuts: J. Da Silva, C. K. Holder.

The margin was similar – another innings defeat – though West Indies did put up marginally sterner resistance at the second attempt. New Zealand again ran up a big score, but this time it was the tourists' catching that let them down, rather than their bowling. For the home side, Southee and Jamieson each took seven wickets, in a fourth successive Test victory.

There was a change at the helm, as Williamson went home for the birth of his first child. Latham stepped in as captain, and collected far happier memories than from his previous Test in charge, at Sydney 11 months earlier, when Australia demolished a side depleted by illness and injury. Watling was back, which meant Blundell moved up to open, and Young took Williamson's spot at No. 3. West Indies introduced Chemar Holder, a fast bowler from Barbados with a high action reminiscent of Jofra Archer, while Joshua Da Silva, a Trinidadian of Portuguese descent, replaced the injured Shane Dowrich behind the stumps. Once again, the conditions were bowler-friendly, with more bounce than usual at Wellington: in a howling northerly wind, Gabriel, Joseph and the Holders ensured the first day started worryingly for the hosts.

Blundell fell in the seventh over, and Latham and Taylor before lunch, though Young hung on nearly three hours for 43. Latham had reeled away when struck on the forearm by a fired-up Gabriel, who also hit Taylor several times, while Nicholls's torso was dotted by bruises when he plunged into the ice bath that evening. Under increasing scrutiny after failing to reach 50 in 13 innings since scoring the Basin's 99th Test century against Bangladesh in March 2019, Nicholls also needed some luck. It came on two, when Da Silva could not quite reach a chance which popped up towards square leg. That was in the first over after lunch, and would have made it 83 for four. Bravo's unhappy series continued when he dropped two straightforward slip catches with Nicholls on 47; five more chances of varying difficulty went down during the innings. Other edges flew wide of the cordon, mistimed skyers fell just out of reach, and Nicholls made hay as his confidence grew. His focus helped lift New Zealand from a precarious spot and, in the lengthening shadows, he raised his bat for the ground's 100th hundred.

As at Hamilton, the hard yards on day one were followed by some fun. This time it was Wagner, winning his 50th cap, who cashed in, while Nicholls advanced to 174, his highest first-class score, in a tick over seven hours. Wagner is better known for dour defence as a nightwatchman, but delighted a hefty Saturday crowd with an unbeaten 66 from 42 balls, his own career-best, studded with four big pulls for six.

It meant that, not long after a par score of around 270 looked on the cards, New Zealand had 460. Gabriel, also in his 50th Test, trudged off with a pained expression – three for 93 were reasonable figures, but nowhere near what they would have been if his fielders had been less fallible.

The vagaries of Wellington's wind mean swing can be elusive, even for exponents such as Southee and Boult – but not this time. Southee again made early inroads, before Jamieson produced an over to live in the memory, going within a whisker of a hat-trick. After Campbell edged to second slip, a searing inswinger knocked over Chase first ball. And the entire team roared a huge appeal when Blackwood was rapped on the pads. Not out, said umpire Chris Brown, a former Auckland seamer standing in his first Test. Replays showed Brown's brave decision was correct, and Blackwood again carried West Indies' innings, with 69. Even so, the tourists were all out for 131, with Jamieson and Southee proving a devastating combination, each snaring five wickets.

As at Hamilton, West Indies were better in the follow-on, though they still could not survive until the second new ball. Campbell resisted for three hours, reaching the sixties, as did Jason Holder, who took the match into a fourth day; there was also a promising 57 from Da Silva. But there was little respite from the seamers. Boult and Wagner took three apiece, while Southee and Jamieson shared the other four. Back at the scene of his debut ten months earlier, Jamieson now had four wins from his first four matches, with a bowling average of 14 and a batting average of 54, in one of the most breathtaking opening stanzas of any New Zealand Test career.

Player of the Match: H. M. Nicholls. *Player of the Series:* K. A. Jamieson.

Close of play: first day, New Zealand 294-6 (Nicholls 117, Jamieson 1); second day, West Indies 124-8 (Da Silva 2, C. K. Holder 5); third day, West Indies 244-6 (J. O. Holder 60, Da Silva 25).

New Zealand

*T. W. M. Latham c Da Silva b C. K. Holder	27
T. A. Blundell b Gabriel	14
W. A. Young c J. O. Holder b Gabriel	43
L. R. P. L. Taylor c Da Silva b Gabriel	9
H. M. Nicholls c Brathwaite b Chase	174
†B-J. Watling b Joseph	30
D. J. Mitchell lbw b C. K. Holder	42
K. A. Jamieson c J. O. Holder b Joseph	20
T. G. Southee b Joseph	11
N. Wagner not out	66
T. A. Boult c Brooks b Chase	6
B 2, lb 7, w 9	18
1/31 (2) 2/63 (1) 3/78 (4) (114 overs)	460
4/148 (3) 5/203 (6) 6/286 (7)	
7/336 (8) 8/359 (9) 9/454 (5) 10/460 (11)	

Gabriel 26–7–93–3; J. O. Holder 27–6–85–0; Joseph 22–2–109–3; C. K. Holder 26–1–110–2; Chase 13–1–54–2.

West Indies

K. C. Brathwaite c Taylor b Southee	0	– c Young b Boult	24
J. D. Campbell c Latham b Jamieson	14	– b Jamieson	68
D. M. Bravo c and b Southee	7	– c Nicholls b Boult	4
S. S. J. Brooks b Jamieson	14	– c Watling b Wagner	36
R. L. Chase b Jamieson	0	– c Latham b Jamieson	0
J. Blackwood c Latham b Southee	69	– b Boult	20
*J. O. Holder c Boult b Jamieson	9	– b Southee	61
†J. Da Silva c Watling b Southee	3	– lbw b Wagner	57
A. S. Joseph c Watling b Jamieson	0	– c Watling b Southee	24
C. K. Holder not out	8	– not out	13
S. T. Gabriel b Southee	2	– b Wagner	0
Lb 3, w 1, nb 1	5	B 1, lb 7, w 1, nb 1	10
1/0 (1) 2/22 (3) 3/29 (2) (56.4 overs)	131	1/37 (1) 2/41 (3) (79.1 overs)	317
4/29 (5) 5/97 (4) 6/111 (6)		3/130 (4) 4/131 (5)	
7/117 (7) 8/117 (9) 9/127 (8) 10/131 (11)		5/134 (2) 6/170 (6) 7/252 (7)	
		8/282 (9) 9/307 (8) 10/317 (11)	

Southee 17.4–6–32–5; Boult 14–5–34–0; Wagner 12–5–28–0; Jamieson 13–4–34–5. *Second innings*—Southee 22–4–96–2; Boult 21–3–96–3; Jamieson 15–4–43–2; Wagner 17.1–4–54–3; Mitchell 4–0–20–0.

Umpires: C. M. Brown and C. B. Gaffaney. Third umpire: W. R. Knights.
Referee: J. J. Crowe.

NEW ZEALAND v PAKISTAN IN 2020-21

ANDREW ALDERSON

Twenty20 internationals (3): New Zealand 2, Pakistan 1
Test matches (2): New Zealand 2 (120 pts), Pakistan 0 (0 pts)

Pakistan's tour almost ended before it began, when six of their 53-strong touring party tested positive for the Covid-19 virus on arrival at their managed isolation hotel in Christchurch. The six were moved to the quarantine arm of the facility, and the New Zealand government issued a threat of expulsion because the tourists had flouted the rules: CCTV footage at the hotel showed them breaching social-distancing protocols, mingling in hallways, and not wearing masks.

Radio phone-ins and social media blazed with indignation, since Pakistan's cricketers had been given special permission to enter the country. Ashley Bloomfield, the normally mild-mannered director-general of health – and the public face of the pandemic response – condemned the behaviour. "It is a privilege to come to New Zealand to play sport," he said. "I take a dim view of what we've seen already, and we'll be taking it very seriously." New Zealand Cricket said: "We will be having discussions with the tourists to assist them in understanding the requirements."

That prompted former Pakistan fast bowler Shoaib Akhtar to mark out his long run on YouTube, claiming NZC should be indebted to his compatriots for agreeing to tour: "You are talking about Pakistan, the greatest country on the planet, so behave yourself." Yet New Zealand's caution was reasonable: thanks to the government's "go hard, go early" approach to lockdown, and public diligence, the virus had been kept at bay. They wanted to keep it that way.

Eventually the ire subsided, and the tour began, albeit after Pakistan altered their warm-up schedule to play a series of intra-squad games in Queenstown, rather than New Zealand A in a four-day match. Dominant performances from Tim Seifert then ensured New Zealand wrapped up the T20 series after two of the three

Michael Bradley, AFP/Getty Images

The sight of summer: Kane Williamson.

games; he finished with 176 runs at a strike-rate of 139. Jacob Duffy's four for 33 on debut at Auckland, and Devon Conway's 63 from 45 balls in the dead rubber at Napier – the tourists' only win – underlined their potential. For Pakistan, the batting of Mohammad Rizwan and Mohammad Hafeez provided highlights, while Fahim Ashraf produced the lowest economy-rate – 5.51 – of anyone to bowl more than four overs.

In the Tests, two players split the match awards as New Zealand rose to the top of the world rankings for the first time. The 6ft 8in Kyle Jamieson interrogated batsmen from a good length, then terrorised them with short-of-a-length deliveries, regularly jarring glove against handle. The pace and bounce at Hagley Oval made him often unplayable in the Second Test, when he took 11 for 117. By the end of a series that brought him 16 wickets at 11, he had 36 in six Tests at 13 apiece, and was yet to finish on the losing side. He was also averaging 56 with the bat.

Meanwhile, Kane Williamson's appetite for runs remained unsated: making good use of a prototype swivel-leave to keep his bat and gloves clear of traffic in the fourth-stump corridor, he collected 388 at 129, including a century and a double. At Mount Maunganui's Bay Oval, he entered during the first over, and made the greentop seem a red herring. Williamson had 24 Test hundreds by the end, equalling Greg Chappell, David Warner, Mohammad Yousuf and Viv Richards, and passed 7,000 runs.

Rizwan again led the way for Pakistan, this time as skipper after Babar Azam broke a thumb before the internationals began. Three half-centuries demonstrated his pluck, as did a fifth-wicket stand of 165 in the First Test with Fawad Alam, who made a century. The partnership gave the visitors a flicker of hope of hauling in a target of 373 during the final session, but New Zealand extinguished those ambitions with 4.3 overs left. By the time the tourists left, the talk was of cricket rather than the coronavirus.

PAKISTAN TOURING PARTY

*Mohammad Rizwan (T/20), Abdullah Shafiq (20), Abid Ali (T), Azhar Ali (T), Fahim Ashraf (T/20), Fawad Alam (T), Haider Ali (20), Haris Rauf (20), Haris Sohail (T), Hussain Talat (20), Iftikhar Ahmed (20), Imad Wasim (20), Imam-ul-Haq (T), Imran Butt (T), Khushdil Shah (20), Mohammad Abbas (T), Mohammad Hafeez (20), Mohammad Hasnain (20), Musa Khan (20), Naseem Shah (T), Sarfraz Ahmed (T/20), Shadab Khan (T/20), Shaheen Shah Afridi (T/20), Shan Masood (T), Sohail Khan (T), Usman Qadir (20), Wahab Riaz (20), Yasir Shah (T), Zafar Gohar (T). *Coach:* Misbah-ul-Haq.

Babar Azam was originally named as captain, but broke his thumb; Mohammad Rizwan took over for the Tests, and Shadab Khan for the T20s. Shadab was then ruled out of the Test squad by injury, and replaced by Zafar Gohar from the reserves. Many of the squad also appeared in the overlapping tour by the Pakistan Shaheens (their A-Team), along with Amad Butt, Danish Aziz, Rohail Nazir and Zeeshan Malik were also on hand, as the Pakistan Shaheens (their A-Team) played six matches between December 17 and January 5.

First Twenty20 international At Auckland, December 18, 2020 (floodlit). **New Zealand won by five wickets.** ‡**Pakistan 153-9** (20 overs) (Shadab Khan 42, Fahim Ashraf 31; J. A. Duffy 4-33, S. C. Kuggeleijn 3-27); **New Zealand 156-5** (18.5 overs) (T. L. Seifert 57, M. S. Chapman 34; Haris Rauf 3-29). *PoM:* J. A. Duffy. *T20I debut:* J. A. Duffy (New Zealand). *The first international from the Southland region since Jeff Wilson in 1992-93, Jacob Duffy made an instant impact, with the best figures by a T20 debutant for New Zealand (previously 3-20, by Nathan Astle and Jeetan Patel in the same game at Johannesburg in 2005-06). Duffy claimed a wicket with his fourth ball, when Abdullah*

Shafiq, undone by extra bounce, spooned a catch to mid-on. By the end of his second over, Duffy had also dismissed Mohammad Rizwan and Mohammad Hafeez. When Scott Kuggeleijn removed Haider Ali with the first ball of the fifth, Pakistan had lost three in three; soon, it was 39-5. But Shadab Khan, captaining his country for the first time after Babar Azam was ruled out with a broken thumb, top-scored with 42, as they crashed 102 from the last nine overs. With Shadab on five, Duffy had almost hauled in a miraculous one-handed catch at third man, only for a finger to brush the boundary. It never felt as if Pakistan had enough. Tim Seifert reduced the pressure with 57 from 43 balls, and Mark Chapman contributed 34 off 20, before Mitchell Santner hit the winning six with seven balls to spare. It was his first win as captain, standing in for Kane Williamson, who had just become a father; his previous chance, against West Indies in November, had been washed out after 14 balls.

Second Twenty20 international At Hamilton, December 20, 2020 (floodlit). **New Zealand won by nine wickets. ‡Pakistan 163-6** (20 overs) (Mohammad Hafeez 99*; T. G. Southee 4-21); **New Zealand 164-1** (19.2 overs) (T. L. Seifert 84*, K. S. Williamson 57*). *PoM:* T. G. Southee. *Playing in place of Duffy, Tim Southee picked up the baton with 4-21 – a decisive intervention as New Zealand claimed the series with a game to spare. After choosing to bat, Pakistan stumbled to 33-3 in the sixth, all to Southee, who returned to remove the dangerous Fahim Ashraf. Amid the wickets, Mohammad Hafeez adjusted well to Seddon Park's bounce to become the fourth player, and the first non-Englishman, to end one short of a T20 international hundred; his career-best 99* came from 57 balls, and included ten fours and five sixes (the fourth and fifth from the last three deliveries of the innings). But Seifert flexed his muscles too, responding with 84* from 63, as he and returning skipper Williamson (57* from 42) put on 129*, a New Zealand record for the second wicket.*

Third Twenty20 international At Napier, December 22, 2020 (floodlit). **Pakistan won by four wickets. New Zealand 173-7** (20 overs) (T. L. Seifert 35, D. P. Conway 63, G. D. Phillips 31; Fahim Ashraf 3-20); ‡**Pakistan 177-6** (19.4 overs) (Mohammad Rizwan 89, Mohammad Hafeez 41). *PoM:* Mohammad Rizwan. *PoS:* T. L. Seifert. *Mohammad Rizwan earned a consolation win for Pakistan with a 59-ball 89 packed with powerful pulls; 70 of his runs came on the leg side. His reward as Player of the Match was a jade pounamu pendant, rather than the customary champagne. But his dismissal in the final over – a fourth wicket in 19 balls from the comfort of 141-2 – threatened to make things tight. When Kyle Jamieson bowled a dot to Iftikhar Ahmed, Pakistan needed three from three, before Iftikhar hit the next for six. Devon Conway's 63 from 45 balls had been the highlight of the New Zealand innings, as he blazed away in front of the wicket, particularly on the off side. For the second season in three, sun stopped play at McLean Park, glaring over the Chapman Stand in the batsman's line of sight around 8pm. Play resumed after a five-minute delay.*

NEW ZEALAND v PAKISTAN

First Test

At Mount Maunganui, December 26–30, 2020, New Zealand won by 101 runs. New Zealand 60pts. Toss: Pakistan.

The spectacle finished as a Test should: in fading light, with fielders camped around the bat, willing on the last wicket. And when Santner leapt high for a left-handed return catch off Pakistan No. 11 Naseem Shah, who had resisted for more than half an hour, New Zealand sealed a hard-fought victory with 27 balls to spare.

It had been a game for the purists – a contest of courage and application to challenge the patience and discipline of players and fans, who streamed in for free. On the fourth afternoon, Williamson toyed with his declaration: was there sufficient bait to tempt a chase, but enough runs to offer insurance? A target of 373 proved just right. The influence of the World Test Championship was at the heart of the decision, too: Williamson said the prospect of qualifying for the final discouraged defensiveness.

New Zealand withdrew at 180 for five before tea, and took two wickets in the five overs before the kettle boiled, the openers gone for ducks. Haris Sohail followed before stumps, as Southee became the third New Zealander, after Richard Hadlee and Daniel Vettori, to take 300 Test wickets. When Pakistan lost Azhar Ali to the ninth ball of the final day, they were 75 for four, and in danger of folding. Instead, Fawad Alam and Mohammad Rizwan put on 165, a stand full of resistance and counter-attack.

Fawad, a 35-year-old left-hander, was arguably playing for his position, having returned to the team in August against England after almost 11 years in the Test wilderness. Since then, he had scored 30 runs in four innings. His unorthodox open stance, pointing to square leg before a huge trigger movement, goaded the bowlers with a full view of the stumps, until he crouched across them at the point of delivery. The method worked, as he ground out his second Test century, 4,188 days after his first, in Colombo, and ate up more than six and a half hours. Rizwan, playing his tenth Test and first as captain, got in line, and forced the bowlers to follow him. Williamson staked catchers on both sides of the wicket, but his opposite number stuck to his guns en route to 60.

The second new ball was taken 12 overs before tea, with Pakistan needing 204 from 48 overs, and harbouring an outside chance. Southee and Boult returned to the attack, but Fawad and Rizwan saw off the ball's hardness and shine. After tea, their attacking intent

LONGEST GAP BETWEEN TEST CENTURIES

Years	*Days*		
13	345	W. Bardsley (Australia).......	Lord's 1912 to Lord's 1926
12	161	Mushtaq Ali (India)..........	Manchester 1936 to Calcutta 1948-49
11	**170**	**Fawad Alam (Pakistan)......**	**Colombo (PSO) 2009 to Mt Maunganui 2020-21**
10	354	F. E. Woolley (England)......	Sydney 1911-12 to Johannesburg 1922-23
10	235	W. U. Tharanga (Sri Lanka)...	Bogra 2005-06 to Harare 2016-17
10	22	V. M. Merchant (India).......	Manchester 1936 to The Oval 1946
10	7	H. Masakadza (Zimbabwe)....	Harare 2001 to Harare 2011-12
9	360	C. G. Macartney (Australia)...	Sydney 1910-11 to Sydney 1920-21
9	351	R. B. Simpson (Australia).....	Melbourne 1967-68 to Perth 1977-78
9	305	W. W. Armstrong (Australia)..	Melbourne 1910-11 to Sydney 1920-21

The gaps shown are between a first and second Test hundred, apart from Bardsley (fifth and sixth), Simpson (eighth and ninth) and Armstrong (third and fourth).

was clear: boundaries came in four of the first six overs. Finally both succumbed, Rizwan lbw to Jamieson, Fawad gloving a short-pitched Wagner delivery down the leg side. They both walked off to standing ovations from their team-mates.

Jamieson maintained the lofty standards he had set throughout the southern summer, while Wagner toiled magnificently, having needed injections to numb two fractured toes on his right foot after he was hit by a yorker from Shaheen Shah Afridi on the second evening. New Zealand chipped away, and the last six Pakistan wickets eventually fell for 31 in 20.5 overs.

Afridi had looked dangerous during a first-innings return of four for 109, never more so than in the opening session against Williamson. The duel deserved star billing, but Williamson – having entered to face the game's fourth delivery – survived to make a first Test century on his home ground. Afridi's left-arm angle tested him from a good length, but Williamson left the ball with authority, and it was clear he had his eye in when he unleashed a swivel-pull behind square which ricocheted off the hoardings. Taylor, playing a New Zealand-record 438th international (beating Vettori's total), passed 50, along with Nicholls and Watling.

Pakistan struggled in reply to 431: by the time Fawad was sixth out, in the 60th over, they had just 80. But Fahim Ashraf and Rizwan stabilised the innings with a stand of 107, during which Jamieson hurled the ball dangerously close to Fahim off his own bowling, and earned a 25% fine. Fahim's Test-best 91 averted the follow-on. The Tom–Tom openers, Latham and Blundell, then helped distract fans from their picnic hampers by upping the tempo, as New Zealand built on a lead of 192. A stand of 111 was their highest in 11 opening partnerships together, and allowed their team complete control. Despite Pakistan's late resistance, they never relinquished it.

Player of the Match: K. S. Williamson.

Close of play: first day, New Zealand 222-3 (Williamson 94, Nicholls 42); second day, Pakistan 30-1 (Abid Ali 19, Mohammad Abbas 0); third day, Pakistan 239; fourth day, Pakistan 71-3 (Azhar Ali 34, Fawad Alam 21).

New Zealand

First innings		Second innings	
T. W. M. Latham c Azhar Ali b Shaheen Shah Afridi	4	– c Abid Ali b Naseem Shah	53
T. A. Blundell c Yasir Shah b Shaheen Shah Afridi	5	– b Mohammad Abbas	64
*K. S. Williamson c Haris Sohail b Yasir Shah	129	– c Mohammad Rizwan b Naseem Shah	21
L. R. P. L. Taylor c Mohammad Rizwan b Shaheen Shah Afridi	70	– not out	12
H. M. Nicholls c Shan Masood b Naseem Shah	56	– c Mohammad Abbas b Naseem Shah	11
†B-J. Watling c Yasir Shah b Shaheen Shah Afridi	73	– run out (sub Imran Butt/ Mohammad Rizwan)	5
M. J. Santner c Mohammad Rizwan b Fahim Ashraf	19	– not out	6
K. A. Jamieson c Mohammad Rizwan b Mohammad Abbas	32		
T. G. Southee b Yasir Shah	0		
N. Wagner c Shan Masood b Yasir Shah	19		
T. A. Boult not out	8		
Lb 5, w 5, nb 6	16	Lb 2, w 1, nb 5	8
1/4 (1) 2/13 (2) 3/133 (4) 4/266 (5) 5/281 (3) 6/317 (7) 7/383 (8) 8/388 (9) 9/421 (6) 10/431 (10) (155 overs)	431	1/111 (2) 2/139 (1) 3/147 (3) 4/165 (5) 5/170 (6) (5 wkts dec, 45.3 overs)	180

Shaheen Shah Afridi 36–7–109–4; Mohammad Abbas 31–14–49–1; Fahim Ashraf 19–8–40–1; Naseem Shah 25–3–96–1; Yasir Shah 37–4–113–3; Shan Masood 2–1–2–0; Haris Sohail 5–0–17–0. *Second innings*—Shaheen Shah Afridi 11–0–47–0; Mohammad Abbas 11–2–33–1; Naseem Shah 12.3–1–55–3; Fahim Ashraf 4–1–18–0; Yasir Shah 6–0–21–0; Shan Masood 1–0–4–0.

Pakistan

First innings		Second innings	
Shan Masood c Watling b Jamieson	10	– c Taylor b Southee	0
Abid Ali b Jamieson	25	– c Watling b Boult	0
Mohammad Abbas c Taylor b Boult	5	– (9) lbw b Santner	1
Azhar Ali c Watling b Southee	5	– (3) c Watling b Boult	38
Haris Sohail c Nicholls b Southee	3	– (4) c Santner b Southee	9
Fawad Alam c Watling b Wagner	9	– (5) c Watling b Wagner	102
*†Mohammad Rizwan run out (Santner)	71	– (6) lbw b Jamieson	60
Fahim Ashraf c Watling b Jamieson	91	– (7) c Watling b Wagner	19
Yasir Shah b Boult	4	– (8) c Southee b Jamieson	0
Shaheen Shah Afridi c Latham b Wagner	6	– not out	8
Naseem Shah not out	0	– c and b Santner	1
B 3, lb 4, w 2, nb 1	10	B 16, lb 7, w 2, nb 8	33
1/28 (1) 2/39 (2) 3/43 (3) 4/51 (4) 5/52 (5) 6/80 (6) 7/187 (7) 8/196 (9) 9/235 (10) 10/239 (8) (102.2 overs)	239	1/0 (2) 2/0 (1) 3/37 (4) 4/75 (3) 5/240 (6) 6/242 (5) 7/251 (8) 8/259 (7) 9/261 (9) 10/271 (11) (123.3 overs)	271

Southee 26–7–69–2; Boult 26–4–71–2; Jamieson 23.2–13–35–3; Wagner 21–5–50–2; Santner 6–2–7–0. *Second innings*—Southee 23–8–33–2; Boult 25–9–72–2; Jamieson 26–13–35–2; Wagner 28–9–55–2; Santner 19.3–3–52–2; Williamson 2–1–1–0.

Umpires: C. B. Gaffaney and W. R. Knights. Third umpire: C. M. Brown.
Referee: J. J. Crowe.

NEW ZEALAND v PAKISTAN

Second Test

At Christchurch, January 3–6, 2021, New Zealand won by an innings and 176 runs. New Zealand 60pts. Toss: New Zealand. Test debut: Zafar Gohar.

The odds of Pakistan levelling the series looked slim when they were sent in on a khaki strip, though a first-day total of 297 was a decent recovery from 83 for four. But any dreams of parity were crushed when New Zealand racked up 659 for six, their fifth-highest total – four of them coming since February 2014.

They had looked vulnerable at 71 for three, until Williamson and Nicholls accumulated 369, the country's highest partnership for the fourth wicket. Brilliantly though they batted, they survived a litany of dropped catches and narrow escapes. The best example came when Williamson avoided being run out for 107, with a bail dislodged from one groove, but not both. Not for the first time, he was metronomically efficient, and impossible to pigeonhole into a segment of the field. His leg glances were the highlight of an epic 238. This was Williamson's 24th Test hundred, and fourth double; he passed 7,000 Test runs. It was his third century in successive Tests, and the first Test double hundred on this ground, where he had previously averaged 28 from 13 innings. When he was finally out, caught at third man trying to ramp Fahim Ashraf for six, after more than nine and a half hours at the crease, his opponents mobbed him in awe. He had faced 364 balls, and hit 28 fours.

HIGHEST TEST PARTNERSHIPS FOR NEW ZEALAND

467	for 3rd	A. H. Jones/M. D. Crowe	v Sri Lanka at Wellington	1990-91
387	for 1st	G. M. Turner/T. W. Jarvis	v West Indies at Georgetown	1971-72
369	**for 4th**	**K. S. Williamson/H. M. Nicholls**	**v Pakistan at Christchurch**	**2020-21**
365*	for 6th	K. S. Williamson/B-J. Watling	v Sri Lanka at Wellington	2014-15
352	for 6th	B. B. McCullum/B-J. Watling	v India at Wellington	2013-14
339	for 6th	M. J. Guptill/B. B. McCullum	v Bangladesh at Hamilton	2009-10
297	for 2nd	B. B. McCullum/K. S. Williamson	v Pakistan at Sharjah	2014-15
276	for 1st	C. S. Dempster/J. E. Mills	v England at Wellington	1929-30
271	for 4th	L. R. P. L. Taylor/J. D. Ryder	v India at Napier	2008-09
265	for 3rd	K. S. Williamson/L. R. P. L. Taylor	v Australia at Perth	2015-16
262	for 3rd	K. S. Williamson/L. R. P. L. Taylor	v Sri Lanka at Colombo (PSO)	2012-13

Nicholls, meanwhile, had hobbled to 157 on a strained left calf, collecting boundaries on instinct, and delighting home fans with his courage. But there was luck too. He was caught behind on three off a Shaheen Shah Afridi no-ball, and almost bowled on seven, inside-edging Naseem Shah to fine leg. On 86, wicketkeeper Rizwan spilled him in the first over of the second new ball, again off Afridi. Throughout, Nicholls was peppered by short-pitched deliveries, with backward square, deep square and long leg lying in wait. But he knuckled down, facing 291 balls across more than six and a half hours, before he was caught at fine leg off Mohammad Abbas.

Watling soon followed, but any hope Pakistan had of defusing the innings at 452 for five proved fruitless. Mitchell continued the momentum with his maiden Test century, accelerating from 50 to three figures in 41 balls.

THINGS CAN ONLY GET BETTER

Most runs conceded in an innings without a wicket on Test debut:

163	A. U. Rashid	England v Pakistan at Abu Dhabi	2015-16
159	**Zafar Gohar**	**Pakistan v New Zealand at Christchurch**	**2020-21**
149	B. E. McGain	Australia v South Africa at Cape Town	2008-09
146	Pankaj Singh	India v England at Southampton	2014
142	J. J. Warr	England v Australia at Sydney	1950-51
136	T. Mupariwa	Zimbabwe v Sri Lanka at Bulawayo	2003-04
132	R. G. Nadkarni	India v New Zealand at Delhi	1955-56
131	Sohail Khan	Pakistan v Sri Lanka at Karachi	2008-09
120	S. J. Benn	West Indies v Sri Lanka at Providence	2007-08
115	G. O. B. Allen	England v Australia at Lord's	1930
114	Musa Khan	Pakistan v Australia at Adelaide	2019-20

Pakistan's chances of survival in the second innings, which they began 362 behind, looked remote as soon as Jamieson took up the attack. In the first innings, he had received a Richard Hadlee-like reception at fine leg from the Hagley crowd – Jamieson used to play for Canterbury – after securing a third five-wicket bag in his sixth Test. The delivery which exploded from back of a length to rap Fawad Alam on the gloves, and balloon to wicketkeeper Watling, would have woken any batsman in a cold sweat. Now, he continued his rise, removing six of the top eight, including opener Shan Masood, who completed a pair, and finishing with match figures of 11 for 117 – the best in eight Tests at the ground. He said he had felt valued ever since his call-up to carry the drinks for the 2019 Boxing Day Test against Australia: "I felt welcome from when I got off the plane in Melbourne. Everyone was willing to get around to help you learn."

In completing a home summer clean sweep of all four Tests, New Zealand also broke the national record of five wins in a row. For the first time, they were ranked the No. 1 Test side in the world, and had a very real chance of reaching the World Test Championship final.

Player of the Match: K. A. Jamieson. *Player of the Series:* K. S. Williamson.

Close of play: first day, Pakistan 297; second day, New Zealand 286-3 (Williamson 112, Nicholls 89); third day, Pakistan 8-1 (Abid Ali 7, Mohammad Abbas 1).

Pakistan

Shan Masood lbw b Southee	0	– c Southee b Jamieson	0
Abid Ali c Southee b Jamieson	25	– c sub (W. A. Young) b Jamieson	26
Azhar Ali c Taylor b Henry	93	– (4) c Watling b Jamieson	37
Haris Sohail c Nicholls b Jamieson	1	– (5) c Watling b Jamieson	15
Fawad Alam c Watling b Jamieson	2	– (6) c Taylor b Boult	16
*†Mohammad Rizwan c Watling b Jamieson	61	– (7) b Jamieson	10
Fahim Ashraf c Taylor b Jamieson	48	– (8) c Watling b Jamieson	28
Zafar Gohar c Jamieson b Southee	34	– (9) c Henry b Boult	37
Shaheen Shah Afridi c Nicholls b Boult	4	– (10) c Taylor b Williamson	7
Mohammad Abbas not out	0	– (3) c Watling b Boult	3
Naseem Shah c Latham b Boult	12	– not out	0
B 2, lb 9, w 6	17	B 1, w 4, nb 2	7
1/4 (1) 2/66 (2) 3/70 (4) (83.5 overs)	297	1/3 (1) 2/17 (3) (81.4 overs)	186
4/83 (5) 5/171 (6) 6/227 (3)		3/46 (2) 4/79 (5)	
7/260 (7) 8/282 (8) 9/285 (9) 10/297 (11)		5/88 (4) 6/98 (7) 7/126 (6)	
		8/145 (8) 9/171 (10) 10/186 (9)	

Southee 23–7–61–2; Boult 20.5–3–82–2; Jamieson 21–8–69–5; Henry 17–2–68–1; Mitchell 2–1–6–0. *Second innings*—Southee 20–8–45–0; Boult 18.4–6–43–3; Jamieson 20–6–48–6; Henry 15–5–25–0; Mitchell 5–1–8–0; Williamson 3–0–16–1.

New Zealand

T. W. M. Latham c Haris Sohail b Shaheen Shah Afridi	33
T. A. Blundell lbw b Fahim Ashraf	16
*K. S. Williamson c Shan Masood b Fahim Ashraf	238
L. R. P. L. Taylor c Shan Masood b Mohammad Abbas	12
H. M. Nicholls c Naseem Shah b Mohammad Abbas	157
†B-J. Watling c Haris Sohail b Shaheen Shah Afridi	7
D. J. Mitchell not out	102
K. A. Jamieson not out	30
B 27, lb 8, w 17, nb 12	64
1/52 (2) 2/52 (1) 3/71 (4) 4/440 (5) 5/452 (6) 6/585 (3) (6 wkts dec, 158.5 overs)	659

T. G. Southee, M. J. Henry and T. A. Boult did not bat.

Shaheen Shah Afridi 35.5–8–101–2; Mohammad Abbas 34–11–98–2; Naseem Shah 26–2–141–0; Fahim Ashraf 28–4–106–2; Shan Masood 2–0–17–0; Zafar Gohar 32–0–159–0; Haris Sohail 1–0–2–0.

Umpires: C. M. Brown and C. B. Gaffaney. Third umpire: W. R. Knights.
Referee: J. J. Crowe.

DOMESTIC CRICKET IN NEW ZEALAND IN 2019-20

MARK GEENTY

On a grey day in March, **Wellington** captain Michael Bracewell and his team gathered at an eerily deserted Basin Reserve to receive the Plunket Shield. Chris Nevin – in the side when they last won the title, in 2003-04, now a Cricket Wellington staffer – made up the presentation party of one. No bubbly was sprayed, and there were no spectators, sponsors or vanquished opponents: only some beaming cricketers and a lone photographer.

Three days earlier, New Zealand Cricket had cancelled the final two rounds of the competition, and declared Wellington champions as Covid-19 crept through the country. A week later, the prime minister, Jacinda Ardern, placed New Zealand in lockdown.

Few could quibble with Wellington's title: after six rounds, they sat 26 points clear of defending champions **Central Districts**, whom they had beaten by nine wickets. Like Central a year earlier, Wellington had already won the Twenty20 Super Smash.

Bracewell, an understated, well-liked captain, with one of the best-known cricket surnames in New Zealand, hoisted both trophies. He had averaged just 26 with the bat in the Shield, but made a most telling contribution with his part-time off-spin, bowling Wellington to an innings victory over Auckland on a parched Colin Maiden Park. Figures of five for 43 doubled his career total, and sealed a fourth win in what would be their final match.

A team-mate with another familiar surname, seamer Michael Snedden, had made headlines in October as the world's first fourth-generation first-class cricketer. He followed in the footsteps of his father Martin, the former Test player and NZC chief executive, grandfather Warwick and great-grandfather Nessie.

But 27-year-old Snedden's debut, against Canterbury, was most notable for the batting of Devon Conway, the versatile South African left-hander. In eight hours five minutes, he plundered 327 not out – the sixth-highest first-class score in New Zealand, and a record for Wellington and the Basin Reserve – against an attack including Test bowlers Matt Henry and Todd Astle. Conway amassed 701 Shield runs at 87, and passed 500 in the 50-over and T20 competitions too; no one else reached 500 in any of them. He was named Domestic Player of the Year for the second time running, and won a central contract; the ICC had confirmed he would become eligible for New Zealand from August 28.

Otago, whose captain Jacob Duffy was the Shield's joint-leading wicket-taker with 22, finished third, two points behind Central, and reached the final of the 50-over Ford Trophy, where they met **Auckland**. Now coached by Heinrich Malan, who had helped Central to back-to-back titles, Auckland were fourth in the Shield but headed the 50-over table before winning a dramatic final: they chased down 284 with two wickets to spare, thanks to a powerful century from Colin Munro. It meant more heartbreak for Otago, who had lost the previous one-day final to Wellington, and this time had two batsmen retire hurt: Hamish Rutherford needed a concussion replacement, though Dean Foxcroft resumed.

Earlier in the Ford Trophy, Rutherford had flayed 155 off 104 balls to help Otago to 407 for four, ten short of the national record, against Central. Conway (553) and Munro (492) topped the tournament's run-charts, while the bowlers were headed by towering Auckland left-armer Ben Lister (23) and the consistent Duffy (21).

Canterbury's one-day captain, former New Zealand all-rounder Andrew Ellis, took 18, often bowling in a baseball catcher's mask for protection; he led them to second place in the 50-over table (they finished fifth in the other competitions), before a narrow defeat by Otago in the elimination final. The 38-year-old Ellis later announced his retirement after a career spanning 18 seasons.

Despite opening their Shield campaign with a team of 11 internationals, and 22 wickets from Test regular Neil Wagner, **Northern Districts,** coached by John Bracewell (Michael's uncle), finished last; like Canterbury, they had a single victory. Their best run was in the Ford Trophy, where they were squeezed out of the play-off on net run-rate.

FIRST-CLASS AVERAGES IN 2019-20

BATTING (250 runs, average 35.00)

		M	*I*	*NO*	*R*	*HS*	*100*	*Avge*	*Ct/St*
1	S. Gill (*India A*)	2	3	1	423	204*	2	211.50	1
2	D. J. Mitchell (*Northern Dists/NZ A/NZ*)	5	6	4	414	170*	2	207.00	2
3	†D. P. Conway (*Wellington*)	6	11	3	701	327*	1	87.62	4
4	M. J. G. Rippon (*Otago*)	4	7	2	364	98	0	72.80	1
5	†L. J. Carter (*Canterbury*)	3	5	1	287	226*	1	71.75	2
6	†M. S. Chapman (*Auckland/NZ A*)	5	8	0	546	146	3	68.25	3
7	K. J. McClure (*Canterbury*)	3	5	0	314	152	1	62.80	3
8	W. A. Young (*NZ A/Central Districts*)	5	8	2	331	133*	1	55.16	4
9	B. D. Schmulian (*Central Districts*)	6	10	2	418	74*	0	52.25	3
10	†T. W. M. Latham (*Canterbury/NZ*)	7	11	1	520	224	2	52.00	9
11	D. Cleaver (*Central Districts/NZ A*)	8	14	1	672	201	2	51.69	33/2
12	B-J. Watling (*Northern Districts/NZ*)	8	11	1	507	205	1	50.70	38
13	H. R. Cooper (*Northern Districts*)	5	10	0	499	149	3	49.90	0
14	G. H. Vihari (*India A/India*)	4	7	1	296	100*	1	49.33	4
15	K. S. Williamson (*Northern Districts/NZ*)	5	7	1	282	104*	1	47.00	0
16	†R. Ravindra (*Wellington/New Zealand A*)	8	13	2	507	101	1	46.09	3
17	M. J. Guptill (*Auckland*)	3	6	0	275	110	1	45.83	4
18	B. J. Horne (*Auckland*)	5	9	3	273	107	1	45.50	22
19	J. F. Carter (*Northern Districts*)	5	10	0	452	169	2	45.20	4
20	L. R. P. L. Taylor (*Central Districts/NZ*)	5	8	2	267	105*	1	44.50	6
21	G. R. Hay (*Central Districts*)	6	11	0	454	83	0	41.27	2
22	N. G. Smith (*Otago/New Zealand A*)	6	10	1	359	114	1	39.88	2
23	†M. J. Santner (*Northern Districts/NZ*)	5	7	0	272	126	1	38.85	3
24	R. R. O'Donnell (*Auckland*)	5	9	2	258	65	0	36.85	4
25	G. D. Phillips (*Auckland/New Zealand A*)	8	13	0	479	116	2	36.84	4

BOWLING (10 wickets, average 35.00)

		Style	*O*	*M*	*R*	*W*	*BB*	*5I*	*Avge*
1	M. J. Nofal (*Wellington*)	SLA	73	19	242	15	4-15	0	16.13
2	B. V. Sears (*Wellington*)	RFM	78.4	10	260	14	6-43	1	18.57
3	W. C. Ludick (*Central Districts*)	RM	154.3	34	411	21	4-51	0	19.57
4	J. G. Walker (*Northern Districts*)	OB	80.3	18	201	10	5-41	1	20.10
5	F. W. Sheat (*Canterbury*)	RM	115	26	367	18	4-52	0	20.38
6	L. H. Ferguson (*Auckland*)	RF	89.3	29	254	12	4-23	0	21.16
7	T. G. Southee (*Northern Districts/NZ*)	RFM	182.1	44	478	22	5-61	1	21.72
8	M. G. Bracewell (*Wellington*)	OB	79.1	18	221	10	5-43	1	22.10
9	J. D. S. Neesham (*Wellington/NZ A*)	RFM	69.4	14	222	10	3-17	0	22.20
10	J. A. Duffy (*Otago/New Zealand A*)	RFM	163.2	39	539	24	7-89	1	22.45
11	M. B. McEwan (*Auckland*)	RFM	131.2	36	369	16	4-39	0	23.06
12	M. J. G. Rippon (*Otago*)	SLW	91.1	18	280	12	5-33	1	23.33
13	N. Wagner (*Northern Districts/NZ*)	LFM	275.5	47	868	37	6-114	4	23.45
14	K. A. Jamieson (*Auckland/NZ A/NZ*)	RFM	116	24	332	14	5-45	1	23.71
15	L. J. Delport (*Auckland*)	SLA	155.4	46	410	17	5-77	1	24.11
16	L. V. van Beek (*Wellington*)	RFM	167.1	44	487	19	4-43	0	25.63
17	S. H. A. Rance (*Central Districts*)	RFM	119.3	23	346	13	3-49	0	26.61
18	W. S. A. Williams (*Canterbury*)	RM	180.1	38	456	17	4-52	0	26.82
19	B. M. Tickner (*Central Dists/NZ A*)	RFM	174.4	35	588	21	5-96	1	28.00
20	T. A. Boult (*Northern Districts/NZ*)	LFM	177	36	572	20	4-28	0	28.60
21	J. D. Baker (*Northern Districts*)	RFM	161.2	41	462	16	5-59	1	28.87
22	S. M. Solia (*Auckland/NZ A*)	RFM	109.4	15	446	15	4-33	0	29.73
23	I. G. McPeake (*Wellington*)	RFM	108	20	344	11	3-80	0	31.27
24	M. J. Henry (*Canterbury/NZ*)	RFM	184.2	37	580	18	4-49	0	32.22
25	A. T. E. Hazeldine (*Canterbury*)	LF	69.1	6	362	11	4-62	0	32.90

PLUNKET SHIELD IN 2019-20

	P	W	L	D	Bonus pts Bat	Bonus pts Bowl	Pts	Net avge runs per wkt
Wellington	6	4	1	1	15	20	83	5.33
Central Districts	6	2	3	1	10	23	57	0.23
Otago	6	2	1	2*	9	18	55	–5.75
Auckland	6	2	1	2*	10	16	54	5.20
Canterbury	6	1	3	2	13	20	45	–3.74
Northern Districts	6	1	3	2	14	16	42	–1.47

* *Plus one abandoned.*

Outright win = 12pts; abandoned = 4pts. Bonus points were awarded as follows for the first 110 overs of each team's first innings: one batting point for the first 200 runs, then for 250, 300 and 350; one bowling point for the third wicket taken, then for the fifth, seventh and ninth.

The final two rounds were cancelled because of the Covid-19 pandemic.

PLUNKET SHIELD WINNERS

1921-22	Auckland	1957-58	Otago	1989-90	Wellington
1922-23	Canterbury	1958-59	Auckland	1990-91	Auckland
1923-24	Wellington	1959-60	Canterbury	1991-92	Central Districts / Northern Districts
1924-25	Otago	1960-61	Wellington	1992-93	Northern Districts
1925-26	Wellington	1961-62	Wellington	1993-94	Canterbury
1926-27	Auckland	1962-63	Northern Districts	1994-95	Auckland
1927-28	Wellington	1963-64	Auckland	1995-96	Auckland
1928-29	Auckland	1964-65	Canterbury	1996-97	Canterbury
1929-30	Wellington	1965-66	Wellington	1997-98	Canterbury
1930-31	Canterbury	1966-67	Central Districts	1998-99	Central Districts
1931-32	Wellington	1967-68	Central Districts	1999-2000	Northern Districts
1932-33	Otago	1968-69	Auckland	2000-01	Wellington
1933-34	Auckland	1969-70	Otago	2001-02	Auckland
1934-35	Canterbury	1970-71	Central Districts	2002-03	Auckland
1935-36	Wellington	1971-72	Otago	2003-04	Wellington
1936-37	Auckland	1972-73	Wellington	2004-05	Auckland
1937-38	Auckland	1973-74	Wellington	2005-06	Central Districts
1938-39	Auckland	1974-75	Otago	2006-07	Northern Districts
1939-40	Auckland	1975-76	Canterbury	2007-08	Canterbury
1940–45	*No competition*	1976-77	Otago	2008-09	Auckland
1945-46	Canterbury	1977-78	Auckland	2009-10	Northern Districts
1946-47	Auckland	1978-79	Otago	2010-11	Canterbury
1947-48	Otago	1979-80	Northern Districts	2011-12	Northern Districts
1948-49	Canterbury	1980-81	Auckland	2012-13	Central Districts
1949-50	Wellington	1981-82	Wellington	2013-14	Canterbury
1950-51	Otago	1982-83	Wellington	2014-15	Canterbury
1951-52	Canterbury	1983-84	Canterbury	2015-16	Auckland
1952-53	Otago	1984-85	Wellington	2016-17	Canterbury
1953-54	Central Districts	1985-86	Otago	2017-18	Central Districts
1954-55	Wellington	1986-87	Central Districts	2018-19	Central Districts
1955-56	Canterbury	1987-88	Otago	2019-20	Wellington
1956-57	Wellington	1988-89	Auckland		

Auckland have won the title outright 23 times, Wellington 21, Canterbury 19, Otago 13, Central Districts 10, Northern Districts 7. Central Districts and Northern Districts also shared the title once.

The tournament was known as the Shell Trophy from 1975-76 to 2000-01, and the State Championship from 2001-02 to 2008-09.

THE FORD TROPHY IN 2019-20

50-over league plus knockout

	P	*W*	*L*	*NR/A*	*Bonus*	*Pts*	*NRR*
AUCKLAND	10	6	4	0	4	28	0.46
CANTERBURY	10	5	4	1	3	25	0.08
OTAGO	10	5	4	1	2	24	0.21
Northern Districts	10	5	4	1	2	24	0.00
Wellington	10	5	5	0	1	21	0.01
Central Districts	10	2	7	1	0	10	–0.83

2nd v 3rd Otago beat Canterbury by six runs.

Final At Auckland (Outer Oval), February 16, 2020. **Auckland won by two wickets.** ‡**Otago 283** (49.4 overs); **Auckland 285-8** (44 overs) (C. Munro 104). *As in the previous final, Otago lost after choosing to bat. This time they avoided a collapse, but two batsmen were tested for concussion: Hamish Rutherford, struck on the helmet, needed a replacement; Dean Foxcroft was able to return some time after colliding with a fielder. But only No. 8 Anaru Kitchen (60) managed a half-century, and Auckland's target was 284. Colin Munro blasted seven sixes in a 60-ball 104, out of 149 in the first 20 overs of the chase. Otago captain Jacob Duffy hit back with 4-58, but Mark Chapman (84* in 78) steered Auckland home with six overs in hand.*

The Dream11 Super Smash has its own section (page 851).

PAKISTAN CRICKET IN 2020

Home comforts

OSMAN SAMIUDDIN

If any nation deserved a break in a blighted year, it was probably Pakistan. And they all but got it. They had not been able to host a full season of international cricket in over a decade, and 2019-20 represented their first opportunity. Had the Covid-19 pandemic struck before it did, the season could have ended in disaster. Instead, by the time the Pakistan Cricket Board were forced to shut down all cricket in March, the home season was nearly done.

The Pakistan Super League's knockout stages were postponed, and so were a Test and a one-day international against Bangladesh. Some loss was unavoidable: the board's chief executive, Wasim Khan, estimated it at $3–4m. But, he said, it could have been much worse. The national side managed to play enough cricket through the year: an important tour of England, hosting

PAKISTAN IN 2020

	Played	*Won*	*Lost*	*Drawn/No result*
Tests	5	1	2	2
One-day internationals	3	2	1	–
Twenty20 internationals	11	7	3	1

JANUARY / FEBRUARY	1 Test and 2 T20Is (h) v Bangladesh	(page 729)
MARCH		
APRIL		
MAY		
JUNE		
JULY		
AUGUST / SEPTEMBER	3 Tests and 3 T20Is (a) v England	(page 355)
OCTOBER / NOVEMBER	3 ODIs and 3 T20Is (h) v Zimbabwe	(page 734)
DECEMBER / JANUARY	2 Tests and 3 T20Is (a) v New Zealand	(page 714)

For a review of Pakistan domestic cricket from the 2019-20 season, see page 737.

Gareth Copley, Getty Images

Coming and going: Babar Azam and Azhar Ali, Pakistan captains present and past.

Zimbabwe, then a trip to New Zealand. Results weren't great, but if ever taking part felt more important than winning, it was in 2020.

The highlight of the year was the fifth edition of the PSL, held for the first time in its entirety in Pakistan. Karachi and Lahore had hosted most of the international and PSL games staged in the country in recent years, but the league spread out to include Rawalpindi and Multan. The move paid off: away from the two metropolises, the smaller venues drew near-full houses.

All told, nearly 600,000 fans attended the 30 matches before the interruption, which forced the last four games, held in Karachi in November, behind closed doors. The postponement drew the competition's sting, but the commercial potential of an entire season at home – as opposed to in the UAE – was finally being realised. The end of the league, with Karachi Kings winning for the first time, came as the PCB pushed ahead with nearly all their domestic commitments. By this stage, the country had been through a cycle of localised, loose lockdowns, and had, according to official figures, avoided the kind of tragic caseloads and deaths seen not only in Europe and the US, but next door in India.

Those figures were often treated with scepticism because of a lack of testing, and uncertainty about the reliability of the data. Undeterred, the PCB hosted Zimbabwe, staged an entire edition of the Quaid-e-Azam Trophy (their reward was a historic tied final), a domestic T20 tournament and a 50-over event, as well as the first visit by South Africa in over 13 years. They also announced plans in 2021 for the first visit by England – both men and women – since late 2005. There were occasional breaches of biosecure bubbles, and some players tested positive, but the cricket did not stand still.

Curiously, it was easier to make deductions about the spread of the disease in Pakistan whenever their cricketers toured. Before flying to England in June, ten players in an expanded squad tested positive. In November, after landing in New Zealand, six did (though two of the results were deemed "historical"). The team were also warned there for contravening protocols while in managed isolation.

A series defeat in England, after draws in 2016 and 2018, was a step back. They should have won the First Test at Old Trafford, but – as so often – a poor session with the bat cost them, before their bowlers failed to defend a target of 277. In New Zealand, their last-wicket pair almost saved one Test, but they lost 2–0. That made it four Test losses in a row in New Zealand, further weighing down an away record that already included other long losing streaks: seven in South Africa, and 14 in Australia.

The England result led, in November, to the removal of Azhar Ali as Test captain, though he probably shouldn't have had the job in the first place. That allowed Babar Azam to take over as captain in all formats, and meant that, after seven years with one leader (Misbah-ul-Haq), Pakistan now had their third in three years. That became four when Babar missed the New Zealand Tests with a fractured thumb, handing the job to wicketkeeper Mohammad Rizwan, and capping a giddy rise for a player who had broken into the Test side only in late 2019. Alongside Babar, Rizwan was Pakistan's player of the year, scoring vital runs in crisis situations and excelling behind the stumps.

There was little solace to be drawn elsewhere, least of all from the bowling. A pace attack of Mohammad Abbas, Shaheen Shah Afridi and Naseem Shah began the year big on promise. A hat-trick for Naseem against Bangladesh at Rawalpindi – at 16, the youngest to record one in Tests – should have been a springboard; instead, he took just seven wickets in five more games. By the time South Africa arrived in early 2021, both he and Abbas had been dropped.

By way of consolation, Afridi was growing into his role as spearhead. But the reliance on him was heavy: among fast bowlers in 2020, only Tim Southee, Jasprit Bumrah and Stuart Broad delivered more than his 220.5 overs across the formats. Pakistan's wasteful modern history of discovering, and swiftly waylaying, fast bowlers after injury or dips in form put that workload into perspective. But last year, perhaps, there were bigger matters to think about.

PAKISTAN v BANGLADESH IN 2019-20

SHAHID HASHMI

Twenty20 internationals (3): Pakistan 2, Bangladesh 0
Test match (1): Pakistan 1 (60pts), Bangladesh 0 (0pts)

The odd shape of this on–off tour was finalised only ten days before it began. In the end, the boards agreed a milking-stool approach: the first leg would comprise three Lahore Twenty20s from January 24–27; the second a Test in Rawalpindi, beginning on February 7; and then a single ODI followed by another Test, both at Karachi in early April. None of the legs was scheduled to last more than a week, while the gap between the second and third was long enough for Bangladesh to host Zimbabwe, and for the Pakistan Super League.

The tripartite nature of the tour was the result of protracted negotiation and frantic correspondence about player safety. While the Bangladesh board were willing to play Twenty20s in Pakistan, they had initially insisted on neutral venues for the Tests, despite their security team apparently being satisfied with the type of precautions usually reserved for heads of state.

Pakistan's determination to play both Tests at home was based on the successful visit by Sri Lanka in 2019. Now, the PCB were prepared to go the extra mile. As well as the heightened security measures, they twice sent chartered planes to Bangladesh to collect the tourists. There would have been a third, had the coronavirus pandemic not halted cricket the world over.

The Bangladeshis were not at full strength. In mid-January, Mushfiqur Rahim confirmed he was pulling out of the tour. "There's no bigger sin for me than not playing for Bangladesh," he said. "But I had denied an offer to play in the PSL after knowing that the tournament will be entirely held in Pakistan. My family didn't agree with it." Other players might have followed suit, but the BCB reminded them of their contractual obligations. They were, though, already without another senior player. Shakib Al Hasan was serving a ban for not reporting fixing offers – and some believed his absence helped explain the board's reluctance to agree the Test schedule.

Bangladesh had not played a match of any type in Pakistan since 2008, and their last Test had been five years before that. All 16 games had brought defeat, but there were hopes of giving the hosts a run for their money. It never happened.

Even though Pakistan had lost six straight Twenty20 internationals since defeating South Africa at Centurion in February 2019, they were clinging on at the top of the ICC rankings. Bangladesh, meanwhile, had beaten India at Delhi in November, and were better value than eighth place suggested. But by the time the third game was washed out, Pakistan had claimed the series. Tamim Iqbal looked comfortable in both matches, but totals of 141 and 136 hardly troubled Pakistan. The experienced trio of Shoaib Malik, Babar Azam and Mohammad Hafeez all hit unbeaten half-centuries.

The Test was similarly one-sided. Four home batsmen passed 50, with Shan Masood and Babar going on to hundreds. For Bangladesh, Mithun Ali's 63

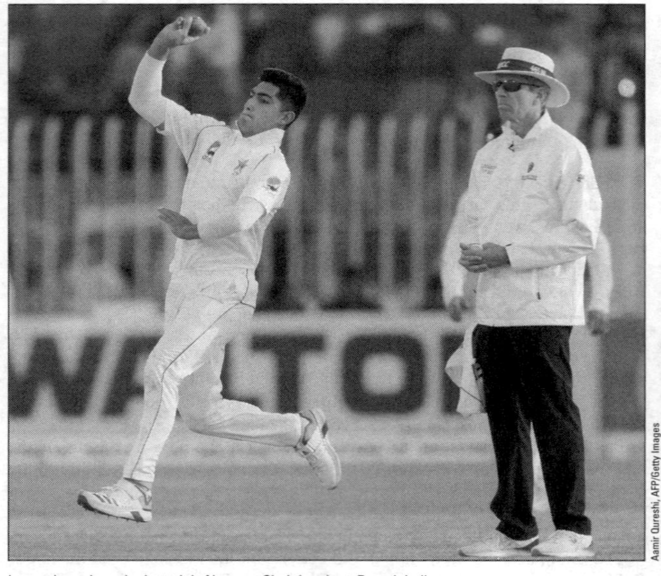

Aamir Qureshi, AFP/Getty Images

Leaps, bounds and a hat-trick: Naseem Shah bowls at Rawalpindi.

was the lone cause for celebration. Throw in a command performance by the latest pair of young Pakistan pace bowlers, Shaheen Shah Afridi and Naseem Shah, and the inevitable result was resounding victory. Afridi, a 19-year-old left-armer, claimed four in the first innings, but was upstaged in the second by Naseem who, a week before his 17th birthday, became the youngest to take a Test hat-trick. With Mohammad Amir recently retired from Test cricket, their arrival was well timed.

Wins in both formats brought relief for head coach Misbah-ul-Haq, who had come under pressure after a disastrous tour of Australia. The opposite was true for Russell Domingo, the South African in charge of Bangladesh, though it probably didn't help that five of his support team were elsewhere. It was a tricky baptism for Ottis Gibson, appointed Bangladesh's fast-bowling coach as the tour began, after Charl Langeveldt had joined South Africa less than five months into the job. However, the successful staging of the games did help persuade overseas players – if not Mushfiqur – to join the PSL.

The abrupt end of the tour brought about by the Covid-19 pandemic meant the Test series was only half completed. Pakistan banked 60 World Championship points, with another 60 at stake whenever the postponed Karachi game could be rearranged.

BANGLADESH TOURING PARTY

*Mominul Haque (T), Abu Jayed (T), Afif Hossain (20), Al-Amin Hossain (T/20), Aminul Islam (20), Ebadat Hossain (T), Hasan Mahmud (20), Liton Das (T/20), Mahmudullah (T/20), Mehedi Hasan snr (20), Mithun Ali (T/20), Mohammad Naim (20), Mustafizur Rahman (20), Nayeem Hasan (T), Nazmul Hossain (T/20), Rubel Hossain (T/20), Saif Hasan (T), Shafiul Islam (20), Soumya Sarkar (T/20), Taijul Islam (T), Tamim Iqbal (T/20). *Coach:* R. C. Domingo.

Mahmudullah captained in the Twenty20 matches. The last leg of the tour, comprising an ODI and a second Test, was called off because of the Covid-19 pandemic.

First Twenty20 international At Lahore, January 24, 2020. **Pakistan won by five wickets.** ‡**Bangladesh 141-5** (20 overs) (Tamim Iqbal 39, Mohammad Naim 43); **Pakistan 142-5** (19.3 overs) (Ahsan Ali 36, Shoaib Malik 58*). *PoM:* Shoaib Malik. *T20I debuts:* Ahsan Ali, Haris Rauf (Pakistan). *This was a ragged encounter, but for Pakistan it ended a run of six defeats. Bangladesh opted to bat on a surface that did not play as easily as predicted, which helped explain a cautious opening stand of 71 in 11 overs; Tamim Iqbal's contribution was a firework-free 39. But canny bowling and smart fielding – Shadab Khan delivered a googly, pursued the false stroke back to long-off, and ran out Liton Das with a direct hit – meant the pace barely quickened. The last nine overs brought a so-so 70-4. Pakistan lost Babar Azam second ball, his first duck in 37 T20 internationals, but the coolness of Shoaib Malik, back in the 20-over side after a year, kept them up with the rate. He gained useful support from the debutant, Ahsan Ali.*

Second Twenty20 international At Lahore, January 25, 2020. **Pakistan won by nine wickets.** ‡**Bangladesh 136-6** (20 overs) (Tamim Iqbal 65); **Pakistan 137-1** (16.4 overs) (Babar Azam 66*, Mohammad Hafeez 67*). *PoM:* Babar Azam. *Pakistan claimed the series, after Bangladesh again chose to bat on a green pitch – and again failed to make a fighting total. Without Tamim, it would have been derisory; he was rarely troubled, and had started to pick up the tempo when he was carelessly run out for a 53-ball 65. Teenage quick Mohammad Hasnain was the pick of the home bowlers, with 2-20, though all the attack played a part. Ahsan could not build on the previous day's promising debut, and departed for a seven-ball duck. From then on, it was all Pakistan: Babar and the 39-year-old Mohammad Hafeez put on a classy 131* in 15 overs.*

Third Twenty20 international At Lahore, January 27, 2020. **Pakistan v Bangladesh. Abandoned.** *PoS:* Babar Azam.

PAKISTAN v BANGLADESH

First Test

At Rawalpindi, February 7–10, 2020. Pakistan won by an innings and 44 runs. Pakistan 60pts. Toss: Pakistan. Test debut: Saif Hasan.

Pakistan's superior pace attack, led by two teenagers, overpowered Bangladesh, who capitulated to an innings defeat on the fourth morning. The result came as no great surprise, given that the visitors were without two experienced players: Shakib Al Hasan was banned, while Mushfiqur Rahim, swayed by the unease of his family, stayed away for security reasons.

But the match will be remembered for a short passage of play late on the third day. Having burst on to the international scene the previous November, 16-year-old Naseem Shah claimed a hat-trick that snuffed out an irritating Bangladeshi fightback. The third-wicket partnership between Nazmul Hossain and Mominul Haque was worth 71, and they had taken the score to 124 for two. The deficit was down to 88, and there was growing hope the Test could be saved.

Bowling at a decent pace, Naseem brought one back sharply in to the left-handed Nazmul. Umpire Llong rejected the appeal, but the review showed the ball knocking over leg. In came nightwatchman Taijul Islam, also a left-hander. He could not lay bat on another beauty that homed in on the stumps – and was so plumb that this time no one needed to check whether Llong had raised his finger. The next ball was full and wide, and Mahmudullah could have left it alone. But he was tempted, and the edge flew to first slip, where Haris Sohail held a smart catch. "I am overwhelmed," Naseem said. "I was later told I am the youngest to record a Test hat-trick – and it's a great feeling."

It ripped the heart out of the Bangladesh resistance, and things soon went from bad to worse: Mithun Ali, who in the first innings had made their only half-century of the game, was bowled by Yasir Shah before the close. Bangladesh had lost four wickets for two runs in 26 balls. (At least they did not have to face Naseem, who managed only two more deliveries before leaving the field complaining of sore ribs; scans revealed no serious injury.) A few hearty blows from Liton Das on the fourth morning did not cause Pakistan much concern, and he was the first of two more victims for Yasir, whose confidence seemed to be returning after a torrid time in Australia. Like Naseem, he finished with four wickets.

YOUNGEST TO TAKE A TEST HAT-TRICK

Years	*Days*			
16	**359**	**Naseem Shah**	**Pakistan v Bangladesh at Rawalpindi**	**2019-20**
19	240	Alok Kapali	Bangladesh v Pakistan at Peshawar	2003-04
20	202	Abdul Razzaq	Pakistan v Sri Lanka at Galle	2000
20	251	Harbhajan Singh	India v Australia at Kolkata	2000-01
21	12	G. M. Griffin	South Africa v England at Lord's	1960
21	12	Mohammad Sami	Pakistan v Sri Lanka at Lahore	2001-02
21	94	I. K. Pathan	India v Pakistan at Karachi	2005-06
21	112	J. J. C. Lawson*	West Indies v Australia at Bridgetown	2002-03
21	197	D. N. T. Zoysa	Sri Lanka v Zimbabwe at Harare	1999-2000
21	198	W. W. Hall	W Indies v Pakistan at Lahore (Bagh-e-Jinnah)	1958-59

* *Split over two innings.*

Back on the first day, Azhar Ali's decision to bowl on a grassy pitch had quickly borne fruit, with both new-ball bowlers claiming a wicket in their first over. The next six batsmen all reached 24, though Mithun alone passed 44, as the lanky Shaheen Shah Afridi, two months from his 20th birthday, caused problems. A total of 233, while far from hopeless, still felt like an opportunity missed.

In the second over of their reply, Pakistan lost Abid Ali, brought back to earth after hundreds in his first two Tests, against Sri Lanka. Azhar departed at 93 and, had Ebadat Hossain not botched a catchable chance off Babar Azam soon after lunch, they would have been an uncertain 104 for three. Babar, whose previous six Test innings had brought three centuries and a 97, made the most of his reprieve, adding 112 with the assured Shan Masood – whose century was his second in a row – then 137 with Asad Shafiq. By the end of the second day, Pakistan were in control at 342 for three, a lead of 109.

YOUNGEST WINNERS OF MATCH AWARD IN TESTS

Years	*Days*			
16	**360**	**Naseem Shah (2; 1-61, 4-26)**	**Pakistan v B'desh at Rawalpindi**	**2019-20**
16	364	Mohammad Ashraful (26, 114; 0-63)	Bangladesh v SL at Colombo (SSC)	2001-02
17	112	S. R. Tendulkar (68, 119*)	India v England at Manchester	1990
17	356	H. Masakadza (9, 119; –, 0-3)	Zimbabwe v West Indies at Harare	2001
18	36	Enamul Haque jnr (0*; 0-55, 6-45)	B'desh v Zimbabwe at Chittagong	2004-05
18	49	D. L. Vettori (4, 6; 4-46, 5-84)	New Zealand v SL at Hamilton	1996-97
18	102	Mohammad Amir (0, 5*; 3-20, 4-86)	Pakistan v Australia at Leeds	2010
18	130	Mohammad Amir (6, 4*; 1-49, 5-52)	Pakistan v England at The Oval	2010
18	197	P. J. Cummins (2, 13*; 1-38, 6-79)	Australia v SA at Johannesburg	2011-12
18	256	Wasim Akram (1*, 8*; 5-56, 5-72)	Pakistan v New Zealand at Dunedin	1984-85

Few Tests had match awards before the 1980s.

Next morning, though, the Bangladesh attack coaxed more from the pitch. Babar departed to the second ball of the day for 143, edging to first slip. Shafiq added only five to his overnight 60, and Pakistan relied on the combative Haris to take the lead past 200. Of the 103 put on by the last six wickets, he scored 70. He enjoyed some luck early on, but grew in fluency: nine runs came from his first 38 balls, 66 from the next 65.

A good day for Bangladesh seemed to be getting better still as runs came from the top order. Saif Hasan, who had made a two-ball duck on the first morning, cracked four fours, before Naseem ripped one through his defences, while three colleagues made at least 34. But then Azhar brought Naseem back for a second spell in fading light. It turned out to be a masterstroke.

Player of the Match: Naseem Shah.

Close of play: first day, Bangladesh 233; second day, Pakistan 342-3 (Babar Azam 143, Asad Shafiq 60); third day, Bangladesh 126-6 (Mominul Haque 37, Liton Das 0).

Bangladesh

First innings		Second innings	
Tamim Iqbal lbw b Mohammad Abbas	3	lbw b Yasir Shah	34
Saif Hasan c Asad Shafiq b Shaheen Shah Afridi	0	b Naseem Shah	16
Nazmul Hossain c Mohammad Rizwan b Mohammad Abbas	44	lbw b Naseem Shah	38
*Mominul Haque c Mohammad Rizwan b Shaheen Shah Afridi	30	lbw b Shaheen Shah Afridi	41
Mahmudullah c Asad Shafiq b Shaheen Shah Afridi	25	(6) c Haris Sohail b Naseem Shah	0
Mithun Ali c Mohammad Rizwan b Naseem Shah	63	(7) b Yasir Shah	0
†Liton Das lbw b Haris Sohail	33	(8) lbw b Yasir Shah	29
Taijul Islam c Yasir Shah b Haris Sohail	24	(5) lbw b Naseem Shah	0
Rubel Hossain b Shaheen Shah Afridi	1	lbw b Mohammad Abbas	5
Abu Jayed run out (Mohammad Abbas)	0	c Asad Shafiq b Yasir Shah	3
Ebadat Hossain not out	0	not out	0
B 6, w 1, nb 3	10	W 2	2
1/3 (2) 2/3 (1) 3/62 (4) 4/95 (3) 5/107 (5) 6/161 (7) 7/214 (8) 8/229 (9) 9/233 (6) 10/233 (10) (82.5 overs)	233	1/39 (2) 2/53 (1) 3/124 (3) 4/124 (5) 5/124 (6) 6/126 (7) 7/130 (4) 8/156 (9) 9/165 (8) 10/168 (10) (62.2 overs)	168

Shaheen Shah Afridi 21.5–3–53–4; Mohammad Abbas 17–9–19–2; Naseem Shah 16–0–61–1; Yasir Shah 22–2–83–0; Haris Sohail 6–2–11–2. *Second innings*—Shaheen Shah Afridi 16–6–39–1; Mohammad Abbas 17.4–6–33–1; Naseem Shah 8.2–2–26–4; Yasir Shah 17.2–3–58–4; Asad Shafiq 3–0–12–0.

Pakistan

Shan Masood b Taijul Islam	100
Abid Ali c Liton Das b Abu Jayed	0
*Azhar Ali c Nazmul Hossain b Abu Jayed	34
Babar Azam c Mithun Ali b Abu Jayed	143
Asad Shafiq c Liton Das b Ebadat Hossain	65
Haris Sohail c Tamim Iqbal b Taijul Islam	75
†Mohammad Rizwan c Mahmudullah b Rubel Hossain	10
Yasir Shah lbw b Rubel Hossain	5
Shaheen Shah Afridi lbw b Rubel Hossain	3
Mohammad Abbas not out	1
Naseem Shah run out (Saif Hasan)	2
B 1, lb 3, w 1, nb 2	7
1/2 (2) 2/93 (3) 3/205 (1) 4/342 (4) 5/353 (5) 6/374 (7) 7/415 (8) 8/422 (9) 9/442 (6) 10/445 (11) (122.5 overs)	445

Ebadat Hossain 25–6–97–1; Abu Jayed 29–4–86–3; Rubel Hossain 25.5–3–113–3; Taijul Islam 41–6–139–2; Mahmudullah 2–0–6–0.

Umpires: C. B. Gaffaney and N. J. Llong. Third umpire: M. Erasmus.
Referee: R. B. Richardson.

Only ODI At Karachi, April 3, 2020. Cancelled.

Second Test At Karachi, April 5–9, 2020. Cancelled.

PAKISTAN v ZIMBABWE IN 2020-21

SHAHID HASHMI

One-day internationals (3): Pakistan 2 (20pts), Zimbabwe 1 (10pts)
Twenty20 internationals (3): Pakistan 3, Zimbabwe 0

The revival of international cricket in Pakistan came almost full circle with another visit from Zimbabwe, who in 2015 had been the first to tour since the attack on the Sri Lankan team bus in Lahore in March 2009. This visit was very different, conducted in a biosecure bubble in Rawalpindi, which staged six white-ball matches in just 12 days. The absence of spectators made the stringent security arrangements a little easier.

Zimbabwe were still emerging from isolation of another kind, after their cricket was disrupted by a brief ICC ban for government interference in 2019. The squad, led by Chamu Chibhabha, was bolstered by the return of the tall 24-year-old opening bowler Blessing Muzarabani, who had spent the previous two English seasons with Northamptonshire as a Kolpak player. There were signs of promise from Wesley Madhevere, a 20-year-old batsman who bowled serviceable off-spin, while there was also a maiden call-up for Faraz Akram, a Saudi Arabian-born seamer. And the tour turned out to be a curtain-call for former captain Elton Chigumbura, who announced his retirement, aged 34, during the T20 series. Zimbabwe's Indian coach, Lalchand Rajput, was advised not to travel to Pakistan; bowling coach Douglas Hondo stepped in.

Pakistan won the first one-day international, despite Brendan Taylor's century, and took the series with a straightforward win in the second. But Zimbabwe salvaged some pride by winning the third after a super over, in which Muzarabani claimed two wickets to take his haul for the day to seven. Pakistan's extra experience gave them the edge in the T20s, which they swept 3–0. That series featured a noteworthy debut, thanks to an ankle injury which sidelined Shadab Khan: Usman Qadir, a 27-year-old leg-spinner who had flirted with qualifying for Australia, followed his famous father, Abdul Qadir – who died in September 2019, aged 63 – into the Pakistan side. Exhibiting a similar bouncy action, and turning his leg-breaks and googlies a long way at times, he claimed eight for 60 in the three matches. "It was quite emotional to remember my father," said Usman. "I was remembering him with every wicket I got, because they are all for him."

The twin series were a triumph for Babar Azam, who followed 77 not out and 125 in the one-dayers with 82 and 51 in the T20s. Already captain in the white-ball formats, he was soon put in charge of the Test team as well.

ZIMBABWE TOURING PARTY

*C. J. Chibhabha, R. P. Burl, B. B. Chari, T. L. Chatara, E. Chigumbura, T. S. Chisoro, C. R. Ervine, Faraz Akram, T. S. Kamunhukamwe, W. N. Madhevere, W. P. Masakadza, C. T. Mumba, R. Mutumbami, B. Muzarabani, R. Ngarava, M. Shumba, Sikandar Raza, B. R. M. Taylor, D. T. Tiripano, S. C. Williams. *Coach:* D. T. Hondo.

First one-day international At Rawalpindi, October 30, 2020 (day/night). **Pakistan won by 26 runs.** ‡**Pakistan 281-8** (50 overs) (Imam-ul-Haq 58, Haris Sohail 71, Imad Wasim 34*); **Zimbabwe 255** (49.4 overs) (C. R. Ervine 41, B. R. M. Taylor 112, W. N. Madhevere 55; Shaheen Shah Afridi 5-49, Wahab Riaz 4-41). *PoM:* B. R. M. Taylor. *ODI debut:* Haris Rauf (Pakistan). *Thanks to a superb century from Brendan Taylor, Zimbabwe threatened an upset at 234-4 in the 46th. But Wahab Riaz removed Wesley Madhevere after a stand of 119, and Taylor fell next over, from the impressive Shaheen Shah Afridi, who added two more in the 49th as Zimbabwe fell short. Earlier, Imam-ul-Haq had batted past halfway for 58, and Haris Sohail also applied himself, before Imad Wasim's breezy 34* ensured a strong total for Pakistan in their first ODI for over a year.*

Second one-day international At Rawalpindi, November 1, 2020 (day/night). **Pakistan won by six wickets.** ‡**Zimbabwe 206** (45.1 overs) (B. R. M. Taylor 36, S. C. Williams 75; Iftikhar Ahmed 5-40); **Pakistan 208-4** (35.2 overs) (Imam-ul-Haq 49, Babar Azam 77*). *PoM:* Iftikhar Ahmed. *ODI debuts:* Haider Ali, Musa Khan (Pakistan). *Pakistan clinched the series thanks to an unlikely destroyer, Iftikhar Ahmed, whose part-time off-breaks produced a five-for. His victims included top-scorers Taylor and Sean Williams. Musa Khan, a 20-year-old seamer, dismissed Craig Ervine with his second ball in ODIs, and finished with 2-21. Pakistan's openers, Imam and Abid Ali (22), had 68 after ten overs, and Babar Azam supervised the rest of the chase, finishing with a six off Madhevere. Haider Ali, another 20-year-old debutant, hit two sixes in a rapid 29, before being given lbw by Aleem Dar, who was umpiring his 210th ODI, breaking Rudi Koertzen's record.*

Third one-day international At Rawalpindi, November 3, 2020 (day/night). **Zimbabwe won the super over, after a tie.** ‡**Zimbabwe 278-6** (50 overs) (B. R. M. Taylor 56, S. C. Williams 118*, W. N. Madhevere 33, Sikandar Raza 45; Mohammad Hasnain 5-26); **Pakistan 278-9** (50 overs) (Babar Azam 125, Khushdil Shah 33, Wahab Riaz 52; B. Muzarabani 5-49). *PoM:* B. Muzarabani. *PoS:* Babar Azam. *ODI debut:* Khushdil Shah (Pakistan). *A clean sweep looked on the cards as Pakistan reached 251-6 in the 47th, with Babar having completed his 12th ODI century. But Muzarabani dismissed Wahab to end a stand of 100, and removed Afridi and Babar with the last two balls of the 49th. Musa and Mohammad Hasnain needed 13 off the last, from Richard Ngarava, and forced a super over when Tendai Chisoro dived over Musa's shot. Muzarabani completed a hat-trick of sorts when Iftikhar cracked the first extra delivery to midwicket, and the fourth-ball departure of Khushdil Shah ended the fun at 2-2; Muzarabani's overall figures were 7-51. Zimbabwe needed three to win, and Sikandar Raza laced the third delivery past mid-off. Earlier, Williams was dropped four times on the way to his fourth ODI century, after Hasnain reduced Zimbabwe to 22-3.*

World Cup Super League: Pakistan 20pts, Zimbabwe 10pts.

First Twenty20 international At Rawalpindi, November 7, 2020 (floodlit). **Pakistan won by six wickets.** ‡**Zimbabwe 156-6** (20 overs) (W. N. Madhevere 70*); **Pakistan 157-4** (18.5 overs) (Babar Azam 82, Mohammad Hafeez 36). *PoM:* Babar Azam. *T20I debut:* Usman Qadir (Pakistan). *Pakistan rested Afridi, but still had enough firepower to contain Zimbabwe, for whom Madhevere scored a career-best 70* in 48 balls. Babar made light of the target, sprinting to 82 from 55, and dominating a third-wicket stand of 80 with 40-year-old Mohammad Hafeez.*

Second Twenty20 international At Rawalpindi, November 8, 2020 (floodlit). **Pakistan won by eight wickets. Zimbabwe 134-7** (20 overs) (R. P. Burl 32*; Haris Rauf 3-31, Usman Qadir 3-23); ‡**Pakistan 137-2** (15.1 overs) (Babar Azam 51, Haider Ali 66*). *PoM:* Haider Ali. *An illustrious name was to the fore as Pakistan clinched the series: Usman Qadir, son of Abdul, returned figures of 24–15–23–3 in only his second international, after Madhevere smacked his nervous opening delivery for six. Two early wickets for Haris Rauf helped ensure Zimbabwe's total would be modest. Babar spanked 51 from 28 balls, and put on 100 with Haider, who finished with 66* from 43.*

Third Twenty20 international At Rawalpindi, November 10, 2020 (floodlit). **Pakistan won by eight wickets.** ‡**Zimbabwe 129-9** (20 overs) (C. J. Chibhabha 31; Usman Qadir 4-13); **Pakistan 130-2** (15.2 overs) (Abdullah Shafiq 41*, Khushdil Shah 36*). *PoM:* Usman Qadir. *PoS:* Usman Qadir. *T20I debuts:* Abdullah Shafiq (Pakistan); M. Shumba, Faraz Akram (Zimbabwe). *Qadir mesmerised the visitors again, and set up another stroll: he had 24–16–13–4 as Zimbabwe slid from 55-2 to 87-7. Their captain Chamu Chibhabha top-scored with 31, which gave him just 65 in six games. When Pakistan batted, a solid start meant Babar did not get a chance to bat, with 20-year-old debutant Abdullah Shafiq settling in for 41* from 33 balls. Khushdil completed the whitewash with a six off another debutant – Faraz Akram, a 27-year-old seamer born in Jeddah, Saudi Arabia. Zimbabwe's players formed a guard of honour to applaud their former captain Elton Chigumbura, who had announced his retirement after 284 international matches.*

MCC IN PAKISTAN IN 2019-20

A strong side, captained by MCC president Kumar Sangakkara, made a flag-waving visit to Lahore early in 2020, as part of Pakistan's attempts to re-establish top-level cricket in the country. Sangakkara had been part of the Sri Lankan team attacked by terrorists in Lahore in March 2009.

The tourists, who included two others with Test caps, as well as several current county players, contested three Twenty20 matches and one 50-over game. They won the two against Pakistan Super League teams, but lost the other two. Ravi Bopara, who had recently announced he was moving from Essex to Sussex to concentrate on T20, led the way with 131 runs in the shorter format, while Sangakkara, now 42, rolled back the years with a 35-ball 52 in the final match.

All in all, the tour helped Pakistan's rehabilitation efforts. "We had a wonderful time," said Sangakkara. "The security has been exceptional, and the cricket highly enjoyable. The hospitality was outstanding, and people were so warm and loving."

MCC TOURING PARTY

*K. C. Sangakkara, R. S. Bopara, M. G. K. Burgess, O. J. Hannon-Dalby, F. J. Klaassen, M. A. Leask, A. M. Lilley, S. R. Patel, I. Qayyum, W. M. H. Rhodes, S. M. Sharif, R. E. van der Merwe, R. A. Whiteley.

At Lahore (Gaddafi Stadium), February 14, 2020 (floodlit). **MCC won by four wickets. Lahore Qalandars 135-5** (20 overs) (Fakhar Zaman 45, Sohail Akhtar 40*); ‡**MCC 136-6** (19.2 overs) (R. S. Bopara 42, S. R. Patel 31). *PoM:* R. S. Bopara. *MCC started their tour with a narrow win, after former England Test players Ravi Bopara (42 from 37 balls) and Samit Patel (31 from 22) had added a crucial 60 for the fourth wicket. Roelof van der Merwe had earlier taken 2-17 – and run out Salman Butt – as Lahore Qalandars failed to make the most of a useful start.*

At Lahore (Aitchison College), February 16, 2020. **Pakistan Shaheens won by five wickets. MCC 204-9** (50 overs) (R. A. Whiteley 51; Ehsan Adil 6-34); ‡**Pakistan Shaheens 205-5** (45 overs) (Imran Rafiq 66*). *PoM:* Ehsan Adil. *Seamer Ehsan Adil, who played the last of his three Tests in 2015, took two early wickets, then returned to dismiss Will Rhodes and Ross Whiteley in successive overs after a stand of 68. Adil finished with 6-34 as MCC reached a modest total. It looked healthier when Oliver Hannon-Dalby took two wickets, but from 114-5 Pakistan Shaheens were steered calmly home by Imran Rafiq (66* from 124 balls) and Hasan Mohsin (49* from 54).*

At Lahore (Aitchison College), February 17, 2020. **Northern Areas won by nine runs. Northern Areas 152-5** (20 overs) (Ali Imran 64; R. S. Bopara 3-14); ‡**MCC 143-7** (20 overs) (S. R. Patel 39*). *The tourists looked on course for victory at 114-4, chasing 153, but 17-year-old off-spinner Mubasir Khan dismissed the dangerous pair of Bopara (19) and Whiteley (21), and Patel was left with too much to do. Earlier, opener Ali Imran had given Northern Areas a good start with 64 from 43 balls, although they were slowed towards the end, when Bopara struck in three successive overs.*

At Lahore (Aitchison College), February 19, 2020. **MCC won by 72 runs.** ‡**MCC 184-4** (20 overs) (K. C. Sangakkara 52, R. S. Bopara 70*); **Multan Sultans 112** (17.4 overs) (Khushdil Shah 45; I. Qayyum 4-9). *MCC ended the tour with a thumping victory against a side captained by Shan Masood, and also including Shahid Afridi, Wayne Madsen and Rilee Rossouw. It was set up by a fourth-wicket stand of 89 between Kumar Sangakkara, whose 52 came from 35 balls, and Bopara, whose 70* from 37 included four sixes and seven fours. Multan Sultans reached 66-2, but then lost eight for 46, with slow left-armer Imran Qayyum taking 4-9 in his four overs, and Patel 2-2 in four balls.*

DOMESTIC CRICKET IN PAKISTAN IN 2019-20

ABID ALI KAZI

The 2019-20 domestic season was the first played under the dramatically revamped structure demanded by Imran Khan after he became prime minister in 2018. After years of the PCB swinging between separate tournaments for regional and departmental sides, and a single competition combining both types, all of them were swept away. The Quaid-e-Azam Trophy was contested by six provincial associations, created by merging the previous 16 regional teams, playing a simple home-and-away league followed by a final. They would also compete in the National T20 Cup and 50-over Pakistan Cup (though the latter was cancelled as the Covid-19 crisis developed), plus Second XI equivalents.

The PCB selected a squad of 32 for each of the six new associations, offering players a central domestic contract with a guaranteed income. Contracted international cricketers were evenly distributed, and leading ex-players assigned as coaches. As in recent County Championships, the visiting side were given the option of bowling first without a toss.

SIXTEEN INTO SIX WILL GO

Baluchistan	Quetta and Dera Murad Jamali
Central Punjab	**Lahore**, Faisalabad and Sialkot
Khyber Pakhtunkhwa	**Peshawar**, Abbottabad and **Federally Administered Tribal Areas**
Northern	**Islamabad**, **Rawalpindi** and Azad Jammu & Kashmir
Sindh	**Karachi**, Hyderabad and Larkana
Southern Punjab	**Multan** and Bahawalpur

Bold signifies teams who played in the 2018-19 Quaid-e-Azam Trophy; the rest were in Grade II.

Critics argued that the streamlined structure, modelled on Australia's, did not take into account the difference in population, and that six teams were not enough for Pakistan. They also said losing the departmental sides left around 400 cricketers without jobs.

But the first season of the reformed system witnessed a marked improvement among the batsmen. There were 77 centuries in 31 Quaid-e-Azam matches, compared with 72 in 69 the previous year, and eight doubles, up from four, headed by Abid Ali's unbeaten 249 for Sindh. Three players – Imran Butt of Baluchistan, and Central Punjab's Kamran Akmal and Salman Butt – passed 900 runs, which no one managed in 2018-19.

The three leading wicket-takers were all spinners, another significant shift from recent trends. Northern's slow left-armer Nauman Ali finished with 54 wickets at 25, ahead of Central Punjab's Bilal Asif (43) and Zafar Gohar (38). Nauman and Zafar took 11 wickets apiece when Northern and Central Punjab met in November, and Bilal repeated the feat when the same teams reached the five-day final in December.

The PCB had allowed for a sixth day, in case five were not enough for both finalists to complete their first innings (in a draw, first-innings lead would be the tie-breaker). But **Central Punjab** won by an innings and 16 runs inside four days: their third innings victory, and their second over Northern. A double-hundred by Umar Akmal, a century from Test captain Azhar Ali, and Zafar's 99 took them to the tournament's highest total – 675 for eight – before Bilal wrecked Northern's second innings with eight for 112.

Northern had already won the National T20 Cup, staged at Faisalabad's Iqbal Stadium in October. They headed the table, winning four of their five qualifying games; and, after a tight semi-final – Khyber Pakhtunkhwa needed eight off the last over, but lost four wickets – crushed Baluchistan by 52 runs in the final. They completed a T20 double by adding the Second XI title, beating Southern Punjab, who did win the non-first-class Grade II Quaid-e-Azam Trophy, on first-innings lead against Khyber Pakhtunkhwa.

FIRST-CLASS AVERAGES IN 2019-20

BATTING (400 runs, average 50.00)

		M	*I*	*NO*	*R*	*HS*	*100*	*Avge*	*Ct/St*
1	Babar Azam (*Central Punjab/Pakistan*)	5	6	2	478	143	3	119.50	6
2	Abid Ali (*Sindh/Pakistan*)	6	9	2	628	249*	3	89.71	4
3	Zohaib Khan (*Khyber Pakhtunkhwa*)	10	13	7	527	133	2	87.83	5
4	†Sami Aslam (*Southern Punjab*)	10	15	4	864	243*	4	78.54	7
5	†Salman Butt (*Central Punjab*)	10	15	3	901	237	3	75.08	3
6	†Zeeshan Ashraf (*Southern Punjab*)	4	7	0	505	141	2	72.14	2
7	Faizan Riaz (*Northern*)	8	15	3	857	211	3	71.41	4
8	†Fawad Alam (*Sindh*)	10	13	2	781	211	4	71.00	4
9	Ashfaq Ahmed (*Khyber Pakhtunkhwa*)	10	14	2	805	173	4	67.08	3
10	Azhar Ali (*Central Punjab/Pakistan*)	9	12	0	786	155	4	65.50	3
11	Umar Akmal (*Central Punjab*)	8	12	0	754	218	2	62.83	0
12	Imran Butt (*Baluchistan*)	9	17	2	934	214	4	62.26	15
13	Kamran Akmal (*Central Punjab*)	11	15	0	906	166	3	60.40	38/3
14	†Imran Farhat (*Baluchistan*)	10	17	2	819	137	3	54.60	5
15	Zeeshan Malik (*Northern*)	8	15	0	780	216	1	52.00	2
16	Adnan Akmal (*Southern Punjab*)	10	13	2	568	113	2	51.63	29/3
17	†Shan Masood (*South Punjab/Pakistan*)	8	10	0	511	135	3	51.10	2
18	Omair Bin Yousuf (*Sindh*)	6	9	1	403	174	1	50.37	3
19	†Umar Siddiq (*Southern Punjab*)	10	15	2	650	130	2	50.00	4

BOWLING (10 wickets, average 40.00)

		Style	*O*	*M*	*R*	*W*	*BB*	*5I*	*Avge*
1	Naseem Shah (*Central Punjab/Pak*)	RF	186.3	30	628	30	6-78	2	20.93
2	Bilal Asif (*Central Punjab*)	OB	307	42	996	43	8-112	2	23.16
3	Sajid Khan (*Khyber Pakhtunkhwa*)	OB	201.4	41	624	25	5-36	1	24.96
4	Nauman Ali (*Northern*)	SLA	414.1	82	1,371	54	8-71	5	25.38
5	Shaheen Shah Afridi (*Northern/Pak*)	LFM	126.4	28	397	15	5-77	1	26.46
6	Usman Shinwari (*Khyber Pakh/Pak*)	LFM	140	26	434	16	3-20	0	27.12
7	Kashif Bhatti (*Sindh*)	SLA	182	53	418	14	4-108	0	29.85
8	Aizaz Cheema (*Central Punjab*)	RFM	142.5	25	497	16	5-81	2	31.06
9	Ehsan Adil (*Central Punjab*)	RFM	209	45	588	18	3-15	0	32.66
10	Mohammad Abbas (*S Punjab/Pak*)	RFM	179.4	48	472	14	4-55	0	33.71
11	Anwar Ali (*Sindh*)	RFM	132	29	407	12	5-75	1	33.91
12	Bilawal Bhatti (*Southern Punjab*)	RFM	106.5	10	420	12	4-23	0	35.00
13	Rahat Ali (*Southern Punjab*)	LFM	198.5	36	696	19	5-49	1	36.63
14	Zafar Gohar (*Central Punjab*)	SLA	433.5	82	1,397	38	7-79	1	36.76
15	Mohammad Asghar (*Baluchistan*)	SLA	285.4	31	1,048	27	6-121	2	38.81
16	Waqas Ahmed (*Northern*)	RF	245.2	48	831	21	6-109	1	39.57
17	Sohail Khan (*Sindh*)	RFM	253.5	50	875	22	4-62	0	39.77

QUAID-E-AZAM TROPHY IN 2019-20

					Bonus pts		
	P	*W*	*L*	*D*	*Bat*	*Bowl*	*Pts*
CENTRAL PUNJAB	10	3	1	6	30	25	133
NORTHERN	10	3	2	5	32	25	130
Khyber Pakhtunkhwa	10	2	1	7	36	21	124
Southern Punjab	10	1	0	9	36	15	112
Sindh	10	0	2	8	27	23	90
Baluchistan	10	0	3	7	28	21	84

Outright win = 16pts; draw = 5pts. Bonus points were awarded as follows for the first 110 overs of each team's first innings: one batting point for the first 200 runs, and then for 250, 300, 350 and 400; one bowling point for the third wicket taken, and then for the sixth and ninth.

Final At Karachi (National), December 27–30, 2019. **Central Punjab won by an innings and 16 runs.** ‡**Northern 254** (Faizan Riaz 116; Fahim Ashraf 5-54) **and 405** (Haider Ali 134; Bilal Asif 8-112); **Central Punjab 675-8 dec** (Azhar Ali 119, Umar Akmal 218). *Central Punjab needed only four days to secure the new-look Quaid-e-Azam Trophy. Northern were on the back foot from the opening morning, when they slumped to 69-5 against Aizaz Cheema and Fahim Ashraf after choosing to bat. Though Faizan Riaz and Rohail Nazir (80) fought back by adding 155, no one else passed 16. Central Punjab charged to a 421-run lead, after Umar Akmal batted more than six hours, hitting eight sixes; he added 215 with Zafar Gohar (99). Opener Haider Ali led a stronger Northern effort second time round, backed by Rohail (70) and Ali Sarfraz (81), but off-spinner Bilal Asif wrapped up the match with five wickets in 20 deliveries to complete a career-best 8-112, and 11-149 in all.*

QUAID-E-AZAM TROPHY WINNERS

1953-54	Bahawalpur	1979-80	PIA	2000-01	Lahore City Blues
1954-55	Karachi	1980-81	United Bank	2001-02	Karachi Whites
1956-57	Punjab	1981-82	National Bank	2002-03	PIA
1957-58	Bahawalpur	1982-83	United Bank	2003-04	Faisalabad
1958-59	Karachi	1983-84	National Bank	2004-05	Peshawar
1959-60	Karachi	1984-85	United Bank	2005-06	Sialkot
1961-62	Karachi Blues	1985-86	Karachi	2006-07	Karachi Urban
1962-63	Karachi A	1986-87	National Bank	2007-08	Sui Northern Gas
1963-64	Karachi Blues	1987-88	PIA	2008-09	Sialkot
1964-65	Karachi Blues	1988-89	ADBP	2009-10	Karachi Blues
1966-67	Karachi	1989-90	PIA	2010-11	Habib Bank
1968-69	Lahore	1990-91	Karachi Whites	2011-12	PIA
1969-70	PIA	1991-92	Karachi Whites	2012-13	Karachi Blues
1970-71	Karachi Blues	1992-93	Karachi Whites	2013-14	Rawalpindi
1972-73	Railways	1993-94	Lahore City	2014-15	Sui Northern Gas
1973-74	Railways	1994-95	Karachi Blues	2015-16	Sui Northern Gas
1974-75	Punjab A	1995-96	Karachi Blues	2016-17	WAPDA
1975-76	National Bank	1996-97	Lahore City	2017-18	Sui Northern Gas
1976-77	United Bank	1997-98	Karachi Blues	2018-19	Habib Bank
1977-78	Habib Bank	1998-99	Peshawar	2019-20	Central Punjab
1978-79	National Bank	1999-2000	PIA		

The competition has been contested sometimes by regional teams, sometimes by departments, sometimes by a mixture of the two, and now by six regional associations. Karachi teams have won the Quaid-e-Azam Trophy 20 times, PIA 7, National Bank 5, Lahore teams, Sui Northern Gas and United Bank 4, Habib Bank 3, Bahawalpur, Peshawar, Punjab, Railways and Sialkot 2, ADBP, Central Punjab, Faisalabad, Rawalpindi and WAPDA 1.

NATIONAL T20 CUP IN 2019-20

20-over league plus knockout

Semi-finals Baluchistan beat Southern Punjab by three wickets; Northern beat Khyber Pakhtunkhwa by three runs.

Final At Faisalabad, October 24, 2019 (floodlit). **Northern won by 52 runs. Northern 167-5** (20 overs); ‡**Baluchistan 115** (18.2 overs). *Northern opener Umar Amin scored 60 in 38 balls, the only half-century of the final, before Mohammad Nawaz and Shadab Khan boosted the total by adding 58 in the last 5.2 overs. Sohail Tanvir (3-27) reduced Baluchistan to 14-2; Awais Zia and Imran Farhat responded by putting on 44, but that remained their best stand, and the last five went down in 20 balls.*

The HBL Pakistan Super League has its own section (page 855).

SOUTH AFRICAN CRICKET IN 2020

Board senseless

COLIN BRYDEN

If 2020 was a year to forget in most cricketing countries, it was especially so in South Africa. By the end, though, there were glimmers of hope: a no-nonsense interim board seemed intent on clearing up the administrative mess of Cricket South Africa, while the national team returned to winning ways.

As almost everywhere else, Covid-19 was hugely disruptive. South Africa's 2019-20 domestic season was brought to a premature conclusion, and tours of India, Sri Lanka and the West Indies were cancelled. Early in 2020-21, England played three Twenty20 internationals – and rather a lot of golf – but went home after an apparent breach of a biosecure bubble at the Cape Town hotel they were sharing with the home team. Three World Cup Super League one-day internationals were postponed.

SOUTH AFRICA IN 2020

	Played	*Won*	*Lost*	*Drawn/No result*
Tests	4	1	3	–
One-day internationals	6	4	1	1
Twenty20 internationals	9	2	7	–

Month	Fixtures	Reference
DECEMBER / JANUARY	4 Tests, 3 ODIs and 3 T20Is (h) v England	(see *Wisden 2020*, page 440)
FEBRUARY / MARCH	3 ODIs and 3 T20Is (h) v Australia	(page 743)
APRIL		
MAY		
JUNE		
JULY		
AUGUST		
SEPTEMBER		
OCTOBER		
NOVEMBER	3 T20Is (h) v England	(page 387)
DECEMBER / JANUARY	2 Tests (h) v Sri Lanka	(page 751)

For a review of South African domestic cricket from the 2019-20 season, see page 758.

Jeffrey Abrahams, Gallo Images/Getty Images

Intervention policy: sports minister Nathi Mthethwa ensured change at Cricket South Africa.

Sri Lanka did fulfil their commitment to two Test matches over the Christmas/New Year period. Four of their players, including two fast bowlers, were injured during the First Test at Centurion, which South Africa won by an innings. It was their only victory of the year, although four Tests was the fewest since 1992, when South Africa returned to the fold. They completed a 2–0 win early in 2021 at the Wanderers, easily accessible from the country club near Pretoria where both sides stayed for the duration of the series. No spectators were allowed for any of these matches.

The captaincy had changed hands early in the year. Faf du Plessis resigned in February, following the home Test defeat by England. Quinton de Kock, the wicketkeeper and the team's most successful batsman of recent times, was appointed white-ball captain and – after worries about his workload – took charge for Tests too, although only for 2020-21.

Just six one-day internationals were played in 2020, also the lowest since readmission. The highlight was a 3–0 home win against Australia shortly before lockdown. There were nine T20 matches, seven of which were lost. South Africa's women won a one-day series in New Zealand, and reached the semi-finals of the T20 World Cup in Australia.

The South African teams in all formats were somewhat experimental, following a slew of retirements. Batting stability was a concern, but capable young fast bowlers began to emerge: Anrich Nortje was the leading wicket-taker on either side in the England Tests, and later Lutho Sipamla looked the part against Sri Lanka. Meanwhile, 22-year-old Wiaan Mulder gave notice that he could be the all-rounder to fill the crucial No. 7 spot in Tests.

Because of the pandemic, the only domestic cricket played in the first half of the new season was at franchise level. The final round of four-day games was postponed, and the Momentum One-Day Cup rescheduled as a shortened tournament later in January 2021, with all the matches in Potchefstroom.

The shortage of actual play meant that, for much of the year, the focus was on the shortcomings of CSA. Thabang Moroe, suspended as chief executive in December 2019, remained on full (and reportedly exorbitant) pay, until he was finally dismissed in August. It became apparent he had supporters both on the board and in the expensive new offices which housed CSA's rapidly expanding staff. There were growing calls for the entire board to resign, not least from the South African Cricketers' Association: the connection between those who played the game, and those charged with administering it, was becoming tenuous.

Chris Nenzani, granted a one-year extension after serving the maximum two four-year terms as president, stood down following a heated board meeting in August, shortly before the formal dismissal of Moroe. Acting-chief executive Jacques Faul also quit, reportedly in frustration after clashing with board members.

The South African Sports Confederation and Olympic Council, recently established as the ultimate governing body of South African elite sport, announced in September that they were conducting an investigation into CSA. The board rejected SASCOC's demand to see the full Fundudzi Forensic Services report on Moroe's alleged misconduct, prompting sports minister Nathi Mthethwa to give two weeks' notice to both CSA and the ICC that he would intervene directly if no progress was made.

The CSA board did resign in October, although five of them remained on the Members' Council, made up of the provincial association presidents. Nominally, at least, it was the CSA's ultimate decision-making authority. On October 30, Mthethwa announced an interim board, headed by retired constitutional-court judge Zac Yacoob. The interim board released the full Fundudzi report, which included damning findings of contraventions of the Companies Act, failures of corporate governance, and questionable credit-card use by Moroe. There were also findings against several other individuals, including company secretary Welsh Gwaza, who had been appointed on Moroe's watch. Gwaza and Kugrandie Govender, acting-chief executive since Faul's resignation, were suspended.

Yacoob said relations with the Members' Council were difficult, and there were tensions within the interim board as well, leading to the removal of two of the nine directors. Yacoob himself resigned in late January, after details were leaked of a phone conversation in which he berated a journalist. But, given an initial three-month deadline, the council were nothing if not committed to their task: while most South Africans were on holiday, the interim board announced on New Year's Day that agreement had been reached on a new domestic structure, following work done by David Richardson, the former Test wicketkeeper and ICC chief executive. The 16-year-old franchise structure was scrapped in favour of a two-tier provincial system, which was due to start in 2021-22.

SOUTH AFRICA v AUSTRALIA IN 2019-20

NEIL MANTHORP

Twenty20 internationals (3): South Africa 1, Australia 2
One-day internationals (3): South Africa 3, Australia 0

All the talk was of the reception the Australians would receive on their return to South Africa, two years after the sandpaper imbroglio. Just how hostile would the crowds be at the notoriously partisan Wanderers – or at Newlands, where Steve Smith, David Warner and Cameron Bancroft had conspired to change the state of the ball? Extra security was employed for the opening game, in Johannesburg, where the raucous Eastern Terrace was unexpectedly closed over safety concerns following torrential rain, less than 24 hours before the start.

It meant Warner's second-ball dismissal was not greeted with uproar. Nor was there much reaction in Cape Town. The fact that South Africa were hammered in both games helped silence the criticism. But, just in case, Australian coach Justin Langer and his players spent much of the tour saying how welcoming the people of South Africa had been.

And so, to a mix of surprise and relief, the fans' behaviour proved nothing to write home about. Almost everybody, it seemed, had moved on, even if a few wags wrote supposedly humorous messages on sheets of sandpaper, or booed Smith and Warner (Bancroft was not selected). The tourists, though, stuck to their roles in a well-choreographed charm offensive and, very soon, the talk was about cricket, and not much else.

In both series, there was an almost exhibition-match atmosphere. The 20-over games, at the start of the tour, were treated more seriously, since there was the focus of the Twenty20 World Cup, scheduled to start in October. They did not foster optimism for South Africa, whose scrambled win at Port Elizabeth was sandwiched by their two heaviest T20 thrashings.

There was little riding on the ODIs so early in the four-year World Cup cycle. The Australians rarely seemed to apply themselves, and South Africa seized the opportunity to placate disillusioned supporters with a rousing clean sweep that took their record against them to 11 wins in their last 12 meetings. Mitchell Starc was hostility incarnate at the start of the innings – only once in five games did he fail to take a wicket in the opening over – but could not sustain his aggression. He was allowed to miss the last ODI to watch his wife, Alyssa Healy, in the final of the women's T20 World Cup at the MCG; the move received more positive media feedback than anything the Australians achieved on the field.

South Africa could look with satisfaction on the performance of several debutants. Opening batsman Janneman Malan – whose brother, Pieter, had recently made his Test debut, against England – followed a first-ball duck with a match-winning century at Bloemfontein. And the series award went to Heinrich Klaasen, whose 242 runs, at better than one a ball, were 90 more than anyone else. After three stop–start years marred by injury and episodes of wretched form, he made an emphatic statement for the future.

For South Africa's new white-ball captain, Quinton de Kock, it proved a challenging few weeks. He made a brisk 70 in the Port Elizabeth T20, but on three occasions across the two series was bowled by Starc in the first over. Yet his side came out comfortably on top in the ODIs, and headed to India with a spring in their step. In the wings, though, lay an unseen enemy that would stop them, and the world, in their tracks.

AUSTRALIA TOURING PARTY

*A. J. Finch (50/20), S. A. Abbott (20), A. C. Agar (50/20), A. T. Carey (50/20), P. J. Cummins (50/20), J. R. Hazlewood (50), M. Labuschagne (50), M. R. Marsh (50/20), J. A. Richardson (50/20), K. W. Richardson (50/20), D. J. M. Short (50/20), S. P. D. Smith (50/20), M. A. Starc (50/20), M. S. Wade (50/20), D. A. Warner (50/20), A. Zampa (50/20). *Coach:* J. L. Langer.

G. J. Maxwell withdrew because of an elbow injury, and was replaced in both squads by Short. J. A. Richardson was initially selected for the Twenty20 games only, but stayed on to cover for Starc, who left early.

SOUTH AFRICA v AUSTRALIA

First Twenty20 International

At Johannesburg, February 21, 2020 (floodlit). Australia won by 107 runs. Toss: South Africa. Twenty20 international debut: P. J. van Biljon.

Ashton Agar became only the second Australian, after Brett Lee, to take a hat-trick in Twenty20 internationals – en route to a format-best five for 24. When he came on for the eighth over, South Africa already cut a ragged figure at 42 for four; six deliveries later, they were in tatters at 44 for seven. They eventually succumbed for 89, their lowest T20 total (beating 98 against Sri Lanka at Colombo in August 2018); the margin of defeat was another unwelcome record. After inducing a mistimed inside-out drive from du Plessis, and trapping Phehlukwayo, Agar produced the perfect ball to the right-handed Steyn: it spun off the edge, and fetched up at slip. Warner had cracked the first delivery of the match from Steyn for four, only to top-edge the next to fine leg – which constituted the entirety of the South Africa highlights package. They dropped several catches, the

---

MOST WICKETS FOR AUSTRALIA IN A T20 INTERNATIONAL

5-24	**A. C. Agar**	**v South Africa at Johannesburg**	**2019-20**
5-27	J. P. Faulkner	v Pakistan at Mohali	2015-16
4-8	B. Stanlake	v Pakistan at Harare	2018
4-15	S. R. Watson	v England at Adelaide	2010-11
4-18	D. P. Nannes	v Bangladesh at Bridgetown	2010
4-20	S. R. Clark	v Sri Lanka at Cape Town	2007-08
4-21	J. P. Behrendorff	v India at Guwahati	2017-18
4-23	A. J. Tye	v New Zealand at Sydney	2017-18
4-29	M. S. Kasprowicz	v New Zealand at Auckland	2004-05
4-30	J. R. Hazlewood	v England at Melbourne	2013-14
4-31	N. M. Coulter-Nile	v England at Hobart	2013-14

costliest Steyn's loss of an upper-cut in the floodlights: Smith, who had yet to score, made the most of the reprieve, as he and Finch feasted on short bowling. They added 80 for the second wicket in eight overs, giving the later batsmen the freedom to swing from the word go; Agar crashed 20 from nine balls. Starc castled de Kock with his third delivery, a snorting inswinger, and in no time a capacity crowd fell silent.

Player of the Match: A. C. Agar.

Australia

		B	*4/6*
1 D. A. Warner *c 11 b 8*	4	2	1
2 *A. J. Finch *c 3 b 11*	42	27	6/1
3 S. P. D. Smith *st 1 b 11*	45	32	5/1
4 M. S. Wade *c 5 b 8*	18	11	2
5 M. R. Marsh *c 8 b 10*	19	14	1/1
6 †A. T. Carey *c 3 b 7*	27	22	3/1
7 A. C. Agar *not out*	20	9	2/1
8 M. A. Starc *not out*	7	3	0/1
Lb 2, w 12	14		
6 overs: 70-1 (20 overs)	196-6		

1/4 2/84 3/114 4/117 5/167 6/171

9 P. J. Cummins, 10 K. W. Richardson and 11 A. Zampa did not bat.

Steyn 24–11–31–2; Ngidi 18–7–37–1; Rabada 18–4–45–0; Phehlukwayo 24–8–35–1; Shamsi 24–6–31–2; Smuts 12–2–15–0.

South Africa

		B	*4/6*
1 *†Q. de Kock *b 8*	2	3	0
2 H. E. van der Dussen *c 8 b 9*	6	10	1
3 F. du Plessis *c 10 b 7*	24	22	3
4 J. T. Smuts *c 11 b 9*	7	5	1
5 D. A. Miller *c 6 b 11*	2	2	0
6 P. J. van Biljon *b 7*	16	15	2
7 A. L. Phehlukwayo *lbw b 7*	0	1	0
8 D. W. Steyn *c 2 b 7*	0	1	0
9 K. Rabada *b 11*	22	19	1/2
10 L. T. Ngidi *c 1 b 7*	1	5	0
11 T. Shamsi *not out*	2	4	0
W 7	7		
6 overs: 38-3 (14.3 overs)	89		

1/2 2/17 3/38 4/40 5/44 6/44 7/44 8/77 9/85

Starc 18–12–23–1; Richardson 18–7–20–0; Cummins 12–6–13–2; Zampa 15–7–9–2; Agar 24–12–24–5.

Umpires: A. T. Holdstock and A. Paleker. Third umpire: B. P. Jele.
Referee: A. J. Pycroft.

SOUTH AFRICA v AUSTRALIA

Second Twenty20 International

At Port Elizabeth, February 23, 2020 (floodlit). South Africa won by 12 runs. Toss: South Africa.

Making light work of a characteristically slow pitch, de Kock was at his sublime, rampaging best: during the powerplay he struck four sixes and sprinted to 43 from 20 balls. Despite South Africa's platform of 59 for none, though, the game was won in the last three overs of the Australian reply, when just 12 runs were scored. Warner had reached a 38-ball fifty when he hit the fourth delivery of the 13th over for his sixth boundary, but thereafter Australia managed just one, a six from Carey. Despite the slowdown, Australia – needing 25 from the last three with seven wickets in hand – seemed certain to prevail. But Ngidi conceded five from the 18th, and Rabada three from the next, both taking a wicket – death bowling at its most clinical. It left Nortje the luxury of defending 17, which he did comfortably. It was the first time Warner had still been batting at the end of the match, yet finished on the losing side. Perhaps the shot of the game was a breathtaking pulled six by de Kock off a length ball from Starc. Superb though de Kock was, it was the range of slower balls from the faster bowlers that won the day, and set up a decider.

Player of the Match: Q. de Kock.

South Africa

		B	4/6
1 *†Q. de Kock *c 8 b 11*	70	47	5/4
2 R. R. Hendricks *c 7 b 10*	14	17	1
3 F. du Plessis *c 10 b 9*	15	14	1
4 H. E. van der Dussen *c 7 b 10*	37	26	2/2
5 D. A. Miller *not out*	11	13	0
6 P. J. van Biljon *not out*	7	3	1
Lb 3, w 1	4		
6 overers: 59-0 (20 overs)	158-4		

1/60 2/81 3/121 4/147

7 D. Pretorius, 8 K. Rabada, 9 A. A. Nortje, 10 L. T. Ngidi and 11 T. Shamsi did not bat.

Starc 24–6–38–0; Cummins 24–8–31–1; Richardson 24–10–21–2; Zampa 24–4–37–1; Agar 24–7–28–0.

Australia

		B	4/6
1 D. A. Warner *not out*	67	56	5/1
2 *A. J. Finch *b 10*	14	12	2
3 S. P. D. Smith *c 3 b 7*	29	26	1/1
4 †A. T. Carey *b 10*	14	10	0/1
5 M. R. Marsh *c 5 b 10*	6	8	0
6 M. S. Wade *c and b 8*	1	2	0
7 A. C. Agar *b 9*	1	5	0
8 M. A. Starc *not out*	2	2	0
B 1, lb 7, w 3, nb 1	12		
6 overs: 54-1 (20 overs)	146-6		

1/48 2/98 3/124 4/138 5/139 6/143

9 P. J. Cummins, 10 K. W. Richardson and 11 A. Zampa did not bat.

Rabada 24–5–27–1; Nortje 24–8–24–1; Ngidi 24–7–41–3; Pretorius 24–5–29–1; Shamsi 24–9–17–0.

Umpires: B. P. Jele and A. Paleker. Third umpire: A. T. Holdstock.
Referee: A. J. Pycroft.

SOUTH AFRICA v AUSTRALIA

Third Twenty20 International

At Cape Town, February 26, 2020 (floodlit). Australia won by 97 runs. Toss: South Africa.

Finch and Warner sped to 75 in a powerplay containing only five balls that did not yield a run (the fewest recorded in Twenty20 internationals), and were not parted until they had reached 120 in the 12th. Shamsi and Ngidi slowed the scoring, and it might have been slowed further had Rabada not overstepped when he bowled Smith on six. Still, de Kock's gamble in opting to chase under lights had clearly failed long before Australia finished on 193 for five – ten more than any side, domestic or international, had made to win at Newlands batting second. Any lingering hopes of South Africa clinching the series were damaged when Starc, just as he had at Johannesburg, clipped the top of de Kock's middle stump in the first over – and dashed when he had du Plessis superbly caught by Zampa on the third-man fence. With combined figures of five for 26, spinners Agar and Zampa dominated the middle overs, and South Africa flirted with setting (for the second time in six days) new marks for their lowest total and heaviest defeat.

Player of the Match: M. A. Starc. *Player of the Series:* A. J. Finch.

INVOLVED IN MOST HUNDRED PARTNERSHIPS IN T20Is

11	R. G. Sharma (India)
10	D. A. Warner (Australia)
8	A. J. Finch (Australia), M. J. Guptill (New Zealand), V. Kohli (India)
7	Babar Azam (Pakistan), A. D. Hales (England), E. J. G. Morgan (England), K. L. Rahul (India)
6	G. J. Maxwell (Australia), Mohammad Hafeez (Pakistan)

Australia

		B	4/6
1 D. A. Warner *c 5 b 9*	57	37	5/2
2 *A. J. Finch *lbw b 11*	55	37	6/1
3 M. S. Wade *c 1 b 10*	10	9	0/1
4 M. R. Marsh *c 11 b 7*	19	16	1/1
5 S. P. D. Smith *not out*	30	15	0/2
6 †A. T. Carey *b 8*	7	6	0
7 A. C. Agar *not out*	1	1	0
Lb 5, w 8, nb 1	14		
6 overs: 75-0 (20 overs)	193-5		

1/120 2/123 3/146 4/155 5/171

8 M. A. Starc, 9 P. J. Cummins, 10 K. W. Richardson and 11 A. Zampa did not bat.

Rabada 24–6–42–1; Nortje 24–6–46–1; Ngidi 24–5–33–1; Pretorius 24–5–42–1; Shamsi 24–8–25–1.

South Africa

		B	4/6
1 *†Q. de Kock *b 8*	5	3	1
2 H. E. van der Dussen *c 11 b 7*	24	19	3
3 F. du Plessis *c 11 b 8*	5	7	0
4 H. Klaasen *b 11*	22	18	1/1
5 D. A. Miller *c 2 b 9*	15	18	0
6 P. J. van Biljon *b 11*	1	4	0
7 D. Pretorius *lbw b 4*	11	9	0/1
8 K. Rabada *lbw b 8*	5	4	1
9 A. A. Nortje *lbw b 7*	2	6	0
10 L. T. Ngidi *b 7*	0	1	0
11 T. Shamsi *not out*	2	4	0
W 4	4		
6 overs: 50-2 (15.3 overs)	96		

1/6 2/23 3/57 4/59 5/65 6/87 7/87 8/90 9/90

Starc 15–6–23–3; Cummins 18–3–27–1; Richardson 12–4–17–0; Agar 24–8–16–3; Zampa 18–9–10–2; Marsh 6–3–3–1.

Umpires: A. T. Holdstock and B. P. Jele. Third umpire: A. Paleker.
Referee: A. J. Pycroft.

SOUTH AFRICA v AUSTRALIA

First One-Day International

At Paarl, February 29, 2020 (day/night). South Africa won by 74 runs. Toss: South Africa. One-day international debuts: J. N. Malan, K. Verreynne.

Coach Mark Boucher's call for the batsmen to "man up", and not rely on de Kock, was heeded by Klaasen, whose brilliant maiden international century put South Africa around 20 ahead of par. Before then, Starc – as was becoming a tradition – broke through in the opening over: Janneman Malan missed a vicious inswinging yorker, and was given out on review, the only player to mark his ODI debut by falling to the first delivery of the match. Neither de Kock nor Bavuma lasted long, so Klaasen teamed up first with Kyle Verreynne, who hit a composed 48 on a happier debut, then Miller. On the ground that yields fewest boundaries in the country, all three ran as hard as their bodies would allow: Verreynne hit only two fours in 64 balls. The Australian openers came and went, but Smith and Labuschagne – playing in his native land for the first time – fiddled and fidgeted their way to a steady 133 for two in the 27th. Aware of the growing need for runs, Labuschagne aimed to clear long-on, and failed. Ngidi removed Marsh with an off-cutter, then Nortje trapped Smith lbw three balls later. No one offered much resistance after that and, in all, the last seven Australian wickets fell for 43.

Player of the Match: H. Klaasen.

South Africa

J. N. Malan lbw b Starc	0
*†Q. de Kock c Carey b Hazlewood	15
T. Bavuma b Cummins	26
K. Verreynne c Marsh b Cummins	48
H. Klaasen not out	123
D. A. Miller c Carey b Cummins	64
A. L. Phehlukwayo run out (Cummins)	0
K. A. Maharaj b Starc	2
A. A. Nortje not out	1
B 1, lb 5, w 6	12
1/0 (1) 2/33 (2) 3/48 (3) 4/126 (4) 5/275 (6) 6/275 (7) 7/286 (8) (7 wkts, 50 overs)	291

10 overs: 50-3

L. T. Ngidi and T. Shamsi did not bat.

Starc 10–0–59–2; Hazlewood 10–0–63–1; Cummins 10–0–45–3; Marsh 5–0–35–0; Short 5–0–35–0; Zampa 10–0–48–0.

Australia

D. A. Warner c Verreynne b Ngidi	25	A. Zampa not out	7
*A. J. Finch c de Kock b Ngidi	10	J. R. Hazlewood b Nortje	1
S. P. D. Smith lbw b Nortje	76		
M. Labuschagne c Ngidi b Maharaj	41	Lb 3, w 4	7
M. R. Marsh b Ngidi	16		——
†A. T. Carey c Verreynne b Shamsi	5	1/23 (2) 2/49 (1) (45.1 overs)	217
D. J. M. Short st de Kock b Shamsi	18	3/133 (4) 4/174 (5) 5/174 (3)	
M. A. Starc run out (de Kock)	5	6/195 (6) 7/203 (8) 8/207 (7)	
P. J. Cummins c Verreynne b Phehlukwayo	6	9/211 (9) 10/217 (11)	10 overs: 58-2

Maharaj 10–0–48–1; Nortje 7.1–0–39–2; Ngidi 8–0–30–3; Phehlukwayo 10–0–52–1; Shamsi 10–0–45–2.

Umpires: A. T. Holdstock and N. J. Llong. Third umpire: R. K. Illingworth.
Referee: A. J. Pycroft.

SOUTH AFRICA v AUSTRALIA

Second One-Day International

At Bloemfontein, March 4, 2020 (day/night). South Africa won by six wickets. Toss: Australia.

Four days after his Paarl trauma, Malan became the first to follow a duck on debut with a hundred in his next innings. More than that, he steered South Africa to victory, giving them their first series win in any format for almost a year. He and Ngidi, who grabbed a superb career-best six for 58 that included three of Australia's illustrious top four, shared the match award. Finch and Warner had made yet another rampant start, before being pegged back by Ngidi: Warner caught at cover, Smith at midwicket, Labuschagne at point – first ball. Short survived two drops before 20 to reach his first ODI fifty, but on 69 he slapped Shamsi to point, to give Malan a third catch. His downfall precipitated a slump, just when a total of 300 seemed likely; Ngidi ripped through the lower order. Starc – yet again – snatched a wicket in the first over. Yet again, though, he failed to make the most of the early momentum, and South Africa regrouped thanks to punctilious innings from Malan and Smuts. Their patience paid dividends and, with Klaasen and then Miller, the increasingly comfortable Malan sped his team home with nine balls to spare.

Players of the Match: J. N. Malan and L. T. Ngidi.

BEST ODI FIGURES FOR SOUTH AFRICA

7-45	Imran Tahir	v West Indies at Basseterre	2016
6-16	K. Rabada	v Bangladesh at Mirpur	2015
6-22	M. Ntini	v Australia at Cape Town	2005-06
6-23	A. A. Donald	v Kenya at Nairobi (Gymkhana)	1996-97
6-24	Imran Tahir	v Zimbabwe at Bloemfontein	2018-19
6-35	S. M. Pollock	v West Indies at East London	1998-99
6-39	D. W. Steyn	v Pakistan at Port Elizabeth	2013-14
6-49	L. Klusener	v Sri Lanka at Lahore	1997-98
6-58	**L. T. Ngidi**	**v Australia at Bloemfontein**	**2019-20**

Australia

D. A. Warner c Malan b Ngidi 35
*A. J. Finch c de Kock b Nortje 69
S. P. D. Smith c Smuts b Ngidi 13
M. Labuschagne c Malan b Ngidi 0
D. J. M. Short c Malan b Shamsi 69
M. R. Marsh b Phehlukwayo 36
†A. T. Carey c de Kock b Ngidi 21
A. C. Agar c Maharaj b Ngidi 9
P. J. Cummins c Smuts b Ngidi 6
M. A. Starc lbw b Nortje 3
A. Zampa not out 3

Lb 3, w 4 7

1/50 (1) 2/81 (3) 3/81 (4) (50 overs) 271
4/158 (2) 5/224 (5) 6/238 (6)
7/257 (8) 8/263 (7) 9/266 (9)
10/271 (10) 10 overs: 73-1

Maharaj 10–0–53–0; Nortje 10–0–59–2; Ngidi 10–0–58–6; Phehlukwayo 10–0–44–1; Shamsi 10–0–54–1.

South Africa

J. N. Malan not out 129
*†Q. de Kock b Starc 0
J. T. Smuts c Cummins b Zampa 41
K. Verreynne c Marsh b Cummins 3
H. Klaasen c Finch b Zampa 51
D. A. Miller not out 37
Lb 4, w 8, nb 1 13

1/1 (2) 2/92 (3) (4 wkts, 48.3 overs) 274
3/103 (4) 4/184 (5) 10 overs: 42-1

A. L. Phehlukwayo, K. A. Maharaj, A. A. Nortje, L. T. Ngidi and T. Shamsi did not bat.

Starc 9.3–0–53–1; Cummins 10–1–59–1; Marsh 9–0–51–0; Agar 9–0–48–0; Zampa 10–0–48–2; Labuschagne 1–0–11–0.

Umpires: R. K. Illingworth and B. P. Jele. Third umpire: N. J. Llong.
Referee: A. J. Pycroft.

SOUTH AFRICA v AUSTRALIA

Third One-Day International

At Potchefstroom, March 7, 2020. South Africa won by six wickets. Toss: South Africa. One-day international debut: D. M. Dupavillon.

On a stiflingly hot day, and with the series decided, Australia looked more interested in the flight home than in scrapping for a consolation victory on a slow, end-of-season pitch. South Africa, though, were rejuvenated, rather than weakened, by another new face: fast bowler Daryn Dupavillon was their ninth white-ball debutant of the season. With no significant contribution from the top three, the tourists were largely unconvincing; the exception was Labuschagne, who batted with organisation and composure. Like Malan earlier in the series, he transformed a golden duck into a maiden one-day international hundred. Nortje, peaking at 151kph, led the attack with controlled hostility in the absence of the injured Rabada and rested Ngidi, while slow left-armers Maharaj and Smuts kept the lid on the scoring. Australia's 254 felt insufficient, even after Hazlewood removed the openers with subtle seam movement. The back of the chase was broken during a third-wicket stand of 96 between the diminutive yet powerful Verreynne and the bulkier Smuts, who lofted Kane Richardson's slower ball to long-on as a century beckoned. Klaasen completed the match – and a coming-of-age series – by smashing Marsh for two fours and a six. A cameraman needed attention from the home physio after a six from de Kock hit him on the head.

Player of the Match: J. T. Smuts. *Player of the Series:* H. Klaasen.

Australia

D. A. Warner c de Kock b Nortje 4
*A. J. Finch c Miller b Dupavillon 22
S. P. D. Smith lbw b Phehlukwayo 20
M. Labuschagne b Nortje 108
D. J. M. Short c Klaasen b Smuts 36
M. R. Marsh run out (Miller/de Kock) 32
†A. T. Carey b Smuts 0
J. A. Richardson not out 24
K. W. Richardson not out 0
B 1, lb 2, w 5 8

1/12 (1) 2/43 (3) (7 wkts, 50 overs) 254
3/55 (2) 4/136 (5)
5/189 (6) 6/189 (7) 7/253 (4) 10 overs: 38-1

J. R. Hazlewood and A. Zampa did not bat.

Nortje 7–0–35–2; Sipamla 8–0–40–0; Dupavillon 6–0–21–1; Phehlukwayo 7–0–49–1; Maharaj 10–0–45–0; Klaasen 3–0–19–0; Smuts 9–1–42–2.

South Africa

J. N. Malan c Carey b Hazlewood. 23
*†Q. de Kock b Hazlewood 26
J. T. Smuts c Warner b K. W. Richardson . 84
K. Verreynne c Labuschagne b Zampa 50
H. Klaasen not out. 68
D. A. Miller not out. 3
Lb 3, w 1 4

1/47 (2) 2/54 (1) (4 wkts, 45.3 overs) 258
3/150 (4) 4/229 (3) 10 overs: 54-1

A. L. Phehlukwayo, K. A. Maharaj, A. A. Nortje, L. L. Sipamla and D. M. Dupavillon did not bat.

J. A. Richardson 10–1–58–0; Hazlewood 10–1–37–2; K. W. Richardson 9–0–63–1; Zampa 10–0–45–1; Marsh 1.3–0–21–0; Finch 2–0–11–0; Short 3–0–20–0.

Umpires: A. T. Holdstock and R. K. Illingworth. Third umpire: N. J. Llong.
Referee: A. J. Pycroft.

SOUTH AFRICA v SRI LANKA IN 2020-21

LUNGANI ZAMA

Test matches (2): South Africa 2 (120pts), Sri Lanka 0 (0pts)

Two years previously, in 2018-19, Sri Lanka had pulled off a stunning heist in South Africa, winning by one wicket at Durban after an incredible innings from Kusal Perera, and completing the job against shocked opponents at Port Elizabeth. The South Africans, after a miserable 2019 – a poor World Cup, followed by Test defeats in India and at home by England – and with a dysfunctional administration placed in the hands of an interim committee, could not afford another setback. These two Tests were staged on the country's quickest and bounciest tracks, at Centurion and Johannesburg, and the home side recorded comfortable victories.

They were helped by a crop of injuries among the tourists, who were already without influential batsman Angelo Mathews; he had injured a hamstring during the T20 Lanka Premier League, which finished three days before the team flew off to their biosecure bubble in Pretoria. And, as seamers fell like flies, Sri Lanka's coach Mickey Arthur admitted the LPL had been a hindrance: "In hindsight, we should have tried to preserve a lot of our main players, but that would have devalued the competition. If I had my time again, we probably would have pulled some of our quicks out of it."

Arthur also suggested the ICC would, in these exceptional times, have to look at their rules about substitutions: "The rigours of the workload are just going to be too much, with coronavirus around." Somehow, he retained a sense of humour: "Luckily we brought 21 players, otherwise it would be batting coach Grant Flower at No. 3 and me at No. 4 in the next Test."

Suranga Lakmal and Oshada Fernando were injured warming up for the First Test, during which seamers Lahiru Kumara, Kasun Rajitha and Dasun Shanaka all picked up knocks; Dhananjaya de Silva badly pulled a thigh muscle, and had to abandon a delightful innings of 79 in an eventual total of 396. "When we started, we had a balanced attack," said Dimuth Karunaratne, the embattled captain. "But in the first innings, we lost that. We had been in a position where we could even have dominated the game."

South Africa had no such worries, their main concern being whether to hurry Kagiso Rabada back after injury; victory in the First Test, allied to a promising display by newcomer Lutho Sipamla, meant he was not risked. After giving up the captaincy, Faf du Plessis made 199 to set up the Centurion win, and Dean Elgar kept the pressure on Sri Lanka's reworked attack at the Wanderers.

It meant Quinton de Kock started his stint as Test captain – he had been installed on a temporary basis, as the selectors were worried about his workload – with a 2–0 victory. "I am sure a leader will pop up somewhere," he said. "I am happy just doing the rest of the summer, but if needs be that I go a little bit longer, then so be it." De Kock said the demands of cricket during

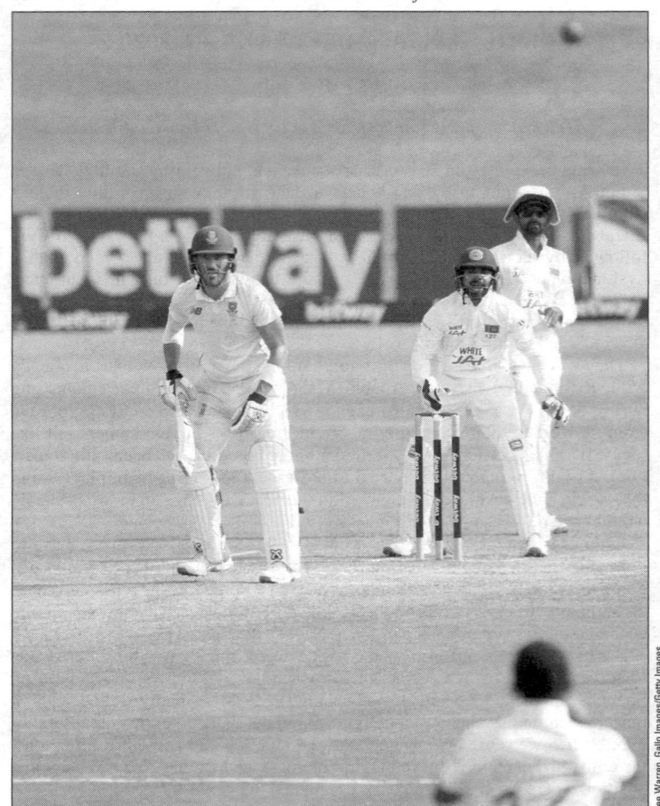

Lee Warren, Gallo Images/Getty Images

One short: Faf du Plessis chips the ball to Dimuth Karunaratne, and falls for 199.

Covid-19 were huge: "Bubbles just make tours longer because of the quarantine period. It's very unsettling. I don't know how long it can last."

Victory at least relieved some of the pressure on Cricket South Africa's beleaguered board. After the government installed an interim committee, there had been a possibility the ICC would sanction CSA for political interference in their administrative affairs. At the same time, the various Covid cancellations – including the mid-tour abandonment by England's white-ball team shortly before this series – meant money was running out, because of a lack of sponsors and broadcast deals. There was also general surprise that the national team did not follow many others in taking a knee in support of the Black Lives Matter movement; given South Africa's chequered history, it stuck out like a sore thumb. The players' decision "to continue to work together in our personal, team and public spaces to dismantle racism" did not silence the critics, though they did raise their fists in a Black Power salute at the start of the First Test.

SRI LANKAN TOURING PARTY

*F. D. M. Karunaratne, P. V. D. Chameera, L. D. Chandimal, D. M. de Silva, P. W. H. de Silva, D. P. D. N. Dickwella, L. Embuldeniya, A. M. Fernando, B. O. P. Fernando, M. V. T. Fernando, S. N. S. Gunathilake, C. B. R. L. S. Kumara, R. A. S. Lakmal, L. M. D. Madushanka, B. K. G. Mendis, M. D. K. Perera, M. D. K. J. Perera, C. A. K. Rajitha, M. B. Ranasinghe, M. D. Shanaka, H. D. R. L. Thirimanne. *Coach:* J. M. Arthur.

A. D. Mathews was originally selected, but withdrew because of a hamstring injury.

SOUTH AFRICA v SRI LANKA

First Test

At Centurion, December 26–29, 2020. South Africa won by an innings and 45 runs. South Africa 60pts. Toss: Sri Lanka. Test debuts: L. L. Sipamla; P. W. H. de Silva.

It takes a spectacular unravelling for a team to score nearly 400 in the first innings of a Test, and lose by an innings. But that is what happened to Sri Lanka at SuperSport Park, as an injury curse ran through their squad, and reduced a potentially tantalising match into a procession for South Africa. For the neutral, it was a shame, because Sri Lanka had started with intent, winning the toss and rattling along at five an over in the opening half-hour, putting an inexperienced home attack under immediate pressure.

The debutant Lutho Sipamla, a 22-year-old seamer from the Eastern Cape, bore the brunt of it, even after Ngidi had bowled Karunaratne for 22 in the fifth over. Nerves got the better of Sipamla, and he sprayed the new ball around. The speedy Nortje was soon in action as first change, and brought a semblance of calm. Still, Sri Lanka were 102 for three by lunch, with Dhananjaya de Silva showing his class. Former captain Chandimal was a willing partner, and the scoring-rate remained a concern for the hosts. But the match – and, arguably, the series – took a decisive turn in the second session, when de Silva was forced to retire after tearing a thigh muscle, and taken off the field on a drinks buggy. He had made a serene 79, and looked in total command, but took no further part in the series.

OUT FOR 199 IN A TEST

Mudassar Nazar	Pakistan v India at Faisalabad	1984-85
M. Azharuddin	India v Sri Lanka at Kanpur	1986-87
M. T. G. Elliott	Australia v England at Leeds	1997
S. T. Jayasuriya	Sri Lanka v India at Colombo (SSC)	1997-98
S. R. Waugh	Australia v West Indies at Bridgetown	1998-99
Younis Khan	Pakistan v India at Lahore	2005-06
I. R. Bell	England v South Africa at Lord's	2008
S. P. D. Smith	Australia v West Indies at Kingston	2015
K. L. Rahul	India v England at Chennai	2016-17
D. Elgar	South Africa v Bangladesh at Potchefstroom	2017-18
F. du Plessis	**South Africa v Sri Lanka at Centurion**	**2020-21**

There have been two scores of 199: A. Flower for Zimbabwe v South Africa at Harare in 2001-02, and K. C. Sangakkara for Sri Lanka v Pakistan at Galle in 2012.*

Sparky contributions from Chandimal, Dickwella and Shanaka propelled Sri Lanka to 396, their highest total in 16 Tests in South Africa. Sipamla, so expensive on the first day, looked a different bowler on the second, and grabbed the last three wickets in 11 balls.

In response, Elgar and the restored Markram combined for South Africa's first century opening stand in 23 Tests. Both playing on their home patch, they seemed in full command, and it was a surprise when they missed out on hundreds. Elgar went for 95, the over after van der Dussen was caught behind off Kumara. The quick demise of de Kock – a first Test wicket for leg-spinner Wanindu Hasaranga de Silva, soon to fall foul of Sri Lanka's injury hoodoo himself – made it 220 for four, but any thoughts of a deficit were banished by du Plessis. The tourists had lost seamers Rajitha, and later Kumara, to strains, and were also lacking Dhananjaya de Silva's tidy off-breaks. Karunaratne looked forlornly to the dressing-room – and all he saw was an equally dismayed coach Mickey Arthur, who was contemplating putting on whites for a stint as an emergency fielder.

Du Plessis took full toll of the thin attack, helping himself to a career-best 199: he was honest enough to admit that his 412-minute knock, which contained 24 fours, was far from his best innings. He put on 179 with Bavuma who, with an elusive second Test century in sight, inexplicably walked when he had 71. He said he heard a sound as he swished at Shanaka, and thought he had been caught at the wicket. Replays showed clear daylight between bat and ball, but a sheepish Bavuma was already off the field.

Mulder made 36, then Maharaj tucked in, collecting a Test-best of his own, and putting on 133 with du Plessis as the total moved past 600. It mattered little that the tail disappeared quickly: South Africa led by 225. They did not need to bat again. Sri Lanka's only resistance came from Perera, who briefly threatened a repeat of his previous-tour heroics, and Hasaranga de Silva, who contributed a run-a-minute 59 late on. South Africa's four seamers took two wickets apiece, but slow left-armer Maharaj finished the match wicketless.

Four wickets in the last hour before lunch on the fourth day hastened the conclusion. A helter-skelter match was probably a fitting way to end an unforgettable year. South Africa were just grateful to win a Test again, while Sri Lanka were left licking considerable wounds going into 2021.

Player of the Match: F. du Plessis.

Close of play: first day, Sri Lanka 340-6 (Shanaka 25, Rajitha 7); second day, South Africa 317-4 (du Plessis 55, Bavuma 41); third day, Sri Lanka 65-2 (Perera 33, Chandimal 21).

Sri Lanka

*F. D. M. Karunaratne b Ngidi	22	– b Ngidi	6
M. D. K. J. Perera c de Kock b Mulder	16	– c de Kock b Nortje	64
B. K. G. Mendis c Ngidi b Nortje	12	– c van der Dussen b Ngidi	0
L. D. Chandimal c du Plessis b Mulder	85	– b Mulder	25
D. M. de Silva retired hurt	79	– absent hurt	
†D. P. D. N. Dickwella lbw b Mulder	49	– (5) c de Kock b Mulder	10
M. D. Shanaka not out	66	– (6) c de Kock b Sipamla	6
P. W. H. de Silva b Sipamla	18	– (7) c Bavuma b Sipamla	59
C. A. K. Rajitha c Elgar b Sipamla	12	– c Maharaj b Nortje	0
M. V. T. Fernando b Sipamla	0	– (8) run out (Mulder/Maharaj)	0
C. B. R. L. S. Kumara c van der Dussen b Sipamla	0	– (10) not out	0
B 16, lb 9, w 6, nb 6	37	B 4, lb 2, nb 4	10
1/28 (1) 2/54 (3) 3/54 (2) 4/284 (4) 5/296 (6) 6/320 (8) 7/387 (9) 8/387 (10) 9/396 (11) (96 overs)	396	1/10 (1) 2/22 (3) 3/85 (4) 4/99 (5) 5/114 (2) 6/142 (6) 7/148 (8) 8/179 (7) 9/180 (9) (46.1 overs)	180

In the first innings de Silva retired hurt at 185-3.

Ngidi 19–3–64–1; Sipamla 16–1–76–4; Nortje 22–3–88–1; Mulder 20–4–69–3; Maharaj 19–3–74–0. *Second innings*—Ngidi 10–2–38–2; Nortje 10.1–1–47–2; Mulder 12–1–39–2; Sipamla 5–0–24–2; Maharaj 6–3–20–0; Markram 3–2–6–0.

South Africa

D. Elgar c and b Shanaka 95
A. K. Markram c Shanaka b Fernando 68
H. E. van der Dussen c Dickwella b Kumara 15
F. du Plessis c Karunaratne
b P. W. H. de Silva . 199
*†Q. de Kock c sub (H. D. R. L. Thirimanne)
b P. W. H. de Silva . 18
T. Bavuma c Dickwella b Shanaka 71
P. W. A. Mulder c Dickwella
b P. W. H. de Silva . 36
K. A. Maharaj c P. W. H. de Silva
b Fernando . 73
A. A. Nortje c Dickwella b Fernando 0
L. L. Sipamla lbw b P. W. H. de Silva 0
L. T. Ngidi not out 2
B 9, lb 18, w 10, nb 7 44

1/141 (2) 2/200 (3) (142.1 overs) 621
3/200 (1) 4/220 (5)
5/399 (6) 6/476 (7) 7/609 (4)
8/610 (9) 9/611 (10) 10/621 (8)

Fernando 31.1–3–129–3; Rajitha 2.1–0–16–0; Shanaka 28.5–2–98–2; P. W. H. de Silva 45–5–171–4; Kumara 21.1–0–103–1; Karunaratne 6.5–0–36–0; Mendis 7–0–41–0.

Umpires: M. Erasmus and A. T. Holdstock. Third umpire: A. Paleker.
Referee: A. J. Pycroft.

SOUTH AFRICA v SRI LANKA

Second Test

At Johannesburg, January 3–5, 2021. South Africa won by ten wickets. South Africa 60pts. Toss: Sri Lanka. Test debuts: A. M. Fernando, M. B. Ranasinghe.

South Africa's Wanderers stronghold loomed into sight too soon for the depleted Sri Lankans. The Bullring, housing the country's fastest pitch, was intimidating, even without the cauldron of noise that normally comes from a packed crowd. And so it proved: the visitors capsized inside three days, and failed to see out 100 overs in total.

Sri Lanka were forced into four changes, with Dhananjaya de Silva a crucial casualty. Chameera and Thirimanne returned, while Asitha Fernando and Minod Bhanuka Ranasinghe made their debuts. There were no such issues for South Africa, who kept the same XI: Kagiso Rabada was brought back into the squad but, with a tour of Pakistan on the horizon, was deemed not quite ready.

Karunaratne again won the toss and batted, but soon fell to the rapid Nortje. Perera, though, dealt primarily in boundaries, collecting 11 on the way to 60 from 67 balls. His driving down the ground was imperious, before he fell victim to Mulder's impeccable line and length. It was only the 22-year-old Mulder's third Test, but already there were whispers South Africa had found a member of that elusive species, the genuine all-rounder. He nicked off C. Perera, Mendis and Thirimanne, and Sri Lanka subsided for 157. Nortje wrecked the middle order, finishing with six for 56, his best Test figures – reward after bowling with less luck in the First Test. There was still half the first day to go.

Markram soon provided Asitha Fernando with his first Test wicket, but Elgar bedded in with the lanky van der Dussen, reaching his 13th Test century early on the second morning. But his dismissal by Chameera precipitated an alarming collapse. Seven balls later, van der Dussen – who had let slip a century against England here in 2019-20 – was snared down the leg side off Shanaka for 67. In all, the last nine wickets fell for 84; no one else managed 20, as the enthusiastic left-arm seamer Vishwa Fernando collected his maiden Test five-for. Even so, South Africa almost doubled Sri Lanka's total, though the slide did show up a fragile middle order.

Sri Lanka were batting again before tea on the second day, and Karunaratne made the most of what was almost a lost cause, with a defiant 103. Thirimanne dug in for an hour and a half, and Dickwella played another of his trademark cameos, but there was little else to bother the bowlers. Ngidi and Sipamla – a quick learner – shared seven wickets as Sri

Lanka were dismissed for 211. Maharaj, South Africa's sole frontline spinner, didn't bowl at all during the match (and finished the series wicketless).

That left a target of 67, which openers Elgar and Markram knocked off soon after lunch on the third day. Elgar's unbeaten 31 gave him 253 runs in the two Tests, and sealed both the match and series awards. South Africa thus swept the series (and the 120 World Test Championship points), and atoned for the shocks induced by Sri Lanka in 2018-19. The unfortunate tourists could not overcome the conditions – or their many niggles, which led to suggestions that, during the pandemic at least, substitutions should be permitted for all injured players, not just those afflicted with concussion.

Player of the Match: D. Elgar. *Player of the Series:* D. Elgar.

Close of play: first day, South Africa 148-1 (Elgar 92, van der Dussen 40); second day, Sri Lanka 150-4 (Karunaratne 91, Dickwella 18).

Sri Lanka

*F. D. M. Karunaratne c de Kock b Nortje	2	– c Mulder b Nortje	103
M. D. K. J. Perera c Markram b Mulder	60	– b Ngidi	1
H. D. R. L. Thirimanne c du Plessis b Mulder	17	– c de Kock b Ngidi	31
B. K. G. Mendis c van der Dussen b Mulder	0	– c de Kock b Ngidi	0
M. B. Ranasinghe c van der Dussen b Nortje	5	– c Maharaj b Nortje	1
†D. P. D. N. Dickwella c de Kock b Nortje	7	– c Bavuma b Ngidi	36
M. D. Shanaka c de Kock b Nortje	4	– c Sipamla b Mulder	8
P. W. H. de Silva c de Kock b Sipamla	29	– b Sipamla	16
P. V. D. Chameera c de Kock b Nortje	22	– c de Kock b Sipamla	0
M. V. T. Fernando not out	2	– not out	1
A. M. Fernando b Nortje	4	– b Sipamla	0
Lb 5	5	B 9, lb 2, w 1, nb 2	14
1/19 (1) 2/71 (2) 3/71 (4) 4/80 (3) 5/84 (5) 6/93 (6) 7/110 (7) 8/149 (8) 9/151 (9) 10/157 (11) (40.3 overs)	157	1/1 (2) 2/86 (3) 3/92 (4) 4/109 (5) 5/176 (1) 6/181 (6) 7/190 (7) 8/209 (8) 9/210 (9) 10/211 (11) (56.5 overs)	211

Ngidi 10–3–44–0; Nortje 14.3–1–56–6; Sipamla 9–3–27–1; Mulder 7–3–25–3. *Second innings*—Ngidi 15–5–44–4; Nortje 19–2–64–2; Mulder 13–3–52–1; Sipamla 9.5–1–40–3.

South Africa

D. Elgar c Thirimanne b Chameera	127	– (2) not out	31
A. K. Markram c Mendis b A. M. Fernando	5	– (1) not out	36
H. E. van der Dussen c Dickwella b Shanaka	67		
F. du Plessis c Dickwella b Shanaka	8		
*†Q. de Kock c Mendis b M. V. T. Fernando	10		
T. Bavuma lbw b M. V. T. Fernando	19		
P. W. A. Mulder lbw b M. V. T. Fernando	7		
K. A. Maharaj c Dickwella b A. M. Fernando	2		
A. A. Nortje c Mendis b M. V. T. Fernando	13		
L. L. Sipamla c Shanaka b M. V. T. Fernando	5		
L. T. Ngidi not out	14		
B 8, lb 14, w 3	25		
1/34 (2) 2/218 (1) 3/218 (3) 4/235 (4) 5/241 (5) 6/257 (7) 7/262 (8) 8/276 (6) 9/283 (9) 10/302 (10) (75.4 overs)	302	(no wkt, 13.2 overs)	67

M. V. T. Fernando 23.4–0–101–5; A. M. Fernando 19–5–61–2; Chameera 14–1–53–1; Shanaka 15–3–42–2; de Silva 4–0–23–0. *Second innings*—M. V. T. Fernando 4–0–23–0; A. M. Fernando 4–1–20–0; de Silva 2.2–0–16–0; Shanaka 3–1–8–0.

Umpires: M. Erasmus and A. T. Holdstock. Third umpire: A. Paleker.
Referee: A. J. Pycroft.

3TC SOLIDARITY CUP IN 2020

NEIL MANTHORP

1 Eagles 2 Kites 3 Kingfishers

The only official cricket played in South Africa between the middle of March and the beginning of the new season in November was an exhibition match involving three teams – all in the same game – randomly selected from South Africa's best available players. The Solidarity Cup took place at Centurion Park on Nelson Mandela Day (July 18), and aimed to raise money for the country's most vulnerable citizens during the pandemic.

There were three teams of eight; each batted for six overs against one opponent, and later for six more against the other. The field was split into six zones, with one fielder allowed in each. The rules also allowed for the final not-out batsman to continue with a runner: he became the "last man standing", but had to hit boundaries or twos to keep the strike. Fortunately, perhaps, that didn't happen in this inaugural contest.

There were no spectators or media (other than the television crew) in the ground, and social distancing was strictly enforced, with hand sanitiser for players and umpires. The ball retrievers were equipped with butterfly nets, to ensure they never handled it.

The players and organisers were upbeat. "There are very few team sports in the world where you get to play more than one opponent in a single fixture – this is going to be a game-changer," said Eagles captain A. B. de Villiers, who later thrashed 61 from 24 balls across both halves of the innings. Graeme Smith, Cricket South Africa's director of cricket, echoed his old team-mate: "It's a thrilling new format, and a match that is working towards a greater good."

The Eagles won – taking "gold" on the day – after de Villiers and Aiden Markram, who hit 70 from 33, lifted them to 160 for four in their split innings, which proved 22 too many for Temba Bavuma's Kites; the Kingfishers, captained by Reeza Hendricks, were a further 25 adrift.

The fast-moving format might be an option at junior level, but seems unlikely to catch on any higher in cricket's food chain.

At Centurion, July 18. **Eagles won by 22 runs. Kingfishers 113-5** (12 overs) (J. N. Malan 31); **Eagles 160-4** (12 overs) (A. K. Markram 70, A. B. de Villiers 61); **Kites 138-3** (12 overs) (J. T. Smuts 48, D. Pretorius 50*). *Kingfishers had 56-2 v Kites at the six-over break, Eagles 66-1 v Kingfishers, and Kites 58-1 v Eagles. But the Eagles took flight in the second half, slamming 94 runs off Kites; in all, Aiden Markram hit 70 (47*+23) from 33 balls, and A. B. de Villiers 61 (11*+50) from 24. Later Dwaine Pretorius faced only 17 balls (all from Kingfishers), and smashed 28 off an over from Tabraiz Shamsi.*

DOMESTIC CRICKET IN SOUTH AFRICA IN 2019-20

COLIN BRYDEN

The South African domestic season was truncated when the Covid-19 pandemic forced the cancellation of the final two rounds of the Four-Day Franchise Series (unsponsored for the second season running) and the knockout stage of the Momentum One-Day Cup.

The defending first-class champions, the Johannesburg-based **Lions**, were declared winners again, because they led the table after eight rounds. But they were only 8.46 points ahead of the **Titans**, who were just over a point ahead of the **Warriors** and the **Knights**. With 16 points for an outright win, and two rounds to go, all four would have been in contention.

The Lions had won four of their first six matches, but faltered, losing what proved to be their last two. No other franchise won more than twice, however, and they also finished second in the one-day tournament. It was a creditable performance under a new coach, Wandile Gwavu – promoted after Enoch Nkwe joined the national team. The Lions also overcame the loss of leading players to call-ups and injuries, while Stephen Cook, their all-time highest run-scorer, had retired after the previous season.

Their first-class batting was dominated by Reeza Hendricks, with 494 runs at 44, and his namesake Dominic Hendricks (480 at 34). Dominic was one of two players to appear in all eight matches, along with seamer Malusi Siboto, their leading wicket-taker with 22 at 27. For the last four, they called up Eldred Hawken, a 30-year-old fast bowler, who earned a place by taking nine for 14 for North West against Easterns in the provincial first-class competition: the fourth-best return in South African cricket. He responded to his franchise debut with 19 wickets at 17 across seven innings.

The leading batsmen in the four-day series were two openers: the Knights' Raynard van Tonder (843 at 70) and the Warriors' Eddie Moore (705 at 50). The wicket-takers were headed by off-spinner Prenelan Subrayen, with 38 at 24 for the Dolphins, and slow left-armer George Linde, with 30 at 20 for the **Cape Cobras** – who finished last, without a win.

The Momentum One-Day Cup went to Durban, because the **Dolphins** headed the round robin stage, though it was disappointing that, as in 2017-18, when they shared the title because of a washout in the final, they could not confirm their success on the field. They had won seven of their ten league matches, to finish two points ahead of the Lions, who should have joined them in the semi-finals alongside the Warriors and the Knights. The Dolphins' Grant Roelofsen was the one-day tournament's outstanding batsman, scoring 588 at 65, with a strike-rate close to a run a ball. They were captained by Test left-arm spinner Keshav Maharaj, who took 16 while conceding only 3.79 an over, winning a recall to the national one-day team.

The first-class provincial three-day title was shared by **Easterns** and **KwaZulu-Natal** (renamed KwaZulu-Natal Coastal, to distinguish them from KwaZulu-Natal Inland), who headed their pools on average points per match when the last round and the final were cancelled. The one-day trophy was shared by **Free State** and **Northern Cape** on the same basis. Easterns, who had already won the provincial Twenty20 tournament, back in September, set a South African first-class all-wicket record when openers Yaseen Valli (230) and Andrea Agathangelou (313) put on 485 against Boland in Paarl.

A controversial move by CSA to reform the domestic season in 2020-21 was overturned. They had proposed dismantling the two-tier system of six franchises fed by provincial teams who also have first-class status, and reinstating something close to the unified system discarded in 2004, with competitions contested by 12 provincial sides. But the South African Cricketers' Association threatened legal action, claiming 70 players would lose their jobs. Instead, CSA retained both tiers, but reduced the number of fixtures to save costs: the six franchises would be divided into two pools in the four-day and one-day competitions, with the pool winners playing off for the title.

FIRST-CLASS AVERAGES IN 2019-20

BATTING (500 runs, average 40.00)

		M	*I*	*NO*	*R*	*HS*	*100*	*Avge*	*Ct/St*
1	†P. Botha (*Free State*)	8	11	2	755	191	2	83.88	6
2	R. van Tonder (*Knights/Free State*)	9	15	2	844	204	2	64.92	5
3	P. J. van Biljon (*Knights*)	7	10	0	633	218	1	63.30	8
4	†E. H. Kemm (*Northern Cape*)	8	12	3	500	161*	2	55.55	5
5	A. G. S. Gous (*Knights/Free State*)	8	12	1	611	256*	1	55.54	11
6	K. Verreynne (*Cape Cobras*)	7	11	1	551	155	2	55.10	16/3
7	†I. Gafieldien (*Boland*)	9	15	2	712	136	3	54.76	8
8	F. Behardien (*Titans*)	7	13	2	591	140	2	53.72	5
9	A. P. Agathangelou (*Titans/Easterns*)	9	14	0	746	313	2	53.28	13
10	A. J. Pienaar (*Northern Cape/Knights*)	9	13	3	529	107*	2	52.90	3
11	†E. M. Moore (*Warriors/E Province*)	10	18	1	883	228	2	51.94	4
12	M. C. Christensen (*Eastern Province*)	10	17	2	776	177	2	51.73	5
13	†D. A. Hendricks (*Lions/Central Gauteng*)	11	19	1	910	187	2	50.55	19
14	W. B. Marshall (*Easterns/Titans*)	10	18	0	884	109	1	49.11	9
15	M. Y. Vallie (*Warriors/Border*)	7	12	0	582	137	1	48.50	0
16	H. E. van der Dussen (*Lions/South Africa*)	7	13	1	581	154*	1	48.41	9
17	G. M. Thomson (*Titans*)	8	14	2	564	103*	2	47.00	13
18	J. F. du Plessis (*South Western Districts*)	7	14	3	517	162*	1	47.00	4
19	R. G. Terblanche (*Boland*)	7	11	0	513	142	2	46.63	5
20	†M. C. Kleinveldt (*Cape Cobras/W Prov*)	12	19	2	791	175	3	46.52	4
21	G. Roelofsen (*Dolphins/KZN Inland*)	8	15	0	665	142	3	44.33	7/1
22	J. F. Smith (*Cape Cobras/W Province*)	10	14	2	527	85	0	43.91	4
23	J. M. Richards (*Central Gauteng/Lions*)	12	22	1	910	161	2	43.33	5
24	†Y. Valli (*Easterns*)	8	14	2	510	230	1	42.50	4
25	†M. J. Ackerman (*Dolphins*)	8	16	0	660	107	1	41.25	11

BOWLING (20 wickets, average 25.00)

		Style	*O*	*M*	*R*	*W*	*BB*	*5I*	*Avge*
1	Z. C. Qwabe (*KwaZulu-Natal Coastal*)	RFM	102.4	38	231	22	7-26	1	10.50
2	R. Klein (*Western Province*)	RFM	124.1	43	260	23	4-34	0	11.30
3	E. L. Hawken (*North West/Lions*)	RF	220.3	60	570	43	9-14	3	13.25
4	Z. Paruk (*KwaZulu-Natal Coastal*)	RFM	127	29	412	25	5-31	1	16.48
5	J. G. Dill (*Western Province*)	RM	220.5	65	535	30	6-25	2	17.83
6	C. J. August (*Easterns*)	LFM	242.1	60	697	39	7-40	2	17.87
7	J. H. Hinrichsen (*North West*)	RFM	121.4	24	404	22	4-40	0	18.36
8	C. G. Classen (*North West*)	RFM	148.1	35	441	24	5-38	1	18.37
9	B. Swanepoel (*Northern Cape/Knights*)	RFM	186.4	44	625	34	7-50	3	18.38
10	B. D. Walters (*E Province/Warriors*)	RF	259.5	67	782	42	6-60	4	18.61
11	P. Fojela (*Border*)	RFM	172.2	41	456	23	4-49	0	19.82
12	G. F. Linde (*Cape Cobras*)	SLA	199.3	41	629	30	7-64	3	20.96
13	S. C. van Schalkwyk (*Free St/Knights*)	RFM	180.5	46	527	25	4-28	0	21.08
14	K. R. Smuts (*E Province/Warriors*)	RFM	185.3	59	498	23	5-50	1	21.65
15	R. A. Cartwright (*Easterns/Titans*)	RF	291.2	73	935	43	4-38	0	21.74
16	G. A. Stuurman (*Warriors/E Province*)	RM	187.3	41	539	24	5-72	1	22.45
17	K. I. Simmonds (*Northerns*)	SLA	248.1	73	658	29	7-65	1	22.68
18	N. R. van Heerden (*Free State*)	RF	142.2	23	529	23	4-19	0	23.00
19	C. A. Dry (*Free State/Knights*)	RFM	251	61	799	34	5-84	1	23.50
20	B. C. Fortuin (*Lions*)	SLA	150.5	18	473	20	5-76	1	23.65
21	D. de Koker (*Northern Cape*)	RFM	159.3	37	527	22	5-45	1	23.95
22	S. Muthusamy (*Dolphins/KZN Coastal*)	SLA	237.3	47	625	26	7-36	1	24.03
23	L. L. Sipamla (*Warriors*)	RF	199	48	591	24	4-53	0	24.62
24	P. Subrayen (*Dolphins*)	OB	317.2	64	937	38	5-105	3	24.65
25	M. Arnold (*Easterns/Titans*)	RF	164	35	518	21	5-93	1	24.66
26	D. Paterson (*Cape Cobras/South Africa*)	RFM	219.5	59	624	25	7-91	1	24.96

FOUR-DAY FRANCHISE SERIES IN 2019-20

					Bonus pts		
	P	*W*	*L*	*D*	*Bat*	*Bowl*	*Pts*
Lions	8	4	3	1	23.62	28	121.62
Titans	8	2	1	5	28.16	23	113.16
Warriors	8	2	2	4	27.10	29	112.10
Knights	8	2	1	5	26.02	24	112.02
Dolphins	8	2	3	3	27.58	21	98.58
Cape Cobras	8	0	2	6	31.20	28	95.20

Outright win = 16pts; draw = 6pts. Bonus points awarded for the first 100 overs of each team's first innings: one batting point for the first 150 runs and 0.02 of a point for every subsequent run; one bowling point for the third wicket taken and for every subsequent two.

The final two rounds were cancelled because of the Covid-19 pandemic.

CHAMPIONS

1889-90	Transvaal
1890-91	Kimberley
1892-93	Western Province
1893-94	Western Province
1894-95	Transvaal
1896-97	Western Province
1897-98	Western Province
1902-03	Transvaal
1903-04	Transvaal
1904-05	Transvaal
1906-07	Transvaal
1908-09	Western Province
1910-11	Natal
1912-13	Natal
1920-21	Western Province
1921-22	Transvaal Natal Western Province
1923-24	Transvaal
1925-26	Transvaal
1926-27	Transvaal
1929-30	Transvaal
1931-32	Western Province
1933-34	Natal
1934-35	Transvaal
1936-37	Natal
1937-38	Natal Transvaal
1946-47	Natal
1947-48	Natal
1950-51	Transvaal
1951-52	Natal
1952-53	Western Province
1954-55	Natal
1955-56	Western Province
1958-59	Transvaal
1959-60	Natal
1960-61	Natal
1962-63	Natal
1963-64	Natal
1965-66	Natal Transvaal
1966-67	Natal
1967-68	Natal
1968-69	Transvaal
1969-70	Transvaal Western Province
1970-71	Transvaal
1971-72	Transvaal
1972-73	Transvaal
1973-74	Natal
1974-75	Western Province
1975-76	Natal
1976-77	Natal
1977-78	Western Province
1978-79	Transvaal
1979-80	Transvaal
1980-81	Natal
1981-82	Western Province
1982-83	Transvaal
1983-84	Transvaal
1984-85	Transvaal
1985-86	Western Province
1986-87	Transvaal
1987-88	Transvaal
1988-89	Eastern Province
1989-90	Eastern Province Western Province
1990-91	Western Province
1991-92	Eastern Province
1992-93	Orange Free State
1993-94	Orange Free State
1994-95	Natal
1995-96	Western Province
1996-97	Natal
1997-98	Free State
1998-99	Western Province
1999-2000	Gauteng
2000-01	Western Province
2001-02	KwaZulu-Natal
2002-03	Easterns
2003-04	Western Province
2004-05	Dolphins Eagles
2005-06	Dolphins Titans
2006-07	Titans
2007-08	Eagles
2008-09	Titans
2009-10	Cape Cobras
2010-11	Cape Cobras
2011-12	Titans
2012-13	Cape Cobras
2013-14	Cape Cobras
2014-15	Lions
2015-16	Titans
2016-17	Knights
2017-18	Titans
2018-19	Lions
2019-20	Lions

Transvaal/Gauteng have won the title outright 25 times, Natal/KwaZulu-Natal 21, Western Province 18, Titans 5, Cape Cobras 4, Lions and Orange Free State/Free State 3, Eagles/Knights and Eastern Province 2, Easterns and Kimberley 1. The title has been shared seven times as follows: Transvaal 4, Natal and Western Province 3, Dolphins 2, Eagles, Eastern Province and Titans 1.

The tournament was the Currie Cup from 1889-90 to 1989-90, the Castle Cup from 1990-91 to 1995-96, the SuperSport Series from 1996-97 to 2011-12, and the Sunfoil Series from 2012-13 to 2017-18. There was no sponsor in 2018-19 or 2019-20.

From 1971-72 to 1990-91, the non-white South African Cricket Board of Control (later the South African Cricket Board) organised their own three-day tournaments. These are now recognised as first-class (see *Wisden 2006*, pages 79–80). A list of winners appears in *Wisden 2007*, page 1346.

CSA PROVINCIAL THREE-DAY CUP IN 2019-20

Pool A	*P*	*W*	*L*	*D*	*Pts*	*Adj pts*	**Pool B**	*P*	*W*	*L*	*D*	*Pts*	*Adj pts*
Easterns . . .	9	2	0	7	138.46	138.46	KZN Coastal	9	5	2	2*	145.42	145.42
E Prov.	10	3	1	6	153.66	138.29	Northerns . .	9	2	0	7	138.14	138.14
Free State . .	9	2	1	6*	125.86	125.86	N Cape	9	3	1	5*	132.96	132.96
C Gauteng . .	9	1	1	7	119.90	119.90	W Prov	9	4	3	2	124.22	124.22
KZN Inland .	10	1	1	8*	107.18	96.46	North West .	9	2	2	5	114.44	114.44
Boland	9	1	3	5	93.66	93.66	SW Dists. . .	10	1	6	3	87.80	79.02
							Border	9	0	6	3	45.04	45.04

* *Includes one abandoned match.*

Outright win = 16pts; draw = 6pts; abandoned = 5pts. Bonus points awarded for the first 100 overs of each team's first innings: one batting point for the first 150 runs and 0.02 of a point for every subsequent run; one bowling point for the third wicket taken and for every subsequent two.

The teams were divided into two pools, one of six and one of seven. Those in Pool A were scheduled to play the other five teams, plus five from the other pool, while those in Pool B played the other six plus four from the other pool; all results counted towards the final table. The pool leaders should have met in a four-day final.

The last round and the final were cancelled because of the Covid-19 pandemic, and the title was shared by Easterns and KwaZulu-Natal Coastal, who led their respective pools. Points were adjusted by multiplying the totals for the three teams who had played ten matches by 0.9, to bring them into line with the remaining teams, who had played only nine.

MOMENTUM ONE-DAY CUP IN 2019-20

50-over league

	P	*W*	*L*	*NR/A*	*Bonus*	*Pts*	*NRR*
Dolphins.	10	7	3	0	2	30	0.69
Lions	10	6	3	1	2	28	0.36
Warriors	10	5	4	1	2	24	0.13
Knights.	10	4	4	2	2	22	–0.36
Titans	10	4	6	0	2	18	–0.08
Cape Cobras.	10	2	8	0	0	8	–0.88

The top four teams should have qualified for the knockout stage in March, but it was cancelled because of the Covid-19 pandemic; the title was awarded to Dolphins.

CSA PROVINCIAL 50-OVER CHALLENGE IN 2019-20

50-over league

Pool A	*P*	*W*	*L*	*A*	*Pts*	*Adj pts*	**Pool B**	*P*	*W*	*L*	*A*	*Pts*	*Adj pts*
Free State . .	9	6	1	2	32	32.0	N Cape. . . .	9	7	1	1	33	33.0
C Gauteng .	9	6	3	0	27	27.0	Northerns . .	9	6	2	1	31	31.0
Easterns . . .	9	5	3	1	24	24.0	SW Dists . .	10	4	5	1	21	18.9
E Province .	10	4	5	1	20	18.0	W Province .	9	4	5	0	17	17.0
KZN Inland .	10	3*	4	2	20	18.0	KZN Coastal	9	2*	5	1	14	14.0
Boland	9	0	6	3	6	6.0	North West .	9	3	6	0	13	13.0
							Border	9	2	6	1	10	10.0

* *Plus one tie.*

The final was cancelled because of the Covid-19 pandemic, and the title shared by Free State and Northern Cape, who led their respective pools. Points were adjusted by multiplying the totals for the three teams who had played ten matches by 0.9, to bring them into line with the remaining teams who had played only nine.

CSA PROVINCIAL T20 CUP IN 2019-20

20-over league plus knockout

Pool A	*P*	*W*	*L*	*Pts*
EASTERNS	4	3	1	13
KZN Coastal	4	3	1	12
Northerns	4	2	2	9
Free State	4	1	3	4
Central Gauteng	4	1	3	4

Pool B	*P*	*W*	*L*	*Pts*
E PROVINCE	4	3	1	14
KZN INLAND	4	3	1	13
Northern Cape	4	2	2	10
SW Districts	4	1	3	5
Boland	4	1	3	4

Pool C	*P*	*W*	*L*	*Pts*
BORDER	4	3	1	14
Limpopo	4	3	1	13
North West	4	2	2	9
Mpumalanga	4	1	3	5
Western Province	4	1	3	4

The three pool leaders and the next-best team advanced to the semi-finals; KwaZulu-Natal Inland qualified ahead of Limpopo on net run-rate. Free State finished above Central Gauteng because they won their head-to-head match.

Semi-finals KwaZulu-Natal Inland beat Eastern Province by 21 runs; Easterns beat Border by nine wickets.

Final At Benoni, September 24, 2019. **Easterns won by five runs. Easterns 178-6** (20 overs); **‡KwaZulu-Natal Inland 173-4** (20 overs). *Wesley Marshall and Yaseen Valli gave Easterns a galloping start, with 118 in 12 overs. Marshall scored a career-best 87 in 53 balls, but the innings later slipped from 150-1 to 164-6, with Kerwin Mungroo seizing three in 11 deliveries. KwaZulu-Natal Inland's openers, Cody Chetty and Grant Roelofsen, responded with their own century stand, and they entered Matthew Arnold's final over needing 15. But they lost two wickets, and fell short.*

The Mzansi Super League has its own section (page 859).

SRI LANKAN CRICKET IN 2020

Joining the party

SA'ADI THAWFEEQ

Even amid the pandemic, cricket found a way to make its presence felt in Sri Lanka, admittedly on a minor scale, with no spectators – and sometimes no media – in attendance. The Sri Lankan board performed a minor miracle by emerging almost unscathed, thanks in large part to the successful launch of the long-awaited T20 Lanka Premier League.

The national team's results were mixed. After T20 defeats in India, they won in Zimbabwe, and followed that with a 3–0 ODI triumph at home against West Indies, who took the T20 series. But that was as far as the good news went. England arrived in March for a two-Test series – part of the World Championship – but by then Covid-19 was beginning to make its presence felt, and they were soon on their way home.

SRI LANKA IN 2020

	Played	*Won*	*Lost*	*Drawn/No result*
Tests	3	1	1	1
One-day internationals	3	3	–	–
Twenty20 internationals	5	–	4	1

JANUARY	3 T20Is (a) v India 2 Tests (a) v Zimbabwe	(page 673) (page 785)
FEBRUARY MARCH	3 ODIs and 2 T20Is (h) v West Indies	(page 766)
APRIL		
MAY		
JUNE		
JULY		
AUGUST		
SEPTEMBER		
OCTOBER		
NOVEMBER		
DECEMBER JANUARY	2 Tests (a) v South Africa	(page 751)

For a review of Sri Lankan domestic cricket from the 2019-20 season, see page 768.

AFP/Getty Images

Getting in on the franchise act: Jaffna Stallions celebrate victory in the first Lanka Premier League.

And that was it for nine months, as tours by South Africa and India were postponed. Bangladesh were due to make a biosecure visit in October, but the Sri Lankan board upset them by laying out different quarantine guidelines from those given to England for their return visit, early in 2021. The Bangladeshis were told the government health authorities were insisting on 14 days' quarantine on arrival; for England, it was relaxed to seven.

After this prolonged inactivity, Sri Lanka finally managed a Test match, visiting South Africa just weeks after England had abandoned their tour there following positive cases at the teams' hotel. The hiatus took its toll: before and during the First Test at Centurion, six players went down with injury. The depleted team were no match for an almost full-strength home line-up – only Kagiso Rabada was missing – and were routed 2–0.

No international cricket meant no television broadcasting revenue, offset slightly by no match fees either. However, Sri Lanka Cricket had to meet the players' contractual payments, plus wages and other expenses. While England and Australia felt the pinch, and cut down on salaries, SLC found a way to keep everyone happy by paying their salaries on time with no deductions – quite a feat considering it involved 30 international players, 50 national contracts and around 250 staff.

SLC secretary Mohan de Silva explained that they had managed their finances prudently, building up reserves from 2017, and prioritising development projects. "The treasurer presented a paper giving three different scenarios – if some or all the tours take place, or if they don't take place at all this year – and how we should move forward," he said. SLC expect 2021 to be a profitable year, if all the inbound tours can be rescheduled.

Between the financial juggling, SLC squeezed in some domestic cricket, finishing the suspended Premier Tier A competition. It proved impossible to complete Tier B, and the major clubs' Under-23 tournament, which was halted with the semi-finals and final unplayed.

SLC were also busy exploring other revenue streams. They secured some sponsorships for the national team, and lined up a host broadcaster for international matches, when other countries were struggling to find one. But the golden goose was a franchise T20 competition. The Lanka Premier League, replete with overseas signings – despite strict health guidelines – finally got under way in November. Jaffna Stallions, captained by white-ball specialist Tissara Perera, came out on top in the final, against Galle Gladiators. All 23 matches were played in Hambantota, and no positive tests were recorded throughout the fortnight-long competition.

It was lapped up on TV by a cricket-starved public, and provided Sri Lanka's players with practice ahead of the tour of South Africa. As the results there proved, a handful of 20-over games was not quite the right preparation for a five-day Test – but most were thankful just to get on to the field.

SRI LANKA v WEST INDIES IN 2019-20

SA'ADI THAWFEEQ

One-day internationals (3): Sri Lanka 3, West Indies 0
Twenty20 internationals (2): Sri Lanka 0, West Indies 2

West Indies' first tour of Sri Lanka for over four years produced a pair of contrasting whitewashes. The hosts won all three one-day internationals, although two could have gone either way, before the visitors won both Twenty20 games with something to spare.

There was not much between the teams ahead of the 50-over matches: Sri Lanka were ranked eighth, West Indies ninth. Sri Lanka scraped home by one wicket in the first game, and by six runs in the third, sandwiching a 161-run triumph. West Indies paid for sloppy fielding and bowling: across the three games, they donated 31 in wides. Sri Lankan opener Avishka Fernando made 206 runs in the series, and put on 239 with Kusal Mendis in the second match. The Player of the Series, though, was 22-year-old all-rounder Wanindu Hasaranga de Silva, who married plucky batting to enticing leg-spin and exceptional fielding.

In the Twenty20s, West Indies were bolstered by the inclusion of several format specialists. They included experienced all-rounders Dwayne Bravo and Andre Russell, who took the Player of the Series award after pummelling 75 runs from 28 balls. Lendl Simmons and Brandon King scored important runs at the top of the order, and Oshane Thomas rattled the batsmen with his pace. Ashantha de Mel, Sri Lanka's chairman of selectors, acknowledged the problem his side had faced: "These guys go around the world playing franchise cricket. They are like the Harlem Globetrotters in basketball. They don't play that many ODIs or Tests – they are T20 specialists, and they know exactly what to do."

WEST INDIES TOURING PARTY

*K. A. Pollard (50/20), F. A. Allen (50/20), S. W. Ambris (50), D. J. Bravo (20), D. M. Bravo (50), R. L. Chase (50), S. S. Cottrell (50/20), S. O. Hetmyer (20), J. O. Holder (50), S. D. Hope (50/20), A. S. Joseph (50), B. A. King (50/20), K. M. A. Paul (50), N. Pooran (50/20), R. Powell (50/20), A. D. Russell (20), R. Shepherd (50), L. M. P. Simmons (20), O. R. Thomas (20), H. R. Walsh (50/20), K. O. K. Williams (20). *Coach:* P. V. Simmons.

First one-day international At Colombo (SSC), February 22, 2020. **Sri Lanka won by one wicket. West Indies 289-7** (50 overs) (S. D. Hope 115, D. M. Bravo 39, R. L. Chase 41, K. M. A. Paul 32*; I. Udana 3-82); ‡**Sri Lanka 290-9** (49.1 overs) (W. I. A. Fernando 50, F. D. M. Karunaratne 52, M. D. K. J. Perera 42, N. L. T. C. Perera 32, P. W. H. de Silva 42*; A. S. Joseph 3-42). *PoM:* P. W. H. de Silva. *Shai Hope's ninth ODI century was at the heart of a decent total, which left Sri Lanka needing the highest chase at the SSC. Avishka Fernando and captain Dimuth Karunaratne shot out of the blocks with 111 in 18 overs. Then, after a slump, Wanindu Hasaranga de Silva entered at 215-6 in the 38th, with 75 still wanted. But the West Indians paid for indifferent bowling (14 wides) and ground fielding: de Silva had the last man for company when the match was completed with a Keemo Paul no-ball in the final over. It was the first time Sri Lanka had successfully chased more than 250 in an ODI since Zimbabwe toured in July 2017.*

Second one-day international At Hambantota, February 26, 2020 (day/night). **Sri Lanka won by 161 runs. Sri Lanka 345-8** (50 overs) (W. I. A. Fernando 127, B. K. G. Mendis 119, N. L. T. C. Perera 36; S. S. Cottrell 4-67, A. S. Joseph 3-57); ‡**West Indies 184** (39.1 overs) (S. D. Hope 51, N. Pooran 31; P. W. H. de Silva 3-30, P. A. D. L. R. Sandakan 3-57). *PoM:* W. I. A. Fernando. *Sri Lanka clinched the series, largely thanks to a stand of 239 between Avishka Fernando and Kusal Mendis – a Sri Lankan record for the third wicket in ODIs, beating 226 by Marvan Atapattu and Mahela Jayawardene against India at Sharjah in October 2000. West Indies captain Kieron Pollard had put down a straightforward slip catch off Mendis which would have made it 12-3. Instead, Sri Lanka surged towards 350, and West Indies were never in touch, slipping from 130-3 to 137-6 as the spinners applied the brakes; de Silva's wickets came from three well-disguised googlies.*

Third one-day international At Pallekele, March 1, 2020 (day/night). **Sri Lanka won by six runs.** ‡**Sri Lanka 307** (50 overs) (F. D. M. Karunaratne 44, M. D. K. J. Perera 44, B. K. G. Mendis 55, D. M. de Silva 51, N. L. T. C. Perera 38; A. S. Joseph 4-65); **West Indies 301-9** (50 overs) (S. D. Hope 72, S. W. Ambris 60, N. Pooran 50, K. A. Pollard 49, F. A. Allen 37; A. D. Mathews 4-59). *PoM:* A. D. Mathews. *PoS:* P. W. H. de Silva. *West Indies made a valiant effort at a consolation victory, but ran up against a revitalised Angelo Mathews. He had rarely bowled in recent seasons because of fitness concerns but, after Nuwan Pradeep Fernando limped off with a leg injury, he got through his full allocation for the first time since July 2015. Mathews took four wickets, including Fabian Allen (37 from 15 balls), who was caught on the boundary from the second delivery of the final over, which started with West Indies needing 13. "Angelo may be the oldest in the team," said Karunaratne, forgetting about Pradeep Fernando, "but he's playing like the youngest." It was hard on Hope, who finished the three-match series with 238 runs.*

First Twenty20 international At Pallekele, March 4, 2020 (floodlit). **West Indies won by 25 runs.** ‡**West Indies 196-4** (20 overs) (L. M. P. Simmons 67*, B. A. King 33, A. D. Russell 35, K. A. Pollard 34); **Sri Lanka 171** (19.1 overs) (M. D. K. J. Perera 66, P. W. H. de Silva 44; O. R. Thomas 5-28). *PoM:* O. R. Thomas. *Sri Lanka were up against it within six overs of their chase, with the fiery Oshane Thomas taking all the wickets as they declined to 56-5. Kusal Perera (66 from 38) and de Silva tried their best, putting on 87, but they had too much to do. Lendl Simmons had batted through the West Indian innings, which was given late oomph by Andre Russell (35 from 14, with four sixes, in his first T20 international for 19 months) and Pollard, who biffed 34 from 15 in his 500th T20 game in all competitions – the first to get there.*

Second Twenty20 international At Pallekele, March 6, 2020 (floodlit). **West Indies won by seven wickets. Sri Lanka 155-6** (20 overs) (M. D. Shanaka 31*); ‡**West Indies 158-3** (17 overs) (B. A. King 43, S. O. Hetmyer 43*, A. D. Russell 40*). *PoM:* A. D. Russell. *PoS:* A. D. Russell. *After restricting Sri Lanka to 155 on a flat track, West Indies were always favourites – and from 103-3 in the 13th over, Russell made sure, blasting 40* from 14 balls with six sixes, including one off Mathews to end the game. Three overs from Lasith Malinga, Sri Lanka's captain, cost 46. He was not helped when de Silva, his in-form spinner, pulled a hamstring while fielding, and was unable to bowl.*

DOMESTIC CRICKET IN SRI LANKA IN 2019-20

SA'ADI THAWFEEQ

When the Covid-19 pandemic brought sport across the world to a standstill in mid-March, Sri Lanka's first-class Premier League looked likely to be one of the casualties. The Tier A group games had just been completed, and the Super Eight and Plate leagues were yet to start. But the competition returned in August, thanks to decisive action from Sri Lanka Cricket's tournament committee. It required an extraordinary general meeting to rewrite the regulations: the Super Eight games, normally scheduled for four days, were cut to three, while promotion and relegation between the two first-class tiers were suspended for one season. The Tier A leagues duly reached a conclusion, helped by the fact that the committee were able to pick neutral venues, where they could stage matches under strict health guidelines. This could not be managed for Tier B, however, and its last four rounds remained unplayed.

In the absence of their usual commitments, most of Sri Lanka's international players were available when the final rounds of the Premier League eventually took place. For some, it was the first time they had appeared in first-class cricket for their clubs in many moons; former national captain Angelo Mathews had managed only three one-day games for Colts in the previous seven years.

Kusal Mendis, who had not featured in any domestic cricket since February 2018, had just been arrested after knocking down an elderly cyclist, and had to pay the dead man's family 1m rupees. But he returned to lead **Colombo** in the Super Eight – and reeled off three centuries in four matches, including a maiden double-hundred, against their nearest rivals, Nondescripts. He retired with cramp on 128, but resumed to guide his team past Nondescripts' 467 – thus claiming eight points for a first-innings lead, which clinched Colombo's second successive Premier League title with a round to go. They won five of their ten matches, more than any other side, and headed the table by 12 points; club chairman Shammi Silva (also president of SLC) attributed their success to retaining a stable squad for five years. Chilaw Marians won four games in all, but finished just behind Nondescripts. **Moors** won the Plate League thanks to two late victories, having been bottom of their Tier A qualifying group. Police led the table in the incomplete Tier B, but no winner was declared.

The Premier League tournament was bookended by triple-centuries. Back in February, Moors' Ramesh Mendis Wanigamuni reached 300 not out against Negombo; in late August, Dinesh Chandimal made an unbeaten 354 for the Army against Saracens – the second-highest first-class innings by a Sri Lankan, after Mahela Jayawardene's 374 for the Test side against South Africa in 2006. That innings took Chandimal to 1,027 runs at 93 in the tournament, in his eighth match. Lahiru Udara Igalagamage had achieved four figures the previous day, amassing 1,039 in nine games for Nondescripts; he had been stranded on 290 in the opening round, against Ragama.

The bowling was dominated by slow left-armers. In Tier A, Duvindu Tillekeratne, son of the Test batsman Hashan, took 61 wickets at 19 in nine matches for Burgher, while Malinda Pushpakumara of Colombo, and Upul Indrasiri of Negombo, had 50 apiece. In Tier B, two more left-arm spinners held sway: Bloomfield's Gayan Sirisoma collected 64 and Ports Authority's Chanaka Komasaru 52, both averaging 14 across seven games. Meanwhile, Test off-spinner Dilruwan Perera, who played for Colts, became only the fifth Sri Lankan to take 800 first-class wickets.

Before the pandemic struck, **Chilaw Marians** had won the final of the SLC Limited-Overs Tournament by a convincing 91 runs, when the spin of Shehan Jayasuriya and the ambidextrous Kamindu Mendis caused Nondescripts to collapse from 119 for one to 204 all out. Chilaw also reached the SLC T20 final three weeks later, when a last-ball victory gave Colombo their first title of the year.

FIRST-CLASS AVERAGES IN 2019-20

BATTING (600 runs)

		M	*I*	*NO*	*R*	*HS*	*100*	*Avge*	*Ct/St*
1	L. D. Chandimal (*Army*)	8	13	2	1,027	354*	3	93.36	5
2	P. N. Silva (*Sri Lanka A/Nondescripts*)	8	12	2	919	192	4	91.90	2
3	L. U. Igalagamage (*SL A/Nondescripts*)	10	15	2	1,059	290*	3	81.46	17/1
4	†P. H. K. D. Mendis (*SL A/Chilaw Mar*)	8	12	3	668	169	2	74.22	17
5	†B. K. E. L. Milantha (*Badureliya*)	8	12	1	692	252	3	62.90	20/2
6	R. T. M. Wanigamuni (*SL A/Moors*)	9	14	1	735	300*	2	56.53	3
7	L. Abeyratne (*Colombo*)	10	16	2	788	153	3	56.28	7
8	†H. D. R. L. Thirimanne (*Ragama*)	9	15	2	726	187*	2	55.84	12
9	A. K. Perera (*Nondescripts*)	10	13	1	656	148	2	54.66	7
10	D. M. Sarathchandra (*SL A/Tamil Union*)	10	15	3	645	163*	3	53.75	27/3
11	K. N. M. Fernando (*Ragama*)	9	14	2	613	169	2	51.08	17/1
12	S. C. Serasinghe (*Moors*)	8	13	0	663	151	3	51.00	6
13	†S. S. D. Arachchige (*Nondescripts*)	10	12	0	603	128	1	50.25	7
14	S. M. A. Priyanjan (*SL A/Colombo*)	11	16	1	740	170	1	49.33	7
15	†P. B. B. Rajapaksa (*Burgher*)	10	18	1	835	115	2	49.11	8
16	S. N. S. Gunathilake (*Colts*)	8	14	0	679	130	2	48.50	3
17	†M. B. Ranasinghe (*Colombo*)	9	15	1	676	114	2	48.28	27/9
18	M. S. Warnapura (*Negombo*)	9	15	2	627	87	0	48.23	4
19	A. R. S. Silva (*Ragama*)	10	15	1	668	165	2	47.71	8
20	L. A. C. Ruwansiri (*Lankan*)	9	15	1	645	165	2	46.07	6
21	†D. S. Weerakkody (*Sinhalese*)	9	16	0	697	114	2	43.56	19
22	†M. D. U. S. Jayasundera (*Ragama*)	10	15	0	630	158	2	42.00	4
23	D. P. W. Diminguwa (*Moors*)	9	15	0	614	132	1	40.93	14
24	E. M. D. Y. Munaweera (*Negombo*)	9	16	0	628	120	1	39.25	3
25	†S. D. Withanawasam (*Burgher*)	10	18	0	623	143	1	34.61	4

BOWLING (28 wickets)

		Style	*O*	*M*	*R*	*W*	*BB*	*5I*	*Avge*
1	R. M. G. K. Sirisoma (*Bloomfield*)	SLA	321.1	62	898	64	7-32	9	14.03
2	N. C. Komasaru (*Ports Authority*)	SLA	284.3	64	768	52	6-54	7	14.76
3	D. K. R. C. Jayatissa (*Panadura*)	OB	208	35	631	36	8-98	3	17.52
4	D. S. Tillekeratne (*Burgher*)	SLA	317	40	1,163	61	8-147	5	19.06
5	M. D. K. Perera (*Colts*)	OB	288	59	786	41	5-31	3	19.17
6	P. A. K. P. Jayawickrama (*Moors*)	SLW	160.4	21	606	31	6-91	3	19.54
7	D. R. F. Weerasinghe (*Ports Auth*)	OB	153.4	17	559	28	5-20	1	19.96
8	W. C. de Silva (*Panadura*)	SLA	270.2	63	775	38	6-48	2	20.39
9	M. W. K. Anjula (*Moors*)	RFM	153.2	26	582	28	6-35	2	20.78
10	M. N. V. Silva (*Chilaw Marians*)	SLA	284	51	925	44	6-62	2	21.02
11	A. M. Fernando (*SL A/Chilaw Mar*)	RFM	310.2	49	1,103	52	7-139	4	21.21
12	K. D. V. Wimalasekara (*Army*)	OB	311	48	896	42	5-20	4	21.33
13	D. S. Auwardt (*Navy*)	SLA	221.5	36	738	34	7-133	2	21.70
14	W. R. C. Fernando (*Negombo*)	RM	215	42	695	32	5-31	1	21.71
15	D. M. N. D. Gunawardene (*Sebast*)	SLA	233	17	869	40	6-57	3	21.72
16	P. M. Pushpakumara (*SL A/Colombo*)	SLA	354.5	47	1,128	51	6-80	4	22.11
17	N. M. Kavikara (*Kurunegala Youth*)	SLA	291.2	46	952	43	8-69	4	22.13
18	A. L. R. Manasinghe (*Negombo*)	OB	209.3	27	904	38	8-57	5	23.78
19	S. M. A. Priyanjan (*SL A/Colombo*)	OB	192	29	673	28	6-24	3	24.03
20	N. G. R. P. Jayasuriya (*SL A/Colts*)	SLA	354.3	52	1,238	49	6-65	4	25.26
21	J. U. Chaturanga (*Kandy Customs*)	SLA	242.1	54	761	28	5-80	1	27.17
22	S. S. M. Perera (*Kandy Customs*)	LB	237.3	30	991	36	6-106	2	27.52
23	S. A. D. U. Indrasiri (*Negombo*)	SLA	407.4	66	1,405	50	7-120	5	28.10
24	M. A. Aponso (*Ragama*)	SLA	314	48	992	33	5-98	2	30.06
25	M. A. Liyanapathiranage (*Tamil U*)	OB	320.4	47	895	29	6-54	1	30.86
26	P. C. de Silva (*Nondescripts*)	SLA	294	20	1,030	33	6-144	2	31.21

THE LAST DAYS BEFORE THE PANDEMIC

Cakes, pens and auto-rickshaws

DOMINIC WOOD

It should have been the final day of England's last tour match before thousands of their fans descended on Galle for the Test series with Sri Lanka. Instead, it proved to be the penultimate day of first-class cricket before coronavirus changed everything. Sunday, March 15, ended with an aspiring Test player's birthday cake littered across a Colombo outfield. As Covid-19 ripped through professional sport, his party morphed into a wake.

Two days earlier, the ECB had postponed the tour, leaving England supporters who had already arrived scrambling for alternative entertainment. Colombo houses many first-class venues, certainly more than any other city. With the first-class season in full swing since January 31 – and set to conclude in mid-April – it was possible to visit four matches in a day.

At the last of the four, Colts Cricket Club, there was only one other spectator. The home side were playing Negombo, who were chasing victory over Colts to leapfrog Burgher Recreation Club in the final round of Premier League group games, and claim a top-four finish in Tier A, and a place in the Super Eights.

That spectator was Burgher's new head coach, Mohammad Reza Thahir, twitching and praying for anything but a Negombo win, and furiously texting wicket updates to his boss. Bespectacled, portly and bearded, with a career in IT behind him, Reza worked under director of cricket Charith Senanayake, who opened the batting in three Tests in New Zealand in 1990-91, and became a popular tour manager with the national team. Charith had plucked Reza from obscurity, because of his attention to detail and aptitude for a motivational speech. This was a sliding-doors moment for Reza: his new career would hang on the next hour.

Negombo were defending 134 in 28 overs, and Colts were battening down the hatches like a Covid-compliant shopkeeper before a curfew. But Negombo's spinners scythed through the batting, and Reza's nascent career was in peril. Then, at 5.36, with the scoreboard reading 81 for six, play was halted: Burgher had made it, and Reza's joy manifested itself in an understated, if finger-shaking, tap of his mobile screen to tell Charith to prepare for the Super Eights. If only for a few days, all was right with their world.

A busy day had begun at Moors Sports Club, close to Colombo's financial district. This time, the other spectator was former Test player and pace-bowling guru Champaka Ramanayake, there to see his son, Himesh, bowl medium-pace for Sinhalese Sports Club. Himesh's team had delayed their declaration, and saw their unlikely hopes of qualification end when Moors held on at 333 for nine.

Twenty-four hours earlier, England's departure had rocked the nation. Although Sri Lanka had, at that point, recorded ten coronavirus cases and no deaths, their government were beginning to take note of global trends. At Colts CC that morning, an odd pall hung over practice: having developed a fear of pens and paper after being told the virus could remain on items for hours, Colts and Negombo players were so spooked they dared not stand next to supporters.

Compared with the raucous affair at the nearby SSC that same day, it could have been another universe: nothing, not even the looming restrictions, would prevent the conclusion of the 141st edition of the Royal–Thomian, one of the world's longest continuously played school matches. With almost 30,000 partying in the stands, it was business as usual. One person with the virus was later said to have attended, and earmarked as a potential super-spreader, leading to a public outcry over the game's staging. Tradition and the lure of profit proved too strong.

A fear of fans had begun on Wednesday, March 11, when the cricket world still seemed naive to the growing threat. With England preparing for their four-day game against a Sri Lanka Board President's XI, one player cheerfully grabbed a pen, and signed for a fan, only then to edgily wonder: "You don't have coronavirus, do you?" Another asked backroom staff: "Signing or not signing?" There was a shake of the head, and England's social-distancing policy had begun. Less than 50 metres away, the President's XI mingled freely with fans.

By the Sunday, local players had slipped back to jovial greetings for English fans, especially for a stray one pitching up at an unfashionable three-day fixture. A tuk-tuk drove me to the day's second venue, a few hundred metres from SSC: the spartan Colombo Cricket Club, where Chilaw Marians and Lankan Cricket Club were at lunch. The only other spectator was a player's mate.

Next up was the Army Ground, Panagoda, 12 miles east of Colombo. Internet updates en route showed Sri Lanka Army Sports Club heading for a shellacking at the hands of table toppers (and eventual competition winners) Colombo Cricket Club. The venue may be among the world's least visited, and it soon became clear why: no one knew where it was.

The tuk-tuk eventually stopped outside a peaceful entrance to what looked like a large park. The ground is buried deep within an army compound, and guarded by two security booths. A soldier forbade entry, and his superior said no one could come in without having passed a security check via their embassy in Colombo a week in advance. Former Test seamer Lahiru Gamage's career-best seven for 47, which took CCC to victory, would remain the one that got away.

Back at Colts' ground, professional cricket with spectators had all but ended for several months. A few hours later, the last rites of a four-day match thousands of miles away in Antigua drifted the sport towards oblivion, while two Sri Lankan domestic games dribbled into Monday; in Bangladesh, a trio of 50-over matches closed the book.

But no one, not even the players, knew it at the time. Colts had claimed second spot, and a boisterous party seemed fitting. Potential Test opener Sangeeth Cooray – who had just made 40 – celebrated his 25th birthday with a traditional Asian-style cake-plastering. As darkness clouded the debris of icing strewn across the outfield, and the ceremonial cheers fell silent, uncertainty had started to take hold.

Nisala Tharaka, a 29-year-old paceman in the selectors' Test thoughts, and fresh from dismissing Joe Denly and Ben Stokes the previous week, was worried his deal with Chesterfield CC would go up in smoke. Now in his prime, after overcoming a serious back injury in his mid-twenties, Nisala saw 2020 as his career springboard. Instead, the year would bring him only four more wickets – another pivotal moment lost to corona.

The frivolous attitude that allowed thousands of fans at the SSC – on the same day first-class players were too scared to meet one – would soon give way to a crushing seven weeks of curfew in the capital. Cricket, as we knew it, died on a steaming hot Sunday in mid-March, with Cooray's birthday lights the last to go out.

PREMIER LEAGUE TOURNAMENT TIER A IN 2019-20

Group A	P	W	L	D	Pts
COLOMBO	6	4	0	2	97.480
COLTS	6	2	2	2	69.745
ARMY	6	2	2	2	61.130
BURGHER	6	1	3	2	55.240
Negombo	6	1	1	4	49.240
Sinhalese	6	1	0	5	47.580
Moors	6	0	3	3	35.435

Group B	P	W	L	D	Pts
CHILAW MARIANS	6	3	2	1	65.700
NONDESCRIPTS	6	1	0	5	62.100
SARACENS	6	1	2	3	60.505
RAGAMA	6	2	1	3	56.455
Tamil Union	6	1	1	4	44.525
Badureliya	6	1	1	4	38.760
Lankan	6	0	2	4	27.970

Super Eight	P	W	L	D	Pts
COLOMBO	7	4	0	3	95.170
Nondescripts	7	2	0	5	83.095
Chilaw Marians	7	2	1	4	81.840
Ragama	7	2	2	3	68.785
Colts	7	1	3	3	58.580
Army	7	1	2	4	51.770
Saracens	7	1	2	4	47.825
Burgher	7	0	3	4	45.965

Plate	P	W	L	D	Pts
MOORS	5	2	0	3	67.880
Negombo	5	1	0	4	58.980
Tamil Union	5	1	1	3	41.440
Sinhalese	5	0	0	5	38.410
Lankan	5	0	2	3	35.135
Badureliya	5	0	1	4	27.565

The top four teams from each group advanced to the Super Eight, carrying forward their results against fellow qualifiers, then played the other four qualifiers. The bottom three from each group entered the Plate competition, run on the same principles. There was no relegation and promotion between Tier A and the (incomplete) Tier B (see next page)..

Outright win = 12pts; win by an innings = 2pts extra; lead on first innings in a drawn game = 8pts. Bonus points were awarded as follows: 0.15pts for each wicket taken and 0.005pts for each run scored, up to 400 runs per innings.

CHAMPIONS

1988-89	Nondescripts / Sinhalese
1989-90	Sinhalese
1990-91	Sinhalese
1991-92	Colts
1992-93	Sinhalese
1993-94	Nondescripts
1994-95	Bloomfield / Sinhalese
1995-96	Colombo
1996-97	Bloomfield
1997-98	Sinhalese
1998-99	Bloomfield
1999-2000	Colts
2000-01	Nondescripts
2001-02	Colts
2002-03	Moors
2003-04	Bloomfield
2004-05	Colts
2005-06	Sinhalese
2006-07	Colombo
2007-08	Sinhalese
2008-09	Colts
2009-10	Chilaw Marians
2010-11	Bloomfield
2011-12	Colts
2012-13	Sinhalese
2013-14	Nondescripts
2014-15	Ports Authority
2015-16	Tamil Union
2016-17	Sinhalese
2017-18	Chilaw Marians
2018-19	Colombo
2019-20	Colombo

Sinhalese have won the title outright 8 times, Colts 6, Bloomfield and Colombo 4, Nondescripts 3, Chilaw Marians 2, Moors, Ports Authority and Tamil Union 1. Sinhalese have shared it twice, Bloomfield and Nondescripts once each.

The tournament was known as the Lakspray Trophy from 1988-89 to 1989-90, the P. Saravanamuttu Trophy from 1990-91 to 1997-98, and the Premier League from 1998-99.

PREMIER LEAGUE TOURNAMENT TIER B IN 2019-20

	P	*W*	*L*	*D*	*Pts*
Police	7	4	0	3	99.105
Ports Authority	7	2	1	4	90.825
Bloomfield	7	4	1	2	82.495
Kandy Customs	7	2	2	3	81.780
Panadura	7	3	1	3	79.420
Galle	7	2	1	4	78.765
Nugegoda	7	3	2	2	78.360
Sebastianites	7	2	2	3	65.435
Kurunegala Youth	7	1	1	5	59.585
Navy	7	1	1	5	41.750
Air Force	7	0	5	2	34.055
Kalutara Town	7	0	7	0	28.945

Outright win = 12pts; win by an innings = 2pts extra; lead on first innings in a drawn game = 8pts. Bonus points were awarded as follows: 0.15pts for each wicket taken and 0.005pts for each run scored, up to 400 runs per innings.

The final four rounds were cancelled because of the Covid-19 pandemic; no winner was declared.

SLC INVITATION LIMITED-OVERS TOURNAMENT IN 2019-20

Four 50-over mini-leagues plus knockout

Quarter-finals Army beat Air Force by five wickets; Chilaw Marians beat Panadura by 130 runs; Nondescripts beat Saracens by three runs; Sinhalese beat Tamil Union by 200 runs.

Semi-finals Chilaw Marians beat Sinhalese by three wickets; Nondescripts beat Army by 22 runs.

Final At Colombo (SSC), December 31, 2019. **Chilaw Marians won by 91 runs. Chilaw Marians 295-8** (50 overs); ‡**Nondescripts 204** (43.3 overs). *Sumit Ghadigaonkar set up Chilaw's total by scoring a 77-ball 79 out of 128 in the first 22 overs; Rumesh Buddika took over the baton with a slightly more sedate 60*, adding 69 in ten overs with Thikshila de Silva (47 in 36). Nondescripts' reply was derailed when they collapsed from 119-1 to 123-6 in four overs, three of them falling to Shehan Jayasuriya's off-spin. Chamika Karunaratne hit four sixes in his 32, but could not deny Chilaw.*

The SLC Twenty20 tournament in 2019-20 can be found on page 867.

WEST INDIAN CRICKET IN 2020

Toil and trouble

VANEISA BAKSH

It was a dreadful end to a dreadful year: in December 2019, the West Indian team returned home after winning one ODI and one T20 game in India. It seemed 2020 had to be better – only for coronavirus to blight a year in which the players spent too much time for their own good cooped up in biosecure bubbles.

The first engagement was expected to be a cakewalk, but Ireland would not roll over: West Indies did win the one-dayers 3–0, but the tenacious tourists won the first T20 match in Grenada and, after rain ruined the second, in St Kitts, West Indies managed to draw the series at the last. That set the tone for a year with rather more downs than ups. The next stop was Sri Lanka, where the ODIs were lost 3–0, but both T20s won. Then it was back to the Caribbean for the regional first-class competition. Barbados came out on top, but the last six of the scheduled 30 fixtures were cancelled, as the pandemic brought everything to a screeching halt.

WEST INDIES IN 2020

	Played	*Won*	*Lost*	*Drawn/No result*
Tests	5	1	4	–
One-day internationals	6	3	3	–
Twenty20 internationals	8	3	3	2

JANUARY	3 ODIs and 3 T20Is (h) v Ireland	(page 777)
FEBRUARY / MARCH	3 ODIs and 2 T20Is (a) v Sri Lanka	(page 766)
APRIL		
MAY		
JUNE		
JULY	3 Tests (a) v England	(page 327)
AUGUST		
SEPTEMBER		
OCTOBER		
NOVEMBER / DECEMBER	2 Tests and 3 T20Is (a) v New Zealand	(page 707)

For a review of West Indian domestic cricket from the 2019-20 season, see page 779.

Mike Hewitt, AFP/Getty Images

Fist things first: Jason Holder and his team start the England summer with a show of solidarity.

Everywhere, sporting organisations were faced with tough decisions: one by one, fixtures and tournaments were rescheduled or cancelled. In the West Indies, where national populations are small, and resources smaller, the dread was exacerbated by the certainty that none of the health services in any of the territories would be able to cope with a major outbreak.

West Indies' tour of South Africa, scheduled for July, was postponed, and a trip to New Zealand shifted to the end of the year. But even as it appeared the players would be idle for months, discussions were taking place between the ECB and Cricket West Indies for a Test series in England in July. The logistics of hosting three matches under the rapidly changing conditions were as daunting as the task of persuading players and officials to take the risk. Eventually, agreements were reached, and a big West Indian squad travelled to England for three Tests (and innumerable Covid tests); only three players declined. Cricket lovers switched on their televisions to witness, for the first time, the spectacle of the game being played without crowds, in a biosecure bubble, a phrase which became mind-numbingly familiar as the year wore on.

The series started in the rain in Southampton, but there was an addition to the usual pre-match razzmatazz. The dignified Jason Holder and his team had asked for a tribute, before each game, to the Black Lives Matter movement. And so, all wearing black gloves on one hand, and the BLM logo on their collars, the tourists took a knee, and raised their clenched fists in solidarity. It was an act of support they maintained throughout the year. Equally notable were the powerful statements of Jamaican player-turned-commentator Michael Holding, whose impassioned account of the devastating impact of racism gained global support.

West Indies' women also looked likely to have a fallow year, before they too braved the bubble, this time in Derby in September. Stafanie Taylor's side were rusty, having not played since the T20 World Cup in Australia in March, and slumped to five defeats against a sparky England.

If the on-field performances of the teams did not yield happy results, Caribbean pride remained intact. At the beginning of December, MCC and the BBC announced that the 2020 Spirit of Cricket Award would go to Cricket West Indies and both their senior teams, in recognition of their courage and the "huge sacrifices and personal risks" they had undertaken to ensure international cricket could resume.

And as the players took a knee on that near-silent day in Southampton, it was clear the significance of the occasion had seeped into the team's core. They played above themselves, and won by four wickets, after being set a tricky target of 200, largely thanks to a defiant 95 from Jermaine Blackwood. It seemed they were fired up, and would compete hard for the rest of the series. But that remained the only Test victory of the year. England won both games at Old Trafford against opponents who seemed increasingly fragile.

The Caribbean Premier League went ahead in mid-August, at two grounds in Trinidad. Again there were no spectators, but it gave those stuck indoors something to watch. Inspired by captain Kieron Pollard, the local Trinbago Knight Riders won all their 12 matches, culminating with the final against St Lucia Zouks. For Pollard, it was a warm-up for the IPL, where his Mumbai Indians side took the spoils as well.

The last engagement was the delayed tour of New Zealand, where the sight of maskless spectators, with barely any social distancing, seemed odd after months of little else. Off the field, life was showing signs of a return to normality. On it, things remained depressingly familiar: only rain stopped New Zealand winning all three T20s, before West Indies were annihilated in the Tests. Both followed a similar pattern: New Zealand ran up a big total, then the West Indian batsmen struggled. And if getting runs was painful, watching the bowlers toil, only for sloppy fielding to ruin their efforts, was worse. A dreadful end to another dreadful year.

WEST INDIES v IRELAND IN 2019-20

IAN CALLENDER

One-day internationals (3): West Indies 3, Ireland 0
Twenty20 internationals (3): West Indies 1, Ireland 1

West Indies won a one-day series at home for the first time since August 2014 after easily outgunning a rusty Ireland, who hit back to share the Twenty20 spoils. Test captain Jason Holder was rested from a powerful West Indies squad that exposed the frailty of Ireland's batting. There was plenty to mull over for their new captain, Andy Balbirnie, on his first assignment since taking over from William Porterfield.

Ireland's previous ODI had been against Zimbabwe in July 2019, and they had not played one in the Caribbean for nearly six years. At first, it showed: West Indies strolled home in the opener, but the Irish regrouped, and took the second game to the penultimate ball – and the last wicket. Ireland were well beaten in a rain-hit third match. Paul Stirling's explosive 95 off 47 balls earned them the lead in the T20 series but, after an unfinished second game, West Indies won the third at a canter.

With 208 runs at 104, Evin Lewis dominated the 50-over matches (the next-highest aggregate on either side was Nicholas Pooran's 112), and he also averaged over 50 in the shorter format. Alzarri Joseph shrugged off an undistinguished ODI record to take eight wickets at 12, with an economy-rate of 3.36. Kieron Pollard, in his first home matches as full-time white-ball captain, was Player of the Series in the 20-over games, taking seven cheap wickets. All-rounder Hayden Walsh, who had played for the United States, was the hero of their backs-to-the-wall victory in the second ODI.

It was a sign of Ireland's eclipse in the one-dayers that Balbirnie was their leading run-scorer with only 97. Simi Singh's off-breaks brought him six wickets at 20, while Stirling and Kevin O'Brien underpinned the T20 batting, which otherwise had little depth. In the opening game, Ireland were 150 without loss after just 11.2 overs, but finished on 208 for seven; in the second, they were 95 for two, also in the 12th, but tumbled to 147 for nine; in the third, 50 for none in the fourth translated to 138 all out.

IRELAND TOURING PARTY

*A. Balbirnie (50/20), M. R. Adair (50/20), G. J. Delany (50/20), G. H. Dockrell (20), J. B. Little (20), A. R. McBrine (50), B. J. McCarthy (50/20), J. A. McCollum (50), K. J. O'Brien (50/20), W. T. S. Porterfield (50), W. B. Rankin (50/20), S. Singh (50/20), P. R. Stirling (50/20), H. T. Tector (20), L. J. Tucker (50/20), G. C. Wilson (50/20), C. A. Young (50/20). *Coach:* G. X. Ford.

First one-day international At Bridgetown, Barbados, January 7, 2020 (day/night). **West Indies won by five wickets.** ‡**Ireland 180** (46.1 overs) (L. J. Tucker 31; A. S. Joseph 4-32); **West Indies 184-5** (33.2 overs) (E. Lewis 99*). *PoM:* A. S. Joseph. *ODI debut:* G. J. Delany (Ireland). *Evin Lewis tried to complete the match – and his hundred – with a six, but his lofted extra-cover drive landed just short of the boundary. After surviving a difficult chance to Kevin O'Brien on 30 off Mark Adair, Lewis assumed command, hitting 13 fours and two sixes in his 99-ball stay (West Indies's next-best* *contribution was 20, from Brandon King). Victory came with nearly 17 overs to spare. Ireland's shot selection had been found wanting as they slipped to 88-6 in the face of a hostile burst from Alzarri Joseph. Lorcan Tucker and Adair added 54, but they could not prevent Ireland's lowest ODI total against West Indies, undercutting 185 at Dublin the previous May.*

Second one-day international At Bridgetown, Barbados, January 9, 2020 (day/night). **West Indies won by one wicket. ‡Ireland 237-9** (50 overs) (P. R. Stirling 63, K. J. O'Brien 31, S. Singh 34; S. S. Cottrell 3-51, A. S. Joseph 4-32); **West Indies 242-9** (49.5 overs) (N. Pooran 52, K. A. Pollard 40, H. R. Walsh 46*; S. Singh 3-48). *PoM:* A. S. Joseph. *Ireland blew two gilt-edged opportunities in the final over, then watched Sheldon Cottrell smash Adair's fifth ball for six. Off the third, Cottrell had been short of his ground when Adair collected Andy McBrine's throw from mid-off, and removed the bails. But, after almost five minutes of replays, third umpire Ruchira Palliyaguruge could not be sure Adair had the ball in his hand. More drama followed, when Cottrell came back for a non-existent second after Hayden Walsh had bunted the ball to long-off. But Barry McCarthy threw to the wrong end, Adair fumbled, and Cottrell scrambled back. Moments later, he launched Adair over cover to secure West Indies' 12th one-wicket win in ODIs. Walsh's cool 46* had dragged them back into a game that seemed lost when, chasing 238, they slumped to 148-7 in the 29th. Ireland ought to have managed more after Paul Stirling and William Porterfield helped them to 110-2 in the 23rd, but they were slowed by Joseph, who again took 4-32.*

Third one-day international At St George's, Grenada, January 12, 2020. **West Indies won by five wickets** (DLS). **Ireland 203** (49.1 overs) (A. Balbirnie 71; O. R. Thomas 3-41, H. R. Walsh 4-36); **‡West Indies 199-5** (36.2 overs) (E. Lewis 102, B. A. King 38, N. Pooran 43*). *PoM:* E. Lewis. *PoS:* E. Lewis. *West Indies completed a whitewash with something to spare. This time, Lewis was not to be denied a third ODI hundred, reaching three figures in 96 balls, before falling to his next as he aimed for his sixth six. Nicholas Pooran ensured West Indies completed the pursuit of a revised target of 197 in 47 overs. Ireland's innings had never got going, save for Andy Balbirnie's battling 71. Oshane Thomas produced a rapid opening spell, but the star performer was Walsh, whose leg-breaks brought him a career-best 4-36, including three for four in 11 balls.*

First Twenty20 international At St George's, Grenada, January 15, 2020. **Ireland won by four runs. ‡Ireland 208-7** (20 overs) (P. R. Stirling 95, K. J. O'Brien 48); **West Indies 204-7** (20 overs) (E. Lewis 53, K. A. Pollard 31; J. B. Little 3-29). *PoM:* P. R. Stirling. *Ireland won a fluctuating match not settled until the final ball. Stirling and O'Brien had launched their innings with two powerplay world records: Stirling's 67, and a total of 93. When Dwayne Bravo, playing his first international since September 2016, bowled O'Brien for a 32-ball 48, Ireland had 154 inside 13 overs, a national first-wicket record, beating the same pair's 126 against Afghanistan at Dehradun in February 2019. Stirling followed next over, for a T20I-best 95 from 47, including an Ireland-record eight sixes (he and O'Brien had both managed seven), and only 55 came in the last eight. Led by Lewis, West Indies reached 105-2 at halfway, and looked favourites when Sherfane Rutherford and Pooran took 27 off the 18th, bowled by McCarthy. They needed 16 off two, with six wickets in hand, but Craig Young removed Pooran in an over costing only three, before Josh Little coolly defended 13.*

Second Twenty20 international At Basseterre, St Kitts, January 18, 2020 (floodlit). **No result** (DLS). **Ireland 147-9** (19 overs) (A. Balbirnie 36, G. J. Delany 44, H. T. Tector 31; K. A. Pollard 4-25); **‡West Indies 16-1** (2.1 overs). *T20I debut:* R. Shepherd (West Indies). *Ireland again faltered in the second half of their innings, after Gareth Delany's 44 off 22 – including four successive sixes off Walsh – had laid a solid platform following an early shower. Pollard brought himself on to halt the charge, and took a wicket in each of his four overs to record his best T20I figures. A second break for rain reduced the innings to 19 overs, though Ireland lost three wickets – two to run-outs – from the three balls they faced after the resumption. West Indies' target was revised to 152 in 19, and they quickly lost Lendl Simmons, but more rain meant the match was abandoned.*

Third Twenty20 international At Basseterre, St Kitts, January 19, 2020 (floodlit). **West Indies won by nine wickets. Ireland 138** (19.1 overs) (K. J. O'Brien 36; K. A. Pollard 3-17, D. J. Bravo 3-19); **‡West Indies 140-1** (11 overs) (L. M. P. Simmons 91*, E. Lewis 46). *PoM:* L. M. P. Simmons. *PoS:* K. A. Pollard. *West Indies responded emphatically to the threat of a series defeat. Simmons lit the fuse, hitting McCarthy for 14 in three balls, then took 16 off four from Young. Two balls after his opening stand of 133 with Lewis (46 off 25) was brought to an end, he wrapped up victory with his tenth six. His career-best 91* had needed only 40 balls. Earlier, Ireland had raced out of the traps again: 50 came up in 20, after O'Brien hit Cottrell for five successive fours. But he fell for 36 off 18 – the first of ten to tumble for 88. When Bravo, who like Pollard finished with three cheap wickets, trapped Stirling, he moved past Samuel Badree's haul of 54 to become West Indies' highest T20 wicket-taker.*

DOMESTIC CRICKET IN THE WEST INDIES IN 2019-20

HAYDN GILL

Barbados denied Guyana an unprecedented sixth successive first-class title by capturing the West Indies Championship in a truncated season. By mid-March, when the competition was halted with two rounds to go in an effort to contain Covid-19, Barbados were runaway leaders. They had won six of their eight matches, twice as many as their closest challengers, stood more than 40 points clear, and were confirmed as champions on March 24.

Rebounding from defeat in their opening fixture, against Windward Islands, they recorded comfortable victories in their next five, before slipping up against Trinidad & Tobago. But they put the title beyond reach in the eighth round, when they visited Guyana and defeated them for the second time, by a massive 235 runs, routing them for 55 and 94 without bowling a single over of spin.

A trio of fast bowlers spearheaded their campaign. The experienced Kemar Roach claimed 30 wickets in five games, while his accomplices Chemar Holder (aged 21) and Keon Harding (23) shared 65; all three finished in the top seven wicket-takers, and they helped Barbados collect 24.8 pace points – the incentive brought in three years earlier to reward wickets earned by speed rather than spin. No other team managed more than 14. In their second fixture against the Windwards, Barbados became the first side to earn a perfect 24 points (12 for the win, five bonus points for batting, three for bowling and four for taking 20 wickets with pace). Among their batsmen, Kyle Mayers, in his first first-class season with his native Barbados after returning from the Windwards, outshone more established players by fashioning two hundreds and five half-centuries on the way to an aggregate of 654 at an average of 50.

Trinidad & Tobago finished second, their best showing in recent seasons, and 21-year-old Joshua Da Silva, who also averaged 50, was one of the tournament's emerging talents. He was among five to pass 500 runs. Two played for **Jamaica** (tied third with Guyana): Jermaine Blackwood was the leading scorer, with 768 at 51, while Nkrumah Bonner's 523 at 58 put him on top of the averages. Blackwood was later recalled to the Test squad for West Indies' tour of England, and Bonner included for the first time.

Guyana, who had won all five previous championships under the franchise system, were a shadow of their former selves. None of their batsmen averaged 40, though left-arm spinner Veerasammy Permaul maintained his dominance, collecting most wickets in the tournament for the third time in six seasons, including 15 for 77 against Jamaica. His 50 at just under 13 put him well ahead of his nearest rivals, Chemar Holder of Barbados and Trinidadian slow left-armer Akeal Hosein, who had 36 apiece.

Windward Islands trailed the pack, winning only once after their opening victory over Barbados, despite 649 runs from former Test batsman Devon Smith. **Leeward Islands** had only one first-class win. Their home match against Barbados was delayed by a day after an overnight burglary at Basseterre, with players' shirts, a pair of glasses and training apparatus stolen from the visitors' dressing-room.

A marginal improvement in batting standards was indicated by seven team totals over 400 (three more than in 2018-19, despite six fewer games), ten under 150 (down from 17) and 24 centuries (up from 21). Additionally, more matches went the distance, with six out of 24 drawn; in 2018-19, it was just one in 30.

Earlier in the season, **West Indies Emerging Players** had upstaged the territorial teams to lift the Super50 Cup, crushing Leeward Islands by 205 runs in the final. Their squad contained 11 players under 25, including four who went on to represent West Indies in the Under-19 World Cup. It was the second year running that a side coached by Floyd Reifer had won the trophy, following Combined Campuses & Colleges (who finished bottom of their group this time, after losing twice to Canada), and prompted calls for Cricket West Indies to expand the first-class championship beyond the six traditional sides.

FIRST-CLASS AVERAGES IN 2019-20

BATTING (250 runs, average 25.00)

		M	*I*	*NO*	*R*	*HS*	*100*	*Avge*	*Ct/St*
1	N. E. Bonner (*Jamaica*)	7	13	4	523	135	2	58.11	4
2	†K. J. Cottoy (*Windward Islands*)	7	12	4	432	103*	1	54.00	3
3	J. Blackwood (*Jamaica*)	8	15	0	768	248	1	51.20	6
4	J. Da Silva (*Trinidad & Tobago*)	8	12	2	507	113*	1	50.70	15
5	†K. R. Mayers (*Barbados*)	8	15	2	654	140	2	50.30	6
6	†D. S. Smith (*Windward Islands*)	8	15	1	649	147*	1	46.35	6
7	†P. Palmer (*Jamaica*)	7	13	3	432	116*	2	43.20	1
8	T. Hinds (*Trinidad & Tobago*)	7	9	3	259	102*	1	43.16	1
9	J. N. Mohammed (*Trinidad & Tobago*)	7	11	1	424	119	2	42.40	3
10	K. A. R. Hodge (*Windward Islands*)	8	13	1	454	100*	1	37.83	13
11	A. D. S. Fletcher (*Windward Islands*)	5	8	0	300	88	0	37.50	3
12	†C. Hemraj (*Guyana*)	6	10	1	329	82	0	36.55	3
13	†L. R. Johnson (*Guyana*)	8	14	1	472	189*	1	36.30	12
14	S. O. Dowrich (*Barbados*)	7	11	1	360	96	0	36.00	21
15	†S. A. R. Moseley (*Barbados*)	8	15	1	490	155*	1	35.00	6
16	†V. A. Singh (*Guyana*)	7	13	2	381	93	0	34.63	2
17	C. D. Barnwell (*Guyana*)	8	14	1	435	107	1	33.46	3
18	K. C. Brathwaite (*Barbados*)	8	15	1	468	84*	0	33.42	9
19	†J. D. Campbell (*Jamaica*)	8	15	0	491	112	2	32.73	7
20	†A. A. Jangoo (*Leeward Islands*)	7	12	0	373	90	0	31.08	6
21	†K. O. A. Powell (*Leeward Islands*)	8	15	1	429	99	0	30.64	4
22	D. C. Green (*Jamaica*)	6	10	1	263	62	0	29.22	1
23	J. N. Hamilton (*Leeward Islands*)	8	14	1	372	67	0	28.61	20
24	A. Bramble (*Guyana*)	8	13	0	339	91	0	26.07	22/5
25	M. V. Hodge (*Leeward Islands*)	8	15	0	390	98	0	26.00	8

BOWLING (12 wickets)

		Style	*O*	*M*	*R*	*W*	*BB*	*5I*	*Avge*
1	A. Phillip (*Trinidad & Tobago*)	RFM	82	20	253	21	6-19	2	12.04
2	V. Permaul (*Guyana*)	SLA	310.4	96	649	50	8-18	3	12.98
3	K. A. J. Roach (*Barbados*)	RFM	140.1	36	411	30	6-84	2	13.70
4	C. K. Holder (*Barbados*)	RFM	207.3	35	681	36	6-47	3	18.91
5	I. Khan (*Trinidad & Tobago*)	LB	87	21	252	13	4-67	0	19.38
6	N. A. Gordon (*Jamaica*)	RFM	102	14	331	17	6-45	2	19.47
7	J. H. Merchant (*Jamaica*)	OB	138.4	33	326	16	3-8	0	20.37
8	A. J. Hosein (*Trinidad & Tobago*)	SLA	318.4	88	742	36	6-62	1	20.61
9	R. R. S. Cornwall (*Leeward Islands*)	OB	239.3	45	632	30	8-51	1	21.06
10	K. A. Stoute (*Barbados*)	RFM	100	27	269	12	3-18	0	22.41
11	M. J. Mindley (*Jamaica*)	RFM	178.1	32	544	24	5-65	1	22.66
12	P. A. S. McSween (*Windward Islands*)	LFM	225	47	706	31	6-64	3	22.77
13	K. J. Harding (*Barbados*)	RFM	180.1	30	673	29	5-19	2	23.20
14	J. A. Warrican (*Barbados*)	SLA	132	39	304	13	4-40	0	23.38
15	D. C. Green (*Jamaica*)	RM	180	38	547	22	5-75	1	24.86
16	K. Sinclair (*Guyana*)	OB	130	33	327	12	2-2	0	27.25
17	K. A. Joseph (*Guyana*)	RFM	119.2	22	344	12	4-75	0	28.66
18	B. N. L. Charles (*Trinidad & Tobago*)	OB	168	34	496	17	5-87	1	29.17
19	N. Smith (*Guyana*)	RM	168	34	586	20	6-55	2	29.30
20	S. Berridge (*Leeward Islands*)	RFM	159	40	538	18	5-22	1	29.88
21	R. A. Reifer (*Guyana*)	LFM	162	41	481	16	3-55	0	30.06
22	P. M. Harty (*Jamaica*)	SLA	252.5	38	709	22	4-43	0	32.22
23	S. Shillingford (*Windward Islands*)	OB	148.4	11	507	15	7-105	1	33.80
24	J. Thomas (*Windward Islands*)	RFM	127	22	470	13	3-83	0	36.15

WEST INDIES CHAMPIONSHIP IN 2019-20

	P	*W*	*L*	*D*	*Bonus points* *Bat*	*Bowl*	*Pace*	*Pts*
Barbados	8	6	2	0	14	24	24.8	134.8
Trinidad & Tobago	8	3	2	3	18	21	10.6	94.6
Guyana	8	3	3	2	16	21	12.8	91.8
Jamaica	8	3	3	2	14	22	13.8	91.8
Windward Islands	8	2	3	3	11	20	14.0	78.0
Leeward Islands	8	1	5	2	6	16	12.8	52.8

Win = 12pts; draw = 3pts. Bonus points awarded for the first 110 overs of each team's first innings: two batting points for the first 250 runs and then one for 300, 350 and 400; one bowling point for the third wicket taken and then for the sixth and ninth. In addition, 0.2pts awarded for every wicket taken by a pace bowler, across both innings.

The final two rounds were cancelled because of the Covid-19 pandemic.

REGIONAL CHAMPIONS

1965-66	Barbados	1983-84	Barbados	2001-02	Jamaica
1966-67	Barbados	1984-85	Trinidad & Tobago	2002-03	Barbados
1967-68	*No competition*	1985-86	Barbados	2003-04	Barbados
1968-69	Jamaica	1986-87	Guyana	2004-05	Jamaica
1969-70	Trinidad	1987-88	Jamaica	2005-06	Trinidad & Tobago
1970-71	Trinidad	1988-89	Jamaica	2006-07	Barbados
1971-72	Barbados	1989-90	Leeward Islands	2007-08	Jamaica
1972-73	Guyana	1990-91	Barbados	2008-09	Jamaica
1973-74	Barbados	1991-92	Jamaica	2009-10	Jamaica
1974-75	Guyana	1992-93	Guyana	2010-11	Jamaica
1975-76	Trinidad	1993-94	Leeward Islands	2011-12	Jamaica
	Barbados	1994-95	Barbados	2012-13	Barbados
1976-77	Barbados	1995-96	Leeward Islands	2013-14	Barbados
1977-78	Barbados	1996-97	Barbados	2014-15	Guyana
1978-79	Barbados	1997-98	Leeward Islands	2015-16	Guyana
1979-80	Barbados		Guyana	2016-17	Guyana
1980-81	Combined Islands	1998-99	Barbados	2017-18	Guyana
1981-82	Barbados	1999-2000	Jamaica	2018-19	Guyana
1982-83	Guyana	2000-01	Barbados	2019-20	Barbados

Barbados have won the title outright 22 times, Jamaica 12, Guyana 10, Trinidad/Trinidad & Tobago 4, Leeward Islands 3, Combined Islands 1. Barbados, Guyana, Leeward Islands and Trinidad have also shared the title.

The tournament was known as the Shell Shield from 1965-66 to 1986-87, the Red Stripe Cup from 1987-88 to 1996-97, the President's Cup in 1997-98, the Busta Cup from 1998-99 to 2001-02, the Carib Beer Cup from 2002-03 to 2007-08, the Headley–Weekes Trophy from 2008-09 to 2012-13, the President's Trophy in 2013-14, the WICB Professional Cricket League from 2014-15 (though it was sponsored by Digicel in 2016-17), and the West Indies Championship from 2018-19.

COLONIAL MEDICAL INSURANCE SUPER50 CUP IN 2019-20

50-over league plus knockout

Zone A	*P*	*W*	*L*	*Pts*	**Zone B**	*P*	*W*	*L*	*Pts*
BARBADOS	8	6	2	24	TRINIDAD & TOBAGO	8	7	1	28
LEEWARD ISLANDS	8	6	2	24	WI EMERGING PLAYERS	8	4	3*	18
Jamaica	8	4	4	16	Guyana	8	4	4	16
Canada	8	2	6	8	Windward Islands	8	2	5*	10
Campuses & Colleges	8	2	6	8	USA	8	2	6	8

* *Plus one abandoned.*

Semi-finals West Indies Emerging Players beat Barbados by three wickets (DLS); Leeward Islands beat Trinidad & Tobago by four wickets.

Final At Port-of-Spain, December 1, 2019 (day/night). **West Indies Emerging Players won by 205 runs. West Indies Emerging Players 293-7** (50 overs); ‡**Leeward Islands 88** (26.5 overs). *The Emerging Players thrashed Leewards, with 18-year-old Leonardo Julien (83) putting them on course for a big total. Their 27-year-old captain, Yannic Cariah, whose leg-breaks returned figures of 5–1–8–3, and 20-year-old off-spinner Kevin Sinclair (4-20) flattened Leewards in barely half their allotted overs.*

The Caribbean Premier League has its own section (page 863).

ZIMBABWE CRICKET IN 2020

A burden eases

LIAM BRICKHILL

Zimbabwe, perhaps the most precarious and vulnerable of the ICC Full Members, somehow found a way to survive the Covid chaos. Surprisingly, their year wasn't all doom and gloom. Their original schedule had included visits by Ireland, Afghanistan, India and the Netherlands, as well as a first tour of Australia for 16 years – a busy itinerary that would have helped salve the lingering disillusionment of their suspension by the ICC in 2019. Durham and Derbyshire had also planned pre-season visits, the first to Zimbabwe by any English county since 2004. But it was all lost to the pandemic, along with the end of the 2019-20 domestic season, leaving the Logan Cup without a winner.

Before the virus really began to bite, however, the Test team managed to squeeze in two home games against Sri Lanka, and a tour of Bangladesh. Sri Lanka had arrived in January, with Zimbabwe still reeling from their suspension. The hosts folded in the First Test – their first against anyone since

ZIMBABWE IN 2020

	Played	*Won*	*Lost*	*Drawn/No result*
Tests	3	–	2	1
One-day internationals	6	1	5	–
Twenty20 internationals	5	–	5	–

JANUARY	2 Tests (h) v Sri Lanka	(page 785)
FEBRUARY / MARCH	1 Test, 3 ODIs and 2 T20Is (a) v Bangladesh	(page 663)
APRIL		
MAY		
JUNE		
JULY		
AUGUST		
SEPTEMBER		
OCTOBER / NOVEMBER	3 ODIs and 3 T20Is (a) v Pakistan	(page 734)
DECEMBER		

For a review of Zimbabwean domestic cricket from the 2019-20 season, see page 790.

November 2018 – but rallied in the Second to secure a draw, thanks to a century by Sean Williams and a seven-for from Sikandar Raza.

The highlight of a winless tour of Bangladesh was the unearthing of Wesley Madhevere, Zimbabwe's most exciting young cricketer in a generation. Lithe, pint-sized and keen-eyed, he was just 19 when he was called up, but soon looked at home in a strong middle order, making a maiden ODI fifty in the second of three games, all at Sylhet. Later in the year, in Pakistan, where Zimbabwe had their first taste of bio-bubbles and empty stadiums, Madhevere top-scored with 70 not out from 48 balls against one of the most waspish attacks in T20 cricket. Their only victory of the year had already come in the one-day series at Rawalpindi, with fast bowler Blessing Muzarabani – back in the mix after two years as a Kolpak at Northamptonshire – taking five for 49, then striking twice more in a super over, to secure precious Super League points.

Perhaps the most important development came in the boardroom, or rather the accountant's office: Zimbabwe Cricket all but managed to clear the debt that had hobbled the sport for over a decade, reportedly spiralling to $27m. A reshuffled, trimmed-down ZC administration, a hands-on approach from the ICC, and a debt re-housing agreement with Zimbabwe's ministry of finance and Central Bank all played vital roles. Counter-intuitively, the pandemic also helped: both players and administration had their salaries slashed, so the wage bill plummeted. ZC spend more than they make on most incoming tours, so the lack of visiting teams further eased financial pressure. The clearing of these debts will remove an enormous encumbrance, and open up new options.

ZC have already changed strategy in some areas. They confirmed the scrapping of their scholarship programme, instrumental in nurturing the likes of Tatenda Taibu, Hamilton Masakadza and many others, and are instead throwing their energies towards revitalising club cricket, and establishing a new national academy. To that end, the National Premier League club competition began in October. There is also a renewed focus on the women's game, with the launch of domestic one-day and T20 tournaments. Amid the pandemic, ZC could well have shelved plans for women's cricket, but have not let this side of the game stand idle.

There are, as ever, hurdles down the road. Zimbabwe will not be part of this year's T20 World Cup in India, having lost their spot at the qualifying tournament because of their suspension, and it was unclear when any of their postponed bilateral engagements would be rescheduled. But cricket in Zimbabwe had at least survived an unprecedented year.

ZIMBABWE v SRI LANKA IN 2019-20

JOHN WARD

Test matches (2): Zimbabwe 0, Sri Lanka 1

This was a tour Zimbabwe could hardly afford, having suffered so drastic a financial cut from the ICC that they struggled to run their domestic season. But it was a tour they desperately needed – to revive public interest in the national team, keep in touch with Test cricket and, it was hoped, show the world the country still had the players to merit Full Member status.

Given the problems at Zimbabwe Cricket, and across the country, this two-match visit by Sri Lanka – who had lost none of the previous 18 Tests between the teams – was a gamble. A weakened and inexperienced home side went into the series with little confidence, without an established opening batsman and one of their two top seamers, the injury-prone Tendai Chatara. The other, Kyle Jarvis, suffered a back strain during the First Test, and missed the Second.

Despite losing, Zimbabwe were competitive on at least eight days out of ten, with the Tests played back-to-back at Harare Sports Club; in the Second, Sri Lanka even had to bat out most of the final day after conceding a big first-innings deficit. Throughout, ZC allowed spectators in for free; on most days, over 1,000 enthusiastic fans created a vibrant atmosphere.

Sri Lanka had strengthened their pace bowling by recalling Suranga Lakmal after illness, and he proved their greatest threat, finishing with ten wickets at 15. Left-arm spinner Lasith Embuldeniya was the leading wicket-taker on either side, with 13, but was often punished by Zimbabwe's batsmen. For the hosts, Sikandar Raza took 11 cheap wickets with his off-breaks – his most successful series with the ball – though among his colleagues only seamer Victor Nyauchi, playing his first Tests, claimed more than two.

Player of the Series, however, was Angelo Mathews, Sri Lanka's patient accumulator and the backbone of their batting: his double-century in the First Test preceded Zimbabwe's fatal third-innings slump. Kusal Mendis, meanwhile, batted for more than 73 overs on the final day of the Second Test to secure a draw, and a 1–0 win.

SRI LANKA TOURING PARTY

*F. D. M. Karunaratne, L. D. Chandimal, D. M. de Silva, D. P. D. N. Dickwella, L. Embuldeniya, B. O. P. Fernando, M. V. T. Fernando, C. B. R. L. S. Kumara, R. A. S. Lakmal, A. D. Mathews, B. K. G. Mendis, M. D. K. Perera, C. A. K. Rajitha, P. A. D. L. R. Sandakan, H. D. R. L. Thirimanne. *Coach:* J. M. Arthur.

> "A new chant was recorded for Rajasthan Royals' Rahul Tewatia, after his unanticipated heroics during a win over Kings XI Punjab."
> Cricket and Technology, page 211

ZIMBABWE v SRI LANKA

First Test

At Harare, January 19–23, 2020. Sri Lanka won by ten wickets. Toss: Zimbabwe. Test debuts: K. T. Kasuza, B. S. Mudzinganyama, A. Ndlovu, V. M. Nyauchi.

This match followed a pattern well known to locals. Their team made a good start, before Sri Lanka fought back steadfastly to take a lead. Then, as Zimbabwe's spirit deserted them, the tourists forced victory with ten overs to spare.

The predicted rain had not arrived, and Williams – in his first Test as captain – chose to bat at a ground where teams often preferred to bowl. But the pitch proved sound. Zimbabwe's openers were Prince Masvaure, whose previous two Tests had been back in 2016, and the debutant Kevin Kasuza, yet they exceeded all expectations, putting on a careful 96 in 50 overs. When Ervine, a little more fluent, also came good, it was the first time Zimbabwe's top three had all reached 50 in the same Test innings. From 208 for two on the second morning, a total of 358 was disappointing, although Sikandar Raza, who alone tried to dominate the bowling, and Tiripano made useful contributions. Embuldeniya showed guile, and found some spin on the second day, to take five wickets from 42 overs of toil.

After losing Fernando on the second evening to Tiripano's first delivery, a sharp nip-backer, Sri Lanka employed similar wearing-down tactics. Mendis made 80, and struck Kasuza on the helmet at short leg; Brian Mudzinganyama, who had played just three first-class matches, later became the first to make his Test debut as a concussion replacement. De Silva and Dickwella each contributed 63, but the reply – which lasted deep into the fourth day – was held together by a monumental effort from Mathews, who never wavered once he had overcome an uncertain start. Occasionally he played a big shot, though he always chose the right ball. Mainly, he knuckled down, reaching his maiden Test double-century – and Sri Lanka's first in five years – with a sweep for four off Raza, from his 468th ball. It had taken him ten hours and, when Rajitha fell two balls later, Karunaratne declared with a lead of 157.

TEST OPENER PARTNERED BY TWO DEBUTANTS

	1st inns	*2nd inns*			
R. G. Barlow	Hon. Ivo Bligh	E. F. S. Tylecote	E v A	Melbourne	1882-83
S. P. Jones	S. Morris	W. Bruce	A v E	Melbourne	1884-85
Naoomal Jeoomal	Dilawar Hussain	Mushtaq Ali	I v E	Calcutta	1933-34
J. D. B. Robertson	W. Place	D. Brookes	E v WI	Bridgetown	1947-48
P. S. Masvaure	**K. T. Kasuza**	**B. S. Mudzinganyama**	**Z v SL**	**Harare**	**2019-20**

Mudzinganyama was the first to make his Test debut as a concussion replacement.

Despite conceding over 500, Zimbabwe's seamers had bowled more impressively than Sri Lanka's. The debutant Victor Nyauchi was the pick, while Jarvis maintained a tight line without any luck, and suffered a back problem that kept him out of the next Test. In 17 overs on the fourth evening, Masvaure and Mudzinganyama survived until stumps, and gave Zimbabwe hope of a draw.

Most of the action, however, came on the final day. Lakmal struck in each of his first three overs and, although Taylor and Williams fought back, they unaccountably threw away their wickets immediately after lunch. Chakabva and Tiripano survived nearly an hour, but Kumara destroyed the tail with the second new ball, leaving Sri Lanka 13 overs to score the 14 they needed.

Player of the Match: A. D. Mathews.

Close of play: first day, Zimbabwe 189-2 (Ervine 55, Taylor 13); second day, Sri Lanka 42-1 (Karunaratne 12, Mendis 6); third day, Sri Lanka 295-4 (Mathews 92, de Silva 42); fourth day, Zimbabwe 30-0 (Masvaure 15, Mudzinganyama 14).

Zimbabwe

First innings		Second innings	
P. S. Masvaure c Karunaratne b Embuldeniya	55	– c Dickwella b Lakmal	17
K. T. Kasuza lbw b Kumara	63		
C. R. Ervine b Lakmal	85	– c Karunaratne b Lakmal	7
B. R. M. Taylor lbw b Lakmal	21	– c Mendis b Lakmal	38
*S. C. Williams c Dickwella b Embuldeniya	18	– c Dickwella b Rajitha	39
Sikandar Raza st Dickwella b Embuldeniya	41	– st Dickwella b Embuldeniya	17
†R. W. Chakabva c Mathews b Embuldeniya	8	– b Embuldeniya	26
D. T. Tiripano not out	44	– lbw b Kumara	6
K. M. Jarvis b Embuldeniya	1	– b Kumara	1
A. Ndlovu c Mendis b Kumara	5	– b Kumara	0
V. M. Nyauchi c sub (P. A. D. L. R. Sandakan) b Lakmal	11	– not out	0
B. S. Mudzinganyama (did not bat)		– (2) lbw b Lakmal	16
Lb 4, nb 2	6	B 2, nb 1	3
1/96 (1) 2/164 (2) 3/208 (4) 4/247 (5) 5/247 (3) 6/266 (7) 7/307 (6) 8/309 (9) 9/328 (10) 10/358 (11) (148 overs)	358	1/33 (1) 2/36 (2) 3/41 (3) 4/120 (4) 5/120 (5) 6/148 (6) 7/159 (8) 8/163 (9) 9/165 (10) 10/170 (7) (92 overs)	170

Mudzinganyama was a concussion replacement for Kasuza.

Lakmal 27–10–53–3; Rajitha 29–9–55–0; Embuldeniya 42–12–114–5; Kumara 29–8–82–2; de Silva 21–8–50–0. *Second innings*—Lakmal 20–8–27–4; Rajitha 14–6–23–1; de Silva 11–6–12–0; Kumara 21–8–32–3; Embuldeniya 26–8–74–2.

Sri Lanka

First innings		Second innings	
*F. D. M. Karunaratne c Ndlovu b Nyauchi	37	– (2) not out	10
B. O. P. Fernando b Tiripano	21	– (1) not out	4
B. K. G. Mendis c Taylor b Nyauchi	80		
A. D. Mathews not out	200		
L. D. Chandimal c and b Williams	12		
D. M. de Silva c Masvaure b Nyauchi	63		
†D. P. D. N. Dickwella lbw b Sikandar Raza	63		
R. A. S. Lakmal st Chakabva b Sikandar Raza	27		
L. Embuldeniya b Sikandar Raza	0		
C. A. K. Rajitha lbw b Williams	1		
B 2, lb 5, nb 4	11		
1/32 (2) 2/92 (1) 3/184 (3) 4/227 (5) 5/325 (6) 6/461 (7) 7/510 (8) 8/510 (9) 9/515 (10) (9 wkts dec, 176.2 overs)	515	(no wkt, 3 overs)	14

C. B. R. L. S. Kumara did not bat.

Jarvis 37–12–84–0; Nyauchi 32–7–69–3; Tiripano 31–3–82–1; Ndlovu 28–3–107–0; Williams 32.2–3–104–2; Sikandar Raza 16–0–62–3. *Second innings*—Tiripano 2–0–8–0; Nyauchi 1–0–6–0.

Umpires: M. Erasmus and N. N. Menon. Third umpire: L. Rusere.
Referee: J. Srinath.

"He thinks in a different currency: not singles and twos, but fours and sixes."
The Leading Twenty20 Cricketer in 2020, page 824

ZIMBABWE v SRI LANKA

Second Test

At Harare, January 27–31, 2020. Drawn. Toss: Zimbabwe. Test debut: C. T. Mutombodzi.

Zimbabwe improved so much that they were ahead almost from start to finish. But they were denied a win by a mixture of determined Sri Lankan batting, another benign pitch, and their own lack of knowhow. With this game starting only four days after the First Test, and on the same ground, there were fears the surface might be underprepared. Those fears proved baseless – ultimately, to Zimbabwe's disadvantage.

They had made a dogged start after batting first once more, with only six runs coming in the first ten overs. Kasuza held firm for 38, made in two and a quarter hours, though on the third morning he would set an unfortunate record, becoming the first to require a concussion replacement in successive Tests. As in the First, he was struck on the helmet at short leg by a pull from Mendis. The ricochet was caught at short fine leg, but for Kasuza – who was stretchered off – that was little consolation.

Before then, Taylor had finally got Zimbabwe's first innings going with a dynamic run-a-ball 62, exemplifying the plan to target Embuldeniya, who went for more than four an over. Williams and Sikandar Raza built on his good work, with Williams reaching his second Test century – the first had come in July 2016 – in fine style. Lower-order contributions lifted Zimbabwe to 406, their highest total since September 2011, when they made 412 against Pakistan at Bulawayo (before that, they had last reached 400 in February 2004). Lakmal was always a menace, despite taking only two wickets.

Sri Lanka responded well at first. Each opener made 44, and Mathews threatened to dig in again. But, from 226 for four shortly before lunch on the third day, they disintegrated against the unheralded off-spin of Raza. Having opened the bowling and taken three of the first four wickets, he now added three more in five overs. And when Mathews was

A SIX OFF THE FIRST BALL OF THE DAY IN A TEST

Batsman	*Bowler*		
K. R. Miller	D. V. P. Wright	Australia v England at Adelaide (*4th day*)......	1946-47
C. H. Gayle	Sohag Gazi	West Indies v Bangladesh at Mirpur (*1st day*)...	2012-13
S. C. Williams	**R. A. S. Lakmal**	**Zimbabwe v Sri Lanka at Harare (*5th day*)...**	**2019-20**

Ball-by-ball data is not available for many early Tests.

strangled down leg for a four-hour 64, handing seamer Carl Mumba his first Test wicket since November 2016 (also against Sri Lanka at Harare), they had lost four for 18. Vishwa Fernando helped them to 293, leaving Raza with seven for 113; only leg-spinner Paul Strang, with eight for 109 against New Zealand at Bulawayo in September 2000, had returned better figures for Zimbabwe. Raza owed much to the accuracy of Tiripano, who bowled 24 overs for 30 (and finished with old-fashioned match figures of 40–22–45–1).

Zimbabwe again batted with discipline in their second innings, determined not to throw away their 113-run advantage, with Taylor again to the fore, hitting 67 off 75 balls. (Kasuza's concussion replacement, Timycen Maruma, was stumped off Embuldeniya for a 14-ball duck.) But bad light and rain on the fourth afternoon frustrated their plans of putting Sri Lanka in before the close, when they led by 354. Next morning, Williams batted on for two reasons: to use the heavy roller and, of secondary importance, to reach his fifty. It took one ball: after swinging a rare leg-stump half-volley from Lakmal over long leg for six, he walked off.

Sri Lanka needed 361 off 96 overs, though they were content to play for a draw. The Zimbabwe bowlers did their best, but on a flat pitch lacked the firepower against a team refusing to take risks. Mendis, in particular, batted in unhurried but masterly style, bringing up his seventh Test century with a straight six off Raza. Mathews and Chandimal, meanwhile, battened down the hatches, making 26 between them from 144 balls. With 45 minutes left, Zimbabwe accepted the draw.

Player of the Match: Sikandar Raza. *Player of the Series:* A. D. Mathews.

Close of play: first day, Zimbabwe 352-6 (Chakabva 31, Mutombodzi 10); second day, Sri Lanka 122-2 (Mendis 19, Mathews 4); third day, Zimbabwe 62-1 (Masvaure 26, Chakabva 14); fourth day, Zimbabwe 241-7 (Williams 47, Tiripano 1).

Zimbabwe

P. S. Masvaure c Dickwella b Kumara	9	– run out (de Silva/Embuldeniya)	35
K. T. Kasuza b Lakmal	38		
C. R. Ervine c B. O. P. Fernando b de Silva	12	– (2) c Dickwella b M. V. T. Fernando	13
B. R. M. Taylor lbw b Lakmal	62	– lbw b Kumara	67
*S. C. Williams b de Silva	107	– (7) not out	53
Sikandar Raza c Mathews b Embuldeniya	72	– lbw b M. V. T. Fernando	34
†R. W. Chakabva c Dickwella b Embuldeniya	31	– (3) c de Silva b Embuldeniya	15
C. T. Mutombodzi lbw b de Silva	33	– b Lakmal	8
D. T. Tiripano c Lakmal b Embuldeniya	13	– not out	1
C. T. Mumba not out	11		
V. M. Nyauchi c de Silva b Embuldeniya	6		
T. Maruma (did not bat)		– (5) st Dickwella b Embuldeniya	0
B 8, lb 3, nb 1	12	B 4, lb 15, w 1, nb 1	21
1/21 (1) 2/49 (3) 3/114 (2) (115.3 overs)	406	1/32 (2) (7 wkts dec, 75 overs)	247
4/133 (4) 5/292 (6) 6/324 (5)		2/64 (3) 3/111 (1)	
7/362 (7) 8/386 (8) 9/394 (9) 10/406 (11)		4/124 (5) 5/151 (4) 6/221 (6) 7/240 (8)	

Maruma was a concussion replacement for Kasuza.

Lakmal 22–9–37–2; M. V. T. Fernando 14–1–45–0; Kumara 20–5–60–1; Embuldeniya 42.3–8–182–4; de Silva 17–1–71–3. *Second innings*—Lakmal 18–5–34–1; de Silva 7–2–32–0; M. V. T. Fernando 20–5–43–2; Kumara 10–2–38–1; Embuldeniya 20–0–81–2.

Sri Lanka

*F. D. M. Karunaratne lbw b Sikandar Raza	44	– (2) c Chakabva b Mumba	12
B. O. P. Fernando c Chakabva b Tiripano	44	– (1) lbw b Sikandar Raza	47
B. K. G. Mendis c Mumba b Sikandar Raza	22	– not out	116
A. D. Mathews c Chakabva b Mumba	64	– c Ervine b Nyauchi	13
L. D. Chandimal c and b Sikandar Raza	6	– not out	13
D. M. de Silva b Sikandar Raza	42		
†D. P. D. N. Dickwella lbw b Sikandar Raza	1		
R. A. S. Lakmal c Mutombodzi b Sikandar Raza	5		
L. Embuldeniya c sub (B. S. Mudzinganyama) b Sikandar Raza	5		
M. V. T. Fernando c Chakabva b Nyauchi	38		
C. B. R. L. S. Kumara not out	3		
B 9, lb 10	19	B 1, lb 1, nb 1	3
1/94 (1) 2/104 (2) 3/134 (3) (119.5 overs)	293	1/26 (2) (3 wkts, 87 overs)	204
4/142 (5) 5/226 (6) 6/228 (7)		2/107 (1) 3/140 (4)	
7/242 (8) 8/244 (4) 9/268 (9) 10/293 (10)			

Mumba 18–4–43–1; Sikandar Raza 43–8–113–7; Tiripano 24–12–30–1; Nyauchi 22.5–7–40–1; Mutombodzi 12–1–48–0. *Second innings*—Sikandar Raza 32–10–63–1; Tiripano 16–10–15–0; Mumba 4–1–13–1; Williams 16–0–49–0; Nyauchi 12–3–43–1; Mutombodzi 7–2–19–0.

Umpires: Aleem Dar and N. N. Menon. Third umpire: L. Rusere.
Referee: J. Srinath.

DOMESTIC CRICKET IN ZIMBABWE IN 2019-20

JOHN WARD

Zimbabwe's domestic season was its most dysfunctional yet. Following the ICC decision to reduce the country's annual grant from $9m to $5m after a brief suspension in 2019, Zimbabwe Cricket halved all employees' salaries, but even this did not leave enough to run the domestic game efficiently, or pay staff on time, though ZC's budgeting was sometimes questionable. A Sri Lankan tour including two Tests, considered vital for Zimbabwe's international progress, took a large chunk of the money.

On the original schedule, the first-class Logan Cup would have taken place from December to February, with the Pro50 in March, and the T20 to follow. But ZC paused the programme twice as they ran out of money, redrawing the fixture list after the next ICC instalment arrived. The final version pushed the season into April – but the coronavirus pandemic brought it to a halt in early March. Only 14 out of 20 Logan Cup games had been completed, and 12 out of 20 Pro50 matches, while the T20 competition had not started. No winners were declared.

For the first time since the 1990s, a couple of English counties had arranged pre-season tours. Derbyshire and Durham arrived, but flew back home, having played a single one-day game between them.

The Logan Cup had introduced a new team, **Rangers**, mostly consisting of young players from the Alistair Campbell High Performance Programme, based at Old Georgians in Harare, and coached by former international all-rounder Gary Brent. The budget cuts rendered this an unaffordable luxury, but the commitment had already been made, and it provided great experience on a steep learning curve. Rangers were boosted by internationals Brendan Taylor and Kyle Jarvis when available, and almost caused an upset in their first match, when the overconfident Eagles scraped home by one wicket. Opening batsman Brian Mudzinganyama scored 320 runs at 53, and jumped from being an unknown to selection in the Test squad against Sri Lanka; he appeared in the First Test as a concussion substitute.

The two strongest Logan Cup teams were the holders, **Mountaineers** (based in Mutare), and **Eagles** (from Harare); either could have won the tournament had it been completed. They met twice: Eagles won the first encounter by six wickets, but Mountaineers responded with an innings victory. Both won all their matches against the other three teams.

On paper, Mountaineers remained the strongest and most experienced all-round side. Opener Kevin Kasuza had a fine season, scoring 314 at 52. He played himself into the Test team, and created history as the first player to require concussion substitutes in his first two Tests. All-rounder William Mashinge made excellent progress (244 runs and 22 wickets in five matches), as did fellow seamer Victor Nyauchi.

The other two teams had their moments, but struggled to field 11 players of first-class standard. Worst hit were **Rhinos**, who lost many of the previous season's team through premature retirements, emigration or transfers. Tendai Chisoro scored 253 runs, including a maiden century, and took 28 wickets, but was omitted by Zimbabwe after falling out with the board.

Tuskers were left to rue their failure to record a surprise win in their second match against Eagles, who were 80 for seven on the final morning, chasing 175. But half an hour of appalling slip fielding saw several catches go down, and Eagles got home by two wickets. Tuskers did have a good run in the Pro50 competition, winning the four matches they played, thanks to the all-round form of Sean Williams.

Overall, standards were disappointing. The general situation in the country and in the board persuaded many capable players that they would be better off in club cricket abroad or outside the game altogether; many who stayed struggled for motivation. The future of the sport in Zimbabwe remains in serious danger, and the ICC's mishandling of the situation must bear a large portion of the blame.

FIRST-CLASS AVERAGES IN 2019-20

BATTING (200 runs)

		M	*I*	*NO*	*R*	*HS*	*100*	*Avge*	*Ct/St*
1	A. D. Mathews (*Sri Lanka*)	2	3	1	277	200*	1	138.50	2
2	B. K. G. Mendis (*Sri Lanka*)	2	3	1	218	116*	1	109.00	2
3	B. R. M. Taylor (*Rangers/Zimbabwe*)	3	6	0	356	143	1	59.33	1
4	†S. C. Williams (*Tuskers/Zimbabwe*)	3	6	1	264	107	1	52.80	1
5	K. T. Kasuza (*Mountaineers/Zimbabwe*)	6	8	0	415	86	0	51.87	2
6	Sikandar Raza (*Tuskers/Zimbabwe*)	3	6	0	302	72	0	50.33	2
7	L. M. Jongwe (*Tuskers*)	5	9	2	343	92	0	49.00	1
8	†B. S. Mudzinganyama (*Rangers/Zim*)	5	8	1	336	128	1	48.00	2
9	N. Madziva (*Rhinos*)	5	9	1	361	117	1	45.12	1
10	R. Nyathi (*Rhinos*)	4	7	0	307	160	2	43.85	2
11	†P. S. Masvaure (*Rhinos/Zimbabwe*)	5	10	1	374	89	0	41.55	5
12	T. S. Kamunhukamwe (*Eagles*)	4	7	0	278	82	0	39.71	2
13	†W. P. Masakadza (*Mountaineers*)	5	8	2	225	70	0	37.50	6
14	R. W. Chakabva (*Eagles/Zimbabwe*)	5	9	0	293	115	1	32.55	16/1
15	W. T. Mashinge (*Mountaineers*)	5	8	0	244	64	0	30.50	5
16	†T. S. Chisoro (*Rhinos*)	5	9	0	253	112	1	28.11	4
17	†J. M. R. Campbell (*Rangers*)	6	12	1	308	73*	0	28.00	2
18	K. O. Maunze (*Eagles*)	5	9	1	212	72	0	26.50	7
19	R. Kaia (*Mountaineers*)	5	9	0	238	82	0	26.44	0
20	J. Gumbie (*Mountaineers*)	5	9	0	237	137	1	26.33	16/1
21	†N. Mpofu (*Tuskers*)	6	12	0	240	79	0	20.00	4

BOWLING (10 wickets)

		Style	*O*	*M*	*R*	*W*	*BB*	*5I*	*Avge*
1	T. N. Garwe (*Eagles*)	RFM	50	16	120	13	4-17	0	9.23
2	C. B. Mpofu (*Tuskers*)	RFM	76.1	28	154	15	6-38	2	10.26
3	T. Chingwara (*Rhinos*)	RFM	98	29	253	18	4-9	0	14.05
4	R. A. S. Lakmal (*Sri Lanka*)	RFM	87	32	151	10	4-27	0	15.10
5	C. K. Tshuma (*Rangers*)	RFM	87.1	26	210	13	4-28	0	16.15
6	W. T. Mashinge (*Mountaineers*)	RFM	107.5	24	378	22	4-92	0	17.18
7	T. S. Chisoro (*Rhinos*)	LFM	154.2	26	482	28	7-31	1	17.21
8	R. Kaia (*Mountaineers*)	RM	93.5	21	273	15	5-44	2	18.20
9	D. T. Tiripano (*Mountaineers/Zim*)	RFM	139.2	39	329	18	5-15	1	18.27
10	T. Mufudza (*Eagles*)	OB	198.5	35	590	30	5-75	1	19.66
11	E. Masuku (*Tuskers*)	RM	104.1	21	374	19	5-23	1	19.68
12	C. T. Mutombodzi (*Eagles/Zimbabwe*)	LB	85.2	10	316	15	5-63	1	21.06
13	V. M. Nyauchi (*Mountaineers/Zim*)	RFM	172.1	40	456	21	4-32	0	21.71
14	K. M. Jarvis (*Rangers/Zimbabwe*)	RFM	85	22	218	10	6-76	1	21.80
15	Sikandar Raza (*Tuskers/Zimbabwe*)	OB	114.3	20	328	15	7-113	1	21.86
16	C. Chitumba (*Rangers*)	RFM	106	23	325	14	4-58	0	23.21
17	R. Ngarava (*Eagles*)	LFM	99	23	241	10	3-42	0	24.10
18	B. A. Mavuta (*Rhinos*)	LB	120.5	9	490	20	5-124	1	24.50
19	J. C. Nyumbu (*Tuskers*)	OB	112.2	30	277	11	3-23	0	25.18
20	S. S. F. Musekwa (*Tuskers*)	RM	87.2	20	278	11	3-31	0	25.27
21	S. D. Chimhamhiwa (*Tuskers*)	RFM	97	16	282	11	3-50	0	25.63
22	C. T. Mumba (*Rhinos/Zimbabwe*)	RFM	95	14	313	12	5-51	1	26.08
23	M. Faraz Akram (*Eagles*)	RM	91.2	22	269	10	2-28	0	26.90
24	K. Macheka (*Rangers*)	RFM	108.4	20	358	13	3-63	0	27.53
25	L. Embuldeniya (*Sri Lanka*)	SLA	130.3	28	451	13	5-114	1	34.69

LOGAN CUP IN 2019-20

	P	W	L	D	1st-inns pts	Pts
Eagles	6	5	1	0	3	28
Mountaineers	5	4	1	0	3	23
Tuskers	6	2	3	1	4	16
Rhinos	5	2	3	0	2	12
Rangers	6	0	5	1	2	4

Win = 5pts; draw = 2pts; lead on first innings = 1pt.

Each team should have played eight matches, but six remained unplayed when the Covid-19 pandemic ended the tournament. No winner was declared.

LOGAN CUP WINNERS

1993-94	Mashonaland U24
1994-95	Mashonaland
1995-96	Mashonaland
1996-97	Mashonaland
1997-98	Mashonaland
1998-99	Mashonaland
1999-2000	Mashonaland
2000-01	Mashonaland
2001-02	Mashonaland
2002-03	Mashonaland
2003-04	Mashonaland
2004-05	Mashonaland
2005-06	*No competition*
2006-07	Easterns
2007-08	Northerns
2008-09	Easterns
2009-10	Mashonaland Eagles
2010-11	Matabeleland Tuskers
2011-12	Matabeleland Tuskers
2012-13	Matabeleland Tuskers
2013-14	Mountaineers
2014-15	Matabeleland Tuskers
2015-16	Mashonaland Eagles
2016-17	Manicaland Mountaineers
2017-18	Manicaland Mountaineers
2018-19	Mountaineers
2019-20	*No winner*

Mashonaland/Northerns/Mashonaland Eagles have won the title 12 times, Easterns/Mountaineers and Matabeleland/Matabeleland Tuskers 6, Mashonaland Under-24 1.

PRO50 CHAMPIONSHIP IN 2019-20

50-over league

	P	W	L	A	Bonus	Pts	NRR
Tuskers	5	4	0	1	2	11	1.89
Mountaineers	5	3	1	1	2	9	1.06
Eagles	5	2	2	1	2	7	–0.22
Rhinos	4	1	3	0	0	2	–0.52
Rangers	5	0	4	1	0	1	–2.34

Each team should have played eight matches, but eight remained unplayed when the Covid-19 pandemic ended the tournament. No winner was declared.

The Domestic Twenty20 Championship was not played.

A-TEAM TOURS IN 2020

INDIA A IN NEW ZEALAND IN 2019-20

A-Team one-day internationals (3): New Zealand A 2, India A 1
A-Team Test matches (2): New Zealand A 0, India A 0

India A shadowed their senior team in New Zealand at the start of 2020. The two parties were, up to a point, interchangeable: Ravichandran Ashwin, Cheteshwar Pujara and Ajinkya Rahane played in the second four-day game as preparation for the full Test series against New Zealand, which started on February 21. New Zealand A took the one-day series with a close victory in the final match, but the two unofficial Tests were high-scoring draws: Shubman Gill's three innings brought him 83, 204 not out and 136, which took his first-class average to 73. Dane Cleaver, the Central Districts wicketkeeper, just missed a double-century in the first game.

Touring party *G. H. Vihari (FC), Aavesh Khan (FC), M. A. Agarwal (FC/50), K. K. Ahmed (50), R. Ashwin (FC), R. D. Chahar (FC/50), A. R. Easwaran (FC), R. S. Gaikwad (50), S. Gill (FC/50), I. P. Kishan (FC/50), S. Nadeem (FC), P. K. Panchal (FC), K. H. Pandya (50), A. R. Patel (50), I. C. Porel (FC/50), C. A. Pujara (FC), A. M. Rahane (FC), W. P. Saha (FC), S. V. Samson (50), S. Sandeep Warrier (FC/50), V. Shankar (FC), P. P. Shaw (FC/50), M. Siraj (FC/50), K. Srikar Bharat (FC), S. A. Yadav (50). *Coach:* S. H. Kotak.

Gill and Agarwal captained in the one-day games.

At Lincoln (Bert Sutcliffe Oval), January 17, 2020. **India A won by 92 runs. India A 279-8** (50 overs) (S. Gill 50, R. D. Gaikwad 93, S. A. Yadav 50; Z. N. Gibson 4-51); ‡**New Zealand XI 187** (41.1 overs) (J. J. N. P. Bhula 50; K. K. Ahmed 4-43). *Ruturaj Gaikwad led a solid batting performance by India A, sharing successive stands of 89 with Shubman Gill and Surya Yadav. The home team made a bright start, reaching 82-0 after 17 overs, but then lost regular wickets; left-arm seamer Khaleel Ahmed took the last four in 12 balls.*

At Lincoln (Bert Sutcliffe Oval), January 19, 2020. **India A won by 12 runs.** ‡**India A 372** (49.2 overs) (P. P. Shaw 150, V. Shankar 58; D. J. Mitchell 3-37); **New Zealand XI 360-6** (50 overs) (J. C. T. Boyle 130, F. H. Allen 87). *Prithvi Shaw pounded 150 from 100 balls, with 22 fours and two sixes, as India A raised a total the New Zealanders could not quite match, despite opener Jack Boyle's run-a-ball 130; his stand of 144 in 21 overs with Finn Allen gave them hope from 27-2.*

First one-day international At Lincoln (Bert Sutcliffe Oval), January 22, 2020. **India A won by five wickets. New Zealand A 230** (48.3 overs) (M. Siraj 3-33); ‡**India A 231-5** (29.3 overs). *A confident all-round display saw India A sail to victory with more than 20 overs to spare. First their bowlers restricted New Zealand A to 230, then – in a match without an individual half-century – their batsmen hit out: Sanju Samson's 39 came from 21 balls, and Yadav's 35 from 19.*

Second one-day international At Christchurch (Hagley Oval), January 24, 2020. **New Zealand A won by 29 runs. New Zealand A 295-7** (50 overs) (G. H. Worker 135, C. E. McConchie 56; I. C. Porel 3-50); ‡**India A 266-9** (50 overs) (K. H. Pandya 51). *New Zealand A looked in trouble at 109-5 in the 25th over, but opener George Worker, who lofted six off-side sixes in his 135, put on 149 with Cole McConchie to set an imposing target. Shaw fell to the second legal delivery of the reply, and India A were soon 88-4; the middle order's rescue work was not quite enough.*

Third one-day international At Christchurch (Hagley Oval), January 26, 2020. **New Zealand A won by five runs. New Zealand A 270-7** (50 overs) (M. S. Chapman 110*, T. D. Astle 56; I. C. Porel 3-64); ‡**India A 265** (49.4 overs) (P. P. Shaw 55, I. P. Kishan 71*; K. A. Jamieson 4-49, A. Y. Patel 3-44). *New Zealand A took the series, after its closest match. From 105-6, they recovered to 270, thanks to a stand of 136 in 21 overs between Mark Chapman, whose 110* came from 98 balls, and Todd Astle. India A made a good start, and were 126-1 in the 23rd, before three quick wickets set them back. Ishan Kishan and Axar Patel (32) took them close by putting on 79 and, when Patel was finally out to his near-namesake (and fellow slow left-armer) Ajaz, the requirement was 14 from ten balls. But Ajaz struck again with his final delivery, and Kyle Jamieson wrapped things up with the third and fourth balls of the last over.*

First Test At Christchurch (Hagley Oval), January 30–February 2, 2020. **Drawn. India A 216** (54.1 overs) (S. Gill 83, G. H. Vihari 51; M. D. Rae 4-54, C. E. McConchie 3-33) **and 448-3** (101.1 overs) (P. K. Panchal 115, S. Gill 204*, G. H. Vihari 100*); **‡New Zealand A 562-7 dec** (160.3 overs) (W. A. Young 54, M. S. Chapman 114, D. Cleaver 196, C. E. McConchie 50*). *Gill and Hanuma Vihari put on 119 for the fourth wicket, but none of the other Indian batsmen reached 20, with Otago seamer Michael Rae collecting four wickets. By the end of the first day, at 105-2, New Zealand A were nearly halfway to a lead, and stretched their eventual advantage to 336, after a sixth-wicket stand of 268 between Chapman and Dane Cleaver, who just missed a maiden first-class double-century (he made sure three weeks later with 201 for Central Districts v Northern Districts at Napier). India A had four sessions to survive, but did rather more than that: Priyank Panchal hit six sixes and put on 167 with Gill, who then added 222* with Vihari.*

Second Test At Lincoln (Bert Sutcliffe Oval), February 7–10, 2020. **Drawn. ‡New Zealand A 386-9 dec** (131.5 overs) (G. D. Phillips 65, D. Cleaver 53, D. J. Mitchell 103*); **India A 467-5** (109.3 overs) (G. H. Vihari 59, S. Gill 136, C. A. Pujara 53, A. M. Rahane 101*, V. Shankar 66). *The loss of the second day condemned this to a draw. Daryl Mitchell batted six hours to guide New Zealand A to 386 before a declaration soon after lunch on the third day, then India A batted out time, thanks to another hundred from Gill and one from Ajinkya Rahane.*

IRELAND WOLVES IN SOUTH AFRICA IN 2019-20

Captained by 20-year-old Harry Tector, and including his brothers Jack, 23, and (briefly) 16-year-old Tim, Ireland's A-Team played five T20 and two 50-over games against Namibia in South Africa early in 2020. They rounded off their tour against Titans, the Centurion-based South African province. The Wolves won the T20s 4–1, but Namibia won both 50-overs matches. A notable addition to the tourists' ranks was Curtis Campher, a 20-year-old all-rounder with an Irish grandmother; he had toured England in 2018 with South Africa Under-19, and had never played a senior game in Ireland. Gary Wilson travelled with the team, but fell ill in South Africa and did not play.

Touring party *H. T. Tector (50/20), J. Cameron-Dow (50), C. Campher (50/20), G. J. Delany (50/20), G. H. Dockrell (50), S. T. Doheny (50/20), M. Frost (50), J. J. Garth (20), S. C. Getkate (50/20), T. E. Kane (50/20), J. B. Little (50/20), J. A. McCollum (50), N. J. McGuire (20), J. I. Mulder (20), N. A. Rock (50/20), J. B. Tector (50), T. H. Tector (20), S. R. Thompson (20), L. J. Tucker (20), G. C. Wilson (50), C. A. Young (50/20). *Coach:* P. Johnston.

T. H. Tector, who was playing club cricket in South Africa, appeared in the fifth T20 match.

At Centurion, February 18, 2020. **Namibia won by three wickets. Ireland Wolves 177-6** (20 overs) (H. T. Tector 73*); **‡Namibia 178-7** (19.4 overs) (M. G. Erasmus 63, J. N. Loftie-Eaton 40). *Harry Tector rescued his side from 106-6 with 73* from 38 balls, including five sixes. Namibia were 17-3 after 13 balls, but their captain Gerhard Erasmus steadied the ship, putting on 80 in six overs with 19-year-old Nicol Loftie-Eaton.*

At Centurion, February 18, 2020. **Ireland Wolves won by 23 runs. ‡Ireland Wolves 170-7** (20 overs) (S. T. Doheny 67*, G. J. Delany 65); **Namibia 147-9** (20 overs) (M. G. Erasmus 43). *Ireland Wolves squared the series, thanks to Stephen Doheny, who batted through their innings, and put on 95 for the third wicket with Gareth Delany in less than nine overs. Namibia were on course at 82-3 in the 11th but, with left-arm seamer Josh Little conceding only 13 runs in his four overs, they ended up well short.*

At Pretoria (Irene Villagers), February 21, 2020. **Ireland Wolves won by 49 runs. Ireland Wolves 196-5** (20 overs) (S. T. Doheny 58, C. Campher 45, G. J. Delany 38; C. G. Williams 3-29); **‡Namibia 147-8** (20 overs) (C. G. Williams 59*; J. I. Mulder 3-23). *Doheny spanked 58 from 33 balls to give his side a good start, then Curtis Campher (in his first senior T20 match) and Delany piled on 75 in 40 balls. Namibia never recovered from 41-4 in the seventh.*

At Pretoria (Irene Villagers), February 23, 2020. **Ireland Wolves won by seven wickets. ‡Namibia 182-5** (20 overs) (Z. E. Green 44, N. Davin 38, C. G. Williams 63*); **Ireland Wolves 185-3** (18.1 overs) (H. T. Tector 91, G. J. Delany 58*). Craig Williams muscled Namibia to 182 with a 30-ball 63*, containing five sixes, but Ireland Wolves skated home on the back of a third-wicket stand of 120 between Tector, who also hit five sixes in his 47-ball 91, and the reliable Delany.

At Pretoria (Irene Villagers), February 23, 2020. **Ireland Wolves won by seven wickets. ‡Namibia 206-5** (20 overs) (N. Davin 73, K. J. Birkenstock 69); **Ireland Wolves 207-3** (19 overs) (S. T. Doheny 37, T. E. Kane 36, N. A. Rock 58*, C. Campher 62*). *A second-wicket partnership of 134 between Niko Davin and Karl Birkenstock helped Namibia past 200 barrier. But a rejigged Irish side (Lorcan Tucker took over as captain from the resting Harry Tector, whose 16-year-old brother, Tim, played) made it 4–1 with an over to spare. Neil Rock and Campher finished things off in a stand of 112*.*

At Centurion, February 26, 2020. **Namibia won by seven wickets. Ireland Wolves 228-8** (50 overs) (G. H. Dockrell 55, C. Campher 54); **‡Namibia 232-3** (40 overs) (S. J. Baard 56, N. Davin 63). *Ireland Wolves paid for slipping to 100-6, before George Dockrell put on 89 with Campher. Namibia had no problems with a modest target.*

At Pretoria (Irene Villagers), February 27, 2020. **Namibia won by seven wickets. Ireland Wolves 149** (39.5 overs) (H. T. Tector 72; B. M. Scholtz 3-25); **‡Namibia 150-3** (26.1 overs) (N. Davin 53, M. G. Erasmus 63*). *Another insipid batting performance by the tourists allowed Namibia to take the 50-over series 2–0; only Harry Tector passed 18.*

At Pretoria (Irene Villagers), February 29, 2020. **Ireland Wolves won by four wickets. Titans 277-7** (50 overs) (G. C. Viljoen 68); **‡Ireland Wolves 281-6** (42.2 overs) (J. B. Tector 60, S. C. Getkate 51*). *Ireland Wolves made up for some poor batting against Namibia with an improved performance against the Titans, captained by former Test player Hardus Viljoen. After Jack Tector's watchful 60, Shane Getkate cracked five sixes in his 39-ball 51*, and Delany (43) four from 18 balls.*

WEST INDIES A IN NEW ZEALAND IN 2020-21

A-Team Test matches (2): New Zealand A 2, West Indies A 0

West Indies A accompanied their senior team to New Zealand, and included players who would go on to appear in the Test side. The results echoed the seniors', too: both A-Team Tests were lost by wide margins. Bright spots for the tourists included the batting of Guyana's Romario Shepherd, who hit 133 in the first match and an unbeaten 77 in the second, and the varied spin attack of Fabian Allen, Rahkeem Cornwall and Hayden Walsh, who picked up 17 wickets between them in the two games.

Touring party *R. Powell, F. A. Allen, N. E. Bonner, R. R. S. Cornwall, J. Da Silva, B. A. King, K. R. Mayers, S. A. R. Moseley, P. A. S. McSween, K. M. A. Paul, N. Pooran, R. A. Reifer, J. N. T. Seales, R. Shepherd, O. R. Thomas, H. R. Walsh. *Coach:* A. Colley.

Powell captained in the first four-day game, and Pooran in the second.

At Mount Maunganui, December 3–6, 2020. **New Zealand A won by an innings and 143 runs. West Indies A 322** (82.1 overs) (R. A. Reifer 65, R. Shepherd 133; J. A. Duffy 4-47, N. G. Smith 3-37) **and 109** (36 overs) (S. C. Kuggeleijn 3-18); **‡New Zealand A 574** (152.5 overs) (G. D. Phillips 136, T. L. Seifert 111, D. Cleaver 85, N. G. Smith 76; F. A. Allen 3-146, H. R. Walsh 3-108). *In the first innings, West Indies A were 113-7 when Raymon Reifer was joined by Romario Shepherd. They put on 199, and Shepherd extended his maiden century to 133, with seven sixes and 14 fours. Glenn Phillips and Tim Seifert then peeled off an opening stand of 226, and contributions down the order swelled the New Zealanders' lead to 252. It proved more than enough, as the tourists could not conjure up another rescue act.*

At Nelson, December 11–14, 2020. **New Zealand A won by 101 runs. ‡New Zealand A 481-7 dec** (134.3 overs) (T. L. Seifert 60, M. G. Bracewell 135, R. Ravindra 144*; R. R. S. Cornwall 3-91) **and 174-7 dec** (27.5 overs) (R. R. S. Cornwall 3-37, H. R. Walsh 3-71); **West Indies A 298** (88.3 overs) (S. A. R. Moseley 110, R. Shepherd 77*; D. A. J. Bracewell 6-42) **and 256** (69.3 overs) (S. A. R. Moseley 54, N. Pooran 69; R. Ravindra 6-89). *Michael Bracewell, whose cousin Doug later demolished the tourists' first innings, put on 161 for the fifth wicket with Rachin Ravindra. The West Indians conceded another big lead, despite Shayne Moseley's century and another eye-catching contribution from Shepherd. Set 358, West Indies A fell victim to Ravindra's left-arm spin: he had never previously taken more than two wickets in a first-class innings, but now scooped up six.*

PAKISTAN SHAHEENS IN NEW ZEALAND IN 2020-21

A-Team Test match (1): New Zealand A 0, Pakistan A 1

Pakistan Shaheens – the A-Team's new name means falcons – travelled alongside the senior side to New Zealand, and undertook one four-day representative match and two T20s, plus some other games which involved more than 11 a side. The first scheduled match of the tour, at Napier on December 10, was cancelled after some of the tourists breached quarantine regulations. Several of those who played in the senior side's T20s and Tests also appeared for the Shaheens.

Touring party *Rohail Nazir, Abdullah Shafiq, Abid Ali, Amad Butt, Azhar Ali, Danish Aziz, Fawad Alam, Haider Ali, Haris Rauf, Hussain Talat, Iftikhar Ahmed, Imran Butt, Khushdil Shah, Mohammad Abbas, Mohammad Hasnain, Musa Khan, Naseem Shah, Shan Masood, Sohail Khan, Usman Qadir, Wahab Riaz, Yasir Shah, Zeeshan Malik. *Coach:* Ijaz Ahmed.

At Whangarei, December 17–20, 2020. **Pakistan Shaheens won by 89 runs. Pakistan Shaheens 194** (73 overs) (Azhar Ali 58; E. J. Nuttall 5-54, N. G. Smith 3-29) **and 329** (96.3 overs) (Fawad Alam 139, Rohail Nazir 100; M. J. Henry 6-53, M. D. Rae 3-85); ‡**New Zealand A 226** (82.5 overs) (R. Ravindra 70, C. D. Fletcher 57; Mohammad Abbas 4-40, Amad Butt 3-22, Yasir Shah 3-54) **and 208** (64 overs) (Naseem Shah 3-44, Amad Butt 3-38). *The decisive stand on a lively pitch at the Cobham Oval came in the Shaheens' second innings, when Fawad Alam and the 19-year-old wicketkeeper/captain Rohail Nazir put on 215. They had come together at 64-4, with their team only 32 in front. Seamers Naseem Shah and Amad Butt then shared six wickets as New Zealand A struggled in pursuit of 298.*

At Hamilton, December 27, 2020. **Northern Districts won by 21 runs. Northern Districts 203-2** (20 overs) (K. D. Clarke 40, T. L. Seifert 99*, A. P. Devcich 38*); ‡**Pakistan Shaheens 182-9** (20 overs) (Haider Ali 51, Zeeshan Malik 52; J. H. Brown 3-42). *Tim Seifert's 55-ball 99* included six sixes, as Northern Districts ran up a total that proved beyond the tourists, despite a lively opening stand of 85 between Haider Ali and Zeeshan Malik.*

At Wellington, December 29, 2020. **Wellington won by nine wickets. Pakistan Shaheens 91** (17.4 overs) (J. D. Gibson 3-30); ‡**Wellington 97-1** (9.5 overs) (D. P. Conway 48*, R. Ravindra 35*). *Pakistan Shaheens crashed to 15-4 in the sixth over, and never recovered. Wellington, the Super Smash champions, cruised home with more than half their overs unused.*

OTHER INTERNATIONAL MATCHES IN 2020

ICC WORLD CUP LEAGUE TWO, 2019–23

The ICC's restructured competition to provide a clearer route to World Cup qualification began in August 2019. The top three in the table will go straight into the Qualifier for the next World Cup, while the other four will face further play-offs against the leading sides from the World Cup Challenge League's two groups. Several of the matches planned for 2020 and early 2021 were called off because of the pandemic, although there was time for the United States – who had topped the table at the start of the year – to lose all their four games, which put them behind Oman. The USA's troubles included being shot out for 35 by Nepal, to equal the lowest total in any one-day international. The tournament was originally supposed to finish in 2022, but the ICC extended it to the end of February 2023, in an effort to squeeze in all the matches. Papua New Guinea and Scotland (who are due to host Namibia and Nepal in July) did not play any in 2020.

WORLD CUP LEAGUE TWO TABLE

	P	*W*	*L*	*A*	*Pts*	*NRR*
Oman	10	8	2	0	16	0.17
United States of America	12	6	6	0	12	–0.31
Scotland	8	4	3	1	9	0.13
Namibia	7	4	3	0	8	0.00
United Arab Emirates	7	3	3	1	7	0.00
Nepal	4	2	2	0	4	0.98
Papua New Guinea	8	0	8	0	0	–0.45

As at December 31, 2020.

At Al Amerat, January 5, 2020. **Oman won by five wickets. United Arab Emirates 170** (47.1 overs) (Mohammad Usman 68; Bilal Khan 3-38, Zeeshan Maqsood 4-15); ‡**Oman 171-5** (37.3 overs) (Jatinder Singh 62, Aaqib Ilyas 80*). *ODI debuts:* M. E. Sanuth (Oman), Zawar Farid (UAE). *A third-wicket stand of 112 between Jatinder Singh and Aaqib Ilyas ensured Oman overhauled a modest target with ease.*

At Al Amerat, January 6, 2020. **United Arab Emirates won by eight runs. United Arab Emirates 222-9** (50 overs) (D. D. P. D'Silva 31, Mohammad Usman 37, Rohan Mustafa 59*); ‡**Namibia 214-8** (50 overs) (S. J. Baard 32, M. G. Erasmus 56, J. N. Frylinck 31; K. P. Meiyappan 4-37). *ODI debut:* B. Shikongo (Namibia). *The UAE bounced back from the previous day's defeat to restrict Namibia, whose middle order was filleted by leg-spinner Palaniapan Meiyappan.*

At Al Amerat, January 8, 2020. **Namibia won by 52 runs.** ‡**Namibia 324-7** (50 overs) (Z. E. Green 62, C. G. Williams 129*, J. J. Smit 31; Bilal Khan 4-49); **Oman 272** (45 overs) (Mohammad Nadeem 41, Suraj Kumar 58, M. E. Sanuth 40, Sandeep Goud 34; J. J. Smit 5-44). *PoM:* C. G. Williams. *ODI debut:* J. I. de Villiers (Namibia). *A maiden ODI century for Craig Williams, who hit six sixes and 13 fours from 94 balls in all, set up a total Oman never threatened. Left-arm seamer J. J. Smit claimed his first ODI five-for.*

At Al Amerat, January 9, 2020. **United Arab Emirates won by eight wickets.** ‡**Namibia 94** (29 overs) (D. D. P. D'Silva 3-22, Ahmed Raza 5-26); **United Arab Emirates 95-2** (19.3 overs) (J. F. John 32*). *PoM:* Ahmed Raza. *Namibia's batsmen, so impressive the previous day, crashed back to earth: they were soon 45-5 and, with left-arm spinner Ahmed Raza (the UAE captain) making regular inroads, struggled to 94. The match was all over in less than half the scheduled playing time.*

At Al Amerat, January 11, 2020. **Oman v United Arab Emirates. Cancelled.** *This match (and the next) was called off after the death of Sultan Qaboos bin Said, who had ruled Oman for almost 50 years.*

At Al Amerat, January 12, 2020. **Oman v Namibia. Cancelled.**

At Kirtipur, February 5, 2020. **Oman won by 18 runs. Oman 197-9** (50 overs) (Mohammad Nadeem 69*, Sandeep Goud 33; K. C. Karan 4-47, S. Bhari 3-14); ‡**Nepal 179** (46.5 overs) (S. Vesawkar 55, D. S. Airee 36; Zeeshan Maqsood 3-30). *PoM:* Mohammad Nadeem. *ODI debuts:* S. Bhari, A. Bohara (Nepal); B. M. Singh (Oman). *When Oman dipped to 124-7 in the 42nd over, hosts Nepal seemed to be coasting to victory in their first official ODI on home soil – but Mohammad Nadeem oversaw the addition of 73, to set up a tricky target, despite figures of 10–1–14–3 from the debutant slow left-armer Sushan Bhari. Nepal were soon 4-2, with their most experienced batsmen – Paras Khadka and captain Gyanendra Malla – departing in five balls. Though Sharad Vesawkar mounted a rescue mission, they fell just short. Oman's captain Zeeshan Maqsood followed 20 runs with 3-30 from ten overs of left-arm spin.*

At Kirtipur, February 6, 2020. **Oman won by six wickets. United States of America 213** (50 overs) (I. G. Holland 65, A. Homraj 44; Mohammad Nadeem 3-43); ‡**Oman 214-4** (49.3 overs) (Khawar Ali 31, Aaqib Ilyas 72, Mohammad Nadeem 55*, Suraj Kumar 33*). *PoM:* Mohammad Nadeem. *Oman completed their second win in two days with another gritty effort: from 87-3, Nadeem shared stands of 64 with Ilyas and 63* with Suraj Kumar to ensure a last-over victory.*

At Kirtipur, February 8, 2020. **Nepal won by 35 runs. Nepal 190** (49.2 overs) (K. Malla 50, B. Bhandari 59; C. A. H. Stevenson 3-30); ‡**United States of America 155** (44.1 overs) (I. G. Holland 75; K. C. Karan 4-15, S. Bhari 3-43). *PoM:* K. C. Karan. *ODI debut:* K. Malla (Nepal). *Nepal were tottering at 49-5 before the left-handed debutant Kushal Malla, a month short of his 16th birthday, made 50 from 51 balls and put on 84 with Binod Bhandari. Malla was the youngest to score an ODI half-century, breaking the record of Rohit Kumar Paudel, whose place he took for this match. Paudel was 16 when he scored 55 against the UAE in Dubai in January 2019. The USA were soon 65-7, and came up short, despite Ian Holland's fighting 75.*

At Kirtipur, February 9, 2020. **Oman won by eight wickets. Nepal 249-8** (50 overs) (G. Malla 56, P. Khadka 38, B. Bhandari 35; Mohammad Nadeem 3-44, Aaqib Ilyas 4-36); ‡**Oman 250-2** (47.2 overs) (Khawar Ali 41, Aaqib Ilyas 109*, Zeeshan Maqsood 68*). *PoM:* Aaqib Ilyas. *ODI debut:* K. S. Airee (Nepal). *Oman showed their earlier victory over Nepal was no fluke, breezing to a target of 250. Ilyas scored their first ODI century, and shared a stand of 167* with Zeeshan, a national record – for two days.*

At Kirtipur, February 11, 2020. **Oman won by 92 runs. Oman 276-6** (50 overs) (Aaqib Ilyas 105, Zeeshan Maqsood 109; S. N. Netravalkar 3-37, J. Theron 3-60); ‡**United States of America 184** (39.1 overs) (A. Jones 47*, N. K. Patel 52; Bilal Khan 3-24, Aaqib Ilyas 3-14). *PoM:* Aaqib Ilyas. *Another good batting display took Oman above the USA in the table: Ilyas and Zeeshan broke their new national record with a third-wicket partnership of 216. They then shared five wickets, though the initial damage to the chase was inflicted by left-arm seamer Bilal Khan, who dismissed Monank Patel and Steven Taylor for ducks. No. 5 Aaron Jones dropped anchor for 79 balls, but he and Nisarg Patel (a maiden fifty from 32 balls, with four sixes) could only narrow the margin.*

At Kirtipur, February 12, 2020. **Nepal won by eight wickets. United States of America 35** (12 overs) (S. Lamichhane 6-16, S. Bhari 4-5); ‡**Nepal 36-2** (5.2 overs). *PoM:* S. Lamichhane. *Nepal ended the round with a stunning victory, demolishing the USA for the joint-lowest total in all ODIs, equalling Zimbabwe's 35 against Sri Lanka at Harare in April 2004. It was also the shortest completed innings, undercutting 13.5 overs by Zimbabwe (54) against Afghanistan at Harare in February 2017. The carnage came courtesy of Nepal's slow men: leg-spinner Sandeep Lamichhane finished with figures of 6–1–16–6, while Bhari's four wickets gave him 11-103 in this round of matches, his first ODIs. The only better figures by an Associate bowler in ODIs were Rashid Khan's 7-18 against West Indies in St Lucia in June 2017, shortly before Afghanistan were promoted to full membership. Lamichhane joked: "Rashid is a Test player now, so forget that – Number One!"*

Later matches, scheduled to be played in the USA in April, were called off because of Covid-19.

ASIA CUP QUALIFYING IN 2019-20

The Asian Cricket Council staged preliminary matches to decide which four teams should progress to the Asia Cup Qualifier, due to take place in Malaysia in August; the winner of that would progress to the Asia Cup proper in September. The United Arab Emirates, Kuwait, Singapore and Hong Kong made the cut – but both later competitions fell victim to Covid-19. The ACC hoped to stage the main event in June 2021, probably in Sri Lanka.

The UAE won the Western Region tournament in Oman. The hosts failed to progress from their group, which hinged on Bahrain's upset of Qatar in the last pool game. The UAE's Chirag Suri headed the run-scorers with 239, ahead of Ravija Sandaruwan de Silva of Kuwait (219) and Qatar's Kamran Khan (201). Mohomad Aslam, a slow left-armer who played first-class cricket for Saracens in his native Sri Lanka, took 12 wickets for Kuwait. Iran played their first official internationals.

In the Eastern Region tournament, held in Thailand, Singapore won all their completed matches, with Sidhant Singh making 153 runs and Hobart Hurricanes' Tim David 150, including an unbeaten 92 from 32 balls against Malaysia. Hong Kong's slow left-armer Aftab Hussain won the bowling award for combined figures of eight for 73, at an economy-rate of 4.43. China had been expected to take part, but withdrew as coronavirus spread, while Bhutan and Myanmar pulled out later, leaving only five competing nations.

Western Region

At Al Amerat, February 23, 2020. **United Arab Emirates won by ten wickets. Iran 61-8** (20 overs); ‡**United Arab Emirates 62-0** (5.3 overs) (Rohan Mustafa 41*). *PoM:* Rohan Mustafa. *T20I debuts:* Ali Mohammadipour, Arshad Mazarzei, D. K. Dahani, Emran Shahbakhsh, Hamid Hashemi, Masood Jayazeh, Nader Zahidiafzal, Naiem Bameri, Navid Balouch, Navid Abdollahpour, Yousef Shadzehisariou (Iran); V. Aravind, Basil Hameed, A. Sharafu (UAE). *Playing their first official international, Iran were soon 15-4, and struggled to 61-8; the UAE openers made short work of the target.*

At Al Amerat, February 23, 2020. **Qatar won by 106 runs.** ‡**Qatar 196-4** (20 overs) (Kamran Khan 88, Muhammad Tanveer 64, Mohammad Rizlan 31*); **Maldives 90-9** (20 overs). *T20I debut:* I. G. T. R. Kumara (Maldives). *A second-wicket stand of 109 in 57 balls between Kamran Khan (88 from 53, seven sixes) and Muhammad Tanveer (64 from 31), set up a total the Maldives never threatened: their highest score was 26, from 41-year-old Sri Lankan-born opener Nilantha Cooray.*

At Al Amerat, February 23, 2020. **Kuwait won by nine wickets. Saudi Arabia 113** (17.5 overs) (Muhammad Ansar 3-35); ‡**Kuwait 114-1** (10.4 overs) (B. R. S. de Silva 84*). *PoM:* B. R. S. de Silva. *T20I debuts:* Aphsal Ashraf, Muhammad Ansar, U. Patel, Sayed Monib (Kuwait); Abdul Wahid, Adil Butt, Imran Yousaf, Mohamed Naeem, Sarfraz Butt (Saudi Arabia). *A 38-ball 84* from Ravija Sandaruwan de Silva – another Sri Lankan-born opener – ensured Kuwait breezed past their target. He reached 50 in 25 balls, and hit five sixes and 11 fours in all.*

At Al Amerat, February 23, 2020. **Oman won by eight wickets.** ‡**Bahrain 83** (17.1 overs) (Bilal Khan 3-8, Khawar Ali 4-16); **Oman 84-2** (13.2 overs) (Khawar Ali 38*, Jatinder Singh 35). *PoM:* Khawar Ali. *T20I debuts:* M. E. Sanuth (Oman); Abdul Majid, Imran Butt, Junaid Aziz, S. Veerapathiran (Bahrain). *Oman's captain Khawar Ali followed four wickets for his leg-breaks by remaining unbeaten in a regulation chase.*

At Al Amerat, February 24, 2020. **Saudi Arabia won by nine wickets. Iran 72-9** (20 overs); ‡**Saudi Arabia 73-1** (5.3 overs) (Abdul Waheed 41*). *PoM:* Abdul Waheed. *T20I debuts:* Adel Kolasangiani, Mehran Dorri (Iran); Khawar Zafar (Saudi Arabia). *Iran again doggedly survived the full 20 overs, before Saudi Arabia lost a solitary wicket in their rapid pursuit.*

At Al Amerat, February 24, 2020. **Qatar won by 34 runs.** **‡Qatar 175-5** (20 overs) (Zaheer Ibrahim 39, Kamran Khan 54); **Oman 141** (19.1 overs) (Khawar Ali 38, Aamer Kaleem 32; Awais Malik 3-28, Mohammed Nadeem 3-34). *PoM:* Kamran Khan. *Qatar upset fancied Oman thanks to a disciplined bowling performance.*

At Al Amerat, February 24, 2020. **Bahrain won by 65 runs.** **‡Bahrain 186-9** (20 overs) (Sarfaraz Ali 50); **Maldives 121-9** (20 overs) (M. N. R. Cooray 40). *PoM:* Sarfaraz Ali. *T20I debut:* Muhammad Younis (Bahrain). *Bahrain made a bright start through Sarfaraz Ali, whose 50 came from 22 balls, with five sixes.*

At Al Amerat, February 24, 2020. **United Arab Emirates won by 47 runs.** **United Arab Emirates 186-5** (20 overs) (C. Suri 51, Rohan Mustafa 51); **‡Kuwait 139** (17.4 overs) (B. R. S. de Silva 49, M. N. M. Aslam 32; Zahoor Khan 3-18, Waheed Ahmed 3-24). *PoM:* Rohan Mustafa. *T20I debut:* Naveed Fakhr (Kuwait). *Chirag Suri and Rohan Mustafa opened with 96 in 11 overs. Kuwait lost touch once Sandaruwan de Silva fell for a 32-ball 49, which included four sixes.*

At Al Amerat, February 25, 2020. **Oman won by ten wickets.** **Maldives 129-7** (20 overs) (Mohamed Rishwan 61, Hassan Rasheed 34); **‡Oman 132-0** (14.2 overs) (Khawar Ali 72*, Jatinder Singh 48*). *PoM:* Khawar Ali. *T20I debut:* Ahmed Raid (Maldives). *The opening stand of 132* was a record for any Oman wicket in T20Is.*

At Al Amerat, February 25, 2020. **United Arab Emirates won by 12 runs.** **‡United Arab Emirates 150** (19 overs) (C. Suri 75, Rohan Mustafa 32; Abdul Wahid 4-14); **Saudi Arabia 138-7** (20 overs). *PoM:* C. Suri. *T20I debuts:* Mohammad Ayaz, A. Tandon (UAE). *Medium-pacer Abdul Wahid abruptly ended the UAE innings with four wickets in ten balls, bowling for some of the time in tandem with leg-spinner Abdul Waheed (2-11). Saudi Arabia's batsmen reached 55-1, before the home spinners applied the handbrake.*

At Al Amerat, February 25, 2020. **Bahrain won by six wickets.** **‡Qatar 106-9** (20 overs) (Kamran Khan 46; Abdul Majid 4-23); **Bahrain 109-4** (11.5 overs) (Sarfaraz Ali 43, Ammad Uddin 41*). *PoM:* Sarfaraz Ali. *T20I debut:* Mohammed Sameer (Bahrain). *Bahrain's victory put them top of the group and into the semi-finals; hosts Oman missed out, on net run-rate.*

At Al Amerat, February 25, 2020. **Kuwait won by eight wickets.** **Iran 108-8** (20 overs) (Yousef Shadzehisarjou 39; M. N. M. Aslam 4-5); **‡Kuwait 109-2** (12.5 overs) (U. Patel 59*, Bilal Tahir 34*). *PoM:* M. N. M. Aslam. *T20I debut:* Mehran Siasar (Iran). *Iran finally made it into three figures, then reduced Kuwait to 24-2 – but wicketkeeper Usman Patel and Bilal Tahir took them into the semis without further alarms.*

Group A: BAHRAIN 4pts, NRR 1.46; QATAR 4pts, NRR 1.39; Oman 4pts, NRR 1.04; Maldives 0pts, NRR –3.79. Group B: UNITED ARAB EMIRATES 6pts, KUWAIT 4pts, Saudi Arabia 2pts, Iran 0pts.

Semi-final At Al Amerat, February 26, 2020. **Kuwait won by 87 runs.** **Kuwait 210-4** (20 overs) (B. R. S. de Silva 67, U. Patel 58, Mohammad Amin 32, Aphsal Ashraf 45*); **‡Bahrain 123** (17 overs) (Fiaz Ahmed 30; Muhammad Ansar 3-27, M. N. M. Aslam 4-23). *PoM:* B. R. S. de Silva. *Kuwait's opening stand of 129, between de Silva and Patel, outscored Bahrain's entire XI.*

Semi-final At Al Amerat, February 26, 2020. **United Arab Emirates won by 28 runs.** **‡United Arab Emirates 122** (18.4 overs) (C. Suri 38; Mohammed Nadeem 3-27, Iqbal Hussain 4-16); **Qatar 94** (20 overs) (Junaid Siddique 4-12, Zahoor Khan 3-17). *PoM:* Junaid Siddique. *An upset looked on the cards as the UAE struggled to 122, with medium-pacer Iqbal Hussain taking four wickets. But Qatar were soon 18-4, and Junaid Siddique booked the hosts' place in the final with 4-12.*

Final At Al Amerat, February 27, 2020. **United Arab Emirates won by 102 runs.** **United Arab Emirates 199-5** (20 overs) (C. Suri 60, Waheed Ahmed 45*); **‡Kuwait 97-7** (20 overs) (Sultan Ahmed 4-9). *PoM:* Sultan Ahmed. *After a nervy semi-final, the UAE had fewer problems. Suri hit 60 in 41 balls, Waheed Ahmed blasted six sixes on his way to 45* in 15, and Kuwait never looked like reaching a target of 200. Their top-scorer was No. 9 Mohomad Aslam, their captain, with 23*. His slow left-armers had claimed 4-23 in the semi, but four overs now disappeared for 57.*

Eastern Region

At Bangkok (Terdthai), February 29, 2020. **Singapore won by 43 runs. Singapore 139-7** (20 overs) (Sidhant Singh 59); ‡**Thailand 96** (19 overs) (K. Subramanian 3-27). *PoM:* Sidhant Singh. *T20I debuts:* S. Desungnoen, R. Raina, N. Senamontree, P. Suanchuai, W. Uisuk (Thailand); K. Subramanian (Singapore). *Singapore opener Sidhant Singh's 59 – the only score above 28 – made the difference. Thailand struggled against accurate bowling, with seamer Karthikeyan Subramanian claiming three wickets on debut.*

At Bangkok (Terdthai), February 29, 2020. **Malaysia won by 22 runs.** ‡**Malaysia 154-6** (20 overs) (Anwar Arudin 31, Ahmed Faiz 30, Syed Aziz 51*; S. Lamichhane 3-22); **Nepal 132** (19.5 overs) (G. Malla 38, D. S. Airee 38; S. Muniandy 4-13). *PoM:* S. Muniandy. *From 89-5 in the 14th, Malaysia rallied thanks to a stand of 63 between Syed Aziz and Aminuddin Ramly (29). Sandeep Lamichhane's three wickets included his 100th in T20 matches, but it was not enough: Nepal slumped to 132, with seamer Sharvin Muniandy taking three wickets in four balls in the final over.*

At Bangkok (Terdthai), March 1, 2020. **Hong Kong won by 43 runs. Hong Kong 154-6** (20 overs) (Nizakat Khan 48); ‡**Nepal 111** (18.1 overs) (G. Malla 46; Haroon Arshad 5-16, Aftab Hussain 3-14). *PoM:* Haroon Arshad. *A second setback for Nepal ended their qualification chances, following another poor batting display: only Gyanendra Malla reached 20. Medium-pacer Haroon Arshad finished with five wickets, three in the 17th over.*

At Bangkok (Terdthai), March 1, 2020. **Malaysia won by eight wickets.** ‡**Thailand 85-9** (20 overs) (H. J. Jordaan 37); **Malaysia 86-2** (11.5 overs) (Virandeep Singh 41*). *PoM:* Pavandeep Singh. *Pavandeep Singh (2-6), Syazrul Idrus (2-11) and Khizar Hayat (2-11) all enjoyed economical four-over spells as Thailand battled vainly to get the total ticking over. Pavandeep's brother Virandeep supervised the chase.*

At Bangkok (Terdthai), March 3, 2020. **Singapore won by 128 runs.** ‡**Singapore 239-3** (20 overs) (Sidhant Singh 77, S. Chandramohan 47, T. H. David 92*); **Malaysia 111** (15.1 overs) (A. Krishna 4-28). *PoM:* T. H. David. *Tim David blasted 92* from 32 balls, with seven sixes and nine fours, after an opening stand of 96 between Sidhant and Surendran Chandramohan. Singapore's highest T20I total (previously 191-6 against Nepal in 2019) was predictably too high a mountain for Malaysia to climb.*

At Bangkok (Terdthai), March 3, 2020. **Hong Kong won by eight wickets.** ‡**Thailand 77-8** (20 overs); **Hong Kong 78-2** (7.4 overs) (Nizakat Khan 36). *PoM:* K. D. Shah. *T20I debut:* Ismail Sardar (Thailand). *Thailand again failed to get the score moving: off-spinners Kinchit Shah and Ehsan Khan both had 2-9 in their four overs, and slow left-armer Aftab Hussain 2-11.*

At Bangkok (Terdthai), March 4, 2020. **Nepal won by nine wickets.** ‡**Thailand 66** (20 overs) (K. C. Karan 3-12); **Nepal 72-1** (5.3 overs) (K. Malla 36*). *PoM:* K. C. Karan. *T20I debut:* B. Karki (Nepal). *For the fourth match running, the Thais almost ground to a halt: Lamichhane (1-9) sent down 22 dot balls in his four overs, and the debutant slow left-armer Bhuvan Karki 1-6 in his, as Nepal finally recorded a win.*

At Bangkok (Terdthai), March 4, 2020. **Singapore won by 16 runs.** ‡**Singapore 168-5** (20 overs) (S. Chandramohan 32, T. H. David 58, Manpreet Singh 42*); **Hong Kong 152-8** (20 overs) (J. J. Atkinson 50). *PoM:* Manpreet Singh. *Singapore secured top spot with their third straight win. They owed a lot to Manpreet Singh's late 42* from 29 balls, after David's 58 from 46. The target proved beyond Hong Kong, who had looked in control at 73-2 after nine overs.*

At Bangkok (Terdthai), March 6, 2020. **Nepal v Singapore. Abandoned.**

At Bangkok (Terdthai), March 6, 2020. **Hong Kong won by six wickets.** ‡**Malaysia 132-6** (20 overs) (Virandeep Singh 33, Syed Aziz 30); **Hong Kong 133-4** (18.5 overs) (Shahid Wasif 50, J. J. Atkinson 33*). *PoM:* Shahid Wasif. *Hong Kong rounded off the tournament by claiming revenge for a recent 5–0 defeat by Malaysia in the T20 Interport Series in Kuala Lumpur. It secured them a place in the Asia Cup Qualifier, though that was later postponed.*

SINGAPORE 7pts, HONG KONG 6pts, Malaysia 4pts, Nepal 3pts, Thailand 0pts.

THE LEADING ASSOCIATE NATIONS IN 2020

Cricket never stands completely still and, despite the coronavirus pandemic extending across the globe, there were developments – and matches – in 2020. At the start of the year, before Covid-19 sank its teeth into the fixture list, World Cup League Two trundled on, with two triangular tournaments. The first (see page 797) was held in Oman in January, when Namibia and the UAE joined in. However, the last two games, both involving the hosts, were cancelled, after the death of Sultan Qaboos bin Said. Each side won and lost at least once. The second triangular, staged the next month at Kirtipur in Nepal (see page 798), included the United States and Oman, and followed a clearer pattern, with Oman winning all their four games, the US losing all four, and Nepal winning two and losing two.

NAMIBIA

The year began with the WCL Two tournament in Oman. Thanks to a maiden one-day century from Craig Williams, who walloped an unbeaten 129 from 94 balls, and a white-ball-best five for 44 from left-arm seamer Johannes Smit, Namibia beat the hosts. But they lost twice to the UAE, before the death of the Sultan of Oman caused the abandonment of the remaining fixtures. Then the pandemic took hold, and cricket dried up; a tour by the Netherlands was an early casualty. Even so, in July, the ICC named Namibia as winners of the Associate Member men's Performance of the Year, in recognition of a stellar 2019: they had hosted – and won – the WCL Division Two tournament, gained ODI status for the first time in 16 years, and qualified for the T20 World Cup. In domestic cricket, Windhoek High School Old Boys broke Wanderers' dominance in March, when they won the 50-over Premier League title, defeating their rivals by six wickets; Wanderers had won the title in eight of the previous ten years.   HELGE SCHUTZ

NEPAL

Had it not taken a better turn in December, the year would have been wholly forgettable. But there was optimism in the appointment of Dav Whatmore, who took Sri Lanka to the 1996 World Cup, as the national coach; and also in three Nepalis – Sompal Kami, Kushal Malla, and KC Karan – being picked in the Abu Dhabi T10 draft. In September, the Cricket Association of Nepal had wisely introduced central contracts for women cricketers, eight years after their male counterparts. There had been a flurry of activity in February and March, just before the pandemic took hold. In the only ODIs played by the national side, Nepal – hosting a round of World Cricket League Two – lost twice to Oman, but twice beat the USA, bowling them out for 35. Then, in a poor performance, they finished fourth out of five in the Asia Cup T20 Qualifiers and failed to progress. Their one victory came against Thailand, the hosts. Leg-spinner Sandeep Lamichhane had an up-and-down year: in the Caribbean Premier League, he claimed 12 wickets for Jamaica Tallawahs, and conceded just 5.27 an over, but he never made it on to the pitch for Delhi Capitals in the IPL. Lamichhane was one of five national players, including ex-captain Paras Khadka, to test positive for coronavirus. Ujjwal Acharya

THE NETHERLANDS

Club cricket was played for six happy weeks, from mid-July until the end of August. The almost complete absence of overseas professionals gave the top leagues a different flavour, with local talent to the fore. There was no official championship, nor promotion or relegation, but the Twenty20 tournament survived, with VRA of Amstelveen triumphing on finals day in September. In the truncated *Topklasse* season, the 36-year-old Stephan Myburgh hit 524 runs at 131, and earned a recall to the national squad. All international matches, including the visit of Pakistan for three ODIs, were postponed. During 2020, VRA, the Netherlands' international home, completed an indoor cricket centre. With hindsight, perhaps a biosecure hotel would have been a good idea, since the visit of England in May 2021 – also for three ODIs – was put back a year. In September, Sterre Kalis, a 21-year-old Dutch international, starred in the Rachael Heyhoe Flint Trophy, hitting a half-century for Northern Diamonds in the final at Edgbaston. The Netherlands won an ICC award their Cricket4kids initiative. Elsewhere, Hermes DVS became the seventh club to lay a grass square, the second in the city of Schiedam. Dave Hardy

OMAN

For Oman, the loss of the beloved Sultan Qaboos in January, after a long battle with cancer, felt like a bigger blow even than the pandemic. The WCL2 triangular involving the UAE and Namibia was promptly abandoned. For Omani cricket fans, the sadness was tempered by the fact that his successor was Sultan Haithem bin Tariq, the government sponsor of the game since 1992. Oman dominated the next round of WCL2 games, in February – winning all four in Nepal – but could not progress from the Asia Cup T20 Qualifier. Covid-19 precautions then brought 12-hour curfews and little cricket. The growing international status of players such as Aaqib Ilyas, Khawar Ali, Zeeshan Maqsood and Jatinder Singh has maintained confidence in Omani cricket and, thanks also to a full domestic programme that began late in the year, there is enthusiasm for the challenges ahead. Paul Bird

PAPUA NEW GUINEA

The pandemic had less of an impact on Papua New Guinea than on many countries – being an island has its advantages – and so domestic cricket survived with minimal interruption. Since the national teams had empty calendars for the first time in a decade, Cricket PNG took the opportunity to address their recent poor record in ODIs. They brought in a series of 50-over matches between three teams comprising the best players in the country. The games were considered a success, and will be repeated in 2021. There was also a women's 40-over series along the same lines, while the domestic T20 cups continued as normal. The hope is this will stand the national teams in good stead for what should be a busy 2021: the men have reached the T20 World Cup (now scheduled for India in October), and have several WCL2 series to complete, while the women will be contesting qualifiers for the ODI World Cup and Commonwealth Games. ANDREW NIXON

UNITED ARAB EMIRATES

The scandal which lanced UAE's chances of qualifying for the T20 World Cup cast a shadow across the whole of 2020. More than a year after they were kicked out of the team, and banned from the game because of alleged corrupt acts, Mohammed Naveed and Shaiman Anwar were found guilty of trying to fix matches at the T20 World Cup Qualifier in 2019, and of failing to report corrupt approaches. Naveed was also found guilty of the same offences at the 2019 T10 tournament in the UAE. A few months earlier, Amir Hayat and Ashfaq Ahmed had been formally charged by the ICC with breaches of the anti-corruption code, taking the tally of banned UAE players to five; Qadeer Ahmed, thrown out at the same time as Naveed and Shaiman, was yet to have his case heard. The national team, with no option but to field a new-look, youthful side, largely weathered the corruption storm, twice beating Namibia in ODIs in WCL2, and qualifying for the next stage of the Asia Cup. There were casualties, though. Coach Dougie Brown lost his job, and was replaced in February by Robin Singh, the former India all-rounder. PAUL RADLEY

For a report on cricket in Scotland, see page 805; for the United States, see page 806.

CRICKET IN SCOTLAND IN 2020

Hanging by a thread

WILLIAM DICK

Majid Haq faced many tough examinations of his physical and mental strength during a long international career. He was one of the most skilful spinners Scotland has produced, though it all ended on a well-documented low when he was sent home from the 2015 World Cup after posting a race-related tweet. Effectively ostracised by Cricket Scotland, he was left battling depression but, with the support of family and friends, pulled through.

But just as he was looking ahead optimistically to the rest of his club career, and a potential future in coaching, Haq faced the biggest battle of his 37 years. After contracting Covid-19 in March, he found himself in the intensive care unit of the Royal Alexandra Hospital, Paisley, his future hanging by a thread. Thanks to the expertise and commitment of medical staff, and his own fighting spirit, Haq again came out the other side. But it was touch and go.

"I'd been down in London in early March, and a few days after getting back I started feeling unwell," he said. "I isolated for seven days, and it still wasn't getting better. I could hardly breathe just walking up and downstairs. I got taken into hospital, and tested positive for coronavirus – I knew there was something seriously wrong, and I ended up in the ICU. At that stage, it's out of your hands.

"For 48 hours, I had to have an oxygen mask most of the time during the day, although I was really lucky and recovered quite quickly. I was moved into a ward after three days, before going home. But it was really scary, especially being unable to breathe properly."

The only consolation for Haq may be that he missed no cricket: thanks to the pandemic, virtually none took place. All domestic competitions were cancelled and, while efforts were made to arrange abbreviated regional series for men and women, it turned into an exercise in futility, with neither tournament reaching a conclusion. A women's international series against Ireland in La Manga, enthusiastically announced in October, was called off in November, just a week before the first match. The men's national side last played competitively in December 2019. Their next matches, marking the resumption of ICC World Cup League 2, were scheduled to take place in Papua New Guinea in April 2021, against the hosts and Oman.

CRICKET IN THE USA IN 2020

Foreigners welcome

PETER DELLA PENNA

After achieving ODI status in 2019, the USA made history for the wrong reason. In February, they finished winless in four ODIs in Kathmandu against Oman and Nepal, and were bowled out by the hosts for 35 – both the joint-lowest ODI total (equalling Zimbabwe against Sri Lanka at Harare in April 2004) and, in 12 overs, the shortest completed innings. Outgoing interim head coach James Pamment didn't hold back: the team had been "exposed" by poor administration, and lacked professionalism, despite being the best-paid in Associate cricket. By July, with Covid emptying the fixture list, the squad's wage packet had taken a heavy hit: from central contracts worth nearly $100,000 a year, players now received $1,800 a month.

Instead, American Cricket Enterprises, the chief commercial partner of USA Cricket, invested in recruiting former overseas internationals, with an eye both to launching the Major League Cricket T20 franchise competition in 2022, and to putting them on a three-year residency pathway to qualify for the USA. Among those who signed on were South Africa's Dane Piedt, Pakistan's Sami Aslam, New Zealand's Corey Anderson and Sri Lanka's Shehan Jayasuriya. The likelihood of developing home-grown players to represent the USA in the near future is increasingly remote.

USAC later unveiled a ten-year plan, including lofty targets such as qualifying for men's and women's T20 World Cups, and Full Member status by 2030. A previous strategic document, from 2015, listed many of the same objectives, with a deadline of 2020. A similar document, put out in 2010 by the USA Cricket Association, had been titled "Project 15", and targeted a top-15 ranking, as well as qualification for T20 World Cups by 2015. None of that happened either.

The year ended with the usual governance issues. A referendum vote sent out to USAC's individual members – fewer than 800 at the time, despite regular boasts by board chairman Paraag Marathe about the nation's "15–20 million cricket fans" – required a two-thirds majority to enact sweeping changes to membership eligibility guidelines. But weeks after the November voting deadline passed, there was no word of the result. Finally, a press release stated that the resolution had passed, based on advice obtained from USAC's legal counsel, though the referendum numbers were not fully disclosed. Multiple sources claimed there had been no two-thirds majority, yet the changes happened anyway. The board also used the referendum to delay elections for the third time since the new governing body were established in 2017. It established a precedent: what other changes might be forced through, while bypassing the constitution? Cricket aficionados don't need to look too far back in the USA's history to know the consequences of such governance.

OTHER TWENTY20 INTERNATIONALS IN 2020

Brussels sprouts a record holder

STEVEN LYNCH

The ICC's decision to extend official international status to all T20 matches between member nations in 2019 had threatened to rewrite *Wisden's* Records section: during that year, the Czech Republic equalled the highest total in T20 internationals by clattering 278 against Turkey, who themselves annexed the three lowest scores in the format (21, 28 and 32) with a side containing four 50-year-olds. But there were fewer statistical somersaults in 2020, with coronavirus preventing several series from taking place.

The Czech Republic did eventually have a chance to shine again, in a tri-series in the unlikely surroundings of Walferdange, Luxembourg, late in August. They struggled to reprise their run-scoring feats in the absence of the not-so-young Turks, but did vanquish the hosts. Belgium won all their four games comfortably to nab the trophy, and possessed the star performer: their 38-year-old captain, Shaheryar Butt, hit 81 not out in the first match, against Luxembourg, and added an unbeaten 125 from 50 balls later the same day against the Czechs. He was the first to score a T20I hundred and a half-century on the same day. "It hasn't hit me yet to be a world-record holder," said Shaheryar, who was born in Pakistan but moved to Belgium after taking a shine to the place when he visited family; he now works in sales in Brussels. "It can be difficult to play back-to-back games. Due to funding and budgets, it's more beneficial to organise two matches a day. It's tiring – but after scoring runs, it's a good fatigue."

Scores of two and 28 in the return matches at least ensured he had an average – 118, and a strike-rate of 212, was enough to put him top of the global lists for T20 internationals for the year, ahead of Quinton de Kock and Eoin Morgan (see page 604).

In bilateral battles in February and March, Malaysia hammered Hong Kong 5–0 at home in the Interport Series, Qatar beat Uganda 2–1, and Spain drew 1–1 with Germany. The first action after the coronavirus break was a one-off game in the Channel Islands on August 21, when Guernsey beat the Isle of Man – in their first official international – by eight wickets. Then Malta despatched Bulgaria 2–0 in a four-match series in soggy Sofia. The Bulgarians towelled down and travelled to Romania for the Balkan Cup, but lost 3–1 after winning the first game, in which the Romanians fielded 14-year-old Marian Gherasim, the youngest male T20I player. Pavel Florin, the internet sensation of 2019, with his high-tossed flighted filth, was at it again for Romania: now 41, he took two wickets in his only over in the second game. And in the final match, Bulgaria's 60 (Florin 1–0–8–1) was the lowest total of the year.

ABU DHABI T10 IN 2019-20

PAUL RADLEY

1 Maratha Arabians 2 Deccan Gladiators

The shortest format (so far) started life with the aim of lasting roughly as long – around 90 minutes – as matches in other major sports, such as football and rugby. Everything about ten-over cricket, though, seems short-lived. Maratha Arabians won the third incarnation of the T10 League, beating Deccan Gladiators by eight wickets in a final that drew a crowd of over 20,000. Remarkably, Maratha were the only survivors of the first tournament, in 2017-18: each of the other seven teams were either completely new, had a new name, or were under new ownership.

The surroundings were different as well. After two seasons in Sharjah, the competition decamped 100 miles down the coast to the UAE's capital. It was rebranded as the Abu Dhabi T10, following a five-year deal for it to be played at the Sheikh Zayed Stadium.

After three seasons, the league was still awaiting a first centurion – although the Australian Chris Lynn repeatedly came close. Opening for Maratha, he thrashed four of the top seven scores: 91 not out (from 30 balls), 89 (from 33), 67 and 61 (both from 30). He looked set for a hundred in the highest of those, in a group game against Moeen Ali's Team Abu Dhabi, but Yorkshire's Adam Lyth took some of the strike in the closing overs.

Lynn finished with 371 runs at a dizzying strike-rate of 236 (Shane Watson was next, with 237 runs at 170), clobbering 31 sixes and 29 fours. Maratha were captained by Dwayne Bravo and coached by Andy Flower, in his first assignment since leaving the ECB. And while T10 might not seem the most natural fit for a former Ashes-winning coach, he was clearly immersed in the challenge, at one point wagging a finger at an official over a perceived infraction of the playing regulations.

Lasith Malinga led Maratha's bowling attack, while Yuvraj Singh was their big-money "international community promoter", satisfying a rule that each side must have one player – like Yuvraj or Zaheer Khan, who played alongside Eoin Morgan for Delhi Bulls – whose presence would sell the league beyond its borders. They were each supposed to feature in at least three matches, but that condition had a brief shelf life: 48-year-old Indian leg-spinner Pravin Tambe – who had taken a hat-trick in the 2018-19 tournament – did not get a game for Northern Warriors.

The popular Yuvraj missed three matches with a bad back, possibly incurred carrying his wages around: he was signed for $200,000, which amounted to $40,000 a game, or $4,545 per run. But the league's bean-counters may have regarded that as money well spent: his presence helped double the share of the TV audience in India.

T10 LEAGUE IN 2019-20

	P	*W*	*L*	*T*	*NR*	*Pts*	*NRR*
MARATHA ARABIANS	6	4	1	0	1	9	1.72
QALANDARS	6	3	2	1	0	7	0.57
DECCAN GLADIATORS	6	3	2	0	1	7	0.57
BANGLA TIGERS	6	3	2	1	0	7	0.48
Team Abu Dhabi	6	2	2	1	1	6	0.01
Northern Warriors	6	3	3	0	0	6	–0.52
Delhi Bulls	6	1	4	1	0	3	–1.12
Karnataka Tuskers	6	1	4	0	1	3	–1.67

Play-offs **1st v 2nd** Maratha Arabians beat Qalandars by seven runs. **3rd v 4th** Deccan Gladiators beat Bangla Tigers by five wickets. **Final eliminator** Deccan Gladiators beat Qalandars by 12 runs. **Third-place play-off** Bangla Tigers beat Qalandars by six wickets.

Final At Abu Dhabi, November 24, 2019 (floodlit). **Maratha Arabians won by eight wickets. Deccan Gladiators 87-8** (10 overs); ‡**Maratha Arabians 89-2** (7.2 overs) (C. A. K. Walton 51*). *The Gladiators made a partial recovery from 34-4 thanks to Bhanuka Rajapaksa (23) and Asif Khan (25*), but a final total of 87 never looked enough; left-armer Mitchell McClenaghan (1-12) and Dwayne Bravo (2-16) led a tight bowling effort. The prolific Chris Lynn departed for 16, but Jamaica's Chadwick Walton cracked 51* from 26 to take Maratha Arabians to a comfortable victory.*

CRICKET ROUND THE WORLD IN 2020

COMPILED BY JAMES COYNE AND TIMOTHY ABRAHAM

ASSOCIATE CRICKET DURING THE COVID-19 PANDEMIC

Veronica Vasquez, the Argentina captain, took a deep breath, checked her protective equipment, then made her way into the thick of things. She should have been walking out to bat for her country in a T20 series with rivals Brazil in March 2020. Instead, Vasquez – an anaesthetist – donned PPE and worked 24-hour shifts at the Fiorito Hospital in Buenos Aires, as the country battled the coronavirus.

Like most Associate cricketers, the 25-year-old Vasquez is an enthusiastic amateur, and saw her chances to represent *Las Flamingos* wiped out by Covid-19: budgets for biosecure bubbles do not extend far down the ICC pyramid. Her concern was saving lives, and sometimes fearing for her own. "Every day, we listen to stories of doctors dying doing their job, and that is very scary," she says. "I think about my playing days, and pray they can come back soon, because that will show me we've fought and won against this awful thing."

The men's, women's and junior South American Championships, which were due to be staged in Rio de Janeiro in October, were postponed because of travel restrictions. Abrupt lockdowns in the region even caught out touring teams: in March, the Oxfordshire village side Stanton Harcourt CC found themselves holed up in a Lima hotel for a fortnight, with international flights suspended, and the Peruvian army patrolling the streets.

Many players turned to social media. Vasquez's Brazilian counterpart, Roberta Moretti Avery, regularly filmed herself netting with her husband in the garage, and was part of a cricket-themed Spice Girls tribute montage video involving players from across Latin America. Cricket Peru held a competition for their youngsters to make cricket bats out of recycled materials.

At the elite end of the Associate spectrum, the ICC Cricket World Cup Challenge League was one of the higher-profile tournaments postponed until 2021. Part of the pathway to the 2023 World Cup, the league was due to be hosted in Uganda and Malaysia, and feature the likes of Kenya, Denmark, Hong Kong and Canada. Regional qualifying tournaments for the 2022 T20 World Cup were postponed, along with a host of bilateral series, invitational tournaments and domestic events. Everything from the inaugural T10 Premier League in Tajikistan, who want to emulate the rise of neighbours Afghanistan, to the Nordic Cup featuring Germany, Denmark and Finland, were off. Even Sweden's light-touch approach, with more relaxed social distancing, did not stop the *Svenska Cricketförbundet* from cancelling chunks of their domestic programme.

Also scrubbed from the calendar was the Wuhan Premier League, an inter-university tournament for South Asian students in the central Chinese city where Covid-19 was first identified. Cricket did eventually re-emerge elsewhere in China, with Beijing Ducks CC travelling to Shenzhen for some friendlies. Their players were screened to enable them to make the trip.

In the South Pacific, the Vanuatu women's T20 tournament was suspended by a pre-emptive lockdown, but the easing of restrictions in late April allowed the completion of the final, and a men's T10 exhibition match. Shane Deitz, the former South Australia left-hander who went on to become Cricket Vanuatu chief executive (and in December was named coach of the Netherlands' women), cobbled together "four cameramen who had never seen cricket, and didn't know where the ball was coming from". The archipelago got its 15 minutes of fame, as half a million people around the world tuned in to watch the live stream. It encouraged Vanuatu to scrap that season's men's 40-over tournament, and switch to a T10 Blast.

Guernsey was the first place in the British Isles to resume playing in the summer, on May 30. Later, they hosted the Isle of Man, who were one of two ICC members to make their T20I debut in 2020 (the other was Iran, in February before lockdown).

The British Overseas Territory of St Helena in the South Atlantic, however, could claim to be the only ICC member to play throughout the pandemic. By early December, St Helena and the Cook Islands were the only ICC member countries yet to report a single case of Covid-19. TIMOTHY ABRAHAM

ÅLAND

Åland is an autonomous group of a thousand Finnish islands featuring log cabins, pine forests and around 30,000 people, mostly Swedish-speakers. Not, perhaps, fertile cricket territory. And yet, for one day in 2015, the sport was front-page news. Graham Robins grew up in Scotland before he moved in 2000 to Mariehamn, capital of the largest island, Fasta Åland. Some years later, he began playing cricket in his garden with his seven-year-old son, Viktor. The pair attended two summer camps on the mainland, run by the Finnish Cricket Association. When they returned, they wanted to drum up interest, and contacted the local newspaper. What followed was an in-depth profile in *Ålandstidningen*, featuring young Viktor – in full whites, pads, gloves and helmet – playing a textbook cover-drive. His photograph appeared under the headline "*Viktor tränar cricket på en gräsmatta*" ("Viktor trains on the lawn"). Even the wicket looked perfect: "Clipping the grass with a push lawnmower felt like part of the fun," said Graham, the *kurator* at the islands' Cultural History Museum. The article led to the discovery of at least one young Ålander with cricket kit – he had learned the game at boarding school in Wales – but sadly not enough interest to develop Åland's first team. For the time being, elk hunting remains a more popular pastime on this archipelago in the Baltic. OWEN AMOS

BRAZIL

Luiz Roberto Francisco, a retired engineer who now works as a carpenter, will follow in the footsteps of the conquistadors by venturing deep into the Amazon. Unlike them, he does not have Inca gold or El Dorado on his mind – but cricket bats. His initial contact with Cricket Brasil came about when he was enlisted to make wooden benches for players at their high performance centre in Poços de Caldas. A spa town in the state of Minas Gerais, around 170 miles north of São Paulo, it is the epicentre of one the most exciting projects in Associate cricket. Around 3,700 children are playing the sport there, while 14 of the country's top women players (but not their men) were handed central contracts in 2020 – unprecedented in the Americas. To meet the growing demand, a container full of equipment was shipped over by the Lord's Taverners, requiring the British ambassador to sign it off at customs. Cricket Brasil's accelerated growth programme is set to bring the game to the satellite towns around Poços. This aims to introduce the sport to a staggering 30,000 youngsters, and has left the governing body with a huge equipment shortfall, especially bats. Enter the wily, grey-haired Francisco, who has become the first bona fide maker of hand-crafted bats – *tacos* in Portuguese. "I presented Luiz with an old bat, and asked if he could make one," says Cricket Brasil president Matt Featherstone. "We needed something light and cheap to produce, which children could use. What came back was superb." The first bats can withstand the real thing, but will mainly be used against a hard plastic ball by youngsters learning the game. Francisco has watched "nearly every YouTube video on bat-making", and fully kitted out his workshop, trademarking his company "Royal Bats", and naming a range of bats after members of the national coaching team. He has since experimented with 11 varieties of wood in an attempt to produce one capable of adult use. *Salix alba caerulea,* the white willow, is not native to South America, so Francisco plans to head to the rainforest to obtain samples of other wood, which he hopes can break willow's monopoly. If successful, he plans to open a factory, and export globally. "Already some of the bats using Brazilian wood are superior to Kashmir willow, in my opinion," says Featherstone, a good club cricketer in Kent before he moved to Brazil two decades ago. The expat-dominated men's teams of Rio and São Paulo used to find it easy going against Poços, but are now given the odd bloody nose by a team made up almost entirely of Brazilians. "It's not going to be long before we see a Brazilian player exported, and maybe playing county cricket," adds Featherstone. When that happens, they will doubtless wield a Royal. TIMOTHY ABRAHAM

EUROPEAN CRICKET SERIES

In the year European governments enacted unprecedented lockdowns, cricket somehow achieved mainstream attention. From June to November, almost 600 club matches from 17 countries across the continent were broadcast free-to-air round most of the world. With little international cricket, the window belonged almost exclusively to the European Cricket Network – the people behind the T10 "Champions League of European cricket", which had begun at La Manga in July 2019.

The second European Cricket League, bolstered by clubs from England, Ireland and Scotland, was kyboshed by travel restrictions. But once governments began easing the rules, there was less to stop the ECN from running domestic series – starting with the Finnish Premier League on June 1. Nimble management was still needed from the man behind it all, Daniel Weston, a hedge-fund manager from Western Australia who had settled in Munich, and now had to navigate frequent policy changes. Where the ECN dared to go, the IPL followed – at least in signing up the Indian fantasy cricket platform Dream11 as their title sponsor.

The European Cricket Series roadshow shone a light on obscure cricketing cultures. There was a married couple playing for Kummerfeld, in northern Germany: Sharanya Sadarangani – who played for Karnataka Under-19s – kept wicket proficiently to the cutters of husband Finn Sadarangani, who had played age-group cricket for Denmark. Then there were the distinctly un-Commonwealth backdrops: Eastern European tower blocks; a glimpse of the 1992 Olympic baseball stadium from the next-door Montjuic Cricket Ground in Barcelona; the futuristic design of the Lutheran church behind the Víðistaðatún ground at Reykjavík (if only a second wave of infections hadn't led Iceland's government to cancel the tournament at the last minute).

The ECS was dominated by migrants from major cricket nations, particularly Pakistan. The closest to a native star – one more substantial than Pavel Florin, who made headlines in 2019 by bowling lobs for Romanian side Cluj – was perhaps Hristo Lakov, the crisp-hitting vice-captain of Bulgaria who had recently relocated from New Zealand. He struck three fifties for Indo-Bulgarian CC, and took the first wicket in the ECS Bulgaria final, broadcast live on state television.

If there had been grumbles during the 2019 ECL that the standard of cricket (and commentary) was uncomfortably low for television, the argument was stronger still in the ECS. Some of it was barely Third XI club standard, and verged on the unwatchable if you weren't personally invested.

That arguably made fixing harder to identify. Any televised cricket is vulnerable to the illegal gambling of the subcontinent, and ECS events looked especially so. As early as July, a player was reprimanded for using his mobile phone to film his side batting – not usually an offence for a recreational cricketer, but cause for alarm in a televised game. Days later, the ECN stopped a match in Cyprus halfway through, and suspended Limassol Gladiators after $2m was traded on one of their games on Betfair. Two men were arrested in Jaipur, India, accused of targeting ECS matches for corruption.

Weston was quick to issue a statement: "We are making use of the latest in big-data analytical software to help us fight to keep cricket clean. T10 is about making the game faster and more entertaining, so as soon as batsmen are not showing intent to score, or bowlers are wastefully sending down significant amounts of extras, alarm bells ring for our investigative team." By the end of the year, the ICC anti-corruption unit were investigating in at least two ECS host countries.

He later admitted it was "uncomfortable at times to broadcast amateur cricket, because we are at the crossroads of taking the game from amateur to professional in Europe. Just like any sport in any era, it has to grow through a transition phase." But ECS tournaments just kept coming, continuing into December in the warm Mediterranean, though rain in Malta disrupted the 33rd event of the year.

Outside the subcontinent, it was all free to watch initially, either on TV or YouTube, and the ECN trumpeted total viewership of 300m by November, with a peak of 2m unique users. Unsurprisingly, once the cricket had grown in value, it disappeared behind a paywall. A deal with the Australian streaming platform Sports Flick kicked in on November 2, though highlights and clips dripped out on social media. It was up to consumers to decide whether a £10 monthly subscription was worth it for 1,000 matches live in 2021 ("by volume, the largest cricket portfolio in the world").

There was regret among Associate fans that the continental game might swiftly return to the margins; some even alleged the ECS was doing little more than fuel online betting. And yet one can-do Australian had achieved more for the visibility of European cricket in two years than the ICC in two decades. JAMES COYNE

GUANTÁNAMO BAY

Land of no umpires

CLIVE STAFFORD SMITH

It was humid in Guantánamo Bay, at the notorious US naval base on the south-east tip of Cuba, the thermometer hovering above 40°C. July 4, Independence Day, is when Americans celebrate casting off the chains of British colonialism. But the Jamaicans were celebrating in a different way – with a game of cricket.

There are many laws that do not apply in Guantánamo, including workers' rights. The wages for more than 100 Jamaican migrants start at $1.25 an hour – and $12 a day is less than the cost of three meals in the navy galley ($13.25). But people must find joy somewhere, and I was present for the first annual Cricket Challenge between teams from the Windward Side and the Leeward Side.

Guantánamo is my Caribbean resort of choice: I have been 40 times to visit clients. I take a cricket ball to practise in the nets – the tennis court next to the Combined Bachelors' Quarters, across the bay from the prisoners in their orange jumpsuits in the detention camp. At the galley, Wallie had explained the shortage of cricket equipment, so I had brought some on the flight in, bemusing the American security guards.

I was not impartial: there were friends on the Leeward Side. But when I offered to umpire, the captains said it was not necessary – there would be no lbws, and a catch would be out only if everyone agreed. The Leeward Side chose to bat, in a 25-over game, with the first ball from the Kitchen Stand End. The stand itself was a 10ft green garbage dumpster, its plastic hinged lid flipped over to provide shade to spectators. There was a well-rolled clay wicket, with the odd tuft of grass in the outfield, yet everyone wore full whites. The Windward Side had no spinners: despite the heat, everyone wanted to be Michael Holding, sprinting in off 30 paces. They tore through the Leeward batting: 85 all out.

The commentator was upbeat, backed by loud reggae. He opined that ten would have been a good score, given the legendary prowess of the Leeward attack. The Windward Side slumped to 42 for seven off 18 overs. Yet Tefari, the No. 7, seemed to have mastered the cracking clay, and smacked two enormous sixes. He brought the target down to 11 off two overs, then took an unwise single, leaving Mario to face the music. Mario was patently a No. 11, and the DJ played the theme tune from a horror film. But Mario used his pads well to keep out a sequence of glaring lbws. Tefari was now facing the final over, and he clouted a short ball into the wall of a disused military bathroom: four needed from three. He missed the next delivery, which was both within a whisper of being struck for six, and gaspingly close to off stump. The bowler bounded in again, raucously accompanied by the commentator. The ball was fast. It was straight. And Tefari missed. Leeward leapt in unison.

Clive Stafford Smith is a British human-rights lawyer and co-founder of Reprieve. He has represented more than 100 detainees at Guantánamo Bay.

MACAU

"Cricket matches are held from mid-October until late January," declared a 1960s guide issued by the Macau tourist board. But visitors to the then Portuguese colony on China's south coast might have been left scratching their heads. The "cricket matches", which date back over 1,000 years, had nothing to do with bat and ball. Instead, they involved pitting teams of insects against each other. This ancient means of settling disputes between warlords was promoted to travellers looking for something to bet on while visiting the so-called Monte Carlo of the East. The bat-and-ball version arrived a little later, thanks to new arrivals who work in a gambling industry that exploded after Macau reverted to Chinese control in 1999. Cricket was initially confined to informal games after Friday prayers at Macau's mosque, until the influx of foreigners created enough interest for an annual six-a-side tournament. It might have lacked the stellar names of the version in nearby Hong Kong, but the competition was just as fierce. The Macau Cricket Association were founded in 2008, and matches took place at the International School in the Taipa district – only for the school's expansion to leave the field beneath a car park. In the most densely populated place on the planet, finding somewhere to play was a challenge. Eventually, the MCA struck a deal to use a multi-sports ground for frenzied Friday-night games, with the 1,100ft Macau Tower a striking backdrop. Association members have coached Macanese children at schools, and are keen to spread the word to the locals, and play teams from mainland China; the international stadium in Guangzhou is only a short drive away. From the buzz of warring crickets, the buzz now is provided by the cricket itself. TIM OSCROFT

RUSSIA

The Kremlin presumably appreciate the sentiment behind *это просто не крикет* ("it's just not cricket"). The day after England's 2019 World Cup triumph at Lord's, Russian media reported that the sports ministry had refused to include cricket on the register of officially recognised sports, unlikle pétanque, draughts and mini-golf. A year later, Anglo–Russian political relations were "close to frozen", according to Andrei Kelin, the Russian ambassador in London. But attitudes to cricket started to thaw. Though *Pravda* and others did not publish the follow-up story, a repeat application by Cricket Russia was accepted by the Kremlin in May 2020, giving them official recognition and, in theory, government support. It is not yet clear if that will lead to direct funding, but it will help introduce cricket lessons at a greater number of schools. That will fulfil one of the key targets identified by Cricket Russia's president, Ashwani Chopra, assisted by Elena Sukhotina, an English teacher, and Sergey Kurchenko, originally a baseball coach. Chopra wants to increase awareness of cricket among Russians, and stock clubs with local players. Already, left-arm seamer Andrey Bogatyrev and his brother Sasha, an all-rounder, are mainstays of the domestic scene, along with wicketkeeper-batsman Sasha Vasiliev. The star batsman is astrologer Pavel Maksimov, who reads spin as well as he does celestial objects. Russia became an ICC member in 2012, but lost their only permanent pitch at Karacharovo, in the Moscow suburbs, and have yet to make their official T20 international debut in either the men's or women's game. That could change in 2021, after Chopra earmarked a site for a new ground. He plans to send reigning champions Moscow Foxes to the European Cricket League in La Manga, where St Petersburg Lions made a respectable debut in 2019. Chopra dreams that his son, Yash, will one day represent Russia in cricket at the Olympics; Cricket Russia even tweeted the ICC urging them to stop dragging their heels on the sport's inclusion. The continued influx of South Asian medical students to universities has sparked action far beyond the traditional bases of Moscow and St Petersburg. This has led to matches in places previously untouched by the game, including the mountainous Siberian republic of Altai. It is also played in Novgorod, the birthplace of *lapta*, a Russian bat-and-ball game with similarities to cricket which dates back to the 14th century. JONATHAN CAMPION

SEALAND

England fans may want Ben Stokes knighted for his various heroics, but he already has aristocratic credentials. He became Lord Benjamin Stokes of Sealand, after Piers Morgan purchased the title (at a cost of £29.99) and presented it to him on breakfast television days after England's 2019 World Cup win. Sealand, seven and a half miles off the coast of Suffolk, was originally HM Fort Roughs – a platform built in 1942 to defend shipping lanes from Nazi mine-laying aircraft, and occupied by up to 300 Royal Navy staff until it was decommissioned in 1956. Eleven years later, former British Army major Paddy Roy Bates seized the abandoned platform. Back then, it lay in international waters, so he declared it the Principality of Sealand on his wife Joan's birthday, and later moved the family in. Michael Bates, the hereditary ruler since Roy's death in 2012, was "delighted to honour" Stokes, who has seemingly embraced Sealander nobility. He revealed in a recent autobiography that he asked his wife, Clare, for approval to use the title when filling out an online form ("Safe to say she didn't grant it"). Might he one day represent Sealand? Given the micronation is an offshore platform measuring 0.0015 square miles – one fifth the size of the average cricket field – it has hosted little more than a knockabout. However, a team representing Sealand – made up of supporters of the principality – have played, and lost, a charity match against Harrow School. Though not in the side on that occasion, Michael was a keen bowler in his school days. Sealand's vibrant history includes pirate radio stations, disputes with the UK government (who do not recognise its sovereignty), and an attempted coup – repelled by the Bates family – by German and Dutch mercenaries in 1978. Only two security personnel live full-time on the fort now. Sealand has its own flag, stamps, currency, anthem and, for one day only so far, a cricket team. Will a Sealand XI take the field again? "We have often considered holding a match for a charity event on a nearby sandbank at low tide," says Michael. Maybe Lord Stokes will play. JACK SKELTON

SINGAPORE

Singapore's status as a cricketing power in South-East Asia grew when it briefly provided the chairman of the ICC. Imran Khwaja, 64-year-old lawyer, former all-rounder and ex-president of the Singapore Cricket Association, became the first from an Associate nation to hold the post when he took over on an interim basis from India's Shashank Manohar in July. Five months later, Khwaja lost the election to Greg Barclay of New Zealand, but has long been a key voice for Associates on the ICC board. In Singapore, the number of registered players has spiralled to 7,000, assisted by the availability of several academies linked to the subcontinent. The CricKingdom Cricket Academy was the brainchild of Chetan Suryawanshi, a former Singapore and Maharashtra Under-19 captain, and launched in partnership with Indian superstar Rohit Sharma, with sister academies across the world. A few years ago, Singapore had 20 cricket grounds, four with turf wickets. But the SCA's lease of Kallang Stadium, where cricketers had trained for two decades, was ended in 2016 by the government, who earmarked it for football. The SCA had to hire facilities across the strait in Johor, Malaysia, until the local Indian Association ground was leased for $S60,000 (about £33,000) a year. Sport Singapore chipped in with $S1m to pay for floodlights and indoor nets for night cricket – a necessity, as many national team players are working professionals, students or on national service. It allowed the ground to stage the T20 World Cup Asia Regional finals in July 2019, won by Singapore ahead of Nepal, and a T20 tri-series in which Singapore pulled off their first win over a Full Member, beating Zimbabwe. Victories over Scotland and Bermuda in the T20 World Cup Qualifier in Dubai helped move Singapore up to 20th in the ICC rankings by the time Covid-19 struck. In less than a year's worth of T20Is, Tim David, the Perth Scorchers batsman whose father, Rod, also represented Singapore, hammered 558 runs at 46. Singapore also boasts probably the most stunning clubhouse and backdrop in the Associate world: the Padang, a historic green space in downtown, home to Singapore Cricket Club since the mid-19th century. In March, Northamptonshire emulated the likes of Bayern Munich by flying in for a pre-season training camp, the first stage in their global partnership with Singapore CC and the SCA, though their trip was cut short by the pandemic. RAVI CHATURVEDI

SWEDEN

Last summer, an email from South African cricketer Jonty Rhodes dropped in the inbox of Benn Harradine, performance director at the *Svenska Cricketförbundet*, asking if there was a long-term position going. "At first I thought he was taking the piss," said Harradine. By September, Rhodes had become Sweden's head coach for at least two years, relocating with his wife, Melanie – "a massive fan of the Swedish schooling system" – and four young children. Rhodes was just starting as fielding coach for IPL side Kings XI Punjab, and had filled short-term coaching roles in Kenya, Nepal and Malawi. He joined at a time when the number of clubs in Sweden had mushroomed from 17 to 78 in two years – boosted by immigration from the subcontinent – and the number of grounds to 25, though with access to just one indoor facility in a country of harsh winters. Rhodes was keen to avoid some of the pitfalls experienced by Associate countries. "Too often you see people not working together in emerging nations," he said. "People almost make excuses: 'We don't have good facilities', or 'It's pointless trying to get high performance because everyone's volunteering.' There's some great work done in many Associate countries, but in isolation." Harradine had thrown Australia to gold in the discus at the 2010 Commonwealth Games, while Rhodes represented South Africa at field hockey as well as cricket. They hoped their varied sporting experiences could help the SCF attract Swedish athletes and coaches with transferrable skills from the likes of ice hockey, floorball and bandy. JAMES COYNE

TUNISIA

A curious throng of Tunisians are gathered on a wall, as Eric Idle, in robes and sandals, with a Roman bust as stumps, gets ready to face a delivery from the distinctively lanky, Speedo-clad frame of John Cleese. Michael Palin, in costume as an ex-leper, is explaining the nuances of cricket to the US-born Terry Gilliam. The match involving the Monty Python troupe outside the Ribat of Sousse, an eighth-century sandstone fort near Monastir constructed by Ibrahim the Great, surely ranks among Tunisia's most unlikely sporting occurrences. *The Life of Brian* was set in AD33 but shot in 1978, with the first game of cricket on Tunisian soil taking place somewhere in between. It may have involved Field Marshal Montgomery's Desert Rats, who played on old landing grounds in Tunis after taking the city from Rommel in 1943. Former Essex captain J. W. A. Stephenson, who armed himself with cricket balls in his pockets on night patrols, was garrisoned in the city. Lt-Col Stephenson went on to play for England in one of the 1945 Victory Tests at Lord's, but at least one first-class cricketer – Geoffrey Fletcher, fleetingly of Oxford University and Somerset – died in the Tunisian campaign. Many more club players perished during bitter fighting in the decisive British victory at Longstop Hill, the heights between Djebel el Ahmera and Djebel Rha named after the least glamorous of fielding positions. Tunisia declared independence from France in 1956, and Shaharyar Khan, later Pakistan foreign secretary and PCB chairman, wrote of regular cricket matches during a stint at his country's embassy from 1962 until 1966. But cricket secured its firmest foothold with the foundation of Carthage CC by Mark Oppe and John Phillips in 2012. They scoured embassies and banks for players, but finding a ground was tricky. "Security issues ruled out school playing fields and the British ambassador's residence," says Oppe. The new club settled for an astroturf football pitch at La Marsa, a coastal resort close to Tunis. Two years later, bolstered by players from an Indian engineering company, Carthage toured Malta. In spite of assurances from the British Embassy, many of the Asian players were deemed a flight risk by the Maltese authorities over visa concerns. On passing through passport control, each player was applauded by team-mates with the same enthusiasm as for a glorious six. The club are still active eight years later, and at least one Tunisian player, Aymen Triki, has ensured newspaper reports on Carthage's cricket have appeared in Arabic, as well as French and English. STEVE MENARY

THE VIETNAM WAR

Birth of the Cinders

BRENDAN SMITH

Last May, because of the pandemic, I was indoors at home in Cootamundra, New South Wales, reading one of my *Wisdens*. On page 1092 of the 2018 edition, I stumbled across "The Test cricketer who served in Vietnam" about fast bowler Tony Dell. It mentioned a match played by Australian airmen of No. 2 Squadron Royal Australian Air Force at the Phan Rang airbase in 1967. I know about that match: I played in it. Our squadron boasted several who played first grade cricket, so it was inevitable some form of the game would take place. It was agreed the Officers would play the Airmen; a trophy was fashioned from a bomber starting cartridge, and christened "the Cinders". Cricket kit was flown in from RAAF Butterworth in Malaysia. Operational requirements dictated when the game could be played, in the least rock-strewn area of a field, in a remote part of the base. The ground was so hard stumps had to be driven into a small box containing wet earth. There was no wicket as such, and the bowlers struggled to generate bounce from an uneven surface. Competition was fierce, and the airmen rejoiced whenever they dismissed an officer. The match attracted a large crowd, including hundreds of US airmen and quite a few Vietnamese. Eventually, after hours in the hot sun, the Airmen narrowly won. That evening, the Officers laid on an evening of festivities, and the Cinders trophy was presented to the Airmen by the commanding officer. Years later, a few of us visited the Australian War Memorial in Canberra. There, among other exhibits, was the Cinders. The hair on the back of my neck stood up. That trophy meant a lot, to a lot.

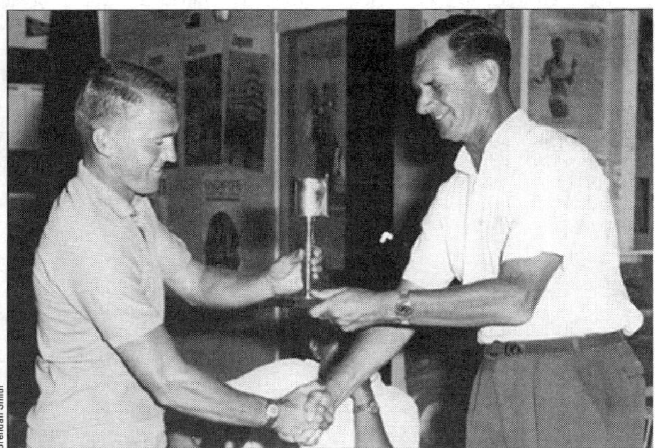

Brendan Smith

Top brass: Brendan Smith, captain of the Airmen XI, receives the Cinders from Wing Commander David Evans, later Air Force Chief of Staff.

YEMEN

Yemen is a failed state, plunged since 2014 into a conflict which has become the planet's worst humanitarian crisis, a proxy war between Saudi Arabia and Iran. Improbably, the first cricket for five years was played in June, in a "Beat Corona" event held by members of the significant Pakistani diaspora in the capital, Sana'a, and has continued under threat of bombardment. Before 2015, there were as many as 12 teams playing a mixture of tapeball and hardball in the Yemen Premier League. "We were actually at our peak when the war began," says Arshad Ali Bajwa, owner of a logistics company who plays in and sponsors the league. The Yemen Cricket Association were in talks with the ICC and Asian Cricket Council about steps to membership. But Sana'a fell under heavy bombing, and the national football stadium, one of three grounds used by the YCA, suffered considerable damage. In 1976, Scyld Berry, a Cambridge graduate in Arabic – and future *Wisden* editor – reported for *The Cricketer* on a match between Sana'a CC (a side of British expats including Berry) and United Sports Club (a team of Pakistanis). They had to beat a hasty retreat after a holy man warned them against playing on sanctified land, and regrouped in the shadow of the Sarawat Mountains on a spot of desert which, as expected, played slow and low. Cricket had its firmest footing down south among British troops in the Isthmus Barracks protecting Aden, a key stopping point between the Suez Canal and India. In late 1963 came the Aden Emergency, leading to the British evacuation, but cricket was still permitted in the Soviet satellite state which emerged in the south. In 1971, while stopping off in Aden en route to East Africa, a strong Hyderabad Blues touring side took on none other than the People's Democratic Republic of Yemen Cricket Association XI. JAMES COYNE

REGIONAL TOURNAMENTS

	Date	*Promoted*	*Others*
Asian E Region T20	Feb	Singapore, Hong Kong	Malaysia, Nepal, Thailand
Asian W Region T20	Feb	UAE, Kuwait	Bahrain, Qatar, Oman, Saudi Arabia, Maldives, Iran

PART SIX

Overseas Domestic Twenty20 Cricket

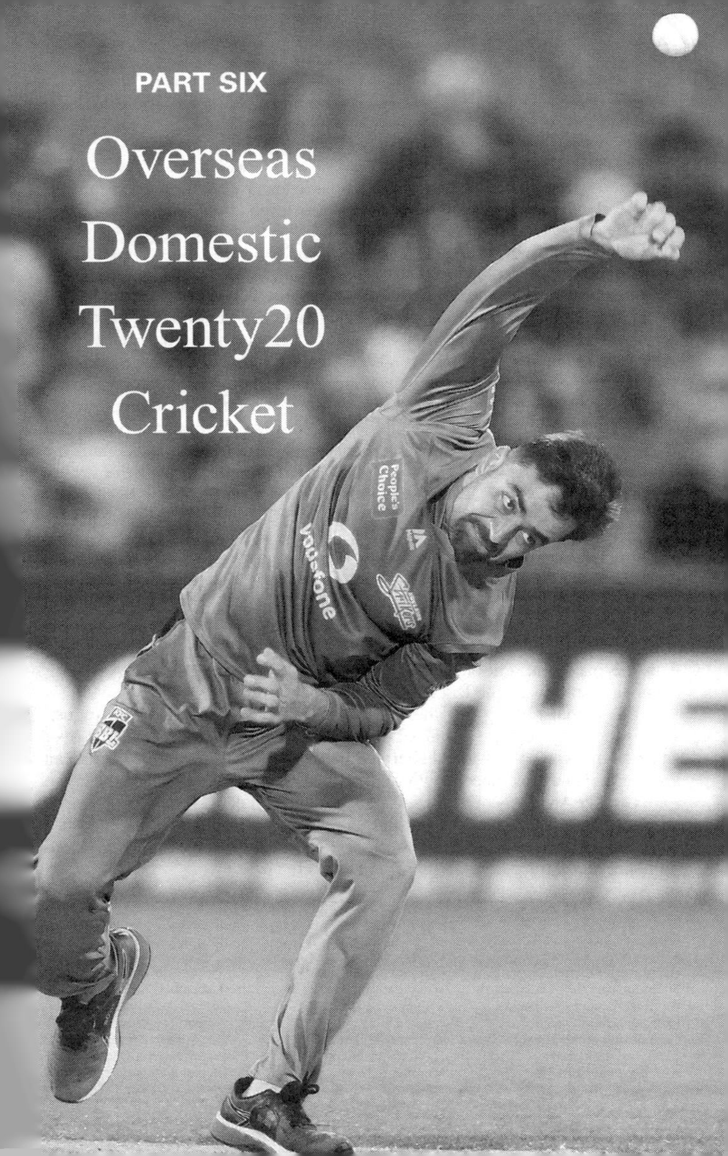

OVERSEAS TWENTY20 FRANCHISE CRICKET IN 2019-20

FREDDIE WILDE

For several years, it had been apparent that the power of domestic T20 cricket, particularly the IPL, was growing relative to the international game. Never was the scale of the shift as clear as in 2020. While the long-term effects of Covid-19 on the sport remained to be seen, the pandemic threw a harsh light on the priorities of world cricket.

At no point was this more obvious than when the T20 World Cup, scheduled for October and November 2020, was delayed a year, and the IPL, postponed during the global lockdown, filled the window left behind. It took place in the UAE, where the virus was less of a threat than in India. Although hosting the World Cup – 16 teams playing in eight Australian cities – was a greater logistical challenge during the pandemic, the swap reflected a simple truth: cricket could not afford the cancellation of the IPL. "With a contribution of around one-third of global revenues generally," wrote Sundar Raman, the tournament's former chief operating officer, "the importance of the IPL to cricket's global economy cannot be overstressed."

It was not the only instance of domestic T20 being given priority. In England, despite an abbreviated season that did not start until August, they played a slightly amended T20 Blast, comprising 97 matches behind closed doors – while the 50-over tournament was cancelled, and the first-class competition significantly curtailed. In the Caribbean and Pakistan, the T20 leagues were the first high-profile matches after lockdown, while the Sri Lankan board announced in July that they would start their 2020-21 season with the inaugural edition of the Lanka Premier League. Cricket Australia, meanwhile, promised the Big Bash would be played in full.

It was perhaps fitting that the T20 circuit rebooted in Trinidad in August: such is the array of talent produced there, it is the spiritual home of the 20-over game, with Dwayne Bravo and Kieron Pollard to the fore. The entire Caribbean Premier League took place at two venues, the Queen's Park Oval and the Brian Lara Cricket Academy. The organisers could not install players in hotels at the grounds, as the ECB did for their international season, so the CPL served as a more achievable template for biosecure cricket. The administrators deserved immense credit for pulling it off with hardly a hitch.

ROLL OF HONOUR

Mzansi Super League (SA)	Paarl Rocks	November–December 2019
Bangladesh Premier League	Rajshahi Royals	December–January 2019-20
Super Smash (New Zealand)	Wellington Firebirds	December–January 2019-20
Big Bash League (Australia)	Sydney Sixers	December–February 2019-20
Pakistan Super League	Karachi Kings	February–November 2020
Caribbean Premier League	Trinbago Knight Riders	August–September 2020
T20 Blast (England)	Nottinghamshire Outlaws	August–October 2020
Indian Premier League	Mumbai Indians	September–November 2020

The Lanka Premier League started in Sri Lanka late in 2020, and will feature in Wisden 2022.

The cricket itself demonstrated the challenges posed by tournament hubs. Pitches became worn and tired, and low-scoring games were dominated by spin; some were turgid, a few intriguing. The 54% of overs sent down by slow bowlers, and a spin economy-rate of 5.98, were records for major T20 leagues.

It was a different story in the UAE. The groundstaff in Abu Dhabi, Dubai and Sharjah produced pitches that remained excellent, and even suited quick bowling. IPL13 was defined by the high pace, swing and aggression of the likes of Jofra Archer (MVP), Kagiso Rabada (leading wicket-taker), Anrich Nortje, Trent Boult and Jasprit Bumrah. It was the second time the Indian board had been forced to take the IPL abroad at short notice, following 2009, when elections led to a relocation to South Africa. Organising a blockbuster tournament during a pandemic was probably an even greater coup.

The IPL was also notable for the manufactured crowd noise applied to the broadcasts. It has always been a made-for-TV product, and the absence of spectators further prioritised the sofa over the grandstand seat. Rather than use universal background noise, Star Sports (the host broadcaster) created a library of specific responses to events, featuring certain players against particular opponents. The tournament was not the same without fans – but no event came as close as the IPL to replicating the real thing.

But there was a familiarity to events on the pitch. The CPL was won by Trinbago Knight Riders, unbeaten en route to their fourth title, while Mumbai Indians claimed a fifth IPL crown. Both teams featured the year's outstanding player: Pollard, still only 33, contributed in all facets of the game, and arguably elevated himself from T20 great to T20 legend, emerging from Chris Gayle's considerable shadow.

Before the pandemic, South Africa's Mzansi Super League was beset by poor weather, with eight of its 32 matches not producing a result. The best team, Paarl Rocks, topped the table, then won the final. Melbourne Stars dominated the Big Bash league stage with a spin-heavy attack, but fell short of their elusive first title in a rain-affected final against Sydney Sixers.

In February, the PSL returned, in full, to Pakistan (the previous season, only the last eight games had taken place there). The group stage played out, before the global lockdown, in front of packed and passionate crowds. One week featured three matches in Multan – all won by Multan Sultans, who topped the league stage – and were the first elite-level games played there since 2008. In a year when cricket became accustomed to matches behind closed doors, it had become clear what the return of live matches meant to Pakistan.

The PSL was halted by the pandemic, and completed in November. Karachi Kings sealed a well-deserved first title, a fitting tribute to their coach, Dean Jones, who had died of a heart attack two months earlier.

THE LEADING TWENTY20 CRICKETER IN 2020

Kieron Pollard

TIM WIGMORE

In 2010, after Kieron Pollard turned down a West Indies contract, a Caribbean administrator asked him: "Do you want to be remembered as a legend or a mercenary?" Pollard long ago rejected this as a false choice: he could both earn the sums his talents deserved, and be one of the most influential cricketers in the modern age. Last year, when he also became the first to 500 T20 appearances, he achieved a new level of mastery.

Pollard's aura was exemplified in a Caribbean Premier League match in August. Trinbago Knight Riders required 53 from 21 balls with four wickets in hand. Yet when Pollard pulled Barbados Tridents leg-spinner Hayden Walsh to deep square leg, he refused a single, apparently intensifying the pressure on his team, and defying a basic dictum of T20: take every run.

But Pollard thinks in a different currency: not singles and twos, but fours and sixes. If you can clear the ropes with his regularity – in 2020, he hit 59 sixes, one every 5.5 balls – you can mock the notion that T20 matches are won by marginal gains. Most are won by the side who score the most fours and sixes. Hence the refused single: Pollard knew that Trinbago's only chance lay in boundaries, and that he was best placed to hit them. He had already launched Walsh for two sixes in the 17th over. Now, he hit two more: a pull over square leg, and a trademark blow down the ground. He was eventually run out, immediately after his ninth six, for 72 from 28 deliveries, but Trinbago were on the brink of an astounding heist. They won with a ball to spare.

> He rejected the traditional T20 trade-off

It was a snapshot of a year in which Pollard emerged from global lockdown as the best T20 batsman around, thriving in the CPL, the Indian Premier League and for West Indies. Just as he had rejected the administrator's trade-off, he now rejected the traditional T20 trade-off, between scoring at high speeds and scoring consistently.

In 2020, Pollard scored faster than everyone – a stratospheric strike-rate of 199 – and averaged 53. His finishing prowess was highlighted by 11 not-outs from 23 innings. He bowled cannily when required, while his boundary catching – another area in which he has been a T20 revolutionary – was as electric as ever.

In the year he turned 33, he was still evolving. He started innings more quickly, and continued to improve against leg-spin: during the IPL, Pollard razed Adam Zampa for 27 in an over, typical of a batsman who targeted bowlers, aiming not for a risk-free single after hitting a six, but for another six, and then another.

Quantity and velocity: Kieron Pollard bends Twenty20 to his will.

Perhaps the best measure of his worth remained the trophy cabinet. He led Trinbago to a uniquely perfect CPL campaign – 12 wins out of 12. Mumbai Indians, where he has played for 11 seasons and is vice-captain, were almost as imperious, winning a fifth IPL out of eight. It was Pollard's 16th T20 title, yet another record for a player who has changed how the game is played. In the West Indies and beyond, his legacy is assured.

THE LEADING TWENTY20 CRICKETER IN THE WORLD

2018 Rashid Khan (Afghanistan)
2019 Rashid Khan (Afghanistan)
2020 Andre Russell (West Indies)
2021 Kieron Pollard (West Indies)

KFC TWENTY20 BIG BASH LEAGUE IN 2019-20

Daniel Cherny

1 Sydney Sixers   2 Melbourne Stars

Chastened by criticism of the previous Big Bash League, the first played as a full home-and-away competition, Cricket Australia made several changes in 2019-20. They tightened the schedule by a week and altered the play-off system, increasing the number of qualifiers from four to five, and providing the top two teams with two chances of reaching the final.

The tinkering had side effects. Such a cramped calendar made for an exhausting schedule, especially for Western Australians. Jamming 56 league matches into 42 days also meant some unfriendly start times, with a few on weekday afternoons outside the Christmas/New Year window. Average crowds fell for a third consecutive season, while television ratings were down on both Fox and Channel Seven. The five-match play-off series was supposed to be the season's climax, yet none of the games drew more than 16,000 fans.

Sydney Sixers won their first title since the inaugural tournament eight years earlier. They were helped hugely by the all-round efforts of Tom Curran, who claimed 22 wickets, though he departed to join England in South Africa ahead of the knockouts. By then, however, the Sixers' Australian internationals Steve Smith, Josh Hazlewood and Nathan Lyon were all available. Hazlewood and Lyon helped bowl out table-toppers **Melbourne Stars** for 99 in a play-off, earning the right to host the final – where the Stars, who rejoined them after winning the last eliminator match, lost again in a rain-shortened game.

Much of the build-up to the tournament had surrounded the big-name acquisitions of Dale Steyn, who played for the Stars in the first half, and his fellow South African A. B. de Villiers, who signed with Brisbane Heat for the second. Steyn was solid if not spectacular, missing two of his scheduled six games through injury. But the Stars signed Pakistani quick Haris Rauf as cover, and he proved a diamond: he took 20 wickets at 13, and was soon catapulted into his national team. The omission of Marcus Stoinis and Glenn Maxwell from Australia's one-day squad in India was another huge boost, and the Stars burst from the blocks to win ten of their first 11 games. Stoinis scored 705 runs, a BBL record, and was named Player of the Tournament, although he was fined $7,500 for a homophobic slur during a Melbourne derby.

A run of five wins in six games in January sealed third place for **Adelaide Strikers**, but four teams found themselves chasing the last two play-off slots with two matches to go. **Hobart Hurricanes**, helped by the explosive batting of Matthew Wade, won both to jump from seventh to fourth. **Sydney Thunder**, who had lost off-spinner Chris Green midway through the tournament after he was suspended for an illegal action, squeezed into fifth, and won two knockout games (both away from home), before being stopped by the Stars in the battle to join the Sixers in the final. All-rounder Daniel Sams was the Thunder's chief destroyer, with 30 wickets – another BBL record.

Perth Scorchers, burdened by the tyranny of distance in a condensed schedule, missed the knockouts for a second straight season after qualifying in the previous seven. Like de Villiers himself, **Brisbane Heat** showed only glimpses of their best; they failed to qualify after being beaten on the last day of the league stage.

That was one of only three wins for defending champions **Melbourne Renegades**, who lost their first nine matches in a horrendous season under new coach Michael Klinger. He had taken over less than a month before the first game, when Andrew McDonald became assistant coach to the national side.

BIG BASH LEAGUE AVERAGES IN 2019-20

BATTING (250 runs)

		M	*I*	*NO*	*R*	*HS*	*100*	*50*	*Avge*	*SR*	*4*	*6*
1	†M. S. Wade (*Hobart H*)	9	8	1	351	130*	1	3	50.14	**171.21**	30	15
2	P. D. Salt (*Adelaide S*)	15	15	1	361	67*	0	4	25.78	**164.09**	45	12
3	J. P. Inglis (*Perth S*)	14	14	0	405	73	0	4	28.92	**153.99**	41	15
4	C. A. Lynn (*Brisbane H*)	14	14	1	387	94	0	2	29.76	**148.84**	36	23
5	G. J. Maxwell (*Melbourne S*)	17	16	6	398	83*	0	3	39.80	**148.50**	28	20
6	M. C. Henriques (*Sydney S*)	14	14	3	267	72	0	1	24.27	**148.33**	12	15
7	A. D. Hales (*Sydney T*)	17	17	2	576	85	0	6	38.40	**146.93**	59	23
8	M. R. Marsh (*Perth S*)	14	14	3	382	93*	0	2	34.72	**145.24**	19	20
9	S. B. Harper (*Melbourne R*)	12	12	1	279	73	0	2	25.36	**144.55**	28	10
10	L. S. Livingstone (*Perth S*)	14	14	0	425	79	0	4	30.35	**142.61**	26	27
11	A. J. Finch (*Melbourne R*)	9	9	1	363	109	1	3	45.37	**139.08**	23	16
12	N. C. R. Larkin (*Melbourne S*)	14	11	3	297	83*	0	2	37.12	**136.86**	29	8
13	M. P. Stoinis (*Melbourne S*)	17	17	4	705	147*	1	6	54.23	**136.62**	62	28
14	J. W. Wells (*Adelaide S*)	15	14	7	478	68*	0	4	68.28	**135.41**	38	9
15	†J. B. Weatherald (*Adelaide S*)	15	15	1	407	83	0	2	29.07	**133.88**	47	13
16	B. J. Webster (*Melbourne R*)	14	14	4	425	67*	0	3	42.50	**131.98**	26	17
17	†D. J. M. Short (*Hobart H*)	9	9	1	357	103*	1	3	44.62	**131.25**	28	14
18	A. I. Ross (*Sydney T*)	17	15	5	372	58	0	2	37.20	**130.06**	25	14
19	J. R. Philippe (*Sydney S*)	16	16	3	487	83*	0	5	37.46	**129.86**	41	16
20	†M. T. Renshaw (*Brisbane H*)	14	14	2	348	65	0	3	29.00	**129.85**	27	13
21	C. J. Ferguson (*Sydney T*)	17	17	4	376	73*	0	3	28.92	**126.59**	35	8
22	†A. T. Carey (*Adelaide S*)	11	11	0	391	55	0	1	35.54	**125.32**	30	13
23	†U. T Khawaja (*Sydney T*)	17	17	0	388	66	0	3	22.82	**124.35**	42	5
24	†D. P. Hughes (*Sydney S*)	16	15	2	267	40	0	0	20.53	**124.18**	28	4
25	†S. E. Marsh (*Melbourne R*)	12	12	0	449	63	0	3	37.41	**124.03**	40	14
26	J. M. Vince (*Sydney S*)	15	15	1	323	51	0	1	23.07	**123.28**	24	9
27	B. R. McDermott (*Hobart H*)	15	14	4	265	51*	0	1	26.50	**122.68**	11	11
28	C. T. Bancroft (*Perth S*)	14	13	3	290	51	0	2	29.00	**112.84**	16	7

BOWLING (10 wickets)

		Style	*Balls*	*Dots*	*R*	*W*	*BB*	*4I*	*Avge*	*SR*	*ER*
1	R. P. Meredith (*Hobart H*)	RFM	123	54	137	10	3-26	0	13.70	12.30	**6.68**
2	Fawad Ahmed (*Perth S*)	LB	324	111	373	15	3-16	0	24.86	21.60	**6.90**
3	K. W. Richardson (*Melb R*)	RFM	187	76	218	10	4-22	2	21.80	18.70	**6.99**
4	G. J. Maxwell (*Melbourne S*)	OB	222	64	260	10	2-15	0	26.00	22.20	**7.02**
5	Haris Rauf (*Melbourne S*)	RFM	227	96	267	20	5-27	1	13.35	11.35	**7.05**
6	J. A. Richardson (*Perth S*)	RFM	318	144	375	15	4-19	1	25.00	21.20	**7.07**
7	L. A. J. Pope (*Sydney S*)	LB	168	60	200	10	3-23	0	20.00	16.80	**7.14**
8	Rashid Khan (*Adelaide S*)	LB	332	120	396	19	4-22	1	20.84	17.47	**7.15**

		Style	*Balls*	*Dots*	*R*	*W*	*BB*	*4I*	*Avge*	*SR*	*ER*
9	P. M. Siddle (*Adelaide S*) .	RFM	289	124	346	19	4-33	1	18.21	15.21	**7.18**
10	A. Zampa (*Melbourne S*)	LB	270	93	324	20	3-21	0	16.20	13.50	**7.20**
11	J. M. Bird (*Sydney S*) . . .	RFM	198	87	240	10	3-33	0	24.00	19.80	**7.27**
12	S. A. Abbott (*Sydney S*) . .	RFM	156	58	190	14	3-20	0	13.57	11.14	**7.30**
13	S. Lamichhane (*Melb S*) . .	LB	270	97	335	15	3-26	0	22.33	18.00	**7.44**
14	C. J. Boyce (*Melbourne R*)	LB	318	80	395	14	4-15	1	28.21	22.71	**7.45**
15	N. M. Coulter-Nile (*Melb S*)	RFM	228	86	286	10	2-14	0	28.60	22.80	**7.52**
16	J. P. Faulkner (*Hobart H*)	LFM	126	51	161	10	3-26	0	16.10	12.60	**7.66**
17	J. D. Cook (*Sydney T*) . . .	LB	252	84	327	13	4-21	1	25.15	19.38	**7.78**
18	D. R. Sams (*Sydney T*) . .	LFM	353	129	461	30	4-34	1	15.36	11.76	**7.83**
19	J. K. Lalor (*Brisbane H*) .	LFM	228	101	301	11	3-21	0	27.36	20.72	**7.92**
20	N. T. Ellis (*Hobart H*). . .	RFM	305	103	404	12	3-15	0	33.66	25.41	**7.94**
21	C. H. Morris (*Sydney T*) .	RFM	319	125	426	22	3-27	0	19.36	14.50	**8.01**
22	B. J. Dwarshuis (*Sydney S*)	LFM	313	128	419	16	2-15	0	26.18	19.56	**8.03**
23	M. G. Neser (*Adelaide S*)	RFM	202	67	273	10	2-14	0	27.30	20.20	**8.10**
24	Qais Ahmad (*Hobart H*) .	LB	300	84	407	12	4-12	1	33.91	25.00	**8.14**
25	S. M. Boland (*Hobart H*)	RFM	228	86	315	15	3-16	0	21.00	15.20	**8.28**
26	C. J. Jordan (*Perth S*) . . .	RFM	258	85	374	15	3-28	0	24.93	17.20	**8.69**
27	B. Laughlin (*Brisbane H*)	RFM	264	81	386	15	3-31	0	25.73	17.60	**8.77**
28	B. C. J. Cutting (*Brisbane H*)	RF	188	47	276	11	2-24	0	25.09	17.09	**8.80**
29	W. A. Agar (*Adelaide S*).	RFM	246	96	365	17	4-33	1	21.47	14.47	**8.90**
30	T. M. Curran (*Sydney S*) .	RFM	283	96	427	22	4-22	1	19.40	12.86	**9.05**

KFC TWENTY20 BIG BASH LEAGUE IN 2019-20

	P	*W*	*L*	*A*	*Pts*	*NRR*
MELBOURNE STARS . . .	14	10	4	0	20	0.52
SYDNEY SIXERS	14	9	4	1	19	0.26
ADELAIDE STRIKERS. . .	14	8	5	1	17	0.56
HOBART HURRICANES .	14	6	7	1	13	–0.35
SYDNEY THUNDER	14	6	7	1	13	–0.44
Perth Scorchers	14	6	8	0	12	–0.02
Brisbane Heat.	14	6	8	0	12	–0.23
Melbourne Renegades	14	3	11	0	6	–0.34

4th v 5th At Hobart, January 30, 2020 (floodlit). **Sydney Thunder won by 57 runs.** ‡**Sydney Thunder 197-5** (20 overs) (U. T. Khawaja 54, A. D. Hales 60, C. J. Ferguson 33); **Hobart Hurricanes 140** (18.3 overs) (D. J. M. Short 37; J. D. Cook 4-21, C. H. Morris 3-27). *PoM:* J. D. Cook. *The Thunder rolled to victory after Usman Khawaja and Alex Hales gave them a platform of 103 inside ten overs. Despite 4–9–18–1 from Nathan Ellis, who didn't concede a boundary, they set a target of nearly 200. Leg-spinner Jono Cook dismissed both Hurricanes openers, and picked up two more in his final over. Chris Morris finished with three, including George Bailey in his final innings before retirement: he hit three fours in six balls, then pulled his seventh to midwicket. Commentating on TV, former Test captain Ricky Ponting accused Hales of "cheating" when he stepped outside the inner circle just after the bowler had delivered the ball – now sanctioned by the revised Law on fielding. Hales later tweeted that Ponting's claim was "pretty average".*

1st v 2nd At Melbourne, January 31, 2020 (floodlit). **Sydney Sixers won by 43 runs. Sydney Sixers 142-7** (20 overs) (J. R. Philippe 34; A. Zampa 3-21); ‡**Melbourne Stars 99** (18 overs) (S. A. Abbott 3-23). *PoM:* S. N. J. O'Keefe. *The Sixers secured a home final by beating the Stars in a low-scoring game. Glenn Maxwell deployed eight bowlers to keep the Sixers off-balance, and Adam Zampa's leg-breaks accounted for three, including Steve Smith for 24. But the Stars succumbed for their lowest all-out total, with only three reaching double figures; Steve O'Keefe took two catches in addition to two middle-order wickets.*

3rd v winners of first play-off At Adelaide, February 1, 2020 (floodlit). **Sydney Thunder won by eight runs. Sydney Thunder 151-7** (20 overs) (A. D. Hales 59); **‡Adelaide Strikers 143-9** (20 overs) (T. M. Head 32, J. W. Wells 34; D. R. Sams 3-26). *PoM:* A. D. Hales. *Sydney Thunder scraped through in the closest of the play-offs. Rain had freshened up the pitch, and only Hales looked comfortable, striking four sixes in his 35-ball 59; Morris provided a late cameo of 21 in 14. Jon Wells had a chance of steering the Strikers to victory from 115-3 but, once Alex Carey was run out, they lost six for 24, concluding with Wells.*

Losers of second play-off v winners of third play-off At Melbourne, February 6, 2020 (floodlit). **Melbourne Stars won by 28 runs. ‡Melbourne Stars 194-2** (20 overs) (M. P. Stoinis 83, N. C. R. Larkin 83*); **Sydney Thunder 166-8** (20 overs) (A. I. Ross 58, A. J. Nair 30; Haris Rauf 3-17). *PoM:* N. C. R. Larkin. *The Stars reached their second successive final on the back of solid batting from Marcus Stoinis and Nick Larkin, who added 117 in 13 overs for the second wicket; Stoinis passed D'Arcy Short's BBL record of 637 runs in a tournament. Their eventual 194-2 was almost double what they had made against the Sixers six days earlier. Haris Rauf returned 4–13–17–3 to pin back the Thunder, and Zampa removed both Alex Ross and Arjun Nair, who put on 58 for the fifth wicket, the only half-century stand of the innings.*

FINAL

SYDNEY SIXERS v MELBOURNE STARS

At Sydney, February 8, 2020 (floodlit). Sydney Sixers won by 19 runs. Toss: Melbourne Stars.

For several days beforehand, it appeared unlikely this match would be played: heavy rain in Sydney forced Cricket Australia to move a bushfire relief match, planned as a curtain-raiser, to Melbourne. To the credit of the SCG groundstaff, the pitch was ready in time for a 12-over game. But there was more heartbreak for the Stars, who lost the final for the second year running; they had played 12 knockout fixtures since 2011-12, and won three. Player of the Match was opener Josh Philippe, who had initially turned down the chance to move from Perth Scorchers the previous season, before a call from Steve Smith convinced him. The Sixers' persistence was vindicated by his mature 52 from 29 balls; he batted throughout the innings, though Zampa bowled him with the final delivery. Chasing 117, the Stars collapsed horribly, after Lyon dismissed their leading batsman, Stoinis, with the fourth ball. They were 25 for four in the fifth over, and 54 for six in the ninth, with two each for Lyon and fellow spinner O'Keefe.

Player of the Match: J. R. Philippe. *Player of the Tournament:* M. P. Stoinis.

Sydney Sixers

		B	*4/6*
1 †J. R. Philippe *b 9*	52	29	4/3
2 J. M. Vince *c 8 b 10*	2	9	0
3 S. P. D. Smith *c 5 b 3*	21	12	2/1
4 *M. C. Henriques *b 9*	7	6	0
5 D. P. Hughes *lbw b 3*	0	1	0
6 J. C. Silk *not out*	27	15	1/1
Lb 3, w 4	7		
3 overs: 26-1 (12 overs)	116-5		

1/15 2/49 3/67 4/68 5/116

7 S. A. Abbott, 8 B. J. Dwarshuis, 9 S. N. J. O'Keefe, 10 N. M. Lyon and 11 J. R. Hazlewood did not bat.

Worrall 12–5–14–1; Coulter-Nile 12–5–22–0; Haris Rauf 18–2–36–0; Zampa 18–5–24–2; Maxwell 12–2–17–2.

Melbourne Stars

		B	*4/6*
1 M. P. Stoinis *c 7 b 10*	10	4	1/1
2 N. J. Maddinson *c 2 b 11*	0	4	0
3 *G. J. Maxwell *lbw b 9*	5	4	1
4 N. C. R. Larkin *not out*	38	26	2/2
5 P. S. P. Handscomb *run out (3/7)*	6	8	0
6 B. R. Dunk *lbw b 10*	11	9	0/1
7 †S. E. Gotch *c 7 b 9*	8	9	0
8 N. M. Coulter-Nile *not out*	19	8	1/1
3 overs: 19-3 (12 overs)	97-6		

1/10 2/14 3/18 4/25 5/40 6/54

9 A. Zampa, 10 D. J. Worrall and 11 Haris Rauf did not bat.

Lyon 12–5–19–2; Hazlewood 18–9–18–1; O'Keefe 18–3–27–2; Abbott 12–4–19–0; Dwarshuis 12–6–14–0.

Umpires: G. A. Abood and P. Wilson. Third umpire: S. A. J. Craig.
Referee: D. J. Harper.

BIG BASH FINALS

2011-12	SYDNEY SIXERS beat Perth Scorchers by seven wickets at Perth.
2012-13	BRISBANE HEAT beat Perth Scorchers by 34 runs at Perth.
2013-14	PERTH SCORCHERS beat Hobart Hurricanes by 39 runs at Perth.
2014-15	PERTH SCORCHERS beat Sydney Sixers by four wickets at Canberra.
2015-16	SYDNEY THUNDER beat Melbourne Stars by three wickets at Melbourne.
2016-17	PERTH SCORCHERS beat Sydney Sixers by nine wickets at Perth.
2017-18	ADELAIDE STRIKERS beat Hobart Hurricanes by 25 runs at Adelaide.
2018-19	MELBOURNE RENEGADES beat Melbourne Stars by 13 runs at Melbourne (Dock).
2019-20	SYDNEY SIXERS beat Melbourne Stars by 19 runs at Sydney.

BIG BASH LEAGUE RECORDS

Highest score	**147***	**M. P. Stoinis**	**Melbourne S v Sydney S at Melbourne**	2019-20
	130*	**M. S. Wade**	**Hobart H v Adelaide S at Adelaide**	**2019-20**
	122*	D. J. M. Short	Hobart H v Brisbane H at Brisbane	2017-18
Fastest 50 – balls	12	C. H. Gayle	Melbourne R v Adelaide S at Melbourne	2015-16
Fastest 100 – balls	39	C. J. Simmons	Perth S v Adelaide S at Perth	2013-14
Most sixes – innings	11	C. H. Gayle	Sydney T v Adelaide S at Sydney	2011-12
	11	C. J. Simmons	Perth S v Sydney S at Sydney	2013-14
	11	C. A. Lynn	Brisbane H v Perth S at Perth	2016-17
	11	**C. A. Lynn**	**Brisbane H v Sydney S at Sydney**	**2019-20**

Most runs – season	**705**	**M. P. Stoinis (avge 54.23, SR 136.62) for Melbourne S**	2019-20
Most sixes – season	**28**	**M. P. Stoinis for Melbourne S**	**2019-20**

Most runs – career	**2,332**	**C. A. Lynn (avge 37.61, SR 150.35)**	**2011-12 to 2019-20**
	2,252	**A. J. Finch (avge 38.82, SR 136.65)**	**2011-12 to 2019-20**
Most 100s – career	**2**	**A. J. Finch (2011-12 to 2019-20), U. T. Khawaja (2011-12 to 2019-20), D. J. M. Short (2016-17 to 2019-20)**, C. J. Simmons (2013-14 to 2015-16), L. J. Wright (2011-12 to 2017-18)	
Best SR – career†	**150.35**	**C. A. Lynn (2,332 runs, avge 37.61)**	**2011-12 to 2019-20**
Most sixes – career	**146**	**C. A. Lynn**	**2011-12 to 2019-20**

Best bowling	6-7	S. L. Malinga	Melbourne S v Perth S at Perth	2012-13
	6-11	I. S. Sodhi	Adelaide S v Sydney T at Sydney	2016-17
	5-14	D. T. Christian	Hobart H v Adelaide S at Hobart	2016-17
Most econ four overs	3-3	M. G. Johnson	Perth S v Melbourne S at Perth	2016-17
Most expensive analysis	**0-61**	**B. J. Dwarshuis**	**Sydney S v Melb S at Melbourne**	**2019-20**

Most wickets – season	**30**	**D. R. Sams (avge 15.36, ER 7.83) for Sydney T**	**2019-20**

Most wickets – career	**110**	**B. Laughlin (avge 22.12, ER 8.00)**	**2011-12 to 2019-20**
	99	**S. A. Abbott (avge 21.21, ER 8.47)**	**2011-12 to 2019-20**
Best ER – career‡	5.40	S. L. Malinga (300 balls, avge 15.00)	2012-13 to 2013-14

Highest total	223-8	Hobart H v Melbourne R at Melbourne (Dock)	2016-17
	222-4	Melbourne R v Hobart H at Melbourne (Dock)	2016-17
Lowest total	57	Melbourne R v Melbourne S at Melbourne (Dock)	2014-15
Highest successful chase	223-8	Hobart H v Melbourne R at Melbourne (Dock)	2016-17
Highest match aggregate	445-12	Melbourne R v Hobart H at Melbourne (Dock)	2016-17

† *Career strike-rate: minimum 500 runs.* ‡ *Career economy-rate: minimum 300 balls.*

BANGABANDHU BANGLADESH PREMIER LEAGUE IN 2019-20

MOHAMMAD ISAM

1 Rajshahi Royals   2 Khulna Tigers

The size of Andre Russell's cheque was undisclosed, although the widely rumoured figure was $350,000, making him the highest-paid player in the Bangladesh Premier League. He lived up to his billing (and bill) with two crucial interventions in the knockout stages that powered **Rajshahi Royals** to the title.

For a time, it seemed the seventh edition of the tournament might not happen. Having failed to reach an agreement with the franchises regarding revenue-sharing, the Bangladesh Cricket Board decided to scrap the franchise model for one year. This resulted in new team names, though at a late stage the board invited corporate backers. Eventually, only Comilla Warriors were completely run by the BCB.

Russell's salary was taken care of by Rajshahi's sponsors, who enjoyed a return on their investment in the final play-off, against Chattogram Challengers, with an unbeaten 54 off 22 balls as Rajshahi sneaked home by two wickets. In the final, he contributed 27 off 16 to an unbroken partnership of 71 with Mohammad Nawaz, then took two Khulna Tigers wickets to set up a comfortable 21-run victory. "They trusted my ability, and I believe in myself to get the job done," said Russell, named Player of the Tournament.

He led a formidable line-up. Ravi Bopara, Mohammad Irfan and Shoaib Malik added to their overseas strength, and the home-grown players appeared determined not to live in their shadows. Liton Das and Afif Hossain made a powerful opening pair, contributing 825 runs between them. And their bowlers formed a cohesive unit, with Irfan and Russell each taking 14 wickets.

Khulna Tigers boasted the competition's top two run-scorers. Rilee Rossouw's 495 runs at 45 made him the most prolific batsman for the second year running, just ahead of Mushfiqur Rahim (491 at 70). In Nazmul Hossain, Khulna also had one of the tournament's three century-makers: he smashed an undefeated 115 off 57 in a huge chase against Dhaka Platoon. But Khulna's outstanding performance came from Pakistan left-arm seamer Mohammad Amir in the 1st v 2nd play-off against Rajshahi. He took six for 17, career-best T20 figures, and the best in BPL history. Amir was one of four bowlers to take 20 wickets, a landmark also reached by his team-mate and fellow seamer, South African Robbie Frylinck.

Chattogram Challengers invested in the fading box-office potential of Chris Gayle, and in four matches he hit 144 runs. Their real stars, however, were home-grown: Imrul Kayes made 442 at 49, while Rubel Hossain was one of the 20-wicket quartet. **Dhaka Platoon**, the fourth qualifiers for the knockout matches, relied on the runs of Tamim Iqbal and the wickets of Mehedi Hasan snr, plus Pakistan duo Shadab Khan and Wahab Riaz.

The top four were comfortably ahead of the pack, though Dawid Malan enjoyed a superb tournament for **Comilla Warriors**, hitting 444 at 49. Against

Rajshahi, he smashed a century off 54 balls (his team's next-highest score was 20), but still finished on the losing side. Team-mate Mujeeb Zadran, the Afghan off-spinner, comfortably proved the tournament's most unhittable bowler, going for barely five an over. Beset by internal strife, **Rangpur Rangers** struggled, despite having one of the competition's most potent strike weapons in Mustafizur Rahman, who took 20 wickets at 15. In his first overseas T20 engagement, England's Lewis Gregory proved a useful acquisition with 262 runs and 15 wickets. His Somerset colleague Tom Abell was one of three players to captain Rangpur.

With just one win, **Sylhet Thunder** had a miserable time, although Grenadian Andre Fletcher slammed a 53-ball hundred against Khulna. They were also the subject of a BCB anti-corruption investigation, after Jamaican seamer Krishmar Santokie bowled a huge no-ball in the opening match, against Chattogram. He was later cleared.

BANGLADESH PREMIER LEAGUE AVERAGES IN 2019-20

BATTING (200 runs)

	M	*I*	*NO*	*R*	*HS*	*100*	*50*	*Avge*	*SR*	*4*	*6*
1 A. D. Russell (*Rajshahi R*)	13	11	7	225	54*	0	1	56.25	**180.00**	12	21
2 Mahmudullah (*Chgram C*)	7	7	2	201	59	0	1	40.20	**170.33**	12	15
3 W. I. A. Fernando (*Chgram C*)	6	6	0	221	72	0	1	36.83	**164.92**	21	14
4 J. Charles (*Sylhet T*).	11	11	0	296	90	0	2	26.90	**164.44**	29	20
5 †R. R. Rossouw (*Khulna T*)	14	14	3	495	71*	0	4	45.00	**155.17**	43	23
6 Mushfiqur Rahim (*Khulna T*)	14	14	7	491	98*	0	4	70.14	**147.00**	51	15
7 †D. J. Malan (*Comilla W*) . .	11	11	2	444	100*	1	3	49.33	**145.09**	35	19
8 †Nazmul Hossain (*Khulna T*)	11	11	2	308	115*	1	1	34.22	**143.92**	28	13
9 C. A. K. Walton (*Chgram C*)	14	14	5	316	71*	0	2	35.11	**141.07**	19	20
10 †Soumya Sarkar (*Comilla W*)	12	12	2	331	88*	0	2	33.10	**140.25**	34	14
11 L. Gregory (*Rangpur R*) . .	11	11	1	262	76*	0	1	26.20	**140.10**	21	13
12 Mehedi Hasan snr (*Dhaka P*).	13	12	1	253	68*	0	3	23.00	**136.02**	17	17
13 Liton Das (*Rajshahi R*) . . .	15	15	1	455	75	0	3	32.50	**134.21**	47	15
14 †Imrul Kayes (*Chattogram C*) .	13	13	4	442	67*	0	4	49.11	**132.33**	37	22
15 †Afif Hossain (*Rajshahi R*) .	15	14	0	370	76	0	1	26.42	**131.20**	41	13
16 L. M. P. Simmons (*Chgram C*)	9	9	0	293	57	0	3	32.55	**130.80**	22	19
17 Mehedi Hasan (*Khulna T*).	14	11	2	290	87*	0	2	32.22	**130.63**	27	11
18 Shoaib Malik (*Rajshahi R*)	15	15	3	455	87	0	3	37.91	**130.00**	40	17
19 A. D. S. Fletcher (*Sylhet T*)	10	10	1	255	103*	1	0	28.33	**129.44**	26	11
20 Mithun Ali (*Sylhet T*)	12	12	2	349	84*	0	2	34.90	**123.75**	19	14
21 †Mominul Haque (*Dhaka P*)	10	8	1	297	91	0	2	42.42	**122.22**	24	7
22 †Mohammad Naim (*Rpur R*)	12	12	1	359	78	0	2	32.63	**115.43**	36	13
23 Sabbir Rahman (*Comilla W*)	11	11	0	204	62	0	1	18.54	**112.08**	19	5
24 †Tamim Iqbal (*Dhaka P*). . .	12	12	2	396	74	0	3	39.60	**109.39**	36	11

BOWLING (8 wickets, economy-rate 10.00)

	Style	*Balls*	*Dots*	*R*	*W*	*BB*	*4I*	*Avge*	*SR*	*ER*
1 Mujeeb Zadran (*Comilla W*)	OB	282	152	238	15	4-12	1	15.86	18.80	**5.06**
2 Mohammad Irfan (*Rajsh R*) .	LFM	282	153	265	14	2-13	0	18.92	20.14	**5.63**
3 Wahab Riaz (*Dhaka P*). . .	LF	154	67	167	10	5-8	1	16.70	15.40	**6.50**
4 Mohammad Nabi (*Rpur R*) . .	OB	246	87	273	11	2-21	0	24.81	22.36	**6.65**
5 Mehedi Hasan snr (*Dhaka P*)	OB	243	129	274	12	3-13	0	22.83	20.25	**6.76**
6 Shadab Khan (*Dhaka P*). .	LB	208	84	240	11	2-14	0	21.81	18.90	**6.92**
7 R. S. Bopara (*Rajshahi R*)	RM	166	56	193	9	2-10	0	21.44	18.44	**6.97**
8 Mustafizur Rahman (*Rpur R*)	LFM	267	139	312	20	3-10	0	15.60	13.35	**7.01**

		Style	Balls	Dots	R	W	BB	4I	Avge	SR	ER
9	Mohammad Amir (*Khulna T*)	LFM	302	131	355	20	6-17	1	17.75	15.10	**7.05**
10	Ebadat Hossain (*Sylhet T*)	RFM	258	125	314	14	3-33	0	22.42	18.42	**7.30**
11	Rubel Hossain (*Chgram C*) .	RFM	293	121	357	20	3-17	0	17.85	14.65	**7.31**
12	R. Frylinck (*Khulna T*) . . .	RFM	318	146	392	20	5-16	1	19.60	15.90	**7.39**
13	Mehedi Hasan Rana (*Chg C*)	LFM	228	108	285	18	4-23	2	15.83	12.66	**7.50**
14	Mashrafe bin Mortaza (*Dhk P*)	RFM	258	111	328	8	2-18	0	41.00	32.25	**7.62**
15	L. Gregory (*Rangpur R*) . .	RFM	234	82	298	15	2-25	0	19.86	15.60	**7.64**
16	Shahidul Islam (*Khulna T*)	RM	294	120	396	19	4-23	1	20.84	15.47	**8.08**
17	Soumya Sarkar (*Comilla W*) .	RFM	203	58	290	12	2-12	0	24.16	16.91	**8.57**
18	A. D. Russell (*Rajshahi R*)	RFM	246	105	359	14	4-37	1	25.64	17.57	**8.75**
19	K. Santokie (*Sylhet T*). . . .	LM	161	67	239	8	3-13	0	29.87	20.12	**8.90**
20	Kamrul Islam (*Rajshahi R*)	RFM	183	64	272	9	2-23	0	30.22	20.33	**8.91**
21	Shafiul Islam (*Khulna T*) .	RFM	288	106	431	9	3-21	0	47.88	32.00	**8.97**
22	Taskin Ahmed (*Rangpur R*) .	RFM	156	55	238	11	4-29	1	21.63	14.18	**9.15**
23	Hasan Mahmud (*Dhaka P*)	RM	247	88	379	10	4-32	1	37.90	24.70	**9.20**
24	Al-Amin Hossain (*Com W*)	RFM	245	80	387	12	3-14	0	32.25	20.41	**9.47**
25	Mukhtar Ali (*Chgram C*) .	RFM	166	49	267	8	3-42	0	33.37	20.75	**9.65**
26	K. O. K. Williams (*Chg C*) . .	RFM	155	40	251	8	2-21	0	31.37	19.37	**9.71**

BANGLADESH PREMIER LEAGUE IN 2019-20

	P	W	L	Pts	NRR
KHULNA TIGERS.	12	8	4	16	0.91
RAJSHAHI ROYALS	12	8	4	16	0.42
CHATTOGRAM CHALLENGERS. . .	12	8	4	16	0.12
DHAKA PLATOON.	12	7	5	14	0.57
Comilla Warriors	12	5	7	10	–0.33
Rangpur Rangers	12	5	7	10	–0.82
Sylhet Thunder.	12	1	11	2	–0.82

3rd v 4th At Mirpur, January 13, 2020. **Chattogram Challengers won by seven wickets. Dhaka Platoon 144-8** (20 overs) (Mominul Haque 31, Shadab Khan 64*; R. R. Emrit 3-23); ‡**Chattogram Challengers 147-3** (17.4 overs) (C. H. Gayle 38, Imrul Kayes 32, Mahmudullah 34*). *PoM:* R. R. Emrit. *A brilliant early bowling performance – backing up Mahmudullah's decision to put Dhaka in – laid the foundations for Chattogram's comfortable progress. Dhaka had been 60-7 before Shadab Khan's 64* off 41 gave them something to defend. Chris Gayle slipped into the unfamiliar anchor role, before Mahmudullah hammered 34* off 14.*

1st v 2nd At Mirpur, January 13, 2020 (floodlit). **Khulna Tigers won by 27 runs. Khulna Tigers 158-3** (20 overs) (Nazmul Hossain 78*, Shamsur Rahman 32); ‡**Rajshahi Royals 131** (20 overs) (Shoaib Malik 80; Mohammad Amir 6-17). *PoM:* Mohammad Amir. *Rajshahi's powerful batting line-up must have been confident of overhauling Khulna's 158-3. But they were blown away by Mohammad Amir. He took four wickets in his first three overs – including Andre Russell for a duck – as Rajshahi slumped to 23-5. Shoaib Malik rescued them from humiliation, but Amir returned to complete figures of 6-17, the best in BPL history, and secure Khulna's place in the final. They were also indebted to Nazmul Hossain's patient 78*.*

Final play-off At Mirpur, January 15, 2020 (floodlit). **Rajshahi Royals won by two wickets. Chattogram Challengers 164-9** (20 overs) (C. H. Gayle 60, Mahmudullah 33, D. A. S. Gunaratne 31); ‡**Rajshahi Royals 165-8** (19.2 overs) (Irfan Sukkur 45, A. D. Russell 54*). *PoM:* A. D. Russell. *A thrilling late intervention from Russell wrestled the game from Chattogram's grasp, and took Rajshahi into the final. He hoisted an Asela Gunaratne no-ball over midwicket for the seventh six of his 22-ball half-century, to win the match with four to spare. Just as critical – if less explosive – was Irfan Sukkur's 45 off 42. Chattogram had been boosted by Gayle's 60 off 24, only his second fifty in his last 18 T20 innings.*

Final At Mirpur, January 17, 2020 (floodlit). **Rajshahi Royals won by 21 runs. Rajshahi Royals 170-4** (20 overs) (Irfan Sukkur 52, Mohammad Nawaz 41*); ‡**Khulna Tigers 149-8** (20 overs) (Shamsur Rahman 52, R. R. Rossouw 37). *PoM:* A. D. Russell. *PoT:* A. D. Russell. *The partnership between Russell (27*) and Mohammad Nawaz proved the difference. After Sukkur had again given Rajshahi a solid base, they added 71* off 34 balls to set a target that proved too steep for Khulna.*

Both then made a key contribution with the ball: Nawaz removed Rilee Rossouw to break a third-wicket partnership of 74 in nine overs with Shamsur Rahman. Then Russell yorked Mushfiqur Rahim. After a tournament of poor attendances, the BCB were cheered by a larger than expected crowd.

BPL FINALS

2011-12 DHAKA GLADIATORS beat Barisal Burners by eight wickets at Mirpur.
2012-13 DHAKA GLADIATORS beat Chittagong Kings by 43 runs at Mirpur.
2015-16 COMILLA VICTORIANS beat Barisal Bulls by three wickets at Mirpur.
2016-17 DHAKA DYNAMITES beat Rajshahi Kings by 56 runs at Mirpur.
2017-18 RANGPUR RIDERS beat Dhaka Dynamites by 57 runs at Mirpur.
2018-19 COMILLA VICTORIANS beat Dhaka Dynamites by 17 runs at Mirpur.
2019-20 RAJSHAHI ROYALS beat Khulna Tigers by 21 runs at Mirpur.

There was no tournament in 2013-14 or 2014-15, following a match-fixing scandal and pay disputes.

BANGLADESH PREMIER LEAGUE RECORDS

Highest score	146*	C. H. Gayle	Rangpur R v Dhaka D at Mirpur	2017-18
	141*	Tamim Iqbal	Comilla V v Dhaka D at Mirpur	2018-19
	126*	C. H. Gayle	Rangpur R v Khulna T at Mirpur	2017-18
Fastest 50 – balls	16	Ahmed Shehzad	Barisal B v D Rajshahi at Mirpur	2011-12
Fastest 100 – balls	40	Ahmed Shehzad	Barisal B v D Rajshahi at Mirpur	2011-12
Most sixes – innings	18	C. H. Gayle	Rangpur R v Dhaka D at Mirpur	2017-18

Most runs – season	558	R. R. Rossouw (avge 69.75, SR 150.00) for Rangpur R	2018-19
Most sixes – season	47	C. H. Gayle for Rangpur R	2017-18

Most runs – career	**2,274**	**Mushfiqur Rahim (avge 37.27, SR 133.92)**	2011-12 to 2019-20
	2,221	**Tamim Iqbal (avge 36.40, SR 120.96)**	**2011-12 to 2019-20**
Most 100s – career	**5**	**C. H. Gayle**	**2011-12 to 2019-20**
Best SR – career†	**165.41**	**A. D. Russell (751 runs, avge 35.76)**	**2011-12 to 2019-20**
Most sixes – career	**132**	**C. H. Gayle**	**2011-12 to 2019-20**

Best bowling	**6-17**	**Mohammad Amir**	**Khulna T v Rajshahi R at Mirpur**	2019-20
	5-6	Mohammad Sami	D Rajshahi v Dhaka G at Mirpur	2011-12
	5-8	**Wahab Riaz**	**Dhaka P v Rajshahi R at Mirpur**	**2019-20**
Most econ four overs	2-5	Shahid Afridi	Sylhet S v Barisal B at Mirpur	2015-16
Most expensive analysis	**2-60**	**Nasir Hossain**	**Chgram C v Dhaka P at Chittagong**	2019-20

Most wickets – season	23	Shakib Al Hasan (avge 17.65, ER 7.25) for Dhaka D	2018-19

Most wickets – career	106	Shakib Al Hasan (avge 17.83, ER 6.73)	2011-12 to 2018-19
	90	**Rubel Hossain (avge 20.85, ER 7.92)**	**2011-12 to 2019-20**
Best ER – career‡	**5.00**	**Mujeeb Zadran (306 balls, 15 wkts)**	**2017-18 to 2019-20**

Highest total	239-4	Rangpur R v Chittagong V at Chittagong	2018-19
	238-4	**Chattogram C v Comilla W at Chittagong**	**2019-20**
Lowest total	44	Khulna T v Rangpur R at Mirpur	2016-17
Highest successful chase	**207-2**	**Khulna T v Dhaka P at Mirpur**	**2019-20**
Highest match aggregate	**460-11**	**Chattogram C v Comilla W at Chittagong**	**2019-20**

† *Career strike-rate: minimum 500 runs.* ‡ *Career economy-rate: minimum 300 balls.*

Team nicknames have varied over the years. Barisal (who did not play in 2019-20) have been known as Burners and Bulls; Chittagong/Chattogram as Kings, Vikings and Challengers; Comilla as Victorians and Warriors; Dhaka as Gladiators, Dynamites and Platoon; Khulna as Royal Bengals, Titans and Tigers; Rajshahi as Duronto Rajshahi, Kings and Royals; Rangpur as Riders and Rangers; and Sylhet as Royals, Superstars and Sixers.

DREAM11 INDIAN PREMIER LEAGUE IN 2020

PAUL RADLEY

In the cold light of a one-sided final, the 2020 IPL felt just like any other: eight teams spend seven weeks playing 60 matches, and at the end **Mumbai Indians** win. This was their fifth title in eight seasons. They finished top of the points table, dominated second-placed **Delhi Capitals** in both the first play-off and the final, and retained the trophy. It seemed fair enough that, amid the pyrotechnics and ticker-tape celebrations staged in front of a few friends, family and sponsors, the question arose of whether they were now the greatest T20 side.

And yet they might not have played at all. The IPL had been forced into exile before: in 2009, the second edition took place in South Africa because of a national election in India, and in 2014 the opening rounds were moved to the United Arab Emirates, for the same reason. At least those tournaments were held at the usual time of year. This time, the Covid-19 pandemic not only drove it back to the UAE, but delayed it six months.

The pandemic created an IPL the like of which had never been seen before. There were no cheerleaders, for a start. Media were not permitted, bar the host broadcasters. The stands in the three venues – Dubai, Sharjah and Abu Dhabi – were empty, because of the stringent safety measures. The only fans anywhere near the live action were the diehards who lined the pavement outside the Sharjah Cricket Stadium, waiting for the ball to be hit over the wall.

The organisers did their best to make things feel normal. Instead of the genteel hum of a Test day at Lord's, used as the baseline soundtrack for TV coverage of the English summer, the IPL tried to match the din of a tournament in India. Noisy ambient sounds were played across the speaker systems, which made for a cacophony under the tented roof of the Dubai stadium. LED screens, 14ft tall, ran the length of the square boundaries at each ground, displaying sponsor messages and images of fans. They must have taken some getting used to, judging by the number of dropped catches in the early games by fielders square of the wicket. Clearly, it was impossible to replicate the frenzy of a packed Wankhede Stadium or Feroz Shah Kotla. After one breathless finish in Sharjah, where he helped the unheralded Rahul Tewatia set up an extraordinary win for **Rajasthan Royals** over **Kings XI Punjab**, Sanju Samson explained the difference. "People who have started playing the IPL this year, I think you should come and play in India," he said. "The fans over there, the atmosphere, the sound – it is amazing."

The measures designed to protect the tournament from Covid-19 were exhaustive. Each of the eight teams chartered a plane to the UAE, with extra flights arranged for late arrivals, such as the England and Australia players who had just finished a white-ball series in Manchester. Next, they checked into biosecure hotels – where most would live for 80 days. Six franchises settled in Dubai, but Mumbai and Kolkata were based in Abu Dhabi, where even stricter regulations demanded that overseas arrivals quarantine in their

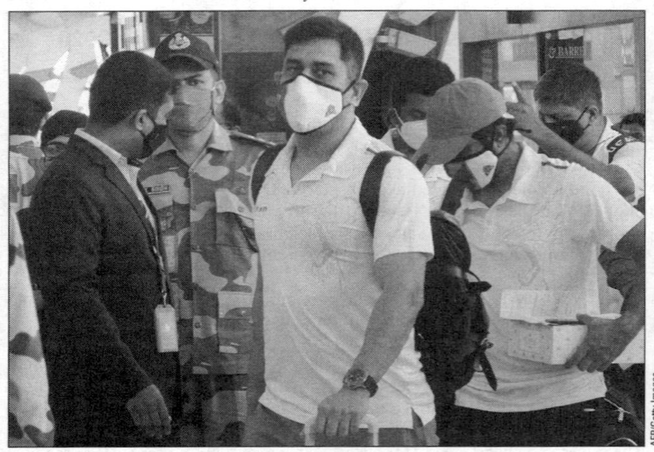

AFP/Getty Images

Cautious start: Mahendra Singh Dhoni prepares to fly to the UAE.

rooms for 14 days. Following discussions with government health authorities, an exemption was secured for the two squads to practise from the eighth day – with extra sterilising precautions, requiring workers in full hazmat suits to fog the net and training areas before and after.

The UAE does not want for five-star opulence, but some sides fared better than others. Rajasthan had rooms with their own patch of lawn, which made the ordeal of their initial solitary confinement more bearable. Later, they had the run of a team room offering table tennis, a pool table, PlayStations and personalised bean bags; they also had their own section of the beach, surrounded by partitions. They shared the swimming pool with other hotel guests, but a timetable gave them exclusive sessions.

On the field, three-time champions **Chennai Super Kings** finished seventh, failing to reach the play-offs for the first time (excluding the two seasons when they were suspended after a betting scandal). There were mitigating factors, and no side were so acutely affected by the Covid crisis: just as they were about to start training after a week's quarantine in Dubai, 13 of their personnel reported positive tests – including two players, Deepak Chahar and Ruturaj Gaikwad, though both made a swift recovery. Meanwhile, star batsman Suresh Raina went home within days of arriving, while veteran off-spinner Harbhajan Singh never made it to the Gulf; both cited personal reasons. Yet Chennai's faltering performance spoke of a deeper issue: their team of high achievers had grown old together, and this was one tournament too many. Shane Watson, the architect of their triumph in the 2018 final, retired as soon as he got back to Australia. But captain M. S. Dhoni – whose powers seemed on the wane –

suggested he would still be around when the rebuilding began, and coach Stephen Fleming said he was looking forward to the challenge of starting a new dynasty.

This was the closest of the 13 IPL tournaments, with only six points between top and bottom. Though Chennai were first to fall by the wayside, they were within a victory of third-placed **Sunrisers Hyderabad**. The winning margins, too, were sometimes gossamer-thin: four matches were tied, and one – between Mumbai and Punjab – needed two super overs. Jofra Archer won the Most Valuable Player award, contributing 20 economical wickets and some useful runs for Rajasthan, who still came last; K. L. Rahul was the leading run-scorer, with 670, but his side, Punjab, were sixth. The leading bowlers, however, belonged to the most successful teams: Kagiso Rabada (Delhi) and Jasprit Bumrah (Mumbai) headed the wicket-takers' lists even before the play-offs, and finished with 30 and 27 respectively. Rashid Khan (Hyderabad), who took 20, conceded less than a run a ball.

Eoin Morgan took over as **Kolkata Knight Riders** captain from Dinesh Karthik midway through, and nearly navigated them into the knockouts. They were beaten to fourth place by **Royal Challengers Bangalore**, led by Virat Kohli and often inspired by the electric batting of A. B. de Villiers. Bangalore initially looked threatening, thanks to the leg-spin of Yuzvendra Chahal and the arrival of stylish young opener Devdutt Padikkal, the Emerging Player of the Tournament. But they went cold in the final throes, and were soundly beaten by David Warner's Hyderabad in the play-offs. Hyderabad, in turn, were no match for Delhi in the last qualifier, despite beating them twice in the league phase.

That victory put Delhi in their first IPL final. But they had already been trounced by Mumbai in three earlier games, and could not gain the upper hand now. From the first ball, they seemed on course for an undignified defeat, when Trent Boult – who had been traded between the sides in the off-season – had Marcus Stoinis caught behind. Mumbai coasted home with five wickets to spare, confirming their batting prowess in a tournament where five of their players – led by the powerful Kieron Pollard –had strike-rates of 140 or more.

INDIAN PREMIER LEAGUE AVERAGES IN 2020

BATTING (250 runs)

		M	*I*	*NO*	*R*	*HS*	*100*	*50*	*Avge*	*SR*	*4*	*6*
1	K. A. Pollard (*Mumbai I*) .	16	12	7	268	60*	0	1	53.60	**191.42**	15	22
2	H. H. Pandya (*Mumbai I*) .	14	13	5	281	60*	0	1	35.12	**178.98**	14	25
3	†N. Pooran (*KXI Punjab*) . .	14	14	4	353	77	0	2	35.30	**169.71**	23	25
4	S. V. Samson (*Raj R*)	14	14	1	375	85	0	3	28.84	**158.89**	21	26
5	A. B. de Villiers (*RC Bang*)	15	14	4	454	73*	0	5	45.40	**158.74**	33	23
6	M. A. Agarwal (*KXI Punj*)	11	11	0	424	106	1	2	38.54	**156.45**	44	15
7	M. P. Stoinis (*Delhi C*) . . .	17	17	3	352	65	0	3	25.14	**148.52**	31	16
8	†I. P. Kishan (*Mumbai I*) . .	14	13	4	516	99	0	4	57.33	**145.76**	36	30

		M	*I*	*NO*	*R*	*HS*	*100*	*50*	*Avge*	*SR*	*4*	*6*
9	S. A. Yadav (*Mumbai I*) . .	16	15	3	480	79*	0	4	40.00	**145.01**	61	11
10	†S. Dhawan (*Delhi C*)	17	17	3	618	106*	2	4	44.14	**144.73**	67	12
11	J. C. Buttler (*Rajasthan R*)	13	12	2	328	70*	0	2	32.80	**144.49**	27	16
12	†B. A. Stokes (*Rajasthan R*)	8	8	1	285	107*	1	1	40.71	**142.50**	36	7
13	F. du Plessis (*Chennai SK*)	13	13	2	449	87*	0	4	40.81	**140.75**	42	14
14	†Q. de Kock (*Mumbai I*). . .	16	16	2	503	78*	0	4	35.92	**140.50**	46	22
15	†R. Tewatia (*Rajasthan R*) .	14	11	5	255	53	0	1	42.50	**139.34**	13	17
16	†N. Rana (*Kolkata KR*). . . .	14	14	0	352	87	0	3	25.14	**138.58**	43	12
17	†E. J. G. Morgan (*Kolk KR*)	14	14	4	418	68*	0	1	41.80	**138.41**	32	24
18	†C. H. Gayle (*KXI Punjab*)	7	7	0	288	99	0	3	41.14	**137.14**	15	23
19	†D. A. Warner (*S Hyd'bad*)	16	16	2	548	85*	0	4	39.14	**134.64**	52	14
20	K. S. Williamson (*S H'bad*)	12	11	4	317	67	0	3	45.28	**133.75**	26	10
21	S. P. D. Smith (*Raj R*). . . .	14	14	2	311	69	0	3	25.91	**131.22**	32	9
22	K. L. Rahul (*KXI Punjab*)	14	14	2	670	132*	1	5	55.83	**129.34**	58	23
23	R. G. Sharma (*Mumbai I*) .	12	12	0	332	80	0	3	27.66	**127.69**	27	19
24	M. K. Pandey (*S Hyd'bad*)	16	15	2	425	83*	0	3	32.69	**127.62**	35	18
25	A. T. Rayudu (*Chennai SK*)	12	11	2	359	71	0	1	39.88	**127.30**	30	12
26	J. M. Bairstow (*S Hyd'bad*)	11	11	0	345	97	0	3	31.36	**126.83**	31	13
27	†D. B. Padikkal (*RC Bang*)	15	15	0	473	74	0	5	31.53	**124.80**	51	8
28	S. S. Iyer (*Delhi C*).	17	17	2	519	88*	0	3	34.60	**123.27**	40	16
29	V. Kohli (*RC Bangalore*) .	15	15	4	466	90*	0	3	42.36	**121.35**	23	11
30	S. R. Watson (*Chennai SK*)	11	11	1	299	83*	0	2	29.90	**121.05**	33	13
31	S. Gill (*Kolkata KR*)	14	14	1	440	70*	0	3	33.84	**117.96**	44	9
32	†R. R. Pant (*Delhi C*)	14	14	3	343	56	0	1	31.18	**113.95**	31	9
33	A. J. Finch (*RC Bangalore*)	12	12	0	268	52	0	1	22.33	**111.20**	28	8

BOWLING (10 wickets)

		Style	*Balls*	*Dots*	*R*	*W*	*BB*	*4I*	*Avge*	*SR*	*ER*
1	Rashid Khan (*S Hyd'bad*)	LB	384	168	344	20	3-7	0	17.20	19.20	**5.37**
2	J. C. Archer (*Rajasthan R*)	RF	334	175	365	20	3-19	0	18.25	16.70	**6.55**
3	C. H. Morris (*RC Bang*) .	RFM	190	91	210	11	4-26	1	19.09	17.27	**6.63**
4	J. J. Bumrah (*Mumbai I*) .	RFM	360	175	404	27	4-14	2	14.96	13.33	**6.73**
5	V. V. Chakravarthy (*KKR*)	LB	312	111	356	17	5-20	1	20.94	18.35	**6.84**
6	Y. S. Chahal (*RC Bang*) .	LB	343	118	405	21	3-18	0	19.28	16.33	**7.08**
7	R. Tewatia (*Rajasthan R*)	LB	276	95	326	10	3-25	0	32.60	27.60	**7.08**
8	S. Sharma (*S Hyd'bad*) . .	RFM	312	119	374	14	3-34	0	26.71	22.28	**7.19**
9	R. Bishnoi (*KXI Punjab*)	LB	306	122	376	12	3-29	0	31.33	25.50	**7.37**
10	M. Ashwin (*KXI Punjab*)	LB	189	70	235	10	3-21	0	23.50	18.90	**7.46**
11	D. L. Chahar (*Chen SK*) .	RFM	312	118	396	12	2-18	0	33.00	26.00	**7.61**
12	R. Ashwin (*Delhi C*). . . .	OB	306	101	391	13	3-29	0	30.07	23.53	**7.66**
13	P. J. Cummins (*Kolk KR*)	RF	312	140	409	12	4-34	1	34.08	26.00	**7.86**
14	T. A. Boult (*Mumbai I*). .	LFM	344	157	457	25	4-18	1	18.28	13.76	**7.97**
15	T. Natarajan (*S Hyd'bad*)	LFM	377	136	504	16	2-24	0	31.50	23.56	**8.02**
16	R. D. Chahar (*Mumbai I*)	LB	318	104	433	15	2-18	0	28.86	21.20	**8.16**
17	S. M. Curran (*Chen SK*) .	LFM	252	91	344	13	3-19	0	26.46	19.38	**8.19**
18	J. O. Holder (*S Hyd'bad*)	RFM	168	58	233	14	3-25	0	16.64	12.00	**8.32**
19	K. Rabada (*Delhi C*)	RF	394	156	548	30	4-24	2	18.26	13.13	**8.34**
20	A. A. Nortje (*Delhi C*) . .	RF	366	160	512	22	3-33	0	23.27	16.63	**8.39**
21	S. N. Thakur (*Chennai SK*)	RFM	194	68	275	10	2-28	0	27.50	19.40	**8.50**
22	R. Shreyas Gopal (*Raj R*)	LB	300	86	427	10	2-28	0	42.70	30.00	**8.54**
23	Mohammed Shami (*KXIP*)	RFM	322	140	460	20	3-15	0	23.00	16.10	**8.57**
24	M. Siraj (*RC Bangalore*)	RFM	163	77	236	11	3-8	0	21.45	14.81	**8.68**
25	J. L. Pattinson (*Mumb I*) .	RFM	213	78	320	11	2-19	0	29.09	19.36	**9.01**
26	M. P. Stoinis (*Delhi C*) . .	RFM	178	50	283	13	3-26	0	21.76	13.69	**9.53**

INDIAN PREMIER LEAGUE IN 2020

	P	*W*	*L*	*Pts*	*NRR*
MUMBAI INDIANS	14	9	5	18	1.10
DELHI CAPITALS	14	8	6	16	−0.10
SUNRISERS HYDERABAD	14	7	7	14	0.60
ROYAL CHALLENGERS BANGALORE	14	7	7	14	−0.17
Kolkata Knight Riders	14	7	7	14	−0.21
Kings XI Punjab	14	6	8	12	−0.16
Chennai Super Kings	14	6	8	12	−0.45
Rajasthan Royals	14	6	8	12	−0.56

At Abu Dhabi, September 19, 2020 (floodlit). **Chennai Super Kings won by five wickets. Mumbai Indians 162-9** (20 overs) (Q. de Kock 33, S. S. Tiwary 42; L. T. Ngidi 3-38); ‡**Chennai Super Kings 166-5** (19.2 overs) (F. du Plessis 58*, A. T. Rayudu 71). *PoM:* A. T. Rayudu. *CSK began by beating the team who had beaten them in the previous final, 16 months earlier in Hyderabad. It meant Mumbai hadn't won their opening match since 2012. Twice they seemed well placed: at 92-2 in the 11th after being put in, then when Chennai were 6-2. But Mumbai had lost seven for 70 in their last 55 balls, and later allowed Faf du Plessis and Ambati Rayudu (71 off 48) to add 115. Still, it needed Sam Curran's six-ball 18 to make things comfortable for CSK.*

At Dubai, September 20, 2020 (floodlit). **Delhi Capitals won the super over, after a tie. Delhi Capitals 157-8** (20 overs) (S. S. Iyer 39, R. R. Pant 31, M. P. Stoinis 53; Mohammed Shami 3-15); ‡**Kings XI Punjab 157-8** (20 overs) (M. A. Agarwal 89). *PoM:* M. P. Stoinis. *An astounding match hinged on the last scheduled over, bowled by Marcus Stoinis. Punjab needed 13, with Mayank Agarwal going great guns; he hit the first three balls for six, two and four to level the scores. But he wafted at the next, and was caught by the sweeper from the fifth, before Chris Jordan clouted a full toss to square leg: three deliveries, two wickets, no runs. Kagiso Rabada needed three balls of the super over to end Punjab's hopes, dismissing batsmen with his second and third, and Delhi waltzed to a target of three. Stoinis had earlier boosted the end of their innings by crashing 49 of the 57 that gushed from the final three overs; Jordan's last cost 30. Agarwal then played a lone hand, and seemed to have done enough – indeed* might *have done enough, had umpire Nitin Menon not imagined a short run in the 19th.*

At Dubai, September 21, 2020 (floodlit). **Royal Challengers Bangalore won by ten runs. Royal Challengers Bangalore 163-5** (20 overs) (D. B. Padikkal 56, A. B. de Villiers 51); ‡**Sunrisers Hyderabad 153** (19.4 overs) (J. M. Bairstow 61, M. K. Pandey 34; Y. S. Chahal 3-18). *PoM:* Y. S. Chahal. *Bangalore's Devdutt Padikkal scored 56 on IPL debut (following half-centuries on first-class, List A and T20 debuts). He put on 90 in 11 overs with Aaron Finch, before A. B. de Villiers hiked the Challengers past 150 with two sixes over extra cover. David Warner was run out in the Sunrisers' second over by a deflection on to the stumps as Umesh Yadav missed a return catch off Jonny Bairstow. But Hyderabad were 121-2, needing 43 off 30, before Yuzvendra Chahal castled Bairstow and Vijay Shankar with successive deliveries; the last eight tumbled for 32. Mitchell Marsh was ruled out of the tournament after twisting his ankle bowling the game's fifth over.*

At Sharjah, September 22, 2020 (floodlit). **Rajasthan Royals won by 16 runs. Rajasthan Royals 216-7** (20 overs) (S. P. D. Smith 69, S. V. Samson 74; S. M. Curran 3-33); ‡**Chennai Super Kings 200-6** (20 overs) (S. R. Watson 33, F. du Plessis 72; R. Tewatia 3-37). *PoM:* S. V. Samson. *Sanju Samson starred for Rajasthan Royals, clattering nine sixes in a 32-ball 74, and putting on 121 in nine overs with Steve Smith. One Piyush Chawla over disappeared for 28. David Miller was run out without facing, then three wickets in seven balls for Sam Curran – taking on brother Tom for the first time in a senior match, after 105 on the same side – seemed to have dragged Chennai back into it. But Jofra Archer (27*) clubbed four successive sixes off Lungi Ngidi, two from no-balls, as the last over cost 30. Du Plessis retaliated with seven sixes of his own in a 37-ball 72, but CSK stalled after Sam Curran and Ruturaj Gaikwad fell in two balls to Rahul Tewatia. M. S. Dhoni surprisingly held himself back to No. 7, by which time they needed 16 an over; he made 29* from 17.*

At Abu Dhabi, September 23, 2020 (floodlit). **Mumbai Indians won by 49 runs. Mumbai Indians 195-5** (20 overs) (R. G. Sharma 80, S. A. Yadav 47); ‡**Kolkata Knight Riders 146-9** (20 overs) (K. D. Karthik 30, P. J. Cummins 33). *PoM:* R. G. Sharma. *Rohit Sharma's powerful 54-ball 80, including six sixes, proved too much for the rusty Knight Riders. Only Sunil Narine (24–8–22–1) went at less than an eight an over as Mumbai racked up 195. Then Trent Boult set the tone with the* *ball, starting with a maiden to Shubman Gill. Kolkata's only headway came when it was too late: Pat Cummins, whose three overs had cost 49, hit four sixes in an over off Jasprit Bumrah, whose first three had cost five.*

At Dubai, September 24, 2020 (floodlit). **Kings XI Punjab won by 97 runs. Kings XI Punjab 206-3** (20 overs) (K. L. Rahul 132*); ‡**Royal Challengers Bangalore 109** (17 overs) (M. S. Washington Sundar 30; R. Bishnoi 3-32, M. Ashwin 3-21). *PoM:* K. L. Rahul. *Rahul's 69-ball 132* – the fourth-best score in the IPL, and the highest either for Punjab or by an Indian – crescendoed brutally with 42 from his last nine. Dale Steyn bore the brunt, with the 19th over costing 26. Rahul, though, could have been caught on 83 and 89; both times the unlikely culprit was Virat Kohli. Needing 207, Bangalore were 4-3 in a trice; leg-spinners Ravi Bishnoi and Murugan Ashwin then shared six wickets to ensure a crushing victory.*

At Dubai, September 25, 2020 (floodlit). **Delhi Capitals won by 44 runs. Delhi Capitals 175-3** (20 overs) (P. P. Shaw 64, S. Dhawan 35, R. R. Pant 37*); ‡**Chennai Super Kings 131-7** (20 overs) (F. du Plessis 43; K. Rabada 3-26). *PoM:* P. P. Shaw. *For the third time in a week, Dhoni chose to chase; for the second time running, it failed. He came in at 98-4, with CSK needing 78 from 26 balls, but scored only 15, as Rabada took three wickets in his last two overs. Earlier, Dhoni had stumped Prithvi Shaw for 64 off 43, after Shaw and Shikhar Dhawan opened with 94 for Delhi in 10.4 overs; Rishabh Pant lifted the target to 176. With Rayudu injured, Chennai relied heavily on du Plessis, but his 43 was not enough.*

At Abu Dhabi, September 26, 2020 (floodlit). **Kolkata Knight Riders won by seven wickets.** ‡**Sunrisers Hyderabad 142-4** (20 overs) (D. A. Warner 36, M. K. Pandey 51, W. P. Saha 30); **Kolkata Knight Riders 145-3** (18 overs) (S. Gill 70*, E. J. G. Morgan 42*). *PoM:* S. Gill. *The Knight Riders' disciplined bowling limited the Sunrisers to 142 after they became the first side in the tournament to choose to bat. Cummins took 1-19 in his four overs, and 29-year-old leg-spinner Varun Chakravarthy 1-25 in only his second IPL match. Kolkata lost Narine for a second-ball duck, but Gill's stand of 92* with Eoin Morgan, who returned to form with 42* from 29, finished the job.*

At Sharjah, September 27, 2020 (floodlit). **Rajasthan Royals won by four wickets. Kings XI Punjab 223-2** (20 overs) (K. L. Rahul 69, M. A. Agarwal 106); ‡**Rajasthan Royals 226-6** (19.3 overs) (S. P. D. Smith 50, S. V. Samson 85, R. Tewatia 53; Mohammed Shami 3-53). *PoM:* S. V. Samson. *A sensational late onslaught by Tewatia inspired the Royals to a record IPL chase, beating their own successful pursuit of 215 against Deccan Chargers at Hyderabad in 2008. Tewatia had laboured to 17 off 23 – "the worst 20 balls I have ever played" – and the requirement was 51 off three overs. But he launched Sheldon Cottrell for five sixes, before Archer hit two more in the 19th, bowled by Mohammed Shami, and Tewatia one. After Tewatia fell for 53 off 31, Tom Curran swatted the winning four with three balls to go. Kings XI appeared to have it sewn up after Rahul (69 off 54) and Agarwal (106 off 50, with ten fours and seven sixes) put on 183 in 16.3 overs, the IPL's third-highest opening stand. Smith (50 off 27) and Samson (85 off 42) then gave Rajasthan an outside chance. But they still needed a miracle – and up stepped Tewatia.*

At Dubai, September 28, 2020 (floodlit). **Royal Challengers Bangalore won the super over, after a tie. Royal Challengers Bangalore 201-3** (20 overs) (D. B. Padikkal 54, A. J. Finch 52, A. B. de Villiers 55*); ‡**Mumbai Indians 201-5** (20 overs) (I. P. Kishan 99, K. A. Pollard 60*). *PoM:* A. B. de Villiers. *Ten games into the tournament came its second tie; never before in the IPL had teams made 200 or more and finished level. With four overs remaining, Mumbai – 80 short of their target – looked out of it. But 49 came from the next two, including 42 by the explosive Kieron Pollard. Ishan Kishan, playing because of injury to Saurabh Tiwary, was almost as destructive, and the pair reached the last needing 19. Kishan perished aiming for the third successive six that would have brought victory, leaving Pollard to take five from the last ball. He managed four, but de Villiers and Kohli kept their heads in the super over. De Villiers had earlier given Bangalore a rousing climax to their main innings too: he and Shivam Dube helped clout 65 from the last four.*

At Abu Dhabi, September 29, 2020 (floodlit). **Sunrisers Hyderabad won by 15 runs. Sunrisers Hyderabad 162-4** (20 overs) (D. A. Warner 45, J. M. Bairstow 53, K. S. Williamson 41); ‡**Delhi Capitals 147-7** (20 overs) (S. Dhawan 34; Rashid Khan 3-14). *PoM:* Rashid Khan. *Warner and Bairstow made a sedate start by their standards – 77 in 9.3 overs – but Kane Williamson, in his first game of the tournament, struck 41 in 26 balls. Then Bhuvneshwar Kumar had Shaw caught behind in Delhi's first over, and Rashid Khan, revelling in a pitch that suited him, collected three top-order wickets for 14. The Sunrisers completed their first victory in three games, which was also the Capitals' first defeat.*

At Dubai, September 30, 2020 (floodlit). **Kolkata Knight Riders won by 37 runs. Kolkata Knight Riders 174-6** (20 overs) (S. Gill 47, E. J. G. Morgan 34*); **‡Rajasthan Royals 137-9** (20 overs) (T. K. Curran 54*). *PoM:* S. P. Mavi. *Despite a rapid spell from Archer, who took 2-18 and hurried Andre Russell (24) and Morgan, KKR reached a solid total, and defended it with ease after another excellent bowling performance. The Royals dipped to 66-6 and, although Tom Curran cracked 54* from 36 (his first IPL half-century), the result was never in doubt. Chakravarthy, fast becoming one of the bowlers to watch, took 2-25 to build on the good work of seamers Shivam Mavi (2-20) and Kamlesh Nagarkoti (2-13).*

At Abu Dhabi, October 1, 2020 (floodlit). **Mumbai Indians won by 48 runs. Mumbai Indians 191-4** (20 overs) (R. G. Sharma 70, K. A. Pollard 47*, H. H. Pandya 30*); **‡Kings XI Punjab 143-8** (20 overs) (N. Pooran 44). *PoM:* K. A. Pollard. *Mumbai won comfortably thanks to Sharma's 45-ball 70 (making him the third player to reach 5,000 IPL runs), followed by blitzes from Pollard (47* off 20) and Hardik Pandya (30* off 11). Pollard hit the last three balls of the innings, from off-spinner Krishnappa Gowtham, for six, as he and Pandya smashed 67* in 3.5 overs. The innings had begun, misleadingly, with a wicket-maiden for Cottrell, whose previous over – against Rajasthan four days earlier – had cost 30. Kings XI were never in the hunt, and only Nicholas Pooran passed 25. Bumrah (24–13–18–2) was all but unhittable.*

At Dubai, October 2, 2020 (floodlit). **Sunrisers Hyderabad won by seven runs. ‡Sunrisers Hyderabad 164-5** (20 overs) (P. K. Garg 51*, A. Sharma 31); **Chennai Super Kings 157-5** (20 overs) (M. S. Dhoni 47*, R. A. Jadeja 50). *PoM:* P. K. Garg. *Hyderabad condemned Chennai to a third straight defeat, their worst sequence since 2014. Not that Hyderabad, labouring to 69-4 in 11 overs, had made an auspicious start. But the 19-year-old Priyam Garg, working like a Trojan in his second IPL innings, crashed 51* off 26. Chennai began disastrously: 42-4 in the ninth, before the experience of Dhoni and Jadeja helped bring 70 from the last four – in vain. For the Sunrisers, Bhuvneshwar suffered a thigh injury that ended his tournament.*

At Abu Dhabi, October 3, 2020. **Royal Challengers Bangalore won by eight wickets. ‡Rajasthan Royals 154-6** (20 overs) (M. K. Lomror 47; Y. S. Chahal 3-24); **Royal Challengers Bangalore 158-2** (19.1 overs) (D. B. Padikkal 63, V. Kohli 72*). *PoM:* Y. S. Chahal. *Kohli returned to form, after 18 in three innings; his 72* steered Bangalore to a big win, and he added 99 in 80 balls with Padikkal, who completed a record three fifties in his first four IPL innings. Earlier, in this tournament's first day game, Mahipal Lomror helped Rajasthan recover from 31-3, before becoming Chahal's third victim. Tewatia and Archer lifted the target to 155, despite a comic incident when Archer, ball-watching, failed to notice Tewatia charging to his end, then charging back; a wild throw prevented a run-out.*

At Sharjah, October 3, 2020 (floodlit). **Delhi Capitals won by 18 runs. Delhi Capitals 228-4** (20 overs) (P. P. Shaw 66, S. S. Iyer 88*, R. R. Pant 38); **‡Kolkata Knight Riders 210-8** (20 overs) (N. Rana 58, E. J. G. Morgan 44, R. A. Tripathi 36; A. A. Nortje 3-33). *PoM:* S. S. Iyer. *After brutal hitting from Shaw (66 from 41) and Iyer (88* from 38, with six sixes) vaulted them to the highest total of the competition, Delhi looked home and dry when Kolkata slipped to 122-6 in the 14th; Russell was already out, as was Nitin Rana, who had made 58 from 35. But KKR kept going, and got closer than expected after needing 78 from four overs: Morgan hit five sixes in an 18-ball 44, and the Capitals could breathe easily only after Rahul Tripathi (36 from 16) was yorked by Stoinis.*

At Sharjah, October 4, 2020. **Mumbai Indians won by 34 runs. ‡Mumbai Indians 208-5** (20 overs) (Q. de Kock 67, I. P. Kishan 31); **Sunrisers Hyderabad 174-7** (20 overs) (D. A. Warner 60, M. K. Pandey 30). *PoM:* T. A. Boult. *The formula that had worked against Kings XI served Mumbai Indians well once more: early runs from an opener (Quinton de Kock, this time, with 67 off 39), then late fireworks from Pollard (25* off 13) and one of the Pandyas. On this occasion, Krunal took up the slack after brother Hardik was yorked by Siddharth Kaul in the final over: Krunal carted the last four balls for 20, leaving Kaul with 2-64, and Mumbai with 208. From 94-1 in the tenth, the Sunrisers fell away, including Warner for a 44-ball 60; Boult finished with 2-28.*

At Dubai, October 4, 2020 (floodlit). **Chennai Super Kings won by ten wickets. ‡Kings XI Punjab 178-4** (20 overs) (K. L. Rahul 63, N. Pooran 33); **Chennai Super Kings 181-0** (17.4 overs) (S. R. Watson 83*, F. du Plessis 87*). *PoM:* S. R. Watson. *Chennai brought a run of three defeats to an emphatic end, thanks to a chanceless opening partnership of 181*, their all-wicket record; Shane Watson and du Plessis each faced 53 balls. The bowler to suffer most was Jordan, back in the Punjab side on his 32nd birthday after a mauling a fortnight earlier. His first over went for 19, as Chennai ended the powerplay on 60-0. Punjab had started strongly too, but from 130-2 after 15, a total of 178-4 felt thin. And so it proved.*

HIGHEST T20 TARGETS REACHED WITHOUT LOSING A WICKET

Target		
184	Kolkata Knight Riders (184-0) beat Gujarat Lions at Rajkot	2016-17
179	**Chennai Super Kings (181-0) beat Kings XI Punjab at Dubai**	**2020**
171	Perth Scorchers (171-0) beat Melbourne Renegades at Melbourne (Docklands)	2015-16
169	New Zealand (171-0) beat Pakistan at Hamilton	2015-16
169	**Limpopo (169-0) beat Western Province at Potchefstroom (University)**	**2019-20**
169	**Wellington Firebirds (169-0) beat Otago Volts at Dunedin**	**2019-20**
166	Barisal Burners (167-0) beat Sylhet Royals at Mirpur	2011-12
166	Free State (166-0) beat Namibia at Kimberley	2017-18
165	Quetta Bears (165-0) beat Larkana Bulls at Karachi	2014-15
163	Mumbai Indians (163-0) beat Rajasthan Royals at Jaipur	2011-12

At Dubai, October 5, 2020 (floodlit). **Delhi Capitals won by 59 runs. Delhi Capitals 196-4** (20 overs) (P. P. Shaw 42, S. Dhawan 32, R. R. Pant 37, M. P. Stoinis 53*); **‡Royal Challengers Bangalore 137-9** (20 overs) (V. Kohli 43; K. Rabada 4-24). *PoM:* A. R. Patel. *Delhi pulled away at the top of the table with their fourth win in five. Shaw and Dhawan shared a third half-century opening stand, before Pant and Stoinis plundered 89 off seven overs. Only Kohli passed 17 in Bangalore's reply. Rabada had him caught behind in a spell of four in 13 deliveries, after the left-arm spin of Akshar Patel (24–10–18–2, and playing because of a finger injury to Amit Mishra) had tied him down. Earlier, Ravichandran Ashwin, who had run out non-striker Jos Buttler in the previous IPL, refrained from doing the same to Finch, but gave him what he said was his "first and final warning for 2020".*

At Abu Dhabi, October 6, 2020 (floodlit). **Mumbai Indians won by 57 runs. ‡Mumbai Indians 193-4** (20 overs) (R. G. Sharma 35, S. A. Yadav 79*, H. H. Pandya 30*); **Rajasthan Royals 136** (18.1 overs) (J. C. Buttler 70; J. J. Bumrah 4-20). *PoM:* S. A. Yadav. *Suryakumar Yadav's IPL-best 79* from 47, and late violence from Hardik Pandya, lifted Mumbai Indians close to 200, even though Pollard never batted. The Royals were 12-3 in the third: Smith fell to Bumrah for his third single-figure score in a row, after starting with two fifties. Buttler organised a recovery, crunching five sixes, but Bumrah returned to complete figures of 24–14–20–4. Mumbai went top.*

At Abu Dhabi, October 7, 2020 (floodlit). **Kolkata Knight Riders won by ten runs. ‡Kolkata Knight Riders 167** (20 overs) (R. A. Tripathi 81; D. J. Bravo 3-37); **Chennai Super Kings 157-5** (20 overs) (S. R. Watson 50, A. T. Rayudu 30). *PoM:* R. A. Tripathi. *CSK's chase was strangled by disciplined Kolkata bowling after they had reached 99-1 in 12 overs, needing just 69 more. Nagarkoti removed Rayudu, before Narine – held back until the business end – conceded only eight off his first two overs, and trapped Watson. With the rate climbing, Dhoni and Curran fell in quick succession to make it 129-5, and 14 from the last three balls – from Russell to Jadeja – made things look closer. Kolkata's innings had hinged on 81 off 51 by Tripathi, opening in place of Narine, whose 17 from No. 4 was the joint-next-best score.*

At Dubai, October 8, 2020 (floodlit). **Sunrisers Hyderabad won by 69 runs. ‡Sunrisers Hyderabad 201-6** (20 overs) (D. A. Warner 52, J. M. Bairstow 97; R. Bishnoi 3-29); **Kings XI Punjab 132** (16.5 overs) (N. Pooran 77; Rashid Khan 3-12). *PoM:* J. M. Bairstow. *When Bishnoi removed Warner to make it 160-1, Punjab had their first wicket in almost 37 overs, containing 408 runs. Others in Hyderabad's brittle middle order soon followed; but, thanks to the vim of Bairstow (97 from 55 balls) and the remorselessness of Warner (his 50th IPL score of 50-plus), they had plenty. Punjab relied entirely on Pooran: his 77 came from 37, while no one else passed 11. When he fell at 126-7, in a double-wicket maiden from Rashid, their goose was cooked.*

At Sharjah, October 9, 2020 (floodlit). **Delhi Capitals won by 46 runs. Delhi Capitals 184-8** (20 overs) (M. P. Stoinis 39, S. O. Hetmyer 45; J. C. Archer 3-24); **‡Rajasthan Royals 138** (19.4 overs) (Y. B. Jaiswal 34, R. Tewatia 38; K. Rabada 3-35). *PoM:* R. Ashwin. *Delhi took control after a doubtful start. Archer removed Dhawan and Shaw, and two run-outs left the Capitals 79-4, before Stoinis and Shimron Hetmyer lashed nine sixes. But Rajasthan's batting line-up could not find their mojo. Ashwin began the damage by dismissing Buttler (uncontroversially, this time, caught at square leg), and seven of the last eight totalled 19.*

At Abu Dhabi, October 10, 2020. **Kolkata Knight Riders won by two runs. ‡Kolkata Knight Riders 164-6** (20 overs) (S. Gill 57, K. D. Karthik 58); **Kings XI Punjab 162-5** (20 overs) (K. L. Rahul 74, M. A. Agarwal 56; P. M. Krishna 3-29). *PoM:* K. D. Karthik. *An opening stand of 115* *between Rahul and Agarwal seemed to have put Kings XI in charge: with three overs to go, they needed only 22, with nine wickets in hand. But Rahul fell to the last ball of the 19th – a third wicket for seamer Prashidh Krishna – which left Narine to defend 14, against two brand-new batsmen. After seven came from the first four deliveries, Mandeep Singh was caught at midwicket, then Glenn Maxwell – needing six to tie – spiralled the last ball over cover, tantalisingly short of the boundary. Narine's joy was brief: he was reported after the match for a suspect action. Earlier, Dinesh Karthik's 29-ball 58 muscled KKR to a decent score.*

At Dubai, October 10, 2020 (floodlit). **Royal Challengers Bangalore won by 37 runs.** ‡**Royal Challengers Bangalore 169-4** (20 overs) (D. B. Padikkal 33, V. Kohli 90*); **Chennai Super Kings 132-8** (20 overs) (A. T. Rayudu 42, N. Jagadeesan 33; C. H. Morris 3-19). *PoM:* V. Kohli. *For Chennai, chasing for a seventh game out of seven, it was a familiar struggle: a slow start (26-2 in the powerplay after Washington Sundar removed the openers), sluggish accumulation in the middle (Rayudu's 42 consumed 40 balls), and an impossible task for the rest. It added up their fifth defeat, leaving Dhoni to lament "too many holes in the ship". Kohli had given Bangalore's innings late oomph with 90* off 52 – glossing over a rare duck for de Villiers – before Chris Morris took 3-19 in his first game of the tournament following a side strain.*

At Dubai, October 11, 2020. **Rajasthan Royals won by five wickets.** ‡**Sunrisers Hyderabad 158-4** (20 overs) (D. A. Warner 48, M. K. Pandey 54); **Rajasthan Royals 163-5** (19.5 overs) (R. P. Das 42*, R. Tewatia 45*). *PoM:* R. Tewatia. *A sticky pitch made life awkward for batsmen, though Tewatia and the 18-year-old Riyan Parag Das showed their illustrious team-mates what could be achieved. They rescued Rajasthan from 78-5 after 12, cracked a thrilling 85*, and brought victory with a ball to spare. Earlier, Archer had revived memories of September's England–Australia games, when he had Warner on a string; it took a little longer this time, but Archer cleaned him up with a beauty. Ben Stokes, newly arrived after visiting his seriously ill father in New Zealand, had a quiet match for Rajasthan: one over for seven, and five runs.*

At Abu Dhabi, October 11, 2020 (floodlit). **Mumbai Indians won by five wickets.** ‡**Delhi Capitals 162-4** (20 overs) (S. Dhawan 69*, S. S. Iyer 42); **Mumbai Indians 166-5** (19.4 overs) (Q. de Kock 53, S. A. Yadav 53). *PoM:* Q. de Kock. *Mumbai edged ahead of Delhi at the top of the table. While Shaw fell to the game's third delivery, fellow opener Dhawan batted throughout the Capitals' innings for his first half-century of the tournament, adding 85 in 62 balls with Iyer. But Stoinis was run out for 13, and there was no late acceleration. Mumbai's chase advanced steadily, thanks to fifties from de Kock and Yadav. Krunal Pandya, after two wickets and a catch, finished it with two fours.*

At Sharjah, October 12, 2020 (floodlit). **Royal Challengers Bangalore won by 82 runs.** ‡**Royal Challengers Bangalore 194-2** (20 overs) (A. J. Finch 47, D. B. Padikkal 32, V. Kohli 33*, A. B. de Villiers 73*); **Kolkata Knight Riders 112-9** (20 overs) (S. Gill 34). *PoM:* A. B. de Villiers. *On a sluggish pitch, a rumbustious 33-ball 73* from de Villiers, including six sixes, propelled RCB to a lofty score. He dominated a stand of 100* with Kohli, whose 28-ball 33* included a solitary four against an attack lacking Narine, left out after his action was reported. It was all too much for KKR, who were sunk at 64-5. Morris finished with 2-17, and Washington Sundar 2-20.*

At Dubai, October 13, 2020 (floodlit). **Chennai Super Kings won by 20 runs.** ‡**Chennai Super Kings 167-6** (20 overs) (S. M. Curran 31, S. R. Watson 42, A. T. Rayudu 41); **Sunrisers Hyderabad 147-8** (20 overs) (K. S. Williamson 57). *PoM:* R. A. Jadeja. *Sam Curran was described by Dhoni as "a complete cricketer" after Chennai, finally batting first, outmanoeuvred the Sunrisers on a tired pitch. First he made 31 off 21 after replacing Watson – who dropped to No. 3 – as opener. Then he claimed the crucial wicket of Warner, caught and bowled for nine. After that, only Williamson (57 off 39) flourished, though the Sunrisers were unhappy when umpire Paul Reiffel appeared to be dissuaded by Dhoni from calling a second successive wide in the 19th over, bowled by seamer Shardul Thakur.*

At Dubai, October 14, 2020 (floodlit). **Delhi Capitals won by 13 runs.** ‡**Delhi Capitals 161-7** (20 overs) (S. Dhawan 57, S. S. Iyer 53; J. C. Archer 3-19); **Rajasthan Royals 148-8** (20 overs) (B. A. Stokes 41, R. V. Uthappa 32). *PoM:* A. A. Nortje. *Archer gave the game an electric start, crashing a first-ball lightning bolt into Shaw's stumps, then doing Ajinkya Rahane – caught at mid-on – for pace next over. But Dhawan and Iyer oversaw a Delhi recovery against Rajasthan's less-discomfiting back-up bowlers and, despite Archer taking another wicket at the death, a target of 162 proved too many. Rajasthan, well placed at 85-2 after ten overs, fell away against the miserliness of Ashwin (1-17) and speed of Anrich Nortje (2-33).*

At Sharjah, October 15, 2020 (floodlit). **Kings XI Punjab won by eight wickets.** ‡**Royal Challengers Bangalore 171-6** (20 overs) (V. Kohli 48); **Kings XI Punjab 177-2** (20 overs) (K. L. Rahul 61*, M. A. Agarwal 45, C. H. Gayle 53). *PoM:* K. L. Rahul. *Punjab beat Bangalore for a second time, but remained bottom: they had lost to the other six. They had been coasting, thanks to five sixes apiece from Rahul and Chris Gayle – who reached 50 in his first match of the tournament, and the first IPL innings in which he hadn't opened since 2012. At the start of the final over, Punjab needed just two, but Chahal conceded one in four deliveries, before Gayle was run out. With the scores level, Pooran came in, and struck a six over long-on. Earlier, Kohli hit only three fours in 39 balls, while de Villiers was kept back to No. 6; arriving in the 17th over, he managed two singles.*

At Abu Dhabi, October 16, 2020 (floodlit). **Mumbai Indians won by eight wickets.** ‡**Kolkata Knight Riders 148-5** (20 overs) (E. J. G. Morgan 39*, P. J. Cummins 53*); **Mumbai Indians 149-2** (16.5 overs) (R. G. Sharma 35, Q. de Kock 78*). *PoM:* Q. de Kock. *Not long after leg-spinner Rahul Chahar (2-18) nabbed Gill and Karthik with successive balls, KKR were 61-5 in the 11th. But Morgan, their new captain, and Cummins, who thrashed a maiden T20 half-century, dragged them to a respectable total. It soon looked insignificant: Sharma shared an opening stand of 94 with de Kock, who finished with 78* from 44 as Mumbai rejoined Delhi at the head of the table.*

At Dubai, October 17, 2020. **Royal Challengers Bangalore won by seven wickets.** ‡**Rajasthan Royals 177-6** (20 overs) (R. V. Uthappa 41, S. P. D. Smith 57; C. H. Morris 4-26); **Royal Challengers Bangalore 179-3** (19.4 overs) (D. B. Padikkal 35, V. Kohli 43, A. B. de Villiers 55*). *PoM:* A. B. de Villiers. *"We just got AB'd there," lamented Smith after a tour de force from de Villiers. Bangalore had needed 76 off 41 balls on a slow pitch when he took guard, and had just lost Padikkal and Kohli in two balls. That became 35 off 12 when Smith handed the 19th over to Jaydev Unadkat, keeping Archer for the 20th. But de Villiers hit his first three deliveries for leg-side sixes in an over eventually costing 25, then swung Archer for another – his sixth – to bring up a 22-ball fifty, and seal a breathtaking win. Rajasthan had managed 177, with Smith's 36-ball 57 following 41 off 22 from Robin Uthappa, promoted to open in a rejigged line-up that had Buttler down at No. 5. But 4-26 from Morris kept them within reach.*

At Sharjah, October 17, 2020 (floodlit). **Delhi Capitals won by five wickets.** ‡**Chennai Super Kings 179-4** (20 overs) (F. du Plessis 58, S. R. Watson 36, A. T. Rayudu 45*, R. A. Jadeja 33*); **Delhi Capitals 185-5** (19.5 overs) (S. Dhawan 101*). *PoM:* S. Dhawan. *Delhi went top again thanks to Dhawan – dropped four times en route to his first T20 hundred. Though he dominated their chase, it was the cool-headed Akshar Patel who administered the coup de grâce. He struck Jadeja for 6626 to win with a ball to spare after Sam Curran had brought Chennai back into the reckoning by conceding only four off the 19th. For Jadeja, it was a dose of his own medicine: he had crashed 33 from 13, including two sixes in the last over, to ensure the Chennai innings ended with a flourish. Du Plessis was their mainstay, before becoming the 50th IPL victim for Rabada, in his 27th game, five fewer than the next-quickest, Narine.*

At Abu Dhabi, October 18, 2020. **Kolkata Knight Riders won the super over, after a tie. Kolkata Knight Riders 163-5** (20 overs) (S. Gill 36, E. J. G. Morgan 34); ‡**Sunrisers Hyderabad 163-6** (20 overs) (J. M. Bairstow 36, D. A. Warner 47*; L. H. Ferguson 3-15). *PoM:* L. H. Ferguson. *In his first outing of the tournament, Lockie Ferguson claimed a boundary-free 3-15 before the match went to a super over – which he effectively settled by bowling Warner and Abdul Samad in his first three deliveries. Warner had almost stolen victory with three successive fours in the Sunrisers' 20th over, bowled by Russell off a short run after a hamstring twinge. But, needing two to win off the last ball, he managed only a leg-bye. Earlier, he had been the first in 12 games to insert the opposition, before becoming the fourth to 5,000 IPL runs – the first non-Indian, and the quickest, in 135 innings to Kohli's 157. The Knight Riders' batting had been solid rather than spectacular: the highest stand was 58 between Morgan and Karthik in the last five overs.*

At Dubai, October 18, 2020 (floodlit). **Kings XI Punjab won the second super over, after a tie.** ‡**Mumbai Indians 176-6** (20 overs) (Q. de Kock 53, K. H. Pandya 34, K. A. Pollard 34*); **Kings XI Punjab 176-6** (20 overs) (K. L. Rahul 77; J. J. Bumrah 3-24). *PoM:* K. L. Rahul. *This was a tale of two super overs. Both teams managed only five runs in the first, with Bumrah taking two wickets; then, after some pinpoint yorkers from Shami, de Kock was narrowly run out diving for victory, thanks to slick glovework from Rahul. Mumbai made 11-1 in the second super over, in which the teams had to use players who had not bowled or been dismissed in the first, but the match was virtually decided when Gayle smashed Boult's first delivery for six; Agarwal hit the third and fourth for four. In the game itself, Rahul top-scored with 77 from 51 as Kings XI chased a total inflated by* *late fireworks from Pollard (34* off 12) and Nathan Coulter-Nile (24*), who piled on 57* in 21 balls. But Rahul again fell in sight of the finish line, and the hairline last-ball run-out of Jordan set up the extended tiebreaker.*

At Abu Dhabi, October 19, 2020 (floodlit). **Rajasthan Royals won by seven wickets. ‡Chennai Super Kings 125-5** (20 overs) (R. A. Jadeja 35*); **Rajasthan Royals 126-3** (17.3 overs) (J. C. Buttler 70*). *PoM:* J. C. Buttler. *Buttler flourished on a grudging surface that defeated almost everyone else, hitting 70* off 48 in a fourth-wicket stand of 98* with Smith (26* off 34) after Rajasthan lurched to 28-3. The result meant Chennai replaced them at the bottom. Later, Dhoni sounded as if he had already written off the season ("we were not really there"), but was generous enough on the occasion of his record 200th IPL appearance to hand Buttler his shirt. Chennai had made an anaemic 125-5, thwarted by leg-spinners Shreyas Gopal and Tewatia (48–23–32–2 between them) and the compelling Archer (24–11–20–1).*

At Dubai, October 20, 2020 (floodlit). **Kings XI Punjab won by five wickets. ‡Delhi Capitals 164-5** (20 overs) (S. Dhawan 106*); **Kings XI Punjab 167-5** (19 overs) (N. Pooran 53, G. J. Maxwell 32). *PoM:* S. Dhawan. *Dhawan had gone 264 T20 innings without a hundred; in his 266th, he became the first in IPL history to hit two in a row, both arriving in 57 balls (he also reached 5,000 IPL runs). The pattern for his team-mates' contributions, though, was set by Shaw, who endured a fourth successive single-figure score; Dhawan aside, no Delhi batsman reached 15. Leading the way for Punjab was Shami, who took 2-13 in the 18th and 20th overs. In reply, Gayle pummelled 29 from 13 balls, and Pooran 53 from 28, nullifying Dhawan's achievement.*

At Abu Dhabi, October 21, 2020 (floodlit). **Royal Challengers Bangalore won by eight wickets. ‡Kolkata Knight Riders 84-8** (20 overs) (E. J. G. Morgan 30; M. Siraj 3-8); **Royal Challengers Bangalore 85-2** (13.3 overs). *PoM:* M. Siraj. *Kolkata's hopes lay in ruins by the fourth over: 14-4 after Mohammed Siraj had swung his way to 3-0. His previous ten overs had cost 102; now, he became the first to bowl two maidens in an IPL game, and the eight he later conceded were all singles. Though Morgan did his best to rebuild, the Knight Riders' 84-8 was the lowest by an IPL side batting 20 overs, and featured four maidens in all, double the previous record. Bangalore openers Padikkal and Finch sauntered to 46-0, before Kohli steered his team home.*

At Dubai, October 22, 2020 (floodlit). **Sunrisers Hyderabad won by eight wickets. Rajasthan Royals 154-6** (20 overs) (B. A. Stokes 30, S. V. Samson 36; J. O. Holder 3-33); **‡Sunrisers Hyderabad 156-2** (18.1 overs) (M. K. Pandey 83*, V. Shankar 52*). *PoM:* M. K. Pandey. *A superb performance from Jason Holder restricted the Royals to 154. Playing only because Williamson was injured, he ran out Uthappa, then took three wickets, including top-scorer Samson. When the Sunrisers batted, Archer removed openers Warner (for the sixth time in 45 balls across formats in 2020) and Bairstow to leave them 16-2. But Manish Pandey took charge, blasting eight sixes in his 47-ball 83*, and putting on 140* with Shankar in what ended up as a stroll.*

At Sharjah, October 23, 2020 (floodlit). **Mumbai Indians won by ten wickets. Chennai Super Kings 114-9** (20 overs) (S. M. Curran 52; T. A. Boult 4-18); **‡Mumbai Indians 116-0** (12.2 overs) (Q. de Kock 46*, I. P. Kishan 68*). *PoM:* T. A. Boult. *CSK's latest humiliation began early, as Boult and Bumrah – for once operating with the new ball – reduced them to 3-4. That was soon 43-7, and only Curran's half-century, and a ninth-wicket stand of 43 with Imran Tahir (13*), dragged them into three figures. Boult's 4-18 were his best T20 figures. With Sharma nursing a hamstring, Kishan opened with de Kock: he launched five sixes in a 37-ball 68*. The win took Mumbai top on net run-rate, ahead of Delhi and Bangalore. Earlier, Deepak Chahar was stumped for a duck off Rahul Chahar, his double first cousin (their fathers were brothers and their mothers sisters).*

At Abu Dhabi, October 24, 2020. **Kolkata Knight Riders won by 59 runs. Kolkata Knight Riders 194-6** (20 overs) (N. Rana 81, S. P. Narine 64); **‡Delhi Capitals 135-9** (20 overs) (S. S. Iyer 47; P. J. Cummins 3-17, V. V. Chakravarthy 5-20). *PoM:* V. V. Chakravarthy. *A blistering stand of 115 in 56 balls between Nitish Rana and Narine propelled Kolkata – 84-8 in their previous game – to a healthy 194-6. They came together at 42-3 in the eighth, and were especially harsh on Ashwin: his three overs cost 45. The Delhi openers soon disappeared in a fiery spell from Cummins, who belied a tournament record of 3-296 to claim 3-17. Yet he was upstaged by the leg-spin of Chakravarthy. Bowling a flat line at a brisk pace, he picked up 5-20, an all-format career-best.*

At Dubai, October 24, 2020 (floodlit). **Kings XI Punjab won by 12 runs. Kings XI Punjab 126-7** (20 overs) (N. Pooran 32*); **‡Sunrisers Hyderabad 114** (19.5 overs) (D. A. Warner 35; Arshdeep Singh 3-23, C. J. Jordan 3-17). *PoM:* C. J. Jordan. *A collapse of seven for 14 handed Punjab a fourth straight win. With the Sunrisers needing 27, sub J. Suchith raced round the boundary to remove*

Pandey (15 off 29) with a leaping catch, off Jordan, who had Holder and Rashid Khan caught off successive deliveries in his next over; meanwhile, Arshdeep Singh extracted three for one in five balls, and the last man was run out. Kings XI had also lost momentum, Rashid's four overs costing only 14. After seven boundaries in the first seven overs, there were no more until Pooran managed a couple at the end.

At Dubai, October 25, 2020. **Chennai Super Kings won by eight wickets.** ‡**Royal Challengers Bangalore 145-6** (20 overs) (V. Kohli 50, A. B. de Villiers 39; S. M. Curran 3-19); **Chennai Super Kings 150-2** (18.4 overs) (R. D. Gaikwad 65*, A. T. Rayudu 39). *PoM:* R. D. Gaikwad. *Victory would have taken RCB top; instead the Super Kings dragged themselves off the bottom. Bangalore battled a slowish pitch to reach 128-2 in the 18th, but de Villiers was the first of four quick wickets, with Sam Curran dismissing Moeen Ali and Kohli in the 19th. Gaikwad and du Plessis ignited the chase with 46 in five overs, and Gaikwad finished things off by pulling Morris for six.*

At Abu Dhabi, October 25, 2020 (floodlit). **Rajasthan Royals won by eight wickets.** ‡**Mumbai Indians 195-5** (20 overs) (I. P. Kishan 37, S. A. Yadav 40, S. S. Tiwary 34, H. H. Pandya 60*); **Rajasthan Royals 196-2** (18.2 overs) (B. A. Stokes 107*, S. V. Samson 54*). *PoM:* B. A. Stokes. *After scores of five, 41, 15, 19 and 30 (and no sixes), Stokes unfurled a destructive 107* off 60 balls (with 14 fours and three sixes), and put on 152* with Samson (54* off 31). They made mincemeat of Mumbai's imposing 195-5, and kept the Royals in the play-off mix, while also ensuring CSK would fail to reach that stage for the first time. "I hope this has given a bit of happiness back home," said Stokes, whose father, Ged, was severely ill in Christchurch. Mumbai's innings had ended with a kick, as Hardik Pandya – dropped on five by Tewatia – mauled seven sixes in a 21-ball 60*, including 26 in the last over, from Kartik Tyagi. He celebrated his half-century by taking a knee in homage to the Black Lives Matter movement.*

At Sharjah, October 26, 2020 (floodlit). **Kings XI Punjab won by eight wickets. Kolkata Knight Riders 149-9** (20 overs) (S. Gill 57, E. J. G. Morgan 40; Mohammed Shami 3-35); ‡**Kings XI Punjab 150-2** (18.5 overs) (Mandeep Singh 66*, C. H. Gayle 51). *PoM:* C. H. Gayle. *The Kolkata innings boiled down to one partnership: after Shami helped reduce them to 10-3, Gill and Morgan picked up the pieces. At 91-3 in the tenth, they had hopes of pushing 200. But Morgan slog-swept to deep backward square, Gill lost the strike, and the rate slowed: against the leg-spin of Bishnoi and Murugan Ashwin, overs 12–16 brought 13 runs and two wickets. A modest target allowed Punjab time to acclimatise, before the 41-year-old Gayle, strutting in at 47-1, walloped his fourth and fifth balls, from Chakravarthy, for six. He departed for a 29-ball 51, but the more circumspect Mandeep (66* off 56) was there when Punjab gained a fifth win in a row.*

At Dubai, October 27, 2020 (floodlit). **Sunrisers Hyderabad won by 88 runs. Sunrisers Hyderabad 219-2** (20 overs) (D. A. Warner 66, W. P. Saha 87, M. K. Pandey 44*); ‡**Delhi Capitals 131** (19 overs) (R. R. Pant 36; Rashid Khan 3-7). *PoM:* W. P. Saha. *Warner celebrated his 34th birthday with 66 in 34 balls, two catches, and a huge win to keep Hyderabad's hopes alive. With Wriddhiman Saha (87 in 45, after replacing Bairstow for his second game of the season) he piled up 77-0, the highest powerplay of the tournament; Ravichandran Ashwin finally broke the stand at 107 in the tenth. Rabada went wicketless for the first time in 26 IPL games since May 2017. The Capitals never threatened a target of 11 an over. Rashid came on straight after the powerplay, removed Hetmyer and Rahane in his first five balls, and finished with 24–17–7–3, this competition's most economical spell.*

At Abu Dhabi, October 28, 2020 (floodlit). **Mumbai Indians won by five wickets. Royal Challengers Bangalore 164-6** (20 overs) (J. R. Philippe 33, D. B. Padikkal 74; J. J. Bumrah 3-14); ‡**Mumbai Indians 166-5** (19.1 overs) (S. A. Yadav 79*). *PoM:* S. A. Yadav. *Once again, Bangalore tripped up at the end of their innings after de Villiers was out, caught for 15 off a Pollard full toss which dipped just below the waist. This time, they added only 33 from the last 28 balls after being 131-2. The main destroyer was Bumrah, whose 24–15–14–3 featured a double-wicket maiden; Padikkal top-scored with 74 from 45. Yadav, who cracked 79* from 43, oversaw the chase. Mumbai's win, coupled with a healthy net run-rate, meant they were all but assured a play-off place.*

At Dubai, October 29, 2020 (floodlit). **Chennai Super Kings won by six wickets. Kolkata Knight Riders 172-5** (20 overs) (N. Rana 87); ‡**Chennai Super Kings 178-4** (20 overs) (R. D. Gaikwad 72, A. T. Rayudu 38, R. A. Jadeja 31*). *PoM:* R. D. Gaikwad. *Jadeja disrupted Kolkata's play-off plans after Chennai needed 27 from nine deliveries. Helped by a high no-ball from Ferguson, he reduced the equation to ten off the last over, though that became seven off two deliveries as Sam Curran struggled to match his team-mate's fluency. But Jadeja deposited a length ball from Nagarkoti over midwicket, then made sure with six more, over wide long-on. His heroics ensured Gaikwad's classy 72 off 53 did not go to waste. Kolkata's middling total centred on Rana's 87 off 61.*

At Abu Dhabi, October 30, 2020 (floodlit). **Rajasthan Royals won by seven wickets. Kings XI Punjab 185-4** (20 overs) (K. L. Rahul 46, C. H. Gayle 99); ‡**Rajasthan Royals 186-3** (17.3 overs) (R. V. Uthappa 30, B. A. Stokes 50, S. V. Samson 48, S. P. D. Smith 31*). *PoM:* B. A. Stokes. *Punjab's winning streak came to a halt on a pitch with little in it for bowlers. Rahul and Gayle put on 120 for their second wicket, with the seventh of Gayle's eight sixes taking his total in T20 cricket to 1,000; Pollard was a distant second, with 690 (at the time), more than 200 ahead of third-placed Brendon McCullum. Gayle, who faced only 63 balls, also became the first player dismissed for 99 in all three formats, when yorked by Archer; like Stokes, he took two wickets. Stokes then gave Rajasthan a roistering start, before falling in the sixth over, having contributed a 26-ball 50 to a score of 60-1. Samson and Buttler (22* off 11) sped Rajasthan home.*

At Dubai, October 31, 2020. **Mumbai Indians won by nine wickets. Delhi Capitals 110-9** (20 overs) (T. A. Boult 3-21, J. J. Bumrah 3-17); ‡**Mumbai Indians 111-1** (14.2 overs) (I. P. Kishan 72*). *PoM:* I. P. Kishan. *Table-leaders Mumbai Indians became the first team to play 200 IPL matches – and clinched their 118th victory when Kishan (72* in 47 balls) lifted his third six, over square leg. Their previous two games in Dubai had ended with super-over defeats. This time, they soon had Delhi in trouble. Boult's third delivery removed Dhawan for a second successive duck; his 12th had Shaw slicing behind. Bumrah grabbed three to leave them 73-6, and finished the innings with a run-out. Kishan scored two off his first eight balls – but once he and de Kock knocked 13 off Nortje's first over, he never looked back.*

At Sharjah, October 31, 2020 (floodlit). **Sunrisers Hyderabad won by five wickets. Royal Challengers Bangalore 120-7** (20 overs) (J. R. Philippe 32); ‡**Sunrisers Hyderabad 121-5** (14.1 overs) (W. P. Saha 39). *PoM:* S. Sharma. *The Sunrisers stayed in the hunt with a good all-round performance. First they restricted RCB to 120, with the new-ball pair Sandeep Sharma (2-20) and Holder (2-27) applying the brakes; then they surged home with almost six overs to spare, doing wonders for their net run-rate. Holder rounded the match off with 26* from ten balls, confirming Bangalore's third straight defeat with his third six.*

At Abu Dhabi, November 1, 2020. **Chennai Super Kings won by nine wickets. Kings XI Punjab 153-6** (20 overs) (D. Hooda 62*; L. T. Ngidi 3-39); ‡**Chennai Super Kings 154-1** (18.5 overs) (R. D. Gaikwad 62*, F. du Plessis 48, A. T. Rayudu 30*). *PoM:* R. D. Gaikwad. *A third successive half-century from Gaikwad took CSK to a third successive win – and ended Kings XI's play-off ambitions. Their own innings had been stifled by the spin of Jadeja and Tahir, who helped turn a promising 48-0 in the sixth over into a wobbly 72-4 in the 12th. Deepak Hooda gave Kings XI something to defend with 62* off 30, but Gaikwad and du Plessis began with 82 inside ten, and the rest was a breeze.*

At Dubai, November 1, 2020 (floodlit). **Kolkata Knight Riders won by 60 runs. Kolkata Knight Riders 191-7** (20 overs) (S. Gill 36, R. A. Tripathi 39, E. J. G. Morgan 68*; R. Tewatia 3-25); ‡**Rajasthan Royals 131-9** (20 overs) (J. C. Buttler 35, R. Tewatia 31; P. J. Cummins 4-34). *PoM:* P. J. Cummins. *IPL-best performances from Morgan and Cummins gave Kolkata the big win that kept qualification possible, if results went their way. Archer's contribution to the powerplay was 1-3 in two overs, but his Rajasthan colleagues failed to match his control and, after six, Kolkata were 55-1. Gopal's three overs cost 44, and Morgan (who finished on 68* from 35) gave England colleague Stokes a battering from the 19th, which went for 24. Five legal deliveries into the reply, the Royals were 19-0, but Cummins had the last laugh. He took four wickets – including Stokes and Smith – in his next 13 to leave them in tatters at 37-5. Defeat meant the end of the road for Rajasthan.*

At Abu Dhabi, November 2, 2020 (floodlit). **Delhi Capitals won by six wickets. Royal Challengers Bangalore 152-7** (20 overs) (D. B. Padikkal 50, A. B. de Villiers 35; A. A. Nortje 3-33); ‡**Delhi Capitals 154-4** (19 overs) (S. Dhawan 54, A. M. Rahane 60). *PoM:* A. A. Nortje. *The teams started tied on 14 points with Kolkata Knight Riders: victory would guarantee second place behind Mumbai, but both would enter the knockouts if the loser's net run-rate remained above Kolkata's. As it was, Delhi won comfortably but, because they took more than 17.3 overs to reach 153, Bangalore advanced too – despite a fourth successive loss. Their total had been disappointing, though Padikkal completed a fifth half-century before becoming the first of Nortje's three victims. When Rabada dismissed Josh Philippe, it was his 24th wicket of the tournament – more than anyone else – but his first in a powerplay. For the Capitals, Dhawan bounced back with 54 in 41 balls, and Rahane saw them most of the way home.*

At Sharjah, November 3, 2020 (floodlit). **Sunrisers Hyderabad won by ten wickets. Mumbai Indians 149-8** (20 overs) (S. A. Yadav 36, I. P. Kishan 33, K. A. Pollard 41; S. Sharma 3-34); ‡**Sunrisers Hyderabad 151-0** (17.1 overs) (D. A. Warner 85*, W. P. Saha 58*). *PoM:* S. Nadeem.

With three matches to go, all against the top three, the Sunrisers' qualification hopes had looked remote. But a third win sent them soaring into the play-offs, at Kolkata's expense, with Warner (85 from 58) and Saha (58* from 45) putting on 151*. It was the third ten-wicket win of 2020, and the 14th in all in the IPL, including the Sunrisers' victory over Gujarat Lions in 2016. Mumbai were already assured of first place, and rested Boult, Bumrah and Hardik Pandya. But their batting was the problem: only Pollard's late 41, which included four sixes, swelled the target, in the face of miserly displays from Sandeep Sharma (who delivered 14 dot balls), Holder (2-25) and slow left-armer Shahbaz Nadeem (2-19).*

Play-offs

1st v 2nd At Dubai, November 5, 2020 (floodlit). **Mumbai Indians won by 57 runs. Mumbai Indians 200-5** (20 overs) (Q. de Kock 40, S. A. Yadav 51, I. P. Kishan 55*, H. H. Pandya 37*; R. Ashwin 3-29); **‡Delhi Capitals 143-8** (20 overs) (M. P. Stoinis 65, A. R. Patel 42; J. J. Bumrah 4-14). *PoM:* J. J. Bumrah. *Mumbai's all-round class was too much for Delhi as they cruised into the final. They began with a powerful batting display: de Kock (40 off 25) and Yadav (51 off 38) paved the way for Kishan (55* off 30) and Hardik Pandya (37* off 14, with five sixes) to cart 60* from the final 23 balls. Without Ashwin's steadying 3-29, Delhi would have been chasing even more. Their target quickly felt irrelevant: eight balls in, Boult and Bumrah had them 0-3. Boult left the field with groin trouble after bowling two overs, but from 41-5 only Stoinis (65 off 46) prospered – until he became the third of Bumrah's four victims. Delhi went into a second play-off, three days later.*

3rd v 4th At Abu Dhabi, November 6, 2020 (floodlit). **Sunrisers Hyderabad won by six wickets. Royal Challengers Bangalore 131-7** (20 overs) (A. J. Finch 32, A. B. de Villiers 56; J. O. Holder 3-25); **‡Sunrisers Hyderabad 132-4** (19.4 overs) (K. S. Williamson 50*). *PoM:* K. S. Williamson. *This game followed form: Hyderabad's fourth win in a row was Bangalore's fifth straight defeat. Kohli promoted himself to open, but gloved a short ball from Holder on six. On a pitch that seamed and turned, patience was essential, and the one Bangalore batsman to prosper was de Villiers. After 19 boundary-less balls, he picked up speed, hitting 41 off his next 23, before being castled by a superb yorker from T. Natarajan. A total of 131 was worth more than its face value, though, and the Sunrisers found little fluency, especially against the leg-spin of Chahal and Adam Zampa, whose combined figures were 2-36. Williamson had seen de Villiers, and matched his sangfroid: his first boundary came from his 25th ball (a six), and he kept going. He and Holder (24*) added an unhurried 65*, and ushered Hyderabad home.*

Final play-off At Abu Dhabi, November 8, 2020 (floodlit). **Delhi Capitals won by 17 runs. ‡Delhi Capitals 189-3** (20 overs) (M. P. Stoinis 38, S. Dhawan 78, S. O. Hetmyer 42*); **Sunrisers Hyderabad 172-8** (20 overs) (K. S. Williamson 67, A. Samad 33; K. Rabada 4-29, M. P. Stoinis 3-26). *PoM:* M. P. Stoinis. *Delhi entered their first IPL final after ending Hyderabad's run. They chose to bat, and Stoinis opened in place of Shaw: he and Dhawan put on 86 in 8.2 overs. Dhawan batted into the 19th, and his 50-ball 78 extended his hit-or-miss record to two hundreds, four half-centuries and three ducks in his last ten innings. Rabada bowled Warner with his first delivery, and Stoinis reduced the Sunrisers to 44-3 with a double-strike in the fifth over. Now their hopes lay in Williamson, who made 67 in 45, but was caught at deep cover in the 17th, Stoinis's third victim. Samad and Rashid struck out until a devastating 19th over: Rabada dismissed both in two balls, then added Goswami after a wide. With Hyderabad needing 22 off six, Nortje conceded four singles.*

FINAL

DELHI CAPITALS v MUMBAI INDIANS

At Dubai, November 10, 2020 (floodlit). Mumbai Indians won by five wickets. Toss: Delhi Capitals.

Mumbai completed their fifth IPL triumph in eight seasons, thanks to their fourth win out of four in this tournament over Delhi. They were in control from the start: Boult had Stoinis caught behind off the game's first delivery, and Delhi were soon listing at 22 for three. Iyer, their captain, and the out-of-form Pant, who went on to his lone half-century of the competition, put on 96, only for the innings to peter out: the last five overs brought a modest 38. Delhi needed early wickets, but Sharma – following Dhoni to 200 IPL appearances – lofted Ashwin's third ball for six, and de Kock helped

Ron Gaunt, Sportzpics for BCCI

Desert storm: Rohit Sharma crashes Mumbai towards victory in the final. Delhi's Rishabh Pant has a prime view.

take 18 off the second over, from South African compatriot Rabada. By the time Sharma departed for a 51-ball 68, his team were nearly there. Kishan supplied the finishing touches, and hit his 30th six – more than anyone else in the tournament – as Mumbai strengthened their claim to be the world's pre-eminent T20 franchise.

Player of the Match: T. A. Boult.

Player of the Tournament: J. C. Archer (Rajasthan Royals).

Delhi Capitals

		B	*4/6*
1 M. P. Stoinis *c 2 b 10*	0	1	0
2 S. Dhawan *b 8*	15	13	3
3 A. M. Rahane *c 2 b 10*	2	4	0
4 *S. S. Iyer *not out*	65	50	6/2
5 †R. R. Pant *c 6 b 9*	56	38	4/2
6 S. O. Hetmyer *c 9 b 10*	5	5	1
7 A. R. Patel *c 12 b 9*	9	9	1
8 K. Rabada *run out (3/9)*	0	0	0
Lb 1, w 3	4		
6 overs: 41-3 (20 overs)	156-7		

1/0 2/16 3/22 4/118 5/137 6/149 7/156

9 R. Ashwin, 10 P. Dubey and 11 A. A. Nortje did not bat.

12th man: L. Yadav.

Boult 24–12–30–3; Bumrah 24–8–28–0; J. Yadav 24–7–25–1; Coulter-Nile 24–10–29–2; K. H. Pandya 18–3–30–0; Pollard 6–2–13–0.

Mumbai Indians

		B	*4/6*
1 *R. G. Sharma *c 12 b 11*	68	51	5/4
2 †Q. de Kock *c 5 b 1*	20	12	3/1
3 S. A. Yadav *run out (10/5)*	19	20	1/1
4 I. P. Kishan *not out*	33	19	3/1
5 K. A. Pollard *b 8*	9	4	2
6 H. H. Pandya *c 3 b 11*	3	5	0
7 K. H. Pandya *not out*	1	1	0
Lb 4	4		
6 overs: 61-1 (18.4 overs)	157-5		

1/45 2/90 3/137 4/147 5/156

8 J. Yadav, 9 N. M. Coulter-Nile, 10 T. A. Boult and 11 J. J. Bumrah did not bat.

12th man: A. S. Roy.

Ashwin 24–8–28–0; Rabada 18–6–32–1; Nortje 16–6–25–2; Stoinis 12–3–23–1; Patel 24–11–16–0; Dubey 18–5–29–0.

Umpires: C. B. Gaffaney and N. N. Menon. Third umpire: A. K. Chaudhary.
Referee: J. Srinath.

INDIAN PREMIER LEAGUE FINALS

2007-08 RAJASTHAN ROYALS beat Chennai Super Kings by three wickets at Mumbai.
2008-09 DECCAN CHARGERS beat Royal Challengers Bangalore by six runs at Johannesburg.
2009-10 CHENNAI SUPER KINGS beat Mumbai Indians by 22 runs at Mumbai.
2010-11 CHENNAI SUPER KINGS beat Royal Challengers Bangalore by 58 runs at Chennai.
2011-12 KOLKATA KNIGHT RIDERS beat Chennai Super Kings by five wickets at Chennai.
2012-13 MUMBAI INDIANS beat Chennai Super Kings by 23 runs at Kolkata.
2013-14 KOLKATA KNIGHT RIDERS beat Kings XI Punjab by three wickets at Bangalore.
2014-15 MUMBAI INDIANS beat Chennai Super Kings by 41 runs at Kolkata.
2015-16 SUNRISERS HYDERABAD beat Royal Challengers Bangalore by eight runs at Bangalore.
2016-17 MUMBAI INDIANS beat Rising Pune Supergiant by one run at Hyderabad.
2017-18 CHENNAI SUPER KINGS beat Sunrisers Hyderabad by eight wickets at Mumbai.
2018-19 MUMBAI INDIANS beat Chennai Super Kings by one run at Hyderabad.
2020 MUMBAI INDIANS beat Delhi Capitals by five wickets at Dubai.

INDIAN PREMIER LEAGUE RECORDS

Highest score	175*	C. H. Gayle . . .	RC Bangalore v Pune Warriors at Bangalore	2012-13
	158*	B. B. McCullum	Kolkata KR v RC Bangalore at Bangalore	2007-08
	133*	A. B. de Villiers	RC Bangalore v Mumbai Indians at Mumbai	2014-15
Fastest 50 – balls	14	K. L. Rahul . . .	KXI Punjab v Delhi Daredevils at Mohali	2017-18
Fastest 100 – balls	30	C. H. Gayle . . .	RC Bangalore v Pune Warriors at Bangalore	2012-13
Most sixes – innings	17	C. H. Gayle . . .	RC Bangalore v Pune Warriors at Bangalore	2012-13
Most runs – season	973	V. Kohli (avge 81.08, SR 152.03) for RC Bangalore . .		2015-16
Most sixes – season	59	C. H. Gayle for RC Bangalore		2011-12
Most runs – career	**5,878**	**V. Kohli (avge 38.16, SR 130.73). . . . .**		**2007-08 to 2020**
	5,368	S. K. Raina (avge 33.34, SR 137.14)		2007-08 to 2018-19
	5,254	**D. A. Warner (avge 42.71, SR 141.54) . . .**		**2008-09 to 2020**
Most 100s – career	**6**	**C. H. Gayle . . . .**		**2008-09 to 2020**
Best SR – career†	**182.33**	**A. D. Russell (1,517 runs, avge 29.74). . . .**		**2011-12 to 2020**
Most sixes – career	**349**	**C. H. Gayle . . . .**		**2008-09 to 2020**
Best bowling	6-12	A. S. Joseph	Mumbai Indians v S Hyderabad at Hyderabad	2018-19
	6-14	Sohail Tanvir	Rajasthan Royals v Chennai SK at Jaipur .	2007-08
	6-19	A. Zampa. . .	Rising Pune S v S Hyderabad at Visakhapatnam	2015-16
Most econ four overs	0-6	F. H. Edwards	Deccan C v Kolkata KR at Cape Town . . .	2008-09
	1-6	A. Nehra . . .	Delhi D v KXI Punjab at Bloemfontein. . .	2008-09
	1-6	Y. S. Chahal	RC Bangalore v Chennai SK at Chennai . .	2018-19
Most expensive analysis	0-70	B. Thampi . .	S Hyderabad v RCB at Bangalore.	2017-18
Most wickets – season	32	D. J. Bravo (avge 15.53, ER 7.95) for Chennai SK		2012-13
Most wickets – career	170	S. L. Malinga (avge 19.80, ER 7.14)		2008-09 to 2018-19
	160	**A. Mishra (avge 24.16, ER 7.34) . . . .**		**2007-08 to 2020**
	156	**P. P. Chawla (avge 27.32, ER 7.87). . . . . .**		**2007-08 to 2020**
Best ER – career‡	**6.24**	**Rashid Khan (1,476 balls, avge 20.49) . . .**		**2016-17 to 2020**
Highest total	263-5	RC Bangalore v Pune Warriors at Bangalore		2012-13
	248-3	RC Bangalore v Gujarat Lions at Bangalore		2015-16
Lowest total	49	RC Bangalore v Kolkata KR at Kolkata		2016-17
Highest successful chase	**226-6**	**Rajasthan R v Kings XI Punjab at Sharjah**		**2020**
Highest match aggregate	469-10	Chennai SK v Rajasthan Royals at Chennai		2009-10

† *Career strike-rate: minimum 500 runs.* ‡ *Career economy-rate: minimum 300 balls.*

DREAM11 SUPER SMASH IN 2019-20

MARK GEENTY

1 Wellington Firebirds 2 Auckland Aces

For a Twenty20 competition lacking international stars, and languishing in the shadow of New Zealand's international schedule and Australia's Big Bash League, a strong back-up cast is essential. **Wellington Firebirds** had the men for the job, bringing the Super Smash trophy back to the Basin Reserve for the third time in six years, and providing instant success for new coach Glenn Pocknall, who had succeeded the retiring Bruce Edgar.

As the countdown continued to his eligibility for New Zealand later in 2020, South African-born Devon Conway shone brightly. His numbers were mind-boggling: 543 runs from 11 innings (140 clear of Auckland Aces' Martin Guptill), with an average of 67 and a strike-rate of 145. Team-mate Jimmy Neesham averaged 45 with the bat and 19 with the ball, and stepped up in some big moments: a cool final over sealed a one-run victory over Otago Volts, which ultimately helped the Firebirds qualify top, ensuring a home final.

The tournament's two leading wicket-takers also wore Wellington's yellow and black. Aged nearly 33, Hamish Bennett topped the charts with 17, and booked an international recall to face India; his canny variations made him the most effective death bowler in the country. Ollie Newton, his new-ball partner, snared 16. Next came two left-arm spinners: Ajaz Patel of Central Stags managed 15, and Auckland's Ronnie Hira 14. Knights seamer Anurag Verma also claimed 14.

It was a tight competition, with just six points separating Wellington and **Knights** (from Northern Districts), who had been finalists in the previous two years, but this time finished last. **Central Stags**, finalists in the previous three, also missed the play-offs, along with **Canterbury Kings**, who at least provided the individual highlight of the competition. With their team chasing 220 to beat Knights at Christchurch's Hagley Park, Leo Carter became the first New Zealander to hit six sixes in an over in top-level cricket, repeatedly launching the left-arm spin of Anton Devcich into the arc between backward square and long-on. He finished with an unbeaten 70 from 29 balls, eclipsing Knights opener Tim Seifert's earlier 74 off 36, and joined Yuvraj Singh, Worcestershire's Ross Whiteley and Afghan batsman Hazratullah Zazai as the only players to achieve the feat in T20 cricket.

Meanwhile, **Otago Volts** looked set to reach their first final for four years, only to blow their chance. Defeat in the concluding round of group matches by the Kings cost them top spot, and they then failed to defend 31 off the last ten balls in the preliminary final against **Auckland Aces** in Dunedin, as Hira and Robert O'Donnell peppered the boundary.

In the decider, on a grey, foggy Wellington afternoon, Conway top-scored with 49 off 37 in what looked a barely par Firebirds total of 168 for seven. Logan van Beek then starred with the ball and in the field, collecting three wickets and two tricky catches in the deep as Auckland's chase faltered. Television pictures caught the joy and wonderment on faces in the crowd behind him. That was soon mirrored by the players as they closed out a 22-run victory, and clutched their winners' medals.

DREAM11 SUPER SMASH AVERAGES IN 2019-20

BATTING (150 runs)

		M	*I*	*NO*	*R*	*HS*	*100*	*50*	*Avge*	*SR*	*4*	*6*
1	†H. D. Rutherford (*Otago V*)	11	11	1	293	81*	0	2	29.30	**173.37**	30	17
2	C. J. Bowes (*Canterbury K*)	10	10	1	358	95	0	3	39.77	**169.66**	42	14
3	J. L. Finnie (*Otago V*)	11	9	2	183	71*	0	1	26.14	**160.52**	20	7
4	†A. P. Devcich (*Knights*)	10	9	0	208	57	0	2	23.11	**148.57**	28	5
5	D. J. Mitchell (*Knights*)	10	8	1	219	58	0	1	31.28	**146.97**	15	9
6	†D. P. Conway (*Wellgtn F*)	11	11	3	543	101*	1	5	67.87	**145.18**	63	12
7	†R. Ravindra (*Wellington F*)	11	9	0	186	39	0	0	20.66	**144.18**	19	6
8	T. L. Seifert (*Knights*)	9	8	0	323	75	0	3	40.37	**143.55**	33	14
9	M. J. Guptill (*Auckland A*)	12	10	1	403	83*	0	2	44.77	**142.40**	38	18
10	G. D. Phillips (*Auckland A*)	11	9	1	206	106*	1	0	25.75	**142.06**	17	9
11	†M. S. Chapman (*Auck A*)	12	10	2	225	63*	0	2	28.12	**139.75**	16	8
12	†N. F. Kelly (*Otago V*)	11	10	1	398	85	0	4	44.22	**139.64**	38	16
13	D. Cleaver (*Central S*)	10	10	0	278	81	0	1	27.80	**139.00**	26	9
14	Craig Cachopa (*Auck A*)	12	9	1	223	66	0	1	27.87	**137.65**	11	14
15	N. T. Broom (*Otago V*)	11	11	0	357	93	0	3	32.45	**136.25**	32	18
16	D. Foxcroft (*Otago V*)	9	9	5	269	82*	0	1	67.25	**135.85**	20	10
17	T. C. Bruce (*Central S*)	10	10	0	273	67	0	2	27.30	**135.82**	20	11
18	†K. Noema-Barnett (*Central S*)	10	10	0	209	58	0	2	20.90	**134.83**	12	14
19	†J. D. S. Neesham (*Well F*)	9	8	3	229	47*	0	0	45.80	**134.70**	16	9
20	†G. H. Worker (*Central S*)	10	10	0	258	62	0	1	25.80	**134.37**	27	13
21	†C. Munro (*Auckland A*)	12	10	0	220	68	0	1	22.00	**133.33**	34	5
22	J. A. Clarkson (*Central S*)	10	10	2	212	36	0	0	26.50	**131.67**	8	12
23	M. A. Pollard (*Wellgtn F*)	11	11	1	291	70	0	3	29.10	**130.49**	24	14
24	C. D. Fletcher (*Canterbury K*)	10	8	4	232	65*	0	2	58.00	**129.60**	16	6
25	J. C. T. Boyle (*Canterbury K*)	10	10	1	231	69*	0	1	25.66	**113.23**	25	3
26	B. R. Hampton (*Knights*)	10	9	0	150	52	0	1	16.66	**112.78**	9	7

BOWLING (7 wickets)

		Style	*Balls*	*Dots*	*R*	*W*	*BB*	*4I*	*Avge*	*SR*	*ER*
1	C. E. McConchie (*Cant K*)	OB	210	78	236	12	3-18	0	19.66	17.50	**6.74**
2	M. S. Chapman (*Auck A*)	SLA	126	45	145	7	2-17	0	20.71	18.00	**6.90**
3	K. Noema-Barnett (*Cent S*)	RM	150	51	180	12	3-10	0	15.00	12.50	**7.20**
4	H. K. Bennett (*Wellgtn F*)	RFM	243	111	292	17	3-27	0	17.17	14.29	**7.20**
5	A. Y. Patel (*Central S*)	SLA	209	84	258	15	3-20	0	17.20	13.93	**7.40**
6	I. S. Sodhi (*Knights*)	LB	233	67	294	10	3-12	0	29.40	23.30	**7.57**
7	M. J. G. Rippon (*Otago V*)	SLW	234	53	309	8	2-20	0	38.62	29.25	**7.92**
8	R. Ravindra (*Wellgtn F*)	SLA	216	60	288	8	2-30	0	36.00	27.00	**8.00**
9	R. M. Hira (*Auckland A*)	SLA	246	64	329	14	3-30	0	23.50	17.57	**8.02**
10	J. A. Duffy (*Otago V*)	RFM	227	75	306	11	2-27	0	27.81	20.63	**8.08**
11	B. M. Wheeler (*Cent S*)	LFM	183	70	248	8	2-30	0	31.00	22.87	**8.13**
12	L. V. van Beek (*Wellgtn F*)	RFM	238	82	325	9	3-28	0	36.11	26.44	**8.19**
13	O. R. Newton (*Wellgtn F*)	RM	246	97	340	16	5-45	1	21.25	15.37	**8.29**
14	J. D. S. Neesham (*Welln F*)	RFM	121	33	171	9	2-24	0	19.00	13.44	**8.47**
15	A. Verma (*Knights*)	RFM	234	82	331	14	3-29	0	23.64	16.71	**8.48**
16	A. M. Ellis (*Canterbury K*)	RFM	162	40	235	9	2-30	0	26.11	18.00	**8.70**
17	E. J. Nuttall (*Canterbury K*)	LFM	196	85	291	7	2-27	0	41.57	28.00	**8.90**
18	B. G. Randell (*Knights*)	RM	168	55	257	11	3-29	0	23.36	15.27	**9.17**
19	M. D. Rae (*Otago V*)	RFM	207	66	319	11	3-23	0	29.00	18.81	**9.24**

		Style	*Balls*	*Dots*	*R*	*W*	*BB*	*4I*	*Avge*	*SR*	*ER*
20	N. G. Smith (*Otago V*) . . .	RFM	116	40	179	11	5-14	1	16.27	10.54	**9.25**
21	W. S. A. Williams (*Cant K*) .	RM	169	49	263	12	5-12	1	21.91	14.08	**9.33**
22	S. C. Kuggeleijn (*Knights*) . .	RFM	234	93	366	9	3-30	0	40.66	26.00	**9.38**
23	K. A. Jamieson (*Auck A*) . .	RFM	132	55	207	8	3-34	0	25.87	16.50	**9.40**
24	M. J. McClenaghan (*Auck A*) .	LFM	252	90	398	10	3-32	0	39.80	25.20	**9.47**
25	D. J. Mitchell (*Knights*) . .	RM	120	37	190	10	4-32	1	19.00	12.00	**9.50**
26	B. M. Tickner (*Central S*) .	RFM	174	70	286	11	4-26	1	26.00	15.81	**9.86**

DREAM11 SUPER SMASH IN 2019-20

	P	*W*	*L*	*NR*	*Pts*	*NRR*
WELLINGTON FIREBIRDS . .	10	6	4	0	24	0.50
OTAGO VOLTS	10	5	4	1	22	0.46
AUCKLAND ACES	10	4	4	2	20	−0.23
Central Stags	10	4	5	1	18	0.37
Canterbury Kings	10	4	5	1	18	−0.18
Knights	10	4	5	1	18	−1.00

2nd v 3rd At Dunedin (University Oval), January 17, 2020 (floodlit). **Auckland Aces won by three wickets. Otago Volts 174-8** (20 overs) (N. F. Kelly 60, D. Foxcroft 31; W. E. R. Somerville 3-25); ‡**Auckland Aces 178-7** (19.5 overs) (M. J. Guptill 43, R. M. Hira 33; M. D. Rae 3-23). *Auckland looked to be heading out when Ronnie Hira, who had just hit Jacob Duffy for 16 off three balls, and Ben Horne fell to successive deliveries. That left them needing 13 off five – only for Robert O'Donnell to smash 16 off seamer Nathan Smith's next four balls. It meant Nick Kelly's 44-ball 60 – the game's only half-century – went to waste, as Otago missed out on a sixth final.*

Final At Wellington (Basin Reserve), January 19, 2020 (floodlit). **Wellington Firebirds won by 22 runs. Wellington Firebirds 168-7** (20 overs) (D. P. Conway 49; M. J. McClenaghan 3-32); ‡**Auckland Aces 146-9** (20 overs) (M. J. Guptill 60; H. K. Bennett 3-34, L. V. van Beek 3-28). *Netherlands and Derbyshire seamer Logan van Beek turned the game Wellington's way after Auckland had reached a promising 103-3 in the 15th. First, he knocked over their middle order with 3-3 in six balls. Then, in a Hamish Bennett over that ended 6W6W, he held two juggling catches on the midwicket boundary to see off the dangerous Martin Guptill and Horne. Earlier, van Beek had contributed a breezy eight-ball 15* as the Firebirds built on Conway's 49 in 37. Their total of 168 proved enough to secure a third title in six years.*

SUPER SMASH FINALS

2005-06 CANTERBURY WIZARDS beat Auckland Aces by six wickets at Auckland.
2006-07 AUCKLAND ACES beat Otago Volts by 60 runs at Auckland.
2007-08 CENTRAL STAGS beat Northern Knights by five wickets at New Plymouth.
2008-09 OTAGO VOLTS headed the table; the final against Canterbury Wizards at Dunedin was washed out.
2009-10 CENTRAL STAGS beat Auckland Aces by 78 runs at New Plymouth.
2010-11 AUCKLAND ACES beat Central Stags by four runs at Auckland.
2011-12 AUCKLAND ACES beat Canterbury Wizards by 44 runs at Auckland.
2012-13 OTAGO VOLTS beat Wellington Firebirds by four wickets at Dunedin.
2013-14 NORTHERN KNIGHTS beat Otago Volts by five wickets at Hamilton.
2014-15 WELLINGTON FIREBIRDS beat Auckland Aces by six runs at Hamilton.
2015-16 AUCKLAND ACES beat Otago Volts by 20 runs at New Plymouth.
2016-17 WELLINGTON FIREBIRDS beat Central Stags by 14 runs at New Plymouth.
2017-18 KNIGHTS beat Central Stags by nine wickets at Hamilton.
2018-19 CENTRAL STAGS beat Knights by 67 runs at Hamilton.
2019-20 WELLINGTON FIREBIRDS beat Auckland Aces by 22 runs at Wellington.

SUPER SMASH RECORDS

Highest score	120*	M. J. Guptill. . . .	Auckland A v Canterbury W at Rangiora	2011-12
	116*	G. D. Phillips . . .	Auckland A v Central S at Auckland .	2016-17
	116	D. P. M. D. Jayawardene . .	Central S v Otago V at New Plymouth	2016-17
Fastest 50 – balls	14	K. Noema-Barnett	Central S v Otago V at Invercargill. . .	2010-11
Fastest 100 – balls	40	T. L. Seifert	Knights v Auckland A at Mt Maunganui	2017-18
Most sixes – innings	9	R. J. Nicol.	Canterbury W v Auckland A at Auckland	2011-12
	9	G. D. Phillips . . .	Auckland A v Central S at Auckland .	2016-17
	9	T. L. Seifert	Knights v Auckland A at Mt Maunganui	2017-18

Most runs – season	584	J. D. Ryder (avge 58.40, SR 174.32) for Wellington F . .	2012-13
Most sixes – season	39	J. D. Ryder for Wellington F	2012-13

Most runs – career	**2,546**	**N. T. Broom (avge 27.97, SR 121.70)**.	**2005-06 to 2019-20**
	2,374	**G. H. Worker (avge 26.97, SR 125.34)** . . .	**2008-09 to 2019-20**
	2,336	R. J. Nicol (avge 30.33, SR 121.09)	2005-06 to 2017-18
Most 100s – career	**2**	**D. P. Conway (2017-18 to 2019-20)**, B. B. McCullum (2005-06 to 2011-12), **G. D. Phillips (2016-17 to 2019-20)**	
Best SR – career*	176.43	C. de Grandhomme (1,595 runs, avge 27.03). .	2006-07 to 2017-18
Most sixes – career	102	C. de Grandhomme	2006-07 to 2017-18

Best bowling	6-7	K. A. Jamieson . .	Canterbury K v Auckland A at Auckland .	2018-19
	6-23	T. S. Nethula . . .	Knights v Central S at Napier.	2018-19
	6-28	I. G. Butler. . . .	Otago V v Auckland A at Dunedin . .	2009-10
	6-28	B. Laughlin . . .	Northern K v Wellington F at Wellington	2013-14
Most econ four overs	6-7	K. A. Jamieson . .	Canterbury K v Auckland A at Auckland .	2018-19
Most expensive analysis	0-70	A. W. Mathieson	Central S v Auckland A at Auckland . .	2015-16

Most wickets – season	22	K. A. Jamieson (avge 12.77, ER 7.33) for Canterbury K	2018-19

Most wickets – career	**125**	**A. M. Ellis (avge 22.35, ER 8.32)**	**2006-07 to 2019-20**
	109	**R. M. Hira (avge 22.48, ER 7.24)**	**2006-07 to 2019-20**
Best ER – career	6.45	D. L. Vettori (682 balls, avge 22.24).	2005-06 to 2014-15

Highest total	249-3	Otago V v Central S at New Plymouth	2016-17
	248-4	Central S v Otago V at New Plymouth	2016-17
Lowest total	72	Wellington F v Northern Knights at Hamilton.	2015-16
Highest successful chase	**222-3**	**Canterbury K v Knights at Christchurch**	**2019-20**
Highest match aggregate	497-7	Central S v Otago V at New Plymouth	2016-17

* *Career strike-rate: minimum 500 runs.* † *Career economy-rate: minimum 300 balls.*

THE HBL PAKISTAN SUPER LEAGUE IN 2019-20

MAZHER ARSHAD

1 Karachi Kings   2 Lahore Qalandars

The fifth edition of the PSL was the first held entirely in Pakistan. Four venues were used, with Multan and Rawalpindi joining Lahore and Karachi, and 15 players from England spearheaded a large overseas contingent. The pandemic cut the tournament in two: the board tried to complete it by closing the doors and reducing the number of matches, but that plan was abandoned just before the first semi-final, on March 17, when news broke that Alex Hales of Karachi Kings had shown Covid-19 symptoms after returning to England.

The tournament resumed – still behind closed doors – eight months later, when **Karachi Kings** secured an emotional first title. They had been guided in the round robin by their new coach Dean Jones, but he died of a heart attack in September, aged just 59. His team paid a warm tribute on the field before the play-offs started – then won the tournament for him. "Dean Jones gets the credit," said Karachi's captain, Imad Wasim. "What he taught us, very few coaches in the world can."

The cricket had resumed with a thrilling encounter in which Karachi upset **Multan Sultans** after a super over. Multan had topped the qualifying table, but crashed out when they lost the elimination play-off to **Lahore Qalandars**, first-time finalists after four wooden spoons. Twenty overseas players – including nine new signings – had travelled to Lahore for the last four games. The highest-profile newcomer was the former South African captain Faf du Plessis, who made his PSL debut for **Peshawar Zalmi**. There were a few hiccups: James Vince and Mahmudullah failed to join Multan after they tested positive for Covid-19.

The final was contested between teams representing Pakistan's two biggest cities – but the only player from either was Babar Azam, born in Lahore but playing for Karachi. His 65 had helped defeat Multan, and he now added 63 not out, to finish with 473 runs, easily the highest aggregate; he was named Batsman of the Tournament. Lahore's Shaheen Shah Afridi was the leading wicket-taker with 17.

It was a forgettable competition for the defending champions, **Quetta Gladiators**, who failed to reach the play-offs for the first time. They at least finished ahead of **Islamabad United**, twice winners but now last, despite the presence of South African fast bowler Dale Steyn, another PSL debutant.

The find of the competition was Haider Ali, a 19-year-old from Peshawar, whose 239 runs came at a strike-rate of 157. Two Australian T20 specialists, both with Lahore, made waves: Chris Lynn powered 284 runs at a strike-rate of 179, while Ben Dunk's 300 at 167 included 23 sixes. Lynn made one of three centuries in the qualifying phase, the others coming from Rilee Rossouw and former Pakistan wicketkeeper Kamran Akmal. Dunk just missed out, with 99 not out – from 40 balls – in the group game against Karachi.

PAKISTAN SUPER LEAGUE AVERAGES IN 2019-20

BATTING (150 runs)

		M	*I*	*NO*	*R*	*HS*	*100*	*50*	*Avge*	*SR*	*4*	*6*
1	C. A. Lynn (*Lahore Q*)...	8	8	1	284	113*	1	1	40.57	**179.74**	32	16
2	†B. R. Dunk (*Lahore Q*)...	11	10	2	300	99*	0	2	37.50	**167.59**	18	23
3	J. M. Vince (*Multan S*)...	5	5	1	155	61*	0	1	38.75	**166.66**	26	3
4	Kamran Akmal (*Peshawar Z*)	9	9	0	251	101	1	0	27.88	**161.93**	31	10
5	Shadab Khan (*Islamabad U*)	9	8	1	263	77	0	3	37.57	**159.39**	16	15
6	S. R. Watson (*Quetta G*) .	9	9	0	247	80	0	2	27.44	**157.32**	26	16
7	Haider Ali (*Peshawar Z*) .	10	10	1	239	69	0	1	26.55	**157.23**	20	14
8	L. Ronchi (*Islamabad U*) .	8	8	1	266	85*	0	2	38.00	**156.47**	31	9
9	†C. A. Ingram (*Islamabad U*)	9	9	2	206	63*	0	1	29.42	**150.36**	18	8
10	A. D. Hales (*Karachi K*)..	9	7	1	272	80*	0	2	45.33	**148.63**	26	12
11	†C. Munro (*Islamabad U*) .	8	8	1	248	87*	0	3	35.42	**147.61**	18	15
12	S. R. Patel (*Lahore Q*) ...	12	9	2	188	71	0	1	26.85	**145.73**	24	4
13	†R. R. Rossouw (*Multan S*)	9	8	2	212	100*	1	0	35.33	**142.28**	21	8
14	C. A. K. Walton (*Karachi K*)	12	10	2	176	45	0	0	22.00	**139.68**	15	8
15	†Khushdil Shah (*Multan S*)	11	10	4	222	70*	0	1	37.00	**139.62**	12	13
16	Shoaib Malik (*Peshawar Z*)	9	8	0	278	68	0	3	34.75	**137.62**	27	8
17	†Sharjeel Khan (*Karachi K*)	12	11	1	216	74*	0	1	21.60	**137.57**	18	16
18	†Imad Wasim (*Karachi K*).	11	8	4	158	50	0	1	39.50	**133.89**	13	7
19	†Azam Khan (*Quetta G*)...	9	9	1	150	59	0	1	18.75	**130.43**	14	6
20	†Zeeshan Ashraf (*Multan S*)	11	11	0	202	52	0	2	18.36	**130.32**	25	6
21	†Fakhar Zaman (*Lahore Q*)	12	12	0	325	63	0	2	27.08	**128.96**	36	10
22	†Shan Masood (*Multan S*) .	11	10	0	283	61	0	1	28.30	**128.05**	30	2
23	Mohammad Hafeez (*LQ*)..	13	12	4	312	98*	0	2	39.00	**125.30**	28	11
24	Babar Azam (*Karachi K*).	12	11	3	473	78	0	5	59.12	**124.14**	55	5
25	†C. S. Delport (*Karachi K*)	8	8	0	178	62	0	1	22.25	**121.08**	13	7
26	Sohail Akhtar (*Lahore Q*)	13	13	4	262	68*	0	2	29.11	**120.18**	24	9
27	J. J. Roy (*Quetta G*).....	8	8	1	233	73*	0	2	33.28	**120.10**	25	6

BOWLING (7 wickets)

		Style	*Balls*	*Dots*	*R*	*W*	*BB*	*4I*	*Avge*	*SR*	*ER*
1	Imad Wasim (*Karachi K*) .	SLA	191	75	225	7	2-14	0	32.14	27.28	**7.06**
2	Shaheen Shah Afridi (*LQ*).	LFM	280	122	332	17	4-18	1	19.52	16.47	**7.11**
3	Imran Tahir (*Multan S*)...	LB	192	63	238	11	3-28	0	21.63	17.45	**7.43**
4	Sohail Tanvir (*Multan S*).	LFM	183	95	230	14	4-13	1	16.42	13.07	**7.54**
5	S. R. Patel (*Lahore Q*)...	SLA	186	65	235	10	4-5	1	23.50	18.60	**7.58**
6	Mohammad Amir (*KK*)...	LFM	257	95	327	10	4-25	1	32.70	25.70	**7.63**
7	Umaid Asif (*Karachi K*) .	RFM	150	57	193	8	2-18	0	24.12	18.75	**7.72**
8	Shahid Afridi (*Multan S*).	LB	138	49	178	7	2-18	0	25.42	19.71	**7.73**
9	Dilbar Hussain (*Lahore Q*).	RFM	207	70	279	14	4-24	1	19.92	14.78	**8.08**
10	Wahab Riaz (*PZ*).......	LF	215	70	292	11	3-21	0	26.54	19.54	**8.14**
11	Shadab Khan (*IU*)......	LB	171	55	235	8	2-14	0	29.37	21.37	**8.24**
12	C. J. Jordan (*Karachi K*) .	RFM	198	60	273	9	2-29	0	30.33	22.00	**8.27**
13	Rahat Ali (*Peshawar Z*)..	LFM	217	83	302	9	3-24	0	33.55	24.11	**8.35**
14	D. Wiese (*Lahore Q*)....	RFM	180	46	252	12	3-27	0	21.00	15.00	**8.40**
15	Arshad Iqbal (*Karachi K*) .	RFM	146	44	206	9	2-15	0	22.88	16.22	**8.46**
16	Hasan Ali (*Peshawar Z*) .	RFM	192	74	275	8	2-36	0	34.37	24.00	**8.59**
17	Mohammad Ilyas (*MS*) ...	RFM	118	45	169	8	2-16	0	21.12	14.75	**8.59**
18	Mohammad Hasnain (*QG*) .	RF	192	75	287	15	4-25	2	19.13	12.80	**8.96**
19	Sohail Khan (*Quetta G*)..	RFM	151	54	235	7	2-21	0	33.57	21.57	**9.33**
20	Haris Rauf (*Lahore Q*)...	RFM	180	65	302	10	3-30	0	30.20	18.00	**10.06**
21	Fahim Ashraf (*IU*)......	RFM	124	37	220	7	2-34	0	31.42	17.71	**10.64**
22	B. C. J. Cutting (*Quetta G*)	RFM	96	21	173	8	3-31	0	21.62	12.00	**10.81**
23	Salman Irshad (*Lahore Q*).	RM	78	30	143	7	4-30	1	20.42	11.14	**11.00**

PAKISTAN SUPER LEAGUE IN 2019-20

	P	*W*	*L*	*NR/A*	*Pts*	*NRR*
MULTAN SULTANS	10	6	2	2	14	1.03
KARACHI KINGS	10	5	4	1	11	−0.19
LAHORE QALANDARS	10	5	5	0	10	−0.07
PESHAWAR ZALMI	10	4	5	1	9	−0.05
Quetta Gladiators	10	4	5	1	9	−0.72
Islamabad United	10	3	6	1	7	0.18

1st v 2nd At Lahore, November 14, 2020. **Karachi Kings won the super over, after a tie. Multan Sultans 141-7** (20 overs) (R. S. Bopara 40); ‡**Karachi Kings 141-8** (20 overs) (Babar Azam 65; Sohail Tanvir 3-25). *PoM:* Babar Azam. *Karachi Kings seemed to be sailing into the final while Babar Azam was stroking 65 from 53 balls. But his dismissal in the 17th over was the first of five to clatter for 18, and it needed Imad Wasim's last-ball four through square leg off Mohammad Ilyas to force a super over. Multan's Sohail Tanvir took two wickets, but Sherfane Rutherford swung a six and a four to set a target of 14; Mohammad Amir's yorkers kept Multan down to nine, despite two wides. Earlier, Ravi Bopara had supervised Multan's recovery from 40-4 in the seventh.*

3rd v 4th At Lahore, November 14, 2020 (floodlit). **Lahore Qalandars won by five wickets. Peshawar Zalmi 170-9** (20 overs) (F. du Plessis 31, Shoaib Malik 39, G. C. Viljoen 37; Dilbar Hussain 3-33); ‡**Lahore Qalandars 171-5** (19 overs) (Mohammad Hafeez 74*; S. Mahmood 3-41). *PoM:* Mohammad Hafeez. *On a night for wise heads, Lahore's 40-year-old Mohammad Hafeez (74* from 46 balls) trumped the Peshawar pair of Faf du Plessis and Shoaib Malik (combined age 74), who were both caught behind by Ben Dunk off the canny Dilbar Hussain. Hardus Viljoen – du Plessis's brother-in-law – biffed 37 from 16 to swell the target. But Hafeez controlled the chase, which was completed when David Wiese (16*) cracked successive sixes off Wahab Riaz.*

Final play-off At Lahore, November 15, 2020 (floodlit). **Lahore Qalandars won by 25 runs. Lahore Qalandars 182-6** (20 overs) (Tamim Iqbal 30, Fakhar Zaman 46, D. Wiese 48*); ‡**Multan Sultans 157** (19.1 overs) (A. Lyth 50, Khushdil Shah 30; Haris Rauf 3-30, D. Wiese 3-27). *PoM:* D. Wiese. *Multan Sultans had topped the league phase, but a second play-off defeat sent them tumbling out, while Lahore Qalandars made the final for the first time. They had been given a good start by Tamim Iqbal and Fakhar Zaman; later, after three wickets fell for 17, Wiese thrashed 48* from 21. That included sixes from the last two balls of the innings, as the usually parsimonious Sohail Tanvir ended up with 1-52. Yorkshire's Adam Lyth caned 50 from 29, but a collapse from 102-2 to 122-7 doomed the Sultans' chase, Wiese rounding off a good day with three wickets.*

Final At Lahore, November 17, 2020 (floodlit). **Karachi Kings won by five wickets.** ‡**Lahore Qalandars 134-7** (20 overs) (Tamim Iqbal 35); **Karachi Kings 135-5** (18.4 overs) (Babar Azam 63*). *PoM:* Babar Azam. *Batsman of the Tournament:* Babar Azam. *Bowler of the Tournament:* Shaheen Shah Afridi (Lahore Qalandars). *Wicketkeeper of the Tournament:* B. R. Dunk (Lahore Qalandars). *Karachi Kings may have mucked up their chase in the play-off, but they made no mistake in the final. Babar guided them home with 63* from 49 – his sixth successive half-century in all matches – with Haris Rauf's wickets from the first two balls of the 18th over only a minor irritant. Lahore Qalandars had been 68-0 at halfway, but managed just 66-7 afterwards, with unheralded seamers Waqas Maqsood (2-18), Umaid Asif (2-18) and Arshad Iqbal (2-26) applying the brakes. "We knew if Babar put on a masterclass, we could effectively put our feet up in the chase," said Imad Wasim, Karachi's captain.*

PAKISTAN SUPER LEAGUE FINALS

2015-16 ISLAMABAD UNITED beat Quetta Gladiators by six wickets at Dubai.
2016-17 PESHAWAR ZALMI beat Quetta Gladiators by 58 runs at Lahore.
2017-18 ISLAMABAD UNITED beat Peshawar Zalmi by three wickets at Karachi.
2018-19 QUETTA GLADIATORS beat Peshawar Zalmi by eight wickets at Karachi.
2019-20 KARACHI KINGS beat Lahore Qalandars by five wickets at Lahore.

PAKISTAN SUPER LEAGUE RECORDS

Highest score	127*	C. A. Ingram. . . .	Karachi K v Quetta G at Sharjah	2018-19
	117*	C. S. Delport. . . .	Islamabad U v Lahore Q at Karachi	2018-19
	117	Sharjeel Khan . . .	Islamabad U v Peshawar Z at Dubai	2015-16
Fastest 50 – balls	17	Kamran Akmal . .	Peshawar Z v Karachi K at Lahore	2017-18
	17	Asif Ali.	Islamabad U v Lahore Q at Karachi	2018-19
Fastest 100 – balls	**43**	**R. R. Rossouw . .**	**Multan S v Quetta G at Multan**	**2019-20**
Most sixes – innings	**12**	**B. R. Dunk. . . . .**	**Lahore Q v Karachi K at Lahore**	**2019-20**
Most runs – season	**473**	**Babar Azam (avge 59.12, SR 124.14) for Karachi K .**		**2019-20**
Most sixes – season	28	Kamran Akmal for Peshawar Z		2017-18
Most runs – career	**1,537**	**Kamran Akmal (avge 29.00, SR 138.34) .**		**2015-16 to 2019-20**
	1,516	**Babar Azam (avge 37.90, SR 117.97) . . . .**		**2015-16 to 2019-20**
	1,361	**S. R. Watson (avge 32.40, SR 138.59). . . .**		**2015-16 to 2019-20**
Most 100s – career	**3**	**Kamran Akmal. . . . .**		**2015-16 to 2019-20**
Best SR – career†	166.24	K. A. Pollard (650 runs, avge 32.50)		2016-17 to 2018-19
Most sixes – career	**81**	**S. R. Watson . . . .**		**2015-16 to 2019-20**
Best bowling	6-16	R. S. Bopara	Karachi K v Lahore Q at Sharjah .	2015-16
	6-19	Fahim Ashraf	Islamabad U v Lahore Q at Karachi	2018-19
	6-24	Umar Gul	Multan S v Quetta G at Dubai. . . .	2017-18
Most econ four overs	2-4	Mohammad Nawaz	Quetta G v Lahore Q at Dubai	2017-18
Most expensive analysis	1-62	Shaheen Shah Afridi	Lahore Q v Islamabad U at Karachi	2018-19
Most wickets – season	25	Hasan Ali (avge 13.64, ER 6.77) for Peshawar Z.		2018-19
Most wickets – career	**76**	**Wahab Riaz (avge 18.71, ER 7.01). . . . . .**		**2015-16 to 2019-20**
	59	**Hasan Ali (avge 20.93, ER 7.47). . . . .**		**2015-16 to 2019-20**
Best ER – career‡	6.22	S. P. Narine (396 balls, avge 20.55)		2016-17 to 2017-18
Highest total	238-3	Islamabad U v Lahore Q at Karachi		2018-19
	214-5	Peshawar Z v Islamabad U at Karachi		2018-19
Lowest total	59	Lahore Q v Peshawar Z at Dubai		2016-17
Highest successful chase	204-4	Lahore Q v Multan S at Sharjah		2018-19
Highest match aggregate	427-12	Lahore Q v Islamabad U at Karachi		2018-19

† *Career strike-rate: minimum 500 runs.* ‡ *Career economy-rate: minimum 300 balls.*

MZANSI SUPER LEAGUE IN 2019-20

COLIN BRYDEN

1 Paarl Rocks   2 Tshwane Spartans

The second edition of the Mzansi Super League showed signs that it was still finding its feet. Like the first, it had no title sponsor and no major television deal, although the matches were broadcast to India, Pakistan, the UK, the Caribbean and the United Arab Emirates. Some overseas players departed mid-tournament for Australia's Big Bash League, which was instructive. The total television audience on SABC, the free-to-air state broadcaster, was 6.4m, down from 10.6m the previous year, which organisers attributed partly to the large number of weather-affected matches: eight out of 32 were ruined by rain. Despite that, total attendances grew from 119,957 in 2018-19 to 206,392.

Paarl Rocks, led by Faf du Plessis, won the title, despite withdrawals and injuries. Yorkshire all-rounder David Willey, their original overseas marquee player, was forced to pull out before the tournament because of the ECB's workload management plan, and was replaced by Sri Lanka's Isuru Udana; J-P. Duminy, their first-round draft pick, was ruled out by a hamstring injury; and Aiden Markram never played after fracturing his wrist punching a "solid object" in frustration during South Africa's tour of India. Hampshire's James Vince left Paarl before the final to join Sydney Sixers, though the fact that he had been a bargain buy at R350,000 (about £18,400) might have been a factor. Overseas and home marquee players earned R1.2m apiece.

Udana proved a respectable acquisition for the Rocks, and took two top-order wickets in the final, as did Tabraiz Shamsi, who collected 16 in all with his left-arm wrist-spin. That was one short of the leading wicket-taker, Imran Tahir, the local marquee player for Port Elizabeth's **Nelson Mandela Bay Giants**. The Giants tied on points with the Rocks, who gained top spot through winning both their head-to-head matches; at the second game, du Plessis explained to a TV interviewer that Hardus Viljoen was not in the Paarl side because "he is lying in bed with my sister" after their wedding the day before.

Tshwane Spartans, from Pretoria, finished third, despite winning only three of their ten league games – rain meant five abandonments or no-results – and beat the Giants in a play-off to qualify for the final. There, impressive all-round bowling by the Rocks restricted the Spartans to 147, despite a fifty from A. B. de Villiers, and Henry Davids led them to a comfortable victory. The match was played in front of an enthusiastic local crowd at Boland Park: all 7,500 tickets had been snapped up once the Rocks clinched top place and a home final. The previous season's finalists, **Jozi Stars** and **Cape Town Blitz**, finished at the bottom of the table; the Stars never won a match in defence of their title, and their overseas marquee player, Chris Gayle, averaged 16. The Blitz had four wins, one more than the Spartans or **Durban Heat**, who were placed above them thanks to points from washouts.

Few of the foreign players were box-office attractions, and few proved value for money. Like Gayle, Alex Hales and Jason Roy hit only a half-century apiece, for the Durban Heat and NMB Giants respectively; Tom Curran bowled tidily – but with little success – for Tshwane, before leaving for the BBL; and neither Wahab Riaz nor Moeen Ali, who covered for him, was electrifying for the Blitz. The most valuable foreign player turned out to be the Giants' Australian batsman Ben Dunk, a bargain at R200,000: he was the leading run-scorer with 415 at 51 and a strike-rate of 149.

MZANSI SUPER LEAGUE AVERAGES IN 2019-20

BATTING (120 runs)

		M	*I*	*NO*	*R*	*HS*	*50*	*Avge*	*SR*	*4*	*6*
1	†W. J. Lubbe (*DH*)	6	6	0	175	83	1	29.16	**184.21**	19	9
2	C. H. Morris (*NMBG*)	11	8	4	122	42	0	30.50	**176.81**	9	6
3	†Q. de Kock (*CTB*)	9	9	0	235	41	0	26.11	**163.19**	31	11
4	†C. S. Delport (*PR*)	10	10	0	264	84	1	26.40	**160.00**	42	5
5	D. Pretorius (*PR*)	5	5	0	152	43	0	30.40	**158.33**	8	10
6	M. Marais (*NMDB*)	9	8	3	146	40*	0	29.20	**156.98**	14	5
7	A. B. de Villiers (*TS*)	9	9	2	325	69*	4	46.42	**152.58**	26	11
8	†B. R. Dunk (*NMBG*)	11	10	2	415	99*	3	51.87	**149.81**	39	17
9	J. N. Malan (*CTB*)	9	9	1	358	99*	3	44.75	**149.79**	26	22
10	D. J. Vilas (*DH*)	6	6	1	134	75*	1	26.80	**147.25**	10	6
11	A. D. Hales (*DH*)	6	6	2	160	97*	1	40.00	**141.59**	17	5
12	J. M. Vince (*PR*)	8	8	2	226	86*	1	37.66	**141.25**	16	7
13	P. J. van Biljon (*TS*)	9	7	3	192	62	1	48.00	**139.13**	16	6
14	H. Davids (*PR*)	10	10	1	275	77*	1	30.55	**135.46**	33	7
15	T. Bavuma (*JS*)	7	6	0	232	62	1	38.66	**134.88**	21	7
16	B. S. Makhanya (*PR*)	8	6	2	121	63*	1	30.25	**132.96**	8	6
17	H. Klaasen (*TS*)	9	9	2	158	36*	0	22.57	**131.66**	14	5
18	F. du Plessis (*PR*)	10	10	2	219	66*	1	27.37	**131.13**	9	13
19	†D. A. Miller (*DH*)	6	5	2	184	50*	1	61.33	**128.67**	7	11
20	L. S. Livingstone (*CTB*)	9	9	0	208	65	1	23.11	**128.39**	7	15
21	J. T. Smuts (*NMBG*)	11	10	1	238	73	2	26.44	**126.59**	22	6
22	R. R. Hendricks (*JS*)	7	7	0	275	80	3	39.28	**125.00**	28	4
23	H. E. van der Dussen (*JS*)	7	7	2	130	31	0	26.00	**120.37**	8	4
24	H. G. Kuhn (*NMBG*)	11	9	1	154	58	1	19.25	**116.66**	12	3
25	†D. Elgar (*TS*)	8	8	2	216	88*	2	36.00	**115.50**	21	2
26	M. P. Breetzke (*NMBG*)	9	8	0	154	64	1	19.25	**114.92**	14	3

BOWLING (5 wickets)

		Style	*Balls*	*Dots*	*R*	*W*	*BB*	*Avge*	*SR*	*ER*
1	Imran Tahir (*NMBG*)	LB	252	88	242	17	3-23	14.23	14.82	**5.76**
2	R. E. van der Merwe (*TS*)	SLA	142	44	148	8	3-15	18.50	17.75	**6.25**
3	M. Morkel (*TS*)	RFM	154	60	163	12	3-21	13.58	12.83	**6.35**
4	B. C. Fortuin (*PR*)	SLA	222	72	238	8	2-13	29.75	27.75	**6.43**
5	K. A. Maharaj (*DH*)	SLA	138	52	152	5	3-15	30.40	27.60	**6.60**
6	J. T. Smuts (*NMBG*)	SLA	193	61	216	6	1-3	36.00	32.16	**6.71**
7	A. M. Phangiso (*JS*)	SLA	121	39	142	5	2-32	28.40	24.20	**7.04**
8	Wahab Riaz (*CTB*)	LF	147	64	173	9	3-19	19.22	16.33	**7.06**
9	D. W. Steyn (*CTB*)	RF	192	91	227	15	3-10	15.13	12.80	**7.09**
10	T. Shamsi (*PR*)	SLW	228	58	270	16	3-16	16.87	14.25	**7.10**
11	N. Burger (*NMBG*)	LFM	161	71	209	5	2-24	41.80	32.20	**7.78**
12	I. Udana (*PR*)	LFM	209	65	274	10	2-24	27.40	20.90	**7.86**
13	L. T. Ngidi (*TS*)	RFM	120	41	164	9	2-2	18.22	13.33	**8.20**
14	C. H. Morris (*NMBG*)	RFM	245	97	335	10	2-8	33.50	24.50	**8.20**

		Style	Balls	Dots	R	W	BB	Avge	SR	ER
15	S. S. B. Magala (*CTB*)	RFM	194	60	266	11	3-17	24.18	17.63	**8.22**
16	K. Rabada (*JS*)	RF	157	67	218	8	3-36	27.25	19.62	**8.33**
17	F. D. Adams (*PR*)	RF	100	26	142	6	3-36	23.66	16.66	**8.52**
18	A. A. Nortje (*CTB*)	RF	158	58	228	6	3-31	38.00	26.33	**8.65**
19	G. F. Linde (*CTB*)	SLA	78	16	118	5	3-23	23.60	15.60	**9.07**
20	M. P. Siboto (*DH*)	RFM	119	37	182	7	2-41	26.00	17.00	**9.17**
21	T. K. Curran (*TS*)	RFM	120	41	187	5	3-30	37.40	24.00	**9.35**
22	K. J. Abbott (*DH*)	RFM	132	48	207	5	2-32	41.40	26.40	**9.40**
23	A. L. Phehlukwayo (*DH*)	RFM	96	30	161	6	2-34	26.83	16.00	**10.06**
24	G. C. Viljoen (*PR*)	RFM	161	43	275	6	2-9	45.83	26.83	**10.24**
25	D. Olivier (*JS*)	RF	102	35	177	7	3-39	25.28	14.57	**10.41**
26	C. J. Dala (*NMBG*)	RFM	162	58	286	12	3-19	23.83	13.50	**10.59**

MZANSI SUPER LEAGUE IN 2019-20

	P	W	L	NR/A	BP	Pts	NRR
PAARL ROCKS	10	6	3	1	1	27	0.64
NELSON MANDELA BAY GIANTS	10	6	3	1	1	27	0.51
TSHWANE SPARTANS	10	3	2	5	1	23	0.51
Durban Heat	10	3	2	5	0	22	0.18
Cape Town Blitz	10	4	5	1	1	19	–0.07
Jozi Stars	10	0	7	3	0	6	–1.89

2nd v 3rd At Port Elizabeth, December 13, 2019 (floodlit). **Tshwane Spartans won by 22 runs. Tshwane Spartans 166-4** (20 overs) (P. J. van Biljon 48*, D. Wiese 31*); ‡**Nelson Mandela Bay Giants 144-8** (20 overs) (B. R. Dunk 35, C. H. Morris 42; D. Wiese 3-30). *PoM:* D. Wiese. *David Wiese swung his first match of the tournament the Spartans' way. He joined Pite van Biljon at 79-4, and added 87* in 52 balls, then took three wickets to sink the Giants' chase. Chris Morris fought hard, but they began the final over needing 28; Wiese removed him for a 23-ball 42, and added Nandre Burger with his next delivery. The Giants managed only five.*

Final At Paarl, December 16, 2019 (floodlit). **Paarl Rocks won by eight wickets. Tshwane Spartans 147-6** (20 overs) (A. B. de Villiers 51); ‡**Paarl Rocks 148-2** (14.2 overs) (H. Davids 77*, D. Pretorius 43). *PoM:* H. Davids. *A. B. de Villiers hit his fourth fifty of the tournament for the Spartans, before becoming the second man bowled by left-armer Isuru Udana, and his side failed to set a challenging target. Henry Davids reached a 22-ball half-century in the Rocks' fifth over, and batted throughout the innings for 77* off 44, with four sixes, though he briefly took a back seat while Dwaine Pretorius whacked 43 off 21 out of a second-wicket stand of 52; captain Faf du Plessis hit the winning run with more than five overs to spare.*

MZANSI SUPER LEAGUE FINALS

2018-19 JOZI STARS beat Cape Town Blitz by eight wickets at Cape Town.
2019-20 PAARL ROCKS beat Tshwane Spartans by eight wickets at Paarl.

MZANSI SUPER LEAGUE RECORDS

Highest score	108*	R. R. Hendricks	JS v NMBG at Port Elizabeth	2018-19
	108	Q. de Kock	CTB v TS at Centurion	2018-19
	104*	R. R. Hendricks	JS v DH at Johannesburg	2018-19
Fastest 50 – balls	18	D. T. Christian	JS v TS at Johannesburg	2018-19
Fastest 100 – balls	49	R. R. Hendricks	JS v DH at Johannesburg	2018-19
Most sixes – innings	**7**	**J. N. Malan**	**CTB v DH at Cape Town**	**2019-20**

Most runs – season	469	H. E. van der Dussen (avge 58.62, SR 138.75) for JS	2018-19
Most sixes – season	23	H. E. van der Dussen for JS	2018-19

Most runs – career	**687**	**R. R. Hendricks (avge 49.07, SR 134.97)**		**2018-19 to 2019-20**
	663	**J. N. Malan (avge 39.00, SR 137.55) . . .**		**2018-19 to 2019-20**
	647	**Q. de Kock (avge 40.43, SR 167.18. . . . .**		**2018-19 to 2019-20**
Most 100s – career	**2**	**R. R. Hendricks . . . .**		**2018-19 to 2019-20**
Best SR – career†	**167.18**	**Q. de Kock (647 runs, avge 40.43) . . . . .**		**2018-19 to 2019-20**
Most sixes – career	**30**	**J. N. Malan. . . . .**		**2018-19 to 2019-20**
Best bowling	6-20	Z. Pongolo	JS v TS at Johannesburg.	2018-19
	4-15	B. C. Fortuin	PR v CTB at Paarl	2018-19
	4-22	B. M. A. J. Mendis	TS v NMBG at Centurion.	2018-19
	4-22	D. T. Christian . . .	JS v CTB at Cape Town	2018-19
Most econ four overs	2-8	K. Rabada.	JS v NMBG at Port Elizabeth. . . .	2018-19
Most expensive analysis	1-63	T. Bokako.	DH v JS at Johannesburg	2018-19
Most wickets – season	20	D. Olivier (avge 13.20, ER 7.88) for JS		2018-19
Most wickets – career	**27**	**D. Olivier (avge 16.33, ER 8.73). . . . . .**		**2018-19 to 2019-20**
	27	**D. W. Steyn (avge 16.81, ER 6.77) . . . .**		**2018-19 to 2019-20**
	26	**T. Shamsi (avge 17.53, ER 6.75). . . . . .**		**2018-19 to 2019-20**
Best ER – career‡	**6.08**	**Imran Tahir (372 balls, avge 17.95). . .**		**2018-19 to 2019-20**
Highest total	239-3	JS v TS at Johannesburg.		2018-19
	230-3	JS v DH at Johannesburg		2018-19
Lowest total	**84**	**CTB v PR at Paarl . . . .**		**2019-20**
Highest successful chase	**197-4**	**DH v PR at Paarl . . . .**		**2019-20**
Highest match aggregate	**411-8**	**JS v CTB at Johannesburg . . . .**		**2019-20**

† *Career strike-rate: minimum 500 runs.* ‡ *Career economy-rate: minimum 300 balls.*

THE HERO CARIBBEAN PREMIER LEAGUE IN 2020

PETER MILLER

1 Trinbago Knight Riders 2 St Lucia Zouks

Like the rest of the world, the Caribbean Premier League was profoundly affected by the Covid-19 pandemic. The self-proclaimed "Biggest Party in Sport" was played behind closed doors, and – for the first time – in a single country, Trinidad & Tobago. By the time it started in August, international cricket had returned, in biosecure bubbles in England, but this was the first T20 franchise featuring overseas players since lockdowns and travel restrictions became the norm. The process of getting 162 players, administrators and broadcast crew into Trinidad was fiendishly complicated. In a normal season, cricketers would be the most valuable contributors; in 2020, it was operations director Michael Hall and his team.

Everyone entering Trinidad had to observe 14 days' quarantine, and for the first eight they were unable to leave their hotel rooms. This was followed by a rigorous testing regime. When the tournament finally began, it was soon clear that home advantage would play a big role. Champions **Trinbago Knight Riders** were the first team to win all 12 matches in a CPL season; the previous year, Guyana had won their first 11, only to fail in the final. Brilliantly led by Kieron Pollard, the Knight Riders fired from the opening day. Their batsmen thrived in bowler-friendly conditions – Lendl Simmons was the leading scorer, with 356, Darren Bravo was third with 297, and Pollard hammered 207 at a strike-rate of 204, miles ahead of the rest. Their only disappointment was the lack of a crowd to cheer them on, though the overall televison and online audience grew by 67% to 523m.

Runners-up **St Lucia Zouks** were a surprise package. Only once, in 2016, had they reached the knockouts, and few fancied them when they lost Chris Gayle in June. He had signed after an acrimonious exit from Jamaica Tallawahs in April, then decided to stay with his family. But the Zouks exceeded the sum of their parts. New Zealand's Scott Kuggeleijn took 17 wickets, more than anyone else, and Afghanistan's Mohammad Nabi 12, with an economy-rate of 5.10. Roston Chase was in fine all-round form, going for just 4.65; Darren Sammy struggled with the bat and rarely bowled, but earned plaudits as captain.

Guyana Amazon Warriors have made the play-offs every season, but their quest for a title continued. Off-spinner Chris Green bowled well with the new ball, while leg-spinner Imran Tahir and Afghanistan seamer Naveen-ul-Haq took 26 wickets between them. Their batting struggled, however, apart from the powerful Shimron Hetmyer, with 267 runs, and Nicholas Pooran, who scored the tournament's only century. They collapsed in the knockouts.

The fourth team to make it through were **Jamaica Tallawahs**, who owed much to New Zealand international Glenn Phillips. He made 316 runs, more than anyone but Simmons, and could both build platforms and push on. Mujeeb

Zadran and Andre Russell showed flashes of their star quality, but couldn't spark when they met Trinbago in the first play-off.

Barbados Tridents became the first defending champions to fail to qualify, despite the services of the world's best T20 bowler, Afghan leg-spinner Rashid Khan. A lack of killer instinct was epitomised when they bowled out the Zouks for 92, but lost after limping to 89 for seven – the first of three games in which they batted 20 overs without reaching three figures.

St Kitts & Nevis Patriots finished last. They never really recovered from the loss of Fabian Allen, who missed the plane to Trinidad; with the borders closed except to charter flights, he could not join the Patriots later on. Some of their brightest moments came from seamer Rayad Emrit, who collected 11 wickets, and went for less than a run a ball.

CARIBBEAN PREMIER LEAGUE AVERAGES IN 2020

BATTING (140 runs)

		M	*I*	*NO*	*R*	*HS*	*100*	*50*	*Avge*	*SR*	*4*	*6*
1	K. A. Pollard (*Trinbago KR*)	11	7	3	207	72	0	1	51.75	**204.95**	9	20
2	†S. P. Narine (*Trinbago KR*)	5	5	0	144	53	0	2	28.80	**148.45**	16	7
3	A. D. Russell (*Jamaica T*)	9	8	3	222	54	0	3	44.40	**141.40**	19	16
4	R. R. S. Cornwall (*St L Z*)	10	10	1	182	32*	0	0	20.22	**141.08**	18	13
5	J. O. Holder (*Barbados T*)	10	10	1	192	69	0	1	21.33	**140.14**	15	12
6	†C. Munro (*Trinbago KR*) .	8	8	2	207	65	0	2	34.50	**133.54**	26	8
7	A. D. S. Fletcher (*St L Z*) .	12	11	1	211	46	0	0	21.10	**127.87**	17	11
8	G. D. Phillips (*Jamaica T*)	11	10	1	316	79*	0	2	35.11	**127.41**	19	18
9	†M. Deyal (*St Lucia Z*). . . .	10	9	1	166	40	0	0	20.75	**126.71**	14	7
10	†S. O. Hetmyer (*Guyana AW*)	11	11	3	267	71	0	3	33.37	**125.94**	21	9
11	Mohammad Nabi (*St LZ*) .	12	10	2	156	35*	0	0	19.50	**124.80**	9	9
12	†N. Pooran (*Guyana AW*). .	11	11	2	245	100*	1	1	27.22	**123.73**	18	12
13	L. M. P. Simmons (*Trin KR*)	11	11	2	356	96	0	3	39.55	**122.33**	26	20
14	†E. Lewis (*St K&N P*)	10	10	1	235	89	0	1	26.11	**120.51**	16	18
15	†D. M. Bravo (*Trinbago KR*)	12	9	4	297	58*	0	3	59.40	**115.11**	12	20
16	†M. J. Santner (*Barbados T*)	9	8	5	145	36	0	0	48.33	**115.07**	9	5
17	J. Charles (*Barbados T*) . .	10	10	0	214	52	0	1	21.40	**115.05**	21	7
18	†K. R. Mayers (*Barbados T*)	9	9	0	222	85	0	1	24.66	**111.55**	10	14
19	†Najibullah Zadran (*St L Z*) .	12	11	0	224	35	0	0	20.36	**110.89**	16	9
20	R. L. Chase (*St Lucia Z*). .	11	9	3	225	66	0	2	37.50	**110.29**	15	6
21	†B. R. Dunk (*St K&N P*) . .	10	9	1	155	34	0	0	19.37	**109.15**	8	5
22	J. Blackwood (*Jamaica T*)	8	7	0	189	74	0	1	27.00	**103.27**	16	7
23	†C. Hemraj (*Guyana AW*) .	8	8	0	140	29	0	0	17.50	**100.00**	8	7
24	T. Webster (*Trinbago KR*)	7	7	2	147	44*	0	0	29.40	**98.65**	15	6
25	D. Ramdin (*St K&N P*). . .	10	9	1	170	46	0	0	21.25	**97.14**	4	7
26	N. E. Bonner (*Jamaica T*)	8	6	1	148	41	0	0	29.60	**94.26**	15	3
27	L. R. P. L. Taylor (*Guy AW*)	11	10	3	164	33	0	0	23.42	**87.23**	10	5

BOWLING (7 wickets)

		Style	*Balls*	*Dots*	*R*	*W*	*BB*	*4I*	*Avge*	*SR*	*ER*
1	R. L. Chase (*St Lucia Z*)	OB	174	88	135	9	3-12	0	15.00	19.33	**4.65**
2	Mohammad Nabi (*St L Z*)	OB	240	128	204	12	5-15	1	17.00	20.00	**5.10**
3	S. Lamichhane (*Jam T*) .	LB	240	129	211	12	2-8	0	17.58	20.00	**5.27**
4	Mujeeb Zadran (*Jam T*).	OB	246	140	217	16	3-11	0	13.56	15.37	**5.29**
5	A. J. Hosein (*Trin KR*) .	SLA	162	89	150	10	3-14	0	15.00	16.20	**5.55**
6	C. J. Green (*Guyana AW*)	OB	225	113	213	9	2-10	0	23.66	25.00	**5.68**
7	Imran Tahir (*Guyana AW*)	LB	246	129	239	15	3-12	0	15.93	16.40	**5.82**
8	J. J. Glenn (*St Lucia Z*) .	LB	60	24	59	7	3-16	0	8.42	8.57	**5.90**

		Style	Balls	Dots	R	W	BB	4I	Avge	SR	ER
9	R. R. Emrit (*St K&N P*).	RFM	192	90	191	11	3-31	0	17.36	17.45	**5.96**
10	Naveen-ul-Haq (*GuyAW*)	RFM	196	98	210	11	4-14	1	19.09	17.81	**6.42**
11	Sikandar Raza (*Trin KR*)	OB	102	50	110	7	3-15	0	15.71	14.57	**6.47**
12	Fawad Ahmed (*Trin KR*)	LB	216	96	236	13	4-21	1	18.15	16.61	**6.55**
13	J. O. Holder (*Barb T*)...	RFM	198	107	219	10	2-10	0	21.90	19.80	**6.63**
14	K. A. Pierre (*Trin KR*)..	SLA	193	92	215	9	3-18	0	23.88	21.44	**6.68**
15	Rashid Khan (*Barb T*)..	LB	218	113	249	11	2-24	0	22.63	19.81	**6.85**
16	Zahir Khan (*St Lucia Z*)	SLW	142	62	164	8	3-25	0	20.50	17.75	**6.92**
17	K. M. A. Paul (*Guy AW*)	RFM	176	84	215	9	4-19	1	23.88	19.55	**7.32**
18	Ali Khan (*Trinbago KR*)	RFM	121	47	150	8	2-25	0	18.75	15.12	**7.43**
19	D. J. Bravo (*Trin KR*) ..	RFM	192	63	240	9	2-7	0	26.66	21.33	**7.50**
20	K. A. Pollard (*Trin KR*).	RM	120	40	151	8	4-30	1	18.87	15.00	**7.55**
21	H. R. Walsh (*Barbados T*)	LB	138	53	176	7	3-19	0	25.14	19.71	**7.65**
22	F. H. Edwards (*Jam T*) .	RFM	180	78	230	9	3-30	0	25.55	20.00	**7.66**
23	S. C. Kuggeleijn (*St L Z*)	RFM	205	102	266	17	4-33	1	15.64	12.05	**7.78**
24	C. R. Brathwaite (*Jam T*)	RFM	182	82	249	10	3-11	0	24.90	18.20	**8.20**
25	R. A. Reifer (*Barbados T*)	LFM	120	38	174	8	2-5	0	21.75	15.00	**8.70**
26	K. O. K. Williams (*St L Z*)	RFM	205	73	305	13	2-12	0	23.46	15.76	**8.92**
27	J. N. T. Seales (*Trin KR*)	RFM	78	33	143	8	2-21	0	17.87	9.75	**11.00**

CARIBBEAN PREMIER LEAGUE IN 2020

	P	W	L	NR	Pts	NRR
TRINBAGO KNIGHT RIDERS.....	10	10	0	0	20	1.29
GUYANA AMAZON WARRIORS..	10	6	4	0	12	0.60
ST LUCIA ZOUKS...............	10	6	4	0	12	−0.02
JAMAICA TALLAWAHS..........	10	3	6	1	7	−0.24
Barbados Tridents..................	10	3	7	0	6	−0.25
St Kitts & Nevis Patriots............	10	1	8	1	3	−1.49

1st v 4th At Tarouba, Trinidad, September 8, 2020. **Trinbago Knight Riders won by nine wickets. Jamaica Tallawahs 107-7** (20 overs) (N. E. Bonner 41, R. Powell 33; A. J. Hosein 3-14); **‡Trinbago Knight Riders 111-1** (15 overs) (L. M. P. Simmons 54*, T. Webster 44*). *PoM:* A. J. Hosein. *The Knight Riders' triumphant progress continued with their 11th successive win. Left-arm spinners Akeal Hosein and Khary Pierre opened the attack, and reduced the Tallawahs to 25-4; Hosein struck in each of his first three overs, while Pierre removed the dangerous Glenn Phillips for two. Jamaica limped to three figures. Though Mujeeb Zadran bowled Sunil Narine cheaply, Lendl Simmons and Tion Webster strolled into the final with five overs in hand.*

2nd v 3rd At Tarouba, Trinidad, September 8, 2020 (floodlit). **St Lucia Zouks by ten wickets. Guyana Amazon Warriors 55** (13.4 overs); **‡St Lucia Zouks 56-0** (4.3 overs) (R. R. S. Cornwall 32*). *PoM:* M. Deyal. *The second knockout was even more one-sided: the Zouks routed the Warriors for 55, the second-lowest total in the CPL's eight editions, and knocked off the runs in 27 deliveries. Guyana were 0-2 after four balls from Scott Kuggeleijn. Only Chanderpaul Hemraj passed 11; he was bowled for 25 by Mark Deyal, who won the match award after taking 2-2 in his only over, catching Nicholas Pooran, and scoring 19* as he and Rahkeem Cornwall rushed St Lucia into their first final.*

Final At Tarouba, Trinidad, September 10, 2020. **Trinbago Knight Riders won by eight wickets. St Lucia Zouks 154** (19.1 overs) (A. D. S. Fletcher 39; K. A. Pollard 4-30); **‡Trinbago Knight Riders 157-2** (18.1 overs) (L. M. P. Simmons 84*, D. M. Bravo 58*). *PoM:* L. M. P. Simmons. *PoT:* K. A. Pollard. *Trinbago's 100% record secured their fourth title in six years. The Zouks had started well – 60-1 in the powerplay – but stumbled when Kieron Pollard dismissed Andre Fletcher and Roston Chase in successive overs, and went on to lose their last five for 17. Pollard finished with four, and also completed a run-out. Any hopes St Lucia retained when they took two early wickets were crushed as Simmons (84* in 49 balls) and Darren Bravo (58* in 47) charged to glory with a stand of 138*, hoisting ten sixes between them.*

CPL FINALS

2013 JAMAICA TALLAWAHS beat Guyana Amazon Warriors by seven wickets at Port-of-Spain.
2014 BARBADOS TRIDENTS beat Guyana Amazon Warriors by eight runs (D/L) at Basseterre.
2015 TRINIDAD & TOBAGO RED STEEL beat Barbados Tridents by 20 runs at Port-of-Spain.
2016 JAMAICA TALLAWAHS beat Guyana Amazon Warriors by nine wickets at Basseterre.
2017 TRINBAGO KNIGHT RIDERS beat St Kitts & Nevis Patriots by three wickets at Tarouba.
2018 TRINBAGO KNIGHT RIDERS beat Guyana Amazon Warriors by eight wickets at Tarouba.
2019 BARBADOS TRIDENTS beat Guyana Amazon Warriors by 27 runs at Tarouba.
2020 TRINBAGO KNIGHT RIDERS beat St Lucia Zouks by eight wickets at Tarouba.

CPL RECORDS

Highest score	132*	B. A. King	Guyana AW v Barbados T at Providence	2019
	121*	A. D. Russell	Jamaica T v Trinbago KR at Port-of-Spain	2018
	116	C. H. Gayle	Jamaica T v St Kitts & Nevis P at Basseterre	2019
Fastest 50 – balls	15	J-P. Duminy	Barbados T v Trinbago KR at Bridgetown	2019
Fastest 100 – balls	40	A. D. Russell	Jamaica T v Trinbago KR at Port-of-Spain	2018
Most sixes – innings	13	A. D. Russell	Jamaica T v Trinbago KR at Port-of-Spain	2018

Most runs – season	567	C. Munro (avge 51.54, SR 140.34) for Trinbago KR	2018
Most sixes – season	37	C. H. Gayle for Jamaica Tallawahs	2016
Most runs – career	**2,436**	**L. M. P. Simmons (avge 33.83, SR 120.41)**	**2013 to 2020**
	2,354	C. H. Gayle (avge 39.23, SR 133.44)	2013 to 2019
	2,081	**A. D. S. Fletcher (avge 29.72, SR 118.30)**	**2013 to 2020**
Most 100s – career	4	C. H. Gayle	2013 to 2019
	4	D. R. Smith	2013 to 2019
Best SR – career†	**173.08**	**A. D. Russell (1,331 runs, avge 32.46)**	**2013 to 2020**
Most sixes – career	162	C. H. Gayle	2013 to 2019

Best bowling	6-6	Shakib Al Hasan	Barbados T v T&T RS at Bridgetown	2013
	5-3	Sohail Tanvir	Guyana AW v Barbados T at Bridgetown	2017
	5-15	**Mohammad Nabi**	**St Lucia Z v St K&N P at Port-of-Spain**	**2020**
Most econ four overs	2-1	Mohammad Irfan	Barbados T v St K&N P at Bridgetown	2018
Most expensive analysis	0-68	J. D. S. Neesham	Trinbago KR v St K&N P at Basseterre	2019

Most wickets – season	28	D. J. Bravo (avge 11.71, ER 7.34) for T&T RS	2015
Most wickets – career	**106**	**D. J. Bravo (avge 21.96, ER 8.57)**	**2013 to 2020**
	96	**R. R. Emrit (avge 22.75, ER 7.64)**	**2013 to 2020**
	85	K. Santokie (avge 19.90, ER 7.59)	2013 to 2019
Best ER – career‡	**5.45**	**S. P. Narine (1,795 balls, avge 20.92)**	**2013 to 2020**

Highest total	267-2	Trinbago KR v Jamaica T at Kingston	2019
	242-6	St Kitts & Nevis P v Jamaica T at Basseterre	2019
Lowest total	52	T&T RS v Barbados T at Bridgetown	2013
Highest successful chase	242-6	St Kitts & Nevis P v Jamaica T at Basseterre	2019
Highest match aggregate	493-7	Jamaica T v Trinbago KR at Kingston	2019

† *Career strike-rate: minimum 500 runs.* ‡ *Career economy-rate: minimum 300 balls.*

OTHER DOMESTIC T20 COMPETITIONS IN 2019-20

SHPAGEEZA T20 TOURNAMENT IN AFGHANISTAN IN 2020

After a delay because of coronavirus concerns, Afghanistan's domestic T20 tournament took place in September. The grounds were allowed to admit up to 30% of their usual capacity; social-distancing measures were enforced, and the Afghan board handed out masks. **Kabul Eagles** lost their first match, to Boost Defenders, but won the rest to top the table; they then narrowly defeated Mis Ainak Knights in the final, helped by three run-outs in a hectic last over. The Knights' Mohammad Shahzad, the former national wicketkeeper-batsman, scored the only century of the competition – an unbeaten 106 against Boost – although 18-year-old Rahmanullah Gurbaz of the Eagles was out for 99 against Amo Sharks. The Sharks were bowled out for 62 by the Knights, with Dawlat Zadran taking five for nine. The Afghanistan Premier League, played in the UAE in October 2018, did not take place in 2019 or 2020.

	P	*W*	*L*	*Pts*	*NRR*
KABUL EAGLES	5	4	1	8	0.35
MIS AINAK KNIGHTS	5	3	2	6	1.77
BAND-E-AMIR DRAGONS	5	3	2	6	1.00
BOOST DEFENDERS	5	3	2	6	0.91
Speen Ghar Tigers	5	2	3	4	–0.60
Amo Sharks	5	0	5	0	–3.48

Preliminary finals 1st v 2nd Kabul Eagles beat Mis Ainak Knights by four wickets. **3rd v 4th** Band-e-Amir beat Boost Defenders by 76 runs. **Final play-off** Mis Ainak beat Band-e-Amir Dragons by five wickets.

Final At Kabul, September 16, 2020. **Kabul Eagles won by nine runs. Kabul Eagles 139** (19.1 overs); ‡**Mis Ainak Knights 130** (19.4 overs). *Kabul Eagles were 12-3 in the second over, but the middle order, led by Younas Ahmadzai (36) and Samiullah Shenwari (32), fought back to 117-6, before another flurry of wickets. Mis Ainak also suffered early losses, but Ghamai Zadran made 40, the match's top score, and they needed 33 off the last three overs with six wickets in hand. Three tumbled to make that 18 off six balls, but three run-outs handed the trophy to Kabul.*

SRI LANKA CRICKET TWENTY20 TOURNAMENT IN 2019-20

Four 20-over mini-leagues plus knockout

The annual domestic T20 tournament occupied a fortnight in January 2020, and was won by **Colombo**, captained by the off-spinning all-rounder Ashan Priyanjan, a former white-ball international. In the final, they came up against Chilaw Marians, whose skipper Shehan Jayasuriya – another recent Sri Lanka player – had hit one of the tournament's three centuries, on the opening day. Chilaw looked likely winners when Colombo reached the last over needing 17 – but Wanindu Hasaranga de Silva hit 15 off the first five deliveries, then Manelker de Silva cracked the last for four. Jayasuriya was the tournament's leading run-scorer, with 385, while Colombo's slow left-armer Malinda Pushpakumara led the wicket-takers with 18. That included three for nine from his four overs as Kandy Customs crumbled for 56. The long-delayed franchise Lanka Premier League finally got under way in November 2020; a report will appear in *Wisden 2022*.

Quarter-finals Chilaw Marians beat Sinhalese by 14 runs; Colombo beat Badureliya by seven wickets; Nondescripts beat Army by six wickets; Ragama beat Colts by five wickets.

Semi-finals Chilaw Marians beat Ragama by 33 runs; Colombo beat Nondescripts by ten runs.

Final At Colombo (SSC), January 21, 2020. **Colombo won by four wickets. Chilaw Marians 162-8** (20 overs) (P. H. K. D. Mendis 46, G. S. N. F. G. Jayasuriya 80); ‡**Colombo 165-6** (20 overs) (M. B. Ranasinghe 59, P. W. H. de Silva 60*). *PoM:* P. W. H. de Silva. *Chilaw Marians had won their quarter- and semi-final after batting first, and seemed set for another victory when, after Kamindu Mendis and captain Shehan Jayasuriya shared a stand of 96 to set up a total of 162, Colombo slipped to 96-6 in the 14th over. But Wanindu Hasaranga de Silva thrashed 60* from 34 balls, and put on 69* with Manelker de Silva. They needed 17 from the last over, bowled by Thikshila de Silva. Hasaranga hit 62421. With two needed, Manelker got the final delivery away for four.*

TEST TRIANGLE INTERPROVINCIAL CUP IN IRELAND IN 2020

Ireland's T20 competition was played in August and September. **Leinster Lightning** completed the first half of a domestic white-ball double, with the 2019 champions Northern Knights second. Only half the scheduled 12 matches escaped the weather, which at least was an improvement on 2019, when only four did. Leinster won all four of their completed games, and the evergreen Kevin O'Brien hit 148 runs at a strike-rate of 182, including the tournament's highest score: 82, with eight sixes – one smashed the back window of his own sponsored car – against North West Warriors. Leinster's off-spinner Simi Singh took eight wickets at 6.62, with an economy-rate just over four. The competition, in its eighth season, was notable for Ireland's leading batsman Paul Stirling playing his first, and so far only, interprovincial innings. Opening for Northern Knights against the Warriors, he had made 41 out of 52 for three when rain ended the game.

	P	*W*	*L*	*A*	*Bonus*	*Pts*	*NRR*
Leinster Lightning	6	4	0	2	2	22	2.60
Northern Knights	6	2	1	3	1	15	0.75
Munster Reds	6	0	2	4	0	8	–4.11
North West Warriors	6	0	0	3	0	6	–2.01

Zimbabwe's usual domestic T20 competition was not played in 2020, because of Covid-19, and there was also no franchise event in Canada. The Pokhara Premier League did take place in Nepal in December 2019 – **Chitwan Rhinos**, captained by Paras Khadka, came out on top of a six-team league, winning all five of their matches, then beat Biratnagar Titans by 32 runs in the final. Rohan Mustafa, the UAE international, won the match award for his 50, and was also Player of the Tournament after making 206 runs, although Puneet Mehra scored more (236) for the Titans. But Mustafa also claimed nine wickets: his team-mate, Nepal seamer K. C. Karan, led the way with 14. The Hong Kong Premier League was not played in 2019-20, but restarted in October 2020; it will be reported in *Wisden 2022*.

PART SEVEN

Women's Cricket

WOMEN'S CRICKET IN 2020

MELINDA FARRELL

March 8 brought the greatest moment in the history of women's cricket: 86,174 fans crammed into the MCG for a box-seat view of the women's T20 World Cup final, won by the dominant Australians, while millions tuned in on television. A few years ago, such an occasion with such an audience would have seemed a dream; a few decades earlier, a delusion. This showpiece was meant to herald a new age of prosperity by proving that the women's game could be a commercially viable arm of the sport.

Alyssa Healy and Beth Mooney ignited fireworks, and Katy Perry sang about them, in the last major sporting beacon as the coronavirus closed in. A week later, the final would not have happened – unless, perhaps, in an empty stadium. The Melbourne Grand Prix scheduled for the following weekend was cancelled, as sport, and so much else, collapsed around the world.

The Covid-19 pandemic ravaged all cricket, from men's Tests to recreational games, but the blow to the women's game, so soon after reaching its highest peak, was enormous. The T20 World Cup should have preceded the 50-over version, due to be held in New Zealand in early 2021; in August, the ICC announced it was being postponed for 12 months, along with the tournament to decide the last three qualifiers. The closing series of the Women's Championship, which determined the initial five, had been cancelled because of the pandemic, and the points split; the ICC extended the same principle to the India–Pakistan series, confirming India's qualification, although Pakistan protested that they should have been awarded the points for a forfeit, as India had declined to play.

The Covid crisis also tested the commitment of domestic boards scrambling to salvage their schedules. The initial forecasts from the ECB were grim: a projected £380m loss. Clare Connor, their managing director of women's cricket, conceded that the more financially lucrative men's series would have to take priority, shunting women to the back of the queue.

"If we have to play less international women's cricket this summer, to safeguard the longer-term future and build the infrastructure for a more stable and sustainable women's game, then that is probably a hit we have to take," she said. "I don't think you can argue with the rationale. For the whole game to survive, the financial necessity rests on many of these international men's matches being fulfilled." For a champion of women's sport such as Connor to accept its relative expendability was sobering.

Ultimately, the ECB did stage some internationals in late September. Although India and South Africa declined to tour, England won five T20s against West Indies in a Derby bubble. There was also a one-off 50-over domestic competition, named the Rachael Heyhoe Flint Trophy after one of the game's pioneers. It was some consolation for the delay of The Hundred, heralded as the centrepiece of the ECB's promotion of women's cricket. But the loss of fixtures was a significant setback, compared with the Herculean efforts that ensured the men's international summer went ahead, along with men's first-class and Twenty20 competitions.

India's women suffered even more. They had been at their best in reaching the T20 World Cup final, but did not play again all year. Their trip to England was cancelled, and their tour of Australia in January 2021 pushed back a season. There was no domestic cricket in India – though the four matches of the Women's T20 Challenge took place in the UAE alongside the closing stages of the IPL in November.

Some boards had the advantage of timing and situation. By September, Australia – who were less badly affected by Covid-19 than many countries – were able to meet New Zealand in three T20s and three ODIs, and even welcomed back small crowds. They also showed significant resolve by creating a biosecure hub in Sydney to stage a full season of the WBBL. Cricket Australia have led the way in professionalising the women's game, but there was the additional pressure of delivering a product for the two television companies with broadcast rights. Channel Seven were pushing for a discount, given the altered summer schedule; any reduction in the agreed number of televised matches would have bolstered their argument.

In New Zealand, which had successfully avoided the worst of the pandemic, the women's domestic competitions resumed alongside the men's in 2020-21. South Africa managed to stage a mini T20 Super League over three days in December, and hosted Pakistan in January. But elsewhere, while boards fought to rescue at least some men's series, the women's game largely ground to a halt. In cricketing nations already scrapping for cash before Covid, its funding is severely threatened.

The Federation of International Cricketers' Associations released their second report into Women's Professional Cricket Global Employment at the start of 2021. Much of it was prepared before the pandemic took hold, but its findings were only magnified by subsequent events. The first report, released in 2018, had highlighted the pyramid of investment in domestic and international cricket by different countries. Australia sat at the top, followed by England and India; New Zealand, South Africa and West Indies formed the next layer of semi-professionalism, above the rest.

The latest report found little change. The hierarchy has been reflected in results, most recently Australia's triumph in the T20 World Cup, where India, England and South Africa also reached the semi-finals. FICA's recommendations included an increase in the volume of women's cricket, professional conditions and fairer representation.

The most inspiring story of the T20 World Cup was the qualification of Thailand, who delighted everyone with their competitive spirit and joyful exuberance. But what does the future hold for emerging countries if more established nations cannot support professionalisation?

The pandemic revealed the worrying reality behind the World Cup euphoria. When cricket is thriving, the women's game can make significant progress, drawing big audiences and commercial success. But when the sport faces financial hardship, equality all too easily slides into expendability, and rhetoric into lip service. The MCG's crowds and hype receded into silence.

ICC WOMEN'S CHAMPIONSHIP IN 2017–2020

In 2014, the ICC introduced a women's Championship as a qualifying tournament for the World Cup, and to create a more meaningful programme for the leading teams. There have been two editions, the first ending in 2016 and the second in 2020; Australia have won both.

Each of the eight sides from the previous World Cup play each other in three one-day internationals over two and a half years (they can arrange more games if they choose, but only the designated three carry points). In 2020, New Zealand – the hosts of the next World Cup – and the top four in the final table advanced directly to the tournament, while the remaining three entered a further qualifying competition with seven others.

In the 2017–2020 cycle, only England and West Indies completed their seven series. Two series in early 2020 – South Africa v Australia and Sri Lanka v New Zealand – had to be cancelled because of the Covid-19 crisis, and the teams were awarded three points each. Meanwhile, India had again declined to play Pakistan; in 2016, the ICC had awarded the six points for the series to Pakistan, but in April 2020 India persuaded them to split the points, on the grounds that their government had not allowed them to fulfil the fixtures. This ensured they secured the fifth direct qualification slot, which would have gone to Pakistan had India been deemed to have forfeited the series. As in 2016, Australia finished several points clear of England at the head of the table.

New Zealand was originally set to stage the World Cup in early 2021, but it was postponed for a year because of the pandemic, and is now scheduled for March 3–April 4, 2022. The qualifying tournament to determine the three remaining participants is due to take place in Sri Lanka in June and July 2021, featuring Pakistan, West Indies and Sri Lanka (non-qualifiers from the Championship), Bangladesh and Ireland (who also have ODI status), and the winners of five regional qualifiers: the Netherlands (Europe), Papua New Guinea (East Asia Pacific), Thailand (Asia), USA (Americas) and Zimbabwe (Africa).

FINAL QUALIFYING TABLE

	P	*W*	*L*	*T*	*NR*	*A*	*Pts*	*NRR*
AUSTRALIA	21	17	1	0	0	3	37	1.83
ENGLAND	21	14	6	0	1	0	29	1.26
SOUTH AFRICA	21	10	6	1	1	3	25	–0.30
INDIA	21	10	8	0	0	3	23	0.46
Pakistan	21	7	9	1	1	3	19	–0.46
NEW ZEALAND	21	7	11	0	0	3	17	–0.20
West Indies	21	6	14	0	1	0	13	–1.03
Sri Lanka	21	1	17	0	0	3	5	–1.61

New Zealand qualified for the World Cup ahead of Pakistan because they are the hosts of the tournament.

South Africa v Australia and Sri Lanka v New Zealand were cancelled because of the Covid-19 pandemic, while India declined to play Pakistan.

"He was holding the ball aloft, not to acknowledge the crowd, since there was none, but in dedication to his father, Bob, who had recently died at a Leicester care home from Covid-related illnesses."

Five Cricketers of the Year, page 73

MRF TYRES ICC WOMEN'S RANKINGS

In 2015, the ICC introduced a table of women's international rankings, which combined results from Tests, one-day internationals and Twenty20 internationals. In 2018, after Twenty20 international status was extended to all Associate women's teams, this was replaced by separate rankings for one-day and Twenty20 cricket.

ONE-DAY INTERNATIONAL TEAM RANKINGS

(As at December 31, 2020)

		Matches	*Points*	*Rating*
1	Australia	15	2,436	162
2	India	15	1,812	121
3	England	14	1,670	119
4	South Africa	16	1,713	107
5	New Zealand	15	1,384	92
6	West Indies	12	1,025	85
7	Pakistan	12	927	77
8	Bangladesh	5	306	61
9	Sri Lanka	11	519	47
10	Ireland	2	25	13

TWENTY20 INTERNATIONAL TEAM RANKINGS

(As at December 31, 2020)

		Matches	*Points*	*Rating*
1	Australia	29	8,438	291
2	England	30	8,405	280
3	India	32	8,640	270
4	New Zealand	23	6,197	269
5	South Africa	24	5,978	249
6	West Indies	26	6,126	236
7	Pakistan	24	5,516	230
8	Sri Lanka	18	3,631	202
9	Bangladesh	26	5,001	192
10	Ireland	13	2,180	168
11	Thailand	26	4,145	159
12	Zimbabwe	11	1,711	156

Remaining rankings: 13 Scotland (149), 14 Nepal (132), 15 PNG (129), 16 Samoa (125), 17 UAE (121), 18 Uganda (120), 19 Tanzania (108), 20 Indonesia (87), 21 Netherlands (83), 22 Kenya (82), 23 Namibia (69), 24 Hong Kong (67), 25 Germany (66), 26 China (63), 27 Brazil (54), 28 Vanuatu (54), 29 Japan (52), 30 France (48), 31 USA (47), 32 Belize (45), 33 Argentina (44), 34 Rwanda (43), 35 Myanmar (42), 36 Kuwait (42), 37 Sierra Leone (41), 38 Malaysia (40), 39 Jersey (40), 40 Botswana (39), 41 Nigeria (32), 42 Oman (26), 43 Bhutan (23), 44 South Korea (18), 45 Malawi (16), 46 Chile (12), 47 Singapore (10), 48 Costa Rica (10), 49 Mozambique (7), 50 Mexico (5), 51 Austria (1), 52= Fiji (0), Lesotho (0), Mali (0), Norway (0), Peru (0).

PLAYER RANKINGS

In October 2008, the ICC launched a set of rankings for women cricketers, on the same principles as those for men, based on one-day international performances. Twenty20 rankings were added in September 2012. There are no Test rankings.

The leading players in the women's one-day international rankings on December 31, 2020, were:

	Batsmen	*Points*		*Bowlers*	*Points*
1	M. M. Lanning (A)	749	1	J. L. Jonassen (A)	804
2	S. R. Taylor (WI)	746	2	M. Kapp (SA)	738
3	A. J. Healy (A)	741	3	M. Schutt (A)	735
4	S. S. Mandhana (I)	732	4	S. Ismail (SA)	717
5	A. E. Satterthwaite (NZ)	723	5	J. N. Goswami (I)	691
6	T. T. Beaumont (E)	716	6	P. Yadav (I)	679
7	E. A. Perry (A)	691	7	S. S. Pandey (I)	675
8	L. Lee (SA)	690	8	E. A. Perry (A)	666
9	L. Wolvaardt (SA)	689	9	A. Shrubsole (E)	645
10	M. D. Raj (I)	687	10	D. B. Sharma (I)	639

The leading players in the women's Twenty20 international rankings on December 31, 2020, were:

	Batsmen	*Points*		*Bowlers*	*Points*
1	B. L. Mooney (A)	748	1	S. Ecclestone (E)	777
2	S. W. Bates (NZ)	745	2	M. Schutt (A)	753
3	S. Verma (I)	744	3	S. Ismail (SA)	743
4	S. F. M. Devine (NZ)	738	4	A. C. Kerr (NZ)	739
5	M. M. Lanning (A)	712	5	J. L. Jonassen (A)	730
6	A. J. Healy (A)	705	6	D. B. Sharma (I)	716
7	S. S. Mandhana (I)	693	7	R. P. Yadav (I)	704
8	S. R. Taylor (WI)	658	8	P. Yadav (I)	698
9	J. I. Rodrigues (I)	643	9	S. Glenn (E)	684
10	N. R. Sciver (E)	629	10	G. L. Wareham (A)	666

WOMEN'S ONE-DAY INTERNATIONAL AVERAGES IN CALENDAR YEAR 2020

BATTING (100 runs)

		M	*I*	*NO*	*R*	*HS*	*100*	*50*	*Avge*	*SR*	*4*	*6*
1	†R. L. Haynes (A)	3	3	0	222	96	0	2	74.00	87.05	28	4
2	L. Wolvaardt (SA)	3	3	1	117	91*	0	1	58.50	62.56	13	0
3	L. Lee (SA)	3	3	0	157	99	0	1	52.33	95.15	22	1
4	A. J. Healy (A)	3	3	0	134	87	0	1	44.66	100.75	21	2
5	S. W. Bates (NZ)	4	4	0	156	53	0	2	39.00	69.95	14	0
6	†A. E. Satterthwaite (NZ)	3	3	0	111	69	0	1	37.00	85.38	15	0
7	K. T. Perkins (NZ)	6	6	1	132	78	0	1	26.40	72.92	11	0
8	S. F. M. Devine (NZ)	6	6	0	150	79	0	1	25.00	66.37	13	0
9	M. M. Lanning (A)	2	2	2	163	101*	1	1	–	98.19	14	5

BOWLING (5 wickets)

		Style	*O*	*M*	*R*	*W*	*BB*	*4I*	*Avge*	*SR*	*ER*
1	J. L. Jonassen (A)	SLA	24.1	0	81	8	4-36	1	10.12	18.12	3.35
2	S. E. Luus (SA)	LB	15	0	67	6	6-45	1	11.16	15.00	4.46
3	S. G. Molineux (A)	SLA	20	3	79	6	2-2	0	13.16	20.00	3.95
4	A. Khaka (SA)	RFM	17	0	75	5	3-43	0	15.00	20.40	4.41
5	M. Kapp (SA)	RFM	20	0	79	5	4-29	1	15.80	24.00	3.95
6	M. Schutt (A)	RFM	25	4	115	5	2-25	0	23.00	30.00	4.60
7	A. C. Kerr (NZ)	LB	50	1	237	7	3-47	0	33.85	42.85	4.74

WOMEN'S TWENTY20 INTERNATIONAL AVERAGES IN CALENDAR YEAR 2020

BATTING (150 runs)

		M	*I*	*NO*	*R*	*HS*	*100*	*50*	*Avge*	*SR*	*4*	*6*
1	S. Verma (I)	10	10	0	265	49	0	0	26.50	**149.71**	33	11
2	A. J. Healy (A)	14	14	0	298	83	0	3	21.28	**141.23**	37	11
3	H. C. Knight (E)	13	13	1	486	108*	1	3	40.50	**135.75**	55	11
4	†A. M. C. Jayangani (SL)	4	4	0	154	50	0	1	38.50	**135.08**	19	7
5	†S. S. Mandhana (I)	9	9	0	265	66	0	2	29.44	**134.51**	41	3
6	†C. M. Gough (Germany)	9	7	3	348	101*	1	3	87.00	**127.47**	41	1
7	S. F. M. Devine (NZ)	11	11	2	492	105	1	4	54.66	**126.47**	41	21
8	A. K. Gardner (A)	14	13	1	337	93	0	2	28.08	**126.21**	42	9
9	L. Lee (SA)	8	8	0	181	101	1	0	22.62	**123.97**	29	3
10	†B. L. Mooney (A)	14	14	3	504	81*	0	6	45.81	**122.92**	64	3
11	L. Wolvaardt (SA)	8	6	2	158	53*	0	1	39.50	**121.53**	19	2
12	†R. L. Haynes (A)	14	13	3	234	60	0	1	23.40	**120.00**	18	5
13	T. T. Beaumont (E)	13	11	0	181	62	0	1	16.45	**119.86**	26	2
14	N. R. Sciver (E)	13	13	1	402	82	0	5	33.50	**116.52**	49	3
15	A. E. Jones (E)	13	13	1	177	55	0	1	14.75	**107.27**	20	3
16	J. E. Ronalds (Germany)	9	7	3	342	105*	1	2	85.50	**106.87**	32	0
17	D. J. S. Dottin (WI)	8	8	0	197	69	0	2	24.62	**105.34**	22	5
18	†D. B. Sharma (I)	10	10	5	158	49*	0	0	31.60	**100.63**	11	0
19	M. M. Lanning (A)	13	12	3	279	49*	0	0	31.00	**100.35**	29	4
20	J. I. Rodrigues (I)	10	10	1	167	34	0	0	18.55	**97.66**	16	1
21	S. W. Bates (NZ)	11	11	2	201	47*	0	0	22.33	**90.54**	14	0
22	S. R. Taylor (WI)	8	8	4	162	43	0	0	40.50	**87.09**	18	2
23	S. V. Shetty (Oman)	9	9	0	158	44	0	0	17.55	**71.17**	12	0

BOWLING (10 wickets)

		Style	*B*	*D*	*R*	*W*	*BB*	*4I*	*Avge*	*SR*	*ER*
1	E. C. Bargna (Germany)	OB	138	101	78	12	5-9	1	6.50	11.50	**3.39**
2	S. Ecclestone (E)	SLA	289	161	236	19	3-7	0	12.42	15.21	**4.89**
3	A. C. Kerr (NZ)	LB	246	108	218	14	2-17	0	15.57	17.57	**5.31**
4	S. Glenn (E)	LB	252	124	224	18	3-15	0	12.44	14.00	**5.33**
5	J. L. Jonassen (A)	SLA	306	135	285	19	5-12	1	15.00	16.10	**5.58**
6	P. Yadav (I)	LB	120	52	119	10	4-19	1	11.90	12.00	**5.95**
7	N. R. Sciver (E)	RM	216	102	215	11	3-23	0	19.54	19.63	**5.97**
8	H. N. K. Jensen (NZ)	RM	174	76	174	11	3-11	0	15.81	15.81	**6.00**
9	B. Shetty (Oman)	RFM	176	33	181	10	2-8	0	18.10	17.60	**6.17**
10	R. S. Gayakwad (I)	SLA	240	113	251	15	3-23	0	16.73	16.00	**6.27**
11	K. H. Brunt (E)	RFM	269	135	289	13	2-21	0	22.23	20.69	**6.44**
12	S. R. Taylor (WI)	OB	140	52	152	10	3-13	0	15.20	14.00	**6.51**
13	D. B. Sharma (I)	OB	240	100	268	11	2-27	0	24.36	21.81	**6.70**
14	M. Schutt (A)	RFM	304	133	346	22	4-18	2	15.72	13.81	**6.82**
15	A. Shrubsole (E)	RFM	228	110	268	12	3-21	0	22.33	19.00	**7.05**
16	S. S. Pandey (I)	RM	238	106	280	10	3-14	0	28.00	23.80	**7.05**
17	S. F. M. Devine (NZ)	RM	179	80	214	11	3-18	0	19.45	16.27	**7.17**
18	R. P. Yadav (I)	SLA	191	74	231	11	4-23	1	21.00	17.36	**7.25**

ICC WOMEN'S TWENTY20 WORLD CUP IN 2019-20

REVIEW BY KALIKA MEHTA

1 Australia 2 India 3= England, South Africa

"You're going to hear me roar!" pop singer Katy Perry bellowed to more than 86,000 spectators rocking the MCG on International Women's Day. You could have been forgiven for thinking that Perry, the first to attract 100 million followers on Twitter, was there to headline a concert. In fact, her call to female empowerment signalled the end of an extraordinary tournament that had showcased record-breaking cricket in front of generous crowds.

The seventh women's T20 World Cup, which ran for 17 days in February and March, proved a landmark event, not least because it was almost the last international cricket, men's or women's, to be played for several months before the coronavirus gripped the world. Some truths remained constant – despite a couple of blips, **Australia** extended their dominance of women's cricket when they were crowned T20 champions for the fifth time – but the quality of all ten teams demonstrated the talent across an ever-growing game. Its followers radiated excitement.

The beaming smiles of **Thailand's** players stole the early limelight as they arrived for their first World Cup in women's or men's cricket. Their government had not recognised the sport until 2008, so this was a feat for which the Cricket Association of Thailand deserved praise. They have created a blueprint for how Associate countries should treat women's teams, giving their 11 core players

Cameron Spencer, Getty Images

Constellation: Katy Perry and the stars of Australia roar after victory in the Twenty20 World Cup.

central contracts, while younger players are able to continue their education alongside cricket scholarships. Despite ending the tournament without a win, Sornnarin Tippoch's team showed glimpses of promise: in their first game, they reduced West Indies to 27 for three; in their last, opening bat Natthakan Chantham struck her country's maiden World Cup half-century, against Pakistan, before the match was washed out, dashing their hopes of victory.

World Cups have often seen a clear gap between the best and the rest, but there was evidence it was beginning to close. **South Africa's** potential was finally converted into success after Mignon du Preez slapped a last-over six in their first victory over England at any women's World Cup for nearly 20 years. **Pakistan**, meanwhile, so often disappointing in the major competitions, produced a near-perfect display to defeat West Indies – champions in 2015-16 – kindling hopes of reaching the knockout stages for the first time. Though it proved their only win, they had good moments in every match.

New Zealand and **West Indies** were both underwhelming, and faced some stark realities. Despite plenty of talent, and a change of captain and coach, the New Zealanders failed to reach the knockout of a world tournament for the third time running; they lost to India by three runs, and to Australia by four. Being skittled for 91, in **Bangladesh's** best performance, was a low for Sophie Devine's side, even though they went on to win. If New Zealand were to make waves when they hosted the 50-over World Cup in 2021, they needed to get to the root of their problems with big tournaments. West Indies were plagued by injury, poor fielding and the failure of their best to fire. A team which looked dangerous on paper seemed to be going backwards on the field.

As in the Caribbean in 2018-19, **Sri Lanka's** only win came against Bangladesh, though there were individual successes for captain Chamari Atapattu Jayangani and, in her final international outing, off-spinner Shashikala Siriwardene, comfortably her country's leading wicket-taker, with 201.

Few cricket events are complete without rain – and when the heavens opened **England** were the biggest losers. Heather Knight, who had smashed a maiden T20I century in their comprehensive win over Thailand, paid a heavy price for that opening defeat by South Africa. A second-place finish in Group B set up a semi-final clash against **India** – already a tough task against an unbeaten side boasting 16-year-old opener Shafali Verma in brilliant touch, and the unrelated spinners Poonam and Radha Yadav bamboozling all before them.

But with both semi-finals taking place on the same day at Sydney, and no reserve day, a downpour saw India through to their first T20 World Cup final, as they had led Group A. It was a bitter pill for England to swallow – many questions were raised about the scheduling – but the regulations had been agreed in advance, so there was little room to complain. An incredible effort from the SCG groundstaff enabled Australia's clash against South Africa to be played that evening. Captain Meg Lanning's unbeaten 49 anchored a challenging total, and Australia held their nerve to reach their sixth successive T20 final, after more rain revised South Africa's target to 98 off 13. Had the rain continued, South Africa would have gone through instead.

That set up a mouth-watering climax between Lanning's Southern Stars – the competition favourites – and Harmanpreet Kaur's India, the combination

Tony Ashby, AFP/Getty Images

Thai fives: Chanida Sutthiruang of Thailand enjoys the dismissal of West Indies' Deandra Dottin.

most likely to realise Cricket Australia's ambition of filling the MCG. In the tournament's opening fixture, India had brushed aside the Australians, whose batters were bewildered by a masterclass from leg-spinner Poonam Yadav: she took four for 19 as they folded for 115.

But in the final, Verma – one of four teenagers in India's 15-strong squad – came unstuck: when she dropped Alyssa Healy in the first over, it set the tone. Fluffed lines in the field had been a theme throughout the tournament; India were the biggest culprits, with nine dropped catches. Healy took advantage of the nerves that seemed to spread through the Indian team, striking a half-century off 30 balls, the fastest in any World Cup final, as Australia piled up the highest total in the final of any T20 World Cup. Healy's opening partner, Beth Mooney, took her tournament aggregate to 259, beating Lanning's record of 257 in 2013-14. In front of a raucous crowd, Australia completed a crushing 85-run defeat.

Despite the disappointment, there was no doubting the strides India had made. Calls grew louder for further investment and greater infrastructure in the domestic game, and a women's Indian Premier League may have come closer.

For Australia, their opening blip aside, the tournament demonstrated their depth – especially as they were forced to play both knockout matches without their talisman Ellyse Perry, who had strained a hamstring. Across each of the six cities in which they appeared, from warm-up matches to group games and the knockouts, the Australians were followed with a fanaticism previously inspired only by the men's team.

Though they were just short of filling the MCG, the 86,174 attending the final constituted the second-biggest official crowd at any women's sporting fixture, after the 90,185 who watched the 1999 football World Cup final at Pasadena. The total attendance of 136,549 was the highest for any women's cricket tournament, and the ICC reported 1.1bn video views across their digital channels.

This World Cup was the biggest sign yet that 2020 was not a turning point for women's cricket: that point had already arrived.

STATISTICS

Leading run-scorers

	M	*I*	*NO*	*R*	*HS*	*50*	*Avge*	*SR*	*4*	*6*
†B. L. Mooney (A)	6	6	2	259	81*	3	64.75	125.12	30	2
A. J. Healy (A).	6	6	0	236	83	3	39.33	156.29	28	9
N. R. Sciver (E)	4	4	1	202	59*	3	67.33	113.48	24	1
H. C. Knight (E)	4	4	1	193	108*	2	64.33	136.87	22	5
S. Verma (I).	5	5	0	163	47	0	32.60	158.25	18	9
†A. M. C. Jayangani (SL) .	4	4	0	154	50	1	38.50	135.08	19	7
S. F. M. Devine (NZ). . . .	4	4	1	132	75*	1	44.00	103.93	11	3
M. M. Lanning (A)	6	5	2	132	49*	0	44.00	99.24	14	1
L. Lee (SA)	4	4	0	119	101	1	29.75	138.37	19	3
†D. B. Sharma (I).	5	5	2	116	49*	0	38.66	95.86	7	0
Nigar Sultana (B).	4	4	0	114	39	0	28.50	88.37	15	0
†R. L. Haynes (A)	6	5	1	106	60	1	26.50	123.25	6	3
N. Chantham (Thai).	4	4	0	103	56	1	25.75	83.73	17	0

The only centuries were H. C. Knight's 108 for England and L. Lee's 101 for South Africa, both v Thailand at Canberra.*

Best strike-rates

	SR	*Runs*		*SR*	*Runs*
S. Verma (I).	158.25	163	S. E. Luus (SA).	125.00	95
A. J. Healy (A)	156.29	236	†R. L. Haynes (A).	123.25	106
L. Wolvaardt (SA).	149.20	94	Aliya Riaz (P)	123.07	80
L. Lee (SA)	138.37	119	N. R. Sciver (E).	113.48	202
H. C. Knight (E)	136.87	193	M. L. Green (NZ)	112.19	92
†A. M. C. Jayangani (SL)	135.08	154	Javeria Khan (P)	106.49	82
†B. L. Mooney (A)	125.12	259	S. F. M. Devine (NZ)	103.93	132

Minimum 75 runs.

Leading wicket-takers

	Style	*B*	*D*	*R*	*W*	*BB*	*4I*	*Avge*	*SR*	*ER*
M. Schutt (A)	RFM	127	60	134	13	4-18	1	10.30	9.76	6.33
P. Yadav (I)	LB	120	52	119	10	4-19	1	11.90	12.00	5.95
J. L. Jonassen (A).	SLA	138	58	140	10	3-20	0	14.00	13.80	6.08
S. Ecclestone (E)	SLA	91	63	49	8	3-7	0	6.12	11.37	3.23
A. Shrubsole (E).	RFM	84	48	85	8	3-21	0	10.62	10.50	6.07
H. N. K. Jensen (NZ)	RM	84	38	73	7	3-11	0	10.42	12.00	5.21
H. A. S. D. Siriwardene (SL)	OB	90	40	99	7	4-16	1	14.14	12.85	6.60
S. S. Pandey (I).	RM	119	48	136	7	3-14	0	19.42	17.00	6.85
S. Glenn (E)	LB	96	52	68	6	3-15	0	11.33	16.00	4.25
A. C. Kerr (NZ)	LB	96	51	74	6	2-21	0	12.33	16.00	4.62
R. P. Yadav (I)	SLA	72	31	82	6	4-23	1	13.66	12.00	6.83
Diana Baig (P)	RM	96	59	85	6	2-19	0	14.16	16.00	5.31
Salma Khatun (B).	OB	80	35	86	6	3-7	0	14.33	13.33	6.45
Aimen Anwar (P)	RFM	72	23	105	6	3-30	0	17.50	12.00	8.75
Nida Dar (P)	OB	96	35	116	6	2-30	0	19.33	16.00	7.25

Most economical bowlers

	ER		*ER*
S. Ecclestone (E)	3.23	S. Ismail (SA)	4.68
K. D. U. Prabodhani (SL)	3.68	A. Mohammed (WI)	4.70
S. Glenn (E)	4.25	N. Mlaba (SA)	4.86
Ritu Moni (B)	4.50	S. E. Luus (SA)	5.00
G. L. Wareham (A)	4.57	N. de Klerk (SA)	5.14
A. C. Kerr (NZ)	4.62	H. N. K. Jensen (NZ)	5.21

Minimum 42 balls.

Leading wicketkeepers

	Dis	*M*		*Dis*	*M*
T. Bhatia (I)	10 (6ct, 4st)	5	A. E. Jones (E)	4 (2ct, 2st)	4
A. J. Healy (A)	7 (3ct, 4st)	6	Nigar Sultana (B)	4 (1ct, 3st)	4
T. Chetty (SA)	4 (2ct, 2st)	4			

Leading fielders

	Ct	*M*		*Ct*	*M*
B. L. Mooney (A)	5	6	N. J. Carey (A)	4	5
A. C. Kerr (NZ)	4	4	M. M. Lanning (A)	4	6

NATIONAL SQUADS

* *Captain.* † *Did not play.*

Australia *M. M. Lanning, †E. A. Burns, N. J. Carey, A. K. Gardner, R. L. Haynes, A. J. Healy, J. L. Jonassen, D. M. Kimmince, S. G. Molineux, B. L. Mooney, E. A. Perry, M. Schutt, M. R. Strano, A. J. Sutherland, G. L. Wareham. *Coach:* M. P. Mott.

T. J. Vlaeminck was ruled out by a foot injury on the eve of the tournament and replaced by Strano.

Bangladesh *Salma Khatun, Ayasha Rahman, Fahima Khatun, Farzana Haque, Jahanara Alam, Khadija Tul Kobra, Murshida Khatun, Nahida Akter, Nigar Sultana, Panna Ghosh, Ritu Moni, Rumana Ahmed, Sanjida Islam, Shamima Sultana, Sobhana Mostary. *Coach:* A. Jain.

England *H. C. Knight, T. T. Beaumont, K. H. Brunt, †K. L. Cross, †F. R. Davies, S. Ecclestone, †G. A. Elwiss, S. Glenn, A. E. Jones, N. R. Sciver, A. Shrubsole, M. K. Villiers, F. C. Wilson, L. Winfield, D. N. Wyatt. *Coach:* L. M. Keightley.

India *H. Kaur, T. Bhatia, †H. Deol, R. S. Gayakwad, R. M. Ghosh, V. Krishnamurthy, S. S. Mandhana, S. S. Pandey, A. Reddy, J. I. Rodrigues, D. B. Sharma, †P. Vastrakar, S. Verma, P. Yadav, R. P. Yadav. *Coach:* W. V. Raman.

New Zealand *S. F. M. Devine, S. W. Bates, †L. R. Down, M. L. Green, †H. R. Huddleston, H. N. K. Jensen, L. M. Kasperek, A. C. Kerr, J. M. Kerr, R. A. Mair, K. J. Martin, K. T. Perkins, A. M. Peterson, R. H. Priest, L. M. Tahuhu. *Coach:* R. M. Carter.

Pakistan *Bismah Maroof, Aimen Anwar, Aliya Riaz, Anam Amin, Ayesha Naseem, Diana Baig, †Fatima Sana, Iram Javed, Javeria Khan, Muneeba Ali, †Nahida Khan, Nida Dar, Sadia Iqbal, Sidra Nawaz, Syeda Aroob Shah, Umaima Sohail. *Coach:* Iqbal Imam.

Bismah Maroof broke her thumb during Pakistan's match against England, and was replaced by Nahida Khan. Javeria Khan took over the captaincy.

South Africa *D. van Niekerk, T. Chetty, N. de Klerk, M. du Preez, S. Ismail, M. Kapp, A. Khaka, †M. M. Klaas, L. Lee, S. E. Luus, N. Mlaba, †T. S. Sekhukhune, †N. Shangase, C. L. Tryon, L. Wolvaardt. *Coach:* H. K. Moreeng.

Sri Lanka *A. M. C. Jayangani, N. N. D. de Silva, W. K. Dilhari, K. A. D. A. Kanchana, H. I. H. Karunaratne, W. G. A. K. K. Kulasuriya, B. M. S. M. Kumari, G. W. H. M. Perera, K. D. U.

Prabodhani, H. M. D. Samarawickrama, P. S. Sandeepani, M. A. A. Sanjeewani, H. A. S. D. Siriwardene, †M. A. D. D. Surangika, U. N. Thimashini. *Coach:* H. de Silva.

Thailand *S. Tippoch, N. Boochatham, N. Chaiwai, N. Chantham, O. Kamchomphu, †R. Kanoh, †S. Khiaoto, N. Koncharoenkai, S. Laomi, S. Lateh, W. Liengprasert, †P. Maya, R. Padunglerd, †T. Putthawong, C. Sutthiruang. *Coach:* H. J. Pathak.

West Indies *S. R. Taylor, A. A. Alleyne, S. A. Campbelle, S. S. Connell, B. Cooper, D. J. S. Dottin, A. S. S. Fletcher, †C. Fraser, †S. S. Grimmond, C. A. Henry, L. G. L. Kirby, H. K. Matthews, A. Mohammed, C. N. Nation, S. C. Selman. *Coach:* A. L. Logie.

Group A

At Sydney (Showground), February 21, 2020 (floodlit). **India won by 17 runs. India 132-4** (20 overs) (D. B. Sharma 49*); ‡**Australia 115** (19.5 overs) (A. J. Healy 51, A. K. Gardner 34; S. S. Pandey 3-14, P. Yadav 4-19). *PoM:* P. Yadav. *Poonam Yadav's loopy spin turned the match after Australia needed 75 off 11 overs with eight wickets in hand. In 13 chaotic balls, she took 4–6, and would have had a hat-trick if wicketkeeper Taniya Bhatia had not dropped Jess Jonassen moments after Ellyse Perry was bowled by a googly. Yadav later bowled Ashleigh Gardner too, but the delivery had bounced twice before reaching the popping crease, and was thus a no-ball. Before a crowd of 13,432 – then a record for a standalone women's game in Australia – the hosts lost nine for 60 in total; only Alyssa Healy and Gardner reached double figures. India had made a lively start, thanks to Shafali Verma's 15-ball 29, before Deepti Sharma's career-best 49* off 46 gave their bowlers something to defend. Yadav accepted the challenge.*

At Perth (WACA), February 22, 2020 (floodlit). **New Zealand won by seven wickets. Sri Lanka 127-7** (20 overs) (A. M. C. Jayangani 41; H. N. K. Jensen 3-16); ‡**New Zealand 131-3** (17.4 overs) (S. F. M. Devine 75*). *PoM:* H. N. K. Jensen. *Sri Lanka began well, as openers Hasini Perera (20) and Chamari Atapattu Jayangani put on 60 inside eight overs. But after Jayangani gave a return catch to Lea Tahuhu in the 12th, they managed only 40 more, with medium-pacer Hayley Jensen*

Flight engineer: Poonam Yadav celebrates the fall of Ellyse Perry with Taniya Bhatia.

equalling her career-best 3-16. Sophie Devine, dropped on 18 (Suzie Bates was also dropped, first ball), spanked 75 from 55 – her sixth successive T20I half-century – to take New Zealand to a convincing victory.*

At Perth (WACA), February 24, 2020. **Australia won by five wickets.** ‡**Sri Lanka 122-6** (20 overs) (A. M. C. Jayangani 50); **Australia 123-5** (19.3 overs) (M. M. Lanning 41*, R. L. Haynes 60). *PoM:* R. L. Haynes. *At 10-3 in the fourth over, Australia were contemplating the unthinkable – a second successive defeat, and elimination from their home tournament. But Meg Lanning and Rachael Haynes dragged things back with a gritty stand of 95, and Lanning's clenched fist when Perry scrambled the winning runs with three balls left spoke volumes. Australia needed some fortune – Haynes was dropped on 26 when the required rate was climbing. "There were nerves," she said. "But we showed our character." Jayangani's 50 off 38 had been the bedrock of Sri Lanka's total, before the left-arm swing of Udeshika Prabodhani exposed Australia's top order.*

At Perth (WACA), February 24, 2020 (floodlit). **India won by 18 runs. India 142-6** (20 overs) (S. Verma 39, J. I. Rodrigues 34); ‡**Bangladesh 124-8** (20 overs) (Murshida Khatun 30, Nigar Sultana 35; P. Yadav 3-18). *PoM:* S. Verma. *Poonam Yadav shone once more, stifling the Bangladesh chase with 24–14–18–3 as India completed a comfortable win. Their batsmen had faltered slightly after Verma's action-packed 39 from 17 balls, including four sixes, and Sharma was run out after a mix-up with Veda Krishnamurthy that involved both batsmen racing to the same end. But Krishnamurthy's late flurry – four fours in 11 balls – turned a shaky 113-6 into a respectable 142, and Bangladesh lacked oomph with the bat.*

At St Kilda, February 27, 2020. **India won by three runs. India 133-8** (20 overs) (S. Verma 46); ‡**New Zealand 130-6** (20 overs) (A. C. Kerr 34*). *PoM:* S. Verma. *India became the first to qualify for the semi-finals, thanks to a third straight win – their tightest yet. Verma made a dynamic start, striking consecutive sixes off Anna Peterson during a half-century stand with Bhatia. But from 68-1 in nine overs, India fell away; Amelia Kerr followed two catches with two wickets, including Verma. New Zealand's top order failed to get going – Devine's run of fifties ended when she fell for 14 – and they needed 34 off the last two overs. Kerr smashed 18, including four fours, off Poonam Yadav; she needed five off the final ball, or four for a super over, but Shikha Pandey's yorker kept her to a leg-bye.*

At Canberra, February 27, 2020 (floodlit) **Australia won by 86 runs.** ‡**Australia 189-1** (20 overs) (A. J. Healy 83, B. L. Mooney 81*); **Bangladesh 103-9** (20 overs) (Farzana Haque 36; M. Schutt 3-21). *PoM:* A. J. Healy. *A national all-wicket record stand of 151 between Healy and Beth Mooney propelled Australia towards an emphatic win. Healy led the charge, racing to 83 off 53, while Mooney finished with 81* off 58. Gardner added 22* off nine as Bangladesh wilted under the assault, dropping three late catches. They soon slipped to 26-3, before Nigar Sultana (19) and Farzana Haque put on 50. But it took more than eight overs, and the match ended with three wickets in three balls, two to run-outs.*

At St Kilda, February 29, 2020. **New Zealand won by 17 runs.** ‡**New Zealand 91** (18.2 overs) (Salma Khatun 3-7, Ritu Moni 4-18); **Bangladesh 74** (19.5 overs) (L. M. Kasperek 3-23, H. N. K. Jensen 3-11). *PoM:* H. N. K. Jensen. *New Zealand looked set to crash out after being rolled over for 91 on a sluggish pitch. Medium-pacer Ritu Moni finished with a career-best 24–12–18–4, and spinners Salma Khatun and Rumana Ahmed a combined 5-24. From 66-2 in the 13th, eight wickets tumbled for 25. No side had defended so low a total in a T20 World Cup, but New Zealand's bowlers strangled Bangladesh to such an extent that only Sultana (21) passed 11. There were 76 dot balls, 18 by Kerr (1-10) and 16 by Devine (1-14). This time, Jensen bettered her career-best, with 3-11.*

At St Kilda, February 29, 2020 (floodlit). **India won by seven wickets.** ‡**Sri Lanka 113-9** (20 overs) (A. M. C. Jayangani 33; R. P. Yadav 4-23); **India 116-3** (14.4 overs) (S. Verma 47). *PoM:* R. P. Yadav. *T20I debut:* P. S. Sandeepani (Sri Lanka). *The only side to win all four of their group games, India got there with more than five overs in hand. Jayangani had chosen to bat, and made a forceful 33 before being caught attempting a second successive six off Radha Yadav, who collected a career-best 4-23. No. 9 Kavisha Dilhari struck 25* in 16 balls, but the target was only 114. Verma's 47 took her tournament aggregate to 161, and India were well on the way when Dilhari ran her out.*

At St Kilda, March 2, 2020. **Sri Lanka won by nine wickets.** ‡**Bangladesh 91-8** (20 overs) (Nigar Sultana 39; H. A. S. D. Siriwardene 4-16); **Sri Lanka 92-1** (15.3 overs) (G. W. H. M. Perera 39*, A. M. C. Jayangani 30). *PoM:* H. A. S. D. Siriwardene. *A one-sided tussle between the group's two winless teams went Sri Lanka's way, allowing Shashikala Siriwardene to end her 17-year international career on a high. Opening the bowling with canny, attacking off-spin, she picked up*

4-16, thanks in part to pressure applied at the other end by left-arm seamer Prabodhani, whose four wicketless overs cost only 13. The one Bangladesh player to muster much resistance was Sultana: her 39 came from 45 balls. Sri Lanka could afford to take their time, but Jayangani sped to a 22-ball 30; Perera anchored them to a nine-wicket rout.

At St Kilda, March 2, 2020 (floodlit). **Australia won by four runs. Australia 155-5** (20 overs) (B. L. Mooney 60); ‡**New Zealand 151-7** (20 overs) (S. F. M. Devine 31, K. J. Martin 37*; M. Schutt 3-28, G. L. Wareham 3-17). *PoM:* G. L. Wareham. *Both sides' defeats by India turned this into a knockout, and Australia scraped through. They were indebted to leg-spinner Georgia Wareham, who removed Bates (14), Devine and Maddy Green (28 from 23) when they appeared set. Then seamer Megan Schutt took three wickets in five balls to reduce New Zealand to 129-7 in the 19th. Australia had it won, before Katey Martin narrowed the margin by swiping the last two balls for four and six. Victory came at a price: Perry limped out of the tournament after tearing her right hamstring in the field. Earlier, Mooney's 50-ball 60 had sustained Australia's total.*

Group B

At Perth (WACA), February 22, 2020. **West Indies won by seven wickets.** ‡**Thailand 78-9** (20 overs) (N. Koncharoenkai 33; S. R. Taylor 3-13); **West Indies 80-3** (16.4 overs). *PoM:* S. R. Taylor. *For a fleeting moment, it looked as if Thailand, in their first match at an ICC global event, might win. Despite a dogged 33 from Nannapat Koncharoenkai, they had managed just 78-9 after opting to bat. However, fielding was always likely to be their strength: Naruemol Chaiwai ran out Lee-Ann Kirby with a direct hit, and Suleeporn Laomi's accurate throw despatched Deandra Dottin. Hayley Matthews had also gone and, when Shemaine Campbelle was ruled lbw, West Indies were teetering at 27-4. But Campbelle was reprieved on review and, with Stafanie Taylor – whose off-spin had claimed three wickets – righted the West Indian ship.*

At Perth (WACA), February 23, 2020 (floodlit). **South Africa won by six wickets. England 123-8** (20 overs) (N. R. Sciver 50; A. Khaka 3-25); ‡**South Africa 124-4** (19.4 overs) (D. van Niekerk 46, M. Kapp 38). *PoM:* D. van Niekerk. *Like Australia, England began with an unexpected defeat – one that would cost them later. But it was a good evening for South African captain Dane van Niekerk, who put England in and took the key wicket of her opposite number, Heather Knight. Only Amy Jones, with 23 of the first 25 runs, and Nat Sciver, who reached 50 before becoming one of Ayabonga*

Ryan Pierse, Getty Images

Final warning: Mignon du Preez and Sune Luus at the moment of South Africa's victory – a result that would knock England out in the semis.

Khaka's three victims, made much headway. Van Niekerk and her wife, Marizanne Kapp, added 84 for South Africa's second wicket, but fell in quick succession to the spin of Sarah Glenn and Sophie Ecclestone. Mignon du Preez, in her 100th T20I, levelled the scores with a six off Katherine Brunt, then finished the job with a single.

At Canberra, February 26, 2020. **England won by 98 runs. England 176-2** (20 overs) (N. R. Sciver 59*, H. C. Knight 108*); ‡**Thailand 78-7** (20 overs) (N. Chantham 32; A. Shrubsole 3-21). *PoM:* H. C. Knight. *England's resounding win gave their run-rate a shot in the arm, though not before Thailand again unsettled illustrious opponents: ten balls in, Jones and Danni Wyatt were both gone for ducks. Normal service then resumed: Sciver crafted a neat 52-ball 59*, and Knight a more brutal 108* from 66. She became the first woman to hit a century in all three formats, and their stand of 169* was an England all-wicket T20 record. Thailand did not entertain a target of 177 and, as they had against West Indies, saw out their overs in reaching 78; Natthakan Chantam compiled a resolute 32, and Anya Shrubsole claimed three wickets.*

HIGHEST PARTNERSHIPS IN WOMEN'S T20 INTERNATIONALS

236* for 3rd	Nigar Sultana/Farzana Haque, Bangladesh v Maldives at Pokhara	2019-20
182 for 1st	S. W. Bates/S. F. M. Devine, New Zealand v South Africa at Taunton	2018
170 for 1st	S. A. Fritz /T. Chetty, South Africa v Netherlands at Potchefstroom (Uni)	2010-11
169* for 3rd	**N. R. Sciver/H. C. Knight, England v Thailand at Canberra**	**2019-20**
163* for 1st	L. Lee/D. van Niekerk, South Africa v Pakistan at Sylhet	2013-14
162* for 2nd	H. K. Matthews/C. N. Nation, West Indies v Ireland at Dublin (Sydney Pde)	2019
151 for 1st	**A. J. Healy/B. L. Mooney, Australia v Bangladesh at Canberra**	**2019-20**
147* for 4th	K. L. Rolton/K. A. Blackwell, Australia v England at Taunton	2005
147 for 1st	L. Winfield/T. T. Beaumont, England v Pakistan at Bristol	2016
147 for 1st	D. N. Wyatt/T. T. Beaumont, England v South Africa at Taunton	2018

Only matches involving at least one ICC Full Member; the overall record for all women's T20 internationals is 257 (1st) by Y. Anggraeni (112) and K. W. Prastini (89) for Indonesia v Philippines at Dasmarinas in 2019-20.*

At Canberra, February 26, 2020 (floodlit). **Pakistan won by eight wickets.** ‡**West Indies 124-7** (20 overs) (S. R. Taylor 43, S. A. Campbelle 43); **Pakistan 127-2** (18.2 overs) (Javeria Khan 35, Bismah Maroof 38*). *PoM:* Javeria Khan. *A sloppy display from West Indies allowed Pakistan to record only their third T20 win against them in 13 matches (including three ties that went to a super over, all won by West Indies). Matthews was adjudged lbw to the first ball of the match, from Diana Baig, and took too long to review; replays showed it sliding down leg. West Indies made only 28-2 in the powerplay, and Dottin was out at the same score. Although Taylor and Campbelle added 63, it took almost ten overs. Pakistan's openers, Muneeba Ali (25) and Javeria Khan, began with 58 in 7.2; after they were separated, captain Bismah Maroof and Nida Dar (18*) calmly steered their side home. Four of the group's five teams now had a win apiece, with Thailand nursing two defeats.*

At Canberra, February 28, 2020. **South Africa won by 113 runs.** ‡**South Africa 195-3** (20 overs) (L. Lee 101, S. E. Luus 61*); **Thailand 82** (19.1 overs) (S. Ismail 3-8, S. E. Luus 3-15). *PoM:* L. Lee. *Lizelle Lee's maiden T20I hundred, from 59 balls, lifted South Africa to the highest total at a women's T20 World Cup, pipping India's 194-5 against New Zealand at Providence in November 2018. She put on 131 with Sune Luus, a national second-wicket record (the same pair had added 103 against England at Taunton in 2018), before Chloe Tryon's 11-ball 24 rubbed salt into Thai wounds. Thailand then staggered from 14-0 to 15-4, including three wickets in three balls – a run-out, plus two bowled by Shabnim Ismail. Her opening partner, left-arm spinner Nonkululeko Mlaba, conceded only four singles in her four overs, while Luus's leg-breaks produced figures of 24–9–15–3. Onnicha Kamchomphu hit van Niekerk for six, a rare highlight for the Thais, who were spared a bigger drubbing by four dropped catches.*

At Canberra, February 28, 2020 (floodlit). **England won by 42 runs. England 158-7** (20 overs) (N. R. Sciver 36, H. C. Knight 62; Aimen Anwar 3-30); ‡**Pakistan 116** (19.4 overs) (Aliya Riaz 41; A. Shrubsole 3-25, S. Glenn 3-15). *PoM:* H. C. Knight. *England took a step closer to the semis with* *their 13th victory in 14 T20 games against Pakistan – they had lost the other by one run, in 2013 – thanks to more runs from Knight and Sciver, and a tight bowling performance from two young spinners. The openers faltered again, before the middle order made good the damage: Sciver hit 36 before being nimbly stumped by Sidra Nawaz, and Knight another crisp half-century. When Pakistan batted, wickets fell regularly. Slow left-armer Sophie Ecclestone (aged 20) and leg-spinner Sarah Glenn (21 the previous day) shared figures of 5-27 from eight overs, while Shrubsole notched her 100th wicket in the format (the third to the mark, after Anisa Mohammed of West Indies and Australia's Ellyse Perry). Aliya Riaz struck out from 50-5, but the game was up.*

At Sydney (Showground), March 1, 2020. **South Africa won by 17 runs.** ‡**South Africa 136-6** (20 overs) (M. Kapp 31, L. Wolvaardt 53*); **Pakistan 119-5** (20 overs) (Javeria Khan 31, Aliya Riaz 39*). *PoM:* L. Wolvaardt. *Laura Wolvaardt powered South Africa into the semi-finals. When she arrived, they were 54-3 from ten, after Baig had struck two early blows, but Wolvaardt hit 53* off 36, including five fours from her last six balls. Pakistan's chase also started slowly, but Javeria, acting-captain after Bismah Maroof had fractured her thumb, initially kept them in the hunt. Then she was run out at the non-striker's end by a deflection from Tryon, sending down her little-used left-arm spin because attack leader Kapp – fighting off a respiratory infection – was unable to bowl. Riaz again offered late resistance, but it was not enough.*

At Sydney (Showground), March 1, 2020 (floodlit). **England won by 46 runs.** ‡**England 143-5** (20 overs) (N. R. Sciver 57); **West Indies 97** (17.1 overs) (S. Ecclestone 3-7). *PoM:* N. R. Sciver. *A third half-century in four innings for Sciver secured England a semi-final at their opponents' expense. The turning point of the West Indian chase came at 41-1, when Taylor injured her groin and was stretchered off. Dottin had already fallen – the first of three victims for the relentless Ecclestone – and West Indies stumbled from 42-1 to 42-4 in 12 balls against England's three-pronged spin attack. Only Kirby reached 20. Earlier, Sciver made a fluent 57 off 56, before Jones – demoted to No. 6 after struggling as an opener – contributed 23* off 13. Her replacement at the top of the order, Tammy Beaumont, had fallen second ball for nought.*

At Sydney (Showground), March 3, 2020. **No result.** ‡**Thailand 150-3** (20 overs) (N. Chantham 56, N. Boochatham 44) **v Pakistan.** *T20I debut:* Ayesha Naseem (Pakistan). *Thailand were deprived of a golden opportunity to end their World Cup adventure with a victory when rain washed out Pakistan's innings. The Thais had amassed 150, their highest total in the format, thanks to an opening partnership of 93 between Chantham – who hit their first fifty against an ODI nation – and Nattaya Boochatham; it was Thailand's only half-century stand in the tournament, and exceeded each of their previous three completed totals. Poor fielding in drizzly conditions helped, but the Thais played some stylish shots, and had high hopes of restricting Pakistan, who had never scored more than 144 batting second in T20Is.*

At Sydney (Showground), March 3, 2020 (floodlit). **South Africa v West Indies. Abandoned.** *The washout meant South Africa finished top of Group B, and would face Australia in the semi-finals.*

GROUP TABLES

Group A

	P	*W*	*L*	*NR/A*	*Pts*	*NRR*
INDIA	4	4	0	0	8	0.97
AUSTRALIA	4	3	1	0	6	0.97
New Zealand	4	2	2	0	4	0.36
Sri Lanka	4	1	3	0	2	–0.40
Bangladesh	4	0	4	0	0	–1.90

Group B

	P	*W*	*L*	*NR/A*	*Pts*	*NRR*
SOUTH AFRICA	4	3	0	1	7	2.22
ENGLAND	4	3	1	0	6	2.29
West Indies	4	1	2	1	3	–0.65
Pakistan	4	1	2	1	3	–0.76
Thailand	4	0	3	1	1	–3.99

SEMI-FINALS

ENGLAND v INDIA

At Sydney, March 5, 2020. Abandoned. India qualified for the final by virtue of a better record in their qualifying group.

India were handed a free pass to their maiden final in this competition by Sydney's weather, which wiped out the first semi-final, and left England ruing their opening-game defeat by South Africa. That left them with an inferior group-stage record to India's – the tie-breaker in such circumstances. Captain Heather Knight said she was "gutted", adding: "You'd hope now there is going to be a rule change, and no other team will have to experience going out of a World Cup purely because of rain." Her Indian counterpart, Harmanpreet Kaur, said: "These are the rules. We can't help it."

AUSTRALIA v SOUTH AFRICA

At Sydney, March 5, 2020 (floodlit). Australia won by five runs (DLS). Toss: South Africa.

Australia overcame South Africa – and the elements – to advance to the final, despite having lost Ellyse Perry to a hamstring injury. Put in, they reached 68 for one early in the ninth, with openers Alyssa Healy and Beth Mooney sharing eight fours. But they never quite made the most of the sound base, and relied on the cool head of their captain, Meg Lanning. She stuck around for 49 balls, and ensured a decent total on a slow SCG pitch that suited Nadine de Klerk's medium-pace. As the innings ended, so the rain returned; if South Africa did not face ten overs, then they – having topped their group – would meet India in the final. The deadline for a resumption was 9.49; with nine minutes to spare, the South Africans began their assault on a target of 98 in 13 overs. By the fifth, they were 24 for three, and sliding out of contention. Laura Wolvaardt threatened to pull it back, but 27 from the last two proved too many.

Player of the Match: M. M. Lanning.

Australia

		B	*4/6*
1 †A. J. Healy *c 2 b 10*	18	13	4
2 B. L. Mooney *b 7*	28	24	4
3 *M. M. Lanning *not out*	49	49	4/1
4 J. L. Jonassen *c 9 b 11*	1	3	0
5 A. K. Gardner *c 8 b 7*	0	2	0
6 R. L. Haynes *b 7*	17	18	0
7 N. J. Carey *not out*	7	11	0
Lb 8, w 6	14		
6 overs: 48-1 (20 overs)	134-5		

1/34 2/68 3/69 4/71 5/103

8 S. G. Molineux, 9 G. L. Wareham, 10 D. M. Kimmince and 11 M. Schutt did not bat.

Ismail 24–14–20–0; Khaka 24–10–29–1; Mlaba 18–9–18–1; van Niekerk 12–3–20–0; de Klerk 24–10–19–3; Tryon 18–3–20–0.

South Africa

		B	*4/6*
1 L. Lee *c 5 b 8*	10	10	2
2 *D. van Niekerk *b 11*	12	12	0/1
3 S. E. Luus *c 2 b 11*	21	22	2
4 M. du Preez *c 3 b 10*	0	4	0
5 L. Wolvaardt *not out*	41	27	3/2
6 C. L. Tryon *c 3 b 4*	1	2	0
7 N. de Klerk *not out*	6	2	1
Nb 1	1		
4 overs: 23-2 (13 overs)	92-5		

1/20 2/23 3/24 4/71 5/79

8 †T. Chetty, 9 S. Ismail, 10 A. Khaka and 11 N. Mlaba did not bat.

Schutt 18–10–17–2; Jonassen 18–6–28–1; Molineux 12–7–16–1; Kimmince 18–7–16–1; Carey 12–4–15–0.

Umpires: K. D. Cotton and N. N. Menon. Third umpire: L. Rusere.
Referee: B. C. Broad.

Strength in numbers: over 86,000 watch as Meg Lanning boosts the Australia total.

William West, AFP/Getty Images

FINAL

AUSTRALIA v INDIA

KALIKA MEHTA

At Melbourne, March 8, 2020 (floodlit). Australia won by 85 runs. Toss: Australia.

A cacophonous, ear-splitting boom reverberated around the MCG at approximately 6.05pm. In the first over, 16-year-old Shafali Verma had dropped Australia's opener Alyssa Healy, who was on nine. You may not be able to win a match of such significance just five balls in. But, for India, that moment signalled what was to come: they were overawed by a heaving crowd – 86,174 was more than three times the number at Lord's for their 2017 World Cup final – and the nous of the Australians.

The final was loaded with records for the hosts, even though they were missing their most valuable player, Ellyse Perry. Having shared the poster for the tournament with her namesake, American pop star Katy, she had torn her hamstring in their last group game. Healy smoked the fastest half-century, off just 30 balls, in a World Cup final – men's or women's, 20 overs or 50 – and racked up five sixes. The first sailed 83 metres into a delirious crowd, but she saved the best for last, moving slightly to the off, opening up her body, and using her power to wallop the ball over cover. She shared a breathtaking 115-run opening stand with Beth Mooney, whose unbeaten 78 off 54 took her tournament aggregate to 259, a record in any women's T20 World Cup.

Even Healy's dismissal created a world record: when she found the hands of long-on, Radha Yadav had taken at least one wicket in 24 consecutive T20 internationals. Mooney continued unfazed, collecting ten fours to guide Australia to 184 for four, the highest total in a T20 World Cup final (the men's best was 161 for six by West Indies in 2015-16).

India were in need of a miracle, but Verma's previously brilliant tournament came to a crashing end, just three balls into the innings; Healy was her nemesis again, pouching a thin edge off Megan Schutt, who went on to pick up an exceptional four for 18. It culminated in the wicket of Poonam Yadav, as India failed to reach three figures; they weren't helped when No. 3 Taniya Bhatia had to be replaced after she missed a sweep and was hit on the helmet. Afterwards, the Australian players danced alongside Katy Perry as she belted out her hit tunes, a signal that this was where they belonged – on top of the world stage.

Player of the Match: A. J. Healy. *Attendance:* 86,174.

Player of the Tournament: B. L. Mooney.

Australia

		B	4/6
1 †A. J. Healy *c 7 b 10*	75	39	7/5
2 B. L. Mooney *not out*	78	54	10
3 *M. M. Lanning *c 9 b 6*	16	15	2
4 A. K. Gardner *st 3 b 6*	2	3	0
5 R. L. Haynes *b 11*	4	5	0
6 N. J. Carey *not out*	5	5	1
B 1, w 2, nb 1	4		
6 overs: 49-0 (20 overs)	184-4		

1/115 2/154 3/156 4/176

7 J. L. Jonassen, 8 S. G. Molineux, 9 G. L. Wareham, 10 D. M. Kimmince and 11 M. Schutt did not bat.

Sharma 24–7–38–2; Pandey 24–6–52–0; Gayakwad 24–12–29–0; P. Yadav 24–5–30–1; R. P. Yadav 24–6–34–1.

India

		B	4/6
1 S. Verma *c 1 b 11*	2	3	0
2 S. S. Mandhana *c 6 b 8*	11	8	2
3 †T. Bhatia *retired hurt*	2	4	0
4 J. I. Rodrigues *c 6 b 7*	0	2	0
5 *H. Kaur *c 4 b 7*	4	7	1
6 D. B. Sharma *c 2 b 6*	33	35	2
7 V. Krishnamurthy *c 7 b 10*	19	24	1
8 R. M. Ghosh *c 6 b 11*	18	18	2
9 S. S. Pandey *c 2 b 11*	2	4	0
10 R. P. Yadav *c 2 b 7*	1	2	0
11 P. Yadav *c 4 b 11*	1	5	0
12 R. S. Gayakwad *not out*	1	3	0
W 5	5		
6 overs: 32-4 (19.1 overs)	99		

1/2 2/8 3/18 4/30 5/58 6/88 7/92 8/96 9/97

Bhatia retired hurt at 5-1. Ghosh was a concussion replacement for Bhatia.

Schutt 19–12–18–4; Jonassen 24–11–20–3; Molineux 24–10–21–1; Kimmince 24–12–17–1; Carey 24–7–23–1.

Umpires: Ahsan Raza and K. D. Cotton. Third umpire: G. O. Brathwaite.
Referee: B. C. Broad.

WOMEN'S T20 WORLD CUP FINALS

2009	ENGLAND (86-4) beat New Zealand (85) by six wickets	Lord's
2010	AUSTRALIA (106-8) beat New Zealand (103-6) by three runs	Bridgetown
2012-13	AUSTRALIA (142-4) beat England (138-9) by four runs	Colombo (RPS)
2013-14	AUSTRALIA (106-4) beat England (105-8) by six wickets	Mirpur
2015-16	WEST INDIES (149-2) beat Australia (148-5) by eight wickets	Kolkata
2018-19	AUSTRALIA (106-2) beat England (105) by eight wickets	North Sound
2019-20	AUSTRALIA (184-4) beat India (99) by 85 runs	Melbourne

WOMEN'S INTERNATIONAL SERIES IN 2020

NEW ZEALAND v SOUTH AFRICA IN 2019-20

One-day internationals (3): New Zealand 0, South Africa 3
Twenty20 internationals (5): New Zealand 3, South Africa 1

South Africa secured their place at the 2021 World Cup with a resounding one-day whitewash, after only two ODI victories over New Zealand in 13 completed matches dating back to 1999. Openers Lizelle Lee and Laura Wolvaardt totalled 274 between them. The hosts hit back in the Twenty20 matches, in which Sophie Devine – the new captain after Amy Satterthwaite had become the first to take advantage of New Zealand's maternity-leave provisions – was supreme. She thrashed 297 runs at 99, with a strike-rate of 150; next came South Africa's Mignon du Preez, 200 adrift. Devine's aggregate was a record for a women's bilateral series or tournament, surpassing Meg Lanning's 257 in six games for Australia at the 2013-14 World T20. While no one else on either side reached 50, Devine did so in all four matches that survived the weather. She hit 16 sixes, one more than everyone else put together, and a record for a women's T20 international series.

First one-day international At Auckland (Outer Oval), January 25, 2020. **South Africa won by seven wickets. New Zealand 259-9** (50 overs) (S. W. Bates 53, K. T. Perkins 78; M. M. Klaas 3-37, A. Khaka 3-43); ‡**South Africa 260-3** (48.3 overs) (L. Lee 99, L. Wolvaardt 91*, D. van Niekerk 37). *PoM:* L. Lee. *Lizelle Lee and Laura Wolvaardt effectively settled the game with an opening stand of 163 inside 32 overs, South Africa's first century partnership for any wicket against New Zealand. Lee fell for a run-a-ball 99, but Wolvaardt steered her country to their second-highest successful chase (behind 265-5 against England at Centurion in February 2016). The meat of the New Zealand innings had been Katie Perkins's career-best 78.*

Second one-day international At Auckland (Outer Oval), January 27, 2020. **South Africa won by eight wickets.** ‡**New Zealand 115** (36 overs) (S. W. Bates 38; M. Kapp 4-29); **South Africa 117-2** (23.5 overs) (L. Lee 38, S. E. Luus 37*, M. du Preez 35*). *PoM:* L. Lee. *ODI debut:* J. M. Kerr (New Zealand). *Four wickets for Marizanne Kapp – the openers, plus Nos 9 and 10 – set up South Africa's series-clinching win. Eight New Zealanders failed to reach double figures, and the last six wickets cascaded for 29 in their lowest all-out total against these opponents (previously 127 at Kimberley in October 2016). Shabnim Ismail, Kapp's new-ball partner, sent down eight overs for just ten. In reply, Wolvaardt fell for a duck, but Lee's good form continued with a brisk 38, before she fell to debutant seamer Jess Kerr, older sister of team-mate Amelia (their grandfather, Bruce Murray, played 13 Tests for New Zealand). Sune Luus and Mignon du Preez (35* from 27 balls) romped home with more than 26 overs to spare.*

Third one-day international At Hamilton, January 30, 2020 (day/night). **South Africa won by six wickets. New Zealand 149** (38.1 overs) (S. W. Bates 51; S. E. Luus 6-45); ‡**South Africa 150-4** (37.2 overs) (D. van Niekerk 30, M. du Preez 35*). *PoM:* S. E. Luus. *PoS:* L. Lee. *Luus starred as South Africa made sure of automatic qualification for the 2021 World Cup. With New Zealand a promising 96-3, she removed Perkins, the first of three stumpings off her leg-spin by Trisha Chetty, then added top-scorer Suzie Bates next over. The collapse gathered pace: seven fell for 53, with Luus – the seventh bowler used – picking up 6-45.*

Women's Championship: South Africa 6pts, New Zealand 0pts.

First Twenty20 international At Mount Maunganui, February 2, 2020 (floodlit). **New Zealand won by nine wickets. South Africa 116-7** (20 overs) (L. Wolvaardt 33); ‡**New Zealand 117-1** (12.2 overs) (R. H. Priest 37, S. F. M. Devine 54*). *PoM:* S. F. M. Devine. *New Zealand hit back in style after their ODI rout, as openers Rachel Priest (37 off 28) and Sophie Devine (54* off 32) thrashed 75 inside eight overs; each hit four sixes. South Africa had been reasonably placed at 72-1 in the 12th, but leg-spinner Amelia Kerr slowed the rate and – like off-spinner Leigh Kasperek – finished with 2-17. The final 52 balls of the innings yielded 44-6, leaving New Zealand a small chase.*

Second Twenty20 international At Hamilton, February 6, 2020. **New Zealand won by five wickets. South Africa 119** (19.4 overs) (M. du Preez 40); ‡**New Zealand 120-5** (18.2 overs) (S. F. M. Devine 61). *PoM:* L. M. Tahuhu. *Another South African collapse, another New Zealand stroll. This time, from 94-3, it was seven for 25, as Lea Tahuhu took 2-10 from four overs. Du Preez slapped 40 from 26, but enjoyed little support. Devine flourished once more, launching five sixes in her 43-ball 61, and adding a decisive 72 for the third wicket with Maddy Green (23).*

Third Twenty20 international At Wellington (Basin Reserve), February 9, 2020. **South Africa won by five wickets.** ‡**New Zealand 153-5** (20 overs) (S. F. M. Devine 77); **South Africa 154-5** (19.5 overs) (D. van Niekerk 42, C. L. Tryon 34*). *PoM:* S. F. M. Devine. *T20I debuts:* L. R. Down, J. M. Kerr (New Zealand). *Devine hit her third successive fifty, then removed both South Africa's openers, but a late cameo from Chloe Tryon kept the visitors in the series. With 17 needed off seven deliveries, she launched Holly Huddleston for six, repeating the dose three balls later off Devine. Earlier, Devine's 57-ball 77 had included 11 of New Zealand's 19 boundaries, with Bates's 23 the next-best. South Africa slipped to 56-3, but Dane van Niekerk managed 42 off 40, before Tryon (34* off 16) ensured only their second T20 win over New Zealand in ten attempts. It was the highest successful chase in a women's T20I in New Zealand, beating the hosts' 143-3 against West Indies at Hamilton in 2017-18.*

Fourth Twenty20 international At Wellington (Basin Reserve), February 10, 2020. **New Zealand won by 69 runs. New Zealand 171-2** (20 overs) (S. F. M. Devine 105, S. W. Bates 47*); ‡**South Africa 102** (17 overs) (A. M. Peterson 3-14). *PoM:* S. F. M. Devine. *New Zealand clinched the series, with the crucial innings coming from a predictable source: Devine took her series haul to 297 with a punishing 105 from 65 balls, having put on 142 (a national second-wicket record) with Bates, New Zealand's only previous T20I centurion. Having made 72 against India a year earlier, Devine had now passed 50 in five successive T20I innings, a record for either gender (Brendon McCullum, Chris Gayle and Mithali Raj had all managed four in a row). South Africa reached 58-2 in the ninth, before seven tumbled for 44 (Ismail was absent injured).*

Fifth Twenty20 international At Dunedin (University Oval), February 13, 2020. **New Zealand v South Africa. Abandoned.** *PoS:* S. F. M. Devine. *Devine added the series award to her three match awards.*

AUSTRALIA TRI-NATION WOMEN'S T20 SERIES IN 2019-20

1 Australia 2 India 3 England

Australia won a tight triangular tournament that served as rigorous preparation for the T20 World Cup. All three teams ended the group stage with two wins apiece, but Australia claimed top spot on net run-rate after winning the last match, by 16 runs against England, who fell eight short of the total they needed to finish above India. Meg Lanning's team then confirmed their World Cup credentials by escaping from a tricky position in the final, Jess Jonassen collecting five for 12 as India faltered with the line in sight. Despite that, the Indians had the competition's leading run-scorer (Smriti Mandhana, with 216) and wicket-taker (slow left-armer Rajeshwari Gayakwad, with ten). But Australia could boast Beth Mooney's tally of 208 (she, Mandhana and England's Heather Knight accounted for seven of the competition's nine half-centuries), as well as seven wickets each for the thrifty pace of Tayla

Vlaeminck, the left-arm spin of Jonassen and the brisk seam of the inevitable Ellyse Perry. England were scuppered by their limp showing in the last group match, while Australia's status as the best all-round team in women's cricket was underlined by the presentation of the ICC Women's Championship trophy after the fifth game. Only wicketkeeper Alyssa Healy seemed off-colour, totalling just 15 in her five innings from the top of the order.

NATIONAL SQUADS

Australia *M. M. Lanning, E. A. Burns, N. J. Carey, A. K. Gardner, R. L. Haynes, A. J. Healy, J. L. Jonassen, D. M. Kimmince, S. G. Molineux, B. L. Mooney, E. A. Perry, M. Schutt, A. J. Sutherland, T. J. Vlaeminck, G. L. Wareham. *Coach:* M. P. Mott.

England *H. C. Knight, T. T. Beaumont, K. H. Brunt, K. L. Cross, F. R. Davies, S. Ecclestone, G. A. Elwiss, S. Glenn, A. E. Jones, N. R. Sciver, A. Shrubsole, F. C. Wilson, L. Winfield, D. N. Wyatt, M. K. Villiers. *Coach:* L. M. Keightley.

India *H. Kaur, T. Bhatia, H. Deol, R. S. Gayakwad, R. M. Ghosh, V. Krishnamurthy, S. S. Mandhana, S. S. Pandey, N. M. Parween, A. Reddy, J. I. Rodrigues, D. B. Sharma, P. Vastrakar, S. Verma, P. Yadav, R. P. Yadav. *Coach:* W. V. Raman.

At Canberra, January 31, 2020. **India won by five wickets. England 147-7** (20 overs) (H. C. Knight 67, T. T. Beaumont 37); ‡**India 150-5** (19.3 overs) (S. Verma 30, H. Kaur 42*). *PoM:* H. C. Knight. *India secured only their fourth win in 18 T20s against England when captain Harmanpreet Kaur lofted Katherine Brunt over cover for six with three balls to spare. Earlier, England had fought back from 9-2 and 59-4, thanks to their own captain, Heather Knight, though she was dropped on five and 13 en route to a 44-ball 67. They then thought they had removed Smriti Mandhana for a duck, only for the third umpire to rule that wicketkeeper Amy Jones had not retained control of the ball as she tried to complete a diving catch. India needed 26 off three overs, then 17 off two, but substitute Mady Villiers dropped Deepti Sharma at long-on, and Harmanpreet took control.*

Knight strike: Megan Schutt fields off her own bowling against England captain Heather Knight.

At Canberra, February 1, 2020. **England won the super over, after a tie. England 156-4** (20 overs) (H. C. Knight 78, F. C. Wilson 39*); ‡**Australia 156-8** (20 overs) (B. L. Mooney 65; N. R. Sciver 3-23, S. Glenn 3-28). *PoM:* H. C. Knight. *T20I debut:* A. J. Sutherland (Australia). *Knight first presided over another England recovery, then hit two boundaries in the super over after Sophie Ecclestone's left-arm spin had limited Alyssa Healy and Ashleigh Gardner to eight. England had laboured to 41-3 in ten overs, with Ellyse Perry bowling her four off the reel, taking 1-9. But Knight, who faced only 45 balls for her 78 (after a lone half-century in 20 T20 innings against Australia), and Fran Wilson thrashed 115. Australia were in contention at 104-3 in the 15th, before Sarah Glenn removed Perry and Rachael Haynes in the same over. Wickets continued to fall, and the runs dried up; with three overs left, Australia needed 40. But 18-year-old debutant Annabel Sutherland, daughter of former Cricket Australia chief executive James, belted Brunt – whose four overs cost 47, her most expensive T20I figures – for three successive fours, and forced a tie with a ninth-wicket stand of 17* from eight balls with Delissa Kimmince. England, though, had the last laugh.*

At Canberra, February 2, 2020. **Australia won by four wickets. India 103-9** (20 overs) (S. S. Mandhana 35; E. A. Perry 4-13, T. J. Vlaeminck 3-13); ‡**Australia 104-6** (18.5 overs) (E. A. Perry 49). *PoM:* E. A. Perry. *Perry starred, to bring the three teams level on one win apiece. She followed figures of 4-13, including three in India's 14th over, with a nerve-settling 49 from 47 balls during an otherwise shaky Australian chase. Her demolition of India's batting was assisted by Tayla Vlaeminck, who touched 75mph and picked up two wickets in the 15th; from 78-3, the Indians lost five in ten balls. At 30-3 in reply, Australia had work to do, but Perry took them within five of their target.*

At St Kilda, February 7, 2020. **England won by four wickets. India 123-6** (20 overs) (S. S. Mandhana 45; A. Shrubsole 3-31); ‡**England 124-6** (18.5 overs) (N. R. Sciver 50; R. S. Gayakwad 3-23). *PoM:* A. Shrubsole. *Nat Sciver's 38-ball 50 proved the difference in a scrappy match. With England 28-3 in pursuit of 124, she put on 37 with the in-form Knight, and 49 with Wilson, eventually hitting seven of her team's 12 boundaries. Earlier, Mandhana had managed eight of India's 14, but their promising 62-1 in the tenth became an underwhelming 123-6, only two fours coming from the last nine. Anya Shrubsole (back from a foot injury) and Brunt (back from her mauling in Canberra) shared five wickets.*

At St Kilda, February 8, 2020. **India won by seven wickets. Australia 173-5** (20 overs) (A. K. Gardner 93, M. M. Lanning 37); ‡**India 177-3** (19.4 overs) (S. Verma 49, S. S. Mandhana 55, J. I. Rodrigues 30). *PoM:* A. K. Gardner. *India gave themselves a chance of the final after their highest T20 chase, beating 168-3 against South Africa at Potchefstroom in February 2018. They were set on their way by a punishing opening stand of 85 inside nine overs by Shafali Verma (49 off 28) and Mandhana, and hurried towards victory by Jemimah Rodrigues (30 off 19); Sharma (11* off four) supplied the icing. Australia had looked set to qualify after Gardner's career-best 93 off 57, and Meg Lanning's 37 off 22, had lifted them to 173.*

At St Kilda, February 9, 2020. **Australia won by 16 runs. Australia 132-7** (20 overs) (B. L. Mooney 50); ‡**England 116-7** (20 overs) (S. G. Molineux 3-19). *PoM:* S. G. Molineux. *Not only did Australia reach the final, they knocked out their opponents in the process. England needed 133 to win the game; failing that, 124 to finish above India on net run-rate. Against disciplined bowling, they managed neither, with slow left-armer Sophie Molineux to the fore. Vlaeminck was hard to hit too, finishing with 2-18, and no one made more than 23. Australia's modest-looking 132 had centred on Beth Mooney's hard-fought 50, after spinners Ecclestone and Glenn shared 4-37.*

AUSTRALIA 4pts (NRR 0.23), India 4pts (NRR –0.07), England 4pts (NRR –0.16).

Final At St Kilda, February 12, 2020. **Australia won by 11 runs.** ‡**Australia 155-6** (20 overs) (B. L. Mooney 71*); **India 144** (20 overs) (S. S. Mandhana 66; J. L. Jonassen 5-12). *PoM:* J. L. Jonassen. *PoS:* B. L. Mooney. *T20I debut:* R. M. Ghosh (India). *India collapsed in sight of victory to the left-arm spin of Jess Jonassen. Chasing 156, they needed 41 more from 35 balls with seven wickets in hand. But Megan Schutt removed the dangerous Mandhana, who had pummelled 12 fours in a 37-ball 66, before Jonassen embarked on a spell of 5-8 in 16 deliveries by trapping Harmanpreet; in 72 previous T20Is, she had claimed more than two wickets in an innings only twice. In all, India's last seven tumbled for 29. Australia's innings had depended on Mooney's expertly compiled 71* off 54, though a late burst from Haynes (18 off seven) lifted their total from middling to challenging. Lanning earned a bizarre reprieve on 18, when Shikha Pandey's accurate throw from mid-off deflected off the lid of the small underground box housing the microphone at the base of the stumps, and ricocheted to safety; Lanning had been out of her ground, but collected an overthrow.*

ENGLAND v WEST INDIES IN 2020

KALIKA MEHTA

Twenty20 internationals (5): England 5, West Indies 0

The Covid-19 pandemic predictably hit women's cricket harder than men's, with India and South Africa both dropping out of scheduled visits before England finally got back on the field. Even as Cricket South Africa confirmed their women's side could not travel – a fortnight before they were due to leave – many of their male colleagues were preparing to fly to the United Arab Emirates to take part in the Indian Premier League.

It could have become the first English summer without a women's international since 1995. But, like their men, West Indies stepped up, agreeing to meet England in five Twenty20 games. Neither team had played since their group match at the T20 World Cup in Sydney on March 1, and it was in a very different world that both sides took a knee – saluting the Black Lives Matter movement – at an empty County Ground in Derby on September 21.

The cricket was lopsided: Heather Knight's team won 5–0 (their first such victory in any format), with the closest result coming in a five-over thrash in the final game. Deandra Dottin, who had needed reconstructive surgery in 2019 after a shoulder injury threatened her career, was the only West Indian to fire with the bat. She was the series' leading scorer with 185 runs, including two half-centuries, lashing 21 fours and five sixes. Four England players managed three figures, but the failures of Dottin's team-mates were another reminder that, without serious investment, West Indies will fall further from the top of the crop. In a positive move, Courtney Walsh, their leading wicket-taker in men's Tests, was appointed head coach two days after the series ended (his fellow Jamaican Andre Coley had served on an interim basis during the tour).

Lisa Keightley's charges, meanwhile, showcased the depth in their ranks. Spin trio Sophie Ecclestone, Sarah Glenn and Mady Villiers easily filled the hole left by Laura Marsh's retirement. Most of the batting line-up contributed at some stage, but the most encouraging sign was that Amy Jones was growing into her role as a finisher, making a quickfire 55 in the fourth match.

England may not have learned much on the field, but in the circumstances what mattered was that the series was played at all.

WEST INDIAN TOURING PARTY

*S. R. Taylor, A. A. Alleyne, S. A. Campbelle, S. S. Connell, B. Cooper, D. J. S. Dottin, A. S. S. Fletcher, C. S. Fraser, S. Gajnabi, S. S. Grimmond, C. A. Henry, L. G. L. Kirby, N. Y. McLean, H. K. Matthews, C. N. Nation, K. Ramharack, K. C. Schultz, S. C. Selman. *Coach:* A. N. Coley.

A. Mohammed declined to tour because of Covid-19 concerns.

First Twenty20 international At Derby, September 21 (floodlit). **England won by 47 runs.** ‡**England 163-8** (20 overs) (T. T. Beaumont 62; S. C. Selman 3-26); **West Indies 116-6** (20 overs) (D. J. S. Dottin 69). *PoM:* T. T. Beaumont. *The last women's international had been the T20 World*

Cup final, played in front of a crowd of 86,174 at the MCG on March 8. Now, 197 days later, England and West Indies met behind closed doors at Derby, in a match as one-sided as Australia's victory over India had been. Opening again after batting down the order for most of the World Cup, Tammy Beaumont was the backbone of England's innings. She smoked Aaliyah Alleyne through midwicket to bring up her eighth score of 50 or more in T20Is, and followed up with a six over mid-off two balls later. She was eventually caught by Afy Fletcher at the second attempt, one of three victims for Shakera Selman, but her 62 off 49 deliveries propelled England towards a challenging 163-8. Captain Heather Knight (25 off 17) and Amy Jones (24 off 16) also made useful contributions. West Indies' chase never properly got off the ground, despite the power hitting of Deandra Dottin, who blasted 69 off 59. No one else managed double figures, as Nat Sciver and Sophie Ecclestone picked up two cheap wickets each.

Second Twenty20 international At Derby, September 23 (floodlit). **England won by 47 runs. England 151-8** (20 overs); **‡West Indies 104-8** (20 overs) (D. J. S. Dottin 38). *PoM:* S. Glenn. *There were moments on this blustery evening when it seemed West Indies might pull level. But every time their hard work prised open an opportunity, a dropped catch or a poor decision saw it slip through their fingers; again, they went down by a demoralising 47 runs. Put in, England had lost regular wickets: Stafanie Taylor secured two stumpings and conceded only 12 in her four overs, and Danni Wyatt was run out when Dottin fired in a sharp throw from backward point. It took some lusty blows from Katherine Brunt (18) and Sarah Glenn (26) to scrape England to 151-8. Despite Brunt's early strike – Hayley Matthews caught off a leading edge – Dottin and Taylor, who became the second woman after New Zealand's Suzie Bates to pass 3,000 T20I runs, built an assured stand of 61, and West Indies were looking good at 72-1. Then Glenn's leg-spin derailed the chase: in successive overs, she trapped Dottin for 38 and had Taylor stumped for 28. Mady Villiers (2-10) and Ecclestone (2-19) rolled up the lower order.*

Third Twenty20 international At Derby, September 26. **England won by 20 runs. ‡England 154-6** (20 overs) (N. R. Sciver 82); **West Indies 134-5** (20 overs) (D. J. S. Dottin 63). *PoM:* N. R. Sciver. *Sciver's career-best 82 off 61 deliveries helped England clinch the series, though the West Indians made a better fist of the chase. Wyatt had a double reprieve in the second over: she hammered the ball back to Selman, who failed to hold on, but parried it to mid-off, where it burst through Lee-Ann Kirby's fingers and into her face, causing her to go off for treatment. Wyatt's luck was short-lived: Shamilia Connell had her and Beaumont caught in the next over, leaving England 13-2. But Sciver kept a cool head. She added 59 with Knight (29), brought up a 40-ball fifty with a powerful four past wide long-on, and struck Taylor for two fours and a six in three deliveries, before Dottin, in her first spell for 18 months, bowled her round her legs. Needing 155, West Indies looked like folding again when Kirby and Shemaine Campbelle went in single figures. Again Dottin rose to the challenge, with 63 in 56; Matthews, now at No. 4, aided her with a pithy 21. But once Dottin fell to Wilson's fine catch at deep backward square, they were heading for a third defeat.*

Fourth Twenty20 international At Derby, September 28 (floodlit). **England won by 44 runs. ‡England 166-6** (20 overs) (H. C. Knight 42, A. E. Jones 55); **West Indies 122-9** (20 overs) (C. N. Nation 30). *PoM:* A. E. Jones. *Batting first for the fourth time, England racked up their highest total of the series. It was Amy Jones's turn to shine, with her first half-century since moving down to No. 5. After an entertaining fourth-wicket stand of 65 with Knight, she reached 50 in 30 balls, and was unluckily run out in the final over: Brunt, caught off a waist-high no-ball at backward square, and still watching the fielder, missed Jones's call for a single. West Indies had made three changes to their attack: Alleyne had Wyatt and Sciver caught behind cheaply, and off-spinner Karishma Ramharack trapped Beaumont with her first delivery of the series, but Shabika Gajnabi's only over cost 17. West Indies' pursuit of 167 seemed doomed from the moment Brunt bowled Dottin with her third ball. Only Chedean Nation reached 30, and the next-best was 24 from Extras. Glenn removed Taylor and Matthews to take her series haul to seven at 12 each, and three run-outs limited the tourists to 122-9.*

Fifth Twenty20 international At Derby, September 30 (floodlit). **England won by three wickets. West Indies 41-3** (5 overs); **‡England 42-7** (4.3 overs) (S. S. Connell 3-14). *PoM:* S. S. Connell. *PoS:* S. Glenn. *T20I debut:* C. S. Fraser (West Indies). *After heavy rain prevented any play before 8.30, England completed the series sweep in a five-over game, though no one reached double figures as seven wickets fell in a chaotic chase. Knight had asked West Indies to bat for the first time, and Dottin smashed a four and a six in the first over, but was caught for 11 in the second. They were 17-3 from their first 15 balls, before Taylor (15*) and Natasha McLean (14*) added 24* off the*

WINNING AN INTERNATIONAL WITH NO ONE IN DOUBLE FIGURES

Men's T20Is		*HS*		
43-7	(9 overs)	7	Ireland v Bermuda at Belfast	2008
Women's T20Is		*HS*		
42-3	(10)	9*	Malawi v Mozambique at Blantyre	2019-20
42-7	**(4.3)**	**9**	**England v West Indies at Derby**	**2020**
18-0	(1.4)	9*	Uganda v Mali at Kigali	2019
16-0	(1.4)	5*	Indonesia v Philippines at Dasmarinas	2019-20
9-0	(1.1)	5*	Nepal v Maldives at Pokhara	2019-20
8-0	(0.4)	5*	Rwanda v Mali at Kigali	2019

Ireland (men) and Malawi (women) were batting first; all other winning teams batted second. There have been no instances in Tests or ODIs.

last 15, thanks to McLean's huge six over midwicket from the final delivery off Ecclestone. England needed 42, and lost two wickets in each of the first, third and fifth overs (plus Beaumont, their top-scorer with nine, in the second). But, after two shambolic run-outs in the last, successive no-balls from Selman took them over the line, an anticlimactic finish to a one-sided series.

AUSTRALIA v NEW ZEALAND IN 2020-21

Twenty20 internationals (3): Australia 2, New Zealand 1
One-day internationals (3): Australia 3, New Zealand 0

Australia continued their domination of the women's game, winning both series at the earliest opportunity. They did slip up in the third T20, but were unstoppable in the 50-over format, extending their unbeaten run to a world record 21 matches since early 2018, equalling the men's mark set by Ricky Ponting's 2003 World Cup winners. "It's a really special effort," said Meg Lanning, the captain. This time, her side did it all without Ellyse Perry, who was making a gradual recovery from surgery after tearing a hamstring during the T20 World Cup earlier in the year. But Australia's depth meant she was hardly missed. Ashleigh Gardner struck 90 runs from 62 balls in the T20s, in which seamer Delissa Kimmince took six wickets, and 21-year-old leg-spinner Georgia Wareham five; New Zealand's highest individual score was just 33, by Suzie Bates. Lanning took control in the ODIs, with undefeated innings of 62 and 101 – her 14th century in the format, taking her back to the top of the ICC rankings, ahead of Stafanie Taylor and team-mate Alyssa Healy – before missing the last match with a hamstring injury of her own. Rachael Haynes contributed 44, 82 and 96, sharing an opening stand of 144 with Healy as Australia breached 300 in the final game, while slow left-armer Jess Jonassen finished with overall figures of eight for 81. All six matches were played in biosecure conditions in Brisbane. Small crowds of under 1,000 were allowed – the first internationals to have paying spectators since Bangladesh's men hosted Zimbabwe on March 11.

First Twenty20 international At Brisbane (Allan Border Field), September 26, 2020. **Australia won by 17 runs. Australia 138-6** (20 overs) (A. K. Gardner 61; S. F. M. Devine 3-18); ‡**New Zealand 121-7** (20 overs) (S. W. Bates 33; M. Schutt 4-23). *PoM:* A. K. Gardner. *Australia lost Beth Mooney in the second over, and Alyssa Healy in the fifth. Had Nicola Carey been given out caught behind first ball in an over from New Zealand captain Sophie Devine that had already* *produced the wickets of Rachael Haynes and Sophie Molineux, they would have been 83-6. But DRS was not available, and Carey hung around as Ashleigh Gardner's 41-ball 61 lifted the Australians to a competitive total. Devine followed figures of 3-18 with a solid 29 but, from 104-3 after 17 overs, New Zealand slipped to 116-7 in the last. "We probably let them get 20–30 more than they should have," she said. "In the field I thought we were poor."*

Second Twenty20 international At Brisbane (Allan Border Field), September 27, 2020. **Australia won by eight wickets.** ‡**New Zealand 128** (19.2 overs) (A. E. Satterthwaite 30; D. M. Kimmince 3-21, G. L. Wareham 3-26); **Australia 129-2** (16.4 overs) (A. J. Healy 33, R. L. Haynes 40*). *PoM:* S. G. Molineux. *Australia wrapped up the series with ease. Delissa Kimmince and Georgia Wareham took three wickets apiece, and Molineux 2-17, to restrict New Zealand to 128 on a surface that helped the spinners. Healy and Mooney shot out of the blocks, pounding 51 from 26 balls, before Meg Lanning and Haynes finished things off with a stand of 65*. Healy had earlier equalled M. S. Dhoni's 91 wicketkeeping dismissals (the record in men's T20 internationals) by stumping Amy Satterthwaite, a hairline decision the third umpire took five minutes to confirm; it was her 50th stumping. She added a 92nd when she caught Lauren Down.*

Third Twenty20 international At Brisbane (Allan Border Field), September 30, 2020. **New Zealand won by five wickets. Australia 123-7** (20 overs); ‡**New Zealand 125-5** (19.3 overs) (A. E. Satterthwaite 30). *PoM:* A. C. Kerr. *PoS:* A. K. Gardner. *With the series won, Australia's cloak of invincibility slipped: Amelia Kerr's loopy leg-breaks accounted for Haynes and Lanning in successive overs, and Gardner's 29 was the highest contribution to an underwhelming total. New Zealand stumbled as Devine and Suzie Bates departed in the eighth over to leave them 44-3, but Satterthwaite and Katey Martin added 52, then Kerr (18* from ten balls) finished the job. It was their first T20 win over Australia in three and a half years, after seven defeats.*

First one-day international At Brisbane (Allan Border Field), October 3, 2020. **Australia won by seven wickets. New Zealand 180** (49.1 overs) (K. T. Perkins 32, M. L. Green 35); ‡**Australia 181-3** (33.4 overs) (R. L. Haynes 44, M. M. Lanning 62*). *PoM:* G. L. Wareham. *ODI debut:* A. J. Sutherland (Australia). *New Zealand struggled to make headway against the varied spin of Molineux, Wareham and Jess Jonassen, who finished with a combined 6-80 from 29.1 overs. Only 11 fours were hit in all, although Maddy Green (down at No. 8 after opening in the T20s) did manage three of their four sixes. After another sprightly opening stand from Haynes and Healy – 41 in 8.3 overs this time – Lanning supervised a leisurely chase with 62* from 70 balls. Bates injured her right shoulder in the field, and missed the rest of the series. Annabel Sutherland, Australia's 18-year-old debutant seamer, dismissed Satterthwaite in her third over.*

Second one-day international At Brisbane (Allan Border Field), October 5, 2020. **Australia won by four wickets. New Zealand 252-9** (50 overs) (N. C. Dodd 34, S. F. M. Devine 79, A. E. Satterthwaite 69; J. L. Jonassen 4-36); ‡**Australia 255-6** (45.1 overs) (R. L. Haynes 82, M. M. Lanning 101*; A. C. Kerr 3-47). *PoM:* M. M. Lanning. *Australia retained the Rose Bowl – their 17th win in 18 series since New Zealand won in 1998-99 (there was a draw in 2008-09). This match was at least more of a contest: after an opening stand of 75 with Natalie Dodd, Devine joined forces with Satterthwaite, and New Zealand reached 168-1 in the 39th, before falling away as Jonassen bagged four. But Haynes, who hit 13 fours and a six, and Lanning turned the chase into another cakewalk, putting on 117 for the second wicket in 20 overs. Australia overcame a minor wobble when Kerr dismissed Molineux and Gardner with successive balls in the 36th, but Lanning finished the match with a four off Hayley Jensen. It brought up her 14th ODI century in her 82nd innings; the fastest man to 14 was Hashim Amla, who took 84.*

Third one-day international At Brisbane (Allan Border Field), October 7, 2020. **Australia won by 232 runs. Australia 325-5** (50 overs) (R. L. Haynes 96, A. J. Healy 87, A. J. Sutherland 35, A. K. Gardner 34; A. C. Kerr 3-50); ‡**New Zealand 93** (27 overs) (A. E. Satterthwaite 41). *PoM:* R. L. Haynes. *PoS:* R. L. Haynes. *An opening partnership of 144 inside 26 overs between Haynes and Healy put Australia on course for the highest total New Zealand had conceded in an ODI (previously Australia's 307-4 at Hamilton in 2008-09); only Kerr went for less than a run a ball. New Zealand lost Devine in the first over, and sank to their heaviest ODI defeat (previously 186 runs by India at Derby in the 2017 World Cup). Haynes stood in as captain as Lanning rested a hamstring strained during her century in the previous game; since Lanning's debut in December 2010, it was Australia's first international in any format – 213 matches in all – without either her or Ellyse Perry. The win was their 21st in succession in ODIs, equalling the world record of their men, between January and May 2003; their last defeat had come by England at Coffs Harbour in October 2017. Gardner, Haynes, Healy and Mooney played in all 21.*

OTHER WOMEN'S TWENTY20 INTERNATIONALS

Goodnight, Vienna

STEVEN LYNCH

It might have been a quiet year, but you couldn't keep a good German down. After four wins earlier in the year, Germany whitewashed Austria in August in Seebarn, on the outskirts of Vienna, in the first women's internationals anywhere after the coronavirus lockdown.

The bowlers did particularly well, restricting Austria to five totals between 50 and 83. In the third match, Anne Bierwisch, a medium-pacer with a PhD in toxicology, proved venomous to the home side with a hat-trick. Later that day, the German captain, Anuradha Doddaballapur, went one better, taking four in four balls, a first for women's T20Is, and finished with five for one. Doddaballapur, who played for Karnataka in India, is a cardiovascular scientist, and joked: "The minimum qualification to make it to our women's national side is a master's degree."

One who hasn't quite graduated yet is Emma Bargna, a 15-year-old off-spinner from Munich, whose ten wickets in Austria included five for nine in the second game, in which the home side folded for 53. It was the first international five-for by any German, man or woman: Bargna was upset she couldn't get a hug from her team-mates, as they were forbidden by Covid regulations.

In that match, Germany had scored 191 for none, thanks to an unbroken stand between Australian-born Janet Ronalds, who made Germany's first century, and Christina Gough; next day, they piled on 198, again without being separated. There has been only one higher opening partnership in women's T20Is, for Indonesia against the Philippines in December 2019. Left-hander Gough, a former Oxford Blue who was born in Hamburg, had three innings against Austria, and made 72, 66 not out and 101 not out. It helped Germany complete a perfect year: nine T20 internationals, nine wins. In February, they had won four out of four in Oman. In the first game, Ronalds and Gough put on 158, again unbroken, this time for the second wicket.

Oman had started the year in Qatar, for a triangular tournament that also involved Kuwait. The teams were well matched: on the first day, Oman beat Qatar by three runs, then Qatar pinched their game against Kuwait off the penultimate ball, with the last pair together. Oman beat Kuwait in the final. But they were no match for the Germans.

REBEL WOMEN'S BIG BASH LEAGUE IN 2019-20

DANIEL CHERNY

1 Brisbane Heat 2 Adelaide Strikers

The fifth edition of the Women's Big Bash League was the first shifted to the start of the season, finishing before the men's began, rather than running in parallel. It was a bold move from Cricket Australia, designed to test whether the women's game could stand on its own two feet in the early summer, when pitted against Spring Racing, the rugby World Cup and the Australian Football League trade period.

The tournament was built around carnival weekends held across state capitals, plus a smattering of midweek matches. Attendances were modest: the October weather was not always spectator-friendly. But Channel Seven again showed 23 matches live, and the average audience for the regular season was 191,000, showing the appetite for women's cricket.

There was a new format, too, for the semis and final, which were held over one weekend, instead of across several days. **Brisbane Heat** earned the right to host all three games at Allan Border Field after topping the table on net run-rate, and went on to retain their title. Their impressive line-up was headed by Beth Mooney, who scored 743 runs, and Jess Jonassen, who combined 419 with 21 wickets.

Adelaide Strikers were runners-up; they matched the Heat with ten league wins, and might have won their first final if New Zealand's Sophie Devine had not suffered a rare failure. The standout player of the tournament, she made nine half-centuries and amassed 769 runs – just short of Ellyse Perry's WBBL record the previous season – and smashed 29 sixes, ten more than her nearest rival, Melbourne Stars' South African batsman Lizelle Lee. Devine also picked up 19 wickets with her seamers, at an economy-rate of 6.77.

Australian captain Meg Lanning finally saw action in a WBBL semi-final, playing several crucial innings as she led **Perth Scorchers** to third place. But their top order collapsed against Devine and Megan Schutt, before Devine led the Strikers' charge to victory.

Melbourne Renegades had a sometimes shaky campaign, and lost all-rounder Sophie Molineux in the closing rounds when she took a break to deal with mental health issues. But the brilliance of 30-year-old batter Jess Duffin and the guile of off-spinner Molly Strano, the season's leading wicket-taker with 24, catapulted them into the semi-finals, only to be undone by Brisbane.

The biggest shock was that **Sydney Sixers**, who had featured in all four previous finals, failed to make the last four. Halfway through, they suffered a heavy blow when Perry injured her shoulder while fielding in mid-November, and missed the rest of the tournament. She was averaging 93 – a fortnight earlier, she had shared an unbeaten 199-run opening stand against the Stars with Alyssa Healy, who smashed 106 not out from 53 balls. The Sixers managed only one win after Perry's departure, and slid down the table.

Boosted by youngsters such as Phoebe Litchfield and Hannah Darlington, **Sydney Thunder** had their moments, but fell short of qualifying, with Rachael Haynes – who averaged just 15 – in uncharacteristically poor form.

After an audacious off-season recruiting spree by **Hobart Hurricanes** – they nabbed Nicola Carey, Belinda Vakarewa and Maisy Gibson from the Thunder, and Tayla Vlaeminck from the Renegades – they needed only two days to equal their two wins the previous season, completing an opening weekend double over **Melbourne Stars**. The Hurricanes' South African batsman was comfortably the fastest scorer in the competition.

But the Hurricanes and the Stars, who were led by Elyse Villani after her defection from Perth, again filled the bottom two spots. The Stars did topple Villani's old team at the WACA, on the back of a century from Lee, but such highlights were few, and they were yet to qualify for the finals.

WOMEN'S BIG BASH LEAGUE AVERAGES IN 2019-20

BATTING (200 runs, strike-rate 100.00)

		M	*I*	*NO*	*R*	*HS*	*100*	*50*	*Avge*	*SR*	*4*	*6*
1	†C. L. Tryon (*Hobart H*) . .	13	13	6	248	46*	0	0	35.42	**178.41**	26	12
2	A. J. Healy (*Sydney S*) . . .	14	14	1	383	106*	1	1	29.46	**155.69**	43	18
3	J. E. Duffin (*Melbourne R*)	14	13	5	544	76*	0	5	68.00	**138.77**	62	15
4	†J. L. Jonassen (*Brisbane H*)	16	15	4	419	63*	0	2	38.09	**133.01**	47	8
5	L. Lee (*Melbourne S*)	14	14	1	475	103*	1	4	36.53	**131.94**	50	19
6	D. N. Wyatt (*Melbourne R*)	14	14	2	468	87	0	4	39.00	**131.83**	61	7
7	S. F. M. Devine (*Adelaide S*)	16	16	6	769	88	0	9	76.90	**130.33**	68	29
8	†B. L. Mooney (*Brisbane H*)	16	16	6	743	86	0	9	74.30	**125.08**	82	2
9	R. H. Priest (*Sydney T*) . . .	13	13	0	296	50	0	1	22.76	**124.36**	46	8
10	E. G. Fazackerley (*Hobart H*)	13	13	0	243	58	0	1	18.69	**123.97**	27	8
11	G. M. Harris (*Brisbane H*)	16	14	2	212	43	0	0	17.66	**123.97**	21	9
12	N. R. Sciver (*Perth S*). . . .	13	13	4	342	55*	0	2	38.00	**123.02**	43	2
13	M. du Preez (*Melbourne S*)	14	14	0	404	88	0	3	28.85	**120.59**	46	6
14	C. L. Hall (*Hobart H*). . . .	13	13	4	237	50*	0	1	26.33	**119.69**	18	0
15	M. Kapp (*Sydney S*)	14	10	3	232	55*	0	2	33.14	**118.97**	27	2
16	M. M. Lanning (*Perth S*) .	15	15	2	531	101	1	4	40.84	**118.26**	59	12
17	B. E. Patterson (*Adelaide S*)	16	16	4	319	60	0	2	26.58	**117.71**	30	6
18	A. K. Gardner (*Sydney S*) .	14	13	0	275	54	0	1	21.15	**115.54**	34	6
19	A. E. Jones (*Perth S*)	13	13	1	391	80	0	3	32.58	**115.33**	44	5
20	E. A. Perry (*Sydney S*) . . .	9	9	4	469	87*	0	4	93.80	**112.47**	51	8
21	M. L. Green (*Brisbane H*)	16	15	0	309	56	0	1	20.60	**112.36**	40	4
22	N. E. Stalenberg (*Sydney T*)	10	10	0	200	37	0	0	20.00	**111.11**	28	2
23	E. A. Osborne (*Melbourne S*)	14	14	4	205	40	0	0	20.50	**110.21**	16	2
24	A. J. Blackwell (*Sydney T*)	13	13	2	317	65	0	2	28.81	**108.56**	31	5
25	T. M. McGrath (*Adelaide S*)	16	16	2	327	65*	0	1	23.35	**106.86**	32	8
26	E. J. Villani (*Melbourne S*)	14	14	0	344	59	0	3	24.57	**103.92**	44	2
27	H. C. Knight (*Hobart H*) .	13	13	1	282	77	0	2	23.50	**102.54**	27	4

BOWLING (10 wickets, economy-rate of 7.50)

		Style	*Balls*	*Dots*	*R*	*W*	*BB*	*4I*	*Avge*	*SR*	*ER*
1	M. Schutt (*Adelaide S*) . . .	RFM	378	188	353	15	2-12	0	23.53	25.20	**5.6[illegible]**
2	S. Ismail (*Sydney T*)	RFM	306	164	300	10	3-14	0	30.00	30.60	**5.8[illegible]**
3	M. Kapp (*Sydney S*)	RFM	302	167	303	15	3-16	0	20.20	20.13	**6.0[illegible]**
4	B. W. Vakarewa (*Hobart H*) .	RFM	311	155	316	20	4-19	1	15.80	15.55	**6.0[illegible]**
5	A. C. Kerr (*Brisbane H*). . .	LB	344	131	357	14	3-8	0	25.50	24.57	**6.2[illegible]**
6	T. J. Vlaeminck (*Hobart H*) .	RFM	298	158	328	10	2-18	0	32.80	29.80	**6.6[illegible]**

		Style	Balls	Dots	R	W	BB	4I	Avge	SR	ER
7	T. M. McGrath (*Adelaide S*) .	RM	288	104	320	14	2-19	0	22.85	20.57	**6.66**
8	S. J. Johnson (*Brisbane H*).	RM	329	156	367	18	2-16	0	20.38	18.27	**6.69**
9	S. F. M. Devine (*Adelaide S*)	RM	348	156	393	19	3-13	0	20.68	18.31	**6.77**
10	K. J. Garth (*Perth S*)	RM	300	141	339	14	3-21	0	24.21	21.42	**6.78**
11	H. J. Darlington (*Sydney T*)	RM	300	113	341	16	3-29	0	21.31	18.75	**6.82**
12	J. L. Jonassen (*Brisbane H*)	SLA	354	154	403	21	4-13	3	19.19	16.85	**6.83**
13	Nida Dar (*Sydney T*)	OB	192	80	220	13	2-15	0	16.92	14.76	**6.87**
14	S. J. Coyte (*Adelaide S*) . .	RM	349	122	404	19	3-9	0	21.26	18.36	**6.94**
15	A. Wellington (*Adelaide S*)	LB	277	93	324	16	3-17	0	20.25	17.31	**7.01**
16	S. L. Bates (*Sydney T*). . . .	RM	312	123	367	15	3-21	0	24.46	20.80	**7.05**
17	H. L. Graham (*Perth S*). . .	RM	283	96	338	15	3-22	0	22.53	18.86	**7.16**
18	G. K. Prestwidge (*Bris H*). . .	RFM	222	86	266	11	3-29	0	24.18	20.18	**7.18**
19	R. M. Farrell (*Sydney T*). . .	RFM	283	117	343	11	2-23	0	31.18	25.72	**7.27**
20	M. J. Brown (*Melbourne R*) .	RFM	290	123	354	16	3-22	0	22.12	18.12	**7.32**
21	M. L. Gibson (*Hobart H*) .	LB	270	103	332	14	3-26	0	23.71	19.28	**7.37**
22	M. R. Strano (*Melbourne R*) .	OB	329	113	406	24	4-28	1	16.91	13.70	**7.40**
23	A. K. Gardner (*Sydney S*) .	OB	216	59	267	11	2-23	0	24.27	19.63	**7.41**

WOMEN'S BIG BASH LEAGUE IN 2019-20

	P	W	L	A	Pts	NRR
BRISBANE HEAT	14	10	4	0	20	0.72
ADELAIDE STRIKERS	14	10	4	0	20	0.60
PERTH SCORCHERS.	14	9	5	0	18	0.02
MELBOURNE RENEGADES .	14	8	6	0	16	0.11
Sydney Sixers	14	7	7	0	14	–0.07
Sydney Thunder	14	5	8	1	11	–0.48
Hobart Hurricanes	14	4	9	1	9	–0.19
Melbourne Stars	14	2	12	0	4	–0.73

Semi-final At Brisbane (Allan Border Field), December 7, 2019. **Adelaide Strikers won by eight wickets. Perth Scorchers 126-7** (20 overs) (G. P. Redmayne 51, J. L. Barsby 31); **‡Adelaide Strikers 130-2** (18.1 overs) (S. F. M. Devine 65*, T. M. McGrath 36). *PoM:* S. F. M. Devine. *Sophie Devine led Adelaide Strikers into their first BBL final as she lifted her tournament aggregate to 764 at 84. Earlier, she and Megan Schutt had taken a couple of wickets apiece. Perth Scorchers relied heavily on Georgia Redmayne and Jemma Barsby, who took them from 23-3 to 111, before another four fell in the last 15 deliveries. In reply, Suzie Bates was run out for one, before Devine – her fellow New Zealander – surged to 65* in 46 balls.*

Semi-final At Brisbane (Allan Border Field), December 7, 2019. **Brisbane Heat won by four wickets. Melbourne Renegades 163-4** (20 overs) (J. E. Dooley 50*, J. E. Duffin 44); **‡Brisbane Heat 165-6** (18 overs) (M. L. Green 46, J. L. Jonassen 38, G. M. Harris 42; M. R. Strano 4-28). *PoM:* J. L. Jonassen. *Title holders Brisbane Heat secured another final with their ninth win in ten games. In reply to 163, Maddy Green hit 46 off 29 balls, before off-spinner Molly Strano struck twice with successive deliveries. Then Jess Jonassen and Grace Harris took over, adding 80 in 7.2 overs. A further double-strike from Strano triggered a collapse of four for 12, but the Heat won with two overs in hand. The Renegades' innings had also been shaped by an 80-run partnership, between Josie Dooley and Jess Duffin.*

FINAL

BRISBANE HEAT v ADELAIDE STRIKERS

At Brisbane (Allan Border Field), December 8, 2019. Brisbane Heat won by six wickets. Toss: Brisbane Heat.

For the second season running, the WBBL decider was a sell-out, with officials forced to lock the gates at Allan Border Field. And it was déjà vu in more ways than one: Brisbane Heat claimed back-to-back titles, while Beth Mooney was again Player of the Final. The crucial moment came early, when Georgia Prestwidge removed the dangerous Sophie Devine for five. Even so, Amanda-Jade Wellington blasted 55 from 33 balls, leading the Strikers to 161 for seven. In the Heat's chase, Mooney concluded her stellar tournament with a ninth fifty, but the decisive innings was Sammy-Jo Johnson's 27 from 11 balls, which included four sixes off five deliveries from Devine, before she gave a return catch off the sixth. Brisbane triumphed with nearly two overs to spare.

Player of the Match: B. L. Mooney. *Player of the Tournament:* S. F. M. Devine.

Adelaide Strikers

		B	*4/6*
1 S. F. M. Devine *c 2 b 11*	5	7	1
2 *S. W. Bates *c 4 b 7*	27	24	2/1
3 T. M. McGrath *c 10 b 3*	33	20	3/1
4 B. E. Patterson *c 8 b 11*	12	13	1
5 K. M. Mack *run out (1)*	6	10	0
6 A. Wellington *run out (1/8)*	55	33	10
7 †T. J. McPharlin *b 4*	18	14	2
8 S. J. Coyte *not out*	0	0	0
Lb 1, w 3, nb 1	5		
6 overs: 54-1 (20 overs)	161-7		

1/5 2/64 3/67 4/79 5/93 6/149 7/161

9 M. Schutt, 10 A. E. Price and 11 A. V. O'Neil did not bat.

Kimmince 24–8–37–0; Prestwidge 18–7–24–2; G. M. Harris 6–1–12–0; Johnson 24–11–35–1; Jonassen 24–8–30–1; Kerr 24–8–22–1.

Brisbane Heat

		B	*4/6*
1 †B. L. Mooney *not out*	56	45	5
2 M. L. Green *c 2 b 3*	11	9	1
3 S. J. Johnson *c and b 1*	27	11	0/4
4 J. L. Jonassen *c 4 b 8*	33	28	5
5 G. M. Harris *b 3*	2	6	0
6 L. M. Harris *not out*	19	11	3
Lb 5, w 8, nb 1	14		
6 overs: 59-2 (18.1 overs)	162-4		

1/27 2/54 3/121 4/134

7 A. C. Kerr, 8 D. M. Kimmince, 9 *K. L. H. Short, 10 M. C. Hinkley and 11 G. K. Prestwidge did not bat.

Schutt 24–6–27–0; Devine 18–4–46–1; McGrath 24–12–34–2; Coyte 24–6–27–1; Bates 7–3–6–0; Wellington 12–3–17–0.

Umpires: C. A. Polosak and B. C. Treloar. Third umpire: D. R. Close.
Referee: D. A. Johnston.

WOMEN'S BIG BASH LEAGUE FINALS

2015-16	SYDNEY THUNDER beat Sydney Sixers by three wickets at Melbourne.
2016-17	SYDNEY SIXERS beat Perth Scorchers by seven runs at Perth.
2017-18	SYDNEY SIXERS beat Perth Scorchers by nine wickets at Adelaide.
2018-19	BRISBANE HEAT beat Sydney Sixers by three wickets at Sydney (Drummoyne Oval).
2019-20	BRISBANE HEAT beat Adelaide Strikers by six wickets at Brisbane (Allan Border Field).

WOMEN'S BIG BASH LEAGUE RECORDS

Highest score	114	A. K. Gardner	Sydney S v Melbourne S at North Sydney	2017-18
	112*	A. J. Healy	Sydney S v Adel S at Sydney (Hurstville)	2018-19
	106*	**A. J. Healy**	**Sydney S v Melbourne Stars at Perth**	**2019-20**
	106	A. J. Healy	Sydney S v Adel S at Sydney (Hurstville)	2017-18
Fastest 50 – balls	22	A. K. Gardner	Sydney S v Melbourne S at North Sydney	2017-18
	22	L. Lee	Melbourne S v Sydney S at North Sydney	2017-18
Fastest 100 – balls	42	G. M. Harris	Brisbane H v Melbourne S at Brisbane	2018-19
Most sixes – innings	10	A. K. Gardner	Sydney S v Melbourne S at North Sydney	2017-18

Most runs – season	777	E. A. Perry (avge 86.33, SR 121.21) for Sydney S	2018-19
Most sixes – season	**29**	**S. F. M. Devine for Adelaide S**	**2019-20**

Most runs – career	**612**	**E. A. Perry (avge 53.20, SR 105.53**	**2015-16 to 2019-20**
	576	**B. L. Mooney (avge 45.19, SR 122.60)**	**2015-16 to 2019-20**
Most 100s – career	**3**	**A. J. Healy**	**2015-16 to 2019-20**
Best SR – career†	**137.4**	**G. M. Harris (1,113 runs, avge 21.40)**	**2015-16 to 2019-20**
Most sixes – career	**88**	**S. F. M. Devine**	**2015-16 to 2019-20**

Best bowling	5-15	M. R. Strano.	Melb R v Melb S at Melbourne . .	2015-16
	5-17	A. E. Satterthwaite	Hobart H v Sydney T at Hobart . .	2016-17
	5-19	H. K. Matthews . .	Hobart H v Brisbane H at Hobart.	2016-17
Most econ four overs	1-7	N. R. Sciver	Melb S v Melb R at Melbourne . . .	2015-16
	1-7	K. M. Beams	Melbourne S v Bris H at Mackay . .	2017-18
	0-7	L. M. M. Tahuhu .	Melbourne R v Sydney S at Geelong	2018-19
Most expensive analysis	2-54	S. G. Molineux . . .	Melbourne R v Bris H at Geelong .	2018-19

Most wickets – season	28	S. E. Aley (avge 11.75, ER 5.68) for Sydney S	2016-17

Most wickets – career	**96**	**M. R. Strano (avge 17.10, ER 6.40)**	**2015-16 to 2019-20**
	83	**S. E. Aley (avge 17.42, ER 6.45)**.	**2015-16 to 2019-20**
Best ER – career‡	5.15	K. H. Brunt (1,011 balls, avge 17.71). . . .	2015-16 to 2017-18

Highest total	242-4	Sydney S v Melbourne S at North Sydney	2017-18
	206-1	Sydney S v Adelaide S at Sydney (Hurstville)	2018-19
	200-6	Sydney T v Melbourne R at North Sydney.	2017-18
Lowest total	66	Hobart H v Sydney S at Brisbane	2016-17
	66	Brisbane H v Melbourne R at Melbourne (Dock)	2017-18
Highest successful chase	**185-4**	**Melbourne R v Brisbane H at Brisbane (AB)**.	**2019-20**
Highest match aggregate	398-11	Sydney S v Melbourne S at North Sydney	2017-18

† *Career strike-rate: minimum 500 runs.* ‡ *Career economy-rate: minimum 300 balls.*

JIO WOMEN'S T20 CHALLENGE IN 2020

PAUL RADLEY

1 Trailblazers   2 Supernovas

In the ratings war, the Women's T20 Challenge never stood a chance. The BCCI had already made the dubious call to shoehorn the third edition of its pared-down women's IPL into a six-day window in Sharjah at the business end of the men's event, also in the UAE. That meant a scheduling clash with Australia's WBBL, which diminished the player pool: the likes of Ellyse Perry, Alyssa Healy, Katherine Brunt, Laura Wolvaardt and Sophie Devine were playing on a different channel, in a different country. There was still some stardust left for Sharjah. Mithali Raj, Smriti Mandhana and Harmanpreet Kaur captained the three teams; Deandra Dottin arrived from the West Indies, while England supplied Sophie Ecclestone, ranked the world's No. 1 T20 bowler, and Danni Wyatt.

But even they could not compete against the drama of the US presidential election. The T20 Challenge started in the hours after polling day, and Joe Biden was confirmed as president-elect as the last qualifier reached an engrossing climax, with Dottin and Mandhana knitting together **Trailblazers'** plucky response to **Supernovas'** 146 for six in an empty stadium. Although they fell just short, every side finished with one win and one defeat, and these two made the final on net run-rate. Raj's **Velocity**, who had beaten Supernovas in the opening game, paid for a disastrous collapse in the second: they were skittled for 47, with Ecclestone collecting four for nine. Supernovas were looking for a hat-trick of titles, but Trailblazers won the rematch. Even so, Supernovas had the tournament's leading run-scorer – Chamari Atapattu Jayangani, with 117 – and the leading wicket-taker, Radha Yadav, whose eight included five in the final.

The climax also provided the image of the competition – a spine-threatening, acrobatic boundary save by Thailand's Natthakan Chantham. She might have been frustrated at facing one ball in three games (she was run out, off Trailblazers' last delivery in the final), but that moment in the field went viral. Shortly after, she held a fine diving catch to dismiss Jemimah Rodrigues. In a low-scoring match on a slow pitch, both felt seminal.

JIO WOMEN'S T20 CHALLENGE IN 2020

	P	*W*	*L*	*Pts*	*NRR*
TRAILBLAZERS	2	1	1	2	2.10
SUPERNOVAS	2	1	1	2	–0.05
Velocity	2	1	1	2	–1.86

Final At Sharjah, November 9, 2020 (floodlit). **Trailblazers won by 16 runs. Trailblazers 118-8** (20 overs) (S. S. Mandhana 68; R. P. Yadav 5-16); ‡**Supernovas 102-7** (20 overs) (H. Kaur 30; Salma Khatun 3-18). *PoM:* S. S. Mandhana. *PoS:* R. P. Yadav. *Smriti Mandhana made 68 from 49 – the tournament's highest score – to lead Trailblazers to 101-1 in the 15th over. Then slow left-armer Radha Yadav, in her last two overs, took the first five-wicket haul in the Challenge's short history to keep the target down to 119. But Supernovas laboured – only Harmanpreet Kaur passed 19, and she was limping with a strained hamstring. Off-spinner Salma Khatun claimed two wickets and a run-out in the 19th over as the defending champions surrendered their title.*

RACHAEL HEYHOE FLINT TROPHY IN 2020

SYD EGAN

1 Southern Vipers 2 Northern Diamonds

With The Hundred scheduled to replace the Kia Super League as England's premier women's domestic competition in 2020, the ECB had already planned a semi-professional regional structure, with eight teams broadly aligned to the Hundred franchises. But the postponement of that competition due to Covid-19 gave new significance to the regional plans: the 50-over Rachael Heyhoe Flint Trophy – honouring the England captain, who died in 2017 – was drawn up, along the lines of the men's Bob Willis Trophy, and continues for 2021.

The structure – eight teams playing double rounds in North and South groups, followed by a final at Edgbaston – was devised with Covid security in mind, minimising travel and the need for hotel stays. Six of the teams had the same (or similar) names as the KSL sides, but there were two new ones: the Central Sparks, primarily drawn from Warwickshire and Worcestershire, and the Sunrisers, focused on Essex, Middlesex and Northamptonshire.

The entire competition was played behind closed doors, but most games were live-streamed, with tens of thousands watching online; the final, televised by Sky, was the first women's domestic 50-over match broadcast in the UK. The winners were familiar: **Southern Vipers** had appeared in three of the four KSL finals, though Yorkshire Diamonds, predecessors of runners-up Northern Diamonds, had never reached finals day.

Once the England squad had disappeared after the first two rounds, opportunities opened up for others, and no one more than Vipers captain Georgia Adams, who finished with 500 runs at 83. Her 154 not out against **Western Storm** at Southampton was the second-highest score by an uncapped player in top-tier women's cricket in England (Barbara Daniels hit 156 for West Midlands in 1992, the year before her ODI debut) and secured the Vipers' place in the final with a round to spare. Then there was little-known off-spinner Charlotte Taylor, whose haul of 15 wickets included six in the final. They finished with six wins from six; the Storm came in second, having won all their games except the two against the Vipers, whereas **South East Stars** beat only **Sunrisers**.

Gareth Copley, Getty Images

Killer bite: the Vipers' Charlotte Taylor was the tournament's leading wicket-taker.

Although **Northern Diamonds** (representing Yorkshire and Durham) led the North Group from start to finish, **Central Sparks** kept things interesting by beating them in the fifth round, successfully chasing 217, thanks to 77 from captain Eve Jones, after seamer Liz Russell's four for 28. That put them five points behind going into the last round – requiring a huge win, for a bonus point and a turnabout in net run-rate, plus a heavy loss for the Diamonds. In fact, the Diamonds beat **Thunder** (from the North-West), while the Sparks lost to **Lightning** (Derbyshire, Leicestershire and Nottinghamshire) for a second time, despite Jones carrying her bat for 115. For Lightning, Scotland's Sarah Bryce hit 136 out of 303 for five – the tournament's only total of 300-plus.

Bryce was one of just three non-England internationals to appear in the competition; the others were her sister Kathryn, also at Lightning, who was the leading wicket-taker in the group stages with 14, and the Netherlands' Sterre Kalis at the Diamonds, who followed three consecutive ducks with three half-centuries.

The six hundreds scored during the tournament showed the benefit of playing all 25 matches on first-class pitches; there had been only ten in the previous five seasons of Division One in the old County Championship (the Royal London Women's One-Day Cup), played mainly on club grounds.

RACHAEL HEYHOE FLINT TROPHY AVERAGES IN 2020

BATTING (160 runs)

		M	*I*	*NO*	*R*	*HS*	*100*	*50*	*Avge*	*SR*	*4*	*6*
1	G. L. Adams (*Southern Vipers*)	7	7	1	500	154*	1	3	83.33	81.69	60	0
2	S. J. Bryce (*Lightning*)	6	6	1	395	136*	1	4	79.00	78.52	48	0
3	S. N. Luff (*Western Storm*)	6	6	1	339	104*	1	3	67.80	75.50	32	2
4	†E. Jones (*Central Sparks*)	6	6	1	334	115*	1	2	66.80	74.05	42	0
5	M. Kelly (*Central Sparks*)	6	6	2	223	59*	0	2	55.75	61.77	22	0
6	C. E. Dean (*Southern Vipers*)	7	6	2	180	60*	0	1	45.00	73.77	16	0
7	S. L. Kalis (*N Diamonds*)	7	6	1	197	87	0	3	39.40	74.62	29	0
8	G. M. Hennessy (*W Storm*)	6	6	0	209	105	1	1	34.83	80.07	28	0
9	A. J. Freeborn (*Lightning*)	5	5	0	167	40	0	0	33.40	69.00	20	1
10	J. L. Gardner (*Sunrisers*)	6	6	0	193	54	0	1	32.16	69.17	19	3
11	N. Brown (*Thunder*)	6	6	0	189	52	0	1	31.50	68.72	25	0
12	M. E. Bouchier (*S Vipers*)	7	7	1	183	50*	0	1	30.50	85.51	22	1
13	H. J. Armitage (*N Diamonds*)	7	7	1	176	54*	0	1	29.33	62.19	21	2
14	E. M. McCaughan (*S Vipers*)	7	6	0	172	63	0	2	28.66	59.10	19	0
15	†G. M. Davies (*Central Sparks*)	6	6	0	169	50	0	1	28.16	68.14	22	0

BOWLING (8 wickets)

		Style	*O*	*M*	*R*	*W*	*BB*	*4I*	*Avge*	*SR*	*ER*
1	C. M. Taylor (*S Vipers*)	OB	44	2	152	15	6-34	2	10.13	17.60	3.45
2	K. E. Bryce (*Lightning*)	RM	55.4	4	216	14	5-29	2	15.42	23.85	3.88
3	A. Hartley (*Thunder*)	SLA	54	6	170	11	4-8	1	15.45	29.45	3.14
4	T. G. Norris (*S Vipers*)	LM	44.5	2	215	12	4-45	1	17.91	22.41	4.79
5	B. A. Langston (*N Diamonds*)	RM	56.1	5	233	12	3-18	0	19.41	28.08	4.14
6	N. E. Farrant (*SE Stars*)	LFM	52	9	177	9	3-24	0	19.66	34.66	3.40
7	C. K. Boycott (*C Sparks*)	RFM	37	1	160	8	4-40	1	20.00	27.75	4.32
8	F. M. K. Morris (*W Storm*)	OB	59	4	240	11	5-26	1	21.81	32.18	4.06

		Style	O	M	R	W	BB	4I	Avge	SR	ER
9	K. A. Levick (*N Diamonds*)	LB	60	5	244	11	3-22	0	22.18	32.72	4.06
10	G. M. Hennessy (*W Storm*)	RFM	53.1	2	257	11	4-31	1	23.36	29.00	4.83
11	J. L. Gunn (*N Diamonds*)	RFM	45.5	3	187	8	2-18	0	23.37	34.37	4.08
12	P. J. Scholfield (*S Vipers*)	RFM	51.1	2	212	9	3-33	0	23.55	34.11	4.14
13	L. F. Higham (*Lightning*)	OB	44	3	195	8	3-38	0	24.37	33.00	4.43
14	A. Patel (*Central Sparks*)	LB	44	3	202	8	3-49	0	25.25	33.00	4.59
15	C. E. Dean (*Southern Vipers*)	OB	58	2	269	9	3-50	0	29.88	38.66	4.63

RACHAEL HEYHOE FLINT TROPHY IN 2020

50-over league

North Group	P	W	L	Bonus	Pts	NRR
NORTHERN DIAMONDS	6	5	1	3	23	1.00
Central Sparks	6	3	3	1	13	–0.28
Thunder	6	2	4	1	9	–0.51
Lightning	6	2	4	0	8	–0.11

South Group	P	W	L	Bonus	Pts	NRR
SOUTHERN VIPERS	6	6	0	3	27	1.01
Western Storm	6	4	2	2	18	0.51
South East Stars	6	2	4	2	10	–0.19
Sunrisers	6	0	6	0	0	–1.36

Win = 4pts; 1 bonus pt awarded for achieving victory with a run-rate 1.25 times that of the opposition.

FINAL

NORTHERN DIAMONDS v SOUTHERN VIPERS

At Birmingham, September 27. Southern Vipers won by 38 runs. Toss: Northern Diamonds.

Southern Vipers' unheralded hero on a chilly day at Edgbaston was bespectacled off-spinner Charlotte Taylor, whose career-best six for 34 – the tournament's best return – wrecked Northern Diamonds' pursuit of 232. They were ahead of the rate for much of the chase, but their batters were undone by the away-drift of Taylor's stock arm-ball, and the Diamonds were bowled out in the 43rd over. Earlier, they had bowled tightly and fielded sharply. A century opening stand between Georgia Adams and Ella McCaughan was followed by a collapse – 150 for one to 191 for eight – though Emily Windsor rallied the tail to reach a score that at the time seemed barely par.

Player of the Match: C. M. Taylor. *Most Valuable Player of the Tournament:* G. L. Adams.

Southern Vipers

*G. L. Adams c Armitage b Levick	80
E. M. McCaughan c Heath b Smith	35
M. E. Bouchier c MacDonald b Armitage	28
C. E. Dean lbw b Levick	2
P. J. Scholfield c Campbell b Armitage	3
E. L. Windsor run out (Kalis)	37
†C. E. Rudd lbw b Levick	1
T. G. Norris run out (Smith/Langston)	5
A. Z. Monaghan c Heath b Langston	1
C. M. Taylor c Armitage b Gunn	7
L. K. Bell not out	6
Lb 8, w 16, nb 2	26
1/100 (2) 2/150 (3) 3/155 (4) 4/158 (5) 5/165 (1) 6/172 (7) 7/188 (8) 8/191 (9) 9/220 (6) 10/231 (10) (49.5 overs)	231
10 overs: 35-0	

Langston 10–2–35–1; Smith 7–0–31–1; Graham 8–0–43–0; Levick 8–1–49–3; Gunn 8.5–0–32–1; Armitage 8–0–33–2.

Northern Diamonds

*L. Winfield-Hill c Windsor b Bouchier	20	P. C. Graham c Scholfield b Adams	16
H. J. Armitage c Dean b Taylor	26	K. A. Levick not out	8
S. L. Kalis c Adams b Taylor	55		
A. Campbell run out (Bell/Dean)	0	Lb 8, w 23	31
A. L. MacDonald hit wkt b Taylor	0		
J. L. Gunn lbw b Taylor	9	1/36 (1) 2/74 (2) 3/78 (4) (42.2 overs)	193
†B. A. M. Heath c Monaghan b Taylor	0	4/79 (5) 5/94 (6) 6/96 (7)	
L. C. N. Smith lbw b Dean	7	7/110 (8) 8/159 (9) 9/172 (3)	
B. A. Langston lbw b Taylor	21	10/193 (10) 10 overs: 49-1	

Bell 9–0–43–0; Norris 4–0–22–0; Bouchier 3–0–13–1; Taylor 10–0–34–6; Scholfield 4–0–25–0; Dean 10–1–35–1; Adams 2.2–0–13–1.

Umpires: N. Pratt and R. A. White. Third umpire: J. D. Middlebrook.
Referee: S. J. Davis.

ENGLISH DOMESTIC CRICKET IN 2020

County sides gradually took to the field in late summer; most matches were friendlies, but some mini-leagues were organised. In July, an inexperienced **Surrey** beat favourites Middlesex to claim their first London Cup (an annual Twenty20 challenge), having lost the previous five. This was followed by a 50-over London Championship, in which they were joined by Essex and Kent. Again, Surrey won the title: they beat Kent and Essex, before their match with Middlesex was ended by rain. Middlesex had a chance of catching up the following week, but their fixture with Kent was washed out. Four more teams – Buckinghamshire, Hertfordshire, Huntingdonshire and Norfolk – contested a 45-over league in August, followed by a T20 competition in September. The first tournament produced a thrilling last day, when Hertfordshire and Norfolk, who had both won their first two matches, tied on 74, and contested a super over: **Hertfordshire** triumphed. **Buckinghamshire**, who lost all their 45-over matches, won their first five T20 games to become champions, before slipping up against Hertfordshire on the final afternoon.

London Cup At The Oval, July 22. **Surrey won by four wickets**. ‡**Middlesex 108-7** (20 overs) (C. L. Griffith 30); **Surrey 110-6** (19.5 overs). *The first match at The Oval in 2020 brought Surrey a maiden London Cup. Amy Gordon dismissed Naomi Dattani with the game's fourth ball and, despite opener Cordelia Griffith (30 in 23) and Gayatri Gole (28* in 24), Middlesex set only 109. At 60-5, that looked tricky, but Kira Chathli (28*) won it with a ball to spare.*

London Championship *50-over league* SURREY 41pts, Middlesex 28, Kent 25, Essex 9.

East of England Women's County Championship *45-over league* HERTFORDSHIRE 54pts, Norfolk 41, Huntingdonshire 18, Buckinghamshire 18.

East of England Women's T20 Championship BUCKINGHAMSHIRE 20, Hertfordshire 16, Norfolk 8, Huntingdonshire 4.

THE UNIVERSITY MATCH IN 2020

At Oxford, September 2. **Oxford University won by 59 runs** (DLS). ‡**Oxford University 175-4** (20 overs) (A. Travers 70, O. Lee-Smith 38); **Cambridge University 57-5** (14 overs). *Oxford overwhelmed Cambridge in the women's T20 Varsity Match, postponed from May and staged the day after the men's 50-over game. The previous Oxford captain, Vanessa Picker, could not get back from Australia because of Covid travel restrictions, so Amy Hearn led the side. Alex Travers (70 in 46 balls) and Liv Lee-Smith stormed to 123 in 13 overs. In reply, only Katie Gibson and the captain, Chloe Allison – in her final appearance for Cambridge, whom she first represented in 2012 – reached double figures; when rain ended play after 14 overs they had limped to 57-5, less than half the retrospective target of 117. A second fixture planned for the same day was abandoned.*

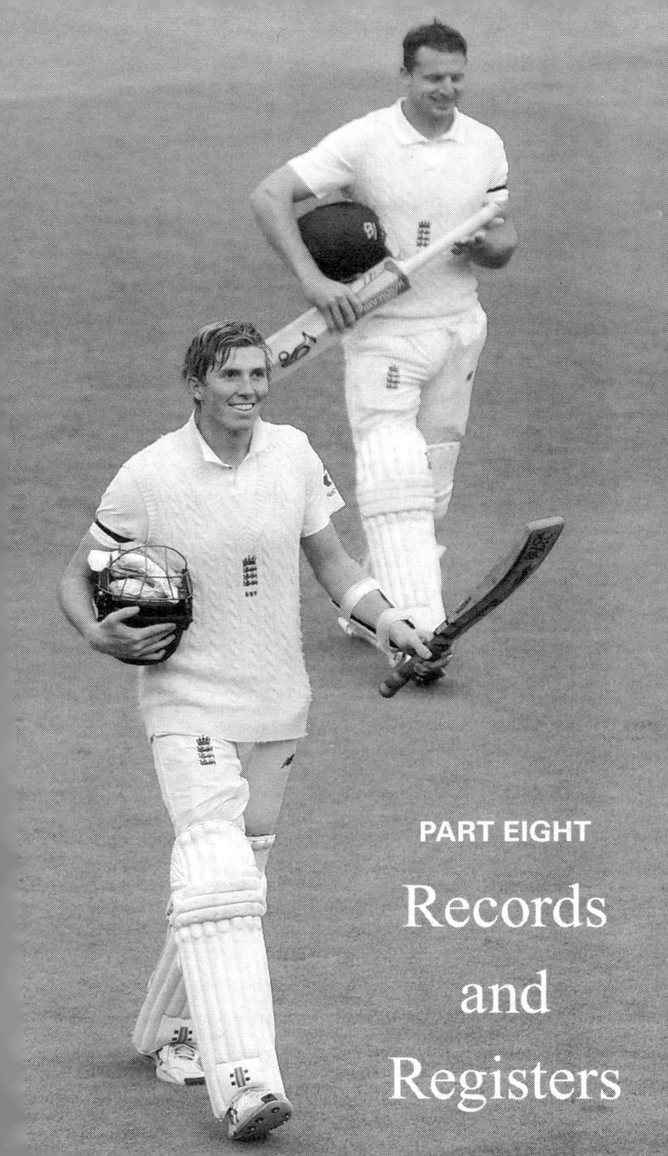

PART EIGHT

Records and Registers

FIRST-CLASS FEATURES OF 2020

This section covers the calendar year. Some of the features listed occurred in series and seasons reported in *Wisden 2020* and some in series and seasons that will be reported in *Wisden 2022*; these items are indicated by [W20] or [W22].

Double-Hundreds (51)

	Mins	*Balls*	*4*	*6*		
354*		391	33	9	L. D. Chandimal....	Army v Saracens at Katunayake.
334*	585	426	42	3	Tamim Iqbal.......	East Zone v Central Zone at Mirpur.
313	621	459	25	4	A. P. Agathangelou .	Easterns v Boland at Paarl.
303*		414	30	5	M. K. Tiwary	Bengal v Hyderabad at Kalyani.
301*		391	30	8	‡S. N. Khan	Mumbai v Uttar Pradesh at Mumbai.
300*		270	28	10	R. T. M. Wanigamuni	Moors v Negombo at Colombo (Moors).
290*		303	28	9	L. U. Igalagamage ..	Nondescripts v Ragama at Colombo (NCC).
267*		329	33	5	R. Dalal...........	Arunachal Pradesh v Nagaland at Dimapur.
267	541	393	34	1	Z. Crawley	England v Pak (3rd Test) at Southampton.
255*	564	386	27	1	‡W. J. Pucovski	Victoria v South Australia at Adelaide.[W22]
254*		228	23	13	R. Sanjay Yadav....	Meghalaya v Mizoram at Kolkata.
253*	396	310	25	9	Nazmul Hossain	Central Zone v South Zone at Cox's Bazar.
253	415	310	33	6	Hussain Talat	Southern Punjab v Northern at Karachi.[W22]
252		314	27	6	B. K. E. L. Milantha .	Badureliya v Lankan at Maggona.
251	624	412	34	2	K. S. Williamson ...	New Zealand v WI (1st Test) at Hamilton.
250		267	26	1	P. Bisht...........	Meghalaya v Arunachal Pr at Dibrugarh.
248		390	24	1	C. A. Pujara	Saurashtra v Karnataka at Rajkot.
248	502	332	33	2	J. Blackwood	Jamaica v Leeward Islands at North Sound.
246	552	400	17	1	K. C. Brathwaite....	West Indians v NZ A at Queenstown.
239	486	399	27	1	M. S. Harris	Victoria v South Australia at Adelaide.[W22]
238*	474	345	27	3	J. M. Cox	Kent v Sussex at Canterbury.
236		195	28	3	S. K. Patel.........	Goa v Mizoram at Calcutta.
236		357	31	0	Jiwanjot Singh	Chhattisgarh v Services at Naya Raipur.
233		268	33	3	Fabid Ahmed	Puducherry v Manipur at Kolkata.
230	508	384	22	1	Y. Valli...........	Easterns v Boland at Paarl.
226*		213	32	4	‡S. N. Khan	Mumbai v Himachal Pradesh at Dharamsala.
226*	519	367	21	3	L. J. Carter	Canterbury v Wellington at Rangiora.
221		402	29	1	H. S. Bhatia	Chhattisgarh v Jharkhand at Jamshedpur.
221		277	23	0	K. W. S. L. Fernando	Air Force v Police at Katunayake.
220*	373	308	29	0	J. A. Leaning	Kent v Sussex at Canterbury.
219*	487	346	27	2	Usman Salahuddin ..	Central Punjab v S Punjab at Karachi.[W22]
219	366	244	28	4	D. J. Malan........	Yorkshire v Derbyshire at Leeds.
215	516	363	19	1	M. Labuschagne....	Australia v NZ (3rd Test) at Sydney.[W20]
213*	529	351	30	1	T. de Zorzi	Titans v Cape Cobras at Cape Town.
212*		273	28	0	U. Kaul...........	Chandigarh v Mizoram at Chandigarh.
207	489	328	22	0	W. M. H. Rhodes ...	Warwickshire v Worcs at Worcester.
206		242	34	0	A. Mukund	Tamil Nadu v Baroda at Vadodara.
204*		260	18	1	D. B. Ravi Teja.....	Meghalaya v Mizoram at Kolkata.
204*	359	279	22	4	S. Gill	India A v New Zealand A at Christchurch.
204*		406	21	1	A. R. Bawne	Maharashtra v Orissa at Gahunje.
204*		398	11	5	A. N. Ghosh	Railways v Himachal Pradesh at Delhi.
203*		239	27	3	U. D. Yadav	Uttar Pradesh v Mumbai at Mumbai.
203*	431	318	28	0	Mushfiqur Rahim ...	Bangladesh v Zim (Only Test) at Mirpur.
202	441	347	27	0	‡W. J. Pucovski	Victoria v Western Australia at Adelaide.[W22]
201	345	223	18	8	D. Cleaver.........	Central Districts v N Districts at Napier.
200*		231	25	3	R. Jonathan........	Nagaland v Bihar at Dimapur.
200*	600	468	16	3	A. D. Mathews	Sri Lanka v Zimbabwe (1st Test) at Harare.
200*		171	23	4	Gurender Singh.....	Chandigarh v Manipur at Kolkata.
200*		300	24	1	B. K. G. Mendis	Colombo v Nondescripts at Colombo (PSO).
200		276	27	4	B. Sharma.........	Chandigarh v Manipur at Kolkata.
200	421	261	25	2	R. van Tonder......	Knights v Lions at Bloemfontein.[W22]

‡ *S. N. Khan and W. J. Pucovski each scored two double-hundreds.*

Hundred on First-Class Debut

118	M. D. Dilshan	Moors v Colts at Colombo (Moors).
122	A. P. Gomel	Mumbai v Madhya Pradesh at Mumbai.
101	Kamal Singh	Uttarakhand v Maharashtra at Baramati.
164	Mubasir Khan	Northern v Sindh at Karachi.W22
150	Y. Rishav	Bihar v Meghalaya at Patna.
106	C. Z. Taylor	Glamorgan v Northamptonshire at Northampton.

Three or More Hundreds in Successive Innings

A. K. Markram (Titans)	149 and 121	v Warriors at Centurion.W22
	113	v Cape Cobras at Centurion.W22
M. D. Rahmatullah (Bihar)	105*	v Meghalaya at Patna.
	140 and 113*	v Arunachal Pradesh at Patna.

Hundred in Each Innings of a Match

Anamul Haque	129	109*	South Zone v East Zone at Cox's Bazar.
J. F. Carter	169	120	Northern Districts v Auckland at Auckland.
M. S. Chapman	143	146	Auckland v Northern Districts at Auckland.
D. P. Hughes	103	136	New South Wales v South Australia at Sydney.W20
A. K. Markram	149	121	Titans v Warriors at Centurion.W22
D. L. Perera	113	112*	Badureliya v Sinhalese at Moratuwa.
M. D. Rahmatullah	140	113*	Bihar v Arunachal Pradesh at Patna.
P. B. B. Rajapaksa	115	110*	Burgher v Nondescripts at Katunayake.
Yasir Ali	165	110	East Zone v North Zone at Chittagong.

Carrying Bat through Completed Innings

K. C. Brathwaite	84*	Barbados (210) v Guyana at Providence.
M. P. Breetzke	77*	Warriors (186) v Knights at Bloemfontein.W22
T. Chanderpaul	66*	Guyana (209) v Barbados at Bridgetown.
P. P. Das	76*	Tripura (144) v Chhattisgarh at Naya Raipur.
T. A. Lammonby	107*	Somerset (193) v Worcestershire at Worcester.
W. A. D. P. Madusanka	63*	Nugegoda (128) v Ports Authority at Dombagoda.
S. N. Rupero	105*	Nagaland (243) v Mizoram at Calcutta.

Hundred before Lunch

P. D. Daneel	116*	Cambridge U v Oxford U at Cambridge on day 3.
G. J. Snyman	109	Knights v Warriors at Bloemfontein on day 1.W22
Y. Valli	107* to 210*	Easterns v Boland at Paarl on day 3.

Most Sixes in an Innings

13	A. K. Kaushik (177)	Chandigarh v Mizoram at Chandigarh.
13	R. Sanjay Yadav (254*)	Meghalaya v Mizoram at Kolkata.
11	P. Dogra (194)	Puducherry v Goa at Puducherry.
11	A. Samad (128)	Jammu & Kashmir v Jharkhand at Ranchi.
10	D. A. Randika (133)	Army v Chilaw Marians at Colombo (PSO).
10	R. T. M. Wanigamuni (300*)	Moors v Negombo at Colombo (Moors).
9	L. D. Chandimal (354*)	Army v Saracens at Katunayake.
9	M. de Lange (113)	Glamorgan v Northamptonshire at Northampton.
9	L. U. Igalagamage (290*)	Nondescripts v Ragama at Colombo (NCC).
9	J. K. Joshi (107)	Sebastianites v Kalutara Town at Horana.
9	Nazmul Hossain (253*)	Central Zone v South Zone at Cox's Bazar.
9	R. J. M. G. M. Rupasinghe (132)	Kalutara Town v Bloomfield at Colombo (Bloomfield).
9	L. A. C. Ruwansiri (124)	Lankan v Negombo at Moratuwa.

Longest Innings

Mins

624 K. S. Williamson (251) . . . . New Zealand v West Indies (1st Test) at Hamilton.
621 A. P. Agathangelou (313) . . . . . . Easterns v Boland at Paarl.
600 A. D. Mathews (200*). . . . . Sri Lanka v Zimbabwe (1st Test) at Harare.

Unusual Dismissals

Obstructing the Field

T. A. Blundell (101) . . . . Wellington v Otago at Wellington.[W22]

Highest Wicket Partnerships

First Wicket

486 W. J. Pucovski/M. S. Harris, Victoria v South Australia at Adelaide.[W22]
485 Y. Valli/A. P. Agathangelou, Easterns v Boland at Paarl.
316 S. P. Amonkar/V. V. Govekar, Goa v Arunachal Pradesh at Porvorim.
256 J. M. Richards/D. A. Hendricks, Lions v Knights at Johannesburg.[W22]

Second Wicket

423* J. M. Cox/J. A. Leaning, Kent v Sussex at Canterbury.
353 Jiwanjot Singh/H. S. Bhatia, Chhattisgarh v Services at Naya Raipur.
344 S. J. Erwee/K. D. Petersen, Dolphins v Lions at Durban.[W22]
305 H. D. R. L. Thirimanne/M. D. U. S. Jayasundera, Ragama v Burgher at Colombo (PSO).
296 Tamim Iqbal/Mominul Haque, East Zone v Central Zone at Mirpur.
263* D. S. Smith/K. A. R. Hodge, Windward Islands v Guyana at St George's.

Third Wicket

394 C. A. Pujara/S. P. Jackson, Saurashtra v Karnataka at Rajkot.
301 S. K. Patel/A. A. Verma, Goa v Mizoram at Calcutta.
287 D. P. Conway/M. G. Bracewell, Wellington v Auckland at Wellington.[W22]
254 M. D. U. S. Jayasundera/A. R. S. Silva, Ragama v Nondescripts at Colombo (NCC).
253 N. C. R. Larkin/M. C. Henriques, New South Wales v Tasmania at Adelaide.[W22]

Fourth Wicket

318 J. D. Libby/B. L. D'Oliveira, Worcestershire v Glamorgan at Worcester.
294 S. C. Serasinghe/R. T. M. Wanigamuni, Moors v Negombo at Colombo (Moors).
275 A. P. Gomel/S. N. Khan, Mumbai v Madhya Pradesh at Mumbai.
260 D. P. Sibley/B. A. Stokes, England v West Indies (2nd Test) at Manchester.

Fifth Wicket

440* D. B. Ravi Teja/R. Sanjay Yadav, Meghalaya v Mizoram at Kolkata.
359 Z. Crawley/J. C. Buttler, England v Pakistan (3rd Test) at Southampton.
296 A. R. S. Silva/K. N. M. Fernando, Ragama v Lankan at Colombo (NCC).
294 Hammad Azam/Mubasir Khan, Northern v Sindh at Karachi.[W22]
279 U. Kaul/A. K. Kaushik, Chandigarh v Mizoram at Chandigarh.

Sixth Wicket

268 M. S. Chapman/D. Cleaver, New Zealand A v India A at Christchurch.
266* A. C. Agar/J. P. Inglis, Western Australia v South Australia at Adelaide.[W22]
252 C. G. Wijesinghe/R. S. Wickramarachchi, Kandy Customs v Bloomfield at Colombo (Bloomfield).
221 U. Kaul/B. Sharma, Chandigarh v Manipur at Kolkata.
205 M. S. Chapman/B. J. Horne, Auckland v Northern Districts at Auckland.
204 P. C. de Silva/S. S. D. Arachchige, Nondescripts v Colombo at Colombo (PSO).

Seventh Wicket

200* A. M. Rossington/L. A. Procter, Northamptonshire v Warwickshire at Birmingham.

Eighth Wicket

204	S. A. D. U. Mihiran/A. G. S. Mayura, Police v Nugegoda at Panadura.
199	R. A. Reifer/R. Shepherd, West Indies A v New Zealand A at Mount Maunganui.
198	R. Dalal/A. R. Sahani, Arunachal Pradesh v Nagaland at Dimapur.
189	R. Ranasinghe/P. L. M. Jayarathne, Kurunegala Youth v Navy at Welisara.
169	R. J. M. G. M. Rupasinghe/A. Perera, Kalutara Town v Bloomfield at Colombo (Bloomfield).
162	Saad Nasim/S. A. D. U. Indrasiri, Negombo v Army at Colombo (Moors).
159*	M. K. Tiwary/A. A. Nandy, Bengal v Hyderabad at Kalyani.

Ninth Wicket

204	B. J. Horne/D. K. Ferns, Auckland v Otago at Auckland.[W22]
192	Fabid Ahmed/S. P. Udeshi, Puducherry v Manipur at Kolkata.
180	S. M. Davies/J. Overton, Somerset v Warwickshire at Birmingham.
168	D. A. Douthwaite/M. de Lange, Glamorgan v Northamptonshire at Northampton.

Tenth Wicket

124	C. Z. Taylor/M. G. Hogan, Glamorgan v Northamptonshire at Northampton.
107	S. M. Davies/J. A. Brooks, Somerset v Glamorgan at Taunton.
103	P. Dogra/S. P. Udeshi, Puducherry v Goa at Puducherry.

Most Wickets in an Innings

9-86	L. Embuldeniya	Nondescripts v Saracens at Maggona.
8-18	V. Permaul	Guyana v Jamaica at Greenfields.
8-31	C. A. K. Rajitha	Saracens v Ragama at Maggona.
8-31	R. Sanjay Yadav	Meghalaya v Puducherry at Mangoldoi.
8-32	E. M. C. D. Edirisinghe	Saracens v Ragama at Maggona.
8-32	T. Shamsi	Titans v Warriors at Port Elizabeth.[W22]
8-51	R. R. S. Cornwall	Leeward Islands v Trinidad & Tobago at Basseterre.
8-56	L. L. Guite	Mizoram v Sikkim at Bhubaneswar.
8-57	A. L. R. Manasinghe	Negombo v Burgher at Colombo (Moors).
8-64	S. R. Harmer	Essex v Surrey at Chelmsford.
8-69	N. M. Kavikara	Kurunegala Youth v Panadura at Kurunegala.
8-76	D. M. Ranasinghe	Moors v Army at Panagoda.
8-98	D. K. R. C. Jayatissa	Panadura v Navy at Panadura.
8-107	Nayeem Hasan	East Zone v North Zone at Chittagong.
8-147	D. S. Tillekeratne	Burgher v Colts at Colombo (Burgher).

Most Wickets in a Match

15-77	V. Permaul	Guyana v Jamaica at Greenfields.
14-131	S. R. Harmer	Essex v Surrey at Chelmsford.
13-118	D. S. Tillekeratne	Burgher v Nondescripts at Katunayake.
13-208	Nayeem Hasan	East Zone v North Zone at Chittagong.
12-73	Parvez Rasool	Jammu & Kashmir v Tripura at Agartala.
12-86	C. J. August	Easterns v South Western Districts at Benoni.
12-100	S. P. Udeshi	Chilaw Marians v Lankan at Colombo (CCC).
12-106	J. D. Unadkat	Saurashtra v Baroda at Vadodara.
12-109	D. M. de Silva	Tamil Union v Moors at Moratuwa.
12-110	R. M. G. K. Sirisoma	Bloomfield v Sebastianites at Colombo (Bloomfield).
12-110	O. J. Hannon-Dalby	Warwickshire v Gloucestershire at Bristol.
12-165	N. Tempol	Arunachal Pradesh v Puducherry at Puducherry.
12-171	R. M. G. K. Sirisoma	Bloomfield v Nugegoda at Colombo (Bloomfield).
12-243	D. S. Auwardt	Navy v Police at Welisara.

Outstanding Innings Analysis

7.5–5–2–6	R. M. G. K. Sirisoma	Bloomfield v Navy at Colombo (Bloomfield).

Hat-Tricks (10)

K. H. R. K. Fernando	Sebastianites v Air Force at Katunayake.
K. W. S. L. Fernando	Air Force v Nugegoda at Katunayake.
J. K. Fuller	Hampshire v Surrey at Arundel.
K. A. Jamieson	Auckland v Central Districts at Auckland.[W22]
S. Kaul	Punjab v Andhra at Patiala.
Naseem Shah	Pakistan v Bangladesh (1st Test) at Rawalpindi.
A. R. Sanganakal	Puducherry v Meghalaya at Mangoldoi.
W. D. A. Senaratne	Sinhalese v Moors at Colombo (Moors).
Shahbaz Ahmed	Bengal v Hyderabad at Kalyani.
R. R. Yadav	Madhya Pradesh v Uttar Pradesh at Indore (*on first-class debut*).

Wicket with First Ball in First-Class Career

S. S. Coomaraswamy	Army v Burgher at Dombagoda.
D. M. N. D. Gunawardene	Sebastianites v Panadura at Katunayake.
Y. B. Kothari	Rajasthan v Andhra at Jaipur.

Most Wicketkeeping Dismissals in an Innings

7 (6ct, 1st)	M. Mosehle	KwaZulu-Natal Inland v Northerns at Pretoria.
6 (5ct, 1st)	P. V. R. de Silva	Colts v Ragama at Colombo (CCC).
6 (6ct)	Kamran Akmal	Central Punjab v Sindh at Karachi.[W22]
6 (6ct)	S. K. Lenka	Orissa v Jammu & Kashmir at Cuttack.
6 (6ct)	S. Masondo	Easterns v Northerns at Pretoria.
6 (5ct, 1st)	Nurul Hasan	South Zone v East Zone at Chittagong.
6 (6ct)	O. G. Robinson	Kent v Hampshire at Canterbury.
6 (6ct)	R. S. Second	Warriors v Cape Cobras at East London.
6 (4ct, 2st)	S. Sharath	Karnataka v Bengal at Kolkata.
6 (6ct)	K. Srikar Bharat	Andhra v Saurashtra at Ongole.

Most Wicketkeeping Dismissals in a Match

11 (8ct, 3st)	K. Srikar Bharat	Andhra v Saurashtra at Ongole.
9 (8ct, 1st)	D. Cleaver	Central Districts v Northern Districts at Napier.
9 (7ct, 2st)	C. B. Cooke	Glamorgan v Worcestershire at Worcester.
9 (8ct, 1st)	P. V. R. de Silva	Colts v Ragama at Colombo (CCC).
9 (8ct, 1st)	M. Mosehle	KwaZulu-Natal Inland v Northerns at Pretoria.
9 (9ct)	D. M. Sarathchandra	Tamil Union v Badureliya at Dambulla.
9 (7ct, 2st)	S. Sharath	Karnataka v Bengal at Kolkata.

Most Catches in an Innings in the Field

5	B. A. Stokes	England v South Africa (2nd Test) at Cape Town.[W20]

Most Catches in a Match in the Field

7	S. J. Mullaney	Nottinghamshire v Yorkshire at Nottingham.
7	S. Qeshile	Warriors v Titans at Centurion.[W22]
6	P. Bisht	Meghalaya v Arunachal Pradesh at Dibrugarh.
6	B. N. L. Charles	Trinidad & Tobago v Leeward Islands at Tarouba.
6	I. Dev Singh	Kandy Customs v Nugegoda at Colombo (Burgher).
6	N. A. N. N. Perera	Galle v Air Force at Katunayake.
6	O. J. D. Pope	England v South Africa (3rd Test) at Port Elizabeth.[W20]
6	B. A. Stokes	England v South Africa (2nd Test) at Cape Town.[W20]

No Byes Conceded in Total of 500 or More

A. L. K. L. Abeyrathne	Lankan v Moors (599-9 dec) at Colombo (NCC).
D. Cleaver	New Zealand A v West Indians (571) at Queenstown.
L. P. P. M. Kumara	Army v Ragama (501-9 dec) at Colombo (CCC).
S. K. Patel	Goa v Gujarat (602-8 dec) at Valsad.
S. L. Sailo	Mizoram v Chandigarh (587-5 dec) at Chandigarh.

Highest Innings Totals

688-7 dec	Mumbai v Uttar Pradesh at Mumbai.
672-8 dec	Chandigarh v Manipur at Kolkata.
662-4 dec	Meghalaya v Mizoram at Kolkata.
652-8 dec	Moors v Negombo at Colombo (Moors).
648-8 dec	Badureliya v Lankan at Maggona.
642-4 dec	Easterns v Boland at Paarl.
642-8 dec	Army v Saracens at Katunayake.
635-7 dec	Bengal v Hyderabad at Kalyani.
625-8 dec	Uttar Pradesh v Mumbai at Mumbai.
625-8 dec	Puducherry v Nagaland at Puducherry.
623	Delhi v Rajasthan at Delhi.
621	South Africa v Sri Lanka (1st Test) at Centurion.
602-8 dec	Gujarat v Goa at Valsad.

Lowest Innings Totals

27	Manipur v Meghalaya at Mangoldoi.
36	Navy v Bloomfield at Colombo (Bloomfield).
36†	India v Australia (1st Test) at Adelaide.
44	Maharashtra v Services at Delhi.
44	Eastern Province v Western Province at Port Elizabeth.
46	Kandy Customs v Navy at Welisara.
51	Windward Islands v Leeward Islands at Gros Islet.
52	Air Force v Sebastianites at Katunayake.
53†	Tripura v Chhattisgarh at Naya Raipur.
54	Otago v Auckland at Auckland.[W22]
55	Guyana v Barbados at Providence.
56	Nugegoda v Kalutara Town at Horana.
60	Jamaica v Windward Islands at St George's.
62	Navy v Bloomfield at Colombo (Bloomfield).
63	Meghalaya v Puducherry at Mangoldoi.
63	Manipur v Chandigarh at Kolkata.
64	New South Wales v Tasmania at Adelaide.[W22]
65	Meghalaya v Puducherry at Mangoldoi.
65	Wellington v Canterbury at Wellington.[W22]
67	Northamptonshire v Somerset at Northampton.
68	Mizoram v Bihar at Patna.

† *One man absent.*

Highest Fourth-Innings Totals

436	Warriors v Lions at Port Elizabeth (set 513).[W22]

Matches Dominated by Batting (1,200 runs at 80 runs per wicket)

1,313 for 15 (87.53)	Uttar Pradesh (625-8 dec) v Mumbai (688-7 dec) at Mumbai.

Four Individual Hundreds in an Innings

Goa (589-2 dec) v Arunachal Pradesh at Porvorim.

Six Individual Fifties in an Innings

Gujarat (602-8 dec) v Goa at Valsad.

Largest Victories

Inns and 425 runs	Meghalaya (662-4 dec) beat Mizoram (114 and 123) at Kolkata.
Inns and 405 runs	Chandigarh (672-8 dec) beat Manipur (63 and 204) at Kolkata.
464 runs	Gujarat (602-8 dec and 199-6 dec) beat Goa (173 and 164) at Valsad.

Victory Losing Only One Wicket

Sussex (332 and 173) v Kent (530-1) at Canterbury.

Most Extras in an Innings

	b	*lb*	*w*	*nb*	
73	38	25	6	4	Karnataka (426) v Madhya Pradesh at Shimoga.
55	18	9	14	14	Nondescripts (511-9 dec) v Lankan at Colombo (NCC).
54	9	7	12	26	Cambridge University (307) v Oxford University at Cambridge.
50	12	22	7	9	Northern Districts (438) v Auckland at Auckland.

Career Aggregate Milestones

10,000 runs	Asad Shafiq, K. C. Brathwaite, U. T. Khawaja, A. Mukund.
500 wickets	V. Permaul, C. Rushworth, R. Vinay Kumar, C. R. Woakes.

LIST A FEATURES OF 2020

Highest Individual Scores

176	Liton Das	Bangladesh v Zimbabwe (3rd ODI) at Sylhet.
163*	A. G. S. Gous.	Knights v Titans at Kimberley.
158	Tamim Iqbal.	Bangladesh v Zimbabwe (2nd ODI) at Sylhet.
157	R. D. Rickelton	Lions v Cape Cobras at Paarl.
156	M. Z. Hamza	Cape Cobras v Lions at Potchefstroom.
155	H. D. Rutherford	Otago v Central Districts at Dunedin.
150	P. P. Shaw	India A v New Zealand XI at Lincoln.

Most Sixes in an Innings

10	G. Roelofsen (147*).	Dolphins v Titans at Centurion.
9	G. J. Snyman (124)	Knights v Cape Cobras at Kimberley.

Highest Wicket Partnerships

First Wicket

292 Tamim Iqbal/Liton Das, Bangladesh v Zimbabwe (3rd ODI) at Sylhet.
258* D. A. Warner/A. J. Finch, Australia v India (1st ODI) at Mumbai.

Second Wicket
224 G. H. Worker/B. S. Smith, Central Districts v Otago at Nelson.
214 P. R. Stirling/A. Balbirnie, Ireland v England (3rd ODI) at Southampton.
200 C. J. Bowes/K. J. McClure, Canterbury v Northern Districts at Christchurch.[W22]

Third Wicket
239 W. I. A. Fernando/B. K. G. Mendis, Sri Lanka v West Indies (2nd ODI) at Hambantota.
216 Aaqib Ilyas/Zeeshan Maqsood, Oman v USA at Kirtipur.

Sixth Wicket
212 A. T. Carey/G. J. Maxwell, Australia v England (3rd ODI) at Manchester.

Most Wickets in an Innings

7-35	K. J. Dudgeon	KwaZulu-Natal Coastal v KwaZulu-Natal Inland at Chatsworth.
7-35	M. D. Rae	Otago v Auckland at Auckland.[W22]

Match Double (50 Runs and Four Wickets)

Aaqib Ilyas	109*; 4-36	Oman v Nepal at Kirtipur.
W. N. Madhevere	57; 4-28	Eagles v Rangers at Harare.
K. A. Maharaj	50*; 4-24	Dolphins v Cape Cobras at Cape Town.
S. C. Williams	61*; 4-44	Tuskers v Rangers at Bulawayo.

Most Wicketkeeping Dismissals in an Innings

6 (6ct)	F. D. de Beer	Boland v Eastern Province at Paarl.

Highest Innings Totals

407-4	50 overs	Otago v Central Districts at Dunedin.

Lowest Innings Totals

35	12 overs	USA v Nepal at Kirtipur.

Largest Victories

210 runs	Otago 354-6 (50 overs) v Auckland 144 (31.2 overs) at Dunedin.
10 wickets	Australia 258-0 (37.4 overs) v India 255 (49.1 overs) (1st ODI) at Mumbai.

Tied Matches

KwaZulu-Natal Coastal 159 (41.5 overs) v KwaZulu-Natal Inland 159 (46.2 overs) at Chatsworth.

TWENTY20 FEATURES OF 2020

Highest Individual Scores

147*	M. P. Stoinis	Melbourne Stars v Sydney Sixers at Melbourne.
132*	K. L. Rahul	Kings XI Punjab v Royal Challengers Bangalore at Dubai.
130*	M. S. Wade	Hobart Hurricanes v Adelaide Strikers at Adelaide.
125*	Shaheryar Butt	Belgium v Czech Republic at Walferdange.

Hundred on Twenty20 Debut

102*	Abdullah Shafiq	Central Punjab v Southern Punjab at Multan.[W22]

Carrying Bat

Mansoor Amjad	52*	Galle (131) v Badureliya at Colombo (PSO).

Most Sixes in an Innings

12	B. R. Dunk (99*)	Lahore Qalandars v Karachi Kings at Lahore.
11	Nazmul Hossain (109)	Rajshahi v Barisal at Mirpur.[W22]
10	B. R. Dunk (93)	Lahore Qalandars v Quetta Gladiators at Lahore.
10	N. Pooran (100*)	Guyana Amazon Warriors v St Kitts & Nevis P at Port-of-Spain.
10	L. M. P. Simmons (91*)	West Indies v Ireland (3rd T20I) at Basseterre.

Highest Wicket Partnerships

First Wicket

207 M. P. Stoinis/H. W. R. Cartwright, Melbourne Stars v Sydney Sixers at Melbourne.
203 M. S. Wade/D. J. M. Short, Hobart Hurricanes v Adelaide Strikers at Adelaide.

Most Wickets in an Innings

6-8	A. M. Fernando	Chilaw Marians v Negombo at Colombo (CCC).
6-17	Mohammad Amir	Khulna Tigers v Rajshahi Royals at Mirpur.

Four Wickets in Four Balls

Shaheen Shah Afridi	Hampshire v Middlesex at Southampton.

Hat-Tricks (6)

A. C. Agar	Australia v South Africa (1st T20I) at Johannesburg.
Haris Rauf	Melbourne Stars v Sydney Thunder at Melbourne.
Kamrul Islam	Barisal v Rajshahi at Mirpur.[W22]
Rashid Khan	Adelaide Strikers v Sydney Sixers at Adelaide.
Shaheen Shah Afridi	Hampshire v Middlesex at Southampton.
W. S. A. Williams	Canterbury Kings v Wellington Firebirds at Wellington.

Match Double (50 Runs and Four Wickets)

Fahim Ashraf	52*;	4-18	Central Punjab v Northern at Rawalpindi.[W22]
Mansoor Amjad	52*;	4-18	Galle v Badureliya at Colombo (PSO).
E. M. D. Y. Munaweera	55;	4-35	Negombo v Kurunegala Youth at Maggona.
S. M. A. Priyanjan	90;	4-11	Colombo v Kandy Customs at Colombo (Colts).

Highest Innings Totals

244-2	20 overs	Chilaw Marians v Kurunegala Youth at Colombo (SSC).
242-3	20 overs	Northern v Khyber Pakhtunkhwa at Multan.[W22]

Lowest Innings Totals

55	13.4 overs	Guyana Amazon Warriors v St Lucia Zouks at Tarouba.
56	15.4 overs	Kandy Customs v Colombo at Colombo (Colts).

RECORDS

COMPILED BY PHILIP BAILEY

This section covers
- first-class records to December 31, 2020 (page 926).
- List A one-day records to December 31, 2020 (page 954).
- List A Twenty20 records to December 31, 2020 (page 958).
- All-format career records to December 31, 2020 (page 961).
- Test records to January 25, 2021, the end of the Sri Lanka v England series (page 963).
- Test records series by series (page 997).
- one-day international records to December 31, 2020 (page 1043).
- World Cup records (page 1054).
- Twenty20 international records to December 31, 2020 (page 1055).
- miscellaneous other records to December 31, 2020 (page 1061).
- women's Test records, one-day international and Twenty20 international records to December 31, 2020 (page 1065).

The sequence
- Test series records begin with those involving England, arranged in the order their opponents entered Test cricket (Australia, South Africa, West Indies, New Zealand, India, Pakistan, Sri Lanka, Zimbabwe, Bangladesh, Ireland, Afghanistan). Next come all remaining series involving Australia, then South Africa – and so on until Ireland v Afghanistan records appear on page 1039.

Notes
- Unless otherwise stated, all records apply only to first-class cricket. This is considered to have started in 1815, after the Napoleonic War.
- mid-year seasons taking place outside England are given simply as 2018, 2019, etc.
- (E), (A), (SA), (WI), (NZ), (I), (P), (SL), (Z), (B), (Ire), (Afg) indicates the nationality of a player or the country in which a record was made.
- in career records, dates in italic indicate seasons embracing two different years (i.e. non-English seasons). In these cases, only the first year is given, e.g. *2020* for 2020-21.

See also
- up-to-date records on www.wisdenrecords.com.
- Features of 2020 (page 910).

CONTENTS

FIRST-CLASS RECORDS

BATTING RECORDS

BOWLING RECORDS

ALL-ROUND RECORDS

WICKETKEEPING RECORDS

FIELDING RECORDS

TEAM RECORDS

LIST A ONE-DAY RECORDS

LIST A TWENTY20 RECORDS

ALL-FORMAT CAREER RECORDS

TEST RECORDS

BATTING RECORDS

BOWLING RECORDS

ALL-ROUND RECORDS

WICKETKEEPING RECORDS

FIELDING RECORDS

TEAM RECORDS

PLAYERS

UMPIRES

TEST SERIES

ONE-DAY INTERNATIONAL RECORDS

TWENTY20 INTERNATIONAL RECORDS

MISCELLANEOUS RECORDS

WOMEN'S INTERNATIONAL RECORDS

NOTES ON RECORDS

Root march

STEVEN LYNCH

Just as the Records section was being finalised, it came under attack from England's captain. After a quiet time in 2020 – he failed to pass 70 in nine successive Tests – Joe Root hit the ground running in 2021. In Galle, he broke the drought with 228 in the First Test against Sri Lanka, added 186 in the Second, and shortly after marked his 100th appearance with 218 against India at Chennai.

Root had started his 99th Test in seventh place on England's run-scoring list with 8,052, but during it leapfrogged Geoffrey Boycott (8,114), Kevin Pietersen (8,181) and David Gower (8,231) to go fourth; in India, he passed Alec Stewart (8,463), with second-placed Graham Gooch (8,900) next in his sights. As *Wisden* includes only each country's top six, it meant one famous Yorkshireman was replaced by another, with Boycott consigned to the best of the rest.

Elsewhere, Kent recorded a rare first-class win while losing just one wicket, and India's domestic season threw up two victories by an innings and more than 400 runs. At the other end of a different scale, the United States were skittled for 35 in Nepal, equalling the lowest score in any one-day international, set by Zimbabwe in 2004.

Another strange characteristic of 2020 was that – like Root – Virat Kohli did not score an international hundred, for the first year since his debut in 2008. With 70 centuries in all, he remains poised to overtake Ricky Ponting's 71 – and then attempt to close in on Sachin Tendulkar's magnificent 100. Meanwhile, as Kane Williamson continued scoring centuries – and doubles – for fun, another New Zealander claimed a unique triple: in February 2020, Ross Taylor became the first to win 100 caps in Tests, ODIs and T20 internationals.

ROLL OF DISHONOUR

The following players have either been banned after being found guilty of breaching anti-corruption codes, or have admitted to some form of on-field corruption:

Amit Singh (I), Ata-ur-Rehman (P), M. Azharuddin (I), A. Bali (I), G. H. Bodi (SA), A. Chandila (I), A. A. Chavan (I), P. Cleary (A), W. J. Cronje (SA), Danish Kaneria (P), L. H. D. Dilhara (SL), H. H. Gibbs (SA), C. L. Hall (A), Haseeb Amjad (HK), Irfan Ahmed (HK), Irfan Ansari (UAE), A. Jadeja (I), S. T. Jayasuriya (SL), H. N. K. Jensen (NZ), Khalid Latif (P), J. Logan (A), K. S. Lokuarachchi (SL), P. Matshikwe (SA), N. E. Mbhalati (SA), M. D. Mishra (I), Mohammad Amir (P), Mohammad Ashraful (B), Mohammad Asif (P), Mohammad Irfan (P), Mohammad Naveed (UAE), Mohammad Nawaz (P), Nadeem Ahmed (HK), Nasir Jamshed (P), Naved Arif (P), M. O. Odumbe (Ken), A. N. Petersen (SA), M. Prabhakar (I), Salim Malik (P), Salman Butt (P), M. N. Samuels (WI), Shafiqullah Shinwari (Afg), H. N. Shah (I), Shaiman Anwar (UAE), Shakib Al Hasan (B), Shariful Haque (B), Sharjeel Khan (P), Ajay Sharma (I), S. Sreesanth (I), S. J. Srivastava (I), T. P. Sudhindra (I), J. Symes (SA), S. K. Trivedi (I), T. L. Tsolekile (SA), L. L. Tsotsobe (SA), Umar Akmal (P), L. Vincent (NZ), M. S. Westfield (E), H. S. Williams (SA), A. R. Yadav (I), Yousuf Mahmood (Oman), D. N. T. Zoysa (SL).

FIRST-CLASS RECORDS

This section covers first-class cricket to December 31, 2020. Bold type denotes performances in the calendar year 2020 or, in career figures, players who appeared in first-class cricket in that year.

BATTING RECORDS

HIGHEST INDIVIDUAL INNINGS

In all first-class cricket, there have been **230** individual scores of 300 or more. The highest are:

501*	B. C. Lara	Warwickshire v Durham at Birmingham	1994
499	Hanif Mohammad	Karachi v Bahawalpur at Karachi	1958-59
452*	D. G. Bradman	NSW v Queensland at Sydney	1929-30
443*	B. B. Nimbalkar	Maharashtra v Kathiawar at Poona	1948-49
437	W. H. Ponsford	Victoria v Queensland at Melbourne	1927-28
429	W. H. Ponsford	Victoria v Tasmania at Melbourne	1922-23
428	Aftab Baloch	Sind v Baluchistan at Karachi	1973-74
424	A. C. MacLaren	Lancashire v Somerset at Taunton	1895
405*	G. A. Hick	Worcestershire v Somerset at Taunton	1988
400*	B. C. Lara	West Indies v England at St John's	2003-04
394	Naved Latif	Sargodha v Gujranwala at Gujranwala	2000-01
390	S. C. Cook	Lions v Warriors at East London	2009-10
385	B. Sutcliffe	Otago v Canterbury at Christchurch	1952-53
383	C. W. Gregory	NSW v Queensland at Brisbane	1906-07
380	M. L. Hayden	Australia v Zimbabwe at Perth	2003-04
377	S. V. Manjrekar	Bombay v Hyderabad at Bombay	1990-91
375	B. C. Lara	West Indies v England at St John's	1993-94
374	D. P. M. D. Jayawardene	Sri Lanka v South Africa at Colombo (SSC)	2006
369	D. G. Bradman	South Australia v Tasmania at Adelaide	1935-36
366	N. H. Fairbrother	Lancashire v Surrey at The Oval	1990
366	M. V. Sridhar	Hyderabad v Andhra at Secunderabad	1993-94
365*	C. Hill	South Australia v NSW at Adelaide	1900-01
365*	G. S. Sobers	West Indies v Pakistan at Kingston	1957-58
364	L. Hutton	England v Australia at The Oval	1938
359*	V. M. Merchant	Bombay v Maharashtra at Bombay	1943-44
359*	S. B. Gohel	Gujarat v Orissa at Jaipur	2016-17
359	R. B. Simpson	NSW v Queensland at Brisbane	1963-64
357*	R. Abel	Surrey v Somerset at The Oval	1899
357	D. G. Bradman	South Australia v Victoria at Melbourne	1935-36
356	B. A. Richards	South Australia v Western Australia at Perth	1970-71
355*	G. R. Marsh	Western Australia v South Australia at Perth	1989-90
355*	K. P. Pietersen	Surrey v Leicestershire at The Oval	2015
355	B. Sutcliffe	Otago v Auckland at Dunedin	1949-50
354*	**L. D. Chandimal**	**Sri Lanka Army v Saracens at Katunayake**	**2020**
353	V. V. S. Laxman	Hyderabad v Karnataka at Bangalore	1999-2000
352	W. H. Ponsford	Victoria v NSW at Melbourne	1926-27
352	C. A. Pujara	Saurashtra v Karnataka at Rajkot	2012-13
351*	S. M. Gugale	Maharashtra v Delhi at Mumbai	2016-17
351	K. D. K. Vithanage	Tamil Union v Air Force at Katunayake	2014-15
350	Rashid Israr	Habib Bank v National Bank at Lahore	1976-77

A fuller list can be found in Wisdens *up to 2011.*

DOUBLE-HUNDRED ON DEBUT

227	T. Marsden	Sheffield & Leicester v Nottingham at Sheffield	1826
207	N. F. Callaway†	New South Wales v Queensland at Sydney	1914-15
	In his only first-class innings. He was killed in action in France in 1917.		
240	W. F. E. Marx	Transvaal v Griqualand West at Johannesburg	1920-21
200*	A. Maynard	Trinidad v MCC at Port-of-Spain	1934-35
232*	S. J. E. Loxton	Victoria v Queensland at Melbourne	1946-47

215*	G. H. G. Doggart	Cambridge University v Lancashire at Cambridge	1948
202	J. Hallebone	Victoria v Tasmania at Melbourne	1951-52
230	G. R. Viswanath	Mysore v Andhra at Vijayawada	1967-68
260	A. A. Muzumdar	Bombay v Haryana at Faridabad	1993-94
209*	A. Pandey	Madhya Pradesh v Uttar Pradesh at Bhilai	1995-96
210*	D. J. Sales	Northamptonshire v Worcestershire at Kidderminster	1996
200*	M. J. Powell	Glamorgan v Oxford University at Oxford	1997
201*	M. C. Juneja	Gujarat v Tamil Nadu at Ahmedabad	2011-12
213	Jiwanjot Singh	Punjab v Hyderabad at Mohali	2012-13
202	A. Gupta	Punjab v Himachal Pradesh at Dharamsala	2017-18
256*	Bahir Shah	Speen Ghar v Amo at Ghazi Amanullah Town	2017-18
203	B. D. Schmulian	C. Districts v N. Districts at Mount Maunganui	2017-18
228	M. Raghav	Manipur v Nagaland at Dimapur	2018-19
267*	A. R. Rohera	Madhya Pradesh v Hyderabad at Indore	2018-19
200*	Hanif Kunrai	Kunar v Kandahar at Asadabad	2018-19
233*	Arslan Khan	Chandigarh v Arunachal Pradesh at Chandigarh	2019-20

TWO SEPARATE HUNDREDS ON DEBUT

148 and 111	A. R. Morris	New South Wales v Queensland at Sydney	1940-41
152 and 102*	N. J. Contractor	Gujarat v Baroda at Baroda	1952-53
132* and 110	Aamer Malik	Lahore A v Railways at Lahore	1979-80
130 and 100*	Noor Ali	Afghanistan v Zimbabwe XI at Mutare	2009
158 and 103*	K. H. T. Indika	Police v Seeduwa Raddoluwa at Colombo (Police)	2010-11
126 and 112	V. S. Awate	Maharashtra v Vidarbha at Nagpur	2012-13
154* and 109*	T. J. Dean	Victoria v Queensland at Melbourne	2015-16
102 and 142	Haji Murad	Amo v Speen Ghar at Ghazi Amanullah Town	2017-18

TWO DOUBLE-HUNDREDS IN A MATCH

A. E. Fagg	244	202*	Kent v Essex at Colchester	1938
A. K. Perera	201	231	Nondescripts v Sinhalese at Colombo (PSO)	2018-19

TRIPLE-HUNDRED AND HUNDRED IN A MATCH

G. A. Gooch	333	123	England v India at Lord's	1990
K. C. Sangakkara	319	105	Sri Lanka v Bangladesh at Chittagong	2013-14

DOUBLE-HUNDRED AND HUNDRED IN A MATCH

In addition to Fagg, Perera, Gooch and Sangakkara, there have been **65** further instances of a batsman scoring a double-hundred and a hundred in the same first-class match. The most recent are:

N. V. Ojha	219*	101*	India A v Australia A at Brisbane	2014
S. D. Robson	231	106	Middlesex v Warwickshire at Lord's	2016
G. S. Ballance	108	203*	Yorkshire v Hampshire at Southampton	2017
B. O. P. Fernando	109	234	Chilaw Marians v Colts at Colombo (NCC)	2018-19
D. P. Sibley	215*	109	Warwickshire v Nottinghamshire at Nottingham	2019
R. Dalal	178	205*	Arunachal Pradesh v Mizoram at Puducherry	2019-20

Zaheer Abbas achieved the feat four times, for Gloucestershire between 1976 and 1981, and was not out in all eight innings. M. R. Hallam did it twice for Leicestershire, in 1959 and 1961; N. R. Taylor twice for Kent, in 1990 and 1991; G. A. Gooch for England in 1990 (see above) and Essex in 1994; M. W. Goodwin twice for Sussex, in 2001 and 2007; and C. J. L. Rogers for Northamptonshire in 2006 and for Derbyshire in 2010.

TWO SEPARATE HUNDREDS IN A MATCH MOST TIMES

R. T. Ponting	8	J. B. Hobbs	6	M. L. Hayden	5
Zaheer Abbas	8	G. M. Turner	6	G. A. Hick	5
W. R. Hammond	7	C. B. Fry	5	C. J. L. Rogers	5
M. R. Ramprakash	7	G. A. Gooch	5		

W. Lambert scored 107 and 157 for Sussex v Epsom at Lord's in 1817, a feat not repeated until W. G. Grace's 130 and 102 for South of the Thames v North of the Thames at Canterbury in 1868.*

FIVE HUNDREDS OR MORE IN SUCCESSION

D. G. Bradman (1938-39)	6	B. C. Lara (1993-94–1994)	5
C. B. Fry (1901)	6	P. A. Patel (2007–2007-08)	5
M. J. Procter (1970-71)	6	K. C. Sangakkara (2017)	5
M. E. K. Hussey (2003)	5	E. D. Weekes (1955-56)	5

Bradman also scored four hundreds in succession twice, in 1931-32 and 1948–1948-49; W. R. Hammond did it in 1936-37 and 1945–1946, and H. Sutcliffe in 1931 and 1939.

T. W. Hayward (Surrey v Nottinghamshire and Leicestershire), D. W. Hookes (South Australia v Queensland and New South Wales) and V. Sibanda (Zimbabwe XI v Kenya and Mid West v Southern Rocks) are the only players to score two hundreds in each of two successive matches. Hayward scored his in six days, June 4–9, 1906.

The most fifties in consecutive innings is ten – by E. Tyldesley in 1926, by D. G. Bradman in the 1947-48 and 1948 seasons and by R. S. Kaluwitharana in 1994-95.

MOST HUNDREDS IN A SEASON

D. C. S. Compton (1947)	18	W. R. Hammond (1937)	13
J. B. Hobbs (1925)	16	T. W. Hayward (1906)	13
W. R. Hammond (1938)	15	E. H. Hendren (1923)	13
H. Sutcliffe (1932)	14	E. H. Hendren (1927)	13
G. Boycott (1971)	13	E. H. Hendren (1928)	13
D. G. Bradman (1938)	13	C. P. Mead (1928)	13
C. B. Fry (1901)	13	H. Sutcliffe (1928)	13
W. R. Hammond (1933)	13	H. Sutcliffe (1931)	13

Since 1969 (excluding G. Boycott – above)

G. A. Gooch (1990)	12	M. R. Ramprakash (1995)	10
S. J. Cook (1991)	11	M. R. Ramprakash (2007)	10
Zaheer Abbas (1976)	11	G. M. Turner (1970)	10
G. A. Hick (1988)	10	Zaheer Abbas (1981)	10
H. Morris (1990)	10		

The most outside England is nine by V. Sibanda in Zimbabwe (2009-10), followed by eight by D. G. Bradman in Australia (1947-48), D. C. S. Compton (1948-49), R. N. Harvey and A. R. Morris (both 1949-50) all three in South Africa, M. D. Crowe in New Zealand (1986-87), Asif Mujtaba in Pakistan (1995-96), V. V. S. Laxman in India (1999-2000), M. G. Bevan in Australia (2004-05) and Zia-ul-Haq in Afghanistan (2017-18).

The most double-hundreds in a season is six by D. G. Bradman (1930), five by K. S. Ranjitsinhji (1900) and E. D. Weekes (1950), and four by Arun Lal (1986-87), C. B. Fry (1901), W. R. Hammond (1933 and 1934), E. H. Hendren (1929-30), V. M. Merchant (1944-45), C. A. Pujara (2012-13) and G. M. Turner (1971-72).

MOST DOUBLE-HUNDREDS IN A CAREER

D. G. Bradman	37	W. G. Grace	13	Younis Khan	12
W. R. Hammond	36	B. C. Lara	13	J. W. Hearne	11
E. H. Hendren	22	C. P. Mead	13	L. Hutton	11
M. R. Ramprakash	17	W. H. Ponsford	13	D. S. Lehmann	11
H. Sutcliffe	17	K. C. Sangakkara	13	V. M. Merchant	11
C. B. Fry	16	J. T. Tyldesley	13	C. J. L. Rogers	11
G. A. Hick	16	P. Holmes	12	A. Sandham	11
J. B. Hobbs	16	Javed Miandad	12	G. Boycott	10
C. G. Greenidge	14	J. L. Langer	12	R. Dravid	10
K. S. Ranjitsinhji	14	**C. A. Pujara**	**12**	M. W. Gatting	10
G. A. Gooch	13	R. B. Simpson	12	S. M. Gavaskar	10

J. Hardstaff jnr	10	D. P. M. D. Jayawardene	10	R. T. Simpson	10
V. S. Hazare	10	I. V. A. Richards	10	G. M. Turner	10
B. J. Hodge	10	A. Shrewsbury	10	Zaheer Abbas	10

MOST HUNDREDS IN A CAREER

(100 or more)

		Total	Total Inns	100th 100 Season	Inns	400+	300+	200+
1	J. B. Hobbs	197	1,315	1923	821	0	1	16
2	E. H. Hendren	170	1,300	1928-29	740	0	1	22
3	W. R. Hammond	167	1,005	1935	680	0	4	36
4	C. P. Mead	153	1,340	1927	892	0	0	13
5	G. Boycott	151	1,014	1977	645	0	0	10
6	H. Sutcliffe	149	1,088	1932	700	0	1	17
7	F. E. Woolley	145	1,532	1929	1,031	0	1	9
8	G. A. Hick	136	871	1998	574	1	3	16
9	L. Hutton	129	814	1951	619	0	1	11
10	G. A. Gooch	128	990	1992-93	820	0	1	13
11	W. G. Grace	126	1,493	1895	1,113	0	3	13
12	D. C. S. Compton	123	839	1952	552	0	1	9
13	T. W. Graveney	122	1,223	1964	940	0	0	7
14	D. G. Bradman	117	338	1947-48	295	1	6	37
15	I. V. A. Richards	114	796	1988-89	658	0	1	10
	M. R. Ramprakash	114	764	2008	676	0	1	17
17	Zaheer Abbas	108	768	1982-83	658	0	0	10
18	A. Sandham	107	1,000	1935	871	0	1	11
	M. C. Cowdrey	107	1,130	1973	1,035	0	1	3
20	T. W. Hayward	104	1,138	1913	1,076	0	1	8
21	G. M. Turner	103	792	1982	779	0	1	10
	J. H. Edrich	103	979	1977	945	0	1	4
23	L. E. G. Ames	102	951	1950	916	0	0	9
	E. Tyldesley	102	961	1934	919	0	0	7
	D. L. Amiss	102	1,139	1986	1,081	0	0	3

In the above table, 200+, 300+ and 400+ include all scores above those figures.
Zaheer Abbas and G. Boycott scored their 100th hundreds in Test matches.

Current Players

The following who played in 2020 have scored 40 or more hundreds.

A. N. Cook	67	C. A. Pujara	50	Azhar Ali	40
I. R. Bell	57	J. C. Hildreth	46	N. T. Paranavitana	40
Wasim Jaffer	57	D. Elgar	42		
H. M. Amla	52	S. P. D. Smith	42		

MOST RUNS IN A SEASON

	Season	I	NO	R	HS	100	Avge
D. C. S. Compton	1947	50	8	3,816	246	18	90.85
W. J. Edrich	1947	52	8	3,539	267*	12	80.43
T. W. Hayward	1906	61	8	3,518	219	13	66.37
L. Hutton	1949	56	6	3,429	269*	12	68.58
F. E. Woolley	1928	59	4	3,352	198	12	60.94
H. Sutcliffe	1932	52	7	3,336	313	14	74.13
W. R. Hammond	1933	54	5	3,323	264	13	67.81
E. H. Hendren	1928	54	7	3,311	209*	13	70.44
R. Abel	1901	68	8	3,309	247	7	55.15

3,000 in a season has been surpassed on 19 other occasions (a full list can be found in Wisden *1999 and earlier editions). W. R. Hammond, E. H. Hendren and H. Sutcliffe are the only players to achieve the feat three times. K. S. Ranjitsinhji was the first batsman to reach 3,000 in a season, with 3,159 in 1899. M. J. K. Smith (3,245 in 1959) and W. E. Alley (3,019 in 1961) are the only players except those listed above to have reached 3,000 since the Second World War.*

W. G. Grace scored 2,739 runs in 1871 – the first batsman to reach 2,000 in a season. He made ten hundreds, including two double-hundreds, with an average of 78.25 in all first-class matches.

The highest aggregate in a season since the reduction of County Championship matches in 1969 was 2,755 by S. J. Cook (42 innings) in 1991, and the last batsman to achieve 2,000 in England was M. R. Ramprakash (2,026 in 2007); C. A. Pujara scored 2,064 in India in 2016-17.

2,000 RUNS IN A SEASON MOST TIMES

J. B. Hobbs	17	F. E. Woolley	13	C. P. Mead	11
E. H. Hendren	15	W. R. Hammond	12	T. W. Hayward	10
H. Sutcliffe	15	J. G. Langridge	11		

Since the reduction of County Championship matches in 1969, G. A. Gooch is the only batsman to have reached 2,000 runs in a season five times.

1,000 RUNS IN A SEASON MOST TIMES

Includes overseas tours and seasons

W. G. Grace	28	A. Jones	23	G. Gunn	20
F. E. Woolley	28	T. W. Graveney	22	T. W. Hayward	20
M. C. Cowdrey	27	W. R. Hammond	22	G. A. Hick	20
C. P. Mead	27	D. Denton	21	James Langridge	20
G. Boycott	26	J. H. Edrich	21	J. M. Parks	20
J. B. Hobbs	26	G. A. Gooch	21	M. R. Ramprakash	20
E. H. Hendren	25	W. Rhodes	21	A. Sandham	20
D. L. Amiss	24	D. B. Close	20	M. J. K. Smith	20
W. G. Quaife	24	K. W. R. Fletcher	20	C. Washbrook	20
H. Sutcliffe	24	M. W. Gatting	20		

F. E. Woolley reached 1,000 runs in 28 consecutive seasons (1907–1938), C. P. Mead in 27 (1906–1936).

Outside England, 1,000 runs in a season has been reached most times by D. G. Bradman (in 12 seasons in Australia).

Three batsmen have scored 1,000 runs in a season in each of four different countries: G. S. Sobers in West Indies, England, India and Australia; M. C. Cowdrey and G. Boycott in England, South Africa, West Indies and Australia.

HIGHEST AGGREGATES OUTSIDE ENGLAND

	Season	*I*	*NO*	*R*	*HS*	*100*	*Avge*
In Australia							
D. G. Bradman	1928-29	24	6	1,690	340*	7	93.88
In South Africa							
J. R. Reid	1961-62	30	2	1,915	203	7	68.39
In West Indies							
E. H. Hendren	1929-30	18	5	1,765	254*	6	135.76
In New Zealand							
M. D. Crowe	1986-87	21	3	1,676	175*	8	93.11
In India							
C. A. Pujara	2016-17	29	4	2,064	256*	7	82.56
In Pakistan							
Saadat Ali	1983-84	27	1	1,649	208	4	63.42

	Season	I	NO	R	HS	100	Avge
In Sri Lanka							
R. P. Arnold	1995-96	24	3	1,475	217*	5	70.23
In Zimbabwe							
V. Sibanda	2009-10	26	4	1,612	215	9	73.27
In Bangladesh							
Tushar Imran	2016-17	16	2	1,249	220	5	89.21
In Afghanistan							
Zia-ul-Haq	2017-18	31	4	1,616	148	8	59.85

Excluding Pujara in India (above), the following aggregates of over 2,000 runs have been recorded in more than one country:

	Season	I	NO	R	HS	100	Avge
M. Amarnath (P/I/WI)	1982-83	34	6	2,234	207	9	79.78
J. R. Reid (SA/A/NZ)	1961-62	40	2	2,188	203	7	57.57
S. M. Gavaskar (I/P)	1978-79	30	6	2,121	205	10	88.37
R. B. Simpson (I/P/A/WI)	1964-65	34	4	2,063	201	8	68.76
M. H. Richardson (Z/SA/NZ)	2000-01	34	3	2,030	306	4	65.48

The only other player to hit ten hundreds in an overseas season was V. V. S. Laxman in India and Australia in 1999-2000.

LEADING BATSMEN IN AN ENGLISH SEASON

(Qualification: 8 completed innings)

Season	Leading scorer	Runs	Avge	Top of averages	Runs	Avge
1946	D. C. S. Compton	2,403	61.61	W. R. Hammond	1,783	84.90
1947	D. C. S. Compton	3,816	90.85	D. C. S. Compton	3,816	90.85
1948	L. Hutton	2,654	64.73	D. G. Bradman	2,428	89.92
1949	L. Hutton	3,429	68.58	J. Hardstaff	2,251	72.61
1950	R. T. Simpson	2,576	62.82	E. D. Weekes	2,310	79.65
1951	J. D. Robertson	2,917	56.09	P. B. H. May	2,339	68.79
1952	L. Hutton	2,567	61.11	D. S. Sheppard	2,262	64.62
1953	W. J. Edrich	2,557	47.35	R. N. Harvey	2,040	65.80
1954	D. Kenyon	2,636	51.68	D. C. S. Compton	1,524	58.61
1955	D. J. Insole	2,427	42.57	D. J. McGlew	1,871	58.46
1956	T. W. Graveney	2,397	49.93	K. Mackay	1,103	52.52
1957	T. W. Graveney	2,361	49.18	P. B. H. May	2,347	61.76
1958	P. B. H. May	2,231	63.74	P. B. H. May	2,231	63.74
1959	M. J. K. Smith	3,245	57.94	V. L. Manjrekar	755	68.63
1960	M. J. K. Smith	2,551	45.55	R. Subba Row	1,503	55.66
1961	W. E. Alley	3,019	56.96	W. M. Lawry	2,019	61.18
1962	J. H. Edrich	2,482	51.70	R. T. Simpson	867	54.18
1963	J. B. Bolus	2,190	41.32	G. S. Sobers	1,333	47.60
1964	T. W. Graveney	2,385	54.20	K. F. Barrington	1,872	62.40
1965	J. H. Edrich	2,319	62.67	M. C. Cowdrey	2,093	63.42
1966	A. R. Lewis	2,198	41.47	G. S. Sobers	1,349	61.31
1967	C. A. Milton	2,089	46.42	K. F. Barrington	2,059	68.63
1968	B. A. Richards	2,395	47.90	G. Boycott	1,487	64.65
1969	J. H. Edrich	2,238	69.93	J. H. Edrich	2,238	69.93
1970	G. M. Turner	2,379	61.00	G. S. Sobers	1,742	75.73
1971	G. Boycott	2,503	100.12	G. Boycott	2,503	100.12
1972	Majid Khan	2,074	61.00	G. Boycott	1,230	72.35
1973	G. M. Turner	2,416	67.11	G. M. Turner	2,416	67.11
1974	R. T. Virgin	1,936	56.94	C. H. Lloyd	1,458	63.39
1975	G. Boycott	1,915	73.65	R. B. Kanhai	1,073	82.53
1976	Zaheer Abbas	2,554	75.11	Zaheer Abbas	2,554	75.11
1977	I. V. A. Richards	2,161	65.48	G. Boycott	1,701	68.04
1978	D. L. Amiss	2,030	53.42	C. E. B. Rice	1,871	66.82
1979	K. C. Wessels	1,800	52.94	G. Boycott	1,538	102.53

Season	*Leading scorer*	*Runs*	*Avge*	*Top of averages*	*Runs*	*Avge*
1980	P. N. Kirsten	1,895	63.16	A. J. Lamb	1,797	66.55
1981	Zaheer Abbas	2,306	88.69	Zaheer Abbas	2,306	88.69
1982	A. I. Kallicharran	2,120	66.25	G. M. Turner	1,171	90.07
1983	K. S. McEwan	2,176	64.00	I. V. A. Richards	1,204	75.25
1984	G. A. Gooch	2,559	67.34	C. G. Greenidge	1,069	82.23
1985	G. A. Gooch	2,208	71.22	I. V. A. Richards	1,836	76.50
1986	C. G. Greenidge	2,035	67.83	C. G. Greenidge	2,035	67.83
1987	G. A. Hick	1,879	52.19	M. D. Crowe	1,627	67.79
1988	G. A. Hick	2,713	77.51	R. A. Harper	622	77.75
1989	S. J. Cook	2,241	60.56	D. M. Jones	1,510	88.82
1990	G. A. Gooch	2,746	101.70	G. A. Gooch	2,746	101.70
1991	S. J. Cook	2,755	81.02	C. L. Hooper	1,501	93.81
1992	{P. D. Bowler {M. A. Roseberry	2,044 2,044	65.93 56.77	Salim Malik	1,184	78.93
1993	G. A. Gooch	2,023	63.21	D. C. Boon	1,437	75.63
1994	B. C. Lara	2,066	89.82	J. D. Carr	1,543	90.76
1995	M. R. Ramprakash	2,258	77.86	M. R. Ramprakash	2,258	77.86
1996	G. A. Gooch	1,944	67.03	S. C. Ganguly	762	95.25
1997	S. P. James	1,775	68.26	G. A. Hick	1,524	69.27
1998	J. P. Crawley	1,851	74.04	J. P. Crawley	1,851	74.04
1999	S. G. Law	1,833	73.32	S. G. Law	1,833	73.32
2000	D. S. Lehmann	1,477	67.13	M. G. Bevan	1,124	74.93
2001	M. E. K. Hussey	2,055	79.03	D. R. Martyn	942	104.66
2002	I. J. Ward	1,759	62.82	R. Dravid	773	96.62
2003	S. G. Law	1,820	91.00	S. G. Law	1,820	91.00
2004	R. W. T. Key	1,896	79.00	R. W. T. Key	1,896	79.00
2005	O. A. Shah	1,728	66.46	M. E. K. Hussey	1,074	76.71
2006	M. R. Ramprakash	2,278	103.54	M. R. Ramprakash	2,278	103.54
2007	M. R. Ramprakash	2,026	101.30	M. R. Ramprakash	2,026	101.30
2008	S. C. Moore	1,451	55.80	T. Frost	1,003	83.58
2009	M. E. Trescothick	1,817	75.70	M. R. Ramprakash	1,350	90.00
2010	M. R. Ramprakash	1,595	61.34	J. C. Hildreth	1,440	65.45
2011	M. E. Trescothick	1,673	79.66	I. R. Bell	1,091	90.91
2012	N. R. D. Compton	1,494	99.60	N. R. D. Compton	1,494	99.60
2013	C. J. L. Rogers	1,536	51.20	S. M. Katich	1,097	73.13
2014	A. Lyth	1,619	70.39	J. E. Root	1,052	75.14
2015	J. C. Hildreth	1,758	56.70	J. M. Bairstow	1,226	72.11
2016	K. K. Jennings	1,602	64.08	S. A. Northeast	1,402	82.47
2017	K. C. Sangakkara	1,491	106.50	K. C. Sangakkara	1,491	106.50
2018	R. J. Burns	1,402	60.95	O. J. D. Pope	1,098	61.00
2019	D. P. Sibley	1,575	68.47	O. J. D. Pope	812	101.50
2020	**A. N. Cook**	**563**	**56.30**	**Z. Crawley**	**522**	**65.25**

The highest average recorded in an English season was 115.66 (2,429 runs, 26 innings) by D. G. Bradman in 1938.

In 1953, W. A. Johnston averaged 102.00 from 17 innings, 16 not out.

MOST RUNS

Dates in italics denote the first half of an overseas season; i.e. *1945* denotes the 1945-46 season.

		Career	*R*	*I*	*NO*	*HS*	*100*	*Avge*
1	J. B. Hobbs	1905–1934	61,237	1,315	106	316*	197	50.65
2	F. E. Woolley	1906–1938	58,969	1,532	85	305*	145	40.75
3	E. H. Hendren	1907–1938	57,611	1,300	166	301*	170	50.80
4	C. P. Mead	1905–1936	55,061	1,340	185	280*	153	47.67
5	W. G. Grace	1865–1908	54,896	1,493	105	344	126	39.55
6	W. R. Hammond	1920–1951	50,551	1,005	104	336*	167	56.10
7	H. Sutcliffe	1919–1945	50,138	1,088	123	313	149	51.95
8	G. Boycott	1962–1986	48,426	1,014	162	261*	151	56.83
9	T. W. Graveney	1948–*1971*	47,793	1,223	159	258	122	44.91

		Career	*R*	*I*	*NO*	*HS*	*100*	*Avge*
10	G. A. Gooch	1973–2000	44,846	990	75	333	128	49.01
11	T. W. Hayward	1893–1914	43,551	1,138	96	315*	104	41.79
12	D. L. Amiss	1960–1987	43,423	1,139	126	262*	102	42.86
13	M. C. Cowdrey	1950–1976	42,719	1,130	134	307	107	42.89
14	A. Sandham	1911–*1937*	41,284	1,000	79	325	107	44.82
15	G. A. Hick	*1983*–2008	41,112	871	84	405*	136	52.23
16	L. Hutton	1934–1960	40,140	814	91	364	129	55.51
17	M. J. K. Smith	1951–1975	39,832	1,091	139	204	69	41.84
18	W. Rhodes	1898–1930	39,802	1,528	237	267*	58	30.83
19	J. H. Edrich	1956–1978	39,790	979	104	310*	103	45.47
20	R. E. S. Wyatt	1923–1957	39,405	1,141	157	232	85	40.04
21	D. C. S. Compton	1936–1964	38,942	839	88	300	123	51.85
22	E. Tyldesley	1909–1936	38,874	961	106	256*	102	45.46
23	J. T. Tyldesley	1895–1923	37,897	994	62	295*	86	40.66
24	K. W. R. Fletcher	1962–1988	37,665	1,167	170	228*	63	37.77
25	C. G. Greenidge	1970–1992	37,354	889	75	273*	92	45.88
26	J. W. Hearne	1909–1936	37,252	1,025	116	285*	96	40.98
27	L. E. G. Ames	1926–1951	37,248	951	95	295	102	43.51
28	D. Kenyon	1946–1967	37,002	1,159	59	259	74	33.63
29	W. J. Edrich	1934–1958	36,965	964	92	267*	86	42.39
30	J. M. Parks	1949–1976	36,673	1,227	172	205*	51	34.76
31	M. W. Gatting	1975–1998	36,549	861	123	258	94	49.52
32	D. Denton	1894–1920	36,479	1,163	70	221	69	33.37
33	G. H. Hirst	1891–1929	36,323	1,215	151	341	60	34.13
34	I. V. A. Richards	*1971*–1993	36,212	796	63	322	114	49.40
35	A. Jones	1957–1983	36,049	1,168	72	204*	56	32.89
36	W. G. Quaife	1894–1928	36,012	1,203	185	255*	72	35.37
37	R. E. Marshall	*1945*–1972	35,725	1,053	59	228*	68	35.94
38	M. R. Ramprakash	1987–2012	35,659	764	93	301*	114	53.14
39	G. Gunn	1902–1932	35,208	1,061	82	220	62	35.96

Some works of reference provide career figures which differ from those in this list, owing to the exclusion or inclusion of matches recognised or not recognised as first-class by Wisden. *A fuller list can be found in* Wisdens *up to 2011.*

Current Players with 20,000 Runs

	Career	*R*	*I*	*NO*	*HS*	*100*	*Avge*
A. N. Cook	2003–2020	24,230	549	42	294	67	47.79
I. R. Bell	1999–2020	20,440	524	55	262*	57	43.58

HIGHEST CAREER AVERAGE

(Qualification: 10,000 runs)

Avge		*Career*	*I*	*NO*	*R*	*HS*	*100*
95.14	D. G. Bradman	*1927–1948*	338	43	28,067	452*	117
71.22	V. M. Merchant	*1929–1951*	229	43	13,248	359*	44
67.46	Ajay Sharma	*1984–2000*	166	16	10,120	259*	38
65.18	W. H. Ponsford	*1920–1934*	235	23	13,819	437	47
64.99	W. M. Woodfull	*1921–1934*	245	39	13,388	284	49
58.24	A. L. Hassett	*1932–1953*	322	32	16,890	232	59
58.19	V. S. Hazare	*1934–1966*	365	45	18,621	316*	60
57.84	S. R. Tendulkar	*1988–2013*	490	51	25,396	248*	81
57.83	D. S. Lehmann	*1987–2007*	479	33	25,795	339	82
57.32	M. G. Bevan	*1989–2006*	400	66	19,147	216	68
57.22	A. F. Kippax	*1918–1935*	256	33	12,762	315*	43
57.15	**S. P. D. Smith**	***2007–2020***	**232**	**27**	**11,717**	**239**	**42**
56.83	G. Boycott	1962–1986	1,014	162	48,426	261*	151
56.55	C. L. Walcott	*1941–1963*	238	29	11,820	314*	40

Avge		Career	I	NO	R	HS	100
56.54	**Fawad Alam**	***2003–2020***	**271**	**44**	**12,835**	**296***	**37**
56.37	K. S. Ranjitsinhji	1893–1920	500	62	24,692	285*	72
56.22	R. B. Simpson	*1952–1977*	436	62	21,029	359	60
56.10	W. R. Hammond	1920–1951	1,005	104	50,551	336*	167
56.02	M. D. Crowe	*1979–1995*	412	62	19,608	299	71
55.90	R. T. Ponting	*1992*–2013	494	62	24,150	257	82
55.51	L. Hutton	1934–1960	814	91	40,140	364	129
55.34	E. D. Weekes	*1944*–1964	241	24	12,010	304*	36
55.33	R. Dravid	*1990–2011*	497	67	23,794	270	68
55.11	S. V. Manjrekar	*1984–1997*	217	31	10,252	377	31

G. A. Headley scored 9,921 runs, average 69.86, between 1927-28 and 1954; V. G. Kambli scored 9,965, average 59.67, between 1989-90 and 2004-05.

FASTEST FIFTIES

Minutes			
11	C. I. J. Smith (66)	Middlesex v Gloucestershire at Bristol	1938
13	Khalid Mahmood (56)	Gujranwala v Sargodha at Gujranwala	2000-01
14	S. J. Pegler (50)	South Africans v Tasmania at Launceston	1910-11
14	F. T. Mann (53)	Middlesex v Nottinghamshire at Lord's	1921
14	H. B. Cameron (56)	Transvaal v Orange Free State at Johannesburg	1934-35
14	C. I. J. Smith (52)	Middlesex v Kent at Maidstone	1935

The number of balls taken to achieve fifties was rarely recorded until recently. C. I. J. Smith's two fifties (above) may have taken only 12 balls each. Khalid Mahmood reached his fifty in 15 balls.

Fifties scored in contrived circumstances and with the bowlers' compliance are excluded from the above list, including the fastest of them all, in 8 minutes (13 balls) by C. C. Inman, Leicestershire v Nottinghamshire at Nottingham, 1965, and 10 minutes by G. Chapple, Lancashire v Glamorgan at Manchester, 1993.

FASTEST HUNDREDS

Minutes			
35	P. G. H. Fender (113*)	Surrey v Northamptonshire at Northampton	1920
40	G. L. Jessop (101)	Gloucestershire v Yorkshire at Harrogate	1897
40	Ahsan-ul-Haq (100*)	Muslims v Sikhs at Lahore	1923-24
42	G. L. Jessop (191)	Gentlemen of South v Players of South at Hastings	1907
43	A. H. Hornby (106)	Lancashire v Somerset at Manchester	1905
43	D. W. Hookes (107)	South Australia v Victoria at Adelaide	1982-83
44	R. N. S. Hobbs (100)	Essex v Australians at Chelmsford	1975

The fastest recorded authentic hundred in terms of balls received was scored off 34 balls by D. W. Hookes (above). Research of the scorebook has shown that P. G. H. Fender scored his hundred from between 40 and 46 balls. He contributed 113 to an unfinished sixth-wicket partnership of 171 in 42 minutes with H. A. Peach.

E. B. Alletson (Nottinghamshire) scored 189 out of 227 runs in 90 minutes against Sussex at Hove in 1911. It has been estimated that his last 139 runs took 37 minutes.

Hundreds scored in contrived circumstances and with the bowlers' compliance are excluded, including the fastest of them all, in 21 minutes (27 balls) by G. Chapple, Lancashire v Glamorgan at Manchester, 1993, 24 minutes (27 balls) by M. L. Pettini, Essex v Leicestershire at Leicester, 2006, and 26 minutes (36 balls) by T. M. Moody, Warwickshire v Glamorgan at Swansea, 1990.

FASTEST DOUBLE-HUNDREDS

Minutes			
103	Shafiqullah Shinwari (200*)	Kabul v Boost at Asadabad	2017-18
113	R. J. Shastri (200*)	Bombay v Baroda at Bombay	1984-85
120	G. L. Jessop (286)	Gloucestershire v Sussex at Hove	1903
120	C. H. Lloyd (201*)	West Indians v Glamorgan at Swansea	1976
130	G. L. Jessop (234)	Gloucestershire v Somerset at Bristol	1905
131	V. T. Trumper (293)	Australians v Canterbury at Christchurch	1913-14

Shafiqullah faced 89 balls, which was also a record.

FASTEST TRIPLE-HUNDREDS

Minutes			
181	D. C. S. Compton (300)	MCC v North Eastern Transvaal at Benoni	1948-49
205	F. E. Woolley (305*)	MCC v Tasmania at Hobart	1911-12
205	C. G. Macartney (345)	Australians v Nottinghamshire at Nottingham	1921
213	D. G. Bradman (369)	South Australia v Tasmania at Adelaide	1935-36

The fastest triple-hundred in terms of balls received was scored off 191 balls by M. Marais for Border v Eastern Province at East London in 2017-18.

MOST RUNS IN A DAY BY ONE BATSMAN

390*	B. C. Lara (501*)	Warwickshire v Durham at Birmingham	1994
345	C. G. Macartney (345)	Australians v Nottinghamshire at Nottingham	1921
334*	W. H. Ponsford (352)	Victoria v New South Wales at Melbourne	1926-27
333	K. S. Duleepsinhji (333)	Sussex v Northamptonshire at Hove	1930
331*	J. D. Robertson (331*)	Middlesex v Worcestershire at Worcester	1949
325*	B. A. Richards (356)	South Australia v Western Australia at Perth	1970-71

*There have been another **14** instances of a batsman scoring 300 in a day, most recently 319 by R. R. Rossouw, Eagles v Titans at Centurion in 2009-10 (see* Wisden *2003, page 278, for full list).*

LONGEST INNINGS

Hrs	*Mins*			
16	55	R. Nayyar (271)	Himachal Pradesh v Jammu & Kashmir at Chamba	1999-2000
16	10	Hanif Mohammad (337)	Pakistan v West Indies at Bridgetown	1957-58
		Hanif believed he batted 16 hours 39 minutes.		
16	4	S. B. Gohel (359*)	Gujarat v Orissa at Jaipur	2016-17
15	7	V. A. Saxena (257)	Rajasthan v Tamil Nadu at Chennai	2011-12
14	38	G. Kirsten (275)	South Africa v England at Durban	1999-2000
14	32	K. K. Nair (328)	Karnataka v Tamil Nadu at Mumbai	2014-15
13	58	S. C. Cook (390)	Lions v Warriors at East London	2009-10
13	56	A. N. Cook (263)	England v Pakistan at Abu Dhabi	2015-16
13	43	T. Kohli (300*)	Punjab v Jharkhand at Jamshedpur	2012-13
13	41	S. S. Shukla (178*)	Uttar Pradesh v Tamil Nadu at Nagpur	2008-09
13	32	A. Chopra (301*)	Rajasthan v Maharashtra at Nasik	2010-11

1,000 RUNS IN MAY

	Runs	*Avge*
W. G. Grace, May 9 to May 30, 1895 (22 days)	1,016	112.88
Grace was 46 years old.		
W. R. Hammond, May 7 to May 31, 1927 (25 days)	1,042	74.42
Hammond scored his 1,000th run on May 28, thus equalling Grace's record of 22 days.		
C. Hallows, May 5 to May 31, 1928 (27 days)	1,000	125.00

1,000 RUNS IN APRIL AND MAY

	Runs	*Avge*
T. W. Hayward, April 16 to May 31, 1900	1,074	97.63
D. G. Bradman, April 30 to May 31, 1930	1,001	143.00
On April 30 Bradman was 75 not out.		

	Runs	Avge
D. G. Bradman, April 30 to May 31, 1938	1,056	150.85
Bradman scored 258 on April 30, and his 1,000th run on May 27.		
W. J. Edrich, April 30 to May 31, 1938	1,010	84.16
Edrich was 21 not out on April 30. All his runs were scored at Lord's.		
G. M. Turner, April 24 to May 31, 1973	1,018	78.30
G. A. Hick, April 17 to May 29, 1988	1,019	101.90
Hick scored a record 410 runs in April, and his 1,000th run on May 28.		

MOST RUNS SCORED OFF AN OVER

(All instances refer to six-ball overs)

36	G. S. Sobers	off M. A. Nash, Nottinghamshire v Glam at Swansea (six sixes)	1968
36	R. J. Shastri	off Tilak Raj, Bombay v Baroda at Bombay (six sixes)	1984-85
34	E. B. Alletson	off E. H. Killick, Notts v Sussex at Hove (46604446 inc 2 nb)	1911
34	F. C. Hayes	off M. A. Nash, Lancashire v Glamorgan at Swansea (646666)	1977
34†	A. Flintoff	off A. J. Tudor, Lancs v Surrey at Manchester (64444660 inc 2 nb)	1998
34	C. M. Spearman	off S. J. P. Moreton, Gloucestershire v Oxford UCCE at Oxford (666646) *Moreton's first over in first-class cricket.*	2005
32	C. C. Smart	off G. Hill, Glamorgan v Hampshire at Cardiff (664664)	1935
32	I. R. Redpath	off N. Rosendorff, Australians v OFS at Bloemfontein (666644)	1969-70
32	P. W. G. Parker	off A. I. Kallicharran, Sussex v Warwicks at Birmingham (466664)	1982
32	I. T. Botham	off I. R. Snook, England XI v C Dists at Palmerston North (466466)	1983-84
32	Khalid Mahmood	off Naved Latif, Gujranwala v Sargodha at Gujranwala (666662)	2000-01

† *Altogether 38 runs were scored off this over, the two no-balls counting for two extra runs each under ECB regulations.*

The following instances have been excluded because of the bowlers' compliance: 34 – M. P. Maynard off S. A. Marsh, Glamorgan v Kent at Swansea, 1992; 34 – G. Chapple off P. A. Cottey, Lancashire v Glamorgan at Manchester, 1993; 34 – F. B. Touzel off F. J. J. Viljoen, Western Province B v Griqualand West at Kimberley, 1993-94. Chapple scored a further 32 off Cottey's next over.

There were 35 runs off an over received by A. T. Reinholds off H. T. Davis, Auckland v Wellington at Auckland 1995-96, but this included 16 extras and only 19 off the bat.

In a match against KwaZulu-Natal at Stellenbosch in 2006-07, W. E. September (Boland) conceded 34 in an over: 27 to M. Bekker, six to K. Smit, plus one no-ball.

In a match against Canterbury at Christchurch in 1989-90, R. H. Vance (Wellington) deliberately conceded 77 runs in an over of full tosses which contained 17 no-balls and, owing to the umpire's understandable miscalculation, only five legitimate deliveries.

The greatest number of runs scored off an eight-ball over is 34 (40446664) by R. M. Edwards off M. C. Carew, Governor-General's XI v West Indians at Auckland, 1968-69.

MOST SIXES IN AN INNINGS

23	C. Munro (281)	Auckland v Central Districts at Napier	2014-15
22	Shafiqullah Shinwari (200*)	Kabul v Boost at Asadabad	2017-18
19	P. B. B. Rajapaksa (268)	Burgher v Ports Authority at Colombo (Moors)	2018-19
19	Najeeb Tarakai (200)	Speen Ghar v Mis Ainak at Asadabad	2018-19
17	B. O. P. Fernando (234)	Chilaw Marians v Colts at Colombo (NCC)	2018-19
16	A. Symonds (254*)	Gloucestershire v Glamorgan at Abergavenny	1995
16	G. R. Napier (196)	Essex v Surrey at Croydon	2011
16	J. D. Ryder (175)	New Zealanders v Australia A at Brisbane	2011-12
16	Mukhtar Ali (168)	Rajshahi v Chittagong at Savar	2013-14

*There have been **six** further instances of 15 sixes in an innings.*

MOST SIXES IN A MATCH

24	Shafiqullah Shinwari (22, 200*)	Kabul v Boost at Asadabad	2017-18
23	C. Munro (281)	Auckland v Central Districts at Napier	2014-15
21	R. R. Pant (117, 131)	Delhi v Jharkhand at Thumba	2016-17
20	A. Symonds (254*, 76)	Gloucestershire v Glam at Abergavenny	1995
19	B. O. P. Fernando (109, 234)	Chilaw Marians v Colts at Colombo (NCC)	2018-19
19	P. B. B. Rajapaksa (268)	Burgher v Ports Authority at Colombo (Moors)	2018-19
19	Najeeb Tarakai (200)	Speen Ghar v Mis Ainak at Asadabad	2018-19

MOST SIXES IN A SEASON

80	I. T. Botham	1985
66	A. W. Wellard	1935
65	Najeeb Tarakai	2017-18
57	A. W. Wellard	1936
57	A. W. Wellard	1938
51	A. W. Wellard	1933
49	I. V. A. Richards	1985
48	A. W. Carr	1925
48	J. H. Edrich	1965
48	A. Symonds	1995

MOST BOUNDARIES IN AN INNINGS

	4/6			
72	62/10	B. C. Lara (501*)	Warwickshire v Durham at Birmingham	1994
68	68/–	P. A. Perrin (343*)	Essex v Derbyshire at Chesterfield	1904
65	64/1	A. C. MacLaren (424)	Lancashire v Somerset at Taunton	1895
64	64/–	Hanif Mohammad (499)	Karachi v Bahawalpur at Karachi	1958-59
57	52/5	J. H. Edrich (310*)	England v New Zealand at Leeds	1965
57	52/5	Naved Latif (394)	Sargodha v Gujranwala at Gujranwala	2000-01
56	54/2	K. M. Jadhav (327)	Maharashtra v Uttar Pradesh at Pune	2012-13
55	55/–	C. W. Gregory (383)	NSW v Queensland at Brisbane	1906-07
55	53/2	G. R. Marsh (355*)	W. Australia v S. Australia at Perth	1989-90
55	51/3†	S. V. Manjrekar (377)	Bombay v Hyderabad at Bombay	1990-91
55	52/3	D. S. Lehmann (339)	Yorkshire v Durham at Leeds	2006
55	54/1	D. K. H. Mitchell (298)	Worcestershire v Somerset at Taunton	2009
55	54/1	S. C. Cook (390)	Lions v Warriors at East London	2009-10
55	47/8	R. R. Rossouw (319)	Eagles v Titans at Centurion	2009-10

† *Plus one five.*

PARTNERSHIPS OVER 500

624	for 3rd	K. C. Sangakkara (287)/D. P. M. D. Jayawardene (374), Sri Lanka v South Africa at Colombo (SSC)	2006
594*	for 3rd	S. M. Gugale (351*)/A. R. Bawne (258*), Maharashtra v Delhi at Mumbai	2016-17
580	for 2nd	Rafatullah Mohmand (302*)/Aamer Sajjad (289), WAPDA v Sui Southern Gas at Sheikhupura	2009-10
577	for 4th	V. S. Hazare (288)/Gul Mahomed (319), Baroda v Holkar at Baroda	1946-47
576	for 2nd	S. T. Jayasuriya (340)/R. S. Mahanama (225), Sri Lanka v India at Colombo (RPS)	1997-98
574*	for 4th	F. M. M. Worrell (255*)/C. L. Walcott (314*), Barbados v Trinidad at Port-of-Spain	1945-46
561	for 1st	Waheed Mirza (324)/Mansoor Akhtar (224*), Karachi Whites v Quetta at Karachi	1976-77
555	for 1st	P. Holmes (224*)/H. Sutcliffe (313), Yorkshire v Essex at Leyton	1932
554	for 1st	J. T. Brown (300)/J. Tunnicliffe (243), Yorks v Derbys at Chesterfield	1898
539	for 3rd	S. D. Jogiyani (282)/R. A. Jadeja (303*), Saurashtra v Gujarat at Surat	2012-13
523	for 3rd	M. A. Carberry (300*)/N. D. McKenzie (237), Hants v Yorks at Southampton	2011
520*	for 5th	C. A. Pujara (302*)/R. A. Jadeja (232*), Saurashtra v Orissa at Rajkot	2008-09
503	for 1st	R. G. L. Carters (209)/A. J. Finch (288*), Cricket Australia XI v New Zealanders at Sydney	2015-16
502*	for 4th	F. M. M. Worrell (308*)/J. D. C. Goddard (218*), Barbados v Trinidad at Bridgetown	1943-44
501	for 3rd	A. N. Petersen (286)/A. G. Prince (261), Lancs v Glam at Colwyn Bay	2015

HIGHEST PARTNERSHIPS FOR EACH WICKET

First Wicket

561	Waheed Mirza/Mansoor Akhtar, Karachi Whites v Quetta at Karachi	1976-77
555	P. Holmes/H. Sutcliffe, Yorkshire v Essex at Leyton	1932
554	J. T. Brown/J. Tunnicliffe, Yorkshire v Derbyshire at Chesterfield	1898
503	R. G. L. Carters/A. J. Finch, Cricket Australia XI v New Zealanders at Sydney	2015-16
490	E. H. Bowley/J. G. Langridge, Sussex v Middlesex at Hove	1933

Second Wicket

580	Rafatullah Mohmand/Aamer Sajjad, WAPDA v Sui S. Gas at Sheikhupura	2009-10
576	S. T. Jayasuriya/R. S. Mahanama, Sri Lanka v India at Colombo (RPS)	1997-98
480	D. Elgar/R. R. Rossouw, Eagles v Titans at Centurion	2009-10
475	Zahir Alam/L. S. Rajput, Assam v Tripura at Gauhati	1991-92
465*	J. A. Jameson/R. B. Kanhai, Warwickshire v Gloucestershire at Birmingham	1974

Third Wicket

624	K. C. Sangakkara/D. P. M. D. Jayawardene, Sri Lanka v SA at Colombo (SSC)	2006
594*	S. M. Gugale/A. R. Bawne, Maharashtra v Delhi at Mumbai	2016-17
539	S. D. Jogiyani/R. A. Jadeja, Saurashtra v Gujarat at Surat	2012-13
523	M. A. Carberry/N. D. McKenzie, Hampshire v Yorkshire at Southampton	2011
501	A. N. Petersen/A. G. Prince, Lancashire v Glamorgan at Colwyn Bay	2015

Fourth Wicket

577	V. S. Hazare/Gul Mahomed, Baroda v Holkar at Baroda	1946-47
574*	C. L. Walcott/F. M. M. Worrell, Barbados v Trinidad at Port-of-Spain	1945-46
502*	F. M. M. Worrell/J. D. C. Goddard, Barbados v Trinidad at Bridgetown	1943-44
470	A. I. Kallicharran/G. W. Humpage, Warwickshire v Lancashire at Southport	1982
462*	D. W. Hookes/W. B. Phillips, South Australia v Tasmania at Adelaide	1986-87

Fifth Wicket

520*	C. A. Pujara/R. A. Jadeja, Saurashtra v Orissa at Rajkot	2008-09
494	Marshall Ayub/Mehrab Hossain, Central Zone v East Zone at Bogra	2012-13
479	Misbah-ul-Haq/Usman Arshad, Sui N. Gas v Lahore Shalimar at Lahore	2009-10
464*	M. E. Waugh/S. R. Waugh, New South Wales v Western Australia at Perth	1990-91
440*	**D. B. Ravi Teja/R. Sanjay Yadav, Meghalaya v Mizoram at Kolkata**	**2019-20**

Sixth Wicket

487*	G. A. Headley/C. C. Passailaigue, Jamaica v Lord Tennyson's XI at Kingston	1931-32
428	W. W. Armstrong/M. A. Noble, Australians v Sussex at Hove	1902
417	W. P. Saha/L. R. Shukla, Bengal v Assam at Kolkata	2010-11
411	R. M. Poore/E. G. Wynyard, Hampshire v Somerset at Taunton	1899
399	B. A. Stokes/J. M. Bairstow, England v South Africa at Cape Town	2015-16

Seventh Wicket

460	Bhupinder Singh jnr/P. Dharmani, Punjab v Delhi at Delhi	1994-9
399	A. N. Khare/A. J. Mandal, Chhattisgarh v Uttarakhand at Naya Raipur	2019-2
371	M. R. Marsh/S. M. Whiteman, Australia A v India A at Brisbane	201
366*	J. M. Bairstow/T. T. Bresnan, Yorkshire v Durham at Chester-le-Street	201
347	D. St E. Atkinson/C. C. Depeiza, West Indies v Australia at Bridgetown	1954-5
347	Farhad Reza/Sanjamul Islam, Rajshahi v Chittagong at Savar	2013-1

Eighth Wicket

433	A. Sims and V. T. Trumper, A. Sims' Aust. XI v Canterbury at Christchurch. . .	1913-14
392	A. Mishra/J. Yadav, Haryana v Karnataka at Hubli	2012-13
332	I. J. L. Trott/S. C. J. Broad, England v Pakistan at Lord's	2010
313	Wasim Akram/Saqlain Mushtaq, Pakistan v Zimbabwe at Sheikhupura	1996-97
292	R. Peel/Lord Hawke, Yorkshire v Warwickshire at Birmingham.	1896

Ninth Wicket

283	A. Warren/J. Chapman, Derbyshire v Warwickshire at Blackwell.	1910
268	J. B. Commins/N. Boje, South Africa A v Mashonaland at Harare	1994-95
261	W. L. Madsen/T. Poynton, Derbyshire v Northamptonshire at Northampton . . .	2012
251	J. W. H. T. Douglas/S. N. Hare, Essex v Derbyshire at Leyton	1921
249*†	A. S. Srivastava/K. Seth, Madhya Pradesh v Vidarbha at Indore	2000-01

† *276 unbeaten runs were scored for this wicket in two separate partnerships; after Srivastava retired hurt, Seth and N. D. Hirwani added 27.*

Tenth Wicket

307	A. F. Kippax/J. E. H. Hooker, New South Wales v Victoria at Melbourne	1928-29
249	C. T. Sarwate/S. N. Banerjee, Indians v Surrey at The Oval	1946
239	Aqeel Arshad/Ali Raza, Lahore Whites v Hyderabad at Lahore	2004-05
235	F. E. Woolley/A. Fielder, Kent v Worcestershire at Stourbridge	1909
233	Ajay Sharma/Maninder Singh, Delhi v Bombay at Bombay	1991-92

There have been only 13 last-wicket stands of 200 or more.

UNUSUAL DISMISSALS

Handled the Ball

There have been **63** instances in first-class cricket. The most recent are:

W. S. A. Williams	Canterbury v Otago at Dunedin	2012-13
E. Lewis	Trinidad & Tobago v Leeward Islands at Port-of-Spain	2013-14
C. A. Pujara	Derbyshire v Leicestershire at Derby	2014
I. Khan	Dolphins v Lions at Johannesburg	2014-15
K. Lesporis	Windward Islands v Barbados at Bridgetown	2015-16
S. R. Dickson	Kent v Leicestershire at Leicester	2016
M. Z. Hamza	Cape Cobras v Knights at Bloemfontein	2016-17

Under the 2017 revision of the Laws, Handled the Ball was subsumed under Obstructing the Field.

Obstructing the Field

There have been **32** instances in first-class cricket. T. Straw of Worcestershire was given out for obstruction v Warwickshire in both 1899 and 1901. The most recent are:

W. E. Bell	Northern Cape v Border at Kimberley	2015-16
ahid Ali	Pakistan A v Zimbabwe A at Bulawayo.	2016-17
hamai Zadran	Mis Ainak v Boost at Ghazi Amanullah Town	2017-18
ashid Zadran	Mis Ainak v Band-e-Amir at Kabul	2017-18
ia-ur-Rehman	Mis Ainak v Amo at Khost.	2017-18
. P. Burl	Rising Stars v Harare Metropolitan Eagles at Harare.	2017-18
. Cotani	North West v Free State at Bloemfontein.	2018-19
. A. Blundell	**Wellington v Otago at Wellington**	**2020-21**

Hit the Ball Twice

There have been **21** instances in first-class cricket. The last occurrence in England involved J. H. King of Leicestershire v Surrey at The Oval in 1906. The most recent are:

Aziz Malik	Lahore Division v Faisalabad at Sialkot	1984-85
Javed Mohammad	Multan v Karachi Whites at Sahiwal	1986-87
Shahid Pervez	Jammu & Kashmir v Punjab at Srinagar	1986-87
Ali Naqvi	PNSC v National Bank at Faisalabad	1998-99
A. George	Tamil Nadu v Maharashtra at Pune	1998-99
Maqsood Raza	Lahore Division v PNSC at Sheikhupura	1999-2000
D. Mahajan	Jammu & Kashmir v Bihar at Jammu	2005-06

Timed Out

There have been **six** instances in first-class cricket:

A. Jordaan	Eastern Province v Transvaal at Port Elizabeth (SACB match)	1987-88
H. Yadav	Tripura v Orissa at Cuttack	1997-98
V. C. Drakes	Border v Free State at East London	2002-03
A. J. Harris	Nottinghamshire v Durham UCCE at Nottingham	2003
R. A. Austin	Combined Campuses & Colleges v Windward Is at Arnos Vale	2013-14
C. Kunje	Bulawayo Met Tuskers v Manica Mountaineers at Bulawayo	2017-18

BOWLING RECORDS

TEN WICKETS IN AN INNINGS

In the history of first-class cricket, there have been **81** instances of a bowler taking all ten wickets in an innings, plus a further three instances of ten wickets in 12-a-side matches. Occurrences since the Second World War:

	O	*M*	*R*		
*W. E. Hollies (Warwickshire)	20.4	4	49	v Notts at Birmingham	1946
J. M. Sims (East)	18.4	2	90	v West at Kingston	1948
T. E. Bailey (Essex)	39.4	9	90	v Lancashire at Clacton	1949
J. K. Graveney (Glos.)	18.4	2	66	v Derbyshire at Chesterfield	1949
R. Berry (Lancashire)	36.2	9	102	v Worcestershire at Blackpool	1953
S. P. Gupte (President's XI)	24.2	7	78	v Combined XI at Bombay	1954-55
J. C. Laker (Surrey)	46	18	88	v Australians at The Oval	1956
J. C. Laker (England)	51.2	23	53	v Australia at Manchester	1956
G. A. R. Lock (Surrey)	29.1	18	54	v Kent at Blackheath	1956
K. Smales (Nottinghamshire)	41.3	20	66	v Gloucestershire at Stroud	1956
P. M. Chatterjee (Bengal)	19	11	20	v Assam at Jorhat	1956-57
J. D. Bannister (Warwickshire)	23.3	11	41	v Comb. Services at Birmingham†	1959
A. J. G. Pearson (Cambridge U.)	30.3	8	78	v Leics at Loughborough	1961
N. I. Thomson (Sussex)	34.2	19	49	v Warwickshire at Worthing	1964
P. J. Allan (Queensland)	15.6	3	61	v Victoria at Melbourne	1965-66
I. J. Brayshaw (W. Australia)	17.6	4	44	v Victoria at Perth	1967-68
Shahid Mahmood (Karachi Whites)	25	5	58	v Khairpur at Karachi	1969-70
E. E. Hemmings (International XI)	49.3	14	175	v West Indies XI at Kingston	1982-8
P. Sunderam (Rajasthan)	22	5	78	v Vidarbha at Jodhpur	1985-8
S. T. Jefferies (W. Province)	22.5	7	59	v Orange Free State at Cape Town	1987-8
Imran Adil (Bahawalpur)	22.5	3	92	v Faisalabad at Faisalabad	1989-9
G. P. Wickremasinghe (Sinhalese)	19.2	5	41	v Kalutara PCC at Colombo (SSC)	1991-9
R. L. Johnson (Middlesex)	18.5	6	45	v Derbyshire at Derby	199
Naeem Akhtar (Rawalpindi B)	21.3	10	28	v Peshawar at Peshawar	1995-9
A. Kumble (India)	26.3	9	74	v Pakistan at Delhi	1998-9
D. S. Mohanty (East Zone)	19	5	46	v South Zone at Agartala	2000-0

	O	*M*	*R*		
O. D. Gibson (Durham)	17.3	1	47	v Hampshire at Chester-le-Street	2007
M. W. Olivier (Warriors)	26.3	4	65	v Eagles at Bloemfontein	2007-08
Zulfiqar Babar (Multan)	39.4	3	143	v Islamabad at Multan	2009-10
P. M. Pushpakumara (Colombo)	18.4	5	37	v Saracens at Moratuwa	2018-19

* *W. E. Hollies bowled seven and had three lbw. The only other instance of a bowler achieving the feat without the direct assistance of a fielder came in 1850 when J. Wisden bowled all ten, for North v South at Lord's.*
† *Mitchells & Butlers Ground.*

OUTSTANDING BOWLING ANALYSES

	O	*M*	*R*	*W*		
H. Verity (Yorkshire)	19.4	16	10	10	v Nottinghamshire at Leeds	1932
G. Elliott (Victoria)	19	17	2	9	v Tasmania at Launceston	1857-58
Ahad Khan (Railways)	6.3	4	7	9	v Dera Ismail Khan at Lahore	1964-65
J. C. Laker (England)	14	12	2	8	v The Rest at Bradford	1950
D. Shackleton (Hampshire)	11.1	7	4	8	v Somerset at Weston-s-Mare	1955
E. Peate (Yorkshire)	16	11	5	8	v Surrey at Holbeck	1883
K. M. Dabengwa (Westerns)	4.4	3	1	7	v Northerns at Harare	2006-07
F. R. Spofforth (Australians)	8.3	6	3	7	v England XI at Birmingham	1884
W. A. Henderson (NE Transvaal)	9.3	7	4	7	v OFS at Bloemfontein	1937-38
Rajinder Goel (Haryana)	7	4	4	7	v Jammu & K at Chandigarh	1977-78
N. W. Bracken (NSW)	7	5	4	7	v South Australia at Sydney	2004-05
V. I. Smith (South Africans)	4.5	3	1	6	v Derbyshire at Derby	1947
S. Cosstick (Victoria)	21.1	20	1	6	v Tasmania at Melbourne	1868-69
Israr Ali (Bahawalpur)	11	10	1	6	v Dacca U. at Bahawalpur	1957-58
A. D. Pougher (MCC)	3	3	0	5	v Australians at Lord's	1896
G. R. Cox (Sussex)	6	6	0	5	v Somerset at Weston-s-Mare	1921
R. K. Tyldesley (Lancashire)	5	5	0	5	v Leicestershire at Manchester	1924
P. T. Mills (Gloucestershire)	6.4	6	0	5	v Somerset at Bristol	1928

MOST WICKETS IN A MATCH

19-90	J. C. Laker	England v Australia at Manchester	1956
17-48†	C. Blythe	Kent v Northamptonshire at Northampton	1907
17-50	C. T. B. Turner	Australians v England XI at Hastings	1888
17-54	W. P. Howell	Australians v Western Province at Cape Town	1902-03
17-56	C. W. L. Parker	Gloucestershire v Essex at Gloucester	1925
17-67	A. P. Freeman	Kent v Sussex at Hove	1922
17-86	K. J. Abbott	Hampshire v Somerset at Southampton	2019
17-89	W. G. Grace	Gloucestershire v Nottinghamshire at Cheltenham	1877
17-89	F. C. L. Matthews	Nottinghamshire v Northants at Nottingham	1923
17-91	H. Dean	Lancashire v Yorkshire at Liverpool	1913
17-91†	H. Verity	Yorkshire v Essex at Leyton	1933
17-92	A. P. Freeman	Kent v Warwickshire at Folkestone	1932
17-103	W. Mycroft	Derbyshire v Hampshire at Southampton	1876
17-106	G. R. Cox	Sussex v Warwickshire at Horsham	1926
17-106†	T. W. J. Goddard	Gloucestershire v Kent at Bristol	1939
17-119	W. Mead	Essex v Hampshire at Southampton	1895
17-137	W. Brearley	Lancashire v Somerset at Manchester	1905
17-137	J. M. Davison	Canada v USA at Fort Lauderdale	2004
17-159	S. F. Barnes	England v South Africa at Johannesburg	1913-14
17-201	G. Giffen	South Australia v Victoria at Adelaide	1885-86
17-212	J. C. Clay	Glamorgan v Worcestershire at Swansea	1937

† *Achieved in a single day.*

*H. Arkwright took 18-96 for MCC v Gentlemen of Kent in a 12-a-side match at Canterbury in 1861. There have been **60** instances of a bowler taking 16 wickets in an 11-a-side match, the most recent being 16-110 by P. M. Pushpakumara for Colombo v Saracens at Moratuwa, 2018-19.*

FOUR WICKETS WITH CONSECUTIVE BALLS

There have been **44** instances in first-class cricket. R. J. Crisp achieved the feat twice, for Western Province in 1931-32 and 1933-34. A. E. Trott took four in four balls and another hat-trick in the same innings for Middlesex v Somerset in 1907, his benefit match. Occurrences since 2007:

Tabish Khan	Karachi Whites v ZTBL at Karachi	2009-10
Kamran Hussain	Habib Bank v Lahore Shalimar at Lahore	2009-10
N. Wagner	Otago v Wellington at Queenstown	2010-11
Khalid Usman	Abbottabad v Karachi Blues at Karachi	2011-12
Mahmudullah	Central Zone v North Zone at Savar	2013-14
A. C. Thomas	Somerset v Sussex at Taunton	2014
Taj Wali	Peshawar v Port Qasim Authority at Peshawar	2015-16
N. G. R. P. Jayasuriya	Colts v Badureliya at Maggona	2015-16
K. R. Smuts	Eastern Province v Boland at Paarl	2015-16

In their match with England at The Oval in 1863, Surrey lost four wickets in the course of a four-ball over from G. Bennett.

Sussex lost five wickets in the course of the final (six-ball) over of their match with Surrey at Eastbourne in 1972. P. I. Pocock, who had taken three wickets in his previous over, captured four more, taking in all seven wickets with 11 balls, a feat unique in first-class matches. (The eighth wicket fell to a run-out.)

In 1996, K. D. James took four in four balls for Hampshire against Indians at Southampton and scored a century, a feat later emulated by Mahmudullah and Smuts.

HAT-TRICKS

Double Hat-Trick

Besides Trott's performance, which is mentioned in the preceding section, the following instances are recorded of players having performed the hat-trick twice in the same match, Rao doing so in the same innings.

A. Shaw	Nottinghamshire v Gloucestershire at Nottingham	1884
T. J. Matthews	Australia v South Africa at Manchester	1912
C. W. L. Parker	Gloucestershire v Middlesex at Bristol	1924
R. O. Jenkins	Worcestershire v Surrey at Worcester	1949
J. S. Rao	Services v Northern Punjab at Amritsar	1963-64
Amin Lakhani	Combined XI v Indians at Multan	1978-79
M. A. Starc	New South Wales v Western Australia at Sydney (Hurstville)	2017-18

Five Wickets in Six Balls

W. H. Copson	Derbyshire v Warwickshire at Derby	1937
W. A. Henderson	NE Transvaal v Orange Free State at Bloemfontein	1937-38
P. I. Pocock	Surrey v Sussex at Eastbourne	1972
Yasir Arafat	Rawalpindi v Faisalabad at Rawalpindi	2004-05
N. Wagner	Otago v Wellington at Queenstown	2010-11

Yasir Arafat's five wickets were spread across two innings and interrupted only by a no-ball. Wagner was the first to take five wickets in a single over.

Most Hat-Tricks

D. V. P. Wright	7	R. G. Barlow	4	T. G. Matthews	4
T. W. J. Goddard	6	Fazl-e-Akbar	4	M. J. Procter	4
C. W. L. Parker	6	A. P. Freeman	4	T. Richardson	4
S. Haigh	5	J. T. Hearne	4	F. R. Spofforth	4
V. W. C. Jupp	5	J. C. Laker	4	F. S. Trueman	4
A. E. G. Rhodes	5	G. A. R. Lock	4		
F. A. Tarrant	5	G. G. Macaulay	4		

Hat-Trick on Debut

There have been **19** instances in first-class cricket. Occurrences since 2000:

S. M. Harwood	Victoria v Tasmania at Melbourne	2002-03
P. Connell	Ireland v Netherlands at Rotterdam	2008
A. Mithun	Karnataka v Uttar Pradesh at Meerut	2009-10
Zohaib Shera	Karachi Whites v National Bank at Karachi	2009-10
R. R. Yadav	**Madhya Pradesh v Uttar Pradesh at Indore**	**2019-20**

R. R. Phillips (Border) took a hat-trick in his first over in first-class cricket (v Eastern Province at Port Elizabeth, 1939-40) having previously played in four matches without bowling.

250 WICKETS IN A SEASON

	Season	*O*	*M*	*R*	*W*	*Avge*
A. P. Freeman	1928	1,976.1	423	5,489	304	18.05
A. P. Freeman	1933	2,039	651	4,549	298	15.26
T. Richardson	1895‡	1,690.1	463	4,170	290	14.37
C. T. B. Turner	1888†	2,427.2	1,127	3,307	283	11.68
A. P. Freeman	1931	1,618	360	4,307	276	15.60
A. P. Freeman	1930	1,914.3	472	4,632	275	16.84
T. Richardson	1897‡	1,603.4	495	3,945	273	14.45
A. P. Freeman	1929	1,670.5	381	4,879	267	18.27
W. Rhodes	1900	1,553	455	3,606	261	13.81
J. T. Hearne	1896‡	2,003.1	818	3,670	257	14.28
A. P. Freeman	1932	1,565.5	404	4,149	253	16.39
W. Rhodes	1901	1,565	505	3,797	251	15.12

† *Indicates 4-ball overs.* ‡ *5-ball overs.*

In four consecutive seasons (1928–1931), A. P. Freeman took 1,122 wickets, and in eight consecutive seasons (1928–1935), 2,090 wickets. In each of these eight seasons he took over 200 wickets.

T. Richardson took 1,005 wickets in four consecutive seasons (1894–1897).

The earliest date by which any bowler has taken 100 in an English season is June 12, achieved by J. T. Hearne in 1896 and C. W. L. Parker in 1931, when A. P. Freeman did it on June 13.

100 WICKETS IN A SEASON MOST TIMES

(Includes overseas tours and seasons)

W. Rhodes	23	C. W. L. Parker	16	G. H. Hirst	15
D. Shackleton	20	R. T. D. Perks	16	A. S. Kennedy	15
A. P. Freeman	17	F. J. Titmus	16		
T. W. J. Goddard	16	J. T. Hearne	15		

D. Shackleton reached 100 wickets in 20 successive seasons – 1949–1968.

Since the reduction of County Championship matches in 1969, D. L. Underwood (five times) and J. K. Lever (four times) are the only bowlers to have reached 100 wickets in a season more than twice. The highest aggregate in a season since 1969 is 134 by M. D. Marshall in 1982.

The most instances of 200 wickets in a season is eight by A. P. Freeman, who did it in eight successive seasons – 1928 to 1935 – including 304 in 1928. C. W. L. Parker did it five times, T. W. J. Goddard four times, and J. T. Hearne, G. A. Lohmann, W. Rhodes, T. Richardson, M. W. Tate and H. Verity three times each.

The last bowler to reach 200 wickets in a season was G. A. R. Lock (212 in 1957).

An expanded and regularly updated online version of the Records can be found at www.wisdenrecords.com

100 WICKETS IN A SEASON OUTSIDE ENGLAND

W		*Season*	*Country*	*R*	*Avge*
116	M. W. Tate	1926-27	India/Ceylon	1,599	13.78
113	Kabir Khan	1998-99	Pakistan	1,706	15.09
107	Ijaz Faqih	1985-86	Pakistan	1,719	16.06
106	C. T. B. Turner	1887-88	Australia	1,441	13.59
106	R. Benaud	1957-58	South Africa	2,056	19.39
105	Murtaza Hussain	1995-96	Pakistan	1,882	17.92
104	S. F. Barnes	1913-14	South Africa	1,117	10.74
104	Sajjad Akbar	1989-90	Pakistan	2,328	22.38
103	Abdul Qadir	1982-83	Pakistan	2,367	22.98
101	Zia-ur-Rehman	2017-18	Afghanistan	1,995	19.75

LEADING BOWLERS IN AN ENGLISH SEASON

(Qualification: 10 wickets in 10 innings)

Season	*Leading wicket-taker*	*Wkts*	*Avge*	*Top of averages*	*Wkts*	*Avge*
1946	W. E. Hollies	184	15.60	A. Booth	111	11.61
1947	T. W. J. Goddard	238	17.30	J. C. Clay	65	16.44
1948	J. E. Walsh	174	19.56	J. C. Clay	41	14.17
1949	R. O. Jenkins	183	21.19	T. W. J. Goddard	160	19.18
1950	R. Tattersall	193	13.59	R. Tattersall	193	13.59
1951	R. Appleyard	200	14.14	R. Appleyard	200	14.14
1952	J. H. Wardle	177	19.54	F. S. Trueman	61	13.78
1953	B. Dooland	172	16.58	C. J. Knott	38	13.71
1954	B. Dooland	196	15.48	J. B. Statham	92	14.13
1955	G. A. R. Lock	216	14.49	R. Appleyard	85	13.01
1956	D. J. Shepherd	177	15.36	G. A. R. Lock	155	12.46
1957	G. A. R. Lock	212	12.02	G. A. R. Lock	212	12.02
1958	G. A. R. Lock	170	12.08	H. L. Jackson	143	10.99
1959	D. Shackleton	148	21.55	J. B. Statham	139	15.01
1960	F. S. Trueman	175	13.98	J. B. Statham	135	12.31
1961	J. A. Flavell	171	17.79	J. A. Flavell	171	17.79
1962	D. Shackleton	172	20.15	C. Cook	58	17.13
1963	D. Shackleton	146	16.75	C. C. Griffith	119	12.83
1964	D. Shackleton	142	20.40	J. A. Standen	64	13.00
1965	D. Shackleton	144	16.08	H. J. Rhodes	119	11.04
1966	D. L. Underwood	157	13.80	D. L. Underwood	157	13.80
1967	T. W. Cartwright	147	15.52	D. L. Underwood	136	12.39
1968	R. Illingworth	131	14.36	O. S. Wheatley	82	12.95
1969	R. M. H. Cottam	109	21.04	A. Ward	69	14.82
1970	D. J. Shepherd	106	19.16	Majid Khan	11	18.81
1971	L. R. Gibbs	131	18.89	G. G. Arnold	83	17.12
1972	T. W. Cartwright B. Stead	98 98	18.64 20.38	I. M. Chappell	10	10.60
1973	B. S. Bedi	105	17.94	T. W. Cartwright	89	15.84
1974	A. M. E. Roberts	119	13.62	A. M. E. Roberts	119	13.62
1975	P. G. Lee	112	18.45	A. M. E. Roberts	57	15.80
1976	G. A. Cope	93	24.13	M. A. Holding	55	14.38
1977	M. J. Procter	109	18.04	R. A. Woolmer	19	15.21
1978	D. L. Underwood	110	14.49	D. L. Underwood	110	14.49
1979	D. L. Underwood J. K. Lever	106 106	14.85 17.30	J. Garner	55	13.83
1980	R. D. Jackman	121	15.40	J. Garner	49	13.93
1981	R. J. Hadlee	105	14.89	R. J. Hadlee	105	14.89
1982	M. D. Marshall	134	15.73	R. J. Hadlee	61	14.57
1983	J. K. Lever D. L. Underwood	106 106	16.28 19.28	Imran Khan	12	7.16
1984	R. J. Hadlee	117	14.05	R. J. Hadlee	117	14.05

Season	*Leading wicket-taker*	*Wkts*	*Avge*	*Top of averages*	*Wkts*	*Avge*
1985	N. V. Radford	101	24.68	R. M. Ellison	65	17.20
1986	C. A. Walsh	118	18.17	M. D. Marshall	100	15.08
1987	N. V. Radford	109	20.81	R. J. Hadlee	97	12.64
1988	F. D. Stephenson	125	18.31	M. D. Marshall	42	13.16
1989	D. R. Pringle	94	18.64	T. M. Alderman	70	15.64
	S. L. Watkin	94	25.09			
1990	N. A. Foster	94	26.61	I. R. Bishop	59	19.05
1991	Waqar Younis	113	14.65	Waqar Younis	113	14.65
1992	C. A. Walsh	92	15.96	C. A. Walsh	92	15.96
1993	S. L. Watkin	92	22.80	Wasim Akram	59	19.27
1994	M. M. Patel	90	22.86	C. E. L. Ambrose	77	14.45
1995	A. Kumble	105	20.40	A. A. Donald	89	16.07
1996	C. A. Walsh	85	16.84	C. E. L. Ambrose	43	16.67
1997	A. M. Smith	83	17.63	A. A. Donald	60	15.63
1998	C. A. Walsh	106	17.31	V. J. Wells	36	14.27
1999	A. Sheriyar	92	24.70	Saqlain Mushtaq	58	11.37
2000	G. D. McGrath	80	13.21	C. A. Walsh	40	11.42
2001	R. J. Kirtley	75	23.32	G. D. McGrath	40	15.60
2002	M. J. Saggers	83	21.51	C. P. Schofield	18	18.38
	K. J. Dean	83	23.50			
2003	Mushtaq Ahmed	103	24.65	Shoaib Akhtar	34	17.05
2004	Mushtaq Ahmed	84	27.59	D. S. Lehmann	15	17.40
2005	S. K. Warne	87	22.50	M. Muralitharan	36	15.00
2006	Mushtaq Ahmed	102	19.91	Naved-ul-Hasan	35	16.71
2007	Mushtaq Ahmed	90	25.66	Harbhajan Singh	37	18.54
2008	J. A. Tomlinson	67	24.76	M. Davies	41	14.63
2009	Danish Kaneria	75	23.69	G. Onions	69	19.95
2010	A. R. Adams	68	22.17	J. K. H. Naik	35	17.68
2011	D. D. Masters	93	18.13	T. T. Bresnan	29	17.68
2012	G. Onions	72	14.73	G. Onions	72	14.73
2013	G. Onions	73	18.92	T. A. Copeland	45	18.26
2014	M. H. A. Footitt	84	19.19	G. R. Napier	52	15.63
2015	C. Rushworth	90	20.54	R. J. Sidebottom	43	18.09
2016	G. R. Napier	69	22.30	J. M. Anderson	45	17.00
	J. S. Patel	69	24.02			
2017	J. A. Porter	85	16.74	J. L. Pattinson	32	12.06
2018	O. E. Robinson	81	17.43	O. P. Stone	43	12.30
2019	S. R. Harmer	86	18.15	J. M. Anderson	30	9.40
2020	**S. R. Harmer**	**38**	**15.86**	**C. Overton**	**30**	**13.43**

MOST WICKETS

Dates in italics denote the first half of an overseas season; i.e. *1970* denotes the 1970-71 season.

		Career	*W*	*R*	*Avge*
1	W. Rhodes	1898–1930	4,187	69,993	16.71
2	A. P. Freeman	1914–1936	3,776	69,577	18.42
3	C. W. L. Parker	1903–1935	3,278	63,817	19.46
4	J. T. Hearne	1888–1923	3,061	54,352	17.75
5	T. W. J. Goddard	1922–1952	2,979	59,116	19.84
6	W. G. Grace	1865–1908	2,876	51,545	17.92
7	A. S. Kennedy	1907–1936	2,874	61,034	21.23
8	D. Shackleton	1948–1969	2,857	53,303	18.65
9	G. A. R. Lock	1946–*1970*	2,844	54,709	19.23
10	F. J. Titmus	1949–1982	2,830	63,313	22.37
11	M. W. Tate	1912–1937	2,784	50,571	18.16
12	G. H. Hirst	1891–1929	2,739	51,282	18.72
13	C. Blythe	1899–1914	2,506	42,136	16.81

Some works of reference provide career figures which differ from those in this list, owing to the exclusion or inclusion of matches recognised or not recognised as first-class by Wisden. *A fuller list can be found in* Wisdens *up to 2011.*

Current Players with 750 Wickets

	Career	*W*	*R*	*Avge*
J. M. Anderson	2002–2020	975	24,315	24.93
T. J. Murtagh	2000–2020	841	20,836	24.77
S. C. J. Broad	2005–2020	808	21,808	26.99
M. D. K. Perera	*2000*–2020	802	21,186	26.41
P. M. Pushpakumara	*2006*–2020	793	15,884	20.03

ALL-ROUND RECORDS

REMARKABLE ALL-ROUND MATCHES

V. E. Walker	20*	108	10-74	4-17	England v Surrey at The Oval	1859
W. G. Grace	104		2-60	10-49	MCC v Oxford University at Oxford .	1886
G. Giffen	271		9-96	7-70	South Australia v Victoria at Adelaide	1891-92
B. J. T. Bosanquet	103	100*	3-75	8-53	Middlesex v Sussex at Lord's	1905
G. H. Hirst	111	117*	6-70	5-45	Yorkshire v Somerset at Bath	1906
F. D. Stephenson	111	117	4-105	7-117	Notts v Yorkshire at Nottingham.	1988

E. M. Grace, for MCC v Gentlemen of Kent in a 12-a-side match at Canterbury in 1862, scored 192 and took 5-77 and 10-69.*

HUNDRED AND HAT-TRICK

G. Giffen, Australians v Lancashire at Manchester	1884
*W. E. Roller, Surrey v Sussex at The Oval	1885
W. B. Burns, Worcestershire v Gloucestershire at Worcester	1913
V. W. C. Jupp, Sussex v Essex at Colchester	1921
R. E. S. Wyatt, MCC v Ceylonese at Colombo (Victoria Park)	1926-27
L. N. Constantine, West Indians v Northamptonshire at Northampton	1928
D. E. Davies, Glamorgan v Leicestershire at Leicester	1937
V. M. Merchant, Dr C. R. Pereira's XI v Sir Homi Mehta's XI at Bombay	1946-47
M. J. Procter, Gloucestershire v Essex at Westcliff-on-Sea.	1972
M. J. Procter, Gloucestershire v Leicestershire at Bristol	1979
†K. D. James, Hampshire v Indians at Southampton.	1996
J. E. C. Franklin, Gloucestershire v Derbyshire at Cheltenham.	2009
Sohag Gazi, Barisal v Khulna at Khulna	2012-13
Sohag Gazi, Bangladesh v New Zealand at Chittagong	2013-14
†Mahmudullah, Central Zone v North Zone at Savar	2013-14
†K. R. Smuts, Eastern Province v Boland at Paarl	2015-16

* *W. E. Roller is the only player to combine 200 with a hat-trick.*

† *K. D. James, Mahmudullah and K. R. Smuts all combined 100 with four wickets in four balls (Mahmudullah's split between two innings).*

THE DOUBLE

The double was traditionally regarded as 1,000 runs and 100 wickets in an English season. The fea became exceptionally rare after the reduction of County Championship matches in 1969.

Remarkable Seasons

	Season	*R*	*W*		*Season*	*R*	*W*
G. H. Hirst	1906	2,385	208	J. H. Parks	1937	3,003	10

1,000 Runs and 100 Wickets

W. Rhodes	16	W. G. Grace	8	F. J. Titmus	8
G. H. Hirst	14	M. S. Nichols	8	F. E. Woolley	7
V. W. C. Jupp	10	A. E. Relf	8	G. E. Tribe	7
W. E. Astill	9	F. A. Tarrant	8		
T. E. Bailey	8	M. W. Tate	8†		

† *M. W. Tate also scored 1,193 runs and took 116 wickets on the 1926-27 MCC tour of India and Ceylon.*

R. J. Hadlee (1984) and F. D. Stephenson (1988) are the only players to perform the feat since the reduction of County Championship matches in 1969. A complete list of those performing the feat before then may be found on page 202 of the 1982 Wisden. *T. E. Bailey (1959) was the last player to achieve 2,000 runs and 100 wickets in a season; M. W. Tate (1925) the last to reach 1,000 runs and 200 wickets. Full lists may be found in* Wisdens *up to 2003.*

Wicketkeeper's Double

The only wicketkeepers to achieve 1,000 runs and 100 dismissals in a season were L. E. G. Ames (1928, 1929 and 1932, when he scored 2,482 runs) and J. T. Murray (1957).

WICKETKEEPING RECORDS

MOST DISMISSALS IN AN INNINGS

9 (8ct, 1st)	Tahir Rashid	Habib Bank v PACO at Gujranwala	1992-93
9 (7ct, 2st)	W. R. James*	Matabeleland v Mashonaland CD at Bulawayo	1995-96
8 (8ct)	A. T. W. Grout	Queensland v Western Australia at Brisbane	1959-60
8 (8ct)†	D. E. East	Essex v Somerset at Taunton	1985
8 (8ct)	S. A. Marsh‡	Kent v Middlesex at Lord's	1991
8 (6ct, 2st)	T. J. Zoehrer	Australians v Surrey at The Oval	1993
8 (7ct, 1st)	D. S. Berry	Victoria v South Australia at Melbourne	1996-97
8 (7ct, 1st)	Y. S. S. Mendis	Bloomfield v Kurunegala Y at Colombo (Bloomfield)	2000-01
8 (7ct, 1st)	S. Nath§	Assam v Tripura at Guwahati	2001-02
8 (8ct)	J. N. Batty¶	Surrey v Kent at The Oval	2004
8 (8ct)	Golam Mabud	Sylhet v Dhaka at Dhaka	2005-06
8 (8ct)	A. Z. M. Dyili	Eastern Province v Free State at Port Elizabeth	2009-10
8 (8ct)	D. C. de Boorder	Otago v Wellington at Wellington	2009-10
8 (8ct)	R. S. Second	Free State v North West at Bloemfontein	2011-12
8 (8ct)	T. L. Tsolekile	South Africa A v Sri Lanka A at Durban	2012
8 (7ct, 1st)	M. A. R. S. Fernando	Chilaw Marians v Colts at Colombo (SSC)	2017-18

*There have been **112** further instances of seven dismissals in an innings. R. W. Taylor achieved the feat three times, and G. J. Hopkins, Kamran Akmal, I. Khaleel, S. A. Marsh, K. J. Piper, Shahin Hossain, T. L. Tsolekile and Wasim Bari twice. Khaleel did it twice in the same match. Marsh's and Tsolekile's two instances both included one of eight dismssals – see above. H. Yarnold made six stumpings and one catch in an innings for Worcestershire v Scotland at Dundee in 1951. A fuller list can be found in* Wisdens *before 2004.*

* *W. R. James also scored 99 and 99 not out.*
† *The first eight wickets to fall.*
‡ *S. A. Marsh also scored 108 not out.*
§ *On his only first-class appearance.*
¶ *J. N. Batty also scored 129.*

WICKETKEEPERS' HAT-TRICKS

W. H. Brain, Gloucestershire v Somerset at Cheltenham, 1893 – three stumpings off successive balls from C. L. Townsend.

K. R. Meherhomji, Freelooters v Nizam's State Railway A at Secunderabad, 1931-32 – three catches off successive balls from L. Ramji.

G. O. Dawkes, Derbyshire v Worcestershire at Kidderminster, 1958 – three catches off successive balls from H. L. Jackson.

R. C. Russell, Gloucestershire v Surrey at The Oval, 1986 – three catches off successive balls from C. A. Walsh and D. V. Lawrence (2).

T. Frost, Warwickshire v Surrey at Birmingham, 2003 – three catches off successive balls from G. G. Wagg and N. M. Carter (2).

MOST DISMISSALS IN A MATCH

14 (11ct, 3st)	I. Khaleel	Hyderabad v Assam at Guwahati	2011-12
13 (11ct, 2st)	W. R. James*	Matabeleland v Mashonaland CD at Bulawayo	1995-96
12 (8ct, 4st)	E. Pooley	Surrey v Sussex at The Oval	1868
12 (9ct, 3st)	D. Tallon	Queensland v New South Wales at Sydney	1938-39
12 (9ct, 3st)	H. B. Taber	New South Wales v South Australia at Adelaide	1968-69
12 (12ct)	P. D. McGlashan	Northern Districts v Central Districts at Whangarei	2009-10
12 (11ct, 1st)	T. L. Tsolekile	Lions v Dolphins at Johannesburg	2010-11
12 (12ct)	Kashif Mahmood	Lahore Shalimar v Abbottabad at Abbottabad	2010-11
12 (12ct)	R. S. Second	Free State v North West at Bloemfontein	2011-12

* *W. R. James also scored 99 and 99 not out.*

100 DISMISSALS IN A SEASON

128 (79ct, 49st)	L. E. G. Ames	1929	104 (82ct, 22st)	J. T. Murray	1957
122 (70ct, 52st)	L. E. G. Ames	1928	102 (69ct, 33st)	F. H. Huish	1913
110 (63ct, 47st)	H. Yarnold	1949	102 (95ct, 7st)	J. T. Murray	1960
107 (77ct, 30st)	G. Duckworth	1928	101 (62ct, 39st)	F. H. Huish	1911
107 (96ct, 11st)	J. G. Binks	1960	101 (85ct, 16st)	R. Booth	1960
104 (40ct, 64st)	L. E. G. Ames	1932	100 (91ct, 9st)	R. Booth	1964

L. E. G. Ames achieved the two highest stumping totals in a season: 64 in 1932, and 52 in 1928.

MOST DISMISSALS

Dates in italics denote the first half of an overseas season; i.e. *1997* denotes the 1997-98 season.

			Career	*M*	*Ct*	*St*
1	R. W. Taylor	1,649	1960–1988	639	1,473	176
2	J. T. Murray	1,527	1952–1975	635	1,270	257
3	H. Strudwick	1,497	1902–1927	675	1,242	255
4	A. P. E. Knott	1,344	1964–1985	511	1,211	133
5	R. C. Russell	1,320	1981–2004	465	1,192	128
6	F. H. Huish	1,310	1895–1914	497	933	377
7	B. Taylor	1,294	1949–1973	572	1,083	211
8	S. J. Rhodes	1,263	1981–2004	440	1,139	124
9	D. Hunter	1,253	1888–1909	548	906	347

Current Players with 500 Dismissals

		Career	*M*	*Ct*	*St*
937	Kamran Akmal	*1997–2020*	247	869	68
584	S. M. Davies	2005–2020	231	551	33
578	Adnan Akmal	*2003–2020*	171	544	34
561	Sarfraz Ahmed	*2005–2020*	160	507	54
561	P. A. Patel	*2001–2019*	194	484	77
511	J. A. Simpson	2009–2020	160	486	25
500	J. M. Bairstow	2009–2020	183	476	24

Many of these figures include catches taken in the field.

FIELDING RECORDS

excluding wicketkeepers

MOST CATCHES IN AN INNINGS

7	M. J. Stewart	Surrey v Northamptonshire at Northampton	1957
7	A. S. Brown	Gloucestershire v Nottinghamshire at Nottingham	1966
7	R. Clarke	Warwickshire v Lancashire at Liverpool	2011

MOST CATCHES IN A MATCH

10	W. R. Hammond†	Gloucestershire v Surrey at Cheltenham	1928
9	R. Clarke	Warwickshire v Lancashire at Liverpool	2011
8	W. B. Burns	Worcestershire v Yorkshire at Bradford	1907
8	F. G. Travers	Europeans v Parsees at Bombay	1923-24
8	A. H. Bakewell	Northamptonshire v Essex at Leyton	1928
8	W. R. Hammond	Gloucestershire v Worcestershire at Cheltenham	1932
8	K. J. Grieves	Lancashire v Sussex at Manchester	1951
8	C. A. Milton	Gloucestershire v Sussex at Hove	1952
8	G. A. R. Lock	Surrey v Warwickshire at The Oval	1957
8	J. M. Prodger	Kent v Gloucestershire at Cheltenham	1961
8	P. M. Walker	Glamorgan v Derbyshire at Swansea	1970
8	Masood Anwar	Rawalpindi v Lahore Division at Rawalpindi	1983-84
8	M. C. J. Ball	Gloucestershire v Yorkshire at Cheltenham	1994
8	J. D. Carr	Middlesex v Warwickshire at Birmingham	1995
8	G. A. Hick	Worcestershire v Essex at Chelmsford	2005
8	Naved Yasin	State Bank v Bahawalpur Stags at Bahawalpur	2014-15
8	A. M. Rahane	India v Sri Lanka at Galle	2015-16

† *Hammond also scored a hundred in each innings.*

MOST CATCHES IN A SEASON

78	W. R. Hammond	1928
77	M. J. Stewart	1957
73	P. M. Walker	1961
71	P. J. Sharpe	1962
70	J. Tunnicliffe	1901

The most catches by a fielder since the reduction of County Championship matches in 1969 is 59 by G. R. J. Roope in 1971.

MOST CATCHES

Dates in italics denote the first half of an overseas season; i.e. *1970* denotes the 1970-71 season.

		Career	*M*
1,018	F. E. Woolley	1906–1938	979
887	W. G. Grace	1865–1908	879
830	G. A. R. Lock	1946–*1970*	654
819	W. R. Hammond	1920–1951	634
813	D. B. Close	1949–1986	786
784	J. G. Langridge	1928–1955	574
764	W. Rhodes	1898–1930	1,107
758	C. A. Milton	1948–1974	620
754	E. H. Hendren	1907–1938	833

*The most catches by a current player is **378** by **R. Clarke** in 256 matches between 2002 and 2020.*

TEAM RECORDS

HIGHEST INNINGS TOTALS

1,107	Victoria v New South Wales at Melbourne	1926-27
1,059	Victoria v Tasmania at Melbourne	1922-23
952-6 dec	Sri Lanka v India at Colombo (RPS)	1997-98
951-7 dec	Sind v Baluchistan at Karachi	1973-74
944-6 dec	Hyderabad v Andhra at Secunderabad	1993-94
918	New South Wales v South Australia at Sydney	1900-01
912-8 dec	Holkar v Mysore at Indore	1945-46
912-6 dec†	Tamil Nadu v Goa at Panjim	1988-89
910-6 dec	Railways v Dera Ismail Khan at Lahore	1964-65
903-7 dec	England v Australia at The Oval	1938
900-6 dec	Queensland v Victoria at Brisbane	2005-06

† *Tamil Nadu's total of 912-6 dec included 52 penalty runs from their opponents' failure to meet the required bowling rate.*

The highest total in a team's second innings is 770 by New South Wales v South Australia at Adelaide in 1920-21.

HIGHEST FOURTH-INNINGS TOTALS

654-5	England v South Africa at Durban *After being set 696 to win. The match was left drawn on the tenth day.*	1938-39
604	Maharashtra (*set 959 to win*) v Bombay at Poona	1948-49
576-8	Trinidad (*set 672 to win*) v Barbados at Port-of-Spain	1945-46
572	New South Wales (*set 593 to win*) v South Australia at Sydney	1907-08
541-7	West Zone (*won*) v South Zone at Hyderabad	2009-10
529-9	Combined XI (*set 579 to win*) v South Africans at Perth	1963-64
518	Victoria (*set 753 to win*) v Queensland at Brisbane	1926-27
513-9	Central Province (*won*) v Southern Province at Kandy	2003-04
507-7	Cambridge University (*won*) v MCC and Ground at Lord's	1896
506-6	South Australia (*won*) v Queensland at Adelaide	1991-92
503-4	South Zone (*won*) v England A at Gurgaon	2003-04
502-6	Middlesex (*won*) v Nottinghamshire at Nottingham	1925
502-8	Players (*won*) v Gentlemen at Lord's	1900
500-7	South African Universities (*won*) v Western Province at Stellenbosch	1978-79

MOST RUNS IN A DAY (ONE SIDE)

721	Australians (721) v Essex at Southend (1st day)	1948
651	West Indians (651-2) v Leicestershire at Leicester (1st day)	1950
649	New South Wales (649-7) v Otago at Dunedin (2nd day)	1923-24
645	Surrey (645-4) v Hampshire at The Oval (1st day)	1909
644	Oxford U. (644-8) v H. D. G. Leveson Gower's XI at Eastbourne (1st day)	1921
640	Lancashire (640-8) v Sussex at Hove (1st day)	1937
636	Free Foresters (636-7) v Cambridge U. at Cambridge (1st day)	1938
625	Gloucestershire (625-6) v Worcestershire at Dudley (2nd day)	1934

MOST RUNS IN A DAY (BOTH SIDES)

(excluding the above)

685	North (169-8 and 255-7), South (261-8 dec) at Blackpool (2nd day)	1961
666	Surrey (607-4), Northamptonshire (59-2) at Northampton (2nd day)	1920
665	Rest of South Africa (339), Transvaal (326) at Johannesburg (1st day)	1911-12
663	Middlesex (503-4), Leicestershire (160-2) at Leicester (2nd day)	1947
661	Border (201), Griqualand West (460) at Kimberley (1st day)	1920-21
649	Hampshire (570-8), Somerset (79-3) at Taunton (2nd day)	1901

HIGHEST AGGREGATES IN A MATCH

Runs	*Wkts*		
2,376	37	Maharashtra v Bombay at Poona	1948-49
2,078	40	Bombay v Holkar at Bombay	1944-45
1,981	35	South Africa v England at Durban	1938-39
1,945	18	Canterbury v Wellington at Christchurch	1994-95
1,929	39	New South Wales v South Australia at Sydney	1925-26
1,911	34	New South Wales v Victoria at Sydney	1908-09
1,905	40	Otago v Wellington at Dunedin	1923-24

In Britain

Runs	*Wkts*		
1,815	28	Somerset v Surrey at Taunton	2002
1,808	20	Sussex v Essex at Hove	1993
1,795	34	Somerset v Northamptonshire at Taunton	2001
1,723	31	England v Australia at Leeds	1948
1,706	23	Hampshire v Warwickshire at Southampton	1997

LOWEST INNINGS TOTALS

12†	Oxford University v MCC and Ground at Oxford	1877
12	Northamptonshire v Gloucestershire at Gloucester	1907
13	Auckland v Canterbury at Auckland	1877-78
13	Nottinghamshire v Yorkshire at Nottingham	1901
14	Surrey v Essex at Chelmsford	1983
15	MCC v Surrey at Lord's	1839
15†	Victoria v MCC at Melbourne	1903-04
15†	Northamptonshire v Yorkshire at Northampton	1908
15	Hampshire v Warwickshire at Birmingham	1922
	Following on, Hampshire scored 521 and won by 155 runs.	
16	MCC and Ground v Surrey at Lord's	1872
16	Derbyshire v Nottinghamshire at Nottingham	1879
16	Surrey v Nottinghamshire at The Oval	1880
16	Warwickshire v Kent at Tonbridge	1913
16	Trinidad v Barbados at Bridgetown	1942-43
16	Border v Natal at East London (first innings)	1959-60
17	Gentlemen of Kent v Gentlemen of England at Lord's	1850
17	Gloucestershire v Australians at Cheltenham	1896
18	The Bs v England at Lord's	1831
18†	Kent v Sussex at Gravesend	1867
18	Tasmania v Victoria at Melbourne	1868-69
18†	Australians v MCC and Ground at Lord's	1896
18	Border v Natal at East London (second innings)	1959-60
18†	Durham MCCU v Durham at Chester-le-Street	2012

† *One man absent.*

At Lord's in 1810, The Bs, with one man absent, were dismissed by England for 6.

LOWEST TOTALS IN A MATCH

34	(16 and 18) Border v Natal at East London	1959-60
42	(27† and 15†) Northamptonshire v Yorkshire at Northampton	1908

† *Northamptonshire batted one man short in each innings.*

LOWEST AGGREGATE IN A COMPLETED MATCH

Runs	*Wkts*		
85	11†	Quetta v Rawalpindi at Islamabad	2008-09
105	31	MCC v Australians at Lord's	1878

† *Both teams forfeited their first innings.*

The lowest aggregate in a match in which the losing team was bowled out twice since 1900 is 157 for 22 wickets, Surrey v Worcestershire at The Oval, 1954.

LARGEST VICTORIES

Largest Innings Victories

Inns and 851 runs	Railways (910-6 dec) v Dera Ismail Khan at Lahore	1964-65
Inns and 666 runs	Victoria (1,059) v Tasmania at Melbourne	1922-23
Inns and 656 runs	Victoria (1,107) v New South Wales at Melbourne	1926-27
Inns and 605 runs	New South Wales (918) v South Australia at Sydney	1900-01
Inns and 579 runs	England (903-7 dec) v Australia at The Oval	1938
Inns and 575 runs	Sind (951-7 dec) v Baluchistan at Karachi	1973-74
Inns and 527 runs	New South Wales (713) v South Australia at Adelaide	1908-09
Inns and 517 runs	Australians (675) v Nottinghamshire at Nottingham	1921

Largest Victories by Runs Margin

685 runs	New South Wales (235 and 761-8 dec) v Queensland at Sydney	1929-30
675 runs	England (521 and 342-8 dec) v Australia at Brisbane	1928-29
638 runs	New South Wales (304 and 770) v South Australia at Adelaide	1920-21
609 runs	Muslim Comm. Bank (575 and 282-0 dec) v WAPDA at Lahore	1977-78

Victory Without Losing a Wicket

Lancashire (166-0 dec and 66-0) beat Leicestershire by ten wickets at Manchester	1956
Karachi A (277-0 dec) beat Sind A by an innings and 77 runs at Karachi	1957-58
Railways (236-0 dec and 16-0) beat Jammu & Kashmir by ten wickets at Srinagar	1960-61
Karnataka (451-0 dec) beat Kerala by an innings and 186 runs at Chikmagalur	1977-78

There have been ***32*** *wins by an innings and 400 runs or more, the most recent being* ***an innings and 425 by Meghalaya v Mizoram*** *and* ***an innings and 405 by Chandigarh v Manipur, both at Kolkata in 2019-20****.*

There have been ***25*** *wins by 500 runs or more, the most recent being 568 runs by Somerset v Cardiff MCCU at Taunton in 2019.*

There have been ***34*** *wins by a team losing only one wicket, the most recent being by* ***Kent v Sussex at Canterbury in 2020****.*

TIED MATCHES

Since 1948, a tie has been recognised only when the scores are level with all the wickets down in the fourth innings. There have been **40** instances since then, including two Tests (see Test record section); Sussex have featured in five of those, Essex and Kent in four each.

The most recent instances are:

Kalutara PCC v Police at Colombo (Burgher)	2016-17
Guyana v Windward Islands at Providence	2017-18
Chilaw Marians v Burgher at Katunayake	2017-18
Negombo v Kalutara Town at Gampaha	2017-18
Bloomfield v Army at Colombo (Moors)	2017-18
Somerset v Lancashire at Taunton	2018

MATCHES COMPLETED ON FIRST DAY

(Since 1946)

Derbyshire v Somerset at Chesterfield, June 11	1947
Lancashire v Sussex at Manchester, July 12	1950
Surrey v Warwickshire at The Oval, May 16	1953
Somerset v Lancashire at Bath, June 6 (H. F. T. Buse's benefit)	1953
Kent v Worcestershire at Tunbridge Wells, June 15	1960
Griqualand West v Easterns at Kimberley, March 10	2010-11

SHORTEST COMPLETED MATCHES

Balls		
121	Quetta (forfeit and 41) v Rawalpindi (forfeit and 44-1) at Islamabad	2008-09
350	Somerset (35 and 44) v Middlesex (86) at Lord's	1899
352	Victoria (82 and 57) v Tasmania (104 and 37-7) at Launceston	1850-51
372	Victoria (80 and 50) v Tasmania (97 and 35-2) at Launceston	1853-54

LIST A ONE-DAY RECORDS

List A is a concept intended to provide an approximate equivalent in one-day cricket of first-class status. It was introduced by the Association of Cricket Statisticians and Historians and is now recognised by the ICC, with a separate category for Twenty20 cricket. Further details are available at stats.acscricket.com/ListA/Description.html. List A games comprise:

(a) One-day internationals.
(b) Other international matches (e.g. A-team internationals).
(c) Premier domestic one-day tournaments in Test-playing countries.
(d) Official tourist matches against the main first-class teams (e.g. counties, states and Board XIs).

The following matches are excluded:

(a) Matches originally scheduled as less than 40 overs per side (e.g. Twenty20 games).
(b) World Cup warm-up games.
(c) Tourist matches against teams outside the major domestic competitions (e.g. universities).
(d) Festival games and pre-season friendlies.

This section covers one-day cricket to December 31, 2020. Bold type denotes performances in the calendar year 2020 or, in career figures, players who appeared in List A cricket in that year.

BATTING RECORDS

HIGHEST INDIVIDUAL INNINGS

268	A. D. Brown	Surrey v Glamorgan at The Oval	2002
264	R. G. Sharma	India v Sri Lanka at Kolkata	2014-15
257	D. J. M. Short	Western Australia v Queensland at Sydney	2018-19
248	S. Dhawan	India A v South Africa A at Pretoria	2013
237*	M. J. Guptill	New Zealand v West Indies at Wellington	2014-15
229*	B. R. Dunk	Tasmania v Queensland at Sydney	2014-15
222*	R. G. Pollock	Eastern Province v Border at East London	1974-75
222	J. M. How	Central Districts v Northern Districts at Hamilton	2012-13
220*	B. M. Duckett	England Lions v Sri Lanka A at Canterbury	2016
219	V. Sehwag	India v West Indies at Indore	2011-12
215	C. H. Gayle	West Indies v Zimbabwe at Canberra	2014-15
212*	S. V. Samson	Kerala v Goa at Alur	2019-20
210*	Fakhar Zaman	Pakistan v Zimbabwe at Bulawayo	2018
209*	Abid Ali	Islamabad v Peshawar at Peshawar	2017-18
209	R. G. Sharma	India v Australia at Bangalore	2013-14
208*	R. G. Sharma	India v Sri Lanka at Mohali	2017-18
208*	Soumya Sarkar	Abahani v Sheikh Jamal Dhanmondi at Savar	2018-19
207	Mohammad Ali	Pakistan Customs v DHA at Sialkot	2004-05
206	A. I. Kallicharran	Warwickshire v Oxfordshire at Birmingham	1984
204*	Khalid Latif	Karachi Dolphins v Quetta Bears at Karachi	2008-09
203	A. D. Brown	Surrey v Hampshire at Guildford	1997
203	Y. B. Jaiswal	Mumbai v Jharkhand at Alur	2019-20
202*	A. Barrow	Natal v SA African XI at Durban	1975-76
202*	P. J. Hughes	Australia A v South Africa A at Darwin	2014
202	T. M. Head	South Australia v Western Australia at Sydney	2015-16
202	K. V. Kaushal	Uttarakhand v Sikkim at Nadiad	2018-19
201*	R. S. Bopara	Essex v Leicestershire at Leicester	2008
201	V. J. Wells	Leicestershire v Berkshire at Leicester	1996
200*	S. R. Tendulkar	India v South Africa at Gwalior	2009-10
200	Kamran Akmal	WAPDA v Habib Bank at Hyderabad	2017-18
200	M. B. van Buuren	Gauteng v Western Province at Johannesburg	2018-19

MOST RUNS

	Career	*M*	*I*	*NO*	*R*	*HS*	*100*	*Avge*
G. A. Gooch	1973–1997	614	601	48	22,211	198*	44	40.16
G. A. Hick	*1983*–2008	651	630	96	22,059	172*	40	41.30
S. R. Tendulkar	*1989–2011*	551	538	55	21,999	200*	60	45.54
K. C. Sangakkara	***1997–2019***	**529**	**501**	**54**	**19,456**	**169**	**39**	**43.52**
I. V. A. Richards	1973–1993	500	466	61	16,995	189*	26	41.96
R. T. Ponting	*1992*–2013	456	445	53	16,363	164	34	41.74
C. G. Greenidge	1970–1992	440	436	33	16,349	186*	33	40.56
S. T. Jayasuriya	*1989–2011*	557	542	25	16,128	189	31	31.19
A. J. Lamb	1972–1995	484	463	63	15,658	132*	19	39.14
D. L. Haynes	1976–1996	419	416	44	15,651	152*	28	42.07
S. C. Ganguly	*1989–2011*	437	421	43	15,622	183	31	41.32
K. J. Barnett	1979–2005	527	500	54	15,564	136	17	34.89
D. P. M. D. Jayawardene	*1995*–2016	546	509	51	15,364	163*	21	33.54
R. Dravid	*1992*–2011	449	416	55	15,271	153	21	42.30
M. G. Bevan	*1989–2006*	427	385	124	15,103	157*	13	57.86

FASTEST FIFTIES

Balls			
12	K. Weeraratne	Ragama v Kurunegala Youth at Colombo (Thurstan)	2005-06
14	R. K. Kleinveldt	Western Province v KwaZulu-Natal at Durban	2010-11
15	Salman Butt	National Bank v Lahore Eagles at Lahore	2008-09
16	A. V. Kale	Maharashtra v Baroda at Vadodara	1994-95
16	A. B. de Villiers	South Africa v West Indies at Johannesburg	2014-15
16	T. C. Bruce	Central Districts v Canterbury at New Plymouth	2015-16
16	Anwar Ali	Baluchistan v Khyber Pakhtunkhwa at Faisalabad	2018

FASTEST HUNDREDS

Balls			
31	A. B. de Villiers	South Africa v West Indies at Johannesburg	2014-15
36	C. J. Anderson	New Zealand v West Indies at Queenstown	2013-14
37	Shahid Afridi	Pakistan v Sri Lanka at Nairobi	1996-97
38	R. Powell	Jamaica v Leeward Islands at Conaree	2019-20
39	D. S. Weerakkody	Sinhalese v Burgher at Colombo (BRC)	2019-20
40	Y. K. Pathan	Baroda v Maharashtra at Ahmedabad	2009-10
43	R. R. Watson	Scotland v Somerset at Edinburgh	2003
44	M. A. Ealham	Kent v Derbyshire at Maidstone	1995
44	M. V. Boucher	South Africa v Zimbabwe at Potchefstroom	2006-07
44	T. C. Smith	Lancashire v Worcestershire at Worcester	2012
44	D. I. Stevens	Kent v Sussex at Canterbury	2013

HIGHEST PARTNERSHIP FOR EACH WICKET

367*	for 1st	M. N. van Wyk/C. S. Delport, Dolphins v Knights at Bloemfontein	2014-15
372	for 2nd	C. H. Gayle/M. N. Samuels, West Indies v Zimbabwe at Canberra	2014-15
338	for 3rd	S. V. Samson/S. Baby, Kerala v Goa at Alur	2019-20
276	for 4th	Mominul Haque/A. R. S. Silva, Prime Doleshwar v Abahani at Bogra	2013-14
267*	for 5th	Minhazul Abedin/Khaled Mahmud, Bangladeshis v Bahawalpur at Karachi	1997-98
272	for 6th	A. K. Markram/F. Behardien, Titans v Cape Cobras at Cape Town	2018-19
215*	for 7th	S. Singh/G. H. Dockrell, Leinster v Northern at Dublin	2018
203	for 8th	Shahid Iqbal/Haaris Ayaz, Karachi Whites v Hyderabad at Karachi	1998-99
155	for 9th	C. M. W. Read/A. J. Harris, Nottinghamshire v Durham at Nottingham	2006
128	for 10th	A. Ashish Reddy/M. Ravi Kiran, Hyderabad v Kerala at Secunderabad	2014-15

BOWLING RECORDS

BEST BOWLING ANALYSES

8-10	S. Nadeem	Jharkhand v Rajasthan at Chennai	2018-19
8-15	R. L. Sanghvi	Delhi v Himachal Pradesh at Una	1997-98
8-19	W. P. U. J. C. Vaas	Sri Lanka v Zimbabwe at Colombo (SSC)	2001-02
8-20*	D. T. Kottehewa	Nondescripts v Ragama at Colombo (Moors)	2007-08
8-21	M. A. Holding	Derbyshire v Sussex at Hove	1988
8-26	K. D. Boyce	Essex v Lancashire at Manchester	1971
8-30	G. D. R. Eranga	Burgher v Army at Colombo (Colts)	2007-08
8-31	D. L. Underwood	Kent v Scotland at Edinburgh	1987
8-38	B. A. Mavuta	Rising Stars v Manicaland Mountaineers at Harare	2017-18
8-40	Yeasin Arafat	Gazi Group Cricketers v Abahani at Fatullah	2017-18
8-43	S. W. Tait	South Australia v Tasmania at Adelaide	2003-04
8-52	K. A. Stoute	West Indies A v Lancashire at Manchester	2010
8-66	S. R. G. Francis	Somerset v Derbyshire at Derby	2004

* *Including two hat-tricks.*

MOST WICKETS

	Career	*M*	*B*	*R*	*W*	*BB*	*4I*	*Avge*
Wasim Akram	*1984–2003*	594	29,719	19,303	881	5-10	46	21.91
A. A. Donald	*1985–2003*	458	22,856	14,942	684	6-15	38	21.84
M. Muralitharan	*1991–2010*	453	23,734	15,270	682	7-30	29	22.39
Waqar Younis	*1988–2003*	412	19,841	15,098	675	7-36	44	22.36
J. K. Lever	1968–1990	481	23,208	13,278	674	5-8	34	19.70
J. E. Emburey	1975–2000	536	26,399	16,811	647	5-23	26	25.98
I. T. Botham	1973–1993	470	22,899	15,264	612	5-27	18	24.94

WICKETKEEPING AND FIELDING RECORDS

MOST DISMISSALS IN AN INNINGS

8	(8 ct)	D. J. S. Taylor	Somerset v Combined Universities at Taunton	1982
8	(5ct, 3st)	S. J. Palframan	Boland v Easterns at Paarl	1997-98
8	(8ct)	D. J. Pipe	Worcestershire v Hertfordshire at Hertford	2001
8	(6ct, 2st)	P. M. Nevill	New South Wales v Cricket Aus XI at Sydney	2017-18

There have been ***15*** *instances of seven dismissals in an innings, the most recent being L. U. Igalagamage (6ct, 1st) for Nondescripts v Army at Colombo (SSC) in 2019-20.*

MOST CATCHES IN AN INNINGS IN THE FIELD

There have been **16** instances of a fielder taking five catches in an innings. The most recent are:

5	A. R. McBrine	Ireland v Sri Lanka A at Belfast	2014
5	Farhad Hossain	Prime Doleshwar v Sheikh Jamal Dhanmondi at Fatullah	2017-18
5	Zahid Zakhail	Amo v Boost at Kabul	2018
5	Mominul Haque	Legends of Rupganj v Abahani at Savar	2018-19

TEAM RECORDS

HIGHEST INNINGS TOTALS

496-4	(50 overs)	Surrey v Gloucestershire at The Oval	2007
481-6	(50 overs)	England v Australia at Nottingham	2018
458-4	(50 overs)	India A v Leicestershire at Leicester	2018
445-8	(50 overs)	Nottinghamshire v Northamptonshire at Nottingham	2016
444-3	(50 overs)	England v Pakistan at Nottingham	2016

443-9	(50 overs)	Sri Lanka v Netherlands at Amstelveen	2006
439-2	(50 overs)	South Africa v West Indies at Johannesburg	2014-15
438-4	(50 overs)	South Africa v India at Mumbai	2014-15
438-5	(50 overs)	Surrey v Glamorgan at The Oval	2002
438-9	(49.5 overs)	South Africa v Australia at Johannesburg	2005-06
434-4	(50 overs)	Australia v South Africa at Johannesburg	2005-06
434-4	(50 overs)	Jamaica v Trinidad & Tobago at Coolidge	2016-17
433-3	(50 overs)	India A v South Africa A at Pretoria	2013
433-7	(50 overs)	Nottinghamshire v Leicestershire at Nottingham	2019

LOWEST INNINGS TOTALS

18	(14.3 overs)	West Indies Under-19 v Barbados at Blairmont	2007-08
19	(10.5 overs)	Saracens v Colts at Colombo (Colts)	2012-13
23	(19.4 overs)	Middlesex v Yorkshire at Leeds	1974
24	(17.1 overs)	Oman v Scotland at Al Amerat	2018-19
30	(20.4 overs)	Chittagong v Sylhet at Dhaka	2002-03
31	(13.5 overs)	Border v South Western Districts at East London	2007-08
34	(21.1 overs)	Saurashtra v Mumbai at Mumbai	1999-2000
35	(18 overs)	Zimbabwe v Sri Lanka at Harare	2003-04
35	(20.2 overs)	Cricket Coaching School v Abahani at Fatullah	2013-14
35	(15.3 overs)	Rajasthan v Railways at Nagpur	2014-15
35	**(12 overs)**	**USA v Nepal at Kirtipur**	**2019-20**
36	(25.4 overs)	Leicestershire v Sussex at Leicester	1973
36	(18.4 overs)	Canada v Sri Lanka at Paarl	2002-03

LIST A TWENTY20 RECORDS

This section covers Twenty20 cricket to December 31, 2020. Bold type denotes performances in the calendar year 2020 or, in career figures, players who appeared in Twenty20 cricket in that year.

BATTING RECORDS

HIGHEST INDIVIDUAL INNINGS

175*	C. H. Gayle	RC Bangalore v Pune Warriors at Bangalore	2012-13
172	A. J. Finch	Australia v Zimbabwe at Harare	2018
162*	H. Masakadza	Mountaineers v Mashonaland Eagles at Bulawayo	2015-16
162*	Hazratullah Zazai	Afghanistan v Ireland at Dehradun	2018-19
161	A. Lyth	Yorkshire v Northamptonshire at Leeds	2017
158*	B. B. McCullum	Kolkata Knight Riders v RC Bangalore at Bangalore	2007-08
158*	B. B. McCullum	Warwickshire v Derbyshire at Birmingham	2015
156	A. J. Finch	Australia v England at Southampton	2013
153*	L. J. Wright	Sussex v Essex at Chelmsford	2014
152*	G. R. Napier	Essex v Sussex at Chelmsford	2008
151*	C. H. Gayle	Somerset v Kent at Taunton	2015
150*	Kamran Akmal	Lahore Whites v Islamabad at Rawalpindi	2017-18

MOST RUNS

	Career	*M*	*I*	*NO*	*R*	*HS*	*100*	*Avge*	*SR*
C. H. Gayle	**2005–2020**	**411**	**403**	**48**	**13,584**	**175***	**22**	**38.26**	**146.72**
K. A. Pollard	**2006–2020**	**531**	**471**	**137**	**10,579**	**104**	**1**	**31.67**	**152.52**
Shoaib Malik	**2004–2020**	**412**	**384**	**104**	**10,387**	**95***	**0**	**37.09**	**125.93**
B. B. McCullum	2004–2018	370	364	33	9,922	158*	7	29.97	136.49
D. A. Warner	**2006–2020**	**298**	**297**	**38**	**9,824**	**135***	**8**	**37.93**	**141.55**
V. Kohli	**2006–2020**	**299**	**284**	**54**	**9,500**	**113**	**5**	**41.30**	**133.95**
A. J. Finch	**2008–2020**	**305**	**300**	**32**	**9,448**	**172**	**8**	**35.25**	**142.22**
A. B. de Villiers	**2003–2020**	**325**	**306**	**63**	**9,111**	**133***	**4**	**37.49**	**150.19**
R. G. Sharma	**2006–2020**	**340**	**327**	**47**	**8,974**	**118**	**6**	**32.05**	**133.50**
S. K. Raina	2006–2018	319	303	46	8,391	126*	4	32.64	138.00
S. R. Watson	**2004–2020**	**343**	**335**	**34**	**8,822**	**124***	**6**	**29.30**	**138.31**
L. J. Wright	**2004–2020**	**325**	**302**	**27**	**7,999**	**153***	**7**	**29.08**	**142.78**
S. Dhawan	**2006–2020**	**279**	**276**	**29**	**7,992**	**106***	**2**	**32.35**	**125.08**
D. R. Smith	2005–2019	337	327	27	7,870	110*	5	26.23	127.44
A. D. Hales	**2009–2020**	**276**	**273**	**19**	**7,536**	**116***	**3**	**29.66**	**143.54**
R. N. ten Doeschate	**2003–2020**	**369**	**329**	**78**	**7,524**	**121***	**2**	**29.97**	**134.09**

FASTEST FIFTIES

Balls			
12	Yuvraj Singh	India v England at Durban	2007-08
12	C. H. Gayle	Melbourne Ren v Adelaide Str at Melbourne	2015-16
12	Hazratullah Zazai	Kabul Zwanan v Balkh Legends at Sharjah	2018-19
13	M. E. Trescothick	Somerset v Hampshire at Taunton	2010
13	M. Ahsan	Austria v Luxembourg at Ilfov	2019

There are nine instances of 14 balls.

FASTEST HUNDREDS

Balls			
30	C. H. Gayle	RC Bangalore v Pune Warriors at Bangalore	2012-13
32	R. R. Pant	Delhi v Himachal Pradesh at Delhi	2017-18
33	W. J. Lubbe	North West v Limpopo at Paarl	2018-19
34	A. Symonds	Kent v Middlesex at Maidstone	2004
35	L. P. van der Westhuizen	Namibia v Kenya at Windhoek	2011-12
35	D. A. Miller	South Africa v Bangladesh at Potchefstroom	2017-18
35	R. G. Sharma	India v Sri Lanka at Indore	2017-18
35	M. J. Guptill	Worcestershire v Northamptonshire at Northampton	2018
35	S. Wickramasekara	Czech Republic v Turkey at Ilfov	2019
35	**Khushdil Shah**	**Southern Punjab v Sindh at Rawalpindi**	**2020-21**

HIGHEST PARTNERSHIP FOR EACH WICKET

236	for 1st	Hazratullah Zazai/Usman Ghani, Afghanistan v Ireland at Dehradun	2018-19
229	for 2nd	V. Kohli/A. B. de Villiers, RC Bangalore v Gujarat Lions at Bangalore	2015-16
213	for 3rd	S. S. Iyer/S. A. Yadav, Mumbai v Sikkim at Indore	2018-19
202*	for 4th	M. C. Juneja/A. Malik, Gujarat v Kerala at Indore	2012-13
171	**for 5th**	**A. J. Hose/D. R. Mousley, Warwickshire v Northants at Birmingham**	**2020**
161	for 6th	K. Lewis/A. D. Russell, Jamaica Tallawahs v Trinbago KR at Port-of-Spain	2018
107*	for 7th	L. Abeyratne/P. S. R. Anurudhda, Colombo v Chilaw Marians at Colombo	2015-16
120	for 8th	Azhar Mahmood/I. Udana, Wayamba v Uva at Colombo (RPS)	2012
69	for 9th	C. J. Anderson/J. H. Davey, Somerset v Surrey at The Oval	2017
63	for 10th	G. D. Elliott/Zulfiqar Babar, Quetta Glad. v Peshawar Zalmi at Sharjah	2015-16

BOWLING RECORDS

BEST BOWLING ANALYSES

7-18	C. N. Ackermann	Leicestershire v Warwickshire at Leicester	2019
6-5	A. V. Suppiah	Somerset v Glamorgan at Cardiff	2011
6-6	Shakib Al Hasan	Barbados v Trinidad & Tobago at Bridgetown	2013
6-7	S. L. Malinga	Melbourne Stars v Perth Scorchers at Perth	2012-13
6-7	K. A. Jamieson	Canterbury v Auckland at Auckland	2018-19
6-7	D. L. Chahar	India v Bangladesh at Nagpur	2019-20
6-8	B. A. W. Mendis	Sri Lanka v Zimbabwe at Hambantota	2012-13
6-8	**A. M. Fernando**	**Chilaw Marians v Negombo at Colombo (CCC)**	**2019-20**
6-9	P. Fojela	Border v Easterns at East London	2014-15
6-11	I. S. Sodhi	Adelaide Strikers v Sydney Thunder at Sydney	2016-17
6-12	A. S. Joseph	Mumbai Indians v Sunrisers Hyderabad at Hyderabad	2018-19

MOST WICKETS

	Career	*M*	*B*	*R*	*W*	*BB*	*4I*	*Avge*	*ER*
D. J. Bravo	***2005–2020***	**471**	**9,187**	**12,611**	**512**	**5-23**	**11**	**24.63**	**8.23**
S. P. Narine	***2010–2020***	**351**	**8,030**	**8,113**	**390**	**5-19**	**12**	**20.80**	**6.06**
S. L. Malinga	***2004–2019***	**294**	**6,484**	**7,653**	**389**	**6-7**	**15**	**19.67**	**7.08**
Imran Tahir	***2005–2020***	**306**	**6,557**	**7,607**	**382**	**5-23**	**12**	**19.91**	**6.96**
Sohail Tanvir	***2004–2020***	**355**	**7,440**	**9,146**	**368**	**6-14**	**9**	**24.85**	**7.37**
Shakib Al Hasan	***2006–2020***	**317**	**6,691**	**7,663**	**360**	**6-6**	**12**	**21.28**	**6.87**
Shahid Afridi	**2004–*2020***	**322**	**6,838**	**7,653**	**342**	**5-7**	**11**	**22.37**	**6.71**
Rashid Khan	***2015–2020***	**243**	**5,593**	**5,869**	**335**	**5-3**	**8**	**17.51**	**6.29**
Wahab Riaz	***2004–2020***	**268**	**5,693**	**6,900**	**316**	**5-8**	**3**	**21.83**	**7.27**
A. D. Russell	***2009–2020***	**348**	**5,718**	**7,933**	**308**	**4-11**	**8**	**25.75**	**8.32**
K. A. Pollard	**2006–*2020***	**531**	**5,246**	**7,188**	**293**	**4-15**	**7**	**24.53**	**8.22**

	Career	*M*	*B*	*R*	*W*	*BB*	*4I*	*Avge*	*ER*
Yasir Arafat	*2005–2016*	226	4,702	6,344	281	4-5	10	22.57	8.09
Saeed Ajmal	*2004–2017*	195	4,338	4,706	271	4-14	8	17.36	6.50
Mohammad Nabi	***2009–2020***	**274**	**5,463**	**6,306**	**270**	**5-15**	**8**	**23.35**	**6.92**
C. H. Morris	***2010–2020***	**218**	**4,612**	**5,966**	**270**	**4-9**	**8**	**22.09**	**7.76**

WICKETKEEPING AND FIELDING RECORDS

MOST DISMISSALS IN AN INNINGS

7 (7ct)	E. F. M. U. Fernando	Lankan v Moors at Colombo (Bloomfield)	2005-06

MOST CATCHES IN AN INNINGS IN THE FIELD

5	Manzoor Ilahi	Jammu & Kashmir v Delhi at Delhi	2010-11
5	J. M. Vince	Hampshire v Leeward Islands at North Sound	2010-11
5	J. L. Ontong	Cape Cobras v Knights at Cape Town	2014-15
5	A. K. V. Adikari	Chilaw Marians v Bloomfield at Colombo (SSC)	2014-15
5	P. G. Fulton	Canterbury v Northern Districts at Hamilton	2015-16
5	M. W. Machan	Sussex v Glamorgan at Hove	2016

TEAM RECORDS

HIGHEST INNINGS TOTALS

278-3	(20 overs)	Afghanistan v Ireland at Dehradun	2018-19
278-4	(20 overs)	Czech Republic v Turkey at Ilfov	2019
267-2	(20 overs)	Trinbago Knight Riders v Jamaica Tallawahs at Kingston	2019
263-3	(20 overs)	Australia v Sri Lanka at Pallekele	2016
263-5	(20 overs)	RC Bangalore v Pune Warriors at Bangalore	2012-13
262-4	(20 overs)	North West v Limpopo at Paarl	2018-19
260-4	(20 overs)	Yorkshire v Northamptonshire at Leeds	2017
260-5	(20 overs)	India v Sri Lanka at Indore	2017-18
260-6	(20 overs)	Sri Lanka v Kenya at Johannesburg	2007-08

LOWEST INNINGS TOTALS

21	(8.3 overs)	Turkey v Czech Republic at Ilfov	2019
28	(11.3 overs)	Turkey v Luxembourg at Ilfov	2019
30	(11.1 overs)	Tripura v Jharkhand at Dhanbad	2009-10
32	(8.5 overs)	Turkey v Austria at Ilfov	2019
39	(10.3 overs)	Netherlands v Sri Lanka at Chittagong	2013-14

ALL-FORMAT CAREER RECORDS

This section covers combined records in first-class, List A and Twenty20 cricket to December 31, 2020. Bold type denotes a player who appeared in 2020. Daggers denote players who appeared in first-class and List A formats, and double daggers players who appeared in all three; all other players appeared only in first-class cricket.

MOST RUNS

	Career	*M*	*I*	*NO*	*R*	*HS*	*100*	*Avge*
G. A. Gooch†	1973–2000	1,195	1,591	123	67,057	333	172	45.67
G. A. Hick‡	*1983*–2008	1,214	1,537	183	64,372	405*	178	47.54
J. B. Hobbs	1905–1934	826	1,315	106	61,237	316*	197	50.65
F. E. Woolley	1906–1938	979	1,532	85	58,969	305*	145	40.75
G. Boycott†	1962–1986	922	1,316	206	58,521	261*	159	52.72
E. H. Hendren	1907–1938	833	1,300	166	57,611	301*	170	50.80
D. L. Amiss†	1960–1987	1,062	1,530	160	55,942	262*	117	40.83
C. P. Mead	1905–1936	814	1,340	185	55,061	280*	153	47.67
W. G. Grace	1865–1908	880	1,493	105	54,896	344	126	39.55
C. G. Greenidge†	1970–1992	963	1,325	108	53,703	273*	125	44.12

MOST WICKETS

	Career	*M*	*B*	*R*	*W*	*BB*	*5I*	*Avge*
W. Rhodes	1898–1930	1,107	184,940	69,993	4,187	9-24	287	16.71
A. P. Freeman	1914–1936	592	154,658	69,577	3,776	10-53	386	18.42
C. W. L. Parker	1903–1935	635	157,328	63,819	3,278	10-79	277	19.46
J. T. Hearne	1888–1923	639	144,470	54,352	3,061	9-32	255	17.75
D. L. Underwood†	1963–1987	1,089	159,571	61,111	3,037	9-28	161	20.12
F. J. Titmus†	1949–1982	941	180,576	67,396	2,989	9-52	171	22.54
T. W. J. Goddard	1922–1952	593	142,186	59,116	2,979	10-113	251	19.84
D. Shackleton†	1948–1973	684	161,071	54,175	2,898	9-30	194	18.69
W. G. Grace	1865–1908	880	126,056	51,545	2,876	10-49	246	17.92
A. S. Kennedy	1907–1936	677	150,917	61,034	2,874	10-37	225	21.23

The figure for balls bowled by Grace is uncertain.

MOST DISMISSALS

	Career	*M*	*Dis*	*Ct*	*St*
R. W. Taylor†	1960–1988	972	2,070	1,819	251
S. J. Rhodes‡	1981–2004	920	1,929	1,671	258
R. C. Russell‡	1981–2004	946	1,885	1,658	227
A. P. E. Knott†	1964–1985	829	1,741	1,553	188
J. T. Murray†	1952–1975	784	1,724	1,432	292
Kamran Akmal‡	***1997–2020***	**852**	**1,643**	**1,382**	**261**
C. M. W. Read‡	1995–2017	801	1,583	1,430	153
P. A. Nixon‡	1989–*2011*	862	1,549	1,360	189
D. L. Bairstow†	1970–1990	888	1,545	1,372	173
A. C. Gilchrist‡	*1992*–2013	648	1,498	1,356	142

Total dismissals include catches taken when not keeping wicket.

MOST CATCHES IN THE FIELD

	Career	*M*	*Ct*		*Career*	*M*	*Ct*
F. E. Woolley	1906–1938	979	1,018	G. A. Hick‡	*1983*–2008	1,214	1,008

TEST RECORDS

This section covers all Tests up to January 25, 2021. Bold type denotes performances since January 1, 2020, or, in career figures, players who have appeared in Test cricket since that date.

BATTING RECORDS

HIGHEST INDIVIDUAL INNINGS

400*	B. C. Lara	West Indies v England at St John's	2003-04
380	M. L. Hayden	Australia v Zimbabwe at Perth	2003-04
375	B. C. Lara	West Indies v England at St John's	1993-94
374	D. P. M. D. Jayawardene	Sri Lanka v South Africa at Colombo (SSC)	2006
365*	G. S. Sobers	West Indies v Pakistan at Kingston	1957-58
364	L. Hutton	England v Australia at The Oval	1938
340	S. T. Jayasuriya	Sri Lanka v India at Colombo (RPS)	1997-98
337	Hanif Mohammad	Pakistan v West Indies at Bridgetown	1957-58
336*	W. R. Hammond	England v New Zealand at Auckland	1932-33
335*	D. A. Warner	Australia v Pakistan at Adelaide	2019-20
334*	M. A. Taylor	Australia v Pakistan at Peshawar	1998-99
334	D. G. Bradman	Australia v England at Leeds	1930
333	G. A. Gooch	England v India at Lord's	1990
333	C. H. Gayle	West Indies v Sri Lanka at Galle	2010-11
329*	M. J. Clarke	Australia v India at Sydney	2011-12
329	Inzamam-ul-Haq	Pakistan v New Zealand at Lahore	2002
325	A. Sandham	England v West Indies at Kingston	1929-30
319	V. Sehwag	India v South Africa at Chennai	2007-08
319	K. C. Sangakkara	Sri Lanka v Bangladesh at Chittagong	2013-14
317	C. H. Gayle	West Indies v South Africa at St John's	2004-05
313	Younis Khan	Pakistan v Sri Lanka at Karachi	2008-09
311*	H. M. Amla	South Africa v England at The Oval	2012
311	R. B. Simpson	Australia v England at Manchester	1964
310*	J. H. Edrich	England v New Zealand at Leeds	1965
309	V. Sehwag	India v Pakistan at Multan	2003-04
307	R. M. Cowper	Australia v England at Melbourne	1965-66
304	D. G. Bradman	Australia v England at Leeds	1934
303*	K. K. Nair	India v England at Chennai	2016-17
302*	Azhar Ali	Pakistan v West Indies at Dubai	2016-17
302	L. G. Rowe	West Indies v England at Bridgetown	1973-74
302	B. B. McCullum	New Zealand v India at Wellington	2013-14

*There have been **67** further instances of 250 or more runs in a Test innings.*

The highest innings for the countries not mentioned above are:

266	D. L. Houghton	Zimbabwe v Sri Lanka at Bulawayo	1994-95
219*	Mushfiqur Rahim	Bangladesh v Zimbabwe at Mirpur	2018-19
118	K. J. O'Brien	Ireland v Pakistan at Malahide	2018
102	Rahmat Shah	Afghanistan v Bangladesh at Chittagong	2019-20

HUNDRED ON TEST DEBUT

C. Bannerman (165*)	Australia v England at Melbourne	1876-77
W. G. Grace (152)	England v Australia at The Oval	1880
H. Graham (107)	Australia v England at Lord's	1893
†K. S. Ranjitsinhji (154*)	England v Australia at Manchester	1896
†P. F. Warner (132*)	England v South Africa at Johannesburg	1898-99
†R. A. Duff (104)	Australia v England at Melbourne	1901-02
§R. E. Foster (287)	England v Australia at Sydney	1903-04
G. Gunn (119)	England v Australia at Sydney	1907-08
†R. J. Hartigan (116)	Australia v England at Adelaide	1907-08

†H. L. Collins (104)	Australia v England at Sydney	1920-21
W. H. Ponsford (110)	Australia v England at Sydney	1924-25
A. A. Jackson (164)	Australia v England at Adelaide	1928-29
†G. A. Headley (176)	West Indies v England at Bridgetown	1929-30
J. E. Mills (117)	New Zealand v England at Wellington	1929-30
Nawab of Pataudi snr (102)	England v Australia at Sydney	1932-33
B. H. Valentine (136)	England v India at Bombay	1933-34
†L. Amarnath (118)	India v England at Bombay	1933-34
†P. A. Gibb (106)	England v South Africa at Johannesburg	1938-39
S. C. Griffith (140)	England v West Indies at Port-of-Spain	1947-48
A. G. Ganteaume (112)	West Indies v England at Port-of-Spain	1947-48
†J. W. Burke (101*)	Australia v England at Adelaide	1950-51
P. B. H. May (138)	England v South Africa at Leeds	1951
R. H. Shodhan (110)	India v Pakistan at Calcutta	1952-53
B. H. Pairaudeau (115)	West Indies v India at Port-of-Spain	1952-53
†O. G. Smith (104)	West Indies v Australia at Kingston	1954-55
A. G. Kripal Singh (100*)	India v New Zealand at Hyderabad	1955-56
C. C. Hunte (142)	West Indies v Pakistan at Bridgetown	1957-58
C. A. Milton (104*)	England v New Zealand at Leeds	1958
†A. A. Baig (112)	India v England at Manchester	1959
Hanumant Singh (105)	India v England at Delhi	1963-64
Khalid Ibadulla (166)	Pakistan v Australia at Karachi	1964-65
B. R. Taylor (105)	New Zealand v India at Calcutta	1964-65
K. D. Walters (155)	Australia v England at Brisbane	1965-66
J. H. Hampshire (107)	England v West Indies at Lord's	1969
†G. R. Viswanath (137)	India v Australia at Kanpur	1969-70
G. S. Chappell (108)	Australia v England at Perth	1970-71
‡§L. G. Rowe (214, 100*)	West Indies v New Zealand at Kingston	1971-72
A. I. Kallicharran (100*)	West Indies v New Zealand at Georgetown	1971-72
R. E. Redmond (107)	New Zealand v Pakistan at Auckland	1972-73
†F. C. Hayes (106*)	England v West Indies at The Oval	1973
†C. G. Greenidge (107)	West Indies v India at Bangalore	1974-75
†L. Baichan (105*)	West Indies v Pakistan at Lahore	1974-75
G. J. Cosier (109)	Australia v West Indies at Melbourne	1975-76
S. Amarnath (124)	India v New Zealand at Auckland	1975-76
Javed Miandad (163)	Pakistan v New Zealand at Lahore	1976-77
†A. B. Williams (100)	West Indies v Australia at Georgetown	1977-78
†D. M. Wellham (103)	Australia v England at The Oval	1981
†Salim Malik (100*)	Pakistan v Sri Lanka at Karachi	1981-82
K. C. Wessels (162)	Australia v England at Brisbane	1982-83
W. B. Phillips (159)	Australia v Pakistan at Perth	1983-84
¶M. Azharuddin (110)	India v England at Calcutta	1984-85
D. S. B. P. Kuruppu (201*)	Sri Lanka v New Zealand at Colombo (CCC)	1986-87
†M. J. Greatbatch (107*)	New Zealand v England at Auckland	1987-88
M. E. Waugh (138)	Australia v England at Adelaide	1990-91
A. C. Hudson (163)	South Africa v West Indies at Bridgetown	1991-92
R. S. Kaluwitharana (132*)	Sri Lanka v Australia at Colombo (SSC)	1992-93
D. L. Houghton (121)	Zimbabwe v India at Harare	1992-93
P. K. Amre (103)	India v South Africa at Durban	1992-93
†G. P. Thorpe (114*)	England v Australia at Nottingham	1993
G. S. Blewett (102*)	Australia v England at Adelaide	1994-95
S. C. Ganguly (131)	India v England at Lord's	1996
†Mohammad Wasim (109*)	Pakistan v New Zealand at Lahore	1996-97
Ali Naqvi (115)	Pakistan v South Africa at Rawalpindi	1997-98
Azhar Mahmood (128*)	Pakistan v South Africa at Rawalpindi	1997-98
M. S. Sinclair (214)	New Zealand v West Indies at Wellington	1999-2000
†Younis Khan (107)	Pakistan v Sri Lanka at Rawalpindi	1999-2000
Aminul Islam (145)	Bangladesh v India at Dhaka	2000-01
†H. Masakadza (119)	Zimbabwe v West Indies at Harare	2001
T. T. Samaraweera (103*)	Sri Lanka v India at Colombo (SSC)	2001
Taufeeq Umar (104)	Pakistan v Bangladesh at Multan	2001-02

†Mohammad Ashraful (114)	Bangladesh v Sri Lanka at Colombo (SSC)	2001-02
V. Sehwag (105)	India v South Africa at Bloemfontein	2001-02
L. Vincent (104)	New Zealand v Australia at Perth	2001-02
S. B. Styris (107)	New Zealand v West Indies at St George's	2002
J. A. Rudolph (222*)	South Africa v Bangladesh at Chittagong	2003
‡Yasir Hameed (170, 105)	Pakistan v Bangladesh at Karachi	2003
†D. R. Smith (105*)	West Indies v South Africa at Cape Town	2003-04
A. J. Strauss (112)	England v New Zealand at Lord's	2004
M. J. Clarke (151)	Australia v India at Bangalore	2004-05
†A. N. Cook (104*)	England v India at Nagpur	2005-06
M. J. Prior (126*)	England v West Indies at Lord's	2007
M. J. North (117)	Australia v South Africa at Johannesburg	2008-09
†Fawad Alam (168)	Pakistan v Sri Lanka at Colombo (PSS)	2009
†I. J. L. Trott (119)	England v Australia at The Oval	2009
Umar Akmal (129)	Pakistan v New Zealand at Dunedin	2009-10
†A. B. Barath (104)	West Indies v Australia at Brisbane	2009-10
A. N. Petersen (100)	South Africa v India at Kolkata	2009-10
S. K. Raina (120)	India v Sri Lanka at Colombo (SSC)	2010
K. S. Williamson (131)	New Zealand v India at Ahmedabad	2010-11
†K. A. Edwards (110)	West Indies v India at Roseau	2011
S. E. Marsh (141)	Australia v Sri Lanka at Pallekele	2011-12
Abul Hasan (113)	Bangladesh v West Indies at Khulna	2012-13
†F. du Plessis (110*)	South Africa v Australia at Adelaide	2012-13
H. D. Rutherford (171)	New Zealand v England at Dunedin	2012-13
S. Dhawan (187)	India v Australia at Mohali	2012-13
R. G. Sharma (177)	India v West Indies at Kolkata	2013-14
†J. D. S. Neesham (137*)	New Zealand v India at Wellington	2013-14
S. van Zyl (101*)	South Africa v West Indies at Centurion	2014-15
A. C. Voges (130*)	Australia v West Indies at Roseau	2015
S. C. Cook (115)	South Africa v England at Centurion	2015-16
K. K. Jennings (112)	England v India at Mumbai	2016-17
T. A. Blundell (107*)	New Zealand v West Indies at Wellington	2017-18
K. J. O'Brien (118)	Ireland v Pakistan at Malahide	2018
P. P. Shaw (134)	India v West Indies at Rajkot	2018-19
B. T. Foakes (107)	England v Sri Lanka at Galle	2018-19
Abid Ali (109*)	Pakistan v Sri Lanka at Rawalpindi	2019-20

† *In his second innings of the match.*
‡ *L. G. Rowe and Yasir Hameed are the only batsmen to score a hundred in each innings on debut.*
§ *R. E. Foster (287, 19) and L. G. Rowe (214, 100*) are the only batsmen to score 300 on debut.*
¶ *M. Azharuddin is the only batsman to score hundreds in each of his first three Tests.*

L. Amarnath and S. Amarnath were father and son.
Ali Naqvi and Azhar Mahmood achieved the feat in the same innings.
Only Bannerman, Houghton, Aminul Islam and O'Brien scored hundreds in their country's first Test.

TWO SEPARATE HUNDREDS IN A TEST

Triple-Hundred and Hundred in a Test

G. A. Gooch (England)	333 and 123 v India at Lord's	1990
K. C. Sangakkara (Sri Lanka)	319 and 105 v Bangladesh at Chittagong	2013-14

The only instances in first-class cricket. M. A. Taylor (Australia) scored 334 and 92 v Pakistan at Peshawar in 1998-99.*

Double-Hundred and Hundred in a Test

K. D. Walters (Australia)	242 and 103 v West Indies at Sydney	1968-69
S. M. Gavaskar (India)	124 and 220 v West Indies at Port-of-Spain	1970-71
†L. G. Rowe (West Indies)	214 and 100* v New Zealand at Kingston	1971-72
G. S. Chappell (Australia)	247* and 133 v New Zealand at Wellington	1973-74
B. C. Lara (West Indies)	221 and 130 v Sri Lanka at Colombo (SSC)	2001-02

† *On Test debut.*

Two Hundreds in a Test

There have been **86** instances of a batsman scoring two separate hundreds in a Test, including the seven listed above. The most recent was by R. G. Sharma for India v South Africa at Visakhapatnam in 2019-20.

S. M. Gavaskar (India), R. T. Ponting (Australia) and D. A. Warner (Australia) all achieved the feat three times. C. L. Walcott scored twin hundreds twice in one series, for West Indies v Australia in 1954-55. L. G. Rowe and Yasir Hameed both did it on Test debut.

MOST DOUBLE-HUNDREDS

D. G. Bradman (A)	12	**V. Kohli (I)**	**7**	S. R. Tendulkar (I)	6
K. C. Sangakkara (SL)	11	M. S. Atapattu (SL)	6	Younis Khan (P)	6
B. C. Lara (WI)	9	Javed Miandad (P)	6	A. N. Cook (E)	5
W. R. Hammond (E)	7	R. T. Ponting (A)	6	R. Dravid (I)	5
D. P. M. D. Jayawardene (SL)	7	V. Sehwag (I)	6	G. C. Smith (SA)	5

M. J. Clarke (Australia) scored four double-hundreds in the calendar year 2012.

MOST HUNDREDS

S. R. Tendulkar (I)	51	M. J. Clarke (A)	28	V. Sehwag (I)	23
J. H. Kallis (SA)	45	A. R. Border (A)	27	M. Azharuddin (I)	22
R. T. Ponting (A)	41	**V. Kohli (I)**	**27**	I. R. Bell (E)	22
K. C. Sangakkara (SL)	38	G. C. Smith (SA)	27	G. Boycott (E)	22
R. Dravid (I)	36	**S. P. D. Smith (A)**	**27**	M. C. Cowdrey (E)	22
S. M. Gavaskar (I)	34	G. S. Sobers (WI)	26	A. B. de Villiers (SA)	22
D. P. M. D. Jayawardene (SL)	34	Inzamam-ul-Haq (P)	25	W. R. Hammond (E)	22
B. C. Lara (WI)	34	G. S. Chappell (A)	24	D. C. Boon (A)	21
Younis Khan (P)	34	Mohammad Yousuf (P)	24	R. N. Harvey (A)	21
A. N. Cook (E)	33	I. V. A. Richards (WI)	24	G. Kirsten (SA)	21
S. R. Waugh (A)	32	**D. A. Warner (A)**	**24**	A. J. Strauss (E)	21
S. Chanderpaul (WI)	30	**K. S. Williamson (NZ)**	**24**	K. F. Barrington (E)	20
M. L. Hayden (A)	30	Javed Miandad (P)	23	P. A. de Silva (SL)	20
D. G. Bradman (A)	29	J. L. Langer (A)	23	G. A. Gooch (E)	20
H. M. Amla (SA)	28	K. P. Pietersen (E)	23	M. E. Waugh (A)	20

The most hundreds for Zimbabwe is 12 by A. Flower, the most for Bangladesh is ***9*** *by* ***Mominul Haque*** *and* ***Tamim Iqbal****, the most for Ireland is 1 by K. J. O'Brien, and the most for Afghanistan is 1 by Rahmat Shah.*

MOST HUNDREDS AGAINST ONE TEAM

D. G. Bradman	19	Australia v England	S. R. Tendulkar	11	India v Australia
S. M. Gavaskar	13	India v West Indies	K. C. Sangakkara	10	Sri Lanka v Pakistan
J. B. Hobbs	12	England v Australia	G. S. Sobers	10	West Indies v England
S. P. D. Smith	**11**	**Australia v England**	S. R. Waugh	10	Australia v England

MOST DUCKS

	0s	*Inns*		*0s*	*Inns*
C. A. Walsh (WI)	43	185	C. E. L. Ambrose (WI)	26	145
C. S. Martin (NZ)	36	104	**J. M. Anderson (E)**	**26**	**217**
G. D. McGrath (A)	35	138	Danish Kaneria (P)	25	84
S. C. J. Broad (E)	**35**	**209**	D. K. Morrison (NZ)	24	71
S. K. Warne (A)	34	199	B. S. Chandrasekhar (I)	23	80
M. Muralitharan (SL/World)	33	164	H. M. R. K. B. Herath (SL)	23	144
I. Sharma (I)	**31**	**129**	M. Morkel (SA)	22	104
Zaheer Khan (I)	29	127	M. S. Atapattu (SL)	22	156
M. Dillon (WI)	26	68	S. R. Waugh (A)	22	260

	0s	*Inns*		*0s*	*Inns*
S. J. Harmison (E/World)	21	86	**S. T. Gabriel (WI)**	**20**	**75**
M. Ntini (SA)	21	116	B. S. Bedi (I)	20	101
Waqar Younis (P)	21	120	D. L. Vettori (NZ/World)	20	174
M. S. Panesar (E)	20	68	M. A. Atherton (E)	20	212

CARRYING BAT THROUGH TEST INNINGS

(Figures in brackets show team's total)

A. B. Tancred	26*	(47)	South Africa v England at Cape Town	1888-89
J. E. Barrett	67*	(176)†	Australia v England at Lord's	1890
R. Abel	132*	(307)	England v Australia at Sydney	1891-92
P. F. Warner	132*	(237)†	England v South Africa at Johannesburg	1898-99
W. W. Armstrong	159*	(309)	Australia v South Africa at Johannesburg	1902-03
J. W. Zulch	43*	(103)	South Africa v England at Cape Town	1909-10
W. Bardsley	193*	(383)	Australia v England at Lord's	1926
W. M. Woodfull	30*	(66)§	Australia v England at Brisbane	1928-29
W. M. Woodfull	73*	(193)‡	Australia v England at Adelaide	1932-33
W. A. Brown	206*	(422)	Australia v England at Lord's	1938
L. Hutton	202*	(344)	England v West Indies at The Oval	1950
L. Hutton	156*	(272)	England v Australia at Adelaide	1950-51
Nazar Mohammad¶	124*	(331)	Pakistan v India at Lucknow	1952-53
F. M. M. Worrell	191*	(372)	West Indies v England at Nottingham	1957
T. L. Goddard	56*	(99)	South Africa v Australia at Cape Town	1957-58
D. J. McGlew	127*	(292)	South Africa v New Zealand at Durban	1961-62
C. C. Hunte	60*	(131)	West Indies v Australia at Port-of-Spain	1964-65
G. M. Turner	43*	(131)	New Zealand v England at Lord's	1969
W. M. Lawry	49*	(107)	Australia v India at Delhi	1969-70
W. M. Lawry	60*	(116)‡	Australia v England at Sydney	1970-71
G. M. Turner	223*	(386)	New Zealand v West Indies at Kingston	1971-72
I. R. Redpath	159*	(346)	Australia v New Zealand at Auckland	1973-74
G. Boycott	99*	(215)	England v Australia at Perth	1979-80
S. M. Gavaskar	127*	(286)	India v Pakistan at Faisalabad	1982-83
Mudassar Nazar¶	152*	(323)	Pakistan v India at Lahore	1982-83
S. Wettimuny	63*	(144)	Sri Lanka v New Zealand at Christchurch	1982-83
D. C. Boon	58*	(103)	Australia v New Zealand at Auckland	1985-86
D. L. Haynes	88*	(211)	West Indies v Pakistan at Karachi	1986-87
G. A. Gooch	154*	(252)	England v West Indies at Leeds	1991
D. L. Haynes	75*	(176)	West Indies v England at The Oval	1991
A. J. Stewart	69*	(175)	England v Pakistan at Lord's	1992
D. L. Haynes	143*	(382)	West Indies v Pakistan at Port-of-Spain	1992-93
M. H. Dekker	68*	(187)	Zimbabwe v Pakistan at Rawalpindi	1993-94
M. A. Atherton	94*	(228)	England v New Zealand at Christchurch	1996-97
G. Kirsten	100*	(239)	South Africa v Pakistan at Faisalabad	1997-98
M. A. Taylor	169*	(350)	Australia v South Africa at Adelaide	1997-98
G. W. Flower	156*	(321)	Zimbabwe v Pakistan at Bulawayo	1997-98
Saeed Anwar	188*	(316)	Pakistan v India at Calcutta	1998-99
M. S. Atapattu	216*	(428)	Sri Lanka v Zimbabwe at Bulawayo	1999-2000
R. P. Arnold	104*	(231)	Sri Lanka v Zimbabwe at Harare	1999-2000
Javed Omar	85*	(168)†‡	Bangladesh v Zimbabwe at Bulawayo	2000-01
V. Sehwag	201*	(329)	India v Sri Lanka at Galle	2008
S. M. Katich	131*	(268)	Australia v New Zealand at Brisbane	2008-09
C. H. Gayle	165*	(317)	West Indies v Australia at Adelaide	2009-10
Imran Farhat	117*	(223)	Pakistan v New Zealand at Napier	2009-10
R. Dravid	146*	(300)	India v England at The Oval	2011
T. M. K. Mawoyo	163*	(412)	Zimbabwe v Pakistan at Bulawayo	2011-12
D. A. Warner	123*	(233)	Australia v New Zealand at Hobart	2011-12
C. A. Pujara	145*	(312)	India v Sri Lanka at Colombo (SSC)	2015-16
D. Elgar	118*	(214)	South Africa v England at Durban	2015-16
K. C. Brathwaite	142*	(337)	West Indies v Pakistan at Sharjah	2016-17

A. N. Cook	244*	(491)	England v Australia at Melbourne	2017-18
D. Elgar.	86*	(177)	South Africa v India at Johannesburg.	2017-18
D. Elgar.	141*	(311)	South Africa v Australia at Cape Town	2017-18
F. D. M. Karunaratne .	158*	(287)	Sri Lanka v South Africa at Galle	2018
T. W. M. Latham.	264*	(578)	New Zealand v Sri Lanka at Wellington	2018-19

† *On debut.* ‡ *One man absent.* § *Two men absent.* ¶ *Father and son.*

T. W. M. Latham (264) holds the record for the highest score by a player carrying his bat in a Test.*
D. L. Haynes and D. Elgar have achieved the feat on three occasions; Haynes also opened the batting and was last man out in each innings for West Indies v New Zealand at Dunedin, 1979-80.
G. M. Turner was the youngest at 22 years 63 days old when he first did it in 1969.

MOST RUNS IN A SERIES

	T	*I*	*NO*	*R*	*HS*	*100*	*Avge*		
D. G. Bradman	5	7	0	974	334	4	139.14	A v E	1930
W. R. Hammond. . .	5	9	1	905	251	4	113.12	E v A	1928-29
M. A. Taylor.	6	11	1	839	219	2	83.90	A v E	1989
R. N. Harvey.	5	9	0	834	205	4	92.66	A v SA	1952-53
I. V. A. Richards. . .	4	7	0	829	291	3	118.42	WI v E	1976
C. L. Walcott	5	10	0	827	155	5	82.70	WI v A	1954-55
G. S. Sobers	5	8	2	824	365*	3	137.33	WI v P	1957-58
D. G. Bradman	5	9	0	810	270	3	90.00	A v E	1936-37
D. G. Bradman	5	5	1	806	299*	4	201.50	A v SA	1931-32

MOST RUNS IN A CALENDAR YEAR

	T	*I*	*NO*	*R*	*HS*	*100*	*Avge*	*Year*
Mohammad Yousuf (P).	11	19	1	1,788	202	9	99.33	2006
I. V. A. Richards (WI).	11	19	0	1,710	291	7	90.00	1976
G. C. Smith (SA).	15	25	2	1,656	232	6	72.00	2008
M. J. Clarke (A).	11	18	3	1,595	329*	5	106.33	2012
S. R. Tendulkar (I).	14	23	3	1,562	214	7	78.10	2010
S. M. Gavaskar (I)	18	27	1	1,555	221	5	59.80	1979
R. T. Ponting (A).	15	28	5	1,544	207	6	67.13	2005
R. T. Ponting (A).	11	18	3	1,503	257	6	100.20	2003

M. Amarnath reached 1,000 runs in 1983 on May 3, in his ninth Test of the year.
The only case of 1,000 in a year before World War II was C. Hill of Australia: 1,060 in 1902.
M. L. Hayden (Australia) scored 1,000 runs in each year from 2001 to 2005.

MOST RUNS

		T	*I*	*NO*	*R*	*HS*	*100*	*Avge*
1	S. R. Tendulkar (India)	200	329	33	15,921	248*	51	53.78
2	R. T. Ponting (Australia).	168	287	29	13,378	257	41	51.85
3	J. H. Kallis (South Africa/World) .	166	280	40	13,289	224	45	55.37
4	R. Dravid (India/World)	164	286	32	13,288	270	36	52.31
5	A. N. Cook (England)	161	291	16	12,472	294	33	45.35
6	K. C. Sangakkara (Sri Lanka)	134	233	17	12,400	319	38	57.40
7	B. C. Lara (West Indies/World) . .	131	232	6	11,953	400*	34	52.88
8	S. Chanderpaul (West Indies)	164	280	49	11,867	203*	30	51.37
9	D. P. M. D. Jayawardene (SL) . . .	149	252	15	11,814	374	34	49.84
10	A. R. Border (Australia)	156	265	44	11,174	205	27	50.56
11	S. R. Waugh (Australia)	168	260	46	10,927	200	32	51.06
12	S. M. Gavaskar (India)	125	214	16	10,122	236*	34	51.12
13	Younis Khan (Pakistan)	118	213	19	10,099	313	34	52.05
14	H. M. Amla (South Africa)	124	215	16	9,282	311*	28	46.64
15	G. C. Smith (South Africa/Wld) . .	117	205	13	9,265	277	27	48.25
16	G. A. Gooch (England)	118	215	6	8,900	333	20	42.58
17	Javed Miandad (Pakistan)	124	189	21	8,832	280*	23	52.57

		T	*I*	*NO*	*R*	*HS*	*100*	*Avge*
18	Inzamam-ul-Haq (Pakistan/World)	120	200	22	8,830	329	25	49.60
19	V. V. S. Laxman (India)	134	225	34	8,781	281	17	45.97
20	A. B. de Villiers (South Africa)	114	191	18	8,765	278*	22	50.66
21	M. J. Clarke (Australia)	115	198	22	8,643	329*	28	49.10
22	M. L. Hayden (Australia)	103	184	14	8,625	380	30	50.73
23	V. Sehwag (India/World)	104	180	6	8,586	319	23	49.34
24	I. V. A. Richards (West Indies)	121	182	12	8,540	291	24	50.23
25	A. J. Stewart (England)	133	235	21	8,463	190	15	39.54
26	**J. E. Root (England)**	**99**	**181**	**14**	**8,249**	**254**	**19**	**49.39**
27	D. I. Gower (England)	117	204	18	8,231	215	18	44.25
28	K. P. Pietersen (England)	104	181	8	8,181	227	23	47.28
29	G. Boycott (England)	108	193	23	8,114	246*	22	47.72
30	G. S. Sobers (West Indies)	93	160	21	8,032	365*	26	57.78
31	M. E. Waugh (Australia)	128	209	17	8,029	153*	20	41.81
32	M. A. Atherton (England)	115	212	7	7,728	185*	16	37.69
33	I. R. Bell (England)	118	205	24	7,727	235	22	42.69
34	J. L. Langer (Australia)	105	182	12	7,696	250	23	45.27
35	M. C. Cowdrey (England)	114	188	15	7,624	182	22	44.06
36	C. G. Greenidge (West Indies)	108	185	16	7,558	226	19	44.72
37	**S. P. D. Smith (Australia)**	**77**	**139**	**17**	**7,540**	**239**	**27**	**61.80**
38	Mohammad Yousuf (Pakistan)	90	156	12	7,530	223	24	52.29
39	M. A. Taylor (Australia)	104	186	13	7,525	334*	19	43.49
40	C. H. Lloyd (West Indies)	110	175	14	7,515	242*	19	46.67

MOST RUNS FOR EACH COUNTRY

ENGLAND

A. N. Cook	12,472	A. J. Stewart	8,463	D. I. Gower	8,231
G. A. Gooch	8,900	**J. E. Root**	**8,249**	K. P. Pietersen	8,181

AUSTRALIA

R. T. Ponting	13,378	S. R. Waugh	10,927	M. L. Hayden	8,625
A. R. Border	11,174	M. J. Clarke	8,643	M. E. Waugh	8,029

SOUTH AFRICA

J. H. Kallis†	13,206	G. C. Smith†	9,253	G. Kirsten	7,289
H. M. Amla	9,282	A. B. de Villiers	8,765	H. H. Gibbs	6,167

† *J. H. Kallis also scored 44 and 39* and G. C. Smith 12 and 0 for the World XI v Australia (2005-06 Super Series Test).*

WEST INDIES

B. C. Lara†	11,912	I. V. A. Richards	8,540	C. G. Greenidge	7,558
S. Chanderpaul	11,867	G. S. Sobers	8,032	C. H. Lloyd	7,515

† *B. C. Lara also scored 5 and 36 for the World XI v Australia (2005-06 Super Series Test).*

NEW ZEALAND

L. R. P. L. Taylor	**7,379**	**K. S. Williamson**	**7,115**	M. D. Crowe	5,444
S. P. Fleming	7,172	B. B. McCullum	6,453	J. G. Wright	5,334

INDIA

S. R. Tendulkar	15,921	S. M. Gavaskar	10,122	V. Sehwag†	8,503
R. Dravid†	13,265	V. V. S. Laxman	8,781	**V. Kohli**	**7,318**

† *R. Dravid also scored 0 and 23 and V. Sehwag 76 and 7 for the World XI v Australia (2005-06 Super Series Test).*

PAKISTAN

Younis Khan	10,099	Inzamam-ul-Haq†	8,829	**Azhar Ali**	**6,302**
Javed Miandad	8,832	Mohammad Yousuf	7,530	Salim Malik	5,768

† *Inzamam-ul-Haq also scored 1 and 0 for the World XI v Australia (2005-06 Super Series Test).*

SRI LANKA

K. C. Sangakkara	12,400	S. T. Jayasuriya	6,973	**A. D. Mathews**	**6,194**
D. P. M. D. Jayawardene	11,814	P. A. de Silva	6,361	M. S. Atapattu	5,502

ZIMBABWE

A. Flower	4,794	A. D. R. Campbell	2,858	G. J. Whittall	2,207
G. W. Flower	3,457	H. Masakadza	2,223	**B. R. M. Taylor**	**2,055**

BANGLADESH

Mushfiqur Rahim	**4,413**	Shakib Al Hasan	3,862	**Mominul Haque**	**2,860**
Tamim Iqbal	**4,405**	Habibul Bashar	3,026	**Mahmudullah**	**2,764**

IRELAND

No player has scored 1,000 Test runs for Ireland. The highest total is **258**, by K. J. O'Brien.

AFGHANISTAN

No player has scored 1,000 Test runs for Afghanistan. The highest total is **298**, by Rahmat Shah.

HIGHEST CAREER AVERAGE

(Qualification: 20 innings)

Avge		*T*	*I*	*NO*	*R*	*HS*	*100*
99.94	D. G. Bradman (A)	52	80	10	6,996	334	29
61.87	A. C. Voges (A)	20	31	7	1,485	269*	5
61.80	**S. P. D. Smith (A)**	**77**	**139**	**17**	**7,540**	**239**	**27**
60.97	R. G. Pollock (SA)	23	41	4	2,256	274	7
60.83	G. A. Headley (WI)	22	40	4	2,190	270*	10
60.80	**M. Labuschagne (A)**	**18**	**31**	**0**	**1,885**	**215**	**5**
60.73	H. Sutcliffe (E)	54	84	9	4,555	194	16
59.23	E. Paynter (E)	20	31	5	1,540	243	4
58.67	K. F. Barrington (E)	82	131	15	6,806	256	20
58.61	E. D. Weekes (WI)	48	81	5	4,455	207	15
58.45	W. R. Hammond (E)	85	140	16	7,249	336*	22
57.78	G. S. Sobers (WI)	93	160	21	8,032	365*	26
57.40	K. C. Sangakkara (SL)	134	233	17	12,400	319	38
56.94	J. B. Hobbs (E)	61	102	7	5,410	211	15
56.68	C. L. Walcott (WI)	44	74	7	3,798	220	15

Avge		*T*	*I*	*NO*	*R*	*HS*	*100*
56.67	L. Hutton (E)	79	138	15	6,971	364	19
55.37	J. H. Kallis (SA/World)	166	280	40	13,289	224	45
55.00	E. Tyldesley (E)	14	20	2	990	122	3

S. G. Barnes (A) scored 1,072 runs at 63.05 from 19 innings.

BEST CAREER STRIKE-RATES

(Runs per 100 balls. Qualification: 1,000 runs)

SR		*T*	*I*	*NO*	*R*	*100*	*Avge*
86.97	Shahid Afridi (P)	27	48	1	1,716	5	36.51
85.61	**T. G. Southee (NZ)**	**77**	**109**	**11**	**1,690**	**0**	**17.24**
82.22	V. Sehwag (I)	104	180	6	8,586	23	49.34
81.98	A. C. Gilchrist (A)	96	137	20	5,570	17	47.60
81.72	**C. de Grandhomme (NZ)**	**24**	**36**	**4**	**1,185**	**1**	**37.03**
76.49	G. P. Swann (E)	60	76	14	1,370	0	22.09
72.68	**D. A. Warner (A)**	**86**	**159**	**7**	**7,311**	**24**	**48.09**
72.25	**M. D. K. J. Perera (SL)**	**22**	**41**	**3**	**1,177**	**2**	**30.97**
71.09	**Q. de Kock (SA)**	**49**	**82**	**5**	**2,962**	**5**	**38.46**
70.98	Sarfraz Ahmed (P)	49	86	13	2,657	3	36.39
70.28	M. Muralitharan (SL)	133	164	56	1,261	0	11.67
68.90	**R. R. Pant (I)**	**16**	**27**	**2**	**1,088**	**2**	**43.52**
67.88	D. J. G. Sammy (WI)	38	63	2	1,323	1	21.68
67.68	**M. A. Starc (A)**	**61**	**91**	**19**	**1,596**	**0**	**22.16**
66.94	S. Dhawan (I)	34	58	1	2,315	7	40.61

Comprehensive data on balls faced has been available only in recent decades, and its introduction varied from country to country. Among earlier players for whom partial data is available, Kapil Dev (India) had a strike-rate of 80.91 and I. V. A. Richards (West Indies) 70.19 in those innings which were fully recorded.

HIGHEST PERCENTAGE OF TEAM'S RUNS OVER TEST CAREER

(Qualification: 20 Tests)

	Tests	*Runs*	*Team Runs*	*% of Team Runs*
D. G. Bradman (Australia)	52	6,996	28,810	24.28
G. A. Headley (West Indies)	22	2,190	10,239	21.38
B. C. Lara (West Indies)	131	11,953	63,328	18.87
L. Hutton (England)	79	6,971	38,440	18.13
J. B. Hobbs (England)	61	5,410	30,211	17.90
A. D. Nourse (South Africa)	34	2,960	16,659	17.76
S. P. D. Smith (Australia)	**77**	**7,540**	**43,290**	**17.41**
E. D. Weekes (West Indies)	48	4,455	25,667	17.35
B. Mitchell (South Africa)	42	3,471	20,175	17.20
H. Sutcliffe (England)	54	4,555	26,604	17.12
K. C. Sangakkara (Sri Lanka)	134	12,400	72,779	17.03
B. Sutcliffe (New Zealand)	42	2,727	16,158	16.87

The percentage shows the proportion of a team's runs scored by that player in all Tests in which he played, including team runs in innings in which he did not bat.

FASTEST FIFTIES

Minutes			
24	Misbah-ul-Haq	Pakistan v Australia at Abu Dhabi	2014-15
27	Mohammad Ashraful	Bangladesh v India at Mirpur	2007
28	J. T. Brown	England v Australia at Melbourne	1894-95
29	S. A. Durani	India v England at Kanpur	1963-64
30	E. A. V. Williams	West Indies v England at Bridgetown	1947-48
30	B. R. Taylor	New Zealand v West Indies at Auckland	1968-69

The fastest fifties in terms of balls received (where recorded) are:

Balls			
21	Misbah-ul-Haq	Pakistan v Australia at Abu Dhabi	2014-15
23	D. A. Warner	Australia v Pakistan at Sydney	2016-17
24	J. H. Kallis	South Africa v Zimbabwe at Cape Town	2004-05
25	S. Shillingford	West Indies v New Zealand at Kingston	2014
26	Shahid Afridi	Pakistan v India at Bangalore	2004-05
26	Mohammad Ashraful	Bangladesh v India at Mirpur	2007
26	D. W. Steyn	South Africa v West Indies at Port Elizabeth	2014-15

FASTEST HUNDREDS

Minutes			
70	J. M. Gregory	Australia v South Africa at Johannesburg	1921-22
74	Misbah-ul-Haq	Pakistan v Australia at Abu Dhabi	2014-15
75	G. L. Jessop	England v Australia at The Oval	1902
78	R. Benaud	Australia v West Indies at Kingston	1954-55
80	J. H. Sinclair	South Africa v Australia at Cape Town	1902-03
81	I. V. A. Richards	West Indies v England at St John's	1985-86
86	B. R. Taylor	New Zealand v West Indies at Auckland	1968-69

The fastest hundreds in terms of balls received (where recorded) are:

Balls			
54	B. B. McCullum	New Zealand v Australia at Christchurch	2015-16
56	I. V. A. Richards	West Indies v England at St John's	1985-86
56	Misbah-ul-Haq	Pakistan v Australia at Abu Dhabi	2014-15
57	A. C. Gilchrist	Australia v England at Perth	2006-07
67	J. M. Gregory	Australia v South Africa at Johannesburg	1921-22
69	S. Chanderpaul	West Indies v Australia at Georgetown	2002-03
69	D. A. Warner	Australia v India at Perth	2011-12
70	C. H. Gayle	West Indies v Australia at Perth	2009-10

FASTEST DOUBLE-HUNDREDS

Minutes			
214	D. G. Bradman	Australia v England at Leeds	1930
217	N. J. Astle	New Zealand v England at Christchurch	2001-02
223	S. J. McCabe	Australia v England at Nottingham	1938
226	V. T. Trumper	Australia v South Africa at Adelaide	1910-11
234	D. G. Bradman	Australia v England at Lord's	1930
240	W. R. Hammond	England v New Zealand at Auckland	1932-33

The fastest double-hundreds in terms of balls received (where recorded) are:

Balls			
153	N. J. Astle	New Zealand v England at Christchurch	2001-02
163	B. A. Stokes	England v South Africa at Cape Town	2015-16
168	V. Sehwag	India v Sri Lanka at Mumbai (BS)	2009-10
182	V. Sehwag	India v Pakistan at Lahore	2005-06
186	B. B. McCullum	New Zealand v Pakistan at Sharjah	2014-15
194	V. Sehwag	India v South Africa at Chennai	2007-08

FASTEST TRIPLE-HUNDREDS

Minutes			
288	W. R. Hammond	England v New Zealand at Auckland	1932-33
336	D. G. Bradman	Australia v England at Leeds	1930

The fastest triple-hundred in terms of balls received (where recorded) is:

Balls			
278	V. Sehwag	India v South Africa at Chennai	2007-08

MOST RUNS SCORED OFF AN OVER

28	B. C. Lara (466444)	off R. J. Peterson	WI v SA at Johannesburg	2003-04
28	G. J. Bailey (462466)	off J. M. Anderson	A v E at Perth	2013-14
28	**K. A. Maharaj (444660)**	**off J. E. Root**	**SA v E at Port Elizabeth**	**2019-20**
	The sixth ball produced four byes.			
27	Shahid Afridi (666621)	off Harbhajan Singh	P v I at Lahore	2005-06
26	C. D. McMillan (444464)	off Younis Khan	NZ v P at Hamilton	2000-01
26	B. C. Lara (406664)	off Danish Kaneria	WI v P at Multan	2006-07
26	M. G. Johnson (446066)	off P. L. Harris	A v SA at Johannesburg	2009-10
26	B. B. McCullum (466046)	off R. A. S. Lakmal	NZ v SL at Christchurch	2014-15
26	H. H. Pandya (446660)	off P. M. Pushpakumara	I v SL at Pallekele	2017

MOST RUNS IN A DAY

309	D. G. Bradman	Australia v England at Leeds	1930
295	W. R. Hammond	England v New Zealand at Auckland	1932-33
284	V. Sehwag	India v Sri Lanka at Mumbai	2009-10
273	D. C. S. Compton	England v Pakistan at Nottingham	1954
271	D. G. Bradman	Australia v England at Leeds	1934

MOST SIXES IN A CAREER

B. B. McCullum (NZ)	107
A. C. Gilchrist (A)	100
C. H. Gayle (WI)	98
J. H. Kallis (SA/World)	97
V. Sehwag (I/World)	91
B. C. Lara (WI)	88
C. L. Cairns (NZ)	87
I. V. A. Richards (WI)	84
A. Flintoff (E/World)	82
M. L. Hayden (A)	82
Misbah-ul-Haq (P)	81
K. P. Pietersen (E)	81
M. S. Dhoni (I)	78
B. A. Stokes (E)	**74**
R. T. Ponting (A)	73
T. G. Southee (NZ)	**73**
C. H. Lloyd (WI)	70
Younis Khan (P)	70

SLOWEST INDIVIDUAL BATTING

0	in 101 minutes	G. I. Allott, New Zealand v South Africa at Auckland	1998-99
4*	in 110 minutes	Abdul Razzaq, Pakistan v Australia at Melbourne	2004-05
6	in 137 minutes	S. C. J. Broad, England v New Zealand at Auckland	2012-13
9*	in 184 minutes	Arshad Khan, Pakistan v Sri Lanka at Colombo (SSC)	2000
18	in 194 minutes	W. R. Playle, New Zealand v England at Leeds	1958
19*	in 217 minutes	M. D. Crowe, New Zealand v Sri Lanka at Colombo (SSC)	1983-84
25	in 289 minutes	H. M. Amla, South Africa v India at Delhi	2015-16
35	in 332 minutes	C. J. Tavaré, England v India at Madras	1981-82
43	in 354 minutes	A. B. de Villiers, South Africa v India at Delhi	2015-16
60	in 390 minutes	D. N. Sardesai, India v West Indies at Bridgetown	1961-62
62	in 408 minutes	Ramiz Raja, Pakistan v West Indies at Karachi	1986-87
68	in 458 minutes	T. E. Bailey, England v Australia at Brisbane	1958-59
86	in 474 minutes	Shoaib Mohammad, Pakistan v West Indies at Karachi	1990-91
99	in 505 minutes	M. L. Jaisimha, India v Pakistan at Kanpur	1960-61
104	in 529 minutes	S. V. Manjrekar, India v Zimbabwe at Harare	1992-93
105	in 575 minutes	D. J. McGlew, South Africa v Australia at Durban	1957-58
114	in 591 minutes	Mudassar Nazar, Pakistan v England at Lahore	1977-78
120*	in 609 minutes	J. J. Crowe, New Zealand v Sri Lanka at Colombo (CCC)	1986-87
136*	in 675 minutes	S. Chanderpaul, West Indies v India at St John's	2001-02
163	in 720 minutes	Shoaib Mohammad, Pakistan v New Zealand at Wellington	1988-89
201*	in 777 minutes	D. S. B. P. Kuruppu, Sri Lanka v NZ at Colombo (CCC)	1986-87
275	in 878 minutes	G. Kirsten, South Africa v England at Durban	1999-2000
337	in 970 minutes	Hanif Mohammad, Pakistan v West Indies at Bridgetown	1957-58

SLOWEST HUNDREDS

557 minutes	Mudassar Nazar, Pakistan v England at Lahore	1977-78
545 minutes	D. J. McGlew, South Africa v Australia at Durban	1957-58
535 minutes	A. P. Gurusinha, Sri Lanka v Zimbabwe at Harare	1994-95
516 minutes	J. J. Crowe, New Zealand v Sri Lanka at Colombo (CCC)	1986-87
500 minutes	S. V. Manjrekar, India v Zimbabwe at Harare	1992-93
488 minutes	P. E. Richardson, England v South Africa at Johannesburg	1956-57

*The slowest hundred for any Test in England is **465 minutes** (312 balls) by **D. P. Sibley**, England v West Indies at Manchester, 2020.*

The slowest double-hundred in a Test was scored in 777 minutes (548 balls) by D. S. B. P. Kuruppu for Sri Lanka v New Zealand at Colombo (CCC), 1986-87, on his debut.

PARTNERSHIPS OVER 400

624	for 3rd	K. C. Sangakkara (287)/ D. P. M. D. Jayawardene (374)	SL v SA	Colombo (SSC)	2006
576	for 2nd	S. T. Jayasuriya (340)/R. S. Mahanama (225)	SL v I	Colombo (RPS)	1997-98
467	for 3rd	A. H. Jones (186)/M. D. Crowe (299)	NZ v SL	Wellington	1990-91
451	for 2nd	W. H. Ponsford (266)/D. G. Bradman (244)	A v E	The Oval	1934
451	for 3rd	Mudassar Nazar (231)/Javed Miandad (280*)	P v I	Hyderabad	1982-83
449	for 4th	A. C. Voges (269*)/S. E. Marsh (182)	A v WI	Hobart	2015-16
446	for 2nd	C. C. Hunte (260)/G. S. Sobers (365*)	WI v P	Kingston	1957-58
438	for 2nd	M. S. Atapattu (249)/K. C. Sangakkara (270)	SL v Z	Bulawayo	2003-04
437	for 4th	D. P. M. D. Jayawardene (240)/ T. T. Samaraweera (231)	SL v P	Karachi	2008-09
429*	for 3rd	J. A. Rudolph (222*)/H. H. Dippenaar (177*)	SA v B	Chittagong	2003
415	for 1st	N. D. McKenzie (226)/G. C. Smith (232)	SA v B	Chittagong	2007-08
413	for 1st	M. H. Mankad (231)/Pankaj Roy (173)	I v NZ	Madras	1955-56
411	for 4th	P. B. H. May (285*)/M. C. Cowdrey (154)	E v WI	Birmingham	1957
410	for 1st	V. Sehwag (254)/R. Dravid (128*)	I v P	Lahore	2005-06
405	for 5th	S. G. Barnes (234)/D. G. Bradman (234)	A v E	Sydney	1946-47

415 runs were added for the third wicket for India v England at Madras in 1981-82 by D. B. Vengsarkar (retired hurt), G. R. Viswanath and Yashpal Sharma. 408 runs were added for the first wicket for India v Bangladesh at Mirpur in 2007 by K. D. Karthik (retired hurt), Wasim Jaffer (retired hurt), R. Dravid and S. R. Tendulkar.

HIGHEST PARTNERSHIPS FOR EACH WICKET

First Wicket

415	N. D. McKenzie (226)/G. C. Smith (232)	SA v B	Chittagong	2007-08
413	M. H. Mankad (231)/Pankaj Roy (173)	I v NZ	Madras	1955-56
410	V. Sehwag (254)/R. Dravid (128*)	I v P	Lahore	2005-06
387	G. M. Turner (259)/T. W. Jarvis (182)	NZ v WI	Georgetown	1971-72
382	W. M. Lawry (210)/R. B. Simpson (201)	A v WI	Bridgetown	1964-65

Second Wicket

576	S. T. Jayasuriya (340)/R. S. Mahanama (225)	SL v I	Colombo (RPS)	1997-98
451	W. H. Ponsford (266)/D. G. Bradman (244)	A v E	The Oval	1934
446	C. C. Hunte (260)/G. S. Sobers (365*)	WI v P	Kingston	1957-58
438	M. S. Atapattu (249)/K. C. Sangakkara (270)	SL v Z	Bulawayo	2003-04
382	L. Hutton (364)/M. Leyland (187)	E v A	The Oval	1938

Third Wicket

624	K. C. Sangakkara (287)/D. P. M. D. Jayawardene (374). .	SL v SA	Colombo (SSC)	2006
467	A. H. Jones (186)/M. D. Crowe (299)	NZ v SL	Wellington	1990-91
451	Mudassar Nazar (231)/Javed Miandad (280*)	P v I	Hyderabad	1982-83
429*	J. A. Rudolph (222*)/H. H. Dippenaar (177*)	SA v B	Chittagong	2003
397	Qasim Omar (206)/Javed Miandad (203*)	P v SL	Faisalabad	1985-86

Fourth Wicket

449	A. C. Voges (269*)/S. E. Marsh (182)	A v WI	Hobart	2015-16
437	D. P. M. D. Jayawardene(240)/T. T. Samaraweera (231) .	SL v P	Karachi	2008-09
411	P. B. H. May (285*)/M. C. Cowdrey (154)	E v WI	Birmingham	1957
399	G. S. Sobers (226)/F. M. M. Worrell (197*)	WI v E	Bridgetown	1959-60
388	W. H. Ponsford (181)/D. G. Bradman (304).	A v E	Leeds	1934

Fifth Wicket

405	S. G. Barnes (234)/D. G. Bradman (234)	A v E	Sydney	1946-47
385	S. R. Waugh (160)/G. S. Blewett (214)	A v SA	Johannesburg	1996-97
376	V. V. S. Laxman (281)/R. Dravid (180)	I v A	Kolkata	2000-01
359	Shakib Al Hasan (217)/Mushfiqur Rahim (159). . . .	B v NZ	Wellington	2016-17
359	**Z. Crawley (267)/J. C. Buttler (152)**	**E v P**	**Southampton**	**2020**

Sixth Wicket

399	B. A. Stokes (258)/J. M. Bairstow (150*)	E v SA	Cape Town	2015-16
365*	K. S. Williamson (242*)/B-J. Watling (142*)	NZ v SL	Wellington	2014-15
352	B. B. McCullum (302)/B-J. Watling (124).	NZ v I	Wellington	2013-14
351	D. P. M. D. Jayawardene (275)/ H. A. P. W. Jayawardene (154*)	SL v I	Ahmedabad	2009-10
346	J. H. Fingleton (136)/D. G. Bradman (270)	A v E	Melbourne	1936-37

Seventh Wicket

347	D. St E. Atkinson (219)/C. C. Depeiza (122)	WI v A	Bridgetown	1954-55
308	Waqar Hassan (189)/Imtiaz Ahmed (209)	P v NZ	Lahore	1955-56
295*	S. O. Dowrich (116*)/J. O. Holder (202*)	WI v E	Bridgetown	2018-19
280	R. G. Sharma (177)/R. Ashwin (124)	I v WI	Kolkata	2013-14
261	B-J. Watling (205)/M. J. Santner (126)	NZ v E	Mt Maunganui	2019-20

Eighth Wicket

332	I. J. L. Trott (184)/S. C. J. Broad (169).	E v P	Lord's	2010
313	Wasim Akram (257*)/Saqlain Mushtaq (79)	P v Z	Sheikhupura	1996-97
256	S. P. Fleming (262)/J. E. C. Franklin (122*)	NZ v SA	Cape Town	2005-06
253	N. J. Astle (156*)/A. C. Parore (110)	NZ v A	Perth	2001-02
246	L. E. G. Ames (137)/G. O. B. Allen (122)	E v NZ	Lord's	1931

Ninth Wicket

195	M. V. Boucher (78)/P. L. Symcox (108)	SA v P	Johannesburg	1997-98
190	Asif Iqbal (146)/Intikhab Alam (51).	P v E	The Oval	1967
184	Mahmudullah (76)/Abul Hasan (113).	B v WI	Khulna	2012-13
180	J-P. Duminy (166)/D. W. Steyn (76)	SA v A	Melbourne	2008-09
163*	M. C. Cowdrey (128*)/A. C. Smith (69*)	E v NZ	Wellington	1962-63

Tenth Wicket

198	J. E. Root (154*)/J. M. Anderson (81)	E v I	Nottingham	2014
163	P. J. Hughes (81*)/A. C. Agar (98)	A v E	Nottingham	2013
151	B. F. Hastings (110)/R. O. Collinge (68*)	NZ v P	Auckland	1972-73
151	Azhar Mahmood (128*)/Mushtaq Ahmed (59)	P v SA	Rawalpindi	1997-98
143	D. Ramdin (107*)/T. L. Best (95)	WI v E	Birmingham	2012

HIGHEST PARTNERSHIPS FOR EACH COUNTRY

ENGLAND

359	for 1st	L. Hutton (158)/C. Washbrook (195)	v SA	Johannesburg	1948-49
382	for 2nd	L. Hutton (364)/M. Leyland (187)	v A	The Oval	1938
370	for 3rd	W. J. Edrich (189)/D. C. S. Compton (208)	v SA	Lord's	1947
411	for 4th	P. B. H. May (285*)/M. C. Cowdrey (154)	v WI	Birmingham	1957
359	**for 5th**	**Z. Crawley (267)/J. C. Buttler (152)**	**v P**	**Southampton**	**2020**
399	for 6th	B. A. Stokes (258)/J. M. Bairstow (150*)	v SA	Cape Town	2015-16
197	for 7th	M. J. K. Smith (96)/J. M. Parks (101*)	v WI	Port-of-Spain	1959-60
332	for 8th	I. J. L. Trott (184)/S. C. J. Broad (169)	v P	Lord's	2010
163*	for 9th	M. C. Cowdrey (128*)/A. C. Smith (69*)	v NZ	Wellington	1962-63
198	for 10th	J. E. Root (154*)/J. M. Anderson (81)	v I	Nottingham	2014

AUSTRALIA

382	for 1st	W. M. Lawry (210)/R. B. Simpson (201)	v WI	Bridgetown	1964-65
451	for 2nd	W. H. Ponsford (266)/D. G. Bradman (244)	v E	The Oval	1934
315	for 3rd	R. T. Ponting (206)/D. S. Lehmann (160)	v WI	Port-of-Spain	2002-03
449	for 4th	A. C. Voges (269*)/S. E. Marsh (182)	v WI	Hobart	2015-16
405	for 5th	S. G. Barnes (234)/D. G. Bradman (234)	v E	Sydney	1946-47
346	for 6th	J. H. Fingleton (136)/D. G. Bradman (270)	v E	Melbourne	1936-37
217	for 7th	K. D. Walters (250)/G. J. Gilmour (101)	v NZ	Christchurch	1976-77
243	for 8th	R. J. Hartigan (116)/C. Hill (160)	v E	Adelaide	1907-08
154	for 9th	S. E. Gregory (201)/J. M. Blackham (74)	v E	Sydney	1894-95
163	for 10th	P. J. Hughes (81*)/A. C. Agar (98)	v E	Nottingham	2013

SOUTH AFRICA

415	for 1st	N. D. McKenzie (226)/G. C. Smith (232)	v B	Chittagong	2007-08
315*	for 2nd	H. H. Gibbs (211*)/J. H. Kallis (148*)	v NZ	Christchurch	1998-99
429*	for 3rd	J. A. Rudolph (222*)/H. H. Dippenaar (177*)	v B	Chittagong	2003
308	for 4th	H. M. Amla (208)/A. B. de Villiers (152)	v WI	Centurion	2014-15
338	for 5th	G. C. Smith (234)/A. B. de Villiers (164)	v P	Dubai	2013-14
271	for 6th	A. G. Prince (162*)/M. V. Boucher (117)	v B	Centurion	2008-09
246	for 7th	D. J. McGlew (255*)/A. R. A. Murray (109)	v NZ	Wellington	1952-53
150	for 8th	N. D. McKenzie (103)/S. M. Pollock (111)	v SL	Centurion	2000-01
		G. Kirsten (130)/M. Zondeki (59)	v E	Leeds	2003
195	for 9th	M. V. Boucher (78)/P. L. Symcox (108)	v P	Johannesburg	1997-98
107*	for 10th	A. B. de Villiers (278*)/M. Morkel (35*)	v P	Abu Dhabi	2010-11

WEST INDIES

298	for 1st	C. G. Greenidge (149)/D. L. Haynes (167)	v E	St John's	1989-90
446	for 2nd	C. C. Hunte (260)/G. S. Sobers (365*)	v P	Kingston	1957-58
338	for 3rd	E. D. Weekes (206)/F. M. M. Worrell (167)	v E	Port-of-Spain	1953-54
399	for 4th	G. S. Sobers (226)/F. M. M. Worrell (197*)	v E	Bridgetown	1959-60
322	for 5th†	B. C. Lara (213)/J. C. Adams (94)	v A	Kingston	1998-99
282*	for 6th	B. C. Lara (400*)/R. D. Jacobs (107*)	v E	St John's	2003-04
347	for 7th	D. St E. Atkinson (219)/C. C. Depeiza (122)	v A	Bridgetown	1954-55
212	for 8th	S. O. Dowrich (103)/J. O. Holder (110)	v Z	Bulawayo	2017-18
161	for 9th	C. H. Lloyd (161*)/A. M. E. Roberts (68)	v I	Calcutta	1983-84
143	for 10th	D. Ramdin (107*)/T. L. Best (95)	v E	Birmingham	2012

† *344 runs were added between the fall of the 4th and 5th wickets: P. T. Collins retired hurt when he and Lara had added 22 runs.*

NEW ZEALAND

387	for 1st	G. M. Turner (259)/T. W. Jarvis (182)	v WI	Georgetown	1971-72
297	for 2nd	B. B. McCullum (202)/K. S. Williamson (192)	v P	Sharjah	2014-15
467	for 3rd	A. H. Jones (186)/M. D. Crowe (299)	v SL	Wellington	1990-91
369	**for 4th**	**K. S. Williamson (238)/H. M. Nicholls (157)**	**v P**	**Christchurch**	**2020-21**
222	for 5th	N. J. Astle (141)/C. D. McMillan (142)	v Z	Wellington	2000-01
365*	for 6th	K. S. Williamson (242*)/B-J. Watling (142*)	v SL	Wellington	2014-15
261	for 7th	B-J. Watling (205)/M. J. Santner (126)	v E	Mt Maunganui	2019-20
256	for 8th	S. P. Fleming (262)/J. E. C. Franklin (122*)	v SA	Cape Town	2005-06
136	for 9th	I. D. S. Smith (173)/M. C. Snedden (22)	v I	Auckland	1989-90
151	for 10th	B. F. Hastings (110)/R. O. Collinge (68*)	v P	Auckland	1972-73

INDIA

413	for 1st	M. H. Mankad (231)/Pankaj Roy (173)	v NZ	Madras	1955-56
370	for 2nd	M. Vijay (167)/C. A. Pujara (204)	v A	Hyderabad	2012-13
336	for 3rd†	V. Sehwag (309)/S. R. Tendulkar (194*)	v P	Multan	2003-04
365	for 4th	V. Kohli (211)/A. M. Rahane (188)	v NZ	Indore	2016-17
376	for 5th	V. V. S. Laxman (281)/R. Dravid (180)	v A	Kolkata	2000-01
298*	for 6th	D. B. Vengsarkar (164*)/R. J. Shastri (121*)	v A	Bombay	1986-87
280	for 7th	R. G. Sharma (177)/R. Ashwin (124)	v WI	Kolkata	2013-14
241	for 8th	V. Kohli (235)/J. Yadav (104)	v E	Mumbai	2016-17
149	for 9th	P. G. Joshi (52*)/R. B. Desai (85)	v P	Bombay	1960-61
133	for 10th	S. R. Tendulkar (248*)/Zaheer Khan (75)	v B	Dhaka	2004-05

† *415 runs were scored for India's 3rd wicket v England at Madras in 1981-82, in two partnerships: D. B. Vengsarkar and G. R. Viswanath put on 99 before Vengsarkar retired hurt, then Viswanath and Yashpal Sharma added a further 316.*

PAKISTAN

298	for 1st	Aamir Sohail (160)/Ijaz Ahmed snr (151)	v WI	Karachi	1997-98
291	for 2nd	Zaheer Abbas (274)/Mushtaq Mohammad (100)	v E	Birmingham	1971
451	for 3rd	Mudassar Nazar (231)/Javed Miandad (280*)	v I	Hyderabad	1982-83
350	for 4th	Mushtaq Mohammad (201)/Asif Iqbal (175)	v NZ	Dunedin	1972-73
281	for 5th	Javed Miandad (163)/Asif Iqbal (166)	v NZ	Lahore	1976-77
269	for 6th	Mohammad Yousuf (223)/Kamran Akmal (154)	v E	Lahore	2005-06
308	for 7th	Waqar Hassan (189)/Imtiaz Ahmed (209)	v NZ	Lahore	1955-56
313	for 8th	Wasim Akram (257*)/Saqlain Mushtaq (79)	v Z	Sheikhupura	1996-97
190	for 9th	Asif Iqbal (146)/Intikhab Alam (51)	v E	The Oval	1967
151	for 10th	Azhar Mahmood (128*)/Mushtaq Ahmed (59)	v SA	Rawalpindi	1997-98

SRI LANKA

335	for 1st	M. S. Atapattu (207*)/S. T. Jayasuriya (188)	v P	Kandy	2000
576	for 2nd	S. T. Jayasuriya (340)/R. S. Mahanama (225)	v I	Colombo (RPS)	1997-98
624	for 3rd	K. C. Sangakkara (287)/ D. P. M. D. Jayawardene (374)	v SA	Colombo (SSC)	2006
437	for 4th	D. P. M. D. Jayawardene (240)/ T. T. Samaraweera (231)	v P	Karachi	2008-09
280	for 5th	T. T. Samaraweera (138)/T. M. Dilshan (168)	v B	Colombo (PSS)	2005-06
351	for 6th	D. P. M. D. Jayawardene (275)/ H. A. P. W. Jayawardene (154*)	v I	Ahmedabad	2009-10
223*	for 7th	H. A. P. W. Jayawardene (120*)/ W. P. U. J. C. Vaas (100*)	v B	Colombo (SSC)	2007
170	for 8th	D. P. M. D. Jayawardene (237)/ W. P. U. J. C. Vaas (69)	v SA	Galle	2004
118	for 9th	T. T. Samaraweera (83)/B. A. W. Mendis (78)	v I	Colombo (PSS)	2010
79	for 10th	W. P. U. J. C. Vaas (68*)/M. Muralitharan (43)	v A	Kandy	2003-04

ZIMBABWE

164	for 1st	D. D. Ebrahim (71)/A. D. R. Campbell (103)	v WI	Bulawayo	2001
160	for 2nd	Sikandar Raza (82)/H. Masakadza (81)	v B	Chittagong	2014-15
194	for 3rd	A. D. R. Campbell (99)/D. L. Houghton (142)	v SL	Harare	1994-95
269	for 4th	G. W. Flower (201*)/A. Flower (156)	v P	Harare	1994-95
277*	for 5th	M. W. Goodwin (166*)/A. Flower (100*)	v P	Bulawayo	1997-98
165	for 6th	D. L. Houghton (121)/A. Flower (59)	v I	Harare	1992-93
154	for 7th	H. H. Streak (83*)/A. M. Blignaut (92)	v WI	Harare	2001
168	for 8th	H. H. Streak (127*)/A. M. Blignaut (91)	v WI	Harare	2003-04
87	for 9th	P. A. Strang (106*)/B. C. Strang (42)	v P	Sheikhupura	1996-97
97*	for 10th	A. Flower (183*)/H. K. Olonga (11*)	v I	Delhi	2000-01

BANGLADESH

312	for 1st	Tamim Iqbal (206)/Imrul Kayes (150)	v P	Khulna	2014-15
232	for 2nd	Shamsur Rahman (106)/Imrul Kayes (115)	v SL	Chittagong	2013-14
236	for 3rd	Mominul Haque (176)/Mushfiqur Rahim (92)	v SL	Chittagong	2017-18
266	for 4th	Mominul Haque (161)/Mushfiqur Rahim (219*)	v Z	Mirpur	2018-19
359	for 5th	Shakib Al Hasan (217)/Mushfiqur Rahim (159)	v NZ	Wellington	2016-17
191	for 6th	Mohammad Ashraful (129*)/ Mushfiqur Rahim (80)	v SL	Colombo (PSS)	2007
145	for 7th	Shakib Al Hasan (87)/Mahmudullah (115)	v NZ	Hamilton	2009-10
144*	for 8th	Mushfiqur Rahim (219*)/Mehedi Hasan (68*)	v Z	Mirpur	2018-19
184	for 9th	Mahmudullah (76)/Abul Hasan (113)	v WI	Khulna	2012-13
69	for 10th	Mohammad Rafique (65)/Shahadat Hossain (3*)	v A	Chittagong	2005-06

IRELAND

69	for 1st	E. C. Joyce (43)/W. T. S. Porterfield (32)	v P	Malahide	2018
33	for 2nd	P. R. Stirling (14)/A. Balbirnie (82)	v Afg	Dehradun	2018-19
104	for 3rd	A. Balbirnie (82)/J. A. McCollum (39)	v Afg	Dehradun	2018-19
14	for 4th	J. A. McCollum (4)/K. J. O'Brien (12)	v Afg	Dehradun	2018-19
32	for 5th	P. R. Stirling (11)/K. J. O'Brien (118)	v P	Malahide	2018
30	for 6th	K. J. O'Brien (118)/G. C. Wilson (12)	v P	Malahide	2018
114	for 7th	K. J. O'Brien (118)/S. R. Thompson (53)	v P	Malahide	2018
50	for 8th	K. J. O'Brien (118)/T. E. Kane (14)	v P	Malahide	2018
34	for 9th	G. C. Wilson (33*)/W. B. Rankin (17)	v P	Malahide	2018
87	for 10th	G. H. Dockrell (39)/T. J. Murtagh (54*)	v Afg	Dehradun	2018-19

AFGHANISTAN

53	for 1st	Ibrahim Zadran (23)/Javed Ahmadi (62)	v WI	Lucknow	2019-20
139	for 2nd	Ihsanullah Janat (65*)/Rahmat Shah (76)	v Ire	Dehradun	2018-19
130	for 3rd	Rahmat Shah (98)/Hashmatullah Shahidi (61)	v Ire	Dehradun	2018-19
120	for 4th	Rahmat Shah (102)/Asghar Afghan (92)	v B	Chittagong	2019-20
37	for 5th	Hashmatullah Shahidi (36*)/Asghar Afghan (25)	v I	Bangalore	2018
		Javed Ahmadi (62)/Nasir Ahmadzai (15)	v WI	Lucknow	2019-20
81	for 6th	Asghar Afghan (92)/Afsar Zazai (41)	v B	Chittagong	2019-20
30	for 7th	Afsar Zazai (48*)/Rashid Khan (24)	v B	Chittagong	2019-20
54	for 8th	Afsar Zazai (32)/Hamza Hotak (34)	v WI	Lucknow	2019-20
31	for 9th	Asghar Afghan (67)/Wafadar Momand (6)	v Ire	Dehradun	2018-19
21	for 10th	Mujeeb Zadran (15)/Wafadar Momand (6*)	v I	Bangalore	2018

UNUSUAL DISMISSALS

Handled the Ball

W. R. Endean	South Africa v England at Cape Town	1956-57
A. M. J. Hilditch	Australia v Pakistan at Perth	1978-79
Mohsin Khan	Pakistan v Australia at Karachi	1982-83
D. L. Haynes	West Indies v India at Bombay	1983-84
G. A. Gooch	England v Australia at Manchester	1993
S. R. Waugh	Australia v India at Chennai	2000-01
M. P. Vaughan	England v India at Bangalore	2001-02

Obstructing the Field

L. Hutton	England v South Africa at The Oval	1951

There have been no cases of Hit the Ball Twice or Timed Out in Test cricket.

BOWLING RECORDS

MOST WICKETS IN AN INNINGS

10-53	J. C. Laker	England v Australia at Manchester	1956
10-74	A. Kumble	India v Pakistan at Delhi	1998-99
9-28	G. A. Lohmann	England v South Africa at Johannesburg	1895-96
9-37	J. C. Laker	England v Australia at Manchester	1956
9-51	M. Muralitharan	Sri Lanka v Zimbabwe at Kandy	2001-02
9-52	R. J. Hadlee	New Zealand v Australia at Brisbane	1985-86
9-56	Abdul Qadir	Pakistan v England at Lahore	1987-88
9-57	D. E. Malcolm	England v South Africa at The Oval	1994
9-65	M. Muralitharan	Sri Lanka v England at The Oval	1998
9-69	J. M. Patel	India v Australia at Kanpur	1959-60
9-83	Kapil Dev	India v West Indies at Ahmedabad	1983-84
9-86	Sarfraz Nawaz	Pakistan v Australia at Melbourne	1978-79
9-95	J. M. Noreiga	West Indies v India at Port-of-Spain	1970-71
9-102	S. P. Gupte	India v West Indies at Kanpur	1958-59
9-103	S. F. Barnes	England v South Africa at Johannesburg	1913-14
9-113	H. J. Tayfield	South Africa v England at Johannesburg	1956-57
9-121	A. A. Mailey	Australia v England at Melbourne	1920-21
9-127	H. M. R. K. B. Herath	Sri Lanka v Pakistan at Colombo (SSC)	2014
9-129	K. A. Maharaj	South Africa v Sri Lanka at Colombo (SSC)	2018

*There have been **79** instances of eight wickets in a Test innings.*

The best bowling figures for the countries not mentioned above are:

8-39	Taijul Islam	Bangladesh v Zimbabwe at Mirpur	2014-15
8-109	P. A. Strang	Zimbabwe v New Zealand at Bulawayo	2000-01
6-49	Rashid Khan	Afghanistan v Bangladesh at Chittagong	2019-20
5-13	T. J. Murtagh	Ireland v England at Lord's	2019

OUTSTANDING BOWLING ANALYSES

	O	*M*	*R*	*W*		
J. C. Laker (E)	51.2	23	53	10	v Australia at Manchester	1956
A. Kumble (I)	26.3	9	74	10	v Pakistan at Delhi	1998-99
G. A. Lohmann (E)	14.2	6	28	9	v South Africa at Johannesburg	1895-96
J. C. Laker (E)	16.4	4	37	9	v Australia at Manchester	1956
G. A. Lohmann (E)	9.4	5	7	8	v South Africa at Port Elizabeth	1895-96
J. Briggs (E)	14.2	5	11	8	v South Africa at Cape Town	1888-89
S. C. J. Broad (E)	9.3	5	15	8	v Australia at Nottingham	2015
S. J. Harmison (E)	12.3	8	12	7	v West Indies at Kingston	2003-04
J. Briggs (E)	19.1	11	17	7	v South Africa at Cape Town	1888-89
M. A. Noble (A)	7.4	2	17	7	v England at Melbourne	1901-02
W. Rhodes (E)	11	3	17	7	v Australia at Birmingham	1902

WICKET WITH FIRST BALL IN TEST CRICKET

	Batsman dismissed			
T. P. Horan	W. W. Read	A v E	Sydney	1882-83
A. Coningham	A. C. MacLaren	A v E	Melbourne	1894-95
W. M. Bradley	F. Laver	E v A	Manchester	1899
E. G. Arnold	V. T. Trumper	E v A	Sydney	1903-04
A. E. E. Vogler	E. G. Hayes	SA v E	Johannesburg	1905-06
J. N. Crawford	A. E. E. Vogler	E v SA	Johannesburg	1905-06
G. G. Macaulay	G. A. L. Hearne	E v SA	Cape Town	1922-23
M. W. Tate	M. J. Susskind	E v SA	Birmingham	1924
M. Henderson	E. W. Dawson	NZ v E	Christchurch	1929-30
H. D. Smith	E. Paynter	NZ v E	Christchurch	1932-33
T. F. Johnson	W. W. Keeton	WI v E	The Oval	1939
R. Howorth	D. V. Dyer	E v SA	The Oval	1947
Intikhab Alam	C. C. McDonald	P v A	Karachi	1959-60
R. K. Illingworth	P. V. Simmons	E v WI	Nottingham	1991
N. M. Kulkarni	M. S. Atapattu	I v SL	Colombo (RPS)	1997-98
M. K. G. C. P. Lakshitha	Mohammad Ashraful	SL v B	Colombo (SSC)	2002
N. M. Lyon	K. C. Sangakkara	A v SL	Galle	2011-12
R. M. S. Eranga	S. R. Watson	SL v A	Colombo (SSC)	2011-12
D. L. Piedt	M. A. Vermeulen	SA v Z	Harare	2014-15
G. C. Viljoen	A. N. Cook	SA v E	Johannesburg	2015-16

HAT-TRICKS

Most Hat-Tricks

S. C. J. Broad	**2**	H. Trumble	2
T. J. Matthews†	2	Wasim Akram‡	2

† *T. J. Matthews did the hat-trick in each innings of the same match.*
‡ *Wasim Akram did the hat-trick in successive matches.*

Hat-Tricks

There have been **45** hat-tricks in Tests, including the above. Occurrences since 2007:

P. M. Siddle	Australia v England at Brisbane	2010-11
S. C. J. Broad	England v India at Nottingham	2011
Sohag Gazi†	Bangladesh v New Zealand at Chittagong	2013-14
S. C. J. Broad	England v Sri Lanka at Leeds	2014
H. M. R. K. B. Herath	Sri Lanka v Australia at Galle	2016
M. M. Ali	England v South Africa at The Oval	2017
J. J. Bumrah	India v West Indies at North Sound	2019
Naseem Shah	**Pakistan v Bangladesh at Rawalpindi**	**2019-20**

† *Sohag Gazi also scored 101 not out.*

M. J. C. Allom, P. J. Petherick and D. W. Fleming did the hat-trick on Test debut. D. N. T. Zoysa took one in the second over of a Test (his first three balls); I. K. Pathan in the first over of a Test. Naseem Shah was the youngest to take a Test hat-trick, aged 16 years 359 days.

FOUR WICKETS IN FIVE BALLS

M. J. C. Allom	England v New Zealand at Christchurch *On debut, in his eighth over: W-WWW*	1929-30
C. M. Old	England v Pakistan at Birmingham *Sequence interrupted by a no-ball: WW-WW*	1978
Wasim Akram	Pakistan v West Indies at Lahore (*WW-WW*)	1990-91

MOST WICKETS IN A TEST

19-90	J. C. Laker	England v Australia at Manchester	1956
17-159	S. F. Barnes	England v South Africa at Johannesburg	1913-14
16-136†	N. D. Hirwani	India v West Indies at Madras	1987-88
16-137†	R. A. L. Massie	Australia v England at Lord's	1972
16-220	M. Muralitharan	Sri Lanka v England at The Oval	1998

† *On Test debut.*

There have been 18 further instances of 14 or more wickets in a Test match.

The best bowling figures for the countries not mentioned above are:

15-123	R. J. Hadlee	New Zealand v Australia at Brisbane	1985-86
14-116	Imran Khan	Pakistan v Sri Lanka at Lahore	1981-82
14-149	M. A. Holding	West Indies v England at The Oval	1976
13-132	M. Ntini	South Africa v West Indies at Port-of-Spain	2004-05
12-117	Mehedi Hasan	Bangladesh v West Indies at Mirpur	2018-19
11-104	Rashid Khan	Afghanistan v Bangladesh at Chittagong	2019-20
11-255	A. G. Huckle	Zimbabwe v New Zealand at Bulawayo	1997-98
6-65	T. J. Murtagh	Ireland v England at Lord's	2019

MOST BALLS BOWLED IN A TEST

S. Ramadhin (West Indies) sent down 774 balls in 129 overs against England at Birmingham, 1957, the most delivered by any bowler in a Test, beating H. Verity's 766 for England against South Africa at Durban, 1938-39. In this match Ramadhin also bowled the most balls (588) in any first-class innings, since equalled by Arshad Ayub, Hyderabad v Madhya Pradesh at Secunderabad, 1991-92.

MOST WICKETS IN A SERIES

	T	R	W	Avge		
S. F. Barnes	4	536	49	10.93	England v South Africa	1913-14
J. C. Laker	5	442	46	9.60	England v Australia	1956
C. V. Grimmett	5	642	44	14.59	Australia v South Africa	1935-36
T. M. Alderman	6	893	42	21.26	Australia v England	1981
R. M. Hogg	6	527	41	12.85	Australia v England	1978-79
T. M. Alderman	6	712	41	17.36	Australia v England	1989
Imran Khan	6	558	40	13.95	Pakistan v India	1982-83
S. K. Warne	5	797	40	19.92	Australia v England	2005

The most for South Africa is 37 by H. J. Tayfield against England in 1956-57, for West Indies 35 by M. D. Marshall against England in 1988, for India 35 by B. S. Chandrasekhar against England in 1972-73 (all in five Tests), for New Zealand 33 by R. J. Hadlee against Australia in 1985-86, for Sri Lanka 30 by M. Muralitharan against Zimbabwe in 2001-02, for Zimbabwe 22 by H. H. Streak against Pakistan in 1994-95 (all in three Tests), and for Bangladesh 19 by Mehedi Hasan against England in 2016-17 (two Tests).

MOST WICKETS IN A CALENDAR YEAR

	T	R	W	5I	10M	Avge	Year
S. K. Warne (Australia)	15	2,114	96	6	2	22.02	2005
M. Muralitharan (Sri Lanka)	11	1,521	90	9	5	16.89	2006
D. K. Lillee (Australia)	13	1,781	85	5	2	20.95	1981
A. A. Donald (South Africa)	14	1,571	80	7	–	19.63	1998
M. Muralitharan (Sri Lanka)	12	1,699	80	7	4	21.23	2001
J. Garner (West Indies)	15	1,604	77	4	–	20.83	1984
Kapil Dev (India)	18	1,739	75	5	1	23.18	1983
M. Muralitharan (Sri Lanka)	10	1,463	75	7	3	19.50	2000

MOST WICKETS

		T	Balls	R	W	5I	10M	Avge	SR
1	M. Muralitharan (SL/World)	133	44,039	18,180	800	67	22	22.72	55.04
2	S. K. Warne (Australia)	145	40,704	17,995	708	37	10	25.41	57.49
3	A. Kumble (India)	132	40,850	18,355	619	35	8	29.65	65.99
4	**J. M. Anderson (England)**	**157**	**33,931**	**16,124**	**606**	**30**	**3**	**26.60**	**55.99**
5	G. D. McGrath (Australia)	124	29,248	12,186	563	29	3	21.64	51.95
6	C. A. Walsh (West Indies)	132	30,019	12,688	519	22	3	24.44	57.84
7	**S. C. J. Broad (England)**	**144**	**29,160**	**14,250**	**517**	**18**	**3**	**27.56**	**56.40**
8	D. W. Steyn (South Africa)	93	18,608	10,077	439	26	5	22.95	42.38
9	Kapil Dev (India)	131	27,740	12,867	434	23	2	29.64	63.91
10	H. M. R. K. B. Herath (SL)	93	25,993	12,157	433	34	9	28.07	60.03
11	R. J. Hadlee (New Zealand)	86	21,918	9,611	431	36	9	22.29	50.85
12	S. M. Pollock (South Africa)	108	24,353	9,733	421	16	1	23.11	57.84
13	Harbhajan Singh (India)	103	28,580	13,537	417	25	5	32.46	68.53
14	Wasim Akram (Pakistan)	104	22,627	9,779	414	25	5	23.62	54.65
15	C. E. L. Ambrose (WI)	98	22,103	8,501	405	22	3	20.99	54.57
16	**N. M. Lyon (Australia)**	**100**	**25,690**	**12,816**	**399**	**18**	**3**	**32.12**	**64.38**
17	M. Ntini (South Africa)	101	20,834	11,242	390	18	4	28.82	53.42
18	I. T. Botham (England)	102	21,815	10,878	383	27	4	28.40	56.95
19	**R. Ashwin (India)**	**74**	**20,391**	**9,628**	**377**	**27**	**7**	**25.53**	**54.08**
20	M. D. Marshall (West Indies)	81	17,584	7,876	376	22	4	20.94	46.76
21	Waqar Younis (Pakistan)	87	16,224	8,788	373	22	5	23.56	43.49
22	Imran Khan (Pakistan)	88	19,458	8,258	362	23	6	22.81	53.75
	D. L. Vettori (NZ/World)	113	28,814	12,441	362	20	3	34.36	79.59
24	D. K. Lillee (Australia)	70	18,467	8,493	355	23	7	23.92	52.01
	W. P. U. J. C. Vaas (SL)	111	23,438	10,501	355	12	2	29.58	66.02

		T	*Balls*	*R*	*W*	*5I*	*10M*	*Avge*	*SR*
26	A. A. Donald (South Africa)	72	15,519	7,344	330	20	3	22.25	47.02
27	R. G. D. Willis (England)	90	17,357	8,190	325	16	–	25.20	53.40
28	M. G. Johnson (Australia)	73	16,001	8,891	313	12	3	28.40	51.12
29	Zaheer Khan (India)	92	18,785	10,247	311	11	1	32.94	60.40
30	B. Lee (Australia)	76	16,531	9,554	310	10	–	30.81	53.32
31	M. Morkel (South Africa)	86	16,498	8,550	309	8	0	27.66	53.39
31	L. R. Gibbs (West Indies)	79	27,115	8,989	309	18	2	29.09	87.75
33	F. S. Trueman (England)	67	15,178	6,625	307	17	3	21.57	49.43
34	**T. G. Southee (New Zealand)**	**77**	**17,387**	**8,670**	**302**	**11**	**1**	**28.70**	**57.57**

MOST WICKETS FOR EACH COUNTRY

ENGLAND

J. M. Anderson	**606**	I. T. Botham	383	F. S. Trueman	307
S. C. J. Broad	**517**	R. G. D. Willis	325	D. L. Underwood	297

AUSTRALIA

S. K. Warne	708	**N. M. Lyon**	**399**	M. G. Johnson	313
G. D. McGrath	563	D. K. Lillee	355	B. Lee	310

SOUTH AFRICA

D. W. Steyn	439	M. Ntini	390	M. Morkel	309
S. M. Pollock	421	A. A. Donald	330	J. H. Kallis†	291

† *J. H. Kallis also took 0-35 and 1-3 for the World XI v Australia (2005-06 Super Series Test).*

WEST INDIES

C. A. Walsh	519	M. D. Marshall	376	J. Garner	259
C. E. L. Ambrose	405	L. R. Gibbs	309	M. A. Holding	249

NEW ZEALAND

R. J. Hadlee	431	**T. G. Southee**	**302**	C. S. Martin	233
D. L. Vettori†	361	**T. A. Boult**	**281**	**N. Wagner**	**219**

† *D. L. Vettori also took 1-73 and 0-38 for the World XI v Australia (2005-06 Super Series Test).*

INDIA

A. Kumble	619	Harbhajan Singh	417	Zaheer Khan	311
Kapil Dev	434	**R. Ashwin**	**377**	**I. Sharma**	**297**

PAKISTAN

Wasim Akram	414	Imran Khan	362	Abdul Qadir	236
Waqar Younis	373	Danish Kaneria	261	**Yasir Shah**	**227**

SRI LANKA

M. Muralitharan† 795	W. P. U. J. C. Vaas 355	**R. A. S. Lakmal** **151**
H. M. R. K. B. Herath . . 433	**M. D. K. Perera** **161**	S. L. Malinga 101

† *M. Muralitharan also took 2-102 and 3-55 for the World XI v Australia (2005-06 Super Series Test).*

ZIMBABWE

H. H. Streak 216	P. A. Strang 70	A. G. Cremer 57
R. W. Price 80	H. K. Olonga 68	B. C. Strang 56

BANGLADESH

Shakib Al Hasan. 210	Mohammad Rafique. . . . 100	Mashrafe bin Mortaza . . 78
Taijul Islam. **114**	Mehedi Hasan 90	Shahadat Hossain 72

IRELAND

T. J. Murtagh 13	S. R. Thompson 10

AFGHANISTAN

Rashid Khan. 23	Yamin Ahmadzai 10

BEST CAREER AVERAGES

(Qualification: 75 wickets)

Avge		*T*	*W*	*Avge*		*T*	*W*
10.75	G. A. Lohmann (E)	18	112	18.63	C. Blythe (E)	19	100
16.43	S. F. Barnes (E)	27	189	20.39	J. H. Wardle (E)	28	102
16.53	C. T. B. Turner (A)	17	101	20.53	A. K. Davidson (A)	44	186
16.98	R. Peel (E)	20	101	20.94	M. D. Marshall (WI)	81	376
17.75	J. Briggs (E)	33	118	20.97	J. Garner (WI)	58	259
18.41	F. R. Spofforth (A)	18	94	20.99	C. E. L. Ambrose (WI)	98	405
18.56	F. H. Tyson (E)	17	76				

BEST CAREER STRIKE-RATES

(Balls per wicket. Qualification: 75 wickets)

SR		*T*	*W*	*SR*		*T*	*W*
34.19	G. A. Lohmann (E)	18	112	45.74	Shoaib Akhtar (P)	46	178
38.75	S. E. Bond (NZ)	18	87	46.76	M. D. Marshall (WI)	81	376
40.66	**K. Rabada (SA)**	**43**	**197**	47.02	A. A. Donald (SA)	72	330
41.65	S. F. Barnes (E)	27	189	**47.15**	**P. J. Cummins (A)**	**34**	**164**
42.38	D. W. Steyn (SA)	93	439	**47.93**	**J. J. Bumrah (I)**	**17**	**79**
43.49	Waqar Younis (P)	87	373	48.78	Mohammad Asif (P)	23	106
44.52	F. R. Spofforth (A)	18	94	**48.92**	**J. L. Pattinson (A)**	**21**	**81**
45.12	J. V. Saunders (A)	14	79	**49.31**	**M. A. Starc (A)**	**61**	**255**
45.18	J. Briggs (E)	33	118	49.32	C. E. H. Croft (WI)	27	125
45.42	F. H. Tyson (E)	17	76	49.43	F. S. Trueman (E)	67	307
45.46	C. Blythe (E)	19	100	**49.99**	**Mohammed Shami (I)**	**50**	**180**

2,000 RUNS AND 200 WICKETS

	Tests	Runs	Wkts	Tests for 1,000/100 Double
R. Ashwin (India)	**74**	**2,467**	**377**	**24**
R. Benaud (Australia)	63	2,201	248	32
†I. T. Botham (England)	102	5,200	383	21
S. C. J. Broad (England)	**144**	**3,346**	**517**	**35**
C. L. Cairns (New Zealand)	62	3,320	218	33
A. Flintoff (England/World)	79	3,845	226	43
R. J. Hadlee (New Zealand)	86	3,124	431	28
Harbhajan Singh (India)	103	2,224	417	62
Imran Khan (Pakistan)	88	3,807	362	30
M. J. Johnson (Australia)	73	2,065	313	37
†J. H. Kallis (South Africa/World)	166	13,289	292	53
Kapil Dev (India)	131	5,248	434	25
A. Kumble (India)	132	2,506	619	56
S. M. Pollock (South Africa)	108	3,781	421	26
Shakib Al Hasan (Bangladesh)	56	3,862	210	28
†G. S. Sobers (West Indies)	93	8,032	235	48
W. P. U. J. C. Vaas (Sri Lanka)	111	3,089	355	47
D. L. Vettori (New Zealand/World)	113	4,531	362	47
†S. K. Warne (Australia)	145	3,154	708	58
Wasim Akram (Pakistan)	104	2,898	414	45

H. H. Streak scored 1,990 runs and took 216 wickets in 65 Tests for Zimbabwe.

† *J. H. Kallis also took 200 catches, S. K. Warne 125, I. T. Botham 120 and G. S. Sobers 109. These four and C. L. Hooper (5,762 runs, 114 wickets and 115 catches for West Indies) are the only players to have achieved the treble of 1,000 runs, 100 wickets and 100 catches in Test cricket.*

WICKETKEEPING RECORDS

MOST DISMISSALS IN AN INNINGS

7 (7ct)	Wasim Bari	Pakistan v New Zealand at Auckland	1978-79
7 (7ct)	R. W. Taylor	England v India at Bombay	1979-80
7 (7ct)	I. D. S. Smith	New Zealand v Sri Lanka at Hamilton	1990-91
7 (7ct)	R. D. Jacobs	West Indies v Australia at Melbourne	2000-01

The first instance of seven wicketkeeping dismissals in a Test innings was a joint effort for Pakistan v West Indies at Kingston in 1976-77. Majid Khan made four catches, deputising for the injured wicketkeeper Wasim Bari, who made three more catches on his return.

There have been ***32*** *instances of players making six dismissals in a Test innings, the most recent being Q. de Kock (6ct) for South Africa v England at Centurion in 2019-20.*

MOST STUMPINGS IN AN INNINGS

5	K. S. More	India v West Indies at Madras	1987-88

MOST DISMISSALS IN A TEST

11 (11ct)	R. C. Russell	England v South Africa at Johannesburg	1995-96
11 (11ct)	A. B. de Villiers	South Africa v Pakistan at Johannesburg	2012-13
11 (11ct)	R. R. Pant	India v Australia at Adelaide	2018-19
10 (10ct)	R. W. Taylor	England v India at Bombay	1979-80
10 (10ct)	A. C. Gilchrist	Australia v New Zealand at Hamilton	1999-2000
10 (10ct)	W. P. Saha	India v South Africa at Cape Town	2017-18
10 (10ct)	Sarfraz Ahmed	Pakistan v South Africa at Johannesburg	2018-19

*There have been **26** instances of players making nine dismissals in a Test, the most recent being J. M. Bairstow (9 ct) for England v Sri Lanka at Leeds in 2016. S. A. R. Silva made 18 in two successive Tests for Sri Lanka against India in 1985-86.*

The most stumpings in a match is 6 by K. S. More for India v West Indies at Madras in 1987-88.

J. J. Kelly (8ct) for Australia v England in 1901-02 and L. E. G. Ames (6ct, 2st) for England v West Indies in 1933 were the only keepers to make eight dismissals in a Test before World War II.

MOST DISMISSALS IN A SERIES

(Played in 5 Tests unless otherwise stated)

29 (29ct)	B. J. Haddin	Australia v England	2013
28 (28ct)	R. W. Marsh	Australia v England	1982-83
27 (25ct, 2st)	R. C. Russell	England v South Africa	1995-96
27 (25ct, 2st)	I. A. Healy	Australia v England (6 Tests)	1997

S. A. R. Silva made 22 dismissals (21ct, 1st) in three Tests for Sri Lanka v India in 1985-86.

H. Strudwick, with 21 (15ct, 6st) for England v South Africa in 1913-14, was the only wicketkeeper to make as many as 20 dismissals in a series before World War II.

MOST DISMISSALS

			T	*Ct*	*St*
1	M. V. Boucher (South Africa/World)	555	147	532	23
2	A. C. Gilchrist (Australia)	416	96	379	37
3	I. A. Healy (Australia)	395	119	366	29
4	R. W. Marsh (Australia)	355	96	343	12
5	M. S. Dhoni (India)	294	90	256	38
6	B. J. Haddin (Australia)	270	66	262	8
	P. J. L. Dujon (West Indies)	270	79	265	5
8	A. P. E. Knott (England)	269	95	250	19
9	**B-J. Watling (New Zealand)**	**257**	**65**	**249**	**8**
10	M. J. Prior (England)	256	79	243	13
11	A. J. Stewart (England)	241	82	227	14
12	Wasim Bari (Pakistan)	228	81	201	27
13	R. D. Jacobs (West Indies)	219	65	207	12
	T. G. Evans (England)	219	91	173	46
15	D. Ramdin (West Indies)	217	74	205	12
16	**Q. de Kock (South Africa)**	**214**	**47**	**203**	**11**
17	Kamran Akmal (Pakistan)	206	53	184	22
18	A. C. Parore (New Zealand)	201	67	194	7

The record for P. J. L. Dujon excludes two catches taken in two Tests when not keeping wicket; A. J. Stewart's record likewise excludes 36 catches taken in 51 Tests, B-J. Watling's ten in eight Tests and A. C. Parore's three in 11 Tests; Q. de Kock played a further two Tests when not keeping wicket but took no catches.

Excluding the Super Series Test, M. V. Boucher made 553 dismissals (530ct, 23st in 146 Tests) for South Africa, a national record.

W. A. S. Oldfield made 52 stumpings, a Test record, in 54 Tests for Australia; he also took 78 catches.

The most dismissals by a wicketkeeper playing for the countries not mentioned above are:

		T	*Ct*	*St*
K. C. Sangakkara (Sri Lanka)	151	48	131	20
A. Flower (Zimbabwe)	151	55	142	9
Mushfiqur Rahim (Bangladesh)	**113**	**55**	**98**	**15**
G. C. Wilson (Ireland)	6	1	6	0
Afsar Zazai (Afghanistan)	6	3	5	1

K. C. Sangakkara's record excludes 51 catches taken in 86 matches when not keeping wicket bu includes two catches taken as wicketkeeper in a match where he took over when the designatec keeper was injured; A. Flower's record excludes nine catches in eight Tests when not keeping wicket Mushfiqur Rahim's six catches in 15 Tests when not keeping wicket; G. C. Wilson played a furthe Test in which he did not keep wicket and took no catches.

FIELDING RECORDS

(Excluding wicketkeepers)

MOST CATCHES IN AN INNINGS

5	V. Y. Richardson	Australia v South Africa at Durban	1935-36
5	Yajurvindra Singh	India v England at Bangalore	1976-77
5	M. Azharuddin	India v Pakistan at Karachi	1989-90
5	K. Srikkanth	India v Australia at Perth	1991-92
5	S. P. Fleming	New Zealand v Zimbabwe at Harare	1997-98
5	G. C. Smith	South Africa v Australia at Perth	2012-13
5	D. J. G. Sammy	West Indies v India at Mumbai	2013-14
5	D. M. Bravo	West Indies v Bangladesh at Arnos Vale	2014-15
5	A. M. Rahane	India v Sri Lanka at Galle	2015-16
5	J. Blackwood	West Indies v Sri Lanka at Colombo (PSO)	2015-16
5	S. P. D. Smith	Australia v South Africa at Cape Town	2017-18
5	**B. A. Stokes**	**England v South Africa at Cape Town**	**2019-20**
5	**H. D. R. L. Thirimanne†**	**Sri Lanka v England at Galle**	**2020-21**

† *Thirimanne caught all five off the same bowler, L. Embuldeniya.*

MOST CATCHES IN A TEST

8	A. M. Rahane	India v Sri Lanka at Galle	2015-16
7	G. S. Chappell	Australia v England at Perth	1974-75
7	Yajurvindra Singh	India v England at Bangalore	1976-77
7	H. P. Tillekeratne	Sri Lanka v New Zealand at Colombo (SSC)	1992-93
7	S. P. Fleming	New Zealand v Zimbabwe at Harare	1997-98
7	M. L. Hayden	Australia v Sri Lanka at Galle	2003-04
7	K. L. Rahul	India v England at Nottingham	2018

*There have been **35** instances of players taking six catches in a Test, the most recent being **O. J. D. Pope for England v South Africa at Port Elizabeth in 2019-20**.*

MOST CATCHES IN A SERIES

(Played in 5 Tests unless otherwise stated)

15	J. M. Gregory	Australia v England	1920-21
14	G. S. Chappell	Australia v England (6 Tests)	1974-75
14	K. L. Rahul	India v England	2018
13	R. B. Simpson	Australia v South Africa	1957-58
13	R. B. Simpson	Australia v West Indies	1960-61
13	B. C. Lara	West Indies v England (6 Tests)	1997-98
13	R. Dravid	India v Australia (4 Tests)	2004-05
13	B. C. Lara	West Indies v India (4 Tests)	2005-06
13	A. N. Cook	England v India	2018

MOST CATCHES

Ct	*T*	
210	164†	R. Dravid (India/World)
205	149	D. P. M. D. Jayawardene (SL)
200	166†	J. H. Kallis (SA/World)
196	168	R. T. Ponting (Australia)
181	128	M. E. Waugh (Australia)
175	161	A. N. Cook (England)
171	111	S. P. Fleming (New Zealand)
169	117†	G. C. Smith (SA/World)
164	131†	B. C. Lara (West Indies/World)
157	104	M. A. Taylor (Australia)
156	156	A. R. Border (Australia)
155	**105**	**L. R. P. L. Taylor (New Zealand)**
139	118	Younis Khan (Pakistan)
135	134	V. V. S. Laxman (India)
134	115	M. J. Clarke (Australia)
131	**99**	**J. E. Root (England)**
128	103	M. L. Hayden (Australia)
125	145	S. K. Warne (Australia)

† *Excluding the Super Series Test, Dravid made 209 catches in 163 Tests for India, Kallis 196 in 165 Tests for South Africa, and Lara 164 in 130 Tests for West Indies, all national records. G. C. Smith made 166 catches in 116 Tests for South Africa.*

*The most catches in the field for other countries are Zimbabwe 60 in 60 Tests (A. D. R. Campbell); Bangladesh 38 in 49 Tests (**Mahmudullah**); Ireland 4 in 3 Tests (P. R. Stirling); Afghanistan 4 in 2 Tests (Ibrahim Zadran) and in 3 Tests (Ihsanullah Janat).*

TEAM RECORDS

HIGHEST INNINGS TOTALS

952-6 dec	Sri Lanka v India at Colombo (RPS)	1997-98
903-7 dec	England v Australia at The Oval	1938
849	England v West Indies at Kingston	1929-30
790-3 dec	West Indies v Pakistan at Kingston	1957-58
765-6 dec	Pakistan v Sri Lanka at Karachi	2008-09
760-7 dec	Sri Lanka v India at Ahmedabad	2009-10
759-7 dec	India v England at Chennai	2016-17
758-8 dec	Australia v West Indies at Kingston	1954-55
756-5 dec	Sri Lanka v South Africa at Colombo (SSC)	2006
751-5 dec	West Indies v England at St John's	2003-04

The highest innings totals for the countries not mentioned above are:

715-6 dec	New Zealand v Bangladesh at Hamilton	2018-19
682-6 dec	South Africa v England at Lord's	2003
638	Bangladesh v Sri Lanka at Galle	2012-13
563-9 dec	Zimbabwe v West Indies at Harare	2001
342	Afghanistan v Bangladesh at Chittagong	2019-20
339	Ireland v Pakistan at Malahide	2018

HIGHEST FOURTH-INNINGS TOTALS

To win

418-7	West Indies (*set 418 to win*) v Australia at St John's	2002-03
414-4	South Africa (*set 414 to win*) v Australia at Perth	2008-09
406-4	India (*set 403 to win*) v West Indies at Port-of-Spain	1975-76
404-3	Australia (*set 404 to win*) v England at Leeds	1948

To tie

347	India v Australia at Madras	1986-87

To draw

654-5	England (*set 696 to win*) v South Africa at Durban	1938-39
450-7	South Africa (*set 458 to win*) v India at Johannesburg	2013-14
429-8	India (*set 438 to win*) v England at The Oval	1979
423-7	South Africa (*set 451 to win*) v England at The Oval	1947

To lose

451	New Zealand (*lost by 98 runs*) v England at Christchurch	2001-02
450	Pakistan (*lost by 39 runs*) v Australia at Brisbane	2016-17
445	India (*lost by 47 runs*) v Australia at Adelaide	1977-78
440	New Zealand (*lost by 38 runs*) v England at Nottingham	1973
431	New Zealand (*lost by 121 runs*) v England at Napier	2007-08

MOST RUNS IN A DAY (BOTH SIDES)

588	England (398-6), India (190-0) at Manchester (2nd day)	1936
522	England (503-2), South Africa (19-0) at Lord's (2nd day)	1924
509	Sri Lanka (509-9) v Bangladesh at Colombo (PSS) (2nd day)	2002
508	England (221-2), South Africa (287-6) at The Oval (3rd day)	1935

MOST RUNS IN A DAY (ONE SIDE)

509	Sri Lanka (509-9) v Bangladesh at Colombo (PSS) (2nd day)	2002
503	England (503-2) v South Africa at Lord's (2nd day)	1924
494	Australia (494-6) v South Africa at Sydney (1st day)	1910-11
482	Australia (482-5) v South Africa at Adelaide (1st day)	2012-13
475	Australia (475-2) v England at The Oval (1st day)	1934

MOST WICKETS IN A DAY

27	England (18-3 to 53 all out and 62) v Australia (60) at Lord's (2nd day)	1888
25	Australia (112 and 48-5) v England (61) at Melbourne (1st day)	1901-02
24	England (69-1 to 145 and 60-5) v Australia (119) at The Oval (2nd day)	1896
24	India (347-6 to 474) v Afghanistan (109 and 103) at Bangalore (2nd day)	2018

HIGHEST AGGREGATES IN A TEST

Runs	*Wkts*			*Days played*
1,981	35	South Africa v England at Durban	1938-39	10†
1,815	34	West Indies v England at Kingston	1929-30	9‡
1,764	39	Australia v West Indies at Adelaide	1968-69	5
1,753	40	Australia v England at Adelaide	1920-21	6
1,747	25	Australia v India at Sydney	2003-04	5
1,723	31	England v Australia at Leeds	1948	5
1,702	28	Pakistan v India at Faisalabad	2005-06	5

† *No play on one day.* ‡ *No play on two days.*

LOWEST INNINGS TOTALS

26	New Zealand v England at Auckland	1954-55
30	South Africa v England at Port Elizabeth	1895-96
30	South Africa v England at Birmingham	1924
35	South Africa v England at Cape Town	1898-99
36	Australia v England at Birmingham	1902
36	South Africa v Australia at Melbourne	1931-32
36†	**India v Australia at Adelaide**	**2020-21**
38	Ireland v England at Lord's	2019
42	Australia v England at Sydney	1887-88
42	New Zealand v Australia at Wellington	1945-46
42†	India v England at Lord's	1974
43	South Africa v England at Cape Town	1888-89
43	Bangladesh v West Indies at North Sound	2018
44	Australia v England at The Oval	1896
45	England v Australia at Sydney	1886-87
45	South Africa v Australia at Melbourne	1931-32
45	New Zealand v South Africa at Cape Town	2012-13

† *One man retired or absent hurt.*

The lowest innings totals for the countries not mentioned above are:

47	West Indies v England at Kingston	2003-04
49	Pakistan v South Africa at Johannesburg	2012-13
51	Zimbabwe v New Zealand at Napier	2011-12
71	Sri Lanka v Pakistan at Kandy	1994-95
103	Afghanistan v India at Bangalore	2018

FEWEST RUNS IN A FULL DAY'S PLAY

95	Australia (80), Pakistan (15-2) at Karachi (1st day, 5½ hrs)	1956-57
104	Pakistan (0-0 to 104-5) v Australia at Karachi (4th day, 5½ hrs)	1959-60
106	England (92-2 to 198) v Australia at Brisbane (4th day, 5 hrs). *England were dismissed five minutes before the close of play, leaving no time for Australia to start their second innings.*	1958-59
111	S. Africa (48-2 to 130-6 dec), India (29-1) at Cape Town (5th day, 5½ hrs)	1992-93
112	Australia (138-6 to 187), Pakistan (63-1) at Karachi (4th day, 5½ hrs)	1956-57
115	Australia (116-7 to 165 and 66-5 after following on) v Pakistan at Karachi (4th day, 5½ hrs)	1988-89
117	India (117-5) v Australia at Madras (1st day, 5½ hrs)	1956-57
117	New Zealand (6-0 to 123-4) v Sri Lanka at Colombo (SSC) (5th day, 5¾ hrs)	1983-84

In England

151	England (175-2 to 289), New Zealand (37-7) at Lord's (3rd day, 6 hrs)	1978
158	England (211-2 to 369-9) v South Africa at Manchester (5th day, 6 hrs)	1998
159	Pakistan (208-4 to 350), England (17-1) at Leeds (3rd day, 6 hrs)	1971

LOWEST AGGREGATES IN A COMPLETED TEST

Runs	*Wkts*			*Days played*
234	29	Australia v South Africa at Melbourne	1931-32	3†
291	40	England v Australia at Lord's	1888	2
295	28	New Zealand v Australia at Wellington	1945-46	2
309	29	West Indies v England at Bridgetown	1934-35	3
323	30	England v Australia at Manchester	1888	2

† *No play on one day.*

LARGEST VICTORIES

Largest Innings Victories

Inns & 579 runs	England (903-7 dec) v Australia (201 & 123†) at The Oval	1938
Inns & 360 runs	Australia (652-7 dec) v South Africa (159 & 133) at Johannesburg	2001-02
Inns & 336 runs	West Indies (614-5 dec) v India (124 & 154) at Calcutta	1958-59
Inns & 332 runs	Australia (645) v England (141 & 172) at Brisbane	1946-47
Inns & 324 runs	Pakistan (643) v New Zealand (73 & 246) at Lahore	2002
Inns & 322 runs	West Indies (660-5 dec) v New Zealand (216 & 122) at Wellington	1994-95
Inns & 310 runs	West Indies (536) v Bangladesh (139 & 87) at Dhaka	2002-03
Inns & 301 runs	New Zealand (495-7 dec) v Zimbabwe (51 & 143) at Napier	2011-12

† *Two men absent in both Australian innings.*

Largest Victories by Runs Margin

675 runs	England (521 & 342-8 dec) v Australia (122 & 66†) at Brisbane	1928-29
562 runs	Australia (701 & 327) v England (321 & 145‡) at The Oval	1934
530 runs	Australia (328 & 578) v South Africa (205 & 171§) at Melbourne	1910-11
492 runs	South Africa (488 & 344-6 dec) v Australia (221 and 119) at Johannesburg	2017-18
491 runs	Australia (381 & 361-5 dec) v Pakistan (179 & 72) at Perth	2004-05
465 runs	Sri Lanka (384 and 447-6 dec) v Bangladesh (208 and 158) at Chittagong	2008-09
425 runs	West Indies (211 & 411-5 dec) v England (71 & 126) at Manchester	1976
423 runs	New Zealand (178 & 585-4 dec) v Sri Lanka (104 & 236) at Christchurch	2018-19
409 runs	Australia (350 & 460-7 dec) v England (215 & 186) at Lord's	1948
408 runs	West Indies (328 & 448) v Australia (203 & 165) at Adelaide	1979-80
405 runs	Australia (566-8 dec & 254-2 dec) v England (312 & 103) at Lord's	2015

† *One man absent in Australia's first innings; two men absent in their second.*
‡ *Two men absent in England's first innings; one man absent in their second.*
§ *One man absent in South Africa's second innings.*

TIED TESTS

West Indies (453 & 284) v Australia (505 & 232) at Brisbane	1960-61
Australia (574-7 dec & 170-5 dec) v India (397 & 347) at Madras	1986-87

MOST CONSECUTIVE TEST VICTORIES

16	Australia	1999-2000 to 2000-01
16	Australia	2005-06 to 2007-08
11	West Indies	1983-84 to 1984-85
9	Sri Lanka	2001 to 2001-02
9	South Africa	2001-02 to 2003
8	Australia	1920-21 to 1921
8	England	2004 to 2004-05

MOST CONSECUTIVE TESTS WITHOUT VICTORY

44	New Zealand	1929-30 to 1955-56
34	Bangladesh	2000-01 to 2004-05
31	India	1981-82 to 1984-85
28	South Africa	1935 to 1949-50
24	India	1932 to 1951-52
24	Bangladesh	2004-05 to 2008-09
23	New Zealand	1962-63 to 1967-68
22	Pakistan	1958-59 to 1964-65
21	Sri Lanka	1985-86 to 1992-93
20	West Indies	1968-69 to 1972-73
20	West Indies	2004-05 to 2007

WHITEWASHES

Teams winning every game in a series of four Tests or more:

Five-Test Series

Australia beat England	1920-21
Australia beat South Africa	1931-32
England beat India	1959
West Indies beat India	1961-62
West Indies beat England	1984
West Indies beat England	1985-86
South Africa beat West Indies	1998-99
Australia beat West Indies	2000-01
Australia beat England	2006-07
Australia beat England	2013-14

Four-Test Series

Australia beat India	1967-68
South Africa beat Australia	1969-70
England beat West Indies	2004
England beat India	2011
Australia beat India	2011-12
India beat Australia	2012-13

The winning team in each instance was at home, except for West Indies in England, 1984.

PLAYERS

YOUNGEST TEST PLAYERS

Years	*Days*			
15	124	Mushtaq Mohammad	Pakistan v West Indies at Lahore	1958-59
16	189	Aqib Javed	Pakistan v New Zealand at Wellington	1988-89
16	205	S. R. Tendulkar	India v Pakistan at Karachi	1989-90

The above table should be treated with caution. All birthdates for Bangladesh and Pakistan (after Partition) must be regarded as questionable because of deficiencies in record-keeping. Hasan Raza was claimed to be 14 years 227 days old when he played for Pakistan against Zimbabwe at Faisalabad in 1996-97; this age was rejected by the Pakistan Cricket Board, although no alternative has been offered. Suggestions that Enamul Haque jnr was 16 years 230 days old when he played for Bangladesh against England in Dhaka in 2003-04 have been discounted by well-informed local observers, who believe he was 18.

The youngest Test players for countries not mentioned above are:

17	78	Mujeeb Zadran	Afghanistan v India at Bangalore	2018
17	122	J. E. D. Sealy	West Indies v England at Bridgetown	1929-30
17	128	Mohammad Sharif	Bangladesh v Zimbabwe at Bulawayo	2000-01
17	189	C. D. U. S. Weerasinghe	Sri Lanka v India at Colombo (PSS)	1985-86
17	239	I. D. Craig	Australia v South Africa at Melbourne	1952-53
17	352	H. Masakadza	Zimbabwe v West Indies at Harare	2001
18	10	D. L. Vettori	New Zealand v England at Wellington	1996-97
18	149	D. B. Close	England v New Zealand at Manchester	1949
18	340	P. R. Adams	South Africa v England at Port Elizabeth	1995-96
23	119	M. R. Adair	Ireland v England at Lord's	2019

OLDEST PLAYERS ON TEST DEBUT

Years	*Days*			
49	119	J. Southerton	England v Australia at Melbourne	1876-77
47	284	Miran Bux	Pakistan v India at Lahore	1954-55
46	253	D. D. Blackie	Australia v England at Sydney	1928-29
46	237	H. Ironmonger	Australia v England at Brisbane	1928-29
42	242	N. Betancourt	West Indies v England at Port-of-Spain	1929-30
41	337	E. R. Wilson	England v Australia at Sydney	1920-21
41	27	R. J. D. Jamshedji	India v England at Bombay	1933-34
40	345	C. A. Wiles	West Indies v England at Manchester	1933
40	295	O. Henry	South Africa v India at Durban	1992-93
40	216	S. P. Kinneir	England v Australia at Sydney	1911-12
40	110	H. W. Lee	England v South Africa at Johannesburg	1930-31
40	56	G. W. A. Chubb	South Africa v England at Nottingham	1951
40	37	C. Ramaswami	India v England at Manchester	1936

The oldest Test player on debut for Ireland was E. C. Joyce, 39 years 231 days,v Pakistan at Malahide, 2018; for New Zealand, H. M. McGirr, 38 years 101 days, v England at Auckland, 1929-30; for Sri Lanka, D. S. de Silva, 39 years 251 days, v England at Colombo (PSS), 1981-82; for Zimbabwe, A. C. Waller, 37 years 84 days, v England at Bulawayo, 1996-97; for Bangladesh, Enamul Haque snr, 35 years 58 days, v Zimbabwe at Harare, 2000-01; for Afghanistan, Mohammad Nabi, 33 years 99 days, v India at Bangalore, 2018. A. J. Traicos was 45 years 154 days old when he made his debut for Zimbabwe (v India at Harare, 1992-93) having played three Tests for South Africa in 1969-70.

OLDEST TEST PLAYERS

(Age on final day of their last Test match)

Years	*Days*			
52	165	W. Rhodes	England v West Indies at Kingston	1929-3
50	327	H. Ironmonger	Australia v England at Sydney	1932-3
50	320	W. G. Grace	England v Australia at Nottingham	189

Years	*Days*			
50	303	G. Gunn	England v West Indies at Kingston	1929-30
49	139	J. Southerton	England v Australia at Melbourne	1876-77
47	302	Miran Bux	Pakistan v India at Peshawar	1954-55
47	249	J. B. Hobbs	England v Australia at The Oval	1930
47	87	F. E. Woolley	England v Australia at The Oval	1934
46	309	D. D. Blackie	Australia v England at Adelaide	1928-29
46	206	A. W. Nourse	South Africa v England at The Oval	1924
46	202	H. Strudwick	England v Australia at The Oval	1926
46	41	E. H. Hendren	England v West Indies at Kingston	1934-35
45	304	A. J. Traicos	Zimbabwe v India at Delhi	1992-93
45	245	G. O. B. Allen	England v West Indies at Kingston	1947-48
45	215	P. Holmes	England v India at Lord's	1932
45	140	D. B. Close	England v West Indies at Manchester	1976

MOST TEST APPEARANCES

200	S. R. Tendulkar (India)	134	K. C. Sangakkara (Sri Lanka)
168	R. T. Ponting (Australia)	133	M. Muralitharan (Sri Lanka/World)
168	S. R. Waugh (Australia)	133	A. J. Stewart (England)
166	J. H. Kallis (South Africa/World)	132	A. Kumble (India)
164	S. Chanderpaul (West Indies)	132	C. A. Walsh (West Indies)
164	R. Dravid (India/World)	131	Kapil Dev (India)
161	A. N. Cook (England)	131	B. C. Lara (West Indies/World)
157	**J. M. Anderson (England)**	128	M. E. Waugh (Australia)
156	A. R. Border (Australia)	125	S. M. Gavaskar (India)
149	D. P. M. D. Jayawardene (Sri Lanka)	124	H. M. Amla (South Africa)
147	M. V. Boucher (South Africa/World)	124	Javed Miandad (Pakistan)
145	S. K. Warne (Australia)	124	G. D. McGrath (Australia)
144	**S. C. J. Broad (England)**	121	I. V. A. Richards (West Indies)
134	V. V. S. Laxman (India)	120	Inzamam-ul-Haq (Pakistan/World)

Excluding the Super Series Test, J. H. Kallis has made 165 appearances for South Africa, a national record. The most appearances for New Zealand is 112 by D. L. Vettori; for Bangladesh, ***70*** *by* ***Mushfiqur Rahim****; for Zimbabwe, 67 by G. W. Flower; for Afghanistan, 4 by Asghar Afghan, Rahmat Shah, Rashid Khan and Yamin Ahmadzai; and for Ireland, 3 by A. Balbirnie, T. J. Murtagh, K. J. O'Brien, W. T. S. Porterfield, P. R. Stirling and S. R. Thompson.*

MOST CONSECUTIVE TEST APPEARANCES FOR A COUNTRY

159	A. N. Cook (England)	May 2006 to September 2018
153	A. R. Border (Australia)	March 1979 to March 1994
107	M. E. Waugh (Australia)	June 1993 to October 2002
106	S. M. Gavaskar (India)	January 1975 to February 1987
101†	B. B. McCullum (New Zealand)	March 2004 to February 2016
98	A. B. de Villiers (South Africa)	December 2004 to January 2015
96†	A. C. Gilchrist (Australia)	November 1999 to January 2008
93	R. Dravid (India)	June 1996 to December 2005
93	D. P. M. D. Jayawardene (Sri Lanka)	November 2002 to January 2013

The most consecutive Test appearances for the countries not mentioned above (excluding Afghanistan and Ireland) are:

85	G. S. Sobers (West Indies)	April 1955 to April 1972
72	**Asad Shafiq (Pakistan)**	**October 2011 to August 2020**
56	A. D. R. Campbell (Zimbabwe)	October 1992 to September 2001
49	Mushfiqur Rahim (Bangladesh)	July 2007 to January 2017

† *Complete Test career.*

Bold type denotes sequence which was still in progress after January 1, 2020.

MOST TESTS AS CAPTAIN

	P	*W*	*L*	*D*
G. C. Smith (SA/World)	109	53	29*	27
A. R. Border (A)	93	32	22	38†
S. P. Fleming (NZ)	80	28	27	25
R. T. Ponting (A)	77	48	16	13
C. H. Lloyd (WI)	74	36	12	26
M. S. Dhoni (I)	60	27	18	15
A. N. Cook (E)	59	24	22	13
S. R. Waugh (A)	57	41	9	7
V. Kohli (I)	**56**	**33**	**13**	**10**
Misbah-ul-Haq (P)	56	26	19	11
A. Ranatunga (SL)	56	12	19	25
M. A. Atherton (E)	54	13	21	20
W. J. Cronje (SA)	53	27	11	15
M. P. Vaughan (E)	51	26	11	14
I. V. A. Richards (WI)	50	27	8	15
M. A. Taylor (A)	50	26	13	11
A. J. Strauss (E)	50	24	11	15

* *Includes defeat as World XI captain in Super Series Test against Australia.* † *One tie.*

Most Tests as captain of other countries:

	P	*W*	*L*	*D*
Mushfiqur Rahim (B)	34	7	18	9
A. D. R. Campbell (Z)	21	2	12	7
W. T. S. Porterfield (Ire)	3	0	3	0
Asghar Afghan (Afg)	2	0	2	0
Rashid Khan (Afg)	2	1	1	0

A. R. Border captained Australia in 93 consecutive Tests.

W. W. Armstrong (Australia) captained his country in the most Tests without being defeated: ten matches with eight wins and two draws.

Mohammad Ashraful (Bangladesh) captained his country in the most Tests without ever winning: 12 defeats and one draw.

UMPIRES

MOST TESTS

		First Test	*Last Test*
132	**Aleem Dar (Pakistan)**	**2003-04**	**2019-20**
128	S. A. Bucknor (West Indies)	1988-89	2008-09
108	R. E. Koertzen (South Africa)	1992-93	2010
95	D. J. Harper (Australia)	1998-99	2011
92	D. R. Shepherd (England)	1985	2004-05
84	B. F. Bowden (New Zealand)	1999-2000	2014-15
78	D. B. Hair (Australia)	1991-92	2008
74	S. J. A. Taufel (Australia)	2000-01	2012
74	I. J. Gould (England)	2008-09	2018-19
73	S. Venkataraghavan (India)	1992-93	2003-04
71	**R. J. Tucker (Australia)**	**2009-10**	**2019-20**
68	**R. A. Kettleborough (England)**	**2010-11**	**2020**
67	**H. D. P. K. Dharmasena (Sri Lanka)**	**2010-11**	**2020-21**
66	H. D. Bird (England)	1973	1996
64	**M. Erasmus (South Africa)**	**2009-10**	**2020-21**
62	**N. J. Llong (England)**	**2007-08**	**2019-20**
62	**B. N. J. Oxenford (Australia)**	**2010-11**	**2020-21**
57	S. J. Davis (Australia)	1997-98	2014-15
51	**P. R. Reiffel (Australia)**	**2012**	**2020-21**
51	**R. K. Illingworth (England)**	**2012-13**	**2020**

SUMMARY OF TESTS

1876-77 to January 25, 2021

	Opponents	*Tests*	*Won by*														*Tied*	*Drawn*
			E	*A*	*SA*	*WI*	*NZ*	*I*	*P*	*SL*	*Z*	*B*	*Ire*	*Afg*	*Wld*			
England	Australia	**351**	110	146	–	–	–	–	–	–	–	–	–	–	–		–	95
	South Africa	**153**	64	–	34	–	–	–	–	–	–	–	–	–	–		–	55
	West Indies	**160**	51	–	–	58	–	–	–	–	–	–	–	–	–		–	51
	New Zealand	**105**	48	–	–	–	11	–	–	–	–	–	–	–	–		–	46
	India	**122**	47	–	–	–	–	26	–	–	–	–	–	–	–		–	49
	Pakistan	**86**	26	–	–	–	–	–	21	–	–	–	–	–	–		–	39
	Sri Lanka	**36**	17	–	–	–	–	–	–	8	–	–	–	–	–		–	11
	Zimbabwe	**6**	3	–	–	–	–	–	–	–	0	–	–	–	–		–	3
	Bangladesh	**10**	9	–	–	–	–	–	–	–	–	1	–	–	–		–	0
	Ireland	**1**	1	–	–	–	–	–	–	–	–	–	0	–	–		–	0
Australia	South Africa	**98**	–	52	26	–	–	–	–	–	–	–	–	–	–		–	20
	West Indies	**116**	–	58	–	32	–	–	–	–	–	–	–	–	–		1	25
	New Zealand	**60**	–	34	–	–	8	–	–	–	–	–	–	–	–		–	18
	India	**102**	–	43	–	–	–	30	–	–	–	–	–	–	–		1	28
	Pakistan	**66**	–	33	–	–	–	–	15	–	–	–	–	–	–		–	18
	Sri Lanka	**31**	–	19	–	–	–	–	–	4	–	–	–	–	–		–	8
	Zimbabwe	**3**	–	3	–	–	–	–	–	–	0	–	–	–	–		–	0
	Bangladesh	**6**	–	5	–	–	–	–	–	–	–	1	–	–	–		–	0
	ICC World XI	**1**	–	1	–	–	–	–	–	–	–	–	–	–	0		–	0
South Africa	West Indies	**28**	–	–	18	3	–	–	–	–	–	–	–	–	–		–	7
	New Zealand	**45**	–	–	25	–	4	–	–	–	–	–	–	–	–		–	16
	India	**39**	–	–	15	–	–	14	–	–	–	–	–	–	–		–	10
	Pakistan	**26**	–	–	15	–	–	–	4	–	–	–	–	–	–		–	7
	Sri Lanka	**31**	–	–	16	–	–	–	–	9	–	–	–	–	–		–	6
	Zimbabwe	**9**	–	–	8	–	–	–	–	–	0	–	–	–	–		–	1
	Bangladesh	**12**	–	–	10	–	–	–	–	–	–	0	–	–	–		–	2
West Indies	New Zealand	**49**	–	–	–	13	17	–	–	–	–	–	–	–	–		–	19
	India	**98**	–	–	–	30	–	22	–	–	–	–	–	–	–		–	46
	Pakistan	**52**	–	–	–	17	–	–	20	–	–	–	–	–	–		–	15
	Sri Lanka	**20**	–	–	–	4	–	–	–	9	–	–	–	–	–		–	7
	Zimbabwe	**10**	–	–	–	7	–	–	–	–	0	–	–	–	–		–	3
	Bangladesh	**16**	–	–	–	10	–	–	–	–	–	4	–	–	–		–	2
	Afghanistan	**1**	–	–	–	1	–	–	–	–	–	–	–	0	–		–	0
New Zealand	India	**59**	–	–	–	–	12	21	–	–	–	–	–	–	–		–	26
	Pakistan	**60**	–	–	–	–	14	–	25	–	–	–	–	–	–		–	21
	Sri Lanka	**36**	–	–	–	–	16	–	–	9	–	–	–	–	–		–	11
	Zimbabwe	**17**	–	–	–	–	11	–	–	–	0	–	–	–	–		–	6
	Bangladesh	**15**	–	–	–	–	12	–	–	–	–	0	–	–	–		–	3
India	Pakistan	**59**	–	–	–	–	–	9	12	–	–	–	–	–	–		–	38
	Sri Lanka	**44**	–	–	–	–	–	20	–	7	–	–	–	–	–		–	17
	Zimbabwe	**11**	–	–	–	–	–	7	–	–	2	–	–	–	–		–	2
	Bangladesh	**11**	–	–	–	–	–	9	–	–	–	0	–	–	–		–	2
	Afghanistan	**1**	–	–	–	–	–	1	–	–	–	–	–	0	–		–	0
Pakistan	Sri Lanka	**55**	–	–	–	–	–	–	20	16	–	–	–	–	–		–	19
	Zimbabwe	**17**	–	–	–	–	–	–	10	–	3	–	–	–	–		–	4
	Bangladesh	**11**	–	–	–	–	–	–	10	–	–	0	–	–	–		–	1
	Ireland	**1**	–	–	–	–	–	–	1	–	–	–	0	–	–		–	0
Sri Lanka	Zimbabwe	**20**	–	–	–	–	–	–	–	14	0	–	–	–	–		–	6
	Bangladesh	**20**	–	–	–	–	–	–	–	16	–	1	–	–	–		–	3
Zimbabwe	Bangladesh	**17**	–	–	–	–	–	–	–	–	7	7	–	–	–		–	3
Bangladesh	Afghanistan	**1**	–	–	–	–	–	–	–	–	–	0	–	1	–		–	0
Ireland	Afghanistan	**1**	–	–	–	–	–	–	–	–	–	–	0	1	–		–	0
		2,405	376	394	167	175	105	159	138	92	12	14	0	2	0		2	769

RESULTS SUMMARY OF TESTS

1876-77 to January 25, 2021 (2,405 matches)

	Tests	*Won*	*Lost*	*Drawn*	*Tied*	*% Won*	*Toss Won*
England	1,030	376	305	349	–	36.50	503
Australia	834†	394†	226	212	2	47.24	420
South Africa	441	167	150	124	–	37.86	210
West Indies	550	175	199	175	1	31.81	286
New Zealand	446	105	175	166	–	23.54	222

	Tests	Won	Lost	Drawn	Tied	% Won	Toss Won
India	546	159	168	218	1	29.12	271
Pakistan	433	138	133	162	–	31.87	207
Sri Lanka	293	92	113	88	–	31.39	159
Zimbabwe	110	12	70	28	–	10.90	64
Bangladesh	119	14	89	16	–	11.76	60
Ireland	3	0	3	0	–	0.00	2
Afghanistan	4	2	2	0	–	50.00	1
ICC World XI	1	0	1	0	–	0.00	0

† *Includes Super Series Test between Australia and ICC World XI.*

ENGLAND v AUSTRALIA

Season	Captains England	Australia	T	E	A	D
1876-77	James Lillywhite	D. W. Gregory	2	1	1	0
1878-79	Lord Harris	D. W. Gregory	1	0	1	0
1880	Lord Harris	W. L. Murdoch	1	1	0	0
1881-82	A. Shaw	W. L. Murdoch	4	0	2	2
1882	A. N. Hornby	W. L. Murdoch	1	0	1	0

THE ASHES

Season	Captains England	Australia	T	E	A	D	Held by
1882-83	Hon. Ivo Bligh	W. L. Murdoch	4*	2	2	0	E
1884	Lord Harris[1]	W. L. Murdoch	3	1	0	2	E
1884-85	A. Shrewsbury	T. P. Horan[2]	5	3	2	0	E
1886	A. G. Steel	H. J. H. Scott	3	3	0	0	E
1886-87	A. Shrewsbury	P. S. McDonnell	2	2	0	0	E
1887-88	W. W. Read	P. S. McDonnell	1	1	0	0	E
1888	W. G. Grace[3]	P. S. McDonnell	3	2	1	0	E
1890†	W. G. Grace	W. L. Murdoch	2	2	0	0	E
1891-92	W. G. Grace	J. M. Blackham	3	1	2	0	A
1893	W. G. Grace[4]	J. M. Blackham	3	1	0	2	E
1894-95	A. E. Stoddart	G. Giffen[5]	5	3	2	0	E
1896	W. G. Grace	G. H. S. Trott	3	2	1	0	E
1897-98	A. E. Stoddart[6]	G. H. S. Trott	5	1	4	0	A
1899	A. C. MacLaren[7]	J. Darling	5	0	1	4	A
1901-02	A. C. MacLaren	J. Darling[8]	5	1	4	0	A
1902	A. C. MacLaren	J. Darling	5	1	2	2	A
1903-04	P. F. Warner	M. A. Noble	5	3	2	0	E
1905	Hon. F. S. Jackson	J. Darling	5	2	0	3	E
1907-08	A. O. Jones[9]	M. A. Noble	5	1	4	0	A
1909	A. C. MacLaren	M. A. Noble	5	1	2	2	A
1911-12	J. W. H. T. Douglas	C. Hill	5	4	1	0	E
1912	C. B. Fry	S. E. Gregory	3	1	0	2	E
1920-21	J. W. H. T. Douglas	W. W. Armstrong	5	0	5	0	A
1921	Hon. L. H. Tennyson[10]	W. W. Armstrong	5	0	3	2	A
1924-25	A. E. R. Gilligan	H. L. Collins	5	1	4	0	A
1926	A. W. Carr[11]	H. L. Collins[12]	5	1	0	4	E
1928-29	A. P. F. Chapman[13]	J. Ryder	5	4	1	0	E
1930	A. P. F. Chapman[14]	W. M. Woodfull	5	1	2	2	A
1932-33	D. R. Jardine	W. M. Woodfull	5	4	1	0	E
1934	R. E. S. Wyatt[15]	W. M. Woodfull	5	1	2	2	A
1936-37	G. O. B. Allen	D. G. Bradman	5	2	3	0	A
1938†	W. R. Hammond	D. G. Bradman	4	1	1	2	A
1946-47	W. R. Hammond[16]	D. G. Bradman	5	0	3	2	A
1948	N. W. D. Yardley	D. G. Bradman	5	0	4	1	A
1950-51	F. R. Brown	A. L. Hassett	5	1	4	0	A
1953	L. Hutton	A. L. Hassett	5	1	0	4	E
1954-55	L. Hutton	I. W. Johnson[17]	5	3	1	1	E

	Captains						
Season	*England*	*Australia*	*T*	*E*	*A*	*D*	*Held by*
1956	P. B. H. May	I. W. Johnson	5	2	1	2	E
1958-59	P. B. H. May	R. Benaud	5	0	4	1	A
1961	P. B. H. May[18]	R. Benaud[19]	5	1	2	2	A
1962-63	E. R. Dexter	R. Benaud	5	1	1	3	A
1964	E. R. Dexter	R. B. Simpson	5	0	1	4	A
1965-66	M. J. K. Smith	R. B. Simpson[20]	5	1	1	3	A
1968	M. C. Cowdrey[21]	W. M. Lawry[22]	5	1	1	3	A
1970-71†	R. Illingworth	W. M. Lawry[23]	6	2	0	4	E
1972	R. Illingworth	I. M. Chappell	5	2	2	1	E
1974-75	M. H. Denness[24]	I. M. Chappell	6	1	4	1	A
1975	A. W. Greig[25]	I. M. Chappell	4	0	1	3	A
1976-77‡	A. W. Greig	G. S. Chappell	1	0	1	0	—
1977	J. M. Brearley	G. S. Chappell	5	3	0	2	E
1978-79	J. M. Brearley	G. N. Yallop	6	5	1	0	E
1979-80‡	J. M. Brearley	G. S. Chappell	3	0	3	0	—
1980‡	I. T. Botham	G. S. Chappell	1	0	0	1	—
1981	J. M. Brearley[26]	K. J. Hughes	6	3	1	2	E
1982-83	R. G. D. Willis	G. S. Chappell	5	1	2	2	A
1985	D. I. Gower	A. R. Border	6	3	1	2	E
1986-87	M. W. Gatting	A. R. Border	5	2	1	2	E
1987-88‡	M. W. Gatting	A. R. Border	1	0	0	1	—
1989	D. I. Gower	A. R. Border	6	0	4	2	A
1990-91	G. A. Gooch[27]	A. R. Border	5	0	3	2	A
1993	G. A. Gooch[28]	A. R. Border	6	1	4	1	A
1994-95	M. A. Atherton	M. A. Taylor	5	1	3	1	A
1997	M. A. Atherton	M. A. Taylor	6	2	3	1	A
1998-99	A. J. Stewart	M. A. Taylor	5	1	3	1	A
2001	N. Hussain[29]	S. R. Waugh[30]	5	1	4	0	A
2002-03	N. Hussain	S. R. Waugh	5	1	4	0	A
2005	M. P. Vaughan	R. T. Ponting	5	2	1	2	E
2006-07	A. Flintoff	R. T. Ponting	5	0	5	0	A
2009	A. J. Strauss	R. T. Ponting	5	2	1	2	E
2010-11	A. J. Strauss	R. T. Ponting[31]	5	3	1	1	E
2013	A. N. Cook	M. J. Clarke	5	3	0	2	E
2013-14	A. N. Cook	M. J. Clarke	5	0	5	0	A
2015	A. N. Cook	M. J. Clarke	5	3	2	0	E
2017-18	J. E. Root	S. P. D. Smith	5	0	4	1	A
2019	J. E. Root	T. D. Paine	5	2	2	1	A
	In Australia		180	57	95	28	
	In England		171	53	51	67	
	Totals		351	110	146	95	

* *The Ashes were awarded in 1882-83 after a series of three matches which England won 2–1. A fourth match was played and this was won by Australia.*
† *The matches at Manchester in 1890 and 1938 and at Melbourne (Third Test) in 1970-71 were abandoned without a ball being bowled and are excluded.*
‡ *The Ashes were not at stake in these series.*

The following deputised for the official touring captain or were appointed by the home authority for only a minor proportion of the series:

[1]A. N. Hornby (First). [2]W. L. Murdoch (First), H. H. Massie (Third), J. M. Blackham (Fourth). [3]A. G. Steel (First). [4]A. E. Stoddart (First). [5]J. M. Blackham (First). [6]A. C. MacLaren (First, Second and Fifth). [7]W. G. Grace (First). [8]H. Trumble (Fourth and Fifth). [9]F. L. Fane (First, Second and Third). [10]J. W. H. T. Douglas (First and Second). [11]A. P. F. Chapman (Fifth). [12]W. Bardsley (Third and Fourth). [13]J. C. White (Fifth). [14]R. E. S. Wyatt (Fifth). [15]C. F. Walters (First). [16]N. W. D. Yardley (Fifth). [17]A. R. Morris (Second). [18]M. C. Cowdrey (First and Second). [19]R. N. Harvey (Second). [20]B. C. Booth (First and Third). [21]T. W. Graveney (Fourth). [22]B. N. Jarman (Fourth) [23]I. M. Chappell (Seventh). [24]J. H. Edrich (Fourth). [25]M. H. Denness (First). [26]I. T. Botham (First and Second). [27]A. J. Lamb (First). [28]M. A. Atherton (Fifth and Sixth). [29]M. A. Atherton (Second and Third). [30]A. C. Gilchrist (Fourth). [31]M. J. Clarke (Fifth).

HIGHEST INNINGS TOTALS

For England in England: 903-7 dec at The Oval 1938
in Australia: 644 at Sydney 2010-11

For Australia in England: 729-6 dec at Lord's 1930
in Australia: 662-9 dec at Perth 2017-18

LOWEST INNINGS TOTALS

For England in England: 52 at The Oval 1948
in Australia: 45 at Sydney 1886-87

For Australia in England: 36 at Birmingham 1902
in Australia: 42 at Sydney 1887-88

DOUBLE-HUNDREDS

For England (14)

364	L. Hutton at The Oval	1938	231*	W. R. Hammond at Sydney	1936-37
287	R. E. Foster at Sydney	1903-04	227	K. P. Pietersen at Adelaide	2010-11
256	K. F. Barrington at Manchester	1964	216*	E. Paynter at Nottingham	1938
251	W. R. Hammond at Sydney	1928-29	215	D. I. Gower at Birmingham	1985
244*	A. N. Cook at Melbourne	2017-18	207	N. Hussain at Birmingham	1997
240	W. R. Hammond at Lord's	1938	206	P. D. Collingwood at Adelaide	2006-07
235*	A. N. Cook at Brisbane	2010-11	200	W. R. Hammond at Melbourne	1928-29

For Australia (26)

334	D. G. Bradman at Leeds	1930	232	S. J. McCabe at Nottingham	1938
311	R. B. Simpson at Manchester	1964	225	R. B. Simpson at Adelaide	1965-66
307	R. M. Cowper at Melbourne	1965-66	219	M. A. Taylor at Nottingham	1989
304	D. G. Bradman at Leeds	1934	215	S. P. D. Smith at Lord's	2015
270	D. G. Bradman at Melbourne	1936-37	212	D. G. Bradman at Adelaide	1936-37
266	W. H. Ponsford at The Oval	1934	211	W. L. Murdoch at The Oval	1884
254	D. G. Bradman at Lord's	1930	211	S. P. D. Smith at Manchester	2019
250	J. L. Langer at Melbourne	2002-03	207	K. R. Stackpole at Brisbane	1970-71
244	D. G. Bradman at The Oval	1934	206*	W. A. Brown at Lord's	1938
239	S. P. D. Smith at Perth	2017-18	206	A. R. Morris at Adelaide	1950-51
234	S. G. Barnes at Sydney	1946-47	201*	J. Ryder at Adelaide	1924-25
234	D. G. Bradman at Sydney	1946-47	201	S. E. Gregory at Sydney	1894-95
232	D. G. Bradman at The Oval	1930	200*	A. R. Border at Leeds	1993

INDIVIDUAL HUNDREDS

In total, England have scored **245** hundreds against Australia, and Australia have scored **318** against England. The players with at least five hundreds are as follows:

For England

12: J. B. Hobbs.
9: D. I. Gower, W. R. Hammond.
8: H. Sutcliffe.
7: G. Boycott, J. H. Edrich, M. Leyland.
5: K. F. Barrington, D. C. S. Compton, A. N. Cook, M. C. Cowdrey, L. Hutton, F. S. Jackson, A. C. MacLaren.

For Australia

19: D. G. Bradman.
11: S. P. D. Smith
10: S. R. Waugh.
9: G. S. Chappell.
8: A. R. Border, A. R. Morris, R. T. Ponting.
7: D. C. Boon, M. J. Clarke, W. M. Lawry, M. J. Slater.
6: R. N. Harvey, M. A. Taylor, V. T. Trumper, M. E. Waugh, W. M. Woodfull.
5: M. L. Hayden, J. L. Langer, C. G. Macartney, W. H. Ponsford.

RECORD PARTNERSHIPS FOR EACH WICKET

For England

323 for 1st	J. B. Hobbs and W. Rhodes at Melbourne	1911-12
382 for 2nd†	L. Hutton and M. Leyland at The Oval	1938
262 for 3rd	W. R. Hammond and D. R. Jardine at Adelaide	1928-29
310 for 4th	P. D. Collingwood and K. P. Pietersen at Adelaide	2006-07
237 for 5th	D. J. Malan and J. M. Bairstow at Perth	2017-18
215 for 6th	L. Hutton and J. Hardstaff jnr at The Oval	1938
	G. Boycott and A. P. E. Knott at Nottingham	1977
143 for 7th	F. E. Woolley and J. Vine at Sydney	1911-12
124 for 8th	E. H. Hendren and H. Larwood at Brisbane	1928-29
151 for 9th	W. H. Scotton and W. W. Read at The Oval	1884
130 for 10th	R. E. Foster and W. Rhodes at Sydney	1903-04

For Australia

329 for 1st	G. R. Marsh and M. A. Taylor at Nottingham	1989
451 for 2nd†	W. H. Ponsford and D. G. Bradman at The Oval	1934
276 for 3rd	D. G. Bradman and A. L. Hassett at Brisbane	1946-47
388 for 4th	W. H. Ponsford and D. G. Bradman at Leeds	1934
405 for 5th‡	S. G. Barnes and D. G. Bradman at Sydney	1946-47
346 for 6th†	J. H. Fingleton and D. G. Bradman at Melbourne	1936-37
165 for 7th	C. Hill and H. Trumble at Melbourne	1897-98
243 for 8th†	R. J. Hartigan and C. Hill at Adelaide	1907-08
154 for 9th†	S. E. Gregory and J. M. Blackham at Sydney	1894-95
163 for 10th†	P. J. Hughes and A. C. Agar at Nottingham	2013

† *Record partnership against all countries.* ‡ *World record.*

MOST RUNS IN A SERIES

England in England	732 (average 81.33)	D. I. Gower	1985
England in Australia	905 (average 113.12)	W. R. Hammond	1928-29
Australia in England	974 (average 139.14)	D. G. Bradman	1930
Australia in Australia	810 (average 90.00)	D. G. Bradman	1936-37

MOST WICKETS IN A MATCH

In total, England bowlers have taken ten or more wickets in a match **40** times against Australia, and Australian bowlers have done it **43** times against England. The players with at least 12 in a match are as follows:

For England

19-90 (9-37, 10-53)	J. C. Laker at Manchester	1956
15-104 (7-61, 8-43)	H. Verity at Lord's	1934
15-124 (7-56, 8-68)	W. Rhodes at Melbourne	1903-04
14-99 (7-55, 7-44)	A. V. Bedser at Nottingham	1953
14-102 (7-28, 7-74)	W. Bates at Melbourne	1882-83
13-163 (6-42, 7-121)	S. F. Barnes at Melbourne	1901-02
13-244 (7-168, 6-76)	T. Richardson at Manchester	1896

13-256 (5-130, 8-126)	J. C. White at Adelaide	1928-29
12-102 (6-50, 6-52)†	F. Martin at The Oval	1890
12-104 (7-36, 5-68)	G. A. Lohmann at The Oval	1886
12-136 (6-49, 6-87)	J. Briggs at Adelaide	1891-92

There are a further 12 instances of 11 wickets in a match, and 17 instances of ten.

For Australia

16-137 (8-84, 8-53)†	R. A. L. Massie at Lord's	1972
14-90 (7-46, 7-44)	F. R. Spofforth at The Oval	1882
13-77 (7-17, 6-60)	M. A. Noble at Melbourne	1901-02
13-110 (6-48, 7-62)	F. R. Spofforth at Melbourne	1878-79
13-148 (6-97, 7-51)	B. A. Reid at Melbourne	1990-91
13-236 (4-115, 9-121)	A. A. Mailey at Melbourne	1920-21
12-87 (5-44, 7-43)	C. T. B. Turner at Sydney	1887-88
12-89 (6-59, 6-30)	H. Trumble at The Oval	1896
12-107 (5-57, 7-50)	S. C. G. MacGill at Sydney	1998-99
12-173 (8-65, 4-108)	H. Trumble at The Oval	1902
12-175 (5-85, 7-90)†	H. V. Hordern at Sydney	1911-12
12-246 (6-122, 6-124)	S. K. Warne at The Oval	2005

There are a further 13 instances of 11 wickets in a match, and 18 instances of ten.

† *On first appearance in England–Australia Tests.*

A. V. Bedser, J. Briggs, J. C. Laker, T. Richardson, R. M. Hogg, A. A. Mailey, H. Trumble and C. T. B. Turner took ten wickets or more in successive Tests.

MOST WICKETS IN A SERIES

England in England	46 (average 9.60)	J. C. Laker	1956
England in Australia	38 (average 23.18)	M. W. Tate	1924-25
Australia in England	42 (average 21.26)	T. M. Alderman (6 Tests)	1981
Australia in Australia	41 (average 12.85)	R. M. Hogg (6 Tests)	1978-79

WICKETKEEPING – MOST DISMISSALS

	M	*Ct*	*St*	*Total*
†R. W. Marsh (Australia)	42	141	7	148
I. A. Healy (Australia)	33	123	12	135
A. P. E. Knott (England)	34	97	8	105
A. C. Gilchrist (Australia)	20	89	7	96
†W. A. S. Oldfield (Australia)	38	59	31	90
A. F. A. Lilley (England)	32	65	19	84
B. J. Haddin (Australia)	20	79	1	80
A. J. Stewart (England)	26	76	2	78
A. T. W. Grout (Australia)	22	69	7	76
T. G. Evans (England)	31	64	12	76

† *The number of catches by R. W. Marsh (141) and stumpings by W. A. S. Oldfield (31) are respective records in England–Australia Tests.*

Stewart held a further six catches in seven matches when not keeping wicket.

SCORERS OF OVER 2,500 RUNS

	T	*I*	*NO*	*R*	*HS*	*100*	*Avge*
D. G. Bradman (Australia)	37	63	7	5,028	334	19	89.78
J. B. Hobbs (England)	41	71	4	3,636	187	12	54.26
A. R. Border (Australia)	47	82	19	3,548	200*	8	56.31
D. I. Gower (England)	42	77	4	3,269	215	9	44.78
S. R. Waugh (Australia)	46	73	18	3,200	177*	10	58.18
G. Boycott (England)	38	71	9	2,945	191	7	47.50

	T	*I*	*NO*	*R*	*HS*	*100*	*Avge*
W. R. Hammond (England).	33	58	3	2,852	251	9	51.85
S. P. D. Smith (Australia) . .	27	48	5	2,800	239	11	65.11
H. Sutcliffe (England)	27	46	5	2,741	194	8	66.85
C. Hill (Australia)	41	76	1	2,660	188	4	35.46
J. H. Edrich (England).	32	57	3	2,644	175	7	48.96
G. A. Gooch (England)	42	79	0	2,632	196	4	33.31
G. S. Chappell (Australia) . .	35	65	8	2,619	144	9	45.94

BOWLERS WITH 100 WICKETS

	T	*Balls*	*R*	*W*	*5I*	*10M*	*Avge*
S. K. Warne (Australia)	36	10,757	4,535	195	11	4	23.25
D. K. Lillee (Australia).	29	8,516	3,507	167	11	4	21.00
G. D. McGrath (Australia)	30	7,280	3,286	157	10	0	20.92
I. T. Botham (England)	36	8,479	4,093	148	9	2	27.65
H. Trumble (Australia).	31	7,895	2,945	141	9	3	20.88
R. G. D. Willis (England).	35	7,294	3,346	128	7	0	26.14
S. C. J. Broad (England).	32	6,512	3,464	118	7	1	29.35
M. A. Noble (Australia)	39	6,895	2,860	115	9	2	24.86
R. R. Lindwall (Australia)	29	6,728	2,559	114	6	0	22.44
W. Rhodes (England).	41	5,790	2,616	109	6	1	24.00
S. F. Barnes (England)	20	5,749	2,288	106	12	1	21.58
C. V. Grimmett (Australia).	22	9,224	3,439	106	11	2	32.44
D. L. Underwood (England).	29	8,000	2,770	105	4	2	26.38
A. V. Bedser (England)	21	7,065	2,859	104	7	2	27.49
J. M. Anderson (England)	32	7,051	3,595	104	5	1	34.56
G. Giffen (Australia)	31	6,391	2,791	103	7	1	27.09
W. J. O'Reilly (Australia)	19	7,864	2,587	102	8	3	25.36
C. T. B. Turner (Australia).	17	5,179	1,670	101	11	2	16.53
R. Peel (England)	20	5,216	1,715	101	5	1	16.98
T. M. Alderman (Australia)	17	4,717	2,117	100	11	1	21.17
J. R. Thomson (Australia)	21	4,951	2,418	100	5	0	24.18

RESULTS ON EACH GROUND

In England

	Matches	*England wins*	*Australia wins*	*Drawn*
The Oval.	38	17	7	14
Manchester.	30	7	8	15†
Lord's.	37	7	15	15
Nottingham	22	6	7	9
Leeds	25	8	9	8
Birmingham	15	6	4	5
Sheffield.	1	0	1	0
Cardiff	2	1	0	1
Chester-le-Street.	1	1	0	0

† *Excludes two matches abandoned without a ball bowled.*

In Australia

	Matches	*England wins*	*Australia wins*	*Drawn*
Melbourne	56	20	28	8†
Sydney	56	22	27	7
Adelaide.	32	9	18	5
Brisbane				
Exhibition Ground	1	1	0	0
Woolloongabba	21	4	12	5
Perth.	14	1	10	3

† *Excludes one match abandoned without a ball bowled.*

ENGLAND v SOUTH AFRICA

	Captains					
Season	*England*	*South Africa*	*T*	*E*	*SA*	*D*
1888-89	C. A. Smith[1]	O. R. Dunell[2]	2	2	0	0
1891-92	W. W. Read	W. H. Milton	1	1	0	0
1895-96	Lord Hawke[3]	E. A. Halliwell[4]	3	3	0	0
1898-99	Lord Hawke	M. Bisset	2	2	0	0
1905-06	P. F. Warner	P. W. Sherwell	5	1	4	0
1907	R. E. Foster	P. W. Sherwell	3	1	0	2
1909-10	H. D. G. Leveson Gower[5]	S. J. Snooke	5	2	3	0
1912	C. B. Fry	F. Mitchell[6]	3	3	0	0
1913-14	J. W. H. T. Douglas	H. W. Taylor	5	4	0	1
1922-23	F. T. Mann	H. W. Taylor	5	2	1	2
1924	A. E. R. Gilligan[7]	H. W. Taylor	5	3	0	2
1927-28	R. T. Stanyforth[8]	H. G. Deane	5	2	2	1
1929	J. C. White[9]	H. G. Deane	5	2	0	3
1930-31	A. P. F. Chapman	H. G. Deane[10]	5	0	1	4
1935	R. E. S. Wyatt	H. F. Wade	5	0	1	4
1938-39	W. R. Hammond	A. Melville	5	1	0	4
1947	N. W. D. Yardley	A. Melville	5	3	0	2
1948-49	F. G. Mann	A. D. Nourse	5	2	0	3
1951	F. R. Brown	A. D. Nourse	5	3	1	1
1955	P. B. H. May	J. E. Cheetham[11]	5	3	2	0
1956-57	P. B. H. May	C. B. van Ryneveld[12]	5	2	2	1
1960	M. C. Cowdrey	D. J. McGlew	5	3	0	2
1964-65	M. J. K. Smith	T. L. Goddard	5	1	0	4
1965	M. J. K. Smith	P. L. van der Merwe	3	0	1	2
1994	M. A. Atherton	K. C. Wessels	3	1	1	1
1995-96	M. A. Atherton	W. J. Cronje	5	0	1	4
1998	A. J. Stewart	W. J. Cronje	5	2	1	2
1999-2000	N. Hussain	W. J. Cronje	5	1	2	2
2003	M. P. Vaughan[13]	G. C. Smith	5	2	2	1

THE BASIL D'OLIVEIRA TROPHY

	Captains						
Season	*England*	*South Africa*	*T*	*E*	*SA*	*D*	*Held by*
2004-05	M. P. Vaughan	G. C. Smith	5	2	1	2	E
2008	M. P. Vaughan[14]	G. C. Smith	4	1	2	1	SA
2009-10	A. J. Strauss	G. C. Smith	4	1	1	2	SA
2012	A. J. Strauss	G. C. Smith	3	0	2	1	SA
2015-16	A. N. Cook	H. M. Amla[15]	4	2	1	1	E
2017	J. E. Root	F. du Plessis[16]	4	3	1	0	E
2019-20	**J. E. Root**	**F. du Plessis**	**4**	**3**	**1**	**0**	**E**
	In South Africa		**85**	**34**	**20**	**31**	
	In England		68	30	14	24	
	Totals		**153**	**64**	**34**	**55**	

The following deputised for the official touring captain or were appointed by the home authority for only a minor proportion of the series:

[1]M. P. Bowden (Second). [2]W. H. Milton (Second). [3]Sir Timothy O'Brien (First). [4]A. R. Richards (Third). [5]F. L. Fane (Fourth and Fifth). [6]L. J. Tancred (Second and Third). [7]J. W. H. T. Douglas (Fourth). [8]G. T. S. Stevens (Fifth). [9]A. W. Carr (Fourth and Fifth). [10]E. P. Nupen (First), H. B. Cameron (Fourth and Fifth). [11]D. J. McGlew (Third and Fourth). [12]D. J. McGlew (Second). [13]N. Hussain (First). [14]K. P. Pietersen (Fourth). [15]A. B. de Villiers (Third and Fourth). [16]D. Elgar (First).

SERIES RECORDS

Highest score	*E*	258	B. A. Stokes at Cape Town	2015-16
	SA	311*	H. M. Amla at The Oval	2012
Best bowling	*E*	9-28	G. A. Lohmann at Johannesburg	1895-96
	SA	9-113	H. J. Tayfield at Johannesburg	1956-57
Highest total	*E*	654-5	at Durban	1938-39
	SA	682-6 dec	at Lord's	2003
Lowest total	*E*	76	at Leeds	1907
	SA	30	at Port Elizabeth	1895-96
		30	at Birmingham	1924

ENGLAND v WEST INDIES

Season	*England* (Captains)	*West Indies*	*T*	*E*	*WI*	*D*
1928	A. P. F. Chapman	R. K. Nunes	3	3	0	0
1929-30	Hon. F. S. G. Calthorpe	E. L. G. Hoad[1]	4	1	1	2
1933	D. R. Jardine[2]	G. C. Grant	3	2	0	1
1934-35	R. E. S. Wyatt	G. C. Grant	4	1	2	1
1939	W. R. Hammond	R. S. Grant	3	1	0	2
1947-48	G. O. B. Allen[3]	J. D. C. Goddard[4]	4	0	2	2
1950	N. W. D. Yardley[5]	J. D. C. Goddard	4	1	3	0
1953-54	L. Hutton	J. B. Stollmeyer	5	2	2	1
1957	P. B. H. May	J. D. C. Goddard	5	3	0	2
1959-60	P. B. H. May[6]	F. C. M. Alexander	5	1	0	4

THE WISDEN TROPHY

Season	*England* (Captains)	*West Indies*	*T*	*E*	*WI*	*D*	*Held by*
1963	E. R. Dexter	F. M. M. Worrell	5	1	3	1	WI
1966	M. C. Cowdrey[7]	G. S. Sobers	5	1	3	1	WI
1967-68	M. C. Cowdrey	G. S. Sobers	5	1	0	4	E
1969	R. Illingworth	G. S. Sobers	3	2	0	1	E
1973	R. Illingworth	R. B. Kanhai	3	0	2	1	WI
1973-74	M. H. Denness	R. B. Kanhai	5	1	1	3	WI
1976	A. W. Greig	C. H. Lloyd	5	0	3	2	WI
1980	I. T. Botham	C. H. Lloyd[8]	5	0	1	4	WI
1980-81†	I. T. Botham	C. H. Lloyd	4	0	2	2	WI
1984	D. I. Gower	C. H. Lloyd	5	0	5	0	WI
1985-86	D. I. Gower	I. V. A. Richards	5	0	5	0	WI
1988	J. E. Emburey[9]	I. V. A. Richards	5	0	4	1	WI
1989-90‡	G. A. Gooch[10]	I. V. A. Richards[11]	4	1	2	1	WI
1991	G. A. Gooch	I. V. A. Richards	5	2	2	1	WI
1993-94	M. A. Atherton	R. B. Richardson[12]	5	1	3	1	WI
1995	M. A. Atherton	R. B. Richardson	6	2	2	2	WI
1997-98§	M. A. Atherton	B. C. Lara	6	1	3	2	WI
2000	N. Hussain[13]	J. C. Adams	5	3	1	1	E
2003-04	M. P. Vaughan	B. C. Lara	4	3	0	1	E
2004	M. P. Vaughan	B. C. Lara	4	4	0	0	E
2007	M. P. Vaughan[14]	R. R. Sarwan[15]	4	3	0	1	E
2008-09§	A. J. Strauss	C. H. Gayle	5	0	1	4	WI
2009	A. J. Strauss	C. H. Gayle	2	2	0	0	E
2012	A. J. Strauss	D. J. G. Sammy	3	2	0	1	E
2014-15	A. N. Cook	D. Ramdin	3	1	1	1	E

Season	England	West Indies	T	E	WI	D	Held by
	Captains						
2017	J. E. Root	J. O. Holder	3	2	1	0	E
2018-19	J. E. Root	J. O. Holder[16]	3	1	2	0	WI
2020	**J. E. Root**[17]	**J. O. Holder**	**3**	**2**	**1**	**0**	**E**
	In England		**89**	**36**	**31**	**22**	
	In West Indies		71	15	27	29	
	Totals		**160**	**51**	**58**	**51**	

† *The Second Test, at Georgetown, was cancelled owing to political pressure and is excluded.*
‡ *The Second Test, at Georgetown, was abandoned without a ball being bowled and is excluded.*
§ *The First Test at Kingston in 1997-98 and the Second Test at North Sound in 2008-09 were called off on their opening days because of unfit pitches and are shown as draws.*

The following deputised for the official touring captain or were appointed by the home authority for only a minor proportion of the series:

[1]N. Betancourt (Second), M. P. Fernandes (Third), R. K. Nunes (Fourth). [2]R. E. S. Wyatt (Third). [3]K. Cranston (First). [4]G. A. Headley (First), G. E. Gomez (Second). [5]F. R. Brown (Fourth). [6]M. C. Cowdrey (Fourth and Fifth). [7]M. J. K. Smith (First), D. B. Close (Fifth). [8]I. V. A. Richards (Fifth). [9]M. W. Gatting (First), C. S. Cowdrey (Fourth), G. A. Gooch (Fifth). [10]A. J. Lamb (Fourth and Fifth). [11]D. L. Haynes (Third). [12]C. A. Walsh (Fifth). [13]A. J. Stewart (Second). [14]A. J. Strauss (First). [15]D. Ganga (Third and Fourth). [16]K. C. Brathwaite (Third). [17]B. A. Stokes (First).

SERIES RECORDS

Highest score	*E*	325	A. Sandham at Kingston	1929-30
	WI	400*	B. C. Lara at St John's	2003-04
Best bowling	*E*	8-53	A. R. C. Fraser at Port-of-Spain	1997-98
	WI	8-45	C. E. L. Ambrose at Bridgetown	1989-90
Highest total	*E*	849	at Kingston	1929-30
	WI	751-5 dec	at St John's	2003-04
Lowest total	*E*	46	at Port-of-Spain	1993-94
	WI	47	at Kingston	2003-04

ENGLAND v NEW ZEALAND

Season	England	New Zealand	T	E	NZ	D
	Captains					
1929-30	A. H. H. Gilligan	T. C. Lowry	4	1	0	3
1931	D. R. Jardine	T. C. Lowry	3	1	0	2
1932-33	D. R. Jardine[1]	M. L. Page	2	0	0	2
1937	R. W. V. Robins	M. L. Page	3	1	0	2
1946-47	W. R. Hammond	W. A. Hadlee	1	0	0	1
1949	F. G. Mann[2]	W. A. Hadlee	4	0	0	4
1950-51	F. R. Brown	W. A. Hadlee	2	1	0	1
1954-55	L. Hutton	G. O. Rabone	2	2	0	0
1958	P. B. H. May	J. R. Reid	5	4	0	1
1958-59	P. B. H. May	J. R. Reid	2	1	0	1
1962-63	E. R. Dexter	J. R. Reid	3	3	0	0
1965	M. J. K. Smith	J. R. Reid	3	3	0	0
1965-66	M. J. K. Smith	B. W. Sinclair[3]	3	0	0	3
1969	R. Illingworth	G. T. Dowling	3	2	0	1
1970-71	R. Illingworth	G. T. Dowling	2	1	0	1
1973	R. Illingworth	B. E. Congdon	3	2	0	1
1974-75	M. H. Denness	B. E. Congdon	2	1	0	1
1977-78	G. Boycott	M. G. Burgess	3	1	1	1
1978	J. M. Brearley	M. G. Burgess	3	3	0	0
1983	R. G. D. Willis	G. P. Howarth	4	3	1	0
1983-84	R. G. D. Willis	G. P. Howarth	3	0	1	2
1986	M. W. Gatting	J. V. Coney	3	0	1	2
1987-88	M. W. Gatting	J. J. Crowe[4]	3	0	0	3

Captains

Season	*England*	*New Zealand*	*T*	*E*	*NZ*	*D*
1990	G. A. Gooch	J. G. Wright	3	1	0	2
1991-92	G. A. Gooch	M. D. Crowe	3	2	0	1
1994	M. A. Atherton	K. R. Rutherford	3	1	0	2
1996-97	M. A. Atherton	L. K. Germon[5]	3	2	0	1
1999	N. Hussain[6]	S. P. Fleming	4	1	2	1
2001-02	N. Hussain	S. P. Fleming	3	1	1	1
2004	M. P. Vaughan[7]	S. P. Fleming	3	3	0	0
2007-08	M. P. Vaughan	D. L. Vettori	3	2	1	0
2008	M. P. Vaughan	D. L. Vettori	3	2	0	1
2012-13	A. N. Cook	B. B. McCullum	3	0	0	3
2013	A. N. Cook	B. B. McCullum	2	2	0	0
2015	A. N. Cook	B. B. McCullum	2	1	1	0
2017-18	J. E. Root	K. S. Williamson	2	0	1	1
2019-20	J. E. Root	K. S. Williamson	2	0	1	1
	In New Zealand		51	18	6	27
	In England		54	30	5	19
	Totals		105	48	11	46

The following deputised for the official touring captain or were appointed by the home authority for only a minor proportion of the series:

[1]R. E. S. Wyatt (Second). [2]F. R. Brown (Third and Fourth). [3]M. E. Chapple (First). [4]J. G. Wright (Third). [5]S. P. Fleming (Third). [6]M. A. Butcher (Third). [7]M. E. Trescothick (First).

SERIES RECORDS

Highest score	*E*	336*	W. R. Hammond at Auckland.	1932-33
	NZ	222	N. J. Astle at Christchurch	2001-02
Best bowling	*E*	7-32	D. L. Underwood at Lord's.	1969
	NZ	7-74	B. L. Cairns at Leeds.	1983
Highest total	*E*	593-6 dec	at Auckland.	1974-75
	NZ	615-9 dec	at Mount Maunganui.	2019-20
Lowest total	*E*	58	at Auckland.	2017-18
	NZ	26	at Auckland.	1954-55

ENGLAND v INDIA

Captains

Season	*England*	*India*	*T*	*E*	*I*	*D*
1932	D. R. Jardine	C. K. Nayudu	1	1	0	0
1933-34	D. R. Jardine	C. K. Nayudu	3	2	0	1
1936	G. O. B. Allen	Maharaj of Vizianagram	3	2	0	1
1946	W. R. Hammond	Nawab of Pataudi snr	3	1	0	2
1951-52	N. D. Howard[1]	V. S. Hazare	5	1	1	3
1952	L. Hutton	V. S. Hazare	4	3	0	1
1959	P. B. H. May[2]	D. K. Gaekwad[3]	5	5	0	0
1961-62	E. R. Dexter	N. J. Contractor	5	0	2	3
1963-64	M. J. K. Smith	Nawab of Pataudi jnr	5	0	0	5
1967	D. B. Close	Nawab of Pataudi jnr	3	3	0	0
1971	R. Illingworth	A. L. Wadekar	3	0	1	2
1972-73	A. R. Lewis	A. L. Wadekar	5	1	2	2
1974	M. H. Denness	A. L. Wadekar	3	3	0	0
1976-77	A. W. Greig	B. S. Bedi	5	3	1	1
1979	J. M. Brearley	S. Venkataraghavan	4	1	0	3
1979-80	J. M. Brearley	G. R. Viswanath	1	1	0	0
1981-82	K. W. R. Fletcher	S. M. Gavaskar	6	0	1	5
1982	R. G. D. Willis	S. M. Gavaskar	3	1	0	2
1984-85	D. I. Gower	S. M. Gavaskar	5	2	1	2
1986	M. W. Gatting[4]	Kapil Dev	3	0	2	1
1990	G. A. Gooch	M. Azharuddin	3	1	0	2

Season	England	Captains India	T	E	I	D
1992-93	G. A. Gooch[5]	M. Azharuddin	3	0	3	0
1996	M. A. Atherton	M. Azharuddin	3	1	0	2
2001-02	N. Hussain	S. C. Ganguly	3	0	1	2
2002	N. Hussain	S. C. Ganguly	4	1	1	2
2005-06	A. Flintoff	R. Dravid	3	1	1	1
2007	M. P. Vaughan	R. Dravid	3	0	1	2
2008-09	K. P. Pietersen	M. S. Dhoni	2	0	1	1
2011	A. J. Strauss	M. S. Dhoni	4	4	0	0
2012-13	A. N. Cook	M. S. Dhoni	4	2	1	1
2014	A. N. Cook	M. S. Dhoni	5	3	1	1
2016-17	A. N. Cook	V. Kohli	5	0	4	1
2018	J. E. Root	V. Kohli	5	4	1	0
	In England		62	34	7	21
	In India		60	13	19	28
	Totals		122	47	26	49

* *Since 1951-52, series in India have been for the De Mello Trophy. Since 2007, series in England have been for the Pataudi Trophy.*

The following deputised for the official touring captain or were appointed by the home authority for only a minor proportion of the series:

[1]D. B. Carr (Fifth). [2]M. C. Cowdrey (Fourth and Fifth). [3]Pankaj Roy (Second). [4]D. I. Gower (First). [5]A. J. Stewart (Second).

The 1932 Indian touring team was led by the Maharaj of Porbandar but he did not play in the Test.

SERIES RECORDS

Highest score	*E*	333	G. A. Gooch at Lord's	1990
	I	303*	K. K. Nair at Chennai	2016-17
Best bowling	*E*	8-31	F. S. Trueman at Manchester	1952
	I	8-55	M. H. Mankad at Madras	1951-52
Highest total	*E*	710-7 dec	at Birmingham	2011
	I	759-7 dec	at Chennai	2016-17
Lowest total	*E*	101	at The Oval	1971
	I	42	at Lord's	1974

ENGLAND v PAKISTAN

Season	England	Captains Pakistan	T	E	P	D
1954	L. Hutton[1]	A. H. Kardar	4	1	1	2
1961-62	E. R. Dexter	Imtiaz Ahmed	3	1	0	2
1962	E. R. Dexter[2]	Javed Burki	5	4	0	1
1967	D. B. Close	Hanif Mohammad	3	2	0	1
1968-69	M. C. Cowdrey	Saeed Ahmed	3	0	0	3
1971	R. Illingworth	Intikhab Alam	3	1	0	2
1972-73	A. R. Lewis	Majid Khan	3	0	0	3
1974	M. H. Denness	Intikhab Alam	3	0	0	3
1977-78	J. M. Brearley[3]	Wasim Bari	3	0	0	3
1978	J. M. Brearley	Wasim Bari	3	2	0	1
1982	R. G. D. Willis[4]	Imran Khan	3	2	1	0
1983-84	R. G. D. Willis[5]	Zaheer Abbas	3	0	1	2
1987	M. W. Gatting	Imran Khan	5	0	1	4
1987-88	M. W. Gatting	Javed Miandad	3	0	1	2
1992	G. A. Gooch	Javed Miandad	5	1	2	2
1996	M. A. Atherton	Wasim Akram	3	0	2	1
2000-01	N. Hussain	Moin Khan	3	1	0	2
2001	N. Hussain[6]	Waqar Younis	2	1	1	0
2005-06	M. P. Vaughan[7]	Inzamam-ul-Haq	3	0	2	1

	Captains					
Season	*England*	*Pakistan*	*T*	*E*	*P*	*D*
2006†	A. J. Strauss	Inzamam-ul-Haq	4	3	0	1
2010	A. J. Strauss	Salman Butt	4	3	1	0
2011-12*U*	A. J. Strauss	Misbah-ul-Haq	3	0	3	0
2015-16*U*	A. N. Cook	Misbah-ul-Haq	3	0	2	1
2016	A. N. Cook	Misbah-ul-Haq	4	2	2	0
2018	J. E. Root	Sarfraz Ahmed	2	1	1	0
2020	**J. E. Root**	**Azhar Ali**	**3**	**1**	**0**	**2**
	In England		**56**	**24**	**12**	**20**
	In Pakistan		24	2	4	18
	In United Arab Emirates		6	0	5	1
	Totals		**86**	**26**	**21**	**39**

† *In 2008, the ICC changed the result of the forfeited Oval Test of 2006 from an England win to a draw, in contravention of the Laws of Cricket, only to rescind their decision in January 2009.*

U Played in United Arab Emirates.

The following deputised for the official touring captain or were appointed by the home authority for only a minor proportion of the series:

[1]D. S. Sheppard (Second and Third). [2]M. C. Cowdrey (Third). [3]G. Boycott (Third). [4]D. I. Gower (Second). [5]D. I. Gower (Second and Third). [6]A. J. Stewart (Second). [7]M. E. Trescothick (First).

SERIES RECORDS

Highest score	*E*	278	D. C. S. Compton at Nottingham	1954
	P	274	Zaheer Abbas at Birmingham	1971
Best bowling	*E*	8-34	I. T. Botham at Lord's	1978
	P	9-56	Abdul Qadir at Lahore	1987-88
Highest total	*E*	598-9 dec	at Abu Dhabi	2015-16
	P	708	at The Oval	1987
Lowest total	*E*	72	at Abu Dhabi	2011-12
	P	72	at Birmingham	2010

ENGLAND v SRI LANKA

	Captains					
Season	*England*	*Sri Lanka*	*T*	*E*	*SL*	*D*
1981-82	K. W. R. Fletcher	B. Warnapura	1	1	0	0
1984	D. I. Gower	L. R. D. Mendis	1	0	0	1
1988	G. A. Gooch	R. S. Madugalle	1	1	0	0
1991	G. A. Gooch	P. A. de Silva	1	1	0	0
1992-93	A. J. Stewart	A. Ranatunga	1	0	1	0
1998	A. J. Stewart	A. Ranatunga	1	0	1	0
2000-01	N. Hussain	S. T. Jayasuriya	3	2	1	0
2002	N. Hussain	S. T. Jayasuriya	3	2	0	1
2003-04	M. P. Vaughan	H. P. Tillekeratne	3	0	1	2
2006	A. Flintoff	D. P. M. D. Jayawardene	3	1	1	1
2007-08	M. P. Vaughan	D. P. M. D. Jayawardene	3	0	1	2
2011	A. J. Strauss	T. M. Dilshan[1]	3	1	0	2
2011-12	A. J. Strauss	D. P. M. D. Jayawardene	2	1	1	0
2014	A. N. Cook	A. D. Mathews	2	0	1	1
2016	A. N. Cook	A. D. Mathews	3	2	0	1
2018-19	J. E. Root	R. A. S. Lakmal[2]	3	3	0	0
2020-21	**J. E. Root**	**L. D. Chandimal**	**2**	**2**	**0**	**0**
	In England		18	8	3	7
	In Sri Lanka		**18**	**9**	**5**	**4**
	Totals		**36**	**17**	**8**	**11**

The following deputised for the official touring captain or was appointed by the home authority for only a minor proportion of the series:
[1]K. C. Sangakkara (Third). [2]L. D. Chandimal (First).

SERIES RECORDS

Highest score	*E*	**228**	**J. E. Root at Galle**	**2020-21**
	SL	213*	D. P. M. D. Jayawardene at Galle	2007-08
Best bowling	*E*	7-70	P. A. J. DeFreitas at Lord's	1991
	SL	9-65	M. Muralitharan at The Oval	1998
Highest total	*E*	575-9 dec	at Lord's	2014
	SL	628-8 dec	at Colombo (SSC)	2003-04
Lowest total	*E*	81	at Galle	2007-08
	SL	81	at Colombo (SSC)	2000-01

ENGLAND v ZIMBABWE

Captains

Season	*England*	*Zimbabwe*	*T*	*E*	*Z*	*D*
1996-97	M. A. Atherton	A. D. R. Campbell	2	0	0	2
2000	N. Hussain	A. Flower	2	1	0	1
2003	N. Hussain	H. H. Streak	2	2	0	0
	In England		4	3	0	1
	In Zimbabwe		2	0	0	2
	Totals		6	3	0	3

SERIES RECORDS

Highest score	*E*	137	M. A. Butcher at Lord's	2003
	Z	148*	M. W. Goodwin at Nottingham	2000
Best bowling	*E*	6-33	R. L. Johnson at Chester-le-Street	2003
	Z	6-87	H. H. Streak at Lord's	2000
Highest total	*E*	472	at Lord's	2003
	Z	376	at Bulawayo	1996-97
Lowest total	*E*	147	at Nottingham	2000
	Z	83	at Lord's	2000

ENGLAND v BANGLADESH

Captains

Season	*England*	*Bangladesh*	*T*	*E*	*B*	*D*
2003-04	M. P. Vaughan	Khaled Mahmud	2	2	0	0
2005	M. P. Vaughan	Habibul Bashar	2	2	0	0
2009-10	A. N. Cook	Shakib Al Hasan	2	2	0	0
2010	A. J. Strauss	Shakib Al Hasan	2	2	0	0
2016-17	A. N. Cook	Mushfiqur Rahim	2	1	1	0
	In England		4	4	0	0
	In Bangladesh		6	5	1	0
	Totals		10	9	1	0

SERIES RECORDS

Highest score	*E*	226	I. J. L. Trott at Lord's	2010
	B	108	Tamim Iqbal at Manchester	2010
Best bowling	*E*	5-35	S. J. Harmison at Dhaka	2003-04
	B	6-77	Mehedi Hasan at Mirpur	2016-17
Highest total	*E*	599-6 dec	at Chittagong	2009-10
	B	419	at Mirpur	2009-10
Lowest total	*E*	164	at Mirpur	2016-17
	B	104	at Chester-le-Street	2005

ENGLAND v IRELAND

	Captains					
Season	*England*	*Ireland*	*T*	*E*	*Ire*	*D*
2019*E*	J. E. Root	W. T. S. Porterfield	1	1	0	0
	In England		1	1	0	0
	Totals		1	1	0	0

E Played in England.

SERIES RECORDS

Highest score	*E*	92	M. J. Leach at Lord's	2019
	Ire	55	A. Balbirnie at Lord's	2019
Best bowling	*E*	6-17	C. R. Woakes at Lord's	2019
	Ire	5-13	T. J. Murtagh at Lord's	2019
Highest total	*E*	303	at Lord's	2019
	Ire	207	at Lord's	2019
Lowest total	*E*	85	at Lord's	2019
	Ire	38	at Lord's	2019

AUSTRALIA v SOUTH AFRICA

	Captains					
Season	*Australia*	*South Africa*	*T*	*A*	*SA*	*D*
1902-03*S*	J. Darling	H. M. Taberer[1]	3	2	0	1
1910-11*A*	C. Hill	P. W. Sherwell	5	4	1	0
1912*E*	S. E. Gregory	F. Mitchell[2]	3	2	0	1
1921-22*S*	H. L. Collins	H. W. Taylor	3	1	0	2
1931-32*A*	W. M. Woodfull	H. B. Cameron	5	5	0	0
1935-36*S*	V. Y. Richardson	H. F. Wade	5	4	0	1
1949-50*S*	A. L. Hassett	A. D. Nourse	5	4	0	1
1952-53*A*	A. L. Hassett	J. E. Cheetham	5	2	2	1
1957-58*S*	I. D. Craig	C. B. van Ryneveld[3]	5	3	0	2
1963-64*A*	R. B. Simpson[4]	T. L. Goddard	5	1	1	3
1966-67*S*	R. B. Simpson	P. L. van der Merwe	5	1	3	1
1969-70*S*	W. M. Lawry	A. Bacher	4	0	4	0
1993-94*A*	A. R. Border	K. C. Wessels[5]	3	1	1	1
1993-94*S*	A. R. Border	K. C. Wessels	3	1	1	1
1996-97*S*	M. A. Taylor	W. J. Cronje	3	2	1	0
1997-98*A*	M. A. Taylor	W. J. Cronje	3	1	0	2
2001-02*A*	S. R. Waugh	S. M. Pollock	3	3	0	0
2001-02*S*	S. R. Waugh	M. V. Boucher	3	2	1	0
2005-06*A*	R. T. Ponting	G. C. Smith	3	2	0	1
2005-06*S*	R. T. Ponting	G. C. Smith[6]	3	3	0	0
2008-09*A*	R. T. Ponting	G. C. Smith	3	1	2	0
2008-09*S*	R. T. Ponting	G. C. Smith[7]	3	2	1	0

Season	Captains: Australia	South Africa	T	A	SA	D
2011-12*S*	M. J. Clarke	G. C. Smith	2	1	1	0
2012-13*A*	M. J. Clarke	G. C. Smith	3	0	1	2
2013-14*S*	M. J. Clarke	G. C. Smith	3	2	1	0
2016-17*A*	S. P. D. Smith	F. du Plessis	3	1	2	0
2017-18*S*	S. P. D. Smith[8]	F. du Plessis	4	1	3	0
	In South Africa		54	29	16	9
	In Australia		41	21	10	10
	In England		3	2	0	1
	Totals		98	52	26	20

S Played in South Africa. A Played in Australia. E Played in England.

The following deputised for the official touring captain or were appointed by the home authority for only a minor proportion of the series:

[1]J. H. Anderson (Second), E. A. Halliwell (Third). [2]L. J. Tancred (Third). [3]D. J. McGlew (First). [4]R. Benaud (First). [5]W. J. Cronje (Third). [6]J. H. Kallis (Third). [7]J. H. Kallis (Third). [8]T. D. Paine (Fourth).

SERIES RECORDS

Highest score	*A*	299*	D. G. Bradman at Adelaide	1931-32
	SA	274	R. G. Pollock at Durban	1969-70
Best bowling	*A*	8-61	M. G. Johnson at Perth	2008-09
	SA	7-23	H. J. Tayfield at Durban	1949-50
Highest total	*A*	652-7 dec	at Johannesburg	2001-02
	SA	651	at Cape Town	2008-09
Lowest total	*A*	47	at Cape Town	2011-12
	SA	36	at Melbourne	1931-32

AUSTRALIA v WEST INDIES

Season	Captains: Australia	West Indies	T	A	WI	T	D
1930-31*A*	W. M. Woodfull	G. C. Grant	5	4	1	0	0
1951-52*A*	A. L. Hassett[1]	J. D. C. Goddard[2]	5	4	1	0	0
1954-55*W*	I. W. Johnson	D. St E. Atkinson[3]	5	3	0	0	2

THE FRANK WORRELL TROPHY

Season	Captains: Australia	West Indies	T	A	WI	T	D	Held by
1960-61*A*	R. Benaud	F. M. M. Worrell	5	2	1	1	1	A
1964-65*W*	R. B. Simpson	G. S. Sobers	5	1	2	0	2	WI
1968-69*A*	W. M. Lawry	G. S. Sobers	5	3	1	0	1	A
1972-73*W*	I. M. Chappell	R. B. Kanhai	5	2	0	0	3	A
1975-76*A*	G. S. Chappell	C. H. Lloyd	6	5	1	0	0	A
1977-78*W*	R. B. Simpson	A. I. Kallicharran[4]	5	1	3	0	1	WI
1979-80*A*	G. S. Chappell	C. H. Lloyd[5]	3	0	2	0	1	WI
1981-82*A*	G. S. Chappell	C. H. Lloyd	3	1	1	0	1	WI
1983-84*W*	K. J. Hughes	C. H. Lloyd[6]	5	0	3	0	2	WI
1984-85*A*	A. R. Border[7]	C. H. Lloyd	5	1	3	0	1	WI
1988-89*A*	A. R. Border	I. V. A. Richards	5	1	3	0	1	WI
1990-91*W*	A. R. Border	I. V. A. Richards	5	1	2	0	2	WI
1992-93*A*	A. R. Border	R. B. Richardson	5	1	2	0	2	WI
1994-95*W*	M. A. Taylor	R. B. Richardson	4	2	1	0	1	A
1996-97*A*	M. A. Taylor	C. A. Walsh	5	3	2	0	0	A
1998-99*W*	S. R. Waugh	B. C. Lara	4	2	2	0	0	A
2000-01*A*	S. R. Waugh[8]	J. C. Adams	5	5	0	0	0	A

	Captains							
Season	*Australia*	*West Indies*	*T*	*A*	*WI*	*T*	*D*	*Held by*
2002-03*W*	S. R. Waugh	B. C. Lara	4	3	1	0	0	A
2005-06*A*	R. T. Ponting	S. Chanderpaul	3	3	0	0	0	A
2007-08*W*	R. T. Ponting	R. R. Sarwan[9]	3	2	0	0	1	A
2009-10*A*	R. T. Ponting	C. H. Gayle	3	2	0	0	1	A
2011-12*W*	M. J. Clarke	D. J. G. Sammy	3	2	0	0	1	A
2015*W*	M. J. Clarke	D. Ramdin	2	2	0	0	0	A
2015-16*A*	S. P. D. Smith	J. O. Holder	3	2	0	0	1	A
	In Australia		66	37	18	1	10	
	In West Indies		50	21	14	0	15	
	Totals		116	58	32	1	25	

A Played in Australia. W Played in West Indies.

The following deputised for the official touring captain or were appointed by the home authority for only a minor proportion of the series:

[1]A. R. Morris (Third). [2]J. B. Stollmeyer (Fifth). [3]J. B. Stollmeyer (Second and Third). [4]C. H. Lloyd (First and Second). [5]D. L. Murray (First). [6]I. V. A. Richards (Second). [7]K. J. Hughes (First and Second). [8]A. C. Gilchrist (Third). [9]C. H. Gayle (Third).

SERIES RECORDS

Highest score	*A*	269*	A. C. Voges at Hobart	2015-16
	WI	277	B. C. Lara at Sydney	1992-93
Best bowling	*A*	8-71	G. D. McKenzie at Melbourne	1968-69
	WI	7-25	C. E. L. Ambrose at Perth	1992-93
Highest total	*A*	758-8 dec	at Kingston	1954-55
	WI	616	at Adelaide	1968-69
Lowest total	*A*	76	at Perth	1984-85
	WI	51	at Port-of-Spain	1998-99

AUSTRALIA v NEW ZEALAND

	Captains					
Season	*Australia*	*New Zealand*	*T*	*A*	*NZ*	*D*
1945-46*N*	W. A. Brown	W. A. Hadlee	1	1	0	0
1973-74*A*	I. M. Chappell	B. E. Congdon	3	2	0	1
1973-74*N*	I. M. Chappell	B. E. Congdon	3	1	1	1
1976-77*N*	G. S. Chappell	G. M. Turner	2	1	0	1
1980-81*A*	G. S. Chappell	G. P. Howarth[1]	3	2	0	1
1981-82*N*	G. S. Chappell	G. P. Howarth	3	1	1	1

TRANS-TASMAN TROPHY

	Captains						
Season	*Australia*	*New Zealand*	*T*	*A*	*NZ*	*D*	*Held by*
1985-86*A*	A. R. Border	J. V. Coney	3	1	2	0	NZ
1985-86*N*	A. R. Border	J. V. Coney	3	0	1	2	NZ
1987-88*A*	A. R. Border	J. J. Crowe	3	1	0	2	A
1989-90*A*	A. R. Border	J. G. Wright	1	0	0	1	A
1989-90*N*	A. R. Border	J. G. Wright	1	0	1	0	NZ
1992-93*N*	A. R. Border	M. D. Crowe	3	1	1	1	NZ
1993-94*A*	A. R. Border	M. D. Crowe[2]	3	2	0	1	A
1997-98*A*	M. A. Taylor	S. P. Fleming	3	2	0	1	A
1999-2000*N*	S. R. Waugh	S. P. Fleming	3	3	0	0	A
2001-02*A*	S. R. Waugh	S. P. Fleming	3	0	0	3	A
2004-05*A*	R. T. Ponting	S. P. Fleming	2	2	0	0	A
2004-05*N*	R. T. Ponting	S. P. Fleming	3	2	0	1	A

Season	Australia	Captains New Zealand	T	A	NZ	D	Held by
2008-09*A*	R. T. Ponting	D. L. Vettori	2	2	0	0	A
2009-10*N*	R. T. Ponting	D. L. Vettori	2	2	0	0	A
2011-12*A*	M. J. Clarke	L. R. P. L. Taylor	2	1	1	0	A
2015-16*A*	S. P. D. Smith	B. B. McCullum	3	2	0	1	A
2015-16*N*	S. P. D. Smith	B. B. McCullum	2	2	0	0	A
2019-20*A*	**T. D. Paine**	**K. S. Williamson[3]**	**3**	**3**	**0**	**0**	**A**
	In Australia		**34**	**20**	**3**	**11**	
	In New Zealand		26	14	5	7	
	Totals		**60**	**34**	**8**	**18**	

A Played in Australia. N Played in New Zealand.

The following deputised for the official touring captain: [1]M. G. Burgess (Second). [2]K. R. Rutherford (Second and Third). [3]T. W. M. Latham (Third).

SERIES RECORDS

Highest score	*A*	253	D. A. Warner at Perth	2015-16
	NZ	290	L. R. P. L. Taylor at Perth	2015-16
Best bowling	*A*	6-31	S. K. Warne at Hobart	1993-94
	NZ	9-52	R. J. Hadlee at Brisbane	1985-86
Highest total	*A*	607-6 dec	at Brisbane	1993-94
	NZ	624	at Perth	2015-16
Lowest total	*A*	103	at Auckland	1985-86
	NZ	42	at Wellington	1945-46

AUSTRALIA v INDIA

Season	Australia	Captains India	T	A	I	T	D
1947-48*A*	D. G. Bradman	L. Amarnath	5	4	0	0	1
1956-57*I*	I. W. Johnson[1]	P. R. Umrigar	3	2	0	0	1
1959-60*I*	R. Benaud	G. S. Ramchand	5	2	1	0	2
1964-65*I*	R. B. Simpson	Nawab of Pataudi jnr	3	1	1	0	1
1967-68*A*	R. B. Simpson[2]	Nawab of Pataudi jnr[3]	4	4	0	0	0
1969-70*I*	W. M. Lawry	Nawab of Pataudi jnr	5	3	1	0	1
1977-78*A*	R. B. Simpson	B. S. Bedi	5	3	2	0	0
1979-80*I*	K. J. Hughes	S. M. Gavaskar	6	0	2	0	4
1980-81*A*	G. S. Chappell	S. M. Gavaskar	3	1	1	0	1
1985-86*A*	A. R. Border	Kapil Dev	3	0	0	0	3
1986-87*I*	A. R. Border	Kapil Dev	3	0	0	1	2
1991-92*A*	A. R. Border	M. Azharuddin	5	4	0	0	1

THE BORDER–GAVASKAR TROPHY

Season	Australia	Captains India	T	A	I	T	D	Held by
1996-97*I*	M. A. Taylor	S. R. Tendulkar	1	0	1	0	0	I
1997-98*I*	M. A. Taylor	M. Azharuddin	3	1	2	0	0	I
1999-2000*A*	S. R. Waugh	S. R. Tendulkar	3	3	0	0	0	A
2000-01*I*	S. R. Waugh	S. C. Ganguly	3	1	2	0	0	I
2003-04*A*	S. R. Waugh	S. C. Ganguly	4	1	1	0	2	I
2004-05*I*	R. T. Ponting[4]	S. C. Ganguly[5]	4	2	1	0	1	A
2007-08*A*	R. T. Ponting	A. Kumble	4	2	1	0	1	A
2008-09*I*	R. T. Ponting	A. Kumble[6]	4	0	2	0	2	I
2010-11*I*	R. T. Ponting	M. S. Dhoni	2	0	2	0	0	I
2011-12*A*	M. J. Clarke	M. S. Dhoni[7]	4	4	0	0	0	A

Captains

Season	*Australia*	*India*	*T*	*A*	*I*	*T*	*D*	*Held by*
2012-13*I*	M. J. Clarke[8]	M. S. Dhoni	4	0	4	0	0	I
2014-15*A*	M. J. Clarke[9]	M. S. Dhoni[10]	4	2	0	0	2	A
2016-17*I*	S. P. D. Smith	V. Kohli[11]	4	1	2	0	1	I
2018-19*A*	T. D. Paine	V. Kohli	4	1	2	0	1	I
2020-21*A*	**T. D. Paine**	**A. M. Rahane**[12]	**4**	**1**	**2**	**0**	**1**	**I**
	In Australia		**52**	**30**	**9**	**0**	**13**	
	In India		50	13	21	1	15	
	Totals		**102**	**43**	**30**	**1**	**28**	

A Played in Australia. I Played in India.

The following deputised for the official touring captain or were appointed by the home authority for only a minor proportion of the series:

[1]R. R. Lindwall (Second). [2]W. M. Lawry (Third and Fourth). [3]C. G. Borde (First). [4]A. C. Gilchrist (First, Second and Third). [5]R. Dravid (Third and Fourth). [6]M. S. Dhoni (Second and Fourth). [7]V. Sehwag (Fourth). [8]S. R. Watson (Fourth). [9]S. P. D. Smith (Second, Third and Fourth). [10]V. Kohli (First and Fourth). [11]A. M. Rahane (Fourth) [12]V. Kohli (First).

SERIES RECORDS

Highest score	*A*	329*	M. J. Clarke at Sydney	2011-12
	I	281	V. V. S. Laxman at Kolkata	2000-01
Best bowling	*A*	8-50	N. M. Lyon at Bangalore	2016-17
	I	9-69	J. M. Patel at Kanpur	1959-60
Highest total	*A*	674	at Adelaide	1947-48
	I	705-7 dec	at Sydney	2003-04
Lowest total	*A*	83	at Melbourne	1980-81
	I	**36**	**at Adelaide**	**2020-21**

AUSTRALIA v PAKISTAN

Captains

Season	*Australia*	*Pakistan*	*T*	*A*	*P*	*D*
1956-57*P*	I. W. Johnson	A. H. Kardar	1	0	1	0
1959-60*P*	R. Benaud	Fazal Mahmood[1]	3	2	0	1
1964-65*P*	R. B. Simpson	Hanif Mohammad	1	0	0	1
1964-65*A*	R. B. Simpson	Hanif Mohammad	1	0	0	1
1972-73*A*	I. M. Chappell	Intikhab Alam	3	3	0	0
1976-77*A*	G. S. Chappell	Mushtaq Mohammad	3	1	1	1
1978-79*A*	G. N. Yallop[2]	Mushtaq Mohammad	2	1	1	0
1979-80*P*	G. S. Chappell	Javed Miandad	3	0	1	2
1981-82*A*	G. S. Chappell	Javed Miandad	3	2	1	0
1982-83*P*	K. J. Hughes	Imran Khan	3	0	3	0
1983-84*A*	K. J. Hughes	Imran Khan[3]	5	2	0	3
1988-89*P*	A. R. Border	Javed Miandad	3	0	1	2
1989-90*A*	A. R. Border	Imran Khan	3	1	0	2
1994-95*P*	M. A. Taylor	Salim Malik	3	0	1	2
1995-96*A*	M. A. Taylor	Wasim Akram	3	2	1	0
1998-99*P*	M. A. Taylor	Aamir Sohail	3	1	0	2
1999-2000*A*	S. R. Waugh	Wasim Akram	3	3	0	0
2002-03*S*/*U*	S. R. Waugh	Waqar Younis	3	3	0	0
2004-05*A*	R. T. Ponting	Inzamam-ul-Haq[4]	3	3	0	0
2009-10*A*	R. T. Ponting	Mohammad Yousuf	3	3	0	0
2010*E*	R. T. Ponting	Shahid Afridi[5]	2	1	1	0
2014-15*U*	M. J. Clarke	Misbah-ul-Haq	2	0	2	0

	Captains					
Season	*Australia*	*Pakistan*	*T*	*A*	*P*	*D*
2016-17*A*	S. P. D. Smith	Misbah-ul-Haq	3	3	0	0
2018-19*U*	T. D. Paine	Sarfraz Ahmed	2	0	1	1
2019-20*A*	T. D. Paine	Azhar Ali	2	2	0	0
	In Pakistan		20	3	7	10
	In Australia		37	26	4	7
	In Sri Lanka		1	1	0	0
	In United Arab Emirates		6	2	3	1
	In England		2	1	1	0
	Totals		66	33	15	18

P Played in Pakistan. A Played in Australia.
S/U First Test played in Sri Lanka, Second and Third Tests in United Arab Emirates.
U Played in United Arab Emirates. E Played in England.

The following deputised for the official touring captain or were appointed by the home authority for only a minor proportion of the series:

[1]Imtiaz Ahmed (Second). [2]K. J. Hughes (Second). [3]Zaheer Abbas (First, Second and Third). [4]Yousuf Youhana *later known as Mohammad Yousuf* (Second and Third). [5]Salman Butt (Second).

SERIES RECORDS

Highest score	*A*	335*	D. A. Warner at Adelaide	2019-20
	P	237	Salim Malik at Rawalpindi	1994-95
Best bowling	*A*	8-24	G. D. McGrath at Perth	2004-05
	P	9-86	Sarfraz Nawaz at Melbourne	1978-79
Highest total	*A*	624-8 dec	at Melbourne	2016-17
	P	624	at Adelaide	1983-84
Lowest total	*A*	80	at Karachi	1956-57
	P	53	at Sharjah	2002-03

AUSTRALIA v SRI LANKA

	Captains					
Season	*Australia*	*Sri Lanka*	*T*	*A*	*SL*	*D*
1982-83*S*	G. S. Chappell	L. R. D. Mendis	1	1	0	0
1987-88*A*	A. R. Border	R. S. Madugalle	1	1	0	0
1989-90*A*	A. R. Border	A. Ranatunga	2	1	0	1
1992-93*S*	A. R. Border	A. Ranatunga	3	1	0	2
1995-96*A*	M. A. Taylor	A. Ranatunga[1]	3	3	0	0
1999-2000*S*	S. R. Waugh	S. T. Jayasuriya	3	0	1	2
2003-04*S*	R. T. Ponting	H. P. Tillekeratne	3	3	0	0
2004*A*	R. T. Ponting[2]	M. S. Atapattu	2	1	0	1

THE WARNE–MURALITHARAN TROPHY

	Captains						
Season	*Australia*	*Sri Lanka*	*T*	*A*	*SL*	*D*	*Held by*
2007-08*A*	R. T. Ponting	D. P. M. D. Jayawardene	2	2	0	0	A
2011-12*S*	M. J. Clarke	T. M. Dilshan	3	1	0	2	A
2012-13*A*	M. J. Clarke	D. P. M. D. Jayawardene	3	3	0	0	A
2016*S*	S. P. D. Smith	A. D. Mathews	3	0	3	0	SL
2018-19*A*	T. D. Paine	L. D. Chandimal	2	2	0	0	A
	In Australia		15	13	0	2	
	In Sri Lanka		16	6	4	6	
	Totals		31	19	4	8	

A Played in Australia. S Played in Sri Lanka.

SERIES RECORDS

Highest score	*SA*	208	H. M. Amla at Centurion	2014-15
	WI	317	C. H. Gayle at St John's	2004-05
Best bowling	*SA*	7-37	M. Ntini at Port-of-Spain	2004-05
	WI	7-84	F. A. Rose at Durban	1998-99
Highest total	*SA*	658-9 dec	at Durban	2003-04
	WI	747	at St John's	2004-05
Lowest total	*SA*	141	at Kingston	2000-01
	WI	102	at Port-of-Spain	2010

SOUTH AFRICA v NEW ZEALAND

	Captains					
Season	*South Africa*	*New Zealand*	*T*	*SA*	*NZ*	*D*
1931-32*N*	H. B. Cameron	M. L. Page	2	2	0	0
1952-53*N*	J. E. Cheetham	W. M. Wallace	2	1	0	1
1953-54*S*	J. E. Cheetham	G. O. Rabone[1]	5	4	0	1
1961-62*S*	D. J. McGlew	J. R. Reid	5	2	2	1
1963-64*N*	T. L. Goddard	J. R. Reid	3	0	0	3
1994-95*S*	W. J. Cronje	K. R. Rutherford	3	2	1	0
1994-95*N*	W. J. Cronje	K. R. Rutherford	1	1	0	0
1998-99*N*	W. J. Cronje	D. J. Nash	3	1	0	2
2000-01*S*	S. M. Pollock	S. P. Fleming	3	2	0	1
2003-04*N*	G. C. Smith	S. P. Fleming	3	1	1	1
2005-06*S*	G. C. Smith	S. P. Fleming	3	2	0	1
2007-08*S*	G. C. Smith	D. L. Vettori	2	2	0	0
2011-12*N*	G. C. Smith	L. R. P. L. Taylor	3	1	0	2
2012-13*S*	G. C. Smith	B. B. McCullum	2	2	0	0
2016*S*	F. du Plessis	K. S. Williamson	2	1	0	1
2016-17*N*	F. du Plessis	K. S. Williamson	3	1	0	2
	In New Zealand		20	8	1	11
	In South Africa		25	17	3	5
	Totals		45	25	4	16

N Played in New Zealand. *S Played in South Africa.*

The following deputised for the official touring captain:
[1]B. Sutcliffe (Fourth and Fifth).

SERIES RECORDS

Highest score	*SA*	275*	D. J. Cullinan at Auckland	1998-99
	NZ	262	S. P. Fleming at Cape Town	2005-06
Best bowling	*SA*	8-53	G. B. Lawrence at Johannesburg	1961-62
	NZ	6-60	J. R. Reid at Dunedin	1963-64
Highest total	*SA*	621-5 dec	at Auckland	1998-99
	NZ	595	at Auckland	2003-04
Lowest total	*SA*	148	at Johannesburg	1953-54
	NZ	45	at Cape Town	2012-13

SOUTH AFRICA v INDIA

	Captains					
Season	*South Africa*	*India*	*T*	*SA*	*I*	*D*
1992-93*S*	K. C. Wessels	M. Azharuddin	4	1	0	3
1996-97*I*	W. J. Cronje	S. R. Tendulkar	3	1	2	0
1996-97*S*	W. J. Cronje	S. R. Tendulkar	3	2	0	1
1999-2000*I*	W. J. Cronje	S. R. Tendulkar	2	2	0	0

Captains

Season	*South Africa*	*India*	*T*	*SA*	*I*	*D*
2001-02*S*†	S. M. Pollock	S. C. Ganguly	2	1	0	1
2004-05*I*	G. C. Smith	S. C. Ganguly	2	0	1	1
2006-07*S*	G. C. Smith	R. Dravid	3	2	1	0
2007-08*I*	G. C. Smith	A. Kumble[1]	3	1	1	1
2009-10*I*	G. C. Smith	M. S. Dhoni	2	1	1	0
2010-11*S*	G. C. Smith	M. S. Dhoni	3	1	1	1
2013-14*S*	G. C. Smith	M. S. Dhoni	2	1	0	1

THE FREEDOM TROPHY

Captains

Season	*South Africa*	*India*	*T*	*SA*	*I*	*D*	*Held by*
2015-16*I*	H. M. Amla	V. Kohli	4	0	3	1	I
2017-18*S*	F. du Plessis	V. Kohli	3	2	1	0	SA
2019-20*I*	F. du Plessis	V. Kohli	3	0	3	0	I
	In South Africa		20	10	3	7	
	In India		19	5	11	3	
	Totals		39	15	14	10	

S Played in South Africa. I Played in India.

† *The Third Test at Centurion was stripped of its official status by the ICC after a disciplinary dispute and is excluded.*

The following was appointed by the home authority for only a minor proportion of the series:
[1]M. S. Dhoni (Third).

SERIES RECORDS

Highest score	*SA*	253*	H. M. Amla at Nagpur	2009-10
	I	319	V. Sehwag at Chennai	2007-08
Best bowling	*SA*	8-64	L. Klusener at Calcutta	1996-97
	I	7-66	R. Ashwin at Nagpur	2015-16
Highest total	*SA*	620-4 dec	at Centurion	2010-11
	I	643-6 dec	at Kolkata	2009-10
Lowest total	*SA*	79	at Nagpur	2015-16
	I	66	at Durban	1996-97

SOUTH AFRICA v PAKISTAN

Captains

Season	*South Africa*	*Pakistan*	*T*	*SA*	*P*	*D*
1994-95*S*	W. J. Cronje	Salim Malik	1	1	0	0
1997-98*P*	W. J. Cronje	Saeed Anwar	3	1	0	2
1997-98*S*	W. J. Cronje[1]	Rashid Latif[2]	3	1	1	1
2002-03*S*	S. M. Pollock	Waqar Younis	2	2	0	0
2003-04*P*	G. C. Smith	Inzamam-ul-Haq[3]	2	0	1	1
2006-07*S*	G. C. Smith	Inzamam-ul-Haq	3	2	1	0
2007-08*P*	G. C. Smith	Shoaib Malik	2	1	0	1
2010-11*U*	G. C. Smith	Misbah-ul-Haq	2	0	0	2
2012-13*S*	G. C. Smith	Misbah-ul-Haq	3	3	0	0
2013-14*U*	G. C. Smith	Misbah-ul-Haq	2	1	1	0
2018-19*S*	F. du Plessis[4]	Sarfraz Ahmed	3	3	0	0
	In South Africa		15	12	2	1
	In Pakistan		7	2	1	4
	In United Arab Emirates		4	1	1	2
	Totals		26	15	4	7

S Played in South Africa. P Played in Pakistan. U Played in United Arab Emirates.

The following deputised for the official touring captain or were appointed by the home authority for only a minor proportion of the series:

[1]G. Kirsten (First). [2]Aamir Sohail (First and Second). [3]Yousuf Youhana *later known as Mohammad Yousuf* (First). [4]D. Elgar (Third).

SERIES RECORDS

Highest score	*SA*	278*	A. B. de Villiers at Abu Dhabi	2010-11
	P	146	Khurram Manzoor at Abu Dhabi	2013-14
Best bowling	*SA*	7-29	K. J. Abbott at Centurion	2012-13
	P	6-78	Mushtaq Ahmed at Durban	1997-98
		6-78	Waqar Younis at Port Elizabeth	1997-98
Highest total	*SA*	620-7 dec	at Cape Town	2002-03
	P	456	at Rawalpindi	1997-98
Lowest total	*SA*	124	at Port Elizabeth	2006-07
	P	49	at Johannesburg	2012-13

SOUTH AFRICA v SRI LANKA

Captains

Season	*South Africa*	*Sri Lanka*	*T*	*SA*	*SL*	*D*
1993-94*SL*	K. C. Wessels	A. Ranatunga	3	1	0	2
1997-98*SA*	W. J. Cronje	A. Ranatunga	2	2	0	0
2000*SL*	S. M. Pollock	S. T. Jayasuriya	3	1	1	1
2000-01*SA*	S. M. Pollock	S. T. Jayasuriya	3	2	0	1
2002-03*SA*	S. M. Pollock	S. T. Jayasuriya[1]	2	2	0	0
2004*SL*	G. C. Smith	M. S. Atapattu	2	0	1	1
2006*SL*	A. G. Prince	D. P. M. D. Jayawardene	2	0	2	0
2011-12*SA*	G. C. Smith	T. M. Dilshan	3	2	1	0
2014*SL*	H. M. Amla	A. D. Mathews	2	1	0	1
2016-17*SA*	F. du Plessis	A. D. Mathews	3	3	0	0
2018*SL*	F. du Plessis	R. A. S. Lakmal	2	0	2	0
2018-19*SA*	F. du Plessis	F. D. M. Karunaratne	2	0	2	0
2020-21*SA*	**Q. de Kock**	**F. D. M. Karunaratne**	**2**	**2**	**0**	**0**
	In South Africa		**17**	**13**	**3**	**1**
	In Sri Lanka		14	3	6	5
	Totals		**31**	**16**	**9**	**6**

SA Played in South Africa. SL Played in Sri Lanka.

The following deputised for the official captain:

[1]M. S. Atapattu (Second).

SERIES RECORDS

Highest score	*SA*	224	J. H. Kallis at Cape Town	2011-12
	SL	374	D. P. M. D. Jayawardene at Colombo (SSC)	2006
Best bowling	*SA*	9-129	K. A. Maharaj at Colombo (SSC)	2018
	SL	7-84	M. Muralitharan at Galle	2000
Highest total	*SA*	**621**	**at Centurion**	**2020-21**
	SL	756-5 dec	at Colombo (SSC)	2006
Lowest total	*SA*	73	at Galle	2018
	SL	95	at Cape Town	2000-01

SOUTH AFRICA v ZIMBABWE

Season	South Africa (Captains)	Zimbabwe (Captains)	T	SA	Z	D
1995-96*Z*	W. J. Cronje	A. Flower	1	1	0	0
1999-2000*S*	W. J. Cronje	A. D. R. Campbell	1	1	0	0
1999-2000*Z*	W. J. Cronje	A. Flower	1	1	0	0
2001-02*Z*	S. M. Pollock	H. H. Streak	2	1	0	1
2004-05*S*	G. C. Smith	T. Taibu	2	2	0	0
2014-15*Z*	H. M. Amla	B. R. M. Taylor	1	1	0	0
2017-18*S*	A. B. de Villiers	A. G. Cremer	1	1	0	0
	In Zimbabwe		5	4	0	1
	In South Africa		4	4	0	0
	Totals		9	8	0	1

S Played in South Africa. *Z Played in Zimbabwe.*

SERIES RECORDS

Highest score	*SA*	220	G. Kirsten at Harare	2001-02
	Z	199*	A. Flower at Harare	2001-02
Best bowling	*SA*	8-71	A. A. Donald at Harare	1995-96
	Z	5-101	B. C. Strang at Harare	1995-96
Highest total	*SA*	600-3 dec	at Harare	2001-02
	Z	419-9 dec	at Bulawayo	2001-02
Lowest total	*SA*	346	at Harare	1995-96
	Z	54	at Cape Town	2004-05

SOUTH AFRICA v BANGLADESH

Season	South Africa (Captains)	Bangladesh (Captains)	T	SA	B	D
2002-03*S*	S. M. Pollock[1]	Khaled Mashud	2	2	0	0
2003*B*	G. C. Smith	Khaled Mahmud	2	2	0	0
2007-08*B*	G. C. Smith	Mohammad Ashraful	2	2	0	0
2008-09*S*	G. C. Smith	Mohammad Ashraful	2	2	0	0
2015*B*	H. M. Amla	Mushfiqur Rahim	2	0	0	2
2017-18*S*	F. du Plessis	Mushfiqur Rahim	2	2	0	0
	In South Africa		6	6	0	0
	In Bangladesh		6	4	0	2
	Totals		12	10	0	2

S Played in South Africa. *B Played in Bangladesh.*

The following deputised for the official captain:
[1]M. V. Boucher (First).

SERIES RECORDS

Highest score	*SA*	232	G. C. Smith at Chittagong	2007-08
	B	77	Mominul Haque at Potchefstroom	2017-18
Best bowling	*SA*	5-19	M. Ntini at East London	2002-03
	B	6-27	Shahadat Hossain at Mirpur	2007-08
Highest total	*SA*	583-7 dec	at Chittagong	2007-08
	B	326	at Chittagong	2015
Lowest total	*SA*	170	at Mirpur	2007-08
	B	90	at Potchefstroom	2017-18

Season	Captains: West Indies	Pakistan	T	WI	P	D
2006-07*P*	B. C. Lara	Inzamam-ul-Haq	3	0	2	1
2010-11*W*	D. J. G. Sammy	Misbah-ul-Haq	2	1	1	0
2016-17*U*	J. O. Holder	Misbah-ul-Haq	3	1	2	0
2016-17*W*	J. O. Holder	Misbah-ul-Haq	3	1	2	0
	In West Indies		26	12	7	7
	In Pakistan		21	4	9	8
	In United Arab Emirates		5	1	4	0
	Totals		52	17	20	15

P Played in Pakistan. W Played in West Indies. U Played in United Arab Emirates.

The following were appointed by the home authority or deputised for the official touring captain for a minor proportion of the series:
[1]C. G. Greenidge (First). [2]Younis Khan (First).

SERIES RECORDS

Highest score	*WI*	365*	G. S. Sobers at Kingston	1957-58
	P	337	Hanif Mohammad at Bridgetown	1957-58
Best bowling	*WI*	8-29	C. E. H. Croft at Port-of-Spain	1976-77
	P	7-80	Imran Khan at Georgetown	1987-88
Highest total	*WI*	790-3 dec	at Kingston	1957-58
	P	657-8 dec	at Bridgetown	1957-58
Lowest total	*WI*	53	at Faisalabad	1986-87
	P	77	at Lahore	1986-87

WEST INDIES v SRI LANKA

Season	Captains: West Indies	Sri Lanka	T	WI	SL	D
1993-94*S*	R. B. Richardson	A. Ranatunga	1	0	0	1
1996-97*W*	C. A. Walsh	A. Ranatunga	2	1	0	1
2001-02*S*	C. L. Hooper	S. T. Jayasuriya	3	0	3	0
2003*W*	B. C. Lara	H. P. Tillekeratne	2	1	0	1
2005*S*	S. Chanderpaul	M. S. Atapattu	2	0	2	0
2007-08*W*	C. H. Gayle	D. P. M. D. Jayawardene	2	1	1	0
2010-11*S*	D. J. G. Sammy	K. C. Sangakkara	3	0	0	3

THE SOBERS–TISSERA TROPHY

Season	Captains: West Indies	Sri Lanka	T	WI	SL	D	Held by
2015-16*S*	J. O. Holder	A. D. Mathews	2	0	2	0	SL
2018*W*	J. O. Holder	L. D. Chandimal[1]	3	1	1	1	SL
	In West Indies		9	4	2	3	
	In Sri Lanka		11	0	7	4	
	Totals		20	4	9	7	

W Played in West Indies. S Played in Sri Lanka.

The following deputised for the official touring captain:
[1]R. A. S. Lakmal (Third).

SERIES RECORDS

Highest score	*WI*	333	C. H. Gayle at Galle	2010-11
	SL	204*	H. P. Tillekeratne at Colombo (SSC)	2001-02
Best bowling	*WI*	8-62	S. T. Gabriel at Gros Islet	2018
	SL	8-46	M. Muralitharan at Kandy	2005
Highest total	*WI*	580-9 dec	at Galle	2010-11
	SL	627-9 dec	at Colombo (SSC)	2001-02
Lowest total	*WI*	93	at Bridgetown	2018
	SL	150	at Kandy	2005

WEST INDIES v ZIMBABWE

	Captains					
Season	*West Indies*	*Zimbabwe*	*T*	*WI*	*Z*	*D*
1999-2000*W*	J. C. Adams	A. Flower	2	2	0	0

THE CLIVE LLOYD TROPHY

	Captains						
Season	*West Indies*	*Zimbabwe*	*T*	*WI*	*Z*	*D*	*Held by*
2001*Z*	C. L. Hooper	H. H. Streak	2	1	0	1	WI
2003-04*Z*	B. C. Lara	H. H. Streak	2	1	0	1	WI
2012-13*W*	D. J. G. Sammy	B. R. M. Taylor	2	2	0	0	WI
2017-18*Z*	J. O. Holder	A. G. Cremer	2	1	0	1	WI
	In West Indies		4	4	0	0	
	In Zimbabwe		6	3	0	3	
	Totals		10	7	0	3	

W *Played in West Indies.* *Z* *Played in Zimbabwe.*

SERIES RECORDS

Highest score	*WI*	191	B. C. Lara at Bulawayo	2003-04
	Z	147	H. Masakadza at Bulawayo	2017-18
Best bowling	*WI*	6-49	S. Shillingford at Bridgetown	2012-13
	Z	6-73	R. W. Price at Harare	2003-04
Highest total	*WI*	559-6 dec	at Bulawayo	2001
	Z	563-9 dec	at Harare	2001
Lowest total	*WI*	128	at Bulawayo	2003-04
	Z	63	at Port-of-Spain	1999-2000

WEST INDIES v BANGLADESH

	Captains					
Season	*West Indies*	*Bangladesh*	*T*	*WI*	*B*	*D*
2002-03*B*	R. D. Jacobs	Khaled Mashud	2	2	0	0
2003-04*W*	B. C. Lara	Habibul Bashar	2	1	0	1
2009*W*	F. L. Reifer	Mashrafe bin Mortaza[1]	2	0	2	0
2011-12*B*	D. J. G. Sammy	Mushfiqur Rahim	2	1	0	1
2012-13*B*	D. J. G. Sammy	Mushfiqur Rahim	2	2	0	0

	Captains					
Season	*New Zealand*	*Pakistan*	*T*	*NZ*	*P*	*D*
1993-94*N*	K. R. Rutherford	Salim Malik	3	1	2	0
1995-96*N*	L. K. Germon	Wasim Akram	1	0	1	0
1996-97*P*	L. K. Germon	Saeed Anwar	2	1	1	0
2000-01*N*	S. P. Fleming	Moin Khan[2]	3	1	1	1
2002*P*‡	S. P. Fleming	Waqar Younis	1	0	1	0
2003-04*N*	S. P. Fleming	Inzamam-ul-Haq	2	0	1	1
2009-10*N*	D. L. Vettori	Mohammad Yousuf	3	1	1	1
2010-11*N*	D. L. Vettori	Misbah-ul-Haq	2	0	1	1
2014-15*U*	B. B. McCullum	Misbah-ul-Haq	3	1	1	1
2016-17*N*	K. S. Williamson	Misbah-ul-Haq[3]	2	2	0	0
2018-19*U*	K. S. Williamson	Sarfraz Ahmed	3	2	1	0
2020-21*N*	**K. S. Williamson**	**Mohammad Rizwan**	**2**	**2**	**0**	**0**
	In Pakistan		21	2	13	6
	In New Zealand		**33**	**9**	**10**	**14**
	In United Arab Emirates		6	3	2	1
	Totals		**60**	**14**	**25**	**21**

N Played in New Zealand. P Played in Pakistan. U Played in United Arab Emirates.

† *The First Test at Dunedin was abandoned without a ball being bowled and is excluded.*
‡ *The Second Test at Karachi was cancelled owing to civil disturbances.*

The following were appointed by the home authority for only a minor proportion of the series or deputised for the official touring captain:
[1]J. M. Parker (Third). [2]Inzamam-ul-Haq (Third). [3]Azhar Ali (Second).

SERIES RECORDS

Highest score	*NZ*	**238**	**K. S. Williamson at Christchurch**	**2020-21**
	P	329	Inzamam-ul-Haq at Lahore	2002
Best bowling	*NZ*	7-52	C. Pringle at Faisalabad	1990-91
	P	8-41	Yasir Shah at Dubai	2018-19
Highest total	*NZ*	690	at Sharjah	2014-15
	P	643	at Lahore	2002
Lowest total	*NZ*	70	at Dacca	1955-56
	P	102	at Faisalabad	1990-91

NEW ZEALAND v SRI LANKA

	Captains					
Season	*New Zealand*	*Sri Lanka*	*T*	*NZ*	*SL*	*D*
1982-83*N*	G. P. Howarth	D. S. de Silva	2	2	0	0
1983-84*S*	G. P. Howarth	L. R. D. Mendis	3	2	0	1
1986-87*S*†	J. J. Crowe	L. R. D. Mendis	1	0	0	1
1990-91*N*	M. D. Crowe[1]	A. Ranatunga	3	0	0	3
1992-93*S*	M. D. Crowe	A. Ranatunga	2	0	1	1
1994-95*N*	K. R. Rutherford	A. Ranatunga	2	0	1	1
1996-97*N*	S. P. Fleming	A. Ranatunga	2	2	0	0
1997-98*S*	S. P. Fleming	A. Ranatunga	3	1	2	0
2003*S*	S. P. Fleming	H. P. Tillekeratne	2	0	0	2
2004-05*N*	S. P. Fleming	M. S. Atapattu	2	1	0	1
2006-07*N*	S. P. Fleming	D. P. M. D. Jayawardene	2	1	1	0
2009*S*	D. L. Vettori	K. C. Sangakkara	2	0	2	0
2012-13*S*	L. R. P. L. Taylor	D. P. M. D. Jayawardene	2	1	1	0
2014-15*N*	B. B. McCullum	A. D. Mathews	2	2	0	0

	Captains					
Season	*New Zealand*	*Sri Lanka*	*T*	*NZ*	*SL*	*D*
2015-16*N*	B. B. McCullum	A. D. Mathews	2	2	0	0
2018-19*N*	K. S. Williamson	L. D. Chandimal	2	1	0	1
2019*S*	K. S. Williamson	F. D. M. Karunaratne	2	1	1	0
	In New Zealand		19	11	2	6
	In Sri Lanka		17	5	7	5
	Totals		36	16	9	11

N Played in New Zealand. S Played in Sri Lanka.

† *The Second and Third Tests were cancelled owing to civil disturbances.*

The following was appointed by the home authority for only a minor proportion of the series:
[1]I. D. S. Smith (Third).

SERIES RECORDS

Highest score	*NZ*	299	M. D. Crowe at Wellington	1990-91
	SL	267	P. A. de Silva at Wellington	1990-91
Best bowling	*NZ*	7-130	D. L. Vettori at Wellington	2006-07
	SL	6-43	H. M. R. K. B. Herath at Galle	2012-13
Highest total	*NZ*	671-4	at Wellington	1990-91
	SL	498	at Napier	2004-05
Lowest total	*NZ*	102	at Colombo (SSC)	1992-93
	SL	93	at Wellington	1982-83

NEW ZEALAND v ZIMBABWE

	Captains					
Season	*New Zealand*	*Zimbabwe*	*T*	*NZ*	*Z*	*D*
1992-93*Z*	M. D. Crowe	D. L. Houghton	2	1	0	1
1995-96*N*	L. K. Germon	A. Flower	2	0	0	2
1997-98*Z*	S. P. Fleming	A. D. R. Campbell	2	0	0	2
1997-98*N*	S. P. Fleming	A. D. R. Campbell	2	2	0	0
2000-01*Z*	S. P. Fleming	H. H. Streak	2	2	0	0
2000-01*N*	S. P. Fleming	H. H. Streak	1	0	0	1
2005-06*Z*	S. P. Fleming	T. Taibu	2	2	0	0
2011-12*Z*	L. R. P. L. Taylor	B. R. M. Taylor	1	1	0	0
2011-12*N*	L. R. P. L. Taylor	B. R. M. Taylor	1	1	0	0
2016*Z*	K. S. Williamson	A. G. Cremer	2	2	0	0
	In New Zealand		6	3	0	3
	In Zimbabwe		11	8	0	3
	Totals		17	11	0	6

N Played in New Zealand. Z Played in Zimbabwe.

SERIES RECORDS

Highest score	*NZ*	173*	L. R. P. L. Taylor at Bulawayo	2016
	Z	203*	G. J. Whittall at Bulawayo	1997-98
Best bowling	*NZ*	6-26	C. S. Martin at Napier	2011-12
	Z	8-109	P. A. Strang at Bulawayo	2000-01
Highest total	*NZ*	582-4 dec	at Bulawayo	2016
	Z	461	at Bulawayo	1997-98
Lowest total	*NZ*	207	at Harare	1997-98
	Z	51	at Napier	2011-12

NEW ZEALAND v BANGLADESH

Season	*Captains* New Zealand	Bangladesh	*T*	*NZ*	*B*	*D*
2001-02*N*	S. P. Fleming	Khaled Mashud	2	2	0	0
2004-05*B*	S. P. Fleming	Khaled Mashud	2	2	0	0
2007-08*N*	D. L. Vettori	Mohammad Ashraful	2	2	0	0
2008-09*B*	D. L. Vettori	Mohammad Ashraful	2	1	0	1
2009-10*N*	D. L. Vettori	Shakib Al Hasan	1	1	0	0
2013-14*B*	B. B. McCullum	Mushfiqur Rahim	2	0	0	2
2016-17*N*	K. S. Williamson	Mushfiqur Rahim[1]	2	2	0	0
2018-19*N*†	K. S. Williamson	Mahmudullah	2	2	0	0
	In New Zealand		9	9	0	0
	In Bangladesh		6	3	0	3
	Totals		15	12	0	3

B Played in Bangladesh. *N Played in New Zealand.*

† *The Third Test was cancelled owing to a terrorist attack on a nearby mosque.*

The following deputised for the official touring captain for only a minor proportion of the series:
[1]Tamim Iqbal (Second).

SERIES RECORDS

Highest score	*NZ*	202	S. P. Fleming at Chittagong	2004-05
	B	217	Shakib Al Hasan at Wellington	2016-17
Best bowling	*NZ*	7-53	C. L. Cairns at Hamilton	2001-02
	B	7-36	Shakib Al Hasan at Chittagong	2008-09
Highest total	*NZ*	715-6 dec	at Hamilton	2018-19
	B	595-8 dec	at Wellington	2016-17
Lowest total	*NZ*	171	at Chittagong	2008-09
	B	108	at Hamilton	2001-02

INDIA v PAKISTAN

Season	*Captains* India	Pakistan	*T*	*I*	*P*	*D*
1952-53*I*	L. Amarnath	A. H. Kardar	5	2	1	2
1954-55*P*	M. H. Mankad	A. H. Kardar	5	0	0	5
1960-61*I*	N. J. Contractor	Fazal Mahmood	5	0	0	5
1978-79*P*	B. S. Bedi	Mushtaq Mohammad	3	0	2	1
1979-80*I*	S. M. Gavaskar[1]	Asif Iqbal	6	2	0	4
1982-83*P*	S. M. Gavaskar	Imran Khan	6	0	3	3
1983-84*I*	Kapil Dev	Zaheer Abbas	3	0	0	3
1984-85*P*	S. M. Gavaskar	Zaheer Abbas	2	0	0	2
1986-87*I*	Kapil Dev	Imran Khan	5	0	1	4
1989-90*P*	K. Srikkanth	Imran Khan	4	0	0	4
1998-99*I*	M. Azharuddin	Wasim Akram	2	1	1	0
1998-99*I*†	M. Azharuddin	Wasim Akram	1	0	1	0
2003-04*P*	S. C. Ganguly[2]	Inzamam-ul-Haq	3	2	1	0

Season	India	Captains Pakistan	T	I	P	D
2004-05*I*	S. C. Ganguly	Inzamam-ul-Haq	3	1	1	1
2005-06*P*	R. Dravid	Inzamam-ul-Haq[3]	3	0	1	2
2007-08*I*	A. Kumble	Shoaib Malik[4]	3	1	0	2
	In India		33	7	5	21
	In Pakistan		26	2	7	17
	Totals		59	9	12	38

I Played in India. P Played in Pakistan.

† *This Test was part of the Asian Test Championship and was not counted as part of the preceding bilateral series.*

The following were appointed by the home authority for only a minor proportion of the series or deputised for the official touring captain:

[1]G. R. Viswanath (Sixth). [2]R. Dravid (First and Second). [3]Younis Khan (Third). [4]Younis Khan (Second and Third).

SERIES RECORDS

Highest score	*I*	309	V. Sehwag at Multan	2003-04
	P	280*	Javed Miandad at Hyderabad	1982-83
Best bowling	*I*	10-74	A. Kumble at Delhi	1998-99
	P	8-60	Imran Khan at Karachi	1982-83
Highest total	*I*	675-5 dec	at Multan	2003-04
	P	699-5	at Lahore	1989-90
Lowest total	*I*	106	at Lucknow	1952-53
	P	116	at Bangalore	1986-87

INDIA v SRI LANKA

Season	India	Captains Sri Lanka	T	I	SL	D
1982-83*I*	S. M. Gavaskar	B. Warnapura	1	0	0	1
1985-86*S*	Kapil Dev	L. R. D. Mendis	3	0	1	2
1986-87*I*	Kapil Dev	L. R. D. Mendis	3	2	0	1
1990-91*I*	M. Azharuddin	A. Ranatunga	1	1	0	0
1993-94*S*	M. Azharuddin	A. Ranatunga	3	1	0	2
1993-94*I*	M. Azharuddin	A. Ranatunga	3	3	0	0
1997-98*S*	S. R. Tendulkar	A. Ranatunga	2	0	0	2
1997-98*I*	S. R. Tendulkar	A. Ranatunga	3	0	0	3
1998-99*S*†	M. Azharuddin	A. Ranatunga	1	0	0	1
2001*S*	S. C. Ganguly	S. T. Jayasuriya	3	1	2	0
2005-06*I*	R. Dravid[1]	M. S. Atapattu	3	2	0	1
2008*S*	A. Kumble	D. P. M. D. Jayawardene	3	1	2	0
2009-10*I*	M. S. Dhoni	K. C. Sangakkara	3	2	0	1
2010*S*	M. S. Dhoni	K. C. Sangakkara	3	1	1	1
2015-16*S*	V. Kohli	A. D. Mathews	3	2	1	0
2017*S*	V. Kohli	L. D. Chandimal[2]	3	3	0	0
2017-18*I*	V. Kohli	L. D. Chandimal	3	1	0	2
	In India		20	11	0	9
	In Sri Lanka		24	9	7	8
	Totals		44	20	7	17

I Played in India. S Played in Sri Lanka.

† *This Test was part of the Asian Test Championship.*

The following were appointed by the home authority for only a minor proportion of the series:

[1]V. Sehwag (Third). [2]H. M. R. K. B. Herath (First).

SERIES RECORDS

Highest score	*I*	293	V. Sehwag at Mumbai (BS)	2009-10
	SL	340	S. T. Jayasuriya at Colombo (RPS)	1997-98
Best bowling	*I*	7-51	Maninder Singh at Nagpur	1986-87
	SL	8-87	M. Muralitharan at Colombo (SSC)	2001
Highest total	*I*	726-9 dec	at Mumbai (BS)	2009-10
	SL	952-6 dec	at Colombo (RPS)	1997-98
Lowest total	*I*	112	at Galle	2015-16
	SL	82	at Chandigarh	1990-91

INDIA v ZIMBABWE

	Captains					
Season	*India*	*Zimbabwe*	*T*	*I*	*Z*	*D*
1992-93*Z*	M. Azharuddin	D. L. Houghton	1	0	0	1
1992-93*I*	M. Azharuddin	D. L. Houghton	1	1	0	0
1998-99*Z*	M. Azharuddin	A. D. R. Campbell	1	0	1	0
2000-01*I*	S. C. Ganguly	H. H. Streak	2	1	0	1
2001*Z*	S. C. Ganguly	H. H. Streak	2	1	1	0
2001-02*I*	S. C. Ganguly	S. V. Carlisle	2	2	0	0
2005-06*Z*	S. C. Ganguly	T. Taibu	2	2	0	0
	In India		5	4	0	1
	In Zimbabwe		6	3	2	1
	Totals		11	7	2	2

I Played in India. Z Played in Zimbabwe.

SERIES RECORDS

Highest score	*I*	227	V. G. Kambli at Delhi	1992-93
	Z	232*	A. Flower at Nagpur	2000-01
Best bowling	*I*	7-59	I. K. Pathan at Harare	2005-06
	Z	6-73	H. H. Streak at Harare	2005-06
Highest total	*I*	609-6 dec	at Nagpur	2000-01
	Z	503-6	at Nagpur	2000-01
Lowest total	*I*	173	at Harare	1998-99
	Z	146	at Delhi	2001-02

INDIA v BANGLADESH

	Captains					
Season	*India*	*Bangladesh*	*T*	*I*	*B*	*D*
2000-01*B*	S. C. Ganguly	Naimur Rahman	1	1	0	0
2004-05*B*	S. C. Ganguly	Habibul Bashar	2	2	0	0
2007*B*	R. Dravid	Habibul Bashar	2	1	0	1
2009-10*B*	M. S. Dhoni[1]	Shakib Al Hasan	2	2	0	0
2015*B*	V. Kohli	Mushfiqur Rahim	1	0	0	1
2016-17*I*	V. Kohli	Mushfiqur Rahim	1	1	0	0
2019-20*I*	V. Kohli	Mominul Haque	2	2	0	0
	In Bangladesh		8	6	0	2
	In India		3	3	0	0
	Totals		11	9	0	2

B Played in Bangladesh. I Played in India.

The following deputised for the official touring captain for a minor proportion of the series:
[1]V. Sehwag (First).

SERIES RECORDS

Highest score	*I*	248*	S. R. Tendulkar at Dhaka	2004-05
	B	158*	Mohammad Ashraful at Chittagong	2004-05
Best bowling	*I*	7-87	Zaheer Khan at Mirpur	2009-10
	B	6-132	Naimur Rahman at Dhaka	2000-01
Highest total	*I*	687-6 dec	at Hyderabad	2016-17
	B	400	at Dhaka	2000-01
Lowest total	*I*	243	at Chittagong	2009-10
	B	91	at Dhaka	2000-01

INDIA v AFGHANISTAN

	Captains					
Season	*India*	*Afghanistan*	*T*	*I*	*Afg*	*D*
2018*I*	A. M. Rahane	Asghar Stanikzai†	1	1	0	0
	In India		1	1	0	0
	Totals		1	1	0	0

I Played in India.

† *Later known as Asghar Afghan.*

SERIES RECORDS

Highest score	*I*	107	S. Dhawan at Bangalore	2018
	Afg	36*	Hashmatullah Shahidi at Bangalore	2018
Best bowling	*I*	4-17	R. A. Jadeja at Bangalore	2018
	Afg	3-51	Yamin Ahmadzai at Bangalore	2018
Highest total	*I*	474	at Bangalore	2018
	Afg	109	at Bangalore	2018
Lowest total	*I*	474	at Bangalore	2018
	Afg	103	at Bangalore	2018

PAKISTAN v SRI LANKA

	Captains					
Season	*Pakistan*	*Sri Lanka*	*T*	*P*	*SL*	*D*
1981-82*P*	Javed Miandad	B. Warnapura[1]	3	2	0	1
1985-86*P*	Javed Miandad	L. R. D. Mendis	3	2	0	1
1985-86*S*	Imran Khan	L. R. D. Mendis	3	1	1	1
1991-92*P*	Imran Khan	P. A. de Silva	3	1	0	2
1994-95*S*†	Salim Malik	A. Ranatunga	2	2	0	0
1995-96*P*	Ramiz Raja	A. Ranatunga	3	1	2	0
1996-97*S*	Ramiz Raja	A. Ranatunga	2	0	0	2
1998-99*P*‡	Wasim Akram	H. P. Tillekeratne	1	0	0	1
1998-99*B*‡	Wasim Akram	P. A. de Silva	1	1	0	0
1999-2000*P*	Saeed Anwar[2]	S. T. Jayasuriya	3	1	2	0
2000*S*	Moin Khan	S. T. Jayasuriya	3	2	0	[illegible]
2001-02*P*‡	Waqar Younis	S. T. Jayasuriya	1	0	1	[illegible]
2004-05*P*	Inzamam-ul-Haq	M. S. Atapattu	2	1	1	[illegible]
2005-06*S*	Inzamam-ul-Haq	D. P. M. D. Jayawardene	2	1	0	[illegible]
2008-09*P*§	Younis Khan	D. P. M. D. Jayawardene	2	0	0	[illegible]
2009*S*	Younis Khan	K. C. Sangakkara	3	0	2	[illegible]
2011-12*U*	Misbah-ul-Haq	T. M. Dilshan	3	1	0	[illegible]

	Captains					
Season	*Pakistan*	*Sri Lanka*	*T*	*P*	*SL*	*D*
2012*S*	Misbah-ul-Haq[3]	D. P. M. D. Jayawardene	3	0	1	2
2013-14*U*	Misbah-ul-Haq	A. D. Mathews	3	1	1	1
2014*S*	Misbah-ul-Haq	A. D. Mathews	2	0	2	0
2015*S*	Misbah-ul-Haq	A. D. Mathews	3	2	1	0
2017-18*U*	Sarfraz Ahmed	L. D. Chandimal	2	0	2	0
2019-20*P*	Azhar Ali	F. D. M. Karunaratne	2	1	0	1
	In Pakistan		23	9	6	8
	In Sri Lanka		23	8	7	8
	In Bangladesh		1	1	0	0
	In United Arab Emirates		8	2	3	3
	Totals		55	20	16	19

P Played in Pakistan. S Played in Sri Lanka. B Played in Bangladesh.
U Played in United Arab Emirates.

† *One Test was cancelled owing to the threat of civil disturbances following a general election.*
‡ *These Tests were part of the Asian Test Championship.*
§ *The Second Test ended after a terrorist attack on the Sri Lankan team bus on the third day.*

The following deputised for the official touring captain or were appointed by the home authority for only a minor proportion of the series:
[1]L. R. D. Mendis (Second). [2]Moin Khan (Third). [3]Mohammad Hafeez (First).

SERIES RECORDS

Highest score	*P*	313	Younis Khan at Karachi	2008-09
	SL	253	S. T. Jayasuriya at Faisalabad	2004-05
Best bowling	*P*	8-58	Imran Khan at Lahore	1981-82
	SL	9-127	H. M. R. K. B. Herath at Colombo (SSC)	2014
Highest total	*P*	765-6 dec	at Karachi	2008-09
	SL	644-7 dec	at Karachi	2008-09
Lowest total	*P*	90	at Colombo (PSS)	2009
	SL	71	at Kandy	1994-95

PAKISTAN v ZIMBABWE

	Captains					
Season	*Pakistan*	*Zimbabwe*	*T*	*P*	*Z*	*D*
1993-94*P*	Wasim Akram[1]	A. Flower	3	2	0	1
1994-95*Z*	Salim Malik	A. Flower	3	2	1	0
1996-97*P*	Wasim Akram	A. D. R. Campbell	2	1	0	1
1997-98*Z*	Rashid Latif	A. D. R. Campbell	2	1	0	1
1998-99*P*†	Aamir Sohail[2]	A. D. R. Campbell	2	0	1	1
2002-03*Z*	Waqar Younis	A. D. R. Campbell	2	2	0	0
2011-12*Z*	Misbah-ul-Haq	B. R. M. Taylor	1	1	0	0
2013-14*Z*	Misbah-ul-Haq	B. R. M. Taylor[3]	2	1	1	0
	In Pakistan		7	3	1	3
	In Zimbabwe		10	7	2	1
	Totals		17	10	3	4

P Played in Pakistan. Z Played in Zimbabwe.

† *The Third Test at Faisalabad was abandoned without a ball being bowled and is excluded.*

The following were appointed by the home authority for only a minor proportion of the series:
[1]Waqar Younis (First). [2]Moin Khan (Second). [3]H. Masakadza (First).

SERIES RECORDS

Highest score	*P*	257*	Wasim Akram at Sheikhupura	1996-97
	Z	201*	G. W. Flower at Harare	1994-95
Best bowling	*P*	7-66	Saqlain Mushtaq at Bulawayo	2002-03
	Z	6-90	H. H. Streak at Harare	1994-95
Highest total	*P*	553	at Sheikhupura	1996-97
	Z	544-4 dec	at Harare	1994-95
Lowest total	*P*	103	at Peshawar	1998-99
	Z	120	at Harare	2013-14

PAKISTAN v BANGLADESH

	Captains					
Season	*Pakistan*	*Bangladesh*	*T*	*P*	*B*	*D*
2001-02*P*†	Waqar Younis	Naimur Rahman	1	1	0	0
2001-02*B*	Waqar Younis	Khaled Mashud	2	2	0	0
2003-04*P*	Rashid Latif	Khaled Mahmud	3	3	0	0
2011-12*B*	Misbah-ul-Haq	Mushfiqur Rahim	2	2	0	0
2014-15*B*	Misbah-ul-Haq	Mushfiqur Rahim	2	1	0	1
2019-20*P*‡	**Azhar Ali**	**Mominul Haque**	**1**	**1**	**0**	**0**
	In Pakistan		**5**	**5**	**0**	**0**
	In Bangladesh		6	5	0	1
	Totals		**11**	**10**	**0**	**1**

P Played in Pakistan. B Played in Bangladesh.

† *This Test was part of the Asian Test Championship.*
‡ *The Second Test at Karachi was postponed because of the Covid-19 crisis.*

SERIES RECORDS

Highest score	*P*	226	Azhar Ali at Mirpur	2014-15
	B	206	Tamim Iqbal at Khulna	2014-15
Best bowling	*P*	7-77	Danish Kaneria at Dhaka	2001-02
	B	6-82	Shakib Al Hasan at Mirpur	2011-12
Highest total	*P*	628	at Khulna	2014-15
	B	555-6	at Khulna	2014-15
Lowest total	*P*	175	at Multan	2003-04
	B	96	at Peshawar	2003-04

PAKISTAN v IRELAND

	Captains					
Season	*Pakistan*	*Ireland*	*T*	*P*	*Ire*	*D*
2018*Ire*	Sarfraz Ahmed	W. T. S. Porterfield	1	1	0	0
	In Ireland		1	1	0	0
	Totals		1	1	0	0

Ire Played in Ireland.

SERIES RECORDS

Highest score	*P*	83	Fahim Ashraf at Malahide	2018
	Ire	118	K. J. O'Brien at Malahide	2018
Best bowling	*P*	5-66	Mohammad Abbas at Malahide	2018
	Ire	4-45	T. J. Murtagh at Malahide	2018
Highest total	*P*	310-9 dec	at Malahide	2018
	Ire	339	at Malahide	2018
Lowest total	*Ire*	130	at Malahide	2018

SRI LANKA v ZIMBABWE

Captains

Season	*Sri Lanka*	*Zimbabwe*	*T*	*SL*	*Z*	*D*
1994-95*Z*	A. Ranatunga	A. Flower	3	0	0	3
1996-97*S*	A. Ranatunga	A. D. R. Campbell	2	2	0	0
1997-98*S*	A. Ranatunga	A. D. R. Campbell	2	2	0	0
1999-2000*Z*	S. T. Jayasuriya	A. Flower	3	1	0	2
2001-02*S*	S. T. Jayasuriya	S. V. Carlisle	3	3	0	0
2003-04*Z*	M. S. Atapattu	T. Taibu	2	2	0	0
2016-17*Z*	H. M. R. K. B. Herath	A. G. Cremer	2	2	0	0
2017*S*	L. D. Chandimal	A. G. Cremer	1	1	0	0
2019-20*Z*	**F. D. M. Karunaratne**	**S. C. Williams**	**2**	**1**	**0**	**1**
	In Sri Lanka		8	8	0	0
	In Zimbabwe		**12**	**6**	**0**	**6**
	Totals		**20**	**14**	**0**	**6**

S *Played in Sri Lanka.* *Z* *Played in Zimbabwe.*

SERIES RECORDS

Highest score	*SL*	270	K. C. Sangakkara at Bulawayo	2003-04
	Z	266	D. L. Houghton at Bulawayo	1994-95
Best bowling	*SL*	9-51	M. Muralitharan at Kandy	2001-02
	Z	**7-113**	**Sikandar Raza at Harare**	**2019-20**
Highest total	*SL*	713-3 dec	at Bulawayo	2003-04
	Z	462-9 dec	at Bulawayo	1994-95
Lowest total	*SL*	218	at Bulawayo	1994-95
	Z	79	at Galle	2001-02

SRI LANKA v BANGLADESH

Captains

Season	*Sri Lanka*	*Bangladesh*	*T*	*SL*	*B*	*D*
2001-02*S*†	S. T. Jayasuriya	Naimur Rahman	1	1	0	0
2002*S*	S. T. Jayasuriya	Khaled Mashud	2	2	0	0
2005-06*S*	M. S. Atapattu	Habibul Bashar	2	2	0	0
2005-06*B*	D. P. M. D. Jayawardene	Habibul Bashar	2	2	0	0
2007*S*	D. P. M. D. Jayawardene	Mohammad Ashraful	3	3	0	0
2008-09*B*	D. P. M. D. Jayawardene	Mohammad Ashraful	2	2	0	0
2012-13*S*	A. D. Mathews	Mushfiqur Rahim	2	1	0	1

Season	*Sri Lanka*	*Captains* *Bangladesh*	*T*	*SL*	*B*	*D*
2013-14*B*	A. D. Mathews	Mushfiqur Rahim	2	1	0	1
2016-17*S*	H. M. R. K. B. Herath	Mushfiqur Rahim	2	1	1	0
2017-18*B*	L. D. Chandimal	Mahmudullah	2	1	0	1
	In Sri Lanka		12	10	1	1
	In Bangladesh		8	6	0	2
	Totals		20	16	1	3

S Played in Sri Lanka. *B Played in Bangladesh.*

† *This Test was part of the Asian Test Championship.*

SERIES RECORDS

Highest score	*SL*	319	K. C. Sangakkara at Chittagong	2013-14
	B	200	Mushfiqur Rahim at Galle	2012-13
Best bowling	*SL*	7-89	H. M. R. K. B. Herath at Colombo (RPS)	2012-13
	B	5-70	Shakib Al Hasan at Mirpur	2008-09
Highest total	*SL*	730-6 dec	at Mirpur	2013-14
	B	638	at Galle	2012-13
Lowest total	*SL*	222	at Mirpur	2017-18
	B	62	at Colombo (PSS)	2007

ZIMBABWE v BANGLADESH

Season	*Zimbabwe*	*Captains* *Bangladesh*	*T*	*Z*	*B*	*D*
2000-01*Z*	H. H. Streak	Naimur Rahman	2	2	0	0
2001-02*B*	B. A. Murphy[1]	Naimur Rahman	2	1	0	1
2003-04*Z*	H. H. Streak	Habibul Bashar	2	1	0	1
2004-05*B*	T. Taibu	Habibul Bashar	2	0	1	1
2011-12*Z*	B. R. M. Taylor	Shakib Al Hasan	1	1	0	0
2012-13*Z*	B. R. M. Taylor	Mushfiqur Rahim	2	1	1	0
2014-15*B*	B. R. M. Taylor	Mushfiqur Rahim	3	0	3	0
2018-19*B*	H. Masakadza	Mahmudullah	2	1	1	0
2019-20*B*	**C. R. Ervine**	**Mominul Haque**	**1**	**0**	**1**	**0**
	In Zimbabwe		7	5	1	1
	In Bangladesh		**10**	**2**	**6**	**2**
	Totals		**17**	**7**	**7**	**3**

Z Played in Zimbabwe. *B Played in Bangladesh.*

The following deputised for the official touring captain:

[1]S. V. Carlisle (Second).

SERIES RECORDS

Highest score	*Z*	171	B. R. M. Taylor at Harare	2012-13
	B	219*	Mushfiqur Rahim at Mirpur	2018-19
Best bowling	*Z*	6-59	D. T. Hondo at Dhaka	2004-05
	B	8-39	Taijul Islam at Mirpur	2014-15
Highest total	*Z*	542-7 dec	at Chittagong	2001-02
	B	**560-6 dec**	**at Mirpur**	**2019-20**
Lowest total	*Z*	114	at Mirpur	2014-15
	B	107	at Dhaka	2001-02

BANGLADESH v AFGHANISTAN

	Captains					
Season	*Bangladesh*	*Afghanistan*	*T*	*B*	*Afg*	*D*
2019-20*B*	Shakib Al Hasan	Rashid Khan	1	0	1	0
	In Bangladesh		1	0	1	0
	Totals		1	0	1	0

B Played in Bangladesh.

SERIES RECORDS

Highest score	*B*	52	Mominul Haque at Chittagong	2019-20
	Afg	102	Rahmat Shah at Chittagong	2019-20
Best bowling	*B*	4-116	Taijul Islam at Chittagong	2019-20
	Afg	6-49	Rashid Khan at Chittagong	2019-20
Highest total	*B*	205	at Chittagong	2019-20
	Afg	342	at Chittagong	2019-20
Lowest total	*B*	173	at Chittagong	2019-20
	Afg	260	at Chittagong	2019-20

IRELAND v AFGHANISTAN

	Captains					
Season	*Ireland*	*Afghanistan*	*T*	*Ire*	*Afg*	*D*
2018-19*I*	W. T. S. Porterfield	Asghar Afghan	1	0	1	0
	In India		1	0	1	0
	Totals		1	0	1	0

I Played in India.

SERIES RECORDS

Highest score	*Ire*	82	A. Balbirnie at Dehradun	2018-19
	Afg	98	Rahmat Shah at Dehradun	2018-19
Best bowling	*Ire*	3-28	S. R. Thompson at Dehradun	2018-19
	Afg	5-82	Rashid Khan at Dehradun	2018-19
Highest total	*Ire*	288	at Dehradun	2018-19
	Afg	314	at Dehradun	2018-19
Lowest total	*Ire*	172	at Dehradun	2018-19
	Afg	314	at Dehradun	2018-19

TEST GROUNDS

in chronological order

	City and Ground	*First Test Match*		*Tests*
1	**Melbourne, Melbourne Cricket Ground**	**March 15, 1877**	**A v E**	**113**
2	London, Kennington Oval	September 6, 1880	E v A	102
3	**Sydney, Sydney Cricket Ground (No. 1)**	**February 17, 1882**	**A v E**	**109**
4	**Manchester, Old Trafford**	**July 11, 1884**	**E v A**	**82**
5	London, Lord's	July 21, 1884	E v A	139
6	**Adelaide, Adelaide Oval**	**December 12, 1884**	**A v E**	**79**
7	**Port Elizabeth, St George's Park**	**March 12, 1889**	**SA v E**	**31**
8	**Cape Town, Newlands**	**March 25, 1889**	**SA v E**	**58**
9	Johannesburg, Old Wanderers	March 2, 1896	SA v E	22
	Now the site of Johannesburg Railway Station.			
10	Nottingham, Trent Bridge	June 1, 1899	E v A	63

	City and Ground	*First Test Match*		*Tests*
11	Leeds, Headingley	June 29, 1899	E v A	78
12	Birmingham, Edgbaston	May 29, 1902	E v A	52
13	Sheffield, Bramall Lane	July 3, 1902	E v A	1
	Sheffield United Football Club have built a stand over the cricket pitch.			
14	Durban, Lord's	January 21, 1910	SA v E	4
	Ground destroyed and built on.			
15	Durban, Kingsmead	January 18, 1923	SA v E	44
16	Brisbane, Exhibition Ground	November 30, 1928	A v E	2
	No longer used for cricket.			
17	Christchurch, Lancaster Park	January 10, 1930	NZ v E	40
	Also known under sponsors' names.			
18	Bridgetown, Kensington Oval	January 11, 1930	WI v E	54
19	**Wellington, Basin Reserve**	**January 24, 1930**	**NZ v E**	**65**
20	Port-of-Spain, Queen's Park Oval	February 1, 1930	WI v E	61
21	Auckland, Eden Park	February 14, 1930	NZ v E	50
22	Georgetown, Bourda	February 21, 1930	WI v E	30
23	Kingston, Sabina Park	April 3, 1930	WI v E	52
24	**Brisbane, Woolloongabba**	**November 27, 1931**	**A v SA**	**63**
25	Bombay, Gymkhana Ground	December 15, 1933	I v E	1
	No longer used for first-class cricket.			
26	Calcutta (*now Kolkata*), Eden Gardens	January 5, 1934	I v E	42
27	Madras (*now Chennai*), Chepauk (Chidambaram Stadium)	February 10, 1934	I v E	32
28	Delhi, Feroz Shah Kotla	November 10, 1948	I v WI	34
29	Bombay (*now Mumbai*), Brabourne Stadium	December 9, 1948	I v WI	18
	Rarely used for first-class cricket.			
30	Johannesburg, Ellis Park	December 27, 1948	SA v E	6
	Mainly a football and rugby stadium, no longer used for cricket.			
31	Kanpur, Green Park (Modi Stadium)	January 12, 1952	I v E	22
32	Lucknow, University Ground	October 25, 1952	I v P	1
	Ground destroyed, now partly under a river bed.			
33	Dacca (*now Dhaka*), Dacca (*now Bangabandhu*) Stadium	January 1, 1955	P v I	17
	Originally in East Pakistan, now Bangladesh, no longer used for cricket.			
34	Bahawalpur, Dring (*now Bahawal*) Stadium	January 15, 1955	P v I	1
	Still used for first-class cricket.			
35	Lahore, Lawrence Gardens (Bagh-e-Jinnah)	January 29, 1955	P v I	3
	Still used for club and occasional first-class matches.			
36	Peshawar, Services Ground	February 13, 1955	P v I	1
	Superseded by new stadium.			
37	Karachi, National Stadium	February 26, 1955	P v I	42
38	Dunedin, Carisbrook	March 11, 1955	NZ v E	10
39	Hyderabad, Fateh Maidan (Lal Bahadur Stadium)	November 19, 1955	I v NZ	3
40	Madras, Corporation Stadium	January 6, 1956	I v NZ	9
	Superseded by rebuilt Chepauk Stadium.			
41	**Johannesburg, Wanderers**	**December 24, 1956**	**SA v E**	**42**
42	Lahore, Gaddafi Stadium	November 21, 1959	P v A	40
43	Rawalpindi, Pindi Club Ground	March 27, 1965	P v NZ	1
	Superseded by new stadium.			
44	Nagpur, Vidarbha CA Ground	October 3, 1969	I v NZ	9
	Superseded by new stadium.			
45	Perth, Western Australian CA Ground	December 11, 1970	A v E	44
	Superseded by new stadium.			
46	Hyderabad, Niaz Stadium	March 16, 1973	P v E	5
47	Bangalore, Karnataka State CA Ground (Chinnaswamy Stadium)	November 22, 1974	I v WI	23
48	Bombay (*now Mumbai*), Wankhede Stadium	January 23, 1975	I v WI	2[illegible]
49	Faisalabad, Iqbal Stadium	October 16, 1978	P v I	2[illegible]
50	Napier, McLean Park	February 16, 1979	NZ v P	1[illegible]
51	Multan, Ibn-e-Qasim Bagh Stadium	December 30, 1980	P v WI	
	Superseded by new stadium.			

	City and Ground	*First Test Match*		*Tests*
52	St John's (Antigua), Recreation Ground	March 27, 1981	WI v E	22
53	Colombo, P. Saravanamuttu Stadium/ P. Sara Oval	February 17, 1982	SL v E	22
54	Kandy, Asgiriya Stadium	April 22, 1983	SL v A	21
	Superseded by new stadium at Pallekele.			
55	Jullundur, Burlton Park	September 24, 1983	I v P	1
56	Ahmedabad, Sardar Patel (Gujarat) Stadium	November 12, 1983	I v WI	12
57	Colombo, Sinhalese Sports Club Ground	March 16, 1984	SL v NZ	43
58	Colombo, Colombo Cricket Club Ground	March 24, 1984	SL v NZ	3
59	Sialkot, Jinnah Stadium	October 27, 1985	P v SL	4
60	Cuttack, Barabati Stadium	January 4, 1987	I v SL	2
61	Jaipur, Sawai Mansingh Stadium	February 21, 1987	I v P	1
62	Hobart, Bellerive Oval	December 16, 1989	A v SL	13
63	Chandigarh, Sector 16 Stadium	November 23, 1990	I v SL	1
	Superseded by Mohali ground.			
64	**Hamilton, Seddon Park**	**February 22, 1991**	**NZ v SL**	**27**
	Also known under various sponsors' names.			
65	Gujranwala, Municipal Stadium	December 20, 1991	P v SL	1
66	Colombo, R. Premadasa (Khettarama) Stadium	August 28, 1992	SL v A	9
67	Moratuwa, Tyronne Fernando Stadium	September 8, 1992	SL v A	4
68	**Harare, Harare Sports Club**	**October 18, 1992**	**Z v I**	**36**
69	Bulawayo, Bulawayo Athletic Club	November 1, 1992	Z v NZ	1
	Superseded by Queens Sports Club ground.			
70	Karachi, Defence Stadium	December 1, 1993	P v Z	1
71	**Rawalpindi, Rawalpindi Cricket Stadium**	**December 9, 1993**	**P v Z**	**10**
72	Lucknow, K. D. Singh "Babu" Stadium	January 18, 1994	I v SL	1
73	Bulawayo, Queens Sports Club	October 20, 1994	Z v SL	23
74	Mohali, Punjab Cricket Association Stadium	December 10, 1994	I v WI	13
75	Peshawar, Arbab Niaz Stadium	September 8, 1995	P v SL	6
76	**Centurion (*ex Verwoerdburg*), Centurion Park**	**November 16, 1995**	**SA v E**	**26**
77	Sheikhupura, Municipal Stadium	October 17, 1996	P v Z	2
78	St Vincent, Arnos Vale	June 20, 1997	WI v SL	3
79	**Galle, International Stadium**	**June 3, 1998**	**SL v NZ**	**35**
80	Bloemfontein, Springbok Park	October 29, 1999	SA v Z	5
	Also known under various sponsors' names.			
81	Multan, Multan Cricket Stadium	August 29, 2001	P v B	5
82	Chittagong, Chittagong Stadium	November 15, 2001	B v Z	8
	Also known as M. A. Aziz Stadium.			
83	Sharjah, Sharjah Cricket Association Stadium	January 31, 2002	P v WI	9
84	St George's, Grenada, Queen's Park New Stadium	June 28, 2002	WI v NZ	3
85	East London, Buffalo Park	October 18, 2002	SA v B	1
86	Potchefstroom, North West Cricket Stadium	October 25, 2002	SA v B	2
	Now known under sponsor's name.			
87	Chester-le-Street, Riverside Ground	June 5, 2003	E v Z	6
	Also known under sponsor's name.			
88	Gros Islet, St Lucia, Beausejour Stadium	June 20, 2003	WI v SL	7
	Now known as Darren Sammy Stadium.			
89	Darwin, Marrara Cricket Ground	July 18, 2003	A v B	2
90	Cairns, Cazaly's Football Park	July 25, 2003	A v B	2
	Also known under sponsor's name.			
91	Chittagong, Chittagong Divisional Stadium	February 28, 2006	B v SL	19
	Also known as Bir Shrestha Shahid Ruhul Amin Stadium/Zohur Ahmed Chowdhury Stadium.			
92	Bogra, Shaheed Chandu Stadium	March 8, 2006	B v SL	1
93	Fatullah, Narayanganj Osmani Stadium	April 9, 2006	B v A	2
94	Basseterre, St Kitts, Warner Park	June 22, 2006	WI v I	3
95	**Mirpur (Dhaka), Shere Bangla Natl Stadium**	**May 25, 2007**	**B v I**	**20**
96	Dunedin, University Oval	January 4, 2008	NZ v B	8
97	Providence Stadium, Guyana	March 22, 2008	WI v SL	2
98	North Sound, Antigua, Sir Vivian Richards Stadium	May 30, 2008	WI v A	8
99	Nagpur, Vidarbha CA Stadium, Jamtha	November 6, 2008	I v A	6

	City and Ground	*First Test Match*		*Tests*
100	Cardiff, Sophia Gardens	July 8, 2009	E v A	3
	Now known under sponsor's name.			
101	Hyderabad, Rajiv Gandhi Intl Stadium	November 12, 2010	I v NZ	5
102	Dubai, Dubai Sports City Stadium	November 12, 2010	P v SA	13
103	Abu Dhabi, Sheikh Zayed Stadium	November 20, 2010	P v SA	13
104	Pallekele, Muttiah Muralitharan Stadium	December 1, 2010	SL v WI	7
105	**Southampton, Rose Bowl**	**June 16, 2011**	**E v SL**	**6**
	Now known under sponsor's name.			
106	Roseau, Dominica, Windsor Park	July 6, 2011	WI v I	5
107	Khulna, Khulna Division Stadium	November 21, 2012	B v WI	3
	Also known as Bir Shrestha Shahid Flight Lt Motiur Rahman/Shaikh Abu Naser Stadium.			
108	**Christchurch, Hagley Oval**	**December 26, 2014**	**NZ v SL**	**8**
109	Indore, Maharani Usharaje Trust Ground	October 8, 2016	I v NZ	2
110	Rajkot, Saurashtra CA Stadium	November 9, 2016	I v E	2
111	Visakhapatnam, Andhra CA-Visakhapatnam DCA Stadium	November 17, 2016	I v E	2
112	Pune (Gahunje), Subrata Roy Sahara Stadium	February 23, 2017	I v A	2
113	Ranchi, Jharkhand State CA Oval Ground	March 16, 2017	I v A	2
114	Dharamsala, Himachal Pradesh CA Stadium	March 25, 2017	I v A	1
115	Malahide (Dublin), The Village	May 11, 2018	Ire v P	1
116	Sylhet, Sylhet Stadium	November 3, 2018	B v Z	1
117	Perth, Optus Stadium	December 14, 2018	A v I	2
118	Canberra, Manuka Oval	February 1, 2019	A v SL	1
119	Dehradun, Rajiv Gandhi Cricket Stadium	March 15, 2019	Afg v Ire	1
120	**Mount Maunganui, Bay Oval**	**November 21, 2019**	**NZ v E**	**2**
121	Lucknow, Ekana Cricket Stadium	November 27, 2019	Afg v WI	1
	Also known as Bharat Ratna Shri Atal Bihari Vajpayee Ekana Cricket Stadium.			

Bold type denotes grounds used for Test cricket since January 1, 2020.

ONE-DAY INTERNATIONAL RECORDS

Matches in this section do not have first-class status.

This section covers one-day international cricket to December 31, 2020. Bold type denotes performances in the calendar year 2020, or, in career figures, players who appeared in one-day internationals in that year.

SUMMARY OF ONE-DAY INTERNATIONALS

1970-71 to December 31, 2020

	Opponents	*Matches*	*Won by*															
			E	*A*	*SA*	*WI*	*NZ*	*I*	*P*	*SL*	*Z*	*B*	*Ire*	*Afg*	*Ass*	*Oth*	*Tied*	*NR*
England	Australia	**152**	63	84	–	–	–	–	–	–	–	–	–	–	–	–	2	3
	South Africa	**63**	28	–	30	–	–	–	–	–	–	–	–	–	–	–	1	4
	West Indies	**102**	52	–	–	44	–	–	–	–	–	–	–	–	–	–	–	6
	New Zealand	**91**	42	–	–	–	43	–	–	–	–	–	–	–	–	–	2	4
	India	**100**	42	–	–	–	–	53	–	–	–	–	–	–	–	–	2	3
	Pakistan	**88**	53	–	–	–	–	–	32	–	–	–	–	–	–	–	–	3
	Sri Lanka	**75**	36	–	–	–	–	–	–	36	–	–	–	–	–	–	1	2
	Zimbabwe	**30**	21	–	–	–	–	–	–	–	8	–	–	–	–	–	–	1
	Bangladesh	**21**	17	–	–	–	–	–	–	–	–	4	–	–	–	–	–	–
	Ireland	**13**	10	–	–	–	–	–	–	–	–	–	2	–	–	–	–	1
	Afghanistan	**2**	2	–	–	–	–	–	–	–	–	–	–	0	–	–	–	–
	Associates	**15**	13	–	–	–	–	–	–	–	–	–	–	–	1	–	–	1
Australia	South Africa	**103**	–	48	51	–	–	–	–	–	–	–	–	–	–	–	3	1
	West Indies	**140**	–	74	–	60	–	–	–	–	–	–	–	–	–	–	3	3
	New Zealand	**138**	–	92	–	–	39	–	–	–	–	–	–	–	–	–	–	7
	India	**143**	–	80	–	–	–	53	–	–	–	–	–	–	–	–	–	10
	Pakistan	**104**	–	68	–	–	–	–	32	–	–	–	–	–	–	–	1	3
	Sri Lanka	**97**	–	61	–	–	–	–	–	32	–	–	–	–	–	–	–	4
	Zimbabwe	**30**	–	27	–	–	–	–	–	–	2	–	–	–	–	–	–	1
	Bangladesh	**21**	–	19	–	–	–	–	–	–	–	1	–	–	–	–	–	1
	Ireland	**5**	–	4	–	–	–	–	–	–	–	–	0	–	–	–	–	1
	Afghanistan	**3**	–	3	–	–	–	–	–	–	–	–	–	0	–	–	–	–
	Associates	**16**	–	16	–	–	–	–	–	–	–	–	–	–	0	–	–	–
	ICC World XI	**3**	–	3	–	–	–	–	–	–	–	–	–	–	–	0	–	–
South Africa	West Indies	**62**	–	–	44	15	–	–	–	–	–	–	–	–	–	–	1	2
	New Zealand	**71**	–	–	41	–	25	–	–	–	–	–	–	–	–	–	–	5
	India	**84**	–	–	46	–	–	35	–	–	–	–	–	–	–	–	–	3
	Pakistan	**79**	–	–	50	–	–	–	28	–	–	–	–	–	–	–	–	1
	Sri Lanka	**77**	–	–	44	–	–	–	–	31	–	–	–	–	–	–	1	1
	Zimbabwe	**41**	–	–	38	–	–	–	–	–	2	–	–	–	–	–	–	1
	Bangladesh	**21**	–	–	17	–	–	–	–	–	–	4	–	–	–	–	–	–
	Ireland	**5**	–	–	5	–	–	–	–	–	–	–	0	–	–	–	–	–
	Afghanistan	**1**	–	–	1	–	–	–	–	–	–	–	–	0	–	–	–	–
	Associates	**18**	–	–	18	–	–	–	–	–	–	–	–	–	0	–	–	–
West Indies	New Zealand	**65**	–	–	–	30	28	–	–	–	–	–	–	–	–	–	–	7
	India	**133**	–	–	–	63	–	64	–	–	–	–	–	–	–	–	2	4
	Pakistan	**134**	–	–	–	71	–	–	60	–	–	–	–	–	–	–	3	–
	Sri Lanka	**60**	–	–	–	28	–	–	–	29	–	–	–	–	–	–	–	3
	Zimbabwe	**48**	–	–	–	36	–	–	–	–	10	–	–	–	–	–	1	1
	Bangladesh	**38**	–	–	–	21	–	–	–	–	–	15	–	–	–	–	–	2
	Ireland	**12**	–	–	–	10	–	–	–	–	–	–	1	–	–	–	–	1
	Afghanistan	**9**	–	–	–	5	–	–	–	–	–	–	–	3	–	–	–	1
	Associates	**19**	–	–	–	18	–	–	–	–	–	–	–	–	1	–	–	–
New Zealand	India	**110**	–	–	–	–	49	55	–	–	–	–	–	–	–	–	1	5
	Pakistan	**107**	–	–	–	–	48	–	55	–	–	–	–	–	–	–	1	3
	Sri Lanka	**99**	–	–	–	–	49	–	–	41	–	–	–	–	–	–	1	8
	Zimbabwe	**38**	–	–	–	–	27	–	–	–	9	–	–	–	–	–	1	1
	Bangladesh	**35**	–	–	–	–	25	–	–	–	–	10	–	–	–	–	–	–
	Ireland	**4**	–	–	–	–	4	–	–	–	–	–	0	–	–	–	–	–
	Afghanistan	**2**	–	–	–	–	2	–	–	–	–	–	–	0	–	–	–	–
	Associates	**12**	–	–	–	–	12	–	–	–	–	–	–	–	0	–	–	–
India	Pakistan	**132**	–	–	–	–	–	55	73	–	–	–	–	–	–	–	–	4
	Sri Lanka	**159**	–	–	–	–	–	91	–	56	–	–	–	–	–	–	1	11
	Zimbabwe	**63**	–	–	–	–	–	51	–	–	10	–	–	–	–	–	2	–

	Opponents	*Matches*	*Won by*															
			E	*A*	*SA*	*WI*	*NZ*	*I*	*P*	*SL*	*Z*	*B*	*Ire*	*Afg*	*Ass*	*Oth*	*Tied*	*NR*
	Bangladesh	**36**	–	–	–	–	–	30	–	–	–	5	–	–	–	–	–	1
	Ireland	**3**	–	–	–	–	–	3	–	–	–	–	0	–	–	–	–	–
	Afghanistan	**3**	–	–	–	–	–	2	–	–	–	–	–	0	–	–	1	–
	Associates	**24**	–	–	–	–	–	22	–	–	–	–	–	–	2	–	–	–
Pakistan	Sri Lanka	**155**	–	–	–	–	–	–	92	58	–	–	–	–	–	–	1	4
	Zimbabwe	**62**	–	–	–	–	–	–	54	–	5	–	–	–	–	–	1	2
	Bangladesh	**37**	–	–	–	–	–	–	32	–	–	5	–	–	–	–	–	–
	Ireland	**7**	–	–	–	–	–	–	5	–	–	–	1	–	–	–	1	–
	Afghanistan	**4**	–	–	–	–	–	–	4	–	–	–	–	0	–	–	–	–
	Associates	**21**	–	–	–	–	–	–	21	–	–	–	–	–	0	–	–	–
Sri Lanka	Zimbabwe	**57**	–	–	–	–	–	–	–	44	11	–	–	–	–	–	–	2
	Bangladesh	**48**	–	–	–	–	–	–	–	39	–	7	–	–	–	–	–	2
	Ireland	**4**	–	–	–	–	–	–	–	4	–	–	0	–	–	–	–	–
	Afghanistan	**4**	–	–	–	–	–	–	–	3	–	–	–	1	–	–	–	–
	Associates	**17**	–	–	–	–	–	–	–	16	–	–	–	–	1	–	–	–
Zimbabwe	Bangladesh	**75**	–	–	–	–	–	–	–	–	28	47	–	–	–	–	–	–
	Ireland	**13**	–	–	–	–	–	–	–	–	6	–	6	–	–	–	1	–
	Afghanistan	**25**	–	–	–	–	–	–	–	–	10	–	–	15	–	–	–	–
	Associates	**50**	–	–	–	–	–	–	–	–	38	–	–	–	9	–	1	2
Bangladesh	Ireland	**10**	–	–	–	–	–	–	–	–	–	7	2	–	–	–	–	1
	Afghanistan	**8**	–	–	–	–	–	–	–	–	–	5	–	3	–	–	–	–
	Associates	**26**	–	–	–	–	–	–	–	–	–	18	–	–	8	–	–	–
Ireland	Afghanistan	**27**	–	–	–	–	–	–	–	–	–	–	13	13	–	–	–	1
	Associates	**56**	–	–	–	–	–	–	–	–	–	–	43	–	9	–	1	3
Afghanistan	Associates	**38**	–	–	–	–	–	–	–	–	–	–	–	24	13	–	–	1
Associates	Associates	**157**	–	–	–	–	–	–	–	–	–	–	–	–	152	–	–	5
Asian CC XI	ICC World XI	**1**	–	–	–	–	–	–	–	–	–	–	–	–	–	1	–	–
	African XI	**6**	–	–	–	–	–	–	–	–	–	–	–	–	–	5	–	1
		4,267	379	579	385	401	351	514	488	389	139	128	68	59	196	6	37	148

Associate and Affiliate Members of ICC who have played one-day internationals are Bermuda, Canada, East Africa, Hong Kong, Kenya, Namibia, Nepal, Netherlands, Oman, Papua New Guinea, Scotland, United Arab Emirates and USA. Sri Lanka, Zimbabwe, Bangladesh, Afghanistan and Ireland played one-day internationals before gaining Test status; these are not counted as Associate results.

RESULTS SUMMARY OF ONE-DAY INTERNATIONALS

1970-71 to December 31, 2020 (4,267 matches)

	Matches	*Won*	*Lost*	*Tied*	*No Result*	*% Won (excl NR)*
South Africa	625	385	216	6	18	63.92
Australia	955	579	333	9	34	63.35
India	990	514	426	9	41	54.63
Pakistan	930	488	414	8	20	54.06
England	752	379	337	8	28	52.90
West Indies	822	401	381	10	30	51.26
Afghanistan	126	59	63	1	3	48.37
New Zealand	772	351	375	6	40	48.36
Sri Lanka	852	389	421	5	37	48.03
Ireland	159	68	80	3	8	46.02
Bangladesh	376	128	241	–	7	34.68
Zimbabwe	532	139	375	7	11	27.35
Oman	11	8	3	–	–	72.72
Asian Cricket Council XI	7	4	2	–	1	66.66
Nepal	10	5	5	–	–	50.00
Netherlands	80	31	45	1	3	40.90

	Matches	*Won*	*Lost*	*Tied*	*No Result*	*% Won (excl NR)*
USA	15	6	9	–	–	40.00
Scotland	115	42	66	1	6	38.99
Hong Kong	26	9	16	–	1	36.00
Namibia	14	5	9	–	–	35.71
United Arab Emirates	59	17	42	–	–	28.81
Kenya	154	42	107	–	5	28.18
Papua New Guinea	27	7	20	–	–	25.92
ICC World XI	4	1	3	–	–	25.00
Canada	77	17	58	–	2	22.66
Bermuda	35	7	28	–	–	20.00
African XI	6	1	4	–	1	20.00
East Africa	3	–	3	–	–	0.00

Matches abandoned without a ball bowled are not included except (from 2004) where the toss took place, in accordance with an ICC ruling. Such matches, like those called off after play began, are now counted as official internationals in their own right, even when replayed on another day. In the percentages of matches won, ties are counted as half a win.

BATTING RECORDS

HIGHEST INDIVIDUAL INNINGS

264	R. G. Sharma	India v Sri Lanka at Kolkata	2014-15
237*	M. J. Guptill	New Zealand v West Indies at Wellington	2014-15
219	V. Sehwag	India v West Indies at Indore	2011-12
215	C. H. Gayle	West Indies v Zimbabwe at Canberra	2014-15
210*	Fakhar Zaman	Pakistan v Zimbabwe at Bulawayo	2018
209	R. G. Sharma	India v Australia at Bangalore	2013-14
208*	R. G. Sharma	India v Sri Lanka at Mohali	2017-18
200*	S. R. Tendulkar	India v South Africa at Gwalior	2009-10
194*	C. K. Coventry	Zimbabwe v Bangladesh at Bulawayo	2009
194	Saeed Anwar	Pakistan v India at Chennai	1996-97
189*	I. V. A. Richards	West Indies v England at Manchester	1984
189*	M. J. Guptill	New Zealand v England at Southampton	2013
189	S. T. Jayasuriya	Sri Lanka v India at Sharjah	2000-01
188*	G. Kirsten	South Africa v UAE at Rawalpindi	1995-96
186*	S. R. Tendulkar	India v New Zealand at Hyderabad	1999-2000
185*	S. R. Watson	Australia v Bangladesh at Mirpur	2010-11
185	F. du Plessis	South Africa v Sri Lanka at Cape Town	2016-17
183*	M. S. Dhoni	India v Sri Lanka at Jaipur	2005-06
183	S. C. Ganguly	India v Sri Lanka at Taunton	1999
183	V. Kohli	India v Pakistan at Mirpur	2011-12
181*	M. L. Hayden	Australia v New Zealand at Hamilton	2006-07
181*	L. R. P. L. Taylor	New Zealand v England at Dunedin (University)	2017-18
181	I. V. A. Richards	West Indies v Sri Lanka at Karachi	1987-88
180*	M. J. Guptill	New Zealand v South Africa at Hamilton	2016-17
180	J. J. Roy	England v Australia at Melbourne	2017-18

The highest individual scores for other Test countries are:

177	P. R. Stirling	Ireland v Canada at Toronto	2010
176	**Liton Das**	**Bangladesh v Zimbabwe at Sylhet**	**2019-20**
131*	Mohammad Shahzad	Afghanistan v Zimbabwe at Sharjah	2015-16

MOST HUNDREDS

S. R. Tendulkar (I)	49	Saeed Anwar (P)	20	**J. E. Root (E)**	**16**
V. Kohli (I)	**43**	D. P. M. D. Jayawardene (SL/Asia)	19	**Q. de Kock (SA)**	**15**
R. T. Ponting (A/World)	30	B. C. Lara (WI/World)	19	Mohammad Yousuf (P/As)	15
R. G. Sharma (I)	**29**	**D. A. Warner (A)**	**18**	V. Sehwag (I/Wld/Asia)	15
S. T. Jayasuriya (SL/Asia)	28	M. E. Waugh (A)	18	W. U. Tharanga (SL)	15
H. M. Amla (SA)	27	**S. Dhawan (I)**	**17**		
A. B. de Villiers (SA)	25	**A. J. Finch (A)**	**17**	*Most hundreds for other Test countries:*	
C. H. Gayle (WI/World)	25	D. L. Haynes (WI)	17	**Tamim Iqbal (B)**	**13**
K. C. Sangakkara (SL)	25	J. H. Kallis (SA/Wld/Af)	17	**W. T. S. Porterfield (Ire)**	**11**
T. M. Dilshan (SL)	22	N. J. Astle (NZ)	16	**B. R. M. Taylor (Z)**	**11**
S. C. Ganguly (I/Asia)	22	A. C. Gilchrist (A/World)	16	Mohammad Shahzad (Afg)	6
H. H. Gibbs (SA)	21	**M. J. Guptill (NZ)**	**16**		
L. R. P. L. Taylor (NZ)	**21**				

Ponting's total includes one for the World XI, the only hundred for a combined team.

MOST RUNS

		M	I	NO	R	HS	100	Avge
1	S. R. Tendulkar (India)	463	452	41	18,426	200*	49	44.83
2	K. C. Sangakkara (SL/Asia/World)	404	380	41	14,234	169	25	41.98
3	R. T. Ponting (Australia/World)	375	365	39	13,704	164	30	42.03
4	S. T. Jayasuriya (Sri Lanka/Asia)	445	433	18	13,430	189	28	32.36
5	D. P. M. D. Jayawardene (SL/Asia)	448	418	39	12,650	144	19	33.37
6	**V. Kohli (India)**	**251**	**242**	**39**	**12,040**	**183**	**43**	**59.31**
7	Inzamam-ul-Haq (Pakistan/Asia)	378	350	53	11,739	137*	10	39.52
8	J. H. Kallis (S. Africa/World/Africa)	328	314	53	11,579	139	17	44.36
9	S. C. Ganguly (India/Asia)	311	300	23	11,363	183	22	41.02
10	R. Dravid (India/World/Asia)	344	318	40	10,889	153	12	39.16
11	M. S. Dhoni (India/Asia)	350	298	85	10,773	183*	10	50.57
12	C. H. Gayle (West Indies/World)	301	294	17	10,480	215	25	37.83
13	B. C. Lara (West Indies/World)	299	289	32	10,405	169	19	40.48
14	T. M. Dilshan (Sri Lanka)	330	303	41	10,290	161*	22	39.27

The leading aggregates for players who have appeared for other Test countries are:

	M	I	NO	R	HS	100	Avge
L. R. P. L. Taylor (New Zealand)	**232**	**216**	**39**	**8,574**	**181***	**21**	**48.44**
E. J. G. Morgan (Ireland/England)	**242**	**225**	**33**	**7,598**	**148**	**14**	**39.57**
Tamim Iqbal (Bangladesh)	**207**	**205**	**9**	**7,202**	**158**	**13**	**36.74**
A. Flower (Zimbabwe)	213	208	16	6,786	145	4	35.34
Mohammad Nabi (Afghanistan)	124	112	12	2,782	116	1	27.82

Excluding runs for combined teams, the record aggregate for Sri Lanka is 13,975 in 397 matches by K. C. Sangakkara; for Australia, 13,589 in 374 matches by R. T. Ponting; for Pakistan, 11,701 in 375 matches by Inzamam-ul-Haq; for South Africa, 11,550 in 323 matches by J. H. Kallis; for West Indies, 10,425 in 298 matches by C. H. Gayle; for England, ***6,854*** *in 219 matches by* ***E. J. G. Morgan****; and for Ireland,* ***4,277*** *in 120 matches by* ***P. R. Stirling****.*

BEST CAREER STRIKE-RATES BY BATSMEN

(Runs per 100 balls. Qualification: 1,000 runs)

SR		Position	M	I	R	Avge
130.22	A. D. Russell (WI)	7/8	56	47	1,034	27.21
123.37	**G. J. Maxwell (A)**	**5/6**	**116**	**106**	**3,230**	**34.36**
119.05	**J. C. Buttler (E)**	**6/7**	**145**	**120**	**3,855**	**39.74**
117.00	Shahid Afridi (P/World/Asia)	2/7	398	369	8,064	23.57
115.43	**H. H. Pandya (I)**	**5/7**	**57**	**41**	**1,167**	**34.32**
114.50	L. Ronchi (A/NZ)	7	85	68	1,397	23.67
112.59	**N. L. T. C. Perera (SL)**	**7/8**	**164**	**131**	**2,316**	**20.13**

SR		*Position*	*M*	*I*	*R*	*Avge*
108.72	C. J. Anderson (NZ)	6	49	44	1,109	27.72
106.87	**S. O. Hetmyer (WI)**	**4/5**	**45**	**42**	**1,430**	**36.66**
106.67	**J. J. Roy (E)**	**1**	**93**	**89**	**3,483**	**40.03**
104.69	C. Munro (NZ)	2/6	57	53	1,271	24.92
104.33	V. Sehwag (I/World/Asia)	1/2	251	245	8,273	35.05
104.24	J. P. Faulkner (A)	7/8	69	52	1,032	34.40
103.71	**J. M. Bairstow (E)**	**2/6**	**83**	**76**	**3,207**	**47.16**
103.22	**M. M. Ali (E)**	**2/7**	**106**	**86**	**1,790**	**24.86**
102.18	**K. M. Jadhav (I)**	**6/7**	**73**	**52**	**1,367**	**42.09**
101.09	A. B. de Villiers (SA/Africa)	4/5	228	218	9,577	53.50
100.62	**D. A. Miller (SA)**	**5/6**	**132**	**114**	**3,211**	**40.38**
100.05	D. J. G. Sammy (WI)	7/8	126	105	1,871	24.94

Position means a batsman's most usual position(s) in the batting order.

FASTEST ONE-DAY INTERNATIONAL FIFTIES

Balls			
16	A. B. de Villiers	South Africa v West Indies at Johannesburg	2014-15
17	S. T. Jayasuriya	Sri Lanka v Pakistan at Singapore	1995-96
17	M. D. K. J. Perera	Sri Lanka v Pakistan at Pallekele	2015
17	M. J. Guptill	New Zealand v Sri Lanka at Christchurch	2015-16
18	S. P. O'Donnell	Australia v Sri Lanka at Sharjah	1989-90
18	Shahid Afridi	Pakistan v Sri Lanka at Nairobi	1996-97
18	Shahid Afridi	Pakistan v Netherlands at Colombo (SSC)	2002
18	G. J. Maxwell	Australia v India at Bangalore	2013-14
18	Shahid Afridi	Pakistan v Bangladesh at Mirpur	2013-14
18	B. B. McCullum	New Zealand v England at Wellington	2014-15
18	A. J. Finch	Australia v Sri Lanka at Dambulla	2016

FASTEST ONE-DAY INTERNATIONAL HUNDREDS

Balls			
31	A. B. de Villiers	South Africa v West Indies at Johannesburg	2014-15
36	C. J. Anderson	New Zealand v West Indies at Queenstown	2013-14
37	Shahid Afridi	Pakistan v Sri Lanka at Nairobi	1996-97
44	M. V. Boucher	South Africa v Zimbabwe at Potchefstroom	2006-07
45	B. C. Lara	West Indies v Bangladesh at Dhaka	1999-2000
45	Shahid Afridi	Pakistan v India at Kanpur	2004-05
46	J. D. Ryder	New Zealand v West Indies at Queenstown	2013-14
46	J. C. Buttler	England v Pakistan at Dubai	2015-16
48	S. T. Jayasuriya	Sri Lanka v Pakistan at Singapore	1995-96

HIGHEST PARTNERSHIP FOR EACH WICKET

365	for 1st	J. D. Campbell/S. D. Hope	WI v Ire	Clontarf	2019
372	for 2nd	C. H. Gayle/M. N. Samuels	WI v Z	Canberra	2014-15
258	for 3rd	D. M. Bravo/D. Ramdin	WI v B	Basseterre	2014-15
275*	for 4th	M. Azharuddin/A. Jadeja	I v Z	Cuttack	1997-98
256*	for 5th	D. A. Miller/J-P. Duminy	SA v Z	Hamilton	2014-15
267*	for 6th	G. D. Elliott/L. Ronchi	NZ v SL	Dunedin	2014-15
177	for 7th	J. C. Buttler/A. U. Rashid	E v NZ	Birmingham	2015
138*	for 8th	J. M. Kemp/A. J. Hall	SA v I	Cape Town	2006-07
132	for 9th	A. D. Mathews/S. L. Malinga	SL v A	Melbourne	2010-11
106*	for 10th	I. V. A. Richards/M. A. Holding	WI v E	Manchester	1984

BOWLING RECORDS

BEST BOWLING ANALYSES

8-19	W. P. U. J. C. Vaas	Sri Lanka v Zimbabwe at Colombo (SSC)	2001-02
7-12	Shahid Afridi	Pakistan v West Indies at Providence	2013
7-15	G. D. McGrath	Australia v Namibia at Potchefstroom	2002-03

7-18	Rashid Khan	Afghanistan v West Indies at Gros Islet	2017
7-20	A. J. Bichel	Australia v England at Port Elizabeth	2002-03
7-30	M. Muralitharan	Sri Lanka v India at Sharjah	2000-01
7-33	T. G. Southee	New Zealand v England at Wellington	2014-15
7-34	T. A. Boult	New Zealand v West Indies at Christchurch	2017-18
7-36	Waqar Younis	Pakistan v England at Leeds	2001
7-37	Aqib Javed	Pakistan v India at Sharjah	1991-92
7-45	Imran Tahir	South Africa v West Indies at Basseterre	2016
7-51	W. W. Davis	West Indies v Australia at Leeds	1983

The best analyses for other Test countries are:

6-4	S. T. R. Binny	India v Bangladesh at Mirpur	2014
6-19	H. K. Olonga	Zimbabwe v England at Cape Town	1999-2000
6-26	Mashrafe bin Mortaza	Bangladesh v Kenya at Nairobi	2006
6-26	Rubel Hossain	Bangladesh v New Zealand at Mirpur	2013-14
6-31	P. D. Collingwood	England v Bangladesh at Nottingham	2005
6-55	P. R. Stirling	Ireland v Afghanistan at Greater Noida	2016-17

HAT-TRICKS

Four Wickets in Four Balls

S. L. Malinga	Sri Lanka v South Africa at Providence	2006-07

Four Wickets in Five Balls

Saqlain Mushtaq	Pakistan v Zimbabwe at Peshawar	1996-97
A. U. Rashid	England v West Indies at St George's	2018-19

Most Hat-Tricks

S. L. Malinga (SL)	3	Saqlain Mushtaq (P)	2	Wasim Akram (P)	2
T. A. Boult (NZ)	**2**	W. P. U. J. C. Vaas† (SL)	2	**K. Yadav (I)**	**2**

† *W. P. U. J. C. Vaas took the second of his two hat-tricks, for Sri Lanka v Bangladesh at Pietermaritzburg in 2002-03, with the first three balls of the match.*

Hat-Tricks

There have been **49** hat-tricks in one-day internationals, including the above. Those since 2017-18:

K. Yadav	India v Australia at Kolkata	2017-18
D. S. M. Kumara	Sri Lanka v Bangladesh at Mirpur	2017-18
Imran Tahir	South Africa v Zimbabwe at Bloemfontein	2018-19
T. A. Boult	New Zealand v Pakistan at Abu Dhabi	2018-19
Mohammed Shami	India v Afghanistan at Southampton	2019
T. A. Boult	New Zealand v Australia at Lord's	2019
K. Yadav	India v West Indies at Visakhapatnam	2019-20

MOST WICKETS

		M	*Balls*	*R*	*W*	*BB*	*4I*	*Avge*
1	M. Muralitharan (SL/World/Asia)	350	18,811	12,326	534	7-30	25	23.08
2	Wasim Akram (Pakistan)	356	18,186	11,812	502	5-15	23	23.52
3	Waqar Younis (Pakistan)	262	12,698	9,919	416	7-36	27	23.84
4	W. P. U. J. C. Vaas (SL/Asia)	322	15,775	11,014	400	8-19	13	27.53
5	Shahid Afridi (Pakistan/World/Asia)	398	17,670	13,635	395	7-12	13	34.51
6	S. M. Pollock (SA/World/Africa)	303	15,712	9,631	393	6-35	17	24.50
7	G. D. McGrath (Australia/World)	250	12,970	8,391	381	7-15	16	22.02
8	B. Lee (Australia)	221	11,185	8,877	380	5-22	23	23.36
9	S. L. Malinga (Sri Lanka)	226	10,936	9,760	338	6-38	19	28.87

		M	*Balls*	*R*	*W*	*BB*	*4I*	*Avge*
10	A. Kumble (India/Asia)	271	14,496	10,412	337	6-12	10	30.89
11	S. T. Jayasuriya (Sri Lanka/Asia)	445	14,874	11,871	323	6-29	12	36.75
12	J. Srinath (India)	229	11,935	8,847	315	5-23	10	28.08
13	D. L. Vettori (New Zealand/World)	295	14,060	9,674	305	5-7	10	31.71
14	S. K. Warne (Australia/World)	194	10,642	7,541	293	5-33	13	25.73
15	Saqlain Mushtaq (Pakistan)	169	8,770	6,275	288	5-20	17	21.78
	A. B. Agarkar (India)	191	9,484	8,021	288	6-42	12	27.85
17	Zaheer Khan (India/Asia)	200	10,097	8,301	282	5-42	8	29.43
18	J. H. Kallis (S. Africa/World/Africa)	328	10,750	8,680	273	5-30	4	31.79
19	A. A. Donald (South Africa)	164	8,561	5,926	272	6-23	13	21.78
20	**Mashrafe bin Mortaza (Bang/Asia)**	**220**	**10,922**	**8,893**	**270**	**6-26**	**8**	**32.93**
21	J. M. Anderson (England)	194	9,584	7,861	269	5-23	13	29.22
	Abdul Razzaq (Pakistan/Asia)	265	10,941	8,564	269	6-35	11	31.83
	Harbhajan Singh (India/Asia)	236	12,479	8,973	269	5-31	5	33.35
24	M. Ntini (South Africa/World)	173	8,687	6,559	266	6-22	12	24.65
25	Shakib Al Hasan (Bangladesh)	206	10,517	7,857	260	5-29	10	30.21
26	Kapil Dev (India)	225	11,202	6,945	253	5-43	4	27.45

The leading aggregates for players who have appeared for other Test countries are:

	M	Balls	R	W	BB	4I	Avge
H. H. Streak (Zimbabwe)	189	9,468	7,129	239	5-32	8	29.82
C. A. Walsh (West Indies)	205	10,882	6,918	227	5-1	7	30.47
Rashid Khan (Afghanistan)	71	3,558	2,467	133	7-18	8	18.54
K. J. O'Brien (Ireland)	**148**	**4,224**	**3,673**	**113**	**4-13**	**5**	**32.50**

Excluding wickets taken for combined teams, the record for Sri Lanka is 523 in 343 matches by M. Muralitharan; for South Africa, 387 in 294 matches by S. M. Pollock; for Australia, 380 in 249 matches by G. D. McGrath; for India, 334 in 269 matches by A. Kumble; for New Zealand, 297 in 291 matches by D. L. Vettori; for Bangladesh, ***269*** *in 218 matches by* ***Mashrafe bin Mortaza****; and for Zimbabwe, 237 in 187 matches by H. H. Streak.*

BEST CAREER STRIKE-RATES BY BOWLERS

(Balls per wicket. Qualification: 1,500 balls)

SR		*M*	*W*
26.46	**Mustafizur Rahman (B)**	**58**	**109**
26.75	Rashid Khan (Afg)	71	133
26.82	**M. A. Starc (A)**	**96**	**184**
27.10	Hamid Hassan (Afg)	32	56
27.22	S. W. Tait (A)	35	62
27.32	**Mohammed Shami (I)**	**79**	**148**
27.32	B. A. W. Mendis (SL)	87	152
27.81	**B. J. McCarthy (Ire)**	**31**	**55**
28.34	**L. H. Ferguson (NZ)**	**37**	**69**
28.48	M. J. McClenaghan (NZ)	48	82
28.72	R. N. ten Doeschate (Netherlands)	33	55

BEST CAREER ECONOMY-RATES

(Runs conceded per six balls. Qualification: 50 wickets)

ER		*M*	*W*
3.09	J. Garner (WI)	98	146
3.28	R. G. D. Willis (E)	64	80
3.30	R. J. Hadlee (NZ)	115	158
3.32	M. A. Holding (WI)	102	142
3.40	A. M. E. Roberts (WI)	56	87
3.48	C. E. L. Ambrose (WI)	176	225

WICKETKEEPING AND FIELDING RECORDS

MOST DISMISSALS IN AN INNINGS

6 (6ct)	A. C. Gilchrist	Australia v South Africa at Cape Town	1999-2000
6 (6ct)	A. J. Stewart	England v Zimbabwe at Manchester	2000
6 (5ct, 1st)	R. D. Jacobs	West Indies v Sri Lanka at Colombo (RPS)	2001-02
6 (5ct, 1st)	A. C. Gilchrist	Australia v England at Sydney	2002-03
6 (6ct)	A. C. Gilchrist	Australia v Namibia at Potchefstroom	2002-03
6 (6ct)	A. C. Gilchrist	Australia v Sri Lanka at Colombo (RPS)	2003-04
6 (6ct)	M. V. Boucher	South Africa v Pakistan at Cape Town	2006-07
6 (5ct, 1st)	M. S. Dhoni	India v England at Leeds	2007
6 (6ct)	A. C. Gilchrist	Australia v India at Vadodara	2007-08
6 (5ct, 1st)	A. C. Gilchrist	Australia v India at Sydney	2007-08
6 (6ct)	M. J. Prior	England v South Africa at Nottingham	2008
6 (6ct)	J. C. Buttler	England v South Africa at The Oval	2013
6 (6ct)	M. H. Cross	Scotland v Canada at Christchurch	2013-14
6 (5ct, 1st)	Q. de Kock	S. Africa v N. Zealand at Mount Maunganui	2014-15
6 (6ct)	Sarfraz Ahmed	Pakistan v South Africa at Auckland	2014-15

MOST DISMISSALS

			M	Ct	St
1	482	K. C. Sangakkara (Sri Lanka/World/Asia)	360	384	98
2	472	A. C. Gilchrist (Australia/World)	282	417	55
3	444	M. S. Dhoni (India/Asia)	350	321	123
4	424	M. V. Boucher (South Africa/Africa)	294	402	22
5	287	Moin Khan (Pakistan)	219	214	73
6	242	B. B. McCullum (New Zealand)	185	227	15
7	234	I. A. Healy (Australia)	168	195	39
8	**223**	**Mushfiqur Rahim (Bangladesh)**	**204**	**179**	**44**
9	220	Rashid Latif (Pakistan)	166	182	38
10	**209**	**J. C. Buttler (England)**	**144**	**177**	**32**
11	206	R. S. Kaluwitharana (Sri Lanka)	186	131	75
12	204	P. J. L. Dujon (West Indies)	169	183	21

The leading aggregates for players who have appeared for other Test countries are:

		M	Ct	St
165	A. Flower (Zimbabwe)	186	133	32
96	N. J. O'Brien (Ireland)	80	82	14
88	Mohammad Shahzad (Afghanistan)	83	63	25

Excluding dismissals for combined teams, the most for Sri Lanka is 473 (378ct, 95st) in 353 matches by K. C. Sangakkara; for Australia, 470 (416ct, 54st) in 281 matches by A. C. Gilchrist; for India, 438 (318ct, 120st) in 347 matches by M. S. Dhoni; and for South Africa, 415 (394ct, 21st) in 289 matches by M. V. Boucher.

K. C. Sangakkara's list excludes 19 catches taken in 44 one-day internationals when not keeping wicket; M. V. Boucher's record excludes one in one; B. B. McCullum's excludes 35 in 75; Mushfiqur Rahim's two in 14; R. S. Kaluwitharana's one in three; A. Flower's eight in 27; N. J. O'Brien's eight in 23; and Mohammad Shahzad's one in one. A. C. Gilchrist played five one-day internationals and J. C. Buttler one without keeping wicket, but they made no catches in those games. R. Dravid (India) made 210 dismissals (196ct, 14st) in 344 one-day internationals but only 86 (72ct, 14st) in 74 as wicketkeeper (including one where he took over during the match).

MOST CATCHES IN AN INNINGS IN THE FIELD

5	J. N. Rhodes	South Africa v West Indies at Bombay	1993-94

*There have been **40** instances of four catches in an innings.*

MOST CATCHES

Ct	*M*		*Ct*	*M*	
218	448	D. P. M. D. Jayawardene (SL/Asia)	127	273	A. R. Border (Australia)
160	375	R. T. Ponting (Australia/World)	127	398	Shahid Afridi (Pak/World/Asia)
156	334	M. Azharuddin (India)	*Most catches for other Test countries:*		
140	463	S. R. Tendulkar (India)	124	301	C. H. Gayle (WI/World)
139	**232**	**L. R. P. L. Taylor (New Zealand)**	108	19	P. D. Collingwood (England)
133	280	S. P. Fleming (New Zealand/World)	86	221	G. W. Flower (Zimbabwe)
131	328	J. H. Kallis (SA/World/Africa)	**64**	**139**	**W. T. S. Porterfield (Ireland)**
130	262	Younis Khan (Pakistan)	**64**	**148**	**K. J. O'Brien (Ireland)**
130	350	M. Muralitharan (SL/World/Asia)	**64**	**188**	**Mahmudullah (Bangladesh**
129	**251**	**V. Kohli (India)**	55	124	Mohammad Nabi (Afghanistan)

Excluding catches taken for combined teams, the record aggregate for Sri Lanka is 213 in 442 matches by D. P. M. D. Jayawardene; for Australia, 158 in 374 by R. T. Ponting; for New Zealand, 132 in 279 by S. P. Fleming; for South Africa, 131 in 323 by J. H. Kallis; and for West Indies, 123 in 298 by C. H. Gayle.

Younis Khan's record excludes five catches made in three one-day internationals as wicketkeeper.

TEAM RECORDS

HIGHEST INNINGS TOTALS

481-6	(50 overs)	England v Australia at Nottingham	2018
444-3	(50 overs)	England v Pakistan at Nottingham	2016
443-9	(50 overs)	Sri Lanka v Netherlands at Amstelveen	2006
439-2	(50 overs)	South Africa v West Indies at Johannesburg	2014-15
438-4	(50 overs)	South Africa v India at Mumbai	2015-16
438-9	(49.5 overs)	South Africa v Australia at Johannesburg	2005-06
434-4	(50 overs)	Australia v South Africa at Johannesburg	2005-06
418-5	(50 overs)	South Africa v Zimbabwe at Potchefstroom	2006-07
418-5	(50 overs)	India v West Indies at Indore	2011-12
418-6	(50 overs)	England v West Indies at St George's	2018-19
417-6	(50 overs)	Australia v Afghanistan at Perth	2014-15
414-7	(50 overs)	India v Sri Lanka at Rajkot	2009-10
413-5	(50 overs)	India v Bermuda at Port-of-Spain	2006-07
411-4	(50 overs)	South Africa v Ireland at Canberra	2014-15
411-8	(50 overs)	Sri Lanka v India at Rajkot	2009-10
408-5	(50 overs)	South Africa v West Indies at Sydney	2014-15
408-9	(50 overs)	England v New Zealand at Birmingham	2015
404-5	(50 overs)	India v Sri Lanka at Kolkata	2014-15
402-2	(50 overs)	New Zealand v Ireland at Aberdeen	2008
401-3	(50 overs)	India v South Africa at Gwalior	2009-10

The highest totals by other Test countries are:

399-1	(50 overs)	Pakistan v Zimbabwe at Bulawayo	2018
389	(48 overs)	West Indies v England at St George's	2018-19
351-7	(50 overs)	Zimbabwe v Kenya at Mombasa	2008-09
338	(50 overs)	Afghanistan v Ireland at Greater Noida	2016-17
333-8	(50 overs)	Bangladesh v Australia at Nottingham	2019
331-6	(50 overs)	Ireland v Scotland at Dubai	2017-18
331-8	(50 overs)	Ireland v Zimbabwe at Hobart	2014-15

HIGHEST TOTALS BATTING SECOND

438-9	(49.5 overs)	South Africa v Australia at Johannesburg (*Won by 1 wicket*)	2005-06
411-8	(50 overs)	Sri Lanka v India at Rajkot (*Lost by 3 runs*)	2009-10
389	(48 overs)	West Indies v England at St George's (*Lost by 29 runs*)	2018-19
372-6	(49.2 overs)	South Africa v Australia at Durban (*Won by 4 wickets*)	2016-17
366-8	(50 overs)	England v India at Cuttack (*Lost by 15 runs*)	2016-17

365-9	(45 overs)	England v New Zealand at The Oval (*Lost by 13 runs DLS*)	2015
365	(48.5 overs)	England v Scotland at Edinburgh (*Lost by 6 runs*)	2018
364-4	(48.4 overs)	England v West Indies at Bridgetown (*Won by 6 wickets*)	2018-19
362-1	(43.3 overs)	India v Australia at Jaipur (*Won by 9 wickets*)	2013-14
361-7	(50 overs)	Pakistan v England at Southampton (*Lost by 12 runs*)	2019

HIGHEST MATCH AGGREGATES

872-13	(99.5 overs)	South Africa v Australia at Johannesburg	2005-06
825-15	(100 overs)	India v Sri Lanka at Rajkot	2009-10
807-16	(98 overs)	West Indies v England at St George's	2018-19
763-14	(96 overs)	England v New Zealand at The Oval	2015
747-14	(100 overs)	India v England at Cuttack	2016-17
743-12	(99.2 overs)	South Australia v Australia at Durban	2016-17
736-15	(98.5 overs)	Scotland v England at Edinburgh	2018
734-10	(100 overs)	England v Pakistan at Southampton	2019
730-9	(100 overs)	South Africa v West Indies at Johannesburg	2014-15
727-13	**(100 overs)**	**Australia v India at Sydney**	**2020-21**
726-14	(95.1 overs)	New Zealand v India at Christchurch	2008-09
724-12	(98.4 overs)	West Indies v England at Bridgetown	2018-19

LOWEST INNINGS TOTALS

35	(18 overs)	Zimbabwe v Sri Lanka at Harare	2003-04
35	**(12 overs)**	**USA v Nepal at Kirtipur**	**2019-20**
36	(18.4 overs)	Canada v Sri Lanka at Paarl	2002-03
38	(15.4 overs)	Zimbabwe v Sri Lanka at Colombo (SSC)	2001-02
43	(19.5 overs)	Pakistan v West Indies at Cape Town	1992-93
43	(20.1 overs)	Sri Lanka v South Africa at Paarl	2011-12
44	(24.5 overs)	Zimbabwe v Bangladesh at Chittagong	2009-10
45	(40.3 overs)	Canada v England at Manchester	1979
45	(14 overs)	Namibia v Australia at Potchefstroom	2002-03

The lowest totals by other Test countries are:

54	(26.3 overs)	India v Sri Lanka at Sharjah	2000-01
54	(23.2 overs)	West Indies v South Africa at Cape Town	2003-04
58	(18.5 overs)	Bangladesh v West Indies at Mirpur	2010-11
58	(17.4 overs)	Bangladesh v India at Mirpur	2014
58	(16.1 overs)	Afghanistan v Zimbabwe at Sharjah	2015-16
64	(35.5 overs)	New Zealand v Pakistan at Sharjah	1985-86
69	(28 overs)	South Africa v Australia at Sydney	1993-94
70	(25.2 overs)	Australia v England at Birmingham	1977
70	(26.3 overs)	Australia v New Zealand at Adelaide	1985-86
77	(27.4 overs)	Ireland v Sri Lanka at St George's	2006-07
86	(32.4 overs)	England v Australia at Manchester	2001

LARGEST VICTORIES

290 runs	New Zealand (402-2 in 50 overs) v Ireland (112 in 28.4 ov) at Aberdeen	2008
275 runs	Australia (417-6 in 50 overs) v Afghanistan (142 in 37.3 overs) at Perth	2014-15
272 runs	South Africa (399-6 in 50 overs) v Zimbabwe (127 in 29 overs) at Benoni	2010-11
258 runs	South Africa (301-8 in 50 overs) v Sri Lanka (43 in 20.1 overs) at Paarl	2011-12
257 runs	India (413-5 in 50 overs) v Bermuda (156 in 43.1 overs) at Port-of-Spain	2006-07
257 runs	South Africa (408-5 in 50 overs) v West Indies (151 in 33.1 overs) at Sydney	2014-15
256 runs	Australia (301-6 in 50 overs) v Namibia (45 in 14 overs) at Potchefstroom	2002-03
256 runs	India (374-4 in 50 overs) v Hong Kong (118 in 36.5 overs) at Karachi	2008
255 runs	Pakistan (337-6 in 47 overs) v Ireland (82 in 23.4 overs) at Dublin	2016

*There have been **55** instances of victory by ten wickets.*

TIED MATCHES

There have been **37** tied one-day internationals. West Indies have tied ten matches; Bangladesh are the only Test country never to have tied. The most recent ties are:

South Africa (230-6 in 31 overs) v West Indies (190-6 in 26.1 overs) at Cardiff (D/L)	2013
Ireland (268-5 in 50 overs) v Netherlands (268-9 in 50 overs) at Amstelveen	2013
Pakistan (229-6 in 50 overs) v West Indies (229-9 in 50 overs) at Gros Islet	2013
Pakistan (266-5 in 47 overs) v Ireland (275-5 in 47 overs) at Dublin (D/L)	2013
New Zealand (314 in 50 overs) v India (314-9 in 50 overs) at Auckland	2013-14
Sri Lanka (286-9 in 50 overs) v England (286-8 in 50 overs) at Nottingham	2016
Zimbabwe (257 in 50 overs) v West Indies (257-8 in 50 overs) at Bulawayo	2016-17
Zimbabwe (210 in 46.4 overs) v Scotland (210 in 49.1 overs) at Bulawayo	2017-18
Afghanistan (252-8 in 50 overs) v India (252 in 49.5 overs) at Dubai	2018-19
India (321-6 in 50 overs) v West Indies (321-7 in 50 overs) at Visakhapatnam	2018-19

In the 2019 World Cup final at Lord's, New Zealand scored 241-8 and England 241, but England won the match on boundary count after a super over was also tied. Similarly at Rawalpindi in 2020-21, Zimbabwe won in a super over after they scored 278-6 and Pakistan 278-9.

OTHER RECORDS

MOST APPEARANCES

463	S. R. Tendulkar (I)	334	M. Azharuddin (I)
448	D. P. M. D. Jayawardene (SL/Asia)	330	T. M. Dilshan (SL)
445	S. T. Jayasuriya (SL/Asia)	328	J. H. Kallis (SA/World/Africa)
404	K. C. Sangakkara (SL/World/Asia)	325	S. R. Waugh (A)
398	Shahid Afridi (P/World/Asia)	322	W. P. U. J. C. Vaas (SL/Asia)
378	Inzamam-ul-Haq (P/Asia)	311	S. C. Ganguly (I/Asia)
375	R. T. Ponting (A/World)	308	P. A. de Silva (SL)
356	Wasim Akram (P)	304	Yuvraj Singh (I/Asia)
350	M. S. Dhoni (I/Asia)	303	S. M. Pollock (SA/World/Africa)
350	M. Muralitharan (SL/World/Asia)	301	C. H. Gayle (WI/World)
344	R. Dravid (I/World/Asia)	300	T. M. Dilshan (SL)

Excluding appearances for combined teams, the record for Sri Lanka is 441 by S. T. Jayasuriya; for Pakistan, 393 by Shahid Afridi; for Australia, 374 by R. T. Ponting; for South Africa, 323 by J. H. Kallis; for West Indies, 295 by B. C. Lara; for New Zealand, 291 by D. L. Vettori; for Zimbabwe, 221 by G. W. Flower; for Bangladesh, ***218*** *by* ***Mashrafe bin Mortaza*** *and* ***Mushfiqur Rahim****; for England, 197 by P. D. Collingwood; for Ireland,* ***148*** *by* ***K. J. O'Brien****; and for Afghanistan, 124 by Mohammad Nabi.*

MOST MATCHES AS CAPTAIN

	P	*W*	*L*	*T*	*NR*
R. T. Ponting (A/World)	230	165	51	2	12
S. P. Fleming (NZ)	218	98	106	1	13
M. S. Dhoni (I)	200	110	74	5	11
A. Ranatunga (SL)	193	89	95	1	8
A. R. Border (A)	178	107	67	1	3
M. Azharuddin (I)	174	90	76	2	6
G. C. Smith (SA/Af)	150	92	51	1	6
S. C. Ganguly (I/Asia)	147	76	66	0	5
Imran Khan (P)	139	75	59	1	4
W. J. Cronje (SA)	138	99	35	1	3
D. P. M. D. Jayawardene (SL/As)	129	71	49	1	8
B. C. Lara (WI)	125	59	59	1	7

> "Watching these debutants was rather like studying the 18th-century British monarchy: three very different Georges (though none went barmy)."
>
> Lancashire in 2020, page 467

WORLD CUP FINALS

1975	WEST INDIES (291-8) beat Australia (274) by 17 runs	Lord's
1979	WEST INDIES (286-9) beat England (194) by 92 runs	Lord's
1983	INDIA (183) beat West Indies (140) by 43 runs	Lord's
1987	AUSTRALIA (253-5) beat England (246-8) by seven runs	Calcutta
1992	PAKISTAN (249-6) beat England (227) by 22 runs	Melbourne
1996	SRI LANKA (245-3) beat Australia (241-7) by seven wickets	Lahore
1999	AUSTRALIA (133-2) beat Pakistan (132) by eight wickets	Lord's
2003	AUSTRALIA (359-2) beat India (234) by 125 runs	Johannesburg
2007	AUSTRALIA (281-4) beat Sri Lanka (215-8) by 53 runs (D/L method)	Bridgetown
2011	INDIA (277-4) beat Sri Lanka (274-6) by six wickets	Mumbai
2015	AUSTRALIA (186-3) beat New Zealand (183) by seven wickets	Melbourne
2019	ENGLAND (241) beat New Zealand (241-8) on boundary count after a super over	Lord's

TWENTY20 INTERNATIONAL RECORDS

Matches in this section do not have first-class status.

This section covers Twenty20 international cricket to December 31, 2020. Bold type denotes performances in the calendar year 2020, or, in career figures, players who appeared in Twenty20 internationals in that year. The ICC extended official international status to Associate Twenty20 matches from the start of 2019.

RESULTS SUMMARY OF TWENTY20 INTERNATIONALS

2004-05 to December 31, 2020 (1,119 matches)

	Matches	*Won*	*Lost*	*No Result*	*% Won (excl NR)*
Afghanistan	81	55	26*	–	67.90
India	137	88‡	45	4	66.16
Pakistan	160	98*	60†	2	62.02
South Africa	124	71*	52	1	57.72
England	126	66†	55	5	54.54
Australia	131	69	59†	3	53.90
New Zealand	137	67†	66§	4	50.37
Sri Lanka	128	60*	66*	2	47.61
West Indies	127	56†	65*	6	46.28
Ireland	98	42*¶	48	7	46.70
Bangladesh	96	32	62	2	34.04
Zimbabwe	79	20†	59	–	25.31
Qatar	22	15†	7	–	68.18
Papua New Guinea	26	17	8	1	68.00
Malaysia	24	13	10	1	56.52
Netherlands	75	39	33*	3	54.16
United Arab Emirates	49	24	24	1	50.00
Nepal	34	16	17	1	48.48
Scotland	65	29¶	32	3	47.58
Oman	36	16	19	1	45.71
Canada	31	12	18*	1	40.00
Kenya	38	15	23	–	39.47
Hong Kong	44	16	28	–	36.36

* *Includes one game settled by a tie-break.* † *Includes two settled by a tie-break.*
‡ *Includes three settled by a tie-break.* § *Includes six settled by a tie-break.*
¶ *Plus one tie.*
Apart from Ireland v Scotland, ties were decided by bowling contests or one-over eliminators.

Matches abandoned without a ball bowled are not included except where the toss took place, when they are shown as no result. In the percentages of matches won, ties are counted as half a win.

A further 53 teams have played Twenty20 internationals, as follows: Argentina (P5 W5); Belize (P3 W3); Malawi (P7 W5 L1 NR1); Spain (P11 W9 L2); Austria (P5 W4 L1); Namibia (P16 W12 L4); Romania (P8 W6 L2); Italy (P8 W5 L2 NR1); Qatar (P22 W15 L7); Germany (P12 W8 L4); Greece (P3 W2 L1); Panama (P3 W2 L1); Singapore (P15 W9 L6); Jersey (P17 W10 L7); Belgium (P7 W4 L3); Denmark (P9 W4 L3 NR2); Malaysia (P24 W13 L10 NR1); Czech Republic (P11 W6 L5); Bahrain (P8 W4 L4); Saudi Arabia (P8 W4 L4); Peru (P4 W2 L2); Portugal (P4 W2 L2); Kuwait (P15 W7 L8); Uganda (P7 W3 L4); Mexico (P8 W3 L5); Vanuatu (P14 W5 L9); Bulgaria (P10 W3 L6 NR1); Guernsey (P10 W3 L6 NR1); Malta (P7 W2 L4 NR1); Philippines (P4 W1 L2 NR1); Bermuda (P15 W4 L10 NR1); USA (P8 W2 L5 NR1); Luxembourg (P8 W2 L6); Brazil (P4 W1 L3); Chile (P4 W1 L3); Samoa (P4 W1 L3); World XI (P4 W1 L3); Nigeria (P9 W2 L7); Finland (P5 W1 L4); Mozambique (P7 W1 L5 NR1); Maldives (P14 W2 L11 NR1); Thailand (P8 W1 L7); Botswana (P7 L7); Cayman Islands (P6 L6); Norway (P5 L5); Ghana (P4 L4); Gibraltar (P4 L4); Turkey (P4 L4); Costa Rica (P3 L3); Iran (P3 L3); Bhutan (P2 L2); Serbia (P2 L2); Isle of Man (P1 L1).

BATTING RECORDS

HIGHEST INDIVIDUAL INNINGS

172	A. J. Finch	Australia v Zimbabwe at Harare	2018
162*	Hazratullah Zazai	Afghanistan v Ireland at Dehradun	2018-19
156	A. J. Finch	Australia v England at Southampton	2013
145*	G. J. Maxwell	Australia v Sri Lanka at Pallekele	2016
127*	H. G. Munsey	Scotland v Netherlands at Malahide	2019
125*	E. Lewis	West Indies v India at Kingston	2017
125*	**Shaheryar Butt**	**Belgium v Czech Republic at Walferdange**	**2020**
124*	S. R. Watson	Australia v India at Sydney	2015-16
124	K. J. O'Brien	Ireland v Hong Kong at Al Amerat	2019-20
123	B. B. McCullum	New Zealand v Bangladesh at Pallekele	2012-13
122	Babar Hayat	Hong Kong v Oman at Fatullah	2015-16
119	F. du Plessis	South Africa v West Indies at Johannesburg	2014-15
118*	Mohammad Shahzad	Afghanistan v Zimbabwe at Sharjah	2015-16
118	R. G. Sharma	India v Sri Lanka at Indore	2017-18
117*	R. E. Levi	South Africa v New Zealand at Hamilton	2011-12
117*	Shaiman Anwar	United Arab Emirates v Papua New Guinea at Abu Dhabi	2016-17
117	C. H. Gayle	West Indies v South Africa at Johannesburg	2007-08
116*	B. B. McCullum	New Zealand v Australia at Christchurch	2009-10
116*	A. D. Hales	England v Sri Lanka at Chittagong	2013-14

MOST RUNS

		M	*I*	*NO*	*R*	*HS*	*100*	*Avge*	*SR*
1	**V. Kohli (India)**	**85**	**79**	**21**	**2,928**	**94***	**0**	**50.48**	**138.43**
2	**R. G. Sharma (India)**	**108**	**100**	**15**	**2,773**	**118**	**4**	**32.62**	**138.78**
3	**M. J. Guptill (New Zealand)**	**94**	**90**	**7**	**2,621**	**105**	**2**	**31.57**	**134.61**
4	**Shoaib Malik (Pakistan/World)**	**116**	**106**	**31**	**2,335**	**75**	**0**	**31.13**	**123.93**
5	**Mohammad Hafeez (Pakistan)**	**99**	**94**	**11**	**2,323**	**99***	**0**	**27.98**	**121.30**
6	**E. J. G. Morgan (England)**	**97**	**93**	**18**	**2,278**	**91**	**0**	**30.37**	**138.98**
7	**D. A. Warner (Australia)**	**81**	**81**	**9**	**2,265**	**100***	**1**	**31.45**	**139.72**
8	**A. J. Finch (Australia)**	**66**	**66**	**9**	**2,149**	**172**	**2**	**37.70**	**154.05**
9	B. B. McCullum (New Zealand)	71	70	10	2,140	123	2	35.66	136.21
10	**P. R. Stirling (Ireland)**	**78**	**77**	**6**	**2,124**	**95**	**0**	**29.91**	**139.27**
11	Mohammad Shahzad (Afghanistan)	65	65	3	1,936	118*	1	31.22	134.81
12	J-P. Duminy (South Africa)	81	75	25	1,934	96*	0	38.68	126.24
13	**L. R. P. L. Taylor (New Zealand)**	**102**	**94**	**21**	**1,909**	**63**	**0**	**26.15**	**122.37**
14	T. M. Dilshan (Sri Lanka)	80	79	12	1,889	104*	1	28.19	120.47
15	**Tamim Iqbal (Bangladesh/Wld)**	**78**	**78**	**5**	**1,758**	**103***	**1**	**24.08**	**116.96**
16	**C. Munro (New Zealand)**	**65**	**62**	**7**	**1,724**	**109***	**3**	**31.34**	**156.44**
17	**K. S. Williamson (New Zealand)**	**62**	**60**	**8**	**1,723**	**95**	**0**	**33.13**	**125.21**
18	Umar Akmal (Pakistan)	84	79	14	1,690	94	0	26.00	122.73
19	**G. J. Maxwell (Australia)**	**67**	**60**	**9**	**1,687**	**145***	**3**	**33.07**	**157.95**
20	**Babar Azam (Pakistan)**	**44**	**42**	**9**	**1,681**	**97***	**0**	**50.93**	**130.00**
21	A. B. de Villiers (South Africa)	78	75	11	1,672	79*	0	26.12	135.16
	K. J. O'Brien (Ireland)	**96**	**89**	**10**	**1,672**	**124**	**1**	**21.16**	**135.93**
23	**S. Dhawan (India)**	**64**	**62**	**3**	**1,669**	**92**	**0**	**28.28**	**128.28**
24	H. Masakadza (Zimbabwe)	66	66	2	1,662	93*	0	25.96	117.20
25	A. D. Hales (England)	60	60	7	1,644	116*	1	31.01	136.65
26	C. H. Gayle (West Indies)	58	54	4	1,627	117	2	32.54	142.84
27	M. S. Dhoni (India)	98	85	42	1,617	56	0	37.60	126.13
28	M. N. Samuels (West Indies)	67	65	10	1,611	89*	0	29.29	116.23
29	S. K. Raina (India)	78	66	11	1,605	101	1	29.18	134.87

Excluding runs for the World XI, the record aggregate for Pakistan is ***2,323*** *in 115 matches by* ***Shoaib Malik****, and for Bangladesh* ***1,701*** *in 74 matches by* ***Tamim Iqbal****.*

FASTEST TWENTY20 INTERNATIONAL FIFTIES

Balls			
12	Yuvraj Singh	India v England at Durban	2007-08
14	C. Munro	New Zealand v Sri Lanka at Auckland	2015-16
16	S. D. Hope	West Indies v Bangladesh at Sylhet	2018-19
17	P. R. Stirling	Ireland v Afghanistan at Dubai	2011-12
17	S. J. Myburgh	Netherlands v Ireland at Sylhet	2013-14
17	C. H. Gayle	West Indies v South Africa at Cape Town	2014-15
17	**Q. de Kock**	**South Africa v England at Durban**	**2019-20**
18	D. A. Warner	Australia v West Indies at Sydney	2009-10
18	G. J. Maxwell	Australia v Pakistan at Mirpur	2013-14
18	G. J. Maxwell	Australia v Sri Lanka at Pallekele	2016
18	C. Munro	New Zealand v West Indies at Mount Maunganui	2017-18
18	C. Munro	New Zealand v England at Hamilton	2017-18
18	E. Lewis	West Indies v Bangladesh at Mirpur	2018-19

FASTEST TWENTY20 INTERNATIONAL HUNDREDS

Balls			
35	D. A. Miller	South Africa v Bangladesh at Potchefstroom	2017-18
35	R. G. Sharma	India v Sri Lanka at Indore	2017-18
41	H. G. Munsey	Scotland v Netherlands at Malahide	2019
42	Hazratullah Zazai	Afghanistan v Ireland at Dehradun	2018-19
45	R. E. Levi	South Africa v New Zealand at Hamilton	2011-12
46	F. du Plessis	South Africa v West Indies at Johannesburg	2014-15
46	K. L. Rahul	India v West Indies at Lauderhill	2016
46	**G. D. Phillips**	**New Zealand v West Indies at Mount Maunganui**	**2020-21**
47	A. J. Finch	Australia v England at Southampton	2013
47	C. H. Gayle	West Indies v England at Mumbai	2015-16
47	C. Munro	New Zealand v West Indies at Mount Maunganui	2017-18
48	E. Lewis	West Indies v India at Lauderhill	2016
48	D. J. Malan	England v New Zealand at Napier	2019-20
49	G. J. Maxwell	Australia v Sri Lanka at Pallekele	2016
49	M. J. Guptill	New Zealand v Australia at Auckland	2017-18
49	P. Khadka	Nepal v Singapore at Singapore	2019-20

HIGHEST PARTNERSHIP FOR EACH WICKET

236	for 1st	Hazratullah Zazai/Usman Ghani	Afg v Ire	Dehradun	2018-19
167*	**for 2nd**	**J. C. Buttler/D. J. Malan**	**E v SA**	**Cape Town**	**2020-21**
184	**for 3rd**	**D. P. Conway/G. D. Phillips**	**NZ v WI**	**Mt Maunganui**	**2020-21**
161	for 4th	D. A. Warner/G. J. Maxwell	A v SA	Johannesburg	2015-16
119*	for 5th	Shoaib Malik/Misbah-ul-Haq	P v A	Johannesburg	2007-08
101*	for 6th	C. L. White/M. E. K. Hussey	A v SL	Bridgetown	2010
91	for 7th	P. D. Collingwood/M. H. Yardy	E v WI	The Oval	2007
80	for 8th	P. L. Mommsen/S. M. Sharif	Scot v Neth	Edinburgh	2015
66	for 9th	D. J. Bravo/J. E. Taylor	WI v P	Dubai	2016-17
31*	for 10th	Wahab Riaz/Shoaib Akhtar	P v NZ	Auckland	2010-11

BOWLING RECORDS

BEST BOWLING ANALYSES

6-7	D. L. Chahar	India v Bangladesh at Nagpur	2019-20
6-8	B. A. W. Mendis	Sri Lanka v Zimbabwe at Hambantota	2012-13
6-16	B. A. W. Mendis	Sri Lanka v Australia at Pallekele	2011-12
6-25	Y. S. Chahal	India v England at Bangalore	2016-17
5-3	H. M. R. K. B. Herath	Sri Lanka v New Zealand at Chittagong	2013-14
5-3	Rashid Khan	Afghanistan v Ireland at Greater Noida	2016-17
5-4	P. Arrighi	Argentina v Brazil at Lima	2019-20

5-4	**Khizar Hayat**	**Malaysia v Hong Kong at Kuala Lumpur**	**2019-20**
5-6	Umar Gul	Pakistan v New Zealand at The Oval	2009
5-6	Umar Gul	Pakistan v South Africa at Centurion	2012-13
5-6	S. L. Malinga	Sri Lanka v New Zealand at Pallekele	2019
5-6	A. Nanda	Luxembourg v Turkey at Ilfov	2019
5-9	C. Viljoen	Namibia v Botswana at Kampala	2019
5-11	Karim Janat	Afghanistan v West Indies at Lucknow	2019-20
5-13	Elias Sunny	Bangladesh v Ireland at Belfast	2012
5-13	Samiullah Shenwari	Afghanistan v Kenya at Sharjah	2013-14
5-13	**D. Muhumza**	**Uganda v Qatar at Doha**	**2019-20**
5-14	Imad Wasim	Pakistan v West Indies at Dubai	2016-17

HAT-TRICKS

Four Wickets in Four Balls

Rashid Khan	Afghanistan v Ireland at Dehradun	2018-19
S. L. Malinga	Sri Lanka v New Zealand at Pallekele	2019

Four Wickets in Five Balls

T. G. Southee	New Zealand v Pakistan at Auckland	2010-11

Hat-Tricks

There have been **13** hat-tricks in Twenty20 internationals, including the above; S. L. Malinga has taken two. The most recent are:

Mohammad Hasnain	Pakistan v Sri Lanka at Lahore	2019-20
Khawar Ali	Oman v Netherlands at Al Amerat	2019-20
N. Vanua	Papua New Guinea v Bermuda at Dubai	2019-20
D. L. Chahar	India v Bangladesh at Nagpur	2019-20
A. C. Agar	**Australia v South Africa at Johannesburg**	**2019-20**

MOST WICKETS

		M	*B*	*R*	*W*	*BB*	*4I*	*Avge*	*ER*
1	**S. L. Malinga (Sri Lanka)**	**84**	**1,799**	**2,225**	**107**	**5-6**	**3**	**20.79**	**7.42**
2	Shahid Afridi (Pakistan/World)	99	2,168	2,396	98	4-11	3	24.44	6.63
3	Shakib Al Hasan (Bangladesh)	76	1,667	1,894	92	5-20	4	20.58	6.81
4	**Rashid Khan (Afghanistan/World)**	**48**	**1,098**	**1,124**	**89**	**5-3**	**5**	**12.62**	**6.14**
5	**T. G. Southee (New Zealand)**	**75**	**1,608**	**2,258**	**87**	**5-18**	**2**	**25.95**	**8.42**
6	Umar Gul (Pakistan)	60	1,203	1,443	85	5-6	6	16.97	7.19
	Saeed Ajmal (Pakistan)	64	1,430	1,516	85	4-19	4	17.83	6.36
8	**G. H. Dockrell (Ireland)**	**77**	**1,370**	**1,624**	**76**	**4-20**	**1**	**21.36**	**7.11**
9	**Mohammad Nabi (Afghanistan)**	**78**	**1,564**	**1,871**	**69**	**4-10**	**3**	**27.11**	**7.17**
10	B. A. W. Mendis (Sri Lanka)	39	885	952	66	6-8	5	14.42	6.45
	K. M. D. N. Kulasekara (Sri Lanka)	58	1,231	1,530	66	4-31	2	23.18	7.45
	C. J. Jordan (England)	**55**	**1,152**	**1,671**	**66**	**4-6**	**2**	**25.31**	**8.70**
13	S. C. J. Broad (England)	56	1,173	1,491	65	4-24	1	22.93	7.62
14	**D. W. Steyn (South Africa)**	**47**	**1,015**	**1,175**	**64**	**4-9**	**2**	**18.35**	**6.94**
15	Imran Tahir (South Africa/World)	38	845	948	63	5-23	4	15.04	6.73
16	**J. J. Bumrah (India)**	**50**	**1,075**	**1,195**	**59**	**3-11**	**0**	**20.25**	**6.66**
	Mohammad Amir (Pakistan)	**50**	**1,079**	**1,263**	**59**	**4-13**	**1**	**21.40**	**7.02**
	Y. S. Chahal (India)	**45**	**1,053**	**1,456**	**59**	**6-25**	**3**	**24.67**	**8.29**
	D. J. Bravo (West Indies)	**71**	**1,151**	**1,600**	**59**	**4-28**	**2**	**27.11**	**8.34**
20	**K. J. O'Brien (Ireland)**	**96**	**903**	**1,134**	**58**	**4-45**	**1**	**19.55**	**7.53**
	Mustafizur Rahman (Bangladesh)	**41**	**901**	**1,191**	**58**	**5-22**	**2**	**20.53**	**7.93**
	N. L. McCullum (New Zealand)	63	1,123	1,278	58	4-16	2	22.03	6.82
23	S. Badree (West Indies/World)	52	1,146	1,180	56	4-15	1	21.07	6.17
	I. S. Sodhi (New Zealand)	**50**	**1,023**	**1,367**	**56**	**3-18**	**0**	**24.41**	**8.01**
25	**W. B. Rankin (Ireland/England)**	**50**	**1,068**	**1,219**	**55**	**3-16**	**0**	**22.16**	**6.84**

The leading aggregates for other Test countries are:

S. R. Watson (Australia) . .	58	930	1,187	48	4-15	1	24.72	7.65
A. G. Cremer (Zimbabwe)	29	570	660	35	3-11	0	18.85	6.94

*Excluding the World XI, the record aggregate for Pakistan is 97 in 98 matches by Shahid Afridi and for Afghanistan **87** in 47 matches by **Rashid Khan**.*

WICKETKEEPING AND FIELDING RECORDS

MOST DISMISSALS IN AN INNINGS

5 (3ct, 2st)	Mohammad Shahzad	Afghanistan v Oman at Abu Dhabi	2015-16
5 (5ct)	M. S. Dhoni	India v England at Bristol.	2018
5 (2ct, 3st)	I. A. Karim	Kenya v Ghana at Kampala	2019
5 (5ct)	K. Doriga	Papua New Guinea v Vanuata at Apia.	2019

*There have been **26** instances of four dismissals in an innings.*

MOST DISMISSALS

			M	*Ct*	*St*
1	91	M. S. Dhoni (India)	98	57	34
2	63	D. Ramdin (West Indies)	71	43	20
3	**61**	**Mushfiqur Rahim (Bangladesh)**	**82**	**32**	**29**
4	60	Kamran Akmal (Pakistan)	53	28	32
5	54	Mohammad Shahzad (Afghanistan).	64	26	28
6	**52**	**Q. de Kock (South Africa)**.	**46**	**41**	**11**
7	45	K. C. Sangakkara (Sri Lanka)	56	25	20
	45	**Sarfraz Ahmed (Pakistan)**.	**59**	**35**	**10**

Mushfiqur Rahim's record excludes one catch in four matches when not keeping wicket. Kamran Akmal played five matches and Mohammad Shahzad and Q. de Kock one each in which they did not keep wicket or take a catch.

MOST CATCHES IN AN INNINGS IN THE FIELD

There have been **13** instances of four catches in an innings. The most recent are:

4	A. M. Rahane	India v England at Birmingham.	2014
4	Babar Hayat	Hong Kong v Afghanistan at Mirpur.	2015-16
4	D. A. Miller	South Africa v Pakistan at Cape Town	2018-19
4	J. W. Jenner	Jersey v Guernsey at Castel	2019
4	L. Siaka.	Papua New Guinea v Vanuatu at Apia	2019
4	C. S. MacLeod	Scotland v Ireland at Malahide	2019
4	T. H. David.	Singapore v Scotland v Dubai	2019
4	C. de Grandhomme	New Zealand v England at Wellington	2019-20
4	**P. Sarraf**	**Nepal v Malaysia at Bangkok**	**2019-20**

MOST CATCHES

Ct	*M*		*Ct*	*M*	
57	**77**	**D. A. Miller (South Africa/World)**	**41**	**77**	**G. H. Dockrell (Ireland)**
50	**94**	**M. J. Guptill (New Zealand)**	**41**	**97**	**E. J. G. Morgan (England)**
50	**116**	**Shoaib Malik (Pakistan/World)**	**40**	**108**	**R. G. Sharma (India)**
46	**102**	**L. R. P. L. Taylor (New Zealand)**	39	64	Umar Akmal (Pakistan)
44	52	A. B. de Villiers (South Africa)	**38**	**75**	**T. G. Southee (New Zealand)**
44	**78**	**Mohammad Nabi (Afghanistan)**	**36**	**71**	**D. J. Bravo (West Indies)**
44	**81**	**D. A. Warner (Australia)**	**36**	**76**	**K. A. Pollard (West Indies)**
42	78	S. K. Raina (India)	35	81	J-P. Duminy (South Africa)
42	**85**	**V. G. Kohli (India)**	**35**	**96**	**K. J. O'Brien (Ireland)**

D. A. Miller's record excludes 2 dismissals (1ct, 1st) in one match when keeping wicket; A. B. de Villiers's excludes 28 (21ct, 7st) in 26 matches and Umar Akmal's 13 (11ct, 2st) in 20 matches.

TEAM RECORDS

HIGHEST INNINGS TOTALS

278-3	(20 overs)	Afghanistan v Ireland at Dehradun	2018-19
278-4	(20 overs)	Czech Republic v Turkey at Ilfov	2019
263-3	(20 overs)	Australia v Sri Lanka at Pallekele	2016
260-5	(20 overs)	India v Sri Lanka at Indore	2017-18
260-6	(20 overs)	Sri Lanka v Kenya at Johannesburg	2007-08
252-3	(20 overs)	Scotland v Netherlands at Malahide	2019
248-6	(20 overs)	Australia v England at Southampton	2013
245-5	(18.5 overs)	Australia v New Zealand at Auckland	2017-18
245-6	(20 overs)	West Indies v India at Lauderhill	2016
244-4	(20 overs)	India v West Indies at Lauderhill	2016
243-5	(20 overs)	New Zealand v West Indies at Mount Maunganui	2017-18
243-6	(20 overs)	New Zealand v Australia at Auckland	2017-18
241-3	(20 overs)	England v New Zealand at Napier	2019-20
241-6	(20 overs)	South Africa v England at Centurion	2009-10
240-3	(20 overs)	Namibia v Botswana at Windhoek	2019
240-3	(20 overs)	India v West Indies at Mumbai	2019-20

LOWEST INNINGS TOTALS

21	(8.3 overs)	Turkey v Czech Republic at Ilfov	2019
28	(11.3 overs)	Turkey v Luxembourg at Ilfov	2019
32	(8.5 overs)	Turkey v Austria at Ilfov	2019
39	(10.3 overs)	Netherlands v Sri Lanka at Chittagong	2013-14
45	(11.5 overs)	West Indies v England at Basseterre	2018-19
46	(12.1 overs)	Botswana v Namibia at Windhoek	2019
52	(15.2 overs)	Serbia v Greece at Corfu	2019-20
53	(14.3 overs)	Nepal v Ireland at Belfast	2015
53	(16 overs)	Germany v Italy at Utrecht	2019
53	(13 overs)	Turkey v Romania at Ilfov	2019
56	(18.4 overs)	Kenya v Afghanistan at Sharjah	2013-14
60†	(15.3 overs)	New Zealand v Sri Lanka at Chittagong	2013-14
60†	(13.4 overs)	West Indies v Pakistan at Karachi	2017-18
60	**(14.3 overs)**	**Bulgaria v Romania at Ilfov**	**2020**

† *One man absent.*

OTHER RECORDS

MOST APPEARANCES

116	**Shoaib Malik (Pakistan/World)**	**97**	**E. J. G. Morgan (England)**
108	**R. G. Sharma (India)**	**96**	**K. J. O'Brien (Ireland)**
102	**L. R. P. L. Taylor (New Zealand)**	**94**	**M. J. Guptill (New Zealand)**
99	**Mohammad Hafeez (Pakistan)**	**87**	**Mahmudullah (Bangladesh)**
99	Shahid Afridi (Pakistan/World)	**86**	**Mushfiqur Rahim (Bangladesh)**
98	M. S. Dhoni (India)	**85**	**V. Kohli (India)**

WORLD TWENTY20 FINALS

2007-08	INDIA (157-5) beat Pakistan (152) by five runs	Johannesburg
2009	PAKISTAN (139-2) beat Sri Lanka (138-6) by eight wickets	Lord's
2010	ENGLAND (148-3) beat Australia (147-6) by seven wickets	Bridgetown
2012-13	WEST INDIES (137-6) beat Sri Lanka (101) by 36 runs	Colombo (RPS)
2013-14	SRI LANKA (134-4) beat India (130-4) by six wickets	Mirpur
2015-16	WEST INDIES (161-6) beat England (155-9) by four wickets	Kolkata

MISCELLANEOUS RECORDS

LARGE ATTENDANCES

Test Series

943,000	Australia v England (5 Tests)	1936-37
In England		
549,650	England v Australia (5 Tests)	1953

Test Matches

†‡465,000	India v Pakistan, Calcutta	1998-99
350,534	Australia v England, Melbourne (Third Test)	1936-37

Attendance at India v England at Calcutta in 1981-82 may have exceeded 350,000.

In England		
158,000+	England v Australia, Leeds	1948
140,111	England v India, Lord's	2011
137,915	England v Australia, Lord's	1953

Test Match Day

‡100,000	India v Pakistan, Calcutta (first four days)	1998-99
91,112	Australia v England, Melbourne (Fourth Test, first day)	2013-14
90,800	Australia v West Indies, Melbourne (Fifth Test, second day)	1960-61
89,155	Australia v England, Melbourne (Fourth Test, first day)	2006-07

Other First-Class Matches in England

93,000	England v Australia, Lord's (Fourth Victory Match, 3 days)	1945
80,000+	Surrey v Yorkshire, The Oval (3 days)	1906
78,792	Yorkshire v Lancashire, Leeds (3 days)	1904
76,617	Lancashire v Yorkshire, Manchester (3 days)	1926

One-Day Internationals

‡100,000	India v South Africa, Calcutta	1993-94
‡100,000	India v West Indies, Calcutta	1993-94
‡100,000	India v West Indies, Calcutta	1994-95
‡100,000	India v Sri Lanka, Calcutta (World Cup semi-final)	1995-96
‡100,000	India v Australia, Kolkata	2003-04
93,013	Australia v New Zealand, Melbourne (World Cup final)	2014-15
‡90,000	India v Pakistan, Calcutta	1986-87
‡90,000	India v South Africa, Calcutta	1991-92
87,182	England v Pakistan, Melbourne (World Cup final)	1991-92
86,133	Australia v West Indies, Melbourne	1983-84

Twenty20 International

84,041	Australia v India, Melbourne	2007-08

Women's International

86,174	**Australia v India, Melbourne (Twenty20 World Cup final)**	**2019-20**

† *Estimated.*
‡ *No official attendance figures were issued for these games, but capacity at Calcutta (now Kolkata) is believed to have reached 100,000 following rebuilding in 1993.*

LORD'S CRICKET GROUND

Lord's and the Marylebone Cricket Club were founded in London in 1787. The Club has enjoyed an uninterrupted career since that date, but there have been three grounds known as Lord's. The first (1787–1810) was situated where Dorset Square now is; the second (1809–13), at North Bank, had to be abandoned owing to the cutting of the Regent's Canal; and the third, opened in 1814, is the present one at St John's Wood. It was not until 1866 that the freehold of Lord's was secured by MCC. The present pavilion was erected in 1890 at a cost of £21,000.

MINOR CRICKET

HIGHEST INDIVIDUAL SCORES

1,009*	P. P. Dhanawade, K. C. Gandhi English School v Arya Gurukul at Kalyan	2015-16
	Dhanawade faced 327 balls in 6 hours 36 minutes and hit 129 fours and 59 sixes	
628*	A. E. J. Collins, Clark's House v North Town at Clifton College	1899
	Junior house match. He batted 6 hours 50 minutes spread over four afternoons	
566	C. J. Eady, Break-o'-Day v Wellington at Hobart	1901-02
556*	P. Moliya, Mohinder Lal Amarnath C Ac U14 v Yogi C Ac U14 at Vadodara	2018-19
546	P. P. Shaw, Rizvi Springfield School v St Francis D'Assisi School at Mumbai	2013-14
515	D. R. Havewalla, B. B. and C. I. Railways v St Xavier's at Bombay	1933-34
506*	J. C. Sharp, Melbourne GS v Geelong College at Melbourne	1914-15
502*	M. Chamanlal, Mohindra Coll., Patiala v Government Coll., Rupar at Patiala	1956-57
498	Arman Jaffer, Rizvi Springfield School v IES Raja Shivaji School at Mumbai	2010-11
490	S. Dadswell, North West University v Potchefstroom at Potchefstroom	2017-18
486*	S. Sankruth Sriram, JSS Intl School U16 v Hebron School U16 at Ootacamund	2014-15
485	A. E. Stoddart, Hampstead v Stoics at Hampstead	1886
475*	Mohammad Iqbal, Muslim Model HS v Government HS, Sialkot at Gujranwala	1958-59
473	Arman Jaffer, Rizvi Springfield School v IES VN Sule School at Mumbai	2012-13
466*	G. T. S. Stevens, Beta v Lambda (Univ Coll School house match) at Neasden	1919
	Stevens scored his 466 and took 14 wickets on one day	
461*	Ali Zorain Khan, Nagpur Cricket Academy v Reshimbagh Gymkhana at Nagpur	2010-11
459	J. A. Prout, Wesley College v Geelong College at Geelong	1908-09
451*	V. H. Zol, Maharashtra Under-19 v Assam Under-19 at Nasik	2011-12

The highest score in a Minor County match is 323 by F. E. Lacey for Hampshire v Norfolk at Southampton in 1887; the highest in the Minor Counties Championship is 282 by E. Garnett for Berkshire v Wiltshire at Reading in 1908.*

HIGHEST PARTNERSHIPS

721* for 1st	B. Manoj Kumar and M. S. Tumbi, St Peter's High School v St Philip's High School at Secunderabad	2006-07
664* for 3rd	V. G. Kambli and S. R. Tendulkar, Sharadashram Vidyamandir School v St Xavier's High School at Bombay	1987-88

Manoj Kumar and Tumbi reportedly scored 721 in 40 overs in an Under-13 inter-school match; they hit 103 fours between them, but no sixes. Their opponents were all out for 21 in seven overs.

Kambli was 16 years old, Tendulkar 14. Tendulkar made his Test debut 21 months later.

MOST WICKETS WITH CONSECUTIVE BALLS

There are **two** recorded instances of a bowler taking nine wickets with consecutive balls. Both came in school games: Paul Hugo, for Smithfield School v Aliwal North at Smithfield, South Africa, in 1930-31, and Stephen Fleming (not the future Test captain), for Marlborough College A v Bohally School at Blenheim, New Zealand, in 1967-68. There are five further reported instances of eight wickets in eight balls, the most recent by Mike Walters for the Royal Army Educational Corps v Joint Air Transport Establishment at Beaconsfield in 1979.

TEN WICKETS FOR NO RUNS

There are **26** recorded instances of a bowler taking all ten wickets in an innings for no runs, the most recent Akash Choudhary, for Disha Cricket Academy v Pearl Academy in the Late Bahwer Singh T20 Tournament in Jaipur 2017-18. When Jennings Tune did it, for the Yorkshire club Cliffe v Eastrington at Cliffe in 1922, all ten of his victims were bowled.

NOUGHT ALL OUT

In minor matches, this is more common than might be imagined. The historian Peter Wynne-Thomas says the first recorded example was in Norfolk, where an Eleven of Fakenham, Walsingham and Hempton were dismissed for nought by an Eleven of Litcham, Dunham and Brisley in July 1815.

MOST DISMISSALS IN AN INNINGS

The only reported instance of a wicketkeeper being involved in all ten dismissals in an innings was by Welihinda Badalge Bennett. Details are disputed, but some sources state that it was for Mahinda College against Richmond College in Ceylon (now Sri Lanka) in 1952-53, and his feat comprised six catches and four stumpings (or vice versa). There are three other known instances of nine dismissals in the same innings, one of which – by H. W. P. Middleton for Priory v Mitre in a Repton School house match in 1930 – may have included eight stumpings. Young Rangers' innings against Bohran Gymkhana in Karachi in 1969-70 included nine run-outs.

The widespread nature – and differing levels of supervision – of minor cricket matches mean that record claims have to be treated with caution. Additions and corrections to the above records for minor cricket will only be considered for inclusion in Wisden *if they are corroborated by independent evidence of the achievement.*

Research: Steven Lynch

RECORD HIT

The Rev. W. Fellows, while at practice on the Christ Church ground at Oxford in 1856, reportedly drove a ball bowled by Charles Rogers 175 yards from hit to pitch; it is claimed that the feat was matched by J. W. Erskine in a match at Galle in 1902.

BIGGEST HIT AT LORD'S

The only known instance of a batsman hitting a ball over the present pavilion at Lord's occurred when A. E. Trott, appearing for MCC against Australians on July 31, August 1, 2, 1899, drove M. A. Noble so far and high that the ball struck a chimney pot and fell behind the building.

THROWING THE CRICKET BALL

140 yards 2 feet	Robert Percival, on the Durham Sands racecourse, Co. Durham	c1882
140 yards 9 inches	Ross Mackenzie, at Toronto	1872
140 yards	"King Billy" the Aborigine, at Clermont, Queensland	1872

Extensive research by David Rayvern Allen has shown that these traditional records are probably authentic, if not necessarily wholly accurate. Modern competitions have failed to produce similar distances although Ian Pont, the Essex all-rounder who also played baseball, was reported to have thrown 138 yards in Cape Town in 1981. There have been speculative reports attributing throws of 150 yards or more to figures as diverse as the South African Test player Colin Bland, the Latvian javelin thrower Janis Lusis, who won a gold medal for the Soviet Union in the 1968 Olympics, and the British sprinter Charley Ransome. The definitive record is still awaited.

COUNTY CHAMPIONSHIP

MOST APPEARANCES

762	W. Rhodes	Yorkshire	1898–1930
707	F. E. Woolley	Kent	1906–1938
668	C. P. Mead	Hampshire	1906–1936
617	N. Gifford	Worcestershire (484), Warwickshire (133)	1960–1988
611	W. G. Quaife	Warwickshire	1895–1928
601	G. H. Hirst	Yorkshire	1891–1921

MOST CONSECUTIVE APPEARANCES

423	K. G. Suttle	Sussex	1954–1969
412	J. G. Binks	Yorkshire	1955–1969

J. Vine made 417 consecutive appearances for Sussex in all first-class matches (399 of them in the Championship) between July 1900 and September 1914.

J. G. Binks did not miss a Championship match for Yorkshire between making his debut in June 1955 and retiring at the end of the 1969 season.

UMPIRES

MOST COUNTY CHAMPIONSHIP APPEARANCES

570	T. W. Spencer	1950–1980
531	F. Chester	1922–1955
523	D. J. Constant	1969–2006
517	H. G. Baldwin	1932–1962
511	A. G. T. Whitehead	1970–2005

MOST SEASONS ON ENGLISH FIRST-CLASS LIST

38	D. J. Constant	1969–2006
36	A. G. T. Whitehead	1970–2005
31	K. E. Palmer	1972–2002
31	T. W. Spencer	1950–1980
30	R. Julian	1972–2001
30	P. B. Wight	1966–1995
29	H. D. Bird	1970–1998
28	F. Chester	1922–1955
28	B. Leadbeater	1981–2008
28	R. Palmer	1980–2007
27	B. Dudleston	1984–2010
27	J. W. Holder	1983–2009
27	J. Moss	1899–1929
26	W. A. J. West	1896–1925
25	H. G. Baldwin	1932–1962
25	A. Jepson	1960–1984
25	J. G. Langridge	1956–1980
25	B. J. Meyer	1973–1997
25	D. R. Shepherd	1981–2005

WOMEN'S TEST RECORDS

This section covers all women's Tests to December 31, 2020. No Tests were played in the calendar year 2020.

RESULTS SUMMARY OF WOMEN'S TESTS

1934-35 to December 31, 2020 (139 matches)

	Tests	*Won*	*Lost*	*Drawn*	*% Won*	*Toss Won*
Ireland	1	1	0	0	100.00	0
Sri Lanka	1	1	0	0	100.00	1
Australia	74	20	10	44	27.02	27
England	95	20	14	61	21.05	55
India	35	5	5	25	14.28	19
South Africa	12	1	5	6	8.33	6
New Zealand	45	2	10	33	4.44	19
Netherlands	1	0	1	0	0.00	1
Pakistan	3	0	2	1	0.00	1
West Indies	11	0	3	8	0.00	10

BATTING RECORDS

HIGHEST INDIVIDUAL INNINGS

242	Kiran Baluch	Pakistan v West Indies at Karachi	2003-04
214	M. D. Raj	India v England at Taunton	2002
213*	E. A. Perry	Australia v England at North Sydney	2017-18
209*	K. L. Rolton	Australia v England at Leeds	2001
204	K. E. Flavell	New Zealand v England at Scarborough	1996
204	M. A. J. Goszko	Australia v England at Shenley	2001
200	J. Broadbent	Australia v England at Guildford	1998

MOST RUNS

		T	*I*	*NO*	*R*	*HS*	*100*	*Avge*
1	J. A. Brittin (England)	27	44	5	1,935	167	5	49.61
2	C. M. Edwards (England)	23	43	5	1,676	117	4	44.10
3	R. Heyhoe-Flint (England)	22	38	3	1,594	179	3	45.54
4	D. A. Hockley (New Zealand)	19	29	4	1,301	126*	4	52.04
5	C. A. Hodges (England)	18	31	2	1,164	158*	2	40.13
6	S. Agarwal (India)	13	23	1	1,110	190	4	50.45
7	E. Bakewell (England)	12	22	4	1,078	124	4	59.88
8	S. C. Taylor (England)	15	27	2	1,030	177	4	41.20
9	M. E. Maclagan (England)	14	25	1	1,007	119	2	41.95
10	K. L. Rolton (Australia)	14	22	4	1,002	209*	2	55.66

BOWLING RECORDS

BEST BOWLING ANALYSES

8-53	N. David	India v England at Jamshedpur	1995-96
7-6	M. B. Duggan	England v Australia at Melbourne	1957-58
7-7	E. R. Wilson	Australia v England at Melbourne	1957-58
7-10	M. E. Maclagan	England v Australia at Brisbane	1934-35
7-18	A. Palmer	Australia v England at Brisbane	1934-35
7-24	L. Johnston	Australia v New Zealand at Melbourne	1971-72
7-34	G. E. McConway	England v India at Worcester	1986
7-41	J. A. Burley	New Zealand v England at The Oval	1966

MOST WICKETS IN A MATCH

13-226	Shaiza Khan	Pakistan v West Indies at Karachi	2003-04

MOST WICKETS

		T	*Balls*	*R*	*W*	*BB*	*5I*	*10M*	*Avge*	*SR*
1	M. B. Duggan (England)	17	3,734	1,039	77	7-6	5	0	13.49	48.49
2	E. R. Wilson (Australia)	11	2,885	803	68	7-7	4	2	11.80	42.42
3	D. F. Edulji (India)	20	5,188	1,624	63	6-64	1	0	25.77	82.34
4	M. E. Maclagan (England)	14	3,432	935	60	7-10	3	0	15.58	57.20
	C. L. Fitzpatrick (Australia)	13	3,603	1,147	60	5-29	2	0	19.11	60.05
	S. Kulkarni (India)	19	3,320	1,647	60	6-99	5	0	27.45	55.33
7	R. H. Thompson (Australia)	16	4,304	1,040	57	5-33	1	0	18.24	75.50
8	J. Lord (New Zealand)	15	3,108	1,049	55	6-119	4	1	19.07	56.50
9	E. Bakewell (England)	12	2,698	831	50	7-61	3	1	16.62	53.96

WICKETKEEPING RECORDS

SIX DISMISSALS IN AN INNINGS

8 (6ct, 2st)	L. Nye	England v New Zealand at New Plymouth	1991-92
6 (2ct, 4st)	B. A. Brentnall	New Zealand v South Africa at Johannesburg	1971-72

MOST DISMISSALS IN A CAREER

		T	*Ct*	*St*
58	C. Matthews (Australia)	20	46	12
43	J. Smit (England)	21	39	4
36	S. A. Hodges (England)	11	19	17
28	B. A. Brentnall (New Zealand)	10	16	12

TEAM RECORDS

HIGHEST INNINGS TOTALS

569-6 dec	Australia v England at Guildford	1998
525	Australia v India at Ahmedabad	1983-84
517-8	New Zealand v England at Scarborough	1996
503-5 dec	England v New Zealand at Christchurch	1934-35

LOWEST INNINGS TOTALS

35	England v Australia at Melbourne	1957-58
38	Australia v England at Melbourne	1957-58
44	New Zealand v England at Christchurch	1934-35
47	Australia v England at Brisbane	1934-35

WOMEN'S ONE-DAY INTERNATIONAL RECORDS

This section covers women's one-day international cricket to December 31, 2020. Bold type denotes performances in the calendar year 2020 or, in career figures, players who appeared in that year.

RESULTS SUMMARY OF WOMEN'S ONE-DAY INTERNATIONALS

1973 to December 31, 2020 (1,183 matches)

	Matches	*Won*	*Lost*	*Tied*	*No Result*	*% Won (excl NR)*
Australia	332	261	63	2	6	80.36
England	348	204	131	2	11	60.83
India	272	151	116	1	4	56.52
South Africa	196	97	88	3	8	52.39
New Zealand	341	170	163	2	6	51.04
West Indies	177	80	91	1	5	46.80
Sri Lanka	167	56	106	0	5	34.56
Trinidad & Tobago	6	2	4	0	0	33.33
Pakistan	165	48	113	1	3	29.93
Ireland	148	39	103	0	6	27.46
Bangladesh	38	9	27	0	2	25.00
Jamaica	5	1	4	0	0	20.00
Netherlands	101	19	81	0	1	19.00
Denmark	33	6	27	0	0	18.18
International XI	18	3	14	0	1	17.64
Young England	6	1	5	0	0	16.66
Scotland	8	1	7	0	0	12.50
Japan	5	0	5	0	0	0.00

Matches abandoned without a ball bowled are not included except where the toss took place, when they are shown as no result. In the percentages of matches won, ties are counted as half a win.

BATTING RECORDS

HIGHEST INDIVIDUAL INNINGS

232*	A. C. Kerr	New Zealand v Ireland at Dublin	2018
229*	B. J. Clark	Australia v Denmark at Mumbai	1997-98
188	D. B. Sharma	India v Ireland at Potchefstroom	2017
178*	A. M. C. Jayangani	Sri Lanka v Australia at Bristol	2017
173*	C. M. Edwards	England v Ireland at Pune	1997-98
171*	H. Kaur	India v Australia at Derby	2017
171	S. R. Taylor	West Indies v Sri Lanka at Mumbai	2012-13
168*	T. T. Beaumont	England v Pakistan at Taunton	2016
168	S. W. Bates	New Zealand v Pakistan at Sydney	2008-09
157	R. H. Priest	New Zealand v Sri Lanka at Lincoln	2015-16
156*	L. M. Keightley	Australia v Pakistan at Melbourne	1996-97
156*	S. C. Taylor	England v India at Lord's	2006
154*	K. L. Rolton	Australia v Sri Lanka at Christchurch	2000-01
153*	J. Logtenberg	South Africa v Netherlands at Deventer	2007
152*	M. M. Lanning	Australia v Sri Lanka at Bristol	2017
151	K. L. Rolton	Australia v Ireland at Dublin	2005
151	S. W. Bates	New Zealand v Ireland at Dublin	2018

MOST RUNS

		M	*I*	*NO*	*R*	*HS*	*100*	*Avge*
1	M. D. Raj (India)	209	189	53	6,888	125*	7	50.64
2	C. M. Edwards (England)	191	180	23	5,992	173*	9	38.16
3	B. J. Clark (Australia)	118	114	12	4,844	229*	5	47.49
4	K. L. Rolton (Australia)	141	132	32	4,814	154*	8	48.14
5	S. R. Taylor (West Indies)	126	123	15	4,756	171	5	44.03
6	**S. W. Bates (New Zealand)**	**125**	**119**	**12**	**4,548**	**168**	**10**	**42.50**
7	S. C. Taylor (England)	126	120	18	4,101	156*	8	40.20
8	D. A. Hockley (New Zealand)	118	115	18	4,066	117	4	41.91
9	S. J. Taylor (England)	126	119	13	4,056	147	7	38.26
10	A. E. Satterthwaite (NZ)	122	116	15	3,932	137*	6	38.93
11	**M. M. Lanning (Australia)**	**82**	**82**	**12**	**3,856**	**152***	**14**	**55.08**

FASTEST ONE-DAY INTERNATIONAL FIFTIES

Balls			
22	N. R. Sciver	England v Pakistan at Worcester	2016
23	M. M. Lanning	Australia v New Zealand at Sydney	2012-13

FASTEST ONE-DAY INTERNATIONAL HUNDREDS

Balls			
45	M. M. Lanning	Australia v New Zealand at Sydney	2012-13
57	K. L. Rolton	Australia v South Africa at Lincoln	2000-01
59	S. F. M. Devine	New Zealand v Ireland at Dublin	2018

HIGHEST PARTNERSHIP FOR EACH WICKET

320	for 1st	D. B. Sharma/P. G. Raut	I v Ire	Potchefstroom	2017
295	for 2nd	A. C. Kerr/L. M. Kasperek	NZ v Ire	Clontarf	2018
244	for 3rd	K. L. Rolton/L. C. Sthalekar	A v Ire	Dublin (Sandymount)	2005
224*	for 4th	J. Logtenberg/M. du Preez	SA v Neth	Deventer	2007
188*	for 5th	S. C. Taylor/J. Smit	E v SL	Lincoln	2000-01
142	for 6th	S. E. Luus/C. L. Tryon	SA v Ire	Dublin (Merrion)	2016
104*	for 7th	S. J. Tsukigawa/N. J. Browne	NZ v E	Chennai	2006-07
104	for 7th	N. R. Sciver/D. Hazell	E v SL	Colombo (RPS)	2016-17
88	for 8th	N. N. D. de Silva/ O. U. Ranasinghe	SL v E	Hambantota	2018-19
73	for 9th	L. R. F. Askew/I. T. Guha	E v NZ	Chennai	2006-07
76	for 10th	A. J. Blackwell/K. M. Beams	A v I	Derby	2017

† *110 runs were scored for West Indies' 7th wicket v Sri Lanka at Dambulla in 2012-13, in two partnerships: S. A. Campbelle and A. Mohammed put on 34 before Mohammed retired hurt, then Campbelle and S. C. Selman added a further 76.*

BOWLING RECORDS

BEST BOWLING ANALYSES

7-4	Sajjida Shah	Pakistan v Japan at Amsterdam	2003
7-8	J. M. Chamberlain	England v Denmark at Haarlem	1991
7-14	A. Mohammed	West Indies v Pakistan at Mirpur	2011-12
7-22	E. A. Perry	Australia v England at Canterbury	2019
7-24	S. Nitschke	Australia v England at Kidderminster	2005
6-10	J. Lord	New Zealand v India at Auckland	1981-82
6-10	M. Maben	India v Sri Lanka at Kandy	2003-04
6-10	S. Ismail	South Africa v Netherlands at Savar	2011-12

HAT-TRICKS

Four Wickets in Five Balls

D. van Niekerk	South Africa v West Indies at Basseterre	2012-13

Hat-Tricks

There have been **11** hat-tricks in one-day internationals, all by different bowlers. Those since 2017:

M. M. Klaas	South Africa v Pakistan at Potchefstroom	2019
M. Schutt	Australia v West Indies at North Sound	2019-20

MOST WICKETS

		M	*Balls*	*R*	*W*	*BB*	*4I*	*Avge*
1	J. N. Goswami (India)	182	8,835	4,835	225	6-31	8	21.48
2	C. L. Fitzpatrick (Australia)	109	6,017	3,023	180	5-14	11	16.79
3	E. A. Perry (Australia)	112	5,110	3,693	152	7-22	4	24.29
4	A. Mohammed (West Indies)	122	5,368	3,098	151	7-14	12	20.51
	Sana Mir (Pakistan)	120	5,942	3,665	151	5-32	8	24.27
6	K. H. Brunt (England)	123	5,970	3,473	150	5-18	7	23.15
7	L. C. Sthalekar (Australia)	125	5,965	3,646	146	5-35	2	24.97
8	S. R. Taylor (West Indies)	126	5,309	3,032	142	4-17	5	21.35
9	N. L. David (India)	97	4,892	2,305	141	5-20	6	16.34
10	J. L. Gunn (England)	144	5,906	3,822	136	5-22	6	28.10
	S. Ismail (South Africa)	**98**	**4,736**	**2,841**	**136**	**6-10**	**5**	**20.88**
12	**D. van Niekerk (South Africa)**	**102**	**4,342**	**2,549**	**130**	**5-17**	**8**	**19.60**

WICKETKEEPING AND FIELDING RECORDS

MOST DISMISSALS IN AN INNINGS

6 (4ct, 2st)	S. L. Illingworth	New Zealand v Australia at Beckenham	1993
6 (1ct, 5st)	V. Kalpana	India v Denmark at Slough	1993
6 (2ct, 4st)	Batool Fatima	Pakistan v West Indies at Karachi	2003-04
6 (4ct, 2st)	Batool Fatima	Pakistan v Sri Lanka at Colombo (PSO)	2010-11

MOST DISMISSALS

			M	*Ct*	*St*
1	**157**	**T. Chetty (South Africa)**	**109**	**109**	**48**
2	136	S. J. Taylor (England)	118	85	51
3	133	R. J. Rolls (New Zealand)	101	90	43
4	114	J. Smit (England)	108	69	45
5	103	M. R. Aguilleira (West Indies)	104	76	27
6	99	J. C. Price (Australia)	83	69	30
7	97	Batool Fatima (Pakistan)	68	51	46
8	**93**	**R. H. Priest (New Zealand)**	**86**	**72**	**21**
9	81	A. Jain (India)	61	30	51

T. Chetty's total excludes two catches in two matches, S. J. Taylor's and M. R. Aguilleira's each exclude two in eight matches and Batool Fatima's three in 15 while not keeping wicket; J. C. Price's excludes one taken in the field after giving up the gloves mid-game. R. J. Rolls did not keep wicket in three matches and J. Smit in one; neither took any catches in these games.

MOST CATCHES IN AN INNINGS IN THE FIELD

4	Z. J. Goss	Australia v New Zealand at Adelaide	1995-96
4	J. L. Gunn	England v New Zealand at Lincoln	2014-15
4	Nahida Khan	Pakistan v Sri Lanka at Dambulla	2017-18

MOST CATCHES

66	**125**	**S. W. Bates (New Zealand)**	53	209	M. D. Raj (India)
64	182	J. N. Goswami (India)	**52**	**102**	**D. van Niekerk (South Africa)**
58	126	S. R. Taylor (West Indies)	52	126	L. S. Greenway (England)
55	144	A. J. Blackwell (Australia)	52	191	C. M. Edwards (England)

TEAM RECORDS

HIGHEST INNINGS TOTALS

491-4	New Zealand v Ireland at Dublin	2018
455-5	New Zealand v Pakistan at Christchurch	1996-97
440-3	New Zealand v Ireland at Dublin	2018
418	New Zealand v Ireland at Dublin	2018
412-3	Australia v Denmark at Mumbai	1997-98
397-4	Australia v Pakistan at Melbourne	1996-97
378-5	England v Pakistan at Worcester	2016
377-7	England v Pakistan at Leicester	2017
376-2	England v Pakistan at Vijayawada	1997-98
375-5	Netherlands v Japan at Schiedam	2003

LOWEST INNINGS TOTALS

22	Netherlands v West Indies at Deventer	2008
23	Pakistan v Australia at Melbourne	1996-97
24	Scotland v England at Reading	2001
26	India v New Zealand as St Saviour	2002
27	Pakistan v Australia at Hyderabad (India)	1997-98
28	Japan v Pakistan at Amsterdam	2003
29	Netherlands v Australia at Perth	1988-89

LARGEST VICTORIES

408 runs	New Zealand (455-5 in 50 overs) v Pakistan (47 in 23 overs) at Christchurch	1996-97
374 runs	Australia (397-4 in 50 overs) v Pakistan (23 in 24.1 overs) at Melbourne	1996-97
363 runs	Australia (412-3 in 50 overs) v Denmark (49 in 25.5 overs) at Mumbai	1997-98

*There have been **37** instances of victory by ten wickets.*

TIED MATCHES

New Zealand (147-9 in 60 overs) v England (147-8 in 60 overs) at Auckland	1991-92
England (167-8 in 60 overs) v Australia (167 in 60 overs) at Christchurch	1981-82
New Zealand (176-9 in 50 overs) v India (176 in 49.1 overs) at Indore	1997-98
South Africa (180-6 in 50 overs) v West Indies (180-8 in 50 overs) at Cape Town	2009-10
Australia (242 in 49.5 overs) v South Africa (242 in 50 overs) at Coffs Harbour	2016-17
South Africa (265-6 in 50 overs) v Pakistan (265-9 in 50 overs) at Benoni	2019

OTHER RECORDS

MOST APPEARANCES

209	M. D. Raj (I)	127	A. Chopra (I)
191	C. M. Edwards (E)	126	L. S. Greenway (E)
182	J. N. Goswami (I)	126	S. C. Taylor (E)
144	A. J. Blackwell (A)	126	S. J. Taylor (E)
144	J. L. Gunn (E)	126	S. R. Taylor (WI)
141	K. L. Rolton (A)	**125**	**S. W. Bates (NZ)**
134	S. J. McGlashan (NZ)	125	N. J. Browne (NZ)
130	**M. du Preez (SA)**	125	L. C. Sthalekar (A)

WOMEN'S WORLD CUP WINNERS

1973	England	1993	England	2008-09	England
1977-78	Australia	1997-98	Australia	2012-13	Australia
1981-82	Australia	2000-01	New Zealand	2017	England
1988-89	Australia	2004-05	Australia		

WOMEN'S TWENTY20 INTERNATIONAL RECORDS

This section covers women's Twenty20 international cricket to December 31, 2020. Bold type denotes performances in the calendar year 2020 or, in career figures, players who appeared in that year. The ICC extended official international status to Associate Twenty20 matches from June 2018.

RESULTS SUMMARY OF WOMEN'S TWENTY20 INTERNATIONALS

2004 to December 31, 2020 (879 matches)

	Matches	*Won*	*Lost*	*No Result*	*% Won (excl NR)*
England	146	105*	40†	1	72.41
Australia	141	95†	46*	0	67.37
New Zealand	127	76*	50*	1	60.31
West Indies	135	74§	59*	2	55.63
India	123	67	54	2	55.37
South Africa	111	49	60	2	44.95
Pakistan	117	47	68‡	2	40.86
Bangladesh	75	27	48	0	36.00
Ireland	71	20	50	1	28.57
Sri Lanka	100	24	72	4	25.00
Thailand	39	25	13	1	65.78
Netherlands	32	5	25†	2	16.66

* *Includes three settled by a tie-break.* † *Includes two settled by a tie-break.*
‡ *Includes three settled by a tie-break.* § *Includes four settled by a tie-break.*
Ties were decided by super overs, apart from one bowling contest between Australia and New Zealand.

Matches abandoned without a ball bowled are not included except where the toss took place, when they are shown as no result. In the percentages of matches won, ties are counted as half a win.

A further 49 teams have played women's Twenty20 internationals, as follows: Zimbabwe (P14 W14); Brazil (P10 W10); Guernsey (P1 W1); Tanzania (P10 W9 L1); Samoa (P12 W10 L2); Belize (P6 W5 L1); France (P6 W5 L1); Nepal (P14 W11 L3); Germany (P13 W9 L4); Scotland (P20 W13 L7); Indonesia (P17 W11 L6); Papua New Guinea (P22 W14 L8); Argentina (P5 W3 L2); Jersey (P7 W4 L3); United Arab Emirates (P16 W9 L7); Namibia (P25 W14 L11); Uganda (P19 W10 L9); China (P16 W8 L8); Vanuatu (P12 W6 L6); USA (P8 W4 L4); Hong Kong (P15 W7 L8); Malawi (P13 W6 L7); Kenya (P11 W5 L6); Rwanda (P20 W9 L11); Chile (P9 W4 L5); Japan (P9 W4 L5); Sierra Leone (P9 W4 L5); Nigeria (P14 W6 L8); Myanmar (P11 W4 L6 NR1); Malaysia (P24 W9 L15); Oman (P9 W3 L6); Botswana (P16 W5 L11); Mexico (P10 W3 L7); Mozambique (P17 W5 L12); Kuwait (P11 W3 L8); Qatar (P4 W1 L3); Austria (P11 W2 L9); Singapore (P12 W2 L9 NR1); Norway (P6 W1 L5); South Korea (P7 W1 L6); Costa Rica (P8 W1 L7); Fiji (P12 L12); Lesotho (P6 L6); Mali (P6 L6); Bhutan (P4 L4); Peru (P4 L4); Philippines (P4 L4); Canada (P3 L3); Maldives (P3 L3).

BATTING RECORDS

HIGHEST INDIVIDUAL INNINGS

148*	A. J. Healy	Australia v Sri Lanka at Sydney	2019-20
133*	M. M. Lanning	Australia v England at Chelmsford	2019
126*	S. L. Kalis	Netherlands v Germany at La Manga	2019
126	M. M. Lanning	Australia v Ireland at Sylhet	2013-14
124*	S. W. Bates	New Zealand v South Africa at Taunton	2018
124	D. N. Wyatt	England v India at Mumbai (BS)	2017-18
117*	B. L. Mooney	Australia v England at Canberra	2017-18
116*	S. A. Fritz	South Africa v Netherlands at Potchefstroom	2010-11
116	T. T. Beaumont	England v South Africa at Taunton	2018
116	P. Alako	Uganda v Mali at Kigali	2019

MOST RUNS

		M	*I*	*NO*	*R*	*HS*	*100*	*Avge*	*SR*
1	**S. W. Bates (New Zealand)**	**122**	**119**	**9**	**3,301**	**124***	**1**	**30.00**	**110.62**
2	**S. R. Taylor (West Indies)**	**108**	**106**	**22**	**3,062**	**90**	**0**	**36.45**	
3	**M. M. Lanning (Australia)**	**107**	**101**	**22**	**2,859**	**133***	**2**	**36.18**	**115.98**
4	C. M. Edwards (England)	95	93	14	2,605	92*	0	32.97	106.93
5	**D. J. S. Dottin (West Indies)**	**118**	**116**	**19**	**2,565**	**112***	**2**	**26.44**	
6	**S. F. M. Devine (New Zealand)**	**94**	**91**	**12**	**2,447**	**105**	**1**	**30.97**	**125.42**
7	M. D. Raj (India)	89	84	21	2,364	97*	0	37.52	
8	**Bismah Maroof (Pakistan)**	**108**	**101**	**21**	**2,202**	**70***	**0**	**27.52**	**92.40**
9	**H. Kaur (India)**	**114**	**102**	**21**	**2,186**	**103**	**1**	**26.98**	
10	S. J. Taylor (England)	90	87	12	2,177	77	0	29.02	110.67
11	**A. J. Healy (Australia)**	**115**	**100**	**16**	**2,107**	**148***	**1**	**25.08**	**131.68**

Balls and strike-rates are not available for all matches.

FASTEST TWENTY20 INTERNATIONAL FIFTIES

Balls			
18	S. F. M. Devine	New Zealand v India at Bangalore	2015
20	Nida Dar	Pakistan v South Africa at Benoni	2019

FASTEST TWENTY20 INTERNATIONAL HUNDREDS

Balls			
38	D. J. S. Dottin	West Indies v South Africa at Basseterre	2010
49	H. Kaur	India v New Zealand at Providence	2018-19

HIGHEST PARTNERSHIP FOR EACH WICKET

257	for 1st	Y. Anggraeni/K. W. Prastini	Indonesia v Philippines	Dasmarinas	2019-20
227	for 2nd	P. Alako/R. Musamali	Uganda v Mali	Kigali	2019
236*	for 3rd	Nigar Sultana/Farzana Haque	B v Maldives	Pokhara	2019-20
147*	for 4th	K. L. Rolton/A. J. Blackwell	A v E	Taunton	2005
119*	for 5th	M. M. Lanning/R. L. Haynes	A v NZ	N Sydney	2018-19
84	for 6th	M. A. A. Sanjeewani/ N. N. D. de Silva	SL v P	Colombo (SSC)	2017-18
72	for 7th	M. I. Pascal/N. N. Saidi	Tanzania v Uganda	Kigali	2019
53	for 8th	I. C. Chuma/A. Monjane	Mozambique v Malawi	Blantyre	2019-20
67*	for 9th	D. Foerster/A. van Schoor	Namibia v Botswana	Windhoek	2018-19
44	for 10th	W. M. Delgado/A. J. A. Campos	Costa Rica v Belize	San Jose	2019-20

BOWLING RECORDS

BEST BOWLING ANALYSES

6-0	A. Chand	Nepal v Maldives at Pokhara	2019
6-3	Mas Elysa	Malaysia v China at Bangkok	2018-19
6-8	B. Mpedi	Botswana v Lesotho at Gaborone	2018
6-8	N. Thapa	Nepal v Hong Kong at Bangkok	2018-19
6-10	Zon Lin	Myanmar v Indonesia at Bangkok	2018-19
6-17	A. E. Satterthwaite	New Zealand v England at Taunton	2007
5-0	N. N. Saidi	Tanzania v Mali at Kigali	2019
5-1	**A. Doddaballapur**	**Germany v Austria at Seebarn**	**2020**
5-3	C. R. Seneviratne	United Arab Emirates v Kuwait at Bangkok	2018-19
5-4	C. Sutthiruang	Thailand v Indonesia at Bangkok	2018-19
5-5	D. J. S. Dottin	West Indies v Bangladesh at Providence	2018-19
5-5	I. D. A. D. A. Laksmi	Indonesia v Philippines at Dasmarinas	2019-20
5-7	K. Arua	Papua New Guinea v Japan at Port Vila	2019
5-7	K. Y. Chan	Hong Kong v China at Incheon	2019
5-8	S. E. Luus	South Africa v Ireland at Chennai	2015-16
5-8	M. M. P. Suwandewi	Indonesia v Philippines at Dasmarinas	2019-20

HAT-TRICKS

There have been **15** hat-tricks in Twenty20 internationals, all by different bowlers. Those since 2019:

C. Aweko	Uganda v Kenya at Harare (*four wickets in five balls*)	2019
O. Kamchomphu	Thailand v Ireland at Deventer	2019
K. Y. Chan	Hong Kong v China at Incheon	2019
A. Bierswich	**Germany v Austria at Seebarn**	**2020**
A. Doddaballapur	**Germany v Austria at Seebarn (*four wickets in four balls*)**	**2020**

MOST WICKETS

		M	*B*	*R*	*W*	*BB*	*4I*	*Avge*	*ER*
1	**A. Mohammed (West Indies)**	**111**	**2,241**	**2,077**	**120**	**5-10**	**7**	**17.30**	**5.56**
2	**E. A. Perry (Australia)**	**120**	**2,261**	**2,209**	**114**	**4-12**	**4**	**19.37**	**5.86**
3	**A. Shrubsole (England)**	**79**	**1,598**	**1,587**	**102**	**5-11**	**3**	**15.55**	**5.95**
4	**S. Ismail (South Africa)**	**92**	**1,931**	**1,847**	**99**	**5-30**	**1**	**18.65**	**5.73**
5	**Nida Dar (Pakistan)**	**102**	**1,957**	**1,756**	**98**	**5-21**	**2**	**17.91**	**5.38**
6	**P. Yadav (India)**	**67**	**1,452**	**1,367**	**95**	**4-9**	**3**	**14.38**	**5.64**
7	**S. R. Taylor (West Indies)**	**108**	**1,684**	**1,587**	**94**	**4-12**	**1**	**16.88**	**5.65**
8	**M. Schutt (Australia)**	**70**	**1,413**	**1,424**	**93**	**4-18**	**3**	**15.31**	**6.04**
9	**S. F. M. Devine (New Zealand)**	**94**	**1,488**	**1,554**	**91**	**4-22**	**1**	**17.07**	**6.26**
10	**K. H. Brunt (England)**	**87**	**1,885**	**1,726**	**89**	**3-6**	**0**	**19.39**	**5.49**
	Sana Mir (Pakistan)	106	2,246	2,066	89	4-13	4	23.21	5.51
12	D. Hazell (England)	85	1,905	1,764	85	4-12	1	20.75	5.55

WICKETKEEPING AND FIELDING RECORDS

MOST DISMISSALS IN AN INNINGS

5 (1ct, 4st)	Kycia A. Knight	West Indies v Sri Lanka at Colombo (RPS)	2012-13
5 (1ct, 4st)	Batool Fatima	Pakistan v Ireland at Dublin	2013
5 (1ct, 4st)	Batool Fatima	Pakistan v Ireland at Dublin (semi-final)	2013
5 (3ct, 2st)	B. M. Bezuidenhout	New Zealand v Ireland at Dublin	2018
5 (1ct, 4st)	S. J. Bryce	Scotland v Netherlands at Arbroath	2019

MOST DISMISSALS

			M	Ct	St
1	**93**	**A. J. Healy (Australia)**	**100**	**42**	**51**
2	74	S. J. Taylor (England)	88	23	51
3	**73**	**R. H. Priest (New Zealand)**	**74**	**41**	**32**
4	70	M. R. Aguilleira (West Indies)	85	36	34
5	**67**	**T. Bhatia (India)**	**50**	**23**	**44**
6	**64**	**T. Chetty (South Africa)**	**76**	**37**	**27**
7	50	Batool Fatima (Pakistan)	45	11	39

A. J. Healy's record excludes two catches in 15 matches and M. R. Aguilleira's excludes two in ten while not keeping wicket. S. J. Taylor did not keep wicket in two matches and R. H. Priest in one; neither took any catches in these games.

MOST CATCHES IN AN INNINGS IN THE FIELD

4	L. S. Greenway	England v New Zealand at Chelmsford	2010
4	V. Krishnamurthy	India v Australia at Providence	2018-19

MOST CATCHES

Ct	M		Ct	M	
64	**122**	**S. W. Bates (New Zealand)**	**43**	**114**	**H. Kaur (India)**
58	104	J. L. Gunn (England)	**40**	**80**	**N. R. Sciver (England)**
54	85	L. S. Greenway (England)			

TEAM RECORDS

HIGHEST INNINGS TOTALS

314-2	Uganda v Mali at Kigali	2019
285-1	Tanzania v Mali at Kigali	2019
260-1	Indonesia v Philippines at Dasmarinas	2019-20
255-2	Bangladesh v Maldives at Pokhara	2019-20
250-3	England v South Africa at Taunton	2018
246-1	Rwanda v Mali at Kigali	2019
226-2	Australia v Sri Lanka at Sydney	2019-20
226-3	Australia v England at Chelmsford	2019
217-2	Indonesia v Philippines at Dasmarinas	2019-20
217-4	Australia v Sri Lanka at Sydney	2019-20
216-1	New Zealand v South Africa at Taunton	2018
213-4	Ireland v Netherlands at Deventer	2019
210-5	Namibia v Lesotho at Gaborone	2018

LOWEST INNINGS TOTALS

6	Mali v Rwanda at Kigali	2019
6	Maldives v Bangladesh at Pokhara	2019-20
8	Maldives v Nepal at Pokhara	2019-20
10	Mali v Uganda at Kigali	2019
11	Mali v Tanzania at Kigali	2019
14	China v United Arab Emirates at Bangkok	2018-19
15	Philippines v Indonesia at Dasmarinas	2019-20
16	Maldives v Nepal at Pokhara	2019-20
17†	Mali v Tanzania at Kigali	2019
18†	Mexico v Brazil at Bogota	2018-19

† *One woman absent.*

LARGEST VICTORIES

304 runs	Uganda (314-2 in 20 overs) v Mali (10 in 11.1 overs) at Kigali.	2019
268 runs	Tanzania (285-1 in 20 overs) v Mali (17 in 12.5 overs) at Kigali.	2019
249 runs	Bangladesh (255-2 in 20 overs) v Maldives (6 in 12.1 overs) at Pokhara . . .	2019-20

*There have been **33** instances of victory by ten wickets.*

OTHER RECORDS

MOST APPEARANCES

122	**S. W. Bates (NZ)**	**107**	**S. A. Campbelle (WI)**
120	**E. A. Perry (A)**	**107**	**M. M. Lanning (A)**
118	**D. J. S. Dottin (WI)**	106	Sana Mir (P)
115	**A. J. Healy (A)**	104	J. L. Gunn (E)
114	**H. Kaur (I)**	**103**	**M. du Preez (SA)**
113	**D. N. Wyatt (E)**	**102**	**Nida Dar (P)**
111	**A. Mohammed (WI)**	**102**	**A. E. Satterthwaite (NZ)**
108	**Bismah Maroof (P)**	**101**	**Javeria Khan (P)**
108	**S. R. Taylor (WI)**		

WOMEN'S TWENTY20 WORLD CUP WINNERS

2009	England	2013-14	Australia	2019-20	Australia
2010	Australia	2015-16	West Indies		
2012-13	Australia	2018-19	Australia		

BIRTHS AND DEATHS

TEST CRICKETERS

Full list from 1876-77 to January 25, 2021

In the Test career column, dates in italics indicate seasons embracing two different years (i.e. non-English seasons). In these cases, only the first year is given, e.g. *1876* for 1876-77. Some non-English series taking place outside the host country's normal season are dated by a single year.

The Test career figures are complete up to January 25, 2021; the one-day international and Twenty20 international totals up to December 31, 2020. Career figures are for one national team only; those players who have appeared for more than one Test team are listed on page 1167, and for more than one one-day international or Twenty20 international team on page 1170.

The forename by which a player is known is underlined if it is not his first name.

Family relationships are indicated by superscript numbers; where the relationship is not immediately apparent from a shared name, see the notes at the end of this section. (*CY 1889*) signifies that the player was a Wisden Cricketer of the Year in the 1889 Almanack. The 5/10 column indicates instances of a player taking five wickets in a Test innings and ten wickets in a match. O/T signifies number of one-day and Twenty20 internationals played.

[1] *Father and son(s).* [2] *Brothers.* [3] *Grandfather, father and son.* [4] *Grandfather and grandson.* [5] *Great-grandfather and great-grandson.*
† *Excludes matches for another Test team.* ‡ *Excludes matches for another ODI or T20I team.*

ENGLAND (696 players)

	Born	*Died*	*Tests*	*Test Career*	*Runs*	*HS*	*100s*	*Avge*	*Wkts*	*BB*	*5/10*	*Avge*	*Ct/St*	*O/T*
Abel Robert (*CY 1890*)	30.11.1857	10.12.1936	13	1888–1902	744	132*	2	37.20	–	–	–/–	–	13	
Absolom Charles Alfred	7.6.1846	30.7.1889	1	*1878*	58	52	0	29.00	–	–	–/–	–	0	
Adams Christopher John (*CY 2004*)	6.5.1970		5	*1999*	104	31	0	13.00	1	1-42	0/0	59.00	6	5
Afzaal Usman	9.6.1977		3	2001	83	54	0	16.60	1	1-49	0/0	49.00	0	
Agnew Jonathan Philip MBE (*CY 1988*)	4.4.1960		3	1984–1985	10	5	0	10.00	4	2-51	0/0	93.25	0	3
Ali Kabir	24.11.1980		1	2003	10	9	0	5.00	5	3-80	0/0	27.20	0	14
Ali Moeen Munir (*CY 2015*)	18.6.1987		60	2014–2019	2,782	155*	5	28.97	181	6-53	5/1	36.59	32	106/34
Allen David Arthur	29.10.1935	24.5.2014	39	*1959*–1966	918	88	0	25.50	122	5-30	4/0	30.97	10	
Allen *Sir* George Oswald Browning ("Gubby")	31.7.1902	29.11.1989	25	1930–*1947*	750	122	1	24.19	81	7-80	5/1	29.37	20	
Allom Maurice James Carrick	23.3.1906	8.4.1995	5	*1929–1930*	14	8*	0	14.00	14	5-38	1/0	18.92	0	
Allott Paul John Walter	14.9.1956		13	1981–1985	213	52*	0	14.20	26	6-61	1/0	41.69	4	13
Ambrose Timothy Raymond	1.12.1982		11	*2007–2008*	447	102	1	29.80	–	–	–/–	–	31	5/1
Ames Leslie Ethelbert George CBE (*CY 1929*)	3.12.1905	27.2.1990	47	1929–*1938*	2,434	149	8	40.56	–	–	–/–	–	74/23	

	Born	*Died*	*Tests*	*Test Career*	*Runs*	*HS*	*100s*	*Avge*	*Wkts*	*BB*	*5/10*	*Avge*	*Ct/St*	*O/T*
Amiss Dennis Leslie MBE (*CY 1975*)	7.4.1943		50	1966–1977	3,612	262*	11	46.30	–	–	–/–	–	24	18
Anderson James Michael OBE (*CY 2009*)	30.7.1982		157	2003–*2020*	1,221	81	0	9.69	606	7-42	30/3	26.60	96	194/19
Andrew Keith Vincent	15.12.1929	27.12.2010	2	*1954*–1963	29	15	0	9.66	–	–	–/–	–	1	
Ansari Zafar Shahaan	10.12.1991		3	*2016*	49	32	0	9.80	5	2-76	0/0	55.00	1	1
Appleyard Robert MBE (*CY 1952*)	27.6.1924	17.3.2015	9	1954–1956	51	19*	0	17.00	31	5-51	1/0	17.87	4	
Archer Alfred German	6.12.1871	15.7.1935	1	*1898*	31	24*	0	31.00	–	–	–/–	–	0	
Archer Jofra Chioke (*CY 2020*)	1.4.1995		11	2019–2020	139	30	0	8.68	38	6-45	3/0	31.10	2	17/7
Armitage Thomas	25.4.1848	21.9.1922	2	*1876*	33	21	0	11.00	0	0-15	0/0	–	0	
Arnold Edward George	7.11.1876	25.10.1942	10	*1903*–1907	160	40	0	13.33	31	5-37	1/0	25.41	8	
Arnold Geoffrey Graham (*CY 1972*)	3.9.1944		34	1967–1975	421	59	0	12.02	115	6-45	6/0	28.29	9	14
Arnold John	30.11.1907	4.4.1984	1	1931	34	34	0	17.00	–	–	–/–	–	0	
Astill William Ewart (*CY 1933*)	1.3.1888	10.2.1948	9	*1927–1929*	190	40	0	12.66	25	4-58	0/0	34.24	7	
Atherton Michael Andrew OBE (*CY 1991*)	23.3.1968		115	1989–2001	7,728	185*	16	37.69	2	1-20	0/0	151.00	83	54
Athey Charles William Jeffrey	27.9.1957		23	1980–1988	919	123	1	22.97	–	–	–/–	–	13	31
Attewell William (*CY 1892*)	12.6.1861	11.6.1927	10	*1884–1891*	150	43*	0	16.66	28	4-42	0/0	22.35	9	
Bailey Robert John	28.10.1963		4	1988–*1989*	119	43	0	14.87	–	–	–/–	–	0	4
Bailey Trevor Edward CBE (*CY 1950*)	3.12.1923	10.2.2011	61	1949–*1958*	2,290	134*	1	29.74	132	7-34	5/1	29.21	32	
[1] **Bairstow** David Leslie	1.9.1951	5.1.1998	4	1979–*1980*	125	59	0	20.83	–	–	–/–	–	12/1	21
[1] **Bairstow** Jonathan Marc (*CY 2016*)	26.9.1989		72	2012–*2020*	4,169	167*	6	35.03	–	–	–/–	–	186/13	83/46
Bakewell Alfred Harry (*CY 1934*)	2.11.1908	23.1.1983	6	1931–1935	409	107	1	45.44	0	0-8	0/0	–	3	
Balderstone John Christopher	16.11.1940	6.3.2000	2	1976	39	35	0	9.75	1	1-80	0/0	80.00	1	
Ball Jacob Timothy	14.3.1991		4	2016–*2017*	67	31	0	8.37	3	1-47	0/0	114.33	1	18/2
Ballance Gary Simon (*CY 2015*)	22.11.1989		23	*2013*–2017	1,498	156	4	37.45	0	0-0	0/0	–	22	16
Barber Robert William (*CY 1967*)	26.9.1935		28	1960–1968	1,495	185	1	35.59	42	4-132	0/0	43.00	21	
Barber Wilfred	18.4.1901	10.9.1968	2	1935	83	44	0	20.75	1	1-0	0/0	0.00	1	
Barlow Graham Derek	26.3.1950		3	*1976*–1977	17	7*	0	4.25	–	–	–/–	–	0	6
Barlow Richard Gorton	28.5.1851	31.7.1919	17	*1881–1886*	591	62	0	22.73	34	7-40	3/0	22.55	14	
Barnes Sydney Francis (*CY 1910*)	19.4.1873	26.12.1967	27	*1901–1913*	242	38*	0	8.06	189	9-103	24/7	16.43	12	
Barnes William (*CY 1890*)	27.5.1852	24.3.1899	21	1880–1890	725	134	1	23.38	51	6-28	3/0	15.54	19	
Barnett Charles John (*CY 1937*)	3.7.1910	28.5.1993	20	1933–1948	1,098	129	2	35.41	0	0-1	0/0	–	14	
Barnett Kim John (*CY 1989*)	17.7.1960		4	1988–1989	207	80	0	29.57	0	0-32	0/0	–	1	1
Barratt Fred	12.4.1894	29.1.1947	5	1929–*1929*	28	17	0	9.33	5	1-8	0/0	47.00	2	
Barrington Kenneth Frank (*CY 1960*)	24.11.1930	14.3.1981	82	1955–1968	6,806	256	20	58.67	29	3-4	0/0	44.82	58	
Barton Victor Alexander	6.10.1867	23.3.1906	1	*1891*	23	23	0	23.00	–	–	–/–	–	0	
Bates Willie	19.11.1855	8.1.1900	15	*1881–1886*	656	64	0	27.33	50	7-28	4/1	16.42	9	
Batty Gareth Jon	13.10.1977		9	*2003–2016*	149	38	0	14.90	15	3-55	0/0	60.93	3	10/1

	Born	*Died*	*Tests*	*Test Career*	*Runs*	*HS*	*100s*	*Avge*	*Wkts*	*BB*	*5/10*	*Avge*	*Ct/St*	*O/T*
Bean George	7.3.1864	16.3.1923	3	*1891*	92	50	0	18.40	–	–	–/–	–	4	
Bedser *Sir* Alec Victor CBE (*CY 1947*)	4.7.1918	4.4.2010	51	1946–1955	714	79	0	12.75	236	7-44	15/5	24.89	26	
Bell Ian Ronald MBE (*CY 2008*)	11.4.1982		118	2004–*2015*	7,727	235	22	42.69	1	1-33	0/0	76.00	100	161/8
Benjamin Joseph Emmanuel	2.2.1961		1	1994	0	0	0	0.00	4	4-42	0/0	20.00	0	2
Benson Mark Richard	6.7.1958		1	1986	51	30	0	25.50	–	–	–/–	–	0	1
Berry Robert	29.1.1926	2.12.2006	2	1950	6	4*	0	3.00	9	5-63	1/0	25.33	2	
Bess Dominic Mark	22.7.1997		12	2018–*2020*	255	57	0	25.50	31	5-30	2/0	33.09	3	
Bicknell Martin Paul (*CY 2001*)	14.1.1969		4	1993–2003	45	15	0	6.42	14	4-84	0/0	38.78	2	7
Binks James Graham (*CY 1969*)	5.10.1935		2	*1963*	91	55	0	22.75	–	–	–/–	–	8	
Bird Morice Carlos	25.3.1888	9.12.1933	10	*1909–1913*	280	61	0	18.66	8	3-11	0/0	15.00	5	
Birkenshaw Jack MBE	13.11.1940		5	*1972–1973*	148	64	0	21.14	13	5-57	1/0	36.07	3	
Blackwell Ian David	10.6.1978		1	*2005*	4	4	0	4.00	0	0-28	0/0	–	0	34
Blakey Richard John	15.1.1967		2	*1992*	7	6	0	1.75	–	–	–/–	–	2	3
Bligh *Hon.* Ivo Francis Walter	13.3.1859	10.4.1927	4	*1882*	62	19	0	10.33	–	–	–/–	–	7	
Blythe Colin (*CY 1904*)	30.5.1879	8.11.1917	19	*1901–1909*	183	27	0	9.63	100	8-59	9/4	18.63	6	
Board John Henry	23.2.1867	15.4.1924	6	*1898–1905*	108	29	0	10.80	–	–	–/–	–	8/3	
Bolus John Brian	31.1.1934	6.5.2020	7	1963–*1963*	496	88	0	41.33	0	0-16	0/0	–	2	
Booth Major William (*CY 1914*)	10.12.1886	1.7.1916	2	*1913*	46	32	0	23.00	7	4-49	0/0	18.57	0	
Bopara Ravinder Singh	4.5.1985		13	*2007*–2012	575	143	3	31.94	1	1-39	0/0	290.00	6	120/38
Borthwick Scott George	19.4.1990		1	*2013*	5	4	0	2.50	4	3-33	0/0	20.50	2	2/1
Bosanquet Bernard James Tindal (*CY 1905*)	13.10.1877	12.10.1936	7	*1903*–1905	147	27	0	13.36	25	8-107	2/0	24.16	9	
Botham *Lord* [Ian Terence] OBE (*CY 1978*)	24.11.1955		102	1977–1992	5,200	208	14	33.54	383	8-34	27/4	28.40	120	116
Bowden Montague Parker	1.11.1865	19.2.1892	2	*1888*	25	25	0	12.50	–	–	–/–	–	1	
Bowes William Eric (*CY 1932*)	25.7.1908	4.9.1987	15	1932–1946	28	10*	0	4.66	68	6-33	6/0	22.33	2	
Bowley Edward Henry (*CY 1930*)	6.6.1890	9.7.1974	5	1929–*1929*	252	109	1	36.00	0	0-7	0/0	–	2	
Boycott *Sir* Geoffrey OBE (*CY 1965*)	21.10.1940		108	1964–*1981*	8,114	246*	22	47.72	7	3-47	0/0	54.57	33	36
Bradley Walter Morris	2.1.1875	19.6.1944	2	1899	23	23*	0	23.00	6	5-67	1/0	38.83	0	
Braund Leonard Charles (*CY 1902*)	18.10.1875	23.12.1955	23	*1901–1907*	987	104	3	25.97	47	8-81	3/0	38.51	39	
Brearley John Michael OBE (*CY 1977*)	28.4.1942		39	1976–1981	1,442	91	0	22.88	–	–	–/–	–	52	25
Brearley Walter (*CY 1909*)	11.3.1876	30.1.1937	4	1905–1912	21	11*	0	7.00	17	5-110	1/0	21.11	0	
Brennan Donald Vincent	10.2.1920	9.1.1985	2	1951	16	16	0	8.00	–	–	–/–	–	0/1	
Bresnan Timothy Thomas (*CY 2012*)	28.2.1985		23	2009–*2013*	575	91	0	26.13	72	5-48	1/0	32.73	8	85/34
Briggs John (*CY 1889*)	3.10.1862	11.1.1902	33	*1884*–1899	815	121	1	18.11	118	8-11	9/4	17.75	12	
[1] **Broad** Brian Christopher	29.9.1957		25	1984–1989	1,661	162	6	39.54	0	0-4	0/0	–	10	34
[1] **Broad** Stuart Christopher John MBE (*CY 2010*)	24.6.1986		144	*2007–2020*	3,346	169	1	19.12	517	8-15	18/3	27.56	47	121/56
Brockwell William (*CY 1895*)	21.1.1865	30.6.1935	7	1893–1899	202	49	0	16.83	5	3-33	0/0	61.80	6	

	Born	Died	Tests	Test Career	Runs	HS	100s	Avge	Wkts	BB	5/10	Avge	Ct/St	O/T
Bromley-Davenport Hugh Richard	18.8.1870	23.5.1954	4	*1895–1898*	128	84	0	21.33	4	2-46	0/0	24.50	1	
Brookes Dennis (*CY 1957*)	29.10.1915	9.3.2006	1	*1947*	17	10	0	8.50	–	–	–/–	–	1	
Brown Alan	17.10.1935		2	*1961*	3	3*	0	–	3	3-27	0/0	50.00	1	
Brown David John	30.1.1942		26	1965–1969	342	44*	0	11.79	79	5-42	2/0	28.31	7	
Brown Frederick Richard MBE (*CY 1933*)	16.12.1910	24.7.1991	22	1931–1953	734	79	0	25.31	45	5-49	1/0	31.06	22	
Brown George	6.10.1887	3.12.1964	7	1921–*1922*	299	84	0	29.90	–	–	–/–	–	9/3	
Brown John Thomas (*CY 1895*)	20.8.1869	4.11.1904	8	*1894*–1899	470	140	1	36.15	0	0-22	0/0	–	7	
Brown Simon John Emmerson	29.6.1969		1	1996	11	10*	0	11.00	2	1-60	0/0	69.00	1	
Buckenham Claude Percival	16.1.1876	23.2.1937	4	*1909*	43	17	0	6.14	21	5-115	1/0	28.23	2	
Burns Rory Joseph (*CY 2019*)	26.8.1990		21	*2018*–2020	1,233	133	2	32.44	–	–	–/–	–	16	
[1] **Butcher** Alan Raymond (*CY 1991*)	7.1.1954		1	1979	34	20	0	17.00	0	0-9	0/0	–	0	1
[1] **Butcher** Mark Alan	23.8.1972		71	1997–*2004*	4,288	173*	8	34.58	15	4-42	0/0	36.06	61	
Butcher Roland Orlando	14.10.1953		3	*1980*	71	32	0	14.20	–	–	–/–	–	3	3
Butler Harold James	12.3.1913	17.7.1991	2	1947–*1947*	15	15*	0	15.00	12	4-34	0/0	17.91	1	
Butt Henry Rigden	27.12.1865	21.12.1928	3	*1895*	22	13	0	7.33	–	–	–/–	–	1/1	
Buttler Joseph Charles MBE (*CY 2019*)	8.9.1990		49	2014–*2020*	2,674	152	2	34.72	–	–	–/–	–	118/1	145/74
Caddick Andrew Richard (*CY 2001*)	21.11.1968		62	1993–*2002*	861	49*	0	10.37	234	7-46	13/1	29.91	21	54
Calthorpe *Hon.* Frederick Somerset Gough-	27.5.1892	19.11.1935	4	*1929*	129	49	0	18.42	1	1-38	0/0	91.00	3	
Capel David John	6.2.1963	2.9.2020	15	1987–*1989*	374	98	0	15.58	21	3-88	0/0	50.66	6	23
Carberry Michael Alexander	29.9.1980		6	*2009–2013*	345	60	0	28.75	–	–	–/–	–	7	6/1
Carr Arthur William (*CY 1923*)	21.5.1893	7.2.1963	11	*1922*–1929	237	63	0	19.75	–	–	–/–	–	3	
Carr Donald Bryce OBE (*CY 1960*)	28.12.1926	12.6.2016	2	*1951*	135	76	0	33.75	2	2-84	0/0	70.00	0	
Carr Douglas Ward (*CY 1910*)	17.3.1872	23.3.1950	1	1909	0	0	0	0.00	7	5-146	1/0	40.28	0	
Cartwright Thomas William MBE	22.7.1935	30.4.2007	5	1964–1965	26	9	0	5.20	15	6-94	1/0	36.26	2	
Chapman Arthur Percy Frank (*CY 1919*)	3.9.1900	16.9.1961	26	1924–*1930*	925	121	1	28.90	0	0-10	0/0	–	32	
Charlwood Henry Rupert James	19.12.1846	6.6.1888	2	*1876*	63	36	0	15.75	–	–	–/–	–	0	
Chatterton William	27.12.1861	19.3.1913	1	*1891*	48	48	0	48.00	–	–	–/–	–	0	
Childs John Henry (*CY 1987*)	15.8.1951		2	1988	2	2*	0	–	3	1-13	0/0	61.00	1	
Christopherson Stanley	11.11.1861	6.4.1949	1	1884	17	17	0	17.00	1	1-52	0/0	69.00	0	
Clark Edward Winchester	9.8.1902	28.4.1982	8	1929–1934	36	10	0	9.00	32	5-98	1/0	28.09	0	
Clarke Rikki	29.9.1981		2	*2003*	96	55	0	32.00	4	2-7	0/0	15.00	1	20
Clay John Charles	18.3.1898	11.8.1973	1	1935	–	–	–	–	0	0-30	0/0	–	1	
Close Dennis Brian CBE (*CY 1964*)	24.2.1931	14.9.2015	22	1949–1976	887	70	0	25.34	18	4-35	0/0	29.55	24	3
Coldwell Leonard John	10.1.1933	6.8.1996	7	1962–1964	9	6*	0	4.50	22	6-85	1/0	27.72	1	
Collingwood Paul David MBE (*CY 2007*)	26.5.1976		68	*2003–2010*	4,259	206	10	40.56	17	3-23	0/0	59.88	96	197/35‡
[4] **Compton** Denis Charles Scott CBE (*CY 1939*)	23.5.1918	23.4.1997	78	1937–*1956*	5,807	278	17	50.06	25	5-70	1/0	56.40	49	

	Born	Died	Tests	Test Career	Runs	HS	100s	Avge	Wkts	BB	5/10	Avge	Ct/St	O/T
[4] **Compton** Nicholas Richard Denis (*CY 2013*)	26.6.1983		16	*2012*–2016	775	117	2	28.70	–	–	–/–	–	7	
Cook *Sir* Alastair Nathan CBE (*CY 2012*)	25.12.1984		161	*2005*–2018	12,472	294	33	45.35	1	1-6	0/0	7.00	175	92/4
Cook Cecil ("Sam")	23.8.1921	5.9.1996	1	1947	4	4	0	2.00	0	0-40	0/0	–	0	
Cook Geoffrey	9.10.1951		7	*1981–1982*	203	66	0	15.61	0	0-4	0/0	–	9	6
Cook Nicholas Grant Billson	17.6.1956		15	1983–1989	179	31	0	8.52	52	6-65	4/1	32.48	5	3
Cope Geoffrey Alan	23.2.1947		3	*1977*	40	22	0	13.33	8	3-102	0/0	34.62	1	2
Copson William Henry (*CY 1937*)	27.4.1908	13.9.1971	3	1939–1947	6	6	0	6.00	15	5-85	1/0	19.80	1	
Cork Dominic Gerald (*CY 1996*)	7.8.1971		37	1995–2002	864	59	0	18.00	131	7-43	5/0	29.81	18	32
Cornford Walter Latter	25.12.1900	6.2.1964	4	*1929*	36	18	0	9.00	–	–	–/–	–	5/3	
Cottam Robert Michael Henry	16.10.1944		4	*1968–1972*	27	13	0	6.75	14	4-50	0/0	23.35	2	
Coventry *Hon.* Charles John	26.2.1867	2.6.1929	2	*1888*	13	12	0	13.00	–	–	–/–	–	0	
Cowans Norman George	17.4.1961		19	*1982*–1985	175	36	0	7.95	51	6-77	2/0	39.27	9	23
[1] **Cowdrey** Christopher Stuart	20.10.1957		6	*1984*–1988	101	38	0	14.42	4	2-65	0/0	77.25	5	3
[1] **Cowdrey** *Lord* [Michael Colin] CBE (*CY 1956*)	24.12.1932	4.12.2000	114	*1954–1974*	7,624	182	22	44.06	0	0-1	0/0	–	120	1
Coxon Alexander	18.1.1916	22.1.2006	1	1948	19	19	0	9.50	3	2-90	0/0	57.33	0	
Crane Mason Sidney	18.02.1997		1	*2017*	6	4	0	3.00	1	1-193	0/0	193.00	0	0/2
Cranston James	9.1.1859	10.12.1904	1	1890	31	16	0	15.50	–	–	–/–	–	1	
Cranston Kenneth	20.10.1917	8.1.2007	8	1947–1948	209	45	0	14.92	18	4-12	0/0	25.61	3	
Crapp John Frederick	14.10.1912	13.2.1981	7	1948–*1948*	319	56	0	29.00	–	–	–/–	–	7	
Crawford John Neville (*CY 1907*)	1.12.1886	2.5.1963	12	*1905–1907*	469	74	0	22.33	39	5-48	3/0	29.48	13	
Crawley John Paul	21.9.1971		37	1994–*2002*	1,800	156*	4	34.61	–	–	–/–	–	29	13
Crawley Zak (*CY 2021*)	3.2.1998		10	*2019–2020*	616	267	1	38.50	–	–	–/–	–	8	
Croft Robert Damien Bale MBE	25.5.1970		21	1996–2001	421	37*	0	16.19	49	5-95	1/0	37.24	10	50
[2] **Curran** Samuel Matthew (*CY 2019*)	3.6.1998		21	2018–*2020*	741	78	0	25.55	44	4-58	0/0	32.52	4	5/8
[2] **Curran** Thomas Kevin	12.03.1995		2	*2017*	66	39	0	33.00	2	1-65	0/0	100.00	0	24/27
Curtis Timothy Stephen	15.1.1960		5	1988–1989	140	41	0	15.55	0	0-7	0/0	–	3	
Cuttell Willis Robert (*CY 1898*)	13.9.1863	9.12.1929	2	*1898*	65	21	0	16.25	6	3-17	0/0	12.16	2	
Dawson Edward William	13.2.1904	4.6.1979	5	*1927–1929*	175	55	0	19.44	–	–	–/–	–	0	
Dawson Liam Andrew	1.3.1990		3	*2016*–2017	84	66*	0	21.00	7	2-34	0/0	42.57	2	3/6
Dawson Richard Kevin James	4.8.1980		7	*2001–2002*	114	19*	0	11.40	11	4-134	0/0	61.54	3	
Dean Harry	13.8.1884	12.3.1957	3	1912	10	8	0	5.00	11	4-19	0/0	13.90	2	
DeFreitas Phillip Anthony Jason (*CY 1992*)	18.2.1966		44	*1986*–1995	934	88	0	14.82	140	7-70	4/0	33.57	14	103
Denly Joseph Liam	16.3.1986		15	*2018*–2020	827	94	0	29.53	2	2-42	0/0	109.50	7	16/13
Denness Michael Henry OBE (*CY 1975*)	1.12.1940	19.4.2013	28	1969–1975	1,667	188	4	39.69	–	–	–/–	–	28	12
Denton David (*CY 1906*)	4.7.1874	16.2.1950	11	1905–*1909*	424	104	1	20.19	–	–	–/–	–	8	
Dewes John Gordon	11.10.1926	12.5.2015	5	1948–*1950*	121	67	0	12.10	–	–	–/–	–	0	

	Born	*Died*	*Tests*	*Test Career*	*Runs*	*HS*	*100s*	*Avge*	*Wkts*	*BB*	*5/10*	*Avge*	*Ct/St*	*O/T*
Dexter Edward Ralph CBE (*CY 1961*)	15.5.1935		62	1958–1968	4,502	205	9	47.89	66	4-10	0/0	34.93	29	
Dilley Graham Roy	18.5.1959	5.10.2011	41	*1979*–1989	521	56	0	13.35	138	6-38	6/0	29.76	10	36
Dipper Alfred Ernest	9.11.1885	7.11.1945	1	1921	51	40	0	25.50	–	–	–/–	–	0	
Doggart George Hubert Graham OBE	18.7.1925	16.2.2018	2	1950	76	29	0	19.00	–	–	–/–	–	3	
D'Oliveira Basil Lewis CBE (*CY 1967*)	4.10.1931	18.11.2011	44	1966–1972	2,484	158	5	40.06	47	3-46	0/0	39.55	29	4
Dollery Horace Edgar ("Tom") (*CY 1952*)	14.10.1914	20.1.1987	4	1947–1950	72	37	0	10.28	–	–	–/–	–	1	
Dolphin Arthur	24.12.1885	23.10.1942	1	*1920*	1	1	0	0.50	–	–	–/–	–	1	
Douglas John William Henry Tyler (*CY 1915*)	3.9.1882	19.12.1930	23	*1911–1924*	962	119	1	29.15	45	5-46	1/0	33.02	9	
Downton Paul Rupert	4.4.1957		30	*1980*–1988	785	74	0	19.62	–	–	–/–	–	70/5	28
Druce Norman Frank (*CY 1898*)	1.1.1875	27.10.1954	5	*1897*	252	64	0	28.00	–	–	–/–	–	5	
Ducat Andrew (*CY 1920*)	16.2.1886	23.7.1942	1	1921	5	3	0	2.50	–	–	–/–	–	1	
Duckett Ben Matthew (*CY 2017*)	17.10.1994		4	*2016*	110	56	0	15.71	–	–	–/–	–	1	3/1
Duckworth George (*CY 1929*)	9.5.1901	5.1.1966	24	1924–1936	234	39*	0	14.62	–	–	–/–	–	45/15	
Duleepsinhji Kumar Shri (*CY 1930*)	13.6.1905	5.12.1959	12	1929–1931	995	173	3	58.52	0	0-7	0/0	–	10	
Durston Frederick John	11.7.1893	8.4.1965	1	1921	8	6*	0	8.00	5	4-102	0/0	27.20	0	
Ealham Mark Alan	27.8.1969		8	1996–1998	210	53*	0	21.00	17	4-21	0/0	28.70	4	64
Edmonds Philippe-Henri	8.3.1951		51	1975–1987	875	64	0	17.50	125	7-66	2/0	34.18	42	29
Edrich John Hugh MBE (*CY 1966*)	21.6.1937	23.12.2020	77	1963–1976	5,138	310*	12	43.54	0	0-6	0/0	–	43	7
Edrich William John (*CY 1940*)	26.3.1916	24.4.1986	39	1938–*1954*	2,440	219	6	40.00	41	4-68	0/0	41.29	39	
Elliott Harry	2.11.1891	2.2.1976	4	*1927–1933*	61	37*	0	15.25	–	–	–/–	–	8/3	
Ellison Richard Mark (*CY 1986*)	21.9.1959		11	1984–1986	202	41	0	13.46	35	6-77	3/1	29.94	2	14
Emburey John Ernest (*CY 1984*)	20.8.1952		64	1978–1995	1,713	75	0	22.53	147	7-78	6/0	38.40	34	61
Emmett George Malcolm	2.12.1912	18.12.1976	1	1948	10	10	0	5.00	–	–	–/–	–	0	
Emmett Thomas	3.9.1841	29.6.1904	7	*1876–1881*	160	48	0	13.33	9	7-68	1/0	31.55	9	
Evans Alfred John	1.5.1889	18.9.1960	1	1921	18	14	0	9.00	–	–	–/–	–	0	
Evans Thomas Godfrey CBE (*CY 1951*)	18.8.1920	3.5.1999	91	1946–1959	2,439	104	2	20.49	–	–	–/–	–	173/46	
Fagg Arthur Edward	18.6.1915	13.9.1977	5	1936–1939	150	39	0	18.75	–	–	–/–	–	5	
Fairbrother Neil Harvey	9.9.1963		10	1987–*1992*	219	83	0	15.64	0	0-9	0/0	–	4	75
Fane Frederick Luther	27.4.1875	27.11.1960	14	*1905–1909*	682	143	1	26.23	–	–	–/–	–	6	
Farnes Kenneth (*CY 1939*)	8.7.1911	20.10.1941	15	1934–*1938*	58	20	0	4.83	60	6-96	3/1	28.65	1	
Farrimond William	23.5.1903	15.11.1979	4	*1930*–1935	116	35	0	16.57	–	–	–/–	–	5/2	
Fender Percy George Herbert (*CY 1915*)	22.8.1892	15.6.1985	13	*1920*–1929	380	60	0	19.00	29	5-90	2/0	40.86	14	
Ferris John James	21.5.1867	17.11.1900	1†	*1891*	16	16	0	16.00	13	7-37	2/1	7.00	0	
Fielder Arthur (*CY 1907*)	19.7.1877	30.8.1949	6	*1903–1907*	78	20	0	11.14	26	6-82	1/0	27.34	4	
Finn Steven Thomas	4.4.1989		36	*2009–2016*	279	56	0	11.16	125	6-79	5/0	30.40	8	69/21
Fishlock Laurence Barnard (*CY 1947*)	2.1.1907	25.6.1986	4	1936–*1946*	47	19*	0	11.75	–	–	–/–	–	1	

	Born	*Died*	*Tests*	*Test Career*	*Runs*	*HS*	*100s*	*Avge*	*Wkts*	*BB*	*5/10*	*Avge*	*Ct/St*	*O/T*
Flavell John Alfred (*CY 1965*)	15.5.1929	25.2.2004	4	1961–1964	31	14	0	7.75	7	2-65	0/0	52.42	0	
Fletcher Keith William Robert OBE (*CY 1974*)	20.5.1944		59	1968–*1981*	3,272	216	7	39.90	2	1-6	0/0	96.50	54	24
Flintoff Andrew MBE (*CY 2004*)	6.12.1977		78§	1998–2009	3,795	167	5	31.89	219	5-58	3/0	33.34	52	138‡/7
Flowers Wilfred	7.12.1856	1.11.1926	8	*1884*–1893	254	56	0	18.14	14	5-46	1/0	21.14	2	
Foakes Benjamin Thomas	15.2.1993		5	*2018*	332	107	1	41.50	–	–	–/–	–	10/2	1/1
Ford Francis Gilbertson Justice	14.12.1866	7.2.1940	5	*1894*	168	48	0	18.66	1	1-47	0/0	129.00	5	
Foster Frank Rowbotham (*CY 1912*)	31.1.1889	3.5.1958	11	*1911*–1912	330	71	0	23.57	45	6-91	4/0	20.57	11	
Foster James Savin	15.4.1980		7	*2001–2002*	226	48	0	25.11	–	–	–/–	–	17/1	11/5
Foster Neil Alan (*CY 1988*)	6.5.1962		29	1983–1993	446	39	0	11.73	88	8-107	5/1	32.85	7	48
Foster Reginald Erskine ("Tip") (*CY 1900*)	16.4.1878	13.5.1914	8	*1903*–1907	602	287	1	46.30	–	–	–/–	–	13	
Fothergill Arnold James	26.8.1854	1.8.1932	2	*1888*	33	32	0	16.50	8	4-19	0/0	11.25	0	
Fowler Graeme	20.4.1957		21	1982–*1984*	1,307	201	3	35.32	0	0-0	0/0	–	10	26
Fraser Angus Robert Charles MBE (*CY 1996*)	8.8.1965		46	1989–*1998*	388	32	0	7.46	177	8-53	13/2	27.32	9	42
Freeman Alfred Percy ("Tich") (*CY 1923*)	17.5.1888	28.1.1965	12	*1924*–1929	154	50*	0	14.00	66	7-71	5/3	25.86	4	
French Bruce Nicholas	13.8.1959		16	1986–*1987*	308	59	0	18.11	–	–	–/–	–	38/1	13
Fry Charles Burgess (*CY 1895*)	25.4.1872	7.9.1956	26	*1895*–1912	1,223	144	2	32.18	0	0-3	0/0	–	17	
Gallian Jason Edward Riche	25.6.1971		3	1995–*1995*	74	28	0	12.33	0	0-6	0/0	–	1	
Gatting Michael William OBE (*CY 1984*)	6.6.1957		79	*1977–1994*	4,409	207	10	35.55	4	1-14	0/0	79.25	59	92
Gay Leslie Hewitt	24.3.1871	1.11.1949	1	*1894*	37	33	0	18.50	–	–	–/–	–	3/1	
Geary George (*CY 1927*)	9.7.1893	6.3.1981	14	1924–1934	249	66	0	15.56	46	7-70	4/1	29.41	13	
Gibb Paul Antony	11.7.1913	7.12.1977	8	*1938–1946*	581	120	2	44.69	–	–	–/–	–	3/1	
Giddins Edward Simon Hunter	20.7.1971		4	1999–2000	10	7	0	2.50	12	5-15	1/0	20.00	0	
Gifford Norman MBE (*CY 1975*)	30.3.1940		15	1964–1973	179	25*	0	16.27	33	5-55	1/0	31.09	8	2
Giles Ashley Fraser MBE (*CY 2005*)	19.3.1973		54	1998–*2006*	1,421	59	0	20.89	143	5-57	5/0	40.60	33	62
[2] **Gilligan** Alfred Herbert <u>Harold</u>	29.6.1896	5.5.1978	4	*1929*	71	32	0	17.75	–	–	–/–	–	0	
[2] **Gilligan** Arthur Edward Robert (*CY 1924*)	23.12.1894	5.9.1976	11	*1922–1924*	209	39*	0	16.07	36	6-7	2/1	29.05	3	
Gimblett Harold (*CY 1953*)	19.10.1914	30.3.1978	3	1936–1939	129	67*	0	32.25	–	–	–/–	–	1	
Gladwin Clifford	3.4.1916	9.4.1988	8	1947–1949	170	51*	0	28.33	15	3-21	0/0	38.06	2	
Goddard Thomas William John (*CY 1938*)	1.10.1900	22.5.1966	8	1930–1939	13	8	0	6.50	22	6-29	1/0	26.72	3	
Gooch Graham Alan OBE (*CY 1980*)	23.7.1953		118	1975–*1994*	8,900	333	20	42.58	23	3-39	0/0	46.47	103	125
Gough Darren MBE (*CY 1999*)	18.9.1970		58	1994–2003	855	65	0	12.57	229	6-42	9/0	28.39	13	158‡/2
Gover Alfred Richard MBE (*CY 1937*)	29.2.1908	7.10.2001	4	1936–1946	2	2*	0	–	8	3-85	0/0	44.87	1	
Gower David Ivon OBE (*CY 1979*)	1.4.1957		117	1978–1992	8,231	215	18	44.25	1	1-1	0/0	20.00	74	114
[2] **Grace** Edward Mills	28.11.1841	20.5.1911	1	1880	36	36	0	18.00	–	–	–/–	–	1	
[2] **Grace** George <u>Frederick</u>	13.12.1850	22.9.1880	1	1880	0	0	0	0.00	–	–	–/–	–	2	

§ *Flintoff's figures exclude 50 runs and seven wickets for the ICC World XI v Australia in the Super Series Test in 2005-06.*

	Born	Died	Tests	Test Career	Runs	HS	100s	Avge	Wkts	BB	5/10	Avge	Ct/St	O/T
[2] **Grace** William Gilbert (*CY 1896*)	18.7.1848	23.10.1915	22	1880–1899	1,098	170	2	32.29	9	2-12	0/0	26.22	39	
Graveney Thomas William OBE (*CY 1953*)	16.6.1927	3.11.2015	79	1951–1969	4,882	258	11	44.38	1	1-34	0/0	167.00	80	
Greenhough Thomas	9.11.1931	15.9.2009	4	1959–1960	4	2	0	1.33	16	5-35	1/0	22.31	1	
Greenwood Andrew	20.8.1847	12.2.1889	2	*1876*	77	49	0	19.25	–	–	–/–	–	2	
[2] **Greig** Anthony William (*CY 1975*)	6.10.1946	29.12.2012	58	1972–1977	3,599	148	8	40.43	141	8-86	6/2	32.20	87	22
[2] **Greig** Ian Alexander	8.12.1955		2	1982	26	14	0	6.50	4	4-53	0/0	28.50	0	
Grieve Basil Arthur Firebrace	28.5.1864	19.11.1917	2	*1888*	40	14*	0	40.00	–	–	–/–	–	0	
Griffith Stewart Cathie CBE ("Billy")	16.6.1914	7.4.1993	3	*1947–1948*	157	140	1	31.40	–	–	–/–	–	5	
[2] **Gunn** George (*CY 1914*)	13.6.1879	29.6.1958	15	*1907–1929*	1,120	122*	2	40.00	0	0-8	0/0	–	15	
[2] **Gunn** John Richmond (*CY 1904*)	19.7.1876	21.8.1963	6	*1901*–1905	85	24	0	10.62	18	5-76	1/0	21.50	3	
Gunn William (*CY 1890*)	4.12.1858	29.1.1921	11	*1886*–1899	392	102*	1	21.77	–	–	–/–	–	5	
Habib Aftab	7.2.1972		2	1999	26	19	0	8.66	–	–	–/–	–	0	
Haig Nigel Esmé	12.12.1887	27.10.1966	5	1921–*1929*	126	47	0	14.00	13	3-73	0/0	34.46	4	
Haigh Schofield (*CY 1901*)	19.3.1871	27.2.1921	11	*1898*–1912	113	25	0	7.53	24	6-11	1/0	25.91	8	
Hales Alexander Daniel	3.1.1989		11	*2015*–2016	573	94	0	27.28	0	0-2	0/0	–	8	70/60
Hallows Charles (*CY 1928*)	4.4.1895	10.11.1972	2	1921–1928	42	26	0	42.00	–	–	–/–	–	0	
Hameed Haseeb	17.1.1997		3	*2016*	219	82	0	43.80	–	–	–/–	–	4	
Hamilton Gavin Mark	16.9.1974		1	*1999*	0	0	0	0.00	0	0-63	0/0	–	0	0‡
Hammond Walter Reginald (*CY 1928*)	19.6.1903	1.7.1965	85	*1927–1946*	7,249	336*	22	58.45	83	5-36	2/0	37.80	110	
Hampshire John Harry	10.2.1941	1.3.2017	8	1969–1975	403	107	1	26.86	–	–	–/–	–	9	3
Hardinge Harold Thomas William ("Wally") (*CY 1915*)	25.2.1886	8.5.1965	1	1921	30	25	0	15.00	–	–	–/–	–	0	
[1] **Hardstaff** Joseph snr	9.11.1882	2.4.1947	5	*1907*	311	72	0	31.10	–	–	–/–	–	1	
[1] **Hardstaff** Joseph jnr (*CY 1938*)	3.7.1911	1.1.1990	23	1935–1948	1,636	205*	4	46.74	–	–	–/–	–	9	
Harmison Stephen James MBE (*CY 2005*)	23.10.1978		62§	2002–2009	742	49*	0	12.16	222	7-12	8/1	31.94	7	58/2
Harris *Lord* [George Robert Canning]	3.2.1851	24.3.1932	4	*1878*–1884	145	52	0	29.00	0	0-14	0/0	–	2	
Hartley John Cabourn	15.11.1874	8.3.1963	2	*1905*	15	9	0	3.75	1	1-62	0/0	115.00	2	
Hawke *Lord* [Martin Bladen] (*CY 1909*)	16.8.1860	10.10.1938	5	*1895–1898*	55	30	0	7.85	–	–	–/–	–	3	
Hayes Ernest George (*CY 1907*)	6.11.1876	2.12.1953	5	*1905*–1912	86	35	0	10.75	1	1-28	0/0	52.00	2	
Hayes Frank Charles	6.12.1946		9	1973–1976	244	106*	1	15.25	–	–	–/–	–	7	6
Hayward Thomas Walter (*CY 1895*)	29.3.1871	19.7.1939	35	*1895*–1909	1,999	137	3	34.46	14	4-22	0/0	36.71	19	
[3] **Headley** Dean Warren	27.1.1970		15	1997–1999	186	31	0	8.45	60	6-60	1/0	27.85	7	13
[2] **Hearne** Alec (*CY 1894*)	22.7.1863	16.5.1952	1	*1891*	9	9	0	9.00	–	–	–/–	–	1	
[1, 2] **Hearne** Frank	23.11.1858	14.7.1949	2†	*1888*	47	27	0	23.50	–	–	–/–	–	1	
[2] **Hearne** George Gibbons	7.7.1856	13.2.1932	1	*1891*	0	0	0	0.00	–	–	–/–	–	0	

§ *Harmison's figures exclude one run and four wickets for the ICC World XI v Australia in the Super Series Test in 2005-06.*

	Born	*Died*	*Tests*	*Test Career*	*Runs*	*HS*	*100s*	*Avge*	*Wkts*	*BB*	*5/10*	*Avge*	*Ct/St*	*O/T*
Hearne John Thomas (*CY 1892*)	3.5.1867	17.4.1944	12	*1891*–1899	126	40	0	9.00	49	6-41	4/1	22.08	4	
Hearne John William (*CY 1912*)	11.2.1891	14.9.1965	24	*1911*–1926	806	114	1	26.00	30	5-49	1/0	48.73	13	
Hegg Warren Kevin	23.2.1968		2	*1998*	30	15	0	7.50	–	–	–/–	–	8	
Hemmings Edward Ernest	20.2.1949		16	1982–*1990*	383	95	0	22.52	43	6-58	1/0	42.44	5	33
Hendren Elias Henry ("Patsy") (*CY 1920*)	5.2.1889	4.10.1962	51	*1920–1934*	3,525	205*	7	47.63	1	1-27	0/0	31.00	33	
Hendrick Michael (*CY 1978*)	22.10.1948		30	1974–1981	128	15	0	6.40	87	4-28	0/0	25.83	25	22
Heseltine Christopher	26.11.1869	13.6.1944	2	*1895*	18	18	0	9.00	5	5-38	1/0	16.80	3	
Hick Graeme Ashley MBE (*CY 1987*)	23.5.1966		65	1991–*2000*	3,383	178	6	31.32	23	4-126	0/0	56.78	90	120
Higgs Kenneth (*CY 1968*)	14.1.1937	7.9.2016	15	1965–1968	185	63	0	11.56	71	6-91	2/0	20.74	4	
Hill Allen	14.11.1843	28.8.1910	2	*1876*	101	49	0	50.50	7	4-27	0/0	18.57	1	
Hill Arthur James Ledger	26.7.1871	6.9.1950	3	*1895*	251	124	1	62.75	4	4-8	0/0	2.00	1	
Hilton Malcolm Jameson (*CY 1957*)	2.8.1928	8.7.1990	4	1950–*1951*	37	15	0	7.40	14	5-61	1/0	34.07	1	
Hirst George Herbert (*CY 1901*)	7.9.1871	10.5.1954	24	*1897*–1909	790	85	0	22.57	59	5-48	3/0	30.00	18	
Hitch John William (*CY 1914*)	7.5.1886	7.7.1965	7	*1911*–1921	103	51*	0	14.71	7	2-31	0/0	46.42	4	
Hobbs *Sir* John Berry (*CY 1909*)	16.12.1882	21.12.1963	61	*1907*–1930	5,410	211	15	56.94	1	1-19	0/0	165.00	17	
Hobbs Robin Nicholas Stuart	8.5.1942		7	1967–1971	34	15*	0	6.80	12	3-25	0/0	40.08	8	
Hoggard Matthew James MBE (*CY 2006*)	31.12.1976		67	2000–*2007*	473	38	0	7.27	248	7-61	7/1	30.50	24	26
Hollies William Eric (*CY 1955*)	5.6.1912	16.4.1981	13	*1934*–1950	37	18*	0	5.28	44	7-50	5/0	30.27	2	
[2] **Hollioake** Adam John (*CY 2003*)	5.9.1971		4	1997–*1997*	65	45	0	10.83	2	2-31	0/0	33.50	4	35
[2] **Hollioake** Benjamin Caine	11.11.1977	23.3.2002	2	1997–1998	44	28	0	11.00	4	2-105	0/0	49.75	2	20
Holmes Errol Reginald Thorold (*CY 1936*)	21.8.1905	16.8.1960	5	*1934*–1935	114	85*	0	16.28	2	1-10	0/0	38.00	4	
Holmes Percy (*CY 1920*)	25.11.1886	3.9.1971	7	1921–1932	357	88	0	27.46	–	–	–/–	–	3	
Hone Leland	30.1.1853	31.12.1896	1	*1878*	13	7	0	6.50	–	–	–/–	–	2	
Hopwood John Leonard	30.10.1903	15.6.1985	2	1934	12	8	0	6.00	0	0-16	0/0	–	0	
Hornby Albert Neilson ("Monkey")	10.2.1847	17.12.1925	3	*1878*–1884	21	9	0	3.50	1	1-0	0/0	0.00	0	
Horton Martin John	21.4.1934	3.4.2011	2	1959	60	58	0	30.00	2	2-24	0/0	29.50	2	
Howard Nigel David	18.5.1925	31.5.1979	4	*1951*	86	23	0	17.20	–	–	–/–	–	4	
Howell Henry	29.11.1890	9.7.1932	5	*1920*–1924	15	5	0	7.50	7	4-115	0/0	79.85	0	
Howorth Richard	26.4.1909	2.4.1980	5	1947–*1947*	145	45*	0	18.12	19	6-124	1/0	33.42	2	
Humphries Joseph	19.5.1876	7.5.1946	3	*1907*	44	16	0	8.80	–	–	–/–	–	7	
Hunter Joseph	3.8.1855	4.1.1891	5	*1884*	93	39*	0	18.60	–	–	–/–	–	8/3	
Hussain Nasser OBE (*CY 2003*)	28.3.1968		96	*1989*–2004	5,764	207	14	37.18	0	0-15	0/0	–	67	88
Hutchings Kenneth Lotherington (*CY 1907*)	7.12.1882	3.9.1916	7	*1907*–1909	341	126	1	28.41	1	1-5	0/0	81.00	9	
[1] **Hutton** *Sir* Leonard (*CY 1938*)	23.6.1916	6.9.1990	79	1937–*1954*	6,971	364	19	56.67	3	1-2	0/0	77.33	57	
[1] **Hutton** Richard Anthony	6.9.1942		5	1971	219	81	0	36.50	9	3-72	0/0	28.55	9	
Iddon John	8.1.1902	17.4.1946	5	*1934*–1935	170	73	0	28.33	0	0-3	0/0	–	0	

	Born	*Died*	*Tests*	*Test Career*	*Runs*	*HS*	*100s*	*Avge*	*Wkts*	*BB*	*5/10*	*Avge*	*Ct/St*	*O/T*
Igglesden Alan Paul	8.10.1964		3	1989–*1993*	6	3*	0	3.00	6	2-91	0/0	54.83	1	4
Ikin John Thomas	7.3.1918	15.9.1984	18	1946–1955	606	60	0	20.89	3	1-38	0/0	118.00	31	
Illingworth Raymond CBE (*CY 1960*)	8.6.1932		61	1958–1973	1,836	113	2	23.24	122	6-29	3/0	31.20	45	3
Illingworth Richard Keith	23.8.1963		9	1991–*1995*	128	28	0	18.28	19	4-96	0/0	32.36	5	25
Ilott Mark Christopher	27.8.1970		5	1993–*1995*	28	15	0	7.00	12	3-48	0/0	45.16	0	
Insole Douglas John CBE (*CY 1956*)	18.4.1926	5.8.2017	9	1950–1957	408	110*	1	27.20	–	–	–/–	–	8	
Irani Ronald Charles	26.10.1971		3	1996–1999	86	41	0	17.20	3	1-22	0/0	37.33	2	31
Jackman Robin David (*CY 1981*)	13.8.1945	25.12.2020	4	*1980*–1982	42	17	0	7.00	14	4-110	0/0	31.78	0	15
Jackson *Sir* Francis Stanley (*CY 1894*)	21.11.1870	9.3.1947	20	1893–1905	1,415	144*	5	48.79	24	5-52	1/0	33.29	10	
Jackson Herbert Leslie (*CY 1959*)	5.4.1921	25.4.2007	2	1949–1961	15	8	0	15.00	7	2-26	0/0	22.14	1	
James Stephen Peter	7.9.1967		2	1998	71	36	0	17.75	–	–	–/–	–	0	
Jameson John Alexander MBE	30.6.1941		4	1971–*1973*	214	82	0	26.75	1	1-17	0/0	17.00	0	3
Jardine Douglas Robert (*CY 1928*)	23.10.1900	18.6.1958	22	1928–*1933*	1,296	127	1	48.00	0	0-10	0/0	–	26	
Jarvis Paul William	29.6.1965		9	*1987–1992*	132	29*	0	10.15	21	4-107	0/0	45.95	2	16
Jenkins Roland Oliver (*CY 1950*)	24.11.1918	22.7.1995	9	*1948*–1952	198	39	0	18.00	32	5-116	1/0	34.31	4	
Jennings Keaton Kent	19.6.1992		17	*2016–2018*	781	146*	2	25.19	0	0-2	0/0	–	17	
Jessop Gilbert Laird (*CY 1898*)	19.5.1874	11.5.1955	18	1899–1912	569	104	1	21.88	10	4-68	0/0	35.40	11	
Johnson Richard Leonard	29.12.1974		3	2003–*2003*	59	26	0	14.75	16	6-33	2/0	17.18	0	10
Jones Arthur Owen	16.8.1872	21.12.1914	12	1899–1909	291	34	0	13.85	3	3-73	0/0	44.33	15	
Jones Geraint Owen MBE	14.7.1976		34	*2003–2006*	1,172	100	1	23.91	–	–	–/–	–	128/5	49‡/2
[1] **Jones** Ivor Jeffrey	10.12.1941		15	*1963–1967*	38	16	0	4.75	44	6-118	1/0	40.20	4	
[1] **Jones** Simon Philip MBE (*CY 2006*)	25.12.1978		18	2002–2005	205	44	0	15.76	59	6-53	3/0	28.23	4	8
Jordan Christopher James	4.10.1988		8	2014–*2014*	180	35	0	18.00	21	4-18	0/0	35.80	14	34/55
Jupp Henry	19.11.1841	8.4.1889	2	*1876*	68	63	0	17.00	–	–	–/–	–	2	
Jupp Vallance William Crisp (*CY 1928*)	27.3.1891	9.7.1960	8	1921–1928	208	38	0	17.33	28	4-37	0/0	22.00	5	
Keeton William Walter (*CY 1940*)	30.4.1905	10.10.1980	2	1934–1939	57	25	0	14.25	–	–	–/–	–	0	
Kennedy Alexander Stuart (*CY 1933*)	24.1.1891	15.11.1959	5	*1922*	93	41*	0	15.50	31	5-76	2/0	19.32	5	
Kenyon Donald	15.5.1924	12.11.1996	8	*1951*–1955	192	87	0	12.80	–	–	–/–	–	5	
Kerrigan Simon Christopher	10.5.1989		1	2013	1	1*	0	–	0	0-53	0/0	–	0	
Key Robert William Trevor (*CY 2005*)	12.5.1979		15	2002–*2004*	775	221	1	31.00	–	–	–/–	–	11	5/1
Khan Amjad	14.10.1980		1	*2008*	–	–	–	–	1	1-111	0/0	122.00	0	0/1
Killick *Rev.* Edgar Thomas	9.5.1907	18.5.1953	2	1929	81	31	0	20.25	–	–	–/–	–	2	
Kilner Roy (*CY 1924*)	17.10.1890	5.4.1928	9	1924–1926	233	74	0	33.28	24	4-51	0/0	30.58	6	
King John Herbert	16.4.1871	18.11.1946	1	1909	64	60	0	32.00	1	1-99	0/0	99.00	0	
Kinneir Septimus Paul (*CY 1912*)	13.5.1871	16.10.1928	1	*1911*	52	30	0	26.00	–	–	–/–	–	0	
Kirtley Robert James	10.1.1975		4	2003–*2003*	32	12	0	5.33	19	6-34	1/0	29.52	3	11/1

	Born	Died	Tests	Test Career	Runs	HS	100s	Avge	Wkts	BB	5/10	Avge	Ct/St	O/T
Knight Albert Ernest (*CY 1904*)	8.10.1872	25.4.1946	3	*1903*	81	70*	0	16.20	–	–	–/–	–	1	
Knight Barry Rolfe	18.2.1938		29	*1961*–1969	812	127	2	26.19	70	4-38	0/0	31.75	14	
Knight Donald John (*CY 1915*)	12.5.1894	5.1.1960	2	1921	54	38	0	13.50	–	–	–/–	–	1	
Knight Nicholas Verity	28.11.1969		17	1995–2001	719	113	1	23.96	–	–	–/–	–	26	100
Knott Alan Philip Eric MBE (*CY 1970*)	9.4.1946		95	1967–1981	4,389	135	5	32.75	–	–	–/–	–	250/19	20
Knox Neville Alexander (*CY 1907*)	10.10.1884	3.3.1935	2	1907	24	8*	0	8.00	3	2-39	0/0	35.00	0	
Laker James Charles (*CY 1952*)	9.2.1922	23.4.1986	46	*1947–1958*	676	63	0	14.08	193	10-53	9/3	21.24	12	
Lamb Allan Joseph (*CY 1981*)	20.6.1954		79	1982–1992	4,656	142	14	36.09	1	1-6	0/0	23.00	75	122
Langridge James (*CY 1932*)	10.7.1906	10.9.1966	8	1933–1946	242	70	0	26.88	19	7-56	2/0	21.73	6	
Larkins Wayne	22.11.1953		13	*1979–1990*	493	64	0	20.54	–	–	–/–	–	8	25
Larter John David Frederick	24.4.1940		10	1962–1965	16	10	0	3.20	37	5-57	2/0	25.43	5	
Larwood Harold MBE (*CY 1927*)	14.11.1904	22.7.1995	21	1926–*1932*	485	98	0	19.40	78	6-32	4/1	28.35	15	
Lathwell Mark Nicholas	26.12.1971		2	1993	78	33	0	19.50	–	–	–/–	–	0	
Lawrence David Valentine ("Syd")	28.1.1964		5	1988–*1991*	60	34	0	10.00	18	5-106	1/0	37.55	0	1
Lawrence Daniel William	12.7.1997		2	*2020*	99	73	0	33.00	0	0-10	0/0	–	1	
Leach Matthew Jack	22.6.1991		12	*2017–2020*	225	92	0	16.07	44	5-83	2/0	30.50	8	
Leadbeater Edric	15.8.1927	17.4.2011	2	*1951*	40	38	0	20.00	2	1-38	0/0	109.00	3	
Lee Henry William	26.10.1890	21.4.1981	1	*1930*	19	18	0	9.50	–	–	–/–	–	0	
Lees Walter Scott (*CY 1906*)	25.12.1875	10.9.1924	5	*1905*	66	25*	0	11.00	26	6-78	2/0	17.96	2	
Legge Geoffrey Bevington	26.1.1903	21.11.1940	5	*1927–1929*	299	196	1	49.83	0	0-34	0/0	–	1	
Leslie Charles Frederick Henry	8.12.1861	12.2.1921	4	*1882*	106	54	0	15.14	4	3-31	0/0	11.00	1	
Lever John Kenneth MBE (*CY 1979*)	24.2.1949		21	*1976*–1986	306	53	0	11.76	73	7-46	3/1	26.72	11	22
Lever Peter	17.9.1940		17	*1970*–1975	350	88*	0	21.87	41	6-38	2/0	36.80	11	10
Leveson Gower *Sir* Henry Dudley Gresham	8.5.1873	1.2.1954	3	*1909*	95	31	0	23.75	–	–	–/–	–	1	
Levett William Howard Vincent ("Hopper")	25.1.1908	1.12.1995	1	*1933*	7	5	0	7.00	–	–	–/–	–	3	
Lewis Anthony Robert CBE	6.7.1938		9	*1972*–1973	457	125	1	32.64	–	–	–/–	–	0	
Lewis Clairmonte Christopher	14.2.1968		32	1990–1996	1,105	117	1	23.02	93	6-111	3/0	37.52	25	53
Lewis Jonathan	26.8.1975		1	2006	27	20	0	13.50	3	3-68	0/0	40.66	0	13/2
Leyland Maurice (*CY 1929*)	20.7.1900	1.1.1967	41	1928–1938	2,764	187	9	46.06	6	3-91	0/0	97.50	13	
Lilley Arthur Frederick Augustus ("Dick") (*CY 1897*)	28.11.1866	17.11.1929	35	1896–1909	903	84	0	20.52	1	1-23	0/0	23.00	70/22	
Lillywhite James	23.2.1842	25.10.1929	2	*1876*	16	10	0	8.00	8	4-70	0/0	15.75	1	
Lloyd David	18.3.1947		9	1974–*1974*	552	214*	1	42.46	0	0-4	0/0	–	11	8
Lloyd Timothy Andrew	5.11.1956		1	1984	10	10*	0	–	–	–	–/–	–	0	3
Loader Peter James (*CY 1958*)	25.10.1929	15.3.2011	13	1954–*1958*	76	17	0	5.84	39	6-36	1/0	22.51	2	
Lock Graham Anthony Richard (*CY 1954*)	5.7.1929	30.3.1995	49	1952–*1967*	742	89	0	13.74	174	7-35	9/3	25.58	59	

	Born	Died	Tests	Test Career	Runs	HS	100s	Avge	Wkts	BB	5/10	Avge	Ct/St	O/T
Lockwood William Henry (*CY 1899*)	25.3.1868	26.4.1932	12	1893–1902	231	52*	0	17.76	43	7-71	5/1	20.53	4	
Lohmann George Alfred (*CY 1889*)	2.6.1865	1.12.1901	18	1886–1896	213	62*	0	8.87	112	9-28	9/5	10.75	28	
Lowson Frank Anderson	1.7.1925	8.9.1984	7	1951–1955	245	68	0	18.84	–	–	–/–	–	5	
Lucas Alfred Perry	20.2.1857	12.10.1923	5	*1878*–1884	157	55	0	19.62	0	0-23	0/0	–	1	
Luckhurst Brian William (*CY 1971*)	5.2.1939	1.3.2005	21	*1970–1974*	1,298	131	4	36.05	1	1-9	0/0	32.00	14	3
Lyth Adam (*CY 2015*)	25.9.1987		7	2015	265	107	1	20.38	0	0-0	0/0	–	8	
Lyttelton *Hon.* Alfred	7.2.1857	5.7.1913	4	1880–1884	94	31	0	15.66	4	4-19	0/0	4.75	2	
Macaulay George Gibson (*CY 1924*)	7.12.1897	13.12.1940	8	*1922*–1933	112	76	0	18.66	24	5-64	1/0	27.58	5	
MacBryan John Crawford William (*CY 1925*)	22.7.1892	14.7.1983	1	1924	–	–	–	–	–	–	–/–	–	0	
McCague Martin John	24.5.1969		3	1993–*1994*	21	11	0	4.20	6	4-121	0/0	65.00	1	
McConnon James Edward	21.6.1922	26.1.2003	2	1954	18	11	0	9.00	4	3-19	0/0	18.50	4	
McGahey Charles Percy (*CY 1902*)	12.2.1871	10.1.1935	2	*1901*	38	18	0	9.50	–	–	–/–	–	1	
McGrath Anthony	6.10.1975		4	2003	201	81	0	40.20	4	3-16	0/0	14.00	3	14
MacGregor Gregor (*CY 1891*)	31.8.1869	20.8.1919	8	1890–1893	96	31	0	12.00	–	–	–/–	–	14/3	
McIntyre Arthur John William (*CY 1958*)	14.5.1918	26.12.2009	3	1950–1955	19	7	0	3.16	–	–	–/–	–	8	
MacKinnon Francis Alexander	9.4.1848	27.2.1947	1	*1878*	5	5	0	2.50	–	–	–/–	–	0	
MacLaren Archibald Campbell (*CY 1895*)	1.12.1871	17.11.1944	35	*1894*–1909	1,931	140	5	33.87	–	–	–/–	–	29	
McMaster Joseph Emile Patrick	16.3.1861	7.6.1929	1	*1888*	0	0	0	0.00	–	–	–/–	–	0	
Maddy Darren Lee	23.5.1974		3	1999–*1999*	46	24	0	11.50	0	0-40	0/0	–	4	8/4
Mahmood Sajid Iqbal	21.12.1981		8	2006–*2006*	81	34	0	8.10	20	4-22	0/0	38.10	0	26/4
Makepeace Joseph William Henry	22.8.1881	19.12.1952	4	*1920*	279	117	1	34.87	–	–	–/–	–	0	
Malan Dawid Johannes	03.09.1987		15	2017–2018	724	140	1	27.84	0	0-7	0/0	–	11	1/19
Malcolm Devon Eugene (*CY 1995*)	22.2.1963		40	1989–1997	236	29	0	6.05	128	9-57	5/2	37.09	7	10
Mallender Neil Alan	13.8.1961		2	1992	8	4	0	2.66	10	5-50	1/0	21.50	0	
[1] **Mann** Francis George CBE	6.9.1917	8.8.2001	7	*1948*–1949	376	136*	1	37.60	–	–	–/–	–	3	
[1] **Mann** Francis Thomas	3.3.1888	6.10.1964	5	*1922*	281	84	0	35.12	–	–	–/–	–	4	
Marks Victor James	25.6.1955		6	1982–*1983*	249	83	0	27.66	11	3-78	0/0	44.00	0	34
Marriott Charles Stowell ("Father")	14.9.1895	13.10.1966	1	1933	0	0	0	0.00	11	6-59	2/1	8.72	1	
Martin Frederick (*CY 1892*)	12.10.1861	13.12.1921	2	1890–*1891*	14	13	0	7.00	14	6-50	2/1	10.07	2	
Martin John William	16.2.1917	4.1.1987	1	1947	26	26	0	13.00	1	1-111	0/0	129.00	0	
Martin Peter James	15.11.1968		8	1995–1997	115	29	0	8.84	17	4-60	0/0	34.11	6	20
Mason John Richard (*CY 1898*)	26.3.1874	15.10.1958	5	*1897*	129	32	0	12.90	2	1-8	0/0	74.50	3	
Matthews Austin David George	3.5.1904	29.7.1977	1	1937	2	2*	0	–	2	1-13	0/0	32.50	1	
May Peter Barker Howard CBE (*CY 1952*)	31.12.1929	27.12.1994	66	1951–1961	4,537	285*	13	46.77	–	–	–/–	–	42	
Maynard Matthew Peter (*CY 1998*)	21.3.1966		4	1988–*1993*	87	35	0	10.87	–	–	–/–	–	3	14
Mead Charles Philip (*CY 1912*)	9.3.1887	26.3.1958	17	*1911–1928*	1,185	182*	4	49.37	–	–	–/–	–	4	

	Born	Died	Tests	Test Career	Runs	HS	100s	Avge	Wkts	BB	5/10	Avge	Ct/St	O/T
Mead Walter (*CY 1904*)	1.4.1868	18.3.1954	1	1899	7	7	0	3.50	1	1-91	0/0	91.00	1	
Midwinter William Evans	19.6.1851	3.12.1890	4†	*1881*	95	36	0	13.57	10	4-81	0/0	27.20	5	
Milburn Colin ("Ollie") (*CY 1967*)	23.10.1941	28.2.1990	9	1966–*1968*	654	139	2	46.71	–	–	–/–	–	7	
Miller Audley Montague	19.10.1869	26.6.1959	1	*1895*	24	20*	0	–	–	–	–/–	–	0	
Miller Geoffrey OBE	8.9.1952		34	1976–1984	1,213	98*	0	25.80	60	5-44	1/0	30.98	17	25
Milligan Frank William	19.3.1870	31.3.1900	2	*1898*	58	38	0	14.50	0	0-0	0/0	–	1	
Millman Geoffrey	2.10.1934	6.4.2005	6	*1961*–1962	60	32*	0	12.00	–	–	–/–	–	13/2	
Milton Clement Arthur (*CY 1959*)	10.3.1928	25.4.2007	6	1958–1959	204	104*	1	25.50	0	0-12	0/0	–	5	
Mitchell Arthur	13.9.1902	25.12.1976	6	*1933*–1936	298	72	0	29.80	0	0-4	0/0	–	9	
Mitchell Frank (*CY 1902*)	13.8.1872	11.10.1935	2†	*1898*	88	41	0	22.00	–	–	–/–	–	2	
Mitchell Thomas Bignall	4.9.1902	27.1.1996	5	*1932*–1935	20	9	0	5.00	8	2-49	0/0	62.25	1	
Mitchell-Innes Norman Stewart ("Mandy")	7.9.1914	28.12.2006	1	1935	5	5	0	5.00	–	–	–/–	–	0	
Mold Arthur Webb (*CY 1892*)	27.5.1863	29.4.1921	3	1893	0	0*	0	0.00	7	3-44	0/0	33.42	1	
Moon Leonard James	9.2.1878	23.11.1916	4	*1905*	182	36	0	22.75	–	–	–/–	–	4	
Morgan Eoin Joseph Gerard CBE (*CY 2011*)	10.9.1986		16	2010–*2011*	700	130	2	30.43	–	–	–/–	–	11	219‡/97
Morley Frederick	16.12.1850	28.9.1884	4	1880–*1882*	6	2*	0	1.50	16	5-56	1/0	18.50	4	
Morris Hugh	5.10.1963		3	1991	115	44	0	19.16	–	–	–/–	–	3	
Morris John Edward	1.4.1964		3	1990	71	32	0	23.66	–	–	–/–	–	3	8
Mortimore John Brian	14.5.1933	13.2.2014	9	*1958*–1964	243	73*	0	24.30	13	3-36	0/0	56.38	3	
Moss Alan Edward	14.11.1930	12.3.2019	9	*1953*–1960	61	26	0	10.16	21	4-35	0/0	29.80	1	
Moxon Martyn Douglas (*CY 1993*)	4.5.1960		10	1986–1989	455	99	0	28.43	0	0-3	0/0	–	10	8
Mullally Alan David	12.7.1969		19	1996–2001	127	24	0	5.52	58	5-105	1/0	31.24	6	50
Munton Timothy Alan (*CY 1995*)	30.7.1965		2	1992	25	25*	0	25.00	4	2-22	0/0	50.00	0	
Murdoch William Lloyd	18.10.1854	18.2.1911	1†	*1891*	12	12	0	12.00	–	–	–/–	–	0/1	
Murray John Thomas MBE (*CY 1967*)	1.4.1935	24.7.2018	21	1961–1967	506	112	1	22.00	–	–	–/–	–	52/3	
Newham William	12.12.1860	26.6.1944	1	*1887*	26	17	0	13.00	–	–	–/–	–	0	
Newport Philip John	11.10.1962		3	1988–*1990*	110	40*	0	27.50	10	4-87	0/0	41.70	1	
Nichols Morris Stanley (*CY 1934*)	6.10.1900	26.1.1961	14	*1929*–1939	355	78*	0	29.58	41	6-35	2/0	28.09	11	
Oakman Alan Stanley Myles	20.4.1930	6.9.2018	2	1956	14	10	0	7.00	0	0-21	0/0	–	7	
O'Brien *Sir* Timothy Carew	5.11.1861	9.12.1948	5	1884–*1895*	59	20	0	7.37	–	–	–/–	–	4	
O'Connor Jack	6.11.1897	22.2.1977	4	1929–*1929*	153	51	0	21.85	1	1-31	0/0	72.00	2	
Old Christopher Middleton (*CY 1979*)	22.12.1948		46	*1972*–1981	845	65	0	14.82	143	7-50	4/0	28.11	22	32
Oldfield Norman	5.5.1911	19.4.1996	1	1939	99	80	0	49.50	–	–	–/–	–	0	
Onions Graham (*CY 2010*)	9.9.1982		9	2009–2012	30	17*	0	10.00	32	5-38	1/0	29.90	0	4
Ormond James	20.8.1977		2	2001–*2001*	38	18	0	12.66	2	1-70	0/0	92.50	0	
Overton Craig	10.04.1994		4	*2017*–2019	124	41*	0	20.66	9	3-105	0/0	44.77	1	1

	Born	*Died*	*Tests*	*Test Career*	*Runs*	*HS*	*100s*	*Avge*	*Wkts*	*BB*	*5/10*	*Avge*	*Ct/St*	*O/T*
Padgett Douglas Ernest Vernon	20.7.1934		2	1960	51	31	0	12.75	0	0-8	0/0	–	0	
Paine George Alfred Edward (*CY 1935*)	11.6.1908	30.3.1978	4	*1934*	97	49	0	16.16	17	5-168	1/0	27.47	5	
Palairet Lionel Charles Hamilton (*CY 1893*)	27.5.1870	27.3.1933	2	1902	49	20	0	12.25	–	–	–/–	–	2	
Palmer Charles Henry CBE	15.5.1919	31.3.2005	1	*1953*	22	22	0	11.00	0	0-15	0/0	–	0	
Palmer Kenneth Ernest MBE	22.4.1937		1	*1964*	10	10	0	10.00	1	1-113	0/0	189.00	0	
Panesar Mudhsuden Singh ("Monty") (*CY 2007*)	25.4.1982		50	*2005–2013*	220	26	0	4.88	167	6-37	12/2	34.71	10	26/1
Parfitt Peter Howard (*CY 1963*)	8.12.1936		37	*1961*–1972	1,882	131*	7	40.91	12	2-5	0/0	47.83	42	
Parker Charles Warrington Leonard (*CY 1923*)	14.10.1882	11.7.1959	1	1921	3	3*	0	–	2	2-32	0/0	16.00	0	
Parker Paul William Giles	15.1.1956		1	1981	13	13	0	6.50	–	–	–/–	–	0	
Parkhouse William Gilbert Anthony	12.10.1925	10.8.2000	7	1950–1959	373	78	0	28.69	–	–	–/–	–	3	
Parkin Cecil Harry (*CY 1924*)	18.2.1886	15.6.1943	10	*1920*–1924	160	36	0	12.30	32	5-38	2/0	35.25	3	
[1] **Parks** James Horace (*CY 1938*)	12.5.1903	21.11.1980	1	1937	29	22	0	14.50	3	2-26	0/0	12.00	0	
[1] **Parks** James Michael (*CY 1968*)	21.10.1931		46	1954–*1967*	1,962	108*	2	32.16	1	1-43	0/0	51.00	103/11	
[1] **Pataudi** Iftikhar Ali Khan, Nawab of (*CY 1932*)	16.3.1910	5.1.1952	3†	*1932*–1934	144	102	1	28.80	–	–	–/–	–	0	
Patel Minal Mahesh	7.7.1970		2	1996	45	27	0	22.50	1	1-101	0/0	180.00	2	
Patel Samit Rohit	30.11.1984		6	*2011–2015*	151	42	0	16.77	7	2-27	0/0	60.14	3	36/18
[2] **Pattinson** Darren John	2.8.1979		1	2008	21	13	0	10.50	2	2-95	0/0	48.00	0	
Paynter Edward (*CY 1938*)	5.11.1901	5.2.1979	20	*1931–1939*	1,540	243	4	59.23	–	–	–/–	–	7	
Peate Edmund	2.3.1855	11.3.1900	9	*1881*–1886	70	13	0	11.66	31	6-85	2/0	22.03	2	
Peebles Ian Alexander Ross (*CY 1931*)	20.1.1908	27.2.1980	13	*1927*–1931	98	26	0	10.88	45	6-63	3/0	30.91	5	
Peel Robert (*CY 1889*)	12.2.1857	12.8.1941	20	*1884*–1896	427	83	0	14.72	101	7-31	5/1	16.98	17	
Penn Frank	7.3.1851	26.12.1916	1	1880	50	27*	0	50.00	0	0-2	0/0	–	0	
Perks Reginald Thomas David	4.10.1911	22.11.1977	2	*1938*–1939	3	2*	0	–	11	5-100	2/0	32.27	1	
Philipson Hylton	8.6.1866	4.12.1935	5	*1891–1894*	63	30	0	9.00	–	–	–/–	–	8/3	
Pietersen Kevin Peter MBE (*CY 2006*)	27.6.1980		104	2005–*2013*	8,181	227	23	47.28	10	3-52	0/0	88.60	62	134‡/37
Pigott Anthony Charles Shackleton	4.6.1958		1	*1983*	12	8*	0	12.00	2	2-75	0/0	37.50	0	
Pilling Richard (*CY 1891*)	11.8.1855	28.3.1891	8	*1881*–1888	91	23	0	7.58	–	–	–/–	–	10/4	
Place Winston	7.12.1914	25.1.2002	3	*1947*	144	107	1	28.80	–	–	–/–	–	0	
Plunkett Liam Edward	6.4.1985		13	*2005*–2014	238	55*	0	15.86	41	5-64	1/0	37.46	3	89/22
Pocock Patrick Ian	24.9.1946		25	*1967–1984*	206	33	0	6.24	67	6-79	3/0	44.41	15	1
Pollard Richard	19.6.1912	16.12.1985	4	1946–1948	13	10*	0	13.00	15	5-24	1/0	25.20	3	
Poole Cyril John	13.3.1921	11.2.1996	3	*1951*	161	69*	0	40.25	0	0-9	0/0	–	1	
Pope George Henry	27.1.1911	29.10.1993	1	1947	8	8*	0	–	1	1-49	0/0	85.00	0	
Pope Oliver John Douglas	2.1.1998		13	2018–2020	645	135*	1	37.94	–	–	–/–	–	14	
Pougher Arthur Dick	19.4.1865	20.5.1926	1	*1891*	17	17	0	17.00	3	3-26	0/0	8.66	2	
Price John Sidney Ernest	22.7.1937		15	*1963*–1972	66	32	0	7.33	40	5-73	1/0	35.02	7	

	Born	Died	Tests	Test Career	Runs	HS	100s	Avge	Wkts	BB	5/10	Avge	Ct/St	O/T
Price Wilfred Frederick Frank	25.4.1902	13.1.1969	1	1938	6	6	0	3.00	–	–	–/–	–	2	
Prideaux Roger Malcolm	31.7.1939		3	1968–*1968*	102	64	0	20.40	0	0-0	0/0	–	0	
Pringle Derek Raymond	18.9.1958		30	1982–1992	695	63	0	15.10	70	5-95	3/0	35.97	10	44
Prior Matthew James (*CY 2010*)	26.2.1982		79	2007–2014	4,099	131*	7	40.18	–	–	–/–	–	243/13	68/10
Pullar Geoffrey (*CY 1960*)	1.8.1935	26.12.2014	28	1959–*1962*	1,974	175	4	43.86	1	1-1	0/0	37.00	2	
Quaife William George (*CY 1902*)	17.3.1872	13.10.1951	7	1899–*1901*	228	68	0	19.00	0	0-6	0/0	–	4	
Radford Neal Victor (*CY 1986*)	7.6.1957		3	1986–*1987*	21	12*	0	7.00	4	2-131	0/0	87.75	0	6
Radley Clive Thornton MBE (*CY 1979*)	13.5.1944		8	*1977*–1978	481	158	2	48.10	–	–	–/–	–	4	4
Ramprakash Mark Ravin MBE (*CY 2007*)	5.9.1969		52	1991–*2001*	2,350	154	2	27.32	4	1-2	0/0	119.25	39	18
Randall Derek William (*CY 1980*)	24.2.1951		47	*1976*–1984	2,470	174	7	33.37	0	0-1	0/0	–	31	49
Ranjitsinhji Kumar Shri (*CY 1897*)	10.9.1872	2.4.1933	15	1896–1902	989	175	2	44.95	1	1-23	0/0	39.00	13	
Rankin William Boyd	5.7.1984		1†	*2013*	13	13	0	6.50	1	1-47	0/0	81.00	0	7‡/2‡
Rashid Adil Usman	17.2.1988		19	*2015–2018*	540	61	0	19.28	60	5-49	2/0	39.83	4	106/52
Read Christopher Mark Wells (*CY 2011*)	10.8.1978		15	1999–*2006*	360	55	0	18.94	–	–	–/–	–	48/6	36/1
Read Holcombe Douglas ("Hopper")	28.1.1910	5.1.2000	1	1935	–	–	–	–	6	4-136	0/0	33.33	0	
Read John Maurice (*CY 1890*)	9.2.1859	17.2.1929	17	1882–1893	461	57	0	17.07	–	–	–/–	–	8	
Read Walter William (*CY 1893*)	23.11.1855	6.1.1907	18	*1882*–1893	720	117	1	27.69	0	0-27	0/0	–	16	
Reeve Dermot Alexander OBE (*CY 1996*)	2.4.1963		3	*1991*	124	59	0	24.80	2	1-4	0/0	30.00	1	29
Relf Albert Edward (*CY 1914*)	26.6.1874	26.3.1937	13	*1903–1913*	416	63	0	23.11	25	5-85	1/0	24.96	14	
Rhodes Harold James	22.7.1936		2	1959	0	0*	0	–	9	4-50	0/0	27.11	0	
Rhodes Steven John (*CY 1995*)	17.6.1964		11	1994–*1994*	294	65*	0	24.50	–	–	–/–	–	46/3	9
Rhodes Wilfred (*CY 1899*)	29.10.1877	8.7.1973	58	1899–*1929*	2,325	179	2	30.19	127	8-68	6/1	26.96	60	
Richards Clifton James ("Jack")	10.8.1958		8	*1986*–1988	285	133	1	21.92	–	–	–/–	–	20/1	22
[2] **Richardson** Derek Walter ("Dick")	3.11.1934		1	1957	33	33	0	33.00	–	–	–/–	–	1	
[2] **Richardson** Peter Edward (*CY 1957*)	4.7.1931	16.2.2017	34	1956–1963	2,061	126	5	37.47	3	2-10	0/0	16.00	6	
Richardson Thomas (*CY 1897*)	11.8.1870	2.7.1912	14	1893–*1897*	177	25*	0	11.06	88	8-94	11/4	25.22	5	
Richmond Thomas Leonard	23.6.1890	29.12.1957	1	1921	6	4	0	3.00	2	2-69	0/0	43.00	0	
Ridgway Frederick	10.8.1923	26.9.2015	5	*1951*	49	24	0	8.16	7	4-83	0/0	54.14	3	
Robertson John David Benbow (*CY 1948*)	22.2.1917	12.10.1996	11	1947–*1951*	881	133	2	46.36	2	2-17	0/0	29.00	6	
Robins Robert Walter Vivian (*CY 1930*)	3.6.1906	12.12.1968	19	1929–1937	612	108	1	26.60	64	6-32	1/0	27.46	12	
Robinson Robert Timothy (*CY 1986*)	21.11.1958		29	*1984*–1989	1,601	175	4	36.38	0	0-0	0/0	–	8	26
Robson Samuel David	1.7.1989		7	2014	336	127	1	30.54	–	–	–/–	–	5	
Roland-Jones Tobias Skelton	29.01.1988		4	2017	82	25	0	20.50	17	5-57	1/0	19.64	0	1
Roope Graham Richard James	12.7.1946	26.11.2006	21	*1972*–1978	860	77	0	30.71	0	0-2	0/0	–	35	8
Root Charles Frederick	16.4.1890	20.1.1954	3	1926	–	–	–	–	8	4-84	0/0	24.25	1	
Root Joseph Edward MBE (*CY 2014*)	30.12.1990		99	*2012–2020*	8,249	254	19	49.39	31	4-87	0/0	47.19	131	149/32

	Born	*Died*	*Tests*	*Test Career*	*Runs*	*HS*	*100s*	*Avge*	*Wkts*	*BB*	*5/10*	*Avge*	*Ct/St*	*O/T*
Rose Brian Charles (*CY 1980*)	4.6.1950		9	*1977–1980*	358	70	0	25.57	–	–	–/–	–	4	2
Roy Jason Jonathan	21.7.1990		5	2019	187	72	0	18.70	–	–	–/–	–	1	93/38
Royle Vernon Peter Fanshawe Archer	29.1.1854	21.5.1929	1	*1878*	21	18	0	10.50	0	0-6	0/0	–	2	
Rumsey Frederick Edward	4.12.1935		5	1964–1965	30	21*	0	15.00	17	4-25	0/0	27.11	0	
Russell Albert Charles ("Jack") (*CY 1923*)	7.10.1887	23.3.1961	10	*1920–1922*	910	140	5	56.87	–	–	–/–	–	8	
Russell Robert Charles ("Jack") (*CY 1990*)	15.8.1963		54	1988–*1997*	1,897	128*	2	27.10	–	–	–/–	–	153/12	40
Russell William Eric	3.7.1936		10	*1961*–1967	362	70	0	21.29	0	0-19	0/0	–	4	
Saggers Martin John	23.5.1972		3	*2003*–2004	1	1	0	0.33	7	2-29	0/0	35.28	1	
Salisbury Ian David Kenneth (*CY 1993*)	21.1.1970		15	1992–*2000*	368	50	0	16.72	20	4-163	0/0	76.95	5	4
Sandham Andrew (*CY 1923*)	6.7.1890	20.4.1982	14	1921–*1929*	879	325	2	38.21	–	–	–/–	–	4	
Schofield Christopher Paul	6.10.1978		2	2000	67	57	0	22.33	0	0-73	0/0	–	0	0/4
Schultz Sandford Spence	29.8.1857	18.12.1937	1	*1878*	20	20	0	20.00	1	1-16	0/0	26.00	0	
Scotton William Henry	15.1.1856	9.7.1893	15	*1881–1886*	510	90	0	22.17	0	0-20	0/0	–	4	
Selby John	1.7.1849	11.3.1894	6	*1876–1881*	256	70	0	23.27	–	–	–/–	–	1	
Selvey Michael Walter William	25.4.1948		3	1976–*1976*	15	5*	0	7.50	6	4-41	0/0	57.16	1	
Shackleton Derek (*CY 1959*)	12.8.1924	28.9.2007	7	1950–1963	113	42	0	18.83	18	4-72	0/0	42.66	1	
Shah Owais Alam	22.10.1978		6	*2005–2008*	269	88	0	26.90	0	0-12	0/0	–	2	71/17
Shahzad Ajmal	27.7.1985		1	2010	5	5	0	5.00	4	3-45	0/0	15.75	2	11/3
Sharp John	15.2.1878	28.1.1938	3	1909	188	105	1	47.00	3	3-67	0/0	37.00	1	
Sharpe John William (*CY 1892*)	9.12.1866	19.6.1936	3	1890–*1891*	44	26	0	22.00	11	6-84	1/0	27.72	2	
Sharpe Philip John (*CY 1963*)	27.12.1936	19.5.2014	12	1963–1969	786	111	1	46.23	–	–	–/–	–	17	
Shaw Alfred	29.8.1842	16.1.1907	7	*1876–1881*	111	40	0	10.09	12	5-38	1/0	23.75	4	
Sheppard *Rt Rev. Lord* [David Stuart] (*CY 1953*)	6.3.1929	5.3.2005	22	1950–*1962*	1,172	119	3	37.80	–	–	–/–	–	12	
Sherwin Mordecai (*CY 1891*)	26.2.1851	3.7.1910	3	*1886*–1888	30	21*	0	15.00	–	–	–/–	–	5/2	
Shrewsbury Arthur (*CY 1890*)	11.4.1856	19.5.1903	23	*1881*–1893	1,277	164	3	35.47	0	0-2	0/0	–	29	
Shuter John	9.2.1855	5.7.1920	1	1888	28	28	0	28.00	–	–	–/–	–	0	
Shuttleworth Kenneth	13.11.1944		5	*1970*–1971	46	21	0	7.66	12	5-47	1/0	35.58	1	
Sibley Dominic Peter (*CY 2021*)	5.9.1995		14	*2019–2020*	748	133*	2	35.61	0	0-7	0/0	–	9	
[1] **Sidebottom** Arnold	1.4.1954		1	1985	2	2	0	2.00	1	1-65	0/0	65.00	0	
[1] **Sidebottom** Ryan Jay (*CY 2008*)	15.1.1978		22	2001–*2009*	313	31	0	15.65	79	7-47	5/1	28.24	5	25/18
Silverwood Christopher Eric Wilfred	5.3.1975		6	*1996–2002*	29	10	0	7.25	11	5-91	1/0	40.36	2	7
Simpson Reginald Thomas (*CY 1950*)	27.2.1920	24.11.2013	27	*1948–1954*	1,401	156*	4	33.35	2	2-4	0/0	11.00	5	
Simpson-Hayward George Hayward Thomas	7.6.1875	2.10.1936	5	*1909*	105	29*	0	15.00	23	6-43	2/0	18.26	1	
Sims James Morton	13.5.1903	27.4.1973	4	1935–*1936*	16	12	0	4.00	11	5-73	1/0	43.63	6	
Sinfield Reginald Albert	24.12.1900	17.3.1988	1	1938	6	6	0	6.00	2	1-51	0/0	61.50	0	
Slack Wilfred Norris	12.12.1954	15.1.1989	3	*1985*–1986	81	52	0	13.50	–	–	–/–	–	3	2

	Born	Died	Tests	Test Career	Runs	HS	100s	Avge	Wkts	BB	5/10	Avge	Ct/St	O/T
Smailes Thomas Francis	27.3.1910	1.12.1970	1	1946	25	25	0	25.00	3	3-44	0/0	20.66	0	
Small Gladstone Cleophas	18.10.1961		17	1986–*1990*	263	59	0	15.47	55	5-48	2/0	34.01	9	53
Smith Alan Christopher CBE	25.10.1936		6	*1962*	118	69*	0	29.50	–	–	–/–	–	20	
Smith Andrew Michael	1.10.1967		1	1997	4	4*	0	4.00	0	0-89	0/0	–	0	
Smith *Sir* Charles Aubrey	21.7.1863	20.12.1948	1	*1888*	3	3	0	3.00	7	5-19	1/0	8.71	0	
Smith Cedric Ivan James (*CY 1935*)	25.8.1906	8.2.1979	5	*1934*–1937	102	27	0	10.20	15	5-16	1/0	26.20	1	
[2] **Smith** Christopher Lyall (*CY 1984*)	15.10.1958		8	1983–1986	392	91	0	30.15	3	2-31	0/0	13.00	5	4
Smith Denis (*CY 1935*)	24.1.1907	12.9.1979	2	1935	128	57	0	32.00	–	–	–/–	–	1	
Smith David Mark	9.1.1956		2	*1985*	80	47	0	20.00	–	–	–/–	–	0	2
Smith David Robert	5.10.1934	17.12.2003	5	*1961*	38	34	0	9.50	6	2-60	0/0	59.83	2	
Smith Donald Victor	14.6.1923	10.1.2021	3	1957	25	16*	0	8.33	1	1-12	0/0	97.00	0	
Smith Edward Thomas	19.7.1977		3	2003	87	64	0	17.40	–	–	–/–	–	5	
Smith Ernest James ("Tiger")	6.2.1886	31.8.1979	11	*1911–1913*	113	22	0	8.69	–	–	–/–	–	17/3	
Smith Harry	21.5.1891	12.11.1937	1	1928	7	7	0	7.00	–	–	–/–	–	1	
Smith Michael John Knight OBE (*CY 1960*)	30.6.1933		50	1958–1972	2,278	121	3	31.63	1	1-10	0/0	128.00	53	
[2] **Smith** Robin Arnold (*CY 1990*)	13.9.1963		62	1988–*1995*	4,236	175	9	43.67	0	0-6	0/0	–	39	71
Smith Thomas Peter Bromley (*CY 1947*)	30.10.1908	4.8.1967	4	1946–*1946*	33	24	0	6.60	3	2-172	0/0	106.33	1	
Smithson Gerald Arthur	1.11.1926	6.9.1970	2	*1947*	70	35	0	23.33	–	–	–/–	–	0	
Snow John Augustine (*CY 1973*)	13.10.1941		49	1965–1976	772	73	0	13.54	202	7-40	8/1	26.66	16	9
Southerton James	16.11.1827	16.6.1880	2	*1876*	7	6	0	3.50	7	4-46	0/0	15.28	2	
Spooner Reginald Herbert (*CY 1905*)	21.10.1880	2.10.1961	10	1905–1912	481	119	1	32.06	–	–	–/–	–	4	
Spooner Richard Thompson	30.12.1919	20.12.1997	7	*1951*–1955	354	92	0	27.23	–	–	–/–	–	10/2	
Stanyforth Ronald Thomas	30.5.1892	20.2.1964	4	*1927*	13	6*	0	2.60	–	–	–/–	–	7/2	
Staples Samuel James (*CY 1929*)	18.9.1892	4.6.1950	3	*1927*	65	39	0	13.00	15	3-50	0/0	29.00	0	
Statham John Brian CBE (*CY 1955*)	17.6.1930	10.6.2000	70	*1950*–1965	675	38	0	11.44	252	7-39	9/1	24.84	28	
Steel Allan Gibson	24.9.1858	15.6.1914	13	1880–1888	600	148	2	35.29	29	3-27	0/0	20.86	5	
Steele David Stanley OBE (*CY 1976*)	29.9.1941		8	1975–1976	673	106	1	42.06	2	1-1	0/0	19.50	7	1
Stephenson John Patrick	14.3.1965		1	1989	36	25	0	18.00	–	–	–/–	–	0	
Stevens Greville Thomas Scott (*CY 1918*)	7.1.1901	19.9.1970	10	*1922–1929*	263	69	0	15.47	20	5-90	2/1	32.40	9	
Stevenson Graham Barry	16.12.1955	21.1.2014	2	*1979–1980*	28	27*	0	28.00	5	3-111	0/0	36.60	0	4
[1] **Stewart** Alec James OBE (*CY 1993*)	8.4.1963		133	*1989*–2003	8,463	190	15	39.54	0	0-5	0/0	–	263/14	170
[1] **Stewart** Michael James OBE (*CY 1958*)	16.9.1932		8	1962–*1963*	385	87	0	35.00	–	–	–/–	–	6	
Stoddart Andrew Ernest (*CY 1893*)	11.3.1863	3.4.1915	16	*1887–1897*	996	173	2	35.57	2	1-10	0/0	47.00	6	
Stokes Benjamin Andrew OBE (*CY 2016*)	4.6.1991		67	*2013*–2020	4,428	258	10	37.84	158	6-22	4/0	31.40	76	95/29
Stone Oliver Peter	9.10.1993		1	2019	19	19	0	9.50	3	3-29	0/0	9.66	0	4
Stoneman Mark Daniel	26.06.1987		11	2017–2018	526	60	0	27.68	–	–	–/–	–	1	

	Born	*Died*	*Tests*	*Test Career*	*Runs*	*HS*	*100s*	*Avge*	*Wkts*	*BB*	*5/10*	*Avge*	*Ct/St*	*O/T*
Storer William (*CY 1899*)	25.1.1867	28.2.1912	6	*1897*–1899	215	51	0	19.54	2	1-24	0/0	54.00	11	
Strauss *Sir* Andrew John OBE (*CY 2005*)	2.3.1977		100	2004–2012	7,037	177	21	40.91	–	–	–/–	–	121	127/4
Street George Benjamin	6.12.1889	24.4.1924	1	*1922*	11	7*	0	11.00	–	–	–/–	–	0/1	
Strudwick Herbert (*CY 1912*)	28.1.1880	14.2.1970	28	*1909*–1926	230	24	0	7.93	–	–	–/–	–	61/12	
[2]**Studd** Charles Thomas	2.12.1860	16.7.1931	5	1882–*1882*	160	48	0	20.00	3	2-35	0/0	32.66	5	
[2]**Studd** George Brown	20.10.1859	13.2.1945	4	*1882*	31	9	0	4.42	–	–	–/–	–	8	
Subba Row Raman CBE (*CY 1961*)	29.1.1932		13	1958–1961	984	137	3	46.85	0	0-2	0/0	–	5	
Such Peter Mark	12.6.1964		11	1993–1999	67	14*	0	6.09	37	6-67	2/0	33.56	4	
Sugg Frank Howe (*CY 1890*)	11.1.1862	29.5.1933	2	1888	55	31	0	27.50	–	–	–/–	–	0	
Sutcliffe Herbert (*CY 1920*)	24.11.1894	22.1.1978	54	1924–1935	4,555	194	16	60.73	–	–	–/–	–	23	
Swann Graeme Peter (*CY 2010*)	24.3.1979		60	*2008–2013*	1,370	85	0	22.09	255	6-65	17/3	29.96	54	79/39
Swetman Roy	25.10.1933		11	*1958–1959*	254	65	0	16.93	–	–	–/–	–	24/2	
[1]**Tate** Frederick William	24.7.1867	24.2.1943	1	1902	9	5*	0	9.00	2	2-7	0/0	25.50	2	
[1]**Tate** Maurice William (*CY 1924*)	30.5.1895	18.5.1956	39	1924–1935	1,198	100*	1	25.48	155	6-42	7/1	26.16	11	
Tattersall Roy	17.8.1922	9.12.2011	16	*1950*–1954	50	10*	0	5.00	58	7-52	4/1	26.08	8	
Tavaré Christopher James	27.10.1954		31	1980–1989	1,755	149	2	32.50	0	0-0	0/0	–	20	29
Taylor James William Arthur	6.1.1990		7	2012–*2015*	312	76	0	26.00	–	–	–/–	–	7	27
Taylor Jonathan Paul	8.8.1964		2	*1992*–1994	34	17*	0	17.00	3	1-18	0/0	52.00	0	1
Taylor Kenneth	21.8.1935		3	1959–1964	57	24	0	11.40	0	0-6	0/0	–	1	
Taylor Leslie Brian	25.10.1953		2	1985	1	1*	0	–	4	2-34	0/0	44.50	1	2
Taylor Robert William MBE (*CY 1977*)	17.7.1941		57	*1970–1983*	1,156	97	0	16.28	0	0-6	0/0	–	167/7	27
Tennyson *Lord* Lionel Hallam (*CY 1914*)	7.11.1889	6.6.1951	9	*1913*–1921	345	74*	0	31.36	0	0-1	0/0	–	6	
Terry Vivian Paul	14.1.1959		2	1984	16	8	0	5.33	–	–	–/–	–	2	
Thomas John Gregory	12.8.1960		5	*1985*–1986	83	31*	0	13.83	10	4-70	0/0	50.40	0	3
Thompson George Joseph (*CY 1906*)	27.10.1877	3.3.1943	6	1909–*1909*	273	63	0	30.33	23	4-50	0/0	27.73	5	
Thomson Norman Ian	23.1.1929		5	*1964*	69	39	0	23.00	9	2-55	0/0	63.11	3	
Thorpe Graham Paul MBE (*CY 1998*)	1.8.1969		100	1993–2005	6,744	200*	16	44.66	0	0-0	0/0	–	105	82
Titmus Frederick John MBE (*CY 1963*)	24.11.1932	23.3.2011	53	1955–*1974*	1,449	84*	0	22.29	153	7-79	7/0	32.22	35	2
Tolchard Roger William	15.6.1946		4	*1976*	129	67	0	25.80	–	–	–/–	–	5	1
[1]**Townsend** Charles Lucas (*CY 1899*)	7.11.1876	17.10.1958	2	1899	51	38	0	17.00	3	3-50	0/0	25.00	0	
[1]**Townsend** David Charles Humphery	20.4.1912	27.1.1997	3	*1934*	77	36	0	12.83	0	0-9	0/0	–	1	
Townsend Leslie Fletcher (*CY 1934*)	8.6.1903	17.2.1993	4	*1929–1933*	97	40	0	16.16	6	2-22	0/0	34.16	2	
Tredwell James Cullum	27.2.1982		2	*2009–2014*	45	37	0	22.50	11	4-47	0/0	29.18	2	45/17
[4]**Tremlett** Christopher Timothy	2.9.1981		12	2007–*2013*	113	25*	0	10.27	53	6-48	2/0	27.00	4	15/1
[4]**Tremlett** Maurice Fletcher	5.7.1923	30.7.1984	3	*1947*	20	18*	0	6.66	4	2-98	0/0	56.50	0	
Trescothick Marcus Edward MBE (*CY 2005*)	25.12.1975		76	2000–2006	5,825	219	14	43.79	1	1-34	0/0	155.00	95	123/3

	Born	*Died*	*Tests*	*Test Career*	*Runs*	*HS*	*100s*	*Avge*	*Wkts*	*BB*	*5/10*	*Avge*	*Ct/St*	*O/T*
[2] **Trott** Albert Edwin (*CY 1899*)	6.2.1873	30.7.1914	2†	*1898*	23	16	0	5.75	17	5-49	1/0	11.64	0	
Trott Ian Jonathan Leonard (*CY 2011*)	22.4.1981		52	2009–*2014*	3,835	226	9	44.08	5	1-5	0/0	80.00	29	68/7
Trueman Frederick Sewards OBE (*CY 1953*)	6.2.1931	1.7.2006	67	1952–1965	981	39*	0	13.81	307	8-31	17/3	21.57	64	
Tudor Alex Jeremy	23.10.1977		10	*1998–2002*	229	99*	0	19.08	28	5-44	1/0	34.39	3	3
Tufnell Neville Charsley	13.6.1887	3.8.1951	1	*1909*	14	14	0	14.00	–	–	–/–	–	0/1	
Tufnell Philip Clive Roderick	29.4.1966		42	*1990*–2001	153	22*	0	5.10	121	7-47	5/2	37.68	12	20
Turnbull Maurice Joseph Lawson (*CY 1931*)	16.3.1906	5.8.1944	9	*1929*–1936	224	61	0	20.36	–	–	–/–	–	1	
[2] **Tyldesley** [George] Ernest (*CY 1920*)	5.2.1889	5.5.1962	14	1921–*1928*	990	122	3	55.00	0	0-2	0/0	–	2	
[2] **Tyldesley** John Thomas (*CY 1902*)	22.11.1873	27.11.1930	31	*1898*–1909	1,661	138	4	30.75	–	–	–/–	–	16	
Tyldesley Richard Knowles (*CY 1925*)	11.3.1897	17.9.1943	7	1924–1930	47	29	0	7.83	19	3-50	0/0	32.57	1	
Tylecote Edward Ferdinando Sutton	23.6.1849	15.3.1938	6	*1882*–1886	152	66	0	19.00	–	–	–/–	–	5/5	
Tyler Edwin James	13.10.1864	25.1.1917	1	*1895*	0	0	0	0.00	4	3-49	0/0	16.25	0	
Tyson Frank Holmes (*CY 1956*)	6.6.1930	27.9.2015	17	1954–*1958*	230	37*	0	10.95	76	7-27	4/1	18.56	4	
Udal Shaun David	18.3.1969		4	*2005*	109	33*	0	18.16	8	4-14	0/0	43.00	1	11
Ulyett George	21.10.1851	18.6.1898	25	*1876*–1890	949	149	1	24.33	50	7-36	1/0	20.40	19	
Underwood Derek Leslie MBE (*CY 1969*)	8.6.1945		86	1966–*1981*	937	45*	0	11.56	297	8-51	17/6	25.83	44	26
Valentine Bryan Herbert	17.1.1908	2.2.1983	7	*1933–1938*	454	136	2	64.85	–	–	–/–	–	2	
Vaughan Michael Paul OBE (*CY 2003*)	29.10.1974		82	*1999*–2008	5,719	197	18	41.44	6	2-71	0/0	93.50	44	86/2
Verity Hedley (*CY 1932*)	18.5.1905	31.7.1943	40	1931–1939	669	66*	0	20.90	144	8-43	5/2	24.37	30	
Vernon George Frederick	20.6.1856	10.8.1902	1	*1882*	14	11*	0	14.00	–	–	–/–	–	0	
Vince James Michael	14.3.1991		13	2016–*2017*	548	83	0	24.90	0	0-0	0/0	–	8	16/12
Vine Joseph (*CY 1906*)	15.5.1875	25.4.1946	2	*1911*	46	36	0	46.00	–	–	–/–	–	0	
Voce William (*CY 1933*)	8.8.1909	6.6.1984	27	*1929–1946*	308	66	0	13.39	98	7-70	3/2	27.88	15	
Waddington Abraham	4.2.1893	28.10.1959	2	*1920*	16	7	0	4.00	1	1-35	0/0	119.00	1	
Wainwright Edward (*CY 1894*)	8.4.1865	28.10.1919	5	1893–*1897*	132	49	0	14.66	0	0-11	0/0	–	2	
Walker Peter Michael	17.2.1936	4.4.2020	3	1960	128	52	0	32.00	0	0-8	0/0	–	5	
Walters Cyril Frederick (*CY 1934*)	28.8.1905	23.12.1992	11	1933–1934	784	102	1	52.26	–	–	–/–	–	6	
Ward Alan	10.8.1947		5	1969–1976	40	21	0	8.00	14	4-61	0/0	32.35	3	
Ward Albert (*CY 1890*)	21.11.1865	6.1.1939	7	1893–*1894*	487	117	1	37.46	–	–	–/–	–	1	
Ward Ian James	30.9.1972		5	2001	129	39	0	16.12	–	–	–/–	–	1	
Wardle John Henry (*CY 1954*)	8.1.1923	23.7.1985	28	*1947*–1957	653	66	0	19.78	102	7-36	5/1	20.39	12	
Warner *Sir* Pelham Francis (*CY 1904*)	2.10.1873	30.1.1963	15	*1898*–1912	622	132*	1	23.92	–	–	–/–	–	3	
Warr John James	16.7.1927	9.5.2016	2	*1950*	4	4	0	1.00	1	1-76	0/0	281.00	0	
Warren Arnold	2.4.1875	3.9.1951	1	1905	7	7	0	7.00	6	5-57	1/0	18.83	1	
Washbrook Cyril CBE (*CY 1947*)	6.12.1914	27.4.1999	37	1937–1956	2,569	195	6	42.81	1	1-25	0/0	33.00	12	
Watkin Steven Llewellyn (*CY 1994*)	15.9.1964		3	1991–1993	25	13	0	5.00	11	4-65	0/0	27.72	1	4

	Born	*Died*	*Tests*	*Test Career*	*Runs*	*HS*	*100s*	*Avge*	*Wkts*	*BB*	*5/10*	*Avge*	*Ct/St*	*O/T*
Watkins Albert John ("Allan")	21.4.1922	3.8.2011	15	1948–1952	810	137*	2	40.50	11	3-20	0/0	50.36	17	
Watkinson Michael	1.8.1961		4	1995–*1995*	167	82*	0	33.40	10	3-64	0/0	34.80	1	1
Watson Willie (*CY 1954*)	7.3.1920	24.4.2004	23	1951–*1958*	879	116	2	25.85	–	–	–/–	–	8	
Webbe Alexander Josiah	16.1.1855	19.2.1941	1	*1878*	4	4	0	2.00	–	–	–/–	–	2	
Wellard Arthur William (*CY 1936*)	8.4.1902	31.12.1980	2	1937–1938	47	38	0	11.75	7	4-81	0/0	33.85	2	
Wells Alan Peter	2.10.1961		1	1995	3	3*	0	3.00	–	–	–/–	–	0	1
Westley Thomas	13.03.1989		5	2017	193	59	0	24.12	0	0-12	0/0	–	1	
Wharton Alan	30.4.1923	26.8.1993	1	1949	20	13	0	10.00	–	–	–/–	–	0	
Whitaker John James (*CY 1987*)	5.5.1962		1	*1986*	11	11	0	11.00	–	–	–/–	–	1	2
White Craig	16.12.1969		30	1994–*2002*	1,052	121	1	24.46	59	5-32	3/0	37.62	14	51
White David William ("Butch")	14.12.1935	1.8.2008	2	*1961*	0	0	0	0.00	4	3-65	0/0	29.75	0	
White John Cornish (*CY 1929*)	19.2.1891	2.5.1961	15	1921–*1930*	239	29	0	18.38	49	8-126	3/1	32.26	6	
Whysall William Wilfrid (*CY 1925*)	31.10.1887	11.11.1930	4	*1924*–1930	209	76	0	29.85	0	0-9	0/0	–	7	
Wilkinson Leonard Litton	5.11.1916	3.9.2002	3	*1938*	3	2	0	3.00	7	2-12	0/0	38.71	0	
Willey Peter	6.12.1949		26	1976–1986	1,184	102*	2	26.90	7	2-73	0/0	65.14	3	26
Williams Neil FitzGerald	2.7.1962	27.3.2006	1	1990	38	38	0	38.00	2	2-148	0/0	74.00	0	
Willis Robert George Dylan MBE (*CY 1978*)	30.5.1949	4.12.2019	90	*1970*–1984	840	28*	0	11.50	325	8-43	16/0	25.20	39	64
[2] **Wilson** Clement Eustace Macro	15.5.1875	8.2.1944	2	*1898*	42	18	0	14.00	–	–	–/–	–	0	
Wilson Donald	7.8.1937	21.7.2012	6	*1963–1970*	75	42	0	12.50	11	2-17	0/0	42.36	1	
[2] **Wilson** Evelyn Rockley	25.3.1879	21.7.1957	1	*1920*	10	5	0	5.00	3	2-28	0/0	12.00	0	
Woakes Christopher Roger (*CY 2017*)	2.3.1989		38	2013–2020	1,321	137*	1	27.52	112	6-17	4/1	29.30	17	104/8
Wood Arthur (*CY 1939*)	25.8.1898	1.4.1973	4	1938–1939	80	53	0	20.00	–	–	–/–	–	10/1	
Wood Barry	26.12.1942		12	1972–1978	454	90	0	21.61	0	0-2	0/0	–	6	13
Wood George Edward Charles	22.8.1893	18.3.1971	3	1924	7	6	0	3.50	–	–	–/–	–	5/1	
Wood Henry (*CY 1891*)	14.12.1853	30.4.1919	4	1888–*1891*	204	134*	1	68.00	–	–	–/–	–	2/1	
Wood Mark Andrew	11.1.1990		18	2015–*2020*	402	52	0	16.75	53	5-41	2/0	33.43	7	53/11
Wood Reginald	7.3.1860	6.1.1915	1	*1886*	6	6	0	3.00	–	–	–/–	–	0	
Woods Samuel Moses James (*CY 1889*)	13.4.1867	30.4.1931	3†	*1895*	122	53	0	30.50	5	3-28	0/0	25.80	4	
Woolley Frank Edward (*CY 1911*)	27.5.1887	18.10.1978	64	1909–1934	3,283	154	5	36.07	83	7-76	4/1	33.91	64	
Woolmer Robert Andrew (*CY 1976*)	14.5.1948	18.3.2007	19	1975–1981	1,059	149	3	33.09	4	1-8	0/0	74.75	10	6
Worthington Thomas Stanley (*CY 1937*)	21.8.1905	31.8.1973	9	*1929–1936*	321	128	1	29.18	8	2-19	0/0	39.50	8	
Wright Charles William	27.5.1863	10.1.1936	3	*1895*	125	71	0	31.25	–	–	–/–	–	0	
Wright Douglas Vivian Parson (*CY 1940*)	21.8.1914	13.11.1998	34	1938–*1950*	289	45	0	11.11	108	7-105	6/1	39.11	10	
Wyatt Robert Elliott Storey (*CY 1930*)	2.5.1901	20.4.1995	40	*1927–1936*	1,839	149	2	31.70	18	3-4	0/0	35.66	16	
Wynyard Edward George	1.4.1861	30.10.1936	3	1896–*1905*	72	30	0	12.00	0	0-2	0/0	–	0	
Yardley Norman Walter Dransfield (*CY 1948*)	19.3.1915	3.10.1989	20	*1938*–1950	812	99	0	25.37	21	3-67	0/0	33.66	14	

	Born	Died	Tests	Test Career	Runs	HS	100s	Avge	Wkts	BB	5/10	Avge	Ct/St	O/T
Young Harding Isaac ("Sailor")	5.2.1876	12.12.1964	2	1899	43	43	0	21.50	12	4-30	0/0	21.83	1	
Young John Albert	14.10.1912	5.2.1993	8	1947–1949	28	10*	0	5.60	17	3-65	0/0	44.52	5	
Young Richard Alfred	16.9.1885	1.7.1968	2	*1907*	27	13	0	6.75	–	–	–/–	–	6	

AUSTRALIA (460 players)

	Born	Died	Tests	Test Career	Runs	HS	100s	Avge	Wkts	BB	5/10	Avge	Ct/St	O/T
a'Beckett Edward Lambert	11.8.1907	2.6.1989	4	*1928–1931*	143	41	0	20.42	3	1-41	0/0	105.66	4	
Agar Ashton Charles	14.10.1993		4	2013–*2017*	195	98	0	32.50	9	3-46	0/0	45.55	0	14/27
Alderman Terence Michael (*CY 1982*)	12.6.1956		41	1981–*1990*	203	26*	0	6.54	170	6-47	14/1	27.15	27	65
Alexander George	22.4.1851	6.11.1930	2	*1880–1884*	52	33	0	13.00	2	2-69	0/0	46.50	2	
Alexander Harry Houston	9.6.1905	15.4.1993	1	*1932*	17	17*	0	17.00	1	1-129	0/0	154.00	0	
Allan Francis Erskine	2.12.1849	9.2.1917	1	*1878*	5	5	0	5.00	4	2-30	0/0	20.00	0	
Allan Peter John	31.12.1935		1	*1965*	–	–	–	–	2	2-58	0/0	41.50	0	
Allen Reginald Charles	2.7.1858	2.5.1952	1	*1886*	44	30	0	22.00	–	–	–/–	–	2	
Andrews Thomas James Edwin	26.8.1890	28.1.1970	16	1921–1926	592	94	0	26.90	1	1-23	0/0	116.00	12	
Angel Jo	22.4.1968		4	*1992–1994*	35	11	0	5.83	10	3-54	0/0	46.30	1	3
[2] **Archer** Kenneth Alan	17.1.1928		5	*1950–1951*	234	48	0	26.00	–	–	–/–	–	0	
[2] **Archer** Ronald Graham	25.10.1933	27.5.2007	19	*1952–1956*	713	128	1	24.58	48	5-53	1/0	27.45	20	
Armstrong Warwick Windridge (*CY 1903*)	22.5.1879	13.7.1947	50	*1901*–1921	2,863	159*	6	38.68	87	6-35	3/0	33.59	44	
Badcock Clayvel Lindsay ("Jack")	10.4.1914	13.12.1982	7	*1936*–1938	160	118	1	14.54	–	–	–/–	–	3	
Bailey George John	7.9.1982		5	*2013*	183	53	0	26.14	–	–	–/–	–	10	90/29‡
Bancroft Cameron Timothy	19.11.1992		10	*2017*–2019	446	82*	0	26.23	–	–	–/–	–	16	0/1
[2] **Bannerman** Alexander Chalmers	21.3.1854	19.9.1924	28	*1878*–1893	1,108	94	0	23.08	4	3-111	0/0	40.75	21	
[2] **Bannerman** Charles	23.7.1851	20.8.1930	3	*1876–1878*	239	165*	1	59.75	–	–	–/–	–	0	
Bardsley Warren (*CY 1910*)	6.12.1882	20.1.1954	41	1909–1926	2,469	193*	6	40.47	–	–	–/–	–	12	
Barnes Sidney George	5.6.1916	16.12.1973	13	1938–1948	1,072	234	3	63.05	4	2-25	0/0	54.50	14	
Barnett Benjamin Arthur	23.3.1908	29.6.1979	4	1938	195	57	0	27.85	–	–	–/–	–	3/2	
Barrett John Edward	15.10.1866	6.2.1916	2	1890	80	67*	0	26.66	–	–	–/–	–	1	
Beard Graeme Robert	19.8.1950		3	*1979*	114	49	0	22.80	1	1-26	0/0	109.00	0	2
Beer Michael Anthony	9.6.1984		2	*2010–2011*	6	2*	0	3.00	3	2-56	0/0	59.33	1	
[2] **Benaud** John	11.5.1944		3	*1972*	223	142	1	44.60	2	2-12	0/0	6.00	0	
[2] **Benaud** Richard OBE (*CY 1962*)	6.10.1930	10.4.2015	63	*1951–1963*	2,201	122	3	24.45	248	7-72	16/1	27.03	65	
Bennett Murray John	6.10.1956		3	*1984*–1985	71	23	0	23.66	6	3-79	0/0	54.16	5	8

	Born	Died	Tests	Test Career	Runs	HS	100s	Avge	Wkts	BB	5/10	Avge	Ct/St	O/T
Bevan Michael Gwyl	8.5.1970		18	1994–1997	785	91	0	29.07	29	6-82	1/1	24.24	8	232
Bichel Andrew John	27.8.1970		19	1996–2003	355	71	0	16.90	58	5-60	1/0	32.24	16	67
Bird Jackson Munro	11.12.1986		9	2012–2017	43	19*	0	14.33	34	5-59	1/0	30.64	2	
Blackham John McCarthy (*CY 1891*)	11.5.1854	28.12.1932	35	1876–1894	800	74	0	15.68	–	–	–/–	–	37/24	
Blackie Donald Dearness	5.4.1882	18.4.1955	3	1928	24	11*	0	8.00	14	6-94	1/0	31.71	2	
Blewett Gregory Scott	28.10.1971		46	1994–1999	2,552	214	4	34.02	14	2-9	0/0	51.42	45	32
Bollinger Douglas Erwin	24.7.1981		12	2008–2010	54	21	0	7.71	50	5-28	2/0	25.92	2	39/9
Bonnor George John	25.2.1855	27.6.1912	17	1880–1888	512	128	1	17.06	2	1-5	0/0	42.00	16	
Boon David Clarence MBE (*CY 1994*)	29.12.1960		107	1984–1995	7,422	200	21	43.65	0	0-0	0/0	–	99	181
Booth Brian Charles MBE	19.10.1933		29	1961–1965	1,773	169	5	42.21	3	2-33	0/0	48.66	17	
Border Allan Robert (*CY 1982*)	27.7.1955		156	1978–1993	11,174	205	27	50.56	39	7-46	2/1	39.10	156	273
Boyle Henry Frederick	10.12.1847	21.11.1907	12	1878–1884	153	36*	0	12.75	32	6-42	1/0	20.03	10	
Bracken Nathan Wade	12.9.1977		5	2003–2005	70	37	0	17.50	12	4-48	0/0	42.08	2	116/19
Bradman *Sir* Donald George AC (*CY 1931*)	27.8.1908	25.2.2001	52	1928–1948	6,996	334	29	99.94	2	1-8	0/0	36.00	32	
Bright Raymond James	13.7.1954		25	1977–1986	445	33	0	14.35	53	7-87	4/1	41.13	13	11
Bromley Ernest Harvey	2.9.1912	1.2.1967	2	1932–1934	38	26	0	9.50	0	0-19	0/0	–	2	
Brown William Alfred (*CY 1939*)	31.7.1912	16.3.2008	22	1934–1948	1,592	206*	4	46.82	–	–	–/–	–	14	
Bruce William	22.5.1864	3.8.1925	14	1884–1894	702	80	0	29.25	12	3-88	0/0	36.66	12	
Burge Peter John Parnell (*CY 1965*)	17.5.1932	5.10.2001	42	1954–1965	2,290	181	4	38.16	–	–	–/–	–	23	
Burke James Wallace (*CY 1957*)	12.6.1930	2.2.1979	24	1950–1958	1,280	189	3	34.59	8	4-37	0/0	28.75	18	
Burn Edwin James Kenneth (K. E.)	17.9.1862	20.7.1956	2	1890	41	19	0	10.25	–	–	–/–	–	0	
Burns Joseph Antony	6.9.1989		23	2014–2020	1,442	180	4	36.97	–	–	–/–	–	23	6
Burton Frederick John	2.11.1865	25.8.1929	2	1886–1887	4	2*	0	2.00	–	–	–/–	–	1/1	
Callaway Sydney Thomas	6.2.1868	25.11.1923	3	1891–1894	87	41	0	17.40	6	5-37	1/0	23.66	0	
Callen Ian Wayne	2.5.1955		1	1977	26	22*	0	–	6	3-83	0/0	31.83	1	5
Campbell Gregory Dale	10.3.1964		4	1989–1989	10	6	0	2.50	13	3-79	0/0	38.69	1	12
Carkeek William ("Barlow")	17.10.1878	20.2.1937	6	1912	16	6*	0	5.33	–	–	–/–	–	6	
Carlson Phillip Henry	8.8.1951		2	1978	23	21	0	5.75	2	2-41	0/0	49.50	2	4
Carter Hanson	15.3.1878	8.6.1948	28	1907–1921	873	72	0	22.97	–	–	–/–	–	44/21	
Cartwright Hilton William Raymond	14.2.1992		2	2016–2017	55	37	0	27.50	0	0-15	0/0	–	0	2
Casson Beau	7.12.1982		1	2007	10	10	0	10.00	3	3-86	0/0	43.00	2	
[2,4] **Chappell** Gregory Stephen MBE (*CY 1973*)	7.8.1948		87	1970–1983	7,110	247*	24	53.86	47	5-61	1/0	40.70	122	74
[2,4] **Chappell** Ian Michael (*CY 1976*)	26.9.1943		75	1964–1979	5,345	196	14	42.42	20	2-21	0/0	65.80	105	16
[2,4] **Chappell** Trevor Martin	21.10.1952		3	1981	79	27	0	15.80	–	–	–/–	–	2	20
Charlton Percie Chater	9.4.1867	30.9.1954	2	1890	29	11	0	7.25	3	3-18	0/0	8.00	0	
Chipperfield Arthur Gordon	17.11.1905	29.7.1987	14	1934–1938	552	109	1	32.47	5	3-91	0/0	87.40	15	

	Born	*Died*	*Tests*	*Test Career*	*Runs*	*HS*	*100s*	*Avge*	*Wkts*	*BB*	*5/10*	*Avge*	*Ct/St*	*O/T*
Clark Stuart Rupert	28.9.1975		24	*2005–2009*	248	39	0	13.05	94	5-32	2/0	23.86	4	39/9
Clark Wayne Maxwell	19.9.1953		10	*1977–1978*	98	33	0	5.76	44	4-46	0/0	28.75	6	2
Clarke Michael John (*CY 2010*)	2.4.1981		115§	2004–2015	8,643	329*	28	49.10	31	6-9	2/0	38.19	134	245/34
Colley David John	15.3.1947		3	1972	84	54	0	21.00	6	3-83	0/0	52.00	1	1
Collins Herbert Leslie	21.1.1888	28.5.1959	19	*1920*–1926	1,352	203	4	45.06	4	2-47	0/0	63.00	13	
Coningham Arthur	14.7.1863	13.6.1939	1	*1894*	13	10	0	6.50	2	2-17	0/0	38.00	0	
Connolly Alan Norman	29.6.1939		29	*1963–1970*	260	37	0	10.40	102	6-47	4/0	29.22	17	1
Cook Simon Hewitt	29.1.1972		2	*1997*	3	3*	0	–	7	5-39	1/0	20.28	0	
Cooper Bransby Beauchamp	15.3.1844	7.8.1914	1	*1876*	18	15	0	9.00	–	–	–/–	–	2	
[5] **Cooper** William Henry	11.9.1849	5.4.1939	2	*1881–1884*	13	7	0	6.50	9	6-120	1/0	25.11	1	
Copeland Trent Aaron	14.3.1986		3	*2011*	39	23*	0	13.00	6	2-24	0/0	37.83	2	
Corling Grahame Edward	13.7.1941		5	1964	5	3	0	1.66	12	4-60	0/0	37.25	0	
Cosier Gary John	25.4.1953		18	*1975–1978*	897	168	2	28.93	5	2-26	0/0	68.20	14	9
Cottam John Thomas	5.9.1867	30.1.1897	1	*1886*	4	3	0	2.00	–	–	–/–	–	1	
Cotter Albert ("Tibby")	3.12.1883	31.10.1917	21	*1903–1911*	457	45	0	13.05	89	7-148	7/0	28.64	8	
Coulthard George	1.8.1856	22.10.1883	1	*1881*	6	6*	0	–	–	–	–/–	–	0	
Cowan Edward James McKenzie	16.6.1982		18	*2011*–2013	1,001	136	1	31.28	–	–	–/–	–	24	
Cowper Robert Maskew	5.10.1940		27	1964–1968	2,061	307	5	46.84	36	4-48	0/0	31.63	21	
Craig Ian David	12.6.1935	16.11.2014	11	*1952–1957*	358	53	0	19.88	–	–	–/–	–	2	
Crawford William Patrick Anthony	3.8.1933	21.1.2009	4	1956–*1956*	53	34	0	17.66	7	3-28	0/0	15.28	1	
Cullen Daniel James	10.4.1984		1	*2005*	–	–	–	–	1	1-25	0/0	54.00	0	5
Cummins Patrick James (*CY 2020*)	8.5.1993		34	*2011–2020*	708	63	0	16.46	164	6-23	5/1	21.59	16	69/30
Dale Adam Craig	30.12.1968		2	*1997–1998*	6	5	0	2.00	6	3-71	0/0	31.16	0	30
Darling Joseph (*CY 1900*)	21.11.1870	2.1.1946	34	*1894*–1905	1,657	178	3	28.56	–	–	–/–	–	27	
Darling Leonard Stuart	14.8.1909	24.6.1992	12	*1932–1936*	474	85	0	27.88	0	0-3	0/0	–	8	
Darling Warrick Maxwell	1.5.1957		14	*1977–1979*	697	91	0	26.80	–	–	–/–	–	5	18
Davidson Alan Keith MBE (*CY 1962*)	14.6.1929		44	1953–*1962*	1,328	80	0	24.59	186	7-93	14/2	20.53	42	
Davis Ian Charles	25.6.1953		15	1973–1977	692	105	1	26.61	–	–	–/–	–	9	3
Davis Simon Peter	8.11.1959		1	*1985*	0	0	0	0.00	0	0-70	0/0	–	0	39
De Courcy James Harry	18.4.1927	20.6.2000	3	1953	81	41	0	16.20	–	–	–/–	–	3	
Dell Anthony Ross	6.8.1947		2	*1970–1973*	6	3*	0	–	6	3-65	0/0	26.66	0	
Dodemaide Anthony Ian Christopher	5.10.1963		10	*1987–1992*	202	50	0	22.44	34	6-58	1/0	28.02	6	24
Doherty Xavier John	22.12.1982		4	2010–2012	51	18*	0	12.75	7	3-131	0/0	78.28	2	60/11
Donnan Henry	12.11.1864	13.8.1956	5	*1891*–1896	75	15	0	8.33	0	0-22	0/0	–	2	
Doolan Alexander James	29.11.1985		4	*2013–2014*	191	89	0	23.87	–	–	–/–	–	4	

§ *Clarke's figures include 44 runs and one catch for Australia v the ICC World XI in the Super Series Test in 2005-06.*

	Born	Died	Tests	Test Career	Runs	HS	100s	Avge	Wkts	BB	5/10	Avge	Ct/St	O/T
Dooland Bruce (*CY 1955*)	1.11.1923	8.9.1980	3	1946–1947	76	29	0	19.00	9	4-69	0/0	46.55	3	
Duff Reginald Alexander	17.8.1878	13.12.1911	22	1901–1905	1,317	146	2	35.59	4	2-43	0/0	21.25	14	
Duncan John Ross Frederick	25.3.1944		1	1970	3	3	0	3.00	0	0-30	0/0	–	0	
Dyer Gregory Charles	16.3.1959		6	1986–1987	131	60	0	21.83	–	–	–/–	–	22/2	23
Dymock Geoffrey	21.7.1945		21	1973–1979	236	31*	0	9.44	78	7-67	5/1	27.12	1	15
Dyson John	11.6.1954		30	1977–1984	1,359	127*	2	26.64	–	–	–/–	–	10	29
Eady Charles John	29.10.1870	20.12.1945	2	1896–1901	20	10*	0	6.66	7	3-30	0/0	16.00	2	
Eastwood Kenneth Humphrey	23.11.1935		1	1970	5	5	0	2.50	1	1-21	0/0	21.00	0	
Ebeling Hans Irvine	1.1.1905	12.1.1980	1	1934	43	41	0	21.50	3	3-74	0/0	29.66	0	
Edwards John Dunlop	12.6.1860	31.7.1911	3	1888	48	26	0	9.60	–	–	–/–	–	1	
Edwards Ross	1.12.1942		20	1972–1975	1,171	170*	2	40.37	0	0-20	0/0	–	7	9
Edwards Walter John	23.12.1949		3	1974	68	30	0	11.33	–	–	–/–	–	0	1
Elliott Matthew Thomas Gray (*CY 1998*)	28.9.1971		21	1996–2004	1,172	199	3	33.48	0	0-0	0/0	–	14	1
Emery Philip Allen	25.6.1964		1	1994	8	8*	0	–	–	–	–/–	–	5/1	1
Emery Sidney Hand	15.10.1885	7.1.1967	4	1912	6	5	0	3.00	5	2-46	0/0	49.80	2	
Evans Edwin	26.3.1849	2.7.1921	6	1881–1886	82	33	0	10.25	7	3-64	0/0	47.42	5	
Fairfax Alan George	16.6.1906	17.5.1955	10	1928–1930	410	65	0	51.25	21	4-31	0/0	30.71	15	
Faulkner James Peter	29.4.1990		1	2013	45	23	0	22.50	6	4-51	0/0	16.33	0	69/24
Favell Leslie Ernest MBE	6.10.1929	14.6.1987	19	1954–1960	757	101	1	27.03	–	–	–/–	–	9	
Ferguson Callum James	21.11.1984		1	2016	4	3	0	2.00	–	–	–/–	–	0	30/3
Ferris John James (*CY 1889*)	21.5.1867	17.11.1900	8†	1886–1890	98	20*	0	8.16	48	5-26	4/0	14.25	4	
Finch Aaron James	17.11.1986		5	2018	278	62	0	27.80	0	0-8	0/0	–	7	132/66
Fingleton John Henry Webb OBE	28.4.1908	22.11.1981	18	1931–1938	1,189	136	5	42.46	–	–	–/–	–	13	
Fleetwood-Smith Leslie O'Brien ("Chuck")	30.3.1908	16.3.1971	10	1935–1938	54	16*	0	9.00	42	6-110	2/1	37.38	0	
Fleming Damien William	24.4.1970		20	1994–2000	305	71*	0	19.06	75	5-30	3/0	25.89	9	88
Francis Bruce Colin	18.2.1948		3	1972	52	27	0	10.40	–	–	–/–	–	1	
Freeman Eric Walter	13.7.1944	14.12.2020	11	1967–1969	345	76	0	19.16	34	4-52	0/0	33.17	5	
Freer Frederick Alfred William	4.12.1915	2.11.1998	1	1946	28	28*	0	–	3	2-49	0/0	24.66	0	
Gannon John Bryant ("Sam")	8.2.1947	5.2.2021	3	1977	3	3*	0	3.00	11	4-77	0/0	32.81	3	
Garrett Thomas William	26.7.1858	6.8.1943	19	1876–1887	339	51*	0	12.55	36	6-78	2/0	26.94	7	
Gaunt Ronald Arthur	26.2.1934	30.3.2012	3	1957–1963	6	3	0	3.00	7	3-53	0/0	44.28	1	
Gehrs Donald Raeburn Algernon	29.11.1880	25.6.1953	6	1903–1910	221	67	0	20.09	0	0-4	0/0	–	6	
George Peter Robert	16.10.1986		1	2010	2	2	0	1.00	2	2-48	0/0	38.50	0	
[2] **Giffen** George (*CY 1894*)	27.3.1859	29.11.1927	31	1881–1896	1,238	161	1	23.35	103	7-117	7/1	27.09	24	
[2] **Giffen** Walter Frank	20.9.1861	28.6.1949	3	1886–1891	11	3	0	1.83	–	–	–/–	–	1	
Gilbert David Robert	29.12.1960		9	1985–1986	57	15	0	7.12	16	3-48	0/0	52.68	0	14

	Born	Died	Tests	Test Career	Runs	HS	100s	Avge	Wkts	BB	5/10	Avge	Ct/St	O/T
Gilchrist Adam Craig (*CY 2002*)	14.11.1971		96§	*1999–2007*	5,570	204*	17	47.60	–	–	–/–	–	379/37	286‡/13
Gillespie Jason Neil (*CY 2002*)	19.4.1975		71	*1996–2005*	1,218	201*	1	18.73	259	7-37	8/0	26.13	27	97/1
Gilmour Gary John	26.6.1951	10.6.2014	15	*1973–1976*	483	101	1	23.00	54	6-85	3/0	26.03	8	5
Gleeson John William	14.3.1938	8.10.2016	29	1967–1972	395	45	0	10.39	93	5-61	3/0	36.20	17	
Graham Henry	22.11.1870	7.2.1911	6	1893–1896	301	107	2	30.10	–	–	–/–	–	3	
Green Cameron David	3.6.1999		4	*2020*	236	84	0	33.71	0	0-10	0/0	–	5	1
[2]**Gregory** David William	15.4.1845	4.8.1919	3	*1876–1878*	60	43	0	20.00	0	0-9	0/0	–	0	
[1,2]**Gregory** Edward James	29.5.1839	22.4.1899	1	*1876*	11	11	0	5.50	–	–	–/–	–	1	
Gregory Jack Morrison (*CY 1922*)	14.8.1895	7.8.1973	24	*1920–1928*	1,146	119	2	36.96	85	7-69	4/0	31.15	37	
Gregory Ross Gerald	28.2.1916	10.6.1942	2	*1936*	153	80	0	51.00	0	0-14	0/0	–	1	
[1]**Gregory** Sydney Edward (*CY 1897*)	14.4.1870	31.7.1929	58	1890–1912	2,282	201	4	24.53	0	0-4	0/0	–	25	
Grimmett Clarence Victor (*CY 1931*)	25.12.1891	2.5.1980	37	*1924–1935*	557	50	0	13.92	216	7-40	21/7	24.21	17	
Groube Thomas Underwood	2.9.1857	5.8.1927	1	1880	11	11	0	5.50	–	–	–/–	–	0	
Grout Arthur Theodore Wallace	30.3.1927	9.11.1968	51	*1957–1965*	890	74	0	15.08	–	–	–/–	–	163/24	
Guest Colin Ernest John	7.10.1937	8.12.2018	1	*1962*	11	11	0	11.00	0	0-8	0/0	–	0	
Haddin Bradley James	23.10.1977		66	2007–2015	3,265	169	4	32.97	–	–	–/–	–	262/8	126/34
Hamence Ronald Arthur	25.11.1915	24.3.2010	3	*1946–1947*	81	30*	0	27.00	–	–	–/–	–	1	
Hammond Jeffrey Roy	19.4.1950		5	*1972*	28	19	0	9.33	15	4-38	0/0	32.53	2	1
Handscomb Peter Stephen Patrick	26.4.1991		16	*2016–2018*	934	110	2	38.91	–	–	–/–	–	28	22/2
Harris Marcus Sinclair	21.7.1992		10	*2018–2020*	428	79	0	23.77	–	–	–/–	–	7	
Harris Ryan James (*CY 2014*)	11.10.1979		27	*2009–2014*	603	74	0	21.53	113	7-117	5/0	23.52	13	21/3
Harry John	1.8.1857	27.10.1919	1	*1894*	8	6	0	4.00	–	–	–/–	–	1	
Hartigan Roger Joseph	12.12.1879	7.6.1958	2	*1907*	170	116	1	42.50	0	0-7	0/0	–	1	
Hartkopf Albert Ernst Victor	28.12.1889	20.5.1968	1	*1924*	80	80	0	40.00	1	1-120	0/0	134.00	0	
[2]**Harvey** Mervyn Roye	29.4.1918	18.3.1995	1	*1946*	43	31	0	21.50	–	–	–/–	–	0	
[2]**Harvey** Robert Neil MBE (*CY 1954*)	8.10.1928		79	*1947–1962*	6,149	205	21	48.41	3	1-8	0/0	40.00	64	
Hassett Arthur Lindsay MBE (*CY 1949*)	28.8.1913	16.6.1993	43	1938–1953	3,073	198*	10	46.56	0	0-1	0/0	–	30	
Hastings John Wayne	4.11.1985		1	*2012*	52	32	0	26.00	1	1-51	0/0	153.00	1	29/9
Hauritz Nathan Michael	18.10.1981		17	*2004–2010*	426	75	0	25.05	63	5-53	2/0	34.98	3	58/3
Hawke Neil James Napier	27.6.1939	25.12.2000	27	1962–1968	365	45*	0	16.59	91	7-105	6/1	29.41	9	
Hayden Matthew Lawrence (*CY 2003*)	29.10.1971		103§	*1993–2008*	8,625	380	30	50.73	0	0-7	0/0	–	128	160‡/9
Hazlewood Josh Reginald	8.1.1991		55	*2014–2020*	445	39	0	12.02	212	6-67	9/0	25.65	19	54/9
Hazlitt Gervys Rignold	4.9.1888	30.10.1915	9	1907–1912	89	34*	0	11.12	23	7-25	1/0	27.08	4	
Head Travis Michael	29.12.1993		19	*2018–2020*	1,153	161	2	39.75	0	0-0	0/0	–	12	42/16
Healy Ian Andrew (*CY 1994*)	30.4.1964		119	*1988–1999*	4,356	161*	4	27.39	–	–	–/–	–	366/29	168

§ *Gilchrist's figures include 95 runs, five catches and two stumpings and Hayden's 188 runs and three catches for Australia v the ICC World XI in the Super Series Test in 2005-06.*

	Born	*Died*	*Tests*	*Test Career*	*Runs*	*HS*	*100s*	*Avge*	*Wkts*	*BB*	*5/10*	*Avge*	*Ct/St*	*O/T*
Hendry Hunter Scott Thomas Laurie ("Stork")	24.5.1895	16.12.1988	11	1921–*1928*	335	112	1	20.93	16	3-36	0/0	40.00	10	
Henriques Moises Constantino	1.2.1987		4	*2012*–2016	164	81*	0	23.42	2	1-48	0/0	82.00	1	13/14
Hibbert Paul Anthony	23.7.1952	27.11.2008	1	*1977*	15	13	0	7.50	–	–	–/–	–	1	
Higgs James Donald	11.7.1950		22	*1977–1980*	111	16	0	5.55	66	7-143	2/0	31.16	3	
Hilditch Andrew Mark Jefferson	20.5.1956		18	*1978–1985*	1,073	119	2	31.55	–	–	–/–	–	13	8
Hilfenhaus Benjamin William	15.3.1983		27	*2008–2012*	355	56*	0	13.65	99	5-75	2/0	28.50	7	25/7
Hill Clement (*CY 1900*)	18.3.1877	5.9.1945	49	1896–*1911*	3,412	191	7	39.21	–	–	–/–	–	33	
Hill John Charles	25.6.1923	11.8.1974	3	1953–*1954*	21	8*	0	7.00	8	3-35	0/0	34.12	2	
Hoare Desmond Edward	19.10.1934		1	*1960*	35	35	0	17.50	2	2-68	0/0	78.00	2	
Hodge Bradley John	29.12.1974		6	*2005–2007*	503	203*	1	55.88	0	0-8	0/0	–	9	25/15
Hodges John Robart	11.8.1855	d unknown	2	*1876*	10	8	0	3.33	6	2-7	0/0	14.00	0	
Hogan Tom George	23.9.1956		7	*1982–1983*	205	42*	0	18.63	15	5-66	1/0	47.06	2	16
Hogg George Bradley	6.2.1971		7	*1996–2007*	186	79	0	26.57	17	2-40	0/0	54.88	1	123/15
Hogg Rodney Malcolm	5.3.1951		38	*1978–1984*	439	52	0	9.75	123	6-74	6/2	28.47	7	71
Hohns Trevor Victor	23.1.1954		7	*1988*–1989	136	40	0	22.66	17	3-59	0/0	34.11	3	
Hole Graeme Blake	6.1.1931	14.2.1990	18	*1950–1954*	789	66	0	25.45	3	1-9	0/0	42.00	21	
Holland Jonathan Mark	29.5.1987		4	2016–*2018*	6	3	0	3.00	9	3-83	0/0	63.77	1	
Holland Robert George	19.10.1946	17.9.2017	11	*1984–1985*	35	10	0	3.18	34	6-54	3/2	39.76	5	2
Hookes David William	3.5.1955	19.1.2004	23	*1976–1985*	1,306	143*	1	34.36	1	1-4	0/0	41.00	12	39
Hopkins Albert John Young	3.5.1874	25.4.1931	20	*1901*–1909	509	43	0	16.41	26	4-81	0/0	26.76	11	
Horan Thomas Patrick	8.3.1854	16.4.1916	15	*1876–1884*	471	124	1	18.84	11	6-40	1/0	13.00	6	
Hordern Herbert Vivian MBE	10.2.1883	17.6.1938	7	*1910–1911*	254	50	0	23.09	46	7-90	5/2	23.36	6	
Hornibrook Percival Mitchell	27.7.1899	25.8.1976	6	*1928*–1930	60	26	0	10.00	17	7-92	1/0	39.05	7	
Howell William Peter	29.12.1869	14.7.1940	18	*1897–1903*	158	35	0	7.52	49	5-81	1/0	28.71	12	
Hughes Kimberley John (*CY 1981*)	26.1.1954		70	1977–*1984*	4,415	213	9	37.41	0	0-0	0/0	–	50	97
Hughes Mervyn Gregory (*CY 1994*)	23.11.1961		53	*1985–1993*	1,032	72*	0	16.64	212	8-87	7/1	28.38	23	33
Hughes Phillip Joel	30.11.1988	27.11.2014	26	*2008*–2013	1,535	160	3	32.65	–	–	–/–	–	15	25/1
Hunt William Alfred	26.8.1908	30.12.1983	1	*1931*	0	0	0	0.00	0	0-14	0/0	–	1	
Hurst Alan George	15.7.1950		12	*1973–1979*	102	26	0	6.00	43	5-28	2/0	27.90	3	8
Hurwood Alexander	17.6.1902	26.9.1982	2	*1930*	5	5	0	2.50	11	4-22	0/0	15.45	2	
Hussey Michael Edward Killeen	27.5.1975		79	*2005–2012*	6,235	195	19	51.52	7	1-0	0/0	43.71	85	185/38
Inverarity Robert John	31.1.1944		6	1968–1972	174	56	0	17.40	4	3-26	0/0	23.25	4	
Iredale Francis Adams	19.6.1867	15.4.1926	14	*1894*–1899	807	140	2	36.68	0	0-3	0/0	–	16	
Ironmonger Herbert	7.4.1882	31.5.1971	14	*1928–1932*	42	12	0	2.62	74	7-23	4/2	17.97	3	
Iverson John Brian	27.7.1915	24.10.1973	5	*1950*	3	1*	0	0.75	21	6-27	1/0	15.23	2	
Jackson Archibald Alexander	5.9.1909	16.2.1933	8	*1928–1930*	474	164	1	47.40	–	–	–/–	–	7	

	Born	Died	Tests	Test Career	Runs	HS	100s	Avge	Wkts	BB	5/10	Avge	Ct/St	O/T
Jaques Philip Anthony	3.5.1979		11	2005–2007	902	150	3	47.47	–	–	–/–	–	7	6
Jarman Barrington Noel	17.2.1936	17.7.2020	19	1959–1968	400	78	0	14.81	–	–	–/–	–	50/4	
Jarvis Arthur Harwood	19.10.1860	15.11.1933	11	1884–1894	303	82	0	16.83	–	–	–/–	–	9/9	
Jenner Terrence James	8.9.1944	24.5.2011	9	1970–1975	208	74	0	23.11	24	5-90	1/0	31.20	5	1
Jennings Claude Burrows	5.6.1884	20.6.1950	6	1912	107	32	0	17.83	–	–	–/–	–	5	
Johnson Ian William Geddes CBE	8.12.1917	9.10.1998	45	1945–1956	1,000	77	0	18.51	109	7-44	3/0	29.19	30	
Johnson Leonard Joseph	18.3.1919	20.4.1977	1	1947	25	25*	0	–	6	3-8	0/0	12.33	2	
Johnson Mitchell Guy	2.11.1981		73	2007–2015	2,065	123*	1	22.20	313	8-61	12/3	28.40	27	153/30
Johnston William Arras (*CY 1949*)	26.2.1922	25.5.2007	40	1947–1954	273	29	0	11.37	160	6-44	7/0	23.91	16	
Jones Dean Mervyn (*CY 1990*)	24.3.1961	24.9.2020	52	1983–1992	3,631	216	11	46.55	1	1-5	0/0	64.00	34	164
Jones Ernest	30.9.1869	23.11.1943	19	1894–1902	126	20	0	5.04	64	7-88	3/1	29.01	21	
Jones Samuel Percy	1.8.1861	14.7.1951	12	1881–1887	428	87	0	21.40	6	4-47	0/0	18.66	12	
Joslin Leslie Ronald	13.12.1947		1	1967	9	7	0	4.50	–	–	–/–	–	0	
Julian Brendon Paul	10.8.1970		7	1993–1995	128	56*	0	16.00	15	4-36	0/0	39.93	4	25
Kasprowicz Michael Scott	10.2.1972		38	1996–2005	445	25	0	10.59	113	7-36	4/0	32.88	16	43/2
Katich Simon Mathew	21.8.1975		56§	2001–2010	4,188	157	10	45.03	21	6-65	1/0	30.23	39	45/3
Kelleway Charles	25.4.1886	16.11.1944	26	1910–1928	1,422	147	3	37.42	52	5-33	1/0	32.36	24	
Kelly James Joseph (*CY 1903*)	10.5.1867	14.8.1938	36	1896–1905	664	46*	0	17.02	–	–	–/–	–	43/20	
Kelly Thomas Joseph Dart	3.5.1844	20.7.1893	2	1876–1878	64	35	0	21.33	–	–	–/–	–	1	
Kendall Thomas Kingston	24.8.1851	17.8.1924	2	1876	39	17*	0	13.00	14	7-55	1/0	15.35	2	
Kent Martin Francis	23.11.1953		3	1981	171	54	0	28.50	–	–	–/–	–	6	5
Kerr Robert Byers	16.6.1961		2	1985	31	17	0	7.75	–	–	–/–	–	1	4
Khawaja Usman Tariq	18.12.1986		44	2010–2019	2,887	174	8	40.66	0	0-1	0/0	–	35	40/9
Kippax Alan Falconer	25.5.1897	5.9.1972	22	1924–1934	1,192	146	2	36.12	0	0-2	0/0	–	13	
Kline Lindsay Francis	29.9.1934	2.10.2015	13	1957–1960	58	15*	0	8.28	34	7-75	1/0	22.82	9	
Krejza Jason John	14.1.1983		2	2008	71	32	0	23.66	13	8-215	1/1	43.23	4	8
Labuschagne Marnus (*CY 2020*)	22.6.1994		18	2018–2020	1,885	215	5	60.80	12	3-45	0/0	41.66	15	13
Laird Bruce Malcolm	21.11.1950		21	1979–1982	1,341	92	0	35.28	0	0-3	0/0	–	16	23
Langer Justin Lee (*CY 2001*)	21.11.1970		105§	1992–2006	7,696	250	23	45.27	0	0-3	0/0	–	73	8
Langley Gilbert Roche Andrews (*CY 1957*)	14.9.1919	14.5.2001	26	1951–1956	374	53	0	14.96	–	–	–/–	–	83/15	
Laughlin Trevor John	30.1.1951		3	1977–1978	87	35	0	17.40	6	5-101	1/0	43.66	3	6
Laver Frank Jonas	7.12.1869	24.9.1919	15	1899–1909	196	45	0	11.52	37	8-31	2/0	26.05	8	
Law Stuart Grant (*CY 1998*)	18.10.1968		1	1995	54	54*	0	–	0	0-9	0/0	–	1	54
Lawry William Morris (*CY 1962*)	11.2.1937		67	1961–1970	5,234	210	13	47.15	0	0-0	0/0	–	30	1
Lawson Geoffrey Francis	7.12.1957		46	1980–1989	894	74	0	15.96	180	8-112	11/2	30.56	10	79

§ *Katich's figures include two runs and one catch and Langer's 22 runs and one catch for Australia v the ICC World XI in the Super Series Test in 2005-06.*

	Born	Died	Tests	Test Career	Runs	HS	100s	Avge	Wkts	BB	5/10	Avge	Ct/St	O/T
Lee Brett (*CY 2006*)	8.11.1976		76§	1999–2008	1,451	64	0	20.15	310	5-30	10/0	30.81	23	221/25
Lee Philip Keith	15.9.1904	9.8.1980	2	1931–1932	57	42	0	19.00	5	4-111	0/0	42.40	1	
Lehmann Darren Scott (*CY 2001*)	5.2.1970		27	1997–2004	1,798	177	5	44.95	15	3-42	0/0	27.46	11	117
Lillee Dennis Keith MBE (*CY 1973*)	18.7.1949		70	1970–1983	905	73*	0	13.71	355	7-83	23/7	23.92	23	63
Lindwall Raymond Russell MBE (*CY 1949*)	3.10.1921	23.6.1996	61	1945–1959	1,502	118	2	21.15	228	7-38	12/0	23.03	26	
Love Hampden Stanley Bray	10.8.1895	22.7.1969	1	1932	8	5	0	4.00	–	–	–/–	–	3	
Love Martin Lloyd	30.3.1974		5	2002–2003	233	100*	1	46.60	–	–	–/–	–	7	
Loxton Samuel John Everett OBE	29.3.1921	3.12.2011	12	1947–1950	554	101	1	36.93	8	3-55	0/0	43.62	7	
Lyon Nathan Michael	20.11.1987		100	2011–2020	1,101	47	0	12.23	399	8-50	18/3	32.12	50	29/2
Lyons John James	21.5.1863	21.7.1927	14	1886–1897	731	134	1	27.07	6	5-30	1/0	24.83	3	
McAlister Peter Alexander	11.7.1869	10.5.1938	8	1903–1909	252	41	0	16.80	–	–	–/–	–	10	
Macartney Charles George (*CY 1922*)	27.6.1886	9.9.1958	35	1907–1926	2,131	170	7	41.78	45	7-58	2/1	27.55	17	
McCabe Stanley Joseph (*CY 1935*)	16.7.1910	25.8.1968	39	1930–1938	2,748	232	6	48.21	36	4-13	0/0	42.86	41	
McCool Colin Leslie	9.12.1916	5.4.1986	14	1945–1949	459	104*	1	35.30	36	5-41	3/0	26.61	14	
McCormick Ernest Leslie	16.5.1906	28.6.1991	12	1935–1938	54	17*	0	6.00	36	4-101	0/0	29.97	8	
McCosker Richard Bede (*CY 1976*)	11.12.1946		25	1974–1979	1,622	127	4	39.56	–	–	–/–	–	21	14
McDermott Craig John (*CY 1986*)	14.4.1965		71	1984–1995	940	42*	0	12.20	291	8-97	14/2	28.63	19	138
McDonald Andrew Barry	15.6.1981		4	2008	107	68	0	21.40	9	3-25	0/0	33.33	2	
McDonald Colin Campbell	17.11.1928	8.1.2021	47	1951–1961	3,107	170	5	39.32	0	0-3	0/0	–	14	
McDonald Edgar Arthur (*CY 1922*)	6.1.1891	22.7.1937	11	1920–1921	116	36	0	16.57	43	5-32	2/0	33.27	3	
McDonnell Percy Stanislaus	13.11.1858	24.9.1896	19	1880–1888	955	147	3	28.93	0	0-11	0/0	–	6	
McGain Bryce Edward	25.3.1972		1	2008	2	2	0	1.00	0	0-149	0/0	–	0	
MacGill Stuart Charles Glyndwr	25.2.1971		44§	1997–2007	349	43	0	9.69	208	8-108	12/2	29.02	16	3
McGrath Glenn Donald (*CY 1998*)	9.2.1970		124§	1993–2006	641	61	0	7.36	563	8-24	29/3	21.64	38	249‡/2
McIlwraith John	7.9.1857	5.7.1938	1	1886	9	7	0	4.50	–	–	–/–	–	1	
McIntyre Peter Edward	27.4.1966		2	1994–1996	22	16	0	7.33	5	3-103	0/0	38.80	0	
McKay Clinton James	22.2.1983		1	2009	10	10	0	10.00	1	1-56	0/0	101.00	1	59/6
Mackay Kenneth Donald MBE	24.10.1925	13.6.1982	37	1956–1962	1,507	89	0	33.48	50	6-42	2/0	34.42	16	
McKenzie Graham Douglas (*CY 1965*)	24.6.1941		60	1961–1970	945	76	0	12.27	246	8-71	16/3	29.78	34	1
McKibbin Thomas Robert	10.12.1870	15.12.1939	5	1894–1897	88	28*	0	14.66	17	3-35	0/0	29.17	4	
McLaren John William	22.12.1886	17.11.1921	1	1911	0	0*	0	–	1	1-23	0/0	70.00	0	
Maclean John Alexander	27.4.1946		4	1978	79	33*	0	11.28	–	–	–/–	–	18	2
[2] **McLeod** Charles Edward	24.10.1869	26.11.1918	17	1894–1905	573	112	1	23.87	33	5-65	2/0	40.15	9	
[2] **McLeod** Robert William	19.1.1868	14.6.1907	6	1891–1893	146	31	0	13.27	12	5-53	1/0	31.83	3	

§ *B. Lee's figures include four runs, two wickets and one catch, MacGill's no runs and nine wickets and McGrath's two runs and three wickets for Australia v the ICC World XI in the Super Series Test in 2005-06.*

	Born	Died	Tests	Test Career	Runs	HS	100s	Avge	Wkts	BB	5/10	Avge	Ct/St	O/T
McShane Patrick George	18.4.1858	11.12.1903	3	*1884–1887*	26	12*	0	5.20	1	1-39	0/0	48.00	2	
Maddinson Nicolas James	21.12.1991		3	*2016*	27	22	0	6.75	0	0-9	0/0	–	2	0/6
Maddocks Leonard Victor	24.5.1926	27.8.2016	7	*1954–1956*	177	69	0	17.70	–	–	–/–	–	19/1	
Maguire John Norman	15.9.1956		3	*1983*	28	15*	0	7.00	10	4-57	0/0	32.30	2	23
Mailey Arthur Alfred	3.1.1886	31.12.1967	21	*1920*–1926	222	46*	0	11.10	99	9-121	6/2	33.91	14	
Mallett Ashley Alexander	13.7.1945		38	1968–1980	430	43*	0	11.62	132	8-59	6/1	29.84	30	9
Malone Michael Francis	9.10.1950		1	1977	46	46	0	46.00	6	5-63	1/0	12.83	0	10
Mann Anthony Longford	8.11.1945	15.11.2019	4	*1977*	189	105	1	23.62	4	3-12	0/0	79.00	2	
Manou Graham Allan	23.4.1979		1	2009	21	13*	0	21.00	–	–	–/–	–	3	4
Marr Alfred Percy	28.3.1862	15.3.1940	1	*1884*	5	5	0	2.50	0	0-3	0/0	–	0	
[1] **Marsh** Geoffrey Robert	31.12.1958		50	*1985–1991*	2,854	138	4	33.18	–	–	–/–	–	38	117
[1, 2] **Marsh** Mitchell Ross	20.10.1991		32	*2014*–2019	1,260	181	2	25.20	42	5-46	1/0	38.64	16	60/15
Marsh Rodney William MBE (*CY 1982*)	4.11.1947		96	*1970–1983*	3,633	132	3	26.51	0	0-3	0/0	–	343/12	92
[1, 2] **Marsh** Shaun Edward	9.7.1983		38	*2011–2018*	2,265	182	6	34.31	–	–	–/–	–	23	73/15
Martin John Wesley	28.7.1931	16.7.1992	8	*1960–1966*	214	55	0	17.83	17	3-56	0/0	48.94	5	
Martyn Damien Richard (*CY 2002*)	21.10.1971		67	*1992–2006*	4,406	165	13	46.37	2	1-0	0/0	84.00	36	208/4
Massie Hugh Hamon	11.4.1854	12.10.1938	9	*1881–1884*	249	55	0	15.56	–	–	–/–	–	5	
Massie Robert Arnold Lockyer (*CY 1973*)	14.4.1947		6	1972–*1972*	78	42	0	11.14	31	8-53	2/1	20.87	1	3
Matthews Christopher Darrell	22.9.1962		3	*1986–1988*	54	32	0	10.80	6	3-95	0/0	52.16	1	
Matthews Gregory Richard John	15.12.1959		33	*1983–1992*	1,849	130	4	41.08	61	5-103	2/1	48.22	17	59
Matthews Thomas James	3.4.1884	14.10.1943	8	*1911*–1912	153	53	0	17.00	16	4-29	0/0	26.18	7	
Maxwell Glenn James	14.10.1988		7	*2012–2017*	339	104	1	26.07	8	4-127	0/0	42.62	5	116/67
May Timothy Brian Alexander	26.1.1962		24	*1987–1994*	225	42*	0	14.06	75	5-9	3/0	34.74	6	47
Mayne Edgar Richard	2.7.1882	26.10.1961	4	1912–*1921*	64	25*	0	21.33	0	0-1	0/0	–	2	
Mayne Lawrence Charles	23.1.1942		6	*1964–1969*	76	13	0	9.50	19	4-43	0/0	33.05	3	
Meckiff Ian	6.1.1935		18	*1957–1963*	154	45*	0	11.84	45	6-38	2/0	31.62	9	
Mennie Joe Matthew	24.12.1988		1	*2016*	10	10	0	5.00	1	1-85	0/0	85.00	0	2
Meuleman Kenneth Douglas	5.9.1923	10.9.2004	1	*1945*	0	0	0	0.00	–	–	–/–	–	1	
Midwinter William Evans	19.6.1851	3.12.1890	8†	*1876–1886*	174	37	0	13.38	14	5-78	1/0	23.78	5	
Miller Colin Reid	6.2.1964		18	*1998–2000*	174	43	0	8.28	69	5-32	3/1	26.15	6	
Miller Keith Ross MBE (*CY 1954*)	28.11.1919	11.10.2004	55	*1945–1956*	2,958	147	7	36.97	170	7-60	7/1	22.97	38	
Minnett Roy Baldwin	13.6.1888	21.10.1955	9	*1911*–1912	391	90	0	26.06	11	4-34	0/0	26.36	0	
Misson Francis Michael	19.11.1938		5	*1960*–1961	38	25*	0	19.00	16	4-58	0/0	38.50	6	
Moody Thomas Masson (*CY 2000*)	2.10.1965		8	*1989–1992*	456	106	2	32.57	2	1-17	0/0	73.50	9	76
Moroney John	24.7.1917	1.7.1999	7	*1949–1951*	383	118	2	34.81	–	–	–/–	–	0	
Morris Arthur Robert MBE (*CY 1949*)	19.1.1922	22.8.2015	46	*1946–1954*	3,533	206	12	46.48	2	1-5	0/0	25.00	15	

	Born	Died	Tests	Test Career	Runs	HS	100s	Avge	Wkts	BB	5/10	Avge	Ct/St	O/T
Morris Samuel	22.6.1855	20.9.1931	1	*1884*	14	10*	0	14.00	2	2-73	0/0	36.50	0	
Moses Henry	13.2.1858	7.12.1938	6	*1886–1894*	198	33	0	19.80	–	–	–/–	–	1	
Moss Jeffrey Kenneth	29.6.1947		1	*1978*	60	38*	0	60.00	–	–	–/–	–	0	1
Moule William Henry	31.1.1858	24.8.1939	1	1880	40	34	0	20.00	3	3-23	0/0	7.66	1	
Muller Scott Andrew	11.7.1971		2	*1999*	6	6*	0	–	7	3-68	0/0	36.85	2	
Murdoch William Lloyd	18.10.1854	18.2.1911	18†	*1876*–1890	896	211	2	32.00	–	–	–/–	–	14	
Musgrove Henry Alfred	27.11.1858	2.11.1931	1	*1884*	13	9	0	6.50	–	–	–/–	–	0	
Nagel Lisle Ernest	6.3.1905	23.11.1971	1	*1932*	21	21*	0	21.00	2	2-110	0/0	55.00	0	
Nash Laurence John	2.5.1910	24.7.1986	2	*1931–1936*	30	17	0	15.00	10	4-18	0/0	12.60	6	
Nevill Peter Michael	13.10.1985		17	2015–*2016*	468	66	0	22.28	–	–	–/–	–	61/2	0/9
Nicholson Matthew James	2.10.1974		1	*1998*	14	9	0	7.00	4	3-56	0/0	28.75	0	
Nitschke Homesdale Carl ("Jack")	14.4.1905	29.9.1982	2	*1931*	53	47	0	26.50	–	–	–/–	–	3	
Noble Montague Alfred (*CY 1900*)	28.1.1873	22.6.1940	42	*1897*–1909	1,997	133	1	30.25	121	7-17	9/2	25.00	26	
Noblet Geffery	14.9.1916	16.8.2006	3	*1949–1952*	22	13*	0	7.33	7	3-21	0/0	26.14	1	
North Marcus James	28.7.1979		21	*2008–2010*	1,171	128	5	35.48	14	6-55	1/0	42.21	17	2/1
Nothling Otto Ernest	1.8.1900	26.9.1965	1	*1928*	52	44	0	26.00	0	0-12	0/0	–	0	
O'Brien Leo Patrick Joseph	2.7.1907	13.3.1997	5	*1932–1936*	211	61	0	26.37	–	–	–/–	–	3	
O'Connor John Denis Alphonsus	9.9.1875	23.8.1941	4	*1907*–1909	86	20	0	12.28	13	5-40	1/0	26.15	3	
O'Donnell Simon Patrick	26.1.1963		6	1985–*1985*	206	48	0	29.42	6	3-37	0/0	84.00	4	87
Ogilvie Alan David	3.6.1951		5	*1977*	178	47	0	17.80	–	–	–/–	–	5	
O'Keefe Stephen Norman John	9.12.1984		9	*2014–2017*	86	25	0	9.55	35	6-35	2/1	29.40	0	0/7
O'Keeffe Kerry James	25.11.1949		24	*1970*–1977	644	85	0	25.76	53	5-101	1/0	38.07	15	2
Oldfield William Albert Stanley MBE (*CY 1927*)	9.9.1894	10.8.1976	54	*1920–1936*	1,427	65*	0	22.65	–	–	–/–	–	78/52	
O'Neill Norman Clifford Louis (*CY 1962*)	19.2.1937	3.3.2008	42	*1958–1964*	2,779	181	6	45.55	17	4-41	0/0	39.23	21	
O'Reilly William Joseph OBE (*CY 1935*)	20.12.1905	6.10.1992	27	*1931–1945*	410	56*	0	12.81	144	7-54	11/3	22.59	7	
Oxenham Ronald Keven	28.7.1891	16.8.1939	7	*1928–1931*	151	48	0	15.10	14	4-39	0/0	37.28	4	
Paine Timothy David	8.12.1984		35	2010–*2020*	1,534	92	0	32.63	–	–	–/–	–	150/7	35/10‡
Palmer George Eugene	22.2.1859	22.8.1910	17	1880–1886	296	48	0	14.09	78	7-65	6/2	21.51	13	
Park Roy Lindsay	30.7.1892	23.1.1947	1	*1920*	0	0	0	0.00	0	0-9	0/0	–	0	
Pascoe Leonard Stephen	13.2.1950		14	1977–*1981*	106	30*	0	10.60	64	5-59	1/0	26.06	2	29
Patterson Kurtis Robert	5.4.1993		2	*2018*	144	114*	1	144.00	–	–	–/–	–	6	
[2] **Pattinson** James Lee	3.5.1990		21	*2011–2019*	417	47*	0	26.06	81	5-27	4/0	26.33	6	15/4
Pellew Clarence Everard ("Nip")	21.9.1893	9.5.1981	10	*1920–1921*	484	116	2	37.23	0	0-3	0/0	–	4	
Phillips Wayne Bentley	1.3.1958		27	*1983–1985*	1,485	159	2	32.28	–	–	–/–	–	52	48
Phillips Wayne Norman	7.11.1962		1	*1991*	22	14	0	11.00	–	–	–/–	–	0	
Philpott Peter Ian	21.11.1934		8	*1964–1965*	93	22	0	10.33	26	5-90	1/0	38.46	5	

	Born	Died	Tests	Test Career	Runs	HS	100s	Avge	Wkts	BB	5/10	Avge	Ct/St	O/T
Ponsford William Harold MBE (*CY 1935*)	19.10.1900	6.4.1991	29	1924–1934	2,122	266	7	48.22	–	–	–/–	–	21	
Ponting Ricky Thomas (*CY 2006*)	19.12.1974		168§	1995–2012	13,378	257	41	51.85	5	1-0	0/0	55.20	196	374‡/17
Pope Roland James	18.2.1864	27.7.1952	1	1884	3	3	0	1.50	–	–	–/–	–	0	
Pucovski William Jan	2.2.1998		1	2020	72	62	0	36.00	–	–	–/–	–	0	
Quiney Robert John	20.8.1982		2	2012	9	9	0	3.00	0	0-3	0/0	–	5	
Rackemann Carl Gray	3.6.1960		12	1982–1990	53	15*	0	5.30	39	6-86	3/1	29.15	2	52
Ransford Vernon Seymour (*CY 1910*)	20.3.1885	19.3.1958	20	1907–1911	1,211	143*	1	37.84	1	1-9	0/0	28.00	10	
Redpath Ian Ritchie MBE	11.5.1941		66	1963–1975	4,737	171	8	43.45	0	0-0	0/0	–	83	5
Reedman John Cole	9.10.1865	25.3.1924	1	1894	21	17	0	10.50	1	1-12	0/0	24.00	1	
Reid Bruce Anthony	14.3.1963		27	1985–1992	93	13	0	4.65	113	7-51	5/2	24.63	5	61
Reiffel Paul Ronald	19.4.1966		35	1991–1997	955	79*	0	26.52	104	6-71	5/0	26.96	15	92
Renneberg David Alexander	23.9.1942		8	1966–1967	22	9	0	3.66	23	5-39	2/0	36.08	2	
Renshaw Matthew Thomas	28.3.1996		11	2016–2017	636	184	1	33.47	0	0-4	0/0	–	8	
Richardson Arthur John	24.7.1888	23.12.1973	9	1924–1926	403	100	1	31.00	12	2-20	0/0	43.41	1	
Richardson Jhye Avon	20.9.1996		2	2018	1	1	0	1.00	6	3-26	0/0	20.50	0	13/9
[4] **Richardson** Victor York OBE	7.9.1894	30.10.1969	19	1924–1935	706	138	1	23.53	–	–	–/–	–	24	
Rigg Keith Edward	21.5.1906	28.2.1995	8	1930–1936	401	127	1	33.41	–	–	–/–	–	5	
Ring Douglas Thomas	14.10.1918	23.6.2003	13	1947–1953	426	67	0	22.42	35	6-72	2/0	37.28	5	
Ritchie Gregory Michael	23.1.1960		30	1982–1986	1,690	146	3	35.20	0	0-10	0/0	–	14	44
Rixon Stephen John	25.2.1954		13	1977–1984	394	54	0	18.76	–	–	–/–	–	42/5	6
Robertson Gavin Ron	28.5.1966		4	1997–1998	140	57	0	20.00	13	4-72	0/0	39.61	1	13
Robertson William Roderick	6.10.1861	24.6.1938	1	1884	2	2	0	1.00	0	0-24	0/0	–	0	
Robinson Richard Daryl	8.6.1946		3	1977	100	34	0	16.66	–	–	–/–	–	4	2
Robinson Rayford Harold	26.3.1914	10.8.1965	1	1936	5	3	0	2.50	–	–	–/–	–	1	
Rogers Christopher John Llewellyn (*CY 2014*)	31.8.1977		25	2007–2015	2,015	173	5	42.87	–	–	–/–	–	15	
Rorke Gordon Frederick	27.6.1938		4	1958–1959	9	7	0	4.50	10	3-23	0/0	20.30	1	
Rutherford John Walter	25.9.1929		1	1956	30	30	0	30.00	1	1-11	0/0	15.00	0	
Ryder John	8.8.1889	3.4.1977	20	1920–1928	1,394	201*	3	51.62	17	2-20	0/0	43.70	17	
Saggers Ronald Arthur	15.5.1917	17.3.1987	6	1948–1949	30	14	0	10.00	–	–	–/–	–	16/8	
Saunders John Victor	21.3.1876	21.12.1927	14	1901–1907	39	11*	0	2.29	79	7-34	6/0	22.73	5	
Sayers Chadd James	31.8.1987		1	2017	0	0	0	0.00	2	2-78	0/0	73.00	1	
Scott Henry James Herbert	26.12.1858	23.9.1910	8	1884–1886	359	102	1	27.61	0	0-9	0/0	–	8	
Sellers Reginald Hugh Durning	20.8.1940		1	1964	0	0	0	0.00	0	0-17	0/0	–	1	
Serjeant Craig Stanton	1.11.1951		12	1977–1977	522	124	1	23.72	–	–	–/–	–	13	3
[5] **Sheahan** Andrew Paul	30.9.1946		31	1967–1973	1,594	127	2	33.91	–	–	–/–	–	17	3

§ *Ponting's figures include 100 runs and one catch for Australia v the ICC World XI in the Super Series Test in 2005-06.*

	Born	Died	Tests	Test Career	Runs	HS	100s	Avge	Wkts	BB	5/10	Avge	Ct/St	O/T
Shepherd Barry Kenneth	23.4.1937	17.9.2001	9	1962–1964	502	96	0	41.83	0	0-3	0/0	–	2	
Siddle Peter Matthew	25.11.1984		67	2008–2019	1,164	51	0	14.73	221	6-54	8/0	30.66	19	20/2
Sievers Morris William	13.4.1912	10.5.1968	3	1936	67	25*	0	13.40	9	5-21	1/0	17.88	4	
Simpson Robert Baddeley (*CY 1965*)	3.2.1936		62	1957–1977	4,869	311	10	46.81	71	5-57	2/0	42.26	110	2
Sincock David John	1.2.1942		3	1964–1965	80	29	0	26.66	8	3-67	0/0	51.25	2	
Slater Keith Nichol	12.3.1936		1	1958	1	1*	0	–	2	2-40	0/0	50.50	0	
Slater Michael Jonathon	21.2.1970		74	1993–2001	5,312	219	14	42.83	1	1-4	0/0	10.00	33	42
Sleep Peter Raymond	4.5.1957		14	1978–1989	483	90	0	24.15	31	5-72	1/0	45.06	4	
Slight James	20.10.1855	9.12.1930	1	1880	11	11	0	5.50	–	–	–/–	–	0	
Smith David Bertram Miller	14.9.1884	29.7.1963	2	1912	30	24*	0	15.00	–	–	–/–	–	0	
Smith Steven Barry	18.10.1961		3	1983	41	12	0	8.20	–	–	–/–	–	1	28
Smith Steven Peter Devereux (*CY 2016*)	2.6.1989		77	2010–2020	7,540	239	27	61.80	17	3-18	0/0	56.47	123	128/45
Spofforth Frederick Robert	9.9.1853	4.6.1926	18	1876–1886	217	50	0	9.43	94	7-44	7/4	18.41	11	
Stackpole Keith Raymond MBE (*CY 1973*)	10.7.1940		43	1965–1973	2,807	207	7	37.42	15	2-33	0/0	66.73	47	6
Starc Mitchell Aaron	30.1.1990		61	2011–2020	1,596	99	0	22.16	255	6-50	13/2	27.57	31	96/35
Stevens Gavin Byron	29.2.1932		4	1959	112	28	0	16.00	–	–	–/–	–	2	
Symonds Andrew	9.6.1975		26	2003–2008	1,462	162*	2	40.61	24	3-50	0/0	37.33	22	198/14
Taber Hedley Brian	29.4.1940		16	1966–1969	353	48	0	16.04	–	–	–/–	–	56/4	
Tait Shaun William	22.2.1983		3	2005–2007	20	8	0	6.66	5	3-97	0/0	60.40	1	35/21
Tallon Donald (*CY 1949*)	17.2.1916	7.9.1984	21	1945–1953	394	92	0	17.13	–	–	–/–	–	50/8	
Taylor John Morris	10.10.1895	12.5.1971	20	1920–1926	997	108	1	35.60	1	1-25	0/0	45.00	11	
Taylor Mark Anthony (*CY 1990*)	27.10.1964		104	1988–1998	7,525	334*	19	43.49	1	1-11	0/0	26.00	157	113
Taylor Peter Laurence	22.8.1956		13	1986–1991	431	87	0	26.93	27	6-78	1/0	39.55	10	83
Thomas Grahame	21.3.1938		8	1964–1965	325	61	0	29.54	–	–	–/–	–	3	
Thoms George Ronald	22.3.1927	29.8.2003	1	1951	44	28	0	22.00	–	–	–/–	–	0	
Thomson Alan Lloyd ("Froggy")	2.12.1945		4	1970	22	12*	0	22.00	12	3-79	0/0	54.50	0	1
Thomson Jeffrey Robert	16.8.1950		51	1972–1985	679	49	0	12.81	200	6-46	8/0	28.00	20	50
Thomson Nathaniel Frampton Davis	29.5.1839	2.9.1896	2	1876	67	41	0	16.75	1	1-14	0/0	31.00	3	
Thurlow Hugh Motley ("Pud")	10.1.1903	3.12.1975	1	1931	0	0	0	0.00	0	0-33	0/0	–	0	
Toohey Peter Michael	20.4.1954		15	1977–1979	893	122	1	31.89	0	0-4	0/0	–	9	5
Toshack Ernest Raymond Herbert	8.12.1914	11.5.2003	12	1945–1948	73	20*	0	14.60	47	6-29	4/1	21.04	4	
Travers Joseph Patrick Francis	10.1.1871	15.9.1942	1	1901	10	9	0	5.00	1	1-14	0/0	14.00	1	
Tribe George Edward (*CY 1955*)	4.10.1920	5.4.2009	3	1946	35	25*	0	17.50	2	2-48	0/0	165.00	0	
[2] **Trott** Albert Edwin (*CY 1899*)	6.2.1873	30.7.1914	3†	1894	205	85*	0	102.50	9	8-43	1/0	21.33	4	
[2] **Trott** George Henry Stevens (*CY 1894*)	5.8.1866	10.11.1917	24	1888–1897	921	143	1	21.92	29	4-71	0/0	35.13	21	
[2] **Trumble** Hugh (*CY 1897*)	12.5.1867	14.8.1938	32	1890–1903	851	70	0	19.79	141	8-65	9/3	21.78	45	

	Born	Died	Tests	Test Career	Runs	HS	100s	Avge	Wkts	BB	5/10	Avge	Ct/St	O/T
[2] **Trumble** John William	16.9.1863	17.8.1944	7	1884–1886	243	59	0	20.25	10	3-29	0/0	22.20	3	
Trumper Victor Thomas (*CY 1903*)	2.11.1877	28.6.1915	48	1899–1911	3,163	214*	8	39.04	8	3-60	0/0	39.62	31	
Turner Alan	23.7.1950		14	1975–1976	768	136	1	29.53	–	–	–/–	–	15	6
Turner Charles Thomas Biass (*CY 1889*)	16.11.1862	1.1.1944	17	1886–1894	323	29	0	11.53	101	7-43	11/2	16.53	8	
Veivers Thomas Robert	6.4.1937		21	1963–1966	813	88	0	31.26	33	4-68	0/0	41.66	7	
Veletta Michael Robert John	30.10.1963		8	1987–1989	207	39	0	18.81	–	–	–/–	–	12	20
Voges Adam Charles	4.10.1979		20	2015–2016	1,485	269*	5	61.87	0	0-3	0/0	–	15	31/7
Wade Matthew Scott	26.12.1987		36	2011–2020	1,613	117	4	29.87	0	0-0	0/0	–	74/11	94/33
Waite Mervyn George	7.1.1911	16.12.1985	2	1938	11	8	0	3.66	1	1-150	0/0	190.00	1	
Walker Maxwell Henry Norman	12.9.1948	28.9.2016	34	1972–1977	586	78*	0	19.53	138	8-143	6/0	27.47	12	17
Wall Thomas Welbourn ("Tim")	13.5.1904	26.3.1981	18	1928–1934	121	20	0	6.36	56	5-14	3/0	35.89	11	
Walters Francis Henry	9.2.1860	1.6.1922	1	1884	12	7	0	6.00	–	–	–/–	–	2	
Walters Kevin Douglas MBE	21.12.1945		74	1965–1980	5,357	250	15	48.26	49	5-66	1/0	29.08	43	28
Ward Francis Anthony	23.2.1906	25.3.1974	4	1936–1938	36	18	0	6.00	11	6-102	1/0	52.18	1	
Warne Shane Keith (*CY 1994*)	13.9.1969		145§	1991–2006	3,154	99	0	17.32	708	8-71	37/10	25.41	125	193‡
Warner David Andrew	27.10.1986		86	2011–2020	7,311	335*	24	48.09	4	2-45	0/0	67.25	69	128/81
Watkins John Russell	16.4.1943		1	1972	39	36	0	39.00	0	0-21	0/0	–	1	
Watson Graeme Donald	8.3.1945	24.4.2020	5	1966–1972	97	50	0	10.77	6	2-67	0/0	42.33	1	2
Watson Shane Robert	17.6.1981		59§	2004–2015	3,731	176	4	35.19	75	6-33	3/0	33.68	45	190/58
Watson William James	31.1.1931	29.12.2018	4	1954	106	30	0	17.66	0	0-5	0/0	–	2	
[2] **Waugh** Mark Edward (*CY 1991*)	2.6.1965		128	1990–2002	8,029	153*	20	41.81	59	5-40	1/0	41.16	181	244
[2] **Waugh** Stephen Rodger (*CY 1989*)	2.6.1965		168	1985–2003	10,927	200	32	51.06	92	5-28	3/0	37.44	112	325
Wellham Dirk Macdonald	13.3.1959		6	1981–1986	257	103	1	23.36	–	–	–/–	–	5	17
Wessels Kepler Christoffel (*CY 1995*)	14.9.1957		24†	1982–1985	1,761	179	4	42.95	0	0-2	0/0	–	18	54‡
Whatmore Davenell Frederick	16.3.1954		7	1978–1979	293	77	0	22.53	0	0-11	0/0	–	13	1
White Cameron Leon	18.8.1983		4	2008	146	46	0	29.20	5	2-71	0/0	68.40	1	91/47
Whitney Michael Roy	24.2.1959		12	1981–1992	68	13	0	6.18	39	7-27	2/1	33.97	2	38
Whitty William James	15.8.1886	30.1.1974	14	1909–1912	161	39*	0	13.41	65	6-17	3/0	21.12	4	
Wiener Julien Mark	1.5.1955		6	1979	281	93	0	25.54	0	0-19	0/0	–	4	7
Williams Brad Andrew	20.11.1974		4	2003	23	10*	0	7.66	9	4-53	0/0	45.11	4	25
Wilson John William	20.8.1921	13.10.1985	1	1956	–	–	–	–	1	1-25	0/0	64.00	0	
Wilson Paul	12.1.1972		1	1997	0	0*	0	–	0	0-50	0/0	–	0	11
Wood Graeme Malcolm	6.11.1956		59	1977–1988	3,374	172	9	31.83	–	–	–/–	–	41	83
Woodcock Ashley James	27.2.1947		1	1973	27	27	0	27.00	–	–	–/–	–	1	1
Woodfull William Maldon OBE (*CY 1927*)	22.8.1897	11.8.1965	35	1926–1934	2,300	161	7	46.00	–	–	–/–	–	7	

§ *Warne's figures include 12 runs and six wickets and S. R. Watson's 34 runs and no wicket for Australia v the ICC World XI in the Super Series Test in 2005-06.*

	Born	Died	Tests	Test Career	Runs	HS	100s	Avge	Wkts	BB	5/10	Avge	Ct/St	O/T
Woods Samuel Moses James (*CY 1889*)	13.4.1867	30.4.1931	3†	1888	32	18	0	5.33	5	2-35	0/0	24.20	1	
Woolley Roger Douglas	16.9.1954		2	*1982–1983*	21	13	0	10.50	–	–	–/–	–	7	4
Worrall John	20.6.1860	17.11.1937	11	*1884*–1899	478	76	0	25.15	1	1-97	0/0	127.00	13	
Wright Kevin John	27.12.1953		10	*1978–1979*	219	55*	0	16.84	–	–	–/–	–	31/4	5
Yallop Graham Neil	7.10.1952		39	*1975–1984*	2,756	268	8	41.13	1	1-21	0/0	116.00	23	30
Yardley Bruce	5.9.1947	27.3.2019	33	*1977–1982*	978	74	0	19.56	126	7-98	6/1	31.63	31	7
Young Shaun	13.6.1970		1	1997	4	4*	0	4.00	0	0-5	0/0	–	0	
Zoehrer Timothy Joseph	25.9.1961		10	*1985–1986*	246	52*	0	20.50	–	–	–/–	–	18/1	22

SOUTH AFRICA (346 players)

	Born	Died	Tests	Test Career	Runs	HS	100s	Avge	Wkts	BB	5/10	Avge	Ct/St	O/T
Abbott Kyle John	18.6.1987		11	*2012–2016*	95	17	0	6.78	39	7-29	3/0	22.71	4	28/21
Ackerman Hylton Deon	14.2.1973		4	*1997*	161	57	0	20.12	–	–	–/–	–	1	
Adams Paul Regan	20.1.1977		45	*1995–2003*	360	35	0	9.00	134	7-128	4/1	32.87	29	24
Adcock Neil Amwin Treharne (*CY 1961*)	8.3.1931	6.1.2013	26	*1953–1961*	146	24	0	5.40	104	6-43	5/0	21.10	4	
Amla Hashim Mahomed (*CY 2013*)	31.3.1983		124	*2004–2018*	9,282	311*	28	46.64	0	0-4	0/0	–	108	181/41‡
Anderson James Henry	26.4.1874	11.3.1926	1	*1902*	43	32	0	21.50	–	–	–/–	–	1	
Ashley William Hare	10.2.1862	14.7.1930	1	*1888*	1	1	0	0.50	7	7-95	1/0	13.57	0	
Bacher Adam Marc	29.10.1973		19	*1996–1999*	833	96	0	26.03	0	0-4	0/0	–	11	13
Bacher Aron ("Ali")	24.5.1942		12	1965–*1969*	679	73	0	32.33	–	–	–/–	–	10	
Balaskas Xenophon Constantine	15.10.1910	12.5.1994	9	*1930–1938*	174	122*	1	14.50	22	5-49	1/0	36.63	5	
Barlow Edgar John	12.8.1940	30.12.2005	30	*1961–1969*	2,516	201	6	45.74	40	5-85	1/0	34.05	35	
Baumgartner Harold Vane	17.11.1883	8.4.1938	1	*1913*	19	16	0	9.50	2	2-99	0/0	49.50	1	
Bavuma Temba	17.5.1990		42	*2014–2020*	1,935	102*	1	31.20	1	1-29	0/0	61.00	19	6/8
Beaumont Rolland	4.2.1884	25.5.1958	5	1912–*1913*	70	31	0	7.77	0	0-0	0/0	–	2	
Begbie Denis Warburton	12.12.1914	10.3.2009	5	*1948–1949*	138	48	0	19.71	1	1-38	0/0	130.00	2	
Bell Alexander John	15.4.1906	1.8.1985	16	1929–1935	69	26*	0	6.27	48	6-99	4/0	32.64	6	
Bisset *Sir* Murray	14.4.1876	24.10.1931	3	*1898–1909*	103	35	0	25.75	–	–	–/–	–	2/1	
Bissett George Finlay	5.11.1905	14.11.1965	4	*1927*	38	23	0	19.00	25	7-29	2/0	18.76	0	
Blanckenberg James Manuel	31.12.1892	d unknown	18	*1913*–1924	455	59	0	19.78	60	6-76	4/0	30.28	9	
Bland Kenneth Colin (*CY 1966*)	5.4.1938	14.4.2018	21	*1961–1966*	1,669	144*	3	49.08	2	2-16	0/0	62.50	10	
Bock Ernest George	17.9.1908	5.9.1961	1	*1935*	11	9*	0	–	0	0-42	0/0	–	0	
Boje Nico	20.3.1973		43	*1999*–2006	1,312	85	0	25.23	100	5-62	3/0	42.65	18	113‡/1
Bond Gerald Edward	5.4.1909	27.8.1965	1	*1938*	0	0	0	0.00	0	0-16	0/0	–	0	

	Born	Died	Tests	Test Career	Runs	HS	100s	Avge	Wkts	BB	5/10	Avge	Ct/St	O/T
Bosch Tertius	14.3.1966	14.2.2000	1	1991	5	5*	0	–	3	2-61	0/0	34.66	0	2
Botha Johan	2.5.1982		5	2005–2010	83	25	0	20.75	17	4-56	0/0	33.70	3	76‡/40
Botten James Thomas ("Jackie")	21.6.1938	14.5.2006	3	1965	65	33	0	10.83	8	2-56	0/0	42.12	1	
Boucher Mark Verdon (*CY 2009*)	3.12.1976		146§	1997–2011	5,498	125	5	30.54	1	1-6	0/0	6.00	530/23	290‡/25
Brann William Henry	4.4.1899	22.9.1953	3	1922	71	50	0	14.20	–	–	–/–	–	2	
Briscoe Arthur Wellesley ("Dooley")	6.2.1911	22.4.1941	2	1935–1938	33	16	0	11.00	–	–	–/–	–	1	
Bromfield Harry Dudley	26.6.1932	27.12.2020	9	1961–1965	59	21	0	11.80	17	5-88	1/0	35.23	13	
Brown Lennox Sidney	24.11.1910	1.9.1983	2	1931	17	8	0	5.66	3	1-30	0/0	63.00	0	
Burger Christopher George de Villiers	12.7.1935	5.6.2014	2	1957	62	37*	0	20.66	–	–	–/–	–	1	
Burke Sydney Frank	11.3.1934	3.4.2017	2	1961–1964	42	20	0	14.00	11	6-128	2/1	23.36	0	
Buys Isaac Daniel	4.2.1895	d unknown	1	1922	4	4*	0	4.00	0	0-20	0/0	–	0	
Cameron Horace Brakenridge ("Jock") (*CY 1936*)	5.7.1905	2.11.1935	26	1927–1935	1,239	90	0	30.21	–	–	–/–	–	39/12	
Campbell Thomas	9.2.1882	5.10.1924	5	1909–1912	90	48	0	15.00	–	–	–/–	–	7/1	
Carlstein Peter Rudolph	28.10.1938		8	1957–1963	190	42	0	14.61	–	–	–/–	–	3	
Carter Claude Padget	23.4.1881	8.11.1952	10	1912–1924	181	45	0	18.10	28	6-50	2/0	24.78	2	
Catterall Robert Hector (*CY 1925*)	10.7.1900	3.1.1961	24	1922–1930	1,555	120	3	37.92	7	3-15	0/0	23.14	12	
Chapman Horace William	30.6.1890	1.12.1941	2	1913–1921	39	17	0	13.00	1	1-51	0/0	104.00	1	
Cheetham John Erskine	26.5.1920	21.8.1980	24	1948–1955	883	89	0	23.86	0	0-2	0/0	–	13	
Chevalier Grahame Anton	9.3.1937	14.11.2017	1	1969	0	0*	0	0.00	5	3-68	0/0	20.00	1	
Christy James Alexander Joseph	12.12.1904	1.2.1971	10	1929–1931	618	103	1	34.33	2	1-15	0/0	46.00	3	
Chubb Geoffrey Walter Ashton	12.4.1911	28.8.1982	5	1951	63	15*	0	10.50	21	6-51	2/0	27.47	0	
Cochran John Alexander Kennedy	15.7.1909	15.6.1987	1	1930	4	4	0	4.00	0	0-47	0/0	–	0	
Coen Stanley Keppel ("Shunter")	14.10.1902	29.1.1967	2	1927	101	41*	0	50.50	0	0-7	0/0	–	1	
Commaille John McIllwaine Moore ("Mick")	21.2.1883	28.7.1956	12	1909–1927	355	47	0	16.90	–	–	–/–	–	1	
Commins John Brian	19.2.1965		3	1994	125	45	0	25.00	–	–	–/–	–	2	
Conyngham Dalton Parry	10.5.1897	7.7.1979	1	1922	6	3*	0	–	2	1-40	0/0	51.50	1	
Cook Frederick James	1870	30.11.1915	1	1895	7	7	0	3.50	–	–	–/–	–	0	
[1] **Cook** Stephen Craig	29.11.1982		11	2015–2016	632	117	3	33.26	0	0-16	0/0	–	6	
[1] **Cook** Stephen James (*CY 1990*)	31.7.1953		3	1992–1993	107	43	0	17.83	–	–	–/–	–	0	4
Cooper Alfred Henry Cecil	2.9.1893	18.7.1963	1	1913	6	6	0	3.00	–	–	–/–	–	1	
Cox Joseph Lovell	28.6.1886	4.7.1971	3	1913	17	12*	0	3.40	4	2-74	0/0	61.25	1	
Cripps Godfrey	19.10.1865	27.7.1943	1	1891	21	18	0	10.50	0	0-23	0/0	–	0	
Crisp Robert James	28.5.1911	2.3.1994	9	1935–1935	123	35	0	10.25	20	5-99	1/0	37.35	3	
Cronje Wessel Johannes ("Hansie")	25.9.1969	1.6.2002	68	1991–1999	3,714	135	6	36.41	43	3-14	0/0	29.95	33	188

§ *Boucher's figures exclude 17 runs and two catches for the ICC World XI v Australia in the Super Series Test in 2005-06.*

	Born	Died	Tests	Test Career	Runs	HS	100s	Avge	Wkts	BB	5/10	Avge	Ct/St	O/T
Cullinan Daryll John	4.3.1967		70	1992–2000	4,554	275*	14	44.21	2	1-10	0/0	35.50	67	138
Curnow Sydney Harry	16.12.1907	28.7.1986	7	1930–1931	168	47	0	12.00	–	–	–/–	–	5	
Dalton Eric Londesbrough	2.12.1906	3.6.1981	15	1929–1938	698	117	2	31.72	12	4-59	0/0	40.83	5	
Davies Eric Quail	26.8.1909	11.11.1976	5	1935–1938	9	3	0	1.80	7	4-75	0/0	68.71	0	
Dawson Alan Charles	27.11.1969		2	2003	10	10	0	10.00	5	2-20	0/0	23.40	0	19
Dawson Oswald Charles	1.9.1919	22.12.2008	9	1947–1948	293	55	0	20.92	10	2-57	0/0	57.80	10	
Deane Hubert Gouvaine ("Nummy")	21.7.1895	21.10.1939	17	1924–1930	628	93	0	25.12	–	–	–/–	–	8	
de Bruyn Theunis Booysen	8.10.1992		12	2016–2019	428	101	1	19.45	0	0-6	0/0	–	11	0/2
de Bruyn Zander	5.7.1975		3	2004	155	83	0	38.75	3	2-32	0/0	30.66	0	
de Kock Quinton	17.12.1992		49	2013–2020	2,962	129*	5	38.46	–	–	–/–	–	203/11	121/47
de Lange Marchant	13.10.1990		2	2011	9	9	0	4.50	9	7-81	1/0	30.77	1	4/6
de Villiers Abraham Benjamin	17.2.1984		114	2004–2017	8,765	278*	22	50.66	2	2-49	0/0	52.00	222/5	223‡/78
de Villiers Petrus Stephanus ("Fanie")	13.10.1964		18	1993–1997	359	67*	0	18.89	85	6-23	5/2	24.27	11	83
de Wet Friedel	26.6.1980		2	2009	20	20	0	10.00	6	4-55	0/0	31.00	1	
Dippenaar Hendrik Human ("Boeta")	14.6.1977		38	1999–2006	1,718	177*	3	30.14	0	0-1	0/0	–	27	101‡/1
Dixon Cecil Donovan	12.2.1891	9.9.1969	1	1913	0	0	0	0.00	3	2-62	0/0	39.33	1	
Donald Allan Anthony (*CY 1992*)	20.10.1966		72	1991–2001	652	37	0	10.68	330	8-71	20/3	22.25	18	164
Dower Robert Reid	4.6.1876	15.9.1964	1	1898	9	9	0	4.50	–	–	–/–	–	2	
Draper Ronald George	24.12.1926		2	1949	25	15	0	8.33	–	–	–/–	–	0	
Duckworth Christopher Anthony Russell	22.3.1933	16.5.2014	2	1956	28	13	0	7.00	–	–	–/–	–	3	
Dumbrill Richard	19.11.1938		5	1965–1966	153	36	0	15.30	9	4-30	0/0	37.33	3	
Duminy Jacobus Petrus	16.12.1897	31.1.1980	3	1927–1929	30	12	0	5.00	1	1-17	0/0	39.00	2	
Duminy Jean-Paul	14.4.1984		46	2008–2017	2,103	166	6	32.85	42	4-47	0/0	38.11	38	199/81
Dunell Owen Robert	15.7.1856	21.10.1929	2	1888	42	26*	0	14.00	–	–	–/–	–	1	
du Plessis Francois ("Faf")	13.7.1984		67	2012–2020	4,108	199	10	41.08	0	0-1	0/0	–	61	143/47‡
du Preez John Harcourt	14.11.1942	8.4.2020	2	1966	0	0	0	0.00	3	2-22	0/0	17.00	2	
du Toit Jacobus Francois	2.4.1869	10.7.1909	1	1891	2	2*	0	–	1	1-47	0/0	47.00	1	
Dyer Dennis Victor	2.5.1914	16.6.1990	3	1947	96	62	0	16.00	–	–	–/–	–	0	
Eksteen Clive Edward	2.12.1966		7	1993–1999	91	22	0	10.11	8	3-12	0/0	61.75	5	6
Elgar Dean	11.6.1987		65	2012–2020	4,141	199	13	40.20	15	4-22	0/0	43.93	68	8
Elgie Michael Kelsey ("Kim")	6.3.1933		3	1961	75	56	0	12.50	0	0-18	0/0	–	4	
Elworthy Steven MBE	23.2.1965		4	1998–2002	72	48	0	18.00	13	4-66	0/0	34.15	1	39
Endean William Russell	31.5.1924	28.6.2003	28	1951–1957	1,630	162*	3	33.95	–	–	–/–	–	41	
Farrer William Stephen ("Buster")	8.12.1936		6	1961–1963	221	40	0	27.62	–	–	–/–	–	2	
Faulkner George Aubrey	17.12.1881	10.9.1930	25	1905–1924	1,754	204	4	40.79	82	7-84	4/0	26.58	20	
Fellows-Smith Jonathan Payn	3.2.1932	28.9.2013	4	1960	166	35	0	27.66	0	0-13	0/0	–	2	

	Born	Died	Tests	Test Career	Runs	HS	100s	Avge	Wkts	BB	5/10	Avge	Ct/St	O/T
Fichardt Charles Gustav	20.3.1870	30.5.1923	2	*1891–1895*	15	10	0	3.75	–	–	–/–	–	2	
Finlason Charles Edward	19.2.1860	31.7.1917	1	*1888*	6	6	0	3.00	0	0-7	0/0	–	0	
Floquet Claude Eugene	3.11.1884	22.11.1963	1	*1909*	12	11*	0	12.00	0	0-24	0/0	–	0	
Francis Howard Henry	26.5.1868	7.1.1936	2	*1898*	39	29	0	9.75	–	–	–/–	–	1	
Francois Cyril Matthew	20.6.1897	26.5.1944	5	*1922*	252	72	0	31.50	6	3-23	0/0	37.50	5	
Frank Charles Newton	27.1.1891	25.12.1961	3	*1921*	236	152	1	39.33	–	–	–/–	–	0	
Frank William Hughes Bowker	23.11.1872	16.2.1945	1	*1895*	7	5	0	3.50	1	1-52	0/0	52.00	0	
Fuller Edward Russell Henry	2.8.1931	19.7.2008	7	*1952–1957*	64	17	0	8.00	22	5-66	1/0	30.36	3	
Fullerton George Murray	8.12.1922	19.11.2002	7	1947–1951	325	88	0	25.00	–	–	–/–	–	10/2	
Funston Kenneth James	3.12.1925	15.4.2005	18	*1952–1957*	824	92	0	25.75	–	–	–/–	–	7	
Gamsy Dennis	17.2.1940		2	*1969*	39	30*	0	19.50	–	–	–/–	–	5	
Gibbs Herschelle Herman	23.2.1974		90	*1996–2007*	6,167	228	14	41.95	0	0-4	0/0	–	94	248/23
Gleeson Robert Anthony	6.12.1873	27.9.1919	1	*1895*	4	3	0	4.00	–	–	–/–	–	2	
Glover George Keyworth	13.5.1870	15.11.1938	1	*1895*	21	18*	0	21.00	1	1-28	0/0	28.00	0	
Goddard Trevor Leslie	1.8.1931	25.11.2016	41	1955–*1969*	2,516	112	1	34.46	123	6-53	5/0	26.22	48	
Gordon Norman	6.8.1911	2.9.2014	5	*1938*	8	7*	0	2.00	20	5-103	2/0	40.35	1	
Graham Robert	16.9.1877	21.4.1946	2	*1898*	6	4	0	1.50	3	2-22	0/0	42.33	2	
Grieveson Ronald Eustace	24.8.1909	24.7.1998	2	*1938*	114	75	0	57.00	–	–	–/–	–	7/3	
Griffin Geoffrey Merton	12.6.1939	16.11.2006	2	1960	25	14	0	6.25	8	4-87	0/0	24.00	0	
Hall Alfred Ewart	23.1.1896	1.1.1964	7	*1922–1930*	11	5	0	1.83	40	7-63	3/1	22.15	4	
Hall Andrew James	31.7.1975		21	*2001–2006*	760	163	1	26.20	45	3-1	0/0	35.93	16	88/2
Hall Glen Gordon	24.5.1938	26.6.1987	1	*1964*	0	0	0	0.00	1	1-94	0/0	94.00	0	
Halliwell Ernest Austin (*CY 1905*)	7.9.1864	2.10.1919	8	*1891–1902*	188	57	0	12.53	–	–	–/–	–	10/2	
Halse Clive Gray	28.2.1935	28.5.2002	3	*1963*	30	19*	0	–	6	3-50	0/0	43.33	1	
Hamza Mogammad Zubayr	19.6.1995		5	*2018–2019*	181	62	0	18.10	–	–	–/–	–	5	
[2] **Hands** Philip Albert Myburgh	18.3.1890	27.4.1951	7	*1913*–1924	300	83	0	25.00	0	0-1	0/0	–	3	
[2] **Hands** Reginald Harry Myburgh	26.7.1888	20.4.1918	1	*1913*	7	7	0	3.50	–	–	–/–	–	0	
Hanley Martin Andrew	10.11.1918	2.6.2000	1	*1948*	0	0	0	0.00	1	1-57	0/0	88.00	0	
Harmer Simon Ross (*CY 2020*)	10.2.1989		5	*2014–2015*	58	13	0	11.60	20	4-61	0/0	29.40	1	
Harris Paul Lee	2.11.1978		37	*2006–2010*	460	46	0	10.69	103	6-127	3/0	37.87	16	3
Harris Terence Anthony	27.8.1916	7.3.1993	3	1947–*1948*	100	60	0	25.00	–	–	–/–	–	1	
Hartigan Gerald Patrick Desmond	30.12.1884	7.1.1955	5	1912–*1913*	114	51	0	11.40	1	1-72	0/0	141.00	0	
Harvey Robert Lyon	14.9.1911	20.7.2000	2	*1935*	51	28	0	12.75	–	–	–/–	–	0	
Hathorn Christopher Maitland Howard	7.4.1878	17.5.1920	12	*1902–1910*	325	102	1	17.10	–	–	–/–	–	5	
Hayward Mornantau ("Nantie")	6.3.1977		16	*1999–2004*	66	14	0	7.33	54	5-56	1/0	29.79	4	21
[1, 2] **Hearne** Frank	23.11.1858	14.7.1949	4†	*1891–1895*	121	30	0	15.12	2	2-40	0/0	20.00	2	

	Born	*Died*	*Tests*	*Test Career*	*Runs*	*HS*	*100s*	*Avge*	*Wkts*	*BB*	*5/10*	*Avge*	*Ct/St*	*O/T*
[1] **Hearne** George Alfred Lawrence	27.3.1888	13.11.1978	3	*1922–1924*	59	28	0	11.80	–	–	–/–	–	3	
Heine Peter Samuel	28.6.1928	4.2.2005	14	1955–*1961*	209	31	0	9.95	58	6-58	4/0	25.08	8	
Henderson Claude William	14.6.1972		7	*2001–2002*	65	30	0	9.28	22	4-116	0/0	42.18	2	4
Hendricks Beuran Eric	8.6.1990		1	*2019*	9	5*	0	9.00	6	5-64	1/0	29.16	0	7/14
Henry Omar	23.1.1952		3	*1992*	53	34	0	17.66	3	2-56	0/0	63.00	2	3
Hime Charles Frederick William	24.10.1869	6.12.1940	1	*1895*	8	8	0	4.00	1	1-20	0/0	31.00	0	
Hudson Andrew Charles	17.3.1965		35	*1991–1997*	2,007	163	4	33.45	–	–	–/–	–	36	89
Hutchinson Philip	25.1.1862	30.9.1925	2	*1888*	14	11	0	3.50	–	–	–/–	–	3	
Imran Tahir	27.3.1979		20	*2011–2015*	130	29*	0	9.28	57	5-32	2/0	40.24	8	107/35‡
Ironside David Ernest James	2.5.1925	21.8.2005	3	*1953*	37	13	0	18.50	15	5-51	1/0	18.33	1	
Irvine Brian Lee	9.3.1944		4	*1969*	353	102	1	50.42	–	–	–/–	–	2	
Jack Steven Douglas	4.8.1970		2	*1994*	7	7	0	3.50	8	4-69	0/0	24.50	1	2
Johnson Clement Lecky	31.3.1871	31.5.1908	1	*1895*	10	7	0	5.00	0	0-57	0/0	–	1	
Kallis Jacques Henry (*CY 2013*)	16.10.1975		165§	*1995–2013*	13,206	224	45	55.25	291	6-54	5/0	32.63	196	323‡/25
Keith Headley James	25.10.1927	17.11.1997	8	*1952–1956*	318	73	0	21.20	0	0-19	0/0	–	9	
Kemp Justin Miles	2.10.1977		4	*2000–2005*	80	55	0	13.33	9	3-33	0/0	24.66	3	79‡/8
Kempis Gustav Adolph	4.8.1865	19.5.1890	1	*1888*	0	0*	0	0.00	4	3-53	0/0	19.00	0	
Khan Imraan	27.4.1984		1	*2008*	20	20	0	20.00	–	–	–/–	–	1	
[2] **Kirsten** Gary (*CY 2004*)	23.11.1967		101	*1993–2003*	7,289	275	21	45.27	2	1-0	0/0	71.00	83	185
[2] **Kirsten** Peter Noel	14.5.1955		12	*1991*–1994	626	104	1	31.30	0	0-5	0/0	–	8	40
Klaasen Heinrich	30.7.1991		1	*2019*	11	6	0	5.50	–	–	–/–	–	3/1	17/13
Kleinveldt Rory Keith	15.3.1983		4	*2012*	27	17*	0	9.00	10	3-65	0/0	42.20	2	10/6
Klusener Lance (*CY 2000*)	4.9.1971		49	*1996*–2004	1,906	174	4	32.86	80	8-64	1/0	37.91	34	171
Kotze Johannes Jacobus ("Kodgee")	7.8.1879	7.7.1931	3	*1902*–1907	2	2	0	0.40	6	3-64	0/0	40.50	3	
Kuhn Heino Gunther	1.4.1984		4	2017	113	34	0	14.12	–	–	–/–	–	1	0/7
Kuiper Adrian Paul	24.8.1959		1	*1991*	34	34	0	17.00	–	–	–/–	–	1	25
Kuys Frederick	21.3.1870	12.9.1953	1	*1898*	26	26	0	13.00	2	2-31	0/0	15.50	0	
Lance Herbert Roy ("Tiger")	6.6.1940	10.11.2010	13	*1961–1969*	591	70	0	28.14	12	3-30	0/0	39.91	7	
Langeveldt Charl Kenneth	17.12.1974		6	*2004–2005*	16	10	0	8.00	16	5-46	1/0	37.06	2	72/9
Langton Arthur Chudleigh Beaumont ("Chud")	2.3.1912	27.11.1942	15	1935–*1938*	298	73*	0	15.68	40	5-58	1/0	45.67	8	
Lawrence Godfrey Bernard	31.3.1932		5	*1961*	141	43	0	17.62	28	8-53	2/0	18.28	2	
le Roux Frederick Louis	5.2.1882	22.9.1963	1	*1913*	1	1	0	0.50	0	0-5	0/0	–	0	
Lewis Percy Tyson	2.10.1884	30.1.1976	1	*1913*	0	0	0	0.00	–	–	–/–	–	0	
Liebenberg Gerhardus Frederick Johannes	7.4.1972		5	1997–1998	104	45	0	13.00	–	–	–/–	–	1	4
Linde George Fredrik	4.12.1991		1	*2019*	64	37	0	32.00	4	4-133	0/0	33.25	0	0/3

§ *Kallis's figures exclude 83 runs, one wicket and four catches for the ICC World XI v Australia in the Super Series Test in 2005-06.*

	Born	Died	Tests	Test Career	Runs	HS	100s	Avge	Wkts	BB	5/10	Avge	Ct/St	O/T
[1] **Lindsay** Denis Thomson	4.9.1939	30.11.2005	19	*1963–1969*	1,130	182	3	37.66	–	–	–/–	–	57/2	
[1] **Lindsay** John Dixon	8.9.1908	31.8.1990	3	1947	21	9*	0	7.00	–	–	–/–	–	4/1	
Lindsay Nevil Vernon	30.7.1886	2.2.1976	1	*1921*	35	29	0	17.50	–	–	–/–	–	1	
Ling William Victor Stone	3.10.1891	26.9.1960	6	*1921–1922*	168	38	0	16.80	0	0-20	0/0	–	1	
Llewellyn Charles Bennett (*CY 1911*)	26.9.1876	7.6.1964	15	*1895*–1912	544	90	0	20.14	48	6-92	4/1	29.60	7	
Lundie Eric Balfour	15.3.1888	12.9.1917	1	*1913*	1	1	0	1.00	4	4-101	0/0	26.75	0	
Macaulay Michael John	19.4.1939		1	*1964*	33	21	0	16.50	2	1-10	0/0	36.50	0	
McCarthy Cuan Neil	24.3.1929	14.8.2000	15	*1948*–1951	28	5	0	3.11	36	6-43	2/0	41.94	6	
McGlew Derrick John ("Jackie") (*CY 1956*)	11.3.1929	9.6.1998	34	1951–*1961*	2,440	255*	7	42.06	0	0-7	0/0	–	18	
McKenzie Neil Douglas (*CY 2009*)	24.11.1975		58	2000–*2008*	3,253	226	5	37.39	0	0-1	0/0	–	54	64/2
McKinnon Atholl Henry	20.8.1932	2.12.1983	8	1960–*1966*	107	27	0	17.83	26	4-128	0/0	35.57	1	
McLaren Ryan	9.2.1983		2	*2009–2013*	47	33*	0	23.50	3	2-72	0/0	54.00	0	54/12
McLean Roy Alastair (*CY 1961*)	9.7.1930	26.8.2007	40	1951–*1964*	2,120	142	5	30.28	0	0-1	0/0	–	23	
McMillan Brian Mervin	22.12.1963		38	*1992*–1998	1,968	113	3	39.36	75	4-65	0/0	33.82	49	78
McMillan Quintin	23.6.1904	3.7.1948	13	1929–*1931*	306	50*	0	18.00	36	5-66	2/0	34.52	8	
Maharaj Keshav Athmanand	7.2.1990		32	*2016–2020*	718	73	0	16.31	110	9-129	6/1	34.04	10	7
Malan Pieter Jacobus	13.8.1989		3	*2019*	156	84	0	26.00	0	0-5	0/0	–	3	
Mann Norman Bertram Fleetwood ("Tufty")	28.12.1920	31.7.1952	19	1947–1951	400	52	0	13.33	58	6-59	1/0	33.10	3	
Mansell Percy Neville Frank MBE	16.3.1920	9.5.1995	13	1951–1955	355	90	0	17.75	11	3-58	0/0	66.90	15	
Markham Lawrence Anderson	12.9.1924	5.8.2000	1	*1948*	20	20	0	20.00	1	1-34	0/0	72.00	0	
Markram Aiden Kyle	4.10.1994		22	*2017–2020*	1,533	152	4	39.30	0	0-0	0/0	–	16	26/2
Marx Waldemar Frederick Eric	4.7.1895	2.6.1974	3	*1921*	125	36	0	20.83	4	3-85	0/0	36.00	0	
Matthews Craig Russell	15.2.1965		18	*1992–1995*	348	62*	0	18.31	52	5-42	2/0	28.88	4	56
Meintjes Douglas James	9.6.1890	17.7.1979	2	*1922*	43	21	0	14.33	6	3-38	0/0	19.16	3	
Melle Michael George	3.6.1930	28.12.2003	7	*1949–1952*	68	17	0	8.50	26	6-71	2/0	32.73	4	
Melville Alan (*CY 1948*)	19.5.1910	18.4.1983	11	*1938–1948*	894	189	4	52.58	–	–	–/–	–	8	
Middleton James	30.9.1865	23.12.1913	6	*1895–1902*	52	22	0	7.42	24	5-51	2/0	18.41	1	
Mills Charles Henry	26.11.1867	26.7.1948	1	*1891*	25	21	0	12.50	2	2-83	0/0	41.50	1	
Milton *Sir* William Henry	3.12.1854	6.3.1930	3	*1888–1891*	68	21	0	11.33	2	1-5	0/0	24.00	2	
Mitchell Bruce (*CY 1936*)	8.1.1909	1.7.1995	42	1929–*1948*	3,471	189*	8	48.88	27	5-87	1/0	51.11	56	
Mitchell Frank (*CY 1902*)	13.8.1872	11.10.1935	3†	1912	28	12	0	4.66	–	–	–/–	–	0	
Morkel Denijs Paul Beck	25.1.1906	6.10.1980	16	*1927–1931*	663	88	0	24.55	18	4-93	0/0	45.61	13	
[2] **Morkel** Johannes Albertus	10.6.1981		1	2008	58	58	0	58.00	1	1-44	0/0	132.00	0	56‡/50
[2] **Morkel** Morne	6.10.1984		86	*2006–2017*	944	40	0	11.65	309	6-23	8/0	27.66	25	114‡/41‡
Morris Christopher Henry	30.4.1987		4	*2015*–2017	173	69	0	24.71	12	3-38	0/0	38.25	5	42/23
Mulder Peter Wiaan Adriaan	19.2.1998		3	*2018–2020*	57	36	0	14.25	10	3-25	0/0	19.70	1	10

	Born	Died	Tests	Test Career	Runs	HS	100s	Avge	Wkts	BB	5/10	Avge	Ct/St	O/T
Murray Anton Ronald Andrew	30.4.1922	17.4.1995	10	*1952–1953*	289	109	1	22.23	18	4-169	0/0	39.44	3	
Muthusamy Senuran	22.2.1994		2	*2019*	98	49*	0	49.00	2	1-63	0/0	90.00	2	
Nel Andre	15.7.1977		36	*2001*–2008	337	34	0	9.91	123	6-32	3/1	31.86	16	79/2
Nel John Desmond	10.7.1928	13.1.2018	6	*1949–1957*	150	38	0	13.63	–	–	–/–	–	1	
Newberry Claude	1889	1.8.1916	4	*1913*	62	16	0	7.75	11	4-72	0/0	24.36	3	
Newson Edward Serrurier OBE	2.12.1910	24.4.1988	3	*1930–1938*	30	16	0	7.50	4	2-58	0/0	66.25	3	
Ngam Mfuneko	29.1.1979		3	*2000*	0	0*	0	–	11	3-26	0/0	17.18	1	
Ngidi Lungisani True-man	29.03.1996		7	*2017–2020*	31	14*	0	6.20	22	6-39	1/0	25.72	4	26/16
Nicholson Frank	17.9.1909	30.7.1982	4	*1935*	76	29	0	10.85	–	–	–/–	–	3	
Nicolson John Fairless William	19.7.1899	13.12.1935	3	*1927*	179	78	0	35.80	0	0-5	0/0	–	0	
Nortje Anrich Arno	16.11.1993		8	*2019–2020*	102	40	0	9.27	30	6-56	2/0	30.73	1	7/5
Norton Norman Ogilvie	11.5.1881	27.6.1968	1	*1909*	9	7	0	4.50	4	4-47	0/0	11.75	0	
[1] **Nourse** Arthur Dudley (*CY 1948*)	12.11.1910	14.8.1981	34	1935–1951	2,960	231	9	53.81	0	0-0	0/0	–	12	
[1] **Nourse** Arthur William ("Dave")	25.1.1879	8.7.1948	45	*1902–1924*	2,234	111	1	29.78	41	4-25	0/0	37.87	43	
Ntini Makhaya	6.7.1977		101	*1997–2009*	699	32*	0	9.84	390	7-37	18/4	28.82	25	172‡/10
Nupen Eiulf Peter ("Buster")	1.1.1902	29.1.1977	17	*1921–1935*	348	69	0	14.50	50	6-46	5/1	35.76	9	
Ochse Arthur Edward	11.3.1870	11.4.1918	2	*1888*	16	8	0	4.00	–	–	–/–	–	0	
Ochse Arthur Lennox	11.10.1899	5.5.1949	3	*1927*–1929	11	4*	0	3.66	10	4-79	0/0	36.20	1	
O'Linn Sidney	5.5.1927	11.12.2016	7	1960–*1961*	297	98	0	27.00	–	–	–/–	–	4	
Olivier Duanne	9.5.1992		10	*2016–2018*	26	10*	0	3.71	48	6-37	3/1	19.25	2	2
Ontong Justin Lee	4.1.1980		2	*2001–2004*	57	32	0	19.00	1	1-79	0/0	133.00	1	27‡/14
Owen-Smith Harold Geoffrey ("Tuppy") (*CY 1930*)	18.2.1909	28.2.1990	5	1929	252	129	1	42.00	0	0-3	0/0	–	4	
Palm Archibald William	8.6.1901	17.8.1966	1	*1927*	15	13	0	7.50	–	–	–/–	–	1	
Parker George Macdonald	27.5.1899	1.5.1969	2	1924	3	2*	0	1.50	8	6-152	1/0	34.12	0	
Parkin Durant Clifford	20.2.1873	20.3.1936	1	*1891*	6	6	0	3.00	3	3-82	0/0	27.33	1	
Parnell Wayne Dillon	30.7.1989		6	*2009–2017*	67	23	0	16.75	15	4-51	0/0	27.60	3	65/40
Partridge Joseph Titus	9.12.1932	6.6.1988	11	*1963–1964*	73	13*	0	10.42	44	7-91	3/0	31.20	6	
Paterson Dane	4.4.1989		2	*2019*	43	39*	0	43.00	4	2-86	0/0	41.50	1	4/8
Pearse Charles Ormerod Cato	10.10.1884	7.5.1953	3	*1910*	55	31	0	9.16	3	3-56	0/0	35.33	1	
Pegler Sidney James	28.7.1888	10.9.1972	16	*1909*–1924	356	35*	0	15.47	47	7-65	2/0	33.44	5	
Petersen Alviro Nathan	25.11.1980		36	*2009–2014*	2,093	182	5	34.88	1	1-2	0/0	62.00	31	21/2
Peterson Robin John	4.8.1979		15	2003–*2013*	464	84	0	27.29	38	5-33	1/0	37.26	9	79/21
Phehlukwayo Andile Lucky	3.3.1996		4	*2017*	19	9	0	9.50	11	3-13	0/0	13.36	2	58/27
Philander Vernon Darryl	24.6.1985		64	*2011–2019*	1,779	74	0	24.04	224	6-21	13/2	22.32	17	30/7
Piedt Dane Lee-Roy	6.3.1990		9	*2014–2019*	131	56	0	11.90	26	5-153	1/0	45.19	5	

	Born	Died	Tests	Test Career	Runs	HS	100s	Avge	Wkts	BB	5/10	Avge	Ct/St	O/T
[2] **Pithey** Anthony John	17.7.1933	17.11.2006	17	1956–1964	819	154	1	31.50	0	0-5	0/0	–	3	
[2] **Pithey** David Bartlett	4.10.1936	21.1.2018	8	1963–1966	138	55	0	12.54	12	6-58	1/0	48.08	6	
Plimsoll Jack Bruce	27.10.1917	11.11.1999	1	1947	16	8*	0	16.00	3	3-128	0/0	47.66	0	
[1, 2] **Pollock** Peter Maclean (*CY 1966*)	30.6.1941		28	1961–1969	607	75*	0	21.67	116	6-38	9/1	24.18	9	
[2] **Pollock** Robert Graeme (*CY 1966*)	27.2.1944		23	1963–1969	2,256	274	7	60.97	4	2-50	0/0	51.00	17	
[1] **Pollock** Shaun Maclean (*CY 2003*)	16.7.1973		108	1995–2007	3,781	111	2	32.31	421	7-87	16/1	23.11	72	294‡/12
Poore Robert Montagu (*CY 1900*)	20.3.1866	14.7.1938	3	1895	76	20	0	12.66	1	1-4	0/0	4.00	3	
Pothecary James Edward	6.12.1933	11.5.2016	3	1960	26	12	0	6.50	9	4-58	0/0	39.33	2	
Powell Albert William	18.7.1873	11.9.1948	1	1898	16	11	0	8.00	1	1-10	0/0	10.00	2	
Pretorius Dewald	6.12.1977		4	2001–2003	22	9	0	7.33	6	4-115	0/0	71.66	0	
Pretorius Dwaine	29.3.1989		3	2019	83	37	0	13.83	7	2-26	0/0	36.00	2	22/11
Prince Ashwell Gavin	28.5.1977		66	2001–2011	3,665	162*	11	41.64	1	1-2	0/0	47.00	47	49‡/1
Prince Charles Frederick Henry	11.9.1874	2.2.1949	1	1898	6	5	0	3.00	–	–	–/–	–	0	
Pringle Meyrick Wayne	22.6.1966		4	1991–1995	67	33	0	16.75	5	2-62	0/0	54.00	0	17
Procter Michael John (*CY 1970*)	15.9.1946		7	1966–1969	226	48	0	25.11	41	6-73	1/0	15.02	4	
Promnitz Henry Louis Ernest	23.2.1904	7.9.1983	2	1927	14	5	0	3.50	8	5-58	1/0	20.12	2	
Quinn Neville Anthony	21.2.1908	5.8.1934	12	1929–1931	90	28	0	6.00	35	6-92	1/0	32.71	1	
Rabada Kagiso	25.5.1995		43	2015–2019	606	34	0	11.43	197	7-112	9/4	22.95	22	75/26
Reid Norman	26.12.1890	6.6.1947	1	1921	17	11	0	8.50	2	2-63	0/0	31.50	0	
Rhodes Jonathan Neil (*CY 1999*)	27.7.1969		52	1992–2000	2,532	117	3	35.66	0	0-0	0/0	–	34	245
[2] **Richards** Alfred Renfrew	14.12.1867	9.1.1904	1	1895	6	6	0	3.00	–	–	–/–	–	0	
Richards Barry Anderson (*CY 1969*)	21.7.1945		4	1969	508	140	2	72.57	1	1-12	0/0	26.00	3	
[2] **Richards** William Henry Matthews	26.3.1862	4.1.1903	1	1888	4	4	0	2.00	–	–	–/–	–	0	
Richardson David John	16.9.1959		42	1991–1997	1,359	109	1	24.26	–	–	–/–	–	150/2	122
Robertson John Benjamin	5.6.1906	5.7.1985	3	1935	51	17	0	10.20	6	3-143	0/0	53.50	2	
Rose-Innes Albert	16.2.1868	22.11.1946	2	1888	14	13	0	3.50	5	5-43	1/0	17.80	2	
Routledge Thomas William	18.4.1867	9.5.1927	4	1891–1895	72	24	0	9.00	–	–	–/–	–	2	
[2] **Rowan** Athol Matthew Burchell	7.2.1921	22.2.1998	15	1947–1951	290	41	0	17.05	54	5-68	4/0	38.59	7	
[2] **Rowan** Eric Alfred Burchell (*CY 1952*)	20.7.1909	30.4.1993	26	1935–1951	1,965	236	3	43.66	0	0-0	0/0	–	14	
Rowe George Alexander	15.6.1874	8.1.1950	5	1895–1902	26	13*	0	4.33	15	5-115	1/0	30.40	4	
Rudolph Jacobus Andries	4.5.1981		48	2003–2012	2,622	222*	6	35.43	4	1-1	0/0	108.00	29	43‡/1
Rushmere Mark Weir	7.1.1965		1	1991	6	3	0	3.00	–	–	–/–	–	0	4
Samuelson Sivert Vause	21.11.1883	18.11.1958	1	1909	22	15	0	11.00	0	0-64	0/0	–	1	
Schultz Brett Nolan	26.8.1970		9	1992–1997	9	6	0	1.50	37	5-48	2/0	20.24	2	1
Schwarz Reginald Oscar (*CY 1908*)	4.5.1875	18.11.1918	20	1905–1912	374	61	0	13.85	55	6-47	2/0	25.76	18	
Seccull Arthur William	14.9.1868	20.7.1945	1	1895	23	17*	0	23.00	2	2-37	0/0	18.50	1	

	Born	Died	Tests	Test Career	Runs	HS	100s	Avge	Wkts	BB	5/10	Avge	Ct/St	O/T
Seymour Michael Arthur ("Kelly")	5.6.1936	18.2.2019	7	1963–1969	84	36	0	12.00	9	3-80	0/0	65.33	2	
Shalders William Alfred	12.2.1880	18.3.1917	12	1898–1907	355	42	0	16.13	1	1-6	0/0	6.00	3	
Shamsi Tabraiz	18.2.1990		2	2016–2018	20	18*	0	20.00	6	3-91	0/0	46.33	0	22/25
Shepstone George Harold	9.4.1876	3.7.1940	2	1895–1898	38	21	0	9.50	0	0-8	0/0	–	2	
Sherwell Percy William	17.8.1880	17.4.1948	13	1905–1910	427	115	1	23.72	–	–	–/–	–	20/16	
Siedle Ivan Julian ("Jack")	11.1.1903	24.8.1982	18	1927–1935	977	141	1	28.73	1	1-7	0/0	7.00	7	
Sinclair James Hugh	16.10.1876	23.2.1913	25	1895–1910	1,069	106	3	23.23	63	6-26	1/0	31.68	9	
Sipamla Lubabalo Lutho	12.5.1998		2	2020	5	5	0	2.50	10	4-76	0/0	16.70	1	4/6
Smith Charles James Edward	25.12.1872	27.3.1947	3	1902	106	45	0	21.20	–	–	–/–	–	2	
Smith Frederick William	31.3.1861	17.4.1914	3	1888–1895	45	12	0	9.00	–	–	–/–	–	2	
Smith Graeme Craig (*CY 2004*)	1.2.1981		116§	2001–2013	9,253	277	27	48.70	8	2-145	0/0	110.62	166	196‡/33
Smith Vivian Ian	23.2.1925	25.8.2015	9	1947–1957	39	11*	0	3.90	12	4-143	0/0	64.08	3	
Snell Richard Peter	12.9.1968		5	1991–1994	95	48	0	13.57	19	4-74	0/0	28.31	1	42
[2] **Snooke** Sibley John ("Tip")	1.2.1881	14.8.1966	26	1905–1922	1,008	103	1	22.40	35	8-70	1/1	20.05	24	
[2] **Snooke** Stanley de la Courtte	11.11.1878	6.4.1959	1	1907	0	0	0	0.00	–	–	–/–	–	2	
Solomon William Rodger Thomson	23.4.1872	13.7.1964	1	1898	4	2	0	2.00	–	–	–/–	–	1	
Stewart Robert Burnard	3.9.1856	12.9.1913	1	1888	13	9	0	6.50	–	–	–/–	–	2	
Steyn Dale Willem (*CY 2013*)	27.6.1983		93	2004–2018	1,251	76	0	13.59	439	7-51	26/5	22.95	26	123‡/47
Steyn Philippus Jeremia Rudolf	30.6.1967		3	1994	127	46	0	21.16	–	–	–/–	–	0	1
Stricker Louis Anthony	26.5.1884	5.2.1960	13	1909–1912	344	48	0	14.33	1	1-36	0/0	105.00	3	
Strydom Pieter Coenraad	10.6.1969		2	1999	35	30	0	11.66	0	0-27	0/0	–	1	10
Susskind Manfred John	8.6.1891	9.7.1957	5	1924	268	65	0	33.50	–	–	–/–	–	1	
Symcox Patrick Leonard	14.4.1960		20	1993–1998	741	108	1	28.50	37	4-69	0/0	43.32	5	80
Taberer Henry Melville	7.10.1870	5.6.1932	1	1902	2	2	0	2.00	1	1-25	0/0	48.00	0	
[2] **Tancred** Augustus Bernard	20.8.1865	23.11.1911	2	1888	87	29	0	29.00	–	–	–/–	–	2	
[2] **Tancred** Louis Joseph	7.10.1876	28.7.1934	14	1902–1913	530	97	0	21.20	–	–	–/–	–	3	
[2] **Tancred** Vincent Maximillian	7.7.1875	3.6.1904	1	1898	25	18	0	12.50	–	–	–/–	–	0	
[2] **Tapscott** George Lancelot ("Dusty")	7.11.1889	13.12.1940	1	1913	5	4	0	2.50	–	–	–/–	–	1	
[2] **Tapscott** Lionel Eric ("Doodles")	18.3.1894	7.7.1934	2	1922	58	50*	0	29.00	0	0-2	0/0	–	0	
Tayfield Hugh Joseph (*CY 1956*)	30.1.1929	24.2.1994	37	1949–1960	862	75	0	16.90	170	9-113	14/2	25.91	26	
Taylor Alistair Innes ("Scotch")	25.7.1925	7.2.2004	1	1956	18	12	0	9.00	–	–	–/–	–	0	
[2] **Taylor** Daniel	9.1.1887	24.1.1957	2	1913	85	36	0	21.25	–	–	–/–	–	0	
[2] **Taylor** Herbert Wilfred (*CY 1925*)	5.5.1889	8.2.1973	42	1912–1931	2,936	176	7	40.77	5	3-15	0/0	31.20	19	
Terbrugge David John	31.1.1977		7	1998–2003	16	4*	0	5.33	20	5-46	1/0	25.85	4	4
Theunissen Nicolaas Hendrik Christiaan de Jong	4.5.1867	9.11.1929	1	1888	2	2*	0	2.00	0	0-51	0/0	–	0	

§ *G. C. Smith's figures exclude 12 runs and three catches for the ICC World XI v Australia in the Super Series Test in 2005-06.*

	Born	*Died*	*Tests*	*Test Career*	*Runs*	*HS*	*100s*	*Avge*	*Wkts*	*BB*	*5/10*	*Avge*	*Ct/St*	*O/T*
Thornton George	24.12.1867	31.1.1939	1	*1902*	1	1*	0	–	1	1-20	0/0	20.00	1	
Tomlinson Denis Stanley	4.9.1910	11.7.1993	1	1935	9	9	0	9.00	0	0-38	0/0	–	0	
Traicos Athanasios John	17.5.1947		3†	*1969*	8	5*	0	4.00	4	2-70	0/0	51.75	4	0‡
Trimborn Patrick Henry Joseph	18.5.1940		4	*1966–1969*	13	11*	0	6.50	11	3-12	0/0	23.36	7	
Tsolekile Thami Lungisa	9.10.1980		3	*2004*	47	22	0	9.40	–	–	–/–	–	6	
Tsotsobe Lonwabo Lennox	7.3.1984		5	2010–*2010*	19	8*	0	6.33	9	3-43	0/0	49.77	1	61/23
[1] **Tuckett** Lindsay Thomas Delville	6.2.1919	5.9.2016	9	1947–*1948*	131	40*	0	11.90	19	5-68	2/0	51.57	9	
[1] **Tuckett** Lindsay Richard ("Len")	19.4.1885	8.4.1963	1	*1913*	0	0*	0	0.00	0	0-24	0/0	–	2	
Twentyman-Jones Percy Sydney	13.9.1876	8.3.1954	1	*1902*	0	0	0	0.00	–	–	–/–	–	0	
van der Bijl Pieter Gerhard Vintcent	21.10.1907	16.2.1973	5	*1938*	460	125	1	51.11	–	–	–/–	–	1	
van der Dussen Hendrik Erasmus ("Rassie")	7.2.1989		6	*2019–2020*	356	98	0	35.60	–	–	–/–	–	12	21/18
van der Merwe Edward Alexander	9.11.1903	26.2.1971	2	1929–*1935*	27	19	0	9.00	–	–	–/–	–	3	
van der Merwe Peter Laurence	14.3.1937	23.1.2013	15	*1963–1966*	533	76	0	25.38	1	1-6	0/0	22.00	11	
van Jaarsveld Martin	18.6.1974		9	*2002–2004*	397	73	0	30.53	0	0-28	0/0	–	11	11
van Ryneveld Clive Berrange	19.3.1928	29.1.2018	19	1951–*1957*	724	83	0	26.81	17	4-67	0/0	39.47	14	
van Zyl Stiaan	19.9.1987		12	*2014*–2016	395	101*	1	26.33	6	3-20	0/0	24.66	6	
Varnals George Derek	24.7.1935		3	*1964*	97	23	0	16.16	0	0-2	0/0	–	0	
Vilas Dane James	10.6.1985		6	2015–*2015*	94	26	0	10.44	–	–	–/–	–	13	0/1
Viljoen G. C. ("Hardus")	6.3.1989		1	*2015*	26	20*	0	26.00	1	1-79	0/0	94.00	0	
Viljoen Kenneth George	14.5.1910	21.1.1974	27	*1930–1948*	1,365	124	2	28.43	0	0-10	0/0	–	5	
Vincent Cyril Leverton	16.2.1902	24.8.1968	25	*1927*–1935	526	60	0	20.23	84	6-51	3/0	31.32	27	
Vintcent Charles Henry	2.9.1866	28.9.1943	3	*1888–1891*	26	9	0	4.33	4	3-88	0/0	48.25	1	
Vogler Albert Edward Ernest (*CY 1908*)	28.11.1876	9.8.1946	15	*1905–1910*	340	65	0	17.00	64	7-94	5/1	22.73	20	
[2] **Wade** Herbert Frederick	14.9.1905	23.11.1980	10	1935–*1935*	327	40*	0	20.43	–	–	–/–	–	4	
[2] **Wade** Walter Wareham ("Billy")	18.6.1914	31.5.2003	11	*1938–1949*	511	125	1	28.38	–	–	–/–	–	15/2	
Waite John Henry Bickford	19.1.1930	22.6.2011	50	1951–*1964*	2,405	134	4	30.44	–	–	–/–	–	124/17	
Walter Kenneth Alexander	5.11.1939	13.9.2003	2	*1961*	11	10	0	3.66	6	4-63	0/0	32.83	3	
Ward Thomas Alfred	2.8.1887	16.2.1936	23	1912–1924	459	64	0	13.90	–	–	–/–	–	19/13	
Watkins John Cecil	10.4.1923		15	*1949–1956*	612	92	0	23.53	29	4-22	0/0	28.13	12	
Wesley Colin	5.9.1937		3	1960	49	35	0	9.80	–	–	–/–	–	1	
Wessels Kepler Christoffel (*CY 1995*)	14.9.1957		16†	*1991*–1994	1,027	118	2	38.03	–	–	–/–	–	12	55‡
Westcott Richard John	19.9.1927	16.1.2013	5	*1953–1957*	166	62	0	18.44	0	0-22	0/0	–	0	
White Gordon Charles	5.2.1882	17.10.1918	17	*1905*–1912	872	147	2	30.06	9	4-47	0/0	33.44	10	
Willoughby Charl Myles	3.12.1974		2	2003	–	–	–	–	1	1-47	0/0	125.00	0	3
Willoughby Joseph Thomas	7.11.1874	11.3.1952	2	*1895*	8	5	0	2.00	6	2-37	0/0	26.50	0	
Wimble Clarence Skelton	22.4.1861	28.1.1930	1	*1891*	0	0	0	0.00	–	–	–/–	–	0	

	Born	Died	Tests	Test Career	Runs	HS	100s	Avge	Wkts	BB	5/10	Avge	Ct/St	O/T
Winslow Paul Lyndhurst	21.5.1929	24.5.2011	5	*1949*–1955	186	108	1	20.66	–	–	–/–	–	1	
Wynne Owen Edgar	1.6.1919	13.7.1975	6	*1948–1949*	219	50	0	18.25	–	–	–/–	–	3	
Zondeki Monde	25.7.1982		6	2003–*2008*	82	59	0	16.40	19	6-39	1/0	25.26	1	11‡/1
Zulch Johan Wilhelm	2.1.1886	19.5.1924	16	*1909–1921*	983	150	2	32.76	0	0-2	0/0	–	4	

WEST INDIES (322 players)

	Born	Died	Tests	Test Career	Runs	HS	100s	Avge	Wkts	BB	5/10	Avge	Ct/St	O/T
Achong Ellis Edgar	16.2.1904	30.8.1986	6	*1929–1934*	81	22	0	8.10	8	2-64	0/0	47.25	6	
Adams James Clive	9.1.1968		54	*1991–2000*	3,012	208*	6	41.26	27	5-17	1/0	49.48	48	127
Alexander Franz Copeland Murray ("Gerry")	2.11.1928	16.4.2011	25	1957–*1960*	961	108	1	30.03	–	–	–/–	–	85/5	
Ali Imtiaz	28.7.1954		1	*1975*	1	1*	0	–	2	2-37	0/0	44.50	0	
Ali Inshan	25.9.1949	24.6.1995	12	*1970–1976*	172	25	0	10.75	34	5-59	1/0	47.67	7	
Allan David Walter	5.11.1937		5	*1961*–1966	75	40*	0	12.50	–	–	–/–	–	15/3	
Allen Ian Basil Alston	6.10.1965		2	1991	5	4*	0	–	5	2-69	0/0	36.00	1	
Ambris Sunil Walford	23.3.1993		6	*2017–2018*	166	43	0	15.09	–	–	–/–	–	2	13
Ambrose *Sir* Curtly Elconn Lynwall (*CY 1992*)	21.9.1963		98	*1987*–2000	1,439	53	0	12.40	405	8-45	22/3	20.99	18	176
Arthurton Keith Lloyd Thomas	21.2.1965		33	1988–1995	1,382	157*	2	30.71	1	1-17	0/0	183.00	22	105
Asgarali Nyron Sultan	28.12.1920	5.11.2006	2	1957	62	29	0	15.50	–	–	–/–	–	0	
[2] **Atkinson** Denis St Eval	9.8.1926	9.11.2001	22	*1948–1957*	922	219	1	31.79	47	7-53	3/0	35.04	11	
[2] **Atkinson** Eric St Eval	6.11.1927	29.5.1998	8	*1957–1958*	126	37	0	15.75	25	5-42	1/0	23.56	2	
Austin Richard Arkwright	5.9.1954	7.2.2015	2	*1977*	22	20	0	11.00	0	0-5	0/0	–	2	1
Austin Ryan Anthony	15.11.1981		2	2009	39	19	0	9.75	3	1-29	0/0	51.66	3	
Bacchus Sheik Faoud Ahamul Fasiel	31.1.1954		19	*1977–1981*	782	250	1	26.06	0	0-3	0/0	–	17	29
Baichan Leonard	12.5.1946		3	*1974–1975*	184	105*	1	46.00	–	–	–/–	–	2	
Baker Lionel Sionne	6.9.1984		4	*2008*–2009	23	17	0	11.50	5	2-39	0/0	79.00	1	10/3
Banks Omari Ahmed Clemente	17.7.1982		10	*2002*–2005	318	50*	0	26.50	28	4-87	0/0	48.82	6	5
Baptiste Eldine Ashworth Elderfield	12.3.1960		10	*1983–1989*	233	87*	0	23.30	16	3-31	0/0	35.18	2	43
Barath Adrian Boris	14.4.1990		15	*2009*–2012	657	104	1	23.46	0	0-3	0/0	–	13	14/2
Barrett Arthur George	4.4.1944	6.3.2018	6	*1970–1974*	40	19	0	6.66	13	3-43	0/0	46.38	0	
Barrow Ivanhoe Mordecai	16.1.1911	2.4.1979	11	*1929*–1939	276	105	1	16.23	–	–	–/–	–	17/5	
Bartlett Edward Lawson	10.3.1906	21.12.1976	5	1928–*1930*	131	84	0	18.71	–	–	–/–	–	2	
Baugh Carlton Seymour	23.6.1982		21	*2002–2011*	610	68	0	17.94	–	–	–/–	–	43/5	47/3
Benjamin Kenneth Charlie Griffith	8.4.1967		26	*1991–1997*	222	43*	0	7.92	92	6-66	4/1	30.27	2	26
Benjamin Winston Keithroy Matthew	31.12.1964		21	*1987–1994*	470	85	0	18.80	61	4-46	0/0	27.01	12	85

	Born	*Died*	*Tests*	*Test Career*	*Runs*	*HS*	*100s*	*Avge*	*Wkts*	*BB*	*5/10*	*Avge*	*Ct/St*	*O/T*
Benn Sulieman Jamaal	22.7.1981		26	*2007–2014*	486	42	0	14.29	87	6-81	6/0	39.10	14	47/24
Bernard David Eddison	19.7.1981		3	*2002–2009*	202	69	0	40.40	4	2-30	0/0	46.25	0	20/1
Bess Brandon Jeremy	13.12.1987		1	2010	11	11*	0	11.00	1	1-65	0/0	92.00	0	
Best Carlisle Alonza	14.5.1959		8	*1985–1990*	342	164	1	28.50	0	0-2	0/0	–	8	24
Best Tino la Bertram	26.8.1981		25	*2002–2013*	401	95	0	12.53	57	6-40	2/0	40.19	6	26/6
Betancourt Nelson	4.6.1887	12.10.1947	1	*1929*	52	39	0	26.00	–	–	–/–	–	0	
Binns Alfred Phillip	24.7.1929	29.12.2017	5	*1952–1955*	64	27	0	9.14	–	–	–/–	–	14/3	
Birkett Lionel Sydney	14.4.1905	16.1.1998	4	*1930*	136	64	0	17.00	1	1-16	0/0	71.00	4	
Bishoo Devendra	6.11.1985		36	*2010–2018*	707	45	0	15.36	117	8-49	4/1	37.17	20	42/7
Bishop Ian Raphael	24.10.1967		43	*1988–1997*	632	48	0	12.15	161	6-40	6/0	24.27	8	84
Black Marlon Ian	7.6.1975		6	*2000–2001*	21	6	0	2.62	12	4-83	0/0	49.75	0	5
Blackwood Jermaine	20.11.1991		33	2014–*2020*	1,789	112*	2	32.52	2	2-14	0/0	97.00	25	2
Boyce Keith David (*CY 1974*)	11.10.1943	11.10.1996	21	*1970–1975*	657	95*	0	24.33	60	6-77	2/1	30.01	5	8
Bradshaw Ian David Russell	9.7.1974		5	*2005*	96	33	0	13.71	9	3-73	0/0	60.00	3	62/1
Brathwaite Carlos Ricardo	18.7.1988		3	*2015*–2016	181	69	0	45.25	1	1-30	0/0	242.00	0	44/41
Brathwaite Kraigg Clairmonte	1.12.1992		64	*2010–2020*	3,727	212	8	32.40	18	6-29	1/0	58.72	28	10
[2] **Bravo** Dwayne John	7.10.1983		40	2004–*2010*	2,200	113	3	31.42	86	6-55	2/0	39.83	41	164/71
[2] **Bravo** Darren Michael	6.2.1989		56	*2010–2020*	3,538	218	8	36.47	0	0-2	0/0	–	51	113/20
Breese Gareth Rohan	9.1.1976		1	*2002*	5	5	0	2.50	2	2-108	0/0	67.50	1	
Brooks Shamarh Shaqad Joshua	1.10.1988		8	2019–*2020*	422	111	1	28.13	–	–	–/–	–	8	
Browne Courtney Oswald	7.12.1970		20	*1994–2004*	387	68	0	16.12	–	–	–/–	–	79/2	46
Browne Cyril Rutherford	8.10.1890	12.1.1964	4	1928–*1929*	176	70*	0	25.14	6	2-72	0/0	48.00	1	
Butcher Basil Fitzherbert (*CY 1970*)	3.9.1933	16.12.2019	44	*1958*–1969	3,104	209*	7	43.11	5	5-34	1/0	18.00	15	
Butler Lennox Stephen	9.2.1929	1.9.2009	1	*1954*	16	16	0	16.00	2	2-151	0/0	75.50	0	
Butts Clyde Godfrey	8.7.1957		7	*1984–1987*	108	38	0	15.42	10	4-73	0/0	59.50	2	
Bynoe Michael Robin	23.2.1941		4	*1958–1966*	111	48	0	18.50	1	1-5	0/0	5.00	4	
Camacho George Stephen	15.10.1945	2.10.2015	11	*1967–1970*	640	87	0	29.09	0	0-12	0/0	–	4	
[2] **Cameron** Francis James	22.6.1923	10.6.1994	5	*1948*	151	75*	0	25.16	3	2-74	0/0	92.66	0	
[2] **Cameron** John Hemsley	8.4.1914	13.2.2000	2	1939	6	5	0	2.00	3	3-66	0/0	29.33	0	
Campbell John Dillon	21.9.1993		11	*2018–2020*	492	68	0	25.89	0	0-10	0/0	–	5	6/2
Campbell Sherwin Legay	1.11.1970		52	*1994–2001*	2,882	208	4	32.38	–	–	–/–	–	47	90
Carew George McDonald	4.6.1910	9.12.1974	4	*1934–1948*	170	107	1	28.33	0	0-2	0/0	–	1	
Carew Michael Conrad ("Joey")	15.9.1937	8.1.2011	19	1963–*1971*	1,127	109	1	34.15	8	1-11	0/0	54.62	13	
Challenor George	28.6.1888	30.7.1947	3	1928	101	46	0	16.83	–	–	–/–	–	0	
Chanderpaul Shivnarine (*CY 2008*)	16.8.1974		164	*1993–2014*	11,867	203*	30	51.37	9	1-2	0/0	98.11	66	268/22
Chandrika Rajindra	8.8.1989		5	2015–2016	140	37	0	14.00	–	–	–/–	–	2	

	Born	Died	Tests	Test Career	Runs	HS	100s	Avge	Wkts	BB	5/10	Avge	Ct/St	O/T
Chang Herbert Samuel	2.7.1952		1	1978	8	6	0	4.00	–	–	–/–	–	0	
Chase Roston Lamar	22.3.1992		37	2016–2020	1,869	137*	5	29.20	71	8-60	3/0	42.29	15	30
Chattergoon Sewnarine	3.4.1981		4	2007–2008	127	46	0	18.14	–	–	–/–	–	4	18
[2] **Christiani** Cyril Marcel	28.10.1913	4.4.1938	4	1934	98	32*	0	19.60	–	–	–/–	–	6/1	
[2] **Christiani** Robert Julian	19.7.1920	4.1.2005	22	1947–1953	896	107	1	26.35	3	3-52	0/0	36.00	19/2	
Clarke Carlos Bertram OBE	7.4.1918	14.10.1993	3	1939	3	2	0	1.00	6	3-59	0/0	43.50	0	
Clarke Sylvester Theophilus	11.12.1954	4.12.1999	11	1977–1981	172	35*	0	15.63	42	5-126	1/0	27.85	2	10
[2] **Collins** Pedro Tyrone	12.8.1976		32	1998–2005	235	24	0	5.87	106	6-53	3/0	34.63	7	30
Collymore Corey Dalanelo	21.12.1977		30	1998–2007	197	16*	0	7.88	93	7-57	4/1	32.30	6	84
Constantine *Lord* [Learie Nicholas] MBE (*CY 1940*)	21.9.1901	1.7.1971	18	1928–1939	635	90	0	19.24	58	5-75	2/0	30.10	28	
Cornwall Rahkeem Rashawn Shane	1.2.1993		3	2019–2020	32	14	0	6.40	13	7-75	1/1	35.23	7	
Cottrell Sheldon Shane	19.8.1989		2	2013–2014	11	5	0	2.75	2	1-72	0/0	98.00	0	35/30
Croft Colin Everton Hunte	15.3.1953		27	1976–1981	158	33	0	10.53	125	8-29	3/0	23.30	8	19
Cuffy Cameron Eustace	8.2.1970		15	1994–2002	58	15	0	4.14	43	4-82	0/0	33.83	5	41
Cummins Anderson Cleophas	7.5.1966		5	1992–1994	98	50	0	19.60	8	4-54	0/0	42.75	1	63‡
Cummins Miguel Lamar	5.9.1990		14	2016–2019	114	24*	0	7.60	27	6-48	1/0	40.14	2	11
Da Costa Oscar Constantine	11.9.1907	1.10.1936	5	1929–1934	153	39	0	19.12	3	1-14	0/0	58.33	5	
Daniel Wayne Wendell	16.1.1956		10	1975–1983	46	11	0	6.57	36	5-39	1/0	25.27	4	18
Da Silva Joshua	19.6.1998		1	2020	60	57	0	30.00	–	–	–/–	–	2	
[2] **Davis** Bryan Allan	2.5.1940		4	1964	245	68	0	30.62	–	–	–/–	–	1	
[2] **Davis** Charles Allan	1.1.1944		15	1968–1972	1,301	183	4	54.20	2	1-27	0/0	165.00	4	
Davis Winston Walter	18.9.1958		15	1982–1987	202	77	0	15.53	45	4-19	0/0	32.71	10	35
de Caires Francis Ignatius	12.5.1909	2.2.1959	3	1929	232	80	0	38.66	0	0-9	0/0	–	1	
Deonarine Narsingh	16.8.1983		18	2004–2013	725	82	0	25.89	24	4-37	0/0	29.70	16	31/8
Depeiza Cyril Clairmonte	10.10.1928	10.11.1995	5	1954–1955	187	122	1	31.16	0	0-3	0/0	–	7/4	
Dewdney David Thomas	23.10.1933		9	1954–1957	17	5*	0	2.42	21	5-21	1/0	38.42	0	
Dhanraj Rajindra	6.2.1969		4	1994–1995	17	9	0	4.25	8	2-49	0/0	74.37	1	6
Dillon Mervyn	5.6.1974		38	1996–2003	549	43	0	8.44	131	5-71	2/0	33.57	16	108
Dowe Uton George	29.3.1949		4	1970–1972	8	5*	0	8.00	12	4-69	0/0	44.50	3	
Dowlin Travis Montague	24.2.1977		6	2009–2010	343	95	0	31.18	0	0-3	0/0	–	5	11/2
Dowrich Shane Omari	30.10.1991		35	2015–2020	1,570	125*	3	29.07	–	–	–/–	–	85/5	1
Drakes Vasbert Conniel	5.8.1969		12	2002–2003	386	67	0	21.44	33	5-93	1/0	41.27	2	34
Dujon Peter Jeffrey Leroy (*CY 1989*)	28.5.1956		81	1981–1991	3,322	139	5	31.94	–	–	–/–	–	267/5	169
[2] **Edwards** Fidel Henderson	6.2.1982		55	2003–2012	394	30	0	6.56	165	7-87	12/0	37.87	10	50/20
Edwards Kirk Anton	3.11.1984		17	2011–2014	986	121	2	31.80	0	0-19	0/0	–	15	16

	Born	*Died*	*Tests*	*Test Career*	*Runs*	*HS*	*100s*	*Avge*	*Wkts*	*BB*	*5/10*	*Avge*	*Ct/St*	*O/T*
Edwards Richard Martin	3.6.1940		5	*1968*	65	22	0	9.28	18	5-84	1/0	34.77	0	
Ferguson Wilfred	14.12.1917	23.2.1961	8	*1947–1953*	200	75	0	28.57	34	6-92	3/1	34.26	11	
Fernandes Maurius Pacheco	12.8.1897	8.5.1981	2	1928–*1929*	49	22	0	12.25	–	–	–/–	–	0	
Findlay Thaddeus Michael MBE	19.10.1943		10	1969–*1972*	212	44*	0	16.30	–	–	–/–	–	19/2	
Foster Maurice Linton Churchill	9.5.1943		14	1969–*1977*	580	125	1	30.52	9	2-41	0/0	66.66	3	2
Francis George Nathaniel	11.12.1897	12.1.1942	10	1928–1933	81	19*	0	5.78	23	4-40	0/0	33.17	7	
Frederick Michael Campbell	6.5.1927	18.6.2014	1	*1953*	30	30	0	15.00	–	–	–/–	–	0	
Fredericks Roy Clifton (*CY 1974*)	11.11.1942	5.9.2000	59	*1968–1976*	4,334	169	8	42.49	7	1-12	0/0	78.28	62	12
Fudadin Assad Badyr	1.8.1985		3	2012	122	55	0	30.50	0	0-11	0/0	–	4	
Fuller Richard Livingston	30.1.1913	3.5.1987	1	*1934*	1	1	0	1.00	0	0-2	0/0	–	0	
Furlonge Hammond Allan	19.6.1934		3	*1954–1955*	99	64	0	19.80	–	–	–/–	–	0	
Gabriel Shannon Terry	28.4.1988		50	2012–*2020*	207	20*	0	4.31	150	8-62	6/1	30.74	16	25/2
Ganga Daren	14.1.1979		48	*1998–2007*	2,160	135	3	25.71	1	1-20	0/0	106.00	30	35/1
Ganteaume Andrew Gordon	22.1.1921	17.2.2016	1	*1947*	112	112	1	112.00	–	–	–/–	–	0	
Garner Joel MBE (*CY 1980*)	16.12.1952		58	*1976–1986*	672	60	0	12.44	259	6-56	7/0	20.97	42	98
Garrick Leon Vivian	11.11.1976		1	*2000*	27	27	0	13.50	–	–	–/–	–	2	3
Gaskin Berkeley Bertram McGarrell	21.3.1908	2.5.1979	2	*1947*	17	10	0	5.66	2	1-15	0/0	79.00	1	
Gayle Christopher Henry	21.9.1979		103	*1999–2014*	7,214	333	15	42.18	73	5-34	2/0	42.73	96	298/58
Gibbs Glendon Lionel	27.12.1925	21.2.1979	1	*1954*	12	12	0	6.00	0	0-2	0/0	–	1	
Gibbs Lancelot Richard (*CY 1972*)	29.9.1934		79	*1957–1975*	488	25	0	6.97	309	8-38	18/2	29.09	52	3
Gibson Ottis Delroy (*CY 2008*)	16.3.1969		2	1995–*1998*	93	37	0	23.25	3	2-81	0/0	91.66	0	15
Gilchrist Roy	28.6.1934	18.7.2001	13	1957–*1958*	60	12	0	5.45	57	6-55	1/0	26.68	4	
Gladstone Morais George	14.1.1901	19.5.1978	1	*1929*	12	12*	0	–	1	1-139	0/0	189.00	0	
Goddard John Douglas Claude OBE	21.4.1919	26.8.1987	27	*1947*–1957	859	83*	0	30.67	33	5-31	1/0	31.81	22	
Gomes Hilary Angelo ("Larry") (*CY 1985*)	13.7.1953		60	1976–*1986*	3,171	143	9	39.63	15	2-20	0/0	62.00	18	83
Gomez Gerald Ethridge	10.10.1919	6.8.1996	29	1939–*1953*	1,243	101	1	30.31	58	7-55	1/1	27.41	18	
[2] **Grant** George Copeland ("Jackie")	9.5.1907	26.10.1978	12	*1930–1934*	413	71*	0	25.81	0	0-1	0/0	–	10	
[2] **Grant** Rolph Stewart	15.12.1909	18.10.1977	7	*1934*–1939	220	77	0	22.00	11	3-68	0/0	32.09	13	
Gray Anthony Hollis	23.5.1963		5	*1986*	48	12*	0	8.00	22	4-39	0/0	17.13	6	25
Greenidge Alvin Ethelbert	20.8.1956		6	*1977–1978*	222	69	0	22.20	–	–	–/–	–	5	1
Greenidge *Sir* Cuthbert Gordon MBE (*CY 1977*)	1.5.1951		108	*1974–1990*	7,558	226	19	44.72	0	0-0	0/0	–	96	128
Greenidge Geoffrey Alan	26.5.1948		5	*1971–1972*	209	50	0	29.85	0	0-2	0/0	–	3	
Grell Mervyn George	18.12.1899	11.1.1976	1	*1929*	34	21	0	17.00	0	0-7	0/0	–	1	
Griffith Adrian Frank Gordon	19.11.1971		14	*1996*–2000	638	114	1	24.53	–	–	–/–	–	5	9
Griffith *Sir* Charles Christopher (*CY 1964*)	14.12.1938		28	*1959–1968*	530	54	0	16.56	94	6-36	5/0	28.54	16	
Griffith Herman Clarence	1.12.1893	18.3.1980	13	1928–1933	91	18	0	5.05	44	6-103	2/0	28.25	4	

	Born	*Died*	*Tests*	*Test Career*	*Runs*	*HS*	*100s*	*Avge*	*Wkts*	*BB*	*5/10*	*Avge*	*Ct/St*	*O/T*
Guillen Simpson Clairmonte ("Sammy")	24.9.1924	2.3.2013	5†	*1951*	104	54	0	26.00	–	–	–/–	–	9/2	
Hall *Sir* Wesley Winfield	12.9.1937		48	*1958–1968*	818	50*	0	15.73	192	7-69	9/1	26.38	11	
Hamilton Jahmar Neville	22.9.1990		1	2019	5	5	0	2.50	–	–	–/–	–	5	
Harper Roger Andrew	17.3.1963		25	*1983–1993*	535	74	0	18.44	46	6-57	1/0	28.06	36	105
Haynes Desmond Leo (*CY 1991*)	15.2.1956		116	*1977–1993*	7,487	184	18	42.29	1	1-2	0/0	8.00	65	238
[3] **Headley** George Alphonso MBE (*CY 1934*)	30.5.1909	30.11.1983	22	*1929–1953*	2,190	270*	10	60.83	0	0-0	0/0	–	14	
[3] **Headley** Ronald George Alphonso	29.6.1939		2	1973	62	42	0	15.50	–	–	–/–	–	2	1
Hendriks John Leslie	21.12.1933		20	*1961*–1969	447	64	0	18.62	–	–	–/–	–	42/5	
Hetmyer Shimron Odilon	26.12.1996		16	*2016–2019*	838	93	0	27.93	–	–	–/–	–	7	45/27
Hinds Ryan O'Neal	17.2.1981		15	*2001*–2009	505	84	0	21.04	13	2-45	0/0	66.92	7	14
Hinds Wavell Wayne	7.9.1976		45	*1999–2005*	2,608	213	5	33.01	16	3-79	0/0	36.87	32	119/5
Hoad Edward Lisle Goldsworthy	29.1.1896	5.3.1986	4	1928–1933	98	36	0	12.25	–	–	–/–	–	1	
Holder Chemar Keron	3.3.1998		1	*2020*	21	13*	0	–	2	2-110	0/0	55.00	0	
Holder Jason Omar (*CY 2021*)	5.11.1991		45	2014–*2020*	2,115	202*	3	32.04	116	6-42	7/1	27.94	42	115/17
Holder Roland Irwin Christopher	22.12.1967		11	*1996–1998*	380	91	0	25.33	–	–	–/–	–	9	37
Holder Vanburn Alonzo	10.10.1945		40	1969–*1978*	682	42	0	14.20	109	6-28	3/0	33.27	16	12
Holding Michael Anthony (*CY 1977*)	16.2.1954		60	*1975–1986*	910	73	0	13.78	249	8-92	13/2	23.68	22	102
Holford David Anthony Jerome	16.4.1940		24	1966–*1976*	768	105*	1	22.58	51	5-23	1/0	39.39	18	
Holt John Kenneth Constantine	12.8.1923	3.6.1997	17	1953–1958	1,066	166	2	36.75	1	1-20	0/0	20.00	8	
Hooper Carl Llewellyn	15.12.1966		102	1987–2002	5,762	233	13	36.46	114	5-26	4/0	49.42	115	227
[2] **Hope** Kyle Antonio	20.11.1988		5	2017–*2017*	101	43	0	11.22	–	–	–/–	–	3	7
[2] **Hope** Shai Diego (*CY 2018*)	10.11.1993		34	*2014*–2020	1,603	147	2	26.27	–	–	–/–	–	47/1	78/13
Howard Anthony Bourne	27.8.1946		1	*1971*	–	–	–	–	2	2-140	0/0	70.00	0	
Hunte *Sir* Conrad Cleophas (*CY 1964*)	9.5.1932	3.12.1999	44	*1957–1966*	3,245	260	8	45.06	2	1-17	0/0	55.00	16	
Hunte Errol Ashton Clairmore	3.10.1905	26.6.1967	3	*1929*	166	58	0	33.20	–	–	–/–	–	5	
Hylton Leslie George	29.3.1905	17.5.1955	6	*1934*–1939	70	19	0	11.66	16	4-27	0/0	26.12	1	
Jacobs Ridley Detamore	26.11.1967		65	*1998*–2004	2,577	118	3	28.31	–	–	–/–	–	207/12	147
Jaggernauth Amit Sheldon	16.11.1983		1	*2007*	0	0*	0	0.00	1	1-74	0/0	96.00	0	
Johnson Hophnie Hobah Hines	13.7.1910	24.6.1987	3	*1947*–1950	38	22	0	9.50	13	5-41	2/1	18.30	0	
Johnson Leon Rayon	8.8.1987		9	*2014–2016*	403	66	0	25.18	0	0-9	0/0	–	7	6
Johnson Tyrell Fabian	10.1.1917	5.4.1985	1	1939	9	9*	0	–	3	2-53	0/0	43.00	1	
Jones Charles Ernest Llewellyn	3.11.1902	10.12.1959	4	*1929–1934*	63	19	0	9.00	0	0-2	0/0	–	3	
Jones Prior Erskine Waverley	6.6.1917	21.11.1991	9	*1947–1951*	47	10*	0	5.22	25	5-85	1/0	30.04	4	
Joseph Alzarri Shaheim	20.11.1996		13	2016–*2020*	253	86	0	11.50	32	3-53	0/0	37.84	8	28
Joseph David Rolston Emmanuel	15.11.1969		4	*1998*	141	50	0	20.14	–	–	–/–	–	10	
Joseph Sylvester Cleofoster	5.9.1978		5	2004–2007	147	45	0	14.70	0	0-8	0/0	–	3	13

	Born	Died	Tests	Test Career	Runs	HS	100s	Avge	Wkts	BB	5/10	Avge	Ct/St	O/T
Julien Bernard Denis	13.3.1950		24	1973–*1976*	866	121	2	30.92	50	5-57	1/0	37.36	14	12
Jumadeen Raphick Rasif	12.4.1948		12	*1971–1978*	84	56	0	21.00	29	4-72	0/0	39.34	4	
Kallicharran Alvin Isaac BEM (*CY 1983*)	21.3.1949		66	*1971–1980*	4,399	187	12	44.43	4	2-16	0/0	39.50	51	31
Kanhai Rohan Bholalall (*CY 1964*)	26.12.1935		79	1957–*1973*	6,227	256	15	47.53	0	0-1	0/0	–	50	7
Kentish Esmond Seymour Maurice	21.11.1916	10.6.2011	2	*1947–1953*	1	1*	0	1.00	8	5-49	1/0	22.25	1	
King Collis Llewellyn	11.6.1951		9	1976–1980	418	100*	1	32.15	3	1-30	0/0	94.00	5	18
King Frank McDonald	14.12.1926	23.12.1990	14	*1952–1955*	116	21	0	8.28	29	5-74	1/0	39.96	5	
King Lester Anthony	27.2.1939	9.7.1998	2	*1961–1967*	41	20	0	10.25	9	5-46	1/0	17.11	2	
King Reon Dane	6.10.1975		19	*1998–2004*	66	12*	0	3.47	53	5-51	1/0	32.69	2	50
Lambert Clayton Benjamin	10.2.1962		5	1991–*1998*	284	104	1	31.55	1	1-4	0/0	5.00	8	11‡
Lara Brian Charles (*CY 1995*)	2.5.1969		130§	*1990–2006*	11,912	400*	34	53.17	0	0-0	0/0	–	164	295‡
Lashley Patrick Douglas ("Peter")	11.2.1937		4	*1960*–1966	159	49	0	22.71	1	1-1	0/0	1.00	4	
Lawson Jermaine Jay Charles	13.1.1982		13	*2002–2005*	52	14	0	3.46	51	7-78	2/0	29.64	3	13
Legall Ralph Archibald	1.12.1925	2003	4	*1952*	50	23	0	10.00	–	–	–/–	–	8/1	
Lewis Desmond Michael	21.2.1946	25.3.2018	3	*1970*	259	88	0	86.33	–	–	–/–	–	8	
Lewis Rawl Nicholas	5.9.1974		5	*1997–2007*	89	40	0	8.90	4	2-42	0/0	114.00	0	28/1
Lewis Sherman Hakim	21.10.1995		2	*2018*	24	20	0	6.00	3	2-93	0/0	54.00	1	
Lloyd *Sir* Clive Hubert CBE (*CY 1971*)	31.8.1944		110	*1966–1984*	7,515	242*	19	46.67	10	2-13	0/0	62.20	90	87
Logie Augustine Lawrence	28.9.1960		52	*1982*–1991	2,470	130	2	35.79	0	0-0	0/0	–	57	158
McGarrell Neil Christopher	12.7.1972		4	*2000–2001*	61	33	0	15.25	17	4-23	0/0	26.64	2	17
McLean Nixon Alexei McNamara	20.7.1973		19	*1997–2000*	368	46	0	12.26	44	3-53	0/0	42.56	5	45
McMorris Easton Dudley Ashton St John	4.4.1935		13	*1957*–1966	564	125	1	26.85	–	–	–/–	–	5	
McWatt Clifford Aubrey	1.2.1922	20.7.1997	6	*1953–1954*	202	54	0	28.85	1	1-16	0/0	16.00	9/1	
Madray Ivan Samuel	2.7.1934	23.4.2009	2	*1957*	3	2	0	1.00	0	0-12	0/0	–	2	
Marshall Malcolm Denzil (*CY 1983*)	18.4.1958	4.11.1999	81	*1978*–1991	1,810	92	0	18.85	376	7-22	22/4	20.94	25	136
[2] **Marshall** Norman Edgar	27.2.1924	11.8.2007	1	*1954*	8	8	0	4.00	2	1-22	0/0	31.00	0	
[2] **Marshall** Roy Edwin (*CY 1959*)	25.4.1930	27.10.1992	4	*1951*	143	30	0	20.42	0	0-3	0/0	–	1	
Marshall Xavier Melbourne	27.3.1986		7	2005–*2008*	243	85	0	20.25	0	0-0	0/0	–	7	24/6
Martin Frank Reginald	12.10.1893	23.11.1967	9	1928–*1930*	486	123*	1	28.58	8	3-91	0/0	77.37	2	
Martindale Emmanuel Alfred	25.11.1909	17.3.1972	10	1933–1939	58	22	0	5.27	37	5-22	3/0	21.72	5	
Mattis Everton Hugh	11.4.1957		4	*1980*	145	71	0	29.00	0	0-4	0/0	–	3	2
Mendonca Ivor Leon	13.7.1934	14.6.2014	2	*1961*	81	78	0	40.50	–	–	–/–	–	8/2	
Merry Cyril Arthur	20.1.1911	19.4.1964	2	1933	34	13	0	8.50	–	–	–/–	–	1	
Miller Nikita O'Neil	16.5.1982		1	2009	5	5	0	2.50	0	0-27	0/0	–	0	50/9
Miller Roy Samuel	24.12.1924	21.8.2014	1	*1952*	23	23	0	23.00	0	0-28	0/0	–	0	

§ *Lara's figures exclude 41 runs for the ICC World XI v Australia in the Super Series Test in 2005-06.*

	Born	Died	Tests	Test Career	Runs	HS	100s	Avge	Wkts	BB	5/10	Avge	Ct/St	O/T
Mohammed Dave	8.10.1979		5	*2003–2006*	225	52	0	32.14	13	3-98	0/0	51.38	1	7
Moodie George Horatio	26.11.1915	8.6.2002	1	*1934*	5	5	0	5.00	3	2-23	0/0	13.33	0	
Morton Runako Shakur	22.7.1978	4.3.2012	15	2005–*2007*	573	70*	0	22.03	0	0-4	0/0	–	20	56/7
Moseley Ezra Alphonsa	5.1.1958	6.2.2021	2	*1989*	35	26	0	8.75	6	2-70	0/0	43.50	1	9
[1]**Murray** David Anthony	29.5.1950		19	*1977–1981*	601	84	0	21.46	–	–	–/–	–	57/5	10
Murray Deryck Lance	20.5.1943		62	1963–1980	1,993	91	0	22.90	–	–	–/–	–	181/8	26
Murray Junior Randalph	20.1.1968		33	*1992–2001*	918	101*	1	22.39	–	–	–/–	–	99/3	55
Nagamootoo Mahendra Veeren	9.10.1975		5	2000–*2002*	185	68	0	26.42	12	3-119	0/0	53.08	2	24
Nanan Rangy	29.5.1953	23.3.2016	1	*1980*	16	8	0	8.00	4	2-37	0/0	22.75	2	
Narine Sunil Philip	26.5.1988		6	2012–*2013*	40	22*	0	8.00	21	6-91	2/0	40.52	2	65/51
Nash Brendan Paul	14.12.1977		21	*2008*–2011	1,103	114	2	33.42	2	1-21	0/0	123.50	6	9
Neblett James Montague	13.11.1901	28.3.1959	1	*1934*	16	11*	0	16.00	1	1-44	0/0	75.00	0	
Noreiga Jack Mollinson	15.4.1936	8.8.2003	4	*1970*	11	9	0	3.66	17	9-95	2/0	29.00	2	
Nunes Robert Karl	7.6.1894	23.7.1958	4	1928–*1929*	245	92	0	30.62	–	–	–/–	–	2	
Nurse Seymour MacDonald (*CY 1967*)	10.11.1933	6.5.2019	29	*1959–1968*	2,523	258	6	47.60	0	0-0	0/0	–	21	
Padmore Albert Leroy	17.12.1946		2	*1975*–1976	8	8*	0	8.00	1	1-36	0/0	135.00	0	
Pagon Donovan Jomo	13.9.1982		2	*2004*	37	35	0	12.33	–	–	–/–	–	0	
Pairaudeau Bruce Hamilton	14.4.1931		13	*1952*–1957	454	115	1	21.61	0	0-3	0/0	–	6	
Parchment Brenton Anthony	24.6.1982		2	*2007*	55	20	0	13.75	–	–	–/–	–	1	7/1
Parry Derick Recaldo	22.12.1954		12	*1977–1979*	381	65	0	22.41	23	5-15	1/0	40.69	4	6
Pascal Nelon Troy	25.4.1987		2	2010–*2010*	12	10	0	6.00	0	0-27	0/0	–	1	1
Passailaigue Charles Clarence	4.8.1901	7.1.1972	1	*1929*	46	44	0	46.00	0	0-15	0/0	–	3	
Patterson Balfour Patrick	15.9.1961		28	*1985–1992*	145	21*	0	6.59	93	5-24	5/0	30.90	5	59
Paul Keemo Mandela Angus	21.2.1998		3	2018–*2018*	96	47	0	16.00	6	2-25	0/0	31.50	2	19/20
Payne Thelston Rodney O'Neale	13.2.1957		1	*1985*	5	5	0	5.00	–	–	–/–	–	5	7
Permaul Veerasammy	11.8.1989		6	*2012*–2015	98	23*	0	12.25	18	3-32	0/0	43.77	2	7/1
Perry Nehemiah Odolphus	16.6.1968		4	*1998–1999*	74	26	0	12.33	10	5-70	1/0	44.60	1	21
Peters Keon Kenroy	24.2.1982		1	*2014*	0	0	0	0.00	2	2-69	0/0	34.50	0	
Phillip Norbert	12.6.1948		9	*1977–1978*	297	47	0	29.70	28	4-48	0/0	37.17	5	1
Phillips Omar Jamel	12.10.1986		2	2009	160	94	0	40.00	–	–	–/–	–	1	
Pierre Lancelot Richard	5.6.1921	14.4.1989	1	*1947*	–	–	–	–	0	0-9	0/0	–	0	
Powell Daren Brentlyle	15.4.1978		37	2002–*2008*	407	36*	0	7.82	85	5-25	1/0	47.85	8	55/5
Powell Kieran Omar Akeem	6.3.1990		40	2011–*2018*	2,011	134	3	26.81	0	0-0	0/0	–	29	46/1
Powell Ricardo Lloyd	16.12.1978		2	*1999–2003*	53	30	0	17.66	0	0-13	0/0	–	1	109
Rae Allan Fitzroy	30.9.1922	27.2.2005	15	*1948–1952*	1,016	109	4	46.18	–	–	–/–	–	10	
Ragoonath Suruj	22.3.1968		2	*1998*	13	9	0	4.33	–	–	–/–	–	0	

	Born	*Died*	*Tests*	*Test Career*	*Runs*	*HS*	*100s*	*Avge*	*Wkts*	*BB*	*5/10*	*Avge*	*Ct/St*	*O/T*
Ramadhin Sonny (*CY 1951*)	1.5.1929		43	1950–*1960*	361	44	0	8.20	158	7-49	10/1	28.98	9	
Ramdass Ryan Rakesh	3.7.1983		1	2005	26	23	0	13.00	–	–	–/–	–	2	1
Ramdin Denesh	13.3.1985		74	2005–*2015*	2,898	166	4	25.87	–	–	–/–	–	205/12	139/71
Ramnarine Dinanath	4.6.1975		12	*1997–2001*	106	35*	0	6.23	45	5-78	1/0	30.73	8	4
Rampaul Ravindranath	15.10.1984		18	*2009–2012*	335	40*	0	14.56	49	4-48	0/0	34.79	3	92/23
Reifer Floyd Lamonte	23.7.1972		6	*1996*–2009	111	29	0	9.25	–	–	–/–	–	6	8/1
Reifer Raymon Anton	11.5.1991		1	*2017*	52	29	0	52.00	2	1-36	0/0	44.00	0	2
Richards Dale Maurice	16.7.1976		3	2009–2010	125	69	0	20.83	–	–	–/–	–	4	8/1
Richards *Sir* Isaac Vivian Alexander (*CY 1977*)	7.3.1952		121	*1974*–1991	8,540	291	24	50.23	32	2-17	0/0	61.37	122	187
Richardson *Sir* Richard Benjamin (*CY 1992*)	12.1.1962		86	*1983*–1995	5,949	194	16	44.39	0	0-0	0/0	–	90	224
Rickards Kenneth Roy	22.8.1923	21.8.1995	2	*1947–1951*	104	67	0	34.66	–	–	–/–	–	0	
Roach Clifford Archibald	13.3.1904	16.4.1988	16	1928–*1934*	952	209	2	30.70	2	1-18	0/0	51.50	5	
Roach Kemar Andre Jamal	30.6.1988		60	2009–*2020*	907	41	0	11.77	204	6-48	9/1	27.66	14	92/11
Roberts Alphonso Theodore	18.9.1937	24.7.1996	1	*1955*	28	28	0	14.00	–	–	–/–	–	0	
Roberts *Sir* Anderson Montgomery Everton CBE (*CY 1975*)	29.1.1951		47	*1973–1983*	762	68	0	14.94	202	7-54	11/2	25.61	9	56
Roberts Lincoln Abraham	4.9.1974		1	*1998*	0	0	0	0.00	–	–	–/–	–	0	
Rodriguez William Vicente	25.6.1934		5	*1961–1967*	96	50	0	13.71	7	3-51	0/0	53.42	3	
Rose Franklyn Albert	1.2.1972		19	*1996*–2000	344	69	0	13.23	53	7-84	2/0	30.88	4	27
Rowe Lawrence George	8.1.1949		30	*1971–1979*	2,047	302	7	43.55	0	0-1	0/0	–	17	11
Russell Andre Dwayne	29.4.1988		1	*2010*	2	2	0	2.00	1	1-73	0/0	104.00	1	56/49
[2] **St Hill** Edwin Lloyd	9.3.1904	21.5.1957	2	*1929*	18	12	0	4.50	3	2-110	0/0	73.66	0	
[2] **St Hill** Wilton H	6.7.1893	d unknown	3	1928–*1929*	117	38	0	19.50	0	0-9	0/0	–	1	
Sammy Darren Julius Garvey	20.12.1983		38	2007–*2013*	1,323	106	1	21.68	84	7-66	4/0	35.79	65	126/66‡
[2] **Samuels** Marlon Nathaniel (*CY 2013*)	5.1.1981		71	*2000–2016*	3,917	260	7	32.64	41	4-13	0/0	59.63	28	207/67
[2] **Samuels** Robert George	13.3.1971		6	*1995–1996*	372	125	1	37.20	–	–	–/–	–	8	8
Sanford Adam	12.7.1975		11	*2001–2003*	72	18*	0	4.80	30	4-132	0/0	43.86	4	
Sarwan Ramnaresh Ronnie	23.6.1980		87	*1999*–2011	5,842	291	15	40.01	23	4-37	0/0	50.56	53	181/18
Scarlett Reginald Osmond	15.8.1934	14.8.2019	3	*1959*	54	29*	0	18.00	2	1-46	0/0	104.50	2	
[1] **Scott** Alfred Homer Patrick	29.7.1934		1	*1952*	5	5	0	5.00	0	0-52	0/0	–	0	
[1] **Scott** Oscar Charles ("Tommy")	14.8.1892	15.6.1961	8	1928–*1930*	171	35	0	17.10	22	5-266	1/0	42.04	0	
Sealey Benjamin James	12.8.1899	12.9.1963	1	1933	41	29	0	20.50	1	1-10	0/0	10.00	0	
Sealy James Edward Derrick	11.9.1912	3.1.1982	11	*1929*–1939	478	92	0	28.11	3	2-7	0/0	31.33	6/1	
Shepherd John Neil (*CY 1979*)	9.11.1943		5	1969–*1970*	77	32	0	9.62	19	5-104	1/0	25.21	4	
Shillingford Grayson Cleophas	25.9.1944	23.12.2009	7	1969–*1971*	57	25	0	8.14	15	3-63	0/0	35.80	2	
Shillingford Irvine Theodore	18.4.1944		4	*1976–1977*	218	120	1	31.14	–	–	–/–	–	1	2

	Born	*Died*	*Tests*	*Test Career*	*Runs*	*HS*	*100s*	*Avge*	*Wkts*	*BB*	*5/10*	*Avge*	*Ct/St*	*O/T*
Shillingford Shane	22.2.1983		16	2010–2014	266	53*	0	13.30	70	6-49	6/2	34.55	9	
Shivnarine Sewdatt	13.5.1952		8	*1977–1978*	379	63	0	29.15	1	1-13	0/0	167.00	6	1
Simmons Lendl Mark Platter	25.1.1985		8	*2008–2011*	278	49	0	17.37	1	1-60	0/0	147.00	5	68/54
Simmons Philip Verant (*CY 1997*)	18.4.1963		26	*1987–1997*	1,002	110	1	22.26	4	2-34	0/0	64.25	26	143
Singh Charran Kamkaran	27.11.1935	19.11.2015	2	*1959*	11	11	0	3.66	5	2-28	0/0	33.20	2	
Singh Vishaul Anthony	12.1.1989		3	*2016*	63	32	0	10.50	–	–	–/–	–	2	
Small Joseph A.	3.11.1892	26.4.1958	3	1928–*1929*	79	52	0	13.16	3	2-67	0/0	61.33	3	
Small Milton Aster	12.2.1964		2	*1983*–1984	3	3*	0	–	4	3-40	0/0	38.25	0	2
Smith Cameron Wilberforce	29.7.1933		5	*1960–1961*	222	55	0	24.66	–	–	–/–	–	4/1	
Smith Devon Sheldon	21.10.1981		43	*2002*–2018	1,760	108	1	23.78	0	0-3	0/0	–	36	47/6
Smith Dwayne Romel	12.4.1983		10	*2003–2005*	320	105*	1	24.61	7	3-71	0/0	49.14	9	105/33
Smith O'Neil Gordon ("Collie") (*CY 1958*)	5.5.1933	9.9.1959	26	*1954–1958*	1,331	168	4	31.69	48	5-90	1/0	33.85	9	
Sobers *Sir* Garfield St Aubrun (*CY 1964*)	28.7.1936		93	*1953–1973*	8,032	365*	26	57.78	235	6-73	6/0	34.03	109	1
Solomon Joseph Stanislaus	26.8.1930		27	*1958–1964*	1,326	100*	1	34.00	4	1-20	0/0	67.00	13	
Stayers Sven Conrad ("Charlie")	9.6.1937	6.1.2005	4	*1961*	58	35*	0	19.33	9	3-65	0/0	40.44	0	
[2] **Stollmeyer** Jeffrey Baxter	11.3.1921	10.9.1989	32	1939–*1954*	2,159	160	4	42.33	13	3-32	0/0	39.00	20	
[2] **Stollmeyer** Victor Humphrey	24.1.1916	21.9.1999	1	1939	96	96	0	96.00	–	–	–/–	–	0	
Stuart Colin Ellsworth Laurie	28.9.1973		6	*2000–2001*	24	12*	0	3.42	20	3-33	0/0	31.40	2	5
Taylor Jaswick Ossie	3.1.1932	13.11.1999	3	*1957–1958*	4	4*	0	2.00	10	5-109	1/0	27.30	0	
Taylor Jerome Everton	22.6.1984		46	2003–*2015*	856	106	1	12.96	130	6-47	4/0	34.46	8	90/30
Thompson Patterson Ian Chesterfield	26.9.1971		2	*1995–1996*	17	10*	0	8.50	5	2-58	0/0	43.00	0	2
Tonge Gavin Courtney	13.2.1983		1	2009	25	23*	0	25.00	1	1-28	0/0	113.00	0	5/1
Trim John	25.1.1915	12.11.1960	4	*1947–1951*	21	12	0	5.25	18	5-34	1/0	16.16	2	
Valentine Alfred Louis (*CY 1951*)	28.4.1930	11.5.2004	36	1950–*1961*	141	14	0	4.70	139	8-104	8/2	30.32	13	
Valentine Vincent Adolphus	4.4.1908	6.7.1972	2	1933	35	19*	0	11.66	1	1-55	0/0	104.00	0	
Walcott *Sir* Clyde Leopold (*CY 1958*)	17.1.1926	26.8.2006	44	*1947–1959*	3,798	220	15	56.68	11	3-50	0/0	37.09	53/11	
Walcott Leslie Arthur	18.1.1894	27.2.1984	1	*1929*	40	24	0	40.00	1	1-17	0/0	32.00	0	
Wallace Philo Alphonso	2.8.1970		7	*1997–1998*	279	92	0	21.46	–	–	–/–	–	9	33
Walsh Courtney Andrew (*CY 1987*)	30.10.1962		132	*1984–2000*	936	30*	0	7.54	519	7-37	22/3	24.44	29	205
Walton Chadwick Antonio Kirkpatrick	3.7.1985		2	2009	13	10	0	3.25	–	–	–/–	–	10	9/19
Warrican Jomel Andrel	20.5.1992		8	*2015–2019*	142	41	0	28.40	22	4-62	0/0	39.63	3	
Washington Dwight Marlon	5.3.1983		1	*2004*	7	7*	0	–	0	0-20	0/0	–	3	
Watson Chester Donald	1.7.1938		7	*1959–1961*	12	5	0	2.40	19	4-62	0/0	38.10	1	
[1] **Weekes** *Sir* Everton de Courcy (*CY 1951*)	26.2.1925	1.7.2020	48	*1947–1957*	4,455	207	15	58.61	1	1-8	0/0	77.00	49	
Weekes Kenneth Hunnell	24.1.1912	9.2.1998	2	1939	173	137	1	57.66	–	–	–/–	–	0	
White Anthony Wilbur	20.11.1938		2	*1964*	71	57*	0	23.66	3	2-34	0/0	50.66	1	

	Born	Died	Tests	Test Career	Runs	HS	100s	Avge	Wkts	BB	5/10	Avge	Ct/St	O/T
Larsen Gavin Rolf	27.9.1962		8	1994–*1995*	127	26*	0	14.11	24	3-57	0/0	28.70	5	121
[1] **Latham** Rodney Terry	12.6.1961		4	*1991–1992*	219	119	1	31.28	0	0-6	0/0	–	5	33
[1] **Latham** Thomas William Maxwell	2.4.1992		56	*2013–2020*	3,929	264*	11	42.24	–	–	–/–	–	59	99/13
Lees Warren Kenneth MBE	19.3.1952		21	*1976*–1983	778	152	1	23.57	0	0-4	0/0	–	52/7	31
Leggat Ian Bruce	7.6.1930		1	*1953*	0	0	0	0.00	0	0-6	0/0	–	2	
Leggat John Gordon	27.5.1926	9.3.1973	9	*1951–1955*	351	61	0	21.93	–	–	–/–	–	0	
Lissette Allen Fisher	6.11.1919	24.1.1973	2	*1955*	2	1*	0	1.00	3	2-73	0/0	41.33	1	
Loveridge Greg Riaka	15.1.1975		1	*1995*	4	4*	0	–	–	–	–/–	–	0	
Lowry Thomas Coleman	17.2.1898	20.7.1976	7	*1929*–1931	223	80	0	27.87	0	0-0	0/0	–	8	
McCullum Brendon Barrie (*CY 2016*)	27.9.1981		101	*2003–2015*	6,453	302	12	38.64	1	1-1	0/0	88.00	198/11	260/71
McEwan Paul Ernest	19.12.1953		4	*1979–1984*	96	40*	0	16.00	0	0-6	0/0	–	5	17
MacGibbon Anthony Roy	28.8.1924	6.4.2010	26	*1950*–1958	814	66	0	19.85	70	5-64	1/0	30.85	13	
McGirr Herbert Mendelson	5.11.1891	14.4.1964	2	*1929*	51	51	0	51.00	1	1-65	0/0	115.00	0	
McGregor Spencer Noel	18.12.1931	21.11.2007	25	*1954–1964*	892	111	1	19.82	–	–	–/–	–	9	
McIntosh Timothy Gavin	4.12.1979		17	*2008–2010*	854	136	2	27.54	–	–	–/–	–	10	
McKay Andrew John	17.4.1980		1	*2010*	25	20*	0	25.00	1	1-120	0/0	120.00	0	19/2
McLeod Edwin George	14.10.1900	14.9.1989	1	*1929*	18	16	0	18.00	0	0-5	0/0	–	0	
McMahon Trevor George	8.11.1929		5	*1955*	7	4*	0	2.33	–	–	–/–	–	7/1	
McMillan Craig Douglas	13.9.1976		55	*1997–2004*	3,116	142	6	38.46	28	3-48	0/0	44.89	22	197/8
McRae Donald Alexander Noel	25.12.1912	10.8.1986	1	*1945*	8	8	0	4.00	0	0-44	0/0	–	0	
[2] **Marshall** Hamish John Hamilton	15.2.1979		13	*2000–2005*	652	160	2	38.35	0	0-4	0/0	–	1	66/3
[2] **Marshall** James Andrew Hamilton	15.2.1979		7	*2004*–2008	218	52	0	19.81	–	–	–/–	–	5	10/3
Martin Bruce Philip	25.4.1980		5	*2012–2013*	74	41	0	14.80	12	4-43	0/0	53.83	0	
Martin Christopher Stewart	10.12.1974		71	*2000–2012*	123	12*	0	2.36	233	6-26	10/1	33.81	14	20/6
Mason Michael James	27.8.1974		1	*2003*	3	3	0	1.50	0	0-32	0/0	–	0	26/3
Matheson Alexander Malcolm	27.2.1906	31.12.1985	2	*1929*–1931	7	7	0	7.00	2	2-7	0/0	68.00	2	
Meale Trevor	11.11.1928	21.5.2010	2	1958	21	10	0	5.25	–	–	–/–	–	0	
Merritt William Edward	18.8.1908	9.6.1977	6	*1929*–1931	73	19	0	10.42	12	4-104	0/0	51.41	2	
Meuli Edgar Milton	20.2.1926	15.4.2007	1	*1952*	38	23	0	19.00	–	–	–/–	–	0	
Milburn Barry Douglas	24.11.1943		3	*1968*	8	4*	0	8.00	–	–	–/–	–	6/2	
Miller Lawrence Somerville Martin	31.3.1923	17.12.1996	13	*1952*–1958	346	47	0	13.84	0	0-1	0/0	–	1	
Mills John Ernest	3.9.1905	11.12.1972	7	*1929–1932*	241	117	1	26.77	–	–	–/–	–	1	
Mills Kyle David	15.3.1979		19	2004–*2008*	289	57	0	11.56	44	4-16	0/0	33.02	4	170/42
Mitchell Daryl Joseph	20.5.1991		4	*2019–2020*	226	102*	1	75.33	1	1-7	0/0	110.00	1	0/12
Moir Alexander McKenzie	17.7.1919	17.6.2000	17	*1950–1958*	327	41*	0	14.86	28	6-155	2/0	50.64	2	
Moloney Denis Andrew Robert ("Sonny")	11.8.1910	15.7.1942	3	1937	156	64	0	26.00	0	0-9	0/0	–	3	

	Born	Died	Tests	Test Career	Runs	HS	100s	Avge	Wkts	BB	5/10	Avge	Ct/St	O/T
Mooney Francis Leonard Hugh	26.5.1921	8.3.2004	14	1949–1953	343	46	0	17.15	0	0-0	0/0	–	22/8	
Morgan Ross Winston	12.2.1941		20	1964–1971	734	97	0	22.24	5	1-16	0/0	121.80	12	
Morrison Bruce Donald	17.12.1933		1	1962	10	10	0	5.00	2	2-129	0/0	64.50	1	
Morrison Daniel Kyle	3.2.1966		48	1987–1996	379	42	0	8.42	160	7-89	10/0	34.68	14	96
Morrison John Francis MacLean	27.8.1947		17	1973–1981	656	117	1	22.62	2	2-52	0/0	35.50	9	18
Motz Richard Charles (*CY 1966*)	12.1.1940	29.4.2007	32	1961–1969	612	60	0	11.54	100	6-63	5/0	31.48	9	
Munro Colin	11.3.1987		1	2012	15	15	0	7.50	2	2-40	0/0	20.00	0	57/65
Murray Bruce Alexander Grenfell	18.9.1940		13	1967–1970	598	90	0	23.92	1	1-0	0/0	0.00	21	
Murray Darrin James	4.9.1967		8	1994	303	52	0	20.20	–	–	–/–	–	6	1
Nash Dion Joseph	20.11.1971		32	1992–2001	729	89*	0	23.51	93	6-27	3/1	28.48	13	81
Neesham James Douglas Sheehan	17.9.1990		12	2013–2016	709	137*	2	33.76	14	3-42	0/0	48.21	12	63/24
Newman *Sir* Jack	3.7.1902	23.9.1996	3	1931–1932	33	19	0	8.25	2	2-76	0/0	127.00	0	
Nicholls Henry Michael	15.11.1991		37	2015–2020	2,152	174	7	43.91	–	–	–/–	–	25	49/5
Nicol Robert James	28.5.1983		2	2011	28	19	0	7.00	0	0-0	0/0	–	2	22/21
O'Brien Iain Edward	10.7.1976		22	2004–2009	219	31	0	7.55	73	6-75	1/0	33.27	7	10/4
O'Connor Shayne Barry	15.11.1973		19	1997–2001	103	20	0	5.72	53	5-51	1/0	32.52	6	38
Oram Jacob David Philip	28.7.1978		33	2002–2009	1,780	133	5	36.32	60	4-41	0/0	33.05	15	160/36
O'Sullivan David Robert	16.11.1944		11	1972–1976	158	23*	0	9.29	18	5-148	1/0	67.83	2	3
Overton Guy William Fitzroy	8.6.1919	7.9.1993	3	1953	8	3*	0	1.60	9	3-65	0/0	28.66	1	
Owens Michael Barry	11.11.1969		8	1992–1994	16	8*	0	2.66	17	4-99	0/0	34.41	3	1
Page Milford Laurenson ("Curly")	8.5.1902	13.2.1987	14	1929–1937	492	104	1	24.60	5	2-21	0/0	46.20	6	
Papps Michael Hugh William	2.7.1979		8	2003–2007	246	86	0	16.40	–	–	–/–	–	11	6
[2] **Parker** John Morton	21.2.1951		36	1972–1980	1,498	121	3	24.55	1	1-24	0/0	24.00	30	24
[2] **Parker** Norman Murray	28.8.1948		3	1976	89	40	0	14.83	–	–	–/–	–	2	1
Parore Adam Craig	23.1.1971		78	1990–2001	2,865	110	2	26.28	–	–	–/–	–	197/7	179
Patel Ajaz Yunus	21.10.1988		8	2018–2019	53	14	0	7.57	22	5-59	2/0	33.31	5	0/2
Patel Dipak Narshibhai	25.10.1958		37	1986–1996	1,200	99	0	20.68	75	6-50	3/0	42.05	15	75
Patel Jeetan Shashi (*CY 2015*)	7.5.1980		24	2005–2016	381	47	0	12.70	65	5-110	1/0	47.35	13	43/11
Petherick Peter James	25.9.1942	7.6.2015	6	1976	34	13	0	4.85	16	3-90	0/0	42.81	4	
Petrie Eric Charlton	22.5.1927	14.8.2004	14	1955–1965	258	55	0	12.90	–	–	–/–	–	25	
Phillips Glenn Dominic	6.12.1996		1	2019	52	52	0	26.00	–	–	–/–	–	1	0/17
Playle William Rodger	1.12.1938	27.2.2019	8	1958–1962	151	65	0	10.06	–	–	–/–	–	4	
Pocock Blair Andrew	18.6.1971		15	1993–1997	665	85	0	22.93	0	0-10	0/0	–	5	
Pollard Victor	7.9.1945		32	1964–1973	1,266	116	2	24.34	40	3-3	0/0	46.32	19	3
Poore Matt Beresford	1.6.1930	11.6.2020	14	1952–1955	355	45	0	15.43	9	2-28	0/0	40.77	1	
Priest Mark Wellings	12.8.1961		3	1990–1997	56	26	0	14.00	3	2-42	0/0	52.66	0	18

	Born	Died	Tests	Test Career	Runs	HS	100s	Avge	Wkts	BB	5/10	Avge	Ct/St	O/T
Pringle Christopher	26.1.1968		14	1990–1994	175	30	0	10.29	30	7-52	1/1	46.30	3	64
Puna Narotam ("Tom")	28.10.1929	7.6.1996	3	1965	31	18*	0	15.50	4	2-40	0/0	60.00	1	
Rabone Geoffrey Osborne	6.11.1921	19.1.2006	12	1949–1954	562	107	1	31.22	16	6-68	1/0	39.68	5	
Raval Jeet Ashokbhai	22.5.1988		24	2016–2019	1,143	132	1	30.07	1	1-33	0/0	34.00	21	
[1] **Redmond** Aaron James	23.9.1979		8	2008–2013	325	83	0	21.66	3	2-47	0/0	26.66	5	6/7
[1] **Redmond** Rodney Ernest	29.12.1944		1	1972	163	107	1	81.50	–	–	–/–	–	0	2
Reid John Fulton	3.3.1956	28.12.2020	19	1978–1985	1,296	180	6	46.28	0	0-0	0/0	–	9	25
Reid John Richard OBE (*CY 1959*)	3.6.1928	14.10.2020	58	1949–1965	3,428	142	6	33.28	85	6-60	1/0	33.35	43/1	
Richardson Mark Hunter	11.6.1971		38	2000–2004	2,776	145	4	44.77	1	1-16	0/0	21.00	26	4
Roberts Andrew Duncan Glenn	6.5.1947	26.10.1989	7	1975–1976	254	84*	0	23.09	4	1-12	0/0	45.50	4	1
Roberts Albert William	20.8.1909	13.5.1978	5	1929–1937	248	66*	0	27.55	7	4-101	0/0	29.85	4	
Robertson Gary Keith	15.7.1960		1	1985	12	12	0	12.00	1	1-91	0/0	91.00	0	10
Ronchi Luke	23.4.1981		4	2015–2016	319	88	0	39.87	–	–	–/–	–	5	81‡/29‡
Rowe Charles Gordon	30.6.1915	9.6.1995	1	1945	0	0	0	0.00	–	–	–/–	–	1	
[1] **Rutherford** Hamish Duncan	27.4.1989		16	2012–2014	755	171	1	26.96	0	0-2	0/0	–	11	4/8
[1] **Rutherford** Kenneth Robert	26.10.1965		56	1984–1994	2,465	107*	3	27.08	1	1-38	0/0	161.00	32	121
Ryder Jesse Daniel	6.8.1984		18	2008–2011	1,269	201	3	40.93	5	2-7	0/0	56.00	12	48/22
Santner Mitchell Josef	5.2.1992		23	2015–2020	766	126	1	25.53	41	3-53	0/0	43.97	16	72/48
Scott Roy Hamilton	6.3.1917	5.8.2005	1	1946	18	18	0	18.00	1	1-74	0/0	74.00	0	
Scott Verdun John	31.7.1916	2.8.1980	10	1945–1951	458	84	0	28.62	0	0-5	0/0	–	7	
Sewell David Graham	20.10.1977		1	1997	1	1*	0	–	0	0-9	0/0	–	0	
Shrimpton Michael John Froud	23.6.1940	13.6.2015	10	1962–1973	265	46	0	13.94	5	3-35	0/0	31.60	2	
Sinclair Barry Whitley	23.10.1936		21	1962–1967	1,148	138	3	29.43	2	2-32	0/0	16.00	8	
Sinclair Ian McKay	1.6.1933	25.8.2019	2	1955	25	18*	0	8.33	1	1-79	0/0	120.00	1	
Sinclair Mathew Stuart	9.11.1975		33	1999–2009	1,635	214	3	32.05	0	0-1	0/0	–	31	54/2
Smith Frank Brunton	13.3.1922	6.7.1997	4	1946–1951	237	96	0	47.40	–	–	–/–	–	1	
Smith Horace Dennis	8.1.1913	25.1.1986	1	1932	4	4	0	4.00	1	1-113	0/0	113.00	0	
Smith Ian David Stockley MBE	28.2.1957		63	1980–1991	1,815	173	2	25.56	0	0-5	0/0	–	168/8	98
Snedden Colin Alexander	7.1.1918	23.4.2011	1	1946	–	–	–	–	0	0-46	0/0	–	0	
Snedden Martin Colin	23.11.1958		25	1980–1990	327	33*	0	14.86	58	5-68	1/0	37.91	7	93
Sodhi Inderbir Singh ("Ish")	31.10.1992		17	2013–2018	448	63	0	21.33	41	4-60	0/0	48.58	11	33/50
Somerville William Edgar Richard	9.8.1984		4	2018–2019	72	40*	0	18.00	15	4-75	0/0	32.46	0	
Southee Timothy Grant	11.12.1988		77	2007–2020	1,690	77*	0	17.24	302	7-64	11/1	28.70	58	143/75
Sparling John Trevor	24.7.1938		11	1958–1963	229	50	0	12.72	5	1-9	0/0	65.40	4	
Spearman Craig Murray	4.7.1972		19	1995–2000	922	112	1	26.34	–	–	–/–	–	21	51
Stead Gary Raymond	9.1.1972		5	1998–1999	278	78	0	34.75	0	0-1	0/0	–	2	

	Born	Died	Tests	Test Career	Runs	HS	100s	Avge	Wkts	BB	5/10	Avge	Ct/St	O/T
Stirling Derek Alexander	5.10.1961		6	1984–1986	108	26	0	15.42	13	4-88	0/0	46.23	1	6
Styris Scott Bernard	10.7.1975		29	2002–2007	1,586	170	5	36.04	20	3-28	0/0	50.75	23	188/31
Su'a Murphy Logo	7.11.1966		13	1991–1994	165	44	0	12.69	36	5-73	2/0	38.25	8	12
Sutcliffe Bert MBE (*CY 1950*)	17.11.1923	20.4.2001	42	1946–1965	2,727	230*	5	40.10	4	2-38	0/0	86.00	20	
Taylor Bruce Richard	12.7.1943	6.2.2021	30	1964–1973	898	124	2	20.40	111	7-74	4/0	26.60	10	2
Taylor Donald Dougald	2.3.1923	5.12.1980	3	1946–1955	159	77	0	31.80	–	–	–/–	–	2	
Taylor Luteru Ross Poutoa Lote	8.3.1984		105	2007–2020	7,379	290	19	45.83	2	2-4	0/0	24.00	155	232/102
Thomson Keith	26.2.1941		2	1967	94	69	0	31.33	1	1-9	0/0	9.00	0	
Thomson Shane Alexander	27.1.1969		19	1989–1995	958	120*	1	30.90	19	3-63	0/0	50.15	7	56
Tindill Eric William Thomas	18.12.1910	1.8.2010	5	1937–1946	73	37*	0	9.12	–	–	–/–	–	6/1	
Troup Gary Bertram	3.10.1952		15	1976–1985	55	13*	0	4.58	39	6-95	1/1	37.28	2	22
Truscott Peter Bennetts	14.8.1941		1	1964	29	26	0	14.50	–	–	–/–	–	1	
Tuffey Daryl Raymond	11.6.1978		26	1999–2009	427	80*	0	16.42	77	6-54	2/0	31.75	15	94/3
Turner Glenn Maitland (*CY 1971*)	26.5.1947		41	1968–1982	2,991	259	7	44.64	0	0-5	0/0	–	42	41
Twose Roger Graham	17.4.1968		16	1995–1999	628	94	0	25.12	3	2-36	0/0	43.33	5	87
Vance Robert Howard	31.3.1955		4	1987–1989	207	68	0	29.57	–	–	–/–	–	0	8
Van Wyk Cornelius Francois Kruger	7.2.1980		9	2011–2012	341	71	0	21.31	–	–	–/–	–	23/1	
Vaughan Justin Thomas Caldwell	30.8.1967		6	1992–1996	201	44	0	18.27	11	4-27	0/0	40.90	4	18
Vettori Daniel Luca	27.1.1979		112§	1996–2014	4,523	140	6	30.15	361	7-87	20/3	34.15	58	291‡/34
Vincent Lou	11.11.1978		23	2001–2007	1,332	224	3	34.15	0	0-2	0/0	–	19	102/9
[1] **Vivian** Graham Ellery	28.2.1946		5	1964–1971	110	43	0	18.33	1	1-14	0/0	107.00	3	1
[1] **Vivian** Henry Gifford	4.11.1912	12.8.1983	7	1931–1937	421	100	1	42.10	17	4-58	0/0	37.23	4	
Wadsworth Kenneth John	30.11.1946	19.8.1976	33	1969–1975	1,010	80	0	21.48	–	–	–/–	–	92/4	13
Wagner Neil	13.3.1986		51	2012–2020	660	66*	0	14.04	219	7-39	9/0	26.32	12	
Walker Brooke Graeme Keith	25.3.1977		5	2000–2002	118	27*	0	19.66	5	2-92	0/0	79.80	0	11
Wallace Walter Mervyn	19.12.1916	21.3.2008	13	1937–1952	439	66	0	20.90	0	0-5	0/0	–	5	
Walmsley Kerry Peter	23.8.1973		3	1994–2000	13	5	0	2.60	9	3-70	0/0	43.44	0	2
Ward John Thomas	11.3.1937	12.1.2021	8	1963–1967	75	35*	0	12.50	–	–	–/–	–	16/1	
Watling Bradley-John	9.7.1985		73	2009–2020	3,773	205	8	38.11	–	–	–/–	–	259/8	28/5
Watson William	31.8.1965		15	1986–1993	60	11	0	5.00	40	6-78	1/0	34.67	4	61
Watt Leslie	17.9.1924	15.11.1996	1	1954	2	2	0	1.00	–	–	–/–	–	0	
Webb Murray George	22.6.1947		3	1970–1973	12	12	0	6.00	4	2-114	0/0	117.75	0	
Webb Peter Neil	14.7.1957		2	1979	11	5	0	3.66	–	–	–/–	–	2	5
Weir Gordon Lindsay	2.6.1908	31.10.2003	11	1929–1937	416	74*	0	29.71	7	3-38	0/0	29.85	3	
White David John	26.6.1961		2	1990	31	18	0	7.75	0	0-5	0/0	–	0	3

§ *Vettori's figures exclude eight runs and one wicket for the ICC World XI v Australia in the Super Series Test in 2005-06.*

	Born	Died	Tests	Test Career	Runs	HS	100s	Avge	Wkts	BB	5/10	Avge	Ct/St	O/T
Whitelaw Paul Erskine	10.2.1910	28.8.1988	2	*1932*	64	30	0	32.00	–	–	–/–	–	0	
Williamson Kane Stuart (*CY 2016*)	8.8.1990		83	*2010–2020*	7,115	251	24	54.31	30	4-44	0/0	39.83	72	151/62
Wiseman Paul John	4.5.1970		25	*1997–2004*	366	36	0	14.07	61	5-82	2/0	47.59	11	15
Wright John Geoffrey MBE	5.7.1954		82	*1977–1992*	5,334	185	12	37.82	0	0-1	0/0	–	38	149
Young Bryan Andrew	3.11.1964		35	*1993–1998*	2,034	267*	2	31.78	–	–	–/–	–	54	74
Young Reece Alan	15.9.1979		5	*2010–2011*	169	57	0	24.14	–	–	–/–	–	8	
Young William Alexander	22.11.1992		2	*2020*	48	43	0	24.00	–	–	–/–	–	1	
Yuile Bryan William	29.10.1941		17	*1962–1969*	481	64	0	17.81	34	4-43	0/0	35.67	12	

INDIA (301 players)

	Born	Died	Tests	Test Career	Runs	HS	100s	Avge	Wkts	BB	5/10	Avge	Ct/St	O/T
Aaron Varun Raymond	29.10.1989		9	*2011–2015*	35	9	0	3.88	18	3-97	0/0	52.61	1	9
Abid Ali Syed	9.9.1941		29	*1967–1974*	1,018	81	0	20.36	47	6-55	1/0	42.12	32	5
Adhikari Hemchandra Ramachandra	31.7.1919	25.10.2003	21	*1947–1958*	872	114*	1	31.14	3	3-68	0/0	27.33	8	
Agarkar Ajit Bhalchandra	4.12.1977		26	*1998–2005*	571	109*	1	16.79	58	6-41	1/0	47.32	6	191/4
Agarwal Mayank Anurag	16.2.1991		14	*2018–2020*	1,052	243	3	45.73	–	–	–/–	–	11	5
[2] **Amar Singh** Ladha	4.12.1910	21.5.1940	7	1932–1936	292	51	0	22.46	28	7-86	2/0	30.64	3	
[1,2] **Amarnath** Mohinder (*CY 1984*)	24.9.1950		69	*1969–1987*	4,378	138	11	42.50	32	4-63	0/0	55.68	47	85
[1] **Amarnath** Nanik ("Lala")	11.9.1911	5.8.2000	24	*1933–1952*	878	118	1	24.38	45	5-96	2/0	32.91	13	
[1,2] **Amarnath** Surinder	30.12.1948		10	*1975–1978*	550	124	1	30.55	1	1-5	0/0	5.00	4	3
Amir Elahi	1.9.1908	28.12.1980	1†	*1947*	17	13	0	8.50	–	–	–/–	–	0	
Amre Pravin Kalyan	14.8.1968		11	*1992–1993*	425	103	1	42.50	–	–	–/–	–	9	37
Ankola Salil Ashok	1.3.1968		1	*1989*	6	6	0	6.00	2	1-35	0/0	64.00	0	20
[2] **Apte** Arvindrao Laxmanrao	24.10.1934	5.8.2014	1	1959	15	8	0	7.50	–	–	–/–	–	0	
[2] **Apte** Madhavrao Laxmanrao	5.10.1932	23.9.2019	7	*1952*	542	163*	1	49.27	0	0-3	0/0	–	2	
Arshad Ayub	2.8.1958		13	*1987–1989*	257	57	0	17.13	41	5-50	3/0	35.07	2	32
Arun Bharathi	14.12.1962		2	*1986*	4	2*	0	4.00	4	3-76	0/0	29.00	2	4
Arun Lal	1.8.1955		16	*1982–1988*	729	93	0	26.03	0	0-0	0/0	–	13	13
Ashwin Ravichandran	17.9.1986		74	*2011–2020*	2,467	124	4	27.71	377	7-59	27/7	25.53	25	111/46
Azad Kirtivardhan	2.1.1959		7	*1980–1983*	135	24	0	11.25	3	2-84	0/0	124.33	3	25
Azharuddin Mohammad (*CY 1991*)	8.2.1963		99	*1984–1999*	6,215	199	22	45.03	0	0-4	0/0	–	105	334
Badani Hemang Kamal	14.11.1976		4	2001	94	38	0	15.66	0	0-17	0/0	–	6	40
Badrinath Subramaniam	30.8.1980		2	*2009*	63	56	0	21.00	–	–	–/–	–	2	7/1
Bahutule Sairaj Vasant	6.1.1973		2	*2000–2001*	39	21*	0	13.00	3	1-32	0/0	67.66	1	8

	Born	*Died*	*Tests*	*Test Career*	*Runs*	*HS*	*100s*	*Avge*	*Wkts*	*BB*	*5/10*	*Avge*	*Ct/St*	*O/T*
Baig Abbas Ali	19.3.1939		10	1959–*1966*	428	112	1	23.77	0	0-2	0/0	–	6	
Balaji Lakshmipathy	27.9.1981		8	*2003–2004*	51	31	0	5.66	27	5-76	1/0	37.18	1	30/5
Banerjee Sarodindu Nath ("Shute")	3.10.1911	14.10.1980	1	*1948*	13	8	0	6.50	5	4-54	0/0	25.40	0	
Banerjee Subroto Tara	13.2.1969		1	*1991*	3	3	0	3.00	3	3-47	0/0	15.66	0	6
Banerjee Sudangsu Abinash	1.11.1917	14.9.1992	1	*1948*	0	0	0	0.00	5	4-120	0/0	36.20	3	
Bangar Sanjay Bapusaheb	11.10.1972		12	*2001–2002*	470	100*	1	29.37	7	2-23	0/0	49.00	4	15
Baqa Jilani Mohammad	20.7.1911	2.7.1941	1	1936	16	12	0	16.00	0	0-55	0/0	–	0	
Bedi Bishan Singh	25.9.1946		67	*1966*–1979	656	50*	0	8.98	266	7-98	14/1	28.71	26	10
Bhandari Prakash	27.11.1935		3	*1954–1956*	77	39	0	19.25	0	0-12	0/0	–	1	
Bharadwaj Raghvendrarao Vijay	15.8.1975		3	*1999*	28	22	0	9.33	1	1-26	0/0	107.00	3	10
Bhat Adwai Raghuram	16.4.1958		2	*1983*	6	6	0	3.00	4	2-65	0/0	37.75	0	
Bhuvneshwar Kumar	5.2.1990		21	*2012–2017*	552	63*	0	22.08	63	6-82	4/0	26.09	8	114/43
[1] **Binny** Roger Michael Humphrey	19.7.1955		27	*1979–1986*	830	83*	0	23.05	47	6-56	2/0	32.63	11	72
[1] **Binny** Stuart Terence Roger	3.6.1984		6	2014–*2015*	194	78	0	21.55	3	2-24	0/0	86.00	4	14/3
Borde Chandrakant Gulabrao	21.7.1934		55	*1958–1969*	3,061	177*	5	35.59	52	5-88	1/0	46.48	37	
Bumrah Jasprit Jasbirsingh	6.12.1993		17	*2017–2020*	38	10*	0	2.71	79	6-27	5/0	21.59	4	67/50
Chandrasekhar Bhagwat Subramanya (*CY 1972*)	17.5.1945		58	*1963*–1979	167	22	0	4.07	242	8-79	16/2	29.74	25	1
Chauhan Chetandra Pratap Singh	21.7.1947	16.8.2020	40	*1969–1980*	2,084	97	0	31.57	2	1-4	0/0	53.00	38	7
Chauhan Rajesh Kumar	19.12.1966		21	*1992–1997*	98	23	0	7.00	47	4-48	0/0	39.51	12	35
Chawla Piyush Pramod	24.12.1988		3	*2005–2012*	6	4	0	2.00	7	4-69	0/0	38.57	1	25/7
Chopra Aakash	19.9.1977		10	*2003–2004*	437	60	0	23.00	–	–	–/–	–	15	
Chopra Nikhil	26.12.1973		1	*1999*	7	4	0	3.50	0	0-78	0/0	–	0	39
Chowdhury Nirode Ranjan	23.5.1923	14.12.1979	2	*1948–1951*	3	3*	0	3.00	1	1-130	0/0	205.00	0	
Colah Sorabji Hormasji Munchersha	22.9.1902	11.9.1950	2	1932–*1933*	69	31	0	17.25	–	–	–/–	–	2	
Contractor Nariman Jamshedji	7.3.1934		31	*1955–1961*	1,611	108	1	31.58	1	1-9	0/0	80.00	18	
Dahiya Vijay	10.5.1973		2	*2000*	2	2*	0	–	–	–	–/–	–	6	19
Dani Hemchandra Tukaram	24.5.1933	19.12.1999	1	*1952*	–	–	–	–	1	1-9	0/0	19.00	1	
Das Shiv Sunder	5.11.1977		23	*2000–2001*	1,326	110	2	34.89	0	0-7	0/0	–	34	4
Dasgupta Deep	7.6.1977		8	*2001*	344	100	1	28.66	–	–	–/–	–	13	5
Desai Ramakant Bhikaji	20.6.1939	27.4.1998	28	*1958–1967*	418	85	0	13.48	74	6-56	2/0	37.31	9	
Dhawan Shikhar (*CY 2014*)	5.12.1985		34	*2012*–2018	2,315	190	7	40.61	0	0-0	0/0	–	28	139/64
Dhoni Mahendra Singh	7.7.1981		90	*2005–2014*	4,876	224	6	38.09	0	0-1	0/0	–	256/38	347‡/98
Dighe Sameer Sudhakar	8.10.1968		6	*2000*–2001	141	47	0	15.66	–	–	–/–	–	12/2	23
Dilawar Hussain	19.3.1907	26.8.1967	3	*1933*–1936	254	59	0	42.33	–	–	–/–	–	6/1	
Divecha Ramesh Vithaldas	18.10.1927	11.2.2003	5	*1951–1952*	60	26	0	12.00	11	3-102	0/0	32.81	5	

	Born	Died	Tests	Test Career	Runs	HS	100s	Avge	Wkts	BB	5/10	Avge	Ct/St	O/T
Doshi Dilip Rasiklal	22.12.1947		33	1979–1983	129	20	0	4.60	114	6-102	6/0	30.71	10	15
Dravid Rahul (*CY 2000*)	11.1.1973		163§	1996–2011	13,265	270	36	52.63	1	1-18	0/0	39.00	209	340‡/1
Durani Salim Aziz	11.12.1934		29	1959–1972	1,202	104	1	25.04	75	6-73	3/1	35.42	14	
Engineer Farokh Maneksha	25.2.1938		46	1961–1974	2,611	121	2	31.08	–	–	–/–	–	66/16	5
Gadkari Chandrasekhar Vaman	3.2.1928	11.1.1998	6	1952–1954	129	50*	0	21.50	0	0-8	0/0	–	6	
[1] **Gaekwad** Anshuman Dattajirao	23.9.1952		40	1974–1984	1,985	201	2	30.07	2	1-4	0/0	93.50	15	15
[1] **Gaekwad** Dattajirao Krishnarao	27.10.1928		11	1952–1960	350	52	0	18.42	0	0-4	0/0	–	5	
Gaekwad Hiralal Ghasulal	29.8.1923	2.1.2003	1	1952	22	14	0	11.00	0	0-47	0/0	–	0	
Gambhir Gautam	14.10.1981		58	2004–2016	4,154	206	9	41.95	0	0-4	0/0	–	38	147/37
Gandhi Devang Jayant	6.9.1971		4	1999	204	88	0	34.00	–	–	–/–	–	3	3
Gandotra Ashok	24.11.1948		2	1969	54	18	0	13.50	0	0-5	0/0	–	1	
Ganesh Doddanarasiah	30.6.1973		4	1996	25	8	0	6.25	5	2-28	0/0	57.40	0	1
Ganguly Sourav Chandidas	8.7.1972		113	1996–2008	7,212	239	16	42.17	32	3-28	0/0	52.53	71	308‡
Gavaskar Sunil Manohar (*CY 1980*)	10.7.1949		125	1970–1986	10,122	236*	34	51.12	1	1-34	0/0	206.00	108	108
Ghavri Karsan Devjibhai	28.2.1951		39	1974–1980	913	86	0	21.23	109	5-33	4/0	33.54	16	19
Ghorpade Jayasinghrao Mansinghrao	2.10.1930	29.3.1978	8	1952–1959	229	41	0	15.26	0	0-17	0/0	–	4	
Ghulam Ahmed	4.7.1922	28.10.1998	22	1948–1958	192	50	0	8.72	68	7-49	4/1	30.17	11	
Gill Shubman	8.9.1999		3	2020	259	91	0	51.80	–	–	–/–	–	2	3
Gopalan Morappakam Joysam	6.6.1909	21.12.2003	1	1933	18	11*	0	18.00	1	1-39	0/0	39.00	3	
Gopinath Coimbatarao Doraikannu	1.3.1930		8	1951–1959	242	50*	0	22.00	1	1-11	0/0	11.00	2	
Guard Ghulam Mustafa	12.12.1925	13.3.1978	2	1958–1959	11	7	0	5.50	3	2-69	0/0	60.66	2	
Guha Subrata	31.1.1946	5.11.2003	4	1967–1969	17	6	0	3.40	3	2-55	0/0	103.66	2	
Gul Mahomed	15.10.1921	8.5.1992	8†	1946–1952	166	34	0	11.06	2	2-21	0/0	12.00	3	
[2] **Gupte** Balkrishna Pandharinath	30.8.1934	5.7.2005	3	1960–1964	28	17*	0	28.00	3	1-54	0/0	116.33	0	
[2] **Gupte** Subhashchandra Pandharinath ("Fergie")	11.12.1929	31.5.2002	36	1951–1961	183	21	0	6.31	149	9-102	12/1	29.55	14	
Gursharan Singh	8.3.1963		1	1989	18	18	0	18.00	–	–	–/–	–	2	1
Hafeez Abdul (see Kardar)														
Hanumant Singh	29.3.1939	29.11.2006	14	1963–1969	686	105	1	31.18	0	0-5	0/0	–	11	
Harbhajan Singh	3.7.1980		103	1997–2015	2,224	115	2	18.22	417	8-84	25/5	32.46	42	234‡/28
Hardikar Manohar Shankar	8.2.1936	4.2.1995	2	1958	56	32*	0	18.66	1	1-9	0/0	55.00	3	
Harvinder Singh	23.12.1977		3	1997–2001	6	6	0	2.00	4	2-62	0/0	46.25	0	16
Hazare Vijay Samuel	11.3.1915	18.12.2004	30	1946–1952	2,192	164*	7	47.65	20	4-29	0/0	61.00	11	
Hindlekar Dattaram Dharmaji	1.1.1909	30.3.1949	4	1936–1946	71	26	0	14.20	–	–	–/–	–	3	
Hirwani Narendra Deepchand	18.10.1968		17	1987–1996	54	17	0	5.40	66	8-61	4/1	30.10	5	18
Ibrahim Khanmohammad Cassumbhoy	26.1.1919	12.11.2007	4	1948	169	85	0	21.12	–	–	–/–	–	0	

§ *Dravid's figures exclude 23 runs and one catch for the ICC World XI v Australia in the Super Series Test in 2005-06.*

	Born	Died	Tests	Test Career	Runs	HS	100s	Avge	Wkts	BB	5/10	Avge	Ct/St	O/T
Indrajitsinhji Kumar Shri	15.6.1937	12.3.2011	4	*1964–1969*	51	23	0	8.50	–	–	–/–	–	6/3	
Irani Jamshed Khudadad	18.8.1923	25.2.1982	2	*1947*	3	2*	0	3.00	–	–	–/–	–	2/1	
Jadeja Ajaysinhji	1.2.1971		15	*1992–1999*	576	96	0	26.18	–	–	–/–	–	5	196
Jadeja Ravindrasinh Anirudhsinh	6.12.1988		51	*2012–2020*	1,954	100*	1	36.18	220	7-48	9/1	24.32	38	168/50
3 **Jahangir Khan** Mohammad	1.2.1910	23.7.1988	4	1932–1936	39	13	0	5.57	4	4-60	0/0	63.75	4	
Jai Laxmidas Purshottamdas	1.4.1902	29.1.1968	1	*1933*	19	19	0	9.50	–	–	–/–	–	0	
Jaisimha Motganhalli Laxmanarsu	3.3.1939	6.7.1999	39	1959–*1970*	2,056	129	3	30.68	9	2-54	0/0	92.11	17	
Jamshedji Rustomji Jamshedji Dorabji	18.11.1892	5.4.1976	1	*1933*	5	4*	0	–	3	3-137	0/0	45.66	2	
Jayantilal Kenia	13.1.1948		1	*1970*	5	5	0	5.00	–	–	–/–	–	0	
Johnson David Jude	16.10.1971		2	*1996*	8	5	0	4.00	3	2-52	0/0	47.66	0	
Joshi Padmanabh Govind	27.10.1926	8.1.1987	12	*1951–1960*	207	52*	0	10.89	–	–	–/–	–	18/9	
Joshi Sunil Bandacharya	6.6.1970		15	1996–*2000*	352	92	0	20.70	41	5-142	1/0	35.85	7	69
Kaif Mohammad	1.12.1980		13	*1999–2005*	624	148*	1	32.84	0	0-4	0/0	–	14	125
Kambli Vinod Ganpat	18.1.1972		17	*1992–1995*	1,084	227	4	54.20	–	–	–/–	–	7	104
1 **Kanitkar** Hrishikesh Hemant	14.11.1974		2	*1999*	74	45	0	18.50	0	0-2	0/0	–	0	34
1 **Kanitkar** Hemant Shamsunder	8.12.1942	9.6.2015	2	*1974*	111	65	0	27.75	–	–	–/–	–	0	
Kapil Dev (*CY 1983*)	6.1.1959		131	*1978–1993*	5,248	163	8	31.05	434	9-83	23/2	29.64	64	225
Kapoor Aashish Rakesh	25.3.1971		4	*1994–1996*	97	42	0	19.40	6	2-19	0/0	42.50	1	17
Kardar Abdul Hafeez	17.1.1925	21.4.1996	3†	1946	80	43	0	16.00	–	–	–/–	–	1	
Karim Syed Saba	14.11.1967		1	*2000*	15	15	0	15.00	–	–	–/–	–	1	34
Karthik Krishankumar <u>Dinesh</u>	1.6.1985		26	*2004*–2018	1,025	129	1	25.00	–	–	–/–	–	57/6	94/31‡
Kartik Murali	11.9.1976		8	*1999–2004*	88	43	0	9.77	24	4-44	0/0	34.16	2	37/1
Kenny Ramnath Baburao	29.9.1930	21.11.1985	5	*1958–1959*	245	62	0	27.22	–	–	–/–	–	1	
Kirmani Syed Mujtaba Hussein	29.12.1949		88	*1975–1985*	2,759	102	2	27.04	1	1-9	0/0	13.00	160/38	49
Kishenchand Gogumal	14.4.1925	16.4.1997	5	*1947–1952*	89	44	0	8.90	–	–	–/–	–	1	
Kohli Virat (*CY 2019*)	5.11.1988		87	2011–*2020*	7,318	254*	27	53.41	0	0-0	0/0	–	84	251/85
2 **Kripal Singh** Amritsar Govindsingh	6.8.1933	22.7.1987	14	*1955–1964*	422	100*	1	28.13	10	3-43	0/0	58.40	4	
Krishnamurthy Pochiah	12.7.1947	28.1.1999	5	*1970*	33	20	0	5.50	–	–	–/–	–	7/1	1
Kulkarni Nilesh Moreshwar	3.4.1973		3	*1997–2000*	5	4	0	5.00	2	1-70	0/0	166.00	1	10
Kulkarni Rajiv Ramesh	25.9.1962		3	*1986*	2	2	0	1.00	5	3-85	0/0	45.40	1	10
Kulkarni Umesh Narayan	7.3.1942		4	*1967*	13	7	0	4.33	5	2-37	0/0	47.60	0	
Kumar Praveen	2.10.1986		6	2011	149	40	0	14.90	27	5-106	1/0	25.81	2	68/10
Kumar Vaman Viswanath	22.6.1935		2	*1960–1961*	6	6	0	3.00	7	5-64	1/0	28.85	2	
Kumble Anil (*CY 1996*)	17.10.1970		132	1990–*2008*	2,506	110*	1	17.77	619	10-74	35/8	29.65	60	269‡
Kunderan Budhisagar Krishnappa	2.10.1939	23.6.2006	18	*1959*–1967	981	192	2	32.70	0	0-13	0/0	–	23/7	
Kuruvilla Abey	8.8.1968		10	*1996–1997*	66	35*	0	6.60	25	5-68	1/0	35.68	0	25

	Born	Died	Tests	Test Career	Runs	HS	100s	Avge	Wkts	BB	5/10	Avge	Ct/St	O/T
Lall Singh	16.12.1909	19.11.1985	1	1932	44	29	0	22.00	–	–	–/–	–	1	
Lamba Raman	2.1.1960	22.2.1998	4	*1986–1987*	102	53	0	20.40	–	–	–/–	–	5	32
Laxman Vangipurappu Venkata Sai (*CY 2002*)	1.11.1974		134	*1996–2011*	8,781	281	17	45.97	2	1-2	0/0	63.00	135	86
Madan Lal	20.3.1951		39	1974–1986	1,042	74	0	22.65	71	5-23	4/0	40.08	15	67
Maka Ebrahim Suleman	5.3.1922	7.9.1994	2	*1952*	2	2*	0	–	–	–	–/–	–	2/1	
Malhotra Ashok Omprakash	26.1.1957		7	*1981–1984*	226	72*	0	25.11	0	0-0	0/0	–	2	20
Maninder Singh	13.6.1965		35	*1982–1992*	99	15	0	3.80	88	7-27	3/2	37.36	9	59
[1] **Manjrekar** Sanjay Vijay	12.7.1965		37	*1987–1996*	2,043	218	4	37.14	0	0-4	0/0	–	25/1	74
[1] **Manjrekar** Vijay Laxman	26.9.1931	18.10.1983	55	*1951–1964*	3,208	189*	7	39.12	1	1-16	0/0	44.00	19/2	
[1] **Mankad** Ashok Vinoo	12.10.1946	1.8.2008	22	*1969–1977*	991	97	0	25.41	0	0-0	0/0	–	12	1
[1] **Mankad** Mulvantrai Himmatlal ("Vinoo") (*CY 1947*)	12.4.1917	21.8.1978	44	1946–*1958*	2,109	231	5	31.47	162	8-52	8/2	32.32	33	
Mantri Madhav Krishnaji	1.9.1921	23.5.2014	4	*1951–1954*	67	39	0	9.57	–	–	–/–	–	8/1	
Meherhomji Khershedji Rustomji	9.8.1911	10.2.1982	1	1936	0	0*	0	–	–	–	–/–	–	1	
Mehra Vijay Laxman	12.3.1938	25.8.2006	8	*1955–1963*	329	62	0	25.30	0	0-1	0/0	–	1	
Merchant Vijay Madhavji (*CY 1937*)	12.10.1911	27.10.1987	10	*1933–1951*	859	154	3	47.72	0	0-17	0/0	–	7	
Mhambrey Paras Laxmikant	20.6.1972		2	1996	58	28	0	29.00	2	1-43	0/0	74.00	1	3
[2] **Milkha Singh** Amritsar Govindsingh	31.12.1941	10.11.2017	4	*1959–1961*	92	35	0	15.33	0	0-2	0/0	–	2	
Mishra Amit	24.11.1982		22	*2008–2016*	648	84	0	21.60	76	5-71	1/0	35.72	8	36/10
Mithun Abhimanyu	25.10.1989		4	2010–2011	120	46	0	24.00	9	4-105	0/0	50.66	0	5
Modi Rustomji Sheryar	11.11.1924	17.5.1996	10	1946–*1952*	736	112	1	46.00	0	0-14	0/0	–	3	
Mohammed Shami	3.9.1990		50	*2013–2020*	498	51*	0	11.06	180	6-56	5/0	27.58	11	79/12
Mohanty Debasis Sarbeswar	20.7.1976		2	*1997*	0	0*	0	–	4	4-78	0/0	59.75	0	45
Mongia Nayan Ramlal	19.12.1969		44	*1993–2000*	1,442	152	1	24.03	–	–	–/–	–	99/8	140
More Kiran Shankar	4.9.1962		49	1986–*1993*	1,285	73	0	25.70	0	0-12	0/0	–	110/20	94
Muddiah Venkatappa Musandra	8.6.1929	1.10.2009	2	*1959–1960*	11	11	0	5.50	3	2-40	0/0	44.66	0	
Mukund Abhinav	6.1.1990		7	2011–2017	320	81	0	22.85	0	0-14	0/0	–	6	
Mushtaq Ali Syed	17.12.1914	18.6.2005	11	*1933–1951*	612	112	2	32.21	3	1-45	0/0	67.33	7	
Nadeem Shahbaz	12.8.1989		1	*2019*	1	1*	0	–	4	2-18	0/0	10.00	1	
Nadkarni Rameshchandra Gangaram ("Bapu")	4.4.1933	17.1.2020	41	*1955–1967*	1,414	122*	1	25.70	88	6-43	4/1	29.07	22	
Naik Sudhir Sakharam	21.2.1945		3	1974–*1974*	141	77	0	23.50	–	–	–/–	–	0	2
Nair Karun Kaladharan	6.12.1991		6	*2016*	374	303*	1	62.33	0	0-4	0/0	–	6	2
Naoomal Jeoomal	17.4.1904	28.7.1980	3	1932–*1933*	108	43	0	27.00	2	1-4	0/0	34.00	0	
Narasimha Rao Modireddy Venkateshwar	11.8.1954		4	*1978–1979*	46	20*	0	9.20	3	2-46	0/0	75.66	8	
Natarajan Thangarasu	27.5.1991		1	*2020*	1	1*	0	–	3	3-78	0/0	39.66	0	1/3
Navle Janaradan Gyanoba	7.12.1902	7.9.1979	2	1932–*1933*	42	13	0	10.50	–	–	–/–	–	1	

	Born	*Died*	*Tests*	*Test Career*	*Runs*	*HS*	*100s*	*Avge*	*Wkts*	*BB*	*5/10*	*Avge*	*Ct/St*	*O/T*
Nayak Surendra Vithal	20.10.1954		2	1982	19	11	0	9.50	1	1-16	0/0	132.00	1	4
[2]**Nayudu** Cottari Kanakaiya (*CY 1933*)	31.10.1895	14.11.1967	7	1932–1936	350	81	0	25.00	9	3-40	0/0	42.88	4	
[2]**Nayudu** Cottari Subbanna	18.4.1914	22.11.2002	11	*1933–1951*	147	36	0	9.18	2	1-19	0/0	179.50	3	
[2]**Nazir Ali** Syed	8.6.1906	18.2.1975	2	1932–*1933*	30	13	0	7.50	4	4-83	0/0	20.75	0	
Nehra Ashish	29.4.1979		17	*1998–2003*	77	19	0	5.50	44	4-72	0/0	42.40	5	117‡/27
Nissar Mohammad	1.8.1910	11.3.1963	6	1932–1936	55	14	0	6.87	25	5-90	3/0	28.28	2	
Nyalchand Sukhlal Shah	14.9.1915	3.1.1997	1	*1952*	7	6*	0	7.00	3	3-97	0/0	32.33	0	
Ojha Naman Vijaykumar	20.7.1983		1	*2015*	56	35	0	28.00	–	–	–/–	–	4/1	1/2
Ojha Pragyan Prayish	5.9.1986		24	*2009–2013*	89	18*	0	8.90	113	6-47	7/1	30.26	10	18/6
Pai Ajit Manohar	28.4.1945		1	*1969*	10	9	0	5.00	2	2-29	0/0	15.50	0	
Palia Phiroze Edulji	5.9.1910	9.9.1981	2	1932–1936	29	16	0	9.66	0	0-2	0/0	–	0	
Pandit Chandrakant Sitaram	30.9.1961		5	1986–*1991*	171	39	0	24.42	–	–	–/–	–	14/2	36
Pandya Hardik Himanshu	11.10.1993		11	2017–2018	532	108	1	31.29	17	5-28	1/0	31.05	7	57/43
Pankaj Singh	6.5.1985		2	2014	10	9	0	3.33	2	2-113	0/0	146.00	2	1
Pant Rishabh Rajendra	4.10.1997		16	2018–*2020*	1,088	159*	2	43.52	–	–	–/–	–	67/2	16/28
Parkar Ghulam Ahmed	25.10.1955		1	1982	7	6	0	3.50	–	–	–/–	–	1	10
Parkar Ramnath Dhondu	31.10.1946	11.8.1999	2	*1972*	80	35	0	20.00	–	–	–/–	–	0	
Parsana Dhiraj Devshibhai	2.12.1947		2	*1978*	1	1	0	0.50	1	1-32	0/0	50.00	0	
Patankar Chandrakant Trimbak	24.11.1930		1	*1955*	14	13	0	14.00	–	–	–/–	–	3/1	
[1]**Pataudi** Iftikhar Ali Khan, Nawab of (*CY 1932*)	16.3.1910	5.1.1952	3†	1946	55	22	0	11.00	–	–	–/–	–	0	
[1]**Pataudi** Mansur Ali Khan, Nawab of (*CY 1968*)	5.1.1941	22.9.2011	46	*1961–1974*	2,793	203*	6	34.91	1	1-10	0/0	88.00	27	
Patel Brijesh Pursuram	24.11.1952		21	1974–*1977*	972	115*	1	29.45	–	–	–/–	–	17	10
Patel Jasubhai Motibhai	26.11.1924	12.12.1992	7	*1954–1959*	25	12	0	2.77	29	9-69	2/1	21.96	2	
Patel Munaf Musa	12.7.1983		13	*2005*–2011	60	15*	0	7.50	35	4-25	0/0	38.54	6	70/3
Patel Parthiv Ajay	9.3.1985		25	2002–*2017*	934	71	0	31.13	–	–	–/–	–	62/10	38/2
Patel Rashid Ghulam Mohammad	1.6.1964		1	*1988*	0	0	0	0.00	0	0-14	0/0	–	1	1
Pathan Irfan Khan	27.10.1984		29	*2003–2007*	1,105	102	1	31.57	100	7-59	7/2	32.26	8	120/24
Patiala Maharajah of (Yadavendra Singh)	17.1.1913	17.6.1974	1	*1933*	84	60	0	42.00	–	–	–/–	–	2	
Patil Sandeep Madhusudan	18.8.1956		29	*1979–1984*	1,588	174	4	36.93	9	2-28	0/0	26.66	12	45
Patil Sadashiv Raoji	10.10.1933	15.9.2020	1	*1955*	14	14*	0	–	2	1-15	0/0	25.50	1	
Phadkar Dattatraya Gajanan	10.12.1925	17.3.1985	31	*1947–1958*	1,229	123	2	32.34	62	7-159	3/0	36.85	21	
Powar Ramesh Rajaram	20.5.1978		2	2007	13	7	0	6.50	6	3-33	0/0	19.66	0	31
Prabhakar Manoj	15.4.1963		39	*1984–1995*	1,600	120	1	32.65	96	6-132	3/0	37.30	20	130
Prasad Bapu Krishnarao Venkatesh	5.8.1969		33	1996–2001	203	30*	0	7.51	96	6-33	7/1	35.00	6	161
Prasad Mannava Sri Kanth	24.4.1975		6	*1999*	106	19	0	11.77	–	–	–/–	–	15	17

	Born	Died	Tests	Test Career	Runs	HS	100s	Avge	Wkts	BB	5/10	Avge	Ct/St	O/T
Prasanna Erapalli Anatharao Srinivas	22.5.1940		49	1961–1978	735	37	0	11.48	189	8-76	10/2	30.38	18	
Pujara Cheteshwar Arvind	25.1.1988		81	2010–2020	6,111	206*	18	47.74	0	0-2	0/0	–	54	5
Punjabi Pananmal Hotchand	20.9.1921	4.10.2011	5	1954	164	33	0	16.40	–	–	–/–	–	5	
Rahane Ajinkya Madhukar	6.6.1988		69	2012–2020	4,471	188	12	42.58	–	–	–/–	–	87	90/20
Rahul Kannur Lokesh	18.4.1992		36	2014–2019	2,006	199	5	34.58	–	–	–/–	–	46	35/45
Rai Singh Kanwar	24.2.1922	12.11.1993	1	1947	26	24	0	13.00	–	–	–/–	–	0	
Raina Suresh Kumar	27.11.1986		18	2010–2014	768	120	1	26.48	13	2-1	0/0	46.38	23	226/78
Rajinder Pal	18.11.1937	9.5.2018	1	1963	6	3*	0	6.00	0	0-3	0/0	–	0	
Rajindernath Vijay	7.1.1928	22.11.1989	1	1952	–	–	–	–	–	–	–/–	–	0/4	
Rajput Lalchand Sitaram	18.12.1961		2	1985	105	61	0	26.25	–	–	–/–	–	1	4
Raju Sagi Lakshmi Venkatapathy	9.7.1969		28	1989–2000	240	31	0	10.00	93	6-12	5/1	30.72	6	53
Raman Woorkeri Venkat	23.5.1965		11	1987–1996	448	96	0	24.88	2	1-7	0/0	64.50	6	27
Ramaswami Cotar	16.6.1896	1.1990	2	1936	170	60	0	56.66	–	–	–/–	–	0	
Ramchand Gulabrai Sipahimalani	26.7.1927	8.9.2003	33	1952–1959	1,180	109	2	24.58	41	6-49	1/0	46.31	20	
Ramesh Sadagoppan	16.10.1975		19	1998–2001	1,367	143	2	37.97	0	0-5	0/0	–	18	24
[2] **Ramji** Ladha	10.2.1900	20.12.1948	1	1933	1	1	0	0.50	0	0-64	0/0	–	1	
Rangachari Commandur Rajagopalachari	14.4.1916	9.10.1993	4	1947–1948	8	8*	0	2.66	9	5-107	1/0	54.77	0	
Rangnekar Khanderao Moreshwar	27.6.1917	11.10.1984	3	1947	33	18	0	5.50	–	–	–/–	–	1	
Ranjane Vasant Baburao	22.7.1937	22.12.2011	7	1958–1964	40	16	0	6.66	19	4-72	0/0	34.15	1	
Rathore Vikram	26.3.1969		6	1996–1996	131	44	0	13.10	–	–	–/–	–	12	7
Ratra Ajay	13.12.1981		6	2001–2002	163	115*	1	18.11	0	0-1	0/0	–	11/2	12
Razdan Vivek	25.8.1969		2	1989	6	6*	0	6.00	5	5-79	1/0	28.20	0	3
Reddy Bharath	12.11.1954		4	1979	38	21	0	9.50	–	–	–/–	–	9/2	3
Rege Madhusudan Ramachandra	18.3.1924	16.12.2013	1	1948	15	15	0	7.50	–	–	–/–	–	1	
Roy Ambar	5.6.1945	19.9.1997	4	1969	91	48	0	13.00	–	–	–/–	–	0	
[1] **Roy** Pankaj	31.5.1928	4.2.2001	43	1951–1960	2,442	173	5	32.56	1	1-6	0/0	66.00	16	
[1] **Roy** Pranab	10.2.1957		2	1981	71	60*	0	35.50	–	–	–/–	–	1	
Saha Wriddhiman Prasanta	24.10.1984		38	2009–2020	1,251	117	3	29.09	–	–	–/–	–	92/11	9
Saini Navdeep	23.11.1992		2	2020	8	5	0	4.00	4	2-54	0/0	43.00	1	7/10
Sandhu Balwinder Singh	3.8.1956		8	1982–1983	214	71	0	30.57	10	3-87	0/0	55.70	1	22
Sanghvi Rahul Laxman	3.9.1974		1	2000	2	2	0	1.00	2	2-67	0/0	39.00	0	10
Sarandeep Singh	21.10.1979		3	2000–2001	43	39*	0	43.00	10	4-136	0/0	34.00	1	5
Sardesai Dilip Narayan	8.8.1940	2.7.2007	30	1961–1972	2,001	212	5	39.23	0	0-3	0/0	–	4	
Sarwate Chandrasekhar Trimbak	22.7.1920	23.12.2003	9	1946–1951	208	37	0	13.00	3	1-16	0/0	124.66	0	
Saxena Ramesh Chandra	20.9.1944	16.8.2011	1	1967	25	16	0	12.50	0	0-11	0/0	–	0	

	Born	*Died*	*Tests*	*Test Career*	*Runs*	*HS*	*100s*	*Avge*	*Wkts*	*BB*	*5/10*	*Avge*	*Ct/St*	*O/T*
Sehwag Virender	20.10.1978		103§	2001–2012	8,503	319	23	49.43	40	5-104	1/0	47.35	90	241‡/19
Sekhar Thirumalai Ananthanpillai	28.3.1956		2	1982	0	0*	0	–	0	0-43	0/0	–	0	4
Sen Probir Kumar ("Khokhan")	31.5.1926	27.1.1970	14	1947–1952	165	25	0	11.78	–	–	–/–	–	20/11	
Sen Gupta Apoorva Kumar	3.8.1939	14.9.2013	1	1958	9	8	0	4.50	–	–	–/–	–	0	
Sharma Ajay Kumar	3.4.1964		1	1987	53	30	0	26.50	0	0-9	0/0	–	1	31
Sharma Chetan	3.1.1966		23	1984–1988	396	54	0	22.00	61	6-58	4/1	35.45	7	65
Sharma Gopal	3.8.1960		5	1984–1990	11	10*	0	3.66	10	4-88	0/0	41.80	2	11
Sharma Ishant	2.9.1988		97	2007–2019	720	57	0	8.37	297	7-74	11/1	32.39	21	80/14
Sharma Karan Vinod	23.10.1987		1	2014	8	4*	0	8.00	4	2-95	0/0	59.50	0	2/1
Sharma Parthasarathy Harishchandra	5.1.1948	20.10.2010	5	1974–1976	187	54	0	18.70	0	0-2	0/0	–	1	2
Sharma Rohit Gurunath	30.4.1987		34	2013–2020	2,270	212	6	45.40	2	1-26	0/0	108.50	36	224/108
Sharma Sanjeev Kumar	25.8.1965		2	1988–1990	56	38	0	28.00	6	3-37	0/0	41.16	1	23
Shastri Ravishankar Jayadritha	27.5.1962		80	1980–1992	3,830	206	11	35.79	151	5-75	2/0	40.96	36	150
Shaw Prithvi Pankaj	9.11.1999		5	2018–2020	339	134	1	42.37	–	–	–/–	–	2	3
Shinde Sadashiv Ganpatrao	18.8.1923	22.6.1955	7	1946–1952	85	14	0	14.16	12	6-91	1/0	59.75	0	
Shodhan Roshan Harshadlal ("Deepak")	18.10.1928	16.5.2016	3	1952	181	110	1	60.33	0	0-1	0/0	–	1	
Shukla Rakesh Chandra	4.2.1948	29.6.2019	1	1982	–	–	–	–	2	2-82	0/0	76.00	0	
Siddiqui Iqbal Rashid	26.12.1974		1	2001	29	24	0	29.00	1	1-32	0/0	48.00	1	
Sidhu Navjot Singh	20.10.1963		51	1983–1998	3,202	201	9	42.13	0	0-9	0/0	–	9	136
Singh Rabindra Ramanarayan ("Robin")	14.9.1963		1	1998	27	15	0	13.50	0	0-16	0/0	–	5	136
Singh Robin	1.1.1970		1	1998	0	0	0	0.00	3	2-74	0/0	58.66	1	
Singh Rudra Pratap	6.12.1985		14	2005–2011	116	30	0	7.25	40	5-59	1/0	42.05	6	58/10
Singh Vikram Rajvir	17.9.1984		5	2005–2007	47	29	0	11.75	8	3-48	0/0	53.37	1	2
Siraj Mohammed	13.3.1994		3	2020	19	13	0	9.50	13	5-73	1/0	29.53	2	1/3
Sivaramakrishnan Laxman	31.12.1965		9	1982–1985	130	25	0	16.25	26	6-64	3/1	44.03	9	16
Sohoni Sriranga Wasudev	5.3.1918	19.5.1993	4	1946–1951	83	29*	0	16.60	2	1-16	0/0	101.00	2	
Solkar Eknath Dhondu	18.3.1948	26.6.2005	27	1969–1976	1,068	102	1	25.42	18	3-28	0/0	59.44	53	7
Sood Man Mohan	6.7.1939	19.1.2020	1	1959	3	3	0	1.50	–	–	–/–	–	0	
Sreesanth Shanthakumaran	6.2.1983		27	2005–2011	281	35	0	10.40	87	5-40	3/0	37.59	5	53/10
Srikkanth Krishnamachari	21.12.1959		43	1981–1991	2,062	123	2	29.88	0	0-1	0/0	–	40	146
Srinath Javagal	31.8.1969		67	1991–2002	1,009	76	0	14.21	236	8-86	10/1	30.49	22	229
Srinivasan Thirumalai Echambadi	26.10.1950	6.12.2010	1	1980	48	29	0	24.00	–	–	–/–	–	0	2
Subramanya Venkataraman	16.7.1936		9	1964–1967	263	75	0	18.78	3	2-32	0/0	67.00	9	
Sunderam Gundibail Rama	29.3.1930	20.6.2010	2	1955	3	3*	0	–	3	2-46	0/0	55.33	0	

§ *Sehwag's figures exclude 83 runs and one catch for the ICC World XI v Australia in the Super Series Test in 2005-06.*

	Born	Died	Tests	Test Career	Runs	HS	100s	Avge	Wkts	BB	5/10	Avge	Ct/St	O/T
Surendranath Raman	4.1.1937	5.5.2012	11	1958–1960	136	27	0	10.46	26	5-75	2/0	40.50	4	
Surti Rusi Framroze	25.5.1936	13.1.2013	26	1960–1969	1,263	99	0	28.70	42	5-74	1/0	46.71	26	
Swamy Venkatraman Narayan	23.5.1924	1.5.1983	1	1955	–	–	–	–	0	0-15	0/0	–	0	
Tamhane Narendra Shankar	4.8.1931	19.3.2002	21	1954–1960	225	54*	0	10.22	–	–	–/–	–	35/16	
Tarapore Keki Khurshedji	17.12.1910	15.6.1986	1	1948	2	2	0	2.00	0	0-72	0/0	–	0	
Tendulkar Sachin Ramesh (*CY 1997*)	24.4.1973		200	1989–2013	15,921	248*	51	53.78	46	3-10	0/0	54.17	115	463/1
Thakur Shardul Narendra	16.10.1991		2	2018–2020	73	67	0	36.50	7	4-61	0/0	23.42	2	12/17
Umrigar Pahlanji Ratanji ("Polly")	28.3.1926	7.11.2006	59	1948–1961	3,631	223	12	42.22	35	6-74	2/0	42.08	33	
Unadkat Jaydev Dipakbhai	18.10.1991		1	2010	2	1*	0	2.00	0	0-101	0/0	–	0	7/10
Vengsarkar Dilip Balwant (*CY 1987*)	6.4.1956		116	1975–1991	6,868	166	17	42.13	0	0-3	0/0	–	78	129
Venkataraghavan Srinivasaraghavan	21.4.1945		57	1964–1983	748	64	0	11.68	156	8-72	3/1	36.11	44	15
Venkataramana Margashayam	24.4.1966		1	1988	0	0*	0	–	1	1-10	0/0	58.00	1	1
Vihari Gade Hanuma	13.10.1993		12	2018–2020	624	111	1	32.84	5	3-37	0/0	36.00	3	
Vijay Murali	1.4.1984		61	2008–2018	3,982	167	12	38.28	1	1-12	0/0	198.00	49	17/9
Vinay Kumar Ranganath	12.2.1984		1	2011	11	6	0	5.50	1	1-73	0/0	73.00	0	31/9
Viswanath Gundappa Rangnath	12.2.1949		91	1969–1982	6,080	222	14	41.93	1	1-11	0/0	46.00	63	25
Viswanath Sadanand	29.11.1962		3	1985	31	20	0	6.20	–	–	–/–	–	11	22
Vizianagram Maharajkumar of (*Sir* Vijaya Anand)	28.12.1905	2.12.1965	3	1936	33	19*	0	8.25	–	–	–/–	–	1	
Wadekar Ajit Laxman	1.4.1941	15.8.2018	37	1966–1974	2,113	143	1	31.07	0	0-0	0/0	–	46	2
Washington Sundar M. S.	5.10.1999		1	2020	84	62	0	42.00	4	3-89	0/0	42.25	1	1/26
Wasim Jaffer	16.2.1978		31	1999–2007	1,944	212	5	34.10	2	2-18	0/0	9.00	27	2
Wassan Atul Satish	23.3.1968		4	1989–1990	94	53	0	23.50	10	4-108	0/0	50.40	1	9
[1,2] **Wazir Ali** Syed	15.9.1903	17.6.1950	7	1932–1936	237	42	0	16.92	0	0-0	0/0	–	1	
Yadav Jayant	22.1.1990		4	2016	228	104	1	45.60	11	3-30	0/0	33.36	1	1
Yadav Kuldeep	14.12.1994		6	2016–2018	51	26	0	8.50	24	5-57	2/0	24.12	3	61/21
Yadav Nandlal Shivlal	26.1.1957		35	1979–1986	403	43	0	14.39	102	5-76	3/0	35.09	10	7
Yadav Umeshkumar Tilak	25.10.1987		48	2011–2020	359	31	0	11.21	148	6-88	3/1	30.54	17	75/7
Yadav Vijay	14.3.1967		1	1992	30	30	0	30.00	–	–	–/–	–	1/2	19
Yajurvindra Singh	1.8.1952		4	1976–1979	109	43*	0	18.16	0	0-2	0/0	–	11	
Yashpal Sharma	11.8.1954		37	1979–1983	1,606	140	2	33.45	1	1-6	0/0	17.00	16	42
[1] **Yograj Singh**	25.3.1958		1	1980	10	6	0	5.00	1	1-63	0/0	63.00	0	6
Yohannan Tinu	18.2.1979		3	2001–2002	13	8*	0	–	5	2-56	0/0	51.20	1	3
[1] **Yuvraj Singh**	12.12.1981		40	2003–2012	1,900	169	3	33.92	9	2-9	0/0	60.77	31	301‡/58
Zaheer Khan (*CY 2008*)	7.10.1978		92	2000–2013	1,231	75	0	11.95	311	7-87	11/1	32.94	19	194‡/17

PAKISTAN (241 players)

	Born	Died	Tests	Test Career	Runs	HS	100s	Avge	Wkts	BB	5/10	Avge	Ct/St	O/T
Aamer Malik	3.1.1963		14	1987–1994	565	117	2	35.31	1	1-0	0/0	89.00	15/1	24
Aamir Nazir	2.1.1971		6	1992–1995	31	11	0	6.20	20	5-46	1/0	29.85	2	9
Aamir Sohail	14.9.1966		47	1992–1999	2,823	205	5	35.28	25	4-54	0/0	41.96	36	156
Abdul Kadir	10.5.1944	12.3.2002	4	1964	272	95	0	34.00	–	–	–/–	–	0/1	
Abdul Qadir	15.9.1955	6.9.2019	67	1977–1990	1,029	61	0	15.59	236	9-56	15/5	32.80	15	104
Abdul Razzaq	2.12.1979		46	1999–2006	1,946	134	3	28.61	100	5-35	1/0	36.94	15	261‡/32
Abdur Rauf	9.12.1978		3	2009–2009	52	31	0	8.66	6	2-59	0/0	46.33	0	4/1
Abdur Rehman	1.3.1980		22	2007–2014	395	60	0	14.10	99	6-25	2/0	29.39	8	31/8
Abid Ali	16.10.1987		8	2019–2020	536	174	2	44.66	–	–	–/–	–	1	6
[2]**Adnan Akmal**	13.3.1985		21	2010–2013	591	64	0	24.62	–	–	–/–	–	66/11	5
Afaq Hussain	31.12.1939	25.2.2002	2	1961–1964	66	35*	0	–	1	1-40	0/0	106.00	2	
Aftab Baloch	1.4.1953		2	1969–1974	97	60*	0	48.50	0	0-2	0/0	–	0	
Aftab Gul	31.3.1946		6	1968–1971	182	33	0	22.75	0	0-4	0/0	–	3	
Agha Saadat Ali	21.6.1929	25.10.1995	1	1955	8	8*	0	–	–	–	–/–	–	3	
Agha Zahid	7.1.1953		1	1974	15	14	0	7.50	–	–	–/–	–	0	
Ahmed Shehzad	23.11.1991		13	2013–2016	982	176	3	40.91	0	0-8	0/0	–	3	81/59
Aizaz Cheema	5.9.1979		7	2011–2012	1	1*	0	–	20	4-24	0/0	31.90	1	14/5
Akram Raza	22.11.1964		9	1989–1994	153	32	0	15.30	13	3-46	0/0	56.30	8	49
Ali Hussain Rizvi	6.1.1974		1	1997	–	–	–	–	2	2-72	0/0	36.00	0	
Ali Naqvi	19.3.1977		5	1997	242	115	1	30.25	0	0-11	0/0	–	1	
Alim-ud-Din	15.12.1930	12.7.2012	25	1954–1962	1,091	109	2	25.37	1	1-17	0/0	75.00	8	
Amir Elahi	1.9.1908	28.12.1980	5†	1952	65	47	0	10.83	7	4-134	0/0	35.42	0	
Anil Dalpat	20.9.1963		9	1983–1984	167	52	0	15.18	–	–	–/–	–	22/3	15
Anwar Hussain	16.7.1920	9.10.2002	4	1952	42	17	0	7.00	1	1-25	0/0	29.00	0	
Anwar Khan	24.12.1955		1	1978	15	12	0	15.00	0	0-12	0/0	–	0	
Aqib Javed	5.8.1972		22	1988–1998	101	28*	0	5.05	54	5-84	1/0	34.70	2	163
Arif Butt	17.5.1944	10.7.2007	3	1964	59	20	0	11.80	14	6-89	1/0	20.57	0	
Arshad Khan	22.3.1971		9	1997–2004	31	9*	0	5.16	32	5-38	1/0	30.00	0	58
Asad Shafiq	28.1.1986		77	2010–2020	4,660	137	12	38.19	3	1-7	0/0	65.33	77	60/10
Ashfaq Ahmed	6.6.1973		1	1993	1	1*	0	1.00	2	2-31	0/0	26.50	0	3
Ashraf Ali	22.4.1958		8	1981–1987	229	65	0	45.80	–	–	–/–	–	17/5	16
Asif Iqbal (*CY 1968*)	6.6.1943		58	1964–1979	3,575	175	11	38.85	53	5-48	2/0	28.33	36	10
Asif Masood	23.1.1946		16	1968–1976	93	30*	0	10.33	38	5-111	1/0	41.26	5	7

	Born	Died	Tests	Test Career	Runs	HS	100s	Avge	Wkts	BB	5/10	Avge	Ct/St	O/T
Asif Mujtaba	4.11.1967		25	1986–1996	928	65*	0	24.42	4	1-0	0/0	75.75	19	66
Asim Kamal	31.5.1976		12	2003–2005	717	99	0	37.73	–	–	–/–	–	10	
Ata-ur-Rehman	28.3.1975		13	1992–1996	76	19	0	8.44	31	4-50	0/0	34.54	2	30
Atif Rauf	3.3.1964		1	1993	25	16	0	12.50	–	–	–/–	–	0	
Atiq-uz-Zaman	20.7.1975		1	1999	26	25	0	13.00	–	–	–/–	–	5	3
Azam Khan	1.3.1969		1	1996	14	14	0	14.00	–	–	–/–	–	0	6
Azeem Hafeez	29.7.1963		18	1983–1984	134	24	0	8.37	63	6-46	4/0	34.98	1	15
Azhar Ali	19.2.1985		83	2010–2020	6,302	302*	17	42.87	8	2-35	0/0	76.37	62	53
Azhar Khan	7.9.1955		1	1979	14	14	0	14.00	1	1-1	0/0	2.00	0	
Azhar Mahmood	28.2.1975		21	1997–2001	900	136	3	30.00	39	4-50	0/0	35.94	14	143
[2] **Azmat Rana**	3.11.1951	30.5.2015	1	1979	49	49	0	49.00	–	–	–/–	–	0	2
Babar Azam	15.10.1994		29	2016–2020	2,045	143	5	45.44	–	–	–/–	–	20	77/44
Basit Ali	13.12.1970		19	1992–1995	858	103	1	26.81	0	0-6	0/0	–	6	50
[3] **Bazid Khan**	25.3.1981		1	2004	32	23	0	16.00	–	–	–/–	–	2	5
Bilal Asif	24.9.1985		5	2018	73	15	0	9.12	16	6-36	2/0	26.50	2	3
Bilawal Bhatti	17.9.1991		2	2013	70	32	0	35.00	6	3-65	0/0	48.50	0	10/9
Danish Kaneria	16.12.1980		61	2000–2010	360	29	0	7.05	261	7-77	15/2	34.79	18	18
D'Souza Antao	17.1.1939		6	1958–1962	76	23*	0	38.00	17	5-112	1/0	43.82	3	
Ehsan Adil	15.3.1993		3	2012–2015	21	12	0	5.25	5	2-54	0/0	52.60	0	6
Ehtesham-ud-Din	4.9.1950		5	1979–1982	2	2	0	1.00	16	5-47	1/0	23.43	2	
Fahim Ashraf	16.1.1994		6	2018–2020	324	91	0	32.40	14	3-42	0/0	32.21	0	25/32
Faisal Iqbal	30.12.1981		26	2000–2009	1,124	139	1	26.76	0	0-7	0/0	–	22	18
Fakhar Zaman	10.4.1990		3	2018	192	94	0	32.00	–	–	–/–	–	3	47/40
Farhan Adil	25.9.1977		1	2003	33	25	0	16.50	–	–	–/–	–	0	
Farooq Hamid	3.3.1945		1	1964	3	3	0	1.50	1	1-82	0/0	107.00	0	
Farrukh Zaman	2.4.1956		1	1976	–	–	–	–	0	0-7	0/0	–	0	
Fawad Alam	8.10.1985		7	2009–2020	400	168	2	33.33	2	2-46	0/0	23.00	4	38/24
Fazal Mahmood (*CY 1955*)	18.2.1927	30.5.2005	34	1952–1962	620	60	0	14.09	139	7-42	13/4	24.70	11	
Fazl-e-Akbar	20.10.1980		5	1997–2003	52	25	0	13.00	11	3-85	0/0	46.45	2	2
Ghazali Mohammad Ebrahim Zainuddin	15.6.1924	26.4.2003	2	1954	32	18	0	8.00	0	0-18	0/0	–	0	
Ghulam Abbas	1.5.1947		1	1967	12	12	0	6.00	–	–	–/–	–	0	
Gul Mahomed	15.10.1921	8.5.1992	1†	1956	39	27*	0	39.00	–	–	–/–	–	0	
[1, 2] **Hanif Mohammad** (*CY 1968*)	21.12.1934	11.8.2016	55	1952–1969	3,915	337	12	43.98	1	1-1	0/0	95.00	40	
Haris Sohail	9.1.1989		16	2017–2020	847	147	2	32.57	13	3-1	0/0	22.61	14	42/14
Haroon Rashid	25.3.1953		23	1976–1982	1,217	153	3	34.77	0	0-3	0/0	–	16	12
Hasan Ali	7.2.1994		9	2016–2018	155	29	0	15.50	31	5-45	1/0	28.90	4	53/30

	Born	*Died*	*Tests*	*Test Career*	*Runs*	*HS*	*100s*	*Avge*	*Wkts*	*BB*	*5/10*	*Avge*	*Ct/St*	*O/T*
Hasan Raza	11.3.1982		7	*1996–2005*	235	68	0	26.11	0	0-1	0/0	–	5	16
Haseeb Ahsan	15.7.1939	8.3.2013	12	*1957–1961*	61	14	0	6.77	27	6-202	2/0	49.25	1	
[2]**Humayun Farhat**	24.1.1981		1	*2000*	54	28	0	27.00	–	–	–/–	–	0	5
Ibadulla Khalid ("Billy")	20.12.1935		4	*1964*–1967	253	166	1	31.62	1	1-42	0/0	99.00	3	
Iftikhar Ahmed	3.9.1990		3	2016–*2019*	48	27	0	9.60	1	1-1	0/0	141.00	1	7/11
Iftikhar Anjum	1.12.1980		1	*2005*	9	9*	0	–	0	0-8	0/0	–	0	62/2
Ijaz Ahmed snr	20.9.1968		60	*1986–2000*	3,315	211	12	37.67	2	1-9	0/0	38.50	45	250
Ijaz Ahmed jnr	2.2.1969		2	*1995*	29	16	0	9.66	0	0-1	0/0	–	3	2
Ijaz Butt	10.3.1938		8	*1958*–1962	279	58	0	19.92	–	–	–/–	–	5	
Ijaz Faqih	24.3.1956		5	*1980–1987*	183	105	1	26.14	4	1-38	0/0	74.75	0	27
Imam-ul-Haq	12.12.1995		11	2018–*2019*	485	76	0	25.52	–	–	–/–	–	7	40/2
[2]**Imran Farhat**	20.5.1982		40	*2000–2012*	2,400	128	3	32.00	3	2-69	0/0	94.66	40	58/7
Imran Khan (*CY 1983*)	25.11.1952		88	1971–*1991*	3,807	136	6	37.69	362	8-58	23/6	22.81	28	175
Mohammad **Imran Khan**	15.7.1987		10	*2014–2019*	16	6	0	2.28	29	5-58	1/0	31.62	0	
Imran Nazir	16.12.1981		8	*1998–2002*	427	131	2	32.84	–	–	–/–	–	4	79/25
Imtiaz Ahmed	5.1.1928	31.12.2016	41	*1952*–1962	2,079	209	3	29.28	0	0-0	0/0	–	77/16	
Intikhab Alam	28.12.1941		47	*1959–1976*	1,493	138	1	22.28	125	7-52	5/2	35.95	20	4
Inzamam-ul-Haq	3.3.1970		119§	1992–*2007*	8,829	329	25	50.16	0	0-8	0/0	–	81	375‡/1
Iqbal Qasim	6.8.1953		50	*1976–1988*	549	56	0	13.07	171	7-49	8/2	28.11	42	15
Irfan Fazil	2.11.1981		1	*1999*	4	3	0	4.00	2	1-30	0/0	32.50	2	1
Israr Ali	1.5.1927	1.2.2016	4	*1952–1959*	33	10	0	4.71	6	2-29	0/0	27.50	1	
Jalal-ud-Din	12.6.1959		6	*1982–1985*	3	2	0	3.00	11	3-77	0/0	48.81	0	8
Javed Akhtar	21.11.1940	8.7.2016	1	1962	4	2*	0	4.00	0	0-52	0/0	–	0	
Javed Burki	8.5.1938		25	*1960–1969*	1,341	140	3	30.47	0	0-2	0/0	–	7	
Javed Miandad (*CY 1982*)	12.6.1957		124	*1976–1993*	8,832	280*	23	52.57	17	3-74	0/0	40.11	93/1	233
Junaid Khan	24.12.1989		22	*2011*–2015	122	17	0	7.17	71	5-38	5/0	31.73	4	76/9
Kabir Khan	12.4.1974		4	*1994*	24	10	0	8.00	9	3-26	0/0	41.11	1	10
[2]**Kamran Akmal**	13.1.1982		53	*2002*–2010	2,648	158*	6	30.79	–	–	–/–	–	184/22	157/58
Kardar Abdul Hafeez	17.1.1925	21.4.1996	23†	*1952–1957*	847	93	0	24.91	21	3-35	0/0	45.42	15	
Khalid Hassan	14.7.1937	3.12.2013	1	1954	17	10	0	17.00	2	2-116	0/0	58.00	0	
[1]**Khalid Wazir**	27.4.1936	27.6.2020	2	1954	14	9*	0	7.00	–	–	–/–	–	0	
Khan Mohammad	1.1.1928	4.7.2009	13	*1952–1957*	100	26*	0	10.00	54	6-21	4/0	23.92	4	
Khurram Manzoor	10.6.1986		16	*2008*–2014	817	146	1	28.17	–	–	–/–	–	8	7/3
Liaqat Ali	21.5.1955		5	*1974*–1978	28	12	0	7.00	6	3-80	0/0	59.83	1	3
Mahmood Hussain	2.4.1932	25.12.1991	27	*1952*–1962	336	35	0	10.18	68	6-67	2/0	38.64	5	

§ *Inzamam-ul-Haq's figures exclude one run for the ICC World XI v Australia in the Super Series Test in 2005-06.*

	Born	Died	Tests	Test Career	Runs	HS	100s	Avge	Wkts	BB	5/10	Avge	Ct/St	O/T
[3] **Majid** Jahangir **Khan** (*CY 1970*)	28.9.1946		63	*1964–1982*	3,931	167	8	38.92	27	4-45	0/0	53.92	70	23
Mansoor Akhtar	25.12.1957		19	*1980–1989*	655	111	1	25.19	–	–	–/–	–	9	41
[2] **Manzoor Elahi**	15.4.1963		6	*1984–1994*	123	52	0	15.37	7	2-38	0/0	27.71	7	54
Maqsood Ahmed	26.3.1925	4.1.1999	16	*1952–1955*	507	99	0	19.50	3	2-12	0/0	63.66	13	
Masood Anwar	12.12.1967		1	*1990*	39	37	0	19.50	3	2-59	0/0	34.00	0	
Mathias Wallis	4.2.1935	1.9.1994	21	1955–1962	783	77	0	23.72	0	0-20	0/0	–	22	
Mir Hamza	10.9.1992		1	*2018*	4	4*	0	–	1	1-40	0/0	67.00	0	
Miran Bux	20.4.1907	8.2.1991	2	*1954*	1	1*	0	1.00	2	2-82	0/0	57.50	0	
Misbah-ul-Haq (*CY 2017*)	28.5.1974		75	*2000–2016*	5,222	161*	10	46.62	–	–	–/–	–	50	162/39
Mohammad Abbas	10.3.1990		23	*2016–2020*	109	29	0	5.73	84	5-33	4/1	22.80	6	3
Mohammad Akram	10.9.1974		9	*1995–2000*	24	10*	0	2.66	17	5-138	1/0	50.52	4	23
Mohammad Amir (formerly Mohammad Aamer)	13.4.1992		36	2009–*2018*	751	48	0	13.41	119	6-44	4/0	30.47	5	61/50
Mohammad Asif	20.12.1982		23	*2004*–2010	141	29	0	5.64	106	6-41	7/1	24.36	3	35‡/11
Mohammad Aslam Khokhar	5.1.1920	22.1.2011	1	1954	34	18	0	17.00	–	–	–/–	–	0	
Mohammad Ayub	13.9.1979		1	2012	47	25	0	23.50	–	–	–/–	–	1	
Mohammad Farooq	8.4.1938		7	*1960–1964*	85	47	0	17.00	21	4-70	0/0	32.47	1	
Mohammad Hafeez	17.10.1980		55	*2003–2018*	3,652	224	10	37.64	53	4-16	0/0	34.11	45	218/99
Mohammad Hussain	8.10.1976		2	*1996–1998*	18	17	0	6.00	3	2-66	0/0	29.00	1	14
Mohammad Ilyas	19.3.1946		10	*1964–1968*	441	126	1	23.21	0	0-1	0/0	–	6	
Mohammad Irfan	6.6.1982		4	*2012–2013*	28	14	0	5.60	10	3-44	0/0	38.90	0	60/22
Mohammad Khalil	11.11.1982		2	*2004*	9	5	0	3.00	0	0-38	0/0	–	0	3
Mohammad Munaf	2.11.1935	28.1.2020	4	*1959–1961*	63	19	0	12.60	11	4-42	0/0	31.00	0	
Mohammad Nawaz	21.3.1994		3	*2016*	50	25	0	12.50	5	2-32	0/0	29.40	2	15/16
Mohammad Nazir	8.3.1946		14	*1969–1983*	144	29*	0	18.00	34	7-99	3/0	33.05	4	4
Mohammad Ramzan	25.12.1970		1	*1997*	36	29	0	18.00	–	–	–/–	–	1	
Mohammad Rizwan (*CY 2021*)	1.6.1992		11	*2016–2020*	588	95	0	39.20	–	–	–/–	–	26/1	35/26
Mohammad Salman	7.8.1981		2	*2010*	25	13	0	6.25	–	–	–/–	–	2/1	7/1
Mohammad Sami	24.2.1981		36	*2000–2012*	487	49	0	11.59	85	5-36	2/0	52.74	7	87/13
Mohammad Talha	15.10.1988		4	*2008–2014*	34	19	0	8.50	9	3-65	0/0	56.00	1	3
Mohammad Wasim	8.8.1977		18	*1996–2000*	783	192	2	30.11	–	–	–/–	–	22/2	25
Mohammad Yousuf (*CY 2007*) (formerly Yousuf Youhana)	27.8.1974		90	*1997–2010*	7,530	223	24	52.29	0	0-3	0/0	–	65	281‡/3
Mohammad Zahid	2.8.1976		5	*1996–2002*	7	6*	0	1.40	15	7-66	1/1	33.46	0	11
Mohsin Kamal	16.6.1963		9	*1983–1994*	37	13*	0	9.25	24	4-116	0/0	34.25	4	19

	Born	Died	Tests	Test Career	Runs	HS	100s	Avge	Wkts	BB	5/10	Avge	Ct/St	O/T
Mohsin Khan	15.3.1955		48	*1977–1986*	2,709	200	7	37.10	0	0-0	0/0	–	34	75
[2]**Moin Khan**	23.9.1971		69	*1990–2004*	2,741	137	4	28.55	–	–	–/–	–	128/20	219
[1]**Mudassar Nazar**	6.4.1956		76	*1976–1988*	4,114	231	10	38.09	66	6-32	1/0	38.36	48	122
Mufasir-ul-Haq	16.8.1944	27.7.1983	1	*1964*	8	8*	0	–	3	2-50	0/0	28.00	1	
Munir Malik	10.7.1934	30.11.2012	3	*1959*–1962	7	4	0	2.33	9	5-128	1/0	39.77	1	
Musa Khan	20.8.2000		1	*2019*	16	12*	0	–	0	0-114	0/0	–	0	2/2
Mushtaq Ahmed (*CY 1997*)	28.6.1970		52	*1989–2003*	656	59	0	11.71	185	7-56	10/3	32.97	23	144
[2]**Mushtaq Mohammad** (*CY 1963*)	22.11.1943		57	*1958–1978*	3,643	201	10	39.17	79	5-28	3/0	29.22	42	10
Nadeem Abbasi	15.4.1964		3	*1989*	46	36	0	23.00	–	–	–/–	–	6	
Nadeem Ghauri	12.10.1962		1	*1989*	0	0	0	0.00	0	0-20	0/0	–	0	6
[2]**Nadeem Khan**	10.12.1969		2	*1992–1998*	34	25	0	17.00	2	2-147	0/0	115.00	0	2
Naseem Shah	15.2.2003		9	*2019–2020*	28	12	0	4.00	20	5-31	1/0	42.45	1	
Nasim-ul-Ghani	14.5.1941		29	*1957–1972*	747	101	1	16.60	52	6-67	2/0	37.67	11	1
Nasir Jamshed	6.12.1989		2	*2012*	51	46	0	12.75	–	–	–/–	–	1	48/18
Naushad Ali	1.10.1943		6	1964	156	39	0	14.18	–	–	–/–	–	9	
Naved Anjum	27.7.1963		2	*1989–1990*	44	22	0	14.66	4	2-57	0/0	40.50	0	13
Naved Ashraf	4.9.1974		2	*1998–1999*	64	32	0	21.33	–	–	–/–	–	0	
Naved Latif	21.2.1976		1	*2001*	20	20	0	10.00	–	–	–/–	–	0	11
Naved-ul-Hasan	28.2.1978		9	*2004–2006*	239	42*	0	19.91	18	3-30	0/0	58.00	3	74/4
[1]**Nazar Mohammad**	5.3.1921	12.7.1996	5	*1952*	277	124*	1	39.57	0	0-4	0/0	–	7	
Niaz Ahmed	11.11.1945	12.4.2000	2	1967–*1968*	17	16*	0	–	3	2-72	0/0	31.33	1	
[2]**Pervez Sajjad**	30.8.1942		19	*1964–1972*	123	24	0	13.66	59	7-74	3/0	23.89	9	
Qaiser Abbas	7.5.1982		1	*2000*	2	2	0	2.00	0	0-35	0/0	–	0	
Qasim Omar	9.2.1957		26	*1983–1986*	1,502	210	3	36.63	0	0-0	0/0	–	15	31
Rahat Ali	12.9.1988		21	*2012*–2018	136	35*	0	7.55	58	6-127	2/0	39.03	9	14
[2]**Ramiz Raja**	14.8.1962		57	*1983–1996*	2,833	122	2	31.83	–	–	–/–	–	34	198
Rashid Khan	15.12.1959		4	*1981–1984*	155	59	0	51.66	8	3-129	0/0	45.00	2	29
Rashid Latif	14.10.1968		37	1992–*2003*	1,381	150	1	28.77	0	0-10	0/0	–	119/11	166
Rehman Sheikh Fazalur	11.6.1935		1	*1957*	10	8	0	5.00	1	1-43	0/0	99.00	1	
[2]**Riaz Afridi**	21.1.1985		1	*2004*	9	9	0	9.00	2	2-42	0/0	43.50	0	
Rizwan-uz-Zaman	4.9.1961		11	*1981–1988*	345	60	0	19.16	4	3-26	0/0	11.50	4	3
[2]**Sadiq Mohammad**	3.5.1945		41	*1969–1980*	2,579	166	5	35.81	0	0-0	0/0	–	28	19
[2]**Saeed Ahmed**	1.10.1937		41	*1957–1972*	2,991	172	5	40.41	22	4-64	0/0	36.45	13	
Saeed Ajmal	14.10.1977		35	2009–2014	451	50	0	11.00	178	7-55	10/4	28.10	11	113/64
Saeed Anwar (*CY 1997*)	6.9.1968		55	*1990–2001*	4,052	188*	11	45.52	0	0-0	0/0	–	18	247

	Born	Died	Tests	Test Career	Runs	HS	100s	Avge	Wkts	BB	5/10	Avge	Ct/St	O/T
Salah-ud-Din	14.2.1947		5	*1964–1969*	117	34*	0	19.50	7	2-36	0/0	26.71	3	
Saleem Jaffer	19.11.1962		14	*1986–1991*	42	10*	0	5.25	36	5-40	1/0	31.63	2	39
Salim Altaf	19.4.1944		21	1967–*1978*	276	53*	0	14.52	46	4-11	0/0	37.17	3	6
[2] **Salim Elahi**	21.11.1976		13	*1995–2002*	436	72	0	18.95	–	–	–/–	–	10/1	48
Salim Malik (*CY 1988*)	16.4.1963		103	*1981–1998*	5,768	237	15	43.69	5	1-3	0/0	82.80	65	283
Salim Yousuf	7.12.1959		32	*1981–1990*	1,055	91*	0	27.05	–	–	–/–	–	91/13	86
Salman Butt	7.10.1984		33	*2003*–2010	1,889	122	3	30.46	1	1-36	0/0	106.00	12	78/24
Sami Aslam	12.12.1995		13	*2014–2017*	758	91	0	31.58	–	–	–/–	–	7	4
Saqlain Mushtaq (*CY 2000*)	29.12.1976		49	*1995–2003*	927	101*	1	14.48	208	8-164	13/3	29.83	15	169
Sarfraz Ahmed	22.5.1987		49	*2009–2018*	2,657	112	3	36.39	–	–	–/–	–	146/21	116/59
Sarfraz Nawaz	1.12.1948		55	*1968–1983*	1,045	90	0	17.71	177	9-86	4/1	32.75	26	45
Shabbir Ahmed	21.4.1976		10	*2003–2005*	88	24*	0	8.80	51	5-48	2/0	23.03	3	32/1
Shadab Kabir	12.11.1977		5	1996–*2001*	148	55	0	21.14	0	0-9	0/0	–	11	3
Shadab Khan	4.10.1998		6	*2016*–2020	300	56	0	33.33	14	3-31	0/0	36.64	3	43/46
Shafiq Ahmed	28.3.1949		6	1974–*1980*	99	27*	0	11.00	0	0-1	0/0	–	0	3
[2] **Shafqat Rana**	10.8.1943		5	*1964–1969*	221	95	0	31.57	1	1-2	0/0	9.00	5	
[2] **Shaheen Shah Afridi**	6.4.2000		13	*2018–2020*	81	14	0	5.06	41	5-77	1/0	33.02	0	22/18
Shahid Afridi	1.3.1980		27	*1998*–2010	1,716	156	5	36.51	48	5-52	1/0	35.60	10	393‡/98‡
Shahid Israr	1.3.1950	29.4.2013	1	*1976*	7	7*	0	–	–	–	–/–	–	2	
Shahid Mahboob	25.8.1962		1	*1989*	–	–	–	–	2	2-131	0/0	65.50	0	10
Shahid Mahmood	17.3.1939	13.12.2020	1	1962	25	16	0	12.50	0	0-23	0/0	–	0	
Shahid Nazir	4.12.1977		15	*1996–2006*	194	40	0	12.12	36	5-53	1/0	35.33	5	17
Shahid Saeed	6.1.1966		1	*1989*	12	12	0	12.00	0	0-7	0/0	–	0	10
Shakeel Ahmed snr.	12.2.1966		1	*1998*	1	1	0	1.00	4	4-91	0/0	34.75	1	
Shakeel Ahmed jnr.	12.11.1971		3	*1992–1994*	74	33	0	14.80	–	–	–/–	–	4	2
Shan Masood	14.10.1989		25	*2013–2020*	1,378	156	4	29.31	2	1-6	0/0	46.00	16	5
Sharjeel Khan	14.8.1989		1	*2016*	44	40	0	22.00	–	–	–/–	–	0	25/15
Sharpe Duncan Albert	3.8.1937		3	*1959*	134	56	0	22.33	–	–	–/–	–	2	
Shoaib Akhtar	13.8.1975		46	*1997–2007*	544	47	0	10.07	178	6-11	12/2	25.69	12	158‡/15
Shoaib Malik	1.2.1982		35	*2001–2015*	1,898	245	3	35.14	32	4-33	0/0	47.46	18	287/115‡
[1] **Shoaib Mohammad**	8.1.1961		45	*1983–1995*	2,705	203*	7	44.34	5	2-8	0/0	34.00	22	63
Shuja-ud-Din Butt	10.4.1930	7.2.2006	19	1954–*1961*	395	47	0	15.19	20	3-18	0/0	40.05	8	
Sikander Bakht	25.8.1957		26	*1976–1982*	146	22*	0	6.34	67	8-69	3/1	36.00	7	27
Sohail Khan	6.3.1984		9	*2008–2016*	252	65	0	25.20	27	5-68	2/0	41.66	2	13/5
Sohail Tanvir	12.12.1984		2	*2007*	17	13	0	5.66	5	3-83	0/0	63.20	2	62/57

	Born	Died	Tests	Test Career	Runs	HS	100s	Avge	Wkts	BB	5/10	Avge	Ct/St	O/T
Tahir Naqqash	6.6.1959		15	1981–1984	300	57	0	21.42	34	5-40	2/0	41.11	3	40
Talat Ali Malik	29.5.1950		10	1972–1978	370	61	0	23.12	0	0-1	0/0	–	4	
Tanvir Ahmed	20.12.1978		5	2010–2012	170	57	0	34.00	17	6-120	1/0	26.64	1	2/1
Taslim Arif	1.5.1954	13.3.2008	6	1979–1980	501	210*	1	62.62	1	1-28	0/0	28.00	6/3	2
Taufeeq Umar	20.6.1981		44	2001–2014	2,963	236	7	37.98	0	0-0	0/0	–	48	22
Tauseef Ahmed	10.5.1958		34	1979–1993	318	35*	0	17.66	93	6-45	3/0	31.72	9	70
[2] **Umar Akmal**	26.5.1990		16	2009–2011	1,003	129	1	35.82	–	–	–/–	–	12	121/84
Umar Amin	16.10.1989		4	2010	99	33	0	12.37	3	1-7	0/0	21.00	1	16/14
Umar Gul	14.4.1984		47	2003–2012	577	65*	0	9.94	163	6-135	4/0	34.06	11	130/60
Usman Salahuddin	2.12.1990		1	2018	37	33	0	18.50	–	–	–/–	–	0	2
Usman Shinwari	1.5.1994		1	2019	–	–	–	–	1	1-54	0/0	54.00	0	17/16
Wahab Riaz	28.6.1985		27	2010–2018	306	39	0	8.50	83	5-63	2/0	34.50	5	91/36
Wajahatullah Wasti	11.11.1974		6	1998–1999	329	133	2	36.55	0	0-0	0/0	–	7	15
[2] **Waqar Hasan**	12.9.1932	10.2.2020	21	1952–1959	1,071	189	1	31.50	0	0-10	0/0	–	10	
Waqar Younis (*CY 1992*)	16.11.1971		87	1989–2002	1,010	45	0	10.20	373	7-76	22/5	23.56	18	262
Wasim Akram (*CY 1993*)	3.6.1966		104	1984–2001	2,898	257*	3	22.64	414	7-119	25/5	23.62	44	356
Wasim Bari	23.3.1948		81	1967–1983	1,366	85	0	15.88	0	0-2	0/0	–	201/27	51
[2] **Wasim Raja**	3.7.1952	23.8.2006	57	1972–1984	2,821	125	4	36.16	51	4-50	0/0	35.80	20	54
[2] **Wazir Mohammad**	22.12.1929		20	1952–1959	801	189	2	27.62	0	0-2	0/0	–	5	
Yasir Ali	15.10.1985		1	2003	1	1*	0	–	2	1-12	0/0	27.50	0	
Yasir Arafat	12.3.1982		3	2007–2008	94	50*	0	47.00	9	5-161	1/0	48.66	0	11/13
Yasir Hameed	28.2.1978		25	2003–2010	1,491	170	2	32.41	0	0-0	0/0	–	20	56
Yasir Shah	2.5.1986		43	2014–2020	774	113	1	13.34	227	8-41	16/3	30.85	23	25/2
[2] **Younis Ahmed**	20.10.1947		4	1969–1986	177	62	0	29.50	0	0-6	0/0	–	0	2
Younis Khan (*CY 2017*)	29.11.1977		118	1999–2016	10,099	313	34	52.05	9	2-23	0/0	54.55	139	265/25
Yousuf Youhana (*see* Mohammad Yousuf)														
Zafar Gohar	1.2.1995		1	2020	71	37	0	35.50	0	0-159	0/0	–	0	1
Zaheer Abbas (*CY 1972*)	24.7.1947		78	1969–1985	5,062	274	12	44.79	3	2-21	0/0	44.00	34	62
Zahid Fazal	10.11.1973		9	1990–1995	288	78	0	18.00	–	–	–/–	–	5	19
[2] **Zahoor Elahi**	1.3.1971		2	1996	30	22	0	10.00	–	–	–/–	–	1	14
Zakir Khan	3.4.1963		2	1985–1989	9	9*	0	–	5	3-80	0/0	51.80	1	17
Zulfiqar Ahmed	22.11.1926	3.10.2008	9	1952–1956	200	63*	0	33.33	20	6-42	2/1	18.30	5	
Zulfiqar Babar	10.12.1978		15	2013–2016	144	56	0	16.00	54	5-74	2/0	39.42	4	5/7
Zulqarnain	25.5.1962		3	1985	24	13	0	6.00	–	–	–/–	–	8/2	16
Zulqarnain Haider	23.4.1986		1	2010	88	88	0	44.00	–	–	–/–	–	2	4/3

SRI LANKA (154 players)

	Born	Died	Tests	Test Career	Runs	HS	100s	Avge	Wkts	BB	5/10	Avge	Ct/St	O/T
Ahangama Franklyn Saliya	14.9.1959		3	*1985*	11	11	0	5.50	18	5-52	1/0	19.33	1	1
Amalean Kaushik Naginda	7.4.1965		2	*1985–1987*	9	7*	0	9.00	7	4-97	0/0	22.28	1	8
Amerasinghe Amerasinghe Mudalige Jayantha Gamini	2.2.1954		2	*1983*	54	34	0	18.00	3	2-73	0/0	50.00	3	
Amerasinghe Merenna Koralage Don Ishara	5.3.1978		1	*2007*	0	0*	0	–	1	1-62	0/0	105.00	0	8
Anurasiri Sangarange Don	25.2.1966		18	*1985–1997*	91	24	0	5.35	41	4-71	0/0	37.75	4	45
Arnold Russel Premakumaran	25.10.1973		44	*1996–2004*	1,821	123	3	28.01	11	3-76	0/0	54.36	51	180/1
Atapattu Marvan Samson	22.11.1970		90	*1990–2007*	5,502	249	16	39.02	1	1-9	0/0	24.00	58	268/2
Bandara Herath Mudiyanselage Charitha Malinga	31.12.1979		8	*1997–2005*	124	43	0	15.50	16	3-84	0/0	39.56	4	31/4
Bandaratilleke Mapa Rallage Chandima Niroshan	16.5.1975		7	*1997–2001*	93	25	0	11.62	23	5-36	1/0	30.34	0	3
Chameera Pathira Vasan Dushmantha	11.1.1992		9	2015–*2020*	91	22	0	6.06	25	5-47	1/0	41.48	4	23/19
Chandana Umagiliya Durage Upul	7.5.1972		16	*1998–2004*	616	92	0	26.78	37	6-179	3/1	41.48	7	147
Chandimal Lokuge Dinesh	18.11.1989		60	*2011–2020*	4,096	164	11	40.55	–	–	–/–	–	77/10	146/54
Dananjaya Akila (Mahamarakkala Kurukulasooriya Patabendige Akila Dananjaya Perera)	4.10.1993		6	*2017*–2019	135	43*	0	16.87	33	6-115	4/0	24.81	1	36/22
Dassanayake Pubudu Bathiya	11.7.1970		11	*1993–1994*	196	36	0	13.06	–	–	–/–	–	19/5	16
de Alwis Ronald Guy	15.2.1959	12.1.2013	11	*1982–1987*	152	28	0	8.00	–	–	–/–	–	21/2	31
de Mel Ashantha Lakdasa Francis	9.5.1959		17	*1981–1986*	326	34	0	14.17	59	6-109	3/0	36.94	9	57
de Saram Samantha Indika	2.9.1973		4	*1999*	117	39	0	23.40	–	–	–/–	–	1	15/1
de Silva Ashley Matthew	3.12.1963		3	*1992–1993*	10	9	0	3.33	–	–	–/–	–	4/1	4
de Silva Dhananjaya Maduranga	6.9.1991		32	2016–*2020*	1,942	173	6	36.64	21	3-25	0/0	51.95	34	45/16
de Silva Dandeniyage Somachandra	11.6.1942		12	*1981*–1984	406	61	0	21.36	37	5-59	1/0	36.40	5	41
de Silva Ellawalakankanamge Asoka Ranjit	28.3.1956		10	*1985–1990*	185	50	0	15.41	8	2-67	0/0	129.00	4	28
de Silva Ginigalgodage Ramba Ajit	12.12.1952		4	*1981–1982*	41	14	0	8.20	7	2-38	0/0	55.00	0	6
de Silva Karunakalage Sajeewa Chanaka	11.1.1971		8	*1996–1998*	65	27	0	9.28	16	5-85	1/0	55.56	5	38
de Silva Pinnaduwage Aravinda (*CY 1996*)	17.10.1965		93	1984–2002	6,361	267	20	42.97	29	3-30	0/0	41.65	43	308
de Silva Pinnaduwage Wanindu Hasaranga	29.7.1997		3	*2020*	153	59	0	25.50	4	4-171	0/0	69.25	2	15/13
de Silva Sanjeewa Kumara Lanka	29.7.1975		3	*1997*	36	20*	0	18.00	–	–	–/–	–	1	11
de Silva Weddikkara Ruwan Sujeewa	7.10.1979		3	2002–2007	10	5*	0	10.00	11	4-35	0/0	19.00	1	
Dharmasena Handunnettige Deepthi Priyantha Kumar	24.4.1971		31	*1993–2003*	868	62*	0	19.72	69	6-72	3/0	42.31	14	141

	Born	*Died*	*Tests*	*Test Career*	*Runs*	*HS*	*100s*	*Avge*	*Wkts*	*BB*	*5/10*	*Avge*	*Ct/St*	*O/T*
Dias Roy Luke	18.10.1952		20	*1981–1986*	1,285	109	3	36.71	0	0-17	0/0	–	6	58
Dickwella Dickwella Patabandige Dilantha Niroshan	23.6.1993		41	2014–*2020*	2,163	92	0	30.90	–	–	–/–	–	97/23	52/23
Dilshan Tillekeratne Mudiyanselage	14.10.1976		87	*1999–2012*	5,492	193	16	40.98	39	4-10	0/0	43.87	88	330/80
Dunusinghe Chamara Iroshan	19.10.1970		5	*1994–1995*	160	91	0	16.00	–	–	–/–	–	13/2	1
Embuldeniya Lasith	20.10.1996		9	*2018–2020*	103	40	0	7.92	45	7-137	3/1	35.75	2	
Eranga Ranaweera Mudiyanselage Shaminda	23.6.1986		19	*2011*–2016	193	45*	0	12.86	57	4-49	0/0	37.50	5	19/3
Fernando Asitha Madusanka	31.7.1997		3	*2020*	4	4	0	1.33	4	2-44	0/0	39.00	0	1
Fernando Aththachchi Nuwan Pradeep Roshan	19.10.1986		28	*2011–2017*	132	17*	0	4.00	70	6-132	1/0	42.90	5	45/14
Fernando Bodiyabaduge Oshada Piumal	15.4.1992		7	*2018–2020*	396	102	1	36.00	0	0-3	0/0	–	7	6/6
Fernando Congenige Randhi Dilhara	19.7.1979		40	2000–2012	249	39*	0	8.30	100	5-42	3/0	37.84	10	146‡/18
Fernando Ellekutige Rufus Nemesion Susil	19.12.1955		5	*1982–1983*	112	46	0	11.20	–	–	–/–	–	0	7
Fernando Kandana Arachchige Dinusha Manoj	10.8.1979		2	*2003*	56	51*	0	28.00	1	1-29	0/0	107.00	0	1
Fernando Kandage Hasantha Ruwan Kumara	14.10.1979		2	*2002*	38	24	0	9.50	4	3-63	0/0	27.00	1	7
Fernando Muthuthanthrige Vishwa Thilina	18.9.1991		10	2016–*2020*	57	38	0	7.12	31	5-101	1/0	33.06	2	8/1
Fernando Thudellage Charitha Buddhika	22.8.1980		9	*2001*–2002	132	45	0	26.40	18	4-27	0/0	44.00	4	17
Gallage Indika Sanjeewa	22.11.1975		1	*1999*	3	3	0	3.00	0	0-24	0/0	–	0	3
Gamage Panagamuwa Lahiru Sampath	5.4.1988		5	*2017*–2018	6	3	0	1.50	10	2-38	0/0	57.30	0	9
Goonatillake Hettiarachige Mahes	16.8.1952		5	*1981–1982*	177	56	0	22.12	–	–	–/–	–	10/3	6
Gunaratne Downdegedara Asela Sampath	8.1.1986		6	*2016*–2017	455	116	1	56.87	3	2-28	0/0	38.00	6	31/12
Gunasekera Yohan	8.11.1957		2	*1982*	48	23	0	12.00	–	–	–/–	–	6	3
Gunathilleke Mashtayage Dhanushka	17.03.1991		8	2017–*2018*	299	61	0	18.68	1	1-16	0/0	111.00	6	38/24
Gunawardene Dihan Avishka	26.5.1977		6	*1998–2005*	181	43	0	16.45	–	–	–/–	–	2	61
Guneratne Roshan Punyajith Wijesinghe	26.1.1962	21.7.2005	1	*1982*	0	0*	0	–	0	0-84	0/0	–	0	
Gurusinha Asanka Pradeep	16.9.1966		41	*1985*–1996	2,452	143	7	38.92	20	2-7	0/0	34.05	33	147
Hathurusinghe Upul Chandika	13.9.1968		26	*1990–1998*	1,274	83	0	29.62	17	4-66	0/0	46.41	7	35
Herath Herath Mudiyanselage Rangana Keerthi Bandara	19.3.1978		93	*1999–2018*	1,699	80*	0	14.64	433	9-127	34/9	28.07	24	71/17
Hettiarachchi Dinuka Sulaksana	15.7.1976		1	*2000*	0	0*	0	0.00	2	2-36	0/0	20.50	0	
Jayasekera Rohan Stanley Amarasiriwardene	7.12.1957		1	*1981*	2	2	0	1.00	–	–	–/–	–	0	2
Jayasundera Madurawelage Don Udara Supeksha	3.1.1991		2	*2015*	30	26	0	7.50	0	0-12	0/0	–	2	
Jayasuriya Sanath Teran (*CY 1997*)	30.6.1969		110	*1990–2007*	6,973	340	14	40.07	98	5-34	2/0	34.34	78	441‡/31
Jayawardene Denagamage Proboth Mahela de Silva (*CY 2007*)	27.5.1977		149	*1997*–2014	11,814	374	34	49.84	6	2-32	0/0	51.66	205	443‡/55

	Born	*Died*	*Tests*	*Test Career*	*Runs*	*HS*	*100s*	*Avge*	*Wkts*	*BB*	*5/10*	*Avge*	*Ct/St*	*O/T*
Jayawardene Hewasandatchige Asiri Prasanna Wishvanath	9.10.1979		58	2000–*2014*	2,124	154*	4	29.50	–	–	–/–	–	124/32	6
Jeganathan Sridharan	11.7.1951	14.5.1996	2	*1982*	19	8	0	4.75	0	0-12	0/0	–	0	5
John Vinothen Bede	27.5.1960		6	*1982*–1984	53	27*	0	10.60	28	5-60	2/0	21.92	2	45
Jurangpathy Baba Roshan	25.6.1967		2	*1985–1986*	1	1	0	0.25	1	1-69	0/0	93.00	2	
Kalavitigoda Shantha	23.12.1977		1	*2004*	8	7	0	4.00	–	–	–/–	–	2	
Kalpage Ruwan Senani	19.2.1970		11	*1993–1998*	294	63	0	18.37	12	2-27	0/0	64.50	10	86
Kaluhalamulla H. K. S. R. (*see* Randiv, Suraj)														
[2] **Kaluperuma** Lalith Wasantha Silva	25.6.1949		2	*1981*	12	11*	0	4.00	0	0-24	0/0	–	2	4
[2] **Kaluperuma** Sanath Mohan Silva	22.10.1961		4	*1983–1987*	88	23	0	11.00	2	2-17	0/0	62.00	6	2
Kaluwitharana Romesh Shantha	24.11.1969		49	*1992–2004*	1,933	132*	3	26.12	–	–	–/–	–	93/26	189
Kapugedera Chamara Kantha	24.2.1987		8	2006–2009	418	96	0	34.83	0	0-9	0/0	–	6	102/43
Karunaratne Chamika	29.5.1996		1	*2018*	22	22	0	11.00	1	1-130	0/0	148.00	1	
Karunaratne Frank Dimuth Madushanka	28.4.1988		68	*2012–2020*	4,657	196	10	36.66	2	1-12	0/0	92.50	53	31
Kaushal Paskuwal Handi Tharindu	5.3.1993		7	*2014–2015*	106	18	0	10.60	25	5-42	2/0	44.20	3	1
Kulasekara Chamith Kosala Bandara	15.7.1985		1	*2011*	22	15	0	11.00	1	1-65	0/0	80.00	0	4
Kulasekara Kulasekara Mudiyanselage Dinesh Nuwan	22.7.1982		21	*2004*–2014	391	64	0	14.48	48	4-21	0/0	37.37	8	184/58
Kumara Chandradasa Brahammana Ralalage Lahiru Sudesh	13.2.1997		22	*2016–2020*	52	10	0	3.46	68	6-122	1/0	37.55	4	13/7
Kuruppu Don Sardha Brendon Priyantha	5.1.1962		4	*1986*–1991	320	201*	1	53.33	–	–	–/–	–	1	54
Kuruppuarachchi Ajith Kosala	1.11.1964		2	*1985–1986*	0	0*	0	–	8	5-44	1/0	18.62	0	
Labrooy Graeme Fredrick	7.6.1964		9	*1986–1990*	158	70*	0	14.36	27	5-133	1/0	44.22	3	44
Lakmal Ranasinghe Arachchige Suranga	10.3.1987		62	*2010–2020*	847	42	0	11.60	151	5-54	3/0	37.62	18	85/11
Lakshitha Materba Kanatha Gamage Chamila Premanath	4.1.1979		2	2002–*2002*	42	40	0	14.00	5	2-33	0/0	31.60	1	7
Liyanage Dulip Kapila	6.6.1972		9	*1992*–2001	69	23	0	7.66	17	4-56	0/0	39.17	0	16
Lokuarachchi Kaushal Samaraweera	20.5.1982		4	2003–*2003*	94	28*	0	23.50	5	2-47	0/0	59.00	1	21/2
Madugalle Ranjan Senerath	22.4.1959		21	*1981*–1988	1,029	103	1	29.40	0	0-0	0/0	–	9	63
Madurasinghe Madurasinghe Arachchige Wijayasiri Ranjith	30.1.1961		3	1988–*1992*	24	11	0	4.80	3	3-60	0/0	57.33	0	12
Mahanama Roshan Siriwardene	31.5.1966		52	*1985–1997*	2,576	225	4	29.27	0	0-3	0/0	–	56	213
Maharoof Mohamed Farveez	7.9.1984		22	*2003*–2011	556	72	0	18.53	25	4-52	0/0	65.24	7	109/8
Malinga Separamadu Lasith	28.8.1983		30	2004–2010	275	64	0	11.45	101	5-50	3/0	33.15	7	226/84
Mathews Angelo Davis (*CY 2015*)	2.6.1987		88	2009–*2020*	6,194	200*	11	45.54	33	4-44	0/0	52.87	68	217/75

	Born	Died	Tests	Test Career	Runs	HS	100s	Avge	Wkts	BB	5/10	Avge	Ct/St	O/T
Mendis Balapuwaduge Ajantha Winslo	11.3.1985		19	2008–2014	213	78	0	16.38	70	6-99	4/1	34.77	2	87/39
Mendis Balapuwaduge Kusal Gimhan	2.2.1995		47	2015–2020	3,022	196	7	34.73	1	1-10	0/0	110.00	71	76/26
Mendis Louis Rohan Duleep	25.8.1952		24	1981–1988	1,329	124	4	31.64	–	–	–/–	–	9	79
Mirando Magina Thilan Thushara	1.3.1981		10	2003–2010	94	15*	0	8.54	28	5-83	1/0	37.14	3	38/6
Mubarak Jehan	10.1.1981		13	2002–2015	385	49	0	17.50	0	0-1	0/0	–	15	40/16
Muralitharan Muttiah (*CY 1999*)	17.4.1972		132§	1992–2010	1,259	67	0	11.87	795	9-51	67/22	22.67	70	343‡/12
Nawaz Mohamed Naveed	20.9.1973		1	2002	99	78*	0	99.00	–	–	–/–	–	0	3
Nissanka Ratnayake Arachchige Prabath	25.10.1980		4	2003	18	12*	0	6.00	10	5-64	1/0	36.60	0	23
Paranavitana Nishad Tharanga	15.4.1982		32	2008–2012	1,792	111	2	32.58	1	1-26	0/0	86.00	27	
Perera Anhettige Suresh Asanka	16.2.1978		3	1998–2001	77	43*	0	25.66	1	1-104	0/0	180.00	1	20
Perera Mahawaduge Dilruwan Kamalaneth	22.7.1982		43	2013–2020	1,303	95	0	18.88	161	6-32	8/2	35.90	19	13/3
Perera Mathurage Don Kusal Janith	17.8.1990		22	2015–2020	1,177	153*	2	30.97	–	–	–/–	–	19/8	101/47
Perera M. K. P. A. D. (*see* Dananjaya, Akila)														
Perera Narangoda Liyanaarachchilage Tissara Chirantha	3.4.1989		6	2011–2012	203	75	0	20.30	11	4-63	0/0	59.36	1	164/77‡
Perera Panagodage Don Ruchira Laksiri	6.4.1977		8	1998–2002	33	11*	0	11.00	17	3-40	0/0	38.88	2	19/2
Prasad Kariyawasam Tirana Gamage Dammika	30.5.1983		25	2008–2015	476	47	0	12.86	75	5-50	1/0	35.97	6	24/1
Prasanna Seekkuge	27.6.1985		1	2011	5	5	0	5.00	0	0-80	0/0	–	0	40/20
Pushpakumara Karuppiahyage Ravindra	21.7.1975		23	1994–2001	166	44	0	8.73	58	7-116	4/0	38.65	10	31
Pushpakumara Paulage Malinda	24.3.1987		4	2017–2018	102	42*	0	17.00	14	3-28	0/0	37.14	2	2
Rajitha Chandrasekara Arachchilage Kasun	1.6.1993		9	2018–2020	35	12	0	3.50	25	3-20	0/0	31.16	4	9/10
Ramanayake Champaka Priyadarshana Hewage	8.1.1965		18	1987–1993	143	34*	0	9.53	44	5-82	1/0	42.72	6	62
Ramyakumara Wijekoon Mudiyanselage Gayan	21.12.1976		2	2005	38	14	0	12.66	2	2-49	0/0	33.00	0	0/3
Ranasinghe Anura Nandana	13.10.1956	9.11.1998	2	1981–1982	88	77	0	22.00	1	1-23	0/0	69.00	0	9
Ranasinghe Minod Bhanuka	29.4.1995		1	2020	6	5	0	3.00	–	–	–/–	–	0	1/2
[2] **Ranatunga** Arjuna (*CY 1999*)	1.12.1963		93	1981–2000	5,105	135*	4	35.69	16	2-17	0/0	65.00	47	269
[2] **Ranatunga** Dammika	12.10.1962		2	1989	87	45	0	29.00	–	–	–/–	–	0	4
[2] **Ranatunga** Sanjeeva	25.4.1969		9	1994–1996	531	118	2	33.18	–	–	–/–	–	2	13
Randiv Suraj (Hewa Kaluhalamullage Suraj Randiv Kaluhalamulla; formerly M. M. M. Suraj)	30.1.1985		12	2010–2012	147	39	0	9.18	43	5-82	1/0	37.51	1	31/7
Ratnayake Rumesh Joseph	2.1.1964		23	1982–1991	433	56	0	14.43	73	6-66	5/0	35.10	9	70
Ratnayeke Joseph Ravindran	2.5.1960		22	1981–1989	807	93	0	25.21	56	8-83	4/0	35.21	1	78

§ *Muralitharan's figures exclude two runs, five wickets and two catches for the ICC World XI v Australia in the Super Series Test in 2005-06.*

	Born	Died	Tests	Test Career	Runs	HS	100s	Avge	Wkts	BB	5/10	Avge	Ct/St	O/T
Samarasekera Maitipage Athula Rohitha	5.8.1961		4	1988–*1991*	118	57	0	16.85	3	2-38	0/0	34.66	3	39
[2] **Samaraweera** Dulip Prasanna	12.2.1972		7	*1993–1994*	211	42	0	15.07	–	–	–/–	–	5	5
[2] **Samaraweera** Thilan Thusara	22.9.1976		81	2001–*2012*	5,462	231	14	48.76	15	4-49	0/0	45.93	45	53
Samarawickrama Wedagedara Sadeera Rashen	30.8.1995		4	*2017*	125	38	0	15.62	–	–	–/–	–	4	7/7
Sandakan Paththamperuma Arachchige Don Lakshan Rangika	10.6.1991		11	2016–*2018*	117	25	0	10.63	37	5-95	2/0	34.48	6	24/17
Sangakkara Kumar Chokshanada (*CY 2012*)	27.10.1977		134	2000–*2015*	12,400	319	38	57.40	0	0-4	0/0	–	182/20	397‡/56
Senanayake Charith Panduka	19.12.1962		3	*1990*	97	64	0	19.40	–	–	–/–	–	2	7
Senanayake Senanayake Mudiyanselage Sachithra Madhushanka	9.2.1985		1	*2013*	5	5	0	5.00	0	0-30	0/0	–	1	49/24
Shanaka Madagamagamage Dasun	9.9.1991		6	2016–*2020*	140	66*	0	14.00	13	3-46	0/0	33.15	4	22/40
Silva Athege Roshen Shivanka	17.11.1988		12	*2017–2018*	702	109	1	35.10	–	–	–/–	–	2	
Silva Jayan Kaushal	27.5.1986		39	*2011–2018*	2,099	139	3	28.36	–	–	–/–	–	34/1	
Silva Kelaniyage Jayantha	2.6.1973		7	*1995–1997*	6	6*	0	2.00	20	4-16	0/0	32.35	1	1
Silva Lindamlilage Prageeth Chamara	14.12.1979		11	*2006–2007*	537	152*	1	33.56	1	1-57	0/0	65.00	7	75/16
Silva Sampathawaduge Amal Rohitha	12.12.1960		9	*1982*–1988	353	111	2	25.21	–	–	–/–	–	33/1	20
Siriwardene Tissa Appuhamilage Milinda	4.12.1985		5	*2015*–2016	298	68	0	33.11	11	3-25	0/0	23.36	3	27/22
Tharanga Warushavithana Upul	2.2.1985		31	*2005*–2017	1,754	165	3	31.89	–	–	–/–	–	24	234‡/26
Thirimanne Hettige Don Rumesh Lahiru	8.9.1989		38	2011–*2020*	1,623	155*	2	23.86	0	0-5	0/0	–	27	127/26
Tillekeratne Hashan Prasantha	14.7.1967		83	*1989–2003*	4,545	204*	11	42.87	0	0-0	0/0	–	122/2	200
Udawatte Mahela Lakmal	19.7.1986		2	2018	23	19	0	5.75	–	–	–/–	–	2	9/8
Upashantha Kalutarage Eric Amila	10.6.1972		2	*1998*–2002	10	6	0	3.33	4	2-41	0/0	50.00	0	12
Vaas Warnakulasuriya Patabendige Ushantha Joseph Chaminda	27.1.1974		111	*1994*–2009	3,089	100*	1	24.32	355	7-71	12/2	29.58	31	321‡/6
Vandort Michael Graydon	19.1.1980		20	*2001–2008*	1,144	140	4	36.90	–	–	–/–	–	6	1
Vithanage Kasun Disi Kithuruwan	26.2.1991		10	*2012–2015*	370	103*	1	26.42	1	1-73	0/0	133.00	10	6/3
Wanigamuni Ramesh Tarinda Mendis	7.7.1995		1	*2020*	16	16	0	8.00	2	1-48	0/0	48.00	0	
Warnapura Bandula	1.3.1953		4	*1981–1982*	96	38	0	12.00	0	0-1	0/0	–	2	12
Warnapura Basnayake Shalith Malinda	26.5.1979		14	2007–2009	821	120	2	35.69	0	0-40	0/0	–	14	3
Warnaweera Kahakatchchi Patabandige Jayananda	23.11.1960		10	*1985–1994*	39	20	0	4.33	32	4-25	0/0	31.90	0	6
Weerasinghe Colombage Don Udesh Sanjeewa	1.3.1968		1	*1985*	3	3	0	3.00	0	0-8	0/0	–	0	
Welagedara Uda Walawwe Mahim Bandaralage Chanaka Asanka	20.3.1981		21	*2007*–2014	218	48	0	9.08	55	5-52	2/0	41.32	5	10/2
[2] **Wettimuny** Mithra de Silva	11.6.1951	20.1.2019	2	*1982*	28	17	0	7.00	–	–	–/–	–	2	1

	Born	Died	Tests	Test Career	Runs	HS	100s	Avge	Wkts	BB	5/10	Avge	Ct/St	O/T
[2] **Wettimuny** Sidath (*CY 1985*)	12.8.1956		23	*1981–1986*	1,221	190	2	29.07	0	0-16	0/0	–	10	35
Wickremasinghe Anguppulige Gamini Dayantha	27.12.1965		3	*1989–1992*	17	13*	0	8.50	–	–	–/–	–	9/1	4
Wickremasinghe Gallage Pramodya	14.8.1971		40	*1991–2000*	555	51	0	9.40	85	6-60	3/0	41.87	18	134
Wijegunawardene Kapila Indaka Weerakkody	23.11.1964		2	1991–*1991*	14	6*	0	4.66	7	4-51	0/0	21.00	0	26
Wijesuriya Roger Gerard Christopher Ediriweera	18.2.1960		4	*1981–1985*	22	8	0	4.40	1	1-68	0/0	294.00	1	8
Wijetunge Piyal Kashyapa	6.8.1971		1	1993	10	10	0	5.00	2	1-58	0/0	59.00	0	
Zoysa Demuni Nuwan Tharanga	13.5.1978		30	*1996*–2004	288	28*	0	8.47	64	5-20	1/0	33.70	4	9

ZIMBABWE (113 players)

	Born	Died	Tests	Test Career	Runs	HS	100s	Avge	Wkts	BB	5/10	Avge	Ct/St	O/T
Arnott Kevin John	8.3.1961		4	*1992*	302	101*	1	43.14	–	–	–/–	–	4	13
Blignaut Arnoldus Mauritius ("Andy")	1.8.1978		19	*2000–2005*	886	92	0	26.84	53	5-73	3/0	37.05	13	54/1
Brain David Hayden	4.10.1964		9	*1992–1994*	115	28	0	10.45	30	5-42	1/0	30.50	1	23
Brandes Eddo André	5.3.1963		10	*1992–1999*	121	39	0	10.08	26	3-45	0/0	36.57	4	59
Brent Gary Bazil	13.1.1976		4	*1999–2001*	35	25	0	5.83	7	3-21	0/0	44.85	1	70/3
Briant Gavin Aubrey	11.4.1969		1	*1992*	17	16	0	8.50	–	–	–/–	–	0	5
Bruk-Jackson Glen Keith	25.4.1969		2	*1993*	39	31	0	9.75	–	–	–/–	–	0	1
Burl Ryan Ponsonby	15.4.1994		1	*2017*	16	16	0	8.00	–	–	–/–	–	1	18/19
Burmester Mark Greville	24.1.1968		3	*1992*	54	30*	0	27.00	3	3-78	0/0	75.66	1	8
Butchart Iain Peter	9.5.1960		1	*1994*	23	15	0	11.50	0	0-11	0/0	–	1	20
Campbell Alistair Douglas Ross	23.9.1972		60	*1992–2002*	2,858	103	2	27.21	0	0-1	0/0	–	60	188
Carlisle Stuart Vance	10.5.1972		37	*1994–2005*	1,615	118	2	26.91	–	–	–/–	–	34	111
Chakabva Regis Wiriranai	20.9.1987		17	*2011–2019*	806	101	1	25.18	–	–	–/–	–	34/4	41/12
Chari Brian Bara	14.2.1992		7	*2014–2018*	254	80	0	18.14	0	0-3	0/0	–	8	14/3
Chatara Tendai Larry	28.2.1991		9	*2012–2018*	90	22	0	6.42	24	5-61	1/0	27.62	0	70/22
Chibhabha Chamunorwa Justice	6.9.1986		3	2016–*2017*	124	60	0	20.66	1	1-44	0/0	162.00	0	107/36
Chigumbura Elton	14.3.1986		14	*2003–2014*	569	88	0	21.07	21	5-54	1/0	46.00	6	210‡/57
Chinouya Michael Tawanda	9.6.1986		2	2016	1	1	0	0.50	3	1-45	0/0	62.66	0	2
Chisoro Tendai Sam	12.2.1988		1	*2017*	9	9	0	9.00	3	3-113	0/0	37.66	0	21/14
Coventry Charles Kevin	8.3.1983		2	*2005*	88	37	0	22.00	–	–	–/–	–	3	39/13
Cremer Alexander Graeme	19.9.1986		19	*2004–2017*	540	102*	1	16.36	57	5-125	1/0	45.68	12	96/29

	Born	Died	Tests	Test Career	Runs	HS	100s	Avge	Wkts	BB	5/10	Avge	Ct/St	O/T
Crocker Gary John	16.5.1962		3	1992	69	33	0	23.00	3	2-65	0/0	72.33	0	6
Dabengwa Keith Mbusi	17.8.1980		3	2005	90	35	0	15.00	5	3-127	0/0	49.80	1	37/8
Dekker Mark Hamilton	5.12.1969		14	1993–1996	333	68*	0	15.85	0	0-5	0/0	–	12	23
Duffin Terrence	20.3.1982		2	2005	80	56	0	20.00	–	–	–/–	–	1	23
Ebrahim Dion Digby	7.8.1980		29	2000–2005	1,226	94	0	22.70	–	–	–/–	–	16	82
[2] **Ervine** Craig Richard	19.8.1985		18	2011–2019	1,208	160	3	35.52	–	–	–/–	–	16	96/25
[2] **Ervine** Sean Michael	6.12.1982		5	2003–2003	261	86	0	32.62	9	4-146	0/0	43.11	7	42
Evans Craig Neil	29.11.1969		3	1996–2003	52	22	0	8.66	0	0-8	0/0	–	1	53
Ewing Gavin Mackie	21.1.1981		3	2003–2005	108	71	0	18.00	2	1-27	0/0	130.00	1	7
Ferreira Neil Robert	3.6.1979		1	2005	21	16	0	10.50	–	–	–/–	–	0	
[2] **Flower** Andrew OBE (*CY 2002*)	28.4.1968		63	1992–2002	4,794	232*	12	51.54	0	0-0	0/0	–	151/9	213
[2] **Flower** Grant William	20.12.1970		67	1992–2003	3,457	201*	6	29.54	25	4-41	0/0	61.48	43	221
Friend Travis John	7.1.1981		13	2001–2003	447	81	0	29.80	25	5-31	1/0	43.60	2	51
Goodwin Murray William	11.12.1972		19	1997–2000	1,414	166*	3	42.84	0	0-3	0/0	–	10	71
Gripper Trevor Raymond	28.12.1975		20	1999–2003	809	112	1	21.86	6	2-91	0/0	84.83	14	8
Hondo Douglas Tafadzwa	7.7.1979		9	2001–2004	83	19	0	9.22	21	6-59	1/0	36.85	5	56
Houghton David Laud	23.6.1957		22	1992–1997	1,464	266	4	43.05	0	0-0	0/0	–	17	63
Huckle Adam George	21.9.1971		8	1997–1998	74	28*	0	6.72	25	6-109	2/1	34.88	3	19
James Wayne Robert	27.8.1965		4	1993–1994	61	33	0	15.25	–	–	–/–	–	16	11
[1] **Jarvis** Kyle Malcolm	16.2.1989		13	2011–2019	128	25*	0	9.14	46	5-54	3/0	29.43	3	49/22
[1] **Jarvis** Malcolm Peter	6.12.1955		5	1992–1994	4	2*	0	2.00	11	3-30	0/0	35.72	2	12
Johnson Neil Clarkson	24.1.1970		13	1998–2000	532	107	1	24.18	15	4-77	0/0	39.60	12	48
Kamungozi Tafadzwa Paul	8.6.1987		1	2014	5	5	0	2.50	1	1-51	0/0	58.00	0	14/1
Kasuza Kevin Tatenda	20.6.1993		3	2019	113	63	0	28.25	–	–	–/–	–	0	
Lamb Gregory Arthur	4.3.1980		1	2011	46	39	0	23.00	3	3-120	0/0	47.00	2	15/5
Lock Alan Charles Ingram	10.9.1962		1	1995	8	8*	0	8.00	5	3-68	0/0	21.00	0	8
Madondo Trevor Nyasha	22.11.1976	11.6.2001	3	1997–2000	90	74*	0	30.00	–	–	–/–	–	1	13
Mahwire Ngonidzashe Blessing	31.7.1982		10	2002–2005	147	50*	0	13.36	18	4-92	0/0	50.83	1	23
Maregwede Alester	5.8.1981		2	2003	74	28	0	18.50	–	–	–/–	–	1	11
Marillier Douglas Anthony	24.4.1978		5	2000–2001	185	73	0	30.83	11	4-57	0/0	29.27	2	48
Maruma Timycen	19.4.1988		3	2012–2019	68	41	0	13.60	–	–	–/–	–	1	21/13
[2] **Masakadza** Hamilton	9.8.1983		38	2001–2018	2,223	158	5	30.04	16	3-24	0/0	30.56	29	209/66
[2] **Masakadza** Shingirai Winston	4.9.1986		5	2011–2014	88	24	0	11.00	16	4-32	0/0	32.18	2	16/7
[2] **Masakadza** Wellington Pedzisai	4.10.1993		1	2018	21	17	0	10.50	2	2-33	0/0	27.00	1	17/13
Masvaure Prince Spencer	7.10.1988		5	2016–2019	235	64	0	23.50	0	0-23	0/0	–	1	2

	Born	*Died*	*Tests*	*Test Career*	*Runs*	*HS*	*100s*	*Avge*	*Wkts*	*BB*	*5/10*	*Avge*	*Ct/St*	*O/T*
Matambanadzo Everton Zvikomborero	13.4.1976		3	*1996–1999*	17	7	0	4.25	4	2-62	0/0	62.50	0	7
Matsikenyeri Stuart	3.5.1983		8	*2003–2004*	351	57	0	23.40	2	1-58	0/0	172.50	7	113/10
Mavuta Brandon Anesu	4.3.1997		2	*2018*	9	6	0	2.25	4	4-21	0/0	59.25	3	7/3
Mawoyo Tinotenda Mbiri Kanayi	8.1.1986		11	*2011–2016*	615	163*	1	29.28	–	–	–/–	–	7	7
Mbangwa Mpumelelo ("Pommie")	26.6.1976		15	*1996–2000*	34	8	0	2.00	32	3-23	0/0	31.43	2	29
Meth Keegan Orry	8.2.1988		2	*2012*	72	31*	0	24.00	4	2-41	0/0	24.50	0	11/2
Mire Solomon Farai	21.8.1989		2	*2017*	78	47	0	19.50	1	1-22	0/0	32.00	0	47/9
Moor Peter Joseph	2.2.1991		8	2016–*2018*	533	83	0	35.53	–	–	–/–	–	9/1	49/21
Mpofu Christopher Bobby	27.11.1985		15	*2004–2017*	105	33	0	5.83	29	4-92	0/0	48.00	4	84/32
Mudzinganyama Brian Simbarashe	9.4.1999		1	*2019*	16	16	0	16.00	–	–	–/–	–	0	
Mumba Carl Tapfuma	6.5.1995		3	*2016–2019*	25	11*	0	8.33	10	4-50	0/0	35.40	2	7/2
Mupariwa Tawanda	16.4.1985		1	*2003*	15	14	0	15.00	0	0-136	0/0	–	0	40/4
Murphy Brian Andrew	1.12.1976		11	*1999–2001*	123	30	0	10.25	18	3-32	0/0	61.83	11	31
Musakanda Tarisai Kenneth	31.10.1994		1	2017	6	6	0	3.00	–	–	–/–	–	0	15/6
Mushangwe Natsai	9.2.1991		2	*2014*	8	8	0	2.00	7	4-82	0/0	62.14	2	6/5
Mutendera David Travolta	25.1.1979		1	*2000*	10	10	0	5.00	0	0-29	0/0	–	0	9
Mutizwa Forster	24.8.1985		1	*2011*	24	18	0	12.00	–	–	–/–	–	0	17/3
Mutombodzi Confidence Tinotenda	21.12.1990		1	*2019*	41	33	0	20.50	0	0-19	0/0	–	1	14/15
Mutumbami Richmond	11.6.1989		6	*2012–2014*	217	43	0	19.72	–	–	–/–	–	17/2	36/24
Muzarabani Blessing	2.10.1996		1	*2017*	14	10	0	14.00	0	0-48	0/0	–	0	21/9
Mwayenga Waddington	20.6.1984		1	*2005*	15	14*	0	15.00	1	1-79	0/0	79.00	0	3
Ncube Njabulo	14.10.1989		1	*2011*	17	14	0	8.50	1	1-80	0/0	121.00	1	1
Ndlovu Ainsley	26.1.1996		2	*2019*	9	5	0	2.25	2	2-170	0/0	138.50	2	2/3
Nkala Mluleki Luke	1.4.1981		10	2000–*2004*	187	47	0	14.38	11	3-82	0/0	66.09	4	50/1
Nyauchi Victor Munyaradzi	8.7.1992		3	*2019*	30	11	0	15.00	6	3-69	0/0	40.83	0	
Nyumbu John Curtis	1.3.1983		3	*2014*–2016	38	14	0	7.60	5	5-157	1/0	75.80	2	19/2
Olonga Henry Khaaba	3.7.1976		30	*1994–2002*	184	24	0	5.41	68	5-70	2/0	38.52	10	50
Panyangara Tinashe	21.10.1985		9	*2003–2014*	201	40*	0	16.75	31	5-59	1/0	26.22	3	65/14
Peall Stephen Guy	2.9.1969		4	*1993–1994*	60	30	0	15.00	4	2-89	0/0	75.75	1	21
Price Raymond William	12.6.1976		22	*1999–2012*	261	36	0	8.70	80	6-73	5/1	36.06	4	102/16
Pycroft Andrew John	6.6.1956		3	*1992*	152	60	0	30.40	–	–	–/–	–	2	20
Ranchod Ujesh	17.5.1969		1	*1992*	8	7	0	4.00	1	1-45	0/0	45.00	0	3
[2] **Rennie** Gavin James	12.1.1976		23	*1997–2001*	1,023	93	0	22.73	1	1-40	0/0	84.00	13	40
[2] **Rennie** John Alexander	29.7.1970		4	*1993–1997*	62	22	0	12.40	3	2-22	0/0	97.66	1	44
Rogers Barney Guy	20.8.1982		4	*2004*	90	29	0	11.25	0	0-17	0/0	–	1	15

	Born	Died	Tests	Test Career	Runs	HS	100s	Avge	Wkts	BB	5/10	Avge	Ct/St	O/T
Shah Ali Hassimshah	7.8.1959		3	*1992–1996*	122	62	0	24.40	1	1-46	0/0	125.00	0	28
Sibanda Vusimuzi	10.10.1983		14	*2003–2014*	591	93	0	21.10	–	–	–/–	–	16	125‡/26
Sikandar Raza	24.4.1986		15	*2013–2019*	1,037	127	1	34.56	32	7-113	2/0	41.81	3	103/36
[2] **Strang** Bryan Colin	9.6.1972		26	*1994–2001*	465	53	0	12.91	56	5-101	1/0	39.33	11	49
[2] **Strang** Paul Andrew	28.7.1970		24	*1994–2001*	839	106*	1	27.06	70	8-109	4/1	36.02	15	95
Streak Heath Hilton	16.3.1974		65	*1993–2005*	1,990	127*	1	22.35	216	6-73	7/0	28.14	17	187‡
Taibu Tatenda	14.5.1983		28	2001–*2011*	1,546	153	1	30.31	1	1-27	0/0	27.00	57/5	149‡/17
Taylor Brendan Ross Murray	6.2.1986		31	*2003–2019*	2,055	171	6	35.43	0	0-6	0/0	–	28	199/43
Tiripano Donald Tatenda	17.3.1988		10	*2014–2019*	299	49*	0	19.93	16	3-91	0/0	52.31	2	35/13
Traicos Athanasios John	17.5.1947		4†	*1992*	11	5	0	2.75	14	5-86	1/0	40.14	4	27
Tshuma Charlton Kirsh	19.4.1993		1	*2019*	3	3	0	1.50	1	1-85	0/0	85.00	0	2/1
Utseya Prosper	26.3.1985		4	*2003–2013*	107	45	0	15.28	10	3-60	0/0	41.00	2	164/35
Vermeulen Mark Andrew	2.3.1979		9	*2002–2014*	449	118	1	24.94	0	0-5	0/0	–	6	43
Viljoen Dirk Peter	11.3.1977		2	*1997–2000*	57	38	0	14.25	1	1-14	0/0	65.00	1	53
Vitori Brian Vitalis	22.2.1990		4	*2011–2013*	52	19*	0	10.40	12	5-61	1/0	38.66	2	24/11
[1] **Waller** Andrew Christopher	25.9.1959		2	*1996*	69	50	0	23.00	–	–	–/–	–	1	39
[1] **Waller** Malcolm Noel	28.9.1984		14	*2011–2017*	577	72*	0	21.37	8	4-59	0/0	27.25	10	79/32
Watambwa Brighton Tonderai	9.6.1977		6	*2000–2001*	11	4*	0	3.66	14	4-64	0/0	35.00	0	
Whittall Andrew Richard	28.3.1973		10	*1996–1999*	114	17	0	7.60	7	3-73	0/0	105.14	8	63
Whittall Guy James	5.9.1972		46	*1993–2002*	2,207	203*	4	29.42	51	4-18	0/0	40.94	19	147
Williams Sean Colin	26.9.1986		12	*2012–2019*	770	119	2	33.47	19	3-20	0/0	48.68	10	136/42
Wishart Craig Brian	9.1.1974		27	*1995–2005*	1,098	114	1	22.40	–	–	–/–	–	15	90

BANGLADESH (96 players)

	Born	Died	Tests	Test Career	Runs	HS	100s	Avge	Wkts	BB	5/10	Avge	Ct/St	O/T
Abdur Razzak	15.6.1982		13	*2005–2017*	248	43	0	15.50	28	4-63	0/0	59.75	4	153/34
Abu Jayed	2.8.1993		9	2018–*2019*	27	7*	0	2.70	24	4-71	0/0	32.45	1	2/3
Abul Hasan	5.8.1992		3	*2012*	165	113	1	82.50	3	2-80	0/0	123.66	3	7/5
Aftab Ahmed	10.11.1985		16	*2004–2009*	582	82*	0	20.78	5	2-31	0/0	47.40	7	85/11
Akram Khan	1.11.1968		8	*2000–2003*	259	44	0	16.18	–	–	–/–	–	3	44
Al-Amin Hossain	1.1.1990		7	*2013–2019*	90	32*	0	22.50	9	3-80	0/0	60.55	0	15/31
Al Sahariar	23.4.1978		15	*2000*–2003	683	71	0	22.76	–	–	–/–	–	10	29

	Born	Died	Tests	Test Career	Runs	HS	100s	Avge	Wkts	BB	5/10	Avge	Ct/St	O/T
Alamgir Kabir	10.1.1981		3	2002–2003	8	4	0	2.00	0	0-39	0/0	–	0	
Alok Kapali	1.1.1984		17	2002–2005	584	85	0	17.69	6	3-3	0/0	118.16	5	69/7
Aminul Islam	2.2.1968		13	2000–2002	530	145	1	21.20	1	1-66	0/0	149.00	5	39
Anamul Haque	16.12.1992		4	2012–2014	73	22	0	9.12	–	–	–/–	–	2	38/13
Anwar Hossain Monir	31.12.1981		3	2003–2005	22	13	0	7.33	0	0-95	0/0	–	0	1
Anwar Hossain Piju	10.12.1983		1	2002	14	12	0	7.00	–	–	–/–	–	0	1
Ariful Haque	18.11.1992		2	2018	88	41*	0	29.33	1	1-10	0/0	24.00	2	1/9
Bikash Ranjan Das	14.7.1982		1	2000	2	2	0	1.00	1	1-64	0/0	72.00	1	
Ebadat Hossain	7.1.1994		6	2018–2019	4	2	0	0.66	6	3-91	0/0	89.33	1	
Ehsanul Haque	1.12.1979		1	2002	7	5	0	3.50	0	0-18	0/0	–	0	6
Elias Sunny	2.8.1986		4	2011–2012	38	20*	0	7.60	12	6-94	1/0	43.16	1	4/7
Enamul Haque snr.	27.2.1966		10	2000–2003	180	24*	0	12.00	18	4-136	0/0	57.05	1	29
Enamul Haque jnr.	5.12.1986		15	2003–2012	59	13	0	5.90	44	7-95	3/1	40.61	3	10
Fahim Muntasir	1.11.1980		3	2001–2002	52	33	0	8.66	5	3-131	0/0	68.40	1	3
Faisal Hossain	26.10.1978		1	2003	7	5	0	3.50	–	–	–/–	–	0	6
Habibul Bashar	17.8.1972		50	2000–2007	3,026	113	3	30.87	0	0-1	0/0	–	22	111
Hannan Sarkar	1.12.1982		17	2002–2004	662	76	0	20.06	–	–	–/–	–	7	20
Hasibul Hossain	3.6.1977		5	2000–2001	97	31	0	10.77	6	2-125	0/0	95.16	1	32
Imrul Kayes	2.2.1987		39	2008–2019	1,797	150	3	24.28	0	0-1	0/0	–	35	78/14
Jahurul Islam	12.12.1986		7	2009–2012	347	48	0	26.69	–	–	–/–	–	7	14/3
Javed Omar Belim	25.11.1976		40	2000–2007	1,720	119	1	22.05	0	0-12	0/0	–	10	59
Jubair Hossain	12.9.1995		6	2014–2015	13	7*	0	4.33	16	5-96	1/0	30.81	2	3/1
Junaid Siddique	30.10.1987		19	2007–2012	969	106	1	26.18	0	0-2	0/0	–	11	54/7
Kamrul Islam	10.12.1991		7	2016–2018	51	25*	0	5.66	8	3-87	0/0	63.00	0	
Khaled Ahmed	20.9.1992		2	2018	4	4*	0	4.00	0	0-45	0/0	–	2	
Khaled Mahmud	26.7.1971		12	2001–2003	266	45	0	12.09	13	4-37	0/0	64.00	2	77
Khaled Mashud	8.2.1976		44	2000–2007	1,409	103*	1	19.04	–	–	–/–	–	78/9	126
Liton Das	13.10.1994		20	2015–2019	859	94	0	26.03	–	–	–/–	–	32/2	36/29
Mahbubul Alam	1.12.1983		4	2008	5	2	0	1.25	5	2-62	0/0	62.80	0	5
Mahmudullah	4.2.1986		49	2009–2019	2,764	146	4	31.77	43	5-51	1/0	45.32	38/1	188/87
Manjural Islam	7.11.1979		17	2000–2003	81	21	0	3.68	28	6-81	1/0	57.32	4	34
Manjural Islam Rana	4.5.1984	16.3.2007	6	2003–2004	257	69	0	25.70	5	3-84	0/0	80.20	3	25
Marshall Ayub	5.12.1988		3	2013	125	41	0	20.83	0	0-15	0/0	–	2	
Mashrafe bin Mortaza	5.10.1983		36	2001–2009	797	79	0	12.85	78	4-60	0/0	41.52	9	218‡/54
Mehedi Hasan	25.10.1997		22	2016–2019	638	68*	0	17.72	90	7-58	7/2	33.12	19	41/13

	Born	Died	Tests	Test Career	Runs	HS	100s	Avge	Wkts	BB	5/10	Avge	Ct/St	O/T
Mehrab Hossain snr.	22.9.1978		9	2000–2003	241	71	0	13.38	0	0-5	0/0	–	6	18
Mehrab Hossain jnr.	8.7.1987		7	2007–2008	243	83	0	20.25	4	2-29	0/0	70.25	2	18/2
Mithun Ali	3.2.1990		9	2018–2019	308	67	0	19.25	–	–	–/–	–	4	27/15
Mohammad Ashraful	9.9.1984		61	2001–2012	2,737	190	6	24.00	21	2-42	0/0	60.52	25	175‡/23
Mohammad Rafique	5.9.1970		33	2000–2007	1,059	111	1	18.57	100	6-77	7/0	40.76	7	123‡/1
Mohammad Salim	15.10.1981		2	2003	49	26	0	16.33	–	–	–/–	–	3/1	1
Mohammad Shahid	1.11.1988		5	2014–2015	57	25	0	11.40	5	2-23	0/0	57.60	0	1
Mohammad Sharif	12.12.1983		10	2000–2007	122	24*	0	7.17	14	4-98	0/0	79.00	5	9
Mominul Haque	29.9.1991		40	2012–2019	2,860	181	9	40.85	4	3-27	0/0	94.00	29	28/6
Mosaddek Hossain	10.12.1995		3	2016–2019	164	75	0	41.00	0	0-1	0/0	–	2	35/14
Mushfiqur Rahim	1.9.1988		70	2005–2019	4,413	219*	7	36.77	–	–	–/–	–	104/15	218/86
Mushfiqur Rahman	1.1.1980		10	2000–2004	232	46*	0	13.64	13	4-65	0/0	63.30	6	28
Mustafizur Rahman	6.9.1995		13	2015–2018	56	16	0	4.30	28	4-37	0/0	35.17	1	58/41
Naeem Islam	31.12.1986		8	2008–2012	416	108	1	32.00	1	1-11	0/0	303.00	2	59/10
[2] **Nafis Iqbal**	31.1.1985		11	2004–2005	518	121	1	23.54	–	–	–/–	–	2	16
Naimur Rahman	19.9.1974		8	2000–2002	210	48	0	15.00	12	6-132	1/0	59.83	4	29
Nasir Hossain	30.11.1991		19	2011–2017	1,044	100	1	34.80	8	3-52	0/0	55.25	10	65/31
Nayeem Hasan	2.12.2000		5	2018–2019	70	26	0	17.50	19	5-61	2/0	20.47	4	
Nazimuddin	1.10.1985		3	2011–2012	125	78	0	20.83	–	–	–/–	–	1	11/7
Nazmul Hossain	5.10.1987		2	2004–2011	16	8*	0	8.00	5	2-61	0/0	38.80	0	38/4
Nazmul Hossain Shanto	25.5.1998		4	2016–2019	201	71	0	28.71	0	0-13	0/0	–	3	5/2
Nazmul Islam	21.3.1991		1	2018	4	4	0	2.00	4	2-27	0/0	19.00	0	5/13
Nurul Hasan	21.11.1993		3	2016–2018	115	64	0	19.16	–	–	–/–	–	5/3	2/9
Rafiqul Islam	7.11.1977		1	2002	7	6	0	3.50	–	–	–/–	–	0	1
Rajin Saleh	20.11.1983		24	2003–2008	1,141	89	0	25.93	2	1-9	0/0	134.00	15	43
Raqibul Hasan	8.10.1987		9	2008–2011	336	65	0	19.76	1	1-0	0/0	17.00	9	55/5
Robiul Islam	20.10.1986		9	2010–2014	99	33	0	9.00	25	6-71	2/0	39.68	5	3/1
Rubel Hossain	1.1.1990		27	2009–2019	265	45*	0	9.46	36	5-166	1/0	76.77	11	101/27
Sabbir Rahman	20.8.1991		11	2016–2017	481	66	0	24.05	0	0-9	0/0	–	3	66/44
Saif Hasan	30.10.1998		2	2019	24	16	0	8.00	–	–	–/–	–	0	
Sajidul Islam	18.1.1988		3	2007–2012	18	6	0	3.00	3	2-71	0/0	77.33	0	0/1
Sanjamul Islam	17.1.1990		1	2017	24	24	0	24.00	1	1-153	0/0	153.00	0	3
Sanwar Hossain	5.8.1973		9	2001–2003	345	49	0	19.16	5	2-128	0/0	62.00	1	27
Shadman Islam	18.5.1995		6	2018–2019	275	76	0	25.00	–	–	–/–	–	3	
Shafiul Islam	6.10.1989		11	2009–2017	211	53	0	10.55	17	3-86	0/0	55.41	2	60/20

	Born	Died	Tests	Test Career	Runs	HS	100s	Avge	Wkts	BB	5/10	Avge	Ct/St	O/T
Shahadat Hossain	7.8.1986		38	2005–*2014*	521	40	0	10.01	72	6-27	4/0	51.81	9	51/6
Shahriar Hossain	1.6.1976		3	*2000–2003*	99	48	0	19.80	–	–	–/–	–	0/1	20
Shahriar Nafees	1.5.1985		24	*2005–2012*	1,267	138	1	26.39	–	–	–/–	–	19	75/1
Shakib Al Hasan	24.3.1987		56	2007–*2019*	3,862	217	5	39.40	210	7-36	18/2	31.12	24	206/76
Shamsur Rahman	5.6.1988		6	*2013–2014*	305	106	1	25.41	0	0-5	0/0	–	7	10/9
Shuvagata Hom	11.11.1986		8	*2014–2016*	244	50	0	22.18	8	2-66	0/0	63.25	8	4/5
Sohag Gazi	5.8.1991		10	*2012–2013*	325	101*	1	21.66	38	6-74	2/0	42.07	5	20/10
Soumya Sarkar	25.2.1993		15	*2014–2019*	818	149	1	29.21	3	2-68	0/0	96.00	21	55/50
Subashis Roy	28.11.1988		4	*2016–2017*	14	12*	0	14.00	9	3-118	0/0	51.66	0	1
Suhrawadi Shuvo	21.11.1988		1	*2011*	15	15	0	7.50	4	3-73	0/0	36.50	0	17/1
Syed Rasel	3.7.1984		6	*2005*–2007	37	19	0	4.62	12	4-129	0/0	47.75	0	52/8
Taijul Islam	7.2.1992		29	*2014–2019*	412	39*	0	10.04	114	8-39	7/1	33.17	16	9/2
Talha Jubair	10.12.1985		7	2002–*2004*	52	31	0	6.50	14	3-135	0/0	55.07	1	6
[2] **Tamim Iqbal** (*CY 2011*)	20.3.1989		60	*2007–2019*	4,405	206	9	38.64	0	0-1	0/0	–	17	207/74‡
Tapash Baisya	25.12.1982		21	2002–2005	384	66	0	11.29	36	4-72	0/0	59.36	6	56
Tareq Aziz	4.9.1983		3	*2003–2004*	22	10*	0	11.00	1	1-76	0/0	261.00	1	10
Taskin Ahmed	3.4.1995		5	*2016–2017*	68	33	0	6.80	7	2-43	0/0	97.42	1	32/19
Tushar Imran	10.12.1983		5	2002–2007	89	28	0	8.90	0	0-48	0/0	–	1	41
Ziaur Rahman	2.12.1986		1	*2012*	14	14	0	7.00	4	4-63	0/0	17.75	0	13/14

IRELAND (17 players)

	Born	Died	Tests	Test Career	Runs	HS	100s	Avge	Wkts	BB	5/10	Avge	Ct/St	O/T
Adair Mark Richard	27.3.1996		1	2019	11	8	0	5.50	6	3-32	0/0	16.33	1	13/18
Balbirnie Andrew	28.12.1990		3	2018–2019	146	82	0	24.33	0	0-8	0/0	–	3	70/43
Cameron-Dow James	18.5.1990		1	*2018*	41	32*	0	41.00	3	2-94	0/0	39.33	2	4
Dockrell George Henry	22.7.1992		1	*2018*	64	39	0	32.00	2	2-63	0/0	60.50	0	87/77
Joyce Edmund Christopher	22.9.1978		1	2018	47	43	0	23.50	–	–	–/–	–	1	61‡/16‡
Kane Tyrone Edward	8.7.1994		1	2018	14	14	0	7.00	0	0-17	0/0	–	0	0/7
McBrine Andrew Robert	30.4.1993		2	*2018*–2019	18	11	0	4.50	3	2-77	0/0	53.00	0	48/19
McCollum James Alexander	1.8.1995		2	*2018*–2019	73	39	0	18.25	–	–	–/–	–	2	9
Murtagh Timothy James	2.8.1981		3	2018–2019	109	54*	0	27.25	13	5-13	1/0	16.38	0	58/14

	Born	Died	Tests	Test Career	Runs	HS	100s	Avge	Wkts	BB	5/10	Avge	Ct/St	O/T
[2] **O'Brien** Kevin Joseph	4.3.1984		3	2018–2019	258	118	1	51.60	0	0-11	0/0	–	0	148/96
[2] **O'Brien** Niall John	8.11.1981		1	2018	18	18	0	9.00	–	–	–/–	–	2	103/30
Porterfield William Thomas Stuart	6.9.1984		3	2018–2019	58	32	0	9.66	–	–	–/–	–	2	139/61
Poynter Stuart William	18.10.1990		1	*2018*	1	1	0	0.50	–	–	–/–	–	2/1	21/25
Rankin William Boyd	5.7.1984		2†	2018–2019	30	17	0	10.00	7	2-5	0/0	31.85	0	68‡/48‡
Stirling Paul Robert	3.9.1990		3	2018–2019	104	36	0	17.33	0	0-11	0/0	–	4	120/78
Thompson Stuart Robert	15.8.1991		3	2018–2019	64	53	0	10.66	10	3-28	0/0	20.40	0	20/41
Wilson Gary Craig	5.2.1986		2	2018–2019	45	33*	0	15.00	–	–	–/–	–	6	105/81

AFGHANISTAN (19 players)

	Born	Died	Tests	Test Career	Runs	HS	100s	Avge	Wkts	BB	5/10	Avge	Ct/St	O/T
Afsar Zazai	10.8.1993		3	2018–*2019*	135	48*	0	27.00	–	–	–/–	–	5/1	17/1
Asghar Afghan Stanikzai	27.2.1987		4	2018–*2019*	249	92	0	35.57	0	0-16	0/0	–	2	111/69
Hamza Hotak	15.8.1991		1	*2019*	35	34	0	17.50	6	5-74	1/0	13.16	0	31/31
Hashmatullah Shahidi	4.11.1994		3	2018–*2019*	138	61	0	34.50	–	–	–/–	–	1	39/1
Ibrahim Zadran	12.12.2001		2	*2019*	148	87	0	37.00	–	–	–/–	–	4	1/3
Ihsanullah Janat	28.12.1997		3	*2018–2019*	110	65*	0	22.00	–	–	–/–	–	4	16
Ikram Alikhil	29.9.2000		1	*2018*	7	7	0	7.00	–	–	–/–	–	4/1	12
Javed Ahmadi	2.1.1992		2	2018–*2019*	105	62	0	26.25	0	0-9	0/0	–	0	44/3
Mohammad Nabi	7.3.1985		3	2018–*2019*	33	24	0	5.50	8	3-36	0/0	31.75	2	124/78
Mohammad Shahzad	15.7.1991		2	2018–*2018*	69	40	0	17.25	–	–	–/–	–	0	84/65
Mujeeb Ur Rahman **Zadran**	28.3.2001		1	2018	18	15	0	9.00	1	1-75	0/0	75.00	0	40/19
Nasir Ahmadzai	21.12.1993		1	*2019*	17	15	0	8.50	–	–	–/–	–	0	16
Qais Ahmad	15.8.2000		1	*2019*	23	14	0	11.50	1	1-22	0/0	28.00	0	0/1
Rahmat Shah	6.7.1993		4	2018–*2019*	298	102	1	37.25	–	–	–/–	–	2	73
Rashid Khan	20.9.1998		4	2018–*2019*	106	51	0	15.14	23	6-49	3/1	21.08	0	71/47‡
Wafadar Momand	1.2.2000		2	2018–*2018*	12	6*	0	6.00	2	2-100	0/0	77.50	0	
Waqar Salamkheil	2.10.2001		1	*2018*	1	1*	0	–	4	2-35	0/0	25.25	0	
Yamin Ahmadzai	25.7.1992		4	2018–*2019*	31	18	0	4.42	10	3-41	0/0	21.10	0	4/2
Zahir Khan	20.12.1998		2	*2019*	0	0*	0	0.00	5	3-59	0/0	31.60	0	1

Notes

Family relationships in the above lists are indicated by superscript numbers; the following list contains only those players whose relationship is not apparent from a shared name.

In one Test, A. and G. G. Hearne played for England; their brother, F. Hearne, for South Africa.
The Waughs and New Zealand's Marshalls are the only instance of Test-playing twins.
Adnan Akmal: brother of Kamran and Umar Akmal.
Amar Singh, L.: brother of L. Ramji.
Azmat Rana: brother of Shafqat Rana.
Bazid Khan (Pakistan): son of Majid Khan (Pakistan) and grandson of M. Jahangir Khan (India).
Bravo, D. J. and D. M.: half-brothers.
Chappell, G. S., I. M. and T. M.: grandsons of V. Y. Richardson.
Collins, P. T.: half-brother of F. H. Edwards.
Cooper, W. H.: great-grandfather of A. P. Sheahan.
Edwards, F. H.: half-brother of P. T. Collins.
Hanif Mohammad: brother of Mushtaq, Sadiq and Wazir Mohammad; father of Shoaib Mohammad.
Headley, D. W. (England): son of R. G. A. and grandson of G. A. Headley (both West Indies).
Hearne, F. (England and South Africa): father of G. A. L. Hearne (South Africa).
Jahangir Khan, M. (India): father of Majid Khan and grandfather of Bazid Khan (both Pakistan).
Kamran Akmal: brother of Adnan and Umar Akmal.
Khalid Wazir (Pakistan): son of S. Wazir Ali (India).
Kirsten, G. and P. N.: half-brothers.
Majid Khan (Pakistan): son of M. Jahangir Khan (India) and father of Bazid Khan (Pakistan).
Manzoor Elahi: brother of Salim and Zahoor Elahi.
Moin Khan: brother of Nadeem Khan.
Mudassar Nazar: son of Nazar Mohammad.
Murray, D. A.: son of E. D. Weekes.
Mushtaq Mohammad: brother of Hanif, Sadiq and Wazir Mohammad.
Nadeem Khan: brother of Moin Khan.
Nafis Iqbal: brother of Tamim Iqbal.
Nazar Mohammad: father of Mudassar Nazar.
Nazir Ali, S.: brother of S. Wazir Ali.
Pattinson, D. J. (England): brother of J. L. Pattinson (Australia).
Pervez Sajjad: brother of Waqar Hassan.
Ramiz Raja: brother of Wasim Raja.
Ramji, L.: brother of L. Amarsingh.
Riaz Afridi: brother of Shaheen Shah Afridi.
Richardson, V. Y.: grandfather of G. S., I. M. and T. M. Chappell.
Sadiq Mohammad: brother of Hanif, Mushtaq and Wazir Mohammad.
Saeed Ahmed: brother of Younis Ahmed.
Salim Elahi: brother of Manzoor and Zahoor Elahi.
Shafqat Rana: brother of Azmat Rana.
Shaheen Shah Afridi: brother of Riaz Afridi.
Sheahan, A. P.: great-grandson of W. H. Cooper.
Shoaib Mohammad: son of Hanif Mohammad.
Tamim Iqbal: brother of Nafis Iqbal.
Umar Akmal: brother of Adnan and Kamran Akmal.
Waqar Hassan: brother of Pervez Sajjad.
Wasim Raja: brother of Ramiz Raja.
Wazir Ali, S. (India): brother of S. Nazir Ali (India) and father of Khalid Wazir (Pakistan).
Wazir Mohammad: brother of Hanif, Mushtaq and Sadiq Mohammad.
Weekes, E. D.: father of D. A. Murray.
Yograj Singh: father of Yuvraj Singh.
Younis Ahmed: brother of Saeed Ahmed.
Yuvraj Singh: son of Yograj Singh.
Zahoor Elahi: brother of Manzoor and Salim Elahi.

Teams are listed only where relatives played for different sides.

PLAYERS APPEARING FOR MORE THAN ONE TEST TEAM

Fifteen cricketers have appeared for two countries in Test matches, namely:

Amir Elahi (India 1, Pakistan 5)
J. J. Ferris (Australia 8, England 1)
S. C. Guillen (West Indies 5, New Zealand 3)
Gul Mahomed (India 8, Pakistan 1)
F. Hearne (England 2, South Africa 4)
A. H. Kardar (India 3, Pakistan 23)
W. E. Midwinter (England 4, Australia 8)
F. Mitchell (England 2, South Africa 3)
W. L. Murdoch (Australia 18, England 1)
Nawab of Pataudi snr (England 3, India 3)
W. B. Rankin (England 1, Ireland 2)
A. J. Traicos (South Africa 3, Zimbabwe 4)
A. E. Trott (Australia 3, England 2)
K. C. Wessels (Australia 24, South Africa 16)
S. M. J. Woods (Australia 3, England 3)

Rankin also played seven one-day internationals and two Twenty20 internationals for England and 68 ODIs and 48 T20Is for Ireland; Wessels played 54 ODIs for Australia and 55 for South Africa.

The following players appeared for the ICC World XI against Australia in the Super Series Test in 2005-06: M. V. Boucher, R. Dravid, A. Flintoff, S. J. Harmison, Inzamam-ul-Haq, J. H. Kallis, B. C. Lara, M. Muralitharan, V. Sehwag, G. C. Smith, D. L. Vettori.

In 1970, England played five first-class matches against the Rest of the World after the cancellation of South Africa's tour. Players were awarded England caps, but the matches are no longer considered to have Test status. Alan Jones (born 4.11.1938) made his only appearance for England in this series, scoring 5 and 0; he did not bowl and took no catches.

CONCUSSION SUBSTITUTES

From 2019, Test regulations provided for a full playing substitute to replace a player suffering from concussion. The following substitutions have been made:

Original player	*Concussion substitute*		
S. P. D. Smith	M. Labuschagne	Australia v England at Lord's	2019
D. M. Bravo	J. Blackwood	West Indies v India at Kingston	2019
D. Elgar	T. B. de Bruyn	South Africa v India at Ranchi	2019-20
Liton Das	Mehedi Hasan	Bangladesh v India at Kolkata	2019-20
Nayeem Hasan	Taijul Islam	Bangladesh v India at Kolkata	2019-20
K. T. Kasuza	B. S. Mudzinganyama	Zimbabwe v Sri Lanka (1st Test) at Harare	2019-20
K. T. Kasuza	T. Maruma	Zimbabwe v Sri Lanka (2nd Test) at Harare	2019-20

Y. S. Chahal was a concussion substitute for R. A. Jadeja in a T20 international for India v Australia at Canberra in 2020-21.

ONE-DAY AND TWENTY20 INTERNATIONAL CRICKETERS

The following players had appeared for Test-playing countries in one-day internationals or Twenty20 internationals by December 31, 2020, but had not represented their countries in Test matches by January 25, 2021. (Numbers in brackets signify number of ODIs for each player: where a second number appears, e.g. (5/1), it signifies the number of T20Is for that player.)

By January 2021, D. A. Miller (132 ODIs/78 T20Is, including three for the World XI) was the most experienced international player never to have appeared in Test cricket. R. G. Sharma held the record for most international appearances before making his Test debut, with 108 ODIs and 36 T20Is. S. Badree had played a record 52 T20Is (including two for the World XI) without a Test or ODI appearance.

England

M. W. Alleyne (10), I. D. Austin (9), T. Banton (6/9), S. W. Billings (21/29), D. R. Briggs (1/7), A. D. Brown (16), D. R. Brown (9), P. R. Brown (0/4), G. Chapple (1), J. W. M. Dalrymple (27/3), S. M. Davies (8/5), J. W. Dernbach (24/34), M. V. Fleming (11), P. J. Franks (1), I. J. Gould (18), A. P. Grayson (2), L. Gregory (0/8), H. F. Gurney (10/2), G. W. Humpage (3), T. E. Jesty (10), E. C. Joyce (17/2), C. Kieswetter (46/25), L. S. Livingstone (0/2), G. D. Lloyd (6), A. G. R. Loudon (1), J. D. Love (3), M. B. Loye (7), M. J. Lumb (3/27), M. A. Lynch (3), S. Mahmood (4/6), A. D.

Mascarenhas (20/14), S. C. Meaker (2/2), T. S. Mills (0/4), P. Mustard (10/2), P. A. Nixon (19/1), M. W. Parkinson (2/2), S. D. Parry (2/5), M. J. Smith (5), N. M. K. Smith (7), J. N. Snape (10/1), V. S. Solanki (51/3), R. J. W. Topley (11/6), J. O. Troughton (6), C. M. Wells (2), V. J. Wells (9), A. G. Wharf (13), D. J. Willey (49/28), L. J. Wright (50/51), M. H. Yardy (28/14).

D. R. Brown also played 16 ODIs for Scotland, and E. C. Joyce one Test, 61 ODIs and 16 T20Is for Ireland.

Australia

S. A. Abbott (2/7), J. P. Behrendorff (11/7), T. R. Birt (0/4), G. A. Bishop (2), S. M. Boland (14/3), C. J. Boyce (0/7), R. J. Campbell (2), A. T. Carey (42/30), D. T. Christian (19/16), M. J. Cosgrove (3), N. M. Coulter-Nile (32/28), B. C. J. Cutting (4/4), M. J. Di Venuto (9), B. R. Dorey (4), B. R. Dunk (0/5), Fawad Ahmed (3/2), P. J. Forrest (15), B. Geeves (2/1), S. F. Graf (11), I. J. Harvey (73), S. M. Harwood (1/3), S. D. Heazlett (1), J. R. Hopes (84/12), D. J. Hussey (69/39), M. Klinger (0/3), B. Laughlin (5/3), S. Lee (45), M. L. Lewis (7/2), C. A. Lynn (4/18), R. J. McCurdy (11), B. R. McDermott (0/12), K. H. MacLeay (16), J. P. Maher (26), J. M. Muirhead (0/5), D. P. Nannes (1/15), M. G. Neser (2), A. A. Noffke (1/2), J. S. Paris (2), L. A. Pomersbach (0/1), G. D. Porter (2), N. J. Reardon (0/2), K. W. Richardson (25/21), B. J. Rohrer (0/1), L. Ronchi (4/3), D. R. Sams (0/2), G. S. Sandhu (2), D. J. M. Short (8/23), J. D. Siddons (1), B. Stanlake (7/19), M. P. Stoinis (45/23), A. M. Stuart (3), M. J. Swepson (0/4), C. P. Tremain (4), G. S. Trimble (2), A. J. Turner (6/11), A. J. Tye (7/28), J. D. Wildermuth (0/2), D. J. Worrall (3), B. E. Young (6), A. Zampa (61/36), A. K. Zesers (2).

R. J. Campbell also played three T20Is for Hong Kong, D. P. Nannes two T20Is for the Netherlands, and L. Ronchi four Tests, 72 ODIs and 26 T20Is for New Zealand..

South Africa

Y. A. Abdulla (0/2), S. Abrahams (1), F. Behardien (59/38), D. M. Benkenstein (23), G. H. Bodi (2/1), L. E. Bosman (13/14), R. E. Bryson (7), D. J. Callaghan (29), G. L. Cloete (0/2), D. N. Crookes (32), C. J. Dala (2/9), H. Davids (2/9), D. M. Dupavillon (1), B. C. Fortuin (1/4), R. Frylinck (0/3), T. Henderson (0/1), R. R. Hendricks (21/25), C. A. Ingram (31/9), C. Jonker (2/2), J. C. Kent (2), L. J. Koen (5), G. J-P. Kruger (3/1), E. Leie (0/2), R. E. Levi (0/13), J. Louw (3/2), J. N. Malan (3/2), D. A. Miller (132/75), M. Mosehle (0/7), P. V. Mpitsang (2), S. J. Palframan (7), A. M. Phangiso (21/16), N. Pothas (3), A. G. Puttick (1), S. Qeshile (0/2), C. E. B. Rice (3), M. J. R. Rindel (22), R. R. Rossouw (36/15), D. B. Rundle (2), T. G. Shaw (9), M. Shezi (1), E. O. Simons (23), J. T. Smuts (5/11), E. L. R. Stewart (6), R. Telemachus (37/3), J. Theron (4/9), A. C. Thomas (0/1), T. Tshabalala (4), P. J. van Biljon (0/5), R. E. van der Merwe (13/13), J. J. van der Wath (10/8), V. B. van Jaarsveld (2/3), M. N. van Wyk (17/8), C. J. P. G. van Zyl (2), K. Verreynne (3), D. Wiese (6/20), H. S. Williams (7), M. Yachad (1), K. Zondo (5).

R. E. van der Merwe also played two ODIs and 30 T20Is for the Netherlands.

West Indies

F. A. Allen (14/16), H. A. G. Anthony (3), S. Badree (0/50), C. D. Barnwell (0/6), M. C. Bascombe (0/1), R. R. Beaton (2), N. E. Bonner (0/2), D. Brown (3), B. St A. Browne (4), P. A. Browne (5), H. R. Bryan (15), D. C. Butler (5/1), J. L. Carter (33), J. Charles (48/34), D. O. Christian (0/2), R. T. Crandon (1), R. R. Emrit (2/4), S. E. Findlay (9/2), A. D. S. Fletcher (25/45), R. S. Gabriel (11), R. C. Haynes (8), C. Hemraj (6), R. O. Hurley (9), D. P. Hyatt (9/5), K. C. B. Jeremy (6), B. A. King (4/11), E. Lewis (51/32), A. M. McCarthy (0/1), O. C. McCoy (2/2), A. Martin (9/1), G. E. Mathurin (0/3), K. R. Mayers (0/2), J. N. Mohammed (28/9), A. R. Nurse (54/13), W. K. D. Perkins (0/1), K. A. Pierre (3/10), K. A. Pollard (113/76), N. Pooran (25/24), R. Powell (34/29), M. R. Pydanna (3), A. C. L. Richards (1/1), S. E. Rutherford (0/6), K. Santokie (0/12), K. F. Semple (7), R. Shepherd (5/3), O. F. Smith (0/2), D. C. Thomas (21/3), O. R. Thomas (20/15), C. M. Tuckett (1), H. R. Walsh (9/9), K. O. K. Williams (8/26), L. R. Williams (15).

New Zealand

G. W. Aldridge (2/1), M. D. Bailey (1), M. D. Bates (2/3), B. R. Blair (14), T. C. Bruce (0/17), C. E. Bulfin (4), T. K. Canning (4), M. S. Chapman (4/6), P. G. Coman (3), D. P. Conway (0/6), A. P. Devcich (12/4), B. J. Diamanti (1/1), M. W. Douglas (6), J. A. Duffy (0/1), A. M. Ellis (15/5), L. H. Ferguson (19/2), B. G. Hadlee (2), L. J. Hamilton (2), R. T. Hart (1), R. L. Hayes (1), R. M. Hira (0/15), P. A. Hitchcock (14/1), L. G. Howell (12), A. K. Kitchen (0/5), S. C. Kuggeleijn (2/16), M. J. McClenaghan (48/28), N. L. McCullum (84/63), P. D. McGlashan (4/11), B. J. McKechnie (14), E. B. McSweeney (16), A. W. Mathieson (1), J. P. Millmow (5), A. F. Milne (40/21), T. S. Nethula

(5), C. J. Nevin (37), A. J. Penn (5), R. G. Petrie (12), G. D. Phillips (0/11), S. H. A. Rance (2/8), R. B. Reid (9), S. J. Roberts (2), T. L. Seifert (3/30), S. L. Stewart (4), L. W. Stott (1), G. P. Sulzberger (3), A. R. Tait (5), E. P. Thompson (1/1), B. M. Tickner (0/6), M. D. J. Walker (3), R. J. Webb (3), B. M. Wheeler (6/6), J. W. Wilson (6), W. A. Wisneski (3), L. J. Woodcock (4/3), G. H. Worker (10/2).

M. S. Chapman also played 2 ODIs and 19 T20Is for Hong Kong.

India

K. K. Ahmed (11/14), S. Aravind (0/1), P. Awana (0/2), A. C. Bedade (13), A. Bhandari (2), Bhupinder Singh snr (2), G. Bose (1), Y. S. Chahal (54/45), D. L. Chahar (3/13), R. D. Chahar (0/1), V. B. Chandrasekhar (7), U. Chatterjee (3), N. A. David (4), P. Dharmani (1), R. Dhawan (3/1), A. B. Dinda (13/9), S. R. Dube (1/13), F. Y. Fazal (1), R. S. Gavaskar (11), R. S. Ghai (6), M. S. Gony (2), Gurkeerat Singh (3), S. S. Iyer (21/24), K. M. Jadhav (73/9), Joginder Sharma (4/4), A. V. Kale (1), S. Kaul (3/3), S. C. Khanna (10), G. K. Khoda (2), A. R. Khurasiya (12), D. S. Kulkarni (12/2), T. Kumaran (8), Mandeep Singh (0/3), M. Markande (0/1), J. J. Martin (10), D. Mongia (57/1), S. P. Mukherjee (3), A. M. Nayar (3), P. Negi (0/1), G. K. Pandey (2), M. K. Pandey (26/39), K. H. Pandya (0/18), J. V. Paranjpe (4), Parvez Rasool (1/1), A. K. Patel (8), A. R. Patel (38/11), Y. K. Pathan (57/22), Randhir Singh (2), S. S. Raul (2), A. T. Rayudu (55/6), A. M. Salvi (4), S. V. Samson (0/7), V. Shankar (12/9), M. Sharma (26/8), R. Sharma (4/2), S. Sharma (0/2), L. R. Shukla (3), R. P. Singh (2), R. S. Sodhi (18), S. Somasunder (2), B. B. Sran (6/2), S. Sriram (8), Sudhakar Rao (1), M. K. Tiwary (12/3), S. S. Tiwary (3), S. Tyagi (4/1), R. V. Uthappa (46/13), P. S. Vaidya (4), Y. Venugopal Rao (16), Jai P. Yadav (12).

Pakistan

Aamer Hameed (2), Aamer Hanif (5), Aamer Yamin (4/2), Abdullah Shafiq (0/3), Ahsan Ali (0/2), Akhtar Sarfraz (4), Anwar Ali (22/16), Arshad Pervez (2), Asad Ali (4/2), Asif Ali (18/25), Asif Mahmood (2), Awais Zia (0/5), Faisal Athar (1), Ghulam Ali (3), Haafiz Shahid (3), Haider Ali (2/7), Hammad Azam (11/5), Haris Rauf (2/11), Hasan Jamil (6), Hussain Talat (1/15), Imad Wasim (55/49), Imran Abbas (2), Imran Khan jnr (0/3), Iqbal Sikandar (4), Irfan Bhatti (1), Javed Qadir (1), Junaid Zia (4), Kamran Hussain (2), Kashif Raza (1), Khalid Latif (5/13), Khushdil Shah (1/7), Mahmood Hamid (1), Mansoor Amjad (1/1), Mansoor Rana (2), Manzoor Akhtar (7), Maqsood Rana (1), Masood Iqbal (1), Mohammad Hasnain (6/10), Moin-ul-Atiq (5), Mujahid Jamshed (4), Mukhtar Ahmed (0/6), Naeem Ahmed (1), Naeem Ashraf (2), Najaf Shah (1), Naseer Malik (3), Nauman Anwar (0/1), Naumanullah (1), Parvez Mir (3), Rafatullah Mohmand (0/3), Rameez Raja (0/2), Raza Hasan (1/10), Rizwan Ahmed (1), Rumman Raees (9/8), Saad Ali (2), Saad Nasim (3/3), Saadat Ali (8), Saeed Azad (4), Sahibzada Farhan (0/3), Sajid Ali (13), Sajjad Akbar (2), Salim Pervez (1), Samiullah Khan (2), Shahid Anwar (1), Shahzaib Hasan (3/10), Shakeel Ansar (0/2), Shakil Khan (1), Shoaib Khan (0/1), Sohaib Maqsood (26/20), Sohail Fazal (2), Tanvir Mehdi (1), Usman Qadir (0/3), Usman Shinwari (9/13), Waqas Maqsood (0/1),Wasim Haider (3), Zafar Iqbal (8), Zahid Ahmed (2).

Sri Lanka

M. A. Aponso (9/3), J. R. M. W. S. Bandara (0/8), K. M. C. Bandara (1/1), J. W. H. D. Boteju (2), D. L. S. de Silva (2), G. N. de Silva (4), P. C. de Silva (7/2), S. N. T. de Silva (0/3), L. H. D. Dilhara (9/2), B. Fernando (0/2), E. R. Fernando (3), T. L. Fernando (1), U. N. K. Fernando (2), W. I. A. Fernando (18/15), J. C. Gamage (4), W. C. A. Ganegama (4), F. R. M. Goonatilleke (1), P. W. Gunaratne (23), A. A. W. Gunawardene (1), P. D. Heyn (2), W. S. Jayantha (17), P. S. Jayaprakashdaran (1), C. U. Jayasinghe (0/5), S. A. Jayasinghe (2), G. S. N. F. G. Jayasuriya (12/18), N. G. R. P. Jayasuriya (2), S. H. T. Kandamby (39/5), S. H. U. Karnain (19), H. G. J. M. Kulatunga (0/2), D. S. M. Kumara (1/2), L. D. Madushanka (4/2), B. M. A. J. Mendis (58/22), C. Mendis (1), P. H. K. D. Mendis (2/4), A. M. N. Munasinghe (5), E. M. D. Y. Munaweera (2/13), H. G. D. Nayanakantha (3), A. R. M. Opatha (5), S. P. Pasqual (2), S. S. Pathirana (18/5), A. K. Perera (6/6), K. G. Perera (1), P. A. R. P. Perera (2), H. S. M. Pieris (3), S. M. A. Priyanjan (23/3), M. Pushpakumara (3/1), P. B. B. Rajapaksa (0/7), R. L. B. Rambukwella (0/2), S. K. Ranasinghe (4), N. Ranatunga (2), N. L. K. Ratnayake (2), R. J. M. G. M. Rupasinghe (0/2), A. P. B. Tennekoon (4), M. H. Tissera (3), I. Udana (18/30), J. D. F. Vandersay (12/10), D. M. Vonhagt (1), A. P. Weerakkody (1), D. S. Weerakkody (3), S. Weerakoon (2), K. Weeraratne (15/5), S. R. D. Wettimuny (3), R. P. A. H. Wickremaratne (3).

Zimbabwe

R. D. Brown (7), K. M. Curran (11), S. G. Davies (4), K. G. Duers (6), E. A. Essop-Adam (1), Faraz Akram (0/1), D. A. G. Fletcher (6), T. N. Garwe (1), J. G. Heron (6), R. S. Higgins (11), V. R. Hogg (2), A. J. Ireland (26/1), D. Jakiel (0/2), L. M. Jongwe (22/8), R. Kaia (1), T. S. Kamunhukamwe (6/2), F. Kasteni (3), A. J. Mackay (3), W. N. Madhevere (6/5), N. Madziva (12/15), G. C. Martin (5), W. T. Mashinge (0/2), M. A. Meman (1), T. V. Mufambisi (6), T. T. Munyonga (0/5), R. C. Murray (5), T. K. Musakanda (1), C. T. Mutombodzi (11/5), T. Muzarabani (8/9), R. Ngarava (12/3), I. A. Nicolson (2), G. A. Paterson (10), G. E. Peckover (3), E. C. Rainsford (39/2), P. W. E. Rawson (10), H. P. Rinke (18), L. N. Roche (3), M. Shumba (0/1), R. W. Sims (3), G. M. Strydom (12), C. Zhuwao (9/7).

Bangladesh

Abu Haider (2/13), Afif Hossain (1/12), Ahmed Kamal (1), Alam Talukdar (2), Aminul Islam (Bhola) (1), Aminul Islam (Biplob) (0/7), Anisur Rahman (2), Arafat Sunny (16/10), Ather Ali Khan (19), Azhar Hussain (7), Dhiman Ghosh (14/1), Dolar Mahmud (7), Farhad Reza (34/13), Faruq Ahmed (7), Fazle Mahmud (2), Gazi Ashraf (7), Ghulam Faruq (5), Ghulam Nausher (9), Hafizur Rahman (2), Harunur Rashid (2), Hasan Mahmud (0/1), Jahangir Alam (3), Jahangir Badshah (5), Jamaluddin Ahmed (1), Mafizur Rahman (4), Mahbubur Rahman (1), Mazharul Haque (1), Mehedi Hasan snr (0/4), Minhazul Abedin (27), Mohammad Naim (1/6), Mohammad Saifuddin (22/15), Moniruzzaman (2), Morshed Ali Khan (3), Mosharraf Hossain (5), Mukhtar Ali (0/1), Nadif Chowdhury (0/3), Nasir Ahmed (7), Nazmus Sadat (0/1), Neeyamur Rashid (2), Nurul Abedin (4), Rafiqul Alam (2), Raqibul Hasan snr (2), Rony Talukdar (0/1), Saiful Islam (7), Sajjad Ahmed (2), Samiur Rahman (2), Saqlain Sajib (0/1), Shafiuddin Ahmed (11), Shahidur Rahman (2), Shariful Haq (1), Sheikh Salahuddin (6), Tanveer Haider (2), Wahidul Gani (1), Zahid Razzak (3), Zakir Hasan (0/1), Zakir Hassan (2).

Ireland

J. Anderson (8/4), A. C. Botha (42/14), J. P. Bray (15/2), S. A. Britton (1), C. Campher (3), K. E. D. Carroll (6), P. K. D. Chase (25/12), P. Connell (13/9), A. R. Cusack (59/37), D. C. A. Delany (0/8), G. J. Delany (5/23), P. S. Eaglestone (1/1), M. J. Fourie (7), S. C. Getkate (3/15), P. G. Gillespie (5), R. S. Haire (2), J. D. Hall (3), D. T. Johnston (67/30), N. G. Jones (14/5), D. I. Joyce (3), G. E. Kidd (6/1), D. Langford-Smith (22), J. B. Little (6/17), W. K. McCallan (39/9), R. D. McCann (8/3), G. J. McCarter (1/3), B. J. McCarthy (31/10), J. F. Mooney (64/27), P. J. K. Mooney (4), E. J. G. Morgan (23), J. Mulder (4/8), A. D. Poynter (19/19), D. A. Rankin (0/2), E. J. Richardson (2), J. N. K. Shannon (1/8), S. Singh (20/24), M. C. Sorensen (13/26), R. Strydom (9/4), H. T. Tector (3/20), S. P. Terry (5/1), G. J. Thompson (3/10), L. J. Tucker (11/17), A. van der Merwe (9), R. M. West (10/5), R. K. Whelan (2), A. R. White (61/18), C. A. Young (17/32).

E. J. G. Morgan also played 16 Tests, 219 ODIs and 97 T20Is for England.

Afghanistan

Abdullah Mazari (2), Aftab Alam (27/12), Ahmed Shah (1), Dawlat Ahmadzai (3/2), Dawlat Zadran (82/34), Fareed Ahmad (5/14), Fazal Niazai (0/1), Gulbadeen Naib (65/48), Hamid Hassan (38/22), Hasti Gul (2), Hazratullah Zazai (16/15), Izatullah Dawlatzai (5/4), Karim Janat (1/24), Karim Sadiq (24/36), Khaliq Dad (6), Mirwais Ashraf (46/25), Mohibullah Paak (2), Najeeb Tarakai (1/12), Najibullah Zadran (67/60), Nasim Baras (0/3), Naveen-ul-Haq (4/5), Nawroz Mangal (49/32), Noor Ali Zadran (51/20), Noor-ul-Haq (2), Raees Ahmadzai (5/8), Rahmanullah Gurbaz (0/10), Rokhan Barakzai (1/3), Samiullah Shenwari (84/64), Sayed Shirzad (2/4), Shabir Noori (10/1), Shafiqullah Shinwari (24/46), Shapoor Zadran (44/36), Sharafuddin Ashraf (17/8), Usman Ghani (15/20), Zakiullah (1), Zamir Khan (0/1), Ziaur Rahman (0/1).

PLAYERS APPEARING FOR MORE THAN ONE ONE-DAY/TWENTY20 INTERNATIONAL TEAM

The following players have played ODIs for the **African XI** in addition to their national side:

N. Boje (2), L. E. Bosman (1), J. Botha (2), M. V. Boucher (5), E. Chigumbura (3), A. B. de Villiers (5), H. H. Dippenaar (6), J. H. Kallis (2), J. M. Kemp (6), J. A. Morkel (2), M. Morkel (3), T. M. Odoyo (5), P. J. Ongondo (1), J. L. Ontong (1), S. M. Pollock (6), A. G. Prince (3), J. A. Rudolph (2), V. Sibanda (2), G. C. Smith (1), D. W. Steyn (2), H. H. Streak (2), T. Taibu (1), S. O. Tikolo (4), M. Zondeki (2). (Odoyo, Ongondo and Tikolo played for Kenya, who do not have Test status.)

The following players have played ODIs for the **Asian Cricket Council XI** in addition to their national side:

Abdul Razzaq (4), M. S. Dhoni (3), R. Dravid (1), C. R. D. Fernando (1), S. C. Ganguly (3), Harbhajan Singh (2), Inzamam-ul-Haq (3), S. T. Jayasuriya (4), D. P. M. D. Jayawardene (5), A. Kumble (2), Mashrafe bin Mortaza (2), Mohammad Ashraful (2), Mohammad Asif (3), Mohammad Rafique (2), Mohammad Yousuf (7), M. Muralitharan (4), A. Nehra (3), K. C. Sangakkara (4), V. Sehwag (7), Shahid Afridi (3), Shoaib Akhtar (3), W. U. Tharanga (1), W. P. U. J. C. Vaas (1), Yuvraj Singh (3), Zaheer Khan (6).

The following players have played ODIs for an **ICC World XI** in addition to their national side:

C. L. Cairns (1), R. Dravid (3), S. P. Fleming (1), A. Flintoff (3), C. H. Gayle (3), A. C. Gilchrist (1), D. Gough (1), M. L. Hayden (1), J. H. Kallis (3), B. C. Lara (4), G. D. McGrath (1), M. Muralitharan (3), M. Ntini (1), K. P. Pietersen (2), S. M. Pollock (3), R. T. Ponting (1), K. C. Sangakkara (3), V. Sehwag (3), Shahid Afridi (2), Shoaib Akhtar (2), D. L. Vettori (4), S. K. Warne (1).

The following players have played T20Is for a **World XI** in addition to their national side:

H. M. Amla (3), S. Badree (2), G. J. Bailey (1), S. W. Billings (1), P. D. Collingwood (1), B. C. J. Cutting (3), F. du Plessis (3), G. D. Elliott (1), Imran Tahir (3), K. D. Karthik (1), S. Lamichhane (1), M. J. McClenaghan (1), D. A. Miller (3), T. S. Mills (1), M. Morkel (3), T. D. Paine (2), N. L. T. C. Perera (4), Rashid Khan (1), L. Ronchi (1), D. J. G. Sammy (2), Shahid Afridi (1), Shoaib Malik (1), Tamim Iqbal (4).

K. C. Wessels played Tests and ODIs for both Australia and South Africa. **D. R. Brown** played ODIs for England plus ODIs and T20Is for Scotland. **C. B. Lambert** played Tests and ODIs for West Indies and one ODI for USA. **E. C. Joyce** played ODIs and T20Is for England and all three formats for Ireland; **E. J. G. Morgan** ODIs for Ireland and all three formats for England; and **W. B. Rankin** all three formats for Ireland and England. **A. C. Cummins** played Tests and ODIs for West Indies and ODIs for Canada. **G. M. Hamilton** played Tests for England and ODIs for Scotland. **D. P. Nannes** played ODIs and T20Is for Australia and T20Is for the Netherlands. **L. Ronchi** played ODIs and T20Is for Australia and all three formats for New Zealand. **G. O. Jones** played all three formats for England and ODIs for Papua New Guinea. **R. E. van der Merwe** played ODIs and T20Is for South Africa and the Netherlands. **R. J. Campbell** played ODIs for Australia and T20Is for Hong Kong. **M. S. Chapman** played ODIs and T20Is for Hong Kong and New Zealand. **Izatullah Dawlatzai** played ODIs and T20Is for Afghanistan and T20Is for Germany. **X. M. Marshall** played all three formats for West Indies and ODIs and T20Is for USA. **G. M. Strydom** played ODIs for Zimbabwe and T20Is for Cayman Islands. **J. Theron** played ODIs and T20Is for South Africa and ODIs for USA. **H. R. Walsh** played ODIs and T20Is for both USA and West Indies.

ELITE TEST UMPIRES

The following umpires were on the ICC's elite panel in February 2021. The figures for Tests, one-day internationals and Twenty20 internationals and the Test Career dates refer to matches in which they have officiated as on-field umpires (excluding abandoned games). The totals of Tests are complete up to January 25, 2021, the totals of one-day internationals and Twenty20 internationals up to December 31, 2020.

	Country	*Born*	*Tests*	*Test Career*	*ODIs*	*T20Is*
Aleem Dar	P	6.6.1968	132	*2003–2019*	211	48
Dharmasena Handunnettige Deepthi Priyantha Kumar	SL	24.4.1971	67	*2010–2020*	105	22
Erasmus Marais	SA	27.2.1964	64*	*2009–2020*	92	26
Gaffaney Christopher Blair	NZ	30.11.1975	37	*2014–2020*	68	22
Gough Michael Andrew	E	18.12.1979	18	2016–2020	63	14
Illingworth Richard Keith	E	23.8.1963	51*	*2012*–2020	69	16
Kettleborough Richard Allan	E	15.3.1973	68	*2010*–2020	90	22
Menon Nitin Narendra	I	2.11.1983	3	*2019*	24	16
Oxenford Bruce Nicholas James	A	5.3.1960	62	*2010–2020*	97	20
Reiffel Paul Ronald	A	19.4.1966	51	2012–*2020*	71	16
Tucker Rodney James	A	28.8.1964	71	*2009–2019*	85	37
Wilson Joel Sheldon	WI	30.12.1966	19	2015–*2019*	66	26

* *Includes one Test where he took over mid-match.*

BIRTHS AND DEATHS

OTHER CRICKETING NOTABLES

The following list shows the births and deaths of cricketers, and people associated with cricket, who have *not* played in men's Test matches.

Criteria for inclusion All non-Test players who have either (1) scored 20,000 first-class runs, or (2) taken 1,500 first-class wickets, or (3) achieved 750 dismissals, or (4) reached both 15,000 runs and 750 wickets. Also included are (5) the leading players who flourished before the start of Test cricket, (6) *Wisden* Cricketers of the Year who did not play Test cricket, and (7) others of merit or interest.

Names Where players were normally known by a name other than their first, this is underlined.

Teams Where only one team are listed, this is normally the one for which the player made most first-class appearances. Additional teams are listed only if the player appeared for them in more than 20 first-class matches, or if they are especially relevant to their career. School and university teams are not given unless especially relevant (e.g. for the schoolboys chosen as wartime Cricketers of the Year in the 1918 and 1919 *Wisdens*).

		Born	*Died*
Adams Percy Webster	Cheltenham College; *CY 1919*	5.9.1900	28.9.1962
Aird Ronald MC	Hampshire; sec. MCC 1953–62, pres. MCC 1968–69	4.5.1902	16.8.1986
Aislabie Benjamin	Surrey, secretary of MCC 1822–42	14.1.1774	2.6.1842
Alcock Charles William	Secretary of Surrey 1872–1907	2.12.1842	26.2.1907
Editor, Cricket *magazine, 1882–1907. Captain of Wanderers and England football teams.*			
Aleem Dar	Umpire in a record 132 Tests by January 2021	6.6.1968	
Alley William Edward	NSW, Somerset; Test umpire; *CY 1962*	3.2.1919	26.11.2004
Alleyne Mark Wayne	Gloucestershire; *CY 2001*	23.5.1968	
Altham Harry Surtees CBE	Surrey, Hants; historian; pres. MCC 1959–60	30.11.1888	11.3.1965
Arlott Leslie Thomas John OBE	Broadcaster and writer	25.2.1914	14.12.1991
Arthur John Michael	Griq. W, OFS; coach SA 2005–10, Australia 2011–13, Pakistan 2016–19, SL 2019–	17.5.1968	
Ashdown William Henry	Kent	27.12.1898	15.9.1979
The only player to appear in English first-class cricket before and after the two world wars.			
Ash Eileen (*née* Whelan)	England women	30.10.1911	
The longest-lived international cricketer.			
Ashley-Cooper Frederick Samuel	Historian	22.3.1877	31.1.1932
Ashton *Sir* Hubert KBE MC	Cam U, Essex; pres. MCC 1960–61; *CY 1922*	13.2.1898	17.6.1979
Austin *Sir* Harold Bruce Gardiner	Barbados	15.7.1877	27.7.1943
Austin Ian David	Lancashire; *CY 1999*	30.5.1966	
Bailey Jack Arthur	Essex; secretary of MCC 1974–87	22.6.1930	12.7.2018
Bainbridge Philip	Gloucestershire, Durham; *CY 1986*	16.4.1958	
Bakewell Enid (*née* Turton) MBE	England women	16.12.1940	
Bannister John David	Warwickshire; writer and broadcaster	23.8.1930	23.1.2016
Barclay Gregor John	ICC chairman 2020–	19.9.1961	
Barker Gordon	Essex	6.7.1931	10.2.2006
Bartlett Hugh Tryon	Sussex; *CY 1939*	7.10.1914	26.6.1988
Bates Suzannah Wilson	New Zealand women	16.9.1987	
Bayliss Trevor Harley OBE	NSW; coach SL 2007–11, England 2015–19	21.12.1962	
Beauclerk *Rev. Lord* Frederick	Middlesex, Surrey, MCC	8.5.1773	22.4.1850
Beaumont Tamsin Tilley MBE	England women; *CY 2019*	11.3.1991	
Beldam George William	Middlesex; photographer	1.5.1868	23.11.1937
Beldham William ("Silver Billy")	Hambledon, Surrey	5.2.1766	26.2.1862
Beloff Michael Jacob QC	Head of ICC Code of Conduct Commission	18.4.1942	
Benkenstein Dale Martin	KwaZulu-Natal, Durham; *CY 2009*	9.6.1974	
Berry Anthony Scyld Ivens	Editor of *Wisden* 2008–11	28.4.1954	
Berry Leslie George	Leicestershire	28.4.1906	5.2.1985
Bird Harold Dennis ("Dickie") OBE	Yorkshire, Leics; umpire in 66 Tests	19.4.1933	
Blofeld Henry Calthorpe OBE	Cambridge Univ; broadcaster	23.9.1939	
Bond John David	Lancashire; *CY 1971*	6.5.1932	11.7.2019
Booth Roy	Yorkshire, Worcestershire	1.10.1926	24.9.2018

		Born	*Died*
Bowden Brent Fraser ("Billy")	Umpire in 84 Tests	11.4.1963	
Bowley Frederick Lloyd	Worcestershire	9.11.1873	31.5.1943
Bradshaw Keith	Tasmania; secretary/chief executive MCC 2006–11	2.10.1963	
Brewer Derek Michael	Secretary/chief executive MCC 2012–17	2.4.1958	
Briers Nigel Edwin	Leicestershire; *CY 1993*	15.1.1955	
Brittin Janette Ann MBE	England women	4.7.1959	11.9.2017
Brookes Wilfrid H.	Editor of *Wisden* 1936–39	5.12.1894	28.5.1955
Bryan John Lindsay	Kent; *CY 1922*	26.5.1896	23.4.1985
Buchanan John Marshall	Queensland; coach Australia 1999–2007	5.4.1953	
Bucknor Stephen Anthony	Umpire in 128 Tests	31.5.1946	
Bull Frederick George	Essex; *CY 1898*	2.4.1875	16.9.1910
Buller John Sydney MBE	Worcestershire; Test umpire	23.8.1909	7.8.1970
Burnup Cuthbert James	Kent; *CY 1903*	21.11.1875	5.4.1960
Caine Charles Stewart	Editor of *Wisden* 1926–33	28.10.1861	15.4.1933
Calder Harry Lawton	Cranleigh School; *CY 1918*	24.1.1901	15.9.1995
Cardus *Sir* John Frederick Neville	Writer	2.4.1888	27.2.1975
Chalke Stephen Robert	Writer	5.6.1948	
Chandorkar Raghunath Ramachandra	Maharashtra, Bombay	21.11.1920	
Believed to be the oldest living first-class cricketer in February 2021.			
Chapple Glen	Lancashire; *CY 2012*	23.1.1974	
Chester Frank	Worcestershire; Test umpire	20.1.1895	8.4.1957
Stood in 48 Tests between 1924 and 1955, a record that lasted until 1992.			
Clark Belinda Jane	Australia women	10.9.1970	
Clark David Graham	Kent; president MCC 1977–78	27.1.1919	8.10.2013
Clarke Charles Giles CBE	Chairman ECB, 2007–15, pres. ECB, 2015–18	29.5.1953	
Clarke William	Nottinghamshire; founded the All-England XI	24.12.1798	25.8.1856
Collier David Gordon OBE	Chief executive of ECB, 2005–14	22.4.1955	
Collins Arthur Edward Jeune	Clifton College	18.8.1885	11.11.1914
Made 628 in a house match in 1899, the highest score in any cricket until 2016.*			
Conan Doyle *Dr Sir* Arthur Ignatius	MCC	22.5.1859	7.7.1930
Creator of Sherlock Holmes; his only victim in first-class cricket was W. G. Grace.			
Connor Clare Joanne CBE	England women; administrator	1.9.1976	
Constant David John	Kent, Leics; first-class umpire 1969–2006	9.11.1941	
Cook Thomas Edwin Reed	Sussex	5.1.1901	15.1.1950
Cox George jnr	Sussex	23.8.1911	30.3.1985
Cox George snr	Sussex	29.11.1873	24.3.1949
Cozier Winston Anthony Lloyd	Broadcaster and writer	10.7.1940	11.5.2016
Dalmiya Jagmohan	Pres. BCCI 2001–04, 2015, pres. ICC 1997–2000	30.5.1940	20.9.2015
Davies Emrys	Glamorgan; Test umpire	27.6.1904	10.11.1975
Davison Brian Fettes	Rhodesia, Leics, Tasmania, Gloucestershire	21.12.1946	
Dawkes George Owen	Leicestershire, Derbyshire	19.7.1920	10.8.2006
Day Arthur Percival	Kent; *CY 1910*	10.4.1885	22.1.1969
de Lisle Timothy John March Phillipps	Editor of *Wisden* 2003	25.6.1962	
Dennett Edward George	Gloucestershire	27.4.1880	14.9.1937
Deutrom Warren Robert	Chief executive, Cricket Ireland 2006–	13.1.1970	
Dhanawade Pranav Prashant	K. C. Gandhi English School	13.5.2000	
Made the highest score in any cricket, 1,009, in a school match in Mumbai in January 2016.*			
Di Venuto Michael James	Tasmania, Derbys, Durham; coach	12.12.1973	
Domingo Russell Craig	Coach South Africa 2013–17, Bangladesh 2019–	30.8.1974	
Eagar Edward Patrick	Photographer	9.3.1944	
Eddings Earl Robert	Chairman of Cricket Australia 2018–	10.12.1967	
Edwards Charlotte Marie CBE	England women; *CY 2014*	17.12.1979	
Ehsan Mani	President ICC 2003–06; Chairman PCB 2018–	23.3.1945	
Engel Matthew Lewis	Editor of *Wisden* 1993–2000, 2004–07	11.6.1951	
Farbrace Paul	Kent, Middx; coach SL 2014; asst coach Eng. 2014–19	7.7.1967	
"Felix" (Nicholas Wanostrocht)	Kent, Surrey, All-England	4.10.1804	3.9.1876
Batsman, artist, author (Felix on the Bat) *and inventor of the Catapulta bowling machine.*			
Ferguson William Henry BEM	Scorer	6.6.1880	22.9.1957
Scorer and baggage-master for five Test teams on 43 tours over 52 years, and "never lost a bag".			
Findlay William	Oxford U, Lancs; sec. MCC 1926–36	22.6.1880	19.6.1953

		Born	Died
Firth John D'Ewes Evelyn	Winchester College; *CY 1918*	21.2.1900	21.9.1957
Fitzpatrick Cathryn Lorraine	Australia women	4.3.1968	
Fletcher Duncan Andrew Gwynne OBE	Zimbabwe; coach England 1999–2007, India 2011–15	27.9.1948	
Ford Graham Xavier	Natal B; coach SA 1999–2002, SL 2012–14, 2016–17, Ireland 2017–	16.11.1960	
Foster Henry Knollys	Worcestershire; *CY 1911*	30.10.1873	23.6.1950
Frindall William Howard MBE	Statistician	3.3.1939	30.1.2009
Frith David Edward John	Writer	16.3.1937	
Gibbons Harold Harry Ian Haywood	Worcestershire	8.10.1904	16.2.1973
Gibson Clement Herbert	Eton, Cam. U, Sussex, Argentina; *CY 1918*	23.8.1900	31.12.1976
Gibson Norman Alan Stanley	Writer	28.5.1923	10.4.1997
Gore Adrian Clements	Eton College; *CY 1919*	14.5.1900	7.6.1990
Gould Ian James	Middlesex, Sussex; Test umpire	19.8.1957	
Grace *Mrs* Martha	Mother and cricketing mentor of WG	18.7.1812	25.7.1884
Grace William Gilbert jnr	Gloucestershire; son of WG	6.7.1874	2.3.1905
Graveney David Anthony	Gloucestershire, Somerset, Durham	2.1.1953	
Chairman of England selectors 1997–2008.			
Graves Colin James CBE	Chairman of ECB, 2015–20	22.1.1948	
Gray James Roy	Hampshire	19.5.1926	31.10.2016
Gray Malcolm Alexander	President of ICC 2000–03	30.5.1940	
Green David Michael	Lancashire, Gloucestershire; *CY 1969*	10.11.1939	19.3.2016
Grieves Kenneth James	New South Wales, Lancashire	27.8.1925	3.1.1992
Griffith Mike Grenville	Sussex, Camb. Univ; president MCC 2012–13	25.11.1943	
Guha Isa Tara	England women; broadcaster	21.5.1985	
Haigh Gideon Clifford Jeffrey Davidson	Writer	29.12.1965	
Hair Darrell Bruce	Umpire in 78 Tests	30.9.1952	
Hall Louis	Yorkshire; *CY 1890*	1.11.1852	19.11.1915
Hallam Albert William	Lancashire, Nottinghamshire; *CY 1908*	12.11.1869	24.7.1940
Hallam Maurice Raymond	Leicestershire	10.9.1931	1.1.2000
Hallows James	Lancashire; *CY 1905*	14.11.1873	20.5.1910
Hamilton Duncan	Writer	24.12.1958	
Harper Daryl John	Umpire in 95 Tests	23.10.1951	
Harrison Tom William	Derbyshire; chief executive of ECB 2015–	11.12.1971	
Hartley Alfred	Lancashire; *CY 1911*	11.4.1879	9.10.1918
Harvey Ian Joseph	Victoria, Gloucestershire; *CY 2004*	10.4.1972	
Hedges Lionel Paget	Tonbridge School, Kent, Glos; *CY 1919*	13.7.1900	12.1.1933
Henderson Robert	Surrey; *CY 1890*	30.3.1865	28.1.1931
Hesson Michael James	Coach New Zealand 2012–18	30.10.1974	
Hewett Herbert Tremenheere	Somerset; *CY 1893*	25.5.1864	4.3.1921
Heyhoe Flint *Baroness* [Rachael] OBE	England women	11.6.1939	18.1.2017
Hide Mary Edith ("Molly")	England women	24.10.1913	10.9.1995
Hodson Richard Phillip	Cambridge Univ; president MCC 2011–12	26.4.1951	
Horton Henry	Hampshire	18.4.1923	2.11.1998
Howard Cecil Geoffrey	Middlesex; administrator	14.2.1909	8.11.2002
Hughes David Paul	Lancashire; *CY 1988*	13.5.1947	
Huish Frederick Henry	Kent	15.11.1869	16.3.1957
Humpage Geoffrey William	Warwickshire; *CY 1985*	24.4.1954	
Hunter David	Yorkshire	23.2.1860	11.1.1927
Ingleby-Mackenzie Alexander Colin David OBE	Hants; pres. MCC 1996–98	15.9.1933	9.3.2006
Iremonger James	Nottinghamshire; *CY 1903*	5.3.1876	25.3.1956
Isaac Alan Raymond	Chair NZC 2008–10; president ICC 2012–14	20.1.1952	
Jackson Victor Edward	NSW, Leicestershire	25.10.1916	30.1.1965
James Cyril Lionel Robert ("Nello")	Writer	4.1.1901	31.5.1989
Jesty Trevor Edward	Hants, Griq W., Surrey, Lancs; umpire; *CY 1983*	2.6.1948	
Johnson Paul	Nottinghamshire	24.4.1965	
Johnston Brian Alexander CBE MC	Broadcaster	24.6.1912	5.1.1994
Jones Alan MBE	Glamorgan; *CY 1978*	4.11.1938	
Played once for England, against Rest of World in 1970, regarded at the time as a Test match.			
Keightley Lisa Maree	Aust women; coach England women 2019–	26.8.1971	

		Born	*Died*
Kerr Amelia Charlotte	New Zealand women	13.10.2000	
Hit 232, the highest score in women's ODIs, against Ireland in 2018, aged 17.*			
Kilburn James Maurice	Writer	8.7.1909	28.8.1993
King John Barton	Philadelphia	19.10.1873	17.10.1965
"Beyond question the greatest all-round cricketer produced by America" – Wisden.			
Knight Heather Clare OBE	England women; *CY 2018*	26.12.1990	
Knight Roger David Verdon OBE	Surrey, Glos, Sussex; sec. MCC 1994–2005, pres. MCC 2015–16	6.9.1946	
Knight W. H.	Editor of *Wisden* 1864–79	29.11.1812	16.8.1879
Koertzen Rudolf Eric	Umpire in 108 Tests	26.3.1949	
Lacey *Sir* Francis Eden	Hants; secretary of MCC 1898–1926	19.10.1859	26.5.1946
Lamb Timothy Michael	Middx, Northants; ECB chief exec. 1997–2004	24.3.1953	
Langridge John George MBE	Sussex; Test umpire; *CY 1950*	10.2.1910	27.6.1999
Lanning Meghann Moira	Australia women	25.3.1992	
Lavender Guy William	Secretary/chief executive MCC 2017–	8.7.1967	
Lee Peter Granville	Northamptonshire, Lancashire; *CY 1976*	27.8.1945	
Lillywhite Frederick William	Sussex	13.6.1792	21.8.1854
Long Arnold	Surrey, Sussex	18.12.1940	
Lord Thomas	Middlesex; founder of Lord's	23.11.1755	13.1.1832
Lorgat Haroon	Chief executive of ICC 2008–12	26.5.1960	
Lovett Ian Nicholas	President of ECB 2018–	6.9.1944	
Lyon Beverley Hamilton	Gloucestershire; *CY 1931*	19.1.1902	22.6.1970
McEwan Kenneth Scott	Eastern Province, Essex; *CY 1978*	16.7.1952	
McGilvray Alan David MBE	NSW; broadcaster	6.12.1909	17.7.1996
Maclagan Myrtle Ethel	England women	2.4.1911	11.3.1993
MacLaurin *Lord* [Ian Charter]	Chair of ECB 1997–2002, pres. MCC 2017–18	30.3.1937	
Mandhana Smriti Shriniwas	India women	18.7.1996	
Manners John Errol DSC	Hampshire	25.9.1914	7.3.2020
Believed to be the longest-lived first-class cricketer, at 105 years 164 days.			
Manohar Shashank Vyankatesh	Pres. BCCI 2008–11, 2015–16; ICC chairman 2015–20	29.9.1957	
Marlar Robin Geoffrey	Sussex; writer; pres. MCC 2005–06	2.1.1931	
Marshal Alan	Surrey; *CY 1909*	12.6.1883	23.7.1915
Martin-Jenkins Christopher Dennis Alexander MBE	Writer; broadcaster; pres. MCC 2010–11	20.1.1945	1.1.2013
Maxwell James Edward	Commentator	28.7.1950	
Mendis Gehan Dixon	Sussex, Lancashire	20.4.1955	
Mercer John	Sussex, Glamorgan; coach and scorer; *CY 1927*	22.4.1893	31.8.1987
Meyer Rollo John Oliver OBE	Somerset	15.3.1905	9.3.1991
Miller David Andrew	210 ODIs/T20s for South Africa and World XI	10.6.1989	
Modi Lalit Kumar	Chairman, Indian Premier League 2008–10	29.11.1963	
Moles Andrew James	Warwicks; coach NZ 2008–09, Afg 2014–15, 2019	12.2.1961	
Mooney Bethany Louise	Australia women	14.1.1994	
Moores Peter	Sussex; coach England 2007–09, 2014–15	18.12.1962	
Moorhouse Geoffrey	Writer	29.11.1931	26.11.2009
Morgan Derek Clifton	Derbyshire	26.2.1929	4.11.2017
Morgan Frederick David OBE	Chair ECB 2003–07, pres. ICC 2008–10, pres. MCC 2014–15	6.10.1937	
Mynn Alfred	Kent, All-England	19.1.1807	1.11.1861
Neale Phillip Anthony OBE	Worcestershire; England manager; *CY 1989*	5.6.1954	
Newman John Alfred	Hampshire	12.11.1884	21.12.1973
Newstead John Thomas	Yorkshire; *CY 1909*	8.9.1877	25.3.1952
Nicholas Mark Charles Jefford	Hampshire; broadcaster	29.9.1957	
Nicholls Ronald Bernard	Gloucestershire	4.12.1933	21.7.1994
Nixon Paul Andrew	Leicestershire, Kent	21.10.1970	
Nyren John	Hants; author of *The Young Cricketer's Tutor*, 1833	15.12.1764	28.6.1837
Nyren Richard	Hants; Landlord Bat & Ball, Broadhalfpenny Down	1734	25.4.1797
Ontong Rodney Craig	Border, Glamorgan, N. Transvaal	9.9.1955	

		Born	Died
Ormrod Joseph Alan	Worcestershire, Lancashire	22.12.1942	
Pardon Charles Frederick	Editor of *Wisden* 1887–90	28.3.1850	18.4.1890
Pardon Sydney Herbert	Editor of *Wisden* 1891–1925	23.9.1855	20.11.1925
Parks Henry William	Sussex	18.7.1906	7.5.1984
Parr George	Notts, captain/manager of All-England XI	22.5.1826	23.6.1891
Partridge Norman Ernest	Malvern College, Warwickshire; *CY 1919*	10.8.1900	10.3.1982
Pawar Sharadchandra Govindrao	Pres. BCCI 2005–08, ICC 2010–12	12.12.1940	
Payton Wilfred Richard Daniel	Nottinghamshire	13.2.1882	2.5.1943
Pearce Thomas Neill	Essex; administrator	3.11.1905	10.4.1994
Pearson Frederick	Worcestershire	23.9.1880	10.11.1963
Perrin Percival Albert ("Peter")	Essex; *CY 1905*	26.5.1876	20.11.1945
Perry Ellyse Alexandra	Australia women; *CY 2020*	3.11.1990	
Pilch Fuller	Norfolk, Kent	17.3.1804	1.5.1870
"The best batsman that has ever yet appeared" – Arthur Haygarth, 1862.			
Pollard Kieron Adrian	Trinidad & Tobago; 189 ODIs/T20Is for WI	12.5.1987	
Porter James Alexander	Essex; *CY 2018*	25.5.1993	
Preston Hubert	Editor of *Wisden* 1944–51	16.12.1868	6.8.1960
Preston Norman MBE	Editor of *Wisden* 1952–80	18.3.1903	6.3.1980
Pritchard Thomas Leslie	Wellington, Warwickshire, Kent	10.3.1917	22.8.2017
Pybus Richard Alexander	Coach Pak 1999–2003, Bang 2012, WI 2019	5.7.1964	
Rainford-Brent Ebony-Jewel Cora-Lee Camellia Rosamond	England women; broadcaster and coach	31.12.1983	
Rait Kerr *Col.* Rowan Scrope	Europeans; sec. MCC 1936–52	13.4.1891	2.4.1961
Raj Mithali Dorai	India women	3.12.1982	
Reeves William	Essex; Test umpire	22.1.1875	22.3.1944
Rheinberg Netta MBE	England women; writer and administrator	24.10.1911	18.6.2006
Rice Clive Edward Butler	Transvaal, Nottinghamshire; *CY 1981*	23.7.1949	28.7.2015
Richardson Alan	Warwicks, Middx, Worcs; *CY 2012*	6.5.1975	
Roberts Kevin Joseph	NSW; CEO Cricket Australia 2018–20	25.7.1972	
Robertson-Glasgow Raymond Charles	Somerset; writer	15.7.1901	4.3.1965
Robins Derrick Harold	Warwickshire; tour promoter	27.6.1914	3.5.2004
Robinson Mark Andrew OBE	Northants, Yorkshire, Sussex; coach	23.11.1966	
Robinson Raymond John	Writer	8.7.1905	6.7.1982
Roebuck Peter Michael	Somerset; writer; *CY 1988*	6.3.1956	12.11.2011
Rotherham Gerard Alexander	Rugby School, Warwickshire; *CY 1918*	28.5.1899	31.1.1985
Sainsbury Peter James	Hampshire; *CY 1974*	13.6.1934	12.7.2014
Samson Andrew William	Statistician	17.2.1964	
Sawhney Manu	Chief executive of ICC 2019–	1.11.1966	
Sciver Natalie Ruth	England women; *CY 2018*	20.8.1992	
Scott Stanley Winckworth	Middlesex; *CY 1893*	24.3.1854	8.12.1933
Sellers Arthur Brian MBE	Yorkshire; *CY 1940*	5.3.1907	20.2.1981
Seymour James	Kent	25.10.1879	30.9.1930
Shepherd David Robert MBE	Gloucestershire; umpire in 92 Tests	27.12.1940	27.10.2009
Shepherd Donald John	Glamorgan; *CY 1970*	12.8.1927	18.8.2017
Shrubsole Anya MBE	England women; *CY 2018*	7.12.1991	
Silk Dennis Raoul Whitehall CBE	Somerset; pres. MCC 1992–94	8.10.1931	19.6.2019
Simmons Jack MBE	Lancashire, Tasmania; *CY 1985*	28.3.1941	
Skelding Alexander	Leics; first-class umpire 1931–58	5.9.1886	17.4.1960
Smith Sydney Gordon	Northamptonshire; *CY 1915*	15.1.1881	25.10.1963
Smith William Charles ("Razor")	Surrey; *CY 1911*	4.10.1877	15.7.1946
Solanki Vikram Singh	Worcestershire, Surrey, England	1.4.1976	
Southerton Sydney James	Editor of *Wisden* 1934–35	7.7.1874	12.3.1935
Speed Malcolm Walter	Chief executive of ICC 2001–08	14.9.1948	
Spencer Thomas William OBE	Kent; Test umpire	22.3.1914	1.11.1995
Srinivasan Narayanaswami	Pres. BCCI 2011–14; ICC chair 2014–15	3.1.1945	
Stephenson Franklyn Dacosta	Nottinghamshire, Sussex; *CY 1989*	8.4.1959	
Stephenson Harold William	Somerset	18.7.1920	23.4.2008
Stephenson Heathfield Harman	Surrey, All-England	3.5.1832	17.12.1896
Captained first English team to Australia, 1861-62; umpired first Test in England, 1880.			
Stephenson *Lt-Col.* John Robin CBE	Secretary of MCC 1987–93	25.2.1931	2.6.2003

		Born	*Died*
Stevens Darren Ian	Leicestershire, Kent; *CY 2021*	30.4.1976	
Studd *Sir* John Edward Kynaston	Middlesex	26.7.1858	14.1.1944
Lord Mayor of London 1928–29; president of MCC 1930.			
Surridge Walter Stuart	Surrey; *CY 1953*	3.9.1917	13.4.1992
Sutherland James Alexander	Victoria; CEO Cricket Australia 2001–18	14.7.1965	
Suttle Kenneth George	Sussex	25.8.1928	25.3.2005
Swanton Ernest William ("Jim") CBE	Middlesex; writer	11.2.1907	22.1.2000
Tarrant Francis Alfred	Victoria, Middlesex; *CY 1908*	11.12.1880	29.1.1951
Taufel Simon James Arnold	Umpire in 74 Tests	21.1.1971	
Taylor Brian ("Tonker")	Essex; *CY 1972*	19.6.1932	12.6.2017
Taylor Samantha Claire MBE	England women; *CY 2009*	25.9.1975	
Taylor Stafanie Roxann	West Indies women	11.6.1991	
Taylor Tom Launcelot	Yorkshire; *CY 1901*	25.5.1878	16.3.1960
Thornton Charles Inglis ("Buns")	Middlesex	20.3.1850	10.12.1929
Timms John Edward	Northamptonshire	3.11.1906	18.5.1980
Todd Leslie John	Kent	19.6.1907	20.8.1967
Tunnicliffe John	Yorkshire; *CY 1901*	26.8.1866	11.7.1948
Turner Francis Michael MBE	Leicestershire; administrator	8.8.1934	21.7.2015
Turner Robert Julian	Somerset	25.11.1967	
Ufton Derek Gilbert	Kent	31.5.1928	
van der Bijl Vintcent Adriaan Pieter	Natal, Middx, Transvaal; *CY 1981*	19.3.1948	
van Niekerk Dane	South Africa women	14.5.1993	
Virgin Roy Thomas	Somerset, Northamptonshire; *CY 1971*	26.8.1939	
Ward William	Hampshire	24.7.1787	30.6.1849
Scorer of the first recorded double-century: 278 for MCC v Norfolk, 1820.			
Wass Thomas George	Nottinghamshire; *CY 1908*	26.12.1873	27.10.1953
Watmore Ian Charles	Chair of ECB, 2020–	5.7.1958	
Watson Frank	Lancashire	17.9.1898	1.2.1976
Webber Roy	Statistician	23.7.1914	14.11.1962
Weigall Gerald John Villiers	Kent; coach	19.10.1870	17.5.1944
West George H.	Editor of *Wisden* 1880–86	1851	6.10.1896
Wheatley Oswald Stephen CBE	Warwickshire, Glamorgan; *CY 1969*	28.5.1935	
Whitaker Edgar Haddon OBE	Editor of *Wisden* 1940–43	30.8.1908	5.1.1982
Wight Peter Bernard	Somerset; umpire	25.6.1930	31.12.2015
Wilson Elizabeth Rebecca ("Betty")	Australia women	21.11.1921	22.1.2010
Wilson John Victor	Yorkshire; *CY 1961*	17.1.1921	5.6.2008
Wisden John	Sussex	5.9.1826	5.4.1884
"The Little Wonder"; founder of Wisden Cricketers' Almanack, *1864.*			
Wood Cecil John Burditt	Leicestershire	21.11.1875	5.6.1960
Woodcock John Charles OBE	Writer; editor of *Wisden* 1981–86	7.8.1926	
Wooller Wilfred	Glamorgan	20.11.1912	10.3.1997
Wright Graeme Alexander	Editor of *Wisden* 1987–92, 2001–02	23.4.1943	
Wright Levi George	Derbyshire; *CY 1906*	15.1.1862	11.1.1953
Wright Luke James	Leicestershire, Sussex, England	7.3.1985	
Young Douglas Martin	Worcestershire, Gloucestershire	15.4.1924	18.6.1993

CRICKETERS OF THE YEAR, 1889–2021

1889 *Six Great Bowlers of the Year:* J. Briggs, J. J. Ferris, G. A. Lohmann, R. Peel, C. T. B. Turner, S. M. J. Woods.
1890 *Nine Great Batsmen of the Year:* R. Abel, W. Barnes, W. Gunn, L. Hall, R. Henderson, J. M. Read, A. Shrewsbury, F. H. Sugg, A. Ward.
1891 *Five Great Wicketkeepers:* J. M. Blackham, G. MacGregor, R. Pilling, M. Sherwin, H. Wood.
1892 *Five Great Bowlers:* W. Attewell, J. T. Hearne, F. Martin, A. W. Mold, J. W. Sharpe.
1893 *Five Batsmen of the Year:* H. T. Hewett, L. C. H. Palairet, W. W. Read, S. W. Scott, A. E. Stoddart.
1894 *Five All-Round Cricketers:* G. Giffen, A. Hearne, F. S. Jackson, G. H. S. Trott, E. Wainwright.
1895 *Five Young Batsmen of the Season:* W. Brockwell, J. T. Brown, C. B. Fry, T. W. Hayward, A. C. MacLaren.
1896 W. G. Grace.
1897 *Five Cricketers of the Season:* S. E. Gregory, A. A. Lilley, K. S. Ranjitsinhji, T. Richardson, H. Trumble.
1898 *Five Cricketers of the Year:* F. G. Bull, W. R. Cuttell, N. F. Druce, G. L. Jessop, J. R. Mason.
1899 *Five Great Players of the Season:* W. H. Lockwood, W. Rhodes, W. Storer, C. L. Townsend, A. E. Trott.
1900 *Five Cricketers of the Season:* J. Darling, C. Hill, A. O. Jones, M. A. Noble, Major R. M. Poore.
1901 *Mr R. E. Foster and Four Yorkshiremen:* R. E. Foster, S. Haigh, G. H. Hirst, T. L. Taylor, J. Tunnicliffe.
1902 L. C. Braund, C. P. McGahey, F. Mitchell, W. G. Quaife, J. T. Tyldesley.
1903 W. W. Armstrong, C. J. Burnup, J. Iremonger, J. J. Kelly, V. T. Trumper.
1904 C. Blythe, J. Gunn, A. E. Knight, W. Mead, P. F. Warner.
1905 B. J. T. Bosanquet, E. A. Halliwell, J. Hallows, P. A. Perrin, R. H. Spooner.
1906 D. Denton, W. S. Lees, G. J. Thompson, J. Vine, L. G. Wright.
1907 J. N. Crawford, A. Fielder, E. G. Hayes, K. L. Hutchings, N. A. Knox.
1908 A. W. Hallam, R. O. Schwarz, F. A. Tarrant, A. E. E. Vogler, T. G. Wass.
1909 *Lord Hawke and Four Cricketers of the Year:* W. Brearley, Lord Hawke, J. B. Hobbs, A. Marshal, J. T. Newstead.
1910 W. Bardsley, S. F. Barnes, D. W. Carr, A. P. Day, V. S. Ransford.
1911 H. K. Foster, A. Hartley, C. B. Llewellyn, W. C. Smith, F. E. Woolley.
1912 *Five Members of MCC's team in Australia:* F. R. Foster, J. W. Hearne, S. P. Kinneir, C. P. Mead, H. Strudwick.
1913 *Special Portrait:* John Wisden.
1914 M. W. Booth, G. Gunn, J. W. Hitch, A. E. Relf, Hon. L. H. Tennyson.
1915 J. W. H. T. Douglas, P. G. H. Fender, H. T. W. Hardinge, D. J. Knight, S. G. Smith.
1916–17 *No portraits appeared.*
1918 *School Bowlers of the Year:* H. L. Calder, J. D. E. Firth, C. H. Gibson, G. A. Rotherham, G. T. S. Stevens.
1919 *Five Public School Cricketers of the Year:* P. W. Adams, A. P. F. Chapman, A. C. Gore, L. P. Hedges, N. E. Partridge.
1920 *Five Batsmen of the Year:* A. Ducat, E. H. Hendren, P. Holmes, H. Sutcliffe, E. Tyldesley.
1921 *Special Portrait:* P. F. Warner.
1922 H. Ashton, J. L. Bryan, J. M. Gregory, C. G. Macartney, E. A. McDonald.
1923 A. W. Carr, A. P. Freeman, C. W. L. Parker, A. C. Russell, A. Sandham.
1924 *Five Bowlers of the Year:* A. E. R. Gilligan, R. Kilner, G. G. Macaulay, C. H. Parkin, M. W. Tate.
1925 R. H. Catterall, J. C. W. MacBryan, H. W. Taylor, R. K. Tyldesley, W. W. Whysall.
1926 *Special Portrait:* J. B. Hobbs.
1927 G. Geary, H. Larwood, J. Mercer, W. A. Oldfield, W. M. Woodfull.
1928 R. C. Blunt, C. Hallows, W. R. Hammond, D. R. Jardine, V. W. C. Jupp.
1929 L. E. G. Ames, G. Duckworth, M. Leyland, S. J. Staples, J. C. White.
1930 E. H. Bowley, K. S. Duleepsinhji, H. G. Owen-Smith, R. W. V. Robins, R. E. S. Wyatt.
1931 D. G. Bradman, C. V. Grimmett, B. H. Lyon, I. A. R. Peebles, M. J. Turnbull.
1932 W. E. Bowes, C. S. Dempster, James Langridge, Nawab of Pataudi snr, H. Verity.
1933 W. E. Astill, F. R. Brown, A. S. Kennedy, C. K. Nayudu, W. Voce.
1934 A. H. Bakewell, G. A. Headley, M. S. Nichols, L. F. Townsend, C. F. Walters.
1935 S. J. McCabe, W. J. O'Reilly, G. A. E. Paine, W. H. Ponsford, C. I. J. Smith.

1936 H. B. Cameron, E. R. T. Holmes, B. Mitchell, D. Smith, A. W. Wellard.
1937 C. J. Barnett, W. H. Copson, A. R. Gover, V. M. Merchant, T. S. Worthington.
1938 T. W. J. Goddard, J. Hardstaff jnr, L. Hutton, J. H. Parks, E. Paynter.
1939 H. T. Bartlett, W. A. Brown, D. C. S. Compton, K. Farnes, A. Wood.
1940 L. N. Constantine, W. J. Edrich, W. W. Keeton, A. B. Sellers, D. V. P. Wright.
1941–46 No portraits appeared.
1947 A. V. Bedser, L. B. Fishlock, V. (M. H.) Mankad, T. P. B. Smith, C. Washbrook.
1948 M. P. Donnelly, A. Melville, A. D. Nourse, J. D. Robertson, N. W. D. Yardley.
1949 A. L. Hassett, W. A. Johnston, R. R. Lindwall, A. R. Morris, D. Tallon.
1950 T. E. Bailey, R. O. Jenkins, John Langridge, R. T. Simpson, B. Sutcliffe.
1951 T. G. Evans, S. Ramadhin, A. L. Valentine, E. D. Weekes, F. M. M. Worrell.
1952 R. Appleyard, H. E. Dollery, J. C. Laker, P. B. H. May, E. A. B. Rowan.
1953 H. Gimblett, T. W. Graveney, D. S. Sheppard, W. S. Surridge, F. S. Trueman.
1954 R. N. Harvey, G. A. R. Lock, K. R. Miller, J. H. Wardle, W. Watson.
1955 B. Dooland, Fazal Mahmood, W. E. Hollies, J. B. Statham, G. E. Tribe.
1956 M. C. Cowdrey, D. J. Insole, D. J. McGlew, H. J. Tayfield, F. H. Tyson.
1957 D. Brookes, J. W. Burke, M. J. Hilton, G. R. A. Langley, P. E. Richardson.
1958 P. J. Loader, A. J. McIntyre, O. G. Smith, M. J. Stewart, C. L. Walcott.
1959 H. L. Jackson, R. E. Marshall, C. A. Milton, J. R. Reid, D. Shackleton.
1960 K. F. Barrington, D. B. Carr, R. Illingworth, G. Pullar, M. J. K. Smith.
1961 N. A. T. Adcock, E. R. Dexter, R. A. McLean, R. Subba Row, J. V. Wilson.
1962 W. E. Alley, R. Benaud, A. K. Davidson, W. M. Lawry, N. C. O'Neill.
1963 D. Kenyon, Mushtaq Mohammad, P. H. Parfitt, P. J. Sharpe, F. J. Titmus.
1964 D. B. Close, C. C. Griffith, C. C. Hunte, R. B. Kanhai, G. S. Sobers.
1965 G. Boycott, P. J. Burge, J. A. Flavell, G. D. McKenzie, R. B. Simpson.
1966 K. C. Bland, J. H. Edrich, R. C. Motz, P. M. Pollock, R. G. Pollock.
1967 R. W. Barber, B. L. D'Oliveira, C. Milburn, J. T. Murray, S. M. Nurse.
1968 Asif Iqbal, Hanif Mohammad, K. Higgs, J. M. Parks, Nawab of Pataudi jnr.
1969 J. G. Binks, D. M. Green, B. A. Richards, D. L. Underwood, O. S. Wheatley.
1970 B. F. Butcher, A. P. E. Knott, Majid Khan, M. J. Procter, D. J. Shepherd.
1971 J. D. Bond, C. H. Lloyd, B. W. Luckhurst, G. M. Turner, R. T. Virgin.
1972 G. G. Arnold, B. S. Chandrasekhar, L. R. Gibbs, B. Taylor, Zaheer Abbas.
1973 G. S. Chappell, D. K. Lillee, R. A. L. Massie, J. A. Snow, K. R. Stackpole.
1974 K. D. Boyce, B. E. Congdon, K. W. R. Fletcher, R. C. Fredericks, P. J. Sainsbury.
1975 D. L. Amiss, M. H. Denness, N. Gifford, A. W. Greig, A. M. E. Roberts.
1976 I. M. Chappell, P. G. Lee, R. B. McCosker, D. S. Steele, R. A. Woolmer.
1977 J. M. Brearley, C. G. Greenidge, M. A. Holding, I. V. A. Richards, R. W. Taylor.
1978 I. T. Botham, M. Hendrick, A. Jones, K. S. McEwan, R. G. D. Willis.
1979 D. I. Gower, J. K. Lever, C. M. Old, C. T. Radley, J. N. Shepherd.
1980 J. Garner, S. M. Gavaskar, G. A. Gooch, D. W. Randall, B. C. Rose.
1981 K. J. Hughes, R. D. Jackman, A. J. Lamb, C. E. B. Rice, V. A. P. van der Bijl.
1982 T. M. Alderman, A. R. Border, R. J. Hadlee, Javed Miandad, R. W. Marsh.
1983 Imran Khan, T. E. Jesty, A. I. Kallicharran, Kapil Dev, M. D. Marshall.
1984 M. Amarnath, J. V. Coney, J. E. Emburey, M. W. Gatting, C. L. Smith.
1985 M. D. Crowe, H. A. Gomes, G. W. Humpage, J. Simmons, S. Wettimuny.
1986 P. Bainbridge, R. M. Ellison, C. J. McDermott, N. V. Radford, R. T. Robinson.
1987 J. H. Childs, G. A. Hick, D. B. Vengsarkar, C. A. Walsh, J. J. Whitaker.
1988 J. P. Agnew, N. A. Foster, D. P. Hughes, P. M. Roebuck, Salim Malik.
1989 K. J. Barnett, P. J. L. Dujon, P. A. Neale, F. D. Stephenson, S. R. Waugh.
1990 S. J. Cook, D. M. Jones, R. C. Russell, R. A. Smith, M. A. Taylor.
1991 M. A. Atherton, M. Azharuddin, A. R. Butcher, D. L. Haynes, M. E. Waugh.
1992 C. E. L. Ambrose, P. A. J. DeFreitas, A. A. Donald, R. B. Richardson, Waqar Younis.
1993 N. E. Briers, M. D. Moxon, I. D. K. Salisbury, A. J. Stewart, Wasim Akram.
1994 D. C. Boon, I. A. Healy, M. G. Hughes, S. K. Warne, S. L. Watkin.
1995 B. C. Lara, D. E. Malcolm, T. A. Munton, S. J. Rhodes, K. C. Wessels.
1996 D. G. Cork, P. A. de Silva, A. R. C. Fraser, A. Kumble, D. A. Reeve.
1997 S. T. Jayasuriya, Mushtaq Ahmed, Saeed Anwar, P. V. Simmons, S. R. Tendulkar.
1998 M. T. G. Elliott, S. G. Law, G. D. McGrath, M. P. Maynard, G. P. Thorpe.
1999 I. D. Austin, D. Gough, M. Muralitharan, A. Ranatunga, J. N. Rhodes.
2000 C. L. Cairns, R. Dravid, L. Klusener, T. M. Moody, Saqlain Mushtaq.

Cricketers of the Century D. G. Bradman, G. S. Sobers, J. B. Hobbs, S. K. Warne, I. V. A. Richards.

2001 M. W. Alleyne, M. P. Bicknell, A. R. Caddick, J. L. Langer, D. S. Lehmann.
2002 A. Flower, A. C. Gilchrist, J. N. Gillespie, V. V. S. Laxman, D. R. Martyn.
2003 M. L. Hayden, A. J. Hollioake, N. Hussain, S. M. Pollock, M. P. Vaughan.
2004 C. J. Adams, A. Flintoff, I. J. Harvey, G. Kirsten, G. C. Smith.
2005 A. F. Giles, S. J. Harmison, R. W. T. Key, A. J. Strauss, M. E. Trescothick.
2006 M. J. Hoggard, S. P. Jones, B. Lee, K. P. Pietersen, R. T. Ponting.
2007 P. D. Collingwood, D. P. M. D. Jayawardene, Mohammad Yousuf, M. S. Panesar, M. R. Ramprakash.
2008 I. R. Bell, S. Chanderpaul, O. D. Gibson, R. J. Sidebottom, Zaheer Khan.
2009 J. M. Anderson, D. M. Benkenstein, M. V. Boucher, N. D. McKenzie, S. C. Taylor.
2010 S. C. J. Broad, M. J. Clarke, G. Onions, M. J. Prior, G. P. Swann.
2011 E. J. G. Morgan, C. M. W. Read, Tamim Iqbal, I. J. L. Trott.
2012 T. T. Bresnan, G. Chapple, A. N. Cook, A. Richardson, K. C. Sangakkara.
2013 H. M. Amla, N. R. D. Compton, J. H. Kallis, M. N. Samuels, D. W. Steyn.
2014 S. Dhawan, C. M. Edwards, R. J. Harris, C. J. L. Rogers, J. E. Root.
2015 M. M. Ali, G. S. Ballance, A. Lyth, A. D. Mathews, J. S. Patel.
2016 J. M. Bairstow, B. B. McCullum, S. P. D. Smith, B. A. Stokes, K. S. Williamson.
2017 B. M. Duckett, Misbah-ul-Haq, T. S. Roland-Jones, C. R. Woakes, Younis Khan.
2018 S. D. Hope, H. C. Knight, J. A. Porter, N. R. Sciver, A. Shrubsole.
2019 T. T. Beaumont, R. J. Burns, J. C. Buttler, S. M. Curran, V. Kohli.
2020 J. C. Archer, P. J. Cummins, S. R. Harmer, M. Labuschagne, E. A. Perry.
2021 Z. Crawley, J. O. Holder, Mohammad Rizwan, D. P. Sibley, D. I. Stevens.

From 2001 to 2003 the award was made on the basis of all cricket round the world, not just the English season. This ended in 2004 with the start of Wisden's *Leading Cricketer in the World award. Sanath Jayasuriya was chosen in 1997 for his influence on the English season, stemming from the 1996 World Cup. In 2011, only four were named, after the Lord's spot-fixing scandal made one selection unsustainable.*

CRICKETERS OF THE YEAR: AN ANALYSIS

The special portrait of John Wisden in 1913 marked the 50th anniversary of his retirement – and the 50th edition of the Almanack. Wisden died in 1884. The special portraits of P. F. Warner in 1921 and J. B. Hobbs in 1926 followed their earlier selection as a Cricketer of the Year in 1904 and 1909 respectively. These three portraits, and the Cricketers of the Century in 2000, are excluded from the analysis below. The latest five players bring the number chosen since 1889 to 610. They come from 42 different teams, as follows:

Australians	75	Sussex	22	New Zealanders	10	Cranleigh School	1
Surrey	52	Somerset	20	Durham	8	Malvern College	1
Yorkshire	47	Gloucestershire	17	Leicestershire	8	Rugby School	1
Lancashire	35	Worcestershire	17	Oxford Univ	7	Staffordshire	1
Kent	30	Hampshire	16	Sri Lankans	7	Tonbridge School	1
Middlesex	30	Indians	16	England Women	6	Univ College School	1
Nottinghamshire	29	Northamptonshire	15	Eton College	2	Uppingham School	1
South Africans	28	Pakistanis	15	Australia Women	1	Winchester College	1
West Indians	28	Derbyshire	13	Bangladeshis	1	Zimbabweans	1
Warwickshire	27	Glamorgan	13	Berkshire	1		
Essex	26	Cambridge Univ	10	Cheltenham College	1		

Schoolboys were chosen in 1918 and 1919, because first-class cricket had been suspended during the war. The total number of sides comes to 642 because 32 players appeared for more than one side (excluding England men) in the year for which they were chosen.

Types of Player

Of the 610 Cricketers of the Year, 302 are best classified as batsmen, 165 as bowlers, 102 as all-rounders and 41 as wicketkeepers or wicketkeeper-batsmen. *Research: Robert Brooke*

PART NINE
The Almanack

OFFICIAL BODIES

INTERNATIONAL CRICKET COUNCIL

The ICC are world cricket's governing body. They are responsible for managing the playing conditions and Code of Conduct for international fixtures, expanding the game and organising the major tournaments, including World Cups. Their mission statement says the ICC "will lead by providing a world-class environment for international cricket, delivering major events across three formats, providing targeted support to members and promoting the global game".

Twelve national governing bodies are currently Full Members of the ICC; full membership qualifies a nation (or geographic area) to play official Test matches. A candidate for full membership must meet a number of playing and administrative criteria, after which elevation is decided by a vote among existing Full Members. The former categories of associate and affiliate membership merged in 2017; there are currently 92 Associate Members.

The ICC were founded in 1909 as the Imperial Cricket Conference by three Foundation Members: England, Australia and South Africa. Other countries (or geographic areas) became Full Members, and thus acquired Test status, as follows: India, New Zealand and West Indies in 1926, Pakistan in 1952, Sri Lanka in 1981, Zimbabwe in 1992, Bangladesh in 2000, and Afghanistan and Ireland in 2017. South Africa ceased to be a member on leaving the Commonwealth in 1961, but were re-elected as a Full Member in 1991.

In 1965, "Imperial" was replaced by "International", and countries from outside the Commonwealth were elected for the first time. The first Associate Members were Ceylon (later Sri Lanka), Fiji and the USA. Foundation Members retained a veto over all resolutions. In 1989, the renamed International Cricket Council (rather than "Conference") adopted revised rules, aimed at producing an organisation which could make a larger number of binding decisions, rather than simply make recommendations to national governing bodies. In 1993, the Council, previously administered by MCC, gained their own secretariat and chief executive. The category of Foundation Member was abolished.

In 1997, the Council became an incorporated body, with an executive board, and a president instead of a chairman. The ICC remained at Lord's, with a commercial base in Monaco, until August 2005, when after 96 years they moved to Dubai in the United Arab Emirates, which offered organisational and tax advantages.

In 2014, the ICC board approved a new structure, under which they were led by a chairman again, while India, Australia and England took permanent places on key committees. But in 2016 the special privileges given to these three were dismantled and, in early 2017, the board agreed to revise the constitution on more egalitarian lines.

Officers

Chair: G. J. Barclay. *Deputy Chair:* I. Khwaja. *Chief Executive:* M. Sawhney.

Committee Chairs – Chief Executives' Committee: M. Sawhney. *Cricket:* A. Kumble. *Audit:* Y. Narayan. *Finance and Commercial Affairs:* Ehsan Mani. *Nominations Committee:* G. J. Barclay. *Code of Conduct Commission:* M. J. Beloff QC. *Women's Committee:* C. J. Connor. *Development:* I. Khwaja. *Disputes Resolution Committee:* M. J. Beloff QC. *Membership:* I. Khwaja. *Medical Advisory:* Dr P. Harcourt. *Anti-Corruption Oversight:* D. Howman. *HR & Remuneration:* I. C. Watmore. *Anti-Corruption Unit Chair:* Sir Ronnie Flanagan. *ICC Ethics Officer:* P. Nicholson.

ICC Board: The chair and chief executive sit on the board *ex officio*. They are joined by I. K. Nooyi (independent female director), E. R. Eddings (Australia), Ehsan Mani (Pakistan), Farhan Yusefzai (Afghanistan), S. C. Ganguly (India), I. Khwaja (Singapore), R. A. McCollum (Ireland), T. Mukuhlani (Zimbabwe), Nazmul Hassan (Bangladesh), R. Richards (South Africa), A. S. S. Silva (Sri Lanka), R. O. Skerritt (West Indies), M. C. Snedden (New Zealand), N. Speight (Bermuda), M. Vallipuram (Malaysia), I. C. Watmore (England).

Chief Executives' Committee: The chief executive, chair and the chairs of the cricket and women's committees sit on this committee *ex officio*. They are joined by the chief executives of the 12 Full Member boards and three Associate Member boards: S. Damodar (Botswana), A. M. de Silva (Sri Lanka), W. R. Deutrom (Ireland), J. M. Grave (West Indies), T. W. Harrison (England), N. Hockley (Australia), W. G. Khan (Pakistan), G. Makoni (Zimbabwe), P. Moseki (South Africa), Nizam Uddin Chowdhury (Bangladesh), Rahmatullah Qureishi (Afghanistan), J. Shah (India), M. Stafford (Vanuatu), D. J. White (New Zealand), plus one further Associate member.

Cricket Committee: The chief executive and chair sit on the committee *ex officio*. They are joined by A. Kumble (*chair*), J. M. Arthur, K. J. Coetzer, R. Dravid, R. K. Illingworth, D. P. M. D. Jayawardene, D. Kendix, R. S. Madugalle, T. B. A. May, S. M. Pollock, J. P. Stephenson, A. J. Strauss, D. J. White.

Chief Financial Officer: A. Khanna. *Chief Commercial Officer:* A. Dahiya. *General Counsel/Company Secretary:* J. Hall. *General Manager – Cricket:* G. J. Allardice. *General Manager – Integrity Unit:* A. J. Marshall. *General Manager – Marketing & Communications:* C. Furlong. *General Manager – Development:* W. Glenwright. *Head of Events:* C. M. B. Tetley. *Head of Internal Audit:* Muhammad Ali. *Senior Manager Broadcast/Executive Producer – ICC TV:* A. Ramachandran.

Membership

Full Members (12): Afghanistan, Australia, Bangladesh, England, India, Ireland, New Zealand, Pakistan, South Africa, Sri Lanka, West Indies and Zimbabwe.

Associate Members* (92):

Africa (19): Botswana (2005), Cameroon (2007), Eswatini (formerly Swaziland) (2007), Gambia (2002), Ghana (2002), Kenya (1981), Lesotho (2001), Malawi (2003), Mali (2005), Mozambique (2003), Namibia (1992), Nigeria (2002), Rwanda (2003), St Helena (2001), Seychelles (2010), Sierra Leone (2002), Tanzania (2001), Uganda (1998), Zambia (2003).

Americas (16): Argentina (1974), Bahamas (1987), Belize (1997), Bermuda (1966), Brazil (2002), Canada (1968), Cayman Islands (2002), Chile (2002), Costa Rica (2002), Falkland Islands (2007), Mexico (2004), Panama (2002), Peru (2007), Suriname (2002), Turks & Caicos Islands (2002), USA (1965/2019).

Asia (16): Bahrain (2001), Bhutan (2001), China (2004), Hong Kong (1969), Iran (2003), Kuwait (2005), Malaysia (1967), Maldives (2001), Myanmar (2006), Nepal (1996), Oman (2000), Qatar (1999), Saudi Arabia (2003), Singapore (1974), Thailand (2005), United Arab Emirates (1990).

East Asia Pacific (9): Cook Islands (2000), Fiji (1965), Indonesia (2001), Japan (2005), Papua New Guinea (1973), Philippines (2000), Samoa (2000), South Korea (2001), Vanuatu (1995).

Europe (32): Austria (1992), Belgium (2005), Bulgaria (2008), Croatia (2001), Cyprus (1999), Czech Republic (2000), Denmark (1966), Estonia (2008), Finland (2000), France (1998), Germany (1999), Gibraltar (1969), Greece (1995), Guernsey (2005), Hungary (2012), Isle of Man (2004), Israel (1974), Italy (1995), Jersey (2007), Luxembourg (1998), Malta (1998), Netherlands (1966), Norway (2000), Portugal (1996), Romania (2013), Russia (2012), Scotland (1994), Serbia (2015), Slovenia (2005), Spain (1992), Sweden (1997), Turkey (2008).

* *Year of election shown in parentheses. Switzerland (1985) were removed in 2012; Cuba (2002) and Tonga (2000) in 2013; Brunei (1992) in 2014; the USA in 2017, though a new USA body were admitted in 2019; and Morocco (1999) in 2019. Croatia and Zambia were suspended in 2019.*

Full Members are the governing bodies for cricket of a country recognised by the ICC, or nations associated for cricket purposes, or a geographical area, from which representative teams are qualified to play official Test matches.

Associate Members are the governing bodies for cricket of a country recognised by the ICC, or countries associated for cricket purposes, or a geographical area, which does not qualify as a Full Member, but where cricket is firmly established and organised.

Addresses

ICC Street 69, Dubai Sports City, Sh Mohammed Bin Zayed Road, PO Box 500 070, Dubai, United Arab Emirates (+971 4382 8800; www.icc-cricket.com; enquiry@icc-cricket.com; Twitter: @ICC).

Afghanistan Afghanistan Cricket Board, Kabul International Cricket Stadium, Kabul Nandari, District 8, Kabul (+93 78 813 3144; www.cricket.af; info@afghancricket.af; @ACBofficials).

Australia Cricket Australia, 60 Jolimont Street, Jolimont, Victoria 3002 (+61 3 9653 9999; www.cricketaustralia.com.au; public.enquiries@cricket.com.au; @CricketAus).

Bangladesh Bangladesh Cricket Board, Sher-e-Bangla National Cricket Stadium, Mirpur, Dhaka 1216 (+880 2 803 1001; www.tigercricket.com.bd; info@tigercricket.com.bd; @BCBtigers).

England England and Wales Cricket Board (see below).

India Board of Control for Cricket in India, Cricket Centre, 4th Floor, Wankhede Stadium, D Road, Churchgate, Mumbai 400 020 (+91 22 2289 8800; www.bcci.tv; office@bcci.tv; @BCCI).

Ireland Cricket Ireland, 15c Kinsealy Business Park, Kinsealy, Co Dublin K36 YH61 (+353 1 894 7914; www.cricketireland.ie; info@cricketireland.ie; @CricketIreland).

New Zealand New Zealand Cricket, PO Box 8353, Level 4, 8 Nugent Street, Grafton, Auckland 1023 (+64 9 393 9700; www.nzc.nz; info@nzcricket.org.nz; @Blackcaps).

Pakistan Pakistan Cricket Board, Gaddafi Stadium, Ferozpur Road, Lahore 54600 (+92 42 3571 7231; www.pcb.com.pk; inquiry@pcb.com.pk; @TheRealPCB).

South Africa Cricket South Africa, PO Box 55009 Northlands 2116; 86, 5th & Glenhove St, Melrose Estate, Johannesburg (+27 11 880 2810; www.cricket.co.za; info@cricket.co.za; @OfficialCSA).

Sri Lanka Sri Lanka Cricket, 35 Maitland Place, Colombo 07000 (+94 112 681 601; www.srilankacricket.lk; info@srilankacricket.lk; @OfficialSLC).

West Indies West Indies Cricket Board, PO Box 616 W, Factory Road, St John's, Antigua (+1 268 481 2450; www.windiescricket.com; wicb@windiescricket.com; @windiescricket).

Zimbabwe Zimbabwe Cricket, PO Box 2739, 28 Maiden Drive, Highlands, Harare (+263 4 788 090; www.zimcricket.org; info@zimcricket.org; @ZimCricketv).

Associate Members' addresses may be found on the ICC website, www.icc-cricket.com.

ENGLAND AND WALES CRICKET BOARD

The England and Wales Cricket Board (ECB) are responsible for the administration of all cricket – professional and recreational – in England and Wales. In 1997, they took over the functions of the Cricket Council, the Test and County Cricket Board and the National Cricket Association, which had run the game since 1968. In 2005, a streamlined constitution replaced a Management Board of 18 with a 12-strong Board of Directors, three appointed by the first-class counties, two by the county boards. In 2010, this expanded to 14, and added the ECB's first women directors. After a governance review, it returned to 12, including four independent non-executive directors, in 2018.

Officers

President: I. N. Lovett. *Chair:* I. C. Watmore. *Chief Executive Officer:* T. W. Harrison.

Board of Directors: K. Bickerstaffe, D. M. Bushell, M. Darlow, A. P. Dickinson, T. W. Harrison, R. M. Kalifa, B. J. O'Brien, L. C. Pearson, S. A. Smith, B. D. H. Trenowden, I. C. Watmore, J. H. Wood.

Committee Chairs – Anti-Corruption: M. Darlow. *Finance, Audit & Risk:* A. P. Dickinson. *Environmental, Social & Governance:* B. D. H. Trenowden. *Cricket:* Sir Andrew Strauss. *Discipline:* T. J. G. O'Gorman. *Recreational Assembly:* J. H. Wood. *Regulatory:* N. I. Coward. *Remuneration:* I. C. Watmore.

Chief Operating Officer: D. J. Mahoney. *Chief Financial Officer:* S. A. Smith. *Chief Commercial Officer:* T. Singh. *Managing Director, Special Projects:* S. Elworthy. *Managing Director, County Cricket:* N. Snowball. *Managing Director, The Hundred:* S. Patel. *Managing Director, England Men's Cricket:* A. F. Giles. *Managing Director, England Women's Cricket:* C. J. Connor. *Director, Communications:* K. Miller. *People Director:* C. F. Dale.

National Selector: E. T. Smith. *Selector:* J. W. A. Taylor.

ECB: Lord's Ground, London NW8 8QZ (020 7432 1200; www.ecb.co.uk; feedback@ecb.co.uk; Twitter @ECB_cricket).

THE MARYLEBONE CRICKET CLUB

The Marylebone Cricket Club evolved out of the White Conduit Club in 1787, when Thomas Lord laid out his first ground in Dorset Square. Their members revised the Laws in 1788 and gradually took responsibility for cricket throughout the world. However, they relinquished control of the game in the UK in 1968, and the International Cricket Council finally established their own secretariat in 1993. MCC still own Lord's, and remain the guardian of the Laws. They call themselves "a private club with a public function", and aim to support cricket everywhere, especially at grassroots level and in countries where the game is least developed.

Patron: HER MAJESTY THE QUEEN

Officers

President: 2019–21 – K. C. Sangakkara. *Club Chairman:* G. M. N. Corbett. *Treasurer:* A. B. Elgood. *Trustees:* P. A. B. Beecroft, M. V. Fleming, R. S. Leigh. *Hon. Life Vice-Presidents:* E. R. Dexter, C. A. Fry, M. G. Griffith, A. R. Lewis, Sir Oliver Popplewell, O. H. J. Stocken, M. O. C. Sturt, J. C. Woodcock.

C. J. Connor was due to succeed Sangakkara in October 2021.

Chief Executive and Secretary: G. W. Lavender. *Assistant Secretaries – Cricket:* J. P. Stephenson. *Finance:* A. D. Cameron. *Membership and Operations:* G. P. E. Curry. *Estates:* R. J. Ebdon. *Commercial:* A. N. Muggleton. *Legal:* H. A. Roper-Curzon.

MCC Committee: J. M. Brearley, R. Q. Cake, A. R. C. Fraser, N. J. C. Gandon, V. K. Griffiths, C. M. Gupte, W. J. House, S. P. Hughes, G. W. Jones, M. C. J. Nicholas, N. M. Peters, G. J. Toogood. The president, club chairman, treasurer and committee chairs are also on the committee.

Committee Chairs – Cricket: S. C. Taylor. *Estates:* A. J. Johnston. *Finance:* A. B. Elgood. *Heritage and Collections:* J. O. D. Orders. *Membership and General Purposes:* Sir Ian Magee. *World Cricket:* M. W. Gatting.

MCC: Lord's Ground, London NW8 8QN (020 7616 8500; www.lords.org; reception@mcc.org.uk; Twitter@MCCOfficial. Tickets 020 7432 1000; ticketing@mcc.org.uk).

PROFESSIONAL CRICKETERS' ASSOCIATION

The Professional Cricketers' Association were formed in 1967 (as the Cricketers' Association) to be the collective voice of first-class professional players, and enhance and protect their interests. During the 1970s, they succeeded in establishing pension schemes and a minimum wage. In recent years, their strong commercial operations and greater funding from the ECB have increased their services to current and past players, including education, legal and financial help. In 2011, these services were extended to England's women cricketers.

President: G. A. Gooch. *Chair:* J. A. R. Harris. *Vice-chair:* H. C. Knight. *President – Professional Cricketers' Trust:* D. A. Graveney. *Non-Executive Chair:* J. R. Metherell. *Non-Executive Directors:* I. T. Guha, P. G. Read, S. N. White. *Chief Executive:* R. K. Lynch. *Director of Member Services:* I. J. Thomas. *Director of Cricket Operations:* D. K. H. Mitchell. *Director of Finance:* P. Garrett. *Commercial Manager:* A. Phipps. *Head of Fundraising:* K. Ford. *Head of Player Rights and Women's Cricket:* E. M. Reid. *Player Rights Manager:* E. Caldwell. *Head of Communications:* L. Reynolds. *Membership Services Manager:* A. Prosser. *Head of Cricket Operations:* R. Hudson.

PCA: *London Office* – The Bedser Stand, The Oval, Kennington, London SE11 5SS (0207 449 4228; www.thepca.co.uk; communications@thepca.co.uk; Twitter @PCA). *Birmingham Office* – Box 108–9, R. E. S. Wyatt Stand, Edgbaston Stadium, Birmingham B5 7QU.

CRIME AND PUNISHMENT

ICC Code of Conduct – Breaches and Penalties in 2019-20 to 2020-21

B. R. M. Taylor Zimbabwe v Sri Lanka, Second Test at Harare.
Expressed dissent, looking at bat when given lbw. 15% fine/1 demerit pt – J. Srinath.

Abu Jayed Bangladesh v Pakistan, First Test at Rawalpindi.
Provocative close celebration on dismissing Azhar Ali. Reprimand/1 demerit pt – R. B. Richardson.

J. B. Little Ireland v England, 2nd ODI at Southampton.
Inappropriate language on dismissing J. M. Bairstow. Reprimand/1 demerit pt – P. Whitticase.

S. C. J. Broad England v Pakistan, First Test at Manchester.
Inappropriate language on dismissing Yasir Shah. 15% fine/1 demerit pt – B. C. Broad.

D. J. Mitchell New Zealand v West Indies, First Test at Hamilton.
Obscene language as J. O. Holder ran between wickets. 15% fine/1 demerit pt – J. J. Crowe.

K. A. Jamieson New Zealand v Pakistan, First Test at Mount Maunganui.
Throwing ball dangerously close to Fahim Ashraf. 25% fine/1 demerit pt – J. J. Crowe.

T. D. Paine Australia v India, Third Test at Sydney.
Swearing at on-field umpire after unsuccessful DRS review. 15% fine/1 demerit pt – D. C. Boon.

Twelve further breaches took place in Associate Member or Under-19 internationals during this period, ten of them in the Under-19 World Cup.

Under ICC regulations on minor over-rate offences, captains and players are fined 20% of their match fee for every over their side failed to bowl in the allotted time. There were ten instances in Full Member men's internationals reported in this edition of Wisden.

V. Kohli/India v New Zealand, 4th T20I at Wellington, 40% – B. C. Broad.

R. G. Sharma/India v New Zealand, 5th T20I at Mount Maunganui, 20% – B. C. Broad.

V. Kohli/India v New Zealand, 1st ODI at Hamilton, 80% – B. C. Broad.

T. W. M. Latham/New Zealand v India, 2nd ODI at Auckland, 60% – B. C. Broad.

Q. de Kock/South Africa v Australia, 1st T20I at Johannesburg, 20% – A. J. Pycroft.

K. A. Pollard/West Indies v Sri Lanka, 1st ODI at Colombo (SSC), 40% – J. Srinath.

E. J. G. Morgan/England v Australia, 1st T20I at Southampton, 20% – B. C. Broad.

V. Kohli/India v Australia, 1st ODI at Sydney, 20% – D. C. Boon.
India were also fined one point in the World Cup Super League.

V. Kohli/India v Australia, 3rd T20I at Sydney, 20% – D. C. Boon.

T. D. Paine/Australia v India, 2nd Test at Melbourne, 40% – D. C. Boon.
Australia were also fined four points in the World Test Championship.

There was one further instance in an Associate Member international.

INTERNATIONAL UMPIRES' PANELS

In 1993, the ICC formed an international umpires' panel, containing at least two officials from each Full Member. A third-country umpire from this panel stood with a home umpire in every Test from 1994 onwards. In 2002, an elite panel was appointed: two elite umpires – both independent – were to stand in all Tests, and at least one in every ODI, where one home umpire was allowed. (During the pandemic, local umpires were used.) A supporting panel of international umpires was created to provide cover at peak times in the Test schedule, second umpires in one-day internationals, and third umpires to give rulings from TV replays. There is also a panel of development umpires, mostly drawn from Associate Members but also including several female umpires from Full Members. The panels are sponsored by Emirates Airlines.

The elite panel at the start of 2021: Aleem Dar (P), H. D. P. K. Dharmasena (SL), M. Erasmus (SA), C. B. Gaffaney (NZ), M. A. Gough (E), R. K. Illingworth (E), R. A. Kettleborough (E), N. N. Menon (India), B. N. J. Oxenford (A), P. R. Reiffel (A), R. J. Tucker (A), J. S. Wilson (WI).

The international panel: G. A. Abood (A), Ahmed Shah Durrani (Afg), Ahmed Shah Pakteen (Afg), Ahsan Raza (P), K. N. Ananthapadmanabhan (I), Asif Yaqoob (P), Bismillah Shinwari (Afg), R. E. Black (Ire), G. O. Brathwaite (WI), C. M. Brown (NZ), M. Burns (E), I. Chabi (Z), A. K. Chowdhury (I), S. A. J. Craig (A), N. Duguid (WI), Gazi Sohel (B), S. George (SA), P. A. Gustard (WI), S. B. Haig (NZ), L. E. Hannibal (SL), M. Hawthorne (Ire), A. T. Holdstock (SA), Izatullah Safi (Afg), P. B. Jele (SA), W. R. Knights (NZ), Masudur Rahman (B), D. J. Millns (E), F. Mutizwa (Z), A. J. Neill (Ire), S. J. Nogajski (A), A. Paleker (SA), R. S. A. Palliyaguruge (SL), C. Phiri (Z), R. M. P. J. Rambukwella (SL), Rashid Riaz (P), L. S. Reifer (WI), P. A. Reynolds (Ire), L. Rusere (Z), M. J. Saggers (E), C. Shamshuddin (I), Sharfuddoula (B), V. K. Sharma (I), Shozab Raza (P), Tanvir Ahmed (B), A. G. Wharf (E), P. Wilson (A), R. R. Wimalasiri (SL).

ICC development panel: L. Agenbag (SA), Akbar Ali (UAE), V. R. Angara (Botswana), S. N. Bandekar (USA), E. Carrington (Bermuda), K. D. Cotton (NZ), R. D'Mello (Kenya), A. J. T. Dowdalls (Scotland), H. Grewal (Canada), D. A. Haggo (Scotland), Harikrishna Pillai (Oman), R. Hassan (Italy), Iftikhar Ali (UAE), M. Jameson (Germany), N. Janani (I), H. K. G. Jansen (Netherlands), J. Jensen (Denmark), V. K. Jha (Nepal), A. Kapa (PNG), H. E. Kearns (Jersey), J. A. Lindo (USA), A. W. Louw (Namibia), D. H. McLean (Scotland), A. R. Maddela (Canada), V. P. Mallela (USA), P. M. Musoke (Uganda), L. Oala (PNG), D. Odhiambo (Kenya), B. Olewale (PNG), I. O. Oyieko (Kenya), C. A. Polosak (A), B. B. Pradhan (Nepal), S. S. Prasad (Singapore), Rahul Asher (Oman), A. K. Rana (Thailand), V. G. Rathi (I), S. Redfern (E), Rizwan Akram (Netherlands), F. T. Samura (Sierra Leone), C. Schumacher (Namibia), E. Sheridan (A), Shiju Sam (UAE), Shivani Mishra (Qatar), D. N. Subedi (Nepal), S. Subramanian (Indonesia), Tabarak Dar (Hong Kong), I. A. Thomson (Hong Kong), C. H. Thorburn (Namibia), A. van der Dries (Netherlands), W. P. M. van Liemt (Netherlands), Vinod Babu (Oman), K. Viswanadan (Malaysia), M. V. Waldron (Ire), J. M. Williams (WI).

ICC REFEREES' PANEL

In 1991, the ICC formed a panel of referees to enforce their Code of Conduct for Tests and one-day internationals, and to support the umpires in upholding the game's conduct. In 2002, the ICC launched an elite panel, on full-time contracts, for all international cricket, sponsored by Emirates Airlines. At the start of 2021, it consisted of D. C. Boon (A), B. C. Broad (E), J. J. Crowe (NZ), R. S. Madugalle (SL), A. J. Pycroft (Z), R. B. Richardson (WI), J. Srinath (I).

A further panel of international referees consisted of Akhtar Ahmad (B), Anis Sheikh (P), G. A. V. Baxter (NZ), S. R. Bernard (A), O. Chirombe (Z), E. T. Dube (Z), S. A. Fritz (SA), K. Gallagher (Ire), Hamim Talwar (Afg), D. O. Hayles (WI), R. E. Hayward (NZ), D. T. Jukes (E), R. D. King (WI), G. F. Labrooy (SL), W. C. Labrooy (SL), G. S. Lakshmi (I), G. McCrea (Ire), Mohammad Javed (P), V. Narayanan Kutty (I), M. Nayyar (I), Neeyamur Rashid (B), W. M. Noon (E), G. H. Pienaar (SA), R. W. Stratford (A), S. Wadvalla (SA), P. Whitticase (E), Zarab Shah Zaheer (Afg).

ENGLISH UMPIRES FOR 2021

First-class: R. J. Bailey, N. L. Bainton, P. K. Baldwin, I. D. Blackwell, M. Burns, N. G. B. Cook, B. J. Debenham, M. A. Gough, I. J. Gould, P. J. Hartley, R. K. Illingworth, R. A. Kettleborough, N. J. Llong, G. D. Lloyd, N. A. Mallender, D. J. Millns, S. J. O'Shaughnessy, P. R. Pollard, R. T. Robinson, M. J. Saggers, B. V. Taylor, R. J. Warren, A. G. Wharf. *Reserves:* Hassan Adnan, T. Lungley, J. D. Middlebrook, M. Newell, N. Pratt, I. N. Ramage, C. M. Watts, R. A. White.

THE DUCKWORTH/LEWIS/STERN METHOD

In 1997, the ECB's one-day competitions adopted a new method to revise targets in interrupted games, devised by Frank Duckworth of the Royal Statistical Society and Tony Lewis (see Obituaries) of the University of the West of England. The method was gradually taken up by other countries and, in 1999, the ICC decided to incorporate it into the standard playing conditions for one-day internationals.

The system aims to preserve any advantage that one team have established before the interruption. It uses the idea that teams have two resources from which they make runs – an allocated number of overs, and ten wickets. It also takes into account when the interruption occurs, because of the different scoring-rates typical of different stages of an innings. Traditional run-rate calculations relied only on the overs available, and ignored wickets lost.

It uses one table with 50 rows, covering matches of up to 50 overs, and ten columns, from nought to nine wickets down. Each figure gives the percentage of the total runs that would, on average, be scored with a certain number of overs left and wickets lost. If a match is shortened before it begins, to, say, 33 overs a side, the figure for 33 overs and ten wickets remaining would be the starting point.

If overs are lost, the table is used to calculate the percentage of runs the team would be expected to score in those missing overs. This is obtained by reading the figure for the number of overs left, and wickets down, when play stops, and subtracting the figure for the number of overs left when it resumes. If the delay occurs between innings, and the second team's allocation of overs is reduced, then their target is obtained by calculating the appropriate percentage for the reduced number of overs with all ten wickets standing. For instance, if the second team's innings halves from 50 overs to 25, the table shows that they still have 66.5% of their resources left, so have to beat two-thirds of the first team's total, rather than half. If the first innings is complete and the second innings interrupted or prematurely terminated, the score to beat is reduced by the percentage of the innings lost.

The version known as the "Professional Edition" was introduced into one-day internationals from 2003, and subsequently into most national one-day competitions. Using a more advanced mathematical formula (it is entirely computerised), it adjusts the tables to allow for the different scoring-rates that emerge in matches with above-average first-innings scores. In 2014, analysis by Steven Stern, an Australian professor of data science, indicated further modification was needed; Stern, based at Bond University in Queensland, became responsible for the method after Duckworth and Lewis retired. The Duckworth/Lewis/Stern method is now used in all one-day and Twenty20 internationals, as well as most national competitions. The original "Standard Edition" is used where computers are unavailable, and at lower levels of the game.

The system also covers first-innings interruptions, multiple interruptions and innings ended by rain. The tables are revised slightly every two years, taking account of changing scoring-rates; the average total in a 50-over international is now 259 (slightly down from 263 – the first time the average has decreased, after a steady rise from 225 in 1999).

In the World Cup semi-final between South Africa and New Zealand at Auckland in March 2015, South Africa were 216 for three from 38 overs when seven overs were lost to rain; after the innings resumed, they finished on 281. With three wickets down, the lost overs constituted 14.85% of South Africa's scoring resources, meaning they used only 85.15%. By contrast, New Zealand's 43-over chase constituted 90% of the resources of a full innings. Their revised target was determined by multiplying South Africa's total, 281, by 90% divided by 85.15% and adding one run: 281 x (90/85.15) + 1 = 298. New Zealand scored 299 for six in 42.5 overs to win, with a six off the penultimate delivery. Had South Africa been two down at the interruption, the lost overs would have constituted a higher percentage of their scoring resources; the revised target would have been 301, and New Zealand would have needed two more runs off the final ball.

A similar system, usually known as the VJD method, is used in some domestic matches in India. It was devised by V. Jayadevan, a civil engineer from Kerala.

POWERPLAYS

In one-day and Twenty20 internationals, two semi-circles of 30-yard (27.43 metres) radius are drawn on the field behind each set of stumps, joined by straight lines parallel to the pitch.

At the instant of delivery in the first ten overs of an uninterrupted one-day international innings (the first six overs in a Twenty20 international), only two fielders may be positioned outside this fielding restriction area. During the next 30 overs no more than four fielders may be stationed outside the area; and in the final ten overs, no more than five. (In Twenty20 internationals, no more than five may be positioned outside the area for the last 14 overs.) In matches affected by the weather, the number of overs in each powerplay stage is reduced in proportion to the overall reduction of overs.

MEETINGS AND DECISIONS IN 2020

ECB – ENGLISH SEASON

On March 20, the ECB Board announced that, after discussions with the first-class counties, MCC and the Professional Cricketers' Association, no professional cricket would be played in England or Wales until at least May 28 because of Covid-19. (Two days earlier, they had recommended the suspension of all recreational cricket.) They were working on possible revised schedules to begin later in the season, delivering as much international and domestic cricket as possible, and were liaising with the government on whether the season could begin behind closed doors, with live broadcasts.

ICC BOARD

The ICC Board met on March 27, by teleconference because of the Covid-19 pandemic. Sourav Ganguly, the current BCCI president, was welcomed as India's new representative on the board.

They discussed the pandemic's effect on cricket across the globe, and the ICC's contingency planning to adapt to the evolving situation. Cricket Australia were thanked for their successful staging of the women's T20 World Cup, which had finished on March 8. The board approved audited financial statements for 2019, and the final accounts for the men's World Cup and T20 World Cup Qualifier, both staged in 2019.

ECB SUPPORT PACKAGES

The ECB announced a £61m interim support package, to help professional and recreational cricket withstand the financial impact of Covid-19, on March 31.

For the professional game, around £40m was made available to support cash-flow challenges, through the early release of the May-to-July distributions to first-class counties and county cricket boards, and two years' worth of funds for facilities maintenance (whose use would not be restricted to facilities maintenance), plus a further £5.5m for counties not currently eligible for this. International staging fees were suspended for four months, and waived where matches could not be played as scheduled.

For the recreational game, an extra budget of just over £20m was available through a club support loan scheme, grants, and a 12-month holiday on clubs' loan repayments.

Meanwhile, the ECB announced cost-cutting measures, including a two-month staff pay cut ranging from 25% (for chief executive Tom Harrison) to 10%, and furloughing some staff, while job recruitment was frozen for all but critical roles.

On April 17, the ECB added further aid for clubs and leagues, as part of the same £61m support package. An emergency loan scheme would help affiliated clubs cover shortfalls in essential day-to-day running and maintenance costs (such as utility costs, rent, security, insurance) for up to 12 months. Clubs with junior sections could apply for £1,000 to £5,000; adults-only clubs were capped at £3,000. A grant scheme provided clubs and leagues with assistance in exceptional circumstances where other sources of support were not available, e.g. because their constitution ruled out loans. Clubs with junior sections could apply for up to £3,000; adults-only clubs up to £1,000; and leagues (open-age or junior) up to £2,000.

A third emergency funding scheme, for leagues, was added on May 7. Open-age and junior leagues affiliated to the ECB (whether directly or via their county cricket board or other bodies) could apply for an interest-free loan of up to £50,000 to assist with the cost of cricket balls and unrecoverable costs such as the hire of grounds, production of league handbooks, purchase of kit and staging events.

ICC CHIEF EXECUTIVES' COMMITTEE

On April 23, the ICC hosted a chief executives' committee meeting via conference call to consider the impact of Covid-19. There were updates from the 12 Full Members plus three of the Associates on the situation in their own countries, and on contingency planning for global events, including the men's T20 World Cup in 2020 and the women's World Cup in 2021.

They agreed to review the Future Tours Programme up to 2023, and to reschedule as many postponed series as possible. Decisions would be made on the FTP, the men's World Test Championship and the men's World Cup Super League when it was clearer how much cricket had been disrupted.

Dr Peter Harcourt, chair of the medical committee, said there was still much to learn about Covid-19, but the committee were working to create a road map for resuming international cricket, including criteria for decision making and a checklist for what needed to happen, from player preparation to government restrictions and biosecure bubbles. The complexity of restarting cricket could not be overestimated; the more teams, venues and cities involved, the greater the risk to be assessed and managed.

Kevin Roberts, the chief executive of Cricket Australia, said he was working with the ICC, the local organising committee and the Australian government to understand what it would take to play the men's T20 World Cup in Australia in October 2020 as planned.

THE HUNDRED

On April 29, the ECB Board decided that their new short-format tournament, The Hundred, due to launch on July 17, should be postponed until 2021. It was expected that most professional cricket in 2020 would have to be played behind closed doors, which would conflict with The Hundred's aim of attracting a new audience. The complexities of planning during social distancing, travel restrictions affecting the tournament's many overseas players and coaches, and the furloughing of staff across 20 host venues sealed the decision. Spectators, who had already bought more than 180,000 tickets, would be refunded.

On May 4, the ECB terminated the contracts of players due to appear in The Hundred in 2020; they said they were working with the PCA on options for 2021.

ICC BOARD

Meeting by teleconference on May 27–28, the ICC Board discussed the process for electing the ICC's next chair, but did not reach any decision. The current chair, Shashank Manohar, confirmed he would not seek re-election. On the second day, the board deferred all agenda items until June 10 after several members raised the issue of confidentiality. It was agreed that the ICC ethics officer should initiate an independent investigation into the confidentiality of board matters.

The board also asked the ICC management to continue exploring options during the Covid-19 crisis, and denied reports that they had already decided to postpone the men's T20 World Cup.

ECB ANNUAL GENERAL MEETING AND NEW CHAIR

The AGM of the England and Wales Cricket Board, held virtually on June 2, ratified Ian Watmore as the board's new chair, to succeed Colin Graves on September 1. The ECB's 41 members (the chairs of the 39 first-class and National Counties – formerly Minor Counties – and of MCC and the National Counties Cricket Association) voted unanimously to appoint Watmore, a senior civil servant and current chair of the Civil Service Commission, who had also served briefly as chief executive of the Football Association.

It was confirmed that senior independent director Lord Kamlesh Patel would step down in September after five years, during which he was involved in the 2018 action plan to engage South Asian audiences, the establishment of the ECB's governance committee, and the Inspiring Generations Strategy.

The ECB reported a record turnover of £228m for 2019-20 (a period including the hosting of the World Cup and the Ashes), up £56m on 2018, and more than £100m above the average. Administrative expenditure rose to £164m, up £22m, largely due to special fees paid to the first-class counties in respect of the World Cup. The resulting profit of £6.5m enabled the ECB to increase their reserves to £17.1m, though the chief financial officer, Scott Smith, described the figures as "somewhat bittersweet" given the impact of Covid-19.

ENGLAND PROGRAMME IN 2020

The ECB announced the revised schedule for West Indies' tour of England on June 2; it had been postponed from May and June because of the pandemic. Following Cricket West Indies' assent, it was agreed the touring squad would arrive on June 9, and quarantine at Old Trafford; after three weeks they would travel to Southampton to prepare for the First Test at the Rose Bowl, beginning on July 8, with two further Tests at Old Trafford later in the month (all subject to government approval). The Rose Bowl and Old Trafford were chosen because they could offer biosecurity, thanks to onsite hotels, access control, room for medical screening sites, and extendable space for broadcast compounds, studios and written media, as well as players and officials. The two grounds would receive administration fees for staging the Tests, with all additional central costs met by the ECB. With all matches now staged behind closed doors, ticket-holders would be entitled to refunds.

On June 22, the ECB said the Tests, which lacked a sponsor, would be named the #raisethebat series, to honour key workers during the Covid-19 crisis; players would wear the names of key workers, nominated by local cricket clubs, on their training shirts.

ICC BOARD

At a teleconference on June 10, the ICC Board agreed to spend a further month exploring contingency plans for the safe staging of the men's T20 World Cup (scheduled for October) and women's World Cup (February–March 2021). They wanted more time to evaluate the rapidly changing public health situation, and explore how the events could be held while protecting health and safety.

The board also discussed tax exemption for ICC events, prompted by the Indian government taxing the World T20 event held in 2015-16; they agreed the deadline given to the BCCI to provide a solution should be extended to December.

There was an update on the investigation into the confidentiality of board matters, led by the ICC ethics officer, and supported by independent director Indra Nooyi and the chair of the finance and commercial affairs committee, Ehsan Mani.

MCC ANNUAL GENERAL MEETING

The 233rd AGM of the Marylebone Cricket Club was held online on June 24, with president Kumar Sangakkara joining via video from Sri Lanka. He announced that his successor, from October 2021, would be Clare Connor, the former England captain and currently the ECB's managing director of women's cricket and chair of the ICC women's cricket committee; she would be the club's first female president. Connor would not take office until 2021, as members approved the extension of Sangakkara's term to two years, because of the Covid-19 crisis.

Members also approved an increase in entrance fees and the introduction of life memberships, for the first time since 1996, to help the club recover some of the revenue lost because most of the season at Lord's had been wiped out, and to continue to fund the rebuilding of the Compton and Edrich Stands. The life memberships would cost between £3,615 and £17,000 for existing full members, depending on the age and location of applicants; the scheme also permitted the election of up to 350 new members, offered to those on the waiting list (or outside it, if the quota was not filled) for an extra payment.

Membership on December 31, 2019, totalled 23,624, made up of 17,947 full members, 5,015 associate members, 364 honorary members, 168 senior members and 130 out-match members. There were 12,105 candidates awaiting election to full membership; 541 vacancies arose in 2019.

ECB – OVERSEAS PLAYERS

On July 3, the ECB Board announced that, from 2021, first-class counties would again be allowed to field two unqualified cricketers in the same match in the County Championship and Royal London Cup. Counties had been restricted to one per match since 2008, except in the T20 tournament, where they were allowed two. (Unqualified cricketers, generally known as overseas players, are neither British nor Irish citizens – excluding Ireland internationals – nor EU, EEA or Swiss citizens with settled status in the UK.)

The move would allow counties to retain the services of some previous Kolpak signings (players from countries which have trade treaties with the EU) who had been able to appear, in addition to overseas players, under EU law, which would no longer apply in the UK from January 2021. It had been recommended by the ECB's performance cricket committee, chaired by Sir Andrew Strauss. He said there was a balance to be struck between the need for good foreign players in county cricket, and providing opportunities for nine England-qualified players in each county team; domestic players benefited from competing with and against leading players from across the world, while county fans enjoyed watching them.

ECB – ENGLAND PROGRAMME AND DOMESTIC SEASON

On July 6, the ECB confirmed that England's men would play three one-day internationals against Ireland in Southampton, starting on July 30, and three Tests plus three Twenty20 internationals against Pakistan (who had already arrived in England) in August. Talks to reschedule their one-day and Twenty20 internationals against Australia were continuing, as were attempts to schedule a women's international tri-series between England, India and South Africa.

On July 7, the ECB announced that, subject to approval by the board, the chairs of the first-class counties had agreed by a majority vote to play a shortened domestic season of first-class and limited-overs cricket, to begin on August 1. All the counties would undergo medical risk assessments and venue compliance approval to ensure safe environments. On July 10, it was confirmed that all 18 counties would compete in a short four-day competition for the Bob Willis Trophy, to be followed by a reduced version of the previously scheduled T20 Vitality Blast.

ECB INCLUSION AND DIVERSITY STRATEGY

On July 7, the ECB announced plans to strengthen inclusion and diversity. These focused on three key areas:

- **Leadership and Governance** – improving representation across administrators and decision makers to embody a modern and diverse society. The ECB Board already met Sport England targets for gender diversity, but sought to advance Black, Asian and Minority Ethnic representation, and to help first-class counties and county boards raise women's representation to at least 30%, and BAME to a target reflecting their local population. There should also be an anti-discrimination charter and code spanning players, coaches, fans, media and clubs.

- **Listening and Education** – broadening understanding and openness. The ECB would support the Professional Cricketers' Association in consulting current and past BAME players to understand their experiences and the action required, and work with Black influencers and stakeholders. They would expand inclusion and diversity education for the board and leaders across the game. Sanjay Patel, managing director of The Hundred, was appointed the ECB's inclusion and diversity champion, charged with shaping programmes to reach and resonate with Black communities and other groups. The ECB would continue the "Roar for Diversity" primary school programme launched with the Premier League in 2019.
- **Opportunity and Visibility** – creating opportunities and highlighting role models for diverse communities. A coaching bursary was introduced for Black coaches. Cricket provision should be increased in primary schools, particularly the most ethnically diverse. The ECB would work with counties to adopt the Rooney Rule, interviewing at least one BAME candidate when shortlisting for coaching roles. They also aimed to develop recruitment processes for a more inclusive and diverse workforce, and an apprenticeship programme focusing on diverse representation.

The measures built on the ECB's five-year Inspiring Generations Strategy, aimed at increasing cricket's reach through projects such as The Hundred, transforming women's and girls' cricket, growing participation in disability cricket, getting more schools playing, increasing cricket provision in the most diverse communities through urban facilities investment, and the South Asian Action Plan.

ECB GUIDELINES FOR RECREATIONAL CRICKET

Following the UK government's decision to allow the return of recreational cricket in England from July 11, the ECB issued practical guidance to players and clubs.

Individuals should undergo checks, and not take part if they had any Covid-19 symptoms. All groups should be limited to a maximum of 30 people, including coaches and officials. Clubs should record attendees and contact details, to support NHS Test and Trace, and ensure facilities met current Covid legislation and guidance. Players should remain socially distanced at all times, with wicketkeepers and slips at least one metre apart; batters should run in distinct lanes, to remain at least two metres away from the bowler and their batting partner. There should be regular hygiene breaks for participants' hands and the ball, e.g. every six overs or 20 minutes. Players should minimise handling the ball by limiting contact while returning it to the bowler; no sweat or saliva should be applied to the ball at any time. Sharing equipment should be limited where possible; if not possible, there should be strict hand hygiene.

On July 17, the ECB added that clubs who had signed up for the NatWest CricketForce initiative would receive packs containing 25 200ml bottles of hand sanitiser, four 750ml bottles of disinfectant, four packs of 50 face masks, 100 wipes and two packs of four sets of disposable gloves.

ICC BUSINESS CORPORATION MEETING

On July 20, the ICC confirmed that the men's T20 World Cup, due to be staged in Australia in October, would be postponed because of the Covid-19 pandemic. A meeting of the board of the ICC Business Corporation (the ICC's commercial subsidiary) agreed windows for the next three ICC men's events:

- Men's T20 World Cup 2021 – October–November 2021 (final on November 14)
- Men's T20 World Cup 2022 – October–November 2022 (final on November 13)
- Men's World Cup 2023 – October–November 2023, in India (final on November 26)

The T20 events would be held in Australia and India, but it was not yet decided in which order. India would stage the men's World Cup in 2023.

The board would continue to evaluate the changing situation before making final decisions on these tournaments and on the women's World Cup, still due to be held in New Zealand in February 2021.

ECB DOMESTIC COMPETITIONS IN 2020

On July 24, the ECB confirmed details of the Bob Willis Trophy to replace the County Championship in 2020. The four-day tournament, beginning on August 1, would have first-class status, but was a separate competition from the County Championship. It would comprise three regional groups of six, each county playing five matches, and the two group winners with most points progressing to a five-day final. In a drawn final, the county leading on first innings would win the trophy; if the two first innings were incomplete, or the match was tied, the trophy would be shared.

Playing conditions were adapted to protect players, particularly fast bowlers, following the long lay-off due to Covid-19: the minimum number of overs in the day was reduced from 96 to 90; each county's first innings was restricted to 120 overs; the follow-on rose from 150 to 200 runs; and the new ball was available after 90 overs, rather than 80. The points for a draw were increased from five to eight, to mitigate against the impact of weather during a shortened competition. The loan system was relaxed so that players could be loaned from one county to another for a minimum of one week.

A shortened version of the Vitality Blast, with the counties in the same three regional groups, playing ten group games rather than 14, would run from August 27 to October 3.

A special women's domestic 50-over competition (later named the Rachael Heyhoe Flint Trophy) would feature the eight new teams in the women's elite domestic structure. It would comprise two regional groups of four, playing six matches each, with the group winners meeting in a final. Each of the eight regions would have a squad of 15, all of whom would be paid, apart from players already on central contracts.

ICC BUSINESS CORPORATION MEETING

On August 7, the ICC announced that, following the postponement of the men's T20 World Cup scheduled for Australia in October 2020, the next tournament would be held in India in late 2021 as originally planned, while Australia would host the competition a year later. The teams who had qualified for the 2020 edition would take part in 2021, and there would be a new qualification process for 2022.

The women's World Cup, scheduled for New Zealand in early 2021, was postponed for 12 months until February–March 2022 because of the pandemic. The qualifying competition to decide the final three teams for the tournament had not yet taken place – no international women's cricket had been played since the end of the T20 World Cup in March – and the delay would give players the best opportunity to prepare.

ENGLAND PROGRAMME IN 2020

On August 14, the ECB confirmed that Australia would travel to England for three Twenty20 internationals at Southampton and three one-day internationals at Manchester. The matches, originally scheduled for July, would take place in September. This meant the England men's team would complete all their home fixtures in 2020, despite losing half the season. The South African women's team cancelled their scheduled tour on August 18, following the Indian women's withdrawal in July. But, on August 25, the ECB announced West Indies women would play a five-match Twenty20 series at Derby in September.

ECB COST-CUTTING MEASURES

On September 15, ECB chief executive Tom Harrison issued a statement on the financial crisis caused by the Covid-19 pandemic. He said the game had already lost more than £100m, which could rise to £200m if there was further disruption in 2021. It had been a remarkable achievement to get cricket back on, thanks to the first-class counties, the recreational game, broadcast and commercial partners, the government and local public health agencies.

The ECB had put in place short-term money-saving measures, which included furloughing staff, pay cuts and a recruitment freeze. But the pandemic's impact would be long-lasting, so to ensure the financial sustainability of cricket in England and Wales the ECB must reduce their own costs. After reviewing structures and budgets, they proposed a 20% reduction in the workforce budget, equating to the loss of 62 jobs, in addition to changing some posts into flexible working roles.

ENGLAND PLAYER CONTRACTS

The ECB currently award separate contracts for Test and white-ball cricket, but players on both types of contract now have their salaries paid in full by the ECB (until February 2020, those on white-ball contracts received a supplement to their county salary).

On September 30, the ECB awarded 12 Test contracts to run for 12 months from October 2020. They went to James Anderson, Jofra Archer, Stuart Broad, Rory Burns, Jos Buttler, Zak Crawley, Sam Curran, Ollie Pope, Joe Root, Dom Sibley, Ben Stokes and Chris Woakes. They also awarded 12 white-ball contracts, to Archer, Buttler, Root, Stokes and Woakes, plus Moeen Ali, Jonny Bairstow, Tom Curran, Eoin Morgan, Adil Rashid, Jason Roy and Mark Wood. Jack Leach retained his incremental contract, and Dom Bess, Chris Jordan and Dawid Malan were given one. Saqib Mahmood, Craig Overton and Olly Stone retained pace-bowling development contracts.

Compared with 2019-20, Crawley, Pope and Sibley had gained Test contracts, and Tom Curran was promoted from an incremental contract to a central white-ball contract. Bairstow lost his Test contract, and Joe Denly his white-ball contract.

Because of the impact of Covid-19 on the ECB's finances, the levels of player remuneration were renegotiated with the Team England Player Partnership; on October 23, it was announced that England's men had agreed to a 15% reduction.

MCC SPECIAL GENERAL MEETING

At a special general meeting held online on October 15, MCC members approved proposals to reduce the club's management committee from 21 to a maximum of 12, and to change the election process to produce a more diverse spread. Of 6,280 votes received, 5,021 (80%) were in favour.

The current committee, elected under a system whereby any full MCC member could stand, contained 18 men and three women, and only two people from BAME backgrounds. Under the new rules, a nominations committee would determine the skills, experience and diversity required on the MCC committee – and its size – on an annual basis, and assess members applying to stand before recommending appointments. Moving towards the ECB's principles for good governance, which the first-class counties were to adopt by 2023, would also improve MCC's position in bidding for ECB funding.

COUNTY CHAMPIONSHIP IN 2021

On October 16, the chairs of the first-class counties agreed a revised structure for the men's domestic first-class season in 2021, to mitigate against the possible further impact of Covid-19.

The County Championship would return but, rather than resuming the two-division structure, the counties would be placed in three seeded groups of six, playing ten matches each. The top two in each group would progress to Division One, the next two in each group to Division Two, and the bottom two to Division Three; counties would then play a further four matches, against qualifiers from the other two groups in their division. The Division One winners would be champions, but would also compete against the runners-up in a five-day final at Lord's for the Bob Willis Trophy. This meant Essex would be defending two first-class titles: the County Championship which they won in 2019 and the Bob Willis Trophy of 2020.

There would be a further consultation with the counties and other stakeholders in 2021 on the men's domestic structure for 2022 and beyond; the Championship structure originally planned for 2020 (ten counties in Division One and eight in Division Two) would start as the default position.

ENGLAND CRICKET OPERATIONS MANAGER

On October 30, it was announced that Phil Neale, the England men's cricket operations manager, was retiring, aged 66. He had served in the role since 1999, under six head coaches and 11 Test captains, and had worked on 257 Tests, 422 one-day internationals and 110 T20 internationals. Neale had also played for Worcestershire from 1975 to 1992, including ten years as captain.

On November 11, Bruce French, the national lead wicketkeeping coach, stepped down after 11 years.

ECB FUNDING INITIATIVE

On November 3, the ECB and LV= General Insurance launched a £1m investment fund, #Funds4Runs, to support areas of recreational cricket hit by Covid-19. It focused on four areas: children from deprived backgrounds, diverse communities, disability groups, and women's and girls' programmes. It was also intended to deliver three wider objectives: connecting communities and improving lives through cricket, increasing the local relevance of cricket, and growing long-term engagement with the game in these communities. Financial support was accessible to affiliated clubs, All Stars cricket centres (for children aged five to eight), community organisations, county cricket boards and Cricket Wales.

The fund started by expanding the existing All Stars programme, and establishing a partnership with the British Film Institute, enabling clubs to apply for a film-maker programme, First Run, to create films showing the character of their community, and video content for their club via the YouTube channel or social media.

COMMONWEALTH GAMES IN 2022

On November 18, the Commonwealth Games Federation and the ICC announced the qualification process for women's cricket teams aiming to take part in the 2022 Commonwealth Games in Birmingham. Hosts England were guaranteed a place, alongside the six other highest-ranked teams in the women's T20 rankings on April 1, 2021, and the winner of a Commonwealth Games qualifying tournament.

As Caribbean athletes represent their countries, and not West Indies, in the Commonwealth Games, there would be a regional tournament to decide which country should compete if West Indies won a place.

ICC BOARD

On November 19, the ICC Board approved a change in the regulations for the World Test Championship. The Covid-19 pandemic meant only half the Championship's scheduled series had been played so far (estimated to rise to about 85% by the end of the competition window in June 2021). Under the original regulations, matches not played were treated as draws, with the points evenly split. Rather than extending the tournament for another year in an attempt to complete the schedule, the Cricket Committee recommended determining the standings only from matches played, ranking teams by the percentage of possible points earned. This would enable the final to take place in June 2021 as planned.

The board also confirmed that the next women's T20 World Cup would move from November 2022 to February 2023. The 50-over women's World Cup had already been postponed to February–March 2022, and the Commonwealth Games, featuring women's cricket, were scheduled for July 2022, whereas there were currently no major women's events planned for 2023.

The board approved an Excluded Persons Policy as part of the ICC Anti-Corruption Code; this would enable the ACU to impose exclusion orders on known corruptors not covered by the code, barring them from any role in cricket including playing, administration, financing, attendance or any involvement in a league, team or franchise.

The board confirmed that, in future, players in men's, women's and Under-19 internationals must be at least 15. In exceptional circumstances, a member board could apply to include a player under 15, where they could demonstrate that the player's experience, mental development and wellbeing would enable them to cope with the demands of international cricket.

ICC CHAIR

On November 24, the ICC announced that Greg Barclay had been elected as their independent chair. An Auckland-based commercial lawyer, he had been a director of New Zealand Cricket since 2012, and was also a director of the men's 2014-15 World Cup in Australia and New Zealand. He gained two-thirds of the votes in the second round to defeat Imran Khwaja of Singapore, who had been acting as interim chair since Shashank Manohar stood down at the end of his second term in July. Khwaja was re-elected as the ICC's deputy chair in February 2021, defeating West Indies' Ricky Skerritt. Martin Snedden replaced Barclay as New Zealand's representative on the ICC Board.

ECB INCLUSION AND DIVERSITY STRATEGY

On November 24, the ECB approved further measures as part of their Equality, Diversity and Inclusion Plan:

- An independent Commission for Equality in Cricket: to assist the ECB Board in assessing the evidence of inequalities and discrimination within cricket, and the action needed. The commission would have an independent chair and members, bringing a diversity of thought and experience.
- A Forum for Race in Cricket: to provide a confidential, safe space through which the ECB can listen to and learn from the experiences of people across the game.
- A new Equality Code of Conduct: to be adopted and enforced by all organisations under the ECB's jurisdiction, enabling discriminatory behaviour to be sanctioned.

The full Equality, Diversity and Inclusion Plan for 2021–2024 was to be launched in 2021, and would be driven by the ECB's senior independent director, Brenda Trenowden.

ECB WOMEN'S CONTRACTS

On December 3, the ECB announced that 41 female cricketers had signed full-time domestic contracts across the eight teams within the new women's regional set-up. In June, 25 players had signed regional retainers; a further 16 had been added to the list of contracted professionals, all 41 on full-time terms. These were in addition to the 17 centrally contracted England women players. Clare Connor, the managing director of women's cricket, described it as "the most significant step forward for the women's game in recent years".

ICC TOURNAMENTS

Between December 12 and 16, the ICC announced details of various future tournaments.

The match schedule for the **women's World Cup** in New Zealand, postponed by a year to early 2022, was released. Eight teams would play 31 matches between March 4 and April 3 in six venues (Auckland, Christchurch, Dunedin, Hamilton, Mount Maunganui and Wellington); the semi-finals would be staged at the Basin Reserve in Wellington and Hagley Oval in Christchurch, and the final under lights at Hagley Oval. New Zealand, Australia, England, South Africa and India had already qualified; the three remaining teams would emerge from a qualifying tournament in Sri Lanka in 2021.

The **women's T20 World Cup**, now postponed to February 2023, would be contested by ten teams: hosts South Africa and the other seven top sides in the T20 rankings at November 30, 2021, plus two more to be selected from 37 through a qualification process starting in August 2021 and involving 115 women's T20 internationals scheduled across seven months. There would be five regional qualifiers (in Africa, the Americas, Asia, East Asia–Pacific and Europe), with the five winners plus the highest-ranked side of the remaining 32 joining the bottom two from the T20 rankings in a qualifier in 2022.

Under the rescheduled qualification process for the **men's Under-19 World Cup**, to be held in early 2022 in the West Indies, 33 teams would be competing for the last five places. The top 11 sides in the 2020 World Cup – Afghanistan, Australia, Bangladesh, England, India, New Zealand, Pakistan, South Africa, Sri Lanka, West Indies and Zimbabwe – had qualified automatically. The remaining five would emerge from seven regional events starting in June 2021 (due to their strength in depth, Africa and Asia would be split into two divisions, but eventually produce one winner per region).

The next-but-one **men's T20 World Cup** was to be held in Australia in October–November 2022 (a year after the edition scheduled for India in late 2021). It would feature 16 teams: hosts Australia, the other 11 top-ranked sides from the 2021 tournament, and four more who would emerge from a qualifying process due to start in April 2021, with 67 Associate Members taking part in 11 qualifiers across five regions. Two teams each from the Americas, Asia and Europe, plus one each from Africa and East Asia–Pacific, would join the bottom four from the 2021 T20 World Cup, plus Nepal, Singapore, the UAE and Zimbabwe, who qualified on their T20 rankings. These 16 sides would be split into two separate global qualifying competitions, and two winners from each of these would supply the final four teams in Australia.

Twenty ODI series in the pathway to the 2023 **men's World Cup** in India, postponed in 2020, were rescheduled, beginning in March 2021 with Oman hosting USA and Nepal in the World Cup League 2. These series would lead up to a World Cup Qualifier in Zimbabwe in June–July 2023, where the three best teams from League 2 would join the bottom five from the World Cup Super League. The two leading sides from the World Cup Qualifier would join India and the other top seven Super League teams in the World Cup, making ten teams in all.

All events were subject to Covid-19 arrangements required at the time.

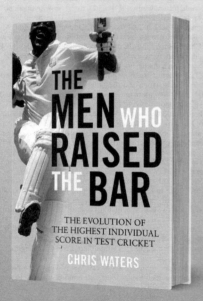

DATES IN CRICKET HISTORY

c. 1550 Evidence of cricket being played in Guildford, Surrey.

1610 Reference to "cricketing" between Weald & Upland and North Downs near Chevening, Kent.

1611 Randle Cotgrave's French–English dictionary translates the French word "crosse" as a cricket staff.
Two youths fined for playing cricket at Sidlesham, Sussex.

1624 Jasper Vinall becomes first man known to be killed playing cricket: hit by a bat while trying to catch the ball – at Horsted Green, Sussex.

1676 First reference to cricket being played abroad, by British residents in Aleppo, Syria.

1694 Two shillings and sixpence paid for a "wagger" (wager) on a match at Lewes.

1697 First reference to "a great match" with 11 players a side for 50 guineas, in Sussex.

1700 Cricket match announced on Clapham Common.

1709 First recorded inter-county match: Kent v Surrey.

1710 First reference to cricket at Cambridge University.

1727 Articles of Agreement written governing the conduct of matches between the teams of the Duke of Richmond and Mr Brodrick of Peperharow, Surrey.

1729 Date of earliest surviving bat, belonging to John Chitty, now in the Oval pavilion.

1730 First recorded match at the Artillery Ground, off City Road, central London, still the cricketing home of the Honourable Artillery Company.

1744 Kent beat All-England by one wicket at the Artillery Ground.
First known version of the Laws of Cricket, issued by the London Club, formalising the pitch as 22 yards long.

c. 1767 Foundation of the Hambledon Club in Hampshire, the leading club in England for the next 30 years.

1769 First recorded century, by John Minshull for Duke of Dorset's XI v Wrotham.

1771 Width of bat limited to 4¼ inches, which it has remained ever since.

1774 Lbw law devised.

1776 Earliest known scorecards, at the Vine Club, Sevenoaks, Kent.

1780 The first six-seamed cricket ball, manufactured by Dukes of Penshurst, Kent.

1787 First match at Thomas Lord's first ground, Dorset Square, Marylebone – White Conduit Club v Middlesex.
Formation of Marylebone Cricket Club by members of the White Conduit Club.

1788 First revision of the Laws of Cricket by MCC.

1794 First recorded inter-school match: Charterhouse v Westminster.

1795 First recorded case of a dismissal "leg before wicket".

1806 First Gentlemen v Players match at Lord's.

1807 First mention of "straight-armed" (i.e. roundarm) bowling: by John Willes of Kent.

1809 Thomas Lord's second ground opened, at North Bank, St John's Wood.

1811 First recorded women's county match: Surrey v Hampshire at Ball's Pond, London.

1814 Lord's third ground opened on its present site, also in St John's Wood.

1827 First Oxford v Cambridge match, at Lord's: a draw.

1828 MCC authorise the bowler to raise his hand level with the elbow.

1833 John Nyren publishes *Young Cricketer's Tutor* and *The Cricketers of My Time.*

1836 First North v South match, for years regarded as the principal fixture of the season.

***c.* 1836** Batting pads invented.

1841 General Lord Hill, commander-in-chief of the British Army, orders that a cricket ground be made an adjunct of every military barracks.

1844 First official international match: Canada v United States.

1845 First match played at The Oval.

1846 The All-England XI, organised by William Clarke, begin playing matches, often against odds, throughout the country.

1849 First Yorkshire v Lancashire match.

***c.* 1850** Wicketkeeping gloves first used.

1850 John Wisden bowls all ten batsmen in an innings for North v South.

1853 First mention of a champion county: Nottinghamshire.

1858 First recorded instance of a hat being awarded to a bowler taking wickets with three consecutive balls.

1859 First touring team to leave England, captained by George Parr, draws enthusiastic crowds in the US and Canada.

1864 "Overhand bowling" authorised by MCC.
John Wisden's *The Cricketer's Almanack* first published.

1868 Team of Australian Aboriginals tour England.

1873 W. G. Grace becomes the first player to record 1,000 runs and 100 wickets in a season.
First regulations restricting county qualifications, regarded by some as the official start of the County Championship.

1877 First Test match: Australia beat England by 45 runs at Melbourne.

1880 First Test in England: a five-wicket win against Australia at The Oval.

1882 Following England's first defeat by Australia in England, an "obituary notice" to English cricket in the *Sporting Times* leads to the tradition of the Ashes.

1889 Work begins on present Lord's Pavilion.
South Africa's first Test match.
Declarations first authorised, but only on the third day, or in a one-day match.

1890 County Championship officially constituted.

1895 W. G. Grace scores 1,000 runs in May, and reaches his 100th hundred.

1899 A. E. J. Collins scores 628 not out in a junior house match at Clifton College, the highest recorded individual score in any game – until 2016.
Selectors choose England team for home Tests, instead of host club issuing invitations.

1900 In England, six-ball over becomes the norm, instead of five.

1909 Imperial Cricket Conference (ICC – now the International Cricket Council) set up, with England, Australia and South Africa the original members.

1910 Six runs given for any hit over the boundary, instead of only for a hit out of the ground.

1912 First and only triangular Test series played in England, involving England, Australia and South Africa.

1915 W. G. Grace dies, aged 67.

1926 Victoria score 1,107 v New South Wales at Melbourne, still a first-class record.

1928 West Indies' first Test match.
A. P. Freeman of Kent and England becomes the only player to take more than 300 first-class wickets in a season: 304.

1930 New Zealand's first Test match.
Donald Bradman's first tour of England: he scores 974 runs in five Tests, still a record for any series.

1931 Stumps made higher (28 inches not 27) and wider (nine inches not eight – this was optional until 1947).

1932 India's first Test match.
Hedley Verity of Yorkshire takes ten wickets for ten runs v Nottinghamshire, the best innings analysis in first-class cricket.

1932-33 The Bodyline tour of Australia in which England bowl at batsmen's bodies with a packed leg-side field to neutralise Bradman's scoring.

1934 Jack Hobbs retires, with 197 centuries and 61,237 runs, both records.
First women's Test: Australia v England at Brisbane.

1935 MCC condemn and outlaw Bodyline.

1947 Denis Compton (Middlesex and England) hits a record 3,816 runs in an English season.

1948 First five-day Tests in England.
Bradman concludes Test career with a second-ball duck at The Oval and an average of 99.94 – four runs would have made it 100.

1952 Pakistan's first Test match.

1953 England regain the Ashes after a 19-year gap, the longest ever.

1956 Jim Laker of England takes 19 wickets for 90 v Australia at Manchester, the best match analysis in first-class cricket.

1960 First tied Test: Australia v West Indies at Brisbane.

1963 Distinction between amateurs and professionals abolished in English cricket.
The first major one-day tournament begins in England: the Gillette Cup.

1968 Garry Sobers becomes first man to hit six sixes in an over, for Nottinghamshire against Glamorgan at Swansea.

1969 Limited-over Sunday league inaugurated for first-class counties.

1970 Proposed South African tour of England cancelled; South Africa excluded from international cricket because of their government's apartheid policies.

1971 First one-day international: Australia beat England at Melbourne by five wickets.

1973 First women's World Cup: England are the winners.

1975 First men's World Cup: West Indies beat Australia in final at Lord's.

1976 First women's match at Lord's: England beat Australia by eight wickets.

1977 Centenary Test at Melbourne, with identical result to the first match: Australia beat England by 45 runs.
Australian media tycoon Kerry Packer signs 51 of the world's leading players in defiance of the cricketing authorities.

1978 Graham Yallop of Australia is the first batsman to wear a protective helmet in a Test.

1979 Packer and official cricket agree peace deal.

1981 England beat Australia in Leeds Test, after following on with bookmakers offering odds of 500-1 against them winning.

1982 Sri Lanka's first Test match.

1991 South Africa return, with a one-day international in India.

1992 Zimbabwe's first Test match.
Durham become first county since Glamorgan in 1921 to attain first-class status.

1993 The ICC cease to be administered by MCC, becoming an independent organisation.

1994 Brian Lara becomes the first player to pass 500 in a first-class innings: 501 not out for Warwickshire v Durham.

2000 South Africa's captain Hansie Cronje banned from cricket for life after admitting receiving bribes from bookmakers in match-fixing scandal.
Bangladesh's first Test match.
County Championship split into two divisions, with promotion and relegation.

2001 Sir Donald Bradman dies, aged 92.

2003 First Twenty20 game played, in England.

2004 Lara is the first to score 400 in a Test innings, for West Indies v England in Antigua.

2005 England regain the Ashes after 16 years.

2006 Pakistan become first team to forfeit a Test, for refusing to resume at The Oval.
Shane Warne becomes the first man to take 700 Test wickets.

2007 Australia complete 5–0 Ashes whitewash for the first time since 1920-21.
Australia win the World Cup for the third time running.
India beat Pakistan in the final of the inaugural World Twenty20.

2008 Indian Premier League of 20-over matches launched.
Sachin Tendulkar becomes the leading scorer in Tests, passing Lara.

2009 Terrorists in Lahore attack buses containing Sri Lankan team and match officials.

2010 Tendulkar scores the first double-century in a one-day international, against South Africa; later in the year, he scores his 50th Test century.
Muttiah Muralitharan retires from Test cricket, after taking his 800th wicket.
England's men win the World T20, their first global title.
Pakistan bowl three deliberate no-balls in Lord's Test against England; the ICC ban the three players responsible.

2011 India become the first team to win the World Cup on home soil.
Salman Butt, Mohammad Asif and Mohammad Amir are given custodial sentences of between six and 30 months for their part in the Lord's spot-fix.

2012 Tendulkar scores his 100th international century, in an ODI against Bangladesh.

2013 150th edition of *Wisden Cricketers' Almanack*.
Tendulkar retires after his 200th Test match, with a record 15,921 runs.

2014 Australia complete only the third 5–0 Ashes whitewash.
India's Rohit Sharma hits 264 in one-day international against Sri Lanka at Kolkata.
Australian batsman Phillip Hughes, 25, dies after being hit on the neck by a bouncer.

2015 Australia win World Cup for fifth time, beating New Zealand in final at Melbourne.

2016 Pranav Dhanawade, 15, makes 1,009 not out – the highest recorded individual score in any match – in a school game in Mumbai.
Brendon McCullum hits Test cricket's fastest hundred, from 54 balls, in his final match, against Australia at Christchurch.

2017 England women beat India by nine runs to win the World Cup at Lord's.
England play their first day/night home Test, against West Indies at Edgbaston.

2018 Three Australians are banned after sandpaper used on the ball in a Test in South Africa.
Afghanistan and Ireland's men play their first Test matches.
Alastair Cook retires after 161 Tests, 12,472 runs and 33 centuries.

2019 England's men win their first 50-over World Cup, after super over against New Zealand.
England (362-9) complete their record run-chase to win Ashes Test, at Leeds.

2020 The coronavirus pandemic forces most cricket behind closed doors.
County Championship suspended; replaced by Bob Willis Trophy.
The Hundred competition is postponed to 2021.
James Anderson reaches 600 Test wickets; Stuart Broad passes 500.

2021 New Zealand go top of the Test rankings for the first time.

FIFTY YEARS AGO

Wisden Cricketers' Almanack 1972

LORD CONSTANTINE: THE SPONTANEOUS CRICKETER, by John Arlott Lord Constantine, MBE, died in London on July 1, 1971. The parents of the child born in Diego Martin, Trinidad, almost 70 years before, may in their highest ambitions have hoped that he would play cricket for West Indies. They cannot have dreamt that he would take a major share in lifting his people to a new level of respect within the British Commonwealth; that along the way he would become the finest fieldsman and one of the most exciting all-rounders the game of cricket has known: and that he would die Baron Constantine, of Maraval in Trinidad and Tobago, and of Nelson, in the County Palatine of Lancaster, a former cabinet minister and high commissioner of his native Trinidad... He made his mark in the only way a poor West Indian boy of his time could do, by playing cricket of ability and character. He went on to argue the rights of the coloured peoples with such an effect as only a man who had won public affection by games-playing could have done in the Britain of that period... As C. L. R. James has written, "he revolted against the revolting contrast between his first-class status as a cricketer and his third-class status as a man". That, almost equally with his enthusiasm for the game, prompted the five years of unremitting practice after which, in 1928, he came to England under Karl Nunes on West Indies' first Test tour as an extremely lively fast bowler, hard-hitting batsman and outstanding fieldsman in any position. Muscular but lithe, stocky but long-armed, he bowled with a bounding run, a high, smooth action and considerable pace. His batting, which depended considerably upon eye, was sometimes unorthodox to the point of spontaneous invention: but on his day it was virtually impossible to bowl at him. In the deep he picked up while going like a sprinter and threw with explosive accuracy; close to the wicket he was fearless and quick; wherever he was posted he amazed everyone by his speed and certainty in making catches which seemed far beyond reach. His movement was so joyously fluid and, at need, acrobatic that he might have been made of springs and rubber... He fought discrimination against his people with a dignity firm but free of acrimony... He remained in England during the Second World War as a Ministry of Labour welfare officer with West Indian workers. In 1944 he fought one of the historic cases against colour prejudice when he won damages from the Imperial Hotel in London for "failing to receive and lodge him". He was... high commissioner for Trinidad and Tobago in London from 1962 until 1964. He was awarded the MBE in 1945; knighted in 1962; made an honorary Master of the Bench in 1963; and created a life peer in 1969. He served various periods as a governor of the BBC, a rector of St Andrews, a member of the Race Relations Board and the Sports Council.

NOTES BY THE EDITOR [Norman Preston] After India's conquests in West Indies and England, one might ask who are the current world cricket champions? True, England regained the Ashes, but India well deserved their success in gaining their first victory either at home or abroad over West Indies, which they followed at The Oval with their first Test victory in England. Small wonder that the flight plans of Ajit Wadekar and his men for the return journey to India were altered at the last minute to take them first to New Delhi, for the prime minister expressed the wish to meet the players and congratulate them personally. When they arrived in Bombay they were taken from the airport to the city in a motorcade, with thousands lining the 17-mile route to cheer the heroes. A leading newspaper raised a fund for the captain and his team. Handsome gifts in cash and kind reached them from people both known and unknown. Following so quickly on success in the West Indies, the public felt that their immense enthusiasm and support for cricket had at last been rewarded with the ultimate prize – a win over England in England. The scene at The Oval was memorable indeed as the cricketers filed in front of the pavilion in a sea of turbans. After 39 years of splendid endeavour, India had at last gained their first victory on English soil.

ONE HUNDRED YEARS AGO

Wisden Cricketers' Almanack 1922

MCC TEAM IN AUSTRALIA, 1920-21 The tour of the MCC's team in the winter of 1920-21 resulted, as everyone knows, in disaster, all the Test matches being easily won by Australia. Never before in the history of English or Australian trips since Test matches were first played had one side shown such an overwhelming superiority. As the news came to hand of defeat after defeat people thought the Englishmen must be playing very badly. Not till the Australians came here in the summer and beat us three times in succession on our own grounds did we fully realise the strength of the combination that had set up such a record… The broad fact remains that the Australians had a vast superiority in bowling – a superiority that made the difference in batting seem greater than it really was. Still, our batting on the big occasions fell far short of what might reasonably have been expected… With Mr F. C. Toone, the Yorkshire secretary, as manager, the tour on the whole passed off very smoothly, but a good deal of friction was caused by cable messages sent home to the *Daily Express* by Mr E. R. Wilson. This led to a resolution passed at the annual meeting of the Marylebone Club in May deprecating the reporting of matches by the players concerned in them.

THE AUSTRALIANS IN ENGLAND, 1921, by Sydney Pardon The Australians had a wonderful tour, and narrowly missed setting up [an unbeaten] record that might have stood for all time… Their final record was almost exactly the same of that of the great team of 1902, the only difference being that they won 22 matches out of 38, and Darling's famous side 23 out of 39. Both teams lost two matches and left 14 unfinished. A comparison between the two records, however, would be very delusive. Last year the summer was one of almost unprecedented sunshine, whereas in 1902 we had an enormous rainfall, and the really fine days were comparatively few… On one point, however, there can be no dispute. In the tour of nearly 20 years ago the Australians were put to a far more searching test, English cricket in 1902 being overwhelmingly strong, and last summer lamentably weak. Allowing for all this, however, one need not hesitate to say that Armstrong had a great side. Their record speaks for itself, but the statistics on the printed page give a poor idea of the consummate ease with which for four months they crumpled up nearly all the teams that opposed them. Only twice did they look at all likely to be beaten, and on one of those occasions they were without Warren Bardsley and Macartney. I cannot think that they were estimated at quite their true value… They could all get runs, even the last man being capable on occasion of hitting up 20 or 30; their fielding was magnificent; and above all they possessed in Gregory and McDonald two very fast bowlers of the highest class. It was the fast bowling more than anything else that brought about our undoing. Never before have English batsmen been so demoralised by great pace… McDonald struck one as being really the finer bowler of the two, but Gregory was by far the more alarming. Gregory was apt when he pitched at all short to get up dangerously high, but old cricketers were inclined to be sarcastic when they saw batsmen frightened by long hops… Of Macartney and Bardsley it would be impossible to say too much. Each in his way was magnificent… [Bardsley] has now gone through three tours in England, and in every one of them he has scored over 2,000 runs – a marvellous record indeed… For the whole tour Macartney beat him both in aggregate of runs and average, but only by a trifle. In point of efficiency the two men stood absolutely on an equality. Macartney was a law to himself – an individual genius but not in any way a model to be copied. He constantly did things that would be quite wrong for an ordinary batsman, but by success justified all his audacities. Except Victor Trumper at his best, no Australian batsman has ever demoralised our bowlers to the same extent… In his various hundreds against the counties he reached almost the extreme limit of brilliancy.

ONE HUNDRED AND FIFTY YEARS AGO

Wisden Cricketers' Almanack 1872

LANCASHIRE v DERBYSHIRE, AT OLD TRAFFORD, MAY 26–27, 1871 This was the first match played by the Derbyshire CC, whose eleven easily won their maiden match... The first innings of Lancashire was a curiosity, being played out in about one hour, for 25 runs, from (less one ball) 25 overs... [Lancashire's Frederick] Reynolds bowled 13 round-arm overs for 14 runs, but all the five wickets booked to his name were due to his slows. The Lancashire men fielded well. For Derbyshire, Mr Sowter's 47 not out was an excellent display of steady batting that included 25 singles. Burnham (Notts born) played capital cricket in his 31; he made three fours – two drives, the other a fine cut. Burnham also long-stopped well. Gregory clean bowled five of the six wickets due to him in Lancashire's first innings. Platts obtained the last three wickets of Lancashire just in time to win the match for his shire, as in less than ten minutes after heavy rain fell, and continued to fall the remainder of that day. Derbyshire won by an innings and 11 runs.

MR W. G. GRACE'S FIRST MATCHES ON GROUNDS In 1871, Mr W. G. Grace played his first match on the West Brompton Ground, on Fenner's, on the Trent Bridge Ground, and on the Mote Park Ground. He played the following innings in those first matches:

- AT WEST BROMPTON: 1st innings, 118 caught; no 2nd innings.
- AT CAMBRIDGE: 1st innings, 162 caught; no 2nd innings.
- AT NOTTINGHAM: 1st innings, 79 caught; 2nd innings, 116 caught.
- AT MAIDSTONE: 1st innings, 81 not out; 2nd innings, 42 not out.

THE GREAT RUN-GETTING MATCH: GENTLEMEN OF THE SOUTH v PLAYERS OF THE SOUTH, AT THE OVAL, JUNE 29–30, JULY 1, 1871 1,139 runs were scored in this affair, the largest number, by three, ever made in a match. Moreover, it was the closest-contested 1,000-run match ever played, as after three days' fine and hard hitting (at the rate of 380 runs per day), the match was won by three runs only – three out of 1,139! The weather and the wickets were in splendid form, and the attendances during the three days great... On Saturday, the pavilion seats were crammed, and the ground thronged by about 7,000 of the most excitable visitors that ever congregated on The Oval.

THE MARYLEBONE CLUB IN 1871 The 85th season of the MCC was one of storms, showers, sunshine, good wickets, splendid batting, great scoring, and one-sided matches. A thunderstorm interrupted the progress of the opening match at Lord's; torrents of rain and hailstones of large size fell during the violent storm that stopped play in the MCC and Ground v Cambridge University match on the old ground; frequent and heavy showers of rain made a mud pond of the wickets, and prevented the completion of that – so far – capitally contested match between the Gentlemen and Players of England; and the continuous heavy rainfall from morn to past mid-day that put cricket on one side for a whole day in Willsher's match, will not readily be forgotten by the very many friends of the Kent bowler who felt interested in the success of the cricket battle between the Benedicts and Bachelors of England. June was nippingly cold, and July was wet and windy, but there are two sides to all tales told, and if the greater portion of the three months up at Lord's in 1871 was unseasonably stormy and showery (and it *was* so), sunshine at other times beamed brilliantly on the famous old turf, most opportunely so at the North v South; at the Oxford v Cambridge; and at the Eton v Harrow matches, and those three attractive contests collectively drew to Lord's audiences more numerous than had ever before been attracted there to three matches in one season.

Compiled by Christopher Lane

HONOURS AND AWARDS IN 2020-21

In 2020-21, the following were decorated for their services to cricket:

Queen's Birthday Honours, 2020: D. B. R. Bowden (Preston Nomads and Sussex Cricket Foundation; services to cricket and the community in Sussex) MBE; D. Gough (Yorkshire and England; services to cricket and charity) MBE; T. W. Higginson (British Association for Cricketers with Disabilities; services to disability cricket) MBE.

Note: In July 2020, Sir Ian Botham was awarded a life peerage, as Baron Botham of Ravensworth, but this was a political nomination after his support for the campaign for the UK to leave the European Union.

Queen's Birthday Honours (Australia), 2020: M. J. Bailey (services to cricket and the community of Charters Towers, Queensland) OAM; K. I. Carroll (services to cricket in Victoria) OAM; M. J. Clarke (New South Wales and Australia; services to cricket and the community) AO; L. A. Larsen (New South Wales and Australia Women; services to cricket) AM; G. J. Price (services to cricket and the community in New South Wales) OAM; G. A. Somerville (services to cricket and the community in New South Wales) OAM.

Queen's Birthday Honours (New Zealand), 2020: C. Daji (services to the Indian community and sport in Auckland) QSM; S. C. Patel (Dannevirke CA; services to the community and sport) QSM; M. A. Walker (Central Western CC; services to sport and education) QSM.

Sitara-e-Imtiaz (Pakistan): Abdul Qadir (posthumously).

Arjuna Awards (India), 2020: D. B. Sharma (Bengal and India Women); I. Sharma (Delhi and India).

New Year's Honours, 2021: S. Bi (Worcestershire women, coach and umpire; services to cricket and diversity in sport) BEM; D. C. Knight and M. J. Knight (Newport CC; services to the club) BEM; D. J. Mahoney (ECB chief operating officer; services to sport) MBE.

New Year's Honours (New Zealand), 2021: D. A. Hockley (Canterbury and New Zealand women; services to cricket) MNZM.

Australia Day Honours, 2021: G. S. Chappell (Queensland and Australia; services to cricket and charity) AO; K. B. Gartrell (Western Australia; services to cricket) OAM; J. A. Howard (Ringwood CC scorer; services to cricket) OAM; K. O'Neill (Carlton CC scorer; services to cricket) OAM; C. J. Reece (Kingston Hawthorn CC scorer; services to cricket) OAM; B. Smith (services to cricket and the community of North Balwyn) OAM; G. A. Voyage (St Kilda CC; services to cricket and Australian rules football) OAM; M. Walsh (Essendon CC and former national team scorer; services to cricket) OAM; P. M. Warner (Camberwell CC; services to cricket and Australian rules football) OAM.

ICC AWARDS

Because of the shortage of international cricket over the previous months, the International Cricket Council's annual awards were replaced by a one-off set of awards for the decade, announced in December 2020. More than 1.5m fans worldwide joined journalists, broadcasters, statisticians, analysts and former cricketers in the voting.

Male Cricketer of the Decade (Sir Garfield Sobers Trophy)	**Virat Kohli** (India)
Female Cricketer of the Decade (Rachael Heyhoe Flint Award)	**Ellyse Perry** (Australia)
Men's Test Cricketer of the Decade	**Steve Smith** (Australia)
Men's One-Day International Cricketer of the Decade	**Virat Kohli** (India)
Women's One-Day International Cricketer of the Decade	**Ellyse Perry** (Australia)
Men's Twenty20 International Cricketer of the Decade	**Rashid Khan** (Afghanistan)
Women's Twenty20 International Cricketer of the Decade	**Ellyse Perry** (Australia)
Men's Associate Player of the Year	**Kyle Coetzer** (Scotland)
Women's Associate Player of the Year	**Kathryn Bryce** (Scotland)
Spirit of Cricket Award of the Decade	***M. S. Dhoni** (India)

* *For recalling Ian Bell after a controversial run-out in the Nottingham Test of 2011.*

The voting academy of journalists and broadcasters selected these ICC World XIs of the decade:

Men's Test team of the decade		*Men's ODI team of the decade*		*Men's T20I team of the decade*	
1	Alastair Cook (E)	1	Rohit Sharma (I)	1	Rohit Sharma (I)
2	David Warner (A)	2	David Warner (A)	2	Chris Gayle (WI)
3	Kane Williamson (NZ)	3	Virat Kohli (I)	3	Aaron Finch (A)
4	*Virat Kohli (I)	4	A. B. de Villiers (SA)	4	Virat Kohli (I)
5	Steve Smith (A)	5	Shakib Al Hasan (B)	5	A. B. de Villiers (SA)
6	†Kumar Sangakkara (SL)	6	*†M. S. Dhoni (I)	6	Glenn Maxwell (A)
7	Ben Stokes (E)	7	Ben Stokes (E)	7	*†M. S. Dhoni (I)
8	Ravichandran Ashwin (I)	8	Mitchell Starc (A)	8	Kieron Pollard (WI)
9	Dale Steyn (SA)	9	Trent Boult (NZ)	9	Rashid Khan (Afg)
10	Stuart Broad (E)	10	Imran Tahir (SA)	10	Jasprit Bumrah (I)
11	James Anderson (E)	11	Lasith Malinga (SL)	11	Lasith Malinga (SL)

Women's ODI team of the decade		*Women's T20I team of the decade*	
1	Alyssa Healy (A)	1	†Alyssa Healy (A)
2	Suzie Bates (NZ)	2	Sophie Devine (NZ)
3	Mithali Raj (I)	3	Suzie Bates (NZ)
4	*Meg Lanning (A)	4	*Meg Lanning (A)
5	Stafanie Taylor (WI)	5	Harmanpreet Kaur (I)
6	†Sarah Taylor (E)	6	Stafanie Taylor (WI)
7	Ellyse Perry (A)	7	Deandra Dottin (WI)
8	Dane van Niekerk (SA)	8	Ellyse Perry (A)
9	Marizanne Kapp (SA)	9	Anya Shrubsole (E)
10	Jhulan Goswami (I)	10	Megan Schutt (A)
11	Anisa Mohammed (WI)	11	Poonam Yadav (I)

ICC CRICKET HALL OF FAME

The ICC Cricket Hall of Fame was launched in 2009 in association with the Federation of International Cricketers' Associations to recognise legends of the game. In the first year, 60 members were inducted: 55 from the earlier FICA Hall of Fame, plus five players elected in October 2009 by a voting academy made up of the ICC president, 11 ICC member representatives, a FICA representative, a women's cricket representative, ten journalists, a statistician, and all living members of the Hall of Fame. Candidates must have retired from international cricket at least five years ago.

The members elected in 2020 were Jacques Kallis (South Africa), Lisa Sthalekar (Australia) and Zaheer Abbas (Pakistan), who brought the total to 93.

ICC DEVELOPMENT AWARDS

The ICC announced the global winners of their 2019 Development Awards for Associate Members in July 2020.

Participation Programme	**Cricket PNG** (projects involving 235,000 people)
Female Participation Programme	**Rwanda Cricket Association** (project for 15–25-year-old women)
Associate Men's Performance of the Year	**Cricket Namibia** (beating Hong Kong to secure ODI status)
Associate Women's Performance of the Year	**Thailand** (beating Ireland in T20 World Cup qualifier)
Digital Engagement of the Year	**Cricket Finland** (live-streaming their T20 series with Spain)
Good Initiative of the Year	**Japan Cricket Association** (Typhoon Hagibis recovery project)

ALLAN BORDER MEDAL

David Warner won his third Allan Border Medal, for the best Australian men's international player of the previous 12 months, in February 2020. He had begun the qualifying period still banned after the ball-tampering scandal in South Africa, and it included a disastrous run in the Ashes, but he fought back with a string of high scores, including a Test triple-hundred against Pakistan. Warner received 194 votes from team-mates, umpires and journalists, one ahead of Steve Smith and nine ahead of the previous year's winner, Pat Cummins. The award has also been won by Glenn McGrath, Steve Waugh, Matthew Hayden, Adam Gilchrist, Ricky Ponting (four times), Michael Clarke (four times), Brett Lee, Shane Watson (twice), Mitchell Johnson, Smith (twice) and Cummins. Warner was also named Twenty20 International Player of the Year. **Marnus Labuschagne** was Test Player of the Year, and the Men's One-day International Player of the Year was national white-ball captain **Aaron Finch**. **Shaun Marsh** of Western Australia was Men's Domestic Player of the Year, and South Australia's **Wes Agar** the Bradman Young Cricketer of the Year. **Ellyse Perry** won the Belinda Clark Award for the leading woman player for the third time, with 161 votes, eight ahead of **Alyssa Healy**, who claimed the One-Day International and Twenty20 International Player of the Year awards for the second year running. **Molly Strano** of Victoria was Women's Domestic Player of the Year, and her team-mate **Taylor Vlaeminck** the Betty Wilson Young Cricketer of the Year. Former Hobart Hurricanes all-rounder **Corrine Hall** won the Community Champion award for her work with education and awareness programmes and grassroots cricket.

AUSTRALIAN STATE CRICKET AWARDS

The Sheffield Shield Player of the Year award for 2019-20 was made jointly to **Moises Henriques**, who scored 512 runs for winners New South Wales, and **Nic Maddinson**, with 780 for runners-up Victoria, after they tied on 16 points. The award, instituted in 1975-76, is adjudicated by umpires over the season. **Ashleigh Gardner**, who had helped Australia's women win the Ashes and the T20 World Cup, was the Taverners Indigenous Cricketer of the Year. The Marsh One-Day Cup award was shared by **Marnus Labuschagne** and **Usman Khawaja** (both Queensland). The BBL Player of the Year was **Marcus Stoinis** (Melbourne Stars) and the WBBL award went to **Sophie Devine** (Adelaide Strikers). Western Australia's **Nicole Bolton** was the Women's National Cricket League Player of the Year. **Paul Wilson** was Umpire of the Year for the third time running, and the **Tasmania** men's and women's teams retained the Benaud Spirit of Cricket Awards for fair play – the women sharing their award with New South Wales and Australian Capital Territory.

CRICKET SOUTH AFRICA AWARDS

South Africa's new captain, **Quinton de Kock**, was named Men's Cricketer of the Year and Players' Player of the Year at the CSA awards, staged online in July 2020. He also retained his title as Test Cricketer of the Year. **Lungi Ngidi** picked up ODI Cricketer of the Year and T20 International Cricketer of the Year; **David Miller** was the Fans' Player of the Year. **Laura Wolvaardt** emulated de Kock with a hat-trick in the women's categories: she was named Women's Cricketer of the Year, Players' Player of the Year and ODI Cricketer of the Year. **Shabnim Ismail** was Women's T20 Cricketer of the Year again. The International Men's Newcomer of the Year was **Anrich Nortje** (Men), who also claimed the award for Delivery of the Year, for the ball that dismissed David Warner in the third ODI against Australia in March. The International Women's Newcomer of the Year was **Nonkululeko Mlaba**. The Streetwise Award went to **Mignon du Preez**, for the six which levelled the scores in South Africa's victory over England in the Women's T20 World Cup.

In the CSA domestic awards, **George Linde** (Cape Cobras) was the Four-Day Domestic Series Cricketer of the Season and also took the SACA Most Valuable Player Award; **Grant Roelofsen** (Dolphins) was the One-Day Cup Cricketer of the Season and Domestic Players' Player. **Wandile Makewetu** (Knights) was the Domestic Newcomer of the Season, and the Coach of the Season was **Wandile Gwavu** (Lions). In the Mzansi Super League, **Tabraiz Shamsi** (Paarl Rocks) was named Impact Player of the Year, and **Janneman Malan** (Cape Town Blitz) Young Player of the Year. The CSA Provincial awards went to **Beyers Swanepoel** (Northern Cape), Three-Day Cricketer of the Year; **Ruan de Swardt** (Northerns), One-Day Cricketer of the Year; **Lerato Kgoatle** (Limpopo) T20 Cricketer of the Year; and **Richard Das Neves** (Easterns), Coach of the Year. **Warriors** won the Fair Play Award. **Adrian Holdstock** was Umpire of the Year as well as Umpires' Umpire, and **Central Gauteng Lions** were the Scorers' Association of the Year.

NEW ZEALAND CRICKET AWARDS

Ross Taylor won his third Sir Richard Hadlee Medal for Player of the Year at the NZC awards, sponsored by banking group ANZ, in April 2020, and was also named Men's T20 Player of the Year. **Tim Southee** was named Test Player of the Year, and also won the Winsor Cup for first-class bowling. New Zealand captain **Kane Williamson** was the Men's ODI Player of the Year, with his role at the World Cup in 2019 singled out. **Suzie Bates** was the Women's ODI Player of the Year, and **Sophie Devine** retained the Women's T20 Player of the Year award, also picking up the Women's Dream11 Super Smash Player of the Year. The Men's Domestic Player of the Year was

Devon Conway again, and he also won the Dream11 Super Smash Men's Player of the Year award; **Tom Latham** won the Redpath Cup for first-class batting. **Katie Gurrey** was the Women's Domestic Player of the Year and also won the Ruth Martin Cup for women's domestic batting while **Jess Kerr** was awarded the Phyl Blackler Cup for women's domestic bowling. **Ian Smith** won the Bert Sutcliffe Medal for Outstanding Services to Cricket.

PROFESSIONAL CRICKETERS' ASSOCIATION AWARDS

The following awards were announced on October 3, 2020, during what should have been the Vitality Blast finals day.

Reg Hayter Cup (NatWest PCA Men's Player of the Year)	**Chris Woakes**
NatWest PCA Women's Player of the Year	**Sarah Glenn**
Vitality PCA Young Player of the Year	**Zak Crawley**
Test Player of the Summer	**Stuart Broad**
Royal London ODI Player of the Summer	**David Willey**
Vitality IT20 Player of the Summer	**Dawid Malan**
Bob Willis Trophy Player of the Year	**Craig Overton**
Vitality Blast Player of the Year	**Will Jacks**
Rachael Heyhoe Flint Trophy Player of the Year	**Georgia Adams**
ECB Special Award	**Nick Peirce** (ECB medical director)

Greene King Team of the Year: **Alastair Cook, Jake Libby, Tom Lammonby, Ben Duckett, Will Jacks, †Chris Cooke, Ryan Higgins, Craig Overton, *Simon Harmer, Darren Stevens, Josh Davey**.

CHRISTOPHER MARTIN-JENKINS SPIRIT OF CRICKET AWARDS

MCC and the BBC introduced the Spirit of Cricket awards in memory of Christopher Martin-Jenkins, the former MCC president and *Test Match Special* commentator, in 2013. In December 2020, the award was made to **Cricket West Indies**, for their courage in sending their men's and women's teams to tour England amid the disruption of the Covid-19 pandemic. MCC and the BBC also commended the Pakistan Cricket Board, Cricket Ireland and Cricket Australia for sending their men's teams, as well as the England and Wales Cricket Board, and everyone involved in the Herculean effort to host a full international programme, which was enjoyed by supporters around the globe.

WALTER LAWRENCE TROPHY

Joe Clarke of Nottinghamshire won the Walter Lawrence Trophy for the fastest century in 2020. Playing Durham in a Vitality Blast game at Chester-le-Street, he reached three figures in 44 balls with his eighth six, which also won the match. Since 2008, the Trophy has been available for innings in all senior cricket in England; before that, it was reserved for the fastest first-class hundred (in 2020, Marchant de Lange's 62-ball century for Glamorgan against Northamptonshire at Northampton). **Georgia Adams**, the captain of Southern Vipers, won the women's award for her 154* against Western Storm at Southampton in the Rachael Heyhoe Flint Trophy, which the Vipers went on to win. The MCCU Universities Award and the Schools Award were not made in 2020 because of the Covid-19 crisis.

CRICKET WRITERS' CLUB AWARDS

The Cricket Writers' Club announced their annual awards in October 2020. Members voted **Zak Crawley** Young Cricketer of the Year (sponsored by NV Play); he had scored 417 runs at 69 for England during the summer, culminating in 267, his maiden Test century, against Pakistan at Southampton, and followed up with hundreds in first-class and Twenty20 formats for Kent. The Bob Willis Trophy Player of the Year (sponsored by William Hill) was **Sir Alastair Cook**; like Simon Harmer, the previous winner, he helped Essex to a first-class title, this time by scoring 563 runs in the BWT. The Women's Cricketer of the year was **Sophie Ecclestone** (Thunder and England); in 2020, she had risen to the top of the ICC's T20I bowling rankings after becoming the youngest woman (at 20) to take 50 wickets in the format. The Lord's Taverners Disability Cricketer of the

Year was **Dan Bowser** from Devon, part of the England Learning Disability Squad, who scored 499 at 99 in England's 8–0 whitewash of Australia in 2019-20. The Peter Smith Memorial Award "for services to the presentation of cricket to the public" went to **Jason Holder and the West Indies men's team**, "a trailblazing tour party that flew into the unknown… As the first sports team to enter a biobubble, they were instrumental in rescuing the international summer." Holder was also praised for his eloquent words on race, racism and the need for education and unity. **Duncan Hamilton's** biography of Neville Cardus, *The Great Romantic*, was the Cricket Book of the Year; *The Unforgiven* by Ashley Gray was highly commended.

A list of Young Cricketers from 1950 to 2004 appears in Wisden 2005, *page 995. A list of Peter Smith Award winners from 1992 to 2004 appears in* Wisden 2005, *page 745.*

FREEDOM OF THE CITY OF LONDON

Michael Holding and **Ebony Rainford-Brent** were awarded the freedom of the City of London in December 2020, in recognition of their powerful advocacy against racism, and their outstanding sporting achievements. Both spoke on Sky Sports during the summer about the racism they and their families had encountered.

MEETINGS INDUSTRY ASSOCIATION AWARD

In December, **Lancashire CCC's Operations Team** were named the Meetings Industry Association's Team of the Year, for their "united effort, innovation through technology, strategic awareness and operational excellence" in safely delivering nine international fixtures in a behind-closed-doors biosecure environment at Old Trafford during the tours by West Indies, Pakistan and Australia.

CRICKET SOCIETY AWARDS

Best Newcomer in First-class Cricket	**Tom Lammonby** (Somerset)
Best Newcomer in the Rachael Heyhoe Flint Trophy	**Charlotte Taylor** (Southern Vipers)
The Perry-Lewis/Kershaw Memorial Trophy (for contribution to the Cricket Society XI)	**Rob Humphreys and Peter Hardy**
The Howard Milton Award for Cricket Scholarship (in association with the British Society of Sports History)	**The Sussex Cricket Museum**

WOMBWELL CRICKET LOVERS' SOCIETY AWARDS

George Spofforth Cricketer of the Year	**Chris Woakes** (England)
Brian Sellers Captain of the Year	**Tom Westley** (Essex)
C. B. Fry Young Cricketer of the Year	**Zak Crawley** (Kent/England)
Denis Compton Memorial Award for Flair	**Dawid Malan** (Yorkshire/England)
Denzil Batchelor Award for Services to English Cricket	**Ian Bell** (Warwickshire/England)
Dr Leslie Taylor Award (best Roses performance)	**Adam Lyth** (Yorkshire)
Les Bailey Most Promising Young Yorkshire Player	**Jordan Thompson**
Ted Umbers Award – Services to Yorkshire Cricket	**David Warner***
J. M. Kilburn Cricket Writer of the Year	**David Warner**
Jack Fingleton Cricket Commentator of the Year	**Isa Guha**

* *David Warner is the former sports editor of the* Bradford Telegraph & Argus*; he has also served as* Wisden's *Yorkshire correspondent, editor of the county yearbook and president of the Cricket Writers' Club. His latest book, about Brian Close*, Just A Few Lines…, *was published in 2020.*

ECB COUNTY JOURNALISM AWARDS

The ECB announced the winners of the annual County Cricket Journalism Awards for the coverage of domestic cricket in March 2020. **Charlie Taylor** of BBC Somerset had a double triumph, as the Christopher Martin-Jenkins Young Journalist of the Year (which he previously won in 2017) and Domestic Cricket Broadcaster of the Year. Paul Martin and Richard Rae were the runners-up as Young Journalist and Domestic Broadcaster respectively. ***The Daily Telegraph*** won the award for

Outstanding Newspaper Coverage, while the 2019 winners, ***The Yorkshire Post***, retained their other title as the Regional Newspaper of the Year, ahead of the *County Gazette* in Somerset and *The Sentinel* in Staffordshire. The Outstanding Online Coverage award went to **thecricketer.com** for the second year running.

ECB OSCAs

The ECB announced the NatWest Outstanding Service to Cricket Awards to volunteers from recreational cricket in October. In 2020, only three awards were made, all to volunteers who had made special contributions to their club and community during the Covid-19 crisis. The winners were:

#RaiseTheBat Award **Jane Reeson** (Cambridgeshire)
Chair of Over CC, Reeson was furloughed, but spent hours every day organising the club and working with the community, including shopping, walking dogs and collecting prescriptions.

Connecting Communities **Jamie Saunders** (Cambridgeshire)
With Isleham CC, organised members to deliver up to 300 fruit and vegetable boxes a week to the elderly and vulnerable, and donated iPads to help villagers in hospital keep in touch with family.

Pro-Active Leadership **Miles Horner** (Cheshire)
Captain of Macclesfield CC's Third XI, Horner set up a club podcast "Get It Whacked" to keep members entertained; it became so popular it has been listened to in 14 countries.

ACS STATISTICIAN OF THE YEAR

In March 2021, the Association of Cricket Statisticians and Historians awarded the Brooke–Lambert Statistician of the Year trophy to **Derek Carlaw**, for his work on an online A to Z of Kent County Cricketers, containing biographical details of 616 players who appeared for Kent in first-class or "important" matches between 1806 and 1939.

2021 FIXTURES

Test	Test match
RL ODI	Royal London one-day international
VT20I	Vitality Twenty20 international
LV=CC	LV= County Championship
LV=CC2	Second group stage of LV= County Championship
BWT	Bob Willis Trophy
RLODC	Royal London One-Day Cup
VB T20	Vitality Blast
RHF	Rachael Heyhoe Flint Trophy
WRC (20)	Women's regional competition
NC	National Counties v fc counties (50 overs)
Univ	University match
💡	Day/night or floodlit game

At the time of going to press, the ECB had not released dates for women's international fixtures, or The Hundred.

Thu Apr 8–Sun 11	**LV=CC**	Essex	v Worcestershire	Chelmsford
		Gloucestershire	v Surrey	Bristol
		Leicestershire	v Hampshire	Leicester
		Middlesex	v Somerset	Lord's
		Northamptonshire	v Kent	Northampton
		Nottinghamshire	v Durham	Nottingham
		Sussex	v Lancashire	Hove
		Warwickshire	v Derbyshire	Birmingham
		Yorkshire	v Glamorgan	Leeds
Thu Apr 15–Sun 18	**LV=CC**	Derbyshire	v Worcestershire	Derby
		Essex	v Durham	Chelmsford
		Glamorgan	v Sussex	Cardiff
		Hampshire	v Middlesex	Southampton
		Kent	v Yorkshire	Canterbury
		Lancashire	v Northamptonshire	Manchester
		Nottinghamshire	v Warwickshire	Nottingham
		Somerset	v Gloucestershire	Taunton
		Surrey	v Leicestershire	The Oval
Thu Apr 22–Sun 25	**LV=CC**	Durham	v Derbyshire	Chester-le-Street
		Hampshire	v Gloucestershire	Southampton
		Kent	v Lancashire	Canterbury
		Leicestershire	v Somerset	Leicester
		Middlesex	v Surrey	Lord's
		Northamptonshire	v Glamorgan	Northampton
		Sussex	v Yorkshire	Hove
		Warwickshire	v Essex	Birmingham
		Worcestershire	v Nottinghamshire	Worcester
Thu Apr 29–Sun May 2	**LV=CC**	Derbyshire	v Nottinghamshire	Derby
		Durham	v Warwickshire	Chester-le-Street
		Glamorgan	v Kent	Cardiff
		Gloucestershire	v Leicestershire	Bristol
		Lancashire	v Sussex	Manchester
		Somerset	v Middlesex	Taunton
		Surrey	v Hampshire	The Oval
		Worcestershire	v Essex	Worcester
		Yorkshire	v Northamptonshire	Leeds

Thu May 6–Sun 9	**LV=CC**	Hampshire	v Somerset	Southampton
		Lancashire	v Glamorgan	Manchester
		Leicestershire	v Surrey	Leicester
		Middlesex	v Gloucestershire	Lord's
		Northamptonshire	v Sussex	Northampton
		Nottinghamshire	v Essex	Nottingham
		Warwickshire	v Worcestershire	Birmingham
		Yorkshire	v Kent	Leeds
Thu May 13–Sun 16	**LV=CC**	Durham	v Worcestershire	Chester-le-Street
		Essex	v Derbyshire	Chelmsford
		Glamorgan	v Yorkshire	Cardiff
		Middlesex	v Hampshire	Lord's
		Somerset	v Surrey	Taunton
		Sussex	v Kent	Hove
Fri May 14	**Univ (T20)**	Camb U women	v Oxford U women	Cambridge
		Cambridge U	v Oxford U	Cambridge
Thu May 20–Sun 23	**LV=CC**	Derbyshire	v Durham	Derby
		Essex	v Warwickshire	Chelmsford
		Gloucestershire	v Somerset	Bristol
		Hampshire	v Leicestershire	Southampton
		Kent	v Glamorgan	Canterbury
		Northamptonshire	v Lancashire	Northampton
		Nottinghamshire	v Worcestershire	Nottingham
		Surrey	v Middlesex	The Oval
Tue May 25–Fri 28	**Tour**	Somerset	v New Zealanders	Taunton
Thu May 27–Sun 30	**LV=CC**	Durham	v Essex	Chester-le-Street
		Lancashire	v Yorkshire	Manchester
		Leicestershire	v Middlesex	Leicester
		Surrey	v Gloucestershire	Guildford
		Sussex	v Northamptonshire	Hove
		Warwickshire	v Nottinghamshire	Birmingham
		Worcestershire	v Derbyshire	Worcester
Sat May 29	**RHF**	N Diamonds	v Central Sparks	Leeds
		S Vipers	v Lightning	Southampton
		Sunrisers	v SE Stars	Chelmsford
		W Storm	v Thunder	Bristol
Mon May 31	**RHF**	Central Sparks	v W Storm	Birmingham
		Lightning	v N Diamonds	TBC
		SE Stars	v S Vipers	TBC
		Thunder	v Sunrisers	TBC
Wed Jun 2–Sun 6	**1st Test**	**ENGLAND**	**v NEW ZEALAND**	**Lord's**
Thu Jun 3–Sun 6	**LV=CC**	Derbyshire	v Warwickshire	Derby
		Essex	v Nottinghamshire	Chelmsford
		Glamorgan	v Lancashire	Cardiff
		Kent	v Northamptonshire	Canterbury
		Leicestershire	v Gloucestershire	Leicester
		Somerset	v Hampshire	Taunton
		Worcestershire	v Durham	Worcester
		Yorkshire	v Sussex	Leeds
Sat Jun 5	**RHF**	S Vipers	v Central Sparks	TBC
		SE Stars	v W Storm	The Oval
		Sunrisers	v N Diamonds	TBC
		Thunder	v Lightning	TBC

Wed Jun 9	**VB T20**	Kent	v Hampshire	Canterbury	💡
		Lancashire	v Derbyshire	Manchester	
		Somerset	v Essex	Taunton	💡
		Worcestershire	v Nottinghamshire	Worcester	
Thu Jun 10–Mon 14	**2nd Test**	**ENGLAND**	**v NEW ZEALAND**	**Birmingham**	
Thu Jun 10	**VB T20**	Glamorgan	v Gloucestershire	Cardiff	💡
		Lancashire	v Leicestershire	Manchester	💡
		Middlesex	v Surrey	Lord's	💡
		Yorkshire	v Warwickshire	Leeds	💡
Fri Jun 11	**VB T20**	Durham	v Yorkshire	Chester-le-Street	💡
		Essex	v Hampshire	Chelmsford	💡
		Gloucestershire	v Sussex	Bristol	💡
		Kent	v Middlesex	Canterbury	💡
		Leicestershire	v Derbyshire	Leicester	💡
		Northamptonshire	v Worcestershire	Northampton	💡
		Nottinghamshire	v Warwickshire	Nottingham	💡
		Somerset	v Surrey	Taunton	💡
Sat Jun 12	**VB T20**	Sussex	v Hampshire	Hove	💡
	RHF	Central Sparks	v Thunder	Worcester	
		Lightning	v Sunrisers	TBC	
		N Diamonds	v SE Stars	Leeds	
		W Storm	v S Vipers	TBC	
Sun Jun 13	**VB T20**	Derbyshire	v Warwickshire	Derby	
		Glamorgan	v Essex	Cardiff	
		Kent	v Gloucestershire	Canterbury	
		Leicestershire	v Durham	Leicester	
		Northamptonshire	v Nottinghamshire	Northampton	
		Worcestershire	v Lancashire	Worcester	
Mon Jun 14	**VB T20**	Surrey	v Glamorgan	The Oval	💡
Tue Jun 15	**VB T20**	Derbyshire	v Lancashire	Derby	💡
		Durham	v Nottinghamshire	Chester-le-Street	💡
		Essex	v Sussex	Chelmsford	💡
		Middlesex	v Hampshire	Radlett	
		Northamptonshire	v Warwickshire	Northampton	💡
		Somerset	v Kent	Taunton	💡
		Yorkshire	v Leicestershire	Leeds	💡
Wed Jun 16	**VB T20**	Glamorgan	v Kent	Cardiff	💡
		Leicestershire	v Warwickshire	Leicester	💡
		Worcestershire	v Yorkshire	Worcester	
Thu Jun 17	**VB T20**	Derbyshire	v Northamptonshire	Derby	💡
		Durham	v Lancashire	Chester-le-Street	💡
		Middlesex	v Gloucestershire	Radlett	
		Surrey	v Sussex	The Oval	💡
Fri Jun 18	**Tour (50)**	Kent	v Sri Lankans	Canterbury	💡
	VB T20	Essex	v Gloucestershire	Chelmsford	💡
		Glamorgan	v Middlesex	Cardiff	💡
		Nottinghamshire	v Derbyshire	Nottingham	💡
		Surrey	v Hampshire	The Oval	💡
		Sussex	v Somerset	Hove	💡
		Warwickshire	v Lancashire	Birmingham	💡
		Worcestershire	v Northamptonshire	Worcester	
		Yorkshire	v Durham	Leeds	💡
Fri Jun 18–Tue 22		**THE WORLD TEST CHAMPIONSHIP FINAL**		**TBC**	
Sat Jun 19	**VB T20**	Somerset	v Glamorgan	Taunton	💡

Date	Competition	Home	Away	Venue
Sun Jun 20	**Tour (20)**	Sussex	v Sri Lankans	Hove
	VB T20	Durham	v Warwickshire	Chester-le-Street
		Gloucestershire	v Hampshire	Bristol
		Kent	v Essex	Canterbury
		Lancashire	v Nottinghamshire	Manchester
		Northamptonshire	v Leicestershire	Northampton
		Yorkshire	v Derbyshire	Leeds
Mon Jun 21	**VB T20**	Surrey	v Essex	The Oval
Tue Jun 22	**VB T20**	Derbyshire	v Leicestershire	Derby
		Gloucestershire	v Kent	Bristol
		Nottinghamshire	v Worcestershire	Nottingham
		Sussex	v Glamorgan	Hove
Wed Jun 23	**VT20I**	**ENGLAND**	**v SRI LANKA**	**Cardiff**
	VB T20	Durham	v Northamptonshire	Chester-le-Street
		Surrey	v Somerset	The Oval
		Yorkshire	v Worcestershire	Leeds
Thu Jun 24	**VT20I**	**ENGLAND**	**v SRI LANKA**	**Cardiff**
	VB T20	Gloucestershire	v Glamorgan	Bristol
		Middlesex	v Essex	Lord's
		Warwickshire	v Derbyshire	Birmingham
Fri Jun 25	**VB T20**	Derbyshire	v Nottinghamshire	Derby
		Essex	v Kent	Chelmsford
		Leicestershire	v Yorkshire	Leicester
		Northamptonshire	v Lancashire	Northampton
		Somerset	v Hampshire	Taunton
		Surrey	v Middlesex	The Oval
		Sussex	v Gloucestershire	Hove
		Worcestershire	v Durham	Worcester
Sat Jun 26	**VT20I**	**ENGLAND**	**v SRI LANKA**	**Southampton**
	VB T20	Nottinghamshire	v Lancashire	Nottingham
		Warwickshire	v Durham	Birmingham
		Yorkshire	v Northamptonshire	Leeds
	WRC (20)	Central Sparks	v S Vipers	Birmingham
		Lightning	v SE Stars	Nottingham
		N Diamonds	v Thunder	Leeds
		W Storm	v Sunrisers	Taunton
Sun Jun 27	**VB T20**	Middlesex	v Glamorgan	Radlett
		Sussex	v Surrey	Hove
		Worcestershire	v Leicestershire	Worcester
Sun Jun 27–Wed 30	**Tour**	Derbyshire	v India A	Derby
Mon Jun 28	**VB T20**	Hampshire	v Middlesex	Southampton
		Kent	v Somerset	Canterbury
	Univ (50)	Oxford U women	v Camb U women	Wormsley
Tue Jun 29	**RL ODI**	**ENGLAND**	**v SRI LANKA**	**Chester-le-Street**
	VB T20	Essex	v Somerset	Chelmsford
		Glamorgan	v Surrey	Cardiff
		Leicestershire	v Northamptonshire	Leicester
		Sussex	v Kent	Hove
Wed Jun 30	**VB T20**	Hampshire	v Surrey	Southampton
		Northamptonshire	v Durham	Northampton
		Warwickshire	v Yorkshire	Birmingham
Thu Jul 1	**RL ODI**	**ENGLAND**	**v SRI LANKA**	**The Oval**
	VB T20	Essex	v Glamorgan	Chelmsford
		Gloucestershire	v Somerset	Bristol
		Lancashire	v Worcestershire	Manchester
		Middlesex	v Sussex	Lord's
		Nottinghamshire	v Leicestershire	Nottingham

Fri Jul 2	**VB T20**	Derbyshire	v Worcestershire	Derby	💡
		Durham	v Leicestershire	Chester-le-Street	💡
		Glamorgan	v Sussex	Cardiff	💡
		Hampshire	v Gloucestershire	Southampton	💡
		Kent	v Surrey	Canterbury	💡
		Somerset	v Middlesex	Taunton	💡
		Warwickshire	v Nottinghamshire	Birmingham	💡
		Yorkshire	v Lancashire	Leeds	💡
	WRC (20)	Sunrisers	v N Diamonds	Chelmsford	
Sat Jul 3	**WRC (20)**	S Vipers	v Lightning	TBC	
		SE Stars	v Central Sparks	TBC	
		Thunder	v W Storm	TBC	
Sun Jul 4	**RL ODI**	**ENGLAND**	**v SRI LANKA**	**Bristol**	
Sun Jul 4–Wed 7	**Tour**	Essex	v India A	Chelmsford	
	LV=CC	Hampshire	v Surrey	Southampton	
		Lancashire	v Kent	Manchester	
		Northamptonshire	v Yorkshire	Northampton	
		Nottinghamshire	v Derbyshire	Nottingham	
		Somerset	v Leicestershire	Taunton	
		Sussex	v Glamorgan	Hove	
		Warwickshire	v Durham	Birmingham	
Mon Jul 5–Thu 8	**LV=CC**	Gloucestershire	v Middlesex	Cheltenham	
	Univ	Oxford U	v Cambridge U	Oxford	
Thu Jul 8	**RL ODI**	**ENGLAND**	**v PAKISTAN**	**Cardiff**	💡
Fri Jul 9	**VB T20**	Durham	v Derbyshire	Chester-le-Street	💡
		Gloucestershire	v Middlesex	Cheltenham	
		Hampshire	v Somerset	Southampton	💡
		Lancashire	v Northamptonshire	Manchester	💡
		Nottinghamshire	v Yorkshire	Nottingham	💡
		Surrey	v Kent	The Oval	💡
		Sussex	v Essex	Hove	💡
		Worcestershire	v Warwickshire	Worcester	
	WRC (20)	Thunder	v Sunrisers	Manchester	
Sat Jul 10	**RL ODI**	**ENGLAND**	**v PAKISTAN**	**Lord's**	
	WRC (20)	Lightning	v Central Sparks	TBC	
		SE Stars	v S Vipers	TBC	
		W Storm	v N Diamonds	Taunton	
Sun Jul 11–Wed 14	**LV=CC**	Derbyshire	v Essex	Chesterfield	
		Durham	v Nottinghamshire	Chester-le-Street	
		Glamorgan	v Northamptonshire	Cardiff	
		Gloucestershire	v Hampshire	Cheltenham	
		Kent	v Sussex	Beckenham	
		Middlesex	v Leicestershire	Northwood	
		Surrey	v Somerset	The Oval	
		Worcestershire	v Warwickshire	Worcester	
		Yorkshire	v Lancashire	Scarborough	
Mon Jul 12–Thu 15	**Tour**	FC Counties XI	v India A	Leicester	
Tue Jul 13	**RL ODI**	**ENGLAND**	**v PAKISTAN**	**Birmingham**	💡
Fri Jul 16	**VT20I**	**ENGLAND**	**v PAKISTAN**	**Nottingham**	💡
	VB T20	Glamorgan	v Somerset	Cardiff	💡
		Gloucestershire	v Surrey	Cheltenham	
		Hampshire	v Essex	Southampton	
		Lancashire	v Durham	Manchester	💡
		Leicestershire	v Nottinghamshire	Leicester	💡
		Middlesex	v Kent	Lord's	💡
		Northamptonshire	v Derbyshire	Northampton	💡
		Warwickshire	v Worcestershire	Birmingham	💡

Date	Competition	Team	Opponent	Venue
Sat Jul 17	**VB T20**	Lancashire	v Yorkshire	Manchester
Sun Jul 18	**VT20I**	**ENGLAND**	**v PAKISTAN**	**Leeds**
	VB T20	Derbyshire	v Yorkshire	Chesterfield
		Essex	v Middlesex	Chelmsford
		Hampshire	v Glamorgan	Southampton
		Kent	v Sussex	Canterbury
		Leicestershire	v Worcestershire	Leicester
		Nottinghamshire	v Durham	Nottingham
		Somerset	v Gloucestershire	Taunton
		Warwickshire	v Northamptonshire	Birmingham
Tue Jul 20	**VT20I**	**ENGLAND**	**v PAKISTAN**	**Manchester**
	NC	Bedfordshire	v Northamptonshire	TBC
		Berkshire	v Middlesex	TBC
		Buckinghamshire	v Surrey	TBC
		Cambridgeshire	v Essex	TBC
		Cheshire	v Warwickshire	TBC
		Cornwall	v Somerset	TBC
		Cumberland	v Lancashire	TBC
		Dorset	v Hampshire	TBC
		Herefordshire	v Worcestershire	TBC
		Lincolnshire	v Durham	TBC
		Norfolk	v Nottinghamshire	TBC
		Northumberland	v Yorkshire	TBC
		Oxfordshire	v Sussex	TBC
		Shropshire	v Derbyshire	TBC
		Staffordshire	v Leicestershire	TBC
		Suffolk	v Kent	TBC
		Wales MC	v Glamorgan	TBC
		Wiltshire	v Gloucestershire	TBC
Wed Jul 21–Sat 24	**Tour**	Indians	v India A	Northampton
Thu Jul 22	**RLODC**	Glamorgan	v Warwickshire	Cardiff
		Hampshire	v Essex	Southampton
		Kent	v Durham	TBC
		Leicestershire	v Derbyshire	Leicester
		Yorkshire	v Surrey	Scarborough
	NC	Devon	v Somerset	TBC
		Hertfordshire	v Middlesex	TBC
Fri Jul 23	**RLODC**	Lancashire	v Sussex	TBC
Sun Jul 25	**RLODC**	Essex	v Middlesex	Chelmsford
		Gloucestershire	v Lancashire	Bristol
		Leicestershire	v Yorkshire	Leicester
		Northamptonshire	v Glamorgan	Northampton
		Somerset	v Derbyshire	Taunton
		Sussex	v Durham	Hove
		Warwickshire	v Nottinghamshire	Birmingham
		Worcestershire	v Kent	Worcester
Tue Jul 27	**RLODC**	Derbyshire	v Warwickshire	Derby
		Gloucestershire	v Worcestershire	Bristol
		Hampshire	v Sussex	Southampton
		Middlesex	v Durham	Radlett
		Surrey	v Nottinghamshire	Guildford
Wed Jul 28	**RLODC**	Kent	v Lancashire	TBC
		Somerset	v Glamorgan	Taunton
		Yorkshire	v Northamptonshire	Scarborough
Wed Jul 28–Sat 31	**Tour**	Indians	v India A	Leicester
Thu Jul 29	**RLODC**	Durham	v Gloucestershire	Gosforth
		Essex	v Worcestershire	Chelmsford
		Warwickshire	v Leicestershire	Birmingham

Fri Jul 30	**RLODC**	Derbyshire	v Glamorgan	Derby
		Middlesex	v Hampshire	Radlett
		Nottinghamshire	v Somerset	Sookholme
		Surrey	v Northamptonshire	The Oval
		Sussex	v Kent	Hove
Sun Aug 1	**RLODC**	Essex	v Kent	Chelmsford
		Hampshire	v Lancashire	Southampton
		Northamptonshire	v Derbyshire	Northampton
		Nottinghamshire	v Leicestershire	Sookholme
		Somerset	v Yorkshire	Taunton
		Sussex	v Gloucestershire	Hove
		Worcestershire	v Middlesex	Worcester
Tue Aug 3	**RLODC**	Glamorgan	v Surrey	Cardiff
		Gloucestershire	v Essex	Bristol
		Lancashire	v Middlesex	Manchester
		Yorkshire	v Warwickshire	York
Wed Aug 4–Sun 8	**1st Test**	**ENGLAND**	**v INDIA**	**Nottingham**
Wed Aug 4	**RLODC**	Hampshire	v Worcestershire	Southampton
		Nottinghamshire	v Derbyshire	Derby
Thu Aug 5	**RLODC**	Durham	v Lancashire	Chester-le-Street
		Leicestershire	v Glamorgan	Leicester
		Surrey	v Somerset	The Oval
Fri Aug 6	**RLODC**	Gloucestershire	v Hampshire	Bristol
		Middlesex	v Kent	Radlett
		Warwickshire	v Northamptonshire	Birmingham
		Worcestershire	v Sussex	Worcester
		Yorkshire	v Nottinghamshire	York
Sat Aug 7	**RLODC**	Leicestershire	v Surrey	Leicester
Sun Aug 8	**RLODC**	Derbyshire	v Yorkshire	Chesterfield
		Durham	v Essex	Chester-le-Street
		Glamorgan	v Nottinghamshire	Cardiff
		Kent	v Hampshire	TBC
		Lancashire	v Worcestershire	Blackpool
		Middlesex	v Gloucestershire	Radlett
		Northamptonshire	v Somerset	Northampton
Tue Aug 10	**RLODC**	Essex	v Sussex	Chelmsford
		Nottinghamshire	v Northamptonshire	Grantham
		Somerset	v Leicestershire	Taunton
		Surrey	v Warwickshire	The Oval
		Worcestershire	v Durham	Worcester
Thu Aug 12–Mon 16	**2nd Test**	**ENGLAND**	**v INDIA**	**Lord's**
Thu Aug 12	**RLODC**	Derbyshire	v Surrey	Derby
		Durham	v Hampshire	Chester-le-Street
		Glamorgan	v Yorkshire	Cardiff
		Kent	v Gloucestershire	TBC
		Lancashire	v Essex	Manchester
		Northamptonshire	v Leicestershire	Northampton
		Sussex	v Middlesex	Hove
		Warwickshire	v Somerset	Birmingham
Sat Aug 14	**RLODC**	**Quarter-final**		
Tue Aug 17	**RLODC**	**Semi-final**		
Thu Aug 19	**RLODC**	**Final**		
Tue Aug 24	**VB T20**	**Quarter-final**		

Date	Competition	Home	Away	Venue
Wed Aug 25–Sun 29	**3rd Test**	**ENGLAND**	**v INDIA**	**Leeds**
Wed Aug 25	**VB T20**	**Quarter-final**		
	WRC (20)	N Diamonds	v Sunrisers	TBC
		S Vipers	v Central Sparks	TBC
		SE Stars	v Lightning	TBC
		W Storm	v Thunder	Cardiff
Thu Aug 26	**VB T20**	**Quarter-final**		
Fri Aug 27	**VB T20**	**Quarter-final**		
Sat Aug 28	**WRC (20)**	Central Sparks	v Lightning	Worcester
		N Diamonds	v W Storm	Chester-le-Street
		S Vipers	v SE Stars	TBC
		Sunrisers	v Thunder	Northampton
Mon Aug 30	**WRC (20)**	Central Sparks	v SE Stars	Worcester
		Lightning	v S Vipers	Derby
		Sunrisers	v W Storm	TBC
		Thunder	v N Diamonds	TBC
Mon Aug 30–Thu Sep 2	**LV=CC2**	TBC	v TBC	(nine matches)
Thu Sep 2–Mon 6	**4th Test**	**ENGLAND**	**v INDIA**	**The Oval**
Sun Sep 5–Wed 8	**LV=CC2**	TBC	v TBC	(nine matches)
Fri Sep 10–Tue 14	**5th Test**	**ENGLAND**	**v INDIA**	**Manchester**
Fri Sep 10	**RHF**	N Diamonds	v W Storm	Chester-le-Street
		SE Stars	v Lightning	TBC
		Sunrisers	v Central Sparks	TBC
		Thunder	v S Vipers	TBC
Sun Sep 12	**RHF**	Central Sparks	v SE Stars	Worcester
		N Diamonds	v Thunder	Chester-le-Street
		Sunrisers	v S Vipers	TBC
		W Storm	v Lightning	Bristol
Sun Sep 12–Wed 15	**LV=CC2**	TBC	v TBC	(nine matches)
Sat Sep 18	**VB T20**	**Final**		
	RHF	Lightning	v Central Sparks	TBC
		S Vipers	v N Diamonds	TBC
		SE Stars	v Thunder	TBC
		W Storm	v Sunrisers	Bristol
Tue Sep 21–Fri 24	**LV=CC2**	TBC	v TBC	(nine matches)
Tue Sep 28–Sat Oct 2	**BWT Final**	TBC	v TBC	Lord's

CRICKET TRADE DIRECTORY

BOOKSELLERS

CHRISTOPHER SAUNDERS, Kingston House, High Street, Newnham-on-Severn, Glos GL14 1BB. Tel: 01594 516030; email: chris@cricket-books.com; website: cricket-books.com. Office/bookroom open by appointment. Second-hand/antiquarian cricket books and memorabilia bought and sold. Regular catalogues issued containing selections from over 12,000 items in stock.

GRACE BOOKS AND CARDS (Ted Kirwan), Donkey Cart Cottage, Main Street, Bruntingthorpe, Lutterworth, Leics LE17 5QE. Tel: 0116 247 8417; email: ted@gracecricketana.co.uk. Second-hand and antiquarian cricket books, *Wisdens*, autographed material and cricket ephemera of all kinds. Now also modern postcards of current international cricketers.

JOHN JEFFERS, The Old Mill, Aylesbury Road, Wing, Leighton Buzzard LU7 0PG. Tel: 01296 688543; e-mail: edgwarerover@live.co.uk. *Wisden* specialist. Immediate decision and top settlement for purchase of *Wisden* collections. Why wait for the next auction? Why pay the auctioneer's commission anyway?

J. W. McKENZIE, 12 Stoneleigh Park Road, Ewell, Epsom, Surrey KT19 0QT. Tel: 020 8393 7700; email: mckenziecricket@btconnect.com; website: mckenzie-cricket.co.uk. Old cricket books and memorabilia specialist since 1971. Free catalogues issued regularly. Large shop premises open 9–4.30 Monday–Friday. Thirty minutes from London Waterloo. Please phone before visiting.

KEN PIESSE CRICKET BOOKS, PO Box 868, Mt Eliza, Victoria 3930, Australia. Tel: (+61) 419 549 458; email: kenpiesse@ozemail.com.au; website: cricketbooks.com.au. Australian cricket's internet specialists. Publishers of quality limited-edition biographies: Turner, Collins, Duff, McDonald, Ironmonger, Loxton and, most recently, *Born Lucky: The Story of Jack Potter, Australia's finest 12th man*.

ROGER PAGE, 10 Ekari Court, Yallambie, Victoria 3085, Australia. Tel: (+61) 3 9435 6332; email: rpcricketbooks@iprimus.com.au; website: rpcricketbooks.com. Australia's only full-time dealer in new and secondhand cricket books. Distributor of overseas cricket annuals and magazines. Agent for Association of Cricket Statisticians and Cricket Memorabilia Society.

ST MARY'S BOOKS & PRINTS, 9 St Mary's Hill, Stamford, Lincolnshire PE9 2DP. Tel: 01780 763033; email: info@stmarysbooks.com; website: stmarysbooks.com. Dealers in *Wisdens*, second-hand, rare cricket books and *Vanity Fair* prints. Book-search service offered.

THE SOMERSET BADGER, River House, Porters Hatch, Meare, Glastonbury, Somerset BA6 9SW. Tel: 0791 232 2620; email: thesomersetbadger@outook.com; website: tinyurl.com/thesomersetbadger. We specialise in buying and selling post-war *Wisdens*. Viewing and valuation by appointment; over 500 editions in stock, and 90% in VGC or better.

SPORTSPAGES, 7 Finns Business Park, Mill Lane, Farnham, Surrey GU10 5RX. Tel: 01252 851040; email: info@sportspages.com; website: sportspages.com. Large stock of *Wisdens*, fine sports books and sports memorabilia. Books and sports memorabilia also purchased. Visitors welcome to browse by appointment.

TIM BEDDOW, 66 Oak Road, Oldbury, West Midlands B68 0BD. Tel: 0121 421 7117 or 07956 456112; email: wisden1864@hotmail.com. Wanted: any items of sporting memorabilia. Cricket, football, boxing, motor racing, TT, F1, stock cars, speedway, ice hockey, rugby, golf, horse racing, athletics and *all* other sports. Top prices paid for vintage items.

WILLIAM H. ROBERTS, Long Low, 27 Gernhill Avenue, Fixby, Huddersfield, West Yorkshire HD2 2HR. Tel: 01484 654463; email: william@roberts-cricket.co.uk; website: williamroberts-cricket.com. Second-hand/antiquarian cricket books, *Wisdens*, autographs and memorabilia bought and sold. Many thanks for your continued support.

WISDEN DIRECT: wisdenalmanack.com/books. *Wisden Cricketers' Almanacks* since 2017 (plus 1864–78 and 1916–19 reprints) and other Wisden publications, all at discounted prices.

WISDEN REPRINTS, email: wisdenauction@cridler.com; website: wisdenauction.com. Limited-edition Willows *Wisden* reprints still available for various years at wisdenauction.com. Secondhand *Wisdens* also sold (see WisdenAuction entry in Auctioneers section).

WISDENWORLD.COM, Tel: 01480 819272 or 07966 513171; email: bill.wisden@gmail.com; website: wisdenworld.com. A unique and friendly service; quality *Wisdens* bought and sold at fair prices, along with free advice on the value of your collection. The world's largest *Wisden*-only seller; licensed by Wisden.

AUCTIONEERS

DOMINIC WINTER, Specialist Auctioneers & Valuers, Mallard House, Broadway Lane, South Cerney, Gloucestershire GL7 5UQ. Tel: 01285 860006; website: dominicwinter.co.uk. Check our website for forthcoming specialist sales.

GRAHAM BUDD AUCTIONS, PO Box 47519, London N14 6XD. Tel: 020 8366 2525; website: grahambuddauctions.co.uk. Specialist auctioneer of sporting memorabilia.

KNIGHTS AUCTIONEERS, Norfolk. Tel: 01263 768488; email: tim@knights.co.uk; website: knights.co.uk. Respected auctioneers, specialising in cricket memorabilia and *Wisden Cricketers' Almanacks*, established in 1993. Three major cricket and sporting memorabilia auctions per year, including specialist *Wisden* sale day in each auction. Entries invited.

WISDENAUCTION.COM. Tel: 0800 7 999 501; email: wisdenauction@cridler.com; website: wisdenauction.com. A specially designed auction website for buying and selling *Wisdens*. List your spares today and bid live for that missing year. Every original edition for sale, including all hardbacks. Built by collectors for collectors, with the best descriptions on the internet.

CRICKET DATABASES

CRICKET ARCHIVE: cricketarchive.com. The most comprehensive searchable database on the internet with scorecards of all first-class, List A, pro T20 and major women's matches, as well as a wealth of league and friendly matches. The database currently has more than 1.25m players and over 700,000 full and partial scorecards.

CRICVIZ: cricviz.com; email: marketing@cricviz.com. CricViz is the largest cricket database, providing predictive modelling and analytics to the ICC, teams and media clients.

CSW DATABASE FOR PCs. Contact Ric Finlay, email: ricf@netspace.net.au; website: tastats.com.au. Men's and women's internationals; major T20 leagues; domestic cricket in Australia, NZ, South Africa and England. Full scorecards and 2,500 searches. Suitable for professionals and hobbyists alike.

WISDEN RECORDS: wisdenrecords.com. Up-to-date and in-depth cricket records from *Wisden*.

CRICKET COLLECTING, MEMORABILIA AND MUSEUMS

CRICKET MEMORABILIA SOCIETY. See entry in Cricket Societies section.

LORD'S TOURS & MUSEUM, Lord's Cricket Ground, St John's Wood, London NW8 8QN. Tel: 020 7616 8595; email: tours@mcc.org.uk; website: lords.org/tours. A tour of Lord's provides a fascinating behind-the-scenes insight into the world's most famous cricket ground. See the original Ashes urn, plus an outstanding collection of art, cricketing memorabilia and much more.

SIR DONALD BRADMAN'S CHILDHOOD HOME, 52 Shepherd Street, Bowral, NSW 2576, Australia. Tel: (+61) 478 779 642; email: hello@52shepherdstreet.com.au; website: 52shepherdstreet.com. The house where Don Bradman developed his phenomenal cricketing skills by throwing a golf ball against the base of a tank stand. Open for tours and special events.

WILLOW STAMPS, 10 Mentmore Close, Harrow, Middlesex HA3 0EA. Tel: 020 8907 4200; email: willowstamps@gmail.com. Standing order service for new cricket stamp issues, comprehensive back stocks of most earlier issues.

WISDEN COLLECTORS' CLUB. Tel: 01480 819272 or 07966 513171; email: bill.wisden@gmail.com; website: wisdencollectorsclub.co.uk. Free and completely impartial advice on *Wisdens*. We also offer *Wisdens* and other cricket books to our members, usually at no charge except postage. Quarterly newsletter, discounts on publications, and a great website. Licensed by Wisden.

WISDENS.ORG. Tel: 07793 060706; email: wisdens@cridler.com; website: wisdens.org; Twitter: @Wisdens. The unofficial *Wisden* collectors' website. Valuations, guide, discussion forum, all free to use. *Wisden* prices updated constantly. We also buy and sell *Wisdens* for our members. Email us for free advice about absolutely anything to do with collecting *Wisdens*.

CRICKET EQUIPMENT

ACUMEN BOOKS, Pennyfields, New Road, Bignall End, Stoke-on-Trent ST7 8QF. Tel: 07956 239801; email: wca@acumenbooks.co.uk; website: acumenbooks.co.uk. Specialist for umpires, scorers, officials, etc. MCC Lawbooks, Tom Smith, other textbooks, Duckworth/Lewis, scorebooks, trousers, over & run counters, gauges, bails (heavy, Hi-Vis and tethered), etc.

BOLA MANUFACTURING LTD, Ravenscourt Road, Patchway, Bristol, BS34 6PL. Tel: 0117 924 3569; email: info@bola.co.uk; website: bola.co.uk. Manufacturer of bowling machines and ball-throwing machines for all sports. Machines for professional and all recreational levels for sale to the UK and overseas.

CHASE CRICKET, Dummer Down Farm, Basingstoke, Hampshire RG25 2AR. Tel: 01256 397499; email: info@chasecricket.co.uk; website: chasecricket.co.uk. Chase Cricket specialises in handmade bats and hi-tech soft goods. Established 1996. "Support British Manufacturing."

CRICKET SOCIETIES

CRICKET MEMORABILIA SOCIETY, Hon. Secretary: Steve Cashmore, 4 Stoke Park Court, Stoke Road, Bishops Cleeve, Cheltenham, Glos GL52 8US. Email: cms87@btinternet.com; website: cricketmemorabilia.org. To promote and support the collection and appreciation of all cricket memorabilia. Four meetings annually at first-class grounds, with two auctions. Meetings attended by former Test players. Regular members' magazine. Research and valuations undertaken.

THE CRICKET SOCIETIES' ASSOCIATION, Secretary: Mike Hitchings, 34 Derwent Drive, Mitton, Tewkesbury GL20 8BB. Tel: 07979 464715; email: mikehitchings@aol.com; website: cricketsocietiesassociation.com. For cricket lovers in the winter – join a local society and enjoy speaker evenings with fellow enthusiasts for the summer game.

THE CRICKET SOCIETY, c/o David Wood, Membership Secretary, PO Box 6024, Leighton Buzzard, LU7 2ZS. Email: davidwood@cricketsociety.com; website: cricketsociety.com. A worldwide society which promotes cricket through its awards, acclaimed publications, regular meetings, lunches and special events.

CRICKET TOUR OPERATORS

GULLIVERS SPORTS TRAVEL, Ground Floor, Ashvale 2, Ashchurch Business Centre, Alexandra Way, Tewkesbury, Glos GL20 8NB. Tel: 01684 879221; email: gullivers@gulliverstravel.co.uk; website: gulliverstravel.co.uk. The UK's longest-established cricket tour operator offers a great choice of supporter packages for the world's most exciting events – including the Ashes in Australia – and playing tours for schools, clubs, universities and military teams.

PITCHES AND GROUND EQUIPMENT

HUCK NETS (UK) LTD, Gore Cross Business Park, Corbin Way, Bradpole, Bridport, Dorset DT6 3UX. Tel: 01308 425100; email: sales@huckcricket.co.uk; website: huckcricket.co.uk. Alongside manufacturing our unique knotless high-quality polypropylene cricket netting, we offer the complete portfolio of ground and club equipment necessary for cricket clubs of all levels.

NOTTS SPORT, Bridge Farm, Holt Lane, Ashby Magna, Leics LE17 5NJ. Tel: 01455 883730; email: info@nottssports.com; website: nottssports.com. With various ECB-approved pitch systems, Notts Sport, the world's leading supplier of artificial grass pitch systems for coaching, practice and matchplay, can provide a solution tailored to suit individual needs and budgets.

ERRATA

Wisden 1923	Page II.523	C. V. Leefe's highest score for Forest School in 1922 was 27, not 277.
Wisden 1943	Page 140	The match between Surrey Home Guard and Sussex Home Guard appears to have taken place on August 17, 1942, not August 18.
Wisden 1965	Page 293	Laurie Johnson, not Ian Hall, was the first man to score a century for Derbyshire against the Australians.
Wisden 1975	Page 446	Kent lost to Hampshire by an innings and 71, not an innings and 51.
	Page 834	The averages given for Yorkshire's Second Eleven derive from a series of friendly matches, not the Minor Counties Championship. C. Johnson did head Yorkshire's Minor Counties averages, too, but his figures were 218 runs at 36.33.
Wisden 1976	Page 336	England scored 225, not 272, off 95 overs on the third day of the Second Test against Australia at Lord's.
Wisden 1977	Page 317	Brian Close was recalled to England's Test team for the first time in nine years, but he had captained England in three one-day internationals in 1972.
	Page 328	In Derbyshire's match against West Indies, Miller batted at No. 4 in the first innings, with Borrington and Morris at Nos 5 and 6. *Wisden* did not give changes in the second-innings batting order at the time, but Morris moved up to open in place of the absent Sharpe, with Borrington at No. 4 and Miller at No. 5.
	Page 937	K. J. Hughes, not J. K. Hughes, appeared for Western Australia v New South Wales on November 1–4, 1975.
Wisden 1978	Page 392	J. Cumbes batted at No. 4, as nightwatchman, in Worcestershire's only innings against Glamorgan; this displaced Hemsley, D'Oliveira, Patel, Humphries, Holder and Gifford to Nos 5 to 10.
	Page 436	Kent's No. 8 against Cambridge University was G. R. Dilley (making his first-class debut), not A. Dilley.
	Page 650	In Hertfordshire's Gillette Cup match against Leicestershire, their No. 9 was B. G. Collins not B. J. Collins.
Wisden 1986	Page 1031	In the Sheffield Shield final in March 1985, it was T. V. Hohns of Queensland who had figures of 24–7–37–0 in New South Wales's first innings, not S. R. Waugh.
Wisden 1995	Page 376	G. A. Gooch scored no hundreds for England v South Africa in 1994.
Wisden 2018	Page 212	Peter Lewington did not owe his Warwickshire recall in 1982 to Eddie Hemmings's Test call-up, as Hemmings had joined Nottinghamshire in 1979.
Wisden 2019	Page 1091	In Australia A's match v India B on August 27, they were 155-5 in the 29th over.
	Page 1200	Chapungu did share first-wicket partnerships in both innings for Midlands Rhinos v Manicaland Mountaineers, but his opening partner in the second innings should have been listed as P. S. Masvaure.
Wisden 2020	Page 188	Jack Bond's funeral was held in Walkden, Salford, not Stafford.
	Page 189	Lord Bramall joined the Army in 1943, and took part in the Normandy Landings the following year.
	Page 212-3	Garry Sobers's six sixes in an over off Malcolm Nash were not broadcast live on BBC Wales: live coverage had stopped earlier in the day. Sobers's innings began at 4.19, not around 5pm. Wooller was BBC Wales's regular commentator.
	Page 219	Livingstone Puckerin's club Spartan played in the Barbados Cricket Association, rather than the less prestigious Barbados Cricket League.

Page 494	B. M. Duckett was also awarded a county cap by Nottinghamshire.
Page 496	In the FA Cup final replay at the Racecourse in 1886, Blackburn Rovers beat West Bromwich Albion 2–0 rather than vice versa.
Pages 616 and 621	Middlesex's matches at Northwood were played on different grounds: they met Oxford MCCU on the Merchant Taylors' School ground, Gloucestershire on the Old Merchant Taylors' club ground nearby.
Page 822	In the scores for MCC Schools v ESCA, J. G. Timms should be J. C. Timms, as in the team list, the batting averages/most runs and the Haileybury statistics.
Page 958	In the fifth A-Team one-day international, England A's last man was Tom Bailey, not Tim.
Page 970	The 365-run opening stand between John Campbell and Shai Hope was at Clontarf, as in the score, rather than Malahide, as in the table.
Page 1161	In the third women's ODI between New Zealand and India, Lea Tahuhu and Anna Peterson shared 7-54 not 7-56.
Page 1205	P. Mogoera scored 100* before lunch for Free State v Boland at Bloemfontein (day 1).
Page 1208-9	Jamal Anwar made seven catches in an innings for Northern Areas v Baluchistan, and ten dismissals (9ct, 1st) in the match.
Page 1211	S. van Zyl, C. L. White and K. S. Williamson have not taken 500 first-class wickets.
Page 1219	Tom Marsden's 227 for Sheffield & Leicester was in 1826, not 1846.
Page 1339	Mohammed Shami's first entry under Best Career Strike-Rates should be deleted. See also *Wisden 2018* page 1297 and *Wisden 2019* page 1333.

A list of Errata in Wisden *since 1920 may be found at www.bloomsbury.com/uk/special-interest/wisden/errata/*

CHRONICLE OF 2020

And now, the rest of the news…

COMPILED BY MATTHEW ENGEL. CARTOONS BY NICK NEWMAN

NEWSHUB — January 2

Australian prime minister Scott Morrison attracted widespread criticism for hosting a game of backyard cricket for the Australian and New Zealand Test teams while devastating bushfires raged across large parts of the country. He had just returned from a holiday in Hawaii, and seemed largely indifferent to the crisis. Morrison, hosting the players on New Year's Day at his official Sydney residence, Kirribilli, said the approaching Test would inspire Australians. Critics said his approach was "abominable" and "bizarre".

LANCASHIRE POST — January 9

Manchester City Council asked the public to help name a fleet of eight gritting lorries. There were 2,000 suggestions, and Spreaddie Flintoff was among those chosen, along with Basil Salty, Grit Astley, Gritter Thunberg, Slushay Away, Snowbi-Gone Kenobi, Snowel Gallagher and Spreaddie Mercury.

CHANGE.ORG — January 14

An online petition has been launched to ban the 2020 edition of *Wisden* from New Zealand to protect its people from having to read of their team's defeat by England in the 2019 World Cup final. This was said to have caused "excessive emotional harm to a large portion of the population of New Zealand"; a ban would provide "the safe space to continue to recover and mend".

THE CRICKETER — January 23

Jayden Regan, fielding for Hastings against Dromana in a Second XI match on the Mornington Peninsula in Victoria, caught Jeff Bluhm for 99 after the pair had exchanged words throughout the innings. In his delight, Regan launched one last tirade, so vociferous he dislocated his jaw. "We got a bit excited and started to carry on, as you do," said Regan. "And then I thought, nah, I'll give it a bit more, and then the jaw just fell out of place." After a doctor reset it in hospital, Regan returned to the ground. "He was having a beer, and I would have – but I couldn't," he said. "We had a bit of a laugh about it."

HALIFAX COURIER February 11

Bridgeholme CC's attractive ground in the Pennines has had its worst flood in living memory thanks to Storm Ciara. "It was bad in 2015, but we put in place all these things to prevent it, like a river wall," said groundsman Keith Hudson. "The wall's still intact but it's been completely flattened. There's sand, silt and sludge everywhere, rubbish all over the field, bricks and boulders." Hudson has been groundsman for 35 years and has lived close by since 1963. "I've never seen anything like it."

DAILY TELEGRAPH February 14

Sir Geoffrey Boycott's wife, Rachel – now Lady Boycott – has appealed to critics to stop "crucifying" her husband over his conviction by a French court for assault on a girlfriend in 1996. The announcement of his knighthood the previous September (*Wisden 2020*, page 1529), which will be conferred by Prince Charles today, reawakened the controversy over the incident which forced Boycott out of media work in the UK for several years; the honour was strongly criticised by women's groups and opposition MPs. Lady Boycott said newly discovered court documents appeared to support her husband's insistence that he did not punch Margaret Moore, whom she described as a "bunny boiler". Ms Moore maintained he had punched her several times.

NEWS & STAR, CARLISLE February 18

Volunteers at Carlisle CC have been trying to rescue fish stranded on the ground after a fourth flood in 15 years. On previous occasions hundreds of fish were found dead after the water from the River Eden receded from the square. (Club chairman Mike Rayson later said local anglers helped restore 375 fish to the river, mainly grayling, but also sea trout, baby salmon and a few flounders.)

THE INDEPENDENT February 24

Donald Trump mispronounced the names of India's two most revered sports stars while addressing a crowd estimated at 100,000 in the rebuilt Motera Stadium in Ahmedabad. Making his first official visit to India, the US president announced: "This is the country where your people cheer on some of the world's greatest cricket players, from Soo-*chin* Tendul-*kerr* to Virot Kohl-*ee*." On the other hand, the Indian prime minister, Narendra Modi, referred to his guest as "Do-land Trump".

THE BUSINESS STANDARD, DHAKA February 25

Bangladesh player Soumya Sarkar has come under fire for sitting on a deerskin during his wedding ritual. Under Bangladeshi law it is illegal to keep any part of a wild animal as a souvenir without a permit. His family said the skin had been theirs for generations.

RUTLAND & STAMFORD MERCURY February 27

Bill Taylor, groundsman at Nassington CC, Northamptonshire, has been given a sack of tiger dung to spread on the pitch by nearby Hamerton Zoo. The smell is supposed to terrify badgers, who have been digging up the outfield.

THE GUARDIAN March 3

Shropshire Council were criticised by the local government ombudsman after a house was built next to a cricket ground without the required consultation. Hinstock CC, faced with the risk of damage or injury, could not play at home for two years and, as players drifted away, the club were expelled from the Shropshire League. The ombudsman obliged the council to reimburse the club's costs, and maintain the 15ft fence needed to protect the new house. "It was David v Goliath," said club secretary Stephen Collins.

THE TIMES March 7

A predominantly Muslim team in Yorkshire have turned down a £2m lottery grant because of the players' religious objections to gambling. Mount CC from Batley was chosen for the award because of their work hosting children's summer camps and food banks. All-rounder Abdul Ravat said the club were unanimous: "We don't believe in gambling, it's as simple as that."

NEWSTRACK April 12

A young man died playing an illicit game of cricket during the Covid lockdown in the Indian state of Chhattisgarh. He collided with another fielder as both went for a catch.

DAILY MAIL April 17

Yorkshire and England cricketer Adil Rashid has been named and shamed by HMRC as a "deliberate defaulter" who failed to pay more than £100,000 in taxes. He was also fined more than £36,000. "It was a simple mistake," he said. "There is nothing else to it. As a player, you just play and leave it to the accountant."

Yesteryear's news

The following, all from the Daily Express, *would certainly have made the Chronicle, had it existed in the 1950s or 1960s.*

AUGUST 19, 1953

The day before England regained the Ashes after 19 years, they had another victory over Australia. On a pitch laid out by the Royal Tank Regiment, British forces in Korea beat the Aussies by 103 runs. Players wore makeshift whites, and the band played during tea.

JULY 26, 1956

The village club at Feniton, Devon, have cancelled fixtures with neighbours Honiton Town after receiving a letter telling them to wear whites. "Our players resent what amounts to an order," said Feniton treasurer Harry Chown. A Honiton player said: "The last time Feniton came here, eight of their men wore grey flannels and some had ordinary shoes."

AUGUST 8, 1959

Hundreds of baby toads stopped the resumption of play after they emerged from a marsh during a thunderstorm; they invaded the pitch at Instow during a match between North Devon and Free Foresters.

OCTOBER 7, 1959

Middlesex captain John Warr (6ft 4in) had his car stolen from outside Lord's. It was found near Maidstone, Kent, having run out of petrol; the suspected thief, a 5ft 4in Hungarian refugee, gave himself up to police. Locals had seen a man wearing a Middlesex blazer and sweater several sizes too big. The culprit was jailed for six months after admitting various offences, including driving while disqualified. He wanted to draw attention to his need for a job, he claimed. Warr said: "Someone suggested we should give him a trial. Nobody ever got his county cap so quickly."

JULY 26, 1960

Film star Trevor Howard got up at 5am yesterday and travelled 180 miles to play cricket at Buxton, Derbyshire. He was out first ball, caught at the wicket.

APRIL 12, 1962

Three live hand grenades were unearthed yesterday from a grass bank at The Nevill Ground in Tunbridge Wells.

JUNE 30, 1962

Four Britons captured by communist guerrillas in Laos said after their release that they had taught their guards cricket. The two doctors and two embassy officials admitted moments of terror, but claimed that they helped establish trust by teaching their captors new skills. "We had some marvellous matches," said diplomat Mervyn Brown. A bamboo pole was the bat, a piece of charcoal the ball, and buffalo posts the stumps.

JULY 23, 1962

A chambermaid confessed yesterday it was her fault Freddie Trueman was dropped from the Yorkshire side against Somerset. She broke a golden rule: never forget to wake the customers at the time they ask. May Swaab, who works at the County Hotel, Taunton, said: "I'm guilty. I knocked on his door, but he didn't answer. I should have gone in, said 'Good morning, sir,' and swished back the curtains."

DECEMBER 12, 1962

A school in the Melbourne suburb of St Albans is naming its houses after England cricketers Dexter, Barrington, Trueman, and Murray, currently engaged in the Ashes series.

JUNE 11, 1963

Everything was set for the presentation. Frank Worrell, having just led West Indies to victory in the Manchester Test, had gone to see his former league team-mates at Radcliffe, and receive a gift from the club. Mr and Mrs Worrell were in the front row, waiting for the curtains to swing open and reveal the surprise: 12 wine glasses, 12 sherry glasses and a decanter, all Irish crystal. But one curtain edge caught the card-table... Four pieces were presented as planned; Worrell will receive replacements for the rest later.

AUGUST 21, 1963

Five prisoners, being coached at cricket on Nottingham jail sports ground, scrambled to freedom through a hole in the new wire fence. They were thought to have been picked up by an Austin Cambridge with false number plates. They were serving long sentences for robbery.

NOVEMBER 14, 1963

An insurance manager depositing the day's takings in the night safe of a bank in High Wycombe yelled for help – and a passing bus driver reported a suspected robbery. The matter was resolved when someone produced a pair of scissors: an MCC tie had got stuck in the mechanism.

JULY 21, 1964

Fast bowler Bob Millar's first delivery grazed batsman Ivan Baker's trousers, igniting a box of matches in his pocket. After hopping about in a cloud of smoke, Baker was saved by a bucket of water from the pavilion. He went on to score the winning run for Smallburgh against Gothic Wanderers in Norfolk.

MARCH 23, 1966

Prime minister Harold Wilson was hit in the eye by a stink bomb at an election meeting in Slough. He was helped off the platform and treated by a doctor, while a 14-year-old boy was detained. "I don't want him prosecuted," Wilson told police. "A boy who can throw like that should be in England's cricket team."

Matthew Engel is researching The Reign*, a book about how Britain has changed since 1952... but is constantly being diverted by cricket stories.*

THE TIMES April 18

The Virtual County Cup, an online cricket tournament organised for Leicestershire & Rutland League teams during lockdown, ended in disarray amid accusations of ballot rigging. While they waited for the real season to begin, clubs were drawn against each other, results decided by voting. However, one club were said to have set up dozens of fake social media accounts to bump up their totals, while others were said to have offered backhanders. "People cheating in made-up cricket, just like the real thing," one player said. The 55-team competition was abandoned at the quarter-final stage.

BBC April 25/26

England fast bowler Jofra Archer lost his 2019 World Cup medal after moving house. He admitted this in a BBC radio interview, adding that he had spent the early weeks of Britain's lockdown looking for it: "There's nothing else to do in isolation." The following day he posted a happy message on Twitter: "Randomly searching the guest bedroom and boom!"

TIMES OF INDIA April 29

A match between rival hamlets near Hardoi in Uttar Pradesh ended in a player being battered to death with a bat and stumps after an argument over the score. Three men were accused of manslaughter, and all the players of breaching lockdown rules.

DAILY MAIL/MSN April 30/May 1

Graham Walters, 72, from Leicestershire, became the oldest man to row the Atlantic solo when he reached Antigua after a 96-day journey – without a support boat – from Gran Canaria. The boat, which he built himself, is called the *George Geary*, after his grandfather, the Leicestershire and England all-rounder. Walters's record hung in the balance because he was blown off course and needed help from the coastguard five miles from the finish. However, the Ocean Rowing Society decided he had done enough.

TIMES OF INDIA June 1

A Covid-19 patient, compulsorily detained at a care hostel, escaped and hid at Maleksaban Stadium, Ahmedabad's oldest cricket ground. The place was unusually deserted due to the lockdown, and the patient, Samir Ansari, 22, grew bored and surrendered to police. "Ansari feared he would die at the hostel," an official said. "But he didn't want to infect his family either." He has been charged with spreading an infectious disease through negligence.

LANCASHIRE POST June 3/November 18

Campaigners in Fulwood, near Preston, have gathered nearly 2,000 signatures to save the old ground at Harris Park. Andrew Flintoff once watched from his pushchair as his father played for Dutton Forshaw, and soon began to show his own talent. Cricket was last played there in 2013. The land had been sold to developers seven years earlier, and they applied to build 83 houses, later reduced to 50. "Harris Park was left to the people of Preston for their enjoyment and education," said Prema Taylor, co-founder of the action group.

THE TIMES June 6

Sir Geoffrey Boycott, 79, was omitted from the *Test Match Special* team for the 2020 Tests after a 14-year stint. The BBC said it was because of the risk to a man of his age and medical history in a confined box during the pandemic. However, one commenter on social media had another explanation: "White, male, straight, Tory and knows about cricket. Surprised he lasted this long at the BBC." Boycott responded "Absolutely right", which he later replaced with a graceful retirement message.

DAILY MAIL June 11

Former Warwickshire opener Andy Moles, 59, has had his left leg amputated after contracting MRSA in hospital. Moles, director of cricket in Afghanistan for the past six years, suffered a foot infection on a training walk in 2019 with the Afghan players in Abu Dhabi. It failed to respond to treatment, and in April 2020 he was told by a specialist in Cape Town, where he is now based, that his leg would have to be amputated below the knee to prevent septicaemia. Moles said he was conscious that elsewhere in the hospital people were dying of Covid. "One or two bodies were already being wheeled out," he said. "The reality is I would only be missing a lower left limb. Is it going to stop me walking? No. Will it stop me coaching? No."

SBS, AUSTRALIA June 13

Streets in Rockbank, a new and distant suburb of Melbourne, have been named after cricketers. The emphasis is on Asian players to attract buyers in an area that already has a large Indian population. The developers said enquiries had doubled after the plan was announced. Streets include Tendulkar Drive, Kohli Crescent and Akram Way. The main street is named Nash Boulevard, after Laurie Nash, who played two Tests for Australia in the 1930s – his grandson was one of the developers. No England players were included.

THE TIMES June 18

Eighty-one-year-old Alan Jones was finally recognised as England Test cricketer No. 696, exactly 50 years after everyone thought he had won his cap. Jones, Glamorgan's long-serving and much-admired left-handed opener, played a single match for England against a mighty Rest of the World team at Lord's in the 1970 series, hastily arranged after South Africa's tour was cancelled due to apartheid. They were treated as Tests at the time, but the ICC later decreed otherwise. Uncharacteristically, Jones was out for five (an "appalling shot", he later admitted) and nought, both times to Mike Procter. He was the only player in the series not to be picked again. To mark the anniversary, the ECB made a sentimental exception and, in a virtual ceremony, he was presented with his cap by former England captain and fellow Welshman Tony Lewis.

ABC June 30

Fourteen-year-old Bradman Thompson, already 6ft 5in, is living up to his name. Playing for Maiden Gully Marist CC in Victoria, he scored 275 runs for the Under-14s, and was out only once in the 2019-20 season. However, owing to a bizarre administrative error, he failed to win a batting prize at the Bendigo District awards: most of his runs had been credited to someone else. "We'll highlight the fact that he did win the award, and it wasn't his fault he didn't get it," club president Neil Byers said. "We are going to speak to the association to make sure it never happens to any other kid."

INDIAN EXPRESS/THE STATESMAN July 3/8

A bogus cricket event staged near Mohali in the north Indian countryside constituted what may have been the most elaborate – if not the most successful – betting scam in cricket history. The "Uva T20 League", furtively held on a remote field hidden by tents with spectators barred "because of the virus", was shown on YouTube, with scores reported on various websites. Commentary was primitive, and players were unidentified. It was billed as coming from Badulla in Sri Lanka, nearly 1,700 miles away, with phoney adverts round the ground and several well-known Sri Lankans supposedly taking part. One, Farveez Maharoof, heard about it, and announced it was fake. Police, hunting for organisers and players, made several arrests.

THEPRINT.IN July 4

The world's best-selling cricket magazine, the Hindi-language monthly *Cricket Samrat*, has closed after 42 years. The pandemic has been blamed.

The Times July 9

Metal detectorists were accused of digging up the pitch at Winchelsea CC, Sussex. Five holes were left in the square, which was fenced off during the Covid summer, and it is thought significant artefacts may have been removed. A local spoke to the interlopers, who were in high-vis jackets and claimed they were from the water board. A major port in medieval times, Winchelsea has a rich archaeological heritage.

Birmingham Mail July 14

Three hundred residents have signed a petition against another cricket pitch being constructed at Blossomfield CC in Solihull. Campaigners say they will lose valuable green space and wildlife habitat. A club spokesman said they needed extra space to meet demand, as nearby grounds were being converted for football use.

West Sussex County Times July 20

Dave Parsons of Hurstpierpoint CC in Sussex was given a socially distanced guard of honour as he led out the first team to mark the 50th anniversary of his debut. For the fixture against Horsted Keynes, club president Parsons took back the captaincy from his son Matthew.

Coventry Telegraph July 23

The chairman of Nuneaton CC, Warwickshire, said "up to 200 kids" have caused havoc on their ground during the Covid lockdown. Gary Cox said teenagers had been tearing up the square on motorbikes and scooters, jumping over new covers and leaving graffiti on the sightscreens. "It has been so difficult for us, not being able to play games, without all of this."

The Times July 24

After five years, 60 matches and almost 200 hours of play, one of English cricket's more depressing losing runs has come to an end. Playing their neighbours Ashley, Bowdon Over-40s from Cheshire needed five to win off the final over, but were not optimistic. Captain Damien Bourke admitted they had often got into winning positions during the bad times. "This game looked no different," he said. "Wides were the biggest scorer, but we'll take all the help we can get."

TIMES OF INDIA July 24

About three dozen youngsters playing beach cricket in defiance of Covid rules at Virar, near Mumbai, left bat, ball and stumps behind when police arrived, and leapt into the sea. They were able to clamber aboard a passing fishing boat.

HASTINGS OBSERVER July 27

Batsmen wore top hats when cricket history met the game's newest and most controversial format in Sussex. The fixture between the Gentlemen of Firle and the Gentlemen of Lewes, which dates back to 1851, was played under the rules of the ECB-concocted Hundred.

THE CRICKETER August

Cynthia Crawford, Worcestershire supporter and Margaret Thatcher's personal assistant, moved in with her employer after Lady T was widowed, and encouraged her to watch cricket on TV, not something that had interested her before. During an Ashes series involving Australian fast bowler Brett Lee, Thatcher remarked: "I like that player. He's got a lovely little face."

BARNSLEY CHRONICLE August 17

Chris Holliday of Hoylandswaine scored 316 off 113 balls against Denby, breaking the Huddersfield League record, despite it being a 30-over fixture played under makeshift pandemic rules. Holliday hit 34 sixes and 21 fours in a total of 456 for three. Denby, not usually in the same division, were bowled out for 78. There was social media chunter that, with normal league competition in abeyance, and Denby clearly outclassed, Holliday should have retired. "I wish I had," he said later, "but even then, I probably would have been called arrogant, so I can't win."

NEW INDIAN EXPRESS August 20

Cricket equipment manufacturers in India say their sales are "70–80%" down because of the pandemic.

BBC August 28

Having started their season late because of the pandemic, Northern Ireland's Dundrum CC had it curtailed when a flash flood wrecked the playing surface. Club official Jeff Maguire was phlegmatic: "We had two pavilions burnt down during the Troubles, but that actually rejuvenated us and allowed us to build new facilities. My heart goes out to the people who have lost their homes. That is a bigger tragedy in my eyes than a bit of grass."

KENT & SUSSEX COURIER September 4

The antique cream-coloured telephone box outside the Nevill Ground at Tunbridge Wells is to be given a makeover, and possibly restored to working use. The box (a Mk1 K236, topped by ornate metalwork) dates from the late 1920s and is said to be one of only four of its type remaining.

OLDHAM TIMES September 7

The Huddersfield League match between Delph & Dobcross II and Birkby Rose Hill was abandoned after alleged unruly behaviour by both teams. The incident was particularly painful for one of the umpires, John Battye, a local councillor and life member of Delph & Dobcross. He had campaigned for the return of recreational cricket during Covid restrictions, calling it "part of the fabric of our society".

HINDUSTAN TIMES September 10

Two teenage Bangladesh cricketers were killed by lightning near Dhaka. Their training session had been interrupted by heavy rain, but several boys stayed outside playing football. Mohammad Nadim and Mizanur Rahman were described as "very promising".

JOE.CO.UK September 14

A cricket match broke out when the M1 was closed near Luton. Four men, trapped in a seemingly interminable hold-up, slipped over the barrier and began an impromptu game on the empty carriageway.

INDIA TODAY September 17

The 40-year-old owner of Kabul Eagles, a team in Afghanistan's Twenty20 Shpageeza League, was banned after a single match. Although not in the squad, Abdul Latif Ayoubi played against Speen Ghar Tigers and bowled one over for 16. He reportedly argued with a commentator, leading to the ban.

LANCASHIRE TELEGRAPH September 21

The Lancashire Council of Mosques beat the Church of England in Lancashire by 66 runs at Ribblesdale CC. The fixture was a repeat of a highly successful inaugural match last year, also won by the imams.

DAILY MAIL September 22

Eight years after revealing he had developed bulimia as a young professional (when his weight was criticised), Andrew Flintoff has said he is still struggling with the eating disorder.

LIVERPOOL ECHO September 28

Supermarket group Aldi, who plan to build a new branch on Huyton CC's former ground, suffered a blow when the half-timbered Victorian pavilion was listed as a Grade II historic building. Huyton were founder members of the Liverpool Competition in 1892, but were relegated in 2008, and folded not long after. Campaigners want the space restored for community use.

ISLE OF WIGHT COUNTY PRESS October 3

Emma Griffiths, sister of former Hampshire and Kent seam bowler David, was said to be recovering well after David, 35, donated a kidney to save her life.

DNA INDIA October 9

Mudassir Gujjar, a fast bowler signed by Lahore Qalandars in the Pakistan Super League, is reportedly between 7ft 4in and 7ft 6in tall. His fellow Pakistani Mohammad Irfan was measured at 7ft 1in.

DAILY MAIL October 14

Dozens of birdwatchers descended on a Yorkshire cricket ground after a hoopoe turned up at Collingham CC. It was thought to have been blown badly off course while trying to migrate from southern Europe to Africa. About a hundred hoopoes a year are sighted in southern England, but this was the first in Yorkshire for 40 years. "Possibly the greatest living thing to grace a Yorkshire cricket pitch since Geoff Boycott," said enthusiast Simon Moody.

BRIDPORT & LYME REGIS NEWS October 15

The lawyer Clive Stafford Smith, who became widely known for his campaign against the death penalty in the US (see page 814), is now leading a drive to save the idyllic ground at Broadwindsor, Dorset, where he is chairman. Stafford Smith said new owners want to sell up, and the club need to raise £35,000. Nearby grounds at Bridport and Melplash have been lost in the past two years.

MAIL ON SUNDAY October 18

Priti Patel, home secretary in Boris Johnson's government, has paid £45,000 (about two-fifths of her salary) to jump the 29-year queue and receive full membership of MCC. This was part of a scheme to recover some of the £30m shortfall in revenue caused by Covid-19, and Patel received no special treatment. Nonetheless the news caused surprise. "I didn't realise Priti was interested in cricket," said one MP.

THE TIMES October 21

The actor due to play Muttiah Muralitharan in a biopic has pulled out of the project, on the player's advice. Vijay Sethupathi, an Indian Tamil, was due to star in *800*, named after Murali's unparalleled number of Test wickets. But Sethupathi came under attack from Tamil nationalists who accuse Murali, also a Tamil, of siding with the Sri Lankan government in the long and brutal war with separatists, which ended in 2009. Murali said he did not want the actor to risk his career "due to the false notions surrounding me".

THE TIMES OF INDIA October 21

A 14-year-old boy was killed by lightning at Bhayander, near Mumbai, while batting on the beach.

DAILY TELEGRAPH November 14

Ian Botham, surprisingly elevated to the House of Lords by Boris Johnson, says he intends to fight for "the ordinary folk who depend on the countryside". He wants to oppose "the grim eco-warriors" of the Royal Society for the Protection of Birds who, he says, are trying to ban pheasant shooting, and are thus themselves threatening the balance of nature.

THE TIMES November 18

Warwickshire CCC have come under fire for appointing a controversial police official to the board of their charitable foundation. Waheed Saleem was made deputy police and crime commissioner of the West Midlands, despite opponents claiming he had links to "numerous scandals". Jon Hunt, leader of Birmingham's Liberal Democrats, said: "It is astonishing the way well-connected individuals in the West Midlands continue to accumulate influential roles, in spite of there being huge unanswered questions."

MID-DAY.COM November 21

Former Mumbai and Maharashtra wicketkeeper-batsman Raghunath Chandorkar celebrated his 100th birthday today, an event recognised only after his passport revealed that he was born in 1920 and not, as previously recorded, 1922. Research by statistician (and *Wisden* contributor) Prakash Dahatonde discovered the error. Chandorkar is the third Indian first-class player to reach 100, after Professor D. B. Deodhar and Vasant Raiji (see page 275). All three played in the same Ranji Trophy match, Maharashtra v Baroda in 1944-45.

SUNDAY TELEGRAPH November 22

Buckingham Town CC found a novel way to break records and raise funds, by scoring 6,805 runs in 12 hours, more than double the previous best. They had their achievement recognised by Guinness World Records. There was no ball involved: participants just had to wear pads, carry a bat and run between the wickets. A total of 187 people took part, ranging from primary schoolchildren to a marathon runner; they raised £8,000 for local cancer charity Alec's Angels.

ST GEORGE & SUTHERLAND SHIRE LEADER November 23

Andrew Walsh scored a double-century from No. 8 to lead St George to a last-ball win over North Sydney in the New South Wales Premier club competition. Walsh came in at 52 for six, facing a target of 356. He fell in the final over, but No. 11 Tom McKenzie drove the last ball for four. Walsh, whose previous best was 53, hit 208 from 209 balls, with 15 fours and 15 sixes. His score ranks equal third with Brian Booth in the club's first-grade history (the record is Don Bradman's 246 in 1931-32). Club coach Dean Gilchrist (brother of the more famous Adam) said: "It's a win for the ages."

THE OBSERVER November 29

James Botham, 22-year-old grandson of Lord Ian Botham, made his debut for the Welsh rugby team as a flanker against Georgia, and kept his place against England a week later. He was born in Cardiff, where his father, Liam, was based during his own rugby career. "This is probably the one thing I have worked for my whole life: to get the red jersey on and play against England," he said. "I am sure my grandad will be backing me 100%, even though I will not have the white jersey."

THE TIMES/VIMPSATTHECREASE.COM November 25, 28/December 2

The Sussex League, the country's biggest, have reversed a decision to make the provision of teas an optional extra at matches in 2021. There were protests after the first vote from clubs deemed to have been in favour, even though they had not been represented at the AGM – and louder protests from sentimentalists across the country. The original 114–82 vote against teas became 114–89 in favour, after a new email ballot. Horsted Keynes had already said they would carry on providing teas for their players and opponents willing to reciprocate: "In fact," the club tweeted, "we are working on a new pavlova recipe." However, there are fears the tradition is still in danger. Earlier in November, the Worcestershire League rejected a motion to scrap the obligation to provide teas by 51% to 49.

SYDNEY MORNING HERALD November 27

Cricket Australia have fined one of the country's leading umpires, George Abood, £2,800 for questioning decisions made in an Under-13s game in Sydney. The punishment was provoked by his behaviour when his son, playing for Inner West Harbour against St George, was given run out for 98 off the final ball of the innings. St George said Abood had tried to intimidate their coach, and had questioned his sportsmanship in condoning the appeal. Abood, who has umpired nine internationals, denied swearing, but accepted he behaved wrongly, and apologised. As well as the fine, he was ordered to do 20 hours' voluntary service educating umpires.

INDIA TODAY December 2

A Gujarat man was allegedly stripped and paraded naked in the busy market place of Khambala after he accused five men of betting on cricket. The five have been arrested and charged for multiple breaches of the criminal code, including "indulging in an obscene act".

DAILY MAIL December 7

The concrete pitch where Don Bradman is thought have honed his skills in his home town of Bowral has been saved from developers. A plan to build town houses and assisted-living homes was rejected. Local historian Nick Corbett believes Bowral's most famous son played there with his high-school team on Wednesdays, which is contested, but the plan was also turned down on environmental grounds.

INDIAN EXPRESS December 27

Different factions of the controversy-ridden Bihar Cricket Association have named separate squads for the Syed Mushtaq Ali tournament (the national Twenty20 competition for Ranji Trophy teams) starting in January. The secretary and president issued separate squads of 20; no player was picked for both. The national board were expected to intervene.

DAILY MAIL December 30

Cricket-loving prime minister John Major rejected a Foreign Office suggestion that Zimbabwean president Robert Mugabe should be made an honorary member of MCC when he came to Britain on a state visit in 1994. According to papers released by the National Archives, Major responded: "I'd leave it. Many MCC members won't like it + it is a dodgy precedent."

This is the 27th year of the Chronicle. Highlights of the first 25 have been published in WHAT Did You Say Stopped Play? *(John Wisden).*

Contributions from readers are always welcome. Items must have been previously published in print or online. Please send weblinks/cuttings to hugh.chevallier@wisdenalmanack.com or post them to Matthew Engel at Fair Oak, Bacton, Herefordshire HR2 0AT.

INDEX OF TEST MATCHES

Nine earlier men's Test series in 2019-20 – Bangladesh v Afghanistan, India v South Africa, India v Bangladesh, New Zealand v England, Australia v Pakistan, Afghanistan v West Indies, Pakistan v Sri Lanka, Australia v New Zealand and South Africa v England – appeared in *Wisden 2020*. WTC signifies that a series formed part of the World Test Championship.

INDEX OF UNUSUAL OCCURRENCES

INDEX OF ADVERTISEMENTS

PART TITLES